FRONT PAGE

Israel

THE JERUSALEM POST

Published by The Jerusalem Post, Jerusalem, Israel

Fifth Edition

ISBN 965-356-027-1

President and Publisher, Yehuda Levy
Executive Editor, David Bar Illan
Compiled by Alexander Zvielli
Cover Design by Ruth Kovel
Cover Photo by Sarit Uziely

Printed at The Jerusalem Post Press, Jerusalem, Israel

In this news-addicted age it is only natural that anthologies of front pages, headlines and all, should be published and avidly scanned by those curious about how our times developed. Middle and back pages of newspapers are something else again. They are likely to carry human interest stories. These are not to be made light of; they are after all the stuff of daily life – the stuff without which one cannot sense the savor, the special nature, of a society.

If there is any national society with a very special nature, it is Israel – problematic and aspiring as it is; past-linked; future oriented; object of theological passion; absorbing groups and individuals from every corner of the world.

The Jerusalem Post has faithfully recorded over 60 years the greatest historic moments and events which reflect the history of Israel and developments in our region.

This book is a remarkable anthology of the front pages of *The Jerusalem Post* which record the history of our people both in Israel and throughout the world in the years leading up to the State; the international struggle, the establishment, development, and defense of the Jewish State.

A large proportion of the inhabitants of Israel and certainly of the Jewish world is unaware of the details of the Jewish Odyssey during one of the most significant periods in the history of our people in which the most terrifying holocaust in the history of mankind took place, wiping out one third of the Jewish people, followed by the rise after 2000 years of an independent Jewish State.

I warmly congratulate *The Jerusalem Post* on this additional gift to the nation, recording great moments, joyous moments, tragic moments and heroic moments in the history of our people.

Chaim Herzog

The Jerusalem Post, an English paper in a Hebrew-speaking country, is a unique publication: it is the only foreign-language paper anywhere which has an international readership and a global reputation. Sold in 103 countries on six continents, it has faithful readers in Papua, New Guinea, and in the US Congress; in the royal court in Amman and in Jewish homes in Wyoming. Recently, the British Broadcasting Corporation named it one of six internationally influential newspapers.

What makes *The Jerusalem Post* an exceptional phenomenon is primarily its place of publication. Israel has been in the center of world attention since its founding. And since 1967 it has been generating more news than almost any other country. A newspaper written and edited by Israelis, which brings news, feature articles, opinions and "slices of life" from Israel, is bound to arouse interest. But what makes it influential is the reputation it has acquired over the years for integrity, meticulous research, fair reporting and the separation of fact from opinion. In recent years it has become known for providing a carefully balanced forum for the whole gamut of Israeli opinion. Few journals in the world are as impartial in providing liberals and conservatives, doves and hawks, rightists and leftists, Arabs and Jews, with an opportunity to express themselves side by side. Virtually no serious Israeli viewpoint is left out of *The Jerusalem Post*.

The paper's world stature would have probably astonished founder Gershon Agron, who established the paper as *The Palestine Post* in 1932. His goal was to provide Israel with "a window to the world." He wanted the authorities in what was then the British Mandate of Palestine to know something about the state of mind of the Jewish community in the country. He wanted newcomers who could not read Hebrew to have a newspaper in an international language. And he wanted the smattering of tourists who visited the country then to know more about the country and its people by reading a home product. It was a modest publication, a reaching-out effort by a community struggling to realize the Zionist dream.

But soon the paper had momentous events to cover. Within a couple of months of its first issue, Hitler came to power in Germany. The influx of refugees from Nazi Germany, many of whom immediately became devoted readers of the *Post*, signaled the beginning of the unspeakable tragedy of European Jewry. In 1936 the Great Arab Revolt, the first Arab "intifada," broke out; it was a blood-drenched terrorist war which for three years took a terrible toll in Arab and Jewish lives. The war against terrorism was accompanied by a relentless political struggle with the British authorities, bent on curbing Jewish immigration and limiting Jewish settlement in the country.

Then came the Second World War and the German advances in North Africa which threatened to overrun the whole Middle East. The country became a major base for British soldiers and sailors, for whom *The Jerusalem Post* was often the only reliable source of news. (Twelve of the 45 permanent workers of the *Post* enlisted in the Palestine units of the British army at that time.) The paper, which as far back as 1934 sent 300 copies to Egypt, could now be seen throughout the region, wherever soldiers were stationed.

When the horror of the Holocaust became known at war's end, *The Jerusalem Post* served as the paper of record for this greatest of Jewish tragedies since the destruction of the Second Temple. And with painful, accurate detail it bore witness to the British effort to choke the flow of refugees from Europe.

The events that followed constituted one of the most dramatic developments in the region's history. The British were forced out by the Jewish underground; the new State of Israel, resisting an invasion by five Arab armies, declared its independence in 1948 and survived a savage, costly war in which one percent of the population was killed (and during which *The Jerusalem Post* offices were bombed by terrorists, killing three workers and wounding many others).

The new state opened its gates to a flood of immigration from Europe and the Arab countries, subjecting the country to an inevitable period of social upheaval and economic hardship; the terrorist campaign against Israelis in Israel and abroad was incessant, interrupted only by conventional battlefield wars; the War of Independence was followed by the Suez Campaign in 1956, the Six Day War of 1967, the War of Attrition of 1969, the Yom Kippur War of 1973, the Peace for the Galilee war of 1982; and the Iraqi Scud attacks of 1991. It was the stuff of legends, creating in a few decades enough drama and news to fill several centuries.

But there were also promising buds of peace. In 1977, peace negotiations began with Egypt, President Anwar Sadat visited Jerusalem, the Camp David Accords brought hope for a new era, and relations with Jordan were almost "normalized" even without a peace treaty. In October 1991, Syria, Lebanon Jordan and the Palestinians agreed for the first time to conduct direct, bilateral negotiations with Israel in Madrid. Last year, official contacts with the PLO culminated in a White House lawn handshake between Prime Minister Yitzhak Rabin and PLO Chairman Yasser Arafat.

The modest newspaper of 1932, printed in 1,200 copies, is now a major force on the world scene. Its international edition, begun as the Weekly Overseas Edition in 1959, has a circulation of 70,000. It is essential reading for anyone abroad interested in Israel and its neighbors. Its French International Edition, launched in November 1990, now sells close to 10,000 copies.

The *Post*'s feature stories and articles are syndicated by *The New York Times* and by the *Post*'s own Foreign Service. The *Jerusalem Post* company also publishes four youth papers, for readers from kindergarten to college.

The paper has the first computerized archives in Israel; the complete contents of every issue since October 1988 are available on CD-ROM. The Book Department provides a mail order service which offers books, video cassettes, compact disks and unique consumer products. The *Post* also sponsors four charitable funds.

In the 62 years of its existence, *The Jerusalem Post* has recorded history as it is seen through Israeli eyes. With authenticity and power, it tells Israel's story. Every major event in Israel's life has been caught on its Front Pages, with the immediacy, drama, tragedy, pain, elation and wonderment that only witnesses to the moment itself can ever hope to capture.

David Bar-Illan

David Bar-Illan, Executive Editor

Founded in 1932 by GERSHON AGRON
Editors: 1932-1955 GERSHON AGRON, 1955-1974 TED LURIE, 1974-1975 LEA BEN DOR, 1975-1989 ARI RATH and ERWIN FRENKEL, 1990-1992 N. DAVID GROSS

THE PALESTINE POST

INCORPORATING The Palestine Bulletin

Vol. VIII. No. 2291. JERUSALEM, THURSDAY, DECEMBER 1, 1932. (Kislev 2 — Shabat 2.) Price: 10 Mils.

SECOND BRITISH NOTE

Weighty Cabinet Meeting

London, Wednesday. — Replying to Mr. Lansbury, in the House of Commons, Mr. Chamberlain briefly announced that the British note in reply to the American debts note of November 23 is now completed and will be transmitted immediately to Washington and published within a few days.

He added that there was no foundation for the newspaper report that gold was being shipped to America in connection with British debts.

The British note is designed to convince the United States Government that unless the December payment is suspended pending a full review of the war debts position, the consequences to international trade must be so harmful as to outweigh, from America's own viewpoint, the benefit to the United States' budget from the receipt of the L.30,000,000 which Great Britain has to pay at the present rates.

GOLD SHIPMENT TO AMERICA
Another Nation's Money

London, Wednesday. — It is authoritatively stated that a shipment of gold from Great Britain to the United States to-day on the liners "Majestic" and "Paris" is not connected with war debts but is gold payment from another country which is being sent from Great Britain as an exchange transaction and amounts to L. 3,000,000, which was held by Great Britain on a foreign account.

The method of payment of the debt instalment is not considered an immediate issue.

U.S. TO ACCEPT INTEREST ONLY
Treasury's Day Of Reckoning

London, Tuesday. (Via Cairo). — It is considered that the United States is practically certain to accept the offer of interest only and to allow the postponement of the principal of the debt instalment due on December 15. The interest amounts to £.13,500,000, which will very probably be remitted in gold, thus saving the difference between the par value of gold dollars and the current sterling value.

The Government will have a huge reckoning day on December 1, when over £.300,000,000 will be disbursed, £.165,000,000 to non-converters of the 5 per cent. War Loan and £.140,000,000 to holders of Treasury Bonds. The Treasury will receive a slightly smaller sum on the same day on account of new loans.

Reuter/P.T.A.

THE KING AND THE CRISIS

London, Tuesday. — The Prime Minister was received in audience by the King at Buckingham Palace this evening.

B.O.W.P.

London Tuesday. (Via Cairo). — Ministerial conferences yesterday on the debt question concluded with a Cabinet meeting lasting two hours and with the Chancellor of the Exchequer being received in audience the King.

Apart from the fact that Ministers are resolved to make the second note to the United States irresistible in argument, it is believed that not only are the terms of the actual note being drafted but the whole of the Government's war debt policy is being reviewed, and it is unlikely that the note will be dispatched before Wednesday.

Divided Opinion

Opinion within the Cabinet is said to be divided. The "Morning Post" ranges Mr. MacDonald, Mr. Baldwin and Mr. Thomas on the one side as declaring that their bond must be honoured without discussion, and Mr. Neville Chamberlain and Sir John Simon on the other as declaring that the prime consideration is the Lausanne Pact, and the French representations must be considered even to the point of default.

Mr. Montagu Norman also called at the Treasury yesterday and according to city circles, advised that default would be disastrous to British credit.

Parliamentary opinion strongly favours payment.

Reuter/P.T.A.

The Premier and his principal Ministers were in close contact most of Tuesday (adds the British Official Wireless) and practically all members of the Cabinet are to meet for further consideration of the question of the American War Debt.

Although it is expected that the note will be confined to setting out the reasons for the proposal briefly made in the original British communication — that the inter-Governmental debts should be re-examined and that the payment due on December 15 should meanwhile be suspended — it is necessary that these reasons should be stated in some detail and supported by facts of incontrovertible accuracy.

Method of Payment

According to the London press, the examination of the situation which is now being undertaken by the British Cabinet is taking also into consideration the effect of the several possible methods of payment, whether by gold sterling or in dollars; and upon these and kindred questions a mass of technical data has been collected.

Among many other considerations which have to be borne in mind there is the effect of the Lausanne agreements: whether Great Britain's payments could conceivably be continued without reopening questions about which settlement had been reached at Lausanne and whether Great Britain could go on paying War Debts to the United States without receiving anything from those countries which owe War Debts to Great Britain. Great Britain has already paid to the United States two hundred million pounds more than she has received from her debtors, in spite of the fact that the amount due to Great Britain was more than the amount due from Great Britain to the United States.

Economic Consequences

It is, however, the economic consequences of inter-governmental debts which are receiving the most attention in the British Press, and newspapers generally take the view expressed to-day in the "News Chronicle" by Sir Walter Layton, who, after pointing out the effect of the American tariff (one of the highest in the world) upon the flow of goods, declares that "there is no device known to the science of economics or to the art of finance which enable the creditor to go on collecting the debts due to him if he will not receive goods and services from his debtors."

B.O.W.P.

Another Hunger March

Washington, Monday. (Via Cairo). — Eight hundred demonstrators have started on a hunger-march to Washington in small parties from different parts of the country in anticipation of the opening of Congress on December 5.

Reuter/P.T.A.

The Palestine Post: Announcement

Today's issue of this newspaper is an attempted forward step in English journalism in Palestine.

The generosity of a number of public-spirited men and women resident here or in England has made it financially practicable to remodel the paper and to adopt a policy of improvement, enlargement and expansion. Our hope is that it will soon be in a position to satisfy more adequately the ever-increasing English-reading public of this country and the neighbouring territories.

The Palestine Post (with which is incorporated *The Palestine Bulletin)* has been entrusted to a new management. The sole object of the new management is to publish a daily paper responding to the needs and tastes of British residents, other Europeans and Palestinians. Their interests served in various degrees by the Arabic and Hebrew Press, the Palestinians, too, may find in this journal certain acceptable features obscured by the specific character of the newspapers in the other languages of the country.

Progress in the development of a newspaper must be gradual, and with an English journal in this country it must be still more gradual. The reading public is limited, the advertising field restricted; but such is the confidence of the Publishers in the future of this enterprise that they are prepared to produce the newspaper at a sacrifice. The Management will do its utmost to enhance the value of the publication for all classes, and will expect thereby substantially to increase the revenue. Time will show whether the country is ripe for a progressive newspaper as nearly as possible approaching the standard to which European readers have become accustomed.

* * *

Published in Jerusalem in the interests of the entire population of the country, nothing Palestinian will be alien to *The Palestine Post*. Whilst endeavouring to bring the outer world nearer both to the Palestinian and to the foreign resident, it will be our constant aim to help the non-Palestinian to acquire a fuller understanding and a deeper affection towards a land which is enshrined in the hearts of most of the races of the earth and in which it is his privilege to live and to work.

The Palestine Post will not seek to promote personal ambitions or party advantage. Its reports will be as objective as is humanly possible, and its criticism informed, legitimate and helpful. In criticism and in reports, the studied purpose will be the present and future welfare of the country and of its people; and the Management will make no attempt to conceal its conviction that such welfare is best assured by a full realisation of the British policy in Palestine as defined in the Mandate. Those supporting law and order, all those standing for progress, all those in sincere sympathy with the clear aims of the Policy, may expect this journal to bring them hope and encouragement. Those who seek by open or devious means to obstruct the policy of the Mandate may count on a fair presentation of their actions and views, but they can be given no other encouragement.

Readers are invited to cooperate in our attempt to make *The Palestine Post* the type of newspaper they would like to see produced in this country. All suggestions and assistance will be gratefully received and carefully considered.

For a number of years, the Jewish Telegraphic Agency has borne alone the heavy burden and grave responsibility of producing Palestine's only English daily paper. To this Agency, the gratitude of the new Management goes out. No smaller degree of recognition is due to Mr. S. Schwartz, who carried on for many years as Responsible Editor, and who only yesterday handed over a difficult task to others.

RATES OF EXCHANGE
NOVEMBER 30

PARIS	80 1/2
NEW YORK	3.15
ZURICH	16.38
TRIESTE	62.
ANTWERP	22 3/4
PRAGUE	107
BERLIN	13.24

(By courtesy of the Anglo-Palestine Bank).

NEW RECORD FOR THE POUND STERLING

London, Tuesday. — Sterling on New York to-day recovered at the opening to 3.19 1/2, but fell later to 3.14 1/2 closing at 3.15 1/2 dollars. Despite the pound's weakness the British funds finished to-day strongly under the lead of War Loan Assented, which rose over one point to 97 1/8.

B.O.W.P.

BRITISH OFFICIALS IN EGYPT

London Tuesday. (Via Cairo). — Questions regarding the filling up of posts in Egypt, vacated by British officials, by other nationals, put by Sir Wardlaw Milne in the House of Commons, evoked a reply from Sir John Simon that there was not the least reason to suppose that any such vacancies were filled by citizens of any other nation than Egyptians.

Mr. Morgan Jones asked whether the appointment of these officials was within the competence of the Egyptian Government.

Sir John Simon asked for notice of this question, saying that he thought he he knew the answer, but it would be better not to make a mistake.

Reuter/P.T.A.

PERSIA CANCELS OIL CONCESSION

Teheran, Tuesday. (Via Cairo). — The Government has officially notified THE ANGLO-PERSIAN OIL COMPANY of the annulment of the d'Arcy Concession. It adds that it is willing to consider fresh terms.

It is learned in London that the Company informed the Persian Government that the concession does not provide for cancellation and they cannot accept the Government's notification.

Reuter/P.T.A.

Car Crash At Railway Crossin

Two R.A.F. Sergeants were injured, one said to be seriously, and two others escaped with bruises, in an accident yesterday evening when a train crashed into a car at the Ramleh Railway crossing.

All four men may be considered to have a lucky escape, since the car which had been hit by the train was carried along by the impact for several yards and was wrecked. The barrier was smashed.

The non-commissioned officers were admitted to the General Hospital at Sarafend.

YASSIN PASHA IN JERUSALEM

Yassin Pasha El Hashemi, leader of the Opposition in Iraq, has arrived in Jerusalem from Baghdad. Many local Arab leaders have called on the Pasha, who is on his way to Egypt for a few days and will return here later.

It is understood that Istaklalist leaders have conferred with Yassin Pasha concerning plans for the pan-Arab Congress which it is proposed to hold in Baghdad in February. Yassin Pasha's visit to Egypt is said to be connected with the proposed meeting.

MARCHIONESS MILFORD HAVEN AND LADY LOUIS MOUNTBATTEN

Flying Visit To Jerusalem

The Marchioness Milford Haven and Lady Louis Mountbatten paid a a flying visit to Jerusalem on Tuesday before sailing for Cyprus from Haifa last night.

Arriving by air at Ramleh from Syria, the unwearied travellers continued to Jerusalem, where they stayed only long enough to arrange for their journey to the island.

MR. BENTWICH RETURNS

Mr. Norman Bentwich returned to Jerusalem yesterday, in time for the Hebrew University semester and his lectures on Mount Scopus.

THE PALESTINE POST

INCORPORATING The Palestine Bulletin

Telephone Numbers 733 & 734

ol. IX. No. 2343. JERUSALEM, TUESDAY, JANUARY 31, 1933 (Sh'vat 4, 5693 — Shawwal 4, 1351.) Price: 10 Mils.

HERR HITLER NEW GERMAN CHANCELLOR

LACK OF PARLIAMENTARY MAJORITY CAUSES APPOINTMENT OF NAZI CHIEF

The New Cabinet Confirmed

Berlin, Monday.— Following a conference of President von Hindenburg, Dr. Alfred Hugenberg, Adolf Hitler, and Fritz von Papen, Hitler was appointed Chancellor of Germany, von Papen declaring that the formation of a government on the basis of a parliamentary majority was impossible.

It is expected in political circles that Hitler will be given the authority to dissolve the Reichstag and set new elections. The new Cabinet is composed of Herr Frick, Minister of Interior, von Neurath, Minister of Foreign Affairs, Seldte (president of the Stahlhelm,) Minister of Labour, and Dr. Hugenberg, Minister of Economics and Agriculture.

All ministerial appointments have been confirmed. Von Papen has been appointed Reichscommissioner of Prussia, and Count Schwerin von Krosigk, Minister of Finance.

Reuter/P.T.A.

Former German Colonies in Africa

Herr Lindequist on the Way to Capetown

London, Sunday. — Herr von Lindequist declares that there is no political significance to be attached to his African visit.

Interviewed by Reuter aboard the Watussi he said that he was going to see old friends in old places. "I do not even know", he added, "how long I shall be there. It may be two months but the trip is a private affair."

Rotterdam, Saturday.— Herr Lindequist, the former German Governor of South West Africa, who is the leader of a movement in Germany for the return of the former German Colonies in Africa, is a passenger aboard the Watussi for Capetown.

He proposes to visit South West Africa and Tanganyika. He resolutely declined to interview Reuter's correspondent, who was not even allowed on board the Watussi. Reuter/P.T.A.

FIRST TURKISH EXPOSITION

The Turkish Ministry of Economy and Finance is occupied now with the preparation and construction of an exposition in Angora in which the minor powers of Europe and the Balkan states are expected to take part.

De Lodier Heads French Cabinet

LEFT WING RADICAL ACCEPTS PREMIERSHIP

Paris, Monday. — Despite the first report stating that he had reserved his reply, which is the usual procedure in such circumstances, M. de Lodier, left wing Radical, who was Minister of War in the Boncour cabinet, has definitely accepted the French premiership.

M. de Lodier, in a statement to the press, declared that he was quite aware of the difficulties of the moment, but believed that their solution was only a question of determination and energy.

Reuter/P.T.A.

Lancashire Cotton

MANCHESTER GUARDIAN ON EXPLOITATION

London, Sunday. — Commenting on the Manchester Chamber of Commerce report, the Manchester Guardian says that the Chamber will only have itself to blame if its word are used to foment Nationalist feeling and to prove that Lancashire is ready for selfish interests to go to the lengths of wrecking the Government's schemes for Indian self-government.

The words of the Chamber's report may be taken to imply that Lancashire is not content with the method of friendly negotiation begun at Ottawa, which bore fruit in preference for Lancashire, but insists that her right to exploit the Indian market is superior to the rights of the Indian Legislature.

Why do not the directors of the Chamber, asks the journal, admit and make the best of the fact that the day has gone when Westminster can dictate what India buys.

Reuter/P.T.A.

PACIFIST ACQUITTED BY FRENCH COURT

Paris, Saturday. — The French Military Court has acquitted the radical pacifist, M. Gilbeaux, of the charges of having spread anti-French propaganda in other countries, and of having inflicted ill-treatment on French subjects when they were in Russia. M. Gilbeaux, who is an ex-officer, a veteran of the French delegation sent to Russia during the war, has since become a bolshevist. In 1919 he was condemned to death for desertion. Since then, he has lived in exile. He had only recently returned to France, to ask a rehearing of his trial. B.P.O.

AUSTRALIAN TENNIS CHAMPIONSHIP

Melbourne, Sunday. — Australian Tennis Championships. Semi-finals— Gledhill beat McGrath 6/4, 6/1 6/1. Crawford and Moon beat Allison and Van Ryn 10/8, 6/3, 6/4. Vines and Gledhill beat Cummings and Hassett 6/2, 6/3, 7/5. Reuter/P.T.A.

INTERNATIONAL SOCCER

Glasgow, Sunday. — Amateur International Soccer. Scotland beat Ireland by six goals to nil.
Reuter/P.T.A.

THE COMING WASHINGTON MEETING

STATEMENT BY MR. ROOSEVELT AND BRITISH AMBASSADOR

Preliminary Understanding

New York, Monday.— Mr. Franklin D. Roosevelt and Sir Ronald Lindsay, British Ambassador in Washington, after a conference, issued a joint statement to the effect that they had conversed satisfactorily concerning tentative arrangements for the meeting with British and other representatives in Washington, which they hoped to begin early in March. Newspapers are of the opinion that Mr. Roosevelt wants to reach a preliminary debt understanding with Britain on the same pattern as the Hoover-MacDonald naval parity agreement.

Reuter/P.T.A.

RAISING WHOLESALE COMMODITY PRICES

U. S. A. and Britain Cooperating

London, Monday (B.O.W.P.)— Sir Robert Horne, a former Chancellor of the Exchequer, in a broadcast speech to the United States last night, said that the British Government had declared its intention to employ all legitimate measures to raise wholesale commodity prices. For, as he could judge, the policy of United States has been directed to the same object. The joint declaration by America and Great Britain that such was their object and that the monetary policy would be designed to that end would of itself start and stimulate the movement in the desired direction.

FOG FOLLOWS FROST IN ENGLAND

Royalty Enjoy Skating

London, Monday (B.O.W.P.)— There was a general thaw throughout Great Britain yesterday, although in some parts it was still possible to skate, and today the frost was succeeded by fog locally.

The Prince of Wales and the Duke of York enjoyed about an hour of skating on Virgina water, Windsor Great Park, on Saturday. They moved freely with hundreds of skaters on the ice which was in an excellent condition. The Prince again watched skating on lake yesterday but did not participate.

ABYSSINIAN EMPEROR AT ADEN

Aden, Saturday. — A great welcome was accorded to Haile Salassie, Emperor of Abyssinia, on his arrival here on board the British sloop Penzance on a brief private visit.

The Emperor, who will visit points of interest in Aden, will leave to-morrow evening on board the Penzance for Djibouti.

Reuter/P.T.A.

Removal of Irish Partition Urged

DE VALERA DISCUSSES ANGLO-IRISH PEACE

Mr. De Valera, interviewed by Reuter, said that the removal of the partition of Ireland was a necessary preliminary to the establishment of true and lasting peace between Ireland and Great Britain. Nevertheless, there would have to be a different temper before proposals were made to the six Northern counties.

Reuter/P.T.A.

Settling the Oil Dispute

UNDERSTANDING REACHED

Geneva, Monday.— It is reported that M. Benes has reached a basis of understanding with both parties in the Anglo-Persian dispute. It is understood that an agreement has been submitted to the two governments, and if they confirm it, the Council of the League will merely have to give its benediction to the arrangement. Reuter/P.T.A.

LADY BAILEY MISSING

London, Monday (B.O.W.P.)— No news has been received of Lady Bailey since early on Saturday. She left San Xavied on the South Coast of Spain, bound for Paris.

GALSWORTHY NOT BETTER

London, Monday (B.O.W.P.)— Mr. John Galsworthy, the famous novelist, who from some weeks has been seriously ill, was reported to be not quite so well this morning following a restless night.

PROGRESS OF HAIFA LAST YEAR

CITY'S PROSPERITY UNAFFECTED BY HARD TIMES

Chamber of Commerce Report

Haifa, Monday.— The world crisis which reached its peak in 1931 although it showed signs of mitigation in 1932, is still sowing its seed of economic evil, Mr. Nathanson, Chairman of the Jewish Chamber of Commerce of Haifa, declared in opening the annual meeting at the Anglo-Palestine Bank last night. His report contained a review of economic conditions in the world in general and in Palestine in particular. The export trade of most countries is still on the downgrade, said Mr. Nathanson, budgets of various governments still show huge deficits, and the world-wide problem of unemployment remains as yet unsolved. Instability of currency, insecurity of stocks and bonds, inability to pay debts, whether national or international, all these circumstances characterise the condition of the world at large today.

In Palestine, however, the reverse is true. Foreign trade is on the increase, the government treasury shows a large surplus and unemployment is at a minimum, despite the constant growth of the population caused by the large influx of immigrants during the past year. Foreign capital has also been streaming into the country, a sign of confidence in the economic future of Palestine.

(Continued on page 5.)

Centenary Of Gordon's Birth

SERVICE IN ST. PAUL'S

London, Saturday. — The base of the statue of General Gordon in Trafalgar Square was decked with flowers to-day on the occasion of the centenary of Gordon's birth.

A special memorial service was held in St. Paul's Cathedral, the congregation including the Duke and Duchess of York, officers and men of the Royal Engineers, Chelsea Pensioners, and several officers and men who served in the relief expedition to Khartoum in 1884-1885. Reuter/P.T.A.

GENERAL WHO FOUGHT WITH BIBLE AND SWORD

Men who took part in the relief expedition to Khartoum in 1885, when British troops fought their way into the town only to find that General Gordon had been killed by the Mahdi after a siege of 317 days, took part in the celebrations of the centenary of Gordon's birth.

They were among the members of the Old Comrades' Association of the Royal Engineers, the corps in which Gordon served for 30 years, who paraded in Trafalgar square on January 28.

Chelsea pensioners and boys from the Gordon Home took part in the centenary celebration and in the evening General Sir Bindon Blood, senior colonel commandant of the R.E.'s, broadcast an appreciation of Gordon, whom he knew in the sixties.

Few events created such a sensation in the England of the last century as the death of Gordon. Gordon, the soldier who fought "with a sword in one hand and a Bible in the other" had won a great hold on the affections of the public and the progress of the expedition for his relief had been followed with the deepest interest.

"Chinese" Gordon was one of the most romantic figures in the annals of British military history. He served against the Chinese in the war of 1860-2 and was subsequently made a commander of their forces and a first class mandarin.

Disgusted, however, by their breach of faith in executing captured rebel leaders, he refused the gifts and honours offered him by the Emperor of China.

His great work was the abolition of the slave trade in the Sudan and it was there that he met his death, at the early age of 51, while the relief expedition was hurrying to his aid.

THE PALESTINE POST

INCORPORATING The Palestine Bulletin

There will be no issue of The Palestine Post to-morrow, the first day of Passover.

Vol. IX. No. 2401 JERUSALEM, MONDAY, APRIL 10, 1933. (Nissan 14, 5693 — Zu (al) l Haj 14, 1351.) Price: 10 Mils

BRITONS' TRIAL IN MOSCOW

RUSSIAN COUNSEL ONLY

Hearing To Begin Wednesday

Five of the six accused Englishmen in Moscow met the Presidium of the Collegium of Defenders on Saturday (according to the British Official Wireless) and provisionally selected counsel to conduct their defence in the trial on the various charges of sabotage and espionage, which is fixed to open on Wednesday.

M. Komadov was appointed as counsel for Monkhouse, M. Bruade for Thornton, M. Lidov for Cushny, and M. Dolmatovski for Nordwall and Gregory. The sixth Englishman, Macdonald, is still in custody but counsel has not yet been allotted him. The British Charge d'Affaires, Mr. Strang arranged to visit him on Saturday evening.

Mr. Robert Turner, legal adviser to Metro-Vickers, has proceeded to Moscow to attend the trial on Wednesday, says Reuter.

The reply given by M. Litvinoff to the effect that a British lawyer might attend the trial as a spectator is regarded as unsatisfactory, and efforts will continue to be made to persuade the Soviet to allow the engineers to have the advice and assistance of British lawyers at the Supreme Court trial.

Sir Austen Chamberlain's Speech

Sir Austen Chamberlain, in a speech at Birmingham on Friday night (continues the Wireless Press) referring to the Moscow arrests said he hoped the strong feeling expressed during the debate in the House of Commons had brought home to the Soviet Government the condition on which alone it was possible to maintain friendly relations or for British citizens to trade with them and so contribute to their prosperity and development as well as that of Great Britain.

BILL TO BAR SOVIET IMPORTS

British Measure To Help Engineers In Russia

London, Friday. — The House of Commons passed the third reading of the Russian imports bill by 291 votes to 41.

The Liberals voted for the bill on the Government assurance that the provisions would be limited to three months as proof that they would not be applied except in connection with the arrested British engineers.

Sir John Simon, winding up the debate, hoped that the bill would never be used, but that, he said, rested with the Soviet authorities.

In response to Sir Austen Chamberlain, Sir Herbert Samuel, and others, Mr. Walter Runciman said he understood that the powers under the bill would only be exercised in connection with the perilous situation of the arrested Metro-Vickers employees in Moscow.

SHUTTING DOWN OIL WELLS

The Railroad Commission has ordered ten thousand oil wells in the East Texas oilfields to close down for five days, says Reuter.

Spirit of Germany

Sir Austen Chamberlain's Denunciation

Racial and Religious Proscription

Alluding to the situation in Germany during his Birmingham address on Friday night, Sir Austen Chamberlain, Chancellor of the Exchequer, said that the utterances of men in authority there had "revived the spirit we hoped had departed from the world," states a B.O.W.P. message.

"It has shocked other nations to see the embers of religious persecution stirring again, and to hear talk of the religious or racial proscription of a great section of the German people," he said.

He asked the German Government to consider the impression their attitude must give to the world.

"Germany," he declared, "had met her fate."

"In her overweening pride and egocentric vanity, she was not willing to allow other people to live as they wished.

"She was determined to dominate and impose her will on the rest of the world.

"We see the same spirit kindling again in her internal affairs, and this at a time when Germany is demanding equality of rights and status at the Disarmament Conference."

Referring to Germany's demands for a revision of the Treaty of Versailles, Sir Austen said,

"Before we can accede to any demands for treaty revision, we must be quite certain that the domineering spirit has departed from Germany.

"Before we can return Germany's equality of armament, we must be certain that they seek that equality for their own security and to maintain peace, and not to threaten the security of other nations."

Jews Barred from Medical Schools

Munich, Saturday.— As a result of the tremendous number of doctors in Germany, enough, it is estimated, to meet any demands for the next nine years, the Reichscommissioner of the Bavarian Ministry of Interior has issued an order limiting the number of medical students to be admitted to the Munich Medical School next term to 345; to the Wurzburg School, 130; and to the Erlanger School, 98.

No Jewish students will be matriculated for the coming season. B.P.O.

"PURGING" THE CIVIL SERVICE

Berlin, Saturday.— The Cabinet to-day approved a law stipulating that all civil service employees appointed since November, 1918, without taking qualifying examinations, may be summarily dismissed. B.P.O.

German Political Violence

WOMAN SOCIALIST BEATEN

The Times has received from a responsible correspondent in Germany the following fully authenticated case of political violence:—

I have seen at the St. Antonius Hospital in Karlshorst, Frau Marie Jankowski, aged 46, who was taken by men in Nazi uniform from her dwelling in Coepenick in the small hours of March 21, stripped and beaten.

Frau Jankowski said that she and her family were awakened by imperative shouts of "Police, open the door," accompanied by threats to shoot. On opening 14 men in Nazi uniform with carbines and revolvers entered and searched the flat and took her to Nazi premises in the Dorotheenstrasse. She was taken to a room where were other men in Nazi uniform — making about 20 in all. They showed her a Republican flag and invited her to call it a foul name, which she refused to do.

On this the leader ordered "20 strokes"; Frau Jankowski was laid over the table and stripped, and while one man held her head four others belaboured her with canes and sticks. This process was repeated four or five times — whenever she answered "No" to such questions as "How much salary do you get from the welfare department?" "Why did you harbour and feed Communists?" "Did you steal shoes from the unemployed?" "Did you prepare a boycott list of Nazi shops?" and so on.

Frau Jankowski, it should be explained, is a Socialist who has long been active in municipal and social work in Coepenick and was head of the local committee which decides applications for municipal relief. She claims to have been on the best of terms with other municipal and social workers, including Nazis, and did not know she had any enemies. She says she can only attribute her treatment to private grudges arising from the

(Continued on page 4.)

Rival Air Women

TWO GERMAN WOMEN FOR THE CAPE

The air woman Miss Elli Beinhorn who left on Thursday for the Cape via Abyssinia and East Africa, is flying in a specially constructed Heinkel, with a petrol supply sufficient for 1800 miles at an average speed of 124 miles an hour, according to a Reuter report from Berlin.

Miss Beinhorn's rival, Miss Von Etzdorg, is following her to South Africa as soon as her machine is ready.

FRENCH AVIATRIX IN INDO-CHINA

Paris, Saturday.— The French aviatrix, Maryse Hilsz, landed in Hanoe in Indo-China on Friday, having covered the distance between Paris and Hanoe in less than seven days. B.P.O.

A GIRL'S SOLO FLIGHT

London, Sunday.— Miss Jean Batten, twenty-three year old New Zealand aviatrix, hopped off from Lympne for Paris to-day on a solo flight to Australia. Reuter/P.T.A.

THE PALESTINE POST WILL NOT BE PUBLISHED TO-MORROW, THE FIRST DAY OF PASSOVER.

COLONIAL SECRETARY AND JERUSALEM WATER FAMINE

The Palestine Post understands that one of the urgent questions to be considered during the visit this week of the Secretary of State for the Colonies will be the problem of the Jerusalem Water Supply.

It is believed in well-informed quarters that Sir Philip Cunliffe-Lister may in all probability bring with him his decision on the big Auja scheme.

A long time must elapse, it is pointed out — at least eighteen months — between the start of the planned construction and the date on which the supply of water from this source will be available.

JERUSALEM TO SPEAK TO SYDNEY

THE PALESTINE POST AND THE SUNDAY SUN

Perhaps the first unofficial radiotelephone conversation between Palestine and Australia will be held on Thursday morning, when the editor of The Palestine Post will speak to the editor of the Sunday Sun in Sydney, at the request of the Australian contemporary.

Arrangements are being made for messages from heads of the leading Christian denominations to be sent in the course of this radiotelephone communication on "Easter Eve in Jerusalem."

The first telephone communication on Friday between Palestine and France was from the French Consulate General when Vicomte and Vicomtesse d'Aumale, spoke from the French Consulate to their family in Paris. The conversation, we are informed, went through without a hitch.

DR. WEIZMANN AND THE SHEIKHS

MEETING OF TRANS-JORDAN AND ZIONIST LEADERS

Dr. Arlosoroff, on behalf of the Jewish Agency executive, on Saturday afternoon entertained at the King David Hotel a number of paramount sheikhs and other leaders of Trans-Jordan at a lunch in honour of Dr. Weizmann, in response to a wish previously expressed by the Tras-Jordanians to make the acquaintance of the Zionist leader.

The guests from Trans-Jordan included Mithgal Pasha al Faiz, (head of the Beni Sakher tribes), Rafifan Pasha (head of the Majal tribes, and member of the Legislative Council), Rashid Pasha (Sheikh of Jebal al Ajlun), Salim Pasha (Sheikh of the Belka tribes), Shamsaddim (a Circassian leader) and Zarikat Pasha (leader of Christians in Trans-Jordan and member of the Legislative Council).

In addition to Dr. Weizmann there were present the members of the executives of the Jewish Agency and of the General Jewish Council.

On the part of both the hosts and the guests great satisfaction was expressed at the changed conditions which made it possible for this meeting to take place. It was primarily due, Dr. Arlosoroff remarked, to the courage of Mithgal Pasha that such a meeting, unprecedented in Palestine-Trans-Jordan history, had been effected.

The feeling expressed by the Trans-Jordan leaders was that hope of developing their country lay in co-operation with Jews. Those attending this function were prepared to extend the Jews a warm welcome, and they were certain this was true of all classes in Trans-Jordan who had the interests of their country at heart.

Dr. Weizmann—whose knowledge of Trans-Jordan dates back to 1918, when in the company of Major Ormsby Gore, he travelled six days and five nights on horseback from Jerusalem to reach the camp of Emir Feisal (now King of Iraq) — recalled that in 1931 he had hoped to meet representative leaders of Trans-Jordan on their own ground and that a meeting had been arranged by their ruler which, owing to circumstances beyond the control of either party, had been postponed. He was naturally delighted that in these two years a change had occurred which facilitated the meeting of people interested in the development of both sides of the Jordan.

The sense of the occasion was expressed by Dr. Weizmann, when he graphically described this as the beginning of a tunnel being dug from both sides, with the working parties destined soon to meet.

Dr. Arlosoroff said that this represented a landmark in the efforts on both sides towards a co-operation of the Jewish and Arab forces of Trans-and Cis-Jordan.

Mr. Emanuel Neumann, of the Jewish Agency Executive, paid a tribute to Dr. Weizmann as the first to entertain the principle of Arab-Jewish co-operation, and to Dr. Arlosoroff for the work he has done in that direction. He said that during the comparatively short time he has spent here, he had been convinced that this was the only road along which the good of both countries would be served.

THE "NEOPOST"

"ALL BRITISH"

THE PALESTINE POST

Vol. IX. No. 2565. JERUSALEM, SUNDAY, OCTOBER 29, 1933.　　(Hshvan 9, 5694 — Ragha'b 11, 1352.)　　Price: 10 Mils.

ROYAL PLOT IN AUSTRIA

SENSATIONAL DISCOVERY IN RAID ON PRINCES' CASTLE

Vienna, Saturday.— A sensational discovery, which is alleged to connect German princes with the recent attempt on the life of Herr Dollfuss, the Chancellor, was made this afternoon in a raid on the Castle of Princes Rainer and Ernst of Sachsen-Coburg-Gotha, at Schladning, Styria, and the residence of Dr. Guenther, the stepfather of Herr Dollfuss. The assailant is stated to be Rudolf Dertil.

A letter has been found from Rudolf Dertil's brother Kurt begging for financial support, the purpose of which is not clear.

Kurt Dertil has been arrested. Two distant relatives of Hitler's are among others arrested on the charge of alleged connivance.

Reuter/PTA.

FRENCH CABINET FORMED

Paris, Friday.— The Cabinet has been composed as follows:—
Premier and Minister of Marine, M. Sarraut.
Foreign Affairs, M. Paul Boncour.
Interior, M. Chautemps.
War, M. Daladier.
Finance, M. Bonnet.
Budget, M. Abel Gardey.
Agriculture, M. Queuille.
Commerce, M. Laurent-Eynac.
Public Works, M. Paganon.
Labour, M. Frot.
Education, M. De Monzie.
Colonies, M. Pietri.
Air, M. Pierre Cot.
Justice, M. Dalamier.
Merchant Marine, M. Jacques Stern.
Health, M. Lisbonne.
The Cabinet is mainly Radical with slight extensions to either wing.
Reuter.

KING'S CHRISTMAS BROADCAST

London, Saturday.— His Majesty the King will broadcast a Christmas message again this year.
Reuter P.T.A.

NAZIS CHARGE BRITISH JOURNALIST

"DAILY EXPRESS" CORRESPONDENT TO BE TRIED FOR TREASON

London, Friday. (BOWP.) — The British Consul-General in Munich, Mr. Gainer, who since Tuesday has been denied access to Mr. Noel Panter, the Munich Correspondent of the "Daily Telegraph," was to-day permitted to visit him at Munich Police Headquarters where he has been held under "protective custody."

Panter is to be charged at Leipzig under Article 92 of the penal code with high treason and espionage the penalty for which is death or penal servitude for life. It is assumed that Panter's arrest is in connection with his descriptive report reproduced in last Monday's "Daily Telegraph" of the parade of storm troops which Chancellor Hitler addressed at Kelheim on Sunday. The German journalist Herr Ackermann has been arrested on a similar charge.

Article 92 of the criminal code provides for punishment by penal servitude for not less than two years of

(Continued on page 4, col. 1.)

ALARM AT LORD RATENDONE'S HOME

London, Friday. The police are investigating a mysterious occurrence at the house in Victoria Square of Viscount Ratendone, the Viceroy's heir, who it is understood will be leaving for India on Monday.

Lord Ratendone's neighbour, Miss Dorota Flattau, the novelist, was giving a party. She went to her study, heard a noise outside the window, and on investigating saw a man, whom she describes as an "Indian" crouching on a flat roof outside Lord Ratendone's bathroom with an eighteen inch curved knife in his hand. She challenged him and he threatened her, whereupon she threw a flower-pot at him and called the police.

A thorough search was made and the knife was found; also some lead piping which the intruder threw at Miss Flattau. Lord Ratendone was not at home at the time.

The police state that "there is no question of any attempt on Lord Ratendone."

After exhaustive inquiries the police no longer entertain the theory of an Indian or coloured man being concerned in the alarm raised at Victoria Square.

PALESTINE POST EXTRA

ORTHODOX JEWS' PROTEST

A delegation of Orthodox Jews who grouped themselves at the door of the pressroom in the Hassolel Building last Friday afternoon and protested against work being done on Sabbath eve, contributed to the difficulties of the Palestine Post in issuing the Government bulletin regarding the situation in Jaffa. They were dispersed by police whom it was necessary to summon to allow the bulletin to be printed.

The cries of the protestors which became uncontrolled as they asked that the publishers should "Have pity on Jerusalem," attracted crowds of passers by to the scene. The necessity for issuing the bulletin in order to quiet the exaggerated rumours which were rife in the city.

was explained to the delegation who would not desist from the demonstration.

The Bulletin, it is believed, had a quieting effect on the population of this city which had received no other reliable news.

We appreciate the comments received, of which the following is one.

Jerusalem, Oct. 27, 1933.

Dear Editor,

Congratulations and appreciation for your prompt issue of the Extra on Friday and thereby relieving an anxious public regarding the result of the demonstration in Jaffa.

A Reader.

ARAB DEMONSTRATIONS CAUSE MANY FATALITIES

Violence And Bloodshed In Jaffa, Haifa, Nablus

DEATH TOLL MAY MOUNT TO FIFTEEN

For about a fortnight the seed of sedition was recklessly sown by the Arab leadership in this country and on Friday the crop of violence and bloodshed was reaped in Jaffa.

Friday's official death toll for Jaffa is one policeman and ten rioters. The number of seriously injured is two policemen and twenty rioters.

These figures are not claimed to be complete, and if to Friday's fatalities and grave injuries in Jaffa are added the gravely and dangerously wounded in Haifa and Nablus, in the former both Friday and yesterday, in the latter on Friday only, the number of killed may well mount to fifteen, with the fate of the injured still in the lap of the gods.

Of the police, at least one other was known to have succumbed in Jaffa on Friday, and the Haifa communique tells of a constable dangerously stabbed yesterday.

A fully authenticated account of what happened in Jaffa may not be had for some time. The police authorities have been far too preoccupied with the situation to take time to prepare a comprehensive report. But what happened in Jaffa had its repercussion elsewhere and, fortified by exaggerations of fatalities which are serious enough without them, the mobs in other places created situations which only the prompt action of the police prevented from becoming as critical as was that at Jaffa.

There have been attacks on police stations at Nablus and Haifa, and attacks on the railway station and trains at Haifa. The attacks have been repulsed not without loss of life and limb, and no serious trouble is reported from other centres.

In Jaffa it was the expected that happened. The official statement which "The Palestine Post" late on Friday afternoon printed in an extra edition, and which appears in this issue, gives the report which we are able to supplement from eye-witnesses' accounts.

A crowd began collecting in and near the Great Mosque in the neighbourhood of the Government Offices at an early hour. By eleven o'clock the mob numbered several thousand. Foot and mounted police were on duty in considerable numbers, with the military in reserve. Access to Government Offices was blocked by barbed wire. The arrival from Jerusalem of a number of women to join in the demonstration caused a disorderly demonstration among the crowd. Police were sent to disperse it, and one constable (No. 870), either was dragged from his horse, or the animal tripped and the rider was thrown. The constable was set upon by the crowd and severely beaten. At this point the first baton charge was made.

At mid-day, it is understood, Mr. Pollock, the Assistant District Commissioner, accompanied by the District Officer, Azmi Eff. Nashashibi, called at the meeting place of the Arab Executive Committee and delivered what was meant to be a final warning, that if the crowd did not disperse quietly, force would be used to disperse them. A large number of the members of the Committee were in conference, but the warning evidently fell on deaf ears, as did the High Commissioner's reminder last Wednesday of "their responsibility as leaders if they did not take all possible measures to stop action which might lead to conflict with the police."

It is believed that following Mr. Pollock's warning, counsel among the Committee became divided.

Whereas the Jaffa people were inclined to do what they could to call off, or at least limit, the demonstration, the Jerusalem agitators insisted on the original plan being carried out.

At 12.30 the crowd poured out of the Mosque, Arab Executive members, the committee of the youth associations and the boatmen, some carrying their oars, in the lead. The crowd formed into what was intended to be two processions — one by way of Salahi Road and Suq el Der to King George's Boulevard, the other through Manshieh. The crowds were ordered to disperse. The mob replied by hurling stones and by

(Continued on page 5.)

POLISH PRESIDENT AND PALESTINE

Warsaw, Saturday.— President Moscicki received Deputy Gruenbaum today and discussed with him the Palestine question, prior to his departure for Palestine as member of the Jewish Agency. The President showed great understanding and sympathy.
PTA.

NO ADVANCE OR NO RETREAT IN NAZI TREATMENT OF JEWS

Berlin, Saturday.— Herr Goebbels, addressing a meeting at Dresden last night, declared that they would not advance but neither would they retreat, with regard to the Jewish question.
PTA.

OFFICIAL STATEMENTS

The first official statement was issued on Friday evening just before sundown as follows:

The Arab Executive Committee announced their intention of holding on Friday, October 27, a political demonstration in Jaffa, similar to that which was disallowed in Jerusalem on October 13. The High Commissioner received the President and members of the Arab Executive on October 25 and informed them that no political procession or demonstration would be allowed in Jaffa; but that members of the Executive would be permitted to proceed to the District Offices and there hand a written protest or manifesto for transmission to His Excellency.

In spite, however, of the High Commissioner's prohibition a procession was formed today at 12.30 p.m. in the neighbourhood of the Government Offices, Jaffa, which moved towards King George Avenue. The procession was ordered to disperse but disobeyed the injunction and assaulted the Police. The Police were compelled to make baton charges, to disperse the mob, who, however, re-formed and again attacked the Police. Shots were fired from the street at the Police, who were compelled in self-protection, to fire a few rounds under control.

By 2 p.m. the rioters had been dispersed by the Police and quiet restored in Jaffa.

All reports show that the Police throughout acted with the greatest control and forebearance.

The Military were not called upon to intervene, as the Police had the situation in hand.

One member of the Police and 3 rioters were killed, and 7 other rioters were reported to be killed.

Two of the Police suffered serious injuries.

The estimated number of rioters seriously wounded is 20. The injured are receiving medical attention.

A large number of arrests have been made.

Complete quiet prevailed throughout Palestine, with the exception of Jaffa.

We understand that curfew has been declared in the Jaffa-Tel Aviv district from 6 p.m. to 5 a.m.

The second communique was issued at noon yesterday as follows:

At about 6 p.m. Friday night a riotous crowd gathered at Nablus

(Continued on page 4, col. 4.)

FEATURED IN LONDON NEWS

London, Saturday.— The reports of unrest in Palestine were most prominently featured in the morning and afternoon issues of the entire London Press, without comment.

A Colonial Office statement says that "the Police throughout acted with the greatest control and forebearance."
PTA.

THE PALESTINE POST

Vol. IX. No. 2566. JERUSALEM, MONDAY, OCTOBER 30, 1933. (Heshvan 10, 5694 — Ragha'b 12, 1352.) Price: 10 Mils.

HE DOLLAR AND STERLING

/ARNING AGAINST DEPRECIATION WAR

New York, Saturday. — A warn- g against a sterling-dollar depre- ation war, which, he said, would ompt Great Britain to do some- ing to defend her trading posi- n was given by Sir Robert Horne a speech here in which he dis- ssed the N.I.R.A. gold scheme. He suggested an informal under- anding with a view to limiting e disparity between the two cur- ncies.

President Roosevelt is inquiring to the question of speculation on e stock and grain exchanges, ap- rently for the purpose of curb- g the wide price fluctuations. It known that President Roosevet preparing to ask Congress for gislation extending the Govern- ent supervision over the New rk exchange. Reuter

MERICA'S GOLD PURCHASES

econstruction Finance Corporation Debentures

Washington, Friday.— Gold will purchased by means of Re- nstruction Finance Corporation bentures, for which it is under- ood there is ready cash in the arket. The debentures will pay terest at one quarter of one per nt and they will be sold to the neral public. Officials are un- le to state how gold transactions ll be executed.

The dollar price of 31.36 is equi- lent to £6. 12. 2 1/2 at the pre- vailing rate of exchange. The ice of gold in London this morn- g was £6 10. 1, including a pre- um of eleven pence over the anc exchange. Reuter.

WASHINGTON DEBT TALKS

Washington, Saturday. — Sir rederick Leith Ross denies the re- orts that the Anglo-American ebt negotiations are making no ogress. Reuter.

CUBAN CABINET RESIGNS

TEN REDS KILLED IN FIGHT IN CUBAN MILL

Havana, Saturday.—At least ten ommunist workers were killed, venty were wounded and three undred arrested during fighting hich occurred in the American wned Jaronu sugar mill in Cama- ey. Reuter.

New York, October 29—Accord- g to the latest Press despatches om Havana, a bomb exploded last ight in the residence of Don Carlos endietta, the leader of the National t Party, destroying part of the uilding, but there were no casualties.

A number of disorders also broke ut in various parts of the city, but he Police finally succeeded in dis- ersing the mob, making about 400 rrests, the greater part of whom are eported to be Communists.

An Associated Press message re- eived later states that the members

(Continued on page 5)

Jewish Immigration Defended

LONDON CONFERENCE FOR RELIEF OF GERMAN JEWISH REFUGEES

London, Sunday. — One hundred delegates of forty-five organisations attended the Conference in London to-day for the relief of German-Jewish refugees.

Mr. Neville Laski, K.C., President of the Board of Jewish Deputies, who presided, stated that the number of refugees are estimated at 65,000, of which 33,000 were business or professional men, with 30,000 dependent women and children, and 2,000 students.

Of the total, 25,000 were in France, and 8,000 of these who were entirely without means, were being supported by the refugee committees.

Palestine was the most suitable country for Jewish immigration, but Palestine alone would not suffice. He hoped that with the help of the good offices of the High Commissioner for German Refugees other countries might be persuaded to admit German Jews.

Mr. Laski revealed that so far £525,000 had been collected for refugees the world over. He insisted that the Conference will deal only with the problem of relief, which is bound to be opposed by various delegations who demand political action including a boycott.

Dr. Chaim Weizmann addressing the opening declared that the present demonstrations in Palestine were unjustified. The Government of Palestine had erred on the side of overcaution in its immigration policy. The country was not being swamped by undesirable immigrants, but its present rate of development had no parallel in the economic history of the world.

The Arab population had largely increased, especially in those districts adjoining Jewish areas of settlement. He hoped the time was approaching when Palestine would be the common country of both races. PTA.

GENEVA AND THE RIOTS

HOW THEY MIGHT HAVE BEEN AVERTED

Geneva, Sunday. — If the ringleaders of the immigration protest in Palestine had been arrested before the demonstrations, it would have been possible to prevent the disturbances. This is the private opinion in the circles of the Permanent Mandates Commission, where it is thought that if arrests had been made instead of warnings being given, bloodshed would have been averted.

The Mandatory Commission now in session will not discuss the present events in Palestine until the report from the Mandatory has been submitted. — PTA.

NAZIS CAUSED DISTURBANCE

German Leader's Boast

Berlin, Sunday. — The Palestine disturbances are a result of the Nazi agitation, is the boast made by the Nazi leader Schoppman while addressing a mass meeting at Coepenick.

The Nazi press generally reports the events in Palestine without comment. with the exception of the "Angriff"

Third Day Of Arab Strike

LEADERS REMANDED AT ACRE

ARABS OF JAFFA TO SUBMIT PROTEST

Mr. I. N. Camp, Land Settlement Officer, sitting as magistrate in Acre, yesterday remanded the Arab leaders who were arrested in Jaffa on Friday. for fifteen days. The detained men include Auni Bey Abdul Hadi, an outstanding Istiklalist, who had proposed to proceed to Geneva to press the Arab case. Among the prisoners is also the Secretary of the Arab Executive, Jamil Eff. Husseini, who is a nephew of Musa Kazim Pasha and cousin to Haj Amin, the Chief Mufti of Palestine, who is still in India.

Whether they will be charged with belonging to an illegal assembly and leading the riot, or the much more serious offence of endeavouring "by armed force or show of armed force to procure an alteration in the Government or law" could not be ascertained.

The prisoners are:

Jamal Al Husseini, Auni Bey Abdul Hadi, Salim Abdul Rahman, Abdul Ghani Ahmad, Tawfik Abdul Razak, Yakoob El Ghussein, Edmond Roch, Talib Arida, Farid Eff. Fakr Al Din, Nimr el Masri, Said Khalil, Mahmud Afghani, Zuhdi Salem Immam, Ghaz Karkur.

(From Our Correspondent)

Jaffa, Sunday. — At a meeting of Arab leaders here today at the office of Mohammed Abdul Rehin, it was decided to protest to the Palestine Government and to the League of Nations against the "cruelty" of the police here on Friday. A delegation is proceeding to Jerusalem tomorrow. It hopes to be received in order to present this protest.

The meeting also decided to call on the Mayor of Jaffa to voice his protest together with that the Mayors of other cities.

Boatmen's Strike

Owing to the strike of the boatmen two steamships, the "Vienna" and the "Sphinx", proceeded to Haifa without landing here. The "Vienna" disembarked passengers there while the "Sphinx" took on about 100 Jaffa passengers who went up to Haifa by rail.

CURFEW IN TEL AVIV

(From Our Correspondent)

Tel Aviv, Sunday. — Although the boatmen are on strike which means considerable dislocation of work at the port, and the majority of the shops in Jaffa are closed, little tension was felt in Jaffa during the day and no disturbance occurred anywhere.

Pickets, self-appointed or otherwise, went about the streets to make sure that no Arabs did business on their premises.

In Tel Aviv work is proceeding normally, as is also traffic. The liveliest concern is shown in developments outside Tel Aviv, and as a result there is very heavy pressure on the telephone service.

Government communiques and municipality bulletins are being eagerly devoured by large crowds. The curfew in Tel Aviv has led to the detention and payment of fines.

2 Dead, 17 Injured In Jerusalem Clashes

SCENE OF UNREST SHIFTED TO HOLY CITY

The following official communique, issued last night reported two fatalities and 17 other casualties as a result of sporadic outbreaks in Jerusalem, as follows:

All was quiet throughout Palestine during the night of the 28th and 29th (Saturday). The strike is general today throughout Palestine.

Shortly after noon a large crowd armed with sticks encountered a police patrol of 2 men at Bab el Silsileh in the old city. The patrol ordered them to disperse but they refused and attacked the patrol attempting to seize the rifle of one of the constables. The patrol had to fire ten rounds to save their lives and disperse the crowd. provised bombs were thrown at

Near Jaffa Gate stones and im the police.

At Damascus Gate the police were fired upon and two shots were fired by the Police at a man who was seen to be shooting at them with a revolver.

The casualties among the crowd in Jerusalem today were two killed and seventeen injured.

The city is now calm. No incident of importance has occurred in Trans-Jordan.

The centre of the disturbances which commenced with the riot in Jaffa on Friday, was diverted to Jerusalem yesterday. During Saturday night shots were heard near the outlying Jewish quarters and shots are reported to have been fired at the British Constables' camp on Mount Scopus. Two unexploded bombs are said to have been found in the Montefiore Quarter which were left by unknown persons.

Rendered idle by the three days' strike which the Arab Executive proclaimed on Friday, youths commenced early yesterday morning to go through the streets in the Old and New City to enforce the closing order on all Arab shopkeepers. No Jews were interfered with, although some took the precaution of not opening their premises.

Just before noon small bands of rioters became active simultaneously in different parts of the town, mainly in the neighbourhood of the city walls. There was an attack on the police at Damascus Gate, opposite which are the Government Offices.

An attempt was made to form a procession soon after mid-day from the Haram-es-Sherif. Those in the procession were evidently intent on breaking through a small police patrol near the Jews' Street. The patrol was attacked and a British non-commissioned officer opened fire on the advancing crowd, which resulted in a some casualties.

Stone throwing from cafes was frequent, also firing from revolvers and sniping. Last night's communique gives the results of the day's unrest.

With the Christian shops closed in observance of the Christian Sabbath, and the Jewish shops also closed because of the feeling of uneasiness, the streets leading to the Old City wore an unusually deserted air.

Fraternisation

The strike of Arab bus and cabmen resulted in a remarkable fraternisation of Arabs and Jews. Arabs were using the Jewish services freely and Arab fezes were prominent in the better-class Jewish cafes outside the Old City.

It was generally expected that the Government would announce a curfew in Jerusalem, as has been done in Jaffa and Haifa. The authorities evidently decided, however, to see first if this step was necessary.

The High Commissioner's interview on Saturday with Musa Kazim Pasha and five other Moslem and Christian Arabs, who were acting as deputies for the members of the Arab Executive who were prevented from being present through their detention in prison, did not indicate what the nature of the charge is likely to be.

"Down With The Effendis"

The funeral in Jaffa on Saturday of the eleven men killed in Friday's disturbances passed without incident. It is reported, however, that the wails of the bereaved women took on the cry of "Down with the Effendis who kill our men." This was directed at the leaders who had guaranteed that the police under no circumstances would use force to disperse the crowd.

The Arab press generally is restrained, though one paper demands that the death of the Arabs should be avenged on the Jews. The Jewish press has published the official communiques and accounts by eye-witnesses of the disturbance in Jaffa. "Davar", the Hebrew Labour daily, earnestly expressed the hope that the clash will not prove a setback to the efforts towards an Arab-Jewish understanding or the economic resilience which the country is at present experiencing.

Among the loiterers in the streets of Jerusalem and elsewhere may be seen numerous Bedouin from the Hauran and Trans-Jordan, who have probably been attracted by prospects of looting in the event of disturbances.

Communist circulars are making their appearance here and there, but it has not been possible to fix responsibility with regard to any outside influences behind the disturbances.

A number of communists, Arabs and Jews, have been arrested.

THE PALESTINE POST

Vol. X. No. 2809, JERUSALEM, FRIDAY, JULY 27, 1934.   Ab 15, 5694—Rabia Tani 17, 1353.   Price 10 Mils

Nazis Foiled in Austria

DOLLFUSS MURDERED — NEW PROVISIONAL CHANCELLOR — VIENNA CALM — MARTIAL LAW

BRITAIN AND ITALY BACKING AUSTRIA

STATEMENTS BY MR. BALDWIN AND SGR. MUSSOLINI

The sensational development of Tuesday's Nazi uprising in Vienna was the assassination of Dr. Englebert Dollfuss, the Chancellor, by a band of Nazis disguised as policemen, who broke into the Chancellery, seized Austria's Dictator and other hostages, and shot Dollfuss through the throat, according to Reuter messages. The Christian Socialist Government has remained in power, and Herr von Schusnigg was appointed Chancellor by President Miklas.

Major Fey, the Minister of Public Security, broadcast a strong statement in which he outlined the continuation of Dr. Dollfuss's policy and sternly announced that the most drastic measures would be taken against those who were trying to overthrow the present regime.

The Army has occupied Vienna, and martial law was declared on Tuesday afternoon. At Innsbruck, the Chief of Police was murdered by two Nazis, according to messages from another source.

All was quiet in Vienna yesterday and last evening, according to Reuter/PTA. cables. It was learned in well-informed circles that no change will be made in the Cabinet before the funeral of Dr. Dollfuss. In the meantime, President Miklas and Prince Von Starthemerg have returned.

The fact that Dollfuss was refused not only medical aid, but also the ministrations of a priest in his last moments, was revealed in a broadcast by the Federal Commissioner, Herr Adam, on Tuesday evening. He declared that the Chancellor died alone among his enemies.

Criminal Violence

"The disastrous events of to-day cannot be regarded as a revolt on a grand scale, but was just a piece of criminal violence carefully planned but nevertheless isolated," said the Commissioner.

Upon the return of President Miklas, he proceeded immediately to the Chancellery to pay his respect to the body of Dollfuss. It is officially announced that the revolt has been suppressed in all provinces except Styria, where rebels in some parts are still active are gradually surrendering.

Only 4 Killed

Only four persons were killed in Vienna besides Dr. Dollfuss. They are two policeman, an actor hit by a bullet when leaving the broadcasting Studio and a porter. The Nazi prisoners of yesterday's coup are being closely guarded. Dollfuss' supposed assailants isolated.

It is generally thought that the President will endeavour to form a new Government on a broader

New Elections

It is reported that elections may be held, as it is unlikely that a table government will be formed unless supported by the majority of the people.
Reuter/PTA.

It was at 11.30 a.m. that a band of 150 Nazis, disguised as policemen, broke into the Chancellery Palace, and seized the Chancellor and other Ministers who were at a special Cabinet meeting. These included Major Fey, the Minister of Public Security, and Herr Karwinsky, the Finance Minister. The Palace was surrounded by troops, who parleyed with the invaders for the release of the hostages. Dr. Dollfuss had already left the room in which the Cabinet meeting was being held, but he must have been shot almost immediately. Herr Fey was conducted by the Nazis to another room where Dollfuss was lying on the sofa, dying from a shot through the throat.

Broadcast Announcer Intimidated

It appears that the official announcer at the Broadcasting Station had a revolver placed at his head, a paper put before his eyes, and ordered to read out that the Government had resigned and Count von Rintelen had taken over power, says Reuter.

While on his death-bed, Dr. Dollfuss ordered that his resignation from the Chancellorship be communicated to the President. He then asked for a Catholic priest to give him absolution, after commending his family to the care of his friends.

Rebels Under Arrest

The fate of the 150 rebels who seized the Chancellery and the Radio Station is still uncertain, and they remain under-arrest. The Cabinet declares that those actually implicated in the murder of Dr. Dollfuss will be punished.

Dr. von Rintelen, who was in Vienna on a visit from Rome where he was Ambassador, was placed under arrest after being asked to attend the Cabinet meeting. He was known to have had strong Nazi sympathies. Later yesterday Rintelen was reported to have committed suicide in prison.

Starhemberg's Stand

Prince von Starhemberg, the young Vice-Chancellor, who flew from Venice to Rome by special aeroplane, might have been appointed the new Chancellor, except for his strong bid for Fascist control of Austria, according to Reuter.

New Chancellor

Upon the return of President Miklas to the capital, it was announced that Herr von Schusnigg, former Minister of Education, had been appointed Chancellor temporarily and taken charge of affairs. Thirty-nine years old, von Schusnigg is a staunch Catholic and an ardent Monarchist.

Vienna Held by Army

Vienna is strongly held by the Army, and martial law has been proclaimed throughout the country. The early morning marketcarts rumbled into the capital as usual yesterday morning, but sentries had been posted everywhere, and strong auxiliary forces of the Heimwehr and a number of postmen and civil servants were being raised.

Major Emil Fey spoke over the wireless on Tuesday evening, and reported the tragic death of Dollfuss. He stressed that the Government, which had been re-formed with the consent of the President, would follow the former policy of Dollfuss and would maintain a rigid regime, as well as impose drastic measures on those who tried to modify the completeness of Austrian independence.

Herr von Schusnigg called for worldwide support for Austria's political stabilisation. With greater force, he said, they would put up a memorial to Dollfuss by maintaining peace, security and culture, the three principles by which Austria had always lived. They, the followers of Dollfuss, had sworn fealty to him and would continue his policy for the regeneration of Austria and its rescue from the hands of its enemies.

Fighting the Nazis

A Government statement declares that any further Nazi insurrection and terrorism would be punished by the severest measures. Curfew has been declared.

(Continued on page 5.)

"LOOK AFTER MY FAMILY!"
Dollfuss' Last Messages

"Look after my family!" and "See that no blood is shed in Austria as a result of my death!" were the two death-bed messages whispered by Dollfuss to Major Fey who had been brought into the room where the Chancellor lay dying on a sofa. Fey was immediately taken out, and the 51-year old Dictator of Austria was left to die alone and unattended.

COMMONS HORROR-STRUCK

London, Thursday. — In the course of a statement on the Austrian situation made in the House of Commons to-day, Sir John Simon said that although Dr. Dollfuss lived for a considerable time after being shot twice at close quarters, he was allowed to bleed to death after being refused medical and spiritual aid.

British to Uphold Autonomy

Sir John said that the British attitude to uphold Austria's independence in accordance with the treaties signed was unchanged.

The members punctuated Simon's recital of the murder of Dr. Dollfuss with exclamations of horror.
Reuter/PTA.

CONDOLENCES IN LONDON
Call at Austrian Embassy

London, Thursday. — The flag was flying at half-mast over the Austrian Embassy here today. Mr. Stanley Baldwin, acting Premier, and Sir John Simon, Foreign Secretary, were among those who called at the Embassy to proffer their condolences. Messages of sympathy have been telegraphed by the British Government to Vienna.
W.

Italy and Austrian Situation

MUSSOLINI RETURNS TO ROME

Rome, Thursday.— Signor Mussolini returned by fast car from Rimini this morning, in order to consult his advisers regarding the situation in Austria.

Prior to leaving Riccione, where he had been awaiting the arrival of Herr Dollfuss at the end of this week, Mussolini declared that the independence of Austria, for which Dollfuss fell, was the principle which would continue to be defended by Italy still more energetically in these exceptionally difficult times.

In a telegram of condolence addressed to Prince von Starhemberg, the Vice-Chancellor, the Italian Dictator adds, "The death of Dr. Dollfuss causes me the deepest grief owing to our personal friendship and the community of our political views."
Reuter/PTA.

HITLER'S CONCERN
Possible Foreign Repercussions

Herr Hitler has arrived at Munich, and is believed to be perturbed over the possible repercussions abroad. The extremist Nazi papers express frank satisfaction. Baron von Neurath's telegram of condolence, however suggests a conflict of opinion in official Nazi circles, says a Reuter/PTA. cable from Berlin.

A Wireless message last night added that the German frontiers have been closed by order from Berlin.

TURKS ATTACK ITALIAN BOAT

MORE "FISHING" BOAT SHOOTING

Athens, July 25. — A telegram from Rhodes says that Turkish sentries fired on an Italian fishing boat off Anatolia, killing one of the crew. The boat was plying near the Italian island of Castelorizo and ran into a creek on the mainland to shelter from a strong wind.
Reuter.

Only last week, some officers of the British Navy were fired on off the Isle of Samos, while on a bathing expedition. One British officer was killed.

HITLER'S 'BLACK GUARDS' PROMOTED
Independent Organisation Honoured For June 30 Services

Berlin, July 25. — Herr Hitler has issued a decree raising the black-uniformed Nazi guards to the status of an independent organisation of the Nazi party, "in view of their great services in connection with the events of June 30".

Thus their leader Herr Himmler will be equal in rank to Herr Lutze and will be responsible only to Herr Hitler instead of as formerly to Herr Lutze. The status of both, becomes that of a Reich departments head.
Reuter.

70,000 JEWS LEFT GERMANY

Berlin, Thursday. — Seventy thousand Jews have left Germany since the advent of the Nazi Government, it is reported. The Jewish exodus is continuing unabated.
PTA.

JEWS SUFFERING IN DANZIG

Danzig, Thursday. — The Nazis are continuing their policy of eliminating Jews from economic life.

"FRANKFURTER ZEITUNG" ASKS FOR REVISION OF JEWISH POLICY

Berlin, Thursday. — The revision of the Jewish question is demanded in an editorial written in the "Frankfurter Zeitung" which states that German economics are not practicable while Jewish firms are not admitted in the labour market.
PTA.

CHANNEL FLOWN UPSIDE DOWN

London, July 24. — Flight Lieutenant Tyson celebrated the 25th anniversary of the first cross channel flight by today making the journey upside down. It took him 14 minutes.
BW.

AMERICA DAVIS CUP CHALLENGERS
U.S. Defeats Australia in Semi Finals

London, July 24. — The United States defeated Australia by three matches to two in inter-zone final of the Davis Cup competition at Wimbledon. Today Wood United States beat Crawford 6/5 9/7 4/6 4/6 and Shields United States beat McGrath 6/2 6/4.

THE PALESTINE POST

Vol. XI. No. 2837.   Price 10 Mils.   Jerusalem, Wednesday, Jan. 2, 1935.

CLASH IN THE SAAR

CATHOLIC MEETING DISPERSED

Saarbrucken, Dec. 31.— Calm which has hitherto prevailed here was broken at Pliesscastel, where a meeting of the Catholic Front was dispersed by the police following a fight in the hall, in which chairs were used as weapons.

The chief speaker, Herr Imbusch, a former Reichstag deputy who is now president of the Christian Trades Unions, was taken to hospital with head wounds.

The police are refusing information, but it is understood that they have arrested the chauffeur of the editor of the anti-German Front journal "Neusaarpost," alleging that he fired a revolver which started the trouble. (R.)

PLEBISCITE MONTH

Radio Telephone to the Saar

Palestine will be able to talk to the Saar territory during the period of the plebiscite. This announcement was made by the Department of Posts and Telegraphs yesterday. The radio telephone service will be extended to the Saar during the present month only.

Particulars of the charges may be obtained at any Post Office.

FRANCO-ITALIAN PACT

Rome, Dec. 31.— Negotiations for a Franco-Italian agreement are rapidly developing, and both Signor Mussolini and the French Ambassador are understood to be optimistic with regard to its satisfactory conclusion in time to enable M. Laval to sign it on his visit to Rome early in 1935.

The agreement it is understood will provide:

1.— That Jugoslavia, Czechoslovakia and Hungary should agree to support Austrian independence with Italy, France and Great Britain.

2.— That France agree to give Italy certain territory in French Somaliland bodering Eritea, which Italy considers important from a military and strategical point of view.

3.— That France agree to let Italy share in the use and working of the railway line from Djibuti to Addis Ababa.

New Year Honours

PROMOTIONS FOR PRINCE OF WALES

London, Tuesday.— Last night's London Gazette announced three promotions in the Navy, Army, and Air Force for H. R. H. the Prince of Wales. His Royal Highness has been advanced to the ranks of Admiral, General, and Air Chief Marshal.

Sir Henry Betterton, former Minister of Labour and now chairman of the Unemployment Asistance Board, has been elevated to a barony. (He will be remembered in Palestine as a member of the Shaw Commission of Inquiry in 1929.)

The Marquis of Linlithgow is the only new Privy Councillor. Sir Josiah Stamp, the famous economist, becomes a K.C.B.   RW.

14 SHOT IN MOSCOW

Nikolayeff and Comrades Executed — Ruthless Soviet Action

Moscow, Dec. 31.—Nikolayeff, together with thirteen others, who were handed over to the supreme military tribunal for trial in connection with the murder of M. Sergei Kirov, Stalin aide, were sentenced to death, and have already been shot and their property confiscated by the state.

It is officially stated that the proceedings established that the accused were formed members of the Zinovieff anti-Stalin group, who formed a secret counter-revolutionary terrorist group in Leningrad aiming at disorganising the leadership of the Soviet Government.

The accused as members of this group were held to have organised and committed the murder of M. Kirov on December 1. (R.)

ANTI-JEWISH CLASHES IN RUSSIA

ECHO OF KIROV MURDER

London, Jan. 1.— Many Jewish workers were taken to hospital as a result of anti-Jewish clashes in factories in Moscow and Leningrad, reports the London "Daily Express." The Jewish workers were accused of being guilty of Kirov's assassination.   PTA.

Jewish Agency Meeting Opens

PALESTINE FLOODS DISCUSSED IN NEW YORK

New York, Jan. 1.— The Palestine floods were mentioned prominently at the opening of the meeting of the Administrative Committee of the Jewish Agency here. Greetings were delivered by Dr. Cyrus Adler, while Mr. Nathan Laski, K.C., of London, delivered the opening address.

The gathering which was attended by 35 persons included Mr. Felix Warburg, Mr. Berl Locker, and Dr. M. B. Hexter.

Reporting on the political and financial situation in Palestine, Mr. Locker described the development of industries, exports, and Jewish employment. A discussion on the non-Zionist role of the Jewish Agency followed.

Dr. Hexter's Review

Dr. Hexter, in reviewing the progress of the country, told of the rate of immigration, and said that all settlements, except one, were self-supporting, orangegroves paying substantial interest on investments.

The session was not a public one, and committees were appointed to deal with political affairs, colonisation, finance, and to draft resolutions.

Mr. Nahum Sokolow, the world Zionist leader, sent a message urging a greater share by American Jewry in Palestine upbuilding works.   PTA.

INDIAN LIBERALS REJECT REPORT

Described as "Illusory"

Poona, Dec. 31.— The annual meeting of the National Liberal Federation unanimously resolved that the Select Committee's report was illusory, and that no enactment based thereon could be acceptable.   (R.)

DEATH OF CARDINAL BOURNE

END CAME SUDDENLY

London, Tuesday.— The death took place at twenty-five minutes after midnight of His Eminence Cardinal Francis Bourne.

Cardinal Bourne, who was in his fiftieth year, became weaker late Monday night, and his death came suddenly. Only a nurse was present at his bedside.

LYING IN STAE

The body of Cardinal Bourne is lying in state in the Westminster Cathedral Hall. The burial will take place on January 4, and the remains ill be interred beneath the altar in the Galilee Chapel at Stedmunds, near Ware, in Hertfordshire, where the late Cardinal celebrated his sacerdotal Golden Jubilee only last June.

Reuter/PTA.

(An appreciation of the leading Catholic divine in Great Britain is given in a leading article on page 4.)

MAYOR TO MEDIATE MINE STRIKE

5,000 Men Out in Durham

London, Tuesday.— The offer of the Mayor of Newcastle to mediate in a colliery strike in Durham has been accepted by both owners and miners. Five thousand men are out on strike. BW.

First Hebrew Telegrams Sent

MR. AMIKAM'S MESSAGE YESTERDAY

An historic event in the annals of the revived Hebrew language was enacted yesterday when the first telegram in Hebrew script was sent, appropriately enough by Mr. Israel Amikam, at 9.30 o'clock in the morning from Afuleh.

Addressed to all the Hebrew newspapers, the message started with the traditional Jewish blessing of "Shehechianu," the ritual benediction upon joyous events, and expressed gratification at the service, which has started between 20 towns and villages of mainly Jewish inhabitants, hoping that it would soon extend to the rest of Palestine.

Mr. Amikam, an ex-soldier in the Jewish Battalions of the Royal Fusiliers, had endeavoured for years to secure telegraphic service in Hebrew characters, submitting petitions to the Palestine Government and the League of Nations on many occasions.

Mr. Dizengoff's Reply

Mr. M. Dizengoff, Mayor of Tel Aviv, in replying to the cablegram addressed to himself, congratulated Mr. Amikam on the enterprise he showed in securing the facility by dint of arduous effort. This message was the first to be dispatched from the Tel Aviv Post Office in Hebrew characters.

JERUSALEM MUNICIPAL COUNCIL QUORUM

FIVE MEMBERS NOT THREE

The five remaining members of the Jerusalem Municipal Council have been recognized as a quorum in the city's administration, The Palestine Post learned yesterday. This is perhaps not quite in accordance with the wishes of the Mayor, Ragheb Bey Nashashibi, who in an interview given to "Doar Hayom" some time ago, had predicted that he and his four remaining colleagues would be permitted to carry on and that any three members present at a meeting would be considered a quorum.

It was this statement, and the absence of any public announcement by the authorities as to the status of the equivocal Municipal Council, that gave rise to the misapprehension that such a quorum had indeed been legalised.

The effect of the District Commissioner's ruling is naturally to render void any decision of the Municipal Council taken in the absence of any one of its five members.

Tel Aviv Election Register

PETITION FOR POSTPONING OPENING DATE

(From Our Own Correspondent)

Tel Aviv, Tuesday.— A delegation of the local Municipal Council were received by the District Commissioner yesterday and asked that the date for the opening of the register of voters be postponed from January to February 15.

The decision of the District Commissioner to open the list of voters on January 6 has caused resentment among certain sections of the population of the city, who regard the action as discrimination against them. It is cited that in Jerusalem the inhabitants were given the period of one month to make payment and that a longer perod was allowed in Haifa.

Owing to the method of tax collection in Tel Aviv, scores of inhabitants have not as yet paid the amount of 500 mils required for the right to vote.

Repairing the Flood Damage

RAILWAY SERVICES RESUMED

RELIEF MEASURES IN TEL AVIV

Activity is proceeding in different parts of the country in repairing the havoc caused by last week-end's torrential downpours and floods.

Reports from The Palestine Post correspondents in different areas disclose problems which are being tackled by official and local authorities.

The railway service between Tulkarm and Zichron-Jacob is being restored to-day following repairs on the line. The early morning goods train from Lydda to Haifa will resume its normal schedule, departing from the junction at five o'clock this morning, instead of four o'clock as has been the case for a week past owing to a shift in the time-table.

The Municipality of Tel Aviv has established that there are 65 families in need of relief as a result of damage to houses, and the relief committee has requested an urgent appropriation of LP. 600 for such measures.

More serious damage is reported from many groves in the Sharon and Emek Hefer vicinities. Efforts were made yesterday by Mr. H. M. Foot, Assistant District Commissioner for Samaria, to reach the inundated areas in the North Sharon and around Nathania (reports our Nathania correspondent), but he was forced to return on account of strong river currents in the Falik.

Among people who are unable to reach Tel Aviv is Mr. E. N. Mohl, general manager of the Jewish Farmers' Bank, who has been at Nathania for the past five days. The first 'bus to proceed to Tel Aviv since road communications were severed will leave to-day, the wadi near the settlement having been filled with sand and stones to make the mud-patch passable.

"Post" by Swimmer

Monday's issue of The Palestine Post was received at Nathania last evening with the rest of the mail after having been taken across the Falik by a porter, who swam across the river. It was the first mail since last Wednesday and several hundred people stormed the Post Office. The first flood supplies arrived at the same time.

Transformers have been repaired by officials of the Palestine Electric Corporation, and power is now available for lighting and machinery.

Road communications to Tulkarm and Hedera are still cut off. Fishermen are finding it difficult to ply their nets as the coast is muddy for miles, earth and other matter having been washed down on the tides.

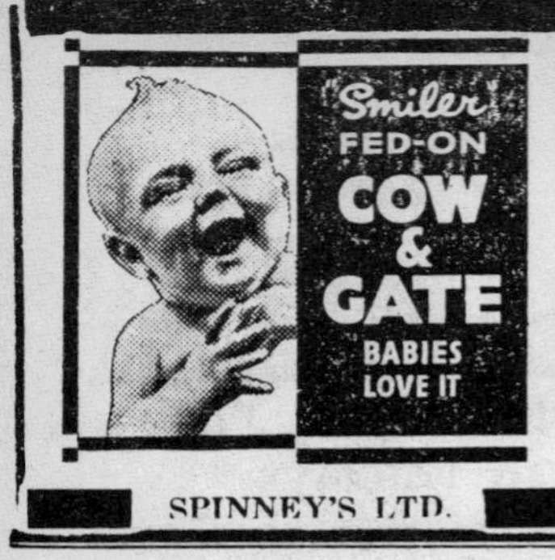

THE PALESTINE POST

JERUSALEM
MONDAY, MAY 20, 1935.

VOL. XI. No. 2635.
PRICE TEN MILS

THE IRAQIAN REVOLT

Heavy Air Bombardments

MORE TRIBAL LEADERS SUBMIT

(From a Special Correspondent)

BAGHDAD, May 16 (By Air Mail). — Heavy bombardment by artillery and aerial operations, carried out by all available machines of the Iraqi Air Force, at the rate of sixty bombs an hour, formed part of the Government's vigorous measures to put down the uprising in the Middle Euphrates area this week.

REVOLT SPREADS

The revolt had spread to a fourth tribe of Shiahs, led by Sheikh Dhawalim Nasriyah, who joined forces with the armed insurgents and raised their number to about ten thousand.

Numerous troops were drafted to the affected area during the past two days, and two regiments left for Rumaitha. The Baghdad railway-station and car parks presented a bustling scene to-day. The authorities had commandeered all lorries and a large number of cars, but the owners were well-paid.

Odds Against Rebels

The new situation means the diffusion of troops over a larger area, but the odds are still in the Government's favour. The affected district is under the absolute control of General Bakir Sidki Pasha, commander-in-chief of the Iraqi forces.

It was this general who, over two years ago, stamped out the Assyrians, and he seems to be as ruthlessly determined to suppress the present rising.

General Bakir Sidki is president of the military tribunal established in the area, and cases of rebel prisoners are being tried continuously.

Raid on Railway Station

Fifteen policemen stormed the railway station at Rumaitha, which was in the hands of the rebels, of whom a number were captured, and took possession of the point the same evening.

Bedouins carried out a counter-raid of the police post in the Nazriyah area, and occupied it.

The main force of the insurgents, however, remain on an island in the middle of the Euphrates, and their tactics are giving the soldiers a rough time.

SURPRISE RAIDS

Past-masters at the art of surprise raids, the rebels traverse the swollen river in canoes under cover of darkness, attack the troops quickly and disappear into the night as silently and as swiftly as they came.

The hospitals at Diwaniyah and Hillah are treating numerous military casualties, many of whom have been victim to this form of guerilla warfare.

Thieves' Chance

Added to the harassing manoeuvres of the tribesmen, thieves are having the time of their lives. A large grain warehouse in the town of Rumaitha owned by Sheikh Kawam, the principal rebel chieftain, was raided by thieves, and they made off with £10,000 worth of cereals.

The Iraqi Air Force is waiting for dry weather before they can utilise incendiary bombs and blow up the rebel hutments.

47 KILLED IN AIR CRASH

WORLD'S LARGEST PLANE DROPS IN MOSCOW

(From a Special Correspondent)

MOSCOW, Sunday. — Forty-seven people were killed outright when the "Maxim Gorki," the largest aeroplane in the world and pride of the Soviet commercial air fleet, broke in three and crashed to destruction after a collision with a smaller machine at mid-day.

There were a party of 36 engineers, workmen and mechanics of the Moscow underground railway and eleven of the crew on board.

The "Maxim Gorki" was flying at about 300 metres, when a smaller 'plane, capable of doing 450 miles an hour, commenced looping the loop in its vicinity. The pilot of the stunting 'plane, Balguin, an instruction machine, had been warned against such aerial tricks but he persisted, apparently to give the passengers on the air liner a thrill.

While in a loop, the small machine struck either the propellor or the wing of the "Maxim Gorki." Eyewitnesses state that the huge 'plane seemed to break up under the impact.

From the ground horrified spectators saw the pilot Uroff making frantic attempts to get the giant machine under control, but first the left wing broke off and then other portions seemed to crumble, and the whole wreckage fell on the roof of a house.

The pilot of the other machine, responsible for the disaster, crashed in the wake of the liner, and was killed.

The authorities have ordered nation-wide mourning for the victims of the disaster, and a State funeral is to be accorded to them. The grief over this appalling loss of life is accentuated by the fact that the machine was the costliest ever built and was convertible into a war 'plane.

The "Maxim Gorki" was built a year ago, and was the gift of the people, workers and peasants, who contributed their "kopeks" towards the construction of the 'plane named in honour of Russia's famous author.

Szurov and Mikhaieff, two of Russia's noted pilots were in the doomed plane. They had the presence of mind, in order to prevent a fire when the plane fell, to hurl the engines to the ground.

"Lawrence of Arabia" Dead

The End of a Legendary Figure

An Orthodox View

By LOWELL THOMAS

(From 'With Lawrence in Arabia')

Among the hundreds of questions we have been asked about Colonel Lawrence, some of the most frequent have been: "What reward has Lawrence received? Does he intend to write a book? Where is he now? How does he earn his living? and what is to become of him? What are his hobbies? Will he ever marry? Is he a normal human being and has he a sense of humour? In fact, just what was the secret of Lawrence's success, and how could a Christian and a European gain such influence over fanatical Mohammedans?"

His Wisdom

There have been a host of factors that have contributed to his success, that gained him his influence, and that enabled him to win not only the respect of the Arabs but their admiration and devotion as well. They respected him because, though a mere youth, he seemed endowed with the wisdom of wise men. They admired him because of his personal prowess, his ability to outdo them in the things in which they excel, such as camel-riding and shooting, and because of his courage and modesty. He usually led them in battle, and under fire he was courageous to a fault. Wounded a number of times, his injuries, fortunately, were never serious enough to keep him out of action. Often he was too far from a base to get medical attention, so that his wounds were obliged to heal themselves. The Arabs became devoted to him because he gained them victories and then tactfully gave all the credit to his companions. That he was a Christian they considered unfortunate, and they decided that it was an accident and in some mysterious way "the will of Allah"; but some regarded him as having been sent from heaven to help free them from the Turks.

To gain his ends it was necessary for Lawrence to be a consummate actor. He was obliged completely to submerge his European mode of living, even at the risk of winning the criticism and ridicule of his own countrymen by appearing in cities like Cairo, where East and West meet, garbed as an Oriental. His critics scoffed and said that he did this merely to gain notoriety. But there was a far deeper reason. Lawrence knew that he was being watched constantly by Sherifs, Sheiks, and tribesmen, and he knew that they would regard it as a very great compliment to them if he went about, even amongst his own people, dressed in the costume of the desert.

In Jerusalem

During those first days which I had spent with Lawrence in Jerusalem he wore nothing but Bedouin garb. Nor did he ever appear to be aware of the curiosity excited by his costume in the streets of the Holy City, for he always gave one the impression that he was engrossed in his own thoughts, hun-

(Continued on Page 8, Column 3)

His Death

After lying unconscious for six days less two hours, T. E. Shaw ("Lawrence of Arabia") died shortly after 8 o'clock yesterday morning at Wool Military Hospital, at Bovington Camp in Dorset.

Lawrence had continued to sink through the early morning. His heart was weakening, and the congestion of his lung increasing, so that the pulse was at a low ebb and breathing was rendered most difficult (says a Reuter/PTA message).

At 7 o'clock artificial respiration was applied as a last desperate resort, but all efforts were unavailing, and he passed away an hour afterwards.

Tributes of Flowers

Throughout Saturday gifts of flowers had been streaming from all parts of the country into the military hospital where Lawrence lay dying. The staff was inundated by telephone inquiries all the time.

Sir E. Farquhar Buzzard, Bart., Physician in Ordinary to the King, one of the leading specialists in the country, and other eminent consultants from London had hurried to Dorsetshire on Saturday morning, but by 7 o'clock yesterday morning his pulse had almost gone.

Lawrence's brother revealed, when he left the hospital after an all-night vigil at the death-bed, that his brain had been irreparably damaged, and that it would have been a tragedy if he had recovered.

GALLANTRY OF A WAR HERO

(From a Staff Correspondent.)

The most romantic figure of the war in the East, Thomas Edward Shaw, who has gone down in history as Colonel Lawrence of Arabia, sacrificed his life to save a boy.

It was on Monday last that, while on his motor-cycle near Bovington Camp, Lawrence was thrown a considerable distance from his machine, although it was only slightly damaged, when he braked hard to avoid a collision with a cyclist.

The accident was witnessed by soldiers of the Tank Corps stationed at the camp, who promptly took him to the military hospital in a lorry. Normally the hospital does not admit civilians, but as he had only left the Air Force in March, and because of his condition, an exception was made.

Youth Not Harmed

Albert Hargreaves, the youth who was riding the pedal-cycle involved in the accident, was also taken to the same hospital, but he was suffering only slight concussion and was not seriously ill.

It was not until two days after the accident that the physicians revealed that Lawrence had concussion and a fractured skull, and was in a serious condition. Up to then it had been stated that the hospital offi-

(Continued on Page 8, Column 2)

An Unorthodox View

Lawrence of Arabia, man of daring, with almost the legendary attributes of a superman, was not to some of his contemporaries the power his worshippers made him out to be.

A volume entitled "Iraq," published ten days ago by Ernest Main, an authority on Iraq, its history and people, points out how the policy associated with the name of Lawrence of Arabia did more harm than good, how the issue of war against Turkey would have been the same Lawrence or no Lawrence, how others in the same sphere and with less colourful methods achieved far more.

Mr. Main admits that the personality, the policies and the money at the disposal of Lawrence, exercised a decisive influence on the future of Iraq, but with reasoned precision shows that the money was the most important factor and that the fancied good which Lawrence accomplished was a "myth."

Dozens of other persons, distinguished soldiers and great leaders, went into the Near and Middle East and became simply by virtue of their greatness, legendary figures among the Arabs. Linguists and travellers, political experts, with little money, bankers and administrators who were impelled only by the desire to be of assistance to the Arabs, likewise went to the Arab countries and achieved genuine fame and affection among these people. Their names are forgotten, (argues Mr. Main), their work known among a limited number of research students but among the people among whom they did most of their work, they remain forever memories.

What are their names?

Gerald E. Leachman, "his extreme nobility...caught the fancy of the Arabs...hundreds of parents called their children by his name"; E. B. Sloane..."his work was every bit as important as that of Lawrence, if less flashy"...Captain W. H. I. Shakespeare..."able and strong."

And Lawrence?

"Lawrence grew into a figure of romantic mystery, soon grew into a legend...finally he set the seal upon his reputation by emerging as one of the great writers of English prose..."

His idea?

"...to develop the Arab guerilla movement, working up the Hedjaz railway and harassing the Turks on the right flank of the British thrust from Egypt across the Canal into Palestine. His implements in forging this new British arm were his persuasive powers, his electric personality and his gold — a crescendo of arguments which no Arab could resist."

He persuaded the leaders of Mecca that they could soon become the rulers of the pleasant land of Syria.

Lawrence, the gold flowing at his bid and command, could "fix" the Sherif to pay each and every man two pounds a month and four for a camel, and for months on end he kept the tribal army in the field.

THE PALESTINE POST
JERUSALEM
MONDAY, OCTOBER 28, 1935
VOL. XI. No. 2870
PRICE TEN MILS.

Dissolution of Parliament
PAGE THREE

Nazis Apply Nuremberg Laws Against the Jews in Germany

Wave of Protest Spreads

"NON-ARYANS" LOSE MUNICIPAL RIGHTS

(From Palestine Telegraphic Agency)

BERLIN, October 25. — Jews in Germany may no longer participate actively or passively in municipal elections, although they must continue to pay municipal taxes, it was announced today. The decision was taken by the authorities on the basis of the Nuremberg laws.

The announcement explained that since the Jews are no longer citizens of the Reich, they are automatically deprived of their municipal citizenships rights.

JEWISH BLOOD PERMISSIBLE

BERLIN. — An Aryan need fear no risk of "racial defilement" if he accepts a transfusion of blood from a Jew.

Professor Loeffler, of the Radical Political Department of the Nazi Party, declares there is no foundation for the belief that such a transfusion would affect the Aryan's "purity of race."

He remarks that persons guilty of spreading such an idea as that Jewish blood is not permissible for transfusions may cause damage to the health of the people since it might result in unnecessary restrictions at a moment when quick action was essential.

"Jews Will Never Forget Nuremberg"

(From Palestine Telegraphic Agency)

LONDON, Sunday. — "Whatever else the Jews may forget, they'll never forget the 'Ghetto' laws of Nuremberg and their authors," Mr. Leonard G. Montefiore, president of the Anglo-Jewish Association, said last night in an address at a meeting here of the Jewish Board of Guardians.

The speaker defended Italy against the charge that anti-Semitism flourishes in that country. He asserted that the movement is non-existent there.

LOCAL PROTEST AGAINST "GHETTO" LAWS

A conference of Jewish youth in Palestine to protest against enactment of the Nuremberg laws and against the persecution of the Jews in Germany will be called, according to a decision taken at a meeting of representatives of all sections of the Jewish youth at the Jerusalem club-house of the Hebrew Students' federation on Wednesday night.

The representative of the German boycott committee proposed that besides the protest conference the Palestinian youth should work towards strengthening the boycott without going into the question of the "transfer."

His motion was carried with only two negative votes, one from the representatives of the Y.W.H.A. and the other from Betar. The Betar representatives left the meeting stating that they would not participate in a conference which would not take a definite stand against the "transfer" system.

18,000 PERSONS ATTEND HYDE PARK DEMONSTRATION

(From Palestine Telegraphic Agency)

LONDON, Sunday.— A huge anti-Nazi demonstration was held here today in Hyde Park. It is estimated that about 18,000 persons attended.

The crowd adopted a resolution condemning the persecutions of the Jews in Germany and Reichsfuehrer Adolf Hitler, and in addition a resolution supporting the boycott of products imported from Germany.

GERMANY VOICES NEED FOR COLONIAL EMPIRE

(From a Special Correspondent)

BERLIN, October 26. — The efforts of the Third Reich to regain Germany's former colonies were again brought to the fore today at the opening of the colonial exhibition at Hanover.

Hitler's slogan "We Need Colonies Like Any Other Country" was the motif of the exhibition and was hung in large letters on all the walls. Dr. Gessner, the President of the Chamber of Commerce, opened the exhibition and stated that Germany suffers from over-population and needs colonies which would supply her with raw materials.

FORMER GERMAN COLONIES UNDER BRITISH AEGIS

(From Our Own Correspondent)

LONDON, October 22. — Correspondence which took place between Lord Apsley, M.P., and the Secretary of State for the Colonies, will be read with interest in Palestine. On October 5 Lord Apsley wrote to Mr. Malcolm MacDonald as follows:

"I notice the enclosed News Agency message in the paper with regard to Germany's Former Colonies.

"You will see that General Ritter von Epp, the speaker at Dusseldorf, seemed to anticipate that the colonial issue would be re-opened either by Great Britain or Germany. May I ask whether there is any likelihood of this, or whether the British Government still maintain the attitude that there is no possibility of the retrocession of German Colonies which are held by Great Britain?"

Surrender Not Contemplated

The Secretary of State replied as follows this week:

"Thank you for sending me the press cutting on the question of the desire of Germany to reopen the Colonial question.

"It has been repeatedly stated in Parliament that His Majesty's Government have never contemplated the surrender of the mandates for the former German colonies which are now under British administration; and as recently as the 9th April the then Prime Minister said, in a reply to a question in the House of Commons, that he had no reason to suppose that the German Government is under any misapprehension as to the attitude of His Majesty's Government on this question.

"I do not think I can usefully add anything to those statements."

SYRIAN ANXIETY OVER INTERNATIONAL SITUATION

(From Our Own Correspondent)

DAMASCUS, Oct. 26.— The panic that arose out of the unstable international political situation has subsided and the price of foodstuffs has returned to normal.

LONDON OPINION DISCOUNTS ARAB ALLEGATIONS

Arms Believed to be Destined for Ethiopia

Following the seizure in Palestine of a consignment of arms concealed in a ship carrying cement, the leaders of the Arab Party in Palestine are accusing the Jews in Palestine of secretly arming against the Arabs, the Morning Post's Diplomatic Correspondent wrote on Oct. 23.

In London this allegation is not taken seriously, the Correspondent added. There is no evidence that the arms in question were intended for use in Palestine and it is thought quite possible that their eventual destination was Abyssinia.

The British authorities are making a thorough investigation into the matter and the High Commissioner has given the Arab leaders complete assurances as to the impossibility of any such plot as they allege materialising.

Anniversary of Bible Translation

The 1500th anniversary of the translation of the Bible into Armenian was celebrated this weekend in Jerusalem.

The three day festival took place at the Armenian Patriarchate of St. James and culminated with a celebration in the hall of the Theological Seminary at which were present His Beatitude the Armenian Patriarch, the Bishops and vartabeds of the community; the Vicar of the Armenian Catholic Patriarch; Archdeacon Stewart, representing the Anglican Bishop; Mr. Shiraganian, representing the British and Foreign Bible Society; and notables of the Armenian lay community.

In his concluding address, the Patriarch reviewed the celebrations which had taken place throughout the world in the Jubilee year, particularly mentioning his gratification with the celebration in London arranged at the request of His Grace the Archbishop of Canterbury and addressed by Bishop Graham Browne of Jerusalem. His Beatitude also commented on the fine unanimity with which Armenian Catholics and Protestant Armenians united to honour the translation made so many centuries ago.

The programme of the Jerusalem festival included addresses by Mr. Shahan Berberian and the Rev. Diran vartabed Uersoyian on the translation of the Bible; a pageant in verse especially composed for the occasion by Mr H. Oshagan; and a number of songs rendered by the theological students.

Fascist Anniversary to be Marked by Huge Offensive

Ethiopian Commanders Warned

NEWS SUPPLY CUT OFF FROM GORAHAI

(Reuter/P.T.A.)

ADDIS ABABA, Sunday. — To mark the thirteenth anniversary of the Fascist march on Rome, which occurs tomorrow, the Italians are preparing a great offensive along the Aksum-Adowa-Adigrat line.

The news of tomorrow's advance was communicated by the Emperor to Ras Seyoum, commander of the troops in the Tigre section.

Orders have also been issued to the Ethiopian commanders on all fronts warning of a general Italian offensive which may be launched tomorrow.

From Harar comes a message that it is believed that the Italians have attacked Gorahai, the nerve centre of the Ogaden district. This is in line of the approach of the Italian troops in the Webbe Shibeli offensive. It is also thought that the wireless station in that town has been bombed and destroyed.

Authorities in Addis Ababa are considerably perturbed over the absence of news from Gorahai. The station usually wirelesses twice a day and for the past twenty-four hours there has been no message.

A RECONNAISSANCE FLIGHT

Major Barnes, Reuter representative at Asmara, who accompanied an Italian squadron led personally by Count Ciano, describes a 300 mile flight over the Northern front with Signor Mussolini's "death or glory boys." The 'planes dived to within a few hundred feet of the Ethiopian machine-gun detachments, opening fire on the soldiers manning the guns. The Ethiopians returned fire but the Italian 'planes were not damaged.

A reconnaissance failed to discover the whereabouts of Ras Seyoum's forces and no large nucleus of the Ethiopian force was observed anywhere.

Rains Handicap Offensive

The Italian offensive which was reported to have started on the Webbe Shibeli river, came to an early standstill last Thursday owing to the sodden character of the country, after the recent heavy rainfall, but is expected to open up again with the general offensive

(Continued on Page Eight)

13TH ANNIVERSARY OF MARCH ON ROME

About fifty Fascists in uniform from Jerusalem, Jaffa and Tel Aviv attended a meeting yesterday morning at the Fascist club in Jerusalem commemorating the thirteenth anniversary of the Fascist era and the march on Rome.

The Italian Consul-General was the first speaker. He was followed by the Secretary of the Fascist club in Jerusalem who delivered a long speech on the Italo-Ethiopian conflict.

(Leader on Page Four.)

CO-ORDINATION PLAN FOR BRITISH MINERS

LONDON, October 25. — As a result of the Government's intervention with the owners, Captain Crookshank, the Secretary of Mines, announced last night to the Executive Committee of the Mine Workers' Federation that he expects to receive next Thursday a definite undertaking that selling organisations will be established in all coalfields with central coordination before next July.

Capt. Crookshank asked the Executive to consider this undertaking very carefully as signifying a substantial and permanent contribution to the structure of the industry as well as to the well-being of work-people in the industry.

Selling organisations, he said, were something practical and held out prospect of benefits to the mine workers more tangible than the arbitration tribunal, which, by itself, would bring them nothing of value.

The Executive privately considered Capt. Crookshank's statement and at midnight issued a reply stating that they regretted the attitude of the Government in declining the miners' offer to submit their claims to an arbitration court and adding that they will therefore proceed with the ballot on the question of a strike as originally suggested.

A further meeting of the Executive was held this morning to consider what other steps should be taken before putting the ballot into operation.

The Miners' Grievances

Following a meeting of the Miners' Federation Executive this morning it was announced that the strike ballot will be taken on November 11, 12 and 13, that is, just before the General Election.

The Executive statement says that they regret no attempt has been made to meet the miners' demands for an increase in wages. They welcome the suggestion for a selling organisation but feel that this alone offers no solution to the problem as it will only succeed in increasing the production costs and thus prevent the owners from making advances in wages. In conclusion they regret that the miners' offer to submit the question to an impartial arbitration tribunal has been rejected.

Last Minute News

The British Government has announced that the sanctions prohibiting loans and credits to Italy will be enforced from Tuesday, October 29. The export of arms and certain raw materials will be prohibited from the same day.

The French Government will not enforce sanctions before the meeting of the Sanctions Committee in Geneva on October 31. French newspapers believe that the early enforcement of sanctions by Great Britain will have a discouraging effect on the peace efforts which are at present being undertaken by M. Laval.

The U. S. State Department has replied to the invitation of the League to join the States applying sanctions against Italy. The U.S. Government, it is stated, has already applied an arms embargo against the states at war, but will not join in sanctions. It will be ready, however, to support the League in any peace efforts.

THE PALESTINE POST

JERUSALEM
THURSDAY, JAN. 30, 1936.

PRICE: TEN MILS
VOL. XII. 2951.

"Salvation of German Jewry Imperative" •

LORD BEARSTED'S APPEAL IN N. Y.

Sir H. Samuel Stresses Urgent Needs

(From Palcor)

NEW YORK, Wednesday. — A meeting was held here today, under the auspices of the joint Distribution Campaign, to welcome Sir Herbert Samuel, Lord Bearstead and Mr. Simon Marks, who have come to America, to co-operate with the various Jewish bodies in evolving a scheme whereby 100,000 German Jews may emigrate to Palestine and other countries.

Lord Bearstead stated that the plan on which they all must concentrate is the annual migration of 25,000 German Jews under 40 years more, for a period of four years.

"We do not want to bring them into any country where they are unwelcome," stated Lord Bearstead, "nor to any country where they would become an economic liability or where their coming would produce anti-Semitism."

"Palestine," continued Lord Bearstead, "owing to the great work yet to be accomplished there, is most suitable for them and offers the greatest opportunity. But that is only one country. The possibilities throughout the world must be studied."

Sir Herbert Samuel, who followed Lord Bearstead, stated that in this campaign which they were inaugurating, they did not want in any way to prejudice the financial campaigns for Palestine to which he had gladly devoted five years of his life.

The need for unity among American Jews was emphasised by Mr. Simon Marks, who appealed for thirty Jews to follow the example set by Lord Bearstead in giving £100,000, thus assuring, the success of the campaign before the return of the Mission to England.

Mr. Marks paid warm tribute to Mr. Felix Warburg whose name he said was revered by American Jews. He traced co-operation with Mr. Warburg in the Palestine Emergency Fund and Emca and hoped that the latter company would be privileged to receive the

(Continued on Page 8, Column 3)

GREEK ELECTIONS

ATHENS, Wednesday. — A sweeping victory for the Venezelists was shown in the final returns of the elections held throughout Greece yesterday.

The Liberals were returned in 142 seats out of 300 while all other parties combined only gained 143 seats. An interesting feature of the elections was the gain of 15 seats by the Communists.

FIVE DEATHS IN CAIRO RIOTING

(From Our Own Correspondent)

CAIRO, Wednesday. (By Telephone). — Egypt is still without a Government and people are becoming gravely considered at the fresh outbreaks of disorder which are caused chiefly by the lack of any central authority.

There have now been five deaths as a result of the recent rioting at Mansura and Damanhour. One of these occurred yesterday during a demonstration at the funeral of one of the schoolboys, who was killed in an earlier demonstration.

In the course of the riots the crowd forced down a fence along the main railway and blocked the line from Cairo to Alexandria for half an hour, holding up two trains. Some of the hooligans stoned the trains, smashing some of the carriage windows.

There was another demonstration in Cairo which centred round the Government Theological Training College. Wafdist students had planned to hold a congress there but police had received orders to prevent them and a two hour battle ensued. The students stoned the police and the police were forced to open fire. No serious casualties are reported.

In dealing with this demonstration the police for the first time employed an armoured tank wagon, which was filled with a coloured liquid. The liquid was squirted on the students, but was ineffectual owing to its lack of force.

Last Minute News

Her Majesty Queen Mary issued a message to the people of the British Empire in which she expresses her deep gratitude for sympathy in her grief.

The Committee of Eighteen resolved at yesterday's meeting to send questionnaires to all League members and also to those not participating in sanctions, for information about their trade with Italy.

Marshal Badoglio's communique reports that there is no news from either front. Italian papers state that Ras Desta's force was reduced from 60,000 men in October 1935 to 10,000 men now by losses, famine and desertions. The Italian Government issued an order last night withdrawing all silver currency from circulation.

A HITCH IN THE FUNERAL PROCESSION

(British Official Wireless Press)

LONDON, Wednesday. — In the detailed arrangements for the burial of King George V yesterday, only one hitch occurred, owing to the unforeseen crowds and the pushing and milling in the streets of London.

It had been intended that the two minutes' silence should coincide with the end of the funeral service at St. George's chapel but the slow progress of the funeral procession to Paddington station took longer than had been expected and the funeral train moved off over half an hour late.

Thus, while the whole Empire observed the silence, the coffin was still on its way from Windsor Station to the Castle.

STABBING OF Dr. M. ELIASH

UNKNOWN ASSAILANT'S ESCAPE

Dr. M. Eliash, a leading Jerusalem advocate, was stabbed by an unknown assailant at about ten minutes to eight last night when walking alone on the unpaved section of Bezalel Road between the Sadovsky Maternity Hospital and King George Avenue.

Dr. Eliash was stabbed twice, once in the right side of the chest near the neck, and once in the head. The second wound penetrated into the ear cavity. He was taken to Hadassah Hospital where his condition is described as not serious although he had suffered considerable loss of blood.

Dr. Eliash's calls for help were answered by Mr. Joseph Stark, a resident of the nearby Beit Atara. Mr. Stark helped him to King George Avenue and took him to the hospital in a taxi.

Mr. Stark stated to the police that he was the first person to speak to the wounded man. Dr. Eliash also remarked that another man had run away on hearing his cries.

Dr. Eliash made a statement

(Continued on Page 5, Column 1)

Busy Days for New King

(From Reuter/Wireless)

LONDON, Wednesday. — The sad ordeal of the past 10 days over, the new King has now to face some very trying weeks.

His Majesty has already received in audience Baron von Neurath, who headed the German representatives to the funeral, Prince Starhemberg, Vice-Chancellor of Austria, and Mr. Anthony Eden, the Foreign Secretary. These interviews, which lasted half an hour each, were followed by interviews with other heads of delegations, in which not only messages of sympathy were conveyed but expressions of faith in the continuation of his father's policy were expressed.

The King also received the Earl of Shaftesbury, who presented to the King the message of condolence passed by the House of Lords.

The Foreign delegates are slowly leaving London. This morning, President Lebrun, together with his party, left for France and was seen off by the Duke of Kent. On reaching Calais, President Lebrun sent another message of sympathy to King Edward.

The Duke of Gloucester saw the King of the Belgians off and the Duke of York was present when the delegation from the State of Piedmont left. Prince Axel of Denmark left by an Imperial Airways liner and Prince Paul of Yugoslavia and Prince George of G——e left London by train.

Land Sales Restrictions Announced by Sir Arthur

LEGISLATION FOR PROTECTION OF SMALLHOLDERS AND TENANTS

Statement to Arab Party Leaders

An important statement in reply to the Arab demands in a recent memorandum for self-government, stoppage of Jewish immigration and prohibition of land sales to Jews, was given by the High Commissioner yesterday morning to representatives of five Arab parties whom His Excellency received at the Government Offices.

Concerning the first demand the High Commissioner referred the deputation to the proposals for the establishment of a Legislative Council.

The High Commissioner made it clear that "there could be no question of the total stoppage of Jewish immigration into Palestine." He reaffirmed the principle of absorptive capacity in the admission of immigrants, but added that he intended to keep in close touch with the changing economic situation, for which purpose a statistical bureau had been established.

As regards the third demand for the prohibition of all sales of lands to Jews the High Commissioner, without rejecting the demand, stated that the Secretary of State had approved of legislation preventing land owners from selling any of their land unless he retained a minimum area sufficient for his and his family's subsistence. This legislation would also preclude collusion between buyer and seller by making the minimum area inalienable. The proposed legislation will not apply in the Beersheba district and urban areas, but otherwise it will be of "general application."

The official communique is given below in full and the supplemetary explanation which Sir Arthur Wauchope gave to the Arab deputation is also summarised. The High Commissioner explained that the Protection of Cultivators Ordinance of 1933 did not assist the small owner or tenant, whose position might be prejudiced, when he has given up his land, by loss of alternative employment, and the natural increase of the population. He stressed that "the process of sale of land by smallholders can no longer safely be allowed to go unchecked. He invited the Arab leaders to help in the application of the protective principles of the scheme which "will inevitably occupy a considerable period of time."

The Arab leaders present at the interview yesterday were Jamaal Eff. el Husseini, representing the Palestine Arab Party; Ragheb Bey Nashashibi, National Defence Party; Ishac Eff. Buleiri, Reform Party; Abdul Latif Bey Salah, National Bloc; and Yacoub Eff. Ghussein, the Youth Organization.

The **Palestine Post** understands that Jamal Eff. Husseini acted as spokesman during this interview which included a free discussion lasting an hour.

To Jamaal Effendi's assertion that the Government's action left things much as they were, the High Commissioner is understood to have replied in the negative, pointing out that the Legislative Council was designed gradually to lead to self-government.

OFFICIAL COMMUNIQUE

It will be recalled that at the end of November the leaders of the Arab political parties submitted a memorandum to the High Commissioner setting out their main demands, namely:

(a) that a democratic government should be established in Palestine;

(b) that Jewish immigration should cease completely;

(c) that all sales of land to Jews should be prohibited.

That memorandum was transmitted by His Excellency the High Commissioner to the Secretary of State who, having given it very careful consideration, communicated to His Excellency by telegraph the following reply: —

Elective Legislative

(a) The demand for the establishment of a democratic Government has been answered by the communication on the part of the High Commissioner to the Arab leaders of proposals for the establishment of a Legislative Council with a large unofficial majority, in the composition of which the elective principle is recognised.

The proposals were made public in Official Communique No. 45/35 of December 22, 1935.

No Total Stoppage

(b) There can be no question of the total stoppage of Jewish immigration into Palestine. The guiding principle as regards the admission of immigrants is a policy of economic absorptive capacity and His Majesty's Government contemplate no departure from that principle.

(Continued on Page Five)

16 Pages

THE PALESTINE POST
JERUSALEM
FRIDAY, MAY 8, 1936
VOL. XII. 3035.
PRICE: TEN MILS

The Negus Returns Home
PAGE SEVEN

Arabs Decide on Civil Disobedience

REFUSAL TO PAY TAXES AFTER MAY 15

A resolution to refuse to pay taxes, if by May 15 the Government does not grant the Arab leaders' demands, was passed at a meeting of some 150 organizers of the Arab strike held in Jerusalem yesterday afternoon.

The Mufti, Haj Amin El Husseini, who is President of the Moslem Supreme Council, presided. The mover of the far-reaching proposal was the Chairman himself, a Government official, and it is understood that there was little discussion and virtually no opposition.

OFFICIAL COMMUNIQUE

THURSDAY, MAY 7, 7:30 P. M.

At about 7.30 last evening a shot was fired at a Jewish bus on the Ramle-Jaffa road near Beit Dajan, and a few minutes later an Arab car was fired on at almost the same spot. No one was injured.

This morning a fire broke out at an envelope factory at Athlit, and was still burning at 4 p. m. Two suspected persons have been arrested.

There are no other incidents to report.

7 Years for Stabbing Constable

The three persons arrested in connection with the trouble at Jenin yesterday were tried by the District Court there today. One, who stabbed a police constable, was sentenced to 7 years' imprisonment, and the others each to 1 year's imprisonment.

CONTINUE STRIKE

The meeting decided also to call upon the Arabs to continue the strike in protest against Government policy.

The Central Strike Committee will visit a number of towns with a view to strengthening the strikers' determination. The first town to be visited is Haifa where breaches in the strikers' ranks have been specially prominent during this week.

During the week's notice which the Mufti and his followers have given the Government, the High Commissioner, in accordance with yesterday's decision, must on pain of having the leaders proclaim a refusal to pay taxes, do the following things:

1. Stop Jewish immigration.
2. Prohibit the sale of land to Jews
3. Form a National (Arab) Government.

THE CHALLENGE
LEADER, PAGE EIGHT

Palestine Greets Emperor Today

Scores of Journalists Congregate at Haifa

by J. L. MELTZER
(Palestine Post Staff Writer)

HAIFA, Thursday. — Elaborate preparations are being taken by the British Admiralty, the Haifa Port authorities and the District Administration in anticipation of the arrival of the Emperor and Empress of Ethiopia and a large suite on board H.M.S. 'Enterprise' tomorrow.

The section of the harbour which fronts the Port Manager's office will be clear of all traffic at ten o'clock in the morning, when the warship is expected to arrive. Only officials, notables and a record gathering of pressmen and photographers will be allowed on a warehouse platform opposite the quay-side at which the ship is to anchor, to watch the Negus and his entourage as they pass by to the special train which will be waiting to take them to Jerusalem.

It is reported here that the party will stay either at the King David Hotel or at the Ethiopian Convent in Abyssinian Street.

Journalists have arrived from all parts to witness the Royal arrival. One London correspondent flew up to Haifa from Cairo, in a specially chartered Misr Airworks'
(Continued on Page Eight)

Negus Passes Through The Suez Canal

SUEZ, Thursday. — When H.M.S. Enterprise, with the Emperor of Ethiopia aboard, arrived here today, the cruiser was granted immediate entrance to the Canal.

There was no sign of the Emperor when the vessel passed here, but several of his suite appeared on the deck.

Business Behind Closed Doors

PEDLARS AND SHOPKEEPERS RESUME WORK

While most of the Arab shops in the country were closed yesterday, many of the shopkeepers in the Old City, Jerusalem, were doing business behind closed shutters.

Hawkers of agricultural products from the villages came to Jerusalem in large numbers yesterday and squatted, as usual, in David Street and the Mahne Yehuda Market with their wares. A new type of hawker selling cuts of meat also made an appearance yesterday in the Old City, and many of the Arab restaurants had meat yesterday for the first time in many days.

Inquiries at the Jerusalem Municipal abattoir revealed that the Arab butchers are not slaughtering there, and it is feared that the meat sold yesterday was not slaughtered under proper sanitary conditions.

Renewal of Municipal Works

Through the efforts of the District Commissioner and the Municipal Engineer, work on sewerage in the Old City was resumed yesterday. Police protection was provided for the 28 labourers who, despite the efforts of several inciters hovering about and attempting to intimidate them, worked throughout the day.

A report that these workers were arrested on attempting to leave their work proved baseless. What actually happened was that the police questioned the labourers as to the identity of the inciters, and they then returned to their work.

Another attempt to resume work on the widening of upper Jaffa Road, the stoppage of which has left the main artery of the city a
(Continued on Page Sixteen)

VILLAGE ELDERS TRIED FOR ARSON

(From Our Own Correspondent)

HEDERA, Thursday. — A collective fine of LP. 10 was today imposed on the Village of Bureika, whose elders appeared before the Assistant District Commissioner, Mr. Pirie-Gordon, on a charge of arson.

The villagers were found guilty of setting fire to haystacks in Zichron Jacob, on the evidence of the police who had traced the tracks of the incendiaries to Bureika.

Jerusalem Mayor Supports Strike

A request to the District Commissioner of Jerusalem to instruct the Mayor, Dr. Khalidi, to "abstain from acts which bring damage to the city of Jerusalem," has been sent by the Agudath Israel, the Orthodox Jewish Association. This action has been taken in protest against the Mayor being a signatory to the appeal urging continuation of the Arab Strike.

The letter was sent on April 30, but submitted for publication only yesterday.

Dr. Khalidi's assistance in the strike is seen as an act which is utterly incompatible with his office of Mayor, the Agudath Israel state.

Losses to City

The strike is inflicting losses on the city especially in that it has caused an interruption in road-work. Its interference with normal commerce and traffic have produced an increase in the cost of living. The strike, continues the Agudath Israel, is also a danger to peace and security and "it is impossible that the head of a Municipality should be permitted to be a direct instrument in bringing harm to the city whose administration he heads."

No Quorum for Meeting

The weekly meeting of the Municipal Council was not held yesterday. The Arab members had previously requested the Mayor to postpone the meeting, because of the strike. The Mayor appears to have acted on this request and advised an out-of-town Jewish member not to come to Jerusalem. The five members resident in Jerusalem were of course available, but in the absence of the sixth Jewish Councillor there would have been no quorum, even if Dr. Khalidi had attended.

One of the Arab Councillors, Hasan Sidky Dajani, was of course "engaged elsewhere," on trial for sedition at the Law Courts not far from the Municipality Building.

A meeting of the Municipal Tenders' Committee was held, though the two Arab members, Anastas Eff. Hanania and Hasan Sidky Dajani were not present. Dr. Khalidi, however, put in an appearance after a conference with the District Commissioner. At the Committee meeting, the District Commissioner was represented by Nasuhi Bey Beydoun.

Jaffa Rioters Sentenced

(From Our Own Correspondent)

JAFFA, Thursday. — Heavy sentences were imposed by the President of the District Court, Mr. Copland, today upon a number of Arabs charged with various crimes in connection with the recent disturbances.
(Continued on Page Nine)

After Midnight

The tribal revolt in Iraq (earlier report, page 12) has been crushed, reports The Palestine Post correspondent in Baghdad.

Mrs. Mollison arrived in Capetown yesterday afternoon, completing the 6,700 flight from England in 78 hours. 28 minutes, beating the world's record by eleven hours, six minutes.

Italy Has a Roman Holiday

Scenes of unbounded rejoicing in Rome and of desolation and ruin in Addis Ababa continue to characterise the end of the East African hostilities.

The Duce has ordered that throughout Italy, the flags be hoisted for three days to celebrate the victory.

An extraordinary meeting of the Fascist Grand Council has been summoned for Saturday. It is expected that this Council, which is the only body competent to consider questions affecting Italy's frontiers, will take important decisions regarding Ethiopia.

It is reported that Jijiga was occupied simultaneously with Mussolini's announcement of the occupation of Addis Ababa.

Marshal Badoglio has taken up residence at the Italian legation in Addis Ababa. Shooting was still going on last night when armed bandits repeatedly raided the shopping quarter, and there was a general outbreak of lawlessness and settlement of private feuds by violence. It is estimated that 500 Ethiopians were killed during the riots.

The British, French, German and Italian legations appear to be the only substantial buildings which have not been wrecked. The French school was looted and burned.

The heads of Foreign Legations in Addis Ababa have received notes from Marshal Badoglio announcing that the legations would enjoy recognised privileges for the representation of their countries' interests and for the protection of their subjects.

The Marshal ensures the security of the personnel, staff and property of the Legations. He expresses confidence that the heads of missions would, in view of the circumstances and the need for ensuring order and discipline, collaborate with him.

In Paris it is stated that, if Signor Mussolini's statement means that he intends to settle the fate of Ethiopia out of court, his view runs counter to the policy of the present French Government.

A competent French authority observes that what is needed is a formula taking account of military realities and the juridical position. An Italian protectorate over Ethiopia, after the model of the French protectorate in Morocco, might be a feasible solution, but this could certainly not be mere annexation.

In This Issue

Sedition Case Adjourned for Day

When His Honour, Judge Plunkett, took his seat in the District Court, Jerusalem, yesterday morning a few minutes after eleven o'clock to resume the hearing of the charge brought against Hasan Sidky Dajani and Saleh Abdu, the Court was crowded. After morning and afternoon sessions, the case was adjourned until tomorrow morning.

The proceedings commenced with the evidence of Tawfik Issa Habbash, the proprietor of the Commercial Press, who stated that he had printed the documents, signed by Hasan Sidky Dajani and Saleh Abdu, the two accused, in respect of which they are charged under Section 9 of the Criminal Law (Seditious Offences) Ordinance, 1929.

"Two Letters"

Cross-examined by Abcarius Bey on behalf of the accused the witness said that the documents in question contained the text of a letter addressed to the first accused from Beirut, and a statement, the tenor of which was a letter to the Supreme Arab Committee from the President (first accused), Vice-President (second accused) and members of the Strike Committee of the Arab Drivers Association.

It would be misleading, submitted Abcarius Bey, addressing the Court, to describe the document in question as a proclamation, it was merely a copy of the above two letters.

The defence cross-examined at length the prosecution witnesses who described the search in Dajani's offices and his arrest outside Major Monroe's Office. Abcarius Bey, for the defence, then stated that he wished to call witnesses for the defence.

Necessity of Defence Witnesses

Abdul Samad for the prosecution objected submitting that the calling of witnesses for the defence, was unnecessary, as the only two questions before the Court were, whether the document in question was distributed and whether it was seditious. The latter, he submitted, was a question for the Court to decide and witnesses were unnecessary. Abcarius Bey, in replying, said that he wished
(Continued on Page Eight)

12 Pages

THE PALESTINE POST

JERUSALEM
SUNDAY, MAY 10, 1936

VOL. XII. 3036.
PRICE: TEN MILS

The Collapse of the Phoenix
PAGE FIVE

GENERAL SITUATION IN PALESTINE QUIET

Fellahin Smuggle Foodstuffs

2 Damascus Papers Banned

The official communiques issued on Friday and yesterday reported that the country was entirely quiet. A small demonstration after the mid-day prayers in Jaffa on Friday, which dispersed quietly, was the only incident officially noted.

Friday's Precautions

What has become routine precaution for Friday, that of having troops and armed police held in readiness, barbed wire barricades at strategic points, and the searching of all pedestrians, was again observed in the Old City, Jerusalem, and at the entrances to Tel Aviv from Jaffa. Jewish clerks, who have returned to their work in Jaffa, were warned not to go to work on Friday and the Jaffa branch of the Anglo-Palestine Bank was closed.

Stores and factories were open as usual in the suburban district near Abu Kebir and other quarters where trouble had occurred. Several Arab labourers were seen at work on the extension of Rehov Herzl and some Arab stores in Abu Kebir were open. Scores of Arabs were also at work on the beach in transporting "zif zif."

Village Hawkers

The fellahin of the villages surrounding Jerusalem did not come into town with their wares on Friday morning, but in the early hours of Saturday morning they began to "smuggle" their goods into the city, each donkey being guarded by three or four villagers armed with stout nabouts. Despite these precautions several parties were attacked and their produce destroyed.

A number of incidents including

(Continued on Page Twelve)

Reinforcements for Palestine Troops

Reinforcements for the troops in Palestine are being sent, presumably from Cairo, and some have evidently already arrived in the country.

The news was conveyed on Friday by the British Official Wireless Press, as follows:

"At the request of the High Commissioner for Palestine, where Arab-Jewish disturbances have recently taken place, troop reinforcements are being sent as necessary."

A Reuter message last night repeated the report in words identical with those of the B.O.W.P.

On Friday, **The Palestine Post** had learned from Cairo that several air carriers had left Egypt with troops.

Official circles in London yesterday informed the P.T.A. that the reinforcements were not due to any grave turn in the Palestine situation. Such reinforcements were available always whenever the High Commissioner asked for them.

Inquiry from official sources in Jerusalem on Friday and Saturday elicited the answer that "No information was available."

London newspapers yesterday gave prominence to the report of the troop movements.

HINDENBURG HAS RECORD ATLANTIC CROSSING

(Reuter/PTA)

LAKEHURST (New Jersey), Saturday.— The German airship Hindenburg arrived here from Germany at 6.10 local time this morning after establishing a record airship flight of 61 hours, 40 minutes.

Civil Disobedience Echoes in Press

To understand the effect of the Arab leaders' decision of last Thursday to recommend to their followers the non-payment of taxes from the coming Friday onwards if their political demands are not met, one must, it seems, now turn to the "Ahram" of Cairo.

This newspaper has become the receptacle for the kind of news which our local Arab contemporaries do not wish, or have been advised not to display too prominently.

The Jerusalem correspondent of "Ahram" speculates whether the decision will be revoked if immigration is stopped. The same source reports that Government officers had tentatively inquired on Friday of some Arab leaders as to the true meaning of this decision. They had found, it is stated, that

(Continued on Page Twelve)

Tribes Save £4,500

(Officially Communicated)

Owing to the failure through drought of the winter crops in Beersheba sub-District, His Excellency the High Commissioner recently recommended to the Secretary of State that half the commuted tithe in this Sub-District should be waived. The Secretary of State has approved of this being done, and the tribes are thus relieved of a payment of LP 4,500.

The Secretary of State has also approved the High Commissioner's recommendation that the Rural Property Tax payable in respect of ground crops in the Auja area of the Jordan Valley, which has suffered from the drying up of springs due to successive years of drought, should be reduced this year by fifty per cent.

The question of the remission of Rural Property Tax on citrus fruits is at present under consideration by Government and a decision will be announced in regard to it later.

After Midnight

General Graziani was yesterday appointed Marshal of the Italian Army.

A daily air-mail service has been arranged between Addis Ababa and Asmara.

The leader of the Wafd party, Nahas Pasha, was yesterday asked to form the Egyptian Cabinet.

The Frankfurter Zeitung commenting yesterday on the Jewish position in Palestine, states that the Jewish population is no longer in danger and advised the Arab leaders to recognize the fait accompli and support Zionist colonization.

Royal Exiles in Jerusalem

Haifa Welcomes the Lion of Judah

MILITARY CEREMONIES MARK SHIP'S ARRIVAL

(From a Special Correspondent)

HAIFA, May 8. — Absence of many of the ceremonies that mark the entrance of monarchs into foreign lands was the outstanding feature of the arrival here this morning of the Emperor and Empress of Ethiopia.

No Ethiopian flags were flown either on the cruiser H.M.S. Enterprise or over the Port Manager's office. The cruiser was escorted by the destroyer Wolsey. A guard of honour of the Loyal Regiment was mounted on the quayside and the military band played an air which many assumed was the Ethiopian national anthem. The strains of this tune rang out three times, once when the Empress and her daughters landed, again when His Imperial Highness came down the gangway and inspected the guard, and

(Continued on Page 12)

WAITING FOR THE NEGUS

Difficult to Obtain Interview

Journalists were waiting in the hall of the King David Hotel throughout yesterday morning to obtain an interview with the Negus. But he kept himself in strict seclusion.

One fortunate man who saw him declared that the Emperor has suffered from gas attacks and that both his health and spirit seemed broken. His hands show the burns of mustard gas.

Selassie May Sail for London

(Reuter/PTA)

LONDON, Saturday.— It has been officially stated here that the Negus is remaining in Jerusalem for the present, but that this does not exclude the possibility of his early visit to London.

It is commonly supposed that the Emperor has been advised not to come until after next week's meeting of the League Council.

Ethiopian Priests Weep at Arrival

ARAB STRIKE COMMITTEE BREAKS STRIKE FOR KING

The arrival of the Negus, the Empress and their party in Jerusalem on Friday afternoon was practically destitute of all ceremony.

As the train steamed in the shutters of the saloon were drawn up, and the crowd of spectators who had been admitted to the platform, on either side of the enclosure, a crowd consisting in the main of newspapermen, press photographers, station staff, their friends and families, was deprived of the opportunity of catching the first glimpse of the Royal exiles.

In the enclosure reserved for the official welcoming party were the A.D.C., representing the High Commissioner; a representative of the Air Officer Commanding; Ruhi Bey Abdul Hadi, for the Secretariat; Mr. Campbell, the District Commissioner; Mr. Mantura, District Officer; Mr. Rice, the Deputy Inspector-General; the Mayor, Dr. Khalidi; and some of the Ethiopian Consulate Staff.

The Royal Party Arrives

To the left of the crowd on the right of the enclosure was the military escort made up of six soldiers of the Loyal Regiment under a sergeant, who, with an officer, had

(Continued on Page 7)

Negus Appeals to World

A three-page communique in French in which a complete history of the East African war was given, beginning with the Wal-wal incident of November 1934, was issued by the Emperor of Ethiopia yesterday evening, and placed on the door leading into the corridor of his suite at the King David Hotel.

According to the statement, the only one made by the Negus since his arrival in this country, the Italian Government had long entertained designs of conquering Ethiopia and the Wal-Wal incident was provoked at what was considered a propitious time. But Ethiopia believed that the incident would be settled by arbitration, in accordance with the 1928 treaty, and upon this procedure failing, she applied to the League of Nations.

Accusations then follow that Italy endeavoured to keep the affair outside the sphere of legal settlement, so as to obtain the delay needed for military preparations. Until the moment aggression occurred, Italy gave the impression that she would find an equitable arrangement satisfactory.

Embargo on Arms

During this period, however, a strict embargo was placed on arms exports to Ethiopia and she was deprived of means of providing for her legitimate defence. Only when Italy had been declared the aggressor by the League, were the Ethiopians able to provide for the defence of their invaded country.

"We carried out this sacred duty by ranging ourselves alongside our humblest soldiers," the Emperor's statement proceeded. "The aggressor, after having trampled on pacts and treaties in order to invade Ethiopia, not content with his superiority of arms and modern organizations, operated his powerful Air Force with full security."

Subsequent points in the communique condemned the breach of League conventions by Italy in bombarding open towns with loss to civilian lives, the use of poison and other gases, the systematic destruction of hospitals and Red Cross units, and the encouragement of pillage and other inhuman acts.

Ethiopia protested to the League against every successive defiance of international pacts, but neither its feeble means nor the League's force could ward off the catastrophe which descended upon a sovereign member-State.

"The Italian Army had already followed up its invasion to the very gates of our capital when, with a sad heart, we decided that we must abandon this unequal war and no longer contribute to a condition under which old men, women and children could be massacred. We preferred to plead the cause of our nation at Geneva, and to appeal to all civilised peoples to help to re-establish peace in Ethiopia.

"We refuse to believe that the League of Nations, the centre of collective security, can allow the independence of one of its members to be brushed aside by another member, who has been unanimously deemed the aggressor thereby creating a dangerous precedent for world security. We demand that justice be done to protect the weaker against the stronger nations."

STOP PRESS

Duce Proclaims Ethiopia Italian Territory

Another mass mobilisation of the whole Italian people heard Signor Mussolini announce the Fascist Grand Council's decision placing Ethiopia under the sovereignty of King Emmanuel.

When the Duce stepped out on the balcony of the Palazzo Venezia in Rome he received a prolonged and enthusiastic ovation by his people. All streets and squares throughout Italy were equipped with loud-speakers.

The Duce announced that the Grand Council had approved by acclamation on May 9 of the 14th year of the Fascist regime the following decision:

1) ***To place the territory and people formerly belonging to the Ethiopian Empire under the full and entire sovereignty of the King of Italy.***

2) ***The King of Italy to assume the title of Emperor for himself and his successors.***

"Italy has finally constructed her Empire," the Duce said, "she will bring to it peace, civilisation and justice in the spirit of the tradition of Rome."

Signor Mussolini emphasized that Italy will be ready, if necessary, to defend her Empire with all her power and at any cost.

"The Empire was re-built on the hills of Rome," the Duce said.

He asked, "Will you be worthy of it?" A thundering "Yes" came in reply.

A salute of 21 guns was fired after the announcement.

12 Pages

The Declaration and the Arabs
"LIFE OF BALFOUR" Page 3

THE PALESTINE POST

JERUSALEM
SUNDAY, MAY 17, 1936

VOL. XII. 3042.
PRICE : TEN MILS

3 Shot Dead in Jerusalem Cinema

Arabs Discuss Strike by Civil Service Workers

Leaders Firm in Demand
Police Warn 'Bus Companies

The proposal to call out Arab civil servants on strike was again discussed by the Arab Higher Committee, held at the house of Auni Bey Abdul Hadi yesterday afternoon, it is understood by The Palestine Post. No decision was reached and the discussion was deferred.

Auni Bey later told a gathering of Arab journalists that the Arab Higher Committee had unanimously decided not to accept any offer from the Government unless Jewish immigration was first suspended.

Whilst the local Arab newspapers have refrained from extensive comment on His Excellency's reported proposals to the Arab leaders on Thursday, Cairo papers have been less reticent.

Thus "Al Ahram" of Friday reported from Jerusalem that the High Commissioner had renewed to the Arab High Committee certain proposals which he had made in the past, and added that the British Government were willing to send a Royal Commission to Palestine to investigate the present position and listen to Arab and Jewish viewpoints, as well as to take evidence from leading Government officials.

The recommendations of this Commission would serve as a basis for consideration by the British Government in relation to its policy in Palestine.

This proposal, says the paper, has been under careful study by the Arab Higher Committee for two days but no decision has yet been reached.

Termination of Strike

"Falastin" yesterday said that the High Commissioner required as a condition for the appointment of such a Commission the immediate breaking off of the strike and the restoration of normal conditions.

"Ahram's" correspondent yesterday, however, pointed out that none of the proposals offered by His Excellency is acceptable to the Arab people. It is now to be hoped, according to this paper, that all strike committees will meet in order to determine the types of taxation which the Arabs should be urged not to pay.

Another Sort of Commission

In discussing General Wauchope's proposal, "Meraat Al Sherk" points out that the Royal
(Continued on Page 7)

Jews Demand Security

DELEGATION VISITS HIGH COMMISSIONER

At their interview with the High Commissioner on Thursday, the delegates representing Palestine Jewry were urgent in their requests for guarantees of security.

After introducing the delegation, Mr. Ben-Zvi declared that they were united in one demand, that the fullest guarantee be given in regard to life and property, and the upbuilding of the National Home. He deplored the effects of the strike which aimed at aggravating racial feeling, besides demoralising the Arabs themselves, many of whom were peaceable and law-abiding and opposed to such tactics.

The lack of security and the refusal of certain Arab elements to recognise that there was a law in the land, were emphasised by Mr. M. Dizengoff, who drew the
(Continued on Page 12)

Flower Show at The Levant Fair

The Levant Fair Flower Show is being held today and tomorrow in the Agricultural Section of the Fair.

Exhibits are invited of roses, carnations, gladiolas, snapdragons, clarkia and flowers in bunches and vases; flowering and foliage plants and for palms and perennials.

Gardeners and flower-lovers, amateurs and professionals, have been invited to submit their choice blooms for competition.

Police Forced to Fire on Crowd

(From Our Own Correspondent)

JAFFA, Saturday. — Demonstrations which took place here following the noon prayers at the Mosque yesterday were dispersed by the police. At one point the police were compelled to fire, killing one Mohammed Mansour, of Gaza, and wounding several others. Among the wounded were two Houranis and one from Kerak, Trans-Jordan.

"Carry Out Resolutions"

Between two and three thousand demonstrated at the Mosque. Fakhri Bey Nashashibi addressed the assembly exhorting his listeners to carry out the resolutions of the Arab Supreme Council (calling for Civil Disobedience) until the Government should be compelled to submit to the Arab demands. He said that while Arabs were giving their lives for their nation the British Government were still permitting hundreds of immigrants to come into the country.

"Mob Dispersed"

At about 12:30 the crowd left the Mosque and proceeded up Ajami Street as far as the bridge over Feisal Street, where it was instructed by Fakhri Bey Nashashibi and the other leaders to disperse.

The mob then broke up into smaller groups some going back towards
(Continued on Page Seven)

War of Extermination?

After the cold-blooded triple murder in the Edison Hall last night, all Jews must ask themselves, "Whose Turn Is It Next?"

For no Jew, however sheltered, is now safe.

Be he a Jew bent on a pious errand in the Old City or one who seeks relaxation in a cinema house, the assassin's bullet is there waiting for him.

The brand of gangsterism to which free rein has been given during the last four weeks, the gangsterism which in one quarter has been abundantly blessed and in another too long suffered, is an indiscriminate gangsterism.

It strikes down old men and snuffs out the lives of young men.

Therefore every Jew must now be on his guard. He must know that the streets are infested with murderers, the public places with assassins whose orders are to kill and maim Jews.

The Jews have shown restraint. Their restraint has been acknowledged and tributed in the highest places. Their moral repugnance for murder has overcome their instinct for self-defence. They hold life dearly, and the life even of their sworn enemy is dear to them. But who can now guarantee that Jews, outraged to their depths, will not undergo a change of outlook on the sacredness of human life?

The Jews have placed their trust in a Government charged with a sacred trust. If now they should lose that faith, seeing that their very lives are held so cheaply, who will blame them?

If this is a war of extermination the Arabs have declared on the Jews, the Arabs had better know that the shooting down of four hundred thousand Jews will not alter the course of history; will not shake the Jews' determination to resettle the land of their fathers.

But if the Jew's life is forfeit, so is the life of every non-Arab. This movement of the Arab Supreme Council seeks not only to terrorise the Jew; it aims to throw this land back into the dark ages.

Jews are no longer safe; Europeans are no longer safe; the British are no longer safe. For the assassin now holds the stage, the assassin calls the tune.

Four weeks ago, after the daylight murders in Jaffa, the Government could have made an example of some murderers which would have stayed the assassin's hand.

Let every man with a spark of humanity in him now pray that it is not yet too late.

MORE JEWISH VICTIMS
ARMED BANDIT FIRES POINT BLANK INTO THEATRE CROWD
Assassin Escapes in Car

Three persons were murdered and two slightly injured by an unknown assailant who fired five shots point blank into the crowd leaving the Edison Theatre in Jerusalem after the first performance at about 9.15 p. m. last night. The Edison is in Zichron Moshe, an exclusively Jewish residential section.

Soon after the lights went on and as the audience was streaming out of the exits, a man, dark moustached, described as of medium height, dressed in European clothes, without a hat, standing inside the hall near the middle exit, pulled out a revolver and fired five shots. All five shots took effect.

("How easily the political agitator could turn the tap on and off. . ." Life of Balfour, Page 3.)

After Midnight

The Italian Senate yesterday enacted the new law of annexation of Ethiopia. An Addis Ababa message announces the organization of a Fascist party there.

The new Polish Cabinet has been installed in Warsaw with the Under-Secretary of War as Premier.

Mr. J. H. Thomas, testifying before the Tribunal investigating alleged leakages in budget information denied yesterday that he had given away any official secrets. (Story, Page Four.)

ALEXANDER POLONSKY, aged 23, was hit in the liver and died on the way to the Hadassah Hospital. He was a student in the Institute of Jewish Sciences of the Hebrew University and came here a year ago from Poland where he had received the degree of Bachelor of Laws.

ISAAC YOLOVSKY, aged 26, was hit in the side, the bullet penetrating the right lung. He died some minutes after he was admitted to the Hadassah Hospital. He was a baker.

DR. ZVI SZABCHOSKI, aged about 30, was hit in the head, the bullet penetrating through the right eye into the brain. He died whilst being operated on in the Hadassah Hospital. He came to Palestine about three months ago and leaves a wife who is expecting a child.

Dr. Szabchovski practised with Dr. Dostrovsky, the well-known skin specialist.

Dr. Plosser, a woman physician, suffered a flesh wound in the arm. She was treated in the Hadassah Hospital and sent home.

Israel Ashkenazi, a youth who was standing about two yards from the assailant, between him and the exit, was grazed in the arm. He was given first aid at the Red Shield Station in the Hadassah Hospital and discharged.

The murderer seems to have escaped in the ensuing panic. The crowd gripped by a wild and uncontrollable fear began pouring out in a panic, rushing into the line of cafes on the street, as the shop-keepers began pulling down their shutters.

Some ten minutes later the theatre was darkened and the crowd was being sent home by armed constables.

There was no second showing of "Happy As the Day" last night.

District Administration officials wished to arrange for the funeral of the three latest victims to be held last night, but the Hadassah Hospital authorities were unable to have the bodies ready in time.

Some of the crowd asserted last night that the car in which the assassin escaped, bore on the wind-shield the permit of the Arab Motor Strike Committee.

For a half hour after the outrage, telephone communication was extremely difficult.

It is believed that curfew will be enforced tonight throughout Jerusalem.

IRAQ REVOLT CRUSHED
(From Our Own Correspondent)

Baghdad, May 14. — The revolt in the Mid Euphrates has subsided and investigation into the uprising is proceeding.

The Minister of the Interior, Sayed Rashid Ali el-Gailani, is expected to return today to Baghdad from Diwaniyah where he has been since the outbreak.

The following official communique has been issued:

"The leaders of the rebellion continue to make their submission to the Government. The Iraq Army unit continued their advance as far as Hajjama Station, clearing the rebels from all the districts traversed. Nothing has happened to necessitate renewed military operations, activity being confined to trifling action by the police and Iraq Air Force. The train service between Baghdad and Basrah has been resumed.

Investigations are proceeding to discover the causes underlying the subversive movement, so that preventive measures may be taken against future outbreaks."

12 PAGES
***The Economist* Page 9, 10, 11, 12**
***Life Of Balfour* PAGE THREE**

THE PALESTINE POST

JERUSALEM
WEDNESDAY, JUNE 3, 1936

VOL. XII. 3056.
PRICE: TEN MILS

THOMAS GUILTY

"Unauthorized Disclosures"

(From Reuter)

LONDON, Tuesday. — "Mr. J. H. Thomas made an unauthorized disclosure in regard to information relating to this year's budget, to Mr. Alfred Bates, whereof the latter made use for his own private gain," declared the Budget Tribunal in a unanimous report.

The identical finding was made in regard to Sir Alfred Butt. After seeing the heads of the Civil Service in the witness box, the Tribunal unhesitatingly accepted their evidence both as regards themselves, their subordinates, and Civil Servants generally.

Mr. Thomas heard the verdict at home in Dulwich, surrounded by his family. He seemed staggered by the report and declared, "It is a cruel verdict. Thank God Leslie is exonerated." Sir A. Butt's secretary said that Sir Alfred was making no intimation to the press. Mr. Bates commented: "I have nothing to say."

Interviewed by "Reuters," Mr. J. H. Thomas affirmed, "My conscience is clear. I made no disclosure as regards Budget secrets, to anybody.

After reviewing the evidence he gave before the Tribunal, Mr. Thomas said that

"nobody will ever know of the indignities my family has suffered. Thousands of letters from all classes of people have given me help and encouragement, and the true comradeship of my loving wife and family enabled me to bear up."

The Budget Leakage Tribunal refers to Mr. Thomas's original statement that he personally did not recollect Sir Alfred Butt's visit to the Colonial Office on Budget morning.

Mr. Thomas had told the Court that only some mention of a Derby winner was made. According to Sir Alfred Butt, he gave Mr. Thomas "Quashed" as a tip for that day's racing, and the Tribunal was informed that Mr. Thomas was a heavy winner in backing the horse that day. "It seems improbable, in the circumstances, that he should have forgotten the whole incident."

New Emergency Measures Gazetted

N. China Moving Towards a Crisis

(From Reuter)

SHANGHAI, Tuesday. — While events in North China were yesterday regarded as moving swiftly towards a crisis, the situation today was confused and ambiguous.

Chinese leaders had been issuing reassuring statements, whilst the Japanese military authorities took no further action either in relation to the railway bombing incident or the return to office of the Mayor of Tientsin.

The Chinese Ambassador at Tokyo protested at the Japanese Foreign Office against the increase of Japanese troops in North China, but this was countered by the Foreign Minister's accusation of unrest and alleged Communist activities there.

Mr. Cheng-fu, chairman of the Foreign Affairs Committee of the Hopei-Chahar Political Council, has gone to Tokyo in an endeavour, it is believed, to compose difficulties with Japan.

The Canton Government in South China, on the other hand, is reported to be pressing the Nanking Central Government immediately to declare war on Japan. The Canton authorities have long been known for their strong opposition to Japanese policy in North China.

While the Japanese report that the Southern Provinces have actually declared war upon Nanking, this is regarded as premature. It is admitted, however, that unusually heavy military preparations are proceeding on both sides.

(*Leader, Page 6*)

After Midnight

Fifty-one more factories in Paris went on strike yesterday in addition to 15 on strike already for a week. The workers have occupied the factories. Similar actions are reported from other towns in France. The new French Senate met for the first time yesterday afternoon, disturbed, like the first meeting of the Chamber by a demonstration of suffragettes.

According to the Official final casualty List, 2,766 white Italians lost their lives in the Ethiopian War. The number of Native troops killed is given as 1,593.

FIVE BATTALIONS IN PALESTINE GARRISON

The first detachment of the battalion of Bedfordshires and Hertfordshires, consisting of about 400 men, arrived in Palestine last night from Cairo. The garrison has now been increased from two to five battalions.

About 200 men of the Seaforth Highlanders are reported to have arrived from Cairo on Monday night and the entire battalion is now in Palestine and is stationed in Nablus.

The new Battalion will be stationed on Mt. Scopus.

Palestine Affairs Before Mandates Commission

(From Palcor)

GENEVA, Tuesday. — A statement on the situation in Palestine was made by Mr. H. H. Trusted, K.C., Attorney-General to the Palestine Government, when the oral examination of the accredited representatives of the British Government was opened before the Permanent Mandates Commission here.

Mr. Trusted affirmed that the British Government would not be deterred from pursuing their policy by terrorist methods. Measures had been taken for the reinforcement of troops and the banishment of agitators.

The Attorney-General referred to the statement by Mr. J. H. Thomas in Parliament on May 18, in which he declared that a Royal Commission would be sent to Palestine when order was restored. In reply to questions from members of the Commission regarding the reason for the unrest, Mr. Trusted said he could not at this stage give information on this point.

Questioned during the afternoon session of the meeting with regard to the present disturbances, Mr. Trusted replied that the Commission met to discuss the report on the year 1935, and that he was unable to furnish information about this year.

The Marchese Theodoli (Italy), who presided, was re-elected chairman by six votes to two with one abstention. The continued participation by Italy in the work of the Commission under the League was the subject of some comment.

OPENING OF SHOPS MAY BE ORDERED

EXTENDED POWERS FOR POLICE AND MILITARY

Strict measures have been enacted under a number of Ordinances, and are published in a Gazette Extraordinary dated June 1 but issued yesterday, vesting powers in various Government officers in dealing with the present disorder in Palestine.

These new regulations provide for

the closing of cafes or public resorts or club premises during or preceding an unlawful assembly, riot or disturbance of the peace;

District Commissioners to order the reopening for "business as usual" of any shops or business establishments closed with a view to coercing the Government;

penalties against persons detained by order of the Government or who escape detention;

certain powers to naval, military and air officers;

the prohibition of the manufacture or import of all explosive substances.

Official Communiques

TUESDAY, JUNE 2, 2 P. M.

Northern District

In Haifa sub-district two buses were fired on between Achuza and Mt. Carmel: no one was injured.

Shots were exchanged between unknown persons and a watchman near Kerkur, and a watchman at Ain Shemen was also fired upon.

Shots were fired from the hills between Nablus and Deir Sharaf. The Police carried out a search at Burqa.

In Tulkarm sub-district three bombs exploded on the outskirts of the town; and a considerable number of trees were destroyed at Even Yehuda, near Tel Mond.

At Nazareth a bomb exploded in the police station, breaking some windows.

There was a crop fire at Tel Adashim, and a hut was burnt near Yavniel.

Jerusalem District

A light engine was derailed on the Jerusalem Lydda line near Artuf. A few shots were fired during the night near Jerusalem, and at the Hebron District offices.

Southern District

A bus was stoned and shot at in Ramle last evening; there were no casualties. Other shots were fired there during the night, and two bombs were thrown. No one was injured.

Shots were fired at the Shemen Soap factory at Rehovoth.

At Ben Shemen shots were exchanged between the police and sev-

(Continued on page Twelve)

IMMEDIATE ENACTMENT

An amendment to the Police Ordinance of 1926 has been enacted immediately as indispensably necessary in the public interest, and provides for the closing by a District Commissioner, Magistrate or superior police officer of any cafe, place of public resort or any club premises when it appears that an unlawful assembly, riot or disturbance of the peace has taken place or may be reasonably apprehended.

Under the Interpretation Ordinance, the Chief Secretary has been deputed by the High Commissioner to exercise on his behalf the powers vested under section 10 of the Press Ordinance.

Regulations gazetted under the Palestine (Defence) Order-in-Council of 1931 provide that a District Commissioner may direct that all or any class of shops or business establishments

"which have been closed in pursuance of any organized or general closure of business directed against or calculated to coerce the Government of Palestine" shall generally reopen and carry on business as usual.

District Commissioners may order that any person named shall be detained for any period (not exceeding one year) where they specify, that such person may be arrested by a police officer without warrant, that if such a person escape from the place of his detention he may be arrested without warrant and taken to any prison for a period not exceeding a year, and that the Inspector-General of Police may give directions or prescribe regulations for the internal management of any place of detention and the discipline of all persons detained therein.

Members of His Majesty's Naval, Military or Air Forces have been vested with certain powers, including powers of arrest and entry or search in suspected premises.

The manufacture of all explosive substances in Palestine has been prohibited by an Order under the 1936 Emergency Regulations, whilst their import has been banned (except under police licence) under the Customs Ordinance.

New York Hails "Queen Mary"

MILLIONS WATCH LINER ARRIVE

(From Reuter)

New York, Tuesday.—Millions of holiday-makers lined the waterfront and gave the giant s. s. Queen Mary an enthusiastic reception when she docked here at 9 o'clock last night. It took the liner exactly 25 minutes to come alongside the £10,000,000 pier.

Deep-throated and shrill sirens sounded from hundreds of craft of all sizes as the liner left quarantine. Windows and skyscraper roofs were black with people, Union Jacks fluttered from all the highest buildings, and hawkers in the streets did a roaring trade in Union Jack pennants, models of the Queen Mary, and even nautical caps.

Twelve aeroplanes dived and dipped dangerously overhead, frequently hidden from view in the dense smoke belching from the funnels of 50 vessels racing alongside the liner.

The enormous crowds delayed the disembarking of passengers, and scores of people, including celebrities, had to wait over two hours. There were 250 Customs inspectors on board. Passengers' tips to stewards were estimated at £5,000.

A Good Crossing

Although the fog which delayed the Queen Mary for nearly 11 hours on her maiden voyage robbed her of a new Atlantic record, the builders and owners are completely satisfied with her performance.

Officials of the Cunard-White Star Company are confident, however, that the Queen Mary will capture the Blue Riband later, possibly on her return journey.

HIGH COMMISSIONER MEETS ULEMA

PROBLEMS OF COUNTRY DISCUSSED

An account of an interview between the High Commissioner and some of Ulema (Moslem clergy) of the country was given in yesterday's issue of "Al Iqdam" of Jaffa, an Arabic weekly, the only Arabic newspaper to appear yesterday.

The delegation was headed by Sheikh Ismail al-Hafez, President of the Sharia Court of Appeal, and consisted of Sheikh Amin al-Ouri, Sheikh Tewfik Thabi, Sheikh Selim al Ghusseini, Sheikh Hassan Abou el Seoud, Sheikh Said al-Khatib, and Sheikh Saad ed Din el Khatib.

The delegation is reported to have complained of the British police and troops, the sheikhs pointing out that "if the use of such force continues, the Arab people will have to protect itself." They protested against the methods employed by the police when searching Arab villages and quarters and passers-by in the streets.

The High Commissioner in replying to the delegation is reported by the Arabic periodical to have referred to the Royal Commission. His Excellency is also reported to have given an assurance that he would give orders that there should be no cause for further complaint about police action.

12 Pages

THE PALESTINE POST

Death for the Death-Dealer
LEADER, PAGE 6

JERUSALEM
SUNDAY, JUNE 14, 1936
VOL. XII. 3065.
PRICE: TEN MILS

Death Penalty for Violence

Fatalities Mount In Spanish Riots

Police Convey Mails; Newspapers Closed

(Reuter)

MADRID, Saturday. — A man was killed, several seriously injured and two children were accidentally shot dead in clashes between rival organizations at Malaga yesterday. The death roll for the past four days is 12 persons.

The situation which has arisen in consequence of the general strike and the conflict between Socialists and Communists, is becoming hourly more serious. The chief of the Municipal Police was recently fired on while walking through the streets.

Rioters are molesting visitors on the outskirts of Malaga. Police in armoured cars have been conveying the mails to Gibraltar. Reinforcements of the Civil Guard and police have arrived at Algeciras from Cadiz owing to the fear of disturbances during the annual fair this Sunday.

Strike Called Off

Members of the National Federation of Labour have called off the general strike, but General Union workers have refused to return, and the outlook is ominous and obscure. No newspapers have been published for the last five days.

A strike is now threatened throughout the Spanish coal industry. The demands are understood to include the replacement of the Ministers of Finance and Labour in the recently formed Cabinet.

Representatives of the Province of Asturias have informed the Government that the strike would commence immediately unless their requests were met.

40-Hour Week Bill Adopted by France

PARIS, Saturday. — French strikers are gradually returning to work, although in some trades further "stay in" strikes have started.

Engineering workers are evidently delighted by the decision to go back, and the strike pickets have been withdrawn and factories are now being evacuated.

Men of the Renault Motor Company formed a giant procession last night and sang songs celebrating the great Labour victory. With employees of the Citroen plant, they are returning to work on Monday.

The return to work continues in the provinces. At Rouen 8,000 textile provinces. At Rouen 8,000 textile workers have gone back, but 1,200 workers of the Nieuport aeroplane works have started a "stay in" strike.

New strikes are beginning to break out in some districts but at Amiens, Toulouse, Toulon and elsewhere, owners of big shops have preferred to give their staffs a holiday and close their premises instead of risking the "stay-in" strike movement which has now spread to Morocco.

40-Hour Week Bill Passed

After a debate which lasted all day, the French Chamber of Deputies passed the Forty Hour Week Bill by a vote of 385 to 175, last evening.

The French "New Deal" — Page 8.

EIGHTEEN INJURED IN BOMB OUTRAGE

Explosion in Haifa Train

(From Our Own Correspondent)

TEL AVIV, Saturday. — Eighteen Jewish passengers were injured, three of them seriously, when a bomb exploded in a third-class coach on the Haifa-Lydda train yesterday morning just as the train was pulling out of Kalkilieh station. The train stopped immediately. Nine of the wounded persons, including four women and a child of six, are still in hospital.

The outrage occurred at about 10.30. There was a rush for the exits when the missile was seen, with its fuse burning, rolling down the floor between the seats. One passenger jumped through a window and received cuts and abrasions.

Terrific Explosion

There was a terrific explosion; the noise was magnified within the restricted space. The passengers were hurled in every direction and lay bleeding on the floor of the coach.

So powerful was the explosion that seats and floor were ripped up, and woodwork and asbestos ceiling were torn away exposing the iron framework, the coach being so badly damaged that it gave the impression of having been hit by a shell.

Reports that an Austrian bomb was used are untrue; the missile was a home-made type of bomb, constructed out of a tin canister filled with explosives and nails. Nor is it true that one woman lost an eye as a result the explosion.

Siesta Almost Fatal

One of the passengers awoke from a siesta only just in time. Tired from his week's work at Haifa, Pesach Schlapobersky, aged 26, a mechanic employed by the Egyptian Engineering Stores, had dozed off after leaving Tulkarm.

Interviewed by a representative of *The Palestine Post*, the man said that he was roused by the noise of people running about. He looked round and noticed, under a seat in the centre of the coach, a slowly rolling canister.

Guessing what had happened, Chlapobersky rushed towards the bomb with the intention of tossing it out of the window. But he saw it was smoking, and realised that it would be foolhardy to touch it.

Suddenly the explosion occurred, and he was thrown to the ground. He

(Continued on Page 12, Column 4)

Britain's Attitude Surprises French

(British Official Wireless Press and Reuter)

LONDON, Saturday. — Considerable surprise, and a flurry in diplomatic and political circles, have been caused by Mr. Neville Chamberlain's speech at a political dinner in London on Thursday night when he criticised suggestions that League sanctions should be continued or intensified.

The French and Belgian Ambassadors visited the Foreign Office today to discuss the speech. It is understood that the changed British attitude as voiced by the Chancellor of the Exchequer has completely surprised both France and Belgium.

The feeling in Whitehall seems to be that it is unbecoming to the dignity and responsibility of a leading Power to seek shelter behind the South American States — in this case, the Argentine — in reference to the raising of sanctions.

Great Britain must therefore take the lead, but even if the raising of sanctions is contemplated, this by no means indicates the recognition of Italy's annexation of Ethiopia.

After Midnight

Scores of shots were fired at Migdal at about midnight last night. Reinforcements for the defenders were sent from Tiberias.

The new Van Zeeland Cabinet in Belgium will take the oath of office today. It closely resembles the last Van Zeeland Cabinet with added Socialist strength.

The strike movement in Belgium has reached the Liege coalfields. There are signs of its spreading to the steel industry. Measures have been taken to maintain order and to prevent the occupation of the factories by strikers. (Reuter).

U. S. A. beat Britain in the Wightman Cup Tennis Tournament, 4 to 3.

The Death Roll

£P.500 REWARD OFFERED FOR EACH MURDERER

Two notices which were posted up in Jerusalem on Friday signed by the Inspector-General of Police offer a reward of £P. 500 to any one giving information leading to the apprehension of the person or persons guilty of the 30 unsolved murders prepetrated since April 19, namely, those of 24 Jews, one British Constable, one Palestinian Constable, three Arabs and one Austrian Christian.

The smaller of the two notices, dated June 12, concerns the murder of M. P. C. Khalif Abdul Latif Idrissi at kilo 19 Jerusalem-Jericho Road on June 8. The other, dated June 8, gives a list of 29 deaths as follows:

Jerusalem District

1. **Rubin Klapholtz**, Jew, killed in the Old City, Jerusalem, on May 13.
2. **Alter Cohen**, Jew, killed in the Old City, Jerusalem, on May 13.
3. **Itzhak Yalovsky**, Jew, killed in Zichron Moshe (Edison Cinema), Jerusalem, on May 16.
4. **Alexander Polansky**, Jew, killed in Zichron Moshe (Edison Cinema), Jerusalem, on May 16.
5. **Dr. Zvi Shabchovsky**, Jew, killed in Zichron Moshe (Edison Cinema), Jerusalem, on May 16.

(Continued on Page 6, Column 4)

POLICE AS BUS DRIVERS

Policemen acted as bus drivers yesterday on the No. 4 route in Jerusalem, plying between the General Post Office and Katamon suburb.

Jewish bus drivers, who at the request of the authorities are carrying on the service during the strike of Arab drivers, were off for the Sabbath.

A.S.P. Sigrist Shot, Escapes Death

ASSAILANT SHOT DEAD; 2 ARAB SUSPECTS ARRESTED

An attempt on the life of a Police Officer was made shortly before noon on Friday by two Arabs crouching just below the level of the Jericho road, a few metres beyond the turn at the northeast corner of the Old City wall, opposite the Rockefeller Museum. They emptied their automatic pistols into the car driven by Mr. Alan E. Sigrist, Acting Assistant Police Superintendent, while he was on a tour of inspection.

Mr. Sigrist was seriously wounded in the shoulder and sustained a slight chest wound. British Constable Edmund Doxat, who was sitting by him, received a slight neck wound and also other injuries when the car swerved into the valley.

Presence of Mind

Constable Doxat showed the most remarkable presence of mind at the moment of the surprise attack as his officer and he had been hit. He whipped out his revolver and fired through the wind-screen at the assailants, mortally wounding one man in the chest.

Just then Mr. Sigrist fainted and

(Continued on Page 6, Column 2)

Official Communiques

SATURDAY, JUNE 13, 8 P. M.

In addition to those injured in the Kalkilieh bomb outrage mentioned in yesterday's communique two Indian Moslems have received treatment as out-patients at the Government Hospital, Jerusalem, for minor injuries.

The Arab reported in this morning's communique to have been wounded in the leg in the course of the disturbance in Bethlehem died in hospital early this afternoon.

Further reports from the Northern and Southern Districts of occurrences during the night are as follows: shots were fired during the night at Pardess Lifshitz, to which police and watchmen replied; a bridge on the Hebron-Beersheba road was blown up; and eighty dunams of melon near Kfar Yona were destroyed. A Syrian watchman near Hedera who ran away when challenged by a party of military in an orange grove was wounded by two shots.

A military patrol operating near Burqa, north-west of Nablus, was fired on by a party of Arabs numbering about 30. The patrol returned the fire, wounding one of their assailants, whom they captured, with his rifle, and took to Nablus hospital. There were no military casualties.

(*Earlier Communiques Page 12*).

NEW DEFENCE REGULATIONS

Grim Powers For Civil Courts

Further regulations to deal with lawlessness have been enacted under or amended in connection with the Palestine (Defence) Order-in-Council 1931 emergency regulations and published in a Gazette Extraordinary dated June 12.

Under the new enactment, civil courts are empowered to inflict the death penalty or life imprisonment on persons convicted of firing at members of the Naval, Air or Military Forces, and the Palestine Police Force, for throwing bombs or other explosives, interference with the working of harbours, railways, waterways, power-stations, transmission lines, or water-supply systems, and for damaging or interfering with any telephone or telephone line, or apparatus or wireless installation, or any other means of communication.

An amendment to regulation 9 provides that any member of the Crown forces may order inhabitants in any place to remove barricades or glass, nails or any other obstructions to traffic from the roads.

Newspaper Restrictions

A new regulation numbered 11-A provides that no newspaper shall be printed or published in Palestine without a permit from the District Commissioner concerned, who may refuse to grant or revoke it without giving any reason. Existing permits are not sufficient, and publishers will have fresh licences issued.

Where a District Commissioner has reason to believe that the inhabitants of any town, quarter or village have committed an of-

(Continued on Page 7, Column 1)

One Killed, Constable Hurt in Bethlehem

INTIMIDATORS CAUSE DISTURBANCES AT MARKET

(From Our Own Correspondent)

BETHLEHEM, Saturday. —One Arab was killed and an Arab constable injured this morning when a disturbance occurred between villagers bringing produce and live stock to the market and intimidators who had come down from the surrounding hills.

The villagers, who refused to listen to the demands of the intimidators to remove their wares, were stoned. The police, who intervened, were also stoned and Constable Farid el Khoury, was struck on the head with a stone.

As he fell, he fired once into the crowd, wounding an Arab, who died later.

The constable's rifle was snatched away by one of the crowd. The military arrived on the scene and retrieved the firearm.

It is reported that the local police did not use a machine gun because of the great number of women in the mob, which numbered close upon two thousand persons.

THE PALESTINE POST

JERUSALEM
THURSDAY, JULY 30, 1936.

VOL. XII. No. 3105
PRICE: TEN MILS

ROYAL COMMISSION APPOINTED

R.C. Composition Criticised in House

"Humiliating Exclusions"

(From Reuter and Palcor)

LONDON, Wednesday. — Upon Mr. Ormsby-Gore concluding his announcement of the composition of the Royal Commission, Colonel J. C. Wedgwood asked why no steps had been taken in Palestine to suppress or deport the committee in Jerusalem who were directing the terrorist activity.

The Colonial Secretary replied that he was satisfied that the High Commissioner would not hesitate to make full use of his powers whenever he thought it necessary.

Colonel Wedgwood then complained of the humiliating, and almost insulting exclusion of members of the House of Commons from the Royal Commission. He asked why the House of Lords were contributing, in the person of Earl Peel, one whose personal convictions were so strongly pro-Moslem..

"I must strongly resent the suggestion that any member of the Royal Commission has been chosen because he is pro-Arab, anti-Jewish, or anti-Arab," the Minister replied.

To include members of the House of Commons would necessitate including members of all parties, which would make the Commission unduly large. No women had been included for religious reasons.

It was most desirable that it should not be thought by the Arabs or the Jews that there was any political aspect in the Commission.

Asked why martial law had not yet been proclaimed in Palestine, the Colonial Secretary replied that martial law has not been enforced because having regard to the extensive powers conferred on the High Commissioner by the Palestine Defence Order in Council, it had not up to now been thought necessary or desirable to do so.

Three questions have been placed on the Order Papers of the House of Commons by Colonel Wedgwood, for reply today.

(Continued on page 5, col. 2)

How Long Will the Commission Wait?

(Palcor)

LONDON, Wednesday. — In a leading article today, the "Daily Mail" comments that it is probable that the Royal Commission will have to wait a very long time before order is restored.

Great Britain's task to establish a National Home for the Jews while at the same time giving the country self-government is an impossible one. Given democratic self-government, the Arabs would legislate against the Zionists, limiting immigration.

In spite of the large British forces, the paper declares, fighting will recur so long as the Arabs fear that they are being outnumbered by Jews.

(BIOGRAPHICAL SKETCHES OF THE MEMBERS OF THE ROYAL COMMISSION, PAGE EIGHT)

NEW PERIL IN SPAIN

REBELS PLAN AIR INVASION

(Reuter)

PARIS, Thursday. — Rebels in Morocco are apparently planning a great aerial invasion of Spain, according to the special correspondent of "L'Intransigeant" in Tetuan.

A big three-engined Junker plane has arrived in Tetuan and 19 more of the same type, as well as 20 big bombers and transport machines, are expected to arrive next week.

Franco in Seville

General Franco has now arrived in Seville which henceforth will be the headquarters of the anti-Government forces.

Interviewed at his headquarters by Reuter's correspondent, General Franco declared that the Spanish question was not merely national, but had become international.

He emphasised that his aim was to help Spain by stamping out Communism, and remarked that surely Great Britain, Germany, and Italy must sympathise with him.

The rebel leader appeared confident, and said that the ability of the Spanish Government to hold out depended upon the amount of help that might be given by Moscow and the "Popular Front" Government in France.

One of a group of Spanish Government submarines guarding the Straits to prevent rebel troops from being transported by sea was bombed and sunk by a seaplane six miles south of the Europa Point Lighthouse.

The lighthouse keepers who watched the encounter assert that they were convinced, from the way the submarine disappeared when she was bombed, that she is lost.

When the police entered the house of Senor Garcia Lerroux, ex-Prime Minister and ex-leader of the Radical Party, they found last night a secret private telephone system connecting his study with every part of Spain. Lerroux himself left the country just before the rebellion started.

BRITISH FIRMS MAY EXPORT ARMS TO SPAIN

Great Britain Maintaining Neutrality

(Reuter)

LONDON, Wednesday. — No difficulties are to be placed in the way of private firms in England wishing to export arms to Spain, it is learned by Reuter.

Actually, however, no applications for export licences have hitherto been made.

Great Britain will maintain her traditional policy of strict neutrality and non-interference in the domestic quarrels of other nations in connection with the Spanish civil war.

"If the Dead Could Come Back to Life"

BALDWIN CONDEMNS WAR

(Reuter)

LONDON, Wednesday. — In a moving address to Canadian pilgrims who attended the Vimy Ridge ceremony, and who are now in London, Mr. Stanley Baldwin condemned the tragedy of war and dwelt upon those who but that they had died in battle might have been leaders today.

"I am confident of this — if the dead could come back today, there would be no war," the Prime Minister said, speaking from the steps of Westminster Hall to the large concourse.

"They would never let the younger generation taste from the bitter cup of war which they drank to the dregs. If Europe and the world can find no other way of settling disputes than by war, even when we are still finding and burying the bodies of those who fell 20 years ago, then the world deserves to perish."

Britain to Establish New Infantry Reserve

(British Official Wireless Press)

LONDON, Wednesday. — The Government's decision to create a new infantry section of the supplementary Reserve, with an initial establishment of 17,000 men, was announced in the House of Commons yesterday afternoon by Mr. Duff Cooper.

Enlistment for general service in the infantry would be for a period of six years with the option of re-engagement for a further four years, and would be open to unmarried men from 17 to 25.

FULL TERMS OF REFERENCE

NO ANNOUNCEMENT MADE ON SUSPENSION OF IMMIGRATION

The Colonial Secretary's statement in the House of Commons yesterday concerning the composition of the Royal Commission for Palestine, was broadcast by the P. B. S. yesterday evening, and at the same time was made available by the Press Bureau.

The announcement gave the terms of reference to the Commission and declared that no further decision has been taken on the question of a temporary suspension of immigration other than that announced on July 22.

The Commission consists of six members and not of five as foreshadowed, and of the six, only three, the Earl Peel, Sir Harris Rumbold, and Professor Coupland, were previously mentioned.

We give below the official communique:

MONDAY, JULY 29

This afternoon the Secretary of State for the Colonies made the following statement in the House of Commons: —

"His Majesty has been pleased to approve the appointment of the following to serve on the Palestine Royal Commission.

The Right Honourable the Earl Peel, G. C. S. I., G. B. E.

The Right Honourable Sir Horace Rumbold, Baronet, G. C. B., G. C. M. G., M. V. O.

Sir Laurie Hammond, K. C. S. I., G. B. E.

Sir Morris Carter, C. B. E.

Sir Harold Morris, M. B. E., K. C.

Professor Reginald Coupland, C. I. E.

Lord Peel will be Chairman of the Commission and Sir Horace Rumbold, vice-Chairman. Mr. J. M. Martin, of the Colonial Office, will be Secretary.

The terms of reference of the Royal Commission will be :—

"To ascertain the underlying causes of the disturbances which broke out in Palestine in the middle of April; to inquire into the manner in which the Mandate for Palestine is being implemented in relation to the obligations of the Mandatory towards the Arabs and the Jews respectively; and to ascertain whether, upon a proper construction of the terms of the Mandate, either the Arabs or the Jews have any legitimate grievances on account of the way in which the Mandate has been, or is being, implemented; and if the Commission is satisfied that any such grievances are well-founded, to make recommendations for their removal and for the prevention of their recurrence."

It is not yet possible to state on what date the Commission will leave for Palestine but it is not proposed that the Commission should begin its work in Palestine until order is restored there. When a Royal Commission has been appointed, it has complete control over its own proceedings, so it would be impossible for me to give even an approximate indication of the time which will elapse before the report of the Commission will become available.

As regards the suggestion that there should be a temporary suspension of immigration while the Commission is carrying out its inquiry, I am unable to add anything to the full reply which I gave on July 22 to the question by the Honourable Member for the Consett Division of Durham."

The following is the text of the Secretary of State's reply in the House of Commons on July 22, referred to above: —

"As I informed the House on June 19, His Majesty's Government can contemplate no change of policy whatsoever with regard to Palestine until they have received and considered the Report of the Royal Commission. As regards, however, the suggestion that there should be a temporary suspension of immigration while the Commission is carrying out its inquiry, I am not at present in a position to make any statement as to the intentions of His Majesty's Government beyond saying that their decision will be taken in due course on the merits of the case, and that there is no question of it being influenced by violence or attempts at intimidation."

All members of the Commission have offered their services to His Majesty's Government and to Palestine gratuitously and will receive no emoluments.

Funeral of Constable Wren

CEREMONY AT MOUNT ZION

A large number of all ranks of the British and Palestinian Police attended the funeral yesterday morning at 10 o'clock of P.C. Christopher Wren, who was shot and killed in action on the Nablus Road at noon on Tuesday.

Among those present were the Inspector-General of Police and Mr. H. M. Foot, Assistant District Commissioner at Nablus. There were wreaths from a number of people.

The firing party was supplied by the British Police, and buglers of the 2nd Bn. The Queen's Own Cameron Highlanders sounded "The Last Post" and "Reveille." The ceremony was held in the Protestant Cemetery on Mount Zion.

The action in which P. C. Wren was killed occurred when, with three other British policemen, he was travelling in a patrol car some five kilometres south of Nablus. A group of armed Arabs ran across the road and refused to halt when challenged. They then opened heavy

(Continued on page 8, col. 4)

After Midnight

A ghaffir named Yehiel Haimovitz, 25, died at midnight last night of wounds received a few hours earlier when he was shot by Arabs from an orange grove near Kfar Saba. He underwent an operation in the Hadassah Hospital, Tel Aviv, succumbing, however, to his wounds. He is survived by a wife and two children. Police are investigating the circumstances of the shooting.

Heavy firing on Tiberias from several sides was reported at 1.15 this morning. Military replied with machine guns.

The Spanish Government claims that all Mediterranean and Atlantic ports are now in Government hands except Cadiz.

THE PALESTINE POST

JERUSALEM

SUNDAY, AUGUST 2, 1936.

VOL. XII. No. 3107

PRICE: TEN MILS

The High Court Judgment

LEADER, PAGE FOUR

Hitler Opens Olympic Festivities in Berlin

53 Countries Represented

100,000 Spectators Crowd Into Stadium

(Reuter)

BERLIN, Saturday.— With the shortest speech of his career, Herr Hitler today opened the greatest sporting event in the world in which 53 countries are represented by over 5,000 athletes.

"I declare the Eleventh Olympiad open," the German Chancellor stated, and then sat down.

There were great scenes of enthusiasm, and rain failed to dampen the ardours of 100,000 spectators crammed into the stadium. The athletes marched past Herr Hitler, some giving the Nazi salute and others the Olympic salute.

Pigeons Released

Thirty thousand pigeons were released to give the news of the opening to the world. The crowd sang the German National Anthem followed by the Horst Wessel song.

The band, conducted by the composer Richard Straus, played the Olympic Hymn, the concourse joining in, while the German runner, carrying the Olympic Torch brought by relay from Olympia in Greece, entered the gate and ran to Herr Hitler's tribune, where he kindled the Olympic fire which will burn throughout the Games.

Next Olympiad in Tokyo

In view of England's refusal of the invitation to hold the 1940 Olympic Games in London, they have now been officially awarded to Japan. They will be held in Tokyo.

A dispute over the merits of two teams which have been sent from Brazil, resulted in the withdrawal of both from the Track, Field, Swimming and Rowing events of the Olympic Games.

The "Gemeindeblatt," the organ of the Federation of German Jews, has warned its members to keep off the streets and public places during the Olympic Games.

Collective Fine on Gaza Held Illegal

Regulation 19A Ultra Vires

The High Court, composed of Their Honours, the Chief Justice, and the Senior Puisne Judge (Manning, J.) on Friday morning gave judgment in the Gaza collective fine case, holding that the fine was illegal.

Once more the Court departed from its usual practice and both Judges gave separate judgments.

The Chief Justice, in a long, reasoned judgment held that Regulation 19A of the Emergency Regulations 1936, was ultra vires, and that it could not be held to be retrospective. Furthermore, the said Regulation purported to empower only a District Commissioner and not an Assistant District Commissioner to impose a collective fine and therefore, the latter had no power to impose any collective fine.

He stated, inter alia.

"... We now come to the most important point as to whether Section 19A was intra vires the power conferred upon the High Commissioner by Article IV of the Palestine (Defence) Order-in-Council 1931. It is clear that that Order-in-Council does not confer unfettered powers upon the High Commissioner in respect of the regulations which he may make thereunder ..."

Mr. Justice Manning, in concurring with the Chief Justice that the rule nisi should be made absolute, held that on the facts before the Court the Assistant District Commissioner was not empowered to impose the fine on Gaza under the said Regulation. This was a good ground for making the order absolute he said and therefore it was not necessary for him to deal with the other grounds on which the action of the Assistant District Commissioner had been challenged.

In his judgment, Mr. Justice Manning stated, inter alia:

"The Regulation is of an unusual nature; it punishes, and is meant to punish, innocent persons without giving them any opportunity of being heard. No Court could construe a regulation of this nature as being retrospective. For the Assistant District Commissioner to have any powers under the regulations, the offences, damages or loss must have occurred on or after the 12th June."

The High Court, composed of the Chief Justice and the Senior Puisne Judge (Mr. Justice Manning) granted an order nisi on Friday in the case of three mukhtars of Suba village, calling upon

(Continued on page 8, col. 2)

After Midnight

The French Government has sent an urgent appeal to all Great Powers not to intervene in the Spanish Civil War.

A member of the crew of the three Italian 'planes (see Page 1, column 5) forced down in Algiers stated that they had been commissioned by an Italian firm to deliver the 'planes to the Spanish rebels.

LORD SEMPILL HALTS FLIGHT

Bad Weather in Persia

(Reuter)

KARACHI, July 31. — Lord Sempill, who is attempting to fly to Australia in 1½ days to prove the superiority of British machines, was compelled today to turn back to Jask (S. Persia) to await better weather conditions.

The machine, which left Hanworth aerodrome on Thursday, made a two-hour stop at Aleppo and left for Bushire (Persia) at 7.20 (British Summer Time) on Friday morning, taking off again at 2.05 from Bushire the same afternoon.

Italy and Germany At Locarno Sittings

DIPLOMATIC PREPARATIONS URGED AS PRELIMINARY

Acceptance in principle of the Locarno Powers' invitation to attend a Five-Power Conference was announced by the Italian and German Governments in Rome and Berlin respectively on Friday.

In an interview with the French Ambassador and the British and Belgian Charge d'Affaires at Rome, the Italian Foreign Minister said that the Italian Government would be glad in principle to participate at a date to be settled.

Count Ciano added that his Government thought it useful that the conference should be properly prepared by an exchange of views through the ordinary diplomatic channels.

Germany Concurs

A similar suggestion that the eventual Locarno discussion needed careful diplomatic preliminaries was made by Baron von Neurath on Friday night to the British and French Ambassadors and the Belgian Minister.

In transmitting to them Germany's official acceptance of the invitation, the German Foreign Minister said that the question of the agenda would have to be carefully considered.

NEW VOLUNTEER RESERVE FOR THE R.A.F.

(British Official Wireless Press)

LONDON, July 31.— The formation of a new volunteer reserve for the Royal Air Force was announced in the House of Lords yesterday by the Secretary for Air.

Fierce Fighting in Northern Spain

Barcelona Faces Siege

(Reuter)

LONDON, Saturday.— Large crowds gathered today on the French side of the frontier at Hendaye in the hope of witnessing an engagement between the Socialists and Fascist rebels in Spain.

A decisive action was expected in the north today. Government forces are attempting to recapture Oyarzun, while the rebels are desperately seeking access to passages to San Sebastian or Bilbao in order to insure supplies.

Every available man has been mobilised by the rebels in Saragossa against Government forces believed to be advancing from Catalonia.

Barcelona Preparing

The town of Barcelona is preparing to resist a siege by the insurgents, and Communists are making house-to-house searches in the city for Fascists or suspected sympathisers.

Big cobblestones are being torn from the roadways to make street barricades and machine-gun emplacements. A definite food shortage is becoming apparent.

Decapitation

Gibraltar, Saturday.— British refugees from Malaga and other small Spanish towns who have arrived here aboard H.M.S. "Bulldog," report that Spanish communists, in order to save their ammunition, are cutting of the heads of fascists and throwing their bodies into the sea. Many decapitated corpses have been seen off the coast of Malaga.

Rout Near Madrid

While Spanish insurgents claim to have reached a point 11 miles from Madrid, the Government states that they were routed 35 miles west of Madrid, losing 63 dead, a number of prisoners, and a large quantity of war material.

Reports from Gibraltar state that a Spanish Government flying-boat which bombed Algeciras this morning, narrowly missing the British Consulate, was disabled by insurgent gunfire and compelled to land in British waters at Gibraltar. The crew of three was brought ashore in a launch.

Today's Programme Of Olympic Games

The many and various festivals and ceremonies connected with the opening of the 11th Olympic Games having been completed last night, the actual Games are due to commence today. The following is the programme for today.

Finals.— High Jump. Shot Put 10,000 metres flat. (Men. Javelin (Ladies).

Finals.— Weight Lifting: Feather-weight and Light-weight.

In addition to the foregoing finals the heats for the 100 metres flat, the 800 metres flat, and the catch-as-catch-can wrestling events will be staged.

The Fencing for foil teams and the eliminating matches in the Hockey championship also start today.

CIVIL WAR BEGUN IN SOUTH CHINA

(Reuter)

NANKING, Saturday. — The civil war which has been threatening for some time in South China, has begun.

The Kwangsi War-lords, Lit-Sung-Jen and Pai-Chung-Hsi have refused to obey a Central Government order to vacate their posts and have launched a surprise attack upon loyal Kwangtung troops on the border of the two provinces.

Severe fighting has been proceeding since Friday morning. The Central Government is rushing troops from Nanking to assist the loyalists.

Italian War Planes Crash in Algiers

BENT ON MYSTERIOUS ERRAND

(Reuter)

ROME, Saturday.— The Italian Government is inquiring into the reported forced landing of three Italian aeroplanes in N. Africa yesterday.

Three out of six Italian aeroplanes were reported from Oran to have made a forced landing on French soil in North Africa en route from Sardinia to Spanish Morocco.

One crashed near Nemours, Algeria, two of the airmen being killed and one injured. Five machine-guns were found on board the plane. The second machine was forced to land near Oran, and the third near Lamoulouya.

Going to the Rebels

One of the crew of the latter stated they were on a mission to Nador, south of Melilla, in Spanish Morocco, held by the insurgents. The machines carried no marks or identification numbers.

King Edward Charters Luxury Yacht

HOLIDAY CRUISE IN MEDITERRANEAN

(Reuter)

LONDON, July 31.— The King has chartered the yacht Nahlin, belonging to the millionairess Lady Yule, for a holiday cruise in the Mediterranean, which will probably begin in ten days' time.

His Majesty plans to cruise along the Adriatic and Eastern Mediterranean coast. The yacht will be escorted by two destroyers.

Luxury Vessel

The Nahlin, which is at present at Southampton, is one of the most luxurious yachts afloat, and an ocean liner in miniature. It is 300 feet over all and has a speed of 17 knots.

She was built in 1930 and cost £278,000. The yacht is equipped with a fine gymnasium and with dining, drawing and smoking rooms, and has a special dance floor.

No Council of State

It is understood that no Council of State will be appointed to act for King Edward. Official documents requiring his signature will be sent by messengers to various points en route and will be picked up probably by the escorting destroyers.

The King will be in constant touch with London from his yacht. If any unforeseen developments occur, rendering His Majesty's presence in London desirable, special arrangements will be made for a speedy return.

Captain Doyle, the master of the Nahlin, has visited St. James's Palace and discussed final arrangements for the cruise with officials of the King's staff.

GEORGE McMAHON COMMITTED

(Reuter)

LONDON, July 31.— George Andrew McMahon, the man who figured in the incident on Constitution Hill on July 16, when the King was passing, was committed for trial at Bow Street today on all three charges against him.

The committal was in respect of his being in unlawful possession of a revolver with intent to endanger life and property, of presenting near to the person of His Majesty a revolver with intent to break the public peace, and of producing a revolver near the person of the King with intent to alarm him.

Sobs in Witness Box

McMahon broke into sobbing

(Continued on Page 8, Col. 2.)

12 PAGES | **The Economist** Pages 9, 10, 11, 12

Cyprus and the Empire PAGE THREE

THE PALESTINE POST

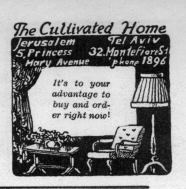
JERUSALEM
WEDNESDAY, SEPTEMBER 30, 1936

VOL. XII. No. 3156
PRICE: TEN MILS

Fliers Reach Cairo After Braving Storms

Portsmouth to Johannesburg

Three Retire from Competition

(Reuter)

At least seven out of the nine competitors in the £10,000 Trophy Air Race from Portsmouth to Johannesburg reached Cairo last night.

Major Miller, flying a Mew Gull, and Alington and Lieut. Booth in a B.A. Eagle machine, were behind the schedule.

BULLETIN

(Reuter)

LONDON, Tuesday.— The first flyer to reach Cairo was Captain Halse in a Mew Gull, who started at scratch. He arrived at 20 07 covering 2,200 miles in 12 and a half hours and received a very animated greeting. The landing-ground was floodlit and the neighbouring desert bathed in beams from thousands of motorcar lights. Flying Officer Clouston flying a Miles Hawk was second arriving at 20.39.

Two more competitors of the Air Race retired. Major Miller, flying a Mew Gull descended on Ruma through shortage of petrol, took four and half hours in order to obtain the necessary supply, reached Belgrade and decided to discontinue the race. Victor Smith was forced to land at Skoplje, in Serbia, owing to oil trouble. He was faced with a long and troublesome repair-job and retired.

BELGRADE-CAIRO HOP

Messages from Belgrade last night reported that the seven machines left between noon and 2.30 yesterday afternoon on the "hop" across the Mediterranean to Cairo.

Captain Halse was first, arriving at 12.08 and leaving at 12.30. Then came Flying Officer Clouston, taxi-ing across the airport at 12.40 and taking off at 12.55. Max Findlay and Kenneth Waller spent only twenty minutes there between 12.50 and 13.10.

Victor Smith shaved their time by one minute when he entered at 14.04 and left at 14.23. C.W.A. Scott and Giles Guthrie arrived at 14.08 and left at 14.23. Tommy Rose followed by arriving at 14.22 and leaving at 14.37, while Llewellyn and Hughesdon were in and out again at 14.23 and 14.37 respectively.

Victor Smith on his arrival declared that he was never so cold in his life as in his open aeroplane, flying at a height of 13,000 feet to cross the Alps. A Yugoslav officer took pity on the young South African and gave him a leather coat. Smith did not even have an overcoat.

Alington and Booth, who had the biggest handicap and were first out from Portsmouth, made a forced landing near Regensburg. The three occupants were not hurt. The machine landed in a field owing to shortage of fuel, damaging the under-carriage.

The first arrivals at Vienna were Tommy Rose at 12.07, and Llwellyn a minute later.

ANOTHER IMPERIAL AIRWAYS LINER LOST

Destroyed by Fire at Delhi

(Reuter)

DELHI, Tuesday. — Another Imperial Airways liner was lost when the eastbound Athena was destroyed by fire at the airport here while taking off this morning.

The passengers and crew of the Athena are safe, and the greater part of its mails has not been damaged.

French Chamber Adopts Gold Bill

ALL NIGHT SITTING ENDS IN VICTORY FOR LEFT WING

(Reuter)

PARIS, Tuesday.— After an all-night sitting, which had to be suspended for half an hour at 11 o'clock owing to an uproar following an offensive Socialist remark, the French Chamber of Deputies this morning adopted the Gold Bill by 350 to 221 votes.

One deputy jeeringly remarked, "M. Blum's franc is not gold but rubber."

Backstage negotiations resulted in the Left Parties accepting M. Blum's offer to withdraw clauses provided a sliding scale of wages and substituting clauses fully empowering the Government to prevent profiteering.

Senate Meets Today

The Senate met and then adjourned until tomorrow to dis-
(Continued on Page 12, Column 3.

INSURGENTS BEGIN ADVANCE ON MADRID

PORTUGAL JOINS NON-INTERVENTION BODY

(Reuter)

LISBON, Tuesday.— Insurgent headquarters at Burgos have issued an announcement that the insurgent advance on Madrid from Toledo has begun.

A Telavera message announces officially that all except 80 of the original population of 1,200 in the Alcazar Citadel at Toledo were rescued alive. Five hundred are wounded.

HERR HESS'S GOOD WISHES

Herr Hitler's deputy, Herr Hess, has telegraphed to the Alcazar defenders,

"The German National-Socialist Party sends its best wishes to the heroes of the Alcazar and their liberators."

NON-INTERVENTION

LONDON, Tuesday.— Portugal was represented at yesterday's meeting of the Commitee for Non-Intervention in Spain by the Portuguese Charge d'Affaires in London, Senhor Monteiro.

In announcing her decision to join, Portugal indicated that she would mainain in entirety the reserve conditions made on August 21 last.

The Committee has agreed that it will be a matter of principle that complaints regarding alleged breaches of agreement will only be considered if submitted on behalf of governments signing that agreement.

It was reported to the Committee today that, since their last meeting, good progress had been made with the preparation of a document summarising legislative and other measures taken by the participating Governments to give effect to the agreement for non-intervention.

PALESTINE MARTIAL LAW ORDER ISSUED

20 Arab Casualties In Jaba Battle

THREE BRITISH WOUNDED

An officer and a private of the Dorsetshire Regiment and a private of the Lincolnshire regiment were wounded in an engagement near Jaba, southwest of Jenin, which lasted throughout yesterday afternoon until dusk.

Detachments from four battalions engaged in a converging movement upon a band whose presence had been reported earlier.

The battalions were the Dorsets, the Lincolns, the Royal Scot Fusiliers and the Beds and Herts, besides aeroplanes and armoured cars.

It is believed that 20 Arab casualties were inflicted by the ground troops while aircraft, which cooperated with the troops, are said to have accounted for further casualties.

The engagement began early in the afternoon following the movements of the troops through the district in search of armed bands.

The Soviet Union is Ready to Fight

RUSSIAN MARSHAL'S ASSERTION

MOSCOW, Sept. 28.— The statement that Soviet Russia was ready to fight any enemy on any front if there were attempts to attack Soviet rule, was made by Marshal Voroshiloff today.

This assertion occurred during a speech towards the end of the Red Army manoeuvres near Moscow.

The reference made by M. Voroshiloff, who is seen in some quarters as successor to M. Stalin at the head of the Soviet Republic, is taken to imply that the Kremlin foresees the possibility of having to fight a coalition of hostile States.

PROCLAMATION TO FOLLOW

Definite Date Not Yet Set

(Reuter)

LONDON, Tuesday.— An Order-in-Council entitled "Palestine Martial Law Order" was issued in tonight's London Gazette.

The Order empowers the High Commissioner to delegate to the General Officer Commanding the Forces powers to make regulations for securing public safety and defence in Palestine.

The new Order will be brought into force by a Proclamation in Palestine, to be promulgated probably, tomorrow.

Later, the High Commissioner will decide, in consultation with Lieut.-General Dill, the Commander-in-Chief, when to issue a further proclamation delegating to General Dill the widest possible powers.

These powers will include the establishment of Military Courts and regulations which cannot be challenged by the ordinary Civil Courts.

Other provisions are for press censorship, arrests and deportations, control of harbours, control of transportation by land, air and water, control of trade and commerce, the infliction of communal fines, and the forfeiture or destruction of property as a punitive measure.

The Mandatory's Jurisdiction

MARTIAL LAW FALLS WITHIN ITS PROVINCE

(By a Legal Correspondent)

Numerous constitutional questions arise from an examination of the Mandate status and the relationship of the Mandatory to the Mandated territory and its population. A telegram from London recently reported on high authority that neither the Administration of Palestine nor the Mandatory Government was allowed to declare Martial Law in Palestine. The authority of the Covenant of the League of Nations was invoked in support of this view, and to vest such power only on the Council of the League of Nations.

Prima facie, however, it seems that the Covenant of the League, far from dealing with the repartition of power in any form of detail, provides (Art. 22) that

"the degree of authority, control and administration to be exercised by the Mandatory shall, if not previously agreed by the members of the League be explicitly defined in each case by the Council."

In examining this issue we are therefore referred to the specific instrument "The Mandate" as it is called, by which the authority of the Mandatory Government is established and defined for every territory to which the Mandatory Regime has been applied.

"Full Powers"

The Mandate for Palestine confers (Art. 1) on the Mandatory "full powers of legislation and administration save as they may be limited by the terms of this mandate."

The intention seems to have been found that in matters of administration, the Mandatory should have a free hand and should not have to invite the Council to deal with any case of emergency, especially as access to the Council involves delay by the very nature of the proceedings.
(Continued on page 6, Col. 4.)

"STATUTORY MARTIAL LAW"

Although the Order, as Reuter says, may be brought into force today it is not likely that any definite steps will be taken immediately (writes a Political Correspondent).

The law will need considerable discussion between the military and the civil authorities and much drafting of regulations.

It is true that preparations have long been made for Martial Law, but it is gathered that what is at present contemplated is not martial law as such but something approaching what experts call "Statutory Martial Law," Lieutenant-General Dill probably dealing with the situation by means of the wide powers to be delegated to him by the High Commissioner.

powers will eventually assume, it is not intended that there should be any general superceding of the civil by the military authority. The civil administration would continue to operate as at present except in so far as it concerns the departments whose activities are closely connected with those of the Army, such as communications, and public security.
(Continued on page 6, Col. 3.)

After Midnight

The Johannesburg air race has turned into a dual battle between Captain Halse and Flying Officer Clouston, the former leaving Cairo a few minutes before the latter.

In a battle between an insurgent cruiser and two Government torpedo boats off the northern Spanish coast, one of the torpedo boats was badly damaged and sank shortly after. Twenty of the crew were saved.

General O'Dufy has left for Burgos where he intends to confer with General Franco about enlisting Irish Blue Shirt volunteers in the insurgent ranks.

FEAST OF TABERNACLES

The Palestine Post will not be published tomorrow, the first day of Tabernacles, but will appear again on Friday morning.

12 PAGES | The Economist Pages 9, 10, 11, 12

Palestine Gives Evidence
TIMES ARTICLE, PAGE 3

THE PALESTINE POST

JERUSALEM
WEDNESDAY, NOVEMBER 11, 1936

VOL. XII. No. 3189
PRICE: TEN MILS

Royal Commission Arrives Today

APPEAL FOR PEACE ISSUED BY BISHOP AND CHIEF RABBI

The Bishop of Jerusalem has issued the following message on the occasion of the arrival of the Palestine Royal Commission today:—

The Royal Commission arrives in Palestine on a day which by many people is observed as marking the end of the greatest war in history. It arrives charged to seek the way to end a lesser but no less deplorable strife in the Holy Land.

As a representative of one of the three great religions of Palestine, which alike believe in one GOD, and in the ultimate certainty that His will must prevail, may I appeal to all the people of Palestine — and to the members of the Royal Commission themselves — to recognise that the land is a Holy Land to all of us, that there can be no solution of our difficulties that is not based on spiritual foundations, and that such a solution can only be attained in an atmosphere of peace, justice, and goodwill.

As a Christian Bishop I would bid all those to whom I have authority to speak to pray constantly during the Sessions of the Royal Commission both for its members and for those who give evidence before them, that under the good hand of GOD this Holy Land may return into the ways not only of prosperity, but of piety and peace.

George Francis
Bishop in Jerusalem.

St. George's Close, Nov. 10.

LORD PEEL, P.C., G.C.S.I., G.B.E., CHAIRMAN.

The Chief Rabbi of the Agudath Israel has published the following appeal:—

The Jewish population in Palestine today welcomes the members of the Royal Commission who have come to Palestine upon a Divinely-inspired mission as representatives of His Britannic Majesty's Government to establish peace among the members of different communities, after a period of serious disturbances which for six months threatened the tranquility of the land and the success of its upbuilding. The Jewish population regards it as a happy augury that the Commission will arrive in this land on the nineteenth anniversary of that day on which the bloodshed of the greatest war in history ceased.

The success of the Royal Commission will depend upon the extent to which its members and those who give evidence before it direct their acts in accord with the exalted aspiration of seeing this Holy Land built up upon the foundation of justice, purity of purpose, and peace between one faith and another.

We therefore request our brethren of this Holy City, to pray for the welfare of the King and his representatives, the members of the Royal Commission, that the hallowed spirit of Zion may rest upon them, to inspire them with wisdom and understanding, to infuse in them good will, to reveal to them the light of truth and justice, and to crown their efforts with success, so that peace may come to the Land of Peace, and the holy prophecy may be fulfilled that "The time of my redemption draweth nigh and my righteousness shall be revealed."

J. Z. Dushinsky.

SIR HAROLD MORRIS, M.B.E., K.C.

SIR MORRIS CARTER, C.B.E., B.A., B.C.L.

RT. HON. SIR HORACE RUMBOLD, P.C., G. C. B., G.C.M.G., K.C.M.G., M.V.O. VICE-CHAIRMAN.

SIR LAURIE HAMMOND, K.C.S.I., C.S.I., C.B.E.

MR. REGINALD COUPLAND, C.I.E.

Passenger Ships In U.S. Stranded

HAWAII HARD HIT

(Reuter)

NEW YORK, Tuesday.—Hawaii has already lost something like $500,000 as a result of the United States shipping strike which continues to paralyse the sea transport and tourist trades.

Seven steamers are at present held up in Honolulu.

In spite of orders from Union leaders at San Francisco asking the strikers to resume work, the latter refuse to comply in the hope of obtaining recognition for local longshoremen.

Meanwhile 600 passengers are stranded, adding to the food problem on the island, which is daily becoming more acute.

The Bethlehem shipbuilding yards at San Francisco will be quiet today following yesterday's walk-out of 6,000 workers.

The strikers claim that 200 ships are idle and that nearly 17,000 men are out, but employers regard the figures as exaggerated.

Steel Ring Around Madrid Tightened

GOV'T HOLDS OUT

(Reuter)

Considerable aerial and artillery bombardments of Madrid occurred yesterday when the insurgents made determined attempts to break down the morale of the inhabitants.

Nevertheless, there was no perceptible change in the situation and the insurgents were kept at bay by the staunch resistance of the loyalist militia.

A small bomb burst over the garden of the British Embassy but caused no damage. There are about 125 people in the Embassy. The building containing the British and American Club was also hit and badly damaged.

Government Offensive

To the south of Madrid the Government troops are reported to have begun a successful counter-offensive. The main brunt of the insurgent attack appears to be
(Continued on page 6, Col. 3.)

"PRAY FOR THE PEACE OF JERUSALEM" — PSALM 122

Two religious leaders in Palestine, the Anglican Bishop in Jerusalem, The Rt. Rev. G. F. Graham-Brown and the Chief Rabbi Joseph Z. Dushinsky of the Agudath Israel, have issued appeals to their respective communities to offer continued prayer during the sessions of the Royal Commission for the success of its task.

(The text of the messages are printed above.)

We understand that the Mufti of Jerusalem considered it to be inappropriate to issue a religious appeal in view of the decision of the Arab Higher Committee not to cooperate with the Royal Commission, since such action might
(Continued on page 7, Col. 2.)

On Inside Pages

British Power as Peace Guarantee

SIR T. INSKIP

(Reuter)

LONDON, Tuesday. — While emphasising the fact that the Navy remained the first line of defence, Sir Thomas Inskip, in reviewing defence problems in the House of Commons this afternoon, emphasised the necessity for collaboration between the Navy and the Air Force. The main purpose of air expansion was to provide a defence against aerial attacks.

"It is our aim and purpose to develop as deterrent and as powerful a striking force as we can," said Sir Thomas.

In speed, capacity and range, British machines were not inferior to any abroad. Behind the Air Force, there were other measures to complete Great Britain's defence — guns, searchlights and other technical equipment. An extensive balloon barrage was contemplated for the protection of London. Next year would see an
(Continued on page 6, Col. 4.)

Arab Leaders Call For Peaceful Day

MANIFESTO ISSUED

(From Our Political Correspondent)

A manifesto calling upon the Arab people to remain peaceful was issued yesterday by the Arab Higher Committee after a six-hour meeting.

Among those present at the meeting besides the members themselves were Sheikh Fuad el Khatib, the personal emissary of H.H. the Emir Abdullah, and Kamal Kassab.

The manifesto states that rumours have been current that a general strike was to be held today, the day of the arrival of the Royal Commission in Palestine. The Committee stated that it had no intention of encouraging such a strike and called upon the Arabs to remain tranquil.

It is understood that both Sheikh el Khatib and Sheikh Kamal pressed forward suggestions for a retraction of the previous
(Continued on page 6, Col. 5.)

THE PALESTINE POST
JERUSALEM
THURSDAY, NOVEMBER 26, 1936
VOL. XII No. 3202
PRICE: TEN MILS

Dr. Weizmann's Statement
LEADER, PAGE FOUR

Russia to Elect Her First Democratic Parliament

New Constitution Adopted

13,721 Amendments to Original Draft

(Reuter)

MOSCOW, Wednesday. — The adoption today by the All-Union Congress of Soviets of the new Constitution of Russia is the prelude to the election of the first democratic Parliament since the Bolshevik Revolution.

At an extraordinary session held at the Kremlin the Congress signed its own death-warrant by abdicating power to a Parliament of two Chambers.

As a result of the discussions of the past few months, attended by 25,000,000 people, the Central Executive Committee made 13,721 amendments to the original draft, affecting every chapter and article.

The grant of full civil rights to all Soviet citizens under this new Constitution was made on June 12 last when the Presidium of the C.E.C. approved of the text now adopted.

The Supreme Legislature was designed to consist of two Chambers — the Soviet of United Republics and the Soviet of Nationalities. The former was to have one representative for every 300,000 population, and the latter 10 representatives from every Federal Republic, five from each Autonomous Republic, and two from each Autonomous Province.

The Legislature was to be elected for four years, and elections, by secret ballot.

Three Germans Arrested

A Berlin message from Moscow says that three more Germans have been arrested by the Soviet authorities.

They are Herr Friedrich Boesherz, Herr Reinhold Schindler, an engineer, and Herr Herman Stammer.

The German Embassy is trying to obtain further information in regard to these arrests which took place on Saturday.

When the German-Japanese agreement to coordinate action against the activities of the Communist International was read to assembled diplomats in Berlin today, it was noteworthy that the Soviet Ambassador was absent.

The absence of an invitation had aroused the belief that the announcement would be much more grave than it actually turned out to be.

A categorical denial is given in British quarters (says BOWP) to a statement that the German Ambassador in London had informed the Prime Minister, Mr. Baldwin, that Germany intended to break off diplomatic relations with Russia if the German engineer Stickling were executed.

BULLETIN

The death sentence of Herr Stickling and of two Russians, MM. Leonenko and Kovalenko, have been commuted to that of ten year's imprisonment each. In the case of the six other Russians accused of "criminal wrecking and diversionist activities of counter-revolutionary groups" the death sentences will be carried out.

Reich - Japanese Military Alliance

ANNOUNCED IN BERLIN

(Reuter)

LONDON, Wednesday. — British circles suspect that the agreement between Japan and Germany, which has been announced in Berlin, goes farther than the published terms.

It may indeed resemble an iceberg — reaching further below the surface than above. Well-informed quarters, however, have no news confirming reports that the two countries have agreed to a defensive military alliance. Such a step, if true, would naturally weaken the position of Great Britain in the Far East.

There is readiness to credit reports of a barter agreement under which German arms would be exchanged for Japanese raw materials.

Taking the published terms alone, it is felt that the agreement does not alter the situation, and it is regarded as an announcement, made for political reasons, of an old-standing affinity between the contracting parties.

Nevertheless, the agreement is not liked by Great Britain insofar as it represents a further accretion to the system of a bloc representing opposing ideologies, and any such alignment runs counter to British policy, as has been frequently made clear by Mr. Eden and Mr. Baldwin.

A message from Rome states that the Italian Government is not affected by the German-Japanese agreement and that no accord exists between Rome and Tokyo although there is an identity of views.

The Acting-Secretary of State in the United States, Mr. Walton Moore, stated yesterday that the United States is only academically interested in the German-Japanese pact.

Spain Rejects Plan For a Neutral Zone

TO BOMB FASCISTS

According to a Lisbon message, the Spanish Government has refused to cooperate in the establishment of a neutral zone in Madrid.

The Government radio station reports that Senor Del Vayo, the Foreign Minister, declared that the suggestion of the International Red Cross to this effect would mean that the Government agreed to the bombardment of the remaining districts of the capital in which anti-Fascists were living.

Mr. Eden informed the House of Commons yesterday that the proposed prohibition of British shipping to carry munitions did not refer to foodstuffs and coal.

Dr. WEIZMANN SPEAKS For the JEWISH PEOPLE

DR. WEIZMANN'S ADDRESS

The Jewish problem was a two-fold problem: it was one that could be expressed in the word "homelessness" and also one of considerable world importance.

There are about 6,000,000 Jews in Central, Eastern, and South-Eastern Europe condemned to be penned up in places where they are not wanted.

Here is a people which is a minority everywhere, a majority nowhere.

Uganda was refused as a Jewish home because "it was never Palestine, it would never be Palestine."

The Jews have conferred, indirectly, considerable benefits on the Arab population.

TESTIFIES BEFORE THE ROYAL COMMISSION

"Gov't Should Introduce Dynamic Development"

(From a Staff Correspondent)

A vivid and profoundly moving account of the world Jewish tragedy of "homelessness" and the moral background and spiritual forces of the Zionist Movement was given to the Royal Commission yesterday morning by Dr. Chaim Weizmann, President of the Jewish Agency and World Zionist Organization.

From 10.30 until after 1 o'clock, Lord Peel and his colleagues listened to Dr. Weizmann's introduction of the Jewish case, which will be later amplified by statistical data and other material submitted by the Jewish experts.

Dr. Weizmann was accompanied by Mr. Moshe Shertok, head of the Political Department of the Jewish Agency Executive, and Mr. Leonard Stein, the Agency's honorary adviser. Visitors included Mr. David Ben Gurion, Dr. Vera Weizmann, Mr. Isaac Ben-Zvi, Mr. Nevill Barbour, Mr. N. Kirschner (of South Africa), and Dr. B. Joseph, Mr. D. G. Harris and Mr. L. Andrews, on liaison duty with the Royal Commission, also attended.

Composition of Jewish Agency

At the request of Lord Peel, the witness described the composition and functions of the Jewish Agency, its constituent bodies, and the method of their election.

Dr. Weizmann then proceeded to give what he called "a bird's-eye view" of the Jewish position and of Zionism. It was a problem, he said, which could best be expressed in the word "homelessness." Individual Jews and individual groups of Jews might have a home and be comfortably placed, but drawing the geographical line across Europe, in the eastern section one found the Jewish populations in a political and economic state which was "something neither life nor death."

No Emigration

The means of migration westwards, mostly to America, had been closed. Only recently Colonel Josef Beck, Polish Foreign Minister, had said in Geneva that there were a million Jews too many (out of 3,000,000) in Poland. Where could they go? Was there a place in the world which could rapidly absorb a million people?

The witness narrated some of the causes which were ousting Jews from economic life in Poland,— principally the migration of poor Polish peasants into the towns.

A similar position existed in other "Succession States," territories formerly part of the old Russian Empire, as well as in Central and Eastern Europe.

"It is no exaggeration on my part to say," declared the Zionist leader, "that there are about 6,000,000 Jews in this part of the world — and I am not speaking of Oriental Communities whose Jews are inarticulate— condemned to live in a place where they

(Continued on Page 4)

"A Certificate for Palestine Is a Certificate for Freedom"

PRESS COMMUNIQUE NO. 13.

Wednesday, November 25.

The Royal Commission sat in public session from 10.30 a.m. to 1 p.m. and heard the evidence of Dr. Chaim Weizmann.

Dr. Weizmann stated that he is the President of the Jewish Agency for Palestine and the President of the Zionist Organization. The Zionist Organization is the Agency referred to in paragraph 4 of the Mandate. Later, in 1929, the Jewish Agency was formed. The Council of the Jewish Agency consists of 50 Zionists and 50 of others who are not Zionists but are interested in the upbuilding of Palestine. The Zionist members are elected by the Zionist Congress and the non-Zionist members are appointed by their respective groups in various countries. The Council of the Jewish Agency has an Administrative Committee, composed also of 50 Zionists and 50 non-Zionists and the Administrative Committee has an Executive Committee in Palestine composed of similar proportions which conducts the current business.

In outlining the background of the Zionist movement Dr. Weizmann stated that the Jewish problem was two-fold. The first one is the homelessness of the Jewish people. Although it may be said that there are individual Jews with homes and many comfortable homes in countries in Western Europe, East of the Rhine, in Poland, Germany, Austria, Rumania, Lithuania and Latvia, there are about 6,000,000 Jews who are condemned to be penned up in places where they cannot live and where they are not wanted.

The Jews and Palestine

The other problem is one of world importance namely, the presence of 6,000,000 people who don't know what will happen tomorrow. The young man in a depressed area in England feels that there is the State which is interested in his welfare and that there is some outlook but the Jew in Eastern Europe has no hope, there is no one who cares for them, they are in despair. A certificate for Palestine is a certificate for freedom and that is why they watch with intensity what is going on here.

In dealing with the past history of the Jews, Dr. Weizmann pointed out that there was not one period where the Jews did not try to come back to Palestine and there have always been movements of Jews into Palestine whenever the opportunity arose. The connection of Great Britain with the return of the Jews to Palestine extends over a period of 300 years and the Balfour declaration is but the final link in the chain.

The Balfour declaration was not lightly made, its form and words were the subject of serious discussion by the British Cabinet, even at a time of stress, and suggestion that it was a mere war-time expediency which might thereafter be whittled down, was unfounded. The Balfour declaration was hailed by Jewry throughout the world as the Magna Carta of the Jewish people and meant, to quote the word of Lord Cecil, "The Jews are restored to Judaea." When he ((Dr. Weizmann) was asked at the Peace Conference "What do you mean by a Jewish National Home?" he replied impromptu "To build up something in Palestine which will be as Jewish as England is English."

Referring to the conditions under which their work was begun, Doctor Weizmann stated that seldom in the history of colonization has work of the kind been carried out by private organization. He spoke from per-

(Continued on Page 8, Col. 2)

After Midnight

Dr. Chaim Weizmann will continue his evidence this morning before the Royal Commission in camera.

Six shots were fired near Napoleon Hill, Ramat Gan, last night. Police are investigating.

The French Government is making an appropriation of 10,500,000,000 francs on armaments in 1937. This is the largest defence budget ever presented in France.

Both the House of Lords and House of Commons approved the Anglo-Egyptian treaty yesterday without division.

16 Pages

THE PALESTINE POST

JERUSALEM
FRIDAY, DECEMBER 11, 1936

VOL. XIII. No. 3215
PRICE: TEN MILS

KING EDWARD ABDICATES

FAREWELL MESSAGE READ BY SPEAKER

"For the Throne, the Empire and the Happiness of My Peoples..."

LONDON, Thursday. —Amid a hushed and painful silence, members of both Houses of Parliament this afternoon listened to the King's own announcement of his abdication read simultaneously by the Speaker in the House of Commons and the Lord Privy Seal in the House of Lords.

The message was as follows:

"After long and anxious consideration I have determined to renounce the Throne to which I succeeded on the death of my father, and I am now communicating this my final and irrevocable decision.

"Realising as I do the gravity of this step, I can only hope that I shall have the understanding of my peoples in the decision I have taken and in the reasons which have led me to take it.

"I will not enter into my private feelings, but I would beg that it should be remembered that the burden which constantly rests upon the shoulders of a Sovereign is so heavy, that it can only be borne in circumstances different from those in which I now find myself. I conceive that I am not overlooking the duties resting on me to place in the forefront the public interests, when I declare that I am conscious that I can no longer discharge this heavy task with efficiency or with satisfaction to myself.

"I have accordingly executed an Instrument of Abdication in the terms following:

I, Edward VIII, of Great Britain, Northern Ireland and the British Dominions beyond the Seas, King-Emperor of India, do hereby declare my irrevocable determination to renounce the Throne for myself and for my descendants, and my desire that effect should be given to this Instrument of Abdication immediately.

In token whereof I have hereunto set my hand this tenth day of December 1936 in the presence of witnesses whose signatures are subscribed.   (Signed) Edward. R. I.,

"The execution of this instrument has been witnessed by my three brothers, Their Royal Highnesses the Duke of York, The Duke of Gloucester, and The Duke of Kent.

"I deeply appreciate the spirit which has actuated the appeals made to me to take a different decision, and I have, before reaching my final determination, most fully pondered them. But my mind is made up. Moreover further delay cannot but be most injurious to our peoples whom I have tried to serve as Prince of Wales and as King, and whose future happiness and prosperity are the constant wish of my heart.

"I take my leave of them in the confident hope that the course which I have thought it right to follow is that which is best for the stability of the Throne and the Empire and the happiness of my peoples.

"I am deeply sensible of the consideration which they have always extended to me both before and after my accession to the Throne and which I know they will extend in full measure to my successor.

"I am most anxious that there should be no delay of any kind in giving effect to the instrument which I have executed and that all necessary steps should be taken immediately to secure that my lawful successor, His Royal Highness the Duke of York, should ascend the Throne.

Edward. R. I."

After Midnight

"His Majesty's Declaration of Abdication Bill" provides that immediately upon Royal signification and Royal Assent thereof, the instrument of abdication shall have effect and thereupon his Majesty shall cease to be King. His Majesty, his issue, if any, and their descendants shall not afterwards succeed to the Throne.

The Abdication Bill will pass through all stages in both houses today. The King will then give his assent which will be his last act as King. Both Houses will meet tomorrow afternoon for swearing-in which will continue on Monday. On Monday, Parliament will receive a message from the new King and will move an address in reply.

On Other Pages

KING EDWARD'S SUCCESSOR

The Successor To the Throne

(From a Staff Correspondent)

In dramatic circumstances without parallel in the history of the British monarchy, H. R. H. the Duke of York becomes King of the United Kingdom and the British Commonwealth and King-Emperor of India by his elder brother's act of voluntary abdication.

The new King, whose full names are Albert Frederick Arthur George, was born at York Cottage, Sandringham, exactly 41 years ago next Monday as the second son of King George V. and Queen Mary.

After passing through Osborne and the Royal Naval College at Dartmouth, he was gazetted a midshipman in September 1913 and though deterred by ill-health from active service during the early years of the World War, he served in the battle of Jutland as a sublieutenant, being mentioned in despatches.

Joins R.A.F.

At the end of 1917 he was attached to the naval branch of the Royal Air Force and, in October a year later, was on the Western Front as a qualified pilot. His Majesty eventually became Wing-Commander in 1920. After the War he entered Trinity College, Cambridge, to take an abridged course in history, economics and civics. He subsequently showed a special interest in industrial questions.

Prince Albert, as he then was, became Duke of York in June, 1920. The popular acclamations that attended his marriage, the first of the late King's four sons to forsake bachelorhood, must still be vivid in the memories of many readers. On April 26, 1923, he was wed to Lady Elizabeth Bowes-Lyon (five years (Continued on page 8, col. 5)

HISTORIC HOURS IN BRITISH PARLIAMENT

Eager Throngs Near Whitehall; Prime Minister Hailed on Arrival

(Reuter)

LONDON, Thursday.—Throughout today an atmosphere of acute tension prevailed in the metropolis and was particularly reflected in and around Whitehall.

This morning was characterised by hectic last-minute conferences and hasty comings and goings in which the Prime Minister, Sir John Simon, Mr. Malcolm MacDonald, Mr. Walter Monckton, and Sir Edward Peacock were prominent.

Integrity of the British Monarchy

BALDWIN'S SPEECH

(Reuter)

LONDON, Thursday. — Immediately after the Speaker had finished reading the King's message, Mr. Stanley Baldwin rose and made one of the most affecting speeches ever heard in the historic chamber.

Moving that the King's message be considered, the Prime Minister told the hushed House that no graver statement had ever been received by Parliament. In simple words, he said that on October 20 he had a private interview with the King.

He told his Majesty of the anxiety which he felt at reports published in the American press. He reminded the King that the Crown today stood for far more than it had ever done in its history. (Cheers.)

"The importance of its integrity is beyond all question, for it is not only the last link of the Empire that is left but a guarantee in this country, so long as it exists in that integrity, against many evils that have afflicted other countries."

Mrs. Simpson's Decree

Mr. Baldwin next saw the King on November 16 when Mrs. Simpson's divorce decree had been pronounced. The King then said he wanted to tell him something that he had long wanted to say.

"I am going to marry Mrs. (Continued on page 16, col. 2)

AT FORT BELVEDERE

Queen Mary, accompanied by the Princess Royal the Earl of Athlone, visited the King yesterday afternoon, and the Duke and Duchess of Kent dined with Queen Mary last evening.

The King had further consultations with the Duke of York yesterday.

His three brothers arrived at Sunningdale at 9.40 this morning separately in their own cars. They looked pale and tired.

Sir John Simon also waited upon the King today.

Large contingents of police were brought into the Westminster area in the morning, 'buses with reinforcements on foot and mounted constables arriving from the suburbs.

Reuter learned on good authority that Mrs. Simpson, who continued to do all in her power to make his Majesty's choice as easy as possible, did not last evening herself know the King's decision.

The Prime Minister received a great ovation as his car slowly progressed to the Parliament buildings. Men waved their hats and women fluttered handkerchiefs. The crowd became so great in front of the Palace Yard that the way became impassable, and police reinforcements were called up to keep people on the move.

The speaker had taken his seat in the House of Commons at 2.45 for the most dramatic sitting in Parliament in recent times. Mr. Baldwin walked to the Bar of the House at 3.30 to hand the Speaker the King's statement.

At its conclusion he rose and commenced his own address.

Message in House of Lords

LONDON, Thursday.— The unusual sight of the House of Lords

MR. EDWARD WINDSOR

LONDON, Thursday.—The Accession Council will meet on Saturday morning and the Duke of York will be proclaimed King on Saturday afternoon. It is understood that he will take the title of George the Sixth.

It is further learned that the King is renouncing all titles and will be known as Mr. Edward Windsor, but the new King may confer a Dukedom upon him.

packed to capacity for an ordinary sitting was presented this afternoon. Some of the peeresses were unable to obtain anything but standing room in their gallery.

Amidst dead silence, Lord Halifax read the King's message in the gravest tones. Many peers and some of the more aged peeresses sat with their heads bowed and grief written across their faces.

Lord Halifax for the Government, Lord Snell for the Labour Party, Lord Crewe for the Liberal Party, and the Archbishop for the Church expressed deep regret at the King's decision and sympathy with Mr. Baldwin and Queen Mary and the Royal Family.

12 Pages

THE PALESTINE POST

JERUSALEM
SUNDAY, DECEMBER 27, 1936

VOL. XIII. No. 3228
PRICE: TEN MILS

3000 Hear Toscanini Lead New Orchestra

Palestine Symphony Launched

Maestro Angered by Photographer

(From Our Own Correspondent)

TEL AVIV, Saturday.—Tonight Tel Aviv witnessed the birth of the Palestine Symphony Orchestra and never was a musical institution inaugurated under more auspicious circumstances.

Almost 3,000 persons, including notables from Tel Aviv, Jerusalem and Haifa, as well as from many of the settlements throughout the country, crowded the Concert Hall in the Levant Fair grounds, which the Orchestra Trust had remodelled from the Foreign Pavilion, to hear and see Toscanini conduct the opening concert.

It was a festive and memorable occasion. The players seemed inspired and the Maestro's baton was like a magic wand calling forth tones of joyous beauty.

Toscanini was greeted as he ascended the podium with thundering applause and cheers, and from the first note of the opening number the audience sat in awed silence. Prolonged applause and cheers of "bravissimo" greeted every selection.

THE PROGRAMME

The programme, which included the Overture "Scala di Setta" (Rossini), the Second Symphony (Brahms), the Unfinished Symphony (Schubert), the Nocturne and Scherzo to Midsummer Night's Dream (Mendelssohn) and the "Oberon" Overture (Weber) seemed to have been especially chosen for the significant occasion.

The Brahms Symphony portrayed the spirit of Spring, which seemed to symbolize the birth of the new Orchestra.

The excitement and ecstasy in the audience were great and were
(Continued on Page 7, Col. 1.)

Arab Rulers Against R.C. Boycott

ABDULLAH ON WAY TO BAGHDAD

No purpose is served by the Arabs of Palestine boycotting the Royal Commission so long as the rulers of Arabia disapprove of the boycott.

This is the burden of a leading article in yesterday's "A' Difaa" suggesting the appointment by Palestine Arabs of "permanent delegates" to Riyadh (capital of Nedj), Sanaa (capital of the Yemen), Damascus and Amman.

"A' Difaa" considers that such delegates would be able to influence the Arab rulers, and that the cost of maintaining them would be small compared to their enormous value.

Once launched, emissaries might also be posted permanently to India, the paper adds.

Appearance Beneficial

"Falastin" also reports that the Arab rulers, including the Emir Abdullah, consider that the appearance of the Arabs before the Royal Commission would be beneficial.

The Emir Abdullah left for Baghdad yesterday, by car, accompanied by Hassan Sidky Dajani of Jerusalem. The purpose of this visit of the Emir's, after the departure from Baghdad last Thursday of Auni Bey Abdul Hadi and the other delegates from Palestine is not known.

The Palestine delegates had an interview with the Foreign Minister and were later received by King Ghazi. The desirability of their giving evidence before the Royal Commission was everywhere impressed on them.

Before Ibn Saud

The delegation has left for Riyadh, to present themselves before King Ibn Saud, probably to canvass his opinion. They are expected back in Baghdad in a week, on their return to Palestine.

A meeting to be devoted to the question of Palestine, during the pilgrimage to Mecca, is proposed at Baghdad, and the Ullema there have decided to apply to King Ibn Saud for permission for such a gathering to which special representatives would be appointed from Iraq.

Woman Identifies Escort as Culprit

HUSSEINI REMANDED IN CHRISTMAS EVE SHOOTING

Shams El Din Eff. Husseini, said to be of the family of Haj Amin el Husseini, the Mufti of Jerusalem, was remanded for 15 days on Friday afternoon pending further investigation by the police into the mysterious shooting on Christmas Eve of Rina Shwiki on Bethlehem Road. Husseini was committed to the custody of the police by the Jerusalem Magistrate, Dr. N. Bardaky.

Mrs. Shwiki, a Syrian Jewess, was brought to the Government Hospital of Jerusalem on Thursday evening by Husseini who reported that while driving to Jerusalem on the Jericho Road his car had been held up by highwaymen who shot his companion, Mrs. Shwiki, and took from him his driving licence.

Statement to Magistrate

At two o'clock on Friday morning, Dr. Bardaky, was summoned by the Police to the bedside of the wounded woman. Mrs. Shwiki gave him a statement alleging that she had been keeping company with Husseini for some time and on the night of the shooting he asked her to accompany him to Bethlehem. They drove there in his car, Mrs. Shwiki declared in her statement, and on their return she said her companion stop-
(Continued on Page 12, Col. 4.)

CHANGE OF GUARD AT CAIRO EMBASSY

With the coming into operation of the Anglo-Egyptian Treaty, the British military guard has been withdrawn from the British Embassy at Cairo and has been replaced by Egyptian Police.

The military guard was on duty for the last time until 10 a.m. last Wednesday. The Police then took over.

Pact with France Ratified by Syria

PROGRAMME OF REFORM

(From Our Own Correspondent)

DAMASCUS, Saturday. — The Franco-Syrian treaty has been unanimously ratified by the House, as was expected, and the Cabinet of Jamil Bey Mardam has gained a unanimous vote of confidence.

Although the treaty was the occasion for a change of government, no opposition was likely to the ratification as every single deputy had been elected with the treaty as his platform.

The home programme of the new cabinet was announced at their first appearance before the House on Wednesday. It is headed by a promise that order will be enforced strictly in all parts of the country and that labour legislation will be prepared.

Progressive Reforms

Other plans include the reform of public finances, and of the Wakf administration, and a more equitable distribution of taxation. The government also intend to further commerce and industry, and to encourage the farmers to employ up-to-date methods.

An early return home has been promised to political exiles. The new Prime Minister has declared that their return is the will of the people, and shall therefore be carried out without delay by his government. It is thought that exiles will be able to come back to Syria within a fortnight.

Alexandretta Problem

Before ending his speech, the Premier extended thanks to France for the valuable services rendered to Syria at the League Council by its defence of Alexandretta last week.

Syria would endeavour to maintain friendly relations with all nations, and particularly with the neighbouring Arab countries, to whom the speaker sent his warmest greetings.

After Midnight

On Other Pages

Liang Offers Life To Redeem China

JAPAN RUFFLED

(Reuter)

NANKING, Saturday. — While rumours are current that Marshal Chang Hsueh Liang's wishes regarding the reconstruction of the Government will be met, other reports state that he will shortly go abroad for some time.

The Marshal, who arrived by 'plane in Nanking only two hours after the arrival of the Premier and is staying at the house of Mr. T.V. Soong, addressed a letter to Marshal Chiang Kai Shek acknowledging the criminal character of his revolt and declaring that he was ready to submit to any punishment, even death.

In some circles this contrite letter is regarded as a move calculated to reassure official opinion in Japan which is beginning to worry about the sudden friendship between the Premier and Marshal Chang Hsueh Liang, in view of the latter's anti-Japanese pronouncements.

Italian Sailors Wreck Spanish Newspaper

(Reuter)

TANGIER, Saturday. — A disturbance was created today in the International Zone when 150 Italian sailors headed by an officer wrecked the plant and the offices of the Spanish newspaper "Democracias."

The paper had printed some articles regarded in Italian circles as derogatory to Italy.

Precautionary Measures

Authoritative quarters in Paris have denied a report current, to the effect that General Gamelin, Chief of the General Staff, had told M. Daladier, Minister of War, that the growth of German intervention in Spain necessitated the consideration of precautionary measures in the Pyrenees and in Morocco.

Special greetings to German warships off the Spanish coast and to Germans in Spain were included in a Christmas broadcast on December 24 by Herr Hitler's deputy, Rudolf Hess.

General Chiang Kai Shek Released by Captors

Chinese Crisis at an End

Government Recalls Troops from Shensi

(From Reuter)

NANKING, Saturday. — The Chinese imbroglio was solved yesterday when General Chiang Kai Shek, the Prime Minister, was released by his captor, Marshal Chang Hsueh Liang, in exchange for certain promises.

After spending two weeks in captivity at Sianfu, the capital of the Shensi Province, General Chiang Kai Shek returned to Nanking today, accompanied by his wife and by Mr. Donald, the Australian journalist who had negotiated his release.

Marshal Chang Hsueh Liang took the same route and arrived in the capital accompanied by Mr. T.P. Soong, the Minister of Finance. It is learnt that he will remain in Nanking for some time in connection with the expected reorganization of the Central Government. A statement issued by the Prime Minister stresses the loyalty of the Marshal "whose action should not be construed as a revolt or a mutiny against the Government."

The Marshal also denied the report that the dispute was settled on a financial basis.

Noisy Welcome

The report of Marshal Chiang Kai Shek's release was enthusiastically received in Shanghai and Nanking. The Premier, who looked well and cheerful, was noisily welcomed by a crowd of 200,000 people. He stated that the success of the negotiations, which secured his release, was largely due to his wife.

It was reported at the time of the opening of the military operations against Shensi by the Central Government that the Generalissimo's wife and her brother, Mr. T.V. Soong, were opposed to a threat of force which they feared would lead to the loss of the captives' lives. Thanks to their efforts, a truce was agreed upon on December 22, during which the release was finally negotiated. The Marshal stated that he revolted because he believed that his troops had not been paid by the Central Government. It has transpired, however, that the money had been misappropriated by a
(Continued on Page 12, Col. 3.)

200 Killed in Boiler Explosion on Steamer

HUNDRED INJURED

ROME, Saturday. — It is just announced that 200 were killed and 100 injured in a boiler explosion on the Italian liner Cesare Battisti at Massawa on December 23. Seventy-three of the injured are in a serious condition and may not survive. The explosion occurred while the ship was unloading.

The liner is now resting at the bottom of the harbour, which is shallow at that point.

SUBSCRIPTIONS: Local: LP.2.250 a year; LP.1.250 a half year;— Abroad: £3.- a year. The rate for display advertisements is 150 mils per column inch. Other rates supplied on request. The right is reserved to make changes in wording or to decline or discontinue any advertisement or to postpone insertions when space is not available.

THE PALESTINE POST

JERUSALEM Hassolel Road P. O. Box 625, Telephone 733-734

Tel Aviv - Jaffa: 65 Allenby Road, P. O. Box 1125, 'Phone 4251-4252

Haifa: New Business Centre, Mushieff Building Jaffa St. P.O.Box 66, 'Phone 1390.

SUNDAY MARCH 13 1938 JERUSALEM VOL. XIV. No. 3597. PRICE 10 MILS

GERMANY INVADES AUSTRIA

SCHUSCHNIGG BREAKS UNDER NAZI THREAT

ARMY'S BLOODLESS OCCUPATION AS FUEHRER ASSUMES CONTROL

Plebiscite Abandoned; Von Schuschnigg's Farewell Message: "God Guard Austria"

BRITISH AND FRENCH GOVERNMENTS' PROTEST AGAINST ACTION DECLARED BY GERMANY AS "INADMISSIBLE"

Moving with ruthless efficiency, Germany has assumed control of Austria, and, backed by a request from Dr. Arthur Seyss-Inquart as the new Austrian Chancellor, German infantry, tanks and aircraft have invaded that country penetrating as far as the Italian Border at the Brenner Pass. Herr Hitler last night arrived at Linz, the capital of Upper Austria, and met Dr. Seyss-Inquart there.

Dr. Kurt von Schuschnigg resigned on Friday night, and the plebiscite to have been held today was postponed, after the receipt of two German ultimatums. The Chancellor announced his resignation in a dramatic broadcast proclamation that ended with the words, "Gott Schuetze Oesterreich — God guard Austria."

Strong protest by the British and French Governments to the German Government were rejected by the latter yesterday as "inadmissible." Thousands of people have fled or are trying to flee from Austria, and there is general uneasiness throughout Europe.

A journey last night by Reuter's Correspondent from the Swiss Frontier to Vienna makes clear that the Nazi regime has come to stay and that it will not meet with any real opposition. Of roughly 80 per cent of the population who 24 hours ago would have voted "yes" in the plebiscite, the great majority were yesterday trying to out-vie one another in Hitler gestures, Hitler greetings and Hitler badges. ... ...

VIENNA, Saturday (R). — Events moved rapidly in the Austrian capital last night following the receipt by Dr. Kurt von Schuschnigg of two ultimatums from the German Government.

At about 9 o'clock, Dr. von Schuschnigg announced his resignation in a broadcast speech in which he declared that Herr Hitler had threatened an armed invasion of Austria unless he resigned, and that the President, Herr Miklas, had ordered him to yield to force. The plebiscite had been postponed.

All representatives of foreign Powers were informed of the German ultimatum, which gave a time-limit of three hours within which to comply. Dr. von Schuschnigg denied the allegation made against him in Germany and concluded with the words:

"So I take my leave at this now from the Austrian people. Gott Scheutze Oesterreich—God Guard Austria."

Dr. Seyss-Inquart, the Pro-Nazi Minister of Interior, was then appointed Chancellor.

Warning to People

In a broadcast speech, he warned the Austrian people against the slightest resistance to the German Army if it marched into Austria. He sent Herr Hitler a telegram, immediately after Dr. von Schuschnigg's resignation, stating that the provisional Austrian Government, which saw as its task the restoration of peace and order in Austria, addressed to the German Government an urgent request to support it in its task and to help in preventing bloodshed.

For this purpose, it asked the German Government to dispatch troops in the earliest possible time.

Nazis without uniforms gathered in Vienna in great force last night and about 3,000 demonstrated in the streets in the evening, with their number swelling every minute. Immediately Dr. von Schuschnigg had announced his resignation, Nazis took control in many towns.

Dr. Schuschnigg Under Guard

Dr. von Schuschnigg was placed under guard and is believed to be in protective custody in his Vienna flat. It is believed that a safe conduct has been offered him to another country.

The Fatherland Front was officially dissolved and many members arrested, including Colonel Adam, the former Press Chief. 'Planes carrying Swastika markings flew low over Vienna throughout the day.

Herr Himmler, head of the German Secret Police, and the Chief of the German Air Staff arrived in Vienna today.

The new Ministers, with Dr. Seyss-Inquart as Chancellor and Minister for Defence, are Herrn Glaise-Horstenau (Vice-Chancellor); Wilhelm Wolff (Foreign Affairs); Hugo Jury (Social Welfare); Anton Reinthaler (Agriculture); Rudolf Neumayer (Finance); Hans Fischbaeck (Commerce); and Secretary of State, Dr. Michael Skubl, Vienna Police President.

Why the German Troops Entered Austria

Hitler's Triumphal Drive to Linz

VIENNA, Saturday (R).—Herr Hitler arrived at Linz, over which several hundreds of aeroplanes circled, at a few minutes before 8 o'clock this evening.

Dr. Arthur Seyss-Inquart, the new Chancellor, went to meet the Fuehrer outside the town. Earlier Herr Hitler had passed through Branau and Ried by car and a fully-equipped German army detachment awaited him in the main square of Linz.

Herr Hitler's arrival was heralded by the calls made through microphones locally by broadcasting announcers. They urged the population to keep open their windows and doors and light all lamps.

"Every lighted window is a friend; every dark window an enemy," were the exhortations. "Put on all lights. Your Fuehrer is coming."

People were strictly forbidden to throw flowers at the Fuehrer's car.

According to an official announcement, Herr Hitler's delay in arriving, amounting to four hours, was due to the fact that all along the route the Fuehrer was held up by admirers and his car was only able to crawl through crowds of adherents. Herr Himmler was among the speakers who addressed the waiting crowd at Linz.

The Fuehrer's Proclamation

Dr. Paul Goebbels, the Minister of Propaganda, in Berlin today read a proclamation to foreign journalists on behalf of Herr Hitler, who had left by air for Munich, and it was later broadcast.

He declared that German troops entered Austria at the request of the new National-Socialist Government in Vienna to ensure "a real plebiscite." He also declared that the frontier had not been crossed until 6.30 this morning, and denied that Dr. Seyss-Inquart had telegraphed requesting help, or that Dr. von Schuschnigg had received an ultimatum from Germany.

The wireless proclamation stated that for years the Austrian regime had suppressed the 6,000,000 Germans in Austria and that many had been imprisoned. The Austrian policy had brought economic ruin to the country.

Herr Hitler had tried for years to convince the Austrian statesmen that the position was untenable and tried to reach an amicable settlement. The last attempt was made a month ago. Soon afterwards, Dr. von Schuschnigg sprang his Plebiscite coup with the obvious intention of taking the people by surprise and obtaining a vote of confidence.

In protest against this ruse, the Austrian people had risen against the Government — which apparently intended to suppress the popular movement by force — and this would have meant civil war. Germany could not tolerate such a state of affairs.

Forces of the Reich

"I have therefore decided to put at the disposal of the millions of Austrians the aid of the Reich," Herr Hitler declared. Since that morning, German troops had been marching into Austria, called by the new Nazi Government.

The troops would be a guarantee for a real plebiscite in the near future, when Austria would be able to decide for herself.

"I myself, as Chancellor of Germany, shall be happy to be able again to visit Austria, the country which is also my home, as a free citizen."

NAZIS "CORRECT POWERS' FALSE INFORMATION"

REPLY TO ANGLO-FRENCH REMONSTRATIONS

BERLIN, Saturday (R).— Germany today rejected the British and French protest against her action in Austria by declaring them to be inadmissible.

A communique issued this afternoon stated that the British and French Governments had made remonstrations through their Ambassadors against the pressure alleged to have been exercised by the Reich on developments in Austria, in which they pointed to certain information they had received from Vienna.

"The German Government rejected these remonstrations as inadmissible and simultaneously corrected the false information in the hands of the two Governments."

Strongest British Protest

Great Britain protested through Sir Nevile Henderson in the strongest terms against the ultimatum to Austria, and declared that such use of coercion, backed by force, against an independent State in order to create a situation incompatible with its national independence, was bound to produce the gravest reactions, of which it was impossible to foretell the issue.

The French Government protested in similar terms.

Instructions were sent to the French Charge d'Affaires in Rome to inquire whether there were any means of Franco-Italian cooperation in regard to Austria, and drew the reply that there was "no such possibility at the moment."

Chamberlain Leaves London

No fresh developments are expected in Downing Street over the weekend and Mr. Neville Chamberlain has left for Chequers, the Prime Minister's official country seat, states a London message.

The Cabinet took the unusual course of meeting on a Saturday morning and, at the conclusion of a conference lasting 1 hour and 40 minutes, an official statement was issued.

"The Cabinet discussed events in Austria," it was declared, "and it is reported that a protest in the strongest terms was made to Berlin. The Prime Minister and the Foreign Minister and the Foreign Secretary had previously made similar representations to Herr von Ribbentrop.

"It was felt that the action of the German Government was bound to have the most disturbing effect on Anglo-German relations and upon public confidence throughout Europe."

Keeping in Close Touch

The statement proceeded that the Government were keeping in close touch with the French Government. Ministers were remaining in reach of

(Continued on Page 7).

THE STOCK EXCHANGE REACTS

LONDON, Saturday (R).— French francs and U.S. dollars were in considerable demand on the Exchange here today. Francs rose from 158 to the £ at the opening to 156, while dollars rose from \$5.00 to \$4.98.

The rise occurred in spite of the intervention of the Equalisation Fund as a seller of francs.

Yesterday, Austrian uncertainties checked business and operators were disinclined to extend commitments over the weekend, as a result of which prices generally were depressed.

HOW INVASION WAS EFFECTED

NAZI TROOPS RAPIDLY SPREAD THROUGHOUT TERRITORY

MUNICH, Saturday (R).—German troops crossed the Austrian frontier at several points at 10 o'clock last night and spread rapidly to various parts of the country, one detachment reaching as far as the southern end of the Brenner Pass this afternoon. Another large party went to Styria and took up positions along the Yugoslav frontier.

It was officially announced in Vienna tonight that Austrian soldiers have evacuated two Vienna barracks which are preparing for the reception of German troops at present approaching.

German troops with field artillery, lorryloads of men and supplies and hundreds of aircraft poured steadily through Bavaria throughout the night.

Two German air squadrons landed at Linz today, while German troops entered Innsbruck, at the head of the Brenner Pass, during the late morning.

Arrival at Brenner Pass

Led by an Alpine infantry commander, the first motorised German troops reached the Brenner Pass at 1 o'clock this afternoon. A regiment lined the road between the Austrian and Italian customs-houses; the commander and officers went to the Italian barrier and told the Italian frontier commander that they were instructed to move with a small detachment of troops to the Italian frontier, where a high Italian officer was expecting them.

The speaker assured the officer that all these undertakings which were being carried out, were done in a thoroughly comradely fashion, corresponding to the friendly relations between Nazi Germany and Fascist Italy and their respective armies:

At Salzburg, the commander of the Austrian garrison visited the German Army Commander and declared that he put himself under the German command.

M. LEON BLUM'S PROSPECTS

"THE SOONER THE BETTER"

PARIS, Saturday (R).— There were increased prospects for M. Leon Blum's success in forming the new French Government as a result of the decision of party leaders to support him in the task. Events in Austria led all French parties to adopt the view that the sooner a Government was formed, the better.

The Socialist National Council this morning adopted a vote of confidence in M. Blum and by the strong majority of 6,500 to 1,600 votes decided in favour of his forming a National Government as

"the rallying of the Republican nation around the Popular Front."

This afternoon, the Socialist leader went to report to President Albert Lebrun of the progress he had made in forming a Cabinet.

M. Leon Blum stated that the developments in Austria were forcing him to hasten a solution of the task he had undertaken.

Yesterday he approached the various parties of the Popular Front. The Radical-Socialists voted a motion proclaiming their attachment to the Popular Front but insisted on receiving some guarantees regarding the maintenance of the non-intervention policy and on the new Cabinet's financial policy — the Radicals being opposed to exchange control which Socialists and Communists favour.

As for the Communists, rather than give up their activity in favour of Republican Spain, they would prefer to support another Popular Front cabinet without however being represented on it.

AFTER MIDNIGHT

The accession to power of the Nazis in Austria has caused dismay in Vatican circles, which see in it the fall of the last stronghold of Roman Catholicism in the German world. It is felt that Catholic Austria will now be subjected to the pagan influences against which the Catholics in Germany are struggling. The 74-year old Archbishop of Salzburg has already been arrested.

Hitler, addressing an enthusiastic crowd before the Linz Town Hall, announced that a plebiscite would be held in Austria on no distant day. Dr. Seyss-Inquart, who welcomed Hitler, said, "We declare Article 80 of the Peace Treaty as no longer valid." Under Article 80, Germany acknowledged and undertook to respect Austrian independence.

AUSTRIAN JEWS ANXIOUS

OUTLOOK FOR FUTURE GLOOMY

VIENNA, Saturday (Palcor).— Grave anxiety exists among the Jewish population of Austria, the bulk of which resides in Vienna, over the rapid developments in the situation.

Several thousands of people have fled from the country, including large numbers of Jews, entering either Italy, Czechoslovakia or Yugoslavia. Those who remain do not leave the Jewish quarter around the Leopoldstrasse.

A message from Budapest states that the Austro-Hungarian Frontiers have been closed to prevent the influx of refugees, while in Belgrade it is officially denied that the Austro-Yugoslav Frontier was closed.

Little doubt is felt as to the Nazi intentions concerning the Jewish community and strict "Aryan" measures are expected in the near future.

Isolated Incidents

P.T.A. states that no anti-Jewish developments are reported from Vienna, with the exception of isolated incidents during the morning, when troops of Nazis on bicycles created some disturbances in the Jewish quarters, while several Jewish shops were attacked last night.

Banks in the Jewish quarters were besieged all day by large crowds seeking to withdraw their savings.

A large number of newspapers has been suppressed or is to be suppressed (adds Reuter). Germany military aeroplanes were flying over Vienna throughout the afternoon, dropping leaflets containing greetings from Germany to the new Nazi Government.

"Horst Wessel" Broadcast

Auxiliary police are watching the country to prevent the escape of people who are wanted for "provocative crimes." The Vienna City police have donned Swastika arm-bands and have begun exchanging the "Heil Hitler" salute. Storm-troops and Black Guards were armed as auxiliary police.

The "Horst Wessel" song was played on the Austria radio for the first time last night. Earlier yesterday afternoon, Police made a sabre charge when 15,000 Nazis demonstrated at Innsbruck. The Police were not sufficiently strong to break up the crowd, which later dispersed.

STRAY SHOT CAUSES DEATH OF SOLDIER

TWO DAYS OF OPERATIONS IN NORTHERN PALESTINE

Private Michael Fury, of the 1st Battalion, Manchester Regiment, was killed on Thursday near the village of Jish in Northern Palestine by a stray shot from an armed Arab band which was trying to break through a military cordon towards the Lebanese frontier. It was stated in a communique issued on Friday night that the bodies of 10 bandits had been picked up as a result of operations during the previous two days.

Other incidents during the week-end were the serious wounding of Michael Akerman, a Jewish hawker, in Haifa on Friday afternoon (reported on page 2) and the puncturing of the oil pipe-line near Kawkab el Hawa, in the Beisan area that night.

Fighting in the North

It was believed in Jerusalem on Friday that the Arab casualties resulting from Thursday's engagements in the North were far higher than officially reported. Infantry and air forces cooperated in the operations.

The communique, which was broadcast on Friday night, read as follows:

"During Thursday and Friday, extensive military operations were carried out in the Tarshiha area against the armed bands which have concentrated there lately.

"On Thursday morning, columns of the 1st Royal Scots, the 1st Border Regiment, the 2nd Royal West Kents, the 1st Manchester Regiment and the 2nd Royal Ulster Rifles, in cooperation with Royal Air Force and Police, quickly gained contact with an armed band near Al Buqueia.

"Troops and aircraft at once attacked the band, which fled into the difficult mountain country of Jebel Jarmaq. The bodies of 10 dead bandits have since been picked up, one of a notoriuos criminal who was shot on Thursday night while entering the village of Majdal Krum. One Arab was also taken prisoner.

"During an interchange of shots between a party of troops and bandits at the village of Safsaf, north of Safad, on Thursday night, one Arab was killed and one Arab and a woman were wounded."

Accidentally Killed

Our Safad correspondent reports that of the three men killed by the military near Beit-Gan, one was identified as Ahmed Shaker Abdul Said, of Majdal Krum, in whose possession a mauser revolver and 15 rounds were found.

Another man, Ahmed Hassan Musa of Safsaf, was accidently killed during the panic which ensued in his village during military operations. At the same time a man and a woman were also wounded and were taken to the Safad Hospital.

One of the unidentified men killed in the same vicinity was found carrying a German rifle and 80 rounds of ammunition.

At 1.30 yesterday morning about 40 shots were reported to have been fired between the Acre Stud Farm and Naharia settlement. The supernumerary constables at both these places heard the shots, but neither they nor the police could locate them.

Villagers Repel Marauders

On Friday night, an armed Arab band fired at a house in Jubeil village, in the Nablus district. Their object was robbery. They fled on the arrival of peasants from neighbouring villages.

A military railway patrol was derailed near Tulkarm on Thursday and some shots were fired at it. Shots were fired at an Arab truck at kilometre 8 on the Jerusalem-Jaffa road (the Kustel bends) and at a lorry on the Nablus-Jenin road, which was blocked, on Thursday.

It is notified that the Migdal police post, in the Tiberias division, has been closed since February 22.

MAX BAER OUTPOINTS TOMMY FARR

15-ROUND FIGHT IN NEW YORK

Max Baer, ex-world heavy-weight champion, outpointed Tommy Farr, British and Empire champion, in 15 rounds at Madison Square Garden, New York on Friday night.

This places Baer in line for a world title fight with the winner of the Max Schmeling — Joe Louis bout which takes place in June.

(Other Sports News — Page 5)

SUBSCRIPTIONS: Local: LP.2.250 a year: LP.1.250 a half year :— Foreign: 23.- a year. The rate for display advertisements is 150 mils per column inch. Other rates supplied on request. The right is reserved to make changes in wording or to decline or discontinue any advertisement or to postpone insertions when space is not available.

THE PALESTINE POST

JERUSALEM Hassolel Road P. O. Box 81, Telephone 4233

Tel Aviv - Jaffa: 65 Allenby Road, P. O. Box 1125. 'Phone 4251-4252.

Haifa: Khayat Sq. opp. the Post Office entrance, P. O. Box 66. 'Phone 1390.

SUNDAY OCTOBER 2 1938 — JERUSALEM — VOL. XIV. No. 3765. — PRICE 10 MILS

SITUATION IN BRIEF; OFFICIAL REPORTS

40 BRIGANDS KILLED; BRITISH POLICE INSPECTOR DEAD

Early yesterday afternoon a police patrol was fired on by a strong armed band in Ramallah and during the attack British Inspector Birch was shot and killed. Reinforcements of troops, aircraft and police proceeded to Ramallah and engaged the band of whom 40 were killed. Three were also taken prisoner and 17 rifles were seized. Two British soldiers were slightly wounded.

TWELVE ARABS KILLED

In an engagement between an armed band and Government forces near Shefa Amr yesterday afternoon, 12 Arabs were killed and a number of rifles captured.

At 4.30 p.m. on Friday, a Jewish bus was fired on between Affuleh and Mes'ha settlement near Mt. Tabor. One of the police escort named Kalman Wolf was fatally wounded, and Dr. Pinzi of the Kadoorie Agricultural school was slightly wounded in the leg. Troops arrived on the scene, and engaged and dispersed the attackers after an encouter lasting half an hour, and killed two of them.

HAIFA

WOMAN SHOT DEAD

An Arab woman was shot dead on Thursday night, in Arab Damayra, near Hadera.

On Friday night, shots were fired at police guarding the pump-house at Ata settlement, near Hadera, and at constables on duty in an orange grove near Benyamina. In both cases the fire was returned and there were no casualties.

A Jewish constable Kalman Darshan, was stabbed in the suq in Haifa yesterday afternoon. His condition is serious but not dangerous.

85 DETAINED AFTER SEARCH

As a result of continued sniping in the neighbourhood, the village of Jaba was searched by troops on Friday and 85 men were detained.

At 2.30 p.m. on Thursday a Jewish Constable arrested an Arab who had assaulted him in the Eastern Quarter of Haifa.

JEWISH SHOP SET ON FIRE

On Thursday afternoon, a Jewish shop was set on fire in Allenby Street, Haifa, but the fire was extinguished before much damage had been done.

Shots were fired at Hanoar settlement on Thursday night. No one was hit.

CAUGHT AFTER ROBBING TILL

Just after 12 noon on Friday, four armed men went to the petrol pump near the I.C.I. building in Haifa and stole LP.3 from the till. They then made off in a taxi. The police were quickly on the trail of the robbers, and, at 1.30 p.m., the taxi was stopped near Kiryat Haim on the Acre Road and its four occupants were arrested.

At Haifa, early yesterday morning, armed men stole a cash-box containing LP.150 from an employee of the Palestine Railways near the Eastern station; and later in the day considerable damage was done by arson to a timber-yard belonging to a Jew in the Jaffa road.

SAMARIA

On Thursday evening, a party of armed men entered the Urban Police Station in Nablus and stole some blankets and documents.

Shots were fired, on Thursday, night, at the Nur esh Shems prison, at the Tulkarm Police Station, at the police billet in the neighbourhood of Tulkarm and at the Nablus Rural Police Station. No one was hit, however, and in all cases the fire was returned.

JERUSALEM

At 7.30 a.m. yesterday a Jew named Nissim Nazri was shot and dangerously wounded in St. Paul's Road, Jerusalem.

At 8.25 a.m. yesterday an Arab of Ramle named Ibrahim Mohammed Fayar was shot and wounded in the Old City of Jerusalem. His condition is serious.

DRIVER DIES OF WOUNDS

Gershon Perl, the Jewish driver wounded near Ataroth on Thursday, has since died.

At 8.15 p.m. on Friday some railway huts on Beit Safafa land were set on fire.

Some wooden huts near the new Hadassah Hospital on Mt. Scopus were burnt on Friday night.

At 7. p.m. on Friday, Neve Yaacov settlement was fired on but no one was hit. At about the same time, an unsuccessful attempt was made to set fire to the corn store of Mann and Berman in Jerusalem. Police quickly arrived, and extinguished the flames before serious damage had been done.

FACTORY DAMAGED BY ARSON

At 9 p.m. on Thursday, a Jewish owned tile factory near Beit Safafa was set on fire and extensively damaged.

CAUGHT WHILE DIGGING ROAD

On Thursday night, a military patrol encountered and engaged a party of men, who were digging up the Jerusalem-Jericho road near km. 10. The saboteurs dispersed on the arrival of the troops. Later, a second party of saboteurs was encountered near Eizariya village; five of them were arrested, one being found in possession of a rifle and ammunition.

A railway bridge at km. 73 on the Jerusalem-Lydda line was damaged on Friday night by explosives.

SOUTHERN

SHOT IN CAFE

At 10.50 a.m. on Friday, an Arab named Mohammed Khaddura was shot and dangerously wounded while sitting in a cafe in the Manshieh quarter of Jaffa.

(Continued on Page 2)

G.O.C. MIDDLE EAST HERE

VISIT OF GENERAL SIR W. E. IRONSIDE

(From Our Political Correspondent)

General Sir W. Edmund Ironside, who was recently appointed Commander-in-Chief of the British Forces in the Middle East, and Major-General A. E. Grasett, his Chief of Staff, arrived in Jerusalem yesterday morning from Alexandria, which they had reached on Wednesday night by Imperial Airways from England.

It may be assumed that the visitors will take an opportunity of examining conditions in Palestine which are, to judge by reports from London, becoming of increasing concern to the British authorities.

It is no secret that certain plans are maturing for execution during the coming month with a view to crushing the terrorism before the winter sets in.

General Ironside is believed to have had a preliminary conference yesterday with the High Commissioner and the General Officer Commanding in Palestine.

(General Ironside, who has been a Colonel-Commandant of the Royal Artillery since 1932, has held several high Army Staff appointments in the past few years, including that of Quartermaster-General in India and G.O.C.-in-C. Eastern Command. He is 58 years old and entered the Army 39 years ago.)

CZECHOSLOVAKIA DISMEMBERED TO SAVE THE PEACE OF EUROPE

GERMAN TROOPS OCCUPY PART OF SUDETEN TERRITORY

Czechoslovakia's dismemberment began yesterday as the result of the full accord reached by the four Great Powers in conference at Munich in the early hours of Friday morning and its acceptance by the Prague Government; under pressure the Polish ultimatum for cession of the Teschen and Silesian areas was also accepted yesterday.

The capitulation by the Czechs under inexorable pressure was followed by the entry of German troops into the districts defined in the Munich Agreement, and the occupation by Polish troops of the areas to the north-east early this morning.

The eleventh-hour avoidance of war brought scenes reminiscent of Armistice Day, 1918, in London and Paris when Mr. Chamberlain and M. Daladier returned to their homes on Friday evening; tumultuous welcomes were also given to signor Mussolini in Rome on Friday night and Herr Hitler in Berlin yesterday morning.

Mr. Chamberlain, announcing the supplementary undertaking that Great Britain and Germany would never go to war with one another again, said he had brought back from Germany "Peace with Honour" for the second time in British history. His homecoming, however, was marred by the resignation of Mr. A. Duff Cooper, First Lord of the Admiralty and a scion of one of England's leading families, owing to his dissatisfaction with the British Government's foreign policy.

CZECHS YIELD TO POLISH PRESSURE

ULTIMATUM ACCEPTED UNDER PROTEST; TROOPS EVACUATE

PRAGUE, Saturday (R).— According to an official announcement made this afternoon, the Czechoslovak Government has accepted under protest the conditions of the Polish ultimatum submitted last night and which expired at noon today.

Polish troops will begin marching in at 2 a.m. tomorrow.

The Note contained two main demands:

(1) The total occupation by noon tomorrow of the Teschen and Silesian territory, in which there is a Polish population including the ceding to Poland of the Czech part of the town of Teschen;

(2) the rest of the territory to be evacuated by the Czech troops and authorities by October 10.

Troops Leaving Teschen

Czech troops began to leave Teschen today, and an official statement at Warsaw said that the Government has discussed the position of other territories, where plebiscites are to be held. Financial questions arising from the frontiers (compensation for Czechoslovak interests) are to be settled by agreement.

All Polish soldiers and political prisoners in Czechoslovakia are to be released. The Polish Government said that it had accepted with deep satisfaction the fact that a satisfactory solution was found in accordance with its own peaceful intentions.

It is stated that negotiations will be opened immediately in regard to the adjacent areas claimed by Poland, and the Czech Government has decided to create a mixed Commission to liquidate matters in connection with this decision.

The amputation of the Teschen

(Continued on Page 2)

"Never to War Again"

Chamberlain—Hitler Pact

MUNICH, Saturday (R).— An historic declaration, "never to go to war with one another again," was the description given by Mr. Chamberlain yesterday of the accord he had signed with Herr Hitler earlier. Receiving the British press, the Prime Minister said that he always had in mind that if England could find a peaceful solution of the problem of Czechoslovakia, they would open the way to a general appeasement in Europe.

Anglo-German Relations

After a further meeting with Herr Hitler, he said, they agreed that recognising "the question of Anglo-German relations was of the first importance to the two countries and to Europe, we regard the agreement signed last night, and the Anglo-German Agreement, as the symbolic desire of our two peoples never to go to war with one another again.

"We are resolved that the method of consultation shall be adopted to deal with any other question concerning the two countries, and are determined to continue our efforts to remove possible sources of difference, thus contributing an assurance of the peace of Europe."

MR. DUFF COOPER RESIGNS POST

AT VARIANCE WITH GOVERNMENT POLICY

LONDON, Saturday (R).—Mr. A. Duff Cooper, M.P., First Lord of the Admiralty, today tendered his resignation from the British Government, owing to his distrust of its foreign policy.

In a letter to the Prime Minister Mr. Duff Cooper stated:

"It is extremely painful to me in the moment of your great triumph to be obliged to strike a discordant note. For reasons with which you are acquainted and which I propose to explain in the House of Commons in due course, I profoundly distrust the foreign policy which the present Government is pursuing and seems likely to continue to pursue.

"Feeling as I do, I consider that honour and loyalty demand that I should offer you my resignation. I do so with profound regret, because I have been so proud to hold my present office, one which I envied more than all others in the State, and I have been so grateful to you for showing me such invariable kindness and patience."

Mr. Chamberlain replied stating:

"I have received your letter with great personal regret, but knowing that you are sincerely convinced that the foreign policy of the present Government is mistaken, I agree with you in thinking that it would not be proper for you to remain a member of the Government.

"Before submitting your resignation to the King, I would like to thank you for your work in the great office which you are now giving up and express the conviction that differences over public policy will make no breach in our personal relations."

Leave of King

The King at Buckingham Palace received Mr. Duff Cooper, who took his leave upon relinquishing his Ministry. The audience lasted nearly half an hour. It is announced that the King and Queen are returning to Balmoral tomorrow evening to complete their holiday, which was interrupted by the crisis.

First Lord's Career

Mr. Alfred Duff Cooper, who has been Conservative M.P. for a Westminster constituency since 1931 and is a nephew of the Duke of Fife (brother of Princess Arthur of Connaught), is 48 years old. He married Lady Diana Manners, a daughter of the Duke of Rutland.

Mr. Duff Cooper has been in Parliament since 1924, after serving during the Great War, and became First Lord in 1937, after having for the two years previously been Secretary of State for War. He is a close personal friend of H.R.H. the Duke of Windsor.

The Munich Agreement

MUNICH, Saturday (R). — After conversations lasting for several hours throughout Thursday night, the leading political representatives of the four Great Powers at Munich reached agreement on the question of Czechoslovakia.

The main features of the agreement were:

(1) the Sudetenland to be evacuated between Friday and October 10 withouth existing installations being damaged;

(2) the conditions of evacuation to be formulated by an international commission representing Germany, Great Britain, France, Italy and Czechoslovakia;

(3) the occupation by stages of predominantly German territory by German troops from Friday, according to four zones marked on a map attached to the agreement, for completion by October 10;

(4) an international commission to determine the territories in which a plebiscite is to be held, these territories to be occupied by international bodies until the plebiscite, which is modelled on that in the Saar and is not to be held later than the end of November, is completed;

(5) the right of option into and out of the transferred territories for a period of six months.

Zone No. 1 was occupied by German troops today, the second zone is to be occupied tomorrow and Monday, the third zone on Tuesday and Wednesday, and the fourth zone on Thursday and Friday.

Under an annexe to the agreement, Great Britain and France immediately guarantee the new status of Czechoslovakia, while Italy and Germany will do likewise when the claims of Poland and Hungary have been satisfied.

If the problem of these minorities is not settled within three months, the signatories of the agreement will re-meet to consider the subject.

NAZI TROOPS TAKE OVER SECTORS

GERMAN ARMY ENGINEERS AS VANGUARD

BERLIN, Saturday (R).— German troops began at 2 o'clock this afternoon the occupation of the two sectors of Czechoslovak territory defined in the Munich Agreement, and German railway authorities took over the rail system of those districts. Czech evacuation of Sector I began last night.

The troops, under the command of General Ritter von Leeb, crossed the Czech frontier into the Bohemian forest between Helfenberg and Finsterau.

Early this morning, German Army engineers crossed the frontier into the Sudetenland to remove "any objectionable material" which might have been left behind near the bridgeheads. They were the first German units to cross.

The Czechoslovak Government has issued instructions to Army commanders to keep an open space of two miles between their units and the advancing German troops to avoid the possibility of clashes. It is learned that Czech troops are also being withdrawn from the Eger district. German sources complain that they are cutting telephone and telegraph wires and causing other damage.

Sudeten Germans who fled into the Reich when the crisis began, are now returning in the wake of the German troops, who are being greeted by Nazi sympathisers in the villages through which they pass.

The Supreme Command in announcing that the German troops marched into Zone 1 according to the plan, states that they were received with jubilation by the liberated population.

The German Social Democrat Party in Bohemia states that many of its members have fled into inner Czechoslovakia but appeals that the Party be kept alive after the cession of the Sudetenland to Germany.

General's Statement

General von Brauschitsch, in an Army order announcing the occupation, said yesterday:

"The German Army enters the liberated territory tomorrow, and is filled with happy pride at being the herald of German discipline and order, and from now on the instrument of its Supreme Commander in offering to its German brothers the strong protection of German arms."

A Prague report says that a regional Nazi leader has already been appointed for the occupied areas. It was added by Reuters correspondent that the Sudeten Free Corps were strictly ordered not to move into Sudeten territory.

(Continued on Page 2)

Prague's "Crown of Thorns"

"DESERTED BY ALL STATES OF EUROPE"—SIROVY

PRAGUE, Saturday (R). — A statement broadcast this afternoon from the Prague wireless station described the Munich Agreement as a great injustice against a nation which had always served in the cause of peace and had gone to extremes in self-denial in order to show its good-will and desire for good relations with its neighbours.

All Czechoslovakia as a nation had received was a crown of thorns. Nevertheless, the life of the Czechoslovak Republic was not closed by the Munich Conference.

Acceptance of Plan

The Czechoslovak Government's acceptance yesterday of the Munich terms came in the form of an official statement issued at Prague to the effect that the Czech Government, "after considering the decisions taken without and against them at the Conference, have no alternative but to accept them."

It was stated that the Czech Government hoped that Great Britain would ensure the economic existence and development of the new Republic.

The Czechoslovak Railways have been placed under the control of the military authorities by a Government decree.

There were attempts to demonstrate in the streets last night against the Four-Power Agreement, and loud-speakers from time to time issued requests to the crowds to move on and to keep calm. The authorities were fully in control of the situation.

General Sirovy, the Czechoslovak Prime Minister, declared in a broadcast yesterday afternoon that "this is the most difficult moment of my life."

A Stronger Nation

Dwelling on the Munich Agreement, he said:

"Superior force compelled us to accept; my duty was to consider everything, and as a soldier I had to choose the way of peace. The nation will be stronger and more united."

"We had to choose between a useless fight and sacrifices. We accepted the unheard-of sacrifices which have been imposed upon us," he went on. "We had to choose between the death of the nation and giving up some territories. The main thing is that we are remaining ourselves.

"I appeal to the people to maintain their confidence in the leaders. There are smaller States than we shall be, but the understanding with our neighbours will be easier. Our main concern will be to rebuild our State."

In the course of his address, he said that Czechoslovakia had been deserted by all the States in Europe.

SEEKING APPEASEMENT

It is understood that the German Government has offered to France to arrange a Franco-German understanding similar to that concluded between Herr Hitler and Mr. Chamberlain. It is hoped that the offer will be accepted within a few days. A report circulated in well-informed Berlin quarters states that negotiations are likely between British and foreign statesmen aboard a yacht in the Mediterranean concerning the Spanish War.

The British Government has been asked by the Czech Government to give urgent and immediate attention to the problem of economic difficulties bound to ensue in Czechoslovakia as a result of the Munich Agreement. Reuter learns that the Czech Government further calls attention to the fact that the Munich Agreement calls for almost the immediate release of all Sudeten German political prisoners, but does not mention the Czech Customs Officers and other civil servants who have been kidnapped and taken into Germany to be held as hostages. The Czech troops have already evacuated Egerland, which was only due to be occupied by the Germans on October 3, 4, and 5.

SUBSCRIPTIONS: Local: LP.2.250 a year; LP.1.250 a half year:— Foreign: £3.- a year. The rate for display advertisements is 150 mils per column inch. Other rates supplied on request. The right is reserved to make changes in wording or to decline or discontinue any advertisement or to postpone insertions when space is not available.

THE PALESTINE POST

JERUSALEM Hassolel Road P. O. Box 81, Telephone 4233
Tel Aviv - Jaffa: 65 Allenby Road, P. O. Box 1125, 'Phone 4251-4252.
Haifa: Khayat Square, opposite the Post Office entrance, P.O.B. 66, 'Phone 1390.

FRIDAY NOVEMBER 11 1938 JERUSALEM VOL. XIV. No. 3797 PRICE 10 MILS.

DEATH OF ATATURK
Creator of Modern Turkey Passes Away at 58
GENERAL INEUNU MAY SUCCEED

ANKARA, Thursday (R). The death took place this morning of Kemal Ataturk, President of the Turkish Republic, at the age of 58.

Abdul Halik Renda, the President of the National Assembly, has assumed the interim Presidency, and the Assembly will elect a new President at 11 o'clock tomorrow morning.

General Ineunu, ex-Premier and for many years Ataturk's right-hand man, is the most likely candidate.

Kemal Ataturk fell ill of a serious liver disease early this year and his condition become grave at the beginning of August last, when seven doctors were in attendance on board his private yacht near Istanbul.

He seemed to be recovering when, on October 18, a relapse set in. Ataturk, however, again showed remarkable vitality and was reported on October 23 to be better.

TURN FOR WORSE

This week, however, his condition took a further turn for the worse, and last night he was reported to have lapsed into a coma. From hour to hour, Turkey waited for news of his condition; and a bulletin issued at 1 o'clock (G.M.T.) last night stated that general weakness was affecting his heart.

Special precautions seemed to have been taken to prevent the news of his death, which took place early this morning, from being known before midday. It was then said that he had died peacefully.

The Lieutenant Who Became President

If ever a man was marked out for greatness and high position in the life of his people, it was Mustapha Kemal, the lowly Army lieutenant who rose to be President of an Asiatic Republic born out of the stress of war and post-War flux; and if ever a man deserved the title of Father of Modern Turkey, it was the first secular Head of State in many hundreds of years of dynastic rule.

Mustapha Kemal or, as he was known in later years, Kemal Ataturk (Great Turk), was born in Salonica in 1880, son of a minor Turkish customs official. Brought up and educated by his mother, a woman of character and ability, young Mustapha entered a military school, where he proved an exceptional student, especially in Mathematics; and his teacher gave him the distinctive surname of "Kemal" (an Arabic word for perfection).

In 1904 he was gazetted lieutenant but, on the same day, was arrested for political intriguing and banished to Damascus where, a year later, he founded the secret political society "Vatan" ("Fatherland").

LIFE AT JAFFA

From Damascus he was transferred to Jaffa and thence made his way secretly to Salonica to organize a similar political movement in the European provinces of Turkey. The society he founded was afterwards affiliated to the Young Turks' Committee of Union and Progress.

After an attempt to re-arrest him, he was forgotten and in 1907 was promoted to a Captaincy and sent to Salonica, where he resumed his revolutionary activities. In 1914 he was appointed Colonel.

When the Great War broke out, he was among those who believed in Germany's ultimate defeat and was not particularly in favour at Turkish H.Q. But he was placed in charge of the Dardanelles defences, and inspired the resistance to the British attack.

Sent to the Caucasus, he was promoted Pasha and fought the Russians successfully. In 1917 he was posted to the Hedjaz and, in the same year, was appointed to command the Seventh Army Corps, under General von Falkenhayn, who was endeavouring to recover Baghdad.

COMMAND IN PALESTINE

After protesting against German military tactics and refusing the commands of the Second and Seventh Corps, he ultimately agreed to take the Seventh Corps command in Palestine in 1918, but it was when Turkish hopes were lost. He kept together the remnants of his corps on the retreat following General Allenby's great victory, and before the end of September was appointed Commander-in-Chief of all the forces constituting the so-called "Yilderim" group.

He opposed the policy of complete surrender at Mudros (October 30, 1937), and retired from activity, but when the Greeks landed at Smyrna in May, 1919, he accepted the Inspector-Generalship of the XIth. Corps. Resuming his political activity, he convened congresses at Erzerum and Sivas in 1919 and secured endorsement of his programme to fight for national existence to the bitter end.

NATIONAL ASSEMBLY

On April 23, 1920, he gathered together the Nationalist members of the Turkish Parliament who had fled from Constantinople and was unanimously elected President of the new National Assembly.

During the summer campaign of 1920-21, the supreme crisis of the Greco-Turkish war, he was appointed generalissimo of the Turkish forces by the National Assembly, and after the battle of Sakaria was given the rank of Field Marshal (at 41) and the traditional title of "Ghazi" (the Victor).

On October 29, 1923, the Republic was proclaimed following the abdication of the Sultan and the abolition of the Caliphate. The National Assembly unanimously elected him first President and in practice, if not in theory, he became Dictator. On November 1, 1927, he was unanimously re-elected.

Kemal was author of "Die Nationale Revolution, 1920-27" (1928) and "Die Neue Turkei, 1919-27" (1929).

MODERNISATION

The history of his rule from 1923 to 1938 was a continuous story of the modernisation of Turkey. He abolished the fez in favour of European headgear; forbade women to wear the veil; introduced the European calendar, and compulsory education; and introduced Latin characters for Turkish. He endeavoured unceasingly to bring Turkey into line on an equal footing with Western Powers, and ruthlessly stamped out all Levantinism in the character of the Turkish people.

A powerful Navy and Army, a pact with Great Britain, friendship for Russia, modern buildings, a five-year Industrial plan, prosperous trade, social hygiene and other public amenities in his own country were part of the achievements which remain as a monument to his untiring industry for his country.

U.S. Republicans Again In the Running
77 SEATS GAINED IN HOUSE OF REPRESENTATIVES

NEW YORK, Thursday (R). — Republican gains in the United States elections have been much larger than expected, with 77 seats in the House of Representatives and eight in the Senate. Further results are still to be declared.

In the State Governorships, Republicans obtained 17 and Democrats 15, and the distribution now is:— 30 Democrats and 18 Republicans.

Republican and other Conservative elements are predicting a substantial Opposition in future to "New Deal" measures in Congress, and while they are talking optimistically concerning the Presidential election of 1940, Democratic circles are inclined to minimize the effect in this respect.

A SETBACK

Observers differ about the extent to which the election results may be regarded as a setback for President Roosevelt. Supporters of the "New Deal" say that some of the successful Republican candidates were more in sympathy with the "New Deal" than some of the Democrats. On the other hand, Democrats elected came from the Conservative wing.

It is thought that the tendency of the elections was a movement towards moderate liberalism. One thing is clear, — the Republicans are again in the running after having been eclipsed for several years.

ROYAL VISIT

It is officially announced in London that Their Majesties will sail on the cruiser, Repulse, to visit Canada and the United States. The Repulse will be escorted by a cruiser squadron.

The date of the sailing has not yet been fixed, but Reuter understands that Their Majesties will arrive in Canada about the middle of May.

NAZI HOOLIGANS VENT WRATH ON THE JEWS THROUGHOUT GERMANY

LONDON PRESS FAVOURS TALKS
GOVERNMENT MUST NOT FORGET IDEA OF NATIONAL HOME

LONDON, Thursday (Palcor & R). Although most of this morning's newspapers refrain from discussing the prospects of the London discussions with representatives of Jews and Palestinian Arabs, as well as of neighbouring Arab states, there is general agreement that, in summoning a conference in a supreme effort to achieve agreement, the British Government has acted wisely.

NO CRITICISM

"The Times" says editorially:

"No criticism can be levelled with any semblance of justice against the Government's decision to promote a conference of Jewish and Palestinian Arab delegates.

"A settlement by consent of the Jewish-Arab quarrel would instantly relieve this country of serious anxieties, and soon restore peace and prosperity to the Holy Land whose inhabitants, all except the professional banditti, desire to see a speedy end to the present period of disorder and uncertainty.

DEBATABLE POINT

"In any case, such a conference would have an inestimable advantage of giving the Jews and Arabs alike, the certainty that the Government would give a fair hearing to their respective cases.

"The most debatable point in the Government's statement is the decision to invite neighbouring Arab States to send their delegates to the Conference."

The editorial recalled that the interference by Arab rulers in 1936 was regarded in Great Britain and by the League of Nations as undesirable and embarrassing.

Referring to Plan C. the article pointed out, "It reduces the Jewish State to microscopic dimensions, leaving out the successful colonies studding the Plain of Esdraelon. It would certainly have been rejected by the Jews, giving the Arabs an excellent opportunity of resisting the policy without concession.

"Fortunately, Plan C. was not adopted by the Government, which based its rejection on economic and financial reasons."

The article regarded it as ironic that, while the Commission admitted that the increase of Jewish immigration has led to improved life within the Arab population and that Palestine had become a paying concern only by the investment of Jewish capital, this should at the same time be an obstacle to the fulfilment of Jewish ambitions.

"MUST NOT FAIL"

"The News-Chronicle," in welcoming the Government's decision, said that the time was ripe for making a supreme effort to bring about an understanding between Jews and Arabs, and the conference deserved every good wish.

"If the Conference fails, the Government will have no recourse but to apply their own solution and enforce it firmly. But the conference must not be allowed to fail." ...

BRITAIN'S POLICY

While more critical of the Government's past handling of the Palestine question, "The Manchester Guardian" regards the Conference with satisfaction, but adds that the Government must not forget that the policy of England is based on the Balfour Declaration and on the idea of a National Home of which less and less has been heard since the days of the Peel report.

(Other London Press Comment on Page 2. Palestine Press Reaction and Jewish Agency Statement on Page 8.)

Negotiations with Arabs and Jews on Basis of the Mandate
STATEMENT IN HOUSE ON FORTHCOMING TALKS

LONDON, Thursday. — Replying to a question by Major Attlee in the House of Commons this afternoon in reference to representation at the London conference on Palestine, Mr. Malcolm MacDonald said that the Government was in a communication with the Governments of Egypt, Iraq, Saudi-Arabia, the Yemen and Trans-Jordan.

It was not proposed to invite the Mufti of Jerusalem as his record over many years made him wholly unacceptable as an Arab representative in London.

The Opposition Leader asked the Colonial Secretary to bear in mind the need for adequate representation of the poorer Arabs and Jewish labour.

PRELIMINARY TALKS

Answering supplementary questions, Mr. MacDonald declared that the Government would enter the Palestine Discussions bound by obligations to both Jews and Arabs under the Mandate, but it would not seek to prevent either party from presenting its arguments for the modification of the Mandate, Mr. MacDonald added that the Government would watch the situation very carefully.

He made it clear that the preliminary discussions in London would be between:

(1) The Arabs of neighbouring countries and the British Government;

(2) The representatives of the Jewish Agency and the British Government.

The discussions, he thought, might well develop into a three-party conference. The conferences would be in the form of purely informal discussions and there was no question of voting.

It was suggested also that invitations might be sent to the United States of America, Poland and Rumania, among others. Mr. MacDonald declined to do so, but stated that if any question arose of the treaty rights of the United States being involved, the Government would enter into immediate discussions with the United States.

In his reply to Major Attlee the Colonial Secretary said:

"As was announced in the Statement which His Majesty's Government published yesterday, it is proposed to invite representatives of the Palestine Arabs and of neighbouring states on the one hand, and of the Jewish Agency on the other. With regard to neighbouring states, we are in communication on the matter with the Governments of Egypt, Iraq, Saudi-Arabia and the Yemen, as well as Trans-Jordan.

CONTACT WITH FRENCH

"Other territories which, by reason of their contiguity, are interested in the Palestine question, are Syria and the Lebanon. They are under French Mandatory control and consequently stand on a different footing. It is not proposed that the representatives of these territories should be invited to the discussions, but His Majesty's Government intend to keep closely in touch with the French Government and to keep them informed of any developments which may be of interest to Syria and the Lebanon.

"With regard to the representation of the Palestine Arabs, I am in consultation with the High Commissioner and I am not at present in a position to indicate what arrangements will be made.

"The House will have observed that the Government reserve the right to refuse to receive leaders whom they regard as responsible for the campaign of assassination and violence. His Majesty's Government must exercise this right in the case of the present Mufti of Jerusalem, whose record over many years makes him wholly unacceptable. With regard to others, I can add nothing at present. The matter must depend on the position in Palestine.

COST OF TROOPS

LONDON, Thursday (R). — Mr. MacDonald in the course of a written reply in the House of Commons revealed that the extra cost of maintaining Army units in Palestine over and above the cost of maintaining them in their normal stations in 1938-39 was estimated to be £1,700,000.

It was not possible to furnish figures of the total cost of the military forces in Palestine, but the additional cost of the Air Force was over the normal expenditure for 1938-39 to date by £11,000.

RESTORING PEACE

"His Majesty's Government made it clear in the Statement which they issued yesterday that they will continue their responsibility for the Government of the whole of Palestine. Their ultimate aim is to give lasting peace and prosperity to the people of the country. Their immediate duty is to establish law and order throughout the land.

"They earnestly hope that they will secure the cooperation of the peoples of Palestine, Jews and Arabs alike, in promoting that state of peace which is so essential for the success of the policy of negotiation which has been announced.

"The Arabs in Palestine are now offered an opportunity of coming to London, in company with the representatives of neighbouring countries, to enter into free and full discussions on the problem of Palestine with His Majesty's Government.

"In these circumstances, His Majesty's Government will expect that rebellious activities should be brought to an end. If they do not cease, His Majesty's Government must continue to take all such measures as may be necessary to put an end to disorders."

NO NEGOTIATIONS WITHOUT LEADERS

The Inter-Parliamentary Palestine Congress delegation (Arab) at present in London has issued a statement declaring that to negotiate about Palestine in the absence of her accredited leaders would not give an authoritative or permanent character to any settlement.

Moslems and Arabs everywhere genuinely desired to be on good terms with Great Britain, said the statement, and the delegation requested the Government not to allow the present opportunity to be spoiled by false notions of prestige.

COUNTRYWIDE POGROMS
SYNAGOGUES RAZED TO THE GROUND; SHOPS WRECKED, LOOTED

BERLIN, Thursday (R).

Since the early hours of this morning, there have been vehement systematic and organized attacks on and destruction of Jewish property in various parts of Germany, shops and synagogues being wrecked and gutted by arson.

The new outburst of anti-Jewish feeling followed the death of Herr von Rath, who is being brought to Frankfurt-on-Main (his native town) tomorrow for a State funeral.

This afternoon, the German Propaganda Minister, Dr. Joseph Goebbels, issued a proclamation calling for an immediate cessation of the attacks on Jewish property, and said that sufficient expression had been given to the German protest.

FRESH DECREES

Reprisals must now stop, and the final answer to the Jews would take the form of fresh legislation and decrees, he declared.

The demonstrations broke out at Munich last night at the conclusion of the three-day anniversary celebrations by the "Old Guard" of the abortive Munich bierhalle "putsch" in 1923.

Almost every Jewish shop in Munich was wrecked, and the sole remaining synagogue was razed to the ground. All Jewish males under 60 were placed under arrest.

The campaign spread this morning to the rest of Germany and Austria, where whole Jewish districts were raided.

In Vienna, only one synagogue escaped destruction by fire. Two were blown up, and several others set on fire. Some 5,000 Jews were arrested, 22 Jews committed suicide this morning, and all Jews waiting outside the British Consulate for emigration visas were taken into custody.

Nine synagogues were burned in Berlin alone, and the fires were got under control only at a late hour. Jewish shop-windows, sometimes as far up as the third storey, were shattered or smeared with slogans, and goods flung into the street.

NO POLICE CONTROL

In the afternoon, gangs of hooligans broke into West End Berlin shops smashed windows and threw the goods inside out into the street, where there were frantic rushes to secure fur, shoes and other articles in the confusion. During the day, said foreign observers, Kurfurstendam littered with glass, wreckage and goods, gave the impression that there had been an air raid or a big explosion.

The Police made no effort to check the hooliganism and smashing of windows, but only controlled the traffic. Crowds of sightseers on foot, in private cars and taxis, thronged the streets.

Foreign observers in Munich and Berlin said that the crowds were mostly silent, and did not approve of what had

(Continued on Page 2)

AFTER MIDNIGHT

The burning of synagogues and the demolition of Jewish stores continued last night throughout Germany. Shops were destroyed from Koenigsberg far in the northwest to towns in the southeast of the Reich. Looting was in full swing in the West End of Berlin last night.

Answering charges of underproduction of aircraft, Sir Kingsley Wood stated yesterday in the House of Commons during the debate on defence deficiencies that next year's Air Estimates would probably be £200,000,000, or £80,000,000 more than this year.

When the Prime Minister was asked to give an assurance in the House of Commons yesterday that the Government would not transfer any British colonies or Mandated territories to other Powers, he declined to add to his previous statements, and refused to be drawn by further questions.

ONLY FEW INCIDENTS REPORTED IN QUIET DAY

There were few incidents throughout the country reported yesterday.

There was a reaction in Tulkarm following the engagement at Irtah village on Wednesday when 19 bandits were killed, and a shop strike was declared yesterday.

An immediate Curfew was imposed on Jaffa as from 7 o'clock yesterday morning, after Mr. Rachwolsky, an employee of the Posts and Telegraphs Department was shot and slightly wounded by an unknown assailant when entering the Post Office. The Curfew was lifted at 4 p.m.

The following reports are taken from the Public Information Officer's bulletin issued yesterday:

BOMBS AND SHOTS AT MILITARY

Two Arab houses were demolished by troops in Nablus yesterday following the throwing of a bomb at the Brigade Headquarters in the town on Wednesday night.

A second bomb was thrown at the military billet at dawn yesterday, but failed to explode.

Military and police billets in Gaza were also the targets of snipers on Wednesday night. There were no casualties, and the fire was returned.

GAZA STATION FIRE

At 10 o'clock yesterday morning a railway trolley was set on fire by unknown persons, in Gaza Railway Station. The flames were extinguished by the Fire Brigade.

Shots were fired at Hefzibah settlement (Haifa District) during Wednesday night, but there were no casualties.

TREES DESTROYED

A small number of eucalyptus trees was uprooted in Rosh Pinah settlement on Wednesday.

Two hundred and fifty orange trees were cut down in a grove in Rishon-le-Zion on Wednesday. The damage is estimated at about LP. 450.

The same afternoon a police car overturned at Km. 24 on the Frontier Road, and two Arab constables were slightly injured.

PASSENGER CUT BY GLASS

Yesterday morning shots were fired at long range at traffic on the Coastal Road near Taba village. One shot broke the window of a car and a Jewish passenger was slightly cut by broken glass.

INJURED SOLDIERS

The names of the soldiers injured in the ambush of a railway trolley near Kalkilya on Wednesday are Lance-Corporal J. Mackintosh; Private A. Easton, Private J. Cairns, and Private A. H. Burton. All the men, who were seriously wounded, belong to the Royal Scots Regiment.

SUBSCRIPTIONS: Local: LP.2.250 a year; LP.1.250 a half year:— Foreign: £3.- a year. The rate for display advertisements is 150 mils per column inch. Other rates supplied on request. The right is reserved to make changes in wording or to decline or discontinue any advertisement or to postpone insertions when space is not available.

THE PALESTINE POST

JERUSALEM Hassolel Road P. O. Box 81, Telephone 4233

Tel Aviv - Jaffa: 65 Allenby Road, P. O. Box 1125, 'Phone 4251-4252.

Haifa: Khayat Square, opposite the Post Office entrance, P.O.B. 66, 'Phone 1390.

SUNDAY NOVEMBER 13 1938 JERUSALEM VOL. XIV. No. 3798 PRICE 10 MILS.

NEW NAZI SAVAGERY SPELLS DOOM OF JEWISH LIFE IN GERMANY

MILITARY AND POLICE ACTION IN SEARCHES

TWELVE KNOWN ARAB CASUALTIES IN 3 DAYS

Military and police operations throughout the country during the past three days included searches in eight different localities.

One member of his Majesty's Forces was killed and three were injured in various localities.

Three Jews have been wounded, and 12 Arabs known to have been killed or wounded including a small girl, as a result of terrorism and military action since Thursday.

PLANE FORCED DOWN

When an R.A.F. machine cooperating with the military in an engagement at Beit Furik village east of Nablus, made a forced landing the pilot, Sergeant Pilot Tebbs, was seriously hurt, while Corporal George Wickens, of the Green Howards, was slightly injured in the same engagement in which heavy casualties were inflicted on the band.

Many arrests were made as a result of these searches, and over a thousand rounds of ammunition seized together with several rifles, bombs and detonators, some documents and a camera.

Shots were fired yesterday afternoon at troops who were on duty at a Traffic Control Post in the Bab Zeitun Quarter of Gaza. One British soldier was killed and another severely wounded. A 24-hour curfew was imposed as from 3 p.m.

EXPLOSION KILLS FIVE

An explosion which occurred on Thursday night in the house of Khalil el Awoor in Al Majdal, north of Gaza, completely wrecked the building, killing the owner and four other persons

Yesterday afternoon a party of British police in a tender were fired on near Jenin police station. They returned the fire and killed an Arab who was subsequently found to be in possession of a rifle and more than 250 rounds of ammunition.

CUSTOMS GUARD SHOT DEAD

Yesterday afternoon a customs guard named Abdul Hafiz of Kalkania was shot dead by unknown assailants while walking in the Nazareth Road, Haifa.

An Arab of Kabatiya village, Samaria, Nasser el Kassem was shot

(Continued on Page 2)

AFTER MIDNIGHT

A decree was issued in Paris last night providing for the revaluation of the gold stock in the Bank of France at the rate of 170 francs to the £. Gold is now valued about 110 francs to the £. Another decree provides that agricultural production be nationalised by agreements to be reached between the parties concerned.

"We shall solve the political Catholic problem with the same consequences as the Jewish question," declared Gauleiter Jury, the Regional Leader of Lower Austria, in addressing a Nazi meeting yesterday in Gaenserndorf.

"A BLACK DAY FOR GERMANY" -- TIMES

BRITISH PRESS CONDEMN NAZI OUTRAGES

LONDON, Saturday (R. and Palcor).— The entire British press devotes space today to the riots and pillaging of Jewish houses and businesses in Germany. Comment takes the form of unprecedentedly strong condemnation, even in journals 'friendly' to Germany.

"The Times" heads its editorial with the words "A Black Day for Germany" and states that no amount of foreign propaganda could have done Germany so much harm as the events which have taken place. Similar views are expressed by other leading morning papers.

CRUELTY AND DESTRUCTION

The Archbishop of Canterbury in a letter to "The Times," expresses the feeling of indignation with which he claims Christians in Britain have "read of the deeds of cruelty and destruction which were perpetrated last Thursday in Germany and Austria."

Adding that whatever provocation may have been given by the deplorable act of a single irresponsible Jewish youth, reprisals on such a scale, so fierce, cruel and vindictive, could not possibly have been justified.

Dr. Lang calls for the remembrance in prayers offered in Churches tomorrow of those who have suffered in this fresh onset of persecution.

Sir Archibald Sinclair, leader of the Liberal Party, in a speech last night said that the treatment of the German Jews was Germany's business only so long as she did not expel them after having robbed them.

Sir Archibald said that the refugee problem must be tackled in a general spirit, and that in the light of recent events British obligations towards the Jewish National Home must be interpreted in a generous spirit.

NAZI ARMS FOR ARABS

He said that the Arabs who were incited by German and Italian propaganda, and aided by German arms, should not be allowed to frighten the British Government from fulfilling its pledges towards the Jewish National Home. He insisted that there was room in Palestine for the Jews, and that the Arab complaints were unreasonable since Jewish immigration had helped development, and the Jews must find a home.

The Foreign Under-Secretary, Mr. R. A. Butler, yesterday received a deputation consisting of Mr. Neville Laski, Chairman of the Board of Jewish Deputies. and Mr. C. G. Montefiore, President of the Anglo-Jewish Association, together with Mr. L. H. Glueckstein, M.P.

PILLAGED OF 84 MILLION POUNDS TO "PAY" FOR MURDER OF GERMAN OFFICIAL

BERLIN, Saturday (R).—Jews in Germany have been ordered to pay one milliard marks (over 80 million pounds sterling) as compensation for the murder of Herr von Rath, the secretary of the German Embassy in Paris.

The indemnity will be levied in the form of a special tax on all Jewish property. Since this property is officially valued at about 10 milliard marks, the tax will be at a rate of ten per cent.

MINISTERS' CONFERENCE

The decision was taken at a conference presided over by Field-Marshal Goering, attended by Dr. Frick, Reich Minister of the Interior, Dr. Goebbels, Minister of Propaganda, Dr. Guertner, Minister of Justice, and Count von Krosigk, the Minister of Finance.

Furthermore, all the damage "caused through the indignation of the people over the agitation by international Jews, on November 8, 9, and 10" must be made good by Jewish occupiers or Jewish businessmen, while sums derived from insurance companies will be confiscated for the benefit of the Reich.

The official communique which announces these decisions also contains the announcement that "further drastic measures for driving the Jews out of Germany's economic life and the elimination of provocative conditions will shortly be taken, in the form of laws and decrees." It is stated that "a number of the most drastic measures will be taken," the first of which have already been announced.

ELIMINATION PROCESS

From January 1, 1939, Jews will not be allowed to engage in

retail trade,
export businesses,
commercial offices or
independent handicraft businesses, and
will not be permitted to occupy managerial posts.

The decree forbidding Jews to own weapons is implemented by new measures announced today.

Further, a decree was issued by Dr. Goebbels, forbidding Jews to visit theatres, concerts, cinemas, music halls, dance entertainments, museums and exhibitions of any kind.

It was stated by Dr. Goebbels that there was no reason why Jews should visit such entertainments or exhibitions since they had their own cultural organizations. The activities of the latter have however been brought to a complete standstill, as all Jewish theatre, concert and cinema performances have been prohibited.

Jewish schools and newspapers have been closed down.

Ruin

EFFECT OF NEW DECREE

(By Our Commercial Correspondent)

The decree ordering Jews in Germany to pay a milliard Reichsmarks and the decision to levy this amount in the form of a ten per cent capital tax clearly reveals the intention to destroy whatever economic assets are left to the Jews.

The execution of this decree means irreparable ruin for every Jewish business in Germany and this apart from the order forbidding Jews to engage any longer in retail trade, since it is normally impossible for owners of businesses to raise ten per cent of their capital in cash.

Landlords, shopkeepers and security holders will thus be compelled to sell their property or shares, provided they can find buyers. To sell buildings has become extremely difficult. The market value is not taken into account, and the price is fixed by an "arbitrator," usually appointed by the Nazis.

In the case of securities the market has contracted to such an extent owing to forced investments in Government securities that small sales inevitably lead to heavy drops in prices. What will happen when large blocks of securities are suddenly offered for sale can readily be imagined.

Altogether the decrees amount to nothing less than the complete spoliation of what property still remains in Jewish hands.

PARIS, Saturday (R). — The funeral service for Herr von Rath took place here today at the Lutheran Church in the German Colony.

The French Foreign Minister, M. Bonnet, was present, and the Government, the President, and the President of the Chamber, were represented.

JEWS HIDING IN BERLIN WOODS

REPORTS OF TORTURE AND MURDER

LONDON, Saturday (R). — Mass arrests of Jews are still the order of the day in Berlin and other German towns. It is estimated that several thousand Jews were arrested in Berlin, while thousands, according to a report received here, are hiding in the woods round Berlin.

In Frankfort-on-Main all Jewish men between the ages of 18 and 60 were arrested and herded into concentration camps, where, like all other Jewish internees, they will have to pay for their own board and lodging, as well as for that of those Jews among them who are without funds.

Further to the demonstrations which took place on Tuesday, Wednesday and Thursday, it is now learned according to reports received here, that the worst disorders occurred in small towns where the entire population took part in smashing and looting Jewish shops. Warnings were published in the local newspapers that anybody who failed to take part would be regarded as an enemy of the regime.

QUESTION IN HOUSE

Notice was given today by Mr. Attlee, Leader of the Opposition, of a question regarding the events in Germany. This fact has caused reports in the German press that Parliament is to debate the riots.

German newspapers react to this report with an outburst of abuse, several stating that if Parliament is to debate the position of the Jews in Germany, the Reichstag will be called to debate British policy in Palestine.

TORTURED TO DEATH

A leading personality who witnessed some of the scenes in Berlin and arrived here yesterday (reports Palcor), stated that no Jewish business was left intact and many Jewish houses were damaged and looted. Scores of Jews, according to him, were not only beaten but literally tortured to death.

Officially it is stated in Berlin that a Polish Jew was killed in Munich, where 1,400 Jews are now stated to have been arrested, over half of whom were brought to Dachau concentration camp.

The announcement that one Jew was killed was made in Munich today by the Gauleiter, Herr Wagner, at a mass meeting. This accident occurred, he said, "because he could not keep his mouth shut."

Herr Wagner also expressed satisfaction that the last synagogue in Munich had now finally been got rid of. "I hope foreigners of all kinds in Munich will now keep out of our affairs," said Herr Wagner.

ATTACK ON CATHOLICS

In another part of his speech he attacked the Roman Catholic Church which he accused of giving shelter to the Jews. Following his speech a mob went to the palace of Cardinal Faulhaber, known as an opponent of the regime, and smashed a number of windows.

Only brief and casual reports of the disturbances were published in the German press. The Berlin streets were cleaned overnight, and apart from paneless windows and closed shops there was nothing yesterday to remind passers-by of the demonstrations. The damage in Berlin alone is estimated at tens of millions of marks.

The Zionist Organization's Offices in Berlin were destroyed by a mob and leading Zionists were arrested.

ONE HUNDRED JEWS FLEE PERSECUTION

LONDON, Saturday. — One hundred Jews, men, women and children, from Germany and Austria sailed from Liverpool last night in the Canadian Pacific liner, Duchess of Bedford, for Montreal on their way to Australia and New Zealand.

All the men are skilled workers and all have received permits to enter the Dominions. Some had sufficient means to pay their fares. Others have been assisted by Jewish Aid Societies.

Some of the women had to leave their husbands in Germany, because they had not enough money for both fares.

RECOGNISES ITALY'S CONQUEST

CAIRO, Saturday (R). — Egypt has decided to recognise the Italian conquest of Abyssinia. An announcement to this effect was made here today.

GEN. INUENU NEW TURKISH PRESIDENT

REGARDED AS ATATURK'S LOGICAL SUCCESSOR

ISTANBUL, Saturday (R).— General Ismet Inuenu, former Prime Minister and close collaborator of Kemal Ataturk, was unanimously elected President of the Republic by the National Assembly in Ankara today.

Following the election, a reshuffle of the Cabinet was announced.

Dr. Rushdi Aras, the Foreign Minister is replaced by the former Minister of Justice, Shukru Aracaghu, while the Minister of the Interior, M. Shukru Kaya is replaced by the former Minister of Health, Refik Saydan.

Dr. Aras has held the post of Foreign Minister continuously since 1925, and was a well-known figure at Geneva where he represented Turkey since she became a member of the League in 1932.

The new President of Turkey was born in 1882 and served a distinguished career in the Army, before joining the Nationalist movement led by Kemal in 1919 and taking over command of the army that defeated the Greeks.

He represented Turkey at the Lausanne Conference in 1923 where she was finally recognised by the former Allied Powers.

In 1925 Inuenu became Prime Minister, a post he occupied for 12 years. He was then known as Ismet Pasha.

His resignation last year was reported to have been due to differences of opinion with the President on Turkey's foreign policy, but his unanimous election is proof that he continues to be regarded as the logical successor to Kemal Ataturk.

In connection with the death of Kemal Ataturk, the Turkish Consulate in Jerusalem on Friday received visits from members of the Consular Corps, including the Consuls of Iran, Iraq and Yugoslavia.

Mr. L. Kohn and Mr. E. Epstein called on behalf of the Jewish Agency and Mr. E. Elmaleh on behalf of the General Council of Palestine Jews.

The latter has also telegraphed to the new President of the Turkish Republic expressing the sorrow of Palestine Jewry on the news of the death of Kemal Ataturk.

The Chief Rabbinate of Palestine has sent the following message signed by Chief Rabbi Herzog and Rabbi Meir to the Prime Minister of Turkey:

"Palestine Jewry's profoundest sympathy and condolence with Turkish nation in serious loss sustained through untimely death of great leader and regenerator of Turkey, Gazi Kemal Ataturk."

INSURGENTS RAID BARCELONA

BARCELONA, Saturday (R). — Barcelona was raided today by Insurgent planes which dropped a number of bombs in the centre of the town. The number of casualties is stated to have been very small.

Fighting on land is progressing, though neither side reports progress on the Segre front. On the Ebro, the Republicans are still defending much of the ground taken in their successful July offensive.

"WE OPEN OUR SESSION TO THE LIGHT OF SYNAGOGUE FIRES"

WEIZMAN OVERCOME WITH EMOTION AT GENERAL ZIONIST MEETING IN LONDON

LONDON, Saturday (Palcor). Meeting under the shadow of the tragic events in Germany, the session of the Zionist General Council opened here at 11 o'clock yesterday morning in the presence of 73 delegates from all parts of the world, including the United States and Palestine.

The Council observed the two minutes' silence customary on Armistice Day, prior to Mr. Ussishkin opening the meeting with a tribute to the victims of the Palestine disturbances, to Dr. F. Rottenstreich and to Mr. L. Motzkin, on the occasion of the fifth anniversary of his death.

Recalling the desecration of the Wailing Wall, Mr. Ussishkin went on to describe the happenings in Europe during the last few days and closed with an appeal for unity.

"Reality overcomes all internal differences," he said, "let us unite for the sole salvation of the Jewish people which is Palestine."

U. S. JEWS THANKED

Mr. Ussishkin paid a special tribute to the Jews of America for their recent great efforts which would not be forgotten in Zionist history. Acting on his suggestion the conference decided to send a telegram of congratulation to Mr. Justice Brandeis on the occasion of his 83rd birthday.

In a hushed silence, Dr. Weizman began his opening address with a reference to the losses recently suffered by the Jews in Palestine, among whom he named with particular sorrow the son of his colleague, Dr. Mossinsohn.

"NO PEACE" — WEIZMAN

Proceeding, Dr. Weizman said that while millions of people of all nations celebrated the Armistice today, there was no peace for the Jews. "We open this session in the light of synagogue bonfires now burning throughout Germany and to the groans of the murdered and cries of thousands of Jews in the concentration camps," he said.

Dr. Weizman was overcome by emotion and a few moments passed before he was able to continue. They had been trying, he said, during the last few days, to influence persons whom them believed to be powerful, but their efforts had been in vain.

They had obtained sympathy but they were unable to do anything. The forces of shameless cruelty could not be checked.

Zionists were not accustomed, however, to weep and wail, he said. The world in which they had been brought up when justice prevailed was breaking up, but there were still elements which justified the view that ultimately the forces of darkness would be withstood, not only so far as the Jews were concerned but for the whole world.

Dr. Weizman then referred to the Palestine situation and said that the partition scheme had been dropped, though they had not been responsible either for its presentation or for its withdrawal. The establishment of a Jewish State would have been impossible now, even if the report of the Partition Commission had been favourable, because the enemies of the Jewish people and of justice were too strong at the moment.

CYNICAL DOCUMENT

He had rarely seen a more cynical document than the Woodhead report, and he was unable to understand the mentality of its members with the exception of one who seemed to possess human feelings. The Report aimed at breaking up what the Jews had already acquired with superhuman effort.

The so-called Jewish State was apparently to be charged with the financial upkeep of the Arabs and British States which were admittedly unable to maintain themselves. Altogether the Report was a sign of the times and significant of the way in which small nations were being treated, of which Czechoslovakia was an example.

The Report, however, was now dead and ignored by the Government. The worst fears which had existed among the Jewish people for several weeks had not materialised

This was to be attributed to the dignified and courageous stand of the Jewish community in Palestine, which, he stated would remain as glorious as the struggle of the Maccabeans, second only to the united efforts of the Jews all over the world, especially in the United States, where Jews had manifested an unexampled unity and reacted to the danger in a manner which was a consolation — if consolation was possible in these days.

MANDATE IN FORCE

Dr. Weizman stressed the fact that the Balfour Declaration and the Mandate were still in force, but they were entering a period of difficulties in continuing and maintaining their work. The central theme of the immediate struggle was the question of immigration, which continued although in a thin stream.

They had received an invitation to negotiate with the Arabs, which they did not wish to refuse, but negotiations were possible only on the basis of the Balfour Declaration and the Mandate.

Concluding, Dr. Weizman said that although the project of a Jewish State had been temporarily dropped, he was convinced that it would come up again in due course. In the meantime Jewry must unite in strengthening the Jewish position in Palestine and its only instrument, the Zionist Organization.

After the close of Dr. Weizman's address, the meeting adjourned until tonight, when Mr. Shertok will give his address which will be followed by the political discussion.

SUBSCRIPTIONS: Local: LP.2.250 a year: LP.1.250 a half year:— Foreign: £3.- a year. The rate for display advertisements is 150 mils per column inch. Other rates supplied on request. The right is reserved to make changes in wording or to decline or discontinue any advertisement or to postpone insertions when space is not available.

THE PALESTINE POST

JERUSALEM Hassolel Road P. O. Box 81, Telephone 4233

Tel Aviv - Jaffa: 65 Allenby Road, P. O. Box 1125, 'Phone 4251-4252.

Haifa: Khayat Square, opposite the Post Office entrance, P.O.B. 66, 'Phone 1390

TUESDAY FEBRUARY 7 1939 JERUSALEM VOL. XV. No 3872 PRICE 10 MILS

TRIPARTITE TALKS ON PALESTINE TONIGHT

Federal Solution of Problem Sought by "The Times"

Another chapter in Palestine's political history will open this afternoon, when the tripartite talks between the British Government, the Arabs, and the Jewish representative will be initiated in St. James's Palace in London.

The Prime Minister, Mr. Neville Chamberlain, will be in the chair. Formalities for the opening ceremony will be completed this morning, and the actual discussions between the British and Arab delegations will begin this evening.

"Diplomatische Korrespondenz," the organ of the German Foreign Office, yesterday in an article on the Palestine talks said that it was quite clear that the development of Jewish influence in Palestine would to some extent affect the general Mediterranean situation. Interest in the talks on Palestine would therefore go beyond those circles directly concerned.

The delegates of the Arab National Defence Party of Palestine arrived in London yesterday evening from Southampton, which they reached from Alexandria by Imperial Airways flying-boat. They were welcomed by Mr. Malcolm MacDonald when they arrived at Waterloo Station in the afternoon.

INFLUENCE OF ARAB STATES

Reuter reported yesterday that the Palestine Conference formed the subject for editorial articles in several London morning papers, notably "The Times", which, while regretfully admitting that the chances of agreement were by no means promising and the demands of Arabs and Jews did not appear to admit of any kind of compromise, felt that there were nevertheless some grounds for the expectation that the influence of some at least of the neighbouring Arab States would be exercised in favour of moderation.

"It is possible," the paper continued, "that a Federal solution of the Palestinian problem, which recognises the rights of the Arab majority in Palestine, will be accepted by these Governments if it were so framed as to pave the way to a wider association of the Arab States extending the present frontiers of Palestine and Trans-Jordan."

At present, however, the attention of His Majesty's Government must remain rivetted to their immediate task of finding a way out of the political impasse in Palestine itself, a task not easily accomplished merely by a coercive policy. "This," "The Times" concluded, "should not prevent the Government from preparing the diplomatic ground for a wider scheme which would do much to ensure political stability and territorial integrity in the Arab East."

The Arab Higher Committee delegates are busily engaged on the case they will present at the talks, according to Reuter. Briefly, their case will be, firstly, recognition of Palestine's complete independence; secondly, the replacement of the Mandate by a Treaty; thirdly, the abolition of the Balfour Declaration; fourthly, the immediate cessation of Jewish immigration and land sales. The question of a possible Confederacy has also engaged attention, but it is felt that this subject could best be broached after the signature of the Treaty with Great Britain.

PRO-MUFTI CABLES

The Higher Committee delegates have received numerous cables from bodies in Egypt and Palestine. Two have particularly insisted that the Defence Party delegates should speak only for themselves and the Higher Committee should solely represent Palestine. The cables tended to stiffen the attitude of the Mufti Party towards the Defence Party and the possibility of an early rapprochement between the two Arab delegations now seems remote.

Mr. Jinnah, President of the Muslim League of India, has published at Bombay a communication received from the Secretary of State for India refusing a request by Indian Muslims to be represented in the London Conference.

Support for the Arab demands has come from the Muslim League of India through their London representatives. A manifesto sympathising with and augmenting the Arab claims to independence was issued last evening. A copy has been placed in the hands of the Marquess of Zetland, who promised to convey its contents to the Government.

(Earlier Reports — Page 2).

STRINGENT OFFICIAL ACTION IN JERUSALEM

CURFEW AND COLLECTIVE FINE IMPOSED

Firm measures were announced by the Military Commander and the District Commissioner for Jerusalem as a result of yesterday's outrages.

They comprised the imposition of a 24-hour Curfew on the Old City, following the attempted murder of a Jewish newspaper-vendor, and the imposition of a collective fine of LP.-300 on the Musrara Quarter.

Other measures include the prohibition of Arab commercial road vehicles from entering or leaving Jaffa, following the derailment of a train on the main Kantara-Lydda line near Rehovoth (reported in another column).

Arab shopkeepers yesterday closed their premises in the Old City and parts of the New City, as the beginning of a three-day strike ordered by followers of the Mufti of Jerusalem and described as "a protest against the presence of the Palestine Arab defence Party delegation at the London talks."

NEWSPAPERS AS SHIELD

As Menasche Nouriel, a newspaper-vendor, was at 7 o'clock yesterday morning standing outside the old G.P.O. building in Allenby Square selling **The Palestine Post**, a young Arab approached him and whipped out a revolver.

Nouriel held up the bundle of papers he was carrying and two bullets ploughed into the wadded sheets. One furrowed the side of the bundle, and the other went through, making a finger-deep hole with a ragged aperture at the other side. Both bullets missed Nouriel.

The 24-hour curfew was imposed from 11.45 yesterday morning in the Old City, excluding the Jewish and Armenian quarters, by the firing of the cannon, as "the assailant, who was not caught, escaped into the Old City."

It will be remembered that another newspaper-vendor selling **The Palestine Post** was fired at and missed near the same spot, and his assailant, who was chased into the New Gate vicinity, was subsequently hanged after conviction by the Military Court.

RECURRENT MURDERS

An order was passed yesterday by Mr. E. Keith-Roach, C.B.E., under the Collective Fines Ordinance, 1936, imposing a communal fine of LP.-300 on the area lying within Allenby-Square, St. Paul's Road, north of Meah Shearim police-station to Nablus Road, east to Damascus Gate, and south to Allenby Square (comprising the Musrara Quarter), but excluding the triangle formed by St. Paul's Road, Street of the Prophets and Queen Melisande's Way, including the Evelina de Rothschild School.

The District Commissioner stated that several crimes had been committed in the area, culminating in an attempt at murder there on February 3 (of Mr. Hugh Bingham), and that investigations made had satisfied Major-General R. N. O'Connor that these crimes were committed by Arabs. The Military Commander had accordingly directed that a fine should be imposed.

Those exempted from payment are male inhabitants below 15, male inhabitants in religious orders irrespective of age, Government officers irrespective of age, and nationals of foreign countries.

REPUBLICAN DEBACLE IN SPAIN

REBELS BREAK GOVERNMENT RESISTANCE

MASS RETREAT; PANIC AND STARVATION

PERPIGNAN, Monday (R). — General Modesta's Army of the Ebro has been defeated and his three Army Corps are pouring into France.

It is estimated that 13,000 men have already crossed the frontier, bringing with them a number of guns and aeroplanes. Altogether 27 Republican war-planes have landed in French territory, notably at Carcassone. As a result of the removal of barricades across the frontier, consequent upon a decision to permit unrestricted entry of troops and refugees, it is believed that between 100,000 and 140,000 soldiers are coming. They are being sent to vast concentration camps at Argeles, Barcares and elsewhere, after being disarmed.

Arrivals today included lorryloads of women and children. All lorries containing 800 cases of art treasures bound for Geneva crossed the frontier undamaged. So far 100,000 refugees have entered France.

SCENES OF TRAGEDY

Reuter reports that the flight of refugees along the frontiers presents a scene of grim tragedy. Beyond Le Perthus, all along the road towards Figueras, there was a solid mass of fugitives of all ages, sexes and classes. Beyond Cerbere and down to Portbou, the road was black with starving people. Thousands of women, children and babies, jammed against the barricades without food or water for two or three days, were suffering intensely, many dying from hunger and exposure.

Ditches on either side of the road for a distance of two miles beyond the frontier are filled with miscellaneous arms. Rifles, light machine-guns, heavy revolvers, with other weapons, lay where they were cast aside by the fleeing Republican troops. This afternoon it was estimated that the Republican forces were entering France at the rate of five or six thousand per hour.

Behind the masses of terrified people pushing on towards the Franco-Spanish frontier, General Franco's forces are advancing rapidly in the completion of their occupation of Catalonia. It was reported this evening that Seo de Urgel and Puigcerda had been captured, and a whole Republican division wiped out.

The Insurgents command practically all the communications through the Pyrenees. Two Republican coastal torpedo boats carrying naval headquarters staff have arrived at Port Vendres, and two smaller craft carrying 15 Republican Army officers were seized by Customs officials, who found a considerable quantity of arms of German origin.

Republican forces were stated to be covering the retreat of the main body, and making a fight-to-the-finish stand behind Seo de Urgel.

A Madrid message says that the application of the mobilisation decree is still actively continuing in the central zone, where all persons up to the age of 40, even though holding important posts, have been incorporated in the army.

BRITISH SAILORS KILLED

The bodies of two British sailors were found after an Insurgent air raid on Cartagena on Monday. Five Italian Savoia planes raided the port, and altogether 40 persons were killed and 60 wounded. One raider was hit by anti-aircraft fire and fell flaming into the sea.

NEARING THE END

Republican resistance to General Franco's advance in Catalonia received a mortal blow yesterday with the departure into France of the entire Catalan Cabinet, led by the Premier, Dr. Negrin. Scores of thousands of soldiers were stated to be on their way to the frontier.

Peace proposals made by the Republican authorities through the mediation of the British and French Ministers, after a conference at Perpignan, were summarily rejected by General Franco.

All frontier barriers into France have been removed, and soldiers as well as refugees were being admitted freely. French newspapers are concerned over the implications of the defeat in Catalonia.

In the pocket at Seo de Urgel, remaining Catalan divisions were preparing yesterday for a fight to the finish.

NEW EMIGRATION PLAN FOR GERMAN JEWS

LONDON, Monday (R). — Assurances against such anti-Jewish measures as "Ghettos," and conditions providing for the livelihood of Jewish residents of Germany unable at present to emigrate, are stated to be part of the new German plan for Jewish emigration brought back to London by Mr. George Rublee, Director of the Inter-Governmental Refugees Bureau, as a result of his negotiations.

According to the Jewish Telegraphic Agency, it is stated that the modified plan drops the export guarantee and international loan provisions of the original plan framed by Dr. Schacht. Conditions for emigration are established, and a fixed number of emigrants provided for annually.

While the exact number cannot be ascertained, it is thought to be less than the 100,000 yearly envisaged at the Evian Conference. All Jewish emigration is to be placed under the direction of a central office, directly controlled by Marshal Goering.

It is emphasized that the memorandum entails no change in the German anti-Jewish programme, and that the Reich Government is determined that all Jews shall leave within a stipulated period, although conditions are provided under which Jews unabe to emigrate or who must wait their turn, may continue to live in Germany.

The general question of the transfer of Jewish capital is left open for further negotiations.

Jewish organizations in Poland have sent a resolution to the British Government asking that Jewish immigration into Palestine be resumed at a higher rate. It was pointed out that of 350,000 Jews who had been allowed to enter since 1927, 190,000 were Polish.

91 FEARED DROWNED IN SUBMARINE WRECK

TOKYO, Monday (R).— Six out of the crew of 97 of the submarine I 63, which sank following a collision while participating in manoeuvres in the Bungo Straits on February 3, have been rescued.

The fate of the remaining members of the crew is not yet known, but the worst is feared.

AFTER MIDNIGHT

Mr. Chamberlain's statement in the House of Commons this afternoon in regard to Anglo-French cooperation has given a shock to Italian political circles who regard it as a more clear-cut expression of Anglo-French unity of interests than Mr. Chamberlain has ever made before. It was suggested in one quarter that Mr. Chamberlain's statement was tantamount to an announcement of a military alliance as binding as that proclaimed by Herr Hitler between Germany and Italy.

FRANCE CAN COUNT ON GREAT BRITAIN

CHAMBERLAIN'S STATEMENT IN COMMONS

LONDON, Monday (R). — Great Britain's immediate cooperation with France in the event of any threat to her vital interests was reaffirmed by Mr. Neville Chamberlain amid cheers in the House of Commons this afternoon, when he answered a question.

The Premier was asked whether M. Bonnet's statement in the French Chamber on January 26 that, in the event of war in which the two countries were involved, all of Britain's resources would be at the disposal of France, just as French assistance would be given to Great Britain, was correct.

That was in complete accordance with the views of the British Government, said Mr. Chamberlain, adding that while it was impossible to examine in detail all the hypothetical cases which might arise, **"nevertheless I feel bound to make it plain that the solidarity and interests by which France and Great Britain are united are such that any threat to the vital interests of France, from whatever quarters it came, must evoke the immediate cooperation of this country."**

A Paris message this evening stated that Mr. Chamberlain's statement is regarded in French political circles as a most important pronouncement, marking the close and indissoluble bonds uniting the two countries. The assurance is regarded as particularly significant in view of the suggestions that Great Britain was not warmly interested in Franco-Italian relations, and was only bound to assist France if she were attacked by Germany.

President Lebrun said in a speech last night that France could not accept the idea that a rule of force in the world could be substituted for a rule of law. "In agreement with peoples remaining true to the principles of Democracy, and echoing the great voice across the Atlantic, France intends to safeguard the fruits of her efforts," he declared.

Stop Press

MR. MACDONALD'S APPEAL

In an address broadcast over the BBC at 00.35 this morning, the Colonial Secretary, Mr. Malcolm MacDonald, referred to today's Palestine Conferences as a discussion between three parties: the British Government, the Arab representatives including those of the Arab States, and the representatives of Palestine and World Jewry, with the object of arriving at an agreed settlement of the Palestine problem.

Declaring that while no problem was insoluble that of Palestine was admittedly difficult, Mr. MacDonald proceeded to describe the historical background of the present situation, with special reference to the Arab opposition to the Mandate. The Colonial Secretary stressed the fact that the Arab delegates represented not only the Palestine Arabs but also the countries neighbouring Palestine which took a natural and inevitable interest in its affairs, just as the Jewish delegates were representative of Jews from many countries.

Referring to the "grim events" of the past two years in Palestine and to the cult of force which had spread in many parts of the world, and whose influence was felt also in Palestine, Mr. MacDonald deprecated the use of violent methods and closed with an expression of hope that the Conference would follow the path of reasoned discussion and agreement, as the only foundation of a lasting settlement.

GOVERNMENT RETREATS TO FRANCE

GENERAL FRANCO REJECTS NEGRIN'S PEACE OFFER

PERPIGNAN, Monday (R). — All members of the Spanish Republican Cabinet, with the exception of Senor Alvarez del Vayo (Foreign Affairs) and Senor Aspe (Finance) who are still in Spain, crossed over into France early this morning in a dramatic retreat from Catalonia.

Dr. Juan Negrin, the Premier and four other Ministers and several officials crossed the frontier at Le Perthus at 3.45 this morning, handing over their pistols and machine-guns as they did so. Their flight was unexpected as it was not known what caused the sudden change in the Premier's plans.

Earlier it had been reported that at a Cabinet meeting near Figueras it was decided that Dr. Negrin should leave immediately for the Madrid-Valencia zone. The Catalan and Basque Presidents, Senors Companys and Aguirre, are also in France, and President Azana is proceeding to Paris.

SERIOUS DIVERGENCES

This morning, it was stated that President Azana's departure was considered in usually well-informed circles in Paris to signify a complete breach with Dr. Negrin and other Republican Ministers, as the President was unwilling to support the line of resistance proposed. These divergences arose after the rejection by General Franco of peace overtures.

Senor del Vayo conferred this afternoon with Mr. Ralph Stevenson and M. Jules Henry, the British and French Ambassadors. Beforehand, Mr. Stevenson was interviewed at Amelie Les Bains, where the British Embassy has been established, and denied that Dr. Negrin has asked him to arrange peace terms. Such a request would be inconsistent with Dr. Negrin's declared intention to continue with the resistance in Central Spain.

He added, however, "Ever since I came to Spain in October, I have tried to find a way of bringing about peace. No negotiations have as yet begun with the Spanish Government, but this afternoon I and M. Jules Henry are meeting Senor del Vayo in Perpignan. That is all I can say at the moment."

President Azana is reported here to have been working for peace for several months in secret.

Steps to bring about a cessation of needless bloodshed in Spain are being taken by Great Britain in close cooperation with France, and endeavours are being made to keep in touch with both sides, according to a message from London.

Reuter understands that the Spanish Republican Government approached the British Government on the subject of mediation, and although no formal Note was sent to General Franco, a suggestion to this effect was turned down by him.

Paris messages today stated that several of the newspapers described peace talks at Perpignan, alleging a split within the Republican Government over the possibility of further resistance. "Echo de Paris" said that long conversations took place at Perpignan on Sunday between the British Minister, Mr. Ralph Stevenson, the French Ambassador, M. Jules Henry, and Senor Del Vayo, and several times they were in telephonic touch with the French Government.

CONCERN OVER CATALONIA

"L'Epoque" said that General Franco refused the peace proposals put forward by Dr. Negrin through Mr. Stevenson, and also rejected the suggestion of a plebiscite, demanding complete capitulation. The paper added that following General Franco's refusal, serious divergences arose among the Republican Ministers, ending in a complete break.

The French press also manifested concern today over the various possibilities of the debacle in Catalonia. It was demanded that political activity of any form by the Republican Ministers in French territory should not be tolerated at any price. A writer in "Le Figaro" insisted that the French Government should be inflexible and treat them as internees.

Road Traffic Stopped After Sabotage

As a result of sabotage of the railway a short distance south of Rehovoth just before noon, when a land mine explosion caused four wagons of the Kantara-bound train to leave the track, Brigadier H.E. de R. Wetherall, Military Commander of the Southern District, yesterday enforced the order issued last Friday with regard to the suspension of Arab traffic.

All Arab commercial road traffic was immediately prohibited from entering or leaving Jaffa, and military pickets and patrols were active in the road leading to Jaffa, stopping all Arab-driven lorries and trucks until by curfew time there was a line of about 70 stationary vehicles with drivers preparing to sleep inside the driving cabs.

UNTIL TODAY

The prohibition on traffic, it is reported, will remain in force until such time as the railway has been repaired and the trains are again running, which is expected to be early this morning.

The explosion occurred some 3 kilometres outside Rehovoth. There were a few passengers in the train, but no one was injured. Two engines were brought from Lydda and Gaza, and the train continued. At dusk last night, the line was still unrepaired.

The original warning, posted on February 3, in conjunction with a similar notice by Major General R. N. O'Connor, Military Commander of the Jerusalem District, stated that "should there be any further cases of damage to the line by evilly disposed persons, I shall take steps either to prohibit or curtail the traffic of Arab owned vehicles and Arab passengers on the road between these two towns — Jerusalem and Jaffa — for as long a period as I deem necessary."

SUBSCRIPTIONS: Local: LP.2.250 a year; LP.1.250 a half year.— Foreign: £3.- a year. The rate for display advertisements is 150 mils per column inch. Other rates supplied on request. The right is reserved to make changes in wording or to decline or discontinue any advertisement or to postpone insertions when space is not available.

THE PALESTINE POST

JERUSALEM Hassolel Road P. O. Box 81, Telephone 4233

Tel Aviv - Jaffa: 65 Allenby Road, P. O. Box 1125, 'Phone 4251-4252.

Haifa: Khayat Square, opposite the Post Office entrance, P.O.B. 66, 'Phone 1390

THURSDAY MARCH 16 1939 JERUSALEM VOL. XV. No. 3904. PRICE 10 MILS

NAZIS ANNEX CZECHO-SLOVAKIA

10,000 JEWS YEARLY IN 5 YEARS-FORECAST

No Statement Issued Yet

INDEPENDENT STATE AND FURTHER IMMIGRATION BY AGREEMENT

LONDON, Wednesday, (Palcor). It was reliably reported this afternoon that the British Government's proposals on Palestine to be submitted to the Arab and Jewish delegations are fundamentally those that had been foreshadowed, namely:

that there is to be a five-year period during which 10,000 to 15,000 Jewish immigrants yearly will be permitted to enter Palestine;

that Arab and Jewish representatives will be invited to join the existing Palestine Executive and Advisory Councils, with an Arab majority; and

that, at the close of five years, further Jewish immigration will depend upon Arab consent, while similarly the independence of Palestine would depend upon Jewish consent.

NO STATEMENT

Answering Mr. Vyvyan Adams in the House of Commons this afternoon, the Colonial Secretary said that he was unable to make any statement on the Palestine Conferences at the present.

Palcor understands that Dr. Weizman's interview with Mr. Neville Chamberlain last night did not change the situation. Dr. Weizman is not expected to be present at tonight's informal meeting with the Government when the Jewish Agency representatives will receive the British proposals.

Tewfik Bey es Suwaidi, head of the Iraqi delegation, gave a reception at Hyde Park Hotel on Tuesday night when members of the other Arab delegations and leading British statesmen were present.

"AL AHRAM" 'S FORECAST

The Cairo "Al Ahram," which reports that Ali Maher Pasha, Fuad Bey Hamza and Tewfik Bey Suwaidi were given access to the British proposals on Tuesday afternoon and later discussed them with the Arab delegations at a meeting in the Egyptian Embassy, makes the following forecast:

recognition of Palestine's independence and the substitution of a Treaty for the Mandate.

formation of a National Government by stages in the coming ten years, beginning with the appointment of Arab and Jewish Ministers without Portfolio under the administration of a High Commissioner, and ultimately the appointment of British Advisers;

a total of 70,000 Jewish immigrants during the first five years, in final fulfilment of the Balfour Declaration;

a conference to be held with participation of the Arab States to discuss whether the second period of five years might be shortened; and the constitution to be framed by an Assembly, with special guarantees for British interests and the Jewish minority.

INESCAPABLE ANALOGY

END OF ANGLO-JEWISH COLLABORATION FORESEEN

By Gershon Agronsky

LONDON, Wednesday. — The hearts that are awaiting the British proposals regarding Palestine this evening have been made heavier by the death of the Czech nation and weighted by the inescapable analogy. The restitution of both the Jews and the Czechs stemmed from the same generous impulse a score of years back when the world seemed on the way to sanity, and the forces responsible for the destruction of the one now menace the other.

The proposals will be public property late tonight when Mr. MacDonald is expected to give the press an authorised summary, after having communicated the Plan separately to the Arabs and the Jews. The Plan which has been divulged piecemeal leaves a great gap in the Arab demands, yet it ought to satisfy them if only because it recognises, however provisionally, their craving for independence.

ELEVENTH HOUR ATTEMPT

For the Jews the Plan offers the possibility for neither further discussion nor future cooperation. This must have been the burden of Dr. Weizman's communication to both the Premier and the Colonial Secretary last evening. The visit to the Premier is seen as an eleventh hour attempt to save the basis for cooperation; if it proved fruitless, it means the end of two decades of Anglo-Jewish collaboration just as the occupation of Prague marks the end of the Versailles era, all except for the precarious position of the colonies.

The Plan will be communicated to the Jews in the absence of Dr. Weizman, for it has been decided that he should be spared the final scene, and therefore only the members of the Political Department of the Agency are attending. The Jewish Panel meets tomorrow perhaps for the last time, since it is most doubtful that there will be any further Anglo-Jewish discussion.

The disintegration of Czecho-Slovakia pours 350,000 more Jews into the overflowing vessel of Jewish misery on the very day that the British Government announces that the admission of Jews into Palestine after a certain period will be subject to Arab consent and for the present will be circumscribed by the Arabs ambition for overlordship.

Anglo-French Attitude 'Calm But Not Complacent'

DEMOCRACIES MUST NOW LOOK TO OWN SECURITY

LONDON, Wednesday (R).—Great Britain and France made formal demarches, through their Ambassadors at Berlin, today regarding the entry of German troops into Czecho-Slovakia, but events moved so swiftly that European opinion generally had scarcely any time to crystallise.

The British attitude was one of complete neutrality, with identical opinion voiced in French circles where, according to a Paris report, feeling was "calm but not complacent." One optimistic leader-writer last night summed up the general view that "the end of Federal Czecho-Slovakia does not increase the risk of general hostilities in Europe or, indeed, put any fresh obstacle in Mr. Chamberlain's path of appeasement."

With the 20-year old Czecho-Slovak State disintegrated, and the Hungarian ultimatum to Ruthenia, the British Cabinet must consider a dramatic change in the face of Europe when it assembles tomorrow for the usual weekly meeting, states a diplomatic observer.

During the recent events, there were close contacts between the British Minister at Prague and Czech officials, but the Czechs made no request for advice from the British Government.

PLANS FOR ALL EMERGENCIES

Although unaware at the time of writing that the annexation of Czecho-Slovakia was so imminent, a leader-writer in "The Times" this morning hit the nail on the head when he stated that while it seemed probable that Dr. Hacha's bold attempt to impose his own authority on Slovakia was unexpected in Berlin, it only showed that the German Chancellor had plans ready for every emergency.

From the moment Dr. Tiso was dismissed as Slovak Premier, the subjugation of Czecho-Slovakia followed with clockwork regularity, the article went on, adding, that British, like French, opinion, could only register reprobation of the ruthless treatment of a small, industrious and friendly nation.

"Herr Hitler's influence, now dominant in Central Europe as it was bound in the end to become, is proving itself consistently hostile to political freedom as the Western democracies understand it. They, on their part, can only continue with increased energy to look to their own security, not only because they wish to prevent the normal growth of a strong Germany, but all the more because the Nazi Reich appears to be determined not only to expand to its full stature, but also to extend its domination, wherever the weakness of other nations may seem to make extension possible."

That there could be no question of British military intervention was the view of the "Daily Telegraph", which pointed out that the Four-Power guarantee of the Czech frontiers never became operative. Nevertheless Germany had "perpetrated an affront to the whole civilised world which will not be readily forgotten."

"The Daily Express" declared that the Czechs are in bondage to Germany. "Faced with menaces and threats on all sides they threw in the towel. It is a sad, bad, wretched moment. Millions of people will come under the heel of foreign masters whose political system they loathe. Their liberty is stripped from them. Their bondage is as complete as that of the Israelites under Pharaoh."

"The New York Times" described Tuesday's events as "the twilight of liberty in Central Europe," adding that it was clear that the old German dream of a Mittel-Europa under the domination of Berlin was closer to realisation today than ever before.

German opinion was probably fairly represented by the statement in "Angriff" concerning the historic necessity of Czecho-Slovakia's collapse. The German papers today delayed publication until they could

(Continued on Page 5)

THE ACME OF REFINEMENT

Flowers to Hacha

BERLIN, Wednesday (R). — When Dr. Emil Hacha, looking tired and grave after having signed away his country to Germany, arrived back at his hotel from the Chancellery early this morning, he found his room a mass of flowers.

They were believed to have been the gift of the German Government.

HUNGARY OCCUPIES RUTHENIA

JOIN WITH POLISH TROOPS TO FORM COMMON FRONTIER

BUDAPEST, Wednesday (R). Acting in apparent agreement with, and possibly with the explicit permission of Germany, Hungarian troops today began the occupation of Ruthenia (Carpatho-Ukraine), after having sent an ultimatum to the Cabinet at Chust to resign. The ultimatum expired at 8 o'clock G.M.T. tonight.

Dr. Volosin, the Premier, was given until tonight to surrender all authority, as Hungary claimed to have received an appeal for aid from the Central National Committee in Ruthenia asking her to intervene to restore order.

The occupying troops joined hands with Polish troops, advancing from their side of the frontier, at 6 o'clock this evening, so that the establishment of a common Hungarian-Polish frontier became an accomplished fact.

"LIFE INSURANCE"

An official spokesman had said in Budapest last night that an ordered Government in Ruthenia was "a life insurance" for Hungary, while the newspapers openly declared that its incorporation in Hungary was an indispensable factor in Hungary's future security. It is also pointed out that Hungary is now the only part of the old Austro-Hungarian Empire that can still claim independence.

Rumania agreed to take common action with Poland and Hungary, according to the Havas correspondent at Bucharest. Such action had the aim, firstly of taking back Rumanian villages in Ruthenia, and secondly, of getting compensation for strategic disadvantages which would be caused to Rumania by the extension of her frontier with Hungary to the north-east.

Hungarian troops crossed the frontier at several points, but no special military precautions were considered necessary on Rumania's frontier and Rumania did not interfere with the joint Hungarian-Polish move for a common border. Some of the population of Ruthenia, however, fled into Rumania and Poland.

Last night it had been officially announced in Prague that "constitutional relations between Prague and Ruthenia having ceased to exist, Prague is no longer obliged to defend the frontiers of that country," and the view was apparently taken that Ruthenia's future was a matter for Hungary to settle with Germany.

GERMAN TROOPS IN BOHEMIA

CZECH GOVT SURRENDERS AS PRAGUE IS OCCUPIED

PRAGUE, Wednesday (R). Bohemia and Moravia — the territory remaining under Czech administration after the secession of Slovakia and Ruthenia — were yesterday occupied by German troops with the clockwork precision which marked the annexation of Austria and the Sudetenland.

Powerful German motorised forces this morning entered both provinces from all directions, and Prague was reached by 7 o'clock, its complete occupation being accomplished by midday. The Czech Government had no alternative but to surrender.

The official German attitude was that the Czechs had made use of their right of self-determination and asked Germany to take the country under their protection. It was held that the Vienna arbitration award, whereby the frontiers of Czecho-Slovakia in the east were fixed, had been superseded by events, and moreover that Germany could have no objection to the incorporation of Ruthenia in Hungary, a step she had hitherto opposed.

HERR HITLER'S ENTRY

Herr Hitler, who left Berlin, by train at 7 o'clock this morning and crossed the frontier this afternoon, made a triumphal entry into Prague at 7.15 p.m. G.M.T.

It was admitted in Berlin that the orders for the occupation were given even before Dr. Hacha reached Berlin, and that while he was talking with Herr Hitler at the Chancellery, German troops were 12 miles inside Czech territory.

German troops began to occupy Bohemia by entering from the south, the first point to be occupied being Maehrisch-Ostrau and environs. The Commander-in-Chief of the German troops immediately ordered a general curfew from 9 p.m. to 6 a.m., and at the latter hour the formal entry, by 14 divisions began. At 5 o'clock in the morning, the Prague wireless station broadcast an appeal to the population to keep calm as the slightest resistance might have "the most brutal consequences."

Prague was occupied in the morning, while Pilsen, Olmütz and Theresienstadt, where the troops allowed some officers to keep their arms, were occupied on the afternoon. German police followed the troops and took charge.

Although this morning Dr. Tiso called up five classes of Hlinka Guard reservists to secure the integrity of Slovak frontiers against Hungarian troop invasions near the Carpatho-Ukraine frontier, the German troops began marching into Slovakia in the afternoon.

TRAFFIC CHAOS

Traffic chaos was caused by the entry of the German troops, as all Czecho-Slovak traffic is on the left (as in England) while the German columns insisted on taking the right (as in the remainder of the Continent).

A snowstorm was raging as the mechanised columns rumbled through the streets to the great Wenceslas Square. Most of the chief administrative buildings including the Ministry of National Defence and the Post Office, were immediately occupied.

Crowds of both Czechs and Germans watched the German troops arrive. In some places the crowds got out of control of the police, but there were no serious disturbances, although two persons were run over by German military cars.

Hostile cries from the Czechs mingled with "Heil"s by the Germans. At some centres, the Czechs sang the Czech national anthem as the armoured lorries drove past. The whole of Bohemia and Moravia are now virtually in German hands but the occupying forces are small. The relations between the Czech Army and police and the German troops have been uniformly courteous and correct.

Generally Prague remained calm. If stunned, the people responding to the wireless appeals broadcast every quarter of an hour to go to work quietly and to send their children to school. The German wireless invited the German population to prepare a fitting welcome for the troops, and also started broadcasting German news, ending with the words, "Heil Hitler."

Under the Eagle's Wings

AGREEMENT SIGNED FOR REICH TO PROTECT CZECHS

The Czech people were placed under the protection of the German Reich under the terms of an agreement reached between Herr Adolf Hitler and Dr. Emil Hacha, the Prague President, and signed in Berlin at 2.55 G.M.T. yesterday morning. The terms of the agreement were as follows:

The Fuehrer today, in the presence of Herr von Ribbentrop, received Dr. Hacha and M. Chvalkovsky at their wish in Berlin. On their arrival, the serious situation which has arisen through the events of the last few weeks in the former Czecho-Slovakian State territory was submitted in all clearness to examination.

Both sides were of the conviction and expressed aim that all efforts must be made for securing quiet, order, and peace in this part of Europe. The Czecho-Slovak President declared that, in order to reach final appeasement, he placed the fate of the Czech people and land trustingly in the hands of the Fuehrer and the German Reich.

The Fuehrer accepted this declaration and gave expression to his decision that he placed the Czech people under the protection of the German Reich and would guarantee it an autonomous development of its national life corresponding to its peculiarities.

(Signed) March 15, 1939.

ADOLF HITLER, EMIL HACHA, JOACHIM von RIBBENTROP, FRANTISEK CHVALKOVSKY.

FINAL PROPOSALS SUBMITTED

LONDON, Thursday, 1.25 a.m. (R).— The final Palestine proposals of the British Government, adopted by the Cabinet at yesterday morning's meeting, were submitted to the Arab Delegation by the British Delegation at St. James's Palace yesterday afternoon.

The leader of the Palestine Arab Delegation asked for time to consider the proposals, and the meeting was adjourned until Friday afternoon.

It is understood that the proposals largely follow the lines of the suggestions already submitted to the delegates by the British Government. The British Delegation met the Jewish Delegation at 9 o'clock and the meeting ended at 9.30.

REICH'S ACTION CONTRARY TO MUNICH

LONDON, Wednesday (R).— When Mr. Chamberlain entered the House of Commons just before the end of question-time this afternoon, in order to make a statement on Czecho-Slovakia, he was greeted by Ministerial cheers and derisive cries from the Opposition benches. After he had made his statement, a general debate opened on a Government motion for the adjournment.

In his statement, the Prime Minister said that the balance of £6,750,000 of the Czecho-Slovak loan now at the Bank of England would in the circumstances be withheld, and that the President of the Board of Trade and the Secretary for Overseas Trade had postponed their projected trip to Berlin.

Mr. Chamberlain began by saying that the Government having failed in their recent endeavour to achieve a guarantee agreement with the other Munich Governments, the British Government regarded the guarantee obligations as no longer binding. After touching upon questions of the Czech loan and the postponement of the visit of Mr. Hudson and Mr. Stanley to Berlin previously announced by Lord Halifax in the House of Lords, Mr. Chamberlain declared that he had no doubt that Munich was right and he believed that it had the approval of the vast majority of the peoples of the world.

The Prime Minister said that he could not believe that anything of the kind now done by Germany was contemplated by any of the Munich signatories. The Munich agreement constituted a settlement and he could not regard the manner and method by which these changes had been brought about as in accordance with the Munich Agreement.

SHOCK TO CONFIDENCE

Now for the first time Germany was in military occupation of a people with whom she had no racial connections. These events could not fail to be a cause of disturbance to the international situation. They were bound to administer a shock to confidence and it was all the more regrettable because confidence was beginning to revive and there was every possibility of concrete measures which could achieve benefit.

Referring to his speech of February 3, the Prime Minister declared that he had said then that he hoped it was time that others could make a contribution which would result in benefits to those immediately concerned.

Mr. Chamberlain added, "It is natural therefore that I should bitterly regret what has now occurred. But do not let us be deflected from our course" (Cheers.) "Let us remember that the desire of all the peoples of the world still remains concentrated on hopes of peace and a return to an atmosphere of understanding and good-will, which had so often been disturbed.

"The aim of this country now as always is to promote that desire and substitute methods of discussion for the method of force in the settlement of differences. Though we may have to suffer checks and disappointments from time to time, the objects I have in mind are of great significance

(Continued on page 2.)

AFTER MIDNIGHT

Mr. Eden, urging the formation of a Government of all parties in his speech in the House of Commons, said that he was convinced that there could be no greater contribution than the knowledge that as a result of these events, the greatest democracy in Europe had decided to make a national effort unparalleled in its history. (Cheers). Then "we must examine the military and strategic position in Europe and consult all nations who are of the same mind as we, wherever and whoever they may be (loud cheers) in regard to what our policy is to be and where to make our stand, and having determined that, to make with them immediately military plans to give effect to our decision." Speaking with great emphasis, Mr. Eden said, "There are times when a great nation has to take great decisions. I believe such a time to be now, and I further believe that only thus shall we banish from our people the haunting fear that shadows our time."

SUBSCRIPTIONS: Local: LP.2.250 a year; LP.1.250 a half year:— Foreign: £3.- a year. The rate for display advertisements is 150 mils per column inch. Other rates supplied on request. The right is reserved to make changes in wording or to decline or discontinue any advertisement or to postpone insertions when space is not available.

THE PALESTINE POST

JERUSALEM Hassolel Road P. O. Box 81, Telephone 4233
Tel Aviv - Jaffa: 65 Allenby Road, P. O. Box 1125, 'Phone 4251-4252.
Haifa: Khayat Square, opposite the Post Office entrance, P.O.B. 66, 'Phone 1390

FRIDAY MARCH 17 1939 JERUSALEM VOL. XV. No. 3905. PRICE 10 MILS

ARABS AND JEWS BOTH REJECT BRITISH PLAN

Hitler Takes Slovaks Under His Wing

FASCIST GENERAL APPOINTED PRAGUE "FUEHRER"; ANTI-JEWISH EXCESSES BEGIN

PRAGUE, Thursday (R). — It was officially announced today that Herr Hitler had taken the Slovak State under his protection. German troops have now occupied the larger part of Bohemia and Moravia without friction.

Herr Hitler today received Dr. Emil Hacha in the Hradschin Castle, where he took up his official residence at 7.45 last night. The Swastika was hoisted over the Castle Tower by a Castle Guard composed of a German infantry regiment. General von Brauchitsch, the German Commander-in-Chief, was commissioned to exercise executive power over Bohemia and Moravia.

The Czech Cabinet resigned last night, and General Rudolf Gajda, chairman of the formerly small Czech Fascist Party, was officially proclaimed as "Fuehrer of the Czech People."

A "DEAD" CITY

Herr Hitler spent the night in a "dead" city, strict curfew having been enforced between 11 o'clock at night until 6 o'clock this morning. No cinemas, theatres, public houses or other public places were open, and the only movement was the passage throughout the night of heavy troop transports partially silenced by the frozen snow coating the streets.

German troops sent in the direction of Ruthenia were recalled. The German War Office had earlier asked for authority to occupy the Slovak-Moravian frontier in order to guard the flank of the army occupying Moravia, and proposed a joint commission to settle the details of the occupation, but the German troops crossed the frontier without waiting for a decision from this body, and detachments entered Slovakia "for protective purposes" this afternoon, cooperating with the Hlinka Guards.

ANTI-JEWISH MEASURES

Anti-Jewish measures were stated to have already started in Prague last night, following the well-tried methods pursued in Germany, Austria and the Sudetenland.

The population, however, accepted the course of events with discipline and calm, and troop movements in Prague streets practically ceased by this afternoon. All munitions and radio sets, except those used by officials, were requisitioned by the military authorities, and food profiteering was rigorously suppressed.

In Bratislava, Dr. Sidor, Minister of Interior in Dr. Tiso's Cabinet, resigned because he was not persona grata with Germany. The Hungarian Consul informed Dr. Tiso of Hungary's decision to recognise the new frontier and to establish a Legation in Bratislava, while the Polish Consul also announced his country's decision to recognise the Slovak frontier.

Herr von Ribbentrop this morning had a long conversation with Signor Fransoni, the Italian Minister in Prague, while Dr. Frick, German Minister of Interior, flew from Berlin to Prague in order "to clarify the international and legal status of Bohemia and Moravia."

Herr Hitler left Prague by car for an unrevealed destination this afternoon, but is thought to be going to Bren, further east, where a big military parade is to be arranged. Before leaving, he received the new Mayor and Municipal Councillors of Prague to whom he promised a long and prosperous career of peace and happiness for the Czech people.

The first German aeroplanes flew over Prague today.

Herr Hitler's announcement respecting Slovakia followed an exchange of telegrams between him and the Slovak President, Dr. Tiso, in which the latter asked the Fuehrer to take the Slovak State under his protection. German troops are advancing into the country, which will receive a constitution similar to that announced for Bohemia and Moravia.

Dr. Tiso has sent Herr Hitler the following telegram: "With the greatest confidence in the Fuehrer of the Great German nation, the State of Slovakia places itself under your protection. We trust that you will grant this appeal." Herr Hitler replied, "I acknowledge receipt of your message of yesterday's date and hereby assume the protection of the Slovak State."

BRITAIN PLAYS DUAL GAME

GIVES EACH SIDE KEY TO OTHER'S ASPIRATIONS

By Gershon Agronsky

LONDON, Thursday. — Reflection on the Government terms submitted to the Arabs and Jews last night clarifies the Cabinet's intention to stimulate inter-racial cooperation, by withholding from each side what it covets most. Although the proposals are officially regarded as secret, today's papers, despite their preoccupation with the murder of Czecho-Slovakia, feature reports of yesterday's meetings at St. James's Palace and reveal the contents of the Plan.

Briefly it amounts to an attempt to induce the Jews during the transitional period to support the constitutional measures leading to ultimate independence, in return for Arab acquiescence to continued immigration after five years. The Arabs are placed in the position of holding the veto on immigration, and the Jews on self-government.

Thus the Palestine State is a matter for the future, dependent on Jewish cooperation, which amounts to an assertion that Palestine is not an Arab country, and Britain is not bound by the MacMahon or any other pledges to give the Arabs independence. If this is an open invitation to the Jews not to cooperate in order to defeat eventual Arab domination, the Arabs possess an equally powerful means of arresting Jewish growth in the future. Yet the Arabs have ample reason for satisfaction in the artificial dwarfing of Jewish growth and the attempt to condemn the Jews to remain one third of the population, unless the Arabs agree to an increase.

The total absence of provisions for political as well as numerical parity renders the plan utterly inadmissible to the Jews, as the Government knows, and therefore the Jews have nothing more to do at the Conference.

In the highest Jewish quarters this turning-point is seen as the end of a chapter, but there is no despair for the future. The Jewish Panel demonstrated the possibility of Jewish cooperation to the last, and its unanimity on fundamental questions. The Palestine Conference, however much feared in advance, and however disappointing its results, has afforded an opportunity for Arabs and Jews to interchange ideas.

All agree that the Palestine Jews have a great responsibility and must maintain, as Dr. Weizman declared today,

"iron discipline, fortitude and moral dignity. What has been accomplished in Palestine was accomplished not with lamentation but with the joy of creation, which will continue though the opportunities have been cruelly circumscribed."

LIMITED IMMIGRATION AND LAND SALES

TRANSITION PERIOD UNDETERMINED

LONDON, Thursday (Palcor & R). — Palcor understood this evening that while the British proposals provided for 10,000 Jewish immigrants annually into Palestine for the next five years, an additional 25,000 refugees would be allowed at any time provided they could be absorbed in the country.

Reuters states, however, that total Jewish immigration in the next five years would be 75,000, while it appeared that the High Commissioner would have power to vary the yearly average in accordance with the absorptive capacity of Palestine in any year, so that the number of immigrants in one year might be above or below 15,000.

At the end of the five years, the question of Jewish immigration would be reviewed. Palcor believes that the worst feature of the Government plan was that the Jews should not exceed approximately a third of the population of Palestine.

The Arab delegates to the Palestine Conference are understood also to have decided that the principles contained in the British proposals were unacceptable. It is anticipated that tomorrow's meeting will be the last of the series.

Reuter understands that the details of the proposals of the British Government make clear that the ultimate objective is an independent Palestine State, possibly of a federal character in treaty relation with Great Britain.

JEWISH REPLY

The Jewish Agency Executive, meeting this afternoon, decided to recommend to the Conference Committee the rejection of the Government proposals as inacceptable and to dissolve the delegation. Lord Reading and Lord Bearsted were present at the Executive meeting.

The Press Association understands, says Reuter, that the Jewish Committee at the Conference has decided that the proposals of the Government's new plan "offer no basis for further discussion or agreement." It is stated that the Conference Committee which has advised the Jewish delegation, has also decided to dissolve and that the Jewish Palestine delegates are leaving for home tonight.

CONSTITUTIONAL ISSUE

Reuter understood that, on the constitutional question of the transition period, no term was set by the Government but it would depend on the peaceful collaboration of the Arabs and Jews. An Executive Council composed of British executive officers would be nominated, with Arab and Jewish members as Ministers without Portfolio. In addition Arab and Jewish members would be co-opted to the Advisory Council to represent the population proportionately, and this Council would carry on the functions of the Government under the control of a British High Commissioner.

The future development of the Constitution would be a matter for decision in Palestine when it was seen that the Arab and Jewish populations were working amicably together.

As regarded land sales, Palestine would be divided into three tracts, firstly, one in which land sales would be permitted, secondly, one in which sales would be restricted, and thirdly, a tract in which sales would be prohibited altogether.

ARABS NOT SATISFIED

Arabs are reported by "Al Ahram" to object strenuously to the provision in the British proposals which makes the independence of Palestine subject to Jewish cooperation. The representatives of the Arab States were to have met Lord Halifax and Mr. MacDonald today (Thursday), while Jamal Al Husseini will meet Mr. MacDonald tomorrow. The whole discussion is to be completed by Saturday at the latest.

Azzam Bey, of the Egyptian delegation, told "Al Ahram" that hopes of an agreement were faint; but the Conference had shown the unity of the Arab delegation and the justness of the Arab cause, the results of which would be far-reaching no matter what happened in the immediate future.

"The Manchester Guardian"'s London correspondent stated that the Foreign Arab envoys were trying to persuade the Palestinian Arabs to accept the proposals. The Egyptian delegation all the time favoured a reasonable attitude, and whilst the Palestinian Arabs were at bottom satisfied with the results, they were inclined to discuss the proposals further, in the belief that it was a mistake to clutch at them immediately as this might be construed as the abandonment of their basic demands.

"IT SHALL NOT COME TO PASS," IS YISHUV'S FIRM REPLY

VAAD LEUMI WARNS OF COMING POLITICAL STRUGGLE

A manifesto calling upon the Jewish population to be prepared for the opening of a political struggle within the next few days was issued yesterday afternoon by the General Council for Palestine Jews (Vaad Leumi) in the following terms:

The Mandatory Government's intention to liquidate the policy of establishing the National Home still forms the basis of its plans.

The imposition of a limit on Jewish immigration for the coming five years, and its complete discontinuance at the end of that period, unless permitted by the Arabs, is tantamount to the crystallisation of the Yishuv as a permanent minority in Palestine and the handing over of the National Home to the Mufti and his bands.

HISTORICAL MISSION

The Yishuv's reply to this proposal was voiced by its representatives at the all-Palestine Conference who clearly affirmed that 'such a thing will not come to pass', and that 'the Yishuv will not submit to the authority of a State so constituted.' This is still its reply. Those who issued the manifesto now call upon you to put this declaration into effect.

Aware of its historical mission, the Yishuv will in the coming days enter upon a political struggle for the rights of the Jewish people and its homeland in a spirit worthy of Jews in the land of the Jewish people.

The Yishuv stands united in faith and discipline and ready to obey the call.

POLAND AND HUNGARY ESTABLISH COMMON FRONTIER

RUTHENIAN LEVIES TRY TO HALT HUNGARIAN TROOPS

BUDAPEST, Thursday (R). — Patrols of Hungarian troops advancing through the blizzard raging in Ruthenia reached the Polish border this morning and were greeted by Polish outposts, thus establishing the accomplished fact of the common frontier desired by Poland and Hungary.

The Hungarians, who also stated that waist-deep snow in the Carpathian mountains had delayed them, said that larger bodies of troops were on their way and would reach the frontier later in the day. The waiting Poles heartily cheered as the patrols appeared in the blinding snow.

The Ruthenian national guard made a big effort to oppose the Hungarian advance. Knowing the ground and accustomed to bitter weather, the local volunteer force, supported by peasants armed with what weapons they had been able to seize, desperately defended the independence of their territory. They were however handicapped by the fact that the Czech military would not hand them weapons and were even resisting them.

Resistance was encountered by Hungarian troops who occupied Chust, but the fighting was stated in Budapest to be sporadic and local. There was no organized opposition, the main difficulties being the weather and lack of roads.

Large numbers of Czech troops have taken refuge in Rumania, where they were disarmed, and into which Dr. Augustin Volosin, the Ruthenian

(Continued on Page 2)

FUEHRER DEFINES STATUS OF BOHEMIA AND MORAVIA

"CZECHO-SLOVAK STATE PROVED IT COULD NOT LIVE"

PRAGUE, Thursday (R). — Standing on the balcony of Hradschin Castle, where Herr Hitler himself later appeared with his raised right arm in salute to assembled thousands of people who shouted, "Fuehrer, we thank you," Herr von Ribbentrop this afternoon broadcast a proclamation by Herr Hitler which outlined the future constitutional status of Bohemia and Moravia.

Dated March 16, the proclamation provided for the organization of the two provinces, and stated:

For 1,000 years, Bohemia and Moravia were part of the living space of the German people. Force and foolishness removed them from their historical surroundings and finally, by incorporating them in the artificial formation of Czecho-Slovakia, created a centre of continual unrest.

From year to year the dangers increased. At any time a new and tremendous menace to European peace might have arisen from this area. The Czecho-Slovak State proved it could not live and fell to pieces.

A "PROTECTORATE"

The proclamation further states that the areas formerly held by the Czechs and occupied by German troops in March, 1939, belong now to the great German Reich and fall under its protection, as the Protectorate of Bohemia and Moravia. The German inhabitants of these areas become German citizens and are placed under German jurisdiction. The Protectorate will be autonomous and administer itself, and will exercise sovereign rights within the limits of the Protectorate.

The head of the Protectorate requires the confidence of the Fuehrer. In the interests of the Reich, the Fuehrer appoints a Reich protector. Membership of the Government of the Protectorate will be subject to the confirmation of the Reich Protector. The Reich Protector can veto measures calculated to harm the Reich and affect foreign affairs taken over by the Reich. The Protectorate will have a representative in Berlin on the Reich Government. The Reich will give the Protectorate its military protection.

The Reich also undertakes the immediate supervision of communications, as well as posts and telegraphs, while the Protectorate will belong to the Customs system of the Reich. So far as general need exists, the Reich may take over any administration in the Protectorate and establish Reich authorities.

FUEHRER'S MANIFESTO

General Rudolf Gajda, the Czech Fascist leader who has been appointed "Fuehrer of the Czechs," has also issued a proclamation establishing a Labour Commission composed of representatives of all classes.

The "Gestapo" (German Secret Police) is already in action, and inhabitants who remained indoors last night communicated only by telephone, and cautiously, because wires were tapped.

It is officially stated that Herr Hitler told Herr Klapa, the new Mayor of Prague, that "a happy future awaits the Czech nation because of its loyal behaviour."

WHO CAN APPEASE A BOA-CONSTRICTOR?

WORLD PRESS CONDEMNS INVASION OF BOHEMIA AND MORAVIA

LONDON, Thursday (R). — Now that the world has recovered from the first shock of the swift German action in annexing Czecho-Slovakia, opinion has crystallised into the sharpest reprobation and accusation of the German methods, and evidence of the severity of the shock caused by the events was reflected in the views expressed in many capitals today.

It is revealed that Sir Nevile Henderson, the British Ambassador in Berlin, sent a written communication to Herr von von Ribbentrop yesterday expressing the British Government's views. The action of the German Government is understood to have been strongly deprecated, the tone of the document being on the lines of the statements by Mr. Chamberlain and Lord Halifax in Parliamen in the afternoon.

Several newspapers believed today that General Sirovy and the Czech Premier, Dr. Rudolph Beran, were among the 11 passengers who landed in mysterious circumstances in Croydon on Tuesday night from a Dutch air-liner which had come from Prague. Among the passengers were also stated to be officials of the Skoda munitions factory in possession of plans brought away so that they should not fall into German hands.

A Washington message says that while the State Department refused to comment on the situation, circles close to President Roosevelt claimed that the events fully justified the President in taking a serious view which some European circles considered alarmist.

At Chicago, the ex-President, Dr. Benes, described the dismemberment of Czecho-Slovakia as "a new and shocking international crime, through which Europe is going to be deprived of her future peace, order and tranquillity."

BRITISH PRESS COMMENT

The British press devoted almost as much space to the subject as during a single day's happenings during the September crisis, and adopted an unrelieved accusatory tone towards Germany rarely seen in British newspaper editorial articles before. The firm conviction that the Democracies must strengthen themselves to be able to put a stop to the ruthlessness of modern map-changing found much expression.

"The Times," in an outspoken leading article, said that the invasion, occupation and annexation of Bohemia and Moravia were notice to the world that German policy no longer sought the protection of a moral case; no decence of any kind and no pretext of the slightest plausibility could be offered for the violent extinction of Czech independence in the historic Czech homelands of Bohemia and Moravia. On the contrary, it violated a whole succession of solemn pledges by the Fuehrer himself. There was nothing left for moral debate in this crude and brutal act of oppression and suppression.

Referring to the "capitulation" of Dr. Hacha, the article said that the world was invited to believe that the Czechs had voluntarily yielded to an alien race their most precious possession — national independence. This last flight of cant at least might have been spared to a people crushed out but, as their demeanour yesterday proclaimed, not yet abject under this load of humiliation and spiritual misery.

"Who can believe that this week's fantastic essay in the obsolete, this

(Continued on Page 2)

AFTER MIDNIGHT

One or two Jewish delegates to London may return this weekend, but the delegation as a whole "will remain until the final word is spoken," states Reuter.

Five thousand men were arrested in Prague last night, including scores of terrorized Jews.

Ukrainian circles in Berlin state that the Ruthenian Government sent a telegram to the four signatories of the Munich Agreement asking them to help and guarantee the independence of Ruthenia.

Chust was occupied at 7.00 p. m. G.M.T., according to a message from Budapest.

SUBSCRIPTION: Local: LP.2.250 a year; LP.1.250 a half year:— Foreign, £3.- a year. The rate for display advertisements is 150 mils per column inch. Other rates supplied on request. The right is reserved to make changes in wording or to decline or discontinue any advertisement or to postpone insertions when space is not available.

THE
PALESTINE
POST

JERUSALEM Hassolel Road P. O. Box 81, Telephone 4233
Tel Aviv - Jaffa: 55 Allenby Road, P. O. Box 1125. 'Phone 4251-4252.
Haifa: Khayat Square, opposite the Post Office entrance, P.O.B. 66. 'Phone 1390.

THURSDAY MAY 18 1939 JERUSALEM VOL. XV. No. 3955. PRICE 10 MILS

NEW POLICY WINDS UP MANDATE AND JEWISH NATIONAL HOME

BRITAIN'S BLOW WILL NOT SUBDUE JEWS

Statement of the Jewish Agency for Palestine

A Statement was issued by the Jewish Agency in Jerusalem last night, in reply to the White Paper, as follows:

The new policy for Palestine laid down by the Mandatory in the White Paper issued on May 17th denies to the Jewish people the right to reconstitute its National Home in its ancestral land. It hands over the government of the country to the present Arab majority and places the Jewish community of Palestine at the mercy of that majority. It decrees the stoppage of immigration as soon as the Jewish inhabitants of the country have become one-third of the total population. It sets up a territorial ghetto for Jews in their own homeland.

The Jewish people regard this breach of faith as a surrender to Arab terrorism, a delivery of England's friends into the hands of its enemies. It widens the gulf between Jews and Arabs and destroys any prospect of peace in the country.

The Jewish people will not acquiesce in such a policy. The new regime envisaged in the White Paper will be a regime of mere coercion devoid of all moral basis and contrary to international law. Such a regime can only be established and maintained by force.

The Royal Commission, invoked by the White Paper, indicated the dangers inherent in such a regime. "Convinced as they (the Jews) are" they wrote "that an Arab Government would mean the frustration of all efforts and ideals, that it would convert the National Home into one more cramped and dangerous ghetto, it seems only too probable that they

(Continued on Page 2)

POLICY IMPOSED UPON JEWS

ZIONIST LEADERS EXPLAIN ATTITUDE

LONDON, Wednesday (Reuter and Palcor). — Professor Brodetsky and Mr. M. Shertok addressed a press conference at the Savoy Hotel here this afternoon in connection with the Government's Statement of Policy. Professor Brodetsky dwelt on the breach of the Government's international obligations and emphasised the fact that the new Policy had not been negotiated with the Jews but imposed on them.

Mr. Shertok, in giving an analysis of the situation, stressed the fact that the White Paper gave expression to a policy of crystallising the National Home instead of developing it in accordance with the obligation under the Balfour Declaration; it restricted immigration, proscribed settlement on the land, subordinated the Jews to Arab domination and completely disregarded the Jewish Agency which possessed an official status under the Mandate.

He announced Jewish resistance which would not be malicious and not unfriendly to Britain but to the Government's Policy.

REUTER COMMENT

The main purpose of the Government's declaration of Palestine policy is to remove uncertainty as to the intentions and objectives of the Government, as uncertainty is felt to be one of the major causes of the trouble in Palestine, Reuters lobby correspondent understands.

The fact that the policy is definite is expected to produce criticisms from both sides. These will be faced, however, in the belief that the proposals represent a just solution which pays regard to the obligations to the Arabs and Jews alike. The Government specifies as an alternative to extreme Jewish and Arab claims an independent state in which Jews and Arabs will share in the authority of Government in a manner serving the interests of both sides.

No arbitrary decision is taken on the form of the new State which can be federal or unitary. It will be shaped in consultation with the League of Nations. The White Paper contains a reference to protecting the interests of foreign countries, which is understood to refer especially to American missions. Under the arrangements for the admission of 25,000 refugees it is expected that 10,000 children will be involved.

The whole scheme is subject to approval by the League and the Permanent Mandates Commission, which is expected to consider it in June and then pass it to the League Council later. The White Paper will be discussed in the House of Commons on Monday and Tuesday, when Mr. MacDonald will explain the Government's reasons for the decisions.

"DAY OF VISITATION"

WHITE PAPER CASTS DARK SHADOW; P.B.S. STAFF TO RAMALLAH IN ARMOURED CAR

At 8 o'clock last night, at the moment when the Arabic broadcast of the summary of the White Paper was to begin, the transmission was interrupted, and the broadcast was not resumed for an hour and a half. Rumours of a last-moment postponement immediately began to circulate, although many people had heard the summary broadcast from Daventry.

The interruption was apparently caused by sabotage to the land line between Jerusalem and Ramallah, where an announcement was immediately made in the three languages that the programme would be given later. It was resumed at 9.25, the P.B.S. Staff, headed by the Programme Director, travelling to Ramallah in armoured cars for the purpose.

"BLACK PAPER"

The White Paper, which the Jewish population, at any rate, on the basis of the numerous forecasts, have dubbed the "Black Paper," cast its shadow over the country yesterday.

The Vaad Leumi (National Council of Palestine Jews) in a statement entitled "Day of Visitation" yesterday said:

"Confronted by the declaration of the British Government announcing its new policy for Palestine and which decrees that the Jewish settlement must never exceed a third of the population, thus degrading the Jewish National Home to a Jewish ghetto in an Arab Palestine State," the Yishuv in its hundreds of thousands declares its opposition to the "policy of betrayal" and to the Government based upon such a policy.

"This is not a day for mourning or lamentations," (the statement proceeds) "but a day of enumeration and consolidation of the Yishuv's forces, a day on which will be demonstrated the determination and the readiness of the people to resist this brutal attack."

"On this day we shall, to a man, enter upon this great political struggle for the fate of our people and homeland — a struggle not for one day, and not of words, but a struggle which may call for heavy sacrifices from us."

The name chosen for the day is from Isaiah 10: 3:

"And what will ye do in the day of visitation, and in the desolation which shall come from far? to whom will ye flee for help?

DAY OF PROTEST

The Vaad Leumi also proclaimed a complete stoppage of work, including transport and schools, but excepting Government services, water and power supply, health services and the Haifa Port.

It was made generally known, by posters on hoardings and through the newspapers, that today would be a day of protest against the new Policy, the protest to take the form

(Continued on Page 2)

LAND RESTRICTIONS OPERATIVE TODAY

No Immigration After Five Years Without Arab Consent

(Reuter's Summary)

The establishment of an independent Palestine State within ten years and the limitation of Jewish immigration to 75,000 over five years with its cessation thereafter, is envisaged in the far-reaching declaration of the Government's intentions contained in the White Paper issued last night.

The new State will be in treaty relations with the United Kingdom, providing satisfactorily for the commercial and strategic requirements of both countries. Consultation with the League would be necessary with a view to the termination of the Mandate. The independent State would be one in which Arabs and Jews will share in the Government (in proportion to their respective population), in such a way as to ensure that the essential interests of both communities are satisfied.

FULL TEXT OF WHITE PAPER ON PAGE 3

TRANSITION PERIOD

The establishment of an independent State would be preceded by a transitional period throughout which His Majesty's Government would maintain responsibility. During the transitional period, the people of Palestine would be given an increasing part in the Government and the process carried on whether or not Arabs and Jews avail themselves of the opportunity.

As soon as peace was sufficiently restored, steps would be taken to give Palestinians an increasing part in the Government with the object of placing Palestinians in charge of all the departments of the Government, with the assistance of British advisers and subject to the control of the High Commissioner. The Palestinian heads of Departments would sit on the Executive Council which advises the High Commissioner, and Arab and Jewish representatives would be invited to serve in proportion to their respective populations.

TOWARDS INDEPENDENCE

Five years from the restoration of peace an appropriate body representing Palestine and His Majesty's Government would be established to review the working of constitutional arangements during the transition period and to make recommendations regarding the constitution of an independent Palestine.

His Majesty's Government would do everything to create conditions enabling the independent State to come into being in ten years, but if the circumstances required a postponement, they would consult with Palestinians and the League of Nations, as well as the neighbouring Arab States, before deciding on a postponement.

MAXIMUM OF 75,000

During the next five years, Jewish immigration would be at a rate to bring the Jewish population to approximately one third of the whole. This would allow as from April of this year of some 75,000 immigrants in the next five years. For each of the next five years a quota of 10,000 would be allowed, and as a contribution towards the Jewish refugee problem an additional 25,000 would be allowed, making an aggregate of 75,000. After five years no further Jewish immigration, would be permitted without the permission of the Arabs.

The High Commissioner is given powers to regulate transfers of land. The Government reject the Arab claim based on the McMahon correspondence that Palestine should be converted into an Arab state and also the Jewish claim that Palestine should become a Jewish State, as this would be contrary to the obligations to the Arabs under the Mandate.

ARABS EXPECTED TO SAY "NO"

FIRST SIGNS OF REJECTING PALESTINE WHITE PAPER

BAGHDAD, Wednesday (R). — It is understood that the Iraqi and Saudi-Arabian Governments have informed the British Government that they consider the British proposals regarding future policy in Palestine as a refusal of the demands of the Arab States.

Writing on Friday last the diplomatic correspondent of "The Times," London, foreshadowed the rejection of the White Paper by the Arab States. Commenting on the wish of the Mufti of Jerusalem, who has been staying with a large suite at Zok, Lebanon, to settle in Baghdad, the correspondent said that important personages in Iraq favoured the visit.

CLAIMING THE KUDOS

The article proceeded that the competition displayed among some of the Arab Governments to take the credit of having extricated the Mufti and his party from their increasing difficulties has been keen, as several incidents during the recent conferences on Palestine indicated.

There are imaginative politicians in Iraq who would like to see an Arab State of Palestine linked in some way to Iraq, in spite of the geographical and political diffculties of such a union.

The Mufti, too, is probably tired of the close surveillance which the French and Lebanese authorities have maintained over his movements for several months, the more so as this has probably become closer since two of his near kinsmen left for Berlin.

NOVEMBER, 1917

Foreign Office,
November 2nd, 1917.

Dear Lord Rothschild,

I have much pleasure in conveying to you, on behalf of His Majesty's Government, the following declaration of sympathy with Jewish Zionist aspirations which has been submitted to, and approved by, the Cabinet.

"His Majesty's Government view with favour the establishment in Palestine of a national home for the Jewish people, and will use their best endeavours to facilitate the achievement of this object, it being clearly understood that nothing shall be done which may prejudice the civil and religious rights of existing non-Jewish communities in Palestine, or the rights and political status enjoyed by Jews in any other country."

I should be grateful if you would bring this declaration to the knowledge of the Zionist Federation.

Yours sincerely,
(Sgd.) *ARTHUR JAMES BALFOUR.*

MAY, 1939

. . . . His Majesty's Government do not read either the Statement of Policy of 1922 or the letter of 1931 as implying that the Mandate requires them, for all time and in all circumstances, to facilitate the immigration of Jews into Palestine subject only to consideration of the country's economic absorptive capacity. Nor do they find anything in the Mandate or in subsequent Statements of Policy to support the view that the establishment of a Jewish National Home in Palestine cannot be effected unless immigration is allowed to continue indefinitely . . .

The alternatives before His Majesty's Government are either (i) to seek to expand the Jewish National Home indefinitely by immigration, against the strongly expressed will of the Arab people of the country; or (ii) to permit further expansion of the Jewish National Home by immigration only if the Arabs are prepared to acquiesce in it . . .

Therefore His Majesty's Government, after earnest consideration, and taking into account the extent to which the growth of the Jewish National Home has been facilitated over the last twenty years, have decided that the time has come to adopt in principle the second of the alternatives referred to above.

T.A. CROWD RAIDS DISTRICT OFFICES

CURFEW DECLARED

TEL AVIV, Wednesday.—Twenty-five persons were injured, four of them seriously, when police dispersed a crowd of 5,000 which stormed the District Offices, at the bottom of Allenby Road, here tonight and set fire to the building. Following the attack, curfew was imposed in Tel Aviv until further notice.

Crowds carrying flags and banners began to collect towards 8 o'clock and converged on the square in front of the Great Synagogue in Allenby Road. There speakers addressed the crowd which had swollen to several thousands, mostly youths. "Hatikvah" was sung and all those present raised their right arm and repeated the words: "If I forget thee, oh Jerusalem, may my right hand forget her cunning."

Shouts of "Down with Weizman" and "Up, Jobotinsky" were raised amongst the crowd.

The demonstration then proceeded to the District Offices, and forced the doors, wrecking the furniture and setting fire to the records, while others hoisted the blue-and-white flag on the roof of the building. Heavy pieces of furniture were hurled into the street and set on fire by the crowd. Considerable damage was also done to the Land Registry and Migration Department Offices.

British police soon appeared on the scene and dispersed the crowd, after firing a volley of shots into the air. Police cars patrolled the streets which remained quiet after a second demonstration which marched down Allenby Road towards 10.30 had been dispersed.

Curfew was imposed at 11.15 until further notice.

(Foreign Cables — Page 5)

BOMBS AND FIRE AT IMMIGRATION OFFICES

A series of loud explosions shortly before 11.30 last night gave the first indication of an attack upon the building of the Government Department of Migration in Queen Melisande Road, Jerusalem. The whole building could be seen lit up by several flashes before fire broke out over the whole of the upper storey.

Police were on the spot immediately, and the alarm siren was sounded continuously for a few minutes. Two bound and unconscious Jewish ghaffirs were found near the gate to the side entrance of the building and taken to the Hadassah Hospital.

After recovering consciousness, shortly after being brought in, one man said that he and his companion had been on duty inside the main entrance, when a rap was heard on the door, and a voice said in English "C.I.D. Inspection. Open the door."

This was a nightly routine, and he went forward to unbar the door. As it opened the ghaffirs distinguished four figures with masked faces, but were then struck over the head and bound, and must have been bundled out of the building by their captors.

Both ghaffirs went to make their reports at the Central Police Station after they had recovered and received first aid.

A motor car battery filled with incendiary material, and with an extingished wick attached, was found on the ground floor of the building by police searchers. It is supposed that the fire in other parts of the building was caused by similar bombs, and a passer-by stated that he had seen the whole of the building light up briefly after each explosion.

The fire brigade arrived shortly after the alarm had been given and succeeded in putting out the flames, though not before the major part of the building had been gutted.

AFTER MIDNIGHT

The Tel Aviv Municipality issued a manifesto at one o'clock this morning, deeply deploring the demonstration in the town as a breach of discipline. Pointing out that the Municipality had assumed responsibility for the maintenance of order, it appealed to all inhabitants to demonstrate their strength through unity and discipline.

The Mayor, Mr. Rokach, was slightly bruised in the leg by a stone thrown at him as he alighted from his car outside the District Offices to persuade the demonstrators to disperse. He did not require medical attention.

Arab circles in London express grave disappointment in the transitional period, expressing the opinion that the utmost limit should have been three years. They stress that the delay in granting independence is not only against Arab interests but against general national interests, in that Palestine is unable to proceed to the objective of an Arab Federation. Indian Moslem opinion is indicated by Moulana Hasrat Mohami, of the All-India Muslim League, who also declares that the transitional period is too long.

INDEFINITE EXILE FOR HAJ AMIN

LONDON, Wednesday (R). — The Mufti of Jerusalem, Haj Amin al Husseini, is to be excluded indefinitely from Palestine.

This statement was made by Mr. Malcolm MacDonald in the House of Commons this afternoon in answer to a questioner who asked if it was the Government's intention to allow the Mufti to return to Palestine.

Replying in the negative, the Colonial Secretary said that His Majesty's Government, in deciding to exclude him from Palestine indefinitely, could not lose sight of the fact that not only was the Mufti the head of the organization held responsible for the campaign of terrorism and the assassination of British and Jews, but also the head of a faction which for many months past had pursued a similar campaign against large numbers of Arabs.

SUBSCRIPTION : Local: LP.2.250 a year; LP.1.250 a half year:— Foreign, £3.- a year. The rate for display advertisements is 150 mils per column inch. Other rates supplied on request. The right is reserved to make changes in wording or to decline or discontinue any advertisement or to postpone insertions when space is not available.

THE PALESTINE POST

JERUSALEM Hassolel Road P. O. Box 81. Telephone 4233

Tel Aviv - Jaffa: 65, Allenby Road, P. O. Box 1125. 'Phone 4251-4252.

Haifa. Khayat Square, opposite the Post Office entrance, P.O.B. 66. 'Phone 1594-1595

WEDNESDAY AUGUST 23 1939 JERUSALEM VOL. XV. No. 4037. PRICE 10 MILS

Nazi-Soviet Pact Stuns World

With only scanty information available until a late hour last night concerning the proposed terms of the Berlin-Moscow non-aggression pact, the world was completely bewildered not only by the surprise announcement that such an alliance was imminent but also by the complete reversal of Nazi and Fascist foreign policies which it betokened. Notwithstanding the implied threat to the success of the Anglo-Franco-Russian agreement, under discussion for the past four months, it was emphasized both in London and in Moscow that a Russo-German "neutrality" pact would not be imcompatible with the tripartite defensive alliance.

Both the British and French Cabinets met yesterday afternoon. The House of Commons will reassemble tomorrow when legislation will be rushed through placing the Government in a position to take any necessary measures without delay, should the situation require it.

International developments had the effect of deciding the Zionist Congress to end its sessions at the latest by tomorrow; Mr. M. Shertok is flying home today.

TOMORROW IS LAST DAY OF CONGRESS

REPORT ON PALESTINE'S ECONOMIC PROGRESS

GENEVA, Tuesday (Palcor).—International developments have cast their shadow over the 21st Zionist Congress, and a joint meeting of the Executive and the Presidium today decided to request all Commissions now in session to expedite their work so as to report to the plenary session not later than Thursday morning.

Last night it was reported that the tendency among all groups was to hasten the conclusion of the Congress, even before Friday as originally scheduled.

Mr. M. Shertok, head of the Political Department of the Jewish Agency Executive in Palestine, is flying to Jerusalem tomorrow (Wednesday).

Another development at the Congress today was the decision taken by the Union of General Zionists (B Group) by 17 votes to 16, not to participate in further proceedings, but they are likely to return to the session tomorrow.

The Commissions have settled down to work. Last night the Political Commission, which Mrs. Blanche Dugdale (niece of the late Lord Balfour) attended, heard Dr. Nahum Goldmann and Dr. Chaim Weizman. Resolutions were drafted for discussion today at a meeting which was again attended by Dr. Weizman. Mr. D. Ben-Gurion delivered a lengthy report on the political struggle against the White Paper.

REPORT ON SETTLEMENT

Dr. Arthur Ruppin reported to the Colonisation Commission last night on work during the past two years. Fifty new settlements had been founded, of which 37 were Palestine Foundation Fund villages, and 1,200 families had already occupied newly-acquired land, while another 900 would settle shortly. He declared that the following funds were now needed:

Consolidation of settlements — £550,000; middle-class settlement — £150,000; final consolidation of older settlements — £2,500; families whose settlement was decided upon by the 19th Congress — £570,000. Total — £1,600,000.

During the 25 years ending 1930, 27,000 Jews had been settled on the land of Palestine, compared with 65,000 in the last eight years.

"I do not believe in White Papers writtin in ink, but I do believe in land made fruitful with sweat and blood," declared Dr. Ruppin.

GROWING FOUNDATION FUND

Mr. E. Kaplan, addressing the Finance Commission, stated that Keren Hayesod (Palestine Foundation Fund) receipts in the past year had been £530,000, or £70,000 more than the estimate. Sixty per cent came from America where steady progress was being made in the fund-raising campaign. Collections in Europe were impeded by currency restrictions.

Five years ago, the budget was only £150,000, said Mr. Kaplan but the tasks had grown correspondingly since then.

Dealing with the citrus industry and manufacturing Mr. Kaplan remarked that the recent census showed that turn-

(Continued on Page 2, Col. 2)

CABINET CONSIDERS NEW TURN IN EUROPEAN SITUATION

PARLIAMENT MAY REASSEMBLE TOMORROW

LONDON, Tuesday (R).— All British Ministers, with the exception of the Lord Chancellor, Lord Maugham, who is in Canada, attended this afternoon's Cabinet meeting which lasted for three hours and agreed to the Prime Minister's proposal for the reassembly of Parliament on Thursday. An official communique to that effect was issued this evening.

Leading Cabinet Ministers were at work in their Departments this morning. The Prime Minister and Mrs. Chamberlain took their customary early morning walk in St. James's Park, and later the Premier received several calls, including Sir John Simon, Lord Halifax and Mr. Stanley Bruce, the Australian High Commissioner.

Mr. Chamberlain conferred with Lord Halifax, Sir Alexander Cadogan (Head of the Foreign Office) and Sir Robert Vansittart (Chief Diplomatic Adviser) this morning. Mr. Arthur Greenwood, Acting Leader of the Opposition, also called at "No. 10", and Sir Archibald Sinclair, the Liberal Opposition Leader, is arriving back from Scotland tomorrow.

GRAVE VIEW

After his interview with the Premier Mr. Greenwood issued a press statement expressing a very grave view of the international situation, and declaring it was the duty of all citizens to remain calm and steadfast in their purpose to withstand any further acts of aggression as the only way to maintain peace in Europe. He hoped that sane counsels would prevail, but even if war came, England would enter upon it, should she be called to do so, with a clear conscience that it was not her action that provoked it.

The National Council of Labour is to meet tomorrow afternoon, and the Parliamentary Labour Party will meet on Thursday morning.

Dr. Kordt, the German Charge d'Affaires, called at the Foreign Office at noon.

It is learned in official circles that Sir Nevile Henderson is not proceeding to Salzburg as arranged owing to the international situation. Sir Nevile will remain in Berlin, but may go to Salzburg later in the week.

(Earlier Cables — Page 5)

Danzig Teeming With Activity

MILITARY LORRIES RUMBLE THROUGH CITY'S STREETS

DANZIG, Tuesday (R). — The city is teeming with military activity, and pursuit planes are arriving hourly. Large numbers of omnibuses are being requisitioned and taken off the streets, through which many heavy military six-wheeled lorries are constantly passing.

Dr. Frank, President of the Academy of Justice, addressing a rally of German lawyers at Zoppot near Danzig today, said that the Reich was prepared, capable and determined to enforce the right of Danzig, from which it was deprived, to belong to the joint German Fatherland.

Dr. Frank enumerated five reasons why Germany does not regard the Articles of the Versailles Treaty regarding Danzig as valid:

(1) It has no legal validity;

(2) The body of Allied and Associated Powers no longer exists;

(3) Germany does not recognise the League of Nations;

(4) The taking over of Danzig does not infringe Polish sovereignty;

(5) The Danzig population long ago decided to belong to the Reich.

RIBBENTROP FLIES TO RUSSIA TO CONCLUDE AGREEMENT

WILL HAVE TO HURRY BACK BECAUSE OF DANZIG

MOSCOW, Tuesday (R). — The German Foreign Minister, Herr von Ribbentrop, accompanied by a party of Foreign Office officials, is expected here tomorrow night to conclude the negotiations for a non-aggression pact between Germany and Russia.

The German Foreign Minister is flying from Salzburg to Koenigsberg, from where he will fly to Moscow tomorrow. He will be accompanied by Herr Gauss, legal adviser to the Foreign Office, who drafted all important pacts in the past; Herr Paul Schmidt, an interpreter; another Paul Schmidt, of the Foreign Office Press Department; and also Herren Hewel and Bruckelman, Foreign Office officials.

Political circles in Berlin do not expect the visit to be long. They emphasize that the crisis is not yet over, that Danzig is still not yet a part of Germany, and important developments are still to come.

It is believed unlikely in competent Moscow quarters that the pact will be signed immediately on Herr von Ribbentrop's arrival, as Berlin messages suggest. A further indication of this view is given in a Tass Agency statement which declares that the Foreign Minister is coming to Moscow to conduct the necessary talks and that these may require some time.

None of the Moscow newspapers commented on the forthcoming visit. The news of the proposed pact came as a shock to Soviet citizens and foreign observers, who were unable to hazard a guess as to the possible effect of the new pact on the Three-Power negotiations.

TEXT OF ANNOUNCEMENT

The Tass Agency revealed Herr von Ribbentrop's impending visit in the following terms:

"After the conclusion of the Soviet-German trade credit agreement, there arose the problem of improving political relations between Germany and Russia. An exchange of views which took place between the Governments of Germany and the U.S.S.R. established that both parties desire to relieve the tension in their political relations, to eliminate the war menace, and to conclude a non-aggression pact.

"Consequently, the German Minister for Foreign Affairs will arrive in Moscow in a few days for the corresponding negotiations."

NOT INCOMPATIBLE

Well-informed Soviet quarters this afternoon expressed the conviction that the Soviet-German non-aggression pact would not be incompatible with the projected defensive alliance between the Soviet Union, Great Britain and France.

The statement is regarded by competent observers as of the highest significance, indicating the Soviet Union Government's desire and intention to continue the Three-Power anti-aggression talks.

GERMANY EXPECTS CLIMAX BY THURSDAY

BERLIN, Tuesday (R).—Having recovered its breath again after Herr Hitler's overnight conjuring trick, Germany today is much more optimistic about the chances of peace, but optimism seems entirely based on the belief that Great Britain will withdraw her guarantee from Warsaw.

According to well-informed quarters here, when Herr von Ribbentrop goes to Moscow developments are likely to come thick and fast. They anticipate that the signature of the non-aggression pact will be only a matter of hours and once it is signed Germany's next step will only be a matter of minutes.

Thursday, on this reckoning, may prove the big day in European history. The German Army will be absolutely ready to move, at a moment's notice.

WANT OLD FRONTIER

Official quarters here refuse to anticipate events, but well-informed German political circles indicate that Germany's desire is to reoccupy her pre-War frontiers and leave it at that. There is much loose talk about the partition of Poland, but best-informed opinion is inclined to anticipate the continuation of an independent Polish state which will be guaranteed an outlet for her trade via Danzig and Gdynia.

If they are assured of no interference from Russia, the Germans are convinced that this programme can be carried out even in the face of active British opposition if necessary.

The news was published without comment, to the mystification of the people who were anxious to learn what had caused the Third Reich to make such a complete volte face, but political circles were well pleased with the pact, which had "taken in the encirclers."

It is pointed out that the comparatively speedy conclusion of a German-Russian trade agreement had already removed the tension which for such a long time divided the two countries, and the impending pact will no doubt help to clear the international atmosphere to the extent of making the "encirclement" powers more cautious in their policy towards Germany.

Reuter understands that the preliminary negotiations between Berlin and Moscow have been running concurrently with the Anglo-French negotiations for a three-power pact. German circles are extremely optimistic regarding the reaction to the news in Europe.

Berliners, too, gasped with astonishment on opening their newspapers today, in which the news of the pact were printed in huge red and black headlines. "Voelkische Beobachter" carried two red headlines eight inches high, underlined in black, across the entire front page.

A wide interpretation of the negotiations is given in Dr. Goebbels' "Angriff," which says, "Herr von Ribbentrop is going to Moscow as the plenipotentiary of the Fuehrer in order to talk with the Soviet Union about this new political relationship of friendship and to examine its further possibilities.

"The man in the street realises that in this resumption of the historic German-Russian policy, Germany did not waste time in talking. Both sides were determined to extend the commercial discussions to the political field. The new agreement offers both countries great possibilities."

CALMER VIEW IN WASHINGTON

PACT SEEN AS SETBACK FOR JAPAN AS WELL AS EUROPE

WASHINGTON, Tuesday (R). — With the first shock of surprise over, officials here are inclined to believe that the announcement of the projected Soviet-German pact is not quite so catastrophic as first appeared.

The State Department has until now withheld comment pending clarification of the announcement. Well-informed circles, however, enumerate a number of points as possibly constituting a "silver lining."

Firstly, it is pointed out that the Soviet Union, which demanded such a high price from Great Britain, can hardly surrender all its bargaining power by giving Germany a free hand in Eastern Europe. Secondly, continued German aggression in that area could hardly be to the Soviet Union's interest. Thirdly, Herr Hitler has certainly paid highly by weakening the Anti-Comintern Pact and exposing Japan to the threat of stronger Russian and Chinese resistance in the Far East.

It is stated that the last point cannot fail to cause some satisfaction here. It is balanced, however, by regret that though aggression in the Far East has received a severe blow, the European peace front has also received a severe setback, particularly the diplomacy of Great Britain, which it has been President Roosevelt's constant desire in recent months to strengthen.

(Press Comment — Page 5)

PARIS REMAINS RESERVED

THREE-POWER TALKS TO CONTINUE

PARIS, Tuesday (R). — The French Cabinet met for an hour this afternoon to consider the international situation, and, according to several reports, to decide whether or not to recall the French military mission from Russia.

There was considerable diplomatic activity here today. M. Bonnet received the British Charge d'Affaires, and other callers included the Polish and Rumanian Ambassadors, the latter having arrived in Paris from Bucharest yesterday.

While the greatest reserve is maintained in diplomatic circles, owing to the scanty information available, attention is drawn to the fact that the conclusion of a plain non-aggression pact between Germany and Russia would not change in a marked degree the juridical relations between them, as these are already bound by the Treaty of Rapallo and the Treaty of Berlin of 1926.

The publicity given in the German press to the matter is thought in Paris to show that the German leaders attach an essentially psychological importance to the event and are seeking to include it in their campaign of intimidation.

CABINET DECISIONS

Following the Cabinet meeting, a communique was issued stating that the Cabinet had examined the international situation, particularly the reports sent to the Government by the representatives of France abroad. The Council of Ministers approved the instructions which had immediately been despatched to the Ambassadors of France abroad. Mr. Daladier had an 85-minute talk with General Gamelin, Chief of the General Staff, after the Cabinet Council.

The Foreign Affairs Committee of the Cabinet has been summoned for a meeting on Friday, when, according to several Deputies, the Chairman, M. Mistler, will explain the international situation. It is likely that M. Bonnet will also make a statement.

(Press Comment — Page 2)

700 REFUGEES AT JOURNEY'S END

TEL AVIV GREETS FUGITIVES LANDING FROM DEATH SHIP

TEL AVIV, Tuesday. — Cheering crowds such as Tel Aviv has not seen for many years gathered on and near the seashore this morning to receive the 700 refugees whose ship, the s.s. Parita, was beached almost opposite the Ritz Hotel about two hours after midnight.

With its 1,100 tons displacement, the s.s. Parita, had on board 524 men, 157 women and 26 children.

S.O.S. calls coming from the ship had been heard for some distance around, and by the time the first of the refugees were taken off the ship in lighters by the police, innumerable residents of neighbouring streets had brought a tangible welcome in the form of food and clothing.

The refugees were disembarked in good order under the supervision of police and troops and later escorted to Sarafand, from where they are to be released again shortly. When the first buses left, the crowds showed some signs of becoming unruly, but were kept in check by the Tel Aviv Civil Guard. There were no incidents.

About 50 of the refugees were taken to hospital by the Magen David Adom ambulances for medical treatment, and many others were given first aid on the beach. Four immigrants were detained at the Hadassah Hospital.

The small steamer, grounded some 40 yards off the beach, was stated to have broken up completely by the evening. A Union Jack was seen hoisted at one of the mastheads, believed to have been run up by the last of the passengers.

CAPTAIN LEAVES SHIP

It was learned that the Captain and crew of the vessel had left in a motor boat shortly before midnight and that the small steamer remained in the hands of the passengers who managed to head it towards the coast. Police who were attracted by distress signals intercepted about 20 persons who had jumped into the sea to swim ashore.

Police, Army, Municipal and Government officials came down to the beach in the early hours of the morning, and under their direction the ragged and famished refugees were brought ashore in lighters. A detachment of the West Yorkshire Regiment threw a cordon around the area. The police and volunteers worked unflinchingly all morning.

The news of the arrival of the ship, whose distress signals had been widely heard, caused considerable excitement in the city and a steady stream of people made for the beach, many of them bringing clothing and food for the refugees which were distributed to them in the Ritz Hotel, the large balconies of which had been converted into an emergency shelter.

Beach lifeguards and police helped the passengers from the lighters, and all were on land by 11 o'clock. The Marine Police then boarded the vessel for a routine search and, after all was reported in order, the transfer of the refugees to Sarafand began.

As they filed out of the hotel into the street, they were acclaimed by the thousands who crowded balconies, roofs and tree-tops in the vicinity. The first party of 250 left to the strains of "Hatikvah" taken up by the crowd and soon echoed by the departing refugees.

Calls of "Not to Sarafand, their place is with the Jews" were heard, and there was some difficulty in controlling the crowds. The procession of cars avoided the main streets, but was recognised and greeted en-

(Continued on Page 2, Col. 4)

AFTER MIDNIGHT

In Britain, further measures of a precautionary character are being taken by all Departments, including the calling up of certain personnel for the Army, Navy and Air Force and for A.R.P. and Civil Defence work. Arrangements are also being made to deal with matters affecting export of essential commodities.

While taking these measures, the British Government considers it necessary at this time to state that they remain of the opinion that there is nothing in the difficulties which have arisen between Germany and Poland which would justify the use of force involving a European war with all its tragic consequences. As the Prime Minister has repeatedly said, there are indeed no questions in Europe which could not be capable of peaceful solution if only conditions of confidence could be restored.

It is understood that no further meetings of the British Cabinet have been arranged. The Ministers have been asked to stand by. It is officially stated that the Cabinet had no hesitation in deciding that the Soviet-German Pact would in no way affect their obligations to Poland, which they had repeatedly stated in public and which they were determined to fulfil.

SUBSCRIPTION: Local: LP.2.250 a year; LP.1.250 a half year:— Foreign, £3.- a year. The rate for display advertisements is 150 mils per column inch. Other rates supplied on request. The right is reserved to make changes in wording or to decline or discontinue any advertisement or to postpone insertions when space is not available.

THE PALESTINE POST

JERUSALEM Hassolel Road P. O. Box 81. Telephone 4233

Tel Aviv - Jaffa: 65, Allenby Road, P. O. Box 1125. 'Phone 4251-4252.

Haifa. Khayat Square, opposite the Post Office entrance, P.O.B. 66. 'Phone 1594-1595

SUNDAY SEPTEMBER 3 1939 JERUSALEM VOL. XV. No. 4046. PRICE 10 MILS

No Negotiations with Invaders

130 POLES KILLED IN FIRST DAY'S AIR ATTACKS

DIFFERING POLISH AND GERMAN VERSIONS

Differing versions of the first day's hostilities on Polish soil on Friday were issued in both Berlin and Warsaw, yesterday.

Official Polish statements present the following picture:

(1) German troops attacked and crossed the Polish frontier between 6 and 7 o'clock on Friday morning from points west and east of the "Corridor of Pomorze," at the same time launching attacks on Polish Upper Silesia from Slovakia and German Silesia.

(2) Soon after the land attack, the German air force bombed seven important Polish towns. By yesterday morning, 92 German air raids on Polish towns and villages had resulted in 130 persons being killed, only 12 of them soldiers, and a large number seriously wounded. Subsequently Gdynia and 18 other towns besides Warsaw were bombed.

(3) Sixteen German 'planes were shot down and two Polish machines lost.

(4) The town of Radom, 60 miles south of Warsaw, was bombed by three German squadrons.

(5) Germany's offensives from Slovakia and East Prussia were replused, and the Poles held their positions at the Westerplatte, on the Danzig coast, in spite of three German attacks. Operations from Slovakia were directed against Zakopane, the well-known Polish winter sports resort. A German armoured train was captured near Danzig territory, and German aircraft bombed a refugee train near Kutnow, Silesia, causing heavy casualties.

(6) Fighting was going on in frontier regions and a most violent battle raged in Kattowice. Polish artillery fire destroyed a German armoured train; seven German tanks were destroyed, and a number of prisoners taken.

(7) The Poles held the Post Office in Danzig, but Germans had taken possession of the railway-station.

(8) Two German bombers were shot down, and the four occupants arrested after a miraculous escape, when 41 German aircraft in formation appeared over eastern Warsaw on Friday afternoon. People watched a thrilling aerial battle over the heart of the city. Several houses caught fire, and the hospital for Jewish defective children was bombed and wrecked. It is claimed that many German bombs did not explode.

The first German war communiques claimed that

(1) Military action in Silesia, Pomerania and East Prusia had brought the expected preliminary successes. German troops had reached the heights of Kattowice. Forces from East Prussia were fighting on Polish soil "for the time being." The air force bombed several Polish aerodromes and gained "the upper hand in the air," and naval units took up positions in the Bay of Danzig. Gdynia was bombed.

(2) German troops were half-way across the Corridor. A large number of aerodromes were bombed.

(3) Polish artillery opened fire on the frontier station at Beuthen, and several shells fell on the station.

(4) The aerodrome at Radom (and not the town) was bombed by German aircraft.

(5) German aeroplanes had not bombed open towns but only military objectives in or near the towns.

German aircraft at dawn yesterday bombed Putch, in the Bay of Danzig, and the towns of Warsaw, Cracow, Radom, Modlin, Pultusk, Kobryn and other cities in Central Poland.

Another entry is claimed into Polish territory at Ostenberg, which is in that part of Czecho-Slovakia which was ceded to Poland last year.

A German war communique states that the German air force today raided a number of Polish towns and on their return journey attacked railway lines and stations and bombed retreating Polish troops. A number of Polish aerodromes were also destroyed, it is claimed, and the *'Polish Air Firce was so seriolsly damaged that the German Air Force is now ready for further measures to protect Germany."*

An air raid of 20 German planes over Warsaw is reported by the Havas correspondent to have taken place at 5.05 yesterday afternoon. It lasted for about 25 minutes.

The raiders flying singly and in formations of threes at a height of about 5,000 feet were engaged by Polish pursuit planes. The result of the raid is not yet known.

A special brigade for the defence of Danzig has been formed by Polish refugees from the Free City at Torun.

The Polish Embassy in London last night announced, that heavy fighting is taking place all along the frontier. The Polish forces were tenaciously holding their positions despite repeated German attacks.

The Third and Fourth German Armies are attempting to cut across the Corridor at the southern end. The Third Army was advancing from East Prussia and the Fourth Army from the west.

The Polish radio stated that 100 German tanks have been put out of action and 34 planes brought down.

ON OTHER PAGES

Mr. Chamberlain's Address to the House on Friday — Page 8.

Summary of White Paper on Anglo-German exchanges — Page 7.

Government Notices concerning restrictions of Trading in essential articles, Maximum Prices, and Censorship of Mails and Telegrams will be found on Pages 2 and 6.

Book Review and Spice of Life — Pages 3 and 4.

AFTER MIDNIGHT

The Germans last night claimed that in upper Silesia they had advanced 30 kilometres into Poland.

The French Senate has passed the Bill opening a credit of £400,000,000 for defence purposes.

At Pretoria General Smuts has introduced an Emergency Bill to enable a new Senate to be constituted while the old one still exists. In reply to a question by the Leader of the Opposition, General Hertzog answered that he would make a statement on the attitude of the Union of South Africa as soon as the new Bill was passed.

The Empire air mail "all-up" scheme has been suspended. Air mails will be sent by ordinary services and routes, and full rates will be payable for air mails, as previously.

POLES URGED TO RESIST INVASION

PRESIDENT MOSCICKI ADDRESSES NATION

WARSAW, Saturday (Reuter). Marshal Edouard Smigly-Rydz, who has been appointed successor to President Ignacy Moscicki, should anything happen to the latter, and also Commander-in-Chief of the Polish Army, has issued a proclamation to the Army stating that the final victory would be with Poland and her allies.

The Polish Government, in a communique, states that several hours before the German armed forces opened hostilities, the Polish Ambassador in Berlin informed the German Government of Poland's attitude of good-will towards the efforts the British Government were making for the maintenance of peace.

The communique accuses Germany of using the allegation of a Polish attack on the Gleiwitz radio station as the pretext for aggression, and declared that no one in the civilised world would doubt who was the real aggressor. This aggression was unparalleled in its brutality and would meet with the firm resistance of the whole Polish nation, which would defend its liberty, rights and honour to the end.

ENVOY RECALLED

The Polish Embassy in Berlin has announced that the Charge d'Affaires had been recalled to Warsaw. The Polish Government has requested the German Ambassador to leave Warsaw at once. The Swedish Legation in Berlin will watch Polish interests, while the Netherlands Legation has undertaken to watch German interests in Poland.

President Moscicki yesterday issued a statement appealing to all citizens of Poland to defend the freedom and honour of the country, and to "give a further reply to the German aggressor as they have done so often in the past".

Evacuation measures for women and children are being taken in Warsaw.

NO WAR

Political circles in Berlin stated today that Germany had not declared war on Poland, and the present condition is therefore not considered one of war.

A German communique states that it is not intended to bring about a complete change of regime in Poland, but merely to rectify Germany's eastern frontier.

1,400 REFUGEES LAND AT TEL AVIV BEACH

THREE KILLED BY MARINE PATROL FIRE

TEL AVIV, Saturday. — A refugee ship, Tiger Hill, with 1,400 passengers aboard, ran ashore at 9.15 last night near Mahloul Quarter, about 300 yards north of the keeled hulk of the s.s. Parita.

As the ship approached the beach, about 185 refugees landed in small boats and were taken into custody by Police. The remainder were landed by the authorities this morning, and all were taken to the Sarafand Detention Camp.

Three of the refugees were mortally wounded when Marine Police fired at the freighter on Thursday night, as she approached the coast south of Jaffa.

The dead are Zvi Bider of Poland, Dr. Robert Schneider, and Mrs. Yona Shimshelevitz, 27, who died at the Hadassah Hospital this afternoon.

The passengers included 680 of the refugees who had been detained for some time at the Quarantine Station in Beirut and who were taken on board the steamer on Wednesday.

Twelve persons were taken to the Hadassah Hospital here.

The ship left Varna, Bulgaria, six weeks ago with 57 passengers, and embarked others at Constanza. The Captain and crew left the ship in a motor boat a few kilometres off the coast, leaving passengers in charge to steer the vessel to the coast.

A representative of *The Palestine Post* walking on the beach at 9.15 last night saw the ship, fully illuminated, approach the coast, the passengers singing "Hatikva." Alongside were three small boats filled with passengers.

News of the landing spread rapidly throughout the town, and food was collected by the Women's Social Service Kitchen. Provisions were sent on board the steamer and more was sent to the detention camp today.

BRIGANDS IN NORTH SUFFER CASUALTIES

ACRE, Saturday. — Casualties were suffered by an armed gang in encounters with the T.J.F.F. troops and R.A.F. in the Northern Area today.

About 6 o'clock a party of 40 brigands armed with rifles and wearing uniforms, were contacted by a detachment of T.J.F.F. near Araba (Jenin District). In the resulting engagement one mounted brigand was killed with his horse and another was wounded and captured and a pistol and a rifle seized

The exchange continued through thick undergrowth and rugged terrain. R.A.F. planes arrived later and in the ensuing action several more brigands are believed to have been killed or wounded.

Another gang of six Arabs were encountered near Kabul by a party of the Leicestershire Regiment, who inflicted additional casualties, killing three and wounding and capturing one bandit. Four rifles, one revolver and 88 rounds of ammunition were seized.

FRANCE WILL STAND BY PLEDGE

M. LEBRUN'S STIRRING ADDRESS TO SENATE

PARIS, Saturday (R). — President Lebrun has sent a stirring message to the Senate and Chamber which was read at this afternoon's sitting. It states,

"You have met at a critical hour in our national life. War has broken out in Central Europe. Men are killing each other, and innocent victims fall, machine-gunned from the air.

How has that come about? Two peoples had differences to settle. They could have done that by free and loyal negotiations as advised from all sides. At a moment when their plenipotentiaries were about to meet, Germany brutally attacked Poland, thus creating a state of war which nothing could justify.

"Great Britain and France, resolutely attached to the policy of prudence, moderation and wisdom, have done everything humanly possible to avert this crisis."

Proceedings in the French Chamber of Deputies opened with a speech by M. Herriot, and the whole House rose to its feet at his reference to their fraternal solidarity with Poland. Deputies listened with the closest attention to M. Daladier, who said:

"Time presses. France and Great Britain will not stand by at the destruction of a friendly people. Aggression against Poland is a new enterprise of violence against Great Britain and France. It is not a question of a German-Polish conflict. It is a question of a new attempt by Hitler at the dictatorship and domination of Europe and the world."

"DEEDS NOT WORDS"

M. Daladier recalled the march into Vienna and Czecho-Slovakia's fate, adding,

"With Hitler it is deeds and not words that count. Poland has been the object of most unjust and brutal aggression. Great Britain and France do not repudiate their signatures."

Reviewing the last minute diplomatic attempts to avert hostilities, M. Daladier said,

"I am happy to render homage to the noble efforts of the Italian Government. Poland the victim of aggression, is assured the help of nations of free men. If the fighting stopped, if the aggressor retained his frontiers if free negotiations could have taken place, the French Government would attempt to facilitate it.

For several days peace had been menaced by the arbitrary demands of Germany. All peaceful means were utilised in order to save the peace of the world. Germany reduced them to nought."

The Chamber was unanimous in approving of the views of the Government, even Communists cheering and applauding M. Daladier. The war credits were voted without debate.

It is now obligatory for all citizens to carry gas masks in the streets, although so far very few people appear to be complying with this order. The police are all equipped with steel helmets and are performing their duties carrying their gas masks. Taxis and buses are scarce.

THE ANGLO-FRENCH ULTIMATUM

FULL TEXT OF DECLARATION

LONDON, Saturday (R). — Acting in pursuance of the instructions received from their respective Governments, the British and French Ambassadors in Berlin yesterday handed a joint declaration to Herr von Ribbentrop concerning the act of aggression committed against Poland. The full text of the declaration is as follows:

"The German Chancellor has issued a proclamation to the German Army which indicated clearly that he was about to attack Poland. The information which has reached His Majesty's Government in the United Kingdom and the French Government indicates that German troops have crossed the Polish frontier and attacks on Polish towns are proceeding.

"In these circumstances, it appears to the Governments of the United Kingdom and France that, by their action, the German Government have created conditions, namely, an aggressive act of force against Poland, threatening the independence of Poland, which call for the immediate implementation by the Governments of the United Kingdom and France of their undertaking to Poland to come to her assistance.

"I am accordingly to inform Your Excellency that, unless the German Government are prepared to give His Majesty's Government an assurance that the German Government have suspended all aggressive action against Poland and are prepared promptly to withdraw their forces from Polish territory, His Majesty's Government in the United Kingdom will without hesitation fulfil their obligations to Poland."

GERMANY MUST WITHDRAW FORCES FROM POLAND FIRST

PREMIER PROMISES DEFINITE STATEMENT TODAY

LONDON, Saturday (R). — Lord Halifax told the House of Lords this evening that the British Government had not yet received any reply to their note to Germany. It was possible that the delay was due to a proposal put forward by the Italian Government that hostilities should cease and that Germany Poland, France, Great Britain and Italy should meet in conference.

While appreciating the efforts of the Italian Government, however, the British Government would find it impossible to take part in such a conference unless the German forces were withdrawn from Polish territory. They were in consultation with the French Government regarding a time limit.

If the German Government were willing to withdraw their forces, then the British Government would be willing to regard the position, but any settlement must have due regard to the fundamental rights of Poland and be ensured by international guarantee.

Action had been taken by the Danzig authorities and the Reichstag with regard to the incorporation of Danzig in the Reich which was the final step in the one-sided repudiation of an international instrument which could only be modified by negotiation.

OPPOSITION CRITICISM

In the House of Commons Mr. Chamberlain made a similar statement. When he sat down Mr. Arthur Greenwood, the Opposition Leader said that the British Parliament would not tolerate delay. It was vital that Poland should not be left without allies, and it was 38 hours since hostilities began.

Mr. Greenwood said that the House was perturbed by the statement of the Prime Minister. He would have preferred Mr. Chamberlain to be able to say definitely tonight whether it was peace or war. "The moment we look like weakening, the Dictatorships know that we are beaten," he declared.

Sir Archibald Sinclair said that the British Parliament would not tolerate delay in the fulfilment of their honourable obligations. A consideration of the conference proposal had caused no delay in the German advance. Parliament feels that a reply must be demanded, unless the advance was promptly stopped.

The Prime Minister, in replying, said that he distrusted a manoeuvre of this kind. The Government was in somewhat of a difficult position. He supposed that there must be difficulties with the allies having to communicate with one another by telephone to synchronise actions so quickly as those in the same room.

"I should be horrified if the House thought for one moment that my statement betrayed the slightest weakening attitude in the decision which we and the French Government have already agreed upon," said the Prime Minister

He would have been very glad if it had been possible to say now that "the French and ourselves have agreed to make the shortest possible limit to the time when action should be taken by both. It is very possible that we may receive a reply from the French Government in the course of the next few hours." *He felt certain that he could make a definite statement in the House tomorrow.*

He was the last man to neglect every serious opportunity to avoid the great catastrophe of war, even at the last moment, but he confessed that in the present case he would have to be convinced of the good faith on the other side in any action they undertook before they could regard the proposition as one from which they could expect a reasonable chance of successful issue.

"I anticipate that there is only one answer I can give the House tomorrow. I hope myself that the issue will be brought to a close at the earliest possible moment so that we may know where we are.

"I trust that the House, realizing the position into which I have been put will believe me that I speak in complete good faith and will not prolong the discussion, which might make our position more embarrassing than it is," concluded the Prime Minister.

Mr. Maxton (I.L.P.) speaking after Mr. Chamberlain, said that if the bombs could be stopped from raining down tomorrow, it would be one of the greatest achievements the world had ever seen. Given time, common sense might begin to function even in Germany and he appealed to the Prime Minister not to let himself be rushed.

The House of Commons then adjourned until noon tomorrow (Sunday)

There was no information available in London last night of any German reply to the British and French notes.

Herr von Ribbentrop received Sir Nevile Henderson in Berlin on Friday night and when he was handed the declaration said that he must refer it to Herr Hitler.

PARLIAMENT PASSES £500,000,000 VOTE

LONDON, Saturday (R).—Royal Assent was given today to 17 Bills and financial resolutions which were passed through all their stages by both Houses of Parliament last night, the most important being a supplementary budget vote of £500,000,000 for securing public safety, the defence of the realm, the maintenance of public order and the prosecution of war. The sum is to be raised by temporary borrowing.

Other Bills included the Currency Defence Bill to amend the regulations regarding the Exchange Equalisation Account and make postal orders and certain bank notes legal tender temporarily in the event of a shortage, and remove the present limit of £550,000,000 as the amount that might be issued to the Exchequer Account.

Other bills apply the Prise Law to aircraft, provide for control of import, export and carriage of certain goods, and forbid dealing with an enemy country.

ITALY TO STAY NEUTRAL

ROME, Saturday (R).—Italy's determination to remain neutral in the present European circumstances was announced yesterday in an official broadcast, which also transmitted Herr Hitler's statement that he did not expect Italian aid in his military operations.

The Fuehrer telegraphed to Signor Mussolini thanking him for past diplomatic and military aid, adding,

"I am convinced that, with the German military forces, I shall be able to fulfil the mission destined for us. I think that in these circumstances I will not need military help from Italy".

A statement made after a Cabinet Council meeting in Rome yesterday declared that Italy would not take the initiative in any military operations. The declaration is considered to be tantamount to a policy of neutrality.

It is declared here that every effort had been made by Italy to reach a peaceful solution, and failing this, Italy's best contribution was to help the conflict by not joining in.

A Tokyo message stated today that all indications continued to point to Japanese neutrality in any general war,

SUBSCRIPTION: Local: LP.2.250 a year; LP.1.250 a half year:— Foreign, £3.- a year. The rate for display advertisements is 150 mils per column inch. Other rates supplied on request. The right is reserved to make changes in wording or to decline or discontinue any advertisement or to postpone insertions when space is not available.

THE PALESTINE POST

JERUSALEM Hassolel Road P. O. Box 81. Telephone 4233

Tel Aviv - Jaffa: 65, Allenby Road, P. O. Box 1125, 'Phone 4251-4252.

Haifa, Khayat Square, opposite the Post Office entrance, P.O.B. 66, 'Phone 1594-1595

MONDAY SEPTEMBER 4 1939 JERUSALEM VOL. XV. No. 4047. PRICE 10 MILS

ANGLO-FRENCH WAR ON HITLER

NAZIS BLAME BRITISH "INTERVENTION"

Wanted 'Reasonable Solution'

BERLIN, Sunday. — The outbreak of war with Great Britain was announced to the German people here today in the form of a broadcast quoting a memorandum which had been handed earlier by the German Government to Sir Nevile Henderson, the British Ambassador.

The statement declares that the German Government and the German people refuse to accept or fulfil any ultimative demands from the British Government and will meet force with force.

It is claimed that a virtual state of war has existed on the eastern frontier of Germany for many months and but for the intervention of Britain a reasonable settlement of the Polish-German dispute would have been found. The memorandum declares,

DEFENCE IN THE WEST

"Germany neither had the intention not has she put forward a demand to annex Poland. The Reich has only demanded the revision of those articles in the treaty of Versailles which farseeing statesmen of all nations regarded at the time it was drafted as intolerable. The memorandum severely attacks Britain's "blank cheque" to Poland and accuses her of being chiefly responsible by this action for Polish terrorism. It is then alleged that Britain rebuffed Signor Mussolini's proposal "which could still have saved the peace of Europe, though the German Government declared itself willing to accept it."

Germany was also unwilling to tolerate further ill-treatment from Poland.

The memorandum continues, adding that therefore the Government refuses all efforts to force Germany by means of ultimatums to recall her troops.

"We shall therefore answer any British aggression with like arms and in a like way."

Herr Hitler in a proclamation to the western army calls on them to protect the frontiers of the Reich "unshakeable as a wall of steel or iron" against every attack. If they did their duty, battle in the east would reach a successful conclusion in a few months. The proclamation concluded "I am going with confidence in you to the army in the east."

A protest against allegations in some foreign newspapers that the German forces had already started using poison gas and incendiary bombs was today issued by the German News Agency, which described the report as the first "atrocity" story in the military sphere.

"Voelkischer Beobachter" stated today that the restrictions on listening to foreign broadcasts were necessary "in order to ensure a German victory in the war of nerves."

BREMEN SEIZED

French wireless stations last night announced that a British warship had seized the German luxury liner, Bremen, on her way back from New York without passengers and was escorting her to an unnamed British port.

THE KING'S MESSAGE TO THE EMPIRE

His Majesty the King broadcast a message to the people of the British Empire at 5 o'clock G.M.T. yesterday afternoon (7 o'clock Palestine time). The message was relayed by the P.B.S. from Jerusalem.

His Majesty said:

"In this grave hour, perhaps the most fateful in our history, I send to every household of my people, both at home and overseas, this message, speaking with the same depth of feeling to each one of you as if I were able to speak to you myself.

"For the second time in the lives of most of us, we are at war. Over and over again we have tried to find a peaceful way out of the differences between ourselves and those who are now our enemies, but it has been in vain.

"We have been forced into a conflict, for we are called with our allies to meet the challenge which, if it were to prevail, would be fatal to any civilized order in the world.

"It is the principle which permits a state in selfish pursuit of power to disregard treaties and solemn pledges, which sanctions the use of force or the threat of force against the sovereignty and independence of other States.

"Such a principle, stripped of all disguise, is merely the primitive doctrine that might is right.

"If this principle were established throughout the world, the freedom of our own country and of the whole British Commonwealth of Nations would be in danger.

"But far more than this, the peoples of the world will be kept in the bondage of fear and all hope of a settled peace and of the security of justice and liberty among nations would be ended. This is the ultimate issue which confronts us.

"For the sake of all that we ourselves hold dear and of the world order and of peace, it is unthinkable that we should refuse to meet the challenge.

"It is for this high purpose that I now call my people at home and my people across the seas who will make our cause their own. I ask them to stand firm and calm, and unite in this time of trial. The task will be hard. There may be dark days ahead. War can no longer be confined to the battlefield. But we can only do the right as we see the right and reverently commit our cause to God.

"If one and all will keep reverently faithful to it, ready for whatever service or sacrifice, then with God's help we shall prevail. One and all we are resolutely faithful to the cause, ready for whatever sacrifice may be demanded. May He bless and keep us all."

WAR CABINET AFTER TWENTY-ONE YEARS

Churchill and Eden Included

LONDON, Sunday (R). —Britain's new War Cabinet was formed today with the inclusion of Mr. Winston Churchill as First Lord of the Admiralty and Mr. Anthony Eden as Dominions Secretary with special access to the Inner Cabinet. The latter is now composed of the following:

Mr. Neville Chamberlain — Prime Minister;
Sir John Simon — Chancellor of the Exchequer;
Lord Halifax — Foreign Secretary;
Lord Chatfield — Minister for the Coordination of Defence;
Mr. Winston Churchill — First Lord of the Admiralty;
Mr. Hore Belisha —Secretary for War;
Sir Kingsley Wood — Secretary for Air;
Sir Samuel Hoare — Lord Privy Seal;
Lord Hankey — Minister without Portfolio.

Sir John Anderson becomes Home Secretary in place of Sir Samuel Hoare and also remains Minister for Civilian Defence. Sir Thomas Inskip becomes Lord Chancellor and Lord Stanhope is moved from the Admiralty to the Lord Presidency. Lord Hankey, the former Sir Maurice Hankey, was Secretary to the Cabinet in the World War.

CONSCRIPTION

In the House of Commons last night, Mr. Ernest Brown, Minister of Labour, moved the second reading of the National Service Armed Forces Bill providing for the enlistment of men between 18 and 41. Mr. Arthur Greenwood supported the second reading of the Bill, which was carried by 340 votes to 7.

The Minister of Pensions introduced the Personal Injuries Emergency Provisions Bill, which is to make loss or damage due to war including accidental injuries sustained while on duty a State liability. Payments are to be immediate to tide the victims over the first emergency, and serious injury or disablement may receive pensions on service lines.

The British Cabinet, which met on Saturday afternoon, was summoned for the second time on Sunday night and sat for 45 minutes.

BRITAIN UNITED AGAINST NAZI TYRANNY

FRENCH ULTIMATUM EXPIRED AT FIVE O'CLOCK YESTERDAY AFTERNOON

LONDON, Sunday (R). — The Commons and Lords were both informed at noon today by the Prime Minister and the Foreign Secretary, respectively, that Great Britain was at war with Germany.

Mr. Chamberlain arrived at Westminster shortly before midday, having 45 minutes earlier broadcast his message (given in an adjoining column) to the United Kingdom, the British Empire and the world.

ALL-DAY CONSULTATIONS

The Premier's statement was as follows:

"When I spoke to the House last night, I could not but be aware that in some parts of the House there were doubts or bewilderment as to whether there would be hesitation or vacillation on the part of His Majesty's Government. But, in the circumstances I make no reproach. If I had been in the same position as members on the other benches, and not in possession of all the information, I might have felt the same.

"We were in consultation all day yesterday with the French Government and we felt that the intensified action which the Germans were taking against Poland allowed of no delay in making our own position clear. Accordingly we decided to send our Ambassador in Berlin instructions which he was to hand at 9 o'clock this morning to the German Foreign Minister."

Mr. Chamberlain then read the terms of the instructions sent to Sir Nevile Henderson, which had been issued earlier in the morning as a communique from No. 10 Downing Street as follows:

11 O'CLOCK THE ZERO HOUR

'On September 1, His Majesty's Ambassador in Berlin was instructed to inform the German Government that unless they were prepared to give His Majesty's Government in the United Kingdom satisfactory assurance that the German Government had suspended all aggressive action against Poland and were prepared promptly to withdraw their forces from Polish territory, His Majesty's Government in the United Kingdom would without hesitation fulfil their obligations to Poland.

'At 9 o'clock this morning, His Majesty's Ambassador informed the German Government that unless not later than 11 o'clock B.S.T. today, September 3, satisfactory assurances to the above effect would

(Continued on Page 2)

German Air Onslaught on Poland

LONDON, Sunday (R). It was announced by the Polish Embassy tonight that the German Government had proposed to Poland that aerial bombardments should be limited to military objectives, but although the Polish Government accepted, German airplanes had bombed 24 towns of Poland.

The Polish Embassy in London claims that the Polish forces are holding their positions, the most serious threat being in the concentration of the main mass of the German Air Force against Poland.

Not only were military objectives being bombed, but it was certain that towns and villages were being indiscriminately and continuously raided although they were of no military importance.

A Warsaw message states that 26 people were killed when 15 bombs were dropped on the town of Lublin 250 miles south-east of Warsaw.

The German radio today claimed that the town of Czenstochowa 130 miles southwest of Warsaw and a famous place of pilgrimage for the Poles had been captured by the German forces.

Last night the Polish Government reported Czenstochowa to be in flames as a result of having been bombed several times by German aircraft on Friday and Saturday.

GERMAN REPORTS

The German Army High Commands in a communique claims that a whole area over the battle area and the hinterland is completely controlled by the German air forces, and asserts that attacks were confined to military objectives.

The communique declares that after units of the German armoured cars reached the Vistula at noon, German forces effectively attacked points for the passage of the river, and asserts that one bridge and another under construction were destroyed by numerous bombs.

An important railway station was also bombed. It adds that while military objectives were being attacked and destroyed, there was resistance by Polish anti-aircraft and pursuit planes.

The new Russian Ambassador to Berlin arrived last night in company of a Russian general and members of his staff.

SUCCESS CLAIMED

Another wireless communication in Germany claims that German troops in the Corridor sector have reached the Vistula and Polish army contingents in the northern part of the Corridor have been cut off and are being mopped up.

The German army is also stated to have reached the Vistula from east Prussia though for several miles the river forms a frontier on this side.

It is believed in London that these claims of successes are probably exaggerated.

HIGH COMMISSIONER'S BROADCAST TODAY

His Excellency the High Commissioner will broadcast to Palestine at 9 p.m. today.

Translations of the address into Arabic and Hebrew will follow immediately.

PALESTINE JEWRY'S STAND

STATEMENT BY JEWISH AGENCY AND VAAD LEUMI

Palestine Jewry's loyalty to Britain and readiness to take its share in the defence of Palestine and support of the British forces was proclaimed yesterday in a statement issued by the Jewish Agency Executive and a joint decision taken by the Jewish Agency and the General Council of Palestine Jews.

The Executive of the Jewish Agency issued the following statement last night:—

His Majesty's Government has today declared war against the Germany of Hitler.

At this fateful moment, the Jewish community has a threefold concern: the protection of the Jewish homeland, the welfare of the Jewish people, the victory of the British Empire.

The White Paper of May, 1939, was a grave blow to us. As heretofore we shall defend to the utmost of our ability the right of the Jewish people in its National Home. Our opposition to the White Paper was, however, never directed against Great Britain or the British Empire.

The war which has now been forced upon Great Britain by Nazi Germany is our war, and all the assistance that we shall be able and permitted to give to the British Army and to the British People we shall render wholeheartedly.

We do not know what will be in store for our country in this war. Our first duty is to ensure the survival and the welfare of the Jewish community, to strengthen it materially and morally, and to prepare it for the great and difficult task which Jewish history has assigned to it.

We have to maintain and strengthen the positions and creative achievements built up by two generations of Jewish pioneers in our Homeland. During two generations we have devoted our forces to constructive effort. If need be, we shall now show our strength in war also.

Let us close our ranks, let us unite in a spirit of responsibility and mutual help, discipline and national devotion, and let us be prepared.

EMERGENCY MEASURES

A joint meeting of the Executives of the Jewish Agency and of the General Council of Palestine Jews, (Vaad Leumi) was held yesterday at the Offices of the Jewish Agency.

The meeting dealt with the emergency created by the declaration of war. Among other matters, it was decided to carry out a registration of volunteers, (men and women) for national service during the period of the emergency. Volunteers will be registered:

(a) to serve the needs of the Jewish Community as regards security, economic life and other public requirements.

(b) to be at the disposal of the British military authorities in Palestine for such services as they may require.

All men and women between the ages of 18 and 50, who register for such voluntary service, will be required to furnish full details of their technical qualifications and special experience, and to indicate the tasks in which they are prepared to serve the Jewish Community or the British Army in Palestine.

Details of the registration will shortly be announced.

It was further resolved to set up, under the auspices of the Jewish Agency, an Economic Council composed of prominent members of the Jewish Community whose function will be to deal with the requirements of the Jewish economy in Palestine in the fields of agriculture, industry, labour, supplies, credit, transport, import, export, etc.

The committees previously established by the Jewish Agency for dealing with the question of supply, banking and transport will continue to function in cooperation with the central Economic Council now to be set up.

Tokyo Staying Out

U.S. EXPECTED TO INVOKE NEUTRALITY ACT

SHANGHAI, —It is reliably learned here that the Japanese Government will give assurances to Great Britain of Japanese neutrality.

WASHINGTON, Sunday (R). —A White House proclamation says that legislation has been drawn up to invoke the Neutrality Act which bans shipment of munitions to belligerents.

President Roosevelt will broadcast tonight at 2.00 a.m. G.M.T. and his speech will afterwards be broadcast in six different languages.

A wonderful impression of calmness and sincerity has been created here by Mr. Chamberlain's speech and the instructions broadcast by the B.B.C., declared a responsible U.S. official today. He added that once again the American people would contrast the voice of Britain with that of Germany "and from such a comparison our people can only draw one conclusion, and the people of Britain know what that conclusion is."

BRUSSELS. — It is officially announced that Belgium has sent a declaration of neutrality to all the countries concerned.

AFTER MIDNIGHT

Australia and New Zealand last night followed the lead of the Mother-country by declaring war on Germany.

Zero hour in France passed quietly without any outward manifestation that France was at war. The weekly rest day has been abolished and a seven-day week has been established in all concerns working for National defence.

"France and Britain are with us," were the cries of thousands of demonstrators outside the British and French Embassies in Warsaw yesterday.

The Admiralty announces that Rear-Admiral the Duke of Kent has taken up a war appointment.

Residents of the United Kingdom have been ordered to sell to the Treasury any gold or foreign exchanges of the following countries at their disposal: U.S. and Canadian dollars, belgas, Swiss and French francs, guilders, Argentine pesos and Swedish and Norwegian crowns.

SUBSCRIPTION: Local: LP.2.250 a year; LP.1.250 a half year:— Foreign, $8.- a year. The rate for display advertisements is 150 mils per column inch. Other rates supplied on request. The right is reserved to make changes in wording or to decline or discontinue any advertisement or to postpone insertions when space is not available.

THE
PALESTINE
POST

JERUSALEM Hasolel Road P. O. Box 81. Telephone 4233
Tel Aviv - Jaffa: 65, Allenby Road, P. O. Box 1125. 'Phone 4251-4252.
Haifa. Khayat Square, opposite the Post Office entrance, P.O.B. 66. 'Phone 1594-1595

MONDAY SEPTEMBER 18 1939 JERUSALEM VOL. XV. 4057. PRICE 10 MILS

REDS JOINING NAZIS IN POLAND

23 Dead in Level Crossing Tragedy

TEL AVIV, Sunday. — Trapped in a burning Egged bus by the protective wire screens over the windows, 23 persons, presumably all Jewish, perished when the vehicle's benzine tank was set ablaze as the result of a collision with a goods train at the railway level crossing near Sarafand shortly after noon today. The bus was travelling from Jerusalem to Tel Aviv.

Six passengers were able to escape from the blazing bus, either through the door or by forcing open wire screens. Four of the survivors were admitted to the General Hospital at Sarafand, and three others were taken to the Hadassah Hospital by a Red Shield Ambulance, which chanced on the scene. Arab passers-by gave the injured what assistance they could.

One of the injured, Yehuda Lehrman (29), succumbed to his injuries at the Hadassah Hospital at 9.30 in the evening. He was a teacher in an evening school in Tel Aviv and was returning from the holidays spent with his parents in Jerusalem.

Joseph Weissfish of Mea Shearim, Jerusalem, was taken to Hospital at Sarafand where he succumbed soon after admission.

The remains of the victims, charred beyond all recognition, were conveyed in lorries to the New Cemetery at Nachlath Yitzhak, where burial will take place tomorrow. An attempt will be made tomorrow morning to establish the identity of the victims, who include a number of women and three children.

Egged Bus Gutted Near Sarafand

Those taken to the Sarafand Hospital are Abraham Litman, D. Levy, Marie Kaufman and the driver, Leon Ludwig. Those admitted to the Hadassah Hospital, Tel Aviv, are Eliahu Ben Haim (22), and Shulamith Lyon, (23). All except the latter are suffering from dangerous burns. Dob Baral, who was also burnt, was able to return to Jerusalem.

The Egged Company towed the remains of the gutted bus to Tel Aviv this afternoon.

Among those who visited the scene of the accident were Mr. C. E. Coulman, of the Palestine Railways, and Messrs. J. Kupperman and Zvi Shimshi, District Officers, and Mr. H. S. Mansfeld.

RAILWAYS ENQUIRY

The following official account was given last night:

At 12.10 p.m. today a serious accident occurred at Sarafand el Amar level crossing on the Jerusalem-Jaffa Road near Ramle when an Egged Bus Number 653, collided with a special train of the Palestine Railways travelling from Lydda to Sarafand.

The bus, which was going from Jerusalem to Tel Aviv, carried 27 persons including the driver. After the collision it overturned and went on fire. As far as it has been possible to ascertain at 9.30 p.m. 21 persons, all of whom are believed to be Jews, have lost their lives.

The remaining six persons, four men and one woman and the driver escaped from the burning vehicle. One man was treated in Ramle for minor injuries and has returned to Jerusalem.

The others, four men including the driver, and one woman were brought to the Military Hospital at Sarafand, all suffering from intensive burns and in a very serious condition.

One of them, Joseph Weissfish of Mea Shearim of Jerusalem, subsequently died of his injuries. The condition of the woman who was injured, Miss Kaufman, who is believed to come from Haifa, is critical.

The other three are the driver, Leon Ludwig of Tel Aviv, David Levy, Jerusalem, and Abraham Litman.

An inquiry into the circumstances of the accident is being opened by the Palestine Railways.

Soviet Army Sweeps Over Border

Soviet Russian troops, who crossed into Eastern Poland in the early hours of yesterday morning, were reported from Riga to have passed Baranowichi, 39 miles from the Soviet frontier. They expect to meet the German troops at Brest-Litovsk in the north and Lwow in the south this morning.

The crossing by vast numbers of the Red Army began at 4 o'clock in the morning along the whole frontier from Polotsk, at the junction with the Latvian border in the north, down to Kamenetz-Podolsk near Rumania in the south.

It was stated at Riga that at points near Latvia, the Russians crossed without meeting any resistance, but Polish troops resisted the Red Army's advance around Molodeczno, south-west of Vilna.

In the course of last night, the Soviet Government handed a Note to the Polish Ambassador declaring that the Polish-German war had so far revealed the rottenness of the Polish State and Government. During ten days, Poland had lost all her industrial districts and cultural positions. Warsaw no longer existed as the capital and the Polish Government was broken up and no longer showed any signs of life.

"Freeing Oppressed Minorities"

"This means that the Polish State and Government no longer exist, and in consequence the agreements between the Soviet Union and Poland are invalidated," the Note continued.

The Polish State, abandoned and deprived of its leadership, had been converted into an easy prey for all manner of events which might constitute a menace to the U. S. S. R.

It was therefore natural that the Soviet Government could not view with indifference the fate of those White Russians and Ukrainians living in Polish territory. In such circumstances it had decided to instruct the Red Army High Command to take all steps necessary to protect the lives and properties of these people.

Simultaneously, the Soviet Government intended to take measures to free the Polish people from the war into which they had been decoyed by their misguided leaders, and give them the opportunity of beginning a peaceful life.

The Polish Ambassador refused to accept the Note but conveyed its contents to his Government, thereafter awaiting further instructions.

MOLOTOV EXPLAINS

M. Molotov, the Premier and Commissar for Foreign Affairs, broadcasting yesterday to the citizens of Russia, explained the invasion in terms similar to that of the Note to Poland. He went on to say that the Soviet Union would continue its policy of neutrality with regard to the major conflict, and appealed for economy of foodstuffs to help the Red Army. Russia had all the supplies she needed but the Red Army must not lack anything so that it could fulfil its duty with honour and glory.

The position of Great Britain, in view of the pledge to defend Polish independence, will need clarification in the light of the Russian neutrality note. The whole position last night remained obscure, and British official reaction was expected some time during the evening.

A statement by the Polish Embassy in London yesterday evening condemned the Russian invasion as a flagrant act of direct aggression, by which the Soviet had flagrantly violated the Polish-Russian Pact of Non-Aggression concluded in Moscow on July 5, 1932, which, by a protocol signed in Moscow on May 5, 1934, was prolonged until December 31, 1945. No consideration of a political, military, economic or any other nature could, under any circumstances, serve as a pretext or an excuse for committing an act of aggression.

Therefore, the statement declared, by the act of wanton aggression committed yesterday morning the Soviet Union stood self-condemned as a violator of its international obligations, thus contradicting all the moral principles on which Soviet Russia had pretended to base her foreign policy since her admission into the League of Nations.

The Polish Government could not enter into any discussion of the pretext which the Soviet Government had invented in order to justify such violation. The Polish Government was continuing to function on Polish soil, and was carrying on the war against the German aggressor by all means in its power.

GERMANY APPROVES

The German News Agency earlier yesterday morning broadcast a statement to the effect that the Soviet measures did not in any way affect U.S.S.R. neutrality in the present conflict.

The announcer repeated the statements from the Soviet Note to Poland, of which he apparently had a copy, concerning Russia's unilateral abrogation of her treaties with Poland, the Russian desire to "re-establish peace and order in Eastern Poland no longer guaranteed as a result of the flight of the Polish Government," and the reference to the protection of national minorities in those areas.

The official organ of the German Foreign Office declares that the Soviet Army has entered Poland to take over the White Russian and Ukrainian minorities which for 20 years have been deprived of their nationality. Moscow has decided to put an end to the terrorism against the White Russians and Ukrainians, which had its counterpart in the ill-treatment of the German minorities in western Poland.

TURKEY AND RUSSIA

It was officially announced yesterday in Ankara that the Turkish Foreign Minister, M. Sarajoglou, had accepted an invitation by the Soviet Government to proceed to Moscow in a few days.

Turkey has always had close friendship with Russia and has maintained this friendship alongside its ties with the Western Powers.

SURRENDER OF WARSAW FEARED AS NAZIS THREATEN TO RAZE CAPITAL

POLISH ENVOY PROCEEDING TO GERMAN HIGH COMMAND

Warsaw was last night expected to surrender as the outcome of a German ultimatum threatening to shell and bombard the city into ruins unless all further resistance ceased.

A threat to annihilate the capital unless it surrendered and a warning to the civilian population to leave along two roads to the south and south-east which were being kept open by the German Army, were contained in leaflets dropped by air at 3.10 on Saturday afternoon. A Polish request for a representative to be received by the German Army Command was granted.

Earlier, according to a German statement, a military officer went through the Polish lines under a white flag and tried to submit the ultimatum to the Military Commander of the capital, but was refused an interview, and other attempts to hand over the demand were similarly unsuccessful.

24 HOURS OF GRACE

The original German ultimatum stated that when the ultimatum expired, at 3.10 yesterday morning, Warsaw would be regarded as a theatre of war, but the population would be given a further 12 hours until the afternoon to evacuate.

The capital was shelled as well as bombed from the air on Saturday, the first time that such a combined attack took place. There were many civilian casualties and much damage was caused to public and private buildings.

The German note claimed that no bombing of the civilian population occurred earlier than Saturday, the leaflets accusing the Polish Army of inciting the civilians to war contrary to international law. It was pointed out in Warsaw, however, that a civil force was formed only a few days ago on a voluntary basis, as has been done throughout history when a town was besieged.

It is stated in Berlin that the negotiations for the surrender of Warsaw have not gone far enough to permit comment on them, but the Polish surrender is thought to be only a matter of hours.

In response to the reported message from Warsaw requesting that a Polish intermediary be received, the German High Command sent a wireless message that they expect the Polish messenger to reach them by 10.00 o'clock to negotiate the evacuation of the city.

The message was sent by the Deutchlandsender to Warsaw and gave instructions as to the lighting of the cars in which the envoys were to travel. For a mile on each side of the roads hostilities should cease, and the Germans would see that there was no firing by them. They asked for confirmation from Warsaw immediately.

At 5.00 o'clock last evening, two hours after the zero hour, the Germans officially stated that there had been no bombardment of Warsaw.

(Continued on Page 2)

AMERICAN VESSEL REPORTED SUNK BY GERMAN U-BOAT

PASSENGERS PICKED UP BY NORWEGIAN BOAT

According to a Rome Wireless report yesterday, an American steamer was sunk in the Atlantic by a submarine and the crew and passengers picked up by a Norwegian boat.

The Italian liner Rex reached New York safely on Saturday carrying 1,500 American passengers. The British liner Aquitania, which carries defensive armaments, has also reached New York.

Commercial circles in Cairo state that the Egypt-American shipping line is to be resumed. Cargo rates have gone up by 50 per cent.

ITALIAN REACTION

The New York correspondent of the Rome "Telegrafo," dealing with the attitude of the United States towards the European conflict, said that it would be much influenced by the way Germany conducted submarine warfare.

If this became wholesale, Germany would alienate formidable sections of public opinion in the United States; America's attitude might then become just as hostile to Germany as it was in 1917, and be ranged alongside "wealthy Britain and France."

DANISH SHIP SUNK OFF HOLAND

It was reported yesterday that the Danish steamer the Ronda, of Bergen, was sunk on Wednesday last when it struck a mine near Terschelling, off the Dutch coast.

Seventeen persons on board, including two Americans, were stated to be missing, while the Italian steamer Providenza rescued 20 people, including four Americans, and brought them to Flushing.

The Hamburg-Amerika Line freighter Odenwald arrived at Yokohama on Saturday after reversing her course in mid-Pacific soon after the outbreak of war.

She was bound for the West Coast of the United States, but the captain put about when only 800 miles from port because he feared that the American authorities would intern her. She had only a few tons of fuel left when she reached Japan.

"POTATO JONES" SHIP

The British collier Bramhill, which under Captain "Potato" Jones became famous for running the Franco blockade in the Spanish civil war, has done it again. Today the Bramhill reached her home port safely after having run the gauntlet of German submarines and mine-fields.

When she berthed with a cargo of wood pulp for paper mills, the skipper, Captain Carter, who was first mate under "Potato" Jones, would not disclose the name of the port from which the Bramhill had left for England.

The crew, equally uninformative, would say nothing else except that it was an exciting voyage.

A damaged Polish submarine has arrived in Swedish territorial waters. The crew has been interned.

PRESIDENT OF POLAND CROSSES INTO RUMANIA

MOSCICKI'S TELEGRAM TO ROOSEVELT

CERNAUTI, Sunday (R). — A number of members of the Polish Government crossed into Rumania and arrived here this morning.

Fifty-five Polish war planes landed here today according to the Havas correspondent. They have been interned. The Germans News Agency reports from Bucharest that President Moscicki together with members of the Polish Government have crossed the Polish-Rumanian frontier at Kuty.

VIA BUCHAREST

A telegram was sent by President Moscicki to President Roosevelt declaring,

"In the past few days German air-craft operating in Poland have deliberately and methodically bombed towns and villages containing no conceivable military objectives. Thousands of civilians have been killed and wounded."

This was sent via the American Minister at Bucharest.

Representatives of 37 countries with Embassies and Legations in Warsaw had reached Cernauti (Czernowitz), on the Rumanian-Polish frontier, and are trying to establish headquarters in the very limited accommodation offered by the town, which is crowded with refugees from Poland.

FOOD SHORTAGE

The Rumanian authorities are allowing refugees across the frontier, but any military formations will be dispersed and interned. The two problems faced by the Rumanian Government were shortage of food and lack of houses.

Polish Foreign Office and other officials left Kuty today in buses, motor cars and wagons, many of which had only enough petrol to take them the few miles over the frontier.

The provisional seat of the Polish Government is reported to be at the frontier town of Zalaszczyki, but owing to the closing of the Polish-Rumanian frontier, communication with Governmental Polish circles has become impossible. The British and French Ambassadors to Poland have arrived here at Cernauti.

GERMAN REINFORCEMENTS TO THE WEST

PARIS, Sunday (R). — German attacks last night on the Western Front, one to the east of the Moselle sector and the other in the centre between the Saar valley and the Vosges, were repulsed by French forces holding positions previously captured on commanding German territory.

An announcement here states that while France has been kept almost free from German planes, French aircraft are actively bombing the German positions everywhere.

Air photographs taken of the Siegfried Line before and after bombardment are most satisfactory. They show that many of the fortifications of the line were constructed hurriedly of inferior concrete.

The French forces still occupy the heights overlooking the Saar valley. Tonight's communique states that there is nothing important to announce. Aerial activity has been reduced owing to weather conditions.

A semi-official survey of the situation on the Western Front at the end of the first fortnight of the war has been issued by Havas. It says,

ATTACKS FAIL TO DISLODGE FRENCH

On the one hand the mobilisation of the French troops is now complete. They are progressing 20 kilometres in front of the Maginot line on the entire front between the Rhine and the Moselle, penetrating German territory everywhere, while ensuring the absolute integrity of the French territory.

On the other hand, the enemy is firmly entrenched in a series of positions on the Siegfried line, in front of posts which he is defending step by step. He is beginning to benefit from the situation on the eastern front, and is now launching a movement of troops from east to west, including certain important units and a section of the air force.

This morning's French communique confirmed the arrival on the Western Front of further reinforcements of German aircraft and field forces from Poland.

A Paris despatch described the repulse of three waves of massed infantry and tanks yesterday, declaring that the offensive had failed to break through the French line at a point half-way between the Luxembourg frontier and Saarbruecken.

French troops withstood the assault in their newly-dug trenches and still hold the hills overlooking the Saar Valley. The German attack was preceded by heavy machine-gun fire and shelling, whilst intense French shelling countered the German tank formations and infantry attacks were repulsed by bayonet charges.

The German communique claimed that the French suffered considerably in several shock attacks near Zweibrucken, five miles north of the frontier.

This was the first admission that French troops were engaged in this sector of German territory.

It was also stated that aerial attacks had not taken place on German territory on the Western Front.

M. Edouard Daladier yesterday visited the French G.H.Q. on the Maginot Line.

AACHEN EVACUATED

A Reuter report from Brussels states that all families in the German frontier town of Aachen (Aix la Chapelle) have been ordered to evacuate. Only old and infirm people will leave by train or motor-car, and all others, including children over 12 and women without children, must travel on foot. Their journey to Cologne will take three days. Each person must carry his own food and a maximum of 33 lbs. of luggage. All other property must be abandoned.

It was emphasised that any efforts to escape into Belgium or Holland would result in the confiscation of all property belonging to the offenders.

It is thought in Brussels that these measures will result in the dispersal of whole families and create a painful impression on the German civil population. Aachen is only three miles away from the southernmost tip of the Luxembourg border, and is the first stop on German territory for travellers by railway from Belgium.

RUMANIA'S GERMAN MINORITY

BUCHAREST, Sunday (R). — Complete agreement has been reached concerning the treatment of German minorities, between the Government and the German Minority leaders according to the official News Agency, which also states that the Minister for the Interior recently visited the German Minority areas accompanied by the German leaders.

Herr Clodius, Chief Economic Secretary of the German Foreign Office has arrived to discuss German-Rumanian commercial arrangements. Emphasising that the visit was not concerned with the war, he said that the existing arrangements expired on October 1, and it was necessary to fix new quotas.

AFTER MIDNIGHT

The British Ministry of Information states that so far operations on the Western front have been of an exploratory character, and no major engagements have yet begun.

Following the Russian invasion of Poland M. Molotov yesterday promised Russian neutrality in the major European conflict to the representatives of 24 states including Great Britain, France, Italy, Germany, Japan and Turkey.

The Polish Embassy in Moscow announces that it is remaining in contact with the Polish Government and denies reports that it is closing down.

IBN SAUD EXPECTED TO SEVER RELATIONS WITH GERMANY

According to the London "Daily Telegraph," King Ibn Saud is expected shortly to sever relations with Germany, as the Governments of Iraq and Egypt have done. Saudi-Arabia has no diplomatic envoy in Germany, and Dr. Grobba, the German Minister at Jedda, returned home recently.

Hitler's efforts to win over Ibn Saud are stated to have failed, in spite of the munificent offers of assistance which he offered for the exploitation of the Al Hassa oil-wells, the concession for which has gone to the Standard Oil Company of California at a much lower price than that offered by Germany.

SUBSCRIPTION: Local: LP.2.500 a year: LP.1.350 a half year:— Foreign, £3.- a year. The rate for display advertisements is 200 mils per column inch. Other rates supplied on request. The right is reserved to make changes in wording or to decline or discontinue any advertisement or to postpone insertions when space is not available.

10 PAGES

THE PALESTINE POST

JERUSALEM Hassolel Road P. O. Box 81. Telephone 4233
Tel Aviv - Jaffa: 65, Allenby Road, P. O. Box 1125. 'Phone, 4251-4252.
Haifa, Khayat Square, opposite the Post Office entrance, P.O.B. 66. 'Phone 1594-1595.

SUNDAY, MAY 12, 1940 — JERUSALEM — VOL. XVI. No. 4254 PRICE 10 MILS

NAZI ADVANCE CHECKED AS ALLIES RUSH TO HELP INVADED; TOTAL AIR WAR UNLEASHED

ALL AIRPORTS RECAPTURED AFTER EPIC STRUGGLE, HEAVY GERMAN AIR LOSSES

Maintaining their stubborn stand against the German "Blitzkrieg," the Dutch and Belgian Armies yesterday brought the full sweep of their well prepared defence tactics into play and not only held up the German advance, but in some places recaptured aerodromes and other points occupied by the surprise landing parties.

The Rotterdam aerodrome, of which German parachutists had gained control, was recaptured after two hours' heavy fighting in which the Dutch troops suffered heavy losses.

German forces are reported to have reached the outer defences of Liege and are making a strong drive towards Roermond. The main German advance appears to be north of the Rhine towards Almelo, Hengelo and Arnhem, and as far north as Groningen.

Effective advances were made by the Allied troops yesterday and Aelon in South Luxemburg, was in their hands in the morning. As the khaki-clad columns began moving into Belgium, crowds of civilians who lined the roads greeted the troops with cheers, pelting them with flowers and running alongside the lorries, offering the men bottles of beer. Long columns of lorries, tanks, armoured cars, motor cycles and motor-cars moved forward in a steady stream as the British Expeditionary Force began its march into Belgium and Holland.

During their advance, British troops were bombed, though without serious casualties, and the Allied air forces retaliated by bombing German troop concentrations and columns on the move. Land fighting has so far not developed on the scale anticipated by the Germans who were frustrated by the swift Dutch action in destroying bridges on the Maas. Only one bridge across the Yssel near Voorseld was not blown up, and the Germans crossed by this route.

It was authoritatively stated last night that the British and French Armies were giving "formidable help" to the Dutch and Belgian forces. The position at the various fronts indicated that French and German advance units are in contact on both sides of the Moselle; the Belgians have fallen back on their main line of defence in accordance with the prearranged plan; and the Dutch plan of demolition and inundation is working successfully.

GERMAN AIR LOSSES

Belgian advance units were in close contact with the enemy yesterday and fighting was proceeding in several places. Most of the German parachutists who landed during Friday night in Belgium were captured, and 15 enemy planes were brought down.

In addition to the Dutch claim to have shot down 100 planes and captured 14 undamaged machines at one of the reconquered aerodromes, the British claim to have destroyed 50 aircraft on the ground and in the air, and the French report 44 German machines "killed" on French soil, making a total of over 200.

A Dutch Military Headquarters communique states:

"Anglo-French forces have come to our assistance and side by side with the Netherlands forces will defend our national territory. Our frontier troops are continually fulfilling their task, and demolition planned was duly carried out by these troops, who were later withdrawn.

"After fierce attacks by our forces lasting for 4½ hours, a village captured by the Germans on Friday was retaken on the same day. During this action the entire personnel of a German armoured train was wiped out."

A Belgian communique issued last night states that "during the day large enemy forces supported by incessant bombing by powerful formations of aircraft and by tanks attacked in the region of Maastricht. They succeeded in gaining a foothold in our defensive positions. Our troops operating in Luxemburg continued their movements according to plan and are vigorously holding up the invaders.

A Belgian High Command communique broadcast by the Brussels radio says,

"During the day of May 10 and the night of May 10/11, our troops made contact with advanced elements of the enemy. Engagements took place at several points. During the night of May 10/11, enemy parachutists landed at several points in the interior of the country. Most of them were captured or put out of action. Several bombing raids were executed against junctions of communications, but without causing important damage. Our own aviation and our air raid protection were extremely active."

British bombers attacked and destroyed German troop-carrying aircraft on the aerodrome at Rotterdam and on the beach near The Hague on Friday. The raid followed so quickly on the German occupation that the enemy had no time to establish an anti-aircraft defence system.

(Continued on Page 2)

AT A GLANCE

Hitler's long-expected blow has fallen, and three more countries were added to the growing list of Germany's victims when German troops early Friday morning invaded Holland Belgium, and Luxemburg, while Berlin proclaimed its intention to "protect" these countries against an "Allied invasion" aimed at western Germany. News of the invasion came almost simultaneously with the announcement that Britain and France had responded to appeals for immediate help from the Dutch and Belgian Governments and that Allied forces were moving.

Repeating the surprise tactics already displayed in the invasion of Denmark and Norway last month, German troops crossed the frontiers, while parachutists clad in Dutch or British uniforms tried to gain control of all aerodromes, and troops smuggled up the Dutch rivers in rubber boats, or concealed in the holds of barges, landed at Rotterdam and other places.

At the same time German planes appeared over Holland and Belgium, as well as Northern France, from 4.30 in the morning, coming over in waves, and raiding aerodromes, railway stations and factories, — Amsterdam, Brussels, Nancy and the Paris region being among the many centres attacked from the air, at heavy cost to the invader, but also to the civilian populations of these towns.

With a million men already mobilized in Holland and Belgium and strong Allied forces moving forward since Friday morning to meet the Germans, the prospect of a tremendous clash between the major belligerent land and air forces loomed for the first time since the beginning of the war. Up till last night, however, the German advance had not penetrated the first Belgian and Dutch defence zones, thus giving time for Allied help and Holland's famed "water-line" to become effective, aided by systematic defensive demolition of bridges to check the invader.

Messages were exchanged between the Sovereigns of Holland and Belgium, King George and the Pope, and a message was also sent by Queen Wilhelmina of Holland to the King of Italy. Italian press comment, however, with the notable exception of the Vatican organ, expressed no sympathy with the victims of Nazi aggression.

In Britain, where Mr. Churchill succeeded Mr. Chamberlain as Prime Minister late on Friday evening, and in France, where the Cabinet was enlarged to include representatives of the Right, political controversy disappeared before the certainty that a decisive clash was at hand.

In Washington, President Roosevelt made it known that in the opinion of the U.S. Government, aggression in Europe represented a definite challenge to American civilization and the interests of all the American Republics. Earlier warnings to Japan appeared on Friday to have had the effect of leading the Tokyo Government to drop any plans for disturbing the status quo in the Dutch East Indies. Precautions are being taken there and in the Dutch W. Indies where Allied units landed.

CHURCHILL AT THE HELM

CHAMBERLAIN REMAINING IN CABINET; LABOUR JOINS

The New War Cabinet

LONDON, Saturday (R). — The new War Cabinet is officially announced as follows:

Prime Minister and Minister of Defence — Winston Churchill;
Lord President of the Council — Neville Chamberlain;
Lord Privy Seal — Clement Attlee;
Foreign Minister — Lord Halifax;
Minister without Portfolio — Arthur Greenwood.

The following are also appointed:

First Lord of the Admiralty — A. V. Alexander;
Secretary of War — Anthony Eden;
Secretary for Air — Sir Archibald Sinclair.

The leaders of the three Parties participating in the Government, whether members of the War Cabinet or not, will be consulted when questions arise affecting the general character and aims of the Government, including the conditions of peace. The remaining appointments will be announced on Monday.

LONDON, Saturday (R). —Political developments in Great Britain since the Parliamentary vote on Wednesday night reached their culmination point yesterday evening when it was announced that Mr. Winston Churchill had succeeded Mr. Neville Chamberlain in the office of Prime Minister and First Lord of the Treasury.

Mr. Chamberlain was received by the King in audience at Buckingham Palace shortly after 5 o'clock yesterday and Mr. Churchill saw the King five minutes after the retiring Premier had left the Palace.

The Executive of the Labour Party met at Bournemouth yesterday, and later announced that they had unanimously decided to share responsibility to the full in a new Government under a new Prime Minister who would command the confidence of the nation.

Mr. Churchill, who is still occupying quarters at the Admiralty and working from there, had conversations today with the Opposition leaders and various Conservatives.

In France, the most general comment on Mr. Churchill's appointment was, "He is the man that Hitler fears most," while a generous welcome was given in Washington where it had long been felt, rightly or wrongly, that the Allied war effort could not attain its maximum drive under the old leadership.

REYNAUD CABINET STRENGTHENED

M. Paul Reynaud re-shuffled his Cabinet last night by including two representatives of the Right as Ministers without portfolio. They are M. Louis Marin, a former Minister and President of the Republican Federation, and M. Ybarnegaray, Vice-President of the French Social Party (Croix de Feu). Both are to be members of the War Cabinet.

M. Reynaud in a broadcast announced that French troops crossed the frontier into Belgium between 5 and 7 o'clock yesterday morning and added:

"Hitler has dropped his mask. Now it is France's turn to show the way with her troops and planes. Everyone is ready to do his duty. France has drawn her sword."

General Gamelin yesterday issued the following Order of the Day to the Army:

'The attack which we have foreseen since last October was launched this morning. Germany has engaged in a war to the death against us. The password for France and all her Allies is 'Courage, Energy and Confidence'."

HEAVY RAIDS ON BELGIAN, DUTCH, FRENCH TOWNS

MANY CIVILIAN CASUALTIES

PARIS, Saturday (R). — Numerous civilian casualties resulted from yesterday's air raids over various parts of France, particularly in the north and north-east, the Loiret and Champagne districts, but the material damage was relatively small.

Among the towns raided were the open cities of Nancy, Lille, Lyons, Colmar, Pontoise, Luxueil, Bethune, Choques, Lens, Dunkirk, Hazebrouck, Calais, Abbeville, Doulens and Albert. Bombs were dropped not only on aerodromes, railway-stations, workshops and mines, but also on purely civilian centres.

Enemy aircraft early yesterday morning also unsuccessfully attacked several aerodromes occupied by the R.A.F. in France. Five German planes at least were shot down, and four others were so badly damaged that they probably did not get home.

Anti-aircraft guns on the Thames estuary and at Dover fired at raiders who appeared off the south-east coast of England, and R.A.F. Fighter Command aircraft were in action at a number of points. While on patrol over the North Sea, Coastal Command planes shot down three Dorniers and damaged a fourth. Four incendiary bombs were dropped at Chilham, near Canterbury.

CAPITALS BOMBED

A serious toll of civilian casualties has been claimed by raiding German aircraft over the Low Countries.

Both Brussels and Amsterdam were yesterday subjected to heavy air attacks as were also the towns of Renaix, Louvain and Verviers, names familiar in the early stages of the German invasion of Belgium in 1914. No military objective was hit in Brussels but there were numerous civilian killed and injured.

Three air raid alarms were sounded in the Belgian capital. Thirty people were killed at Cappellen, near Antwerp, as the result of the crash of a German bomber. Thirty-seven were killed and 61 injured, many of them women and children, in the air attack on the Brussels aerodrome district on Friday.

Amsterdam was bombed for 25 minutes early yesterday morning, massed German bombers coming over the airport and surrounding buildings. Twenty minutes after the first attack, the bombers appeared over the city again. One plane was brought down in a suburb.

Both in Belgium and Holland the raids failed to affect the morale of the people, and city streets maintained their normal busy appearance.

RETALIATION THREAT

Both the British and French Governments last night proclaimed that they reserved to themselves the right to take any action they thought appropriate in the event of the bombing by enemy planes of the civilian populations of the United Kingdom, France or their Allies. The reply to President Roosevelt's appeal sent last September was recalled.

The British Home Office has warned residents of the United Kingdom of the possibility of German parachute landings, similar to those in Belgium and Holland, where the Nazis wore uniforms calculated to deceive observers. Citizens were asked to report immediately to the nearest police-station any such attempt, which were most likely to be made during black-out hours.

All R.A.F. leave has been stopped and all personnel already on leave recalled. The 29th Air Ministry casualty list records that 33 have been killed in action or otherwise, 10 wounded, 12 died, and 37 missing.

AFTER MIDNIGHT

Mr. Stephen Early, President Roosevelt's secretary, stated that the President was gratified at the reaction to his speech when he said that aggression abroad had presented a definite challenge to American civilization. The speech has brought several thousand telegrams to the White House. Nine out of ten were favourable and the remaining ten per cent favoured "Peace at any price."

Before the Italian liner, Rex, sailed from New York yesterday, Signor Italo Verrando, the General Manager of the Italian Line, said that he had received private advices from Rome which "assured him that Italy would not enter the war," according to the Dow Jones Agency.

Other Reports of the Invasion—P.5

ALLIED TROOPS IN DUTCH W. INDIES

LONDON, Saturday (R). — It is learned in authoritative quarters that the Netherlands, British and French Governments have been in consultation on the steps to be taken to prevent possible German attempts to sabotage the important oil refineries at Curacao and Aruba in the Dutch West Indies.

In view of the danger that the local authorities might not have sufficient forces at their command to deal with attacks it was decided that an Allied force should at once be dispatched to cooperate with the local administration in the execution of the necessary measures for security.

Allied troops have already landed and been welcomed cordially. The United States Government is being informed of the position by Allied diplomatic representatives in Washington.

"RALLY BEHIND NEW LEADER"—CHAMBERLAIN

OVERTHROWING THE "WILD BEAST"

LONDON, Saturday (R). — Urging the fullest support for his successor, Mr. Neville Chamberlain broadcast at 8 o'clock last night a statement over the B.B.C. home and overseas stations on the reasons for his resignation.

With deep emotion he spoke of the fight against the "wild beast that has sprung upon us out of his lair."

The full text of Mr. Chamberlain's address was as follows:

"Early this morning without warning or excuse, Hitler added another to the horrible crimes which have already disgraced his name by a sudden attack on Holland, Belgium and Luxemburg.

"In all history no other man has been responsible for such hideous total human sufferings and misery as he.

"He has chosen a moment when perhaps it seemed to him that this country was entangled in the throes of a political crisis and when he might find it divided against itself. If he has counted on our internal differences to help him, he has miscalculated the mind of this people.

RESTORING CONFIDENCE

"I am not now going to make any comment on the debate which took place on Wednesday and Tuesday last, but when it was over I had no doubt in my mind that some drastic action must be taken if confidence was to be restored to the House of Commons and the war carried on with vigour and energy which are essential to victory. What was that action to be? It was clear that in this hour of the war what was needed was the formation of a Government that would include members of the Labour and Liberal Opposition and thus present a United Front to the enemy.

"What had to be ascertained were the conditions necessary to enable such a Government to be formed and to this question I devoted myself with the assistance of some colleagues yesterday afternoon. By the afternoon of today it was apparent that the essential unity could be secured under another Prime Minister, though not under myself.

"In these circumstances my duty was plain. I sought an audience with the King this evening and tendered to him my resignation, which His Majesty has been pleased to accept. His Majesty has now entrusted to my friend and colleague, Mr. Winston Churchill, the task of forming a new administration on a national basis, and in this task I have no doubt he will be successful.

WILL REMAIN IN CABINET

"For this purpose my other colleagues in the Government have intimated to me that they will place their resignations in Mr. Churchill's hands, but they will of course retain their present offices pending the appointment of a new Government. I should perhaps say that Mr. Churchill has expressed to me his strong desire that I should be a member of the War Cabinet and I have told him that I will gladly give him any assistance I can in that capacity.

"Now as this is my last message to you from No. 10 Downing Street, there are one or two things I should like to say to you.

A HEAVY LOAD

"During the period, it is almost exactly three years, that I have been Prime Minister, I have borne a heavy load of anxiety and responsibility. As long as I believed that there was a chance of preserving peace honourably, I strove to take it. When the last hope vanished and the war could not longer be avoided, I strove equally hard to wage it with all my might.

"Perhaps you will remember that in my broadcast of September 3, I told you we should be fighting against evil things. My words proved to be insufficient to describe the vileness of those who now staked everything on the great battle just beginning. Perhaps it may be at least some relief to know that this battle, though it may last for days and even weeks, has ended the period of waiting and uncertainty.

"For the hour has come when we are to be put to the test as the innocent people of Holland, Belgium, and France are being tested already, and you and I must rally behind our new leader and with our united strength and with unshakeable confidence, fight and work until this wild beast that has sprung upon us out of his lair be finally disarmed and overthrown."

PALESTINE'S WORLD FAMOUS PRODUCTS

KABRIA PURE TABLE-WATER

Bottled only by Spinney's Ltd.

SUBSCRIPTION:
Local: LP.2.500 a year; LP.1.250 half year: For-eign, 25.- a year.
The rate for display advertisements is 200 mils per column inch.
Other rates supplied on request.
The right is reserved to make changes in wording or to decline or discontinue any advertisement or to postpone insertion when space is not available.

JERUSALEM
Hassolel Road
P. O. Box 81.
Telephone 4233

Tel Aviv - Jaffa:
65, Allenby Road,
P. O. Box 1126,
'Phone, 4251-4252.

Haifa. Khayat
Square, opposite
the Post Office en-
trance, P.O.B. 44.
'Phone 1594-1595.

Order your copy of the
MIDDLE EAST SUPPLEMENT
NOW
From your Newsdealer.
To be published shortly.

THE
PALESTINE POST

THE PALESTINE POST

WEDNESDAY, JUNE 5, 1940   JERUSALEM   VOL. XVI. No. 4275 PRICE 10 MILS

FRENCH HOLD DUNKIRK AS WEYGAND PLANS
ARTIFICIAL SWAMP AIDED ALLIES

Large French forces were still vigorously resisting in the Dunkirk area today and undertaking local counter-offensives, thus compelling the Germans to retain at least 15 divisions in that area at a period when time is of the greatest value to General Weygand in making his preparations.

The possibility of a German attack between Abbeville and Amiens must not be overlooked, although it may not be necessary for General Weygand to wait to be attacked.

The French positions, stretching from the sea to the Maginot Line, have strong natural river obstacles except at certain places: there being a gap of 12 miles between the Somme and the Oise and another of 18 miles between the Aisne and the Meuse.

PARIS, Tuesday (R).—The French military spokesman today said that in Monday's air raid, the whole of the Paris region as well as Paris itself was attacked. Futile German attacks were continuing against the Dunkirk fortified area, but in spite of artillery and air bombardment, the embarkation of troops was continuing.

Describing the fight for Dunkirk, the spokesman said that water defences had been the greatest help. The water had thoroughly saturated the soil not only where it showed on the surface but also far in advance of the so-called "water line." The result was that every shelter-hole dug by the Germans was filled with water and liquid mud. Tanks became embedded in the morass.

Allied infantrymen and Marines held the dry ground covering the artificial marshes with automatic arms and pinned down to the shifting soil the waves of attacking Germans. The dunes provide safe shelters for defenders. Germans managing to get a foothold on the solid ground were immediately flung back into the marsh, and meanwhile the troops on the beaches continued their embarkation in perfect order.

R. A. F. STRIKES HARD

Marshalling yards were bombed, oil-tank wagons set alight, and troop convoys machine-gunned by low-flying bombers during extensive British raids on Sunday night over north-west Germany.

Moving trains at Soest, an important railway junction east of Dortmund, were hit and brought to a standstill, and direct hits registered on loaded goods waggons. Road and rail junctions at Osnabruck were heavily attacked for the second night.

Enemy air bases at Rotterdam, Deventer and Wesel were also visited, and at Wesel bombs burst on a large hangar used by German bomber squadrons. A violent explosion and a fierce fire seemed as though they came from a petrol dump.

A long convoy of armoured vehicles near Aachen, located by parachute flares, was heavily bombed and then machine-gunned. Heavy explosions continued as ammunition or petrol lorries were ignited by incendiary bombs and blew up.

A similar tale of damage and havoc caused by French aircraft was contained in a Paris war Ministry communique giving an account of violent bombardments of several airfields in Germany on Sunday night by large French bomber squadrons which dropped more than 30 tons of high explosives.

Considerable losses were inflicted on enemy motorized columns, which were attacked several times. All French aircraft returned safely.

Early on Monday afternoon, a strong force of German bombers operating over French territory was engaged by fighters and anti-aircraft batteries, and many enemy machines brought down.

AFTER MIDNIGHT

The War Office announces that General Ironside is organizing for home defence small groups of highly mobile and strongly armed troops who will be called the "Ironsides." There will be many hundreds of these formed from the Regular Army.

The French Admiralty in a communique states that the last land and naval forces defending Dunkirk were embarked during Monday night. The port has been rendered unusable. Throughout the operations the French navy lost 7 destroyers and a supply ship.

It is revealed that Mr. Cordell Hull has written to Mr. Sol Bloom heartily approving the resolution concerning the transfer of Western Hemisphere territory from one non-American nation to another. He added that he would be glad to recommend the resolution to a favourable consideration by Congress.

President Roosevelt has submitted a request to Congress to sanction expenditure of $1,277,000,000 for defence purposes, including the construction of 68 naval vessels and a large number of army aeroplanes.

335,000 MEN SAVED FROM DUNKIRK
PREMIER TELLS HOW FLANDERS DEFEAT TURNED TO VICTORY

LONDON, Tuesday (R). — The full story of the evacuation of the Allied troops from Dunkirk and the fall, after stubborn defence, of Calais, was given in the House of Commons this afternoon by Mr. Winston Churchill who announced that 335,000 of the B.E.F. and the French had been saved, leaving only about 30,000 British casualties in Flanders.

After briefly describing the invasion of Holland, the Prime Minister said that from the moment that the French defences at Sedan and on the Meuse were broken in the second week of May, the only thing that could have saved the French and British troops who entered Belgium at the request of the Belgian King was a rapid retreat to Amiens and the south.

But this strategic fact was not immediately realized. The French High Command first thought that they would be able to close the gap, and the armies of the north were under their orders. Moreover, retirement then would have involved the almost certain destruction of the fine Belgian Army of over 20 divisions and the abandonment of the whole of Belgium.

THE GERMAN SWEEP

Therefore, when the force and scope of German penetration was realized, and when the new French Generalissimo, General Weygand, assumed command in place of General Gamelin, an effort was made by the French and British armies in Belgium to keep on to the hold of the right hand of the Belgians and to their own right hand to the newly formed guard on the Somme in great strength to clasp it.

The Germans, however, swept to the rear and right of the armies of the north. Eight or nine armoured divisions each of about 400 armoured vehicles of different kinds were employed. This force cut off all communications between the British and the main French armies. It severed all communications for food and ammunition, which reached the troops from Amiens at first and afterwards through Abbeville. It then swept off to the coast to Boulogne and Calais and almost to Dunkirk.

Behind this armoured and mechanized onslaught came numbers of German divisions in lorries and behind them again there plodded the comparatively slow mass of the ordinary German army — the German people always so ready to be led to trampling down in other lands the liberties and comforts they had never known themselves.

"This armoured scythe stroke almost reached Dunkirk — almost, but not quite. Boulogne and Calais were the scene of desperate fighting. The Guards defended Boulogne for a while and were withdrawn by orders from this country. The Rifle Brigade, the 16th Rifles and the Queen Victoria Rifles, with a battalion of British tanks and Frenchmen, in all about 4,000 strong, defended Calais to the last (Cheers).

"The British Brigadier was given an hour to surrender. He spurned the offer (cheers) and after four days of intense street fighting silence reigned over Calais, which marked the end of the memorable resistance. Only 30 unwounded survivors were brought off by the Navy and we do not know the fate of their comrades.

Their sacrifice, however, was not in vain.

At least two armoured divisions, which would otherwise have been turned against the B.E.F., had to be sent to overcome them. They have added another page to the glories of the light division and the time gained enabled the waterline as far as Gravelines to be opened and to be held by the French troops.

Thus it was that the port of Dunkirk was kept open. When it was found impossible for the armies in the north to reopen the communications through Amiens with the French armies, only one choice remained. It seemed indeed forlorn. The British, French and Belgian armies were almost surrounded. Their sole line of retreat was to the neighbouring beaches. They were pressed on every side by heavy attacks and far outnumbered."

AIR VICTORY

"We must not assign to this deliverance the attributes of victory; wars are not won by evacuations, (hear, hear) but there was a victory inside this deliverance which should be noted and it was gained by the Air Force.

"Many of our soldiers coming back had not seen the Air Force at work. They only saw the bombers which escaped their protective attack. They underrate its achievements. I have heard much talk of that, and that is why I go out of my way to tell the House about it.

"This was a great trial of strength between the British Air Force and the German. Can you conceive of any greater military objective for the power of Germany in the air than to make all evacuation from those beaches impossible and to sink the ships which were displayed almost to the number of 1,000? Could there have been an objective for the whole purpose of the war of greater military importance, of greater military significance than this? They tried hard and they were beaten back; they were frustrated in their attacks. We got the army away, and they paid fourfold for any losses they inflicted upon us.

"Very large formations of German aeroplanes — and we know this is a very brave race — have turned on several occasions from an attack by one quarter their number of the R.A.F. and dispersed in different directions. Twelve aeroplanes have been hunted by two. One aeroplane was driven into the water and cast away by the mere charge of a British aeroplane which had no more ammunition. (Cheers).

KNIGHTS OF THE AIR

"All our types and all our pilots have been vindicated, Hurricanes, Spitfires and Defiants. Let us now define what they at present have to face. When we consider how much greater would be our advantage in the defence of the air above these islands than overseas, I must say I find in these facts a sure basis upon which a practical and reassuring thought may rest, and I pay my tribute to these young airmen. (Cheers).

"There never has been, I suppose, in all the history of war such opportunity for youth. The Knights of the Round Table, the Crusaders, all fall back into the past, not only distant but prosaic.

"These young men going forth every morning to guard their native land, to guard all that we stand for, these men going forward holding in their hands these instruments of colossal and shattering power, for whom it may be said that every morning brought forth the noble chance, these young men deserve our gratitude and deserve to rank among the highest of all brave men who in so many ways and on so many occasions are ready and will continue to be ready to give their all for their native land."

DISASTER SEEMED CERTAIN

"When a week ago I was asked by this House to pick this afternoon for a statement, I feared that it would be my hard lot to announce the greatest military disaster in our long history.

"I thought — and some good judges agreed with me — that perhaps twenty or thirty thousand men might be reembarked, but it certainly seemed that the whole First French Army and the whole British Expeditionary Force north of the Amiens-Abbeville gap would be broken up in the open field or might have to capitulate for lack of food and ammunition.

"These were the very hard and heavy tidings for which I called on this House and the nation to prepare themselves. The whole root, core and brain of the British Army on which and around which we were to build and are to build (cheers) the great British armies of the later stages of the war, seemed about to perish on the field, or to be led into ignoble and starving captivity.

"That was the prospect a week ago, but another blow which might well have proved fatal was yet to fall upon us. The King of the Belgians had called upon us to come to his aid. Had not this ruler and his Government severed themselves from the Allies who rescued their country from extinction in the last war, had they not sought refuge in what has proved fatal neutrality, then the British and French armies from the very outset might not only have saved Belgium but perhaps even Poland. Yet at the last moment when Belgium was already invaded, King Leopold called upon us to come to his aid and even at the last moment we came.

KING LEOPOLD'S SURRENDER

"He and his strong and efficient army of nearly half a million guarded our eastern flank and thus kept open our only line of retreat to the sea. Suddenly, without prior consultation, without the least possible notice, without the advice of his Ministers, and upon his own personal act, he sent a plenipotentiary to the German High Command, surrendered his forces and exposed our whole flank and means of security. (cries of Shame.).

(Continued on Page 5)

(Continued on Page 5)

War Communiques
275TH AND 276TH DAYS
FRENCH — Monday Night

The enemy continued to attack ferociously our positions around Dunkirk where they encountered vigorous resistance and unceasing counter-attacks by our troops. The French Navy, like the British Navy, is co-operating under enemy fire in the defence of Dunkirk and has successfully proceeded with the embarkation of troops ordered by the Command, giving throughout an example of the greatest bravery.

The enemy today without success launched a local attack against our advance posts in the region of Saint Avold. He is bringing up reinforcements on the right bank of the Aisne and making closer contact with our positions to the west of the Saar.

In the course of last night (Sunday), our bombing aviation attacked numerous fields as well as lines of communications.

Paris and the Paris region were attacked early this afternoon by a considerable bombing expedition strongly protected by German fighters. This expedition came up against the defence of our fighters and anti-aircraft batteries, which inflicted on it heavy losses. Most of our pilots were equipped with the most modern machines.

According to the first information to hand, 17 enemy planes were brought down as already counted.

Tuesday Morning

During the night embarkation went on actively in the Dunkirk region thanks to the resistance of our troops and despite the ceaseless difficulties caused by enemy pressure. On the rest of the front, nothing to report.

FRENCH THREATEN REPRISALS FOR BOMBING PARIS

Paris, Tuesday (R). — Retaliatory action against German towns for yesterday's violent aerial bombing of Paris was forecast by the Paris wireless in a German-language broadcast late last night. The announcer said:

It is to be expected that the German action will not remain unanswered and German towns will have to bear the consequences of this bombardment, which was contrary to the laws of warfare.

Considered the biggest air raid yet carried out by the Germans, who used heavy bombers capable of carrying several tons of explosives, the attack took a toll of 254 killed and 652 injured; 195 of the dead were civilians and 59 military, while 545 of the wounded were civilians and 107 military; 25 German planes were brought down.

The region of Le Havre was also bombed for three hours between 10.15 last night and 1.30 this morning, high-explosive bombs being dropped. Private houses were hit and victims were taken from the wreckage.

INDISCRIMINATE BOMBING

The purpose of the raid on Paris apparently was not only to inflict damage of a military nature but to cause panic among the population. But as an attempt to cause panic, the raid failed, and Parisians soon resumed their normal pursuits after the "All Clear" was sounded.

At least six schools were hit, and a school-building turned into a hospital suffered hits by 15 bombs, two orderlies being killed. The dead include an American.

Some bombs fell inside the city on private houses and others in the suburbs. Countless bomb craters, ruined buildings, smashed windows, streets littered with debris and glass, and other scenes of havoc were watched in the affected areas by large and curious crowds.

Most of the victims apparently were caught owing to their own temerity or carelessness in not seeking shelter when the alarm was sounded.

MR. BULLITT'S ESCAPE

The fact that Mr. William Bullitt, the American Ambassador, was almost killed in the raid came as a shock in Washington, as it indicated the indiscriminate nature of the German bombing. There was much speculation as to what the effect would have been if the Ambassador had been killed, especially in view of the recent ebb of "isolationist" feeling.

The French press today stigmatizes the attack as a flagrant violation of the solemn undertaking by belligerents at the outbreak of war that air attacks would not be made on civilians.

Radio stations in Berlin, Hamburg, Stuttgart, Munich and Nuremberg were off the air at 11.40 last night but the latter two were back again shortly after midnight.

A statement by the German News Agency asserting that 53 civilians, including 20 children, were killed when Allied bombers raided Freiburg is stated by the British Air Ministry to be obviously a German attempt to justify their bombing of Paris. The alleged raid was not given a date and the same allegation that Freiburg was bombed and several children killed was made some weeks ago, when it was denied by the British and French authorities.

War Fever in Italy Mounts as Cabinet Holds Routine Meeting
Momentous Decision Not Announced

ROME, Tuesday (R). — Bills presented by various Ministries regarding measures of ordinary administration are stated in an official communique to have been the main business discussed at a Cabinet meeting held for 1½ hours this morning under Signor Mussolini's chairmanship.

Among other measures, the Cabinet passed a decree extending to Italian Africa the law on national organization in time of war. Other measures approved include bills concerning employment of women to replace men called to the Colours and the allocation of fresh credits for naval construction.

The announcement caused surprise as the eagerly-awaited meeting was thought to be concerned with more momentous issues, and took place at a time when the conviction was growing among Italians that their country was about to enter the war.

It was generally assumed that the session would be marked by a momentous decision for war or peace, although whether the Duce would announce Italy's entry or wait a few days remained a subject of considerable conjecture.

EXHIBITION POSTPONED

The atmosphere in Rome today was very calm, at least outwardly. It was rumoured that a meeting of the Fascist Grand Council was been fixed for tonight as had a meeting of the Supreme Defence Council. There was little belief in Paris reports that the Italian Government's next move would be a final proposal for an international conference.

Rome papers have been allowed to reproduce these reports, with the alleged negative reaction from London and Paris.

Yesterday's postponement of the Rome World Exhibition was regarded by the public as further evidence of coming intervention. The same impression was created by the announcement that military doctors and veterinary surgeons are to be called up on Thursday.

The press today was still filled with anti-Allied reports and despatches.

STOP PRESS
NEW YORK, Tuesday (R). —

After some days suspension the Italian Line has resumed advertisements of trans-Atlantic passenger sailings.

patches from Tangier alleging that the Allies are planning an attack there. Other reports claimed that Italians were being persecuted in Algeria.

The press also predicted a great German offensive against the French line along the Somme and the Aisne, declaring that the attack would be supported by 8,000 planes. "Popolo di Roma" wrote,

"Germany has succeeded in dividing the enemy's forces. Now she is preparing to conquer each one separately."

The fact that the Italian Cabinet adopted only administrative measures did not surprise French official circles, who believe that the Duce is still hesitating over the final decision.

It is pointed out that relations between the thousands of Italians living in France and the French people are excellent, and no incident had occurred which would warrant the tension in Rome. All French approaches to Rome to establish contact have met with complete indifference, while Italy has never officially formulated her demands.

It is stressed that everything leads to the belief that Germany is about to attempt a new offensive against France. In these circumstances it would be important from the German point of view that as large a French force as possible be kept in another sector.

Undoubtedly, if Italy entered the war, French troops would have to be sent to the south-east, but France would have to be certain of Italy's entry before sending them. Some observers are even asking themselves whether Italy's insistence that she is about to enter the war is not aimed at convincing France of this, thus rendering Germany an important service.

EGYPT WATCHES ITALY
TAKING FINAL PRECAUTIONS

CAIRO, Tuesday (R). — While the world press seems of the opinion that Italy will enter the war shortly, Egyptian opinion on Italian intentions is divided, largely owing to the display of Allied military and naval strength in the Near East.

Many observers here believe that it would be madness for Italy to challenge such well-equipped and strategically-placed forces, whose first action would be the closing of the Suez Canal and the isolation of Ethiopia from Italy.

Nevertheless the Egyptian Government is putting the final touches to precautionary measures for the country's defence.

NO PASSENGERS

It was stated today that the Italian steamer Galilean (4,013 tons), due to sail from Alexandria tomorrow for Syria to pick up passengers, is leaving tomorrow direct for Naples without passengers.

BLACK-OUT CONTINUES
PEDESTRIANS URGED TO WEAR WHITE

It was notified yesterday that the black-out arrangements as practiced on Monday night are to be maintained in force throughout Palestine until further notice. The hours are from 9 p.m. to 4 a.m.

Between 9 o'clock and 11 o'clock this morning there will be anti-aircraft firing practice in Haifa.

A notice issued last night advises motorists to use cars as little as possible during the black-out to avoid accidents and not to leave vehicles parked in any main thoroughfare where other motorists could not see them.

Pedestrians are urged to wear white or light-coloured clothing at night, as motorists could not see them otherwise, and also to keep off the road unless crossing it. Pedestrians could not see the motorist but the motorist could not see pedestrians.

The notice added, "Watch your step!"

DON'T BE VAGUE---ASK FOR HAIG
NO FINER WHISKY GOES INTO ANY BOTTLE

THE
PALESTINE
POST

FRIDAY
DECEMBER 13, 1940

VOL. XIV No. 4435.
PRICE 10 MILS

SMASHING BRITISH VICTORY IN AFRICAN WAR

DEATH OF LORD LOTHIAN

British Ambassador in Washington

WASHINGTON, Thursday (R). — The death took place this morning of the Marquess of Lothian, C.H., M.A., the British Ambassador to Washington, at 58. The District of Columbia coroner announces that Lord Lothian died at the British Embassy at Washington at 3 o'clock this morning, local time.

The British Embassy announced that the cause of Lord Lothian's death was uremic infection (a form of blood poisoning.) The delay in announcing his death may be explained by the desire formally to notify President Roosevelt first. The President is at present cruising in the Caribbean.

Last Statement

The Marquess of Lothian's last statement was read on Wednesday evening by Mr. Neville Butler, Counsellor of the British Embassy, at the American Farm Bureau Association dinner at Baltimore. It had been stated that Lord Lothian was unable to attend himself owing to illness.

With American help in aeroplanes, munitions, ships on the sea and in the field of finance, Britain was sure of victory, the statement declared, and it ended with a graphic account of the past, present and possible future course of the war by saying:

If you back us, you will not be backing a quitter. The issue depends largely on what you decide to do.

A Hard Year Ahead

In the course of his speech, Lord Lothian declared that Hitler had lost the second round, but 1941 would be a hard and dangerous year. He held the opinion that the Axis-Japan Pact made it nakedly clear that the ultimate objective was one of military strategy.

If Britain's control of the Atlantic should be sufficiently weakened to cause doubt where the American Fleet should be stationed, a two-ocean attack on us both in the Atlantic and the Pacific will be simultaneously launched. We are therefore both vitally interested in decisively and rapidly defeating a naval attack on the communications of the British Isles.

The British Ambassador declared that the young nations of the British Commonwealth were fast getting into their stride.

Victory will follow Hitler's failure to destroy Britain from the air and sea. With an uninterrupted flow of American munitions, we are confident that we can win, and win decisively, in 1942, if not before.

(Biographical Note and Picture—Page 6)

ALLIED WAR COMMUNIQUES

BRITISH G.H.Q. CAIRO.

British advanced troops in the Western Desert are in contact with the Italian Forces which are continuing their withdrawal to the west. Meanwhile, the clearing of the battlefield is proceeding. It is impossible to give accurate figures, but the latest estimate of prisoners taken exceeds 20,000, with tanks, guns and equipment of all types. One Corps Commander, and two General Officers Commanding divisions are among the hundreds of Italian officers prisoner now in British hands.

In the Sudan British patrols continue successfully to harass the enemy.

BRITISH ADMIRALTY

Thursday Morning. — British naval forces have been harassing the enemy retreating along the coast during the night of December 10. On December 11 they also bombarded enemy columns on the roads round Sollum.

GREEK H. C. No. 46.

Thursday Morning. — The advance is continuing on several parts of the front in spite of powerful enemy resistance. Prisoners and war material have been taken. No enemy air raids on Greek territory have taken place.

AFTER MIDNIGHT

A Hungarian-Yugoslav friendship pact was signed in Belgrade last night, according to the German News Agency.

"A civil war hatching in France is forestalled only by the Army of Occupation," says the Paris correspondent of the Madrid "Ya," who adds, "A further cabinet reshuffle is being discussed in Paris."

The movement in favour of granting financial aid to Britain received powerful and unexpected support yesterday from Mr. Winthrop Aldrich, one of America's leading bankers, who said that funds should now be made available "promptly and generously" for Great Britain's financial needs.

ITALIAN COUNTER-DRIVES FAIL IN ALBANIA

Heavy Fighting in Pogradetz Sector

BELGRADE, Thursday. — Heavy fighting continues in the Pogradetz sector, from the town itself on Lake Ochrida to Moskopolis, some 30 miles to the south-west. Guns of all calibres have been used by both sides in continued artillery duels, and it has been noticed that the Italians are using new heavy guns.

In one sector, the Italians continually counter-attacked and the Greeks here were forced to relinquish some unimportant positions for better ground a few hundred yards back.

Severe fighting is also taking place on the northern flanks of the Motsa mountains near Pogradetz, where Italian resistance is said to have been heartened by rumours of the approach of the first reinforcements. A column of Italian armoured motor-cycles passing through a line north of Pogradetz was ambushed by the Greeks, and 11 motorcycles captured.

Violent fighting also continued today in the Teveli sector, where the Italians, who have been reinforced, are making desperate efforts to prevent the Greeks from descending into the river valley.

In the Skumbi valley, which leads to El Basan, the Greeks advanced to positions in front of Vrepka. Desperate Italian counter-attacks intended to hold up Greek progress have failed. North of Pogradetz, where fierce fighting is progressing, the Greeks are maintaining their positions, despite all attacks.

Along Lake Ochrida and the coast road, the Greeks have advanced slightly, despite snow and rain. Groups of Italians are crossing the border to surrender to the Yugoslav authorities.

SOVIET EYES

MOSCOW, Thursday (R). — Two "Pravda" headlines — "British Offensive in Western Desert" and "Italians Retreat in Albania" — signify Soviet interest in the present fighting. The "Pravda" maintains that the war in Greece and the attack on Taranto are really having effect on the Italian army in Libya.

GREEKS GATHER IN FRUITS OF SUCCESS

NEW MOVEMENT IN PREPARATION

ATHENS, Thursday (R). — While the Greek Army continues methodically to gather in the results of recent successes, reports from the front today suggest that a major tactical movement designed to produce new gains is steadily developing.

The Greeks are now meeting stubborn opposition from the Italians, especially in the north, but they are systematically pursuing the methods which have hitherto brought them victory.

The Italian left wing is retreating towards the heights of Khiamarra and all attempts to resist have failed. In the region of [illegible] troops advancing further into the interior of Albania have taken heights of great strategic value.

Still further north, the Italians have been driven from strongly fortified heights which are so valuable strategically that they tried to re-take the positions but suffered the most severe losses. The Greeks are giving the Italians no breathing space to build a new fortified line and are advancing like a steam-roller.

Behind-Lines Confusion

Reports of growing confusion behind the Italian lines, received mainly from Italian prisoners, are becoming increasingly frequent.

It appears that the Italian failure to stabilize any concentrated series of positions is due to the disputes between the commanders of the various units, who are trying to put the blame for the continued failure on each other. The uncertainty is further increased by the number of changes in the High Command during the actual fighting.

It is generally confirmed by officer prisoners that the command has been given to shoot any soldiers retreating without orders. Some Italians who recently came up as reinforcements were unaware that they were fighting on Albanian territory, having been told that they were inside Greece.

Air Force Inactive

Largely as a result of bad flying conditions and the damage done to Durazzo and Tirana aerodromes by bombing, Italian planes, apart from the Northern front, have played little part in checking the Greeks.

It has been necessary to requisition some Italian planes to provision the large rear-guard which has been holding on to its position until the very last moment in order to slow down the Greek advance.

DEMONSTRATIONS IN JEBEL DRUZE

It is reported that pro-British demonstrations of a spontaneous and widespread character were held this week in Suwaida, capital town of the Jebel Druze, in Syria.

Demonstrators marched through the streets openly carrying the Union Jack and shouting, "Long live Britain!" and "We Want England!"

They were dispersed by French military and police and it is reported that a number was injured.

M. PUAUX LEAVES

M. Gabriel Puaux, former High Commissioner for Syria and the Lebanon, left Beirut yesterday afternoon for France on board the s. s. Athos.

Secrecy about General Dentz
— Report on Page 3

THE DASH TO SEA

RUTHLESS DESERT BATTLE

By Gordon Young,
Reuters Special Correspondent in Egypt

CAIRO, Thursday. — The dull monotonous booming of the guns of the British Fleet many miles away is clearly audible here. The warships are pounding Italian coastal positions.

The battle for the Sidi Barrani area has been bitter and ruthless. The eventual outcome of the present operations is impossible to forecast because of the rapidity with which the situation is changing. But a positive balance has already been achieved by the British, as is indicated by the capture, as one Officer expressed it, of "many prisoners," together with quantities of war materials, most of which is in good condition.

Despite days of gruelling fighting — some of which took place in thick sandstorms — the advance British troops are now in the highest spirit, jubilant at the successes achieved after months of waiting.

Blitzkrieg Method Adopted

It is not yet possible to give a detailed account of the course of the action, the outstanding features of which has been the clock-work coordination of the activities of the Army, Navy and Air Force.

The British advance against the Italians has been similar in method to the German advance in France. They have executed a swift extensive flanking movement, encircling one enemy position after another. The Air Force concentrated on keeping Italian bombers and fighters out of the war by incessantly bombarding and machine-gunning aerodromes.

The mobile column ran like a rapier through the desert to El Am Nibeiwa. This Italian encampment on the escarpment fell within two hours of the initial operations: it was taken completely by surprise. Here General Maletti was killed.

During the morning a whole series of small Italian forts were captured, and then the British mobile forces made a rush towards the coast west of Sidi Barrani as swiftly as the Germans rushed to Boulogne.

Continuous Bombardment

Artillery, infantry, armoured forces and the Navy all contributed to the 12-hour bombardment of Sidi Barrani, while the part of the R.A.F. was to bomb it for sixteen hours almost continuously on Monday. Severe casualties were inflicted on the Black Shirt divisions. Nevertheless they offered fierce resistance to the British onslaughts.

Despite the dust storm which persisted throughout yesterday, making parts of the desert, including aerodromes, look like London in a pea soup fog, the R.A.F. flew out unceasingly on their harassing tasks. At times returning bombers were unable to see their aerodromes and were forced to land on emergency ones elsewhere.

Their bombardment of Benina, which is the Italian advanced air striking base, was probably the heaviest bombing raid ever carried out on Italian hangars and machines out in the Near East and it left shattered wrecks.

JEWISH SOLDIERS' WELFARE
Gift from British Comforts Fund

We acknowledge gratefully the gift of LP.50 to the Jewish Soldiers Welfare Committee's Fund, from the British War Comforts Fund, Jerusalem Branch of which Mr. E. Keith Roach, District Commissioner, is chairman.

The 19th list of subscriptions is on Page 2, showing a total to date of more than LP.1650 raised in this country since Nov. 15, when the subscription opened.

ROME MINIMIZES LOSSES

FASCIST ATROCITIES IN DODECANESE

ATHENS,—Fascist propaganda has from time to time endeavoured to stress the enthusiastic cooperation which the Italian forces fighting in Albania are receiving from the Albanians themselves. It is strange, therefore, that the first official casualty list which was published in Rome this week mentions, among the killed, the names of 681 Italians and only a single Albanian.

This suggests that the degree of Albanian participation in the struggle may be somewhat less than the Italians have been pleased to assert.

The "Estia" also observes that the Rome announcement admits to only 731 Italians missing, and remarks that this figure compares strangely with the fact that in Athens alone several thousand Italian prisoners are already interned.

Fascist Atrocities

An official statement draws attention to the inhuman behaviour of the Italians now beleaguered in the Dodecanese Islands. It says:

The Central Dodecanese Committee brings to the knowledge of the civilised world that, according to absolutely verified reports received from the Dodecanese, the Italians are pursuing their policy of extermination of the islanders with increasing ferocity. They have arrested all the male inhabitants of the island from 18 to 60 years of age and thrown them into open moats and trenches dug near their encampment, where they are submitted to incredible hardships and suffering.

The Italian Army has requisitioned all flocks of sheep and every kind of domestic animals and fowls belonging to inhabitants, as well as all stocks of foodstuffs available".

The cheerful and happy isles of the Dodecanese are now being turned into a vast cemetery in the bloody chaos of Fascist Italy. With broken hearts for the lot of our brothers we denounce before the civilized world this horrible and iniquitous act and proclaim before God and man that civilisation has known no more diabolical enemy than Fascist Italy.

PATRIA QUESTION IN COMMONS

LONDON, Thursday (Palcor). — Answering a question by Colonel Wedgwood in the House of Commons yesterday afternoon concerning the victims of the s.s. Patria, and as to whether the ship could still be raised and repaired and whether the survivors were still at the Athlit detention camp, Mr. George Hall, the Colonial Under-Secretary stated that the number of dead then was 55, leaving 198 persons still not accounted for.

The Under-Secretary added that the ship would probably be salvaged. The survivors were being maintained at the expense of the Palestine Government.

PATRIA ENQUIRY OPENED

HAIFA, Thursday. — The Commission of Enquiry appointed to investigate the sinking of the s.s. Patria held its first regular session this morning.

Evidence was given by Mr. J.H.H. Pollock, O.B.E., the District Commissioner; Captain Holiday, master of the s.s. Patria; Mr R. Spinney; and Lieut. Commander E.M.V. James, D.S.P. in charge of the Port Marine Police.

BRITISH GUARANTEE TO EGYPT FULFILLED

Premier's Statement Cheered

LONDON, Thursday (R). — Speaking with considerably less caution than on Tuesday, Mr. Churchill told the House of Commons this afternoon of the "victory which in the African theatre of war is of the first order."

The Prime Minister alluded to his previous statement when he indicated that a British column had reached the coast between Buqbuq and Sidi Barrani, cutting the principal road by which the main body of the Italian army could retreat.

The question then was, he said, whether the encircling position which General Sir Maitland Wilson's forces captured after a brilliantly executed desert march could be effectively maintained and whether the net so drawn could be forced at all points to the seashore.

"The strong position of Sidi Barrani and the various fortified posts in the neighbourhood appeared to be a formidable obstacle, but Sidi Barrani was captured and the whole coastal region except one or two points is in the hands of the British and Imperial troops."

Three Divisions Smashed

Seven thousand prisoners have already reached Mersa Matruh —so far. We do not yet know how many Italians were caught in the encirclement, but the best part of three divisions including Black Shirt formations, was destroyed or captured in the victory.

"As the Sidi Barrani position was the advance base for all Italian Forces which invaded Egypt and were penetrating further into it, it seems probable that considerable masses of material may be found there.

"The pursuit to the west continues with the greatest vigour. The Air Force is bombing and the Navy shelling the principal road open to the retreating enemy, and considerable captured have already been reported besides those which fell within the original encirclement.

Anxieties Removed

While it was too soon to measure the scale of these operations, it was clear that they constituted a victory which in this African war was of the first order and reflected the highest credit upon General Wavell, General Wilson and the Staff Officers who planned this exceedingly complicated operation and the troops who had performed a remarkable feat of endurance and courage.

The whole episode must be judged upon the background of the fact that only three or four months ago anxieties for the defence of Egypt were acute. These anxieties were now removed, and the British guarantee that Egypt would be effectively defended against all comers had been in every way made good, concluded the Prime Minister amid loud and prolonged cheers.

LIBYAN ARMY IN A JAM

ITALIAN FLEET MUST FIGHT TO SAVE IT

By Fergus J. Ferguson
Reuters Chief Diplomatic Correspondent

LONDON, Thursday. — The crushing blows inflicted on Mussolini's armies in Africa are calculated to have an almost decisive effect upon the course of the war.

The Italian Fleet must now either accept battle or the Duce's Legionaries in North Africa can be considered lost. Their offensive powers have been destroyed at one blow, while the menace to the Nile Valley no longer exists. The effects of the Italian defeat will be felt politically not only in Europe but all over the East.

Japan must now have cause to reconsider her hasty action in joining the Tripartite Pact. Even assuming that violent domestic reactions do not upset the Fascist Regime, it is unlikely that the Duce will get much help from Germany, and Japanese aid can be ruled out. Indeed the question arises whether the Pact holds if one of the parties collapses.

Inspiring Effect

The effect of the Italian reverses will be most inspiring in the Balkans. The Greeks will be encouraged to further acts of valour and the extent of help Britain is able to give may be increased, while Yugoslavia's hands will be strengthened, the wisdom of Turkish policy justified, and Axis propaganda in Bulgaria suffer a severe setback.

Many friends of Britain in France will derive fresh hope and encouragement from this British victory. It will increase France's value in German eyes but will make Laval's policy more unpopular and distasteful to the French people in general and the Army in particular.

CONGRATULATIONS TO GEN. A. WAVELL

MR. EDEN AND SIR J. DILL

LONDON, Thursday (R). — Mr. Anthony Eden and General Sir John Greer Dill, the C.I.G.S., have telegraphed congratulations to General Sir Archibald Wavell. The message says,

On behalf of all ranks of the Army serving at home and in other theatres, we send to you and all under your command, congratulations on your victory. Your brilliant stroke delighted us all and filled us with pride.

Well-Planned Strategy

The success at Sidi Barrani was the outcome of well-planned strategy. British armoured forces first attacked the enemy's right flank and then forced their way to the rear, while a fierce frontal attack was launched against enemy positions at Maktilla, 15 miles west of Sidi Barrani. On finding themselves cut off, the Italian divisions became disorganized when attacked from all sides.

The part taken by the Free French forces was described in a communique from General de Gaulle's H.Q. which stated that advanced French units had taken a number of prisoners and war material.

Effective assistance was given by the British Navy, which heavily bombarded Sollum and Bardia, focal points of the Italian retreat. Both heavy and light units took part.

Other British naval units bombarded Kismayu, in Italian Somaliland, inflicting damage on Italian supplies, and enemy coastal batteries replied ineffectively.

America's Reaction

What America thinks of Sidi Barrani's capture is shown by a sharp rise on the Stock Markets. Radio commentators are vying with each other in praise of the secrecy with which the British preparations were made; the speed of the attack, and the brilliance of British Staff work. Newspapers splashed the story in banner headlines.

FASCIST EMPIRE TOPPLING

By Kenneth Anderson,
Reuters Special Correspondent in the Western Desert

CAIRO, 11.45 p.m. — The British offensive in the Western Desert of Egypt is developing so fast that rumours of a headlong Italian retreat are circulating in Cairo and Alexandria.

It is realized that British G.H.Q. communiques tend to minimize our successes rather than make claims until they have been confirmed beyond doubt. It is thus reasonable to suppose that the figure of 20,000 prisoners give in the latest communique is an underestimate.

The speed of the offensive has meant that communiques are hardly issued before fresh important advances and captures are taking place. It will be days before the exact number of prisoners, guns and tanks taken is known.

As the picture of the first three days of the offensive is gradually fitted together at G.H.Q. from reports arriving from the Desert front, it becomes evident that the Middle East Command, with a brilliant piece of strategy planned for many weeks, has delivered a blow against the Italians that will rock the foundations and topple the edifice of the Fascist Empire.

ABYSSINIA MAY COLLAPSE

There is already general speculation in Cairo in regard to whether the Italians will have to relinquish their hold on Abyssinia. For months Italian morale in East Africa has been bolstered up by the empty assurance that Mussolini's army was ready to march to the Nile Delta at any moment and open up the Suez Canal.

But if the British offensive continues as satisfactorily as at present, the Italian army in Abyssinia may, it is suggested, throw up the sponge because of the pressure being exerted by the British Forces already hammering at the frontier.

20,000 TAKEN PRISONER

Enemy Forces In General Retreat

CAIRO, Thursday (R). — Royal Air Force reconnoitring planes reported this morning that a general Italian retreat was developing in the Western Desert. This report coincided with an official estimate that 20,000 prisoners had been captured, together with tanks, guns and other material.

Operations are stated to be proceeding satisfactorily thanks to close cooperation between all the fighting services. The Navy is pounding the coastal road west of Buqbuq, while the R.A.F. continues ceaselessly to subdue the efforts of the Italian Air Force and bomb them out of their aerodromes.

The news that four Italian Generals have been rendered hors de combat is significant. The death of General Maletti in action gains an added importance for it suggests that the Italian armoured flying column was among the first victims of the British onslaught.

For months this column has had a certain nuisance value and been regarded as a possible threat to the British southern flank. The Italian position as a whole has been very adversely affected by the blow given to this force.

The three Generals taken prisoner are General Sebastiano Gallina (Corps Commander) and Generals Amando Pescator and Mezzari (Divisional Commanders).

Hide and Seek War

The difficulty of establishing a clear picture of the operations now in progress is heightened by the "hide and seek" nature of the fighting along parts of the front and the number of duels fought between tanks and machine-gun posts.

The present offensive demonstrates a new kind of warfare in which there are no definite lines to break through but rather a number of strongly-defended posts dotted along the desert. The camps are roughly circular, with field-guns arranged in perimeter, behind which tanks are ready to dash out and engage the attackers. Behind the tanks are machine-guns and infantry protecting the transports and stores.

The defenders naturally have the advantage since their artillery has the exact range of all surrounding points from which an enemy could appear. British armoured units, however, are making most of the element of surprise and are using the familiar counters of the desert.

They have been able with determined attacks to break down the resistance of some camps and force their way to the coast. Nevertheless, it takes time to eliminate the various hidden machine-gunners who opened fire from the rear of the advancing tanks, and a number of exciting individual charges up one sandhill and down another by British mechanised cavalry units against enemy gunners have already taken place.

Egyptian Tribute

"Truly magnificent" was how a high Egyptian Government official described the success. "This smashing Italian defeat removes any possible doubt concerning the safety of Egypt," he said.

Tremendous enthusiasm greeted the announcement at places of entertainment throughout Cairo last night. "Al Ahram" used for its headline a verse from the Koran, "Our possession has returned to us."

TURKEY LIFTS BLACKOUT

Tension in Balkans Subsiding

SOFIA, Thursday. — Turkish-Bulgarian relations continue to be the subject of active discussion in political circles.

It is learned that the Bulgarian Minister to Turkey, M. Kiroff, has arrived from Ankara with concrete Turkish proposals for a pact of mutual assistance. His interview with the Foreign Minister, Mr Popoff, has evoked much speculation in political and diplomatic circles.

Meanwhile, the lessening of tension in the Balkans is described as the reason for the Turkish Government's decision to suspend the total blackout announced earlier this month. Nevertheless, Turkish mobilization will continue and the "state of siege" recently decreed in European Turkey will be maintained.

The view taken here is that Turkish mobilization is not directed against Bulgaria, which could not by itself attack Turkey, but is of a purely defensive character.

Russian Warning

It is now learned (says an Al Ahram Message) that M. Soboleff, the Soviet delegate at the Danubian conference, told King Boris that if Bulgaria allowed foreign troops to cross her territory against Greece or Turkey, Russia would have no alternative but to seize the Bulgarian Black Sea ports of Varna and Borgas.

King Boris thereupon informed the Soviet envoy that Hitler had made such a suggestion, but had been told that Bulgaria's attitude would largely depend upon the stand which Soviet Russia would take.

BULGARIAN PROTEST AGAINST ANTI-SEMITISM

ISTANBUL, Thursday (Palcor) Several speakers at a recent closed session of the Bulgarian Government Party are known to have criticised the surrender of the authorities to Axis influence to the extent of introducing the anti-Jewish laws.

These measures, it was pointed out, were a disguised curtailment of civil liberties which would ultimately threaten the security of the State. The loyalty of the Jews to the State was undoubted, and the removal of the dictated disabilities was declared to be imperative to the political independence of the country.

BLACKOUT: Sunset in Jerusalem, 5.36 Sunrise 7.31

THE PALESTINE POST

WEDNESDAY
MAY 14, 1941

VOL. XVII. No. 4565
PRICE 10 MILS

BRITISH MAINTAIN DESERT INITIATIVE

Gen. Blamey Reports Improvement in Libya

CAIRO, Tuesday (R). — Notwithstanding the intense heat, Imperial forces in the Western Desert are maintaining the initiative and continually attacking with very satisfactory results, according to military circles here.

It is rumoured that the Germans have solved the heat problem by the use of air-conditioned tanks, but this is thought to be very unlikely. The actions around Tobruk and Sollum, though sharp, are quite localized.

Fewer than 20 miles now separate the Indian and South African forces operating around Amba Alagi, in Abyssinia, and the southern force has already reached Mai Ceu.

The district is precipitous and reminiscent of Keren, so that the advance is bound to be slow; but the enemy position is being more and more restricted by the double advance from the north and south.

British troops in Southern Abyssinia have continued their advance in the Wadara neighbourhood, where the last enemy position has now been occupied. Contact with the enemy has been made north of Sciacamanna.

Libyan Position Improved

General Sir Thomas Blamey, in dispatches to the Australian Army Minister, Mr. Spender, has reported a substantial improvement in conditions in Libya, particularly Tobruk, in the last few days, according to a Canberra message.

Mr. Spender said that General Blamey had informed him that two factors were contributing to the improvement; firstly, the greater freedom which the Navy enjoyed in assisting land operations since the withdrawal from Greece, and secondly, the increasing difficulties of the enemy in maintaining supplies owing to increase and storms.

Considerable damage was done to civilian property when enemy aircraft attacked Malta on Sunday night. There were few civilian casualties.

Four alarms were sounded yesterday when aircraft were reported to be in the vicinity.

Malta has had over 600 Alerts during the 11 months since Italy entered the war, including over 100 in the past month.

Communiques

G.H.Q. MIDDLE EAST.

TUESDAY. — Libya-Tobruk: No change in the situation. In the Sollum area, the enemy carried out a reconnaissance in force advancing eastwards in five small columns. When met by advanced elements of our mechanized forces in the area west and south of Sofafi the enemy turned back. Our air forces have been afforded particularly good targets by the withdrawing enemy.

Abyssinia: A further two hundred Italian prisoners have been captured by British troops advancing on Amba Alagi. The operations in this area continue to develop satisfactorily. In the south, in spite of heavy rains, our forces are continuing to advance in all areas. In the lakes district south of Addis Ababa, our troops successfully assaulted an enemy position inflicting heavy casualties and capturing 13 Italian and 143 African prisoners.

DICTATORS CALL A CONFERENCE

Hitler to See Stalin and Mussolini

LONDON, Tuesday. — It is regarded here as highly probable, on the strength of reports from Berlin, that Hitler and Mussolini will meet again in the near future.

It is learned that for several days the Duce has been soliciting such an interview owing to his alarm over possible developments in Italo-German relations. If a rapprochement comes about between Germany and the U.S.S.R., Italy would be left with a minor role, while any deal between Germany and Vichy would deprive her of long-coveted territory in the Western Mediterranean.

Mussolini is thought to be especially anxious to know the purport of Hitler's conversation with Darlan officially reported in Berlin today.

Meanwhile, the diplomatic correspondent of the 'Sunday Dispatch' reports that Hitler may meet Stalin on a ship in the Black Sea if present negotiations between the two countries lead to a deadlock. Hitler's most important lever for forcing Stalin to cooperate with him is obviously the threat to seize the Ukraine wheat areas and the Baku oilfields, a threat which is now being worked all it is worth.

In this connection it is of interest that a front-page editorial in the "Kokumin Shimbun," the Japanese Army organ, yesterday declared that Japan could not look on with folded arms in the event of a German-Soviet agreement granting Russia a free hand in Asia in return for larger Soviet supplies to Germany.

The paper urged that Japan must guard against unilateral and opportunist territorial measures like the transfer of hegemony by any foreign power or combination of foreign powers before the fundamental conditions for a new world order had been realized.

Hitler's Alternative

Germany apparently still feels that Russia will elect to fulfil every demand rather than resist, but at the same time Hitler is making every preparation against the eventuality of Stalin's refusal to comply with his demands. About two million troops have been concentrated along the Russian border. It is even anticipated in some quarters that Hitler will make his first move of aggression before the end of the spring harvest season in the Ukraine.

Speculation is current on Russia's stand should Germany attack Turkey. It is generally believed that while Russia will make every effort to preserve her neutrality and guard the Black Sea and the Dardanelles, she will not be able to come to satisfactory agreements with both Germany and Turkey.

In some quarters it is believed that Russia's trade relations with the United States may be severed shortly. Russia's difficulty in securing permission for the import from America of materials vital to the American defence scheme may contribute to such a break. On the other hand, Russian shipments to the U.S. have been irregular since the Black Sea was closed to traffic with the inclusion of the Balkans in the war theatre.

It is also pointed out that Iran diplomatic relations between the two countries have cooled considerably since the signing of the Russo-Japanese pact.

ROOSEVELT TO ADDRESS NATION

Will Broadcast 'Chat'

TALK TO PAN-AMERICAN CONFERENCE CANCELLED

WASHINGTON, Tuesday (R). — President Roosevelt has cancelled his scheduled speech to the Pan-American Conference which begins its session tomorrow, and will instead broadcast a "Fireside Chat" to the American people on May 27.

The reason why the President cancelled the speech is unknown, but is believed to be not because of his recent indifferent health. The circumstances were such that only a very important speech could have been delivered.

The situation has been successively primed by Mr. Cordell Hull, Colonel Knox, Mr. Stimson and Mr. Willkie, and any ordinary post-dinner speech would obviously have been a severe let-down to the country and for the President.

Apparently, Mr. Roosevelt is not yet ready to make the next important pronouncement in a world at war, and refuses to be pushed by public sentiment and expressions in the press and on public platforms into what has been openly expected as a momentous speech.

Public Outcry

Mr. Roosevelt apparently is not ready to live up to this expectation — yet the press continues in editorials, cartoons, and by other means to stress the seriousness of the shipping situation, and some writers emphasize that a policy of providing ships for Great Britain without producing protection for them is merely the adoption of the least satisfactory expedient of the improvident — spending capital — and precious capital, because ample shipping next year is absolutely essential for the expansion of the war effort, if Great Britain is not to remain permanently on the defensive.

A columnist in the "Washington Post" says, "Unless protection for shipping is quickly arranged, Britain must continue to submit to the present process of grinding attrition, and there can only be one end to that."

America Must Choose Now

Meanwhile, the Secretary of the Navy, Colonel Knox, declared in a speech to the American Society of Military Engineers last night that America must choose now.

America has three courses: One is to face the aggressor with force, the second is to become isolated from the rest of the world, and the third is to surrender. We are reduced to the first choice, — to oppose the aggressor with enough to scare him off or defeat him.

Referring to the question of convoys, Colonel Knox said that possibly they were not the answer to the problem.

Perhaps we must develop a new defence to assure the arrival of our goods on the other side.

Red Sea Service

Inter-coastal steamship operators have been requested by the U. S. Maritime Commission to contribute 50 of their large coastal vessels for the transport of material to the Red Sea under the Lease and Lend Act. The vessels will bring back freights of strategic materials from Africa and the Far East for use in the United States.

American ships manned by American crews are expected to begin carrying war materials into the Red Sea within a few weeks. Seven vessels have already been tentatively assigned, and 20 more are being assembled.

HITLER RECEIVES DARLAN

BERLIN, Tuesday (R). — Hitler is reported by the German News Agency to have received Admiral Darlan.

The interview took place in the presence of Ribbentrop, but no information is given of the place of the meeting.

Refugee Ship Sunk in Black Sea

GENEVA, Tuesday (Palcor). — A ship carrying Jewish refugees from Central European countries is reported by the Rome radio to have foundered in the Black Sea some 30 miles south of Constantza.

No details have yet been received of the number of passengers on board or of the circumstances of the disaster.

The crew was saved, but it is not known how many of the refugees survived.

AFTER MIDNIGHT

Mr. Churchill was received in audience by the King yesterday.

Berlin is anxiously waiting to learn what revelations Herr Hess will make to the British authorities, according to information reaching the neutral press. Berlin is intimating that Hess was progressively being relieved of responsibilities and attempting to stress the "tragedy" of his case. In Stockholm it is thought that executions may now occur, but if only imprisonment then the whole affair will appear a clever trick on the part of the Nazis.

MOSLEM WORLD GIVES GAILANI COLD SHOULDER

SAUDIA ARABIA AND IRAN DISAPPROVE

LONDON, Tuesday. — It was stated in Cairo today that there was nothing further to report from Iraq since last night's statement that the situation had been stabilized.

Other reports from Cairo indicate that the overtures made by Rashid Ali to Saudi Arabia have met with a cold reception and that no success attended the mission of one of his envoys to Teheran, where the attitude of the Iranian Government to events in Iraq is one of complete disapproval.

Questioned at a press conference yesterday, an official German spokesman answered in the negative an enquiry as to whether Germany recognized Rashid Ali as the legal ruler of Iraq and regarded the Regent, the Emir Abdul 'Illah, as definitely deposed.

He replied evasively when asked whether Rashid Ali had applied to Germany for help and whether any such help had been sent, was forthcoming, or contemplated.

The Turkish Angle

Reports from Ankara quote the Moscow radio on Sunday night as sharply criticizing the attitude of Rashid Ali Gailani's adherents, who were described as instruments of foreign powers.

Responsible Turkish circles emphasize that the Government is by no means pleased with the visit of the Iraqi Defence Minister, Naji Shawkat Bey, who was at first thought to have come with logical proposals for a termination of the dispute.

It has, however, emerged from conversations which he had with the Turkish Foreign Minister, M. Sukru Sarajoglou, that he was more concerned with explaining Iraq's attitude towards Turkey. The real object of his visit is believed to be to contact von Papen, who returned yesterday evening.

A Russian Threat

The Turkish Government has cancelled all Army, Air Force and Navy leave. This may or may not be connected with the fact that the Erivan Soviet Republic is reported to have addressed a request to the Supreme Soviet at Moscow urging the annexation from Turkey of certain frontier districts, which would be incorporated in Erivan.

A Teheran report states that Iran would maintain complete neutrality in the event of an attack on Turkey, since the Saadabad pact of mutual assistance is regarded as having no further practical value.

Von Papen, whose return from Germany, where he had been having consultations with Nazi leaders had been expected for some time, arrived in Ankara this evening. He came by air from Salzburg, where, according to German sources, he saw Hitler yesterday. Von Papen was accompanied by his wife and daughter.

MR. CHURCHILL TO MAKE FURTHER STATEMENT

LONDON, Tuesday (R). — It was announced by Mr. Churchill today, when the House of Commons met in new surroundings, that a further statement would shortly be made on the subject of Rudolf Hess' arrival in England.

"Obviously a further statement will be made in the near future regarding the flight to this country of this very high important Nazi leader," said Mr. Churchill when invited to make a statement about Hess.

The Labour Member, Mr. Lawson, raised the question of the German wireless reference to his "mental instability," and asked whether the Prime Minister had any information on this point, while another Member asked whether the Prime Minister was taking steps with the Minister of Information to see "this piece of news dealt with skill and imagination."

Mr. Churchill said that this was one of those cases in which imagination was somewhat baffled by the facts as they presented themselves. (Laughter.)

Other supplementary questioners begged Mr. Churchill to bear in mind Hess's record of devotion to the evil genius of Europe (cheers) and questioned the prudence of announcing that Hess was, as being unfair to the people of Glasgow, who might possibly expect to become the target of bombs.

The Prime Minister declared, "He will not always be in Glasgow."

"Good News at a Good Time"

When asked at a London meeting today if he could say why Hess had come to Britain, the Minister of Information, Mr. Duff Cooper, said:

"It is suggested that I should tell you something about the rather unexpected arrival of a guest who, whatever his qualities may be, is, by no means unwelcome.

"I am afraid I am not in a position to give information, but can only say that his arrival here shows the first breach in the Nazi Party since Hitler murdered a huge bloc of his own followers on June 30, 1933.

Tired But Comfortable

"Here is a man who was so obviously in possession of his confidence since he was able to accomplish the flight successfully, a man who, with the advantages he must have been enjoying in Germany, and we all know what the advantages are of a tyrant's strength, yet prefers to leave that unhappy, miserable country and fly at a tremendous risk to himself in order to land on what is still a country of the free. That is good news and it comes at a good time."

Hess is in bed in hospital and save for tiredness, is comfortable and in good spirits, it is authoritatively stated in London.

The Deputy Fuehrer has been issued with army pyjamas and army equipment such as a toothbrush, etc. Though suffering pain from his injured ankle, he is quite well. A British officer is on guard looking after him, and he spends most of his time resting, dozing and reading mainly the English "Geographical Magazine." He has been given some novels and writing paper, pencils and ink and is writing quite a lot. He is receiving the usual hospital food, such as boiled chicken and rice for lunch.

Herr Hess conveyed the impression to Mr. Kirkpatrick that he was not having as much outdoor exercise as formerly and spending much time in office work. His tiredness is understandable, considering that he carried out a remarkable 800-mile flight, landing in the dark at the end and parachuting for the first time in his life, nor had he flown a Messerschmitt 110 before.

HESS A REFUGEE IN BRITAIN

HOW HITLER'S SUCCESSOR ESCAPED TO SCOTLAND

LONDON, Tuesday (R). — Rudolf Hess, who has been described as Hitler's "Man Friday," was nominated by the Fuehrer as his successor-designate after Goering, and was responsible to Hitler alone — above Himmler, Goebbels, Ribbentrop and Goering.

Hess was Hitler's private secretary in the old Munich "beer-garden" days and was interned with him in Landsberg fortress. There, treated with paternal latitude by an

"Whatever, he does is right; whatever he does is necessary; and whatever he does is successful... Thus manifestly the Fuehrer has the divine blessing." — Rudolf Hess quoted in "We Make History" by Robert Ziller published by George Allen and Unwin.

indulgent Government, he took down the first part of "Mein Kampf" at Hitler's dictation.

When Hitler came to power, Hess, at the head of the Verbindungsstab (Liaison Staff), brought to the Fuehrer every bit of information which Hitler required from a State about to be over-run.

Hess spent his boyhood in Egypt and went to an English public school (Victoria College) at Alexandria. The outbreak of war in 1914, when he was 18, prevented him from going to an English University. He was a 100 per cent Party man and never wore any other uniform but the brown shirt of the Storm Troopers or the black coat of the S.S. Hitler's Black Guard.

Gossiped with Farmer

It was revealed today that when Hess landed by parachute near the cottage of a Scottish ploughman, David McLean, the latter found him lying injured in a field and assisted him to his house, where the Nazi leader gossiped with McLean's mother and sister for almost an hour before he was taken away.

McLean told the following story: "I was in the house and everyone else was in bed late at night when I heard a plane roaring overhead. As I ran to the back of the farm, I heard a crash and saw the plane burst into flames in a field about 200 yards away. I was amazed and a bit frightened when I saw a parachute dropping slowly downwards through the gathering darkness. I immediately concluded that it was a German airman baling out and raced back to the house for help. They were all asleep, however.

"I looked round hastily for some weapon, but could find nothing except a hay-fork. I hurried round to the back of the house and in a field there saw a man lying on the ground with a parachute nearby, but I could see that he had injured his foot in some way. I helped him into the house

"By this time, my old mother and my sister had got out of bed and made tea. The stranger, however, declined tea and said, 'I never drink tea as late as this. I will only have a glass of water.'

"Word had meanwhile been sent to the military authorities, and the man chatted freely to us, showing us pictures of his little boy of whom he spoke very proudly. He told us that he had left Germany about four hours previously and had landed because nightfall was approaching. He was a man of culture. His English, although it had a foreign accent, was very clear and he understood every word we said.

"He was a striking-looking man, standing over six foot in height and wearing a very magnificent flying suit. He seemed quiet and confident that he would be well treated, and repeatedly expressed how lucky he had been in landing without mishap. He certainly was most gentlemanly in his attitude to my mother and sister and stiffly bowed to them when he came in and before leaving.

"He thanked us most profusely for what we had done for him. He was anxious about only one thing' his parachute. He said to me, 'I should like to keep the parachute, for I think I owe my life to it.' He would not tell us who he was and we assumed that he was just another German airman who had been brought down.

"When officials came on the scene, he greeted them with a smile and assured them that he was unarmed, and stood up and held his arms out to allow them to assure themselves of this. He was then taken away.

"As soon as news came from Germany that Hess had disappeared in a plane, photographs of him were shown to McLean and his family. The McLeans had heard the story on the radio and had come to the conclusion that the visitor of Saturday night had been Hess. As soon as he was shown the picture of Hess saluting Hitler, McLean said, 'That's the man, there is no doubt about it.'"

Had No Bombs

During his stay at the McLean farmhouse, Hess was in the custody of two British Home Guards, Jack Peterson and Robert Gibson, it is now revealed.

The Guards declared that Hess said, "I had no bombs in my plane so do not worry." He had a map on which his route from Augsburg to Scotland was marked in blue pencil. Hess said he had never been in Britain before but did not seem at all worried.

"He was the calmest man in the party," declared one of the men guarding Herr Hess at the McLean farmhouse. "When offered a cigarette he said he did not smoke.

"We were surprised to find that we had plenty of milk and drank half a glassful. He complained that he felt somewhat cramped after being in the plane so long and that his ankle was very painful. He had a camera strapped around his neck but assured us he had not taken any photos."

Before leaving the farm Herr Hess thanked the Home Guards for their kindness and presented one of them with a drinking cup as a souvenir. A collection of compressed food was found on him by the military escort. He told them he had fitted an extra petrol tank to the plane to ensure that it would cover the journey and had dropped the extra tank into the sea as he approached the Scottish coast.

Herr Hess circled over the spot where he landed a long time but in the gathering darkness could not find a suitable landing place. He then climbed several thousand feet, drove the plane over on its back and switched off the engine. Just as he was falling out of the upturned machine he again switched on the engine and sent the plane hurtling earthwards while he himself fell clear.

Held in Secret Place

Hess is being treated as a prisoner, but has been removed to a place which will be kept secret and no one will be allowed to see him. Except for an injury to his leg, the doctors who saw Hess found him healthy and sane.

NEPHEW IN U.S. ARMY

NEW YORK, Tuesday. — A message from Bristol, Virginia, states that Gustav Adolf Hess, a nephew of Rudolf Hess, is now serving with the U.S. anti-aircraft batteries in the Panama Canal zone. His father Gustav, the brother of Rudolf, died in America in 1920.

HITLER'S SHADOW NOW PRISONER OF WAR

LONDON, Tuesday (R). — Leaving behind a farewell note, Rudolf Hess, Hitler's Deputy, has fled from Germany and is now in Scotland. He parachuted from a German plane, which significantly would not have had enough petrol to return to Germany.

The most amazing story of the war was told last night in a communique from No. 10 Downing Street a few hours after Hess had left a note showing traces of mental disorder and had either committed suicide or fallen from a plane.

Hess, who broke his ankle when he landed, brought photographs of himself at different ages to establish his identity, and has been recognized by several people who knew him well. Among others he was seen by Mr. Ivone Kirkpatrick, who was at the British Embassy in Berlin from 1933 to 1938. Mr. Kirkpatrick was closely acquainted with Hess, and had no difficulty at all in identifying him when he saw the prisoner last night.

There was an atmosphere of tense drama in the Ministry of Information last night when the remarkable announcement was made by a high official, in the presence of the Minister, Mr. A. Duff Cooper and the Director-General, Sir Walter Monckton, that the Fuehrer's Deputy had landed in Scotland.

The statement, which was issued from No. 10 Downing Street at 11.20 British summer time, read as follows:

Rudolf Hess, Deputy Fuehrer of Germany and Party Leader of the National Socialist Party, landed in Scotland under the following circumstances.

On the night of Saturday, May 10, a Messerschmitt 110 was reported by our patrols to have crossed the coast of Scotland and to be flying in the direction of Glasgow. Since a Messerschmitt 110 would not have fuel to return to Germany, this report was at first disbelieved.

Later on, a Messerschmitt 110 crashed near Glasgow with its guns unloaded. Shortly afterwards, a German officer who had baled out was found with his parachute in the neighbourhood suffering from a broken ankle. He was taken to hospital in Glasgow where he at first gave his name as Horn, but later on he declared that he was Rudolf Hess. He brought with him various photographs of himself at different ages, apparently in order to establish his identity. These photographs were deemed to be photographs of Hess by several people who knew him personally. Accordingly, an officer of the Foreign Office who was closely acquainted with Hess before the war has been sent up by aeroplane to see him in hospital.

The Core is Rotten

Regarding the question why Hess came to Britain it is thought in London that his flight was presumably the result of a disagreement with other prominent Nazis or possibly a natural revulsion towards other members of the gang. The opinion in the same circles is that Hess's flight shows that the core of Germany is rotten.

It can be stated definitely that Hess is not on a mission and does not carry a message from anyone. The possibility that the episode is a Nazi trick is considered extremely remote in view of the attitude adopted by the German radio towards Hess. During the meeting between Hess and Mr. Kirkpatrick it is understood the Hess conversed freely. It is recalled that Mr. Kirkpatrick participated in the meetings at Godesberg, Berchtesgaden and Munich.

Authoritative circles add that Hess knew that if he had gone to a neutral country, he would have been in imminent peril of being assassinated by some of the Nazi representatives in those places.

NAZIS TRY TO "EXPLAIN" HESS FLIGHT

BERLIN, Tuesday (R). — A detailed "explanation" of Herr Hess's flight to Scotland was issued this evening in the form of a Party bulletin, which declared,

The removal of papers left behind by Herr Hess discloses that he laboured under the delusion that a step taken on his personal initiative with Englishmen whom he formerly knew would lead to an understanding being reached between Germany and Britain.

He has actually, as has been confirmed by a report from London, landed in Scotland by parachute near the place he wished to visit and was presumably picked up there injured.

Herr Rudolf Hess, who, as was known to the party, has for years suffered increasingly in a physical sense, took refuge in various forms of hypnotism, astrology, etc. Attempts to elucidate to what extent these (astrologers etc.) are to blame for causing Herr Hess's mental disturbance, which led him to take this step, are being made. It is also conceivable that Hess in the end led into a trap by the

British, the whole manner of his action confirms, however, the fact already given in the first report that he suffered from delusions. He better than anyone else knew of the many peace offers made by the Fuehrer, which came from the bottom of his heart. Apparently he laboured under the impression that by a personal sacrifice he could prevent the continuation of the war. Herr Hess, whose sphere of activity, as is known, lay exclusively within the party, did not have any clear notion about this act or its consequences, as may be deduced from the notes he left. The National Socialist Party regrets that this idealist fell victim to fateful delusions. By this act nothing has been changed in the prosecution of the war against Britain. It will be continued as the Fuehrer announced in his last speech.

Germany Hears The News

The news of Hess's flight was broken to the German people over the radio today. After saying that Hess was injured after baling out from his plane at Glasgow, the Berlin announcer said that the papers he left behind tended to show that Hess thought he could achieve an understanding with England through Nazi acquaintances.

The announcer then went on to say that Hess was suffering from a disease and had lately been consulting a surgeon, and this might account for his derangement.

"RUDY NOT MAD"

CAIRO, Tuesday. — "I refuse to believe that Rudy is insane: there is either a serious Nazi split or else he has formed a far-reaching plan," declared Frau Paula, an old nurse of Herr Rudolf Hess, in an exclusive interview with Reuter.

Frau Paula added, "I nursed him until he was a grown up boy. He was broadminded, of strong character, and extremely honest. From early childhood he vaunted German invincibility and always fought for the top place, whether at school or elsewhere. He often used to discuss political questions with his father."

BLACKOUT: Sunset 7.31
Jerusalem, 7.37 Sunrise, 5.48

MONDAY JUNE 9, 1941

THE PALESTINE POST

VOL. XVII. No. 4586
PRICE 10 MILS

BRITISH AND FREE FRENCH MOVE INTO SYRIA

Free French troops, with the support of Imperial forces, crossed the frontier from Palestine into Syria and the Lebanon at 2 o'clock yesterday morning.

A manifesto published by General Catroux, in the name of General de Gaulle and with the official endorsement of the British Government, contained a guarantee of liberty and independence for the territories now under French Mandate.

Later it was stated that the operations are proceeding according to plan. It is emphasized that they are political, rather than military, and primarily intended to prevent the Germans from using Syria as a base for operations. In official circles hope was expressed that as a result of the operations which began with a military advance, both French and Arabs will help the British drive out the Germans attempting to establish themselves in that territory. Whether the outcome of the advance will be a military operation depends entirely on the reactions of the French.

VICHY FORCED ALLIED MOVE

NAZI INFILTRATION MUST BE STOPPED

The move by the British and Free French to prevent the Germans from assuming control of Syria and turning it into a battleground was taken in the nick of time, as evidence was accumulating of growing German infiltration, including the arrival planned for next Sunday of a German mission at Aleppo to take over the administration and control of that district, according to a Cairo military spokesman last night.

GOVERNMENT STATEMENT

The British Government has issued the following communique.

In their declaration of July 1, 1940, His Majesty's Government stated that they would not allow Syria and the Lebanon to be occupied by any hostile power or to be used as a base for attack upon those countries in the Middle East which they are pledged to defend.

Despite this clear warning, the Vichy Government, in pursuance of their policy of collaboration with the Axis Powers, have placed air-bases in Syria and the Lebanon at the disposal of Germany and Italy, and have supplied war materials to the rebel forces in Iraq.

German infiltration into Syria has begun, and the Vichy Government are continuing to take measures whose effect must be to bring Syria and the Lebanon under full German control.

His Majesty's Government could not be expected to tolerate such actions which go far beyond anything laid down in the terms of the French armistice and are in flagrant conflict with the recent declaration of Marshal Petain that honour forbade France to undertake anything against her former Allies.

The Free French forces have, therefore, with the support of Imperial forces, entered Syria and the Lebanon at an early hour this morning.

At the same time a declaration has been issued by General Catroux, on behalf of General de Gaulle, guaranteeing the liberty and independence of Syria and the Lebanon, and undertaking to negotiate a treaty to ensure these objects. His Majesty's Government support and associate themselves with this promise of independence.

Lifting Blockade

Other developments in this dramatic move on the part of the British Government are the lifting of the blockade, and enabling Syria to enter the sterling block immediately. The necessary instructions have been given to the British Navy.

There is no doubt, it was stated in Cairo, that the Germans have been using Syria and the Lebanon as an air base for an attack on the British forces in Iraq. There is evidence also of the infiltration into Syria of Germans which goes beyond even the use of air bases.

This situation was immediately discussed between the British authorities and Generals de Gaulle and Catroux, and it was fully agreed on both sides that the situation could not be tolerated.

DARLAN PLACED ALLIES IN DILEMMA

WHOLE RESPONSIBILITY ON VICHY

LONDON, Sunday. (R). — Admiral Darlan's policy of gradually giving the French Empire to Germany and of military collaboration with Germany must bear the entire responsibility for any fighting that may occur in Syria. That is the view of Free French Headquarters in London.

A communique issued from General de Gaulle's Headquarters this afternoon says:

"The Hitler-Darlan policy has placed Britain and her Allies in a grave dilemma. They had either to remain inactive and allow the Germans to establish themselves in Syria with Vichy's compliance, which meant for Syria the loss of independence and for France the abandonment of its position there and the possibility of the transformation of Syria into a powerful military air and naval base threatening Turkey, Iraq, Palestine and Egypt — or to act against the Germans already in Syria and prevent the coming of new German forces at the risk of collision with the forces remaining still loyal to Vichy and acting as auxiliaries and accomplices to the German forces.

"The second alternative was forced upon them. In these conditions, Admiral Darlan's policy of gradually giving the French Empire to Germany and of military collaboration with the enemy bears the whole responsibility for any fighting that may occur in Syria.

"So far as the French forces are concerned, their aim has always been and remains that of hitting the enemy — German or Italian — wherever they meet him, the safeguarding of the French patrimony, and helping Britain wherever and to the fullest extent they can in hastening by a common victory the liberation of France."

VICHY'S "DEFENCE"

Syria will be defended 'to the utmost limit of our forces," according to the Vichy Government.

Announcing that the Allied forces have crossed the Syrian frontier, the Vichy Government in a statement quoted by a German News Agency message, says:

"The British and de Gaullists have attacked Syria, which, according to their assertion, is occupied by German troops.

"A certain Monsieur Catroux has issued a proclamation in which he incites the population in the territory under French Mandate to revolt against France.

"The French Government has already affirmed repeatedly that there are no German troops in Syria.

"Great Britain thus commits a new and unjustifiable attack against France's Empire. We shall defend this, our Empire, to the utmost limit of our forces."

AFTER MIDNIGHT

Petain and Darlan hurriedly conferred as soon as the news of the advance into Syria reached Vichy, states the Rome radio.

GENERAL CATROUX'S PROCLAMATION, ENDORSED BY BRITAIN, TERMINATES MANDATE CONFERS INDEPENDENCE

Declarations by His Majesty's Government and by General Catroux, in the name of General de Gaulle, were dropped by British aircraft flying over the Lebanon and Syria yesterday. The following is the text of His Majesty's Government's declaration:

General Catroux, on behalf of General de Gaulle, Chief of the Free French, has issued a declaration to the inhabitants of Syria and the Lebanon before advancing with the object of expelling the Germans. In this he declares the liberty and independence of Syria and the Lebanon. He undertakes to negotiate a treaty to ensure these objects.

I am authorized by His Majesty's Government in the United Kingdom to declare that they support and associate themselves with the assurance of independence given by General Catroux on behalf of General de Gaulle to Syria and the Lebanon.

I am also authorized to give you the assurance that should you support and join the Allies, His Majesty's Government in the United Kingdom offer you all the advantages enjoyed by free countries who are associated with them.

You may immediately enter into relations with the sterling group which will give you enormous and immediate advantages from the point of view of your exports and imports. You will be able to sell your products and to buy freely in all free countries.

(Signed) MILES LAMPSON, His Britannic Majesty's Ambassador in Cairo, on behalf of His Majesty's Government in the United Kingdom.

General Catroux's declaration was as follows:

Inhabitants of Syria and the Lebanon!

At the moment when the forces of Free France, united to the forces of the British Empire, her Ally, are entering your territory, I declare that I assume the powers, the responsibilities and the duties of the representative of 'La France en Levant.'

This, in the name of Free France which identifies itself with the traditional and real France and in the name of her Chief, General de Gaulle. In this capacity, I come to put an end to the regime of the Mandate and to proclam you free and independent.

You will, therefore, be from henceforward sovereign and independent peoples and you will be able either to form yourselves into separate States, or to unite into a single State. In either event, your statute of independence and sovereignty will be guaranteed by a treaty in which our mutual relations will be defined.

This treaty will be negotiated as soon as possible between your representatives and myself. Pending its conclusion, our mutual situation will be that of Allies closely united in the pursuit of a common ideal and aim.

Inhabitants of Syria and the Lebanon!

You will see from this declaration that if the Free French and the British forces are crossing your frontiers, it is not to suppress your liberty. It is to ensure it. It is to drive out of Syria the forces of Hitler. It is to prevent the Levant from becoming against the British and against ourselves an offensive base of the enemy.

General Catroux

We cannot allow, we who are fighting for the liberty of peoples, that the enemy should submerge your country step by step, obtain control of your persons and your belongings, and turn you into slaves.

We cannot allow that populations which France has promised to defend should be thrown into the hands of the most pitiless master that history has known. We cannot allow that the agelong interests of France in the Levant should be handed to the enemy.

Inhabitants of Syria and the Lebanon!

If, in answer to my appeal, you rally to us, you should know that the British Government, in agreement with Free France, has promised to grant you all the advantages enjoyed by free countries who are associated with them. Thus, the blockade will be lifted and you will enter immediately into relations with the sterling bloc which will open the widest possibilities for your imports and exports. You will be able to buy and sell freely with all free countries.

Inhabitants of Syria and the Lebanon!

A GREAT MOMENT HAS ARRIVED IN YOUR HISTORY. FRANCE, THROUGH THE MOUTHS OF THOSE OF HER SONS WHO ARE FIGHTING FOR HER LIFE AND FOR THE LIBERTY OF THE WORLD, DECLARES YOU INDEPENDENT.

The statement issued by the British Foreign Office on July 1, 1940, and to which reference is made in the communique of H.M. Government (given in another column):

His Majesty's Government understand that General Mittelhauser has stated that hostilities have ceased in Syria. His Majesty's Government assume that this does not mean that if Germany or Italy sought to occupy Syria or the Lebanon, and were to try to do so in the face of British command of the sea, no attempt would be made by the French forces to oppose them.

In order, however, to set at rest doubts which may be felt in any quarter, His Majesty's Government declare that they could not allow Syria or the Lebanon to be occupied by any hostile Power or to be used as a base for attacks upon those countries in the Middle East which they are pledged to defend or to become the scene of such disorder as to constitute a danger to those countries.

They therefore hold themselves free to take whatever measures they may in such circumstances consider necessary in their own interests. Any action which they may hereafter be obliged to take in fulfilment of this declaration will be entirely without prejudice to the future status of the territories now under French Mandate.

SYRIA MAY BE SCREEN for LIBYA

TURKISH OPINION

ANKARA, Sunday (R). — Well-informed circles here are wondering whether German provocation in Syria is not designed to distract the British, while the main attack on Egypt is launched from Libya.

It is pointed out that air-borne troops would be useless in Syria in the face of the heavy tanks which the British are able to bring into action, while the task of supplying the Germans in Syria would be extremely hard owing to the proximity of numerous British air bases.

Therefore, the Turks argue, the British should take over Syria as quickly as possible before the German preparations for a Libyan attack are complete.

Turkey's own position has benefited by the withdrawal of German troops from Greece and Bulgaria, mainly to Moldavia, and military experts express the opinion that it will take the Germans at least a month to build up armies in these areas to their former strength.

Nazis Fly High

German planes are rumoured to have been seen flying very high over Hatay, the former Sanjak of Alexandretta. A German bombing plane made a forced landing yesterday near Istanbul, and the crew were sent to an internment camp.

It is reported from Nicosia that Axis planes at present flying over Cyprus do so only if forced across from what is apparently the regular route between Greece and Syria via the Dodecanese, and then they fly high over the island to avoid trouble.

Enemy planes were over Cyprus yesterday morning, but no bombs were dropped.

Cypriots are moving into country districts. Voluntary evacuation has included a small group of Americans connected with the mines who stayed on despite the U.S. warning which was given months ago.

BLACKOUT: Jerusalem, 7.43 Sunset in / Sunrise, 5.33

Wilson and Catroux

General Sir Maitland Wilson, the General Officer Commanding in Palestine, is in charge of the whole Syrian operation, in which the Allied troops are supported by aircraft and include British, Australians, Indians and Free French.

He was in immediate command of the British Army in Libya, when mechanized forces advanced from Sidi Barrani to Benghazi.

Later he was in charge of the British forces in Greece. Recently he was appointed Commander-in-Chief of the British Forces in Palestine and Trans-Jordan.

He is regarded by many as the master tactician of the British Army. General Wilson is member of a family famous in British military history. His ancestors include Lord Cardigan, of "The Charge of the Light Brigade" fame.

General Georges Catroux was former Commander of the French Foreign Legion. He is 62 and is Commander of the Free French forces in the Middle East.

He was appointed High Commissioner of Free France last November. The field of action then entrusted to him covered Egypt, the Sudan, Syria, Asia Minor and the Balkans. He knows Syria with detailed thoroughness.

No name stands higher throughout the French Empire than General Catroux's. He is the son of a General, is tall and wiry, was born in Algeria, spent many years in Morocco while head of the Foreign Legion, and most of his brilliant military career has been spent in the French Colonies where he quickly established a reputation for courage and great administrative ability.

When Governor-General of French Indo-China, he was organizing resistance against possible Japanese attack when Vichy signed the armistice. He repudiated "the Men of Vichy" who have since sentenced him to death.

FRANCE of DARLAN AND DENTZ

CATROUX AS LIBERATOR

A broadcast to Frenchmen and Syrians, recalling the past career of General Catroux and contrasting it with the record of General Dentz, was made in French over the Palestine Broadcasting Service last night.

General Catroux, the commentator said, had been entrusted with the task of liberating Syria from the Germans to whom the Vichy Government had betrayed the country.

That choice was all the more fitting because he had been far more successful in pacifying Syria after the last War than either General Sarrail, the High Commissioner at the time of the Druse rebellion, or General Dentz.

The speaker recalled General Catroux' brilliant military record, from the days of the last War to his close collaboration in Morocco with Marshal Lyautey which resulted in the pacification of the major part of that territory.

The present High Commissioner, General Dentz, had been sent to Syria by the Vichy Government despite the black record of his previous command in that country because the Germans regarded him as sufficiently servile to carry out their orders. In contrasting General Catroux's record with that of General Dentz, he appealed to Frenchmen and Syrians alike to regard him as the bringer of honour and liberty, "without which, whatever Admiral Darlan and General Dentz may say, there can be no life for a Frenchman."

NO OPPOSITION TO R.A.F.

CAIRO, Sunday (R).— Fighter support for the Allied troops in Syria is revealed in a special R.A.F. Middle East communique tonight which states,

Aircraft of the R.A.F. gave full support to the British, Imperial and Allied troops which crossed into Syria at dawn on Sunday. Fighter aircraft which patrolled the sky over our advancing troops met with no opposition.

ARAB COUNTRIES WERE IN DANGER

HOPE FOR FRENCH AND ARAB COOPERATION

The special character of the operations in Syria was described briefly in last night's war communique from Middle East Headquarters which (as given in full below) stated that Allied forces had crossed the frontier into Syria with the object of eliminating German personnel and influence from certain areas in which they were securing a dominating position. The establishment of these German bases might endanger the security of the Allied situation in the Middle East and lead to Arab countries being seized by the Axis powers, it was stated, and it was hoped to secure both French and Arab cooperation in this task. R.A.F. fighters covered the advancing troops and encountered no opposition.

ALLIED HONOUR AGAINST AXIS PERFIDY

THE DIE IS NOW CAST IN SYRIA

By FERGUS J. FERGUSON,
Reuters Diplomatic Correspondent

LONDON, Sunday. — The die has been cast in Syria. At 2 o'clock this morning, Free French troops, supported by Imperial forces, crossed the frontier to bring to an end the growing Germanization of that country.

It is a move of vital importance which affects the whole position in the Eastern Mediterranean. There is no going back until the situation has been liquidated once and for all. The only criticism that the British action is likely to meet is that the decision has been reached too slowly.

It is unknown yet what forces are being employed or what resistance is likely to be encountered. The French forces in Syria are variously estimated at betwen 30,000 and 60,000, but only about 15,000 are French and the rest Colonials.

It is believed that there is dissatisfaction among some officers, especially those who had not taken kindly to the policy of complete subservience to Germany. The recent appeals to General Dentz for more "trustworthy" troops and the flight of Colonel Collet and other officers to British military lines bear witness to the feeling among the military.

But it would be unwise to rule out the likelihood of strong resistance especially at aerodromes, where German infiltration will supply an element of stiffening to the opposition to the Free French and British advances. Germany is also likely to rush what troops she can by air and, even, if feasible, by sea.

Appeal to Syrians

It is probable that an important section of the population in Syria will be on the side of General de Gaulle and the British. Not only have they the bitterest memories of German military methods during the last war, but they have a strong grievance against the French Government which failed to implement the solemn pledge to give Syria and the Lebanon complete independence.

The proclamation of General Catroux supplemented by the declaration of the British Ambassador in Cairo on behalf of the British Government, guaranteeing liberty to the peoples of Syria and the Lebanon will have a determining effect upon any waverers who may have clung

(Continued on Page 3, Column 3)

SOME RESISTANCE.

HAIFA, Sunday. — News received here from various parts of the border during the afternoon indicate that some resistance was offered by French troops at some points along the front but so far there are no reports of any major resistance.

Reports not yet confirmed state that a number of bridges were blown up by the French to impede the Allied progress along the Nakura-Beirut road.

Operations from Palestine started from a number of points practically along the whole frontier, many columns moving up simultaneously, while the Navy is covering the left flank of the invading forces.

The news of Allied intervention in Syria and the Lebanon spread like wildfire in Haifa today, where great enthusiasm was expressed among all circles of the population at the removal of the threat of Nazi infiltration into French-Mandated Territory.

Arab circles commented most favourably on General Catroux's declaration, and the atmosphere in the town is one of considerable relief following days of nervousness.

Zero Hour

When military traffic became almost continuous throughout the past two days and nights and the war correspondents were seen to leave their temporary headquarters on Mount Carmel for the front yesterday afternoon, there was no longer any doubt among the population that zero hour had come.

Although only some 25 miles from the frontier, Haifa had its first indication that things had started moving up only after work had begun as usual in offices, workshops and in the port, and the subject was eagerly discussed by small groups in the street while the news bulletins displayed at the offices of *The Palestine Post* were frequently consulted by many who were sceptical of rumours.

It was variously reported that distant gunfire could be heard during the day, but apart from repeated flights of planes zooming overhead, Haifa remains much as usual.

Map of Syria — Page 4.

WEYGAND RETURNS TO AFRICA

General Weygand returned to North Africa by air yesterday following his visit to Vichy, says a Vichy dispatch.

The Nazi-controlled Paris radio also reports that Laval is actually going to his estate near Vichy, and may be expected to go to Vichy itself.

Communiques Vigorous Patrols at Sollum

G.H.Q. MIDDLE EAST

Syria Early this morning Allied forces under the command of General Wilson crossed the frontier into Syria with the object of eliminating German personnel and influence from certain areas in which they are securing a dominating position through continued infiltration. If allowed to proceed unchecked, the establishment of German bases in these areas might endanger the security of the Allied situation in the Middle East and lead to Arab countries being seized by the Axis powers. It is hoped to secure both French and Arab cooperation in this task.

Libya Tobruk: Artillery on both sides has been active. Sollum Area: Vigorous patrolling is continuing.

Abyssinia After crossing the river Omo in two places, East and West African troops are pressing forward. At the Northern crossing alone the enemy lost over a hundred dead, leaving a thousand or more prisoners in our hands. In addition we captured 20 guns, 200 lorries, many machine-guns and quantities of other war material. The retreating enemy forces are being vigorously pursued.

R.A.F. MIDDLE EAST

Libya Bomber aircraft of R.A.F. carried out heavy attacks during night of June 6/7 on harbour and other military objectives at Benghazi. Fires were started on central mole, near the telephone exchange, and among military buildings. Aircraft which arrived later over the target bombed the fires causing such an increase in area and intensity that they were visible at 50 miles distance. The aerodrome and satellite landing grounds at Derna were also bombed. Several large fires were started, and a number of aircraft destroyed on the ground. Bombs were also dropped on nearby barracks.

Abyssinia In the Jimma area retreating enemy columns were bombed and machine-gunned by aircraft of S.A.A.F. A number of vehicles were destroyed by direct hits.

Alexandria One enemy aircraft was shot down by machine-gun fire over Alexandria last night. Our fighter aircraft carried out protective patrols over shipping in the Mediterranean. One enemy aircraft was driven off by a South African fighter and forced to jettison its bombs.

All our aircraft returned safely from the above operations.

AMERICA ENDORSES MOVE

ADMIRAL LEAHY WARNS PETAIN

MADRID, Sunday.— The U.S. Ambassador at Vichy, Admiral Leahy, has handed Marshal Petain a memorandum prepared by President Roosevelt, and is reported to have warned the Marshal of the danger facing France from Darlan's machinations.

Admiral Leahy added that Germany was interested in bringing about war between France and Britain, and declared that if any link were traced between the French Colonies and alleged German influence, immediate U.S. action would be taken.

The Admiral also said that evidence in possession of the United States showed that owing to German infiltration, Syria had ceased to become neutral territory, and **the United States could only justify any British action taken in Syria.**

An arrangement with the French Government providing for daily patrols by United States planes and boats of Martinique and Guadeloupe was announced in Washington last night.

The arrangement, disclosed in a letter from Mr. Cordell Hull to Senator Mead, which the latter has published, also

provides certain guarantees regarding the movement of French vessels in United States waters and commits the French Government to prior notification regarding any gold shipments.

A naval observer stationed at Fort de France checks the observance by the United States patrols.

HEAVY RAID ON ALEXANDRIA

CAIRO, Sunday (R). — An air raid on Alexandria in which it is feared that casualties may have been heavy, took place last night (Saturday) when several bombs were dropped and considerable damage caused, states a communique issued by the Egyptian Ministry of the Interior.

It is not yet possible to determine the exact number of casualties. One enemy aircraft was shot down.

THE PALESTINE POST

MONDAY
JUNE 23, 1941

VOL. XVII. No 4598
PRICE 10 MILS

BRITAIN GOES TO SOVIETS' AID AS HITLER'S ARMY INVADES RUSSIA

MAIN PUSH THROUGH BUKOVINA

Italy 'Considers Herself at War' Too

LONDON, Sunday (R). — German mechanized forces, which have crossed the Russo-German border at a number of points, are moving forward particularly in the Bukovina province of Rumania in conjunction with Rumanian forces, which claim to have crossed the River Pruth into Bessarabia and occupied the town of Bolgrad.

This announcement was broadcast this morning by the Rome radio which also added the scarcely surprising statement that Italy considered herself at war with Russia and had notified the Soviet Government to that effect.

A German High Command communique today announced that "fighting broke out on the Soviet border in the early hours of today" and claimed that enemy attempts to fly over East Prussia were "repulsed with heavy losses" by German fighters who "shot down a number of bombers."

The High Command has also broadcast a special warning to the civilian population to be on guard against parachutists "singly or in groups." A warning to shipping that dangers will be encountered in the Arctic Sea northward of Finland, and in the Black Sea except in specified passages leading from the Bosporus, was also broadcast.

Along the Dniester

With both sides apparently massing their strongest forces on the Rumanian front, great masses of Russian troops are reported from various capitals to be arriving in a steady stream behind the line of the Dniester River, while strong concentrations of the Russian Air Force have been moved up from Kiev to newly constructed airfields behind the line.

On the long Polish border, the Russians are understood to have completed the evacuation of all civilians from a zone 60 miles wide in Soviet Poland, and bridges in that region are ready to be blown up. The bridges across the River Pruth which divides Bessarabia from Rumania are similiarly reported ready for dynamiting.

Hitler Courts A Bear Hug

(By a Political Correspondent)

Germany has at last shown Russia the value of her friendship. At dawn yesterday with her Rumanian and Finnish helpers she invaded the Soviets along a 1,500 mile front.

This aggression will come as a surprise to few. Nor will anyone be surprised that once again Hitler has broken his pledged word. The events of yesterday are merely further examples of his policy of *Blitz-krieg* and *Blitz diplomatik*. Nevertheless it is of interest — albeit academic seeing that Hitler is Hitler — to recall his comments about the German-Russian pact which he sprung on the world on August 23, 1939. This is an extract from the approved text of a verbal communication made by him to Sir Neville Henderson two days after Stalin and Ribbentrop had signed the pact in Moscow:

> Agreement with Russia was unconditional and signified a change in the foreign policy of the Reich which would last a very long time. Russia and Germany would never again take up arms against each other. Apart from this, the agreements reached with Russia would also render Germany secure economically for the longest possible period of war.

It is a waste of printer's ink to comment on Hitler's standards of honour; but comment on other lines is not out of place. The two last dictators who went to Russia were Napoleon in 1812 and the Kaiser in 1918. Neither stayed there long.

Ukraine Grain, Baku Oil

Hitler now in his turn proposes to take the Ukraine for grain and Baku for oil to make himself "secure economically for the longest period of war." But even if his aggression succeeds militarily, no military success will solve his ensuing probems.

He would have to transport his booty back to Germany; and when he had got it away by force, the Russian proletariat which already is living at standards little above starvation levels would be faced with a further lowering of these standards, and that would entail a vast German army of occupation to prevent revolt.

Lastly Hitler is already holding down more than half Europe — including Italy. Russia if she falls into his hands, will double his commitments.

Russia has always been a mysterious country. No one knows much about her, except, perhaps that she breeds bears. But every one does know that the hug of a Russian bear means death.

HITLER "FORESTALLS STAB-IN-THE-BACK ATTEMPT"

Reverts to Anti-Bolshevist Policy

Hitler announced in a proclamation over the German radio at 3.30 yesterday morning that the German Army had begun to march against Soviet Russia, assisted by the Finns in the north and the Rumanians in the south.

This sensational outcome of he recent circumstantial reports of rising tension between Germany and her short-lived, powerful war ally Russia was read to German listeners, after only a quarter of an hour's warning by Goebbels, who said:

"The Fuehrer has ordered the German forces to oppose this menace with all the might at their disposal. In the coming struggle, the German people are fully aware that they are called upon not only to defend their native land, but to save the entire civilized world from the deadly dangers of Bolshevism and to clear the way for true social progress in Europe."

Soviet Encroachment

In his proclamation, Hitler said that he sent Ribbentrop to Moscow in 1939 because he thought that he could come to an understanding with Russia.

"The result of that treaty concluded by me (the Soviet-German non-aggression pact) resulted in the disappearance of thousands of German subjects from Lithuania."

But he still kept silent, hoping to arrive at a "lasting" agreement. Germany had had no intention of attacking Lithuania, but on the contrary only to send her troops there to protect it.

After stating that despite all this, he had agreed to the Russian demand to annex Lithuania, he turned to the question of Poland and said that the victory in Poland, which was carried out entirely by German troops, gave him an opportunity of making an offer of peace to the Western Powers, but this offer was rejected. Hitler continued.

"In the autumn of 1939 and the spring of 1940, Russia tried to bring not only Finland but also the Baltic States under her yoke. This could only have been directed against Germany. In 1940, Russia had 22 divisions in the Baltic States. The purpose of this was obviously a demonstration against Germany."

Soviet Demands

Hitler then gave four subjects which, he said, M. Molotov had put to him when he visited Berlin. These questions Hitler enumerated as follows:

1) Would Germany give a guarantee to Rumania in case of an attack by Russia against Rumanian Bessarabia and Bukovina?

2) As Russia felt herself again threatened by Finland, was Germany prepared to aid Finland by sending troops?

3) Was Germany willing that Russia should grant a guarantee and send troops to Bulgaria?

4) Russia required a free passage through the Dardanelles and the establishment of land and naval bases on the Bosporus.

After giving his replies on these points, Hitler insisted.

"The German Army and German home front know that up to now, not a single German tank or motorized division has been on its eastern frontier, whereas Russia had by now 160 divisions facing Germany across that frontier.

"Russia had broken the German-Soviet non-aggression agreement by organizing a 'putsch' in Yugoslavia and promising to send planes and munitions to the Serbs through Salonika.

"Stab in the Back"

"Bolshevism is opposed to National Socialism in deadly enmity. Bolshevist Moscow desires to stab National-Socialist Germany in the back while she is engaged in a struggle for her existence. Germany has no intention of remaining inactive in face of this grave threat to her eastern frontier.

I, therefore, today decided again to place the fate and future of the German Reich and of our people in the hands of our soldiers. May God help us in the battle.

"At this moment, the greatest march in the history of the world is taking place. German troops, together with Finnish divisions and the conquerors of Norway under the command of the Commanding Officer of Norway, are marching together from East Prussia to the Carpathians.

"The German and Rumanian forces extend from the Carpathians to the south. This front is a protection not only of single countries, but of Europe."

Message to Army

"The fate of Europe, the future of the German Reich and the existence of our people lie in your hands alone," Hitler declared in a special message addressed to the German troops on the Eastern Front, according to the official news-agency.

He added, "You are entering into a struggle fraught with difficulties and responsibilities May God help us all in this fight."

Ribbentrop today received the Italian, Japanese, Turkish and Spanish Ambassadors, and the Hungarian, Swedish, Bulgarian, Slovakian, Finnish, Rumanian and Croat Ministers and gave them the latest information concerning events on the eastern borders.

NAZI ATTACK IS ALSO PROPAGANDA DRIVE

LONDON, Sunday (R). — In all probability, the attack on Russia was conceived for a twofold purpose, — to secure material aid from Russian wheatfields and oil and mineral deposits, and at the same time to make a tremendous propaganda drive in Britain and America in order to divide opinion there, in the view of authoritative circles here.

It is significant that the German Transocean News Service today sent out news in code which might easily have been instructions to German agents and Fifth Columnists.

Although the immediate force of Hitler's latest blow may be against Russia, there is no doubt that its ultimate direct purpose is to defeat all Democracies. Exaggerated optimism merely on the grounds that another Great Power has been forced into the war against Germany would, therefore, be very short-sighted.

With tremendous confidence in his Army's powers, Hitler believes that he can crush the Soviet Union in his greatest campaign of all, set up a puppet Government in Moscow, and then, freed of all economic worries, turn his whole attention to the attempted defeat of Britain and her associates.

It is notable that in his proclamation, Hitler put Finland and Rumania, which are small countries with grievances, in the forefront of his propaganda drive. This is a palpable attempt to divide world opinion to cover up his own calculated and unscrupulous scrapping of the Russo-German Pact and to justify his act of blatant and unprovoked aggression.

"UNPROVOKED ATTACK BY BLOODTHIRSTY FASCISTS"

Molotov Calls on Russians to Beat Invaders

LONDON, Sunday (R). — The Foreign Minister, M. Viacheslav Molotov, announced the German invasion of Russia to the Soviet peoples at 11.15 this morning in a broadcast address. He said:

"The Soviet Government and its leader, Comrade Stalin, have commissioned me to make the following announcement:

"Today, at 4 o'clock in the morning, without giving any reason to the Soviet Government and without a declaration of war, the German forces attacked our country, invaded our frontier at many places and raided our towns of Zhitomir, Kiev, Sebastopol Kaunas and several others. More than 200 people were killed and wounded. Flights of enemy aircraft as well as artillery fire were made from Finnish and Rumanian territory.

"This unheard-of attack on our country is without example in the history of civilized nations. The attack on our country has been made in spite of the fact that there is a non-aggression pact between Germany and the U.S.S.R., which was conscientiously kept in every detail. The attack on our country has been made in spite of the fact that, throughout this time, this pact was valid and the German Government could not furnish proof that the Government of the U.S.S.R. has ever infringed a single one of the clauses of the pact.

"All responsibility for this robber attack on the Soviet Union falls on the German Fascist leader. After the attack, the German Ambassador in Moscow, Schulenberg, at 5.30 in the morning gave me as People's Commissar for Foreign Affairs a Note in the name of his Government that the German Government had decided to proceed against the Soviet Union because of the concentration of units of the Red Army on the western German frontier.

Germany the Aggressor

"In answer to this, I declared in the name of the Government of the U.S.S.R. that until the last minute, the German Government had made no representation to the Soviet Government. Germany decided to attack the Soviet Union in spite of the peaceful attitude of the Soviet Union and because of this very fact, Fascist Germany became the aggressor.

"By the desire of the Soviet Government, I have also to announce that at not a single point have our forces or our Air Force allowed any frontier to be violated, and because of that the allegations of the Rumanian radio that the Soviet Air Force raided Rumanian aerodromes is nothing but a lie and a provocation.

"In the same way, the whole of Hitler's declaration published today is nothing but a provocation.

"Now when this attack on the Soviet Union has taken place, the Soviet Government has given our forces the following order:

Beat back the enemy's invasion and do not allow enemy forces to hold the territory of our country. This war has been forced upon us not by the German people, not by the German workers or intelligentsia whose problems we thoroughly understand, but by a clique of bloodthirsty Fascist leaders of Germany who have oppressed the French, the Czechs, the Poles, the Netherlands, the Belgians, Dutch, Danes, Greeks and other nations.

The Government of the Soviet Union are firmly convinced that our gallant Army and Navy supported by the Soviet Air Force will honourably fulfil their duties to the Soviet people and will deal a complete blow to the aggressor.

The Fate of Napoleon

"This is not the first time that our country has had to deal with an arrogant invader. When Napoleon invaded Russia, our country answered with courage and Napoleon was beaten and met his doom. The same thing will happen to the arrogant Hitler, who has started a new attack on our country.

"The Red Army and the whole country will once again wage a victorious war for the nation's honour and liberty. The Government of the Soviet Union are convinced that the whole population of our country, all the workers, peasants and intelligentsia, men and women, will act with a complete understanding of their duties and work.

"All our people must be united as never before. Everyone must demand from himself and from others discipline, organization and a self-sacrifice worthy of the true Soviet patriot in order to fulfil all the needs of the Red Army, Fleet and Air Force, to guarantee victory over the enemy. The Government relies upon all men and women of the Soviet Union."

"Nazi Note" — Page 4.

RUSSIA WELL PREPARED

By MAURICE LOVELL,
Reuters Moscow Correspondent

Germany's deliberate aggression does not find the Soviet Union unprepared.

Throughout the past month, there have been the constant preparations of the armed forces and civilian auxiliary services based on the experience of war conditions and on lessons learnt as a neutral observer of war elsewhere during the past two years.

Since last Spring, the Soviet Army has undergone a considerable overhauling and strengthening, while Marshal Timoshenko's slogan has throughout been "Training under War Conditions."

Hundreds of thousands of anti-parachutists and other air-raid workers in every region of the Soviet Union have been practising throughout the Spring period in warding off mock attacks on their towns and villages.

Blackout Ordered

Throughout Russia, a complete blackout and other precautions have been ordered by the Moscow radio. The blackout also applies to all road and rail transport.

Young Soviet patriots just home from high school are appearing at the local War Commissariats in large numbers asking to be accepted for military service, states the Moscow radio today.

RUSSIA'S ARMED MIGHT

RED ARMY

THE only unanimity achieved by military correspondents in writing of the size, organization and efficiency of the Red Army is in stating that any estimate is "very largely based on conjecture" (according to Reuters' London Bureau).

Compulsory military service has been continuously maintained since 1917, and Russia has always considered herself in a state of war and maintained a high pitch of defensive preparedness.

As recently as a month ago, Stalin declared, "The Red Army has been reorganized and re-equipped in the light of the experience of the present war," and it is well known that the chiefs of the Soviet forces have been closely following many new phases of modern warfare, especially by the Nazis and always with the view in the back of their minds that one day they might well be up against these methods themselves.

There seem to be two schools of thought in foreign military circles — one is that Russia's machines are all right, but her soldiers are no good, and the other that her men are fine fighters, but her machines will drop to pieces.

Unfortunately, much of the world's critical attention on the Finnish war was obsessed with the fact that gallant little Finland was fighting the Russian Colossus, and it was only at the end of the war, when the penetration of the Mannerheim Line brought the battle to a rapid conclusion, that it was realized that the Red Army had achieved what no other Power had achieved, — namely, smashing its way through a fortified line reckoned nearly as strong as the Siegfried and Maginot, which even Hitler decided to go round.

Under the most adverse weather conditions, Russia, with an army trained solely for defensive purposes on a very different terrain, achieved this, according to military correspondents, by very accurate artillery, which undermined the Mannerheim forts till they toppled over and their guns could not be operated, and then, at the right time and in the right place, by perfect cooperation between dive-bombers, tanks, armoured vehicles and infantry breaking through the line — and the war was over.

That her military chiefs are not lacking in enterprise or ingenuity is evidenced by that daring attack on the Finnish mainland by a light armoured column across 60 miles of the frozen Gulf of Finland.

Finally, in assessing the position, it must be remembered that fighting is now taking place across just that frontier which has been strategically enlarged solely for defence purposes against just such an attack and at the risk of being charged by the rest of the world with "Imperialist expansion."

AIR FORCE

WORLD speculation as to the strength and striking power of the Soviet Air Force will at last be brought to an end as her machines go into action against the Luftwaffe and Russia's real strength is revealed in actual battle.

Any estimate of "Red" strength in the past has been largely conditioned by political circumstances at the time of writing; but it has been universally agreed that, from the point of view of numbers, the Soviet Air Force is, if not the largest in the world, at least very close to that of Germany, who is now fighting on a number of fronts, and at the moment Russia is on one only.

As to the efficiency of her Air Force, Russia has released very few details, but it is certain that a power which was the pioneer of parachute troops and glider trains, and was capable of producing planes that made a sensational transport flight to the American Continent a few years ago is fully aviation-conscious.

So are the Russian people. Parachute jumping-towers are as familiar sights in Russian parks as roundabouts and swings in Britain's. Women pilots are as normally accepted as men, and children at early ages participate in flying courses.

Speaking of the "Red" Air Force recently, a Soviet statesman declared:

This mass of lethal metal, which can be flown an enormous distance, could serve as a good 'Soviet strait-jacket' for aggressors, should they in a fit of madness attack the Soviet land.

Four main types of planes are listed in "Jane's All World's Aircraft" The maximum speed of the fastest is given as about 300 miles an hour, but is doubtful if this is anything like their present maximum speed or that Russia's performance in Finland over a year ago is necessarily, any basis for judging her present capabilities.

The total number of first-line machines is usually estimated at between four and five thousand and a similar number in reserve. Russia's aircraft industry employs some hundreds of thousands of workers and her factories are widely spread over the whole of her vast territory.

In making any attempt to estimate Russia's strength in the air, it must finally be remembered that she has the material, the experience, the mechanics, the designers and, above all, rightly or wrongly, 24 years during which, night and day, she as been anticipating and prospecting and preparing for June 22, 1941.

RED FLEET

JUST about as much is known of the Soviet Navy as of her Army and Air Force, namely, practically nothing.

What is known, however, is that she has a very considerable fleet of submarines of the very latest types, many of them believed to have been developed even beyond those of some of the major sea-powers of the world.

It is possible that Hitler may hope to bottle them up in the Baltic or Black Sea, but in that case, he would do well to remember that the Russians have a habit of picking their submarines up and carrying them across land with about as much difficulty as transporting a shipment of fish.

It must also not be forgotten that in the Arctic the Russians are completely at home and have carried out continuous and unique exploration for a great many years, so that they now know these waters like the palms of their hands.

Motor torpedo craft have also been highly developed and produced in considerable numbers, and Russia has quite an effective fleet of modern destroyers. As in other branches of warfare, Russia is here again fighting in circumstances for which she has long prepared.

Already the German radio has announced the warning that Soviet territorial waters in the Arctic and almost the whole of the Black Sea are danger areas by reason of mines, and also that the Nazis have laid mines in specified areas of the Baltic.

Russia's Caspian Fleet has just completed a comprehensive series of naval manoeuvres on a full wartime basis, and is now "ready for war," according to its commander, Admiral Melkitov. Perhaps this is the keynote of the whole position of the Soviet Union's armed forces — ready for war.

AMERICAN HELP CONSIDERED

WASHINGTON, Sunday. — Germany's declaration of war on Russia caused a great sensation here this morning. It is stated that Government officials were caught unprepared for a development of such far-reaching significance, but President Roosevelt, Mr. Cordell Hull and Lord Halifax were immediately informed.

Referring to possible American aid for Russia, radio commentators generally take the view that as that would obviously involve much time, Washington will probably continue to concentrate for the present on maintaining and increasing the delivery of supplies to Britain.

Dispatches from American correspondents in Germany indicate that the news came as a complete surprise to the public and evoked none of those scenes of enthusiasm which were noticeable in Rumania.

Reports from Moscow equally stress the suddenness of the event, so far as the general public is concerned, and the rapidity of the change in the atmosphere. M. Molotov's broadcast was listened to by huge crowds who gathered everywhere around the loudspeakers. Meetings were held all over the country immediately afterwards, and the customary, resolutions passed expressing readiness to defend the country.

There is as yet no trace of hostility in the Soviet press against Japan, with whom a non-aggression pact was recently concluded. Political observers are of the opinion that Japan will for the time being adopt a waiting attitude, but the possibility that she will forward economic demands and ultimately join Germany is not excluded.

BLACKOUT: Jerusalem, 7.47 — Sunset in — Sunrise, 5.34

PRELUDE TO ATTACK ON BRITAIN

Soviet Danger is Our Danger — Churchill

Great Britain will give every possible help and assistance to Russia in her struggle against Germany, and will call upon the Dominions and upon Britain's Allies and friends to adopt the same policy.

This solemn promise was given by the Prime Minister in an address broadcast to the world from No. 10 Downing Street at 7 o'clock G.M.T. last night, when he revealed that the British Government had already offered to supply Russia with every technical and economic aid that was needed.

This new cataract of horrors which Hitler had launched upon the people of Russia would not deflect the Allies from their purpose, said Mr. Churchill. They would never enter into negotiations with Hitler, or with any member of his gang, and any State which found itself face to face with Nazi Germany was their ally.

Britain's Decision

I have to declare the decision of His Majesty's Government. We have but one aim and one single, irrevocable purpose. We are resolved to destroy Hitler and every vestige of the Nazi regime. We shall give whatever help we can to Russia and to the Russian people. We shall appeal to all our friends and allies in every part of the world to take the same course and pursue it steadfastly to the end.

It is not for me to speak for the actions of the United States but if Hitler imagines that his attack on Russia will cause the slightest division of aims or slackening of effort in the great democracies who are resolved upon his doom, he is woefully mistaken.

They would fight Germany by land, on sea, and in the air to the bitter end. The R.A.F., now constantly growing in strength, would redouble its efforts to strike at Germany's heart.

We shall bomb Germany by day as well as by night, making the German people gulp each month a sharper does of the miseries which they have showered upon mankind.

Vast Enterprise

The Prime Minister, who spoke at times with deep emotion, described the German attack on Russia as a turning-point comparable to the fall of France, the Battle of Britain and the Lease-Lend Act. By this act, he said, Hitler was trying not only to destroy the Russian power but to plunge all Asia, above all China and India, into the war which he had begun. The fate of a thousand million human beings was at stake.

Even the carnage and ruin, which Hitler's victory, should he gain it — he has not gained it yet — would bring on the Russian people, would only be a stepping stone to an attempt to plunge four or five hundred million people who live in China and 350 million people who live in India into a bottomless pit of human degradation over which the diabolic emblem of the Swastika flaunts itself.

But even this gigantic enterprise was only the preparation for something yet bigger: the attempt to invade Britain before American intervention became decisive, and ultimately, to subjugate the Western Hemisphere as well. Therefore, in this attack on Russia, the lives of Britain and the United States were equally at stake.

Russia's danger is our danger and the danger of the United States.

"I would not unsay a word I have spoken," said Mr. Churchill referring to his past attitude towards the Soviet regime. But the tragedies of the past paled before the horror which Hitler, "that bloodthirsty guttersnipe", and his gang had unleashed upon mankind. Now it was the Russian people, not long ago allied to Britain in a fight against the same foe, which was defending its peaceful hearths and homes against the monstrous Nazi war machine. In that struggle, Britain was at their side.

Mr. Churchill's speech was relayed from Jerusalem and was broadcast from the B.B.C. in Russian at 8.45 G.M.T.

AFTER MIDNIGHT

Twenty-seven German fighters were destroyed by Hurricanes and Spitfires during another R.A.F. offensive sweep over the Northern coast of France yesterday (Sunday). On Saturday they had destroyed 28 German fighters.

Lord Halifax made an unusual Sunday call yesterday, conferring with Mr. Sumner Welles for hours.

THE PALESTINE POST

FRIDAY
DECEMBER 12, 1941

VOL. XVII. No. 4742
PRICE 10 MILS

AMERICA AT WAR WITH GERMANY

AXIS FOLLOWS TOKYO -- CONGRESS' UNANIMOUS REPLY

President Roosevelt at 3.05 p.m. Eastern Time yesterday (11.05 in Palestine) signed America's Declaration of War Against Germany and at 3.06 Against Italy. Both resolutions were voted unanimously by Congress, following Hitler's and Mussolini's declarations of war against the U.S.

"ITALIANS' DECISION"

GENEVA, Thursday.— Speaking from the balcony of the Palazzo Venezia in Rome today to a mass meeting assembled in the square below, Mussolini announced Italy's "decision" to follow Germany and Japan in declaring war on the United States.

Neither the Axis Powers nor Japan had desired this latest extension of the war, said the Duce, adding that "only one man wanted it and has been working for it with diabolical tenacity for two years — the American despot, Franklin Delano Roosevelt."

Italy, he continued, was making a solemn decision today in the face of great and memorable events which would change the history of mankind. She was ranging herself by the side of Germany and Japan in a tripartite alliance of 250 million people "united in their determination to bring the Anglo-Saxon tyranny to an end."

Russia Not Mentioned

"Italy is proud to fight shoulder to shoulder with Japan," Mussolini concluded. "Italians — you are on your feet again. You are worthy of this great hour. We shall win!"

No mention is made in the tripartite military alliance announced by both Mussolini and Hitler of the war against Russia. The document contains three clauses as follows:

Article one. Italy, Germany and Japan will wage the common war which was imposed on them by the United States and Great Britain by all the means at their disposal until the conclusion of hostilities.

Article two: Japan, Germany and Italy undertake to conclude neither an armistice nor any peace whatever with the United States or Great Britain without a full reciprocal agreement.

Article three: "Japan, Germany and Italy [illegible] even after the victorious conclusion of the war to collaborate very closely in the sense of the Tripartite Pact which they concluded in September, 1940, with the object of accomplishing an equitable order.

PREMIER REVIEWS POSITION ON FOUR FRONTS

HOW THE ALLIES STAND

LONDON, Thursday (R). — Following are the main points made by Mr. Churchill in the House of Commons this afternoon on the position of Britain, the United States and her Allies:

Libya The Libyan offensive did not take the expected course, but General Auchinleck set out to destroy the entire armed forces of the Germans and Italians. Now it seems very probable that he will do so. From the viewpoint of drawing weight from the vast Russian front, the continuance of the fighting in its severity is not to be regarded as evil.

"The first phase is over. The enemy has been swept out of the positions which barred our western advance. Tobruk is definitely disengaged. Substantial British reinforcements and fresh troops are close at hand."

Atlantic November fully maintained the great recovery of the previous four months, as regards shipping losses in the Atlantic.

Russia Paying tribute to Russia's "glorious steadfastness," Mr. Churchill said, "German losses have been immense. The Russians have now regained definite superiority in the air over large parts of the front.

"Although our position has changed in important ways, not all favourable, we must faithfully and punctually fulfill the very serious undertakings that we have made to Russia."

Far East "The Japanese onslaught has brought upon the United States and Britain very serious injuries to our naval power. I cannot remember a naval blow so heavy as the sinking of the Prince of Wales and Repulse. The naval power of Britain and the United States is still largely superior to the combined forces of the three Axis Powers.

"For the next few months at any rate, we must expect that the volume of American supplies reaching Britain and the degree of help given by the United States Navy will be reduced."

Marked Improvement in Atlantic Battle; Russian Air Superiority Over Nazis; Libya Drew Weight from Eastern Front, Auchinleck's Great Battle; Reduced Help from America, Serious Blows in The Pacific but Naval Superiority Maintained

LONDON, Thursday (R). — Mr. Churchill, making his review of the war situation in the House of Commons today, said that the military spokesman in Cairo had been pretty well justified in what he said having regard to how things seemed to stand when he said it. If anybody based his hopes on what he said, that man would find today that he had not been misled. The Prime Minister went on:

"The Libyan offensive did not take the course that General Auchinleck and others expected, though it will reach the end at which they aimed. Still, when all is said and done, on November 18 General Auchinleck set out to destroy the entire armed forces of the Germans and Italians in Cyrenaica and now on December 11, it seems very probable that he will do so.

"The Commanders beforehand had an idea that the whole German armoured forces would be encountered by our armoured forces in mass at the outset. However, the sudden surprise and the success of our advance prevented any such main trial of strength.

"Almost at the first bound, we reached right up to Sidi Razegh, dividing the enemy armoured forces and throwing them into confusion. In consequence, a very large number of fierce detached actions took place over an immense space of desert country, and the battle, though equally intense, became both dispersed and protracted.

"For us the foundation of everything was supply and mechanized transport, and this was provided on what has until now been considered a fantastic scale. Also we had to rely on our superiority in armour and in the air.

Generals and Men

"Most of, well, everything depended for us upon the absolutely unrelenting spirit of the offensive, not only in the generals, but in the troops and every man. That has been forthcoming and is still forthcoming. All troops have fought all the time in every circumstance of fatigue and hardship with one sincere and insatiable desire to engage the enemy and destroy him if possible.

"But behind all this has been the persisting will-power of the Commander-in-Chief, General Auchinleck. Without that will-power, we might easily have subsided to the defensive and lost the precious initiative to which here in this Libyan theatre we have for the first time felt ourselves strong enough to make claim.

"On November 24, General Auchinleck proceeded to Battle Headquarters and on the 26th he decided to relieve General Cunningham and appoint Major-General Ritchie, a comparatively junior officer, to command the Eighth Army in his stead.

"General Cunningham rendered a brilliant service in Abyssinia and was also responsible for the planning and organization of the present offensive in Libya, which be-

General Auchinleck — "a military figure of the first order."

gan with a surprise and success, and which has now definitely turned the corner. He has since been reported by the medical authorities to be suffering from serious overstrain and has been granted sick-leave. Since November 26, therefore, the Eighth Army has been commanded with vigour and skill by General Ritchie.

Although the battle is not yet finished, I have no hesitation in saying that for good or ill it is General Auchinleck's battle. I believe we have found in him, as we have also found in General Wavell, a military figure of the first order.

"British armoured corps, the New Zealand Division, the South African Division, and the Indian Division, the British 17th Division and the rest of Tobruk garrison, including the Poles, all played an equally valiant and active part.

"At the beginning of the offensive I told the House that we should for the first time be fighting the Germans on equal terms in modern weapons. This was quite true.

"Naturally there have been some unpleasant surprises and some awkward things have happened. Those who fight the Germans fight a stubborn and resourceful foe — a foe in every way worthy of the doom prepared for him.

Tanks Four-Pounders

"Some of the German tanks carried as we know, a six-pounder gun, which, though it fires much fewer shots, is sometimes more effective than the gun with which our tanks are mainly armed," continued Mr. Churchill.

"Our losses in tanks were a great deal heavier than we expected and it may be that at the outset, before it was disorganized, the enemy's recovery process for damaged vehicles worked better than ours. I am not so sure of it, but it may be so. We had good superiority in the numbers of armoured vehicles. We gradually obtained mastery as far as the first phase of the battle is concerned.

Our air force was undoubtedly superior throughout in number and quality, and although the Germans have drawn in a most extravagant manner upon reinforcements from many quarters, including the Russian front, that superiority has been more than maintained.

"The greatest satisfaction is expressed by the troops and by the military authorities about the way in which they have been helped and protected by the action of the R.A.F. None of the complaints of the previous enterprises have reached us here upon that score.

"It may be that this wearing down battle will be found in the end to have inflicted deeper injury upon the enemy than if it had all been settled by manoeuvre and in a few days. In no other way in this Libyan attack could a second front have been brought into action under conditions more costly to the enemy and more favourable to ourselves. Remember that about half, and sometimes more, of everything, men, munitions and fuel, which the enemy sends to Africa is sunk before it gets there by our submarines, cruisers, destroyers and our Air Force acting from Libya and Malta.

From the viewpoint of drawing weight from the vast Russian front, the continuance of fighting in its severity is not to be regarded as an evil.

"The first stage of the battle is now over. The enemy has been driven out of the positons which barred our Western advance. Everything has been swept away except certain pockets at Bardia and Halfaya which are hopelessly cut off.

"It may definitely be said that Tobruk has been disengaged. The enemy is still strong but severely mauled and largely stripped of his armour and is retreating to a defensive line west of Tobruk fortress. The clearance of the approaches to Tobruk by the establishment of our air power this far forward to the west in the new air fields, enables the great supply depots of Tobruk which have been carefully built up to furnish support for the [illegible] phase of our offensive with great economy on our lines of communication.

"Substantial reinforcements and fresh troops are available close at hand. It may be that the second phase will gather more easily the fruits of the first than has been our experience in the fighting that has taken place so far.

All the dangers of the Army of the Nile not being able to celebrate Christmas and the New Year in Cairo have been decisively removed.

Mr. Churchill went on to say that the Atlantic Battle in November and the first ten days of December had fully maintained the great recovery of the previous four months.

Turning to Russia, the Prime Minister said that Hitler was not only brought to a standstill everywhere but his losses had been immense — and this was only the beginning of the winter. The Russians had now regained definite superiority in the air over large parts of the front.

The launching of the Nazi campaign on Russia was one of the outstanding blunders of history. "Nevertheless, we must remember the great munition capacities which have been lost to Russia by the German invasion and our pledges to the Russians for heavy monthly quotas of tanks, aeroplanes and vital raw materials."

(Continued on Page 3)

Jap Battleship, Cruiser And Destroyer Sunk

NEW YORK, Thursday (R). The Navy Department has confirmed the sinking of the Japanese battleship, Haruna.

The U.S. Navy also sank one Japanese cruiser and one destroyer [illegible] Wake Island. Four separate attacks on Wake Island have been repulsed during the past 48 hours.

Three hits were scored on the 29,000 ton Japanese battleship Haruna which was set on fire north-east of Northern Luzon. The warship was burning fiercely as the planes left the scene.

The attack occurred ten miles north-east of Northern Luzon.

The Haruna has a displacement of 29,330 tons and a complement of 980. She was launched in 1933 and belongs to the Kongo class of four ships.

Her armament includes eight 14-inch guns, 16 six-inch guns and 8 5-inch anti-aircraft guns. The warship was refitted between 1926 and 1930. Three planes were added to her equipment.

Making the official announcement at a press conference, Mr. Stimson, the Army Secretary, said that determined resistance by American Forces confined the Japanese landings on Luzon to the vicinity of Aparri at the extreme northern tip of the island. (A Manila report, however, states that parachutists have landed near Iligan, in Eastern Luzon).

Mr. Stimson said that there were continued attacks by Japanese aircraft in the vicinity of Manila yesterday. Losses in planes during the attack on Hawaii, on Sunday, although heavy, are already being replaced. "They can be made good and are being made good."

Mr. Stimson said that a flight of four-engined bombers arrived in Hawaii during the Japanese attack. The first was shot down but the crews of the remainder, with a few seconds warning, landed safely in various air fields, only two suffering damage.

Regarding the attack on Hawaii, Mr. Stimson said that the War Department itself had not yet a complete report, but this was no time for recrimination or accusations of blame. "It seems to me that anything like, that is the sign of an immature Government and people.... The present time is one for action and preparation."

Luzon Landing

Mr. Stimson added that the Army was engaged in strengthening its defences everywhere — "In Hawaii and everywhere else."

It was reported from Manila earlier that the Japanese troops which landed early on Wednesday on Luzon Island were immediately engaged by American and Phillipine troops.

A large fire was seen emanating from Nicholls airfield. Moderate anti-aircraft fire was put up, and one plane was seen to be brought down with smoke issuing from its tail.

After the first two attacks, nine more bombers, flying at a high altitude, bombed Cavite and merchantmen anchored in the harbour. The final assault was made eight minutes later by eight more bombers. More than 100 bombs were dropped at Manila and Arza. Citizens watched the raiders without any signs of panic.

It is also announced that a Filipino division has repulsed an attack by Japanese troops 100 miles from Manila. The attack, which was not heavy, was made in the neighbourhood of Lingayen, on the West coast of Luzon. Apart from this fighting, the situation is completely in hand.

ENEMY WITHDRAWING WESTWARD, BUT STILL UNBROKEN

By B. Z. GASTER,
Our Cairo Correspondent

CAIRO, Thursday Evening.— The enemy is still moving west and northwest in Libya, but shows no sign of breaking.

The movement is still orderly, and controlled, though the main concentration forces are spreading out; smaller columns thus avoid affording too marked a target for bombing attacks.

One of these tank columns attempting to halt a southwest flanking movement being carried out by a mixed force of Sikhs, Punjabis and the Royal Sussex Regiment was engaged by a group of our armoured forces which came up in time to drive them off.

Further south other pockets of enemy infantry and armoured cars are being mopped up.

The Germans have been sending a certain amount of air reinforcements to Libya and air attacks against Tobruk, despite a raging duststorm, are somewhat stronger, though largely ineffective. Reports *that these reinforcements are being sent from the Russian front are unconfirmed, though the news that any of our moves in this part of the world would help relieve the pressure of the Soviet front by forcing them to send machines elsewhere would naturally be welcome.*

Earlier Dispatch—Page Three

M.E. Communiques

G.H.Q., CAIRO — Thursday

Throughout the day our mobile forces continued successfully to attack the enemy, whose general trend of movement was northwest and west from El Adem. A number of engagements took place, but owing to the wide area covered and difficulties of communications detailed reports have not been received.

Enemy troops and transport sheltering behind defences immediately west of El Adem were attacked by British armoured units, while further to the west British and South African mobile columns pressed the enemy back all day in a north-westerly direction. Small pockets of enemy infantry and armoured cars left in the area north of Bir Hakeim are being dealt with.

In the late afternoon our armoured forces attacked and drove off a number of German tanks which were endeavouring to interfere with operations being carried out west of El Adem by Sikhs, Punjabis and the Royal Sussex Regiment. Some miles southwest of Acroma, British armoured units shelled a concentration of enemy motor transport, burning some and damaging others.

At Tobruk, Polish units maintaining pressure on the enemy, captured two posts on the Western Defences. Enemy air action against Tobruk yesterday was on a somewhat increased scale, but ineffective.

Further east, South African troops continued to clear up the area north of Trigh Capuzzo, where a few enemy stragglers are being captured. New Zealanders are also engaged in mopping-up operations in the area immediately east of Tobruk.

In addition to the 27 abandoned German tanks found between Bardia and Tobruk the day before yesterday, a further ten German tanks have been discovered.

In the frontier area our artillery is persistently harassing enemy detachments isolated in various defended localities.

Supporting our ground forces, our air forces carried out continual sweeps over the whole area of operations. Enemy concentrations and motor transport were attacked and near Acroma a particularly large number was damaged and set on fire. Ground troops shot down one German ME 110.

R.A.F. MIDDLE EAST—Thursday

Bomber aircraft of the Royal Air Force raided objectives at **Tripoli** and the landing grounds at **Derna** and **Gazala** during Tuesday night.

At **Tripoli**, considerable damage was caused to military buildings and many explosions occurred. A number of fires which broke out developed into a blaze which was seen many miles from the target.

Our aircraft also machine-gunned motor transport vehicles and bombed storage buildings. At **Derna** and Gazala the results of the raids could not be observed owing to unfavourable conditions of visibility.

During yesterday, bad weather seriously hampered operations but in the course of fighter patrols a number of enemy aircraft was damaged.

From these and other operations three of our aircraft are missing, but two pilots are safe.

AFTER MIDNIGHT

Edinburgh will replace both the Prince of Wales and Repulse. The Admiralty previously agreed to allocate the battleship Howe, sister ship of the Prince of Wales, to Edinburgh which has now expressed the intention of replacing the Repulse also. The money invested during Edinburgh's Warships Week last night reached £12,500,000. The original aim was £10,000,000.

BLACKOUT: Jerusalem, 5.36 — Sunset in Sunrise, 7.30

JAP TRANSPORT SUNK

ATTEMPTED LANDING

U.S. War Communiques—Thursday

Out of six Japanese transports escorted by a large naval force which attempted a landing between Vigan and San Fernando (Philippines), three received direct hits, one capsizing and sinking. It is presumed that other attempts were made at various points.

On Wednesday morning all communications with Aparri, Vigan and Toguegarao were interrupted. The news of the fighting caused great excitement in Manila, but there was no panic, business in the city continuing normally, though some people fled to the hills.

Military and naval installations on Luzon Island have been subjected to intermittent Japanese air attacks throughout the day with particularly heavy attacks on the naval base at Cavite.

Initial Japanese attacks against the West coast of Luzon, north of San Fernando, were repulsed with apparent heavy enemy losses, but the Japanese effected landings along the northern coast of the island. The Japanese attacks are of considerable strength and are supported by heavy naval forces.

No action is reported in the Hawaiian Islands since the initial attack on December 7.

BLAMEY BACK IN M.E.

General Sir Thomas A. Blamey, Deputy Commander-in-Chief, Middle East Forces, arrived back in Beirut on Wednesday.

Gen. Blamey in Australia, — Picture — Page 2.

AUSTRALIA'S FIRST WAR COMMUNIQUE

The first war communique ever issued in Australia comes from the R.A.A.F. It states:

There is nothing of major importance to report. Seaward reconnaissances have been carried out by the R.A.A.F. since the Pacific hostilities broke out. One of our aircraft has failed to return.

THAILAND SIGNS

LONDON, Thursday (R). — The conclusion of an alliance between Japan and Thailand was announced today in a Tokyo statement which said:

"It is reported that an agreement of views concerning the conclusion of an offensive and defensive alliance between Japan and Thailand was reached between the Japanese Ambassador at Bangkok, Teiji Tsubokami and the Thai Prime Minister, Luang Pibul Songgram."

2,330 SAVED FROM BATTLESHIPS

ADMIRAL PHILLIPS MISSING

LONDON, Thursday (R). — The Admiralty announces that approximately 130 officers and 2,200 ratings have been saved from the Prince of Wales and Repulse.

It is also announced that Admiral Sir Tom Phillips is reported missing, from H.M.S. Prince of Wales.

The survivors have arrived at Singapore.

At least seven aircraft were destroyed during the attack.

It is now learned that the Prince of Wales and the Repulse were sunk by bomber attacks and three waves of torpedo planes.

The total complement of both ships was approximately 2925 officers and ratings.

WAR FLASHES

President Roosevelt's message to Congress yesterday asking for a Declaration of War against Germany and Italy said in part: "The forces endeavouring to enslave the entire world are now moving toward this hemisphere. . . A rapid and united effort by all the peoples of the world who are determined to remain free will ensure world victory for the forces of justice and righteousness over the forces of savagery and barbarism."

According to Manila newspapers, 30 were killed and 300 wounded in Wednesday afternoon's raids.

The U.S. Senate's declaration of war against Germany was 90 votes to nil, and the House of Representatives 393 to nil. The Senate also passed a Bill enabling American expeditionary forces to be sent to any part of the world. The vote was 86 to nil.

Japanese troops are reported to have landed at the airport six miles from Llagan in Isabela Province 80 miles south of Aparri. The Filipino Constabulary are organizing to repel them.

TIRADE ON ROOSEVELT

By a Staff Correspondent

Hitler's speech to the Reichstag yesterday, delaying for some minutes the announcement of his and Mussolini's declaration of war on the United States, was another exercise in the art of trying to picture himself as an ardent lover of peace whom the wickedness of the Democracies had forced to fight for "a new world order."

Starting out with a survey of the feats accomplished by the Axis armed forces, among which he was careful to include the Italians and the small vassal states which have sent contingents to the Russian front, he gave a detailed time-table of the course of the war since the collapse of France and some highly fanciful accounts of the fighting in Russia.

The most remarkable point of his speech was the fact that the lion's share of praise went not to the much-advertised Panzer divisions which, oddly enough, were not even mentioned, but to the infantry. While carefully avoiding any mention of the recent reverses suffered in Russia, he also announced that the peculiarities of the Russian climate made it necessary for military operations to come to a standstill during the winter.

"Self-Defence"

This uninspiring opening was followed by what must have been an intolerably boring part for even his most devoted listeners, namely a lengthy account of the negotiations on the Polish question which took place immediately prior to the outbreak of the war. Hitler did not spare his audience the reading of a long and complicated document designed to show that in attacking Poland, Germany acted only in self-defence and after having made the most generous offers for a peaceful arrangement between the two countries.

But while acting in self-defence Germany at the same time fought not only for her own interests but for those of Europe as a historical and cultural entity. To prove this point, Hitler ventured into the intricacies of ancient, medieval, and modern history, claiming that what he called his "European Crusade" was in line with, and of a similar importance as the fight of the Greeks against the Persians, and of Rome against Carthage.

Here he took occasion to announce that Europe cannot be limited by political or geographical frontiers in the East. It was incorrect to say that it ended at the Ural Mountains; the Europe of the future would be as large as the "European Spirit" can make it.

Roosevelt the Arch Scoundrel

At this point, Hitler finally came round to the villain of the piece. In the beginning there was some doubt whom he meant, but soon it became clear that Mr. Churchill had now been relegated to second place, while President Roosevelt has advanced to the role of arch-scoundrel.

It was at that point that Hitler, who had spoken up to then with an emotional and oratorical restraint unusual with him, reverted to the pristine purity of his Beer Cellar style. President Roosevelt was deliberately taking the U.S.A. into war to save himself and his "Jewish advisers" from the political and economical bankruptcy of their regime.

In referring to the President and incidentally to Mrs. Roosevelt as well, Hitler became his old ego again. He sentimentalized about the difference between himself and the President whom he pictured as, of all things, the representative of the American plutocracy.

By a long chain of unlawful and dishonourable acts, he declared, President Roosevelt had step by step brought the United States into a ostate of quasi-belligerency, until his shooting order to the U.S. Navy had brought things to a climax. From his interference and his overbearing meddling into affairs which were none of his concern, all the authoritarian countries had had to suffer likewise, though straining their patience and love of peace to the utmost.

It was therefore with deep satisfaction that he and the German people had received the news that Japan had decided to defend herself against the attempts of the United States to cripple her existence and to deny what Japan regarded as her right to live. Even were he not compelled to do so by existing treaties, he would not hesitate to range Germany at the side of those who had called President Roosevelt's bluff, thus making the struggle for the "New Order" truly world-wide. Hitler declared that he was burdened with his task by the will of God by whom he was inspired to fulfil it.

Palestine's
World Famous Products
KABRIA
PURE TABLE WATER
Bottled only by Spinney's Ltd.

LATE Edition

THE PALESTINE POST

TUESDAY
JULY 7, 1942

VOL. XVII. No. 4916
PRICE 10 MILS

THE LESS THE WASTE
THE GREATER THE
HASTE TO VICTORY
FOOD CONTROL

GIGANTIC BATTLE ON 160-MILE FRONT

GERMANS INCREASE PRESSURE

MOSCOW, Monday. — The situation remains difficult and complicated along the 160-mile front from Kursk to Kupyansk, where German pressure has continued in the last 24 hours.

German attacks were especially forceful on the Byelgorod front, where one arm of the two-pronged Nazi drive is trying to thrust north-east in order to link up with the other arm at Kursk. The Germans, at the cost of enormous losses, have succeeded in driving a wedge in positions held by one Russian unit.

Fighting has also continued without respite on the Kursk front where a Russian withdrawal was announced earlier and where the enemy continues to press forward. How far the Red Army has retired on this vital front, which protects the all-important rail junction of Voronezh, midway on the main Moscow-Rostov railroad, was not indicated.

Three times since the beginning of July, Soviet war correspondents have reported German advances achieved by force of superior numbers on several sectors of the Kursk front.

Frenzied Enemy Efforts

A correspondent of the "Pravda" on the spot this morning described the situation. Russian tanks have been thrown into the battle in most of the threatened sectors to limit the enemy's freedom of manoeuvre over a broad front. They have now been in action for five successive days striking hard at what is described as "frenzied" German pressure.

The Germans are using new methods in the onslaught in the Eastern Ukraine. Dive-bombing is being used far more than last year in order to economize in tanks.

The Germans are also making a considerable impression with mobile artillery of all sizes, from ultra-rapid firing machine-guns and anti-tank guns firing explosive shells of high penetrating capacity to heavy artillery.

The hard-pressed Russians have held the enemy in some sectors and counter-attacked elsewhere, taking a mounting toll of tanks, planes and men, but the Germans pierced the defences in one sector, brought up operational and tactical reserves, and began to widen the gap.

Fierce Tank Battles

Fighting in the most difficult conditions against overwhelming numbers, the Russians retired to new positions. Then the Soviet tanks entered the most dangerous positions and manoeuvring skilfully, launched a daring counter-attack and pushed the enemy some distance, stemming the advance on a wider front. According to preliminary reports the tanks destroyed by our infantry regiments and one artillery regiment alone amounted to 60.

The fiercest battle is raging on the banks of an unnamed river (the Germans claim to have crossed the Don), where 50 Panzers succeeded in forcing a crossing. Several hours later Soviet tanks counter-chargd, flung back the enemy to the west bank, kept up the pursuit, and reoccupied several important points.

Despite his terrific losses von Kleist brought up considerable Panzer reserves and re-attacked in the Central sector. Small mechanized groups crossed the river, followed by infantry in collapsible boats, and according to "Pravda"'s correspondent, mechanized troops are continuing the offensive in the Central sector.

Heavy Tanks Thrown In

Heavy Russian tanks called "KV", arfter Marshal Klim Voroshilov, are being thrown in on the Kursk front. They are playing a role of the greatest importance in keeping the terrific German thrust within bounds and permitting the withdrawal of Soviet troops in good order to new positions.

At one point, 20 of these tanks went in to attack German mechanized groups which had succeeded in crossing a water line and drove them back. Only part of the enemy groups managed to regain their own side safely.

Moving always to the most heavily threatened sectors, these tanks by skilful manoeuvres have so far succeeded in preventing what is described by Pravda's correspondent as a "serious situation" from getting out of hand. Captured Germans are referring with the greatest respect to the execution they have done against the German infantry.

Four infantry regiments and one artillery regiment of General von Kleist's troops were wiped out in one day on the Kursk front. Fifty to sixty tanks were destroyed on the same day.

(Reuter and United Press)

NAZIS HEADING FOR MAJOR DISASTER

ONLY 12 WEEKS LEFT FOR DECISION

NEW YORK, Monday. — American military observers in Russia believe that Marshal Timoshenko will for a considerable time to come be fighting a delaying action in the Kursk, Volchansk and Byelgorod sectors, making the enemy pay dearly for every yard gained.

While it is known that von Bock has been throwing large reserves into the battle in the last few days, there are no indications that the Russian Commander has used any of his reserves in the present battle, and it is generally assumed that he is keeping them in readiness for the big counter-offensive planned for a later date.

Maj. George Fielding Elliott, the well-known military commentator, writes today that the German claim to have crossed the Don should not be taken at its face value. The crucial problem facing the Germans at the present is that of time; they have no more than 12 weeks to press on their Russian campaign to a "finish," but they have neither the strength nor the capacity to do so.

The Germans, according to the writer, are heading towards a major disaster in Russia, unprecedented even by that of 1918 in the West, unless they are able to achieve the impossible and gain a decisive victory before the autumn sets in.

Inadequate Preparation

It is noted here that Paul Wolff, Chief of the German Army Medical Corps, has contributed to the "Boersenzeitung" a remarkably blunt criticism of German preparations for the Russian campaign.

The complete inadequacy of the preparations made by the Medical Corps resulted in a "terrific death roll" among the German troops in Russia in the last winter campaign, according to him.

Turkey Unruffled As War Nears Borders

ANKARA, Monday (R). — Though the fall of Sevastopol has brought war nearer to Turkey's borders, complete calm reigns here.

The fact that the Prime Minister and Foreign Minister are on holiday in Istanbul shows that the Government does not expect any immediate problems.

One result of the fall of Sevastopol was the arrival at the Turkish Black Sea coast of a motor-boat containing 40 Soviet soldiers and seven civilians. Two patrol boats also arrived at Sinope, further along the Black Sea coast.

AFTER MIDNIGHT

The Red Army is using a new trench mortar which hurls a small shell developing terrific heat after it explodes, according to the Helsinki correspondent of the Swedish paper "Aftonbladet." These mortars are being used on the Murmansk front, where Russian artillery barrages have been very intensive. About 1,000 shells were fired during one night.

Americans manned American tanks in combat during part of the battle of Libya on June 11/12. They were part of a group of American Armoured Force observers in North Africa, it is announced by the War Department.

Better Outlook in Egypt; But Crisis In Russia

GERMAN THREAT TO VITAL RAILWAY

Military Commentary by ANNALIST

LONDON, Monday. — Ground for fresh hope continues to be afforded by the military situation in Egypt.

Apart from the main fact that the Axis has made no progress since the first attack on the British positions at El Alamein and has in fact slightly lost ground, a number of indications show that we are slowly but perhaps surely doing better.

The Axis losses in guns and tanks so far from their base are serious. Moreover, two points in the battlefield that the enemy has had to give up — the ridge running east and west along the north side of the Quattara Depression, and the strong point lost by him as reported in today's communique — are of consequence and may be the prelude to further German yields. Our superiority in the air is unquestionable and may prove decisive.

The Russian Front

On the Russian front, the German offensive is now in full swing. The dependence of the Soviet High Command on the Moscow-Voronezh-Rostov railway for communication between the northern and southern defence systems is obvious. There is no certainty that the Germans have, as they claim, reached the Don. Even so far north the Don should form a serious obstacle, and Voronezh with the railway lies to the east of the river. The cession of the Don would mean not only that this vital railway was lost to the Russians, but also a direct menace to their armies to the south-west between Kharkov and Rostov. It must be seen as part of a double move on the Caucasus, the other part of which will be launched from the Crimea, probably mainly by air, with the object of taking Marshal Timoshenko in the rear and forcing him to retire towards the Volga.

"Chetnik" Threat Worries Axis

YUGOSLAV FIGHTING REACHES CLIMAX

(From a Special Correspondent)

Fighting in Yugoslavia has reached a climax. With the "Second Front" threat hanging over their heads, the Germans are apparently endeavouring to "pacify" Yugoslavia before the sword of Damocles falls.

The main feature of the present fighting is provided by the large-scale use of aeroplanes by the Germans and Italians for reprisal action. The "Invisible Army" hiding in the forests remains invulnerable to air attacks, and the Germans are therefore giving vent to their rage by razing peaceful villages. Twelve villages in Bosnia were destroyed to the last house by Italian bombers during last week alone.

Unable to send further reinforcements to Yugoslavia, the Germans are tr;ing in vain to fight against the Serbs "to the last Croat." Pavelich has received orders from his German masters to send the Croat Home Guards, his last reserves, into battle.

He has done so, appealing to them to help the regular Croat Army, but most of the Home Guards were so little impressed with the appeal that they deserted by hundreds.

China Will Bear The Burden of The Main Battle

GEN. CHIANG TO THE NATION

"Final Collapse of Enemy is Near"

CHUNGKING, Monday. — China will shoulder the responsibility for the main battle in the Far East, Generalissimo Chiang Kai Shek told the nation today on the eve of the beginning of the sixth year of the Sino-Japanese war.

"We may face worse reverses in the next few months," he continued, "but these will be short and the final collapse of our enemies is near.

"Let none think that the United Nations are without a strategy. China will bear the burden of the main battle in the Eastern Continent, and like the United States is determined to crush Japan, while the British and the Soviets will be responsible for the war in other theatres.

"We must be grateful for the sympathy and assistance of the Allies but the Chinese must help themselves and be worthy of their gallant Allies."

China's Claims

Dr. Sun-Fo, the Foreign Minister in a message to the nation, declares that triumphant China will demand the return of the status prior to 1894, including the restoration of Formosa, the Pescadores, Port Arthur, Dairen and Manchuria. The message adds,

China will be entitled under the armistice and peace terms to demand the complete disarmament of Japan, in order to safeguard her hard-won victory and future security.

The message predicts that China will be able to drive out the invaders if the navies of the United Nations destroy the Japanese Fleet.

Dr. Sun-Fo adds, in referring to internal reconstruction, that China will still be far from "the consummation of democracy," and also that the war's financial burden has been inequitably distributed, while State control of commodities must be increased in order to assist the welfare of the common people.

(Reuter and UP)

U.S. DESTROYERS SCORE ON INDEPENDENCE DAY

WASHINGTON, Monday (R). — Four Japanese destroyers were sunk by U.S. submarines on Independence Day, July 4.

The Navy Department's communique reads:

North Pacific area: On July 4, United States submarines torpedoed four Japanese destroyers in the Aleutian Islands. Three of these destroyers were attacked at Kiska. Two were sunk. The third when last seen was burning fiercely.

A fourth destroyer was torpedoed and sunk at Agattu, where enemy transports and escorting vessels were located on July 2, and attacked by army bombers.

Kiska and Agattu are islands at the westernmost tip of the Aleutian chain which were recently occupied by the Japanese.

Mr. CHURCHILL'S MESSAGE TO CHINA

"WE ARE NO LONGER FIGHTING ALONE"

LONDON, Monday (R).— Mr. Churchill, in a message to the people of China on the fifth anniversary of the Japanese attack, says:

"Both China and the British Commonwealth have known what it is to stand alone against aggression, but they are now fighting side by side against the common enemy together with the tremendous resources of the United States.

"We are determined to extend to the Chinese people every material, moral and spiritual help in our power. Of ultimate victory we are sure. When it was won, our present association will have laid the foundations of lasting friendship."

Allies Will Fight Together

ROOSEVELT'S MESSAGE TO CHIANG KAI SHEK

WASHINGTON, Monday (UP). — President Roosevelt has sent a message to Marshal Chiang Kai Shek, pledging that the United Nations will fight on to the end with China "to secure the establishment of peace, justice and freedom throughout the world."

President William Green of the American Federation of Labour, and President Philip Murray of the Congress of Industrial Organizations, have called on American workers to aid in the relief of China's war sufferers.

BRITISH DESERT COUNTER-ATTACK IN FULL SWING

HUNDREDS OF VEHICLES DESTROYED

RAF Attack Supply Transports

ALEXANDRIA, Monday (R) — The RAF struck one of its biggest blows in the campaign when British planes destroyed hundreds out of 3,500 vehicles, including bowsers containing petrol for Axis Panzers, during an attack on an encampment parked in a sausage-shaped area south of El Alamein.

Naval planes dropped flares and bombs. Then a large formation of heavy bombers roared in showering bombs. They set many vehicles alight and blasted many others.

A naval pilot who took part in the attack said:

Soon we saw many hundreds of fires burning fiercely. The bomb blast must have smashed many more.

Naval pilots also dropped flares at El Daba during the past three nights to guide the heavy bombers. Big explosions and fires were caused. One explosion was visible 70 miles away. Watchers saw two huge sheets of white flame presumably coming from an ammunition dump which was hit.

These naval "night hawks" have been cooperating in attacks on Axis transport for the past ten days without losing a single plane.

Cup Pilot Scores

One of the five German bombers shot down over Alexandria and the Suez Canal area on Saturday night fell to a former Schneider Cup pilot, Wing Commander Stainforth.

Aged 44, Wing Commander Stainforth is the oldest British pilot flying in actve operations in the Middle East. He was piloting a night fighter when he shot down a [illegible] in flames.

Wing Commander Stainforth won the Schneider Cup in 1931, raising the world's speed record to 407½ miles per hour. In 1939 he flew a Spitfire from the south of England to Scotland and back again at an average speed of 273 miles per hour. He is a crack revolver and rifle shot and was in the King's Hundred" at Bisley in 1928.

Egypt Stands Fast Behind Resolute Leadership

"THE TIMES" PRAISES NAHAS PASHA

LONDON, Monday. — In a leading article entitled "Egypt Stands Fast," "The Times" this morning writes:

"The British alliance with Egypt, which has stood and stands between that country and the designs of the totalitarian combine, is fortunate in the clear-minded and resolute leadership of Nahas Pasha.

"While German and Italian forces seek to burst through into the Nile Delta, Rome is putting forth a frantic spate of propaganda to persuade the Egyptians of Mussolini's and Hitler's friendly intentions. For years Mussolini has been swinging the sword of Islam with the intention of wooing the Sphinx more successfully than his model Napoleon.

"But his pretensions are viewed in Egypt — and, it should be added, in Turkey and elsewhere throughout the Moslem world — with a contempt bred both of familiarity and of his present subordination to a more formidable tyrant. Throughout the whole length of the Mediterranean no people, Christian or Islamic, wishes to see this monstrous partnership achieve its ambitions"

(Reuter and BOP.)

DEFENCE TALKS WITH CABINET MEMBERS

CAIRO, Monday. — General Napier-Clavering, head of the British military mission in Egypt, called on the Prime Minister at his office yesterday during a meeting of the Egyptian Cabinet and had a long talk with the Minister of Defence, Hamdi Seif An-Nussar Pasha.

Several members of the military mission were present.

According to reports reaching here from Alexandria, the number of people leaving the city for the country has decreased. Many evacuees have already returned to Alexandria.

PANZERS SHOW SIGNS OF WEAKENING

All Is Not Well Within the Axis Camp

By WILLIAM FORREST and RALPH WALLING, Reuters Correspondents in Egypt

CAIRO, Monday. — There have been indications for some days that all is not well within the Axis camp. Two Panzer divisions showed they have lost much of their former punch.

Attacks that were laid on failed to come off. An intercepted message from the commander of one of the divisions said he could not carry out his allotted task without the help of the other division.

The German infantry division — the famous 90th Light — has also shown signs of having had some of the stuffing knocked out of it. A week ago its losses in killed, wounded and prisoners were estimated at 60 per cent.

Since then the remnants have not been given a moment's rest. They have been continuously on the move and thrown into a series of unsuccessful attacks, bombed and strafed from the air, harassed by our hard-hitting mobile columns and their nights have been made a torment by Allied bombers.

Italians Avoid Action

As for the Italians, the Littoria Division, never quite recovered from the blow administered by our First Armoured Brigade on the last day of June. That was the Littorio's first real taste of fire and it has not sought another. The Italian motorised and infantry divisions — Trieste, Trento, Pavia and Brescia — are hardly taken into account either by the Allies or by the Germans, although they are all up forward.

There is still another Italian infantry division in North Africa — Bologna — which was used to hold the softest sector of the Tobruk perimeter during the siege, but the quality of the Bologna is best described in the words of Italian prisoners who, whenever mention is made, shake their heads and say: "Bologna no good."

Only a thin trickle of reinforcements brought by lighters to Tobruk and Mersa Matruh are reaching the front — nothing like sufficient to rebuild the battered Afrika Korps.

Short of Water

An indication that the enemy's Army is short of water comes from Italian prisoners who say that their ration has been brought down to three quarters of a pint daily.

As they withdrew towards Alexandria, the British Army destroyed the pipeline across the Western Desert and, apart from the muddy liquid available at Tobruk, there is little fresh water to be got between Gazala and the point the Axis troops have now reached. Most of the enemy's water supply has to be brought over 300 miles of desert from the Libyan Djebel country.

Wall of Fire

Both the tank thrust carried out by some 20 Mark III.'s and the infantry advance which the Axis made from the centre of the battle area yesterday morning and afternoon were halted by the Allied wall of fire.

The men of the 15th Panzer Division who made both sorties left behind six blazing tanks. They soon ran into the customary screen of anti-tank guns and fell back to former positions, while guns in the rear continued shelling the Axis.

The Italian Ariete armoured division has cause to regret its first encounter with the New Zealanders, whose inland positions it set out to reduce on Friday. It was the New Zealanders who captured or destroyed 44 guns in that encounter.

The R.A.F. whose fighters I saw today weaving their way back like swallows low over the coast road after strafing the Axis, have shown many people a thing or two since a week ago when Alexandria and the Nile Valley faced the most serious threat of the war. They did as much to [illegible] the Axis dash as the big reinforcements General Auchinleck wisely decided to throw in during the last few critical days.

Morocco Feeds Axis Troops

LONDON, Monday. — According to Lisbon messages, the Axis forces in Africa is receiving 75 per cent of their food supply from Morocco across the land and railway route to Tripoli. There is a shortage of meat, butter and wines in Morocco owing to the large-scale despatches to the Axis forces.

GERMANS SHOW FEAR OF NEW ZEALANDERS

"GET ALL AVAILABLE AMBULANCES"

WELLINGTON, Monday — New Zealand casualties in Egypt up to now have been fairly light, according to war correspondent messages.

An officer told one of the correspondents that the boys were in great heart and had never been fitter. They were in the forefront of the battle at El Alamein, where they staged a spectacular and highly successful counter attack following a terrific German onslaught.

A story is told in Cairo that when the Germans knew the New Zealanders faced them, the following message was flashed back to the German support groups: "Get all available ambulances."

A New Zealand battle group caught the Italian Pavia Division completely by surprise in a new bayonet charge on Saturday night. The Italians were panic-stricken and suffered a great number of casualties.

The Italians had replaced the German infantry of the 90th Light Armoured Division after an earlier charge by the New Zealanders on Wednesday.

New Zealanders have captured the first German war correspondent taken prisoner in northern Africa (as reported earlier.) He had been in the desert only two weeks. He approached a tank to ask the time. An officer looked out politely to answer the request, but, unfortunately for the German, he was a British officer.

The tank crew could not take the German with them, so he was handed over to a gunner. The gunner was later cut off and had to walk 90 miles to regain the British lines. He took the German with him. He slipped past Rommel's headquarters at so close a distance that the German journalist remarked, "That is our Field Marshal's bivouac."

(Reuter and A.I.F. News)

U.S. TANKS AND GUNS ACTIVE IN EGYPT

WASHINGTON, Monday. — While the rumours which have been circulating in Washington and other world capitals that American troops are in the Middle East, particularly Egypt, are not confirmed here, there is no doubt that U.S. arms are being used in Egypt.

Lieut.-General B. B. Somervell, chief of the Army Supply Services, speaking to American newsmen on Saturday said:

"We have a weapon to stop the 88 mm. cannon used by Rommel in Libya and the Western Desert." He refused to say more.

Major-General Levin Campbell, chief of the U.S. Army Ordnance, said at North Carolina, that the American tanks and guns taking part in the battle for Egypt were superior to the German weapons. Type for type, American tanks had heavier guns and armament and greater speed.

The German 88 mm. dual purpose gun which had been credited with much of Rommel's success, was limited in effectiveness. The United States had outmatched it with several field and anti-tank guns.

The War Department today announced regulations permitting United States Army forces in oversea theatres of war, or separate bases, to acquire services, facilities, supplies and equipment under a new Lease-Lend Act without the payment of cash to the foreign Governments concerned.

(Reuter and AIF News)

AXIS DRIVEN FROM STRONG POINT

Growing Allied Initiative

CAIRO, Monday (R). — Fighting was resumed yesterday in roughly the same area, west and south of El Alamein and west of the ridge, and was just as intense in the air as the previous days.

Fighting today is described here as "satisfactory for the Allies." The Axis forces have now been driven back west of a line running due south from El Alamein.

It has been an active day, with General Auchinleck retaining the initiative. The bulk of the enemy forces are now south-west of El Alamein.

Tobruk was again raided last night, while Naval aircraft attacked shipping at Mersa Matruh.

The Middle East joint war communique says:

"The battle in the El Alamein area continued yesterday. Our land and air forces attacked the enemy throughout the day. In one sector our troops in a night attack drove the enemy from a strong point inflicting heavy casualties. Our casualties were slight.

"Medium bombers of the R.A.F. and South African Air Forces again successfully attacked enemy concentrations in the battle area. Our fighters shot down three Junkers 88s, two Messerschmitt 110s and one Messerschmitt 109 and damaged many others.

"Fighter-bombers carried out effective attacks on the landing grounds at the [illegible] area, where at least [illegible] enemy aircraft were damaged on the ground. Six of our aircraft failed to return."

British, Dominion and Allied artillery are still seeking out the enemy and punching him hard in non-stop engagements.

The strong-point mentioned in today's communique is situated to the south of the left flank of our positions around El Alamein, which remain intact.

All British arms have been engaged in fighting during the last few days, and with mighty air support, General Auchinleck's Army has been gradually slowing down and wearing down the Afrika Korps' drive on the Nile.

According to the latest reports the ridge south of El Alamein has been completely cleared of enemy forces.

Battle groups of the South African First Division in many days' continuous action around El Alemein have been inflicting considerable casualties on the Afrika Korps' armoured forces.

Formed now, like other units, into mobile hard-hitting columns, they have carried out regular and successful raids on the enemy as the battle for Egypt swings madly back and forth round the firmly held El Alamein positions.

Helping the Army

CAIRO, Monday (R). — Air Chief Marshal Tedder, Commander-in-Chief of the Middle East, replying to Mr. Churchill's message of Saturday, says:

"I send you the most sincere thanks of the Royal Air Force in the Middle East for your inspiring message. We are all resolved to strive to our utmost and more to assist the Army to clear Africa of the enemy."

Fortitude in Face of Peril

American Jews' Message of Encouragement to Yishuv

A message of encouragement and assurance of support during the time of crisis was received by the Executives of the Jewish Agency and the General Council (Vaad Leumi) of Palestine Jews yesterday from Dr. Stephen Wise, Chairman of the American Zionist Emergency Committee in New York.

On the same day, the Jewish National Fund of America cabled $100,000 to the Head Office in Jerusalem, accompanying the remittance with a similar message of solidarity. Dr. Wise's cable ran

In this hour of crisis and trial, our thoughts and hearts go out to you, our brethren of the Yishuv in warmest affection. We here are doing our utmost to insure for you the means of defence and survival. Your achievements throughout the years and your splendid courage have been a light for all Israel. We know you will not fail.

The message from the Jewish National Fund in New York to the Head Office in Jerusalem, signed by Dr. Israel Goldstein, in part stated:

We are cabling $100,000 and at the same time, wish to convey, on behalf of the Jewish National Fund of America, our admiration of your fortitude in the face of peril and your determination to mobilize the maximum resources to resist the enemy. We will endeavour to prove worthy of your high example by doing what we can to strengthen your hands.

V
Drink
SPINNEY'S MINERALS
PURE AND REFRESHING
SODA WATER
LEMONADE
GINGER BEER
TONIC WATER
GINGER ALE
ORANGE SQUASH
LIME JUICE & SODA
PALESTINE'S PERFECT PRODUCTS
V

THE PALESTINE POST

LATE Edition

WEDNESDAY
NOVEMBER 25, 1942

VOL. XVII. No. 5035
PRICE 12 MILS

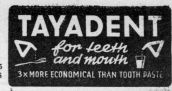
ALLIES ADVANCE ON TUNIS, BIZERTA

HOPE OF 'GERMAN DUNKIRK'

ALLIED HEADQUARTERS, NORTH AFRICA, Tuesday. — Fighting spread over the greater area of Tunisia today in the form of local engagements.

An Anglo-French force drove back the German "advance screen" south-west of Tunis, while the British battered a similar screen along the coast.

Tonight's U.S. communiqué reads:

Local engagements were reported by forward troops of the Allied Force. French patrols report continued activity in the southern sector.

In the southern sector also Allied paratroop units repulsed an enemy mechanized column and captured prisoners. Our fighter planes shot down four enemy aircraft and attacked an enemy troops train near Gabes. Bombers have carried out night raids on Bizerta and Tunis. None of our aircraft is missing from these operations.

Allied columns advancing along the valley of the Nedjerda River have encountered and overcome the resistance of a German light armoured column, while small German detachments are reported to be infiltrating between Kairouan and Gafsa.

The persistence and tenacity of these German landings in the Gabes and Sfax regions would seem to indicate that Rommel is determined to establish land communication between Tripoli and Tunisia. It is also believed that many German troops are coming from Rommel's camp.

Speaking at a press conference here today, General Clark after asserting that the Allied position was better than expected, with the prospect of North Africa becoming a "German Dunkirk," also revealed that the Allies intend to make Oran a gigantic supply base as it is comparatively out of range of German planes.

Referring to the present operations, he said: "Now we are greedy and we want Tunisia without a fight. But we must realize that we can't have it that way."

He added that while the situation ... because the Germans had been able to reinforce their positions.

General Clark was interviewed during a conference with General Fredendall, Commander of the Tarian zone. Brigadier General Doolittle, who led the bombing raid on Tokyo last April, piloted General Clark.

(United Press and Reuter)

U-BOAT TORPEDOED BY BRITISH PLANE

ORAN, Tuesday. — An Allied anti-submarine patrol operating some miles off Oran by depth charges forced a U-boat to the surface, after which a British plane blew it up with a torpedo. Two members of the crew were rescued.

The Seafire, a slight modification of the Spitfire used for aircraft, carriers, has been playing an important part in protecting Allied troopships.

(United Press and Reuter)

DAKAR TO BE USED AS ALLIED BASE

MADRID, Tuesday (UP). — It is reported that Darlan's first order to the Governor of West Africa, M. Boisson, was to forbid any ship to leave Dakar harbour. The warships there include the battleship Richelieu, a cruiser, and 21 submarines.

Darlan is also dispatching a special staff mission to Dakar to establish cooperation and to grant facilities to the British and Americans.

A dispatch which took 13 days in transmission, sheds some light on the situation in West Africa before Boisson joined up with Darlan.

Donald Coe, U.P. correspondent at an Allied base in West Africa, cabling on November 13, said that four young French aviators arrived at the base on that day in a battered American-built plane after incapacitating other planes on an airfield near Dakar and dismantling the aerodrome's radio-station.

They said that for many weeks they had planned to escape from Vichy rule when the American occupation of North Africa gave them a chance, and requested permission to join the United States Air Force.

The flyers asked that their comrades at Dakar be informed of the warm reception they had received, and expressed the hope that many would join the Americans.

MR. EDEN DENIES DIFFERENCES WITH PREMIER

LONDON, Tuesday (R). — Mr. Eden, who was loudly cheered on entering the House of Commons this afternoon for the first time as Leader of the House, dealt with the allegation that the script of a proposed broadcast by General de Gaulle was suppressed by Mr. Churchill after Mr. Eden himself had approved it.

Mr. Eden promised a full reply at the earliest moment to this allegation, adding that there was no difference whatever between Mr. Churchill and himself.

The British Government is not aware that the former French ministers M. Pierre Flandin and M. Pierre Pucheux, both formerly connected with Vichy, have arrived in North Africa, said the Leader of the House of Lords, Lord Cranborne, answering questions today in the House of Lords.

He added, "They have certainly received no assistance or encouragement to proceed there from any British authority."

THOSE IN COMMAND

CAIRO, Tuesday (R). — The names of the Eighth Army Corps Commanders were disclosed in Cairo today. They are: Lieutenant-General H. Lumsden, commanding the 10th Corps, Lieutenant-General Sir O.W.H. Leese, commanding the 30th Corps, and Lieutenant-General B.G. Horrocks, commanding the 13th Corps.

FIGHTING WEST OF EL AGHEILA

CAIRO, Tuesday (R). — The Allied forces have entered Jedabya and occupied Jalo oasis, on the road to Agheila while the Axis forces have continued to withdraw.

Fighting is now going on 30 miles west of El Agheila, according to one report.

Today's joint Middle East war communiqué reads:

LAND: Our forces entered JEDABYA early yesterday and are maintaining contact with the enemy who are continuing their withdrawal towards EL AGHEILA.

The enemy has evacuated JALO Oasis which has been occupied by our troops.

AIR: Air activity over Cyrenaica yesterday was on a small scale. On the night of November 27/28 our torpedo aircraft successfully attacked an enemy merchant vessel south-east of Sardinia. The ship received a direct hit amidships and was subsequently sunk.

BIZERTA was bombed on the same night and dispersed aircraft at PALERMO, Sicily, were also successfully attacked. Yesterday at least three large enemy aircraft were shot down by our fighters off the east coast of TUNISIA, and a fourth was seriously damaged. Anti-aircraft fire destroyed one Axis cannon fire.

From the above operations, two of our aircraft did not return.

The Bizerta Raid

Royal Air Force medium bombers operating from Malta in the raid on Bizerta harbour, reported in today's communiqué, defied German anti-aircraft fire and swooped down to release their bombs. A number of fires were left burning on the docks and a particularly heavy bomb was seen to burst near a dockside goods station.

Other aircraft, which attacked the aerodrome at Palermo in Sicily, shot up several planes dispersed on the ground. Hundreds of wrecked aircraft found on aerodromes captured in Libya have shown the effectiveness of such tactics.

(Flying conditions were still bad in the Tunisia battle area yesterday and reduced air activity to a minimum.)

KNOX HOPEFUL OF SOLOMONS ISSUE

U.S. FORCES KEEP SHARP LOOKOUT

WASHINGTON, Tuesday (UP).—Colonel Frank Knox, the Secretary for the Navy, told the press here today that it was unlikely that the Japanese would now be able to get reinforcements ashore at Guadalcanal due to the United States forces maintaining a day and night watch.

The enemy might be able, he said, to get in small reinforcements and aircraft at night, but while this was possible, it was improbable.

The Secretary said that the Solomons situation appeared to be progressing satisfactorily along the lines which he had outlined at his last press conference when he said that the operations were progressing satisfactorily with the United States forces holding a firm grip on Guadalcanal.

The U.S. forces were widening their area of control to west of Henderson Field, although they actually controlled only three per cent of the total area of the island.

The western front line lay along 20 miles from Cape Esperance, at the south-western tip of the island, where the Japanese had earlier landed their largest concentrations.

(Asked whether he believed that the Japanese forces could be wiped out, he replied, "That is our objective."

ALLIES STORM NEW GUINEA KEYPOINTS

By CURTIS HINDSON
Reuter Special Correspondent at General MacArthur's Headquarters.

Australian forces have entered Gona in strength following the first penetration by their patrols on Sunday afternoon.

There is still some resistance, according to General MacArthur's spokesman, though it should be only a matter of time before the village is completely in Allied hands.

On the right, flank, a U.S. column, after capturing a landing strip at Buna, pressed on to Cape Endaidere. This position was taken against strong opposition, the Japanese having well-prepared machine-gun positions and snipers hidden in the trees.

Fighting is now narrowed down to focal points at Buna village and Buna mission, which are being stormed jointly by the Australian and United States forces. The resistance here is officially stated to be heavy. Some Japanese are attempting to escape down the Kumusi river on rafts have been wiped out.

Marauders and Havocs have again bombed and machine-gunned Japanese positions, especially those at Sanananda Point.

Japanese on Timor

It is now revealed that the Japanese have occupied the villages of Beco and Raimean on the south coast of Timor. This is the first mention of Japanese forces on the south coast of the island. A spokesman disclosed that the Japanese came over from the interior of the island a few days ago.

Beco — on the south-west coast—and Raimean—one mile south-west of Beco—were both bombed and strafed by Hudsons and Beaufighters.

The Allied H.Q. communiqué this morning says:

BUNA-GONA: On the left, our troops entered Gona, advancing on Sanande; on the night of November 22, Cape Endaidere was captured. Heavy resistance around Buna itself continues. Our air forces are supporting the attack.

VITIAZ STRAITS: An Allied reconnaissance unit shot down a Zero Japanese aircraft which attempted interception. TIMOR: Allied medium bombers raided the enemy-occupied Beco and Raimean. (Vitiaz Straits are between New Guinea and New Britain).

AFTER MIDNIGHT

General Zigouris has taken over the command of all Greek forces in the Middle East after a spectacular escape from Greece.

Lieutenant-General Sir Hubert Huddleston, the Governor-General of the Sudan, and Lady Huddleston have arrived in Cairo by air from Khartoum.

SOVIET ARMY SCORES SMASHING VICTORY

It was officially announced in Moscow last night that the Russians have captured three enemy divisions, which had been previously surrounded, together with three German generals and their staffs. Sweeping away all German resistance, Russian troops north-west of Stalingrad have continued their successful advance. In a north-westerly direction the Russians advanced 40 kilometres. South of Stalingrad they advanced between 15 and 20 kilometres. Russian forces yesterday took 12,000 prisoners, bringing the total to 36,000. Fifteen thousand Germans were killed in the latest fighting. The Germans in their retreat are abandoning large quantities of supplies including ammunition, fuel and food dumps.

GERMANS FACE DISASTER

By Reuters Special Correspondent
STOCKHOLM, Tuesday.—If the Germans cannot check the Russian advance north and south of Stalingrad, some 400,000 Axis troops who for the past three months have been bled white at the doors of the Volga fortress will be trapped and annihilated, it is believed here.

Some observers think that the Germans no longer try a position to do real damage, others that they may launch counter-attacks in order to halt the progress of the Russian advance.

If the Russians continue their advance or even if they only succeed in maintaining their positions acquired in the past four days, it is felt that the Germans will not be able to establish a winter line either on the Don or the Chir.

In the Russian advance yesterday, one success overshadowed all others—the capture of Cherryshevskaya on the Chir river. Describing the plight of the Rumanians fighting in this sector the Germans say, "They fought until the last man and the last hand grenade."

The Last Outlet

The gap between Kalach and Abganerovo is probably the only outlet through which the Germans in the Don-Volga corridor can escape. The Russians are now in an excellent position to close the German "sack" before Stalingrad. But the closing up of this "sack" may take some time, because the Germans will probably put up a desperate defensive fight.

At the southern end of the Soviet advance has brought the Red Army 60 miles back along the German rear. Though decisive are not yet to hand, the German communiqué makes it clear that in many places the German defeat has been a total rout.

The big lines of the operational strategy of the Red Army are unfolding themselves as the rapid advance across the Don steppes continues.

It is significant that the latest report is that the Germans are retreating, indeed fleeing precipitately southward from Cherryshevskaya. On Monday night, one army already stood no further than 40 miles from Kotelnikovo and during the night of Monday-Tuesday, this army made a further successful advance. German divisions heading for the south bank of the Southern Don may find their retreat cut off.

Good Staff Work

The course of the Red Army offensive demonstrates without doubt, according to the impression of all observers, the high manoeuvring skill of all ranks of the Soviet Command.

Soviet engineer pontoon detachments from the Volga flotilla brought across the gradually freezing Volga tens of thousands of troops, lorries, guns and tanks practically all by night.

The offensive did not start under the most favourable conditions. For one thing, aircraft were largely grounded on the first day owing to fog and low clouds and therefore did not take part in the initial break of the German defensive line.

The Soviet artillery, on the other hand, played a most important role. Its accurate and concentrated barrages managed the German strong points and systems of communications so effectively that a sapped advance of the motorized infantry and the tanks became possible. Not infrequently artillery fire destroyed German divisional and regimental staff headquarters, leaving many German units without effective direction.

Close cooperation between tanks and infantry was achieved, in breaking through the German defence lines. Light guns all the time followed the tanks South of Stalingrad the German division of 42,000 men ...

Trophies captured by the end of November 23 were 657 guns, 2,826 lorries, 1,200 railway trucks, 2,625 machine-guns, 32 aircraft in working order, 32 tanks in working order, and a large quantity of small arms and ammunition which has not yet been ascertained.

Seventy aircraft, 157 tanks, and 186 guns were destroyed. Enemy losses on the battlefield during the day were 12,000 dead officers and men.

300,000 NAZIS TRAPPED AT STALINGRAD

By HAROLD KING, Reuters Special Correspondent

The armies of Generals Romanenko and Batov are smashing their way from north and south to close the iron ring which the victorious Soviet forces are throwing round the Germans at Stalingrad.

The movement has been beautifully timed and excellently carried out, and the double Soviet attack appears completely to have overwhelmed the enemy and disorganized him.

Three armies are now swiftly and inexorably closing round German forces estimated at some 300,000 men. Cut off from their far-away bases, the Germans in the 40-mile strip of steppe between the Don and Volga at Stalingrad now appear to be hopelessly trapped.

The original blows struck at the vital eastern and southern railroad supply lines for the Germans attacking the Volga city have been reinforced threefold, and the heroic garrison inside Stalingrad, after three months of grim defensive battles, has joined in the offensive in the last 24 hours. General Rodimtsev's troops are slowly advancing westward from the northern factory belt as well as from the southern suburbs of the city.

Advance Continues

Meanwhile the main offensive is going according to plan and the tempo of the Russians is not slackening. The troops of Major-General Chistiakov are chasing the Germans at top speed. Inside the Don elbow, after the big tank battles, the Germans are being rolled back in the direction of the southern arm of the Don.

At the southern end of the Soviet advance has brought the Red Army 60 miles back along ... practically entirely in German hands.

A German communiqué says that Soviet troops have broken through the defensive front south-west of Stalingrad and in the great Don bend. In the Caucasus area unfavourable weather conditions prevented large scale fighting.

"Counter-measures are now in progress. In the last two days, several hundred enemy tanks have been destroyed," states the communiqué, adding that in Stalingrad itself there was only local fighting.

MUSSOLINI SEEKS A WAY OUT

GERMAN GENERALS CONFLICT AMONG

LONDON, Tuesday (ANA). Reliable information reaching London suggests that Mussolini is trying to set up a National Defence Cabinet, now that he doubts his ability to maintain the unity of Italy and the prolongation of resistance at a time when the Allied threat to Italy is growing.

The Fascist leader Viduzoni, the former Liberal Minister Orlando, and Catholic leaders have been contacted for this purpose, it is stated.

Mussolini is also reported to have established contact with the leaders of the former trade union movement, as well as with some leaders of the banned Socialist Party, but the latter at any rate have declined to cooperate.

In the meantime, increased German pressure is being brought to bear on Italy. Mass arrests are taking place throughout the country.

Hitler and Rommel

While trouble is thus brewing in Italy, there are indications that a serious conflict exists among Germany's military leaders.

For reasons of personal prestige and in an attempt to maintain the myth with which Rommel's alleged military genius had been surrounded Hitler has been obliged to sanction the organization of a propaganda campaign intended to explain away the defeat inflicted on the Afrika Korps.

Official German propaganda continues to strike the familiar note that Rommel is invincible, and that the British have been surprised by his western retreat, the pursuit of which has been beyond their power.

The motive underlying this campaign is understood to be Hitler's desire to maintain his leadership of the Army, as Rommel is the only general held in high esteem by Hitler and he is represented to the public as an outstanding strategist.

DECISIVE BATTLE RAGING

By HENRY SHAPIRO
U.P. Correspondent in Moscow

Great possibilities are foreseen for the decisive battle now raging in the Stalingrad region as the battered German forces, fearing entrapment in the Red Army's iron ring, are trying to rally for a counter-attack.

The Soviet offensive meanwhile is gaining momentum. One army moving southward has reached the village of Pogodinsky, well inside the Don River bend, in a drive to achieve a junction with the Russian forces hammering the enemy to the west, while a third army, advancing from the southern sector has cut the railroad to Rostov.

While the Russians have resisted many German divisions, others are still concentrated in the Stalingrad area, occupying fortified villages and other strong-points where the extermination will grow increasingly difficult should Marshal Timoshenko's ... momentum. But General von Roth's attempts to make a counter-offensive have thus far failed with the virtual loss of two divisions.

The situation has apparently become a race between General von Hoth's effort to make a counter-attack and the Soviet ability to reinforce the two principal advance columns in order to prevent a German break-out.

Artillery and Infantry

Aviation played a minor role in the last day's fighting operations, however weather ... cellent cover for artillery and advancing infantry.

Front-line dispatches indicate that the Russian offensive was carried out with divisionary attacks, whereby the enemy was deceived, causing him to throw large forces against unimportant sectors. The Russians then pressed forward in two principal directions.

Soviet forces massed southward of Stalingrad, on the east bank of the Volga, only a few days ago heavily crossed the river in pontoons thrown across the freezing water and struck early in the morning following an intensive 24 hours' artillery bombardment. The fighting cleared the minefields for the passage of tanks which enabled one after another. Mobile heavy and medium-shell artillery played an important part in widening the breach.

After a full day of these operations, Soviet cavalry stormed out cut the railroad to Tikhoretz, smashed numerous German groups, and advanced 14 miles. From then on there was no stopping them.

Freezing Prisoners Surrender

In the steppes south of Stalingrad, the roads are now clustered with overturned and burned-out enemy machines and thousands of green-uniformed bodies.

Endless columns of frostbitten prisoners conveyed by Russian cavalrymen stream to the rear, while the victors are picking up propaganda leaflets such as "Hitler has never been beaten; the German Army remains invincible."

The entire steppe is now frozen and covered with snow. Large German and Rumanian units, poorly clad and wrapped in blankets, are roaming the icy steppes, frequently surrendering without a fight.

REINFORCEMENTS RUSHED TO ITALY

By DANA SCHMIDT
U.P. Staff Correspondent in Ankara

Reports from the Balkans quoted in military quarters here show that all the indications of hurried German troop and air movements after the Allied landings in North Africa and the British break-through in Libya boil down to the fact that reinforcements have been almost exclusively directed towards Italy.

These indications contain only one specific report involving three German divisions which moved through the Balkans from Russia to Africa. These reached Greece too late for their transport to Cyrenaica and have been shipped on to Italy.

It is considered though unestimated number of Italians was withdrawn from Russia and flown across the Balkans to Italy and Sicily.

Reliable sources understand that the German movements from the Balkans to Italy and Sicily were greatly hindered by Chetnik raids.

An 80 per cent increase in the price of civilian rail transport was announced in Sofia this week-end and similar increases are scheduled for Hungary and Croatia from January.

Mass-Butchery of Poland's Jews

LONDON, Tuesday (R). — The most ruthless methods are being used in Poland to give effect to the order made, by Himmler himself, that the whole Jewish population must be exterminated by the end of the year, says a report reaching the Polish Government in London.

Special battalions commanded by SS men seize the victims, including all people and others, who are taken to cemeteries and shot there.

(The remainder are loaded into goods trucks at the rate of 150 to a truck intended for 40. The floor is covered with a thick layer of lime or chlorine sprinkled with water, and the doors of the trucks are sealed. Wherever the trains pull up half the people arrive dead.

(Those surviving are sent to specialized camps. Once there, the so-called "settlers" are massacred. Only the young and relatively strong are left alive for they provide valuable slave labour for the Germans. By the end of September a quarter of a million Jews had thus been "eliminated."

Norwegian Clergy Condemn Pogroms

STOCKHOLM, Tuesday (R). — Norwegian churchmen have sent to Quisling a solemn protest against the persecution of Norwegian Jews and by the Swedish-Norwegian Press Bureau.

The protest is signed by the Provisional Church Council of all affiliated Church organizations and the Theological Faculty of Oslo University. It states:

"These measures have provoked unheard-of sorrow throughout the country. We do not intend to start any political action or to defend Jews who have committed crimes, but if they are guilty, they must be tried according to Norwegian law."

Norwegian Government circles in London (quoted by Palcor) report that 2,300 Norwegian Jews aged 15 and over have been interned by the Nazi authorities and are to be sent for employment in forced labour gangs partly in the far north and partly in Poland.

All Jewish property in Norway has been confiscated.

ARRESTS IN TANGIER

LONDON, Tuesday (Palcor). — Many arrests among the Jewish community in Tangier, now part of Spanish Morocco, have followed the Allied landings in North Africa as reported in a message which has just arrived here.

The arrested persons were sent to concentration camps on the ground that "a movement was discovered among the Jews of Spanish Morocco to cross the border clandestinely and join the Allies in occupied territory."

TEL AVIV MEETING

TEL AVIV, Tuesday. — Local journalists met here today to express their indignation and horror at the unspeakable atrocities inflicted on European Jewry by the Nazis.

In the presence of leaders of Polish Jewry, the pressmen heard authenticated reports of the mass butchery of hundreds of thousands of men, women and children under the German yoke and of the veritable hell under which others live.

Even the findings of an Allied fact-finding committee, it was stated, "protested against the inferno treatment of Jews in Warsaw.

FEEDING THE LIBERATED AREAS

(WASHINGTON, Tuesday (R) President Roosevelt gave a clear intimation today that he will explain his programme for the rehabilitation of liberated countries in a radio speech shortly.

He defended his policy of feeding liberated areas and said that the policy would continue. He added that it would prove sound both from the standpoint of the American pocketbook and from that of defence.

Author of Political Thriller Arrested

NEW YORK, Tuesday (UP).—Upon the order of the Attorney General, Julius Herman Krebs, who under the name of Jan Valtin wrote the best-seller "Out of the Night", describing Gestapo methods, has been arrested for the duration of the war, after the termination of which he is scheduled to be deported.

According to a Chicago message, the father of one of the recently convicted German saboteurs, Hans Haupt, a certain Walter Frehling, and one Otto Wergin, have all been sentenced to death for treason after having been convicted of aiding Herbert Haupt in leaving from a U-boat.

His mother, Mrs. Wergin, and Mrs. Frehling, were sentenced to 25 years' imprisonment.

It will be recalled that Haupt was recently executed at Washington together with five other saboteurs. The Chicago sentence pronounced on six naturalized German-born accused has now climaxed the greatest treason trial in U.S. history.

GOVERNMENT TO BUY CITRUS

At least 25,000 tons of citrus will be purchased at a price for good quality fruit of LP.3.500 per ton on the tree by the Food Controller this season. The object of this step is to absorb any surplus citrus by stimulating consumption, it is officially announced.

In view of the altered citrus marketing circumstances according to a communiqué just issued, the Government has decided with the approval of the Secretary of State to abandon the Disposal Permit Scheme as from November 29. This was inaugurated at a time when supply was far in excess of demand and was aimed at raising the price level of that portion of the crop which could be marketed.

Normal Trading Resumed

Four days' grace are given from today to enable those who have bought fruit on which the fee has been paid to dispose of their stocks. After November 29 the normal channels of trade will operate unrestricted so far as internal civilian requirements are concerned.

The Citrus Marketing Board will afford any necessary and practicable assistance in this and other directions.

Intermediate charges will be subject to strict regulations to ensure a maximum benefit. It is hoped that the fullest and most beneficial use of the fruit will be made and that the necessity for the destruction of any portion of the crop will no longer arise.

The Food Controller will publish shortly details of the methods of purchase and distribution.

The first consignment of Palestinian citrus, consisting of about 1,000 cases, was dispatched by Arab citrus-growers this week in accordance with their agreement with the military authorities.

CHEERFUL WELCOME HOME FOR SMUTS

PRETORIA, Tuesday (R). — Field Marshal Smuts returned home today from his visit to London. In an interview with Reuter on his arrival, he said:

I am very glad to be back and pleased to see everybody looking so cheerful. I am very satisfied and pleased with my visit overseas and my visit to troops in North Africa.

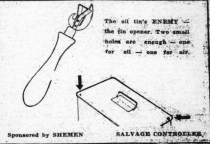

The oil tin's ENEMY the tin opener. Two small holes are enough — one for oil — one for air.

Sponsored by SHEMEN   SALVAGE CONTROLLER

V | V EFFORT IS THE GREATER PART OF WAR EFFORT

GOVERNMENT SAVINGS CERTIFICATES ARE THE EASIEST AND SAFEST WAY OF INVESTING SMALL SUMS OF MONEY

LATE Edition

THE PALESTINE POST

5 A.M.

WEDNESDAY JANUARY 27, 1943

VOL. XVIII. No. 5089 PRICE 12 MILS

WOLFSCHMIDT'S KUMMEL FAMOUS SINCE 1847

WAR FOR UNCONDITIONAL SURRENDER OF AXIS; CHURCHILL-ROOSEVELT MEETING IN MOROCCO

10 DAY SESSION OF COMBINED ALLIED STAFFS FOR 1943 WAR PLANS

GIRAUD AND DE GAULLE FOR UNION OF ALL FRENCHMEN

The BBC programmes at 3 o'clock this morning, London time (4 o'clock Palestine time) were interrupted for what was described by the announcer as "news of great importance".

The news, eagerly awaited the preceding 48 hours, was the meeting at Casablanca, Morocco, between Mr. Churchill and President Roosevelt for 10 days, beginning Jan. 14 and ending Jan. 24.

The result of these deliberations, later described by Mr. Roosevelt as "unprecedented", was the plan for a great offensive in 1943 aiming at the "unconditional surrender of Germany, Italy and Japan".

The combined Staffs of the United States and the British Empire were in constant session, day and night, during the 10 days of the conference, and the whole war picture, theatre by theatre, was carefully examined, and complete agreement reached.

Mr. Stalin was invited, and had he been able to come the conference would have taken place further east, but the Premier of the USSR, who as Commander-in-Chief of the Soviet forces is personally directing the Russian offensive, was unable to leave Russia. He was kept minutely informed of the proceedings, and the decisions reached, amidst expressions of unqualified enthusiasm for the successes of the Russian arms.

Similarly, General Chang Kai Shek was kept in constant touch with the Casablanca deliberations.

Parallel with the meetings, General Giraud and General de Gaulle met, later issuing a combined communique concerning their agreement on the "union in war of all Frenchmen and their Allies." The African and Middle East Commanders, Generals Eisenhower and Alexander, also came to the Casablanca suburb

The spirit of the historic talks, with the resultant global picture of the war, is the determination of the United Nations to maintain the initiative in Russia, the Pacific and Africa, making use in the war plans for 1943, of the "markedly favourable events at the end of 1942."

The world was fully prepared for this announcement. American radio stations throughout yesterday told the public to tune in at 10 p. m. Eastern Time (4 o'clock this morning in Palestine) for a most important announcement of a nature which could not yet be disclosed. amusement arranged to broadcast the news.

The American public, especially, was on tip-toe, prepared by the newspapers and broadcast commentators, to learn of "momentous decisions regarding the Allies' grand strategy."

On the eve of the 10th anniversary of Hitler's regime, Axis radio stations contributed to the general excitement by continued broadcast claiming that Mr. Churchill some the meetings were held.

Wood Asks House For Two More Credit Votes

Extension of Price Control Foreseen

War Costs Britain £14,000,000 a Day

LONDON, Tuesday (R). — The war now costs Britain about £14,000,000 daily, the Chancellor of the Exchequer, Sir Kingsley Wood, announced in the House of Commons today when he presented two further Votes of Credit.

One of these was for £900,000,000 to cover additional costs to the end of the present financial year. The second was for £1,000,000,000, (one thousand million sterling) for future war expenditure.

War expenditure had recently risen by £1 250,000 daily, stated Sir Kingsley Wood This was mainly due to expenditure in North Africa, Libya and other overseas areas.

Estimates Exceeded

He estimated the year's expenditure to be about £4,900,000,000 instead of the original budget estimate of £4,500,000,000. Estimates regarding duties on liquor, tobacco, entertainments and the purchase tax would be exceeded

He foreshadowed the extension of price control, pointing out that prices of uncontrolled goods had risen appreciably.

"In this great struggle for freedom, the general soundness of our finances is definitely adding to our material and moral strength," the Chancellor concluded

The two votes of credit for £1,900,000,000 were agreed to without division.

Commandos Raid Norway Coast

LONDON, Tuesday (R). — An extremely successful commando raid was made on the Norwegian coast, it is stated in authoritative quarters in London today.

According to the German-controlled Oslo radio, the raid was made on Saturday night on Laervik, on Stordoe island, not far south of Bergen, (not Larvik, in the Oslo fjord.)

ADVANCE FORCES TAKE ZAWIA; RAF HITS ZUARA

Rommel Reported in Tunisia

By Reuters Special Correspondent with the American Forces at Allied Headquarters, North Africa

Rommel is reported to have crossed the border into Tunisia, but official confirmation is lacking.

The Morocco radio said this (Tuesday) afternoon that Rommel is finding it difficult to disengage his forces from the Eighth Army's advancing vanguard.

In Cairo it was merely announced today that Allied forward troops made local advances, occupying Zawia, while the R.A.F. attacked retreating enemy units near Zuara. Today's communique states:

Yesterday, local advances were made by our forward troops. In the northern sector our troops occupied Zawia, 30 miles west of Tripoli.

During the night of January 24/25, the Medenina landing-ground was attacked by our bombers, which also scored a hit on targets nearby. Yesterday, enemy supply lines in Sicily and Tunisia were bombed and machine-gunned. All our aircraft returned from these operations."

The attacks made by Allied air forces day and night against the Axis base of Medenina reveal that this strong covering point has become one of the centres of Axis resistance.

British 9-Point Plan for Tripoli

CAIRO, Tuesday (R).— A nine-point plan for the British Military Government in Tripolitania has been posted up in Tripoli in the form of a proclamation to the people, said the Minister of State, Mr. Casey, today.

Plans for a "firm and just British military rule" were prepared before the Eighth Army's advance, Mr. Casey said They emphasize that British military courts have been set up, and war crimes such as sabotage and obtaining military information have been listed.

Arrangements have been made for food supplies and medical treatment for civilians. The Military Government will adopt a "firm but just attitude" towards the Italian population.

Fascist leaders will be interned, Fascist clubs will be closed, and the teaching of the Fascist ideology will be forbidden. The existing Italian courts of justice will continue to function under the control of the military court

Freedom for the Jews of Tripoli

By HENRY GORELL,
Unied Press Correspondent

TRIPOLI, Tuesday. — The happiest people in this city today are the thousands of Jews, many of whom had been imprisoned for many months in the ramshackle Ghetto, surrounded by barbed wire and closely guarded.

The Ghetto Law has been rescinded by an Order of the British Army, and Jews have mingled with Italians and Arabs on an equal footing.

I interviewed several leading Jews who said they had been unaware of the African war situation until the actual entry of the Eighth Army They added hat **the night before the enemy fled, armed guards had entered the Ghetto apparently under the orders of the Germans, and had shot down in cold blood leaders of the Community who the Germans thought might be useful to the Allies.**

8TH ARMY WELCOMED BY JEWS AND ARABS

PTA says that, in a description of General Montgomery's entry into Tripoli, "The Times" mentioned the undisguised pleasure and eloquent feelings of Arabs and Jews in the town.

HINSLEY URGES HELP FOR NAZI VICTIMS

LONDON, Tuesday (R). — On behalf of the Catholic hierarchy of England and Wales Cardinal Hinsley, Archbishop of Westminster, in a letter to "The Times" today declares:

Whatever can be done to save or help the victims of Nazi persecution, we most urgently support.

Commenting that "a multitude of Christians are among the victims but the Jews are singled out for extermination," Cardinal Hinsley says, "Blind racial hate, as Cardinal Faulhaber has repeatedly declared, is the motive of these unparalleled barbarities."

Nazis Use Tanks And Artillery Against French

Street Fighting At Marseilles

ZURICH, Tuesday (R). —German artillery and tanks are being hurried to the old port of Marseilles where French "rebels" are reported to have barricaded themselves inside houses from which they are firing in a determined manner on all approaching.

The German soldiers are literally besieging the houses in a street battle arising out of recent frequent clashes between the "rebels" and French police allied with the German troops.

The Vichy radio announced today that the authorities have proclaimed a state of siege in Marseilles. Nobody is permitted to enter the buildings now being "evacuated" until further notice.

Anyone disobeying the order or attempting to use fire-arms would be arrested and sentenced to death, the announcer said. Members of the "Sol" (Service d'Ordre Legionnaire) have been instructed to use firearms against all who disregard the orders.

The evacuation of the port area is said to have been completed on Sunday evening. Only police and Mobile Guards and municipal officers are now allowed to enter the evacuated district. The warning that the authorities have been ordered to make use of arms immediately, if opposed, was announced all over the city by loud speakers.

All persons who remained in the evacuated area were told to assemble on the Quai Petain by 630 in the evening. They are to be allowed to return some time this week to collect some of their furniture. The authorities are also considering the possible return of young people to Marseilles but not to the evacuated area.

Political Arrests

The German radio said last night that the latest arrests in Marseilles had been carried out under the personal direction of the Chief of the Secretariat-General for Police, Bosquet, and "were directed not only against ordinary criminals but against various secret organizations in the city."

HELL COMES TO MARSEILLES

By RALPH FORTE
U.P. Correspondent in Madrid

Reports describing the evacuation of Marseilles speak of a sad spectacle as thousands of poorly-clad men, women and children push their heavy loads of household effects to the concentration camp at Frejus.

The evacuation is going forward very slowly because of the difficulty of moving thousands of unwilling civilians and women, even though rifle butts are used. The whole district is still cordoned by the police and house to house searches are progressing. Many people are hiding in cellars.

The death roll is reported to be mounting and there are many suicides. A number of older folk have died of shock and the exhaustion of trudging some 35 kilometres to Frejus.

It is pointed out that the 6,000 people who were arrested were luckier than the 40,000 evacuees because they were sent to jail-houses and barracks, while at the Frejus camp no preparations were made to welcome the people from the red-light district, and the place was so crowded that some 10,000 have already been hustled further on to Piers Cuerfeu, formerly an old naval aviation camp now occupied by the Axis Air Force.

When the evacuees reached Piers Cuerfeu, pouring rain greeted them.

The police have ordered all doors and windows of the port district to remain open and also stated that any worthwhile furniture and belongings would be auctioned and credited to the owners. If the belongings were estimated to be valueless, they would be set on fire.

GERMANS AT STALINGRAD LIQUIDATED BY RED ARMY

NEW RUSSIAN OFFENSIVE AT VORONEZH

MOSCOW, Tuesday (R).— The liquidation of the German forces cut off in the Stalingrad area has been completed, states a special communique tonight.

Several important centres of resistance, including Peschankam, have been captured between January 17 and 26 in addition to those previously announced. The list of places captured also includes Kuporoskaya. Soviet troops have occupied the railway station of Voropevova.

Only two small isolated groups totalling about 12,000 in the Stalingrad area remain to be mopped up. Both are doomed to destruction in two or three days.

Since the start of the Soviet offensive against the encircled Germans in Stalingrad, 45,000 Germans have been killed and 28,000 taken prisoner. War material captured includes 1,297 tanks, 2,978 guns, and 523 aircraft.

The Red Army has entered a new phase of its offensive by the latest attacks west of Voronezh (writes Harold King, Reuters Moscow Correspondent). Soviet troops are now approaching the great centres of resistance on line Rostov-Voroshilovgrad-Kupiansk-Byelgorod-Kursk.

A German communique announcing the new Soviet offensive south of Voronezh states that the Russian onslaught against large parts of the eastern front have again increased in fury. In Stalingrad the defenders, who include a small Croatian unit as well as Rumanian divisions, are concentrated in a narrow area in the Southern and central part of the ruins of the city. They "are continuing to offer heroic resistance," add the Germans.

AXIS VASSALS ALMOST WIPED OUT

By HENRY SHAPIRO
U.P. Correspondent in Moscow

The Red Army is striking mercilessly at the disorganized and desperate group of German and other Axis forces on the Voronezh front, wiping out those refusing to surrender, while the main Soviet force moved west to join the direct attack on Kursk, on the main Kharkov-Moscow railway.

According to the "Red Star," more than half the 60 Italian, Rumanian and Hungarian divisions, representing one-fourth of the total Axis armies on the Soviet-German front in the summer of 1942, have by now been smashed or routed. Total Axis losses in the two months' offensive are more than 500,000 in dead alone, while there are over 200,000 prisoners.

In the Voronezh region alone, nine out of a total of 13 Hungarian divisions have been smashed, while in the course of the past two months, 18 out of a total of 22 Rumanian divisions were wiped out, leaving only five or six divisions inside Rumania

Lieut.-Colonel Denisov, "Red Star"'s observer in the Northern Caucasus, reports that the Luftwaffe's losses have been so great that it is now unable to hamper the action of the advanced Soviet troops. The Soviet Air Force has achieved superiority in most sectors, enabling the most active support to be given to the ground troops as well as the most merciless strafing of the retreating Axis forces to be carried out.

These victories coincide with reports in diplomatic quarters that British and American supply deliveries have improved dramatically. It is stated that convoy losses have been reduced sharply due to better protection, and that a large American convoy arrived recently without the loss of a single ship.

ROAD CLEAR FOR DRIVE TO KURSK

Victors

MOSCOW, Tuesday (R). — Stalin, in his capacity as Supreme Commander of the Red Army, issued an Order of the Day last night to the troops on the South-Western, Southern, Don, Northern, Caucasus, Voronezh, Kalinin, Volkhov and Leningrad fronts, in which he said:

As the result of two months of offensive operations, the Red Army has broken through the defences of the German Fascist troops on a wide front, routed 102 enemy divisions and captured more than 200,000 prisoners and 13.000 guns. During this period Soviet troops have advanced about 250 miles. Our troops have won a resounding victory. The offensive of our troops continues.

The Order, which was signed by Stalin as Supreme Commander-in-Chief, also congratulated the commanders and troops on having routed Hitler's armies, and outlined a list of the towns from which the siege had been lifted and which had been recaptured by the Russians.

"Forward — to rout the German invaders and to drive them out beyond the limits of our country," the Order concluded.

Vanquished

The German public are at last learning the truth of what is happening in Russia.

The military correspondent of the German News Agency, quoted by the German radio, writes today that the German High Command plans to shorten the Russian front, and that "a new main defence line is about to materialise"

General Dietmar, the German war commentator, declared on the German radio last night that it was his duty to inform the German people the extent of the defeat suffered by the German Armies in Russia.

"But," he said, "can anybody believe that an army like ours after three years victories could perish from one reverse?"

General Dietmar added that at Stalingrad and in the Don bend, the situation is "far from being a catastrophe or even a turning-point." Referring to the Germans in the Stalingrad area, he said:

Without a chance of retreat they can only hold out or perish. But whatever their fate, their weeks of heroic resistance have warded off heavier calamities for our armies.

By HAROLD KING,
Reuters Moscow Correspondent

MOSCOW, Tuesday. — The remnants of Hitler's 10[...] routed divisions in Southern Russia rolled back to the west with gathering momentum today as the Red Army made important new gains on all sectors of the [...]000-mile front between Voronezh and the Kuban steppes.

The Russians are now conducting active operations along two-thirds of the Eastern front. The only relatively calm sectors are Murmansk, Karelia, and the Kalinin and Briansk fronts.

Considerable strategical significance is attached to the Red Army's mastery over the Voronezh area and the east bank of the Don. With Voronezh cleared entirely of the Axis, the Soviet Command is free to develop a full-scale offensive towards Kursk

The whole left wing of the German Armies on the southern front is now bending under the day and night hammer blows of the Red Army. Kharkov, as well as Kursk, is threatened as General Golikov's forces drive west and northwest from their new positions south-west of Voronezh.

On the lower Don front, General Rokossovsky's army is meeting savage resistance in its three-point drive on the Rostov front. In their race to bottle up Hitler's army in the Caucasus the Soviet columns after a 50-mile advance from Salsk have captured Byelaya-Glina, only 35 miles east of Tikhoretsk, the key junction through which most of the Caucasus Germans must pass to escape to Rostov.

As the Red Army continues its great offensive along a [...]-mile front from Voronezh to the Kuban steppes, harassed German infantrymen trying to defend Kharkov, Kursk and Rostov look for help to the Luftwaffe, but that help does not come.

The Richthofen "circus," the once mighty and "all-conquering" air army operating from Stalingrad to the Caucasus, is practically prostrate. During the past two months, which includes the battle of Stalingrad, the Luftwaffe's losses have been very severe, more than 1,000 machines having been reduced to scrap metal. It is incapable throughout the Caucasus of offering serious resistance to Soviet air activity.

MIHAILOVICH DEFECTION DENIED

Royal Yugoslav Government's Statement

A statement denying certain charges against General Mihailovich was issued recently in London by the Yugoslav Government. The following are excerpts taken from this statement which was given us for publication by the Yugoslav Consul-General in Jerusalem and which bears on the subject discussed in the article published in yesterday's issue of **The Palestine Post.**

A campaign has been launched against the Minister of War, and Chief of Staff of the Yugoslav Army General Draga Mihailovich, on the ground that the units of the Yugoslav Army under his command are inactive, and that he himself is cooperating with the Axis Powers.

The Royal Yugoslav Government, on the basis of reliable information at its disposal, is in a position to issue the following statement:

General Mihailovich's units are organized practically throughout the country, good liaison exists among those units, and they are under excellent leadership. His units are very active on the whole Yugoslav territory from Slovenia to the Greek frontier. The other fighting forces, which operate independently of General Mihailovich, are insignificant in comparison to General Mihailovich's Army, both as regards their numerical strength and the scale of their activity.

The activity of the units under General Mihailovich's command has never ceased for a moment, notwithstanding certain allegations to the contrary which emanate from sources either ill-informed or ill-intentioned. The centre of this struggle has been moving from one part of the country to another, according to circumstances, but the struggle has all the time been a continuous one. The activity of General Mihailovich's units alone is keeping 30-40 Axis divisions tied up in Yugoslavia.

In the course of the autumn 1941 and the winter 1942 the centre of the operations was in Serbia, in the spring 1942 it was moved to Montenegro and Bosnia, and in the autumn of the same year it was moved again to Western Bosnia and Croatia. At the present moment, operations are proceeding in the Sava valley from Zagreb to Belgrade, in accordance with the general Allied strategical plan.

These operations are still proceeding, in accordance with the general Allied strategical plan, and it is therefore impossible to give any details. We can say, however, that all fighting activity in Yugoslavia is connected with General Mihailovich, with the exception of the Western part of Bosnia, of Croatia and of Slovenia, where there are other units which are struggling against the Axis independently. These forces, however, are unimportant both as regards their numerical strength and the scale of their activity.

In the parts we have just mentioned, there exist units of the so-called partisans who are inspired by a certain political ideology, and are known either as the partisan army, Croatian Western Bosnia or, as the Slovene movement of national liberation.

In these parts, there are also Serbian Nationalist units which are fighting against the Ustasi in order to prevent, as far as possible, the extermination of the Serbs which is being systematically carried out in Pavelic's State. But even in these parts, with all the medley of fighting forces, it is the troops under General Mihailovich which are the principal Yugoslav force and are most usefully resisting the Axis. Many actions, which are in reality Mihailovich's, are erroneously attributed to other forces.........

War Flashes

Awaiting the expected international announcement, the London Stock Market was quiet yesterday.

Over 250 persons have been shot in Marseilles, according to a dispatch to the "Journal de Geneve." They include 180 men and 70 women.

The United States Navy had informed the Senate Military Committee of plans to have a strength of 2,220,000 by December of this year. This would make the United States Armed Forces total 10,420,000 by the end of the year.

Victories Stir Bulgaria

People Prefer Imported Information

By CHRISTO PETKOV
Special to The Palestine Post

KUIBYSHEV, Tuesday. — While the whole world stands in awe at the prodigious victories of the Red Army, there is one Government which is doing everything in its power to keep its people in ignorance of these and other events: the Bulgarian Government.

The people of Bulgaria have not been told even as much as the German people of the latest developments in Russia and Africa. The Bulgarian press and radio, as well as speeches and lectures by public men, have tried to hide from their people the defeat of Rommel's Afrika Korps. More: Bulgarian propaganda asserts that Rommel still threatens the Suez Canal and the Persian Gulf.

Not content with denying the exploits of the Red Army, the Bulgarian pen-pushing generals, all those Lukovs, Szekovs, Vulkovs and their ilk, speak of "the brilliant German successes on the Soviet-German front" and assert that "the Bolshevik winter offensives have ended in defeat."

Small wonder that today there are but a few fools left in Bulgaria who attach any credence to Goebbels' propaganda and its Bulgarian variety.

Practically the entire Bulgarian people knows by now that its interests have been betrayed and its very future jeopardized by the present rulers of Bulgaria who have followed a pro-Nazi policy.

It is admitted that the Bulgarian people prefer to listen to what foreign papers and radio stations have to say rather than have their minds poisoned by lying stories. The Sofia radio only a few days ago fulminated against foreign radio stations and newspapers which "are creating discontent by their continuous assertions that Bulgaria has chosen the wrong path and that the country has been sold out and plundered."

The Bulgarian Minister of Finance, Bozhilov, made a clumsy attempt to shift the blame for Bulgaria's impending catastrophe on "defeatist rumours" a few days ago, while presenting the 1943 State budget to the Sobranje. This Hitlerite tax-collector said:

"I appeal warmly to the population not to believe the sundry tendentious defeatist rumors and the black radio stations which are sowing confusion and defeatism and are weakening the morale of our people."

What are the rumours that have so upset Hitler's accomplices in Bulgaria? What are these "continuous assertions" that have so stirred the Bulgarian people?

We can answer these questions without any fear of contradiction: These "rumours" are the remarkable victories of the Red Army and its offensives against the Germans in Russia, and the landing of American and British forces in North Africa and the brilliant campaign of the British Eighth Army which has just captured Tripoli.

SLOVAK RABBIS IN CONCENTRATION CAMPS

LONDON (Palcor). — Agudath Israel circles in London have received authenticated reports that most of the rabbis in Slovakia are now interned in concentration camp at Zilina.

THE DRINK YOU NEED

NO SUGAR FOR

ORANGE JUICE IS

SUGARED BY NATURE

DRINK IT DAILY

FOOD CONTROL

V HAVE YOU INSTALLED AN AUSTERITY LIFE IN YOUR HOME? V

LATE Edition

THE PALESTINE POST

TUESDAY
MARCH 30, 1943

Vol. XVIII. No. 5142
PRICE 12 MILS

ROMMEL IN FULL RETREAT

BRITISH BREAK AND OUTFLANK MARETH LINE

ALLIED HEADQUARTERS IN N. AFRICA, Monday (R). — With the Mareth Line broken and the Afrika Korps in full retreat to the north to avoid encirclement, British, American and French troops are attacking in all sectors on a 300-mile front.

Rommel is falling back to the Gabes area, under tremendous ground and air pressure and with the loss of much equipment and thousands of prisoners. Mareth, Matmata and Toujane are in British hands. At El Hamma, on his flank, first-class German troops were defeated and yielded control of the town to the Eighth Army, while the Gabes area has been heavily bombarded by Allied naval forces.

French and American troops are converging on Kairouan and the American column which took Fondouk continues to advance towards the coast. In the north the First Army continues its offensive in the Djebel Abiod region.

Thaw Holds Up Major Fighting At Smolensk

Russians Reach Main Defences

MOSCOW, Monday. — The Russians have now reached the main defence line of the Smolensk fortifications system and scouts are already probing into the enemy positions.

Reports related steady progress by both Soviet forces in the two-pronged Smolensk drive — one thrusting from Byeli and the other southwestward along the Moscow-Smolensk railway. But the spring thaw and the generally deteriorating climatic conditions are likely to become the predominant factor in the central front operations for several more weeks.

It is admitted that it is now problematical whether the Red Army will undertake an assault on the main enemy line before the weather improves. New gains have been made by the Soviet forces striking for Smolensk but because of thaw fighting has been reduced to local operations.

In a frontal advance towards the great German base, the Russians during the night occupied an inhabited locality in hand-to-hand fighting. Using hand grenades and bayonets, they killed over 100 Germans. Three places south of Byeli were occupied by Soviet troops engaged in a thrust from the north-east, and Guardsmen defeated a German counter-attack in this sector, killing 150 Germans.

In the Middle Donetz area, the Russians flattened out a wedge driven into their lines at one point. By encircling movements on flanks the Germans were surrounded and over 200 wiped out. Elsewhere another German attempt to cross a river was repulsed.

(UP and Reuter)

Nazis Raze Country in Retreat

MOSCOW Monday (UP) — The Metropolitan Nicolai of Kiev, one of the most prominent leaders of the Russian Orthodox Chuch, who has just returned from an extensive tour of the reoccupied area in the Smolensk district, states that the retreating Germans have carried out a devastating "scorched earth" policy.

The Germans, he said, systematically massacred thousands of civilians, burned down hundreds of towns and villages, and destroyed churches, schools, and other public buildings.

A vast area had been turned into a wilderness and many historic towns and villages levelled to the ground.

Puppets to Pay

LONDON, Monday (R). — A Czechoslovak officer broadcasting from London last night said that the puppet Government of Slovakia, as well as the German Army would be held responsible for the decimation of the Slovak Regiment which recently mutinied on the Russian front.

Reports reaching Czechoslovak circles in London state that the regiment decided to go over to the Russians when the Slovak division to which it belonged was ordered to retreat in the Tuapse sector. The Germans were warned of the plan and every tenth man of the regiment was shot.

Underground Army Ready

A leading article in "The Times" today says:

"The underground struggle in Europe is taking on a fiercer note. Premature risings can only serve German ends, but once the moment has been chosen and the call given, there is no doubt that the assault on the enemy from the front will be powerfully assisted from within Hitler's so-called European fortress.

"All over Europe, a great army is preparing to take the field when the hour strikes for a decisive blow."

LEASE-LEND SHIPMENTS IN FEBRUARY

WASHINGTON, Monday (R). — The Lend-Lease Administrator, Mr. Stettinius reports that almost all Lease-Lend food shipped to America's allies during January and February went to Russia and Britain in about equal proportions.

Shipments over this period, he said, showed an increase in items and a decrease in 9, compared with last year.

QUARTER CENTURY OF AIR ARM

Air Minister Pays Tribute to RAF

LATEST RAID ON BERLIN 'A SHATTERING ASSAULT'

LONDON, Monday. — The Secretary for Air, Sir Archibald Sinclair, in a broadcast tribute to the R.A.F. last night on its silver jubilee — the service will be 25 years old on Thursday — described Saturday night's R.A.F. raid on Berlin as "a shattering assault."

"British and Dominion airmen, with their superb British aircraft and equipment, have established their ascendancy over the airmen of the Axis," said the Air Minister. "The present role of the R.A.F. is destructive. It may yet win fame and laurels in constructive work for the service of mankind."

Sir Archibald traced the growth of the R.A.F. from the Royal Naval Air Service and Fleet Air Arm, and paid a tribute to Lord Trenchard, "whose genius, foresight, leadership, and driving force fused the naval and military elements of air power into one mighty service" and to "three other great men of action"—Lloyd George, Field Marshal Smuts, and the Prime Minister, Mr. Churchill, for the part they played in the formation of the service 25 years ago.

Panic in Berlin

The Berlin press now admits that panic and inefficiency was responsible for much of the damage caused during the last R.A.F. raid on Berlin.

Newspapers are admonishing the citizens of Berlin for their behaviour, openly stating that if the people had kept their heads and gone about their fire-fighting duties in a proper manner there would have been much less damage and loss of life.

Following this raid the municipal authorities in Berlin were forced to grant a special allocation of clothing coupons to the thousands of homeless Berliners.

So great was the damage that professional workers were mobilized to clear the blocked roads and repair damaged buildings.

Nuremberg Hard Hit

More facts have now come to light showing how extensively Nuremberg's factories were damaged during the big R.A.F. raid on the night of March 8.

Fire appears to have been the chief cause of the devastation. One area with timber and goods covering 16 acres and another of 30 acres were set ablaze. At the Siemen's plant, two-thirds of the main workshops covering five acres have been destroyed.

The Air Ministry announced tonight that when the Brown House the headquarters of the Nazi Party was hit in the raid on Munich on March 9 the top floor was burned out.

On this floor was Hitler's office. A bust of Mussolini used to stand in the wall facing the door and a head of Napoleon used to be on a small bookcase behind the Fuehrer's chair.

(Reuter and ANA)

Eden-Hull Talks Concluded

WASHINGTON, Monday (UP) — Mr. Anthony Eden is concluding his conferences here, the atmosphere indicating that great progress has been made towards Anglo-American understanding on the issues of war and peace.

The Foreign Secretary will be Mr. Hull's guest of honour at a banquet tonight. He is scheduled to arrive at Ottawa tomorrow.

A War Department statement says: "Meetings have been arranged by the Joint Chiefs of Staff to acquaint the Commanders in the Pacific with the policies and plans decided upon at the recent Casablanca conference which concerned future action in which their theatres will be involved.

"At the same time, the Chiefs of Staff will be able to obtain first-hand knowledge of the developments in the Pacific to learn the views of the commanders in the field."

Half Million Jews Killed in Warsaw

BALTIMORE, Monday. — According to Rabbi Maurice Perlzweig, President of the British Section of the World Jewish Congress, all Warsaw's half a million Jews have been killed by the Germans.

Addressing a mass meeting here yesterday, he declared that the destruction of the entire Jewish population of Warsaw and millions of other Jews by the Nazis had been substantiated by both the British Foreign Office and the U.S. State Department. This was the last phase of Hitler's drive to exterminate European Jewry.

Minority Rights

The U.S. Government and the United Nations generally were urged to clarify the position regarding the restoration of rights of Jewish minorities in European countries by Dr. Israel Goldstein, speaking at a dinner given in his honour in New York today, at which Dr. Weizman spoke.

Senator Barkley backed Dr. Weizman's demand for a national home in Palestine, while Governor Dewey sent a message hailing Palestine's contribution to the war effort.

(Reuter and PAT)

ONLY 20 MILES TO GABES

8th Army Hurdles Another Obstacle

By ALAN HUMPHREYS
Reuters Special Correspondent

For the third time since the Eighth Army started from El Alamein, General Montgomery has overcome a very difficult prepared defence line by an outflanking movement. He used these tactics at El Agheila, at Wadi Zeumzem before Tripoli, and now at Mareth.

Battering its way forward against very fierce opposition in the El Hamma sector, the British column was so threatening to the rear of the Axis forces in the Mareth position that they were compelled to withdraw in the direction of Gabes.

This is not a rout. The Axis Command is making a withdrawal which, though forced, is nevertheless in some order, and the Eighth Army is still having to fight its way forward. At El Hamma, the British are opposed by first class German troops. Pockets of resistance which have been left behind by the retreating enemy make the rearguard fighting very tough.

It is generally believed that Rommel will retreat to a line north of Sousse since his position in the plains bounded by the Shott Djerid, Kairouan, Sousse and Gabes is undefendable.

On the northern front, the First Army's attack in the hilly sector after going like clockwork in its initial stages up to last night, was temporarily slowed down by the weather, rain and hail storms being experienced. On the flank the British troops are being heavily engaged.

On the southern front, fighting went on in the El Guettar valley, where Axis resistance appears to be stiffening. The Americans made some headway in the hills on either side of the valley but Axis strong points are making progress difficult.

Brisbane Cheers The Ninth

BRISBANE, Monday (R).— Elements of the A.I.F. Ninth Division recently home from two years' campaign in the Middle East paraded through the main streets of Brisbane today.

Thousands lined the route, cheering and waving flags and breaking the police cordons to scatter confetti over column after column of bronzed troops.

Sir Leslie Wilson, Governor of Queensland, took the salute from the steps of Brisbane's beflagged Town Hall.

Twenty-three Service personnel, including three members of the R.A.A.F., were killed when an R.A.A.F. transport plane crashed in the darkness near Brisbane early on Saturday.

The victims included 17 R.A.A.F. men one Australian Army officer, and two United States Army officers. There were no survivors.

Squadron Leader Keith Truscott is reported missing believed killed. He crashed off the Australian coast today during a practice flight.

NEW ZEALAND DEFENCE MINISTER HERE

New Zealand's Minister of Defence, the Hon. Frederick Jones, arrived in Jerusalem yesterday at the conclusion of his tour of the Middle East.

Mr. Jones, who brought greetings and messages to troops from the Government and people of New Zealand, previously visited Egypt, Syria and the Lebanon.

W.A.A.F. Recruiting in M.E. Soon

CAIRO, Monday (R). — It is learned that young British women living in Middle East countries, including Egypt and Palestine, may shortly be recruited for service in the Women's Auxiliary Air Force.

AMERICANS DRIVE ON TO COAST

By VIRGIL PINKLEY U.P. Correspondent at Allied H.Q. North Africa

The pressure of the Allied flanking movement behind the Mareth Line has forced Rommel to abandon his positions and the Eighth Army, smashing through the fortifications, has rolled on to capture Matmata, only 22 miles from the big Axis base of Gabes.

All along the battle-front, even in the far north where the British First Army had been biding its time, the Allies are on the march. The American forces continue to advance to the east from El Guettar, and altogether there are six columns pressing the Afrika Korps relentlessly towards the sea.

Nazis Plough Up Gabes Field

By BERTHA GASTER
Our Cairo Correspondent

The threat to Rommel's rear represented by the advance of two Allied columns from Fondouk and El Hamma respectively, is strikingly confirmed by the report that the west and main landing grounds at Gabes have been ploughed up by the Germans.

Whether that indicates preparations for an early withdrawal or only that the landing grounds are now useless under the day and night hammering of Allied planes is not clear. What is clear is that they have no further hope of using them again.

While news of the Mareth battle front has flared up dramatically into the headlines the air offensive over the Gabes area continues in spite of bad weather and swirling dust-storms.

The battle is now over, with Rommel retreating through the Gabes gap, while the British force on his flank which took El Hamma is harassing his columns. The Mareth victory was won largely by this outflanking movement in which the air force played a large part.

(UP).

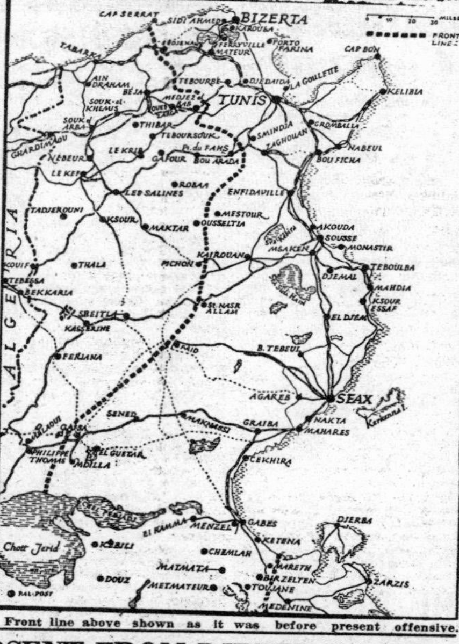

Front line above shown as it was before present offensive.

General Montgomery inflicted a heavy defeat on Rommel in his battering-ram attack on the Southern Tunisian defence system when the enemy was forced to give up the entire Mareth Line and retire towards Gabes. The combination of a frontal attack against the main Mareth Line, a heavy drive against El Hamma, and pressure on the El Guettar, Maknassy and Fondouk areas, forced Rommel to pull out of Mareth and start for Gabes, which is now really a bottleneck, with the Eighth Army driving from the south and other forces at the edge of El Hamma, only 16 miles away.

Combined Blitz

The pressure of combined land and air attack and the gains at El Hamma have caused Rommel to leave a considerable quantity of undamaged guns, tanks and motor transport behind. The air forces and artillery pounded the region so hard that the enemy — mostly crack German troops of the Afrika Korps — were forced to flee before they could destroy their equipment.

The Americans continue to hold the initiative in the El Guettar, Maknassy and Fondouk sectors. Much of this terrain of rocky hills and semi-desert is covered in some places with scrub. The pressure from these American field areas played a great part in the Eighth Army advances against El Hamma and the forcing of the Mareth Line.

Allied air power, built up painstakingly in the past three months, is making itself felt throughout the front as the Axis forces are harassed and threatened on all sides. This power is being applied methodically in accordance with the over-all master plan worked out carefully by General Eisenhower and General Alexander with their affiliated land, air and sea commanders.

The air forces teamed with the ground forces to keep pressure on Rommel from every direction — land and air. It was a magnificent power-house attack. The retreating Axis forces were blasted, bombed and hammered by the air forces which, in addition to strafing and bomb-plastering the ground troops, continued their attacks against landing grounds, harbours, docks, railways, highways and Axis bases in Sicily, Sardinia, and Italy.

The New Line

In the far north, British and French troops pushed deeper into Axis territory as they advanced some miles north and north-east of Djebel Abiod. Allied forces recaptured important parts of the Tamera-Sedjanene roads. North Moroccan "Goums" commanded by French officers fought exceedingly well in this action.

The Allies today hold a huge inverted horse-shoe position starting at the sea end of the Mareth Line, swinging round south-west, and then north-east to El Hamma. Inside this horse-shoe are Rommel's forces. Still further north, the Americans hold a large arc, swinging through points east of El Guettar, Sened and Maknassy, and a similar arc in Central Tunisia, west of the "holy city" of Kairouan, running roughly through Fondouk, Pichon and Ousseltia.

The Americans are less then 40 miles at their forward positions east of Maknassy to Mahares on the coast. From Fondouk to Kairouan is 20 miles while from Pichon to Kairouan is 25 miles. Kairouan and Sousse are 32 miles air-line and about 41 miles by road.

LUFTWAFFE ABSENT FROM DJEBEL BATTLE

By PHIL AULT
U.P. Correspondent with the U.S. Forces beyond El Guettar
(Delayed)

The American troops, opening the big push to the sea, struck the German mountain line at three places on Sunday in an attempt to break through the last hill barriers before the Tunisian coastal plain.

The biggest attack was a strong thrust through the hills along both sides of the Gabes road, nine miles south-east of El Guettar. At the southern end of the sector, American troops developed a threat to Kairouan in a second attack.

The third action involved an artillery duel for the high ground east of Maknassy where the troops crept forward over the naked hills up the ravines under mortar and shell fire south-east of El Guettar and slowly gained ground against stubborn German resistance which lasted all day. The Germans who were favoured by rugged terrain obviously intend to resist to the utmost.

From a captured Italian observation post on top of a wind-blown dusty ridge I watched the Americans edge forward under a German barrage from guns concealed on the north side of the Gabes road. The attack began at dawn. Some troops advanced along the northern slope of Djebel Berda towards the low hills overlooking the road where the supply road south to Kevili crosses the salt lake and joins the Gabes road. Others infiltrated over the high ground skirting the bases of the mountains forming the northern edge of the valley.

Djebel Mcheltat Fight

The key point in this sector — a German stronghold — is the Djebel Mcheltat a bald 1,500-foot hill forming a horse-shoe with its points eastward. The rock is deeply cut by ravines. At dusk the Americans had captured the northern half of the horse-shoe and the Germans were stubbornly holding the southern end. The troops then swung south to aid those trying a frontal assault.

The German air force was entirely absent from the battle while American planes were handicapped by a mist covering the ground for much of the day. In my observation post, lying on an Italian overcoat left by a former occupant when he fled hurriedly several days ago, I could look forward across the semi-arid valley to the southern shoulder of Mcheltat. To the right rose the Djebel, barren-topped. The American vehicles crept forward along the foot of the mountains, raising clouds of dust and dodging into a gully as German artillery laid salvoes along their path.

During a one-minute period in mid-morning, a concentrated American barrage laid on Mcheltat 1,000-lbs. of explosives dropped on the heights but the Germans clung to the position.

The Germans, on higher ground than the Americans, had the advantage of superior observation posts and gun positions enabling them to lay direct fire on jeeps and trucks scouting across the valley. Captain Percy L. Smith, assistant regimental surgeon, told of driving in a jeep around a bend into an exposed position, immediately after which a shell burst 40 yards away. He hopped from the jeep and took cover, several other bursts following quickly.

Capt. Smith said: "Our boys taking cover behind the rocks in small natural caves and gulleys were trying to work forward against the German shell-fire but it was tough going. A number of them were injured and lay in the valley but the shell-fire was so intense that stretcher-bearers were unable to reach them. They had to lie there until dark."

Axis Runs Tunisian Gauntlet

By FERGUS J. FERGUSON,
Reuters Military Correspondent

LONDON, Monday. — It was the threat to the Gabes bottleneck from the British outflanking column at El Hamma that forced Rommel's hand. The German Commander must now draw out as fast as he can if he does not wish to be cornered.

He is believed to have with him the remains of two German armoured divisions and some motorized troops of the 90th Light Division who have had abundant experience in making a quick get-away.

At all costs he has to try to hold his flank between El Hamma and Gabes while the withdraws to the north, but this is going to be a costly experience involving the sacrifice of much material and many prisoners. If he does get through the bottleneck, he has a long and narrow coastal road to traverse before he joins forces with von Arnim in the north.

Here too his flank is threatened at four points, where the roads lead through the coastal range to the coastal plain. The Americans are at Maknassy, at Faid Pass, and now at Fondouk, south-west of Kairouan so that Rommel will find himself beset by the Allies practically along the whole 150 miles to Sousse where he may hope to link up with von Arnim.

It is of course possible that General Alexander may also have some surprise up his sleeve that will make Rommel's route more onerous than his retreat from El Alamein to Tripoli.

Premier of Bengal Dismissed

CALCUTTA, Monday.— Mr. Fazlul Huq, formerly General Secretary of the Indian National Congress, has resigned as Prime Minister of Bengal.

In a statement, Mr. Fazlul Huq said that various proposals were put forward during talks with the Governor last night, some of which he could not accept consistently with self-respect, whereupon the Governor suggested that he should resign.

The growing strength of the Moslem League has just been shown in Bengal, where in six elections for Moslem seats in the Legislative Council five were won by the League.

The Ministry, which is based on a coalition of non-League Moslems and Hindus, survived a motion of censure last week in the Assembly by 30 votes in a House of 202.

The motion accused the Ministry of weakening the administration by not accepting responsibility for the actions of its officials. It was supported by the Moslem League, which is in opposition and by the European group, which is independent but generally supports the Ministry.

(Reuter and ANA)

Curtin Foresees Long War

SYDNEY, Monday (UP).—The Prime Minister, Mr. Curtin, in a speech here today, warned that the war would probably last three more years.

He pointed out that "Japan, tireless, formidable and unrelenting, knows that if she cannot win this time, it will be impossible for her to win in centuries."

The Premier also stressed Australia's vital military importance for the Allies.

War Flashes

A police inspector and another policeman were among ten Belgian hostages shot by the Germans for the killing of several members of the German Army Transport Corps, an SS. man, and a Rexist (Belgian Fascist).

Several German E-boats were sunk in a clash in the Channel yesterday in which light British naval forces suffered no losses.

Ventura bombers with fighter escort yesterday attacked shipping at Rotterdam, industrial objectives in Holland and railway yards at Abbeville, without loss.

AIR BLITZ PAVED THE WAY

Gen. Montgomery Thanks R.A.F.

ALLIED H.Q., NORTH AFRICA, Monday (R). — General Montgomery has signalled the following message of thanks to Air Vice Marshal Broadhurst, Air Officer Commanding the Western Desert Allied Air Force:

I would like to convey to you my great appreciation of the support to the land battle that has been given by the air forces under your command yesterday and, in fact, every day since the battle began. Such intimate support has never to my knowledge been achieved before and it has been an inspiration to all troops. The results have been first-class.

I sincerely trust that you have not suffered many losses. Please convey to all concerned the grateful thanks of myself and the whole Army for the truly magnificent effort.

The air action which General Montgomery singled out was a 2½ hours' intense attack on Axis positions at El Hamma on Friday afternoon. Three big attacks by light bombers and seven strafing and bombing attacks by large formations of fighter-bombers and fighters were made in that time — an average of one every quarter of an hour.

Before the 2½ hours were ended, the Axis forces were in retreat and the British troops had broken through the German positions. The last few attacks were switched on to the road north of El Hamma, which was jammed with retreating enemy transport.

Heaviest Combined Attack

This was the heaviest and most concentrated air attack which the Air Force had ever delivered in combination with Army operations. It was more devastating than anything which had been achieved during the Battle of Egypt at El Alamein. A conservative estimate is that 80 to 100 vehicles were destroyed and another 200 damaged.

Damage to Axis shipping and vital supply lines in rear areas inflicted last week by Flying Fortress, Marauder and Mitchell aircraft was the heaviest of any week in the campaign. Nine ships were sunk in convoys or harbours and 60 others badly damaged.

These losses were inflicted despite the bad weather. A total of 16,496 bombs were dropped on Axis targets during the week.

Today's Communique also pays a special tribute to the Air Force. It says:

Eighth Army Front: The attack which was launched on the afternoon of March 26 on the enemy's strong positions south of El Hamma has forced the enemy to withdraw from the Mareth area. This attack, with powerful and very effective support from our Air Forces, caused the enemy heavy losses in tanks, guns, motor transports and men. Many Germans were taken prisoner.

Fierce fighting continued in this area during March 27 with our troops making good progress. The whole of the strongly organized defences of the Mareth positions are now in our hands and our troops on March 28 occupied Mareth, Toujane and Matmata. Prisoners taken by the Eighth Army since March 20 now total over 6,000.

East of El Guettar, our troops made progress yesterday in difficult country. In the Maknassy and Fondouk areas, our patrols were very active. In the north in the Djebel Abiod, successful advances were made and a considerable number of prisoners were taken.

In spite of bad weather over the Tunisian front, fighters and fighter-bombers of the Western Desert Air Force maintained their attacks on enemy transport in the Gabes area. In the course of these operations, four enemy aircraft were destroyed. Fighters carried out sweeps in the central sector and made attacks on enemy positions and vehicles. From all these operations, two of our aircraft are missing.

RUMOURED RECALL OF SPANISH SHIPS

WASHINGTON, Monday (UP). — State Department and Spanish Embassy officials have both disclaimed any knowledge of unconfirmed radio reports that all Spanish vessels at sea have been called home.

LATE Edition

THE PALESTINE POST

JERUSALEM
FRIDAY, SEPT. 10 1943

PRICE 15 MILS
VOL. XVIII. Number 5280

ALLIES INVADE ITALY AS GERMAN TROOPS CLASH WITH ITALIANS

ANGLO-AMERICAN LANDINGS AT MANY POINTS REPORTED

With British, Canadian and American troops enlarging their bridgehead at Naples after a landing in the early morning hours yesterday, and other Allied forces reported to have landed at points so widely scattered as Sardinia, Genoa, Leghorn and Pisa, Italy yesterday also became the scene of sanguinary conflicts between the German army of occupation and Italian troops who refused to let themselves be disarmed or go over to the side of the Germans and their new puppet Government, under the reputed leadership of Farinacci.

Berlin officially described Badoglio's capitulation as a "stab in the back" and claimed that Northern Italy was under German control, local Italian resistance having been broken, while neutral reports from Switzerland asserted that no German troops remained in Milan and Turin, that railway communications between Germany and Italy had been cut, and that three German divisions stationed in the Verona and Trentino areas of Northern Italy returned to Germany across the Brenner on Wednesday. The Italians officially claimed to have driven out the Germans. Outside Italy, the Germans claimed to have disarmed all Italian troops in Yugoslavia and Greece, while some Italians in Savoy crossed the frontier into Switzerland and were interned.

Political moves included the establishment by the Germans of a Fascist puppet Government, reputedly under Roberto Farinacci, on Austrian soil; a forecast that King Victor Emmanuel might displace Marshal Badoglio; and a statement by Badoglio giving the reasons for his surrender.

Allied aircraft are landing in air fields in southern Italy in almost continuous procession according to reports reaching Washington from the Mediterranean theatre of operations. Well-informed American quarters say that preparations for a sustained attack on Berlin, industrial Germany and the vassal countries from these fields are being completed, while Turkish quarters believe that Italy's surrender is likely to be followed within the next 48 hours by important military developments in Western Europe.

Germans Attack Italians And Try to Seize Control

LONDON, Thursday (R). — While German troops are clashing with Italian forces or disarming them, Hitler has made his first move to counter the Italian Government's defection. The German radio early this morning broadcast a proclamation by a self-styled "National Fascist Government" announcing the establishment of a Government acting in the name of Mussolini.

The Italian Embassy in Berlin has been cordoned off by police, and all leading Italian personalities in Berlin have been taken to police headquarters.

The Germans would defend parts of Italy indispensable for the defence of Europe, declared Dr. Schmidt, the Chief of the Press Department. No change would take place in the European war situation.

"The Italian Government went so far in its treason as to attempt to involve even the German Government as far as possible in the catastrophe of the armistice," he said. "They attempted, after the capitulation had been concluded, to lure German formations into areas where they would be in a fatal position after the Anglo-American landing."

"Stab in the Back"

The Italian capitulation was today officially described by the German News Agency as a "Stab in the back" of the German troops in Italy. The deputy press chief to the Government, Helmut Suendermann, said that the capitulation was the "most indecent and spineless act of a clique of traitors" which would have grim repercussions on the traitors themselves.

Italian units had been concentrated on the German frontier, but the German Command's counter-measures to these developments and the hostile attitude of the Italian troops had been functioning like clockwork says an official statement, adding:

"The most important lines of communications are safeguarded by German troops or Italian troops loyal to the Axis. This is particularly true of the important railway net in North and Central Italy.

"The measures put into force in Italy immediately after Badoglio's capitulation are everywhere proceeding according to plan. Generally speaking, Italian units were disarmed without any major incidents. Only those Italian units were disarmed which did not declare themselves ready to continue fighting under the German Command. There was local resistance which was quickly broken. The important communication lines are usable in their entirety."

Why Italy Surrendered

The Italian News Agency today issued the text of a telegram sent by Marshal Badoglio yesterday to Hitler and other Axis leaders giving the following reasons for Italy's surrender:

Italy's defences collapsed, the Allied advance could not be stemmed, industry had been paralysed, resources were completely exhausted, and railways and shipping had been annihilated. In order to avoid her total ruin, Italy is therefore compelled to ask her enemy for an armistice.

The enemy was able to land now, where and when he wanted with powerful forces, breaking every resistance and growing day by day in quantity and power, ruining the country. It cannot be demanded of any people to continue to fight when every legitimate hope — to not say of victory, but even of defence—has vanished.

Disarming the Italians

The "Free German" broadcasting radio station "Atlantic" was heard last night to say that Marshal Kesselring has ordered the Germans in Italy to hold their positions. Italian Carabinieri are reported to be fighting the Germans. German engineer troops are now repairing the bridges on the Brenner railway.

The German Overseas Radio quoted a military spokesman today for the report that the Italian Army in Greece had agreed to hand over their heavy material and then march to the coast where they would place themselves at the orders of the German Army. It also announced that Croatian troops supported by Germans have occupied Dalmatia which "by consent of Germany" has been incorporated into the Croatian State.

Crossing Into Switzerland

The German radio further announced that Italian troops of the occupation army in French Savoy crossed into Switzerland and marched through the streets of Geneva for several hours this morning. They have not been interned. They crossed the frontier with all their arms, equipment and transport.

The only news of successful Italian resistance comes from Corsica where according to Stockholm reports the Italian garrison overpowered the German troops.

Information from Italian military circles, which lacks confirmation, is to the effect that Italian troops have taken up positions in and around Milan to defend the city from German attempts at occupation. A Berne report says that German forces have taken over the control in Milan and other large towns in North Italy.

The Italians themselves assert that the Germans have been driven from Milan.

The Stockholm "Dagens Nyheter" reports from "a most reliable source" that until yesterday evening German troops were still in Rome. "German cars, motorcycles and patrols were seen in the capital throughout the day. The German headquarters for the Rome district at Frascati were bombed by the Allies yesterday morning."

TENSION IN REICH

By BERNARD VALERY,
Reuters Special Correspondent

STOCKHOLM, Thursday. — S.S. men are patrolling the streets of Berlin today, according to the correspondent of "Allenhanda," who says that "an atmosphere of tension prevails in the city."

Skirmishes are alleged to have taken place in Munich in front of the Brown House, the Nazi Party Headquarters. The correspondent adds that there is also tension in Central Germany. Great excitement is reported among Italian workers in the Reich.

Hitler today held an important war council at which it was decided to reinforce the Po line and fight in Italy to the last man, according to the same correspondent.

Hitler's council was held at Berchtesgaden and Field Marshal Kesselring, the German Commander-in-Chief in Italy, was brought to it by special plane, according to the correspondent. Goering, Himmler, Ribbentrop, Field Marshal Keitel, the Chief of Staff, and Professor Speer, the Minister of Armaments, were also present.

The correspondent further says that at a recent stormy conference several Generals accused Hitler of surrounding himself with second-rate people instead of efficient military men, and blamed the Nazi Party for recent military defeats. They are reported to have described the military situation as extremely strained.

ITALIAN COLLAPSE RESOUNDS THROUGH THE WORLD

LONDON, Thursday (R). — From all over Europe come reports indicating how deep are the repercussions of Italy's surrender.

Citizens of the French province of Upper Savoy paraded through beflagged streets amid ringing church bells. The commander of the Italian occupying troops there has requested the Vichy authorities to facilitate the withdrawal of his forces back into Italy. Some have crossed into Switzerland.

In Budapest, the news caused a sensation, says the Hungarian radio. Newspapers refrain from comment, but according to Stockholm reports from Budapest, Admiral Horthy discussed the new situation with the Hungarian Prime Minister and the Chief of Staff. In Bulgaria also, the Cabinet is reported to have sat until a late hour debating the event.

Soviet Comment

In Russia, "Pravda" observed that is was no mere coincidence that Italy's capitulation followed so closely on the Red Army's great victories. Over 200,000 of Italy's best troops failed to return home from the Russian front, and by holding 300 German divisions the Red Army made the Allied victory in North Africa possible and prevented Germany from helping Italy in Sicily.

"Red Star" published a cartoon showing Hitler having his Italian leg sawn off, with the headline "serious amputation."

Japan is taking Italy's defection badly. The Japanese News Agency stated today:

"The Japanese authorities in Shanghai, following the news of Italy's surrender, immediately started taking over all Italian vested interests in Shanghai according to international law."

The Tokyo radio today was bitter in its comment: "Italy's act is a violation of the tripartite pact. Japan had already taken all necessary measures in anticipation of such an event. Italy's capitulation will have no effect on the war situation."

Londoners Keep Calm

Britain took the news of Italy's collapse with its usual phlegmatic calm. Piccadilly Circus last night was as quiet as on any other night in the blackout.

Typical reaction was reflected in the remark of a passer-by, "Well it's something to get on with."

An American soldier on leave could not understand the calm of Londoners and a Sergeant from Baltimore expressed his disappointment by saying "You Britishers don't react. You're happy enough, though, because you're smiling more than usual."

FARINACCI TO HEAD PUPPET GOVERNMENT

NEW YORK, Thursday (R). — Roberto Farinacci, the former Fascist Party Secretary is believed to be the head of the Fascist "Government" which is reported to have been set up in Austria.

Reports from the Italian frontier received in London via Zurich say there were frantic demonstrations of joy in Milan, Turin, Como and other towns in North Italy as the news of the armistice spread.

The news is published under enormous headlines in today's Italian press, states the Italian News Agency. "Popolo di Roma" writes: "Marshal Badoglio has had the courage to realise the tragic truth."

The Turin "Stampa" observes: "If the Badoglio Government had continued the war, it would have committed a crime against the nation."

The German News Agency says that the German-Italian frontier has been closed to all civilians.

A Swiss telegraphic dispatch from Chiasso says that German and Italian troops are fighting in the streets of Tortona. The Germans are said to have disarmed the Italians guarding a bridge at Boghera and occupied Tessin bridge near the town.

"There are also reports of fighting between Germans and Italians near Pavia and Certosa.

BATTLE FOR PO RIVER VALLEY EXPECTED

By JOHN LEONARD,
Reuters Special Correspondent

WASHINGTON, Thursday Washington is agog with reports that another "big news break" is expected. Meanwhile despite Italy's surrender, military observers here expect the Germans to persist in their plan of holding Northern Italy along the line of the River Po.

They are reported to have between 15 and 20 divisions there. Whatever new drain on their manpower, the view is taken that they cannot lightly surrender the approaches to the Brenner Pass.

Speculation centres on whether the Allies, after securing the whole of Central and Southern Italy, will attempt a direct assault or try to circumvent Hitler's defences.

There is a growing conviction that the air offensive which undermined Italian resistance is to be carried out against Hungary, Rumania and Bulgaria. It is also reliably reported that Finland will follow Italy's example as soon as possible.

Further Landings Expected

Military observers here consider that the Allied landings near Naples do not exclude the possibility of other landings in the next few hours. It is authoritatively stated that General Eisenhower appears to have a definite "partitioning plan" designed to isolate the German troops in sections.

The disclosure that it is the American Fifth Army which landed in Naples has revived speculation on Allied plans for General Patton's Seventh Army. The absence of all mention of this force since the fall of Messina is linked by observers here with the similar silence surrounding General Giraud's troops which may reasonably be supposed to be awaiting the moment for an attack on France.

Mr. Henry Stimson, the War Secretary, told a press conference today that satisfactory progress was being made in the Naples area where the Allies were in contact with the Germans The landing forces included considerable units of the American Fifth Army. The entire operation was under the command of General Clark.

Mr. Stimson estimated that there were from 15 to 20 German divisions in Italy — a greater number of troops than they had in Tunis or in Sicily.

Roosevelt Counsels Caution

President Roosevelt, in a nationwide broadcast opening the drive for the third War Loan last night sounded a warning against premature optimism when he said:

"An armistice with Italy was concluded today. This was a great victory for the United Nations — but it was also a great victory for the Italian people. After years of war and suffering and degradation, the Italian people are at last coming to the day of liberation from their real enemies — the Nazis.

"But let us not delude ourselves that this armistice means the end of the war in the Mediterranean. We must drive the Germans out of Italy as we have driven them out of Tunisia and Sicily; we must drive them out of France and all the other captive countries, and we must strike them on their own soil from all directions.

FULL-SCALE AMPHIBIOUS EXERCISE.

LONDON, Thursday (R).— A joint communique issued by the Admiralty, War Office and Air Ministry today discloses that a full-scale amphibious exercise has recently taken place in the English Channel.

Effective protection for naval and military units engaged in the amphibious operations were provided by fighters, it is officially stated today. Two ensure the success of the operations, 2,000 fighter sorties were flown over Northern France and the Engish Channel during the last 24 hours, while the U.S. and R.A.F. medium bombers carried out 1,000 sorties.

By midday today, over 1,000 fighter sorties had been made without a single loss. These were the climax to a period of intensive operations both by medium bombers and fighters in the last ten days during which the Allies have had undisputed control of the skies.

No bomber or fighter attacks were made by the Germans on the Allied land and sea forces and the number of air combats were few, even when Allied fighters were escorting bombers on offensive operations.

While the German News Agency says that Paris was bombed this morning, it is announced in London that bombers attacked targets in the Boulogne area, last night.

GERMANS ON THE RUN

By HAROLD KING,
Reuters Correspondent

MOSCOW, Thursday.— The German Army in the Southern Ukraine is on the run on a 100-mile front from Malaya Komishevakha, eight miles south of Izyum, to south of Stalino.

Thirty miles south-west of Kharkov, General Koniev's troops are hammering away at one of the strongest of German defence positions and are steadily pressing the enemy back.

With the road opened by the smashing of German resistance in the Donbas, twin forces are now pushing quickly from Krasnoarmeisk along the two railways which run to the great industrial city of Dniepropetrovsk.

Advanced units of one of these forces are only 40 miles from Pavlograd itself, 30 miles north-east of Dniepropetrovsk. The capture of Pavlograd would cut the vital railway from Kharkov which crosses the Donbas-Dniepropetrovsk line and runs south to Zaporozhe, Melitopol and the Crimea.

In the Northern Ukraine, the Soviet drive towards Chernigov and the Middle Dnieper continues to make good progress, the vital junction of Bakhmach, controlling the main lateral railway communications between the German's central and southern armies, having now been captured.

Allied Troops in Contact with Germans in Naples Area

LONDON, Thursday (R). — Italy's surrender has been followed by an all-out Allied assault on the German troops in the country. General Eisenhower's forces, who landed in the Naples area early today under cover of British and U.S. warships are now fighting against the Germans and have taken a number of prisoners, states a special communique from Allied Headquarters.

Satisfactory progress is being made by the Allied forces which, after racing across the plains north of Naples, encountered the German rearguard A considerable concentration of German troops is believed to be in the Naples area and on the beaches.

Unofficial reports say that landings were also made at several other points along the Italian coast, including localities north and south of Rome and near Leghorn and Genoa General Eisenhower is believed to be carrying out a "partitioning plan" designed to cut the German forces into sections and destroy them.

The announcement of the new landings in Italy was made by the Tunis radio in a broadcast to the Italian people which said:

"Powerful British, American and Canadian armies are landing at various points in the heart of Italy. The arrival of these armies, powerfully equipped and protected by the invincible Allied air force and by the full might of the Mediterranean Allied naval forces gives you Italians your last great opportunity."

Sardinia, Genoa, Leghorn

Unconfirmed reports of Allied landings at various places apart from Naples are pouring in from all points of the compass.

Thus the Stockholm "Svenska Dagbladet" correspondent on the Italian frontier telegraphed, "American troops are reported here to have landed in Genoa, Naples and Sardinia," while a report from the frontier to the "Dagens Nyheter" described as "absolutely reliable" said that Allied troops had landed at Gaeta, Civita Vecchia and Pisa.

The Swiss radio said that large forces of the American Seventh Army landed on the Tyrrhenian coast of Italy and at Leghorn. The speaker added,

"Hundreds of Allied planes are about to land on Italian air-fields."

Heavy firing off the French coast was heard late last night, according to a report received from San Sebastian, in Northern Spain. The gunfire, the report added, led to speculation that Allied warships might be firing at coastal batteries.

Fighting at Naples

At Naples so far the Allies are known to have captured two airfields. An American correspondent broadcasting from Allied Headquarters, North Africa, said this morning: "German forces are known to be in the Naples area where we have landed. Military men at Allied Headquarters expect strong resistance.

"Not only have the Germans got a number of divisions in Italy but some are actually in the area where the landing took place — crack divisions which saw action in Russia."

NAPLES OPENS DOOR TO ROME AND THE ADRIATIC COAST

By HAIG NICHOLSON,
Reuters Special Correspondent in North Africa

ALGIERS, Thursday. — The landing near Naples means business. From there the Allies will be able to move north along good roads towards Rome or strike across to the Adriatic.

It remains to be seen how far south the Germans intend to spread their forces, especially as Italian civilians will be more anti-German than before.

The capture of Naples would mean the possession of one of the best harbours in Italy in which the invading forces could continue to be landed. It is, in fact, the only good harbour until Spezia is reached in the north, and it is possible that the Italian Fleet may have been able to get away from Spezia to Naples.

Meanwhile it is pointed out here that from Italian air fields, which in the central and southern parts of the country alone number at least 100, Germany and other enemy countries in Europe will be within easy bombing range. From Foggia—one of the main groups of airfields — Flying Fortresses which have already shown themselves capable of a 1,500 miles round-trip could easily bomb the whole of Bulgaria, Hungary, Austria, and go deep into Germany. The Ploesti oil fields, Warsaw and Berlin would be within range.

From the Lombardy plain, which is also well supplied with good airfields, Fortresses could reach Copenhagen and Brest, and would be only 515 miles from Berlin.

Frascati was bombed by Fortresses for six hours before the announcement of Italy's surrender. Just before noon, three waves of planes dropping several hundred tons of bombs demolished the town.

The villa where German officers lived and worked got a direct hit. Twenty-eight of fifty fighters which tried to prevent the attack were destroyed by Fortresses.

The Italian News Agency says that Field Marshal Kesselring, the German Air-Commander-in-Chief in Italy, narrowly escaped with his life when his house was hit during yesterday's raid on German headquarters in Frascatti.

ITALIAN PLANES COME OVER

CAIRO, Thursday (R). — A certain number of Italian aircraft from the Balkans arrived today at pre-arranged Allied air bases in Cyprus, Tobruk, El Adem, just south of Tobruk, and Derna, it is officially announced.

ITALIAN FLEET TOLD TO MAKE FOR HAIFA

CAIRO, Thursday (R).—An official broadcast last night by a representative of Sir Henry Maitland Wilson, Commander-in-Chief of the Middle East, told the Italian armed forces in the Balkans and the Aegean Sea to cease all hostile acts, resist the Germans and take possession by force of all points occupied by the Germans in the Dodecanese.

Units of the Italian mercantile fleet at any point east of 17 degrees were told to proceed directly to Alexandria. Warships were told to proceed direct to Haifa. Italian planes were told to fly immediately to Nicosia, Derna, Tobruk and El Adem.

Sir H. Maitland Wilson, in a special broadcast to the Greek and Yugoslav peoples said:

"To all of you who are our friends, I say, 'Do not prevent the Italians from returning home.' The Germans will seek to cause bloodshed between you and the Italians in order to strengthen their position. Do not be misled by this and do not play the German game."

The Italian surrender has removed 65 divisions from the enemy ranks, said Sir Henry Wilson, addressing a press conference here tonight.

War Flashes

Persia had declared war on Germany, it is announced in Teheran.

A Paris radio commentator said last night: "German and Italian troops are locked in vicious fighting all over Italy. The German High Command has attempted to gain control over the communications system. But at many points the Italians were driven on by their pro-Allied officers and fierce fighting resulted.'

Radio France reported last night that further reinforcements are being disembarked in the Naples area, where the Germans claim to have localised the Allied landing and inflicted heavy losses on the Anglo-American forces.

The Vatican radio last night denied reports of a telephone conversation between the Pope and President Roosevelt, and also asserted that no political mission had gone to Washington.

The German radio last night issued a warning to the public against possible landings by Allied parachutists.

THE PALESTINE POST

LATE Edition

JERUSALEM SUNDAY, APRIL 2, 1944.

PRICE: 15 MILS

VOL. XIX. Number 5451

BOMBERS OVER S.W. REICH

Strong Force Out in Daylight

LONDON, Saturday (R). — U.S. heavy bombers in great force hammered targets in south-west Germany today, the exact identity of which has not yet been disclosed.

Waves of Allied planes in considerable force crossed the south-east coast between eight and nine o'clock this morning, flying in the direction of the Continent.

At nine o'clock the German radio reported: "Single enemy planes over western and central Germany," and half an hour later, Cologne radio announced: "Strong enemy bomber formations are approaching Southern Germany."

At 10 o'clock faded out in the middle of a sentence after broadcasting Munich: "Achtung, strong bomber forces are approaching southern and south-western Germany."

Last night mosquitoes of the Bomber Command without loss attacked objectives in Western Germany, the Air Ministry announced late this morning. The Air Ministry also stated that one R.A.F. fighter was missing from an offensive patrol in daylight yesterday.

SWISS TOWN HIT

BERNE, Saturday (R). — The Swiss radio, quoting an official statement on a reported American raid, said today that several fires were started in Schaffhausen town, including the area of the railway station.

Railway traffic on all lines leading to Schaffhausen has been temporarily suspended.

U.S. TO APOLOGISE

WASHINGTON, Saturday (UP). — The bombardment of the Swiss town of Schaffhausen which, according to an official Berne statement, was attacked erroneously this morning by American bombers who caused considerable damage and some 150 casualties, is greatly regretted in the United States.

It is expected that the Government will apologise very soon for the bombing.

BRITAIN'S NEW BOFORS GUN DESCRIBED

LONDON, Saturday (R). — What may be one of Britain's new "Second Front" weapons — the Bofors 40-mm. self-propelled gun — was officially described for the first time last night.

Produced in Canada, Britain, the gun has for long been a mainstay of the Home Country's A.A. defences and is mounted on a truck chassis in its new form. Canadian Ordnance experts and the British Ministry of Supply and War Office are cooperating in its output.

The chassis is driven by a 70-h.p. engine giving it a road speed of 40 m.p.h. and good cross-country performance. The gun's best feature is its rapid rate of fire — it can fling up to two pounder shells to the height of 9,000 feet at the rate of 120 a minute. The gun is equipped with a new sight and can be elevated and traversed by power.

R.A.F. Has New Super-Fighter

LONDON, Saturday (R). — Britain has a sensational new fighter plane in production to throw into the air conflict over Britain in the spring, it was disclosed today.

Great secrecy envelops its performance and even its name is not revealed, but Reuter is able to say that this "bomber killer" is even more powerful and faster than the famous Spitfire Mark IX and it was the Spitfire Mark IX whose performance is still on the official secret list, which chalked lengthened and beat the Fockewulf 190 last year—the only German machine seriously to threaten British superiority in the fighter design.

Rocket Guns

The Commander-in-Chief of Anti-Aircraft Command, General Sir Frederick Pole, said on Friday night that Britain's deadly rocket-guns would undoubtedly be the anti-aircraft gun of the future, entirely replacing the present heavy guns.

"Rocket propulsion is opening enormous vistas for us," General Pole said. He added that the Germans "may have something" planned for the future of rocket types — either a rocket or remote controlled aeroplane or both.

Mr. Churchill's son-in-law, Mr. Duncan Sandys, played an important part in rocket development and in the early part of the war was put in charge of rocket experimentation.

War Flashes

Berlin last night admitted that the Russians had broken into Tarnopol.

Chinese and American forces have routed the Japanese in the Laban area of North Burma, said an official Chinese announcement picked up in New York.

The Russians have captured Podhajce, a district centre of the Tarnopol region, as well as Troilovo, a district centre of the Odessa region, and 100 localities near Odessa.

Radio France (Algiers) last night reported that General Giraud had visited Italy to review French troops.

ALLIED TALKS TO TAKE PLACE SOON

Soviet Views on Italy Broadcast

LONDON, Saturday (R). — New Anglo-U.S. talks are foreshadowed here in the report that Mr. Adolph Berle, the U.S. Assistant Secretary of State, is coming to London shortly for an exploratory exchange of views.

The U.S. State Department, in disclosing this yesterday, added that similar talks with a representative of the Soviet Union were expected to take place in Washington within the next fortnight.

In the meantime the British Government's reply to the Soviet proposal that the Badoglio regime should be maintained and broadened by the inclusion of representatives of all democratic parties has now been communicated to Moscow, learns Reuter's Diplomatic Correspondent. Its terms have not been disclosed.

The Soviet Proposals

The Moscow radio yesterday gave prominence to "Izvestia's" article on the subject which contained the following passage:

"The forces of the Badoglio Government and of the Executive Junta have not yet achieved unity, and things in Italy have obviously drifted into an impasse. This state of affairs is bound to affect the Allied cause and the struggle against Hitlerite Germany.

"Where then is a way out of the present situation? The obvious way out is for the Allied Powers, by joint efforts, to direct the political developments in Italy into channels conforming with the tasks of the struggle of the Allies against the common enemy — Hitlerite Germany."

It is reported today from Naples that Marshal Badoglio and his Minister of the Interior, Vitto Reale, flew to Palermo yesterday in connection with the recent appointment of an Italian High Commissioner for Sicily.

Communists Toe "Izvestia" Line

By CECIL SPRIGGE
Reuter's Correspondent

NAPLES, Saturday. — The Italian Communist Party has decided to propose to the other Italian opposition parties that they should waive their insistence on King Victor Emmanuel's abdication and proceed forthwith with the formation of a Government having the support of all parties.

This was announced today by Ercoli, the Italian Communist leader who returned to Naples from Moscow a week ago after having lived in exile for 18 years.

The Communist Party's new programme as announced by Ercoli includes three principal points: (1)... the unity of the anti-Fascist parties must be maintained. (2). The postwar institutions of the Italian State must be decided upon Democratically. (3). A National Government must be formed on a wide basis.

War Comes First

In a statement published in the Communist organ "Unita," Ercoli urges the union of all national forces. He describes the purging of Fascism as an "elementary necessity for the purposes of war and the primary basis of national recovery," but adds: "There is no question of eliminating from the Army the class of experienced and capable officers who are attached to the King. The possibility of another leap-frog landing, perhaps in the Civita Vecchia area, or 'even further north, is not being overlooked by the German commanders."

This fear was expressed by Karl Praeger the German News Agency war reporter in Italy, who said : "The possibility of another leap-frog landing, perhaps in the Civita Vecchia area, or 'even further north, is not being overlooked by the German commanders."

Germans Expect New Landings

ALGIERS, Saturday (R). — The German High Command is now worrying about the danger of new Allied amphibious landings on the Italian north of Rome, where Allied air attacks have recently been intensified.

MT. MARRONE FALLS TO ALLIES

By REYNOLDS PACKARD
U.P. Correspondent

NAPLES, Saturday.— Fifth Army troops have driven forward a mile and captured the 5,840-foot Mt. Marrone in a surprise three-pronged attack which threatens to outflank the deadlocked Cassino front.

Ending the long lull on the mountainous central front, Allied troops attacked under cover of a heavy artillery barrage and, overwhelming the strong German defences, scored their most important success since they reached the outskirts of Cassino in February.

The assault indicates that Generals Alexander and Clark may have decided to shift the main weight of their offensive northward, following their failure to break through the Cassino front.

From Mt. Marrone the Allies are in a position to pose a grave threat to the German positions just behind both Cassino and Monastery Hill. The snow-capped mountain dominates the German-held Atina Colli highway. In addition to Mt. Marrone, the Allies also attacked nearby San Michele and Pizzone, but the outcome of these thrusts is not yet known.

Maj-Gen. Wingate Killed in Burma Air Crash

Death Ends Short, Brilliant Career

By ALFRED GRANT
Reuter's Staff Correspondent

LONDON, Saturday. — The death of Major-General Orde Charles Wingate, D.S.O. & two Bars, leader of the Allied air-borne invasion force behind the Japanese lines in Burma, was announced late last night when it was disclosed that he was killed in a plane crash on March 24 during a severe storm.

Everyone in the plane, including the American crew of five, as well as one or two other passengers, was killed. Major-General Wingate, had been on a tour of inspection in one of Lieutenant Colonel Cochran's Mitchell bombers, with a Mustang escort. Lt. Col.

Major-Gen. Wingate

Cochran was the officer in charge of the glider invasion of Burma. After the inspection General Wingate took off homeward bound, but his bomber never arrived.

That night an American pilot sighted and reported a blaze on a mountain ridge behind the British lines. At dawn the next day, Lt.-Col. Cochran sent out every available light plane but it was some time before the wreckage was spotted.

Major-General Wingate's death came as a shock to most people in the South East Asia Command, as the news was broken to the radio before the official announcement was released.

The Wingate Stamp

Last Monday — two days after his disappearance — it was disclosed that he had planned and led the airborne invasion of Burma which, 150 miles behind the Japanese lines, cut the Mandalay-Myitkyina railway, an essential supply line of the Japanese 18th Division. The secret of his new equipment was well kept for many months, and even his promotion to Major-General was not published. But when the airborne landing was announced, it carried the unmistakable Wingate stamp.

The story has already been told of his training and leadership of the famous "Ghost Army" which he led in 1943 for over 1,000 miles around Japanese positions in Burma, hidden in the jungle, destroying bridges, railways, ammunition dumps, killing large numbers of Japanese and bringing back invaluable information. No sooner had he brought his army out of Burma, than he was on his way to "meet with the Prime Minister, Mr. Churchill."

He said of the Japanese Generals that they were third class, but the Japanese soldier is another matter. It is a matter of training. He can be outwitted easily enough." And certainly he proved it.

His Career

Major-General Wingate was born in February, 1903, the son of Colonel George Wingate who had 32 years of service in the Indian Army. He entered the Royal Artillery as a Second Lieutenant in 1923 and became the rank of Captain by the outbreak of war. He was a nephew of Sir Reginald Wingate who at one time was High Commissioner in Egypt.

Before that, he had fought terrorists in Palestine with their own weapons of ambush and guerilla raids. Within a very short time he had cleaned up the terrorists and restored order. For this he got the Distinguished Service Order.

General Wingate was a puritanical Christian who carried his Bible everywhere and frequently used texts from it in messages to his men.

Tributes to Major-General Wingate were featured today in the American press and were over the broadcasting systems of both countries. Speakers and writers laid stress upon his qualities of generalship and his mastery of guerilla tactics.

The "News Chronicle" commented that the Japanese might easily count this a major victory for themselves, but it would be mistaken because Wingate lived on among the flood of ardent officers and men whom he had trained in the Burma campaign.

(Appreciation by Mr. Ben Gurion — Page 4)

DRIVE TO ODESSA

MOSCOW, Saturday (U.P.) — Upwards of 100,000 Germans in the Southern Ukraine, suddenly abandoning their stubborn defence, have fled in a race to escape from the Soviet drive to Odessa which threatens to cut their last routes of retreat.

The German retreat in some sectors has become a panic-stricken rout. It seems possible that the entire Ukraine, including Odessa, will be cleared of the enemy within a matter of days.

SOVIET-JAP TRADE PACT EXTENDED

MOSCOW, Saturday.—A Soviet Japanese trade agreement published in Moscow yesterday morning is regarded in Allied diplomatic circles as a great triumph of Soviet diplomacy and as a notable and significant tribute to the success of Soviet arms.

Under the new agreement Japan will not get any oil from the Oka oilfields while the war lasts except for existing Japanese owned oil which by agreement they can remove.

During the five years following the end of the present war the Soviet Government will supply on commercial terms 50,000 metric tons of oil to Japan.

New Fisheries Pact

Important new reservations are also introduced into the fisheries agreement, which for the first time since 1936 has been renewed for more than a year at a time.

Under the five-year pact the Japanese undertake not to exploit the fishing concessions rented by them along the east coast of Kamchatka and in Olutorski region until the Pacific war is ended. Japanese subjects and other foreigners are prohibited from fishing in sea areas in the Far East before the end of the present war.

These areas include those near the great Soviet base of Vladivostok.

SHARP FIGHT FOR KOHIMA

By DARRELL BERRIGAN
U.P. Correspondent

NEW DELHI, Saturday. — British and Imperial forces are reported to be putting up stiff resistance to the Japanese drive to Kohima, the important supply centre 60 miles northward of Imphal.

Should the enemy, who is using surprisingly strong forces, succeed at this point, he would force the entire British Army on the Central Burma front to rely on air supplies and depots established earlier.

Fighting at Manipur is reported to be severe. An enemy road-block across the Tamu-Palel road south of Imphal has already isolated from land supply the Allied forces in the Kabaw Valley but it is assumed that air transports and emergency reserves permit troops to hold out until the road is cleared.

Meanwhile another enemy column is trying to break into the Manipur valley from the Ukhrul area east of Imphal, and small patrols who succeeded in penetrating the Imphal plains have come within 16 miles of that city. It is not known how strong these advance units are.

Tanks supported the Allied forces which captured two enemy positions on the river bank northward of Buthidaung on the Arakan peninsula, but today's communiqué warns that enemy forces still remain and offer resistance in that area.

Tokyo radio claims that the Japanese are "relentlessly attacking" in the Buthidaung sector and denies the report that they have lost that town.

Palestine Solution Cannot Wait Until End of War

WASHINGTON, Saturday (PTA). — Pointing out that President Roosevelt's statement last week indicated that it was only military considerations and not political, economic or other reasons which involved the Government's opposition to the Palestine Resolution, Dr. Israel Goldstein, addressing a press luncheon at the Hotel Statler here today, said:

"If the military advise deferment, we accede, but at the first available moment when the military situation improves we expect the resolutions to be considered on their merits.

"American Zionists will not passively accept the view of British official circles that a definite situation of the Palestine problem should wait until the end of the war."

He stressed the fact that the United Nations are making permanent commitments in the Middle East every day.

Some 1,500 university professors have sent a petition to President Roosevelt to intervene in order to secure the free entry of Jews into Palestine. The petition declares that the United States Government has a legal and moral right to intercede on behalf of the Jewish people.

S.E. Europe in the Melting-Pot

LONDON, Saturday. — As the Red Army rolls westward, all south-eastern Europe has been thrown into the melting-pot.

Contact has been established between the Soviet Air Force covering the German army towards the Carpathians, and Czechoslovak guerillas operating inside Ruthenia.

Particularly intense guerilla activities are reported from the districts of Bardejov and Michalovce, north and east of the great junction of Kosice. Slovak and Hungarian — and German frontier posts, military stores, railway lines and bridges have been successfully attacked. According to latest reports reaching here, the occupation of the Carpathian passes is not yet complete.

Leaving Bucharest

From Rumania comes the news that foreign legations in Bucharest are reported to be leaving the capital for the western part of Rumania on the advice of the Rumanian Government. Civilian rail reserves are still pouring into the country through Hungary by road and by way of the Danube.

The Rumanian radio broadcast today's Rumanian Communique stating:

"In North Bessarabia, German troops continue to carry out heavy offensive and defensive fighting. The town of Hotin is in the hands of the German forces.

"Between the Pruth and Jijia, there was local activity. In Central Bessarabia, a German counter-attack is developing successfully and the enemy is being thrown back north of the Kishinev-Jassy railway line."

Yugoslavia and Bulgaria

A communiqué from General Tito's headquarters, broadcast by the Free Yugoslav radio today, reports continued fighting battles in East Bosnia. In Slovenia, there was violent fighting near Idrija and Gorica.

The Radek-Ljubyljana railway was put out at several places. On March 27, the railway station at Risovac was stormed and captured. All the buildings were blown up, the station was burnt and trains of over 100 wagons loaded with food for Germany were burnt.

From Ankara it is reported that four Bulgarian divisions are guarding German orders on the Dobruja to cross the Rumanian frontier and occupy defence positions on the Danube.

Meanwhile Bulgarian partisans are increasing their sabotage and are said to have blown up a bridge near Oboriste, on the Varna-Constanza railway line, resulting in a wreck in which 240 Bulgarian soldiers were killed and about 1,000 injured.

(R. & UP.)

Political Raids

NAPLES, Saturday (R). — "Our air attacks in the Balkans are linked not only with the Russian advance but with the whole Balkan situation. They have definite political aspects," a high Allied air officer told the press here yesterday.

Hitler Calls Up the Last Man

ZURICH, Saturday (R).— For months before Hitler gave his order that every man in Germany must be trained to shoot, there was an intense combing of civilians for the Wehrmacht which even the most hardened members of the population found sensational, state reliable first-hand reports from the German frontier.

Women especially are resentful, for while active members of the Nazi Party are exempt, still more and more war wounded are being recalled and serious physical disabilities are being disregarded.

Of two men from Stuttgart who were recalled a few days ago, one had a stiff leg from a war wound and the other had a bullet in his back. But even these disabilities are insufficient to secure exemption from further active service.

140,000 Jews Left in Bucharest

BEIRUT, Saturday (R). — The Chief Rabbi of Rumania, Shabbetai Jair, who arrived here on Thursday, declared in an interview that there are about 140,000 Jews still left in Bucharest — half of the Jewish population of Rumania.

He said the widely-held belief in Rumania was that Bucharest was not bombed by the Allies owing to the presence of Jews there. He gave as an example Sofia, which he said was bombed only after the Jews had been expelled. The Rabbi appealed urgently for help for those Jews still in Bucharest.

He is on his way to Palestine where he will present to the Rabbinate a prayer shawl (talith) on which is inscribed "soaked in the sacred blood of Rumanian Jewish victims."

"CONTROL OF CARDS"

STOCKHOLM, Saturday (R). — The official explanation for the recall of Finnish military personnel on leave is "control of the card system" — apparently confirmed reports of resumed Finnish-Russian contacts.

Swedish newspapers suggest that there is evidently some relationship between this "control" and the report of resumed Finnish-Russian contacts.

RUSSIANS 30 MILES FROM CITY

By HAROLD KING
Reuter's Special Correspondent

MOSCOW, Saturday.—Three mighty Soviet army groups are rolling forward on a 300-mile front from the Carpathians to the Black Sea. On their left wing the Red Armies are closing in swiftly on Odessa and the latest messages put the Soviet spearheads only 30 to 35 miles from the great Black Sea port.

In the Carpathians, Marshal Zhukov has a stranglehold on the Carpathian passes and Russian troops are at the head of the Tisa valley in Hungary. Thus for the fifth successive week Marshal Stalin's Army continues from victory to victory.

An overwhelming mass of Soviet men, guns and armour is pressing in on Odessa around an arch which at some point north-east of the city is now only 30 miles distant. General Malinovsky's spearhead is flung at right angles across Odessa's two rivers, the big and little Kugalnik, in a thrust for Tiraspol, the junction for the single-track railway back to Galatz in Rumania.

Apart from this line the Germans in Odessa now have only the railway from Ackerman and this must be reached by ferrying across the broad Dniester estuary. On the right wing of these forces are Marshal Koniev's men pouring down the east bank of the Dniester. By smashing German resistance in the Slabodka defences, where the Germans made a force estimated at seven divisions and put up powerful resistance, Marshal Koniev's army has opened the flood gates towards Odessa. They can pour down from the north without meeting any notable opposition.

Towards Tiraspol

Meanwhile on the west bank of the Dniester the enemy has momentarily switched the main weight of his pressure from the Pruth by striking south to complete the isolation of Odessa from the rest. He has already cut the Odessa-Tiraspol-Jassy trunk line between Kishinev and Balti at a point only 33 miles north-west of Tiraspol. Now he is pressing on fast towards Tiraspol itself. At Tiraspol and at the Moldavian capital of Kishinev, the Germans are likely to offer the best resistance they can muster.

Everywhere, in the Odessa plains, in Moldavia, and in Sub-Carpathia, the German Command has tried to break off contact with the Red Army. Nowhere has it succeeded. Russian troops are storming into villages before the retreating Germans can get away. German troops falling back across yet another river line are finding the Red Army at river crossings before them.

JEWISH POLICE SERGEANT KILLED IN HAIFA

Grenade Thrown by Wounded Man; Cache in Garage

From Our Own Correspondent

HAIFA, Saturday. — British Inspector Coles was wounded and P/Sgt. Itzhak Polany fatally injured by a hand-grenade thrown by an unidentified assailant in a house at 22 Tiberias Street, where they were investigating a case shortly before 9 o'clock this morning.

They were taken to the Rothschild Hospital where Sergeant Polany died at 9 o'clock tonight. Inspector Coles is stated to be out of danger.

According to eyewitnesses, a woman living in the house, which stands in a wadi where Mountain Road branches off through Tiberias Street to Massada Street, noticed a suspicious-looking man Saturday, and immediately scaled the balcony and jumping to the ground ten feet below, made their escape.

At the same time, the wounded man withdrew a small hand grenade from his pocket, extracted the pin, and hurled it into the room from which the three men had escaped. Inspector Coles received injuries which are not considered to be serious but Sergeant Polani was critically wounded.

The wounded man escaped over the balcony.

While investigations were in progress, it was reported that a civilian had been admitted to the Hadassah Hospital with a bullet wound in the abdomen and enquiries at that institution revealed that the patient was identical with the person who had thrown the bomb.

Investigations also revealed that a Haifa medical practitioner had received a telephone call shortly after 9 a.m. requesting his attendance at a case requiring urgent attention, and he was informed that a taxi would be sent to collect him. Approximately the same time a taxi driver who has now been detained was requested to go to No. 70, Tiberias Street.

When the driver reached the main bus stop at the top of Mount Carmel, he was hailed by three men who asked him if he was going to the doctor's house. When he replied in the affirmative the three men entered the taxi which he carried on to the house of the doctor who was waiting for them.

The party then travelled to a small garage in Tiberias Street, where three of the three men alighted from the taxi and paid the shutter of the garage, and remarked that the man had gone. He thereupon re-entered the taxi and was carried on from there to the house at 70, Tiberias Street.

The garage was searched and following items were seized: a number of stencils, in course of preparation; a Gestetner duplicator; 12 military uniforms, including officers uniforms; an assortment of small arms, ammunition; a large quantity of

ed man withdrew a small hand grenade from his pocket, extracted the pin and hurled it into the three men had escaped. Inspector Coles received injuries which are not considered to be serious but Sergeant Polani was critically wounded.

Inspector's Wounds

The wounded gangster, while waiting for medical aid, is thought to have moved to the spot where he was seen by the woman.

Prior to the incident, a number of arrests had been carried out on Hadar Hacarmel during the night.

Inspector Coles, who is wounded in the body and leg, was taken to the Rothschild Hospital to the Government Hospital this afternoon.

Sergeant Polany, who was 39, was born in Breslau in Poland, and joined the Palestine Police in 1927. He leaves a wife and two children.

The doctor, who is a well-known surgeon living on Mount Carmel, told The Palestine Post that three men had come to his house around 8.30 in the morning and had taken him in a taxi to a house in Tiberias Street. Shortly after his arrival, the Police came, and the outrage took place.

It is reported that a false identity card in the name of Joseph Rosenberg was found on the assailant, who is now under Police guard at Hadassah Hospital. His wound is believed to have been due to an accident which happened while he or someone else, possibly the man who summoned the doctor, were handling a revolver, probably during a scuffle of the gunmen in the garage where the police later made the seizures.

LATE Edition

THE PALESTINE POST

JERUSALEM
WEDNESDAY, June 7, 1944

PRICE: 15 MILS
VOL. XIX. Number 5506

ALLIES STORM ATLANTIC WALL

The Allied invasion of Western Europe, which got under way early yesterday morning after a 24-hour delay due to bad weather, had by last night broken through the first enemy barrier all along the landing front in Northern France. Protected by an armada of hundreds of warships of all kinds, including British and American battleships, and by a vast air canopy drawing upon the total first-line Allied air strength of 11,000 bombing and fighting planes, the assault troops poured ashore from more than 4,000 ships and landing barges, while whole divisions of paratroopers and air-borne forces were dropped behind the Atlantic Wall and, in Mr. Churchill's words, the sea passage was made "with far less loss than we apprehended."

With the main landings between Le Havre and Cherbourg, in Normandy, but also further to the east, in the direction of Rouen, the enemy-controlled radio stations last night reported ferocious fighting at Caen and north of Rouen, where powerful formations of Allied parachutists took the Atlantic Wall in the rear. From Allied Headquarters came the announcement that an enormous Allied naval fleet was cruising off Cherbourg, where the sea was reported to be very stormy. It was also announced that there were now four distinct centres of fighting in the Manche and Calvados Departments, with German resistance stiffening every hour.

PREMIER REPORTS VICTORIES

LONDON, Tuesday (R). — The Prime Minister, Mr. Churchill, was received with tumultuous applause when he rose in the House of Commons today to make a special statement on the fall of Rome and the Western Invasion. Dealing first with Italy, he said:

"The House should take formal cognizance of the liberation of Rome by the Allied armies under the command of General Alexander (cheers) with General Clark of the United States services and General Oliver Leese, in command of the Fifth and Eighth Armies respectively. This is a memorable and glorious event which rewards the intense fighting of the last five months in Italy.

"The original landing made on January 22 at Anzio has in the end borne good fruit. In the first place, Hitler was induced to send to the south of Rome eight or nine divisions which he might well have needed elsewhere. Secondly these divisions were repulsed and their teeth broken by the successful response of the Allied bridgehead force in an important battle in the middle of February.

"The losses on both sides were heavy, the Allies losing about 20,000 and the Germans about 25,000 men. Thereafter the Anzio bridgehead was considered by the enemy to be impregnable.

"Meanwhile a great regrouping of the main army had to take place before the attack could be renewed. On May 11, General Alexander began his present operations, and after unceasing and intense fighting by the whole army, broke into the enemy lines and entered the Liri valley.

"It is noteworthy that, counting from left to right, Polish, British, French and United States forces all broke the German lines in front of them by frontal attacks, and that has an important bearing on the other aspects which I shall come to later.

The Bridgehead Offensive

"At what was judged to be the right moment, the bridgehead forces, which by this time totalled 150,000 men, fell on the retreating enemy's flank and threatened his retreat. The junction of the main army with the bridgehead forces drove the enemy off his principal lines of retreat to the north, forcing a great part of his army to retire in considerable disorder.

"The Allied forces, with great rapidity were grouped with special emphasis to their left flank which soon deployed against Rome after cutting an important highway. American and other forces of the Fifth Army broke through the enemy's last lines and entered Rome where Allied troops have been received with joy by the population. This entry and liberation of Rome means that we shall have power to defend it from hostile air attacks and deliver it from the famine with which it was threatened.

"However, General Alexander's supreme object has never been the liberation of Rome—as great as are the moral, political and psychological advantages of that episode. The Allied forces, with the Americans in the van, are driving ahead northward in relentless pursuit of the enemy.

"We must await further developments in the Italian theatre before it is possible to estimate the magnitude or quality of the gains, great and timely though they certainly are (cheers).

The Western Invasion

I have also to announce to the House that during the night and early hours of this morning the first of series of landings in force upon the European Continent has taken place (cheers). The liberating assault in this case fell upon the coast of France.

"An immense armada of upwards of 4 000 ships, together with several thousand smaller craft, crossed the Channel. A mass of airborne landings have been successfully effected behind the enemy's lines(cheers). Landings on the beaches are proceeding at various points at the present time. The obstacles which were constructed in the sea have not proved so difficult as was apprehended.

The Anglo-American Allies are sustained by about 11,000 first-line aircraft which can be drawn upon as may be needed for the battle.

"I cannot, of course, commit myself to any particular details, as reports are coming in in rapid succession. So far the Commanders who are engaged report that everything is proceeding according to plan—and what a plan!

"This vast plan is undoubtedly the most complicated and difficult that has ever occurred. It involves tides, wind, waves and visibility, both from air and sea standpoint, and the combined employment of land, air and sea forces in the highest degree of intimacy, and with conditions which could not and cannot be fully known. There are already hopes that an actual tactical surprise has been attained and we hope to furnish the enemy with a succession of surprises during the course of the fighting.

High Spirits

"The battle which has now begun will grow constantly in scale and intensity for many weeks to come and we shall not attempt to speculate on its course, but this I may say — that complete unity prevails. Throughout the Allied armies there is a brotherhood in arms, between us and our friends of the United States. There is complete confidence in the Supreme Commander, General Eisenhower, and in his lieutenants and also in the Commander of the Expeditionary Force, General Montgomery.

"The ardour and spirit of the troops, as I saw for myself when they were embarking in these last few days, was splendid to witness. Nothing that equipment, science or forethought can do has been neglected and the whole process of opening this great new front will be pursued with the utmost resolution both by the Commanders and by the United States and British Governments whom they serve."

Battle Going Well

In a later statement to the House of Commons tonight, Mr. Churchill said: "I can state that this operation is proceeding in a thoroughly satisfactory manner.

"Many dangers and difficulties which this time last night appeared extremely formidable are behind us.

The passage of the sea has been made with far less loss than we apprehended. The German batteries had been greatly weakened by the bombing of the air force or the bombardment of our ships, which quickly reduced their fire to dimensions which did not affect the attack.

Mr. Churchill added that landings on a broad front — along the whole front — had been effective and the troops were by now operating some miles inland.

"The outstanding feature has been the landing of air-borne troops on a scale far larger than has ever been seen before. These landings took place with extremely little loss. Airborne troops are still being established and landings and follow-ups are all proceeding with very much less loss than expected. These paratroops have landed behind the Atlantic Wall Defences.

"Fighting is proceeding at various points and various bridges of importance have been captured. There is even fighting proceeding in the town of Caen inland. The Allies are over the first four or five hurdles of their operations.

Great Risks Taken

"Particular anxiety attached to the air-borne invasion because of the conditions of light prevailing in a very limited period just before dawn. Conditions of visibility made all the difference. It might easily have been that something might have happened at the last minute which would not enable air borne troops to play their part.

"A very great degree of risk had to be taken in respect of the weather, but General Eisenhower's courage was equal to all the necessary decisions that had to be taken in all these extremely difficult and uncontrollable matters.(Cheers)

"But all these very valuable first steps, the essential first steps, of course give no indication whatever of what may be the course of the battle in the next days and weeks, because the enemy will now probably endeavour to concentrate on this area, and in that event heavy fighting will soon begin and will continue without any end as fast as we can push troops in and the enemy can bring other troops up.

"It is therefore a most serious time we are entering upon, and we enter upon it with our great Allies all in good heart and in good friendship." (Cheers).

ARMIES AND PEOPLES GET THEIR ORDERS

LONDON, Tuesday (R). — When the assault troops had embarked for Europe in the early hours of this morning, each man was handed a Stirring Order of the Day from General Eisenhower, which was also read to all the other troops. It ran as follows:

Soldiers, sailors and airmen of the Allied Expeditionary Force:

Your are about to embark upon the great crusade towards which we have striven these many months. The eyes of the world are upon you. The hopes and the prayers of liberty-loving people everywhere march with you.

In company with our brave allies and brothers in arms on other fronts, you will bring about the destruction of the German war machine, the elimination of Nazi tyranny over the oppressed peoples of Europe, and security for ourselves in a free world.

Your task will not be an easy one. Your enemy is well-trained, well-equipped, and battle-hardened. He will fight savagely. But this is the year 1944. Much has happened since the Nazi triumphs of 1940 to 1941. The United Nations have inflicted upon the Germans great defeats in open battle, man to man.

Our air offensive has seriously reduced their strength in the air and their capacity to wage war on the ground. Our home fronts have given us overwhelming superiority in weapons and munitions of war, and placed at our disposal great reserves of trained fighting men.

The tide has turned. The free men of the world are marching together to victory. I have full confidence in your courage, devotion to duty, and skill in battle. We will accept nothing less than full victory. Good luck. And let us all beseech the blessing of the Almighty God upon this great and noble undertaking.

Message to the People

In a message broadcast to the people of Western Europe, General Eisenhower said:

People of Western Europe. A landing was made this morning on the coast of France by troops of the Allied Expeditionary Force. This landing is part of a concerted United Nations plan for the liberation of Europe, made in conjunction with our great Russian Allies. I have this message for all of you. Although the initial assault may not have been made in your country the hour of liberation is approaching.

I say, do not needlessly endanger your lives. Wait until I give you the signal to rise and

(Continued on Page 3 col. 5)

DISORDERLY FLIGHT FROM ROME

ALLIES POURING OVER TIBER

By DAVID BROWN,
Reuters Special Correspondent

ROME, Tuesday.—The Germans are falling back in some disorder north of Rome and east of the Tiber.

Allied armour and infantry were able to cross the river easily in the Rome area and fan out over a wide area five miles west of the city, and other infantry and mechanized forces are across the Tiber about midway between Rome and Ostia. French troops have crossed Highway 5 — the main road from Rome to Pescara on the Adriatic — at Tivo, a strategic point at the foot of the Sabine Hills.

West of the Tiber the Germans are falling back in some disorder. British troops, advancing along the coast, have reached the Tiber at several points and have already taken more than 2,090 prisoners. Others are pouring in with the Germans trapped, as all the bridges down the stream from Rome have been destroyed. It was officially stated today that the Vatican City was completely by-passed during all the Rome action.

Eighth Army Front

The Eighth Army front now stretches over 70 miles and has linked up with the Fifth Army in the Rome sector. General Leese's men advancing up the centre of the Peninsula are meeting stubborn resistance in the mountain sector where the Germans are still fighting 20 miles east of Rome Guarcino, 11 miles north of Frosinone, has been occupied, while tanks have sped forward to Serrone, halfway between Guarcino and Palestrina.

S.H.A.E.F. COMMUNIQUE

NUMBER TWO, JUNE 7 1.30 a.m.

Reports of operations so far show that our forces succeeded in the initial landings, says Communique Number 2 from Supreme Headquarters of the Allied Expeditionary Forces, issued at 1.30 a.m. this morning. The communique adds that light, heavy and medium Allied bombers continued their attacks in very great strength throughout the day.

The following is the text:

Shortly before midnight on June 5, 1944, Allied night bombers opened the asasault. Their attack in very great trength continued until dawn.

Between 6.30 and 7.30 hours this morning, two naval task forces commanded by Rear Admiral Sir Philip Vian, flying his ag in His Majesty's ship Scylla (Captain T.M. Brownrigg), and Rear Admiral Alan Goodrich Kirk, United States Navy, in the U.S.S. Augusta (Captain E.N. Jones) launched their assault force at enemy beaches.

Naval forces which had previously assembled under the overall command of Sir Bertram Ramsay made their departure in fresh weather and were joined during the night by bombarding forces which had previously left northern waters. Channels had to be swept through large enemy minefields. This operation was completed shortly before dawn, and while mine sweeping flotillas continued to sweep towards the enemy coast, the entire naval force followed down the swept channels behind them towards their objective. Shortly before the assault three enemy torpedo boats with armed trawlers in company attempted to interfere with operations but were promptly driven off. One enemy trawler was sunk and another severely damaged.

The assault forces moved towards the beaches under cover of a heavy bombardment from destroyers and other support craft, while heavier ships engaged enemy batteries which had already been subjected to a bombardment from the air. Some of these were silenced. Allied forces continued to engage other batteries.

Landings were effected under cover of the air and naval bombardment and air-borne landings involving troop carrying aircraft and gliders carrying large forces of troops were also made succesfully at a number of points. Reports of operations so far show that our forces succeeded in their initial landings. Fighting continues. Allied heavy, medium, light and fighter bombers continued the air bombardment in very great strength throughout the day with attacks on our gun emplacements, defensive works and communications.

Continuous fighter cover was maintained over the beaches and for some distance inland and over naval operations in the Channel. Our night fighters played an equally important role in protecting shipping and troop carrying forces and in intruder operations. Allied reconnaissance aircraft maintained continuous watch by day and night over shipping and ground forces. Our aircraft met with little enemy fighter opposition. Little anti-aircraft gunfire was encountered. Naval casualties were regarded as being very light, especially when the magnitude of the operation is taken into account.

First Shots Echo Round the World

LONDON, Tuesday (R). — British, American and Canadian troops under General Montgomery opened their attack against Hitler's Fortress this morning, and within a few hours the news had reverberated round the globe.

(The B.B.C. began its 8 o'clock news-bulletin this morning with quotations from the Supreme Headquarters "Urgent Warning" to the inhabitants of enemy-occupied countries living near the coast. Shortly before this broadcast, the German News Agency reported that Le Havre, Calais and Dunkirk were being heavily bombarded and that German naval units were engaged with Allied landing craft. It also said that the air-borne landings in Normandy were made in great depth.

Shortly afterwards Berlin announced that at least four British and American parachute and air-borne divisions were taking part. It also claimed that Hitler had moved his headquarters to "Somewhere in Northern France" in order to be nearer to the scene of operations."

It was stated that Hitler had taken over the Supreme Command.

Shortly before noon G.M.T., the German News Agency, reported these additional landings: On the island of Guernsey and Jersey in the Channel; in the area of Arromanches, which is on the coast of Cherbourg peninsula, about 20 miles north-west of Caen and at Ouistreham, also on the coast.

AFTER MIDNIGHT

Ninth Air Force bombers, fighter-bombers, fighters and troop carrying aircraft flew more than 4,750 individual missions yesterday, June 6, up to 10.00 p.m.

Prince Umberto yesterday accepted the resignation of the Badoglio Government and instructed Marshal Badoglio to form a new Government including political leaders now in liberated Rome.

President Roosevelt stated last night that operations in France were "up to schedule." American naval losses were only two destroyers and one landing ship for tanks. He also disclosed that the approximate invasion time was set at Teheran and that Marshal Stalin was satisfied with the date, but the precise date was determined only in the past few days.

Admiral Ramsay said last night: "We attained a tactical surprise. The enemy had no reconnaissance planes out and he did not know if we were on our way until paratroops landed. The opposition of coastal batteries was much less than expected. Naval ships landed all their cargoes 100%.

It was stated last night that there was a feeling of optimism at Headquarters that all was going well "They are very pleased indeed with the way the airborne operations have gone,"

Gen. De Gaulle's Broadcast

LONDON, Tuesday (R). — General de Gaulle in a broadcast to the French nation from London today, following his sudden and secret arrival, said:

"The supreme battle has begun. This is the decisive blow. This is the battle of France and France's battle."

Declaring that it was the duty of all Frenchmen to fight with every man at their disposal General de Gaulle said that good order in battle required these three conditions:

(1). — The orders given by the French Government and local leaders appointed by it must be followed exactly.

(2). — Action in the rear must be in conjunction with that by Allied and French armies.

(3). — Frenchmen must not allow themselves to be taken prisoners, as "nothing is more bitter than being put out of action without having fought."

Vast Armada Covers Landings

By SIDNEY MASON,
Reuters Special Correspondent at Headquarters, Allied Expeditionary Force.

The extent and scope of the Allied operations is incredible. The air is filled with the continuous thunder of broadsides and the crash of bombs. Great spurts of flame come up from the beaches in long, snakelike ripples and shells ranging from 16 inches to four inches find their mark.

In the last 10 minutes alone more than 2,000 tons of high explosive shells have gone down on the beachheads. It is now exactly 7.25 a.m. and through my glasses I can see the first wave of assault troops touching down on the water's edge and fanning up the beach.

Battleships, monitors and cruisers are steaming up and down, drenching the beaches ahead of the troops with withering broadsides. Guns flash and great clouds of yellow cordite smoke curl into the air. Great assault vessels are standing out to sea in their hundreds, and invasion craft are being lowered like beetles from davits and head towards shore in long lines. They are crammed with troops, tanks, guns and armoured fighting vehicles of all types. The tin-hatted British and Canadian forces in this sector are cheerful and smiling as they go in.

Weather conditions are not ideal. A fairly high sea is running and the sky is overcast.

Bombers are passing over us in their thousands: we cannot see them as they are well above cloud level But the air reverberates with the roar of Fortress engines.

FIRST BARRIERS OVER-RUN

LONDON, Tuesday.— Allied armies transported by a mighty armada of over 4,000 ships and protected by thousands of aircraft, landed in Northern France today, and by mid-afternoon the Berlin radio admitted that the invaders had succeeded in sending landing barges into two estuaries behind the Atlantic Wall.

An hour after the first British, American and Canadian units had hit the beaches, the Allies had won complete mastery of the skies over the landing area. By midday, the air-borne landings behind the German lines were reported to have succeeded and enemy shore batteries were largely silenced, while amphibious forces continued to swarm ashore at numerous points.

Many secret weapons were used for the first time by Allied troops invading France, it is officially disclosed tonight in London, where it is also announced that the invasion was postponed for 24 hours because weather held up the operations.

The first reports indicate that success attended the initial stages of the invasion. Casualties among the air-borne troops were light, notwithstanding a German boast that a paratroop regiment had been wiped out.

The Germans admitted considerable penetrations between Le Havre and Cherbourg,and also the occupation of a number of Channel Islands, including Guernsey and Jersey. They further reported that 80 medium-sized warships were a proaching Ouistreham in th early afternoon, while earli landing barges penetrated th estuaries of the Orme and Vi in the rear of the Atlant Wall. Particularly large lan ings were made at St. Vaa La Hougue.

German broadcasts annou ing that Allied tanks had c several kilometres inland b tween Caen and Isigny, co ceded penetrations ranging to 15 kilometres.

The German military corre pondent, Sertorious, wrote to night: "Enemy landings a Archmanches (29 miles north west of Caen) where America tanks were shelled during th disembarkation, are proceedin with particular strength an intensity. The airborne cou de main on the town of Ca has failed.

"The Allies will now try t gain footholds at vario places along the Atlantic coast."

The German-controlled Par radio said this afternoon:

The Germans are putting very stiff resistance in the Ca area. The town area itself h been sorely tried. The enem appears to be penetratin deeper inland.

It has now become clear th the main Allied blow is n directed against Le Havre, b that General Eisenhower is co centrating his efforts to ca ture Cherbourg. Allied par troops are now striving capture airfields in Normand

> ### King's Broadcast
>
> *LONDON, Tuesday (R). — King George VI, in a broadcast to the nation and the British Commonwealth, called on his people to "prayers and dedication" throughout the present crisis of the liberation of Europe.*
>
> *"Once more a test has to be faced,"* the King said. *"This time the challenge is not to fight to survive, but to fight to win final victory for a good cause. Once again what is demanded from us all is something more than courage and endurance: we need a revival of spirit, a new unconquerable resolve. After nearly five years of toil and suffering we must renew that crusading impulse on which we entered the war and met its darkest hour...*
>
> *"We are not unmindful of our own shortcomings, past and present. We shall not ask that God may do our will, but that we may do the will of God. And we dare to believe that God has used our nation and Empire as an instrument for fulfilling his high purpose."*

Giant Air Onslaught

Between midnight and 8,0 o'clock this morning (loca British time). 10,000 tons o bombs were dropped by th Allied Air Force on the targ area of Northern Franc Thirty one thousand Allied a men were in the air over Franc in that period, not includi air-borne troops.

German opposition on th beaches was patchy and le than was expected while th Allies managed to get asho with the coast guns being n nearly as effective as th might have been. The convoy were not seriously attacked b coastal guns, nor by aircraft German surface vessels. Alli fighters roared across th Channel in a constant patr and the Luftwaffe made litt or no effort to interfere.

More than 1,000 heavy bo bers continued attacks on th French coastal defences in da light today.

This terrific onslaught wa probably the largest and mos concentrated in history. Du ing the night 7,500 sorties we flown and losses in aircra were extremely small.

The giant German nav guns and howitzers along th French coast were bombed b over 1,300 aircraft during th hours of darkness just befor the Allied invasion. Later ov 640 naval guns from 16 inc to four inch bombarded th beaches and enemy stron points in support of th armies.

(R. & UP

Defensive Success Claimed by German

LONDON, Tuesday (R).—Be lin tonight issued its fir "success" bulletins. After a mitting that "the Allied inva sion forces have secured coastal bridgehead at Bayeu (20 miles west of Caen about 20 kilometres in leng and a few kilometres depth," the radio continued.

"Although they brought up inforcements from the wa around Le Havre, the Allies co not prevent the Germans fr sealing off the bridgehead on sides and even from narrowi it down locally. All other lan ings in the region between t estuaries of the Orne and V rivers were eliminated by pow ful counter-attacks.

"The greatest German succe of the day, which ended with complete defensive success the German Command, was t smashing of a large Allied la ing bid at Saint Vaast de Hougue, by air-borne tro dropped between Le Havre a Cherbourg. One particula strong formation gained a h on both sides of the Carent Valognes road. This format received reinforcements from air, including apparently main body of air-borne units w were landed from gliders dur the early morning. Bitter fig ing is in progress along the rentan-Valognes road."

"It is between the lo reaches of the Orne and the a north and north-west of Bay that the enemy has appare put the main weight of his p sure. The bridgehead he set is situated on both sides of mouth of the Orne and no west of Bayeux. Another Bri and American group compri light tank and tank rec naissance cars is opera a few miles farther to the on the dunes north-east of yeux and is trying to join fo with the larger bridgehead."

BIG NEWS OVERHEATS PALESTINE WIRES

When the invasion news broke in Tel Aviv yesterday morning, the telephone wires became so overheated, with almost all the town's 5000 subscribers on the line at once, that the Exchange had to be closed down for an hour, owing to risk of fire.

The telephone service functioned on an A.R.P. basis from 10.30 in the morning, but an hour later, communications were restored in sections. By the afternoon traffic on the switches was normal.

The news certainly came as "a tactical surprise" to the general public in Palestine.

Two handbill news-bulletins were put out in Jerusalem at 10 o'clock and noon yesterday by *The Palestine Post* and displayed in various parts of the city. Similar bulletin placards were put out by our offices at Tel Aviv and Haifa. Nevertheless the offices were inundated with telephone calls from people who still refused to lend credence to the "rumour."

Crowds gathered in the streets to read bulletins and discuss the great news.

Gold prices declined by 170 mils and the Sovereign dropped to LP4.700.

Six Hebrew dailies published special bulletins in Tel Aviv and some published two editions during the day.

In Tel Aviv Synagogues, there were prayers for victory. The Hassidic Rabbi of Belz offered special prayers of intercession for King George and the heads of the Governments and Armies of the United Nations.

Russians Overjoyed with News

By MEYER HANDLER
U.P. Correspondent

MOSCOW, Tuesday. — The invasion news has electrified Russia. Word spread throughout the country with an enthusiasm such as has been rarely seen in this country since the war began. People exploded with joy and shook hands with Britons and Americans.

The special Moscow radio announcer, who usually reads only Marshal Stalin's Orders of the Day, read General Eisenhower's communique and a special bulletin at noon G.M.T. in a voice as solemn and triumphant as that given to Marshal Stalin's most outstanding victory announcements. Soviet marches and the "Yankee Doodle," as well as the usual triumphant music following Marshal Stalin's Orders, were played.

LATE Edition

THE PALESTINE POST

JERUSALEM
SUNDAY, JULY 9, 1944.

PRICE : 15 MILS
VOL. XIX. Number 5533

ADVANCE ON REICH ON 3 FRONTS

By JOHN KIMCHE, Reuters Military Correspondent

LONDON, Saturday. — Three Allied Armies are today 300 miles from the frontier of Greater Germany.

General Montgomery in Normandy, is 300 miles from the Rhine at Cologne, General Zhukov, before Lwow, is 300 miles from Silesia. General Alexander, outside Leghorn, is the same distance from Villach and Innsbruck.

General Bagramyan's advance on East Prussia is a case by itself.

The German High Command now faces its greatest threat. Its overriding need is to stop the leak in the front in the East.

The Germans have lost 20 divisions in a fortnight. Troops must be sent to stiffen the Russian front. Kesselring's armies in Italy are the obvious hope. Given time for reorganization Kesselring should be able to produce 20 to 22 divisions. Italy is a secondary theatre of the war. Therefore troops must somehow be spared from the Italian front.

From the Italian frontier come reports which tend to confirm this suspicion. Widespread German preparations for the total evacuation of Northern Italy are said to be under way, the bulk of the Luftwaffe has been withdrawn.

General Alexander's order to the Partisans on Monday was couched in a language of importance and urgency. If Alexander and the Partisans succeed, they will disorganize German communications so as to make a big transfer of troops almost impossible and certainly too late to have much effect on the present crisis.

Alternatively, the Germans may pull out of Italy using the present stubborn defence of the Gothic Line screen. This would provide General Alexander with a first-rate opportunity as his armies are no further from the borders of Austria than either Marshal Zhukov or General Montgomery is from the Reich frontier.

RUSSIANS FIGHT IN VILNA STREETS

BARANOVICZE JUNCTION LIBERATED

MOSCOW, Saturday Midnight (R).— The capture of Baranowicze, the important junction of the Minsk-Warsaw railway, a break-through into the city of Vilna, where street-fighting is taking place, and the loss to the Germans of 43,000 killed and prisoners in the past four days, including three German generals who surrendered, are announced here tonight.

After reporting the capture of Baranowicze, tonight's Soviet Communique states:

Our troops developing their offensive fought their way forward into more than 500 inhabited localities including 11 railway stations. Thus our troops have cut the railway line from Vilna to Dvinsk.

Our troops have broken into the town of Vilna and engaged the enemy in street fighting. North of Baranowize our troops continuing their offensive, captured Lyubsha, and Gorodische, district centres of the Baranowicze region, and fought their way into more than 150 other inhabited localities. East of Minsk our troops continued the mopping up of the encircled enemy group.

According to preliminary reports, the enemy lost in this area between July 4 and 7 56 tanks, 219 guns of various calibres, 915 machine-guns, and 1,674 lorries. The enemy left more than 28,000 dead on the battlefield; 15,102 German officers and men were taken prisoner.

During the same period, our troops captured the following booty: 34 tanks, 278 guns of various calibre, 24 mortars, 860 machine-guns, 1,635 lorries, 60 tractors and trailers, 930 carts with war material and 1,567 horses.

On July 7 the following German officers surrendered: —The Commander of the 41st German Tank Corps, Lieutenant-General Hoffmeister; the Commander of the 60th German Motorized Division Major-General Steinkeller; the Commander of the 381st German Infantry Regiment Major-General Hirt.

The fighting for the extermination of isolated and dispersed German troops continues.

The communique then repeats the Order of the Day and adds that the Russians occupied a number of places east of Pinsk.

The fall of Baranowicze paves the way for a Soviet drive west to Bialystok and southward toward the approaches to Warsaw.

General Chernyakovsky's tanks and storm troops have moved on Vilna along a 50-mile front while heavily-armoured spearheads thrust ahead to threaten the Germans with encirclement from the north-east and south-east. The Russians are rolling on at an average speed of at least ten miles a day.

It is the same above Polotsk on the Dvinsk front, where the Germans are counter-attacking fiercely. Every wood is thick with mines and the undergrowth is festooned with barbed wire. North-west of Minsk the Russians have their spearhead within 35 miles of the key junction of Lida.

Due west of Minsk the front is 50 miles away. Most of the German front has crumbled and the Germans will be fortunate to extricate the remnants of their garrison, as strong groups of Cossacks are thrusting round the town to cut their escape routes.

Bitter fighting continues in the trap sectors east of Minsk where Red Army men's fury is rising at the reports now confirmed, that encircled units were told by the German Command to go forward with one arm raised in surrender and the other grasping a weapon to open fire on the Russians.

In a fortnight of uninterrupted fighting in which it has moved 150 miles the Red Army has taken nearly 100,000 prisoners and left over 180,000 German dead in marshlands.

Adding a conservative estimate of not less than 250,000 to 300,000 wounded makes the grand total well over half a million German casualties.

The Finnish Front

In the north, the recent progress of the Red Army in advancing west of Petrozavodsk places them within striking distance of the important communications centres of Suojarvi and Sortavala. The capture of these two towns would greatly simplify the movement of supplies and reinforcements for developing the offensive into Finland proper.

RUSSIA SEEN AS MAIN FRONT

LONDON, Saturday (BOP). — The latest dispatches from the Eastern front give the impression of an overwhelming advance, in spite of German efforts to slow the Russian drive and to save their retreating supply columns by throwing in fresh troops, (writes "The Times").

The chief spokesmen in Berlin are now declaring that the Eastern front, for the time being, is front number one. They frankly state that the defence system in White Russia has broken down with far greater speed than the Nazi Command had expected, but that counter-measures have already been taken and that developments in the next few days are likely to be as dramatic as in the preceding fortnight. What these will be is left obscure.

One Berlin report dwells on the nearness of East Prussia to the present front, pointing out that General Bagramyan has little more distance to cover to Koenigsberg than the distance already covered since the advance started east of Vitebsk a fortnight ago. This is true, but it indicates the direction in which the German mind is now working.

All Arms Cooperate

A feature of the whole Russian offensive so far has been the masterly coordination of all arms. Thus Stormoviks are giving such close support to the infantry that Red Army men are following up within 500 to 1,000 yards of ground-strafing formations, and Soviet artillery is always at hand to prepare the ground for a special break-through.

The speed of the advance has resulted in the occupation of numerous great bases and railway centres intact so providing sufficient rolling-stock to nourish the needs of the advancing armies without the usual delays imposed by the necessities for changing the gauge.

The chances are that the only supplies of Russian origin that it will be necessary to bring forward will be oil, fuel and ammunition. All the other needs of the pursuing Russian forces will be satisfied from abandoned enemy sources.

Attack in South Reported

LONDON, Saturday. — The launching of a new Red Army offensive on a wide front at the approaches to the Carpathians in Rumania and east of Lwow was reported tonight by the German News Agency correspondent, Colonel Ernst von Hammer. The correspondent stated:

"At least five Soviet rifle divisions and a tank corps are being hurled against the German positions in a bid to breach their lines and shatter the southern wing of the German Eastern Front."

400,000 Hungarian Jews Sent to Death Camps

LONDON, Saturday (R). —The Polish Government has received from its delegate in Poland details of the fate of more than 400,000 Hungarian Jews who were sent to Poland, mainly to the concentration camp in Oswiecim.

On May 15 the Germans sent from Hungary 62 railway carriages loaded with Jewish children aged between 2 and 8 years. Every day since, for a considerable period, six railway transports with Jewish adults passed through the stations of Plaszo and Krakow. They were sent to Oswiecim where most of them have been put to death in gas chambers. Before deportation they were told that they would be exchanged in Poland for prisoners of war.

This report has been confirmed in despatches received by the Polish Council for the Rescue of Jews in Poland and a Jewish member of the Polish National Council. The Germans erected in Oswiecim, in 1942, gas chambers with installations enabling them to kill 6,000 and even more of their victims daily. Later two more death camps were erected. In these three camps the bulk of the over 2,000,000 Polish Jews, who have died since, 1939, were murdered.

Surete Transfer In Lebanon

BEIRUT Saturday. — The transfer of the Sureté from the French to the Lebanese and Syrian authorities was the subject of a protocol signed yesterday at Sofar by representatives of the three parties.

The Acting Delegate-General M. Yves Chataigneau, and the French delegate to the Syrian Government represented the French authorities; the Syrian Premier, Saadallah Bey Al-Jabiry, and the Foreign Minister, Jamil Bey Mardam, represented the Syrians; while their Lebanese "Opposite Numbers," Riadh Bey es-Solh and Saleem Bey Tackla, signed for the Lebanese Republic.

"German Nation In Danger"

LONDON, Saturday (R).— Speaking in a "town in Eastern Germany" today the Propaganda Minister Goebbels, said: "The German nation is in danger."

"Germany's enemies," Goebbels said, intend to "eradicate the German people and its way of life, root and branch. There is no possibility for us to renew this conflict say in 10, 20, or 50 years if we should prove incapable of resisting the onslaught in this decisive time.

"The major untapped reserves in the unbombed areas of Germany must be now mobilized and each German must now take as a measure of his own way of life the much reduced standard of living which prevails in the districts threatened by the air war."

The Prime Minister, when asked in the House of Commons on Thursday if the Government would inform the German people that if the Nazi government was displaced by a democratic regime in which the Allies had faith the way would be opened toward a settlement on the basis of the Atlantic Charter, replied:

"So far as His Majesty's Government is concerned it repeatedly made it clear in public statements that we shall fight until Germany is forced to capitulate, until Nazism is extirpated and it is for the German people to draw a logical conclusion."

German Civilians Flee from Lithuania

LONDON, Saturday (R). — German officials and settlers and their families are fleeing panic-stricken from Vilna area where Soviet troops are breaking though in their new offensive, it is stated by the Polish Telegraphic Agency today. Vilna railway station is packed with refugees and their belongings, and special evacuation trains are being run.

The agency adds that the speed of the Soviet offensive has taken the Germans by surprise. Roads are full of cars and horse-drawn vehicles laden with possessions of Germans fleeing westward. The Germans are looting everywhere, carrying furniture from factories, offices and private houses as well as household goods and clothing.

Chaos on the roads is increased by the activities of Polish underground army units carrying out sabotage on railway lines and roads, causing even more anxiety among the terrified German residents.

State of Siege

M. Paleckis, the President of the Lithuanian Supreme Soviet, states in the Moscow "Izvestia" that the Lithuanian countryside is in a state of turmoil and attacks by partisan detachments and acts of sabotage are increasing rapidly. Assassinations of German soldiers are increasing in Kaunas. Twenty bodies of soldiers were found in March alone.

In the past two months Lithuanian patriots have killed several dozen German officials. Following large-scale disturbances the Germans arrested 5,000 people in Vilna

Florence Held by Italian Partisans

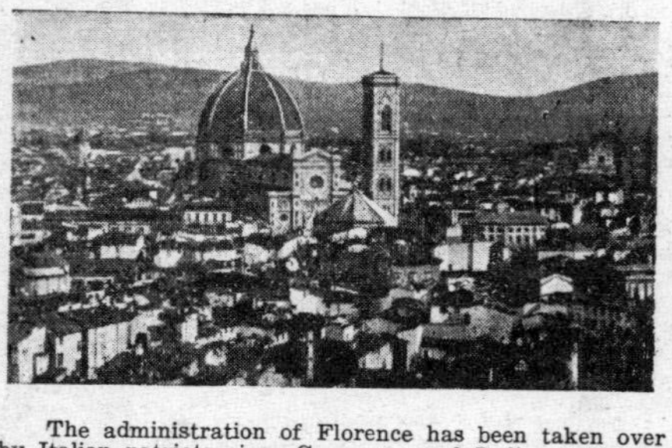

The administration of Florence has been taken over by Italian patriots since Germans and Italian Fascists evacuated the city, according to reports from the Italian frontier published in Berne newspapers.

Allied troops have captured Rosignano, Catellina, and Colledivalle, three outposts of the German defence line below Florence, in bitter hand-to-hand fighting with high casualties on both sides. Volterra is now under assault.

Eighth Army forces still maintain pressure on Arezzo and have made small gains of about six miles, repulsing three counter-attacks.

In the Tiber valley, the village of Carpini, six miles north-east of Umbertide, was captured by Indians who also took Monte Cuzzo and forced the Germans out of Montone also. Polish forces are four miles north-west of Osimo, within 5½ miles of Ancona.

Today's communique states:

ARMY: After overcoming protracted enemy resistance, American troops of the Fifth Army have occupied Rosignano and Castellina and have now progressed just south of Poggibonsi. Troops of the Eighth Army have repulsed a number of counter-attacks in the vicinity of Arezzo and have made further limited gains. In the upper Tiber Valley, Indian troops of the Eighth Army, advancing beyond Umbertide, are now in the outskirts of Montnone. In the Adriatic sector an advance has been made north-west from Ossimo against the enemy who is stubbornly defending the port of Ancona.

AIR: Strong forces of fighters escorted bombers yesterday which attacked three synthetic oil plants in German Silesia, and Blechsamer and another at Odertal, as well as aerodromes and railyards at Zagreb in Yugoslavia. Medium bombers struck at rail bridges and fuel supplies in Northern Italy. Fighter bombers were active against communications and gun positions in or near the battle area.

Rocket firing fighters attacked railways and rolling stock in Salonica (Greece) area. In the day's operations 51 enemy aircraft were destroyed. Twenty-four of our heavy bombers and three other aircraft are missing. In night operations on July 6/7, five enemy aircraft were destroyed and 13 of ours are missing. The MAAF flew approximately 2,200 sorties.

(UP and Reuters)

VIENNA BOMBED

ROME, Saturday (UP). — Over 500 heavy bombers attacked oil plants and airfields in the Vienna area today.

Japan Raided By Super-Bombers

WASHINGTON, Saturday No planes were lost when the Japanese naval base at Sasebo was attacked by Super-Fortresses last night.

Bombs were also dropped on industrial objectives at Yawata, which was the target of Super-Fortresses on June 16. Both cities are on the island of Kyushu, part of the Japanese mainland

The mission was flown from Chinese bases on the seventh anniversary of China's declaration of war against Japan.

The Domei News Agency states that Nagasaki, as well as Sasebo and Yawara, were attacked. It added that three American planes were shot down by air defence units. The Agency reports that the raiders dropped incendiary bombs, but claimed that "practically no damage was done."

First Raid on Yawata — Pg. 4

Jap Losses on Saipan

WASHINGTON, Saturday (P). The Americans who landed on Saipan Island have buried 8,914 Japanese dead since the campaign began, the Commander-in-Chief of the Pacific, Admiral Nimitz, reported last night.

American forces are now within two miles of the north-east tip of the island.

Northern Italy Boils Over

CHIASSO, Saturday (R). — Partisans in Tuscany have begun a general attack on German lines of communication, it is announced by their High Command. At Leghorn, street fighting is taking place and all Fascist chiefs have left the town.

The strikes at Turin have spread to a new centre in Piedmont and Lombardy. Patriots have taken over the administration of Florence since the Germans and Fascists evacuated the city, according to frontier reports.

NEW YUGOSLAV CABINET

By ALFRED GRANT
Reuters Balkan Correspondent

LONDON, Saturday. — A Yugoslav Cabinet of six members under the premiership of Doctor Ivan Subasic was formed last night, I understand. Two of Marshal Tito's associates are joining the Cabinet. They are now on their way from liberated Yugoslav territory.

The two are Sretn Vukosavlyevich, professor of Belgrade University and member of the executive committee of the Independent Democratic Party, well-known as an expert on agricultural questions, and Drago Marusic, a Slovene politician and examiner and Governor of Slovenia.

Vukosavlyeich will hold the important Ministry of Supply as well as the former Ministry of Agriculture. Forests and Mines in the new Cabinet, while Marusic will be Minister of Justice and Communications.

Doctor Subasic, in addition to retaining the Premiership, will hold the portfolios of Foreign Affairs and War. The Serbian ex-Minister Sava Kosanovic becomes Minister of the Interior, Social Welfare, Health and Public Works. He is at present in the United States.

The Slovene University professor and member of the Slovene Catholic Party, Izidor Cankar, becomes Minister of Education. He was Yugoslav Minister to Canada, but resigned office in protest against the policy of the Purich Government. Doctor Juraj Sutej, a leading member of the Croatian Peasant party becomes Minister of Finance.

Altogether the Cabinet consists of two Serbs, two Croats and two Slovenes. A declaration of policy by M. Subasic is expected today.

High Commissioner Says Goodbye at School Prize-Day

Distributing the prizes and certificates at the Bishop Gobat School in Jerusalem on Friday, H.E. the High Commissioner announced that he was leaving Palestine in a month's time

After prayers in Arabic led by Archdeacon A.C McInnes, the principal, the Rev. R. Iliff, reviewed the year's scholastic achievements. There were 10 nationalities and 12 religious denominations among the pupils, he said, and the school was contributing towards international understanding. Music had been introduced as a voluntary subject, there had been many academic distinctions, and the school had excelled in sports as well.

The Anglican Bishop in Jerusalem, said that almost all Arabic Anglican clergy in this country were graduates of the Bishop Gobat School. Mr. Nikola Saba, District Officer at Ramle and an Old Boy, addressed the students, in Arabic and Wadi Rumman made the valedictory address.

AFTER MIDNIGHT

The Russians have again heavily bombed Brest Litovsk. Dozens of fires were started.

BID TO CLEAR ROAD TO PARIS

WHY RUNDSTEDT STEPPED DOWN

By ROBERT LLOYD, Special to The Palestine Post

LONDON, Saturday. — Von Rundstedt had to abandon his command because he considered that Germany has lost the war and said so. This, and not quarrels about the conduct of the campaign in France, was the issue, in the view of experts who follow German affairs closely.

Their opinion is based on these facts and considerations:

(1) According to reliable Allied intelligence reports, a highly-placed German General told officers of one coastal defence regiment on an inspection visit shortly after D-Day; "Unless we can expel the Allies from France within one month, Germany has lost the war." Rundstedt's fall was announced precisely one month after D-Day.

(2) The public announcement that the C.-in-C. had been deposed in the middle of Germany's most critical battle must have been a terrific shock to the German Army and people, and particularly to the officers' corps. Even Hitler would do his utmost to avoid it if at all possible.

For the past two months the Nazi leaders have, indeed, been most careful to spare the susceptibilites of the military. Even now Rundstedt has not been replaced by his old rival Rommel, who would be the obvious candidate for "a strategy of intuition," but by a man of the same tradition as Rundstedt who has a reputation for successful defensive fighting.

(3) Rundstedt is the most far-sighted of the German Generals. He was the man who asked for a transfer to the West in the spring of 1942 because he did not believe in the second Russian offensive and was convinced that timely preparation against invasion was of decisive importance. After one month of fighting he is quite capable of judging coolly that German plans have miscarried and that his armies cannot be expected to hold once the Russians enter Reich territory from the East

GERMANS SHOOT BRITISH PRISONERS

By MARSHAL YARROW,
Reuters Special Correspondent with British Forces in Normandy. — (Delayed).

Authenticated statements by French civilians show that small groups of captured British soldiers have been shot by Germans as reprisals for the alleged shooting of German prisoners by British.

Such incidents have been definitely reported from Audrieu and Bronay where bodies discovered by civilians leave no doubt of the soldiers' fate. The numbers killed are not great.

Paris and Berlin Raided

By IAN MUNRO
Reuters Special Correspondent

S.H.A.E.F., Saturday — A few hours after a smashing attack on German positions outside Caen last night in which 450 Lancasters and Halifaxes dropped 2,300 tons of bombs, Bomber Command heavies went out again to plaster railway yards at Vaires on the eastern outskirts of Paris

Conditions were good and soon the whole area was seething with explosions which later lay hidden by a huge pall of smoke thousands of feet high. The Germans sent up many night fighters in an unsuccessful attempt to beat off the bombers.

At the same time as the attack on Vaires was on squadrons of Mosquitoes, carrying 4,000-lbs bombs were over Berlin. The bombers had come and gone before the defences had had a chance to ward off the attack.

Big Air Battle Over Central Reich

LONDON, Saturday (R). — Yesterday's air fighting over Central Germany cost the Luftwaffe 114 planes—75 shot down by fighters and 39 by bombers. Allied losses were 36 bombers and six fighters.

It was the greatest kill since before D-Day— and over 1,000 bombers took part. One American fighter pilot shot down six single-handed.

It is stated at SHAEF today that the Luftwaffe has been losing 250 planes weekly since D-Day, but the Allies have been losing more heavily.

Some Germans Leave Paris

LONDON, Saturday (R) The Germans are evacuating their civil services from Paris to Nancy, according to French sources. The evacuation began a few days ago. So far it includes the archives of the Gestapo, of the Todt organization and of the Economic Control.

Storms Almost Caused Disaster

By RONALD CLARK,
U.P. Correspondent with the Allied Forces

A high naval authority revealed yesterday that unbelievably bad weather nearly terminated Allied invasion plans in catastrophe two weeks after D-Day.

In the first comprehensive description of the mid-June gale that swept the beach-head positions for four days this spokesman said that there had been some losses in small craft. A large number of river barges equipped with motors were sent to the beaches for unloading tasks and a few of these were lost. Repair of essential craft damaged in this storm is now going on apace.

The four-day gale came at the high tide period and consequently carried some craft so high on the beaches that refloating was a major problem.

The speaker indicated that the weather was still more of a problem to the Allies than enemy operations. German E-boats caused some trouble but Allied activities gradually reduced the threat. The capture of Cherbourg was of material assistance in this respect.

Advance in Carentan Sector

S.H.A.E.F., Saturday (R) — Tonight's communique No. 66 says:

Steady gains have been made on all the active portions of the front. Our patrols are now in the town of La Haye du Puits and we command all the high ground in this area. The bridgehead over the Vire river has been extended beyond Saint Jean de Daye, and between that village and Carentan Allied troops have advanced to the Vire et Taute canal. North of Caen, in heavy fighting the enemy has been driven from the villages of Saint Contest, Epron and Horouville.

Our progress everywhere owns much to the Allied air forces which operated in strength. Medium and light bombers delivered low-level attacks with good results on troop concentrations, batteries, and strong points just ahead of our troops near Caen, and on communication targets as far south as Nantes.

Others reported hits on a railway bridge over the [illegible] at Nojent le Roi and [illegible] spanning the Loire river [illegible] mur. One medium [illegible] missing. Escorting fighters destroyed three enemy aircraft. Heavy day bombers with strong escort of fighters searched for openings in the clouds and bombed targets of opportunity east of the Seine.

Early on Friday morning a force of enemy E-boats and R-boats with two M-Class minesweepers and one other identified vessel was intercepted in an attempt to enter the eastern anchorage and was brought into action. One German vessel was seen to blow up. One E-boat or R-boat was sunk and another set on fire.

BRITISH DRIVING ON CAEN

By VIRGIL PINKLEY
U.P. Correspondent

S.H.A.E.F., Saturday. — The British Second Army began an assault at dawn today on the defences of Caen in an all-out offensive evidently designed to clear the road to Paris. They are reported to be battling deep into the enemy lines against fierce resistance.

General Montgomery has unleashed his offensive against the strongest-held sector on the Normandy front, defended by nearly seven crack enemy Panzer divisions. He is credited with never attempting a full-scale effort unless he has a better-than-even chance to succeed, and he has had five weeks to build up his force.

It is understood that the Germans are moving big guns and armour south of Caen. Reports show heavy movements of German vehicles along the two Caen roads which they still hold. The British and Canadians have now cut 12 out of the 14 roads leading into and out of Caen.

The attack began early today after bombing by hundreds of planes last night. Early this morning artillery began to bombard the German barbed-wire, minefields, strong-points, and other defence positions. The barrage surpassed anything heard on this front since the assault on the beaches on D-Day.

The size of the operations can be gauged from yesterday's German estimate that "over 400,000 men and 2,000 tanks are engaged in a bitter battle on a frontal arc of 12 miles."

S.S. Divisions Identified

By JAMES McGLINCY and SAMUEL HALES
U.P. Correspondents

NORMANDY, Saturday, 7 p.m. — British forces advanced today within half a mile of Caen from the north after the air forces had dropped 2,000 tons of bombs on the German front and another 2,000 tons on the German rear lines.

The ease with which the Lebisey area was taken was one of the biggest surprises in today's British and Canadian assault which may be described as a big operation moving nearer Caen, straightening and tightening the ring of steel around it to the north-west and north.

By mid-afternoon one force had mown its way into the village of Galmanche and were fighting around Epron. Another force was similarly cleaning up busily at Buron and Gruchy and fighting around Authie.

American forces who captured St. Jean de Daye advanced south to the next village of Gruchy while patrols again entered La Haye du Puit. The Americans completed their penetration of the west side of the Foret de Montcastre while through the east side, lying west of Carentan, slow advances were achieved against stout resistance.

The American front is generally static, with strong resistance all along the line.

The Germans are straining to throw in reserves "Das Reich" S.S. Division has now been identified at several spots opposite the Americans. A total of three S.S. divisions, some from Russia, are fighting in Normandy

LATE Edition

THE PALESTINE POST

JERUSALEM
THURSDAY, August 24, 1944

PRICE 15 MILS
VOL. XIX. Number 5573.

PARIS AND MARSEILLES LIBERATED

Paris was liberated yesterday, August 23, after four days of savage street fighting in the course of which 50,000 armed and many more unarmed Frenchmen ove- came the resistance of the garrison left in the city by the Germans to cover the retreat of their main forces, now fleeing across the Seine. The news coincided with a new landing on the coast near the Franco-Spanish border, aimed at Bordeaux, and the capture of Marseilles and Grenoble.

AMERICANS TAKE GRENOBLE.

ADVANCE ON LYONS

ALLIED H.Q., MEDITERRANEAN, Wednesday (R). — American armoured motorized columns driving swiftly northward from the Riviera beach-head have entered the city of Grenoble, a centre of the French resistance movement, situated in the French Alps, some 150 miles north of Toulon.

American spearheads are now only 55 miles south-east of Lyons, in the heart of the Rhone valley industrial belt which is only 180 miles south of the last reported point of the advance of General Patton's forces driving southward at Sens. Less than 240 miles now separate the Northern and Southern France forces over an area where enemy resistance has been markedly weak or entirely lacking.

The capture of Grenoble, a town of 85,600 inhabitants and capital of the Isere department, represents a great leap forward for the Allied invasion force. It was reported to have been surrounded several days ago by the French forces of the interior.

French troops have closed in on Toulon from the east. Heavy fighting continues inside Toulon.

More than 17,000 prisoners have now been taken in the South of France since original landing

Outside Avignon

Allied troops, pushing in an easterly direction, are now less than 11 miles from the French-Italian frontier. An American commentator broadcasting today from advance headquarters, stated "reconnaissance elements are reported just outside Avignon. Another American column is eight miles west of Aix. The Germans are reported to be falling back towards country held by strong French Maquis forces."

In the direction of the Spanish frontier, French forces of the Interior have taken Perpignan, while the German News Agency says that an American landing was made yesterday at Saint Jean de Luz, near Biarritz, close to the Franco-Spanish border on the Bay of Biscay.

The German News Agency said: "Backed by French partisans, American forces on August 22, after a heavy naval bombardment, landed a small group Near Saint Jean de Luz, on the French-Spanish frontier. An attempt to reinforce this group under naval cover failed in the face of strong resistance."

DE GAULLE TO RUN FRANCE

LONDON, Wednesday (R). — The United States and Britain are about to hand over the administration of France to General de Gaulle's Provisional Government.

With the swelling tide of Allied military victory, political circles are anxious to know what are the chances of General de Gaulle succeeding in setting up an effective administration of the country.

Already Frenchmen inside France have occupied, in an organized and competent manner, a number of administrative and political functions and it is pointed out here that the claims advanced by Algiers to complete popular support in France have been substantiated by the general acceptance of the provisional government as the only recognizable authority and by the cooperation of local administrative personnel.

LANDINGS AT BORDEAUX

NEW YORK, Wednesday (R). — A third Allied landing in France began last night in the area of Bordeaux. The landing was coordinated with an attack by American and French columns from inland.

Bordeaux, a city of 260,000 inhabitants, lies 185 miles south of the Loire which an American column crossed at Nantes and Orleans. There has been no official news of this column for more than a week.

An Associated Press despatch from the Franco-Spanish frontier today says that U.S. and French forces are attacking the city. The Allied forces met on the outskirts of Bordeaux about noon yesterday and immediately began a coordinated attack.

The intense aerial and naval bombardment at Bordeaux could be distinctly heard today in the Irun—Hendaye frontier region.

The occupation of Marseilles was today achieved by the French, after the Allies had yesterday driven to within three miles of the great port. Most of the port fell without much resistance. Marseilles fell with a miminimum of resistance as it was completely encircled and all escape routes cut.

MR. CHURCHILL TO MEET POPE

ROME, Wednesday (UP). — Rome's Catholic "Quotidiano", second in importance only to the "Osservatore Romano" in expressing the Vatican's viewpoint, today writes that "Catholic circles attach great importance to Mr. Churchill's forthcoming meeting with the Pope," which the paper hopes will have an important bearing on the peace terms and post-war organization of Europe.

The Christian Democratic (Catholic Conservative) "Popolo" likewise expresses satisfaction that "the forthcoming meeting between Mr. Churchill and the Pope .... which has a particular importance at the present moment when decisive events are taking place ... indicates that the Pontiff will not cease to exert his high influence towards a peace with justice."

Some sources have reported Marshal Tito as demanding that the Yugoslav frontier be extended to Tagliamento, thus putting Fiume, Trieste, Pola and Gorizia inside Yugoslavia.

PARIS ONCE MORE SEES BARRICADES

By JOHN A. PARRIS U.P. Staff Correspondent

LONDON, Wednesday. — In street fighting such as the capital of France has not seen for many years. French patriots routed the bulk of the German occupation forces and massacred the doomed rearguards left to cover the evacuation.

The first reports give few details but the sketchy accounts make it clear that the trapped enemy rearguards had dug in behind barricades at scores of points and battled to the death against the vengeance of the hungry Parisians

Patriots yesterday shelled the Germans at various points of the city with light artillery. Simultaneously the police joined the patriots, and occupied the Ile de la Cité. The Germans spent their last strength in a series of bloody but unavailing attempts to re-take the Seine Island but at nightfall all organized resistance had ceased.

Quislings and collaborationists who remained behind were rounded up and turned over to the F.F.I. for trial and almost certain death. Among those who escaped was the Vichy-appointed Mayor of Paris.

Long Prepared Revolt

Preparations for the revolt date back 18 months and began with the parachuting of arms and ammunition into France on a considerable scale. In recent weeks guns and ammunition, as well as light artillery, were parachuted on a large scale to the Maquis.

The Allied air forces also played a prominent role in the liberation of Paris. German positions, convoys, and communications in all directions leading east from the capital were pounded by Allied bombers, making it impossible for the Germans to bring up reinforcements

Military experts regard the liberation of Paris as a strategical manoeuvre mapped by General Eisenhower and General Koenig to enable the Maquis to strike at the greatly-weakened German garrison while the Americans pushed the bulk of the Germans out of the capital with the threat of encirclement. Not more than 15,000 to 20,000 Germans were in Paris when General Koenig launched his final attack.

VON KLUGE SACKED, TOO

STOCKHOLM, Wednesday. — According to the "Aftonbladet" von Kluge has been relieved by Hitler of his command of the German forces in northern France. The paper adds that his probable successor will be Field Marshal Model, now commanding the German armies in East Prussian and Polish fronts who, in turn will be succeeded by Field Marshal von Brauchitsch with von Halder as Chief of Staff. Brauchitsch is reported to have been given full powers in this new job, going as far as to exempt him from referring to Hitler's General Headquarters before taking major decisions.

If this report is correct it would mean that Hitler has had to give up some of his military prerogatives. This becomes still the more interesting since in his commentary last night, General Dittmar criticized on the Berlin radio the German strategy in Normandy.

Germans Suffer Inland Dunkirk

By WILLIAM STEEN
Reuters Special Correspondent

S.H.A.E.F., Wednesday.—Reports indicate that the German retreat west of the Seine is becoming a rout as the great Allied envelopment movement takes shape. While General Patton is pushing on beyond Sens and strengthens his bridgehead across the Seine at Mantes-Gassicourt, the Germans are stepping up the tempo of their inland Dunkirk.

Disorganization and confusion are increasing among the remnants of the German Seventh Army as they race back towards the crossings of the Seine. They are moving so fast that there is no evidence of any real delaying action or even the usual extensive mining to slow the pursuit. The Seventh Army has collapsed as an organized fighting unit.

American tanks are now on the road to Berlin. General Patton's men have captured and advanced beyond the town of Sens, 60 miles south-east of Paris, on the direct route to Berlin through Troyes and Nancy.

This new outflanking thrust south of Paris is described here as one of the boldest of the war — a fitting continuation of the plan which has already eliminated any German army in being in France. This thrust takes the Allied forces to within 170 miles of the German border — 20 miles less than from Cairo to El Alamein

Another great massacre of the routed German divisions has begun in the 30-mile long "killing ground" between the rivers Aisne and Seine. Hundreds of guns have been throwing an enormous weight of fire-power into the box bounded by Paris, Breteuil, the Foret de Laigle, and Bernay. Allied troops here are using maps marked "killing ground" with boundaries drawn in blue pencil.

Americans lining the west bank of the Seine are behind the Germans, and British guns have already started their dry beat of death. They strike at the battered remnants of the German Seventh Army which escaped from the Falaise trap and the thousands of other Germans who crossed the Seine to help their hard-pressed comrades and walked straight into the trap.

The front is moving at incredible speed. We are now holding a solid and secure line several miles east of the Touques and are across the Aisle in strength at Laigle.

Germans Admit Flight

The German communique today reports that the Allies are hotly pursuing the German "disengaging movement" west of the Seine. The communique says:

"West of the lower Seine, the enemy is hotly pursuing our disengaging movements toward the river Touques sector on either side of Lisieux. At Evreux and west of the town, as well as between the Eure and the Seine, our divisions are offering tenacious resistance.

German forces south of the Seine have been taken back to shorten positions which can be more easily manned by their number. American motorized and tank formations, still further reinforced, continue their attempts at encircling and annihilating the German troops south of the Seine. To that effect they have launched a far-flung movement up to the area of Conches, whence they intend to push ahead in a northerly direction, but they have been halted there.

"DAILY WORKER" NOT ACCREDITED

ALLIED H.Q., Mediterranean, Wednesday (R). — The British War Office has ordered the accreditation of the "Daily Worker" war correspondent, Mr. Clemens Dutt, to be withdrawn.

Reuter understands that Dutt's credentials were issued by the French Committee of National Liberation and authenticated by qualified officials at Allied Force Headquarters.

War Flashes

The Allies are on the road to Berlin and Tokyo, says President Roosevelt in his latest Lend-Lease report to Congress.

The Russians have occupied Dembitsa, in Rumania, says an Order of the Day.

The Americans are reported to have reached the Marne at Meux.

Rumania — In and Out of the Axis

LONDON, Wednesday (R). — Rumania lost the province of Bessarabia and parts of Bukovina and Moldavia to Russia in June, 1940. Two months later Hitler in Vienna imposed an agreement with Hungary on Rumania by which Rumania lost great portions of the province of Transylvania.

This loss of territory was followed by the abdication of King Carol in September, 1940. A few months later, on November 23, 1940, Rumania under her Dictator, Marshal Antonescu, joined the Axis and broke with the Allies.

In June, 1941, when Germany attacked Russia, Rumania declared war on Russia six days after the German invasion—on June 28. From that time the Rumanian Army fought by the side of the German Army, first under Rundstedt, to regain the province of Bessarabia, and then in the advance across the Ukraine and on to Stalingrad.

Several Rumanian divisions were trapped with Paulus' Sixth Army in the Stalingrad debacle. The loss of a great part of the Army was regarded as a national disaster. Rumanian troops also suffered heavily in the Crimea and at Odessa.

Great Britain declared war on Rumania on December 7, 1941, and the United States on December 12.

STOP PRESS

Rumania Capitulates to Russia

The acceptance by Rumania of the peace terms offered by Russia was announced just before midnight, last night, in the form of a Royal Proclamation broadcast from Bucharest.

The news coincided with the announcement by Marshal Stalin of fresh spectacular advances by the Red Army in Rumania.

The Proclamation added that Rumania, taking her fate in her own hands, was joining the United Nations.

A new national government was being formed under General Constantin Senatescu, with the Liberal leader Bratianu and the Peasant Party leader Maniu as members, and its first step was the rejection of the 'Vienna Award' made by Hitler in 1940, under which Rumania lost Transylvania to Hungary.

The King's Proclamation added: "Rumanians: I have decided for the salvation of the fatherland on the immediate cessation of hostilities with the United Nations and I call upon the Government of National Union to fulfil the determined will of the country to conclude a peace with the United Nations. From this moment, all hostilities against the Soviet armies and the state of war with Great Britain and the United States will cease.

"All Rumanians must rally around the Throne and the Government. He who does not assist the Government and resists the will of the nation is a traitor to the country. The United Nations have guaranteed the independence of Rumania and recognized the injustice of the Diktat of Vienna under which Transylvania was torn from us. At the side of the Allies and with their help we will cross the frontiers unjustly imposed upon us at Vienna."

RED ARMY MARCH TO THE DANUBE

By DUNCAN HOOPER, Reuters Special Correspondent

MOSCOW, Wednesday.—The Red Army is on the march towards the Danube in the first of the new offensive ushering in the autumn campaign.

The towns of Akkerman and Benderi, two important strongholds in the German defences on the Lower Dniester have fallen to the Soviet onrush on the Rumanian front, it is announced tonight.

General Tolbukhin's tanks are sweeping on in Moldavia under the protection of a mighty air umbrella which has taken over the function of flying artillery.

Stormoviks and dive bombers are swarming over the front and their effect is seen in the large number of prisoners brought suffering from blast and bombsplinter wounds.

General Tolbukhin's forces are now less than 60 miles from the Danube's lower reaches, the one great Eastern river which up till now has remained outside the battle zone. Meanwhile General Malinovsky's army is driving south through East Rumania towards the "Galatz Gap" area between the Carpathians and the Danube, the natural gateway to Bucharest and Ploesti. Kishinev and the Moldavian town of Bender are benig encircled by these two Ukrainian armies. Akkerman is being rapidly isolated.

Vaslui, an important communication centre and a German strongpoint, was captured by Russian tanks and infantry today, says an Order of the Day by Marshal Stalin. Vaslui lies between the Sepeth and the Pruth rivers.

Rumanians are creeping out from cellars in Jassy to find the city running smoothly under Soviet occupation. The power station and water works are intact, and at the railway station everything was found in complete order with telephones ready to hand and tickets piled up neatly on tables.

Battle of the Bug

In the Polish sector, the combined forces of Marshal Rokossovsky and General Zakharov are grinding ahead in a new offensive which has grown out of the local battles of the past weeks between Warsaw and Bialystok. The struggle for Warsaw has been temporarily pushed into the background by their threat to the German positions in the former Polish corridor.

The Germans are switching reserves to the north bank of the Bug, which is now as important to the security of north-east Germany as the Vistula is to Central Germany. The gradual loosening up of the front along the Warsaw-Bialystok railway is now showing results and facing the Germans with a new crisis.

Further north, General Maslennikov is launching mass attacks against the last stable sector in the Baltic between the sea and Lake Peipus which is still blocking General Govorov's attempts to throw his decisive weight into the northern battleground. His advance towards Tartu is slowly wearing down the flanks of this key German position.

BERLIN ADMITS BREACH

LONDON, Wednesday (R). The German News Agency announces today that the Red Army had made a breach in the German lines between the Bug and Narew rivers, north of Warsaw.

Colonel Ernst von Hammer says tonight that the Russians have launched their expected new large-scale offensive west of Bialystok and that the Germans have retreated to new main defence lines.

APPEAL FOR AID TO WARSAW

WASHINGTON, Wednesday (R). — Claiming to represent six million American citizens of Polish descent, the Polish-American Congress has appealed to President Roosevelt to send help to the members of the Underground movement fighting in Warsaw.

50,000 PATRIOTS LED THE FIGHT

CITIZENS WIN 4-DAY BATTLE

LONDON, Wednesday (R). — Paris is liberated. Her own people have risen against the Germans and seized the City from within. The honour of announcing this unique victory fell to 46-year-old General Joseph Koenig, Commander of the French Forces of the Interior and newly appointed Governor of Paris.

General Koenig today issued a special communique which was first broadcast from Paris itself. Fittingly relayed to the world by the radio of the French capital-in-exile, Algiers, the communique told how the heroic citizens of Paris overthrew the German garrison and their Vichyite collaborators after a four days' struggle battle.

On Saturday morning, August 19, 50,000 armed patriots went into action. They were supported by hundreds of thousands of unarmed Parisians who re-enacted the tradition of the storming of the Bastille in 1789 and the Commune in 1871. The police, who had earlier gone on strike, returned to work for their own people and took over the Prefecture.

General Koenig reported the rising in these triumphant words:

On Saturday morning, August 19, the National Resistance Council and the Paris Committee of Liberation, in agreement with the National Delegates representing the Provisional Government of the French Republic, decreed a general uprising in Paris and in the Paris area.

French Forces of the Interior, 50,000 strong, armed and supported by hundreds of thousands of patriots, unarmed, went into action. The Paris police, which had previously gone on strike, took over the Prefecture of Police and the 'City' island of Paris (the administrative part of the town) was turned into a bastion before which German attacks broke down.

Yesterday, August 22, after four days of fighting, the enemy was beaten everywhere. Patriots have occupied public buildings. Representatives of Vichy have been arrested or have taken to flight. Thus the people of Paris have taken a decisive part in the liberation of the capital.

Parisians first knew the liberation of their city was at hand when last Thursday they heard the rumble of guns as General Patton's American army approached the city on the road from Chartres.

When News Came Out

The first public indication that an uprising was in progress came on Sunday night when the Paris radio broke four days' silence to issue a proclamation from the German Military Commander announcing severe measures against "a revolt." The measures failed and today the French capital has snapped the shackles of serfdom and its inhabitants are now preparing a triumphal reception for the Allied forces at their gates.

Paris has been in German hands since 7.00 a.m., June 14, 1940, when German motorized units moved in and the city surrendered without a shot being fired. Since then, first Bordeaux and then Vichy have been capitals of France, while Paris, under the German heel, has waited for four years to come into her own again.

During that time German control clamped down more and more tightly. Parisians were deported to work in Germany. Those who remained were short of food. Separate restaurants and separate cinemas were set aside for German troops. Sometimes bombs went off in those cinemas.

The world tonight awaits the news of the triumphal entry of the Allied armies into Paris. General Eisenhower's men, who by their hard fighting made possible the liberation of the Capital by its citizens, are closing in from all sides, but have not yet entered the city.

Tonight it is stated that Allied troops are in Fontainebleau about 22 miles to the south-east. Other formations are reported at Melun, Versailles and points to the north-west. The great enveloping move to trap all German forces still west of the Seine is being executed at high speed. Allied troops, including Polish and Belgian formations, are pushing ahead.

ALGIERS BEFLAGGED

ALGIERS, Wednesday. — Twenty-one salvos were fired and Algiers was beflagged today to mark the liberation of Paris. Many thousands of people parade the streets singing the Marseillaise, many of them weeping. In the harbour, British and United States ships are beflagged.

The delegates of the Consultative Assembly were at lunch when the liberation of Paris was announced, and all rose and sang the Marseillaise.

General Catroux has ordered every public and private building to be flagged throughout Algeria. Church bells will chime in every Algerian town. Military music will be played and civilian bands are to play the Marseillaise.

The Algiers radio in a broadcast at 12.35 today gave the first news. The announcer broke into the news bulletin with the words: "Stand by, everyone. The BBC has just announced that the FFI has liberated Paris."

Tomorrow, the bells of St. Paul's in London, including two bells which sounded the victory over the Spanish Armada in 1588, will celebrate the liberation of Paris.

At the same time as the Algiers radio was announcing the liberation of Paris, the German News Agency war correspondent, Schmallfuss, reported: "In Paris, as a result of stern measures taken by the Germans, the city has been pacified. There is no saying, however, that fresh disorders will not break out in the immediate future."

It is now disclosed that two days before the general insurrection began, railwaymen showed immense courage. They went as far as lying down bodily on the rails to prevent trains from running. On Friday, shooting occurred in the Rue Saint Denis and its continuation, the Faubourg Saint Denis, when the S.S. began to fire and there were several victims. In the fashionable Rue de Rivoli which runs along the Tuileries Gardens and the Louvre, the Germans used field guns on that day.

Warning Against Looting

Algiers has broadcast the following warning against looting: "The Government of the Republic is well aware of the extraordinary privations suffered by the population of Paris during the last few weeks. The Government has but one aim — to stop these hardships at the earliest.

"It must, however, be realized that several days will pass before reorganization will permit the arrival of the necessary supplies. Whoever under these circumstances touches stores endangers the supplies for all. Every looter is threatening the people with starvation.

"The authorities, which have the confidence of the resistance movement and which represent the Provisional Government of the French Republic, will assure an equitable distribution of food. The Provisional Government of the Republic appeals to the entire population to watch that supplies are safeguarded."

(UP and R)

V-2 SITES CAPTURED

ON THE CAEN — FALAISE ROAD, Wednesday (R). — A large stone quarry beside this road was intended to be used as a launching site for the "V-2" (rocket-propelled bomb).

At the bottom of the quarry there is provision for three concrete launching platforms while a maze of underground tunnels was obviously intended for the storage of projectiles.

A similar quarry was discovered near Bretteville sur Laize. In the Caumont area, south of Balleroy, a whole wood has been fitted with blast bays.

HEAVY FLY-BOMB ATTACKS

LONDON, Wednesday (R). — Two flying-bomb attacks launched against Southern England from the Pas de Calais before and after dawn today were more sustained than usual.

In each attack, the Germans fired a stream of robots across the Channel for about an hour.

Anti-aircraft gun-fire in one coastal area was the heaviest and most concentrated yet, and a good number of bombs were destroyed, some of them being blown to pieces in the air.

GEN. HAUSSER WOUNDED

NEW YORK, Wednesday (UP). —According to a German broadcast, Col.-General Hausser, of the Waffen S.S., commander of the German Seventh Army, has been wounded in Normandy fighting west of the Upper Dives.

Hausser led German forces temporarily cut off in the western Upper Dives but they have now joined the main German fighting line at Vermoutiers.

THE PALESTINE POST

LATE Edition

JERUSALEM THURSDAY, Nov. 9, 1944

PRICE: 15 MILS

VOL. XIX. Number 5634

MR. EDEN REPORTS ON MIDDLE EAST

PROBLEMS OF GREECE DESCRIBED

LONDON, Wednesday (R). — Mr. Eden told the House of Commons this afternoon of his recent visits to Egypt, Greece and Italy.

"In Egypt," said the Foreign Secretary, "I met the newly-appointed Egyptian Prime Minister, who assured me of his Government's loyalty to the alliance with this country, an alliance, as the House will member, which is enshrined in the Anglo-Egyptian Treaty of 1936 — an instrument which has well stood the test of time, emergency and war.

"In the three or four days I spent in Cairo, I also had an opportunity for discussion with Lord Moyne, whose brutal and tragic assassination in such a way to us all. I discussed with him all the manifold political and administrative problems which were in the area of his responsibility.

"On October 25, I left with Lord Moyne by air for Athens. I should explain that at an earlier stage, our Ambassador to Greece had telegraphed the same Minister and myself, urging one or both of us to go to Athens on the way home to meet the Ministers of the Greek Government and to see for ourselves the situation and the problems which today confront us in liberated Greece.

"Mr. Churchill agreed that it should be my task."

Conditions in Greece

Describing conditions in Greece, Mr. Eden declared that he did not believe that immed British opinion yet fully understood how complete, merciless and dastardly had been the devastation inflicted by the Germans on Allied lands as they were compelled to withdraw.

The purpose underlying this barbarity was clearly to bring the whole life of the nation to a standstill. That was what the Germans had told the weeks they would do as they left. All communications, bridges, telegraphs, and lorries were destroyed, and the essential parts of factories and docks of raw materials were either destroyed or removed.

Substantial progress had been made with the immense complex problems facing the Government regarding civil supplies. The port of Piraeus was slowly working again, thanks to the Navy, the civil population and the Royal Engineers, and a corps which did not always get all the public credit it deserved.

The truly remarkable figure of 3,000 tons a day was being unloaded in Piraeus by the end of October. A substantial part of this was foodstuffs for civilians. When the remaining obstacles were overcome, it was expected to unload in Greece 40,000 tons monthly, of which 30,000 tons would be foodstuffs and 6-70,000 tons medicines and relief goods.

Replying to a question, Mr. Eden said that the Government had not opposed the formation of a Regency Council in Greece, which they regarded as a matter to be settled between the King of Greece and the Greek Government.

"The Greeks are very political-minded. They have many shades of difference, but could find one subject on which they all agreed—to join whole-heartedly in welcoming the British forces."

Mr. Eden told the House in reply to another question that "Fascist political organizations known to the Allied authorities in liberated Italy had been liquidated. "Every effort is being made to obtain information regarding underground Fascist political organizations and these are being guarded as soon as they are discovered," he said.

Storms in Italy

Speaking of his visit to Italy, Mr. Eden said it was unfortunate that his stay coincided with phenomenal storms the like of which the Italians invariably said they had never known since 1880, or thereabouts.

"The rivers were soon torrents and low-lying land a quagmire, much more like Flanders than Italy of the Florentine picture, and all movement was a matter of the utmost difficulty.

"Even with a day's hard work transferring from a jeep to a three-ton lorry, even with fiddling about and cursing and struggling a good deal, even with that, we were only able to cover a small part of the mileage we had planned to cover, that was naturally disappointing, but it did enable me to understand the conditions under which our Allied armies are living and fighting in Italy. No praise that we can utter can be too high for these men. They have had a prolonged struggle with a stubborn foe."

Lord Moyne To Be Buried in England

Ceremonial Funeral Held in Cairo

CAIRO, Wednesday. — Silent, sympathetic crowds of civilians, including many Jews, and members of the Allied forces lined the streets of Cairo this afternoon as the funeral procession of Lord Moyne and his driver, L/Cpl. A. H. Fuller passed slowly from Kasr el Nil Barracks to All Saints' Cathedral.

Lord Moyne was not buried in Egypt. The body is to be embalmed and then flown to England for interment.

The coffins, draped in Union Jacks, were borne on gun-carriages in a procession nearly a mile long which included Navy, Army, R.A.F., Egyptian Army, Allied contingents, and Allied diplomats. Senior officers in the British Forces and leading British civilian representatives were the pall-bearers. The double service was conducted by Bishop H. A. Gwynne.

The burial of L/Cpl. Fuller took place with military honours at the Heliopolis cemetery after the service.

Lord Moyne recovered consciousness for a brief interval after the operation at 5 o'clock on Monday afternoon, when a bullet was extracted from his stomach. His son, Captain the Hon. Bryan Guinness, arrived too late yesterday to see his father alive.

Assassins Confess

Lord Moyne's assassins today gave their names as Moshe Cohen Itzhak and Ch. Salzmann, and said they were members of the Stern group. Their confession, as officially published, was as follows:

"We are members of the Fighters for Freedom of Israel organization (Stern group) and what we have done was done on the instructions of this organization.

The prisoners stated that they were sent down by their organization for the express purpose of murdering Lord Moyne. The reason they gave was that he was head of the Political Department of the British Government in the Middle East, and was carrying out a policy which was contrary to Jewish interests. His attitude, they said, brought him to the notice of the organization which decided to kill him.

The men are understood to have arrived in Egypt at the end of October to make a careful study of Lord Moyne's movements. Investigations were conducted yesterday and today by members of the Military Police and the Palestine Police, and A.N.A. adds that some Jewish officers were present.

Public Reaction

All Cairo newspapers have published lengthy comments on Lord Moyne's death.

After paying tribute to Lord Moyne's sincere sympathy with Middle East problems, "Al-Misri" says: "The authors of this mad action apparently thought that resort to political assassination would be advantageous. It is, however, the worst and the meanest instrument one may use. Political murder has never frightened anybody and has never forced a retreat upon an opponent.

Zionist leaders in Cairo are horrified. "No anti-Zionist or anti-Semite could possibly have thought of a better way to bring discredit on us," said one of them.

In Baghdad yesterday, the Iraqi Foreign Minister visited the British Embassy and expressed the Government's and Nation's condolences and sincere sympathy on the assassination of Lord Moyne.

"The crime deeply touches Iraqis and Arabs for the loss of a great friend," according to one of the local newspapers.

MURDERERS ARE TRAITORS

"We execrate the murderers of Lord Moyne as traitors to the Jewish people," stated Mr. D. Ben-Gurion and Mr. M. Shertok, in a cable sent yesterday on behalf of the Jewish Agency Executive to the Egyptian Prime Minister, Ahmed Maher Pasha. They expressed sympathy with the Egyptian Government at the "grave embarrassment" caused it by the murder.

The Chief Rabbinate in Jerusalem declared in a statement last night:

"We deem it our duty again to appeal to all those who have the terrible tragedy of our people at this time laid bare out of their minds, and who have wantonly gone along the dreadful path of terrorism, to cease at once these revolting crimes forbidden by Holy Command, and to stand, at the same time a peril to our community and the vital interests of the whole of Israel.

Their Eminences appealed to Palestine Jewry to exert its utmost; to guide these erring persons from their evil ways, and to halt their criminal career.

At the Chief Secretary's Press conference at Jaffa-Tel Aviv yesterday, Mr. J. Heftman, on behalf of the Editors of the Jewish press, asked Mr. Shaw to convey to H.M. Government their deep sympathy on the great loss sustained in Lord Moyne's death. Mr. Shaw, stating he was grateful for the expression, promised to convey it, on his return to Jerusalem, to the High Commissioner.

Nothing to Report On Hungary's Jews

LONDON, Wednesday (R). — Mr. Eden expressed regret in the House of Commons today that he had no progress to report on the deliverance of the Jewish community in Hungary.

He was replying to a question by a Conservative member, Mr. Hammersley, who asked whether the undertaking given by Admiral Horthy's Government to grant exit permits or any Jews who could show a visa to Palestine, and any Jewish child under 10 for whom entry could be secured to any Allied country, was being implemented by the present regime in Hungary and the United Nations, respectively.

Mr. Eden said that the Government stood by the terms of the joint Anglo-U.S. declaration of August 17 on which the Horthy Government offer was accepted. He assured Mr. Hammersley that no opportunity had been or would be over-looked to achieve the purpose referred to.

7 KILLED IN TRAIN ACCIDENT

Seven persons were killed and 50 injured in a train accident which occurred at 6.16 yesterday morning on the Kantara-Lydda line. The casualties reported so far are believed to be nearly all military personnel.

Six of the men killed were members of the R.A.F. and one was a soldier. One officer and ten other ranks are among the injured.

Passenger train No. 2, proceeding from Egypt, ran into a wash-out at kilo 196 (at a point between Deir el Balah and Khan Yunis) where approximately 100 metres of the embankment had been swept away by flood waters resulting from the recent heavy rains.

Break-Down Train

Two coaches were partly telescoped, three were derailed but remained standing upright, while the other 11 coaches were not seriously affected.

Medical assistance was at once available, as doctors and ambulances turned out from some military camps nearby. The injured received first-aid and the serious cases were taken to hospital. The military camp personnel also provided food to the passengers.

Two breakdown trains were immediately dispatched to the scene, one from Haifa, and the other from the south, where it had been busy on a derailment which had occurred yesterday involving two locomotives.

The undamaged part of the train was taken south to Khan Yunis, while the passengers were taken north to Gaza, continuing their journey to Lydda and Haifa this afternoon.

Though the damage to the rolling-stock was extensive, it is expected that the block will be cleared by 10 o'clock this morning.

Train services between Haifa and Cairo are being resumed, cancelled yesterday. Amongst those held up were two special trains with pilgrims for Mecca.

Rockets Fired Against South England

Berlin Claims "V-2" In Action Now

LONDON, Wednesday (R). — The new German secret weapon, labelled V-2, is now in action against Southern England, according to a German communique, which claims that it has been in use for some weeks.

The communique says: "The area of Greater London has been under fire by V-1 since June 15, with short interruptions and varying at length. The fire has been intensified for some weeks past by the use of the second and far more effective explosive missile, V-2."

The new weapon is a powerful rocket, according to reports from Sweden and other neutral countries. Some of these reports have credited V-2 with a range of between 200 and 300 miles and a warhead containing something under a ton of high explosive.

One or two of the missiles are said to have been found in Sweden after being fired across the Baltic from the "secret weapon research station" at Peenemunde.

50 Feet Long

Swedish reports describe V-2 as a fairly long rocket projectile with tail fins like ordinary bombs. Some are said to be as long as 50 feet "like a flying telegraph pole with a trail of flame behind it" and faster than sound, so that they hit the objective before they can be heard arriving.

Bases in Germany, Holland, Denmark and Norway have been reported as feasible for attacks on Britain. From Paris have come stories that the V-2 was used against the city but this was later denied. Obviously the use of rocket projectiles over a much greater range is perfectly feasible, though whether an economic load of explosive can be employed is another matter.

FRESH DRIVE IN LORRAINE

S.H.A.E.F., Wednesday (R). — The Allies have opened a new drive in Lorraine. There was some fighter-bomber support for the attack between Nancy and Metz which opened after a heavy artillery barrage.

The attack is officially described as an improvement of positions. It was apparently made on a frontage of two or three miles up to the Seille which is not a wide river. Resistance is described as moderate despite the fact that the weather curtailed extensive air operations.

The old Maginot Line winds along the boundary in front of the Siegfried Line considerably to the east of the Third Army's present position.

Third Army infantry have captured 13 towns between Metz and Nancy and crossed the Seille in three places.

Finishing Touches To Maas Clean-up

S.H.A.E.F., Wednesday (R). — American troops of the Canadian First Army wedging their way into Moerdijk yesterday put the finishing touches to Field Marshal Montgomery's Maas clean-up which has cost the Germans 43,000 men — the equivalent of three fully complemented divisions — at a time when Germany's greatest need is for men to defend the Reich's frontiers.

40,000 Prisoners

"We have cleared the Scheldt and the approaches to Antwerp," said an official spokesman tonight. "We have freed an area of Holland some 20 miles deep on a 40 mile front.

"We have taken prisoner between 38,000 and 40,000 men and perhaps inflicted the same number of casualties. We have destroyed the 64th division south of the Scheldt and the 70th on Walcheren.

Soviet-Norway Agreement in the Air

By RANDAL NEALE
Reuters Diplomatic Correspondent

LONDON, Wednesday. — There are a number of questions which the Norwegian Foreign Minister, Mr. Trygve Lie, may wish to discuss with the Soviet Government in Moscow, to which he has gone from Stockholm.

For the first time since 1918, Norway and Russia are again immediate neighbours. The Civil Affairs agreement between Norway and Russia of May 16 last established the framework within which the Soviet military command and the Norwegian civil authorities agree cooperate in the event of the Red Army invading Northern Norway in pursuit of the Germans.

Now that the Russians are actually on Norwegian soil, west of Kirkenes, the detailed application of the May agreement is bound to raise practical problems calling for an early discussion between the two Governments.

Use of Norwegian Police

The question of the transfer to Northern Norway of Norwegian police trained in Sweden was settled during Mr. Lie's stay in Stockholm. Russia will doubtless look after the men's transportation to their destination.

Norwegian quarters observe that relations between the Soviet and Norwegian Governments are excellent, and they look to the successful outcome of Mr. Lie's conversations in Moscow.

This is his first visit to Russia as Foreign Minister. He visited Washington early last year.

Poles Deny Curzon Line Report

LONDON, Wednesday (PAT). The report that the Polish Government is ready on principle to accept the Curzon Line is denied by the official "Dziennik Polski" which has published the following statement:

"One of London's morning papers (the "Daily Telegraph") published on November 7 sensational news concerning the course of international conversations on the Polish frontiers. The "Dziennik Polski" does not intend to attempt a discussion from the Polish side about this question until the Polish Government discloses its attitude and as long as this question is subject of preparatory talks and explanations.

"Nevertheless, the "Dziennik Polski" has not been able to ascertain from authoritative sources that the attitude attributed to the Polish Government by the London paper does not correspond to the facts."

ISOLATION DEFEATED AT POLLS

By JOSEPH HENNESSY, Reuters Special Correspondent

WASHINGTON, Wednesday.— The re-election of President Roosevelt gives the administration a "go ahead" signal for a new international facts to prevent future war. The new Senate, which must approve the treaties, will be predominantly Democratic.

The general opinion is that the President's re-election means a definite breakaway by American voters from their traditional isolationism. Senators Gerald P. Nye (Republican) of North Dakota, and John A. Danaher (Republican) of Connecticut, both isolationists, have been defeated in their attempts at re-election, though Senator Robert A. Taft (Republican) of Ohio, another isolationist, has been re-elected. Mr. Hamilton Fish, New York's leading isolationist, was also beaten.

Mrs. Clare Booth Luce, a Republican "internationalist" after trailing behind her opponent, Margaret Connors, most of the night was re-elected by a bare majority of 400 votes out of a total of 200,000.

Victory for Labour

Labour, spearheaded by the Congress of Industrial Organization's Political Action Committee, takes the greatest credit for the President's victory. It got out a tremendous vote for President Roosevelt in the large industrial areas and enabled him to carry the pivotal States.

Mr. Sidney Hillman, of the Political Action Committee of the Congress for Industrial organization, declared today: "The election is a stunning repudiation of anti-labour and isolationist elements."

Mr. John L. Lewis, President of the United Mineworkers Union, did not have much success in trying to get his coal miners to vote for Governor Dewey.

Cooperation Assured

International collaboration after the war has been assured by President Roosevelt's re-election, according to informed and unbiased opinion. It is widely believed here that the next major development will be a conference with Mr. Churchill and Marshal Stalin, probably before the New year. Mr. Churchill is understood to have discussed this detail during his visit to Moscow, but the President himself may have some news on the subject at his next press conference.

The main points in the summing-up made by sober members of both the Republican and Democratic Parties are these:

(1). — Despite claims to the contrary, foreign policy and the peace of the post-war world have been major issues in the elections.

(2). — What the American people have decided is not whether the Americans will collaborate to keep the peace but how much effort and sacrifice they will make to prevent another war.

Mr. Dewey undoubtedly would have done much for world collaboration, but rightly or wrongly America has decided that President Roosevelt is prepared to go further and act with greater swiftness.

Weather Slows Soviet Drive

By DUNCAN HOOPER, Reuters Special Correspondent

MOSCOW, Wednesday. — The resumption of the Red Army's general offensive against Budapest is believed in Moscow to be imminent, with only very difficult weather holding the hand of the Soviet Command.

Further bitter fighting is expected, with the entire Danube sector, from Budapest southwards, exposed to the blows of the Soviet forces.

At the northern end of the front, the Red Air Force has joined with Soviet land forces in the fight to finish off the German divisions encircled in Western Latvia.

Russian tanks and infantry are massing for a double pronged drive against German Silesia and the Polish city of Cracow, according to a German military spokesman. Other Russian troops are now within two miles of the centre of Budapest.

The Military correspondent of the German Overseas News Agency said that in the neighbourhood of Budapest, German counter-attacks pushed the Russians out of several localities.

HONGKONG TO STAY IN BRITISH EMPIRE

LONDON, Wednesday (R). — Hong Kong is to remain in the British Empire, it was indicated by Mr. C. R. Attlee in the House of Commons.

When asked whether Hong Kong or any other part of the Empire was excluded from the Prime Minister's declaration that it was "not proposed to liquidate the British Empire," the Deputy Prime Minister declared amid cheers:

No part of the British Empire or Commonwealth of Nations is excluded from the scope of the declaration referred to.

440 Jap Planes Wrecked in 2 Days

PEARL HARBOUR, Wednesday. (R). — A communique from the Commander-in-Chief of the Pacific reports that U.S. carrier aircraft destroyed 249 Japanese planes in Manila.

Japanese losses in the raids on November 4 and 5 are now 440 aircraft. Shipping losses total six ninth and 24 damaged, reported the communique. It was also reported that additional "heavy damage" was inflicted on ground installations.

Rumania Swings To the Left

Palestine Post Special

LONDON, Wednesday. — The new Rumanian Government represents a complete victory of the newly formed left-wing "National Democratic Front."

A large number of the generals and officials who formed the Sanatescu Cabinet are out, and the old leaders of the National Peasant Party and the National Liberal Party, Julius Manin and Constantine Bratianu, are no longer members of the Cabinet.

The Democratic Front has seven representatives in the new Government — three Communists, two Socialists, one delegate of the Agrarian Front and one of the Patriot Front — while the National Peasant Party has six, and the Liberals have four.

Although the two old leaders of the Peasant and the Liberal parties are not in the Cabinet, both parties are prominently represented by their respective Secretary-General.

New York Stayed Up All Night

By STANLEY BURCH, Reuters Special Correspondent

NEW YORK, Wednesday.— The conviction that President Roosevelt would stay at the White House for another four years swept like a wave soon after midnight through hundreds of thousands of people massed deep in the streets of New York—the city of myriad lights.

For long, restless, impatient hours they had packed the streets which were split into huge patches of glaring light and dusky shadow. As the night lengthened into morning the exciting assertion: "Roosevelt wins" sped through the streets, the distribution of midnight papers rounding off the incessant flow of election returns flashing along the famous electric sign of the "New York Times" building.

The main victory began late at night did not deter the crowd — estimated at a quarter of a million which was cheering the election results. Newspaper sellers shouted: "Roosevelt wins by a knockout" and: "Roosevelt the winner," than the vendors did a brisk business in buttons inscribed: "I told you so."

Hundreds of papers rushed specials to the streets carrying headlines reflecting the hour by hour electoral gains. Roosevelt gains here changed to precisely the opposite, when President Dewey had caught up in the neck and neck race.

Many papers stressed the labour vote with such headlines as "record vote cast in industrial cities". The coal mines in West Virginia and elsewhere closed down as the miners went to the polls.

Dewey Concedes Defeat

At 3.14 this morning Governor Dewey conceded President Roosevelt's re-election for a fourth term in these words: "It is clear that President Roosevelt has been re-elected for a fourth term".

Governor Dewey, who was making the announcement over the national radio network declared: "I extend to President Roosevelt my hearty congratulations. I am confident that all Americans will join me in the hope that Divine Confidence will guide and protect the President. I hope his next term will bring a speedy victory and the establishment of lasting peace and the return of tranquility among our people. The Republican party emerges from the election revitalized and a great force for the good of the country and for the preservation of free government in America."

Mrs. Dewey was at her husband's side all night at Republican headquarters and stood by him as he broadcast, while a battery of camera men took their pictures. Governor Dewey was all smiles. He made this statement after late returns had made it clear that his last chances for victory were slipping away. New York went decidedly to President Roosevelt and Missouri and New Hampshire slipped from the Dewey column. Defeat was then certain.

Roosevelt Hears Result

President Roosevelt telegraphed Governor Dewey at 3.30 saying: "I thank you for your statement which I heard over the air a few minutes ago". The President was at his worktable throughout the night. At the time of Governor Dewey's statement conceding defeat the count of the popular vote was: Roosevelt, 14,411,960 and Dewey 12,265,760. President Roosevelt, studying the returns at Hyde Park radiated confidence and happiness at the prospect of entering the White House for the fourth term, though he did not immediately claim a victory. Later he told neighbours at Hyde Park: "It looks very much like I will have to be coming up here by train from Washington for another four years."

ROOSEVELT WINS SOLID VICTORY

DEMOCRATS CONTROL CONGRESS

NEW YORK, Wednesday (R).— President Roosevelt has been re-elected with a reduced popular majority, and a big Electoral College majority. The latest returns are as follows: President Roosevelt — 412, Mr. Dewey — 119.

Tabulations show that almost 100,000 of the nation's 130,810 voting units give President Roosevelt a popular plurality of little more than 2,500,000, compared with about five million in 1940. The figures are: President Roosevelt, 19,700,000, Mr. Dewey, 17,200,000. It is clear, however, that the Democrats have swept to victory with Mr. Roosevelt.

Democratic successes have cut down the Republican membership in the House of Representatives which during the past two years nearly amounted to a majority, while a Democratic Senate majority is definitely assured.

Returns for the Senate and House up to about 3.00 p.m. local time were: Senate: Democrats 17 elected and 36 whose terms have not expired, making a total of 53 seats. Republicans: 10 elected, 24 not expired, making a total of 34. There are 9 results to be still declared.

House of Representatives: Democrats: 223, Republicans: 142.

Latest figures in the Governors contest in 32 States are: Democrats 11, Republicans 10. In the election for Governors, the Democrats have captured three States previously held by the Republicans and are threatening Republican seats at Washington, Ohio and Illinois.

The Race

The returns up to eight p.m. last night from scattered points in 22 States, showed President Roosevelt ahead in 13 and Dewey in nine, but most returns were too small to give a real indication.

At 9 p.m. President Roosevelt was ahead in 20 states with 225 electoral votes and Governor Dewey in 13 with 122 votes.

The President was ahead in the key States of Illinois and Pennsylvania. Governor Dewey was leading in the pivotal states of Ohio, Michigan, Missouri and also in Massachusetts.

At 11.30 the first tabulation of returns from all 48 States could be made but they were still far from complete. President Roosevelt then had 366 electoral votes against Governor Dewey's 165.

A midnight tabulation showed 6,580,000 votes for President Roosevelt and 5,670,000 votes for Governor Dewey. At 1.15 hours incomplete returns showed President Roosevelt leading in 32 States with 387 electoral votes and Governor Dewey ahead in 16 States with 144 votes. At 2 o'clock President Roosevelt, although far ahead in the Electoral College vote, was leading Governor Dewey by less than two million votes.

One of the surprises of the election was the Governor's poor showing in his home State, and especially in the city of New York, which he lost by 769,841 votes; President Roosevelt got 2,390,932 votes. Mr. Dewey obtained 1,770,088. The President carried New York state by over 325,000 votes.

Foreign Policy Upheld

A Democratic headquarters official told Reuter at 4 G.M.T.: "At the moment the trend is definitely towards the re-election of President Roosevelt, which means full participation of the United States in a world organization for peace. It also means continued cooperation between Great Britain, France and China."

Mr. Joseph Ball, the Republican Senator, who asked for the President's re-election, told Reuter: "President Roosevelt has won on the conduct of the war and foreign policy issues.

A large number of the generals and officials who formed the Sanatescu Cabinet are out.

The New York radio last night broadcast a report which said that Metz had already been outflanked.

The German News Agency reports that a British destroyer and a submarine sank by German patrol vessels during engagements in the Aegean.

The usual Munich beer cellar performance at which Hitler would have spoken last night was postponed "until some later date" owing to the "total mobilization" ban on celebrations of any kind.

Provide for Your Future
and insure with
MIGDAL INSURANCE CO. LTD.

LATE Edition

THE PALESTINE POST

8 PAGES

JERUSALEM
FRIDAY, APRIL 27, 1945

PRICE: 25 MILS
VOL. XX. No. 5777

JERUSALEM, OPPOSITE G.P.O.
ALL ELECTRICAL SUPPLIES
Our service — your satisfaction!
JOHN LIFSHITZ

U.S. AND SOVIET ARMIES LINK UP

S.H.A.E.F., Thursday (R). — A large-scale link-up between the Americans and the Russians along a broad belt of the Central German front appears to have taken place. At the same time, General Patton's troops have crossed the Danube at three points on the fringe of the Nazis' southern redoubt. The battle of Berlin is coming to an end. In Italy, German resistance is rapidly collapsing and the main industrial centres are falling.

Column One

By David Courtney

THE way of retribution in Germany is marked clearly. Foul crime has been done there, and those who did it will be brought to justice; so, let us hope, will their accessories. State or war exigencies, raised to justify or at least extenuate so many odious deeds, cannot be raised by the Germans to justify or extenuate a single one of theirs. They are condemned, not by judgments devised hastily or in vengeance, but under the existing common law of every civilized State and under the law of pre-Nazi Germany itself.

Daily one sees how different that matter is in the liberated territories; where urgent, heart-deep indignations, pent-up during hideous years of oppression, have been loosed like a flood. The flood is destined to engulf not only those who outlawed themselves by active treachery and crime, but also those who brought shame upon their race and state by 'collaboration'; and, destined or not, it will engulf innocent men as well, unless a courageous effort is made to direct it. I am brought to this uneasy, even hazardous problem, by evidence from Greece and Rumania, and by the widely publicized details of Marshal Petain's surrender.

PETAIN, though not by any means the cause, is the symbol of France's shame. Whatever he might say in his defence — and we can be sure there will be plenty of evidence to shake the State Prosecutor — he acquiesced in the humiliation of France, he acquiesced in, and actively furthered, the metamorphosis of France from the traditional asylum of the oppressed to a partner in merciless persecution. If the Dreyfus affair shamed France, the acquiescence of Marshal Petain humiliated her and fouled her good name ten times over.

That is his crime — not the fact that he capitulated, nor even that he let the resources of France be used against the old Allies of France; and certainly not the fact that he detested, as many silly old men do, Britain and the Soviet equally. He is the self-chosen symbol of France's shame; his repudiation in the highest courts of France, is essential to the national repudiation of that shame itself: the issue is too big historically to be influenced by the grey hairs of 89 unheroic years.

THE problem lies not in the Petains of liberated territories; or in such puny figures as Quisling of Oslo, Mussert of the Hague, Pavelitch of Zagreb and Hacha of Prague. These are simple matters. So are the gaolers who modelled their technique on Buchenwald. The problem lies in the tendency of retributive justice, as it disperses downwards from the major to the minor personality, to merge imperceptibly with politics. As time goes on, the crowds inside and outside the courtrooms of Europe will get bigger and noisier; and justice, blind as she may be, is not deaf.

In half a dozen countries already, Right has begun to inform against Left and Left against Right; and both have taken justice into their own hands when justice moved too slowly for their passionate indignation. Many a technical 'collaborator', innocent of anything but timidity, has been executed or imprisoned; and many another, whose guilt was political rather than treasonable, has been arraigned and sentenced. And the heresy hunt is not over: it has hardly begun.

Athens, Bucharest, Belgrade, Brussels, Paris and the rest will gain nothing from this except prolonged hatred and a new fear. Gain will only be to the real traitors and the real criminals, who will edge their way beyond the immediate gallows, and in the surfeit that must come at length to a people tired of vengeance, contrive their acquittal. The wretched little men, the timid followers, the bewildered victims of cajolery by press and wireless — merciless judgment upon them is no substitute for judgment on the instigators, the big men, the evil-doers and their masked confederates of army and industry.

Jerusalem, April 27.

NATIONS CONFRONT BIG ISSUES

POLISH DEADLOCK UNBROKEN

By LYLE E. WILSON, U.P. Bureau Chief

WASHINGTON, Thursday. — With the United Nations conference getting down to work today after yesterday's formal opening, it is considered possible that the delicate Polish problem may reach an early climax.

The conference opened in an atmosphere of solemnity which was heightened by the dispatches from Washington and Europe bearing strong hints of great events in the European war in the immediate offing. An undertone of urgency echoed in the 90-minute meeting of Mr. Stettinius, Mr. Eden, M. Molotov, and Mr T. V. Soong just before the formal opening.

The American delegation is standing firm in opposition against admitting the Warsaw Government to the conference. President Truman is described here as "adamant" in rejecting the Soviet demands on behalf of the Warsaw Poles. But it is also indicated that the British might be more willing now to compromise for the sake of getting the embarrassing Polish issue out of the way.

Among delegates there is a belief this afternoon that M. Molotov has received new instructions from Marshal Stalin on the Polish issue. He is reported to be ready to meet again with Mr. Stettinius and Mr. Eden.

U.S. Delegates Meet

The U.S. delegation met for two hours last night and thereafter became uncommonly silent. There is frank anxiety over the Polish dispute. An international compact against aggression undoubtedly will come out of this conference but it will come with much more force and significance if the misunderstanding among the three major Powers is adjusted to the mutual satisfaction of all concerned.

All delegations are interested in the prestige position of their own nations, and thus there are already efforts to expand the conference executive from 11 to 14 or more members. China, France, Britain and Russia are assured of places. Others who might be elected include Brazil, Chile, Canada, Australia, Holland, Yugoslavia, and Iran.

M. Molotov last night gave a banquet in honour of Mexico, which was attended by the chairmen of other Latin American delegations of the countries which have recognized Russia. It would not be surprising if the Latin Americans utilized the banquet to let the Russians know how much they want to see Argentina allowed to come to San Francisco.

Official Opening

Delegates of 46 nations attended the official inauguration yesterday afternoon. They heard pleas from President Truman and Mr. E. R. Stettinius that their course be so guided that big and small Powers in future generations would live in peace.

Mr. Stettinius introduced the President after formal greetings by Governor Earl Warren of California and Mayor Lapham of San Francisco. Neither President Truman nor Mr. Stettinius gave any hint of suggestions for a settlement of the Polish question.

Mr. Stettinius, in an address to the conference today, said: "There will have to be many other conferences and many other decisions, both national and international. We have no time to lose. We are united not only for survival and not only for military victory.

"At Mexico City the Inter-American conference strengthened the ties between the republics of the western hemisphere and prepared the way for close integration between the Inter-American system with the world organization.

Famine Looms in Occupied Holland

By CHARLES LYNCH, Special Correspondent with the First Candian Army in Holland

The food situation inside the Fortress of Holland is growing worse almost hourly. The impression is strong in liberated Holland that only the dropping of food from the air, as proposed by General Eisenhower, would avoid a tragedy overshadowing even the horrors of Buchenwald and Belsen.

The full effects of the flooding and the cutting off of Northern Holland are now beginning to be felt in the Rotterdam. Amsterdam and The Hague areas. Only swift outside action can help the situation.

Unless General Eisenhower's plan is followed, it is feared that thousands of Dutch men, women and children, if they do not die before the food arrives, will be too far gone to be revived when the food is finally delivered overland or by sea. Two months ago the daily death rate in The Hague was 400 and in Amsterdam from 500 to 600.

A wave of hope swept through liberated Holland when General Eisenhower's proposal was made known. It changed almost to despair on Wednesday afternoon when the German reply was picked up by wireless:

"We agree in principle to the supplying of food to Dutch civilians, but we cannot agree to have it delivered by air," the spokesman said, arguing that such a drop would be inaccurate, food might get into the wrong hands and be swallowed up in the black market, and Allied aircraft flying low over the fortress of Holland would be able to make a close-hand study of German defences.

NO MORE ROCKETS

LONDON, Thursday (R). — When asked in the House of Commons today if he was now able to make any statement with regard to German rocket attacks, Mr. Churchill replied: "Yes, sir, they have ceased." (loud laughter).

When asked for an assurance that there was no prospect that they were likely to be resumed, the Prime Minister said: "It is my duty to record facts rather than to indulge in prophesy, but I have recorded such facts with very considerable optimism which I trust will be brought into mockery by events."

V-Weapon Terror Now Ended

By MICHAEL RYERSON, special to The Palestine Post

LONDON, Thursday. — After five years of bombs and flying bombs, capped by a final orgy of hundred of rockets, the Londoner can today walk the streets and sleep in his own bed without the fear of sudden death striking without warning from the skies.

Hitler's last fling took the form of a major assault by rocket bombs, the worst of which killed 167 people in a single second. Flying bombs of the improved type are believed to travel at nearly 800 miles per hour. The total number of rockets which reached Britain, was 1,050. They killed 2,754 people and seriously injured over 6,500.

The first rockets were radio-controlled until they started falling. The latest type had an automatic device to cut off the fuel supply at a determined point. The attack reached its highest intensity during February, when 71 dropped on Southern England in one week. Many of these hit London, but despite German boasts of their accuracy the rockets fell over a very wide area causing serious damage in Essex.

MANDATES COMMITTEE

SAN FRANCISCO, Thursday (P.T.A.). — The appointment of a special body, to be known as "Committee No. 4," to deal with the question of international trusteeships for Mandated areas may be regarded as an initial step toward an eventual decision on Palestine.

The appointment of such a Committee in no way contradicts Mr. C.R. Attlee's statement that no specific reference to Palestine will be made during the conference. For although the British and American delegations will not mention Palestine, the Committee will no doubt have Palestine in mind when preparing recommendations for trusteeship machinery.

The Arabic delegations, which are attracting much press attention because of their colourful appearance, have so far abstained from any statements regarding Palestine. U.S. oil interests have placed an experienced public relations adviser at the disposal of the Saudi-Arabian delegation.

It is known that the Arab delegations were much impressed by Mr. Attlee's statement on Tuesday, especially since he suggested that the question of trusteeship "be put up to Palestinians," which was interpreted as an indication that the British Government might seek a plebiscite in Palestine.

Zionist leaders were taken by surprise by Mr. Attlee's statement. It is believed that if this is the final British word, it means that Britain is determined not to agree to international trusteeship for Palestine. The situation, therefore, remains in the hands of Committee No. 4.

TRUMAN BACKS F.D.R.'S STAND ON ZIONISM

WASHINGTON, Thursday (R). —Representative Emanuel Celler, of New York, discussed the Zionist question with President Truman at the White House yesterday. Mr. Celler told correspondents:—

The President stands four-square behind the pronouncement of the late President Roosevelt. He will not deviate one iota from the Palestine plank in the Democratic party platform which he and I both helped to frame.

YUGOSLAVS GO HOME

CAIRO, Thursday (ANA). — The fourth group of Yugoslav refugees, consisting of 1,720 people, has left the Middle East for home.

They have been living at the UNRRA camp at Shatt near Suez since the early days of last year. Yugoslav and Greek refugees so far repatriated from the Middle East now total 5,000.

Enlarged Council Urged by Egypt

SAN FRANCISCO, Thursday (R). — Abdul Hamid Badawy Pasha, the Egyptian Minister for Foreign Affairs, urged yesterday on behalf of the Egyptian Delegation to the United Nations Conference that the membership of the proposed World Security Council be increased from eleven to 14, thus giving the smaller powers a larger representation.

The Minister said: "We suggest earnest consideration of the principle of territorial representation by zones so that all areas apart from the territories of the five great powers might be embodied into and share in the duties of the Security Council.

"We ask for an increase to 14 of the membership of the Council so as better to provide for small and medium power representation and have a suggestion relating to the vote system in matters of enforcing arrangements when a big power is not involved."

CENTRE OF BERLIN IN FLAMES

By HENRY SHAPIRO, U.P. Correspondent

MOSCOW, Thursday. — On the sixth day of furious fighting inside encircled Berlin, the Red Army is fighting its way towards the Alexanderplatz, in the centre of the city. They have captured the huge Tempelhof aerodrome where they found planes with their motors warmed up, ready to take high Nazi functionaries to safety.

German reports which maintain that Hitler, Goebbels and General Guderian are directing the defence of the city, admit that fighting is going on near the eastern approaches of the Alexanderplatz police headquarters, where thousands of policemen are trying to stem the tide. Soviet assault units swarming across the Spree, south of the Silesian railway station, and followed by tank-borne infantry and artillery, are plunging in the direction of the Tiergarten.

"Red Star" reports that a group of German women dressed as scouts and carrying rucksacks arrived at one Soviet command post, saying: "Life in Berlin under the bombing and shelling is intolerable. We decided to cross the lines to escape the shells." The paper adds that there are many disguised saboteurs and spies among the refugees, carrying radio transmitters and signal flares.

Whole Groups Surrender

"Pravda" reports that whole groups, companies and platoons are surrendering with increasing frequency. At one point on the Spree, sappers had just completed the erection of a pontoon bridge when 18 German soldiers appeared on the west bank and asked permission to cross to the east.

The paper's correspondent saw a group of sullen, punch-drunk, terrified German civilians gazing at a stream of Soviet tanks and guns, and heard one of them saying: "How many of you there are! There is no room in Berlin for so many Russians."

Little more than a stone jungle remains of Berlin where savage fighting proceeds above and below the ground, behind shattered walls and rubble heaps, and in the darkened tunnels of the city's underground railways.

Berlin is going down with many German units still underground in the subways.

Unconfirmed reports say that the Russians have already bagged a large number of Nazi war criminals and Gestapo-men by closing the gap around the city.

Pacific Bases Plan Dropped

By PAUL SCOTT RANKINE, Reuters Special Correspondent

SAN FRANCISCO, Thursday.— Following strong pressure by the War and Navy Departments, the U.S. Government has decided to drop its proposal to place all Pacific islands taken from the Japanese under "international trusteeship," I am reliably informed.

The U.S. delegation will, it is expected here, advocate to the Conference Committee that a distinction be made between Colonial and Mandated areas, and areas essential to the defence of peace and security.

Russia is reported to have indicated her sympathy for the proposal that the United States should take over some Japanese- Mandated islands, but is said to have reserved her position regarding the possibility of some of these being allocated to Russia for her defence.

PETAIN "DELIVERS HIS BODY"

PARIS, Thursday (R). — Marshal Petain surrendered to the French authorities on the Franco-Swiss frontier this afternoon, according to well-informed quarters, though no official statement has yet been made.

A special train taking the officers and staff of General Koenig, the Military Governor of Paris, left for a frontier town whose name is still kept secret. This is in accordance with the precedent created when Marshal Bazaine was arrested in 1871 by an officer of the Military Governor of Paris.

Petain's trial will take place on the date fixed originally for his trial by proxy, according to the public prosecutor in charge of this case.

Official quarters are maintaining their original silence about the arrangements for Petain's arrival on the French frontier. When he does reach it he will be taken in charge by a Police Colonel, who will tell him that he has been ordered to "deliver his body" to the French authorities. Those accompanying Petain are not subject to any warrants for arrest, except General Debeny, the Vichy War Minister, and Admiral Blehaut, the Vichy Minister for Colonies and the Navy.

Dr. Menetreal, who for years has been in attendance of Petain and whose father was Petain's personal physician, does not appear to be accompanying Petain on this occasion. Menetreal, who throughout the Vichy reign, saw Petain three or four times daily, is supposed to have had great influence with the old Marshal and to have used it in favour of Laval's pro-German policy.

Milan and Turin in Partisans' Hands

GENEVA, Thursday. — Milan has been taken over by the Partisans, who are also in control of most of Turin and Genoa, while Allied troops have captured Verona.

The Rome Radio, relaying a recorded broadcast from the Genoa Radio today said: "The German garrison in Genoa has surrendered to Italian partisans." This followed Swiss radio reports that partisans have liberated Turin, the biggest industrial city in Northern Italy after Milan. Partisans have been in complete control of Milan since this morning and the city has been cleared of Germans, according to reliable reports from the Italian frontier.

Meanwhile, U.S. troops are now north of Mantua and have captured Reggio and Parma. Other troops pushed on north-west of Spezia. Eighth Army troops are across the Po along almost the entire front. East of Ferrara Vietinghoff has retreated hastily and has abandoned at least 1,000 motor transport vehicles.

The Germans have also handed over the administration of Como town and lake, near the Swiss frontier, to the Italian partisans, and the Lake Constance Flotilla, consisting of nine ships, has surrendered to the Swiss authorities in Swiss ports on the lake.

On the Run

Unconfirmed reports today speak of a big revolt sweeping large areas of Northern Italy, and it is hinted that Mussolini may be trying to make a deal with the partisans if he is allowed to escape. One report heard by the British radio suggests that Mussolini sent a flag of truce to the Socialist party leaders in Milan, and offered to let them take over on condition that the Germans and Fascists be allowed to leave.

Rome broadcasts say that fighting is going on in Genoa, while the Germans who are leaving Turin are being hammered in their flight. The Fascists are on the run everywhere and one of their principal leaders, Farinacchi, is reported to have fled.

(Reuter and UP)

GERMANS WRECK FIUME

BELGRADE, Thursday (R).— The Germans are demolishing the important Adriatic port of Fiume as Yugoslav troops continue to battle their way into the town against desperate resistance

Farther east, Marshal Tito's troops advancing between the Drava and Sava rivers in Northern Yugoslavia, have reached the line of the Ilova river, only 50 miles south-east of Zagreb.

LP.3,000,000 More Premium Bonds

By Our Financial Editor,

A third issue of LP10 Premium Bonds to total LP3,000,000, instead of the LP1,000,000 for each of the previous issues, is announced by the Government. This follows quickly on the distribution of the last series which was heavily oversubscribed, the bonds being sold privately above their face value even before they were issued. New demand is already reported to be large.

A first prize of LP5,000 will be drawn every three months while 86 other bonds will be drawn as follows: one at LP1,000, one LP500, four LP250 each and 80 at LP100 each. The highest quarterly prizes in the first and second series is LP1,000.

It is presumed, though the official communique does not mention it, that the premiums will not be chargeable with income tax.

It may be expected that the announcement will result in a fall in the price at which the first and second issues have been changing hands. Dealers and speculators who have been paying high prices in the expectation of large profits may now incur losses.

(Official Notice on Page 3)

"Purge" Trials Continue

ROME, Thursday (UP). — The trial of four Fascist Ministers opened today with the revelation that one of them, Guiseppe Bottai, ex-Minister of Corporations and Education, is fighting in France with the Allies.

Of the four — Bottai, Rossoni, (Corporations) Federzoni, (Interior) and Giacomo Acerbo (Agriculture) — the latter was the only one present. The others were tried in absentia.

The defence lawyer, Pasquale Marsano, said that Bottai had been fighting for the past eight months in France and Germany, and asked for his trial to be postponed. But the High Court over-ruled the contention on the ground that there was insufficient evidence to corroborate the defence statement. The Court thn adjourned until May 7.

FASCIST PLOT FOILED IN ARGENTINA

MONTEVIDEO, Thursday. — The discovery of a Fascist plot with countrywide ramifications, designed to nullify the recent Argentine declaration of war against the Axis and adherence to the Chapultepec pact, has led to numerous arrests in Buenos Aires.

Troops have been sent into the city to prevent agitators from interfering with public order when the fall of Berlin is announced. The War Council will deal with the people already arrested.

Reports say that Colonel Juan Peron, Vice-President and actual ruler, submitted his resignation on Tuesday.

(UP and R.)

French Pour Into Constance

ZURICH, Thursday (R). — French armour is tonight rumbling across into Constance, the German lake-side town on the Eastern Swiss border, which was recently proclaimed an open town by the local civilian authorities.

The town is undefended and the population is panick-stricken. Hundreds of soldiers and civilians are thronging towards the border, where they have broken the barriers on the German side and are being held in check by Swiss troops.

DANUBE CROSSED IN FORCE

LONDON, Thursday (R). — The final assault on the twin centres of German last-ditch resistance has begun. While Russian shock troops today are throwing the full weight of their onslaught on the centre of Berlin, General Patton's Third Army has broken through the outer crust of Hitler's southern redoubt after a mass crossing of the Danube.

The crossing of the Oder and the capture of Stettin are reported tonight by Marshal Stalin who also announced the capture of Brno, capital of Moravia.

Patton's troops have stormed Regensburg, while General Patch's Seventh Army is racing for Munich, less than 30 miles away. In the north, British troops have dealt the final blow to resistance in the great port of Bremen, which the Mayor has now handed over.

Patton's drive into the Berchtesgaden redoubt runs at three points east and west of Regensburg, outflanking Munich from the north. The American forces are within 75 miles of the Fuehrer's bomb - shaken mountain eyrie, heavily raided yesterday.

Leaving Berlin to become a giant death trap, the Russians are rapidly narrowing the gap and only a 30-mile corridor separates Marshal Stalin and General Eisenhower on this sector. When it is closed northern Germany will be completely cut off from Hitler's southern nucleus of resistance by a 150-mile long belt of Allied armour.

Goering Quits

STOCKHOLM, Thursday (R). — Goering, who is suffering from "heart's disease," has relinquished command of the Luftwaffe, according to a Hamburg radio announcement which says:

Marshal Goering is suffering from a heart disease which has now entered an acute stage. He has therefore asked to be relieved of the command of the Luftwaffe and all duties connected therewith.

The Fuehrer has granted this request and appointed Colonel-General Ritter von Grimm to be the new Commander-in-Chief of the Luftwaffe, promoting him at the same time to be the rank of Field Marshal.

Stop Press

MUSSOLINI CAPTURED

ROME, Friday (R). — The capture of Mussolini by Italian patriots is reported on good authority in a message received here from the Swiss Telegraph Agency.

Deep in the Heart of Berlin

STOCKHOLM, Thursday (R).— The Hamburg radio announced tonight that Soviet forces, after crossing the Spree river, have reached the Jannowitz Bridge station. This is the deepest penetration into inner Berlin yet reported.

The bridge is only a few hundred yards from the start of Unter Den Linden.

GALA NIGHT
ON MAY 1
at the
CAFE EUROPE
JERUSALEM
Opening of the season with the best orchestra in Palestine conducted by the famous violinist
LISA SCHMITZ
SURPRISES & PRIZES
CONCERT MUSIC DAILY FROM 5.30 p.m.
Dancing nightly. Our beautiful garden is open.

PEACE IN SIGHT!
NOW FOR YOUR FUTURE.
FOR those in Temporary War-Time jobs the joy of peace will be spoilt by fear of an uncertain future. You must, therefore, insure yourself now against low pay and even unemployment. You must read "ENGINEERING OPPORTUNITIES," the well-known Guide to Successful Careers, which shows how you can secure a permanent and highly paid post.
This valuable handbook has been specially prepared by career experts for men like you in the post-war years. It shows you your opportunities and how to use them. It outlines home study courses for recognized qualifications like Matriculation, B. Sc., A.M.I.E.E. etc., which are usually regarded as essential for promotion and high paid posts in Government Service and large companies.

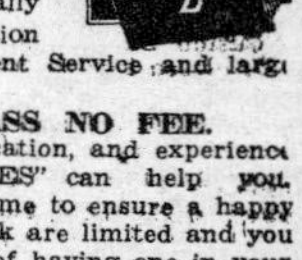

Our Guarantee is: NO PASS NO FEE.
No matter what be your age, education, and experience "ENGINEERING OPPORTUNITIES" can help you. You can use your spare time at home to ensure a happy future. Copies of this valuable book are limited and you cannot afford to miss this chance of having one in your hands. You can have a copy FREE if you apply NOW to:
BRITISH INSTITUTE OF ENGINEERING TECHNOLOGY (N.E.) LTD.
Dept. P.E.10 Sansur Bldg., Jaffa Road, Jerusalem.

V VISIT SPINNEY'S RESTAURANT V
JAFFA ROAD, HAIFA — MAIN ROAD, GAZA
FIRST CLASS CUISINE EXCELLENT. SERVICE

Classifieds
Everyone's Column
Effective and Economical

LATE Edition

THE PALESTINE POST

JERUSALEM
Wednesday, May 2, 1945

PRICE: 15 MILS
VOL. XX. No. 5781

The suit with the beautiful fit — as cut by ROSENBLUM ladies & mens garments 44 HERZL ST., HAIFA

HITLER'S DEATH ANNOUNCED

DOENITZ SUCCEEDS FUEHRER: SAYS GERMANS WILL FIGHT ON

LONDON, Tuesday (R.) — Hitler died this afternoon, and the former C.-in-C. of the German Navy, Admiral Doenitz, is his successor, the German radio announced tonight. Doenitz, speaking over the radio later, said: "The Fuehrer has fallen at his command post. My first task is to save the German people from destruction by Bolshevism. If only for this task the struggle will continue."

The announcement which preceded the proclamation by Doenitz said: "It is reported from the Fuehrer's headquarters that our Fuehrer, Adolf Hitler, has fallen this afternoon at his command post in the Reich Chancellery fighting to the last breath against Bolshevism and for Germany. On April 30 the Fuehrer appointed Grand Admiral Doenitz as his successor. Our new Fuehrer will speak to the German people." Then followed a talk by Doenitz.

Column One

By David Courtney

SAN Francisco is full of problems and vexations already and there is a feeling among the small countries that they are in danger of being rushed. It looks as if the Big Three had left too many preliminaries undone before they set out for California. It is also felt that security decisions cannot be taken on the basis of a Europe much of which, at the moment, is little more than a charred jigsaw puzzle. It would probably be as well if the delegates went home to deal with unconditional surrender on their own ground and came back again when things have sorted themselves out a bit. The brief sojourn in San Francisco will have done them no harm; it has at least raised the kind of preliminary problem, like Poland and Argentina, which the Great Powers ought to be able to solve among themselves. A series of disputes which create "bloks" (with ideological foundation) around the major contestants, as in the case of Argentina, will do post-war security no good. The idea of San Francisco was more valuable than the fact. For the fact, more and better preparation is essential.

WHATEVER may be happening in Denmark, there is still a lot of fighting inside Germany. With the red flag of the Soviets hoisted above the Reichstag, Berlin can be regarded as captured. The "death battalions of wild-eyed women" resisting fanatically at the order of Goebbels are hardly likely to delay the end It would be interesting to know what Russia proposes to do when Berlin is definitely in her hand. Having settled the political affairs of Vienna to her own satisfaction, will she be as hasty in Berlin? Military occupation will be more severe in Germany proper than in Austria. Germany, let us hope, for a long time to come will not be given the opportunity to answer back.

With the Fifth Army at the Southern approaches to the Brenner and the Seventh coming down on Innsbruck at the northern end, Vietinghof cannot hope to get more than a handful of his men through the Alps. The speed and completeness of the Italian move are prime factors in Himmler's despairing conclusion that the game is up; and we should never forget it. Meanwhile the Eighth is on its way to Trieste, where Yugoslav troops are now battling for control of the port. The Romans are choosing this moment to shout slogans reminiscent of d'Annuzio. The Yugoslavs, in possession, don't need to shout slogans Anyway, the grim fact remains, for all the horrid details of Mussolini's end, that Italy is an ex-enemy State; and the Yugoslavs have a big score up against her.

ONE of today's most striking news items is that the heavy bomber offensive in Europe has come to an end. The targets have been overrun. R.A.F. Bomber Command finished off its long and obdurate campaign last week with a load of 12,000-pound bombs on Berchtesgaden. That was the end of four years' terrific effort to break, by strategic air operations, the power of the enemy to wage war. The success of the campaign has been obvious in the rapid diminution of the Wehrmacht's resources, until today it has neither oil nor adequate arms; and in the slowing down of communications to a point where the High Command could no longer maintain cohesion or prevent those disastrous encirclements in the East and in the West, which robbed it of whole armies at a time.

THE end of the heavy bomber offensive in Europe is no pleasant omen for the Japanese. The Fourteenth Army in Burma, and the American Fleet in the Pacific, can do with the long-range heavy bombers from European airfields. The miraculous advance of the Fourteenth from the Indian frontier to within a few miles of Rangoon naturally has not had the bomber support given to our armies in the West: and when such support comes it is hard to see how the Japanese can avoid a disintegration very like that of the German armies. It is the effect on Japan proper, however, that should provide the drama. The Americans in the Pacific have seen to it that airfields within range are availabe. The transfer of the U.S. and British fleets from the West to the East will help to spell for Japan a doom as great as that of her European partner's. Will Japan, for all her spirit of hara-kiri, submit to the obvious doom or to the equally obvious warning?

Jerusalem, May 2, 1945

HELPING HOLLAND

LONDON, Tuesday (UP).— About 400 Eighth Air Force Fortresses today dropped food supplies to the Dutch in the vicinity of The Hague and Rotterdom.

NO OFFER FROM HIMMLER

STOCKHOLM, Tuesday (R) — During his latest visit to Copenhagen, from which he returned today, Count Bernadotte met not Himmler, but Werner Best, the German Minister to Denmark. He was not given any surrender terms.

Count Bernadotte told a press conference today: "I have not seen Himmler during my last visit to Germany and Denmark, and I have not forwarded any message from Himmler or any other authoritative German to the Allies."

The Swedish radio, shortly after denying reports of the German evacuation of Denmark, reported in a broadcast in Danish the "partial withdrawal" of German troops from the towns of Zealand — the island between the mainland and Sweden on which Copenhagen stands, while Free Danish underground sources at Malmoe report that the Germans have begun to move out of Copenhagen today with the apparent intention of abandoning Denmark.

Last night it was expected that the withdrawal from the towns — which would also include the capital — would be continued during the night.

So far it is only the military who are withdrawing from the towns. German police are still functioning. A Danish spokesman in a broadcast from Sweden said: "German forces are still remaining ready for action in Denmark. Avoid provocation and quietly await immediate developments."

Nazi Day of Atonement

LONDON, Tuesday (R). — Lord Vansittart, who advocates a "hard peace" for Germany, wants January 30, the anniversary of Hitler's accession to power, to be observed in Germany as a day of national repentence or atonement.

He made this proposal today in the Lords debate on German atrocity-guilt in which Lord Denham urged that the whole German race must be made to feel remorse for their responsibility for Nazi crimes.

PALESTINE POLICY ATTACKED

WASHINGTON, Tuesday—England had forfeited the trust placed in her by the League of Nations in administering the Palestine Mandate, and Palestine should be placed under international trusteeship, wrote Representative Emanuel Celler (Democrat, New York) to the American delegation at the San Francisco Conference.

Mr. Celler stated that England was no longer entitled to be the sole administrator of Palestine, adding:

An international trusteeship instead of a sole trusteeship of Mandates has awakened widespread interest. Such an international trusteeship of Mandated territories applies most significantly to Palestine.

Another strong attack on British policy in Palestine was launched at yesterday's mass Zionist demonstration by Senator Robert F. Wagner at the Lewisohn Stadium in New York (as reported briefly).

"The power which is preventing the development of a Jewish Commonwealth in Palestine is the British power," he said. "Britain's policies in Palestine are the tragic survival of the disease of appeasement."

Urging that the nations of the world should "put their hand to the neglected task of constituting a Jewish Commonwealth in Palestine," Senator Wagner added:

"I say to our British friends and allies, — You have not fulfilled your obligations to Palestine. The American people believe that it is high time that you redeem your pledge."

Concluding, he said: "While the primary responsibility for the development of Palestine is British, I have never forgotten that America has a responsibility as well to make known its position on the Palestine question."

Wise-Silver Reunion

An outstanding feature at the demonstration was the tremendous reception given to Rabbi Abba Hillel Silver when he was introduced by Dr. Stephen Wise. The great gathering rose spontaneously and sang "Hatikvah." It is thought that this appearance marked Rabbi Silver's return to the American Zionist Emergency Committee.

(R., UP & JWN)

Resistance Broken Everywhere

LONDON, Tuesday.— With the Soviet flag flying from the Reichstag building in Berlin, and Marshal Stalin declaring in his May Day Order to the fighters and workers of Russia, "The collapse of Hitlerite Germany is a matter of the very near future," a Hamburg radio speaker announced today:

The war will probably last only a few more hours.

The latest cables show that there is still stubborn resistance in fragments of the Reich particularly at the northern edge around the ports. But in the south, Munich has been captured undefended and American troops could find nobody in authority.

From the main Elbe bridgehead, British Second Army patrols have thrust out 10 miles and the bridgehead area is seven miles wide and six miles deep. The new bridgehead achieved yesterday 10 miles west of Lauenburg by the U.S. Airborne Division is now two miles wide by two deep. Field Marshal Montgomery's armies are moving in for the kill and the big ports of Hamburg, Bremerhaven, Wilhelmshaven and Emden are entering their last days of life.

Red Army troops are sweeping across the northern plain and have taken important towns west of Stettin, including Neustrelitz in the lake country, and Geifswald, a Baltic port. Marshal Rokossovsky is now 50 miles from Rostock.

In Czechoslovakia, Russian forces took the arms centre of Moravska Ostrava, a key point in the German defence system.

In the south, United States tanks are attacking along a 20-miles' stretch of the Austrian border between the Danube and the Swiss frontier. The American Seventh Army is reported 18 miles north of Innsbruck.

French and Third Army troops and armour have clambered into the northern fringes of the redoubt without meeting the hysterical opposition which would be expected if the Bavarian Alps were planned to be the scene of a "do or die" last stand. Difficult country, road blocks and demolitions are proving more of an obstacle than the Germans, leading to the belief that the plan to establish a Bavarian fortress has been nipped in the bud by the swift and daring Allied sweep.

LEAVING THE NORTH

LONDON, Tuesday (R). — The "Evening News" understands that the Count Bernadotte's negotiations referred to the question of withdrawal from Denmark and the surrender of 300,000 German fighting men in Norway and that the Swedish Government, in agreement with the Allies, is ready to send Swedish armed forces to supervise the German capitulation.

Certain German forces in Norway are understood already to have approached the Norwegian Government in London through a Swedish intermediary regarding their capitulation.

German Naval Last-Ditchers

By PAUL SCOTT RANKINE
Reuters Correspondent

WITH THE CANADIANS, Tuesday. — The German Navy has refused to take any part in Himmler's peace negotiations, according to unconfirmed rumours filtering from Western Holland and N.W. Germany.

The centres of Germany's naval establishments, such as the E-boat bases at Ijmuiden in Holland and the submarine bases like Wilhelmshaven, do not want to yield. German naval officers who want to fight to the end claim they have enough supplies to carry on for another two months from Denmark and Norway if necessary.

2,500,000 LIBERATED

S.H.A.E.F. Tuesday (R). — More than 2,500,000 refugees, displaced persons and liberated prisoners of war have been recovered since the Allied entry into Germany.

The Russians constitute 40% of its total, the French 25%, the Poles 15%, the Belgians 4 per cent, the Dutch 4%, the Italians 8%. The rest are largely, Czechs and Yugoslavs.

It is estimated that between three and six million displaced persons remain in German hands.

TRUSTEESHIP TALKS BEGIN

SAN FRANCISCO, Tuesday. — The Big Five have begun their long-awaited consultations on the problem of international trusteeships.

The first meeting was held last night, and another is scheduled for tomorrow night. The discussions are on the "technical level" but delegates from each nation have been invited. Commander Harold Stassen heads the U.S. delegation on discussions of the question.

The U.S. group last night presented the American plan for trusteeships to Russia, Britain , France and China. It is understood that the plan is designed to provide for control of territory captured from the Japanese in the Pacific.

None of the other Powers has so for presented any trusteeship plan to take care of territory taken from the enemy or territory placed under the League of Nations after the last. They expect, however, to have a lot to say about the U.S. plan at the next meeting.

ARABS SEEK PLACES ON REGIONAL COUNCIL

By FAY BICK,
Palcor Correspondent

SAN FRANCISCO, Tuesday. — Arab delegations at the United Nations Conference here are seeking places not only on the International Trusteeships Commission, but also on the Regional Council likely to be set up in Mandated areas.

The object of the Regional Council is to provide an instrument for consultation among Powers with interests in a given area, and with the Mandatory Power entrusted with the actual administration of that area.

NIGHT LIKE DAY IN BURNING BERLIN

ROCKETS AND FLAMES LIGHT UP DESTRUCTION

By DUNCAN HOOPER,
Reuters Special Correspondent

MOSCOW, Tuesday. — Katushas, rockets and flames from fires blazing in the city make the nights like day in Berlin. With the main sections of Berlin in the hands of the Red Army, the struggle through the streets of the Capital has become a mopping up battle with every hour speeding the complete annihilation of the remnants of the German garrison.

The roar of battle is still resounding through the central streets of the city, as the Red Army storms them. The German defence is disorganized and broken and its fire everywhere is being smothered by the overwhelming concentrations of Soviet artillery and small arms.

German transport planes are attempting to break through to the central area of Berlin to parachute supplies to the defending forces, but few have succeeded.

The Germans are still fighting on like automatons. White flags, and then red flags are going up over the city each time Russian troops approach buildings. The final stage of this greatest of all street battles is marked by such destruction as few cities have endured since the days of Pompeii. It is becoming simpler to pick out the relatively undamaged buildings rather than those which are wrecked.

So far the Red Army does not appear to have reached the German Headquarters, but its location is believed to be known, and every effort will be made to secure any German war leaders remaining in the capital when the last shots are fired.

The Berlin battle has developed into a gigantic mopping-up operation. The defenders are disorganized and broken, although some Germans still fight on fanatically. Volkssturm units are laying down their arms in increasing numbers and sometimes lining whole streets with white surrender flags. Some S.S. battalions, however, have made suicide pacts to go down with the buildings they are defending.

1918—1945

END OF A MYTH

By a Staff Correspondent

Hitler's death marks the end of an epoch and, for all Doenitz' ranting about a last-ditch fight, the end of German resistance. It does not matter that the "Fuehrer" in all probability did not die a soldier's death in Berlin but a gangster's death in some Gestapo cellar. Even if it should turn out that he was not despatched by Himmler's gangsters but spirited away, it would not matter. For the Germans, and the world, he is dead. And that means that his followers have been released from their obligation to fight on. Himmler and Doenitz — the German Badoglio — can now capitulate if they choose.

Hitler had to die when the Third Reich died. If he refused to die he had to be killed. For Hitler had declared that he would never surrender, and surrender has become inevitable. Therefore Hitler died or was despatched, and Doenitz, Admiral of the Fleet and a "respectable" German nationalist, steps forward to declare that he is only fighting against "Bolshevism," while Himmler remains silent and probably organizes his underground. That is the political meaning of the announcement that Hitler is dead.

But Hitler's death is more than the formal dissolution of the alliance between the German Army, which fought this war, and the Nazi Party, which prepared it and is already preparing the next one. It is the final apotheosis of the Hitler myth. The pervert from the slums of Vienna who covered Germany with filth before drenching Europe in blood is destined by the Nazi propagandists to become their biggest asset after his death. His "heroic" death in Berlin is his last and biggest lie, uttered from the grave. It is also his most dangerous lie.

Full Circle

At the very end, Hitler returns to his beginnings. He began as a slum boy in Vienna who hated his socialist fellow-workers. He started his political career in Vienna as a spy set to ferret out ex-soldiers holding radical views. He rose by exploiting the reaction against the Republic and the Peace. He came to power by claiming to deliver Germany from a "Communist danger" which never existed until he created the myth that every anti-Nazi must be a Communist. He won power for Germany by proclaiming himself the bulwark against Bolshevism. He reached the high point of his career when, with all Europe at his feet and the reactionaries hailing him as their saviour, he attacked Russia. Now that the Red Army has hoisted the Red Flag over the flaming ruins of Berlin, he repeats from the grave that his mission consists in defending Germany against the "Red Peril." Having with his own hands torn down every bulwark against the flood, he proclaims himself, or is proclaimed by his lieutenants, the dyke-builder of Europe.

The arch-nihilist who planned to erect a slave state on the ruins of European civilization is dead. His dictatorship has lasted 12 years. For six year he prepared war, then for six years he waged it until every corner of Europe had been turned into a slaughter-house. In the final phase he brought the war to Germany where it had started and thus fulfilled his destiny and that of the deluded nation which followed him into the abyss.

HORTHY IN "PROTECTIVE CUSTODY"

S.H.A.E.F., Tuesday (R). — The former Regent of Hungary, Admiral Nicholas Horthy, and his family have been taken into protective custody by troops of the U. S. Seventh Army, it was announced today.

They were found in a castle at Weilheim, in Bavaria.

RED PERIL STILL THE KEYNOTE

LONDON, Tuesday (R). — "The Fuehrer has appointed me as his successor," said Doenitz, in his broadcast tonight. "Fully conscious of the responsibility I take over the leadership of the German people at this fateful hour. It is my first task to save the German people from destruction by the Bolshevists and it is only to achieve this that the fight continues.

"As long as the British and Americans hamper us on reaching this end we shall fight and defend ourselves against them as well. Britain and America do not fight for the interests of their own people but for the spreading of Bolshevism.

"I shall do my utmost to make life bearable for our brave men, women and children. To achieve all this I need your help. Trust me. Keep order and discipline in town and the countryside. Everybody must do his duty. Only thus we shall be able to alleviate the sufferings which the future will bring to each of us and avoid collapse."

Twilight

The announcement of Hitler's death was preceded by the playing of solemn Wagnerian music including the "Twilight of the Gods." Then came "Achtung: in a few minutes you will hear a serious and important message to the German people. We are now going to play the slow movement of Bruckner's seventh symphony." Finally came the report of Hitler's death. At this time the Southern German radio network went on broadcasting light music.

Where is Goering?

In the event of his death, Hitler, on the historic date of September 1, 1939, before leaving Berlin for an "undisclosed destination"—the Polish front—appointed Goering as his successor. If Goering was not available, Hess was to have succeeded Admiral Doenitz is the man who launched the U-boat warfare against the Allied Atlantic lifeline.

The last German reference to Hitler was in today's German communique which said: "In the heart of Berlin the gallant garrison gathered round the Fuehrer and herded together in a very narrow space is defending itself heroically."

Count Bernadotte today said in Stockholm he was sure Hitler was in Berlin, but whether he was dead or alive he did not know. Himmler is said to have told him that Hitler was dying of cerebral haemorrhage, while Dittmar told his captors on Wednesday that Hitler refused to leave Berlin and would die there.

Duce Buried in 'Potter's Field'

By JAMES ROPER,
U.P. Correspondent

MILAN, Tuesday. — Benito Mussolini, Clara Petacci and Achille Starace were secretly buried in unmarked graves in the "Potter's Field" in Milan's Maggiore cemetery at 6.15 yesterday evening.

The only witnesses were 10 members of the cemetery staff, and the exact locations are being kept secret in order to prevent the mob from exhuming the remains. Officials also filled several empty graves to thwart possible attempts of this kind.

It is now known that the partisans placed Mussolini and his mistress in the bedroom of a peasant's house, where they stayed 14 hours, after which they were taken out and stood against a wall. When the executioner announced the death sentence, Clara Petacci threw her arms around Mussolini. They were separated and then killed by several shots. Mussolini slumped when shot through the chest, and the executioner gave him the coup de grace by shots through the head. His brain has taken from the body for study by psychiatrists and criminologists.

111,000 LIBERATED

MUNICH, Tuesday. — Seven high-ranking Russian officers were freed when Third Army tanks burst into the great "United Nations" prison camp at Moosburg on the banks of the Isar river north of Munich and freed 111,000 war prisoners.

MOLOTOV WILL GO HOME

CONFERENCE TO CARRY ON

By PAUL SCOTT RANKINE,
Reuters Correspondent

SAN FRANCISCO, Tuesday — The Soviet Foreign Commissar, M. Molotov, informed Mr. Stettinius, Mr. Eden and Mr. Soong at a meeting late last night that he would like to return to Moscow at the end of this week or the beginning of next week in view of the war situation, I am authoritatively informed today.

It is understood that the Soviet delegation will continue to use its full rights and privileges as a sponsoring nation and will act on direct instructions from Moscow after M. Molotov's departure. M. Molotov stated that he would stay until the main problems of the conference had been settled but he hoped they would be settled by the beginning of next week.

Mr. Eden is understood to be planning to stay here for the three or four weeks which he originally fixed for his visit, unless some totally unlooked-for situation arises, while Mr. Stettinius is expected to stay for the duration of the conference.

Informed quarters express themselves satisfied with the progress made today and the Big Four are reported to be in an optimistic mood regarding the speed with which matters are proceeding.

Argentina Invited

In a scene of extraordinary emotion, the United Nations today accepted Argentina as a member of the World Security Conference.

It was an open defeat for the Soviet Foreign Commissar, M. Molotov, and in the final vote, which was an exciting climax to a debate of intense fervour, only three delegates voted with Russia— Czechoslovakia, Greece and Yugoslavia. Immediately after the vote had been taken, M. Molotov left the theatre where the conference is taking place.

Answering a request from the president of the session — the British Foreign Secretary, Mr. Eden—whether there were "any observations" on the Steering Committee's proposal that the Argentine be immediately admitted to the conference, M. Molotov, speaking through an interpreter, declared that Argentina's admission to the conference should be postponed for a few days.

Poland's Right

M. Molotov added that several Latin-American countries thought the situation in Argentina had changed for the better but "I think our delegation should be given time to be shown that the situation has changed. I think that will take some time."

Referring to Poland's right to be present at the conference, M. Molotov affirmed that it was well known that Poland had been one of the most active participants on the side of the Allies. He recalled that the Poles made immense sacrifices and added:

"We must not forget that, and if we invite Argentina, which helped the enemy throughout, and do not invite the Polish Provisional Government, we will prejudice the prestige of this conference."

Giving a possible hint that a Polish solution might be produced if the Argentine matter were delayed, the Soviet Foreign Commissar said:

"We should at any rate provide a seat for Poland at this conference no later than we do with regard to Argentina.

"It might perhaps be said that Argentina committed certain sins and they may be forgotten. May be that is true but I wonder why we should forget the sins committed by Argentina and, on the other hand, forget the services rendered by Poland to the common cause."

He noted that India and the Philippines were participating in the conference, although not fully independent, and that Russia had not objected, adding:

"Up to now all invitations for this conference were accepted unanimously by the four sponsor governments. This we consider a very good rule and should not like to depart from it."

Support for Argentina was also given by the leader of the Peruvian delegation, Manuel Gallagher, and Carlos Alberto Liaras, chief of the Colombian delegation. M. Henri Spaak, the Belgian Foreign Minister, spoke in favour of M. Molotov's protest.

War Flashes

The Rome radio has broadcast a proclamation by Marshal Graziani, now in Allied hands, calling to the trapped Ligurian Army of three German and three Fascist-Italian divisions to lay down their arms.

General Patton's tanks have pushed 25 miles south today to reach the river Inn on the Austrian-German frontier near Braunau, Hitler's birthplace.

NAZIS FLED FROM MUNICH

The American Seventh Army completed the occupation of Munich last night against surprisingly light resistance.

Munich was so relieved that the war was over for it that people greeted the Seventh Army with cheers. The Nazi leaders had long since fled, and only a few small fry remained in the Party buildings around the famous Beer Cellar where Hitler and his henchmen plotted the "putsch" which brought them control of Germany.

V — A WIDE SELECTION OF LADIES DRESSES AT SPINNEY'S OUTFITTING DEPARTMENTS — V
JAFFA ROAD, HAIFA. MAMILLAH ROAD, JERUSALEM. KING GEORGE AVE., JAFFA.

Classifieds

Everyone's Column
Effective and Economical

LATE Edition

THE PALESTINE POST

JERUSALEM TUESDAY, MAY 8, 1945.

PRICE: 15 MILS

VOL. XX, No. 5786

YOUR MARINE AND OVERLAND TRANSPORTS INSURED THROUGH

BARNETT Bros. & BORCHARD Ltd.

HAIFA — TEL AVIV — JERUSALEM

EUROPEAN WAR OVER; VICTORY DAY TODAY

Today will be treated as Victory-in-Europe Day, it is officially announced. Mr. Churchill will broadcast at 1 p.m. G.M.T. (4 p.m. Palestine Time), while His Majesty the King will broadcast to the peoples of the British Empire and Commonwealth at 7 p.m. G.M.T. (10 p.m. Palestine Time). Parliament will meet at the usual time, when Mr. Churchill is expected to announce the end of the European War to the House. The six years' war in Europe has ended with the greatest surrender in history. It is estimated that about 10 million Germans are prisoners.

Column One

By David Courtney

THE guns have stopped firing. It is peace in Europe. It is not how many of us expected peace to come; the war was not how many of us expected it to be; and what does it matter, how peace comes, if it is surely and for good? That is why it is not as many of us expected: none of us could have expected the insensate rulers of Germany to fight on, long after the war had been lost, until their whole state and all its panoply of armed men and complex Government machinery, were shattered more completely than any war has ever shattered any nation. That has made peace sure enough; and whether it is for good is no affair of Germany's; it is our affair, and only if we fail is it not for good.

THERE is still grief over Europe; and still many tasks undone; but no man will grudge us two days' rejoicing. This is not a nation's victory, but a people's. When, at the beginning of the war, its issues were clarified, leading observers pointed out that what was happening was a great civil war. That was true. It was a rising of the people of all free nations to defend their liberty; but above all to defend the very ideas of liberty. The victory, therefore, is not the victory of this or that nation or group of nations; but of all people's peoples, including the German people. The German people are humiliated now. Their pride and their power have been ground in the European dust; but the happiness and security of their future generations has been won by the victory signalized today.

THERE was a time in 1940 when more than half the world was ready to deny this world. France had fallen, Britain stood alone; and between her and conquest was little more than the will of her people. That was when Britain utterly alone. She had steadfast allies who drew strength from her unarmed strength; and in Greece, Norway, Poland, Holland, Belgium, France, people recognized their comrades in the people of Britain and drew close to her in a new found unity of defiance to the thing that threatened the good that was common to them all. From the fall of France to Pearl Harbour, Britain's allies were the partisans of Europe: God grant that we may be kept in peace. 1940 and 1941 bore a marvellous brotherhood; and if we keep it the world will be the better for it.

WE glorify today because the guns have ceased, and fear of death has ended. We glorify it because no more shall the nights be hideous and the days a heart-breaking anxiety. But among these blessings, so near to each man's heart and body, the greater glory rises: we have had the courage to strike for an ideal, and that the ideal of the common man. We have had the courage to offer all we had in its defence; and have fought for what we knew or felt in our bones, to be the good — not our good only but all men's good. That is the great glory we celebrate today. Let us not in our rejoicing, in our relief and our nostalgic longings, forget that greater glory. It will be easy to forget it. It will be easy to tarnish the noblest trophy ever won by men's blood and sweat, with the little strife of minor ambitions; the conflict of group with group, community with community, impelled only by prejudice and the exclusive conceptions of men who refuse to accept their comradeship with all peoples.

Jerusalem, May 8, 1945.

More P.W.'s than Allied Troops

LONDON, Monday. — With 10 million Germans in captivity the Western Allies will hold more of them than they have troops in the field.

They may remain prisoners for years under the rules of war, prisoners are not held until the signing of the peace which is not anticipated for a considerable time. Some of them, however, will be released early for work on land to ease the economic difficulties in Central Europe.

The Russians have again said that German prisoners should be used to make good some of the damage they have done. It is believed that the Russian view is that camps should be combed for suitable men for this work but that there should be no general conscription of German labour.

ITALIAN DEMOCRACY IN ACTION

ROME, Monday (UP). — After two days of conferences of the North of Italy and members of the Liberation Committee from the of the present Government, an authoritative Italian spokesman said today that "a shake-up of the Bonomi Government can be expected in two or three days."

Among the demands put forward by the Northerners are:

(1) Confiscation of profits accumulated under Fascism;

(2) Agrarian reforms to break up big landed estates;

(3) The abandonment of Nationalism — both Fascist and pre-Fascist — in foreign policy.

It is also learned that some members of the Northern delegation wanted legislation to enable factories taken over by the partisans to be nationalized. They also made it clear that they wanted new men in the Government capable of understanding and enforcing throughout the country a whole programme of democratic legislation worked out in the North which is much more advanced than the laws in force in the South.

While it appears that the Bonomi Coalition will be able to survive all these demands, in the compromise may break down over the question of the Monarchy against which Leftist attacks have been increasing.

DUCE TRIED TO FORM REPUBLICAN FRONT

By Cecil Sprigge

MILAN, Monday. — I learn on good authority that Mussolini on April 24 tried to negotiate with the Milan Socialist Party with a view to fusing the Fascist Republicans with them. He visited an old Socialist, Signor Silvestri, and told him that he (Mussolini) was a Republican and had prepared the forming of a common front between the Socialists, the Action Party and the Republican fascists against the Royalists. Silvestri sent Mussolini's proposals to his Party. This incident helped the liberation movement to decide that the time for insurrection was ripe.

FRENCH TREATIES WITH LEVANT STATES

PARIS, Monday. — General de Gaulle has given instructions to the French envoy in the Levant States, General Etienne Beynet, to conclude treaties with the Syrian and Lebanese Governments for the determination of their independence, it is announced.

The treaties will safeguard French cultural, economic and strategic interests in these countries.

BERLIN IN RUINS, CITIZENS STARVE

MOSCOW, Monday. — The Soviet Command in Berlin has ordered all members of Nazi organizations to present themselves within three days. The order specifically mentions all members of the Gestapo, the S.S., the S.A., the Nazi Party and all affiliated organizations. At the same time, all these organizations have been declared dissolved and illegal.

Anyone disregarding these orders, will be liable to the death penalty.

The Red Army in Berlin is living under field conditions. Very little of the city remains in a position to provide shelter for either residential or office quarters. The few buildings still remaining fit have been requisitioned by the Soviet military authorities. The civilian population is living among the ruins and in semi-collapsed caves. The Soviet authorities provide them with no food whatsoever, and the Berliners are, for the time being, existing upon the meat of dead horses. On the other hand, the former foreign slave workers, particularly the Russians, Poles, Czechs, and Yugoslavs, are using Red Army facilities for food and shelter, and are expecting to be repatriated.

Search for Hitler

The search for the body of Hitler is going on throughout the ruins, but with no results. Scores of thousands of people are said to be employed in these searches, while great numbers of captured German officers and men, and German civilians, are being interrogated by the Soviet military authorities.

It is understood that for the time being, no survey is being undertaken in connection with the ruins in Berlin, nor is it considered likely that the ruins will be rebuilt in the immediate future. It seems doubtful whether the Inter-Allied Control Commission will be able to be in Berlin in view of the complete destruction.

Soviet military sources state that complete order and security now prevail in Berlin, the Soviet State Security forces having eliminated the last possibility of incidents.

REFORMS IN POLAND

MOSCOW, Monday (R). — The head of the Polish Provisional Government, M. Osabka-Morawski, has told the Polish National Home Council that reforms of the greatest importance have been postponed until the calling of a diet formed on the basis of free elections.

Replying to criticism that the Government has employed officials of the old Polish State, M. Morawski said that the results had been satisfactory.

GOEBBELS "FOUND"
MOSCOW, Monday (R). — Unconfirmed reports reaching Moscow today state that the bodies of Goebbels and his family have been found in an air raid shelter near the Reichstag in Berlin.

NO POLISH SOLUTION IN SIGHT

By Harrison Salisbury
U.P. Correspondent

SAN FRANCISCO, Monday. — Official British circles here are convinced that no solution of the Polish problem can be worked out at the conference, as no further reply has come from Marshal Stalin in response to the requests of Mr. Stettinius and Mr. Eden for further details on the seizure of 16 Polish underground leaders.

Neither the British nor the Americans, however, regarded the issue as paramount to the success of the conference. However, the Polish question continues to hold top-place in discussions. The British feel that even if Marshal Stalin replies eventually to the inquiries on the fate of the missing Poles there is little or no prospect of solving the issue here. It will have to go to Marshal Stalin.

The U.S. delegates are more concerned over Latin-American dissatisfaction with the identical amendments to regional amendments which the United States, Britain and China have submitted. The Latin-Americans fear arrangements which would contravene the Monroe Doctrine which has been the backbone of Western Hemisphere policies since 1823.

Generally, the work of the Conference is progressing. Twenty-two amendments submitted by the Big Four will be sent to the Steering Committee today for allocation to various committees for processing before coming up before the conference sessions for adoption. The Russians have not made known whether they will support the United States, British and Chinese amendments on trusteeships and regional arrangements.

TRUSTEESHIP PLANS DIFFER

SAN FRANCISCO, Monday. — The policy of the "Big Four" with regard to trusteeships is being mapped out behind the doors of Mr. Stettinius' Fairmont Hotel apartment, while Jewish Agency leaders are scrutinizing the American and British plans.

From the British draft, it is obvious that Britain favours the plan whereby she would remain the sole trustee for Palestine, while the American draft indicates that the United States would favour a mixed trusteeship.

Other important differences between the British and the American plans are that American advocates requiring a Trustee to report annually to the General Assembly of the proposed world organization, while the British urge that Trustees should report annually to the Social-Economic Council of the Organization on social and economic affairs only, thus absolving it from a report on political affairs in territories such as Palestine.

From the British draft, it is obvious that Britain favours the plan whereby she would remain the sole trustee for Palestine, while the American draft indicates that the United States would favour a mixed trusteeship.

Other important differences between the British and the American plans are that American advocates requiring a Trustee to report annually to the General Assembly of the proposed world organization, while the British urge that Trustees should report annually to the Social-Economic Council of the Organization on social and economic affairs only, thus absolving it from a report on political affairs in territories such as Palestine.

The most striking difference, however, is that the British always discuss "territorial trusteeships" while the Americans speak of "international trusteeships." Thus, if the British plan is accepted, Palestine will have no international trusteeship. Both plans provide that trusteeship arrangements for areas must be agreed upon by the states concerned. Thus Britain must agree to any change in Palestine's status. The American plan provides also that not all mandated territories shall necessarily be placed under trusteeships.

The American Jewish Committee announced that it had written to Mr. Stettinius supporting the demands of the American Jewish Conference that nothing should be done to prejudice present Jewish rights in regard to Palestine and the right of Jews to immigrate to Palestine. — PTA

HOW THE BIG NEWS WAS RECEIVED

The news awaited for many days, Nazi Germany's acknowledgment of defeat, was at first soberly received in Palestine, both by civilians and servicemen yesterday.

Excitement gathered after the "extras" — including The Palestine Post — were rushed out into the streets in the evening and people crowded around kiosks and hoardings, really to make sure.

Government and Army authorities held special celebration, waiting for confirmation from London, but shops and offices and private houses hung out their flags.

Children too considered the news official enough, and walked through the streets waving the Union Jack, Stars and Stripes, the Russian flag and Zionist colours, and in no time at all there were queues wherever flags were being sold. In Jerusalem outside the Y.M.C.A. loudspeakers were set up late in the afternoon for the transmission of the speeches by His Majesty the King and the Prime Minister today.

Towards evening Jerusalem roads seemed to turn to Zion Circus where masses of people gathered about the traffic island. Around the lamp-post youngsters began enthusiastically dancing the "Hora," and the crowds burst into song. The first building to be lit-up was the Evelina de Rothschild School which had coloured bulbs festooned on its roof. Other buildings will be illuminated tonight.

There was a spontaneous demonstration in the interval at the Palestine Orchestra concert. Four flags — Union Jack, the Stars and Stripes, the Soviet flag and the Zionist colours—were unfurled from the balcony, and the Orchestra played the four national anthems while the audience sang with great warmth.

Young people had a riotous time in the Tel Aviv until late in the night, jamming the traffic in Magen David Square, climbing on cars which tried to pass and decorating them with flags which they carried.

There was a huge gathering in front of the Mograbi, where a parade was formed and hundreds of soldiers and civilians swung into step together and marched down Allenby Street, from which all traffic was diverted.

In the afternoon bulletins were broadcast at two minutes' intervals in Hebrew and English, at the News and Reading Centre of the Public Information Office. Matinee performances in cinemas were interrupted and the great news was announced to the audiences.

An unidentified R.A.F. Sergeant Major and a 17-year-old boy, Yehiel Mizrahi, were killed, and seven civilians and three soldiers injured, when a lorry only which V-day revellers had climbed overturned in Allenby Road, Tel Aviv, at 1 o'clock this morning.

(Today's Programme—Pg 3)

VICTORY WOODLAND

A "Victory Forest," for which the funds will be raised among Palestine Jewry during the two-day Victory celebrations, will be planted by the J.N.F. its National Committee announced.

Palestine Jews are urged to subscribe on V-day for trees, groves and woodlands in honour of Jewish soldiers, leaders of the democracies, and great generals who took an active part in vanquishing the common foe.

World Jewry should observe the Victory by a special Thanksgiving effort under the slogan of "Rescue, Reconstruction, Revival and Redemption" the Jewish National Fund and the Palestine Foundation Fund at Jerusalem have appealed.

DOENITZ SURRENDERS

GERMANS LAY DOWN ARMS

A Reuter cable from Rheims at 5.05 p.m. yesterday afternoon stated that the Allies had officially announced that Germany had surrendered unconditionally. The surrender took place at 2.41 a.m. (French time).

Colonel-General Gustav Jodl signed for Germany.

The surrender took place at a little red school house, which is General Eisenhower's headquarters.

New York Radio, in giving an account of the signing ceremony, said that General Bedell Smith, General Eisenhower's Chief of Staff, signed for the Supreme Allied Command and General Ivan Suslaparoff signed for Russia and General Francois Savez for France.

Nazis in Prague Carry On

LONDON, Monday (UP). — A few hours after the German Foreign Minister, von Krosigk, had broadcast to the German nation that Doenitz had ordered the unconditional surrender of all German troops, the German-controlled radio at Prague said that it involved only the troops fighting the Western Allies.

"In our area, the struggle will be continued until the Germans of the East have been saved and until our way back into the homeland is secured," the speaker said, adding:

"The report broadcast at midday today by the enemy station at Flensburg saying that the Reich Government has capitulated unconditionally to the Soviet Union as well does not correspond to the facts. It is clearly enemy propaganda intent on breaking our troops' will to resist. The Reich Government has only ceased to fight against the Western Powers."

Immediately afterwards the same announcement was repeated in Czech.

Yet at the same time the Prague radio reported that all fighting has ceased in the Silesian capital of Breslau, one of the German pockets deep behind the Allied lines, where the Russians have been waging street battles in the city for some weeks.

Earlier today the German controlled radio in Prague said "The rebellion in Prague renders it impossible to spare the city from destruction of war, although it had been declared a hospital city by the German state and military leaders."

BLUM, SCHUSCHNIGG RECOVERED

ROME, Monday (R). — The former French Prime Minister, M. Leon Blum; Pastor Niemoeller; Dr. Schuschnigg, the former Austrian Premier; Kallay, the former Hungarian Premier; and the former German Commander-in-Chief in Belgium and Northern France, General von Falkenhausen, are among prominent prisoners freed from a German prison camp.

GERMAN ANTI-NAZISM CALLED A FARCE

By Marcel Picard AFP War Correspondent

WITH THE U.S. FIRST ARMY, Monday.— I have just met the "Anti-Nazi Committee" of Weimar. I have seen poor folks, whom I wish to believe sincere; old fellows waiting for clients in their very clean offices.

The first thing they do is to show their certificate of internment in Buchenwald concentration camp or elsewhere. But if you look for the date you see that they left these camps in 1936 or '37. Then you ask yourself what they have been doing since.

It's quite simple: they were very well-behaved little children, trying their utmost not to set up a resistance movement. Now, on the strength of their internment they wave the banner of democracy with the tips of their fragile fingers.

I question them as to what they count on to remodel Germany. They are relying on the German youth, at present in uniform… that is to say, upon that youth which for years and years has been fed on Nazi doctrines. How are they to be re-educated? By those teachers who have remained unsullied — who are still Democrats. How many are there of these? Some 5 per cent perhaps.

They then show a list of Thuringian Nazi leaders, a fat little volume, and they complain of the excessive gentleness of the Americans. Oh! If they would only let their offices work.

What is their programme? A big, new, free Germany. How are they going to bring this about? They haven't the faintest idea. It will certainly not be the Anti-Nazi committees which are going to save Germany — nor are they going to.

I walked out of the office with a strengthened feeling that the Allies must take these matters into their own hands. For this very reason, a lengthy period of occupation is absolutely necessary. For the so-called Anti-Nazis are not sincere, and if by chance they are sincere, they are powerless.

Awaiting Signal

By Michael Ryerson, Reuters Correspondent

LONDON, Monday. — Urgent last-minute talks before Germany's surrender as announced today kept the radio lines humming between London, Moscow and Washington.

The exact moment at which Mr. Churchill goes into the Cabinet room at number 10, Downing Street, to declare over his private microphone that the war is ended was only announced this evening.

Although the war is over, there will be no official announcement of this until tomorrow afternoon. As Parliament will be sitting tomorrow, Mr. Churchill may make his announcement first in the House of Commons.

The delay in announcing V day was occasioned by the agreement reached between Mr. Churchill, President Truman and Marshal Stalin that the announcement, when it come, should be made simultaneously in London, Washington and Moscow.

The Cabinet met this morning and ever since there were comings and goings of Ministers in Whitehall. A large crowd formed at the end of Downing Street, and by six o'clock this evening, great pennants and flags had been strung across the face of many office and hotel buildings in many parts of London. In the fore-court of Buckingham Palace, workmen were busy putting into position batteries of powerful electric lamps which will floodlight the Palace building on V-night.

At street corners throughout central London, loudspeakers are already in place to relay to the public the announcement. Hundreds of men of the Metropolitan Police are standing by ready to deal with the huge crowds that are expected.

Much of London already has a peace-time appearance. Blast curtains are gone. The blackout has gone. Blast curtains and last disappearing from tubes and trams. Tube and subway stations are being cleared of shelters everywhere; workmen are clearing away sandbags.

The German Official Announcement

LONDON, Monday (R). — The German surrender was first officially announced today by the Flensburg radio which reported that Admiral Doenitz had ordered the unconditional surrender of all German fighting troops.

Speaking over the radio, the Foreign Minister, Schwerin von Krosigk, said:

"German men and women — The High Command of the armed forces has today, at the order of Grand Admiral Doenitz, declared the unconditional surrender of all fighting German troops.

"As the leading Minister of the Reich Government which the Admiral of the Fleet has appointed for dealing with the war tasks, I turn at this tragic moment of our history to the German nation. After heroic fight of almost six years of incomparable hardness, Germany has succumbed to the overwhelming power of her enemies.

"To continue the war would only mean senseless bloodshed and futile disintegration. The Government, which has a feeling of responsibility for the future of a nation, was compelled to admit the collapse of its physical and material forces and to demand of the enemy the cessation of hostilities.

Save the Remnant

"It was the noble task of the Admiral of the Fleet, and of the Government supporting him, after the terrible sacrifices which the war demanded to save in the last phase of the war the lives of the maximum number of fellow countrymen. That the war was not ended immediately, simultaneously in the West and the East, is to be explained by this reason alone.

"In this gravest hour of the German nation and its Reich we now stand in deep reverence before the dead of this war. Their sacrifices place the highest obligations on us. Our sympathy goes above all to the wounded and to bereaved, and to all on whom this struggle has inflicted blows

"No one must be under any illusions about the severity of the terms imposed on the German people by our enemies. We must now face our fate squarely and unquestioningly. Nobody can be in any doubt that the future will be difficult for each one of us and will exact sacrifices from us in every sphere of life. We must accept this burden and loyally by our obligations which we have undertaken But we must not despair and fall into mute resignation. Once again we must find the way through the dark future.

Plea for Unity

"From the collapse of the past let us preserve and save one thing—only in the ideas of the national community, which in the years of the war have found their highest expression in the spirit of comradeship at the front. Let us prove to the German nation, in this connection, in the readiness to help one another in all distress which has afflicted the homeland.

"In our nation justice shall be the supreme law and guiding principle. We must also recognize the law as the basis of all relations between nations. We must recognize it and respect it from inner conviction. Respect for treaties will be as sacred as the aim of our nation to belong to the European family of nations. We want to mobilize all human, moral and material forces in order to heal — dreadful wounds which the war has caused. Then we may hope: that the atmosphere of hatred which today surrounds Germany all over the world will give place to a spirit of reconciliation among the nations which; without world cannot recover.

"Only then may we hope we shall again receive the freedom without which no nation can lead a bearable and dignified existence. Let us devote to the future of our nation to meditation on the internal and best forces of the German spirit which has given the world lasting achievement and values. To our pride in the heroic struggle of our nation let us join the determination of belonging, as we do, to the world of Christian Western civilisation, to make to the honest work of peace a contribution which shall be worthy of the best traditions of our nation. May God not leave us in our efforts. May he bless our difficult task."

After the speech there was a silence of three minutes on the Flensburg radio.

KING AND PREMIER TO BROADCAST

LONDON, Monday (R). — In accordance with arrangements between the three Great Powers, an official announcement will be broadcast by the Prime Minister at 1.00 p.m. G.M.T. tomorrow, says an official statement, adding:

In view of this fact tomorrow, Tuesday, this day will be treated as V(ictory) Day and will be regarded as a holiday. The day following, Wednesday, May 9, will also be a holiday.

His Majesty the King will broadcast to the peoples of the British Empire and Commonwealth tomorrow at 7 p.m. G.M.T. Parliament will meet at the usual time tomorrow.

E. Fraser Wighton, Reuters Political Correspondent, writes: The preliminary instrument of surrender has been signed between the Germans and Allies, but the signing of the surrender instrument proper has yet to take place. The venue at this moment cannot be made public and the signatories on both sides are equally secret.

The preliminary instrument is, however, a monumental affair, running, I understand, to 15 pages and taking care of every contingency likely to arise out of the laying down of German arms. It gives directions for the formal handing over of the German Navy with its great fleet of U-boats and goes into considerable detail in dealing with the dispositions of the German armed forces as a whole

News Swept World

The news that the war was over was greeted with immense relief in the principal capitals of the world yesterday.

In New York, the streets were filled with happy crowds, while the flow of ticker tape from torn-up telegrams and forms was so thick that a brigade of street cleaners had to use water hoses to clear the streets of the paper deluge.

In London and Paris, the news of the German surrender brought crowds into the streets to buy extra editions of the newspapers, while in Rome the reaction was quieter, than elsewhere, due to the previous excitement over the liberation of Northern Italy and the death of Mussolini. The British and American troops, on the other hand, let themselves go to the full.

AFTER MIDNIGHT

Rhodes and Crete are reported to have been occupied by British and Greek forces.

Breslau has been captured, said Marshal Stalin in an Order of the Day last night. Over 40,000 prisoners were taken.

British troops have entered the Dutch city of Utrecht the entire population welcomed the Allies and arrested the chief Dutch Nazi, Anton Mussert. The German Command in Norway has given orders to surrender and the British Fleet has steamed into Oslo

Czech military quarters last night reported street fighting between German forces and Czech patriots in Prague. German aircraft bombed the districts held by patriots.

Classifieds
are always read
They More Than Pay

LATE Edition

THE PALESTINE POST

JERUSALEM
TUESDAY, AUGUST 7, 1945

PRICE: 15 MILS
VOL. XX No. 5863

ATIB NAVIGATION CO. LTD.
The
NATIONAL SHIPPING COMPANY

ATOMIC POWER TO HIT JAPAN

WASHINGTON, Monday.— The sensational disclosure that the "atomic bomb" is being used against Japan, with power equal to 20,000 tons of T.N.T. was made here today in a statement issued from the White House by President Truman. The President said that 15 hours earlier—some time on Sunday — an American aircraft had dropped one of the new bombs on Hiroshima, an important Japanese Army base. The bomb, which represents the basic energy of the universe, is 2,000 times more powerful than the giant high explosive bombs previously dropped from planes.

Column One
By David Courtney

THE Spanish Press is indignant. Poland celebrates the extension of its frontiers to the Oder-Neisse line and proclaims Generalissimo Stalin as its Godfather. The Italian Press speculates anxiously on the still unpublished Armistice terms; and the mighty Mr. Grew says there is no question of big credits to Britain; and the "News Chronicle" reveals a black market scandal in British involving the diversion of big American Army supplies. The Petain trial drags on; and Kramer, the Belsen criminal, has made a confession. The news from Europe this morning is along those unsatisfactory lines; it is the clouded window though which we look upon the scene. We are vaguely conscious of great and tragic deeds on the other side of the window.

WE are vaguely conscious of impending disaster to tens of millions of human beings; and of a flurry of ministers, generals and state officials bustling around at tasks only partially comprehended. And because we ourselves are only vaguely conscious of it all, we become disinclined to believe, in its existence. In short, slowly but inexorably, and perhaps unintelligently, after the fearful strain of war, public apathy grows up again. The public apathy that was as much responsible for 1939 as much responsible for non-intervention in Spain as M. Laval; as much responsible for Munich as Mr. Chamberlain; as much responsible for 1939 as Adolf Hitler. Whatever may be said for having any government to the appointed governors, experience has shown that without the constant pressure of informed public opinion, even the most representative of governments gradually and sometimes deliberately, become, like Marshal Petain, hard of hearing.

THE one sure safeguard against public apathy is a free press served by correspondents performing, usually with more forthrightness and less prejudice, for the general public the same kind of service which ministers and ambassadors are charged to perform for their respective governments. The Soviet concession at Potsdam, by which Allied correspondents are to be allowed to visit Soviet occupied territory, including the sponsored States of South-East Europe, is therefore important. How important, we shall only learn when the correspondents get to their posts, and the extent of the censorship imposed upon them by the local authorities is known. Since the end of the war in Europe, half the Continent has been under a complete blackout; a vast humanity and a congeries of States from the Baltic to the Black Sea are in complete isolation from the rest of the world; and what we see through darkness we see fearfully and with faint back from it to tell of monstrous things which, if the truth were really known, might be no more than the goblins of our imagination.

THE truth can only be known, and the darkness lightened, if the press — the plain, honest news-reporters, who are out to do a straight job of work and nothing more or less — is allowed in. Today's news is like than half the news. The indignation of the Spanish newspapers; the strikes in Trieste; the demonstrations in Warsaw — these items, and their like, leave us as ignorant of what is really happening in Spain, Venezia Giulio, Poland and the rest as we were at the start. Little more than that the great stultifier, public apathy, descends upon us once more. The atomic bomb which is to splinter the foundations of Japan — and is the only piece of real news this morning — in the long run is hardly less destructive.

DURING the course of the Pétain trial it has been said more than once that the Vichy Government got in touch with the British Government at various times and sought, among other things, a lessening of the B.B.C. campaign against the Marshal. The truth of this it is not my business to know; but it is a fact that the B.B.C., for some time waxed alternatively hot and cold in its treatment of Pétain. By the end 1941 it had made up its mind to attack him as little as possible. This was not due to Government pressure, but largely to a decision reached by a group of brilliant men directly responsible for the B.B.C. French transmission. Gillie, at one time Paris correspondent of the old "Morning Post," was at the head of the French transmissions — a queer, brooding, yet tempestuous and lovable genius. He believed the Marshal to be a doddering fool, and as such a menace to France and the Allies; but supported by his French staff and by members of General de Gaulle's entourage — he was convinced that Pétain, for all his stupidity and weakness, embodied in his character so much of the average Frenchman that to attack half France was to attack the villain, Pétain. Laval the tool. The trial will not have changed Gillie's views.

Jerusalem, August 7

BRITISH PIONEERED IN BOMB RESEARCH
ATTLEE ISSUES CHURCHILL'S STATEMENT

LONDON, Monday (R). — The Prime Minister, Mr. Attlee, in a statement from 10, Downing Street tonight, says: "The problems of the release of energy by atomic fission have been solved and an atomic bomb has been dropped on Japan by the U.S. Army Air Force.

"President Truman has described the nature and the vast implications of this new discovery. Some account is now required of the part which Britain played in this remarkable scientific advance which has now come to fruition.

"Before the change of Government, Mr. Churchill had prepared a statement which follows and I now issue it in the form in which he wrote it:

"By the year 1939, it had become widely recognized among the scientists of many nations that the release of energy by Atomic Fission was a possibility. The problems which remained to be solved before this possibility could be turned into practical achievement were however manifold and immense; and few scientists would at that time have ventured to predict that the atomic bomb would be ready for use by 1945.

"Scientists Mobilized

"Nevertheless, the potentialities of the project were so great that His Majesty's Government thought it right that research should be carried on in spite of the many competing claims on our scientific man power. At this stage research was carried out mainly in our Universities — principally at Oxford, Cambridge, London (Imperial College), Liverpool and Birmingham. At the time of the formation of the Coalition Government, the responsibility for coordinating the work and pressing it forward lay in the Ministry of Aircraft Production, advised by a committee of leading scientists presided over by Sir George Thomson.

"At the same time, under the general arrangements then in force for pooling scientific information, there was a full interchange of ideas between the scientists carrying out this work in the United Kingdom and those in the United States. Such progress was made that by the summer of 1941 Sir George Thomson's committee was able to report that in their view there was a reasonable chance that the atomic bomb could be produced before the end of the war.

"At the end of August, 1941, Lord Cherwell, whose duty it was to keep me informed on all these and other technical developments, reported the substantial progress which was being made. The general responsibility for the scientific research carried on under the various technical committees lay with the then Lord President of the Council, Sir John Anderson."

Mr. Churchill adds that the Chiefs of Staff recommended immediate action with the maximum priority and it was decided to set up within the Department, a scientific and industrial division to direct the work. Imperial Chemical Industries agreed to release Mr. W.R. Akers to take charge of this directorate which for the purposes of secrecy was called the Directorate of "Alloys".

When Sir John Anderson became Chancellor of the Exchequer, Mr. Churchill asked him to continue to supervise this work for which he has special qualifications. To advise him there was set up a consultative council. Under Mr. Akers there was a technical committee originally composed of Sir James Chadwick (Nobel Prize winner and discoverer of neutron), Dr. Halban, Dr. Simon (both Jewish refugees) and Mr. Slade. Later it was joined by Sir Charles Darwin and Professors Cockcroft, Oliphant and Feather.

"Pooling Information

"On October 11, 1941, the late President Roosevelt suggested that any extended efforts might usefully be coordinated. Accordingly, all British and American efforts were joined and a number of British scientists concerned proceeded to the United States. Complete secrecy guided all these activities. By the summer of 1942 the time had come when a decision must be made whether or not to proceed with the construction of large-scale production plants. Great Britain at this period was fully extended in war production and we could not afford such grave interference with the current munition programmes on which our warlike operations depended. Moreover, Great Britain was within easy range of German bombers.

"The United States, however, where similar progress had been made, was free from these dangers. The decision was therefore taken to build full-scale production plants in America. The main practical effort and virtually the whole of the prodigious cost now fell upon the United States as authorities who were assisted by a number of British scientists. The Canadian Government, whose contribution was most valuable, provided both the indispensable raw material for the project as a whole and also the necessary facilities for the work on one section of the project which has been carried out in Canada by the three Governments in partnership."

Germans Outpaced

"By God's mercy British and American science outpaced all German efforts. These were on a considerable scale but far behind. The possession of these powers by the Germans at any time might have altered the result of the war and profound anxiety was felt by those who were informed.

"Every effort was made by our intelligence service and by

(Continued on page 3)

Nuclear Energy Released
By Our Science Correspondent

No details as to the working of the atomic bomb have been revealed up to now but is is clear that nuclear reactions are involved; in other words, physical process changing the structure of the core of the atom, where its heavy particles are concentrated.

In all the ordinary chemical reactions, including the explosion of bombs hitherto used, energies are released which originate from the electronic shell of the molecules or the atoms constituting the molecules. It has been "known" for the last two decades that nuclear energies are of an order representing a million-fold multiplication of power as compared with these ordinary chemical energies. Thus the energy irradiated by the sun is based on the transmutation of hydrogen into helium within the kernel of the sun. The atomic process underlying this transmutation was clarified only as recently as four years ago by a Russian scientist working in the United States, Gamov, and independently by the German-Jewish refugee, Bethe.

The new bomb would appear to be the famous uranium bomb, based on the work of O. Hahn and H. Strassmann, of Berlin, whose work was published early in 1939. The bombardment of uranium with certain elementary particles, known as neutrons, results in a splitting up of the nucleus of the uranium atom.

Apart from uranium there are only two elements capable of undergoing such fission. Uranium can be slowed down, and the resulting energy controlled and put to constructive uses, though it is easier to construct an atomic bomb than an atomic "oven." It is not without interest that the term "fission" has not appeared in American scientific journals since 1941 — for reasons which are now clear.

AFTER MIDNIGHT

General Eisenhower told the German people in a broadcast last night that their power to make war would be destroyed and called on them to rebuild their lives on a democratic basis and to rejoin the family of the nations. A similar statement was issued by General Montgomery.

STRAITS DEADLOCK CONTINUES
By William Hardcastle
Reuters Correspondent

WASHINGTON, Monday. — Three important issues, chiefly affecting Britain and Russia and having the Mediterranean as their focal point, were discussed at Potsdam without a solution being reached, it is learned.

They have been passed on to a coming meeting of the Council of Foreign Ministers in London, according to usually reliable sources in Washington today.

The most surprising was the question of international trusteeship for Italy's African empire, which, as hinted in the Potsdam communique, was raised by Russia but left over to be decided along with the drawing up of a peace treaty for Italy which will be one of the Foreign Ministers' first tasks. Russia is understood to have referred specifically to Italian Somaliland, Libya and Tripolitania, which are now under British control. Marshal Stalin is said to have recommended that they should be placed under the trusteeship of the United Nations, including Russia.

Montreux Convention

Russia is also reported to have brought up the question of the Montreux Convention which regulates the right of passage through the Dardanelles between the Black Sea and the Mediterranean. So far as is known in Washington this subject was not pursued but the Russians made a point of putting on record what they feel are their vital economic and security interests involved, and no doubt these will be further discussed by the Foreign Ministers.

Within 24 hours of the Potsdam communique, reports reached Washington of a break-down in the talks between Russian and Turkish Governments in which the Russians are said to be seeking privileges in the Dardanelles as a basis for the renewal of the treaty of friendship between the two countries broken off early last year.

Persian Requests

The third unsolved issue was brought up by Britain. This is the question of meeting the Persian Government's request for the withdrawal of all foreign troops from Persian soil. The United States is not directly affected by this question either, as her forces in Persia, at one time numbering many thousands, have been reduced to a few hundred.

The original agreement was that the Allies should have use of transport facilities through Persia until six months after the end of the war with Germany and her associates. Since Russia is not at war with Japan, she is not in a position to dispute the Persian contention that Japan is not an "associate" of Germany. No agreement was reached on this subject either.

ITALY'S FUTURE STILL OBSCURE
By Reuters Diplomatic Correspondent

LONDON, Monday. — There is still no intention of making public the terms of the Italian armistice, a Foreign Office spokesman stated this morning.

Reports purporting to reveal the full text, which have been published in the press, are in fact not more than a short summary of the conditions already published, in September, 1943. It is out of consideration for the Italian Government that the full text of the armistice terms has not yet been published.

Informed quarters believe that the armistice gave the Allied Powers authority to enforce very much more severe conditions than have been found necessary in view of the cooperative policy pursued by the Government of both Signor Bonomi and Signor Parri. It is expected that the meeting of the Council of Foreign Ministers set up at Potsdam, which is to take place in London at the end of the month, will immediately set about drawing up the peace treaty with Italy.

KRAMER CONFESSES

HANOVER, Monday (R).—The chief of the notorious Belsen concentration camp, Kramer, who is awaiting trial here, has signed a statement confessing his war crimes.

The text of his confession cannot be disclosed at present for fear of prejudicing his trial, but it will be read as evidence at the forthcoming trial to be held at Nuremberg.

TRUMAN REVEALS WAR'S BIG SECRET
BIG FACTORIES BUILT IN U.S.

WASHINGTON, Monday. —
"The harnessing of the basic power of the Universe has been accomplished. The force from which the sun draws its power has been loosed against those who brought the war to the Far East," says President Truman's dramatic announcement on the beginning of atomic warfare.

"Before 1939 it was the accepted belief of scientists that it was theoretically possible to release atomic energy. But no one knew any practical method of doing it. By 1942, however, we knew that the Germans were working feverishly to find a way to add atomic energy to the other engines of war with which they hoped to enslave the world. But they failed. We may be grateful to Providence that the Germans got V-1 and V-2 late and in limited quantities, and even more grateful that they did not get atomic bombs at all."

The "battle of the laboratories," the statement went on, held "fateful risks" for the United States. "But we have now won the battle of the laboratories as we won other battles."

British Cooperation

At the beginning of 1940, the United States and Britain pooled all their scientific knowledge that could be used in war, and "many priceless helps to our victories" came from that arrangement. With American and British scientists working together, "we entered a race of discovery against the Germans." Mr. Churchill and President Roosevelt agreed that research should be carried out in the United States because Britain was exposed to constant air attack.

"We have now two great plants and many lesser works devoted to the production of atomic power. Employment during the peak production period numbered 125,000 and even

over 65,000 individuals are now engaged in the operation of the plants. Many have worked there for two and a half years, few know what they have been producing. They see quantities of material coming and they see nothing coming out of these plants, for the physical size of the explosive charge is exceedingly small. We have spent two billion dollars on the greatest scientific gamble in history — and won.

Destruction of Japan

"We are now prepared to obliterate more rapidly and completely every productive enterprise the Japanese have above ground in any city. We shall destroy their docks, factories and their communications. Let there be no mistake; we shall completely destroy Japan's power to make war.

"It was to spare the Japanese people from utter destruction that the ultimatum of July 26 was issued at Potsdam. Their leaders promptly rejected the ultimatum.

If they do not now accept our terms, they may expect a rain of ruin from the air the like of which has never been seen on this earth. Behind this devastating air attack will follow up sea and land forces in such numbers and power as they have not yet seen, with a fighting skill of which they are already aware.

Reviewing the fearful potency of the missile, Mr. Truman said that he would recommend to Congress to consider the establishment of an appropriate commission to control production and use in the United States. "I shall give further consideration and make recommendations to Congress as to how atomic power can become a powerful and forceful influence in the maintenance of world peace."

Science and industry worked together under the U.S. Army on the production. The Army achieved "a unique success in managing so diverse a problem in the advancement of knowledge in so amazingly short a time."

Science and Industry

The "greatest marvel" was not the size of the enterprise, its secrecy or cost, he said, but the achievement of scientific brains in putting together infinitely complex pieces of knowledge held by many men in different fields of science into a workable plan.

"Although the workers at the sites have been making materials to be used in producing the greatest destructive force in history, they have not themselves been in danger beyond that of many other war occupations, for the utmost care has been taken for their safety. Hardly less marvellous is the capacity of the industry and design, has been that of labour to operate the machines and methods, to do things never done before, so that the brain child of many minds came forward in physical shape and performed as it was supposed to do," went on the President.

Mr. Stimson today made public the information that the atomic production centres were at Oak Ridge near Knoxville, Tennessee, at Richland near Pasco, Washington, and near Santa Fe, New Mexico.

(UP & R)

Chinese-Soviet Talks Resumed

MOSCOW, Monday (R). — Mr. T.V. Soong, the Chinese Prime Minister, and Mr. Wang Shi Chieh, the newly appointed Foreign Minister, are expected to arrive here by air within the next 24 hours to resume the Chinese-Soviet discussions interrupted by the Potsdam Conference.

Mr. T.V. Soong, who then held the office as Foreign Minister in addition to being the Prime Minister, had several talks with Generalissimo Stalin in Moscow last month. An official communique issued in Moscow when the talks were broken off on the eve of Stalin's departure for Potsdam, stated: "The aim of the negotiations was the improvement of Soviet-Chinese relations in connection with which most important questions affecting both sides were discussed." No mention was made of the subjects brought under review.

JAPANESE RED CROSS PART OF WAR MACHINE

OKINAWA, Monday (R). — Documents discovered here disclose that the Japanese Red Cross is virtually an adjunct of the Japanese war machine.

Partially destroyed papers found in the ruins of an office showed that with the outbreak of the war the military took charge of the organization. Red Cross literature is devoted to encouraging the Japanese women to take factory jobs. One report in salvaged papers told of an annual meeting of the Red Cross in Tokyo in May 1944 which was attended by military heads.

DEATH OF SENATOR JOHNSON

WASHINGTON, Monday (UP). — The death is announced of Senator Hiram Johnson, who helped to keep the United States out of the League of Nations over two decades ago. He would have been 79 on September 2.

Senator Johnson, a Californian, entered the Senate in 1917. His death leaves vacancies on five Senate Committees, the most important of which is Foreign Relations.

U.S. Defence of Hemisphere

WASHINGTON, Monday (UP) — The suggestion that the American Republics should take over the executive policing of the hemisphere as an instrument of the United Nations— post-war security organization, is made by Senator Arthur Vandenberg (Republican, Michigan), who was a member of the U.S. delegation at San Francisco.

In a letter to the Secretary of State, Mr. J. F. Byrnes, Senator Vandenberg outlines a seven-point programme:
(1) The American delegate to the Security Council should be nominated by the President, subject to the Senate's confirmation.
(2) The delegate, who would rank as Ambassador, should not at times act pursuant to the President's instructions.
(3) The President should immediately report to Congress immediately when he authorizes the delegate to vote on the use of military or economic sanctions.
(4) The President should not be required to report to Congress on cases involving peaceful settlements of disputes.
(5) The President should obtain explicit authorization from Congress before committing the American forces over and above the quota fixed in forthcoming military agreements.
(6) Either in the delegate agreements, the United States jointly with her American sister-republics should assume exclusively responsibility for any armed forces needed to keep the peace in the Western Hemisphere.
(7) The American delegates to the Assembly should be appointed by the President for one-year terms, subject to Senate confirmation.

VIENNA SCIENTIST DESTROYS WONDER APPARATUS

Special to The Palestine Post

VIENNA, Monday. — Pro-Allied partisans were just too late to prevent a Nazi Professor from killing a hammer and smashing one of the world's most remarkable instruments of science — the electronic ultra-microscope — to prevent it from falling into Allied hands.

Professor Johann Lange will go on trial next week as a war criminal on the charge of killing two research experts who tried to stop him from destroying the instrument which was the result of 17 years' research. It took two years above to install the delicate mechanism in the Zoological research institute in the secluded Boltzmannplatz. Special springing insulated it from the vibration of passing traffic. By means of its rays of electronic particles, researchers could see objects such infective viruses too small to be picked up by ordinary light waves.

Lange was sent specially from Berlin to take charge. The assistant was an anti-Nazi, Dr. Horeischy, who knew Lange planned to destroy the microscope. When the partisans rushed to the laboratory Lange

drew a gun and killed Dr. Foh, man another anti-Nazi. He then methodically smashed the unique microscope to pieces with a hammer and chisel.

Mr. Shertok Reviews Jewish War Effort

LONDON, Monday. — A vivid report of political and other developments in and concerning Palestine since 1939, coupled with many dramatic "Now It Can Be Told" episodes in the Yishuv's contribution to the British and Allied war effort, was given by Mr. Moshe Shertok, Head of the Jewish Agency's Political Department in Jerusalem, in a three-hour address to the Zionist Conference yesterday. Mr. Barnett Janner, M.P., was in the chair.

Outstanding points of Mr. Shertok's report were:
(1) The Jewish Agency is now negotiating regarding the future of the Jewish Brigade;
(2) The Brigade had contacted Jewish survivors who might soon be proceeding to Palestine;
(3) The Palestine question, regarded as "closed" after the issue of the White Paper in 1939, had now been reopened.
(4) The victory of Labour in Britain opened up new vistas for the Zionists' political struggle;
(5) An understanding between the Jews and Arabs on the basis of the Zionist programme could only be reached after decision by the Great Powers favourable to the National Home.

Waiting for Decision

"One of the heads of the Arab States told me that we could not now but must wait for a decision by the Powers," Mr. Shertok stated. "We did not mention the White Paper in the whole of our talk."

He flatly rejected the idea of a bi-national Arab-Jewish state, and concluded that the political departments of the Jewish Agency in Jerusalem, London and Washington must be reorganized to work as one unit to counter the political offensive the Arabs were planning.

Mr. Shertok began by recalling that at the outbreak of the war, it had been assumed that the British Government would not proceed with the implementation of the White Paper. But this was not to be. While the Constitutional part remained inoperative, the Land was now promulgated in February 1940, compelling the Jewish Agency to enter upon a fight against the White Paper as if there were no war.

Importance of Land

Mr. Shertok emphasized the far-reaching importance the land factor in view of the catastrophic shrinkage of the Jewish land potential to an insignificant fraction. Recounting the concrete difficulties with which land purchases had now to contend, he pointed to the imperative necessity of a major political break-through to get out of the impasse.

The main battlefield, however, he continued, had been immigration, which during the war had become, in the literal sense, a question of life and death. He enumerated the exertions for a substantial allocation of permits to save European Jews in time, which had been rejected by the Government, apparently on the ground that Jewish fears were exaggerated or invented to defeat the White Paper policy.

Every single allocation of permits had to be wrenched and wrested from the authorities, since Government was obviously anxious to prolong the distribution of certificates as far as possible with a view to postponing a test over the realization of the White Paper.

The mere fact that the White Paper Administration had but continual spokes in their wheel and tried very hard to belittle the recruiting efforts was the measure of its

they were faced with an overwhelming, large-scale demand for permits which only a new departure from the present immigration policy could satisfy.

Blood Circulation

Answering criticism raised during the political discussion, Mr. Shertok explained that there was no dilemma as between the concentration of their efforts on immigration and major policy. It was no good being told to concentrate on high policy instead of immigration, which meant stopping the blood circulation while keeping the heart going. There was an immediate organic connection between immigration and State policy.

But this act in the war drama — the immigration chapter — showed the Jew in the role of victim: there was another act in which they were the fighters. And he then proceeded to outline the principles on which the Jewish Agency's recruiting policy was based, and their achievements, culminating in the formation of the Jewish Brigade.

Mr. Shertok deplored the shallowness of those asking what the Jews had got in return for their efforts. The answer was very simple: self-respect, and the respect of others. "It did not diminish the estimation of our potential capacity to defeat the White Paper policy that could turn out without compulsion, and against heavy material and psychological odds, over 30,000 men and women, ready for the utmost exertions and for the supreme sacrifice," he declared.

The fact that the White Paper Administration had put continual spokes in their wheel and tried very hard to belittle and curtail the recruiting effort

political value; but, above all, these boys had been desperately anxious to fight Hitler and join hands with their brethren in Europe.

Commandos and Paratroops

Mr. Shertok went on to describe the covert forms of Jewish participation in the war of which, for security reasons, could not be published before, such as the organizing of special Commando expeditions at the behest of the British military authorities — from one of which, consisting of 23 specially selected young men, none returned — and attempts to send parachutists into the heart of Europe.

Here Mr. Shertok disclosed for the first time that in 1942 the Jewish Agency proposed sending a contingent by parachute into Poland with a view to stimulating the then existing Jewish resistance. The offer was repeated after the news of the ghetto revolt reached them, but was rejected as impracticable and likely to cause more harm than good to the Jews.

A much more modest offer made in February, 1944, regarding the Balkans was likewise declined. Finally, in July, 1944, a somewhat similar scheme concerning Hungary was approved on the highest level, but when the offer had already reached the implementation stage it was vetoed because it was thought that the political disadvantages outweighed the military advantage.

While all these schemes to form autonomous Jewish military groups were turned down, the Jewish Agency nevertheless succeeded, with the cooperation of certain military authorities, in sending 30 men

(Continued on Page 3, Col. 1)

QUADS IN S. AFRICA

DURBAN, Monday (R). —Quadruplets, all of them girls, were born today to a native woman, Anna Humala, aged 22.

August 7, 1945   61

LATE Edition

THE PALESTINE POST

JERUSALEM
Wednesday, August 15, 1945

PRICE: 15 MILS
VOL. XX. No. 5870

2 A.M. Palestine Time

JAPAN SURRENDERS TO ALLIES

LONDON, Tuesday 12 midnight GMT (R). — "Japan has surrendered." This announcement was made here from No 10, Downing Street tonight by the Prime Minister, Mr. Attlee, who read the text of an Imperial rescript (signed by Togo) declaring that the Emperor had decided to accept the Potsdam declaration and to ensure the execution of its terms, starting with the immediate ending of military resistance.

Mr. Attlee, after saying "the last of our enemies has been laid low," paid a tribute to the fighting men in Britain, the Dominions and Colonies whose efforts made the victory possible; and expressed gratitude to "our splendid allies," especially the United States, without whom the war would have taken much longer.

The Prime Minister announced that Wednesday and Thursday would be days of holiday in Great Britain — "Let all who can relax and enjoy themselves."

He ended with the words, "Thank God for the great deliverance and His mercy. Long Live the King." The British National Anthem was then played.

Mr. Attlee's announcement, which took five minutes to deliver, was preceded by repeated broadcast 'warnings' by the B.B.C. announcer that an important statement by the Prime Minister was to follow. Tension was acute as listeners heard Big Ben leisurely striking 12 bells, the hour of midnight, at which Mr. Attlee came to the microphone with the momentous news.

THE ALLIED TERMS

LONDON, Tuesday (R). — These are the terms which Japan was asked to accept:

1. The Japanese Emperor and Government are to subject their authority to that of an Allied Supreme Commander. General Douglas MacArthur has been unofficially tipped for the post.

2. The Emperor is to order the surrender of Japanese troops in all theatres.

3. The Japanese Government is immediately to transport prisoners and civilian internees to places of safety.

4. The Japanese people are to be free to decide their ultimate form of Government.

5. Allied troops are to remain in Japan for a specified period.

These terms were sent to the Japanese Government through Switzerland on Saturday afternoon in reply to the Japanese offer to accept the Potsdam terms, on condition that the Emperor was allowed to remain. The Potsdam terms, set out in a declaration by President Truman, Mr. Churchill and Marshal Chiang Kai Shek on July 26, and since adhered to by Marshal Stalin, included these clauses:

1. Japanese Sovereignty is to be limited to four main home islands and other islands to be determined by the Allies.

2. The Allies are to occupy points in the country until a new order has been established.

3. The Japanese armed forces are to be disarmed and sent home.

4. The Japanese war industries are to be destroyed and reparations exacted in kind.

World Welcomes Good News

WASHINGTON, Tuesday (R). — The news of today's Tokyo radio report on Japan's forthcoming capitulation came too late for the morning papers and too early for the evening papers. People began the day by going quietly to work, unaware of the latest developments. Later, however, hilarious crowds gathered in the streets, of New York, expressing their enthusiasm by kissing and hugging the nearest servicemen.

Patriotic songs were sung. Many converged on the main thoroughfares without paying any attention to traffic lights or police. Pedestrian cheers and blasts from car horns brought people out of bed throughout Manhattan.

In San Francisco, milling crowds went through the streets cheering and singing in celebration mood. Servicemen climbed to the tops of tramcars and stopped cars in the streets to climb aboard.

At Washington, there was nobody at the White House or State Department this morning for comment when the Japanese News Agency report was broadcast.

The news came to Guam shortly after the announcement of the launching of new Super-Fortress blows against Japan, cables David Brown, Reuters Special Correspondent. General Spaatz confirming that two Super-Fortress missions had not yet returned, grimly stated: "Operations are still continuing."

Admiral Nimitz refused to make any comment on his reported offer to the Japanese to communicate through Guam.

Impromptu celebrations and hand-shaking and back slapping could be seen through the open sided, flat-topped buildings where naval officers have been directing the operations of the world's most powerful fleets.

The lights of Pearl Harbour reinforced by 40 searchlights went on again on Monday night after the Japanese surrender forecast had been picked up here. Rockets and flares filled the air for 20 minutes.

Broadcasts at breakfast time by South African radio stations of the Tokyo acceptance forecast caused wild demonstrations in Johannesburg. Clouds of torn-up directories and ticker tape showered down on the streets from office buildings as hundreds of cheering people gathered outside the United States Consulate.

WAR FLICKERS OUT

By FRANK TREMAINE
U.P. Correspondent

PEARL HARBOUR, Tuesday. — Soviet troops today thrust deeper into Western Manchuria and over 800 Super-Fortresses and fighters ripped into Central Japan, as Tokyo reported that Japan had decided to surrender unconditionally.

The Super-Forts dropped 3,200 tons of bombs and left two arsenals and railway-yards on Honshu wreathed in flames, while Russian tanks and Mongol horsemen swept across the Manchurian plains for over 120 miles in the fifth day of their offensive.

Less than an hour after the last Super-Fortress had turned home, a Tokyo broadcaster announced that Japan had decided to accept the Potsdam declaration. At the same time, the Japanese claimed that suicide planes had made another assault against Admiral Halsey's Third Fleet.

Tokyo's surrender broadcast came a little over two hours later, with the Japanese also claiming that five other suicide planes crashed into an American aircraft carrier off Okinawa last night.

Russia, broadcasting three hours after Tokyo's surrender message, exhorted the advancing Manchurian armies to overtake the fleeing forces and "to show no mercy." Chungking reported that Chinese forces were driving toward the Kwangtung coast and had captured the road centre of Hweilai on the Kwangtung coastal plain five miles from the sea.

Gen. MacArthur to March on Tokyo

By WILLIAM HARDCASTLE, Reuters Correspondent

WASHINGTON, Tuesday. — General MacArthur, Admiral Nimitz and possibly President Truman will put out to the Pacific and obtain the Japanese signature aboard an Allied warship, it is disclosed here today.

No doubt is felt that the end of the Japanese war is only a matter of two or three days formalities. Speculation is now centring on which means the Allies will employ to contact the isolated Japanese garrisons for the surrender signature.

Reports current here suggest that General Mac Arthur will land an army force on the Japanese mainland to seize strategic points and will then march on Tokyo to get the signature of the war lords.

Tokyo announced today that the Emperor Hirohito had addressed a message in that sense to a crowd assembled outside the Tokyo Imperial Palace. The agency said:

"On August 14, 1945, the Imperial decision was granted and the weeping people who had gathered before the Niku Bashi (Double Bridge) outside the Imperial Palace, bowed, to the very ground in shame because their efforts were not enough. His Majesty's subjects are moved to tears by His Majesty's boundless and infinite solicitude."

The broadcast, however, did not say clearly what the decision was and broke off with words implying that what was being broadcast was not for use until later when the Emperor's decision was made public.

Shanghai to be Liberated

By GRAHAM BARROW
Reuters Correspondent

CHUNGKING, Tuesday — Every step is being taken by the highest authorities in China to guard against the possibility of civil war breaking out, but I learn that the attitude of the Chinese Communists will not be allowed to interfere with the peaceful reoccupation of Shanghai and other liberated cities.

It is not impossible that the American-trained Chinese of the Sixth Army which fought in Burma and have since been standing by in China will be flown to the Shanghai area as soon as possible to take part in the city's liberation.

Japanese behaviour in many occupied areas has left a legacy of hate that will not easily be forgotten and one of the first tasks of the army of occupation will be to keep order and prevent a massacre of the Japanese and their Chinese puppets. Earlier reports from Shanghai stated that several high-ranking puppets had made plans to fly to Russia but this refuge has been denied them as a result of the Soviet entry into the Far Eastern war.

Tentative arrangements have been made for feeding the population in the liberated areas and for accommodating the thousands people who will move back from West China. It is not yet known what steps have been taken to meet the currency problem but the steadily strengthening national dollar is worth many times the puppet currency in use in Shanghai.

BRITISH ENVOY SEES SPANISH MINISTER

MADRID, Tuesday (R).— The new British Ambassador, Sir Victor Mallet, had a talk lasting about 90 minutes with the Spanish Foreign Minister, Senor Alberto Martin Artajo.

YENAN GIRDS FOR ACTION

NEW YORK, Tuesday (R). — The Chinese Communist radio at Yenan today called on the Chinese people and the Allies to support its claim that Chinese forces in all liberated areas should participate with the Allies in receiving the Japanese surrender.

The radio said that Generalissimo Chiang's orders to the Communist Generals not to take independent action was further proof of his preference for the Japanese and their puppets rather than the democratic forces in China, and of his active preparation for civil war.

AUSTRALIA ANNOYED

SAN FRANCISCO, Tuesday (UP). — The Melbourne radio reports "growing indignation" in Australia over the management of the surrender negotiations with Japan.

It is pointed out that while Australia was told only perfunctorily about Mr. Byrnes' note, she was not given proper time to study it or to suggest amendments, while Japan was apparently given unlimited time to decide its attitude.

The broadcast said that this was "regarded as curt treatment of Australia which has a war record in the Pacific second only to that of the United States."

RESIGNATION IN U.S. STATE DEPARTMENT

NEW YORK, Tuesday (R). — Mr. Dean Acheson has resigned his post as Assistant Secretary of State which he has held since January, 1941. Many other resignations are expected soon, it is reported in this connection.

Stop Press

NEW YORK, Tuesday (R). — It is officially announced that the Japanese reply has been received in Washington.

The N.B.C. correspondent in Basle says: "The Japanese note accepts the Allied terms in principle."

THE LAST RAIDS

GUAM, Tuesday (R). — The Allied attacks on Japan continued today when Super-Forts raided the Merifu railway yards and ships off the Japanese coast south of Kure. It was the first Super-Fort raid since the Japanese made their surrender offer on Friday.

TALKS IN MOSCOW

MOSCOW, Tuesday (R). — Generalissimo Stalin received the Chinese Prime Minister, Dr. T. V. Soong, and the Foreign Minister, Dr. Wang Shih-Chieh, in the Kremlin this morning. M. Molotov was present and a long conference took place. This was the third meeting between the Chinese Ministers and Generalissimo Stalin since they arrived last week.

Lebanese Vote Of Confidence

BEIRUT, Tuesday (R). — In an extraordinary session today the Lebanese Chamber declared its confidence in the Government of M Abdul Hamid Karameh by 34 votes against 9 There were two abstentions.

The vote took place after a heated debate on the Government's foreign policy. Speaking of the Lebanese Government's achievements in the field of foreign affairs, the Foreign Minister, M. Pharaon, declared that the last two months had been the most important in Lebanese history and reminded the Chamber of Article 78 of the United Nations Charter which gives the official seal the Lebanese independence.

The Minister of the Interior, M. Wadia Naim, who headed the Lebanese delegation to San Francisco, asked the House to ratify the United Nations Charter

The Premier, M. Karameh, then passed the situation in review and revealed that "when we saw our independence threatened, we appealed to the Arab League — but its intervention was not needed because we won.

"The French troops will leave the Lebanon immediately the British troops leave — I was told by Count Ostrorog (the French Assistant Delegate General and Plenipotentiary in the Levant) on July 2," declared the Foreign Minister in answer to a question by the former Vice Premier, M. Habib Azishalah. No answer was given to another question regarding negotiations for concessions for oil refineries and air lines

The vote of confidence in the Karameh Government ends the months long controversy between the Government and the opposition led by the ex-Premier M. Riad el Solh.

CABINET CHANGES

BEIRUT, Tuesday (ANA). — Two Cabinet Members, Sayyed Wadi' Na'im, Minister of Interior and Dr. Jamil Talhouq, Minister of Supply, tendered their resignations at the conclusion of today's session of the Chamber, in compliance with the decision of the Constitutional Bloc party to which they are affiliated.

The withdrawal of the two Ministers will enable the Government to broaden its composition.

Exiles Find Return Barred

POLISH AND YUGOSLAV POLITICAL REFUGEES

By JOHN TALBOT,
Reuters Special Correspondent

ROME, Tuesday. — Within the whole vast problem of sorting out and sending home millions of Europeans uprooted by the Germans lies a hard core which is causing some embarrassment to the Allied authorities. This core is composed of those displaced persons who for political or other reasons will not or dare not return to their native land.

What is to become of these people is a question to which British and American experts are trying to find an answer. In Italy there are nationals of two countries in particular — Poland and Yugoslavia — who for their own reasons do not wish to return to their homeland. Altogether there are about 300,000 of these people consisting of some 100,000 Yugoslavs and 200,000 Poles.

The Polish Army

The majority of the Polish refugees are men of the Polish corps which fought so magnificently with the Eighth Army. Very few of these veterans want to go back to Poland under what they consider — rightly or wrongly — to be a government inimical to them.

Regarding the Yugoslavs in Italy, the position is that the majority are or were supporters of Mihailovich, regarded by Marshal Tito's partisans as the ace Quisling of Yugoslavia, and are thus regarded as traitors to their country through their association with him. Some of these Yugoslavs have taken active part in the fighting with the Germans, while at the same time professing loyalty to King Peter in London. It is perhaps possible that Marshal Tito's recent amnesty will prompt some of them to return.

I was told by an official that for the time being both Poles and Yugoslavs would continue to live under Allied care, drawing their food from Allied sources. Ultimately the whole problem would have to come up for decision before an inter-Government Committee for Refugees.

DEEP SOVIET DRIVE IN MANCHURIA

By ERIC DOWNTON,
Reuters Correspondent

MOSCOW, Tuesday. — General Meretskov's forces pushing into Manchuria from the east today made forward progress towards Harbin after smashing determined Japanese attempts to resist the Soviet advance.

A heavy encounter resulted when Kwantung Army troops tried to hold the Russians in one sector, using artillery, mortars and entrenched infantry. Japanese bombers also put in an appearance but Red Army men eventually overran the position.

The Soviet forces are driving across mountain sides covered with dense woods and criss-crossed by deep rivers. In some sectors the Japanese are retreating so rapidly that they are not destroying railways, roads and bridges.

Nearing Capital

Tokyo admits today that a big new Soviet advance has been made into Manchuria, bringing the Russians to within about 150 miles of the capital, Hsingking.

All in all, Marshal Vassilevsky's three front advance towards the central plain of Manchuria has been continuing at a surprising pace in view of the roughness of the terrain and the suicide stands of pockets of the Kwantung Army. The forces pushing north-westwards yesterday gained 30 miles along the general direction of the railway leading to Harbin, the strategic communication centre in the heart of Manchuria. Other Red Army units advancing from the north between the Sungari and Ussuri rivers pushed forward up to 27 miles.

Marshal Malinovsky's army from Transbaikal front made a further breach of the mighty Khingan mountain range, a natural defence barrier for northern Manchuria, and captured Solun, on the railway leading north and west of Hsinking, the Manchurian capital some 270 miles to the south-west.

There is no news today of the flying vanguards of Marshal Malinovsky's army which by yesterday advanced 400 miles in four days. There is a general impression in Moscow that when they are heard of again they will report a sensational leap forward. It is thought they are probably well past the ancient wall of Ghenghis Khan running for more than 100 miles along the eastern foothills of the Khingan mountains.

Invasion of Sakhalin

Tonight's Soviet communique gives the first Soviet mention of the invasion by the Red Army of the island of Sakhalin.

The communique, which announces a fresh 95 mile advance by troops of the Transbaikal Command attacking east of the great Khingan mountains, reports that ships and units of the Pacific Fleet fought their way into and took the Korean port of Seishin. Over 8,000 Japanese officers and men have been captured.

Mopping Up May Take Long

S. E. A. C. HEADQUARTERS, Tuesday (R). — There is not the slightest indication here yet of the Japanese surrendering said Lieutenant-General F. N. Browning today.

He warned against an easy assumption that the moment peace arrived all men in this theatre could go home. It was likely to be at least six to nine months before S.E.A.C. could hand over the occupied territories to civil governments.

The several hundred thousand Japanese in this theatre may well continue to fight on despite the central surrender at Tokyo, it is thought here.

U.S. Plan for Control of Japan

By GWEN MORGAN,
U.P. Correspondent

WASHINGTON, Tuesday (UP). — The United States Government is understood to have completed a directive outlining the policy to govern the military occupation of Japan.

Informed quarters state that the order, now being circulated for final approval among the various Government agencies involved, will be ready when U.S. troops move into Japan. It is described as a formula for "corrective but not punitive" occupation. Some 2,000 specially-trained officers are ready to take over the administration of the enemy homeland.

Officials emphasize that the directive is intended only for the initial period of occupation. It is in no way comparable to the control programme for Germany. More detailed plans for Japanese economic disarmament and control are still being formulated.

Joint Occupation

It is suggested that the United States, Britain, China, and Russia might decide to undertake joint occupation, with each of the Big Four responsible for one of the main home islands — Hokkaido, Honshu, Hikoku, and Kyushu — and that because of her great role in the Pacific war, the United States is expected to have the dominant influence in any such programme. America will be assigned the major home island of Honshu.

The procedure is that the Allies are to designate the military officers who will meet the Japanese surrender signatories. The place of the meeting and the Allied supreme commander of the occupation force must be selected. General Douglas MacArthur is widely reported to have been chosen.

CELEBRATIONS IN MANILA

MANILA, Tuesday (UP). General MacArthur declined to comment on the Tokyo radio report that Japan had decided to accept the Allied surrender terms. He had announced previously that he would not comment until notified officially that the war was over.

Officers and G.Is. yelled themselves hoarse, however, as the news spread through Manila. In the centre of the city, ticker tape and waste paper were thrown from the windows and covered Manila streets like snow. Twenty-four newspapers published extra editions with the U.P. flash of the surrender.

French Socialists Against Fusion

By HAROLD KING, Reuters Correspondent

PARIS, Tuesday. — The Party leaders of the Socialist Congress today scored a major victory over the minority which favours a fusion of the Communist and Socialist parties.

A motion submitted by the General Secretary of the Party, M. Daniel Meyer, which proposes a close alliance between the Socialist Party and the "Democratic Socialist parties of the Resistance movement" won the day by 6,104 votes against 2,718, with 1,801 abstentions.

There was a violent uproar when the Party leaders tried to rule out of order a motion carried last night urging that the Socialist ministers should resign unless General de Gaulle's Government modified its election scheme. This motion was put through by the delegates from the northern mining areas and is in direct conflict with the view of the Party leaders who are largely responsible for the Government's electoral plans. Order was restored when an undertaking was given to consider the motion again tomorrow

The Radicals pointed to the British example and argued that the withdrawal of Labour members from the Coalition Government on the eve of election had "proved very successful tactics."

While it seems extremely unlikely that the Government will consent to a change in the electoral scheme adopted at the last Cabinet meeting, the chances are slight that the northern delegates can carry the Socialist Congress as a whole with them.

BANK ROBBERY IN BARCELONA

BARCELONA, Tuesday (R). — Armed with tommy guns and hand grenades, a group of men rushed the police on guard at a bank here today, locked them in the waiting room and drove off with half a million pesetas without firing a shot.

Defence Calls Petain a Patriot

PARIS, Tuesday (R). — Continuing his defence in the Petain trial, Maitre Payen declared today that Petain had made no essential concessions to Germany and was horrified when he heard Laval in a broadcast say that he hoped for a German victory.

Maitre Payen denied that Petain congratulated Hitler and von Rundstedt, as was alleged by the Prosecution. "Marshal Petain's guiding thought was to prepare for a resumption of the struggle at a later date," he said. "For that he tried to conceal and camouflage arms. From the beginning of the occupation, Marshal Petain fought against German propaganda in the French forces."

Petain's Last Words

After Petain's Counsel had finished speaking Petain rose to make his own statement. He said:

"During this trial I have kept deliberately silent after having explained to the French people the reason for my attitude. My only thought was to remain with the French people on the soil of France according to my promise in order to try to protect them and ease their suffering. Whatever happens now the people of France will not forget. The people know that I defended them as I defended Verdun.

"Dispose of me according to your conscience My own conscience is clear. After my long life and having reached the threshold of death I affirm that I have had no other ambition than to serve France."

Some clapping and applause greeted this statement but was quickly suppressed.

No Bigger Rations

LONDON, Tuesday (R). — There was no prospect of any improvement in the rations of the British people, declared Sir Ben Smith when he held his first conference as Food Minister in London today.

He described the present position as "not a cheerful picture" but expressed the view that the country should know the worst side of things.

It was too early to say what benefit Great Britain would derive from the end of the Pacific war, but the first claims were those of the rice consuming peoples. They would have to make further economies in the use of sugar but he would not reduce the domestic sugar ration below half a pound weekly.

V-J Day Arrangements in Palestine

The two days following the announcement of Victory over Japan will be observed in Palestine as general holidays by both the military authorities and the Government.

The official celebrations will conform closely to those arranged for V-E Day, when church bells were rung throughout the country to herald the day of thanksgiving.

In Jerusalem, the flags of the Allied Nations will be flown from the roof of the King David Hotel.

At 6.30 p.m. on the day following V-J Day, the Pipes and Drums of a Highland regiment will "Beat Retreat" outside the King David Hotel. The military band of an English County Regiment will also play.

The section of Julian's Way between Mamillah Road junction and King George Avenue will be closed to vehicular traffic from 6 p.m. until 10 p.m.

During the ceremony the Union Jack and the flags of the U.S.A. and USSR will be lowered.

As soon as possible after the Prime Minister's announcement of the cessation of hostilities, a special carrillon will be rung from the YMCA.

There will be an extension of licensing hours until midnight on V-J Day only.

The official Thanksgiving Service will be held in St. George's Cathedral at 10 a.m. on the Sunday following V-J Day. Informal dress will be worn.

Paid Holiday

All Government and WD employees, with the exception of those whom it is necessary to retain on duty for the maintenance of essential services and security precautions, will be released from duty on V-J Day and for the whole of the day following. The whole of this period will be regarded as a paid holiday. Any employee whom it is necessary to retain on duty for any part of this period will be given equivalent time off with pay at the first convenient opportunity. (—Communicated)

"FLYING TIGER" ON WAY HOME

General Chennault Says Mikado Must Go

By M. BRILLIANT,
Our Own Correspondent

TEL AVIV, Tuesday. — Only by removing the Japanese Imperial Family completely can victory for democratic ideals be assured, declared Major-General Claire L. Chennault, Commanding General of the American 14th Air Force in China, in an exclusive interview with *The Palestine Post* yesterday.

General Chennault, who is flying home to his family in Louisiana, spent two days in Palestine this week while his plane was undergoing a check. He visited the Holy Places on Sunday and continued on his flight yesterday.

"Final victory is assured, but I don't know about victory for our ideals," declared the General, who in 1937 became Chiang Kai Shek's air adviser and who before Pearl Harbour, recruited the American Volunteer Group known as "Flying Tigers" to fight the Japs.

"I don't think they have changed their ideology or political principles. I don't think they've repented. The Emperor is the symbol behind all the ideology of the Japs," the General said, "and unless the Imperial Family is removed completely, the Japs will retain their symbol of hero-worship. As long as the Imperial Family remains, it will be impossible to get down to the principles of equality of man, freedom of worship, and all those ideals for which we have fought for eight years."

Beaten Before the Atom Bomb

On General Chennault's Chinese front, the Japs were definitely on the run, he said. They were low on supplies, never tried to take the offensive, their air force was destroyed and they were trying to retreat to save what they could.

General Chennault was indignant at the American press reports that he had quarrelled with Generalissimo Chiang Kai Shek and General Wedemeyer. He had spent his last days in China as a guest of the Generalissimo and General Wedemeyer, he asserted.

"There are no two men I admire more, nor have I ever had happier relations with any men." General Chennault learned here for the first time of these reports. His astonishment was obvious. He recalled that his parting words in Chungking were that he was proud to have been a member of the Sino-American team that these great soldiers had formed.

The General, who before the last war was a student of scientific agriculture, said that he was amazed during his visit here at the great variety of vegetables cultivated in Palestine. He had imagined that the land was more barren, and was interested to see that the hills were not naturally wasteland, but had only been neglected. "You could do wonders here if you could bring water."

As for Tel Aviv, the General had read about the city in China, "some good reports and some bad." Today he was amazed at the progress made in Tel Aviv in such a short time and thought it was a "wonderful city."

General Chennault, who has four rows of ribbons, has a square jawed, leathery, weather beaten face. He was remarkably free and unassuming in his relations with his junior officers. The General and his staff stayed at the Yarden Hotel.

(Picture on Page 4)

LATE Edition

THE PALESTINE POST

8 PAGES

JERUSALEM
Friday, October 19, 1945

PRICE 25 MILS
VOL. XX. No. 5924

TRIAL OF NAZI CHIEFS FORMALLY OPENED

INDICTMENT PRESENTED TO COURT

By CHARLES LYNCH
Reuters Special Correspondent

BERLIN, Thursday. — The opening session of the International Military Tribunal held in Berlin this morning was completed in 50 minutes, when the indictment against the 24 top-ranking Nazis was received and the tribunal adjourned to meet "within 30 days" in Nuremberg.

The Soviet Judge Niketchenko, who presided today, announced that Lord Justice Lawrence, of Britain, would preside at the trial at Nuremberg.

Judge Niketchenko said: "Individual defendants in custody will be notified that they must be ready for trial within 30 days after the service of the indictment upon them. Promptly thereafter, the tribunal shall fix and announce the date of the trial at Nuremberg to take place not less than 30 days after the service of indictment and the defendants shall be advised of such a date as soon as it is fixed."

The indictment in German is being served upon the defendants in Nuremberg today — all, that is, except Bormann, who is not yet in custody.

The Locale

The session was held in the same Berlin Assize Court-room where the Nazis last year sentenced to death several participants in the July 20 bomb plot against Hitler. The room was crowded with Allied servicemen, few German civilians, journalists of the four major powers in Germany, the prosecutors and their assistants, a large staff of interpreters, and the Court itself.

The actual proceedings could have been completed in 15 minutes, but the delay was due to the fact that anything said had to be translated three times.

The session opened at 10.30 when the Court entered the crowded chamber and took their seats — the Americans on the right, the Russians to their left, the French next, and then the British on the extreme left of the long table which was raised up above floor level.

The Soviet judge read the opening words of the trial:

"In pursuance of the agreement between the U.S.S.R., the Provisional Government of the French Republic, the Government of the United States of America, and the Government of the United Kingdom of Britain and Northern Ireland, for the prosecution and punishment of major war criminals of the European Axis dated London, August 8, 1945, and of Article 22 of the Charter annexed thereto, constituting this International Military Tribunal, this meeting is held at Berlin for the reception of the indictment under the agreement and charter."

Judges Take Oath

Then all the four judges and their deputies took the oath: "I solemnly declare that I shall exercise all my powers and duties as member of the International Military Tribunal honourably, impartially and conscientiously.

Sir W. H. Shawcross, the British Attorney General, addressing the Court on behalf of all the prosecutors, said that the indictment had been unanimously approved by the committee of chief prosecutors, representing Britain, France, the U.S.S.R. and the United States. He then invited M. Rudenko to present the Russian text of the indictment.

After Sir W. H. Shawcross' announcement was translated, M. Rudenko rose and said:

"On behalf of my Goverment, I have the honour of presenting the Russian text of the indictment against the main war criminals signed by the prosecutors of the four nations."

This was translated into French, English and German, and M. Rudenko handed the indictment in a pink cover to a uniformed attendant who delivered it to the judges' table. Then followed the French translation, presented by M. Dubost, the deputy French prosecutor and the English copy was presented by Mr. Francis Shea, deputy American prosecutor.

Judge Niketchenko then spoke on behalf of all judges, saying: "The indictment has now been lodged with the Tribunal by the committee of the chief prosecutors setting out the charges made against the following defendants:

Hermann Wilhelm Goering, Rudolf Hess, Joachim von Ribbentrop, Robert Ley, Wilhelm Keitel, Ernst Kaltenbrunner, Alfred Rosenberg, Hans Frank, Wilhelm Frick, Julius Streicher, Walter Funk, Hjalmar Schacht, Gustav Krupp von Bohlen-Halbach, Karl Doenitz, Erich Raeder, Baldur von Schirach, Fritz Sauckel, Alfred Jodl, Martin Bormann, Franz von Papen, Artur Seyss-Inquart, Albert Speer, Constantin von Neurath, and Hans Fritsche.

Rights of Defence

Judge Niketchenko used the Russian pronunciation of the names. He continued:

"Copies of the charter and of its accompanying documents will be served upon the defendants in the German language immediately. Notices will also be served upon them in writing drawing their attention to Articles 16 and 23, of the charter which provide that they may either conduct their own defence or be defended by any counsel professionally qualified to conduct the cases before the courts of his own country or by any other person who may be especially authorized thereto by the Tribunal. A special clerk of the Tribunal has been appointed to advise the defendants of their rights and take instructions from them personally as to their choice of counsel and generally to see to it that their rights of defence are made known to them.

"If any defendant who desires to be represented by counsel is unable to secure such assistance, the Tribunal will appoint counsel to defend him.

"Individual defendants in custody will be notified that they must be ready for the trial within 30 days after the service of the indictment upon them. Promptly thereafter the Tribunal shall fix and announce the date of the trial in Nuremberg, to take place not less than 30 days after the service of the indictment and the defendants shall be advised of such a date as soon as it is fixed. It must be understood that the Tribunal which is directed by the charter to secure an expeditious hearing of the issues raised by the charges will not permit any delay, either in the preparation of the defence or of the trial.

Criminal Organizations

"Notice will also be given under Article 9 of the Charter that the prosecution intends to ask the Tribunal to declare the following organizations or groups of which the defendants or some of them were members, to be criminal organizations and any member of any such group or organization will be entitled to apply to the Tribunal for leave to be heard by the Tribunal upon the question of the criminal character of such a group or organization.

"The organizations referred to are the following: 'Die Reichsregierung (the Reich Cabinet); das Korps der Politischen Leiter der Nationalsozialistischen Deutschen Arbeiterpartei (the Political Leadership Corps of the Nazi Party); Die Schutzstaffeln der Nationalsozialistischen Deutschen Arbeiterpartei (commonly known as the S.S.); and including den Sicherheitsdienst (commonly known as S.D..); die Geheime Staatspolizei (Secret State Police, commonly known as Gestapo); die Sturmabteiungen der NSDAP (commonly known as the S.A.); and the General Staff and the High Command of the German armed forces."

The Judge's address was translated into French, English and German, and Judge Niketchenko then announced: "This session of the military Tribunal is over." No photographs were permitted to be taken during the session, but after the adjournment photographers took over the court-room and requested so many poses of the judges that Judge Niketchenko waved his hands in impatience.

The room in which the session was held is about 80 by 30 feet, newly redecorated by American engineers. There are marble columns in the four corners and huge windows letting in bright sunlight

("Suffering Supermen"—Page 3)

Column One

By David Courtney

THE Russian text of the indictment against the main Nazi war criminals, "wrapped in a pink cover", and the French, British and American texts, in covers of no specified colour, were lodged with the international tribunal at its sitting in the Berlin Assize Court yesterday. The indictment in German was then served upon the accused men in Nuremberg, who will come to trial within thirty days. Yesterday's proceedings were swift and formal. They took only fifty minutes and that could have been reduced to fifteen if it had not been for the need to translate everything three times. It is too much to hope that the trial will be as speedy. The nomination of Lord Chief Justice Lawrence to preside is promising. He is a learned High Court judge with whom counsel can play no tricks; he has a short way with irrelevancies and a damping manner towards eloquent fustian. Whether or not he will be able to preserve these qualities in four different languages it is difficult to tell. The interminable drone of interpreters is likely not only to prolong beyond its merits a trial that would be dangerously dilatory in any case, but also to dull the wits of those who conduct it. There will be much shuffling of feet and blowing of noses and wiping of eyeglasses at Nuremberg; but outside the courtroom, in the wide world, interest will be intense as skilfully edited versions of the trial divert the public; and divert it, one fears, from a score of urgent problems embarrassing a Europe victimized by the accused men and their wicked system. This trial calls for a judgment more solemn, more terrifying, than was ever before pronounced in the history of human justice; and if it warns as awfully as it condemns, its moral effect upon men and states alike may be one of the profound influences in human destiny.

MEANWHILE, the world cries for something to eat; and a hopeful response is the establishment of a World Food and Agricultural Organization, the delegates to which met yesterday in Quebec. It is evidence of a tendency to pool problems if not to pool resources. As a first step it gives grounds for hope in the second. President Truman's message to the conference admits that the new organization will not be enough to ensure a world distribution of adequate food supplies or the enjoyment of the good things of life by those who draw wealth from the earth and sea; but that is the goal and we are thankful for it. The riches of earth and sea to which President Truman refers will apparently continue to be unevenly distributed. They are subject to geographical accident and the variable economic policies of states sovereign and self-centred. To have want on one side of a frontier and plenty on the other is not rare. Chaotic production and still more chaotic distribution under a system of go-as-you please, have been the rule and probably will continue to be for a long time. While this method prevails the World Food and Agricultural Organization will be sadly hampered. World planning of food production and supply is as necessary to the Four Freedoms adumbrated by Mr. Truman's predecessor as the pooling and planned distribution of the world's raw materials.

WE shall come to it one day perhaps. There is a lot of prejudice and muddle to overcome first; but with the best and most constructive will in the world, it is hard not to be angrier at the prejudice and muddle than hopeful at the few signs of progress. What, for example, are we to think of the incredible election muddles in Greece, Bulgaria, Hungary, Yugoslavia and Portugal? Hungary, after an experiment in free voting, the results of which convinced the Communists that they were surprisingly unpopular, has decided to issue joint lists for the November general elections and thus ensure the government Marshal Voroshilov wants. It is questionable tactics. Even in politics half a loaf is better than no bread, and it looks like being a long time before South-East Europe will get more than half a loaf of freedom. There is a great deal more to all this than the muddle of uncertain democracies and the mischievous policy of their self-appointed suzerain; and something of it is exemplified in General George Marshall, American army Chief of Staff: he has just declared that the United States should maintain a military strength capable of impressing foreign governments and forcing them to take note of the American point of view. That was Hitler's way, I seem to remember; and since General George Marshall had Russia, not Honduras, in view when he made his statement, he and his like probably have had a lot to do with what is happening now in South-East Europe.

Jerusalem, October 19.

NEW PARTITION PLAN RUMOURED

Decision by Britain Only

LONDON, Thursday (UP). — The British Government is considering plans for a settlement of the Palestine question on the broad lines of the recommendations of the Peel Report of 1937, i.e. to partition the country into independent Arab and Jewish states, the United Press was told today by a well qualified source.

It was added, however, that no final decision has yet been taken, but the idea to pass the Palestine question on to the United Nations has definitely been abandoned.

TRUMAN-ATTLEE EXCHANGES

WASHINGTON, Thursday (R). President Truman confirmed at a press conference today that he had asked Mr. Clement Attlee to allow 100,000 Jews into Palestine.

The President said that he considered such a request a reasonable one, but the British Prime Minister did not wish to admit that number.

The President added that there had been no recent correspondence between him and Mr. Attlee, but there had been quite a voluminous exchange of letters at one time.

He had made some suggestions which were still under consideration. He did not want to disclose details or comment further, lest Mr. Attlee thought thought he was being unduly pushed.

The Executive Council of the American Federation of Labour, in a statement issued yesterday at Cincinnati, Ohio, urged Britain "to hear and adopt President Truman's recommendation to increase immediately the Jewish immigration quota for Palestine", and asking for the establishment of a democratic Jewish State (says PTA).

Statement Still 'At an Early Date'

LONDON, Thursday (R).—The Prime Minister, Mr. Clement Attlee, when questioned in the House of Commons today about the Palestine situation, said that he had nothing to add to his reply to a question on October 9, when he stated that he hoped to make a statement "at an early date."

Squadron-Leader P. Donner (Conservative) said that it was eight weeks since he first asked this question, and he wanted to know how much longer the Government was going to take before making a statement.

Mr. Attlee: I hope a statement will be made in the near future.

Earl Winterton (Conservative): It is a very lengthy delay, and is it not the case that every day there is delay means that the protagonists in the struggle — the Arab League—and the Zionists — improve their organization in every way, and that it will therefore make the eventual solution much harder than if the Government had taken courage?

Mr. Attlee: It is not a question of taking courage but of taking thought first. (Cheers and laughter).

Reuter adds; political quarters in London are hopeful that the British Government will be able to make a statement on the Palestine situation within the next two weeks.

GOOD NEIGHBOURS

LONDON, Thursday (PTA). — Arabs and Jews are mixing freely in Tel Aviv and Jaffa and peace reigns in Arab villages, reported the London "Evening Standard" correspondent from Tel Aviv yesterday.

"There is nothing in the air to forecast Arab-Jewish troubles," nothing of the atmosphere of 1933/36, when relations between Jews and Arabs were cut, and no Jews dared to go to Jaffa and no Arabs to Tel Aviv. The war has brought the populations in closer touch."

PAN-ARAB CONGRESS POSTPONED

LONDON, Thursday (AFP). — The Pan-Arab Congress, which should have opened in Cairo on October 29, is to be postponed, according to authoritative Arab circles in London today.

This decision taken by the members of the Arab League is destined to allow Azzam Bey, General Secretary of the League, to be present at the workings of the Congress without in any way interfering with the mission he is to carry out in America.

U.S. COAL STRIKE CALLED OFF

WASHINGTON, Thursday (R). The soft-coal strikes in the United States were called off today, with effect from Monday, by the President of the United Mine Workers Union, John L. Lewis, as "in the public interest."

The strikes began on September 21 and spread to more than a thousand mines by today, with more than 200,000 soft-coal miners idle.

ARABS FEAR JEWS, SAYS IBN SAUD

Arab fear of massacres by the Zionists, who are preparing to create a form of Nazi-Fascism and who, moreover, would be one of the main causes of dissension between the Arabs and the Allies, is expressed in a long memorandum dated March 10 which King Ibn Saud sent to the late President Roosevelt.

A translation of the memorandum and the late President's reply, dated April 5 (a week before his death), is released by Saudi-Arabian Legations and Consulates today in the capitals of Middle East countries.

The Saudi Arabian ruler devoted the major part of the memorandum to an historical review of Palestine, beginning with the year 3,500 B.C. when the country's first inhabitants were the Cannanites, "an Arab tribe which emigrated from the Arabian Peninsula and had its first abode in the lowlands."

After tracing subsequent events, including the Israelite conquest under Joshua and the Moslem conquest in the year 637 A.D., the king declared that the Jewish reign did not exceed "380 confused and sporadic years." The solution of the problem of persecuted Jews in the world, in his view, differed from "the fictitious problem of Zionism." He thought that Palestine had done much more than its full share in providing homes for scattered Jews.

Zionist Danger

"To help Zionism in Palestine not only means to endanger Palestine but all neighbouring countries," the Note went on. "The Zionists have given clear evidence of their intentions in Palestine and in all neighbouring countries. They have organized dangerous military formations, which at present hold in Palestine all the arms and military equipment they require.

If the Allied Governments, of whose friendship the Arabs were aware, wished to see the "fires of war" kindled between Arabs and Jews, their support of the Zionists would surely lead to this result.

The King then dwelt on his and Arab countries' fears of massacres of Arabs by Zionists and of Jewish ambitions not confined to Palestine alone: "Preparations they have made show that they intend to take hostile action against neighbouring Arab countries."

King Ibn Saud continued that the formation of a Jewish State in Palestine would be "a deadly blow to the Arabs and a constant threat to peace, for disturbed conditions are bound to prevail between the Jews and the Arabs. If the patience of the latter is one day exhausted and they despair of their future, they will be obliged to defend themselves and future generations against this aggression."

The President's Reply

President Roosevelt, in his reply from the White House dated April 5, said that he had given the closest attention to the King's opinion on the Palestine case. His Majesty would recall (the President went on) that on previous occasions he had informed him of the U.S. Government's attitude regarding Palestine.

Mr. Roosevelt also recalled that he had explained the U.S. administration's view against any decisions affecting existing conditions without full consultation with Arabs and Jews, and that in their recent conversation he had given further assurance that, as Chief Executive, he would take no decision, inimical to the Arabs. He renewed the assurance that his Government's policy in the matter remained unchanged.

VERBATIM REPORT NOT PUBLISHED

By ROY ELSTON
Reuters Special Correspondent in Jerusalem

In addition to the correspondence between King Ibn Saud and President Roosevelt on the subject of Palestine, a further document, stated to be the verbatim report of the conversations on board the British cruiser in the Red Sea between the two Heads of State was prepared for publication, but was withdrawn at the last moment, it is said reliably, on the request of the United States Government.

I have seen the withdrawn document which underlines the pledge given in the late President's memorandum to King Ibn Saud to do nothing regarding Palestine, which might "antagonize" the Arabs.

President Roosevelt's letter, in reply to Ibn Saud's lengthy statement of the Arab case for Palestine, promises not to take part in decisions affecting the existing status of Palestine without full consultation with the Arabs and Jews and renews the assurance that he and his Government will take no action which might make enemies of the Arab people. Only the Arabic version of Mr. Roosevelt's letter is available here.

THE RUHR MAKES STEEL AGAIN

German Industry Recovers

By ROSS MUNRO
Reuters Canadian Press Correspondent

ESSEN, Thursday. — Steel production in the Ruhr, stopped by the Allied invasion of Germany, is now being resummed on a small scale to provide girders for bridges and building in Germany's reconstruction.

Production is under rigid British control and only about 100,000 tons monthly are being produced, a negligible amount compared with 1,500,000 tons monthly turned out by the Germans in 1939 and 1,000,000 tons at the beginning of 1944.

The, at least partial, recovery of the Ruhr steel industry, has an important bearing on the coal crisis and is part of a vicious circle of shortages in which German economy is enmeshed.

Vicious Circle

To step up the Ruhr coal production food must be brought here, and to bring food in the bridges must be repaired. Steel is required for these repairs and steel will have to come from the industries here. Coal distribution also requires that the railway and road bridges be rebuilt, so that trains and lorries can roll to the other parts of Germany and the neighbouring countries.

Until recently only 1% of iron and steel plants in the Ruhr was operating and to obtain even 100,000 tons of steel monthly permission had to be given to open up other plants.

At the Potsdam discussion of an overall policy for eliminating Germany's war potential it is believed that Britain and the United States wanted her producing capacity reduced by 40—50 percent while the Russians wanted it cut down to 15 percent of the normal.

Peace Through Strength

WASHINGTON, Thursday (R). — So far as the continued peace of the world was concerned, the United States must impress the military staffs of foreign Governments with America's military strength, said the US. Army Chief of Staff, General George Marshall, in testimony to the House of Representatives Appropriations Committee made public today.

General Marshall added:

"If we have a readily available, great military potential—which means men trained up to a certain point, though not actually in the ranks — then when Congress or the President speaks in regard to international relationships, the world will — the world must listen attentively."

Declaring that the atomic bomb was primarily psychological and would not necessarily reduce the number of men required for defence, General Marshall urged that for defence, and to influence the peace of the world, America must be able to mobilize four million men in one year after the development of a national emergency.

6 Killed in Buenos Aires

By U.W. COPELAND
U.P. Correspondent

BUENOS AIRES, Thursday. — Six persons were reported to have been killed and nearly 50 wounded in shooting affrays today as supporters of Argentina's resurrected "strong man," Colonel Juan Peron, sought to enforce a general strike in celebration of his return to power.

"La Prensa" said that three Navy vessels left Buenos Aires shortly before midnight carrying Vice-Admiral Hector Vernengo Lima, one of the leaders of the abortive coup which deposed Peron a week ago, on board of one of them. All transport — buses, trolly-cars, and taxis — in Buenos Aires halted in response to Col. Peron's call for a 24-hour strike.

Reports from the interior said that the general strike was complete in both Rosario and Santa Fe. Shooting broke out in the municipal fruit and vegetable market in Buenos Aires today, as Peronists tried to prevent other employees from working.

Earlier, eight persons were shot and wounded seriously after Peronists laid siege to the offices of the democratic newspaper "Critica," the largest afternoon daily in the capital.

AFTER MIDNIGHT

President Truman has denied categorically the current rumours, that a new Big Three meeting was contemplated.

An appeal to the governments of Eastern Europe to discontinue deporting Germans until the winter is over, is contained in a motion signed by 126 members of Parliament.

Mass Murder -- Main Charge

WASHINGTON, (U.P.) — Twenty four top ranking Nazis from Goering down to Propagandist Hans Frische were formally charged today with plotting and starting World War II, and with barbarous mass atrocities, murders, persecution, destruction, pillage and devastation unmatched in scope and savagery in the history of mankind.

Hitler is considered dead and is therefore not among the twenty-four. Neither are Goebbels or Himmler who committed suicide rather than face their punishment. But the twenty-four—the first batch of Nazi ringleaders to be taken to account for their crimes — were left under no misapprehension in regard to their share of responsibility for World War II, and for the mass bestiality that bled Europe, laid cities waste and doomed whole countries to misery which will be felt for generations to come.

Crime of Conspiracy

The defendants are charged on four counts. Part one of the Indictment deals with the "common plan of conspiracy". The common objectives of the conspiracy were, according to the indictment, to "abrogate and overthrow the Versailles Treaty, acquire territories lost by Germany, acquire still further territories in Europe and elsewhere." The methods used included "deceit, threats and intimidation by propaganda, violation of international treaties, agreements and assurances."

Extermination of Jews

The Nazis are accused of "implementing a race policy with a programme of relentless persecution of Jews aimed at their extermination, an intent which the conspirators succeeded in carrying out in many localities of Europe. Of 9,600,000 Jews, 5,700,000 have disappeared. Only remnants of the Jewish population in Europe remained.

Crime of Aggression

Then came a series of foreign aggressions launched by diabolical machines and in violation of treaties. The defendants are charged with 65 of such treaty violations. "With the first aggression successfully consummated the conspirators obtained the much desired resources and bases and were ready to undertake further aggressions. It was recognized that Poland would fight if attacked. Accordingly it was determined to isolate Poland first and, if possible, prevent a simultaneous conflict with the Western Powers. It was agreed that Britain was the enemy to their aspirations. Therefore, every attempt was made to overwhelm her by a "Blitzkrieg."

The aggressive war against Russia was launched after "Nazi conspirators had caused Germany falsely and deceitfully to enter into a non-agression pact with the U.S.S.R."

Subsequently, "the Nazi conspirations exhorted Japan to seek a new order of things".

Part Two charges the defendants with "crimes against peace," it observes that it was the defendants "who waged the war of aggression."

Wanton Mass Murder

Part Three of the indictment deals with war crimes proper; it piles up the data against the defendants who were responsible for the sea of blood that flooded Europe". All the defendants acting in concert with each other formulated and executed the plan of conspiracy to commit their crime:" — wanton mass murder.

"Murder and ill-treatment were carried out by diverse means and included:

Shooting, hanging, gassing, starvation, gross over-crowding, systematic under-nutrition, kicking, beating, brutality, torture of all kinds including the use of hot water, pulling off fingernails, performance of experiments by means of operations and otherwise on living human beings, the immersion in icy water, asphyxiation, torture of limbs and the use of instruments of torture, such as an iron helmet, electric current and other means practised in all prisons, and in torture chambers fitted at Gestapo centres."

The rate of mortality attained in concentration camps reached such figures as — French dead: Buchenwald — 22,761; Dachau — 11,500; 780 priests died from exhaustion in Mauthausen. Of 228,000 French political and racial deportees in concentration camps only 28,000 survived.

From Denmark to Italy

In Denmark 600 Danish subjects were killed in the course of "a premeditated campaign of terrorism initiated in the latter part of 1943." About 500 Danish subjects were murdered in German prisons and concentration camps.

In Belgium, tortures were carried out between 1940 and 1944 in Brussels, Liege, Ghent, Namur and other cities.

In Holland 400 persons were murdered when the Vught camp was evacuated.

In Luxemburg 500 persons were murdered and another 521 "illegally imprisoned, of whom at least 400 were murdered."

In Italy, at least 7,500 men, women and children ranging from teens to extreme old age were murdered by German soldiery.

From Greece to Russia

"The blood of innocents flowed in torrents in East Russia, Poland, Czechoslovakia, Yugoslavia and Greece "From the first of September 1939 when they invaded Poland, and from the 22 June 1941 when they invaded the U.S.S.R., the German Government and High Command adopted a systematic policy of murder and ill-treatment of the civilian population of the eastern countries, as they were successively occupied by German armed forces."

One million five hundred thousand and five hundred persons out of the four million in Auschwitz were murdered. Among them were citizens of Poland, Russia, U.S.A., Britain, Czechoslovakia and others, 700,000 persons mostly Russians and Poles, were exterminated in Lwow where, in addition 133,000 Jews were shot or tortured in the local ghetto.

In Czechoslovakia, as a result of torture, beating, hanging and shooting, thousands were annihilated in Gestapo prisons in Brno, and other places, totalling 20,000 persons. Moreover, many thousands internees were subjected to criminal treatment. Thousands of Czech patriots, Protestants, lawyers, doctors, teachers, etc. were arrested as hostages and a large number killed.

25 Million Homeless

"On the territory of the Soviet Union, Nazi conspirators destroyed or severely damaged 1,710 cities and over 70,000 villages and hamlets, 6 million buildings, — making homeless 25 million people. As evident from official memoranda of the German Command, the Nazi conspirators planned the complete annihilation of entire Soviet cities.

"Crimes Against Humanity"

In Part Four the defendants are accused that "they all committed crimes against humanity in Germany and in all countries and territories occupied by the German forces since the first of September 1939, in Austria, Czechoslovakia, Italy, and on the high seas."

Murders, enslavements and deportations are outlined again together with the persecution of Jews before and during the war. The defendants are charged with the murder of Dollfus, the Social-Democrat Breitscheid and the Communist Thaelmann; the imprisonment of Schuschnigg and Pastor Niemoeller and numerous other political and religous personages.

Four Countries in Election Fever

Election ferment was reported from four European countries in Reuters dispatches yesterday.

Bulgaria: Following the decision of the Opposition groups to boycott the elections, the Fatherland Front, a five-party coalition, will be the sole body taking part.

Distribution of seats among the five parties is: Communists—98; Agrarians—98; Zveno (led by Premier Kimon Georgiev)—46; Fatherland Front Social Democrats—31; Radicals—11.

The total number of seats has been increased by nine to provide sufficient seats for the newly-admitted Radical Party.

Portugal: President Carmona on Wednesday night refused to intervene to grant free elections in Portugal. Opposition leaders had a 50-minute talk with him in a last hour appeal to intervene with the Premier, Dr. Salazar.

The President strongly expressed his admiration for Dr. Salazar's regime. Nominations for the polling began yesterday. The Opposition repeated their previous threat not to submit any names of candidates.

Yugoslavia: The Belgrade Government is carrying on a whirlwind campaign throughout the country, with polling day a month away, holding hundreds of mass meetings addressed by Ministers, Generals, and local candidates.

Government supporters say that the Opposition has made a tactical mistake in deciding to abstain from the elections as they will afterwards have no right to speak on behalf of any section of the people.

The Opposition claim that they were prevented from competing on equal terms with the People's Front and therefore abstained in order not to give the Government a chance of proclaiming that it had won in fair elections.

The Government declares it has the support of at least 80 per cent of the Yugoslav people.

Hungary: Reports are confirmed of the issue of instructions by Marshal Klementi Voroshilov, Soviet Commander, that the Hungarian political parties are to issue joint lists for the general elections due to be held on November 4.

In London, the British official view is understood to be one of considerable regret since these instructions are held to interfere with the free conduct of the elections in Hungary.

It is not yet known whether this step will affect the British intention to recognize any Hungarian Government resulting from the general elections.

The Soviet move follows striking gains by the Smallholders Party in the recent municipal elections. The causes of the unrest which led to the imposition of a state of siege throughout the country some 48 hours ago still remain obscure.

LATE Edition

THE PALESTINE POST

JERUSALEM
SUNDAY, DEC. 16, 1945

PRICE: 15 MILS
VOL. XX, No. 5973

Column One

By David Courtney

WASHINGTON and Mr. Byrnes are apparently insuring against failure at Moscow. Their utterances are intended to give the impression that discussions will be informal and decisions merely provisional. They say in effect that if nothing decisive comes of Moscow no one should be surprised. Nobody will be. At the same time, despatches from London make it clear that Mr. Bevin expects something to happen, and has a pretty full dossier to draw out when he sits in front of M. Molotov. He intends to raise the central problem of Germany and, it is believed, to insist upon reaching a workable basis for the final disposal of Italian colonies and other debatable territories formerly under Italian rule. One report says that Mr. Bevin is in obstinate mood and, ready himself to lay all sorts of surprising cards on the table, is determined to force M. Molotov to display his. A Reuter message from Moscow provides further evidence to discount the American suggestion that the meeting is only to exchange views, not to unify them. It says that Persia and a settlement of the Persian problem is definitely on the agenda; and that the Russians will call for a realignment of policies in the Far East.

WHAT Moscow anticipates is indicated to a certain degree by her official and semi-official press and radio. Since the announcement of the conference of the three Foreign Secretaries, press and radio campaign have been opened affecting Persia, the Far East, Turkey, Spain, Poland and South-East Europe. The line on Persia has become much clearer. In simple terms it is this: Russia has as much right to keep her troops there as Britain to keep hers in Egypt, Palestine or Iraq, not to mention Indonesia; and since the withdrawal of all troops from Persia means virtually the political status quo, with Britain exercising supreme diplomatic influence at Teheran, the British demand that all foreign troops should clear out of the country is suspect anyway. The argument, of course, is weak; but only to those who know the facts — and even then its weakness is probably legal rather than moral. On Persia, Russia has at any rate the advantage of going to the Conference with, as it were, Azerbaijan in her pocket. Tabriz, the second town of Persia, has fallen to the Democrats and practically the whole rich province is now independent of the capital.

WHAT Russia seems to be seeking all over the world is not a balance of power on the basis of old-fashioned political and strategic values, but an equilibrium of forces designed to create stability. She regards world stability as her main defence, and probably is less avid of imperial power than anxious to diminish the imperial power of her major competitors. It is probable that she has no desire to occupy Persia; but would rather do that than submit to a frontier State under what she conceives to be the subjection of Britain. Some circles trace Russia's policy in China to the same negative source — a desire to reduce Anglo-Saxon hegemony rather than impose Soviet hegemony. If these are the facts, and there is a lot to be said for them, it looks as if there is a clear basis for international unity and collaboration; and if they are put that way to Mr. Bevin, instead of in the petulant tabulation of British troop movements appearing in Friday's "Pravda", there is some reason to hope that Britain will react. It has been said in this column before, and I repeat it now, that Britain, for all her impoverishment and financial vassalage to the United States, is still the key to world unity. She has greater flexibility than the other great powers, and her present Government has a foot in both camps. If Mr. Bevin uses the opportunity, he can raise his country's prestige and advance world progress and security. There is still a chance that he may.

WHAT, meanwhile, are we to say of the happenings in Indonesia? Not Mr. Bevin or Mr. Attlee or any other member of the Labour Government will find that easy to explain away. "Pravda" may exaggerate concerning the purpose behind the presence of British troops in Indonesia, Saigon, Egypt, Palestine and elsewhere; but nothing that can be said in malice is as bad in its effect on public opinion as such factual reports as have been published the last day or two on the burning and bombing of villages in Indo China and Java. These punitive acts cannot fail to shock progressive opinion everywhere, and to cast suspicion upon British foreign policy wherever it is applied. To be sure, far worse has been done, and is being done, by other powers; but that is not the point: the point is that far better is expected of Britain and is needful if she is to retain her voice as a moral factor in world affairs.

Jerusalem, December 16.

U.N.O. JOB FOR MRS. ROOSEVELT

WASHINGTON, Saturday (UP) Mrs. Eleanor Roosevelt is being considered by President Truman for a post with the United Nations Organization.

It is learned that the Senate Democratic leader, Senator Barkley, is sounding Senators on the possible appointment of the former First Lady.

NAZIS ADMIT MURDERING 6 MILLION JEWS IN EUROPE

NOT ENOUGH TO SATISFY HIMMLER

By ERIC BOURNE,
Reuters Special Correspondent

NUREMBERG, Saturday. — The Germans killed 6,000,000 Jews in the East, according to an S.S. Sturmbann-fuehrer (Major), Dr. Wilhelm Hoettl, whose affidavit was offered as evidence before the War Crimes Tribunal yesterday.

Hoettl's affidavit said that in August last year, he talked in Budapest with S.S. Obersturmbann-fuehrer (Lt.-Col.) Adolf Eichmann (Hebrew-speaking Nazi German born in Sarona near Tel Aviv), who "certainly had the best record of Jews who had been murdered."

Eichmann told Hoettl that he reported to Himmler that approximately 4,000,000 Jews had been killed in various extermination camps, while an additional 2,000,000 met their deaths in other ways, the majority being shot by the Security Police.

Himmler was not satisfied with this report, since in his opinion the number of Jews who had been killed must have been more than 6,000,000. "I have reasons to believe, however, that Eichmann's information was correct," Hoettl added.

Major Walsh, U.S. Deputy prosecutor, cited evidence that 1,765,000 Jews were exterminated at the Auschwitz and Birkenau death-camps, between April, 1942, and April, 1944.

According to a document from the U.S. President's War Refugee Board files, the Jews murdered were of the following nationalities:

900,000 Poles; 100,000 Dutch; 45,000 Greeks; 150,000 French; 50,000 Belgians; 60,000 Germans; 50,000 Yugoslavs, Italians and Norwegians; 50,000 Lithuanians; 30,000 Bohemians, Moravians and Austrians; 30,000 Slovaks; and 300,000 of various nationalities taken from scattered camps in Poland.

Starving of Millions

Major Walsh introduced a new series of German documents and directives clearly showing the calculated plan to starve millions of Jews to death by shutting them off from all sources of supply and certain areas, and forbidding them to participate in agriculture where they might get food.

So widespread did the executions of the Jews become that the S.S. police at Berlin wrote to Rosenberg complaining that some 5,000 Jews killed by the police and S.S. might have been used for forced labour.

The document added that it should be possible "to avoid atrocities and bury those who have been liquidated. To lock men, women and children into barns and set fire to the structures, does not appear to be a suitable method of combating these bands, even if it is desired to exterminate the population. This method is unworthy of the German cause and hurts our reputation."

S.S. Death Vans

S.S. death vans were mentioned by Major Walsh in his evidence when he produced a report on their operations at Kiev, written by S.S. officials on May 16, 1942. Another report from Riga complained that the existing three death vans were incapable of handling the Jews being brought in for execution, and requested another five vans to cope with the numbers.

Major Walsh then gave details of the German extermination camp for Jews at Treblinka, in Poland. This was part of the indictment of Hans Frank by the Polish Government for *establishing in March, 1942, an extermination camp at Treblinka intended for mass killings of Jews by suffocating them in steam-filled chambers.*

The Polish charge added: "It may be assumed that several hundreds of thousands of Jews have been exterminated at Treblinka. Exposed to the most cruel sufferings of body and soul, their death in the steam chambers must have come almost as a welcome relief.

"Their only crime consisted in fact of belonging to a race condemned by Hitler to death."

Major Walsh read an extract from a British War Office report stating that, during an interrogation, a French student deposed: "During July 1944 at the Auschwitz concentration camp, Hungarian Jews were being liquidated at the rate of 12,000 daily, and the crematoria could not deal with such numbers. Many bodies were thrown in large pits and covered with quick-lime."

"Germanizing Europe"

When Major Walsh closed the case on the murder of six million Jews, another U.S. assistant prosecutor, Mr. Sam Harris, took up the evidence on the spoliation and "Germanization" of the occupied countries.

The first document underlined the German intention to make the conquered Poles slaves of Germany and to rob the country of all its industrial assets.

Frank in a report explained how he intended to govern Poland under Hitler's directive which provided that Poland could only be administered by utilizing the country through the means of ruthless exploitation of all supplies of raw materials, machines and factory installations; making available all labour for work in Germany; and reducing Polish economy to the bare minimum for existence.

It also provided for the closing of all educational Institutions lest they breed a new race of intellectuals, and for reducing Poland to "the status of a German colony, with the Poles becoming the slaves of the Great German world empire."

Poland as Test Ground

Poland was used as a testing ground, said Mr. Harris. Secret documents, introduced in Court, showed that the Nazis had plans for wholesale migrations and re-shuffling of European populations to provide a solid German race for the Reich. The Czech problem was to be solved by absorbing half of the population into Germany and stripping the other half of power and shipping it off.

This last order agreed it would take years to "Germanize" Czechoslovakia, but "any elements which resist the planned 'Germanization' are to be handled roughly and should be eliminated."

At the conclusion of yesterday's hearing, Mr. Justice Jackson, the U.S. prosecutor, announced that he proposed to seek a declaratory judgment by the Tribunal that the six Nazi organizations named in the indictment — the Reich Cabinet, the Leadership Corps of the Nazi Party, the S.S., including the Sicherheitsdienst (S.D.), the Gestapo, the S.A., and the General Staff and High Command of the German armed forces — be named in the indictment as criminal organizations.

Such findings, he pointed out, might constitute the basis for proceedings against individuals in other Courts.

The United States was anxious to present as much as possible of the evidence against these organizations before the Christmas recess, he said, in order that the defence might have an opportunity for examining it.

Court Shown Grim Exhibits of Terror

By GEORGE LICHTHEIM,
Palestine Post Correspondent

NUREMBERG, Dec. 13 (delayed) — Lampshades made of the human skin of victims slain for this purpose by concentration camp guards, and shrunken human skulls used as mascots by Nazis in the same camp, figured among the exhibits when the prosecution this afternoon concluded its case against Nazi terrorism. A new chapter was then opened when the Nazi extermination of the Jewish people was detailed by Major Walsh, the American Military prosecutor, with the aid of captured evidence, including photographs of the Ghetto liquidation taken by an S.S. member.

Going back to the original Nazi programme and outlining the gradual intensification of the campaign against the Jews, the Prosecutor gradually prepared the Court for the climax of the extermination campaign in the actual liquidation of the Polish ghettoes.

Campaign of Horror

Showing the gradual development of the anti-Jewish campaign, beginning with Streicher's ritual murder ravings 20 years ago, and ending with a diary entry of Governor Frank of Poland on August 24, 1942, "that we sentenced 1,200,000 Jews to die of hunger should be noted only marginally," the prosecutor built up a case notably against Frick, who signed most of the early anti-Jewish decrees; Goering, who organized the 1938 confiscations; Streicher and Rosenberg, who supplied the ideological basis; and Frank, who directed the massacres in Poland.

Despite the somewhat sketchy and superficial presentation of the evidence, which mostly ignored the historical background of the campaign, leaving the sources of this outburst unexplained, the prosecutor succeeded in impressing upon the Court the full horror of the final extermination drive, which served the double purpose of ridding the Reich of superfluous consumers, and serving the Nazi political purpose as well as the insatiable bloodlust of Himmler's S.S.

The full S.S. report on the liquidation of the Warsaw ghetto was also issued, giving a detailed day-by-day account of the extermination, resulting in the killing of many tens of thousands of Jewish civilians, mostly unarmed.

A marked feature of this report, which was prefaced by the words, "For the Fuehrer and their Country: The following fell in the battle for the destruction of the Jews and bandits in the former ghetto of Warsaw" followed by fifteen names and then the words "They gave their utmost, their lives. We shall never forget them!" is the apparent conviction of the S.S. murderers that their "operation" with tanks, flame-throwers, and grenades against helpless humanity was a serious and dangerous military action.

Though many of the Jews were armed with primitive weapons smuggled in by Poles and others, the great majority were simply slaughtered, as evidenced by the comparison of losses on both sides.

The accused lost lots of their buoyancy during the recital but showed no sign of shame.

Truman Sees U.S. Inquiry Members

WASHINGTON, Saturday (PTA). — The six American members of the Committee of Inquiry are being received by President Truman today, the White House press secretary announces.

They are impressed with the importance of taking up their work with all possible despatch (he said) and therefore wished to talk over the whole matter with the President.

LONDON, Saturday (Reuter). —The constitution of the Joint Anglo-American Committee of Inquiry on Palestine into the Palestinian problem was the subject of an exchange of Notes between the British Ambassador, Lord Halifax, and the Secretary of State, Mr. James F. Byrnes. The text was published here yesterday.

Mr. Byrnes wrote to Lord Halifax on December 10:

"I have the honour to inform Your Excellency with reference to our conversations on the subject that the Government of the United States agrees to constitute, in co-operation with the Government of the United Kingdom, a joint Anglo-American Committee of Inquiry with the following terms of reference:

"The Committee should be composed of six nationals of the United States appointed by the Government of the United States, and six nationals of the United Kingdom appointed by the Government of the United Kingdom, and shall operate under a rotating chairmanship.

"The Governments of the United States and the United Kingdom shall urge on the Committee the need for the utmost expedition in dealing with the subject committed to it for investigation and shall request that they may be furnished with its reports within 120 days of the inception of the inquiry.

Committee's Procedure

"The procedure of the Committee shall be determined by the Committee itself and it will be open to it, if it thinks fit, to deal simultaneously through the medium of sub-committees with any of the subjects entrusted to its consideration.

"Each Government shall be responsible for compensating its own members of the Committee and other personnel selected by it and for paying such other expenses as are not susceptible of being jointly shared by the two Governments. All other expenses of the Committee shall be borne jointly by both Governments in equal proportions."

Lord Halifax wrote to Mr. Byrnes on December 10:

"I have the honour, under instructions from the Secretary for Foreign Affairs, to inform Your Excellency that the British Government in the United Kingdom are in agreement with the terms of the Note of December 10 about the Joint Anglo-American Committee of Inquiry to report on the position of Jews in certain countries of Europe and in Palestine."

(American comment, Page 3)

LORD CHORLEY

Lord Chorley, who took part in the debate on Palestine in the House of Lords last Monday, is Professor Robert Samuel Theodore Chorley, M.A., occupying the Chair of Commercial and Industrial Law at London University (and not as stated). Lord Chorley is a Labourite.

TRUMAN URGES TRUCE IN CHINA

WASHINGTON, Saturday (R). — President Truman today called for an immediate end to hostilities in China between the National Government and the Communist forces, and the summoning of a national conference of representatives of all major political elements of the Chinese nation to seek an early solution to the present internal strife.

The President issued a comprehensive statement of United States policy towards China within two hours of the departure of General George C. Marshall, new American diplomatic envoy to Chungking.

President Truman reiterated that America would continue to recognize Generalissimo Chiang Kai Shek's Government as the only legal Government of China.

"It is the proper instrument to achieve the objective of unifying China," he said.

ELEVEN BELSEN BANDITS HANGED

HAMBURG, Saturday (Reuter). — All eleven men and women of the Belsen concentration camp staff sentenced to death were hanged on Thursday, it was announced yesterday.

The executions took place in the presence of the prison governor and one British doctor. Only one scaffold was used and the executions were carried out in accordance with British practice. Witnesses from the Court at Lueneburg were present to identify the condemned persons.

German Catholic and Protestant prison chaplains were in attendance. All eleven went quietly to their death and there were no scenes outside the prison.

Chief of those executed were Josef Kramer, commandant; Irma Grese, 21 year old S.S. woman; Elisabeth Volkenrath, an S.S. guard at the camp; Fritz Klein, the camp doctor who made gas-chamber selections; and Juana Bormann, stated at the trial to have turned a dog loose on prisoners.

Five days before the executions Field-Marshal Montgomery rejected an appeal for mercy. Sentences of death were passed on November 16.

POLICE SWOOP IN LONDON

Palestine Post Cable

LONDON, Saturday. — The results of last night's police round-up was announced as follows by Scotland Yard tonight:

Total number of persons stopped — 15,161;

Deserters handed over to military escort — 32;

Arrests for alleged house-breaking — 2;

Arrests for alleged larceny — 4;

Arrests for alleged unlawful possession — 9.

In addition to these arrests, one person was detained on a charge of being found on enclosed premises, two others were R.A.F. personnel said to be wearing false decorations, and another was an escaped Italian prisoner of war. (Earlier Story, Page 3.)

U.N.O. CHOOSES U.S. FOR HEADQUARTERS

LONDON, Saturday (R). — The United Nations executive committee's recommendations that U.N.O. headquarters should be in the United States was today endorsed by the Preparatory Commission with the requisite two-thirds majority, by 30 votes to 14, with six abstentions.

The vote was later made unanimous on a motion by the Canadian delegate seconded by Mr. Philip Noel-Baker, for the United Kingdom, who had led the case for Europe.

Voting was by roll-call after a motion to vote by secret ballot had been defeated.

The Commission's decision for the United States was reached after prolonged and, in some cases, bitter debates.

BRITISH DOCKERS ACCEPT TERMS

LONDON, Saturday (Reuter). British dockers have accepted proposed terms of settlement of their wage dispute made under the Government investigation committee's report, and authorized union representatives to enter into an agreement with the employers.

Dockers' delegates from all over Britain, at a conference in London yesterday, accepted the basis of a 19/- minimum daily wage to date back to November 26, new piece rates, and a medical scheme.

The question of a 48-hour week was left in abeyance because it is being dealt with by the trade unions on a national basis.

MIDDLE EAST ACCORD HAILED IN LEVANT

French Schools in Syria to Reopen

By YEHUDA HELMAN,
Palestine Post Correspondent

BEIRUT, Saturday (By Telephone). — The Syrian Government announced today its decision that all private schools, notably French schools, would reopen immediately. A French spokesman here expressed hope that normal political relations would be established between Syria and France, such as obtained between the Lebanon and France.

Commenting on the Franco-British agreements for the Middle East the spokesman told your correspondent today that it reaffirmed France's recognition of Syro-Lebanese independence proclaimed in 1941 by General Catroux. As at that time France had no constitutional government, it was highly important that the legally-elected French Government should now confirm the independence of the Levant States.

It was the aim of the signatories to help Syria and the Lebanon enter a new era of stability and development, and all progressive people would benefit by the new agreement, the spokesman went on. However, certain politicians would be disappointed that Great Britain and France were co-ordinating their policies in the Middle East which would thwart their policy of exploiting Franco-British differences for their personal ends.

Wider Implications

The agreement also had broad international implications, the spokesman continued. It had been discussed for many weeks in Paris and London, and was the subject of most serious study covering the whole area of the Middle East which actually meant all territory west of India up to the Russian border.

The text of the document was communicated to Russia and the United States, and American support for it had been secured.

The agreement, said the spokesman, marked a point of departure for a common Anglo-French international policy, and it was to be hoped that other Middle East problems still unsolved might be seen in a new light.

The French press is more reserved in its comment on the Anglo-French agreement on the Middle East than official circles in Paris have been. While most papers welcome the clarification in the relations between the two Powers, they observe that the agreement does not imply a common Middle Eastern policy.

"One should remember," writes the extreme right "Epoque" (Paris) "that after the Franco-British Agreement of 1904 in North Africa a quarter of a century was needed for local agents to adopt the new state of mind indicated in their Governments' policies. It is not slandering our British friends to note that in these regions a tradition of suspicion exists towards France, and it would be unwise to expect this to disappear between one day and another".

In Beirut the agreement has been criticized as a settlement of the Levant question without the Levant States having any part. On the other hand, Sayyed Abdullah el-Yafi, Deputy for Beirut and a former Prime Minister, finds that the agreement leaves no doubt that the independence of the Levant has become secure.

In Damascus it is pointed out by a number of Deputies that under cover of organizing the withdrawal of foreign troops they might actually be concentrated in the Lebanon.

(R. and ANA)

PATTON IMPROVING

FRANKFURT, Saturday (R).— Today's bulletin on the state of health of General George Patton, Commander of the U.S. 15th Army in Germany, who was injured in a car accident last Sunday, said that his general condition was excellent.

"There has been a slight but significant improvement in sensation during the past 24 hours," the bulletin added. The General continues alert and cheerful."

BRITISH ADVANCE IN BATAVIA

By NOEL BUCKLEY,
Reuters Correspondent

BATAVIA, Saturday. —British forces have taken over the Batavian railways and telephone exchange at Buitenzorg, about 40 miles from Batavia along the Bandoeng road. The Indonesian "Resident" had left the town after declaring himself unable to maintain order.

On the whole, the present Indonesian administration is doing its utmost to end the disturbances, especially in West Java. The Indonesian Peace Preservation Corps at Bandoeng, a hill station and internee centre in Western Java, are cooperating in full military action against extremists.

Leading members of the Indonesian "Republican" Government will shortly undertake a tour of Central and Eastern Java to induce the local leaders, who wield real power, to accept its discipline.

In Eastern Java, British troops continue to fan out south and west of the Naval base of Sourabaya, and are now clearing towns about 15 miles from the port against slight opposition.

Dr. Van Mook Leaves

Dr. Hubertus van Mook, Lieutenant-Governor of the Netherlands East Indies, left Batavia today for The Hague by air, on his way to confer with his home Government. He was expected to return in about three weeks to resume his talks with Indonesian leaders.

A British paratroop battalion which won fame at Arnhem and two companies of Gurkhas have arrived in Batavia. Allied military police arrested the editor of the popular Indonesian newspaper "Merdeka" and his wife, a graduate of Columbia University. The editor was later released but his wife was detained.

Restitution from Siam

At Singapore, Mr. Moberly Dening, British Foreign Office adviser, stated that it was necessary that Siam "should make restitution for the damage done to British interests, and in particular to the interests of territories bordering on Siam, for the welfare of which Britain is responsible. Siam must realize that treaties are not to be lightly broken."

Mr. Dening has resumed negotiations at Singapore to end the hostilities between Britain and Siam. Britain's armistice proposal are designed to ensure cooperation in dealing with the Japanese remaining in Siam.

TALKS BEGIN IN MOSCOW

INTEREST CENTRES ON PERSIA

MOSCOW, Saturday. — Both Mr. Ernest Bevin, British Foreign Minister, and Mr. James Byrnes, U.S. Secretary of State, have arrived in Moscow after delay and some anxiety due to bad flying weather, and have already been received by the Foreign Commissar, M. Molotov.

Though official statements have specified only atomic energy as one of the subjects to be discussed, it is definite that Persia will be on the agenda, Sir Reader Bullard, the British Ambassador to Iran, and Mr. J. D. Jernegan, U.S. Embassy Representative, having left Teheran for Moscow by Soviet plane.

Another major question up for discussion appears to be Allied relations in the Far East centring round control of Japan.

The talks were "an exploratory exchange of views" and need not necessarily lead to the announcement of any major decisions, Mr. Byrnes told the press.

Meanwhile, at least as far as Persia is concerned, facts are being created which might in themselves become decisions. The latest news from Teheran is that insurgent forces have captured Tabriz, the chief town of Azerbaijan, and Ardabil, the Caspian port 20 miles from the Soviet frontier. All Persian battalions were stopped by the Red Army from moving into the "trouble province" and have returned to the capital on orders from their headquarters.

Azerbaijan Lost,

"Azerbaijan seems definitely lost to Persia," said Nurteza Qualkhan Bayatt, Governor of the province, who arrived in Teheran from Tabriz on Friday and who stated that he had been advised to leave by Jafar Pishevari, president of the newly formed provincial government and leader of the Democratic Party. It appears, states one commentator, that the insurgents hope to confront the Government with a fait accompli before the Moscow Conference can make any decision.

In Teheran itself, although everything looks calm, measures have been taken to prevent disturbances, it being rumoured that several illegal groups are in existence. In spite of this, M. Hakimi, the Iranian Prime Minister, is reported to be optimistic and great hopes are placed on his coming visit to Moscow accompanied by his Foreign Minister. Whether the visit will coincide with or impinge on the talks of the three Allied Foreign Ministers remains for the latter to decide.

The actual military operations in Azerbaijan are expected to develop in intensity in the Spring.

Persian Government circles point out that the province's present rulers are neither Democrats nor Central Government, but Russian occupation authorities. Since these are pledged to evacuate Iran by March 2 at the latest the situation then is likely to develop to a grim climax.

If the Foreign Ministers in Moscow agreed that the foreign forces leave Iran appreciably in advance of that date, it is claimed that the Iran Government would be capable of restoring order, even if it involved a certain amount of fighting.

The next week or two would show to what lengths Russia is prepared to go. It is believed in Teheran that that has already been indicated by the Soviet reply of November 26 to the Iran Government's Note, when it was stated in effect that should the Iran Government despatch troops to Azerbaijan and precipitate bloodshed, it would be necessary to send additional Red Army forces from Russia to restore order.

A strong case to be consulted and represented at talks at which decisions affecting Persia are taken, was advanced by the Iranian Government two days ago. The State Department disclosed in Washington the text of a British Note expressing agreement with the American view that Persia should be able to use her own forces wherever and in whatever manner necessary to preserve its authority and security, but reiterating that British troops could not be withdrawn without similar action on the part of Russia.

U.S. Interest

The United States would prefer a solution of the Iranian question within an international frame rather than by agreement between two countries, well-informed circles in Washington state.

The Iranian crisis is part of the general situation in the Middle East, and its solution will influence public opinion in that part of the world as to the real intentions of the Big Powers in the international questions of the future. It is the United States' wish, according to these circles, that the Moscow discussion of the Iran problem should be only preliminary, and that the final solution should be left to the Security Council of the U.N.O. Although the United States did not sign the agreement fixing the date of the Anglo-Russian evacuation, American Government circles take great interest in the Persian question and also in Russian aims in the Near and Middle East.

(Reuter, U.P. and AFP)

American Securities Suffer Setback

(Reuters Economic Service)

NEW YORK, Saturday. —Wall Street this week suffered its biggest setback since mid-July. Undoubtedly, the market was discouraged by the lack of a conciliatory attitude among either labour or management. The fact that the setback was led by steels and motors was indicative of the market's temper, and the factors affecting these groups spread their depressing influence to other sections.

If the slump was technical, as some assert, the market should partly regain its equilibrium, but if it represents mounting fear about the unsolved labour and price riddle, reaction may extend.

AFTER MIDNIGHT

A Persian Cabinet reshuffle is reported from Teheran, where a former Premier, Ghavam Sultaneh, may succeed Ibrahim Hakimi.

Carlo Scorza, former Fascist Party secretary and member of the Fascist Grand Council, was arrested yesterday at his hiding-place after weeks of search.

An important religious festival at Teheran was interrupted yesterday by a secret session of the Mejlis (Parliament). This is regarded as indicating the gravity of the present situation.

RUSSIANS CLAIM RIGHTS IN PERSIA

LONDON, Saturday (R). — The presence of British troops in Palestine, Egypt, the East Indies, and several European countries was challenged today by a "Pravda" commentator, David Zaslavski, according to the Moscow radio.

M. Zaslavski stated that the U.S.S.R. had the right to station its troops in Persia under its treaty with that country, continuing:

"Just as simple is the answer concerning Soviet troops in other countries. This can arouse no doubt or perplexity.

"It may seem that the question concerning the presence of British troops in Persia, in accordance with the 1942 agreement is relatively simple. Are there not in Persia British troops who were stationed there before the 1942 agreement?

"If so, when did they appear? For what purpose? Where are they stationed? What is their number? What are they doing? Do the conditions of the 1942 agreement extend to them also? We do not hear the answers to these questions.

Other Countries

"The Egyptian press almost daily raises the same question: 'When will Great Britain at last withdraw her troops from Egypt?' Truly, ancient Oedipus encountered less difficulty in extracting a reply from the Egyptian State than contemporary Egypt has in receiving an answer from the British State," the writer added.

RDITI LTD.
EL-AVIV · JERUSALEM · HAIFA
Complete Automotive Service
MOUTH · CHRYSLER · DE SOTO CARS

LATE Edition

THE PALESTINE POST

JERUSALEM
WEDNESDAY, MAY 1, 1946

PRICE 15 MILS
VOL. XXI., No. 6088

"ALISA"   BABY'S DREAM --
A RUBBER DOLL
RUBBER FACTORY
FRANZ LEVI LTD.
P.O.B. 787 HAIFA TEL. 5551, 30 Jaffa Rd

ALL POLITICAL CLAIMS REJECTED

INQUIRY COMMITTEE RECOMMENDS IMMIGRATION OF 100,000 JEWS THIS YEAR; REPEAL OF LAND LAWS; MANDATE ADMINISTRATION TO REMAIN; NO JEWISH OR ARAB STATE, BUT UNO TRUSTEESHIP

The unanimous report of the Anglo-American committee on Palestine recommends that 0,000 Jews be permitted to enter Palestine from Europe this year, if possible,

The Government of Palestine be continued under the present Mandate until a trusteeship agreement is reached under the United Nations and

the existing land transfer regulations be replaced by others based on a policy of freedom of sale, lease or use of land irrespective of race or community.

The Committee declare that Palestine should be-

come neither an Arab nor a Jewish state but a state safeguarding the rights and interests of Moslems, Jews, and Christians alike.

The mandatory, or trustee, should proclaim that Arab economy, education and political advancement in Palestine is of equal importance with that of the Jews. Until a trusteeship agreement has been made, Palestine should be administered according to the Mandate which declared that "the administration of Palestine should ensure that the rights and position of other sections of the population are not prejudiced, and shall facilitate

Jewish immigration under suitable conditions."

The report runs into many thousands of words, covering recommendations for the present, and future possibilities for Palestine.

Urging the Jewish Agency immediately to assume active co-operation with the Mandatory in suppressing terrorism and illegal immigration, the Committee expresses the hope that the Government of the U.S.A. will vigorously and generously participate with the Government of Great Britain in assisting in the movement of the immigrants.

The European Problem

...recommending that our ...ments, in association ...er countries, should be ...r to find new homes ...laced persons," we do ...gest that any country ...be asked to make ...ndamental change in its immigration policy. The conditions, ...we have seen in Europe are unprecedented, and unlikely to arise again that ...were convinced that special ...action could and should be ...e in arising immigration ...to meet this unique and ...larly distressing situation. Furthermore, we believe ...much could be accomplished — particularly in relation to those "displaced persons" including Jews, who ...ll relatives in countries out...de Europe — by a relaxation ...administrative regulations. ...investigations have led ...to believe that a considerable number of Jews will continue to live in Central European countries. In our view the ...emigration of all European Jews would be of service ...ther to the Jews themselves ...for Europe. Every effort ...ould be made to enable the ...to rebuild their shattered

communities, while permitting those Jews, who wish to do so, to emigrate. In order to achieve this, restitution of Jewish property should be effected as soon as possible. Our investigations showed us that the Governments chiefly concerned had for the most part already passed legislation to this end. A real obstacle, however, to individual restitution is that the attempt to give effect to this legislation is frequently a cause of active anti-Semitism. We suggest that, for the reconstruction of the Jewish communities, restitution of their corporate property, either through reparations payments or through other means, is of the first importance.

Nazi occupation has left behind it a legacy of anti-Semitism. This cannot be combated by legislation alone. The only really effective antidotes are the enforcement by each Government of guaranteed civil liberties and equal rights, to the very young and also to skilled workmen whose services will be needed for many months on work rendered necessary by the large influx. It should be made clear that no advantage in the obtaining of a certificate is to be gained by migration from one country to another, or by entering Palestine illegally.

Receiving so large a number will be a heavy burden on Palestine. We feel sure that the authorities will shoulder it and that they will have the full co-operation of the Jewish Agency.

Refugee Immigration Into Palestine

...number of Jewish sur...rs of Nazi and Fascist ...ution with whom we ...ceed to indeed there are more ...that number in Germany, ...ria and Italy alone. Al...ugh nearly a year has ...ed since their liberation, ...jority of these in Germany and Austria are still living ...in assembly centres, the ...alled "camps," siated con...tions in the midst of those ...hose hands they suffered so much.

...their interests and in the ...erests of Europe, the con...on should be closed and their ...camp life ended. Most of them ...have cogent reason for wish...ing to leave Europe. Many are ...the sole survivors of their fa...milies, and few have any tie ...binding them to the countries ...in which they used to live.

...Since the end of hostilities, ...ttle has been done to provide ...for their re-settlement else...where. Emigration laws and ...restrictions bar their entry to ...ost countries and much time ...just pass before such laws ...and restrictions can be alter...and effect given to the ...tentions. Some can go to ...Austria where the laws re...fever, others may secure ad...ission in certain quota. Their ...number is comparatively small.

We know of no country to ...which the great majority can ...go in the immediate future ...other than Palestine. Further...more that is where almost all ...them wanted to go. They ...are sure that they will receive a ...welcome, denied them else...where. There they hope to en...joy peace and rebuild their homes.

We believe it is essential ...that they should be given an ...opportunity to do so at the ...earliest possible time. Fur...thermore we have the assur...ances of the leaders of the ...Jewish Agency that they will ...be supported and cared for.

We recommend the author...zation and issue of 100,000 ...certificates for these reasons ...and because we feel that their ...immediate issue will save a ...great salutary effect upon the ...whole situation.

...In the awarding of these ...certificates priority should as ...far as possible be given to ...those in the centres, and to ...liberated in Germany.

and Austria who are no longer in the centres but remain in those countries. We do not desire that other Jewish victims who wish or will be impelled by their circumstances to leave the countries where they now are, or that those who fled from persecution before the outbreak of war, should be excluded. We appreciate that there will be difficulty in deciding questions of priority, but none the less we urge that so far as possible such a system should be adhered to, and that, in applying it, primary consideration should be given to the aged and infirm, to the very young and also to skilled workmen whose services will be needed for many months on work rendered necessary by the large influx.

Difficult problems will confront those responsible for organizing and carrying out the movement. The many organizations — public and private — working in Europe will certainly render all the aid they can; we mention UNRRA especially. Co-operation by all throughout is necessary.

We are sure that the Government of the United States, which has shown such keen interest in this matter, will participate vigorously and generously with the Government of Great Britain in its fulfilment. There are many ways in which help can be given.

Those who have opposed the admission of these unfortunate people into Palestine should know that we have fully considered all that they have put before us. We hope that they will look upon the situation again, that they will appreciate the considerations which have led us to our conclusion, and that above all, if they cannot see their way to help, at least they will not make the position of these sufferers more difficult.

Principles of Government: No Arab, No Jewish State

THROUGHOUT the long and ...bloody struggle of Jew ...and Arab for dominance in ...Palestine, each crying fiercely: ...'This land is mine' — except ...the brief reference in the ...report of the Royal Commis...on [hereafter referred to as ...the Peel Report] and the little ...notice, written and oral, ...we received on this point of ...view. World in Palestine ...been completely overlook...ed, glossed over or brushed

...aside, emphatically ...that in Palestine is a Holy ...Land to Christian, to the ...Moslem alike; and is ...same way, affirm that the

fact that it is the Holy Land, sets Palestine completely apart from other lands, and dedicates it to the precepts and practices of the Brotherhood of Man, not those of narrow nationalism.

For another reason, in the light of its long history, and particularly its history of the last thirty years, Palestine cannot be regarded as either a purely Jewish land.

The Jews have a historic connection with the country. The Jewish National Home, though embodying a minority of the population, is today a reality established under international guarantee. It has a right to continued existence, protection and development.

Yet Palestine is not, and never can be, a purely Jewish land. It lies at the crossroads of the Arab world. Its Arab population, descended from

COMMITTEE'S TEN RECOMMENDATIONS

The Committee made ten recommendations:

1) *The European Problem:* We have to report that such information as we received about countries other than Palestine gave no hope of substantial assistance in finding homes for Jews wishing or impelled to leave Europe.

But Palestine alone cannot meet the emigration needs of the Jewish victims of Nazi and Fascist persecution. The whole world shares responsibility for them and indeed for the resettlement of all "Displaced Persons".

We therefore recommend that our Governments together, and in association with other countries, should endeavour immediately to find new homes for all such "Displaced Persons", irrespective of creed or nationality, whose ties with their former communities have been irreparably broken.

Though emigration will solve the problems of some victims of persecution, the overwhelming majority, including a considerable number of Jews, will continue to live in Europe. We recommend therefore that our Governments endeavour to secure that immediate effect is given to the provision of the United Nations Charter calling for "universal respect for and observance of, human rights and fundamental freedoms for all without distinction as to race, sex, language, or religion."

2) *Immigration into Palestine:* We recommend (a) that 100,000 certificates be authorized immediately for the admission into Palestine of Jews who have been victims of Nazi and Fascist persecution and (b) that these certificates be awarded, as far as possible, in 1946, and that their actual immigration be pushed forward as rapidly as conditions will permit.

3) *Principles of Government:* No Arab, no Jew is in order to dispose once and for all of the exclusive claims of Jews and

Arabs to Palestine, we regard it as essential that a clear statement of the following principles should be made:

(1) That Jew shall not dominate Arab and Arab shall not dominate Jew in Palestine.

(2) That Palestine shall be neither a Jewish state nor an Arab state.

(3) That the form of government ultimately to be established shall, under international guarantees, fully protect and preserve the interests in the Holy Land of Christendom and of the Moslem and Jewish faiths.

Thus Palestine must ultimately become a state which guards the rights and interests of Moslems, Jews and Christians alike; and accords to the inhabitants, as a whole, the fullest measure of self-government, consistent with the three paramount principles set forth above.

4) *Mandate and United Nations Trusteeship:* We have reached the conclusion that hostility between Jews and Arabs and, in particular, the determination of each to achieve domination, if necessary by violence, make it almost certain that now and for some time to come any attempt to establish either an independent Palestinian state or independent Palestinian states would result in civil strife such as might threaten the peace of the world.

We therefore recommend that until this hostility disappears, the Government of Palestine be continued as at present under Mandate pending the execution of a trusteeship agreement under the United Nations.

5) *Equality of Standards:* Looking towards a form of ultimate self-government consistent with three principles laid down in recommendation No. 3, we recommend that the Mandatory or Trustee should proclaim the principle that Arab economic, educational and political advancement in Palestine is of equal importance with that of the Jews and should at once prepare

measures designed to bridge that gap which now exists and raise the Arab standard of living to that of the Jews and so bring the two peoples to a full appreciation of their common interests and common destiny in the land where both belong.

6) *Future Immigration Policy:* We recommend that pending the early reference to the United Nations of the execution of a trusteeship agreement, the Mandatory should administer Palestine according to the Mandate which declares with regard to immigration that "the Administration of Palestine, while ensuring that the rights and position of other sections of the population are not prejudiced, shall facilitate Jewish immigration under suitable conditions."

7) *Land Policy:* (a) We recommend that the Land Transfer Regulations of 1940 be rescinded and replaced by regulations based on a policy of freedom in the sale, lease or use of land, irrespective of race, community or creed; and provide adequate protection for the interests of small owners and tenant cultivators. (b) We further recommend that steps be taken to render nugatory and to prohibit provisions in conveyances, leases and agreements relating to land which stipulate that only members of one race, community or creed may be employed on or about or in connection therewith. (c) We recommend that the Government should exercise such close supervision over the Holy places and localities such as the Sea of Galilee and its vicinity, as well as protect them from desecration and from uses which offend the conscience of religious people; and that such laws as are required for this purpose be enacted forthwith.

8) *Economic Development:* Various plans for large-scale agricultural and industrial development in Palestine have been presented for our consideration;

these projects, if successfully carried into effect, could not only greatly enlarge the capacity of the country to support an increasing population, but also raise the living standard of Jew and Arab alike.

We are not in a position to assess the soundness of these specific plans; but we cannot state too strongly that, however technically feasible they may be, they will fail unless there is peace in Palestine. Moreover their full success requires the willing cooperation of adjacent Arab states, since they are not merely Palestinian projects. We recommend, therefore, that the examination, discussion and execution of these plans be conducted, from the start and throughout, in full consultation and co-operation not only with the Jewish Agency, but also with the Governments of the neighbouring Arab states directly affected.

9) *Education:* We recommend that, in the interests of the conciliation of the two peoples and of general improvement of the Arab standard of living, the educational system of both Jews and Arabs be reformed including the introduction of compulsory education within a reasonable time.

10) *The Need for Peace in Palestine:* We recommend that, if this Report is adopted, it should be made clear beyond all doubt to both Jews and Arabs, that any attempt from either side by threats of violence, by terrorism, or by the organization or use of illegal armies to prevent its execution, will be resolutely suppressed.

Furthermore, we express the view that the Jewish Agency should at once resume active cooperation with the Mandatory in the suppression of terrorism and of illegal immigration, and in the maintenance of that law and order throughout Palestine, which is essential for the good of all, including the new immigrants.

Palestine, the number of immigrants to be admitted within any given period.

In Palestine there is the Jewish National Home, created in consequence of the Balfour Declaration. Some may think that that Declaration was wrong and should not have been made: some that it was a conception on a grand scale and that effect can be given to one of the most daring and significant colonization plans in history. Controversy as to which view is right is fruitless. The National Home is there. Its roots are deep in the soil of Palestine. It cannot be argued out of existence: neither can the achievements of the Jewish pioneers.

The Government of Palestine in having regard to the well-being of all the people of Palestine cannot ignore the interests of so large a section of the population. It cannot ignore the achievements of the last quarter of a century. No Government of Palestine doing its duty to the people of that land can fail to do its best not only to maintain the National Home, but also to foster its proper development and such development must in our view involve immigration.

The well-being of all the people of Palestine, be they Jews, Arabs or neither, must be the governing consideration. We reject the view that there shall be no further Jewish immigration into Palestine without Arab acquiescence, a view which would result in the Arab dominating the Jew. We also reject the insistent Jewish demand that forced Jewish immigration must proceed apace in order to produce as quickly as possible a Jewish majority

and a Jewish State. The well-being of the Jews must not be subordinated to that of the Arabs: nor that of the Arabs to the Jews. The well-being of both, the economic situation of Palestine as a whole, the degree of execution of plans for further development, all have to be carefully considered in deciding the number of immigration for any particular period.

Palestine is a land sacred to three Faiths and must not become the land of any of them to the exclusion of the others, and Jewish immigration for the development of the National Home must not become a policy of discrimination against other immigrants. Any person, therefore, must not become a qualified under applicable laws to enter Palestine must not be refused admission or subjected to discrimination on the ground that he is not a Jew. All provisions respecting immigration must be drawn, executed and applied with that principle always firmly in mind.

Further, while we recognise that any Jew who enters Palestine *in accordance with its laws* is there of right, we expressly disapprove of the position taken in some Jewish quarters that Palestine has in some way been ceded or granted as their State to the Jews of the world, that every Jew everywhere is, merely because he is a Jew, a citizen of Palestine and therefore can enter Palestine as of right without regard to conditions imposed by the Government upon entry, and that therefore there can be no illegal immigration of Jews into Palestine. We declare and affirm that any immigrant Jew who enters Palestine contrary to its laws is an illegal immigrant.

LAND POLICY

THE Land Transfers Regulations of 1940 sought to protect the Arab tenant and small owner by prohibiting the sale of land save to a Palestinian Arab in one zone, by restricting such sales in another, and allowing unrestricted sale of land only in the third zone. Their effect has been such as to amount to discrimination against the Jews; their tendency is to segregate and keep separate Arabs and Jews. In the zones where sales are prohibited or restricted they have protected the Arab from the temptation to dispose of his land, on which his livelihood and that of his family so often depend, for a sum out of all proportion to its real value. Though made with the object of maintaining the existing standard of living of Arab cultivators, and of preventing the growth of a landless landless Arab population, they afford no protection to the Arab living in the free zone. He may sell his land for a fantastic price and add to the congestion in the other zones by moving there. An Arab living a short distance away, just across the zone boundary, cannot obtain anything approximating the same sum for land of equal quality.

We are opposed to any legislation or restrictions discriminating against Jew or Arab. We recognize the need for protection of the Arab small owner and tenant, for providing against a large landless Arab population, for maintaining, indeed for raising the Arab standard of living. This necessity was also recognized in the Peel Report (Chapter IX, paragraph 10) which endorsed the following principles of earlier reports, that (i) unless there is a marked change in the methods of cultivation the land in Palestine is unable to support a large increase in population, and (ii) there is already congestion on the land in the hill districts. Those principles are as true, if not truer, today.

We do not believe that the necessary protection for the Arab can be provided only by controlling the sale of land to particular portions of Palestine. Such a policy, suggested by the Peel Commission, is consistent with our proposed solution, particu-

tion, but scarcely with that put forward by us.

The leases granted by the Jewish National Fund contain a provision that no labour other than Jewish shall be employed by the lessee on or about or in connection with the land subject to the lease, and a further provision that a sub-lease shall contain similar terms.

As we have said we are opposed to such discrimination. We appreciate that one of the reasons for such provisions was to secure employment for Jews and lands, and jobs immigrants on that land which they buy. We do not think that that object justifies the retention of such stipulations which are harmful to co-operation and understanding between Arab and Jew.

Land acquired by the Jewish National Fund or for a Waqf by the Supreme Moslem Council becomes inalienable. The Peel Commission suggested the view in its Report (Chapter IX, paragraph 80) that caution on the part of the Government in disposing of State domain to these bodies was advisable. The situation requires watching. It would not be to the interests of the inhabitants of Palestine if too large a proportion of the land should become inalienable whether held by one, organisation or another.

In the small, thickly populated country of Palestine, with its rapidly increasing population, it is in the interest of Jews and Arabs alike that all land should be developed and put to the fullest possible use. The settlement of title to land should proceed as quickly as possible and the development of St'ne lands, not required for public purposes and capable of use, should be facilitated.

The Holy Land of Palestine contains within its borders and throughout its territorial places sacred to the followers of three great religions. The "Lido" with its dancing and swing music on the shore of the Sea of Galilee offends the sensibilities of many Christian people. Reports came to our notice of other projects the completion of which would be equally objectionable. We therefore feel it right by our recommendation to emphasize the necessity for close supervision and to recommend the strengthening of the law that should be required.

Economic Development

THE building of the Jewish National Home has enjoyed the advantage of abundant capital, provided on such terms as to make economic return a secondary consideration. The Arabs have had no such advantage. In principle, we do not think it wise or appropriate that plans, such as the project for a Jordan Valley Authority, should, if judged technically sound, be undertaken by any private organization, even though that organization, as suggested by the Jewish Agency, should give an assur-

Refugee Immigration Into Palestine

(see left column)

Principles of Government: No Arab, No Jewish State

(see left column)

Mandate and Uno Trusteeship

WE recognize that in view of the powerful forces both Arab and Jewish, operating from outside Palestine, the task of Great Britain, as Mandatory, has not been easy. The Peel Commission declared in 1937 that the Mandate was unworkable, and the Permanent Mandates Commission of the League of Nations thereupon pointed out that it became almost unworkable once it was publicly declared to be by such a body. Two years later the British Government, having come to the conclusion that the alternative of Partition proposed by the Peel Commission was also unworkable, announced their intention of taking steps to terminate the Mandate by the establishment of an inde-

pendent Palestine State. Our recommendations are based on what we believe at this stage to be as fair a measure of justice to all as we can find in view of what has gone before and of all that has been done. We recognize that they are not in accord with the claims of either party, and furthermore that they involve a departure from the recent policy of the Mandatory. We recognize that, if they are adopted, they will involve a long period of trusteeship, which will mean a very heavy burden for any single Government to undertake, a burden which would be lightened if the difficulties were appreciated and the Trustee had the support of other members of the United Nations.

NO STATEMENT OF POLICY

No statement of policy by H.M. Government is being published with the Inquiry Committee's report today, and it will be considered and announced later, according to Official Communiqué No. 59 (printed below).

In connection with the Report of the Anglo-American Committee of Inquiry, which is being released for publication on May 1, it should be understood that His Majesty's Government in the United Kingdom have not as yet issued a Statement of their policy in regard to the Committee's recommendations.

This Report, dealing with a delicate and complicated subject, has been in the hands of

His Majesty's Government for only a few days. They have not yet determined their attitude to it, and will need time to consider it carefully. Furthermore, since the report was prepared by a Joint Committee of two Governments, His Majesty's Government cannot make a public statement on it until they have consulted the United States Government.

Owing to the short time during which the Report has been in Palestine it has not yet been practicable to translate it into Arabic and Hebrew. This will be done as soon as possible. Neither has it been possible to include the Appendices in the first printed issue. They will be inserted in later issues.

Future Immigration Policy

WE have recommended the admission of 100,000 immigrants, victims of Nazi persecution, as soon as possible. We now deal with the position after the admission of that number. We cannot look far into the future. We cannot construct a yard stick for annual immigration. Until a Trusteeship Agreement is executed it is our clear opinion that Palestine should be administered in accordance with the terms of the Mandate quoted above.

Further than that we cannot go in the form of a recommendation. In this disordered world speculation as to the economic position of any country a few years ahead would be a hazardous proceeding. It is particularly difficult to predict what, after a few years have passed, will be the economic and political condition of Palestine. We hope that the present friction and turbulence will soon die away and be replaced by an era of peace, absent so long from the Holy Land; that the Jew and Arab will soon realize that collaboration is to their mutual advantage, but no one can say how long this will take.

Arab standard of living be raised to that of the Jews. In stressing the need for such a policy we would particularly call attention to the discrepancies between the social services, including hospitals, available in Palestine for Jews and Arabs.

We fully recognize that the

Jewish social services are financed to a very great extent by the Jewish community in Palestine, with the assistance of outside Jewish organizations; and we would stress that nothing should be done which would bring these social services down to the level of those provided for the Arabs, or halt the constant improvements now being made in them.

We suggest that consideration be given to the advisability of encouraging the formation by the Arabs of an Arab community on the lines of the Jewish community which now largely controls and finances Jewish social services. The Arabs will have to rely, to a far greater extent than the Jews, on financial aid from the Government. But the Jews in Palestine should accept the necessity that taxation, raised from both Jews and Arabs, will have to be spent very largely on the Arabs in order to bridge the gap which now exists between the standard of living of the two peoples.

The possibility of the country sustaining a largely increased population at a decent standard of living depends on its economic future, which in turn depends largely on whether or not plans referred to in Recommendation No. 8 can be brought to fruition.

The Peel Commission stated that political as well as economic considerations have to be taken into account in regard to immigration, and recommended a "political high level" of 12,000 a year. We cannot recommend the fixing of a minimum or of a maximum for annual immigration in the future. There are too many uncertain factors.

We desire, however, to state certain considerations which we agree should be taken into account in determining what number of immigrants there should in any period. It is very independent whether we can Jewish...

Equality of Standards

OUR examination of conditions in Palestine led us to the conclusion that one of the chief causes of friction is the great disparity between the Jewish and Arab standards of living. Even under conditions

of war, which brought considerable financial benefits to only a few days, this disparity has not been appreciably reduced. Only by a deliberate and carefully planned policy on the part of the Mandatory can the

ance of Arab benefits and Arab participation in the same.

Such proposals, by reason of *(Continued Overleaf)*

May Day in Palestine

May Day, today, is being observed by organized Labour in Palestine.

Because of the publication of the Inquiry Report, however, press workers have reported for work in order to enable the morning papers to appear in reduced form — two pages

May 1, 1946   65

"AIRMEC" RADIO
Latest Model
Obtainable on instalments at
ELECTRO RADIO
6 Chancellor Road, Jerusalem

LATE Edition

THE PALESTINE POST

JERUSALEM
SUNDAY, JUNE 30, 1946

PRICE 15 MILS
VOL. XXI., No. 6138

Never say CHERRY BRANDY
say: Wolfschmidt's CHERRY BRANDY

ARMY SEIZE JEWISH AGENCY, HOLD LEADERS, 1,000 OTHERS IN DAWN SWOOP

Palestine Post Staff

In a sudden swoop which began before dawn yesterday, and during day-long operations in many parts of Palestine the Army, acting under the orders of the Commander-in-Chief, Middle East, took four members of the Jewish Agency Executive into custody; searched and occupied the offices of the Jewish Agency in Jerusalem, and virtually all offices of leading institutions throughout the country, including the Histadrut in Tel Aviv; cordoned and searched a large number of agricultural labour settlements for arms and rounded up and arrested about 1,000 men.

The day's cost in lives was at least three dead and a number of injured on the part of the Jewish Community and the accidental death of a British soldier.

In the afternoon, Dr. Chaim Weizmann, President of the Jewish Agency, came from Rehovoth to see the High Commissioner at Government House. He was accompanied on the journey by Mrs. Weizmann and his physician.

A curfew of unspecified duration was imposed in practically all Jewish areas throughout the country in an action against what was described by the High Commissioner in a statement first broadcast at 7.45 in the morning, as "one section of the Jewish community." This section, to judge of the leading men under arrest, comprises the whole of the Jewish community, including organized Labour and most others represented in the organized Yishuv.

Of the members of the Jewish Agency Executive, Rabbi J. L. Fishman, Acting Chairman (in the absence in London of Mr. D. Ben Gurion) was arrested in his house in the Montefiore Quarter; Mr. Isaac Gruenbaum at his home in Rehavia; Mr. M. Shertok was traced to his hotel in Tel Aviv and Dr. B. Joseph to his Nathanya home.

LEADERS AT LATRUN

They, together with Mr. David Hacohen, of Haifa, head of Solel Boneh, are lodged together in Latrun, where many of those arrested in various parts of the country during the day were also taken, after being confined in hurriedly improvised cages. Mr. Hacohen, organizer under the military of the sabotage directed from Palestine against the Vichy authorities in Syria, was apprehended in Tel Aviv.

lestine Jews (Vaad Leumi), and for many years General Secretary of the Labour Federation (Histadrut) was arrested at Kinnereth. Other persons in custody include Mr. Bar Rav Hai, Vice Chairman of the Haifa Jewish Community Council; Mr. B. Repetor, member of the Histadrut Executive; Mr. Haim Halperin, Chief Municipal Inspector; Mr. D. Shinkaverski, Secretary Port Section Haifa Labour Council.

The Jewish Agency offices, at the corner of King George Ave. and Keren Kayemeth Street, remained surrounded by Bren Carriers and armoured cars during the whole of the day and night, the entrance to the garden barred by coils of barbed wire.

Present at the Jewish Agency during the search in the early morning were Mr. Giles, and Mr. Catling, of the C.I.D.; and Mr. Newton and Mr. Musgrave of the Secretariat.

Historic Files

These officers occupied the Conference Room, whose wooden panels were dismantled in search, evidently, for arms or papers, while Army officers combed the other rooms, including the basement, where some 50 years of Zionist history is kept, with the more precious documents in safes.

To open these safes, Dr. Herlitz, the Keeper of the Archives, and some of his assistants, were summoned, but were not permitted to be present during the examination of the papers. Nor was Mr. S. Eisenberg, General Secretary, invited to assist in any way beyond giving information on the use of various rooms. Mr. Eisenberg was escorted from his house at 5 o'clock, and permitted to return three or four hours later.

Three trucks full of cupboards and boxes of files were removed by police and Army. Documents found in desk drawers of Jewish Agency officials were also removed. A correspondent who was permitted by the guard to enter the building, was turned out when he entered the meeting hall of the Jewish Agency Executive.

Plane Over Jerusalem

Jerusalem was awakened to the fact that something was amiss by a 'Dawn Patrol' — a spotter plane circling at almost roof-top height over the city.

About the same time, loudspeakers from armoured cars cruised through the streets in Jewish quarters announcing the curfew, in English and Hebrew, and ordering all persons to stay indoors.

The fact that it was Sabbath morning led many people to dismiss the possibility of any serious military action being undertaken, though many remained awake to tune on their wireless sets at 7 a.m., which commenced with the Communique beginning; "At 0415 hrs. this morning, the Army occupied the Jewish Agency's building in Jerusalem and certain buildings in Tel Aviv which are being searched."

Shortly before 10 o'clock, Sir John Shaw received the press and replied to a number of questions arising out of the High Commissioner's broadcast statement. He announced a censorship of outgoing press cables for 24 hours.

The Jerusalem homes both of Mr. Shertok and Dr. Joseph were visited about 5 o'clock in the morning. The caretaker at Mr. Shertok's flat was obliged to accompany the police party that went to Tel Aviv to make the arrest.

Mr. Shertok had gone to Tel Aviv to attend a memorial meeting on the first anniversary of the death of his brother-in-law, Eliahu Golomb. Dr. Joseph's house at Nathanya was surrounded at 7.30. The arrest was made by Mr. H.E. Gould, Assistant Superintendent of Police, who, on being told that he had no legal right to be in the house, withdrew. Dr. Joseph then came out and turning to The Palestine Post correspondent, who was a witness to the scene, and to another person, said: "You two are witnesses to my illegal arrest."

A.S.P. Gould: You are being arrested under the Emergency Regulations.

Dr. Joseph: You can only do so if you have evidence of my having committed a crime, and you have not.

He was driven off in a military car.

HIGH COMMISSIONER'S STATEMENT

The following statement by His Excellency the High Commissioner, Lieut.-General Sir Alan Cunningham, was broadcast three times by P.B.S. yesterday:

It has been repeatedly and consistently stated by His Majesty's Government that the Palestine problem is not one to be settled by force and that there could be no question of allowing the issue to be forced by violent conflict. They have moreover given constant warning that the use of force by either community would be resolutely dealt with.

In spite of these warnings there has been over a considerable period a campaign of vilification, incitement and threats of violence, which has not been confined to only one community. Furthermore, on the part of some members of the Jewish community, there has been carried out a series of outrages against life and property, which has resulted in the loss of numerous lives including many innocent persons and in damage to property amounting to a sum of great magnitude.

In face of the most intense provocation the measures taken for the suppression of violence have up to now been of localised nature conducted with the greatest tolerance and restraint, not through weakness, but in the earnest hope that reason and conciliation would prevail, and that the country would be saved from the weight of large scale operations.

Law and Order

I have now to inform the people of Palestine that, especially while discussions are proceeding about the future of the country, His Majesty's Government are determined that law and order are to be maintained in the territory; and to repeat that they will not tolerate the use of force *by either community.*

It is therefore my duty to give solemn warning that it is firmly resolved to root out terrorism and violence. Lawlessness *from whatever source it may arise,* will in future be dealt with with the utmost vigour and determination. The obective is to restore those conditions of order without which no progress can be made towards the solution of the problem of Palestine.

The operations at present in progress under direction of the C-in-C Mid East are being undertaken as a first step with this end in view. They are not directed against the Jewish community as a whole, but solely against those who are taking an active part in the present campaign of violence and those who are responsible for instigating and directing it. They are not reprisals; they are not punitive; they are being undertaken against one section of the Jewish community merely because it is from that section that present violence has emanated. They will cease at the earliest possible moment after their object has been achieved.

Temporary Occupation

It has been necessary temporarily to occupy the premises of the Jewish Agency, owing to the evidence in our hands as to the part it has played in the organization and direction of, and in co-operation with, the forces that have carried out acts of violence against the Government. It is not the intention at this time to proscribe or close the Agency.

In taking the present wide scale measures it is intended studiously to refrain, as far as possible, from interfering with the well-being of the law-abiding citizens of Palestine and its economic life. Therefore I call upon all those who have the true interests of Palestine at heart to cooperate with the Government in the maintenance of administration and in assisting the return to normal of the life of the country and its preservation thereafter.

It is not the intention to leave either community or any part of a community without protection, but in so far as it may be expedient for such protection to be provided by the communities themselves it must be brought under proper control of the Government.

If any should be contemplating armed resistance or further violence I would commend them most earnestly to consider the misery which they may bring to a country which is dear to all of us, the loss of innocent lives which may be entailed and the destruction they may bring to much that has been built up with such devotion and skill.

Finally I would repeat that the operations which are at present proceeding are directed to one end only, the suppression of violence. The door of negotiation and discussion is not shut.

The situation which has arisen demands calm and order on all sides, not precipitate, rash or irresponsible action. I rely on the good sense of what I feel must be the majority opinion in this country to cooperate in the task of restoring peaceful conditions at the earliest possible moment.

CENSORSHIP IMPOSED

The announcement of a complete black-out on all communications from Palestine, so far as press cables were concerned, between 4 o'clock and 10 o'clock yesterday morning, the temporary censorship of cables and the reimposition of pre-censorship on the local press, was made by the Chief Secretary, Sir John Shaw, at a press conference at the P.I.O. Press Room at 9.45 yesterday morning. It was announced that telephone communications with neighbouring countries had been cut off.

Sir John, who was accompanied by Lt.-Colonel Martin Charteriss of Palestine H.Q., Mr. John Gutch, Under-Secretary (Political), and Mr. R. Stubbs, Public Information Officer, answered a number of questions asked by about 40 local and foreign press representatives present.

Asked whether it was the Palestine Government or the British Government that had directed the action, Sir John said that the two Governments were one, and that the military forces were one, and the operations were actually under the orders of the Commander in Chief, Middle East.

Jewish Sabbath

He was then asked whether Government was aware of the fact that the operations were carried out on the Jewish Sabbath and that this would offend Jewish religious feeling throughout the world. The newspapermen referred to the case of Rabbi L. Fishman, who when arrested early yesterday had been forced against his religious law to ride in a vehicle on the Sabbath, although he asked to be allowed to walk.

Sir John said that Government was aware of the fact that it was Sabbath, but he could not accept the implication that Jewish religious feeling would be offended. He had not been informed of the incident involving Rabbi Fishman but thought it was "probable".

He added that he was not yet in a position to give details regarding the Jewish leaders arrested at the outset, nor could he give any information as to the period for which they were likely to be detained.

The Chief Secretary stated that the premises of the Jewish Agency would be occupied for so long as was necessary to achieve the purposes of the operations.

A correspondent read out the passage in His Excellency's statement that "the door to negotiation and discussion was not shut," and asked with whom the Government would negotiate, if members of the Jewish Agency were arrested. Sir John answered that not all members had been arrested, and added that Dr. Weizmann was not detained.

According to his information at the time, he declared, no resistance had taken place at any of the settlements searched except at one place, where a shot had been fired.

The question was then put: "Were the searches in the settlements a result of the sabotage a fortnight ago or were they general operations?"

Sir John: "The operations are the result of a decision to restore the country from the state of anarchy into which it has fallen to a state of civilization, and to enable law-abiding people to go about their business without fear."

He went on to state that the operations were not directed against law-abiding citizens and instanced the recent outbreaks, explosions, shootings, and kidnappings as acts of violence which His Majesty's Government would not tolerate.

The conference lasted half an hour and ended with Sir John again expressing the hope that cables sent by foreign press correspondents would not be unduly delayed.

America Informed

Authoritative circles in London state that the American Government has been informed of the action against the Jewish Agency, reports PTA, which adds that the discussions at present proceeding between British and American experts on the Inquiry Committee's recommendations will not be interrupted as a result.

LATE NEWS

The Syrian Ministry of the Interior yesterday received reports that the Palestine Authorities have closed their frontiers until further notice.

Two persons were killed and others injured in a clash which took place in Beirut between the employees of the Tobacco Company, who have been on strike for the past few days, and the Police.

HAIFA

"COMPLETE SURPRISE"

Palestine Post Staff

HAIFA, Saturday. — Except for a few officials "blitz curfew" came as a complete surprise to everyone here. A number of Jewish Labour and community leaders were summoned out of their beds at dawn and arrested by Army personnel, who called at houses on Hadar Hacarmel and Mount Carmel, according to prepared lists. The premises of the Jewish Agency in Haifa were not occupied nor searched.

No curfew passes were issued and Government officials' cards were not accepted in lieu. The Officer in charge of the Public Information Office was detained at the Western Police Station while on his way to the office and was kept in a cage for half an hour together with some 200 others.

Port Closed

Several Government offices were not functioning owing to lack of staff, and Barclays Bank closed for the same reason. In Haifa Port the public did not take any deliveries of cargo and though there was no shortage of labour in the morning, the docks were without internal transport and about a dozen ships were idling, while some were being discharged at the breakwater. At 2 p.m. the Port was cleared of all civilians and work stopped completely.

Only essential work could be carried out at the Consolidated Refineries, as none of the daily labourers were available, while the Iraq Petroleum Company discharged tankers as usual and kept the oil flowing with only half the normal number of employees working.

Barbed wire was laid through Prophets Street on the outskirts of Hadar Hacarmel and there were strong military guards on all roads leading to the quarter. Aircraft patrolled the town throughout the morning.

News from the settlements in this district was meagre, with many of them not answering the telephone. It is understood that telephone connections were cut off during the searches.

Tear Smoke at Yagour

At Yagour clashes were reported when settlers resisted the search, and several settlers are believed to have been injured. Tear smoke was used by the troops to make their way in. The search is thought to have been completed at 6 p.m. when a number of military lorries carrying detained persons were seen on their way towards Haifa. The settlement could not be contacted by phone throughout the day and there is therefore no confirmation of this report. It is officially stated that 20 rifles and 30,000 rounds of ammunition were found in this kibbutz.

Shaar Haamakim, further north east, was cordoned off at 4 a.m. and the search there was completed in 4½ hours. The mukhtar was told by the O.C. that the forces were look-

Continued on Page 3 Col. 4

TEL AVIV

"SPORADIC SHOOTING"

Palestine Post Staff

TEL AVIV, Saturday. — One man, Eliezer Mallhi (25), was shot and killed here at 9 o'clock tonight.

In general, there was no resistance to the all-day searches when public buildings were combed, and leading personalities arrested by police and troops.

In the evening, troops dug in at street corners. Pavements were ripped up and Bren gun emplacements established. There were similar nests on roof tops at strategic corners.

The authorities declined to disclose the result of the searches. The army withdrew from the town after midnight tonight, and turned over the enforcement of the curfew to the police.

There was sporadic shooting all morning after curfew was imposed. In the afternoon, there was a lull, but the shooting began again after dark.

When military and police arrived at the Headquarters of the Women's International Zionist Organization in Beit Hashoeva Lane, where the door was barred, they threw bombs through the door and forced an entry. No one was in the building. Safes were forced open and searched.

The watchman at the Workers' Bank at Rehov Montefiore who was asked to open the door objected, saying that the building was a bank. Explosives were used to force open the door.

Shop windows along the whole street were smashed.

Other public buildings searched included the offices of the Jewish Agency, the Histadrut, the Agricultural Workers' Society. The War Needs Fund ciety, the War Needs Fund and the Keren Hayesod. Troops remained billetted in the buildings.

At the Histadrut, sacks of documents were removed.

Some documents were also removed from the room in Pension Brandstetter where Mr. Shertok was staying. The homes of Mr. David Remez, who was arrested in Kinneret, and of Dr. M. Sneh of the Jewish Agency Executive, were also searched.

Water Supply Out

Passengers who arrived by rail from Jerusalem were taken off to Citrus House, where they were given passes to get home.

The water supply in town failed this morning and in the afternoon Municipal workers were escorted by Military Police to restore the service.

The staff of the Hadassah Hospital was not given passes and the Fire Brigade and the Red Shield ambulances had to obtain permission for each trip.

In the Sharon colonies there were no incidents. Curfew announcements were made in Ramat Gan in the morning, af-

Continued on Page 2 Col. 1

Official Communique

NO.67, JUNE 29, 6 a.m.

At 0415 hours this morning Saturday, June 29, the Army occupied the Jewish Agency's building at Jerusalem and certain buildings in Tel Aviv which are being searched.

Searches are also being carried out in the settlements of Kfar Giden, Ashdod Yaacov, Meshek Yagur, Ein Harod, Maabarot, Givat Brenner and Ramat Rahel. Numbers of persons are being detained. The operations are proceeding.

Curfews have been imposed over wide areas. Details will be published as soon as possible.

UNO TRUSTEESHIP FOR PALESTINE URGED

LOS ANGELES, Saturday (PTA). — Direct Uno trusteeship for Palestine was demanded in a resolution sent to President Truman by 21,000 people who jammed Hollywood Bowl in a protest meeting here tonight.

NUREMBERG: FRITZSCHE RECALLED

By WILLIAM HAMPSHER, Reuters Correspondent

NUREMBERG, Saturday. — Fritzsche was recalled to be questioned about a statement by Goebbels in the autumn of 1944 that "there was no longer any objection to the handing over of crews of crashed Allied planes to the wrath of the people."

Fritzsche denied he had ever advocated such treatment.

Goebbels announced at a conference that 40,000 people had been killed in the raid on Dresden adding that Hitler was determined to have a similar number of British and United States fliers shot in Dresden.

Fritzsche said he had approached a represenative of Switzerland — the protecting power — asking him to advance arguments counteracting Hitler's order. This action led to the suggestion for an exchange of British and German prisoners.

"I thought that if two warring powers got to talking about an exchange of prisoners the other plan would be overlooked," Fritzsche said.

The case of Martin Bormann, the missing former Fuehrer's deputy the last of the accused, was stopped this morning without any of the expected evidence.

Bormann was last seen alive on the day of Hitler's death in April, 1945. It was reported that he was killed, but the report was never confirmed.

TENSION MOUNTS IN ATOM ZONE

By JOSEPH LAITIN, Reuters Correspondent on board the U.S.S. Appalachian off Bikini Atoll

Tension mounted high among the 40,000 scientists, technicians and observers at this mid-Pacific atom testing zone yesterday as the seconds ticked by to zero hour — 22.30 hrs. G.M.T. (0130 hrs. Palestinian time Monday — for the launching of the world's fourth atom bomb which will unleash an explosion of cataclysmic force against a prepared target of 75 naval vessels.

It will be dawn on Monday when U.S. scientists and military and naval experts and all the specialists on board the big fleet of observation vessels will be listening by radio to the gentle ticking of the metronome aboard the bulls-eye battleship Nevada. Suddenly the ticking will cease. There will be the sound of a great explosion, but it will not come over the radio.

The microphone on board the Nevada will have disintegrated. "Operation Crossroads" will have begun.

Vice-Admiral Blandy, Commander of the task force, denies reports that bacteriological warfare would be tested during the atom test, adding however that germs had been placed on board one of the vessels for determining the effect on them of radiation.

Admiral Blandy was speaking at a joint press conference with Mr. James Forrestal, U.S. navy secretary, on the open deck of the correspondents' ship anchored in Bikini Lagoon; he added: "We insisted that the germ specimens should be of a harmless variety because we did not want dangerous germs running around the ship when our men went back aboard."

There was a 50-50 chance that the first test would be held on Monday as scheduled (Sunday night, GMT), he said.

PALESTINE British-U.S. Talks

LONDON, Saturday (R). — Preliminary conversations relating to Palestine have, during the past ten days, been taking place between officials of the British and U.S. Governments led by Sir Norman Brook, one of the two secretaries of the British Cabinet, and Mr. Averell Harriman, U.S. Ambassador in London, stated a Foreign Office announcement.

Certain technical problems arising from the recommendations of the Anglo-American Committee of Inquiry that 100,000 Jews enter Palestine before the end of the year have been examined with a view to preparing the ground for further discussions with a group of U.S. officials representing the President's Cabinet Committee on Palestine and Related Problems, which is expected to arrive in London shortly.

The preliminary conversations have now been completed and the U.S. advisers to Ambassador Harriman have returned to Washington.

There is good reason to believe, writes Reuters Diplomatic Correspondent, that this expert committee (whose terms of reference included the technical problems of transport, selection and settlement of a further 100,000 immigrants if Britain finally decides to implement the Palestine report) reached substantial agreement.

One main point at the next stage of discussions may also be the question of American military assistance.

The second group of American experts is now expected in London to discuss also on a technical level the financial and military problems involved. Neither of these groups is empowered to raise the fundamental question of policy whether or not the recommendations of the Report are to be implemented.

The question of policy remains to be decided on the highest level, but no decision is expected until Mr. Attlee, Mr. Bevin, President Truman, and Mr. Byrnes are in possession of the technical report now in preparation.

"TWO INDIAN CARETAKERS"

NEW DELHI, Saturday (R). — The appointment of a temporary caretaker government in India pending further negotiations with the Indian parties was announced here today.

Of the eight members of the new Viceroy's Executive Council formed for this purpose two will be Indians. They are Sir Gurunath Bewoor and Sir Akbar Hydari. The former is expected to have the Commerce and Commonwealth Relations portfolio, and the latter will be responsible for Labour, Works, Mines and Power, Information, Arts and Health.

Field Marshal Sir Claude Auchinleck, Commander-in-Chief, India, will continue to serve as War Member.

"Growing Appreciation"

By GEORGE LICHTHEIM, Palestine Post Correspondent

LONDON, June 28. — Lobby opinion in the House of Commons yesterday, after Mr. Attlee's reply to Mr. Churchill, expressed qualified satisfaction regarding the promised statement next week, mingled with apprehension at the growing evidence of tension in Palestine.

It is noted that although Mr. Churchill expressly referred to the Report stressing the delay in the decision, Mr. Attlee did specifically promise a statement on Government policy. Nevertheless, in spite of the suggestion by the Diplomatic Correspondent of "The Times" today, the statement is likely to deal only with the Palestine incidents, and a policy decision will be delayed a further three or four weeks.

It is believed that the Prime Minister may go beyond commenting on the security situation. The outlook is thought to be slightly improved since Mr. Bevin's letter explaining his Bournemouth speech, in which he denied having opposed the immigration of 100,000 in principle.

Technical Talks Successful

It is now suggested that the Attlee statement is likely to be somewhat more favourable than expected. The winding up of the experts' talks, though not implying a political decision, means that the Government is now in possession of the relevant facts and is able to make up its mind. There is no reason to believe that the technical talks revealed any grounds to modify the Anglo-American Commission's immigration proposals.

Meanwhile, the press gives prominence to the Palestine incidents and the trials, although "The Times" in the past few days has been printing only very brief reports. Other papers gave lengthy descriptions of the Court-room scenes, contributing to the general feeling, which was also noticeable in the House of Commons yesterday that the present uncertainty cannot continue much longer.

FOUR POINTS OF INTEREST

Opportunity is a signpost pointing the way to success: The secret of success in life is for a man to be ready when his opportunity comes.

1. ARE YOU READY FOR TODAY'S OPPORTUNITIES? There are some who are unable to read the signpost pointing to success, others who can but who are unprepared. Both these classes must remain lost in the common herd and hope for little more than a mere existence. There is no excuse today for saying "I never had a chance."
2. YOUR CHANCE IS HERE! The unique and successful system of correspondence tuition by the British Institute of Engineering Technology gives you that chance, and you can have the best books to study in the comfort of your own home, just as if your Tutor were beside you.
3. YOUR SUCCESS IS GUARANTEED! You can, therefore, be prepared for your opportunity when it comes and be able to rise above the crowd. No matter what your age or previous experience, the B.I.E.T. can help you to obtain such valuable qualifications as A.M.I.C.E., A.M.I. Mech. E., A.M.I.E.E., etc. Courses are outlined in all Branches of Engineering, Building, Architecture, Surveying, C. & G. Certificates, B.Sc. and Matriculation, etc., and out of the hundreds of courses available HERE there is one to suit you.
4. OUR GUARANTEE IS — NO PASS — NO FEE! Your next step is to write for our prospectus or call at:-

THE BRITISH INSTITUTE OF ENGINEERING TECHNOLOGY (N.E.) LTD.

Dept. P.E.14, Sansur Bldg., Jaffa Road, and Silberstein's Bldg., Storrs Ave., Jerusalem.

Today's your day for KHAYAT BEACH.

LATE Edition

THE PALESTINE POST

JERUSALEM
Wednesday, July 17, 1946

PRICE 15 MILS
VOL. XXI., No. 6153

Column One

By David Courtney

EDWIN Pauley, who is one of President Truman's less happy appointments, made declarations yesterday on the subject of Germany which may have unfortunate results. He was discussing reparations in the manner of a big-businessman addressing his competitor; and if Russia chooses to play, well and good; if not, America has her own plan and Russia and the Russian Zone can go to the devil. Mr. Byrnes at Paris and again in his broadcast to the American people said much the same thing; and it is clear that the State Department is leading the German issue for the Western Powers, with Mr. Bevin glad to be out of it with his generalization on the need for economic unity. The clash over Germany will prove to be the supreme Big Power test. The preliminaries and their implications have already dwarfed the Peace Conference, which is dependent for the validity of its decisions on a final settlement of the German question.

■

IT is the second time Mr. Byrnes has threatened to isolate Russia. He did so after the first Paris Conference of Foreign Ministers when he declared his intention of calling a Peace Conference with or without Soviet agreement. It may be argued that the threat to isolate Russia succeeded then; it doesn't follow that it will always succeed, and it doesn't follow that the merits of Mr. Byrnes' German Plan are great enough to justify the take-it-leave-it attitude expressed by the Secretary of State and his colleagues. What does follow is that Russia becomes confirmed in her suspicions of Anglo-American fundamental antagonism to the Soviet. True, she does little enough to allay the antagonism; but there is small comfort in that. And for those who, willy-nilly, are within the Anglo-American orbit, it is Britain and America who must find the way out, not Soviet Russia. There is no way out in threats, even when the threats are backed by the atom bomb. Not, perhaps, until the atom bomb is a forgotten nightmare will there be any way out.

■

THE fellah has learned to strike. The so-called Arab awakening is not the restricted affair understood by Mr. Bevin and Chatham House. There are two sides to the Middle East bed; and if the Pasha are getting into their slippers from the one side, the masses are tumbling out of the other and yelling hungrily for their rights. The scale of the strike in the Persian oil fields is indicated by curfew and martial law; the scale in Iraq by the extent of violence and bloodshed; and the fear of similar "awakenings" in Egypt is manifest in the grim measures against all Left-Wing movements and activities taken during the past few days. The claim that Moscow is at the bottom of it is probably sound; but the Middle East worker is not likely to be impressed by that. He has no strong reason for submitting to social conditions which are among the worst in the world, merely as an expression of loyalty to his exploiters and to those who make treaty with them. The British Government has overlooked these factors except where they touch the incipient conflict between Russia and the West; and have been blinded to the social portents in the Middle East by the dust of an antiquated policy of princely alliances. There was a time when British Governments protested at such high-handed tyranny as Sidky Pasha's. There was a time when the Socialist Party, in Opposition, called for adjournments to discuss sharply such events as the strikes in the Iraq and Persian oilfields. Today the protests are kept for the Left-Wing Governments of Poland Bulgaria and Rumania. What has happened to change the conscience of British Labour?

■

THE Labour Government, like most other Governments, is nervous. The nervousness of the world today is exemplified in the revival of spy-scares. We had nothing like it even between the two wars. There is official talk of a Soviet "Fifth Column" in Canada and the United States, and a mountain of mystery is being piled up about the Russian officers said to have been found on American "installations" in Germany. The trouble surely is that there are too many soldiers still about and too much to spy into. Half the world is under direct military control and the other half dares not move in international matters without first consulting its Chiefs of Staff. These are hardly the conditions for the growth of confidence among nations or of progress among men.

Jerusalem, July 17.

WEIZMANN'S MESSAGE

Dr. Chaim Weizmann, on leaving Palestine today, has sent the following message to the Jewish Community:

On leaving Palestine today to continue our exertions in the Metropolis of the Empire, I am experiencing the sadnss I always feel on taking leave of the Yishuv, whether for a long period or a short one.

This feeling is today more oppressive than at any other time, after the attack on the Yishuv's institutions, the arrest of its leaders, the siege of the agricultural settlements and the imprisonment of thousands of our best sons and daughters.

It is a mistake to think that the Yishuv has been numbed by this blow, it is true that the Yishuv has been tried as it has never been tried before, but its disciplined behaviour has honoured it, for the Yishuv knows it must continue in its restraint and not permit itself to be provoked, from whatever quarter.

There is a hard struggle ahead of us, both in Palestine and other centres. The terrible experiences of recent years, down to the massacre at Kielce, have apparently not yet demonstrated to the world where the only solution to this problem lies.

Justice

But whichever way the present consultations may lead, whether of this or succeeding phases, my hope remains firm that justice will triumph and that our tortured people will be enabled to make their home here.

No consultations are possible, however, so long as the elected leaders of the Yishuv are behind barbed wire. Therefore I urge in the first place the immediate release of these leaders as a necessary preliminary to the renewal of confidence in the intentions of Great Britain, a renewal which we all so much desire.

Day of Stoppage

And may it be granted us that this day of stoppage in protest against these arrests and detentions, the day on which I am obliged to leave Palestine, may be the last of our days of trial and suffering, whether for those interned in camps in Palestine and outside Palestine, or for out people as a whole.

YISHUV STRIKE TODAY: LEADERS JOIN RAFA FAST

Palestine Post Staff

The entire Jewish Community in Palestine, with certain permitted exceptions, will cease work today from 9 a.m. to midnight in protest against the continued detention at Rafa of 1,650 men taken from their settlements during the military searches 19 days ago.

Held under guard, behind barbed wire, no charge has been proffered against them. They have been on hunger strike since 7 o'clock Monday evening.

At the same time, the 450 men and women at Latrun yesterday afternoon declared a hunger strike in solidarity with those at Rafa, bringing the total number of fasters to over 2,000.

They include the members of the Jewish Agency Executive and other Yishuv leaders at Latrun camp, namely Messrs. M. Shertok, I. Gruenbaum, and B. Joseph, of the Jewish Agency Executive; David Remez, Chairman of the Vaad Leumi; David Hacohen, Haifa Municipal Councillor; Mordehai Shattner and Yitzhak Ben Aharon, members of the Vaad Leumi (who were transferred from Rafa); David Shingarevsky, of Haifa; and Haim Elperin, of Tel Aviv.

DAVID REMEZ, Chairman of the Vaad Leumi, who is fasting for the second time in 4 months.

Shops Closing

Today all Jewish shops, businesses and places of entertainment throughout Palestine will be closed. Restaurants will be open only from midday to 2 p.m. and from 7 to 8 p.m. Urban and inter-urban road traffic, insofar as it is Jewish, will cease at 10 a.m. Public services such as electricity and water supply, and work in hospitals, Government offices and military establishments will continue normally. Newspapers will appear.

In Haifa, a mass meeting will be held in front of the Funds Building in Herzl Street, Hadar Hacarmel, at 10 o'clock. The Jewish population of Haifa is also requested by the Community Council to maintain a 4-hour voluntary curfew by remaining indoors from 2.30 to 6.30 p.m.

Today's general strike by the Yishuv is only indirectly connected with the political situation. Its purpose is to express the solidarity of the entire community with the 1,650 hunger strikers at Rafa and to express the demand for their immediate release. It is a specific reaction to a specific development in the present situation.

The general strike has been called by the General Council for Palestine Jews (Vaad Leumi), which has been in closest contact with the Jewish Agency throughout the present crisis.

The general political situation arising out of the delay in implementing the Inquiry Committee's recommendations, the occupation of the Jewish Agency buildings, the arrest of the Jewsh leaders and the military searches is under continuous consideration by the Jewish authorities.

Details of a plan of action decided on by the representatives of the Yishuv and endorsed by the Zionist Inner Council are being examined by the various bodies concerned and will doubtless form the subject of conversations between Dr. Weizmann, who is leaving for London today, and the members of the Jewish Agency Executive there.

The hunger strike declared by the 1,650 detainees at Rafa at 7 o'clock on Monday evening was continued throughout the day yesterday. There were no releases of the 550 men who gave their names at the beginning of last week.

During the day cultural and educational activities continued as usual in the camp, and the detainees were reported to be disciplined and cheerful.

In addition to soldiers and ex-servicemen there are among them a number of young people from the death camps, with their camp numbers stencilled on their forearms, and others who arrived only on the latest refugee ships, and had not been released from detention at Athlit for more than a few days before they were rounded up in the settlements where they had gone to work.

Conditions Deteriorate

In the overcrowded camp, sanitary conditions are deteriorating, and almost 600 men are accommodated in a store formerly used for cement. All the detainees sleep on canvas cots without mattresses, and raised only a few inches off the ground.

One of the main hardships is presented by the sandy water, and the small number of taps available.

PALESTINE: FOUR LONDON CABLES

Mr. George Hall, the Colonial Secretary, made it clear in the House of Commons that he expected to be able to publish the evidence against the Jewish Agency in Palestine before the Commons debate on Palestine.

The date of the debate is not yet fixed, but is expected to be before the summer recess.

■

Mr. Hugh Dalton was asked what was the estimated cost of maintaining order in Palestine during the current financial year. He replied that it was impossible to say as "no one could foresee the course of future events."

■

No action has been taken by the British Government in view of the recent statement of the Arab countries that they intended to intensify their boycott of Jewish goods.

This was stated yesterday by a Foreign Office spokesman.

■

The London correspondent of the "New York Herald Tribune" says that the Anglo-American delegation conferring on Palestine has discussed the British proposal that the United Nations should appeal to all countries to accept as immigrants a proportion of the European Jews who wish to leave Europe.

Pauley Accuses Soviet Russia

LONDON, Tuesday (Reuter). —Mr. Edwin Pauley, President Truman's reparations adviser, said on arrival in Frankfurt that the Soviet Union had "violated the Potsdam agreement by effecting the removal of essentials before vital imports were available."

Mr. Pauley said: "The plans of the United States concerning the removal of reparations from Germany must be changed considerably if the Soviet Union continues her present policy.

"The question of reparations from the American zone must be reviewed in the light of the Russian attitude made apparent at the Paris conference.

5,000 JEWISH VETERANS' MARCH

WASHINGTON, Tuesday. — Jewish veterans from both world wars, men and women, many with high decorations for bravery, some limping on crutches or with heads in iron frames, marched up Constitutional Avenue yesterday to the White House, carrying slogans against British policy in Palestine (as reported).

Large crowds witnessed the march of the veterans, who numbered some five thousand, coming from all parts of the country.

The parade was the climax of two days of demonstrations which began with a protest meeting last night. It was almost a mile long and ended with ceremonies honouring the war dead.

After half an hour with the President, a spokesman said that they had been cordially received.

Lost Friendship

At the British Embassy a committee of six submitted a statement to Lord Inverchapel, the British Ambassador, warning Britain that they have lost and will continue to lose the friendship of Americans, who will not remain silent while all principles for which they fought the greatest of all wars was scrapped by a government which represents itself as progressive and liberal. They declared that as long as Britain continues to deny European Jews the right of free immigration into Palestine, "all right-thinking Americans, Christians and Jews, white and black, will have nothing but scorn for your government."

Lord Inverchapel, commenting on the petition, said, "Britain has been the best friend of the Jews." He said that the statement would be forwarded to London.

Other members of the group visited Dean Acheson and charged the State Department with adopting "tactics for delay and evasion, initiated by the British Government by failure to implement President Truman's policy regarding the hundred thousand." They stated that some officials of the State Department acted in direct opposition to the President's policy. The group demanded that the State Department implement President Truman's request for action to save the Jewish survivors.

Mr. Acheson pointed out that President Truman had made it clear that the United States "favoured action without delay," and had asked "for the immediate implementation of the policy to move the 100,000 Jews to Palestine."

(UP, Palcor, PTA)

MASS FLIGHT

PRAGUE, Tuesday (Reuter) — Nine thousand Polish Jews have crossed the Czechoslovak border for UNRRA camps in the U.S. zone, Mr. Israel Jacobson, in charge the American Joint Distribution Committee here, stated tonight.

This number is expected to reach 20,000 by the end of this month, he added.

Refugees are reported as saying that nearly 100 Jews have been murdered in Poland in the last ten days, and that no Jews are able to live there.

The refugees, according to Mr. Jacobson, cross the Czechoslovak border at various points on foot and then cross the Russian and U.S. zones of Austria to Germany. They flee without property and few clothes.

The refugees are also reported to have said that there are nearly 150,000 Jews in Poland, including 100,000 who had returned from Russia.

TRUMAN SPEAKS ON LOAN

WASHINGTON, Tuesday (R). — President Truman in a statement today on the signing of the agreement with Britain said: "This is a major step in carrying out our programme for reviving and expanding international trade.

"The loan serves our immediate and long-range interest by helping to restore world trade. At the same time it enables Britain to co-operate in creating a pattern of mutual, beneficial and economic relations among the nations of the world. It goes far to remove the danger of any rival, antagonistic bloc.

"No one should think that this agreement between the United States and Britain is directed against any other country."

The President ended: "It is fortunate and gratifying that this action both serves our own interests and helps to solve the problems which Britain faces as a direct consequence of having devoted her human and spiritual resources so fully to the common cause."

America Lowers Conscription Age

WASHINGTON, Tuesday. (R). — President Truman today lowered the minimum conscription age in the United States from 20 to 19 years.

Men between the ages of 19 and 29 are now eligible for conscription into the United States armed forces.

Russians Release Missing Couple

BERLIN, Tuesday (Reuter).— Warrant-Officer Samuel Harrison and his wife Helen returned to the U.S. Sector of Berlin early today after being released from Russian custody. They had been held since July 1, when they wandered into the Russian area to buy a dog and had been held as hostages for several Russian officers whom the Russians charge the Americans with detaining.

Brigadier General Sibert, intelligence chief of the United States forces in Germany, left hurriedly and unexpectedly for London today.

Major General Keating, Commander of the Berlin United States district, has now admitted — following his denial yesterday — that two Russian officers, their driver and a Russian soldier, all dressed in civilian clothes, have been arrested and are now in American custody. He alleges that the Russians were spying on U.S. installations.

Nothing has been heard so far about the other two missing Americans.

Despite the Russian claim that they were not carrying proper papers, Harrison had his Adjutant General's identification card and proper identification for his wife.

Mrs. Harrison told press correspondents: "My husband and I were separated for the first two days and grilled repeatedly. We did not get much food — and what there was tasted terrible."

MIHAILOVICH APPEAL OUT: FACES FIRING SQUAD TODAY

BELGRADE, Tuesday (R). — General Mihailovich's appeal against the death sentence passed on him yesterday has been rejected by the Presidium of the Yugoslav National Assembly. It is expected that he will be executed at dawn tomorrow.

The former Foreign Secretary, Mr. Eden, asked Mr. Bevin in the Commons today whether in view of the fact that General Mihailovich was the first to wage guerilla warfare against the enemy and that the British Government supported him for over two years in this struggle, he would now request the Yugoslav Government to take his services during this period into consideration in connection with the death sentence imposed upon him.

Mr. Bevin replied that the British representative in Belgrade had in May communicated to the Yugoslav Government the evidence drawn up by five British liaison officers who served with Mihailovich until the middle of 1944, showing that in their experience he actively fought against the enemy.

The British Government did not consider that they had any right to intervene further in a trial conducted according to the laws of the sovereign state.

TITO SAYS "REACTION SENTENCED"

BELGRADE, Tuesday (Reuter). — Marshal Tito, in a speech last night described the death sentence passed on the Chetnik leader, General Mihailovich, as a "sentence on international reaction."

In the course of a bitter attack Marshal Tito said that certain statesmen, trying to take their revenge, were attempting to deny Yugoslavia Istria, Trieste and the Julian provinces.

In Washington, Mr. Constantin Fotich, who was sentenced to 20 years' imprisonment in his absence, has appealed to President Truman to use all his authority with the Yugoslav Government to set aside what he considers the "monstruous sentence" on General Mihailovich.

M. Fotich, who was former Yugoslav Ambassador to the United States, said that the death sentence, if carried out, would "greatly affect the tranquillity and internal peace of Yugoslavia and consequently the peaceful consolidation of that part of Europe."

The "Manchester Guardian" this morning appeals for clemency for Mihailovich.

In many respects, it says, it would be easy to regard this trial as a normal action of the winning side against the loser in the Yugoslav civil war. But even for the Yugoslavs the issues go deeper than that. One of the deeper issues is the old one between Serb domination and the conception of a Federal Yugoslavia.

"From documents read at the trial and from what has lately been written by the Serbs in the defence of Mihailovich, there is little doubt that certain Chetnik leaders in Yugoslavia and a number of politically interested people abroad are furthering the Greater Serbian Movement with some ugly racialist features," continues the editorial.

"Mihailovich has been made personally responsible for political misuse of the movement which he began with a noble military aim. But he and his work, as he eloquently put it, were carried away by the 'gale of the world'.

"Even if there were no deeper grounds of policy, is there not enough truth in this to have induced the generous victor, having proved his case against the movement, to stay his hand against the man?" the paper concludes.

"Victim of Fate"

The Conservative 'Daily Telegraph' says: "Even though Mihailovich was found guilty, this central paradox still remains. Why should a man who resisted the Axis invader at the darkest hour collaborate with him when the tide of the battle had turned and Allied victory was in sight?

"In the long perspective of history the true stature of this controversial figure may be seen more clearly. His contemporaries can do little but conclude that he was a victim of fate caught in the whirlwind of events which he could not control."

Peter Appeals To Allies

LONDON, Tuesday (R).— Telegrams requesting their intervention to save the life of General Mihailovich have been sent by Ex-King Peter of Yugoslavia, who is now in London, to King George VI, President Truman and the French Premier, M. Bidault.

RUSSIA, FRANCE VIOLATE POTSDAM -- SAYS BYRNES

WASHINGTON, Tuesday (UP). — In a nation-wide radio address on the Paris conference last night, Mr. Byrnes indirectly accused Russia and France of violating the Potsdam agreement to treat Germany as an economic unit.

He revealed that the United States military representative in Germany will be instructed this week to cooperated with any one, or all, of the three occupying governments in essential administrative and economic matters. He said:

He will either secure economic cooperation between the zones or place the responsibility for the violation of the Potsdam agreement upon those who prevent it.

Mr. Byrnes explained that he proposed at Paris that the Control Commission should be instructed to take the necessary steps to administer Germany as a unit and lower the barriers between the zones. Only the British agreed without qualifications. Then Mr. Byrnes proposed "as a last resort" to administer the American zone with any one, or more, of the other zones as an economic unit. The British Government indicated that they were prepared to agree, but neither Russia nor France expressed any views. Mr. Byrnes announced his determination to follow the proposal through to the last resort.

Armed Threat

He indicated that the threat of armed action by Yugoslavia was considered by the "Big Four" in its discussion of the explosive Trieste question — even though it was not mentioned openly. He stated that the greatest struggle of the conference had been over the Italian treaty. "We were," he said, "in a more serious dilemma than most people realized. We could make a separate treaty with Italy leaving her Trieste, but the Soviet and Yugoslav Governments — and possibly others — would never have accepted it. A disarmed Italy could hold Trieste against an armed Yugoslavia only so long as our troops held it for her."

Mr. Byrnes said that at first no one liked the French proposal for the internationalization of Trieste, "but the more it was studied the more it seemed to offer a reasonable basis for agreement." He said he was convinced that control by the United Nations may prove the best means of preventing an armed conflict and relieving tension; that he was convinced the agreed solution "was fair and workable if the peoples most concerned worked together to make it so."

Hope for Signatures

Mr. Byrnes gave an indication for the first time that he hoped to "clean up" completely the treaties for the five Axis satellites at the Peace Conference. He said it was his hope that the Council of Foreign Ministers would consider recommendations to be made to the 21-Nations Conference, "and will agree on the final text so that the treaties may be signed by the delegates before the conference adjourns." Drafts of the treaties agreed upon, said Mr. Byrnes,

are not the best which human goodwill could devise but they are the best which human wit could get the four principal allies to agree upon.

Mr. Byrnes contended that his ten months' struggle to harmonize the views of the great powers on the treaties and call a peace conference had been brought to a successful conclusion. He promised to use all the United States' best influence to keep all Conference meetings open to the press.

Turning to the German peace treaty discussions, Mr. Byrnes said: "I do not believe that the Soviets realize the doubts and suspicions they have raised in the minds of those in other countries, who want to be their friends, by the aloofness, coolness and hostility with which they have received Amercia's offer to guarantee jointly the continued disarmament of Germany.

"Is German militarism going to be used as a pawn in the struggle between east and west, and is German militarism again to be given a chance to divide and conquer?" It is no secret that the four-power control of Germany is not working well from the point of view of any one of the four powers.

Trusteeships

WHITE PAPER ISSUED

LONDON, Tuesday (R). — A White Paper on Trusteeship issued today states that the former mandated territories of Togoland and the Cameroons will continue to be administered as an integral part of the Gold Coast and Nigeria respectively.

The White Paper says that Britain proposes to administer the territories so as to achieve the basic objective of the international Trusteeship system as laid down in the United Nations Charter. She will collaborate fully with the trusteeship council.

Britain will be entitled to establish naval, military and air bases, to erect fortifications, station her own forces there and make use of volunteer forces to ensure that the territories play their part in the maintenance of international peace and security.

North Borneo Joins Empire

SINGAPORE, Tuesday (R).— British North Borneo — the fourth largest island in the world — with a population of over 270,000 administered by a chartered company since 1882, was formally incorporated in the British Empire yesterday.

The directors of the British North Borneo Company decided to hand the country to the Crown at the end of June, after ten months of discussion with the British Government.

The development follows the cession to the Crown by Sir Charles Vyner Brooke, the White Rajah, of the neighbouring territory of Sarawak, for which the Crown is paying him £1,000,000.

75 Arrested In Bombay

POONA, Tuesday (Reuter). — The police today arrested 75 "passive resisters" of the Federation of Untouchables who had defied the ban on demonstrations in the front of the Chamber of the Bombay provincial legislative assembly.

The Untouchables are protesting against the British proposals for Indian independence, saying that the suggested guarantees for their protection are insufficient.

Doenitz Defence At Nuremberg

NUREMBERG, Tuesday (R). — The final plea for Grand Admiral Doenitz and Grand Admiral Raeder was continued today before the International War Crimes Tribunal.

Speaking in the defence of Doenitz, counsel complained that his order of September, 1942, which stated that "rescue is contradictory to the most primitive requirements of warfare which are the annihilation of ships and crews" had appeared in the world press as "a command to murder."

It was in fact, counsel claimed, a measure demanded by the mounting submarine losses.

43 Wehrmacht Men To Hang

DACHAU, Tuesday (Reuter). — A United States military court here today passed sentence of death by hanging on 43 German officers and men convicted of murdering American prisoners during the "battle of the bulge" at Christmas 1944.

Of the remaining 30 accused, 22 were sentenced to life imprisonment and the other eight to between 10 and 20 years.

S.S. Colonel General Dietrich was among those sentenced to life imprisonment. He is the former commander of Hitler's bodyguard.

AFTER MIDNIGHT

Seventeen persons were killed and 150 injured in a clash that followed the lynching of an Arab merchant during the general strike at the Anglo-Iranian Oil Company plants in Persia. The general strike ended yesterday.

The British Food Minister, Mr. Strachey, said yesterday that if bakers refused to operate the bread rationing scheme which begins next week, legal action would be taken against them, with severe penalties of up to a maximum of seven years' imprisonment and a fine of £5,000. .... A general strike was proclaimed in Turin yesterday. .... Vittorio Mussolini, son of the Duce, last reported hiding in Northern Italy, has escaped to Spain. .... A free fight took place in the Italian Constituent Assembly yesterday between deputies of the extreme Right and the Left.

LATE Edition

THE PALESTINE POST

JERUSALEM
TUESDAY, JULY 23, 1946

PRICE 15 MILS
VOL. XXI. No. 6158

41 DEAD, 53 INJURED, 52 MISSING, IN TERRORIST ATTACK ON SECRETARIAT

NOON-HOUR OUTRAGE BY GANG; BOMBS IN MILK CANS; SIR JOHN SHAW AND SOME SENIOR OFFICERS SAFE

At least 41 men and women were killed, 53 were injured, and another 52 were still reported missing at midnight, as a result of a terrorist attack shortly after noon yesterday which destroyed a large section of the offices of the Secretariat of the Palestine Government housed in the south-west corner of the King David Hotel.

Senior and Junior Civil Servants — British, Jewish, and Arab — are among the dead. Of those identified, the names of 23 Palestinians were released for publication, but the identity of five British officials and seven Army and Police personnel will not be disclosed until tonight, after their next-of-kin have been notified.

It was officially announced last night that the following officers in the Secretariat at the time of the morning's outrage were known to be safe.

Sir John Shaw, Mr. Gibson, Mr. J. Gutch, Ruhi Bey Abdul Hadi, Mr. J. Cornes, Mr. A.M. Dryburgh, Mr. J. Smith, Mr. M. Browne, Mr. Bradley, Mr. Ford, Mr. N.W. McClellan, Mrs. Small, Miss M. King, Mrs. Cassell, Miss R. Walsh, Mr. Antippa, Mr. Forrest, Mr. Bayliss, Mr. R. Newton.

The dead whose bodies have so far been recovered and identified include :

Mr. Z. Shimshi ; Mr. Yanowsky; Mr. E. Sperling; Mr. Mughannam; Mr. I. Farraj; Mr. Y. Mormilstein; Mr. L.J. Barder; Mr. Jamil Barder; Mr. A.M. Suleiman; Mr. E. Krantz; Mr. M. Atizeh; Mr. D.M.A.S. Khatib; Mr. Eissa Isis; Mr. G. Paragenian; Mr. T. Mansour; Mr. M.A. Khadir; Mr. S. Yitshaiah; Mr. Bada Abdul Farrah Abu Lahab; Mr. Mohammed H. Salah; Mr. R.S. Tamimi; Mr. F. Stein; Mr. S. Kharougfi ; Miss R. Salman.

The Civil Service Second Division Association has called for the observance of a 15-minute silence by all officers at noon today in sign of mourning.

Arrangements have been made to answer inquiries concerning those missing as a result of the explosions at the King David building. Inquiries may be made by telephone to Number 4437 Extension 5.

Troops and civilian workers were digging in the debris under the glare of searchlights in the early, post-midnight hours of this morning. An R.A.F. bulldozer was brought up early in the evening to remove wreckage, as several people were believed to be still alive beneath the debris.

Curfew was imposed from 12.45 on the whole municipal area of Jerusalem but was later in the afternoon restricted to the central area of the city in which most Jewish residential quarters are situated. The curfew lasted until 5 o'clock this morning, when it was lifted completely.

Patrol wireless cars and armoured cars assisted in the hunt for suspect cars. Within a few minutes of the explosions, as the sirens went, the police had telephoned all Government buildings and ordered the complete evacuation of staffs until searches for further bombs could be carried out.

THREE EXPLOSIONS.

There was first an explosion about 12 o'clock, some 50 yards from the southern end of the hotel building. Almost simultaneously another detonation took place in the lane along the northern end of the hotel, leading to the French Consulate General. Shop-fronts and windows were blown in.

At the same time, a truck drove into the sunken driveway which leads from the northern lane to the service entrance to the basement and kitchens. A number of men — put variously at four or five to seven or eight — alighted and several began unloading milk-cans and buckets. Others went inside and held up the kitchen staff — cooks, waiters, mechanics and dishwashers.

The men deposited the milk-cans and buckets, now known to have been full of explosives, in the hallway outside the Regence cafe at the southern end of the long corridor and then escaped, leaving the hotel staff to scramble to safety as best they could.

According to one report, an anonymous woman caller telephoned to the switchboard operator at the King David and told him that the building must be evacuated as there would be an explosion "in a few minutes." About 12.35, The Palestine Post was told, also by a woman, in English, that the Government offices were about to be blown up, and that the people there had been warned to evacuate the building.

A mysterious women caller telephoned the French Consulate General and said, "In a few minutes there will be an explosion in your neighbourhood. We suggest that you open all your windows." This was done and no one was hurt there.

The third explosion came at 12.37 with a heavy shattering roar. An eye-witness at a window in the P.I.O. office high up in the David Building, across the field, stated that after the explosion, the walls of the south-west corner seemed to bulge, there was a thick and heavy cloud of brown-grey smoke, and then the masonry swayed and collapsed. The screaming of men and women trapped by the debris rose above the din of crumbling stone, iron girders and woodwork.

GAPING HOLE

The dense column of acrid smoke spiralled several hundred feet into the air, completely hiding the southern wing of the hotel. When the billowing smoke started to drift off into the sunny, cloudless sky, there was a huge, gaping chasm where the six-storey corner had been. Wounded troops and civilians, their clothes spattered with blood, their faces covered with white dust and streaked with blood, staggered out of the wreckage dazed by shock.

Inside the hotel, all electric clocks had stopped at 12.37. The entire southern wall at the end of the corridor was blown out and the wall behind the bar was demolished. The bar itself was a shambles of broken bottles, windows and furniture.

The lobby was caked with dust and a good deal of sand blown up through the loosened marble floor, which was covered with glass splinters. A whole row of tiles from the entrance hall to the south wing was raised a few inches. Broken woodwork was scattered about pell-mell in the lobby.

LEAKING PIPES

Down the stairs, in the basement, water pipes were twisted and leaking, the whole looking like the interior of a torpedoed ship.

The annexe building in the southern grounds, where the War Supply Board offices were housed, had its roof knocked in by falling stones. A large iron safe was hurled by the blast into Julian's Way, killing a passer-by.

Within a few minutes after the first explosion, police radio cars, armoured cars, and jeep-borne infantry converged on the spot. The anti-terrorist sirens had sounded and traffic halted, at first somewhat uncertainly. A few minutes later, as C.I.D. experts and Army sappers were examining the wreckage of shop-windows and fronts, the All Clear sirens went and traffic was resumed. The police and infantry withdrew some distance, but then came the third and heaviest explosion and the sirens went again.

Automatic weapon fire was heard a few minutes before the explosion as the gunmen—believed to be members of the Irgun Zevai Leumi or Stern Gang — made their get-away. One station officer in the B.O.A.C. offices said that he saw a closed car speeding away and a sack being flung from the window. Police later found it contained a Sten-gun.

A sentry who saw a man throw the first bomb fired at him and the man, throwing away a sub-machine gun, limped towards a car which disappeared towards Jaffa Gate. The car was later found abandoned at the foot of the Tower of David. In it, according to one report, were two sticks of gelignite, a revolver, and an Arab garment.

Officer Fired On

An army major was in a wash-room assisting another officer wounded in the earlier explosion. He was just above the tradesmen's entrance where the terrorists' truck stood was fired on through the window and fired back. Near the truck the police were later reported to have found a hand-barrow with three or four buckets filled with explosives with fuse-wires attached, but the detonators unset.

All passengers in a passing No. 4 bus were injured, and inside the lounge of the hotel, guests who were having pre-luncheon aperitifs were blown from their places by the blast. There were blood stains on the floor of the corridor afterwards.

Rescue Work

Military and civilian ambulances carried a long succession of bodies, some blanketed and still, others writhing and moaning, to the Government and Military Hospitals. One army doctor crawled with his medical kit into a large hole in the debris — resembling a blitzed London building after an air raid — to treat a man who had been heard calling out. Then three bodies were brought out.

Units of the Argyll and Sutherland Highlanders which arrived on the scene within 15 minutes, with picks, shovels, acetylene blow-torches and hand-operated winches, were joined by about 200 Arab postal linesmen and later by other men recruited by the P.W.D. to remove the wreckage. Searchlights were set up before dark so that the rescue work could continue into the night.

The hall of the Y.M.C.A. was turned into an emergency first-aid station to treat the injured, including many guests evacuated from the hotel, many suffering slight injuries from flying glass or dazed with shock.

The C.I.D. set up temporary investigating offices in the hotel dining room where they took eye-witness statements from hotel personnel. Statements were also taken from B.O.A.C. staff.

In the kitchen below food ready on trays was covered with a layer of dust. One member of the kitchen staff told *The Palestine Post* that he was held up by two men dressed as Arabs who entered the basement door, and told him in Arabic to keep still and not move.

Sir John Shaw permitted press photographers to take pictures at all angles, and it is understood that a special 'plane was flown to Cairo for pictures to be radio-wirelessed to England. One high military officer on the scene was heard to say, "This is mass murder."

The Jerusalem Fire Brigade and Army Fire Service engines were on the scene to cope with possible outbreaks of fire.

Thirty-one bodies were brought to the Government Hospital at 7 o'clock yesterday evening, but only 21 could be identified. According to the P.B.S. at 9.30, five Britons and 23 Palestinians had lost their lives. The radio also stated that 15 Britons and 27 Palestinians were injured, and that a number of persons were not yet accounted for.

The following persons were admitted to hospital:

Government Hospital:

Mr. A. Southworth, Crown Counsel; Emile Marroum; Farid Abu Ghosh; Azar Aref Musha'sha; P/C Mahmud Abdul Sake; Gablan Mitlek; Youssef Mustapha Jeddah; Jabra Bader; Abdullah Maghrabi; Mussa Hussein Ali Tourt; Muhammed Abdul Haj; and an unidentified person.

French Hospital:

George Rushad; Yacub Abdul Muneim; Ribhi Hassan Hamudeh; Muhammad Fattouh Rabbah; Awad Abdul Sayed Mantoul; Hassan Abdul Rahman; and Herman Feldman.

16th General Military Hospital:

Miss Louba Wahbe; Miss Julia Jouzeh; Miss Victoria Hafsapian; Miss Marie Greenberg; Miss Rose-Anne Titinski; Miss Joan Khoury; Miss Adi Bitar; Miss Jose Greenberg; a man named Artin; and Mr. Richard Mower.

More than 50 persons were given first aid treatment at Government Hospital, the French Hospital, and the Hadassah clinic and were sent home.

ATTACKERS OUTLAWED BY JEWISH HEADS

The following joint statement was issued last night by the Jewish Agency and Vaad Leumi.

The Executive of the Jewish Agency and the Executive of the Vaad Leumi express their horror at the dastardly crime perpetrated by the gang of desperadoes who today attacked the Government offices in Jerusalem, and shed the innocent blood of Government officers and other citizens, British, Jewish and Arab.

They express their deepest sympathy to the relatives of those who have been murdered and to those who have been injured.

The Yishuv in Palestine is called upon to rise up against these abominable outrages.

Statements by Tel Aviv Municipality and Histadrut Page 3

'Monty' Summoned to Cabinet on Palestine

LONDON, Monday. — Field Marshal Montgomery, Chief of the General Staff, was summoned to Downing Street today when the British Cabinet met to consider the critical Palestine situation.

While it is doubtful whether the Cabinet had yet received details of the blasting of the Palestine Administration's Headquarters in Jerusalem, Mr. Attlee is believed to have given an account of recent developments in Palestine.

Informed quarters now confirm that there will be both an official statement and a White Paper on Palestine before Parliament rises, probably in the first week of August.

The Government has still to fix a date for the statement, which will be of an interim character so far as general policy is concerned, but will cover the "public order" side of the present situation about which most of the facts are now known.

It is understood that documents found in the Jewish Agency offices in Jerusalem will be published in a white paper nevt week.

Federalism Lesser Evil

There are signs that the Joint Palestine Report's vision of a unitarian Palestinian state is proving impossible of fulfilment, says the "Daily Telegraph", referring to the suggestion of a federal Palestine with Jewish, Arab and "mixed" cantons.

The paper says : "It is idle to object to a federal or indeed to any solution unwelcome to either the Arab leaders or the more extreme Zionists among the Jews. No ingenuity could devise a scheme to satisfy either. Therefore, the first duty of the Mandatory Power must be to restore order as has been done ; and the second, to apply some scheme morally and materially defensible. If there is only a choice of evils, we must choose the lesser."

A federal system for Palestine, dividing the country into Arab and Jewish states, is also forecast as the solution towards which the British and United States experts have been moving during their meetings in London, by the London Correspondent of the 'Yorkshire Post'.

The correspondent adds : "Their examination of the problem is not yet complete, and it remains to be seen whether a federation will be their final verdict, and whether this solution will be favoured by the British Government."

LP.100,000 Damage

The King David Hotel was built in 1929 and opened in 1931. It cost a quarter of a million pounds at that time, but the value is now of course considerably more.

The section of the building destroyed yesterday is valued at LP100,000.

Rental paid by Government to the hotel management is LP1,000 monthly.

Mr. Benjamin Chaikin, F.R.I.B.A., who designed the building, was brought yesterday to examine the damage after the explosion.

Guests were allowed to return last night to sleep there.

Official Army H.Q. Account

In a statement issued from H.Q., Palestine late last night, it was stated that at 12.10 on Monday a civilian truck drove up to the basement of the King David Hotel and a number of Jews dressed as Arabs got out and held up the civilian doorkeeper at the service entrance.

This party of Jews then entered the hotel and held up the kitchen staff before unloading several milk-churns through the service door into the hotel.

They pushed these milk-churns along towards the far end of the building, past the Signal exchange, and deposited them by the Regence restaurant, directly below the Secretariat. A Royal Signals officer working in the exchange, hearing a good deal of noise, came out to investigate and was confronted by a man dressed as an Arab, pointing a revolver at him.

Before the officer had time to make a sound, the man with the revolver shot him twice in the stomach, wounding him severely.

At 12.20 hours, a party of four or five Jews dressed as Arabs was seen escaping from the basement of the hotel. Several shots were fired at them and one man was wounded. This party was seen to escape in a car which had been parked about 200 yards from the King David Hotel.

At 12.25 hours there occurred, presumably as a diversion, a small explosion in the road between the Y.M.C.A. and the King David Hotel. This was followed at 12.37 hours by a tremendous explosion which ripped off a whole corner of the King David Hotel building, destroying some 25 rooms on five floors. These rooms accommodated the Secretariat of the Government of Palestine and offices of the Defence Security office of H.Q. Palestine.

Known casualties up to 9.30 p.m. were 41 dead, including eight unidentified bodies, 53 injured and 52 missing.

The missing persons, presumably buried under the huge pile of debris, include 12 senior British officers of the Secretariat, two senior Palestinian officers of the Secretariat, and two senior Palestinian officers of the Attorney General's Department.

The work of removing the debris continued after dark, powerful electric lamps being used to make the operation possible.

Attlee Statement Expected Today

LONDON, Monday. — The Prime Minister will be asked in the House of Commons tomorrow if he can make a statement on the blowing up by Jewish terrorists of the British Army Headquarters at the King David Hotel in Jerusalem.

Mr. Attlee will, almost certainly, make a statement on the situation, though this may be fairly short pending the completion of the inquiries and the receipt in London of an official report on what has occurred.

There will be no demand for a debate at once, as it is already known that the Government propose to have a full debate on Palestine next week.

Mr. Hall, in a written reply today, refused Mr. Crossman's demand for a statement on the release of the Jewish leaders detained without charge, either entirely or pending their committal for trial.

(Reuter & PTA)

SUBMARINES OFF HAIFA

HAIFA, Monday.—The Cruiser HMS Liverpool, which has been in Haifa since Thursday, left today for Tel Aviv and Jaffa.

Two submarines, the HMS Templar and HMS Tantivy are off Port, and are here for a few days for exercises.

EYE-WITNESS STORIES

The Officer Administering the Government, Sir J.V.W. Shaw, was sitting in his office at the south-eastern corner of the hotel when the explosion occurred. Immediately afterwards, he was seen rushing from one room to another in the hotel and later carrying a ladder to take part in the rescue work. The O.A.G. was joined by the Inspector-General of Police, Colonel W. N. Gray. The G.O.C., Lt.-General E.H. Barker, and members of the Staff were also soon on the scene.

Sir John had been trapped in his room but was rescued after the door was broken open. His office was not damaged as it was in the opposite wing, but the desk and floor were covered with falling plaster.

The Superintendent of Police, Jerusalem District, Mr. K.P. Hadingham, was investigating the cause of the first two apparently diversionary, explosions when the third occurred. He was badly injured about the hands and later returned to the scene bandaged. He also received a cut under the right eye.

Mr. Dan Ben-Dor, R.E. garrison engineer, who was driving by at the time of the explosion, escaped with minor cuts, while his Great Dane, which was sitting at his side, was so badly hurt by fragments that it had to be destroyed. The motor of his car was smashed.

Two correspondents who were standing in the main lounge of the hotel had a narrow escape. Mr. T.S. Steele, "Daily Telegraph," and Mr. Stanley Bishop, "Daily Herald," threw themselves to the ground, and were unhurt. Mr. R. Catling, Deputy Superintendent at the C.I.D., who had arrived to investigate was with them but was also unhurt.

Mr. Richard Mowrer, "New York Post", correspondent, was walking across the street in front of the hotel when he was hit and suffered a broken leg.

One man who emerged from the Secretariat with only slight cuts was praying aloud and weeping. "My sister is under there. Lord, send her out alive." he repeated. He, his father and his sister were all employed in the Secretariat. His father was alive. He was still repeating his prayer half an hour later.

Mr. Robert Newton, of the political section of the Secretariat, said: "The whole side of my room fell away to the ground six stories below and I was left suspended above the wreckage." He made his escape and helped to take charge of the rescue work.

As the "Daily Telegraph" correspondent was standing with Sir John Shaw, the figure of a civilian covered in dirt and with torn clothes emerged from the wreckage, walked up to the O.A.G., and said, "I have got the cyphers and locked the safe, sir."

Responsible Jewish sources put the blame for the attack on the Irgun Zevai Leumi or Stern Gang (according to a news agency report from Jerusalem). The Haganah was absolved of blame by both the Jews and the British, the message added.

The police reported they had arrested two men on suspicion a short distance from the hotel but would give no further details.

One Jewish source quoted by a news agency stated the attack was "an attempt to hamper Dr. Weizmann in the present talks with the British Government."

Column One

By David Courtney

THE dust of irresponsible bombs raises a curtain through which the events of the larger world are seen dimly. The bloody foreground to yesterday's events is foreground only to those near at hand; and the perspective on the other side of the curtain will be less distorted than on this side. The world today comprehends violence as violence only: it has suffered too much of it to be deceived by the extenuations of its fraudulent politics. The outrage committed yesterday in Jerusalem has neither sense nor apology. It was unqualified evil and will be judged as such by honest men in every part of the world. At this moment, it is nothing less than a challenge to the Jewish cause itself, a challenge that must be taken up in the interest of the cause.

■

IT is permissible to argue that the events of yesterday are of a piece with the chaos of a world groping frantically for values. If other world events of the last twenty-four hours have been less spectacular, their implications have been in many cases hardly less terrifying. It is a tale of violence from Trieste to Manchuria and of unwisdom from Berlin to Athens. No one event excuses the other and all of them are symptoms of a Peace which is little more than an uncontrollable projection of the war. It is obvious that Hitler has had greater success in his long-term plans than in his short-term ambitions. That fact needs to be borne in mind. The tendency to consider the German war as over and the penalty largely paid grows alarmingly.

■

THE latest evidence of this is the Anglo-American plan to flout the Soviet and, bowing to the pressure of Big Business in Britain and the United States, to re-establish a west German economic system on lines which can lead to nothing else but the renewed domination of industrial Germany over a large part of Europe. General McNarney talks plain American. If the Russians won't collaborate in a scheme of economic unity for the whole of Germany and largely to the benefit of German heavy industry, their acquiescence will not be sought for a scheme of partial union. One gets the impression from General McNarney's statements of a too-eager readiness to profit by the apparent intransigence of the Soviet.

■

THE Anglo-American case has persuasive merits. Administration of the two western zones is a heavy financial liability on the British and American taxpayer, and may well remain so until a scheme of German inter-zonal and international trading is adopted and applied. In practice this can only mean west German sovereignty based on the revived heavy industries of the Ruhr and therefore fundamentally opposed to the terms of the Potsdam agreement. It is not sufficient to argue that the Soviet itself has failed to honour the Potsdam agreement. It has not been honoured by any one of the occupying Powers. The Russians have claimed that Britain and America's interpretation of the agreement has been contrary to its spirit; and that even with the American twenty-five year plan added to it, the only ultimate result would be the restoration of a Germany little different from the one that has gone to war twice in the last twenty-two years.

■

AT successive conferences of the Big Three during and immediately after the war, it was laid down as a unified principle that the victorious Allies would accept the responsibility for the demilitarization of Germany in every sense including the economic; and for the rehabilitation of the country in a fashion that would make it a welcome and peaceful member of the community of nations. It was, and is, a tremendous job: it may be a forlorn job. But the war has been over barely a year and it is too soon to grow tired or even parsimonious in the task which, if unfulfilled, would make a mockery of Allied victory. It is natural that the British, and especially the Americans, should want to get quit of such a responsibility at a time when their own internal problems are almost unbearable; but Germany in defeat is still the major problem of international security. That problem will only be exacerbated if General McNarney and those who advise from Wall Street and the City of London get their way.

Jerusalem, July 23.

ALEX BOMB CONFESSIONS

CAIRO, Monday (R).— Eleven members of the Misr el Fattah, the Green Shirt organization with extreme nationalist aims, were arrested today in connection with the grenade throwing incident on July 17 at the British Warrant Officers' and Sergeants' Club in Alexandria, it was reliably learned.

Six of the arrested men, it was stated, have already confessed, not only to the club incident, but to other recent acts of violence against British Service personnel.

Forty persons, including British service men and women, were injured in the July 17 incident.

Sidki Phones Stansgate

Sidky Pasha, the Egyptian Prime Minister, received the news by telephone while still in bed early today. He immediately telephoned it to Lord Stansgate, leader of the British treaty mission.

The Misr el Fattah was started by Ahmed Hussein, a young Egyptian lawyer who visited Germany before the War and came under the influence of Nazi ideology and methods.

On his return to Egypt he tried to apply them to the Egyptian youth who were members of his organization. He was arrested during the War on the ground that his beliefs and actions were detrimental to the Allied cause.

Press Comment Page 3

Arab Boycott In Commons

LONDON, Monday (R). — The Chairman of the Zionist Federation of Great Britain, Mr. Barnett Janner (Labour), drew the Foreign Secretary's attention in the House of Commons today to the decree by the Syrian Government on June 23, about the boycott of Zionist good which he said provided for the death penalty to be awarded in certain cases of infringement.

He asked whether in view of the fact that such legislation violated the provisions of the United Nations Charter, designed to prevent racial discrimination, he would make representations to protect the interests of Palestinian citizens against the decree.

Mr. Noel Baker, Minister of State, who replied, said that the Syrian law which dealt with the boycott of Zionist goods provided for certain penalties to persons who violated the boycott, but no death penalty was imposed. The British Government had already expressed to the Syrian Government their strong disapproval of the Arab boycott of Zionist goods.

Mr. Janner: "Is the Syrian Government a member of the United Nations, and is this not contrary to the Charter of the United Nations?"

Mr. Noel Baker: "We have made our representation. We think it is contrary to neighbourly conduct and common sense, and I think we had better leave it at that for the present."

2,000 Killed In Bolivian Revolt

NEW YORK, Monday (R). — Two-thousand persons were killed in Bolivia where the anti Government revolt culminated in the hanging of the 37-year old President, Colonel Villarroel and the killing of several Cabinet Ministers, according to reports received here today.

(More on Page 3)

THE PALESTINE POST

LATE Edition

JERUSALEM
WEDNESDAY, July 31, 1946

PRICE: 15 MILS
VOL. XXI. No. 6165

PALESTINE'S BIGGEST CITY BESIEGED

TEL AVIV'S 200,000 BEING CHECKED BY TWO DIVISIONS

Palestine Post Staff

TEL AVIV, Tuesday. — Nearly 20,000 British troops and Palestine Police were engaged here today in the most intensive and most complete search operation ever undertaken in Palestine or perhaps in any other part of the world, with the object of finding members of terrorist gangs.

Some 25,000 persons were estimated to have been interrogated by evening, of whom 133 men and 10 girls were sent to Rafa and Latrun camps for further investigations. The G.O.C., Sir Evelyn Barker, and the Inspector General of Police, Colonel W. N. Gray, inspected the operations.

The search was so thoroughly planned that every adult in Tel Aviv will be questioned, every building searched, and even patients in hospitals examined during the four or five days it will last. X-ray photographs will be taken of patients in plaster casts to determine if their injuries are genuine.

Completely cut off from the rest of Palestine by land and sea, the city was placed under an absolute curfew from 5 o'clock in the morning.

Residents were warned that anyone breaking the curfew was liable to be shot on sight.

The troops and police appeared to know for whom they were looking. They had been furnished with a long alphabetical list of suspected members of the Irgun Zevai Leumi and the Stern Gang, and with photographs of some of the leading members of the two groups.

NO RESISTANCE

As far as could be observed in Tel Aviv yesterday by visiting press correspondents, there was no resistance to the search, not even passive. Men and women submitted quietly, and seemingly without resentment.

Before dawn, troops of the Sixth Airborne Division placed a cordon around the entire city. All traffic was prevented from entering or leaving. Traffic jams piled up at the cross-roads outside. All telephone and telegraph communications were cut off at about 6.30 a.m. Government launches patrolled off the coast to prevent any boats from leaving the harbour.

Within the city, a series of inner cordons were established. At 4.55 the search began, house by house, shop by shop, building by building and block by block. When the foreign press correspondents arrived on a conducted tour from Jerusalem they found Tel Aviv to be a dead city, at first glance appearing to be entirely deserted except for the red-bereted troops and an occasional scavenging dog. Correspondents of the local press were prevented from joining the tour, though they were given special permit authorising them to move freely in the town.

Every shop and office, including newspaper offices, was closed and not a single civilian could be seen on the streets except under escort of soldiers or in barbed-wire pens.

Troops Patrols

Patrols of troops moved down one street of Tel Aviv after another, entering every door. Every ablebodied man between 15 and 50 years and every woman between 15 and 35 years, with the exception of pregnant women or mothers with small children, were ordered out of their homes to the nearest "screening" point.

Although intolerance reared its ugly head at times on all sides during the day and tempers frequently frayed, there was evident also genuine co-operation by both searched and searchers.

In Salameh Road, however, our correspondent saw soldiers armed with heavy clubs, forcing detainees to double and prodding stragglers. In Last Monday were there was a very serious, murderous outrage against the community as a whole.

For every "Get back inside there!" harshly yelled by police or Tommies to curious spectators standing on flat balconies over the quiet streets, however, there was always a harmonious counter, such as a young cherry-bereted paratrooper offering a "screened" girl a half hearted "Shalom" for her homeward way.

Searchers Civil

The searchers were civil and polite, on the whole, and an attempt was made to keep husbands, wives and children together.

Small groups shepherded the streets made a queer collection — orthodox Jews in long coats and round hats, men in shorts and shirts, women in house-dresses — and one lady in a dressing gown carrying a parasol.

Except for those detained for further interrogation, the screening took only a few minute, sometimes a minute only. Each company of troops had its own "screening" team of

(Continued on Page 2 Col. 3)

THE TWO COMMUNIQUES

No. 76, July 30.

The following communication was received from H.E. the High Commissioner (General Sir Alan Cunningham) this morning:—

I wish to make it clear that the military operations now proceeding in the Tel Aviv area have as their objective the search for and detention of terrorists and are a direct result of the vile and horrible crime committed in Jerusalem on Monday, July 22, 1946, through which over one hundred innocent civilians lost their lives, including women and boys, of British, Arab and Jewish birth.

There is clear evidence of the existence of terrorists in Tel Aviv and that some if not all of those who took part in the Jerusalem crime come from that town.

In making this announcement I do not depart one jot from my statement of June 29. It has been and is my earnest wish that if as a result of violence directed against the Government, military action is forced on us, it should have as its objective the forces responsible for that violence, and that military operations and restrictions should interfere as little as possible with the normal life of the country.

The remedy, therefore, is plain to see. Should violence be eschewed, normal occupations will take no harm, and the endeavour of all for the betterment of the future of Palestine can continue in peace. However, I would remind all the peoples of Palestine of the great and urgent activity now proceeding to find an early solution of the Palestine problem.

Discussions are to be held with both Arabs and Jews. Violence can only make the task more difficult and lengthy, if not impossible.

Habimah Theatre Is Brigade H.Q.

TEL AVIV, Tuesday. — A Brigade Headquarters was established in the Habimah Theatre, which was surrounded by barbed wire. Police and army interrogators sat at a table in the entrance to the question. suspects brought for a second screening. Back stage, wigs were laid out on tables erected from the theatre's props for "Hamlet."

In this instance a shameful and barbarous crime has been committed. It must be evident to every right-minded man that mere protests are not sufficient to remove stains of this kind.

No movement of terrorist character would have a chance of survival against the wishes of the people from whom it springs. Preventive measures have been set in motion. It lies with the Yishuv to decide whether they will help or hinder the design of routing out a canker which, if it remains, can only recoil on the heads of the Yishuv under whatever conditions the future may hold.

No. 77 July 30, 9.30 p.m.

Following the outrage at the Secretariat on July 22, the most extensive operations yet carried out against Jewish terrorists commenced at dawn today when some twenty thousand British troops of the 6th Airborne Division and the 1st British Infantry Division, working in conjunction with the Palestine Police, established close inner and outer cordons around Tel Aviv, isolating the town from the remainder of Palestine. Within the cordons a thorough search is being conducted.

The operations are under the command of Major-General A.J.H. Cassels, C.B., D.S.O., G.O.C., 6th Airborne Division.

A complete curfew has been imposed and all telephone communication has been suspended. All traffic in and out of the town has been suspended. Seaborne traffic has also been stopped. Searches proceeded throughout the day according to plan. Large numbers of Jews were screened and of these 133 males and 10 females have so far been held for further questioning. Apart from minor cases of stone throwing by Jews no incidents occurred. There were no casualties. The operations were attended by a large party of foreign correspondents.

FEDERATION: TRUMAN'S TALK

WASHINGTON, Tuesday (R) — President Truman today examined the full report and recommendations of the London Anglo-American conference for 40 minutes with a party of New York Congressmen, headed by Mr. Emanuel Celler, Democratic representative from Brooklyn, and with members of his special Cabinet committee on Palestine.

While press reports published here today said that Mr. Byrnes in his conference with Mr. Attlee in Paris over the week-end had already approved the plan and had agreed to recommend it to Mr. Truman, Mr. Celler left the White House condemning the scheme as "outrageous".

"The report is dead before it is published, because it has already been rejected in advance by both Arabs and Jews," he said, today.

Referring to the proposed provision of a loan to the Arab world, Mr. Celler said: "This is outrageous when the Arabs did not lend a penny or a donkey to the war effort. Why should we reward them with 300,000,000 dollars? The American people will not stand for it."

He was confident that Congress would not approve such a proposal.

(More on Page 3 Col. 1)
Debate Prospects — Page 4.

"PRELIMINARY STEP" -- CASSELS

The search operations begun in Tel Aviv yesterday were "a preliminary step" towards wiping out the terrorist gangs, declared tall, youthful-looking Major-General A. J. H. Cassels, Area Commander and commander of the Sixth Airborne Division, to foreign press correspondents at "Lydda" Police Headquarters in Jaffa yesterday morning.

Major-General Cassels acknowledged that the search would involve serious inconvenience to large numbers of people. Nineteen units of battalion strength, totalling 14,000 to 15,000 men, and some 600 British police were participating in the search. They would enter "every house, every shed, and every place where a man might be."

The commander explained that arrangements were being made to bring food into the city, that persons ill in bed were not being moved, and that a central pool of ambulances had been formed to assist the sick during the searches.

Jewish policemen were engaged in finding people needed to maintain essential services and staffs of sappers were sent to the Power Houses and water supply to keep the services running.

Hospitals were being searched but they would thereafter be given special facilities to continue their work. He added that plaster casts on hospital patients would be X-rayed to determine whether they covered up genuine injuries. Even hospital nurses would be interrogated.

"Rough Idea"

Giving foreign correspondents "a rough idea of what's behind the house-to-house search," General Cassels said: "It is not a task that anyone would be put "to serious inconvenience within the next few days," he said, adding: "To that I can only say I'm sorry."

But I feel that any steps that can be taken to deal with these terrorists and to stop the outrages which have been going on are well worth while."

The object was, he summed up, to check up on everybody in Tel Aviv with the hope of removing as many members of the Irgun Zevai Leumi and the Stern Gang as we can." Major-General Cassels indicated that the operations were not directed against the "Haganah".

Asked whether British soldiers had been given any special orders concerning their behaviour to the public during the operation, he replied; "Five thousand times."

"I'm Sorry"

As a result of the search, a great many people in Tel Aviv would be very serious, murderous outrage against the community as a whole. It was determined that by hook or by crook we must try and find, and detain, these terrorist gangs.

As a preliminary step, I was given orders to institute a speedy and detailed search of Tel Aviv, the idea being to go through every building in the city with the help of experts in the police force, in the hope of capturing some of these terrorists.

It is not a task that anyone wants to do, but I hope you'll all agree that it's a task which has to be done.

PEACE CONFERENCE OPENS WITH

EVATT-MOLOTOV CLASH ON RULES

By FRASER WIGHTON, Reuter's Special Correspondent

PARIS, Tuesday. — The conference of the 21 nations opened its second day with a clash at the first meeting this morning of the Procedure Committee.

Dr. Herbert Evatt of Australia proposed M. Paul Henri Spaak (Belgium) as chairman of the committee, but was promptly opposed by the Soviet Foreign Minister, M. Molotov, who declared that in his view the leader of the Yugoslav delegation, M. Edvard Kardelj, was better qualified for the office.

OPPOSING VIEWS

A warm discussion is believed to have followed reflecting the opposing views of the followers of Dr. Evatt and those of the Soviet Union on the Big Powers' right in drawing up the peace treaties. Greece, Holland and Britain supported the nomination of M. Spaak, and the Ukraine and Poland supported M. Kardelj.

"ONE OPERATION"

The Chinese delegate, M. Wang Shih Chih advanced that the President and Vice-President be elected in one operation — the one with the majority vote being the President and the other the Vice-President.

A vote on this proposal resulted in its rejection and subsequently a ballot was taken resulting in the election of M. Spaak, who took the chair and proposed that M. Kardelj be elected Vice-President. This proposal was passed unanimously.

DISCUSSION

The discussion over the election of office holders occupied the major portion of the proceedings and apparently the question of a two-thirds majority — proposed by the "Big Four" — as the basis of voting on all matters has not yet been broached.

SOVIET CONFERENCE PLAN FOILED

PARIS, Tuesday (Reuter). — The Soviet delegation attempted to arrange a conference of the heads of all the delegations half an hour before the procedure committee met this morning, presumably to discuss in advance the procedural questions raised by Dr. Evatt at yesterday's opening session, but their plan had to be abandoned because not all heads of delegations were available at such short notice.

This morning's committee meeting carried with it the first real challenge facing the conference. The issue is whether the smaller powers, championed by Dr. Evatt, will agree to the draft rules of procedure drawn up by the "Big Four" or not.

"Very Seriously"

Dr. Evatt made it clear at yesterday's session that the Australian delegation at least is prepared to take very seriously the duties and rights of these Allied powers so far excluded from the active share in the peace-making. The discussion of the rules of procedure will provide the first opportunity for the lesser powers to challenge the joint decisions of the "Big Four".

The basic question is whether the "Big Four" will feel bound to present a united front in defence of the draft rules of procedure, including that which proposed voting by a two-thirds majority on all questions of substance.

Britain's position is of particular interest. On the one hand, being a member of the "Big Four," she is so that extent committed to support the "Big Four" proposals.

On the other hand, she is under heavy pressure from the majority of the members of the British Commonwealth who follow the lead of Dr. Evatt, in seeking to secure a simple majority as the basis of the conference voting procedure.

Draft Treaties, Page 2 Col. 7

K.D. DEATH TOLL NOW 85

With the recovery of the body of Mr. F.W.G. Blenkinsop on Monday the King David bomb toll stood at

**85 DEAD
19 MISSING**

Mr. Blenkinsop was the last of the British victims to be found.

The search of the wreckage

will be continued until the bodies of all victims of last Monday's outrage have been recovered, it is officially stated.

The demolition yesterday was carried out in order to remove part of the building which was endangering the work of excavation, and the search was resumed as quickly as possible.

TRANSFERS TO SECRETARIAT

Five officers in other branches of the Public Service have been transferred to posts in the Secretariat to take the places of men killed in the King David Hotel explosion on July 22.

In addition, Mr. D.H. Mackay has been appointed to act as Postmaster General. During Sir John Shaw's absence, Mr. R. Scott, C.M.G., will act as Chief Secretary and Mr. J. Gutch as Financial Secretary, with Mr. R. Newton as Under Secretary. Mr. C.M. Pirie Gordon, formerly of the Haifa District Administration who has been Assistant British Resident in Trans-Jordan since January,

becomes an Assistant Secretary. Transfers from the District Administration include Mr. A.J. Dalgleish, Deputy District Commissioner in Galilee, to act as Principal Assistant Secretary and Mr. J.V. Prendergast, Gaza Administrative Officer, as Assistant Secretary.

Two transfers have been made from other departments, Mr. D.R. Lockhart, Assistant Controller of Heavy Industries, and Mr. H. Beldes, Assistant Intelligence and Research Officer, Department of Labour, becoming acting Administrative Assistants. Mr. M. Bachrach, of the Secretariat staff, whose sister was killed in the explosion, has received a similar acting appointment.

T. A. Mayor Sees General

The Mayor of Tel Aviv, Mr. Israel Rokach, was summoned at midday yesterday to Major-General Cassels' headquarters at Jaffa, where the Military Commander explained to him the reason for the curfew and searches in Tel Aviv and asked him to urge the inhabitants to cooperate with the authorities in the arrest of the terrorists.

Mr. Rokach strongly objected to the allegation that the terrorist attack on the King David Hotel had been committed by residents of Tel Aviv. He asked to be allowed to convene a meeting of the Municipal Council and also to ensure the city's food supply during the curfew period.

The commander agreed to allow a meeting of the Council at 11 o'clock this morning, and told Mr. Rokach that arrangements had been made for the delivery of bread and milk to residents, with the assistance of the military, as from today.

Dangerous Corner

REPRISALS Rd.

LATE Edition

THE PALESTINE POST

JERUSALEM
TUESDAY, AUGUST 13, 1946

PRICE: 15 MILS
VOL. XXI. NO. 6175

REFUGEES NOT TO BE LANDED IN PALESTINE

LONDON ORDERS ILLEGAL IMMIGRANTS TO BE SENT TO "CYPRUS OR ELSEWHERE" PENDING DECISION ON THEIR FUTURE

LONDON, Tuesday Morning (Reuter). — The British Government have given instructions to the Palestine authorities that reception into Palestine of illegal immigrants must cease, an official Government statement declares. Immigrants arriving illegally will be conveyed to Cyprus or elsewhere and housed in camps there until a decision can be taken as to their future.

GOVERNMENT STATEMENT

Continuance of illegal immigrant traffic at the present time, the statement says, "is likely to have an adverse effect on the hope of a general settlement in Palestine. In announcing this decision, the British Government wish to make it clear that while they cannot tolerate this attempt by a minority of Zionist extremists to exploit the sufferings of the unfortunate people in order to create a situation prejudicial to a just settlement, they are deeply sensible of the sufferings undergone by the Jewish community and are anxious to bring them to an end as soon as possible."

The statement adds that recent developments had revealed illegal immigrant traffic as a "widely ramified and highly organized movement supported by very large financial contributions from Zionist sources, which has been built up and put into operation by unscrupulous persons in an attempt to force the hand of the British Government and anticipate their decision on future policy in Palestine.

UNDERGROUND RAILWAY

"The organizers maintain a closely knit network of agents in countries of Eastern and Southern Europe by whom considerable numbers of Displaced Jews are moved from points of departure as far distant as Poland down to the Mediterranean seaboard. Thence, herded into overcrowded and unseaworthy ships with insufficient food and in conditions of utmost privation and squalor, they are brought across the Mediterranean, inspired by the conviction carefully instilled into them that this is their only road to safety.

"In all this process, the laws and regulations of the countries concerned are ignored; identity and ration cards, travel documents etc. are forged on a large scale; food, clothing, medical supplies and transport provided by UNRRA and other agencies for the relief of suffering in Europe, are diverted to the maintenance of what is openly described as 'the underground railway to Palestine'."

The other points made were: Illegal immigration "threatens both civil war and a breakdown of the Government in Palestine."

From Eastern Europe

The British Government was concerned at the reports of prosecution and pogroms against the Jews in Eastern and South-Eastern Europe, and hoped that the countries concerned would "bring this shame to a sharp and decisive end."

The statement also expressed concern that a large proportion of these immigrants came from Eastern Europe and not from Displaced Persons centres in Germany, Austria and Italy, which it was hoped to empty.

Illegals

The statement added: apart from its illegality, immigration and traffic to Palestine is a source of grave danger to law and order in Palestine. The reception and guarding of large numbers of illegal immigrants places a severe strain on the administration.

Their arrival has greatly increased the tension between the Arab and Jewish communities in Palestine. And since there is evidence that the terrorist element among the Jews has been reinforced from the ranks of illegal immigrants, their promiscuous introduction clearly cannot be tolerated any longer. As the mandatory power for Palestine, H.M. Government have responsibilities towards the population of that country.

It is obviously not in the interests of Palestine generally that such illegal activities should be allowed to continue.

The recent increase in illegal immigration, which sets aside considerations of priority and equity, the statement continues, is also operating with great unfairness towards those Jews who would otherwise have been able to enter Palestine legally under the quota. All potential legal immigration has been pushed aside by this illegal traffic.

The statement recalls that the British Government has accepted as basis for negotiation the plan drawn up by the British and American experts in London, which is designed to "provide for increased immigration into Palestine under conditions which would not disturb the peace and economy of the country."

Giving the background of their decision about illegal immigration into Palestine, the British Government in their statement say:

Not a country in the world has been a better or more consistent friend of the Jewish people than Britain. Wherever Jews were persecuted, the voice of Britain was lifted in protest, and wherever possible action was taken to mitigate their lot.

The statement says that under the British Mandate, nearly 500,000 Jews settled legally in Palestine. In December 1945, the quota of 75,000 Jewish immigrants permitted to enter Palestine under the provisions of the White Paper, was exhausted. Nevertheless, pending final decision on the future policy for Palestine, the British Government authorized the continuance of Jewish immigration at the rate of 1,500 monthly.

Yet there has been an increasing flow of illegal immigration and their numbers have to be set off against the monthly quota. Those already held in camps in Palestine or on ships in Haifa Harbour are more than sufficient to absorb the whole quota for many months ahead. Moved by sympathy for the suffering of the Jewish people in Europe, the British Government have hitherto allowed illegal immigrants to land, in spite of the great embarrassment caused to the Palestine authorities.

"The patience, forbearance and humanity thus shown by the British Government has, however, been interpreted by those responsible for the traffic as a sign of weakness and as an encouragement to redouble their efforts to increase the flow of illegal immigrants still further.

Harmonizing Claims

"A point has now been reached when it is clear that the present illegal traffic is not, as has been maintained, a movement arising spontaneously among European Jews who see in Palestine their only hope for the future. Nor are those who encourage and direct it inspired solely by the sympathy which is so widely felt for their suffering."

Concluding the statement says: "It is clear that a permanent solution of this complicated question can only be brought about if Jews and Arabs are prepared to enter upon discussions in a realistic and constructive spirit in order to evolve a practical scheme for harmonizing the claims of these two historic peoples."

STOP PRESS

CURFEW IN HAIFA

The High Commissioner announced at 2.30 this morning that those illegal immigrants who arrived at Haifa before August 11 will be sent to Athlit and not to Cyprus.

(This means that passengers in the Hagana and Hahayal Haivri, who are still on board ship in Haifa Harbour, will be landed, but those who arrived yesterday in the Yagour and Henrietta Szold will be deported.)

Curfew has been imposed on the entire Haifa Municipal Area as from one o'clock this morning until further notice. The announcement was made by loud-speaker cars touring the town shortly after one.

Column One

By David Courtney

THAT swift-flowing channel of contention, the Dardanelles, is about to overflow its banks: nothing else was to be expected. The Foreign Office has confirmed the announcement from Ankara that Russia has made a formal demand for the revision of the Montreux Treaty; and without or within any existing international machinery, a conference will be called soon: the chant of Macbeth's witches will be heard over still another cauldron. The Dardanelles in its immediate implications, link with the Danube; but like the Persia problem, which will probably stay quiescent for a week or two, its future status is a matter of very real interest to Palestine: the two problems together are gradually shifting the powder barrel of international politics from the Balkans to the Middle East. Behind them rival interests are assembling with modern manuals of strategy in their pockets and conflicting ideologies with which to bribe their way among the people.

■

THE validity of the Montreux Treaty lies in the assumption that the Straits are a dividing line, not a bridge, between Russia and the West. By reducing Russia's belligerent rights in the Straits to an equality with those of Britain and France and their lesser Allies, it ignored the special position of Russia as a State dependent on the Dardanelles for outlet and missed the natural, inevitable and legitimate tendency of the industrializing Soviet to extend its interests to the Eastern Mediterranean. The treaty revision which the Russians are demanding is likely to amount to a virtual scrapping of the original terms; and a new treaty will be proposed under which the Soviet would be given privileges on a par with those which Britain is relinquishing in Egypt and taking up in Trans-Jordan.

■

DOUBTLESS, the Sovereignty of Turkey is threatened: that is the line Ankara will take; and it is probable that Britain and the United States will toe it also, with a great show of moral indignation. It is as good, or as bad, an argument as the line of security along which the Russians will marshal their forces. But however much they keep their tongues in their cheeks, in their minds will be the problem of strategy in relation to possible Danube, Middle East and Mediterranean developments. The current that races turbulently down the Straits divides at Cyprus to sweep on the one side to the Persian Gulf and on the other to Trieste; in short, the Mediterranean and its pendant problems are gradually, portentously taking their old shape. The legacy of Czarist and Tory Imperialism is too much for its Socialist inheritors; and neither Britain nor Russia has the courage to experiment in its own faith. There is one sensible answer to the problems of these great waterways: it is the same answer for the Straits as for the Suez Canal, for the Danube as for the Rhine — their full and positive internationalization. But if the old order is to remain, Russia has as much right to favoured treatment in the Dardanelles as America to favoured treatment through the Panama Canal; and on much the same principles as those which animate the Monroe Doctrine.

■

THE Dardanelles, with their direct and immediate bearing on the Danube and their indirect but unmistakeable bearing on the Middle East as a whole; the oil and Southward highways of Persia: these are part of the terrifying concatenation of portents through which the delegates to the Paris Conference have to pick their way, as through barbed wire, to the problems set them. Whether the addition of Albania, Cuba, Egypt and Mexico to their counsels will help or hinder there is no knowing; but it is clear that Russia has had to pay a trifle heavily for its championship of Albania. Dr. Evatt, bent on his role as the White Knight of small nations, keeps his vizor closed so tightly that he fails to see that at a certain stage of their smallness, the small states are little more than food for the bellies of the Big Powers. Neither Albania, Cuba, Egypt nor Mexico are in Paris as independent units; and half the voices raised at the Luxembourg Palace are no better confusing echoes. They play their part in Big Power politics as diligently as their masters; and if Dr. Evatt feels he has a crusade to lead, let it be rather for the weeding out of the Conference than for its cluttering up.

Jerusalem, August 13.

Mr. Acheson's Recommendations

U.S. COMPROMISE PLAN

The American compromise plan for Palestine, said to have been prepared under the supervision of Mr. Dean Acheson, is reported to provide for a Jewish zone of 4,900 sq. kilometres, instead of 2,900 sq. kms., as in the British plan. Another source speaks of an increase in the area of only 30 percent over the British proposal.

Larger local autonomy is also proposed, with the powers of the British High Commissioner limited, the immigration quota to be fixed by the Jews themselves, and the United States to help finance the execution of the entire plan — for both the Arab and Jewish provinces — for a period still to be decided on.

According to the New York correspondent of the London "Evening News," the experts are urging the quickest acceptance by President Truman of these suggestions, in order to avoid the grave consequences which might result from the measures taken by the British Government against illegal immigration.

"Yedioth Ahronot" reports from "a source close to the White House" that America will demand the addition of the Negev to the Jewish zone and make it a prior condition of American participation that 100,000 Jews be allowed to immigrate immediately.

From the same quarter it is said that America would agree to federalization only as a step towards definite partition of Palestine into independent Jewish and Arab States within two or three years, with bases for Britain by treaty on the lines of the Anglo-Iraqi Treaty.

The British Ambassador, Lord Inverchapel, is reported to be leaving shortly for London with details of this American scheme.

On the other hand, UP reports from London that British circles are sceptical about President Truman approving the Federal Plan.

In Baghdad, Jamil Bey el Madfai, President of the Iraqi Senate, described the partition plan as an act against the Arab world and a help to the Zionists in the use of Palestine for spreading their influence in the Arab world. "I believe Arabs will definitely refuse to attend the London conference, he added, especially after the British declaration approving the partition proposals."

In a note handed by the British Minister in Damascus to the Syrian Foreign Minister yesterday it is stated that the partitioning of Palestine would not form the basis for discussion at the London conference, and the Arab Governments would be able to make any suggestions for the solution of the Palestine problem (says AFP).

The American Labour Committee for Palestine, which has the support of both the A.F.L. and the C.I.O., has sent a telegram to the British Labour Party protesting against the present Palestine policy of the Labour Government: "So long as it continues with its present policy it cannot count on the support of the American Labour movement".

(R., PTA., Palcor, AFP., UP.)

Rundstedt in Box

By WILLIAM HAMSHER,
Reuters Special Correspondent

NUREMBERG, Monday (R) — Field Marshal von Rundstedt, Hitler's commander-in-chief on the Western Front during the Ardennes counter offensive of Christmas, 1944, told the tribunal today that he was opposed to this attack because "all the conditions for success were lacking despite the stroke of genius behind the idea."

Von Rundstedt explained his own idea was to attack the American troops east of Aachen from several sides. This idea was turned down in favour of the Ardennes offensive which had to start with inadequate forces.

"In my opinion the war could not be won after Stalingrad. It was lost, I consider, after the Allies had established a strong bridgehead on French soil."

Rundstedt said that he and Field-Marshal Rommel wanted to bring the front back to Germany, but Hitler would not listen. Declaring that he had never entertained the idea of overthrowing Hitler by violence, Rundstedt said that such an attempt would not have been successful. If he had brought it about with the aid of the Allies, it would have been exactly the same, and he would have been considered for all time a traitor to the Fatherland.

Haifa Bulletin

HAIFA, Tuesday (3 a.m.). — The two small vessels, Yagour and Szold, are still anchored outside the breakwater, and two cruisers, the Ajax and the Mauritius (the latter had arrived today from Malta) have left the harbour and are anchored near them.

The "deportation ships" are still at their moorings and are brightly illuminated.

Some shops were opened on Hadar Hacarmel after the curfew announcement, and people are queueing up to buy food.

Pauley Scheme

2ND EXODUS

By GEORGE LICHTHEIM
Palestine Post Correspondent

LONDON, Monday. — A minor sensation was caused today by Washington cables concerning a report to President Truman by Mr. E.D. Pauley, U.S. Reparations Commissioner.

Mr. Pauley apparently suggested that pending an over-all solution of the refugee problem, in which America must play a part, the European Jews now trekking west might well organize their own exodus to Italy in "caravans," carrying their own medical supplies, etc. Mr. Pauley, reportedly, feels there is no reason why Germany should not contribute reparations to the Jews in the form of building materials useable in Palestine and elsewhere for the rapid construction of houses.

Generally, the Pauley Report suggests that half a million or a million Jews might well be settled during the coming year in the United States and other overseas countries, including Palestine. There has been no comment here so far. The mere fact that someone is capable of approaching the problem in other than nagging and pettifogging terms seems to have struck Whitehall and Printing House Square alike.

An interesting contrast to Pauley was provided by Miss Maude Royden in a letter prominently displayed by "The Times" on Saturday, wherein, after declaring that all countries must share the burden, she adds that there is no reason why, for example, "Jewish Communists" who are now shooting British soldiers in Palestine might not be sent to Siberia, while others could find homes in East Africa and other tropics.

The prominence lent by "The Times" to these aberrations bears out the impression created by earlier excursions into a political no-man's land. Concerning the major issue, earlier predictions that President Truman is likely to sponsor a modified Federation scheme are now supported by the latest despatches from Washington and unofficial information.

Agency Marking Time

It is understood that the Agency Conference in Paris is awaiting publication of the American views this week before considering the possibility of attending a round-table, but little doubt is felt that President Truman will accept the scheme in principle, but with substantial modifications, stressing the urgency of immediate entry of the immigrants and also for a larger area of the Jewish province and greater Jewish control of immigration.

Observers believe that the scheme with these modifications is acceptable as a basis for discussion as far as the Agency is concerned, while the British reaction is doubtful. The failure of the original attempt to rush Washington into an acceptance of the original scheme is still rankling in Whitehall, where a fortnight ago Jews were already regarded as a negligible factor.

The new development may necessitate greater activity on the part of the Arab League moderates to curb the extremists' wild talk of dragging Russia into the controversy.

"Optimism" In London

From Our Political Correspondent

News from Jewish Agency quarters in London yesterday had a quality of astringent "optimism" as regards the future. In part, this was based on more hopeful news, from the Jewish point of view, brought from Washington by Dr. Nahum Goldman, the member of the Executive who had flown over to confer with President Truman's Cabinet Committee.

As reported in another column, the more hopeful outlook is based on not much more than somewhat better proposals, or rather counter-proposals, from the White House.

But a matter causing grave concern in London is the continued detention of the Jewish Agency members in Latrun. The absence from the present important consultations of Mr. Shertok and Dr. Joseph, who have been responsible for the Agency's political work for several years, is acutely felt. To this lack must be added the complication that the Agency is precluded from entering into any official consultations with the Government so long as the Jewish leaders are incarcerated.

This complication, to which Dr. Weizmann, while still in Palestine, referred as a "vicious circle," not only hampers or prevents consultations with the Colonial Office concerning the proposed Round-Table, but is also in the way of urgent, if less important, day-to-day questions that have to be negotiated with the authorities, whether in London or Jerusalem.

Other Nations to State Their Views

PARIS DELEGATES ACTUALLY AGREE

PARIS, Monday (UP). — The Peace Conference today unanimously agreed to invite Albania, Mexico, Cuba and Egypt to "state their views" here at the plenary sessions and the Commissions on the Italian peace treaty.

The vote came after more than two hours' wrangling over procedure and how to vote on various amendments.

Britain tried to amend the resolution to include Austria among the invited states but it withdrew the proposal and no one moved to include Iran on the list. Both Austria and Iran had made a belated request to be admitted.

Persia's Application

Iran's application was received by the Conference Secretariat late on Saturday night and was made public this morning just before the plenary session opened.

The conference session ended a two days' debate on methods of permitting nations outside the 21 to express their views. The action almost certainly opens the flood-gates to other requests, probably from most of those nations which declared war on the Axis.

General Agreement

Originally Yugoslavia had asked that Albania should be admitted with full voting privileges. This request was withdrawn early in the Conference and there was general agreement that additional states should be invited to state their views on the Italian treaty.

The Conference proceeded by acclamation to elect M. Fouques du Parc of France as permanent Secretary-General.

Vyshinsky vs. Australia

PARIS, Monday (Reuter).— When Australia was proposed as a member of the Conference secretariat, M. Vyshinsky (U.S.S.R.) objected, declaring:

"Australia has shown herself a rather temperamental member of our meeting and has taken part with great energy in our debates. It would perhaps be better to have at the secretariat, for which other qualities are required, a representative of a calmer nation and therfore I propose Ethiopia."

The Ethiopian delegation indicated that it did not wish to stand. Norway, proposed by Byelo-Russia, also declined and ultimately the British proposal that Australia, Brazil, China and Yugoslavia be represented on the secretariat in addition to the "Big Four" was accepted without a vote.

Diplomatic Moves against Refugees

GREEK PORTS TO BE BLOCKED

Palestine Post Staff

Greece has been added to the list of countries requested by Britain to assist in controlling illegal Jewish immigration to Palestine, a Foreign Office spokesman announced yesterday.

No reply has yet been received by Britain from the Soviet Union. The majority of the countries approached are said to have promised to do all in their power to help.

Last week the Mexican and Panama embassies in London were requested to make a careful check on the issue of visas to Jewish refugees in Europe.

In view of more reassuring reports reaching leading Jewish circles at present in Paris regarding American measures connected with the entry of Jewish refugees into the American zone of Germany, the proposed visit of Dr. Stephen Wise to Frankfort has been postponed.

It is understood that the Salzburg-Munich route used by refugees entering the American zone of Germany from the American zone of Austria is now open again. The frontier between Czechoslovakia and the American zone remains, however, temporarily closed. The Czech authorities appear to want guarantees that the number of Jewish refugees allowed to enter the American zone will not be deducted by the Americans from the number of Sudeten Germans which the Czechs are permitted to send across the border.

The Americans, on the other hand, apparently considered that the arrival of Jewish refugees from across the Czech border complicated their task of screening of the Sudeten Germans before the latter are allowed to proceed further inland. In these circumstances, the only route open to refugees from Czechoslovakia to Vienna — from where they are sent to the American zone of Austria — is across the Russian zone of Austria. On several occasions recently, the Russians have interfered with refugees crossing their zone, but it is not certain whether this is a settled policy.

Approach to America

As part of her diplomatic campaign, Britain has made representations to the U.S.A. about the publication of Zionist appeals for money to transport Jewish refugees which have been appearing in American papers. While the network which has been passing Jews illegally into Palestine has grown up inside Europe, writes Reuters Diplomatic Correspondent, there is reason to believe that most of the funds which have financed the movement have come from Zionist organizations in the U.S.A. who have been conducting their appeals quite openly in columns of American newspapers. It is believed that the U.S. authorities have agreed to look into the matter.

A categorical denial of reports that refugees reaching Palestine were terrorists was made by a Jewish Agency spokesman yesterday at a press conference in Jerusalem with foreign newspaper correspondents.

"On the contrary, they are people who oppose terrorism in any form," the spokesman said. He added that there were 3,700 people on board the refugee ships at Haifa, and not 8,000 as was stated by the B.B.C. Over half of the refugees at Haifa were children.

When asked how many more refugees were known to be at sea, the spokesman replied that it was believed there were another 1,300 on their way to Palestine.

The Public Information Officer, Mr. R. Stubbs, told journalists at his weekly Press Conference in Tel Aviv yesterday that the Palestine Government still had no confirmation of reports that camps were being prepared in Famagusta, Cyprus, for Jewish immigrants. He also stated that he had no information about the floating cages in the Haifa Port.

3rd Ship Sighted

1,298 ARRIVE

HAIFA, Monday. — "Yagur" and the "Henrietta Szold," two sailing vessels carrying illegal immigrants arrived in Haifa Port this morning. The two ships, have a total of 1,298 men, women and children on board.

A third vessel, believed to be carrying 1,300 refugees, is also reported to be approaching Haifa.

First to be escorted into port was the "Yagur," which anchored outside the main breakwater among the warships there at about 7.30 this morning.

Though for the first time Jewish Agency officials were not allowed to board the ship, some facts were ascertained by an official who spoke to the passengers from the police launch which took police officers alongside.

Aboard the ship are 758 immigrants consisting of 350 women, 10 old people and about 400 younger people, some of whom are members of the Youth Aliyah.

Among the women 50 are expectant mothers, 13 of them being in the last month of pregnancy.

The ship is reported to have been at sea for 20 days. The crew of about 10, including several Turks and one Lebanese, have been arrested.

The Henrietta Szold, a smaller sailing ship with an auxiliary motor, was sighted about two hours later. She has 540 passengers on board, including some 150 women and 250 young people, 30 infants and 15 old men and women. Fifteen of the women are expectant mothers. The trip from the port of embarkation is said to have taken 15 days.

Preparations which are believed to presage the deportation of the refugees are meanwhile progressing in Haifa Port. The cargo jetty has been cleared of all civilians and placed under army guard.

Two Liberty ships, the Empire Rival and the Empire Weywood, are moored to the jetty and barbed wire cages have been constructed on the decks and around the hatches.

The ships have also been fitted with searchlights which are used to illuminate the port at night. Work on the landing barges which, as reported yesterday, have been converted into floating cages, has now been completed, and the craft are at the western end of the Harbour where they have been camouflaged. It is assumed that the expected transfer will take place within the next 24 hours.

One of the new arrivals, a 25-year-old woman from Greece named Naomi Furt, was rushed today at noon by a Red Shield Society Ambulance to the Moladah Maternity Hospital on Mt. Carmel, suffering from childbirth complications.

USSR ASKS BRITAIN FOR STRAITS TALKS

By Reuter's Diplomatic Correspondent

LONDON, Monday. — The Soviet Government has informed Britain that it wishes the Montreux Straits Convention of 1936 to be revised, a Foreign Office spokesman stated in London this morning.

This announcement follows the unconfirmed reports from Ankara during the week-end that the Turkish Government had been informed that the Soviet Union intended to secure the revision of the terms.

The Montreux Convention, which since 1936 has governed navigation conditions in the Dardanelles, is valid for a period of 20 years from November 9, 1936, the date on which it came into force through the ratification by all the signatories, except Japan.

THE PALESTINE POST

JERUSALEM
Wednesday, Sept. 4, 1946

PRICE 15 MILS
VOL. XXI., No. 6195

Column One

By
David Courtney

DETAIL in Paris is running ahead of principle. Both special Committees and the Foreign Ministers' Deputies have made progress. This is all to the good and when Mr. Molotov comes back the way will have been cleared for some at least of the basic questions. Of these, the disposition and status of the International Commission for the control of Trieste is likely to be the first issue, and if agreement is found on that, the rest should be fairly easy. It is not believed that agreement will be found. In that case, the other major issues and especially the Danube question, will remain unsolved and may become further complicated by unilateral decisions. The upshot of the strenuous work now being done by the Committees and Deputies can only be the settlement of relatively minor matters, ultimately dependent on the settlement of main problems, which have been suspended to give the Conference a breathing-space. Molotov has taken advantage of the occasion to consult with his leader, and Mr. Bevin will take advantage of it to deal with the Palestine problem in London. One hopes that it will not last long enough for Marshal Tito to want to take advantage of it.

■

IT is proper that Mr. Bevin should be in London and should preside at the Round Table, however small, warped and rickety that piece of furniture may have become; and it is natural that he should want to. He is aware by now that his Palestine references at Bournemouth lost him considerable ground, and if there is half a chance of recovering it next week at Lancaster House, he will seize it. It is clear also that Mr. Byrnes, however half-heartedly, has been making certain things plain to the Foreign Secretary. Mr. Bevin is also reported to have become alarmed at the way certain issues are slipping away from the Foreign Office to the War Office and may be prepared to put up a fight to get them back. These are signs, nothing more; and it needs plenty of faith to read either hope or charity into them.

■

GREECE is one of the key States of a world system based on the prospect of another war and I cannot ignore it, however humbling the comments of Mrs. Kapsambelis in her letter published yesterday in *The Palestine Post*. The King will go back. The voting was overwhelmingly in his favour, but no one with a knowledge of what goes on every day throughout the length and breadth of Greece will deny that at least one out of every three votes for the king was cast under duress. Trained men with no axe to grind except the axe of truth have confirmed that large tracts of the Greek countryside are under Royalist pressure and that towns and villages have several times undergone what was virtually a rehearsal of the Plebiscite, with armed men reinforcing the Gendarmerie in the job of carrying out the rehearsal. Lamia, which is claimed to have polled eighty per cent for the King, was an example. One cannot escape the belief that the forces of "law and order" are nothing more than a Royalist bodyguard and that their official directive is precisely that of the old but far from forgotten Security Battalions.

■

THE Greek people have become an easy prey to terror. They have been terrorized for more than ten years. They emerged from the Metaxas terror to the Italo-German terror; and had superimposed upon that the terror of resistance gangs both Right and Left in their politics. In spite of it all they have remained one of the bravest and most lovable peoples of the earth; but repression tells in the long run and many of them have got to the point where they are willing to take anything for the sake of peace. The British Government's part in this humiliating martyrdom has been one of the strangest episodes of its history; and is in origin the personal doing of Mr. Churchill. His interference in the early stages of political reconstruction in Athens was largely the cause of the riots, feuds and gang-politics which followed, and brought about the present ascendancy of Reaction. Already then he foresaw himself in the role of his Fulton, Missouri, speech; and his policy saw in prostrate Greece an appropriate field of coming battle. When the Labour Government came along they took Mr. Churchill's Greek policy bag and baggage, and made it their own, with unhappy results for the Greeks and one day for themselves. That is the background to the return of King George. He will probably reign more cautiously than when Metaxas propped up his throne; but his presence in Greece, however benevolent in personal intention, cannot be other than an influence consolidating the forces of reaction and repression.

Jerusalem, September 4.

FROM 'FOUR FREEDOMS' TO EMPIRE HEYWOOD

1.000 IMMIGRANTS TRANSFERRED

Palestine Post Reporter

HAIFA, Tuesday.—The transfer to the "Empire Heywood" of the thousand illegal immigrants who arrived on board the 400-ton "Four Freedoms," was completed at 6 o'clock this afternoon, to the accompaniment of screams of protest and constant machine-gun fire from the cruiser H.M.S. Mauritius. The fire was not directed at the deportees.

"And so that's what you call a Liberty Ship"
From "Fraternite," Paris

The transfer took place about two miles from land.

A large party of local and foreign correspondents were invited to be present during part of the transhipment, and were taken by police launch out into the bay, where the operation was taking place.

As the launch approached the "Empire Heywood," the small, drab caique could be seen tied alongside a landing craft used to bridge the gap between her and the deportation ship. A child was heard screaming for her sick mother, who had been taken ashore as the journalists arrived.

A raised platform had been built on the landing craft, level with the deck of the immigrant ship, and a slow stream of half-dressed and exhausted people was being pushed onto the platform, which was rising and falling with the swell. Many had to be lifted bodily over the rail of the "Four Freedoms" and down the steps to the landing craft. The ship had been without water for four days, and many of the refugees who had been taken ill were lying on stretchers or on the decks of the landing craft. One man who is said to have drunk salt water on the way was raving and had to be held down by two other immigrants.

A few struggled and had to be forced up the ramp to the Heywood, while many were too weary to go up alone. Army launches were kept busy taking stretcher cases aboard and conveying them ashore where ambulances were waiting to take them to the Athlit Hospital.

After climbing wearily up the ramp, the people entered the enclosed foredeck of the Heywood and descended to the hold, being sprayed with D.D.T. on the way. The immigrants' rucksacks and bundles had been taken from them, lifted on board by cranes and dumped in a pile amidships.

Part of the operation was watched by the correspondents from the bridge of the landing craft. While police launches vigilantly circled the scene to pick up any of the people who might try to jump overboard, one man broke through the cordon of soldiers and, shouting to make himself heard to the pressmen, cried out:

"My father, mother and sister were destroyed in Europe; for seven years I was in a camp. Now I have come to my country, my homeland, and you take me away. I would rather die."

He was led away by two soldiers, just as he bared his breast, as if welcoming death. Many crowded the steps leading to the bridge and asked for water, saying that they had gone without for three days. A woman who had obtained some, ran to the side of a man on a stretcher and tried to make him drink. Some just stood and stared vacantly at the neatly dressed men and women come to look at them.

The operation seemed to be in its final stages when the press party arrived and some correspondents visited the "Four Freedoms," though she still had a number of immigrants on board. When questioned, one man stated that the ship had been at sea for 12 days, but he would not say which had been their port of embarkation.

Told to Lower Flag

They had been intercepted as soon as they entered territorial water, and were ordered by the destroyer to heave to and to lower the Zionist colours which they had been flying. This order was refused.

Machinegun fire was then opened across the bows of the ship, and some of the men pointed to bullet holes in the after-cabin on deck and stated that these had been made by the firing.

A first attempt to board the ship was repulsed by the immigrants. A hose pipe was then played on the ship, and a second boarding party managed to get on board. Force had to be used, and some men stated that many had been hit with rifle butts.

Six men jumped into the sea, but were caught with the aid of a motor-boat. While this was going on another two jumped into the water.

A large hole could be seen in the stern of the ship, apparently made when the destroyer came alongside. The whole starboard side of the ship had a series of deep gashes in the woodwork due to the same cause.

One naval rating was seriously injured during the boarding yesterday, and a number of Jews and other seamen received minor injuries.

The "Four Freedoms" is the fifth immigrant ship whose passengers have been deported. The transhipment was completed shortly after the press had left, and the empty craft was being towed into harbour.

A total of 30 patients were transferred to hospital including the woman who left her three children on board. Brigadier McNeill Graham, who was in charge of the operation is understood to have undertaken personally to see that they join their mother at Athlit.

With the operation taking place some distance from shore, only a small detachment of troops was used — not more than 150 — and they were mostly unarmed.

Swam Home

Jumping from the "Four Freedoms" in a dash for freedom, a refugee succeeded in swimming ashore somewhere in Palestine in the early hours of Tuesday morning.

After completing the last lap of his trip, he expressed anxiety for the fate of a friend who had jumped with him at 8 o'clock the previous evening, but who had disappeared in the waves about 2 o'clock in the morning, shortly before he himself gained shore.

He had eluded the small boats sent by destroyers to collect refugees who had jumped off their ship near Tel Aviv.

The refugee stated that when sighted by a plane, the immigrants had signalled that they were unarmed.

In the first attempt by naval ratings to board the vessel, he added, the refugees disarmed several of them and tossed their rifles into the sea.

It was only after the boarding party had damaged the engines that they were able to stop the vessel.

He also said that an American newspaperwoman had made the trip with the refugees.

Back to the Starting Point

LONDON, Tuesday (PTA). — Professor Brodetsky and Mr. Locker, of the Jewish Agency Executive, have returned from Paris to confer with Dr. Weizmann on Mr. Bevin's reply. Although its exact contents have not yet been disclosed, it is reported to bring the situation back to the starting point of retaining the Federal plan as the "point from which the discussions must start."

Agency circles seem surprised and disappointed, since the expected change in the Government attitude has apparently not materialized.

AGENCY MAY STAY AWAY

By Our Political Correspondent

The British Government's refusal of the Jewish Agency's demand that the Zionist plan for an autonomous Jewish State in Palestine be made the basis for the discussion at the Palestine Conference next week, was confirmed by London Correspondents last night.

As a consequence, both British and Jewish Agency spokesmen unofficially predicted that the Agency would decide to boycott the conference.

A Colonial Office spokesman in London yesterday indicated that Britain would, however, invite prominent non-Agency Jews to represent Palestine Jewry in the event of the Agency's formal rejection of the invitation.

This would parallel the British action in inviting four non-members of the Arab Higher Executive to represent Palestine Arabs — which followed the Higher Executive refusal to attend the conference, he said.

The Government spokesman emphasized British determination to go ahead with the conference, and said that the possibility that the Agency and the Arab Higher Executive would decide to participate at a later date could not be ruled out.

Meanwhile, reliable Arab sources said that Arab League leaders had urged the Palestine Arab Higher Executive to reconsider its refusal to attend the conference. They said that "face-saving" proposals were being drafted in an effort to get the Palestine Arabs to reverse their decision. The Executive met in Jerusalem yesterday to hear Dr. Khalidi's report on his interview with King Abdullah. While the London "News Chronicle" yesterday reported that Mr. Bevin in Paris had approved the British Government's rejection of the Jewish Agency's proposals for the basis of the discussions, according to other reports, Mr. Bevin was making last minute efforts to secure the attendance of both the Jews and the Palestinian Arabs and also of the United States.

A high Foreign Office official is quoted as saying that the subject was discussed by Mr. Bevin and Mr. Byrnes on Monday, the former urging that American participation in the conference would enhance its value. The U.S. Secretary of State is understood to have reiterated his earlier refusal.

Mr. Attlee will open the conference with two speeches, one to the morning session of Jewish delegates and the other to the afternoon session of Arabs, according to authoritative sources.

Mr. George Hall saw the Prime Minister yesterday and, it is understood, discussed with him arrangements for the conference. The Iraqi delegation to the conference was expected in London yesterday.

The Chief Rabbi of Palestine, Dr. I. Herzog, too, was requested by Mr. Bevin last Friday to persuade the Jewish Agency to take part in the conference on the basis of the federal scheme, reports "Yedioth Ahronot" from Paris. Mr. Bevin is reported to have said that in five years' time it might be possible to take a further step towards Jewish independence. To this Dr. Herzog replied that acceptance of the federal plan may result in the final ending of Jewish hopes.

The conversation is stated to have lasted an hour, after which Dr. Herzog wrote a letter to the Foreign Secretary upholding the Jewish Agency's demand for statehood, emphasizing that a Jewish State was the only means for the revival of the Jewish people.

China's Civil War

PEACE TALKS IN NANKING

PEIPING, Tuesday (UP). — The Chinese Nationalist armies are today reported to be closing in on the Communist stonghold of Chihfeng in Northern Jehol province. One Government column is said to be in the city's suburbs.

Other Government forces are reported to be threatening the Communist city of Kalgan, north of Peiping, in a drive to surround all the Communist troops in North China.

In Nanking, where peace talks reopened today, the newspaper "Ta Kung Pao" said that the Communists in Jehol province were facing the greatest military reverses of the civil war. Kalgan is expected to fall in a week.

Other reports reaching Peiping indicate that the Nationalists are surrounding the Communists in Manchuria generally. They have driven the Chinese Communists into a rectangular area in the vicinity of Tientsin and are ready to spring the trap.

Other unconfirmed dispatches say that large-scale Nationalist operations are proceeding near the Korean border, 40 miles east of the city of Kirin. In Northern Shansi province, Tatung is apparently still in Nationalist hands although the Communists have not raised the siege.

Bombay Death Roll Now 85

BOMBAY, Tuesday.— Renewed rioting occurred in Bombay today and casualties continued to mount, with 85 deaths and 350 persons injured reported up to late this evening in the Moslem-Hindu clashes which started on Sunday when Moslems went into mourning on the eve of the convening of the new interim Government.

Between 1 and 4 o'clock today alone, 79 casualties were admitted into Bombay hospitals, and officials said that casualties were increasing.

At least four textile mills have been closed.

The police opened fire three times here this morning in the course of clashes in which two persons were killed and nine injured. Forty-one persons were arrested for curfew-breaking.

A Bombay Government communique stated there had been no improvement in the situation as a whole since last night.

British troops are reported to have opened fire in the curfew area early this morning — the first report today of British troops taking action.

(U.P. and Reuter).

NO CLAIMS FOR PALESTINE

PARIS, Tuesday (PTA).— The British delegation's enumeration of the Empire's reparations claims from Italy for war damage does not include Palestine, it was revealed in Conference circles today.

A British delegation spokesman said that this did not mean that no claims had been made for Palestine, but he was unable to explain their omission from the list presented to the Conference.

It is known that Italian bombing, particularly of Tel Aviv in the summer of 1940, had cost considerable loss of life and damage.

AFTER MIDNIGHT

Premier Tsaldaris Flies to London

REGENT REPORTS TO GREEK KING

LONDON, Tuesday (Reuter). — It is not yet known when King George II of the Hellenes will return to Greece, but the Greek Premier, M. Tsaldaris, who was expected in London from Athens by air tonight, is believed to be bringing a request for the King's speedy return.

Prince Paul of Greece, the king's brother and heir-apparent, sent a message to the Greek people today saying that the King and himself were "eagerly awaiting the moment when we shall be able to set foot on the beloved soil of Greece again."

Ovewhelming Vote

Official returns received up to 1 o'clock this morning in Athens showed that 1,019,801 voted for the King's return out of 1,394,677 votes cast in Sunday's plebiscite.

Archbishop Damaskinos, the Regent, in a message of congratulation to King George on the results, is reported to have asked for instructions about his Regency.

A Moscow radio commentator, M. Linetzky, alleging that the will of the Greek people "was subjected to pressure of the harshest kind" in the plebiscite, said:

"The Tsaldaris Government which, under the control of British troops, has destroyed the most elementary rights and liberties of man, is dragging the country towards civil war."

The Royalist press in Athens today came out with reports alleging new fighting between Government troops and Opposition forces not far from the Albanian frontier, but there was no confirmation of the outbreaks in any reliable quarter, says the United Press.

The newspapers charge that 400 men identified as Communists attacked the town of Contili, near Kastoria, and fought a four-hour battle with Government troops. The reports added that 16 soldiers were killed and two wounded.

The Communists were reported to have fallen back towards the Albanian border where another battle is said to have occurred near Mount Broukia.

While the country as a whole gave King George II 72 per cent of the votes cast, Salonika gave the monarchy 55,428 and the Republic 52,304.

With the exception of the Comunist "Daily Worker" the British press today struck a cautious note on the result of the Greek plebiscite.

"The Times," declaring that the king will "be prudent not to mistake his mandate," warned that his return must not mean a repetition of "government by repression. Social stability and economic restoration are not secured by a single success at the polls.

"Nor can any remedy for the perpetual instability of Greek politics be found in the old and tempting slogans. Because of the special responsibility British diplomacy and British troops have undertaken in Greece, the British Government must make these issues plain to the returning King and his ministers."

The *"Manchester Guardian"*, after referring to the "present Slav and Albanian campaign to vilify the Greek Government," comments: "The more discreditable the action of the Greek Government, the more Britain can be discredited as long as it can plausibly be argued that what happens in Greece has British approval. In this sense, the result of the plebiscite and its probable effects make our position more difficult than before."

"Kingdom of Bevin"

The *"Daily Worker"* roundly denounces the plebiscite results, declaring: "Democracy in Greece has been murdered and the assassin is the Labour Government in London. The return of the King symbolizes the triumph of the Fascist Monarchists who have deliberately been placed in power by the Foreign Secretary, Mr. Bevin.

"Greece is no longer an independent country; it is a British colony where the ruling clique, containing a large number of Quislings, has been installed in office by the occupying power. A land that might have been a democratic republic has become a kingdom of Bevin."

Italian Claims Denounced

By R.H. SHACKFORD
U.P. Correspondent

PARIS, Tuesday. — Yugoslavia took the campaign to overrule the "Big Four" compromise and to obtain all Venezia Giulia, including Trieste, before the Peace Conference today with a slashing oratorical assault on Italy.

The Yugoslav delegate, Alex Debler, in an hour's speech to the Italian Political Commission charged Italy with lying, making unjust claims, and displaying an aggressive spirit. M. Debler delivered a scathing personal attack on Signor Bonomi, who presented Italy's claim to the Commission yesterday.

Attacking the Italian claim to the Trieste area, M. Debler denounced the "Big Four" agreement to accept the French line for the Italo-Yugoslav frontier and to establish an international zone in Trieste. He charged that the "Big Four" agreement on Venezia Giulia abandoned all ethnic principles by leaving large numbers of Yugoslavs under Italian rule and an equal number of Italians in Yugoslavia.

If the principle of ethnic equilibrium were fully carried out, he declared, Italy would have the right to claim colonies in the United States, Brazil, and Australia, all of which have large Italian minorities. He contended that the present Italian regime was a continuation of the Italian Imperialism of earlier years.

The Italian Premier, Signor de Gasperi, who arrived by air today, plans to spend several days pressing the Italian case on the treaty-makers.

Burst of Speed.

Meanwhile, the Military Commission put on a burst of speed today. Yugoslavia and Australia withdrew their amendments to the military clauses and the Commission unanimously approved the "Big Four" proposals on the Italian army and air force.

These provide for an army of 185,000 combat and service troops, 65,000 carabinieri, 200 tanks, 200 fighter planes, 150 transport planes, and 25,000 air and ground personnel.

Naval personnel will be limited to 25,000.

The Balkan Economic Commission adopted three clauses in the Rumanian treaty after deciding that Rumania must restore all the legal rights in Rumania of United Nations countries and their nationals as they existed on September 1, 1939, instead of on June 22, 1941.

Poland proposed that a date be set to begin the discussion of the U.S. proposal for full restoration by Rumania of United Nations property damaged or lost in that country. The U.S. delegate Mr. Willard Thorp pointed out that restitution differed from reparations, since it was not a drain on the country.

Italian C.o.L. Protest

MILAN, Tuesday (Reuter). — A protest against the continued increase in the cost of living and black market activities, as well as unscrupulous speculative operations, was adopted at a mass meeting of 5,000 people in Milan last night.

The meeting was called by the local Confederation of Labour.

Industrial shares have trebled in value in the last two months.

One Milan left-wing paper said yesterday that unless the Government enforced its authority and maintained some kind of economic discipline, it would be most difficult to prevent an explosion of popular indignation.

The Prime Minister, Signor de Gasperi, arrived in Milan last night for a special meeting of North Italian prefects to discuss measures to deal with the serious food situation and rising prices. The cost of living has risen from 20 to 40 per cent in the last few weeks.

Communist Objections

In an interview in Venice yesterday, the Finance Minister, Signor Scoscimarro, declared that the Italian Communist Party will leave the present Government and join the Opposition unless drastic measures are taken to face the problems harassing the economic life of the country.

The economic policy so far followed by the Government, the Minister said, had resulted in utter failure.

Russians Rejoice

STALIN CLAIMS HE BEAT JAPS

By MEYER HANDLER
U.P. Correspondent

MOSCOW, Tuesday. — Generalissimo Stalin in an Order of the Day declared today that the Russians and their armed forces a year ago "victoriously ended the war against imperialist Japan."

Simultaneously, the Government organ "Izvestia" charged that the "international forces of reaction are trying to attain positions to hurl mankind again into a new bloody war."

Stalin's Order told the people: "Japan signed an unconditional surrender. The Soviet people and their armed forces gained the victory, and by this victory made a huge investment in the establishment of peace in the world."

Every city, town and village in Russia celebrated the Soviet victory today. All public pronouncements credit Russia with the victory over Japan.

With all newspaper editorials stressing the theme that Russia won the war against Japan, "Pravda," organ of the Communist Party, says that "the American military administration has not, after a full year, effected any real fundamental changes in Japanese mentality or Japanese politics."

"American reactionary circles do not conceal their intention to maintain Japanese militarism and transform Japan into a bridgehead for various Far Eastern adventures," declared "The New Times."

"Izvestia" the organ of the Government hails "the triumph of the national might of the U.S.S.R.," and says, "The convincing lesson taught the German-Japanese aggressor must be a stern warning to those who are cherishing thoughts of a new war."

Yugoslavs Send U.S. New Note

BELGRADE, Tuesday (UP).— The Yugoslav Government has announced that a new note to the United States was despatched on August 30 asking for a guarantee that no further flights of American planes would take place over Yugoslavia, and citing continued flights between August 23 and 27 inclusive.

The note said that Yugoslavia had once again asked the U.S. Government to reply that it had undertaken to put an end to unauthorized and deliberate flights over Yugoslav territory on the part of the American military and civilian planes and what guarantees it would give that these would not be repeated.

The note was given front-page prominence in the morning papers. London reports stated that Mr. Bartley Crum, Republican leader, who was on the Anglo-American Palestine Commission, said after a tour of Europe that the incidents "represent the end of a long series of reconnaissance flights during which we tried to photograph the Yugoslav defences."

Radio Belgrade said that the note denied responsibility for the deaths of the five U.S. flyers shot down on August 19. The broadcast added that Marshal Tito had promised the U.S. Ambassador, Mr. Richard Patterson, that Yugoslav planes would in future refrain from firing on planes crossing the frontier.

H.E. PAYS SURPRISE VISIT TO NEGBA

Palestine Post Staff

The hope that further searches in Jewish villages would be avoided was voiced by the High Commissioner during a surprise visit to Negba settlement yesterday. Negba is about 12 miles north of Dorot.

His Excellency also promised that if searches should be made, everything possible would be done to reduce dislocation.

General Cunningham added that he regretted he was unable to visit Dorot and Ruham. He promised that complaints of damage by search parties would be investigated, but in this connection recalled that terrorist activities had cost the lives of British personnel.

During His Excellency's visit to Gaza later in the day, Mayor Rushdi eff. Esh-Shawa requested that Government charge the reparation of damage resulting from sabotage to Jews, and not to general Government funds.

He expressed the hope that Anglo-Arab friendship would be strengthened and that "Arabs would be justified."

The Mayor also asked His Excellency for a Government loan of LP.50,000 for town-planning and badly-needed improvements in Gaza, and requested more schools.

General Cunningham also visited the Government Hospital at Gaza. Earlier in the day, he inspected the textile factories at Majdal, where an exhibition of cloth had been organized.

(Govt. House Bulletin—Pg. 2)

LATE Edition

THE PALESTINE POST

JERUSALEM
TUESDAY, DEC. 10, 1946

PRICE: 15 MILS
VOL. XXI. No. 6274

PERSIAN DISPUTE COMES TO HEAD

FIGHTING BREAKS OUT IN KURDISTAN HILLS

TEHERAN, Monday. — Tanks, artillery and trench-mortars have been used in a battle between Persian Government troops and Azerbaijan forces, Radio Tabriz stated tonight.

The battle took place in the mountainous district of Qardasht in Kurdistan, which the Central Government troops occupied after it had changed hands twice.

"Our casualties were one killed and 17 wounded," the Azerbaijan radio station said. "According to villagers, the Government troops lost 30 men, who were killed in the first offensive. Two peasants were seriously injured in the aerial bombardment of a village near the town of Miyanduas.

"During the battle villages and industrial enterprises were continuously bombed by Government planes," Radio Tabriz added.

Radio Tabriz also stated that Persian Government planes are "mercilessly bombing Kurd villages," adding that many peasants' houses had been destroyed, but that the casualties were not yet known.

Planes of the Central Government have again flown over Tabriz and dropped leaflets signed by M. Ghavam Sultaneh which said: "If Azerbaijan really belongs to Iran then the soldiers of the Central Government have the right of free movement in their own house."

The Iranian Government is following "a dangerous path suggested to it from the outside" in sending troops to Azerbaijan, writes "Pravda" today. The troops are not being sent, "Pravda" asserts, "for the purpose of securing order but with the intent to liquidate the national democratic freedoms of Azerbaijan, to disband the Democratic Party there and to prevent the election of its representatives to the Central Parliament."

The new development, "Pravda" says, is welcomed not only by Iranian reactionaries but also by certain foreign circles. As an instance for this "Pravda" quotes a public statement by the American Ambassador to Iran in which he said that there is "nothing unusual in sending troops for the maintenance of order during elections." The Azerbaijan government had invited the Central Government to send observers and journalists to the elections but "the Iranian Government did not accept this sensible suggestion" "Pravda" concludes.

(U.P. and Reuter)

TREATY TALKS CRISIS

By JON KIMCHE
Palestine Post Cable

LONDON, Monday. — Hopes of an early conclusion of the Anglo-Egyptian treaty were dashed today when a Foreign Office spokesman read a dramatic communique to a crowded press conference, thus virtually ruling out the possibility of any revision of the treaty unless either the British or Egyptians drastically change their present standpoints.

"The Governor of the Sudan, Sir Hubert Huddleston", said the spokesman, "was compelled to make his statement—assuring the Sudanese that nothing in the proposed new Egyptian treaty could prejudice their right to achieve independence nor bind a people in search of liberty—owing to partial disclosures in Egypt of the Sidky-Bevin talks.

Continued silence by the British Government, in view of one-sided interpretations, might have led to bloodshed or even worse in the Sudan. In these circumstances neither H.M. Government nor the Sudanese Government can be blamed for clearing up the situation.

"It should be noted that all the British Government want to do is to establish a situation under which, when the time is ripe, the Sudan can choose to become an independent state. Clearly, this is only one of several choices open to the Sudan.

"They can seek union with Egypt if they wish. It would be manifestly impossible for the British Government in its treaty discussions with Egypt to deny the rights of a free people to the Sudan".

This statement is considered in diplomatic circles as writing "finis" to the treaty discussions. It is considered unlikely here that any Egyptian Government can renew the talks in the present atmosphere.

Boycott of Conference

There has been some discussion here with the embassies of other Arab States, but there is no definite indication of what attitude they will take in view of the Arab League's commitment to support Egypt.

One form of Arab reaction considered possible is an Arab boycott of the Palestine Conference next month. The other most likely is reference to Uno

Parliamentary circles, particularly in the Labour Party, are surprised by the firmness of the British statement, but not altogether displeased by it.

Statement on Sudan

The statement by Sir Hubert Huddlestone to which the Egyptian Government has taken exception read as follows:

"Whatever the results of the Anglo-Egyptian negotiations, Mr. Attlee has authorized me in writing to give the Sudanese assurances that the British Government is determined that nothing shall be permitted to deflect the Sudanese Government from preparing the Sudanese for self-government.

"The Sudanese protocol provides that the Sudanese when ripe for self-government shall be free to choose the future status of the Sudan. H.M. Government considers that, in the words used by the Egyptian Premier to the British Foreign Secretary, nothing in the proposed treaty can prejudice the right of the Sudanese to achieve independence."

T.-J. STUDENTS AGAINST MONARCHY

BEIRUT, Monday (A.F.P.). — Trans-Jordan students from the universities of Beirut and Damascus at a meeting held here today passed a resolution affirming their determination to work for the replacement of King Abdullah by a republic.

750 DEPORTEES LEAVE CYPRUS

Palestine Post Correspondent

KYRENIA, Monday. — Seven hundred and fifty immigrants of the January quota, three hospital cases from the December quota, and three people with individual entry permits embarked on the Ocean Vigour at 6 o'clock this evening and sailed for Palestine.

Another 750 deportees were transferred to winter quarters at Xylotymbou today, and the remainder of the first batch of 2,000 are expected to be transferred tomorrow.

REST of the NEWS

CHRISTMAS MAIL will be flown by R.A.F. Transport Command to the tune of fifty tons per week to ensure that troops everywhere are receiving it on time.

THE U.S. CRUISER FARAGO, the aircraft carrier Randolph, the destroyer Perry and a landing craft have left Piraeus harbour after a three-days' visit to Greece.

PASTEUR. — The fiftieth anniversary of the death of Louis Pasteur, the founder of modern bacteriology, is celebrated by French scientists this week.

Owing to the slight indisposition of David Courtney "Column One" will not appear for the next two or three days.

Lebanese Cabinet Goes

BEIRUT, Monday (Reuter). — Saadi el Mulla, Premier of the Lebanon, today confirmed that his Cabinet would resign tomorrow (as already reported on Sunday).

According to parliamentary circles the resignation is due to the severe criticism of the Government's economic policy and to the intention of some deputies to press for a vote of non-confidence.

WEIZMANN OPENS FIRST POST-WAR ZIONIST CONGRESS

NATIONAL HOME MUST BECOME JEWISH STATE

WHITE PAPER DIRECTLY RESPONSIBLE FOR PALESTINE TROUBLES

BASLE, Monday.— Dr. Chaim Weizmann, President of the World Zionist Organization and the Jewish Agency for Palestine, opening the 22nd Zionist Congress this afternoon, declared that if Britain could not return to the original spirit of the Mandate she should, before retiring, vest the Jewish National Home with the full authority and status of a Jewish State. He rejected the Morrison federal plan "without hesitation or reserve, in principle and in detail", since it entirely excluded 85 percent of Palestine from the scope of Jewish colonization without even assuring complete freedom in the remaining 15 percent. The Jewish community, he said, will never surrender its national attributes and tradition in order to merge them into the attributes and traditions of another people. He held the White Paper of 1939 largely responsible for the present desperate situation of the Jewish people and directly responsible for the present troubles in Palestine. "Few documents in history have worse consequences for which to answer".

The Zionist President began his address, which lasted an hour, at this turning point in Jewish history, in a quiet voice that carried to the ends of the great Exhibition hall, the Mustermesse, in which were seated close on 400 delegates, representing the Jewries of 61 countries of the world, and over 2,000 visitors. The hundreds who could not find place in the main hall overflowed into one adjoining, to which the speech was relayed by radio.

Seated on the platform behind the President were the leaders of the Zionist Organization and representatives of the Swiss Federal Government, the Cantonal authorities and Basle Municipality. In a special gallery were the diplomatic representatives of 23 countries. Special interest was aroused by the presence of the Soviet, United States, and Vatican representatives, but regrets at his inability to attend had been received from the British Minister through the Vice-Consul in Basle. A party of refugees from camps in Germany arrived at the last moment.

Dominating the assembly was a huge portrait, flanked by the Jewish blue-white colours, of Theodor Herzl, founder of the Zionist Movement, who had opened the first Congress in the same city in 1897; while significant of the changes wrought on the Jewish people by the intervening fifty years were the massed delegations from Palestine and the United States contrasting with the handful from the once great communities of Eastern Europe.

Dr. Weizmann recalled that the condition stipulated for the National Home by Arab leaders such as King Feisal and British advisers such as Colonel Lawrence, was that the Arabs outside Palestine should be enabled to achieve independence. The Arabs now possess seven independent sovereignties and a generous measure of international representation.

How can it be moderate for them to claim seven States and extreme for us to claim one? By what tortuous logic can our morsel be stolen and added to their feast?

Other nations are liberated and can rebuild their ruins, **but the survivors of our holocaust languish without liberty and hope, and when, in desperate bid for these, they strike out towards their homeland, they are barred from its shores and herded behind barbed wire, once again on foreign soil,** Dr. Weizmann said.

Turning to Britain, he said that the bond of friendship between the Jewish people and Britain had been all but destroyed, but not by the Jews, and it could not be healed by the Jews themselves but the strain could be eased by the Government's undertaking to carry out the provisions of the Mandate in its spirit and letter.

STERN WARNING AGAINST TERRORISM

The Zionist President uttered a stern warning against the effects of terrorism. Terrorist acts, he said, are morally abhorrent and also barren of all advantage. Against suicidal 'heroics' he urged the courage of endurance and the heroism of superhuman restraint.

Finally, after a tribute to the American nation and to President Truman for their unfailing understanding of the Jewish problem, Dr. Weizmann said:

Believing as we do that our claim to establish a Jewish State is justified by the Mandate and by the relative positions of the Arab world and ourselves, we cannot contemplate a solution falling short of that claim. The Jews must be vested with the privileges and responsibilities of direct government. Once secure in possession of full national status, we shall strive to enter into a free and harmonious relationship with the other States in the Middle East.

Dr. Weizmann was followed by Mr. David Remez, Chairman of the Vaad Leumi, who said the Jews wanted peace and not conditions of war in Palestine. They wanted an alliance with the Arabs. He invited the next Congress to meet in Palestine.

(Full text of Dr. Weizmann's address begins on Page Two)

Nokrashy Forms Government

CAIRO, Monday. — Nokrashy Pasha, the leader of the Saadist Party, tonight formed a coalition Cabinet of Saadists and Liberals. The Wafd are excluded.

The Cabinet was approved by King Farouk.

When he was asked whether any change would take place in the Egyptian Government's attitude towards the Anglo-Egyptian Treaty Draft, Nokrashy replied: "This question will be studied by the new Cabinet."

Police Stand By

Troops and police stood by in Cairo today. The city was calm but some anxiety was felt lest the resignation of Sidky Pasha should lead to disorders.

Political talk centred round the question whether Sidky Pasha's resignation in effect meant a breakdown in the Anglo-Egyptian negotiations for the revision of the treaty. Circles in close touch with Sidky suggest that he interpreted the statement by the Governor General of the Sudan as tantamount to the breaking off of the negotiations by Britain.

U.S. Army Was Ready for D.P.'s

LONDON, Monday (Palcor). — "In May and June of this year, the U.S. Army was prepared, under President Truman's direction, to move the D.P.s from Europe's pest-holes to Palestine within 30 days," stated Mr. Bartley Crum, speaking to 2,000 Jews and non-Jews at the Portland (Oregon) Municipal Auditorium.

"Mr. John Dugdale, Financial Secretary of the British Admiralty, recently expressed on several occasions his grave concern about those Jews who were brave enough to try to reach Palestine by underground route, and were risking their lives in unseaworthy hulks which were likely to founder in the winter gales.

"Since I am somewhat familiar with the situation, Mr. Dugdale's words fail to move me, and I think that if Mr. Dugdale will consult British intelligence, he will find that the determination of these stateless and oppressed people is unshakeable and that, if necessary, they will go to Palestine on rafts.

"I respectfully suggest to Mr. Dugdale that American ships, perfectly seaworthy and still available in sufficient numbers, transport these people in safety and comfort to Palestine."

General Zionists Debate Partition

BASLE, Monday. — The most important of the pre-Congress party debates, that of the Confederation of General Zionists, developed on Sunday into sharp differences of opinion regarding participation in the London Conference and future Zionist policy.

Rabbi Abba Hillel Silver (as reported in *The Palestine Post* yesterday) and Mr. M. Sneh attacked the trend of the Jewish Agency Executive's recent talks with the British Government, while Dr. Nahum Goldmann and Professor S. Brodetsky advocated participation.

Recalling that in 1939 he had opposed Partition, Professor Brodetsky said that now he saw no solution except in a Jewish State wherein Jews would be masters of their destiny.

Dr. Goldmann said that Jews could not force the British to allow such mass immigration as was needed. Even the friends of Zionism in the Government were not prepared to agree to 100,000 immigrants except as part of a final solution. There were three alternatives: Britain might give up the Mandate and undertake a trusteeship instead, which would perpetuate the present situation; or there would be a joint trusteeship, making the Jews a pawn in the game between the Great Powers; or the Jews could bring forward their plan for a viable state. The last was "a tragic compromise", but it would be a historic decision which would bring rejoicing to the Jewish people, Dr. Goldmann concluded.

Mr. Sneh opposed participation in the London Conference on such terms. Why, he asked, should Jews serve as ornaments at a British conference which only sought an anti-Zionist decision?

Changes of Front

Possibility of a change of front of those members of the Zionist Organization of America who have hitherto opposed partition is indicated in a decision of the Organization to agree to Jewish participation in negotiations at the London Conference "with the purpose of discussing the creation of a Jewish State." The significance in this decision is that it does not insist on the inclusion of all Palestine in such a State. Mr. Daniel Frisch, one of the principal members until now against the Jewish Agency's present leadership, said that he accepted Dr. Weizmann's thesis of a "viable State capable of absorbing the remnants of European Jewry in ten years."

(PTA, Palcor, U.P., Reuter)

TERRORIST TRUCE REPORTED

It was reported from Tel Aviv yesterday that both the Irgun Zvai Leumi and the Stern Group would cease all terrorist activities until after the close of the sessions of the Zionist Congress.

CONGRESS OPENING CELEBRATED

TEL AVIV, Monday. — To mark the opening of the Zionist Congress at Basle, over 1,000 people attended a ceremony in the Ohel Shem hall here tonight, arranged by the Jewish National Fund, the Palestine Foundation Fund and the Municipality.

Speakers were the Mayor, Mr. I. Rokach; Dr. A. Shalit, who was Dr. Herzl's secretary; Dr. A. Goldstein; and Dr. A. Gelber.

A programme of Zionist songs was given by the choirs of the Histadruth and the Teachers' Seminary.

AFTER MIDNIGHT

MR. LA GUARDIA will announce his resignation as Director-General of UNRRA today, when the council of the organization holds its sixth and final meeting in Washington.

15,000 CHINESE Communist troops have crossed the frozen river Sungari in what a Nanking message describes as the beginning of the Communist winter offensive.

1000-MILE MISSION OF MERCY

R.A.F. FLIES TO AID OF STRANDED REFUGEES

Palestine Post Reporter

Despite bad flying weather, six tons of food, medical supplies and clothing for the ship-wrecked immigrants on the Dodecanese island of Syrina, 500 miles from Haifa, were dropped at dawn yesterday by a flight of three four-engined Halifax transports of No. 113 Royal Air Force Airborne Support Squadron.

'READY AND GENEROUS ASSISTANCE'

Describing the relief measures that had been taken and were being planned, a Jewish Agency spokesman in Jerusalem yesterday said,

"We should like to put on record the ready and generous assistance which we have received from the Palestine Government Secretariat, the security authorities, the R.A.F., the people who deal with passports, and others.

"We have been helped very considerably and with great readiness by everybody concerned. We should like that to be made known."

A British tanker was reported late last night to have reached the islet, where she stood by waiting for the arrival of H.M.S. Chevron which left Haifa last night.

The Chevron, which was accompanied by a minesweeper, is expected to arrive at 8 o'clock this morning with doctors, nurses, medical supplies and food on board.

A medical mission consisting of three doctors and two nurses is to leave Palestine by air for Rhodes this morning, and will sail for Syrina to attend the refugees, some of whom are likely to have been injured during the shipwreck.

The planes took off from Aqir airport at 4 a.m. and returned at 11.45 after the 1000-mile journey. A fourth Halifax left just after noon with a further two tons of supplies.

Working all night, the R.A.F. ground crews prepared the machines for their special mission and the handling and packing of the stores was carried out by men of the 6th Airborne Division. Two paratroopers flew in each plane to carry out the actual dropping of the supplies, which included a six volt wireless battery in case the stranded refugees have a radio transmitter.

The story of the trip was told by F/Lt. Alan Ross, of Wembley, Middlesex, who was in command of the flight, a few minutes after he had touched down.

"It was pitch-black when we took off from Aqir," the Flight Lieutenant said, "and, though weather conditions were very bad — the worst I've ever known — we sighted the island just after first light."

The airmen saw no trace either on the shores of the island or at sea of the vessel that had foundered. They noticed a few white stone houses and barns in which they thought some of the refugees might have found shelter.

Tree-less and barren, Syrina's 650 ft. hills are split by a valley in which the R.A.F. observers could see the immigrants — 400 or 500 was the estimate — sheltering.

With only 200 or 300 yards in which to drop their supplies, the aircraft had to make several runs over the wadi and the job took just under an hour. They came down as low as 50 feet over the hill-tops to do it.

Smoke-Fires Lit

"As soon as the people in the wadi saw us," the R.A.F. officer continued, "they spread out, lit bonfires, waved and signalled to us. The smoke from the fires gave us our course and in we went to drop the supplies. We landed everything that

(Continued on Page 3 Col. 1)

BRITISH WANT ARMS CENSUS AUDIT

FLUSHING MEADOW, N.Y., Monday (Reuter). — In a five-hour night session the Uno General Assembly last night held a debate on the census of troops, during which Sir Hartley Shawcross (Britain) urged that information furnished should be verified by an "auditing committee" and M. Molotov asked that the question of troops at home should be kept separate from that of troops abroad. A census of troops at home without a tally of armaments, he said, would give an incomplete picture.

When Britain submits her return on troops, Sir Hartley promised, there would be a surprise at the smallness of the forces she maintains. "But," he added, "we should like our figures certified, so that nobody will be able to challenge them.

"If we are not prepared to agree to the simple process of verification now, in regard to this comparatively unimportant matter, what confidence could remain in the world that when the time comes we shall be ready to put into operation a far more rigid and far more elaborate system of control for the prohibition of atomic warfare?", Sir Hartley asked.

"Test of Sincerity"

"This is perhaps a test of our sincerity in the matter," he said. A perfectly simple system of international audit could be set up quickly by the Military Staffs Committee. "Who ever heard of the requirement that accounts should be submitted and compared with other accounts without a provision that they should also be audited?" The job of the auditing committee would be to put figures which meant different things in different countries on a comparable basis, which could present them in the proper perspective.

M. Molotov, who started speaking after midnight, said:

"We put forward the suggestion that all member States should report to the United Nations on their armed forces stationed outside their country. According to our proposal, all States would have to report on the forces which they still have on territories of other Uno members. The presence of foreign troops on other nations' territory can be used by a State to exert pressure on the internal affairs of another and in influencing relations between the occupied State and its neighbours. It is obvious that such a situation cannot be permitted to last."

M. Molotov repeated the Soviet argument that the question of troops at home should not be mixed up with the census of troops in foreign territories. Home troops, he said, should be dealt with separately when the United Nations took up the whole wider issue of disarmament.

M. Molotov pointed out that the request for a census of home troops did not include the census of armaments, and therefore it would give an incomplete picture.

Yesterday at U.N.

The South African demand that the dispute between India and the Union should be referred to the International Court of Justice was defeated in the General Assembly. First the Assembly decided by 29 votes to 24 that the South African amendment should require a two thirds majority. After that the amendment was defeated by 31 votes to 21 with two abstentions.

The American proposal on Franco Spain was amended by the political sub-committee to include the demand for the breaking off of diplomatic relations with Franco. The American version of the resolution had called on Franco to surrender his power to a provisional government but had refrained from demanding the rupture of diplomatic relations. Sunday night's amendment, submitted jointly by Mexico, Venezuela, Guatemala, Panama, and Chile demands the break-off as well. It was carried by 11 votes to 6 with one abstention.

Overriding Russian objections the Political and Security Committee yesterday decided to call upon the Security Council to curb the use of the veto.

INDIAN CONSTITUENT ASSEMBLY MEETS

NEW DELHI, Monday (R). — The Indian Constituent Assembly met here this morning in the brilliantly lit domed circular library hall of the Central Legislature under the chairmanship of the 75 years old Dr. Sinha.

The 74 Moslem League members did not attend owing to the League's decision to boycott the Assembly. The 205 members present made a colourful gathering dressed in the many different garbs of Indian provinces.

In his inaugural address Dr. Sinha strongly recommended the United States Constitution to the Assembly for careful study.

He held it up to the members as an ideal constitution, one "built for immortality, and adamantine strength which will outlast and overcome all destructive forces."

FRANCO STAGES PROTEST

MADRID, Monday (UP). — General Franco today addressed a crowd of 100,000 people on the occasion of the "Day of National Protest" against what is called the "interference of Uno in Spain's internal affairs." The movers of the motion to break off diplomatic relations with Spain were called by General Franco "enemies of our crusade."

He was speaking from the balcony of the Oriente Palace and said that Spain would not tolerate any foreign interference in her internal affairs. Spain had the right to benefit from her internal victory, he said.

Many thousands had marched in procession for two miles along Madrid's avenues until they reached the plaza before the Oriente Palace. At the climax of the rally, Franco appeared on the balcony and received a long ovation. He spoke for only five minutes.

"Forced Demonstration"

Many workers were given half tickets and ordered to retrieve the other half at certain assembly centres of the procession so as to assure their attendance. Unidentified persons phoned the United Press offices at Madrid and shouted: "Tell the world that this is a forced demonstration."

Members of the American and British Embassies were warned by their chiefs to avoid the streets where demonstrations were scheduled to be held and the wives of Embassy officials were instructed to remain indoors.

Despite today's demonstrations reliable diplomatic observers believe that General Franco may accept mediation by the Latin American Republics in his differences with the United Nations. The Spanish Foreign Office is reported to be in favour of the Colombian resolution submitted at Uno which recommends that the Latin American nations should offer their good offices towards the solution of the Spanish question by the Spaniards themselves. Although the resolution was rejected in the Political and Security Sub-Committees on Sunday, Colombia is planning to submit it again to the full committee.

M.R.P. WIN POLL

PARIS, Monday (R). — The Popular Republicans (M.R.P.) beat the Communists by exactly 1500 votes to the first place in the Council of the Republic — the new French Upper House — in the elections held yesterday.

The elections were for the first 214 out of 315 members to be chosen for the Council. The struggle between the M.R.P. and the Communists has thereby been taken a step further, the M.R.P. emerging as the strongest party — though by one seat only — in the Upper House, while the Communists are the strongest in the Chamber.

Results published this morning (including North African seats) were as follows:

Popular Republican	*62 seats*
Communists	*61 seats*
Socialists	*37 seats*
Radicals	*25 seats*
Independent Republicans	*12 seats*
Liberty Party (Right-wing)	*8 seats*
Other Metropolitan Parties	*2 seats*
Algerian Manifesto List	*4 seats*
Franco Muselman	*3 seats.*

Nearly 89,000 electors were chosen in the primary elections a fortnight ago. They gave 27,280 votes to the Communists.

The remaining 101 members are to be elected by electoral colleges. The National Assembly will elect 42 of them; another 51 will be chosen by overseas assemblies, some of which have not yet been constituted, while eight will be appointed by means yet to be determined to represent Frenchmen living in Tunis.

LATE Edition

THE PALESTINE POST

JERUSALEM
MONDAY, MARCH 3, 1947

PRICE 15 MILS
VOL. XXII. No. 6345

Column One

By

David Courtney

THE right of the individual to preserve his spiritual integrity may be the last right he has. It is the biggest. It preserves a people's national character and in the end becomes the spring of men's social rights. When Government and leadership fail, the nation is held secure in the heart of the people. Nothing can wreck it, neither physical nor psychological aggression nor ill-will nor stupidity within and without. Powerful overlords have steadily ignored that factor in their relationships with the peoples in their charge since the time of the Babylonians; and it is a fair chance that they will go on ignoring it for as long as overlordship may exist. That won't be much longer. The world has moved into a revolutionary phase which affects every person of every race and colour: the sun on his face and the earth under his feet are his, and he knows it and not a hundred thousand armed men can persuade him to deny that truth. Once the taste of his own earth is in his hungry mouth and the feel of his own sun upon his limbs, a man cannot forget: those things are himself, his nation, his integrity as a free man. It is as simple as that. The great problems of the world are very simple when you come to think of them. The trouble is that many people never come to think of them except in their artificial relationship with each other: in their complexity, therefore.

■

NOT a hundred thousand men nor a hundred million dollars are enough to stop the inevitable, revolutionary progress of the common man. The United States has just expressed its willingness to finance a Greek Government that suits it; and is said to have asked the British Government to keep its soldiers on the soil of Greece to reinforce whatever regime Anglo-American policy may elect. Basically, the notion is pernicious and ultimately unworkable. At the same time it is clear that the proposals of the United States are not merely for the purpose of maintaining in Athens a Government which a big section of the Greek people would like to see on the way out. The Greeks need work and bread. They cannot get it without the dollars that only the United States can provide. It is a pity that the United States should also feel it necessary to supply the Government as well.

■

IT becomes obvious that Britain and the United States regard Greece as a key political element in the affairs of the Balkans and of the Middle East. It is obvious that they are profoundly fearful of what might happen there and its consequences over a wide area: what is it? Is it simply the formation of a Left Wing Government in Greece or is there sound evidence of aggressive intentions, in which a Communist Greece would play a prominent role, and which threaten Turkey? If there is anything of this sort the facts ought to be made known in good time and if necessary they should be put before U.N. Perhaps the report of the Commission at present investigating events along the Greek frontiers will help to clarify the whole Greek and Balkan situation: meantime, the prospect of the Greek people joining up with their Slav neighbours on behalf of Soviet Russia and marching into Turkey, is hard to credit. One cannot help thinking that what the Greeks really want is a good, progressive Government.

Jerusalem, March 3.

TEL AVIV OUTLAWED

MARTIAL LAW OVER HALF YISHUV

PARALYSIS TILL TERROR IS ENDED; PART OF JEWISH J'LEM BESIEGED

Palestine Post Staff

Tel Aviv, Ramat Gan, Bnei Brak and Petah Tikva, with about a quarter of a million inhabitants, together with a small area of northeast Jerusalem have been completely isolated and outlawed since dawn yesterday, when 10,000 troops of the First Infantry Division and the Ninth Infantry Brigade launched "Operation Hippo".

The curfew imposed on Tel Aviv at midnight on Saturday is to be lifted at 5 o'clock this morning, the Area Commander, Brigadier J.W.R. Moore, announced last night.

The nature and background of Operation Hippo was described at his Divisional Headquarters in Tel Litwinsky to a party of local and foreign correspondents by Major-General R. N. Gale, in command of the operation. "For some time past the authorities had been preparing to take vigorous steps to put down illegal activities against the State," the General declared.

"Certain preliminary steps, such as cantonment and evacuation of British subjects, have already taken place, but the problem which faces us now is to know what to do in the event of sabotage and murder, and, obviously, our purpose is to get hold of the perpetrators with as little inconvenience as possible to the public. Yet, unfortunately, indirectly, the community must suffer. This is regretted as much by us as by them," he said.

The isolated area has been completely cut off from the rest of the world. Communications have ceased. The railway system, with the exception of certain food and through trains, has been dislocated, and road transport has been stopped. Posts, telegraphs and telephones have ceased functioning, and the distribution of food will be made through the Food Control authorities, with military transport at their disposal. Tel Aviv Port has ceased functioning, and six freighters waiting to be unloaded must go elsewhere.

A number of destroyers were seen patrolling off the shore today.

A special system of Military Courts will be set up to deal with all offenders. This, however, was not Martial Law, the General emphasized, and the military were only assisting the police in this operation, which was primarily directed towards the search for individuals.

Essential Services

All facilities would be given to essential services as well as to the press, whose duty it was to "make it clear that this operation was not a punitive measure, but a drastic step against illegal organizations which must be paralyzed.

General Gale told the hushed press conference that measures will continue until the terrorists have been run to earth, even if this takes weeks. This most drastic action ever taken in Palestine was the Government's answer to Saturday's terrorist attacks on the military and the police.

All evidence we have as to who carries out these attacks tends to show that they come from the area we have isolated. In order to eradicate them, we shall try to prevent as far as is humanly possible any movement in or out of the area. The objective of this plan is to search for and arrest the law-breakers within it, however long that may take.

"The operation's objective is not punitive," the General emphasized. "There is absolutely no quarrel with the community as a whole. In fact, what I know of the community, which is quite a lot, makes me think they would be as glad to get rid of the bad souls."

No Large Searches

The General made it clear that he was not going to have any wide-scale searches, such as the four-day house-to-house search last July which *angered the population and achieved next to nothing. The police have their suspicions, and I have told them to go after the men they want. They cannot get out of the area except by sea, and the Navy is looking after that. This means a terrific paralysis, I know, but it cannot be helped. This thing has got beyond the control of the police, and we have got to help them.*

When asked what would happen if the terrorists lay low during the operation, and what would happen in fact if the plan failed, the General said:

Frankly, I don't know. We can only hope that is the answer, and it will work, but how soon is imponderable. It may take a week or a month, I just don't know.

Traffic between Jaffa and Haifa yesterday was diverted through Beit Dajan, and roads leading into the Controlled Area were blocked by tanks and barbed-wire barriers. Wire entanglements were stretched across fields and troops were posted every few hundred metres around the perimeter.

A number of Hebrew newspapers, normally printed in Tel Aviv, have transferred their offices to Haifa and will publish one-sheet editions.

RED HIPPO

Special orange-coloured identification cards, labeled "Hippo" and stamped across the back, with the picture of a hippopotamus in red, have been issued to 16 residents of the Controlled Area in Jerusalem.

The cards, which permit entry and departure from the zone, must be held overhead in clear view of the patrols. They have been issued to mukhtars of the Quarter, Government officials, and two doctors.

Deserted City

Palestine Post Reporter

A deathly stillness reigned in the streets of Tel Aviv yesterday. Patrols closely checked the military vehicles circulating in the city but both police and troops, worn out by the khamsin, *sought shade whenever possible. Even roving cats seemed to sense the new order and hardly ventured on the streets.*

In some parts of town, as patrolling was relaxed towards evening, people began to move cautiously about.

Of the city's 6,000 telephones, only two lines were operating— one to the Public Information Office and the other to the Mayor's residence. Neither nurses nor doctors were allowed on the streets. Sanitary and other services were suspended.

Very few screenings or searches were carried out and, with the announcement that the curfew would be lifted at 5 o'clock this morning, it seemed unlikely that intensive searches would take place.

Instead of the usual 80 buses on the Tel Aviv-Petah Tikva route, 25 will be allowed to operate daily between 6 and 8 o'clock in the morning, and from 4 to 8 in the evening. No other buses will leave Tel Aviv.

By 11 o'clock no order had been received instructing factories and other industrial undertakings to close, and employees will walk to work this morning. Schools will function as fully as possible.

25,000 ISOLATED IN JERUSALEM QUARTERS

Palestine Post Staff

Statutory Martial Law was brought into force in the north-eastern quarters of Jerusalem at 8 o'clock yesterday — Mea Shearim, Bokharian Houses, Sanhedria, Beth Israel, Beth Israel Hahadasha, Geulah and Kerem Avraham.

The announcement that the measure had been applied to the large area which includes, Tel Aviv, Bnei Brak, Ramat Gan and Petah Tikva and a number of Arab villages came five hours later, at 1.15 p.m.

The official figure of the number of people affected by Operation Hippo is 238,210 : 180,000 in Tel Aviv; 17,250 in Petah Tikva; 10,200 in Ramat Gan; 5,760 in Bnei Brak, and 25,000 in Jerusalem.

The New Order was enacted in a supplement to the "Palestine Gazette" yesterday and announced in two official communiques.

The curfew imposed on other Jewish quarters of Jerusalem at 7 o'clock on Saturday night was lifted at 1 o'clock yesterday afternoon, 18 hours later, but in the Martial Law area remains in force until 10 o'clock tomorrow morning, when it will be lifted for only three hours.

Statutory Martial Law differs from full martial law in that it prescribes the powers and regulations by which a Military Commander can govern certain areas. These powers are

Continued On Page 2, Col. 1.

VAAD LEUMI STOPPAGE CALLED OFF

The self-imposed curfew which the Jewish communities of Haifa and Jerusalem had planned for last night was cancelled, and cafes and restaurants were open.

Communists Accuse Chiang Kai Shek

NANKING, Sunday (Reuter). — In a telegram to Generalissimo Chiang Kai Shek from General Chou En-Lai, the Communist leader, the Generalissimo is accused of "bolting the door to any negotiations," and is charged with determination to wage civil war to the end.

This follows the order that Communist representatives leave Nationalist territory, signed, according to General Chou En-Lai, by Marshal Chiang Kai Shek himself.

The first group of Communist liaison officials left Nanking for Yenan in an American plane today. About 160 men, women and children are to be evacuated by March 7.

20 KILLED ON SATURDAY

Palestine Post Staff

Terrorist activities throughout Palestine on Saturday took toll of 20 lives — two British officers, eight British other ranks, a British police clerk and nine civilians. Twenty-five other people were wounded — seven British officers, 10 British other ranks, two British policemen and six civilians.

In addition to the series of outrages reported yesterday, two soldiers were killed when the scout car in which they were patrolling was blown up north of Petah Tikva on Saturday night. One soldier on road patrol nearby was killed and another wounded.

Two soldiers were wounded, one seriously and the other slightly, yesterday afternoon when the truck in which they were travelling struck a mine on the Tel Aviv-Haifa highway two kilometres south of the Hadera junction.

A third member of the party of four Military Police lance-corporals, whose jeep was blown upon on Mountain Road, Haifa, late on Saturday, died yesterday.

The fourth N.C.O. is not out of danger and has been transferred to the Military Hospital at Sarafand.

The funeral of Mr. George Beynon, a police clerical officer, who was killed in the Goldsmith Club outrage, took place at the Zion cemetery in Jerusalem yesterday afternoon.

The three British Army victims of the same outrage will be buried at the Military Cemetery in Ramle this morning.

The identities of the seven NAAFI employees killed in the Club have now been established. They are —

Germano Mazzoti, the manager;
Emil Gandour, assistant manager;
Olga Padovracynski, receptionist;
Hassan Yussef el Bakhri;
Elias Yussef Korro;
Hanna Elias Sashan; and
Mussa Mohammed Abu Diab.

The two NAAFI employees injured are — Stadios Andronizi and Rushid Murrad Massud.

CHILD KILLED

A four-year-old girl, Ketti Shalom, was fatally injured when she was shot in the head as she appeared on the balcony of her parents' house in the Stauri Building in the Mea Shearim Quarter of Jerusalem (in the Controlled Area) at 3 o'clock yesterday afternoon.

The child died almost immediately after admission to hospital.

Her older sister, Mrs. B. Mazon (22), was shot in the leg, but was not permitted to go to the Red Shield Society clinic for treatment.

It was stated later that a court of inquiry is to be held to investigate the circumstances in which the girl was killed. The P.I.O. said that the shot was fired at the girl's father when he tried to leave the house. The bullet "penetrated the balcony wounding Mrs. Mazon in the leg, and the child was hit by the ricochet."

Another official statement, issued at 6 o'clock, said that warning shots were fired during the day in the Mea Shearim Quarter under Statutory Martial Law, and that no casualties occurred.

'RESULT of LACK of COOPERATION'

OFFICIAL COMMUNIQUE
No. 110, March 2, 7.45 a.m.

Following on extensive outrages on March 1, 1947, the High Commissioner has made regulations under the Palestine (Defence) Order in Council, 1937, which provide for the imposition of statutory martial law in areas specified by the High Commissioner. These Regulations are considered by the High Commissioner to be expedient for the maintenance of public order and their effect, in areas to which they are applied, is to provide for the withdrawal from the population of such areas of the normal facilities of civil government. Government offices and courts will be closed; banks may be closed by order of the military commander; telephone and postal services may be suspended. The movement of persons and vehicles may be prohibited. Exclusive jurisdiction in respect of criminal offences committed in areas specified by the High Commissioner is vested in military courts.

These regulations have been applied with effect from 8 a.m. on March 2, 1947 to the following area of Jerusalem:—

From a point in Mea Shearim Street at the southeast corner of the Syrian Orphanage property, in a northerly direction along the eastern boundary of the Syrian Orphanage property to a point adjacent to Survey cairn No. 799, 2: thence in a northeasterly direction following the middle of the road to a point on the Nebi Samwil road approximately 100 metres northwest of Survey cairn No.764.6: thence in a southeasterly direction in a straight line to the culvert on the Nablus road in the Sheikh Jarrah quarter: thence in a southerly direction along the middle of Saint George's Road to its junction with Mea Shearim Street: thence along Mea Shearim Street to the point at the southeast corner of the Syrian Orphanage property.

OFFICIAL COMMUNIQUE
No. 111, March 2, 1.15 p.m.

A month ago the Government invited the Jewish Agency and the Vaad Leumi to call upon the Yishuv to cooperate in bringing to justice members of the terrorist groups. These institutions refused their cooperation. Renewed warnings were therefore given of the serious consequences which any further outbreaks of terrorism would entail. The severer measures now necessary are the result of the lack of cooperation against bloodshed and terrorism which these institutions have themselves condemned.

Since the invitation to cooperate was issued, 48 outrages have occurred in which 20 people have lost their lives and 31 people have been injured, including 18 killed and 25 injured in yesterday's incidents. Included in these casualties are 15 civilians.

There is distinct evidence to link the attacks carried out on March 1 with the Tel Aviv area, from which it is well known that operations by the dissident groups are conducted. For instance, the vehicles used in the attacks in Jerusalem and Haifa were stolen yesterday in Tel Aviv.

The regulations providing for the imposition of Statutory Martial Law are therefore being applied with effect from 1.15 p.m. today, March 2, to an area including Tel Aviv, Ramat Gan, Bnei Brak and Petah Tikva.

"Fight Against Terror Will Be Intensified"

OUTRAGES A "NUMBING SHOCK"

Expressing the Yishuv's "numbing shock" at the latest outrages, a statement issued by the Jewish Agency and the Vaad Leumi last night declared the determination of the Yishuv to intensify its fight to stamp out terror.

Both bodies point out that they have made consistent efforts to combat terrorism, but the failure of the Government to ease the immigration restrictions had not helped to relieve the tension in the country. The statement reads as follows:

The Jewish Agency and the Vaad Leumi are filled with horror at the outrages which have been perpetrated in Palestine during the past 24 hours. These murderous and senseless crimes have come as a numbing shock to the entire Yishuv and its leaders. For some considerable time past the disciplined elements in the Yishuv, hampered though they have been by lack of adequate powers, have been making efforts to combat the terrorist groups and to undermine their organization. These efforts are continuing and will be intensified, for the Yishuv is determined that the shedding of innocent blood shall play no part in its national struggle.

The Executive of the Jewish Agency and the Executive of the Vaad Leumi deplore the loss of life caused by these latest crimes and share to the utmost the grief of the bereaved families, British, Arab and Jewish alike.

The Jewish Agency and the Vaad Leumi would not have prolonged their statement beyond this point, or ventured to raise these terrible happenings to a political plane, if the Government in its official statement had not linked the "severer measures now necessary" with the Jewish National Institutions' "lack of cooperation."

They would point out, for their part, that the Jewish Agency has, as stated above, made consistent efforts to combat terrorism. It regrets however that in the course of lengthy negotiations it has failed to secure from the Government any measure of help in solving the burning question of immigration, a matter which, apart from its intrinsic urgency, would no doubt also have relieved the existing tension. The Government has steadily refused concessions of any kind, and no amount of pleading nor even the hard facts of the situation have so far availed to move the Government an inch. The Government is now retaliating against the Yishuv as a whole for the crimes of a few desperate gunmen, and is seeking by the imposition of martial law, which is unlikely to deter the terrorism, to punish an entire community.

The Jewish Agency and the Vaad Leumi wish to stress once again that the disciplined forces of the Yishuv will intensify their action against terrorism so as to bring to an end all murder and bloodshed in this country. They call upon the Yishuv in this hour of crisis to rally round the National Institutions. Those sections of Palestine which are now under martial law remain an integral part of the Yishuv, which declares its complete solidarity with them both in the common fight against terrorist outrages and in the fate which they have been called upon to endure as scapegoats for an evil that is not their making.

Tel Aviv Mayor Urges Courage

Nothing will be allowed to stop the building of Palestine and of Tel Aviv, declared the Mayor of the city, Mr. I. Rokach, in a statement last night.

Referring to the restriction on movement and the withdrawal of Government services, the Mayor warned that "other severe blows may follow," and were likely to weaken the economic position of the Yishuv, on which further development depended.

Mr. Rokach said that the Municipal Council was about to take steps, in conjunction with the economic and public institutions, to prevent or at least reduce the suffering of the population.

Calling on the citizens to refrain from panic action likely to weaken efforts to overcome the present difficulties, the Mayor declared that the private individual was "from now on at the disposal of the public — and the public will look after the individual."

Export-Import Bank Stops Credits

WILL CONTINUE TO FINANCE TRADE

WASHINGTON, Sunday (Reuter). — The Export-Import Bank has informed the U.S. Congress that it "had decided to bring to an end its programme of emergency reconstruction credits, and this decision would apply especially to countries which have access to facilities of the International Bank."

In its third semi-annual report to Congress, it states, however, it would continue to consider, in accordance with its general powers and policies, credits to finance trade with countries undergoing reconstruction as well as with other countries. "It is the policy of the Bank that credits which it authorizes shall be for specific purposes; shall contribute in a most direct manner to a balanced long-range expansion of foreign trade; and shall be on terms appropriate to circumstances in each case," the Bank says.

The report discloses that "credits authorized by the Export-Import Bank from July 1, 1945, to December 31, 1946, amounted to approximately 2,250 million dollars.

(World Bank — Page 3.)

America's Terms For Greek Aid

LONDON, Sunday (Reuter). — Receipt of an aide-memoire from the U.S. outlining the terms on which it would be prepared to provide economic assistance for the Greek Government, was confirmed by a Foreign Office spokesman tonight.

The communication is now being considered. The U.S. is reliably understood to have urged that British troops should continue to stay in Greece, if economic assistance is to be supplied from Washington.

Germans Escape To S. America

LONDON, Sunday (Reuter). The International Committee for the Study of European Questions, in a fresh report issued today on underground Nazi plots, says many Germans are still escaping to South America through Sweden and Italy, some having changed their passports, identity and nationality as many as three times.

The report has been sent to the Prime Ministers and Foreign Secretaries of Britain, France, Belgium, Denmark, Norway, the U.S. and Russia. "In spite of recent denials," it says, "a great part of the economic potential hidden abroad by the Axis powers has neither been handed over to former Allied countries nor liquidated. The Argentine Government, after having supported Axis policy during the war, definitely refuses to hand over their assets to former Allied nations.

Invitation

ATLANTA, (Georgia), Sunday (Reuter). — A proposal that England, Scotland, Ireland and Wales should be admitted as member states of the U.S.A. was made by Senator Richard Russel, Georgia (Democrat) in an interview with Ralph McGill, the editor of the "Atlanta Constitution," a Democratic morning paper.

The newspaper quoted the Senator as saying that his proposal was based on the threatened break-up of the British Empire and its probable inability to carry out world commitments. He proposed that the commonwealths within the Empire should consider some form of association with the U.S., if Britain acted to become part of the U.S.

Senator Russel added that the King and Queen would be able to retire on their incomes "and the King could, if he wished, remain in politics and run for the Senate as could Mr. Churchill."

Anglo-French Alliance

BRITAIN'S SECOND STEP

PARIS, Sunday (Reuter). — Mr. Bevin and M. Bidault, the British and French Foreign Ministers, are both expected to make speeches when they sign the Anglo-French Treaty of Alliance at Dunkirk on Tuesday.

The pact will be signed at the Sub-Prefecture at 1500 hrs G.M.T. and three hours later the text will be published.

The "Observer" says in a leading article today the alliance with France was the "second big step to improve things Britain has taken since the end of the war" — the first having been her agreement with the U.S. to unite their two zones in Germany. A diplomatic correspondent of the "Sunday Times" makes the suggestion that the formula used in the Treaty may serve as a model for a revised Treaty of Alliance with Russia which Mr. Bevin is expected to negotiate in Moscow.

France Welcomes Pact

An enthusiastic welcome to the Treaty was also given in editorials of the French press, which were broadcast to the nation today as the Paris newspaper workers' strike is still going on.

United Nations Army Under Discussion

LAKE SUCCESS, Sunday — (AFP). — The Committee appointed to study the deployment of the armed forces to be controlled by the United Nations has completed its work, and is now examining the organization of these armed forces.

Speaking at a reception given by the League for Industrial Democracy in New York yesterday, Mr. Trygve Lie said that the United Nations would have succeeded in its aims if belief in the possibility of another war were banished for ever from the minds of men.

The German and Japanese peace treaties should be signed as soon as possible, he said, to avoid antagonisms between the big and small nations.

Mr. Lie said that workers of the world should know that the United Nations was their organization, and have confidence in it. Their fate was linked to that of the U.N.

BIG 4 MAY DISCUSS DARDANELLES

ANKARA, Sunday (Reuter). — Turkey's dispute with Russia over the control of the Dardanelles will "most probably" be discussed at the Big Four meeting in Moscow, Turkish political quarters stated today.

The possibility of direct talks between the two countries has now been excluded, but a conference of all the signatories of the Montreux Convention might take place some time soon.

Eight days before the opening of the conference, the Embassies of the participating powers had not been informed today where the meeting was to take place.

MR. BEN-GURION IN HOSPITAL

Mr. David Ben-Gurion, Chairman of Jewish Agency Executive who arrived in Palestine on Thursday, was admitted to the Surgical Section of the Hadassah Hospital in Jerusalem yesterday morning. He was brought from the Kallia Hotel in an ambulance to be treated for a leg ailment.

Dr. Milevitzky said that his condition is not serious, and that while a week or 10 days of treatment and rest are necessary, it is unlikely that an operation will be needed.

MAXIMUM PRICES FOR BEEF

(mils per kilo)	Ordinary	Kosher
Boneless (excluding fillet, tongue and liver, but including brain and inner organs)	520	580
Fillet & tongue	620	680
Liver	560	620
Bones	50	60

PAY NO MORE

FOOD CONTROL

THE PALESTINE POST

LATE Edition

JERUSALEM THURSDAY, APRIL 17, 1947

PRICE 15 MILS   VOL. XXII. No. 6383

THE psychological effect of shrewd bookkeeping softens the practical effects of empty pockets. Dr. Dalton's analysis of Britain's financial position was a masterly example of good propaganda. Press and public reaction to the Budget speech suggests that the astute Chancellor of the Exchequer has got away with it: Socialism says, Gilt edged securities should rise on the stock exchange and the next by-election should maintain the Labour vote at its 1945 level. In short, one gathers, there is not much to worry about in the internal position of Great Britain except exports, which, Dr. Dalton agreed, were the key to the future but of which, be found that, he had little to say except in terms of exhortation. It boils down to this: the apparently favourable outlook depends on two uncertain factors — the stepping up of output and the goodwill of the United States Congress in the matter of dollars. Dalton's exposition was probably intended as much for America as for Britain. It was designed to show the basic solvency of the country and to convince Congress that 3 per cent dollar loans to Britain would be a sound investment.

HENRY Wallace was present at Tuesday's debate. He could hardly have been unaware of the present dependence of British economy on the United States, however carefully and patriotically Dr. Dalton may have paraded the figures. He might even have seen the parallel between the Chancellor's conspicuous effort and the Greek Government's spectacular campaign against the guerrillas — both to impress the United States Congress, which directs today's world with the authority if not the wisdom of the Roman Senate of Augustine times. Mr. Wallace has attacked this development. He sees in it a new form of Imperialism and an impediment to human progress, and he was said to in plain words. We should thank our stars for Mr. Wallace. The supporters of the Truman doctrine describe him as idealist, sentimentalist and even traitor: good men have been called that before and their influence has outlived the policy they contemptuously denounced.

ADMISSION to the Wallace meetings in Britain was by ticket. In the biggest hall which London and Manchester could provide, the seats were sold out days in advance and people waited outside to catch what they could. It is clear that this man in his ill-fitting clothes and with his formless hat has come to be heard and that out of them he has brought a message welcome to the common people. You cannot take a single sentence from a single one of his addresses delivered in Britain and find fault with it on grounds of simple, plain sense. It is unlikely that he will turn out to be the leader the world awaits. It may even be too much to hope that he is the precursor; but there is no doubt that in the era of what he calls the common man, no more apt spokesman has yet put in an appearance. His words, bitterly opposed as they are to the present mood of his President and Congress and perhaps to the temper of the greater part of the United States, have a truly American ring to them, which harmonizes with the basic Americanism of a Roosevelt, a Lincoln or a Jefferson. He is now on the European continent which will be the better for what he has to say. And one big advantage is that it has put him back into the middle of the American picture: he has again become front page news.

GENERAL de Gaulle has formalized his re-entry into politics. There is no knowing at this stage what will be the strength of his party and no judging its effect on the electorate until the municipal voting in the winter. Much will depend on whether the Vichyites of the Right wing parties maintain their resentment of the General and the General his resentment of them. This factor is likely to play a big part in the development of the de Gaullist movement and to the traitor, the House of Lords was allowed to hear Joyce's appeal before he was hanged.

Jerusalem, April 17.

JEWISH COMMUNITY IMMOBILIZED BY COUNTRY-WIDE CURFEWS
4 HANGED IN SECRET AT ACRE; FUNERAL AT SAFAD

Palestine Post Staff

While the Yishuv was immobilized by a sudden curfew "until further notice," the four Jews under sentence of death in Acre Prison were led out of the condemned cells and hanged two hours before dawn yesterday.

The four men, Dov Gruener, Dov Rosenbaum, Eliezer Kashani and Mordehai Alkoshi, were the first Jews to be executed for crimes with political backgrounds since the hanging of Shlomo Ben Yossef in 1938.

They had been transferred from the Jerusalem Central Prison to Acre on Monday, No announcement of the executions had been made, and the secrecy in which they were shrouded still prevails, so that few details are known.

The relatives of the executed men were informed about four hours later, and were taken to Safad to attend the burial. The Chief Rabbinate had not been informed.

A layman, the only Jew living in Acre, who had been appointed acting Chaplain' to be able to lead prayers for Jewish prisoners, was summoned by the authorities to attend the executions, but declined to do so, and the four men went to their death without a rabbi's ministrations.

Wide Curfew

A wide curfew was clamped on all Jewish towns and Jewish quarters of mixed cities, and a nightly 12-hour road curfew for vehicles and pedestrians went into effect at 6 o'clock yesterday.

For the second time in six weeks, the normal life of over half a million people was brought to a standstill by the house-arrest and the closure of all urban schools and places of work.

From Acre, where night workers in the prison were not allowed to leave until the bodies of the four men were removed, it was reported yesterday that a party of Army and Police officers arrived shortly after midnight, presumably with the orders for the executions. The condemned men were taken from their cells to a room where they were informed that their sentences would be carried out almost at once. They quickly regained their composure after the initial shock, it is said, and sang "Hatikvah," the initial national anthem. At 3 o'clock Dov Gruener was hanged, and the other executions followed.

Safad Cordoned

Later, the Jewish quarter of Safad was cordoned off by the Army, and at 7.30 the Assistant District Commissioner, Mr. W.J.A. Livingstone, accompanied by the District Superintendent of Police, Mr. A.S. Barham, and the District Officer, Mr. M. Kahane, informed the Chairman of the Safad Jewish Community Council, Mr. M. Podhorcer, of the executions and of the Government's decision to have the men buried there.

It was reported later that the four men themselves had asked to be buried at Rosh Pina, where the body of Shlomo Ben-Yossef lies.

Mr. Podhorcer was asked to make the necessary preparations for the burial. Curfew had been imposed as a precautionary measure, Mr. Livingstone said.

Meanwhile the bodies had left Acre before 7 o'clock in a police tender escorted by a large number of Bren-carriers and armoured cars. The convoy arrived in Safad at 9 o'clock, and the bodies, wrapped in sheets, were kept at Mount Canaan Police Headquarters until the arrival of the dead men's relatives. Shortly after 3 o'clock the bodies were delivered to the Safad Jewish Community Council at the edge of the cemetery.

The mourners were Mrs. Helen Friedman, Gruener's sister; Kashani's parents, a brother and a sister; and Alkoshi's father and sister. Alkoshi's mother was ill and unable to come. There were no relatives of Rosenbaum.

The men were buried near the graves of the victims of the disorders in 1929 and 1936. More than 300 men and women attended the funeral, and Rabbi J. Silberman and Mr. M. Podhorcer spoke at the graveside.

The 120 Jewish prisoners in Acre Prison fasted yesterday as a sign of mourning.

The authorities were satisfied that in the circumstances everything possible had been done to provide last religious rites to the four men, a Government spokesman said in Jerusalem yesterday.

The executed men had not been allowed to bid farewell to their relatives for security reasons, he added.

Questioned on the legal aspect of Gruener's case, for whom an appeal before the Privy Council was pending, the spokesman recalled that the Colonial Secretary had recently told the House of Commons that he had been advised by the Attorney-General that Governors and High Commissioners were not obliged to stay executions longer than they thought advisable in the circumstances, even when an appeal to the Privy Council was pending.

('Families Not Told'—Pg.2 Col.1)

Executions Meant to "Aggravate Conditions"

LAKE SUCCESS (UP). — The execution of Dov Gruener "furnishes new evidence to the U.N. of the disastrous results" of the British administration of the Holy Land, a Jewish Agency spokesman said here today.

"It is a cruel act which seems to be calculated to aggravate the already intolerable situation in Palestine," he added.

The American section of the Jewish Agency, with its H.Q. in New York, has been entrusted with the task of piloting the Jewish case through the forthcoming special session, which the General Assembly will hold on April 28, to begin the mapping of Palestine's future.

'SHOCKING RETROGRESSION'

LONDON, Wednesday (R).—A member of the London Committee for Aid to Jewish Prisoners, Mr. Jehuda Benari, commenting on Dov Gruener's execution, told Reuter: "In our opinion it was not an execution of sentence. This is the very first time that death sentences have been carried out within the British Empire when legal appeals were pending. Even in the case of Joyce the traitor, the House of Lords was allowed to hear Joyce's appeal before he was hanged.

"We believe that this execution is a shocking retrogression in the British judicial administration — even if one goes back to the time prior to the Magna Carta."

After declaring that a petition for special leave to appeal to the Privy Council had been lodged on April 14, Mr. Benari said the authorities knew perfectly well that the question was sub judice and added: "We fully anticipate that the whole question of the execution will be ventilated in the House of Commons."

Curfew Lasted 25 Hours

The first intimation the public had that the four men transferred to Acre Prison were being hanged yesterday came with the blaring of loudspeaker cars which toured the streets of Jewish cities and quarters after 4 a.m. and announced that a curfew had been imposed and it was enforced from 4.30. A broadcast announcement later proclaimed the usual road restrictions, though these have now been extended to include movement on foot or horseback on the roads affected.

The house curfew in Jerusalem would be lifted at 5.30 this morning, but continued for 11 hours at 6.30 this afternoon, it was announced last night. The 6.30 p.m. — 5.30 a.m. curfew would be imposed nightly until further notice. In Tel Aviv, curfew was to be lifted at 6.

Yesterday's curfew was imposed on parts of Jerusalem and Haifa, the Municipal areas of Tel Aviv and the urban area of Petah Tikva.

The curfew area in Jerusalem was strongly patrolled by military and police, and only a few passers-by were going about their business. Early in the morning, bread vans escorted by soldiers toured the area, bringing bread to housewives.

Boy Shot

Shortly after one o'clock a 12-year-old boy, Gedalya Ben (Continued on Page 2 Col. 1)

No British, U.S. Committee Place

By GEORGE LICHTHEIM, Palestine Post Correspondent

LONDON, Wednesday. — Gruener's execution and Palestine's country-wide curfew were banner-headed by early editions of the afternoon papers here today.

Simultaneously, the "Evening Standard" reports from Washington that neither the Americans nor the British will seek a place on the U.N. fact-finding committee. Nor apparently will the Arabs obtain British support for their preposterous request that an Arab delegate be included.

More important than these skirmishings are the impending conversations between Jewish representatives and French Government circles scheduled for this week-end. These talks should clarify both the French attitude next September, and the immediate measures to be taken by the French authorities in accordance with the British request for closer supervision of Jewish emigration via France.

French Attitude

So far, there is nothing in the official French attitude which suggests that the French have changed their minds on such subjects as the undesirability of allowing the Arab League to dictate the attitude of the Western Powers in the Middle-East.

French reaction to certain happenings in Algiers and Morocco — whose Sultan this week proclaimed Pan-Arab objectives — are regarded as a sign that the Radmadier Government, with the fullest support from M. Blum, intends to maintain a firm attitude in face of Pan-Arab agitation.

League Rejection

The note pointed out that one of the last acts of the League's Permanent Mandates Commission had been to declare the 1939 White Paper to be contrary to the terms of the Mandate granted to Britain. Violation of the Mandate had been carried through only because the League had ceased to exist without leaving any international forum to which the Jewish people could have appealed.

A British spokesman at Lake Success said that the British favoured a U.N. committee because all previous commissions had been suspect.

Canada will be represented at the special Assembly session by Mr. Lester B. Pearson, but the general attitude of the Canadian Government has not yet been clarified. For Britain, Mr. Ivor Thomas, Under-Secretary for the Colonies, has been named as an alternate for Sir Alexander Cadogan.

M. Andre Gromyko is expected to represent Russia, though he has not yet received instructions from Moscow.

'We Owe Solution To Jews, Arabs'

NEW YORK, Wednesday (UP). — While the Palestine problem remains unsolved, "Britain, the U.S. and to some extent the U.N. are in a moral bankruptcy", says Henry Wallace, writing in the current issue of the "New Republic".

He asserts the basic step toward a solution of the Palestine problem would be the development of a sound economic programme for the entire Near East. All nations concerned should give financial support to large scale reclamation of land, irrigation, and industrialization.

Mr. Wallace observes Palestine "occupies a unique strategic position in the power struggle between Anglo-American and Russian interests in the Mediterranean. Is all this part of an Anglo-American drive against Russia?" he asks, adding: "Yet, Russia is against Zionism. The Communists are stirring up the poorer Arabs against the Jews, by declaring their land is being taken from them by people from alien lands."

Any new mandate over Palestine should be under the U.N., Mr. Wallace concludes. "We must have confidence that there is a solution. We owe both to the Jews and the Arabs."

Secret Arms Factory Reported in T.-J.

BEIRUT, Wednesday (ANA). — The Trans-Jordanian Legation here today denied the report that a secret factory operated by Syrians and producing arms had been discovered at Irbid in Trans-Jordan.

NEUTRAL COMMITTEE AT U.N. FAVOURED

LAKE SUCCESS, Wednesday. — The United States will ask the U.N. Assembly to limit its special session to the appointment of the fact-finding committee and to refrain from discussing the Palestine issue itself, it is reported here.

It also favours a neutral membership for the committee with American, British, Arab and Jewish representatives all excluded.

The Jewish Agency note to the United Nations asking for an interim decision permitting the immediate large-scale immigration of Jews to Palestine (briefly reported yesterday) recalled that most of the U.N. member States had been members of the League of Nations and had signed the covenant establishing the right of the Jewish people to its Homeland within the framework of the Mandate.

BRITISH FORCES TO LEAVE IRAQ

LONDON, Wednesday — Reports from Baghdad that all British Army units will be withdrawn from Iraq by autumn of this year were confirmed by a Foreign Office spokesman in London this afternoon.

British air force contingents, including ground staffs, which are under the terms of the Anglo-Iraqi Treaty of Alliance of 1930 are stationed at the Habbaniyah and Shaibah airfields, are not affected by the withdrawal, whose effect will be to restore the pre-war position regarding the dispositioning of British troops in Iraq.

During the war, British military dispositions in the Middle East were strengthened by the stationing in Iraq of a number of army units, additional to the air force contingents normally held there under the terms of the Treaty.

Dr. Jamali told Parliament that Iraq will approach Britain for revision of the Treaty. The revision will be based on an equal footing and will be within the U.N. Charter to which both Iraq and Britain are bound.

Arab Opposition

The Arab States will oppose the setting up of a fact-finding committee, announced Faris El Khoury, Syrian delegate to the U.N. Instead of a committee, the Arabs want the immediate establishment of an independent Arab republic.

Foreign Ministers of the Arab States flew today from their respective capitals to Damascus to attend the meeting of the political committee of the Arab League. Azzam Pasha, Secretary-General of the League, arrived this afternoon.

A communique issued at the close of tonight's meeting of the Arab League's Political Commission stated that the Arab League would press for an independent Palestine, abolition of the Mandate and the stoppage of Jewish immigration. The meeting is to be resumed tomorrow evening.

Azzam Pasha declared that the Arab states should send the best possible delegates to defend the Palestine Arab. He stated that the Arab League would fight with all its force against Britain and the Zionists, and added that this victory could not be achieved by mere protestations.

(PTA, Palcor, Reuter & AFP)

Telephone Hoax at Scotland Yard
BOMB FOUND IN DOVER HOUSE; GRUENER CASE LINK DENIED

LONDON, Wednesday (Reuter) — A home-made bomb, composed of a number of sticks of gelignite with a fuse attached, and wrapped in brown paper to resemble a parcel, was found early this morning in a cloakroom of Dover House, part of the Colonial Office in Whitehall.

The bomb was discovered an hour before it was due to go off. It has been described as "most powerful" and had it exploded, it would have completely wrecked the building.

Dover House, where normally a hundred people work, deals with economic matters, principally Palestine economic affairs. It receives many callers during the day interested in the export of goods to Palestine.

Scotland Yard officers were rushed to Whitehall this afternoon, following a telephone message from an anonymous caller, who said: "There is an organization which is going to blow up the War Office at four o'clock this afternoon."

A Colonial Office spokesman denied press statements to the effect that Colonial Office officials believed the attempt was a Palestine terrorist outrage. No such remark has been made, he said. While admitting that the bomb had been planted and discovered before the secrecy of Gruener's execution had reached London, the spokesman pointed out the coincidence between the bomb and the execution.

The Colonial Office stated this afternoon that there was not considered to be any link between this incident and the execution of Dov Gruener.

The building was searched, but it is understood that nothing suspicious was found.

Mystery Woman Sought

LONDON, Wednesday (UP). — Scotland Yard agents are combing London and their "top-secret" intelligence files tonight in an endeavour to obtain information about a well-dressed "mystery woman of Jewish appearance," believed to have left the powerful home-made time bomb in Dover House, only 100 yards from No. 10 Downing Street.

Following examination of the bomb by Home Office and Scotland Yard experts, an official announcement said it had been determined that the explosives were of French manufacture.

A woman who spoke broken English had made a brief visit to the ladies' lavatory on the pretext of having to fix a run in her stocking. She was carrying a package.

The "heroine of London" set off the bomb was timed to explode at about eleven o'clock this morning. More than 100 persons have already been questioned. A number of clues have been found outside London, and it is proposed to carry the investigation to France.

DALTON BUDGET WINS LIBERAL APPROVAL; LABOUR COOL

Palestine Post Correspondent

LONDON, Wednesday. — Dr. Dalton's budget has somewhat improved relations between the Chancellor and his critics outside his own party, especially amongst the Liberals and other middle-of-the-roaders.

This is clear from today's "Times" and "Manchester Guardian" leaders, and will probably be reflected in the "Economist's" week-end comment.

Since the main issue between the Chancellor and this group of critics was the danger of inflation, its refusal to grant extensive tax relief and reduce the food subsidies, now costing £425 million annually, are not taken tragically, as it is understood that such reductions will probably follow the forthcoming publication of a revised up-to-date cost of living index.

The critics of luxury spending are satisfied by the increased tobacco tax which it is hoped will reduce the tobacco purchases from America, now totalling as much as Britain's entire exports to the U.S.A.

Labour Not Enthusiastic

By contrast, Labour opinion is not enthusiastic. The "Daily Herald" only points to the exemption of the low income groups from this, though welcome, does not meet the wide spread T.U. demand for a tax on overtime earnings often described as the biggest obstacle to higher productivity.

Next month's Labour Party conference at Margate will probably not see a repetition of last year's enthusiastic cheering of Dr. Dalton by the Left wing, but his position and the Cabinet has probably been strengthened by his refusal to consider toward those such as Stafford Cripps and Mr. Herbert Morrison, now forming a very strong team.

(Other Cable—Page 3)

TOBACCO FALLS ON MARKET

LONDON, Wednesday (UP). — Over £18,000,000 was knocked off the market value of Imperial Tobacco £1 ordinary shares following the Chancellor of the Exchequer's budget announcement, which is expected to have a marked effect on tobacco profits.

Left-wing Labour M.P.'s are reported to be planning a protest against Dr. Dalton's increased customs duties on tobacco which will operate against the poorer people.

Three Death Sentences In Hungary

BUDAPEST, Wednesday (Reuter) — The People's Court here today sentenced to death the retired Generals Lajos Dalnok Veres and Samdor Andros, and a third officer, for their part in the big conspiracy to overthrow the Hungarian Government and restore Admiral Horthy.

Istvan Szentmilkossy, for whom a milder sentence was requested "in view of his frank confession," was sentenced to hard labour for life.

Thousand Dead in Texas Blast

NEW YORK, Wednesday (R). — A death roll of 1,200 is feared from the explosion which rocked the Texas City today, starting fires and sending poison gas sweeping through the streets.

A New York Coast Guard report says between 2,000 and 8,500 persons were injured.

The disaster, which started with an explosion on a ship and spread to a chemical factory and oil tanks, was tonight described as one of the greatest in the history of the U.S.

Rescue workers trying to reach the dead are being hurled back by the roaring flames as 50 oil storage tanks blazed and buildings were enveloped in what the Police Chief described as a "holocaust."

Hours after the explosion the streets were jammed with thousands of people still dazed by the blast while about them masonry crashed and tall buildings were levelled.

Red Cross workers trained in disaster relief work were last night flying from Washington to Texas City, while emergency stocks of morphia and blood plasma were being rushed to the spot.

Blazing City

A clear picture of the disaster was still obscured tonight by conflicting reports from the blazing city where all telephone circuits had been shattered. But this is what has been established so far: Early today the 7,176-ton Liberty Ship "Grand Camp," said to have been taking on a cargo of ammonium nitrate fertilizer at Texas City docks, was discovered to be on fire. Efforts to control the fire failed, and while the ship was being towed out of the docks the first terrific explosion occurred. This set up a chain of explosions which spread from the ship until they reached the new million-dollar buildings of the Monsanto Chemical Company, which in turn exploded.

The plant was completely wrecked, reports said, and the "Grand Camp" is a total loss. One report said fragments of the ship were hurled for 25 kilometres.

New Explosions

Full details of the dead and injured will not be known for many hours, since hundreds of people were working on the dock at the time of the explosion. Reports from Galveston say new explosions are being touched off by the fires raging in the town. Rescue workers under police orders are pouring in and out of the city to prevent further loss of life. No direct contact has yet been made between the Red Cross and the strike ken city. Mr. Basil O'Connor of the American Red Cross has made 250,000 dollars immediately available for relief.

The Monsanto Chemical Company plant which was on fire as a result of the explosion was making a liquid used in synthetic rubber and plastics. While not as rapidly a petrol.

The Police said tonight the raging fires were nearing a large store of dynamite at waterfront warehouse.

Gandhi, Jinnah, Appeal

NEW DELHI, Wednesday (Reuter). — Mahatma Gandhi and the President of the Moslem League, Mohammed Ali Jinnah, last night issued a joint appeal on the initiative of the new Viceroy, Lord Mountbatten, declaring: "We deeply deplore the recent acts of lawlessness and violence that have brought utmost grief and disgrace on the fair name of India.

"We denounce for all time the use of force to achieve political ends, and we call upon all communities of India, whatever persuasion they may belong, not only to refrain from all acts of violence and disorder, but also to avoid, in speech and writing, any incitements to such acts."

No Appeal From Military Courts

Judgments and sentences passed by the Military Courts in Palestine or by the G.O.C. will henceforth not be subject to appeal and may not be questioned or challenged before any Court, according to an amendment of the Defence (Emergency) Regulations, 1945, published today in the Palestine Gazette.

A second amendment lays down that certain of the Prison Rules shall not henceforth apply in the case of death sentences passed by Military Courts. It also empowers the G.O.C. to issue directions relating to the time and place of executions, the custody of persons under sentence pending execution, and other matters arising out of such sentences, including the disposal and burial of the bodies.

Both amendments are retroactive and apply to sentences passed prior to 1947.

They were dated April 14 and came into effect yesterday although first published in the Palestine Gazette dated April 17.

1,600 MORE ARRIVE AT CYPRUS

By SHAHE GUEBENLIAN

NICOSIA, Wednesday. — The 16th batch of immigrants to be deported to Cyprus since last August arrived at Famagusta this morning on board the deportation ships Empire Comfort, Lifeguard, Rest and Shelter. The 1,600 refugees, made up of 848 men, 616 women and 136 children were disembarked without incident, and sent by lorry to the fourth Xylotymbou winter camp, which was recently built.

With the fifth camp nearing completion, the winter camps will eventually be able to hold 10,000 refugees.

The deportation ships returned immediately to Haifa for the 1,000 refugees still awaiting transhipment there.

Curfew Lasted 25 Hours

Eliahu, was seriously wounded in the head while standing on the balcony of his house in the Zichron Yosef Quarter, when shots were fired into the air by a military patrol at a group of young persons who were breaking the curfew, according to an official statement. He was removed to the Shaarei Zedek Hospital and immediately operated on. His condition last night was stated to be serious.

The boy's father said that he was crossing the balcony to a lavatory when he was hit.

Tel Aviv

There were no sounds of music from windows in Tel Aviv, as there had been during previous curfews.

The day was quiet, and no warning shots were fired by troops. Only a few armoured vehicles cruised in the streets and stopped pedestrians to check curfew passes.

The Acting Mayor, Mr. E. Perlson, and the Town Clerk, Mr. Y. Nedivi, were summoned this morning by the O.C. troops, who informed them that the curfew had been imposed following the execution of four Jews in Acre Prison.

The Magistrate, Mr. Zuckerman, toured police stations to (Continued on Page 2 Col. 1)

LATE Edition

THE PALESTINE POST

JERUSALEM
MONDAY, MAY 5, 1947

PRICE: 15 MILS
VOL.XXII. No. 6398

Column One
By David Courtney

SOCIAL progress creates prosperity, not the other way about. Last night the British coal-miners began the five-day week: five days out of seven are long enough for a man to dig away in the guts of the earth and breathe dust. There has been bitter criticism of the new measure from the Conservatives; and the Cabinet itself is a bit nervous about it. The coal output still shows no sign of rising to the 200 million tons set as this year's goal by the Government, and the warning of bigger fuel cuts next winter has not created an atmosphere likely to popularize the shorter working week. The Government's decision is therefore an act of courage and imagination, and Shinwell has done well to push it through. If the five-day week fails to reduce absenteeism and increase output, the Minister will get into very hot water and may not get out of it; but he has taken the risk and stands a fair chance of succeeding. Shinwell is a fighter and his weathering of the fuel crisis during the winter has added to his reputation in the Party. He is liked by the miners and well-supported by their Union: that is why Mr. Attlee decided against throwing him to the Opposition wolves at a time when the whole country, except his own miners, was ready enough to attribute to him everything from the cold grate in the home to the smokeless chimneys in the Midlands.

■

THE introduction of the five-day week for the miners is new evidence of the Government's renewed confidence in home matters. It is clear that the Unions are still solidly behind it; and in the industries already nationalized or about to be, the workers are just as solidly behind the Unions. There is still the risk that the Union Executives, up to their eyes in political work and too much inclined to regard themselves as a Department of Government, may lose intimate touch with the workers and provide further cause for "unofficial" strikes. But as long as the Government is far-seeing enough to concede, in the nationalized industries, such basic claims as the five-day week now introduced in the coal mines, the Unions will keep their hold on the workers and the Party on the Electorate.

■

THE output problem in the whole industrial field is still Britain's main preoccupation. She is still spending many more dollars than she can afford, and is already 100 million sterling ahead of estimated expenditure out of the American Loan. But nothing is to be gained by making tired workers still more tired or by keeping working hours at the point where it ultimately must reduce working capacity. What the British worker needs to increase output is an assurance that the Socialist schemes prated about by the Party will be carried into effect without compromise and that he, in the long run, will profit from them. The Government's decision to go ahead with the nationalization of steel, in spite of the terrific opposition of the industry itself, is sure to make a good impression on Labour as a whole. Steel represents the hard core of British industry and of the British Capitalist system; its nationalization will will be a greater triumph for Socialist principles than anything yet done by the Labour Government.

■

IT is pitiful that in foreign affairs the Government should ignore the Socialism it serves with real if cautious loyalty at home. The larger issues abroad seem only to perplex and frighten it; and in its perplexity and fear it leaves the smaller issues to take care of themselves. What, for example, is its policy in the matter of that peculiar element of Displaced Persons who remain homeless because they are at political loggerheads with the Governments of their respective countries? There are some eleven thousand Yugoslavs in Italy, who are to be moved today into Germany to swell the problems of the British Zone. Most of them are anti-Tito and some 900 of them are regarded by the Belgrade Government as former collaborationists who should be brought to trial. They represent considerable cells of Reaction and are nursed in their prejudices by the authorities set to watch over them. They and their like should be dispersed, and that quickly.

Jerusalem, May 5.

U.S. WARSHIPS CALLS AT LATTAKIA

DAMASCUS, Sunday. — An American warship, on a courtesy cruise in the Eastern Mediterranean, arrived at Lattakia during the week-end.

The cruiser fired a salvo of 21 guns when the Syrian Defense Minister and the Minister of the Interior visited the ship. Today, the American Captain was received by President Kowatly in Damascus.

LATIN-AMERICANS SEEK COMPROMISE
JEWS' ATTENDANCE AT U.N. STILL IN BALANCE

By RALPH HEINZEN, United Press Correspondent

FLUSHING MEADOW, Sunday. — A Latin-American compromise, that would be based on changing the wording of the American motion so as to instruct the Chairman, Mr. Lester Pearson, to call on the Jewish Agency to present its case before the First Committee (Political) instead of leaving the hearing to the discretion of the Committee and primarily its Chairman, is in the offing.

It is not known whether such a compromise would satisfy the Russians, as their demand went much further. They are solid behind the Polish motion that the Jewish Agency be given a vote-less voice and a seat in the General Assembly itself.

During the week-end interruption, unofficial polls showed that the Russian effort would be overwhelmingly defeated. The United States motion could find a majority, if there are not too many abstentions, and if the Latin American bloc does not secure a compromise. A compromise such as the Latin Americans seek, would almost certainly win a heavy majority.

(U.N. observers are also quoted by Reuters as forecasting a compromise plan to to give Jewry some voice in the General Assembly discussions.)

M. GROMYKO'S PLEA

FLUSHING MEADOW, Sunday. — The U.N. Assembly is meeting again tomorrow (Monday) to hear eight more speakers in the debate on the Polish motion to grant the Jewish Agency a hearing in the Assembly itself.

After Sir Carl Berendsen for New Zealand opened the debate on Saturday (reported yesterday), Dr. A. Federkiewicz (Poland) appealed to the Assembly to reverse the Steering Committee's decision against the proposal that the Jewish Agency be admitted to the Assembly. He pointed out that there were no differences in working procedure between the Assembly and its Political Committee and said that arguments for barring the Agency from the former were therefore unconvincing. Mere sympathy for the Jews was not enough, he said.

In opposing the Polish proposal, Mr. Warren Austin (United States) reiterated that non-Governmental bodies could not appear before the Assembly. Claimants, he said, should be patient. None of them would be denied his privileges and rights.

M. Gromyko (Soviet Russia) said that he could not understand why an invitation to the Jews should be thought to impair the dignity of the U.N. Assembly. So far they knew the Jewish case only partially and from biased sources.

It was true that they had no precedent to go by, but they were too young to be bound by precedents. The Jewish population of Palestine and also others might misunderstand failure to invite the Jewish Agency.

M. Gromyko also pointed out that the American resolution which had been adopted by the Steering Committee spoke only of the memoranda from the Jewish organizations being referred to the Political Committee. The resolution did not provide for the organizations themselves to appear, and he would support their personal appearance.

Chairman's Plan

Mr. Lester Pearson, the Canadian delegate who occupies the important position of chairman of the Political Committee, indicated that in that Committee's hearing he would try to eliminate debate on the substance of the Palestine issue, since its only function was the appointment of a fact-finding commission. He would not be bound by the declaration made in the Steering Committee by Dr. Aranha, President of the U.N. Assembly, that full debate would be permitted.

If Mr. Pearson carries out his intention, it means that even if the Jewish Agency is invited to attend the Committee it will not be free to present its case at any length.

(Palcor PTA & Reuter)

Senators Urge Commonwealth

WASHINGTON, Sunday. — Senator Robert Wagner and James Murray have telegraphed to President Truman and to Senator Austin urging them to use United States influence for securing large scale Jewish immigration into Palestine, and also for the removal of land-sales restrictions as an interim policy pending the U.N. decision.

They urged the United States to support in the U.N. Assembly a programme calling for the establishment of a free and democratic Jewish commonwealth in Palestine. They recalled that the Republican and Democratic parties as well as both Houses of Congress were on record in favour of such a Commonwealth and of free Jewish immigration into Palestine.

They also urged that the Jewish Agency be granted full representation in the Assembly deliberations:

A negative or even neutral attitude by the United States Government may seal the fate of the proposal and deprive the Jewish people of representation and a voice in the proceedings of such vital and historic importance to the Jewish future. Such negative or neutral action would be a harmful action and would shock the conscience of every fair person.

Congressman Emmanuel Celler has denounced the United States stand with regard to the Jewish Agency's demand for a seat, and has asked Mr. Marshall to state clearly American policy on Palestine.

(PTA & UP)

White Paper on "Greater Syria"

AMMAN, Sunday (ANA). — A 294-page White Paper on "Greater Syria" has been issued by the Trans-Jordan Government, outlining the history and developments of this question from the Crane Commission's plebiscite in 1919 until the present day.

The document quotes from correspondence exchanged between King Abdullah and leading Syrian statesmen and refers to negotiations which took place at several "Syrian" congresses held in the capitals of Arab countries, in European cities and at Arab League sessions.

The White Paper also stresses the "Zionist Danger in Palestine", and in conclusion outlines that Trans-Jordan's foreign policy was based on the unity of the "Syrian" countries within the framework of an Arab union, and Eastern collaboration in accordance with the aims of the U.N.

RUSSIA'S GRIP ON PERSIA SLIPPING

TEHERAN, Sunday (U.P.). — Almost everyone in Persia, including Government officials and industrialists, believe that Russia's hold on Persian politics is slipping, while only the Tudeh left-wing Party seems to be looking to Moscow for support.

Ghavam Es Sultaneh's Government is now openly punishing "traitors" who are alleged to be backed by Soviet Russia.

The American Ambassador, Mr. George Alden, stated here recently that the U.S. was considering to let Persia have 25,000,000 dollars worth of surplus army equipment, "presuming that Persia's use of these supplies will be toward the naintenance of internal security and the defence of the country against any foreign aggression".

20 Years for Czech Nazi Journalist

PRAGUE, Sunday (PTA). — Vladimir Breter, a journalist charged with editing publications supporting Nazism and incitement against Jews, and with founding the Czech anti-Semitic League, was today sentenced to 20 years' imprisonment by the Prague People's court.

The same sentence was pronounced on Gerard Guenel, an S.S. officer and Vice-Chief of the Central Jewish office in Prague, for participating in the registration of Jews.

Paul Rafaelson, a former inmate of Sozen labour camp, was sentenced to death and immediately hanged, having been found guilty of cruelties against Jewish fellow prisoners. He is the first Jewish criminal to be hanged for atrocities.

BRITAIN LIFTS BAN ON CUT DIAMONDS

LONDON, Sunday (Reuter). — According to the "Evening Standard", the British Government has decided to abolish immediately the ban on the importation of cut diamonds.

It is expected that cut diamond prices will be lowered as a result of this decision.

SENATORS DEMAND ROOSEVELT FILES

WASHINGTON, Sunday (UP). — The executors of the estate of the late President Roosevelt have been invited to a private conference with a Senate committee to discuss the surrender of certain Roosevelt papers on the Saudi-Arabian oil inquiry.

Senator Brewster said yesterday that the committee plans to meet the executors behind closed doors on Thursday, to find out whether they are prepared to give up certain documents now on file in the Roosevelt Memorial Library. He inferred that he may issue subpoenas for the records, which some Senators hope will throw some light on the Navy's wartime purchases of Saudi Arabian oil. The committee's actions are apparently aimed at by-passing President Truman, who has turned over photos relating to the inquiry, but said he could not grant the additional request to let investigators look through President Roosevelt's files.

NO URANIUM FOUND IN PALESTINE

Palestine Post Staff

The Geological Department of the Government of Palestine has denied rumours that uranium deposits have been discovered in Palestine.

Conflicting reports concerning the alleged discovery appeared in the press yesterday. "Haaretz" said that Government geologists were investigating possible radium deposits about 45 kilometres northeast of Akaba. The paper also stated that oil had been discovered in this area. Manganese salt was found there in 1938.

"Hamashkif" wrote that uranium deposits were found near the Gulf of Akaba.

RUSSIANS FAIL TO UNDERSTAND WEST

By GEORGE LICHTHEIM, Palestine Post Correspondent

LONDON, Sunday. — Fuller reports of the Stassen interview with Generalissimo Stalin were received here with interest, chiefly for the light they throw on last week's unofficial but authoritative disclosures regarding Mr. Bevin's conversation with Generalissimo Stalin on Anglo-Russian relations.

These disclosures which were prominently featured by the Paris "Herald Tribune," but ignored by the British press, except for the "Manchester Guardian," gave the impression that Generalissimo Stalin was badly informed on Western policies, an impression which deepened when, following their conversation, detailed discussions began between M. Vyshinsky and Sir Maurice Peterson, the British Ambassador to Moscow.

These quickly showed that the Kremlin was aiming at the conversion of the present Anglo-Soviet Treaty into a much more precise instrument of cooperation, including such amiable features as a mutual ban of "unfair" public criticism in the press and radio.

For this reason, it is considered interesting that Marshal Stalin should have laid stress in his talk with Mr. Stassen on the desirability of refraining from hostile criticism.

No doubt the Soviet view of the nature of American "Monopoly Capitalism" encourages the belief that such interference with the freedom of speech was easily practicable, if the right steps are taken in the proper quarters. The matter of course does not present a problem to Russia, but it can be said that the British negotiators were somewhat startled by M. Vyshinsky's naive assumption that the British Government is in a position to silence criticism of foreign governments.

Such requests, however cautiously phrased, do not only evoke unpleasant memories of certain German proposals during the Thirties which had helped to undermine Ribbentrop's popularity during his brief ambassadorship in London, but they also raise the question whether the Kremlin is really alive to the realities of the situation in the West.

Conquered Ruhr

Similar doubts were caused here by Premier Stalin's staggering suggestion to Mr. Bevin that Britain should try to overcome her coal crisis by treating the Ruhr as a conquered province, forcing the Germans to go without coal and also depriving other Western countries of their rightful share.

These and other suggestions made by Stalin, as well as his clumsy attempt to convince Mr. Stassen that Hitler's Germany and America had come to blows although their social systems were identical — by way of proof that identity or difference in this respect need not determine international relations — are finally beginning to convince observers here of what has long been suspected; namely, that the Soviet Leader is both badly informed of Western conditions and unable to form an accurate mental picture of the outside world.

By contrast, some of his colleagues seem better informed only in proportion to their lesser readiness to seek ways of understanding with the West.

French Crisis
COMMUNISTS REPLACED

PARIS, Sunday (Reuter). — The Communist Ministers ceased to be members of the French Government tonight, following a Cabinet meeting which decided to ask the President of the Republic, M. Vincent Auriol, to replace them as a result of their voting against the Government in the National Assembly earlier today.

This followed a meeting of the Executive Committee of the Socialist Party, which decided to support the immediate exclusion from the Government of the Communist Ministers.

An impassioned speech by the veteran Socialist leader, M. Leon Blum, in favour of this course, helped to sway the decision.

The Ministries held by Communists are — National Defence, Labour, Reconstruction, and the Vice-Presidency, so far occupied by M. Maurice Thorez.

Although M. Ramadier received a substantial majority in the confidence vote — 360 in favour to 186 against with 62 abstentions — he declared that he would not accept the presence of Ministers in the Government who did not support it.

ATTLEE LOOKS TO SUNSIHNE

LONDON, Sunday (Reuter). — The Prime Minister, Mr. Attlee, speaking at a May Day celebration in London tonight, sent a "message of goodwill" to the peoples of all the lands, when he said: "It is our belief that their happiness and prosperity are also our concern.

"We are still in the difficult transition period of springtime, coming out of darkness into light," Mr. Attlee declared. "We have the promise of a good summer, but the seeds which have been sown are only beginning to spring up, and there will be much hard work before they are reaped. Like the English spring, there is sunshine, warmth and chill."

Reviewing his Government's programme, the Prime Minister said: "We are engaged in making great changes in the social and economic structure of this country. We are making them without disturbance and with due regard to the rights of the individual and the community. The nationalization of the basic industries, social insurance schemes, a just division of wealth are only means to an end.

"Many of the attributes of freedom were formerly the prerogatives of the privileged few, though spiritual freedom was possible for all. There is great danger of the people being contented with material advance alone."

Appealing to all "men and women of goodwill" to realize the part they were playing in British national life, Mr. Attlee concluded with these words: "I should like the message of May Day to all in our movement and to the nation at large to be — work, for the day is dawning."

Glasgow Dock Strike Over

GLASGOW, Sunday (Reuter). — Dockers here by an overwhelming majority today decided to end the six week old strike over the dismissal of "redundant" men and returned to work. This was made known this afternoon when the result of a week-end ballot was published.

Just over half of the 3,800 men affected participated in the vote.

The decision to hold the week-end vote was made by the Union Executive, following last Saturday's rejection of the proposal to end the dispute and return to work.

Last week, 9,800 London stevedores, lightermen and other dock workers struck in sympathy with the Glasgow men, but on Friday they began to return, and the docks are expected to be fully at work again tomorrow. The men are putting in extra-hours to make up for lost time.

P.O.W.'S LEAVE EGYPT

CAIRO, Sunday. — The British military authorities have started the evacuation of prisoners of war from camps in Egypt.

The operation will be concluded by the end of the year, when the 82,000 P.o.W.'s will have been evacuated at the rate of 8,000 a month. Those who are still enthusiastic Nazis and Fascists, numbering 5,000, will be the last to be removed.

15 DEAD; 251 ESCAPE IN ACRE PRISON BREAK

PALESTINE POST BUREAU

HAIFA, Sunday.— Leaving a trail of land mines behind them on the Haifa-Acre road, a large party of terrorists this afternoon attacked the Acre Prison and freed 251 prisoners — 131 Arabs and 120 Jews.

The glass-studded domed roof of Acre's old Turkish bath-house

At least 15 men, prisoners and attackers, are known to have been killed, and about 23 others wounded, among them service personnel and civilians. Nineteen of the prisoners have been recaptured.

In the confusion of diversionary attacks with automatic fire at the prison guards, on the police station nearby and in other parts of Acre town, one of the walls was blown in. There were 400 Arab and 120 Jewish prisoners in the gaol.

The attackers arrived shortly after four o'clock in a large number of lorries, preceded by a uniformed party in two jeeps. It is reported from an Arab source that the men wore khaki and some were in blue shirts. There were several women reportedly among the party.

A few minutes after the exchange of fire with the guards, at 4.25, a bomb was thrown at one of the prison walls from the roof of the Basha Bath House, and the prisoners rushed out. Detonations were heard throughout Haifa Bay area, Haifa town, and on Mt. Carmel.

It is thought that most of the prisoners got away in the lorries and cars which were apparently waiting on the main road and the terrorists fought it out with the military and police, giving cover to the prisoners until they were able to escape themselves. From 4.30 until late in the evening there were intermittent explosions, apparently from landmines which were being detonated by the authorities.

Bomb in Playground

A disaster was averted when a large bomb was discovered near the Sports Ground in Kiriat Bialik, where many schoolchildren were playing. It was found by one of the electricians of the Ahava School, who brought police to remove it.

Electricity was cut off from the Haifa Bay area and Naharia after a military car had crashed into a pylon, and the water supply, wherever it was electrically pumped, was also interrupted. The electricity was restored at 9 o'clock.

There was no telephone connection with Acre for several hours.

Two No. 14 buses which were on their way to Naharia at 4.30 were unable to continue because the bridge over the Naaman River on the Haifa-Acre road had been blown up. Children among the passengers were brought to Kiriat Haim by military escort, while the adults had to remain in the buses all night.

Refusing to hand over his truck to the terrorists, a driver, Abdul Hamid Baghdadi, was severely injured.

About the same time as the prison break took place, five British soldiers were slightly injured when the truck in which they were travelling blew up on a land mine on the Haifa-Acre road about a kilometre from Kiriat Haim.

In August, 1946, when special security measures were taken in Acre Prison, Arab inhabitants in nearby houses were warned against looking out of their windows or walking on their rooftops, from which it was possible to look into the prison court.

One of the Arab prisoners was Fakri Maraka, a rebel leader sentenced to life imprisonment during the 1936-39 disturbances. He took a leading part in the recent Arab hunger strike in Acre Prison.

COEUR DE LION'S FORTRESS

The Citadel in Acre, now used as one of Palestine's two Central Prisons, was rebuilt by Abdallah Pasha about 1820 The fortress was used by Sir Sidney Smith in the defence of Acre against Napoleon in 1799. Some of the stones used in the construction are said to have been taken from the Crusader fortress at Athlit.

Underneath the Citadel is the crypt of the residence of the Knights of St. John, built in the 12th century, and recaptured by Richard Coeur de Lion in 1193 from Saladin.

BATH-HOUSE USED AS BASE

ACRE, Sunday. — In today's prison break four Jewish and one Arab prisoners were killed, while 10 of the attackers are also dead.

Eight Jewish prisoners, six of them injured, have been recaptured, while 11 of the escaping Arabs have also been rounded up, two of whom are hurt. Fifteen other terrorists were captured, seven of them injured. One of the dead terrorists was found to be wearing the uniform of a Captain of the Royal Engineers.

A tight cordon was immediately thrown round the town and search parties quickly rounded up 19 of the prisoners. Military and police reinforcements were rushed here and all exits of the town blocked.

Intercepting a jeep and a 15-cwt truck north of Haifa after the attack, troops found two dead men and ten other Jews, three of them injured, in the vehicles.

A number of criminal lunatics were slightly injured when grenades were thrown as part of a diversionary attack into their section of the prison.

A section of the attackers parked near the Hammam el Basha, the Turkish baths, close to the prison. It appears that some of the men then climbed to the roof of the baths and from there reached the wall of the prison, where they placed bombs. Explosions then occurred near the prison, and the men in the two vehicles opened fire near the main gate to create a diversion. One British constable was hit in the leg and five Arab civilians, caught in the cross-fire, were also hurt.

Escape Through Hole

Police and soldiers immediately took up strategic positions, but in the first confusion a large number of prisoners streamed through the gap in the wall. The attack took place at a time when the prisoners were at exercise in the yard. Three unexploded bombs were later picked up in front of the prison.

In the operations following the attack and escape one Bren gun, two Sten guns, a tommy-gun as well as some bombs and ammunition were found. A party of paratroopers of the 1st Parachute Bn. returning from bathing near Acre, were fired upon and, replying, killed five men. There were no British casualties.

About five o'clock a 15-cwt. truck drove up to 2nd Parachute Bn. camp at Naharia and six bombs were hurled into the compound from the vehicle. There were no casualties.

Prisoners Give Up

LEAVENWORTH, (Kansas), Sunday (Reuter). — The commander of the military prison here reported last night that the "white prisoners rioting" at the U.S. Army Disciplinary Barracks here capitulated after 6 hours and were being removed in small groups to the lower floor.

They were instructed to discard their clothing first.

SICILIAN RIOTERS ARRESTED

ROME, Sunday (Reuter). — After a violent gun battle, police yesterday captured 22 men believed to be responsible for the Sicilian May Day incidents, it was reported from Palermo.

They were discovered hiding in an isolated farm. A number of machine guns, rifles and ammunition was also found. So far, 120 persons have been detained by the Sicilian police.

"MOTHERS' DAY"

Palestine Post Correspondent

BAGHDAD, Sunday. — On the occasion of "Mothers Day" (the first Sunday in May), the Queen Mother of Iraq, broadcasting over Baghdad radio, stressed the importance of the day and said the position of the mother was a "cornerstone in the structure of social life."

She promised all possible help to make the day a success.

Lebanese Elections

BEIRUT, Sunday.— Abdul Hamid Karami, a former Prime Minister, has announced that he will take part in the Lebanese elections to be held this month.

It is recalled that his supporters were involved in a clash in Tripoli on March 5, following the return to his home town of Fawzi el Kaukji, a member of Karami's party.

TREBITSCH LINCOLN REPORTED ALIVE

COLOMBO, Sunday (Reuter).— Trebitsch Lincoln, a former British M.P. suspected of having been a German spy during the first world war, and whose death in Shanghai was reported by the Japanese in 1943, is still alive, according to a report in the "Times of Ceylon" today.

The report said that a local journalist had received a letter from Lincoln, dated March, 1947, with a Bengal postmark. "You might be glad to hear that I am not dead," the letter said.

The journalist believes that Lincoln, who after World War I, turned Buddhist, is living in a monastery in Tibet. Born in Hungary in 1879, of Jewish parents, Lincoln, who had been described as "one of the strangest characters in modern times" became a naturalized British subject in 1910 and was elected Liberal M.P.

During the 1914 war, he was suspected of being a German spy. In 1916, he was sentenced to three years imprisonment on a forgery charge and later went to America. In 1918, he lost his British citizenship.

TRUMAN AID PLAN

WASHINGTON, Sunday (UP). — The House Rules Committee decided last night by a narrow margin to send the 400 million dollar Greek and Turkish Aid Bill to the House floor tomorrow with debate limitations which may permit final action by Thursday.

CYPRIOT GREEKS ELECT ARCHBISHOP

By SHAHE GUEBENLIAN, Palestine Post Cable

NICOSIA, Sunday. — The police were on the alert today, when the entire adult Greek population of Cyprus, numbering well over 100,000, went to the polls for the first time since 1933, to elect 1,000 representatives as the first step in the election of an Archbishop and Ethnarch for the Autocephalous Church of Cyprus, left vacant since the 1933 disturbances, as the British Government had not since then permitted new elections.

Today's electorate is sharply divided into leftist and rightist camps, and minor clashes have been reported from villages.

CONSCRIPTION FOR EGYPT

CAIRO, Sunday (ANA). — According to press reports, the Egyptian Government proposes to ask foreign—including American — military, naval and air experts to train the Egyptian forces, now that the British military mission has been liquidated.

Conscription which will provide the country with 500,000 troops within 10 years is to be introduced in Egypt. New defence taxes are to be imposed, and the Government is shortly going to set up war industries.

ANGLO-EGYPTIAN FINANCE TALKS

CAIRO, Sunday (ANA).— According to the Cairo weekly "Akhbar el Yom", agreement has been reached between Britain and Egypt for a resumption of the Sterling balances talks.

The negotiations will take place in London in June, and the Egyptian delegation will include the Finance Minister, Mahmoud Bey el-Darwish, the Under-Secretary of Finance, and a representative of the Bank of Egypt.

THE PALESTINE POST

LATE Edition

JERUSALEM
Wednesday, July 9, 1947

PRICE 20 MILS
VOL. XXII. No. 6453

Column One
By David Courtney

IT is not often, in these days, that a great cause is raised above the squalor of disputatious ambition and petty rivalries, to the level of its own virtue. That was done yesterday by Dr Chaim Weizmann. His was the simplification of the cause: the truth and the wisdom of it; and the deep cognizance of its promise. He said in telling effect: "We Jews are like any other people in our hopes and our needs; but not a bit like other people in the frustration of our hopes and the withholding of our needs. We need a home and our own undisputed latchkey just as any other men of flesh and blood need a home and a latch-key: in fact, we have been homeless for so long that most of us have perished; the survivors must be got into a home of their own quickly. quickly — time is of the essence; speed, only speed can save the lives of most of my people. One saw behind the simple, improvised and often exquisitely-chosen words of Dr Weizmann, the miserable trail of persecution and periodic doom that winds away from the beginning of this era, through dispersal and ghetto, racialism and pogrom, gas chamber and the bitter silence of multitudinous death, to wretched little ships in a remote Mediterranean harbour and the last desperate, heart-sickening ride to the land of the Balfour Declaration, the White Paper, the misapprehensions of Mr Bevin and now, one last hope, the majestic judgment of the United Nations.

DR WEIZMANN disclaimed the authority of the historian. He could not disclaim the authority of a statesman who has lived intimately the recent history of his people and taken primary part in the weaving of its threads among the threads of British history. His easy, sometimes careless and untidy, obiter dicta from the Past, restored the atmosphere of a generous and rational Liberalism, which seems to have gone, to make way for Mr. Molotov's suspicions, Mr Truman's doctrine and the peculiar insensibilities of Mr Bevin. He embodied the ghosts — and the pledges — of great men who were wise in their day and whose wisdom, it can be said, stands up exceedingly well to the Memorandum on the Administration of Palestine under the Mandate.

THIS elder statesman's moving expression of gratitude to the British Nation of that day was the measure of his accusation against the British Government of this and of the calamitous White Paper; and his grounds for hope: the British Nation has not changed except from the added weight of its burdens; the change is a matter of Government, which seems to have reached a point where it devises in perplexity and rules in confusion. The historical analysis potently submitted by Dr. Weizmann was free from the bogey of Soviet Russia. Russia was not present as the Balfour Declaration and nowhere in the background. Today, it is terrifyingly close; just over the border; deep within Mr. Bevin's calculations. It has become the exigency by which pledges are broken and people denied their rights, even to the right of a man to live equal among other men and to the equal among other men, in the comfort of happy issue upon the soil of his fathers and in the security of his historic home.

DR Weizmann said that he may not again appear before a Committee of Inquiry, and besides, in the authority of this present Committee is the prospect of a final decision and the fulfilment of a responsibility which weighs upon the conscience of every civilized and democratic nation. Not because he proves old but because of that conscience, one hopes that this, indeed, is the last occasion on which this great and good man will be called upon to speak for pity and for justice in the name of men and women and little children, who have neither peace nor quiet nor any equal rights among their fellow men. Not because he grows old, but because there is no time to waste, one realizes, that this should be the last Commission before which Dr. Weizmann is asked to appear. He has served his people well and he has served well the conscience of the whole world; and now the time has come to pay tribute to him and to his people by the performance of pledge and the fulfilment of justice. Britain has failed. Let the world not fail in this human and historic problem: its own future is no less than the future of the Jews is bound up in the act of retribution and mercy which, yesterday, it was charged in gentle and forgiving terms to perform. The opportunity is great and the good that may come out of it greater; and the end will be justice.

Jerusalem, July 9.

After Midnight

TWENTY-NINE people were reported killed and about 160 injured up to mid-day in Calcutta yesterday as armed marauders roved the city for the second successive day.

DR. WEIZMANN URGES UNSCOP TO PRESS FOR PARTITION

Palestine Post Staff

Free from the fetters of office, Dr. Chaim Weizmann, for nearly 25 years President of the Zionist Organization, which was later to form part of the Jewish Agency of which he is the architect, yesterday morning gave evidence before the United Nations Special Committee on Palestine, with drops of distilled wisdom and items of personal experience from a long record as negotiator, draftsman and recipient of the Balfour Declaration.

Towards the end of his address, Dr. Weizmann came out firmly for Partition as the solution of the Palestine dilemma — an act of surgery to which he had been driven to resort, though he was "not a cruel mother" who liked "cutting her baby into two."

In support of this solution, Dr. Weizmann read a personal letter he had recently received from Field Marshal Smuts, who had also hoped Palestine might remain undivided, but who now propounded Partition.

The letter from the Prime Minister of the Union of South Africa was but one of the striking features in his statement. It contained, besides, a number of little-known documents, notably the message in 1917 from the Foreign Office to the British Ambassador in Russia, announcing the Declaration to "re-establish the Jewish State in Palestine," and the letter which General Bols, head of the Occupied Enemy Territory Administration in Palestine, sent in 1919 to General Allenby, the Commander-in-Chief, outlining financial and other measures for the swift beginning of Jewish mass immigration.

Dr. Weizmann Before UNSCOP

Because of difficulty, owing to imperfect eye-sight, in following his prepared notes, there were many spontaneous and welcome additions to Dr. Weizmann's own text, and both Delegates and public made no effort to conceal their pleasure at his asides, as he "ad-libbed," always adding anecdotal point to the formal phrase, delivered with conversational ease and in a resonant voice.

Shortly after 10 o'clock, many in the audience received the news of the announcement that the three pending death sentences had just been confirmed. The shadow of death fell to coincide, though the speaker could not be aware of it, with his tragic denunciation of terrorism, out of which he plainly indicated a better way than the scaffold.

The sounds of blasting for a foundation nearby came at 11 o'clock, and there were many in the packed auditorium who wondered whether the interruption of seconds — it was not more — was not due to something more sinister than builders' explosions.

OBITER DICTA

Dr. Weizmann yesterday declared that one should not try to be a prophet in this country, *There is great competition.*

In his introductory remarks to the Committee he said he believed *he understood the mind of the British Government—at least I have been trying to do so the whole of my life.*

What is a Jew? He is a man who has to offer a long explanation of his existence and is therefore always suspect.

Why Palestine?—Blame Moses who acted obviously on Divine inspiration.

He could have brought us to the United States, and then we would have had the Mississippi instead of the Jordan but he chose to stop here.

Of Gromyko's speech at U.N. — "It could have been made by a Zionist. I am sure he is not a Zionist and would be offended if called one."

On the Palestine Administration:—"These Jews are troublesome and never take 'no' for an answer. If you throw them out through the door they come back through the window."

About the White Paper:— *"Appeasement only brings Dead Sea Fruit."*

The Syrian Prime Minister, Jamil Mardam Bey, belongs to the category of people who declare, *We are friends, but don't salute me in Piccadilly. Nobody must know that we know each other.*

Partition is a la mode. In India — you can do it with a big knife, here it has to be done with a microscope.

Partitioned Palestine must be big enough, must not be just "standing room only."

About previous Commissions, *You can almost cover the surface of Palestine with excellent reports.*

Of Arab discrimination — It is only when an Arab is very ill that he calls in a Jewish doctor to operate, and I am thankful to say that the operation is usually very successful.

About possible contradictions in British promises:—
There are cases when one Government Department does not know what the other is doing; that even happens in the Zionist Organization, which is not yet a Government.

'PEEL AREA' PLUS NEGEV

Palestine Post Reporter

Dr. Weizmann's plea for partition came at the conclusion of his evidence. He urged UNSCOP to recommend a solution of the Palestine problem based on finality, justice and equality, and offered Partition — the "Peel Area" plus the Negev — as meeting these requirements.

As he had been associated with the authorities who issued the Balfour Declaration, he said, he felt he was "somewhat competent" to speak of its meaning, which was a matter of heart-searching and controversy. Even now, although he held no office, he added, he believed he knew, more or less, what the Jewish people thought.

"Unpleasant Intermezzo"

Dr. Weizmann expressed gratitude to Britain for having inaugurated the Mandate, and pointed out that had it not been for the conquest and rule of Palestine by the British, there would now have been a thriving community here. He termed the deterioration of relations between the Jews and Great Britain, which he, with a great many Jews, deplored, "a temporary thing which in the light of historical perspective is rather an unpleasant intermezzo."

Dr. Weizmann reviewed the birth and history of the Mandate until the White Paper of 1939, which was branded by the League of Nations' Permanent Mandates Commission as incompatible with the Mandate.

"I may be permitted," he continued, "to say, for lack of a better parliamentary expression, that a great deal of nonsense is spoken about it, and perhaps here is the time and place to put it right."

One of the two main purposes of the Balfour Declaration, he said, was idealistic, to give restitution to the Jews for the contribution they had made to civilization for thousands of years. Mr. Lloyd George had told him at the time,

You talk to me about Palestine. This is the only geography I know, and I am acquainted with it almost better than with the geography of the present front.

A second motive was utilitarian, although not in a purely materialistic sense, and was directed at winning the sympathy of U.S. Jewry for Britain, which was at war with Germany.

"I may be forgiven for having dwelt on this," Dr. Weizmann said, "but I think now is the time. I am advanced in years and may not have the opportunity of clearing it up again, so I am taking the opportunity now of submitting it to you for what it may be worth."

He referred to the abnormal positions of the Jews in the world due to their common homelessness.

"There are groups of Jews who have comfortable homes, but as a collectivity they are homeless. They are and they are not. They are a people and they lack the props of a people. They are a disembodied ghost... if you ask, what is a Jews?—he is a man who has to offer a long explanation, such a man is always suspect. From suspicion there is only one step to hatred."

Dr. Weizmann explained why the Jews had returned to Palestine instead of choosing another country, and recalled that efforts to establish Jewish colonies in the Argentine had not been successful. When he travelled from Tel Aviv to Jerusalem in 1918, he said, Allenby had remarked,

"I thought you were a reasonable fellow. Do you really think anybody can come and settle this country?"

His reply had been,

"Well, General, let us wait 20 years, and perhaps we will meet again and rediscuss the subject."

"We did meet," he continued, "and we did re-discuss the subject, and he did change his mind, and he did announce it publicly...."

The rocks and marshes and sands of Palestine became a precious possession into which we pour our sweat and blood and effort and ingenuity to make it what it is,

Dr. Weizmann repeated his warning to the Anglo-American Commission that time was of the essence, that to the Jewish people Palestine was a question of survival which brooked no delay. He had never believed that Palestine could be built with Jeremiahs, he continued, but briefly stressed the sombre position of the Jews today. He pointed out that in other countries the Jews were accused of "coming into the second floor of the building" after the foundation had been laid, that they were therefore branded as parasites.

"Given a Chance."

"Here in Palestine there are marshes and we drained them, sands and we planted them, there were no houses and we built them. It was ridden with disease and we cleared them... This gives us a certain amount of pride. Given a dog's chance we can do as well as anybody else. We did the best with our chance."

Comparing Jewish settlement in Palestine with imperial colonization, Dr. Weizmann pointed out that it was even admitted by the Palestine Administration, "which cannot be suspected of very much bias in favour of our work," that others had benefited by the work of the Jews. He rejected the contention of the Government's memorandum to the Committee that the Jews should have moved more slowly.

"We are driven by all the furies of the world," he said. *"We cannot afford to be slow. Slowing down means destruction to us."*

He recalled the origin of the phrase "National Home," a conception which succeeded the idea of "chartered companies."

The Jewish Agency had been, while carrying out its work, caught between the anvil and the hammer. The Government protested that it was going too fast, the Jews that it was too slow. There was a vicious circle; in order to create absorptive capacity ("which does not grow on trees") governmental power was needed; in order to have a government it was necessary to have immigration on a scale only a government could handle.

The 1939 White Paper, which nullified the Mandate, he continued, had two fatal effects. It convinced the Arabs that with very little violence they could get what they wanted and more, and thus spoiled Arab-Jewish relations. Too, the White Paper had released certain phenomena in Jewish life which were un-Jewish, contrary to Jewish ethics and tradition.

"I hide my head in shame when I have to speak of it here," Dr. Weizmann said of terrorism, "I hope international action will clear out this disease."

The Mandate was born of hope, the White Paper of fear. The British paid for appeasement with a devastating war, and the Jews paid for it in the form of the White Paper. Appeasement brought only Dead Sea fruit.

Dr. Weizmann denied that the Balfour Declaration had been given "behind the backs of the Arabs." Sir Mark Sykes had reported every step of the negotiations to King Hussein. In 1918, Dr. Weizmann came to Palestine by way of Egypt, where he met with Arab leaders, and later became friends with Emir Feisal, whom he had helped him to negotiate a treaty with France through Leon Blum.

"Why, if you could come to Trans-Jordan, we could probably do the same thing here (as in Palestine)."

Jamil Mardam Bey, he added, was another of his early acquaintances, and Dr. Weizmann had helped him to negotiate a treaty with France through Leon Blum.

"There were many more examples. There was never a year when an attempt was not made to come to an agreement with the Arabs. The Mufti is one of the men who bears a heavy responsibility in that he has never allowed these relations to come to anything... Jews and Arabs seem to be working in harmony until something steps in and breaks it up... Devils are active in Palestine quite often. These attempts will not stop until we begin to understand one another. One of the most important prerequisites is to establish a definite, clear and equal status between the Arabs and the Jews."

He pointed out that the Feisal-Weizmann agreement contained a post-script saying that Feisal would carry it out if and when he obtained his demands, namely independence for the Arab countries.

Federalism Not Final

Asked concerning his views on a federal state, Dr. Weizmann replied that he had arrived at "the conclusion that Partition was the best solution by a process of exclusion. Its

DOCUMENTS REVEALED

A letter from Field Marshal Smuts to Dr. Chaim Weizmann advocating Partition was read by him to the U.N. Committee in Jerusalem yesterday. It was one of three documents, never before published, which Dr. Weizmann revealed in the course of his statement. The other two dated back thirty years.

One was a letter to General Allenby from General Louis Bols, dated December 21, 1919, when the writer was military administrator in Palestine, and the other, a telegram sent by the British Government in 1917 to Sir George Buchanan, who was then British Ambassador to Russia. This telegram sent for the information of the Russian-Jewish community read:

The British Government has issued an official declaration regarding the re-establishment of a Jewish State in Palestine.

General Bols' letter, which Dr. Weizmann personally carried from Palestine to Allenby who was then in London, read:—

The country is in need of development quickly in order to make the people content. At present we are suffering from famine and the people must be made to budget balance.

The moment the Mandate is given we should be ready to produce a big loan, part of which should be absorbed by inhabitants.

I want Sir Herbert Samuel here for advice on this matter, and I want a much bigger financial adviser than you have been able to send us as yet. With such a loan, say 10 to 20 millions, I feel certain I can develop the country quickly and make it pay and gradually the population should increase from the present 900,000 to 2½ million.

There is plenty of room for this. The Jordan Valley should hold a million instead of the present 1,000.

But we must have water. The northern and eastern frontiers must be arranged to ensure control of the Litani and the Jordan.

These matters are of no use to our northern and eastern neighbours and they are essential to us.

F.M. Smuts' Letter

The letter from Field Marshal Smuts is dated Capetown, May 29, and Dr. Weizmann spoke of the writer as one of the authors of the Balfour Declaration. It read:—

I can imagine your anguish in a world which was so full of hope, and today has nothing but despair to show for itself.

We cannot undo the past, and can only try to find a better way to the future. As I told you in London last year I see now, as this sad stage, no escape except by way of Partition. I was long for an undivided Palestine, but after all these failures and missed opportunities I see no other way out of the present impasse.

Only yesterday, speaking in our Parliament, I expressed myself publicly in favour of this solution—if solution it is. Palestine never was undivided in the great past, and perhaps a fair share of it for Jewry may once more be the nucleus of a National Home and a Holy Land. Now that a UNO Commission has been appointed to assemble the facts for their recommendations my expression of opinion, as one of the original authors of the Balfour Declaration, may carry some weight with the Commission. At any rate it is something concrete and definite, and not another and further postponement of a decision which can brook no further delay.

It must be a heartbreaking misery for you to live amid all that scene of frustration and suffering—of lawlessness and counter-lawlessness. You who have laboured so hard and so long to enter upon the Promise....

I blame no one, I praise no one. I only pray that the Great Mercy will once more come, and wash out even the memory of these years....

Ever Yours affectionately
(Signed) JAN SMUTS

FEDERALISM NOT FINAL

Repeating some of the questions he had put to Mr. Ben Gurion on the previous day, the Chairman asked Dr. Weizmann whether he thought "that the reservation concerning the rights of the inhabitants might make the Mandate unworkable."

Dr. Weizmann replied that he did not think so, unless one wanted to read that meaning into it. All were agreed that the Arabs had benefited economically, materially, morally. Politically- they never had a position in Palestine.

Chairman: Do you believe that force should have been used against Palestine?

Dr. Weizmann: If the Mandatory had proceeded with firmness from the beginning, there would have been no need for force. As I indicated, the Arabs were quite ready to have us come to Palestine. The moment they saw vacillation they made the position of the Mandatory difficult.

Chairman: Did not Feisal in his agreement with you make a condition that the promise of independence to the Arabs must be carried out?

Weizmann: These promises were not carried out at the time, but now, the Arabs have all the independence they claim under Feisal.

Federalism Not Final

Asked concerning his views on a federal state, Dr. Weizmann replied that he had arrived at "the conclusion that Partition was the best solution by a process of exclusion. Its

advantage was that it would be final and definite, and leave no room for differences. A federal state would mean a third party again, in another form. Even under Partition there would be many common interests; but it would be better to be separated politically, and to leave governmental cooperation to a process of evolution."

Replying to the Indian delegate, Sir Abdur Rahman, who feared that both parties might later try to break the line of demarcation, Dr. Weizmann said that it would be foolish to think that passions would die out in a day. But if the solution was proclaimed by the United Nations, on the whole it would be kept. Partition had come in India at the end of a long road of suffering, and still people were being killed every day, he continued.

Of course it is a drop in the ocean in India, but a drop of blood goes a long way. Give us time and benevolence, the opportunity of making more friends with the Arabs and the neighbouring countries, and I think that in time it will be all right.

To the charge of Jewish discrimination against Arab labour, Dr. Weizmann explained at some length how absorptive capacity had been created in Palestine, in the first place by the pennies of Jews abroad who wished to help on the re-

G.O.C. CONFIRMS ACRE DEATH SENTENCES

Confirmation of the three death sentences passed by the Jerusalem Military Court on June 16 in the Acre Prison break trial was announced in an official communique at 10.30 yesterday morning.

The communique was issued by the Secretariat, while across the street in the Y.M.C.A. Dr. Weizmann was giving his evidence before the United Nations Committee.

The High Commissioner still has the right to commute the sentences, but his approval is not required for their execution, which may under the Regulations passed last April, be carried out at any moment, now that they have been confirmed by the General Officer Commanding.

The Communique, No. 122, reads as follows:—

ACRE TRIAL AND SENTENCES

On 16th June 1947, Meir Ben Kaddourie Nakar, Yaacob Ben Yoseph Weiss, Avshalom Eliezer Habib, Amnon Ben Nuriel Michaelov, and Nachman Ben Reuven Ziterbaum were tried by the Military Court, Jerusalem, on charges in connection with the attack on Acre Prison on 4th May 1947: (1) Discharging Firearms at H.M. Forces and the Palestine Police; (2) Carrying Firearms, ammunition and grenades; (3) Unlawfully wearing uniform; (4) Depositing bombs with intent to cause damage to Acre Prison.

All the accused were found Guilty of all the charges with the exception of Habib who was found Guilty of the first three charges but not Guilty of depositing bombs.

Nakar, Weiss and Habib were sentenced to death. Michaelov and Ziterbaum were sentenced to fifteen years imprisonment and to be detained during His Excellency's the High Commissioner's pleasure.

The findings and sentences have been confirmed by the General Officer Commanding.

It will be remembered that as a result of the attack on Acre Prison on 4th May 1947, 251 convicted criminals were freed and loosed on to the community.

An appeal for a stay of execution is being made to the G.O.C. by Mr. Asher Levitzky, the Jerusalem lawyer, on behalf of the three condemned men, as well as on behalf of Miss Edith Weiss, Yaacob Weiss' sister, who arrived from Czechoslovakia during the weekend.

Speaking in Jerusalem yesterday, she said that her brother, while an officer in the Czechoslovak underground, smuggled anti-typhoid serum to a Jewish camp where a typhoid epidemic had broken out.

The Chief Rabbinate and Mr. I. Rokach, the Mayor of Tel Aviv, are also lodging appeals to the High Commissioner.

Mr. Levitzky's application to the G.O.C. has been made in order to enable "the High Commissioner to have time and opportunity to study all applications which have been, or may be, put forward for clemency."

New C.-in-C. in Fayid

Gen: Sir John Tredinnick Crocker, K.C.B., K.B.E., D.S.O., M.C., has arrived at G.H.Q. Fayid to take up his appointment as Commander-in-Chief, M.E.L.F., in succession to Gen. Sir Miles Dempsey.

Gen. Crocker who is 51, served as a private for some time during the first world war, receiving a temporary commission in the Machine Gun Corps in 1917.

Demobilized in 1919, he returned to the colours about a year later and accepted a regular commission with the Middlesex Regiment. Since joining the Tank Corps in 1923, Gen. Crocker has been closely identified with the development of British armoured formations and with the training of tank officers.

Promoted to the rank of Major-General, he was entrusted with the formation and training of a new armoured division in September, 1940.

Twelve Answers 3 MORE TO GO TO PARIS

LONDON, Tuesday. — Three more countries have notified of their acceptance of the Anglo-French invitation to the "Save Europe Talks," which open in Paris on Saturday, bringing the total to 12. They are Austria, Iceland and Switzerland.

Czechoslovakia still remains the only East European country which has so far accepted the invitation. There is, however, no confirmation of the Soviet reports that Rumania, Poland and Yugoslavia would attend the talks. Indeed, the news agency quotes a Bucharest dispatch which, it says, "provides strong new evidence of a diplomatic tug of war is in progress over the Soviet satellites in Eastern Europe."

Mr. Bevin declared in London today that there was a "very happy prospect now" of approaching the problem of Europe on an economic basis which, if built upon rightly and worked out properly, might yet make the biggest contribution to the unity of the principles of Europe.

(Reuter and U.P.)

U.S. Miners Sign Contract

WASHINGTON, Tuesday (UP) — John L. Lewis today signed his best contract ever with over half of the nation's soft coal industry and predicted that the rest of the owners — the Westerners and the Southerners — would fall in line in a few days.

The one-year contract grants the miners 13.05 dollars an hour basic daily wage for 120 dollars-an-hour day, which is 12.20 dollars higher than what they had been receiving for nine hours up till now. More than 195,000 of the country's 400,000 miners will go back to work immediately.

UNSCOP WON'T VISIT CYPRUS

The United Nations Special Committee at a private meeting yesterday decided neither to send a sub-committee to the deportee camps in Cyprus, nor to grant a hearing to representatives of the Cyprus detainees.

It was agreed, in another resolution, to invite Arab States to give evidence now and also to reiterate the invitation to the Arab Higher Committee to cooperate.

The text of the letter to the AHC. was adopted on the proposal of the Yugoslav delegate, while the invitation to the Arab States was agreed upon following a proposal by the Indian representative.

By six votes (Australia, Canada, Czechoslovakia, India, Peru and Sweden) to three (Guatemala, Uruguay, Yugoslavia), with Iran and the Netherlands abstaining, it was decided not to send a sub-committee to Cyprus. Iran and Czechoslovakia abstained on voting when Australia, Canada, India, Peru and Sweden defeated Guatemala, Netherlands, Uruguay and Yugoslavia on the question of hearing deportees from Cyprus.

A 24-hour hunger-strike was due to begin at midnight last night by the 5,599 detainees in the Caraolos camps in Cyprus in protest against the fact that the U.N. Committee had not acknowledged several messages by the Cyprus deportees, inviting the Committee to visit the camps and investigate conditions there.

Detainees in the five Xylotymbou camps held a one-day hunger-strike on Monday in protest against the conditions in the camps.

(Continued on Page 3)
(Continued on Page Four)

THE PALESTINE POST

LATE Edition

JERUSALEM Wednesday, July 30, 1947

Tel. 4846, HAIFA

PRICE: 20 MILS VOL. XXII. No. 6471

HOTEL SHOSHANAT HACARMEL

Column One
By David Courtney

MR. Attlee will have to stand up to some sharp heckling when he faces the Parliamentary Labour Party today. Morrison will be there to help and can be relied upon to crack his whip. Between them, the Prime Minister and the Leader of the House will make it clear that the country's crisis is the Party's crisis and that the ranks had better stay solidly in formation unless willing to risk defeat in the Commons and a sharp reaction against the Government outside. Driven by the fear of bankruptcy and of failure in Germany and the rest of Europe, the lukewarm support of the Liberals for the Government's planned economy schemes is turning to hostility; and the big Middle Class vote, which gave Labour the extra seats that made the difference between a bare, perhaps unworkable majority and mastery with hardly any risk of defeat as long as the Party voted together, is getting ready to turn back to its old, safe loyalties. Whether this will frighten the conscientious Socialists of both front bench and back into acceptance of a compromise policy of go-slow in the home-schemes of nationalization remains to be seen. Those who refuse to admit the need of subservience to the American demand that Britain should quit its plans for nationalization in the Ruhr and should share control of its zone with the United States.

SHORTLY after the elections in the summer of 1945, Mr. Attlee, as much frightened by some of the elements which made up his own majority as by the problems ahead of him, decided upon a policy of gradualness. "We need at least one full term of office to work ourselves in," he is reported to have said. "He is a modest man," Mr. Churchill has said of the Prime Minister. "His modesty and his policy of Socialist gradualness would have served well enough in fair weather. In the foul tempests to which Britain has been subjected, in common with the rest of the old world, they have not been enough. Some of his Cabinet colleagues and an increasing number of his supporters on the back benches have become critical." If, in the present crisis, gradualness is to become still more gradual and modesty to develop into appeasement to the Tory Opposition as well as subjection to the Marshall planners, ructions will start in the Labour Party. It looks as if Mr. Attlee must decide today between more Socialism and less, and whatever the decision, it cannot fail to bring about big Ministerial changes.

JON Kimche says that Aneurin Bevan, Minister for Health and Housing, has his resignation in his pocket. Kimche is the editor of the political weekly, "Tribune," which is largely owned by Bevan and has consistently warned the Government against giving in to the steel interests on the question of the nationalization of the industry they control, and against selling the Ruhr trade unionists down the river at the behest of Americans. Bevan's prestige is high. He has done more than he might have done in the field; and in the field of Public Health has carried out some of the most important reforms in the social legislation of the present Government. He is politically more consistent than a Crossman, has more skill and experience than Michael Foot, and none of the pseudo-Communist taint attributed to that conscientious and courageous politician, Zilliacus.

FOREIGN policy, apart from the future of the Ruhr and the necessity to apply such policy at crippling cost in men and money, may not be a major subject today. Critics will keep most of their fire for the debate. But it is a process of self-accounting has set in among the members of the Labour Party, it is difficult to see what Mr. Bevin can escape the consequences. His long record of failure has brought him the sympathy of an easy-going people ready to forgive much for the sake of at least one vivid personality among a drab collection of apparent dullards. But no people will go on being made a fool of for very long; and it begins to look as if Mr. Bevin is by way of doing just that.

Jerusalem, July 30.

"NONE BUT DEAD MEN WILL BE LANDED HERE", SAY EXILES

REFUGEES REFUSE TO LEAVE THE SHIPS

PORT DE BOUC, Tuesday.— Saying that they wanted to go to Palestine, the 4,500 Jewish immigrants of the "Exodus 1947," who arrived here today in three British transports, refused to land and, thanking the French for their hospitality, declared, "None but dead men will be landed here." A French official said that his Government would not force the Jews to disembark.

The three British vessels anchored half a mile apart, a mile off this tiny harbour. The French health officer who went aboard the first transport, quickly ran up a flag signalling that no signs of an epidemic had been found.

The French had intended to register the refugees at the rate of one shipload a day. They prepared invitations to land in French, Hebrew, and Yiddish, and promised each refugee that he would be fed, given medical attention and moved swiftly to camps or hospitals. Trucks, field kitchens and ambulances gathered at the docks before dawn to attend to the refugees' needs.

The harbour area was cordoned off to prevent incidents, but hundreds of Frenchmen crowded into this little holiday village. The first of the refugee freighters arrived just before 8 o'clock. French authorities did not permit either newsmen or representatives of Jewish aid associations to board the ships.

FLOATING CAGES

The ships were described as "floating cages" by eye-witnesses who approached them in small craft. The cargo holds had been converted into dormitories and the decks surrounded by 12-feet high barbed wire.

M. Rene Colaveri, the Secretary-General of the local prefecture, went out to meet the ships, and on his return spoke to the French Premier, M. Paul Ramadier, in Paris by phone. He is understood to have delivered a message from the emigrants that they were unwilling to land.

According to a PTA message, a British Colonel on the Runnymede Park told the head of the French delegation to "return tomorrow morning when more than a thousand refugees would be willing to get off."

The ships had been cruising the French waters, just out of sight of land for three days, awaiting instructions.

As soon as the first of the three ships entered the roads a special police boat left the harbour with a boarding party of French officials and M. S. E. Kay, the British Consul-General in Marseilles, who is representing the British Government. In the wake of the police boat was another small craft carrying French medical officers.

M. Colaveri declared that the launch conveying representatives of the Foreign Affairs, Interior and Public Health Ministries, M. Guineau of the "Entr'aide Française," M. Blumer, special Government Delegate, Admiral Decoux and the adviser to the British Embassy in Paris, first proceeded to the "Runnymede Park" and then to the "Ocean Vigour," anchored a few hundred metres farther.

"We were greeted on board by a British Officer, and by Col. Gregson, to whom we expressed our desire to speak to the immigrants. They were assembled behind grilles on the forecastle. They apparently did not understand what it was all about, as they all went to starboard and port, where we followed them in the company of British officers. In the holds, where it was terribly hot, I read to the five hundred men and women the French Government's declaration offering them hospitality in the following words:

The French Government informs the immigrants on board the Exodus 1947 that, with their consent, they will be given asylum on the national soil, where they will enjoy all the liberties which France traditionally endows upon all citizens who long for the freedoms of the human being. Immediately after landing ashore, they will be provided with food and immediate material needs.

One of the immigrants, on

(Continued on Page 2)

"We Would Rather Starve than Land"

By BOYD FRANCE, Reuters Special Correspondent

PORT DE BOUC, Tuesday.— The Jewish refugees aboard the British ship Ocean Vigour who arrived here today told me that they refused to land.

When I pulled alongside the ship and asked the immigrants, through a Hebrew interpreter, whether they would land, there was a deathly silence. Then as one man, they chorused, "No."

"We would rather starve to death than land anywhere except in Palestine," they shouted.

Although my boat was unable to approach the other two immigrant ships lying outside the port, I was told that the immigrants there, too, were refusing to land.

Only one immigrant had landed by this afternoon a woman suffering from tuberculosis, whose condition made it necessary to send her to Marseilles Hospital.

The control of ships' movements in and out of the port was strict. Privately owned vessels were told that they would not be allowed to get out to sea. My boat ran the police blockade, but as we tried to approach the "Runnymede Park," lying one kilometre off the entrance of the port with refugees on board, we were overtaken by the police boat and threatened with a fine of 15,000 francs and a term of imprisonment if we persisted in our attempt.

Instead, we proceeded to follow the Ocean Vigour which had weighed anchor and was making for the open sea. About 15 miles offshore we overtook the ship and drew alongside.

We asked them four times "Are you going to get off?" Suddenly the crowd burst into a loud cry of "Nein, nein," and began to sing "Hatikvah."

At strategic points along the railing of the ship's deck British Paratroopers with red be-rets stood in silent guard over their unwilling passengers.

About 32 kms. offshore we could distinguish the outlines of the four British warships which had escorted the immigrants back to France. With them was the third immigrant ship, Empire Rival.

BRITAIN ASKED WHAT WAS GAINED

LONDON, Tuesday.— The whole press has given prominence to the arrival at Port de Bouc of the deportation convoy and also to this morning's execution in Palestine and the Irgun Zvai Leumi's threats of reprisals.

There might be ugly scenes around Marseilles, apart from a new wave of terrorism in Palestine, whose "unscrupulous temper is clear from their clamour to board the British transports to inspect living conditions," while "the people who raise this cry are those who condemned 4,000 of their co-religionists to the squalor of the Exodus 1947."

"In such an atmosphere," the "Chronicle" continued, violence may be avoided by a miracle, but bitterness and recrimination will be planted in many hearts and minds. We have fanned the flames in Palestine. We have thrust friendly France into a situation which at the very least must be most embarrassing to her."

The "Chronicle" then asked: "What have we gained by this sudden decision about one shipload of Jews among the many? What did we think we were going to gain? It is high time somebody told us."

The "Daily Mail" featured an article by Mr. Maurice Jaffa, formerly Jewish chaplain to the British Forces in the Far East, answering charges levelled against the conditions in which refugees are being brought to Palestine. Explaining the tragic position of the Jewish DPs, he said that they were escaping from Gehenna, not, as described, being placed on the road to Gehenna.

The Paris correspondent of the B.B.C. criticized the decision of the British authorities not to allow press representatives at the disembarkation.

800 DISEMBARK IN CYPRUS

By SHAHE GUEBENLIAN

NICOSIA, Tuesday.— The Empire Shelter and Comfort arrived here this morning with 187 men, 228 women and 187 children from the two ships "Return to Zion" and the "Fourteen."

They were taken to Caraolos Camp by road. About 400 of the party are Arabic-speaking Jews from North Africa.

There is still no news of the fate of the remainder of the July quota of repatriates, some of whom had already embarked for the return journey on July 23, but were removed from the ship again.

The "Empire Comfort" returned to Haifa late last night and took on board 223 refugees from the "Fourteen"—165 men, 54 women and four children. They were due to leave at midnight for Cyprus.

Twenty-one refugees from the same ship have been taken to the hospital at Athlit.

FRANCE DENIES DEAL TO LIMIT MIGRATION

Palestine Post Reporter

The Jewish Agency was officially informed by the French Government yesterday that no agreement had been made by France with Britain to limit Jewish immigration to Palestine. The full text of the message, which was given to correspondents at a press conference in Jerusalem yesterday morning, is as follows:

"According to a growing number of rumours coming from the foreign press it would appear that the taking to France of the refugees on board the "Exodus 1947" by the British authorities has been done in agreement with the French Government. Foreign correspondents also maintain that France and Great Britain have concluded a secret agreement limiting Jewish immigration into Palestine. In reply to these rumours, the French Ministry of Foreign Affairs stresses that, following upon repeated British notes, the Government of the Republic has simply issued the following order to the relevant authorities:

(1) To verify the authenticity of visas for any destination.

(2) To assure the application of the conventions concerning the safeguard of human lives at sea."

"These orders are obviously applicable without distinction of race or religion to any emigrants leaving French territory.

"An exchange of letters between France and Great Britain is the only document on board the "Exodus 1947" by which the two Governments have treated the question of Jewish refugees. There is no foundation to the statement by some news agencies concerning an agreement for the limitation of Jewish immigration into Palestine, in connection with decisions taken solely by the British authorities.

"I would like to add that the French Government is about to apply to the refugees on board the "Exodus 1947" the liberal attitude which has already been publicly announced."

PLEAS FOR 2 SERGEANTS

A strongly-worded warning against possible reprisals against the two kidnapped sergeants was issued by the Executive of the Vaad Leumi at its meeting in Jerusalem yesterday morning.

Appeals for the release of two British Army Sergeants were voiced yesterday by the Chief Rabbis, Dr. I. H. Herzog and Rabbi B. Z. Uziel, the Vaad Leumi Executive and the Hebrew press, while an appeal from Sgt. Paice's father was transmitted to the Jewish Agency for publication by the Zionist Federation in London.

The Vaad Leumi's statement ran as follows:

The Yishuv, which has been hurt and shocked by the Government's lack of response to all the appeals for clemency and by the execution of the three young men sentenced to death for the attack on Acre Prison, will regard any act of reprisal taken against the two innocent Britons as a bloodthirsty deed contrary to all standards and an unforgivable sin against the Yishuv and the Jewish people.

Sgt. Paice's appeal was transmitted at 2.45 by telephone from the Chief Secretary's Office to the Jewish Agency:

Most immediate. Following from Zionist Federation of Great Britain to the Jewish Agency Jerusalem: Just received telephone call from Mr. Paice, father of one of the two British sergeants held as hostages by the Irgun, who asks us if humanly possible to transmit message to Palestine in attempt to save life of son stressing that neither he, nor son ever anti-Zionists and completely innocent participants in tragic political situation. Have explained to him how strongly you and we disapprove action Irgun and deplore present terrible situation. Promised transmit this message urgently for publication Palestine in last minute attempt influence Irgun to exercise compassion.

The Chief Rabbis expressed deep grief that the appeals of the Yishuv and its leaders for the commutation of the death sentences of the three Jewish youths had not been heeded. These men had not been convicted of murder, they stressed, and that the sentences were carried out at a time when the Jewish and Palestine problems were being judged by the United Nations.

Not to Blame

"Hasretz" also appealed "to the comrades of the executed men."

"They have done all they could to save their comrades' lives; they even trespassed the limit; and failed. They know as well as we do that the two British boys who have fallen into their hands by chance are not to blame for this morning's tragedy. They too are but victims of the hidden hand that has engineered all this."

They called on them to release the two men immediately and to sanctify their religion, people and land.

In a leading article, "Davar" wrote that if there was still a vestige of common sense and national responsibility in the minds of those who directed the acts of the dissidents, they must now release the two men.

Prison Raiders Hanged at Acre

Palestine Post Bureau

HAIFA, Tuesday.— "Do not grieve too much, what we have done we did out of conviction." This last message from the three men executed this morning to their families was given to Acre by Chief Rabbi Nissim Ohana, who was brought to Acre by the police last night at the request of the condemned men.

The parents and brother of Nakar, the mother, father and sister of Habib, and Weiss' sister were not permitted to see the men before they died, but, having been brought to Haifa in the middle of the night, were kept at C.I.D. Headquarters until morning. Rabbi Ohana, who did not know that the hanging was imminent, was awakened after midnight by a Police Inspector accompanied by constables, who told him why he was needed.

When he arrived at Acre, the three men were awakened. He was brought first to the cell of Nakar, who was alone, and heard his confession through the heavy grilled door, with a prison inspector and two Arab policemen standing by. He gave Nakar a skull-cap for the prayer. He was then taken to Habib and Weiss who were together in one cell, and again carried out the last rites with the men on the other side of bars.

All three men were composed and steadfast, the Rabbi told The Palestine Post, and their main concern was for their families.

The prison authorities asked Rabbi Ohana to wait and witness the execution, but he chose to return to Haifa where he saw the Police Inspector before going home.

A police sergeant came to the house where Edith Weiss lives in the Neve Shaanan Quarter here shortly before 11 o'clock, where they found that Weiss' sister had gone to friends in Ramat Gan. She last saw her brother on Saturday.

There was a guard of about 200 soldiers and police outside the Haifa H.Q. at Mt. Cana'an. The taxis bringing the relatives were thoroughly searched from top to bottom after the people alighted.

The bodies were accompanied to Safad by a convoy of two H.Q. and 10 armoured cars, but arrived unescorted at the cemetery.

There were no casualties when an explosion wrecked a pill-box at the Acre check post last night.

BURIALS AGAIN AT SAFAD

Palestine Post Reporter

SAFAD, Tuesday.— For the second time this year Safad was designated as the burial place for Jews executed at Acre, and at four o'clock this morning, Rabbi M. Podhorzer, Chairman of the Jewish Community Council, was officially informed that the bodies of the three condemned men would be brought here.

The four men executed in April, Dov Gruner, Rosenbaum, Kashani and Alkoshi, had also been sent here for burial.

The families of the three men executed today—Nakar's parents and brother, Habib's parents, brother and sister-in-law, and Weiss' sister, his only surviving relative, arrived at seven o'clock this morning and were taken to police headquarters on Mount Cana'an where the bodies were brought from Acre at 8.15, each in a separate police tender. The Haifa Burial Society came at the same time.

Small bundles consisting of the men's clothing and articles found on them at the time of their capture were handed over to the relatives.

The funeral set out at 10 o'clock from Mt. Cana'an to the cemetery, headed by the police tenders bearing the three bodies. The streets of the Jewish quarter through which it passed were shuttered and lined with silent men and women, while hundreds waited at the cemetery. The Prayer for the Dead for Nakar and Habib was spoken by their fathers, and for Weiss the prayer was recited by Mr. Podhorzer.

The families left the town at one o'clock to return home. Only Jewish constables and special police were on duty at the funeral. The town has been cut off for the day, no traffic being permitted in or out from early morning until evening.

Searches for N.C.O. Hostages

Palestine Post Staff

Eighteen days after the kidnapping of Sergeants Paice and Martin, no trace has yet been found of them, although searches were carried out with renewed vigour in various parts of Palestine yesterday. The Nordiah Quarter in Tel Aviv was cordoned off and searched in the afternoon, but nothing was found. In the morning, Kfar Avihayil, near Nathanya, was also searched.

Civilian patrols were also formed all over the Nathanya area last night to conduct renewed searches for the two missing men.

Throughout the day rumours that the two men had been found were current all over the country, but none of them was substantiated.

British Policemen and Military Police guarded Zion Square in Jerusalem all day, taking up positions early in the morning and leaving them only after the curfew came into force.

In Tel Aviv, people continued to buy food against possible curfews, and there were long queues at ice factories and bakeries.

Cinema and theatre performances were stopped and cafes and restaurants closed.

In Nathanya, a memorial service was held in the afternoon for the three men executed in the morning.

"UNNECESSARY DANGER"

LONDON, Tuesday (PTA).— The House of Commons watches with anxiety and sympathy the position of our men in Palestine, and with horror the danger to which they are unnecessarily exposed," declared the Rt. Hon. Oliver Stanley, during a brief reference to Palestine in a debate on the Colonies today.

Cabinet to Review Military Needs

EARLY SHOWDOWN IN CRISIS EXPECTED

By JON KIMCHE, Special to The Palestine Post.

LONDON, Tuesday.— Field-Marshal Montgomery's sudden recall from his Pacific tour is said to be due to the Cabinet's request to the War Office for an immediate reassessment of British military requirements in the Middle East and Germany, with a view to drastically cutting them down.

The crisis atmosphere lessened somewhat today with an inspired editorial in the "Daily Herald" entitled "Crisis" which acknowledged the seriousness of the situation, but stated categorically that there will not be a coalition.

Meanwhile, Mr. Attlee has had discussions with leading Ministers and received a long letter signed by Messrs. Crossman and Ben Levy, making serious categorical demands. In Downing Street it is stated that there is no Cabinet crisis as such, but it is known that on a number of specific issues serious differences have arisen among the Ministers.

The campaign in the Conservative press and also among some Trade Union M.P.'s for "Bevin for Prime Minister" is discounted in Government circles, where it is suggested that whatever changes Mr. Attlee may make, it is not of the question that he will give up the Premiership.

City Reacts

The crisis is also reflected in a general unsettling of the stock exchange and the marking down of all types of shares, but there is nothing that can be called panic-selling. The Government still has the financial situation firmly in hand, although there is now also a propaganda campaign in certain Opposition circles for the devaluation of the sterling.

In view of the accumulation of these factors, an early showdown between the Government and the Opposition is expected, and tomorrow's meeting may take the form of an appeal by Mr. Attlee to the Party, to unite to face this Opposition drive against the Labour Government. Critics are, however, at present not in the mood to accept this, unless it is combined with undertakings by the Government to take firm measures on outstanding domestic and foreign policy issues.

New York Stocks Break

NEW YORK, Tuesday (UP).— Stocks broke sharply on a heavy volume of late afternoon trading.

Shortly after 2 p.m. the tape was two minutes behind, with prices down one to four points. Wheat broke as much as 5-5/8 cents a bushel. Cotton lost $4.50 a bale.

INDONESIANS BOMB 2 DUTCH-HELD TOWNS

BATAVIA, Tuesday.— The Indonesian "Air Force," in its first combat operation, bombed two Dutch-held towns on the North Coast, and the other Salatiga, in the eastern sector of the island. This was announced by Jogjakarta radio, which stated that the raiding aircraft had evaded two Dutch fighter planes and returned to their base undamaged. Pamphlets as well as bombs were dropped on Semarang, it is stated.

An Indonesian communiqué said that Republican ground troops had shot down two Dutch fighter planes near Mantoep, in Eastern Java, and that the area north of Mantoep was now in control of Indonesian troops.

Russia Accepts Invitation

By SYLVAIN MANGEOT, Reuters Diplomatic Correspondent

LONDON, Tuesday.— The Soviet Government has accepted Britain's invitation to a conference of the Foreign Ministers Deputies, to meet in London at the beginning of October, it was officially stated by a Foreign Office spokesman today. The invitation was sent simultaneously three weeks ago to Washington, Paris and Moscow.

The Russian reply is the first official answer, though the French Government has given its approval in principle to the Deputies' meeting in London, without the mention of a fixed date. No American reply has yet been made.

U.P. & Reuter.

NO UNSCOP COMMENT ON TRIPLE HANGING

GENEVA, Tuesday (UP).— Members of the U.N. Special Committee on Palestine refrained from official comment on the execution of the three Irgun members at Acre this morning. Individual delegates said that the matter was an internal Palestine issue.

The Yugoslav member said, however, that he personally regretted the executions, especially since the three condemned men had not killed anybody while attempting to aid the escape of prisoners from the Acre fortress.

After Midnight

A Dutch spokesman said yesterday his Government saw no reason to postpone the moves to bring the Indonesian conflict before the U.N.

M. Gromyko, in the Security Council, yesterday vetoed the entire U.S. proposal to keep the Border Investigating Commission on the Balkans.

Reversing its declaration of independence made over six weeks ago, Travancore, has decided to join the Dominion of India.

Pandit Nehru, will be the Indian Union's first Prime Minister, Mahatma Gandhi told a prayer meeting last night.

THE GRESHAM
Life Assurance
Society Ltd.
COMPETITIVE TERMS
FOR ENDOWMENT
ASSURANCE PLANS

LATE Edition

THE PALESTINE POST

JERUSALEM
TUESDAY, SEPT. 9, 1947

PRICE: 20 MILS
VOL. XXII No. 6506

WE ARRANGE SHIPPING SPACE FOR YOU FROM AND TO ALL PARTS AND PORTS OF THE WORLD
ATID NAVIGATION Co. Ltd.
HAIFA— JAFFA—TEL AVIV—JERUSALEM

Column One

By David Courtney

THE London ratification of the Anglo-French Treaty will have no meaning in France. The usual diplomatic twaddle from Mr. Bevin and M. Massigli made hardly a pretence at patching up the ravelled cloak of an alliance which, it now seems, was never intended to keep anybody warm. The French people are today far more concerned about the Ruhr coal talks, which begin today in Berlin. After the way France was snubbed at the London Conference on the industrial level of Germany, she need expect little from the talks opening today. It is this fact which has given weighty significance to the speech delivered by General de Gaulle on Sunday.

■

THE General, although for sinister reasons, points to the swing further into Communism. The Communist Party has a good case. It can show that the present French Government has thrown away the chance of alignment with the strongest Continental Power and has been rewarded by its British and American sponsors with a plan for the resurgence of industrial Germany at France's expense. Even under the Marshall Plan, it is clear that Germany is to get priority, whilst France, taking her place in the beggarly European queue, has virtually been forbidden by the State Department from establishing industries of a defensive military character as partial security against a revived and vengeful Germany. She has been told, for example, not to make agricultural tractors, which are badly needed in France. The plant can too easily be put to making tanks.

■

MR. BEVIN'S ratification ambiguities are hardly an alternative. He has never given France any reason to believe in his sincerity; and what might have been an alliance for the good of all Europe was nothing better than a wayside diversion on the Foreign Secretary's road to Moscow. Willing or driven, he has plaited the German basket into which Mr. Snyder is willing to put the Treasury's eggs. France, with neither basket nor eggs, must fend for herself. It is pretty certain that she will not get a single dollar or a single sack of coal until the October Municipal Elections have shown whether the Electorate's trend is toward Communism or towards the Truman Doctrine. It is even doubtful if Bevin's betrayal of France will help England. Snyder is in London and will want some clarification of the Foreign Secretary's Southport speech; and as it is he, and not Mr. Marshall, who seems to run General Clay, he may also demand assurances in the matter of Ruhr coal and nationalization of German industry in return for accepting full bi-zonal financial responsibility. If he should gain that point, Britain will have taken the first step towards withdrawal from all real authority in the Ruhr.

■

THE Cabinet meets in London today. Dalton's visit to America and Snyder's to London are likely to be the main subjects of discussion. It is clear that the Government's recent measures for self-sufficiency were little more than window-dressing and that it is banking on a release of dollars. "The Times" has put the matter in a cynical nutshell: no dollars, no more support for the Truman Doctrine. In other words, the Americans had better beware or the Socialist Government may turn in despair to Socialism. Economics aside, the Cabinet is expected to get down to some definition of the policy it intends to follow at the U.N. meeting, which opens on the 15th. There is strong feeling that it will take the line of least resistance and offer no serious objections to the UNSCOP recommendations provided it gets an assurance of help in carrying them out. Bevin will do all he can to throw the onus on the United States and to make that country responsible for anything that may go wrong. But an apparent willingness to make a virtue of necessity is likely: for one thing, it would help to put into the background such stupid and consciousless acts of policy as the sending of the Exodus refugees to Hamburg.

Jerusalem, September 9.

JAZZ FROM LOUDSPEAKERS BACKGROUND TO OPERATION

REFUGEES FORCED TO LAND AT HAMBURG

HAMBURG, Monday.—With more than 1,000 British troops armed with machine guns, rifles, tommyguns, tear-gas pistols, steel-tipped truncheons and high-pressure hosepipes on the cage-lined dock, British officers at first told pressmen that the disembarkation of the 1,400 refugees from the Ocean Vigour — first of the three "Liberty" ships carrying Jewish refugees back from Palestine — had "generally proceeded well" and that they had been "highly pleased with the Jews' cooperation."

A British press release later in the afternoon said, however, that forceful action against the Jews began when, after several hundred had disembarked quietly, some young Jews in one of the holds resisted and military police had to be brought aboard to assist the escort troops.

The reporters themselves tell of steel-helmeted soldiers of the Sherwood Foresters having to go aboard to silence the Jews singing hymns; of men and some women and children resisting, clinging to the ship's rails; of the steel-tipped truncheons being applied; of a group of about 30 young refugees struggling for half-an-hour before they could be overcome and dragged across the gangway; of one man, whose head was bleeding and who tried to show his wounds to journalists, being hustled off the quayside by soldiers who rushed to surround him.

All but five minutes of the hour's time limit given the deportees to leave the ship without force passed in grim silence. Then, at nearly 7 a.m., women and children and a few men started wearily across the gangway.

Trouble began when about a third of the 1,400 refugees, mostly women, children and old people, had landed. Then a company of troops went into the evil-smelling holds to push and drag off those who were holding up the proceedings.

At one point German workers began to put up a covered gangway so that spectators should not see what force was to be applied.

RESISTANCE OVERCOME

The resistance of the younger men overcome, the rest of the refugees landed quietly, disembarkation being completed by 10.35. Some of the soldiers helped women across, led children by the hand and assisted with the refugees' packages — "all that they had left," as one soldier said. In a number of instances the offer of assistance was refused by deportees, who spat in the soldiers' faces and called them "dirty Fascists."

On the dock itself an incongruous touch was added by loudspeakers blaring out dance music, as the Jews, after being searched, filed to the waiting trains. Some of them were still wearing old Allied uniforms. About 25 sick people were placed on ambulances and a child with measles was taken to Hamburg hospital.

A woman photographer, one of a group of foreign correspondents held in specially prepared press boxes, was arrested for having photographed the disembarkation.

Women and Children First

A few of the refugees were able to call across to the journalists before they entered the trains. One said that, seeing nobody but soldiers on the quays, they thought the world had forgotten them. Another said that disembarkation had begun with the Ocean Vigour because, it having more women and children on board than the other two ships, the British considered it likely to offer least resistance. He expected greater trouble on the other ships.

The entraining was not carried out quietly. Shouting defiance, over 100 had to be carried bodily to the coaches, while from the trains a hail of missles, mostly packets of food, rained suddenly through the barred windows at the guards. Military police entered the the coaches and hustled several men across the pier to a temporary post erected on the dock.

On the way to Poppendorf camp, near Luebeck, a lavatory door was wrenched from its hinges and rammed through a window, knocking off and injuring several Germans clinging to the sides of an overcrowded, passing passenger train.

Soldiers and Red Cross representatives toured the cars offering coffee, milk and sandwiches, some of which was thrown back at them.

At Poppendorf

Detraining at Poppendorf camp, which is heavily guarded, with two rows of triple-stranded barbed wire, was completed in the afternoon. Newsmen were forbidden to approach the camp, despite special passes that had been issued to them earlier. The dusty roads in the neighbourhood swarmed with British troops, taking over guard duty from Germans. The unloading of the trains was supervised by troops of the 7th Armoured Division wearing the famous Desert Rat emblem.

The second of the deportation ships, the Empire Rival, was expected to dock later today, for offloading early tomorrow, with the turn of the Runnymede Park on Wednesday.

British officials expressed fear that there would be further violence tomorrow if any of the reufgees refused to get off the ship quickly and quietly. They said that the troops again had orders to drag and haul off any who resisted.

In the American Zone in Germany, 3,000 Jewish DPs. in Zeilsheim camp, near Frankfurt, began a sit-down strike in protest against the forced landings.

(Reuter, UP, AP ,AFP, Palcor.)

BEVIN WILL NOT GO TO LAKE SUCCESS

By JON KIMCHE,
Special to The Palestine Post

LONDON, Monday.— Although Mr. Bevin will head the British delegation to the U.N. Assembly, he will not go to Lake Success, a Foreign Office spokesman said today.

The Government has decided that the Colonial Secretary, Mr. Creech Jones, and not Mr. Bevin's second-in-command, Mr. Hector MacNeil, will represent Britain at the Uno Assembly, when the Palestine report is discussed.

This last minute change follows consultations in London between Mr. Bevin, Mr. MacNeil, and Mr. McGillivray, the Government's Liaison Officer with UNSCOP. It appears that the British Government has now been convinced that the UNSCOP report will present a serious problem at the Assembly, and that it would be unfair on Mr. MacNeil to expect him to deal adequately with it.

Mr. Creech Jones has therefore been chosen, in his absence in the West Indies, to present Britain's case.

No Decision Yet

No decision has been taken so far on what this case will be. The UNSCOP report is still being studied on Departmental levels by the Foreign Office, the Colonial Office, and Service Departments. It has not yet reached Ministerial regions, and at tomorrow's Cabinet meeting there will be the first survey by the Ministers of the new situation created by the report.

From the Arab side, there is also lively activity. This weekend Mr. Bevin dined with Abdul Illah, the Regent of Iraq, privately at the Regent's suite.

Among those present was Musa eff. Alami, who is handling Arab Office affairs in connection with the report.

FULL CABINET MEETS TODAY

By FRASER WIGHTON,
Reuters Diplomatic Correspondent

LONDON, Monday—The Prime Minister, Mr. Attlee, is back from his holiday in Wales to preside over tomorrow's first full Cabinet meeting since Parliament adjourned for the summer recess early in August.

Leading Ministers have already begun to prepare for a week of intense activity in domestic and foreign affairs, beginning tomorrow and ending on Friday with the announcement of the Government's plans for increasing Britain's exports to meet the dollar famine. The announcement will be made to an important meeting in London, of representatives of both sides of industry, by Sir Stafford Cripps, the President, of the Board.

Palestine on Agenda

The Cabinet faces four big problems. It must—

(1) consider new measures to end the Yorkshire coal strike which has so far cost the country 350,000 tons of coal;

(2) approve the "Cripps Plan" to raise exports by 40 percent during the month;

(3) decide Britain's Palestine policy at the U.N. General Assembly, opening in New York on September 16;

(4) examine the proposals which the Chancellor of the Exchequer, Dr. Dalton, will put before Mr. John Snyder, the Secretary of the U.S. Treasury, to ease the dollar shortage. Mr. Snyder was due in London today.

The House of Lords is returning from holiday for a oneday debate on the crisis tomorrow.

G.O.C. FOR U.K.

The G.O.C., Lt.-General G. H. A. MacMillan, left Palestine for the United Kingdom on Sunday to attend a course there. He will see an exercise carried out by Airborne troops and will spend a few days on leave.

During his absence, the Acting G.O.C. will be Major-General R. Gale.

features and fashions

OUT TOMORROW — SEPTEMBER 10

THIS ISSUE CONTAINS:

Special Rosh Hashanah Feature
Cookery Page
Exclusive Paris Fashion Service
Design for Living
Pets Corner, Gardening hints, and articles of interest to men as much as to women.

Distributed free with tomorrow's issue.

Order your copy in advance.

THE PALESTINE POST

What Happened?

HAMBURG, Monday (Reuter).— Disembarkation was held up because some of the refugess refused to land, and continued cheers and shouts were heard from the hold of the ship.

Troops in steel helmets boarded the Ocean Vigour, and soon afterwards, the peaceful disembarkation was resumed.

MAYORS' RELEASE WHEN THEY 'TALK'

Palestine Post Staff

The release of the three mayors, Mr. I. Rokach, Mr. O. Ben Ami and Mr. A. Krinizi, was dependent "on their willingness to reply to questions put to them by the security authorities," a Government spokesman said in Jerusalem last night when asked if they would be released before Rosh Hashana.

If the Mayors agreed to talk, each case would later be reviewed in the light of information already in the hands of the police and which may be obtained as a result of the interrogation, the spokesman added.

Meanwhile, Noah Zevuloni, of the "Hamashkif" office in Jerusalem, and Daniel Yanovsky, a clerk at the Jerusalem Jewish Community Council, who were arrested on Friday night, were released yesterday.

Trying to Reverse "Polly"

British Women's Sit-Down Strike

Palestine Post Bureau

HAIFA, Monday. — Twelve British women and five children are camping in a disused police barrack at the Ras en Nakura Frontier Post, where they are waiting for a reply from Jerusalem to their appeal to be permitted to re-enter Palestine to re-join their husbands, most of whom are officials of the Iraq Petroleum Company. The Russian-born wife of a Briton and her child were allowed to cross the border into Palestine.

The party arrived in a bus from Beirut, where they had been living since Operation "Polly" last February. They were turned back by the Frontier Control, but refused to leave and remained at the post. Despite a decision by the central authorities in Jerusalem not to permit them to enter, they sent a special appeal through the Frontier Control to the Acting Chief Secretary, asking that their seven months' exile from their homes and their separation from their husbands be ended.

Eleven of the women are wives of I.P.C. officials, while the husband of the twelfth is employed by the Cable and Wireless Company.

The Manager of the I.P.C., Mr. G.H. Herridge, drove up

(Continued on Page 3)

FREEDOM OF MOVEMENT

Within a few days, British civilians will again be allowed to walk about unescorted in various parts of the country. The escort system was introduced when the Security Zones were established in February.

It is understood that District Commissioners are preparing a number of "Out of Bounds" areas. Elsewhere, British cicivilians will be allowed to move about freely.

Civilians will, however, still have to live in security zones.

Refugees Into D.P.'s: Yishuv's Protest

Palestine Post Staff

A two-hour stoppage of work was observed throughout Palestine yesterday — "Hamburg Day" — as a protest against the British Government's taking the refugees back to Germany and turning them into D.P.'s again. The Zionist colours were flown at half-mast, draped in black, from public buildings. All shops, offices and places of entertainment were closed, and all urban traffic was stopped, as mass meetings were attended by thousands.

A message of solidarity was sent to the refugees by the Vaad Leumi, which also appealed to the Jews of America and Britain to help them.

The names of the refugees are to be inscribed in the Golden Book of the Jewish National Fund. Subscriptions will be collected from the public by members of youth movements.

JERUSALEM: Speakers at a meeting at the Orion Hall included Mr. I. Ben Zvi, President of the Vaad Leumi, Chief Rabbi B. Z. Uziel, and Dr. I. Thon, of the Jewish Community Council. While the meeting was in progress, an Army patrol of three reconnaissance cars and a heavy armoured car stopped near the hall for a few minutes during its tour of the city.

TEL AVIV: Thousands gathered in the square before the Habimah Theatre to demonstrate against Britain's immigration policy. From a dais on the theatre's broad steps, Mrs. Goldie Myerson, Head of the Jewish Agency's Political Department, warned Mr. Bevin not to be misled by the tameness of the Jewish reaction to his provocative action. The Jewish people were still prepared to break the ban on immigration to Palestine, she said.

Jews have been herded behind barbed wire in Germany before, but this time the persecutors were the British, who only recently were themselves mobilized for war against the Germans, with whom they were now collaborating in this outrage.

Lashing out against the British Foreign Minister, Mrs. Myerson pointed out that it was Mr. Bevin who had ini-

(Continued on Page 3)

Full UNSCOP Text Released

LAKE SUCCESS, Monday. — The text of the UNSCOP report, summarized last week in reports from Geneva, and now available in full, states that the basic conflict in Palestine "is the clash of two intense nationalisms. The claims of the Arabs and the Jews both possess validity and are irreconcilable." Partition, therefore, appeared to be the "only means available by which political and economic responsibility can be placed squarely on both." Further, it hoped that the "implicit limitations on immigration" set by Partition would allay Arab suspicions of an expanding Jewish State.

(U.P., & A.P.)

Arabs Veto UNSCOP

LAKE SUCCESS, Monday. — The Palestine Arab Higher Committee issued a statement here tonight declaring that the U.N. Special Committee's report on Palestine was "absurd, impracticable and unjust" and the Arabs would never accept it.

The statement said: "The Arabs will never allow a Jewish State to be established in one inch of Palestine.

"Not a single Jew will be allowed to migrate to Palestine. Any attempt to impose a solution contrary to the Arabs' birthright will only lead to trouble, bloodshed and probably a third world war".

Drew Pearson, the well-known radio commentator, broadcasting today, challenged the State Department to release its document about some of the Arab leaders' war record. This was most important, he said, in view of the Arab determination to sabotage the UNSCOP report.

Pearson added that if the State Department refused to publish the paper he would from his own duplicate.

(Palcor, Reuter)

JAMAL EFF. SEES SIR HENRY

The Deputy Chairman of the Arab Higher Executive, Jamal eff. Husseini, was received yesterday by the O. A. G., Sir Henry Gurney. The Arabs' stand at the forthcoming U.N. session is believed to have been dicussed, but no details have been released.

Jamal eff. is leaving Palestine for Cairo this morning, and is expected to fly from Egypt tomorrow for Lake Success to head the Arab delegation at the U.N. session. It is not yet known if Emile eff. Ghoury, who left for Egypt with him, will be a member of the delegation.

PLAN TO BOMB LONDON PROBABLY A HOAX

PARIS, Monday. — The alleged Jewish terrorist plot to drop leaflets and then home-made bombs on London may have been a hoax or a propaganda stunt to coincide with the landing of the Exodus 1947 deportees, well-informed quarters here believed today.

Although the plot had been given the appearance of a Stern Group terrorist affair, it is now considered to be entirely a personal venture of Rabbi Baruch Korff, co-chairman of the body calling itself the American Political Action Committee for Palestine.

A spokesman of the Hebrew Committee of National Liberation, which is connected with the Irgun Zvai Leumi, described the affair as a "spectacular foolish stunt" and said that neither the Irgun nor the Stern Group was connected with "this fantastic matter."

Reginald Gilbert, former U.S. Air Force pilot, who was arrested with Rabbi Korff, is believed to have been released by the French police, although the latter refused to confirm this. He is said to have given the information which led the authorities to the airfield near Paris as Korff was about to enter his plane, though this is denied by the police. Four others of the 14 arrested in Paris in connection with the plot have also been freed after questioning.

Among the people detained are said to be three women; one described as a "former employee of the Tel Aviv Municipality," named Braun; a man said to have been formerly a Polish Army officer; and a 19 year old student named Martinsky, who is reported to have been arrested last June when anti-British pamphlets were found during a search and who was subsequently released.

Charges which might, after investigation, be made against the detainees are: possession of pamphlets of foreign origin likely to endanger the security of the country, and presumption of possession of arms and ammunition.

(R., U.P., A.P., PTA, AFP)

(Comment — Page 3)

After Midnight

The British reply to the U.S. request for concessions on imperial preferences will be presented this morning.

NEW COAL CRISIS COULD WRECK GOVT. -- Horner

LONDON, Monday (Reuter). — A new coal crisis such as Britain suffered last winter could bring down the Labour Government, Mr. Arthur Horner, the Secretary of the National Union of Mine Workers, warned tonight.

Addressing a press conference, he denounced the Grimethorpe miners who have decided to continue their strike, thus giving impetus to the tie-up of the South Yorkshire mines which by tonight involved 43,000 men in 31 pits. Today's coal loss alone was officially given as 40,000 tons, bringing the total for the strike to almost 400,000 tons.

"It is not even the fate of the Government which is involved," Mr. Horner said, "it is the fate of the country." The present situation was driving the Miners Union into discussions about lengthening the working day or the working week, he added.

Mr. Shinwell, the Fuel Minister, today held a special conference with members of the National Coal Board which administers the state-owned coal mines. Though no details were available, it was suggested that he may be considering the possibility of taking legal action against the men on the grounds that the strike is unofficial and they are acting against the advice of their union leaders.

Meanwhile, coal is being rushed to Yorkshire from neighbouring coal mines, but vital steel furnaces and textile mills in Yorkshire have closed down for lack of fuel, and other industrial concerns are expected to be affected this week.

Refugees Leave Under Escort

MORE THAN 300 DEAD IN DELHI CLASHES

NEW DELHI, Monday. (R)—Fresh communal clashes broke out within two kilometres of the centre of Delhi today and Indian troops, led by British officers as well as the police, engaged the rioters. Sikhs and Hindus fought Moslems with Sten guns, bombs, rifles and shot guns.

An unofficial figure gave today's dead as 300 to 400.

Hysterical civilians, Hindus and Moslems, classified as refugees, were being shepherded out of the Old City, where fighting was going on, under heavy military escort.

British officers said they believed the opposing communities were fairly evenly matched in arms. Many rioters were rounded up, but large groups escaped.

Dr. N.C. Joshi, one of India's foremost surgeons, was shot dead by a mob which collected outside his home.

Meanwhile, the Delhi Province was officially declared "dangerously disturbed" and instructions were issued to the police and armed forces that "when you shoot at law breakers, you must shoot to kill, and not merely to disable."

The India Cabinet tonight announced the setting up of a joint police and military sub-area command H.Q. to restore communications and coordinate necessary measures to restore law and order.

An India Cabinet Emergency Committee was also called to increase the police force and to form a volunteer motor squad for reconnaissance in New Delhi.

50 MOSLEMS BUTCHERED

By JAMES MICHAELS,
U.P. Correspondent

NEW DELHI, Monday. — Bearded Sikhs, wielding three foot swords, today attacked the Lahore train at the main Delhi station and hacked to death at least 50 Moslem men, women and children. The Sikhs literally cut the Moslems to death, while Hindu troops and police watched, making no effort to intervene.

The attack came as the Indian Government announced new emergency regulations under which anyone caught looting or killing could be shot at sight. I counted at least 50 Moslem bodies, cut up like so much dogmeat, piled on baggage handcarts, lying in train compartments or stretched across the tracks. Flies swarmed on the undried blood.

On the train inside the station lay the body of a 12-year old Moslem youngster, his head severed. Next to him was an old man, his throat ripped, but still alive. As I appealed for help for him, tall Sikhs came up, stared at the suffering man, spat and turned away.

A grey-bearded Moslem, his skull split by a Sikh's sword but still alive, was about to be slung by Hindu policemen on the corpse heap, when he was extricated at the last minute by a British officer passing by.

Order was finally restored at the station when a company of Gurkhas under the command of a British Lieut. Colonel arrived and supervised the removal of bodies and confiscated the swords of the Sikhs. Indian troops and police stood by idly watching.

Anglo-French Treaty Ratified in London

LONDON, Monday (Reuter).— The Anglo-French Treaty of Alliance, signed by the British Foreign Secretary, Mr. Bevin, and the French Foreign Minister, M. Bidault, at Dunkirk in March, was ratified at the Foreign Office today. Mr. Bevin signed for Britain and Ambassador Massigli for France.

The Treaty, which runs for 50 years, aims at creating an alliance against the revival of possible German aggression and at developing economic ties in both countries' interests. It comes into force immediately.

After the ceremony, Mr. Bevin told M. Massigli: "This Treaty is really the culmination of Anglo-French cooperation which began in 1906, and which has seen us through two world wars." It also provided the framework for Anglo-French cooperation to be developed in all spheres. "To that end we are working now on the economic side. We must get closer and closer to assist each other out of the morass the war has left behind."

KING IBN SAUD SERIOUSLY ILL

CAIRO, Monday (AFP).— King Farouk has sent three well-known Cairo doctors to Riad, to attend King Ibn Saud, who, according to his son, the Emir Feisal, is seriously ill.

The doctors left on Sunday by special plane.

STOP PRESS

TROOPS TAKE UP POSITIONS ON QUAY

HAMBURG, Tuesday 1 a.m. (R) At dawn today, about 1,000 British troops trained in close-range combat will take up their positions on the quayside to deal with the expected resistance from the "rough and tough" Jews on board.

Among the headlines yesterday in the American press were these:

"BRITISH BATTLE REFUGEES" (N.Y. Journal)

"EXODUS JEWS RESIST LANDING" (World Telegram)

"BRITISH CLUB JEWS AT HAMBURG" (N.Y. Post).

for the future

LUXURY COSTS LESS!

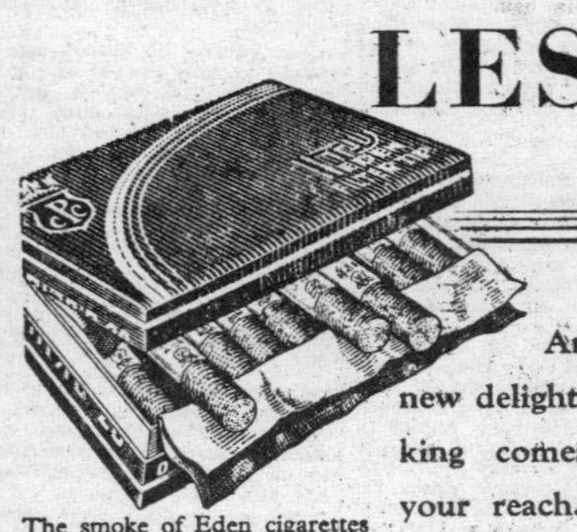

An entirely new delight in smoking comes within your reach. A new fragrance, a new flavour, the true flavour of the heart of the ripened leaf is revealed by the exclusive Eden filter tip. And the price is now no more than 105 mils for Twenty.

The smoke of Eden cigarettes is smoke freed from everything that could taint or conceal its natural richness. Irritants which form whenever tobacco is burned are trapped by the filter tip. And when it is thus cooled, made smooth, refined and cleansed— cigarette smoke has a fragrance and flavour never before enjoyed.

EDEN

Filter tip cigarettes
NOW 105 MILS FOR 20

MADE BY THE PALESTINE CIGARETTE COMPANY LIMITED

JACOB ROSE
General Agent for
UNITED STATES LINES
Travel and Shipping
Correspondent for
THE AMERICAN EXPRESS
COMPANY INC.
TEL AVIV: 12 Herzl Street
HAIFA: 59 Harbour Street

LATE Edition

THE PALESTINE POST

JERUSALEM
SUNDAY, SEPT. 28, 1947

PRICE 20 MILS
VOL. XXII. No. 6519

AS GOOD AS EVER
JOHNNIE WALKER
BORN 1820—STILL GOING STRONG
John Walker & Sons Ltd. Scotch Whisky Distillers, Kilmarnock, Scotland.
Agent:- Joseph P. Albina, Jerusalem, Palestine.

BRITAIN REJECTS UNSCOP, ANNOUNCES WITHDRAWAL

LAKE SUCCESS, Saturday. — In the long awaited British statement of policy, the Colonial Secretary, Mr. Arthur Creech Jones, told the 55-nation Special Palestine Committee of the U.N. yesterday that Britain will not implement by herself or probably with other nations jointly, any United Nations solution which is not agreeable to both Jews and Arabs. He announced Britain's intentions to abandon the 25 year old Mandate over Palestine and to pull out her military and Government forces in the area at "an early" date.

The Palestine Committee, under the chairmanship of the Australian delegate, Mr. Herbert Evatt, listened in profoundest attention, in conformity with the importance of the declaration by Mr. Creech Jones. He spoke with his hands clasped on the front of his breast, slowly reading from a three-page manuscript spread before him on the horseshoe table. Deep silence descended on the committee room as he delivered the statement of his Government's attitude which avoided setting a dead-line for the withdrawal and reserved the right to judge the Assembly's final decision thereby reserving to herself the right to act unilaterally regarding Palestine.

(Full text of Statement on Page 4)

The Chairman of UNSCOP, Judge E. Sandstrom, spoke after Mr. Creech Jones and the session then adjourned until Monday when the Palestine Arab Higher Committee is to state its case. The Jewish case is to be presented on Tuesday, probably by Dr. A.H. Silver and Mr. Shertok.

Dr. Emanuel Neumann was yesterday seated at the Committee table as the Jewish Agency representative and Jamal eff. Husseini on behalf of the Arab Executive.

Challenge To U.N.

LAKE SUCCESS, Saturday. — The United Nations was presented with the greatest challenge of its career when Britain declared its new Palestine policy, in the opinion of delegates of the most important countries.

The British move poses at least four problems, observers agree: Does Britain consider the UNSCOP partition plan unworkable and unjust? Has Britain any alternative proposal? Does it seriously intend to leave Palestine, whether the United Nations finds a solution or not? How can the United Nations enforce its partition proposals?

Two salient impressions emerged form internal talks, Reuters correspondent said: 1. The Arabs were not displeased with the main lines of Mr. Creech Jones' speech. 2. The Jews were definitely disappointed at some of its implications. In the final analysis, the only country able to take Britain's place in maintaining order was the U.S.A., and there was no indication now that America was prepared to send troops to Palestine.

Important Implications

A reference in the speech which was puzzling the Arabs slightly was Mr. Creech Jones' use of the term "independence in Palestine," instead of the more usual "independence of Palestine." They felt that this small point might conceal important practical implications.

Zionist circles expressed disappointment that the British gave no indication of an immediate policy towards immigration, fearing that Britain might try to sidetrack the whole of the Palestine immigration problem. Zionists also felt that Britain's insistence on supporting a solution acceptable to both Jews and Arabs placed a virtual "veto" in Arab hands.

A question being asked here is whether the British threat to leave Palestine whatever happened was not intended to exert pressure on the Jews and Arabs to come to agreement among themselves, with the fear of possible chaos when the troops withdraw, the example of India being fresh in delegates' minds.

Wise Decision

The "New York Herald Tribune" wrote that the British decision was as wise as it was honourable. Grave as were the issues with which the British withdrawal confronted all concerned, it provided the best hope of achieving a viable solution.

The "Daily Worker" (Communist), on the other hand, saw in the statement that Britain would have to take into account the "inherent justice" of any solution, an implied threat of a veto if Britain did not like it or if the British did not get a suitable *quid pro quo* from America.

The paper pointed out that while Britain demanded an advance commitment from Bulgaria and Albania to abide by the U.N. decision on Greece, it reserved the veto if it did not like the U.N. decision on Palestine.

The "New York Post" suggested an interim administration of Palestine by one Power, preferably the U.S.A. backed by the United Nations and a police force recruited from the signatory countries of the UNSCOP majority report.

(Reuter and U.P.)

Mr. Arthur Creech Jones

TWO COURSES OPEN TO U.S.

By GEORGE LICHTHEIM,
Palestine Post Correspondent

LONDON, Saturday. — Informed circles here are wondering what effect Britain's opening gambit at Lake Success is likely to produce on the Americans.

Theoretically, two courses are open to them — they can either treat Mr. Creech Jones' statement as an invitation to step in and carry out UNSCOP's majority report, or carry out a prompt retreat from the advanced position taken up by Mr. Marshall in his preliminary remarks.

Mr. Creech Jones' speech is generally regarded as a heavy setback for hopes of a settlement on the basis of UNSCOP's findings, not because it announces the termination of the Mandate, but because even British cooperation in applying a scheme approved by the U.N. and actively backed by other U.N. members, is made conditional on the British view of "its inherent justice and the force required to effect it."

"Cowardice"

The "Manchester Guardian" describes this as "carrying caution to the point of cowardice," and aptly remarks that "the scruples of the British Government would be more impressive if it had not during the past two years been trying to impose on the Jews a solution acceptable to the Arabs."

Even "The Times" remarks that the Government will shortly be compelled to study afresh "the irrefutable arguments originally mustered by the Peel Commission" in favour of Partition.

Plainly, however, the Foreign Office's view that Britain should pull out completely rather than undertake any responsibilities likely to harm the "friendship" with the Arab world, has more weight in Cabinet circles than was thought.

(More on Page 3, Col. 2)

HOLD TIGHT

LAKE SUCCESS, Saturday (Palcor). — The obliqueness of Mr. Creech Jones' statement was noted by some observers here. A Hungarian journalist quoted a Hungarian proverb:

Here is nothing. Hold on tight.

FIRST DAY OF SUCCOTH

The Palestine Post will not appear tomorrow, the first day of the Jewish festival of Succoth. The paper will be published as usual on Tuesday.

DISCRIMINATING WOMEN WILL ALWAYS PREFER
ELIZABETH ARDEN'S PREPARATIONS
BECAUSE THEY ARE THE RESULT OF LONG AND CAREFUL RESEARCH WORK.
OBTAINABLE AT:—
The NEW BRITISH PHARMACY
ex. Norton & Co., Zion Cinema St.,
Tel. 3374, Jerusalem.

BRITISH WILL LEAVE AS SOON AS POSSIBLE AFTER DEBATE

LONDON, Saturday (Reuter). — Britain's withdrawal from Palestine will take place as soon as practicable after the present debate in the U.N. General Assembly, in the absence of a settlement, a Foreign Office spokesman reaffirmed today.

He added that it was possible that Britain might agree to take part in some international force instructed by the United Nations to take up its station in Palestine, in which case it would be a question of reducing rather than completely evacuating the present forces.

Asked what policy regarding Jewish immigrants Britain would enforce in the present interim period, the spokesman said: "I think the period will be a very short one, and the question of policy will hardly arise." (A maximum of two months was mentioned.)

He said that details of the withdrawal, which in any case is dependent on the outcome of the U.N. debates, such as the future ownership of British military installations in Palestine, remained unclear, but he emphasized that Britain's decision to terminate the Mandate would certainly hold good if the Assembly failed to come to any conclusion at its present session.

The spokesman had said last night that Britain's announcement was "decisive and considered."

Anarchy Predicted

It is no secret that British officials do not believe that the United Nations can produce a solution where Britain has failed over a quarter of a century. In the view of usually well informed quarters in London, the sequence of events is now likely to be:

1.—**Britain would start preparations to leave Palestine as soon as the present Assembly discussions are complete;**

2.—**The subsequent withdrawal would take place as soon as is technically and physically possible, and**

3.—**Britain would not concern herself with the handing over of authority to any racial group in Palestine and that a period of anarchy might follow.**

The spokesman emphasized that the decision to withdraw from Palestine did not mean that Britain was pulling out of the Middle East as a whole. The evacuation of Palestine, it was understood, will be part of a general rearrangement of British forces in that area.

According to usually reliable sources this will involve the development of bases in East Africa and will lend critical interest to the forthcoming Big Four discussions on the future of the Italian Empire. The spokesman said that the British position in the Middle East would to some extent be strengthened by the termination of the extensive Palestine commitment, where British forces have needed to be virtually on a war footing.

MARSHALL RECEIVES SHERTOK, SILVER

LAKE SUCCESS, Saturday (United Press).—Mr. George Marshall, who earlier this week conferred with Arab leaders, this morning received the American Zionist leader, Dr. Abba Hillel Silver, and Mr. Moshe Shertok, of the Jewish Agency, for a 40-minute conference to discuss the entire Palestine problem.

QUICK U.N. SOLUTION ESSENTIAL

The decision announced by Mr. Creech Jones made it all the more imperative for the U.N. Assembly to find a solution for Palestine without delay and to devise means for its implementation, says a Jewish Agency statement in New York.

Fortunately, the Assembly had before it the UNSCOP report and it was logical that the majority recommendations should be adopted as a basis. The Agency hoped that in view of Britain's failure to carry out the Mandate the withdrawal from Palestine would be carried out speedily.

It characterized as "singular" Mr. Creech Jones' assertion that the British Government refused to carry out any Palestine policy by force of arms, since that is what Britain was doing at present. It warned Britain not to persist in using force during the evacuation period.

The Arab Office in London issued a statement welcoming the British decision to withdraw from Palestine and to grant it independence, but denouncing Britain's "intention to escape the consequences of the problem she created by handing the country to the United Nations or to any other State or group of States."

The Arab statement considered Britain's virtual rejection of the UNSCOP report as "wise and practical," and approved the British decision not to participate in the enforcement of any recommendations "which are against the interests of the Arabs," even if made by the United Nations. *(Reuter, PTA, ANA)*

SANDSTROM PRESENTS UNSCOP REPORT

LAKE SUCCESS, Saturday. — After Mr. Creech Jones' statement yesterday, Judge Emil Sandstrom of Sweden presented UNSCOP's report to the Ad-Hoc Committee.

He explained that it had been necessary to reach a compromise solution, in order to honour as far as possible the pledges already made to both Jews and Arabs. No solution could possibly satisfy all interested parties.

Mr. Sandstrom recalled that the Palestine problem was a "legacy of the First World War and the League's Mandate" under which Britain had agreed to do her best to establish a Jewish National Home in Palestine without prejudice to the rights of the non-Jewish communities.

He pointed out that Jewish immigration had been increasing in recent years, and that at the same time, the Arab population had swelled by 500,000, thus making the Jews a considerable minority. Jewish immigrants, who had brought with them the Western way of life, had "achieved things in material aspects which call for the admiration of everyone." Colonies had been established on land previously uncultivated, and huge industries had been built up.

Farmers had settled along the coastal plain not following a coherent plan, but in pockets among Arab agricultural settlements. Thus, "the presence of a minority in the country aroused nationalism which is liable to create complications and difficulties," he stated.

Judge Sandstrom told the Ad-Hoc Committee that Jewish nationalism was being partly fed by the DP problem and "outside influences— support in the U.S.A. specifically". and Arab nationalism by the Arab States. The Arabs were also being placated by the British to oppose Jewish immigration, he alleged.

The claims of both the Jews and the Arabs had validity, but a solution should be reached honouring pledges made. UNSCOP attempted, but had been unable to reach unanimity due to the complexities of the problem.

(UP, PTA, Palcor and Reuter)

BOMB EXPLODES IN SWEDISH CONSULATE

Palestine Post Staff

A violent explosion shattered the windows of the Swedish Consulate in Nablus Road in Jerusalem, as well as those of neighbouring buildings, just before 8 o'clock last night. There were no casualties. The bomb had been placed in the gateway of the Consulate.

The sirens sounded immediately and all traffic remained at a standstill for 25 minutes until the All Clear.

An official of the Consulate told *The Palestine Post* that the first sign that anything was wrong was the barking of his two dogs. Shortly afterwards, the explosion rocked the house, throwing furniture about and showering glass on the floors.

Some damage was caused to St. George's School across the street.

Noticing suspicious movements in the garden of the Swedish Consulate at 49 Rothschild Blvd. in Tel Aviv about 8.30 tonight, the Consul informed the Police. A patrol was sent out and a guard was put on the building all night.

Octuplets

SHANGHAI, Saturday (AFP). — A young Chinese woman in the Communist territory of Ning Chun in Hopei Province, has given birth to eight children, all boys, according to press reports. One of the babies has died, while the other seven are stated to be in perfect health.

From Moscow comes the news that a young Caucasian woman in Oulanoude has given birth to quins — three boys and two girls, all of whom are said to be doing fine.

A Speech and 3 Sentences

By JESSE ZEL LURIE,
Palestine Post Correspondent

LAKE SUCCESS, Saturday. — Mr. Creech Jones' statement yesterday required careful analysis and reactions to it varied according to what paragraph was stressed.

First reading gave the impression that Britain was getting out, and last night's late editions carried streamer headlines such as "Britain to Quit Palestine."

Upon second reading, you may find the catches, and Victor Bernstein's dispatch in this morning's "PM" was headlined "British Claim Right to Veto Palestine Decision." He wrote that Britain had amplified their earlier statement to the Special Session that they would not implement a solution they did not like and were now refusing to assist in the implementation of a distasteful solution.

In its context with the rest of the statement, that may mean distasteful to the Arabs. In the present state of the world it is almost unthinkable that troops can be sent to Palestine without British approval and assistance. Therefore, if Britain stands by yesterday's statement, the Arabs will virtually have the power of veto on the Palestine decision, "PM" says.

Soviet Stand

Another statement yesterday by M. Vyshinsky, consisting of three short sentences, may in the long run prove as important as Mr. Creech Jones' announcement. Asked for comment on the British announcement of withdrawal from Palestine, M. Vyshinsky said:

It is not clear whose withdrawal is meant. I fear the meaning of the statement is the ultimate withdrawal of the Jews. To that we are, of course, opposed.

M. Vyshinsky will be amazed that reporters interpreted his statement as meaning it was necessary for Britain to protect the Jews from annihilation. The hard core of Soviet policy in Palestine is the withdrawal of "imperialist powers." M. Vyshinsky, of course, meant opposition to the final withdrawal of Jewish rights to Palestine.

This statement of support for the Zionists at a time when it is most needed foreshadows that the Soviet Union may again play a crucial role as at the last session, in achieving a decision. If America and Britain continue to sit on the fence, the Soviet Union may take the lead in proposing a solution which will force the Western Powers to follow along, thus achieving a two thirds majority for the termination of the British Mandate.

Another optimistic note is the indication that the Assembly will rule that abstentions are not to be counted in figuring the two thirds majority. Thus, the Arab strategy of trading favours for Latin American abstentions would not help.

Officials' Lot

The position of Government officers and Police in Palestine in the event of British evacuation is the subject of the following special communique issued yesterday:

OFFICIAL COMMUNIQUE NO. 128
September 27, 1947

The Secretary of State has approved an announcement in the following terms in connection with the statement made by him on behalf of His Majesty's Government to the United Nations Committee on Palestine on September 26, 1947.

2. Officers of the Palestine Government will desire to know at once that their interests will be adequately safeguarded in the event of constitutional changes. Any announcement must necessarily be in general terms until the actual conditions to be met are known and until compensation benefits to be granted have been worked out in detail.

3. (a) Every effort will be made to absorb expatriate officers serving in permanent appointments by their voluntary transfer to suitable posts elsewhere in the Colonial Service.

(b) Expatriate officers serving in permanent appointments whom it is not possible to absorb elsewhere, or who do not wish to accept transfer, will be permitted to retire with suitable compensation for loss of office.

(c) Steps will be taken to secure the rights of the non-expatriate officers to retiring benefits earned under pensions and provident fund ordinances. Further consideration of the position of non-expatriate officers must necessarily await clarification of constitutional arrangements which would replace the British administration on its withdrawal.

(d) British Police whose normal retiring benefits are provided for under the Police Ordinance will be granted enhanced benefits on premature termination of service.

(e) The question of the terms to be granted under (b) and (d) is now under active consideration.

4. The Officer Administering the Government trusts that all officers will appreciate that nothing more on this subject can be said at the moment and that in the meantime it is of great importance that the administration of Palestine should be maintained with energy and efficiency and without discouragement.

CHOLERA IN EGYPT GROWS

Both Britain and the U.S. are rushing anti-cholera serum to Egypt to help fight the disease which has spread in the Nile Delta area and in districts just north of Cairo.

It was officially announced in Jerusalem on Friday that normal quarantine restrictions, as permitted under the International Sanitary Convention, have been imposed against passengers and traffic from Egypt by all routes.

Passengers from Egypt by any route will be required to present a valid certificate of inoculation against cholera.

After arrival in Palestine, passengers will be subjected to surveillance for a period of not less than five days.

An Extraordinary Gazette, published on Friday bans the import from Egypt of fresh and salted fish; fresh and preserved fruit, and vegetables other than canned.

MARONITE FOR JEWISH STATE

Palestine Post Correspondent

BEIRUT, Saturday. — The creation of a Jewish State in Palestine and a Christian State in the Lebanon was urged in a memorandum submitted to UNSCOP in Geneva last August by Mgr. Ignatz Moubarak, the Maronite Archbishop of Beirut.

This was revealed today by the Arabic paper "Biar" which published the full text of the memorandum. Mgr. Moubarak, who was in Rome when the Committee visited the Lebanon, has recently returned to Beirut.

Palestine is the centre of two great religions, — Judaism Christianity — he said. The Moslem population had entered the country only by force or arms. The inclusion of Palestine and the Lebanon in a complex of Arab states would be contrary to history and would disturb the equilibrium of the Near East, the Archbishop claimed.

440 MORE SENT TO CYPRUS
REFUGEE SHOT DEAD ON SHIP

Palestine Post Bureau

HAIFA, Saturday. — One man killed and at least 10 wounded — that was the price which 446 men, women and children paid today to reach the shores of Palestine on their small tank landing craft of several hundred tons, which they had named "Af Al Pi Khen" — "In spite of it all."

Intercepted about 8 o'clock this morning by British destroyers off the south coast of Palestine, the vessel was boarded by a naval party which forced its way to the strategic points of the ship, killing in the operation one man, apparently by revolver shots, and wounding several men and women by charging with their batons.

The refugee was killed, it is officially stated, when a number of Jews, brandishing crowbars, surrounded a sailor.

Two other Jews were shot and wounded and seven more hurt in the 20-minute fight that followed the boarding. A sailor had his finger broken in the struggle.

The approach to the cargo jetty in the port here tonight resembled an armed camp teeming with jeeps, lorries, wireless cars and projectors, and strong detachments of the 6th Airborne Division.

At 8.30 the ship was brought in by a tug and moored along the quayside with its railings broken, the blue and white Zionist colours fluttering from its wheelhouse on the wall of which "Haganah Ship — Af Al Pi Khen" was written. Her original name, "Farida," was painted in English and Arabic on the bows. The refugees fell to singing "Hatikvah," with the muffled explosions of depth charges puctuating the song.

Angry Shouts

A gang-plank was moved in place and Airborne soldiers, armed with wooden clubs and wearing steel helmets, went aboard to relieve the naval boarding party.

The refugees were told in Hebrew over loud-speakers, that they would be taken to Cyprus and that their baggage would be returned to them after it had been searched.

First two sick women were brought down on stretchers and taken to the Government Hospital, one of them followed by her husband who was allowed to remain with her. Two soldiers carried down a man who had suffered a fit.

The refugees then came down the gangplank in single file, glum and weary, dressed in shabby clothes, their bundles slung over their shoulders. There were few children. Several men and women had fresh bandages around their heads.

They marched quietly to the disinfection tent, and were thoroughly searched. Their bundles were thrown on a large heap on the quay and examined by a party of soldiers who opened every box, scanned every paper and looked into every water bottle.

The refugees were marched aboard the two deportation ships which had been standing by since the afternoon. The first, the Empire Comfort, left at 9.30 with 203 men and 88 women. The Empire Rest followed soon after with 113 men, 25 women and eight children. Four women, one pregnant and three ill, were taken to the Government Hospital, and three husbands were allowed to land with them. Two men were also taken to hospital.

EXODUS REFUGEES DEMONSTRATE

By ROBERT GARY,
ONA Correspondent

LUEBECK, Saturday. — Demonstrations of protest against the British ultimatum were repeated in both camps yesterday. In Am Stau, people tore down the tent where registration of volunteers for France should have taken place and threw it over the barbed-wire enclosure.

In Poppendorf, a huge parade was staged, people marching with banners demanding the re-opening of the gates of Palestine.

4 Killed in Bank Robbery

Palestine Post Bureau

TEL AVIV, Saturday. — Four British constables, the crew of a police armoured car and members of a foot patrol, were killed here yesterday morning, and two constables and two civilians were wounded, by terrorists who stole two sacks with LP.150,000 which were being taken from Barclays Bank under armed escort to Jerusalem.

But the larger sack, containing LP.105,000, so heavy that four men dragged it away, was abandoned a block from the bank and later recovered by the police. The robbers are believed to have escaped in a white jeep with the other sack, with LP.45,000.

The four dead constables were:

J. J. Murray, 20, Newton Daly, Lough Rea, County Galway, Ireland;

A. D. Mitchell, 19, Sandfield House, High Street, Sutton-on-Sea, Lincs.;

P. Bould, 26, 63 Platt Street Hightown, Hednesford, Staffs; and

A. J. Ford, 18, 34, Royal Hill, Greenwich, London.

The wounded: B/Const. John Harbison (19), P/Const. Eliahu Mizrahi (28), Mr. Hans Bar (23), a passing driver; and Mr. Haim Cohen (17), a passing cyclist.

The armoured car parked before the main entrance of the bank in Rehov Allenby, at the corner of Rehov Ahad Haam, shortly before 9 o'clock. The driver remained at the wheel and a gunner at his post in the turret, while two other members of the crew entered the bank to escort the porter who was to take the sacks out of the bank.

The porter, Moshe Tevach, first took the smaller sack with LP.45,000 and placed it in the armoured car. He again entered the bank and came out with the heavier sack over his shoulder. Suddenly, pistol fire was opened from three directions. The armoured car driver and the gunner were shot dead and one of the escort was fatally injured.

Four men then rushed at Tevach and sent him sprawling with a blow in the head. They dragged the heavy sack around the corner into Rehov Ahad Haam and disappeared behind a smoke screen. Scare bombs and smoke bombs thrown by the gang added to the confusion. Other gangsters removed the smaller sack from the armoured car.

One agile terrorist climbed into the turret of the armoured car and removed the gun. A white jeep passed the scene and is believed to have picked up the bandits with the smaller sack. It sped southwards in the direction of Rothschild Boulevard.

A police patrol of two British and one Jewish constables rushed to the scene from the corner of Rehov Ahad Haam and Rehov Yavneh. They were shot before they could fire. One British constable died later in the hospital and his two companions were wounded, one of them seriously.

The entire operation was executed with lightning speed. But there was one hitch. The vehicle which was to have picked up the sack at the cor-

(Continued on Page 2, Col. 2)

CONSTABLES' FUNERAL

RAMLEH, Saturday. — The funeral of the four constables took place at the Military Cemetery here today. The men were buried with full honours in the presence of Col. W.N. Gray, Inspector-General of Police, and a large number of senior officers and men.

Europe's Empty Shelves

By ROBERT MUNSON, A.P. Correspondent

PARIS, Saturday. — Europe opened its cupboard doors tonight to display its empty shelves in a 20,000 word detailed Report of the delegates to the Marshall Plan Conference here, but the event was dimmed by the statement of the U.S. President on Thursday that he hoped to avoid calling a special session of Congress to discuss European Aid.

The Report contains the details of a basic plan announced on Monday in which the 16 nations of Western Europe agreed they could restore their own industrial and farming productivity provided they were not hampered by a lack of dollars. They asked the U.S. for more than 19 billion dollars to cover purchases in the well stocked western hemisphere, but did not specify how the money was to be repaid.

Observers believed the delegates to the Conference had been reminded of earlier statements coming from U.S. Treasury officials that any sum to aid the recovery of Europe would be an outright gift.

Volume One of the Report blames the Second World War for the critical situation. "The destruction of European economic life was far greater than that which Europe experienced in the First World War," the report declared pointing out that more than half of Europe's two million goods wagons had been destroyed or damaged, bread grain crops had fallen off by one third and industrial production in Belgium, France and the Netherlands was reduced by 30 to 40%.

It estimates that between now and 1951 the countries of Western Europe can recover from the war if they are allowed to run up a bill of 15,810 million dollars with the U.S.

As suggested by the U.S. Assistant Secretary of State the Report contains a plan for organizing a customs union and a study group has been formed to examine the problems involved.

LATIN PATRIARCH OF PALESTINE DEAD

We regret to announce the death in Jerusalem last night of Mgr. Louis Barlassina, the Latin Patriarch of Palestine, Trans-Jordan and Cyprus, at the age of 76. His Beatitude died suddenly after a heart attack.

Mgr. Barlassina, who was born in Turin, came to Palestine in 1917. He was ordained at the age of 22 and, when he was 40, he was appointed Curate of St. Jean de Lateran, one of the largest parishes in Rome.

He was sent to Jerusalem in 1918, and was appointed the fifth Latin Patriarch in 1920.

SINCE 1925
Portadyne Radio
ALL WAVE A.C. SUPERHETERODYNE
5 VALVE RECEIVER LP. 33.000
This new Portadyne Model is one of the finest post-war receivers yet produced.
For particulars apply to your Radio Dealer or to SOLE AGENTS & IMPORTERS
STEEL BROTHERS & CO. LTD.
43 Kingsway HAIFA

THE PALESTINE POST

JERUSALEM
SUNDAY, NOV. 30, 1947

PRICE: 20 MILS
VOL. XXII. No. 6571

PARTITION APPROVED BY MORE THAN 2/3; 33 TO 13

FLUSHING MEADOW, Saturday (U.P.) — When the plan for the Partition of Palestine and the setting up of Jewish and Arab States appeared certain of enough votes to pass the General Assembly today, the Arab States in a last-ditch effort to prevent this, proposed the establishment of a federated state based on the canton system in which the Jews and Arabs would be separated as far as possible.

The Arab motion, which was attacked as a move to sabotage the U.N. Partition plan, was opposed by the rapporteur of the Ad Hoc Committee, Mr. Thors, and by the delegate of the United States, Mr. H. Johnson, who asked the Chairman, Dr. Aranha, to call for a vote on the Ad Hoc Committee's recommendation for Partition. Mr. Aranha ruled that the delegates would have to vote on the partition plan after hearing last minute appeals by Iran and Syria. Mr. Johnson, said:"There is nothing conciliatory in this," and he was supported by the Soviet Delegate. The vote was taken; 33 said Yes, 13 No and 10 abstained; One was absent.

24-Hour Delay Follows Colombian Resolution

FLUSHING MEADOW Saturday. — The Colombian delegate, Senor Alfonso Lopez, opened yesterday afternoon's session of the U.N. Assembly with a surprise manoeuvre, suggesting that the U.N. defer its vote and make a last-minute attempt at guiding the Arabs and Jews to a settlement.

"With so many abstentions and negative votes registered in the Ad Hoc Committee," he said, "Partition will remain a minority plan, even if it got the required two-thirds majority in the Assembly." It was irrelevant at the last minute to try and influence another few delegates to endorse the proposal — that would not give it world backing. One should not ignore the fact that the Moslem delegations opposed it en bloc, and it was significant in the Ad Hoc Committee. China and France had not seen eye to eye with the U.S. and U.S.S.R. His new plan would leave the question of Palestine in the consideration stage until well into Spring next year.

His proposal was to give the Ad Hoc Committee the character of an interim subsidiary organ of the General Assembly, to carry on the study of the Palestine question with a view to finding a satisfactory solution. This Committee should be authorized

to take necessary steps to bring about agreement between the Arabs and Jews as to the future Government of that country;

to request, if it deems necessary, the advisory opinion of the International Court of Justice;

to formulate complete recommendations as to the manner in which the U.N. may give effect to its unanimous recommendations and to report on its work not later than February 29, 1948.

He proposed that member states shall advise not later than April 15, 1948, whether they wish to consider the matter at a special Assembly session.

"We have limited but ample time, as the Mandatory will not complete the evacuation until August next year." Thus, if the Palestine Committee was allowed to continue its work and report before the end of February, that would give ample time to convene — if necessary — a special session in Spring.

When the Colombian delegate left the rostrum, the President of the Assembly, Dr. Aranha, announced that the proposal would be put to the vote later in the session.

M. Alexandre Parodi, of France, then sprang the second surprise in proposing a 24-hour adjournment in the hope of some last-minute conciliatory move. He based his proposal on the statements of Sir Mohammed Zafrullah Khan (Pakistan) and Dr. Fahdil Jamali (Iraq) who earlier in the debate had suggested that the door to conciliation was still open.

"This overture comes quite late in the game, and it might be asked whether it is not merely an attempt to delay the moment of decision," he said later. However, he considered the question too grave and complicated to allow any chance to be left aside, "even a faint one," of making a peaceful settlement based on agreement.

M. Parodi opened his short statement with explaining the present position was — either Partition or nothing, and that he did not like being pushed to this extremity.

After the Ethiopian delegate declared he would abstain, the Chairman declared the debate closed and put the French proposal to the vote. The Assembly decided by 25 votes to 15 votes to adjourn for 24 hours, after M. Oscar Lange of Poland had made a short but ardent plea against the deferment, and so did the Colombian delegate — for different reasons.

(Reuter, UP, Palcor)

ARABS PROPOSE ALTERNATIVE

FLUSHING MEADOW, Saturday. — The tenseness of the last few hours at the U.N. Assembly when it was believed that voting on the Palestine question would finally be taken was evidenced tonight by the packed public galleries, with crowds larger than ever in the chequered history of the United Nations.

For the first time in the history of the United Nations, uniformed police appeared at all strategic points of the public and press galleries.

M. Chamoun's soft spoken approach reportedly did not have the support of Jamal Eff. Husseini, who as spokesman for the Arabs of Palestine, recently threatened to hurl the entire Arab world of 70 million persons against anv Jewish State created in the Middle East. The Arabs had held off until the last possible moment and until passage of partition seemed assured.

Mr. Johnson said: "I submit that the conditions outlined by the delegate of France have not been fulfilled. The purpose of the adjournment was to permit conciliation. No conciliation plan is before the Assembly now. The Lebanon "has no more to do with conciliation than Austria or China. There is no mention of conciliation between the Jewish Agency and the Arab Higher Committee."

The Iran delegate suggested that the question should be referred back to the Ad Hoc Committee for further study during a "number of weeks." The Chairman ruled the proposal to be put in writing and called on Faris Bey el Khoury, Syria, who appealed to the delegates to look for a solution other than Partition, which he said was impossible of implementation.

The Syrian delegate read a letter from Dr. Evatt to Prince Feisal of Saudi Arabia dated November 1, inviting him to confer with Mr. George Marshall on conciliation efforts. The Saudi reply accepted the suggestion but, Faris Bey maintained, nothing was done, the Ad Hoc Committee concentrating on partition. He therefore appealed for further time for conciliation efforts, in order to avert violenve and bloodshed.

The Chairman announced he could not put the Iranian motion — which he considered a new one — until the Partition proposal was voted and decided. "Now we proceed to vote" said Dr. Aranha, at 12.20 a.m. (Palestine time) when M. Chamoun for the Lebanon was given the floor on "a point of order."

Dr. Aranha ruled that the Lebanese proposal was out of order. Voting began at 12.27 a.m. Palestine time and was concluded by 12.30 a.m.

Mr. Gromyko was the last speaker pending the written translation of the Iranian adjournment motion. He said nothing was changed in the 24 hours during which the Assembly stood adjourned: it was a question that had remained unsettled for 25 years. The Lebanese proposals did not change the position "one iota," although it was the same proposal as the UNSCOP alternative which the Arabs, for reasons of their own, had not even wished to discuss. The U.N. had taken the question on itself and must settle it; the Assembly must proceed to a vote without delay. The Soviet delegation would support Partition in the Assembly as it had done in the Ad Hoc Committee.

The Chairman then read the Iranian motion asking for adjournment until January 15,1948.

ARAB STATES PREPARE TO FIGHT ABDULLAH

By JON KIMCHE, Special to The Palestine Post

LONDON, Saturday.—Representatives of the Arab States here express serious disquiet following reports that King Abdullah's Arab Legion will occupy the Arab State sector of Palestine when the British withdraw. One British source normally very close to these representatives has stated, however, that what will happen, according to his information, is rather different.

The Arab Legion, together with a token force from Iraq will occupy, he said, the central sector of the Palestine Arab State. Syria and the Lebanon will occupy the coastal stretch of the Arab State north of Acre, and Egypt, with a token Saudi Arabian force, will occupy parts of the Negev and the desert frontier area.

What will happen after such a "partition of partitioned Palestine," he added, is anybody's guess, but one thing is certain: that the Arab States will not accept Trans-Jordan taking over by itself, and that Trans-Jordan will oppose Syrian and Lebanese inroads.

British Personnel

This has raised again more acutely the question of the position of British officers and personnel seconded for service in Trans-Jordan. The position is that the status of these military and civilian officials is still not decided. When the British Administration leaves Palestine, a new agreement with Trans-Jordan is to be negotiated on lines similar to that negotiated with India, which would allow for continued service by British officials in Trans-Jordan. Special consideration, however, is to be given to the position of Glubb Pasha.

The Colonial Office is at present engaged in straightening out this situation, but a Foreign Office source today stated categorically that the British Government would not allow a situation to arise where a high British officer would be responsible for leading a foreign army against either the prospective Jewish State or against other Arab States or against a U.N. force. This has been interpreted as foreshadowing the probable early withdrawal of Glubb Pasha and other high-ranking officers in executive positions in the Trans-Jordan army. The possibility, however, that they may remain in Trans-Jordan's service in a purely advisory capacity is now under consideration.

PAKISTAN, IRAQ TALK OF RECONCILIATION

FLUSHING MEADOW, Saturday. — The first speaker in yesterday's debate was the delegate of Pakistan, Sir Mohammed Zafrullah Khan, who recalled the "mortal struggle" in which the Allies had been drawn not long ago, when the Arabs were called upon to redress the balance in the Middle East, and they threw in their lot with the Allies.

What legal right had the world to cut up Palestine, he asked, warning the nations of the West that tomorrow they might need friends and allies in the Middle East. "I appeal to you," he said, "not to wrong your friends."

From North Africa to Central Asia, Sir Mohammed said, there were doubts and distrust of the motives and statements of the Western Powers. "You take the gravest risks of impairing any chance of real cooperation between East and West by thus forcibly driving what amounts to a western wedge into the heart of the Middle East."

UNSCOP had recommended that all UN members take refugees and D.P.'s to alleviate their lot. What had the General Assembly done in that respect? Sub-Committee Two had put forward the same recommendation; it had asked that D.P.'s and refugees "shall be distributed among member states according to their capacity to receive them." The U.S., which was "so humanitarian" had made no effort to take refugees but recommended that they go to Palestine. That was the contribution to the solution of the problem by that "august power."

The proposed Jewish and Arab States would each consist of three parts. Was that justice? And Jerusalem would remain forever under international jurisdiction. The Holy City would never belong to the Arabs, she would always be different. "What authority, legal authority, have you to do this," he asked. The whole scheme lacked legal and constitutional authority, Sir Mohammad asserted, imploring delegates not to accept it. "Will you take the responsibility?"

Economic Board

The Joint Economic Board was as illegal as the U.N. administration of Jerusalem. Sir Mohammad then went into detail as concerns boundaries, minorities etc. to claim that injustice was being done to the Arabs, and he drew particular attention to the Negev where far more Arabs were now living, but which was to be given to the Jews.

He also invited the attention of delegates to "that eminent, highly respected Jew," Dr. Magnes, who had always stood for political unity. It was a fallacy, he said, to think that once economic unity was established, political unity would follow. But the Arabs of Palestine and the Arab States would not cooperate.

Mr. Johnson of the U.S., he said, had expressed the hope that, given the support of the surrounding Arab States and the people of Palestine, the experiment might work. "But the Arabs of Palestine have declared that they are not going to cooperate—and remember," he warned, "this is not an experiment; it is proposed as a permanent solution."

"The United Nations was in honour bound to seek to unite and bring together, rather than divide," he concluded. Let it make a last attempt at bringing together. "Let us decide here today to promote and foster peace, prosperity and welfare for all, Jew, Arab and Gentile alike, which shall redound to our glory forever."

In a brief statement, the Chinese delegate informed the Assembly that as per instructions received from Nanking, China would not support Partition, but abstain from voting. His country maintained that any solution of the problem must be based on the consent of the peoples immediately concerned.

China's Abstention

China had right from the beginning of the Ad Hoc Committee's work sought to bring about cooperation between the Jews and the Arabs in search of a settlement. Unfortunately, the two plans submitted by the Sub Committees represented a set of diametrically opposed views that could not be reconciled. It had then been hoped that the plan of Sub-Committee One could be modified in such a way as to be "if not satisfactory to both, at least less objectionable to either." That, too, had not been achieved.

Dr. G. Granados, of Guatemala recalled that the Arab Higher Executive would not even listen to UNSCOP's chairman, Judge Sandstrom, and had intimated that they did not seem to be in favour of conciliation. "UNSCOP went out to call at the doors of the Arabs and were received in villages, where it did not notice the hostility accorded to them by Arab leaders."

He gave instances of the Arab boycott against the Jews, to prove that conciliation was not possible, not because the Jews did not want it, but because of the Arabs' animosity.

The unitary system proposed by the Arab Higher Executive and supported by the other Arab States would mean immediate persecution and enslavement for the Jews. A Jewish State had to be established; the world owed that to the Jews. There was no alternative, he concluded.

Mr. Ernest Dihigo announced that Cuba would oppose Partition "despite the pressure brought to bear upon us." Cuba had shown sympathy to the Jews and appreciated their qualities. "We have allowed into our own territory thousands of Jews, and they live amongst us free and without discrimination of any kind. We cannot, however, vote here according to their wishes, because we consider the partition of Palestine goes contrary to right and justice," he declared.

The Jews were aliens in Palestine, he added, Partition would place those into a "subordinate position" who had previously been the rightful owners of the country. Cuba urged that the Assembly should wait a few months, rather than hurry a bad solution.

Dr. Fahdil Jamali, the Iraqi delegate, spoke for over an hour alleging that "great pressure" was being brought to bear on the anti-Partitionists and that power politics were "playing havoc" with the independence of UN members.

Laughter broke out, and Dr. Aranha pounded his gavel on the table, when Dr. Jamali asserted that 150,000 Jews in Iraq shared "equal rights with the Arabs," and again when he asserted that some power was using "infiltration methods as the Nazis did in the past"; and that immigrants from Black Sea ports were "subversive discordant elements."

He warned that any injustice imposed on Palestine "will have serious effects on the harmony between the Jews and non-Jews of Iraq." Palestine was a Holy Land, and Partition would only dissect its holiness. Why did the Jews not fight for the retention of Jerusalem in their State, he asked. Jerusalem was said to be their Holy City, and if the Jews "acquiesce in having Jerusalem separated from the Jewish State, then why don't they want to establish their Jewish State in another part of the world, such as the U.S., Australia or Birobidjan?"

Three times during his speech, Dr. Jamali referred to great power pressure trying to make the Partition plan work. Asserting that no serious attempt had been made at conciliation, Dr. Jamali referred to Article 14 of the Charter which recommended peaceful adjustment. "No member here present can claim that an effort at peaceful settlement has been made," he declared.

Where, he asked, would the armed force to implement Partition come from. The States who would be asked to send troops to Palestine would be considered enemies of the Arab world. Thus, the plan would achieve nothing but breed prejudice and hatred.

Was it not better to let both parties sort out their disputes by themselves? That could not produce more chaos, not only in Palestine, but all around it. However, Dr. Jamali asserted, it was not necessary that there should be chaos and disorder. Conciliation between the Arabs and Jews was still possible, he concluded.

The Assembly then adjourned for lunch.

MASS ESCAPE TUNNEL FOUND IN LATRUN

A tell-tale crack in the floor of a hut led to the uncovering on Friday morning of a mass-escape plan from the Latrun Detention Camp.

Inspecting the camp shortly before noon, a Senior Police Officer noticed a crack in the flooring of one room. Probing, he found an escape chamber linked to a shaft, about 100 metres long, leading to the perimeter fence. Inside were an electric drill, electric lighting and air ventilation.

The Officer raised the alarm, and some of the detainees stoned the Police, slightly injuring a British Sergeant and Constable.

Meanwhile, four detainees were released from Latrun on Friday after their parents had posted LP.500 bonds for each of them. They are to remain under police supervision.

Three are from Haifa and one from Jerusalem.

Lebanese Mission Arrives in Baghdad

BAGHDAD, Saturday. — The Lebanese President, Sheikh Bishara Khouri, arrived here this morning accompanied by his Premier, Riad Bey es Solh, the Defence Minister, Emir Majid Arslan and a number of other Deputies.

The party was met at the airport by the Regent of Iraq, Emir Abdul Illah, the Premier, Saleh Jabr, and other Senators and Deputies. It is understood

Talking to the press at the airport, the Iraqi Premier said that the U.S. would "regret its unjust attitude at the U.N.," adding that the Jews themselves would regret it.

Paris Police Get Reinforcements
FRANCE CONSIDERS ANTI-STRIKE BILL

PARIS, Saturday (Reuter). — Paris police were reinforced and on the alert for trouble tonight as news was received of four big Communist meetings to be held in the capital while the Assembly debated the Government's new severe anti-strike bill.

This followed police confiscation of special editions of the Communist newspapers "Humanite" and "Ce Soir." The latter described the bill as "a reactionary coup d'etat" and announced in bold headlines "the republic is in danger."

"Humanite" said: "The 'American party' is about to tear up the Constitution. A coup d'etat is to be carried out tonight at midnight. Workers, Democrats, Patriots—you have the power to prevent this crime."

In the Assembly, Premier Schuman, introducing the Bill to restrain strikers, declared that responsibility for it lay with the Communists. They in turn claimed that it was "worse than anything Napoleon thought of."

With about two million workers idle, crippling industries and public services, Mr. Schuman asked for an immediate passage of the Bill which provides for the call up of 80,000 more reservists to service in the Mobile Republican Guard, and prison terms and fines of up to 500,000 francs for people found guilty of obstructing workers.

Official sources said that the Bill, if passed today, would become effective at 2300 hours GMT tomorrow, November 30, and remain in force until 2300 hours, GMT., May 31, 1948.

The door for renewed negotiations between the Government and the General Confederation of Labour was left open by M. Pierre Lebrun, the Secretary General of the C.G.T., who indicated that there might be negotiations between the Government and the Confederation before the Assembly began debating the anti-strike Bill. Many informed observers believed that the Government might accept the overture.

CAIRO PAPER COMES OUT FOR PARTITION

CAIRO, Saturday.—While Azzam Pasha, Secretary-General of the Arab League, repeated his threat of the use of force against Partition if it is decided on by the United Nations, the influential daily "Al Mokattam" came out today with an editorial supporting Partition.

This is the first time that any important Arab voice in the Middle East has pronounced publicly for Partition, and Arab circles in Cairo are reported to be amazed at the article.

The paper wrote: "We stand for Partition because we believe that it is the best final solution for the problem of Palestine. If rejection of Partition would solve the problem we would have welcomed it, but in fact it will lead to further complications and will give the Zionists another space of time to complete their plans of defence and attack."

Failure of the U.N. to come to a decision now would, "Al Mokattam" considers, lead to a delay of one more year, which would not benefit the Arabs but would benefit the Jews, especially after the British evacuation, when, the paper thinks, the U.N. would be unable to keep order in the country.

Azzam Pasha, who returned to Cairo from Saudi-Arabia, told pressmen that a decision in favour of Partition would lead to war in the Middle East.

Activity has been evident at Arab League headquarters here in connection with the forthcoming meeting of the League's Council. Sheikh Sami El Khoury, the Lebanese Minister, consulted his Government by telephone on Thursday. Dr. Fawzi Bey El Mulky, the Trans-Jordan Minister, had a long conference at the League's offices. It is reported that Faris Eff. El Khoury, the Syrian delegate at Lake Success, and Camille Eff. Chamoun, the Lebanese representative, have been called to the Arab League Council's meeting.

In Damascus, a communique from the Ministry of the Interior reminds the press that no news concerning troop movements may be published.

(ANA, Reuter, AFP)

("Al Mokattam" is owned and published by Dr. Nimr, father of Lady Smart, whose husband was for many years Oriental Secretary at the British Embassy in Cairo, and of Mrs. Kate Antonius of Jerusalem).

British Lobbying

FLUSHING MEADOW, Saturday (UP). — Feverish last-minute lobbying is going on in the Assembly hall and the corridors.

Although Britain has officially professed a position of neutrality, a tall blond Britain busily mingled with the Latin American delegation urging them to refrain from supporting Partition.

The Briton was the British Legation's liaison officer for the Latin American nations.

CAIRO STUDENTS STONE POLICE

CAIRO, Saturday (AP). — Students shouting against capitalism, the Egyptian Prime Minister, Nokrashi Pasha, and the "Truman-Attlee Axis" engaged in a stone throwing bout with the police today at Fouad University which opened this morning after being closed during the cholera epidemic.

The police tried to limit the students admitted to the small number who have paid University fees and had identity cards, but the remainder forced the police cordon at one of the University's iron doors.

Inside they roamed the halls shouting "Capitalism evacuate... education for all... long live Russia our ally . . . mobs are the leaders of the people . . . no education by dollars . . . down with the Truman-Attlee Axis... Nokrashi, enemy of the people . . . where is evacuation?"

A force of about 500 police, armed with rifles and clubs, was attacked by stone-throwing students and some policemen threw the stones back despite contrary orders from their officers. The exchange lasted for 15 minutes until a police officer raised a white handkerchief and a truce was arranged.

1,420 VISALESS IMMIGRANTS COME BACK TO PALESTINE

Palestine Post Bureau

HAIFA, Saturday. — Their number carefully checked, 1,420 mothers, fathers and infants had boarded the Ocean Vigour in Cyprus on a special transfer to Palestine, but 1,421 left Haifa Harbour yesterday.

One of them was born in the Port itself, in the Quarantine Section of the Health Department.

His mother, Mrs. Simha Nahmani, was rushed over in a lighter while the ship was still standing in the roadstead, and later she was taken to Moladah Hospital.

The morning was high, and hot as midsummer, by the time the Ocean Vigour (on its first trip here since Hamburg) was moored, its caged human cargo singing and cheering. There was a large party on the jetty to meet the young parents and their babies, who had been sent out of their turn through the generosity of other refugees. Ambulances of the Red Shield Society waited alongside the ship as an oblong wooden "bucket" was slowly lowered by a boom, with a cargo of three — a mother, her three-day-old baby and a soldier who held the stretcher steady. To avoid the jarring trip down the long, steep gangplank, eight such loads of women and their babies born this week were swung off in a smooth transfer. Four were taken to the Ezra Hospital here and four to Moladah. Six infants were sent to the Hadassah Hospital in Tel Aviv.

Tubs from Tins

Then the refugees marched down the gangplank, fathers holding tightly to well-padded tubs made from petrol tins in which babies bobbed up and down. Mothers, many with childish faces themselves, followed. Soldiers carried the bigger children. One man, balancing a tub with a baby on his head, oriental-fashion, brought watchers hearts to their mouths, but he seemed to know what he was about. Some of the women were met by their husbands, who, for reasons of health, had not been deported to Cyprus.

An old woman waited for hours on the jetty. She wore a heavy black dress, a black woollen coat and a long black lace shawl. She told how seven sons and daughters had been killed in Poland, by bayonets, bullets, gas-chamber. An eighth son, Mordechai Sorin, had fled. She had come to Palestine only a few weeks ago "on a proper ship, like a princess," because she had been told her son was here. And now he was coming, on this ship. Someone asked her how old she was. "Ninety, or a 1,000. I don't know. Ever since the Germans came, every day was like a 1,000 years."

At least a man who resembled her came down the gangplank, and then he held her hard in his arms, and kissed her mouth to stifle her wailing, and everyone turned away. Her daughter-in-law and granddaughter were among those sent to hospital.

Cheering Rhythm

The cheerful rhythm of refugees filing down the gangplank was resumed, and the fleet of 33 Egged buses filled with quietly contented people and squalling babies. At 2.30 the first bus reached Raanana, where the Jewish Agency transit camp had been prepared for their arrival. Thirty six nurses and assistants, graduates of the WIZO Mothercraft School and the institutions of the Working Mother's Organization, will take care of the babies, and 40 women from Raanana and nearby kibbutzim have been enrolled. Dr. J. Roth, pediatrician of the Hadassah Hospital in Jerusalem will spend the first 10 days there, and medical service will be provided by the Jewish Agency.

The Government has waived immigration certificates for the 467 babies under two who came yesterday, but deducted them for the 912 parents and 41 older children.

The Jewish Distribution Committee, which had been responsible for the Cyprus Children's Camp, will continue to take care of the more than 150 babies who remained there and the newborns who are coming at the rate of two and three a day.

The immigrants were accompanied from Cyprus by Dr. W. Falk and five Palestinian nurses. On the quay they were met by Mrs. Goldie Myerson, Mr. Eliahu Dobkin, Dr. Grushka, and Mr. P. Litvak of the J.D.C.

(Raanana — Page 3)

TWO DEAD IN PLANE CRASH

Palestine Post Reporter

NATHANYA, Saturday.— Two men were killed when a private Czech-made "Bi-Bi" single-engined bi-plane, belonging to Mr. Z. Levinson, co-owner of the "Michsaf" silverware plant, crashed near Beit Itzhak smallholders settlement shortly after noon today. The victims were Mr. Levinson, who piloted the aircraft, and his friend, Mr. Ernst Mendelson, a BOAC engineer who took the flight while off duty.

The plane took off from Lydda Airport before noon and turned towards Beit Itzhak, 25 kilometres away. Mendelson had informed his brother, Walter, a settler there, that he would be flying over.

The plane cruised over the houses, and settlers came out of their homes waving. While the plane was in a steep bank, and flying low, its engine stopped suddenly.

The machine was then seen to rise to about 50 metres, and then crashed to the earth between the village well and central stores. Both men were thrown out of the plane, Mr. Mendelson being killed instantly. Mr. Levinson died shortly afterwards.

"Hunch" Disregarded

Mr. Levinson, who was a R.A.F. engineer during the war, purchased the plane some years ago and used it at least twice weekly. It was tested twice before it took off this morning. A pilot friend P. Constable Gruenberg, of Tel Aviv Div. H.Q., who flew along on the test flight, insisted that he had a "hunch" and begged Levinson not to fly. The two friends discussed the matter heatedly, and finally Levinson pushed Gruenberg aside and switched on the engine. Thirty minutes later, Gruenberg, who was waiting at the airport for the plane to return, was informed that it had crashed.

Levinson leaves a wife and three children.

KAPLAN LEAVES FOR U.S.

Dr. Moshe Sneh, of the Jewish Agency Executive, returned by Air France to Palestine from Paris on Friday morning.

Mr. Eliezer Kaplan, the Agency Treasurer, left by air for America, where he is to take part in the United Jewish Appeal conference.

After Midnight

THE PALESTINE POST

LATE Edition

JERUSALEM Wednesday, Dec. 3, 1947
PRICE: 20 MILS
VOL. XXII. No. 6674

Features and Fashions DISTRIBUTED WITH THIS ISSUE

Column One By David Courtney

WINDOWS have been broken, Jews have been killed, buses stoned, property has been set on fire and some looted. Police and soldiers were out holding a watching brief. There was always the risk that heads would be bashed in; but the mob suffered little hurt and went home. When dusk fell, there was nothing more the demonstrators could do. Curfew barred their way and they stayed home. It is easy to guess what the London papers will say of it this morning; and the type they will say it in. Adding the Jerusalem incidents to the broken windows, the chanted slogans, the processions of Damascus, Aleppo, Baghdad and Alexandria, the occasion has served the promise that the Middle East would "go up in flames." The Middle East has done its duty by the pained prophets of Whitehall and Fleet Street; and has every right, today, to revert to that milder cliché, a tense situation.

WHAT happened yesterday in Jerusalem was ugly; but not a single Arab spent the night behind bars because of it. A few Jews did. What happened was ugly and unnecessary. It is a pity one cannot know, but must guess, why an Arab went to prison for stabbing, arson, looting. It is always bad to leave public matters of this sort to guesswork. We should know better by the end of today. We should know whether the mob rule has had its day in this perplexed and perplexing city.

THE Arab goes out and stones a bus, burns a house, stabs a poor Jew. He is got together in a crowd and worked up to a desire to break, burn, loot, kill. He is persuaded that to do so is to be a patriot. He is persuaded that to do so is to serve Freedom. He cannot, surely, be persuaded that to do so is to ensure for himself and his family bread, work, good wages, the produce of his labour in the fields, a better standard of life, and peace, without which, what is the substance or the use of freedom? Now and then in history men have had the right to go out with a weapon and break heads, even kill and be killed, for freedom. That was his own freedom: the freedom of himself and his common fellows to live in dignity, peace and prosperity, equal with other men and with their neighbours. Freedom is no more a matter of frontiers than it is an interest of landlords or a purpose of sectional politicians. The Moslems and the Hindus of the Punjab, urged on to fratricidal murder by the cupidity of landlordism, found that out to their cost. The overlords with their vested rights have never been on the side of the common people; and never will be.

THE Arab is as good a man as another; and his rights are as good as another's: let no man forget that, in his criticism of a leadership which seemed barren of statesmanship at U.N. and today seems to have no resource but threat and incitement. As the Jews have emerged to freedom from centuries of persecution and ostracism, so the Arab peoples are rising from centuries of oppression and exploitation to a consciousness of their rightful place among their fellows. Political and social equilibrium has yet to be achieved. Rabble-rousers have yet to be replaced by leaders of the people; group dominance by mass interest; passion by understanding and sectionalism by the general welfare. The Arabs of Palestine are probably in a better position to lead towards these replacings than any other Arab people. They are settled, they have experience of modern and democratic usages, and they are fundamentally progressive. Those who support and encourage them in their intransigent refusal to co-operate with world authority in the solution of Palestine's problems, have no mind to press and enlarge these advantages. And the foreign interests which the Arabs believe to be sympathetic to their policy of all or nothing, may desire only their return to exploitable dependence and romantic isolation from a world of real and equitably-distributed freedom. The Arab crisis today is less a matter of the whole or part of Palestine, than of true freedom or a return to the deadening twilight of traditionalism.

Jerusalem, December 3.

RIOTS MARK START OF STRIKE; 5 JEWS, 3 ARABS DEAD

The three-day Arab strike in protest against the Partition plan began yesterday with arson, bloodshed and rioting by Arab mobs. Jerusalem and the Tel Aviv-Jaffa border area were most seriously affected. The total dead were five Jews — one in Haifa, one at Ramle, and three outside Tel Aviv — and three Arabs — one near Safad and two near Tel Aviv. Six Jews were seriously injured and about 30 slightly hurt, and ten Arabs were injured, mostly in Jerusalem. Damage to property was estimated at several hundred thousand pounds.

FOR THE FIRST TIME, THE HAGANAH CAME OUT OPENLY IN DEFENCE OF JEWISH LIVES AND PROPERTY IN JERUSALEM WHERE 16 OF ITS MEMBERS WERE ARRESTED. CURFEW WAS IMPOSED ON ARAB PARTS OF JERUSALEM.

ARAB MOB LOOTS, BURNS AND STABS

Palestine Post Staff

A mob of 200 Arab hooligans between 10 and 20 years of age began the trouble in Jerusalem in the morning. They surged in ragged ranks past the shuttered shops of Mamillah Road and broke into Princess Mary Avenue, where the first casualties occurred. In full view of British Police they smashed windows, looted shops and stabbed a number of people, including Mr. Asher Lazar, the Jerusalem correspondent of the Hebrew daily "Ha'aretz" who was taken to hospital in a serious condition. A line of British Police edged the mob back but took no forceful action; even when his face was slapped by an Arab, one policeman merely shoved back his attacker.

Troops nearby told one newspaper correspondent that they "had orders not to take any action until they received further orders." Half-a-dozen 50-gallon barrels were placed to form a road block in Princess Mary Avenue, where an armoured car also took up position while members of the Jewish civic guard stopped Jewish civilians from going down the street.

Retreating, the mob burst into the Commercial Centre, assaulted a number of persons and looted shops in Julian's Way. They then forced their way into textile and trade shops in the Commercial Centre, where the proprietors and workers had barricaded themselves, and set goods on fire. Stacks of textiles were piled in the road and turned into blazing bonfires. Police, steel-helmeted and carrying shields, and some troops moved into the wrecked area.

Workers Hemmed in

Meanwhile, about 20 Jewish workers, hemmed in by an Arab mob armed with sticks and stones, tried to get into the Police Traffic Office in Mamillah Road, but the barbed-wire barricade was closed against them. They held off their attackers with stones while British officials in the building appealed to the Police to open the barrier. For more than 30 minutes the men outside were left to defend themselves as best they could, although at one particularly ugly moment an armoured car fired a burst into the air.

With spirals of black smoke curling above the Commercial Centre, police armoured cars came through into the Jewish section of the town carrying workers and residents who had been stranded. On the front of one car a young man held a handkerchief to a cut on his forehead. Another truck drove through with a man holding a baby beside the Police driver, while in the back one of the rescued women clasped a dog in her arms. From the roof of a Princess Mary Avenue building, ambulances and police vehicles could be seen dashing to the scene, but hardly a pedestrian was in the street. The deep ugly roar of the
(Continued on Page 3)

(Continued on Page 3)

THANKS

Drivers of the Hamekasher Bus Company asked *The Palestine Post* to express their thanks to the British Police Inspector and his men who looked after five buses and passengers on their way to Talpioth and Mekor Haim last night. The buses were convoyed through Zone A and then rescued when attacked by an Arab mob. Three men, including a driver, were hurt.

About noon, while the tension was at its highest, a small Arab boy wandered through Zion Square leading a couple of goats.

He was not molested.

Smoke pouring from the Rex Cinema after it had been set ablaze by rioters in Jerusalem yesterday.
—*Palestine Post Photo (L.D.)*

Deadly Barricades in Jaffa

Palestine Post Bureau

JAFFA, Tuesday. — Four Jews and two Arabs were killed in this region in a series of Arab attacks on Jewish traffic. One of the Arabs was killed at a barricade when he was knocked down by a truck at the approach to Abu Kebir Quarter on the Jaffa-Jerusalem road.

Today's Arab disturbances appear to have been the work of unorganized mobs. The organized Arab bands were stated by observers to be awaiting orders from abroad, and members of the Arab Youth Organization in Ramleh were seen attempting to restrain Arab boys from stoning Jewish vehicles.

The streets here were filled with villagers wandering about aimlessly. Britons who ventured into the shuttered streets said they had not encountered any animosity. There were several demonstrations during the morning. The largest comprised 400 schoolboys who paraded with banners and slogans.

Sporadic shooting continued in the border areas in the night. A dead Egyptian and six wounded Arabs, all of them shot, were brought to the Jaffa Government Hospital. Constable Yehuda Navon, 24, was hit in the hand by a stray bullet while on patrol in Neve Shalom at 10.30 tonight.

Shops Raided

Two Jewish shops were raided in the afternoon. Rioters entered the Gamzu Photography Studio in King George Avenue, dragged the fittings out and set fire to them. A paint shop around the corner was also raided and cans were stoned in the street. In both cases police charged the mob with batons and dispersed it. The most serious incident of the day occurred this evening at Hassan Bey Square. A military pick-up travelling from Qastina sped towards the barricade, and the driver, Gershon Praga, 25, tried to crash through it. An excited mob of Arabs heaped barrels, rocks and wire against the barricade and the truck was brought to a halt. One of the Arabs who manned the barricade was knocked down by the truck and killed outright.

The mob then swarmed over the vehicle, set it afire and stabbed the driver and two passengers. The driver was killed outright. The hacked body of one passenger, Gershon Levy, 34, of Tel Aviv, was later found by police some distance away, while Cpl Ben Shalom 25, was brought unconscious to the Hadassah Hospital, where he died at 11 o'clock.

Patrols of the Jewish Settlement Police in tenders, armed with Lewis guns, found roads barricaded near Faluja village this morning. They cleared the road and there were no disturbances.

Our correspondents in Southern Judea and Samaria reported no disturbances, but Arab families were still loading their belongings on donkeys and moving to Jaffa.

Egyptian and Haurani workers in Petah Tikva came to work in Jewish orange groves this morning, but workers of the Abu Kishek tribe stayed away.

Fellaheen worked as usual in the fields, and in many Arab
(Continued on Page 3)

(Continued on Page 3)

Passenger Killed

Near Ramleh this morning a taxi of the Atid Cooperative travelling from Jerusalem to Tel Aviv was stoned and Mr. Max Pin, 40, head of the Jewish Agency's Trade and Transfer Office, was mortally injured. Another passenger, Mr. Friedrich Zitterman of Jerusalem, was also hurt.

Police patrols cruised the highways today and the streets of Jaffa were heavily patrolled. Witnesses stated that most of the stoning on the highways was done by boys. Bombs thrown at traffic were primitive. Traffic was suspended at noon while police organized convoys of vehicles which were given armed escort.

In the Gaza area, an Arab driver was wounded when the W.D. vehicle belonging to the Mauritius Pioneer Company which he was driving was shot at 7 a.m. Three hours later another Mauritius driver was injured when his vehicle was stoned in the same area.

Shots were fired by soldiers at a mob near Gaza this morning after stones were thrown.

SAFETY

The convoy system was introduced again on highways yesterday. Police armoured cars escorted cars from Tel Aviv to Jerusalem, and dispersed a threatening crowd in Ramle.

Convoys also took food into the Old City of Jerusalem and brought out a number of families.

At a convoy taking the equipment of the REME Workshop in Tel Aviv to Egypt, there were no casualties.

At Sawafir village, a government with a licensed paint purser a mob which had stoned his vehicle. He is an Englishman, who was an Army Major and is now a member of the Negbah settlement. The mob got away but the Major was seized by Military Police. He produced his licence and the matter was closed.

At Ramleh this morning a taxi of the Atid Cooperative travelling from Jerusalem...

Bunche May Head U.N. Secretary Staff

LAKE SUCCESS, Tuesday (Reuter). — The head of the U.N. Secretariat staff on the Palestine Commission would, it was strongly expected tonight, be Dr. Ralph J. Bunche, 43-year-old Director of the U.N. Trusteeship Division.

Dr. Bunche, who was Assistant Secretary of UNSCOP, is regarded by experts here as one of the most capable officials to deal with minority and colonial matters. Considerable reluctance was noticed among U.N. Secretariat members to serve on the Palestine Commission.

JEW KILLED IN HAIFA

Palestine Post Bureau

HAIFA, Tuesday. — There was comparative quiet today in the mixed town of Haifa, with about 15 light casualties reported, most of them injured by stones thrown at trucks and cars passing Nazareth Street and the Suq. But tonight the body of Abraham Katzengold about 20 years of age, was found in Shukri Street with an expended cartridge case beside it.

Katzengold lived in Kfar Hanoch settlement.

The bus companies reported that their vehicles had been stoned and their windows broken. Trucks of the Tnuva Co-operative and the Shemen Company and lorries bringing supplies from the kibbutzim were also stoned. Out-of-town trucks bound for Haifa Bay drove through Hadar Hacarmel, avoiding the town proper.

About 8.30 this morning, in Lower Kingsway, a crowd of about 300 Arabs stoned passersby, injuring Manfred Butner of Tel Aviv. In the Suq, at the same time, Moshe Rosenberg was cut about the face, but escaped and received first aid at the Government Hospital. A crowd also gathered at Palmer's Gate near the Port, but was dispersed when a policeman fired into the air.

Although British and Arab police were stationed in Nazareth Street and there was frequent patrolling by armoured and wireless cars, stones kept flying when Jewish vehicles passed.

After prayers in the Mosque, a large group of hot-heads wanted to go up into the Jewish quarters, but were restrained by responsible leaders of the Community.

Five bullets were fired at Haim Cohen, a taxi-driver, who was also stoned as he drove out of the Port's east gate this morning, and he was slightly hurt about the head. Shots were also heard near the Eastern Railway Station.

Others who were slightly injured were a No. 6 bus-driver named Karlebath; Ezra Weinstein, a taxi-driver, hit in the head by a stone; Benyamin Ingres and Mizrachi Rahmim, of the Namal Hehadash Trucking Co.; a driver from Tel Aviv named Steklov; and Haim Hellman, who received a stone in his forehead.

Apart from the attacks, which were sporadic and concentrated in one district, work was carried on as usual by Arab labourers in the Port, on railways, in W.D. camps and on public works. Arab shops and cafes were closed, however.

Shortly after 8 p.m., fires broke out in two Jewish carpentry shops, one in Iraq Street, belonging to Mr. Kandinovsky, and the other at 36 Stanton Street. Little damage was caused, as the Fire Brigade came down immediately. Arson is suspected.

A fewer cooperative bus bringing workers from the Nesher Cement factory was shot at near Balad Esh-Sheikh at 9:30 tonight. No one was hit.

JEWS LEAVE HAIFA'S ARAB QUARTERS

HAIFA, Tuesday. — Afraid to remain cut off from the Jewish quarters in the midst of an Arab neighbourhood, about 70 families left their homes in Nazareth Street here and came in a group to the offices of the Jewish Community Council for help.

The Council assured them it would take care of those who in their opinion were situated in danger spots, and most of these families are spending the night in the Community Council building until accommodation can be found for them tomorrow. A number have also been given quarters in Akiva Street.

They said they had been advised to move out by their Arab neighbours.

ARAB STATES ASK FOR CALM

Palestine Post Correspondent

BEIRUT, Tuesday. — The Governments of the Arab States have decided to call off all strikes and Arab all demonstrations from tomorrow morning, it was learned here tonight from official sources. Students have been instructed to return to their lessons.

Aleppo was quiet today, with military and police patrolling the streets and guarding Jewish shops and houses. Loud-speaker vans went through the streets instructing the inhabitants to remain calm and to respect Jewish property. A number of youngsters tried to repeat yesterday's demonstrations, but were stopped by the army, and about 200 men found to be in possession of firearms and grenades were arrested.

The Government has ordered an inquiry into yesterday's incidents, to ascertain if "foreign elements" were among the demonstrators.

APOLOGY

WASHINGTON, Tuesday. (UP). — The Syrian Government has apologized to the U.S. Government for the mob attack on the American Legation in Damascus on Sunday, the State Department announced today.

Damascus was quiet today observing a complete strike after an eventless day. Thousands gathered in the great Omayyad Mosque in a meeting organized by the newly formed Palestine Liberation Committee.

The Syrian Chamber of Deputies, at a special session on Palestine, referred a Bill for compulsory military service to a special national defence committee. The Bill is to be voted on next Thursday, and the Chamber authorized the Government to make an immediate payment of L.S. 2,000,000 from the country's reserve fund as their first instalment of the sum allotted by the Arab League for the liberation of Palestine.

From many parts of Iraq, similar demonstrations were reported. The Iraqi Foreign Ministry has sent messages of sincere thanks to all non-Moslem and non-Arab States which rejected Partition in the Assembly vote.

Demand Arms

In Cairo, demonstrators went to Abdine Palace and shouted for King Farouk, demanding that he command his Ministers to mobilize assistance for Palestine.

In Zagazig, where there are no Jews, the British Institute was completely gutted by fire and Cypriot-owned cars and a Greek-owned cinema were broken up.

Students in Alexandria called at Ras el Tin Palace and handed over a memorandum asking King Farouk for a Royal Rescript confiscating all Jewish funds and property in Egypt. The Egyptian press, while protesting against Partition, gives no indication that the Egyptian Government is prepared to take part in any convert action against Jewish Palestine. The "Journal d'Egypte" writes that while the armies of the Arab States were not strong at present, they could become strong in four or five years, when they will represent a serious threat if the Jewish State had to rely on its own defence forces.

The Chief of the Egyptian General Staff, Marshal Nurn Attala Pasha, is reported to have gone by air to the Sinai Peninsula on an inspection tour of the frontier with Palestine.

In Asmara, all the Arab shops were closed in a one-day strike.

(AFP, AP, R, UP).

Agency to Negotiate Two Huge Loans

LAKE SUCCESS, Tuesday. (Reuter). — Plans for the negotiation of a U.S. loan of about 135,000,000 dollars to aid the immigration of Jewish D.P.'s into Palestine are being made by Jewish Agency officials here, it was reliably learned today. The negotiations, which are in a very early stage, were also understood to concern a larger loan from the World Bank to finance the first part of the Lowdermilk irrigation scheme.

Complications. It is understood have arisen over the actual date when the Mandate is to be given up. There was considerable pressure that this should not be done too early, to avoid making extra difficulties for the military during the evacuation phase.

Sir Alexander Cadogan is now expected to make a statement of the actual date tomorrow or Thursday, and to invite the Palestine Commission to a detailed discussion on an interim policy on immigration and the creation of Jewish and Arab militia. The supply of arms to both militias and their immediate return.

The question of the entry of the Jewish State and possibly also the Arab State into the British Empire was considered, but no decisions were taken. It is understood.

After Midnight

Galon settlement in southern Palestine was attacked by an Arab band last night. A mobile Auxiliary Police patrol engaged the brigands and routed them.

CABINET DISCUSSES WITHDRAWAL PLANS

By JON KIMCHE, Special to The Palestine Post

LONDON, Tuesday. — Today's Cabinet meeting considered the further steps to be taken to carry out the withdrawal from Palestine.

Complications, it is understood, have arisen over the actual date when the Mandate is to be given up. There was considerable pressure that this should not be done too early, to avoid making extra difficulties for the military during the evacuation phase.

Sir Alexander Cadogan is now expected to make a statement of the actual date tomorrow or Thursday.

6-NATION WORKING GROUP FOR JERUSALEM PLAN

LAKE SUCCESS, Tuesday. — A six-nation working group including all the Big Powers except Russia, was today appointed to formulate plans for a Government of Jerusalem. The countries named were: U.S., Britain, France, China, Mexico and Australia.

The final choice for the position of Governor of Jerusalem is expected to be made from among the nationals of one of the small powers. He will have an annual salary of $20,000.

The Security Council at its meeting on Thursday, will be officially notified by the Secretariat of the Assembly's decision on action by the Council if the peace in Palestine is threatened. *(AP and PTA)*

Upper Chamber Passes Strike Bill

FRENCH STRIKERS COUNTER-ATTACK

PARIS, Tuesday. — France's 2,000,000 Communist led strikers, falling back before Government forces which seized occupied factories, railway stations and mines, today launched an apparently retake their lost strongholds.

These moves began in the morning and a number of premises previously cleared of strikers in different cities were re-occupied.

The most serious clash occurred here today when an estimated 3,000 strikers of the Renault car factory broke into the Salmson motor plant by pulling down part of the wall with a tractor in an effort to oust occupying police forces. A pitched battle ensued, which ended with the dispersal of the mob at a cost of three Mobile Guardsmen wounded and an undetermined number of strikers injured.

In Nice, striking postmen driven out of the central post office yesterday marched back into the post office. At St. Roch railway station was retaken by strikers after police forces had evacuated them while police forces retook the Nice central post office for the second time shortly after the lunch hour.

Police using tear gas tonight cleared strikers from the railway station at Limoges after clashes lasting for hours.

The Upper Chamber of the National Assembly today adopted the Government's anti-strike bill for calling up 80,000 Reservists, by 209 vote to 84. *(A.P. & Reuter)*

Marshall-Bevin Palestine Talks

LONDON, Tuesday (Reuter). — The Big Four Foreign Ministers have decided to examine tomorrow a report submitted to them today by the Special Deputies for Austria.

This document records a broad rejection by Russia of a French compromise proposal for defining German assets in Austria and acceptance of the plan by the British and U.S. Governments.

The Ministers devoted most of today's session to examining a document dealing with Allied Powers in the negotiations of the German Peace Treaty. Some agreement was reached, but many unagreed points remained, which will come up at a later session.

Tomorrow evening, the King will receive the four Ministers at Buckingham Palace. On Friday, Mr. Marshall will have lunch with Mr. Bevin.

According to PTA, Mr. Marshall and Mr. Bevin lunched together today and it is believed that the Palestine question was the main topic of their conversation.

Immigration Rise Mooted

LONDON, Tuesday (AP). — It is "safe to assume" that Britain will authorize a minimum 50 per cent increase in the rate of Jewish immigration into Palestine between now and her scheduled evacuation deadline on August 1, a Government source said today.

While no decision has yet been taken, the informant said that the purpose of the increase would be to clear the 16,000 Jews at present held in camps in Cyprus.

Entry Priority For D.P.'s

LAKE SUCCESS, Tuesday (Reuter). — Plans to accommodate nearly 1,000,000 Jewish immigrants from Europe and the Middle East in the new Jewish State in Palestine were discussed last night by Zionist leaders conferring in New York on the practical aspects of Partition.

Top priority, it is understood, will be given to about 200,000 displaced Jews at present in Europe and Cyprus, and afterwards it is planned to transfer about 700,000 more Jews from Central European and Arab countries, probably at the rate of 100,000 a year.

Jewish leaders are planning an appeal to the British Government to lift the immigration restrictions immediately, instead of waiting until August, in order to build up a strong defence force.

Meanwhile, the Jewish Agency is proceeding with high-level talks to determine the amount of aid the Jewish State will require. The National Administrative Council of the Zionist Organization of America, comprising all Zionist groups there, will hold an extraordinary Jewish Palestine. The "Journal d'Egypte" conference in New York on Saturday and Sunday, to formulate plans.

1,500 QUOTA INTOLERABLE

Palestine Post Bureau

TEL AVIV, Tuesday. — Holding that the continuation of the 1,500 a month immigration quota was not commensurate with the establishment of the Jewish State, Dr. Moshe Sneh, of the Jewish Agency Executive, said today that the restrictions should not be tolerated.

He was speaking at the general meeting of the Association of Palestine Journalists in the Tel Aviv Museum.

Immigration and security were the most urgent tasks confronting the Jewish people, he said. The overwhelming majority of Jews in D.P. camps, Rumania and North Africa wish to come to Palestine, he said, reporting on his tour to Europe.

The convention was opened by the President, Mr. Joseph Heftman, who appealed to Arab journalists to co-operate to achieve peace and settle. The Mayor, Mr. Israel Rokach, urged the press to educate the public to maturity as citizens of the Jewish State and the formation of an immaculate civil service.

U.S. Asked to Supply Arms

By JESSE ZEL LURIE, Palestine Post Correspondent

NEW YORK, Tuesday. — Swinging into its new role of supporting the legal Army of the Jewish State, the Americans For Haganah yesterday called on the U.S. to supply arms to the Haganah.

Mr. Bartley C. Crum, member of the Anglo-U.S. Inquiry Commission of 1946 and chairman of the Americans For Haganah National Council, declared that "in keeping with American foreign policy, pledged to support democracy throughout the world, all Americans are obliged to see to it that the Jewish Defence Army is supplied with the necessary equipment and technical assistance to carry out its functions."

He also asked the U.N. to prevent attacks on Christians and Jews in the Arab States.

The following additions have been announced to the National Council: Mr. Sumner Welles; Mr. Herbert Lehman (former head of UNRRA); Congressman Robert Wagner; Congressman Emanuel Celler; Eddie Cantor; and Mr. James G. Patton (President of the National Farmers' Union).

U.P. reports from Washington that Senator Owen Brewster today proposed that the U.S. and other U.N. members should set up a "Foreign Legion" of volunteers to prevent violence in the Middle East over the Partition of Palestine.

"In the event of an uprising," Senator Brewster said, "Russia will be prepared to move in with armed forces. If no one else is ready to go in and restore order, we would not be able to veto the use of Russian troops."

Senator Brewster said that he was willing to have Russian soldiers as members of his Foreign Legion, provided that the unit was directed by the U.N.

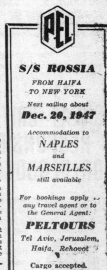

THE PALESTINE POST

JERUSALEM
Monday, Feb. 2, 1948
PRICE: 20 MILS
VOL. XXIII No. 6627

SPECIAL EDITION

Printed for the Jerusalem Press Ltd. at Hamadpis Liphshitz Press Jerusalem

COLUMN ONE

By **David Courtney**

THE truth is louder than TNT and burns brighter than the flames of arson. It will win in the end. Last night's bomb smashed machinery, burned precious records, made people homeless, injured some; but the target was plain truth. It is surprising what some men will do to destroy truth. The tyrant, the Fascist, the fool and the ignorant victims of any one or all of these have tried to suppress the truth since history began; and tried vainly. They are still at their monstrous folly.

WHAT was done last night is an incident among many in the brutal history of this land. It was nothing new to see flames and hear the groans of hurt men. It was nothing new to see little children and old women and stumbling men silhouetted against fire as they hurried silently away from their homes. That is the modern history of Palestine. It is the recent history of the Mandate. It will be said in London that it is the consequence of the judgment of the earth's United Nations. To say just that accusingly, is to be in part responsible for the evil that is done.

THE bomb in Hassolel Street for a moment closed the mouths of the messengers of the world; and shut off, as a telephone is shut off, the news from a score of capitals. It did but throw into still sharper relief, and sound with still farther-reaching voice, the truth of this land and the sureness of its triumph. And that truth will be told. The men who did last night's deed probably overlooked that. There is nothing they can do about it now or at any time. It has escaped them. It makes their triumph short-lived and hollow.

Jerusalem, February 2.

COMMISSION'S FIRST REPORT

Palestine Post Correspondent

LAKE SUCCESS, Sunday. — Tomorrow will be a crucial day for the Yishuv — as the Five-Nation Palestine Commission hands its first report to the Security Council.

If the Commissioners are determined to see the Assembly's resolution implemented, the report will contain a strong indictment of Britain, who has in all her actions obstructed the Commission's work rather than helped.

The five Commissioners will hold a press conference at 3 o'clock in the afternoon (10 p.m. Palestine time)).

At the same time, the sixth session of the U.N. Social and Economic Council opens tomorrow, and Dr. Charles Malik of the Lebanon is certain to be elected Chairman. The only opposition will come from countries of the Slav Bloc and some Latin American Republics who want to see a delegate of their blocs elected.

Dr. Malik has long been held in great esteem by U.N. members, because of his intellectual abilities and wide experience. As chairman of the Social and Economic Council he will be responsible for the establishment of economic unity in partitioned Palestine.

Dr. Malik's appointment as such would not be of vital importance to the Jews, but the fact that his candidacy is being supported by the U.S., may be another pointer of America's intention to follow a bi-partisan policy which would in the end bring about some sort of Morrison-Grady plan.

The Jerusalem Working Committee has been busy completing its report which is due to be submitted to the Trusteeship Council on February 11. Here the Jerusalem delegates, Dr. Eliash and Mr. Auster have done a great deal of constructive work and sheer logic has succeeded to some extent in face of the considerable lack of enthusiasm of the delegates which has been evident there.

PALESTINE POST PRESS AND OFFICES DESTROYED

Bomb and Fire Gut Three Buildings

EXPLOSION ROCKS JERUSALEM

The Palestine Post and two adjacent buildings at the top of Hassolel Street were wrecked by an explosion and a fire that followed last night. A five-ton army-type lorry drove up the narrow street shortly after 10.45 and parked outside the press room. An explosion a few minutes later rocked a large part of the city and smashed windows and doors within a radius of almost a mile.

As *The Palestine Post* goes to press this morning, prepared in borrowed office space, its editorial offices and the Jerusalem Press are smoking ruins.

About 20 persons were hurt by the blast and flying glass, nine of them seriously. It is not yet known whether the United Press wireless operator who is usually in the building at that time reached safety or not.

The pressmen seriously hurt are: Zalman Levin, Shimshon Lifshitz, Aharon Tanachi, Yitzhak Tawil and Nathan Rabinovitz.

Others wounded are: Benjamin Meyuhas, Victoria Meyuhas, Judith Ash, Zipora Shimoni, Banin Tamanni, Weinberg (watchman), Harry Mardler, Zina Mardler, Jaacov Shtrevneh, and Ruth Shtrevneh.

The blast came with a dull red flash that reached the level of the upper stories of the two buildings, sending glass spinning across the rooms, shaking workers and tenants, cutting them about the face and toppling furniture. On some floors the lights went out adding to the confusion.

Workers and tenants hurried out of the buildings. The slightly wounded and uninjured helped the seriously hurt to the Hadassah Clearing Clinic a few metres up the road, edging past a blazing ambulance. In the Jerusalem Press, on the ground floor of the building, the blast sent pieces of lead flying through the air.

The last injured man to be brought out of the press, when it was thick with smoke and dust and stiflingly hot, was rescued by Mr. John Donovan, the Jerusalem corespondent of the N.B.C., who was on his way to *The Palestine Post* when the explosion occurred. Another foreign correspondent who helped in the rescue work was Mr. Fitzhugh Turner of the "New York Herald-Tribune," who climbed the stairs into the burning building in search of victims, together with three British constables and had to jump from an upper story when he was cut off from the stair

(*Continued on page 2*)

Nehru Weeps For Gandhi

NEW DELHI, Sunday (AP). — Pandit Nehru wept tonight when he placed a floral tribute beside Gandhi's ashes.

Part of Gandhi's ashes will be cast into the sacred Jumma River at Delhi near where he was cremated, but some of the bones will be carried later to other sacred rivers and cast there to symbolize the universal love between him and the people.

Crowds gathered today near Birla House. Some knelt down to touch the ground with their heads as an indication of grief and as a symbolic act signifying their desire to transfer to themselves what they consider to be Ghandi's saintliness.

MAHASABHA ACCUSED

Police refused to discuss anything which might have been told them by Narayan Vinayak Godse, who is held as Gandhi's assassin. They identified him as active in the Hindu Mahasabha leadership and as a vigorous critic of Gandhi.

Delhi newspapers carried stories today asserting that they had learned that Godse had made statements implicating several persons in several parts of India as members of a conspiracy to kill Gandhi. His statement was said to have uncovered the existence of a gang operating in Delhi, Bombay, East Punjab and West Bengal. The newspaper alleged that this group was responsible for placing the bomb which exploded near Gandhi not many days before the assassination.

The paper also linked this group with the man found with a hand grenade in his pocket who was arrested at a meeting addressed in Amritsar recently by Nehru. Both men are still held incommunicado.

Bombay Police Fire at Rioters

BOMBAY, Sunday (Reuter). — Police opened fire early today to disperse angry crowds which persisted in attacking the residences of Hindu Mahasabha leaders and supporters in northern Bombay. A tense situation was reported to have developed and police reinforcements, supported by military, were sent to the areas.

Gandhi's accused assassin, Naturam Vinyak Godse, once belonged to the Mahasabha. Rioting, looting and burning of Mahasabha members' homes and business premises ocurred in Bombay, Poona and Kolhapup, after Ghandi's cremation yesterday.

In north Bombay, several casualties were reported and police opened fire several times.

At Poona today, an angry crowd attempted to set fire to the house of a leader of a militant Hindu organization soon after the curfew in the city was lifted. Troops and police intervened.

280 Deported To Cyprus

HAIFA, Sunday. — On the day on which Britain was to have opened a free port to Jewish immigration, as recommended by the United Nations General Assembly, the Royal Navy today intercepted a small schooner with 280 men, women and children on board. The Navy was more vigilant in maintaining its blockade than the Army in guarding the land frontiers across which a steady stream of armed Arabs has been coming for the past month.

The ship, called the "35 Heroes of Kfar Etzion," was boarded without incident early this morning. It was brought into Haifa shortly after noon. Transhipment to the Empire Rival was a sea-borne operation. The refugees were taken from the schooner aboard the cruiser, Phoebe, alongside which they were moored, and after passing through fumigation tents, were taken across to the Empire Rival which sailed for Cyprus in the afternoon.

CABLES IN BRIEF

STUDENTS from the Farouk I University in Alexandria yesterday staged anti-Government demonstrations and stoned the police who fired at them.

A TURKISH motor-boat was attacked and boarded by an armed motorboat of unknown nationality off Samos island yesterday. Turkish coastguards opened fire and the ship escaped out to sea.

THE FRANCO-SPANISH frontier will probably be reopened in the next fortnight. The desirability of a change in Spanish-French relations is understood to have been agreed upon in semi-official talks in Madrid.

ITALY and the U.S. will today sign a trade and financial agreement which will re-open economic cooperation between the two States after a lapse of ten years.

SOVIET revenue exceeded expenditure in 1947 by 24,000 million roubles, said the Soviet Finance Minister in a budget speech to the Supreme Soviet yesterday.

THREE THOUSAND Singapore workers struck yesterday as a protest against the new federation of Malaya.

THE NEW IRAQI Cabinet has lifted censorship on the national press and on foreign correspondents.

Syrian Currency Breaks from Franc

DAMASCUS, Sunday (AP). — The Syrian currency was separated definitely from the French franc as from this morning, and it is now intended to create a purely national currency backed by a healthy export-import policy.

Rumours that this separation was sought in order to attach Syria to the sterling area were authoritatively denied. The Syrian pound, it was stated, will conserve its equivalent with the sterling rate.

In Beirut, the Lebanese Premier issued a communique last night regarding a financial agreement now being negotiated with France. It stated that France had not fulfilled her obligations and that the Lebanon was determined to recover the debt due to her.

GREAT BRITAIN "RESPONSIBLE FOR BLOODSHED"

LONDON, Sunday (Reuter). — The Zionist Federation Conference here today passed a resolution deploring the "present attitude of the British Government to the implementation of the United Nations Palestine decision."

"By impeding the defence of the Yishuv (the Jews of Palestine), allowing Arab preparations for warfare, refusing to permit a gradual transference of power and failing to cooperate with the U.N. Commission, the British Administration is responsible for avoidable bloodshed and chaos," the resolution added.

NEW YORK SHORTAGE OF OIL CRITICAL

NEW YORK, Sunday. — Offices in New York had to close down on Friday, when Mayor O'Dwyer banned the supply of fuel oil to all but private homes and certain priority industries.

This is a hard blow to business, coming as it does in one of the coldest winters in U.S. history.

The reason for the shortage is said to be the expansion of home building, but even during the war, when half of America's oil supplies were reserved for the forces, no such breakdown ever occurred.

Observers think that one of the causes may be the Administration's determination to drive home to the public the great importance of Middle East oil, said to be endangered by the U.N. decision to partition Palestine.

Cominform Meets In Secret

BELGRADE, Sunday (AP). — The Cominform held its first meeting in Yugoslavia in the middle of January, according to a communique published in the sixth issue of the Cominform Bulletin, which appeared on the streets of Belgrade today.

The meeting was held in the closest secrecy, and it is believed that the formation of a permanent editorial board was the major issue under discussion.

None of the top Communist leaders of the nine countries belonging to the Cominform attended the meeting.

USTACHIS JOIN ARABS

By SAM SOUKI, U.P. Correspondent

BEIRUT, Sunday. — Twenty-five Yugoslav Moslems, said to have been members of Pavlevitch's Ustachis who during the war fought alongside the Nazis against the Allies, have arrived in Beirut and have gone on to Syria for training as volunteers to fight against the Jews of Palestine.

One of them, however, has been arrested, as it was alleged that he was a "Jewish spy."

Altogether there are now 40 Yugoslav Moslems in camps in Southern Syria. The Syrian authorities are determined to keep them there, despite Marshal Tito's repeated demands for their extradition, as they are on the "wanted" list, to be tried in Yugoslavia as war criminals.

THE PALESTINE POST
JERUSALEM
Monday, Feb. 23, 1948
PRICE 20 MILS
VOL. XXIII. No. 6644

STREET BOMBED BY UNIFORMED MEN IN ARMY CONVOY; 44 KNOWN DEAD, MORE THAN 130 HURT

PALESTINE POST STAFF

In the rubble and wreckage of Ben Yehuda Street in Jerusalem pioneer squads of the Haganah and the Jewish Civil Guard, volunteers and members of the Jewish Fire Brigade, were still working early this morning searching for survivors or bodies and clearing the buildings blasted in the shattering explosion which destroyed nearly all of Ben Yehuda Street in the heart of the residential and business centre of the city early yesterday morning.

AT A LATE HOUR LAST NIGHT THE CASUALTY LIST TOTALLED 44 DEAD AND 132 WOUNDED, OF WHOM 57 ARE DETAINED IN HOSPITAL.

The murderous assault on a thickly populated area of the city just stirring for the day's work was carried out by a group of men in British police and army uniforms who drove to the scene in three vehicles, lit the fuse of their deadly load and then scuttled away in a waiting armoured car, shooting dead two watchmen and leaving helpless unsuspecting men, women and children to die and be maimed as the violent blast brought down three and four storey buildings, and shattered dozens of shops and houses over a radius of several hundred metres.

The blast — exactly three weeks after the attack on **The Palestine Post** — wrecked Ben Yehuda Street from Zion Circus to King George Avenue. The Army-type trucks which blew up had been placed at the corner of Ben Yehuda and Hillel Ha'cohen streets. The Atlantic Hotel — a building owned by a Christian Arab — the Amdursky Hotel, the modern Vilentchik building and the Halvaa Ve'hisachon block were the most seriously damaged.

About 30 people, including Mr. Warshawsky, the proprietor, and his family, had a few brief seconds to escape to safety before one wing of the Atlantic Hotel, shuddering under the force of the explosion, crumbled into a mass of powdery rubble and twisted metal. Mr. Y. Amdursky, the owner of the Amdursky Hotel, had left the building a few seconds earlier on his way to the morning service when he heard the blast and ran back to help the people in his ruined hotel. Nearly everyone got out before the interior caved in.

Out of the Ruins — other picture, Page 4

Road to Hadassah

Numbed by the shock of the explosion, dazed people wandered aimlessly about the streets in their night clothes not knowing where to take refuge, but a degree of confidence was restored as Haganah squads and members of the Civil Guard raced to the spot and began the rescue work. Red Shield and Army ambulances, cars and trucks were used to take the dead and wounded to Jewish hospitals throughout the city. First-aid posts were set up in wrecked shops, and troops of the Highland Light Infantry moved into the Sheikh Jarrah Quarter to ensure a safe passage for traffic bound for the Hadassah Hospital on Mt. Scopus. Doctors and nurses were swiftly mobilized and an appeal for blood donors brought queues of people to replace the stocks of blood plasma stored by the Workers Sick Fund, which used the refrigerators of the wrecked Lucullus Cafe to increase its capacity.

Within a few minutes the Jewish Volunteer Fire Brigade and Army fire tenders sped to the scene and began to tackle blazes which had broken out on both sides of Ben Yehuda Street. For some minutes the fires spread fiercely and the firemen were unable to cope with the flames owing to a lack of water, but R.A.S.C. mobile tanks kept up a shuttle service and within an hour the fires were under control. The Jewish Brigade men stayed on, under the command of Mr. Gutinsky and Mr. Lieberman, and joined in the rescue work.

Human Chains

While people clambered to safety down drain-pipes, step-ladders and ropes knotted from bedclothes and canvas, rescue workers began to tackle the huge mound of rubble into which the Atlantic Hotel had been reduced. Using acetylene torches, engineers cut through metal and squads of volunteers formed human chains to transfer building stones and buckets of rubble to a fleet of hastily summoned lorries.

Occasionally there was the cry of "stretcher" as an injured person, or the mangled remains of a body, was brought from the wreckage.

About noon, five-year-old Rahel Meyouhas was rescued alive from the remains of her home at 15 Ben Yehuda Street. She had injuries to an eye and a finger, but a doctor said she was not seriously hurt. Near her was found the body of her two-year-old brother. Yoav. He bore no injury but had been suffocated. Her father and mother and her sister Ruth 12, all perished.

By about 8 o'clock the streets began to fill with people on their way to work, but chains of Civil Guard cordons manned by men and women barred their way and, with the help of appeals from loudspeakers mounted on cars, Ben Yehuda was practically cleared of all but essential workers by 10 o'clock. All British troops and Police were ordered by their headquarters to withdraw from the area after angry crowds shouted to them to go. All Jewish Police, including men who had just gone off duty, were called out.

Street Canteen

Women members of the Civil Guard set up a street canteen and a first-aid post for the rescue workers. They handed out cups of tea, cigarettes and sandwiches to workers who toiled without a break. Many people carried salvaged belongings to the car park near the Orion Cinema and sat patiently until emergency accommodation was found for them. The cinema's corrugated roof was badly damaged, and shutters were twisted and windows smashed at the Eden Hotel. The roof of the Tel Or Cinema caved in, and the building itself, housing the Labour Federation offices and a restaurant, was badly damaged.

Four hours shopkeepers and cafe owners in Ben Yehuda Street, King George Avenue, Jaffa Road and side-streets worked among the ruins to which their premises had been reduced and by the early afternoon a number of premises, mainly food shops and restaurants, were open again.

On a building above the Atara Cafe one of two crossed blue-and-white Zionist Flags had been blown away, but the other remained fluttering. Close to the four-metre deep crater blown by the bomb was a crumpled Union Jack.

Saw Whole Incident

Three eye-witnesses, all wounded by the explosion gave a graphic picture as they lay in the Shaare Zedek Hospital. One of them, who had been walking to his work in Ben Yehuda Street, said that about 6.20 he heard a shot and saw three Army-type trucks, at least one of which bore the dagger insignia of Palestine Army Headquarters, and a Police armoured car.

"One of the trucks was standing still at the corner of Hillel Ha'Cohen Street with its engine running and the

(Continued — Page 2, Col. 7).

OFFICIAL ACCOUNT

Just after 6 a.m. the crew of a Police armoured car patrolling the Mustashfa area of Jerusalem observed a convoy of three vehicles and an armoured car pass the Police billet travelling towards the centre of the town, it was officially reported. The armoured car, which bore the number 597 preceded the other vehicles and a man wearing a brown great-coat and a blue police cap was occupying the turret of the vehicle.

The other vehicles forming the convoy were two Dodge 15 cwt. trucks and one three ton Dodge truck, all canvas covered and of military type. Two persons, dressed as soldiers, were occupying the cab of each truck.

The crew of the patrolling armoured car became suspicious and the driver turned round his vehicle and proceeded towards Zion Square and then along Ben Yehuda Street. Near the Atlantic Hotel in Ben Yehuda Street, the crew observed the three trucks they had previously seen, parked at the roadside facing towards Zion Square; the doors of the trucks were open and the vehicles were apparently unoccupied.

The driver of the police armoured car stopped beside the first vehicle, and smoke was seen to be coming from the rear of it. Fearing an explosion the driver carried on towards King George Ave. A few seconds later a heavy explosion occurred throwing the police vehicle forward.

All military ambulances in Jerusalem were ordered to the scene of the incident to render such assistance as was possible.

Jewish Civil Guards at a road-block near the junction of the Beth Hakerem and Jaffa roads have stated (the official account continues) that, at about 6 a.m., a Police armoured car and three military-type trucks passed through the road-block travelling towards Jerusalem. After the explosion this same armoured car was observed by a Police patrol car returning at great speed out of Jerusalem in a westerly direction.

Thorough police enquiries are in progress.

Yesterday's Victims

Of the 44 dead whose bodies had been found by late last night only the following 25 had been identified: Eliahu Fisher (owner of the Ora Cafe), Aliza Danal, Simha Levi, Miriam Bricker, Mr. and Mrs. Bracha Castan and their daughter Miriam, Malka Opatowski, Shulamit Bauman, Rivkah Parnés, Jacqueline Abutbul, Mr. Philipowitch, Albert Sasson and Israel Gadiel (the watchmen who were shot and killed), David Schiffer, Mrs. Mina Hochberg (her husband, Zvi, was badly hurt), Ruth Meyouhas (12), Mr. and Mrs. Ben Zion Meyouhas, Yoav Meyouhas (2), Elimelech Moridetsky (8 months), Ita Moridetsky (4), Mrs. Zahava Hollander, Haim Manfred Goldman, and Haim Schoenberg.

The wounded:

At the Bikur Holim Hospital: Richard Karpan, Adolph Burstein, Avraham Mizlavsky, Yaacov Yehoshua, Shmuel Zuckerberg, Yaacov Bricker, Pinhas Shvili, David Abutbul, Zalman Hurvitz, Ovadya Yehoshua, Itzhak Glazer, Nissan Landner, Miriam Goldman, Yehudit Levi Zleit, Hannah Mizrahi, and three children — Aharon Abutbul, Hanoch Lizkovsky, and Dan Kaplan.

At the Hadassah Hospital: Avraham Hirsch, Hillel Friaki, Shmuel Sack, Yenta Hurvitz, Itzhak Dinovitz, Shmuel Abutbul, Gofriti, Shmuel Sherenshi, Yaacov Hudnick, Shmuel Ashkenazi, Shuster, David Russo, Avraham Sofer, Rahel Ben Yaacov, Esther Yenuka, Dr. Shomert, a baby, Avraham Seroka and Shmuel Auerbach.

At the Shaarei Zedek Hospital: Rahel Matalon, Garfinkel, Edith Shachner, Shoshana Levi, Yafa and Rivka Ordenlich, Flora Cohen, Yaacov Mizrahi, Hanny Zani, Frieda Modetzky, Tova Mizrahi, Penina Feffer, Dr. Leah Kolner, Mordechai Binyamin, Michael Gordon, Rahamim Kladbond, Zvi Hochberg, Rahel Meyouhas, Julia Zen, Shmuel Greenbaum, Alexander Kasyon, David Ganon, Shmaryahu Mintz, Yisrael Fisher, and Yosef Kadosh.

ARMY VEHICLES FIRED ON

RISHON LE'ZION, Sunday. — Two Army vehicles which attempted to crash through an authorized road-block near here today, were fired on by Jewish guards, it is officially reported.

There were no casualties.

20 Greeks Executed

ATHENS, Sunday (Reuter. — Twenty Greeks, including one woman, were shot outside the Athens barracks at dawn yesterday, 11 of whom tried before the Athens Assize Court, had been under sentence of death for two years.

Column One

By David Courtney

WHO did this thing? It is better to wait and make sure; but make sure. Whatever the heart feels, it is better to wait until the mind knows; but see that the mind knows. Nothing is unbelievable: if the infamy of Ben Yehuda is possible what should there be that is unbelievable? But let nothing be believed until the mind is without a doubt; and even if a man sit with his dead in his arms and his tears hot upon a cheek coated with the street's dust, let him be as the scales of justice: without mercy, if it must be; but just. There is no other way: that man with his dead in his arms and his tears hot on a dust-caked cheek, has no other way: he has too many enemies, who will chill his passion with logic and flay his instinctive reasoning with contempt. The bare, blinding truth should be the urge of every just man now; for the awful guilt of yesterday's deed cannot stand upon complaint, or quibble or bureaucratic device, or impulsive revenge, or disbelief. The truth is there and it had better be found and acknowledged or worse evils will follow.

UNBELIEVABLE . . . : that word is not surprising; it is not to be scoffed at. It possesses in this context the sense of a dreadful nostalgia; and what the final judgment may be or not, the deep condemnation of the London Government is in that word. British policy, like all the bitterness that has come of it, is unbelievable. Yesterday it seemed more like a nightmare: that broken street, the horror of death and pain and heart-rending loss; and the mourning of a whole people, who had come from death and fire in Europe to be at peace in this land. The report of it must have been on the early morning news of the B.B.C. Mr. Bevin will have heard it before going to chapel. One cannot help wondering if he thought the deed unbelievable, let alone the rumoured charges; for surely no man, in his vanity, and his Ministerial power, could comprehend such tragedy and remain unmoved. A people has been cruelly hurt. In the way they bear their hurt will lie their strength and the strength of their cause.

Jerusalem, February 23.

Morgenthau Opens U.J.A. Drive

WASHINGTON, Sunday — (PTA). — Jewish leaders throughout the U. S. launched the $250 million United Jewish Appeal drive today at a two-day conference opened by Mr. Henry Morgenthau Jr., who declared that neither Palestine nor peace was possible if the U.N. fails to check the war which the Arabs have declared against the U.N.

J.C. APPEAL

Appealing to the Jews of Jerusalem to close their ranks while the ruins were still smouldering, the Jewish Community Council called on them yesterday to begin the work of reconstruction at once. Consumers and employers were urged to do what they could to help those who had suffered loss.

The Council called for discipline and restraint.

CALL FOR RESTRAINT

A call to the Jews of Jerusalem and of Palestine to refrain from "irresponsible action" was issued jointly by the Jewish Agency and the Vaad Leumi in Jerusalem last night.

"A horrible crime was perpetrated this morning," the statement continued, adding that the Jewish national institutions were investigating the attack and were in constant contact with the authorities as well as with Jewish representatives abroad.

Over a dozen eye-witnesses had reported to the Jewish Agency that they saw a number of Army trucks and a Police armoured vehicle approach Ben Yehuda Street just before the explosion, a Jewish Agency spokesman said at a conference in the Agency's Information Bureau in Ben Yehuda Street just after noon yesterday.

"Eye-witness evidence corroborates fully one point — that is, that the trucks were Army and Police, and the people who alighted from them were in Army and Police dress," the spokesman continued.

The Jewish Agency, he said,

(Continued on Page 3)

ARAB LEAGUE MEETINGS END

CAIRO, Sunday (AP). — The Arab League Council held the final session of its current Cairo meetings tonight, and at the close the following decisions were announced:

1) The Council's Political Committee will accept the "economic coordination of the Arab Middle East with the U.N. in principle.

2) The Council considers Iraq's proposal for the unification of the Arab countries' currencies a word of encouragement and refers the proposal to the Arab Governments for their consideration, asking them to send replies at the earliest possible date.

3) In view of the internal war prevailing in Palestine and the resulting casualties in lives and homeless victims, the Syrian delegation proposed that a tax be imposed on the populations of the League States to be called "The Saving of Palestine Tax." This proposal was also referred to the Arab Governments for their individual execution as deemed suitable.

Agency Charges Britain

LAKE SUCCESS, Sunday — (AP). — The Jewish Agency charged today that British policy in Palestine was strengthening Arab attacks against the Partition decision.

In their first formal indictment of the British regime, in a 12,000-word memorandum to the Security Council, the Agency blamed British policy for weakening Jewish defence and seriously threatening peace and security in the Holy Land.

The Agency rejected the recent statements by Sir Alexander Cadogan and Mr. Creech Jones as "untenable" and declared that the Palestine Government was not only obstructing the Palestine Commission of the United Nations, but also failed in its elementary obligation to maintain law and order.

"It seems inevitable," the Agency declared, "that unless preventive action is taken internationally and at an early date, there will be a full-scale Arab attack on the U.N. decision countered by a whole-hearted Jewish effort to defend that decision."

The attack would be stronger and the defence weaker as a direct consequence of the Mandatory policy and administrative practice.

The memorandum cited evidence which, it said, demonstrated that the Arabs were "powerfully encouraged" in their battle against Partition by the "atmosphere of tolerance and relative impunity in which they have been able to operate."

CZECH TRADE UNIONS FAVOUR COMMUNIST PREMIER

PRAGUE, Sunday (AP). — Organized labour today pledged a one-hour strike throughout Czechoslovakia on Tuesday in support of Premier Gottwald's bid to form a new Cabinet of Communists, Social Democrats and representatives of trade union, farm and ex-service organizations.

The Communist Premier demanded for the fourth time in three days that President Benes accept the resignations of the 12 Ministers who resigned on Friday. They belong to the Socialist Party, the Catholic Peoples Party and the Slovak Democratic Party.

The President's refusal to accept the resignations has on the face of things kept the Government from falling apart. He will confer with leaders and Ministers of the Slovak Democratic Party tomorrow.

The Slovak Democrats are the dominant Party in Slovakia. They formed one group which refused to continue in the Government until the Communist withdrew an order promoting eight Communists to high posts in the security police.

WILD SHOOTING FOLLOWS BOMB

The murderous attack in Ben Yehuda Street yesterday began a chain of incidents in which three Jews, seven soldiers and two airmen were killed, and an Army Padre, seven soldiers and 15 Jews were wounded. Heavy firing and explosions were heard all day. In the late afternoon, as the firing reached its heaviest, streets in the centre of the town cleared, people going home sought the shelter of walls, and persons in Jewish buses were wounded by shots from Police armoured cars.

The first incident occurred just before 11 a.m., when an Army Chaplain was shot and wounded and his driver was killed in King George Avenue. About 45 minutes later two R.A.F. men were killed near the Halbreich House and a Police armoured car which arrived at the scene reported that it was fired on. This car and several others in the vicinity opened fire.

About 4 o'clock in the afternoon heavy fire was directed at Jewish quarters by Arab snipers, and the Haganah replied, claiming casualties among Arabs in the Musrara Quarter.

Shortly after British Police were seen evacuating their billets at Mustashfa Police Station, an attack was launched by the Stern Group. The sirens sounded at 5.40 p.m., and a few minutes later an Army truck loaded with explosives and ammunition blew up on a landmine in St. George's Road. Five soldiers were killed and six others were injured, and the truck was wrecked. Troops in the area immediately opened wild fire, during which 10-year-old Itzhak Deutsch was killed, Shimon, 15, his brother was seriously hurt, and Azriel Brauer, 22, was fatally wounded.

A girl was killed and four persons were hurt when a No. 12 bus came under fire from a Police armoured car at the corner of Alliance Street and Jaffa Road. The injured are Gideon Stern, 29, Sarah Lauskovski, 19, Miriam Jano, 25, and Dvora Zelkind, 17, The dead girl had not been identified last night.

About the same time, Shlomo Ezra Cohen, 10, and Bechor Mizrachi, 70, were wounded near the English Mission Hospital, while Mr. E.

(Continued — Page 3, Col, 1)

CLEAR-CUT U.S. STAND AT S.C. NOT EXPECTED

By Palcor's Political Correspondent

NEW YORK, Sunday. — It is not anticipated that a clear-cut American statement will be forthcoming when the Security Council meets tomorrow to discuss the Palestine Commission's security report.

The Syrian delegate, Faris Bey el Khoury, will again try filibuster tactics by querying the legality of the proposal submitted by the Canadian chairman, General McNaughton, to have Jewish Agency representatives join in the Council's Palestine discussions. Faris Bey will also question the legality of the General Assembly's decision in general.

The final American position is unlikely to be revealed until President Truman returns from his Caribbean trip in a fortnight's time, it is believed. Votes are decisive; if America stands firm, Colombia and even China. might be favourably influenced, while Argentina continues to exhibit belligerent indolence in UN voting.

Democrats' Pleas

New York Democratic leaders last week asked the President to liberalize his actions so as to bring them into line with his declarations. His sit-down policy on Palestine constituted political suicide for the Democrats, they told him.

Mr. Paul FitzPatrick, Democratic leader of New York State, pleaded for four hours with Mr. James V. Forrestal, the Defence Secretary, last week. Mr. Truman's aides were so impressed by the urgency of these pleas that they claim the President had in mind also the Arab States' defiance of the Palestine decision when he scored in his recent annual report on UN those States that were blocking UN's decisions.

Tom Reynolds of the "Washington Sun" states that the White House decision on Palestine would be to support the Palestine Commission's demand for an international police force, but not to provide contingents.

At the same time, he says the U.S. was still most anxious to achieve a postponement and hoped that Britain would delay the withdrawal from Palestine. Britain would be ready to agree to this, provided her troops maintained only the **status quo** and that Partition is eventually modified, he adds.

Cooling Off

In Lake Success, too, there are rumours that a "cooling off" period has been proposed by the US. The Arabs are canvassing delegates to obtain support for a Special Assembly session before May 15.

Mallory Brown, UN correspondent of the "New York Times," states that the US is likely to propose an international police force to be composed of volunteers from regular armed services. Most credence, however, is given to yet another report that the U.S. will back a proposal to appeal to all nations to lift the arms embargo and to recruit a UN force composed of Palestine residents.

MARSHALL SHAPES PALESTINE POLICY

By JOHN HIGHTOWER
AP Correspondent.

WASHINGTON, Sunday. — American policy on Partition will be forged into final shape tomorrow by Mr. George Marshall, Secretary of State, Mr. Warren Austin, the U.N. delegate, and other high American officials.

The State Department is maintaining secrecy on the matter. Nevertheless, statements by President Truman himself have led to speculation that the U.S. will support the recommendation of the Palestine Commission for an international armed force to implement Partition.

Mr. Austin's report is expected to be a major factor in determining whether the Security Council itself eventually orders an armed force to take over when the British surrender authority on May 15.

BRITAIN'S "GREAT WORK" HERE

NEW YORK, Sunday (AP).— "Britain has been traduced and judged less than generously, but I think later generations will acknowledge the great work she has done in Palestine," said Mr. Creech Jones in a broadcast here tonight.

Speaking over the N.B.C. network in a debate on Palestine the British Colonial Secretary declared Britain had paid "a great price" in carrying out the Mandate during the past 25 years.

After Midnight

About 12.30 a.m. a loud explosion was heard from the Sheikh Jarrah Quarter.

Iraqi Parliament To Be Dissolved

BAGHDAD, Sunday (AP). — After a three-hour meeting of the Council of Ministers, the dissolution of the Iraqi Parliament has been officially decided.

Premier Mohammed A-Sader returned this morning from a two-day visit to Surseng in Northern Iraq, where the Regent spends his vacation, and immediately the Council of Ministers convened and took the decision dissolving Parliament.

An official communique will be made shortly.

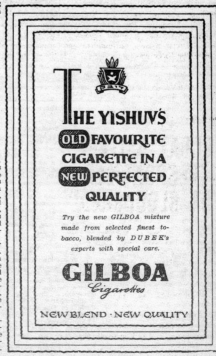

CeDe
TRULY FINE CHOCOLATE
CeDe LTD

JERUSALEM
Tuesday, May 11, 1948

THE PALESTINE POST

PRICE: 25 MILS
VOL. XXIII. No. 6710

GRESHAM
Life Assurance
Society Ltd.
Transacts the largest
LIFE ASSURANCE business
in the Middle East

HAGANAH WRESTS SAFAD FROM IRAQIS AND SYRIANS IN BITTER FIGHTING

GANGS FLEE TO HILLS IN WEST

Safad, key centre in the Galilee, fell to Jewish forces yesterday morning, when Arab gangs, numbering approximately 3,000, fled on foot in full retreat to the west following some of the bitterest fighting that has yet taken place in Palestine. The Arab forces, which included about 700 Iraqis and Syrians, were reported by the Haganah to have suffered 90 killed, while Jewish losses were eight and a number of wounded.

Preceded by 10 days of skirmishes, a full-scale battle broke out on Sunday night when Jewish forces launched a three-pronged assault on well-entrenched positions.

Under cover of a heavy mortar bombardment, one Haganah column stormed the outer positions, but a desperate defence forced them to fall back. Regrouping, the Jews moved in again, and this time silenced the opposition. A squad of pioneers moved in immediately to re-fortify the emplacements against possible counter-attacks.

Room-To-Room Fighting

Another Haganah unit assaulted an abandoned Jewish school which Arabs had taken over. The school, overlooking the Arab Quarter and the entrance to the town, was defended bitterly by its occupants. For every metre of ground hundreds of bullets from automatic weapons and rifles were spent. The battle raged from room to room and floor to floor until, overpowered, the Arabs withdrew, leaving 15 dead behind.

The Police Station, meanwhile, was the scene of a third attack. Every man of a squad which hit the perimeter defences was wounded, and fresh forces were sent up and breached the fence.

In stiff hand-to-hand fighting in the halls and corridors, the Arabs were overcome by 7 a.m., and the last strategic point in the town was in possession of the Haganah.

During the operation, the headquarters of the Nejada was destroyed, as well as several other houses. Jewish quarters came under heavy shelling from Arab positions during the night and early morning.

Military Rule

When the Jewish victory was assured, the town was placed under Haganah administration, and a Military Government was appointed. No one was permitted to enter the Arab area without permission.

The last of the 8,000 Arab inhabitants of Safad, who had begun to evacuate early last week, were reported to be leaving hastily as the battle got under way. Safad has 2,000 Jewish inhabitants.

Searches of Arab strongholds and buildings uncovered large quantities of munitions and other military equipment.

Arab sources admitted the loss of Safad yesterday, but tried to soften the blow with other claims. The Arab Radio at Ramallah announced that the "Liberation Army's" forces withdrew at 3.45 a.m. on Monday, but only after it had "completely destroyed" the Jewish quarters.

The Cairo daily "Al Misr" said yesterday that British troops were expected to prevent Safad from falling to the Jews, the Associated Press reported. Syria had advised British authorities, the paper said, that the capture of Safad by Jews would threaten Syria's security. She could not remain with her "hands tied" in the face of such danger, and Britain should intervene.

JERUSALEM ROAD CLEARED BY JEWS

By J. L. MELTZER

The Haganah last night firmly held the entire 15-mile stretch of mountain highway from Bab el Wad eastwards to Jerusalem. Late in the afternoon, Jewish troops brought to a climax two days of stiff fighting 2,300 feet above sea level with the capture of the commanding ridges and strongpoints overlooking the five-mile long ravine.

An Arab village was surrounded and isolated, the only remaining major centre of Arab resistance. Haganah patrols were last night operating fanwise around the ravine in pursuit of the Arabs who fought them.

Arab village boys were selling dried sunflower seeds and cigarettes to Jewish soldiers, when I visited the battle command post. Unlike the nearby villages of Beit Iksa, Beit Sureik, and Nebi Samwil, Abu Ghosh is virtually unscarred. Its two monasteries have not been touched.

The first indication that the battle for the highway was over came when three truckloads carrying Jewish "Civil Guard" volunteers raced along past a headquarters in the field. Staid businessmen, professional men and storekeepers were among these road gangs on full-time duty in erecting fortifications and clearing roads in the Jerusalem area.

"The road is clear," they shouted as they passed. Actually a number of small stone barriers remained in position across the road. They consisted of only two or three courses half a metre high.

Among the troops in the armoured cars outside the battle headquarters, 10 miles west of Jerusalem, were girls wearing battle-dress tunics and slacks.

Neutral Version

The following account of the fighting was produced by the Public Information Office.

Approximately 400 Jews attacked Beit Mahsir early this morning. The attacks were repulsed by about 600 Arab irregulars, and the local Arab Commander has applied for reinforcements from Ramallah.

The main body of the Jews is reported to be around Beit Mahsir and appear to hold a bridge in that area.

RED CROSS PLAN FOR HOLY CITY

To Be a "Hospital" Respected By Armies

M. Jaques de Reynier, the I.R.C. delegate in Palestine, told a press conference in Jerusalem yesterday afternoon that he hoped the Red Cross flag would go up over the entire town-planning area of Jerusalem the moment the Union Jack was hauled down at midnight on Friday — when the British Mandate over Palestine ends.

He had received verbal agreement, M. de Reynier stated, from the "highest Arab and Jewish authorities within and without Palestine" that Jerusalem be demilitarized, that all fighting forces be withdrawn and that the City become entirely separated from the fighting now going on in the country.

Before this scheme (to which the Palestine Government indicated on Sunday that it agreed) comes into operation, however, written requests from various Jewish and Arab political, religious and medical organizations and personalities must reach M. de Reynier, not later than Friday morning, and if one of the specified bodies fails to do so, the whole plan will come to nothing.

The Red Cross delegate explained that under this scheme the City of Jerusalem would, if all parties handed in their requests in time, be considered as a "hospital or place of refuge," to be respected by all armies. The **status quo** prevailing when the flags go up would be maintained, meaning both Jews and Arabs would keep the positions they now occupied and continue to man their roadblocks — unarmed — until such time as they felt the obstructions served no useful purpose.

Parts of Jerusalem now occupied by the Haganah would be cleared of all troops, he explained, and the former residents would, he hoped, trickle back.

One of the biggest problems, bringing supplies to Jerusalem from outside the area, would be solved in this way —

Moral Force

Unarmed convoys would proceed to Jerusalem under the Red Cross flag. They would not be searched, but Red Cross officials would make snap inspections to satisfy themselves that no arms or ammunition were being conveyed. Since the I.R.C. was only a 'moral force," consisting of a few officials, M. de Reynier explained that the whole scheme was based on mutual trust and confidence, which would in due course bring real peace to Jerusalem.

Four Red Cross flags would be hoisted on top of the Y.M.C.A. tower, clearly visible from most parts of the city, and banners would also go up at all entrances of the city.

Special provision is contemplated for food convoys, through the Red Cross, to the

(Continued on Page 2, Col. 2)

TRUCE TRIO IN TOUCH

Reports that the U.N. Consular Truce Commission and the Palestine Government were not working together were unfounded, the Commission stated yesterday. The two have been "in close touch since the Commission's appointment," the statement said. It added:

"It will be remembered that the Mandatory Power has certain responsibilities under the Security Council's resolution of April 17, 1948."

The resolution requested the Mandatory Power to supervise and "give effect with all means at its disposal" to the carrying out of a truce in Jerusalem. It also held the Mandatory responsible for taking "all steps necessary to maintain" law and order.

STILL NO TALKS

The truce negotiations due to have opened yesterday between the High Commissioner and the Jewish Agency were again postponed, as neither Mr. Ben Gurion, Mrs. Myerson nor Mr. Kaplan had returned to Jerusalem.

The Jewish Agency briefed two senior officials at present in the city, but Sir Alan preferred to await the arrival of one of the three representatives specified by him.

Column One

By

David Courtney

U.N. cannot fail because it dare not. This is the substance of an article written by Mr. Trygve Lie and published a few days ago. Trygve Lie is that rare person, a liberal with constructive views and positive sympathies, whose conscience does more than gently prick at the touch of wrong, and whose reason asks something better than a universal armchair for the peoples of the world to relax in. His article points out that U.N. has not failed; and implies that certain States, which should have known better, have endangered both the Charter and the instruments of U.N., for selfish purposes. Mr. Lie did not name Russia. He did not name America or Britain. But it is clear that if he had the first in his mind, he had also the other two.

*

COMING during the course of the most humiliating session of U.N. since its foundation, the Secretary-General's words are timely. It has been said that the behaviour of Britain and America over Palestine may wreck U.N.; and there has been good cause to say it. Whatever may be the apologetics and expostulations of British spokesmen, there can no longer be any doubt that Britain has deliberately obstructed U.N. in its attempt to solve the Palestine problem. Its refusal to accept the U.N. Commission in time; its condoning of aggressive action from across the frontiers; and even the snatching of a Jerusalem truce from under the noses of the Consular authorities charged from Lake Success to arrange a truce, are not the actions of a loyal unit of U.N. But Mr. Trygve Lie writes: "No nation can maintain, for any length of time, an attitude which cannot be defended before world public opinion." Let us say, for Democracy's sake, that he meant Russia; and for Truth's sake, that he also meant Britain and the United States.

*

IT is probable that Russia's use of the veto was, on occasion, more than an irritant; and no one will pretend that Russia has done all she might have done to build U.N. into the majestic and impregnable authority it should be. But there was never a misuse of the veto by Russia to equal in its callous disregard of the purpose and dignity of U.N.. the veto implied in America's powerful pressure upon U.N. to follow the "whirling dervish" politics of the State Department and reverse its own solemn decision of a few months ago. If America were to succeed in her attempt, and if Soviet Russia were in fact bent on the evil practices attributed to her in Washingon and London, then, as surely as that the sky will remain above us though the atom bomb destroy all below, U.N. would not have a single moral finger left to raise against any act Soviet Russia might choose to perform.

*

YOU can fool all of the people some of the time, etc; but sooner or later you get found out. That is Mr. Lie's opinion. A majority of the nations at U.N. have no profound love for the Jews and have never been seriously troubled in conscience by the plight of the Jews. But it seems more than probable that the small nations are tired of being fooled and resent being made to look ridiculous in the service of the Foreign Office and the State Department. At any rate, it is clear that although the influence of Britain and the U.S. at Lake Success may still be strong, the prestige of those countries has sagged. Neither of them is likely again, for some considerable time, to try to impose its own policy above the judgment of the nations. A few boys with a good cause and a strong heart have been enough to tear the high-falutin' trappings from a piece of shoddy intrigue, which cared neither for U.N. nor for the good of Jew or Arab. Mr. Trygve Lie, therefore, may be fully justified in his optimism; for now that the stark facts of Palestine are plain to see, it is unlikely that the ponderous mummery of Mr. Creech Jones and Mr. Warren Austin will impress the Assembly.

Jerusalem, May 11.

The second instalment of Herzl's "Jewish State" appears on p. 4 of today's issue.

Draft Resolution Seeks to Withhold Permission To Maintain Autonomy

LAKE SUCCESS, Monday. (Palcor). — Dr. Pablo Azcarate, member of the Palestine Commission's Secretariat who was in Palestine before, left New York today to return to Jerusalem, where he will join the Consular Truce Commission.

When the 12-man Palestine Sub-Committee resumed its secret meetings today, M. Finn Moe, Norwegian Rapporteur of the Political Committee, presented his draft resolution for a provisional regime in Palestine. He denied his personal and his Government's responsibility for the draft, saying he had shaped the report in the form of a resolution, in order to facilitate the work.

The document was a five-page working paper which, informed sources say, calls for the creation of a six-member agency, called the "Temporary Central Commission for Palestine," and to be composed of representatives of the US, France and Belgium and three as yet unnamed members.

While the draft is still being withheld from the press, it is said to be along the lines put forward by Mr. Creech Jones, of Britain, who today left for England.

M. Katz-Suchy (Poland) and M. Panushkin (Russia), surprised at the resolution, pointed out that M Finn Moe had gone beyond his assignment, since the resolution did not incorporate the discussions held hitherto.

Basis For Discussion

The Norwegian delegate, Mr. Philip Jessup (U.S.) and M.A. Parodi (France) said that the resolution was a mere basis for discussion, and their support of the document did not necessarily commit their governments to it.

M. Katz-Suchy is said to have objected to the fact that the document makes no mention of the Arab and Jewish States, and refers only to Arab and Jewish authorities. This implies that the document goes beyond the mere suspension of Partition and seeks to withhold permission to maintain the autonomy already attained.

The Committee decided by nine votes to three to continue in closed session. While Poland, Soviet Russia and Guatemala insisted on holding public meetings, Dr. Granados supported the decision that the document be withheld from publication, apparently in order not to publicize it as a constructive proposal before May 15.

All three wanted the Jews and Arabs to receive a copy of the plan immediately for consideration, but they were overruled.

The Sub-Committee is likely to require two or three more days of private discussion before handing to the General Assembly their specific proposal, embodying Britain's suggestion for a shadow Government to succeed the Mandatory.

In the afternoon, the Sub-Committee was due to meet to

(Continued on Page 2, Col. 1)

Russia To Open Consulates

LONDON, Monday (PTA) — It is reported from Istanbul that Russia has decided to open Consulates in Jerusalem and Tel Aviv.

Three members of the Soviet Embassy staff at Ankara have been ordered to leave for Palestine at once for the purpose, the report said.

Two Possibles For Jerusalem Mayor

LONDON, Monday (UP). — A Foreign Office spokesman said that Britain was considering at least two men for possible appointment as "emergency mayor" of Jerusalem. He mentioned the name of Mr. A.P.S. Clark of Barclays Bank, but would not name the other.

Mr. Clark is reported to have called at the Foreign Office this morning.

Britain's final choice would be advised to the United Nations within a day or two, the spokesman indicated.

(U.P. and A.P.)

WHEN DOES THE MANDATE END?

By JESSE ZEL LURIE,
Palestine Post Correspondent

LAKE SUCCESS, Monday. — With only four days to go, a dispute has arisen here as to when exactly the British Mandate over Palestine is to end.

Some suggest one hour after midnight on Friday, others say 12 o'clock noon on Saturday. This would mean Jewry would celebrate Sunday, May 16, as "Independence Day."

Sir Alexander Cadogan, the British delegate to the UN, asked about this matter, said: "What difference does it make at what hour the Mandate ends?"

While all indications are that Partition is a **fait accompli** which cannot be undone, M. Trygve Lie, the UN Secretary-General, is making feverish last-minute efforts to set up an interim committee to carry on the administration of Palestine until the next regular session of the UN in autumn — a revolutionary departure from the original idea that May 15 should be Palestine Independence Day.

'GHOST AUTHORITIES'

LAKE SUCCESS, Monday. — A dispirited United Nations moved towards the appointment of the ghost authorities for Jerusalem and for Palestine as a whole, with neither having any power to back up their decisions if the Jews or the Arabs chose to scorn their orders.

In Lake Success circles it was reported that the most likely name put forward for the U.N. "emergency mayor" of Jerusalem was Mr. A. P. S. Clark, Local Director of Barclays Bank and a well-known resident of the city during the past 30 years. Complete secrecy surrounds the U.N. negotiations on the appointment, and a Jewish Agency spokesman refused to say which of the three men proposed by the Arabs (Mr. Clark, Mr. A. Miller, secretary of the Jerusalem Y.M.C.A., and Father Eugene, an Irish Franciscan) was considered acceptable.

The announcement of the name finally decided on would be made in Jerusalem by Sir Alan Cunningham, the High Commissioner, said Mr. Andrew Cordier, executive assistant to the Secretary-General of the U.N.

For Palestine as a whole, the

(Continued on Page 2, Col. 1

JAFFA CAPITULATES: AN OPEN CITY

In what amounts to unconditional capitulation, Jaffa, largest Arab town in Palestine, has asked to be declared an open city and has undertaken that it would not be used for military purposes.

Following the complete breakdown of municipal services and the evacuation of most of its 70,000 inhabitants, the Jaffa Emergency Committee, in an almost abject letter sent on Sunday to the Government, invited supervision of its status.

The Committee (the three members of the National Committee who are still in Jaffa — Ahmad eff. Abu Laban, Saleh eff. Nasr, and A. Andrawis) requested the Palestine Government to appoint without delay a neutral observer acceptable to Jews and Arabs to supervise the now "undefended town."

Its letter to the "Lydda" District Commissioner, Mr. W. V. Fuller, was published officially yesterday. The Committee stated that it was asking that Jaffa be declared open and undefended because the British Army would no longer be responsible for its defence.

The Government pointed out yesterday that only some 4,000 Arabs were left in Jaffa following the recent fighting. A quorum of the Municipal Council was no longer available, and before Mayor Haikal's departure, he appointed three men to ensure the safety of the town. Of these three only one, Haj Ahmad Abu Laban, remained, the official report said.

A copy of the letter was sent to the Chairman of the U.N. Truce Commission in Jerusalem. The letter read:

May 9, 1948
District Commissioner, Jaffa.
Sir,

On April 30, 1948, as a result of representations on the part of Tel Aviv made to Major-General H. Murray, Commanding the First Infantry Division, a cease fire was ordered by the British Military Commander.

This was followed not by a truce, such as might have been expected, but by an order of the commander to both sides that there should be no aggressive action of any sort in the Jaffa area. In view of the fact that such an order is unlikely to remain in force after May 15, when Britain will terminate the Mandate, and in view of the fact that the town of Jaffa is no longer defended, we, the members of the Emergency Committee of Jaffa, hereby declare that this town will not be used for military purposes, and we request the Government of Palestine to ensure that this decision is made known by radio and other means to the U.N. Organization and the general public, and to appoint without delay a neutral observer acceptable to both parties who may see to it that the state of an undefended town shall be observed and respected.

DIRECT APPROACH

A British offer to mediate a truce in Jaffa was refused by the Haganah yesterday, the U.P. reported.

"We are willing to negotiate with the Arabs directly," the Haganah told the "Lydda" District Commissioner, Mr. W. J. Fuller, who had made the offer. "We no longer need British mediation."

War Loan A Hit

TEL AVIV, Monday. — To-night, even before the opening of the subscription lists for the Jewish national LP.5 m. loan, LP. 1 m. had been offered in this city alone. Among the first to enter his name was Mr. Quentin Reynolds, the well-known American war correspondent and author, for a unit of LP.100. One Tel Aviv resident subscribed LP. 25,000.

The proceeds of the loan are to be devoted to war needs and the immediate purposes of the Jewish State administration.

In Jerusalem it was reported last night that the loan subscription forms had not yet arrived. The fear was expressed that the whole loan might be taken up before Jerusalemites had the chance of joining in.

Jerusalem Still Without Water

Jerusalem was still without water yesterday. The two pipelines from Ras el Ein which were blown up by Arabs between Latrun and Bab el Wad on Friday have still to be repaired.

Crews are scheduled to leave under Army escort this morning to continue repair work, and barring further trouble, repairs may be completed today. Water may be pumped into Jerusalem within a few days, according to one municipal water official.

No repairs were made yesterday, because sections for the damaged lines had to be made ready in the city.

Road Truce in Western Galilee

The first Jewish convoy from Haifa to the north, under the terms of the road-truce effected between Jews and Arabs in that region was held up at Acre for 24 hours, the United Press reported yesterday.

The convoy, which reached Acre on Sunday, was delayed to give the Arabs a chance to notify their outposts in the north of its departure.

Jewish sources said that once before such a truce had been arranged — and violated by the Arabs. The Haganah would therefore act with the utmost caution.

The first Arab convoy is reported by the Baghdad Radio to have reached Haifa safely from Acre.

Ibn Saud Promises To Intervene "At Time Agreed Upon"

CAIRO, Monday. — King Ibn Saud has "decided that his country will participate with other Arab countries in the military defence of Palestine at a time which has been agreed upon," the Saudi Arabian Legation announced tonight.

Allaying fears of some Arabs that the Arabian King would oppose the Palestine invasion plans of King Abdullah of Trans-Jordan, the Legation issued the following communique.

"Following Talks which took place in Cairo and Amman, Jamil Mardam Bey and Riad es Solh, the Syrian and Lebanese Prime Ministers, arrived in Riadh, capital of Saudi Arabia.

"They conveyed to King Ibn Saud a summary of the situation in Palestine.

"The King expressed full support of all the decisions taken to defend Palestine, maintain its Arabism and prevent Partition or the creation of a Jewish State.

"His Majesty decided that his country will participate with other Arab countries in the military defence of Palestine at points which have been agreed upon. He will cooperate with other Arab countries until Palestine regains her freedom and Arabism, however long it may take."

No Discharges

The Egyptian Cabinet has postponed all regular discharges from the army and appropriated LE.4 m. to finance the fighting in Palestine, according to official sources. It is said that the postponement of army discharges is effective "until the situation has been restored to normal."

The Defence Minister, Mohammed Heidar Pasha, said that the appropriation was "only the first instalment" and that the Premier had agreed to arrange for other preparations for a war in Palestine in the future.

Officially it was explained that the money will be used "to face the expenditure necessitated by the stationing of Egyptian forces on the Palestine border." It will be taken from the Treasury reserves and

Continued on Page 2, Col. 3)

British Threat To Block Finances

LAKE SUCCESS, Monday (PTA). — Assurances regarding the protection of British and other foreign economic interests in Palestine after termination of the Mandate have been requested by the British Government in a communication to the U.N. Palestine Commission, reliable sources here state, adding that implied in the request was a threat that the funds of the Palestine Currency Board and other assets of the Palestine Administration might otherwise not be released.

Among the British economic interests mentioned in the communication were the oil pipe line from Iraq, civil aviation rights to the use of Palestinian airports, the Dead Sea Potash Works, and citrus groves and packing plants. The guarantees asked for concerned mainly movable property.

A second communication discussed British Army stores. It is understood that the Palestine Commission made no reply since its functions expire shortly.

The "New York Times" recalls that the Palestine Commission strongly disapproved of Britain's treatment of the financial assets of Palestine, especially in connection with the charging against them of the cost of maintaining the Cyprus refugee camps.

Arab States May Have Martial Law

Rumours are circulating in the Middle East that the Arab States are on the verge of proclaiming martial law on or near May 15, for the purpose of suppressing those sections of the population who are not in agreement with their governments' policies, a Jewish Agency spokesman said in Jerusalem yesterday.

The Trans-Jordan Minister of the Interior, on the other hand, announced on Sunday that such measures were unnecessary there, since the whole country was united on its aims and agreed on the Government's policy.

Arab Parts Only

Meanwhile, the Minister of the Interior in the Lebanese Government, M. Camille Chamoun, declared on Sunday night that when the Arab Armies invaded Palestine, they would first occupy only the Arab parts of the country, stopping at the borders of the Jewish areas.

The Agency spokesman, commenting on this announcement, said it indicated that the Lebanon seemed to have territorial ambitions in Palestine and would try and occupy those parts nearest to the Lebanon — Western Galilee.

After Midnight

Paris Radio reported last night that the British naval blockade would be lifted at the end of the Mandate.

Britons Leave As "E-Day" Nears

HAIFA, Monday. — Three Government-chartered Dakotas brought 60 British civilians from Kalandia Airport to Haifa today en route for Britain.

The passengers were escorted to Kalandia by the Army. The British liner Samaria will arrive here on Thursday to take 500 British policemen and a number of troops to Britain.

The Empress of Australia is expected on Sunday.

Across the River

Large units of the British Army are crossing the Allenby Bridge from Palestine into Trans-Jordan, the Baghdad Radio reported last night.

Jews Not Acceptable

GENEVA, Monday (AP). — Guatemala announced today a colonization scheme for 15,000 European D.P.'s in the interior forests of the country. The terms of the scheme indicated that Jews would not be acceptable.

If you can't come to town,
please telephone 4607

Lighting, Heating, Cooking, Refrigeration

CARL MARX
3 PRINCESS MARY AVE., JERUSALEM

THE PALESTINE POST

JERUSALEM
SUNDAY, MAY 16, 1948

PRICE: 25 MILS
VOL. XXIII. No. 6714

THE PALESTINE POST
THE SUBSCRIPTION DEPARTMENT has returned to The Palestine Post offices, Hassolel Street, Jerusalem, Tel. 4233.

STATE OF ISRAEL IS BORN

The first independent Jewish State in 19 centuries was born in Tel Aviv as the British Mandate over Palestine came to an end at midnight on Friday, and it was immediately subjected to the test of fire. As "Medinat Yisrael" (State of Israel) was proclaimed, the battle for Jerusalem raged, with most of the city falling to the Jews. At the same time, President Truman announced that the United States would accord recognition to the new State. A few hours later, Palestine was invaded by Moslem armies from the south, east and north, and Tel Aviv was raided from the air. On Friday the United Nations Special Assembly adjourned after adopting a resolution to appoint a mediator but without taking any action on the Partition Resolution of November 29.

Yesterday the battle for the Jerusalem-Tel Aviv road was still under way, and two Arab villages were taken. In the north, Acre town was captured, and the Jewish Army consolidated its positions in Western Galilee.

Most Crowded Hours in Palestine's History

Between Thursday night and this morning Palestine went through what by all standards must be among the most crowded hours in its history.

For the Jewish population there was the anguish over the fate of the few hundred Haganah men and women in the Kfar Etzion bloc of settlements near Hebron. Their surrender to a fully equipped superior foreign force desperately in need of a victory was a foregone conclusion. What could not be known, with no communications since Thursday morning, was whether and to what extent the Red Cross and the Truce Consuls would secure civilized conditions for prisoners and wounded, and proper respect for the dead. Doubts on some of these anxious questions have now been resolved.

On Friday afternoon, from Tel Aviv, came the expected announcement of the Jewish State, and its official naming at birth, "Medinat Yisrael"—State of Israel, with the swearing in of the first Council of Government. The proclamation of the State was made at midnight, coinciding with the sailing from Haifa of Britain's last High Commissioner. Within the hour, President Truman announced in Washington that the Government of the United States had decided to give *de facto* recognition to the Jewish State, with all that such recognition implied. The Assembly of the United Nations, meeting since the middle of April for "further study" of the Palestine problem was thus left, by one means or another, to ratify the Two-States decision of November last year, or dissolve with nothing concrete to its credit. The Assembly adjourned with the resolution to appoint a mediator between the Jews and Arabs, to cooperate with the Security Council's Truce Commission in Jerusalem.

Russian Recognition Awaited

Russia and her allies had given early assurance of their intention to recognize the Jewish State, whoever else did or did not. As a result of Washington's action and the Eastern Bloc's stand, other countries are expected to extend their recognition to the newly born state.

Nor did the Arab Bloc remain idle. True to their promises, or threats, the members of the Arab League completed their plans for a full-scale invasion of Palestine in what has been described as a Moslem "crusade" against the Jews. Tel Aviv was bombed twice yesterday by Egyptian war planes. One of the enemy planes was shot down by a Jewish fighter plane, and the pilot taken prisoner, showing that this move against the civilian population was not a surprise, and that the Jewish preparations include anti-aircraft defences.

A black-out has been ordered for the whole of Jewish Palestine Tel Aviv itself having blacked out on Friday.

At the same time, the air was filled with reports of two Egyptian columns on the move from the south towards Gaza and Beersheba, and of intensified shelling from across the northern border of Jewish settlements in North-Eastern Galilee.

The Security Council met yesterday in a special session to consider action on the invasion of Palestine by member states of the U.N.

In the afternoon, Jerusalem was subjected to shelling from the northwest.

Haganah forces throughout the country continued mopping up, and Jewish sources claimed most of Western Galilee safe against attack. Naharayim, near Jisr el Majamie, inside Trans-Jordan, where the Jordan River works of the Palestine Electric Corporation are, is claimed by the Arab Legion. The battle for the Tel Aviv-Jerusalem Road at Bab el Wad is still on, Haganah taking two villages — Abu Shusha and Kubab — between Ramleh and Latrun.

Converging on Old City

In Jerusalem the "cease fire" observed on both sides for six days was broken on Friday, although the more strategic buildings in Princess Mary Avenue, the Russian Compound, and Jaffa Road passed to the Jews without a shot being fired, as did the David Building commanding the road to the German Colony and Railway Station. By yesterday evening, Jewish forces were approaching some of the gates of the Old City. The Police Training School on Mt. Scopus and Sheikh Jarrah are in Jewish hands.

On Friday morning, the Truce Commission met at the French Consulate and invited Jewish and Arab representatives to confer with them. Jewish Agency delegates agreed that the "cease fire" be extended in Jerusalem for eight days. Arab representatives could not attend, they said, because of the firing in Julian's Way, and a two-hour respite was arranged from 5 to 7 in the evening. Whether they agreed or not, became academic as by that time the battle for Jerusalem had been renewed.

To Jerusalem's tension was added the aggravation of electric power failing in most parts of the city, as nearly all of the Electric Corporation's lines had been shot down. This meant, on top of the other heardships to a fuel-less city, no broadcast news yesterday, when there were no newspapers. For more than a week the city was also without piped water.

JEWS TAKE OVER SECURITY ZONES

The Battle for Jerusalem, which began when the British forces withdrew on Friday morning, continued all day Friday and yesterday. The crackle of small-arms fire and explosions of mortar shells were still being heard in the early hours of this morning as the battle entered its third day.

Repeated efforts on Friday evening and again on Saturday by the U.N. Truce Commission to bring about a "cease fire" were brought to nought when the Arab representatives failed to agree within the specified time limit.

On Friday morning, Jewish forces entered the Russian Compound and Zone C to reoccupy the buildings requisitioned from Jews last year. This operation was almost bloodless, but beyond the western edge of Zone C, Arabs engaged the Jews in Jaffa Road. The Arabs were forced back and the Barclays Bank area was taken.

In other parts of the city fighting flared up. Jews overran one after another the areas evacuated by the British. By last night, the quarters and strongpoints held by Haganah included the German Colony and part of the Baka'a Quarter in Zone A, all of Zone B except for the Red Cross area, Sheikh Jarrah (where the Jewish flag was flown from the Mufti's House), the Mea Shearim Police Station and Allenby Barracks on the Bethlehem Road. The I.Z.L. were in occupation of the Scopus Police Billet.

Yesterday afternoon eight cannon shelled Jewish Jerusalem from the Arab village of Nebi Samwil, more than 100 shells falling in the northwestern quarters. Several persons were injured.

Jewish casualties in the two days of fighting were eight killed and a number of wounded. Arab casualties are not known.

EMERGENCY

A state of emergency in the Jerusalem area was declared to exist by the Haganah Area Commander as from yesterday in what is the first Order of the Day to be issued in almost 2,000 years by a Jewish Military Commander of the city.

The Order said:

With the declaration of the establishment of Medinat Israel (the State of Israel) and the setting up of its Provisional Council of Government, the Jews of Palestine have entered upon the decisive phase of the war.

In order to obviate any disturbance during the difficult time that confronts us, I hereby declare a state of emergency to exist in the Jerusalem District as from 00.01 hours on Saturday, May 15, and I hereby give the following instructions:

1. Every inhabitant must place himself at the disposal of the authorized security forces of Medinat Israel and obey their orders.
2. All property required for the needs of the Military Command may be expropriated by the security forces acting through officers carrying proper documents. Compensation for such expropriated property will be paid according to evaluation by the Jerusalem Committee and at such time as the latter shall decide.
3. The areas evacuated by the forces of the Mandatory Government and now held by the security forces are hereby declared to be Military Occupation Areas under the authority of Military Governors.
4. No person may enter any such area without permission of the Military Governor.
5. Any person found looting or committing any criminal act will be brought before a Military Court and punished with all the rigour of the law.

The Palestine Post

Despite the power failure in Jerusalem, the Electric Corporation succeeded in providing these offices with power about 10.15 last night. There was another failure about 11.15 but again the Corporation was able to restore the current.

Before the linotype machines could begin to work, however, it was 1 a.m., and in order to be able to appear this morning, The Palestine Post is published, for the third time in as many weeks, in two pages.

Egyptian Air Force Spitfires Bomb Tel Aviv; One Shot Down

Kol Israel, the Tel Aviv broadcasting station, reported at 2 o'clock yesterday afternoon that Tel Aviv had been bombed three times in the previous evening and morning, and that one plane had been shot down and its Egyptian pilot taken prisoner.

In the first raid, four planes attacked from a height of 300 feet. Two dropped bombs, while the others strafed the city. Little damage was caused. In the second attack two hours later, the airport to the north of the city was bombed, and an Air France plane parked there was damaged. The third raid was launched shortly before midday, but the planes were driven off without causing any damage.

Two settlements in the Negev had also been attacked from the air, the radio reported.

A country-wide blackout was ordered by Air Raid Precaution Headquarters in Tel Aviv.

Mr. David Ben Gurion, the Prime Minister, broadcast from Tel Aviv to the people of America yesterday morning. As he spoke, Egyptian planes were bombing the city.

In the north, the settlements of Ein Gev and Shaar Hagolan and Dan had been shelled, but no further details were available.

Kalandia airfield was taken by the Jewish army on Friday morning, shortly after the High Commissioner had left there by plane for Haifa. The field was evacuated, together with the neighbouring settlement of Ataroth, on Friday night. The settlement itself was burnt by Arabs yesterday.

2 Columns Cross Southern Border

By WALTER COLLINS
U.P. Correspondent

CAIRO, Saturday. — A communique issued today by the Egyptian Ministry of National Defence reported that two columns of Egyptian troops, including infantry and artillery, had struck across the Palestine border, preceded by aircraft.

One column was reported to have crossed the frontier 30 miles inland and to have attacked the "Jewish village of Auja on the road to Beersheba, wiping it out because its inhabitants had refused to surrender." (Auja is a police post near the frontier, about 25 miles from the nearest Jewish settlement). The column then entrenched itself on heights east of Gaza.

Meanwhile, according to this Cairo report, another column crossed the border at midnight, travelling north along the coast road towards Gaza.

Egyptian sources later reported that their forces had reached the Negev settlements of Nirim and Kfar Darom, but could give no further details.

In Cairo, at midnight, 2,000 Egyptian Police, commanded by 370 Officers, started a round-up of suspected Zionist sympathizers and arrested 600 persons within six hours.

According to Haganah sources, Jewish soldiers beat off an Egyptian "amphibious operation," an attempt to land troops near Ashdod, 20 miles north of Gaza. The ship which attempted to make the landing was forced to turn back, these sources said.

Arab Legion Cross Border

It was reported in Jerusalem last night that troops of the Arab Legion had crossed the border into Palestine in two places, over Allenby Bridge and near the Palestine Electric power station at Naharaim.

According to Reuters, the long convoy of the first route of lorry-borne troops, artillery and armoured cars, was headed by King Abdullah, who fired a symbolic pistol shot towards Palestine and wished his troops success in their campaign.

In Cairo, a group of journalists have asked the Egyptian Premier, Nokrashi Pasha, for an interview to discuss the proposed blackout of news, the Cairo Radio has reported.

A Good Thing

CAIRO, Saturday (UP). — The Egyptian Premier, Nokrashi Pasha, told the press that advance units of the Egyptian army had entered Gaza 12 hours after crossing the frontier.

"This is a very good thing," he added.

Etzion Settlers Taken P.O.W.

Fighting in the Kfar Etzion bloc continued throughout Friday, after Kfar Etzion itself had surrendered to the Arabs on the previous day. The wounded from the settlement were evacuated to Massuot Itzhak.

The fighting was broken off on Friday on the intervention of a Red Cross representative, accompanied by a Jewish Medical Officer, who went out to the settlements and supervised the transfer of the Jews from Revadim and Ein Zurim, the wounded and women being taken to Bethlehem, and the other settlers to prison.

The settlers from Massuot Itzhak, including the wounded from the first day's fighting at Kfar Etzion, were removed yesterday.

The terms of surrender agreed on by the Jews and Arabs were:

All able-bodied soldiers to be taken as prisoners of war, and kept in special camps, to be supervised by the International Red Cross.

Women, non-combatants and wounded to be brought to Jerusalem by the Red Cross.

War Office Says Legion Had Left

LAKE SUCCESS, Saturday. — Sir Alexander Cadogan, Britain's delegate to the UN, ...read in the Security Council a telegram from the War Office today, stating that *all units of the Arab Legion had left Palestine for Trans-Jordan prior to the end of the Mandate.*

U.S. RECOGNIZES JEWISH STATE

WASHINGTON, Saturday. —Ten minutes after the termination of the British Mandate on Friday, the White House released a formal statement by President Truman that the U.S. Government intended to recognize the Provisional Jewish Government as the *de facto* authority representing the Jewish State.

The U.S. is also considering lifting the arms embargo but it is not known whether to Palestine only or the entire Middle East, and the establishment of diplomatic relations with the Jewish Provisional Government.

The White House press secretary, Mr. Charles Ross, told correspondents today that reaction so far to the recognition had been overwhelmingly favourable. He said this step had been discussed with Mr. Marshall and Mr. Lovett before action was taken, and it had their complete support.

Mr. Ross said that the President had decided several days ago to grant American recognition to the new Jewish State, but due to protocol regulations he could not announce his policy until a formal letter arrived. "We were able to move very quickly when the messenger brought the letter," he said, "because the President had already determined the course of action to be taken."

Provisional Government

A few minutes before five (midnight Palestine time), Mr. Eliyahu Epstein, of the Jewish Agency's Washington Office, handed a letter to the White House, requesting the U.S. to recognize the new Jewish State.. "With the full knowledge of the deep bond of sympathy which existed and has been strengthened over the past 30 years between the U.S. Government and the Jewish people of Palestine," the letter said, "I have been authorized by the Provisional Government of the new State to tender this message and express the hope that your Government will recognize and welcome Israel into the community of nations."

In Frankfurt, General Lucius D. Clay, the U.S. Military Commander of Germany, said today that Jews in Germany and Austria would be assisted to leave for the State of Israel as soon as official word of America's recognition was to hand.

EGYPTIAN INVASION BEFORE U.N. SECURITY COUNCIL

LAKE SUCCESS, Saturday. — Israel today appealed to an emergency meeting of the Security Council to order a halt to Arab invasions into Palestine and, if necessary, to impose economic and military sanctions.

Dr. Mordechai Eliash, representing the day-old Jewish State, appealed to the Council to act fast against the invading Arab States, because "every hour counts." He stated that King Abdullah of Trans-Jordan, through the instrument of the Arab Legion, was clearly committing an act of aggression.

At the beginning of the session, Dr. Issa Nakhleh, of the Arab Higher Committee, declared that Egyptian forces had been invited by the A.H.C. to assist in the establishment of law and order. He asked: "What right has the Jewish Agency, which represents world Jewry, to complain against this action before the Security Council?"

Mahmoud Bey Fawzi, of Egypt, declared in explanation of a cable which he had earlier read to the Council that Egyptian troops had entered Palestine by invitation and with the unequivocal consent of the Palestine people. Egyptian forces were not going to Palestine to conquer anybody, but just to restore peace.

The invasion was "not directed against the Palestine

(Continued on Page 2, Co. 7)

GROMYKO TO BE REPLACED

LAKE SUCCESS, Saturday. (UP). — M. Andrei Gromyko, the Soviet Deputy Foreign Minister and his country's representative at the U.N., will soon be replaced — probably permanently.

The 38-year-old Soviet diplomat will be replaced by M. Jacob A. Malik Deputy Foreign Minister and a major figure in the conduct of Russian Foreign policy in the Far East. M. Malik, is already en route here by plane from Berlin.

Proclamation by Head Of Government

The creation of "Medinat Yisrael", the State of Israel, was proclaimed at midnight on Friday by Mr. David Ben Gurion, until then Chairman of the Jewish Agency Executive and now head of the State's Provisional Council of Government.

David Ben Gurion, Prime Minister

The first act of the Council of Government, as announced by its head, was to abolish all legislation of the 1939 White Paper of the late Mandatory Power, particularly the Ordinances and Orders relating to immigration and land transfer.

In the declaration of independence, Mr. Ben Gurion called on the Arabs of Palestine to restore peace, assuring them full civic rights and full representation in all governmental organs of the State.

Mr. Ben Gurion prefaced the declaration with a review of the historic connection of the Jewish people with the Land of Israel and of their efforts to return, which never ceased throughout the generations of their dispersal, until the Nazi holocaust proved anew the urgency of the need for a Jewish State.

The Balfour Declaration of 1917, confirmed by the League of Nations, had given explicit international recognition to the right of the Jewish people to reconstitute its National Home in Palestine, he said.

"On November 29, 1947," continued the declaration, "the United Nations decided on the establishment of a Jewish State and an Arab State in Palestine and called upon the inhabitants of the country to take all steps necessary for the establishment of the two States.

Historic Rights

"This decision cannot now be changed. Accordingly, we, the members of the Provisio-

(Continued on Page 2, Col. 6)

Special Assembly Adjourns

FLUSHING MEADOWS, Saturday. — The Special U.N. Assembly, called four weeks ago to discuss the U.S. proposal for a temporary Trusteeship for Palestine, adjourned yesterday until its next regular meeting in September without taking any decision to alter the resolution of November 29, which called for the setting up of two states in Palestine. The Assembly adopted only one motion — to appoint a special mediator to go to Palestine and cooperate with Truce Commission.

President Truman's announcement that the U.S. was proposing to recognize the new Jewish State reached newsmen during the session before the American delegation itself knew about it.

All the afternoon, the Assembly had been tied up in knots. After much filibustering it rejected the Franco-U.S. proposal for a special administration for Jerusalem. As the debate dragged on, correspondents sat with stopwatches to see whether a decision would be taken before the six o'clock deadline (N.Y. Summer Time) when the Mandate terminated. As zero hour was reached without a vote, they rushed to the booths, and about ten minutes later, the tickers in the local news agency offices flashed President Truman's recognition.

Gromyko and Jessup

The Assembly floor was half deserted and the American delegation had not been officially informed. The first to mention the Jewish State from the restrum was M. Gromyko, who said he saw no need for further action on the American mediator proposal, since the Jewish State had been recognized as a reality by the U.S. He asked what was being proposed for the Arab area of Palestine which was still without a government.

Shortly afterwards, Mr. Philip Jessup, the anti-Partition fighter, mounted the rostrum and officially announced U.S. recognition of the Jewish State, insisting, however, that the passage of the American mediator proposal was more necessary now than ever.

The Assembly passed it.

Between the flash from the White House and the final vote there was an eerie atmosphere in Flushing Meadows. The lights of the television cameras played on the rostrum, lighting up one Arab speaker after another who mounted the steps and expressed in a low voice frustration and anger.

To the last minute, officials of the State Department had been lobbying right on the floor against the Jewish State, even while the President's statement was already on the wires.

The Assembly did not adopt any resolution at all which altered the U.N. decision of November 29, 1947,

2 Villages Taken In Road Battle

In the battle for the Tel Aviv-Jerusalem road, the Haganah on Friday night took Kubeib and Abu Shusha villages between Latrun and Ramle. In engagements elsewhere along the route positions near Latrun and Bab el Wad changed hands.

Jewish casualties in this area in the last two days are about 40 killed. The Iraqis suffered greater losses, but their exact number is unknown.

It was reported that Iraqi troops had entered the Trappist Monastery at Latrun, and had set up strongpoints on the grounds and the building itself.

Sir Alan Sails From Palestine

The High Commissioner's departure from Palestine on Friday went according to plan — he appeared on the steps of Government House at 8 o'clock in the morning, wearing a full General's uniform. There he reviewed a guard of honour, consisting of 50 men of the Highland Light Infantry, the last British troops to leave Jerusalem.

Sir Alan Cunningham then drove to Kalandia airfield and boarded a plane for Haifa. Spitfires and Lancasters covered his short car journey.

The last British civil servants left Jerusalem together with Sir Alan: including Sir William Fitz-Gerald, the Chief Justice, and Sir Henry Gurney, the Chief Secretary.

Sir Alan's plane was piloted to Haifa by the Air Officer Commanding in Palestine, Air Commodore Dawson.

ACRE CAPTURED

Acre, the sea-coast town across the bay from Haifa, was captured by Jewish forces yesterday, the Haganah Radio reported. The surrender of the town, and subsequently two villages to the north, came after a strong Jewish attack.

Arms dumps containing enormous quantities of military equipment were captured.

The B.B.C. stated yesterday that almost all of Western Galilee was in Jewish hands, but that Naharayim, on the Jordan, had been occupied by the Legion.

Double Summer Time in Jerusalem

At midnight tonight all clocks in Jewish Jerusalem will be advanced two hours.

The Emergency Committee has instituted double summer time in order to save fuel. The measure does not apply to the rest of the country.

The Jerusalem Electric Corporation will cut off current to the Jewish Quarters from 1 to 9 p.m. as from today.

THE PALESTINE POST

FIVE A.M.

JERUSALEM
SUNDAY, MAY 30, 1948

PRICE: 25 MILS
VOL. XXIII. No. 6724

THE PALESTINE POST
SUBSCRIPTION RATES

Monthly	LP. 0.675
Three Months	LP. 2.000
Six Months	LP. 3.900
One Year	LP. 7.500

Column One
By David Courtney

THE blandness of Sir Alexander Cadogan lies thinly upon the surface of his embarrassment. He is a man with a code, born of a family with a code; and the code must conflict painfully with Sir Alexander's loyalty to a master who distorts, falsifies and deceives; and whose performance of his Ministry is a corruption not merely of the Parliamentary traditions, but also of the public life of England. The plan put up to the Security Council by Sir Alexander Cadogan was a transparent move to neutralize that body and at the same time to provide a foxhole for Bevin to hide in. The Chinese delegate, with the leisurely whimsy of his race, gave the plan his blessing; but the British Cabinet, even with the full strength of the Kuomintang behind it, once more has failed to get itself taken at its word: the word of England, which this Government has made a lie. And time is getting short, for the British Government. There sits Mr. Bevin in his Whitehall chambers. He strains his ears for sound of the messenger with news of the victory of his Allies; and fills in the anxious time doodling time-savers for U.N., to which Sir Alexander Cadogan, drawing comfort from the tireless encouragement of the Chinese delegate, gives the accent if not the substance of his training as a Christian Gentleman. But time, quite definitely, is getting short. Mr. Bevin's messenger seems much delayed. The planned victory, on which the Government depends to save its thick skin, seems a very uncertain prospect. Even Cadogan's blandness is no longer an effective covering to the sham piety of London. The world sees through it.

*

THE other day Mr. Bevin recalled Britain's strategic interests in the Middle East. We are getting our soldiers out, he said, but that doesn't mean that we have not a deep commitment in the Middle East. He has lost Palestine and lost the whole Middle East. By the manner of his losing Palestine, he has lost Britain's influence in every part of Arabia and the Eastern Mediterranean; for it is no use being wicked and stubborn if you are unsuccessful; and no use offering treaties to countries you have led into disaster. Mr. Bevin has persuaded himself that his policy is a flail to beat the Jews with. It has proved itself to be a lie to fool the Arabs with; for the British Government, and the British Government alone, is responsible for the extravagant adventure into which the States of the Arab League have plunged. How will Mr. Bevin get them out of their fix? It is his own fix as well as their fix. It is the British people's fix as well as the Arabs'. Mr. Bevin had better resign. He cannot go on boasting of his failures: even "The Times" begins to count the cost and resent the tedium of this puffed-up and perfidious ignoramus.

*

AGAINST the background of London's cheap manoeuvring and U.N.'s whistling of every tune it can think of, to keep up its spirits, the battle scorches the earth of the Holy Land and welds the future with blood and fire. The word is not with London or with Lake Success but with the man gasping under the hot sun and the woman waiting at dawn. The chatter of London and Lake Success is like pebbles thrown against the Homeric shield raised by young men in the name of a people's freedom. Whatever, from now on, politics may do or say, the problem of Palestine has become, grimly, Palestine's problem and the solution lies here, in the hands and hearts of the people. Bevin has forfeited his country's right to any part in the counsels of this land; and what part has U.N. deserved? Or the Archbishop of Canterbury, or His Holiness the Pope: or any of these magnificent gentlemen who speak holiness and condone desecration; and would preserve a stone but stand aside indifferently at the slaying of souls? No matter. The proud men and nations have been stripped to their nakedness: one knows them; and that, for the future should be half the battle. They go about naked and men, increasingly, will turn from them in disgust. This, then, is a cleansing war. Its implications may be greater than any of the great wars of the past; and their greatness will be in what is done on the land's holy soil, not in the schemes and formulas of mighty powers.

Jerusalem, May 30.

OLD CITY DEFENDERS YIELD AFTER EPIC RESISTANCE

Exhausted after two weeks of incessant lane-to-lane and house-to-house fighting, and overcome by fresh Arab troops who greatly outnumbered them, the Jewish garrison in the Old City of Jerusalem accepted the Arab Legion's surrender terms on Friday afternoon, while 290 able-bodied men from 15 to 50 were taken prisoner, and 1,200 women, children and aged were passed to the Jewish lines outside the walls with the cooperation of the U.N. representative and the Red Cross. Among the prisoners were 54 slightly wounded, including four nurses.

GARRISON'S LAST DITCH STAND

By AP & Reuter Correspondent in the Old City

The surrender of the Jews in the Old City, after 14 days of house-to-house fighting, was offered before noon on Friday when two men of the religious community came out with a white flag, and asked for terms. The terms were accepted in the afternoon.

The evacuation went on through the night. The Jews appeared to be reassured when the Legion threw a strong protective cordon round them, brought in the Red Cross, and provided food, water, and attention for the sick, wounded and aged.

A convoy of 14 buses from the Jordan Valley reached the Old City at dawn yesterday to take prisoners to a prisoners' camp in Trans-Jordan for screening. During the night, 294 men of military age had been held temporarily in the Jaffa Gate (Kishleh) Police Station. In the Armenian School, 150 wounded were sorted out, the seriously wounded to be delivered to the Jewish lines, the others to be kept as prisoners of war.

Weapons Seized

The Legion Headquarters reported the seizure of about 400 assorted Jewish weapons. The Commander claimed that the Jews mined the last buildings they held on surrendering, and when the mines exploded they caused big fires.

Long queues of civilians — women, children, and the aged —passed through Zion Gate, held by the Legion, crossed the shell-scarred garden of the Church of Dormition, and entered the Haganah lines. It required more than six hours for the 1,200 people to leave the walls of the Old City and return to Jewish care, carrying bundless of their few wordly goods.

Many sad-eyed Jewish grandfathers, women and children who were sealed up, living on meagre rations for weeks, carried small bags holding personal belongings. But other personal things, like children's toys, clothes, shoes, photographs, combs and books, were left behind.

A Legion soldier was wounded at 8.30 p.m. at Zion Gate, when sniping suddenly broke out there. Dr. Pablo Azcarate, representing the Secretary General of the United Nations in Palestine, was at the side of the Legion's Old City Commander when word came of the soldier casualty.

"It is only provocation. Please keep pushing the civilians right along," Dr. Azcarate pleaded, and the Arab Officer complied.

"Sticking to the Rules"

Armed women were among the Jews captured, the Legion Commander said, but had been allowed to go. Mr. A. M. Weingarten, Mukhtar of the Jewish Community, was also among those released. The Legion Commander said: "These people were told we would massacre them. I am letting such men as Weingarten go because we want the Jews as a whole to know that the Arab Legion is sticking to the rules and abiding by international conventions." (Later, reports stated that Weingarten had been taken prisoner.)

"It was quite a job protecting 2,000 Jews from the 40—50,000 Arabs, but the Legion saw to it that not a single Jew was harmed on the way out," he said.

(For more than an hour, Reuter's Correspondent, Doon Campbell, tramped over the stumps of walls that were once homes, and piles of rubble that were once a synagogue. It must have been like life in Belsen in this crowded, fly-ridden and shell-ripped quarter towards the end. The scene was like Stalingrad or Berlin. Roofless walls leaned crazily. Alleys were wrist-high with debris.

A Swiss official of the International Red Cross who remained with the Jewish wounded overnight, voluntarily declared: "I have never seen anything finer than the conduct of the Trans-Jordan soldiers towards the Jews."

At 11 a.m. on Friday, Rabbis Reuven Hazan, 70 and Israel Mintzberg, 83, walked from one of the Jewish positions toward the Arab lines. They carried a white flag made out of a bit of once-festive table cloth tacked to a stick. Although he was shot at and wounded by a sniper, Rabbi Hazan called out in Arabic, "Good morning. We have come to talk to you, and we want to see your commander."

They were led into the Armenian Convent of St. James, the Arab H.Q., where they were given cigarettes and tea. The Commander appeared, followed by about 30 Britons, many of them tattooed, and wearing only khaki shorts.

The Arabs asked for the Haganah chief and Mr. A. M. Weingarten, Chairman of the Jewish Community of the Old City. Rabbi Hazan replied that he and his colleague had come to negotiate, but were not authorized to conclude terms.

Rabbi as Hostage

Holding Rabbi Mintzberg as hostage, the Arabs sent Rabbi Hazan back to the Jewish lines to return with a Haganah representative. When the Haganah man appeared, the Arab demands were presented. All able-bodied men from 15 to 50, including the slightly wounded, were to collect at the Armenian School, with their arms, as prisoners of war. Non-combatants were to be evacuated out of the Old City, and the Legion was to accept responsibility for protecting the Jews from Arab mobs.

Informed by the Jewish Agency of the negotiations, the Red Cross delegation in Jerusalem, which was meeting with the World President, Mr. Paul Ruegger, at the time, sent three men into the Old City, including, at the Agency's request, Dr. K.S. Krikorian of the Red Crescent Society

The Legion's terms were accepted, and through intervention of the Red Cross "cease fire" was agreed upon to evacuate the non-combatants.

The evacuation of civilians through Zion Gate began on Friday evening, and lasted until 2 o'clock on Saturday morning. At the same time, the prisoners of war, among whom were 39 men carrying arms, were taken to the Armenian School. Fifty-one of the captives were wounded, and three physicians and four nurses volunteered to accompany the prisoners.

Another "cease fire" was arranged for 5.30 p.m yesterday, and Red Cross ambulances and

(Continued on Page 3, Col. 8)

HELD OUT UNTIL AMMO RAN OUT

By DANIEL DE LUCE, AP Correspondent

INSIDE THE OLD CITY, Saturday. — In a shadowy prison near Jaffa Gate an Arab Policeman chatted pleasantly with a Haganah Commander early this morning — blood enemies, but observing the ancient formalities after the surrender.

A few feet away Eric J. Apter, a Jewish agricultural expert before he became a Haganah Liaison Officer, leaned wearily against the steel bars and tried to reconstruct the history of the battle which had made him a captive.

"Our fighting men were too few—our arms were too few—finally our position was hopeless and our casualties very heavy," said Mayer, the Haganah Commander." "We kept hoping for a new linkup with our people outside Zion Gate." We had this link on the evening of May 17, and brought in new fighters and ammunition. But when the Legion came into the Old City on May 18, the link-up was broken and never restored. We surrendered yesterday because we were at the end of our resources. We were finished.

Short of Drugs

"Our greatest shortage was weapons and ammunition. We had three physicians from the Hadassah Hospital and rather large stocks of medical supplies, although we ran short of some drugs towards the end.

"Our biggest burden was civilians, 1,500 of them. They kept below ground most of the time so that their casualties were low, but they were a heavy weight on us."

Wounded American

Mayer said the Jewish garrison had learned to spot all types of shells which the Legion hurled into the siege zone. He said demolitions were most feared, "because you never knew when your house would tumble down around you."

He said that one American Jew, who had served in the U.S. Navy and had a family in San Francisco, had been wounded in the fighting and was in the hospital when surrender came.

ISRAEL CHARGES VANDALISM

TEL AVIV, Saturday (Reuter). — Israel today accused the Arabs of deliberately destroying the Hurva Synagogue in Jerusalem's Old City, where the Jews made their last stand before surrender.

They said it was the first time a Holy Place had been destroyed deliberately, and not hit by accident during fighting.

LEBANESE UNITS ROUTED BY JEWS

ROSH PINAH, Saturday — In a combined operation last night, Israel's Army — artillery, armour and infantry — captured the Lebanese border villages of Malkieh and Kadesh after a fierce engagement with units of the Lebanese Army there. Three enemy armoured cars and a number of supply vehicles were destroyed.

Jewish forces pursued the Lebanese soldiers fleeing from these two key points on the road to northern Galilee, penetrated about three kilometres inside the Lebanon. Thirty of the Lebanese were killed and large quantities of arms and ammunition were captured. One Jew was killed and 13 were wounded.

The Haganah reported that the whole of the Western Galilee was safe from invasion following this operation.

The Lebanese villages of Eitarou, Ein Abel and Aalma were bombed by the Air Force. Jewish infantry later cleared the area of Eitarou, and other units silenced enemy resistance in two Police Posts on the Syrian frontier. Both stations — near Lehavoth Hazashan and Amir — put up stiff resistance. A quantity of arms and ammunition was captured, and the buildings were blown up.

Jewish forces raided enemy concentrations in the Banias area, over the Syrian border, and villages in the area were evacuated.

A bridge near the Arab village of Meron has been blown up by Jewish forces, which conquered and are now in occupation of the village itself. Two Arabs were killed.

Further south, the Arab village of Zara'in, in the Valley of Jezreel, was captured on Thursday night. The enemy had fortified the village as a strongpoint on the northern edge of the Jenin-Tulkarm-Nablus triangle, and the Jewish forces met stiff opposition. Israel's soldiers broke through the fortifications and remained in possession despite counter-attacks by guns and armoured vehicles.

Arabs Try To Fan Out From Old City

Arab forces tried to break into Jewish Jerusalem in two sectors on Friday night, under cover of a barrage, but both attempts were fought off.

The Arabs struck out simultaneously from Sheikh Jarrah toward the northern quarters, and from the Damascus Gate toward the New Gate, but withdrew when they met heavy fire.

Meanwhile, the shelling of Jerusalem continued on Friday and yesterday.

Local and foreign correspondents were yesterday shown Jewish hospitals which had received direct hits during the past week. Most severely hit was the Hadassah Clinic. Other hospitals badly damaged were Bikur Holim and the Hadassah at the English Mission

The dome of the Abyssinian Church has received six direct hits, while the Ethiopian Consulate had been hit 30 times in one day recently. The church has been badly damaged.

Marshall's Wishes To State Of Israel

In a telegram to Mr. Moshe Shertok on Friday, Mr. George Marshall expressed the hope that the new Jewish State would prosper in the years of peace.

Mr Marshall formally acknowledged the appointment of Mr Eliahu Epstein as Israel's representative in Washington

TRIANGLE BOMBED

The Jewish Air Force made daylight air raids yesterday on the three apexes of the "dangerous Triangle" —Nablus, Jenin and Tulkarm.

Direct hits on troop concentrations were observed in the first two towns, the Haganah reported. In Tulkarm, a fuel dump in the Arab Legion camp went up in flames.

Earlier, Kfar Yona and Ein Vered settlements west of Tulkarm had been attacked by artillery and infantry, but both attacks were repulsed. An attack on Friday on the settlement of Kfar Yaavetz was also beaten off.

At one point in the fighting, Bnei Geulim settlement in this area was overrun by Arabs, but was re-taken by the Haganah.

A U.P. despatch from Amman, quoting 'frontline advices,' said that Iraqi troops had occupied Kfar Yona, marking "the first Iraqi push towards Nethanya in an effort to puncture the Jewish coastal strip between Tel Aviv and Haifa."

Jewish aircraft yesterday and on Friday night bombed Arab Legion artillery positions in the Jerusalem area and transport north of the city. Troop concentrations at Ramallah were also raided, and fires were started there.

In the south, Jewish aircraft bombed an Egyptian ammunition train coming from Egypt.

All Israelean planes returned safely.

A twin-engined Anton Iraqi bomber was brought down over the Jordan Valley on Friday

Bombs dropped by the enemy in the Dan sector failed to explode.

Ramat Naphtali was bombed on Friday. Our planes raided Kuneitra, El Hama and Lubia, scoring a number of direct hits.

There was a fighter-bomber attack on Tel Aviv on Friday.

IRAQIS CONQUER ARAB TOWNS

KYRENIA, CYPRUS, Saturday (Reuter). — Iraqi forces today claimed they had advanced to within 15 miles of Tel Aviv, reports said here,

The Iraqi troops, advancing from the northeast, occupied Nablus, Tulkarm and "Kalkilya," the reports said.

Syrian and Iraqi troops raided Degania, the large Jewish settlement to the south the Sea of Galilee, and dropped leaflets on Tiberias.

In the fighting on the Tel Aviv-Jerusalem road, Jewish troops had encircled a large force of Arabs south of Latrun.

SECURITY COUNCIL ADOPTS BRITISH FOUR-WEEK TRUCE

Cadogan Proposed World-Wide Arms Embargo

By RICHARD WITKIN, UP Correspondent

LAKE SUCCESS, Saturday. — At Thursday night's session of the Security Council, Britain suggested a world-wide embargo on arms shipments to the Middle East and asked the U.N. Security Council to appeal once again for a truce in Palestine.

Britain offered to cut off the flow of British armaments to Iraq, Trans-Jordan and Egypt, if the U.N. laid down an effective and universal ban on arms to both Jews and Arabs. Sir Alexander Cadogan, the British delegate, formally proposed a four-weeks' cessation of hostilities in Palestine, during which time both Jews and Arabs should stop importing arms and men of military age into Palestine.

During the "cease-fire" period, Britain suggested, the U.N. mediator, Count Bernadotte, should try to work out a settlement between the Arabs and Jews. If this new appeal were to fail Britain would be willing to go along with the American and Russian view that the Palestine war should be declared a "breach of the peace" under the punitive sections of the U.N. Charter. This theoretically would open the way to the use of economic blockades or military sanctions force against the Arabs or Jews, in case either or both failed to comply with the "cease fire" order—a tougher measure than a mere "appeal."

Britain's delegate said his country would review subsidy payments to the Trans-Jordan Government "in the light of decisions by the U.N." and would immediately withdraw 21 of the 37 British officers at present helping to direct the operations of the Arab Legion. Sir Alexander said that Britain had no power to withdraw the other 16 officers, including Brigadier Glubb Pasha, since they were employed by King Abdullah as private individuals.

He heatedly denied statements that Britain had the power to halt the Legion's operations if it wanted to. Saying that Russia and the Jewish Agency had particularly charged "that the foreign policy of King Abdullah ... is controlled by my Government," Cadogan declared "I entirely repudiate this misconception. Trans-Jordan is a Sovereign State."

Britain Accuses Jews

He bitterly attacked the Jews at several points in his speech and charged that the Stern Group was responsible for the breakdown of the "cease-fire" agreement in force for a short time last month in Jerusalem. He also accused the Jews for responsibility for the failure of the Red Cross attempt to arrange a truce with King Abdullah for the evacuation of doctors and patients from the Hadassah Hospital.

A Jewish spokesman, rejecting the new British proposal, said that "the British Government's aim is to tie Israel's hand behind its back so that the Arabs can be free to strike Israel down."

He said that Sir Alexander Cadogan "apologetically repeated Arab excuses for not observing the "cease fire, and associated his Government with them. The alliance between the British Government and the Arab aggressors, now complete both in the political and military spheres, can be no better expressed than in the suggestion for a world-wide arms embargo. This is not a neutral proposal ... it is an attempt to perpetuate the advantage which the Arab States gained through stock-piling British arms for months and years, while denying the State of Israel, claim any access to the means of defence."

The Jewish spokesman said the British proposal was a "manebuvre to create the best conditions for the Arabs to pursue their aggression successfully for the next four weeks and at the same time to twist the U.N. Charter, so that the punitive section of the Charter becomes a weapon against the State of Israel, instead of an instrument for its defence."

225 BRITONS IN LEGION—EBAN

LAKE SUCCESS, Saturday (UP) — The number of British officers and technicians serving with the Arab Legion was 225, and not, as stated by Mr. Bevin recently 37, said Mr. Aubrey Eban, Israel's representative at Lake Success, today. He was referring to Sir Alexander Cadogan's announcement yesterday that 21 British officers serving with Abdullah's Army had been recalled

That announcement was an empty gesture, Mr. Eban said, which "should not lead the public into believing the U.K. is effectively withdrawing support from Abdullah's drive to rule and ruin Jerusalem."

Without those British officers and technicians, he declared, the Legion could not effectively maintain and operate its destructive equipment. "Top British officers remain in command," he added.

STOP PRESS —5 A.M.

The Security Council called on the Jews and Arabs to send their acceptance of the cease-fire by 2200 GMT on Tuesday and stating that the Council would take direct action under Chapter 7 of the Charter against whichever party rejected it. The Soviet and the Ukrainian delegates consistently abstained on all the parts of the British resolution. The Council adjourned until Wednesday.

SOVIET MOTION FOR SANCTIONS DEFEATED

LAKE SUCCESS, Saturday. — The British proposal for a 4-week cease-fire in Palestine was adopted by the Security Council by eight votes, with three abstentions, tonight (3.15 a.m. Sunday Palestine Time).

The Council adopted by seven votes, with four abstentions, a French amendment to the British text calling on all governments and authorities concerned to undertake that "they will not introduce fighting personnel into Palestine, Egypt, Iraq, the Lebanon, Syria, Trans-Jordan, Saudi Arabia and the Yemen during the Cease Fire," and calling on all governments and authorities, "if men of military age are introduced into the countries or territories under their control during the cease fire not to mobilise or submit them to military training during that period."

By nine votes with two abstentions the Council adopted an American amendment to the British text calling on all governments and authorities concerned "to refrain from importing or exporting war material into or to Palestine, Egypt, Iraq, the Lebanon, Syria, Trans-Jordan, Saudi Arabia and the Yemen during the cease-fire." The Council adopted unanimously a clause urging "all governments and authorities to take every possible precaution for the protection of thes Holy Places and the City of Jerusalem, including access to all shrines and sanctuaries for those who have an established right to visit and worship at them."

Earlier, the Soviet Resolution calling for an unconditional cease-fire within 36 hours and the imposition of Sanctions under Article 7 of the Charter obtained only five votes and failed to pass.

The continuing aggression of the Arabs and their failure to obey the Council's previous cease fire orders constituted a direct threat to international peace, the Soviet resolution said.

France put forward a proposal for a cease fire for Jerusalem only.

Both Senator Austin and the Colombian delegate last night recalled that on five different occasions had the Council already tried to negotiate a truce and failed. Stronger measures were now imperative, they said.

"Scandalous Mockery"

Today, the American delegate vigorously attacked the British attitude in the Security Council and denounced Britain's deeds in Palestine. Mr. Aubrey Eban, the representative of Israel, called Britain's attitude to the U.N. a scandalous mockery, aimed against the very existence of the Jewish State and the UN's Partition decision, and giving weapons to the Arabs to destroy Israel.

There was a heated exchange between M Gromyko and Sir Alexander at this morning's session. The Soviet delegate made a bitter attack on Britain's Middle East policy, charging that her latest proposal —if adopted — would "not only complicate the situation in Palestine, but intensify the struggle and intensify the bloodshed."

Moreover, the proposal would be illegal, as "the Security Council had no power to adopt any decision except one which would implement the decision of the General Assembly."

Sir Alexander Cadogan dismissed the Soviet charge that Britain was pursuing a policy of "hypocrisy and cynicism" as a "vulgar, base and general vilification." He counter-charged that the Soviet demand for an unconditional "cease fire" would only worsen the situation.

This afternoon, Fares el Khoury defended the "legality" of the Arab invasion of Palestine, claiming that the Arab armies had been "invited" by the Palestine Arabs to help.

The U.S. and Russia had power to suppress whatever they wanted to suppress, he charged, adding: "They suppressed Germany." However, force could not solve the problem, el Khoury said. "When you base peace on justice, you may get it," he added.

Criticizing the British resolution, Mr. Eban declared: "No other State in the world would allow its immigration to be interfered with." And he asked: "Would Israel be well advised to neglect her defence for four weeks?" If five armies were invading Britain, would the British people allow such a thing?" (PTA & UP)

SMUTS DEFEATED; MALAN HEADS GOVERNMENT

LONDON, Saturday. — Following his victory at the polls, Dr. D.F. Malan, leader of the South African Nationalist Party, has been invited by the Governor-General, Mr. Van Zeel, to form a new Government.

Field Marshall Jan C. Smuts, who tendered his resignation as soon as the results were announced, will remain in office until the new Government is formed.

General Smuts' United Party was defeated by a narrow majority of five seats, although it polled more individual votes in the country as a whole than its opponents. The arrangement of the constituencies, however, is such that the United Party gained 65 seats and the Nationalist Party 70. Supporting General Smuts are also three Labour members and six Coloured Africans, while supporting Dr. Malan are nine members of the Afrikaner Party so that the grouping in the House of Assembly is 79 to 74.

The defeat of General Smuts came as a surprise after the first polls, which had convinced observers that he would have a large majority. The rural counts later changed the picture.

The principal issue of the elections was the colour question. It is now feared that Dr. Malan will introduce a strict colour bar and that he might even force the coloured people of the cities back into their reserves. Other issues were the rising cost of living and the housing shortage.

In the outgoing House of Assembly, elected in 1943, mainly on the war issue, General Smuts had the support of 110 members against the Opposition's 43.

AP quotes political observers in Johannesburg as saying that another general election in South Africa is inevitable in the next few months.

They pointed out that the nationalist Afrikaner coalition majority of only five seats in Parliament will become increasingly embarrassing for the Government.

Field Marshal Smuts is not likely to avail himself of offers by elected members of Parliament to stand down in his favour, said newspaper reports today. More than a score of successful United Party candidates offered their seats to their defeated leader.

The "Rand Daily Mail" states that it is doubtful whether Marshal Smuts will go to Capetown at all during the next parliamentary session, and Mr. J. H. Hofmeyr, the former Deputy Prime Minister, is expected to be the new leader of the Opposition.

Speculation about the legislative programme of the victorious and traditionally anti-British Nationalists in the new Parliament was marked by returning confidence today.

Financiers and manufacturers generally consider that no drastic changes will be made in the immediate future, and say there is no reason why industrial firms wanting to establish factories in South Africa should not do so.

Dr. Malan's accession to power in South Africa will save 218 Germans from deportation from the Union to Germany.

The Government of Field Marshal Smuts appointed a commission to examine the cases of 5,000 Germans, mainly resident in South Africa, who had been interned during the war and recommended 218 for deportation. The deportations were confirmed on the day that Dr. Malan came into power.

In Parliament, as leader of the opposition, Dr. Malan had pleaded vigorously against the proposed deportations. Now he can simply wash out the whole thing.

WORLD BANK LOAN

WASHINGTON, Saturday (PTA).— The Security Council requested the arms embargo several months ago, and the U.S. could not modify the ban until the Council lifted the embargo, President Truman told a press conference yesterday.

Mr. Truman said that Israel had not formally requested a loan, and if made, such a request would have to be dealt with like any other loan application, through the World Import and Export Bank.

The President shrugged his shoulders when a reporter pointed out that the Bank's Charter prevented arms purchases with money obtained through the Bank. He said that British shipments to the Arabs made no difference to the American position.

HUMBER HAWK
1947 — 14 H.P. SALOON
Moise Carasso & Sons Ltd.
TEL AVIV
Edmund Astruc, Jerusalem
Isaac Loulou, Haifa

JERUSALEM
Thursday, July 1, 1948.

THE PALESTINE POST

PRICE: 25 MILS
VOL. XXIII. No. 6751

For and ET a glass Carmel
Rishon le Zion and Zichron Yaacov Wine Cellars

Column One
By
David Courtney

THE British Army has gone. When the war ended in 1945, no one, then, could have foreseen that the British Army would one day leave like that. It is not the way the British Army usually leaves. The British Army has a tradition and is proud of it. It broke the tradition in Palestine and by the manner of its flight from Haifa seemed half ashamed. Perhaps that was why General MacMillan was rude to the Haifa Mayor and Councillors: embarrassment makes not for gentle manners. All in all, it is not the fault of the Army. The British soldier under the Labour Government has become a kind of political agent; and from military leadership, most of the officers have been turned into a species of commissar. They have been used to serve the niggling schemes of Mr. Bevin and to uphold the conspiracies of his agents. They have been coached in a form of anti-Semitism and taught to regard the Jew as fair game; and in the process of withdrawal since early May have been encouraged to render unto the Arabs many things that were Jewish and unto the Jews as little as possible.

*

IN this process the British Army has been used by the Government as an instrument. There can be as little regret among the soldiers, therefore, at their departure, as there is among the Jewish people. It should be plainly understood that a very large proportion of the Army in Palestine has consisted of good, sound, fair-minded men; and that even among the officers there have been many who had little heart for the contemptible task assigned them by the Government. But policy is policy and directives are directives and service privileges and pensions are not things to be thrown away lightly even for a principle. Here and there, even in Jerusalem, and as at Haifa during the battle which gave that port to the Jews, British Army Commanders and men have acted well. But their part, on the whole, has been a small one. The Army does not allow for much individual decision and performance. Policy is laid down directly where possible, and by careful innuendo where it is unwise to run the kind of risk General Barker ran with his notorious letter.

*

THE purpose to which the British Army has been put in the Holy Land is consistent with the general lowering of the standards of British public life under the Labour Government. It should not be surprising, therefore, to know that the Arab Legion is virtually under British command and that British officers gave the orders to wreck the Holy City with British guns, and may again give such orders. It seems to surprise no one in the British Army. It seems to be accepted by the House of Commons as fair and honourable. It seems to worry none of the Press barons of Fleet Street. Why, then, should it surprise those of this country.

*

THE end of the British Army in Palestine is not the end of Britain in the land; but that end will come, with still more profound humiliation unless the disastrous foreign policy of the Attlee Cabinet is soon adjusted to facts and soon takes note of the rising disgust of world public opinion. It won't look well to be beaten by a little people whose very freedom is a defiance of British policy.

Jerusalem, July 1.

יהודה חברה לאחריות ובטוח בע"מ
THE JUDEA INSURANCE CO. LTD.
announce herewith the appointment of
Messrs. HAMISHMAR INSURANCE SERVICE
33 Rothschild Blvd., Tel Aviv
as their General Agents for Eretz Israel of their
FIRE — ACCIDENT — and MARINE DEPARTMENTS
with effect from July 1, 1948.

MORE RUMOURS FROM RHODES

Conflicting reports of Count Bernadotte's proposals for Palestine came yesterday from the capitals of several countries. So far, the plan has been kept secret, and both Jews and Arabs were last night discussing the proposals.

At Lake Success, UP. quotes an "authoritative source" that the Mediator's peace settlement would give the Arabs control of Jerusalem provided they gave up their fight against the State of Israel. Jerusalem would be used by the Arabs as their capital, and special arrangements would be made to provide some degree of autonomy for the Jews living there, this report said.

While it was believed at U.N. headquarters that the present plan would be rejected by both sides, it was thought that it offered at least a basis for discussion of a final settlement. The Mediator would try to extend the truce period for this purpose, it was stated.

Count Folke Bernadotte

"Hellish"

In Cairo, a spokesman of the Arab League complained that the proposals put forward favoured the Jews, and Fauzi Mulki Pasha, the Trans-Jordan Foreign Minister, described them as "Hellish."

Another "well-informed source" in Cairo said the Mediator had proposed a Federal State in Palestine, with the Jewish section under U.N. Trusteeship pending a permanent settlement. The same source claimed that U.N. officials would prevent "illegal immigration" into Palestine, the Mediator believing that this would "guarantee the Arab nations against an attack by the Zionists."

In Baghdad, the Iraqi Premier, Muzakam al Pachachi, said he understood that Count Bernadotte's plan was "contrary to Arab desires" and would be rejected.

Before leaving Beirut to attend the meeting of the Political Committee of the Arab League in Cairo, Riad Bey es Solh, the Lebanese Premier, told a press conference yesterday that the Arab policy was to resume the fighting as soon as the truce ended, if "nothing happened to satisfy Arab aspirations."

(U.P. and A.P.)

LIE'S ASSISTANT FLIES TO RHODES

RHODES, Wednesday (UP).—Commander R.G.A. Jackson, Australian Assistant U.N. Secretary-General, arrived here today for talks with Count Bernadotte.

ARAB LEAGUE DISCUSSES PLAN

CAIRO, Wednesday. (AP).—Some of the delegates left the conference room an hour after the start of the Arab League Political Committee meeting at the Egyptian Foreign Office today. Azzam Pasha, the League's Secretary-General, told reporters that the heads of the delegations were consulting in a separate room.

Abdullah Arrives In Baghdad

BAGHDAD, Wednesday. — The firing of 21 salvoes, the playing of the Trans-Jordan and Iraqi national anthems and the mounting of a guard of honour today heralded the arrival of King Abdullah at Baghdad Airport.

The Trans-Jordan King, who arrived from Riad, will spend four days in the Iraqi capital as the guest of his nephew, the Regent Abdul Ilah.

Earlier today, a communique, issued simultaneously at Riad and the Arab League H.Q. in Cairo, announced that King Abdullah and King Ibn Saud had re-pledged themselves to use "all possible means" to attain "complete Arab independence and control" in Palestine. The Kings were in "complete agreement regarding the Arab national aspirations," the communique stated, adding that they based their unity on two principles — "worship of God and the defence of our existence."

They were also "in complete agreement on the support of the Arab League and all its decisions made within the provisions of its Charter and the limits of its responsibilities," the communique stated.

"We have faith in the Arab League's aims, which are to ensure the consolidation of peace in the Middle East. This can only be achieved by the maintenance of the Arabs' rights and a guarantee of independence of their countries. We are convinced that the Arab League is defending fundamental Arab interests, Arab honour, freedom and peace," the communique continued.

Before leaving Riad last night, King Abdullah was presented with golden swords and choice pearls by his host, King Ibn Saud.

TITO'S SECOND CHALLENGE

By R.H. SHACKFORD, U.P. Correspondent

LONDON, Wednesday. — A few hours after he had called all Cominform charges against him false and unjustified, Marshal Tito again challenged the Kremlin by renewing his appeal for a Balkan Bloc, uniting Albania, Bulgaria and Yugoslavia "on the principle of national equality," which, he is well aware, is bitterly opposed by Russia.

This idea was contained in a formal programme, published today in "Borba," the Communist newspaper in Belgrade, which reported that a programme had been drawn up at a meeting of the Central Committee on June 14, and that it had now been sent to local Communist Committees for suggestions, prior to the Party's planned convention on July 21.

The programme calls for the "strengthening and furthering of political unity of the Yugoslav peoples" and for "strengthening and furthering development in all respects of cooperation" with Russia.

The Tito-led group said that it is willing to deal with the West as well as the Soviet East on terms of "peaceful cooperation."

Western diplomats are elated over these developments, but none are prepared to suggest that Tito could resist Russia very long without risking civil war or armed Russian intervention.

(Earlier Stories, Page 3)

U.S. TO FREE YUGOSLAV GOLD

WASHINGTON, Wednesday. (UP) — The U.S. and Yugoslavia have reached agreement on the freeing of over $50m. of Yugoslav gold held in the U.S. since the war, the authorities here have reported.

It is emphasized that the agreement was not the result of the friction between Marshal Tito and Moscow, but the authorities did not discount its future bearing on possible improved relations between the two countries.

PLAN TO UNIFY WEST GERMANY

By DON DOANE, AP. Correspondent

FRANKFURT, Wednesday. — A plan to create a new central German Government in Western Germany was worked out here today by the top U.S., British and French occupation authorities.

The Western Allied commanders will meet with the German State Premiers tomorrow morning, to discuss the details and set the plan in motion. The oft-postponed meeting with the German officials was announced this afternoon after a two-hour conference of the three Western Military commanders.

ISRAEL FLAG OVER HAIFA HARBOUR AS LAST BRITISH SOLDIER SAILS

By JUDITH AVRUNIN, Palestine Post Correspondent

HAIFA, Wednesday. — Haifa port is now the main port of the State of Israel, the military occupation of Palestine by Britain having ceased today with the release of the harbour city.

FRIENDSHIP OFFERED TO BRITAIN

HAIFA, Wednesday. — With a sharp awareness of new freedom, Haifa today celebrated its full possession of its greatest asset — the port.

A crowd burst through the gate of the port to watch the ceremony. In the presence of the Prime Minister, Mr. David Ben Gurion, the Mayor, Mr. Shabetai Levy, the Town Commander, the Chief Rabbinate, and the Port authorities, the flag of Israel and of the Israel Navy were raised in the harbour and on three corvettes which had entered the port.

Mr. Ben Gurion, who came from Tel Aviv by sea, addressed the parade of sailors and soldiers and the civilians who had gathered. He recalled the "Balfours" of England who had helped Israel and he offered Israel's friendship to Britain, conditional on her abandoning the war she was waging on the Jewish State through Arab mercenaries. He continued

Jewish Jerusalem is Israel's spiritual centre, Haifa its political and commercial heart.

As Mr. Ben Gurion concluded, the parade snapped to attention, and the national anthem was played by the Fire Brigade band.

As the Union Jack was slowly lowered from the Port Authority's building early this afternoon, the Last Post was sounded and the Jews and Englishmen on the pier, for whom it was the time for rejoicing and hope, or for regrets and bitterness, stood gravely rigid.

The last British soldier had just sailed on the troopship, L.S.T. Striker, and General MacMillan handed the Union Jack to the British Consul, Mr. Cyril Marryat. The departure of the last 5,000 British troops began at midnight, with the cargo jetty teeming with men, tanks and equipment, the same pier which two years ago was named "the refugees' via dolorosa," the place of many violent and bloody deportations. Now, young and fresh-faced English boys marched there, knowing nothing of the undertaking of their statesmen a generation ago, knowing little of what has happened to force them to go, but simply glad to get away.

They embarked on the vessels, Altoona; Eastern Prince; Ocean Vigour; (The latter's cages for Cyprus-bound prisoners were still on the deck, but this time there were soldiers ludicrously crowded into them); the hospital ship, Oxfordshire, the L.S.T. Humphrey Gale; Reginald Kerr; Messina; Dieppe; and finally, the covering party and rear-guard of the Royal Marine Commandos in the L.S.T. Striker.

U.N. Observers

The white jeep of the U.N. observers' team, headed by Lieutenant Richley, toured the field and saw British reconnaissance planes circle the harbour. The smartly turned out Jewish Port Authority Police stood watching.

The last inspection of the port was made at 10 o'clock by Lieut. Col. R. Hawkins, M.C., O.C. Commandos, accompanied by the Port Authority and Police, after which he handed the keys of the harbour to the Manager, Mr. Amos Landman, the Superintendent of Port Property, Mr. D. Shiloh, and A.S.P. Spiegel, who have been in charge of the Port Police since May 3.

The harbour gates were closed with lock and key at noon, as the rear-guard of Royal Marine Commandos left to board their ship, and at the same time, General MacMillan disembarked from the cruiser, H.M.S. Phoebe. He watched the last of the operation, took leave of the British Consul. To the foreign newspapermen he said he had no last words except goodbye:

I am very sorry to leave the Holy Land. It is a lovely country, and I am most sad.

At the last minute there was a hunt for a missing marine. He was found sleeping in a shed.

Flags Come Down

It was when the L.S.T. Striker left the quay that the British flag was taken down, after which General MacMillan and his party boarded a launch returning to the Phoebe. He sailed shortly after with an escort of four destroyers and the aircraft carrier, Triumph.

Meanwhile, in town, the people had watched the evacuation of the airport, Bat Galim, and the Police Headquarters, and cheered when the flag of Israel was hoisted over that partially-blasted building at noon.

We looked down from Panorama Road. The silver blue harbour was free of British boats and warships. The Pan Crescent and Pan York were there with the 40 small vessels of the "illegal fleet."

The first cargo and passenger ship, the Campidoglio, expected in the Haifa harbour of the State of Israel, is due shortly.

Cabinet Postponed

The Israel Cabinet will meet in Tel Aviv this morning to discuss the Mediator's proposals.

No meeting was held yesterday because the Prime Minister had gone to Haifa.

The Provisional Council is due to hold its weekly session this evening.

MILITARY RULE FORMALLY ENDS

HAIFA, Wednesday. (AP, UP) — All last night flares and explosions lit the port area as the British destroyed records and equipment. In the harbour itself depth charges exploded every half-hour to blast any frogmen who might try to attach limpet mines to the hulls of the British ships.

The last British troops to leave, the Royal Marine Commandos deployed from the town to the port area fully armed and with orders to shoot to kill if there were any interference. There was none.

The evacuation of the British who had first arrived in 1917 under Allenby was a quiet one. In small groups, the rear-guard commandos withdrew from their posts on Mt. Carmel, and then withdrew from the gates of the port, until the only beachhead was a small barbed-wire enclosure around the gaping mouth of a landing ship through which the troops filed.

The last soldier to leave, General MacMillan, issued a proclamation formally ending Britain's "military jurisdiction" in Palestine at midnight. The proclamation said that the port would be left in Jewish hands, but would be under U.N. supervision for the duration of the truce.

Most of the British troops are being evacuated to the Suez Canal Zone, but some are going to Tripoli and Malta, an Army spokesman said.

While Spitfires roared overhead, General MacMillan shook hands with the British Consul and the American Consul, Mr. Audrey Lippincot; the Jewish Mayor and notables, who had been expected, were conspicuously absent, a silent retort for General MacMillan's boycotting the Municipal lunch on Tuesday on discovering that three tanks had disappeared.

Since the end of the Mandate on May 15, 17,150 British soldiers were evacuated from Palestine, the last 4,800 leaving yesterday. With them went 41,000 tons of equipment and supplies.

During the last year of the Mandate 13 British officers and 161 enlisted men were killed, and 37 officers and 380 enlisted men were wounded. In the last stages of the evacuation the death of four Britons and injury to 15 others were reported.

Most Arab radio stations reported the withdrawal from Haifa in yesterday's broadcasts, but few had any comment. The Baghdad Radio said,

After 25 years of miserable and tragic rule over the Holy Land, the last British troops have eventually withdrawn from the country, leaving it to its own people.

The Minister of War, Mr. Emanuel Shinwell, sent a telegram to General McMillan saying that the British Government had fully appreciated how unpleasant had been the task the British forces in Palestine had had to carry out. "We admire you for the good job you have always done," the Minister said.

Last of Britain's Prisoners Freed

PETAH TIKVAH, Wednesday. — The last 12 Jewish prisoners, who were turned over by the British on Monday, were released from prison here today after the British left Palestine.

The 12 men, six of whom had received death sentences, left for their homes in Tel Aviv, Nathanya and Haifa.

Among them were two who were suspected of taking part in the King David Hotel bombing and six who had raided the Haifa Railway Workshop. One man had a leg amputated following injuries sustained in that attack. Others had been detained after the hanging of the two sergeants at Nathanya.

TO SERVE DURING CONGRESS RECESS

WASHINGTON, Wednesday (AP). — President Truman today appointed Mr. James Grover McDonald, special U.S. Representative to Israel, to serve during the recess of Congress.

Congress adjourned on June 20, without confirming the President's nomination of Mr. McDonald.

MARCUS' BODY ARRIVES IN U.S.

NEW YORK, Wednesday (PTA). — The body of Colonel David Marcus, Haganah Divisional Commander, arrived at LaGuardia Airfield at noon today.

Mr. Moshe Dayan, a high Haganah officer who was military adviser to the British against the Vichy-French in Syria, and Mr. Joseph Hamburger, Captain of the Exodus 1947, escorted the bier.

After Midnight

A vote by the Italian Socialist Party Congress on continued alliance with the Communists was hoped for last night, leaders of the three factions but it may be delayed while the jockey for control of the new Party Directorate.

Russians Add Water Blockade to Berlin's 10-Day Siege

BERLIN, Wednesday. (AP). — The Russians apparently added a water blockade of Berlin today to their 10-day siege by land. A British officer in Hamburg said that the Russians had halted the movement of supply barges along the Elbe river. These previously had filtered through to Berlin, 26 of them arriving since the land blockade began.

The Soviet Commander in Germany, Marshal Sokolovsky, today informed his British counterpart, General Sir Brian Robertson, that he hoped it would be possible to resume rail traffic between Berlin and the Western Zones before the city's food supplies run out.

While the Marshal did not say on what he based his hope, it was noted that his letter was conciliatory in tone. He said he appreciated the "energetic" American and British efforts to supply the isolated city by air adding, however: "I most earnestly hope that all flight safety regulations will be completely and thoroughly observed."

House Told

In London, Mr. Bevin predicted today that the Western Allies could defeat the Russian blockade of Berlin with planes, but warned that the decision to try and do so might bring real trouble with Russia.

He made this statement on behalf of the Government at the opening of the debate on the Berlin crisis, and assured the House that the West was throwing all its available aircraft into the job of feeding Berlin. Reaffirming Britain's intention to stay in Berlin, the Foreign Secretary said the U.S. was pursuing the same policy. But he made no reference to France's intention.

Flouting Agreement

He charged Russia with flouting the Potsdam Agreements on fundamental freedoms and subjecting the Germans to mass deportation, arbitrary arrest, the liquidation of independent political parties and the suppression of free speech. Russia was paying "lip service" to the idea of German unity, but at the same time insisting upon policies which made such unity impossible, he added.

Earlier, Mr. Anthony Eden, Deputy Leader of the Opposition, charged that the Soviet blockade was an "act openly directed against the Allies." It also carried a "callous threat of untold suffering and hardship" to more than 2,000,000 Germans in the Western sectors, Mr. Eden declared, adding: "It is not an occasion upon which this House should keep silent."

"Basic Question"

Russia's action in blockading Berlin raises "basic questions of serious import with which we expect to deal promptly," Mr. Marshall said in Washington yesterday. "We are in Berlin to stay," he added.

The Secretary of State hinted that it might be possible to keep the Western sector of Berlin going for some time longer than was at first expected, when he said that it had been found possible to carry more food in by air than was originally thought possible.

The State Department, after several days of silence, issued the Marshall statement aligning the U.S. publicly with Britain in her determination to stay in Berlin against all Russian actions.

BALLOON SCARE EXPLODED

FRANKFURT, Wednesday (AP). — A barrage balloon scare over the Russian Zone of Germany exploded this afternoon, when excited American Air Force officials who thought that their air lifeline to Berlin was threatened found that a supposed mass of obstacles was just one old balloon that had been in the corridor between Berlin and the British Zone for a long time.

This was the second time in a fortnight that the solitary relic of the last war touched off a scare in Allied Air Force circles.

American fliers returning to Frankfurt from their "mercy missions" to Berlin were switched to the British air corridor last night to avoid congestion in the American corridor between Frankfurt and Berlin. The Rhine-Main's air flight service warned these pilots to fly above 5,000 feet to avoid the barrage at Dolle, 75 miles west of Berlin. The warning, new to American pilots, apparently caused alarm and rumours that the Soviets had warned the Anglo-Americans that balloons would be flown in the British and American corridors yesterday.

When the rumours reached U.S. Air Force H.Q. at Wiesbaden, a spokesman for Lieut-General Curtis LeMay, said that he knew nothing about them but was checking. A few minutes later, however, the Air Force's public information office told correspondents flatly that balloons were reported over Dolle and that a warning to planes was going out "in a few minutes." A formal P.I.O. release was being prepared that American pilots had been warned. Thirty minutes later, however, there were some questions.

Berlin and the R.A.F. notified Wiesbaden that it was the same old balloon of which the Russians had given the Allies full warning. Then the Air Force began to deny its report, and there were a lot of red faces.

"The Air Flight Service was just doing its job, warning all pilots," an officer said.

It was later explained that the troublesome balloon was part of a Russian artillery range north of Magdeburg, and was used for spotting. They have informed Berlin's Four-Power air safety centre about it periodically and stated that it is never up for more than one hour at a time.

YOU
HAVE YOU SUBSCRIBED TO THE NATIONAL FUND?
DON'T DELAY!
YOUR PARTICIPATION IS NEEDED FOR THE MAINTENANCE OF THE ARMY AND TO FORTIFY ITS POSITIONS.
THE CEASE-FIRE PERIOD IS A PERIOD OF PREPAREDNESS!
THE ARMY NEEDS YOUR MONEY TODAY. IT WILL BE REFUNDED TO YOU IN A SHORT TIME, WITH GOOD INTEREST AND GUARANTEED BY DOLLARS.
SUBSCRIBE TO THE NATIONAL LOAN

Jerusalem's Purchasing Centre for the whole family
המשביר לצרכן
HAMASHBIR LATZARKAN
JAFFA ROAD near 'EGGED'

THE PALESTINE POST

JERUSALEM
SUNDAY, Sept. 19, 1948

PRICE: 25 MILS
VOL. XXIV. No. 6816

ORDER A Gift Subscription of THE PALESTINE POST
See Advertisement on Page Four

Column One

By

David Courtney

IT is nothing new. Count Bernadotte was shot and killed in a Jerusalem street by men who had lain in ambush with the sole idea of shooting and killing Count Bernadotte. It is nothing new. That is the tragic pity of it.

*

EVERY Jew in the land with his wits and his heart about him, had believed that the days of stealthy death and bloody conspiracy were over; and that terror had ended itself by helping to end the days of national subjection. Israel had come out into the open as a free people, and had no need to kill in the dark.

*

THE habit of thinking with a gun is hard to throw off. The habit of bitter enmity is hard to be rid of. The habit of vengeance corrupts the avenger until he becomes his own victim. The State of Israel, which was succour for its Jews and triumph over their enemies, was the victim of Friday's ambush. It staggers into the unfinished contest with a shameful burden on its back.

*

THE people of Jerusalem and of the State of Israel have been shot at, bombed, and shelled for months. They have seen death and felt the agony of wounds. They have suffered bravely as a people conscious of their just cause and have fought heroically as a people conscious of their new, inspiring dignity. This they have borne and will bear without fret until the end. But the madness of their own crazed sons, whose overweaning pride sets them above the spirit and the purpose of the nation, cannot be borne.

*

THE State of Israel has not come about as a mere climax in the performance of inevitable history. It has come as a retribution and an absolution; to comfort and dignify a whole people, and in their restored comfort and dignity to absolve the world of a mortifying sin against itself. Let the nations today ponder their own sin against themselves, through their sin against the Jews, before judging the loathsome fruit of it in the vengeance of Friday evening.

*

THE assassination of Count Bernadotte has probably undone the work of the defenders of Jerusalem. It is useless for politics to ignore the perversities of human psychology or to set the blood of a thousand brave and nameless people, who died in the Holy City's streets, against the blood of one who died named. Count Bernadotte was twice named. He stood not only as a man, nor only as a symbol of his own people; but also in the name and the writ of an international aggregate of nations among which Israel itself aspires to be.

*

ISRAEL'S voice in the Assembly at Paris cannot but falter before the shock of this grievous misfortune. But though it falter in tone, in the shaping of a people's rights it must continue steadfast. The very wrong that has been done the world, and Israel, by a wicked deed, should remind both Israel and the world of the urgency of the Jews' cause. Forced into battle, to defend with life and limb their birthright of earth and God's air, the Jews have but little time to heal the hurts of centuries and cleanse the national soul. Peace is in the world's gift and it is the bounden duty of the world to give peace to Israel, as it is the bounden duty of Israel to give itself honour and righteousness among the peoples.

*

ON this sad day there is a lump in the throat of Israel. Men and women have been made heavy of heart. But in the balance of good and evil, courage and cowardice, strength and weakness, the people are not shamed. Their way as a people has been the good way, and though with heavier steps, they must go no other. At the end is quiet, and friendliness, and healing.

Tel Aviv, September 19.

HYDERABAD SURRENDERS

NEW DELHI, Saturday (AP). — Hyderabad State troops surrendered to the Indian Army under General J.B. Chauphury at 12 noon today, according to Hyderabad Radio.

Official reports received in New Delhi from the Indian Agent General's office in Hyderabad said the Indian army has not yet entered Secunderabad, as the area between Hyderabad City and Secunderabad, about 40 miles to the west, had been "heavily mined."

The Agent-General's office reported from Hyderabad the situation as normal and said that India had resumed control over Hakimpet aerodrome in the vicinity of Secunderabad.

India Replies

It was officially announced in New Delhi that the Indian Governor-General, Rajagopalachari, replying to the Nizam of Hyderabad's telegram announcing his surrender, said: "I thank you for your message and we are all thankful that the event has ended speedily. I join your regret that your Exalted Highness' Government did not act rightly in time, and caused complication of all the issues. My Government is giving the most careful attention to your Exalted Highness' message to me, as well as to your broadcast published in the newspapers."

Unconfirmed reports said that the Government of India had sent conditions of surrender to the Nizam for acceptance. The Nizam has been asked to hand over the administration to the Area Commander, Rajendra Sinhji, pending a final settlement.

Attempt on Burma Police Officer

RANGOON, Saturday (AP). — Brigadier U Tin Tut, Inspector-General of the Burmese Auxiliary Forces, was injured last night when a hand grenade was thrown into his car by an unidentified man who escaped, it was officially stated today. He was taken to hospital in a "most grave" condition.

Night workers of the "New Times" of Burma gave the A.P. an eyewitness account of the explosion which occurred outside their office. They said that the explosion took place as U Tin Tut's car was driving off and he and his two Gurkha bodyguards were wounded in the legs and the upper parts of their bodies.

The workers said they saw no.one nearby after the explosion, and gave their opinion that the explosive, which appeared to be locally made, was planted in the car while it stood outside the "New Times" office.

U Tin Tut's daughter is the editor of the paper. U Tin Tut himself until recently was a member of the Burmese Cabinet, holding the portfolio of Foreign Affairs. He resigned to devote his service to the Army. There were reports that he was due to become Burmese Ambassador to London.

Lundstroem's Eye-Witness Account of Slaying

Count Folke Bernadotte, U.N. Mediator for Palestine since May 16, was murdered in cold blood at 5.05 p.m. on Friday in the Kiryat Shmuel Quarter of Jerusalem, on his fifth visit to the city.

The Mediator and his party were driving in a convoy of three cars from Government House, where he was to have set up his winter headquarters, to a meeting with the Military Governor, Dr. Bernard Joseph. Two of the cars were flying the U.N. flag, and the third a Red Cross flag.

Jeep Across Road

As the party, which was accompanied by Captain Moshe Hillman, an Israel Army Liaison Officer, drove up to a road-block, they found a jeep (believed to be one stolen from the U.N. several weeks ago) parked across the road. Two of the three men in it, disguised in Army uniforms and heavily armed, jumped from their vehicle, while the driver remained at the wheel.

General Lunstroem, giving the U.N. staff in Haifa an eyewitness description of the assault, said that after the conference with the Arabs in Ramallah, Bernadotte was told that cars were often shot at, and it was suggested to him that it might be safer to go to the Jewish area by a roundabout route.

"I would not do that," Count Bernadotte answered. "I have to take the same risk as my Observers, and moreover, I think that no one has the right to refuse me permission to cross the line."

They then went on through the neutralized Red Cross zone, lunched at the Y.M.C.A., visited Government House and proceeded to the Jewish area. The first car was driven by Major Massart (French) with a Jewish Liaison Officer beside him in the front seat. In the rear were Miss Barbara Wessel, Count Bernadotte's personal secretary, Lt.-Col. M. Flachs, and Major DeGeer, all Swedish.

Driven By Begley

The second car was driven by Colonel Frank Begley of the U.N. Secretariat. Commander Cox (U.S.) was sitting beside him, while Count Bernadotte, Colonel Serot and General Lundstroem were in the rear.

The cars went from the neutral zone to Jewish territory, and proceeded further into the new city of Jerusalem. General Lundstroem continued.

In the Katamon Quarter we were held up by a Jewish Army-type jeep placed in a road-block and filled with men dressed in Jewish Army uniform. At the same moment, I saw a man running from the jeep, but I took little notice because I thought it was merely another check-point. However, he pushed a tommy-gun through the open window at my side of the car and fired point blank at Count Bernadotte and Colonel Serot.

I also heard shots fired from other points, and there was considerable confusion. The Jewish Liaison Officer told Begley to drive away as quickly as possible. In the meantime, the assailant was still firing. Colonel Serot fell in the seat towards me, and I saw immediately that he was dead. Count Bernadotte went forward and I thought at the time that he was trying to take cover. I asked him 'Are you wounded?' He merely nodded and fell back. I helped him to lie down in the car, and I now understand that he was severely wounded as there was a considerable amount of blood on his clothes, especially around the heart.

General Lundstroem then ordered the cars to rush to the Hadassah Hospital, which they reached in a few minutes, but the doctors could only confirm that both men were dead.

Three of the bullets hit the Mediator, two of them just above the heart. Colonel Andre Pierre Serot, of the French

(Continued on Page 3, Col. 3)

ISRAEL ARMY TAKES SWIFT ACTION TO WIPE OUT DISSIDENT MURDERERS OF BERNADOTTE

The Israel Government took swift action yesterday to trace the murderers of Count Bernadotte, who was killed in Jerusalem on Friday afternoon by men disguised in the uniform of the Israel Army. Count Bernadotte and a French Observer, Colonel Andre Serot, were murdered as they drove from Government House to an appointment with the Military Governor of Jerusalem. Widespread searches were carried out, L.H.Y. bases were raided and over 200 suspects were arrested. All ports and airfields in the country were closed, as were roads leading out of Jerusalem, where a 15-hour curfew was imposed, ending at 5 o clock this morning. While the I.Z.L. disclaimed all connection with the crime, responsibility for it was claimed by a group calling itself "Fatherland Front" which an official spokesman described as a sham splinter group of the L.H.Y. The intention of the Government to root out the dissidents was clearly expressed in the Army's firm action yesterday, and was backed by the unanimous condemnation of the killing of the distinguished representative of the United Nations. Both the Israel Cabinet in Tel Aviv and the Security Council in Paris met in special session, and the U.N. staff in Haifa announced that the Mediator's work would go on with Dr. R. Bunche acting as Mediator.

Palestine Put on UN Assembly Agenda

By A.P. Special Correspondents.

PARIS, Saturday. — The U.N. Secretary-General, M. Trygve Lie, today placed the Palestine problem before the full U.N. General Assembly, opening in Paris on Tuesday afternoon.

He announced this action to the Security Council, which met today in special session to discuss the situation arising out of the assassination of the Mediator and Colonel Serot, and to debate whether sterner measures should now be taken in Palestine in the light of the latest crisis.

Israel's representative to the U.N., Mr. Aubrey S. Eban, told the press just before the Council met that his Government was "now conducting a vast purge" of terrorists. Later he joined in condemning the killing. He had prepared an address for delivery to the Council, if invited to do so. However, the invitation was not forthcoming.

Mr. Eban said later that he would "demand the right to present our views" and issued a revised statement to the press as-

(Continued on Page 3, Col. 2)

Count Folke Bernadotte

COUNT'S REPORT BEFORE U.N.

HAIFA, Saturday.—Count Bernadotte completed his report to the U.N. Assembly on September 16, just before he set out on his tour of Arab capitals and Jerusalem. The 35,000-word report has been submitted to the Assembly.

It was most unlikely, the U.N. spokesman here told the press, that General Lundstroem would recommend any changes in the basic conclusions of his report.

The report is expected to be made public this week.

A U. P. message stated that the report called for "prompt action" on

certain decisions relating vitally to peaceful settlement of the Palestien question, and humanitarian measures required by the desperate conditions of more than 300,000 Arab refugees.

Truce Continues As Before

HAIFA, Saturday. – It must be fully understood that despite the terrible tragedy, the truce continues, and supervision of its terms will be carried out precisely as heretofore, General Lundstroem told Observers at a U.N. Staff meeting held here at 3 o'clock this afternoon.

In his statement to the Staff, General Lundstroem, saying that he was shocked beyond measure at the assassination of Count Bernadotte and Colonel Serot, described Count Bernadotte as "the fairest apostle of the United Nations," struck down by a cowardly hand while working tirelessly and devotedly to bring peace to Jerusalem and to all of Palestine.

He declared that the deliberate murder of two international officials constituted a breach of the truce of utmost gravity and was a "black page in Palestine's history" for which the United Nations would demand full accounting.

TEL AVIV STUNNED

TEL AVIV, Saturday.— The news of Count Bernadotte's murder stunned the city, and crowds of people gathered to listen to news broadcasts at public radio sets.

About 50 arrests were made in Tel Aviv and the vicinity and 10 persons were interrogated in the south in a combined police and military operation which started at 2 o'clock this morning. During the day, soldiers were seen leaving town as the stand-to order was issued in both Army and Police Forces. Traffic on the roads was checked and all men, civilians and military alike, were screened.

GOVERNMENT WILL USE ALL FORCE AT ITS COMMAND

TEL AVIV, Saturday. — The Government of Israel issued the following statement today:

The Government of Israel is outraged by the appalling crime committed yesterday in Jerusalem, when the U.N. Mediator, Count Bernadotte, and his assistant, Colonel Serot, were assassinated within the area under the control and defence of the State of Israel.

This murder is an attack on the authority of the U.N. and a calculated assault on the sovereignty of the State of Israel. It is an act of treachery against the Israel Defence Army. It is a desecration of the Holy City of Jerusalem.

The Government of Israel will use all the force at its command to suppress this insane attempt by gunmen to wreck Israel's relations with the U.N.

The perpetrators of this crime are traitors to the people and enemies of its liberty. The Government is mobilizing the entire force of the State to track down the murderers and their accomplices and bring them to justice. It will uproot the criminal gang responsible for the outrage.

The Government calls on the nation to rise as one man against the enemy within its midst. Every citizen and resident of Israel will give active and unhesitating assistance to the Army and Police in apprehending the assassins and their accomplices and expunging the stain of terrorism from the soil of our country.

JEWS MEET GRAVE CHALLENGE

By Our Diplomatic Correspondent

HA'KIRYA, Saturday. — The Government regards the murder of Count Bernadotte as a challenge graver than the Altalena incident. It intends to react now as forcefully as it did then, and will show the world that it has gained complete mastery in its own house.

The assassins are believed to be members of a terrorist elite which was created by the Stern Group with the object of keeping a clandestine cadre in being if, as was expected, the Group as an open movement should be suppressed by the Government. The present army and police operations are countrywide, and will continue until the movement and its ramifications are wiped out.

The Foreign Ministry has been active without respite in an effort to repair the damage done internationally to the cause of Israel by the treacherous murder of Count Bernadotte and Colonel Serot. Full details and special instructions have been sent to the Israel delegate in Paris, who will be able to show the Security Council that the Government moved swiftly and to the fullest extent of its powers to apprehend the assassins and root out their organization.

Sweden May Hesitate

While it is recognized here that the chances of U. N. membership have been lessened, it is not believed that the dastardly crime of yesterday will be permitted, by responsible member states of U.N., to influence their judgment on major issues of the dispute between Israel and the Arabs.

The event may check the recognition of the State by some Governments which were believed to be on the verge of granting recognition, notably Sweden, where an Israel representative, who arrived in Stockholm four days ago, was already in negotiation. There is no question of the withdrawal of recognition by any of the States already in diplomatic relations with Israel.

Reports from Paris which attribute to U.N. officials the statement that the Council may consider voting Article 11, under which sanctions can be applied, are not taken seriously here. There are absolutely no legal grounds for any punitive action against Israel, whose Government has reacted in full accordance with the Security Council's requirements, which in this incident cannot be more drastic than the requirements of the Government itself. Dr. Bunche's letter to Mr. Shertok, to part of which exception may be taken, does not alter this fact.

I learn also that there is not a shred of truth in the report cabled from Tel Aviv which asserts that U. N. Observers had been under orders to leave Israel, but that the orders were rescinded after the murder of Count Bernadotte in order to prevent giving the impression that the withdrawal was the consequence of the murder. The Observers were at no time under orders to leave Israel, and there is therefore no question of such orders having been given.

The withdrawal was said to have been decided upon because it was believed that the Arabs would launch an offensive in a matter of hours.

These inaccurate reports may have originated in the fact that General Lundstroem, as a first reaction to the murder of his chief, proposed the withdrawal of all Observers from Jerusalem but later, on the advice of Col. Begley, gave up the idea. In the interval, Israel Forces began to occupy the neutral Zone around Government House, but started to move out when it was decided to maintain the machinery of U.N. Observation.

PRESIDENT'S STATEMENT

President Weizmann said in Geneva yesterday that he was "broken down" by the "infamous murder in Jerusalem," although it was well-known that the Stern gang which had perpetrated it was a "very small group and the Jewish public has no contact with them."

17th RECOGNITION

SAN SALVADOR, Saturday (PTA). — El Salvador, the first of those countries which abstained from voting when the U.N. decided on Partition last November, has recognized Israel, it was officially announced here yesterday.

This Latin American Republic is the 17th country to recognize the Jewish State.

Jerusalem Curfew; LHY Bases Raided

The Israel Government's declaration that it would take "the most vigorous and energetic measures to bring the assassins to justice and eradicate the evil" was translated into action yesterday when full-scale operations were launched in Jerusalem. The Cabinet met in extraordinary session last night.

Orders were given on Friday night to the military commander in Jerusalem which gave him full authority to use all the means at his disposal to take whatever action necessary.

A curfew was imposed on the entire city at 2.15 in the afternoon, and all exits from the city were barred. All L.H.Y. bases in Jerusalem were surrounded and searched. Arms dumps were found and seized, in Talbieh and elsewhere; 150 suspects were taken into military custody. None of them is a member of the Israel Army.

Invited To Line-Up

The operation was not confined to Jerusalem, and all ports and airfields in the country were closed to arrivals and departures. In other parts of the country, over 50 persons were arrested, including some who are believed to be leading members of the L.H.Y.

General Lundstroem has been informed by the military authorities that he and other U.N. personnel who were eye-witnesses of the crime would be invited to an identification parade of the suspects.

Curfew

Army trucks patrolled the streets of Jerusalem warning the public over loudspeakers to stay indoors. At first persons breaking the curfew were cautioned by Policemen who were stationed at nearly every street corner. Mishmar Ha'am personnel joined civil police on curfew patrols. Military Police were reinforced by squads from Tel Aviv. Later, curfew-breakers were arrested, and by late last night about 250 were arrested. They are to be tried before the Magistrate's Court today.

The curfew was lifted at 5 o'clock this morning.

As precautionary measures, Jewish Policemen were stationed outside the American, Belgium, and French Consulates. All U.N. cars in Jerusalem were accompanied by M.P. escort

Hunt for Murderers

The Military Governor, Dr. B. Joseph, said almost immediately after the murder was made known, that "the perpetrators of this dastardly act" would be hunted down.

The Foreign Minister, Mr. Moshe Shertok, cabled the U.N. that "Israel, is adopting the most vigorous and energetic measures to bring the assassins to justice and eradicate the evil" in the country.

Mr. Shertok cabled condolences to the King of Sweden and Countess Bernadotte.

In Jerusalem yesterday the Mayor, Mr. Daniel Auster, expressed the condemnation of the murders at a public meeting. The Labour Council, called into extraordinary session, adopted resolutions calling on the Government to use every means possible to bring the perpetrators to justice.

DR. RALPH J. BUNCHE

Bunche in Charge

HAIFA, Saturday. — Dr. Ralphe Bunche, Special Representative in Palestine of U.N., was asked today in a cable from Mr. Trygve Lie to take charge of affairs here pending the appointment of the new Mediator. In his statement to a C.B.S. correspondent, Dr. Bunche said:

"If Bernadottte could be with us today, he would say: 'I want you to carry out the mission for which I have given my life'."

Dr. Bunche continued:

Our number one task now is to carry out the posthumous command of the man who died for peace and decency. The truce in Palestine must go on, and everyone connected with the U.N. will do his best to see to it that this truce will go on. If this task succeeds, then I feel the chances are good that the opportunity to reach a peaceful settlement through U.N. intervention will not be lost.

On being informed of his appointment as Acting Mediator, Dr. Bunche wrote the following to the Chairman of the U.N. Truce Commission, Mr. John J. Macdonald:

In temporarily assuming this heavy responsibility under such sorrowful circumstances, I wish you to know that I have but one objective, namely to exert every possible effort to maintain the truce in pursuance of the instructions of the Security Council, and to that end to keep the truce observation machinery intact and in full operation.

I will, of course, work closely with the Truce Commission in this effort, and earnestly hope that the Commission will continue to accept a special responsibility for Jerusalem during these difficult times.

One of Dr. Bunche's first tasks will be to complete an inquiry into the circumstances of the murder and to wire the results to Paris, according to a request made by the U.N. Secretariat yesterday.

TO WHOM IT MAY CONCERN

The Executive of the Jewish Agency for Palestine herewith notify that they will not be bound — as they are not and have never been in the past — in respect of any obligation professed to be incurred in their name or on their behalf, unless such obligation is, or has been, countersigned by the Treasurer of the Jewish Agency for Palestine, or the Deputy Treasurer, or any substitute specially authorised in writing by the Treasurer.

Until further notice the Treasurer is Dr. Israel Goldstein, the Deputy Treasurer is Mr. David Bahral.

THE PALESTINE POST

JERUSALEM
Thursday, Feb. 17, 1949

PRICE: 25 MILS
VOL. XXV. No. 6940

LEBANESE TALKS BEFORE T.-J.

By Our Diplomatic Correspondent, Copyright, The Palestine Post

Ha'KIRYA, Wednesday. — It is thought probable that the Lebanon may precede Trans-Jordan as the next Arab State to negotiate an armistice agreement with Isral. The conditions of armistice are understood to have been considered at length between Israel and Lebanese representatives some weeks ago, and to present relatively few difficulties.

On the other hand, protracted and delicate discussions are anticipated with Trans-Jordan, especially as agreement between this Arab state and Israel, covering military problems affecting a long and vital area, including Jerusalem, is regarded as of the utmost importance from the political angle. It is expected in some quarters that these talks will be raised at a later stage to Ministerial level.

Same Level

In the earlier phases of the talks with Trans-Jordan, which may begin toward the end of next week, Israel will probably be represented at a level similar to that of the Delegation now at Rhodes. Dr. Walter Eytan, who led the present Israel delegation, will not, it is thought, take part, as his services are greatly needed at the Foreign Office Ministry, of which he is Director-General. Among the military leaders expected to go to Rhodes for the talks with Trans-Jordan is Lt.-Col. Dayan, Commander of the Jerusalem Area.

Great satisfaction is felt at the fortunate turn of events in the Israel-Egyptian talks at Rhodes. The concluding phase of the negotiations will almost certainly take another week and perhaps longer. While the main outstanding problem, which covers the military future of Auja, has been settled in principle, a good deal has yet to be ironed out before the agreement, which is now in draft form, will have been filled in and made ready to sign.

Important questions are said to be:

a. Whether the armistice agreement is to be temporary or of a permanent nature;
b. how far, if at all, it can be regarded as of political consequence;
c. what is to be the extent of the area subject to the same arrangement as for the post of Auja itself;
d. how much of the area on both sides of the Gaza-Rafa strip should be subject to the demilitarization terms; and
e. the extent of that demilitarization.

It is thought that it may take at least a full week before these details are satisfactorily worked out.

Fierce Battles In Burma

RANGOON, Wednesday (AP). — A fierce battle was fought today on the outskirts of Karen-held Intsein, north of Rangoon, in which strongpoints changed hands several times as Government forces sought to penetrate the hard core of the Karen defences.

Government troops were in possession of a monastery which is a strategic point, but the Karens were preparing yet another counter-offensive, official sources said this afternoon. Karens have established a series of road blocks behind the monastery.

The town of Bassein, 70 miles west of Rangoon, is now "infested with Communist insurgents, who are harassed by Government troops," according to a Government communique released tonight. The Karens are reported to be regrouping east and west of Bassein. Fifty Karens were killed during the fighting at Hlegu, 26 miles north of Rangoon, the communique said.

Arms Dump Explodes

SHANGHAI, Wednesday, (UP). — The northern suburbs of Shanghai were shaken by a series of explosions of anti-aircraft shells and bombs tonight when a Chinese army munitions dump caught fire and burned for six hours.

CLAY AGAINST ANTI-SEMITISM

FRANKFURT, Wednesday, (PTA). — General Lucius D. Clay, U.S. Military Commander here, addressing a press conference today, vigorously denounced members of the U.S. Military Government who show anti-Semitic inclinations.

If persons in the army were found guilty of anti-Semitic statements they would be subject to official disciplinary action, he said. If there were civilian members of the occupation forces they would be asked to resign.

Egypt Must Refer Text to Cairo

RHODES, Wednesday (Reuter). — Although Israel-Egyptian agreement on an armistice is expected to be reached next week, a slight delay in the signing is expected, as the Egyptians have to send the completed text to Cairo for approval. This should, however, not take more than 24 hours, and the Egyptian delegation is reported to have told Dr. Ralph Bunche that it was a "formality."

Both delegations were today putting the finishing touches to that part of the agreement affecting Auja, and are next due to consider the question of Beersheba, where Israel forces are expected to remain. An Egyptian demand for a civil administration in Bir Asluj is reported to have been dropped, after the Israel delegation had convinced the Egyptians that the place was little more than a few huts, needing no "administration."

Jerusalem's Place

While no details are known about the composition of the Trans-Jordan delegation which is expected here next week, Israel circles have pointed out that they would refuse to meet it if it included any British officers such as Glubb Pasha or Brigadier, Norman Lash.

A source close to the Israel delegation said here today that an armistice with the Lebanon was "very close," the main point of dispute between the two countries — the return of nine Israel-held Lebanese villages — having been settled by Israel's agreement to hand them back. An agreement between the two sides had been "virtually drafted," it was said. (Reuter.)

RED CROSS CHIEF COMES TO ISRAEL

Dr. Paul Ruegger, President of the International Red Cross, arrived in Israel on Tuesday, visited Jerusalem yesterday and was the guest of the Foreign Minister, Mr. M. Shertok, at lunch.

Other guests were the Middle East directors of the Red Cross; Dr. Avraham Katznelson, Director of the Government Health Department; Mr. Bert Locker, chairman of the Jewish Agency Executive; Mr. Juda Gaulan, of the Foreign Ministry; and Dr. Steinberg and Dr. Hochman, Israel Army Liaison Officers with the Red Cross.

Dr. Ruegger had earlier erroneously been reported missing in a flight from Beirut to Amman.

Dr. Ruegger later went to the Old City and met Lt.-Col. Abdullah el-Tel.

SEARCH FOR U.N. PLANE

HAIFA, Wednesday. — U.N. and Israel Air Force planes continued to search today for the missing U.N. Consul plane. (One plane, and not two, as reported earlier, is missing.)

The craft left Beirut for Amman on Monday, piloted by a Briton, Mr. Whitehead; its radio operator was Mr. Borden.

Several Israel planes carried on the search this morning over Israel territory and two U.N. Dakotas scoured the snow-covered mountains to the north. U.N. Headquarters here did not make any statement to the press.

THREAT TO ISRAEL'S LONDON OFFICE

LONDON, Wednesday (PTA). — Scotland Yard detectives were called to the Israel delegation offices in Manchester Square this afternoon following the receipt of an anonymous letter that the building would be blown up.

The letter was taken away by C.I.D. for further examination.

WEIZMANN FIRST PRESIDENT OF ISRAEL

Jerusalem Will Come Into Its Own

After a dramatic debate, the Knesset decided last night to hold a special session in Tel Aviv after the new Government was formed to discuss the possibility of transferring the seat of the Knesset and the Government to Jerusalem.

During the debate on the "small constitution," Mr. Menahem Begin proposed a clause naming "Jerusalem, the capital, as the seat of the Knesset and of the Government." When this motion had been brought before the ad hoc Legislative Committee, the majority decided that the question was not one to be resolved in the "small constitution."

When he addressed the plenary session in the evening, Mr. Begin referred to his late mentor, Zeev Jabotinsky, and recalled that his proposal for a Jewish State formula at the 17th Zionist Congress had been turned down by the majority; the State was nevertheless forged. So, too, if the majority voted against Mr. Begin's current proposal, history would show that in any case Jerusalem would come into its own.

Jerusalem's Place

Mr. Shertok replied that those who had voted against Jabotinsky's motion at the 17th Zionist Congress had in the final analysis established the Jewish State. Thus, those who voted against Mr. Begin's proposal, would in the end ensure that Jerusalem received its due place in the State of Israel. This was not a matter to be decided in interim legislation, the Foreign Minister declared.

Nevertheless, a considerable part of the House appeared reluctant to vote against Mr. Begin's motion. There was something of a commotion and a number of Members pleaded for the floor, despite the fact that a general debate on a question that had been through a sub-committee was against procedure.

Compromise Proposed

Rabbi Avraham Zvebner (Mizrahi), white-bearded and dignified in his knee-length black cloak, proposed a compromise formula. He said he could not vote against the Herut proposal but suggested instead a resolution calling on the Government to do everything possible to establish Jerusalem as the seat of the Knesset and the Government.

Mr. Eliahu Eliachar (Sephardim) criticized Mr. Belgin for having caused the stir in the House.

Finally, Mr. Pinkas, one of the shrewdest parliamentarians in the defunct State Council, showed the chairman a way out of the impasse. He suggested that the issue be reverted to the ad hoc Committee on the ground that Rabbi Zvebner, a Member, had been unable to participate in the discussion at that point.

Mr. Pinkas's suggestion was received with laughter. His view, however, was strengthened when the chairman, Mr. Sprinzak, gratefully picked it up. He put it to a vote and the Knesset passed it unanimously, with the Herut faction and Mr. Friedman-Yellin (Fighters) abstaining.

KNESSET ADOPTS "SMALL CONSTITUTION"

Before choosing the new President, the Knesset, at a five-hour session adopted a "Small Constitution," which also defined his powers and duties. With the approval of the Knesset or the minister concerned, he will sign treaties, make diplomatic appointments, receive foreign diplomats and confirm foreign diplomatic representations. He will also have the power of amnesty. Every presidential act, however, will require the counter-signature of the Prime Minister.

The President's duties will not necessarily be limited to these. This was made clear during the debate by Mr. Israel Idelson (Mapam), chairman of the ad hoc parliamentary Legislative Committee. He said that these powers were defined in the "small constitution" because they concerned urgent matters. But when the State Constitution is adopted, it may give the President broader powers.

Mr. Idelson made this statement when he replied to Mr. Menahem Begin (Herut) who had proposed that the State President should be empowered to veto and return bills to the Knesset if he did not wish to sign them. Only after they passed the Knesset a second time, would they become law against the President's wishes, according to Mr. Begin's proposals.

The Knesset defeated the Herut motion (69-13) and upheld the view expressed by Mr. Idelson that the people's chosen representatives should

INAUGURATION CEREMONY

A delegation of Members of the Knesset, led by the Praesidium, will travel to Rehovot this morning to invite Dr. Chaim Weizmann to come to Jerusalem to take the oath of office as first President of Israel.

A Military and Police Guard of Honour, and an escort of representatives of the Army, Navy and Air Force, will accompany Dr. Weizmann.

exclusively enjoy powers of legislation.

Mr. Begin also sought to amend the text of the Presidential oath, in which the President is to pledge allegiance to "the State of Israel and its laws." Mr. Begin proposed the substitution of "people" for "State" and objected to the pledge of allegiance to the State laws, on the grounds that some emergency laws had been carried over from the British Administration.

Mr. Idelson opposed these amendments on the grounds that not all the people of Israel were Jews and not all the Jews were in Israel. He further said that the pledge

to uphold the laws referred to the laws which the Knesset would enact. In the vote on these points, Herut obtained some support from Orthodox members, but their motions were defeated (78-18).

A motion by a Progressive Member, Mr. Izhar Harari, designed to give the President the sole power of signing bills was defeated by an overwhelming majority. Hence, bills will require the signatures of the Prime Minister as well as the ministers charged with their execution.

The President will receive the resignation of the Provisional Government and will ask them to remain in office until a new Government is formed. He will then ask Mr. David Ben Gurion to form a new Government.

Mapam sought to introduce a clause which would allow the man charged to form a government only seven days in which to bring his recommendations to the Knesset for a vote of confidence. If he were then unable to do so, the President should charge someone else, according to the proposal. Mapam was backed by Herut and the Communists, but the motion was defeated (52-31).

There was a close vote on the question of whether persons who were not members of the Knesset could be included

in the Cabinet. The Provisional Government had recommended that others be eligible, but the ad hoc Legislative Committee confined its recommendation only to Knesset members. Mr. Shertok defended the Government view which prevailed (49-39). Another Herut motion for a Cabinet of eight was decisively defeated.

Second Thoughts

At the second reading of the draft "small constitution," the Knesset passed a motion giving the name of "Megilot Hamedina" (State Scrolls) to Official Gazettes. It was passed unanimously.

A few hours later, however, Mr. David Pinkas (Mizrahi) reconsidered and objected to the name. "Megilot" was the Hebrew name for the Books of the Bible, and Mr. Pinkas thought it was improper to use the same nomenclature for a publication which would report such mundane things as bankruptcies.

He received unexpected support from the Mapai benches when Dr. Yosef Lamm proposed that this question was not so urgent that it had to be included in the interim legislation. Other Assemblymen offered alternative names, and it was decided to postpone the decision for a week.

(Constitution Text — Page 3)

Silver and Neumann Resign from Agency

By JESSE ZEL LURIE
Copyright, The Palestine Post

NEW YORK, Wednesday. — Dr. Abba H. Silver, Chairman of the American Section of the Jewish Agency, and Dr. Emanuel Neumann, President of the Zionist Organization of America, resigned from the Agency Executive today but their resignations have not yet been accepted.

Dr. Silver cancelled a trip to see Mr. Henry Morgenthau, former Chairman of the United Jewish Appeal, when Mr. Morgenthau wired that he could not change his minimum demand to be given full control of the U.J.A. campaign if he resumed the Chairmanship. The Agency proceeded to vote on returning to office Mr. Morgenthau and Mr. Henry Montor, former Executive Director of the campaign, and the vote is still going on. All absent members are being polled by cable.

Only the Z.O.A. representatives opposed acceptance of Mr. Morgenthau's terms, while

the Mizrahi members of the Agency abstained from voting. The votes of members absent from the sessions are expected to increase the majority for Mr. Morgenthau, and unless Dr. Silver and Dr. Neumann withdraw their resignations, they will be announced when the final vote is published.

Dr. Silver and Dr. Neumann intimated that they will appeal to the Zionist General Council. A statement which they issued declared that they "cannot accept the responsibility for the consequences if the U.J.A. campaign is headed by a divisive personality such as Mr. Montor, who has created ill-will in the Jewish communities and whose appointment to high office is sure to jeopardize the success of the campaign."

Dr. Silver returned to Cleveland today. Meanwhile the Agency resumed its sessions in camera. An official spokesman indicated that there is a feeling of optimism regarding the eventual solution of the new crisis.

Commission Revises Schedule of M.E. Tour; Now in Saudi Arabia

The Conciliation Commission's schedule has been revised, and it will complete its tour of the Middle East on February 26, when it will return to Jerusalem, it was announced by the Commission's Press Officer, Mr. Hamilton Fischer, at a press conference in Jerusalem yesterday. The Commission has as yet no detailed plan for its future programme.

The Commission visited Jedda yesterday, and will go to Riadh today to continue official talks with Saudi Arabian representatives. Mr. Fischer was unable to say whether members of the Commission had been received by King Ibn Saud. From Riadh the Commission will fly to Baghdad for conversations with the Iraqi Government, and on February 20 it will begin official talks with the Trans-Jordan Government at Amman. The Commissioners will fly to Damascus on February 21, and then to Beirut.

They will visit Tel Aviv on February 24 for official talks with the Israel Government, returning to Jerusalem two days later.

Asked whether the Commission had had talks with the Egyptian Government or the

Arab League, Mr. Fischer stated that the programme called for official talks with the Egyptian Government, and it was possible that the members had met "other factors" also.

He denied reports that a decision to partition Jerusalem had been reached, and stated that the sub-committee on Jerusalem was continuing its work. The Commission has reached no final decision with regard to the Legion's demand for a road from the Old City to the former Government House, but the Commission is considering the possibility of alternate approaches from the Old City.

THREE MORE RECOGNITIONS

Three states announced their recognition of Israel yesterday — Argentina, Peru and Sweden. The Argentine and Peruvian recognitions were de jure.

The Argentine recognition was announced by the Argentine Government in Buenos Aires. In Lima, members of the Jewish mission called on the President and thanked him for his government's recognition.

The Swedish recognition, which was de facto, was communicated to the Foreign Minister, Mr. Shertok, by the Swedish Consul-General in Jerusalem, Mr. WidarBagge.

Wins over Klausner on first Ballot-83:15

DR. CHAIM WEIZMANN WAS ELECTED ISRAEL'S FIRST PRESIDENT AT 1.15 THIS MORNING ON THE FIRST BALLOT IN THE KNESSET (the new official name for the Constituent Assembly). HE OBTAINED 83 VOTES AGAINST 15 FOR PROFESSOR YOSEF KLAUSNER, WHOSE CANDIDACY WAS SPONSORED BY HERUT AND SUPPORTED BY MR. FRIEDMAN-YELLIN.

The result was announced by the Knesset Speaker, Mr. Yosef Sprinzak, who rapped three times with his gavel and announced "Chaim Ben Oser Weizmann has been elected first President of the State of Israel."

The meeting then rose and sang the national anthem, and the Knesset adjourned until today, when Dr. Weizmann will be ceremoniously inaugurated.

Fifteen envelopes were empty to represent opposition to both candidates. One vote was not valid, and six Assembly members were absent.

The midnight session lasted an hour and 24 minutes, and was packed with drama and studded with heated outbursts. There had been intense lobbying after the adjournment of the evening session at 9 o'clock to ensure that Dr. Weizmann would get the required 61 votes on the first ballot. The meeting had been called for 10.15 but no agreement had been reached, and it was postponed for an hour. However, there was a further delay until five minutes before midnight, when the chairman of the Steering Committee, Mr. Zalman Rubashov, announced that there were two candidates: Professor Chaim Weizmann and Professor Yosef Klausner.

Party leaders then made brief statements explaining how they would vote, although the actual balloting was secret. Mr. Eliezer Praki (Mapai) read a declaration that his party would vote for Dr. Weizmann out of recognition of his stature in the Zionist Movement, especially in his support for pioneering. It also wanted to show its determined opposition to the candidate of the Herut Party. At the same time, it declared that it did not agree with Dr. Weizmann's policy.

Uproar in House

When the Herut spokesman, Mr. Arieh Ben Eliezer, concluded his declaration nominating Professor Klausner with the words "We won't argue with collaborators," there was an uproar. Mapai members rose in their seats calling "Shame" at the Herut group seated on benches directly behind them, and the Herut members shouted back for several minutes until the Chairman succeeded in restoring order.

There followed declarations by Mr. Meir Wilner (Communists) and Mr. Nathan Friedman-Yellin, both of whom expressed opposition to Dr. Weizmann. The Communists also opposed Professor Klausner, and indicated that his party would abstain.

Ballot by Roll Call

The roll call of 120 names took a quarter of an hour, each Member casting his vote into the ballot-box as his name was called. There were six absentees, including the Prime Minister who was confined to bed with a chill, the Finance Minister, Mr. Eliezer Kaplan, who is in Washington, and Mrs. Goldie Myerson, Envoy to Moscow. It took 15 minutes to count the votes and the results were announced.

A few minutes later, the Presidential Private Secretary, Mr. Yigal Kimche, was on the phone to Rehovot informing Dr. Weizmann of his election. Dr. Weizmann will come to Jerusalem today for his inauguration.

810,000 Refugees From Palestine

LONDON, Wednesday (AP). — The Minister of State, Mr. Hector McNeil, said today that there were about 810,000 Arab refugees from the Palestine fighting.

In a written reply in the House of Commons to Brigadier R. Rayner (Cons.), Mr. McNeil said that there were 210,000 in the Gaza area, 320,000 in Palestine and 280,000 in neighbouring Arab states.

Mr. McNeil said that the U.N. Relief groups were aiding about 600,000.

U.S. Minister to Leave Hungary

BUDAPEST, Wednesday (AP). — The U.S. Minister to Hungary, Mr. Selden Chapin, is considered "persona non-grata" by the Hungarian Government, and will leave Budapest tomorrow morning, a spokesman for the U.S. Legation revealed today.

Mr. Chapin's plans were not disclosed, but it is believed that he will stay in Paris for a time. The spokesman said that the Minister will return to Washington for talks with the U.S. State Department.

2 MORE HANGED IN IRAQ

BAGHDAD, Wednesday (Reuter). — Two more men, Zakki Mohammed Basim and Yahuda Ibrahim Sedik, under sentence of death for security offences, were hanged yesterday.

Two others, Yusif Salman Yusif and Hussain Mohammed al Shabiby, were executed on Monday on the same charges — "activities aimed at destroying the State's foundations and instigating certain elements of the armed forces to join their subversive organization, their object being anarchy."

THE PALESTINE POST

JERUSALEM
FRIDAY, Feb. 25, 1949

6 PAGES
PRICE: 45 MILS
VOL. XXV. No. 6947

SIGNING OF ARMISTICE ENDS WAR WITH EGYPT

Column One
By David Courtney

ARGENTINA is a huge and powerful country. It comes first among the world's exporters of beef and mutton and third in the list of grain-exporting countries: in other words, the world cannot do without it. It is the chief trading country of Latin America. A serious economic and political crisis in Argentina would perilously upset the supply system of a large part of Europe. President Peron is dependent for the security of his regime on the combination of working-class and extreme Right-wing Army support. Until January of this year his Richelieu was Senor Miguel Miranda, a subtle if Fascist-minded Minister who believed in Lenin's theory that successful revolution is a question of electrification. He decided that Argentina should stop being almost exclusively a cattle and grain producing country and should industrialize itself; and with that object in view, an exuberant and enormously costly Five-Year Plan was laid down. The workers liked it. They cheered Senor Peron when he appeared on decorated balconies and Senora Peron when she went shopping. But in spite of taking advantage of the world food shortage to wring every penny they could from the grain-hungry and beef-hungry countries, the Perons and Senor Miranda began to find themselves short of money and faced with rising prices. So did the workers. Miranda was then made the scapegoat, and dropped: some say that he has only been dropped temporarily, and will come back again as soon as the crisis is over.

■

IT is probable that Senor Peron will have to end his pretence of being the workers' friend. He is beginning to ask for harder work, longer working hours and the freezing of wages; and if he insists, he may have to take measures against the disillusioned Trade Unions. His effective control over Labour in the first years of his Presidency is what endeared him to the Right-wing Army, which is his main line of defence. He can afford to lose the loyalty of the workers if he can regain effective control over them and thus ensure the Army's continued support. At the same time, it is obvious that he will have to pull in the horns of the Five Year Plan and try to balance Argentina's overseas payments. The gold holdings of the Central Bank dropped from 1,072 million American dollars' worth in 1946 to 322 million at the end of 1947 and 196 million in August of last year. It is fairly obvious that in these conditions the heavy imports of capital goods, upon which the Five Year Plan is based, and for which, as a rule, dollars have to be paid, must be curtailed.

■

PERON might do better for himself and his country if he were less of a skinflint in his dealings with buyers of Argentinian goods. The world food shortage has been very considerably eased. What is more, the Third World War on which Miranda banked has not come off. The long and short of it seems to be that if the Perons want to stay in power and to keep their country solvent, they had better develop an honest conscience and bank on fair international trading conditions instead of the desperation of hungry nations, and on world peace instead of world war.

Tel Aviv, February 25.

Truman Gratified By News of Signature

WASHINGTON, Thursday. — President Truman told a press conference here today that he was "immensely gratified" by the news of the signing of the Israel-Egyptian armistice agreement.

The President's statement said: "I am immensely gratified over the news from Rhodes that representatives of Egypt and Israel have signed an armistice agreement. This act is a tribute to the restraint and statesmanship of the two Governments.

"I wish also to congratulate the U.N. Mediator, Dr. Ralph Bunche, whose untiring efforts have so greatly contributed to the success of these negotiations. I hope that now that a formal armistice has been agreed upon between Egypt and Israel, this pattern for peace will be followed rapidly by the conclusion of similar agreements between Israel and the other Arab states. A general armistice will then, I trust, lead to the attainment of permanent peace, thus freeing the talents of these Near Eastern peoples for constructive work in the development of their respective countries.

"As a member of the Palestine Conciliation Commission, the U.S. stands ready to assist all parties to a rapid conclusion of a just and honourable peace."

Under U.N. Auspices

From Lake Success, the U.N. Secretary-General, Mr. Trygve Lie, sent congratulations to Dr. Bunche and the Israel and Egyptian Governments. "This agreement marks a long step forward to better relations in the Middle East and represents a solid accomplishment for peace under U.N. auspices," he said.

Arab World Has Accepted State of Israel as Fact

TEL AVIV, Thursday. — The signing of the armistice was warmly received here. At the moment it was signed in Rhodes, the Foreign Minister, Mr. Moshe Shertok, faced newspaper editors on the veranda of the Ministry. He hailed the agreement as the first "since the historic Weizmann-Feisal pact to have been signed jointly by official Arab and Jewish representatives." He added: "It is the first accord reached between Israel and a neighbouring Arab State."

Mr. Shertok said that the signing of the armistice bore out the oft-repeated contention that only equality of political status would bring the Arab world to recognize and accept Israel as a fact.

Terming the armistice as "the first link in a new chain of evolutions," Mr. Shertok said it would go down in history as a far-reaching departure in Israel foreign relations and a momentous event in the Middle East.

In the six weeks of close contact with the Egyptians, he said, very useful contacts had been made. An identity of views had emerged on future problems both concerning mutual relations and those with the outside world.

The Foreign Minister paid tribute to "the realism and courage of the Egyptian Monarch and Government, their breadth of vision and bold statesmanship which have made the present agreement possible." He continued:

Israel will not forget that among the neighbouring countries which had waged a war of aggression against her, Egypt was the first to respond, albeit belatedly and partially, to her call for peace and to comply with the Security Council Resolution on an armistice. Israel is confident that Egypt will never have

(Continued on Page 3, Col. 4)

THE NEGEV'S FUTURE

BEERSHEBA, Thursday. — At the first meeting of the Negev settlement representatives which opened here today while the armistice was being signed in Rhodes, Mr. J. Weitz of the Jewish National Fund outlined a scheme to provide this part of the country with water.

Plans for the Negev call for the establishment of 120 new settlements in the near future.

Mr. A. Zisling, Minister of Agriculture, addressed the settlers.

ARAB CIVILIANS CAN STAY

There was agreement in Rhodes on two points not actually included in the general armistice agreement:

1. **Those of the 3,200 Arab civilians in the Falujja pocket who wish to remain in their villages will be permitted to do so and will be granted the full right of Israel citizens. The others will be permitted to leave with the Egyptian Brigade, except for those who had taken up arms against Israel, who would be treated as prisoners of war;**
2. **If Egypt decides to withdraw her forces from Hebron and Bethlehem, Israel will permit them to cross her territory.**

These points are provided for in letters to Dr. Bunche from Dr. W. Eytan, which are attached to the agreement.

The eastern front in the Negev is not affected by the armistice, and as far as the agreement is concerned, Israel has complete freedom of movement down to the Gulf of Akaba. The question of the eastern line is a matter for negotiation between Israel and Trans-Jordan. These talks will begin in Rhodes on Monday.

Cairo Stresses Agreement is "Purely Military"

CAIRO, Thursday (AP) — The Egyptian Prime Minister, Abdel Hadi Pasha, told newsmen today that the Palestine armistice concerned "purely military questions." He declared that the agreement did not deal with the political future of Palestine and "has no political nature."

Hadi Pasha said: "In compliance with the Security Council decision of November 16, 1948, which appealed to the Egyptian Government and the Jews to negotiate an armistice which would serve as a transition from a cease-fire to a permanent truce in Palestine, the Egyptian Government sent a military delegation to Rhodes on January 12."

Negotiations lasted six weeks, he added, during which time both sides more than once sent delegates back for consultation with their respective Governments.

Following the negotiations, Dr. Ralph Bunche drafted a plan for an armistice "constituting a compromise between the different viewpoints, and, after discussing all the aspects of this plan, the two parties approved it."

In London, a Foreign Office spokesman said that Britain welcomed the concessions made by Egypt in reaching an agreement with Israel.

Britain, he added, was glad that the two sides have been able to agree, because the settlement of the Palestine conflict would contribute to the restoration of stability in the Middle East.

Short Ceremony Laid Basis For Permanent Peace

RHODES, Thursday. — The Israel-Egyptian armistice was signed at 10.30 this morning in the Yellow Room of the Hotel des Roses, in a 22-minute ceremony which laid the basis for permanent peace in Palestine. The signing automatically signified Egypt's de facto recognition of Israel.

The Egyptian Brigade at Falujja will begin to evacuate wounded, infantry and heavy equipment — in that order — at 0500 G.M.T. on Saturday.

One of the most important points in the agreement is the concession by the Egyptians that the October 14 lines would not serve as the "purpose and spirit" of the armistice. These were the lines before Israel launched the October offensive.

The agreement was signed for Israel by Dr. Walter Eytan and Colonel Yigael Yadin and for Egypt by Colonel Seif ed-Din and Colonel Mohamed Kamel el Rahmani. Signatures were affixed on five leather-bound copies of the document — one for each delegation, two for the U.N. Security Council and Assembly and one for Dr. Ralph Bunche.

Coloured markers showed the pages where the signatures were to be written. When this had been done by the two delegations, Dr. Bunche turned to the page where he and Brigadier-General William Riley, his Chief of Staff, signed for the United Nations.

Bunche's Speech

The Acting Mediator then complimented the two delegations on the conclusion of the agreement: "Important history is being recorded here today," he said.

You have now made a significant contribution to the cause of world peace. For this, the international community, the Near East and the people of Palestine shall fervently thank you.

In the past six weeks on the island of Rhodes you have worked hard and earnestly. It was not an easy task you were called upon to do. Wars are much more easily made than unmade, but you succeeded, and you have done so only because you, as delegates, and the Governments you represent were imbued with the will and the determination to find the road to peace. Once having found it, you resolutely set on keeping to it.

History will owe you a great debt for this noble and successful effort.

Egypt's Thanks

On behalf of the Egyptian delegation, Colonel Seif ed-Din thanked Dr. Bunche "who never lost hope." He also thanked the people of Rhodes for their hospitality, and concluded with the assurance that the agreement would be carried out in good will and all sincerity:

The agreement we have just signed must be implemented in a spirit of mutual understanding and goodwill in order to secure the ultimate end at which it aims. We are hopeful that it will not raise any difficulty, and that the stability of this part of the world will thus be secured.

Eytan's Address

Dr. Eytan, for the Israel delegation, said: "We should like to express our satisfaction at the conclusion of the armistice agreement and at the fact that each has shown understanding for the other's viewpoint.

I think everybody will share my view that the agreements are fair and honourable for both sides and augur well for peaceful relations between them in the future, I am certain that the armistice provisions will be scrupulously observed, and that their scrupulous observance will lead to an intensification on a national scale of these friendly relations which we have been privileged to form at Rhodes with the Egyptian delegation.

Turning to Dr. Bunche, Dr. Eytan said: "If it had not been for your unfailing kindness and patience and your ample fund of constructive ideas, your almost superhuman capacity for hard work, the result of this conference might have been different.

The chief Israel delegate also thanked General Riley and the U.N. staff and concluded: "We end one chapter today, but are confident that this is merely the beginning of a new volume in the history of the relations between our peoples and the pacific development of the Middle East.

"We thank you, Colonel Seif ed-Din and all the members of your delegation for the good will and cooperation shown in the execution of a task that was never easy and would have been even more difficult if it were not for the spirit of harmony and understanding that prevailed."

When the meeting was over, Dr. Bunche invited both delegations to stay for an informal talk. The members of the Egyptian delegation left for Cairo soon afterwards. The Israel delegation is expected to return to Tel Aviv tomorrow.

In a prepared statement distributed to the press, after the meeting, Dr. Bunche declared that "for the first time in the long history of the Palestine dispute, Arab and Jewish representatives have met, negotiated and signed a formal agreement."

"On the whole," he continued, "it may be said that the negotiations were outstanding for the restraint and dignity manifested throughout by both delegations, even when the most important matters were under consideration.

"In my view, this is a very fair and honourable agreement. In it both parties are taken as equals. It affords very great safeguards for the security of both parties, and incorporates in Article One a declaration which is very much akin to a non-aggression pact. It provides for a substantial withdrawal and reduction of armed forces on both sides.

"It virtually eliminates any possibility of future armed conflict between the two. There is no doubt in my mind that this agreement will pave the way for an early and peaceful settlement of all outstanding differences between Egypt and Israel."

News of the armistice and the reading of the various articles and appendixes took up the major portion of the transmissions over Arabic radio stations yesterday. No comment on the armistice was voiced, however.

(UP, AP and PTA)

RELAXED

RHODES, Thursday. — The basic agreement was signed first and then the annexes, each delegate signing his name 24 times with his own pen.

Throughout the signing, Dr. Walter Eytan, head of the Israel delegation, sat with an unlighted pipe in his mouth. When the signatures were affixed, he pulled out a match and lighted his pipe. Colonel Seif ed-Din, leader of the Egyptian delegation, wiped his glasses and then also lighted a cigarette.

Final Peace Settlement Not Seen as Urgent

By Our Diplomatic Correspondent
Copyright, The Palestine Post

Ha'KIRYA, Thursday. — Satisfaction at the signing of the armistice agreement with Egypt has probably been slightly marred by the nature of the conversations this afternoon between the members of the Conciliation Commission and the Foreign Minister, Mr. Shertok.

No report of the conversations has been issued, but from hints let fall unofficially and from the carefully guarded statement made to the press by Mr. Ethridge, one gathers that the Commission came to Tel Aviv holding the view that no final settlement between Israel and the Arab States was possible without a prior agreement on the part of Israel to take back all Arab refugees desiring to return.

It is understood that the Government here has not changed its stated policy on this question. It is believed to regard the refugee problem as one which can only be satisfactorily solved within a scheme for the exchange of populations, and to regard the wholesale return of refugees as re-creating the conditions of instability and potential strife of which agitators among the Arabs have from time to time made so much use.

Scheme for Resettlement

The Government is believed to be willing to contribute, in relation to its capacity and within the ultimate arrangements for the satisfaction of rightful claims on both sides, to an international scheme for the resettlement of the refugees.

One gathers also that the Arab States take the view that once armistice agreements have been signed, the final peace settlement need not be regarded as a matter of urgency. It is noted that the agreement signed at Rhodes between Israel and Egypt leaves the time factor indeterminate, and that there is nothing to prevent this instrument remaining in force for a period of many years.

On the other hand, Mr. Shertok's statement to the press this morning suggests that he is hopeful of settling political problems with Egypt step by step, and it is probable that Mr. Sassoon's visit to Paris will be at least partly with the object of sounding out the Egyptian Government, through its emissaries there, on outstanding matters of a political nature, including the refugee problem.

A further promising sign is the fact that direct formal talks at Rhodes beween Israel delegates and the Egyptian Foreign Office observers who were attached in an advisory capacity to the official delegation were many and fruitful.

It is understood that the

(Continued on Page 4 Col. 1)

Full Text of Armistice Agreement

PREAMBLE

THE Parties to the present Agreement, responding to the Security Council resolution of 16 November 1948 calling upon them, as a further provisional measure under Article 40 of the Charter of the United Nations and in order to facilitate the transition from the present truce to permanent peace in Palestine, to negotiate an Armistice; having decided to enter into negotiations under United Nations Chairmanship concerning the implementation of the Security Council resolutions of 4 and 16 November 1948; and having appointed representatives empowered to negotiate and conclude an Armistice Agreement;

THE undersigned representatives, in the full authority entrusted to them by their respective Governments, have agreed upon the following provisions:

ARTICLE I

With a view to promoting the return of permanent peace in Palestine and in recognition of the importance in this regard of mutual assurances concerning the future military operations of the Parties, the following principles, which shall be fully observed by both Parties during the Armistice, are hereby affirmed:

1. The injunction of the Security Council against resort to military force in the settlement of the Palestine question shall henceforth be scrupulously respected by both Parties.
2. No aggressive action by the armed forces — land, sea, or air — of either Party shall be undertaken, planned, or threatened against the people or the armed forces of the other; it being understood that the use of the term "planned" in this context has no bearing on normal staff planning as generally practised in military organizations.
3. The right of each Party to its security and freedom from fear of attack by the armed forces of the other shall be fully respected.
4. The establishment of an armistice between the armed forces of the two Parties is accepted as an indispensable step toward the liquidation of armed conflict and the resoration of peace in Palestine.

ARTICLE II

1. In pursuance of the foregoing principles and of the resolutions of the Security Council of 4 and 16 November 1948, a general Armistice between the armed forces of the two Parties —land, sea and air—is hereby established.

2. No element of the land, sea or air military or para-military forces of either Party, including non-regular forces, shall commit any warlike or hostile act against the military or para-military forces of the other Party, or against civilians in territory under the control of that Party; or shall advance beyond or pass over for any purpose whatsoever the Armistice Demarcation Line set forth in Article VI of this Agreement except as provided in Article III of this Agreement; and elsewhere shall not violate the international frontier; or enter into or pass through the air space of the other Party or through the waters within three miles of the coastline of the other Party.

ARTICLE III

1. In pursuance of the Security Council's resolution of 4 November 1948, and with a view to the implementation of the Security Council's resolution of 16 November 1948, the Egyptian Military Forces in the AL FALUJA area shall be withdrawn.

2. This withdrawal shall begin on the day after that which follows the signing of this Agreement, at 0500 hours GMT, and shall be beyond the Egypt-Palestine frontier.

3. The withdrawal shall be under the supervision of the United Nations and in accordance with the Plan of Withdrawal set forth in Annex I to this Agreement.

ARTICLE IV

With specific reference to the implementation of the resolutions of the Security Council of 4 and 16 November 1948, the following principles and purposes are affirmed:

1. The principle that no military or political advantage should be gained under the truce ordered by the Security Council is recognized.
2. It is also recognized that the basic purposes and spirit of the Armistice would not be served by the restoration of previously held military positions, changes from those now held other than as specifically provided for in this Agreement, or by the advance of the military forces of either side beyond positions held at the time this Armistice Agreement is signed.
3. It is further recognized that rights, claims or interests of a non-military character in the area of Palestine covered by this Agreement may be asserted by either Party, and that these, by mutual agreement being excluded from the Armistice negotiations, shall be, at the discretion of the Parties, the subject of later settlement. It is emphasized that it is not the purpose of this Agreement to establish, to recognize, to strengthen, or to weaken or nullify, in any way, any territorial, custodial or other rights, claims or interests which may be asserted by either Party in the area of Palestine or any part or locality thereof covered by this Agreement, whether such asserted rights, claims or interests derive from Security Council resolutions, including the resolution of 4 November 1948 and the Memorandum of 13 November 1948 for its implementation, or from any other source. The provisions of this Agreement are dictated exclusively by military considerations and are valid only for the period of the Armistice.

ARTICLE V

1. The line described in Article VI of this Agreement shall be designated as the Armistice Demarcation Line and is delineated in pursuance of the purpose and intent of the resolutions of the Security Council of 4 and 16 November 1948.

2. The Armistice Demarcation Line is not to be construed in any sense as a political or territorial boundary, and is delineated without prejudice to rights, claims and positions of either Party to the Armistice as regards ultimate settlement of the Palestine question.

3. The basic purpose of the Armistice Demarcation Line is to delineate the line beyond which the armed forces of the respective Parties shall not move except as provided in Article III of this Agreement.

4. Rules and regulations of the armed forces of the Parties, which prohibit civilians from crossing the fighting lines or entering the area between the lines, shall remain in effect after the signing of this Agreement with application to the Armistice Demarcation Line defined in Article VI.

ARTICLE VI

1. In the GAZA-RAFAH area the Armistice Demarcation Line shall be as delineated in paragraph 2.B(i) of the Memorandum of 13 November 1948 on the implementation of the Security Council resolution of 4 November 1948, namely by a line from the coast at the mouth of Wadi Hasi in an easterly direction through Deir Suneid and across the Gaza-Al Majdal Highway to a point 3 kilometers east of the Highway, then in a southerly direction parallel to the Gaza-Al Majdal Highway, and continuing thus to the Egyptian frontier.

2. Within this line Egyptian forces shall nowhere advance beyond their present positions, and this shall include Beit Hanun and its surrounding area from which Israeli forces shall be withdrawn to north of the Armistice Demarcation Line, and any other positions within the line delineated in paragraph 1 which shall be evacuated by Israeli forces as set forth in paragraph 3.

3. Israeli outposts, each limited to platoon strength, may be maintained in this area at the following points: Deir Suneid, on the north side of the Wadi (MR 10751090); 700 X SW of Sa'ad (MR 10500982); Sulphur Quarries (MR 09870924); Tall-Jamma (MR 09720887); and KH AL Ma'in (MR 09320821). The Israeli outpost maintained at the Cemetery (MR 08160723) shall be evacuated on the day after that which follows the signing of this Agreement. The Israeli outpost at Hill 79 (MR 10451017) shall be evacuated not later than four weeks following the day on which this Agreement is signed. Following the evacuation of the above outposts, new Israeli outposts may be established at MR 08360700, and at a point due east of Hill 79 east of the Armistice Demarcation Line.

4. In the BETHLEHEM-HEBRON area, wherever positions are held by Egyptian forces, the

(Continued on Page 2, Col. 2)

THE PALESTINE POST

JERUSALEM
Monday, April 4, 1949

PRICE: 30 MILS
VOL. XXV. No. 6979

Column One
By David Courtney

THE Atlantic Pact will be signed today. Portugal, Italy and Norway will sign alongside the U.S.A., Great Britain, France, and the Benelux Group. An armed attack against any one of these signatories will in future be regarded as an attack against them all. For that matter, an armed attack against any Atlantic territory (including the Western Zones of Germany) north of the Tropic of Cancer, where the interests of any one of the signatories are involved, may prove to be enough to set the atom ball rolling. What constitutes an armed attack is not clearly defined; but from today, the risk of war becomes not less but more. That is to say, warlike circumstances which normally would be localized, now introduce the risk of an invocation, by a signatory of the Atlantic Pact, of the terms and awful commitments of the Pact. For example, serious trouble in Trieste might with some show of reason be attributed to Soviet Russia who might then be declared as aggressor by Italy. The other signatories, doubtless, would argue Italy out of her invocation, but in the process we would come near to world war. What it means is that tension, henceforth, will sharpen; and that the world will be on perpetual tenterhooks.

■ AT the best, the Atlantic Pact must confirm the cold war. Soviet Russia, against whom the alliance has been formed, is unlikely to surrender to a treaty. The Russian people are different in many fundamental respects from the German people; but not in their readiness to react with nationalistic loyalty to what their Government can show to be an imperialist attempt to encircle Russia and the "new democracies" and to build up an aggressive alliance against them. Any action of a preventive nature which Russia might feel called upon to take as a result of the Atlantic Pact would be likely to have the whole of the Russian and East European peoples behind it, not to mention the considerable mass of pro-Soviet opinion in Germany, Italy and France.

■ THE official Soviet complaint against the Pact may be exaggerated; but it is not without solid basis. Abundant references in the Pact, and by its sponsors, to the United Nations, are not enough to do away with the charge that the alliance contravenes the U.N. Charter. These abundant references are an attempt to define the powers of U.N. to suit the Pact. It is claimed that the Pact comes within the meaning of Articles 51 and 52 of the U.N. Charter, which allow for regional groupings intended to provide collective security. On the other hand, the Charter requires that such regional groupings, and above all any decisions they may take, shall have the authorisation of the Security Council. It is clear that the sponsors of the Atlantic Pact have no intention of consulting the Security Council and risking the Soviet Veto either now or in the event of a decision to go to war. In short, it would seem that the signatories of the Atlantic Pact have taken over from the U.N. the right to decide what is or is not an act of aggression against any of them.

■ WHAT, now, will the Soviet do? It will probably not take the preventive action which many people fear, except in the diplomatic field. It is almost certain to do everything it can, from the Elbe to the Yangtze, to draw together a military alliance which, barring America's atomic weapon, may look as good on paper as the Atlantic Pact. It may attempt to being the new alliance before U.N., if for no other reason than to air its views in public; and whatever U.N. may do about it, the Soviet will almost certainly continue to be a member and to try to show itself faithful to the Charter. But the chief worry is not what the Soviet will do, but what will be brought about by mere international accident, now that the West has discarded the restrictions of U.N.

Tel Aviv, April 4.

ATLANTIC PACT SIGNING TODAY

WASHINGTON, Sunday (Reuter).— The stage is now set for tomorrow's signing of the North Atlantic Pact.

The Foreign Ministers of the 12 North Atlantic Powers formally approved the text of the Pact without alteration when they met here together for the first time yesterday.

They issued at the same time a joint reply rejecting the Russian note criticizing the Pact, which they emphasized, was "of a completely defensive nature."

The Pact was "not directed against any nation or group of nations, but only against armed aggression", they said. It conforms "with both the spirit and letter of the U.N. Charter"

Yesterday's meeting, in the auditorium where the signing ceremony will take place tomorrow, was attended by the Foreign Ministers of Belgium, Canada, Denmark, France, Iceland, Italy, Luxembourg, the Netherlands, Norway, Portugal, the U.K. and the U.S. Secretary of State.

They will sign in that alphabetic order tomorrow, M. Paul-Henri Spaak, of Belgium, being the first to put his name to the document.

GREECE ON AGENDA OF WASHINGTON TALKS

By GEORGE LICHTHEIM.
Copyright, The Palestine Post

LONDON, Sunday. — Although Greece is not a member of the Atlantic Pact, its problems are on the agenda of the current Washington talks. Observers here believe that Anglo-American diplomacy will increasingly concentrate on whittling down whatever support the rebels are still receiving from Marshal Tito. Such support has declined but a trickle is still going through.

Albania is, however, fast becoming the main operations base against Greece, while the Greek rebel movement itself is gradually assuming a new character. Broadcast appeals are now being made on behalf of the "National Leberation Front of Macedonia" to Macedonian people in Greece and Yugoslavia. These appeals have a definitely anti-Yugoslav character and represent an intensification of the Soviet-directed campaign against Tito.

Diplomats here are convinced that the guerrilla movement is no longer aiming at the capture of all Greece, and is now directed against Belgrade as much as against Athens. As this campaign develops, the chances of securing Yugoslav neutrality in the Greek internal struggle are increasing.

Against East and West

Considerable attention has been given to Marshal Tito's remark, addressed to a delegation of Croats, Slovenes and Italians who visited him at Brioni yesterday. While repudiating the rumours of secret negotiations with Britain and America, he took the opportunity of referring to the "lies and calumnies" spread against Yugoslavia "both in Western Capitalist and Eastern Socialist States." This juxtaposition is unusual and in the opinion of observers here portends the gradual establishment of a neutral position, although both Marshal Tito and his chief lieutenants continue to refer to Yugoslavia as a member of the Socialist camp.

Rumours of possible Bulgarian or Hungarian military action against Tito are discounted here. Military quarters are convinced that the Yugoslav Army represents the only real force in south-eastern Europe and could easily deal with foreign incursions, unless disaffection in Macedonia went much further than seems likely. That sheer self-preservation will shortly compel Greece and Yugoslavia to cooperate, at least passively, is no longer doubted.

ATTEMPTED COUP IN COSTA RICA

SAN JOSE, Sunday (AP). — Costa Rican rebels surrendered this morning after a short lived attempt to overthrow Senor Jose Figueres' Government. The last group of rebels in Bella Vista barracks surrendered after heavy bombardment.

Eye witnesses said that many dead and wounded were carried from the barracks after the surrender, but so far there has been no official estimate of the casualties.

The Security Minister in the Costa Rican Government, Colonel Edgar Cardona, seized two public buildings in San Jose yesterday afternoon, while the President established anti-revolt headquarters at the Pacific Railway terminal and kept control of the city's airport.

NEW E.R.P. LOANS ANNOUNCED

WASHINGTON, Sunday (AP). — On the eve of the expiry of its present funds, the Economic Cooperation Administration today announced new loans totalling $29 m. under the European Recovery Programme to Sweden, Belgium and Turkey, to finance the purchase of recovery commodities.

Under the agreements worked out with the Government by the ECA and the Export-Import Bank, Turkey will borrow $8 m. The loans are in addition to outright foreign aid grants made by the ECA under provisions of the ERP.

40 SENTENCED TO DEATH IN GREECE

ATHENS, Sunday (AP). — Twenty-eight guerrillas captured during recent operations in the Peloponnesus were sentenced to death, some of them on three or four counts, by a Military Tribunal at Tripolis today for participation in armed Communist guerrilla bands, sabotage or slaying.

Twelve saboteurs were also sentenced to death by a Military Tribunal in Athens today. All members of OPLA, a Communist execution squad, they were found guilty of setting fire to a Government garage near Athens last year.

U.S. LEGATION MAN KILLED

DAMASCUS, Sunday (UP). — The police reported today that Mr. William Parker, First Secretary of the American Legation here, was killed yesterday when his jeep ran off the road and plunged into the Barada River in Damascus.

ISRAEL'S ENTRY EXPECTED SOON

LAKE SUCCESS, Sunday (AP). — Most diplomats at Lake Success predict that Israel will become the 59th U.N. Member in the early days of the General Assembly session opening next Tuesday.

Little opposition is expected outside the delegations for the six Arab countries and perhaps the British. A spokesman indicated that Britain still was not satisfied that Israel should be admitted to the U.N. now. It was not known, however, whether she would abstain or vote No.

The date of the final vote has not yet been set. This is one of the questions to be considered by the Assembly's 14-nation Steering Committee as soon as the session begins. The normal practice is for the Steering Committee to send Council-approved membership bids direct to a plenary meeting of the Assembly for final action.

It is possible that either the Steering Committee or the Assembly itself may send the application to the 58-nation political Committee for a full debate, but this is considered unlikely.

Mr. Moshe Sharett, Israel's Foreign Minister, is in the U.S. at the moment. If Israel is admitted, he will act as head of the Israel delegation during the remainder of the session.

Britons Lobby

By JESSE ZEL LURIE
Copyright, The Palestine Post

LAKE SUCCESS, Sunday. — The British delegation is increasing its lobbying to postpone the vote on Israel's admission to the U.N., stating that Burma should be the first item on the Assembly's agenda.

The British argument is that admission should be held back as a club to secure concessions from Israel on the question of Jerusalem and the refugees.

It is understood that the Conciliation Commission is cooperating by sending revisions to its earlier report which was couched in generalities.

ARABS DISCUSS SITUATION

BEIRUT, Sunday. — The delegates to the Conciliation Commission's conference met at the Lebanese Foreign Office today to discuss the Syrian situation and their own answer to the choice of a neutral country for an Israeli-Arab meeting. No final decision was taken, but it was generally agreed that the Syrian coup d'état was a purely internal question.

Reuters reports that the Arab countries were last night said to be split over their attitude to the P.C.C.'s invitation to meet Israel representatives "on neutral ground" for a "further exchange of views."

Syria, Egypt and Saudi Arabia were reported likely to decline the invitation, because it would "imply recognition of the State of Israel". Iraq, the Lebanon and Trans-Jordan were said to be in favour.

One U.N. official said last night that the Commission would remain in Beirut for a few more days to "clear the work up" before leaving for Tel Aviv in mid-week to consult the Israel Government.

CURFEW LIFTED IN SYRIA

DAMASCUS, Sunday. — The Syrian curfew was lifted today in all parts of the country except Damascus, where it will remain in force nightly between 10 p.m. and 7 a.m.

Two high-ranking Egyptian officers were expected here by special plane today with a message from King Farouk to Colonel el Zaim.

A message promising the support of the entire Jebel Druze area was today conveyed to Colonel el Zaim by the el Atrash family. Observers take this as a sign that el Zaim's movement has the backing of King Abdullah.

The Trans-Jordan Premier, Tewfik Abul Huda, is expected to visit Cairo shortly, accompanied by the Defence Minister, Fawzi Pasha el Mulki, to confer with the Egyptian Government on the recent events in Syria, according to an AFP message from Amman.

First Broadcast

Colonel el Zaim tonight made his first broadcast, in the name of the new Syria." He said that the freedom and liberty enjoyed by the people of Syria was due to the courage and bravery of the army, "who elevated the name of their country in the recent battles in Palestine."

He thanked the people for their support and said he was deeply moved by the sympathetic attitude of foreign powers to the new regime. Addressing the countrypeople of Syria, he said that he was always ready to hear their complaints, but said that he would "strike" hard against Communist and demoralising elements," while endeavouring to improve the standard of living by progressive labour legislation.

In conclusion, Col. Zaim pledged Syria's support for the Lebanon and said he would continue to support the Arab League and all international bodies and organizations.

(AP, UP, Reuter and AFP)

Approved Without Reservation

By RUTH CALE
Copyright, The Palestine Post

RHODES, Sunday. — It was a solemn moment when Colonel Ahmed el Jundi and Mr. Reuven Shiloah told Dr. Ralph Bunche that they "approved this general armistice without reservation" and then smilingly affixed their signatures on Page 17 of the black leather-bound book passed them by Senior U.N. staff officers.

Colonel el Jundi wrote his name in careful Latin letters, while Lieut.-Col. Mohammed Muaytah scribbled swiftly in Arabic, and both Mr. Shiloah and Sgan-Aloof Moshe Dayan signed both in Hebrew and Latin characters.

Dr. Bunche read a prepared congratulatory speech, but did not always stick to his text: but he called the Trans-Jordanians the Hashemite Kingdom of Jordania, which may be interpreted as U.N. recognition of King Abdullah's claim to Eastern Palestine.

SYRIAN TALKS TOMORROW

RHODES, Sunday (UP). — United Nations officials reported here today that Col. Husni el-Za'im, who assumed power in Syria last week, has agreed to negotiate an armistice with Israel.

Brig.-Gen. William Riley, U.N. Chief of Staff, has informed the Acting Mediator, Dr. Ralph Bunche, that Col. Za'im has agreed to start the negotiations on Tuesday.

The Near East Arab Broadcasting Station said yesterday that the signing of the Israel-Trans-Jordan armistice marked an important step towards peace in Palestine and the solution of the Arab refugees problem.

"It must be admitted that Israel cannot accept back all the refugees, owing to the present high rate of Jewish immigration...The blame for the present plight of the refugees is not all Jewish; it must not be forgotten that the Arab Higher Committee encouraged the refugees to flee from their homes in Jaffa, Haifa and Jerusalem, and that certain Arab leaders have tried to make political capital out of their miserable situation."

Job Finished, Team Goes Home

RHODES, Sunday (UP).— Dr. Ralph Bunche gave a dinner here tonight to celebrate the signing of the armistice. U.N. officials scoured the island for wine, and the acting Mediator finally cabled to Haifa, asking for champagne to be flown over.

The U.N. team will begin to disperse tomorrow. Brigadier-General Riley is flying to Syria shortly to help in the Israel-Syrian talks, and Dr. Bunche is to fly to Beirut on Tuesday for consultation with the Conciliation Commission. He will then go on to Paris and possibly Stockholm to visit the widow of the late Count Bernadotte. After that, he will return to his home in the U.S., his mediation task done.

TRANS-JORDAN ARMISTICE SIGNED
Triangle, Latrun, Scopus, Holy Sites All Included

RHODES, Sunday. — The Israel-Trans-Jordan armistice agreement was signed here at 7.30 local time tonight, ending a month of negotiations.

The agreement, which is valid for a year and renewable thereafter, calls for a reduction of forces to a distance of 10 kilometres from each side of the demarcation lines "except where geographical considerations make this impracticable."

A special Joint Armistice Commission is to be set up "to enlarge the scope of this agreement and to provide improvements in its application." The Commission is to supervise, among other things: free movement on the Bethlehem and Latrun roads; the opening of the road to Mount Scopus and the Jewish cemetery on the Mount of Olives; the operation of the Latrun pumping station and the provision of electricity to the Old City, the resumption of operation of the railway to Jerusalem and free access to the Holy Places.

In addition, the front lines are to be rectified to give Israel the Wadi Ara road and the road and railway running west of Tulkarm-Kalkiliya, in exchange for "substantial concessions in the Hebron area."

The Akaba area is not specified by name in the agreement. Iraqi forces in the "triangle" come under the complete control of the Arab Legion.

After the signatures were penned, Colonel Jundi, speaking Arabic, extended "deep thanks" to Dr. Bunche and his staff. Mr. Shiloah replied and the Acting Mediator's efforts to get the two sides to confer without a mediator. He continued:

This has always been our contention: we believe that this is the only way to solve problems in the Middle East. Mr. Shiloah expressed appreciation for "our friends of the Trans-Jordan delegation for personal friendly relations and their sincere desire to reach a peaceful settlement."

After 55 minutes, Dr. Bunche's gavel came down in general exodus is to begin tomorrow after which will probably be an all-night celebration in the hotel's ballroom.

"ZIONIST ATTACK" ALLEGED

AMMAN, Sunday (AFP). — "Zionist forces" last night attacked Iraqi forward positions in the region of Jaljuliya, it is claimed here. Supported by mortar fire, the attack is reported to have continued until dawn, when it was repulsed by Iraqi forces.

The Iraqi Defence Minister, Shaker el Wadi, and the Chief of Staff Saleh Sa'eb, have left Amman for Baghdad after conferring with the Trans-Jordan authorities.

It is understood that the situation in the Triangle was discussed.

Full Text of Agreement

PREAMBLE

The Parties to the Agreement,

Responding to the Security Council's Resolution of 16 November, 1948, calling upon them, as a further provisional measure under Article 40 of the Charter of the U.N. and in order to facilitate the transition from the present truce to permanent peace in Palestine, to negotiate an armistice;

Having decided to enter into negotiations under U.N. Chairmanship concerning the implementation of the Security Council Resolution of 16 November, 1948; and having appointed representatives empowered to negotiate and conclude an armistice agreement;

The undersigned representatives of their respective Governments, having exchanged their full powers found to be in good and proper form, have agreed upon the following provisions:

ARTICLE ONE

With a view to promoting the return of permanent peace in Palestine and in recognition of the importance in this regard of mutual assurances concerning the future military operations of the parties, the following principles, which shall be fully observed by both parties during the armistice, are hereby affirmed:

1. The injunction of the Security Council against resort to military force in the settlement of the Palestine question shall henceforth be scrupulously respected by both parties.

2. No aggressive action by the armed forces — land, sea or air — of either party shall be undertaken, planned, or threatened against the people or the armed forces of the other; it being understood that the use of the term planned in this context has no bearing on normal staff planning as generally practised in military organisations.

3. The right of each party to its security and freedom from fear of attacks by the armed forces of the other shall be fully respected.

4. The establishment of an armistice between the armed forces of the two parties is accepted as an indispensable step toward the liquidation of armed conflict and the restoration of peace in Palestine.

ARTICLE TWO

With a specific view to the implementation of the Resolution of the Security Council of 16 November, 1948 the following principles and purposes are affirmed:

1. The principle that no military or political advantage should be gained under the truce ordered by the Security Council is recognised.

2. It is also recognized that no provision of this agreement shall in any way prejudice the rights, claims and positions of either party hereto in the ultimate peace settlement of the Palestine question, the provisions of this agreement being dictated exclusively by military considerations.

ARTICLE THREE

1. In pursuance of the foregoing principles and of the Resolution of the Security Council of 16 November, 1948, a general armistice between the armed forces of the two Parties — land, sea and air — is hereby established.

2. No element of the land, sea and air military or para-military forces of either Party, including non-regular forces, shall commit any warlike or hostile act against the military or para-military forces of the other Party, or against civilians in territory under control of that Party; or shall advance beyond or pass-over for any purpose whatsoever the Armistice Demarcation Line set forth in Articles Five and Six of this agreement; or enter into or pass through the air space of the other Party.

3. No warlike act or act of hostility shall be conducted from territory controlled by one of the Parties to this Agreement against the other Party.

ARTICLE FOUR

1. The lines described in Articles Five and Six of this agreement shall be designated as the Armistice Demarcation Line and are delineated in pursuance of the purpose and intent of the Resolution of the Security Council of 16 November, 1948.

2. The basic purpose of the Armistice Demarcation Line is to delineate the line beyond which the armed forces of the respective Parties shall not move.

3. Rules and regulations of the armed forces of the Parties, which prohibit civilians from crossing the fighting lines or entering the area between the lines, shall remain in effect after the signing of this agreement with application to the Armistice Demarcation Line defined in Articles Five and Six.

ARTICLE FIVE

1. The Armistice Demarcation Lines for all sectors other than the sector held by Iraqi forces, shall be as delineated on the map in Annex 1 to this Agreement, and shall be defined as follows:

a. In the sector Kh. Deir 'Arab (MR159—1574) to the northern terminus of the line defined in the 30th November, 1948, Cease-Fire Agreement for the Jerusalem area, the Armistice Demarcation Line shall follow the truce line as certified by the U.N. Supervision Organisation.

b. In the Jerusalem sector, the Armistice Demarcation Line shall correspond to the lines defined in the 30th November, 1948, Cease-Fire Agreement for the Jerusalem area.

c. In the Hebron-Dead Sea sector, the Armistice Demarcation Line shall be delineated on Map 1 and marked "B" in annex 1 to this Agreement.

d. In the sector from a point on the Dead Sea (Mr1925-0928) to the southernmost tip of Palestine, the Armistice Demarcation Line shall be determined by existing military positions as surveyed in March, 1949, by United Nations Observers, and shall run from north to south as delineated on Map 1 Annex 1 to this Agreement.

ARTICLE SIX

1. It is agreed that the forces of the Hashemite Jordan Kingdom shall replace the forces of Iraq in the sector now held by the latter forces, the intention of the Government of Iraq in this regard having been communicated to the Acting Mediator in the message of March 20 from the Foreign Minister of Iraq authorizing a delegation of the Hashemite Jordan Kingdom to negotiate for the Iraqi forces and stating that those forces would be withdrawn.

2. The Armistice Demarcation Line for the sector now held by Iraqi forces shall be as delineated on Map 1 in Annex 1 to this Agreement and marked "A".

3. The Armistice Demarcation Line provided for in paragraph 2 of this Article shall be established as follows, pending which the existing military lines may be maintained:

a. In the area west of the road from Baqa to Jaljulia and thence to the east of Kafr Qasim within five weeks of the date on which this Armistice Agreement is signed.

b. In the area of Wadi Ara north of the line from Baqa to Zubeiba: within seven weeks of the date on which this Armistice Agreement is signed.

c. In all other areas of the Iraqi sector: within 15 weeks of the date on which this Armistice Agreement is signed.

4. The Armistice Demarca-

tion Line in the Hebron-Dead Sea sector, referred to in Paragraph C of Article Five of this Agreement and marked "B" on Map 1 in Annex 1, which involves substantial deviation from the existing military line in favour of the forces of the Hashemite Jordan Kingdom, is designed to offset the modification of the existing military line in the Iraqi sector set forth in Paragraph 3 of this Article.

5. In compensation for the road acquired between Tulkarm and Qalqilya the Government of Israel agrees to pay to the Government of the Hashemite Jordan Kingdom the cost of constructing 20 kilometres of first class new road.

6. Wherever villages may be affected by the establishment of the Armistice Demarcation Line provided for in Paragraph 2 of this Article, the inhabitants of such villages shall be entitled to maintain, and shall be protected in, their full rights of residence, property and freedom. In the event that any inhabitants should decide to leave their villages, they shall be entitled to take with them their livestock and other movable property, and to receive without delay full compensation for the land which they have left. It shall be prohibited for Israeli forces to enter or to be stationed in such villages, in which locally recruited Arab police shall be organized and stationed for internal security purposes.

7. The Hashemite Jordan Kingdom accepts responsibility for all Iraqi forces in Palestine.

8. The provisions of this Article shall not be interpreted as prejudicing, in any sense, any ultimate political settlement between the Parties to this agreement.

9. The Armistice Demarcation Line defined in Articles Five and Six of this Agreement are agreed upon by the Parties without prejudice to future territorial settlement or boundary lines or to claims of either Party relating thereto.

10. Except where otherwise provided, the Armistice Demarcation Line shall be established, including such withdrawal of forces as may be

(Continued on Page 2, Col. 3)

8 DAYS TO THE DRAW
להגרלה
היום הזה אתה
OF THE POPULAR LOAN

SUNDAY, JULY 22, 1951

THE JERUSALEM POST

PRICE: 35 PRUTA
VOL. XXVII. No. 7314

Marginal Column

By "COMMENTATOR"

FIGURES recently published in Moscow show that in most fields Soviet industrial and agricultural developments are going according to plan. There is, however, one project which has not been completed, and somebody will be called to account for it one of these days. The Communist party executive decided early in 1946 that Josef Stalin's writings were to be published in 16 volumes. Every two or three months a new volume was to appear, and the series should have been completed some time in 1949. When this deadline arrived, the editors (headed by Molotov) were somewhat behind schedule; they had only produced 12 volumes.

■

SIX months passed, war broke out in Korea, and General Razmara was killed. Two years after the deadline, there was no indication that Volume 13 of Joseph Vissarionovitch Stalin's works was soon to appear. Thirteen is considered an unlucky number by many people, but it would be preposterous to assume that good Leninist-Stalinists would be influenced by popular superstition. The real reason for this most unexpected delay was the considerable difficulty involved in the publication of the works of the Soviet leader.

■

THE works do not contain everything Stalin ever said or wrote. They are a well-edited and frequently rewritten selection of those of his writings which can serve as a basis for Soviet ideology today. Why should Stalin be compelled to re-issue those articles and speeches which contained mistaken views? If he wrote for instance (on November 7, 1918) that Trotsky was the man chiefly responsible for the Russian revolution or if he congratulated Hitler as the beloved leader of the German people (September, 1939) or if he declared that England and the U.S. were very democratic states and that those who vilified them as "plutocrats" were mere fascists (November 6, 1941)—why should these statements be recorded in the new edition?

■

THE other day Volume 13 suddenly appeared in Moscow bookshops and "Pravda" devoted one and a half of its four pages to this historic event; and "Izvestia" was not to be outdone. Searching for the reason for the delay, one finds scores of debatable political points, for 1930-34 were very interesting years.

■

DOES Stalin believe that a third world war could be prevented? His answer was in the affirmative, when a "Pravda" correspondent asked him last February. His writings and speeches show, however, that literally dozens of times he had dwelt on the inevitability of further world wars. He told "Comerad Ivanov" for instance in 1938: "The co-existence of the Soviet Union and the Imperialist states is unthinkable for the duration. A series of terrible clashes will occur before the end comes." More recently, in February, 1946 Stalin said: "The Second World War was not incidental and cannot be explained as a result of the mistakes of diplomats. It was the inevitable result of the development of the political and economic forces on the basis of monopoly capitalism..."

Truce Talks Off Till Wednesday

TOKYO, Saturday (Reuter). — The U.N. cease-fire team arrived in Tokyo by air tonight to discuss with General Ridgway the latest developments in the armistice talks at Kaesong, now recessed for three days. The delegates acceded to the Communist request for a break until July 25, but gave notice they would still refuse to agree on the inclusion on the agenda of the withdrawal of foreign troops from Korea.

A report from the U.N. Advanced Camp said the Communists wanted the adjournment to give them time to consider the U.N. stand on this point and other controversial issues.

The Chief Allied delegate, Vice-Admiral Charles Turner Joy, told the Communists he had no need of a recess to reconsider the U.N. position and an Allied statement described the adjournment as unnecessary "in view of the agreement reached on points necessary for an agenda."

After the return of the delegates from the eighth session of the talks, a spokesman aknowledged officially for the first time that the conference had been unable to agree on the withdrawal of "foreign troops" from Korea.

Complete Agenda

Admiral Joy conferred with General Ridgway immediately on his arrival in Tokyo. The General was reported by reliable sources neither optimistic nor pessimistic over the new turn of events.

At the brief one hour meeting today Admiral Joy told the Communists he felt the items already agreed upon by the two delegations were a complete agenda and that the conference should proceed with the task of arranging an end to the shooting war in Korea.

The U.N. stand seemed to leave it in Communist hands whether the talks would break down or whether they would retreat from their demand for a discussion of the withdrawal of foreign troops.

It was noticed that last night and during today the Communist radio stopped their earlier frequent references to Communist insistence on the withdrawal of foreign troops as an essential point for consideration.

According to U.N. officers present at today's session the two Chinese Communist delegates took a leading role in the discussion for the first time. They interrupted the discussion twice to hold private consultations without their North Korean colleagues. General Nam Il, the Chief North Korean delegate, appeared tense and relatively subdued, the officers said.

The Communist representatives asked for assurances that they could travel freely between Kaesong and Pyongyang, the North Korean Capital, without being attacked by aircraft. The U.N. delegation guaranteed this on condition the Communist gave notice of their movements during the next few days and distinctly marked their vehicles.

Admiral Joy asked that radio contact between the two delegations be maintained in the event of the Communists wishing to resume talks here on Wednesday.

The briefing officer said after the meeting: "No tangible progress was made — yet I think it would be erroneous to say no progress was made. There was a general air of reasonableness about the Communist delegation."

He said Admiral Joy was patient and resigned. "He wasn't brusque but there seemed to be a certain air of finality in his general attitude," he added.

ELECTION ROUNDUP:

'Citizens of Israel First'

TEL AVIV, Saturday.—"You can't stop speaking Hungarian overnight, but you should now think of yourselves in the first place as Jews and citizens of Israel," Mr. Ben Gurion said, addressing a Mapai meeting of Hungarian Immigrants' Associations in Tel Aviv.

Referring to the differences within Hungarian Jewry, Mr. Ben Gurion recalled that both Herzl and Stampfer (who founded the first agricultural settlement at Petah Tikvah 75 years ago) were born in Hungary. Mass immigration, he said, would not cause unemployment, because immigrants brought with them their creative abilities. The lag between present needs and rising production would be overcome with the help of Jews in the Diaspora. Welcoming the Prime Minister, Dr. J. Kastner said that Hungary's 100,000 Jews waited for the opportunity to come to Israel.

Mr. Ben Gurion had cut short his visit to Kfar Saba when the news of King Abdullah's assassination was brought to him by special messenger.

Dollar or Rouble

Within a few days, 20,000 persons had registered for the popular housing scheme, stated Mrs. Golda Myerson, speaking before a capacity crowd this morning. Mapai had always supported mass immigration, but the General Zionists were frightened of it. Turning to Mapam, Mrs. Myerson recalled that Dr. Sneh had shortly before the U.N. decision in 1947 declared that an independent State was Utopian and had advocated a mandated regime under a triumvirate of a U.S., British, and Soviet High Commissioner.

Contrary to the Kremlin itself, he seemed to prefer the Russian rouble to the U.S. dollar.

Mass immigration was a bloodless revolution proceeding at a much lower price than any revolution in history, said Mr. P. Lavon, Minister of Agriculture. There could be no slackening in the Ingathering process. The Mapam trend towards the Cominform was unacceptable, if only because it would lead to severance from Jews in free countries. Similar to Mapam, the old veterans in the General Zionist Party found themselves today in opposition to other groups, notably the rightist capitalists of Ihud Ezrahi, and the Club of the "Jeunesse Doree." It was no mean achievement that within the last year water supply for irrigation had been doubled and no one was hungry.

Addressing a huge open-air rally in the new immigrants' housing area near Rishon le Zion on Friday night, Mr. M. Sharett delivered five separate addresses in five languages — Yiddish, Turkish, Arabic, French and Hebrew.

Mr. Sharett's Iraqi listeners were warned, particularly, against the Communist Party, which Mr. Sharett described as the "inveterate enemy of Zionism."

He admonished his listeners from Turkey and North Africa not to be misled by those who were fomenting communal discord instead of fostering national unity.

In Haifa, yesterday morning, at the Orah Cinema, Mr. Sharett spoke to a large audience of women. They were crossing (he said) a stormy sea, and there were many who were suffering ill effects. They should not, however, allow this to turn them against the navigators.

"You have a skilful captain and a brave and loyal crew," he said.

"If you change them in mid-voyage something far worse may befall you than mere sea-sickness. Your ship may founder and you may not reach haven at all. Remember that when the ship rocks, it is the fault of the storm and not of the capain."

Last night Mr. Sharett

(Continued on Page 2, Col. 1)

AFTER MIDNIGHT

M. Rene Meyer, Radical leader, informed President Auriol late last night that he would ask the French Parliament to confirm his Premiership as head of a right-wing and centre coalition.

Murder of Arab King Shock to World
Amman in Mourning as Old City Riots

WORLD REACTS

Messages from heads of state from all over the world have been pouring into Amman, while political leaders and pressmen mourned Abdullah's murder as gravely affecting peace and stability in the Middle East.

London: King George VI sent a message of condolence to Emir Na'if on Friday. Representatives of the British Foreign Office called on the Jordan Minister in London to express the condolences of the Foreign Secretary of State Herbert Morrison.

Washington: President Truman sent a message of sympathy yesterday to Prince Talal, saying that "King Abdullah's name will live as one of the greatest personages in the history of the Arab peoples." Secretary of State Dean Acheson sent a message of regret to the Jordan Prime Minister, Samir Pasha Rifai.

Reuters reported that diplomatic circles here thought the assassination might strike a blow at prospects of an early settlement of the Arab-Israel dispute by strengthening the hand of extremist leaders in the Arab League.

New York: Dr. Ralph Bunche, former Palestine mediator, stated that he was shocked by the news, calling the assassination "another tragic episode in the history of the Near East."

The "Times" and "Herald Tribune" here feared that conflict might flare up and spread beyond Jordan.

Beirut: Troops were called out on Friday to keep order when news of the assassination reached here. Demonstrators tried to start street riots similar to those after the assassination four days ago of Riad el-Solh.

Crown Prince Abdul Illah, regent of Iraq, and Emir Abdul Majid Haidar, Jordan Minister in London, left here tonight by air for Amman.

Damascus: The Cabinet will meet today to discuss the implications of the assassination.

Syrian political leaders believed it would have widespread repercussions in the Arab world and in Arab-Jewish relations.

New Delhi: Dr. Rajandra Prasad, President of India, conveyed India's condolences in a message to Prince Na'if. Flags were flown at half-mast at Government House and Government buildings.

Cairo: The Foreign Minister issued a statement deploring the "new wave of political crimes."

Baghdad: The Iraqi press said yesterday that the assassination "represents the gravest turning point in Arab's modern history."

Harriman Makes New Oil Proposals

TEHERAN, Saturday (Reuter). — President Truman's oil envoy, Mr. Averell Harriman, tonight presented the Persians with a series of proposals designed to settle the oil dispute, it was learned from an authoritative Persian source. The proposals were made at a special meeting between Mr. Harriman and his advisers and the Persian Oil Commission.

The source said one of Mr. Harriman's proposals was a compromise suggestion to settle the problem of the form of receipt required from the masters of tankers leaving Abadan. It was not immediately known what the others were.

An authoritative Persian source revealed, however, that Mr. Harriman's proposals were "mainly satisfactory" to the Persians and held out the prospect that they might eventually lead to resumed negotiations with the British.

Both the Americans and Persians indicated that the British had not yet been informed of the Harriman proposals.

Persian police here yesterday ordered two senior officials of the Anglo-Iranian Oil Company to report to the passport office in Teheran "within a day or two" to be expelled.

Russia Invited To Meeting on Japan

MOSCOW, Saturday (Reuter) — The British and U.S. Ambassadors in Moscow, Sir David Kelly and Admiral Alan Kirk, yesterday handed notes to the Soviet Deputy Foreign Minister, Mr. Andrei Gromyko.

Admiral Kirk handed Mr. Gromyko a joint Anglo-American note and the text of the draft Japanese treaty. The note invited Soviet comment on the draft treaty before August 13, and extended an invitation to Russia to attend the peace conference.

During the day, the U.S. Government invited 52 nations to attend the Conference at San Francisco on September 4.

Murder Motives

Press comment all over the world, stressing that King Abdullah's assassination was a major blow to peace and stability in the Middle East, largely concurred that his assassination was the direct result of his pro-British policy and his believed preparedness to negotiate peace with Israel.

These policies were known to be violently opposed by members of the Mufti clique, as well as by followers of the King's eldest son, Emir Talal.

Foreign Diplomats in Jerusalem, however, completely ruled out the possibility of the assassination having been carried out by Talal's supporters. They pointed out that the assassin, Mustapha Shukri Ushu, was known to have participated in outrages against the Polish and Swedish consulates in Jerusalem perpetrated by the "Firqat el Tadmir lil Jihad el Muqades" (The Sappers of the Holy Jihad) — a violently pro-Mufti organization.

Other observers pointed out that Riad Bey e-Solh, assassinated last Monday, was a supporter of the Mufti's, and that the latest assassination might well be an act of revenge "evening the Mufti score."

Although extremely varied in background and character, opposition to King Abdullah had been growing steadily since his annexation of the Arab-held part of Palestine.

Parliament has several times demanded the resignation of Glubb Pasha, British Commander of the Arab Legion, the cancellation of the Jordan-British Treaty of Friendship and the suspension of the armistice agreement with Israel, and a succession of Premiers have had to resign. Early this year, King Abdullah finally dissolved Parliament because of its incessant opposition on the above points.

Jordan's first elections brought a majority of anti-Abdullah elements into Parliament, comprising the entire representatives of the Palestinian section and some Amman delegates. Among them were such active Mufti supporters as the former commander in chief of the Husseini "El Fatuwah" semi-military youth movement.

King's Respect For Jews

On a number of occasions in the past King Abdullah expressed himself in favour of Jewish efforts in Palestine and advocated a settlement between the Arabs and Jews through peaceful means.

"The disturbances in Palestine are the result of incitement from outside the Holy Land," he once declared at the Amman Town Hall.

In his memoirs which were published in 1946 he said, "I was astonished at what I saw of the Jewish settlements. They have colonized the sand dunes, drawn water from them, and transformed them into a paradise."

In April, 1948 he was the first to recognize the right of the Jews to have their own administration in Palestine, albeit under Arab sovereignty.

Before the outbreak of the Arab war King Abdullah received Mrs. Golda Myerson, now Minister of Labour, at Shuneh, site of his winter home, in a last-minute effort to prevent hostilities.

In November, 1948 he was the first Arab ruler to declare that "further fighting in Palestine is useless," and in 1949 he offered peace in exchange for a port on the Mediterranean Sea. In November, 1949 he permitted pilgrims to enter Jordan from Israel.

Last year he admitted that the Jews have rights to their Holy Places in the Old City.

ELATH STATEMENT

LONDON, Saturday. — Mr. Eliahu Elath, Israel Minister to Britain, said on Friday that "the assassination of King Abdullah has not only deprived the people of Jordan of its monarch, but constituted a serious blow to peace and stability in the Middle East."

Heavily-armed guards patrolled the tense streets of the Old City yesterday, as a severe curfew followed looting and riots after the assassination of King Abdullah on Friday. The 69-year-old monarch of the Hashemite Kingdom of the Jordan, was assassinated at 11.45 a.m. (12.45 Israel time) inside the El Aksa Mosque in the Old City of Jerusalem, a short distance from the tomb of his father, Hussein Ibn Ali. He died instantly from a bullet wound in the head.

King Abdullah

A half-hour following the murder the Council of Jordan Ministers met at Amman and there declared Crown Prince Naif, King Abdullah's 38-year-old younger son, as Regent.

King Abdullah had arrived in the Old City on Thursday night and was due to eulogize Riad e-Solh at the noon prayers. The former Lebanese Premier was the victim of assassins' bullets in Amman on Monday.

The assassin, Mustafa Shukri Ushu, 21, is reported to have been in the employ of King Abdullah's old rival, Haj Amin Hussini, former Mufti of Jerusalem. The murderer was shot and killed by the King's guard.

In the general shooting that followed Colonel Radi Bey Hindawi, Arab Legion Commander in the Old City, and Major Radi Bey Anab, Police Commander of the Old City, were hit and wounded.

The King had already entered the mosque ahead of his bodyguard who were still busy taking off their shoes and putting on the slippers worn during services when the shots were fired. The Haram es-Sharif compound, which also includes the Dome of the Rock, is regarded in the Moslem world in holiness second only to the towns of Mecca and Medina.

Funeral Tomorrow

Very shortly after the killing, the King's body was flown to Amman. The funeral will take place tomorrow in Amman.

Crowds that had gathered in the area of Damascus Gate were dispersed by fire from Arab Legion machine guns.

The Council of Ministers declared martial law in Amman and the Old City. A period of mourning was set for three months.

The country-wide curfew was lifted at 5.30 a.m. yesterday, and only bakers, grocers and chemists shops and other vital services were open.

Government offices, excepting the Premier's office, the Foreign Ministry, the Post and Telegrams Ministry and the Security Ministry have been closed for three days on official orders.

Street traffic was at a minimum. The Old City and neighbourhood were under a 12-hour curfew from 6 p.m. to 6 a.m. and the military has taken the area over.

Quiet reigned throughout Jordan.

Legion Searches

The Arab Legion continued searching towns and villages throughout Jordan for "extremists."

Mandelbaum Gate was sealed.

The manhunt in Jordan was believed to be for extremists belonging to the Syrian Nationalist Party, held responsible for the assassination of former Premier Riad e-Solh in Amman last Tuesday.

The assassin, a tailor from the Old City, was a member of the "dynamite squad" of the irregular force which was associated with Haj Amin Husseini during Israel's War of Independence. He had been hiding behind the main

(Contiued on Page 3, Col. 6)

From Mecca To Amman

Born in Mecca in 1882, the second son of the Sheriff Hussein, King of Hedjaz, King Abdullah was educated privately in Istanbul, later assisting his father as Sheriff of Mecca. In 1909 he was appointed member of Mecca in the Ottoman Parliament and, in 1912, was invited by the Khalif to Istanbul to discuss the rights of the Sheriff's office.

Returning home at the outbreak of World War I he served as a liaison man between his father and British politicians in Egypt. In 1916 Abdullah raised the flag of revolt against the Turks and fought with the British alongside Lawrence of Arabia. An Arab Congress in Damascus proclaimed him King of Iraq but on British advice he returned to Mecca.

In 1920, the French crossed the Syrian frontier from the Lebanon, captured Damascus and drove Abdullah's brother, Feisal, from the throne. Abdullah, bent on evicting the French, arrived at Ma'an in Transjordan at the head of 1,000 tribesmen. At the same time, a British Middle East conference was assembling in Cairo, under the presidency of Mr. Winston Churchill, the Colonial Secretary. After a meeting in Jerusalem with Mr. Churchill, Abdullah agreed to call off the expedition and to accept the sovereignty of the "unwanted" territory of Transjordan. On April 7, 1921, the Parliament of Transjordan was formally founded.

Seven years later Abdullah signed a Treaty of Friendship with Britain and undertook to be guided by her in all matters concerning Transjordan's foreign policy, as well as permitting the British Government to maintain armed forces in Transjordan.

Finally the agreement was superseded by the Treaty of Alliance signed by Mr. Bevin and Ibrahim Pasha in London on March 22, 1946, which recognized Trans-Jor-

(Continued on Page 3, Col. 8)

Emir Naif — The New Regent

The Emir Naif Ibn Abdullah, second son of the late King, was born in Mecca in 1913. He was educated at the Men's Elementary Training College, Jerusalem, and received military training from Major E. W. Northfield Bey, Second-in-Command of the Arab Legion.

After his appointment as Judge in the Tribal Courts he assumed the Presidency of the Court on the death of the Emir Shakeer. He was commissioned in the Arab Legion in 1938.

Ten Murders In 6 Years

The death of King Abdullah marks the 10th Arab political assassination in the Middle East during the past six years.

- **Ahmed Maher Pasha,** Egyptian Premier, killed by the Moslem Brotherhood in February, 1945 immediately after having read Egypt's declaration of war on Germany and Japan to the Egyptian parliament.
- **Immam Yahya, King of Yemen,** was assassinated in February, 1948, by his Chief Minister and Secretary. Two of his sons were killed in the ensuing conflict.
- **Mustapha Fihmi Nokrashi Pasha,** Egyptian Premier, assassinated by the Moslem Brotherhood in December 1948, four days after he had ordered the outlawing of the Organization.
- **Sheikh Hassan el Bannah,** leader of the Moslem Brotherhood, was himself assassinated, two months later.
- **General Husni A'Za'im,** self-proclaimed dictator after the first Damascus coup d'etat, killed in August, 1949, by his successor, Col. Sami Hinnawi.
- **Dr. Muhsin Bey Barazani,** Syrian Premier under the Za'im regime, also executed in August, 1949, together with Za'im.
- **Col. Hinnawi,** assassinated in October, 1950, by a cousin of Dr. Barazani.
- **General Ali Razmara,** Prime Minister of Persia, was shot and killed on March 7, 1951, by a member of the Fidayan Islam terrorist sect for alleged connivance with the Anglo-Iranian Oil Company
- **Riad e-Solh,** pro-Mufti, ex-Premier of the Lebanon, was assassinated in Amman, last Monday.

E-Solh's Daughter Asks Blood Revenge

"Swear that you will avenge my father's death and see that his assailants do not escape," Alia, eldest daughter of Riad Bey e-Solh, cried to the crowds of mourners who followed her father's funeral in Beirut, on Thursday, Damascus Radio reports.

Clashes that occurred during the funeral ceremony were suppressed by the police. The Lebanese Foreign Minister, Charles Bey Hilu, who fainted during the proceedings, was later admitted to hospital.

Iraq Regent to Amman

LONDON, Saturday (Reuter). — The regent of Iraq, Abdul Illah, and the Jordan Minister in London, Amir Abdul Majid Kaidar, flew to Amman as a result of King Abdullah's assassination.

THE JERUSALEM POST

TUESDAY, JANUARY 8, 1952

PRICE: 40 PRUTA
VOL. XXVIII. No. 7154

200 HURT AS POLICE DEFEND KNESSET FROM HERUT RIOT

IN THE FACE OF AN ORGANIZED ATTEMPT BY THE HERUT PARTY OF FORMER IRGUN ZVAI LEUMI TERRORISTS TO PREVENT A PARLIAMENTARY DISCUSSION, THE KNESSET YESTERDAY BEGAN A TEN-HOUR DEBATE ON THE SUBJECT OF ISRAEL'S CLAIM FOR REPARATIONS FROM GERMANY. POLICE RIOT SQUADS, WEARING STEEL HELMETS AND GAS-MASKS, BATTLED WITH MORE THAN 1,000 DEMONSTRATORS WHO USED TEAR-GAS TO BREAK THROUGH CORDONS AND BARBED-WIRE BARRIERS, AND THEN STONED THE KNESSET BUILDING, SMASHING WINDOWS AND FILLING THE CHAMBER WITH CLOUDS OF TEAR-GAS. THE RIOTERS WERE DISPERSED AFTER A TWO-HOUR BATTLE BY POLICE USING TEAR-GAS AND BATONS. PLATOONS OF TROOPS IN FULL BATTLE KIT WERE CALLED OUT BUT STOOD BY WITHOUT GOING INTO ACTION. NINETY-TWO POLICEMEN WERE INJURED, OF WHOM TEN WERE HOSPITALIZED, AND 70 RIOTERS WERE ARRESTED. OVER 30 CIVILIANS WERE TREATED FOR INJURIES BY THE MAGEN DAVID ADOM AND FIVE WERE TAKEN TO HOSPITAL, BUT IT IS BELIEVED THAT ABOUT 100 MORE WERE TREATED PRIVATELY TO EVADE THE POLICE. THE DEBATE IN THE KNESSET WAS OPENED BY THE PRIME MINISTER AT 4.30, BUT ABOUT AN HOUR LATER IT BECAME STORMY AND HECTIC WHEN HERUT AND COMMUNIST MEMBERS CALLED OUT FROM THE FLOOR THAT POLICE WERE BEHAVING SAVAGELY OUTSIDE. EYEWITNESSES OF THE RIOTING, HOWEVER, PRAISED THE POLICE'S RESTRAINT IN THE FACE OF VIOLENT PROVOCATION. THE DEBATE WILL BE RESUMED THIS AFTERNOON.

Police in 2-Hour Street Battle

Violence surged in the streets of Jerusalem for two hours yesterday in the wake of a Herut demonstration opposing the Knesset debate on negotiations with Germany. Police barbed-wire barricades were broken through, parked cars overturned and rocks thrown into the Knesset chamber and at police protecting the building. Injuries had reached 92 policemen and 36 civilians by 7 p.m. when an army detachment arrived on the scene and drew up in formation alongside the Knesset. By 7.30 order had been restored and the littered streets before the Knesset building were virtually abandoned.

Several hundred people stood in a thin drizzle at the mass meeting in Zion Square to hear Herut leader Menahem Begin and Professor Joseph Klausner, speaking from a balcony of the Tel Aviv Hotel, voice sharp opposition to any negotiations with Germany for reparations payments to Israel. Professor Klausner, who had been the Herut candidate for first president of the State, asserted that, whereas the Jewish people has remembered its ancient enemies, it has forgotten the Nazis in a matter of only five years.

Mr. Begin spoke with emotion, frequently shouting, interspersing his words with many Biblical quotations. He referred to the Government statement in support of German reparations discussions as the culmination of the policies of "that maniac who is now Prime Minister."

Gas from Germany

Midway through his harangue, Mr. Begin pulled a note from his pocket, held it aloft dramtically and said:

I have not come here to enflame you; but this note which has just been handed to me states that the police have grenades which contain gas made in Germany — the same gas which was used to kill your fathers and mothers. — We are prepared to suffer anything, "torture chambers, concentration camps and subterranean prisons — so that any decision to deal with Germany will not come to pass.

No policeman were to be seen in Zion Square during the meeting which closed with the singing of the national anthem. Then groups of youths led the march up Ben-Yehuda Road in the direction of the Knesset building. A number carried haversacks loaded with stones. Many openly bragged that they had come from Tel Aviv and Haifa and had brought "our arms with us."

Earlier in the day, police had cordoned off a large section of the city's centre, running from Jaffa Road to Terra Sancta College. Barbed wire concertinas blocked the roads, and bus routes were temporarily changed. Pedestrians with business in the area were permitted to pass the barriers, although they were kept away from the immediate Knesset environs. Heavy detachments of police, estimate to number over 600, patrolled the cordoned area. Most were armed with shields, batons, steel helmets and gas-mask kits.

The lower barrier on Ben-Yehuda Road at the corner of Rehov Hapo'alim was broken through in short order, with little police resistance apparent. As the crowds of demonstrators swelled, however, and violence became evident, groups of police went to the roofs of nearby buildings and lobbed down tear-gas bombs in an attempt to disperse the mob.

District Police Superintendent Levi Avrahami reported, however, that the tear gas was first employed by the demonstrators who, by this means, were able to break past the first barrier. The light wind wafted the gas into the faces of the police, away from Ben-Yehuda Road and in the direction of the Knesset.

Police Self-Restraint

The shrieking sirens of Magen David Adom ambulances, the billowing clouds of tear-gas and the ring of pistol shots fired by police above the heads of the mob soon gave the area the semblance of a street battle.

As road blocks were removed forcibly by the marchers, the police, who had been ordered to observe extreme self-restraint in dealing with the demonstrators, fell back to positions around the Knesset. The crowd showered the police with stones; and even

Magen David Adom ambulances rushing first aid to the injured were stoned and halted. Attempts were also even made to drag out the injured.

During the first hour of the demonstrations, 13 policemen were injured, among them Deputy Superintendent Israel Maiber and Assistant Superintendent Moshe Ayalon, who sustained a serious eye injury from a flying rock.

A car parked outside the Knesset was overturned by the demonstrators. As the gasoline poured out of the tank, a tear-gas bomb apparently ignited it. The blaze was put out by the Jerusalem Fire Brigade. A number of cars parked along King George Avenue, between Jaffa Road and the Jewish Agency compound, were also damaged.

At this point no one was permitted to enter or leave Knesset building, which was in fact in a state of siege.

15 in Hospital

Only wounded policemen were admitted for treatment. Mrs. Paula Ben Gurion who was a nurse before she married the Prime Minister, assisted in giving them first aid.

Ten of the 92 injured policemen and five civilians were hospitalized at Hadassah. Magen David Adom gave first aid to 69 policemen and 31 civilians, many of these firemen. Twenty policemen were treated by Kupat Holim and private physicians. Because of shortage of space, many policemen were transferred from M.D.A. to police headquarters in the Russian Compound, where a temporary infirmary was set up.

Police arrested 70 demonstrators during the day.

A statement was issued last night by Mayor Shragai, expressing shame at "the descretion of the name of Jerusalem and Israel by... those who lifted their hands against the guardians of law and order ... Even the most proper emotions do not justify abominable deeds like these and do not permit taking the law into one's own hands."

Small Demonstrations In T.A. and Haifa

TEL AVIV, Monday.—A small demonstration organized by Mapam and Communists, attended by about 200 persons, was held near the Mograbi Cinema here this evening in protest against direct talks with the Bonn Government on restitution. There were no incidents.

Dr. Moshe Sneh, the Mapam leader, declared, "the decision will be made by the people, not the Knesset."

A loudspeaker van was in attendance, but few people stopped to listen and traffic continued normally throughout the meeting.

In Haifa, a small crowd at Rehov Herzl, corner Arlosoroff, listened to three Communist speakers denounce restitution negotiations.

Bonn Welcomes Expected Knesset Decision

BONN, Monday (INA). — As the Knesset opened the German reparations debate, Government circles here welcomed the expected outcome—a decision to negotiate directly with Germany.

A German Chancellory spokesman said that the German Government welcomed every step taken by Israel towards direct negotiations; it was, however, up to Israel to determine the best way of carrying out these negotiations.

Officials point out that reparation negotiations with Jewish organizations in Germany, and preparations for a reparations law made by the Federal Ministry of Finance, have considerably eased the ground for official contact between Israel and Germany.

"The Times" Tel Aviv correspondent, outlining today's debate in the Knesset, said, "opposition critics, except the most extreme, compromise their moral objections by suggesting that Israel, instead of negotiating directly, should get her reparations through the agency of the present occupying powers."

Debate in Atmosphere of Violence

The question of an approach to Bonn for reparations was debated yesterday in the Knesset in an atmosphere of violence unprecedented in Israel parliamentary life. The shouting of a mob not far off, the intermittent wail of police cars and ambulance sirens, sporadic explosions of gas grenades and the glow of flames from a burning car came through the windows of the Knesset building, and later the window panes were splintered, by rocks, and fumes of tear-gas bombs from the battle-scarred street outside permeated the chamber. One member was hit in the head by a stone.

Through all this disturbance, the meeting went on. The section of the hall where stones and glass splinters fell, the Mapam, General Zionist and Hapoel Hamizrahi benches, was vacated and members stood around elsewhere. But later the proceedings were interrupted by obstruction within the Knesset itself when Mr. Menahem Begin (Herut) called the Prime Minister "a hooligan" and refused to recant. He also declined to leave the platform when ordered to do so by the Deputy Speaker, saying "If I don't speak, no one will speak." The meeting was closed by the Deputy Speaker amidst an uproar.

This marked Mr. Begin's return to the political scene from his semi-retirement, which followed the setback to his party in the last Knesset elections. It was his first appearance in the Second Knesset, and in fact, he took the oath of office only some two hours before he began his speech.

Begin's Apology

After the recess, Mr. Begin returned to the platform and apologized. He added that he was waiving his Knesset immunity and that this would be his last appearance in the Knesset, and made what most listeners thought was a threat to go underground if an attempt is made to negotiate with Germany:

Some things are dearer than life. Some things are worse than death. We are willing to leave our families and die... People went to the barricades for lesser things... I know we will be dragged to concentration camps... We will die together.

The proceedings of the day opened calmly enough with Mr. Ben Gurion's introductory statement. The Prime Minister reviewed the history of Israel's approach to the four occupying powers in Germany. He said that Russia had not replied and no indication had been received about the reaction of the East German Government. The Western powers, he went on, had expressed support for the principle but said that they were bound by treaties not to make additional claims upon Germany for themselves or on behalf of others. Mr. Ben Gurion read from the text of the American Government's reply and he added that Great Britain and France had answered in the same vein.

Under pressure of public opinion and after friendly intercession by official British circles and others, the Chancellor of Western Germany wrote a few weeks ago on behalf of his Government that they were ready to discuss with the State of Israel and Jewish representatives the question of reparations on the basis of the claims set forward by Israel in her note of March 12, 1951.

"The Government regards itself as bound, together with representatives of world Jewry and without undue delay to make every effort to restore as quickly as possible the maximum loot to individual Jews and to the Jewish people," the Prime Minister said. "Let not the murderers of our people be also their inheritors."

Opposition Speakers

This was taken to mean that the Government had decided to deal directly with Germany. The decision was attacked by three Opposition speakers, all of whom spoke passionately. Two had lost their parents in the Nazi exterminations.

Mr. Elimelech Rimalt (General Zionists) argued that as Hitler's extermination of the Jews had not been logical, so was the current issue not one of logic but of emotions. He declared that the argument that murderers should not inherit did not apply here because the Nazis had not murdered for the legacy. He quoted his small son as asking him: "What price will we get for grandpa and grandma?"

The Mapam speaker, Mr. Yaakov Hazan, said that reparations could be justified if it were possible to restore all the property or if the Germans themselves had destroyed the Nazis. He implied that the whole thing was a trick by the Western powers designed to facilitate the grooming of Western Germany as the spearhead of new hordes to attack Russia.

During Mr. Hazan's speech, Dr. Yohanan Bader (Herut) burst into the chamber crying, "Gas against the Jews! With that you will win!" He had just returned from the demonstration outside. Other Herut members joined in the denunciation, and with some difficulty the Speaker, Mr. Yosef Sprinzak, restored order.

During a speech by Mr. Itshak Raphael (Hapoel Hamizrahi), Mr. Meir Wilner followed by Mrs. Esther Wilenska, both Communists, entered the chamber excitedly. "We sit here, and argue while people are being murdered outside. They're shooting!" Mr. Wilner shouted.

Shortly afterwards, the first stones came crashing through the windows. They entered over the heads of Mapam members, who took shelter from glass splinters. More stones came crashing through and the fumes of tear gas moved slowly across the hall. At the cabinet table and in the U-shaped tiers occupied by members, men and women rubbed swollen eyes with handkerchiefs. An outstanding exception was the Prime Minister, who throughout did not reach for a handkerchief.

Members' Discipline

Some members made a bold effort to remain in their places. Mr. Rustum Bastuni (Mapam) stayed in his seat in an exposed part of the hall during the stoning. Later, Dr. Hanan Rubin returned to his place but he was hit in the head and left, holding a handkerchief over his wound. Dr. Benzion Harell (General Zionists), the only physician in the House (Dr. Moshe Sneh was absent) raced after Dr. Rubin to treat his colleague. Mrs. Shoshana Persitz also remained in her place but was later overcome, and Mr. Ben Gurion went up to her and helped her out. The Mapai members who were in the far side of the hall away from the windows for the most part remained in their places.

The stoning continued when Mr. Begin took the platform. He took issue with the Prime Minister's statement that the wrath had been "staged.' He read a list of rabbis, scholars and poets who had signed a petition opposing negotiations with Germany. Mr. Ben Gurion, who had been remarkably quiet throughout, rose from his place and pointed to the windows. "They are not identified with your hooligans in the street," he said.

It was here that Mr. Begin said to the Prime Minister: "You are a hooligan." This had not been the worst epithet hurled across the floor. In the frequent exchanges, Mr. Be-

(Continued on Page 3, Col. 6)

Column One

By David Courtney

THERE are three world personalities whose influence and even authority extend beyond their own sovereign domains to government, communities, and the family hearth as well, of other races and nations. They are His Holiness the Pope, Mr. Joseph Stalin and the President of the United States of America. Next autumn a new American president will be elected. He will be elected by the citizens of the United States, but in effect the electorate directly concerned extends over half Europe, most of the Middle East, including Israel, and a considerable slice of Asia. Except where formal treaties exist, there is no written bond between any of these countries and the United States; but in present circumstances every one of them is dependent, in real and definable terms, on American policy; the dependence may be economic, it may be a matter of military security, it may be recognition of the plain fact that America, in or out of U.N. is always in a position to enforce her judgements at least upon those who accept her leadership. Her currency is needed by everyone; her food, her machines, her arms; and there is no alternative source.

■

THEREFORE, the presidential and congressional elections this year are the business of us all. For the selfsame reason some of us have claimed the right to analyse and criticize American Policy; like it or not, we are to be bound up with a specific form of world leadership assumed by a great and powerful nation, we have the right and duty to check upon the course of such leadership and find it good or bad as our intelligence directs. It has been said that the rival, Communist leadership forbids, within its wide realms, the exercise of independent conscience and criticism. No doubt it does. Until it is similarly forbidden on this side, the intelligent man of conscience and critical faculty cannot be expected voluntarily to stop thinking for himself. The next president and his Congress, and the United States as a whole, will be none the worse for a little independent thinking on the part of those who are likely to be subject to the policies that will come out of Washington after the November elections.

■

SOMETHING of a mystery has been allowed to fog presidential prospects. General Eisenhower, supreme Commander of the NATO forces, personifies the mystery. He has been set down by Governor Dewey, the "Herald-Tribune," and a good many other influential Republicans as the obvious Republican candidate and the one man likely to break the Democratic succession. Some Democrats have claimed that he was of their persuasion and it was stated by a columnist of the "New York Times" that Mr. Truman had as good as offered the Democratic candidacy to the General. Now we are told, by the word of Senator Lodge, who is a more valid and respected Republican spokesman than some, that he has entered General Eisenhower to be candidate for the Republican presidential nomination in the N... ampshire primary.
... days, that being
... ry limit, General
... vill have to accept
... n or cause it to
... , and we shall
... e we are at least
... of the future of
... at of Republi-
... n the contest.

... enhower's
... ican rivals
... i Mr. Stas-
... tified his
... nly the
... when
... vith
... at
... t

West Proposes To Shelve PCC

By MAURICE CARR POST Correspondent

PARIS, Monday.—A resolution with the avowed object of resolving nothing for the time being in Israel-Arab relations, and of waiting on major developments elsewhere, was jointly introduced by France, Turkey, Britain and the U.S. this morning at the opening of a full-dress debate on Palestine in the Ad Hoc Political Committee.

The gist of the resolution is to place the P.C.C., as it were, on the "retired list," but to make it available for active service whenever required. It is proposed to transfer P.C.C. Headquarters to the U.N. Building in New York, but maintain a representative in Jerusalem. The P.C.C. would be required to submit reports on its progress periodically, thus keeping Palestine as a permanent item on the agenda.

The P.C.C. would, under this resolution, be authorized to designate a representative or representatives to assist it in carrying out its functions.

Sees Useful Basis

M. Leon Marchal, who opened the discussion with a 10-minute statement urging the retention of the Commission, stressed that "it is necessary to reserve possibilities for immediate action in Palestine." He absolved the Commission's failure to bring about peace, blaming the unwillingness of the disputing parties to "negotiate among themselves on a basis of mutual concessions."

M. Marchal proclaimed his conviction that the comprehensive five-point proposals submitted to the two sides by the P.C.C. at the recent abortive Paris conference "might be a useful basis for the conditions of restoring peace in Palestine." Thus he made quite clear the intention of petrifying the political aspects of the situation, like the principal character in the "Sleeping Beauty," until the right moment comes for awakening.

Mr. Philip Jessup, U.S. delegate, expressed support of the P.C.C. comprehensive proposals. Regarding the four-power resolution, he admitted it was not an attempt to solve the complex Palestine problems at the present U.N. session, and appealed to delegates to confine themselves to what the Turkish delegate previously described as the "procedural or administrative nature" of the quadripartite resolution."

Arabs Reject West's PCC Resolution

PARIS, Monday (UP). — The Arab states yesterday unanimously decided to reject the four-power resolution recommending the creation of a new body to replace the P.C.C. The resolution was introduced at the Ad Hoc Political Committee today, but was yesterday circulated privately among the Arab representatives.

It was decided the resolution ignored previous U.N. resolutions on the problem and did not put sufficient emphasis on, the enforcement and implementation of earlier resolutions.

This appeal was ignored by Lebanese Foreign Minister Charles Helou, who launched an extremely violent and familiar diatribe against Israel, "whose mystic immigration policy predestined it to territorial expansionism." Helou demanded the implementation of earlier Assembly resolutions — unrestricted repatriation of Palestine Arab refugees, internationalization of Jerusalem and the withdrawal of Israel within the partition frontiers."

Arab Motion Due

He announced that the Arabs would introduce their own resolution.

France spoke briefly in favour of the resolution. China, also supporting the resolution, nearly summed up the basic idea of the Western powers at the present stage: "It is no use shaking the kettle to stop the water boiling," said the Chinese delegate, Mr. Shuhsi Hsu, "You must put out the fire."

The Western powers regard the refugee problem as the fire which must first be extinguished before emotions can be sufficiently cooled for the restoration of peace.

Accordingly, the second part of the Palestine debate, when Mr. John Blandford's report comes up for discussion, promises to provide a dynamic contrast to the static opening."

Mr. Abba Eban had not yet arrived. (Mr. Eban left for Paris from Lydda airfield today.—Ed.).

A Jordan representative was admitted as an observer.

By arrangement with the "Jewish Chronicle," London.

Big 3 Back USSR On Council Meeting

PARIS, Monday (Reuter). — The three Western powers and Brazil today supported Russia's proposal to hold a "periodic" Security Council meeting to help relieve international tension, but only when a "useful" purpose would be served by such a meeting.

They tabled an amendment to the Soviet resolution calling for a Council meeting which would discuss international tension, and specifically Korea.

PARIS, Monday (AP). — Soviet Foreign Minister Andrei Vyshinsky told the U.N. today the Korean armistice talks are "deadlocked" after "foundering" for six months. He urged that a special meeting of the Security Council attempt to help end the negotiations successfully.

The U.S. delegate, Mr. Benjamin Cohen, and the British Minister of State, Mr. Selwyn Lloyd, rejected the idea in a declaration to the U.N. Political Committee. Mr. Cohen branded it as an attempt to "confuse, impair and delay those talks." He said that "U.N. soldiers are not dying in Korea to return the fate of that country to the Soviet veto (in the Security Council)." Mr. Lloyd said transfer of the Korean talks to the U.N. would mean "delay and complication."

Gloomy Reaction

Some delegations gloomily observed that Mr. Vyshinsky's declaration in the Political Committee that the Korean talks are "deadlocked," obviously meant that they would remain deadlocked until the ...oviet Union changes its mind.

Mr. Lloyd denounced Mr. Vy...nsky's proposal as a dodge ...get a new platform for vit...ation and abuse against the ... He said the Russian plan ...t indeed break up the Korean ...

... Vyshinsky replied that he ... see no alternative but a ...ity Council session for an ...pt to ease tensions. He said ... is the worst "sore spot" ...ppealed to everyone to tackle ...t.

...ey have got themselves into ...llock," Mr. Vyshinsky said, ...ng to the Korean talks, ... the Security Council ...own and talk, let us help ... If the talks do not come ...thing, we can end them. But ... try. You say you do not ... your boys to die. Neither ... We have heard here that (USSR) do not want peace — ...orrible slander.

"The sinister spot of war is in ...rea and that is where we ...uld like to liquidate it," Mr. ...shinsky said.

Korean Truce Talks Remain Deadlocked

TOKYO, Monday (Reuter). — Cease-fire talks at Panmunjom progressed little today.

The chief U.N. delegate, Vice Admiral Charles Turner Joy, who returned to Tokyo today, charged: "Each passing day there is less reason to think the Communists really want a stable armistice."

The U.N. spokesman, Brigadier-General William Nuckols, said Communist delegates and their interpreter showed no interest in today's 90-minute session of the cease-fire supervision subcommittee. He said the Communist interpreter "giggled and snickered frequently."

The spokesman described today's atmosphere as "the strangest since the talks started." He said General Hsieh Feng of China read a magazine and passed it back and forth to other delegates. The Communists behaved "as if a load had been taken off their minds."

The prisoners subcommittee had a morning and afternoon session, but made no progress.

A few miles from Panmunjom, U.N. forces and communists were fighting for a hill position west of Korangpori. The Communists, defending the hill, were strongly supported by artillery.

Pleven Cabinet Falls on Issue Of State Rlys.

PARIS, Monday, (Reuter).— The French coalition government of M. Rene Pleven fell today after five months in office. Its downfall came when the Socialists turned against the government for its plans to economize on the state railways.

On the first of the eight votes of confidence demanded by M. Pleven, the official count gave the voting as 341 to 243 against the government.

M. Pleven and his Ministers then left the chamber to draft their letter of resignation, which they handed to the President later tonight.

The decisive vote came on a clause in the Government's budget bill, giving it powers to keep the railway deficit to 80,000 million francs. Without these economies, the Government estimated the deficit would rise to 100,000 million francs.

The Socialists, who abstained when Pleven's Ministry narrowly gained a confidence vote last Thursday, decided today to vote against the planned economies.

M. Pleven's coalition, formed last August, was France's 15th Government since the war. His own party is the Democratic and Socialist Resistance Union, affiliated to the Radicals. His cabinet included other Radicals, Popular Rebublicans (MRP), Peasant Party members and Independents.

The Socialists were not in the Government, but had lent it support in critical votes during its brief life.

Big Two Await Steel Report

WASHINGTON, Monday, (AP). — President Truman and Mr. Churchill today instructed a special committee of economic experts to examine the problem of raw materials — including British steel requirements — and report back to them tomorrow.

That was the most significant question discussed by the two statesmen in the first of their four proposed meetings at the White House.

Their first meeting today lasted 65 minutes. They met again later this afternoon, Mr. Churchill being accompanied by his Foreign Secretary, Mr. Eden, and the British Ambassador to the U.S., Sir Oliver Franks.

Britain has been reported to be seeking large quantities of American steel, but persons familiar with Monday's proceedings said no figure was mentioned.

During the afternoon session it was expected that the military problems of the Western — and specifically the European—defence drive would be looked into in some detail, presumably covering the development of atomic energy and weapons.

SUEZ CANAL CO.'S EMPLOYEES STRIKE

PORT SAID, Monday, (AP). — The British Navy announced tonight that it will continue its efforts to maintain shipping traffic through the Suez Canal despite the strike today of 2,500 Egyptian employees of the Suez Canal Company.

Captain L.F. Durnford Slater, Commander of the British cruiser "Gambia," told correspondents: "Regardless of the outcome of the strike, our aim remains the same — to maintain shipping through the canal."

The strike was precipitated by demands from workers over how certain work should be done.

Talal-Na'if Feud Flares Anew

The 25-year-old feud between the two sons of the late King Abdullah, King Talal, the elder, and Emir Na'if, flared up anew yesterday when, according to an ANA dispatch from Baghdad, Na'if announced that he would permanently reside in Baghdad, at the side of Iraqi Regent Emir Abdul Illah, his cousin.

The announcement followed the return to Iraq from Jordan of former Premier and President of the Iraqi Senate, Jamil Pasha Madfa'i, after his failure to reconcile the two brothers. Madfa'i arrived in Amman at the beginning of the week in an effort to mediate between the Jordan ruler and his brother.

Long Standing Rivalry

The rivalry between Abdullah's two sons dates back to their early childhood, when it became clear that the father preferred Emir Na'if to his elder brother and made him his "pet." Ever since Talal had been described as an "obstinate and difficult" son, while his brother used to accompany Abdullah on his various tours.

In 1948 Abdullah placed Talal under house arrest for siding with the opposition, and threatened to deprive him of his succession to the throne.

Since then, Talal has suffered from a number of mental attacks, believed to be due, partly, to his father's conduct and the mounting of rivality and envy between the two brothers.

When King Abdullah was assassinated in the Old City last July, it was Na'if who was proclaimed by the Jordan Cabinet as Regent, while Talal, then undergoing medical treatment at a Swiss mental home, was not called back immediately.

Disapproves of Na'if

Since Talal's return to Amman and his coronation as King of Jordan, he had taken a number of steps to show his disapproval of the arrangements made by his brother during the latter's short regency. One of the first was to dissolve the Jordan Senate, appointed by Emir Na'if, and dismiss a number of its members, including a former Foreign Minister and for years a personal adviser of King Abdullah, Mohammed Shureiki Pasha.

During the past few months of Talal's reign, Na'if resided abroad most of the time, and the Palace and Government, as well as the press, rarely referred to him.

It is believed that as a result of the fresh outbreak of hostility between the brothers, Jordan-Iraqi relations will further deteriorate shortly.

FROM TOWN TO TOWN
Express Parcels Service
Jerusalem Tel Aviv Haifa Nahariya
Tel. 2350-2554 3535-5822 2824-4141 36

THE JERUSALEM POST
SUNDAY, JULY 27, 1952
PRICE: 70 PRUTA
VOL. XXVIII, No.7321

RADIO ERES
HAIFA 57, REHOV HERZL
4, PALMER'S GATE
TEL-AVIV 94, REHOV ALLENBY
A. GERSCFELD

Stevenson, Sparkman Chosen by Democrats

North, South Factions Joined

CHICAGO, Saturday. — The Democratic National Convention early today chose Illinois Governor Adlai Stevenson as its candidate to oppose Republical General Dwight Eisenhower in November's presidential election.

The choice came on the third ballot after nearly 12 hours of voting.

Senator Joseph W. Sparkman of Alabama received the nomination for Vice-President in a roaring shout of acclamation. Governor Stevenson picked the non-drinking, non-smoking senator as his running-mate to give the Deep South a place on the Democratic ticket for the first time in modern politics.

Mrs. India Edwards of Maryland, Vice-Chairman of the Democratic National Committee, and Judge Sarah Hughes of Texas, withdrew their candidacies so that Sen. Sparkman could take the nomination unopposed.

President Truman, addressing the Convention, confidently predicted that the Democrats would defeat the Republicans in the election. "You have picked a winner," he told delegates who chose the 52-year-old lawyer as their candidate after a last-minute landslide for the Truman-backed selection. "I am going to take my coat off and do everything I can to help him."

Before balloting bgean Mr. Jack Kroll, Political Action Director of the Congress of Industrial Organizations, asked all delegates who are C.I.O. members to vote for Mr. Stevenson.

Mr. Stevenson was nominated by 617.5 votes against 275.5 polled by his nearest rival, racket-busting Senator Estes Kefauver from Tennessee who had topped the poll in the first two ballots but failed to get the necessary majority for nomination.

The swing towards Mr. Stevenson came at the start of the third ballot when Mr. Averell Harriman, fighting as an all-out advocate of the Truman "Fair Deal" and who had received 121 votes in the second ballot, announced he was throwing his support over to Mr. Stevenson.

Even at the end of the roll-call in the third ballot Mr. Stevenson had only 611 votes—4.5 short of the total needed for victory. Then Utah and Tennessee switched their votes and ensured his nomination.

In his address to the Convention Mr. Truman declared that the Democratic programme for strengthening the U.S. would improve the life of every person in it. Under it the country would not turn to "men who would sacrifice the Army to protect the privileges of the few — and that is the Republican policy from start to finish."

"We will carry on the fight for fair wages and good working conditions for American labour," he added, "and we will fight for the repeal of the good-for-nothing Taft-Hartley Act. We are determined to avoid a third world war."

(Reuter, UP)

Democrats' Running Mates

Gov. Stevenson

A member of a family prominent in politics for four generations, Adlai E. Stevenson, born in Los Angeles, California 52 years ago, is a lawyer, administrator and diplomat. He became Governor of Illinois in 1949.

His great-grandfather was an adviser to Lincoln. His grandfather, for whom he was named, was vice-president under Grover Cleveland, and his father was a former secretary of the state of Illinois.

He was appointed an assistant secretary of the Navy and served under the late Frank Knox from July, 1941 to June 1944.

Stevenson achieved fame for his work in the U.N. In 1945 he was appointed special assistant to the Secretary of State and served as press officer during the U.N. conference in San Francisco. In August of that year he went to London as deputy delegate, under Edward R. Stettinius, to the U.N. meeting there.

The following year he was senior adviser to the U.S. delegation at the first general assembly of the U.N. in London and served as alternate delegate in 1946 and 1947.

Sen. Sparkman

Long considered one of the Democratic Party's stalwarts, Senator John J. Sparkman started his political career in 1936 when he was elected to Congress.

Born in 1899 of tenant-farmer parents, Sparkman borrowed money to begin law studies at the University of Alabama, later won a fellowship and graduated with honours.

As a member of the Military Affairs Committee, Sparkman was an advocate of civilian control of atomic energy. In 1951 he supported an amendment put forward by Senator Paul Douglas to restore the cuts made in the overall Foreign Aid Bill providing for a $50m. grant-in-aid to resettle Jewish refugees.

He became a Senator in 1946 to fill an unexpired term of the late Senator John Bankhead, and was re-elected in 1948. Sparkman is a member of the Senate Foreign Relations Committee and Chairman of the Senate's Small Business Committee.

He is married and has one daughter

Governor of Illinois Drafted Against Will

By JESSE ZEL LURIE
POST Correspondent

NEW YORK, Saturday. — For the first time in the memory of living men, a Presidential nominating convention has drafted a candidate against his will.

Adlai (named for a minor biblical character: Chronicles I 27:29) finally agreed to accept the nomination early this morning, after Mr. Harriman and other northern liberals broke the Stevenson-Kefauver-Russel deadlock and started a Stevenson stampede on the third ballot. Togther with General Eisenhower, who was reluctant to run but finally fought hard to win the Republican nomination, the professional politicians of both parties have given the country two middle-of-the-road candidates, whose abilities, integrities, and records would be hard to match anywhere, and of which the nation can well be proud.

Stevenson

On the top levels the campaign will probably be the cleanest in a century, although crackpots have already begun spreading obscene stories about both men, and Senators McCarthy and Nixon can be expected to make the most of the deposition which Mr. Stevenson made for Alger Hiss at the request of the Federal Court.

Independent voters will probably judge between the two candidates on the basis of their parties' records which would give the Democrats the Liberal vote and another victory.

One of the happiest men in Chicago today is Jacob ("Jake") Arvey, the first Jewish political boss to make the "big time"; he discovered Stevenson when he needed someone to clean up the State capital and he master-minded the draft nomination.

Portuguese Clash With Chinese On Macao Frontier

HONG KONG, Saturday (Reuter).—Portuguese and Chinese Communist troops exchanged machine-gun fire today across the border of the tiny Portuguese colony of Macao on the Chinese mainland, 65 kms. south-west of Hong Kong.

They began to fight last night after a dispute over the position of a barbed-wire barricade. By noon today two Portuguese soldiers and a Chinese civilian had been killed and five Portuguese soldiers wounded. Chinese Communist casualties were not known.

A Portuguese gunboat with heavy machine-guns mounted on her deck stood by in case the situation worsened, according to eye-witnesses arriving in Hong Kong aboard a crowded ferry steamer.

Troops Alerted

Chinese newspaper reports in Hong Kong said Portuguese troops had been recalled from leave last night to take up defence positions. Other reports said China had rushed a battalion of troops to the area of the fighting and was concentrating troops at a village 15 miles north of Macao.

Machine-guns kept up intermittent fire on the frontier during the afternoon but the situation was reported here to be no worse. No further casualties were reported.

The Chinese-owned ferry Golden Star from Canton was turned back by the Macao harbour authorities when it tried to dock.

(See Truce Talks, Col. 1)

Secret Truce Talks End: No Progress

PANMUNJOM, Saturday (Reuter).—General William Harrison, chief U.N. delegate, roundly denounced the Communists and stalked out of the Korean truce meeting here today. Staff officers then talked for 39 minutes without making any progress and adjourned until tomorrow.

At the first open meeting of the full delegation in three weeks General Nam Il, the chief Communist negotiator, had attacked the U.N. delegation for their refusal to repatriate all prisoners of war. He also opposed a week's recess of the negotiations.

General Harrison replied that the meetings of the full delegations had been futile. "In these meetings," he said, "we have been restrained in our statements and have tried to be absolutely factual. Your statements, on the other hand, have demonstrated utter hypocrisy.

"You have said we want to retain your personnel. What we know and what the world knows as a fact is that those prisoners are afraid to be returned as slaves to the tender mercies of Communist control.

Octogenarian to Fight Rhee for Presidency

PUSAN, Saturday (Reuter).—A third condidate entered the lists against President Syngman Rhee in the presidential elections here on August 5.

He is 82-year-old Lee Sui Yung, considered the most likely candidate to get the support of the Democratic Nationalists—the main party opposing President Rhee's supporters.

The other candidates besides President Rhee himself are Cho Bong Ahm, former Communist leader who stands as an independent, and Shin Hueng Woo, also an independent.

Mossadegh Premier And War Minister

TEHERAN, Saturday (Reuter). — Premier Mohammed Mossadegh's new nine-man Cabinet was sworn in at the Shah's Palace here today, with himself also the War Minister. He had resigned the premiership a fortnight ago after the Shah had rejected his request for this post.

The new Foreign Minister is Hussein Navab, who is at present Persian Minister at The Hague. The former Foreign Minister, Bagher Kazemi, is now Finance Minister. The Ministers of National Economy, Education and Post and Telegraph will be appointed later.

In a broadcast to the nation over Teheran Radio yesterday Mossadegh pledged himself to carry out reforms "now that the solution of the tangled oil question has taken a turn for the better." But he said no reforms could begin until order and security were restored. He appealed to the people "not to repeat the events of the last days" and to collaborate with the security forces in maintaining order.

British Charge d'Affaires George Middle called on Mossadegh yesterday at the Premier's request. The interview lasted nearly three hours, and the strictest secrecy was maintained by both parties. The only indication available was that "oil was discussed."

Semi-official sources said the Premier indicated he would be prepared to discuss compensation to be paid to the Anglo-Iranian Oil Co. and to let the British take up any disputes with a Persian court of law now that The Hague Court had ruled itself incompetent to judge the Anglo-Persian controversy.

Meanwhile, the American Officers Club is remaining closed until the situation completely returns to normal. All foreigners, especially Americans and Britons, have been cautious about appearing on the streets since the riots of the Wednesday and Thursday.

Spiradic groups of pro-Communists have been the only demonstrators seen in the streets during those two days. Some of them shouted anti-Shah and anti-American slogans.

Ben Aharon Quits Mapam Executive

TEL AVIV, Saturday. — Mr. Itzhak Ben Aharon, Mapam M.K., has resigned from the Mapam Central Committee, following a decision of the "Sneh group," Mapam's left wing faction, last Thursday, to demand from the Le'ahdut Haavoda faction that it cease its separate activities within the party, it was learned here today.

Le'ahdut Haavoda, which is in a minority opposition within Mapam and is the right wing faction of the party, has in recent months come into strong conflict with other factions within Mapam and has been holding separate meetings and issuing its own conclusions.

At Thursday's meeting the left wing group threatened Le'ahdut Haavoda members with expulsion from the party if they did not cease their activities.

U.S.-British Note On F.M Shown to Rifa'i

DAMASCUS, Saturday (AP).—The U.S. and British Charges d'Affaires here today visited the Minister for Foreign Affairs, Dr. Safer Rifa'i to show him the text of the Anglo-American note to Israel objecting to the transfer of the Israel Foreign Office from Tel Aviv to Jerusalem.

The note confirms the U.S. and British Governments' refusal to transfer their Embassies and their adherence to the U.N. resolutions concerning the "Internationalization" of Jerusalem.

According to a report in the London Jewish Observer, the British Government has made an oral representation to Israel concerning the move.

Repairmen to Leave For Potash Works

The first steps for renewing operations at the potash works will be taken this week, Dead Sea Works sources disclosed in Jerusalem yesterday. A group of electricians, carpenters, and other repairmen will start then to refurbish the living quarters for plant workers. Required materials have almost all been brought to the plant via the Ein Husub road.

The next step is to ensure sufficient fresh water for the workers and for the plant. Although a water line is planned, it will be brought at first in tanker cars. This method of supply, however, will not suffice to clean the evaporation basins.

Experts claim, however, that this cleaning can be done by salt water although much more labour and pumping is required. It was pointed out that when work first began at the plant, there was no fresh

(Continued on Page 3. Col 1)

7 Jailed, 2 for Life in East German Espionage Trial

BERLIN, Saturday (Reuter). — The East German supreme court today passed two life sentences and a total of 59 years' imprisonment on seven Germans found guilty of spying for U.S. and West Berlin "espionage groups."

All seven admitted collecting economic, military and political information about East Germany and Soviet installations and transmitting it to a West Berlin anti-Communist group, the "Free Jurists." This group, mainly composed of former East German lawyers, is one of several groups collecting information about East Germany.

Passed on to U.S.

Dr. Ernst Melsheimer, State Attorney-General who prosecuted in this trial,—the biggest spy trial in East Germany since the war—said information provided by the seven was passed on by the jurists to the U.S. secret service.

The court was presided over by Frau Hilde Benjamin, East Germany's only woman judge, who has already passed several death sentences on alleged spies.

The two men sentenced to life imprisonment are Fritz Krefeld, chief constructor of the Heinrich Rau heavy machine-building works at Wildau, Brandenburg, and Fritz Schmelzer, engineer in the Building Union works at Staalsung.

Others sentenced were: Karl Neubauer, director of an East Berlin state-owned electric bulb factory—15 years; Gerhard Schneider, official of the Central Construction Bureau in the Ministry of Machinery—12 years; Paul Schallon, official of a cooperative dairy at Stralsunk—10 years; Rudolf Fissler, accountant in the Trade Ministry—12 years, and Gerhard Pape, mechanic in the state-owned EKM machine works at Gourlitz—10 years.

The East German Government is to set up a uniformed semi-military youth labour corps on the lines of those in other Communist countries. It is to be called "Service for Germany" and will channel East German youth into works of national importance. A law setting up this corps was passed by the Cabinet on Thursday.

The Soviet authorities in East Germany have imposed restrictions on the U.S. military mission there as a reprisal for U.S. restrictions on the Soviet military mission in West Germany, the East German ADN news agency announced on Thursday.

FAROUK FORCED OUT

Abdicates in Favour of Infant Son

CAIRO, Saturday. — King Farouk's 16-year reign came to a sudden and dramatic end today. He left the country at 6 o'clock this evening — nine hours after Army units headed by Field Marshal Mohammed Najib surrounded his summer residence in Alexandria, the Ras el Tin Palace and served an abdication order on the 32-year-old monarch. The Cabinet proclaimed Ahmed Fuad II King of Egypt and the Sudan and assumed the powers of the Throne pending the appointment of a Regency Council.

Before sending his troops to surround the Palace, Najib sent a warning to the King against any attempt to flee the country by sea or air. The warning said that the Royal Yacht or any plane taking the King out of the country before he had abdicated would be sunk or shot down. A crowd whose feelings had not yet taken definite shape watched in silence along Alexandria's waterfront as Farouk walked up the gangplank of his yacht, Al Mahroussa, en route to his exile. His destination was believed to be the Italian port of Genoa, from where he may fly to the U.S. But the U.S. Embassy denied knowldege of this.

Uncertainty seemed to surround the whereabouts of Farouk's wife, ex-Queen Narriman, and their 7-month-old son, Prince Ahmed Fuad, in whose favour Farouk abdicated. While *Reuter* reported that Narriman and the child, as well as Farouk's eldest daughters by his first wife Farida, were also on board the Mahroussa, A.P. quoted an army announcement that Farouk sailed alone, leaving the 18-year-old ex-Queen and the child behind. The army announcement said Narriman had wanted to follow Farouk into exile, but was prevented from doing so "because she must take care of the baby Crown Prince and bring him up."

Najib announced at six o'clock (local time) tonight that Farouk had accepted an ultimatum this morning demanding that:

- **He sign his abdication before noon and**
- **He leave the country before six o'clock this evening**

In a nation-wide broadcast Najib declared that "everything is proceeding quietly and in order." He appealed to Egyptians and foreigners alike and in particular to the inhabitants of Alexandria to remain calm and disregard misleading rumours.

"Our foreign brethren must rest assured of the safety of their lives and property," he said, adding, "I trust no demonstration of any kind will take place. Such demonstrations will be dispersed, whatever their nature."

"This is the conclusion of a national struggle which has lasted for several decades," he said, announcing that he was giving up the rank of Field Marshal and the post of Minister given to him by Farouk in order to save money in time of economic crisis.

Ali Maher later announced that Farouk had left with him two sealed envelopes, one addressed to the Cabinet and the second to Parliament, containing his suggestions for the Regency Council. The letters will be opened in the presence of members of Parliament, which was dissolved in February.

Position Hopeless

Farouk's position became hopeless when before dawn today strong units of the army led by Field Marshal Najib surrounded the Ras el Tin Palace. While Najib's forces and the Royal bodyguard faced each other across the railings of the Palace courtyard, Najib and Premier Ali Maher went into conference. No resistance was offered by the bodyguard, which capitulated after a few shots were fired into the air. No one was hurt.

Farouk's three other main Palaces—the Abdin and Koubbeh (in Cairo) and the Montazah in Alexandria, were also cordoned off, and the Royal guards here also surrendered without fighting.

While "Operation Palace" — Najib's second bloodless *coup*—was being carried out in Alexandria, Cairo bristled with military activity. Sherman tanks, armoured cars and other mechanized forces raced through the streets and squares. Troops in full battle-dress guarded strategic centres. Air force planes roared low over the two Alexandria palaces and over the capital.

Citizens lining the streets of Cairo cheered the troops, men embraced and kissd each other. There were shouts of "Najib—liberator of Egypt."

Punctually at 6 o'clock, as the Royal Yacht weighed anchor at Alexandria, a colonel at the General H.Q. of the Egyptian Army in Cairo smashed a portrait of the ex-King hanging in the entrance hall. All portratis of Farouk in Government offices, barracks and public buildings were also smashed.

Mr. Jefferson Caffery, U.S. Ambassador, was the only foreign diplomat who saw Farouk between his abdication and departure. Mr. Caffery was among the people who saw Farouk off at Alexandria.

A few minutes before the appearance of Farouk, clad in the white uniform of Admiral of the Fleet, crowds cheered Egyptian tanks, infantrymen and guards posted all around the Ras el Tin Palace. Then Farouk appeared and silence fell like a shroud. With him was Premier Aly Maher Pasha. A few minutes later Najib arrived to bid the former King good-bye. He gave the ex-King a military salute, then the King walked aboard the Yacht.

As he stood on the deck of the Mahroussa while it pulled away from the dock, tears came to the ex-King's eyes.

The detention of seven members of Farouk's Royal Cabinet who had earlier resigned, was reported tonight. They include Elias Andraos Pasha, industrialist who had previously announced his resignation from his posts as honorary Economic Counsellor and delegate on the board of the Suez Canal Company.

Others are Brigadier Mohammed Hilmy Hussein Bey, Commander of Palace transport Commodore Akef Bey, Farouk's Personal Pilot; Italian-born Antonio Pulli Bey, Private Secretary; Jussef Rashad Bey, Commander of the Royal Yacht; Mohammed Hassan Bey, Private Chamberlain. Also detained was Karim Tabet Pasha, Royal Press Counsellor who resigned some time ago. Hafez Afifii Pasha, chief of the Royal Cabinet, also confirmed his resignation today. He was reported still at liberty.

Yesterday Najib paraded his tanks through the capital's main streets in a show of force following reports of a counter-plot by high police officers, five of whom were arrested.

(AP, Reuter, UP)

U.K. Suez Troops On Alert; Navy Moves

LONDON, Saturday (Reuter). — The Foreign Office and the Admiralty announced tonight that precautionary moves were taken by British troops in the Canal Zone and by the Mediterranean Fleet in view of the unsettled position in Egypt.

Britain would not hesitate to take action to protect British subjects in Egypt, the Foreign Office said earlier.

It is understood that the precautionary measures did not indicate any change in the general policy of non-intervention in the Egyptian domestic crisis. Such measures include the general alerting of British troops in the Canal Zone and changes in the Mediterranean Fleet's summer cruise.

Officials of the Foreign Office went into hurried conference earlier today and were unavailable for comment. A spokesman later hinted that the abdication might delay the return of Sir Ralph Stevenson to Cairo. The Ambassador, who had been recalled for consultations last week, was planning to return to his post in a few days.

Only First Phase

It is now realized here that the clash between the King and General Najib may only be the first phase of a continuing revolution which only came to the surface last week.

The abdication was expected as the logical outcome of last Thursday's *coup*. The birth of the Crown Prince had made it possible to force Farouk's abdication while still adhering to the formula for unity with the Sudan under the Crown.

The questions now are first whether Najib will remain in control of the movement which he has launched and secondly, how far the Wafd, the Moslem Brotherhood and the Communists will exploit the unstable situation for their own political ends.

Soviets See Plot For Mid East Comand

MOSCOW, Saturday (AP).—Soviet commentators take the line that the Egyptian coup is part of a plot to bring Egypt into the Middle East Command.

'Crust of Peace Cracking'—Nehru

NEW DELHI, Saturday (Reuter). — Commenting on events in Egypt and Persia, Prime Minister Nehru said in Parliament yesterday that the current of history was moving rapidly. He said:

We seem to be living on a thin crust of peace and that crust threatens to crack up often enough and does crack sometimes... The happening in some of the states in Western Asia, the coup d'etat and the rest reveal a picture of instability.

Not Likely to Seek Asylum in U.S.

WASHINGTON, Saturday.—U.S. officials said today that they doubted whether King Farouk will seek political asylum in America. The deposed monarch conferred with the U.S. Ambassador Mr. Jefferson Caffery shortly before he fled from Alexandria, it was not thought that the question of asylum was discussed.

State Department officials indicated that the U.S. would have no objections to the King taking up exile in the country, but they guessed he would prefer his more familiar haunts on the continent.

The U.S. Government was aware of a substantial build-up of the Egyptian Royal Family's investments in America in recent months.

The State Department announced that Mr. Caffery told Ali Maher Pasha this morning in Alexandria that while the U.S. considered the change of government an internal matter the U.S. wishes to make it clear that it was following the situation with the closest attention and would expect the constituted authorities to exert every effort to maintain law and order.

The State Department said the Prime Minister gave Mr. Caffery all these assurances.

Officials added that the question of recognition presumably will not arise if the King has legally abdicted and transferred authority to his son.

(U.P., Reuter)

Unpopular King

CAIRO, Saturday (Reuter).—King Farouk was one of the youngest and richest of the world's monarchs, but at the end of his reign probably the most unpopular. When he ascended the throne in 1936 at the age of 16 he was a handsome prince adored by his people. At 30 his looks and prestige had faded. He looked far more than his years and had become the centre of a national and personal controversy.

Returning in 1950 from a visit abroad he was greeted by a warning from Egypt's opposition parties. "The patience of Your Majesty's public has come to an end," the petition said. "We are afraid a revolt will take place in the country which will not only destroy those who are unjust but will leave the country in a state of financial, moral and political bankruptcy."

Arms Scandal

Signed by the Saadists, Liberals, Nationalists, Kotlists and several independent leaders, the petition sought a renewed respect for the constitution and the dismissal of all who "have wronged the country." It referred specifically to the "arms scandal" — a long-standing point of argument in Egypt following allegations that useless arms and ammunition had been bought for the Egyptian forces during the Palestine war, mainly through intermediaries in Italy.

When Farouk's marriage to Queen Farida, who had borne him three daughters, was dissolved in 1948, his subjects expected him to remarry, as his desire for a son was generally known. But few could have guessed who the new Queen would be. Narriman Sadek, daughter of the late Hussein Fahmi Sadek Bey, former Secretary-General of the Ministry of Communications, was engaged to Zaki Hachem, an Egyptian diplomat at U.N. Headquarters. But rumour had it that Farouk met her a few days before the wedding in a Cairo jeweller's shop — it was said to be "love at first sight."

The engagement was broken, and early in 1951 Narriman's betrothal to

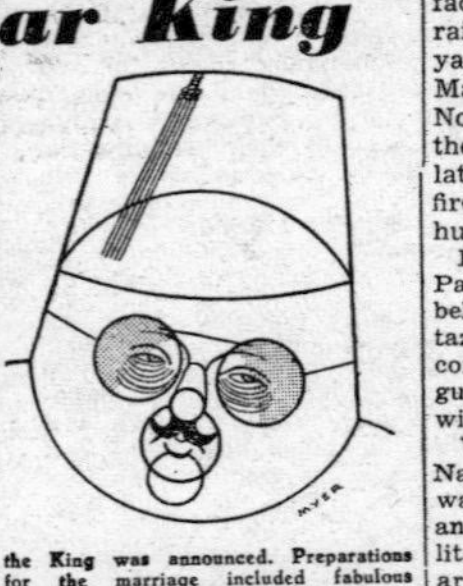

the King was announced. Preparations for the marriage included fabulous gowns for the young bride. One evening dress had a 10m. franc diamond shoulder strap. The wedding gown, encrusted with diamonds, took 4,000 hours to make.

This splashing of luxury before a population which was struggling in vain to meet the soaring cost of living with incredibly low incomes was the last blow to whatever popularity Farouk still had in the eyes of his subjects. Criticism of the King became more open. Complaints now were voiced aloud in trams, cinemas and everywhere.

Only son of King Fuad I and of Queen Nazli, Farouk was born in Cairo on February 11, 1920. His name means "the one who carefully distinguishes between good and evil." His son Ahmed Fuad II was born on January 16, this year.

AFTER MIDNIGHT

The condition of Senora Eva Peron was considerably worsened late yesterday.

Reports of African Intimidation

LONDON, Saturday (Reuter). — Colonial Secretary Oliver Lyttelton said in the House of Commons last night he had received reports that Africans were being intimidated not to support proposals for a Central African Federation of Nyasaland and North and South Rhodesia.

The Governor of Nyasaland had told him that Africans in the southern province had said they dared not support the Federation under fear of death. There were also allegations of widespread intimidation in both the southern and central provinces.

1,600 Tons Sulphur To Israel Authorized

WASHINGTON, Saturday (INA). — Negotiations have been concluded here for the supply of 1,100 long tons of crude and 500 tons of refined sulphur.

The announcement by the Department of Commerce covers the period October to December 1952. It is the first time that the U.S. has authorized an allocation of refined sulphur to Israel.

Under the new allocation Israel will receive more refined sulphur than any other country in the Middle East or Africa. She also gets more crude sulphur than any of the Arabs

Wafd Watches in Geneva

GENEVA, Saturday (Reuter).—Mustafa Nahas Pasha, former Prime Minister and leader of the Wafd, discussed the new situation in Egypt with Fuad Seraj e-Din Pasha, Secretary-General of the Party and Senator Mahmud Abdul Fath, owner of the newspaper "Al Misri."

Nahas Pasha said he was expecting a visitor from Cairo tomorrow and would then decide whether it is necessary to return to Egypt.

TUNIS INTERNEES FREED

TUNIS, Saturday (Reuter).—One hundred persons interned in camps under the state siege were set free on Thursday, it was disclosed here today. All those held at Ben Gardane in Southern Tunisia have been transferred to the north.

From flat to flat
by our own reliable
and well trained
packers and
porters.

EXPRESS SERVICE
TRANSPORT LTD
For 20 years noted
for faithful service...
Head Office:
TEL AVIV: 4 Rehov Mikve Israel
HAIFA: 63 Harbour Street
JERUSALEM: 1 Rehov Habavazeleth

JUDEA
INSURANCE
COMPANY LTD.
THE FIRST ISRAEL
INSURANCE COMPANY

THE JERUSALEM POST

THURSDAY,
SEPTEMBER 11, 1952

PRICE: 70 PRUTA
VOL. XXVIII, No. 7360

The Daily News
All Israel Views
THE JERUSALEM POST

Marginal Column
By A. V. SHERMAN

AZZAM'S resignation is a measure not only of Egypt's crisis but also of the Arab League's. His resignation was not unforeseen. During the past few years he has been engaged in a series of conflicts, partly political, partly personal, with many delegations, governments, and personalities; only recently the representatives of Libya, his second homeland, declared him persona non grata. Even had the internal Egyptian scene not changed as abruptly as it has done, it is doubtful whether a reform movement inside the League which has met so many defeats under Azzam's leadership, would not have pushed him out sooner or later.

BECAUSE Azzam was a prominent and representative figure, almost an institution in the Arab world, his rise and fall in themselves epitomize its recent unhappy history. He was born in 1891 in Egypt still nominally part of the Ottoman Empire. A brilliant but emotionally unstable youth he went to England to study medicine, but found the discipline of continued study irksome, and soon was caught up in the Arab nationalist movement which was gaining strength at that time among the young intellectuals. Even at that time the basis of the movement was largely negative; the young men felt that they and their people were undervalued, and that independence was the thing. But they lacked a general philosophy and orientation to guide them amid the rapid world changes which were soon to come about. For most Syrians and others under Turkish rule the Turk was the main enemy, the blight which held back their countries from progress. For Azzam, however, the Europeans were the enemy, and Turkey was to spearhead the East's revival. While other Arab nationalists aided the Entente against the Turks, Azzam joined the Turkish Armies in Libya, showing himself a talented chief but poor collaborator.

AFTER the 1936 Anglo-Egyptian Treaty he served as Minister to several Middle Eastern countries, later joining the Cabinet as Minister for Social Welfare. He was one of the generation which took up high posts in the administration, as a reward for years of successful opposition. But they had become far too set in their habits and could only oppose, cherish old enmities and make new ones. His policy with regard to Palestine illustrated the duality of his character. His claim that the Jews were his "cousins" and that he desired peace and co-operation with them were no less sincere than his fire-eating oratory, when he threatened that Arab power would push the Jews into the sea. Even his fellow-orators complained that he was carried away by his own oratory.

THE Palestine defeat was only one of the causes which led to the League's splintering and his own growing unpopularity. Indulging in his old feud against the Senussi, Azzam used his position and power to try to gain for himself the post of "Viceroy of Tripolitania," thereby setting up a barrier between Egypt and Libya, which has remained outside the League. In 1949 the feud between him and Iraq grew nearly strong enough to make his position untenable, and only Egyptian intervention saved him. After 1951, when the Wafd brought the Anglo-Egyptian crisis to a head, Azzam's efforts to embroil the whole Arab League in Egypt's troubles led to further League crises, with Iraq, Syria, Lebanon and Jordan objecting on one score or another and Azzam becoming ever fiercer and more irreconcilable in his imprecations against Imperialism and Zionism. His removal opens the way for a changed attitude on the part of the Arab League, if it survives. There is no reason why the League under sober guidance could not become an instrument of Arab co-operation and political stability in the Middle East, but this can come about only if Azzam's mistakes are not repeated. Peace with Israel is only one of the steps the League needs to take now that Azzam — who, like one of his collaborators, staked his reputation on Palestine — has gone.

Jerusalem, September 11.

Azzam Quits: New Secretary Sought

CAIRO, Wednesday (Reuter). — Leading candidates for the vacant post of Secretary-General of the Arab League are former Egyptian Foreign Ministers Mohammed Salah e-Din and Abdul Khalek Hassuna, it was reported here.

Abdul Rahman Azzam announced his resignation from the position last night on the eve of the important meeting of the League's Council opening here tonight under the presidency of former Premier Ali Maher, but gave no precise reasons for it.

The first business of the Council is likely to be the acceptance of Azzam's resignation and the choice of a successor. Both candidates for the post have wide experience in Arab and international affairs.

It was understood that Azzam's reasons for resigning were he felt he did not represent the spirit of Egypt's new regime, and was too closely associated in the public mind with Egypt's former rulers.

In a formal letter of resignation to be presented to the Council today Azzam said he had considered giving up his post several times in the past, "but my conscience prevented me from withdrawing from the field while a battle was still being waged against imperialism."

"But now I think God wants me to cast off this responsibility," Azzam's letter added. He declared that he would not change his mind under any circumstances.

Imperialism and Zionism

His letter went on to say that the League had struggled against immense enemies of imperialism and Zionism, and he prayed it would continue its fight for the liberty, freedom and dignity of the Arab world, and that Arab states would realize unity and cooperation between themselves.

Azzam later told Reuter, "I wish my country and the Arab world a blessed renaissance. The Egyptian Army movement opens a new and better future for the Egyptian people."

An Egyptian Foreign Office spokesman said earlier last night: "The significance of this Council session lies in the fact that it is the first meeting since the Arab League collective security pact of 1949 came into force last August 23 after its ratification by four member states."

(Abdul Rahman Azzam, 59, was a scholar who studied medicine in London, but interrupted his career to rally the Arabs of Libya against the Italians in World War I and after, and to fight the British.

(When further resistance was hopeless he returned to Egypt and became the youngest member to be elected to the Egyptian Parliament. It was then he began his campaign for Arab independence through Arab unity, being unanimously elected Secretary-General of the League when it was formally constituted in 1945.)

Egypt Plans New Approach to U.K.

CAIRO, Wednesday (Reuter). — Egypt is planning a new approach to solve the Anglo-Egyptian question, an Egyptian Foreign Office spokesman said last night.

He said that although no immediate action was contemplated, because the Egyptian government is busy implementing social, political and economic reforms at home, "we shall turn to foreign affairs in the not too distant future."

The spokesman made this comment after British Ambassador Sir Ralph Stevenson paid a courtesy call on the new foreign Minister, Ahmed Farag Tayeh.

The Wafd's executive today announced the formation of a three-man committee to draw up the rules for the Party's reorganization in accordance with the new law governing political parties.

Searches Continue

Special Army and police squads, continuing the search for "hostile elements" in Egypt, have raided scores of houses in Cairo and Alexandria in the past 48 hours, it was disclosed today.

They seized masses of documents which are now being studied. One of the main objectives raided was the premises of the Royal Automobile Club in the two cities. The homes of many prominent personalities under the old regime, many of them under arrest since last Saturday, were also searched.

The Government today ordered three clubs where ex-King Farouk and his associates used to meet to close down immediately. They are the Royal Automobile, the Mohammed Aly and the Nile Boat clubs.

General Nagib last night announced the appointment of Brigadier Mohammed Ibrahim, Director of Military Training, as Deputy Commander in Chief of the Army.

Brigadier Ibrahim will carry out the day to day military routine of the commander in chief which General Nagib, as Premier, no longer looks after owing to his political duties.

Mexico Proposes Korea Compromise

MEXICO CITY, Wednesday. — President Aleman, of Mexico, has formulated a compromise proposal on Korea which was officially submitted yesterday to the U.N. The proposal is designed to break the bottleneck preventing an armistice in Korea, and provides a compromise on the question of prisoners of war. Its main points are as follows:

1) Prisoners detained by either side, and who have expressed the wish to return to their country of origin, will be exchanged.

2) Other prisoners will be given the right to work and will be received by U.N. member countries which approve this step.

3) After restoration of a normal regime in Korea, the governments of the countries of origin of these prisoners will extend the assistance and facilities necessary for their immediate return; these Governments will also agree to repatriate prisoners, who wish to return to their country of origin before the restoration of normal conditions in Korea. In this latter event, the U.N. will provide the necessary assistance.

Mr. Trygve Lie, U.N. Secretary-General, said at his press conference at the U.N. today that he supported the Mexican plan.

Freezing of C-o-L Considered

Jerusalem POST Reporter

Commodity prices and the cost-of-living index featured in a series of conferences in Jerusalem yesterday.

Mapai, Government and Histadrut leaders met for several hours in the morning at the Ministry of Finance. It was reported that the C-o-L allowance was thoroughly aired, with Cabinet members generally favouring a halt in further increases, and Histadrut representatives reluctant to agree to such a policy.

Among those who participated in the conference were Minister of Finance Levy Eshkol, Minister of Commerce and Industry Dov Joseph, Minister of Agriculture Peretz Naphtali, Minister Without Portfolio Pinhas Lavon; Mr. A. Becker and Mr. Z. Onn, of the Histadrut, and Mr. H. Dan, of Solel Boneh.

At a meeting of Finance Ministry and Commerce Ministry representatives a difference of opinion arose over sugar and oil prices. Finance officials are reportedly of the opinion that under the present exchange arrangement the two items are virtually subsidized.

No Shoe Tenders

At still another meeting, shoe manufacturers accepted a Commerce Ministry proposal for the production of 40,000 pairs of shoes at last April's prices, thus guaranteeing no immediate increase. A Ministry spokesman declared that the tender system had been rejected in this instance because of a "shortage of materials," although it was reported that the tenders had begun to be stencilled. Another Ministry source stated that although a tender for the shoes "probably would have dropped the price," it was important that several manufacturers would have been forced to close down for lack of materials.

Dr. Joseph also conferred with Mr. A. Shenkar, President of the Manufacturers Association, on the "problems of industry." Among the questions discussed were the difficulty of business to pay wages and the continuing raw material shortage.

Manoeuvres End in South
By Sraya Shapiro
POST Military Correspondent

TEL AVIV, Wednesday. — The southern war games ended at 4.15 p.m. today. They formed the fifth and last link in the summer manoeuvres this year, which included three Army war games and large-scale Navy and Air Force manoeuvres. In autumn, a test of the preparedness of area defences will be held, while on the higher Army level there will be an internal trial of combined staff operations without the participation of soldiers.

These will virtually end a three-year plan, intended to test the preparedness of the Israel Defence Forces, their composition, training and war-fare principles, the Chief of the General Staff, Rav Aluf Yigael Yadin, told military correspondents today. To learn the lessons of the manoeuvres and translate them into proper instructions in the Army Training Depots is a matter of weeks.

Nobody was more conscious of the defects revealed than Headquarters, Rav Aluf Yadin said. There was a marked improvement over last year's performance.

Parachutists' Ability

The Air Force and the Navy, in particular, deserved praise for their technical ability and the fighting spirit of the crews — whose job was almost as perilous in peacetime as it is in war. The parachute unit was able to stand comparison with any group abroad, according to expert testimony.

Unreserved praise from the Chief of Staff also went to the Reservists. They proved to be as tough and dependable as regular soldiers. The same compliment went to the owners of the civilian vehicles which had been drafted for the war games.

The Deputy Chief of Staff, Aluf Mordecai Makleff, said he could see "enormous progress" in the Army after a seven month absence abroad.

In the last day of the southern war games, the Green armoured column was given the task of exploiting to the former position in face of increasing Blue pressure. The Greens had some casualties and vehicles, the umpires declared, but were able to fulfill their mission.

SHARETT, ADENAUER SIGN PACT IN MUTE, SECRET 13-MINUTE CEREMONY

'Blow to Nazism, Triumph for Israel'

WASHINGTON, Wednesday (Reuter). — Official and diplomatic quarters here regard the West German-Israel agreement as a personal triumph for Chancellor Adenauer.

These sources point out that in the negotiations was played by Dr. Adenauer, who had the support of democratic and liberal groups in Germany, but was strongly opposed by neo-Nazi elements.

One source stated that the signing of the agreement "is also a triumph for the forces genuinely anxious to promote the cause of Democracy in Germany."

Historic Achievement

The agreement is also regarded in diplomatic quarters here as an historic achievement for the new State of Israel in that it has been able to emphasize the changed status of Jews and defend their rights in Europe.

It is further pointed out here that recompense for confiscated Jewish property is to be paid by a foreign state for the first time since ancient days.

Acheson Hopes For Quick Ratification

WASHINGTON, Wednesday (AP). — Secretary of State Dean Acheson said today that West Germany's agreement with Israel to compensate the Jewish victims of Nazi persecution is proof that the "vast majority of the German people intend to make redress for the sufferings of the Jews under the Nazis."

Mr. Acheson said that the U.S. hoped the agreements signed in Luxembourg today will be ratified without delay. He told a news conference that the U.S. is pleased the negotiations ended in success.

German Envoy in U.S. 'Deeply Satisfied'

WASHINGTON, Wednesday (AP). — West German Charge d'Affaires Dr. Heinz Krekeler today issued a statement expressing his "deep-est satisfaction" at the successful outcome of the Hague negotiations.

"I am very well aware of the fact that human suffering has no relation to material claims and their restitution," the statement said, "but material means are often a way to express an attitude of mind and spirit, and this is exactly what is happening here."

Referring to the crimes of Hitler and his associates against the Jewish people, Krekeler said, "We cannot undo the crimes, but we can and must see to it that they may never happen again. It is with profound respect for the victims of terror and persecution that we present this pledge before the people of the world."

Preamble to Agreement

WHEREAS unspeakable criminal acts were perpetrated against the Jewish people during the National Socialist regime of terror

AND WHEREAS by a declaration in the Bundestag on September 27, 1951, the Government of the Federal Republic of Germany made known their determination, within the limits of their capacity, to make good the material damage caused by these acts

AND WHEREAS the State of Israel has assumed the heavy burden of resettling so great a number of uprooted and destitute Jewish refugees from Germany and from territories formerly under German rule and has on this basis advanced a claim against the Federal Republic of Germany for global recompense for the cost of the integration of these refugees.

NOW THEREFORE the State of Israel and the Federal Republic of Germany have agreed:

(The preamble is followed by the 11 articles of the agreement which are summarized on Page 4 and which will be published textually tomorrow.)

First Goods to Arrive In 1953, Oil in Few Weeks

TEL AVIV, Wednesday. — The first German goods under the reparations agreement will probably arrive in Israel at the beginning of next year, shortly after formal ratification of the agreement, but oil purchased with German Sterling balances will probably come within the next few weeks.

At a press conference here tonight, Dr. Jacob Robinson, Legal Adviser to the Israeli delegation to the U.N. and Legal Adviser to the Reparations Delegation, said that the Government's formal ratification would follow a day or so after ratification by the German parliament, probably about the end of November. The instruments of ratification will then be exchanged by the representatives of the two Governments before the Secretary-General of the U.N. in New York. An unofficial Israel delegation will probably start administrative work in Germany preparing for the establishment of the official Israel mission even before the formal ratification.

Agency and Malben

Part of the 450m. marks to be paid to Israel for the benefit of the Conference on Jewish Material Claims Against Germany will be spent by the Jewish organizations, principally the Jewish Agency and the American Joint Jewish Committee, in Israel for the absorption and rehabilitation of Jewish refugees.

Two-thirds of the entire sum of 3,450m. marks will be used directly by Israel, while 18.3 per cent will be used by the Jewish Agency and the Joint, through Malben, in Israel. The balance of about 15 per cent will be used abroad by the 20 Jewish organizations for the relief of former victims of the Nazis.

Germany still being under the control of the Occupying Powers, the agreement, as all contracts entered into by Germany, must be sent to the three High Commissioners. If no objections are raised by them within 21 days, the agreement is regarded as having the consent of the Occupying Powers.

In an exchange of letters between the two delegations, and contained in a special annex to the agreement, arrangements are made for reparations goods to be shipped to Israel in Israel vessels, in which case shipping charges are to be paid by Israel, or by ships of a third party, with payment to be made in German marks out of the sum set aside for services. In no case will goods be brought to Israel in German vessels.

Eban and Blaustein Sign Contract
By Jesse Zel Lurie
POST Correspondent

NEW YORK, Wednesday (Reuter). — The reparations agreement signed with West Germany is "a moral victory, a victory of conscience over the dictates of brute force," Israel Ambassador Abba Eban said this morning. He was speaking after ratification by the three occupying powers. The initial reply was positive, and Dr. Nahum Goldmann, chairman of the Conference on Material Claims, and Mr. Nahum Goldmann signed a contract with the Jewish Conference on Material Claims Against Germany providing for Israel's payment to the Jewish organizations of their share of the reparations.

"The Germans, who wanted to wipe the Jews off the face of the earth, are now signing a contract of compensation with a sovereign Jewish State," Mr. Eban said.

Mr. Jacob Blaustein, President of the American Jewish Committee, stated that it was the Conference's intention to use its share of the reparations for relief of victims outside Israel, but it did not exclude spending some of the funds in Israel.

Much of the Conference's funds, he said, will probably be given to the Joint Distribution Committee.

(Continued on Page 3, Col 4)

3,450m. Marks in Reparations

LUXEMBOURG, Wednesday. — At a secret, silent ceremony that lasted 13 minutes, Israel and Germany signed an agreement here today under which the Bonn Government agrees to pay 3,450m. marks as reparations for material damage suffered by the Jews at the hands of the Nazis.

The treaty was signed in a large anteroom of the main salon of Luxembourg's City Hall. The two delegations sat opposite each other across a long table, Foreign Minister Moshe Sharett and Chancellor Konrad Adenauer facing each other in the centre. Mr. Sharett had seven advisers and Dr. Adenauer five.

Mr. Sharett and Dr. Adenauer signed the agreement which had been initialed here yesterday. Before entering the room the two Ministers met briefly and shook hands.

The ceremony, which lasted 13 minutes, was conducted in complete silence. Not a single word was exchanged across the table until, the signing over, Dr. Adenauer leaned forward and suggested to Mr. Sharett that they should rise.

Two Protocols

Later Dr. Adenauer and Dr. Nahum Goldmann, chairman of the Praesidium of the Conference on Jewish Material Claims against Germany, signed two protocols. The first deals with the extension of compensation and restitution legislation for individuals now in force in Germany. In it Germany undertakes as soon as possible to take all steps within her power to ensure that the Cabinet would present a full report to the Knesset after the summer recess and might then initiate a debate on the subject. West German law, on the other hand, lays down that such agreements must be ratified by the Parliament.

The second protocol provides for the payment of 450m. marks to Israel for the benefit of the Conference.

A small group of reporters representing world news agencies, who had been conveyed to the building in official cars without being told of their destination, stood at the end of the room to witness the signing. Stringent security measures were imposed throughout the ceremony to meet a possible threat to the lives of the two statesmen.

Private Talk

After signing the treaty Mr. Sharett, Dr. Adenauer and Dr. Goldmann talked in a small room for 30 minutes. No one was allowed in the room, which was guarded by armed detectives.

Mr. Sharett was accompanied by his advisers Dr. G. Josephtal and Dr. F. E. Shinnar, joint heads of the Israel delegation, Mr. Gershon Avner and other delegation members and by Dr. M. Amir, Minister Blackhorn, Member of the Bundestag Altmeyer, Professor Franz Boehm, head of the German delegation and Abraham Frohwein.

In an exchange of letters accompanying the agreement Israel declared that the will advance no further claims against Germany. Individual claims of Israel nationals are not affected by the agreement. Israel also undertook to give preference to the industry of West Berlin when purchasing commodities.

At a joint press conference given by the two delegations following the signing a German spokesman said that the goods would be delivered to Israel who will not necessarily be of German origin only but could come from countries with which West Germany has a credit surplus.

Speaking of possible reactions from Arab countries, the spokesman said that while it is important the agreement has provoked "a certain anxiety and even upset in Moslem countries," there is no direct connection between the treaty and the Arab States, with whom West Germany entertains friendly relations.

He said it was West Germany's intention to speed up the ratification of the treaty.

Asked if the agreement will improve Israel-German relations, an Israel spokesman said, "We cannot say that this treaty has any connection with political relations between the two States."

(Reuter, INA)

Contacts First Made 18 Months Ago
POST Political Correspondent

TEL AVIV, Wednesday. — The signing of the German reparations agreement by the Israel Foreign Minister and the head of the West German Federal Government was in accordance with the wish of the Israel Government to underline the historic importance of the agreement, regarded as unique in that it represents restitution by a plunderer for past actions.

The agreement follows 18 months of contacts and negotiations. It was completed seven years after the end of the war. Without the establishment of the State of Israel, it is pointed out in Hakirya, such agreement would have been impossible.

Ratification by the West German Parliament is expected by the end of this year. As for Israel, the agreement requires the ratification of the Cabinet alone, but it is understood that when Foreign Minister Sharett returned to the Knesset Foreign Affairs Committee on the agreement he stated that the Cabinet would present a full report to the Knesset after the summer recess and might then initiate a debate on the subject.

Payments to Gird State and Lead To Economic Freedom — Lavon

The reparations agreement — a great moral and political victory — will strengthen the country and help make us economically independent, Mr. Pinhas Lavon, Minister without Portfolio, told the nation last night over Kol Yisrael.

No amount of reparations could wipe out the wrong done to the Jewish people, he emphasized, and noted that reparations would increase the State's future safety by placing it on a firmer economic basis. "Weakness arouses the lust of tyrants and extortioners," he said.

Mr. Lavon noted the benefits the nation could draw from $715m. to be paid directly and the $110m. given to world Jewry, by comparison with the $800m. the nation has received from all sources in the past four years — appeals, private and national loan, grants, private investments, property of new immigrants, and non-payment imports. With the latter sum, he said, we fought and were victorious in the War of Liberation; we re-equipped our Defence Forces; we brought 650,000 Jews from different countries and assured accommodation to hundreds of thousands; we established hundreds of agricultural settlements and equipped older settlers with all needed equipment; we built new cities in various parts of the country; we laid pipelines and built irrigation works on hundreds of thousands of dunams; and we enlarged Haifa harbour and built Kishon port.

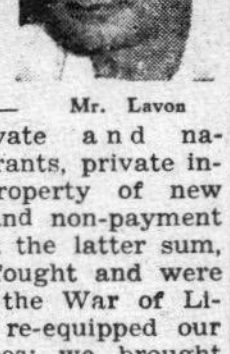

The Minister emphasized that the goods to be received from West Germany would further the process of development. They would permit us to exploit the Negev mines, broaden agriculture, develop transportation, shipping and fishing, increase electrical output, develop basic industries, and build homes for ma'abarot residents.

Mr. Lavon reminded the nation that "the people which wanted to exterminate us is forced to bear some of the burden involved in creating a new Jewish centre of strength and a place of rebirth."

It was not by chance that some Germans, those openly and those secretly anti-Semitic, tried to block the agreement. It was not by chance that the Arab countries tried many times to prevent the signing. Both knew that this agreement would strengthen the State of Israel and the feeling of security of world Jewry.

This is the first time in the history of mankind that an unwritten law was broken — the law that only force can assure just claims. The agreement establishes a new principle in international relations, he said.

"Our renewed strength gave birth to the possibility of obtaining reparations; the reparations will give birth to new forces of strength," Mr. Lavon concluded.

Tension at Signing
By Nora Beloff
Special to The POST

LUXEMBOURG (OFNS). — An atmosphere of tension created by threats of Jewish extremists and the need for security measures enveloped the ceremony of signature of the Israel-German reparations agreement here today. Nevertheless, when the silent ceremony was ended and the text signed, Mr. Sharett accepted Chancellor Adenauer's invitation to a private talk, which could no longer have been just a matter of terms of payments since those had been settled, but must have covered a wider political field.

The contents of the agreement were in no way surprising. The six months of negotiations which started in The Hague and ended in Luxembourg today were carried through in part by technicians and economists, many of whom are university professors whose job was to set Israel's claims against Germany's capacity for payment and to formulate an acceptable compromise.

The background of the talks which brought Jews and Germans together was memories of the kind of evil which cannot be paid for in cash: the evil of gas-chambers and the mass slaughter of six million men, women and children, the horrors of Belsen and Buchenwald concentration camps.

There were still unrepentant Nazis loose in the country denouncing the talks, but the Germans concerned with the talks did not disguise that they had received "encouragingly few" letters of opposition since the talks began.

AFTER MIDNIGHT

Mr. Sharett and Dr. Goldmann are staying at a hotel from Luxembourg this evening.

SOCIALISTS SAY ALL GERMANS CONCERNED

BONN, Wednesday (Reuter). — The press service of the Social Democratic (opposition) Party said today the German Israel reparations agreement should be ratified by the West German Parliament as soon as possible.

Material and moral reparation to the Jews concerned all Germans. The German people would only then be reconciled with its neighbours when it had brought proof of its good will in making good the crimes of the Third Reich, the statement said.

But there remained the task of fighting and killing all movements whose liking for dictatorship, including its excesses, made them unsuitable to serve mankind and the German people. This was an obligation which could not be laid down in the heart, but must come from within, it added.

ELECTION EXTRA

THE JERUSALEM POST

ELECTION EXTRA

WEDNESDAY,
NOVEMBER 5, 1952

PRICE: 70 PRUTA
VOL. XXVIII. No. 7404

EISENHOWER IS U.S. PRESIDENT

BULLETIN

SPRINGFIELD, ILLINOIS, WEDNESDAY (8.50 a.m. Israel Time). — GOVERNOR STEVENSON HAS CONCEDED THE ELECTION TO GENERAL EISENHOWER.

States conceded to Eisenhower at 8 a.m. Israel time, indicating how the State voted in 1948 and the number of electoral votes.

California	Dem	32
Connecticut	Rep.	8
Florida	Dem	10
Illinois	Dem	27
Indiana	Rep	13
Kansas	Rep	8
Maryland	Rep	9
New Jersey	Rep	16
New York	Rep	45
Ohio	Dem	25
Pennsylvania	Rep	32
Virginia	Dem	12
Wisconsin	Dem	12

Column One

By
David Courtney

IS it Stevenson or Eisenhower? The Americans know by now; and it is their business, it is their responsibility. But bound up with it is the fate of millions of people who had no vote, no say in the matter — whole countries, whole peoples, who have stood by and wordlessly appealed to the American electorate to keep them in mind, alongside the Tidelands Oil and the Taft-Hartley Act and the "coddling of Communists." It was terribly important to those countries and peoples whether Mr. Eisenhower or Mr. Stevenson was chosen. And that fact is no matter for American vanity, but for American pride — that is to say, if the American voters have indeed kept in mind the unenfranchised world outside.

●

THINK how rich is America. It has all the gold in the world, nearly; half the oil in the world; more atomic bombs than anyone else; more aeroplanes, tanks, guns, rockets, everything. The Americans can go where they like and take as many dollars as they like; buy refrigerators, automobiles, washing-machines; give grants-in-aid to needy nations; blankets to refugees; scholarships to poor scholars. Think how powerful is America. Alone of all the non-Communist world it has the means to fight great wars and stop little ones and by the same token to spread the balm of peace over the aching limbs of the world. Small wonder it matters so terribly whether Mr. Eisenhower or Mr. Stevenson is President this morning.

●

IT matters to the oddest of people, who have never heard of Kansas City or Fort Knox or the Daughters of the Revolution: common, unknown people all over the world, probably in Russia, too.

●

IT is hard on the American people and their President that so much of the world outside should look to them for more than the price of a meal and a gun — for more than economic aid; and for more than an ideology. What the world looks for is an end to sterile hatreds. It is all very well to prepare for war. Human nature being what it is, or even supposedly being what the realists think it is, it may be necessary to prepare for war. But there is always the chance that human nature, wisely prodded, may be better than it seems. It wants to be. It wants to be something better than a soldier trained to kill or a scientist trained to destroy; and, therefore, it looks to be guided towards peace of mind and the works that can arise out of peace of mind. And because the Americans hold so much of the world's resources in the hollow of their hands it is felt that they must also have much of the wisdom of the world in their heads. It is quite natural that whole peoples should look to them for a sign.

●

HAS America given the sign?

●

OF course, there will be plenty of people to say that it makes no difference whether Mr. Eisenhower or Mr. Stevenson is President. Mr. Stevenson has shown that he possesses the mark of world statesmanship and we know that Mr. Eisenhower is a great leader of men. Mr. Stevenson has shown a profound understanding of mankind; Mr. Eisenhower a true understanding of men and women. All the same, there is a difference. It is odd how people all over the world have seized upon the difference with almost desperate hope. With the American voters the issues were not quite the same, of course — not quite as simple. But their choice, whatever it may have been, is fateful.

Jerusalem, November 5.

Premier Tables W.Z.O. Status Bill in Knesset

By Moshe Brilliant,
POST Parliamentary Correspondent

Prime Minister Ben Gurion introduced a bill in the Knesset yesterday recognizing the World Zionist Organization as the agency authorized to coordinate the activities of all Jewish bodies engaged in development of Israel and in the integration of immigrants.

This bill was almost passed in August. It was withdrawn by the Government after the Knesset, during the final reading, amended it in a snap vote to accord recognition as "the organized representatives of the Jewish nation in all matters relating to the development of Israel."

The formula which had upset the Government three months ago had been more in line with what the Zionist Congress had requested in 1951. Mr. Ben Gurion, however, rephrased it after representations from non-Zionist supporters of Israel in the United States. The measure he introduced yesterday had been drafted in consultation with the Jewish Agency Executive in Jerusalem and was approved by the Zionist General Council.

A last minute amendmant of the draft was announced by Mr. Ben Gurion, who said that the expression the State of Israel "represents its citizens only" would be eliminated. The clause had been inserted originally to allay the fears of non-Zionists that they would be accused of dual allegiance if they supported Israel. In the debate in August, Mr. Ishar Harari (Progressive) had fought for the deletion of the clause, arguing that it might jeopardize the Government's position when it demanded permission for Jews in countries like Russia to migrate to this country. Mr. Harari's proposed amendment had been defeated in August, by the votes of the coalition.

In the debate, which will be concluded today, the focal issue was again the Government's formula of "authorized agency" versus that of "organized representatives" which a snap majority had passed three months ago.

Mr. Ben Gurion said that the State of Israel had no right to name representatives of world Jewry, since its jurisdiction was confined to its boundaries. He added that it would be preposterous for the Knesset to designate the World Zionist Organization as the representatives of the 2,000,000 Jews in Soviet Russia, where Zionism is outlawed, or of the 5,000,000 Jews in the U.S., only a minority of whom were organized in the Zionist Movement.

Mr. Harari, who together with Mr. Israel Bar Yehuda (Mapam) had introduced the motion which had upset the Government in August, defended his formula. He said that the Zionist Organization was the only group supporting Israel in an organized way.. His proposed formula would not be construed as a snub by any other group.

Politics was seen as Mr. Ben Gurion's motive by Mr. Yosef Serlin (Geenral Zionist), who said that the Prime Minister wanted to curb the authority and influence of the Zionist Organization, because his party did not control it as they did the Government.

Mr. Ben Gurion said that the status he was proposing would enable the World Zionist Organization to act in place of the State in matters of immigration and settlement. Government supporters said this had in effect been the status of the Movement before Israel's independence. Mr. Zalman Shazar (Mapai), who is a member of the Jewish Agency Executive, said the measure was in the spirit of the Zionist Congress' request.

Opposition to granting the Movement a special staus was voiced by spokesmen of two anti-Zionist parties. Mr. Meir Wilner (Communist) said the status would create a "state within a state" and he opposed relinquishing sovereignty to a body not elected by the people of Israel. Dr. Avraham Deutch (Agudat Israel) praised the Movement's immigration, settlement and political activities but said they had no business dealing with spiritual and cultural matters. He called for the establishment of an enlarged Jewish Agency including non-Zionist parties, which he said should get the status.

Senators and Representatives

Senator Joseph McCarthy was setting the pace in Wisconsin for the Republican candidates who are leading in most of the contests. The controversial Senator from Wisconsin gained a lead of nearly two and a half to one over his Democratic opponent, Thomas Fairchild.

In Connecticut, both Democratic candidates for the Senate, the incumbent Senator Benton and Representative Ribacoff, conceded defeat to their Republican opponents at an early hour. Among the other Senators who were re-elected at an early hour were Knowland of California who ran on both parties; and Byrd of Virginia who was unopposed.

In Massachusetts, Senator Lodge, who was one of the first to back Eisenhower for president, was losing to his Democratic opponent John Kennedy.

In other Senate races, Smith (Republican) of New Jersey was leading Alexander; Bricker (Republican) was leading Di Salle in Ohio; and Senator Jenner was leading in Indiana.

The first results of the elections to the Senate came from California where Senator William F. Knowland standing on both the Republican and Democratic tickets was re-elected against slight opposition from an Independent.

In Texas, Mr. Price Daniel, formerly State Attorney General, was elected Senator in the place of Mr. Tom Connally, former Chairman of the Senate's Foreign Affairs Committee, who did not seek reelection. Mr. Daniel stood as a Republican as well as a Democrat and had no opposition.

In the 435 contests for the House of Representatives the Democrats had won 79 seats (mostly in the South) at 6 a.m. (Israel time) while the Republicans had won 13.

Democratic candidates for the House of Representatives were elected unopposed in nearly 40 electorates in southern States. They were four in Mississipi (other two seats contested) seven in Alabama (two others contested) seven in Louisiana (one other contested), five in Tennessee (4 others contested) 4 in Virginia (6 others contested) in addition to all 10 in Georgia.

Brooklyn borough president, Mr. John Cashmore, Democrat, was defeated by incumbent Senator Irving Ives, Republican, in a Senate race.

The Winning Team

Dwight David Eisenhower ... Born in Denison, Texas, October 14, 1890... Grew up in Abilene, Kansas... Graduated from Abilene High School in 1909... Entered United States Military Academy at West Point, New York, in 1911... Commissioned as 2nd Lieutenant, 1915... Married Mamie Geneva Doud on July 1, 1916 in Denver, Colorado. They attend the Presbyterian Church. Their one son, Major John Eisenhower, has just returned from Korea.

Between 1915 and 1941, Eisenhower served in many U.S. military posts: Panama (where he helped plan its defences); Philippines (under General MacArthur) and in France, with the Battle Monuments Commission. In 1942, became commanding general of European Theatre of Operations... Planned invasion of North Africa and invasion of France which began June 6, 1944.

Remained in Europe until November, 1945, then returned to Washington to become Chief of Staff of U.S. Army... Retired in October, 1948 to become President of Columbia University in New York City... In December, 1950, was recalled to military service to head SHAPE (Supreme Headquarters, Allied Powers, Europe). In May, 1952, resigned from SHAPE... A month later Eisenhower resigned from U.S. Army to accept Republican nomination... Conservative on domestic matters, strongly internationalist.

Richard Nixon, 39, lawyer... Married, three children... After war-service in the U.S. Navy entered Californian politics and became Congressman, and in 1950, Senator. In domestic politics strongly conservative; internationalist voting record.

Republicans Claim Landslide; Ike Breaks 'Solid South'

NEW YORK, Wednesday, 8.40 a.m. — With half the votes counted, General Eisenhower has a two million lead over Governor Stevenson in the popular vote, assuring his election as 34th President of the United States.

The vote was 14,100,000 to 12,300,000 assuring Eisenhower 249 electoral votes from thirteen States. He was also leading in 22 other States with a total of 144 votes (266 are needed for election).

Gov. Stevenson is ahead in only 13 States with 134 electoral votes.

Stevenson's top aides said at 7.25 a.m. Israel time: "It is all over but the concession to Ike."

This adviser said there was no doubt that Eisenhower had won, and there is not much use in "hanging on" to the outside possibility that Stevenson still had a chance to win.

At 7.30 Israel time, Gen. Eisenhower led the popular return with 12,800,000 votes as against 11,300,000 for Mr. Stevenson. He had to his credit eight states with a total of 111 electoral college votes.

Eisenhower took an early lead and held it as the votes rose rapidly into the millions. The first state which was won by a candidate was Maine, traditionally Republican, which gave its five electoral votes to Eisenhower.

The Republicans predicted a landslide for their nominee soon after their candidate jumped into the lead. At 5.30 a.m. (Israel time) an assistant to Governor Stevenson said, "The news is not so good, and looks pretty grim."

This pessimism was generated by the fact that Eisenhower took early leads in such traditionally Democratic southern states as South Carolina, Virginia, Alabama, Florida, Texas and Oklahoma. He was also leading in his home state of Kansas, Ohio, New Jersey, Indiana, Massachusetts, and Maryland.

Stevenson took an early lead in North Carolina, Illinois, Pennsylvania, and Tennessee.

This was at an early stage of the voting when only 12 per cent of the total vote had been counted.

The Democrats conceded Florida's 10 electoral votes to Eisenhower. It was the first time the Republicans captured this State since 1928.

Virginia and Florida also gave their electoral votes to Eisenhower. It was the first time that these traditionally Democratic states had done so since the bitter Smith-Hoover campaign in 1928.

At 7.30, Israel time, Mr. Jacob Arvey, the Democratic campaign manager in Chicago conceded Illinois.

Eisenhower also won Maryland's nine electoral votes. Maryland went Republican in 1948.

Eisenhower took a strong hold on the Presidency at 6.15 a.m. (Israel time) when New York state was conceded to him by the Democratic chairman there, Mr. Fitzpatrick. New York has 45 electoral votes, the largest of any state.

At that time the popular vote was Eisenhower 6,845,033; Stevenson 6,117,538. The Republican also carried such important states as Pennsylvania, Illinois, New Jersey, Maryland, Ohio, Indiana, and Wisconsin.

The Democratic State Chairman conceded Ohio's 25 electoral votes to General Eisenhower in face of his commanding lead with 30 per cent of the polling places reported.

Eisenhower virtually assured Oklahoma's eight electoral votes for President on the basis of a 36,000 vote lead in the normally Democratic state with 70 per cent of the vote counted. Unofficial returns from 2,678 precincts of 3,859 gave Eisenhower 284,456 and Stevenson 248,195.

Record-breaking voting was reported all across the nation. A spot check showed that 85 per cent of Manhattan and Bronx registered voters had cast their ballots by 5 p.m. In some heavily populated districts the count reached 90 per cent. The same was true in Illinois, Mr. Stevenson's home state which has gone Democratic since 1932.

California pitched into the election with determined enthusiasm, and predictions were that more than 5 m. would go to the polls. Other key states such as Ohio, Senator Taft's baliwick, Pennsylvania, and Missouri, President Truman's home, were reporting record counts.

The amazing thing, on which both sides could agree, was that people were turning out in tremendous numbers. Bright, sunny weather combined with the heat of the campaign to produce what will probably be a record total.

Record-Breaking Vote Interpreted

New York, Wednesday (Reuter) The record-breaking size of the early vote in the presidential election was claimed by the Republicans to represent a nationwide upsurge of independent, new and formerly indifferent voters in support of the crusade of their candidate, General Dwight Eisenhower.

The record vote can also be explained non-partisanly as due to the exceptional measures which have been taken this time to get out the vote. National leaders from the President downwards have expressed their shame that the proportion of the voters casting ballots is so much lower in the U.S. than in other free countries.

Many people had to stand in line an hour or more to vote. Many polls were swamped from the opening hour..

Stevenson stood in a queue for half an hour this morning, refusing offers for him to go straight in, at the hamlet of Half-Day, Illinois, which adjoins his farm. The Governor then drove to his official mansion in Springfield to await the results.

Eisenhower voted with his wife in New York and then went "into seclusion" at his Morningside Heights residence on the Columbia University campus. He expressed weariness after his 52,000-mile campaign, which he called "the toughest fight of my life."

Election Sidelights

At Newburyport, Mass., 101-year-old Henry Bailey stopped on his way to work to vote in his 21st presidential election. He first voted in 1872 when President Ulysses Grant was re-elected.

An unidentified woman had to take off her skirt outside a Miami Beach, Florida polling station before the officials would allow her to vote. The skirt bore an embroidered slogan "I like Ike," and it was illegal to take propaganda into the station. She calmly removed her skirt, stood in line in her slip for 15 minutes, and then voted.

In Boston, a woman drove up to vote in a sleek limousine, ordered her chauffeur to stand in queue, and a half hour later as his turn came up she took his place, voted and drove off.

In Tarentum, Penna., a woman was driven in an ambulance to a booth six hours after giving birth to a son.

A Soldier's Revenge

A survey of the preferences of 500 "typical" American soldiers on duty in Korea gave a two-to-one vote for Stevenson, according to a "New York Times" correspondent.

Their reason was "I have been with the Army for a year. Would you expect me to vote for a General?"

Tidal Wave

Tidal waves hit the Hawaiian Islands flooding buildings and wrecking moored houseboats, but otherwise causing little damage.

Panic stricken people who rushed into streets halted traffic. Police were dispersing them, reports said. Wake Island had been alerted for tidal waves. Other reports said four waves had struck the Hawaiian islands ofKauai and Oahu flooding roads and killing cattle. Oahu's windward shore was being evacuated but no deaths were so far reported.

Quake Report — Page 3

Backstage Talks On Korean Issue

UNITED NATIONS, Tuesday. — While the debate on Korea has been postponed until tomorrow, active behind-the-scenes moves are taking place in atttempts to achieve a compromise between the Soviet and U.S. views.

The 14-nation Arab-Asian bloc is meeting tonight to prepare a resolution for the Committee aimed at ending the war. Peru has presented a resolution calling for the appointment of a commission specifically directed to settle the war prisoners issue which has blocked the Panmunjom talks.

The Peruvian delegate explained that his proposed commission would be headed by Switzerland and contain all states with armed forces in Korea, plus one neutral state from the Far East and one from Europe or the Americas.

Non-Discriminatory Trusts

The Trusteeship Council voted without opposition last night to urge states administering trust territories to abolish laws and practices contrary to the U.N. Charter and the Universal Declaration of Human Rights. With 46 votes for and India and France abstaining, the committee asked the Assembly to recommend administering authorities to open up all public facilities to indigenous inhabitants of their territories without race distinction.

In last night's debate on India's complaint of South African discrimination against Indian nationals in the Union, Iraq and Pakistan voiced their support to the complaint, embellishing their speeches with general attacks on the whole South African Apartheid system.

The Arab-Asian bloc is endeavouring to set up a three-man Good Offices Commission to bring India, Pakistan and South Africa to resume negotiations on the issue.

A Soviet proposal to prevent the use of press, radio and other information media for promoting "aggression and war" was defeated in the Social Committee last night.

Korean Front Quiet, Chinese Repulsed

SEOUL, Tuesday (Reuter). — Leaving their dead on the battlefield, Chinese attackers drew back on the east flank during the night and "all-quiet" was restored all along the Korean front.

About 1,000 Chinese had stormed forward near Heartbreak Ridge during the night after laying down a heavy artillery barrage. They were knocked back to their starting point, leaving 131 dead on the battlefield. About 50 more were believed wounded.

An Eighth Army spokesman said tonight that there had been "little fighting" along the front since this attack.

Bonn Disturbed by Prospect Of Arab Boycott Over Reparations

By GEORGE LICHTHEIM, POST Correspondent

LONDON, Tuesday. — Reports from Bonn suggest that the West German government is disturbed by the prospects of an Arab boycott should the reparations agreement with Israel be ratified. Government circles have been alarmed by the cancellation of some German contracts in Saudi Arabia and the formal Egyptian note of protest has stimulated uneasiness among the government coalition's right wing which is composed chiefly of business groups interested in exports.

Their political unit, the Free Democratic Party, includes elements like Mende who told reporters yesterday that good relations with the Arab world were vital to Germany. Various many have been active, chiefly Arab delegations to West Ger- among industrialists and their main argument, that firms exporting reparations goods to Israel would be boycotted elsewhere in the Middle East, is shrewdly designed to frighten business circles on whose support the government relies.

There is also a somewhat more pronounced ideological opposition to the reparations agreement among conservative nationalist circles whose strength is not entirely negligible.

The argument that Israel is still at war with its neighbours, and that Germany would thus be taking sides against the Arabs, has scared the Bonn Foreign Ministry which is super-sensitive to anything affecting Germany's reviving export trade.

Ratification Assured

Despite this concerted campaign, against ratification of the agreement, most observers in Bonn and in London believe that Adenauer will stand firm. His personal prestige is involved and he has long experience in wearing down parliamentary opposition. Besides, both major parties, Christian Democrats and Social Democrats, firmly support ratification.

It is a misfortune, on this and on other grounds that the Social Democrats are outside the government, especially since they are fairly close to the left-wing of Adenauer's party which fortunately holds most key posts.

The danger lies in a "compromise" under which the Bundestag would ratify the agreement, but with some proviso making its execution dependent upon prior agreement over property restitution to the Arab refugees. A hint that the Arabs would drop their opposition if a proportion of the German funds were employed for this purpose was contained in the Syrian note of September 8 which inaugurated the chorus.

'Mission Has Failed,' Delegation Head Says

"Our mission to convince Germany to reverse its stand on reparations to Israel has failed," Ahmed Daouk, leader of the Arab League's delegation to Bonn, told the correspondent of "Falastin," the Old City daily, in the West German capital yesterday. "Our delegation arrived too late to convince Germany," Daouk said.

In Beirut, the Union of Lebanese Chambers of Commerce yesterday morning decided to proclaim a strict boycott of German goods.

Bonn Proposes U.N. To Supervise Reparations

BONN, Tuesday (UP). — West Germany has suggested to the Arabs that shipments to Israel under the reparations agreement be supervised by the United Nations.

Parliamentary sources here said that the proposal was raised last week during the talks with the Arab protest delegation in an effort to allay Arab fears that Israel would be receiving war materials from Germany.

The Arabs are understood to be pleased with the suggestion. It is pointed out here that the proposal cannot be carried out without Israel approval and the attitude of the Israel government has not yet been made known.

Belgrade Protests Rome Measures in Trieste

BELGRADE, Tuesday (Reuter) — Yugoslavia today handed a note to the Italian Minister here protesting against the gradual annexation by Italy of the "A" zone of the Free Trieste territory, according to Tanjug, Yugoslav news agency.

The note claimed Italian measures in the zone violated the peace treaty, prevented the possibility of an agreement on Trieste and damaged the cause of peace in Europe.

Yugoslavia reaffirmed her readiness to continue exchanging views with the aim of settling the question on the basis of a "reasonable agreement."

In Italy today Premier Alcide de Gasperi asked Yugoslavia for "one act of goodwill to settle the question of the Trieste Free Territory."

Egyptian Actor Gets 15 Years' Hard Labour

CAIRO, Tuesday (AFP). — Ra'afat Shalabi, Egyptian actor convicted for conspiring against the Government, was sentenced to 15 years' hard labour by a military court here today.

This sentence, the verdict pointed out, was mitigated by General Mohammed Nagib, whose approval was sought by the military court. The original verdict entailed life imprisonment.

Egypt Soon to Get British Jets

LONDON, Tuesday (Reuter).— Britain is on the point of resuming the supply of jet aircraft to Egypt, a usually well informed source said here tonight. Resumption of supply would be on the basis of contracts interrupted by a British Government decision in September, 1950, it is understood here.

The form of announcement on the resumption of supply has not been finally decided. It may be made in the House by Foreign Secretary Anthony Eden before he leaves London for New York next Friday.

The jet planes Egypt will get are expected to be Gloster Meteors.

After the improvement in relations between the two countries since General Mohammed Nagib came to power in Egypt last July, Britain recently resumed the supply to Egypt of non-warlike material including training aircraft and spare parts.

News Blackout On Jordan Parliament

The Jordan Parliament held the first meeting of its new session yesterday afternoon to debate a motion of confidence in Abu'l Huda's Cabinet after hearing his policy statement.

Until late last night no news of the result of the vote was given by any Arab radio station or news agency. This suggests that censorship had been imposed on the proceedings of the House.

All Radio Ramallah would say was that the House had drafted a reply to the Regency Council's Speech from the Throne on Saturday and that they had elected a committee to present the reply to the Council this morning.

Majlis Passes Bill For Prosecution of Ghavam

TEHERAN, Tuesday (Reuter).— The Persian Majlis today passed a bill authorizing the Government to prosecute and punish ex-Premier Ghavam e-Sultaneh for the incidents on July 21.

The bill was submitted to the Majlis by Premier Mossadegh last week and said Ghavam, who is 75, was responsible for the deaths that occurred on that day, during his term as Premier. Earlier, in a letter to the Senate, Ghavam announced that he was prepared for trial by a court.

(Ghavam resigned on the evening of July 21 after a premiership lasting four days following disturbances which local observers at the time described as "the bloodiest ever." By the time his resignation was announced it was estimated that more than 20 people had been killed in clashes with the police and army, about 1,000 injured and more than 200 arrested.)

ARGUS
The National Insurance Co. Ltd.
Fire ★ Accident
Workmen's Compensation ★ Marine

THE JERUSALEM POST
MONDAY, NOVEMBER 10, 1952
PRICE: 70 PRUTA
VOL. XXVIII. No. 7408

Keep Abreast Of Affairs
Have THE JERUSALEM POST sent to your home address

DEATH OF PRESIDENT CHAIM WEIZMANN

Column One
By
David Courtney

THERE is profound reason for grief. Something more than the State's first President has died; something more than a venerable leader of Zionism. How much more is not possible to tell; but in the first shock, muffled as it may have been by expectation, it is as if an era had passed — the era of Zionist vision. That may have been why Mr. Ben Gurion, in a wise and moving eulogy, put Dr. Weizmann among the patriarchs, the judges, the prophets and the kings, from whose deeds and teachings was formed what now we call the Jewish spirit, which outlasted the statehood of antiquity.

●

GREATNESS is not subject to precise definition. It is a pervasive quality seldom recognized in its own generation. For there is littleness even in great men, and a tendency among contemporaries, whose understanding is limited by the stress and hurt of current history, to set up the littleness in denial of the greatness, forgetting that greatness is a quality of men intensely human, who may be as prone to the silly frailties of our kind as any man. One day, I hazard, the historians will call Chaim Weizmann great. The integrity, the vision, and the profound ideal drawn from the true spirit of the Jews rather than from their ambitions, will have come into their own.

●

I SAW Dr. Weizmann for the first time at a session of the Anglo-American Committee of Inquiry in Jerusalem. Seated well behind, I could see only broad, stooping shoulders, the bald, freckled pate with its fringe of iron-grey hair, the occasional gesture of expressive hands. The voice, slow and gently dignified, hesitant as it searched for a telling phrase or a persuasive image, spoke almost an Elizabethan English. In the stooped back, the fervently gesturing hands, the searching words, was a tangible sincerity, an urgent, inevitable manifestation of the truth of a whole people: the man and his words took on the grandeur of the cause he pleaded.

●

OTHERS came to whom the cause was history and only the solution remained to argue. They did not plead the cause but the rights of the Jews. Perhaps therein lay the difference between Weizmann and his Zionist colleagues. Where he strove for the redemption of the Jews in the land of their fathers, they strove for the sovereignty of the Jews in a Jewish territorial state; and from that distinction came the distinction between the man of peace and the men of action. Both were needed, but in the final event there was room only for the men of action, by whose deeds a war was won and a State founded. From then on, Chaim Weizmann was to remain a lonely figure on the Presidential eminence; but it can be said that if Israel was founded by the deeds of the men of action, it will survive only by the principles and wisdoms of which Dr. Weizmann was, perhaps, the last of an impressive line of preceptors.

●

HE was an aged man when he died, and his last years were cruelly enfeebled. He will not be remembered for his service as the first President of Israel. The honour fell naturally to him as it could have done to no other living man; but an honour it remained and that alone. And yet his passing is not the breaking off of a withered branch of Zionism. Rather will it be felt as the loss of something profoundly important, which was personified in his frail body and which gave to the highest office of the State a decorum it can ill afford to lose. Politically inactive as he may have been at the last, he was more than a national figure, more even than a great Zionist: he was a great Jew, and by that greatness a figure of international stature. Not only Israel, but the world, has need of such men and of their vision.

Jerusalem, November 10.

Army Stops Work

All entertainment and fatigues in Army units, excepting the most essential tasks, were suspended as soon as the news of the President's death was received. Parades will be resumed only after the funeral.

The national flag was lowered to half mast at all units, and at the time of the funeral special parades will be held.

In all Defence Force synagogues, after the reading of the Torah on Monday, Thursday and Saturday, which fall during the seven days of mourning, special remembrance prayers are to be held.

At all morning parades, during the seven days, unit commanders will order one moment of silence as the flag is lowered to half mast.

'He Wore Crowns of Learning And Statesmanship'—Ben Gurion

The Cabinet met in special session at 11 o'clock yesterday morning in Jerusalem to hear a memorial address by the Prime Minister. The meeting, which was attended by heads of the Jewish Agency, was broadcast by Kol Yisrael, and a recording was broadcast several times during the day.

Mr. Ben Gurion said:

Members of the Israel Government and the Zionist Executive — that which we feared has come: the President of the State, Dr. Chaim Weizmann, passed away this morning at his home in Rehovot. I will not attempt to describe fully the achievements and the personality of the Chosen One of the Nation, to whom there has not been an equal since Herzl. For such a description many volumes would be necessary, for Weizmann carried two crowns on his head — a crown of Statesmanship and a crown of Learning. He was at once the first of our Nation and among the greatest in science.

Even in the few years when he had not been elected as President of the Zionist Organization, Dr. Weizmann was the first citizen of the Jewish People and symbolized our stivings for national renaissance, which has been called Zionism. His magnetic personality, his hallowed achievements over tens of years, his special position among the Jewish People and among the whole of the civilized world — all these reasons made him the natural choice of the people. And even as Dr. Weizmann carved for himself an everlasting niche in Jewish history, so has he attained a place of glory in the world of science.

One can only wonder at the fact that the man who devoted his entire life, his strength and his time to the Zionist Movement and the upbuilding of the Yishuv and the State, did not for one moment cease his scientific research. He not only built up a Zionist school of thought with its great accomplishment, he also established a Scientific Institute of great excellence.

For Dr. Weizmann these two activities—his political and practical efforts on the one hand, and his scientific achievements on the other — were not separate aspects of his life, but were twin activities emerging from a single root — his Jewish spirit.

Dr. Weizmann recognized the profound and simple truth that the renewal of our life and our independence, that the security of our existence and its future, and that the upbuilding of our homeland and our culture all depend on science as the central pillar of the structure we are forging. For Weizmann, his great scientific deeds were an organic and central part of his historic contribution to the upbuilding of the State of Israel.

Thus even his greatest achievements in the field of international politics — the Balfour Declaration — was, as is well known, not unrelated to his scientific work.

Dr. Chaim Weizmann will take his place in the everlasting history of the Hebrew Nation together with the greatest figures of our past—our forefathers, Judges, Prophets, Kings and all the leading figures who wove the fabric of the nation for four thousand years.

In the name of the Government of Israel, we send to the bereaved family of Dr. Weizmann, his widow, Dr. Vera Weizmann, and his son, as well as to the Executive of the World Zionist Organization, our heartfelt and deep sorrow at their loss.

The State of Israel and the Jewish people the world over will join in this deep mourning at the passing of the last President of the Zionist Organization and the first President of the State of Israel.

Order of the Day

The Chief of Staff has issued this Order of the Day:

The Defence Army of Israel stands in salute. The Defence Army of Israel lowers its flag. The pennants of its corps and brigades are lowered. Israel's first President Chaim Weizmann has departed. He began as the emissary of an exiled people, dispersed and divided; and as President of an independent people in a sovereign state he completed his years.

He symbolized the driving force of vision, the wisdom of science, the joy of upbuilding and the creative power of a generation of pioneers, of those who brought their dreams to fulfilment. He was the symbol of our revival and renaissance—beloved, renowned, illustrious.

In solemn awe the Defence Army of Israel salutes the memory of the President.

Agency Heads Hear Locker, Goldmann

The Jewish Agency Executive held a special meeting in Jerusalem yesterday immediately upon hearing of the death of the President.

Mr. Berl Locker, Chirman of the Executive who opened the meeting, described the historic role of the President in the history of the Zionist movement and the Jewish people from the days of Herzl to the establishment of the State.

"Let us recall that President Weizmann was one of those fortunate statesmen who saw the fulfilment of the great vision toward which he had strived throughout his life," Mr. Locker said.

The Chairman called the late President a great scientist, a great Jewish patriot, and a wise and cautious statesman.

Dr. Nahum Goldmann Chairman of the Executive, spoke on the genius of the late President, his personal charm and how he had synthesized East European Jewish culture with Western learning.

President Weizmann had lived not only to become the President of Israel, but also to witness something that few merit: he became a legend during his own lifetime.

After the meeting, Mr. Locker and Dr. Goldmann called on Prime Minister Ben Gurion and expressed the sorrow of the Zionist movement. They also attended the special session of the Cabinet yesterday morning.

Youth Aliya Message

A condolence message to Mrs. Vera Weizmann, the late President's wife, has been sent by the Youth Aliya Department of the Jewish Agency. "We all mourn deeply and we are with you in these difficult hours," the message said. It was signed by Mr. Moshe Kol, Director of the Department, and Mrs. Bertha Schoolman, chairman of Haddasah's Youth Aliya Committee.

The Histadrut's Executive held a special meeting in the morning: Mr. M. Namir, Secretary-General, said that the "Era of Chaim Weizmann has just ended — a glorious era of historic struggle and achievement."

Dr. Weizmann saw in Jewish Labour a partner. He had a deep understanding for the working man, the pioneer and the builder. The Israel Labour movement had lost a faithful friend, he said.

Shock to American Jewry

By JESSE ZEL LURIE

NEW YORK, Sunday. — President Chaim Weizmann's passing, though long expected, still came as a shock to the American Jewish community.

At a memorial service held today by the United Israel Appeal Conference Mr. Arthur Lourie, Weizmann's close friend and associate for decades, delivered a moving eulogy. Israel Ambassador Abba Eban cancelled his planned appearance at the Conference and is carrying on diplomatic duties in connection with the President's death in Washington.

A mass memorial meeting in the New York area is planned next Sunday and will be addressed by Mr. Eban and others. Special memorial services will be held in all synagogues next Saturday.

The U.I.A. Conference has decided that the best tribute to the President would be to carry on its work, which envisions providing funds for 265,026 new immigrants in the next five years.

The five-year budget presented by the Chairman, Mr. Rudolf Sonneborn, totalling $625m. includes a provision increasing the number of settlements to 825 from the present figure of 575 and doubling the number of trained farmers from 7,200 to 14,500.

A quarter of a million permanent housing units for immigrants are projected by 1958, quintupling the present figure of 57,000.

The success of these plans depends on United Jewish Appeal increasing collections. The 1953 budget which will be presented to the U.J.A. annual meeting next month totals $102.2m.

The 1952 figure is slightly larger. The U.J.A. adopted the 1952 quota on this basis and the Joint Distribution Committee needs $151m., of which almost half will be raised this year.

The expenditures of the Jewish Agency and Keren Hayesod in the first 10 months of 1952, according $67,125,563, the bulk of it from U.J.A.

KNESSET TO MEET THIS AFTERNOON

The Knesset is to meet at 4 o'clock this afternoon for a memorial session.

Israel flags at all Government and Municipal offices will be flown at half mast during the seven-day mourning period. All schools will be open today, the Ministry of Education announced. Classes were stopped at noon yesterday.

The meeting of the Economic Council to have met this morning has been postponed.

Queen Cables Condolences

LONDON, Sunday. — Queen Elizabeth II, statesmen, the press and organizations in many countries paid tribute today to the qualities of Dr. Weizmann.

Messages spoke of the grief occasioned by the passing of one who had dedicated an inspired life to Jewry.

Queen Elizabeth telegraphed to the Acting President of Israel, "I have learned with deep regret of the death of Dr. Chaim Weizmann who devoted his life so wholeheartedly to the welfare of his people. Please convey my sincere sympathy to the family."

News of the death reached British Jewry through the B.B.C. news broadcasts. The Home Service bulletins opened with an appreciation of Dr. Weizmann's role as the leader of the Zionist movement, and stressed his friendship with Mr. Churchill and other great British leaders. It made special mention of the fact that he was at one time a British citizen.

British Jews yesterday expressed their "profound grief" on the death of President Weizmann.

A message to Ambassador Eliahu Elath said, "The Board of Deputies of Britain's Jews request Your Excellency to convey to the Government of Israel and to the family of the late President the deepest condolences and the expression of profound grief at the death of Dr. Weizmann.

"No tribute can adequately convey the debt which world Jewry owes to the late President whose life-long endeavours and determination, combined with statesmenship of the highest order, culminated in the creation of the State of Israel, a homeland and refuge for oppressed Jewry from all corners of the world.

"British Jewry recalls with special pride that it was in this country with the cooperation of the British Government that Dr. Weizmann was able to lay the foundations of the State.

The message ended saying, Dr. Weizmann's name "will be engraved forever on the hearts of world Jewry of which he was a noble and dauntless champion throughout his distinguished life." It was signed by Dr. A. Cohen, president of the Board of Deputies, and Mr. H. E. Rotman, secretary.

In a statement, Dr. S. Levenberg, Jewish Agency representative in London, said that "with the death of Dr. Weizmann has disappeared the greatest Jewish political figure of our generation. His prodigality has dominated the world Zionist Movement for almost four decades."

The Zionist Federation issued the following statement:

"We are heart-broken at the passing of Dr. Weizmann, and deaply mourn the irreplaceable loss which the whole Jewish nation has suffered. Dr. Weizmann's blessed memory will remain enshrined forever in Jewish hearts. Through his wise statesmanship as President of the Zionist Organization, he directed the constructive effort that inspired Halutziut and the planners and builders of the Yishuv."

Churchill: 'World Lost A Distinguished Citizen'

Premier Churchill's telegram to Prime Minister David Ben Gurion read:

"I am deeply grieved to hear of the death of my old friend Dr. Chaim Weizmann. The world has lost a distinguished citizen and Israel a faithful son. I should be grateful if you would convey my sympathy to Mrs. Weizmann."

World Capitals Send Messages

A French Foreign Ministry spokesman said that "France heard the news of the death of Dr. Weizmann with deep sorrow. The French people will share the grief of the people of Israel at the passing of this great figure."

The Chief Rabbi of Paris said, "President Weizmann was destined from the start for a great part in the history of Jewry. His name will always remain linked with the miraculous resurrection of Israel, a resurrection in which he played a great and noble part.

"French Jewry joins with the world in paying tribute to the great scientist and statesman, and in the grief of the people of Israel."

Special services in French synagogues will be held next week.

Flags at Half-Mast

Swiss Federal authorities, in Berne yesterday expressed their profound sorrow over the death of Dr. Weizmann. Both the Legation and the Swiss Foreign Office lowered their flags to half-mast. The Legation announced that a Condolence Book was opened yesterday.

The Norwegian Government has forwarded its condolences to the Government of Israel, it was officially announced in Oslo yesterday.

West Berlin's Mayor, Mr. Ernst Reuter, said in Berlin yesterday that news of the death of President Weizmann "will be received with deep sorrow by the German people.'

Our sympathy will be the deeper because of the inmeasurable sorrow caused both to him and to millions of our dead Jewish fellow citizens by the injustice of the past."

Messages were received from Mr. Trygve Lie, the Secretary-General of the U.N. One was addressed to Mrs. Weizmann and the other to the Foreign Minister.

Cables of condolence were also received from the Minister of Iceland, Mr. Helgi Briem, who is in Stockholm; the Netherlands Minister, Jonkheer M.P.M. Van Karnebeek; M. Rene Mayer, former member of the French Government, and from the Jewish Organizations of the town of Sfax, Tunisia.

The "New York Times" said yesterday that Dr. Weizmann's life was "sufficiently full of adventure, romance, accomplishment and fulfilment to have been lived by a dozen men. He was a world famous scientist, a statesman, a leader of a forceful political movement, an intellectual and, above all, a great huamnitarian."

The paper said that in his 78 years he "experienced every emotion: reward for priceless scientific achievement, despair when the great prize seemed lost and triumph when the prize, his lifelong dream, was won."

The "Times" also devoted more than half a page to the achievments of the late President and to his biography. The "New York Herald Tribune" lauded the great role played by the President in the struggle for the establishment of the State.

With deep sorrow, the Government of Israel announces the death of the President of the State, Dr. Chaim Weizmann.

Chaim Weizmann, the son of Ozer and Rahel Weizmann, died at his home in Rehovot at 5:55 on the morning of the 21st of Heshvan, 5713 — November 9, 1952. His wife was at his bedside.

The House of Israel mourns the loss of the elect of his people. The Government has set up a committee with full powers to carry out the funeral arrangements.

Funeral Tomorrow in Rehovot

By HUGH ORGEL, Jerusalem POST Correspondent

REHOVOT, Sunday. — The body of President Weizmann is tonight lying in state on a black-draped catafalque beneath a blue and white canopy, in the open space before the President's residence here as thousands of citizens of all ages and all walks of life file slowly past to pay their last respects to the statesman-scientist, the first President of the State of Israel.

The funeral is to take place at 2 p.m. on Tuesday afternoon, on a consecrated spot in the olive grove of 75 trees planted in honour of Professor Weizmann's 70th and 75th bithdays. The site some 50 metres from his home was chosen by the late President for his grave.

The public will be permitted to file past the coffin throughout today, and tomorrow until 10 a.m.

Tomorrow, between the hours of 12 a.m. and 2 p.m. only those invited will be admitted to the grounds of the President's house, for the funeral; members of the Diplomatic Corps will arrive at 1.30.

Public Files Past

At 6 o'clock this evening, as the widow and other members of the President's family, close friends, and members of his household stood silently on the terrace before the house, members of the public began entering the grounds, passing long lines of soldiers forming a guard of honour along all roads leading to the Residence. First to file past were the Staff of the Weizmann Institute of Science, who had formed a subdued group before the entrance from late this afternoon.

The coffin containing the remains of Dr. Weizmann draped in a silk-tassled blue and white flag stands on a tall black-draped catafalque in the centre of the circular driveway before the main entrance to the Residence. The severe, sombre hue of the platform is relieved by large gilt grape-leaves. Above the catafalque is a tall blue and white canopy suspended by iron chains from four tall pylons, swathed in the national colours and entwined with black ribbon.

The pylons holding up the canopy are each topped by a gilt Magen David.

A guard of honour of four junior officers and officer-cadets is mounted at the corners of the bier; the still, silent guards, standing rigidly to attention, are relieved at half hour intervals through the long watch from this afternoon until the interment on Tuesday. Electric lamps on tall candlesticks will remain lighted at the head and foot of the coffin until it is removed to its last resting place.

By ten o'clock to night, four special trains had arrived in Rehovot. Two additional trains were expected by midnight.

Standard Lowered

At six o'clock this morning, the President's standard, which has flown over the residence continually since his election to high office, was lowered and the national flag run up to half-mast in its place. President Weizmann's driver, Mr. Yehoshua Harlap, veteran resident of Rehovot, left the house to warn the police guard and pass the tragic news to the Secretary of the Government, Mr. Z. Sharef. A few minutes before 9 o'clock the Acting President, Mr. Y. Sprinzak, Ministers Dov Yoseph and Pinhas Lavon accompanied by Mr. Moshe Rosette, Secretary to the Knesset, arrived at the house. "What is there to say? The first President of Israel is no more," was all Mr. Sprinzak could say.

At 9.30 the body was removed from the bed and placed on the floor, in accordance with Jewish custom. An honour guard of policemen and household attendants was mounted. Meanwhile, members of the family in Tel Aviv and Haifa were informed and the news conveyed to the President's son, Mr. Benjamin Weizmann, by phone to London. The Chief Army Chaplain, Sgan-Aluf Shlomo Goren, took charge of the prescribed death ritual.

During the morning the Foreign Minister, and Mrs. Sharett; the Chief of Staff, and Mrs. Eliezer Kaplan called at the residence. Other visitors were asked to leave their names at the gate. All members of the Cabinet, headed by Prime Minister Ben Gurion, called this afternoon to express condolences to Mrs. Weizmann and members of the family. They then passed before the bier which had meanwhile been brought to the President's study.

During the morning the military authorities, who have been made responsible for carrying out the arrangements, took over the [illegible] A guard of honour was mounted along the roads and tracks leading from the surrounding roads, and Army sappers strung ropes along the roadways to control the crowds; Army communications men laid special telephone wires.

At 4.15 the coffin was brought out from the house by Army officer pall-bearers and carried between two lines of soldiers to the catafalque. The intimate procession was headed by Mrs. Weizmann, the President's three sisters, Mrs. Haya Lichtenstein, Miss Hannah Weizmann and Mrs. Gittel Dunya; and his brothers, Professor Moshe Weizmann and Mr. Yechiel Weizmann; and included the Acting President and the Secretary to the Government. A short service was conducted by the Army cantor.

The ground in which the President is to be laid to rest is to be consecrated at a special ceremony to be conducted by Sgan-Aluf Shlomo Goren, Chief of Army Chaplains, and 10 other rabbis on Tuesday morning.

Illness Began Year Ago

President Weizmann's last illness began just a year ago, on November 13, 1951, and fears were then expressed for his life. He then made a good recovery, which was of but short duration. His last public appearances had been in response to processions of Rehovot residents who came to his house on Independence Day, 1950, and on the fiftieth anniversary of the foundation of the Jewish National Fund in 1951.

On both occasions, he came out onto the terrace before his house and warmly greeted his well-wishers.

In recent weeks no change had been reported in the President's condition, which continued weak. Dr. Weizmann, however, continued to take a lively interest in affairs of state, foreign affairs and especially all matters appertaining to the work of the Science Institute which bears his name and with which he had been actively associated until forced to take to his bed.

During the presidential elections in the U.S. last week Dr. Weizmann continually asked for the lastest news. In a conversation with his sister, Mrs. Lichtenstein, last night, he had said that he had high hopes for continued aid to Israel from the future President of the U.S., Mr. Dwight Eisenhower.

When his brother, Yechiel, called on him on Friday, the President was cheerful and had chatted with him about the weather and other topics, in the joking manner which had become famous.

Dr. Weizmann's temperature had risen during the day, yesterday, but not sufficiently to alarm his physicians. When the nurse who brought him his supper last night asked how he felt, he replied, "Like a poor old Jew."

(New Election—Page 3; Biography by Louis Lipsky and Editorial—Page 4.)

News Spread Swiftly Throughout Nation

Jerusalem POST Staff

Throughout the country yesterday there was spontaneous reaction to the quickly spreading news of the death of President Weizmann.

People on their way to work stopped to talk in small groups, and early queuers in grocery and vegetable shops were the first to grasp that the man whose name had been a household word had passed away. In most public places pictures of the President were displayed bordered with black ribbon, and flags were draped in black and lowered to half mast.

All public meetings scheduled for last night were cancelled. The Tel Aviv Municipality posted mourning notices throughout the city, and the Mayor scheduled a special Council meeting for Tuesday night, when most of the Local and Regional Councils will hold memorial sessions. All places of amusement are to be closed until after the funeral, it was announced yesterday.

Israel embassies, legations and consulates were informed yesterday morning of the death of the President in a special bulletin issued by the Foreign Ministry. The Ministry also informed foreign representatives in Israel.

Among the first of the Diplomatic Corps to call at the Foreign Ministry yesterday to express condolences were the Australian Minister, Mr. O.C.W. Fuhrman; the Argentine Minister, Dr. Pablo Manguel; the Brazilian Minister, Sr. H. de Olievira Baiao; the Swedish Charge D'Affaires, Mr. M. G. Hendengren; the French Charge D'Affaires, M. Yves Debroise; the Austrian Consul, Mr. Karl Hartl; and the Finnish Consul, Mr. Kalla.

Flying to Funeral

The President's son and his wife are expected at Lydda Airport by special El Al plane this morning.

Sir Simon Marks, Lord Nathan, Mr. and Mrs. Sigmund Gestetner, and Mrs. Blumenfeld, sister of Mrs. Weizmann, are travelling by the same service.

Mrs. Rose Halperin, member of the Jewish Agency Executive, is on the way from New York by air for the funeral, as are Mr. and Mrs. M. Weisgal.

Death Came At 5.55 After Two Seizures

The bulletin on the President's death stated that the President had died at 5:55 a.m. as a result of a heart attack (*angina pectoris*). It was signed by the late President's chief physician, Dr. S. Zondek, and by Dr. M. Yoel.

The President's physicians stated that the disease of the heart and the arteries which developed last year had became gradually worse. Despite a certain stabilizing of his condition, in recent weeks he could not leave his bed.

After the first heart attack in the early hours of yesterday morning he made a slight recovery. Dr. Yoel, who was summoned to his bedside, remained with him throughout the night. At 5.55 he was again seized and all the efforts of Dr. Yoel and Prof. Zondek failed to revive him, and within three minutes he died.

The Governors and Staff of the
Weizmann Institute of Science
and the
Daniel Sieff Research Institute
deeply mourn the death of their beloved
President and teacher.
Dr. Chaim Weizmann
and are in deep sympathy with the bereaved family

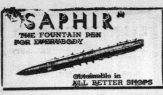
"SAPHIR"
THE FOUNTAIN PEN
FOR EVERYBODY

Obtainable in
ALL BETTER SHOPS

THE JERUSALEM POST

TUESDAY, NOVEMBER 18, 1952

PRICE: 70 PRUTA
VOL. XXVIII. No. 7415

The Daily News
All Israel Views
THE JERUSALEM POST

Column One
By David Courtney

THE newspapers give it a decoded name — the Hydrogen Bomb; and say quite plainly that the first hydrogen bomb has been exploded: "an awful weapon" adds Dr. Kaya, nuclear scientist of Tokyo, which constitutes "the greatest threat to the human race since the black death" according to the "New York Times." The official announcement hesitates to speak the word or claim the deadly secret. It says that tests were made at Eniwetok atoll in the Marshall Islands which "included experiments contributing to thermonuclear weapons research." The results were satisfactory. "Everyone at U.N. will be very greatly impressed," said Mr. Lester Pearson, of Canada; "but we may be impressed in different ways." His point is clear.

THE newspapers go on to say that the official statement contains a threat to Russia. After all, Dr. Kaya, the Tokyo scientist, says that a 50-ton "thermonuclear" bomb could crush the world to bits. A fifth that size would be enough to crush Russia to bits. What the official announcement actually says is that "in the presence of threats to the peace of the world and in the absence of effective and enforceable arrangements for the control of armaments, the U.S. Government must continue studies looking toward the development of these vast energies for the productive uses of the world." Threats, in fact, convey upon humankind from every quarter of the globe. If the newspapers' interpretation of the official statement is correct, then latest threat is gone before. But the newspapers also say that Russia should be able to follow along in good time with a hydrogen bomb. Why not? It is the natural sequence.

THE scientists are satisfied. The newspapers say they are pleased. Perhaps the newspapers exaggerate. One hopes that for the sake of the scientists and one's belief in their great role, which, at school, we were taught was a healing, enlightening, noble role. And, to be sure, at the end of the official announcement about the Eniwetok tests there is reference to experiments for the benefit of mankind. There would be comfort in that idea if we could feel the fact that the bombs have been got ready first and that some of them may go off before we have a chance to enjoy such benefits as there may be in nuclear fission and thermonuclear fusion. There is nothing to do but wait; and to hope that the "effective and enforceable arrangements for the control of armaments," which the American announcement says is now missing, will be found.

WE are supposed, also, to take comfort from the fact that the American experiments threaten an enemy with such appalling catastrophe that the enemy will never dare reveal himself as such. That is to say, Russia will stand rebuked and contrite; or at any rate cautious; and at least until she has a hydrogen bomb of her own when the whole business will start all over again. There may, of course, be something in this. There may also be something in the fairly general belief that the hydrogen bomb is such a monstrous thing that no one would ever dare use it, even if the other side could only respond with an atomic bomb of the good old-fashioned kind. In that case it seems reasonable to ask: Why bother about the weapon?

IT is no use trying to be reasonable about bombs. They have reached a stage today where the simple reason of ordinary people is confounded by their mere existence. Their probable effect is outside normal human experience and comprehension. The peril is horror which cannot be imagined and with which few will who fear death is a familiar and sensible opinion prods them. We are in the hands of the scientists and the statesmen. If the latter were as clever as the former we might sleep soundly and greet the day light-heartedly.

Jerusalem, November 18.

COST-OF-LIVING UP 4 POINTS

The cost-of-living index rose by four points during the month of October to 173, the Bureau of Statistics and Economic Research has announced. This figure is relative to September, 1951, when the cost-of-living index was readjusted to 100. During the previous month the index had also risen four points.

All Parties Unite In Praise of Weizmann

Tributes to President Chaim Weizmann were paid in the Knesset yesterday by spokesmen of all parties. The eulogies were heard by the President's widow, Dr. Vera Weizmann, who sat in the black-draped President's box with Dr. Weizmann's secretary, Miss Eiga Shapiro, and his military aide, Sgan-Aluf David Arnon. Other members of the President's family were seated in the well of the House behind the Cabinet members' table.

Mr. Zalman Shazar (Mapai) recalled in a moving speech that Dr. Weizmann had risen in the Zionist ranks as a rebel, but he knew the secret of bringing the extremes together. He said his generation had not been of a uniform opinion, but Dr. Weizmann, like Dr. Herzl had been able to unite them through the magic of his personality. Mr. Shazar cited as examples the late President's conciliation with the Orthodox parties in 1902 and his consistently positive attitude toward labour.

On behalf of the General Zionists, Mr. Israel Rokach said that Dr. Weizmann had belonged to the group which placed public interest before the interests of groups, and who put the national interest before those of sections of the nation. In this respect, General Zionism was always close to his heart.

Mr. Aharon Zisling (Mapam) said although his party was not politically in conflict with Dr. Weizmann they had always been on friendly terms. The Minister of Interior, Mr. Moshe Shapiro, spoke for Hapoel Hamizrahi and recalled the story of how Dr. Weizmann had sat in an air raid shelter during the "blitz" of London reading Isaiah.

The Progressive leader, Mr. Pinhas Rosen, compared Dr. Weizmann to Massaryk and Cavour.

Mrs. Esther Raziel-Naor (Herut) recalled that the President had helped the Revisionist Leader Zeev Jabotinsky to form the Jewish Legion during World War I.

Mr. Meir Wilner (Communist) injected the party line into his tribute when he said the most fitting honour to the President would be if military rule in the Arab areas would be abolished, and his scientific discoveries would be used for peace instead of war.

Rabbi Yitzhak M. Levin, of Agudat Israel, said that Dr. Weizmann in his last years leaned toward traditional Judaism.

Seif of Bin Zuabi, speaking for the Arab parties, recalled that when he was first introduced to Dr. Weizmann as the representative of the Arabs in the Knesset, the President said in Arabic "El Hamd'lilah" (Praise the Lord.)

Mr. David Livshitz (Mapai Avodah) talked of the associations of Dr. Weizmann with labour, and Rabbi Mordecai Nurock (Mizrahi), the Minister of Posts, referred to his cooperation with the religious parties. The Speaker, Mr. Yoseph Sprinzak, presided and said in his opening remarks that the realization of the extent of the loss was growing.

Mrs. Weizmann's Message

The profound gratitude of Mrs. Vera Weizmann and her son, Benjamin, for the messages of sympathy from all over the world was expressed yesterday in a statement issued by Mrs. Weizmann as follows: In this hour of grief, I want to express my deep and profound gratitude to the people of Israel, its elected representatives, its Defence Forces and the Government; to the Jewish communities everywhere; to the nations of the world and their leaders; and to our personal friends in all lands who, by their actions of sympathy, have sustained me and my son Benjamin in these hours of sorrow.

I wish I could thank personally each and every one of the hundreds of thousands, who came from all corners of the land to pay homage to my husband's memory.

I hope that by my services for the welfare of the people of Israel in the days to come I shall prove, at least in a small measure, worthy not only of the memory of my husband, but also of the great outpouring of love and affection which has been shown to me and my son in these difficult and trying days.

MemorialServiceHeld At President's Grave

A short memorial service was held yesterday morning at the grave of the late President to mark the end of the traditional seven days of mourning.

Those attending included Mrs. Weizmann and family of the late president, the Acting President, the Prime Minister and members of the Cabinet, the Chief and Deputy Chief of the General Staff, the State Comptroller, the Chairmen of the Jewish Agency, the Inspector General of Police, representatives of the Weizmann Institute of Science and of Kfar Hanassi, the President's physicians, the household staff and friends.

After the singing of "El Male Rahamim" and Psalm 16 by the opera singer, M. Wilkomirsky the President's brother, Mr. Yehiel Weizmann, said "Kaddish".

The Prime Minister then announced the decision of the Government and the Jewish Agency to perpetuate the President's memory by the "Yad Chaim" memorial in Rehovot.

Wreaths were laid in the name of the President's son, Benjamin who is indisposed and is confined to bed with a child, and by other members of the family, the Zionist Executive and the household staff.

At 11 a.m., the grounds of the Residence were opened to the public who began to file past the grave.

Streets Renamed

Haifa's most beautiful road, Rehov Zinobar on Mt. Carmel, will be renamed Rehov Hanassi in honour of the late President. This was announced at the beginning of the Municipal Council's meeting last night by the Mayor. The Council stood in silent tribute to the memory of Dr. Weizmann.

Rehov Hasharon, the main street in Kfar Saba, was renamed after President Weizmann at a memorial meeting of the Municipality yesterday.

Armenian Service

The Armenian Church in Haifa held a special memorial service for the President after Mass on Sunday. The vicar, the Rev. Dertad Berian, spoke briefly on Dr. Weizmann's life.

Solemn Services Held InSynagoguesAbroad

Memorial Services for the late President were held yesterday by many Jewish communities in the Diaspora.

High officials and diplomats attended a service at the synagogue in Rome. The chief rabbi officiated. An Italian army guard of honour was drawn up in front of the synagogue.

The diplomats included Israel minister Moshe Ishai and the ambassadors of Britain, France and the Soviet Union.

High Turkish officials and foreign diplomats attended a memorial service in the chief Istanbul synagogue.

In the Berne Synagogue, numerous Swiss and diplomatic personalities were present. The funeral address was delivered by Chief Rabbi Eugen Meissinger of Berne.

A solemn service was celebrated at the Synagogue of the Rue de la Victoire in Paris.

Services were also held in Amsterdam and The Hague synagogues.

Premier Daniel Malan and three other South African cabinet members attended a memorial service in the New Synagogue, Pretoria. The Governor of Transvaal also attended.

Knesset to Vote For New President On December 8

By Moshe Brilliant, POST Parliamentary Correspondent

The election of a successor to President Chaim Weizmann will take place in the Knesset on December 8, it was announced yesterday by the Acting President, Mr. Yosef Sprinzak, in his capacity as Knesset Speaker.

In accordance with the President's Tenure Law which provides that he must announce the time at least twenty days before the election date, Mr. Sprinzak circulated a note to Knesset Members yesterday. The elections, according to the law, must be held within 30 days after the President's death.

The deadline for nominations will thus be November 28, as the law provides that nominations shall close ten days before the election date. The list of candidates will be posted by the Speaker on December 1.

Gruenbaum, Bart Backed

Two parties have thus far decided to promote candidates, but in neither case has the candidate formally agreed to stand. Mapam will offer the nomination to Mr. Izhak Gruenbaum, the veteran Zionist who was Minister of Interior in the Provisional Government of 1948 when he was a member of the

There were strong rumours in the Knesset lobbies yesterday that the Prime Minister Mr. David Ben Gurion, had cabled Professor Albert Einstein in Princeton asking him whether he would be available for the presidency. Cabinet members and officials of the Premier's Office could not confirm the report.

"A" General Zionists. When the party merged with Aliyah Hadashah and Oved Zioni to form the Progressive party, Mr. Gruenbaum did not go along and he stood for the First Knesset in the 1949 elections as an independent, but was defeated. He later became active in the Peace Movement and began contributing to "Al Hamishmar" but he has not joined Mapam.

Hapoel Hamizrahi's candidate is Dr. Aharon Barth, Managing Director of the Bank Leumi. As a member of the Mizrahi party, Dr. Barth had been active in Zionist politics, but has played no part in political affairs since 1948, owing to his poor health. Hapoel Hamizrahi who have only eight Knesset Members, would require support from other parties to nominate Dr. Barth, as a minimum of ten sponsors is needed for each candidate. Mizrahi, and probably Agudath Israel and Poalei Agudat Israel would back the nomination, if Dr. Barth agrees to stand. The Mizrahi party itself is now divided as some of their leaders back the Minister of Posts and Telegraphs, Rabbi Mordecai Nurock. However, Mizrahi would have to go along with Hapoel Hamizrahi, since with only two members in the House they could not put up a candidate of their own.

The Mapai Political Committee will meet on Wednesday night in Jerusalem. The outstanding Mapai candidate is Mr. Sprinzak, who has been Acting President for almost a year since President Weizmann's illness. The Mapai decision is expected to be decisive, as they control 50 of the 120 votes in the Knesset. They would need outside support, however, to elect their candidate. The winning candidate must have at least 61 votes to be elected on the first ballot, or a majority of the members participating in the vote on subsequent ballots.

The possible nomination of Mr. Pinhas Rosen is linked with the negotiations between Mapai and the Progressives for the broadening of the coalition. Mapai has offered the Progressives only the Commerce and Industry portfolio, while the Progressives demand a second Cabinet seat. The offer of the presidency to Mr. Rosen may break the deadlock. Dr. Barth is also a possible coalition choice.

A caucus of the General Zionists yesterday but reached no decision. There was a proposal to nominate Dr. Peretz Bernstein, the party leader who was Minister of Commerce and Industry in the Provisional Government.

Iraq Oil Firm Renounces Prospect Rights

While the final touches are now being added to the agreement between the Anglo-Iranian Oil Company and the Israel government on the status of the Consolidated Refineries in Haifa, the Iraq Petroleum Company has formally confirmed the renunciation of its oil prospecting claims in Israel.

In a letter dated November 7, 1952, the Palestine Petroleum (Development) Company, an affiliate of the I.P.C., informed the Oil Commissioner, Mr. Y.R. Kossoff, that the Company does not intend to engage in oil prospecting in Israel. Consequently, the company renounces all its rights accruing from the four licences granted it by the Mandatory Government. By approving the Oil Law, the Knesset in any event revoked all Mandatory oil licences.

The agreement on the Haifa Refineries will be presented to the Knesset for ratification.

One of the basic clauses of the agreement states that the Refineries must aid in the development of the petro-chemical industry of Israel and must supply as much raw material as possible to that industry. An agreement has been reached between the Refineries and the Chemicals and Fertilizers, Ltd., of Haifa, which will be the main recipients of the Refineries' by-products.

The Israel company will provide up to 30 per cent of the total local consumption, but in the first year it will expand its operation by another five per cent, on condition that during that year the total oil consumption in Israel rises by at least five per cent. Other clauses in the draft agreement define the various questions of land possession, water supply, payment arrangements, and reexport facilities. A special provision allows the Israel Fuel Company to pay for the services of the Refineries in Israel currency.

During his stay in London, Mr. Kossoff made certain arrangements for banking procedure in connection with the use of some of Germany's sterling balances for payment of Israel's oil supplies.

AFTER MIDNIGHT

The Supreme Court again refused a hearing to Julius and Ethel Rosenberg, the New York couple condemned to death for giving atom bomb secrets to Russia. Only a commutation by the President can save them.

First Hydrogen Bomb Explosion Quakes Earth, Disintegrates Isle

'A Remarkable Feat of Precision'

WASHINGTON, Monday, (UP). — The following is the text of the official announcement on the hydrogen bomb:

Joint Task Force 132, operating for the Department of Defence and the U.S. Atomic Energy Commission, has concluded the third series of weapons development tests at Eniwetok Atoll in the Marshall Islands.

Like the Greenhouse series in 1951, it was designed to further the development of various types of weapons. In furtherance of the President's announcement of January 31, 1950, the test programme included experiments contributing to thermo-nuclear weapons research.

Scientific executives for the tests have expressed satisfaction with the results. Leaders and members of military and civilian components of the Task Force have accomplished a remarkable feat of precision in the planning and in the operations, and have the commendation of the Department of Defence and the Atomic Energy Commission.

In the presence of threats to the peace of the world and in the absence of effective and enforceable arrangements for the control of armaments, the U.S. Government must continue studies looking towards the development of these vast energies for the defence of the free world.

At the same time this Government is pushing, with wide and growing success, its studies directed towards utilising these energies for the productive purposes of mankind.

Arab Protests to Bonn Only Meant to Extort More Trade

By GEORGE LICHTHEIM, POST Correspondent

LONDON, Monday. — The expansion of German-Arab trade is now considered here to be the most likely outcome of the current dispute over the reparations issue. This paradoxical result seems indicated by the German offer to "compensate" the Arabs by stepping up imports from the Middle East. In return for this concession, which is quite clearly suggested in the latest Arab note, the Germans propose to eliminate cash payments for oil imports, substituting material deliveries.

Since oil now accounts for the bulk of Germany's imports from the Middle East, and since payment is largely in dollars or sterling, this ingenious scheme kills several birds simultaneously; Germany saves foreign currency and the Arabs obtain more German goods through barter.

The losers are Britain and America whose Middle Eastern oil companies now earn sterling and dollars for their respective governments. The proposed deal therefore raises complex payments problems between Germany and the Western powers.

Boomerang on Rivals

Even if this point is settled, German-Arab trade seems destined for expansion at a moment when British exports are encountering growing difficulties. If it is a fact, as the Germans suspect, that recent Arab protests were partly instigated by Germany's commercial competitors, the final outcome seems likely to boomerang.

Apart from Egypt, the principal field of this economic expansion is Iraq, where the imminent arrival of a German diplomatic and commercial mission under Van Scherpenberg coincides with a mounting wave of Anglophobic opposition to Nuri Said. If Germany is able to deliver the goods the threatened rupture of relations seems unlikely to occur.

Bonn government quarters now indicate that they dislike the tone of the latest Arab note, but believe that it was principally designed to extort commercial concessions which Germany is quite willing to discuss. The fact that the Arabs kept quiet until the reparations agreement was signed and are now threatening a rupture only if Germany fails to open trade talks before ratification, has finally convinced Bonn that his whole campaign is quite a piece of blackmail which the Germans feel able to convert to their own ends.

Goldmann Sure Of Ratification

LYDDA AIRPORT, Monday (ITIM). — The West German parliament in Bonn will begin to discuss ratification of the reparations agreement next month and should complete its work on this by the end of December or the beginning of January, Dr. Nahum Goldmann, chairman of the Jewish Agency Executive in New York and chairman of the World Jewish Claims Committee, said here today, Dr. Goldmann returned by B.O.A.C. this morning from London, after talks in Bonn with the West German Chancellor, Dr. Konrad Adenauer.

"I am convinced that the agreement will be ratified despite Arab threats and other difficulties," Dr. Goldmann said. The first goods under the agreement should thus be received in Israel during the first month of next year.

45-Minute Talk

Dr. Goldmann's talk with Dr. Adenauer, which lasted 45 minutes, was the seventh between the two. It was devoted to proposals to speed up implementation of the reparations agreement, and the date the purchasing mission is to begin its work in Germany.

While in Germany, Dr. Goldmann paid a courtesy call on the American High Commissioner for Germany, Mr. Walter J. Donnelly. The U.S. was putting no pressure on Germany regarding reparations, the Jewish leader said.

Arab influence was not to be felt in Germany, Dr. Goldmann said. The German Government was determined to carry out the reparations agreement. He shared with the Arabs, stressing that they would be shared only between the State of Israel and the Jewish Claims Committee. There was no change in the arrangements whereby Israel is to receive fuel from Britain against reparations payments, Dr. Goldmann said. He is to spend a few days in London shortly in this connection.

Dr. Goldmann said that he would probably visit Germany again soon with regard to the erection of a memorial at the site of the Bergen Belsen camp in memory of Jews killed by the Nazis.

LandslideVoteSweeps Papagos Into Office

ATHENS, Monday. — King Paul gave Field Marshal Alexander Papagos a mandate to form a new Greek government today after the right-wing leader's Greek Rally won a landslide victory in the country's general election yesterday.

The Rally secured almost 50 per cent of the popular vote but with is 241 of the 300 parliamentary seats. The voting was, for the first time, on a direct constituency basis instead of proportional representation. Final figures give 779,982 votes to the Greek Rally, Marshal Papagos 577,678 to the centre parties which formerly constituted the government coalition, and 164,848 to the left-wing EDA. The centre groups have 59 seats and the EDA none.

Observers consider that the victory over the Liberal-Progressive coalition was due to the nation's longing for political stability. All members of the last cabinet, except M. Venizelos, were defeated.

(AP, Reuter)

U.S. Made Tests in Pacific

WASHINGTON, Monday (UP). — The U.S. has exploded the first hydrogen bomb at the Eniwetok proving grounds in the Pacific, the Atomic Energy Commission announced here today in a statement that was bare of details. It did not even state when the explosion took place, but letters from eyewitnesses in the area placed it at 7.15 a.m. (Eniwetok time) on November 1.

The Commission announced that scientists were pleased with the results. While it did not mention the word hydrogen bomb in so many words, the Commission employed the technical phrase "thermo-nuclear weapons." Scientists define a thermo-nuclear reaction as the reaction between nuclei of atoms induced by extremely high temperatures. In the atom bomb, heat is not a factor.

The wording of the announcement suggested that several explosions might have been set off. The Commission accompanied the report on the secret "experiments" with a warning to Russia that the U.S. will continue "its studies toward the development" of the awesome bomb. It said that the lack of any "effective and enforceable arrangements for control" of atomic armaments demands it.

Intense Heat

Seismographs throughout the world recorded major tremors in the Pacific Ocean on November 4. These were followed by a great tidal wave.

Almost all eyewitness letters reported a sudden intense flash of heat sharply felt at distances up to 35 miles. The tremendous intensity of the flash heat is one respect in which the H-bomb is far superior to the A-bomb.

Another is blast. Some letters reported that an island onequarter of a mile in width disappeared following the explosion.

Servicemen's letters reported that the bomb was transported to San Francisco under heavy guard. It was loaded on a Navy vessel and placed in a special compartment. The door was welded shut and chains were welded across the door.

Looks to Be Probed

The Commission's statement apparently means that the U.S. has beaten Russia in the race for the first hydrogen bomb. Simultaneously, Mr. Gordon Dean, Chairman of the Commission, said that investigations are under way that may "lead to the possible disciplinary action or prosecution" of members of the test task force who sent home eyewitness reports of the explosion.

Mr. Dean said there would be no amplification of the official announcement, because "any amplification might give aid to potential enemies. Making public further information as to the nature and results of the test might injure the interest of the U.S."

President Truman gave the order for the development of the hydrogen bomb on January 31, 1950 "to see to it that our country is able to defend itself against any possible aggressor." As the experiments proceeded the "hell bomb" was described by Mr. William L. Laurence, science correspondent of the "New York Times," known to be in close touch with the work, as capable of releasing the destructive energy of the human race since the black death (the 14th century plague which ravaged Europe and killed one-fourth of Europe's population, 25 million persons). The bomb gains its tremendous destructive force through fusion rather than fission.

(Continued on P. 3, Col. 7)

Japanese Receive News with Concern

TOKYO, Monday (UP). — The Japanese people could think today only of the terrible consequences which would result from the use of the hydrogen bomb in warfare.

The news of the trial explosion was received here with fearful concern by the only people who have experienced the horror of atomic war.

The mayor of Hiroshima, Mr. Shinzo Hamai, whose city was the first devastated by an atom bomb, said "Once the U.S. employs the hydrogen bomb, it won't be long before Russia and Britain also have it and both sides in any future war will suffer terrible consequences. If the bomb gets out of hand, it may destroy mankind."

Pearson Greatly Impressed

UNITED NATIONS, Monday (UP). — The President of the General Assembly, Mr. Lester Pearson, of Canada, said in reply to a question in a radio interview today, that he did not think the presence of Russia at U.N. increased the danger to the secrecy of the H-bomb. He said he thought everyone at U.N. would be "very greatly impressed" by the fact that the hydrogen bomb has been exploded but we may be impressed in different ways.

India Proposes Plan For Korea Peace

UNITED NATIONS, Monday (UP). — India laid before the U.N. today a detailed formula for settling the deadlocked Korean P.O.W. issue.

It called for the creation of a four-nation repatriation commission, which would take charge of prisoners in the demilitarised zones. It also tried to bridge the gap between Communist and non-Communist positions by declaring against using force to send prisoners home and at the same time putting off until later a decision as to what would happen to those who do not want to be repatriated.

The resolution was presented to a closed meeting of top-level diplomats, including Secretary of State Dean Acheson and Britain's Minister of State Mr. Selwyn Lloyd. The Soviet countries have also been consulted on it privately.

While the western delegates declined to comment immediately on Communist diplomat said it did not go far enough. The question of what to do about prisoners who do not want to return to their own countries would be left up to an international conference which would consider other broad political problems after a cease-fire had been obtained, the resolution provided.

Poland, Sweden, Chechoslovakia and Switzerland would comprise the commission under the long awaited resolution made public just before the General Assembly Political committee resumed debate on the question.

Four Killed In Iraq Riots

BAGHDAD (AP). — Iraqi police killed four university students and seriously wounded three more during demonstrations in Baghdad on Sunday.

The week-long protests against Mustapha el Omari's government have spread to Basra and other towns in Iraq where ANA describes the situation as a "primed powder-keg."

Strikes are being staged daily by Basra dockers and by other workers demanding the cancellation of the Anglo-Iraqi treaty and an immediate end to government corruption.

According to ANA, Hikmet Suleiman, a former Premier, had declined the Regent's request to form a new caretaker cabinet pending the elections.

The Government is expected to announce this week that elections will take place as planned in spite of the declared boycott of four of the new Iraqi parties. Nuri es-Said's Liberal Constitutional Party will be the only list.

THE JERUSALEM POST

FRIDAY, NOVEMBER 28, 1952

8 Pages

PRICE: 100 PRUTA
VOL. XXVIII, No. 7424

Prague Verdict: 11 to Die, 3 Others Jailed for Life

Defendants Accept Sentences

VIENNA, Thursday, (UP). — Czechoslovakia today sentenced 11 of her former leaders to death and three to life imprisonment. This was the verdict of the biggest Communist trial since the purge of the "old Bolsheviks" in the USSR in the 30s.

Prague Radio said that all the defendants "accepted" their sentences, thus apparently eliminating the possibility of appeals to the Supreme Court and paving the way for early executions.

The presiding judge, the Prague Radio commentator stated, said the accused could seek advice from their defence lawyers and appeal if they wished to do so. After a short whispered conversation between the accused and their lawyers the prisoners stepped forward in turn and stated in monotonous, lifeless tones that they accepted the sentences and would not appeal.

The trial was the first since the rise of the Nazis in which the Jews and Zionism were openly attacked. It apparently signals the start of even greater purges and trials throughout the satellite countries and will serve as a springboard for more accusations of espionage and sabotage directed at the West. The trial also seems to solve the mystery of the American brothers, Herman and Noel Field, who vanished without trace in 1949.

Throughout the trial the 11 Jewish defendants, most of the witnesses and those named in court were described as Jews. Slansky's entire "conspiracy" was said to have been a "Jewish bourgeois nationalist" plot.

The President of the court, Jaroslav Novak, mentioned that Slansky, Frank and Reicin had during the Second World War provided the enemy with information, a charge which had not been mentioned before.

Those sentenced to death were:
Rudolf Slansky, 51, former Secretary General of the Communist Party and "chief engineer" of the coup of February, 1948. He was arrested exactly a year ago after being "kicked upstairs" to the post of Vice Premier. Like ten of the other defendants he was described in the indictment as a Jew. His original name was Salzmann.
Bedrich Geminder, 51, also a Jew, was former deputy to Slansky. He was personal secretary to Georgi Dimitroff when the late Bulgarian Premier was leader of the Cominform. He later became Czech delegate to the Cominform. Reputedly the "grey eminence" of the Czech Party, he was said to have been the Kremlin's chief agent in the country.
Vladimir Clementis, 50, former Foreign Minister, a Slovak intellectual who followed Communism all his life. He was removed from his post in March, 1950, and denounced at Party congresses. While his "self-criticism" was not accepted, he was given a job in the National Bank until his arrest in January 1951. Clementis succeeded the late Jan Masaryk as Foreign Minister and is believed to be one of the few men who knew the facts of Masaryk's mysterious death.
Andrei Simone, 57, a Jew, born Otto Katz, former editor of "Rude Pravo," official Party newspaper, and leading Czech propa-

(Continued on P. 3, Col. 5)

Prague Radio Refers To Knesset Debate

The Prague Radio commentator yesterday referred to the Knesset discussion of th Prague trial as a "Provocative debate in which Communist and Mapam members "actively intervened."

He said that Mr. Meier Wilner had effectively replied to Mr. Menahem Begin, who was elected by the "fascist Irgun Zvai Leumi." Mr. Wilner had confirmed Mr. Mordecai Oren's guilt, the radio claimed, and added that the reactionaries were so upset by his speech that the Speaker of the House ordered the Communist member to leave the Knesset.

E. German Papers Launch Anti-Payments Drive

By GEORGE LICHTHEIM, POST Correspondent

LONDON, Thursday. — The anti-Zionist campaign started in the Prague trial is now spreading to Eastern Germany, where Communist newspapers have launched a concerted drive against the West German-Israel Reparations Agreement.

The campaign takes two forms. On the one hand it is argued that the agreement merely camouflages the persistence of "Fascist" tendencies in West Germany. On the other hand, it is suggested that Germany is providing a means for America's policy of consolidating its hold in the Middle East by bolstering Israel. By a further twist, this American policy is described as being aimed at Britain and the Arabs.

There has been no sign as yet that the hunt for Zionist "agents" has been extended to East Germany, but three committees have been appointed to look into the past of doubtful members of the Communist Party and that may be the first step. German observers believe that the campaign's tone suggests that in addition to the above-mentioned motives, the regime has been genuinely mortified by the Federal Government's initiative in clearing Germany's reputation and would like to counteract the effect on world opinion.

(See Column Six)

'Jews Have Always Been Plotters'

The Jordan press commented editorially on the Prague trials for the first time yesterday, when "A-Diffa," under the headline "The Spoiled Jewish Nature," wrote that the trials revealed only one more link in the century-old chain of Jewish plotting against nations, religions and human institutions in general.

Israel to Counter Prague Offensive

By JESSE ZEL LURIE, POST Correspondent

UNITED NATIONS, Thursday. —Mr. Abba Eban, senior Israel delegate to the U.N., yesterday met representatives of Jewish organizations to decide on concerted action to counteract Prague efforts to revive the Protocols of Zion.

The Israelis are looking for an opportune moment to answer Czechoslovak attacks on the Zionist liberation movement from the U.N. podium, and Mr. Eban may refer to the Prague trial during the Political Committee's scheduled discussion on Austria.

Israel, again in consultation with Jewish organizations, opposes the Austrian request for the relinquishing of military controls, expressing dissatisfaction that Austria has not equalled Germany's minimum actions in restitution and denazification.

In the Ad Hoc Committee tomorrow, Mr. Eban will not devote more than scant paragraphs in answering the Arabs' rehashed juridical and historical arguments. This will be a reference to Paragraph 11 of the U.N. resolution on Palestine on responsibility for refugees.

After five years, delegates have heard all the arguments in which both sides are skilful. But in keeping with the desire of the majority of nations for a new start Mr. Eban will paint a broad picture of the development of conditions in the Middle East for peace and not war. He may suggest amending the six-power resolution submitted yesterday to substitute a U.N. mediator for the P.C.C., which is appointed by the big powers, and thus eliminate a possible excuse for Soviet opposition or the chance of the Arabs hiding behind the P.C.C.'s skirts.

Meanwhile, the Arab threat is unabated and the Israelis are working intensively in Washington to secure American arms to match the weapons the Arabs are receiving under British treaties. They are also asking for American intervention in London to stop Arab rearmament.

Repercussion of Prague Trial in East Germany

BERLIN, Thursday (Reuter).— Former East German State Secretary Paul Merker has been arrested in connection with the Prague treason trials, the German-language paper "Neue Zeitung" said here today.

It said Merker had been arrested by East German state security police after several of the accused in the Prague trial had said they maintained connection with "the Trotskyist Merker." The arrest was also reported by the North-West German radio.

Merker, who was a member of the East German Politburo, was relieved of his secretaryship in September, 1950, for "cooperation with a Western spy organization." He was not arrested but worked as a barkeeper in a state-owned inn.

Adenauer Wins As Bundestag Votes Treaty Debate

BONN, Thursday (Reuter). — West German Chancellor Konrad Adenauer won a triumph today when the Bundestag (Lower House) agreed by a large vote of 220 to 160 to vote next week on the ratification of the West German Peace Treaty and the European Army pact under which Germany will conscript an army of 500,000 men.

Government leaders said they believed that the treaties will be approved by about the same majority next Friday.

His unexpectedly heavy 60-vote majority wiped out his defeat by 13 votes on the same issue last week, when a group of some 200 coalition deputies rebelled.

Full House

Scarcely a seat in the house was empty after strict order to attend was sent out to deputies throughout the country, including the sick. Dr. Franz Etzel, a Christian Democrat, who has not occupied his seat since being appointed Vice-Chairman of the Schuman Plan higher authority, was called back from Luxemburg.

The one-hour debate, which started as a discussion on procedure, was packed with incident and tension.

Jessup Confers with Arabs At Private Meeting

UNITED NATIONS, Thursday, (UP). — The senior American U.N. delegate, Mr. Philip Jessup, discussed with the leaders of the Arab delegations the Palestine, Tunis, and Moroccan questions at a long, private meeting here today.

It is not known how France will behave when the last two issues come up not later than next Monday. So far, France has held that the U.N. is not competent to discuss what she feels to be French internal matters. A British spokesman said today that his country supported France in this contention.

The Arab-Asian resolution, not yet ready, is expected to ask the U.N. to help Tunisia and France to renew negotiations on the former's claim for independence.

JORDAN ABSENT FROM M.A.C.

The Jordan delegation absented itself from an emergency meeting of the Mixed Armistice Commission held yesterday. The meeting had been convened by the Chairman of the Commission, General B. de Ridder, at the request of Israel, in connection with the document found on the body of a marauder last week revealing that he had been on active duty.

An Israel policeman and an Army officer gave evidence at the meeting, at which the acting head of the Israel delegation, Rav-Seren Nutov, represented Israel. The meeting will be continued at the beginning of next week. The Chairman promised he would take steps to bring the Arab Legion Commander, who had signed the document, to the meeting as a witness.

A.Z.C. Says Prague Trial Held to Stir Anti-Semitism

NEW YORK, Thursday (INA). — The American Zionist Council, in a statement condemning the Prague trial, said today it was being enacted "with the aim of arousing anti-Jewish and anti-Israel hatred in the satellite states of the Soviet empire.

"The injection of the classic libel of an international Jewish conspiracy has been built up on elaborate trumped-up evidence in order to stir the dark currents of anti-Semitism throughout Eastern Europe."

At an emergency meeting of the Executive of the Zionist Federation of Gt. Britain and Ireland, tonight, the Prague trial was condemned as "a slanderous and provocative attack upon Zionism and the State of Israel."

A resolution said, "The exploitation of the Jewish origin of the men concerned is a viciously deliberate attempt to stir up anti-Semitism and is bound to have the effect of encouraging reactionaries throughout the world to renew their onslaught on the Jewish people."

Column One

By David Courtney

SLANSKY, Clementis, and nine others are to die.

●

MORE and more, in a world full of sentiment and empty of pity, the space between life and death becomes narrowed. More and more, in the name of merciless ideologies, the State itself becomes a savage conspiracy against justice.

●

A GREAT deal has been written and spoken about the Prague trial. Its resort to the worst kind of racialism has revolted honest men and shocked thoughtful people into a search for some logical explanation. "It can only be understood," writes one London commentator, "if it is regarded, not as a trial in the western sense but as the last stage in a battle for power between two rival groups of Communists." The defeated group consists mainly of Jews. From that fact may derive the decision of the victors to raise anti-Semitism to the dignity of a policy of State.

●

SLANSKY went into the dock as good a Communist as his judges. With Geminder, Reicin and London, his novitiate in the faith had been served in Moscow. Geminder had been for years an official of the Comintern and an agent of the Soviet secret police. As recently as July, 1951 Slansky was fulsomely praised by Gottwald for his services to communism in Czechoslovakia. Within four months of that date, he lost his job and now he is to lose his life. In the internecine ruthlessness of revolutionary statecraft it is not unusual for the lives of ambitious men to become forfeit to the power-lust of other ambitious men. What is unusual is that the grim process should have been broadened to make forfeit to that lust a principle of which communism has never failed to boast; and to bring into the service of the State one of the most ancient and most vile of racial superstitions.

●

THE death sentences have been passed. The rival group of Communists presently will have been got rid of. In the Middle Ages, a phial of poison, a stiletto in the dead of night, a hired killer in a flowing cape, would have done. Today, the State judiciary has taken the place of the hired killer in the flowing robe. There the tragedy lies. Not Slansky's life alone, and the life of the others, and not merely the boasted absence of racialism from the Czechoslovak system, but the rule of law as the basis of man's freedom within the community, has been forfeited to the ambitions of the present rulers of the State.

●

COMMUNISTS in this country, infuriated by the bitter protests of others, and perhaps hurt in their consciences, have retorted: But what of the Rosenbergs and Miami? If there had been a hundred Rosenberg sentences and all of them unjust, and a hundred Miamis, the evil done at Prague would still have been grossly evil.

●

ARGUMENT and parallel aside, Slansky, Clementis and nine others are to die; Zionism to be outlawed; the Jews to be suspect: for this reason or that; but a reason that already exposes fatal weakness in the present Communist regime of Czechoslovakia.

●

IT need not be said that the men who are to die are martyrs for a cause that will triumph. There is no cause and no martyrdom here in the person of any man. The trial itself is the cause. It was a mockery and a martyrdom of justice. Mr. Gottwald and his friends have made themselves safe from Mr. Slansky and his. But their black day inevitably must come. A ruling clique established on the negation of law and forced to buttress itself with racial superstitions will need to keep its hangmen pretty b u s y. And hangmen, on the evidence of history, usually keep a halter ready for those who have overworked them.

Jerusalem, November 28.

Progressive Exec. Vote to Join, But Approval Needed

TEL AVIV, Thursday. — The Executive of the Progressive Party voted 17 to 15 tonight to return to the Ben Gurion coalition. The decision requires the approval of the 130-man Party Council which will meet next week.

The vote was taken by secret ballot after a dramatic meeting in which Mr. Moshe Kol and Mr. Ishar Harari spoke in favour of joining the Government, and Dr. Herbert Foerder, Mr. Pinhas Rosen and Mr. Yehuda Shari spoke against. Dr. Foerder is slated to be Minister of Commerce and Industry and Mr. Rosen, a former Minister of Justice, will return to the Government without a portfolio, if the Council approves the move.

Dr. Nahum Goldmann, Chairman of the Jewish Agency Executive, joined in later and spoke in favour of returning to the Government.

Those who favoured entering the coalition argued that the Party could exercise more influence within the Government than by remaining in opposition. Mr. Kol said that the party was intrinsically collaborationist and must cooperate, particularly if it could show achievement.

The opponents said that Mapai had made no fundamental concessions on basic issues of economic and educational policies.

Cyprus RAF Searching For Israel Sailboat

POST Correspondent

NICOSIA, Thursday. — The R.A.F. in Cyprus has been searching for a missing Israel sailing boat since dawn this morning. The missing boat is understood to have left Haifa on November 18 and has been unheard of since. The search was intensified this afternoon when four Meteor-7's, two Beaufighters and one Valetta were added to the search party. Altogether 26 RAF planes have been engaged in the biggest search ever from Cyprus.

The first sortie from here this morning was made up of 13 jet Vampires, who searched the area around the island's coast and between Cyprus and Lebanon.

The jets have now withdrawn, but the search is continuing with five R.A.F. Vallettas. They are searching the area along the Lebanese and Israel coasts and further south towards Canal Zone.

Five R.A.F. Vallettas planes from the Canal Zone are also searching the Egyptian coast.

The Army spokesman announced in Tel Aviv that two Israel sailboats with 15 sailors aboard were driven out to sea by a heavy storm and did not report back at the appointed time. Sea and Air Forces of the Israel Defence Army began search operations immediately, it was said.

On November 24 the Lebanese delegation to the Mixed Armistice Commission reported that one Israel sailboat with a crew of eight was picked up along the Lebanese coast. The sailors were taken to Beirut, where they are reported to be in good health.

THE JERUSALEM POST

On the occasion of its 20th anniversary, The Jerusalem Post *will publish a special Economic Supplement on Monday.*

The 24-page Supplement contains authoritative articles on a variety of topical subjects and instructive statistical studies, reflecting some of the developments during these 20 years and vital problems of Israel's economy today. It is introduced by an important article, "The Road to Stabilization," by Mr. Peretz Naphtali, Minister of Agriculture.

Subscribers will receive the Supplement with Monday's issue. Others interested are advised to place their order immediately as the edition is limited.

4 Candidates Named To Run for Presidency

Four candidates have been nominated for the presidential elections to be held in the Knesset on December 8. Entries closed at midnight tonight. The candidates are:

1) Yitzhak Ben Zvie (Mapai), who headed the National Council for Palestine Jews (Va'ad Leumi) for 17 years.
2) Dr. Peretz Bernstein (General Zionist), who was Minister of Commerce and Industry in the Provisional Government of 1948, and now heads the General Zionist opposition in the Knesset.
3) Rabbi Mordecai Nurock (Mizrahi), the Minister of Posts and Telegraphs, who became the candidate of the four religious parties yesterday after Dr. Aharon Barth, Managing Director of Bank Leumi, finally declined to stand.
4) Yitzhak Gruenbaum (unaffiliated, but nominated by Mapam), who was Minister of Interior in the Provisional Government and for many years previously was a key figure in the Jewish Agency Executive.

Mr. Ben Zvie is favoured to win the election on the third ballot. Neither the parties to the Right or the Left of Mapai have enough votes to elect a candidate, unless Mapai switches its vote from Mr. Ben Zvie. However, if all the other parties continue to oppose Mr. Ben Zvie they can block his election and create a deadlock. In such an event, the election of Rabbi Nurock with the support of Mapai is possible. The other two candidates have been put up for demonstrative purposes only and have no chance of election.

61 Votes Needed

Unless one of the candidates withdraws, none of them could mathematically be elected on the first or second ballot when 61 votes in the 120 member Chamber are needed. On the third and subsequent ballots, a majority of the votes cast will be sufficient.

There are six General Zionists and two members each from Mapai, Herut and the Communists absent from the country. Assuming that the three candidates who are members of the Knesset will not participate in the election and that all members who are present in the country will attend, approximately 105 votes will be cast. Thus, some 53 votes will be needed for election on the third ballot, but of course the final number depends upon the actual participation.

Mapai and their Arab affiliates control 50 votes on paper, but Police Minister Behor Shitreet and Mr Zalman Aranne are in the U.S. and Mr. Ben Zvie will probably abstain. Thus they would have 47 votes.

Herut Measure

The Herut party, which lacks the necessary 10 members to sponsor a candidate, will seek to introduce a measure in the Knesset on Wednesday, five days before the election date, broadening the presidential powers. The Herut bill, which is being drafted by Dr. Yohanan Bader, would give the president veto powers, would authorize him to appoint Army commanders-in-chief and judges, and would permit him to preside over meetings of the Cabinet, but without a vote.

Unless the General Zionists and Herut swing behind Rabbi Nurock and make him a serious contender, Hapoel Hamizrahi will swing their eight votes to Mr. Ben Zvie on the third ballot and secure his election. Ahdut Avodah are also expected to cast their two votes for the Mapai candidate.

Mr. Ben Zvie is personally popular with the rival parties. He is acceptable to the moderate religious groups because he is a traditional Jew. As a member of a parliamentary committee investigating complaints of discrimination against religious education in ma'barot he upheld some of the complaints of the religious groups.

However, there is a strong feeling that Mapai should be content with the Premiership and the Speakership of the House, and that another party should get the Presidency. If all parties outside Mapai stand firmly on this point, they could block Mr. Ben Zvie's election.

Dr. Barth, who had been considered a serious contender, declined to accept the nomination of the religious parties yesterday morning when it became clear that he would not be the candidate of most of the parties. He had earlier declined to run, but was inclined to reconsider when he was told by Hapoel Hamizrahi leaders that, as a man who had been above party politics for a decade, he could unite behind him the entire Knesset except the Mapam and Communist members. When Dr. Barth saw that Mapai had put up Mr. Ben Zvie, he finally refused to stand.

Zionist Council Ends Session

The adoption of a score of resolutions aimed at strengthening the Zionist Movement and extending its work in Israel brought to a close yesterday the eight-day conference of the Zionist General Council in Jerusalem.

By adjourning as early as 7:30 in the evening, in a subdued and sombre mood, the meeting broke with the tradition of Zionist conferences of not ending on the scheduled time and having a final late hour session.

Noting that the conference had been marked by a minimum of polemics and a maximum of practical discussion, Mr. Yosef Sprinzak, Chairman of the Council, called upon the delegates to redouble their efforts in making Zionism the "leading force in uniting Jewry."

The needs of Jews, he said, are still "self-defence and self-determination," the one where Jews are imperilled and the other for them in Israel.

Mr. Berl Locker, Chairman of the Jewish Agency in Jerusalem, prefaced his final summation with a warm tribute to the late Chaim Weizmann.

The Government's grant of status to the Zionist Movement Mr. Locker termed the second most vital ruling for Jewry after the Law of Return. "It is now up to us to prove whether we are strong enough to enlist the Jewish masses in the Movement," he asserted.

'Barbaric Attack'

Mr. Locker described the Prague trial as a "barbaric attack on our national liberation movement," and reinforced the Movement's rejection of charges that it ever participated in any form of subversion. Declaring that there could only be one Movement he demanded the "total identification of every Zionist party" with it. He disclosed that Mapam's stand on the trial had been discussed by the Executive yesterday. It was learned that a number of delegates from the West had demanded immediate action to curtail Mapam's influence and activities particularly in the fields of education and organizing of youth. No decision was taken but the issue, it is believed, will remain under constant study.

All the resolutions were approved speedily and practically as submitted by the four commissions. The IL.73,750,000 budget was passed after authorizing the permanent Budget Committee, in consultation with the Agency Executive, to decide on the allocation of a IL.3m. reserve and on other reserve funds that may be forthcoming.

A proposal by the commission on the Agency's activities in Israel urging the Executive to increase the immigration flow was adopted. It was interpreted as giving the "go-ahead" sign to the plan to relax the provisions of the selectivity programme. A series of proposals to increase the number of agricultural settlements, welcoming steps being taken to liquidate the ma'barot and to expand Youth Aliya work, were also passed.

The Council recommended the establishment of Zionist Advisory Regional Councils in "areas where they may prove helpful" and would consist of organizations in several countries. This proposal was made by the Commission on Diaspora Activities, which also offered resolutions on the need for pioneering and educational work abroad.

A constitution for the Council, as submitted by the fourth commission, was adopted and outlined the composition and jurisdiction of the body, as well as listing orders of procedure.

The Council voted to send a congratulatory cable to the Rev. Y.K. Goldbloom of England on his 80th birthday, and a cable wishing speedy recovery to Prof. S. Brodetsky in England.

The singing of Hatikva, followed by the experienced gavel-rapping of Mr. Sprinzak, ended the conference.

Yehiel Off to Bonn

LYDDA AIRPORT, Thursday (ITIM). — Dr. Haim Yehiel, deputy head of the Israel Purchasing Mission in West Germany, left here for Frankfurt by PAL today, on his way to Bonn. He said he was going to Germany for a short visit of only two or three weeks, to watch developments on ratication of the agreement by the West German parliament.

Asked if he would deal with political propaganda in connection with Arab threats, Dr. Yehiel, who until his present appointment served as director of the Information Division of the Foreign Ministry, said his duties had not yet been defined, apart from his appointment as deputy head of the Mission.

AFTER MIDNIGHT

Dr. Nahum Goldmann left by Air France last night for Bonn where he will meet Dr. Adenauer. On Sunday he will unveil a monument at Bergen Belsen and will then fly to London to attend a World Jewish Congress meeting to deal with the problem arising out of the Prague trial.

THE JERUSALEM POST
SUNDAY, MARCH 8, 1953
PRICE: 80 PRUTA
VOL. XXIX, No. 7509

Malenkov Succeeds Stalin; Molotov, Beria, Bulganin, Kaganovitch are Deputy Premiers

Marginal Column

By "COMMENTATOR"

ONE of the closest and most reliable observers of the Russian scene in the 'twenties, Paul Scheffer, once wrote that a new period in Soviet history began in the days immediately following Lenin's death. The deification of Lenin, his embalment, the pilgrimages to the mausoleum and the entire Lenin cult opened a new era. Such a development appears unlikely after Stalin's death; he had been deified in his own lifetime: "Thou who didst give birth to man, thou who didst make fertile the earth, thou who dost rejuvenate the centuries, thou who givest blossom to the spring..." Capital letters were the order of the day for all pronouns and attributes where Stalin was concerned. There had been nothing like it in human history since Nectanebo the Third, Pharaoh of all Egyptians.

■

WE shall soon be told that there is a new *primus inter pares* — the best, closest and most faithful disciple of the immortal Stalin. This disciple will slowly emerge as Omniscient, Illustrious and Victorious, and in the end it will be his turn to give birth to man and make fertile the earth. To build up such a leader, to transfer all the attributes of Stalin to his successor, will take some time, but it is not too difficult a task in a regime with its monopoly of all propaganda channels and of mass communication.

■

AND then the big purge will start again. The other day I saw a book published in Moscow in March, 1924, and dedicated to the memory of Lenin. It contained contributions from the 26 Soviet leaders closest to Lenin. All but five died an unnatural death. Of those five, all but two, Stalin and Yaroslavski, had left politics "for good" after Lenin's death. It would be highly unrealistic to expect a very different development now, or rather during the next two or three years. The man to emerge as the ruler of all Russia and of Progressive Mankind will have to eliminate all those who had been at one time closer to Stalin than himself, also all his one time equals until the *primus* purges the *pares*.

■

ONE should not assume, however, that these internal developments in Russia will cause the new Leader to withdraw, even partially or temporarily, from world politics. On the contrary: He will feel obliged to prove that he is a worthy successor of the great Stalin, at all times the guardian of the Empire. Stalin could afford to be conciliatory at times, at least outwardly, particularly if it cost him nothing. Stalin could even make minor concessions, but it is doubtful whether his successor will. It is to be feared that Russia's internal crisis will not lead to lessening of world tension; on the contrary...

■

AFTER Lenin's death, Stalin appeared at the Second Soviet Congress and promised in a solemn and extremely detailed oath that he would faithfully preserve and carry out the will of the founder of the party. (Lenin's political testament, to be sure, has not been published to this day.) We shall know in due course about the fate of Stalin's political testament: Everybody will do his utmost in the coming years to show that he is in the tradition of the great Stalin and acting in the spirit of his teaching. But many interpretations are possible, and the future development of Stalinism might be not less startling than what became of Marxism-Leninism in Soviet Russia.

Jerusalem, March 8.

Anglo-U.S. Accord Reached on Persia

WASHINGTON, Saturday (UP). — A joint communique on Anglo-American political talks issued here today said the U.S. and Britain were agreed that the proposals presented to Iran on the oil problem "are reasonable and fair." It also said that Iran, if agreement is reached, would have funds placed at her disposal to meet her "immediate financial problems."

It added that Foreign Secretary Anthony Eden and Secretary of State John Foster Dulles reaffirmed the importance of preventing the shipment of strategic materials to Communist China and that Britain has decided to "take additional steps designed to ensure that no ships of the Soviet bloc or any other nationality carrying strategic cargoes to China should be accommodated in a British port."

Britain has decided to introduce a new system of licensing British vessels so that strategic materials from non-British sources could not be carried to China in British ships.

In addition to discussions on economic and financial problems, the two Ministers discussed international political developments that have taken place since their conversations in London early in February. One such exchange of views, regarded developments in the Soviet Union, and another was the proposed treaty for the European Defence Community. Both countries are concerned that the treaty be ratified as soon as possible so as to provide further continental unity which is essential to the most effective operation of NATO, the communique said.

They also considered the situation in the Middle East with particular reference to the major problems in the area and were in agreement on the urgency of furthering constructive solutions in the interests of all concerned.

The communique said that under arrangements made for common defence, the U.S. has the use of certain bases in the U.K. A prior understanding was confirmed, it was said, that the use of these bases in an emergency would be a matter for joint decision by the U.K. and the U.S. in the light of circumstances prevailing at the time.

Martial Law In Lahore

KARACHI, Friday (Reuter). — Martial law was today proclaimed in riot-torn Lahore, where Police again fired on violent religious demonstrators. Other riot squads and troops in battle order struggled to control the situation with baton charges and tear gas.

Shouting crowds paraded through the streets calling for the resignation of Foreign Minister Sir Mohammed Zafrullah Khan and demanding that the "modernist" Ahmadiya sect to which he belongs be declared a minority. Some of the demonstrators attacked vehicles and their occupants. Others tried to set fire to buildings.

Troops were deployed all over the paralyzed city. Shops were barred and shuttered, transport almost completely dislocated. Employers of the telegraph and other public services came out on strike and troops took their place.

The Ahmadiya sect which the demonstrations are against is regarded as heretical by some orthodox Moslems. It was formed 50 years ago to interpret the Koran on modern lines.

India M.P.'s Arrested For Hindu Agitation

NEW DELHI, Saturday (Reuter). — Police here yesterday arrested three leaders of Indian political parties — all members of Parliament — and 19 others who tried to lead a mass procession in support of Hindu agitation in Jammu Kashmir.

Tear gas bombs were used to break up the crowds of about 1,000. Those arrested were Syamaprased Mockerjee, head of the Jansangh party; Mr. N. C. Chatterjee, president of the Hindu Mahasa party, and Nandual Sharma, General-Secretary of the Ram Rajya Parishad party. All three parties are Hindu right wing.

Organizers of the demonstration had announced they would carry in the processions urns containing the ashes of 11 people killed by Police in Jammu during the past three months.

About 1000 people have been arrested in Jammu since the Hindu agitation began.

East Germany, Egypt Sign Trade Treaty

CAIRO, Saturday (UP). — A one-year bilateral trade agreement was signed by Foreign Minister Mahmoud Fawzi and Fritz Kich, head of the East German delegation, here today. The agreement, which will be automatically renewed after a year unless either side advises to the contrary, includes the export to Germany of Egyptian cotton, flax, linen, phosphate and other goods, and the import of German products such as electrical equipment, chemicals, transport equipment, paper, fertilizers, etc. The two countries will grant each other most favoured nation treatment, but Egypt made her treatment to the Arab League states and to Lybia an exception, while East Germany excluded certain unspecified countries.

The agreement is effective as from today.

'53 BOND DRIVE OPENS IN U.S.

By Jesse Zel Lurie, POST Correspondent

WASHINGTON, Saturday. — Forces in America wanting to compete with the Soviet Union for the favour of the Arab states by "sacrificing Israel" may influence the Administration to change its Middle East policy, Senator Herbert Lehman warned 400 Jewsh leaders at the Bond Conference here tonight.

The three-day conference, which opened yesterday, inaugurated the 1953 campaign for the sale of Israel Bonds.

Ambassador Abba Eban, at the Executive Committee meeting yesterday, is understood to have told the leaders that the highest officials in the Administration assured him that American friendship and aid for Israel would continue. But well-based reports by writers with close contacts in the lower echelons of the State Department say assistance to Israel must be reduced in order to improve relations with the Arabs. These reports prove, as Mr. Lehman said, a change of a "deadly serious nature" which we must combat "not as Jews but as Americans dedicated to freedom, democracy and humanity."

Mr. Lehman as well as other speakers tonight — Dr. Dov Joseph, Minister without Portfolio, Professor Nelson Glueck, President of the Hebrew Union College in Cincinnat, Mr. Benjamin Abrams, Chairman of the New York Bond Sales Committee; and Mrs Judith Epstein, Chairman of the Bonds' Women's Division, — stressed the importance of Bonds in strengthening Israel's economy and in meeting Soviet and Arab threats.

While world attention is centred on the change of power in the Soviet Union and its continued offensive against the Jews and Israel, Mrs. Epstein warned, "We must not lose sight of an intensified anti-Israel propaganda war launched in recent weeks by the Arab states".

Arab propagandists, however, have not been too successful in securing the lengthy list of arms demanded by Egypt. After intensive efforts by the Israelis, the Americans cut out jet planes, tanks and other offensive weapons, and reduced the remainder to $11m. to be purchased on credit. While this victory is due to Israel's diplomacy, the primary objective of Israelis is to convince Americans not to sell any arms to the Arabs until peace is negotiated.

Mr. Lehman said tonight that those who sell arms to Arabs without assuring peace in the Middle East "are playing fast and loose with America's security".

EBAN SEES BYROADE

WASHINGTON, Saturday (UP). — The Israel Ambassador, Mr. Abba Eban, called on Assistant Secretary of State for Near Eastern Affairs, Mr. Henry Byroade yesterday for a 50-minute talk. Mr. Eban said that the meeting was routine.

AFTER MIDNIGHT

Australians continued their swing towards Labour in State elections yesterday, the Labour Party holding Queensland with an increased majority and gaining seats in South Australia.

Stalin Dies After Four Days In Coma; Funeral Set for Tomorrow

MOSCOW, Saturday. — Marshal Joseph Vissarionovitch Stalin, 73, Secretary of the Central Committee of the Communist Party and Chairman of the Council of Ministers, died in his Kremlin apartment at 9.50 on Thursday evening, four days after he was struck by a cerebral hemorrhage. He never regained consciousness. The funeral will be held at noon on Monday, climaxing a four-day mourning period.

Relatives at his bedside when he died were his third wife, Rosa, sister of Deputy Premier Lazar Kaganovitch; his daughter, Svetlana, and his son, Vassili, the children of his second wife who died 20 years ago.

The coffin was borne yesterday 300 metres from the Kremlin to the glittering Hall of Columns in the House of Trade Unions where many Communist leaders, including Lenin, have lain in state. An hour later thousands of mourners began to climb the long-carpeted staircase to the first floor hall where the coffin rests on a high bier under floodlights.

A funeral commission was appointed, and is headed by Nikita Krushev, President of the Ukrainian Council of the People's Commissars. Other members include Deputy Premier Kaganovitch, the President of the Soviet Union, Nikolai Shvernik, the Mayor of Moscow, A. Yasnov, the Moscow Military Commandant, Marshal A. Vasilevsky, General Artemyev and N. Pegov, of the Communist Party Presidium.

Stands Guard

Georgi Malenkov, Russia's new Premier, was the first to stand guard over the body. He was followed at five-minute intervals by the members of the new 10-man Presidium. Music played continually – Chopin's funeral march was played over and over again. At one point a boys' choir sang a requiem, reminiscent of those sung for the dead Czars of the old regime.

The line of mourners stretched 16 kilometres through Moscow's streets waiting to pay their last respects. They moved 16 abreast in orderly silence from points in the city suburbs that converged on Red Square. It was believed to be the greatest demonstration of mourning ever seen in the capital.

As they approached the building they saw hung outside the Hall a huge portrait of their dead leader framed in gold. The mourners entered two abreast.

The staircase on which were potted palms decorated with red bunting led up to the long marble-columned vestibule lined with a forest of wreaths, some as large as a man. Dozens of crystal chandeliers lighted the vestibule and the main hall which were draped in transparent black crepe.

Military Dress

Stalin's body was visible from the waist upward in the open coffin. The Marshal's service and order ribbons formed two rows on the left breast of the tan military tunic in which he was dressed.

Flowers blanketed the coffin from the waist down and were banked around the bier. A giant portrait gilded in a black-bordered frame hung behind the coffin. An enormous spotlight on the picture cast a shadow over the deceased's face.

Around the coffin four soldiers represetning the branches of the armed services stood at attention flanked by a dozen civilians, wearing black armbands, who made up the civilian guard of honour.

The air was saturated with the scent of the flowers.

The diplomatic corps led by the doyen, Mr. Rolf Sohlman, of Sweden, gathered in the bitter sub-zero weather in the square opposite the Kremlin gate The American group of 100 was led by the Charge d'Affaires and included the wives and children of the Embassy employees.

The diplomatic procession look more than an hour to pass through the slow-moving tens of thousands of mourners. The walk ordinarily takes two minutes. The procession passed the American Embassy where the Stars and Stripes fluttered at half staff.

Throughout the capital black-bordered red flags fluttered at half mast. The streets were white with snow. The people of Moscow had kept an all-night vigil by their radios which first told them the news at 6.05 a.m. yesterday. But by then the news was already in the rest of the world's newspapers. It had been picked up through the reports to Russian provincial newspapers broadcast by Tass, the official Soviet news agency.

The autopsy performed on Stalin indicated that no doctor could have saved his life after the massive hemorrhage struck the left side of his brain, Moscow Radio said today. The findings confirmed the diagnosis made by the nine professors and physicians attending Stalin. The hemorrhage destroyed the vital functions of the brain, and affected his breathing and blood circulation. There were also numerous hemorrhages in the heart muscles and in the mucous membranes of the stomach and intestines. The autopsy report was signed by the Minister of Health, A. F. Tretyakov, and eight other leading medical authorities. *(UP, Reuter)*

(Communique—Pg. 3; Leader—Pg.4)

Round-the-World Reaction

LONDON, Saturday (Reuter). — Reaction in the non-Communist world to Stalin's death ranged from deep sympathy to "official" regrets among those who considered Stalin a tyrant.

President Eisenhower sent a one-sentence message of "official" condolences to the Soviet Government with the coldest possible formality.

In contrast India's Premier Jawaharal Nehru termed Stalin a man of great "stature" whose influence "was generally exercised in favour of peace." His message of regret said, "A personality of exceptional gifts and great achievements" had been removed from the world.

Pope Pius prayed in his private chapel for the soul of the "great persecutor who is now dead."

Prime Minister Churchill, now the last of the wartime "Big Three," made no comment and officials said indications were that he was unlikely to make a statement.

Attlee Comment

Mr. Clement Attlee, leader of the British Labour Party and former Socialist Prime Minister, said there would be "world-wide sympathy with the Russian people at the loss of a great national leader who by his courage and tenacity brought his country through the perils of the Second World War and played a great part in defeating the Nazis."

These were the comments from world leaders:

Mr. Lester Pearson (Canada) as President of the United Nations General Assembly: "With his passing the United Nations has lost one of its founders and the Soviet peoples the man who was their indomitable leader in the common struggle against Nazi aggression."

Chaing Kai-Shek, the Chinese nationalist leader: "We believe Stalin's death will bring no immediate change in the course of world affairs. Russian Communists work to an iron-bound time table which Stalin made".

French Premier, Rene Mayer expressed the sympathy "which is called for by the disappearance of the great statesman and leader of the glorius Soviet army".

M. Paul Henri Spaak, leader of the European Assembly: "The impact of this event cannot be grasped and assessed immediately. For us Europeans the change in the East is an added incentive to unite Europe".

West German Chancellor Konrad Adenauer said nobody could predict Russia's political development now He called on the free peoples of Europe to stand by each other. "The uncertainty of the new situation forces the free peoples more than ever before to conduct a clear and decided policy".

Former President Truman who met Stalin at the 1944 Potsdam Conference said: "I am always sorry to hear of the passing of an acquaintance of mine. Further than that I have nothing to say".

Mr. Tage Erlander, Swedish Prime Minister, said Stalin was "the object of devoted worship of millions of people. Millions of others have regarded him with bitterness and fear. No one was indifferent to him".

Egyptian Premier Nagib told reporters, "I beg Almighty God to bless the soul of the great man beloved by 200m people. Stalin was a rare hero and his name shall remain among history's heroes of extraordinary talent. What he did for the glory and greatness of his country in the Second World War shall never be forgotten. It was well known he loved a policy of peace and I believe the entire world will be sorry for the death of a great man who devoted his life to the last for the service of his people".

The British Chancellor of the Exchequer, Mr. A. Butler, would only comment," There will always be a Russia".

Pantheon to House Stalin, Lenin Coffins

MOSCOW, Saturday (UP). — A pantheon is to be built to house the stone coffins of Joseph Stalin and V. I. Lenin, Mocow Radio reported today.

Presidium Reduced to 10 Members

MOSCOW, Saturday. — The Soviet Union today enters a new era with a "streamlined" hierarchy under 51-year-old Georgi Malenkov, appointed Prime Minister within 24 hours of Stalin's death. Round-faced, heavy-jowled and corpulent, Mr. Malenkov is known as the man with the "card-index" brain. He already holds the key position of senior Secretary in the Soviet Communist Party which rules Russia. His swift appointment was followed equally rapidly by sweeping changes in the Government with the creation of a ten-man Presidium instead of the 36 under Stalin.

All ten are over 50. Premier Malenkov is the youngest of the lot. Marshal Klimenti Voroshilov at 72 is the oldest. The latter was one of Stalin's closest associates in the revolutionary days and builder of the Red Army. He becomes President of the Presidium of the USSR Supreme Soviet, a post which corresponds loosely to President of the USSR and in which he replaces Mr. Nikolai Shvernik.

MALENKOV

These are the other eight men who will rule Russia:

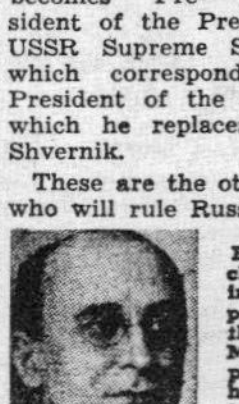
BERIA

Mr. Lavrenti Beria, 53, "Stalin's closest comrade-in-arms," is Deputy Chairman of the Council of Ministers and Deputy Premier. He headed the Soviet political police and internal security organization for eight years and is now Minister for Internal Affairs.

Mr. Vyachaslev Molotov, 62, the U.S.S.R.'s mouthpiece to the rest of the world as Foreign Minister from 1939-49. Western powers nicknamed him "Mr. No," because he was scarcely ever heard to say "yes." He gets back his post of Foreign Minister and is a Deputy Premier.

Marshal Nikolai Bulganin, 57, another Deputy Premier, becomes also War Minister. He is a "political General" and diplomat. He holds the rank of Marshal but never commanded an army in the field. Organizing ability and loyalty to the Party won him high office. He "made" himself in 1941 when, as a member of the Military Council for the western front, he organized the defence of Moscow. His father was a factory clerk.

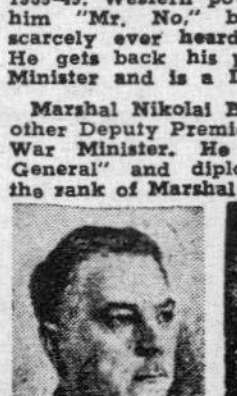
VOROSHILOV

MOLOTOV

Mr. Lazar Kaganovich, 59, the fourth Deputy Premier is the only Jew left in the "upper ten." He is reported to be Stalin's brother-in-law. His reputation for energy and ruthless efficiency made him known as the Kremlin's "human dynamo" and the "trouble shooter."

Mr. Nikita Khrushchev, 59, holds the Order of Lenin and comes from a Ukrainian mining family. As Secretary of the Moscow Committee of the Communist Party he criticized Party members last October for failing to pay proper attention to ideological work. He is now relieved of the secretaryship to concentrate on his work on the Central Committee.

Mr. Maxim Saburov takes over the new Ministry of Machine-Building which combines the old Ministries of Motorcar and Tractor industries, Machine-Building and Tool and Instrument Making, Agricultural Machinery and Machine Tools. He is a planner, Chairman of the State Planning Commission since 1949 and "author" of the fifth Soviet five-year plan presented last October.

(Continued on Page 3 — Col. 7)

Power Concentrated In a Few Hands

POST Political Correspondent

The sweeping reshuffle in both party and state leadership in Moscow — less than 24 hours after Stalin's death — reveals a clear tendency towards the concentration of power in a few hands and the almost complete fusion of state and party leadership. Georgi Malenkov, who has taken over from Stalin (with Lavrenti Beria as a close second), appears to have very different notions from those of the late Soviet leader with regard to the organization of work and the distribution of functions. Otherwise, such wholesale changes would hardly be necessary, even if Mr. Malenkov really wished to prevent "panic", as stated in an official communiqué.

Fourteen of the 25 members of the party presidium elected last October have been ousted, as have seven of the 11 alternate members. The all-powerful secretariat of the party has been virtually abolished: three of the 10 Communist leaders who formed it remain, but none of them belong to the central party leadership.

'Old Bolsheviks' Out

Among those ousted two groups can be easily discerned: one consists of "old Bolsheviks" like Kuusinen and Shkiryatov, whose loyalty to Stalin was the main reason for their appointment. The same goes for Marshal Voroshilov who has remained in the presidium, but is demoted to Deputy Prime Minister and appointed to the utterly unimportant post of President of the Supreme Soviet.

A second group consists of the young "ideologues," such as Suslov and Chesnokov, who have also been ousted from the presidium, probably because of Malenkov's known aversion to people who quote Marx, Engels, Lenin and Stalin too frequently.

The newcomers are V. V. Kuznetzov, who has been appointed Deputy Foreign Minister and Marshal Zhukov who is back (after a prolonged period of disgrace — 1946-52 — caused by his great popularity) as Deputy Minister of Defence under the former head of the Soviet State Bank, Marshal Bulganin. Nothing is known of the head of the State Planning Commission, Kosmychenko, who was the only minister not to be elected a member of the party central committee last October.

Four Return

Beria, Molotov, Bulganin and Mikoyan, who left their executive posts in the Soviet Government in 1949 in a campaign launched by Marshal Stalin to draw a dividing line between the state and the party apparatus, have all returned to their former positions — suggesting that Mr. Malenkov regards the division as artificial and anachronistic.

The changes probably have been long in preparation;—Marshal Stalin's death has provided the occasion for their implementation.

The fusion of the two Soviet security services (MVD and MGB) under Beria is likewise in clear contradiction to Stalin's line, which was one of **divide et impera** even in his own party This step is clearly a personal victory for Beria, who is now advanced to undisputed second place in the Soviet hierarchy, after having been dropped to fifth in the last months of Marshal Stalin's life.

The decisions published yesterday will have legal force only after they are approved by the Supreme Soviet, which has been summoned to meet on March 14.

Molotov Ministry To Seek Peace

LONDON, Saturday (Reuter). — The Soviet Foreign Ministry said today Soviet diplomats would aim at developing cooperation with all countries "against a war and for peace in the whole world.

This first statement from the Ministry since Mr. Vyacheslav Molotov returned to his post of Foreign Minister was reported in a TASS message received in London today.

It said, "the immortal name of Stalin will always inspire Soviet diplomats, whose aim will be to strengthen the prestige of the peace-loving Soviet Union, to strengthen and cultivate brotherly friendship with the people's democracies, to develop cooperation and business-like ties with all countries against a war and for peace in the whole world."

Soviet Stand On Korea Unchanged

UNITED NATIONS, Saturday (Reuter). — In the first Russian political speech in the United Nations since the announcement of the new regime in Moscow, Soviet delegate Valerian Zorin today reiterated in the Political Committee Soviet demands for ending the Korean war.

He again demanded an immediate cease-fire and the transfer of the war prisoners issue, now in stalemate, to a political conference.

U.S. delegate Cabot Lodge said, "We refuse to support a cease-fire which will leave thousands of prisoners in Communist hands."

Mr. Lodge said the non-Communist world intended to stand by the Indian resolution adopted by the General Assembly last December.

Indian delegate Krishna Menon said the most important characteristic of the Indian resolution had been that the release and repatriation of prisoners of war should be effected in accordance with the Geneva convention.

Soviet Ambassador to Britain Andrei Gromyko arrived here today to head the Russian delegation to the U.N. General Assembly in the absence of former Foreign Minister Andrei Vyshinski who returned home yesterday aboard the s.s. Liberte. Mr. Vyshinsky sailed just as Moscow announced that he is to be the new penrmanent U.N. envoy.

The former Foreign Minister accompanied by Mr. Georgi Zarubin, Ambassador to the U.S. and Mr. A. Soldatov, member of the U.N. delegation, appeared before the U.N. Political Committee before leaving.

The opening of the meeting was delayed while delegates lined up to shake Mr. Vyshinski's hand and to express their condolences. The Committee stood for one minute of silence out of respect to Stalin.

The Committee chairman, Joao Muniz of Brazil said:

"I ask the distinguished Foreign Minister of the Soviet Union to accept and to convey to his government and people our condolences for the passing of Generalissimo Joseph V. Stalin, Chairman of the Council of Ministers of the U.S.S.R."

Afterwards, Mr. Vyshinsky addressed the Committee and expressed the "great sorrow of the peace-loving peoples and of progressive mankind."

"The foreign policy of the Soviet Union and our party inspired by a great leader and teacher has been and continues to be unswerving policy of maintenance and strengthening of peace of the struggle against the unleashing of a new war and of developing business-like relations with all countries."

Request Council Meeting

Britain and France today requested the U.N. Security Council to meet early next week to consider the nomination of a new Secretary-General of the world organization.

Israel Sends No Official Regrets

TEL AVIV, Saturday. — Israel will be one of the few countries in the world not to be represented at the funeral of Marshal Stalin. No official cables have been sent by the Government to the Kremlin because no diplomatic relations now exist between the two countries.

Israel flags are not being flown at half-mast over Government buildings here. Buildings housing diplomatic representations of East European countries are flying large black flags under their national colours.

Headquarters of the Communist Party and Mapam here also flew black mourning streamers upon the announcement of Stalin's death, while mourning posters issued by Maki, the Communist Youth League, Mapam and Sneh's "Left Faction" were posted up in town.

Maki leaders here tonight would not state wether they had tried to go to Moscow to attend the funeral.

KESHER
DIRECT CARS
JERUSALEM - HAIFA - JERUSALEM
Tel. 2350 — Jerusalem • Tel. 2824 Haifa

THE JERUSALEM POST

SUNDAY, APRIL 5, 1953

PRICE: 80 PRUTA
VOL. XXIX, No. 7532

RADIO ERES
HAIFA: 57, REHOV HERZL
4, PALMER'S GATE
TEL-AVIV: 94, REHOV ALLENBY
A. GERSCFELD

Soviets Surprise World by Releasing Doctors; Malenkov Move Welcomed as Step to Peace

Marginal Column

"COMMENTATOR"

IN January 1939 a short item published in "Pravda" somewhere on its back page announced that the leading G.P.U. official in the Moldavian Republic had been arrested after having been found guilty of extracting false confession by using force against their prisoners. The item, ludicrous as it appeared, was of momentous importance. It meant the end of the big purge, or rather the signal for the arrest of the jailers. Yesterday's announcement which came in a more dramatic manner might be even more important. This time the announcement came not at the end, but at the beginning of a big purge. It might mean not more and not less than the beginning of the end of Stalinism in Russia, the first big effort to show that the Soviet regime can exist without confessions, mass purges and concentration camps — and perhaps even without thought control and the distortion of history. It might mean the liquidation of the totalitarian regime though we have the most serious doubts indeed whether this can be done. But it is no longer good to deny that the first genuine effort in that direction has been made, whatever the outcome.

STALINISM has been a theory and a practice. Great play has been made with regard to the former, which fulfilled about the same function as the Emperor's clothes in Andersen's fable. The really important thing which impressed the world about Stalinism was its practice, not its theory which remained somewhat less than formidable notwithstanding all efforts of the Kremlin's hagiographers. Malenkov and his colleagues continue to pay lip service to Stalin's theory, but are trying to drop his practices; it was Stalin who okayed the physicians' trial, as it appears now. Yesterday's official announcement might have incalculable results, and Malenkov cannot be unaware of this. If the "former M.G.B. people" as they are called in the official communiqué, used illegal means to extract false confessions (and according to the Soviet press the doctors had already confessed!) then it will of course be asked what happened in the Slanski trial and in all other trials and purges. The totalitarian state is based on the principle of infallibility. Once you deviate from this basic tenet, once you admit a mistake, there is an end to absolute rule.

NOR should it be forgotten that the Kremlin must have known that the Communist leaders abroad would be discredited by yesterday's announcement. All our local Timashuks — the Mikunises, Snehs and Rilfins who congratulated the Kremlin on the arrest of the "terrorist doctors," who uttered contemptible lies pretending their conviction in the guilt of the physicians — they have all now become the laughing stock of their respective countries.

IT will be hoped that yesterday's announcement foreshadows the end of the anti-Jewish and anti-Israel drive, just as recent Soviet statements and actions in foreign affairs tend to show that the Soviet leaders are really interested in Cold Peace rather than Cold War in the immediate future. Of course there are ultimate intentions, mental reservations, and secondary objectives about which more will have to be said on later occasions. But there is nothing surprising in that; the real thing is that Stalin's death has improved the chances of peace for the next few years, as Foster Dulles predicted it would. And as everybody seems to admit errors and mistakes nowadays we may as well add that we too have luckily been proved wrong for the time being, in our apprehensions as to the political implications of Stalin's death and his heritage.

Jerusalem, April 5.

THE JERUSALEM POST will not appear tomorrow, the last day of Passover. The next issue will be on Tuesday, April 7.

IL. 100
and more
at your disposal for your purchases by instalments, through
Irgun Ashrai B.M.
4 Rehov Hess,
P.O.B. 4813, Tel Aviv

75 Perish as Turkish Sub Sinks in Collision

ISTANBUL, Saturday (Reuter). — Seventy-five Turkish sailors perished after the 1,526-ton submarine Dumplinar collided with the Swedish ship Naboland and plunged 35 metres to the bottom of the sea off the West coast of Turkey.

Radio Ankara said tonight that only 22 of the 96 trapped inside the submarine were alive.

One man on the sub's deck was drowned at the time of the collision. Five others on the deck were saved and taken to hospital.

The 22 men reported to be still alive were in a watertight compartment of the damaged submarine. From that compartment earlier today came a dramatic radio message: "We can survive another 24 hours."

An American destroyer arrived on the scene to attempt a rescue of the survivors after efforts to lower a diving bell by the Turks failed in the swift current. A Turkish ship, the Kurtaran, was in touch with the sub through a telephone attached to a buoy sent up by the sunken craft.

The Dumlupinar, formerly the U.S. submarine Bumper, was turned over to Turkey under the military aid programme.

The Commander of the Turkish Navy, Admiral Altuncan, and National Defence Minister Kurtbek were at the scene directing rescue operations.

League Deserts Egypt On Suez Evacuation

POST Special Correspondent

The Arab League appears to have deserted Egypt in its coming struggle with Britain, and there will be no united Arab front to meet U.S. Secretary of State John Foster Dulles on his forthcoming Middle East visit.

This is made clear by a statement by a spokesman of the Lebanese Foreign Ministry who said yesterday that the Foreign Ministers of his country and Jordan, Syria, Iraq and Saudi Arabia had declined Cairo's invitation to attend the current League session because they refused to be dragged into a strong anti-West line over Egypt's demand for the evacuation of the Suez Canal zone.

The spokesman, quoted by ANA, said that although the members of the League supported Egypt's demand in principle, the matter was one which did not concern the League as such. He advised Egypt that it would be in vain for her to try to bring pressure on her fellow League members and recommended that she solve the Suez problem through diplomatic channels instead of by a bitter anti-West campaign.

NEABS said yesterday that Arab observers felt that Egypt has failed to establish a united Arab front in preparation for Mr. Dulles' visit. It seems most likely, the station thought, that each state will conduct its own conversation with Mr. Dulles in line with its own interests.

According to ANA, the Political Committee which met yesterday after a three-day recess, struck from its agenda items on the Suez Canal, the attitude to Germany following the ratification of the Israel reparations agreement and the Dulles visit.

These items, the only serious matters under discussion this session, are referred to the meeting of the Foreign Ministers of member states, whenever that may be.

McDaniel Sees Mill and Farm As Ways to Economic Freedom

POST Special Correspondent

RAMIM, Upper Galilee, Saturday. — Allocation of another $7m. from the current year's $70m. U.S. grant to Israel was announced here yesterday, towards the close of the two-day tour of the North by Mr. Bruce McDaniel.

With this release, $11m. are left to come from the 1952-53 Grant-in-Aid. The announcement was made on Mr. McDaniel's behalf by Mr. J. Bach, Grant-in-Aid Director of the Israel Treasury, who said the money was intended for food, fuel, feeding stuff, raw materials, and building material for housing of people shifting from town to country. In addition, IL.4m. are being released from the Counterpart Fund, for approved projects, with this, some 50 per cent of this Fund will have been authorized for withdrawal.

Mr. McDaniel as Point Four Director has blank clearance of grant funds, within the total voted by the U.S. Congress. His present tour was designed to enable him and one of his staff to see for themselves how the money was being used, and to examine projects to be financed by the present or future grants.

Ramim was a happy choice for the announcement, which came after a close examination of the water works scheme to control the Banyas River flow, one of the three streams which feed the Jordan.

Ramim is the new name for the once all but inaccessible Minara, the Kibbutz Hameuhad collective on top of a hill commanding an unparalleled view of the Huleh, the Huleh Plain, its swamps, and the several large fish ponds.

It was from Ramim-Minara that Operation Hiram was launched in the autumn of 1948, after Kaukji's Syrian "Irregulars" infringed the Cease Fire. Commanded by Moshe Carmel and Haim Laskov, the Operation ended in the freeing of the whole of Eastern Galilee and the capture of a number of villages inside Lebanese territory, which under the Armistice Agreement were later restored to the Lebanon. Lebanese cultivators are now working their lands not more than 50 yards from Ramim.

Yesterday, at noon, the Galilee

(Continued on Page 3. — Col. 8)

ITALIAN MINISTER TO ISRAEL NAMED

ROME, Saturday (INA). — Sr. Benedetto Capomaza is to be Italian Minister to Israel, it was announced here today.

Sr. Capomaza has been Italian Representative in Eritrea and was formerly Charge d'Affaires in Madrid.

Korean PoW Talks Open Tomorrow

TOKYO, Saturday (Reuter). — U.N. and Communist liaison officers meet at Panmunjom, site of the deadlocked truce talks, on Monday to discuss the exchange of sick and wounded prisoners of war.

Some allied officers today believed that the Communists — who recently agreed to the U.N. suggestion for such an exchange — will try to rush the sick prisoners through Panmunjom as quickly as possible after the meeting.

The U.N. Command did not say today whether Monday's talks would lead to a resumption of full-scale armistice meetings, as the Communists proposed recently. Official circles here predicted that General Mark Clark, the U.N. Commander, would see first if the Communists were sincere about the sick prisoners before discussing resumption of the full armistice talks which the U.N. broke off last October.

Arrangements went on today to receive the prisoners at the "Freedom Village" hospital camp near the wrecked town of Munsan, the Allied negotiators' base. U.S. Marine engineers working day and night have almost finished the village — a canvas camp in a valley where prisoners will live while they receive attention from army doctors and nurses. The camp is surrounded by barbed wire, but nothing like the high impassable wire walls of prison camps. It is a single strand of wire about three feet high marking the camp boundaries.

Salem Warns British: Egypt Will Sabotage

CAIRO, Saturday (UP). — In one of his most bitter attacks on Britain, Major Salah Salem, said today that the 1936 Anglo-Egyptian treaty was "not worth a dime." He threatened to deny Britain all wartime facilities if she does not evacuate the Suez Canal zone.

Salem, who is Nagib's agent in the Sudan, told members of the Liberation Rally at Mehalla el Kubra in the Nile Delta, "The treaty no longer exists. If British troops remain and we are forced to collaborate in wartime we shall blow up communication lines and bridges to prevent their using them. We will lead the people to fight against the British."

He said that the Egyptian Government would not negotiate on the evacuation of Suez unless it knew beforehand that its demands would be accepted.

New Tourist Rate Today—IL.1.800:$1

The new IL.1.800 per dollar exchange rate for tourists will go into effect today. A premium of IL.20 will be paid on each IL.25 of a letter of credit.

A joint announcement by the Ministries of Finance and Commerce yesterday stated that in accordance with a decision taken by the Government a fund had been set up to encourage tourism and that grants to tourists exchanging foreign currency would be covered out of that fund.

Other benefits hitherto enjoyed by tourists will end — purchases in special shops, for example. Letters of credit purchased with foreign currency before today and which have not been used or used only in part can be exchanged for foreign currency by the tourists upon their departure from the country or through authorised banks at the rate at which the letters were purchased.

Under the new arrangement tourists will be allowed to buy back foreign currency at the time of their departure for a sum not greater than IL.10 (at the C rate) on condition that they return the proportional premium received from the fund. Tourists will still be prohibited from taking Israel currency out of the country.

Hotels, tourist shops' proprietors and tourist transport companies dealing in letters of credit had received no instructions from the Government last night. The Hotel Keepers' Association told its members not to make any transactions on letters of credit until after a meeting in Tel Aviv this afternoon. In the meantime the Secretary of the Association will seek clarification on the Ministry of Finance new arrangements this morning.

When the Norwegian motor ship Brand V (whose arrival is reported on page 3) entered Haifa Port on Friday orders were received from the Finance Ministry in Jerusalem to leave in force the old exchange rate of one pound for the tourist dollar, countermanding earlier instructions that the visitors be granted an advance in Israel pounds pending the instructions of the new exchange rate.

As the control officials were already aboard, the Foreign Exchange Controller for Northern District, Mr. David Freeman, came to the quay in person to ensure that it was the latest change of mind and not the exchange rate that was put into effect.

Moscow Press Plays Up Ike's Comment

MOSCOW, Saturday (Reuter). — Moscow newspapers displayed on their foreign news pages a statement by President Eisenhower reporting his "favourable comment" at a press conference on Thursday on the recent peace moves in Korea by Soviet Foreign Minister Vyacheslav Molotov and Prime Minister of Communist China Chou En-lai. Yesterday they gave similar prominence to British Prime Minister Churchill for his statement in the Commons on Wednesday on the Chinese Prime Minister's offer on the prisoners of war issue in Korea.

Ike Urges West's Unity in Strength

WASHINGTON, Saturday (Reuter). — President Eisenhower said today that the North Atlantic Treaty Organization was "an instrument of peace" but that the Western world must be united in strength because "peace cannot be defended by the weak."

He made his remarks in a statement commemorating the fourth anniversary today of the signing of the North Atlantic Treaty by the original 12 nations.

NATO, he declared "endangers none who will respect freedom." "It serves all who love freedom and wish to enjoy it in peace. We have learned from bitter and conclusive experience that peace cannot be defended by the weak. It demands strength — the strength of our armies, the strength of our economies and above all the strength of our spirit."

NATO was far from complete, he said, and urged that the anniversary be made the signal for all member nations to dedicate themselves with renewed vigour to the work still to be done, remembering that "the faint of heart and the slow of deed are the first and the surest to invite the torment of aggression."

The 200 million people of the NATO countries of Europe were indispensible to the defence of freedom everywhere, Mr. Eisenhower said. If they and their resources ever were captured and exploited by an aggressor, he added, "there would be no corner of safety anywhere in the world."

Britain to Meet Any Genuine Offer

LONDON, Saturday (Reuter). — Foreign Secretary Anthony Eden declared here tonight that Britain would meet half-way any genuine attempt to ease the existing tension between the Eastern and Western worlds. "Today we see signs that some lessening of tension between East and West may become possible," he told the nation in a broadcast.

At the same time Mr. Eden warned, "We must not make the mistake of thinking that we can relax our efforts to build an effective defence. We must not allow ourselves to be divided from our friends. That would be to lose all that we have gained.

"And so, we must continue the work of the North Atlantic Treaty in every sphere. Our own safety and the peace of the world depend upon it".

The Foreign Secreary was speaking on the fourth anniversary of the signing of the Atlantic pact. He said, "This treaty and the organization built up around it has built up our defence in the West. More than anything else it has helped to guard our security and to keep the peace in recent years.

"As the West has grown in strength and unity we have begun to create a deterrent to aggression. When we staged the North Atlantic treaty we declared that it was purely defensive. So it has proved. It threatened no one.

"This community of the North Atlantic is the key to future relations between the countries of Western Europe and of North America," Mr. Eden said. "Our cooperation there with Canada, with the U.S. and with our European partners offers the best prospect of a settled and prosperous future."

Deep Satisfaction Voiced by Israel

TEL AVIV, Saturday. — The Government of Israel has heard with deep satisfaction of the official announcement made in Moscow that the charges brought against the Jewish doctors have proved false, and that the so-called confessions by the doctors were obtained by improper means, the Foreign Ministry spokesman said today in the name of the Government.

Thus the attitude of the Government of Israel in this matter as announced in the Knesset on January 19, 1953 has been fully vindicated, the spokesman said.

In connection with the accusations made against the doctors, false charges were also levelled against Jewish world organizations such as the Joint and the Zionist Organization. The false accusations against the doctors also served as a basis for an anti-Jewish campaign, one step in which was the severance by the Soviet Union of diplomatic relations with Israel.

The Government of Israel hopes that the redress of the injustice will be completed by the termination of the anti-Jewish campaign and will welcome the resumption of normal relations between the Soviet Union and Israel, the Government statement concluded.

Hope for Resumption of Relations and Open Doors

POST Diplomatic Correspondent

TEL AVIV, Saturday. — Diplomatic circles here regard the latest Moscow move as a continuation of the Soviet Union's current peace offensive, and as a step towards ending the cold war and removing friction between East and West.

Observers here believe that the Soviet Union decided to drop the charges against the doctors so as to avoid acrimonious debate in the U.N. and to obviate charges of anti-Semitism anywhere in the Soviet orbit.

It was a bold step; it is to be hoped that it may be followed by further bold steps and the policy continued to its logical conclusion including admission of the innocence of the Joint and of the Zionist Movement.

It is thought not improbable that the Soviet leaders will show sufficient statesmanship to renew diplomatic relations with this country.

The lead given by Moscow is expected to be followed by similar conciliatory moves in other Eastern bloc countries. It is not to much to hope that emigration of Jews may be permitted by Czechoslovakia, Rumania, Hungary and Poland, and that Zionist leaders now in prison in some of the Soviet satellites may be released.

It is felt here that the stand taken by the Government in calling the world's attention to anti-Zionist and anti-Semitic tendencies in the Soviet bloc, and the world-wide response to this move, have been noted by Soviet leaders and may have contributed to their surprise decision.

'U.S. Still Friendly Towards Israel'—Joseph

LYDDA AIRPORT, Saturday (ITIM). — Dr. Dov Joseph, Minister without Portfolio, returned by El Al yesterday after a visit to the U.S. and Canada on behalf of the Bond Drive and the U.J.A. He was accompanied by his wife, who had also taken part in the campaign.

Dr. Joseph said that he had been assured by a "central figure in the American Government" that there were no grounds to fear any changes in the friendly attitude of the U.S. towards Israel because of America's desire for friendship with the Arab States. The Minister said this declaration had been made in view of reports that U.S. friendship for the Arabs meant a worsening of the relationship with Israel.

Dr. Joseph expressed satisfaction at the results of both the Bond Drive and the U.J.A. this year, but said that more remained to be done. In Canada, the Minister had launched the Bond Drive in that Dominion and had also discussed Israel purchases from there.

RUMANIA GRANTS PARTIAL AMNESTY

LONDON, Saturday (Reuter). — The Presidium of the Rumanian Grand National Assembly has granted an amnesty to certain classes of offenders, the official Rumanian news agency announced tonight.

Among the classes covered are women prisoners with children under seven years old, pregnant women and prisoners aged over 60.

SOCIALIST JUSTICE 'VINDICATED' — SNEH

TEL AVIV, Saturday. — Asked to comment on the Moscow statement tonight Dr. Moshe Sneh, leader of the Left Faction, said that this was "additional proof of socialist justice." "It was a decisive blow to the false agitation about anti-Semitism in Soviet countries, he added."

Ex-King Carol Dead in Portugal

LISBON, Saturday (Reuter). — Ex-King Carol of Rumania died of a heart attack at the seaside resort of Estoril, near Lisbon early today.

Princess Helena of Rumania, the former Mme. Lupescu was at Carol's bedside when he died.

Marshal Urdarianu, former Rumanian Royal Court Minister, said the ex-King felt quite well until half an hour before midnight when he was suddenly taken ill. A doctor was called but despite his utmost efforts he could not save Carol's life.

Ex-King Carol lived in Estoril, a fashionable seaside resort about 15 miles from Lisbon, since October 1947.

Carol would never admit that his love for Madame Lupescu cost him his throne in 1925 and again in 1940. He would say, "The story that I renounced my claim to the throne because of her is a lie. I was compelled to leave Rumania for purely political motives because I was the enemy of graft and bribery. She stood by me as nobody else did."

Carol, who was 59, is to be buried with Portuguese Kings in the pantheon of the monastery of Sao Vicente, here on Tuesday. The body will be embalmed tomorrow.

In Lausanne, former King Michael of Rumania, in a communique issued by his entourage tonight, said he would not attend the funeral of his father. It is known that there had been a noticeable coolness between father and son for years. During the several years Michael lived in Lausanne after his abdication he was at no time visited by his father although his mother, former Queen Helena, was a frequent visitor.

PUSHES NEW ELECTIONS ITALIAN RIGHT-WING

ROME, Saturday (Reuter). — Italy's general elections are to be held on June 7 and 8. The cabinet today dissolved the Chamber of Deputies and the Senate, the latter, one year before its six-year term expires.

'Confession' Extractors Arrested

LONDON, Saturday (Reuter). — The USSR today astonished the world by announcing that the group of doctors, many Jewish, accused of murdering Soviet leaders had been exonerated and freed while the people who extracted false confessions from them had been arrested. The Order of Lenin was stripped from the woman physician, Dr. Lydia Timashuk, who had been honoured for "unmasking" the doctors.

The unprecedented state admission of error and illegal methods used to obtain confessions was seen in the capitals of the world as one of the most significant acts to date of Premier Georgi Malenkov's month old regime. Commentators said it might not merely be a gesture of conciliation towards the West but also a move to withdraw Soviet justice from the realm of politics and to safeguard individual liberty.

The communique from the Soviet Ministry of Internal Affairs published in "Pravda" and "Izvestia" today named 15 liberated doctors and spoke of the release of "the others implicated in the case." At the time of the accusations last January only nine doctors were mentioned. Observers in Moscow identified the additional six as all distinguished medical practitioners, most of them members of the USSR Academy of Medical Sciences.

The announcement said the Ministry of Internal Affairs had made a thorough investigation and found the doctors were wrongfully arrested and without any legal grounds. The charges were false, the documentary data unfounded and the alleged confessions were obtained "through the use of methods of investigation which are inadmissible and most strictly forbidden by Soviet law."

"The accused had been "fully cleared of the charges of wrecking, terrorist and espionage activities" and had been released, while "the persons guilty of the improper conduct of the investigation have been arrested and are held criminally responsible."

The Supreme Soviet has annulled the granting of the Order of Lenin to Dr. Timashuk as "incorrect," the Moscow press announced later.

Special Probe Body

The announcement said that this innocence was established by an investigation commission specially set up by the USSR Ministry of Internal Affairs.

The 15 doctors include the original nine named in January — Professors M.S. Vovsi, V.N. Vinogradov, M.B. Kogan, B.B. Kogan, P.I. Yegorov, A. Feldman, I.S. Etinger, A.M. Grinstein and B.I. Mayorov, and six others who had not been previously mentioned: Professor V. Vasilenko, V. Zelenin, V. Zakusov, N. Shereshevsky, N.A. Popova and V. Zakusov.

Of the latter group Prof. Zakusov was one-time delegate to the U.N. Social and Economic Commission, while Prof. Vasilenko was one of the physicians who signed a medical statement on the death of Andrei Zhdanov, Cominform leader whose end was said to have been deliberately hastened by the doctors.

Observers in London said that Premier Malenkov has made history, for never before has the Soviet state officially admitted a major mistake — and one of the gravest character. Never before have "criminals" denounced in Soviet newspapers as "fiends in human form" been not only freed but completely vindicated. Neither is there a precedent for the withdrawal of the Order of Lenin, highest Soviet civilian decoration.

One of the most significant aspects of the affair is the statement that the investigation methods had been "impermissible" and "strictly forbidden under Soviet law."

The observers saw in the announcements evidence that the Malenkov Government is carrying through the measures outlined in the Stalin funeral orations on the protection of individual rights.

Five of the nine doctors originally named were specifically named in January as belonging to a "terrorist group connected with an international Jewish bourgeois national organization, the Joint." In addition to being charged with hastening Zhdanov's death they were accused of trying to "eliminate" the then Army Minister Marshal Vasilevsky, General Shtemenko who succeeded him as Chief of Staff, Marshal Koniev, Marshal Govorov and Admiral Levchenko. The "terrorists" were also accused of being linked with British and U.S. intelligence services.

Freed Physicians Back with Families

MOSCOW, Saturday (AP). — The wrongly arrested medical men were reported back with their rejoicing families today while those who conducted the investigation that led to their arrest were under indictment on criminal charges. A number of the arrested doctors were Jews and the fact that they have been released and it has been admitted they were falsely accused has broad significance. It should be welcomed by Jews everywhere and it may have far-reaching importance.

Locker Lauds USSR Courageous Action

Describing the Soviet repudiation of the charges against the Russian doctors as a "very rare occurrence," Mr. B. Locker, Chairman of the Jewish Agency, in a statement in Jerusalem last night, congratulated the Government of the USSR on its courage in admitting that the libel which had shocked the Jewish world and non-Jewish world alike, had been baseless.

Mr. Locker added that the withdrawal of the accusation showed how justified those had been who had taken a severely critical stand towards the libel and had focused the world's attention on it; nor had the reaction of the physicians' associations been in vain.

"With all our satisfaction at the Soviet statement, Mr. Locker continued, it must be emphasized that this is but a first step. The exploding of this charge itself points to the baselessness of all that Soviet and Communist quarters had alleged against such Jewish organizations as the J.D.C., the Zionist Organization and the Jewish world as a whole."

Mr. Locker expressed the hope that the Soviet authorities would agree to this, and would also review the "extreme measure" of breaking off relations with Israel — a revision which would strongly appeal to people in Israel and to peace-loving people throughout the world.

The libels against Jews neither began with the accused physicans, nor do they end there, Mr. Locker concluded. He recalled that there had been the Prague trial and the Communist attacks on the Zionist Movement and on Israel in the countries attached to the USSR — Poland Hungary and Rumania. "We have never faltered in our claim for the emigration of Jews from those countries."

RIFT REVEALED IN SECURITY MINISTRIES

POST Political Correspondent

The wording of the Moscow statement revealed for the first time the existence of a rift between the Ministry of State Security (MGB) and the Ministry of the Interior (MVD).

Mr. Lavrenti Beria, who had been in charge of the latter until 1949 returned to it only after the death of Stalin when it was merged with the MGB. After the arrest of the doctors in January, the MGB was given fullsome praise while the MVD was criticized for incompetence. Yesterday's statement shows that the trend has been reversed, perhaps irrevocably.

Sharett Welcomes USSR Relations Renewal

NEW YORK, Saturday (Reuter). — Moshe Sharett, Israel Foreign Minister told reporters yesterday that his country would welcome a resumption of diplomatic relations with the Soviet Union.

Mr. Sharett who arrived here by plane from Amsterdam, will go to Washington on Tuesday to confer with President Eisenhower and Secretary of State Dulles. With Mr. Dulles he is to exchange views on "the question of peace in the Middle East as a contribution to world peace."

French Civilians Freed

PARIS, Saturday (Reuter). — All 14 French civilians interned in North Korea have been freed and will reach Moscow shortly, according to the Soviet Government.

Togal
QUICK RELIEF FROM:
Pains in the Joints and Limbs, Lumbago, Rheumatism, Sciatica, Colds, Neuralgia. TOGAL dissolves uric acid, and helps even in chronic diseases. More than 7,000 doctors recommend TOGAL for its amazing action in relieving pain.
ONE TRIAL WILL CONVINCE YOU!

TOURISTS!
Before Going Home...
Buy Your Souvenirs and Bezalel Jewellery
at FREUND
LIC. TOURIST SHOP
41 Allenby Rd., Tel Aviv opp. Allenby Cinema.

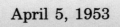

THE JERUSALEM POST
FRIDAY, FEBRUARY 26, 1954
8 Pages
PRICE: 140 PRUTA
VOL. XXX, No. 7803

SHISHAKLY FLEES AFTER ARMY REVOLT; NASSER GRABS POWER, NAGIB HELD

Simultaneously in the early hours of yesterday morning, Syrian and Egyptian army officers overthrew their respective heads of state, General Adib Shishakly and General Mohammed Nagib. Shishakly, who climbed to power in a coup in November, 1951, submitted his resignation to the House of Deputies last night and fled the country following an insurrection that began in Aleppo and engulfed the country, 28 days after Shishakly crushed a Druze revolt. Hashem el-Attasi, of Homs, is now President. Nagib, who headed the Revolutionary Council after the overthrow of King Farouk in July 1952, was succeeded by his aide, Lieut-Col. Gamal Abdul Nasser, and placed under house arrest.

Guards Surround Cairo Villa

CAIRO, Thursday (Reuter). — General Mohammed Nagib, overthrown in Cairo today by "the man-behind-the-scenes," 36-year-old Lieut.-Col. Jamal Abdul Nasser, tonight was being held incommunicado in his suburban Cairo villa. Heavily armed troops kept guard outside.

RECORD OF VIOLENCE

Achmed Maher Pasha, Egyptian Premier, killed by Moslem Brotherhood in February, 1945.

Mustapha Tihmi Nokrashi Pasha, Egyptian Premier, assassinated by Moslem Brotherhood in December, 1948.

Sheikh Hassan el Banna, leader of Moslem Brotherhood, assassinated in February, 1949.

General Husni a-Za'im, self-proclaimed Syrian dictator, killed in Damascus in August, 1949.

Colonel Sami a-Hinawi, hero of Syria's second coup d'etat, assassinated in October, 1950.

Riad e-Solh, Lebanese Premier assassinated in Amman in June, 1951.

King Abdullah of Jordan, assassinated in the Mosque of El Aqsa, Old City, in July, 1951.

King Farouk of Egypt deposed in July, 1952.

King Talal of Jordan deposed in Amman, in August, 1952.

B'shara el Khoury, President of the Lebanon, forced to resign in Beirut, September 1952, as a result of a coup d'etat.

Mustapha el Omari, Iraqi Premier, forced to resign in Baghdad, in November, 1952, as a result of a coup d'etat.

Posters and portraits of Nagib, who ousted King Farouk in July, 1952, were being ripped from offices and public buildings in the city which had been dominated by his image ever since the Army revolt two years ago.

The ruling Revolutionary Council announced that it had been fighting for some time against demands by General Nagib for wider personal powers.

The first act today of the new Premier, Colonel Nasser, was to send troops to reinforce guards outside the city's broadcasting studios.

An Army officer outside General Nagib's house told reporters, "You cannot see him," but a spokesman of the Revolution Council denied a report which he said had gained currency abroad that General Nagib was dead. "He is fit and well."

Palestine Hero

General Nagib, 53-year-old Palestine war hero, was stripped of his offices by the Revolutionary Council in the early hours today while Cairo still slept.

The strapping six-foot Colonel who is now Premier presided at an extraordinary meeting of the Council, and later conferred with his Director of Intelligence, Lieutenant-Colonel Zakaria Mohammed e-Din and with Army and Police chiefs.

Major Salah Salem, Minister of National Guidance, then announced that the Council had accepted General Nagib's resignation, and that Colonel Nasser, who was Vice-Premier, had assumed full powers as chief of the military junta "until liberation of the country from imperialistic forces."

The post of President would remain open with the return of parliamentary life in Egypt, he said.

Colonel Nasser was head of the Liberation Rally which was set up in place of the political parties abolished under the Nagib regime in January 1953.

The Revolution Council communique announced today that Nagib had presented his resignation knowing full well that "any rift within the Council in such circumstances could lead to a regrettable consequence."

"The Council had put up with Nagib's continuous pressure for wider powers at a time when the country faced serious problems inherited from the previous regime," the communique stated. "He went through a psychological crisis from which he suffered a great deal, despite our efforts to present him to the world as the real leader of the Revolution and its Council."

Absolute Rule

(Cairo Radio quoted the communique as adding, "We have exploited all possible ways for the sake of past sentiments to dissuade him from these requests which would return the country to absolute rule by an individual and thereby possibly sacrifice our Revolution.")

Major Salem told reporters that General Nagib had tried to face the Council with a *fait accompli* by offering his resignation three days ago and seeking to demand the authority to veto the Council's right to appoint and dismiss Cabinet Ministers and the right to promote and transfer members of the armed forces.

He had threatened to resign because of "feigned sickness" several times in the past ten months, the Minister alleged.

Nagib had cancelled all his engagements in the past two days. He had presided over his final Cabinet meeting last night and had then driven home to his villa.

The Revolutionary Council has declared that it will continue to exercise its powers until the Revolution has achieved "its principal aim—the evacuation of imperialists."

The first news of Nagib's departure from power provoked a few demonstrations, for the fatherly looking, soft-spoken general was an idol. More than that, he was the symbol of Egypt's new freedom from centuries of monarchy and, in many eras, of utter oppression.

More than 1,000 students were waiting in the hall of Ibrahim University for Nagib to make one of his popular appearances when they were told of his resignation. The news turned the hall into a mass of confused and milling youth, hundreds of whom shouted, "We want Nagib."

(Nasser Profile, — P. 4)

Salem: Cairo In 'Severe Crisis'

CAIRO, Thursday (Reuter). — Egypt's Minister of National Guidance, Major Salah Salem, in a broadcast over Cairo Radio tonight said that the Egyptian nation "was passing through a severe crisis" as a result of the split between the Revolution Council and General Nagib.

He stated that the issue was not a personal one, but a question of principles placing the interest of the State above all. He disclosed that when Nagib asked for wider powers, officers of the Revolution Council planned to abandon the political scene and go back to their units.

Salah Salem

"But Army officers who had carried the standard of the revolution and lighted its torch would not accept such a solution, for the responsibility was too great to be borne by any one person whoever he might be," he added.

Mission Accomplished

The Army officers decided to carry on their mission.

Salem, who is also Minister in charge of Sudan affairs, said that relations between Egypt and the Sudan would not be affected by the changes in Cairo. He warned the Sudanese people against "conspirators who may exploit the occasion to further their own ends."

Major Salem accused General Nagib of "sabotaging" the work of the Revolution Command Council, and said, "We could have killed Nagib but we decided to let him live — as we did with ex-King Farouk and Lieutenant-Colonel Rashad Mehanna before him."

Major Salem said that Nagib had not been arrested but "we asked him to stay at home for one or two months".

We Must Be Alert, Dayan Tells Cadets

TEL AVIV, Thursday. — Pinning wings onto the tunics of a group of Air Force cadets — one of them a woman — at a passing-out parade today of new pilots and air members at an air base somewhere in Israel, the Chief of Staff, Rav-Aluf Moshe Dayan, stressed the necessity for the Army to be on the alert. Aluf Dan Tolkowsky, O.C. Air Force, was present.

"This morning, we heard of the rebuff to Israel's efforts for peace with our neighbours, while at midday came the news of a revolt in Egypt and of disturbances in Syria," he said.

Yaffi Seeks Cabinet

BEIRUT, Thursday (UP). — Abdullah el Yaffi, who resigned as Premier twice in the past few days, began consultations today on the formation of a new Government for Lebanon.

El Yaffi has been under considerable pressure in Parliament on both domestic and foreign issues, and has been given very narrow votes of confidence.

Reported on Plane to Egypt

General Adib Shishakly resigned as President and Prime Minister last night "in order to avoid serious bloodshed," Damascus Radio announced in its 11.15 p.m. news bulletin. He submitted his resignation to the House of Deputies. It was the first mention by Damascus Radio of the country-wide crisis in Syria that came to a head in the early hours of yesterday morning following an insurrection against General Shishakly by Army officers.

General Shishakly (left) and General Nagib, both deposed as the heads of their respective countries, are shown here attending services in El Azhar Mosque, Cairo.

Following the terse announcement, General Shawkat Shukeir, a Druze and Commander-in-Chief of the Army, broadcast a proclamation:

"The Army is one and continues to be united. We call upon the population of Syria to remain calm. The Army will care for the security of the country."

(UP quotes Beirut reports that Shishakly flew to Egypt late last night.)

Until the announcement was made the country appeared to be in a state of siege with all main cities except Damascus, the capital, in the hands of the insurrectionist Army officers.

Shishakly had been given 24 hours to resign and leave the country, and the rebellious officers have declared 80-year-old former President Hashem el Attasi as legal President in his home town of Homs.

The Commanders of the Northern, Western, Central and Eastern districts issued a press statement in Aleppo last night announcing that the movement "aims at sending the Army back to its barracks one day and leaving the country's administration to manage its own affairs according to the wishes of the people expressed according to democratic principles."

EL-ATTASI
New President

It added that the movement would in no way interfere with Syria's international obligations. The commanders had "no personal or political ambitions for the present or for the future."

An earlier broadcast from the rebel radio in Aleppo appealed directly to the Jebel Druze to join the "national front," particularly in view of the savage suppression by Shishakly of their attempted revolt last month.

According to reports reaching Beirut, Shishakly sent a plenipotentiary to the rebels in Homs urging them to call off their struggle.

Less than 12 hours after the proclamation of the insurrection, the northern cities of Homs, Aleppo, Hama, Latakia, the provinces of Jezirah, Hauran and the South as far as Dara, on the Jordan border, had joined

(Continued on Page 3, — Col. 5)

Bennike's Chances May Improve

UNITED NATIONS, Thursday (INA). — The revolt against the Shishakly regime, it is believed here, may improve General Bennike's chances to secure an Israel-Syrian understanding on the Jordan River waters.

Colonel Shishakly has been the most aggressive among Arab rulers with regard to Israel. General Bennike is under instruction from the U.N. Security Council to report back on his attempt to mediate on the spot the dispute between Israel and Syria.

As a result of the revolts in Egypt and Syria, it is expected here that the Jordan Cabinet may also face a serious crisis on the eve of its reply to the U.N. invitation to meet with Israel. It is known that some members of the Jordan Cabinet favour its acceptance.

In Washington, State Department spokesman Henry Suydam at his press conference today declined to comment on the reported Syrian revolt pending receipt of fuller information by the U.S. Government.

Reactions From World Capitals

LONDON, Thursday. — While the British Foreign Office announced today that it was awaiting a report from Ambassador Sir Ralph Stevenson in Cairo, other official sources said that Mr. Selwyn Lloyd, Minister of State, would make a brief stop in the Egyptian capital on Saturday to confer with Mr. Stevenson. Mr. Lloyd will be on his way to Khartoum to open the Sudanese parliament on Monday.

Authoritative sources stated that the overthrow of General Nagib has dashed hopes of agreement on the evacuation of the Suez Canal.

"There can be no treaty with the hotheads of the military junta who are now in power in Egypt," one source quoted by U.P. said.

Reuter quotes diplomatic sources as saying that the change to Colonel Nasser is not expected to affect Egypt's internal or external policy. They added that since Nagib seized power in 1952 there was always speculation whether he or Nasser was the key personality. As long as the military which forced the abdication of King Farouk remains in control, no major policy change can be expected.

Britain will continue to seek a settlement with the Nasser Government as it has done with all Egyptian Governments for the past eight years, it is understood by Reuter.

No Effect at UN

WASHINGTON, Thursday (UP). A State Department spokesman said it was believed that developments in Egypt were unrelated to Egypt's international policies. "It is our opinion that the question of the Suez base negotiations was not involved in these developments."

Not International

UNITED NATIONS, Thursday — The resignation of General Nagib "will have absolutely no effect" on Egypt's U.N. delegation, Dr. Mahmoud Azmi, special Egyptian envoy to the United Nations, announced today. "As far as we are concerned, there has been no change in our government — only a personnel change."

American officials stated today that they did not believe the resignation of General Nagib would have any effect whatsoever on Egyptian-American relations.

They added that they had foreseen an eventual split between Nagib and Nasser, but had thought that it would be longer in coming than had proved to be the case.

The official attitude here is that the events of the past 24 hours in Cairo are a "purely internal political affair" and of no concern to the U.S. Nagib was regarded here as more "pro-Western" than his successor, but officials did not believe that this would have any real effect on Egyptian policy.

The Turkish Ambassador here stated that the news from

(Continued on Page 2, — Col. 7)

Jordanians Fire On Israelis

Jordanians opened fire on Israelis in the Jerusalem and "Little Triangle" areas yesterday, the Army spokesman announced.

In the Valley of Hinnom, near Mt. Zion, Army sappers were dismantling mines when they came under fire from Arab Legion positions in the Old City — despite a previous announcement to the Jordan authorities that the soldiers would be in the area for this purpose, it was said.

A shepherd from Yarhiv village, near Kalkilya, was fired on from Halba village, across the border, while he was grazing his flock yesterday, it was announced. The Yarhiv villagers laid down covering fire and the shepherd managed to escape and to extricate his flock. The exchange of fire lasted for 15 minutes.

Israel has submitted complaints on both incidents to the Mixed Armistice Commission and has demanded on-the-spot investigations.

The chairman of the Israel Egyptian Mixed Armistice Commission yesterday postponed until Sunday and emergency meeting scheduled for today to discuss the murder of an Israel soldier on February 19, the Army spokesman announced. The soldier was killed when armed Egyptian Bedouin entered Israel and clashed with an Israel unit.

Column One

BY **David Courtney**

IT is too early to predict the consequences of the dramatic events reported from Egypt and Syria and indirectly connected with Iraqi signs and portents hardly less dramatic. The political seismograph has recorded something more than a tremour in these lands. It indicates a wide area of serious disturbance, the shock of which is likely to be felt as far away as London and Washington; but it would be idle to guess at the outcome until the dust has settled. Some of the dust may settle thickly on certain western plans said to have been drawn up and got ready for application in the lands that are now giving dramatic evidence of their instability. In any event, it is clear that the fall of General Nagib, the outbreak of fresh rebellion in Syria, and Fadil el Jamali's hints that Iraq may decide to plough its own furrow outside the Arab League and in association with the West, have upset a great many calculations and posed a new set of questions affecting the Arab League and the relationships between its members and the Powers.

●

GENERAL Nagib's overthrow came as a surprise, although some Cairo and London observers have been warning us for some time of the ambitions of Colonel Abdul Nasser and the danger of a conflict between him and General Nagib. General Nagib was a good soldier and a sound patriot with a genuine feeling for his people and, it would seem, a genuine desire to better their lot. But his was not a forceful personality and he appears to have had few of the qualities necessary to impose his authority upon his ardent and impatient colleagues. For a long time it had been evident that Colonel Nasser was the effective ruler and that General Nagib had become little more than a figure to be cheered at railway stations. He seems to have rebelled against the role. That, at any rate, is the deduction to be made from Colonel Nasser's claim that General Nagib had been forced to resign all his offices because he had demanded powers which the Revolutionary Council thought excessive.

●

IT is assumed in London that an Anglo-Egyptian settlement has now become remote; and certainly the statements made in Cairo yesterday in the name of the Revolutionary Council gave the impression that Egypt, under its new ruler, would be even less conciliatory in its external disputes than it was under Nagib. The mood that has now got the upper hand will doubtless have its effect upon such issues as the one now before the Security Council, at Israel's bidding, as well as upon the larger issue of Anglo-Egyptian relations. If the West expects less from Nasser's Egypt than it hoped from Nagib's, it may be more uncompromising in its demand for the freeing of the Suez Canal and the Gulf of Akaba to all international shipping wherever bound. But what will be the use of such a gesture if Egypt decides to take no notice of it? Indeed, the question now is whether Colonel Nasser rid himself of General Nagib merely because he wants the power for himself or because he felt that General Nagib stood in the way of a policy of unbridled nationalism.

●

THE fact that General Nagib has been got out of the way and that Colonel Nasser seems to have taken over without bloodshed or tumult is not evidence that the Revolutionary Council is firmly set. It is evidence that the Egyptian regime is on a pretty unsteady foundation. The many people outside Egypt who drew from General Nagib's *coup d'état* and his subsequent behaviour the hope that Egypt had at last got itself on to a straight and progressive path, will draw no such hopes from Colonel Nasser's rise: not because General Nagib was necessarily a better leader than Colonel Nasser but because his overthrow has revealed fundamental weakness in the revolutionary movement itself.

●

FROM the Nile to the Tigris and to the rivers of Damascus, the Arab peoples are having a bad time one way and another. They are the sport of petty rulers and the victims of a grotesque nationalism fed them in the stead of bread. One day, surely, they will grow tired of it.

Jerusalem, February, 26.

AFTER MIDNIGHT

The U.S. Government last night told Poland to close its Consulates General in New York, Chicago and Detroit. Secretary of State Dulles told Polish Ambassador Jozef Winiewicz that the Consulates "serve no useful purpose in the conduct of relations between the U.S. and Poland at the present time."

US Gives Pakistan Aid, Offer to Nehru

WASHINGTON, Thursday. — President Eisenhower announced today that the U.S. will grant military aid to Pakistan. He did not specify the amount. The white House also made public a letter from Mr. Eisenhower to Indian Prime Minister Nehru justifying the American action, and offering arms to India.

A military mission will be sent to Pakistan soon to determine its military needs. The military aid would be provided under the Mutual Security Act.

The President said that the U.S. Government has been "gravely concerned" over the defensive weakness of the Middle East.

"The U.S. earnestly desires that there be increased stability and strength in the Middle East, as it has desired this same thing in other parts of the free world.

"It believes that aspirations in this area for maintaining and developing their way of life and for realizing the social advances close to their hearts will be best served by strength to deter aggression and to reduce the fear of aggression. The U.S. is prepared to help in this endeavour, if its help is wanted."

In Karachi, Pakistan Prime Minister Mohammed Ali, announcing the granting of aid, said that the only condition imposed by the U.S. was that Pakistan would not engage in aggressive action. "That condition we willingly accept," he told Parliament.

In London, the Foreign Office welcomed the grant of aid as "strengthening the general security of the Middle East."

Treaty with Karachi Open to All--Koprulu

ANKARA, Thursday (Reuter). — Turkish Foreign Minister, Fuat Koprulu told the National Assembly yesterday that Turkey's proposed defence pact with Pakistan constituted an automatic invitation to all countries wishing to strengthen peace and security.

Speaking in a debate on the Foreign Ministry budget Mr. Koprulu said that although the pact would not have the form of a military alliance, its aim was to strengthen peace and security.

"Any countries interested in this pact because of their geographical position, may join it whenever they desire in any way they wish" he declared.

Turkey wished to develop the existing good relations with India, which had a great role to play in world affairs, he added.

Berlin Cleared Way for Future Peace by Diplomacy—Dulles

WASHINGTON, Thursday (Reuter). — Secretary of State Dulles, in a nationwide broadcast today, said that the Berlin Conference had two results which would profoundly influence the future. Berlin cleared the way for other things to happen, he stated.

Mr. Dulles added "First, as far as Europe was concerned, we brought Mr. Molotov to show Russia's hand. It will be seen as a hand that held fast to everything it had, including East Germany and East Austria, and it also sought to grasp some more.

"Secondly, as far as Korea and Indo-China were concerned, we brought Mr. Molotov to accept a resolution which spelled out the American position that Red China might in these two instances be dealt with, but not as a Government recognized by us.

"There is no reason, however, why we should refuse to seek peacefully the results we want merely because of fear that we will be outmanoeuvred at the conference table.

"No informed observers believe that we were outmanoeuvred at Berlin.

"We need not out of fright lay down the tools of diplomacy and the possibilities which they provide. Our cause is not so poor, and our capacity not so low, that our nation must seek security by sulking in its tent."

CHURCHILL WANTS TRADE WITH RUSSIA

LONDON, Thursday. — Prime Minister Sir Winston Churchill announced today that Britain favours a "substantial relaxation" in regulations affecting trade with Russia and will take up the matter with the U.S.

The Prime Minister also declared that a meeting of the Heads of State of the Great Powers still "should not be ruled out."

Army Sec'y Asks Ike's Aid Against McCarthy

WASHINGTON, Thursday (UP). —Army Secretary Robert Stevens telephoned the White House today seeking presidential backing in his feud with Senator Joseph McCarthy. But he "categorically denied" that he intends to resign or has asked for any public statement of support from President Eisenhower.

A high Administration source said that Mr. Stevens was apparently seeking a personal appointment with Mr. Eisenhower to determine how far the Administration will go to support his stand against Mr. McCarthy's "unwarranted abuse" of Army officers.

The source stated that Mr. Stevens had discussed with the White House yesterday's "memorandum of understanding" with Mr. McCarthy in which Mr. Stevens reversed this attitude and agreed to let Army officers testify before Mr. McCarthy's Senate permanent Investigating Subcommittee on alleged Communist penetration of the service.

This source added that the Army Secretary also talked with the White House on the widely interpreted view that he had "capitulated" to Mr. McCarthy. Mr. Stevens was pictured as "steaming mad" over this interpretation, and as seeking Presidential assurance that he would not be "sacrificed" to Mr. McCarthy "for the sake of politics."

Stevens 'Submits'

NEW YORK, Thursday. — "Under severe Party pressure, Secretary of the Army Robert Stevens surrendered to Senator Joseph McCarthy, who had humiliated and bullied an Army General and who had spread the most infamous insinuations touching upon the Army's very loyalty and patriotism," the Republican "Herald Tribune" editorializes this morning.

Once again, the Party rescued Senator McCarthy from the consequences of his rashness, giving him renewed strength, the paper asserts, adding, "His assault of the Army was the supreme test of the ability of men in high office to meet a threat which in other parts of the world has been fatal to liberty itself. They failed to meet that test."

('Eisenhower Helpless' — P. 4)

DIAL PHONE EQUIPMENT

TEL AVIV, Thursday. — Equipment and cables for "direct dialling" telephone contacts between the main cities in Israel are to be purchased immediately according to an agreement signed in Cologne yesterday by the Reparations Purchasing Mission there, the Israel Postal Service and one of the biggest industrialists in Germany, the Shilumim Corporation announced here today.

Oscar Levant Fails In Suicide Attempt

BEVERLY HILLS, California, Thursday (UP).—Concert pianist Oscar Levant, who attempted to commit suicide early today by swallowing two teaspoonsful of an embalming fluid because his wife had left him, was reported out of danger this afternoon and resting comfortably.

Mr. Levant, who was one of the closest friends of the late composer, George Gershwin, said that he had swallowed the poison "just to be dramatic" and force his wife to return to him. Mrs. Levant left him yesterday and took their three daughters with her.

Hussein to See Feisal

AMMAN, Thursday (Reuter). — The Royal Court here announced tonight that King Hussein will pay a "family visit" to King Feisal of Iraq on Sunday.

'THE BEST MOMENT'

LONDON, Thursday (UP). — Labourite Harold Wilson, referring to President Nagib's resignation, brought cheers from Socialists in the Commons today when he told the Government:

"It may well be that the best moment for seeking the agreement that the Foreign Secretary wanted (on the Suez dispute) has come."

THURSDAY, MARCH 18, 1954

THE JERUSALEM POST

PRICE: 100 PRUTA
VOL. XXX, No. 7820

Marginal Column

By GEORGE LEONOF

SOMETHING must have yielded in the Anglo-Egyptian stalemate over the Suez Canal base if Cairo has requested resumption of negotiations, as announced by a British Foreign Office spokesman; and judging from Colonel Nasser's brusque denial of the announcement, it was the Egyptians who did at least some of the giving. The new development comes close on the heels of persistent if unauthenticated reports that the military junta may be willing to compromise on what up to the present has been a major obstacle to a settlement—the condition that British troops may reoccupy the base in case of an attack on Turkey. As to the other rock on which the talks appeared to have foundered last October — the "prestige" squabble over whether British technicians who stay behind wear khaki or mufti — the tides of five months seem to have eroded it to its proper pebble proportions.

•

EGYPT'S objection to the "Turkish" clause was that it conspired to lure her away from her oft-avowed preference for a strictly regional defence organization and into a much broader Western military grouping which she had repeatedly declined to join. Since Turkey is a member of the North Atlantic Treaty Organization and the Balkan pacts, it was claimed an attack on any NATO nation, or even Western Germany, Greece or Yugoslavia, would bring Turkey into the war, thus automatically involving Egypt once British troops returned to the base.

•

THE oscillating fortunes of Nasser and Nagib have revealed to the world that the Egyptian army's mailed fist has of government. But they also brought Britain face to face with the problem of whether the Revolution Command Council is not the most stable government Egypt could hope for, and whether its fall would necessarily be to Britain's advantage. If the answer is negative, then it is obvious that a Suez settlement would strengthen the Council's hand. As for Egypt — the threat of war is receding, and if reactivation of the base could be made dependent on a direct attack on Turkey, avoiding the latter's commitments in Europe, it is not unlikely that the clause may be more palatable to the Egyptians. In addition there is always the starkly realistic viewpoint that once war breaks out and the Suez is indeed threatened, it would take more than a treaty to keep Allied forces from defending what their governments consider a vital lifeline.

Jerusalem, March 18.

British Protest Wave Of Terror in Suez Zone

LONDON, Wednesday. — Britain has protested to Egypt over attacks against British servicemen in the Suez Canal zone base in the past 24 hours, a Foreign Office spokesman said here today.

According to reports reaching London, two British soldiers have been killed and five wounded.

Sir Ralph Stevenson, British Ambassador in Cairo, made the protest when he was asked to call on the Egyptian Foreign Minister Mahmud Fawzi today.

The spokesman said Sir Ralph protested about the disappearance of two signalmen on the morning of March 15 and the murder of two servicemen and the wounding of two others on the same night.

In consequence of these two incidents British forces made a number of enquiries and started tracking the assaults, the spokesmen said. Dr. Fawzi asked the Ambassador to call on him and described these measures as a "reign of terror" loosed by the British against the Egyptian population.

(Last Monday Fawzi had summoned Sir Ralph and handed him a protest against the killing of an Egyptian officer in the Canal Zone last week.)

Rejects Allegation

"The Ambassador rejected the allegation and expressed resentment at the failure of the Egyptian authorities to maintain order," the British spokesman added.

Earlier, a British spokesman said that the prospect of reaching agreement with Egypt on the base must depend on the prevailing atmosphere. The atmosphere would naturally be affected by attacks on British personnel. He emphasised that recent attacks were "not a contribution to the improvement of relations we should like to see."

In Cairo, Minister of National Guidance Major Salah Salem today confirmed that Egypt is not seeking to resume the deadlocked Suez Canal discussions with Britain.

The internal situation would not "prevent us taking action against the British now," Salem told journalists.

After a six-hour joint meeting of Cabinet and Revolution Council members, Salem told reporters early today that they had discussed British "transgressions in the Canal Zone and are determined to take drastic measures to put an end to them."

One thousand students shouting slogans against Vice Premier Gamal Abdul Nasser demonstrated on Cairo University campus today, demanding release of Professors jailed for activities connected with the outlawed Moslem Brotherhood.

'Top Secret' Talks Held on Cyprus

By IRIS K. RUSSELL,
Jerusalem Post Correspondent

NICOSIA, Wednesday. — General Sir Charles Keightley, C.-in-C. Middle East Land Forces, and Air Chief Marshal Claude Pelly, C.-in-C. Middle East Air Forces, flew here from the Suez Canal zone today for a "top secret" conference with service chiefs from Britain.

This evening they met at the Cyprus Garrison Headquarters with General Sir Ouvry Roberts, Quartermaster General, and Air Chief Marshal Sir John Whitworth Jones, who had arrived from Britain on Monday. A number of other senior Army and Air Force officers also attended the meeting.

It is believed the talks are connected with the major military and R.A.F. construction projects in Cyprus, but it is also strongly rumoured that they dealt with the possible transfer of British Middle East headquarters from the Suez Canal zone to Cyprus.

This transfer, which some British papers have described as "imminent," has been denied by a military spokesman here.

Military construction projects at present under way in Cyprus include the building of an army camp at Dekhelia in Southeastern Cyprus, facing the coast of Israel. The first stage of this £13m. project has just been completed and while the camp is not expected to be ready before 1959, it is well known that the plans could easily be modified to accommodate troops at short notice.

Another army cantonment is being built at Episcopi, near Limassol in Southwestern Cyprus, while 13 kms. away, at Akrotiki, is the site of a new RAF airfield which is to become a huge bomber base. Limassol port is to be improved radically to make it into one of the best harbours in the Middle East. It is also rumoured that the Limassol salt lake will be converted into a submarine base.

BOTVINNIK LEADS

MOSCOW, Wednesday (UP). — Mikhail Botvinnik won the first of a series of matches for the world chess championship when the challenger, Vassily Smyslov, resigned after the 52nd move.

French Order All Planes to Aid Of Beleaguered Fort

SAIGON, Wednesday.—General Henri Navarre, French Commander-in-Chief in Indo-China, today ordered all available planes into the air to assist the beleaguered garrison of Dien Bien Phu on the eve of the second and probably decisive round of the biggest battle of the Indo-China war.

With improved weather conditions, French transport planes braved Communist anti-aircraft fire to drop massive supplies of food and ammunition to the French defenders after a 380 kms. flight from Haiphong air base.

Military authorities in Hanoi disclosed today that Vietminh artillery has knocked out several airlift planes. A spokesman lifted the veil on French airlift losses after the Vietminh claimed having shot down or destroyed on the ground 12 planes, including a big C-119 Flying Boxcar and several Dakota transports.

Decisive Round

French Union defenders of the mountain fortress tonight prepared for a second and probably decisive round in the biggest battle so far in the Indo-China war.

The Vietminh rebels under General Vo Nguyen Giap are closing in north and west of the fortress. Gen. Giap is believed to be massing thousands of his best shock troops for an all-out assault.

The battle-weary French Union defenders, meanwhile, have been reinforced by several hundreds of paratroops dropped by the French Air Force yesterday.

(Reuter, UP)

JOINT ANGLO-RUSSIAN MOTION ON TRADE

GENEVA, Wednesday (Reuter). — Britain and Russia tonight tabled in the U.N. Economic Commission for Europe a joint draft resolution on the expansion of East-West trade.

The draft, worked out in private meetings between the two delegations, will be discussed tomorrow by a commission. It invites the Executive Secretary of the E.C.E. to consult governments in the light of East-West trade talks due to open here on April 20, to ascertain by June 30, 1954, their opinion about reviving the E.C.E. Trade Committee this year.

It was reliably learned here today that a high-level conference of economists from all European countries — both East and West — has been suggested.

11 Bus Passengers Are Massacred By Arab Marauders on Negev Road

Attack a 'Clear Warlike Act'

All necessary measures within the Government's power will be taken to ensure security of movement in the Negev, declared the official statement issued by the Government last night. The statement refers to the ambush as "a clear warlike act."

"The Government of Israel expresses its revulsion and horror at the murderous attack by an organized Arab force on a passenger bus in the Negev, which was carried out as a military operation and which resulted in the cold-blooded killing of eleven men, women and children and the wounding of three others," the Government declared.

"The Government of Israel regards this attack as a clear warlike act, responsibility for which falls squarely upon the Government from whose territory this unit of murderers was sent forth across the border into Israel territory to carry out this dastardly deed.

"The series of wanton acts of hostility by neighbouring Arab states against Israel has reached a new climax with this latest outrage.

"The Government of Israel will take all necessary measures within its power to ensure that the blood of Israel citizens will not be shed with impunity. All steps will be taken to safeguard the security of travellers along the roads of the Negev so that movement will continue without hindrance.

"The deepest sympathy of the people of Israel goes out to the families of the victims of the massacre.

"Gravest Attack Ever By Marauders"

The Army spokesman said last night that the Scorpions' Ascent attack was the gravest ever perpetrated by marauders in years. The attackers, whose numbers are not yet known, acted as a well-trained military unit.

The Army was unable to comment further until the full story of the murder is known.

Jordan Disclaims Any Knowledge

An official Jordan communique alleged that the Mixed Armistice Commission emergency meeting, scheduled for 3.30 p.m. yesterday, was postponed due to an Israel charge that a bus was ambushed on the road to Eilat.

The communique added the Jordan authorities were surprised to hear that an alleged ambush deep in Israel territory, 50 kilometres from the nearest Jordan border, an incident in which Jordan could not possibly have been involved should have resulted in the postponement of the meeting.

The communique ended by stating that in spite of these circumstances, the Jordan authorities have ordered competent authorities to investigate this matter. *(ANA)*

VICTIMS CAUGHT IN AMBUSH

By H. BEN-ADI, Jerusalem Post Reporter.

BEERSHEBA, Wednesday. — Arab gunmen, attacked an oncoming Eshed Bus in the Negev at 11.45 a.m. today, murdering 11 persons and wounding two. The killers who had been lying in ambush behind the Eilat Liberators' Monument entered the vehicle, which backed into the hill, and pumped automatic fire into the passengers. Three persons escaped unharmed.

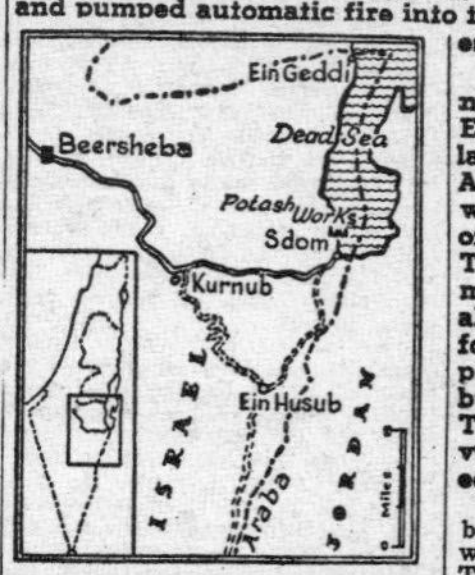

The cold-blooded murder took place where the road twists and turns between Kurnub and Ein Husub.

The bus bearing the banner "Hail Negev Builders on Eilat Day", was coming up the last bend of the steep Ma'ale Akrabim (Scorpions' Ascent) when the Arabs came out of hiding and shot the driver. The vehicle backed up 20 metres and leaned against the almost perpendicular wall formed by the mountain. Four passengers jumped from the bus and were killed outright. The killers then entered the vehicle and brutally murdered the passengers.

The driver, Ephraim Fistenberg, was shot and killed. His wife is also among the dead. Their daughter, 5, escaped unhurt. Their son, 11, fell on his back when the bus crashed into the mountain. While lying on his back near Esther Levy, an Army nurse on leave in Eilat, he was shot in the head at less than fifty centimetres. The nurse was shot in the abdomen and although wounded seriously managed to extend some first aid to the boy.

The boy was operated upon in Hadassah Hospital, Jerusalem, tonight by Dr. A. J. Beller, head of the Hospital's Neurosurgery Department. His condition is extremely grave.

Another of the murdered is Kalman Esroni, also a driver.

Besides the child, among those who escaped unhurt was a worker at the Eilat canteen and an Army sergeant.

An Army car, which passed the spot ninety minutes after the incident, picked up the survivors and wounded and took them to Beersheba. Police and Army immediately went to the scene. Planes were directed to search for marauders.

The scene at 4.30 this afternoon was ghastly. The bodies of the dead had not been touched by the investigators until the arrival of the U.N. Observers at about 6 p.m.

Two soldiers were killed. One was found lying not far from the monument. By the side of a woman was a smashed bottle of eau-de-cologne. The inside of the bus was littered with coral and other souvenirs which tourists usually bring from Eilat. The weapons of the four soldiers, who were aboard to guard the bus, were gone.

The cartridges found on the spot were of German rifles and machine-guns. According to one source, the killers were dressed in khaki. A small black Arab cap, worn by Jordan Arabs, was found on the spot.

A complaint has been filed with the Israel-Jordan MAC. The U.N. observers are due to visit the scene of the crime at dawn tomorrow.

Eyewitness Account

BEERSHEBA, Wednesday. — "As the bus approached the monument," Miss Miriam Lesser, 28, a survivor of the murderous attack, told reporters at the local police station tonight, "men clad in khaki overalls, with red belts and carrying daggers appeared, shooting in our direction. They spoke Arabic.

"We all fell on the floor. Two of the men entered the bus, firing their weapons. For one and a half hours I didn't move a limb," she said.

Ninety minutes later a jeep passed, taking her and the five-year-old girl to the police station here.

Miss Lesser is from Holland and has been in the country for seven years. She works at the Eilat canteen.

"We left Eilat early. We were all holiday makers who had been taking part in the celebrations. Whilst on the Ma'ale Akrabim we asked the driver to take pictures. When he drove on and we were just on the last turn we heard firing. Our first thought was that one of the soldiers in the bus had fired his gun. A minute later most of the passengers were dead and others were lying under the dead bodies. I lay on the floor while machine-gun firing went on. The driver was hit and fell out of the window. One passenger after the other fell and I found myself on the floor."

The two men who entered the bus armed pulled out one body after another and on finding signs of life fired at short range. One of the men pulled her by the hair and searched her for arms, but she played dead and the bullet just missed her. Two men removed all the arms and possessions of the soldiers, but did not loot the passengers' luggage, she said.

The place of the murder is 80 kilometres south of Beersheba, about 10 kilometres from the phosphate mines.

US Awaits Details Of Negev Incident

WASHINGTON, Wednesday (INA). — The State Department is awaiting details of the Negev bus incident while closely observing the continued friction on Lake Kinneret, State Department sources said today.

Meanwhile, the Israel Embassy here announced that Mr. Reuyen Shiloah, Israel Minister, met with Acting Assistant Secretary of State Mr. John Jernegan this afternoon.

Knesset Security C'tee

The Knesset Foreign Affairs and Security Committee will meet in the Ministry of Defence at Hakirya at noon tomorrow. Prime Minister Moshe Sharett and the Minister of Defence Mr. Pinhas Lavon, will be present.

Prime Minister Sharett and Defence Minister Lavon are expected to leave for Beersheba tomorrow (Thursday) morning.

Patrol Fired Upon

An Israel army patrol, made up of a number of officers and soldiers, was shot at by a Jordan unit of 15 men, east of the Beersheba-Hebron road, near the Israel-Jordan Armistice line, at 2:45 p.m. yesterday the Army spokesman announced. The Israel patrol fired back. There were no casualties.

LUCKY TELEGRAM

Dr. A. Shamir of the Hadassah in Jerusalem, and his wife, who were vacationing in Eilat had tickets to return to Beersheba on the fatal bus. A telegram from Jerusalem, however that their son had met with an accident while playing with a pair of scissors caused them to change their plans and instead they returned home by plane.

Syrians Again Open Fire Near Kinneret

Jerusalem Post Reporter

TIBERIAS, Wednesday. — Fire was directed at a cowherd at Tel Katzir settlement from Syrian positions half a kilometre away at eleven o'clock this morning.

The cowherd, Gideon Geisler, 21, was grazing his cattle about 500 metres from the kibbutz when several single shots and one burst of automatic fire were directed at him from 600-metres range.

The volley passed over his head. He drove the cattle out of sight behind a hill and ran to the settlement to alarm the members.

Earlier he had noted Arab shepherds on the Syrian side making off from the area, a sign that they knew what was about to happen. He noted one Arab running away with a gun in his hand.

He had been grazing his cattle at the same place for the past three weeks, always between 10 a.m. and 1.30 p.m., and the Arabs had apparently noted this and laid an ambush for him. Apparently the attackers were regular soldiers. Late this afternoon Arab shepherds returned to the area to graze their flock.

Israel has submitted a complaint to the Israel-Syrian Mixed Armistice Commission, the Army spokesman announced.

In the Rambam Hospital in Haifa, Zakaria Ibrahim, a Circassian Frontier policeman, died today of wounds received while on patrol at Baka el Gharbiya, in the Little Triangle, on March 7.

Ibrahim, a mounted policeman, was shot by Jordan Legionnaires from across the border.

On Tuesday, the Israel-Jordan M.A.C. blamed Jordan for the incident.

CANNON REMOVED

TEL AVIV, Wednesday. — Orders were issued today to dismantle the guns from the police craft on Lake Kinneret, the Army spokesman said today. This was done in pursuance to the decision of the Israel-Syrian Mixed Armistice Commission yesterday.

"We are not interested in arming police boats with cannon," the spokesman said. "All we want is that Israel fishermen be safe in Israel waters."

Bennike Visits Site Of Jordan Canal

General Vagn Bennike, U.N. Chief of Staff, his advisers, the U.N. chairman of the Israel-Syrian Mixed Armistice Commission, and the senior Syrian M.A.C. delegate, Major Tewfik Shatilah, visited the scene of the Jordan river diversion canal on Wednesday morning, NEABS reports. The visit took place at the request of the Syrian Government.

They later toured the two Syrian posts on the eastern side of Lake Kinneret and inspected the damage caused by Israel guns.

It was understood that an emergency meeting of the Israel-Syrian MAC on the March 15 incident on the Lake will take place within two days.

Eban Seeks Change In Munro Resolution

By JESSE ZEL LURIE,
Jerusalem Post Correspondent

NEW YORK, Wednesday. — Israel Ambassador Abba Eban and Mr. Mordechai Kidron of the Israel U.N. delegation, today saw the New Zealand U.N. delegate, Mr. Leslie Munro, to suggest improvements in the New Zealand resolution.

This reaffirms the Security Council's resolution of 1951, condemning Egypt's blockade of the Suez Canal, expresses concern at Egypt's disregard of the resolution but makes no provision to follow it up.

"The New York Times" today stated that this was as far as the Western powers were prepared to go. The paper added that the West felt anything more might both wreck the imminent Anglo-Egyptian Suez negotiations and induce a Soviet Union veto.

Mr. Munro intends to lodge his draft resolution with the Security Council tomorrow. It is probable that it will be debated by the Council at a meeting next Tuesday.

NEW MID-EAST BLOC IN MAKING—DULLES

WASHINGTON, Wednesday (Reuter). — U.S. Secretary of State Dulles said last night that collective arrangements were now in the making in the Middle East with Turkey and Pakistan as the nucleus.

Ike Favours Quick Retaliation

WASHINGTON, Wednesday (Reuter). — President Eisenhower said today that any President of the United States should be hanged if he did not take immediate action to repel an attack on the U.S. whether Congress was or was not available to declare war.

Mr. Eisenhower was discussing at his weekly press conference the implications of America's defence policy of instant "massive retaliation" against aggression directed at the territory of the U.S. or its allies.

The President said the "new look" military programme which has been under attack by some Democrats represented the best efforts to use modern weapons and to conserve manpower in any war that might break out.

The President said he thought there was too much hysteria. There was a multiplicity of fear—fear of the men of the Kremlin, fear of what they might do, fear of depression, fear of loss of jobs, and fear of unwise investigators.

All this made Americans almost hysterical, he said, and it was necessary for everything to be put into its proper perspective.

AFTER MIDNIGHT

The Soviet Government last night announced its agreement that the Geneva conference on the Far East should be opened in the Palais des Nations, former headquarters of the League of Nations, on April 26 as arranged.

Paris Would Prefer Prior Consultation

PARIS, Wednesday (Reuter). France is to ask the U.S. the exact meaning of Mr. John Foster Dulles' statement in a Washington press conference last night that any attack on London or Paris would be followed automatically by retaliation by U.S. forces, it was learned at the French Foreign Ministry today.

French officials are awaiting a full official text of the U.S. Secretary of State's press conference, but a French Foreign Ministery spokesman said tonight that the Government's point of view was "consultation must precede retaliation".

HORE BELISHA WANTS NEGEV PIPELINE

LONDON, Wednesday (AFP). — Lord Hore Belisha yesterday recommended in the House of Lords the construction of a pipeline connecting the Gulf of Akaba to the Mediterranean.

THE JERUSALEM POST

TUESDAY,
FEBRUARY 1, 1955

PRICE : 100 PRUTA
VOL. XXXI, No. 8081

Marginal Column
By ZE'EV LAQUEUR

THE Supreme Soviet of the USSR has been convoked for an extraordinary session this Thursday. On the same day, incidentally, M. Mendes-France will have to fight for survival in the National Assembly and might be defeated. The Moscow meeting, it is believed, is connected with the recall of the Soviet envoys from the Western capitals for consultations last week. This, it was noted, was a highly unusual, perhaps even an unprecedented step, some observers believe the Russian Government may well carry out its threat and renounce the friendship treaties with France and Britain dating back to World War II. A major foreign political statement on that occasion would not come as a great surprise. Western statesmen have long argued that the existence of these treaties has not mattered for years past, anyway.

IT is more difficult to understand that the Western Governments have ignored the Soviet note of January 16, too, in which, for the first time, proposals approximating to the Western demand for all-German free elections were contained. This may be an important event and it is certainly a matter of regret that the West has not even tried to find out how serious the new offer is. They appear to be so preoccupied with the creation of the new West-German Army, as unrealistic in their approach to German affairs, that they refuse to consider the very possibility of some alternative solution. It was obvious from the very beginning that a substantial Soviet offer would be made, if at all, at the last possible moment. This moment may now have come, and the Western allies, deterred by so many past disappointments, refuses even to consider the possibility of a debate with Russia over Germany. They are taking a grave responsibility upon themselves.

MEANWHILE in Russia, some reshuffle in the top leadership appears to be in the offing. The names of Marshals Vassilevski, Zhukov and Budyenny, for the first time in many years, do not appear on the lists of candidates for the Supreme Soviet. Perhaps they are not interested in politics just now; perhaps they are preoccupied elsewhere — nobody knows. It may also have some political significance. Mr. Malenkov has been silent for six months, watching his colleague, Krushchev, and noting his frequent speeches in public: in Prague, in Peking, at the conventions of the tractor drivers, architects, Sotkhoz workers and cotton experts, and most recently at a big youth meeting. Mr. Krushchev was also the moving spirit at the November 7 reception, and some weeks later at the Yugoslav Embassy. They may be collaborating closely, but they are watching each other closely, too.

MR. Mikoyan's resignation from his post as Minister for Foreign Trade was foreshadowed by a curious incident last September. "Partinaya Shizn," a fairly restricted Party periodical, announced that A. Krutikov, Mr. Mikoyan's deputy, had been excluded from the Party because he had misused his position by helping relatives, thus putting private interests above the interests of State and Party. The news item, not reprinted in the rest of the Soviet press, also charged the Party organisation and the Ministry with having covered up Krutikov's behaviour. Krutikov's purge came in the wake of a resolution of the Party Central Commission adopted earlier in 1954 on "serious inadequacies in the Party and State apparatus." However, as things are at present in Moscow demotion is by no means identical with total purge and trial. Even in Stalin's time, Andreyev, a member of the Politboro until 1950, was removed from the supreme party body but continued to be employed in a subordinate capacity. Mr. Mikoyan, despite his resignation from foreign trade, may well continue to be active in some other field.

Jerusalem, February 1.

SWEDISH AIR FORCE GENERAL COMING

STOCKHOLM, Monday (Reuter). — The Deputy Commander-in-Chief of the Swedish Air Force, Major-General Gustaf Adolf Westring, left for Israel by air today. He has been invited by the Israel Government to lecture on the organization and equipment of a modern Air Force.

UN Chief to Urge Peking Presence For Truce Debate

UNITED NATIONS, Monday (UP). — New Zealand announced today that it would ask Secretary-General Dag Hammarskjold to urge China to participate in the Security Council's debate on a Chinese cease-fire in the Formosa area. Sir Leslie Knox Munro, Chief New Zealand representative who is Council President for January, said he would ask the Council to agree to an invitation to the Chinese as soon as it adopts its agenda. The agenda contains proposals from both New Zealand and Russia, aimed at achieving a cease-fire in the China fighting. Sir Leslie made his announcement after the Council rejected a Soviet demand, made at the outset of the historic meeting of the 11-nation body, that Nationalist China be barred from the debate.

By a 10-1 vote, with Russia against, the Council approved a motion presented by the United States prohibiting any action to bar the Chinese Nationalists or seat the Chinese Communists. The Russian delegate, Mr. A.A. Soboliev, said acts of aggression by the United States against China had been expressed in unprovoked armed attacks, the concentration of naval and air forces in the area, and the threatening use of armed force against the Peoples Republic of China.

He complained that the New Zealand proposal "has reduced everything to a cease-fire—and that only in a small group of coastal islands."

"A cease-fire in the area of the coastal islands is nothing in reality, but a clumsy manoeuvre to force the Peoples Republic of China to give up their sovereign rights to age-old Chinese territory and to reinforce the illegal seizure of these islands by the United States." Mr. Soboliev said.

The U.S. delegate, Mr. Henry Cabot Lodge, declared that international Communism would take over "Formosa or any other place on this earth if it could" and labelled Russian manoeuvres in the United Nations a "smoke screen" to conceal a "Communist refusal to agree to a China cease-fire."

He made the declaration after Nationalist China's Dr. Tingfu F. Tsiang had asked the Council to deal with the Chinese crisis as a "problem of Soviet aggression in the Far East."

"I wish" the Security Council "for once at least, to meet fully the enormity of the master plan designed to destroy us," Dr. Tsiang said. "For this reason, I am of the opinion that Council should consider primarily the problem of Soviet aggression in the Far East."

War Danger Seen By Molotov

MOSCOW, Monday (Reuter). — The British Ambassador Sir William Hayter tonight called on the Foreign Minister Viacheslav Molotov who handed him a statement.

"Tass" reported that the statement arose from a conversation which took place on January 28 between Sir William and Mr. Molotov. Sir William at that time asked Russia's support for a cease-fire in Formosa. Today, Mr. Molotov expressed concern over the situation in the Formosa area which he said had been intensified by "aggressive" American actions.

"The Soviet Government shares the opinion of the British Government about the necessity of discussing that question in the Security Council," he said.

Moscow Radio said that Mr. Molotov in a talk with two American journalists on Saturday said he regarded the situation in the Formosa area as a serious threat to world peace and that it presented a danger of war. The newspapermen were Mr. William Randolph Hearst, Jr., newspaper publisher and proprietor, and Mr. J. Kingsbury Smith, European manager of the International News Service.

Jerusalem, February 1.

New IL.631m. Budget Tabled in Knesset

Jerusalem Post Reporter

The IL.631.1m. draft budget for the 1955/56 fiscal year was tabled in the Knesset yesterday. Ordinary expenditure amounts to IL.311.6m., and of this almost half—IL.149.3m.—is allotted to security, special budgets (including police and courts), and reserves.

WHERE THE MONEY GOES

Here is how the Government proposes to spend each Pound of the IL.311.6m. allocated for "ordinary expenditure" in next year's Budget:

	pruta
Security, special budgets and reserves	480
Social services	200
Administration	130
Economic services	90
Interest	80
Subsidies	20

Interest on loans takes IL.25.4m., eight per cent of ordinary expenditure.

Education and social services receive IL.61.8m. Included in this heading are health, education, social welfare, local authorities, and invalids' pensions. The administrative expenses of all Government Ministries taken together come to IL.36.8m.

Economic services — including agriculture, commerce and industry, labour and development — take IL.28.3m., while IL.10m. goes for subsidies.

On the revenue side, slightly more than half of all ordinary income — IL.152.1m. — is expected to come from indirect taxes. Direct taxes account for IL.130m., interest for IL.16m., and service fees for IL.7.5m.

Compared with the 1954/55 Budget, ordinary expenditure takes IL.311.6m. instead of IL.279.4m. Extraordinary expenditure with IL.14.6m. last year. Posts and communications receive IL.39.7m. in place of IL.35.1m., and the capital budget (development and special expenditure) stands at IL.262.5m. as compared with IL.243.4m.

("Budget Increase"—P. 4)

GZ Executive Votes To Oppose Budget

Jerusalem Post Reporter

The General Zionist Party Executive which met in joint session with the Party's Knesset faction in Jerusalem last night decided that the Party will not support the proposed 1955-56 budget when it comes up for the vote in the Knesset.

In view of the fact that this move would entail the Party's leaving the Coalition, it was agreed to refer the matter to the Party's Council for a final decision. The Council is to meet tomorrow in Tel Aviv.

Despite last night's decision, it was not thought in the Knesset lobbies that a Government crisis was imminent, mainly because the majority of the General Zionist Ministers are known to be opposed to leaving the Government at this time.

In Tel Aviv yesterday (before the General Zionist Party caucus had taken place), the Minister of Justice, Mr. P. Rosen, told the Progressive Party Executive Board that the Coalition crisis is "practically over." The Progressive Party, the Minister said would consider adhering to the solution, because it is the Party's stand that the broad coalition must be maintained.

Mr. Rosen said that, in his opinion, there will be no electoral reforms before the general elections next summer.

Position of Foreign Investors Improved

Six more Knesset members spoke yesterday in the third continuation of the debate on the amendments to Encouragement of Foreign Investments Bill. Mr. Eshkol is now due to wind up at a fifth and final session, probably tomorrow.

Mr. Z. Susayeff (General Zionist), the Deputy Minister of Commerce and Industry, who was largely responsible for the framing of the amendment, said that a committee had studied the proposals for 18 months, and felt they had removed most of the remaining obstacles.

He observed that the entire position of foreign investors had changed, because Israel industry could now obtain foreign currency for equipment and raw materials for essential enterprises. But in most cases there was not sufficient capital in Israel currency, while a few years back there was no shortage of local currency for investment. This meant that the investor was asked only to transfer dollars for conversion into pounds. Previously he could send equipment that he might be able to obtain on favourable terms.

He said he saw a little prospect for the development of industry while there was such a shortage of money in Israel that banks were able to charge 20 per cent interest. Under such conditions nobody would embark on investments which could never bring such interest, but would lend the money where it brought in most.

Formosa Issue Leads Commonwealth Talks

LONDON, Monday (Reuter). — Sir Winston Churchill stressed to other Prime Ministers of the Commonwealth here today that the Formosa crisis was of the utmost delicacy and urged the greatest care in any joint efforts to ease the tension. His reference to Formosa came in a brief speech welcoming the visiting Prime Ministers and reviewing the international situation.

Foreign Secretary Sir Anthony Eden then addressed the statesmen and dealt specifically with the Far East. He said that Britain differentiates between Formosa and the Peoples off-shore islands on the one hand, and small coastal islands, occupied by the Nationalists, on the other because the peace treaty under which Japan ceded Formosa made no provision for its transfer to any other nation. The legal position is therefore indeterminate.

The Commonwealth leaders will discuss a wide range of foreign questions grouped under four heads — Europe, the Middle East, South-East Asia and the Far East.

ISRAELIS IN PEKING

HONG KONG, Monday (Reuter). — An Israel trade delegation of six headed by the Minister to Burma, Mr. David Hacohen, arrived in Peking by air today, the New China news agency reported. The delegation was welcomed by officials of the Ministry of Foreign Trade and of the National Export-Import Corporation.

Syria Ignores UN Bid for Release Of Israel Captives

The Chief of Staff of the U.N. Truce Supervision Organization, General E. L. M. Burns, yesterday morning informed Sgan-Aluf Aryeh Shalev, General Staff Officer in charge of the Israel delegations to the Mixed Armistice Commissions, and Mr. Joseph Tekoa, head of the Foreign Ministry's division for Armistice Affairs, of the Syrians' ignoring of his appeal for the early release of the Israel soldiers captured on December 9.

According to a U.N. communique issued in Jerusalem last night, General Burns sent a cable on January 18, to General Shawkat Shukier, Chief of Staff of the Syrian Army, in which he stated that he felt it was his duty to appeal through the Syrian Chief of Staff to the Syrian Government.

General Burns wrote that his appeal was in conformity with the second resolution adopted on December 12 by the Israel-Syrian M.A.C., calling on the Syrian authorities to release and return the Israel patrol at the earliest date, through the Commission. Such a measure, General Burns pointed out, would contribute to the relaxation of tension along the Israel-Syrian Demarcation Line.

'Cause of Tension'

On January 27, according to the U.N. communique, the Syrian Chief of Staff replied that the real cause of the tension along the Demarcation Line was to found in the character of the mission of the Israel patrol, captured while operating in Syrian territory. Consequently the Syrian authorities could not be held responsible for the tension, and called on General Burns to stop such actions by Israel.

General Shukeir further stated that, "notwithstanding the fact that the Syrian authorities in a spirit of concession, had agreed to treat the prisoners of war according to the regulations embodied in the Geneva Convention of 1949 on the treatment of prisoners of war, it should be remembered that the Israel soldiers did not carry with them any marks or papers which would have permitted the Syrian authorities to identify them. The Syrian authorities might therefore have dealt with them as spies."

Negotiations for the release of the Israel prisoners are proceeding, the U.N. communique concluded.

JORDANIAN KIDNAP ATTEMPT FOILED

An attempt by Jordanians to kidnap an Israel Arab from Kafr Kasim near Rosh Ha'ayin was foiled on Sunday night, the Army spokesman announced yesterday.

Armed Jordanians crossed the armistice lines and tried to kidnap the Arab who was on the village lands. When he resisted, the Jordanians fled beyond the armistice line. Israel has lodged a complaint with the Israel-Jordan Mixed Armistice Commission.

French Gov't Loses Vote in Assembly

PARIS, Monday (Reuter). — The Mendes-France Cabinet was defeated in the National Assembly today when its demand for a renewal of one month's credits for February for its civil servant budgets was rejected by 325 against 286.

The defeat does not involve the resignation of the Government, but was seen in the lobbies as a serious warning that the Government's life will be in danger on Friday night when a confidence vote is due to be taken following an important debate on North Africa.

A vote was necessary on a one month's temporary credits because the 1955 Budget has not yet been fully approved by the Assembly. The Government is expected to resubmit its request shortly for temporary credits.

The various Conservative groups voted solidly against the Government today and may do so again in Friday's vote on North Africa. Some Radicals, a few Gaullists as well as the Communists and Populists constituted the remainder of the anti-Government majority.

Anti-Jewish Violence In Tunis Rising

TUNIS, Monday (INA). — Hardly a day has passed recently without two or three violent attacks on Jews, with the attackers using a variety of weapons. Official statistics show that of every 30 reported acts of violence, 26 are against Jews.

Observers note that Arabic newspapers, in contrast to the French publications, make no protest against such actions.

The growing attacks on Jews and the uncertainty of the political situation are reflected in the number of Jews who have left for Israel in recent months. In November, 1954, 788 persons immigrated to Israel, compared with 190 in July. The figure dropped last month, but is expected to rise again in April.

AFTER MIDNIGHT

The United States has agreed to equip, train and support a South Vietnam Army of about 150,000 men.

Egypt Sends Jewish Doctor, Teacher to Die on Gallows

Nation Denounces Martyrs' Execution

By a Special Correspondent

Before a hushed and solemn House and packed public galleries, and in the presence of the President and the Chief Rabbi, Mr. Moshe Sharett, the Prime Minister and Foreign Secretary, yesterday afternoon denounced in the name of the nation the execution of Moshe Marzouk and Shmuel Azzar. As Mr. Sharett began his statement, members and spectators rose spontaneously and stood in silence.

The Israel Nation, the Jewish people everywhere and lovers of justice and peace the world over, said the Prime Minister, heard with indignation and moral revulsion the terrible news of the carrying out of the death sentences passed by a Military Court in Cairo on two young Jews, Moshe Marzouk, physician, and Shmuel Azzar, schoolmaster, who died a martyr's death yesterday morning.

The number of Jewish victims of the odious trial in Cairo has now reached four. Mr. Sharett continued.

One, Eli Cremona, was beaten to death; another, Max Bennet, took his own life, according to the Egyptian authorities, in the nightmare which enveloped the trial; and two were put to death this morning. We rise in respect to their memory and convey our deep-felt sympathy to their families.

The Egyptian junta has decided to try to strengthen its position against its antagonists within and its opponents abroad by the shedding of Jewish blood, Mr. Sharett declared. Many regimes have followed the same pernicious course in the past and in the end have sealed their own doom. Egypt has chosen to avenge itself on Jews devoted in their hearts to Israel. The Military Court imposed savage sentences, and the Head of the State confirmed the execution of two, and penal servitude for life or long terms for others.

Victims of War

These Jewish martyrs, the Prime Minister said, are victims of the same criminal war which is launched against Israel at the moment of her emergence, and which her rulers continue to wage to this day with whatever means they find suitable. Egypt cannot cleanse her self of the blood which she has thus wantonly shed. Israel and the Jewish people will not forget their martyrs. The devotion to Zion of untold numbers of Jews was never extinguished by persecution and terror in the past, nor will it be in the future. Their love for their people will triumph over the hatred which rages around them.

The Government of Israel pays tribute, Mr. Sharett concluded, to the efforts which were made all over the world — in Europe, Asia and the Americas — by Governments, organizations and individuals, including eminent leaders of nations, to save the condemned men. In denouncing before the world the heartless rejection by the rulers of Egypt of the urgent representations made to them, a rejection accompanied in some cases by misleading assurances, the Government of Israel wishes to express its profound appreciation to all those who raised their voices to save human lives and protested openly the death sentence.

(Continued on Page 2, Col. 5)

Grief, Protests All Over Country

Black-draped national flags were hung yesterday outside houses in Ramle, the chief centre of immigrants from Egypt, as a sign of mourning for the two Jews put to death in Cairo. Sons born in the near future into the congregation of former Egyptian nationals in Ramle are to be named Moshe and Shmuel after the two victims.

In Tel Aviv, the grief of the workers of the city following the hanging was expressed by Mr. Z. Shechter, Secretary of the Tel Aviv-Jaffa Labour Council at a meeting of the Secretariat yesterday. He warned the murderers that "those who spilled the innocent blood of others, should not think that the blood-spilling finished there."

The Haifa Labour Council opened its session last night with a one-minute silent tribute.

The Municipalities of Ramat Gan and Beersheba decided to name two streets after Dr. Mo-

(Continued on Page 5, Col. 7)

Cairo Unmoved by Clemency Pleas

CAIRO, Monday. — Dr. Moshe Marzouk, 26, and Samuel Azzar, 26, charged as spies for Israel, were hanged this morning. They were condemned to death after a trial by a high military tribunal which sentenced six other Jews to imprisonment with hard labour. Dr. Marzouk, Tunisian-born French citizen and house-surgeon of the Jewish Hospital here, his eyes shackled, was the first to go to the gallows. He was hanged at 7 o'clock this morning. Azzar, teacher, followed him half-an-hour later.

The sentences were carried out despite strong protest from abroad, especially from Israel, France, and numerous Jewish organizations and bodies.

Three battalions of Egyptian soldiers will guard the stores and the 1,500 British civilians who will remain. These plans were outlined here today by Sir John Duncanson, chairman of the Suez Contractors Management Company, which is coordinating the activities of contractors in the Canal base for the British Government.

UK to Leave 50,000 Tons Of Ammunition at Suez

LONDON, Monday (Reuter). — The maximum level of stores to be maintained in the Suez Canal base following the evacuation of British soldiers late in 1956 will include 50,000 tons of ammunition, 300,000 tons of ordnance and engineer stores, 2,000 vehicles, 30 locomotives, 100 railway wagons and 1,300,000 lorry cans of petrol.

Egyptian Envoy Called To Quai d'Orsay

PARIS, Monday (Reuter).—Foreign Minister Edgar Faure called the Egyptian Ambassador to the Foreign Ministry to tell him of the "feeling" provoked in France and Tunisia by the execution of Dr. Marzouk on spy charges in Cairo today, Foreign Office sources said.

M. Faure recalled that this execution was carried out "despite repeated moves by French authorities in Paris and Cairo to obtain a measure of clemency in favour of the accused."

Political Considerations Prompted Hangings

By MAURICE CARR, Jerusalem Post Correspondent

PARIS, Monday. — The Quai d'Orsay explained tonight on the Cairo executions, but unofficially it is recognized that the hangings were prompted not by considerations of justice but by politics. It was pointed out that Abdul Nasser is in difficulties at home and with the Arab League, and could not afford to reprieve the Jews after executing several members of the Moslem Brotherhood.

Directly after the sentences were pronounced, M. Massigli, Secretary-General of the Foreign Ministry, summoned the Egyptian Ambassador. In Cairo, the French Charge d'Affaires likewise presented a demarche and hope for clemency for humanitarian reasons and because Dr. Moshe Marzouk was a French protege. But it was stressed that France did not want to meddle in Egyptian domestic affairs.

The Quai d'Orsay, like the State Department, conducted all moves for intercession quietly, on the plea that publicity was harmful. It was felt then that lives would not be saved if the Powers were less discreet and protested openly the death sentence.

Shows No Emotion

The condemned men's last walk was through a long dimly-lit, iron-pillared hall lined on both sides with auxiliary policemen. After Dr. Marzouk heard the reading of the sentence in a cold, deeply unruffled manner Warden, Major Fuad Hassan signalled to the two executioners Mohammed Zanfal and Abdullah Zaidan, who strapped his prisoner's arms. He then walked into the execution chamber slowly, not showing the slightest sign of emotion.

Lieut.-Gen. Ahmed Moussaila and other officers, entered the room to witness the execution. Dr. Marzouk's pulse stopped beating three-and-a-half minutes after the two-door was dropped after the execution. The bodies were left hanging on the gibbet long enough for the son doctor, Mohammed Abd Meguid, to declare that they were dead.

The bodies were put in a special van and taken away. Marzouk's mother went...

(Continued on Page 5, Col. 6)

Final Meeting Held On Water Scheme

Mr. Eric Johnston, President Eisenhower's special representative, is leaving Israel this morning for conversations in Cairo with representatives of the Arab states on the Jordan Valley development programme. He expects to return to Israel at an early date, the Foreign Ministry's spokesman announced at 1:15 this morning at the end of a three-hour meeting between the Israel and America teams in the conversations.

The spokesman said that during his stay, Mr. Johnston explored with representatives of the Government all questions involved in the proposed Valley development plan.

Earlier in the afternoon, Mr. Levi Eshkol, Minister of Finance, and the Israel delegation met with Mr. Johnston and his experts in the Prime Minister's Office.

Later, leading members of the Cabinet, together with Rav-Aluf Moshe Dayan, the Chief of Staff, and expert advisers met in the Prime Minister's Office to discuss policy in connection with the negotiations. Among those who took part were Prime Minister Sharett; Mr. Eshkol; Mr. Pereta Naphtali, Minister of Agriculture; Mr. Pinhas Lavon, Minister of Defence; Mr. Zalman Aranne, Minister without Portfolio, Mr. T. Kollek, Mr. Pinhas Sapir and Mr. Simha Blass, Water Adviser to the Government.

The presidential envoy will spend a short time in the Old City, for conversations with the Foreign Operations Mission there and will then leave from Kalandia airport for Cairo.

League Pressure On Iraq to Delay Pact

The four-man delegation sent by the Arab Premiers' conference in Cairo last night handed Iraqi Premier Nuri e-Said a message from Lebanese President Camille Chamoun, Egyptian Premier Abdul Nasser, and Syrian Premier Fares el Khoury which appealed for a practicable and acceptable solution to the dispute over the proposed Turco-Iraqi pact.

The message reportedly asked Nuri to ease the task of the special delegation which is to plead with Iraq not to proceed with plans for an alliance with Turkey. The mission was sent after the conference in the Egyptian capital had broken up in utter disagreement, and after Egypt was reported to have threatened to walk out of the Arab League if Iraq insists on going ahead with her plans.

President Chamoun also sent a cable to King Faisal and Nuri asking for the postponement of the signing of the pact. The cable was sent after the Arab League mission had conferred for two hours this morning with the President and the Cabinet during its stopover in Beirut.

The leader of the mission, Lebanese Premier Sami el Solh, said in Baghdad last night that he "hopes to be able to influence" Nuri at least to postpone the signature of the treaty "for some time." He pointed out that were it not for the "strenuous efforts" of the Syrian, Lebanese, and Jordan delegations, the Arab League would have "collapsed" in the middle of the Cairo conference.

Also present at last night's meeting with Nuri were the three Iraqi participants in the Cairo conference, ex-Premier Dr. Fadhel Jamali, Vice-Premier Ahmed Mukhtar Baban, and acting Foreign Minister Burhan e-Din Bashayan.

Earlier yesterday, an urgent meeting of the Iraqi Cabinet heard a report from the Iraqi officials who had just arrived from Cairo ahead of the League delegation.

The Egyptian Propaganda Minister, Major Salah Salem, member of the League delegation, on landing from the plane, was met by Bashayan on behalf of the Iraqi Government and ostentatiously walked hand in hand with him to the airport building.

(NEABS, ANA, Reuter, UP)

THE JERUSALEM POST

FRIDAY, FEBRUARY 18, 1955

8 Pages

PRICE: 150 PRUTA
VOL. XXXI, No. 8096

BEN-GURION BACK IN CABINET AS DEFENCE HEAD; LAVON OUT

Mr. David Ben-Gurion will return to the Government as Minister of Defence, it was announced last night following a statement, a few hours earlier, that Mr. Pinhas Lavon had resigned this post. Mr. Ben-Gurion, Israel's war-time leader and first Prime Minister, resigned from his position as head of the Government in October 1953, and has since been working at the Negev settlement of Sde Boker.

Mr. Ben Gurion's appointment will become effective only after formal approval by the Knesset, which must approve any member co-opted by the Cabinet It is expected that the Prime Minister, Mr. M. Sharett, will detail the reasons for Mr. Lavon's resignation at the Cabinet meeting on Sunday, which is also to hear a statement by Mr. Lavon himself.

The Cabinet will presumably on this occasion also approve the return of Mr. Ben Gurion, so that this may be presented to the Knesset at the next meeting, on the following day (Monday.) Mr. Lavon's resignation does not require Knesset approval, but Mr. Ben Gurion's joining does.

The first hint of impending changes in the Cabinet came on Wednesday, when the Prime Minister published a statement that Mr. Lavon had asked for an inquiry to be held. The report stated that the enquiry committee's findings had been communicated to the Ministerial Foreign Affairs and Defence Committee, and followed on the heels of a press report the same morning which had suggested that Mr. Lavon had been required to appear before an inquiry committee.

Lavon Statement

The news of Mr. Lavon's resignation came in the form of an announcement published on his behalf by the Government Press Office at 7 o'clock in the evening. It stated that the Minister of Defence had made the following statement:

On February 2, I submitted my resignation from the Cabinet to the Prime Minister in writing. Following continued discussions since then, I today (Thursday), informed the Prime Minister that my decision to resign was final.

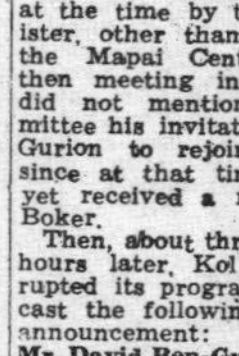

Mr. Lavon

I will submit the reasons for my decision to the Cabinet and to the Foreign Affairs and Defence Committee of the Knesset.

No announcement was made at the time by the Prime Minister, other than his report to the Mapai Central Committee then meeting in Tel Aviv. He did not mention to the Committee his invitation to Mr. Ben-Gurion to rejoin the Cabinet, since at that time he had not yet received a reply from Sde Boker.

Then, about three and one half hours later, Kol Yisrael interrupted its programme to broadcast the following two-sentence announcement:

Mr. David Ben-Gurion has agreed to the request of the Prime Minister, Mr. Moshe Sharett, to accept the post of Minister of Defence.

His appointment will be brought before the Cabinet for approval at its meeting on Sunday.

Back to Politics

Thus was announced the return from semi-retirement to active political life of Mr. Ben-Gurion who, from his retreat in the Negev, had in recent weeks been in more active contact with his former Cabinet colleagues. Only two weeks ago, for example, he was visited by Mr. Sharett, Mr. Eshkol and Mrs. Golda Myerson. As this visit coincided with Mr. Lavon's original resignation (February 2), it may be assumed that the two things were not unconnected.

Mr. Lavon, who is 50, was Secretary-General of the Histadrut from July 1949 until October, 1950 when he was appointed Minister of Agriculture. In 1952 he was appointed Minister without Portfolio, and served for various periods as Acting Foreign Minister and Acting Defence Minister until his appointment as Minister of Defence in January, 1954.

HOW BEN-GURION GOT THE NEWS

Prime Minister Sharett's invitation to Mr. Ben-Gurion to assume the post of Minister of Defence was conveyed to him at Sde Boker late yesterday afternoon by the Minister of Labour, Mrs. Golda Myerson.

By pre-arrangement, she met the Prime Minister on her return from the Negev, about 9 o'clock at Kibbutz Netser, near Be'er Ya'acov, where they both had planned to attend a memorial meeting for the late Uri Avigad. There Mrs. Myerson gave the Premier Mr. Ben-Gurion's affirmative answer, and Mr. Sharett wrote out the official announcement which was telephoned to Jerusalem.

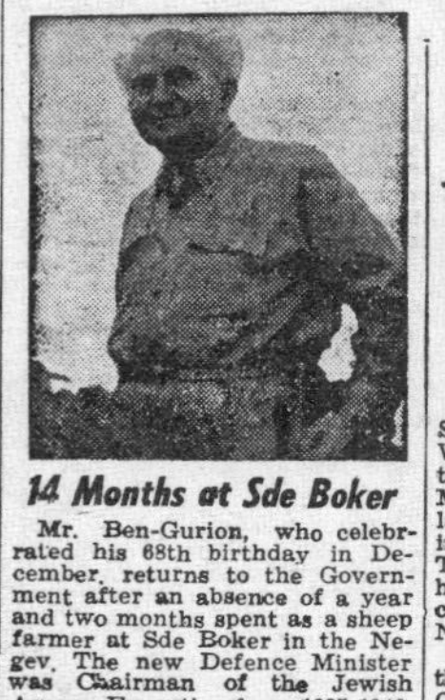

14 Months at Sde Boker

Mr. Ben-Gurion, who celebrated his 68th birthday in December, returns to the Government after an absence of a year and two months spent as a sheep farmer at Sde Boker in the Negev. The new Defence Minister was Chairman of the Jewish Agency Executive from 1935-1948, and was in supreme charge of the Haganah until the creation of the Israel Defence Army. He became head of the Provisional Government of Israel after proclaiming on May 14, 1948 the Independence of the State of Israel, and became also first Minister of Defence. He held the posts of Prime Minister and Minister of Defence until he and Mrs. Ben Gurion took up residence at Sde Boker in December 1953.

Lavon Asks to Be Relieved of Post

From Our Political Correspondent

The resignation of Mr. Pinhas Lavon will have come as no surprise to those who read with care Wednesday's announcement that, at Mr. Lavon's own request, there had been an inquiry recently.

A statement from the Prime Minister's Office on Wednesday said that the Ministerial Committee on Foreign Affairs and Defence had been made acquainted with the nature of the inquiry and also the conclusions that were reached.

It would appear that this caused Mr. Lavon to ask Mr. Sharett finally to relieve him of his portfolio and to announce that he will offer more detailed reasons for his decision to the Cabinet, probably on Sunday, and to the Foreign Affairs and Defence Committee on an early occasion. Last night's official announcement from Mr. Lavon revealed only that he had first asked to be allowed to resign about a fortnight ago, on February 2.

Mr. Sharett informed the Mapai Central Committee of Mr. Lavon's resignation shortly after his own comprehensive review of Israel's foreign relations in which was included an appraisal of the negotiations with Mr. Johnston concerning the right to the waters of the principal rivers shared by Israel with three of its neighbours, and of the present prospects in this regard.

Mutilated Remains of Two Hikers Handed Over in Jerusalem

Jerusalem Post Reporter

The dismembered remains of Shoshana Har-Zion and Oded Wagmeister were handed over to the Israel authorities at Mandelbaum Gate at 11 p.m. last night. The remnants were immediately transferred to the Tel Hashomer Hospital. They had been missing since December, when they went on a Negev hike.

The remains were brought by the Jordanians to Mandelbaum Gate in two mail sacks about 9.30 p.m. One sack contained a torso so decomposed that it was difficult to say immediately what sex it was. The other contained a head which has not yet been definitely identified, and various separate decomposed limbs.

Dr. Klasner, of the Jerusalem District Health Office, carried out a preliminary examination in the presence of the Chairman of the Israel-Jordan Mixed Armistice Commission, Colonel Charles Brewster. Israel representatives present included the Jerusalem Area Commander, Aluf-Mishne Haim Herzog, and Seren Salant. Jordan was represented by Major M. Itzhak and a physician.

Police photographer Samal Tamari, who photographed the remains, said that he had never seen such a sight in all his experience. The skull, he said, showed several holes which lookel to him like bullet holes.

The policemen were white-faced and tense, as they carried the sacks on two stretchers from the MAC building to the waiting ambulance over the rough track illuminated by the headlights of a waiting jeep.

The constables reported that of all those present the Jordanians appeared quite unperturbed. "Tomorrow we'll bring you some more," Major Itzhak was said to have told one of the constables.

Earlier yesterday, U.N. officers waited in vain at Kilometre 69 on the Beersheba-Hebron road for Jordan representatives to conduct them to the place where the bodies of the two hikers were found three days ago.

The U.N. officers had set out for Hebron with an Israel Beduin early in the morning. From there they were to ride on horseback to Wadi Ghar to look for the remains.

Our Beersheba correspondent reports Israel Beduin as saying that they heard "from the other side" that the young couple were attacked by a band of Beduin robbers and that they fought back "like devils" until they were overpowered and killed. Negev residents have praised local Beduin for their loyalty and help in the search for the missing couple at the risk of their own lives.

Bayar's Karachi Talks 'To Save Arab Unity'

KARACHI, Thursday (Reuter).— Important decisions on a Middle East defence system are expected to be taken during the 10-day visit of Turkish President Celal Bayar to Pakistan which begins tomorrow. The presidential yacht Savrona, escorted by a mixed flotilla of Pakistan and Turkish warships is due to arrive here tomorrow morning.

Foreign Ministry sources here said the decisions would cover ways of bringing Arab countries and Persia into a collective security system and plans for expediting the Turco-Pakistan pact signed last April. These sources said Pakistan was anxious to avoid the break-up of Arab-Moslem unity following Egypt's opposition to the proposed Turco-Iraqi pact.

Pakistan might now try to overcome the Arabs' objections by an approach through Saudi Arabia with whom she has very cordial relations. Such a move might be made after consultations with President Bayar, they said.

Legion Guilty Of Beit Awwa Firing

The Israel-Jordan Mixed Armistice Commission yesterday found an Arab Legion force guilty of opening rifle and mortar fire on an Israel patrol near Beit Awwa village on February 12, killing one Israel soldier and wounding two, one of whom died of his wounds.

The U.N. chairman, Col. Charles Brewster, upheld this charge. He also voted with a Jordan complaint that an Israel force estimated at 50 strong directed rifle and automatic fire at Beit Awwa for five hours, culminating in a burst of mortar fire.

The Chairman appealed strongly to both parties to cooperate in demarcation of the line, which is insufficiently marked in the area. The Chairman abstained from voting on paragraphs of the resolution which condemned the parties for firing on U.N. officers.

"I cannot believe that this fire was deliberately aimed at the U.N.," he said.

The Chairman had abstained from voting on an Israel complaint that heavy fire from Beit Awwa had prevented the investigation team in a white U.N. jeepster coming from the Israel side to a pre-arranged meeting on the demarcation line. He also withheld his vote from a Jordan charge that U.N. Observers approaching from Jordan "were pinned down before they reached their destination."

Nevertheless, Colonel Brewster agreed that an Arab force which had taken up positions inside Israel foiled a second attempt of the U.N. team to approach the lines.

The Chairman abstained from

(Continued on Page 3, — Col. 4)

Scelba Talks Include Middle East Problems

LONDON, Thursday (Reuter). — The Italian Premier, Mr. Mario Scelba, and his Foreign Minister, Mr. Gaetano Martino, today concluded their talks with Government leaders here. The discussions included the Middle Eastern situation, diplomatic sources revealed.

The Foreign Secretary, Sir Anthony Eden, was believed yesterday to have outlined his hopes that the Egyptian-Iraqi breach regarding the pact with Turkey could be avoided. The Italian Minister later had an extra meeting with Sir Anthony on foreign policy.

UK to Make H-Bomb, Cut Defence Budget

LONDON, Thursday (Reuter). — **Britain** is to develop and produce a Hydrogen bomb, it was announced today. A Government White Paper on defence said that Britain had the ability to produce thermonuclear (Hydrogen) weapons.

"After fully considering all the implications of this step, the Government have thought it their duty to proceed with their development and production," the White Paper said.

The document, presented to the House of Commons by the Minister of Defence, Mr. Harold MacMillan, said that if the West did not use "the full weight of our nuclear power, Europe can hardly be protected from invasion and occupation — with all that this implies both for Europe and the U.K."

An estimated £1,537,200,000 would be spent on defence in the 1955-56 financial year, a drop of £102,000,000 on the estimate for the current year, it was announced. The overall strength of all three fighting services would be about 788,000 by April, 1956, a decrease of 35,300 on the current year's estimated figures.

Russia was clearly following the U.S. in proceeding with full-scale production of Hydrogen weapons — though it could not be said when they would have them available for operational use.

The report said that development of air-to-air guided weapons had reached an advanced stage. The main effort in the development of guided weapons was being devoted to defence against bombers flying at high speeds and at great heights.

In Pittsburgh today, General Nathan Twining, Air Force Chief of Staff, said that U.S. defence chiefs have given high priority to the development of a guided missile which can reach overseas targets. . .

He added that the Air Force would soon be equipped with new "one hit" missiles which could be launched from a fighter plane and guided to any enemy bomber.

General Twining also said that construction would begin this year of the "Texas Tower" radar net, running from Nova Scotia to New York.

Swiss Refuse Extradition Of Rumanian Gunmen

BERNE, Thursday (Reuter). — Switzerland today refused to extradite to Rumania the anti-Communist gunmen who seized the Rumanian Legation here and held it for 36 hours before surrendering yesterday.

The Federal Department of Justice and Police said in a communique that the acts for which the four gunmen had been arrested were committed on Swiss territory. Switzerland was bound by no extradition treaty with Rumania, which has demanded that the men be handed over.

All Swiss police and frontier guards have been alerted to watch for the remnants of the gang. Detectives believe that two men may have got away during the siege by troops and police. Four are in prison facing charges arising out of the death of a Legation chauffeur, of house breaking and destruction of property. Armed with automatics, three men held out to the last, yesterday afternoon. One surrendered a few hours after the siege began.

Food, Fodder Bought in Turkey

Jerusalem Post Reporter

The main purpose of the Israel trade delegation to Turkey, which returned on Tuesday, was to make immediate purchases there and to prepare the ground for further purchases in the future, it is learned from an informed source in Jerusalem. This purpose was achieved to a considerable degree, it is stated.

Israel trade with Turkey involves the problem of maintaining a balance between the amount of both countries import and export, and the difficulty at present lies in the limited amount of suitable Turkish offers of goods for sale to Israel.

The delegation made purchases of foodstuffs and fodder and made preliminary arrangements for additional imports in sizable amounts. It is expected that the letters of credit for these transactions will be issued in the near future, and when the purchases are completed, the continuation of Israel exports to Turkey will be made possible in accordance with Turkey's credit balance in the clearing account.

Of the $4.5m. "swing" provided for in the trade agreement between the two countries, Turkey has used only $3.6m. The credits which she will acquire from the orders just placed will make possible the continuation of Israel exports, but the extent cannot yet be stated precisely.

During its stay in Turkey the delegation also discussed the steps to be taken in order to coordinate the issue of import licences by the Turkish authorities with the issue of export licences here.

There are now $12m. worth of unutilized import licences in the hands of Turkish importers.

Mr. Sefkati Istinyeli, the Turkish Minister, will see the Prime Minister, Mr. Moshe Sharett, today at the latter's request.

FIRING AT QUEMOY

TAIPEH, Thursday (Reuter). — Chinese batteries fired more than 90 rounds at the Nationalist island of Quemoy early today.

Nationalist guns returned the fire and "succeeded in silencing the enemy," it was announced.

U.S. 'Reappraising' Middle East Policy

The U.S. is to review and make a fresh appraisal of the effect of the Turco-Iraqi pact and Egypt's new friendship with the neutralist Indian Premier, according to the Cairo newspaper "Al Ahram" **Washington correspondent.**

He cabled that Washington is convinced that the Nasser regime is pro-West and anti-Communist, and feels that the present crisis can be worked out.

Sir Anthony Eden will stop in Cairo on Sunday on his way to the NATO conference in Bangkok; he will also report to Secretary of State John Foster Dulles when both meet there, regarding his talks with the Egyptian Premier. Mr. Dulles is leaving Washington today for the Bangkok conference.

A State Department source said that only after the Eden-Dulles talks on this subject, will the new appraisal be made, the Cairo newspaper declared.

Mr. Nehru declared on his arrival that his country will take the initiative in making informal approaches for an international conference on Formosa "if the necessity arises," U.P. reported. He told reporters that he envisaged a conference of the "Geneva type." He reiterated that the "only alternative to war" in the Formosa Straits is "some kind of peaceful approach by negotiation."

(Reuter, UP)

Syrians Fire on Gonen

A Syrian force penetrated into Israel territory at noon yesterday and opened machinegun fire on Gonen, the kibbutz five kilometres north of Lake Hula, the Army spokesman announced.

When members of the settlement returned fire, the Syrians retreated to positions across the lines and continued firing with medium machineguns. The firing ceased only after the Isarelis trained heavy fire at the Syrian positions.

This is the second attack this week on Gonen which lies close to the frontier. On Tuesday both the kibbutz itself and some of its animals grazing in the fields were fired on.

One Jordanian was killed and another injured at Jaba, in the Hebron area, on Wednesday morning in a clash with Israelis NEABS reported last night.

Jordan Said Agreeing To Johnston Plan

The last in the series of talks with Arab countries by Mr. Eric Johnston, President Eisenhower's special envoy to the Middle East, will open today in Beirut. The U.S. envoy arrived in the Lebanese capital last night from Aleppo where he had gone following the conclusion of his talks in Damascus, according to NEABS last night. He is due in Israel again on Sunday.

A Jordan report yesterday said that the Cabinet has decided to accept the Johnston scheme for the Jordan River project. It was said that two Jordan ministers will participate in the Beirut meeting today.

The Jordan press reacted sourly to reports that Jordan would consider acceptance of the Johnston plan. Such an acceptance, it was pointed out, is one reason for Arab disunity, another being the projected Turco-Iraqi pact. While the pact makes Russia and not Israel the Arabs' first enemy, the Johnston plan will signal the start of Arab cooperation with Israel, it was stated.

Arab sources said that Jordan would probably be willing to make concessions regarding her share of water if Mr. Johnston would guarantee a dam higher up the Yarmuk River than the one proposed.

The Damascus correspondent of "The New York Times" cabled his paper yesterday that agreement has been reached between Israel, on the one hand, and Jordan, Syria and the Lebanon, on the other, to use Lake Kinneret as the main reservoir in the proposed Jordan Valley development project.

Mr. Johnston said in the Syrian capital on Tuesday that he personally felt it was "inopportune" to comment under the present circumstances. But sources close to the mission's activities, including Arab spokesman, reported that differences between the Arab and Israel positions had "narrowed very much." It was said that Mr. Johnston's planned fourth trip to the Middle East within a few months is expected to bring final agreement from the two sides.

Both Israelis and Arabs were said to have accepted without reservation the necessity for both a comprehensive plan for the Jordan Valley project and international supervision for water distribution.

REPORT DOUBTED

It is very doubtful, writes *The Jerusalem Post* Diplomatic Correspondent, whether the Damascus report on agreement to use the waters of Lake Kinneret as a storage reservoir for the regional water scheme has any foundation. There is no confirmation here of any such agreement which is very unlikely as Israel would require substantial guarantees from the Arab states that no reflection on her complete sovereignty over the Lake would be involved in its use in the project.

On the other hand, the Arabs are afraid that if the Lake is used as a reservoir Israel would be able to cut off the flow when she wished.

In general it can be taken that press reports from the Arab capitals on the progress of the negotiations are most unreliable. It is learned here that so far the talks have continued to be exploratory and no decisions have been made. There may be some progress when Mr. Johnston returns to Israel on Sunday for further discussions but so far the gap between the parties cannot be said to have narrowed.

In the same way there is no foundation for the rumours that Israel has accepted the Arab proposals on the ratio of distribution of the water.

Kinneret to Remain Sweet Water Lake

Jerusalem Post Reporter

TEL AVIV, Thursday. — The Kinneret will remain a sweet-water lake even after the main stream of the Jordan is diverted to irrigate the Negev, Mr. S. Blass, of Tahal (Israel Water Planning), told reporters here today in reply to reports that the lakes water may become saline, if the plan is carried out. The salinity of Lake Kinneret will be maintained at its present level of 250 milligrammes of chlorine per litre, or less.

The source of the 132,000 tons of salt which enter the Kinneret annually are the numerous mineral springs around the lake, Mr. Blass said. Most of them, particularly those situated at Tabgha and Tiberias — will be guided into a specially built canal around the lake, and the salt water will enter the Jordan somewhere south of Dagania. The Jordan waters, part of which will be tapped near Gesher Bnot Ya'acov have a minimum salinity—about 20 mgs. The water which will reach the Negev will have a salinity of about 40 mgs. per litre. The maximum salinity of good irrigation water is considered to be slightly over 400 mgs. per litre, Mr. Blass stated.

The Jordan, whose waters are salted in any case by the many springs which join it on its course, will thus be still more saline. The Arabs' plan, moreover, is to utilize the water of the Yarmuk, which will be brought to the irrigated areas through pipes, as in the Tahal plan for Israel.

"We do not work in hiding", Mr. Blass commented. "The schemes for tapping the Jordan waters have been outlined in books, and the actual plans are supervised by the best minds in the water engineering world, both here and abroad," he added.

Egypt Says 'No' To Burns on Bat Galim

Egypt has informed General E.L. Burns, Chief of Staff of the Truce Supervision Organization, that it cannot accede to Israel's demand, transmitted through him, that the Bat Galim be allowed to proceed together with her cargo through the Suez Canal to Haifa.

The reply was handed over to Israel by General Burns yesterday.

It will be recalled that on January 18 General Burns called on Mr. Walter Eytan, Director-General of the Foreign Ministry, at the latter's invitation and agreed to use his good offices to put Israel's demands to the Egyptian authorities.

(It is understood that the Egyptian reply to General Burns suggests that they are ready to send the Bat Galim cargo on to Israel through the Suez Canal and the appointment of an agency for the purpose should be discussed in the Mixed Armistice Commission. The Egyptians were prepared to release the ship to a non-Israeli crew who would take it to Israel by the southern (non-Suez) route.)

INA reported from the United Nations last night that the President of the Security Council, Mr. Victor Belaunde (Peru), was conferring with the Egyptian delegation, at Israel's request, on the release of the Bat Galim.

Jordan Accepts Burns Proposals on POW's

Jordan has agreed to the principle of treating prisoners of war in accordance with the Geneva Convention and of exchanging them within a fortnight, as suggested by General Burns, the Jordan Defence Minister, Anwar Nuseibeh, said in Amman on Wednesday night, the Old City "El Jihad" reported.

Nuseibeh added that the Convention still had to be adapted to local conditions. General Burns' proposals on the Jerusalem commanders, agreement were logical, but he opposed the suggestion that the agreement for the entire frontier should be on a higher level than that of area commanders.

Hussein Prepares For Mediation in Cairo

King Hussein was back in Amman yesterday after being briefed in Baghdad for two days by Iraq's King Faisal and Government leaders on the Turco-Iraqi act in preparation for his scheduled three-day visit to Cairo tomorrow.

They explained to the Jordan boy-king why Iraq is determined to conclude the treaty and why she was anxious that all Arab League states should participate. Hussein is expected to present to Premier Abdul Nasser Iraqi views in an attempt to bridge Cairo-Baghdad differences.

Meanwhile, in Beirut, Foreign Minister Alfred Naccache declared yesterday that unless Egypt ceased her persistent anti-Iraqi radio and press campaign, all Lebanese efforts to mediate between the two countries would be fruitless.

Newly-Weds Slain as They Sleep

Jerusalem Post Reporter

ACRE, Thursday. — A young Arab couple was murdered last night in their home at Kfar Yasif, in Western Galillee. The unknown murderer strangled his victims while they were in bed, hit them on the head with an axe and then set their bed afire.

Ahmed Salah Safiya, 26, and his 19-year-old wife, Kaukab, were cousins and had been married for a fortnight. Yesterday, they attended a wedding in the village.

Sometime after they returned home neighbours noticed smoke rising from the house. They forced the door open and found the bed and some other furniture on fire.

The husband was already dead. His wife had a deep head wound and died on the way to the Rambam Hospital in Haifa. The neighbours put out the fire and called the police.

This morning a police dog was put on the trial, but lost it on rocky ground. The tracker later found a blood-stained axe not far from the house and unearthed some gold jewellery which belonged to the wife. Neighbours and relatives could give no clues, but police are convinced that it was a crime of passion.

Column One

BY

David Courtney

THE question is whether the Great Powers are as reat as they think. There may ven come a time when the uestion will be: who, indeed, re the Great Powers? Dr. denauer, rummaging in the Iohenzollern cupboard, has ragged out the grisly skeleton f the Yellow Peril and shakn its bones in the face of Iarshal Bulganin. But the arning may not be simply a haracteristic example of Gerianic bogey-building. China ost certainly has the makgs of a great Power, which, aning its weight against the siatic frontiers of the Soviet, ould set up a friction damagg to Moscow's nerves. The me for that is not yet. Mao d Chou want their share of r. Kruschev's heavy industry rst. For that matter and for verybody's comfort, the time challenge in a territorial nse may never come. In the eat Power sense of "spheres influence" and the like, it is most certain to come.

GENERALLY throughout the political world there have ismic warnings, most of them ntered in far and near Asia, cluding what is commonly eant by the Middle East and rtain parts of Europe that one time looked eastward, ithin the Ottoman Empire, d which, through the Balan alliance, still have one ot on the Asiatic side of the sphoros. What, for example, one to make of the Nehruasser-Tito axis? It is, at the oment, a tenuous, informal fair; but it might be unwise sneer at it. At first glance, ehru's attitude to world probms may seem wishy-washy utralism; Nasser's may seem e negativism of a man afraid commit himself; and Tito's e flamboyant ambiguities of shrewd political tradesman. it these judgments are too nple. Nehru has an enormous pulation and wide political fluence behind him; Nasser, r all his and Egypt's weakss, is a new force in Arab fairs and has, throughout abia, the prestige of a sucssful revolution. He has neier the cunning nor the conence of a Nuri es-Said. But the long run — perhaps not very long run at that — the assers of the Arab world will ke over from the Nuris.

IT has been said that hatred of Israel can be depended on unify the Arabs. It has been pretty doubtful unity so far. th little of substance to comend it to the Arabs themves. What Nehru represents ay be, for middle and near ia, a larger, unifying quany, capable of bringing into ing an uncommitted force th an enormous bargaining wer in relation to each of e two defined world blocs. It s not reached that stage yet. present the amiable cups of ffee taken together by Neh- Nasser and Tito leave only e impression of easy genalities shared in common, th all three men opposed in inciple to letting themselves tied to the apron strings of e fairy godmother whose unty they desire. But the d fact is that they have a ry good chance of receiving e bounty without getting tied in the apron strings. In ort, the non-committal polis of India, Egypt and Yuslavia can probably made to y; and the more unified the ree countries become in their proach to world affairs—that to say, the nearer they, with ch other countries of the ian and Arab world as may n in, reach a condition of Power influence — the gher the pay they will be le to extort.

THE matter is being fought out in the diplomatic arena d, until now, the victory ould seem to have gone to e Asian and Arab countries ich are content to hook emselves on to an existing oc. India failed to keep Pakan uncommitted. Now it oks as if Egypt has failed to ep Iraq uncommitted. But at position can easily change. may in any event, and conary to earlier predictions, ive Egypt farther away from rmal association with the est and encourage her ingue against the Arab Govnments favouring such asciation. Much will depend on ether the Nehru-Nasser-Tito is can be turned into someng substantial instead of ing mere solace for disapinted ambition.

rusalem, February 18.

THE JERUSALEM POST

TUESDAY, DECEMBER 13, 1955

PRICE: 100 PRUTA
VOL. XXXI, No. 8374

THE LAND OF THE BOOK
Hand-coloured greeting cards.
Antique maps and views.
The most appreciated gifts
The Universitas-Booksellers
9 Princess Mary Ave., Jerusalem, Tel. 4050.

Marginal Column

By Our Diplomatic Correspondent

CIVILIAN eyes in Israel have been so firmly focussed on the south and on the constant danger of war with Egypt that news of a major action in the north came as a double shock. A first reaction that it was just as well that the Israel Army at least has eyes in the back of its head was mixed with a certain feeling that surely there has always been shooting on Lake Tiberias? Had the shooting been worse than usual lately, but overlooked in the pressure of events on the Egyptian border?

THERE have indeed been periods when shooting at Israel fishing boats from the Syrian shore was, if not worse, then more accurate and claimed more victims; for though some bullet may reach its mark and another may fail to do so, the intention with which it is fired is always the same. The difference is not so much in the other side, as in Israel's present determination that the Armistice Agreements shall no longer be totally one-sided. You would not attempt to play even a game with the rules different for the two sides, and border warfare is not a game. The reason for sharp retaliation this year where there was none last year is that neither the U.N. nor any other outside factor has been able to stop Syria shooting on the lake.

BOATS do not go out on treacherous Lake Kinneret in winter for pleasure. They go out in groups of four and five to place and haul in huge nets into which the fish are attracted by powerful lights. The lights make the fisherman a pitifully easy target, and when shooting starts he has no choice but to cut the nets adrift and make for home. During last season there was a loss of about IL100,000 in this way, a burden the industry cannot bear. If there was to be a choice between removing the Syrian gun posts from the shore, and giving up fishing the lake, it may perhaps be understood that an independent country will choose to defend its own citizens' rights before it weighs the possible heavy loss to the enemy.

ISRAEL announced her decision to enforce the Armistice Agreements, but not to abrogate them, and accordingly withdrew from Syrian territory as soon as the concrete fortresses had been blown up. After a speechless day, Syrian spokesmen took a leaf from Egypt's book and declared that they had forced the Israel Army to retire, and had caused a hundred casualties. "Ambulances were seen travelling to and fro all day," as a Damascus spokesman claimed. But even this tale will be cold comfort to the Syrian commander who knows that his force was outwitted and outfought and his officers caught playing cards. It is likely that this phantom victory will remain the extent of the Egyptian military aid to Egypt's new ally, Syria. Short of the unlikely event of a full-scale Syrian retaliatory war on Israel, Damascus will scarcely be able to invoke Egyptian military help. It is possible, in consequence, that this sharp warning blow may also have knocked some of the gilt off this piece of gingerbread and make the defensive pact with Egypt look to some Syrians like an added danger rather than a protective device. Even wavering Jordan may decide to seek shelter on the far side of the fence from Egypt after all.

IN a few months' time work must be resumed on the Jordan Canal where it was stopped two years ago at the request of the U.N., and in the hope that Syria would in time let reason prevail and take part in some agreed distribution of the Jordan waters. When the Johnston Plan was close to acceptance not long ago, it was finally rejected through Syrian agitation in Egypt and pressure in Jordan. For Israel, both water from the Jordan and fish from the Kinneret are not only a necessity but almost a matter of life and death. The right to peace in Israel territory is not a political gambit like Syrian pretentions in the demilitarized zone. If our neighbours were half as concerned with bringing water to dry fields and catching fish to feed people as Israel is, we could have this peace tomorrow.

Jerusalem, December 13.

IRAQ BUDGET UP

BAGHDAD, Monday (Reuter). — The Iraqi Finance Minister, Dia Jafar, today submitted a record budget for 1956 estimating government expenditure at 65,185,-923 dinars — an increase of 12m. dinars over the current budget.

Both Sides Nibbling At Eden Plan—Macmillan

LONDON, Monday (Reuter). — Foreign Secretary Harold Macmillan declared at the opening of the Commons debate on the Middle East today that both Israel and Arab leaders were nibbling at the recent proposal for mutual concessions made recently by Sir Anthony Eden. Speaking to a packed chamber, with world ambassadors listening intently, the Secretary defended the Prime Minister's speech against the Labour opposition's criticism that it demands one-sided concessions by Israel.

Mr. Macmillan said that "serious Arab leaders" have begun to realize that they must live with Israel, and that Israel is making more careful consideration of what Sir Anthony said about making some sacrifice.

He pointed out that the Russians will try to block any settlement and keep alive the hatreds in the region, and expressed doubt that a new security guarantee to Israel, coming after a long list of declarations and guarantees already given, would settle the problem.

It would be foolish of the West, he asserted, to start an arms race by sending arms to Israel to balance the Soviet bloc shipments to Egypt. Mr. Macmillan said he was not convinced that the U.N. was the right machinery now to turn the Palestine truce into a peace.

Sir Winston Churchill attended the debate in one of his now infrequent visits to the House—the third since he resigned.

Policy 'Utter Failure'

Mr. Herbert Morrison, former Labour Foreign Secretary and candidate for the party's leadership, said that Mr. Macmillan's statement was a confession of the Government's "utter failure" regarding its Middle East policy.

He accused the Government of "isolating" Israel and leaving her in great difficulties. British Labour objected to the exclusion of Israel, although Britain's agreements with the Arab states were all right in themselves, he said, adding that if the borders of Iraq and other Arab countries were to be guaranteed by Britain, then Israel's borders should be similarly guaranteed — otherwise "there is a danger of war which may lead anywhere."

Mr. Morrison said it was natural for Prime Minister David Ben-Gurion to think Sir Anthony called for substantial concessions by Israel, as the Guildhall speech had been vague. But he pointed out that Israel is still willing to consider minor border adjustments, which he termed "sensible" on her part. At one point he referred to a speech by Sir Winston Churchill on May 11, 1953, that Israel would never be placed at an unfair disadvantage regarding the supply of arms to the Middle East. He invited — amid laughter—the elder statesman to "have a go" in spite of the fact that the Government did not want him to speak. Sir Winston smiled, but did not comment.

Urges Peace Talks

Mr. Morrison said that the West should work to bring Israel and the Arabs together for peace talks.

Mr. Hugh Dalton, former Labour Chancellor of the Exchequer, said that Egypt now should get "nothing more from us," but that arms should be diverted to countries like Israel, and not to those "who spit and spurn us, or humiliate us on every possible occasion." He likened the situation with that of Munich before the last war, and urged the Prime Minister, when he goes to Washington, not to take with him some project for a second Munich at the expense of Israel.

Goldmann Reports To Agency Executive

Dr. Nahum Goldmann, Chairman of the Jewish Agency Executive, surveyed the activities of the Zionist Organization in the U.S. and its special problems at a meeting of the full Executive in Jerusalem yesterday.

The session was opened by the Chairman of the Executive, Mr. Berl Locker, M.K., who eulogized Dr. Mayer Ebner, member of the First Zionist Congress who died yesterday in Tel Aviv.

Mr. Yosef Sprinzak, Chairman of the Zionist General Council, participated in the meeting.

Dr. Goldmann reported to the Executive on the meeting of 400 Jewish and non-Jewish dignitaries which has been called in Washington next month by the "Presidents' Club" (heads of community organizations) to discuss the urgent problems facing Israel.

The advancing of the date of the Zionist Congress to February was also discussed, but a decision was postponed until the full Executive's meeting on Thursday.

ARISTON

is the new Filter-Cigarett put on the market by the DUBEK Factory today.

3 factors make the ARISTON-FILTER superior:

1. More puffs per Cigarette and longer, better filtering due to ARISTON'S extra long size —
2. Highly effective Filter Protection through ARISTON'S special (shred) filter —
3. Full and rich aroma thanks to ARISTON'S superb tobaccos — specially blended for filter-smoking.

Filter-smokers, try ARISTON! Here at last is the fully satisfying Filter-Cigarette you have been looking for. (480 Pruta for 20 Cigarettes). *(Advt.)*

B.-G. Said Ready To Meet Nasser at Xmas

NEW YORK, Monday (Reuter). — An American newspaper correspondent who has been reporting on the Middle East situation for several weeks said today that the Israel Premier, Mr. Ben-Gurion, had offered to meet Egypt's Prime Minister, Abdul Nasser, on Christmas Day to discuss peace between the two countries.

Mr. William Longgood of the New York "World-Telegram and Sun" reported the offer in a dispatch from Jerusalem. He said the Israel Premier had suggested that he and Abdul Nasser should meet at Kilometre 95, where the U.N. Mixed Armistice Commission meets between the Egyptian and Israel lines, or in Geneva. "Mr Ben-Gurion said that the time, place and date were suggestions, and he would abide by Abdul Nasser's preference," the correspondent said, adding that he learned of the offer during an exclusive interview with Mr. Ben-Gurion, who also made these points.

"Unless a peace settlement comes, he believes that Egypt may attack Israel within five or six months.

"Israel will not make war unless attacked.

"Israel will continue to meet force with force.

"Abdul Nasser is the only Arab leader with enough strength to make peace with Israel.

"External pressure has nothing to do with Israel's decision not to start a so-called preventive war.

"Israel does not seek another inch of territory, nor will she give up an inch of her own territory."

Egypt Will Not Budge On Nitzana Issue

CAIRO, Monday (Reuter). — Egypt has told Major-General E.L.M. Burns, Chief of Staff of the U.N. Truce Supervision Organization, that "Egypt demands the withdrawal of all forces from the El Auja (Nitzana) demilitarized Zone as it was before last September," an Egyptian spokesman said here today.

Gen. Burns visited Cairo last week to continue discussions with Egyptian leaders on the proposals of U.N. Secretary-General Dag Hammarskjold to end border tension between Egypt and Israel.

Israel has accepted the proposals in principle.

U.N: Urges Study Of Ike, Bulganin Plans

UNITED NATIONS, Monday (UP). — The U.N. Political Committee today approved a Western resolution giving top priority to President Eisenhower's "open skies" inspection plan in disarmament talks.

The resolution calls upon the five major atomic powers, meeting as a subcommittee of the U.N. Disarmament Commission, also to consider the plan submitted by the Soviet Premier, Marshal Nikolai Bulganin.

The Bulganin plan, submitted by the Soviet Union last May, proposed reduction of conventional arms, prohibition of atomic weapons and establishment of ground control check points.

The subcommittee is expected to resume its secret meetings in London in February.

The Political Committee killed an Indian amendment, which would have enlarged the 12-nation Disarmament Commission, which now comprises the members of the Security Council and Canada.

Immediate Cuts Rejected

It also voted down another Indian amendment calling for an immediate Big Power agreement on arms reduction.

The U.S., before the vote, called on the world's military powers to "take every action now feasible" as a first step toward disarmament.

Mr. Henry Cabot Lodge (U.S.), who introduced the resolution, said it proposed "such initial reductions as can be adequately controlled at the earliest opportunity."

Mr. Lodge said the resolution also requested the Governments concerned to "start now" to carry out the Eisenhower and Bulganin plans. The earlier version had urged that "priority" should be given to the implementation of these plans."

Brentano to Visit U.S. in February

BONN, Monday (Reuter). — Foreign Minister Heinrich von Brentano will visit the U.S. in February as guest of the American Government, Foreign Ministry officials announced today. His visit will follow soon after that of the British Prime Minister, Sir Anthony Eden, and Foreign Secretary Harold Macmillan.

Chancellor Adenauer is planning to visit the U.S. in the early summer but not before, they said when commenting on a report in the newspaper "Die Welt" of Hamburg that the Chancellor would himself go to the U.S. in February.

Templer Awaiting Jordan Reply On Baghdad Alliance

Gen. Sir Gerald Templer, Chief of the British Imperial General Staff, yesterday again postponed his departure from Amman, to await a final Jordan reply on his proposals concerning defence, the Arab News Agency reported. He was to leave today.

Reuter yesterday quoted reliable Amman sources as stating that Gen. Templer had offered most favourable terms in exchange for Jordan's participation in the Baghdad pact (METO).

The Jordan Cabinet, meanwhile, had an intensive round of discussions yesterday. After the first session, lasting four hours in the morning, the Ministers left for King Hussein's Palace, where they conferred for three hours in the afternoon.

Gen. John Glubb on Sunday night twice met with Premier Said el Mufti in connection with the Templer proposals.

The Old City daily, "El Jihad," reported that one question that was subjected to hard scrutiny during the talks of the past two days was doubling the strength of the Arab Legion, and modernizing its armaments and equipment.

Arabs Warn Dulles Of Strained Relations

WASHINGTON, Monday (Reuter).—Eight Arab diplomatic representatives today jointly warned Secretary of State John Foster Dulles that the activities of Israel in the Middle East and of Zionist groups in the U.S. were causing strained American-Arab relations. The envoys, who conferred for an hour with the Secretary, were the Ambassadors of Egypt, Iraq, Jordan, the Lebanon, Libya, Saudi Arabia, and Syria, and the Charge d'Affaires of the Yemen.

The Iraqi Ambassador, Musa Shabander, acting as spokesman, told reporters that the Arab nations did not want to interfere in the U.S. political situation, but they had told Mr. Dulles how they felt about such activity and how, if it continued, it would affect future relations between the Arab states and the U.S.

He said Mr. Dulles had told them that the U.S. had a policy of "friendly impartiality" in the Middle East *vis-a-vis* the Arabs and other states.

Asked if this position satisfied the Arabs, Shabandar replied, "We shall be very satisfied if this impartiality is based on the number and the size of the people involved." He said that Israel's request for arms was not discussed at the meeting.

The Syrian Ambassador, Farid Zein e-Din, stated that the U.S. was indirectly subsidizing Israel, because it did not take taxes on financial contributions made by Zionist organizations. "This money is said to be for philanthropic purposes, but it really is going to build up the State for political reasons."

Goedhart: Refugees Must Settle Where They Are

OSLO, Monday (Reuter). — Dr. G. J. van Heuven Goedhart, U.N. High Commissioner for Refugees, said in his Nobel Peace Prize lecture here tonight that most refugees would have to look for integration into their countries of present residence.

Dr. Goedhart, who on Saturday received the 1954 Nobel Peace Prize on behalf of the U.N High Commission for Refugees, said that there were only three ways of solving refugee problems: by voluntary repatriation, resettlement overseas, and integration either in the country of present residence or in combination with intra-European migration.

There were practically no refugees today who wished to return to their countries of origin, he said, and the possibilities of resettlement overseas by the International Refugee Organization (I.R.O.) were largely exhausted.

SUDAN IRKED BY ANGLO-EGYPTIAN SNUB

KHARTOUM, Monday (Reuter). — The Government has protested to Britain and Egypt that it was not consulted when these two countries agreed on the procedure for Sudan's self-determination.

On December 3, Britain and Egypt, as condominium powers, signed an agreement in Cairo providing for the Sudanese to vote in a plebiscite to decide whether the territory should become an independent state or have a form of union with Egypt.

In Cairo today, the British Ambassador, Sir Humphrey Trevelyan, conferred with Premier Abdul Nasser on "current affairs, including the Sudan." In London, the Foreign Office announced today that Sir Alexander Knox Helm has announced his wish to resign the governorship of the the Sudan "for personal reasons." It said that the British Government does not intend to nominate another candidate for the post when it becomes vacant, probably in the spring.

NOTORIOUS INFILTRATOR JAILED IN JORDAN

Abd Ibn Mohammed Abu Arar, a notorious Jordan infiltrator and smuggler, was detained in Jordan this week when returning from Israel, according to the Old City daily, "El Jihad." He was sentenced to three years in jail by the Hebron District Commissioner.

Wanted to rent
Factory Premises
for immediate occupancy
1,500 (or more) sq.m., in Tel Aviv or suburbs
Mark envelopes "Factory Premises," and send to: P.O.B. 3094, Tel Aviv.

50 Syrians Killed, 30 Captured As Army Action Clears Kinneret Shore

Peace in Galilee is Up to Syria

"This morning (Monday) Israel fishermen cast their nets as usual in Lake Kinneret ... Quiet reigns throughout Galilee at present, and it will not be disturbed by Israel," the Foreign Ministry spokesman said in Jerusalem yesterday. "If Syria refrains from aggression, there is no reason why quiet should not prevail permanently to the benefit of peaceful citizens on both sides of the border as they go about their occupations."

The spokesman ridiculed the Syrian claim of 100 Israel casualties in Sunday night's action. "The spurious Syrian claim appears to be modelled on Egyptian lines," he remarked. (Following the Nitzana action three weeks ago Egypt claimed 200 Israel dead.)

The spokesman went on to say it was inconceivable that the Israel people were presented with anything but the whole truth about Army casualties.

"The figures on dead and wounded made public by the Israel authorities, are accurate and full. Israel has never had the ambition to compete with Syria in the field of lies."

The spokesman recalled that Israel had offered to make room on Lake Kinneret for Syrian fishermen if they cared to apply for fishing permits, but this offer was never accepted. Instead, for years Syria has interfered with the peaceful fishermen plying their trade on the lake.

Entire Shore Israel Territory

"No part of the lake shore belongs to Syria," he stressed, "nor any part of the lake itself. Yet Syria has erected and maintained strong military positions in her territory on the hills overlooking Lake Kinneret. Syrian troops occupying these positions have regularly shelled the unarmed Israel fishing fleet as soon as it has put out its nets."

The spokesman reiterated Israel's desire to make the lake safe for the fishermen who "are entitled to the protection of their Government under all circumstances, and particularly when they come under enemy attack. Israel cannot allow the Syrian Army to continue its aggression against her fishermen from the cover of its fortified positions on the ridges and slopes dominating Lake Kinneret."

A communique from the U.N. Truce Supervision Organization said yesterday that a provisional list of Syrian casualties "mentions 41 killed."

The Chief of Staff of the T.S.O said that he "regrets this retaliatory action which brought about such a heavy loss of life. He expresses his sympathy to the wounded and to the relatives of the dead."

Attack Synchronized

From preliminary reports, the U.N. said, "the Israel attack apparently took place at all points at the same time. Explosives were used for the destruction of positions."

The reports of the U.N. Observers noted that Ein Gev was shelled by artillery during the night, and the settlers "returned the fire with 81 mm. mortars."

The attack stretched between Buteiha Farm and El Kursi, the communique stated. It said that a force of company strength attacked the former area: one group in two boats landed south-east of the Farm, while another forded the Jordan River and attacked at the mouth of the Jordan.

The residence of the Farm, the employees' mess hall and one civilian truck were blown up, the communique added.

The Observers said that the Syrian casualties at the Farm were reported to be nine soldiers and one civilian dead, one soldier wounded, one officer and three soldiers missing.

In the El Kursi area, the Observers saw two Syrian officers and 15 soldiers dead.

"Evidence has been found that a small Israel force had penetrated as far as Skoufiye and ambushed a Syrian detachment. Eight Syrians were reported killed and five wounded."

Syrians Rebuilding Wrecked Positions

EIN GEV, Monday. — Ein Gev settlers this morning observed Syrian forces returning to the positions which were blown up by an Israel force last night. They began rebuilding their destroyed posts and dug communication trenches. They also moved up cannon and mortars and tested the range with machinegun fire.

The settlement was calm today after a wakeful night. The children and infants were taken to shelters yesterday. The older children were in high spirits this morning when the full news of the successful operation became known. Because of the sleepless night, only the most essential work, including the cowshed chores, was done this morning. Reinforcements arrived from Jordan Valley settlements to help the tired men. The settlers wistfully recalled today that they were to have held their traditional Hanukka celebration last night.

The four or five Syrian shells which hit the settlement during the night caused negligible damage. One shell hit a corner of the cowshed, another a paved walk and the rest made small craters in the earth, 50 cms. in diameter. Some settlers watched part of the battle.

Ein Gev was informed of the impending action yesterday afternoon and immediately undertook emergency arrangements, including removal of the children to shelters and organization of medical teams.

Majority of Prisoners Regular Soldiers

TIBERIAS, Monday. — During the night, 23 Syrian prisoners were taken to a settlement. The majority were regular soldiers. They were given fish to eat and later moved on. Some of the wounded were given first aid before being taken to hospital. The booty included a six-pounder, French machineguns and rifles. By 5 a.m., all our forces had been withdrawn in a smooth operation.

Soldier Escorts Syrian Woman, Child Home

Orders were to spare women and children during the operation, but this sometimes made for difficulties. There was the case of a woman and child who were frightened into the field by the appearance of a soldier. It took some diplomatic persuasion to assure the woman that she would be much better off if she returned to her village — to which she was carefully escorted by the armed Israeli.

Kinneret Clash Worries French Officials

PARIS, Monday (Reuter).—Official circles here are expressing anxiety about the situation in the Middle East following the Israel-Syrian border clash yesterday.

They refused to take sides about the final responsibility of either party for the incidents near Lake Kinneret, but deplored Israel's action against Syria, which was closely linked to France by bonds of friendship.

CAIRO'S GIFT TO SYRIAN ARMS FUND

Egypt has contributed LS500,-000 to the Syrian arms fund which now stands at LS4m., "El Jihad" reported yesterday.

Maltese May Sit In House of Commons

LONDON, Monday (Reuter). — A report by leading politicians of all parties will recommend this week that Malta should become the first colony to have seats in the Commons, usually well-informed political sources said today.

Israel Loses 6 Dead, 10 Wounded

SOMEWHERE IN THE NORTH, Monday. — Within two hours last night, some 300 Israel soldiers cleared the north-eastern bank of Lake Kinneret of Syrian troops and fortifications. Enemy casualties were at least 50 dead and about 30 taken prisoner. Our troops suffered six dead and 10 wounded, two of them seriously. One of the dead was an officer.

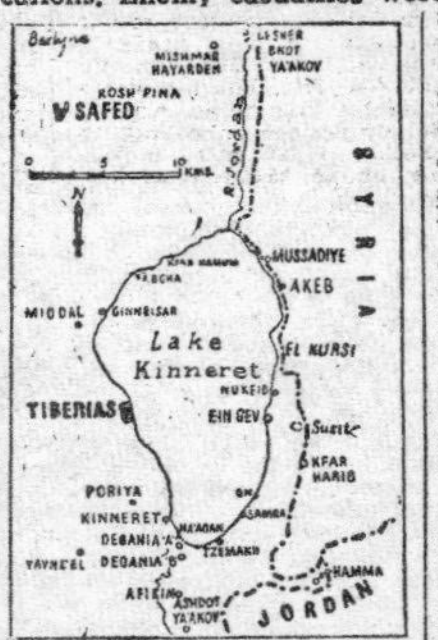

Four of the dead fell in battle. Two others died of their wounds after they were brought back to Israel territory.

Aluf Moshe Zadok, O.C. Northern Command, told newsmen at noon today that the operation was considered one of major importance, proving the Israel soldier's ability and courage under most difficult conditions. It was, if anything, a tougher proposition than the El Sabha operation in the Nitzana area last month.

The immediate cause of the action last night was the attack on an Israel patrol boat on the lake by a Syrian anti-tank gun on Saturday morning, in which the vessel was damaged. Syrian interference with fishing on the lake, which is wholly in Israel territory, is not new, especially at this time of the year which marks the beginning of the fishing season. However, Aluf Zadok said, in the past Syrian troops usually employed rifles or light machineguns. Yesterday, they used artillery — and the Army promptly countered, as it did last year when Syrians similarly violated Israel suzerainty over the lake. On the previous occasion Syrian forts in Kursi, on the eastern shore of the Lake, were silenced by Israel artillery. This time, the operation was mainly an infantry show.

Attack in Two Columns

The attacking force was split roughly in two, one operating from the north, the other from the south. The former had the more difficult task. Starting at nightfall, they descended in total darkness to the Jordan River, some distance north of where the river flows into the lake.

"Someone, probably a Beduin, heard us, and cried out 'Min hada?' (Who's that?),"—a junior officer who took part in the operation told reporters. "We had strict orders not to tangle with civilians unless they attacked us, so we took no notice of the Beduin, and he probably fled."

Swelled by recent rains, the Jordan was running high — "Whirlpools were what we feared most." Several soldiers forded the swift, ice-cold current, to stretch ropes across. The rest of the unit crossed the river holding fast to the ropes. The shorter men struggling submerged to their necks. Guns and ammunition were also transported by ropes.

The southern column had a dry passage, but a long one. Some units had to walk up to 8 kms. to reach their objective. The watchmen of Nukeib, the Syrian-held village on the northern tip of the Demilitarized Zone, fired a few shots at the passing troops, then became silent. Adhering to the instructions not to touch civilians, the troops by-passed the villagers, who followed the action from the front row.

The attack started almost simultaneously along the whole front, which stretched for about 11 kms. The Syrians were caught by surprise almost everywhere, Aluf Zadok said. While stiff opposition was encountered in a few places, at some points the Syrians preferred to surrender and, in many instances, to flee.

Intelligence reports estimate that some 200 Syrian regulars defended the prepared positions at several points along the shore. Fortified positions, with concrete pillboxes, barbed-wire entanglements and communication trenches were found near the Jordan mouth, at the Bek house — an isolated building which once belonged to the owner of the surrounding lands — at

(Continued on Page 3, Col. 3)

Kinneret Action Is Lauded in Knesset

Sunday night's action against Syrian forces was mentioned in the Knesset yesterday during the concluding speeches in the budget debate.

The first speaker of the day, Mr. Binyamin Mintz (Poalei Agudat Yisrael) lauded the action of our troops and said that if Syria wished to be Israel's enemy, as of old, Israel would be able to deal with her. Israel did not want war, but any infringement of her boundaries would be stopped.

Mr. Menahem Begin (Herut), said that if there was any consolation for the relatives of the men who died in the action it was that they had not fallen as victims of a slaughter but had given their lives in an heroic battle.

Arms Too Late

He declared that even if the U.S. agreed to supply arms to Israel, it would probably take a year before we receive them. But now, before Egypt received her MIG's and Stalin tanks, we still had the chance to crush her. He concluded with an appeal to France to halt arms shipments to "our enemies, who are your enemies as well."

Mr. Emile Habibi (Communist) stated that some of the speeches he had heard reminded him of similar speeches addressed to the Palestine Arabs in 1947. They had been warned then that if they did not start a war against the Jews, they would be destroyed, and that those who were not in favour of such a war were traitors.

The Six Who Fell

The six Israelis who fell in the attack on the Syrian positions on Sunday night are: Seren Yitzhak Ben-Menahem, 26, of Ramatayim; Raphael Yair, 19, Jerusalem; Yoram Katz, 19, Jerusalem; Avraham Kabiri, 20, Kfar Ono *ma'bara*, Shalom Kimmel (Selikovitch), 18, Moshav Mevo Betar; and Avraham Shababo, 19, Haifa.

Seren Ben-Menahem will be buried at 2 p.m. today at Ramatayim. The funeral of Yair and Katz will take place at 1.30 this afternoon at the Mt. Herzl Military Cemetery, Jerusalem.

Seren Ben-Menahem was the son of Gita and Yehezkel Ben-Menahem, veteran settlers of Givatayim. He was born there and completed the Kfar Saba secondary school before studying law at the Hebrew University.

A veteran of the War of Independence, he was wounded in the Battle of Latrun, and after the war was sent by the Army on a mission to the U.S. He is survived by his parents and a brother. His funeral will take place at 2 p.m. today in Ramatayim.

The other two were Jerusalem boys. Raphael Yair was the only son of Mr. Shlomo Yair, owner of a wrought iron workshop in Yoel Salomon St., near the Zion Cinema. Yoram Katz was the son of Dr. and Mrs. Walter Katz, owners of the knitwear shop, also near the Zion Cinema.

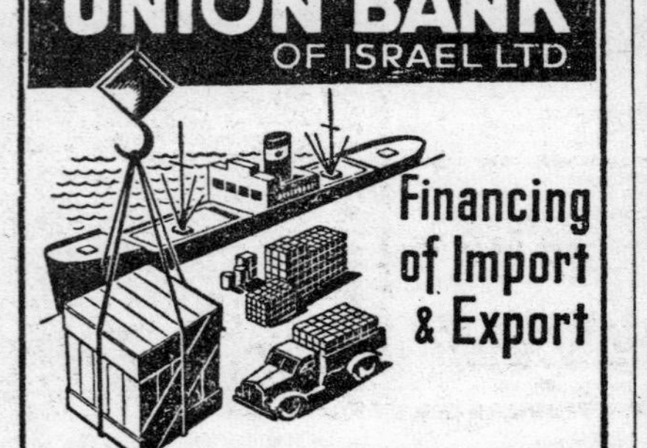

THE JERUSALEM POST
FRIDAY, APRIL 6, 1956
8 Pages
PRICE: 100 PRUTA
VOL. XXXII, No. 8471

Six Israelis Wounded as Cairo Provokes Gaza Strip Duel; 140 Egyptian Casualties

Egypt's Folly Cause of Tragedy

"The reported regrettable loss of life at Gaza is the inevitable boomerang effect of Egyptian reckless folly," the Foreign Ministry spokesman said in Jerusalem last night.

"In the face of repeated warnings the Egyptian forces have harassed the Israel border day in, day out for many months. Despite repeated admonitions by the United Nations the Egyptian Government obstinately refused to issue a cease-fire order.

"Egyptian fortified positions along the Gaza border persistently opened fire without the slightest provocation on Israel patrols moving on foot along their customary beat inside Israel territory and on Israel's stationary observation posts.

"On Wednesday such a patrol was taken under machine-gun and mortar fire. Two soldiers were killed outright and one mortally wounded. Artillery had to be used to extricate the survivors from the death-trap.

"The day before another soldier lost his life in an Egyptian ambush. Today a similar unprovoked attack occurred and several Israel villages were shelled from Egyptian positions suffering casualties and destruction.

"Return fire became imperative and unavoidable."

Sharett Protests to Burns

Jerusalem Post Reporter

A cease-fire effected at 6.45 p.m. yesterday brought to an end an artillery and mortar battle that flared up along most of the Gaza Strip border after incessant fire from Egyptian positions had attacked Israel patrols up and down the line and pummelled five Negev settlements from 8.30 a.m.

The Army spokesman announced that six Israelis — four soldiers and two civilians — were wounded. One of the civilians is in a serious condition.

U.N. Military Observers in Gaza reported to U.N. Truce Supervision Organization headquarters in Jerusalem last night that about 40 Egyptians were killed and more than 100 wounded.

Soon after the Egyptians began their attacks on Israel patrols yesterday morning—attacks that have been continuing for weeks—Foreign Minister Moshe Sharett in Jerusalem dispatched an urgent letter to Maj-Gen. E. L. M. Burns, the U.N. Chief of Staff, in which he underlined the "murderous character of the Egyptian acts of provocation along the Gaza Strip." Mr. Sharett demanded action to stop them.

In the afternoon Mr. Sharett invited Gen. Burns to the Foreign Ministry. The Foreign Minister placed the responsibility for the attacks and for the lives lost squarely on the shoulders of the Egyptians, who had "obstinately refused to issue the cease-fire order as demanded by the U.N."

Stresses Gravity

The Foreign Minister pointed to the grave consequences liable to result from the unceasing Egyptian attacks if they were not stopped. He stated that Israel "must reserve to herself, as a matter of course, freedom of action in self-defence."

Following this conversation Gen. Burns issued a request for a complete cease-fire along the demarcation line surrounding the Gaza Strip, effective at midnight, should the efforts being taken for a cease-fire by the Chairman of the Egyptian-Israel Mixed Armistice Commission, Col. Robert Bayard, be ineffective before that time.

Gen. Burns in his request to both Governments said, "It is of the utmost importance that the situation along the demarcation line surrounding the Gaza Strip be brought under control immediately and all forms of firing across the demarcation line be stopped."

Meanwhile, negotiations for a cease-fire had already been initiated by Col. Bayard. At 5 p.m. Sgan-Aluf Y. Nursella, head of the Israel delegation to the Mixed Armistice Commission, informed Col. Bayard that Israel was prepared to conform to the cease-fire call on condition that the Egyptians discontinue their fire as well.

Israel Orders

Shortly afterwards, Col. Bayard informed Sgan-Aluf Nursella that the Egyptians promised to stop their fire at 6 p.m. and the Israel representative said that Israel fire would be halted at the same hour.

Despite their promise, however, the Egyptians continued the attack for another 30 minutes.

At 6.30 p.m. Sgan-Aluf Nursella in a radio-telephone conversation told Col. Bayard: "I suggest you contact the senior Egyptian delegate and inform him it would be well for him to control his troops."

Col. Bayard replied: "I understand this, but it applies to both sides."

Sgan-Aluf Nursella: "Israel troops don't fire unless they are fired upon."

Col. Bayard: "Is this an official statement?"

Sgan-Aluf Nursella: "The Israel Government has stated on repeated occasions that the Israel Defence Army is under orders not to fire unless fired upon."

Fire along the line was stopped 15 minutes later at 6.45 p.m.

Egypt Notifies U.N. of Clash

NEW YORK, Thursday (Reuter). — Egypt charged in the U.N. today that Israel forces had killed 33 civilians and injured 99 other persons in an attack today in the Gaza Strip. The list of casualties was according to a "preliminary" report, it was said.

(Cairo later announced the casualties as 42 civilians killed and 103 wounded. Nine members of the armed forces were also reported wounded.)

News of the alleged attack was given in an urgent letter sent by the permanent Egyptian delegate, Omar Lutfi, to the Secretary-General, Mr. Dag Hammarskjold, on the eve of his departure for the Middle East.

Lutfi's letter said Israel armed forces had attacked at 12.30 a.m. local time today. All the 33 dead were said to be civilians. Ninety-two other civilians were said to have been injured, together with seven Egyptian soldiers, including an officer.

Lutfi said he would keep Mr. Hammarskjold informed about developments and reserved the right of his delegation "to pursue the matter further."

The Egyptian delegation spokesman said the Israel alleged attack was "an act of atrocious assault."

The Egyptian spokesman said the "atrocious assault" provided irrefutable proof of Israel's intentions towards the Secretary-General's mission.

Lutfi asked his letter be directed to the President of the Security Council, who for April is Mr. Henry Cabot Lodge of the U.S.

Lutfi's comment reserving his right to pursue the matter further was taken by observers to mean that he might ask later for a meeting of the Security Council on the issue.

The places attacked were said to be Gaza, Deir el Balah, Abasan and Khoza.

The Israel U.N. delegation yesterday declared the Israel casualties in yesterday's battle in the Gaza Strip, when three Israel soldiers were killed, were "a direct result of Premier Abdul Nasser's refusal to order a cease-fire as he was requested to do a few months ago."

A statement issued by the delegation described the incident as a "wanton attack" on an Israel patrol by an Egyptian fixed position. It said the attack "contrasts grimly with the Egyptian delegate's professions of peace."

New Shelters Help Settlers

Jerusalem Post Reporter

Defence fortifications that have been constructed recently in frontier settlements along the Gaza Strip by volunteers served their purpose in yesterday's shell duel, and helped keep Israel casualties to a bare minimum. Although the Egyptians sustained heavy losses, according to Cairo, Israel casulaties were light — six wounded—because settlers took to their shelters as soon as the attacks began.

The Egyptian attacks began at 8.30 a.m. when an Israel patrol near Kisufim sustained rifle and machinegun fire. The patrol returned the fire and the exchange continued for about 20 minutes.

At 9.25 a second exchange occurred between Egyptian positions and the patrol.

Egyptian infiltrators penetrated into the Be'eri area at 10.15, but ran back across the border into the Gaza Strip when they were met by a patrol.

At 11.30 Egyptians fired on a patrol in the Mefalsim area. Again the fire was returned.

Machineguns were opened up from Egyptian positions on a patrol in the Kisufim area. The exchange lasted for 30 minutes. It was resumed again at 1.35 p.m.

Kisufim and Ein Hashlosha settlements came under 120 mm. mortar barrages at 3 p.m. Nohal Oz and Yogev were battered by mortars at 4.30 p.m. and Nirim at 5.10 p.m.

Mortars rained on Nahal Oz again at 6 p.m.

Fifteen minutes later the Egyptians again aimed machinegun fire and mortars on Israel positions in the Kisufim area.

Mission 'Useful,' Says U.N. Chief

NEW YORK, Thursday. — Mr. Dag Hammarskjold, U.N. Secretary-General, said today on the eve of his departure for the Middle East that he would not have undertaken the mission given him by the Security Council if he did not feel "something useful could be done."

The Secretary-General said at a press conference that he might prolong his stay in the Middle East if his discussion with Israel and Arab leaders showed promise. In that case, he might delay his final report to the Council beyond the month allowed him to report back on the tense situation, and would submit a "progress" report within the allotted time.

Mr. Hammarskjold stated that in the view of the governments concerned, and in his own, a somewhat prolonged discussion would be helpful and promising. He did not think that it would be departing from the Security Council's intentions if he gave the discussions all the time that seemed necessary.

Mr. Hammarskjold said that the Security Council's mandate to him was "very clear in its limitation." It "undoubtedly" did not include questions such as a possible arms ban.

Has More Freedom

"On the other hand," Mr. Hammarskjold added, "you must not forget that the Secretary-General remains the Secretary-General and, quite apart from the Security Council action, I have, of course, my regular right to bring up with governments points which I think are worth consideration."

From that point of view, he said, the arms issue was "not outside the scope of my interests."

Mr. Hammarskjold reiterated the call he made yesterday before the Council for "restraint on all sides" while he was engaged on his mission.

He said that the mission would not be a test of the U.N.'s effectiveness. It was just an episode on the long road. Dramatic results should not be expected and were not warranted by anything said, done or intended in this case.

Mr. Hammarskjold said that there was no reason to talk in "a desperate mood" about the Middle Eastern situation. If there were any risk of an outbreak of war it would be an added reason for him to go there.

Centre in Beirut

Outlining his travel arrangements, the Secretary-General stated that he would fly direct to Rome (where he is due on Saturday) with a refuelling stop in London. He would not confer with any British officials during his stay. He said he would be met in Rome by Major-General E. L. M. Burns, Chief of Staff of the U.N. Truce Supervision Organization, and M. Henry Labouisse, Director of the U.N. Works and Relief Agency for Palestine Refugees.

Mr. Hammarskjold explained that it was not an affair in which M. Labouisse's agency was involved, but he was one of the U.N.'s top men in the region with a deep knowledge of Middle Eastern problems.

Also meeting him in Rome would be M. Henri Vigier Political Adviser to the U.N. Truce Supervision Organization.

The Secretary-General added that he would stay in Rome for three days, then go on to Beirut, a centre from which it was easy to reach all the main capitals. From then on, he said, his plans "were rather loose."

The first place he would go to from Beirut would be Cairo, probably on Wednesday next, he concluded.

Saudia Gets 'Surplus' Jets from Egypt

WASHINGTON Thursday (UP). — Saudi Arabia has informed the U.S. that she is buying British-built Vampire jet planes from Egypt, Administration officials disclosed tonight.

Information on the deal was given by King Saud to U.S. Ambassador George Wadsworth, who relayed it to Washington some time ago.

The planes, King Saud said, were declared surplus by Egypt after she had received newer Communist-built Mig-15 jet fighters and bombers. King Saud assured Mr. Wadsworth, it was said, that he was not purchasing Soviet bloc arms.

The plane deal was signed in Cairo several weeks ago when King Saud met there with Premier Gamal Abdul Nasser The exact number of planes involved was not learned but officials understood that it was 12 to 20.

The U.S. is preparing to enter important negotiations with Saudi Arabia for a new five-year lease for the Air Force and the Dhahran air base. The present agreement expires on June 18. Negotiations are expected to begin later this month.

The U.S. has been training some Saudi Arabian airmen and ground personnel.

Cairo Denies Report On Russian Offer

CAIRO, Thursday (Reuter).— The Egyptian Information Office said today that it knew nothing of a Damascus report that Russia had offered military aid to the Arab states in case of any Western armed intervention.

The Damascus report said that Russia would extend aid to all Arab states neighbouring on Israel in the event of Western intervention in "violation of the U.N. Charter" to prevent an Arab-Israel war.

The alleged offer had been made in response to Syrian and Egyptian inquiries.

The Damascus report was treated with reserve in official quarters in London, especially in the absence of official Syrian confirmation. It was noted, however, that such a move would follow the pattern of Soviet reaction to suggestions that the three Western powers act outside the framework of the U.N. against the threat of an Arab-Israel conflict.

Silver Takes Ben-Zvi Message to Ike

LYDDA AIRPORT, Thursday. — Dr. Abba Hillel Silver, the American Zionist leader, took a message from President Ben-Zvi to President Eisenhower when he left today on the completion of his short visit.

Dr. Silver expressed his heartfelt thanks to the Government and the people of Israel for the hospitality they had extended to him. He hoped to be able to return soon, but could not say when.

In a statement, Dr. Silver had prepared for the U.S. press, the American General Zionist leader said he had found peace and quiet in Israel. "I found no signs of panic, though there are signs of apprehension at the supply of arms to the Arab states."

Dr. Silver was seen off by Mr. Ya'akov Herzog, chief of the U.S. Division of the Foreign Ministry, and leaders of the General Zionist Party headed by its President, Mr. Peretz Bernstein, M.K. (Itim)

SHARETT SEES U.S., CANADIAN ENVOYS

The Foreign Minister, Mr. Moshe Sharett, on Wednesday received Mr. Edward Lawson, the American Ambassador. Yesterday, the Minister met the temporary Canadian Charge d'Affairs, Mr. George Kidd.

Both appointments were made at Mr. Sharett's instigation.

PINEAU LEAVING FOR ISRAEL ON MONDAY

PARIS, Thursday (INA). — Foreign Minister Christian Pineau is leaving for Israel on Monday for a four-day stay.

U.S. Not Yet Able to Agree To British Call for M.E. Action

By GEORGE LICHTHEIM, Jerusalem Post Correspondent

LONDON, Thursday. — The great Anglo-American muddle has now reached the point where it is possible for the American Embassy here to confirm and for the Foreign Office simultaneously to deny that Sir Anthony Eden has recently sent a crisis message to Mr. Eisenhower.

Much depends, of course, on the definition of "recently." That letters have been exchanged was stated yesterday by President Eisenhower after his Press Secretary, Mr. James Hagerty, had tried earlier to suppress the news. But basically, this quibble about the timing and content of Sir Anthony's latest message no longer matters.

The real news today is that Mr. Eisenhower has indicated privately his inability to answer Britain's appeal for action in the Middle East for at least a month. This delay, in the official view here, could make the difference between saving the Baghdad Pact or watching it collapse.

It could also determine whether Britain may have to take unilateral action to defend her Red Sea positions against Saudi Arabian and Yemenite attacks.

The worst aspect of yesterday's statement by the U.S. President, from the British point of view, is that it places Britain in the position of being the only country committed to military intervention if war breaks out around Israel or if civil war occurs in Jordan.

The President's remarks are interpreted as meaning that he recognizes neither the explosive nature of the situation nor that Britain is in danger of being driven into isolation. This view is shared not only by Conservative papers which, for the second day running, assail American inactivity, but by the "Manchester Guardian." The "Guardian" however, couples its criticism of Washington's inability with a wholesale condemnation of British policy in the Middle East, including the lighthearted decision to join the Baghdad Pact without making sure of American support.

Yet, while conceding that the Americans may be right to dissociate themselves from British policy, in view of its spectacular failure, the "Guardian" adds: "At this moment neither the anti-colonial issue nor the Anglo-Egyptian quarrel is the dominant theme in the Middle East. The emergency has come about from another cause — the Arab resolve to destroy Israel."

The paper wonders whether Mr. Eisenhower and Mr. Dulles by their recent declarations may not have weakened the Tripartite Declaration and given Egypt the

(Continued on Page 2, Col. 5)

AFTER MIDNIGHT

General Franco and Sulan Mohammed Ben Yussef, Sultan of Morocco, last night officially opened talks in Madrid to lead to the incorporation of the Spanish zone of Morocco in a united Morocco.

Column One By DAVID COURTNEY

THE papers say: "Sir Anthony Eden's dramatic appeal (to President Eisenhower) for instant action to salvage the Baghdad Pact..."; and elsewhere: "President Eisenhower denied that he had received any recent letter from Sir Anthony Eden on the urgent need for a common Middle East policy"; and somewhere else the papers say: "A steady stream of messages is now flowing across the Atlantic..."

•

A LONDON paper says: "American influence has been exerted directly or indirectly, knowingly or unknowingly, to get (Britain) out of Egypt and to weaken us in Jordan and Persia. And when Britain comes out, Russia walks in." A local paper says: "There may be some grounds for believing that British blunders have contributed to raising American caution," the American caution being read at U.N. as an incredible "abandonment of collective action in the Middle East area." This is a reading of the statement of Mr. Dulles according to which America's refusal of arms to Israel is "most conducive to our particular ability to exert influence for peace and independence in that area. But the same considerations which apply to the U.S. do not necessarily apply to other countries."

•

THE papers say......

•

AND heaven knows what the intelligent reader can make of it all. The fact seems to be that everyone, from Secretaries of State to newspaper commentators, is busy just now "re-appraising" policy. Editorial writers who have been in the habit of suggesting that Sir Anthony Eden was the one who wanted to "appease" Colonel Abdul Nasser while America would have liked to do something for Israel but was being prevented from doing it by its British ally, have reappraised their judgment to fit an assumption that Britain's policy has been a succession of mistakes which have so horrified Mr. Dulles that he has decided to "go it alone" and leave Britain and France to stew in their own North African and Middle East juices and if they want to give a few arms to Israel, why, let them.

•

IN other words, it is still Britain's fault. But some papers are pointing out (a trifle exaggeratedly but, in the main, accurately) that America wanted Britain out of Abadan, out of the Suez Canal Zone, and that after Abadan and the evacuation of Suez, developments like the dismissal of Sir John Glubb were inevitable. Were the Abadan affair and the evacuation of the Canal Zone mistakes? Definitely there were mistakes of method and timing in Britain's dealing with Persia and Egypt, and the greatest mistake of all was not that Britain gave in to Persian demands and withdrew from Egypt but that she waited until Persian and Egyptian pressure forced action that should have been taken before the element of compulsion entered into it.

•

THE fact remains that if the British "retreat" from the Middle East has been a mistake, the alternative could only have been something like British military occupation of Persia and Egypt in the good old-fashioned imperialistic sense; and it is difficult, in the present state of world opinion and temper, to imagine a worse mistake than that. Anyway, the situation calls now for exactly that "re-appraisal" by the British Government which the papers say is going on; and it seems to me that if the papers are correct then the British Government deserves some credit for an attempt to correct a policy which everybody has been saying was calamitous.

•

BUT the papers say....; and however inconsistent and conflicting the despatches may be the correspondents who send them obviously have "reliable sources" — whose perplexity we all must share.

Jerusalem, April 6.

Paris Speeds Call-Up For Algerian Action

PARIS, Thursday. — The War Ministry announced today that conscription would be speeded up and that volunteers would be accepted to fight in Algeria. The announcement followed the arrival here of the Minister Resident in Algeria, M. Robert Lacoste, and may be a prelude to the recall of reservists.

M. Lacoste said that Premier Guy Mollet has assured him "all the military means necessary to keep peace in Algeria." The Minister did not elaborate, but his words indicated that Mollet was definitely decided on calling up another 40,000 men, including up to 25,000 reservists. M. Lacoste had asked for 100,000 reinforcements, but informed sources said that there were no immediate plans for raising that many.

The draft, which until now has worked on the basis of two intakes a year into the armed forces, is to be speeded up, and there will be six calls yearly, the Secretary of State for War announced.

M. Lacoste announced social reforms to accompany the military drive in Algeria. He told reporters that Moslems would be put at the head of some civil service departments, including health services, ex-servicemen's affairs and the service which deals with Moslem farmers.

Cadet Deserts

Meanwhile, in Algeria, a young European officer cadet went over to the Algerian rebels yesterday with a truckload of arms, ammunition and hand grenades, according to unofficial reports in Algiers today.

Police were searching the Casbah today for the arms —132 light machineguns, 140 pistols, and large quantities of grenades and ammunition —which were stolen 10 kms. outside Algiers.

In the Kabylie mountains French *gendarmes* shot dead 18 prisoners—all rebel suspects—who tried to escape during a rebel raid on a police outpost, authorities said today. The prisoners made a break for the back wall of the post during the commotion of the attack. When they refused to halt, they were shot down.

At Saint-Arnaud, 105 kms. southeast of Bougie, terrorists threw a grenade into a downtown bar, killing two Jews, Abraham Zaoui, 70, and Salomon Nabet, a rural policeman.

A Canadian immigration spokesman said yesterday in Ottawa that about 3,000 inquiries have been received in the past six months from residents of French North Africa who wish to settle in Canada. Most of the requests are from European-born colonists. *(UP, Reuter)*

Algerians Ambush Seven Lorries

NEMOURS, West Algeria, Thursday (Reuter). — Algerian rebels tonight tipped seven lorries into a ravine near Nemours and machinegunned the occupants.

The casualties were not immediately known. The machinegun attack was believed to have followed an ambush.

China Joins In Attack on Stalin

HONG KONG, Thursday (Reuter). — The Communist Party of China today joined in denunciations of Stalin and laid a new charge at his door — of neglecting agriculture and the material welfare of the peasantry.

The charge came in a long statement issued after a meeting of the top leaders of the Chinese Party.

The statement was the first direct comment by China's leaders on the Soviet campaign against Stalin's "errors."

It was published in today's Peking "People's Daily," organ of the Communist Party, and issued fully by the New China News Agency service received here.

Premier Chou En-lai told Executive Council members of the World Federation of Scientific Workers at a banquet he gave in their honour yesterday that China was economically and culturally backward, and needed the help of scientists of advanced countries, the New China News Agency reported.

Soviets Agree to Meet Britain on Vietnam

LONDON, Thursday (Reuter) — The Soviet Government has agreed in principle to a meeting between the representatives of Britain and Russia to discuss the situation in partitioned Vietnam, the Foreign Office spokesman said today.

Britain and Russia were joint chairmen of the Geneva peace conference on Indo-China. Britain proposed such a meeting to Russia in a note delivered in Moscow on March 9.

Diplomatic quarters said that the meeting would probably take place at the Foreign Office on Wednesday between the Soviet Deputy Foreign Minister, Mr. Andrei Gromyko, and the Marquis of Reading, the British Minister of State.

Meanwhile, TASS announced today that the Soviet Union has sent a new note to Britain complaining about South Vietnam's non-compliance with the Geneva conference decisions on Vietnam. The note was addressed to the British Embassy in Moscow on March 30.

GUNMEN WOUND CYPRIOT GREEK

PAPHOS, Cyprus, Thursday (Reuter). — Unknown gunmen shot and seriously wounded a Cypriot Greek at Lysson Village, 40 kms. from here, last night.

It is understood that he was shot during a local feast, but the villagers were afraid to report the shooting to the police, and he was brought to hospital here only this morning.

Malenkov Denies Russia Seeks British Amity at U.S. Expense

LONDON, Thursday (Reuter). — Mr. Georgi Malenkov declared today that although Russia wants to improve relations with Britain, she is not trying to do so at the expense of this country's relations with the U.S.

People who thought so were in error, the Soviet Minister for Power Stations told a crowded Press conference.

"Our aim is to bring about a programme of good relations between the Soviet and British peoples, and at the same time between the Soviet, American and British peoples."

Mr. Malenkov met reporters towards the close of his three-week tour of Britain. He defended the recent Russian denunciation of Stalin, saying that "the cult of personality" was against the morale of the Communist Party. "We believe that our Party should not conceal its shortcomings. We have always exposed our shortcomings to criticism and we believe that this is a source of our strength."

Reporters put blunt questions to the portly Soviet Minister after he had read out a formal statement declaring Russia's peaceful intentions. One was, "Do you have any feelings of guilt for the work you carried out under Stalin in the great purges of the 1930's?"

"We collectively always feel responsible for such errors as we have made, and we openly admit them to our people," he replied.

Another report asked whether Mr. Malenkov thought that the sale of arms to Egypt helped to prevent war. "The cause of tension in this part of the world is not Egypt," he said. "It is the situation created by war alliances. We know that the people of the Middle East, who long for independence, are entitled to choose their own policy in getting their independence, and this applies to their foreign policies."

Asked what he thought of reports published here about Mr. Khrushchev's speech at the Communist Party Congress denouncing Stalin, Mr. Malenkov replied that he was not able to read British newspapers, but it was said there was "a lot of nonsense" in the translations of Mr. Khrushchev's speech.

"For correct answers to what is happening in Russia, you should read the Soviet Press," he said.

Bonn Attacks Mollet's Views On Reunification

BONN, Thursday (Reuter).— The Foreign Ministry declared here today that it strongly disapproved of the views reported to have been expressed by the French Prime Minister M. Guy Mollet, that disarmament should take precedence over the problems of European security and German reunification.

In a statement issued after consultation with Foreign Minister Heinrich von Brentano, who is on leave, the Foreign Ministry said that M. Mollet's interview with an American magazine had aroused "surprise and criticism" in West Germany.

It recalled that the West German Government had repeatedly declared "in full agreement" with the French, British and the U.S. Governments that reunification and the creation of a security system acceptable to all states was the prerequisite to talks on disarmament if the latter were to have any promise of success.

"If the head of the French Government now describes as false the policy adopted by the three Western governments in general and expresses the view that disarmament should precede the solution of the problem of reunification and the question of security, he appears to suggest a certain readiness to accept the order of priority demanded by the Soviet Union," the Foreign Ministry said.

"The Federal Government will not leave any doubt that it does not share this view."

Byroade Sees Fawzi On Aswan Project

The American Ambassador to Cairo, Mr. Henry Byroade, last night met the Egyptian Foreign Minister, Mahmoud Fawzi, to discuss U.S. aid for the Aswan Dam project, NEABS reported last night.

Later, Mr. Byroade was closeted with Premier Abdul Nasser for one hour. He told correspondents after the meeting that he had congratulated Egypt in the name of the U.S. Government on Egypt's "noble" attitude during the recent U.N. Security Council debate.

I.C.A. AUTHORIZES $4m. FOR ISRAEL

WASHINGTON, Thursday (INA). — The International Cooperation Administration yesterday announced that procurement authorizations totalling $4.25m. had been approved for Israel.

Goods included for purchase are crude oil and petroleum products and motor vehicles, engines and parts.

Weak Attendance At Arab League Session

The Syrian and Lebanese Foreign Ministers were the only two of the Arab League's nine members to put in an appearance at the opening of the 25th session of the League Council in Cairo yesterday afternoon, according to "El Jihad", the Old City daily.

The meeting, which was to have been attended by all Foreign Ministers, was presided over by the Egyptian Deputy Foreign Minister, Ahmed Kheirat Said.

Bulgaria Asks U.S. To Restore Relations

WASHINGTON, Thursday (Reuter) — The State Department is giving "serious and active" consideration to "overtures" by the Bulgarian Government on the possibility of resuming diplomatic relations between the two countries, severed six years ago, officials said last night.

The U.S. broke off relations with Bulgaria in 1950 when the Bulgarian Government attempted to implicate the American Ambassador, Mr. Donald Heath, in the Kostov case.

Ceylonese Elections

COLOMBO, Thursday (UP). — Heavily armed police stood by today while orderly voters lined up for Ceylon's national elections. There were no incidents.

The Government posted armed police for fear of violence in the elections which centre around the touchy issues of a national language and the price of rice.

Women outnumbered men at the voting, which is to continue on April 7 and 10.

SWEDISH PREMIER OFF TO GEORGIA

MOSCOW, Thursday (Reuter). — The visiting Swedish Prime Minister, Mr. Tage Erlander, and his party left Moscow airport today for Sukhumi, Georgia — Stalin's homeland — at the start of a one-week tour in the Soviet Union.

He was seen off by Prime Minister Nikolai Bulganin, Foreign Minister Vyacheslav Molotov and other Ministers.

6 U.S. Firemen Killed

NEW YORK, Thursday (Reuter). — A brick wall crashed on at least 12 firemen in a fire here last night. Six firemen were reported killed.

EGYPTIAN PORT PILOT HELD IN HAIFA

HAIFA, Thursday. — An Alexandria harbour pilot arrived aboard a Norwegian freighter today. He had taken the vessel out of his port and a storm prevented his launch from returning home.

The freighter, Elisabeth Jensen, was scheduled to call at Cyprus, but received orders *en route* to proceed to Haifa instead.

The pilot is being held by the port police pending the departure of the ship.

With deep sorrow we announce the sudden death of our dear friend and colleague

Dr. Sigbert Feuchtwanger

legal adviser of our firm.

The memory of his noble personality shall ever remain with us.

The Management and Staff
I. L. Feuchtwanger Bank Ltd.

Tel Aviv, April 5, 1956.

The funeral will leave from the Hadassah Hospital Rehov Mane, Tel Aviv. As the time has not yet been fixed kindly telephone our office for information.

THE JERUSALEM POST

TUESDAY, OCTOBER 30, 1956

PRICE: 120 PRUTA
VOL. XXXII, No. 8642

ARMY ATTACKS BASES IN HEART OF SINAI

MARGINAL COLUMN

By ARTHUR SAUL SUPER

WHAT possessed President Eisenhower at this particular juncture to call upon the Israel Premier to stop the partial mobilization of Israel's reserve forces? It is true that the statement was also accompanied by an offhand reference to the Arab states and a very much less urgent appeal to them not to jeopardize the peace. When the Egyptians took over virtual control of Jordan's territory and actual control of her armed forces, making it clear that the aim was to crush Israel, he said nothing. When Syria, Egypt and Jordan formed a closely knit anti-Israel alliance and seriously endangered the *status quo* in the Middle East, he said nothing. When Iraq began to mass her troops on Jordan's borders, he said nothing. But when Israel, seeing the vultures gather, took measures in the defence of her security and the integrity of her frontiers, the U.S. President suddenly came up with a statement asking Mr. Ben-Gurion to call off the mobilization.

•

IN this way the Arabs will be encouraged in their stand. They will deduce that the State Department thinks that, now that the Soviet Union is seriously preoccupied nearer home, the time has come for a new campaign of appeasement of Nasser, and if Israel is to be the victim, then that will do very well.

•

NEITHER President Eisenhower nor his advisers can really believe that Israel has major aggressive intentions. As a general of no mean skill, Mr. Eisenhower must be aware of the true balance of forces in the Middle East. He must know that when Mr. Ben-Gurion repeatedly claims that Israel wants peace, he must have information enough at his disposal to know that he means what he says. Israel is heavily outnumbered by Egypt alone, without taking into account Iraq's British-trained army, Syria's French-trained cadres, Jordan's Arab Legion—weakened though it be in recent months, and the tribesmen of Saudi Arabia. All these countries have been heavily armed, either by Egypt out of her supplies from Eastern Europe, or by Britain and the U.S. in their pursuit of appeasement cloaked under the euphemism of fulfilment of treaty obligations. The Arabs number 40 millions against Israel's 1,700,000.

•

IT should be clear that a country which would deliberately and without need pit itself against such odds would be completely irrational. Even assuming that Israel was crazy, and sought the conquest of the Arab world, what would she do with it afterwards? Britain's Foreign Office must be in a position today to tell the State Department what is the position of a foreign power seeking to maintain itself by force inside a hostile land. Britain had to scurry out of Egypt the moment popular opposition broke out in the Canal zone; she has gone from Jordan and is on her way out in Cyprus. And she has a vast empire still behind her. France with her 45 millions has had to abandon sovereignty in Tunis and Morocco and has only a precarious hold on Algeria. Is it not therefore a calculated falsification of self-evident truth for President Eisenhower and his advisers to nourish the myth of Jewish aggressiveness and to base upon that myth statements like that which he issued on Saturday?

•

IF Israel is armed to the limit of her heavily outnumbered population and if she is now compelled to move is it not clear that she is doing so in a heroic effort; and let no enemy underestimate her striking power, to protect herself against the total massacre which is daily threatened by all the Arab states. It is a sad world in which the shout of the aggressor could not be heard because those who should have heeded it were too busy trying to talk the potential victim into silence.

Jerusalem, October 30.

France's Top Leaders View M.E. Crisis

By MAURICE CARR
Jerusalem Post Correspondent

PARIS, Monday. — Three of the principal French ministers, Premier Guy Mollet, Foreign Minister Christian Pineau, and Defence Minister Bourges-Manoury, held an hour-long meeting this afternoon to examine the Middle East situation.

For the past two days the Government has been studying what measures to take, on the one hand, in the light of the anti-French pogroms in Morocco and the anti-French outbreaks elsewhere in the Arab world, and on the other hand against the eventuality of an Israel-Arab war.

While there is a general tendency to be helpful to Israel, based on the recognition of common Franco-Israel interests, French leaders are understood to be divided on certain aspects of higher policy.

Right-Wing View

Right-wingers ardently desire an Israel-Arab war, hoping this would eliminate Abdul Nasser and enable the French to "reconquer" North Africa — not only Algeria, but Tunisia and Morocco.

The Socialists and Liberals, however, fear that war on Nasserist Fascism — and Abdul Nasser's nationalism is seen by democratic left-wingers as real Fascism — may give the French Fascists, including the Poujadists who have lately greatly strengthened their grip on the French policy and on the Army, a longed for opportunity to overthrow the parliamentary regime and install fascism at home.

Meanwhile, official French quarters, while welcoming President Eisenhower's proposal for tripartite talks on the Middle East, deplore his "one-sided intervention to the detriment of Israel."

ARABS SHARE BLAME

The United Press reports from Paris that Quai d'Orsay officials said the security measures taken by Israel followed the decisions taken by Egypt and Syria to strengthen their links with Jordan, thus creating a joint military command.

These sources said the French Government was disturbed by President Eisenhower's letter to the Israel Premier, Mr. David Ben-Gurion, and feel that Israel should not be the only state blamed for causing tension in the Middle East. "We feel the Arab states bear a large share of the responsibility," the source said.

They added that the Government disapproved of any mobilization moves in the Middle East. However, the Government wanted to initiate multilateral efforts to ease the tension rather than just issue warnings to one of the parties.

West Holds Hurried Talks on Mid-East

WASHINGTON, Monday. — The British and French envoys held an emergency meeting tonight with Secretary of State John Foster Dulles, within minutes of news of Israel's drive into Egypt.

Earlier, Mr. Dulles had called three members of the Senate Foreign Relations Committee for a talk on the situation. State Department officials said Mr. Dulles arranged the meeting to brief the Senators on U.S. policy in the Middle East crisis.

British Charge d'Affaires John Coulson and Charles Lucet, of the French Embassy, asked for a joint meeting with Mr. Dulles in the absence from the capital of the Ambassadors.

First reports of Israel's attack on Egyptian positions today was radioed to President Eisenhower aboard his plane on an election tour of the southern U.S.

A White House spokesman said the official Israel report was sent immediately to the President who yesterday sent an appeal to Premier Ben-Gurion for restraint in the tense Middle East situation.

There was no immediate comment from the White House or the State Department.

Mr. Eisenhower was flying between Jacksonville, Florida, and Richmond, Virginia, when the White House radioed the news to his plane. He is due to return to Washington today after an election campaign trip, a State Department spokesman said.

Washington officials received the first intimation of the Israel move from news agency reports. The Department was awaiting details from the American Embassy in Israel, the spokesman said.

Earlier today in Miami, the President said on his arrival from Washington that there was "no more critical danger to peace at present than in the Middle East."

He added, "In such a critical situation we cannot expect to erase suddenly the bitter heritage of the ages. We can — and must and we shall — go on strying to do all in our power to heal old wounds, rather than let them open in bloodshed."

This afternoon, the Israel Embassy had received no official word of the fighting. Neither had the Egyptian Embassy received any dispatch from its Government. An Egyptian spokesman said that apparently "an exceedingly serious situation" was developing.

At U.N. Headquarters, representatives of the Western Big Three met privately tonight in the office of Secretary-General Dag Hammarskojld presumably to discuss the Israel action.

(Reuter, INA)

Two Jordan Rioters Die of Wounds

Two of the 15 Jordanians wounded when a mob attacked the French Consulate outside the Old City on Sunday afternoon, died in hospital during the night, it was reported yesterday.

The Old City press asserted that the French security guards at the Consulate, two of whom were wounded during the clash, were responsible for all the Jordanian casualties. It said that the French guards possessed five automatic rifles, two cases of hand grenades, a quantity of ammunition and tear-gas bombs.

In the building at the time of the attack were four Frenchmen, including security guards, and three Jordanian employees, one of them a woman. It was also reported that the car of the French Vice-Consul was set on fire.

In Amman, total casualties were three civilians and two police injured and detained in hospital, and another 12 police slightly wounded.

(In Jerusalem, it was learned that the two wounded French guards would probably be evacuated from Augusta Victoria Hospital to Hadassah. One of them, who was shot through the cheek, is reported to be in a critical condition. The other, who was wounded by a burst of bullets in his leg, faces either amputation of the limb or paralysis. It is believed that the leg may be saved if he is brought to Hadassah.)

Meanwhile, France yesterday protested to both Syria and Jordan against the attacks on French institutions and civilians in the two countries.

In Aleppo, Syria, where French buildings were attacked and burned on Sunday, the authorities instituted a dusk-to-dawn curfew, which is being enforced by troops which were brought to the town. Three Cabinet Ministers were hurriedly dispatched to Aleppo from Damascus to conduct an investigation. The Governor has already been dismissed.

(Reuter, A-Diffa)

Kuwatly, Top Syrian tatesmen to Moscow

President Shukri Kuwatly of Syria, accompanied by General Tewfik Nizam e-Din, and the Ministers of Foreign Affairs and Defence, Salah e-Din Bitar and Abdul Hasib Raslan, left for Damascus last night for a state visit to Moscow.

They are flying in three special Russian planes which had arrived in the Syrian capital on Monday morning.

U.S. SOVIET ENVOYS IN CAIRO CONFER

CAIRO, Monday (Reuter). — Mr. Raymond Hare, the U.S. Ambassador, and Mr. Dmitri Sobolev, the Soviet Chargé d'Affaires, met at the American Embassy yesterday, Cairo Radio has reported.

Abdul Nasser later received Mr. Hare, the Radio said.

New Jordan Gov't Is Sworn In

Suleiman Nabulsi, pro-Egyptian leader of the National Socialist Party, yesterday completed formation of a new Jordanian Cabinet which was sworn in by King Hussein.

Nabulsi, who was not returned to Parliament in the election although his party gained 11 seats, put in five other National Socialists in his Cabinet, and also took over the foreign portfolio.

The 11-man Cabinet includes seven Palestine Arabs. The full list:

Suleiman Nabulsi (Palestinian and National Socialist) Premier; Abdullah Rimawi (Palestinian, El Ba'ath) Foreign Minister; Abdul Halim Nimr e Humud (Jordanian, National Socialist) Defence and Interior; Shafik Irshidat (Jordanian, National Socialist) Justice and Education; Naim Abdul Hadi (Palestinian, National Socialist) National Economy; Abdul Kader Saleh (Palestinian, National Bloc) Agriculture; Anwar Khatib (Palestinian, National Socialist) Public Works; Saleh Majali (Jordanian, pro-Communist Independent) Posts and Aviation; Sam'an Daoud (Palestinian, Independent) Reconstruction; Salah Muashar (Jordanian, National Socialist) Health and Social Welfare; Salah Toukan (Palestinian, Independent) Finance.

ANGLO-FRENCH IN CYPRUS ALERTED

NICOSIA, Monday (Reuter). — British and French servicemen were today reported to be "on the alert" at an air base near Limassol as the tense Middle East situation deteriorated.

There was no official indication whether any special moves were afoot, but today's activities at the base were generally ascribed to the Middle East situation.

Thousands of British paratroopers who have been engaged on an anti-terrorist operation in West Cyprus since last Thursday, were today reported returning to their bases.

In London, a spokesman of the Ministry of Transport and Civil Aviation said all British aircraft were advised today that Israel had been declared a "prohibited area."

Must Ask Lydda

The spokesman said that the following notice has been issued to all British aircraft "Civil aircraft flying to Lydda will contact Lydda control prior to reaching the Israel control area and will proceed to Lydda as directed by the Air Traffic Control. All corridors are cancelled and the entire territory of Israel is declared prohibited."

The spokesman said he was not certain but believed that all countries would be issuing the same warning to their aicraft.

Arab Armies Said Partly Mobilizing

Premier Sabri el Assali of Syria said last night that the armies of Syria, Egypt and Jordan are "partly mobilizing" as a counter-measure to Israel's mobilization, NEABS has reported.

The Arabs, he asserted, would "reply to aggression with aggression."

The Syrian Defence Minister has stated that the Israel mobilization "was no surprise" and that the Arabs "had expected it since the signing of the three-power military agreement in Amman last week."

NAHAL OZ SHELLED

Egyptian positions opened fire with mortars on Kibbutz Nahal Oz, near the Gaza Strip, yesterday afternoon, the Army spokesman announced last night. Several shells fell on the settlement, but there were no casualties.

The shelling followed an attack on an Army patrol in the vicinity. The patrol returned the fire

Americans See M.E. Situation Ominous

By JESSE ZEL LURIE
Jerusalem Post Correspondent

NEW YORK, Monday. — News of Israel's mobilization with the implication of imminent war is deeply disturbing the American Jewish community.

Additionally, observers say the situation must be very serious for President Eisenhower to admonish Mr. David Ben-Gurion publicly just before the elections. But others believe that what Mr. Eisenhower really said was, "Don't spoil my peace and prosperity slogan."

Steps Defensive, Eban Tells Dulles

WASHINGTON, Monday (UP). — The Israel Ambassador to the U.S., Mr. Abba Eban, was summoned to the State Department late yesterday for an emergency meeting with Secretary of State Dulles.

Mr. Eban told reporters after the meeting that Mr. Dulles was concerned with the "significance of defensive measures Israel has taken in the last 48 hours." The Ambassador said that he was able to assure the Secretary of State that the "sole motive" of the mobilization was "vigilance and preparedness" in view of an anticipated attack on Israel by the neighbouring Arab states.

Mr. Eban said that his country's fear of an attack "has been intensified by certain developments in Arab policy in the past few days." He referred to the "joint action by Syria, Jordan and Egypt," and said that Israel had received recent reports of further troop concentrations along the Jordan-Iraqi frontier.

Speaking at a Jewish National Fund dinner last night, Mr. Eban said that Israel "will start no war but cannot surrender the inherent right of self-defence for all sovereign states as upheld by the U.N. Charter."

(U.P. Reuter)

Soviet Arms to Egypt Top Initial Estimates

NEW YORK, Monday (INA). — The Egyptian Army Command and its signals, maintenance, supply and training branches have not yet managed to master the modern arms they have received from Russia, Mr. Hanson Baldwin, Military Correspondent of "The New York Times," reported yesterday.

However, he said, arms supplies to Egypt exceed all initial estimates.

Mr. Baldwin, who had received permission to tour Egyptian Army installations, stated that Soviet arms supplies to Egypt in September alone were worth \$250m. to \$300m. at "bargain" prices. The transport of the supplies had kept busy 15 vessels flying Soviet bloc flags.

The number of Egypt's tanks has been doubled, the correspondent said, while her merchant fleet has also grown more than twofold and the Egyptian Air Force now has jet fighter planes and modern type bombers.

(INA)

Forces Half Way to Suez Canal

The Israel Defence Forces struck into the heart of the Sinai Peninsula last night, and were more than half way to the Suez Canal, an Army communique issued at 9 o'clock last night indicated.

"Units of the Israel Defence Forces have penetrated and attacked fedayeen bases in the Kuntilla and Ras el Nakb area, and have taken up positions to the west of the Nakhl road junction on the approaches to the Suez Canal," said the announcement.

"This operation was necessitated by the continuous Egyptian military attacks on citizens and on Israel land and sea communications, the purpose of which was to cause destruction and to deprive the people of Israel of the possibility of a peaceful existence," it concluded.

It was announced later that road junctions west of Nakhl were taken in the operation.

During the past 36 hours, Israel's Premier and Foreign Minister have been in close contact with the envoys of the U.S., U.K. and France.

Mr. Ben-Gurion yesterday received the French Ambassador, M. Pierre E. Gilbert. The British Ambassador, Sir John Nicholls, called on Mrs. Golda Meir at his request.

At 5 a.m. yesterday the second of two letters from President Eisenhower was delivered by a high U.S. Embassy official to Prime Minister Ben-Gurion in Tel Aviv. It followed a letter presented by Ambassador Edward B. Lawson on the previous evening.

In both letters Israel was asked by the President to exercise restraint and to avoid doing anything which might disturb the peace in the Middle East. It was understood that a reply to President Eisenhower was being drafted last evening.

During the day yesterday, Egyptians opened mortar fire on Nahal Oz opposite the Gaza Strip. There were no casualties.

Two Fedayeen gangs were captured near Kibbutz Erez while a third managed to escape. The Fedayeen said they had been sent on errands of murder and sabotage.

It was further reported that two Egyptian destroyers and three or four other warships had weighed anchor at Alexandria. It was believed that they had headed in the direction of the Israel coast.

One Year Later

Yesterday's attack by Israel on Kuntilla came exactly one year to the day of a retaliatory raid on an army camp at the very same spot. At that time 10 Egyptians were killed and 29 prisoners were taken. The reprisal last October came following the Egyptian incursion into Israel's Demilitarized Zone at Nitzana.

The Jerusalem Municipal Council decided to empower its Finance Committee, which contains representatives of all parties, to act as an "Emergency Committee" during the crisis.

Mandelbaum Gate was open as usual during the day, although transit was described as "almost non-existent." Another American evacuee, Mr. John A. Sabini, Consul, crossed into Israel yesterday with his family and belongings. On Sunday, Mr. Edward Bird, Vice-Consul, crossed.

LEGION OPENS FIRE IN JERUSALEM

A burst of sub-machinegun fire was opened on the Musrara quarter in Jerusalem at about 9 o'clock last night from Arab Legion posts. No one was hit.

Aim to Destroy Fedayeen Nests

The Foreign Ministry spokesman announced last night: "Israel this evening took security measures to eliminate the Egyptian fedayeen bases in the Sinai Peninsula. These units, organized some two years ago by the Egyptian Government as a part of the Egyptian Army to spread terror in Israel by acts of indiscriminate murder, mining, and sabotage, were quiescent for a few weeks on the Egyptian border during the period of Egypt's deep involvement with the maritime nations of the world on the Suez Canal issue. With the conclusion of the Security Council deliberations, Col. Nasser felt himself immediately free to authorize the fedayeen units to renew their incursions into Israel territory. Within the last week 24 Israel casualties, dead and wounded, were caused by mines planted by the fedayeen in the Southern Negev.

Following the earlier capture of two other gangs in Erez and Sde Boker respectively, today a further group was apprehended in Israel territory by the Israel security forces.

"Col. Nasser has persistently declared that despite the explicit provisions of the Israel Armistice Agreement his country remains in a state of war with Israel. He has carried on a war of limited liability. It is not Israel which has sent murder gangs into Egypt; it is Egypt which week after week and month after month, sent such gangs into Israel. It is not Israel which has sought to strangle Egypt's economy and life by illegal blockade of the Suez Canal and Akaba; it is Egypt which in its pursuit of a one-sided state of war has done these things. It is not Israel which has sought to encompass Egypt with a ring of steel with the announced and flaunted purpose at the appropriate moment of annihilating her; it is Egypt which has gloried in this effort crowned a few days ago by a Syrian-Jordan-Egyptian military command under the Egyptian commander-in-chief.

"On top of all this Col. Nasser has ignored his international obligations under the Charter of the United Nations, has flouted his duty under the Constantinople Convention of 1888 and the Security Council resolution of September 1, 1951, to permit free passage through the Suez Canal for the vessels of all nations at all times; and most recently, after the resolution of the Security Council adopted barely two weeks ago once again reaffirming the duty to afford such free passage to all, the Egyptian Government has again reiterated its determination to block the passage of Israel shipping through the Canal.

"Israel has done all in its power to achieve peace with Egypt. Its leaders have declared their readiness at any time and at any place to meet with Egyptian representatives and to discuss a settlement of the mutual problems of the two countries.

"The proffered hand of peace has always been brutally and even derisively rejected. Egypt's response has been to heighten the propaganda of hate and the hostile activities directed against the very existence of Israel.

"All this has been a central part of the comprehensive plan of subversion and imperialist expansion pursued by the Egyptian dictatorship throughout the countries of the Middle East and on the African continent.

"Israel seeks a relationship with the people of Egypt based upon mutual respect of rights, free from the threat of attack on its citizens, of blockade and of interference with its communications whether by land or sea."

Israel army units were last night reported west of El Nakhl, in the centre of the Sinai Peninsula, shown above. Other Israel forces occupied the fedayeen centres of Kuntilla, 60 kms. north of Eilat along the border, and Ras el Nakb (not indicated on the map) 10 kms. north of Eilat. *(Large-Scale Map — P. 4)*

Nakhl is located at the geographical centre of the Sinai peninsula, 100 kms. in a straight line from the Israel border. It is half way to the Suez Canal at the junction of three roads. One leads to the Gulf of Akaba, another to Nitzana in the Negev, and the third to Suez itself.

Hilly country surrounds Nakhl. From the Negev to Nakhl the terrain is mountainous. The spot itself faces a decline which then rises into more rugged country. The roads are good in dry weather.

Four Fedayeen from Gaza Caught in Negev Ambush

TEL AVIV, Monday. — Four *fedayeen* from Egypt were caught near Erez, north of the Gaza Strip last night. One of them by his accent and appearance seemed to be an Egyptian officer, but refused to give his identity.

No Egyptian officer has ever been captured among the *fedayeen* so far.

A well was blown up by infiltrators in the same area during the night.

The four were apprehended some eight kilometres from the demarcation lines.

The officer who commanded the Israel ambush told correspondents this afternoon that his men were ordered to take up ambush positions and at 3.30 a.m. a group of infiltrators was heard coming from the direction of Gaza.

When challenged, the infiltrators opened fire which was returned. When the firing died down a search revealed two *fedayeen* lying, unscathed, in the sand. Two wounded men were found nearby. Their equipment was scattered around, and included the Egyptians' standard submachinegun, the Karl Gustav, 200 rounds of ammunition per person, hand grenades and substantial quantities of explosives.

A fifth Karl Gustav indicated that the group had contained more than these four men. Tracks and blood-strains revealed that some wounded persons had escaped. It is possible that the group comprised more than six members, the Israel officer said.

The prisoner, who appeared to be an officer, was very clean, had well-groomed hands, and he wore shoes and dark woollen trousers. He said he was a soldier, but would not give his name. He would not answer any questions.

The other, unwounded, *fedaye*, who gave his name as Mustafa Osman, was a Palestinian, a native of Bureir village (now Bror Hayil) near Erez. He said he was summoned from the *fedayeen* base at midnight and hurried to headquarters in Gaza, where he and his comrades were told to obey the man in the dark trousers whose name, he said, was Yussef. They crossed the border later in the night.

Mustafa was barefooted and like the other captives, wore the dark-green *fedayeen* uniform.

Burns Says Egypt May Complain to UN Council

The Chief of Staff of the U.N. Truce Supervision Organization, Maj.-Gen. E.L.M. Burns, told an Associated Press correspondent in Jerusalem at 10 p.m. yesterday that he had no complaint from Egypt on the Israel attack. He said that he expected any such complaint would be directed straight to the U.N. Security Council.

Gen. Burns added that there were no U.N. Observers in the area where the attack was made.

By midnight the U.N. T.S.O. still had heard nothing from either side and the information they had at their disposal came from Kol Yisrael and Israel news sources. Nor had there been any mention of the events on Cairo radio.

U.S.O.M. Evacuates Dependents by Air

About 60 dependents of U.S.O.M. staff took off yesterday from Lydda Airport in a two-engined plane on their way back to the U.S.

The C-119 military transport plane's first scheduled stop was Athens. It had originally come to take away the American display at the recent Atoms for Peace Exhibition.

The American Embassy has inserted advertisements in today's press advising American citizens, who have no pressing business in Israel, to leave.

The British Embassy also announced yesterday that it was advising British subjects to leave Israel if there was no compelling reason for them to remain.

Cabinet Continues Security Talks

The Cabinet yesterday continued its discussion of foreign affairs and the security situation. The discussion will be concluded at today's meeting.

The Cabinet approved a draft law regulating the granting of compensation to invalidated former inmates of Nazi concentration camps.

Histadrut Forms Emergency Council

TEL AVIV, Monday. — At its special meeting today the Central Committee of the Va'ad Hapoel elected an emergency council. The members are: B. Reftor (Organizer), S. Blass, M. Bitan, N. Verlinsky, B. Linn and Y. Meshel.

The Central Committee also decided to postpone the meeting of the Histadrut Council from November 21, to December 5.

Because of unforeseen circumstances,

The meeting of the

Histadrut Public Health Committee

which was scheduled to take place on Wednesday, October 31, 1956, at the Vaad Hapoel,

HAS BEEN POSTPONED

A new date will be announced in invitations.

Notice To All American Citizens

Because of increased tension in the Middle East area the United States Government considers it advisable for American citizens to leave Israel without delay. It is suggested, therefore, that you place your passports in order at once, making sure that they are valid for travel, and make immediate commercial transportation arrangements for your departure. Please inform the consular section of the American Embassy, Tel Aviv, or the American Consulates in Haifa or Jerusalem of your travel plans wherever possible.

The American Ambassador

October 29, 1956.

THE JERUSALEM POST

FRIDAY, NOVEMBER 2, 1956

PRICE: 200 PRUTA
VOL. XXXII, No.8645*

MARGINAL COLUMN
By ZE'EV LAQUEUR

WHAT is going to happen next in Eastern Europe? There is no immediate danger to Russia's position. The situation is under control. But it is equally certain that the Soviet brand of Socialism is unsuitable for the more developed countries of Eastern Europe and will be gradually replaced by something different. Eastern Europe is lost not only to Stalinism, but most probably to Leninism as well. The Russian leaders should not be envied. Stalin and his heirs have tried so hard to export to Eastern Europe what they sincerely believed was the best form of government. But the peoples of Eastern Europe have not been very grateful and as a result Russia has found itself in an awkward position. It bears an uncomfortable resemblance to Czarist Russia: Shades of 1846, 1848 and 1863, of Suvorov and Paskevitch, of "Order reigns in Warsaw" and "Hungary lies at the feet of your Majesty," of Russia as the gendarme of Europe. It is all very well to talk about "counter-revolutionary elements." But it so happens that the counter-revolutionaries are students, workers and peasants, and the "revolutionaries" are mainly entrenched bureaucrats.

THE basic mistake of the Soviet leaders was their assumption that a system which may have its merits when applied in backward countries would function equally well in Europe. Stalinism was a terrorist regime, it was based on the assumption that a permanent purge would go on, that a certain percentage of the population would be killed and that the rest would be frightened into submission. Once the terror has ceased there is little to hold the system together. Its ideology is not sufficient (as the more intelligent Leninists such as G. Lukacs now admit) to hold its own in the free market of ideas — in Europe that is. In Korea, China and in Jordan the situation may be different. If the ideological ferment has not yet affected Russia the explanation is perfectly simple: Russia has had 30 years of Stalinism, the East European countries less than ten. But there cannot be the slightest doubt that in a couple of years there will be a new generation in Russia less afraid than their parents. The students will no more accept unquestioningly the dogmatism of the teachings presented to them. This ideological ferment of the nineteen sixties is bound to have the most far-reaching political consequences.

THIS does not mean the end of Marxism. It certainly does not mean the end of Socialism, which in one form or another is likely to prevail in the whole world. But it does mean that the era of Stalinist socialism, and of Leninism, a political theory and practice adapted to the Czarist Russia of 1905, is drawing to a close. It may persist for many years in Asia, but its end is in sight in Eastern Europe and the Soviet Union. It will not be an easy process, especially in the Soviet Union. There is undoubtedly a large element which believe quite correctly, from their point of view, that the regime in due to disintegrate unless a monopoly of power is maintained. And this, as Stalin has shown convincingly, can be done only through permanent terror. There may be setbacks on the long road towards democratic socialism for Europe and the Soviet leaders will probably continue to argue for years to come that they have done just now vis-a-vis the Poles) that all those who do not agree with their mistaken belief that there can be a socialist regime without political freedom, that all critics of this fatal theory which is rooted in Russia's backward past, are automatically "anti-Socialist." But despite the setbacks which are undoubtedly in store, Eastern Europe and the Soviet Union are now on the move. However strong the conservative forces to prevent this and to perpetuate the *status quo*, they are not strong enough to hold up what seems more and more to be an irresistible movement.

London, October 1956.

Cairo Arrests Five Jews for Espionage

CAIRO, Thursday (Reuter). — The Egyptian police arrested today three men and three women on charges of spying for the enemy, according to the Cairo daily, "A-Sha'ab".

Five of those detained were said to be Jews and the sixth an Egyptian named Azizi Youssef, a Finance Ministry official whose Jewish wife was said to be one of the women arrested.

Hungary Says She Will Quit Warsaw Pact

VIENNA, Thursday (UP). — Budapest Radio announced tonight that Hungary is quitting the Warsaw Pact, is declaring her neutrality and will ask for a four-power guarantee of its neutral status.

It was further stated that the Hungarian Premier, Imre Nagy, informed the Soviet Ambassador of these decisions of his Government and protested the behaviour of Soviet troops in Hungary. The Ambassador replied merely that he would inform the Soviet Government of the Premier's declaration.

At the same time, Budapest Radio said, Nagy called the U.N. Secretary-General, Mr. Dag Hammarskjold, asking that the Hungarian crisis be placed on the agenda of the General Assembly's next regular session, beginning November 12, as a priority issue for debate.

Soviets Said Returning

The West German news agency said tonight that Mr. Nagy had told reporters in Budapest that strong Soviet forces were advancing on the Hungarian capital.

The Agency's correspondent in Budapest said the Soviets had reoccupied Budapest airfields this afternoon.

Earlier today, it was announced that Premier Nagy has taken over the post of Foreign Minister, while also retaining the Premiership. It was not revealed what would happen to Hungary's previous Foreign Minister, Mr. Imre Horvath, who left Budapest this week to represent Hungary at the U.N.

These announcements were broadcast by Budapest Radio even as correspondents inside the shattered city reported that Soviet tank forces are still surrounding it.

Dominions Split On Intervention

LONDON, Thursday (Reuter) — The British Commonwealth is sharply split over the Anglo-French attack on Egypt, according to Government statements and press comment in Commonwealth countries today.

Australia, New Zealand and the Rhodesian Federation rallied to Britain's support, but India and Ceylon strongly opposed intervention in the Middle East.

Canadian public opinion as reflected in the press was mainly hostile to the Anglo-French action although some newspapers saw it as a means to end large-scale conflict in the area.

Prime Minister Nehru declared in Hyderabad today that self - respecting independent nations in Asia and Africa were not going to tolerate the aggression by the British and French in Egypt.

Mr. Nehru added, "In my experience of foreign affairs I have not come across a grosser case of naked aggression than what England and France are trying to do."

Students from six British universities today took part in demonstrations in their university towns against the British Government's policy in the Middle East.

In Oxford, two students were arrested and charged after a demonstration. Another group of 100 students from Ruskin College presented members of Parliament in London with a resolution condemning the Government's policy.

In Manchester, some 700 students marched through the streets with banners urging that there should be no war over Suez. In Birmingham, students who made a similar protest march through the city were re-routed by the police.

Iraq Declares Martial Law

BAGHDAD, Thursday (Reuter). — Iraq today declared martial law throughout the country.

Foreign Minister Burhanuddin Bashayan summoned Sir Michael Wright, the British Ambassador, and Baron Silagas, the French Chargé d'Affaires, to protest strongly against Anglo-French military operations in the Suez Canal area, it was announced.

Prime Ministers and Foreign Ministers of four member countries of the Baghdad Pact — Iraq, Turkey, Persia and Pakistan — will meet in Teheran soon to discuss the Middle East situation, Baghdad Radio announced.

The Shah of Persia and President Iskander Mirza of Pakistan will also attend the meeting.

EGYPT'S SINAI ARMY IN FULL FLIGHT

U.K., French Navies Converging on Suez

LONDON, Thursday. — British and French naval forces approached the Suez canal from north and south today after a 24-hour offensive against Egyptian military airfields by warplanes of the two nations.

The announcement said that warships were moving on the waterway from the Mediterranean and through the Gulf of Suez came from the French Defence Ministry.

Allied Forces Headquarters in Cyprus announced that carrier-borne aircraft joined island-based bombers in the Allied offensive renewed by daylight after a short overnight lull.

The Commander-in-Chief Allied Forces, General Sir Charles Keightley, told reporters allied forces had at their disposal strength to "deal severe blows in these operations. Our only hope is that we shall not need to use them."

A spokesman of the French Defence Ministry said that all operations were designed to make Egyptian airfields unusable and to destroy as many Egyptian planes on the ground as possible.

The French Ministry of Defence in Paris yesterday announced that French and British naval forces are approaching the Suez Canal. The Ministry said these forces were approaching the Canal from the north from the Mediterranean side and in the south through the gulf of Suez.

In London, the Admiralty announced that the 8,800-ton British cruiser Newfoundland sank an Egyptian frigate in the Gulf of Suez last night after it failed to stop when called upon. Survivors from the Egyptian vessel were taken aboard the Newfoundland. (An official Egyptian communique in Cairo said the sinking of a frigate, by Anglo-French aerial bombing in the Suez Canal Zone has caused the suspension of all navigation in the Canal.)

The British Air Ministry said yesterday that British Venom fighter attack planes have strafed five Egyptian airfields since dawn. Britain today claimed 14 enemy aircraft destroyed, including some Mig-15's.

Earlier it was announced that all bombers under Franco-British command which attacked Egyptian airfields Wednesday night have returned to their base. The bombers met to operation from Egyptian fighters and the Egyptian anti aircraft fire did not appear very effective, according to a French Defence Ministry spokesman.

Egypt in 'State of War' With Britain and France

An Egyptian spokesman at the U.N. Headquarters in New York said yesterday that Egypt considers herself to be "in a state of war" with Britain and France.

The statement, issued at U.N. Headquarters, said that "Britain and France have joined Israel in declaring war against Egypt." The French and British bombers are fighting side by side with Israel forces in the Sinai desert," he said.

Earlier, President Nasser told the Egyptian people in a radio broadcast that the Egyptian High Command had decided to concentrate Egyptian armed forces in Egypt proper to defend it against an invasion by French and British forces.

Nasser said that the decision not to reinforce the forces figting the Israel Defence Army in the Sinai Peninsula was made so as not to expose the main body of troops to the danger of being cut off from the mainland. General Abdul Hakim Amer, the Egyptian Chief of Staff, had been entrusted with implementing the order, he said.

Proclaiming martial law in Egypt, Nasser appointed himself Military Governor-General.

Nasser accused Britain, France and Israel of conspiring against Egypt, who was "attacked without any reason." The aggressor joint aim is the destruction of our main forces, he said. "But we shall fight and we shall not surrender," he declared.

Speaking in what were for him unusually modulated tones Nasser said that the friendly relations with France and U.K. would not be affected by the "aggressive attack against Egypt" was delivered by the Jordanian Minister for Foreign Affairs, Abdulla Rimawi, to the British and French Ambassadors in Amman.

In an address over Radio Ramallah today, King Hussein called for a stand by all Arab nations "by the side of justice" and in support of Egypt. "The present battle taking place in Egypt is not Egypt's battle alone but the battle of all Arab nations," the King said.

Last night, the Jordan cabinet held a meeting until after midnight and called a secret session of parliament to hear a government statement on the present situation to be taken. At the parliament meeting, Premier Suleiman Nabulsi reported to the parliament meeting today and the new cabinet was given an unanimous vote of confidence on its policy.

(Reuter, U.P., Radio Ramallah)

Egypt Takes Over UK, French Oil Plants

CAIRO, Thursday (UP). — The Government today took over French and British owned oil installations in Egypt.

The Minister of Commerce and Industry said that Egypt had confiscated facilities owned by the Shell Petroleum Company, the Anglo-Egyptian Oil Company and the French-Egyptian Petroleum Company.

Russia Urges Second Bandung Conference

MOSCOW, Thursday (Reuter). — Russia announced today she had called for a second Bandung conference which would demand the withdrawal of British, French and Israel troops from Egypt.

It was also officially announced in Moscow today that a letter has been sent to President Eisenhower from the Soviet Union dealing with Egypt.

Sen. George Sees Finish of NATO

AUGUSTA, Georgia, Thursday (UP). — Senator Walter F. George, President Eisenhower's personal representative to the North Atlantic Treaty Organization, said today he believed that the outbreak of the conflict in the Middle East had dealt a "death blow" to NATO.

Eden Says Action 'Police Operation'

LONDON, Thursday (Reuter). — Prime Minister Sir Anthony Eden told the Commons tonight that the Anglo-French move on Egypt "is essentially a police operation. We do not want or intend to stay one moment longer than necessary."

Sir Anthony, trying to make himself heard above the interruptions from the Opposition benches, declared that Britain does not seek to impose by force a solution of the Israel-Egypt or Suez Canal disputes. If the U.N. were willing to undertake the practical task of maintaining peace in that area, "no one would be better pleased than we," he said.

The British Government issued its ultimatum and began its military operations because "we were convinced that, if we had not, the state of war in the region would have spread over an infinitely wider area," Sir Anthony continued.

He refused to answer what he called a hypothetical question when asked by a Labour member if Britain would withdraw her troops if asked to do so by the U.N. General Assembly.

63-Vote Majority

At the end of the debate, the Government tonight defeated the Labour opposition move to censure it on military action against Egypt by 324 votes to 255 votes.

Earlier the sitting of the House was suspended for half an hour when the Labour Opposition refused to permit debate to continue on a motion to censure the Government, calling instead for an answer to the question whether the Government had declared war on Egypt.

Repeatedly the Speaker, Mr. William Morrison, tried to get the House to deal with the censure motion, which Labour had put forward on the military intervention in Egypt. But the Opposition bellowed, "No, no, no," insisting on an answer to their question.

The point pressed by the Labour benches was that if no state of war existed, then British soldiers had no protection under the Geneva Convention if they fell into Egyptian hands.

As the Prime Minister and his Cabinet walked out of the chamber following the Speaker's suspension of the sitting, they were followed by loud calls of "resign, resign" from the Labour side and equally strong cheers from the Conservative benches.

Pressed for an answer after the intermission, by the *(Continued on Page 2, Col. 3)*

2 Killed, 3 Hurt By Fedayeen Mines

ASHKELON, Thursday. — Simha Korichman, District Manager of Mekorot in the Negev, and his assistant, Shlomo Glickstein, were killed this afternoon near Ashkelon while pursuing a *fedayeen* gang the with security forces they hit a mine.

The bodies were taken to the Forensic Medicine Institute in Abu Kabir.

Mr. Korichman, 46, was a resident of Tel Aviv and leaves a wife, a seven-year-old child and a married daughter. Mr. Glickstein, 31, lived in Ashkelon, and is survived by a wife and a three-year-old daughter.

Four *fedayeen* were killed and one captured after being wounded in a battle which took place on Monday evening between Israel security forces and an enemy gang near Nitzanim, north of Ashkelon. It appears that this was the gang which carried out sabotage activities in the area the night before when a railway truck and an electric transformer were blown up.

Three Solel Boneh workers were slightly wounded yesterday afternoon near the water line connecting Tekuma and Magen in the Western Negev when their car set off a mine which had been laid by fedayeen.

AFTER MIDNIGHT

A ten-minute alert was sounded in Tel Aviv some time after midnight. There were no incidents.

Israel Forces Seal Off Gaza Strip

Israelis Bag 100 Tanks

WASHINGTON, Thursday (Reuter). — The Israel Embassy said today that Egyptian forces in the Sinai Peninsula, now in "full and disorderly retreat," were abandoning most of their equipment.

The statement, based on an official Israel Government dispatch to the Embassy, reported "complete success" of the Israel military operations in the area. It said Colonel Abdul Nasser personally ordered the general retreat.

The statement said Egyptian equipment abandoned by Israel forces included some 100 tanks, mostly of Soviet and Czech manufacture, including Stalin tanks. It added that "10 Egyptian jet planes, including Soviet MIG's, have been shot down."

Egyptian casualties — killed, wounded and captured — are estimated at 5,000. Israel casualties are extremely light, including less than 100 killed.

"Israel's Air Force is intact. Only two light reconnaissance planes (Piper Cubs) have been lost," the statement added.

TEL AVIV, Thursday. — The general collapse of the Egyptian army in the Sinai Peninsula was announced by the Army and Government spokesman, Sgan-Aluf Moshe Pearlman, this evening. The bulk of the northern half of the Sinai Peninsula was in our hands, and Egyptian troops are withdrawing in disorder towards the Suez Canal, he said.

Israel forces sealed off the Gaza Strip by taking stations which had served as the key points in the invasion of Palestine by General Allenby during the First World War.

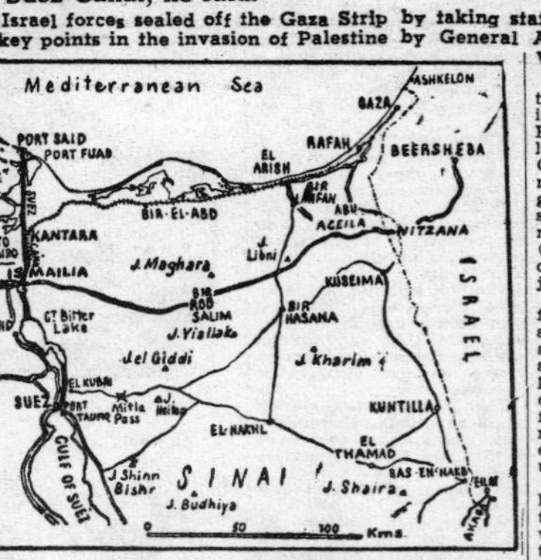

The greatest armoured battle in the campaign was raging this afternoon south of Bir Gafgafa and Bir Rodl Salem, some 70 kms. east of the Canal on the main Sinai Road. The battle was progressing satisfactorily by sunset, the spokesman said. A number of captured T-34 (Stalin) tanks were taken over by Israel crews and rejoined the battle on our side.

The bulk of the Egyptian forces in the Sinai was estimated at two divisions, one armoured brigade group and a number of armoured auxiliary units. There were "tens of thousands" of Egyptians facing the Israelis in the Sinai, he said, though Egyptian prisoners were "many," but no figures are available at present.

The Egyptians were still holding out in several pockets, the spokesman said. There was little Egyptian air activity during the day.

Leaflets in Arabic were dropped over the Gaza Strip in the evening, urging the civilian population to stay at home as the roads were being bombed. "Do not touch any weapon, stay where you are with your family. You will not be molested. The Israel Army is here to drive out the Egyptians from Palestine and will not touch you."

The casualties of the Israelis were "a minor fraction of what the Egyptians claim," the spokesman said. The only known casualty in the raid was a jet fighter hit, which managed to reach its base safely. However, the spokesman stressed, the impression that the campaign has been a walk-over, which seems to be current among civilians, was absolutely wrong.

The air battle yesterday was confined to harassment of armoured cars and other vehicles. The Air Force supported the Army's advance against a large number of tanks, armoured cars, and other vehicles in the heart of the Sinai Peninsula.

Paratroop Descent 60 Kms. East of Suez Described
By URI DAN
Military Correspondent Attached To The Airborne Force in Sinai

Quiet wind blowing into the whole length of the road. It is nine o'clock. We are witnessing a tremendous spectacle. A string of lights approaches us from three days of retreat. With the capture of Abu Aweigila yesterday, the road to El Arish and east to Ismailia were opened — the best roads in the peninsula. Rafah was captured today, and in the afternoon it was reported that our troops had reached the outskirts of El Arish.

But the main thrust, it seems, is directed westwards. The Egyptians brought in the bulk of their armoured brigade 70 kms. east of the Canal and there made their main counter-attack.

Fighting in Sinai is a tough job. The terrain is varied but high rocky mountains in the southern half of the Peninsula, and vast expanses of desert — dry, pulverised earth littered with stones.

Water is a greater problem than ammunition and food. The few accounts of front-line action that have been released speak eloquently of the toil and sweat of the troops fighting battles far greater than ever before.

The military objective of Israel, though undeclared, now *(Continued on Page 2, Col. 4)*

(Middle section) Quiet wind blowing into the desert. Ambushes and listening posts are set up. Darkness soon envelops us and we march westwards carrying our equipment on our backs. We reach a crossroads and occupy the surrounding heights. The ground is hard and rocky, but the "Hevra" dig in energetically as never before. By midnight the jeeps and supplies have been dropped. The jeeps prove a boon in picking up the packages all around.

By sunrise we are ready to face the enemy. On Tuesday at 9 a.m. the enemy appears. Our Vampires make a reconnaissance and are closely followed by two silvery Migs, who strafe us and fly away.

Two hours later our outposts report: "A big convoy is approaching from the Canal. It includes command cars and half-tracks, and carries mortars."

Mortars Mounted

We put out our own mortars in readiness behind a range of hills to stop the convoy, but we are beaten to it by two of our jet planes which appear from nowhere and wreak havoc among them. The enemy nevertheless manages to set up his mortars and starts sensing them in, but our jets come back to give them another dose. this time with rockets, too. Before dusk our planes have attacked the road from Matla, 30 kilometres east of Suez, right up to our positions. Afterwards we receive a report that burning cars line

---

Roads to El Arish, Ismailia Open
By SRAYA SHAPIRO
Jerusalem Post Correspondent

TEL AVIV, Thursday. — A decimated Egyptian Army is fighting its way out of the Sinai after three days of retreat. With the capture of Abu Aweigila yesterday, the road to El Arish and east to Ismailia were opened — the best roads in the peninsula. Rafah was captured today, and in the afternoon it was reported that our troops had reached the outskirts of El Arish.

But the main thrust, it seems, is directed westwards. The Egyptians brought in the bulk of their armoured brigade 70 kms. east of the Canal and there made their main counter-attack.

Good News

The arrivals bring us good news; it took only a few minutes to capture Kuntilla. The conquest of the Themed road junction, which is the nerve centre of Sinai, cost the enemy fifty dead and then they seized Nakhl, where the Egyptians had a fortified position — dry, pulverised earth littered with stones.

A lightning thrust took Nakhl, where dozens of vehicles and armaments, some command cars and half-tracks, and carries mortars.

The new arrivals dispersed in the plain. On Wednesday at dawn, four Vampires swoop down on us and almost immediately two Mysteres appear over them. They shoot down a couple of the Vampires, a third we see in flames heading for the Canal, followed by the fourth.

U.K. Not to Use Bases In Jordan, Libya

LONDON, Thursday. — Britain has given assurances to Jordan and Libya that British bases in those countries will not be used for operations against Egypt, the Foreign Office spokesman said here today.

Asked whether Iraq had asked for similar assurances, the spokesman pointed out that Britain does not have air or military bases in Iraq. Britain had the use of certain facilities at Iraqi bases but the position is different from that in Jordan and Libya and consequently the question of the use of bases there against Egypt "did not arise."

U.N. Assembly Votes To Debate M.E. Crisis

NEW YORK, Thursday — The emergency session of the U.N. General Assembly to debate the Middle East crisis got under way tonight after seven abstentions, to include on its agenda the U.N. resolution, vetoed in the Security Council by Britain and France, calling for a cease-fire in Egypt, the withdrawal of Israel troops and non-interference in the area by other states. The abstaining voters were New Zealand, Turkey, the Netherlands, Australia, South Africa, Canada and Israel.

It was the Assembly's first emergency session in its 11-year history.

Peking Supports Hungarians, Poles

TOKYO, Thursday (UP). — China announced her wholehearted support for the Hungarian and Polish demands for independence, democracy and equality, according to Peking Radio monitored here.

Jordan Severs Ties with France

AMMAN, Thursday. — Jordan has severed diplomatic relations with France and will withdraw her ambassador and staff from Paris, it was announced today. Jordan's official protest against the

Iraq Declares Martial Law
(see above)

THE JERUSALEM POST

SUNDAY
NOVEMBER 4, 1956

PRICE: 120 PRUTA
VOL. XXXII, No. 8646

Nagy Forms New All-Party Gov't

BUDAPEST, Saturday. — Premier Imre Nagy formed a new Government today and opened negotiations with Russia on withdrawing the Red Army from Hungary. The new Government is said to contain all major Hungarian parties and is "truly representative."

These parties include the Conservative Smallholders Party, the Social Democrats, the Liberal Peasants Party and the Communists, who this week changed their name to the Socialist Workers Party.

With the formation of the new Cabinet, it was announced that negotiations had been opened with a Soviet military mission on the withdrawal of the Red Army. The Soviet delegates consiste of three Russian generals and four colonels.

There were no reports of fighting today although news of Soviet troop movements was widespread.

In New York, the U.N. Security Council met today, over the objections of Russia, to discuss the situation in strife-torn Hungary.

The U.S. delegate, Mr. John Cabot Lodge, said, "We must give honest consideration to what the U.N. can do that will help the brave Hungarian people in their struggle for freedom."

The use of Soviet armies' might against the Hungarians was "shocking to the whole world." He said Hungarians had earned the "admiration and respect of all free peoples."

He suggested that the Secretary-General, Mr. Dag Hammarskjold, communicate with the Budapest Government so that members could be sure the Hungarian delegate here was "truly representative."

Dr. Carlos Blanco, of Cuba, said he could not believe that any member would resist the demands of the Hungarian people for self-determination. He recalled that the Soviet delegate yesterday spoke eloquently during the Middle East debate of the right of all people to choose their own governments and against armed intervention by foreign powers.

Dr. Blanco suggested a resolution to appeal immediately to Moscow to withdraw Soviet troops from Hungarian territory; to reiterate the right of the Hungarian people to determine by free elections the type of government they wanted; and to establish a Commission of the Council to supervise and see that these measures were carried out.

US Tempts Hungary With $20m. Aid

WASHINGTON, Saturday (Reuter)). — The U.S. yesterday offered an initial allocation of $20m.-worth of food and medical supplies to Hungary.

The White House Press Secretary, Mr. James Hagerty, said the offer would be transmitted immediately to the Hungarian Government. President Eisenhower took the final decision to make this offer at a meeting yesterday afternoon.

The U.S. protested to Russia that dependents of American legation officials being evacuated from Budapest were turned back at the Austrian-Hungarian border at Soviet military road blocks yesterday.

Russian troops armed with tommyguns turned back four American mothers and 10 children for the second straight day today when the dependents of U.S. Legation personnel in Budapest tried to reach haven in Austria.

A State Department spokesman said that the Depuy Under-Secretary of State, Mr. Robert Murphy, summoned the Soveit Ambassador, Mr. Georgi Zarubin, and "protested energetically against the interference with American official personnel."

DULLES TAKEN TO HOSPITAL

WASHINGTON, Saturday (Reuter). — Mr. John Foster Dulles, Secretary of State, entered the Walter Reed Army Hospital early today and doctors reported that he might be suffering from appendicitis.

The State Department said 68-year-old Mr. Dulles "is resting comfortably," and was carrying on some of his work by telephone from his hospital bed. The Under-Secretary of State, Mr. Herbert Hoover, Jr., was in charge at the State Department as Acting Secretary.

A later announcement said that Mr. Dulles would have an immediate operation for acute appendicitis.

Dulles Would Like Bonn To Halt Reparations

WASHINGTON, Saturday (INA).—The State Department has notified West Germany that the U.S. Government would take a sympathetic view if Germany was to withhold reparations shipments to Israel. This was made known here yesterday by State Department sources.

Such a move would be seen by the State Department as clearly in spirit with the U.N. General Assembly resolution adopted on Thursday night and would be consistent with the efforts of the international community to restrain Israel.

It was made known that earlier this week the matter had been discussed in a meeting between the German Ambassador, Mr. Heinz Krekeler, and Mr. Robert Murphy, Deputy Under Secretary of State.

Eden Promises Israel Withdrawal

LONDON, Saturday (Reuter). Prime Minister Sir Anthony Eden in a nation-wide broadcast tonight said, "Once British and French forces have occupied the key points on the Canal, the Government will the Government will ensure that the Israel forces withdraw from Egyptian territory.

"I have no doubt that that is their intention, but they will not do so unless we are there to keep the peace, to give the necessary guarantee and prevent a repetition of these events."

CABINET MEETS

The Cabinet met yesterday to discuss the U.N. General Assembly resolution and the security situation.

Fedayeen Make Last Attacks

REHOVOT, Saturday. — The remnants of the *fedayeen* gangs fleeing from Gaza cimmitted acts of sabotage on Friday and tonight, in the Rehovot area.

A woman member of Kibbutz Givat Brenner was knifed three times early tonight by an assailant who jumped out of a wood near the kibbutz school. He tried to drag her away and when she flashed her torch he stabbed her. She is being treated for her injuries at the hospital.

The railway line from Tel Aviv to Beersheba was blown up near Kfar Yavneh on Friday evening, but workers soon came to repair it. Telephone lines were also cut in the vicinity. Police and defence forces have gone to comb the whole area for *fedayeen*.

The Army spokesman announced that on Friday night a number of shots were fired on a bus on the Wadi Ara road. A Border Police car which rushed to the place hit a mine. There were no casualties.

On Thursday night a considerable number of *fedayeen* bands were active in the Negev, the spokesman said. A number of vehicles were attacked, and waterlines were blown up.

Uri Osen, aged 23, a member of Kibbutz Erez died today from wounds sustained when his car hit a mine laid by *fedayeen* on Thursday last. He leaves a pregnant wife.

Osen is the third victim of this attack. The other two, Simha Korichman and Shlomo Glickstein, were killed instantly.

Battle for Gaza— Edgar Hirshbain, photographer of The Jerusalem Post, went into action with his camera along with Israel troops on Friday morning in their attack on Gaza. Top photo shows Israelis advancing on strongpoint at Al Mashahira, north of Gaza. Smoke rises from exploding Israel mortars. After the action was over, Hirshbain took picture (below) of Egyptians captured at the outpost. (See other photos on Page 3.) The Post photographer was forced to take cover behind a tank when cross-fire was opened up on Army jeep in which he was riding.

SINAI BATTLE WON

TEL AVIV, Saturday. — The Sinai Campaign is virtually over. Israel troops are within sight of the Suez Canal. In the South, the capture of the village, Tor, on the Gulf of Suez, 250 kilometres south of the Canal on the western banks of the peninsula, was announced this morning.

The two islands which block the Tiran straits are included in the term "the whole of the peninsula" used by the army spokesman tonight, although their occupation was not yet officially announced today.

The campaign was won by brilliant planning and hard hitting. As it now emerges, the plan consisted of performing the obvious, that is, in opening the three or four available roads across the Peninsula as quickly as possible. The campaign started rather dramatically by parachuting a force into the middle of the desert, west of el-Nakhle last Monday. After dark, fighting started at two points on the Southern border, which opened the way for two columns moving along most difficult roads.

The real problem was to open the middle road, the rest of all the available routes across Sinai. It was tackled by taking Kuseima first and moving to the El-Ageila crossroads. Very tough opposition was encountered in this place, the Egyptian troops having been lucky in having a good commanding officer who reminded one of Major El-Taha of Faluja fame.

The Egyptians here did not succeed in holding the crossroads, but managed to concentrate on a range which was difficult to take.

"Obviously, they were led by some officers who wished to die heroes. We did our best to fulfil their wish," as an Israel officer said yesterday. The Abu-Ageila pocket did not capitulate until yesterday.

An Israel column pushing northwards, captured El Arish without much opposition. The column moving to the east was halted for a day by the Egyptian armoured brigade, which gave it a battle near Bir Gafgafa. According to preliminary reports, it was a most remarkable battle which will be studied in the military academies not only of Israel, a G.H.Q. officer said.

On Thursday night, the Egyptians received a general order to withdraw. This they did in the most disorderly fashion. The task of the Israel forces was then to overcome them and destroy as much of the army as possible.

But it seems that the bulk of the military stores the Egyptians had in the Sinai have fallen ino Israel hands. It was worth tens of millions of dollars, according to a wild estimate. It included everything a modern army should have in order to stage a large attack: tanks, guns, ammunition, food. Most of the supply dumps were near the Israel frontier, mainly in Rafa and El Arish.

The presence of these enormous dumps of military supplies serves as the best proof of Egypt's preparations for the war on Israel. It is now clear beyond doubt, even without waiting for the publication of the many documents which may be found to support this, that the Egyptian attack on Israel was a matter of short delay. It was, indeed, high time for Israel to strike. If she had waited, the world would have been appalled and condemned Egypt for a dastardly attack, but that would hardly have helped, and Israel wants to live.

Two Tiran Islands Next to Fall

TEL AVIV, Saturday. — The Government and Army spokesman said this evening that the whole of the Sinai Peninsula is "or shortly will be" occupied by the Israel Army. This included the two Tiran islands blocking the entrance to the Gulf of Akaba, the spokesman said.

Israel troops, moving along three fairly parallel roads across the Peninsula, have halted some 15 kilometres from the Suez Canal, the spokesman added. "I am sure reconnaissance patrois have come up to the Canal itself," he said.

There was no Egyptian air activity today. Asked if the Government intended to keep the troops one kilometre nearer the Canal than the 16 kilometres mentioned in the Anglo-French ultimatum, the spokesman said he did not know.

The number of Israel casualties in the campaign may be announced in a day or two. The only indication of the number of enemy prisoners was that they were "thousands." Comparatively few officers were among them, and it appears from what Egyptian soldiers said that the bulk of the officers fled as quickly as they could, leaving their troops behind.

Arabic "Mein Kampf"

About 100 tanks and self-propelled guns have been taken as booty. They were mostly T-34's, with a number of Shermans among them. The self-propelled guns were mostly SU 100's (Russian-made). The number of vehicles of various makes runs into hundreds. Very large dumps of ammunition were discovered near the frontier.

Among the standard equipment of the Egyptian officers captured there was a two volume paper-back edition in Arabic of Hitler's "Mein Kampf."

Nasser Says Army Has Left Sinai

CAIRO, Saturday (UP).— Abdul Nasser announced today that Egyptian forces had completed their withdrawal from the Sinai Peninsula, leaving only suicide commandos behind.

Meanwhile, in London, British Defence Minister, Mr. Anthony Head, said that latest reports "indicated that Egyptian forces were withdrawing in some disorder in Kantara and Suez, and that some have reached the Canal."

500 Cairo Jews Said Arrested

More than 500 Jews have been rounded up by the Egyptian authorities in Cairo and its suburbs and sent to concentration camps, Beirut Radio reported on Friday. The Jews were said to be "well-known for their Zionist sympathies."

The same source declared that 450 British technicians who remained in Egypt to tend the Suez Canal Zone military bases after the British evacuation, were also arrested and sent to detention camps.

More than 100 British firms and some 30 French businesses registered in Egypt have been confiscated and their assets placed under the control of the Egyptian Government, the Radio reported.

Nutting Quits As Minister of State

LONDON, Saturday (Reuter). —Mr. Anthony Nutting, Minister of State at the Foreign Office, has resigned because he disagrees with the policy of the Conservative Government on Egypt.

Two days ago Mr. Nutting denied reports that he was going to resign. Nutting, 36, became Minister of State two years ago — then the youngest-ever man to hold the post of second in command at the Foreign Office.

In that capacity he negotiated the 1954 agreement with Egypt on the British evacuation of the Suez Canal Zone base. He was Foreign Under-Secretary from the age of 31.

Iraq Orders Army Into Jordan

The Iraqi Government yesterday ordered its troops to enter Jordan immediately to reinforce the Arab Legion against a possible Israel attack.

The order followed an urgent request from King Hussein of Jordan, it was reliably learned in Baghdad. The troops would come under the orders of the Jordan Commander-in-Chief, who would dispose of them according to his requirements.

According to Reuter correspondent Ronald Batchelor, who left Jordan for Syria with a U.N. convoy on Friday, Syrian tanks were moving over the border in a steady stream.

Meanwhile, the Syrian Embassy in Washington informed the U.S. Government on Friday that Syria had "decided to implement immediately the joint Egyptian-Syrian defence pact."

The note said that the Syrian forces are now under the command of the Egyptian Chief-of-Staff, General Abdul Hakim Amer. Syria's armed forces "and all her resources are from this moment on devoted to the common cause," it concluded.

In Damascus, Acting Foreign Minister Khalil Kallas announced yesterday that Syria has broken off consular relations with Britain and France.

The Soviet President, Marshal Klementi Voroshilov, told President Kuwatly of Syria yesterday in Moscow that Russia is "ready to supply the necessary assistance to help Syria surmount the vestiges of colonialism and reinforce its independence."

Speaking at a reception for the Syrian President, who cut short his visit to the Russian capital, Marshal Voroshilov said that "aggression against Egypt by one of the founders of the Baghdad Pact proves once again that the alliance is an aggressive bloc."

The Old City daily "Falastin" reported on Friday that the Arab Legion had taken over Mafrak Airport near the Iraqi border. Earlier, the paper had reported that the R.A.F. had evacuated Amman Military Airport. *(Reuter, UP)*

Holland to 'Protect' Israel P.o.W.'s

THE HAGUE, Saturday (UP) — The Netherlands will act as "protecting nation" for Israel prisoners-of-war in Egypt, it was officially announced here this afternoon.

I.P.C. Stops Pumping Oil Through Syria

BAGHDAD, Saturday (Reuter). — The Iraq Petroleum Company today suspended the pumping of crude oil through Syria, a company spokesman announced here. He said that owing to a breakdown in the company's transport between Iraq and Syria it was thought wise under present circumstances to stop pumping from Iraq to Mediterranean seaports through Syrian territory.

An I.P.C. spokesman said tonight he had received unconfirmed reports that three of the Company's pumping stations in Syria had been blown up.

Eden: We'll Stop If U.N. Force Enters

LONDON, Saturday (Reuter). — Sir Anthony Eden told an extraordinary session of the House of Commons today that Britain has informed the United Nations she will willingly stop military action in Egypt if the U.N. will put in a force to keep peace between Egypt and Israel. A condition will be that both Egypt and Israel agree to accept a U.N. force to keep the peace. A third condition was that until the U.N. force is constituted, both Israel and Egypt would agree to accept forthwith limited detachments of Anglo-French troops to be stationed between the combatants.

The Prime Minister said he had been in consultation with the governments of Australia and New Zealand. "I have good reason to believe that these governments will welcome my statement" he said. The substance of the statement had also been communicated to Canada, the United States, and the United Nations Secretary-General.

Sir Anthony began by saying that this sitting of the Commons had been arranged so that he could make a statement on the reply Britain proposed to send to the resolution of the U.N. Assembly.

The House will first recall the statement which I made in the course of my speech on November 1, when I said that the first and urgent task is to separate the combatants and to stabilize the position. That is our purpose. If the U.N. were then willing to take over the official task of maintaining peace in the area nobody would have been better pleased than I.

"Since that statement was made I have had consultations in London with the French Foreign Minister. As a result the British and French Governments are sending the following reply to the resolution of the U.N. General Assembly:

The British and French Governments have given careful consideration to the resolution passed by the General Assembly on November 2.

They maintain the view that police action must be carried through urgently to stop hostilities which are now threat-

(Continued on Page 3, Col. 2)

AFTER MIDNIGHT

The United States warned Britain and France that they must not use against Egypt arms provided by the United States under military aid agreements.

The Egyptian Embassy in Bonn issued an Egyptian Government statement declaring that war was raging between Egypt and Britain and France, not between Egypt and Israel.

France Elated by Israel Victory

By MAURICE CARR, Jerusalem Post Correspondent

PARIS, Saturday. — Franco-British determination to bring their military move into the Suez Canal to a successful and speedy conclusion remains "absolute," it was authoritatively learned here. Nothing happening at the U.N. or elsewhere in the diplomatic sphere can change that determination, it was said.

A team of technicians and appropriate equipment is already being assembled for the clearance of the blocked Canal with a minimum of delay as soon as the occupation of the Canal Zone is completed. It is intended that the French and British forces will serve as the spearhead and nucleus of future U.N. police, paving the way for international control of the Canal and an Israel-Arab peace settlement.

Expressing "very great satisfaction" with the brilliantly successful Israel operations, the same sources pointed out that the apparent slowness of the Franco-British landing is due to the fact that for reasons of international propriety it was impossible to embark troops, let alone order troopships to sail, before the expiration of the ultimatum.

The Egyptian Air Force is described as "virtually dead." Its installations are destroyed, rendering Egyptian night flights impossible, and by day the Egyptians are capable at most of individual sorties, but not of coherent actions. The first phase of the Franco-British campaign is regarded as successfully terminated.

(An Israel Embassy spokesman in Paris reported the Army had got within 15 kilometres of the Suez Canal at one point.

(He also said Israel had taken about 15,000 Egyptian prisoners in the Sinai Peninsula and captured about 100 tanks, 500 guns of various calibres and considerable stocks of munitions and petrol. Final figures had not yet been established.)

The Quai d'Orsay officially refuses to take a tragic view of the American attitude, underlining the more positive aspects of Eisenhower's television address, notably his allusion to friendship for Britain and France and recognition of Israel's action under serious provocation.

The French press, however, is exceedingly critical of the U.S. attitude. Thus, Roger Massip, diplomatic editor of the Conservative "Figaro." writes: "Mr. Dulles has deliberately permitted aggravation of the menace which has pressed on Israel since the accession of the military dictatorship in Cairo."

Assembly Meets On U.K.-France Rebuff

NEW YORK, Saturday. — The United Nations General Assembly will meet in emergency session at 3 a.m. Israel time tomorrow, Sunday.

A "new approach" to a solution in the Middle East is contained in two separate resolutions which will be submitted to the General Assembly by the U.S. on the Israel-Arab dispute and on Suez, the White House announced.

Egypt asked for an urgent meeting to discuss the Anglo-French rejection of the Assembly's call for a Middle East cease-fire. The Egyptian request was supported by the Asian-African group.

The British and French qualified rejection of the United Nations cease-fire demand today was expected to spur moves by the Arab and Asian nations to have the Assembly censure the two Western Powers, impose sanctions and possibly expel them from the United Nations.

In advance of today's announcements from London and Paris most of these states had been cool towards the idea of setting up a United Nationh force to keep peace in the Middle East.

France and Britain said today they will halt their military operations against Egypt only when Israel and Egypt accept intervention of a United Nations police force until peace is achieved and a "satisfactory arrangement" for the Suez Canal arrived at.

Landing in Canal Expected

LONDON, Saturday (Reuter). — British and French amphibious landings at each end of the Suez Canal were expected this weekend after Britain and France jointly reaffirmed their determination to go ahead with their "police action" in Egypt.

A junior Minister in the Government declared in a public speech at Wolverhampton last night that within a few hours British and French troops would be occupying territory in the Suez Canal Zone. But spokesmen for the Prime Minister and the Ministry of Defence both declined to comment on the speech by Mr. Enoch Powell, Parliamentary Secretary to the Ministry of Housing.

Mr. Anthony Head, the Minister of Defence, told the House of Commons today that no landing had taken place so far by the Anglo-French forces.

He said reports indicated that Egyptian forces were withdrawing in some disorder to Kantara and Suez. There were also indications that some had reached the Canal area. He added that the Egyptians had sunk four block ships so far in the Port Said approach to the Suez Canal.

Mr. Head reported that "Egyptian armoured units are moving from the Delta to the Canal area."

He reported that the plan to neutralize the Egypian Air Force had been largely accomplished by means of bombing atacks on airfields by Valiant and Canberra jet bombers followed by low-level ground attacks.

The plan was devised to achieve maximum destruction of Egyptian aircraft with the minimum loss of Egyptian life. "A very high degree of accuracy was achieved."

He said that after this phase, attacks were being switched to other purely military targets, particularly armour, and successful attacks had been made in the past 24 hours. Many hundreds of sorties were flown. He added that repeated warnings had been given to the Egyptian civil population to keep away from purely military installations and airfields.

Allied Air Forces suffered their first casualty in the Middle East conflict today when a Royal Air Force "Venom" failed to return from dawn strikes against Egyptian military objectives.

Allied Headquarters in Nicosia said a heavy attack by R.A.F. Valiant and Canberra jet bombers from Cyprus and Malta pin-pointed Luxor Airfield on the Nile about 400 miles south of Cairo. An indefinite night curfew has been imposed on all Cyprus main towns as from tonight following a fresh outbreak of bomb incidents on the island.

On Friday British Canberra bombers attacked Cairo Radio's transmitters.

A French Defence Ministry spokesman said on Friday that 105 Egyptian planes were believed destroyed or badly damaged.

A British Ministry of Defence communique said on Friday night that French naval aircraft attacked and set on fire an Egyptian destroyer of the Russian "Skoryi" class off Alexandria on Thursday morning. The "Skoryi" class destroyers are of 3,000 tons.

Develop Israel with Israel Bonds

THE JERUSALEM POST

FRIDAY
MARCH 8, 1957

8 Pages

PRICE: 200 PRUTA
VOL.XXXIII, No.8755*

Every 25-30 minutes on the Tel Aviv-Haifa route
by a Direct
EGGED BUS
No advance bookings.
No additional payment.

MARGINAL COLUMN

By ELIEZER LIVNEH

ONE of the more spectacular developments resulting from the failure of the British Suez venture is the complete withdrawal of Britain from the Hashemite Kingdom of Jordan. The exhilaration felt by the Amman crowds and the more short-sighted politicians at the abrogation of the British-Jordanian treaty may not be fully shared by the young King and the Hashemite dynasty in general. It is surely no accident that the cancellation of the treaty was immediately followed by a carefully laid plot to replace the Hashemite monarchy by a republic. The "republicans" did not succeed this time, but it is an omen. Everybody knows who these ardent republicans are and where they look for help, counsel and encouragement. A republican regime in Amman may be no more than a brief interval before the "*Anschluss*" with Egypt, or possibly Syria, under some federal cover. What such a development portends is abundantly clear: a general free-for-all, with every one of Jordan's Arab neighbours doing his best (or his worst) to get his share of the spoils. And the despoiled will be alone responsible for its plight.

THINGS look better from the British angle. During the last two decades Britain attempted a task in the Middle East that was beyond her powers. The U.K. was (and is) vitally interested in the Arabian oil and tried to safeguard her interests by relying on her diminishing imperial powers. The discrepancy between needs and means tended in practice to make Whitehall dependent on the whims and pressures of diverse Arab governments. This precluded any constructive, imaginative and non-partisan British contribution to the solution of Middle Eastern problems. It was a perpetual retreat; orderly but quite hopeless. Old half-friends turned into sullen and open enemies. New friends were not sought and indeed avoided. The status and stature of Britain in this part of the world suffered both politically and morally. The short-lived experiment to ride the American buffalo down the old imperial trails ended in a complete failure. The buffalo threw off its hesitant rider and went grazing in the well prepared pastures on its own account.

THE constructive answer to this basically unhealthy situation was to pool the British potentialities into a common European endeavour. Free Europe depends on Mid-Eastern oil no less than Britain, and in future will do so even more. Both the short-range interests and the more distant aims of Britain and free Europe are identical: to prevent the exclusive and unfettered Arabian dominion over those oil resources and their transportation, upon which the existence of European civilization and freedom may depend until atomic power (or some other unforeseen fount of energy) replaces Middle Eastern oil. Some form of European co-responsibility *vis-a-vis* the Arabian oil — developed by European initiative, knowledge, capital and skill — is imperative unless Europe resigns itself to being ruthlessly exploited, pressured and bullied, both financially and politically, by a chequered set of irresponsible and megalomanic Arab rulers.

A MERGER of British and European policies in the Middle East was for long obstructed by the hopes based upon the British positions in Arabian lands, although those positions turned out to be more in the nature of liabilities rather than assets. Still, their sentimental value was immense. They helped preserve an illusion that Britain might be able to safeguard its vital and legitimate oil interests through its own power. The Anglo-Egyptian Suez agreement, the Anglo-Jordanian treaty and various Anglo-Iraqi entanglements performed this dubious role; obstructing and befogging the good and reliable road towards European solidarity both at home and in the Middle East. Even Sir Winston Churchill was not free from this delusion when he helped to undermine French prestige in the Levant in 1945. The chickens are coming home to roost. Now the Egyptian and Jordanian positions are gone. If Britain succeeds in getting rid of her exclusive Iraqi "responsibilities" she will leave behind an assemblage of shaky and lonely make-believe castles — in order to stage a come-back at the head of a powerful European bloc, largely independent of American pressures and collusions. A wise tactical retreat in due time is probably a condition for a broad strategic advance on the royal road of European solidarity.

Jerusalem, March 8.

Congress Backs Ike to Use Force in M-E

WASHINGTON, Thursday (Reuter). — The House of Representatives today passed and sent to President Eisenhower a resolution declaring that the U.S. was willing to resist possible Communist aggression in the Middle East by force if necessary.

The House acted by quickly adopting the Senate version of the resolution which Mr. Eisenhower sought on an urgent basis two months ago. The Senate finally passed the bill on Tuesday night 72 to 19.

The measure also gives Mr. Eisenhower great discretion in sending $200m. in military and economic aid in the area between now and July 1.

The House Democratic leader, Rep. John McCormack, said it was up to Mr. Eisenhower to carry out the Middle East resolution.

"It's his responsibility," Mr. McCormack said, adding, "The Democratic control of Congress has given to the country and to the free world leadership of an outstanding and courageous nature. Let us hope the President, who is the sole authority of foreign affairs under our form of Government, will proceed affirmatively with sound judgment and with courage."

No U.S. Pledge To Israel, Syria Told

DAMASCUS, Thursday. — American Ambassador James Moose yesterday called on Premier Sabri Assali to assure him that the U.S. has given no pledge or promise to Israel in return for her withdrawal from the Gaza Strip and the Gulf of Akaba, reliable sources said today.

Assali said relations would not be resumed with Britain until the latter compensated Egypt for damage suffered through her "aggression."

De Valera Wins Eire Elections

DUBLIN, Thursday (Reuter). — Mr. Eramon De Valera's Fianna Fail Party today won the Irish Republic's general election.

With 78 seats in the Dail (parliament) the 74-year-old former revolutionary leader was assured of a workable majority.

The declared intention of four Sinn Fein members to boycott the Dail reduces effective membership to 143 — a figure which gives absolute power to any party with 72 or more seats.

Sinn Fein is the political wing of the outlawed Irish Republican Army which uses violence in its campaign for the unity of Eire with Northern Ireland.

With Finna Fail holding 78 seats, the position of the other parties was, Fine Grel 36, Labour 12, Farmers, three, Sinn Fein, four, Independents, nine, Republicans, one.

De Valera, once jailed by Britain during Ireland's fight for independence, fought the present election on the argument that single party government was better than a coalition for solving the country's economic problems. These include an unemployment figure of 92,000 and a high rate of migration to Britain.

De Valera had been in opposition for three years to the retiring Government, a coalition led by Mr. John Costello of the Fine Grel Party. His victory means he will again be Prime Minister, a role he has occupied for about 20 of the last 25 years.

Meanwhile, in Derrylin, Northern Ireland, last night raiders of the I.R.A. fought a half-hour gun battle with police.

The objective of the raiders was the village police station, and a constable was wounded in the action. The I.R.A. men, armed with sten guns, were reported to have crossed the border from the Irish Republic.

NARROW GOV'T WIN IN THAI ELECTIONS

BANGKOK, Thursday (Reuter). — Final results in Thailand's first national elections held on February 26 showed the Government won a small but absolute majority in the National Assembly.

The Government party won 85 of the 160 seats contested. The Government nominates a further 160 seats in the Assembly. A Government spokesman said today the state of emergency which was proclaimed on March 2 is likely to be lifted in the next few days.

AFTER MIDNIGHT

The death occurred in Tel Aviv yesterday of Rabbi M. Levene, aged 91. He was the grandfather of Mr. Herman Wouk, noted American author of "The Cain Mutiny," who visited Israel in April, 1955.

Ike: U.S. Will Use Tiran As Int'l Route

WASHINGTON, Thursday. — President Eisenhower, at his news conference today, said that the U.S. is prepared to declare and use the Straits of Tiran, as an international waterway.

At the same time, the President said that he thought that the outlook for peace in the Middle East was brighter. He went into no details.

He did say, however, that the U.N. has not yet come to grips with the basic problems which disturb the peace of that area. The underlying difficulties, by which he apparently referred to the long-standing Israel-Arab dispute, must be solved, he declared.

Mr. Eisenhower made it clear that he had told King Saud of Saudi Arabia that the Arab world must learn to live with Israel. When asked whether he had told Saud that "Israel is here to stay," Mr. Eisenhower replied that ever since 1948 he has told everyone he talked with about the situation that it must be recognized that Israel is an historical fact and her problems must be dealt with.

The President's remark about a brighter outlook in the Middle East came at the beginning of his conference when he was asked whether he intended to go to the south-western U.S. for relief of a persistent cough. He replied that he was being kept in Washington by the Middle East situation — which, however, had brightened — as well as by Secretary of State Dulles' trip to Australia for the SEATO Council meeting, and Vice-President Richard M. Nixon's tour of Africa.

He declined to give a personal appraisal of the situation in the Middle East, particularly as it related to Israel and Egypt. He would merely say that from the beginning he and Secretary of State Dulles had insisted that the mere solution of one or two of the preliminary phases of problems brought on since last July 26 (when Egypt nationalized the Suez Canal Company) would not solve the underlying cause of the difficulty. *(UP, Reuter)*

B-G REPLIES

The U.S. Ambassador, Mr. Edward B. Lawson, called on the Prime Minister in Jerusalem yesterday evening to receive Mr. Ben-Gurion's reply to President Eisenhower's letter to him of last Saturday.

Czechs Sell Egyptian Cotton 10% Cheaper

BONN, Thursday (INA).— A West German official has given confirmation that his country is buying Egyptian cotton from Soviet bloc countries at 10 per cent less than the normal Egyptian price.

Dr. Albert Degener, Secretary-General of the German-Egyptian Chamber of Commerce, said in Cairo that the Czechs are reselling to West Germany Egyptian cotton that they had got in exchange for arms. He said that this policy has seriously interfered with West German-Egyptian trade and has contributed to a big trade imbalance in West Germany's favour.

China Allows Abortion To Control Population

HONG KONG, Thursday (Reuter). — It was announced in Peking today that China is to legalize abortion and sterilization to keep her population of over 600 million people within bonds.

The New China News Agency quoted Mrs. Lee Teh-chuan, Health Minister, who in a speech to a Chinese Peoples Political Consultative Conference made a strong plea for birth control and planned families to improve welfare and the health of the people. From now on these operations would be performed on request without restriction, she said.

The Chinese Health Minister said that if China's population increase is not planned "we will not be able to get rid of poverty in a short period and become prosperous and strong."

She predicted a population of 700 million in China by 1962, an addition of 15 million yearly, if means are not urgently taken to control this increase. China could never satisfy the needs of such a large population, she added.

Cairo Sabotage of Suez Canal Opening Now Urgent Issue

By GEORGE LICHTHEIM, Jerusalem Post Correspondent

LONDON, Thursday. — Petrol rationing is unlikely to be ended until the Canal has been reopened, and this is now becoming the most urgent issue between Egypt and the Western powers, especially Britain.

There is considerable anger in Parliament and elsewhere over the continued Egyptian sabotage of the Canal clearance operations. This sentiment erupted yesterday at question time and is reflected in today's press, which gives prominence to the Egyptian refusal to let the U.N. salvage team proceed with its work.

There is also skepticism over the statement made by the U.S. Secretary of State, Mr. John Foster Dulles, to the effect that the Canal could be opened within 10 days, a doubt apparently shared by the U.N. officer in charge of the clearance operations, Gen. Raymond Wheeler.

Oil Flow Resumption

Meanwhile, some satisfaction is expressed here at reports from Baghdad and Damascus suggesting that an emergency oil flow at a rate of 11 million tons annually could be secured through Iraq Petroleum Company pipelines by next week, rather less than half the total before Syrian pumping stations were destroyed, but enough to ease the petrol situation and reduce costly dollar imports from the Western hemisphere. The major oil companies are expected to divert some tankers from the Cape or Western hemisphere routes to take advantage of the Syrian flow. A large part of the supplies from Banias is likely to go to Mediterranean ports, such as Marseilles, thus effecting a considerable tanker saving.

As far as Suez is concerned, the best guess here is that if the Egyptians prove more cooperative, the Canal may be operative for normal traffic by the month's end. No progress has been made on an interim arrangement on Canal fees proposed to Egypt through the U.N. Secretary-General, Mr. Dag Hammarskjold, by the U.S., Britain, France and Norway last month, and talks are now progressing between the Western governments concerned over a common attitude to be adopted if the Egyptians prove uncompromising.

In the meantime, long term considerations are coming into play. City commentators today drew attention to the lessons learned by Europe in recent months, chief of which is that dependence on Middle East oil must be lessened.

While there is emphasis on the need for new supply lines, such as a pipeline through Turkey, there is a growing tendency to stress the advantage of building giant tankers which will not only make the Cape route almost competitive with the Canal route, but will also make the Atlantic Ocean route considerably cheaper than either Cape or Suez traffic.

Promising Oil Source

This leads to Canada as the most promising source of oil for Europe. An expert is quoted in today's "Manchester Guardian" as stating that the total cost incurred in carrying oil from Alberta to Europe need not be greater than the cost of transporting Persian Gulf oil via the Cape.

There is reason to believe that this is more than just talk by an individual, and that the Canadian Government's attitude in recent months has had some bearing upon the whole question of reducing Europe's dependence on Middle Eastern suppliers.

GHANA TO JOIN U.N. TODAY

UNITED NATIONS, Thursday (Reuter). — The Security Council today unanimously approved Ghana's application for admission as the 81st member of the U.N.

The Assembly is expected to vote likewise tomorrow.

The formal application was presented yesterday, immediately after the former Gold Coast Colony, now a British Dominion, acquired independence.

The application was sponsored by Britain and Australia.

Italian Gov't Crisis Again Threatened

ROME, Thursday (Reuter).— The Secretary of the Italian Socialist Democratic Party, Mr. Matteo Matteotti, today tendered his resignation and demanded that the Party leave the coalition Government. The move brought the Government to the verge of a new crisis after it had received a confidence vote in Parliament last week with a narrow majority.

Mr. Matteotti presented his resignation to a meeting of the party's directorate which is convening again tonight to decide whether to accept it.

Israel to Send Chartered Ship Through Suez

Post Diplomatic Correspondent

The question of freedom of passage for Israel ships through the Suez Canal will be put to the test next month —always providing the waterway is made ready for use again by that time—when the s.s Mars, a 3,500 ton foreign vessel under charter to the Zim Navigation Company, will leave Haifa for Burma via the Suez Canal.

In the negotiations and discussions which followed the Sinai Campaign during the past four months, the issue of freedom of passage for Israel ships through the Suez Canal was not directly raised by Israel.

The view taken here was that the legal right of ships bound for or from Israel whether of foreign register, under charter to her, or flying the Israel flag is fully established both by the Constantinople Convention of 1888 and the resolution passed by the Security Council in September 1951.

Cairo Opens Canal For Small Ships

CAIRO, Thursday. — With Israel's Gaza Strip evacuation almost completed, the U.N. Canal clearance force was tonight awaiting Egyptian permission to remove the last obstacle from the Suez waterway, the tug Edgar Bonnet, laden with explosives.

Egypt announced tonight that the Canal will be open from tomorrow for navigation by vessels up to 500 tons.

The Egyptian and Syrian Governments were reported by the authoritative Egyptian newspaper "A-Sha'ab" today to have "jointly decided that Suez Canal clearance should be resumed and Syrian pipelines repaired after the Israel withdrawal from Gaza."

A spokesman for Gen. Raymond Wheeler, in charge of clearance operations, said today, "We hope to receive permission to start clearance of the Edgar Bonnet. So far it has not been received."

The chief public relations officer of the Egyptian Canal Authority, Mustafa Niazi, was asked if British and French ships would be allowed to go through the Canal. He replied, "All ships who pay tolls to Egypt will be allowed transit."

Shipping circles anticipated that permission for clearance of the Edgar Bonnet would be given very soon.

At U.N. Headquarters, Secretary-General Dag Hammarskjold turned his attention today to the problem of reopening the Canal. He was getting full reports from Gen. Raymond Wheeler in charge of clearance work, and he has been consulting with the Egyptian Foreign Minister, Mahmoud Fawzi.

British experts estimated that if the work of raising the last two obstacles is started his weekend, a clear channel for ships up to 30,000 tons will be ready by the end of this month.

Authoritative U.N. sources denied that Mr. Hammarskjold planned to visit Cairo for talks with Abdul Nasser within the next few days. They indicated that such reports were premature.

Meanwhile, two British engineers left Baghdad by air today to join the Iraq Petroleum Company's repair teams which are due to enter Syria tomorrow to repair pipelines to the Mediterranean. *(Reuter, UP)*

Dutch Leader Lauds Israel's Struggle

THE HAGUE, Thursday (Reuter). — Tribute was paid today to Israel's "struggle for bare survival," by Mr. E. Vermeer, Chairman of the Dutch Labour Party.

Speaking at the three-day Congress of the party here, which is also being attended by foreign socialists, Mr. Vermeer said: "There is no difference of opinion in our ranks about the conflict between Israel and the Arab states. I believe that we, as Socialists, sympathize with the Israel people in their struggle for bare survival. Israel is fighting for her existence and it is the duty of the West to support this small nation. We ask the Government to support a policy which will make life possible for Israel and all small nations."

(Mr. Moshe Sharett, M.K., left Lydda today to represent Mapai at the conference.)

Eli is back!

Eli, whose observations on the country's weekly worries entertained readers of the **Post** for a number of years, reappears on page four today. His creator, Meir Ronnen, has just returned from South Africa where he served as Patwa Director.

Last Israel Contingents Move Smoothly Out of the Gaza Strip

Israel troops leaving Gaza.
Photos by Hirshbain

U.N. Briefed On Gaza Problems

LYDDA AIRPORT, Thursday. — The handing over of Israel civilian administration of the Gaza Strip to the UNEF was discussed between Israel and U.N. officials at a four-hour meeting here today.

The first to arrive were UNEF officers, who had flown from their headquarters in el-Arish; they were followed by UNRWA delegates in cars. Officials representing all the Israel Ministries which had operated in Gaza reached the airfield shortly afterwards.

The Chief of Staff, Rav-Aluf Moshe Dayan, and his aides were present for a short time at the start of the proceedings. The U.N. bodies were represented by the Legal Advisor to the UNEF administration, Norwegian, Swedish and Canadian officers, American civilian officials of UNEF, and the area director of UNRWA, Mr. N. Lucas, and his assistants.

The U.N. officials were given detailed instructions on the operation of postal, legal and administrative services. They were also briefed on the special economic and agricultural problems of the new "U.N. Colony."

Most of the discussion dealt with the maintenance of commercial relations between Israel and the Strip. The U.N. officials said they were prepared to make Israel their main source of supply, but they would decide only after considering possibilities of supplies from Egypt and England. The main consideration would be the price. They added that obviously, there were many goods that could only be obtained from Israel.

The U.N. officials would also try to obtain English language newspapers from Israel. It seems that copies of *The Jerusalem Post* will be supplied at their request.

The U.N. administration is seriously considering issuing permits to foreign journalists to enter the Strip from Israel. *(Itim)*

1,113 Egyptian Jews Arrive in Greece

ATHENS, Thursday (INA). — A total of 1,113 Jews forced out of Egypt arrived here yesterday aboard the Egyptian ship Mecca. All will go to Israel.

This brought to about 13,000 the number of Jews who have left Egypt. The first passengers transferred from the Mecca will sail for Israel tomorrow.

Jordan Getting British Bases 'Almost Free'

Britain has transferred to Jordan "almost free of charge" installations, equipment and surplus stocks in the British bases at Mafrak and Akaba, the Old City "Falastin" reported yesterday.

Britain withdrew her request of £14m. for the installations, estimated by a joint British-Jordan committee of experts, and has agreed to accept £1m. from Jordan, it was stated.

The paper added that agreement has been reached whereby the British forces would leave Jordan within less than three months, instead of the six months originally specified.

U.N. Assembly Meets Today

UNITED NATIONS, Thursday (Reuter). — The General Assembly will meet tomorrow at 20.00 G.M.T. (10 p.m. Israel time) to resume its Middle East debate

Secretary-General Hammarskjold is expected to have ready a new report on the withdrawal of Israel troops and civil administration from the Gaza Strip and from the Gulf of Akaba area.

Meir Seeing Tsur In Paris Today

By MAURICE CARR
Jerusalem Post Correspondent

PARIS, Thursday. — The Israel Ambassador, Mr. Ya'acov Tsur, has postponed his appointment with Foreign Minister Christian Pineau from tomorrow until Monday because of the arrival of the Israel Foreign Minister, Mrs Golda Meir.

Mrs. Meir is stopping over here tomorrow for a few hours, and possibly longer, on her return home from the U.N.

In the meantime, Mr. Tsur today had long friendly talks with the Political Director of the Foreign Ministry, Mr. Daridan, and the Secretary General, M. Joxe, who had accompanied Premier Mollet and M. Pineau to Washington.

I have learned that Mr. Levi Eshkol is to meet his French counterpart, Finance Minister Paul Ramadier, when he visits Paris in about a fortnight.

The President of the Senate Foreign Affairs Commission, M. Plaisant, stated today: "It is France's absolute duty to support Israel, not because of love, but because Israel is today's champion of freedom of the seas, and freedom of navigation in the Gulf of Akaba is the key to freedom of navigation in the Suez Canal."

M. Emile Roche, President of the French Economic Council, has accepted an invitation from Mr. Tsur, to visit Israel next month.

He will leave France on April 15 and will be accompanied by his wife, daughter and representatives of the Ministry of Finance and Economy, as well as a party of French industrialists and bankers.

First German Army Games in 18 Years

BONN, Thursday (Reuter). — German Army manoeuvres will be held in West Germany this summer for the first time in 18 years, Defence Ministry sources said today.

They said the exercises would be held as soon as the first three infantry divisions are at about 80 per cent of the full strength. West Germany's army has about 9,000 men. By the end of this year it is planned to reach a strength of 120,000 men including two armoured divisions. The final target of 350,000 men is expected to be reached in 1961.

UNEF in Control, Keeps Gaza Curfew

CAIRO, Thursday. — Complete quiet is prevailing throughout the Gaza Strip today except for a few demonstrations by Arabs cheering U.N. troops, (Picture Page 3), a UNEF spokesman declared today.

He said that UNEF imposed a curfew in the Strip at dawn today as Danish and Norwegian soldiers guarded food stores, hospitals, and other public buildings.

Newsmen were told that UNEF would not bring Egyptian officials into the Strip—at least in the initial stages.

UNEF Headquarters at El Ballah said that Mr. Dag Hammarskjold's special envoy, Dr. Ralph Bunche, is expected to visit the new UNEF Headquarters in Gaza on Sunday.

Gen. E.L.M. Burns, UNEF Commander, has appealed to the the Gaza Strip people not to carry arms and explosives. In a proclamation after his forces took over control from Israel troops, he asked the population to "help UNEF maintain quiet." The proclamation said that UNEF will conduct the civil affairs of the Strip until further arrangements are made, and that UNRWA will continue relief services.

In Ottawa, Defence Minister Ralph Campney, told the Commons that additional Canadian reconnaissance and administration troops will leave tomorrow to serve with UNEF. *(Reuter, UP)*

UNEF NOT TO TAKE OVER TIRAN ISLES

CAIRO, Thursday (Reuter). — A spokesman at U.N.E.F. Headquarters in El Ballah announced tonight that the U.N. force would not occupy the Tiran Islands (controlling the entrance to the Gulf of Akaba) after the Israelis evacuate them.

The Israel evacuation is due to take place by Saturday. The U.N.E.F. spokesman said "The U.N.E.F. forces will be stationed on the shore facing the islands."

PINEAU SEES GAZA SCENE 'UNCERTAIN'

PARIS, Thursday (Reuter). — Foreign Minister Christian Pineau today described the solution found for the Gaza Strip as "uncertain and imprecise" as it did not guarantee that Egyptian raiders would not resume attacks on Israel.

Addressing the Foreign Affairs Commission of the National Assembly, M. Pineau said he considered the solution for the Gulf of Akaba as satisfactory since under the U.N. Charter, Israel could plead self-defence if her shipping was held up in the Gulf.

Border Settlers Watch Grimly

By MACABEE KASKIN
Jerusalem Post Reporter

NIR YITZHAK. — At the crisp command of their officer, the last Israel soldiers in the Gaza Strip clambered aboard their vehicles shortly before dusk today, and moved out towards Israel, leaving a company of Swedish troops in the Rafah area to maintain law and order.

The Swedish company, commanded by Major G. Bergstrom, had entered this sector, a cross-roads four kilometres from Rafah, earlier in the day. It had pitched its dark-green tents, above which the U.N. flags floated lazily in the wet, cold breeze, on a small grass-covered bluff overlooking the rolling flats.

When the Swedes moved into the bivouac area, they were greeted by the Israel major in charge.

The two officers and their subordinates shook hands, and the Israelis pointed out the location of a nearby mine field. The Israelis packed their equipment and sat on it, waiting patiently and emotionlessly for the word to leave. The area had a quiet, pastoral peacefulness.

The command was given at 5 p.m.

No Flags Flown

Without benefit of ceremony, the Israelis mounted their half-tracks and jeeps, which flew no flags, and began moving down the narrow road, two-and-a-half kilometres to this border settlement.

At the unmarked border, they caught up with a column of Israel tanks, lumbering away.

The soldiers, infantry and armoured, were neither happy nor glum, but seemed to be performing a routine job with a minimum of boredom. On the last half-track to leave the Gaza Strip was a girl soldier, Esther of Tel Giborim, in the Negev.

Here, the settlers, and their children, lined the side of the road, solemnly watching the soldiers pass. Even the small children, instinctively feeling the seriousness of the situation, would not smile. "Can't you smile?" a soldier asked a little girl.

"What do we have to smile about?" her father answered. Another farmer chimed in: "This is *fedayeen* country."

When the Israel Defence Forces moved into the Strip in November, the settlers said they had breathed a sigh of relief. Now the daily nightmare of endless night watches and death-dealing shadows had returned.

Today, they cleaned up the bunkers, oiled their guns and tested the perimeter wire. Tonight, for the third consecutive time in the past four months, the searchlights will lay white protective swathes around the settlement.

"We have returned to October, 1956," one settler said. "What we prayed would never happen, has taken place."

Shortly before the convoy left the Gaza Strip, an Israel officer had explained to a Swedish captain how the fedayeen operated.

The Swedish officer replied:

(Continued on Page 3, — Col. 3)

Khan Yunis Notable Accepts Asylum

Jerusalem Post Reporter

ASHKELON, Thursday. — A Khan Yunis notable and his family of eight were brought here yesterday by the withdrawing Israel forces. After staying the night at the Pink House Pension here, they drove off this morning in a relative's car to an unstated part of Israel.

It is understood that he has both money and family in this country.

Joseph Dinai
F.E.I.A.
Consuela Abrams
Married
Tel Aviv, March 1957.

Heartiest Congratulations to
Mr. Joseph Dinai
on the occasion of his marriage.
A Group of Auditor Friends

הועד הפועל
המרכז לתרבות ולחנוך
מכון ישראלי להשכלה בכתב
משרד החינוך והתרבות
המחלקה להנחלת הלשון
ולהשכלה

Learn Hebrew at Home
Correspondence Courses
3,500
people from all parts of the country,
learned Hebrew in Correspondence Ulpan Courses
Intermediate and Advanced Levels
Special courses:
LANGUAGE IMPROVEMENT • SPELLING
Special Reduction to
Readers of The Jerusalem Post
Cut and mail coupon to the Institute

Correspondence Ulpan
P.O.B. 373. Tel Aviv
Reduction coupon to readers of The Jerusalem Post
Kindly send me your curriculum and list of reductions
My name .... Address ....
J.P. 24

THE JERUSALEM POST

SUNDAY, OCTOBER 6, 1957

PRICE: 140 PRUTA
VOL. XXXIII, No. 8931*

Russians Launch 1st Man-Made Satellite To Speed Around Earth at 29,000 K.P.H.

MARGINAL COLUMN

By NISSIM REJWAN

BY now almost everybody has gone on record as saying that the real cause of unrest and trouble in the Middle East is the Arab-Israel dispute or, in other words, the mere existence of Israel. Colonel Abdul Kader Hatem, Director of the Egyptian Information Services, last week went so far as to claim that "peace and tranquillity reigned in the Middle East until Israel was created in 1948;" King Hussein of Jordan, in his Speech from the Throne last Tuesday, called the Palestine question "the most important topic" in Jordan's foreign policy; the British Government in their latest Note to the Soviet Union reiterated the contention that it is the chief cause of tension in the area; even some Israelis have come to believe it. As far as can be ascertained, the only dissenting voice has come from the Soviet Union, and this rather unconvincingly, since, if anything, that Power has been leaning on very little else in her unscrupulous manoeuvring in the area.

•

THE logical conclusion of this view is, of course, that it would have been so simple had Israel never come into being; that it would be quite convenient, even at this juncture, not to have her around. In a way Ahmed Shukeiri, the Wandering Palestinian who, after working for some time as Syria's chief delegate to the U.N., has now decided to accept King Saud's offer to work for him in the same capacity, was the only exponent of the theory who had the courage of his convictions, asking the U.N. Assembly to supervise the liquidation of this country and submitting fairly concrete proposals and appointing a chief executor. By comparison, Egyptian Foreign Minister Mahmoud Fawzi's references to the Palestine question in his own speech before the Assembly may have sounded sweet reasonableness itself. But anyone familiar with the subtleties of Egyptian diplomacy can discern that Fawzi's hints at Israel's having to comply with past U.N. resolutions were only a more delicate way of voicing Shukeiri's ideas.

•

THE claim that the Middle East of pre-Israel times was blessed with peace and serenity is of course so blatantly false that it hardly needs refuting; its only importance is that it has been made at all. But the idea that the creation of Israel in 1948 was alone responsible for all, or at any rate most, of the trouble and unrest has become so widely accepted that it seems to call for some examination. The first step toward clarifying the problem is to establish a distinction between the Palestine Arabs and the *Pan*-Arabs; what is called the Israel-Arab dispute has in reality been a dispute not between the inhabitants of Palestine and the Jewish settlers — as such, a solution would not have proved so difficult; the dispute has become one between Pan-Arabism and Zionism. Moreover, the forces of Pan-Arabism were on the scene considerably before 1948, and it was these, not the Arab population, which took over, making a settlement of the question quite impossible. Mandatory Government statistics on casualties during the 1938 period of Arab disturbances show that there were 503 Arabs killed compared to 77 Britons and 255 Jews. It may be argued that the Arab dissidents were engaged in liquidating "traitors" in their own ranks, but the fact remains that here was a new force, an almost foreign element, that had gate-crashed the theatre.

•

IN an article published in the "Spectator" some time ago Mr. Elie Kedourie, author of "England and the Middle East," had this to say on the subject: "Had the invasion of Palestine by the Arab League States been successful, the difficulty would have emerged at one remove; there would have been the spoils to divide, and Britain would still have had to take sides. And had Egypt triumphed in Palestine, would she have been less insistent on the evacuation of the Suez Canal base, or the annexation of the Sudan? And would a Middle East defence pact have been easier to negotiate? The illusion that a particular outcome of the Zionist-Arab League quarrel would be more favourable to (Britain's) position in the Middle East than another has led to great tragedies. The Arab refugees uprooted from Palestine, and the Jewish communities uprooted from the Arab countries, stand witness to what may happen if quarrels are intermixed and exacerbated by each other. Zionism or no Zionism, then, Israel or no Israel, a power which has interests in the Middle East has to reckon with a condition of society in which extremism is endemic, and with a doctrine sustained by the infiniteness of its ambition and the inevitability of its triumph."

•

IT is the unholy union between an ambitious, dynamic and triumphant doctrine of Arab Nationalism and the real grievances of the Palestine Arabs that has bedevilled the whole subject. And it is not as though there is even the dimmest prospect of ever separating the two.

Jerusalem, October 6.

Tear-Gas Used in 3rd Day of Warsaw Riots

WARSAW, Saturday (Reuter). — Steel-helmeted militiamen used tear-gas grenades again in Warsaw tonight for the third consecutive night of disorders over the banning of the student newspaper "Po Prostu."

Earlier, one person died from injuries sustained in clashes which had begun on Thursday night.

Polish students today addressed an open letter to the Communist Party leader, Mr. Wladyslaw Gomulka, to ask why their newspaper had been banned. The students, badly mauled by militiamen in two days of rioting, stood sullenly in Workers Unity Square for hours before the Polytechnic school, scene of full-scale riots for two days.

Casualty estimates varied but it was known that several police and students were hospitalized. About 200 students were arrested.

The clashes followed last night's protest meeting attended by 7,000 students at the Polytechnic School and addressed by Mr. Bukhowski, a deputy of the Sejm.

Trams and buses stopped running for 90 minutes during the fighting and unconfirmed reports said all traffic was stopped from entering the capital, with traffic from Poznan and Cracow held up on the city boundary.

About 2,000 militiamen used tear-gas shells as well as rubber truncheons to break up the crowd of several thousand marching on the eight-story building of the Communist Party Headquarters.

Students battled with stones and even boulders. Shouts of "Fascist swine" were hurled at the militia.

Western sources estimated that throughout the city hundreds of tear-gas bombs were exploded in an effort to disperse the yelling and booing crowd. Western reporters saw several dozen incidents of police using truncheons.

At last night's protest meeting a delegation of five students was elected to see Minister of Higher Education Stefan Zolkiewski. It was urging the release of students imprisoned after the big demonstration on Thursday.

Experienced observers said Warsaw had never known such a sight since the war. The general atmosphere throughout the city was one of tenseness and possible crisis. Crowds got almost to the main doors of the Central Committee headquarters before they were driven back by truncheon-wielding police.

By 8.30 p.m. the centre of the city appeared to have been cleared by the police. Fighting between stone-throwing civilians and militia armed with truncheons and tear-gas grenades was reported from the side streets. *(Reuter, U.P.)*

Greek Businessman Held As Spy Suspect

TEL AVIV, Saturday. — A Greek businessman was remanded into custody for 14 days by the Magistrate's Court yesterday on charges of being an Egyptian spy.

The suspect, Yohanis Alkyados Kukas, 36, was arrested several days ago in Tel Aviv. The police are concluding their investigation and believe that within two weeks they will be able to bring him up for a preliminary examination.

From police circles it was learned that Kukas used to visit Israel frequently on business. In the past he had been here on four separate occasions, each time for several weeks.

A search of his living quarters revealed documents testifying to his espionage activities, the sources said.

The suspect is well acquainted with the country, having been stationed here during World War II as a soldier in the Greek Army.

Hoffa Chosen Head Of Teamsters Union

MIAMI BEACH, Saturday (UP). — James R. Hoffa, the Detroit labour leader who has been accused of mishandling union funds, was yesterday voted into the presidency of the biggest U.S. union, the International Teamsters, in defiance of the AFL-CIO, the courts, and Senate investigators.

Mr. Hoffa's salary will be $50,000 a year, and he succeeds Mr. Dave Beck, also under fire from Congress investigation. Mr. Beck retires on December 1 at $50,000 a year.

However, Mr. Hoffa has been in control of the 1,400,000-member union since top officers gathered here two weeks ago to prepare for the convention. Not once were any of his suggestions voted down in committee meetings or convention sessions.

Meanwhile, the Senate Labour Rackets Committee served a subpoena on the Teamsters Union, demanding records of the Credentials Committee which screened delegates who elected Mr. Hoffa. It was claimed that more than half of the delegates were not chosen in accordance with the union's constitution.

Emergency Rule After B'Aires Labour Unrest

BUENOS AIRES, Saturday (Reuter). — Argentine metal workers will start an indefinite strike on Monday following the reported arrest of seven union leaders among 270 people detained in a police round-up.

Delegates of the Metalworkers Union who attended an emergency meeting said the strike will be called to secure the release of the seven leaders.

Workers at the Swift and Armour meat-packing plants walked out today following news of the arrest of two labour leaders who were detained "at the Government's pleasure" and taken aboard the troopship Paris in Buenos Aires Port.

Three hundred union leaders were reported to have received similar treatment.

The Government last night proclaimed a state of siege in the city and province of Buenos Aires. The proclamation, by the Under-Secretary for the Interior, Mr. Garcia Puente, suspended constitutional guarantees for 30 days. He said its object was to "defend the normal development of the Government's political plan, jeopardized through sabotage and social unrest."

U.S. Pledges $21m. to UNRWA

NEW YORK, Saturday (Reuter). — The U.S. alone yesterday pledged more than half the total of $40m. requested to finance U.N. aid for Palestine refugees.

Britain said she would contribute nearly $3m.

The U.N. General Assembly had, for the first time, been turned into a special committee to raise funds for the Palestine Arab refugees programme and for the U.N. Refugee Fund. The Assembly President, Mr. Leslie Munro, of New Zealand, said the financial situation of U.N.R.W.A. (United Nations Relief and Work Agency for Palestine) was "extremely grave."

M. Henry Labouisse, Director of the Agency, said only 31 member governments had contributed in 1957 towards the minimum Relief Budget and "some $2m. more than we can expect to receive will be needed for relief in 1958, even on the assumption that the rate of current contributions will continue."

He appealed for contributions towards the Agency's $15m. Rehabilitation Programme — up to last June it had received only $3.4m., contributed by Britain and the U.S. — and said the minimum Relief Budget would require $25.7m.

M. Labouisse added: "It is obvious that if the General Assembly wishes the Agency to continue its current relief operations, arrangements must be made so that there will be either new contributions from members who have never contributed, or else increased contributions from those who have been supporting us year after year.

The American pledge for over $21m. was given by former Hollywood film star Miss Irene Dunne, now a U.S. delegate to the U.N. She was authorized to pledge $17.5m. towards the relief budget and $4m. towards the Rehabilitation Programme.

Britain's Minister of State for Foreign Affairs, Commander Allan Noble, said the U.K. would contribute $2.2m. for relief in the first six months of 1958, and $500,000 for rehabilitation, with another $200,000 for either relief or rehabilitation.

HEAVY DEATH TOLL IN TUNISIAN QUAKE

TUNIS, Saturday (Reuter).— Many people were killed last night, according to first reports, when a severe tremor shook the Kerkenna islands off Sfax on the east coast of Tunisia.

Eleven people were killed, 135 injured and 150 boats destroyed by the earthquake in the small island of Kraten, the reports said.

The earthquake was followed by a violent storm which made many people homeless.

Tunis Cancels Recall Order To Paris Envoy

PARIS, Saturday (Reuter).— President Habib Bourguiba of Tunisia has cancelled his decision to recall his Ambassador from Paris. A statement by the Tunisian Embassy said he had decided to do so "in view of the conciliatory moves by the French authorities and owing to the government crisis in Paris."

President Bourguiba said earlier this week that he was withdrawing the Ambassador because "at the present stage it is impossible for me to maintain friendly relations with France."

Earlier today the French Ministry of Defence said in a statement, referring to alleged attacks by French aircraft on Tunisian territory bordering on Algeria, that French planes had been fired on 19 times from the Tunisian side of the border in 12 days.

"In no case was there any provocation on our part," the statement quoted Defence Minister Andre Morice as saying.

The Tunisian Ambassador, Mohammed Mahmoudi, today saw the outgoing Prime Minister Bourges-Maunoury and the French Ambassador to Tunisia, M. Georges Gorse, who is at present in Paris making arrangements for a Franco-Tunisian conference to settle outstanding issues.

Two Infiltrators Killed by Patrols

Two infiltrators were killed on Friday night in two separate incidents, the Army spokesman announced. One was apparently from Jordan and the other from the Gaza Strip.

The Jordan infiltrator, a sergeant in the Jordan Army, was shot and killed by an Israel patrol lying in ambush near the fish ponds of Kibbutz Ashdod Ya'akov in the Jordan Valley at midnight last night.

Eight other infiltrators who were with the sergeant got away across the border.

He was not armed. The body was taken to the Poriya Hospital.

The ambush was laid following several cases of theft of fish from the ponds by infiltrators during the past few nights. The group was discerned at midnight and the patrol opened fire after the infiltrators attempted to escape when challenged.

A report of the incident has been made to the Jordan-Israel M.A.C.

The second incident took place near M'falsim, when an Israel patrol came upon a group of four infiltrators carrying stolen pipes.

When the infiltrators became aware of the patrol, they opened fire with submachineguns. In the exchange of fire, one of them was killed. The rest of them escaped to the Gaza Strip.

It is learned that the infiltrator killed near M'falsim was wearing a khaki uniform and rubber shoes. Near his body there was found a Karl Gustav sub-machinegun and a magazine with bullets.

U.K. Labour Confident Of Return to Power Soon

BRIGHTON, Saturday (Reuter). — The 1,500 delegates to the British Labour Party's annual conference, which ended here yesterday with the singing of "The Red Flag," dispersed today, confident that the new policies they have hammered out will help put a Labour Government in power soon.

If they are right, it will be a government with the party leader, Mr. Hugh Gaitskell, as Prime Minister and his former rival for power, Mr. Aneurin Bevan, at his side as Foreign Secretary.

A new unity between the leaders and the transformation of Mr. Bevan from a fiery left-wing rebel to a seasoned statesman were the highlights of the conference.

The pattern of Britain under a future Labour government is fixed as follows:

- Foreign Affairs — retention of the H-bomb as a necessary instrument of policy but seizure of the initiative in proposing world-wide suspension of nuclear tests.
- Welfare State — Half-pay pensions up to £15 a week for all workers at their retirement at the age of 65, and an increase in the basic old age pension from £2 to £3 a week.
- Public Ownership — Government purchase of stock market shares in key industrial firms, instead of the traditional Socialist policy of outright nationalzation. But firms judged to be failing the nation may be taken over and the steel and road haulage industries, which the Conservatives handed back to private ownership, will be renationalized.
- Housing — repeal of the Rents Act, by which the Conservative Government has enabled the landlords of hundreds of thousands of middle class houses and flats to raise rents and evict tenants. Eventually, all rented property will be taken out of the hands of landlords and handed over to town and city authorities.
- Colonies — self-determination for the troubled island of Cyprus and progress for the colonial and backward territories.

The conference has been regarded as the most successful for years, although some delegates regret that "old-fashioned" nationalization has given way to the stock-market scheme which seems to be a compromise with capitalism. The left-wingers feel leaderless now that, as they complain, "Bevan is no longer a Bevanite."

A resolution calling for the resignation or expulsion of the French Socialist Party from the Socialist International, in view of the party's attitude towards Algeria, was yesterday passed to the Labour Party's executive committee for its consideration. It was not voted on by the conference.

Djilas Given More Years in Jail

SREMSKA MITROVICA, Yugoslavia, Saturday (Reuter).— A judge today imposed a new seven-year jail term on Milovan Djilas, former Yugoslav Communist leader once tipped to succeed President Tito, for making "hostile propaganda" against the Tito regime.

Today's sentence was tacked on to the three-year term passed on Mr. Djilas last December on a similar charge. He has already been in jail for nearly a year, so the sentence means he has nine more years to go.

The judge told Mr. Djilas that after serving his sentence he would be deprived of civil rights for five years because "he does not deserve to take part in the public life of this country for that period."

Mr. Djilas was stripped of all Yugoslav decorations, including the Yugoslav wartime honour of "People's Hero" because he "committed serious mistakes against the achievements of the people's revolution."

He was condemned for publishing and distributing "The New Class," his book condemning the Communist system, which was smuggled out of the country and published in New York. The 46-year-old Montenegrin stood stiffly at attention in the district courthouse as Judge Nokolin read the sentence. A slight smile crossed his tired, lined face.

Yesterday, before the judge ordered a secret hearing, Mr. Djilas jumped to his feet and said, "If there is a secret trial, I refuse to answer any questions at all, either by the judge or prosecutor. I should like to state that I stand by my book in the way it is written, from the first to the last letter."

The secret trial was ordered after the prosecutor said that it would be in the public interests to have a closed hearing, because Mr. Djilas' book "served certain reactionary circles and individuals abroad as a means for an organized campaign directed against Yugoslavia, with the object of interfering in her internal affairs and doing damage to her reputation."

Earlier, two foreign press correspondents and a Yugoslav representing the United Press were banned from the trial.

In London, the publishing firm of Methuen said today that a second book by Mr. Djilas will be published in the West. The new book is entitled "Land Without Justice." A spokesman for the publishers said the manuscript had been smuggled into the U.S. and was being translated.

ZHUKOV ON VISIT

ISTANBUL, Saturday (Reuter). — The Soviet Defence Minister, Marshal Georgi Zhukov, passed through the Bosphorous today aboard the Soviet cruiser Kuibyshev on his way to Yugoslavia.

Satellite Signals Heard in Israel

TEL AVIV, Saturday. — Signals from the space satellite launched by Russia yesterday were picked up today by the Post Office radio services.

The Post Office was notified to be on the lookout for the impulses by the Itim-Reuter office here shortly after word was received of the satellite's launching.

The first faint impulse was picked up at 2.12 p.m. today. It gradually became stronger and clearer, then fainter again. Within nine minutes of the time it was first detected, the signals faded out completely. *(Itim)*

Dulles and Gromyko Meet on Mid-East

WASHINGTON, Saturday. — — Mr. Andrei Gromyko, the Soviet Foreign Minister, today called on Secretary of State Dulles to discuss means of easing international tensions.

Mr. Dulles in anxious to sound out the Soviet statesman on Russian attitudes to the problems of the Middle East, disarmament and German reunification, and to convey some of his own thinking to Moscow.

A U.P. report quoting reliable sources in Washington said Mr. Dulles intends to ask Mr. Gromyko whether Russia seeks a major war. Mr. Dulles is reported to have expressed the fear that the Soviet Union may try to get all the Arab states together for a war against Israel and thus provoke a major conflict.

The Secretary of State, it was said, believes it would be difficult for other Arab countries not to join in such a conflict if Russia could persuade one or more Arab nations to start fighting Israel. *(Reuter, UP)*

Meir Tells Gromyko To See for Himself

At their meeting last week, Foreign Minister Golda Meir invited the Soviet Foreign Minister, Mr. Andrei Gromyko, to visit Israel, according to the "Yediot Aharonot" correspondent in New York, quoting authoritative Western sources on Friday.

The invitation reportedly came as a reply to Mr. Gromyko's accusations that Israel's intentions are aggressive and that she is serving as a tool in the hands of imperialist states.

"Come to Israel and see for yourself whether Israel is preparing any act of aggression," Mrs. Meir is reported to have said.

Mr. Gromyko did not state whether he would accept the invitation, but declared that "Russia knows everything that is happening in Israel" and knows that her foreign policy is "bad and dangerous."

He said that Israel had been a disappointment to Russia, while the Arabs had proved a pleasant surprise, the correspondent added.

Nehru, Kishi Confer On Middle East

TOKYO, Saturday (Reuter). — The Indian Prime Minister, Mr. Nehru, began his nine-day official visit to Japan with a two-hour conference with Prime Minister M. Kishi.

Mr. Nehru, who arrived yesterday, also outlined to Mr. Kishi his views on recent developments in the Middle East, the sources said.

The Chief Japanese Cabinet Secretary, Mr. Aichi, said that Mr. Nehru's assessment of the present situation in the Middle East, with emphasis on Syria and the Baghdad Pact, "was of particular importance."

HUNGARIAN REBEL LEADER GETS DEATH

BUDAPEST, Saturday (Reuter). — Laszlo Balogh, described as commander of an insurgent crowd in Budapest in last year's rising, was sentenced to death today for plotting to overthrow the regime. Four others were jailed for life.

BUDAPEST AMNESTY FOR EMIGRE LEADER

BUDAPEST, Saturday (Reuter). — The Hungarian presidential council has granted amnesty to the former Hungarian refugee leader, Miklos Szabo, who returned here from Vienna last month after nearly two years in the West.

U.S. 'Not Surprised' By Artificial Moon

WASHINGTON, Saturday. — The White House said today that the Russian launching of the world's first earth satellite "did not come as any surprise" to the U.S. Government, and that the successful Soviet effort woud not have any effect on U.S. plans to launch a satellite next spring.

The White House also said the launching of the satellite was of "great scientific interest" and should contribute much to scientific knowledge.

"We never thought of our programme as one which was in a race with the Soviets," White House Press Secretary James C. Hagerty told reporters.

He evaded a question whether the Soviet satellite was of great military and defence as well as scientific interest.

Leaders of the U.S. satellite programme said it appeared to them that the Russians put their satellite into its globe-girdling orbit with a rocket "close to an intercontinental ballistic missile."

Though dismayed by the Soviet victory in the friendly race to establish the first earth satellite, U.S. scientists were lavish in their praise of the accomplishment last night and the conference session today.

When the news was announced at a Soviet Embassy reception to scientists in Washington attending a special International Geophysical Year conference, the Russian scientist, Dr. A. Blagonravov, said the satellite might stay aloft up to a month depending on the density of the air 800 kms. up.

Dr. I. M. Levitt, Director of Fels Planetarium in Philadelphia, told Reuters today the satellite could remain in the sky "a thousand or a million years, and there is nothing man can do to bring it down." He said that when it does begin to fall it will

(Continued on Page 3, Col. 7)

Attendance Up At Little Rock School

LITTLE ROCK, Arkansas, Saturday (UP). — An incident at a school dance yesterday was the only serious one following the suspension of "hard core" anti-integrationist students from the Central High School. The incident was caused when a youth who had been drinking called a paratrooper "Nigger lover," the Army announced.

Attendance at the school rose yesterday to 1,725 students out of a total enrolment of 1,990. White students who gathered on the front steps made no demonstration as the nine Negro students came and went with their usual escort of troops. The suspension of 50 white students who took part in the abortive "mass walk-out" appeared to have removed the most aggressive agitators from the school.

Projectile Sent 800 Kms. Up

LONDON, Saturday (Reuter). — Russia took the Western world by surprise again yesterday, when she launched the world's first man-made satellite by rocket into outer space. The artificial moon was tracked by official watchers and heard by radio stations all over the world today as it hurtled through space at nearly 29,000 kms. an hour — or round the world every 96 minutes.

U.S. Test Launching 'Within Few Days'

WASHINGTON, Saturday (Reuter). — The third test firing in the U.S. earth satellite programme is expected to be made "within a few days," the Defence Department announced today.

The satellite, sent up without any preliminary tests, captured the world headlines. The launching was toasted in vodka at a Soviet Embassy party in Washington today.

"Moon watching" teams of the International Geophysical Year — of which the Russian launching of the satellite was a part — have been alerted throughout the world.

Not only experts, but the man in the street, equipped with ordinary binoculars or spy glasses, will be able to see the satellite in the rays of the rising and setting sun as it careens on its oval-shaped orbit, ranging up to a maximum height of 900 kms.

U.S. Concedes Victory

American press and radio reception of the event acknowledged that Russia had beaten the U.S. in a race to be the first to launch the satellite. The U.S. plans to launch its first moon early next spring.

Moscow Radio reported today that its receiving station is picking up signals from the earth satellite "very clearly." The radio, quoting the Ministry of Communications, said the signals grew stronger as the satellite approached, "and gradually faded out" as it passed the receiving station.

The radio said that the launching of the satellite was the first step in space travel and flight to the moon. More satellites carrying special equipment would be launched to investigate the highest parts of the earth's atmosphere, it said.

The radio said a special observatory to follow the satellite's course had been established at Leningrad. Each appearance would be automatically recorded and timed.

Moscow Radio said today the power of the rocket device used for launching the satellite is fully comparable with the power of the greatest hydro-electric power stations in the world.

TASS said, "The satellite is at present describing an elliptical trajectory around the earth. It is in the form of a sphere and carries a radio transmitter. It is 58 cms. in diameter and weighs 83.6 kilograms, and was launched from a carrier rocket. The carrier rocket had imparted to the satellite the required orbital velocity of about 8,000 metres a second."

The orbit of the satellite

(Continued on Page 3, Col. 3)

Moon Missile Seen In 'Near Future'

PARIS, Saturday (UP). — The French space pioneer, Alexander Ananov, said today that the job of rocketing a missile into an earth-circling orbit is more difficult than shooting a missile to the moon.

The Russian achievement shows the moon-missile is coming in the "very near future," he stated, adding that the U.S. may catch up and launch a missile soon.

M. Ananov, 47, a Russian-born French scientist, said, "From my talks and letters with Russian scientists, I knew they were ahead of the Americans but I didn't know they were that far ahead. The American lag is undoubtedly in the rocket carrying the satellite rather than the satellite itself."

Syria, Iraq Sign Oil Agreement

BAGHDAD, Saturday (Reuter). — Syria is to cooperate with Iraq to facilitate Iraq's oil exports from her northern oilfields, the Iraqi Minister of Economics, Nadim el Pachachi, said here last night on his return from talks in Damascus.

He added, "This will enable Iraq to induce the oil companies operating in our country to maintain the present Arab oil routes, which is the Iraq Government's policy."

In New York on Thursday, Iraq's delegate told the U.N. General Assembly that "certain powers" were using the threat of possible Communist infiltration in the Middle East as "a pretext for their infernal designs."

Dr. Mousa Al Shabandar, the Iraqi delegate, assailed Western policies and said there was no Communism in the Arab world.

"The phenomenon we are witnessing is nothing but the expression of bitterness caused by injustice and partialities favouring Israel, to the detriment of Arab rights and aspirations," he declared.

Fishermen's Union Undeterred By Cairo Action Against Doron

HAIFA, Saturday. — Israel's trawler fishermen pledged at an emergency meeting held yesterday that they would not be deterred by Egypt's illegal detention of the fishing boat Doron, and would continue their operations in the same area.

The fishermen appealed to public opinion in Israel and throughout the world against the detention, which was made well outside Egyptian territorial waters. They termed it an act of piracy, against a harmless fishing boat carrying a crew of six.

Israel fishermen will continue operating in the same area in which the Doron was detained, as they were entitled to by international law, the meeting decided.

This week a new trawler, the Kadesh, would enter service, while two others, now under repair, would be speedily returned to service, it was disclosed.

According to usually reliable sources in Geneva, the Red Cross delegate in Egypt has received assurances from the Egyptian authorities that he will soon be permitted to visit the crew of the Doron. It was also disclosed that the Egyptians have refused to reveal the place of detention of the fishermen or to permit them to send the usual Red Cross messages to their families.

Meanwhile, U.P. and Reuter reported that two U.N. officers from Gaza arrived in Port Said on Thursday to investigate the case of the Doron. They held a long meeting with Egyptian officials. No details were released.

(The Israel Army spokesman in Tel Aviv tonight denied news agency reports from Athens that the Israel Navy last Tuesday intercepted and captured a 1,000-ton Egyptian freighter with an 11-man crew. The spokesman said that no ship at all had been captured.)

Right Foils Mollet Try at Cabinet

PARIS, Saturday. — The Socialist leader, M. Guy Mollet, said tonight he was giving up his attempt to form France's 24th post-war government.

He laid full blame for his decision on the right-wing Independents, who threw him out of the Premier's post three and one-half months ago on a higher-taxes bill.

This time again the stumbling block was financial. The Independents refused to agree to give M. Mollet special economic and financial powers.

Unofficial reports last Thursday that M. Mollet had declined to undertake the formation of a government at the present time were later found to be premature. Yesterday the Socialist leader announced that he had "reluctantly" agreed to make the attempt, adding "I must admit I am sceptical of my chances."

TO THE BEREAVED FAMILY

We deeply mourn with you the untimely death of our dear

DANNY GOV

Cargal Company
Management and Employees.

The funeral cortege will leave the Beilinson Hospital today at 2 p.m. for the Kiryat Shaul Cemetery. Buses will leave the Hospital at 2 p.m. sharp.

Attention overseas visitors
YOUR BANK IN ISRAEL
BRANCHES ALL OVER THE COUNTRY
ISRAEL DISCOUNT BANK LTD.

WEDNESDAY, JULY 16, 1958

THE JERUSALEM POST

VOL. XXXIV. No. 9170
PRICE: 150 PRUTA

59 New
JUST OUT
IMPROVED MECHANISM IN THE NEW MODEL
Price: IL2.490
ROLEX 59

ORTHODOX JOIN OPPOSITION

Gov't Gets 60:41 Confidence Vote

By ARYEH RUBINSTEIN, Jerusalem Post Knesset Reporter

The National Religious Party on Tuesday night supported a motion of non-confidence in the Government, and their spokesman later announced that the Party was now going over to the Opposition.

The non-confidence motion was defeated by 60 votes to 41. It was supported by Herut, the General Zionists, the National Religious Party, Agudat Yisrael, and Poalei Agudat Yisrael. Voting against the motion were Mapai, Ahdut Ha'avoda, Mapam and the Progressives. The Communists abstained.

The Knesset debate on the Cabinet crisis ended in the afternoon, and the Prime Minister's reply was announced for 8 p.m.

At 8.13, Mr. Ben-Gurion mounted the rostrum and informed the Knesset that the Cabinet had decided in the morning to appoint a Committee of Three consisting of himself, the Minister of Interior (Mr. Bar-Yehuda) and the Minister of Justice (Mr. Rosen) to examine and formulate rules for the registration of children of mixed marriages whose parents wish to register them as Jews.

After Mr. Ben-Gurion's statement — which took exactly three minutes (see col. X) — Mrs. Esther Raziel-Naor (Herut), Dr. I. S. Rosenberg (speaking for the National Religious, Aguda and Poalei Aguda parties, and Mr. Israel Rokach (General Zionist) presented their parties' motions.

In identical and apparently pre-arranged wording, each of them proposed: "In summing up the debate, and in the light of the Prime Minister's reply, we move that the Knesset express non-confidence in the Government."

After the non-confidence motions were defeated, a Communist motion submitted by Dr. Moshe Sneh was put to a vote. It called upon the Government to follow the principle of the complete separation of State and religion. It received only the vote of Dr. Sneh.

The Prime Minister's motion that the Knesset take note of his statement was adopted by a vote of 59-40. The party division being the same as on the non-confidence motion.

At a press conference called by the National Religious Party immediately after the Knesset session, Dr. Zerah Warhaftig declared that the Prime Minister's statement represented nothing new at all on the point at issue.

He said that two of the three members of the new Committee (presumably Mr. Ben-Gurion and Mr. Bar-Yehuda) had made their positions so clear in the last few weeks that the committee's appointment could not be

(Continued on Page 3, Col. 3)

C-o-L Allowance Up IL 7 to IL 18

Monthly wages of persons earning up to IL500 will be increased by 3.6 per cent following a rise of nine points in the cost-of-living Index in the last quarter. The increase is exempt from income tax.

The Index had risen by 18 points up to the month of June but fell by nine points during June itself, mainly due to a reduction in vegetable prices, according to the Central Bureau of Statistics report on Tuesday. The Index now stands at 267 (100 in September 1951).

The 3.6 per cent increase is to be calculated on the basic wage plus the cost of living allowance paid until 1956 but not including the 3.2 percent c-o-l allowance payment made in July 1957. According to these calculations persons earning IL200 monthly will receive an additional IL7.200, while persons earning IL500 monthly will get the maximum of IL18.

The rise in the Index was kept at nine points for the period by the liberal use of subsidies on food products. The subsidies on fruits and vegetables have now been rescinded and it is not expected that they will be reactivated that they will be reactivated.

It is learned that Mr. Aharon Becker the head of the Histadrut Trade Union Department, declared on Tuesday that the Histadrut's agreement that c-o-l allowance payments be made in the future only in case the Index rose by three per cent in a six month period pertained only to 1959, and it was still possible that another c-o-l allowance payment would be made in 1958 if the Index were to rise by five per cent or more in the next three months.

News on Other Pages

Special dispatches on the fast-moving Middle-East developments, cabled to *The Jerusalem Post* yesterday, from H.A.R. Philby, "Observer" correspondent in Beirut, and E. Crankshaw, the paper's Soviet expert in London, appear on Page 2.

A review of the rise and fall of the Hashemite dynasty by our columnist on Mid-East affairs, Amnon Bartur, is on Page 4.

Ben-Zvis Lunch with Royalty

President and Mrs. Ben-Zvi were on Tuesday the luncheon guests of Queen Juliana and Prince Bernhard of the Netherlands at Soestdijk Palace, in what was undoubtedly the highlight of the President's unofficial visit to Holland. The President was scheduled to tender an official dinner in honour of the Queen, the Prince and Prime Minister Dr. Willem Drees at the Israel Embassy on Tuesday night.

On their arrival in Holland on Monday afternoon, the President and Mrs. Ben-Zvi received an official welcome and reviewed a unit of gaily uniformed gendarmes who stood at attention with drawn swords. They later drove into the Hague where they met with Jewish community and Zionist Organization leaders.

At a press conference with newspaper, radio and television reporters at the airport, the President and the Director General of the Foreign Ministry, Mr. Walter Eytan, who is accompanying him, were asked for their reaction to the events in the Middle East. The President replied that his schedule would remain unchanged by the disturbed situation in the Middle East.

On Tuesday morning, the President was received by Prime Minister Drees, and later met with representatives of underground organizations which rendered wartime assistance to Jews in Holland. He also received members of the Israel colony in Holland.

The President was accompanied to his meeting with the Prime Minister by the Israel Ambassador, Mr. Hanan Cidor, and by his Military Aide, Sgan-Aluf Yosef Carmel. He later visited the noted Hague art museum "Maurithuis" under the guidance of its director, Dr. A.B. De Vries. The museum is noted for its collection of Rembrandt paintings.

According to the Israel Ambassador, President Ben-Zvi's visit has caused a stir in the local press and has received widespread publicity even in the provincial press, with each paper stressing the Presidential couple's pioneering background.

First Group of Soviet Tourists Arrive

LYDDA AIRPORT. — The first organized group of tourists from the Soviet Union arrived here Tuesday evening by Air France. The group, comprising 12 tourists, mostly professional men and women, left Moscow Monday morning and reached here via Prague and Paris.

The well-dressed tourists were met at the airport by Mr. A. Glebov, Attache at the Russian Embassy, representatives of the Mapai-sponsored Israel-USSR friendship league and a delegate of the Communist-controlled Israel-Soviet Friendship Movement.

The visitors paid 4,000 roubles (app. $1,000) each to Intourist for fares and accomodation. Their 10-day stay here is being handled by Peltours.

6 GERMAN AIRMEN DIE IN CRASH

BONN, (Reuter). — All six crew were killed when a West German Air Force transport plane crashed in flames on Tuesday near Berchtesgaden, according to a Defence Ministry spokesman. The plane was on a training flight.

The Executive
Of the World Zionist Organization
expresses its deepest sympathy
to the RAZIEL (Raczkowski)-SOKOLOW families
on the death of
SOPHIA RAZIEL
daughter of the late Nahum Sokolow,
President of the World Zionist Organization

Rassia Asks For Friendship Pacts

LONDON (Reuter). — A Foreign Office spokesman said Tuesday night that the Soviet Union has proposed in a note to the U.S. and all European nations a treaty of friendship and collective security.

A summary of the note had been received in London. The note had been handed over in Moscow earlier in the day to the envoys of Western powers.

France Sees Hope In Counter-Revolt

By MAURICE CARR
Jerusalem Post Correspondent

PARIS. — The Quai d'Orsay spokesman stated Tuesday that it would be realistic on the part of the Western powers "to do something" to safeguard Israel on the same principle as they are doing something to preserve the independence of Lebanon.

Feelings have been expressed privately in Foreign Ministry circles that, even if the Baghdad rebellion succeeds, Iraq will not dare to launch with the U.A.R. a combined attack on Israel and that for the moment at any rate there is still a good chance that Iraqi troops, including one division stationed in Jordan which remained loyal to Nuri Said, will restore the situation. It is evident that the degree of determination now shown by the Western powers to halt the pro-Nasser movement throughout the Middle East will influence wavering Arab elements.

The Quai d'Orsay spokesman announced that French warships cruising in the East Mediterranean were ready to intervene to protect the 3,000 French residents of Lebanon, any moment the Government may deem this necessary.

British Troops To Persian Gulf

LONDON (Reuter). — The Defence Ministry announced Tuesday that three Army brigades — one in Britain and two in Cyprus — have been alerted as part of precautionary measures and that reinforcements have been sent to Aden and the Persian Gulf area. British naval units were on the move in the Mediterranean and the Persian Gulf.

At Malta, Naval Headquarters announced that ships of the British Mediterranean Fleet were standing by ready to sail at 24 hours' notice "as a precautionary measure" in view of the situation in the Eastern Mediterranean."

Reports in Nairobi, Kenya, said that "important movements of British troops from Kenya and East Africa had been planned," and that "indications are that an airlift is urgently pending."

It is learned at the Ad-

(Continued on Page 3, Col. 6)

French and British Units Stand By in Mid-East As U.S. Marines Land in Lebanon, Take Over Airport

B-G Warns of 'Grave Events'

Grave events are about to take place in Israel's neighbourhood, the Prime Minister declared Tuesday evening.

Replying to the Knesset debate on the resignation of the National Religious Party Ministers, Mr. Ben-Gurion said:

"Perhaps I may surprise the members of the Knesset — I do not know whether they will be disappointed or pleased — if I tell you that I shall not make on this occasion the speech I had intended to make in winding up this unfortunate debate, for in the meantime grave events have taken place and are about to take place in our area, events which were discussed this morning in the Cabinet and will be discussed tomorrow in the Foreign Affairs and Security Committee.

"I shall therefore content myself with informing you of the Government's decision, to which I will preface only two sentences on my own behalf:

"In my opinion there does not exist anywhere in the world a Jewry so firmly rooted, true, full of content and authentic as in Israel. I have declared more than once in the name of the Government that this is a State governed by the Rule of Law, and not a State governed by Religious Law, and all the parties participating in it obliged themselves, by their signatures to the Foundation Scroll of the State on May 14, 1948, to freedom of conscience and religion.

Cabinet's Plan

"The Government's decision is as follows:

"'To appoint a Committee of Three, consisting of the Prime Minister, the Minister of Interior and the Minister of Justice, to examine and formulate rules for the registration of children of mixed marriages whose parents wish to register them as Jews. The Committee of Three shall hear the opinion of Jewish sages in Israel and abroad on this question, and shall formulate registration rules, which will be in keeping both with the accepted tradition in all circles of Jewry, including all trends, both orthodox and non-orthodox, and with the special conditions prevailing in Israel, as a sovereign Jewish State in which freedom of conscience and religion are assured, and as a centre for the ingathering of the exiles.'

"Accordingly I propose that the Knesset should take note of the Government's decision and reject the Herut party's non-confidence motion.

Premier Calls In Western Envoys

POST Diplomatic Correspondent

Israel's activity during the present crisis is being limited to maintaining close contact with friendly governments in an attempt to gather a clear picture of events and to make clear its own views on developments to these governments.

The Cabinet heard a report on the situation from the Prime Minister on Tuesday morning. Mr. Ben-Gurion received the French Ambassador, M. P.E. Gilbert, in the evening, and the British Charge d'Affaires, Miss B. Salt, in the morning. The British Ambassador is abroad on leave.

On Wednesday (today) the Foreign Affairs and Security Committee of the Knesset will meet to hear a report.

The Ambassador to the U.S., Mr. Eban, is due immediately on what was scheduled to be an extended home leave. Whether he will return to the U.S. after consultations, cutting short his leave, will only be decided after his arrival.

Foreign Minister Meir remained at home all day Tuesday after an exhausting day on Monday when she actively participated in the round of

(Continued on Page 3, Col. 2)

The End of Nuri

Nuri Said, 70, Iraq's strong man for the past 30 years, has been shot dead, Baghdad Radio announced on Tuesday. Earlier, it had said that he had escaped from the insurgent forces.

The radio said, "The people arrested the dog of imperialism, Nuri Said, and insisted on executing him. His body has been handed over to the authorities."

The broadcast said that information was received that Nuri was hiding in a house in one of the old parts of Baghdad.

A military patrol drove to the house and an "old woman" emerged wearing a black cloak. The "woman" produced a rifle from under her clothes, and opened fire on the soldiers, the statement said.

The soldiers shot back and killed "her." When the body was examined, it was found to be that of Nuri, the statement said.

The Baghdad junta had put a price of £10,000 on the head of the former Premier.

(Arabic radio monitors in Jerusalem on Tuesday night said the news about Nuri's killing was broadcast by Cairo Radio 15 minutes before Baghdad Radio made the announcement. Cairo Radio quoted the Baghdad station as the source for the item.)

U.K. Opinion Along Party Lines

By GERDA L. COHEN, Jerusalem Post Correspondent

LONDON. — British reaction to the Iraqi *coup* was hardening on Tuesday from the outraged bewilderment and recrimination which characterized Monday's unofficial comments. The attitudes expressed are divided according to party lines as was the case in previous Middle Eastern crises.

Although holding no illusions as to the grim possibilities of a Cairo stranglehold on the entire Middle East, left-wing spokesmen consider Western intervention politically fruitless: the use of armed force to suppress the Lebanese rebels would not have prevented the Iraqi revolt nor would immediate action in Iraq now succeed in restoring the overthrown regime.

The dilemma of Britain's position regarding Israel is exemplified by the chorus of eulogies for Nuri Said, always accompanied by reminders that the Iraqi leader had always begged the Western leaders to enhance their standing in the region by extorting concessions from Israel. On the other hand Israel's increased peril in the new situation provides an additional argument for those advocating firm action.

Despite the initial nose-dive of oil share prices on the London Exchange, the City remains calm as no immediate danger to Britain's oil supplies from the Middle East is envisaged. Iraq supplied only 11 per cent of Britain's crude oil needs this year following Kuwait's stepping-up of oil shipments. The Iraqi Government was actually negotiating a favourable agreement with the Iraq Petroleum Company when the revolt broke out.

Were the Cabinet to decide to intervene it would command wholehearted support of the Tory backbenchers and of the popular press: the sacking of the British Embassy in Baghdad shocked opinion here more than the imminent eclipse of Western influence in the Middle East. There would in all likelihood be a loud outcry if the Government did nothing to safeguard the lives of the 5,600 Britons in Iraq including the personnel at the R.A.F. Base there.

Tory Middle East experts are predicting the extension of the conflict either to the Turkish-Iraqi frontier or to Israel and are assuming that Israel may well take advantage of King Hussein's state of helplessness to launch an attack to avoid future encirclement by a single Arab command under Nasser.

Israel Ambassador Eliahu Elath on Tuesday met with the Deputy Under-Secretary of State, Sir William Hayter, at his own request, to discuss the situation following President Eisenhower's announcement of the dispatch of U.S. troops to Lebanon.

Akaba Quiet, Only Civilian Unloading

Jerusalem Post Reporter

EILAT.—Two civilian freighters Tuesday afternoon joined the three other American ships unloading in Akaba port, the cargoes appearing entirely non-military.

This was the only increased activity which followed news of the American Marine landing at Beirut. Two of the ships have been unloading since last week.

Akaba was observed to be entirely tranquil with no unusual movements noticed.

Shepherds and farmers of border settlements on Israel's northern border told The Jerusalem Post *late Tuesday night that no increase in activity had been noted on the Lebanese side of the border and that no U.S. Marines had been seen so far.*

U.S., Britain Deny Troops in Jordan

The Egyptian Government-sponsored Middle East News Agency said Tuesday that U.S. and Turkish troops had arrived in Jordan at the request of King Hussein. In Beirut, a Lebanese Government source said British paratroopers had landed in Jordan.

The reports were denied in both Washington and London. The White House Press Secretary in Washington added that he could not speak for Turkey.

American, British and French air, land and sea forces stood by in the Middle East Tuesday to back the landing by 5,000 U.S. Marines off Beirut. Loyalist Iraqi troops were said b[y] Amman to be marching toward Baghdad to crush the Nasserite revolt which sparked t[he] American move. Although news from the interior of Iraq remains scanty, it [is] thought possible that the rebel officers who overthrew the Faisal-Nuri regime in a lightning coup on Monday hold only the capital.

In Washington, the Defence Department announced early Tuesday that a number [of] military transport planes have been sent to "an undisclosed European Air Force bas[e]" and that the Tactical Air Command has sent a striking force to an undisclosed destinati[on]. Fifteen ships of the U.S. Sixth Fleet, including the aircraft carrier Wasp, left Napl[es] during the day, while 11 of the Fleet's 12 ships in Nice left that harbour, presumabl[y] for the Eastern Mediterranean.

5,000 Marines Land in 24 Min.

BEIRUT. — Five thousand fully-equipped U.S. Marines from the Sixth Fleet — more than half of the size of the Lebanon's standing army of 9,000 men—landed on the beach here Tuesday and were deployed close to the Lebanese capital in the course of a single afternoon, ready for any action.

The Marines, landing swiftly and smoothly from ships which appeared off the coast a little earlier, left no doubt that Beirut airport, eight kilometres down the coast from Beirut, was the main strategic target.

Advance units dashed into the airfield and immediately took control of the tower, hangars and service installations. Other units deployed and surrounded the field to guard against infiltration. Once on the airfield, the Marine force regrouped by companies and started organizing a vast cantonment.

Giant Globemaster troop transport planes were expected soon. The Marines also moved on to Khaled military airfield, about five kms. from Beirut. However, there were no immediate indications that the troops intend to enter Beirut itself

Waiting Four Days

Once ashore, Marines reported that they had been circling offshore "for several days" awaiting the landing order. One Marine said their ships left Greece four days ago.

After the first wave of Marines hit the shore and found everything calm, the second and third waves brought up tanks, trucks and jeeps.

The first hint of major action came in mid-morning when American nationals were told to get off the streets. Then came word for them to report to a staging area in the suburbs — a precaution against rebel vengeance. Finally, Beirut International Airport closed down. All air traffic ceased shortly before the landing force appeared from the sea directly off the big field.

The landing was carefully coordinated with Lebanese troops. The Lebanese Army took over the airport as well as the docks.

The Marines came ashore in waves of about 500 men each. They came from a fleet of about 40 small boats about a mile offshore, coming from ships which included at least nine units of the 6th Fleet. The ships comprised an aircraft carrier, two cruisers, two destroyers and four amphibious craft.

The order to land was signalled to the Marines in the small craft at 1330 GMT. Sightseers crowded around, shouting greetings in English as the first wave took up positions on sand dunes behind the beach, while the boats went back again towards the landing fleet. When the last wave had landed the Marines moved on to the airport. The operation was complete 24 minutes after the first wave landed.

People were bathing on the beach just a kilometre from the landing point. Many cars drove along the coast road and pulled up to watch the landing. When the landing ships started loading alongside the big grey transports, Marine Air Arm jet fighters zoomed in from the main carrier force, flying down the coast out of sight.

Unconfirmed reports said other Marine units went ashore at Tripoli, Sidon, and Jounieh, all of them key coastal points. *(UPI, Reuter)*

Russia Demands U.S. Evacuation

The Security Council was summoned into emergency session Tuesday afternoon at President Eisenhower's request to hear an explanation of why the U.S. sent forces to the Lebanon.

After the U.S. delegate had stressed that the troops would be withdrawn "when the U.N. is ready to take over" to save the Lebanese Government, the Soviet delegate presented a resolution demanding immediate American evacuation of the country.

The session was adjourned until Wednesday (4 o'clock this afternoon Israel time).

In order to avoid the procedural debate which must precede the inclusion of a new item on the Council's agenda, the U.S. summoned the session officially to continue its debate on Lebanon's complaint of massive intervention by the U.A.R.

The American delegate, Mr. Cabot Lodge, told the Council that the territorial integrity of Lebanon was increasingly threatened by insurrection "stimulated and assisted from outside."

Plots against the Kingdom of Jordan in the past few months were "another sign of serious instability in the relations between nations in the Middle East." Now came the overthrow in an exceptionally brutal and revolting manner of the legal Government of Iraq.

He said Lebanese President Chamoun asked for help and the U.S. "responded affirmatively and positively to this request in the light of the need for immediate action." The U.S. was also considering economic assistance to Lebanon.

Mr. Lodge declared: "Our forces are not there to engage in hostilities of any kind and even less to fight a war... The despatch of U.S. forces to Lebanon is not the ideal way to solve the problem."

They would be withdrawn as soon as the U.N. took over and the U.S. hoped the U.N. would soon be able to take over its responsibilities.

After Sir Pierson Didon announced full British support for the U.S. action, Mr. Arkady Sobolev introduced a formal resolution.

The Soviet resolution reads: "The Security Council, having heard the communication of the representative of the U.S. on the introduction of armed forces in Lebanese territory, and considering that this action is a gross intervention in the domestic affairs of the peoples of the Arab countries and because of that is contrary to the aims and principles of the U.N. as expressed in the Charter and specifically in Paragraph Seven of Article Two which prohibits intervention in affairs which are essentially within the domestic jurisdiction of States, and bearing in mind that this action of the U.S. constitutes a serious threat to peace and security.

"Calls upon the Government of the U.S. to cease armed intervention in the domestic affairs of the Arab countries and to withdraw forthwith its troops from Lebanese territory."

Mr. Sobolev branded the American action as "an act of aggression against the peoples of the Arab world." He said it was a "gross violation of the Charter which prohibits the use of force as a means of foreign policy."

U.S. Warns Against Travel to Middle East

WASHINGTON (INA). — The State Department issued what its spokesman, Mr. Lincoln White, described as "general caution" to tourists and others planning "unnecessary trips" to the Middle East, particularly to the Lebanon and Iraq.

Mr. White said that 288 Americans are in Israel on official business at this time, and 5,800 are there unofficially. In Jerusalem, he said, 52 Americans are present officially. He gave similar statistics on Americans in Iraq, the Lebanon, Jordan, Syria, Egypt and other Middle Eastern states.

American Tourists Are Cordially Invited to a
RECEPTION
In honour of the 10th Histadrut Folk Delegation
From the U.S.A. and Canada
With the participation of H.E. the U.S. Ambassador, Representatives of the Israel Government and the Vaad Hapoel of the Histadrut
THURSDAY, JULY 17, 1958, 8 p.m.
in the Garden of the Farband-Hamlin House,
26 Rehov Weizmann, Tel Aviv

While British warships gathered around Cy[prus] from the Western Mediterranean, British Army [units] moved toward the Persian Gulf. The French Minist[ry of] Information announced that the Lebanese Govern[ment] had been informed of French forces which coul[d be] put at its disposal. Units of the French Fleet wer[e in] the Eastern Mediterranean in agreement with [the] Lebanese Government.

The Soviet news agency, TASS, described [the] American landings at Beirut as "an act of aggressi[on]" while in the U.N. Security Council, the Soviet U[nion] demanded immediate evacuation of the Marines.

Ike Prefers To Forget Suez

WASHINGTON, (INA). — President Eisenhower has indicated that the U.S. possibly erred in rushing to the U.N. to save the Egyptian regime from the Anglo-French Suez campaign in 1956 and the Israel drive through Sinai.

When he met on Monday with Congressional leaders, the President was reportedly asked if it had not been a mistake to have prevented the military actions against Abdul Nasser from running their course.

Mr. Eisenhower was quoted as replying that it was now "water over the dam."

Ike: 'We Know The Risks

WASHINGTON (Reuter). — President Eisenhower in a message to Congress Tuesday night said the dispatch of 5,000 Marines to the Lebanon "will be augmented as required."

The message said, "It is recognized that the step now being taken may have serious consequences. I have, however, come to the considered and sober conclusion that, despite the risks involved, this action is required to support the principles of justice and international law upon which peace and a stable international order depend.

"About two months ago, a violent insurrection broke out in the Lebanon, particularly along the border with Syria. This revolt was encouraged and strongly backed by the official Cairo, Damascus and Soviet radios which broadcast to the Lebanon in the Arabic language."

Earlier, the President said that the troops were sent to the Lebanon to protect American lives and encourage the defence of the Lebanon's sovereignty and integrity.

These forces have not been sent as any "act of war," the special White House statement said. They had been dispatched in response to an urgent plea from President Chamoun received Monday.

He added, "President Chamoun made it clear that he considered an immediate U.S. response imperative if the Lebanon's independence, already menaced from without, were to be preserved in the face of the grave developments which occurred Monday in Baghdad, whereby the lawful Government was violently overthrown and many of its members martyred."

Atlantic, Pacific Fleets Alerted

WASHINGTON (Reuter). — The U.S. Pacific and Atlantic Fleets Tuesday announced all their units and men had been placed on alert and said all units "have been made ready for extended operations at four hours' notice."

Amman Radio annou[nced] that the loyalist Iraqi Se[cond] Division marched Tue[sday] from Mosul and Kirkuk [in] northern Iraq, to coun[ter-]attack those who carried [out] the military coup in B[agh]dad. The division is no[t ex]pected to reach Baghdad [for] 24 hours. Mosul is about [...] kilometres north of the I[raqi] capital.

Amman radio said that [the] uprising in Baghdad is [con]fined to a limited area o[f the] city."

"It added "Loyal Iraqi fo[rces] began at noon Tuesday to [ad]vance from various par[ts of] the country towards Bag[hdad] to wipe out the element[s of] sedition and restore sec[urity] and order."

Reports from Amman [said] King Hussein held ano[ther] Cabinet meeting in his pa[lace]. Top Army advisers were [pre]sent.

One Battalion of Reb[els]

The B.B.C. diplomatic [cor]respondent said Tue[sday] night in the Arabic broa[dcast] that the rebel officers [and] men constituted one batt[alion] of the Iraqi Army. He [said] this battalion had rec[ently] returned from Jordan, [which] was the reason why the [...] authorities did not know [any]thing about what we[nt on] within the ranks of this [...]

Other reports said that [the] plot to overthrow Faisal [was] planned in Jordan by [this] battalion in coordination [with] certain elements of the [Jor]dan Army, and that the [ori]ginal plot envisaged the [over]throw of Faisal and Hu[ssein] simultaneously.

An Amman report [said] that King Faisal was now [un]der house arrest in Bag[hdad] although a foreign diplo[mat]ic source in Washing[ton] quoted by U.P.I., stated [that] Faisal had been killed by [a] mob. Other diplomatic sou[rces] could not confirm the re[port]. The State Department sa[id it] had conflicting and unc[on]firmed reports.

Warning to Rebels

Ramallah Radio in its [...] broadcast Tuesday ni[ght] warned the rebel Iraqi au[tho]rities that if any harm [is] done to members of [the] royal family, [or] to Jordan officials [who] are in Baghdad (there ar[e se]veral Jordan Ministers o[f the] Union Cabinet there) [they] would be held responsible [for] their actions and would fa[ce] "heavy reckoning."

The U.S. State Departm[ent] spokesman said at a p[ress] briefing that, according [to] reports still unconfirme[d, a] group of Europeans wa[s at]tacked by a mob in Ba[gh]dad Tuesday, and two [...] businessmen were repo[rted] killed, according to Re[uter].

Jews Enter Lebanon

WASHINGTON (INA). — [De]fence Department source[s said] Tuesday that U.S. Ma[rine] Corps personnel of Je[wish] faith are among the 5,[000-]man contingent landed in Lebanon.

Pentagon officials sai[d no] effort had been made [to] screen Jews out of the [mili]tary units that are attac[hed] to the U.S. Sixth Fleet.

"Why don't we [do] this more often...?"
is one of the popular [...] tunes on the program[me] of Duci-Carlo's [...] which plays tonight [and] every night on the [...] terrace of the Ramat A[viv] Night Club.
"Why don't we do th[is] more often?" is what [you] will ask yourself after [an] evening at this latest [ad]dition to Tel Aviv's nig[ht] life: the popular open-[air] nightclub, where a dish [of] 'Kebab' costs only IL1.[...] and the taxi-fare is [in]cluded in the week-d[ay] price of the first dri[nk] IL2.500 per person!
Why don't we?

WATCH
YOUR CHILDREN'S HEALTH
—let them drink
MALTON
THE PASTEURIZED BEVERAGE WITH BOILED WATER

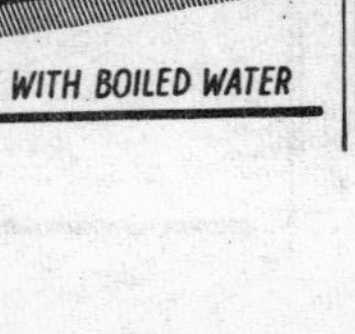

THE JERUSALEM POST
Published daily except on Saturday by The Palestine Post Ltd. Founded in 1932 by GERSHON AGRON.
Registered at the G.P.O. for transmission by post as a newspaper; reproduction of all material reserved; reproduction permitted only by arrangement.

Editor: TED R. LURIE
Head Office: 9 Rehov Havatzelet, Jerusalem, P.O.Box 81, Tel. 4233.
Tel Aviv: 52 Rehov Nahlat Binyamin, P.O.Box 1125, Tel. 64251/2.
Haifa: 34 Rehov Herzl, Tel. 4594/5.
Annual Subscription: IL 52.
Single Copy: 17 Agora.

THURSDAY, MAY 12, 1960
15 Iyar, 5720. 16 Zi el Ka'ada, 1379
Vol. XXXVI, No. 9725*

THE JERUSALEM POST

OPEN DIPLOMACY

IN the absence of an "open skies" agreement, President Eisenhower has resorted to "open diplomacy." Future historians — we are going on the assumption that humanity does not destroy itself — may come to regard the American President's statement of policy yesterday as an unprecedented, a revolutionary departure in international affairs. Before the bar of world opinion, the Head of a Great Power saw fit to unburden himself of the truth, the whole truth, and nothing but the truth.

President Eisenhower's total frankness had a startling effect. Most of all, it shook Mr. Khrushchev. From the outset of the "spyflight" incident, the Soviet Premier had been publicly proclaiming his belief that President Eisenhower knew nothing about it. Here was a broad hint, which by dint of repetition became almost a pathetic plea. "You pretend ignorance, and I'll pretend you're not pretending," was the gist of Khrushchev's message to Eisenhower.

Moscow and Washington are both angry, and making no bones about it. At the same time, however, and this is what really counts, neither side is allowing itself to be deflected from the tortuous path that leads to the Summit.

The present crisis will, after all, have served a useful purpose if it forces the Great Powers at their forthcoming meeting in Paris to tackle first things first. Here and now the primary need is to devise foolproof safeguards against an accidental outbreak of atomic warfare. As matters stand, it would appear that the people whose fingers are hovering over the pushbutton controls that could bring civilization down in ruins are not homicidal maniacs. They want to live, even if that involves letting the other fellow live as well. But with the constant state of alert in an atmosphere poisoned by mutual suspicions, a technical mistake or foolish miscalculation could bring on disaster, which will be none the less complete for being unpremeditated. The danger has to be faced and overcome, and if the "open skies" scheme is unacceptable to Mr. Khrushchev then some effective alternative must be found, and soon.

While President Eisenhower, in his sincerity, administered a shock, he also gave comfort to Mr. Khrushchev. The Soviet leader's recent irascibility cannot be wholly or even mainly attributed to the incursion of unarmed American reconnaissance planes over Russia. He must have been aware of this practice for some considerable time. What certainly upset him far more was the announcement made last week that President Eisenhower would not stay overlong at the Summit. Mr. Khrushchev's political position could be rendered untenable if he were left alone at Paris, and was made to look ridiculous in the eyes of his Stalinist opponents within the Communist camp. It must have been quite a relief to him to hear that President Eisenhower will remain at the Summit as long as substantial hope of success.

The "Big Four" will have their appointment with fate — ours as well as their own — in the French capital. If all goes reasonably well there, we shall not be surprised if President Eisenhower will then proceed to visit the Soviet Union, as planned. We must wait and see.

Did She — Or Didn't She...

11 Bar Kochba Letters Found in Dead Sea Cave

By SHALOM COHEN, POST Reporter

A dramatic announcement of the discovery of letters despatched by Bar-Kochba, leader of the Jewish revolt against the Romans in the second century C.E., was made in Jerusalem last night by Prof. Yigael Yadin. He was reporting to President Ben-Zvi on the archaeological expedition to the Judean Desert six weeks ago, at a large reception given the expedition at Beit Hanassi.

Eleven letters from "Shimon Bar Kosba" were found. Seven have been opened completely and four only partially. The letters, which open clearly with the words, "From Shimon Bar Kosba," are addressed mainly to Yehonatan Bar Ba'yah and to Masbala. They consist of orders, often phrased in a direct and brusque manner. "Send me Eliezer Ben Hitta immediately," states one missive. In others, he orders crops to be delivered and names persons to be brought in under guard.

Another letter begins, "From Shimon Bar Kosba, Nasi al Yisrael (Prince over Israel)," and instructs: that an amount of corn be taken from a certain person. It ends with a warning that non-compliance will be followed by punishment.

The same letter orders certain Yehoshua Bar Tadmori to be arrested and brought in under custody, noting with caution that "his sword should not be overlooked."

Note of Caution

The letters, written on papyrus and wooden slats, were found in a cave by Nahal Hever on the western bank of the Dead Sea by Dr. Yadin's team — one of four groups participating in the expedition.

The papyri were folded over many times with thin slats of wood between the folds. Because the bundle was found together with an assortment of feminine items, such as wool and beads, Dr. Yadin had earlier predicted that the unopened papyrus might contain magic formulae to exorcise evil spirits. These items, together with the papyri, were in a goatskin found deep in a crevice in the cave and had probably been overlooked by scroll-seeking Beduin. (Picture — Page 3)

In Cursive Aramaic

The letters, written in cursive Aramaic, conclude with "composed by ...," the name is given) indicating that the letters were dictated to a scribe.

The edges of the wooden slats were marked with a cross — perhaps by the Yehonatan referred to, or his wife, Dr. Yadin said—to show where they should be joined to reconstruct the letters.

Two letters from Bar Kochba were found in 1952. The Beduin say they found it in nearby wadi Meruba'at, which is in Jordan territory. They were published the following year by Père Milik.

Dr. Yadin believes the letters were written before the Jews went underground, since they refer to such items as crops, fields, and houses. He said that the letters would help clear up certain Hebrew language questions.

Dr. Yadin's dramatic announcement came at the end of reports given by the three other leaders of the expedition teams, Dr. N. Avigad, Prof. Y. Aharoni, and Mr. P. Bar-Adon and by the co-ordinator, Mr. Y. Aviram.

Hush in Audience

Since there had already been rumours of a dramatic revelation, there was a hush in the large gathering when Dr. Yadin declared "I have the great and unusual honour of..." His disclosure was followed by a spontaneous burst of applause.

The reception was attended by Prime Minister Ben-Gurion, Foreign Minister Golda Meir, the Knesset Speaker, the Chief of Staff, scores of soldiers, kibbutz settlers and students who took part in the expedition, and by a galaxy of leading personalities. Prof. B. Mazar, President of the Hebrew University, presided.

The Bar-Kochba letters as found in the Judean Desert.

FULBRIGHT MAY VISIT ISRAEL ON M-E TOUR

By JESSE ZEL LURIE, Jerusalem Post Correspondent

NEW YORK — Senator J.W. Fulbright left here yesterday for Cairo, on the first leg of his fact-finding mission in the Middle East for the Foreign Relations Committee, of which he is the Chairman.

He is accompanied by Mrs. Fulbright and his aide, Mr. Carl Marcy.

The Senator told reporters that he expects to meet with Abdul Nasser and discuss with him the amendment Congress voted into the Foreign Aid Bill, giving President Eisenhower discretionary authority to withhold mutual security assistance to the U.A.R. if it continued to restrict Israel shipping.

Mr. Fulbright, who strongly opposed the amendment, said he would "have a look at refugee camps" in Jordan, and that he would probably go on to Israel.

His secretary added that the full itinerary is still not decided, but will presumably include Israel, Jordan and possibly the Lebanon and Iraq.

(In Jerusalem, it was learned that Mr. Fulbright contacted the Israel Embassy only a few hours before his departure to request that arrangements be made for his possible visit to Israel next week, at the same time recalling the invitation for a visit made by Mr. Ben-Gurion at their meeting in Washington last March. Final details for Mr. Fulbright's visit are expected to be made in Washington today after the Foreign Ministry has given its confirmation. Mr. Fulbright is expected to meet with Mr. Ben-Gurion and Foreign Minister Golda Meir.)

'Dangerous' Spies Seized in Lebanon

BEIRUT. — A "dangerous" spy ring has been unearthed by Lebanese security men, according to a statement issued by the Directorate of Public Security here on Wednesday. A Lebanese, a Syrian and a Turk have been arrested while other members of the gang are still at large outside the Lebanon.

Four Lebanese women have also been arrested for allegedly going to Israel from Turkey.

The statement did not say for whom the alleged spies worked. It said they were to plan assassinations of politicians and forge identity cards.

A military court has questioned two chief suspects on the arrest for allegedly forming a Lebanese underground ring for Communist activities. Dr. Jamil Badour, a Jordan physician, and Ibrahim Tawwal, were said to have admitted they received messages originating from the "Central Communist Agency for the Middle East" with headquarters in Leipzig, East Germany. (Reuter, UPI)

Eshkol Warns Against Pressure Groups

By PHILIP GILLON, Post Reporter

KFAR WARBURG. — The Minister of Finance, Mr. Levi Eshkol, warned last night that pressure groups working to raise the standard of living unduly were endangering the nation.

Speaking at the 10th congress of the Moshav Movement, Mr. Eshkol said: "I told the doctors, the engineers, the civil servants, the teachers and I am telling you, the farmers — if the Jews don't want there to be a State of Israel, there won't be."

In a long, hard-hitting speech, Mr. Eshkol replied one by one to complaints by dozens of speakers throughout the day.

Although the movement is entirely Mapai, there was considerable criticism of the policy of the Government and the Jewish Agency. One of the most outspoken critics was Mr. Shmuel Dayan, father of the Minister of Agriculture, a former Member of the Knesset and one of the founders of Nahalal. Mr. Dayan complained that money was always available outside the budget for everything except agriculture, and that it was no good promising future solutions to people in dire need today.

Mr. Eshkol dealt with all criticisms, but he had to concede that the farmers and the authorities did not seem to have adequate contact nor to be aware of what the other was doing. (Picture — Page 3)

Communist Cells Raided in Congo

BRAZZAVILLE, Congo Republic (Reuter). — Security police swooped at dawn on suspected Communist cells in all the Congo Republic's main towns on Tuesday, taking in several suspects for questioning. Further arrests are expected.

A Government communique yesterday, revealing the searches and seizures of documents which are still being studied, said police had uncovered "an affair affecting the security of the state," and that "important developments in this affair can be expected."

The Government of this West African Republic, which is an autonomous member of the French Community, had proof of a plot involving the Communist-dominated World Federation of Trade Unions. The National Assembly gave quick approval to a new law restricting subversive organizations, banning subversive publications and providing for the arrest without warrant and expulsion of suspects.

HUSSEIN IN NAIROBI

NAIROBI (Reuter). — King Hussein of Jordan flew into Nairobi on Wednesday for a two-day informal visit to Kenya.

Mid-East Arms Curb Secondary, Is London View

LONDON (Reuter). — The Government made it clear yesterday that at present it thought it was more important to make progress on general disarmament than to limit arms in the Middle East.

This emerged from exchanges in the Commons between Mr. Denis Healey, one of the Labour spokesmen on foreign affairs, and Mr. David Ormsby-Gore, Minister of State at the Foreign Office.

Mr. Healey asked what proposals Foreign Secretary Selwyn Lloyd had made at the recent meeting of the Central Treaty Organization to seek agreement with the Soviet Union and other interested powers on the limitation of Middle East armaments.

Hope for Progress

Mr. Ormsby-Gore replied: "None, Sir. The general question of disarmament was, however, discussed and the Council expressed the hope that real progress would be made at the 10-power conference.

Mr. Healey: "But in view of the fact that the Government is already committed, by the Tripartite Agreement, to try to limit armaments in the Middle East without Soviet help and that, in the Prime Minister's communique to Mr. Khrushchev last year, he agreed to try to limit arms in Europe with Soviet agreement, why is the Government so unwilling to try to seek to explore this possibility so far as the Middle East is concerned?"

More Important

Mr. Ormsby-Gore: "We think it more important to make progress on general disarmament. I think you asked the Prime Minister a rather similar question the other day and the Prime Minister did say that he was bearing those considerations in mind."

C'wealth Premiers Air M-E Problems

LONDON (Reuter). — Problems of the Middle East were reviewed at yesterday's session of the Commonwealth Prime Ministers' conference here.

The 10-day conference, which is due to end on Friday, also discussed international developments in South-East Asia and the situation in the Far East.

Gilbert Seen as New Intelligence Chief

By ISRAEL NEUMANN, Jerusalem Post Correspondent

PARIS. — The former French Ambassador to Israel, M. Pierre Gilbert, is shortly to replace Gen. Grossin, Chief of the counter-espionage service, it was learned here on Wednesday.

Gen. Grossin, known as a supporter of M. Jacques Soustelle, who was recently expelled from the Gaullist party, is reported to have lost President de Gaulle's confidence.

'Would Not Like to be Ike' In Moscow, Khrushchev Declare

Soviet 'Provocation' Charge Ridiculous, Says Eisenhower

WASHINGTON (UPI). — President Eisenhower on Wednesday rejected as ridiculous Soviet charges of "provocative" espionage by the U.S. He said U.S. intelligence efforts such as the recently downed U-2 plane in Russia were distasteful but vitally necessary defence measures. Mr. Eisenhower told the 274 correspondents at his news conference that there were discrepancies in the Soviet version of how the plane was brought down.

For one thing, he did not believe that the U-2 plane was shot down from a high altitude as claimed by Premier Khrushchev. The President also said that Russian photographs of the plane debris were not pictures of the U.S. aircraft.

Mr. Eisenhower brought up the case of the Soviet spy convicted in the U.S., Col. Rudolph Abel, who was sentenced to 30 years in prison for spy activities in the U.S. Brusquely, he said that before the Russians accuse the U.S. of being provocative, they had better look at their own record.

The President spoke only from notes. Copies of his remarks were not made available for immediate quotation. These were his essential points:

§ He said no one wants another Pearl Harbour and it is essential for the U.S. to (Continued on Page 3, Col. 7)

Humphrey Quits Presidential Race

CHARLESTON, West Virginia (Reuter). — Senator John Kennedy, 42-year-old Roman Catholic millionaire, on Thursday won a landslide victory in the primary (popularity) election in this state over Protestant "Bible-belt" state and now has high hopes of being Democratic candidate for the Presidency.

His opponent, Senator Hubert Humphrey, a congregationalist,running as the "poor man's candidate," was so badly beaten that he announced: "I am no longer a candidate for the presidential nomination."

Senator Kennedy told the people of West Virginia: "I had no doubt you would cast your vote on the basis of the issues and not on any religious prejudice."

With returns in from 1,702 of the 2,750 polling centres, totals were: Kennedy 173,113; Humphrey 108,893.

Senator Kennedy's clearcut victory thrusts him into direct conflict with Republican Vice-President Richard Nixon, and the combined forces of rivals in the Democratic Party. Mr. Nixon is now disposed to treat Mr. Kennedy as his certain rival for the White House and to plan his campaign on that basis.

But Mr. Humphrey's withdrawal brings back into the running Mr. Adlai Stevenson, who has been twice defeated for the Presidency but this time would no longer favour Mr. Eisenhower as his opponent. Senator Humphrey's "liberal" wing may now give him its support.

Humphrey

Swiss Expel 2 Soviet Spies

BERNE (Reuter). — Two officials of the Soviet Embassy here have been ordered to "leave Switzerland immediately" for spying, it was officially announced on Wednesday.

The two Russians were arrested in Zurich Tuesday night as they left a restaurant with an agent in the pay of the Soviet espionage system. They were to have received from the agent, against payment, plans of Swiss radar establishments and information on the organization of the Swiss Army, as well as plans on rocket bases in West Germany.

The names of the two officials and the agent were not given, and police refused to say whether the agent had been arrested on the spot.

This led to speculation that he may have been a double agent who led the Soviet officials into a trap and whose identity the police wish to keep secret.

Will be Asked Many Questions

LONDON (Reuter). — Prime Minister Khrushchev said in Moscow yesterday that President Eisenhower's endorsement of spy-flying he "would not like to be in his shoes when he comes to the Soviet Union."

The Premier was surrounded by correspondents during a surprise visit to Gorki Park, where the wreckage of the plane shot down on May Day was on view, and asked if he still wanted President to come.

He made a long pause stared solemnly at the questioner, then said, "when would you like me to reply Get up here and reply me."

He said people would be a lot of questions to ask Eisenhower and they'd be right. But "there will be no excesses," he added.

Asked whether the incident changed his estimation of Mr. Eisenhower, the Soviet leader said, "It does, of course. I was not aware of the fact that this plane not the caprice of an irresponsible officer ... rified to learn that the President had endorsed the acts."

He said he would be going to the Summit conference and did not think it would be appropriate forum in which to raise the aircraft issue.

Two of America's allies were sore, condemned her action, "and that reflects honourable position."

Observers here felt that the tone of Mr. Khrushchev's marks indicated that his enthusiasm was waning (Continued on Page 3, Col.)

Denies 'Limit'

WASHINGTON (UPI). — At his press conference Wednesday President Eisenhower sought to correct any misunderstanding about the possible role of Vice-President Nixon as his substitute in case he must temporarily leave the Summit meeting.

He said his critics evidently missed the point that he always intended to return to the conference after two or three days of absence, if the meeting were still going on. He had not imposed, as Mr. Khrushchev had implied, a unilateral one-week time limit on the negotiations and was willing to keep talking at Paris as long as there was any possibility of agreement.

As to Premier Khrushchev's denunciation of the possible substitution of Mr. Nixon for the President at the meeting, Mr. Eisenhower commented that the Soviet Premier had never asked his opinion about some of Mr. Khrushchev's associates.

Experts Meet On Underground Tests

GENEVA (Reuter). — Experts from the U.S., Britain and the Soviet Union opened talks here yesterday on methods of detecting underground nuclear explosions.

U.S. Economy Tops $500,000m. Mark

WASHINGTON (Reuter). — President Eisenhower on Wednesday announced at his press conference that the economy of the U.S. had for the first time passed the $500,000m. mark.

He said that the biggest April rise in employment since World War II occurred last month when the number of people with jobs increased by 1,900,000 to 66,200,000. At the same time unemployment decreased by more than half a million.

Wreck on View

MOSCOW (Reuter). — Twisted hunks of metal, two huge virtually unmarked plane wings, equipment, and the personal contents of the wallet of Francis Gary Powers, the pilot of the downed American plane, were on show here yesterday.

The Soviet Government staged the exhibition in the Gorki Park's Chess Club, surrounded by gardens and a fun fair.

The complete sea-blue wings of the plane were propped up in the middle of the room with their surfaces in perfect condition, except for small holes peppering the surface as though the plane had been hit by shrapnel. Also shown were the engine, the ejector seat, the tail part of the fuselage and the oxygen containers.

The pilot's high-altitude suit and all his "bandit" equipment — the silent pistol, dagger and the suicide pin — were also on show, with the Soviet rouble and other currency which he had with him. Visitors also listened to recordings, said to have been made by Powers, of Soviet radar signals.

Published daily except on Saturday by The Palestine Post Ltd. Founded in 1932 by GERSHON AGRON
Registered at the G.P.O. Copyright of material reserved; reproduction permitted only by arrangement.
Editor: TED R. LURIE
Head Office: 6 Rehov Havatzelet, Jerusalem, P.O.Box 81, Tel. 4233.
Tel Aviv: 52 Rehov Nahlat Binyamin, P.O.Box 1125, Tel. 64251/2.
Haifa: 34 Rehov Herzl, Tel. 4594/5.
Annual Subscription: IL.57.
Single Copy: 17 Agora.

THE JERUSALEM POST

Gromyko Asks U.N. To Condemn Spying

UNITED NATIONS. — The Soviet Union yesterday asked the Security Council to condemn the American U-2 flights over its air space as aggression and to state that "such actions create a threat to universal peace."

In addition, a resolution tabled in the Council by the Soviet Foreign Minister, Mr. Andrei Gromyko, would have the 11-member body request the U.S. Government to "take steps forthwith to put an end to such actions and to prevent their recurrence."

In his reply, U.S. Ambassador Henry Cabot Lodge, offered to negotiate an "open skies" treaty with Russia and other countries to "obviate forever such measures of self-protection" as the admitted U-2 spy flights.

Mr. Lodge said: "The U.S. has not committed any aggressive act against the Soviet Union or any other country, neither through its air force nor any other agency of the U.S. Government."

Mr. Gromyko charged the U.S. with "unprecedented cynicism" in claiming that the "aggressive spy flights" over Russia were both justified and endorsed by President Eisenhower.

Spying for Years

He declared that the U.S., "without batting an eyelash," had admitted that espionage was an integral part of its foreign policy and that President Eisenhower's administration had been pursuing it for years.

The Foreign Minister said the murder of the Jews of Europe also gives grounds for the profound satisfaction. The desire to destroy the Jews could serve, even in the closest sense, as the only means of enabling the Jews to establish their equality of status as Jews. The State exists, and it has proved its fitness to defend those to wish to become part of it.

It is a punishment strangely fitting to the crime that it is here, in Israel, that Eichmann should stand trial for his crimes. — it cannot be doubted that the Soviet Union "has the facilities to defend its borders," he told the Council meeting which began its debate on the U-2 spy flights.

Ike to Broadcast On Summit Tomorrow

WASHINGTON (Reuter). — President Eisenhower will make a 30-minute coast-to-coast radio-television address tomorrow night on the abortive Summit talks, the White House announced yesterday.

Mr. James Hagerty, the White House Press Secretary, said: "He will make a report to the American people on the events at Paris and the future aims and goals of the U.S., and indeed, of its allies in the free world."

Gaitskell Defends Stand on A-Bomb

GREAT YARMOUTH (Reuter). — Mr. Hugh Gaitskell, leader of the British Labour Party, said here yesterday the urgent necessity for Britain was to remain in Nato and to keep nuclear weapons to be available as long as Russia has them.

But he told the annual conference of the General and Municipal Workers' Union (as he wanted to see a greater reliance on conventional and a smaller reliance on nuclear weapons in Europe.

"I want to be sure that nuclear weapons are effectively subject to control by the governments concerned and not just left in the hands of the generals," he added.

Mr. Gaitskell continued: "We believe that if Western Europe does not stand together and stand with America, we should each one of us be hopelessly weak in the face of any possible Soviet threat."

He did not think much of the point of view which said: "We will have nothing to do at all with nuclear weapons" and "Yank go home, but please protect us if there is any trouble."

To the Labour Party split over defence matters, Mr. Gaitskell said the Party must decide clearly questions of principle.

Demonstrators Clash With Tokyo Police

TOKYO — Police on Monday clashed with over 1,000 students who tried to break into the Diet (Parliament) grounds in a demonstration against the U.S.-Japanese security treaty.

Eighty-two policemen and more than 50 students were injured.

The leader of the students — most of whom were members of the fanatic and violent Zengakuren Student Federation — vowed that the students would burn down the official residence of Premier Kishi and the Foreign Ministry building "when the time comes."

NEHRU TO BURIAL FOR 2-DAY STAY

Premier Nehru of India will arrive in the Lebanese capital from Istanbul today for a two-day visit, according to Beirut Radio last night.

MOROCCAN KING BECOMES PREMIER

RABAT, (Reuter) — King Mohammed V of Morocco announced last night that he himself would take over government of the country.

In a radio message to the Moroccan people, the king said. "It is difficult to form a government. We will take the government in hand and preside over it."

He announced that Crown Prince Moulay Hassan would be his deputy Premier.

New Tremors Shake Chile

SANTIAGO (Reuter). — Another strong earthquake rocked southern Chile yesterday after a weekend of terror, adding new casualties to a reported toll of 400 dead and over 500 injured.

New fires were started in the partially-destroyed city of Castro on Chiloe Island, and fire fighters lacking water had to use dynamite to control them.

Ancud, in the north of the island, where 100 persons were believed swept away in Sunday's tidal wave, suffered at least 100 severely injured there.

Massive aid by ship and plane is being rushed to the thousands left homeless by the weekend quakes, fires and tidal waves.

The army provided tents for the panic-stricken population of Concepcion, a town of 180,000 persons 440 km. south of here, who fled to the woods and fields when the second quake struck the area early Sunday night.

Many trying to escape were trapped in their crumbling homes. Bridges, roads, railway and telephone lines were cut, and the desolated city was cut off from the world. Many smaller communities were devastated in an area of 70,000 square miles between Santiago and Chiloe Island.

A six-foot tidal wave, thought to have been triggered off by the Chilean earthquakes, struck the tropical paradise of Hawaii early yesterday, bringing death to the palm-ringed islands.

The main brunt of the rushing waters was borne by Hilo, largest city on the island, where at least four persons were known to have lost their lives.

There were also tidal waves in San Francisco Bay, but no damage was caused.

Four Murdered in Congo Elections

LEOPOLDVILLE, Belgian Congo (Reuter). — Four African voters were hacked to death at Kamina, near Jadotville, during the last major round of the Belgian Congo's general election on Monday.

Fourteen other voters were injured during a clash between tribesmen belonging to rival political parties. The authorities immediately clamped a military occupation regime over the area. Minor incidents were also reported in Elisabethville. Jadotville and Leopoldville, the capital.

Results in the three cities — described as "test areas" by election organizers — will be known today.

Eichmann Found by Security Services; To be Tried Here for Crimes Against Jews

Adolf Eichmann, one of the most notorious Nazi war criminals, who has been in hiding for 15 years, was found recently by the Israel Security Services and is now under arrest in Israel, where he will shortly be put on trial. This dramatic announcement was made by the Prime Minister in the Knesset yesterday afternoon. It caused unprecedented excitement in the Chamber and shortly thereafter in the streets outside.

ADOLF EICHMANN, YOU ARE CHARGED...

Jerusalem Post Reporter

TEL AVIV. — Clean-shaven, well groomed, and looking younger than his 54 years, S.S. Colonel Adolf Eichmann appeared before Chief Magistrate Yedidya Halevy in Jaffa at 11 o'clock yesterday morning, to hear the charges against him.

"Adolf Eichmann, you are charged with causing the death of millions of Jews in Germany and the occupied countries in the years 1938 to 1945. Are you he, Adolf Eichmann?" he was asked.

This was translated to the accused by Rav-Pakad Shmuel Roth, head of the C.I.D. at police headquarters. Rav-Pakad Roth told The Jerusalem Post that Eichmann was composed, but turned pale as he heard the charge.

He replied distinctly:
"Ich bin Adolf Eichmann."

He had nothing more to say at present, other than that he would ask to be defended. Eichmann speaks no language but German, Rav-Pakad Roth said.

Chief Magistrate Halevy remanded the accused for 14 days. The proceedings, at which the Inspector-General of Police, Mr. Yosef Nahmias, was present, lasted 20 minutes.

Eichmann had been brought to Jaffa in handcuffs. These were removed as he appears before the Magistrate. He stood to rigid attention, and was escorted by armed police guards.

Penalty is Death

Paragraph 1 of the Nazis and Nazi Collaborators (Punishment) Law 1950 stipulates that: persons, who during the period of the Nazi regime committed crimes against the Jewish people and humanity in general or during the Second World War committed war crimes, will be liable to the death penalty.

A crime against the Jewish people is defined as the commission of any of the following with the intent of destroying the Jewish people in whole or in part:

- killing Jews;
- causing serious bodily or mental harm to Jews;
- placing Jews in living conditions calculated to bring about their physical destruction;
- imposing measures intended to prevent births among Jews;
- forcibly transferring Jewish children to another national or religious group;
- destroying or desecrating Jewish religious or cultural assets or values;
- inciting to hatred against Jews.

The above crimes are excluded from the provisions of the later law abolishing the death penalty in Israel.

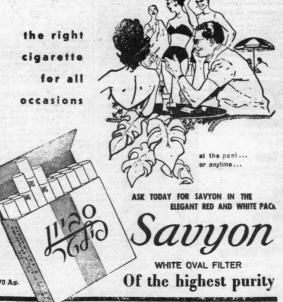

Eichmann in the uniform of an S.S. Colonel

'Most Wanted' In Germany

FRANKFURT, (AP). — Adolf Eichmann is the Nazi wartime criminal most wanted in Germany. He once headed a Nazi office named after him. It was charged with the systematic extermination of Jews.

An arrest warrant for the German-born former Lt. Colonel of the S.S. for murder had been circulated through the country for years. German prosecution officials dealing with wartime crimes asked Israel officials last year to check reports that Eichmann was in the Middle East, possibly in Israel.

El Al Plane Delayed Three Hours in Brazil

LYDDA AIRPORT. — The El Al plane that took the Israel delegation to the Argentine independence celebrations, returned early on Sunday morning from Buenos Aires.

En route to Argentina, crew members related, the plane made a brief stop at Recifa airport in Brazil. The aircraft was held up three hours by the airport manager there who, for reasons that are unclear, tried to prevent the plane from taking off.

After the seriousness of his action was pointed out, in view of international aviation regulations, the manager allowed the plane to proceed on its way. (Itim)

Chief Rabbi Asks Stern Justice

Chief Rabbi Nissim, in a statement last night, described Eichmann as a criminal "whose like had not been known in all Israel's history of persecutors and enemies."

"Hundreds of thousands of the children of Israel who were bereaved and tortured by this oppressor look to the courts to judge him with all the severity of the law."

Meir Stands by Statement On Dag's Suez Assurance

Jerusalem Post Knesset Reporter

Foreign Minister Golda Meir yesterday stood by her statement of last December 22, when she told the Knesset of Mr. Hammarskjold's advice to Israel regarding the shipment of cargoes through the Suez Canal. She was reviewing the activities of the Foreign Ministry, in the context of the debate on the State Budget for 1960/61.

Mrs. Meir quoted from Mr. Hammarskjold's press conference of May 5, in which he said:

"The fact is that there has never been any agreement (with Nasser on the shipment of Israel cargoes). And that is well known to all parties... No understanding preceded the despatch of the Astypalea."

The Foreign Minister noted that she had been asked time and again concerning the apparent contradiction between this and her statement, which she quoted as follows:

"Following on these efforts with the Egyptian authorities, the U.N. Secretary-General told us that he had reason to believe that, if Israel would agree to send her export cargoes through the Canal in the ownership of the purchaser (that is, f.o.b.), and to import goods intended to pass through the Canal towards her own ports under the ownership of the seller (that is, c.i.f.) the U.A.R. authorities would not obstruct the passage of ships carrying these cargoes."

"That is how I then summed up what was said to us by Mr. Hammarskjold, and I

Relations with U.S.S.R.

Referring to our relations with the Soviet Union, Mrs. Meir said that, despite all our efforts, the U.S.S.R. has not permitted relations of substance with us. In this it has displayed a marked attitude of discrimination in contrast with its declared policy of willingness to maintain commercial and cultural relations with all countries.

Mrs. Meir noted that our attempt to have talks with the heads of the Soviet Government were unsuccessful. The reason given by the Soviet Government when it refused to agree to a meeting between Mr. Ben-Gurion and Mr. Khrushchev was that meetings allegedly made in Israel which were not conducive to peace.

With regard to the last sentence of the U.S.S.R. reply, which states that "the U.S.S.R. wishes good relations with all countries of the Middle East, if mutual aspiration and mutual interest of that kind exist," the Foreign Minister
(Continued on Page 3, Col. 8)

Official Government sources have so far declined to release any details on the circumstances that led to Eichmann's apprehension. However, at a press conference one hour after Mr. Ben-Gurion's statement, the Minister of Justice, Mr. Pinhas Rosen, repeated his reply to a parliamentary question several months ago. which quoted a British denial of reports that the notorious Nazi criminal was hiding in Kuwait. The only other reports on Eichmann's whereabouts during recent years spoke of his hiding in a Latin American country.

Mr. Rosen said that no request had been made for Eichmann to be extradited to this country.

Mr. Ben-Gurion's announcement read as follows:

"I have to inform the Knesset that a short time ago one of the greatest of the Nazi war criminals, Adolf Eichmann, who was responsible, together with the Nazi leaders, for what they called "the final solution of the Jewish question," that is, the extermination of six million of the Jews of Europe, was found by the Israel Security Services.

"Adolf Eichmann is already under arrest in Israel, and will shortly be placed on trial in Israel under the terms of the Law for the Punishment of Nazis and Nazi Collaborators, 5710-1950."

The news of Eichmann's arrest spread quickly to Jerusalem's adjacent business centre and at 4.30, only half-an-hour after Mr. Ben-Gurion's announcement, both evening papers came out in Tel Aviv with special editions which were in demand faster than newsboys could sell them.

With the five o'clock news over Kol Yisrael, the entire nation could listen to the Prime Minister's statement and the story of Eichmann's capture had become the talk of the country.

At 3.30 p.m., half-an-hour prior to yesterday's Knesset session, the Cabinet convened in special session so that the Prime Minister could inform all his colleagues of the news.

Speculation Rife

Speculation on the content of Mr. Ben-Gurion's statement began when the Prime Minister entered the Knesset building accompanied by the Inspector-General of Police and the Chief of the Security Services.

"I have nothing to add or detract," Mrs. Meir declared yesterday.

Mr. Rosen stressed that everything would be done to hasten Eichmann's trial. He presumed that he would be charged with crimes against the Jewish people, under the Law of Punishment of Nazis and their Collaborators, for which the penalty is death.

Mr. Rosen said that West Germany was the only other country to have issued a warrant of arrest against Eichmann. Asked whether another country could ask for Eichmann's extradition, Mr. Rosen said that he would first have to serve the sentence pronounced against him here before an extradition request could be considered.

Eichmann is entitled to and will receive, full legal defence, even if he should request legal counsel from abroad, Mr. Rosen said. Up to now he has not been fully interrogated and the charge sheet against him would soon be prepared, Mr. Rosen added.

Other States Not Told

No other government has been officially informed of Eichmann's arrest, Mr. Rosen said, and Mr. Ben-Gurion's statement in the Knesset should be considered as an official announcement to all interested governments.

Mr. Nahmias stated that Eichmann was "absolutely fit" and that special security precautions are being taken for his custody. The press would not be allowed to meet him for the time being, Mr. Nahmias stated.

Mr. Rosen declined to say how long the place of Eichmann's arrest would be kept secret, saying only that he was from now on in the hands of the police.

The 14-day remand order would be renewed whenever necessary, Mr. Rosen said.

Leading members of all Knesset factions were unanimous in terming the arrest a "tremendous operation." Dr. Y. Bader (Herut) said the security services deserve high praise, and Mr. M. Ya'ari (Mapam) said that the arrest proved the organization was outstanding.

Mr. Y. Bar-Yehuda (Ahdut Ha'avoda) said that he had been deeply moved when he heard the news of the arrest and added his praise to that expressed by other M.K.'s.
(Portrait of a Killer—Page 4)

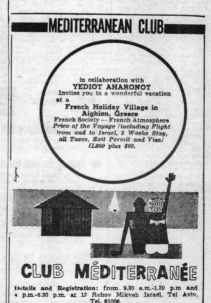

POST
Published daily except on Saturday by The Palestine Post Ltd. Founded in 1932 by GERSHON AGRON

Registered at the G.P.O. Copyright of all material reserved; reproduction permitted only by arrangement.

Editor: TED R. LURIE

Head Office: 9 Rehov Havatzelet, Jerusalem. P.O.Box 81, Tel. 24233. Tel Aviv: 52 Rehov Nahlat Binyamin, P.O.Box 1125, Tel. 64251/2. Haifa: 34 Rehov Herzl, Tel. 4594/5. Annual Subscription: IL. 57. Single Copy: 17 Agora.

Vol. XXXVI. No. 9876*

THE JERUSALEM POST

THURSDAY. NOVEMBER 10. 1960. 20 Heshvan, 5721. 21 Jamad Awal. 1380.

SENATOR Kennedy has been elected President of the United States, and with him America may expect to enter a new phase of initiative and leadership.

A NEW PRESIDENT

He has been generally welcomed on many sides, by Conservative Mr. Macmillan in England, by the French Socialist leader, M. Guy Mollet and by both the Nenni Socialists and the near-Fascists in Italy: Mr. Khrushchev sent an unwelcome compliment, saying that Mr. Kennedy's election represents the American People's rejection of the U2 policies of the Eisenhower administration, but offering renewed friendship. He is wrong in his election analysis. The U2 incident shook the United States. but not so much because it was anti-Russian." but because it was seen as badly mismanaged.

If Senator Kennedy represents an American wish, it is that he shall re-vivify the American nation, that he shall give them the leadership and the planning and the training needed to compete with a Soviet Russia that is rapidly forging ahead in political prestige and technical achievement. It is a courageous choice and in no sense a warlike one, but rather a choice directed at maintaining the strength needed to make war as unattractive a proposition as possible for any rival.

Inevitably, other countries will consider what this election means for themselves. Where political parties range from extreme right to extreme left, the two non-ideological American colossi seem hard to tell apart, but in the past, at least in foreign affairs, the Republicans have leant more to the practical approach and the preserving of America's favourable *status quo,* if no longer to actual isolationism, while the Democrats are inclined to proffer an ear to political change.

Both parties no doubt wish us well and envisage a continuation of the present active cooperation in times of peace. At a time of major crisis the longer-term planning of the Democratic approach is perhaps more likely to produce understanding of our point of view. It is not impossible that Democratic intervention in Egypt in 1956 might have taken a different form to that of the Republicans, with more logic and less opportunism as regards Nasser. At the same time the inherent plight of Egypt, as well as of the other Arab countries, is more likely to appeal to the Democrats, and there is no knowing to what use at least Nasser might put increased aid.

Senator Kennedy has outlined more imaginative help for the Middle East and shown that he has a good grasp of the area's essential problems, such as a need for systematic regional development rather than the encouraging of feuds for political negemony. To help solve these problems will require vision and courage and much critical intelligence. These are the qualities that the new American President will bring to his task, and there is good reason to applaud his nation's hard-fought decision.

Balubas Kill Ten Irish UN Soldiers

ELISABETHVILLE (AP). — An Irish U.N. patrol, seeking possible survivors of a rebel ambush on Tuesday on another Irish patrol which left 10 known dead. failed to report at its checkpoint late yesterday.

A Katanga Government spokesman said the detachment had left Albertville on the shores of Lake Tanganyika early on Wednesday heading for Niemba, about 16 miles away, where Tuesday's ambush occurred.

By 3 p.m. local time the patrol had not reported in and fears were being voiced for its safety, the spokesman added.

A U.N. spokesman declined to comment immediately on the apparently missing patrol. Meanwhile, U.N. Irish and Ethiopian troops threw a dragnet over the bush country.

The attack on the first patrol by Balube tribesmen took place late Tuesday evening as the 11 Irishmen, driving in two jeeps, crossed a bridge over a small river in north Katanga.

In Leopoldville, meanwhile, Cleophas Kamitatu pro-Lumumba head of the Leopoldville Provincial Government, again challenged President Kasavubu's right to speak for the Congo at the U.N. General Assembly.

At the United Nations yesterday, the General Assembly's Credentials Committee wrangled for more than an hour without getting down to the purpose of the meeting—consideration of a request by Congolese President Joseph Kasavubu to have his delegation seated in the world forum.

The nine-member committee finally agreed to postpone discussion until this afternoon.

Majority of Minorities Went to Kennedy

By JESSE ZEL LURIE, Jerusalem Post Correspondent

NEW YORK. — The key to the Kennedy victory lay in the overwhelming majority of what is called the minority vote — Catholics, Jews and Negroes, who are concentrated in the industrial States of the North-East, Illinois and California. All these States were won by Mr. Eisenhower in 1956 and all are in the Kennedy column today.

An analysis of the vote in Jewish districts in New York City shows the Jewish vote for Senator Kennedy to have been 10 per cent higher than that for Mr. Stevenson in 1956.

While most Jewish leaders personally favoured Mr. Kennedy, all Jewish organizations adopted a non-partisan attitude and Jewish leaders refrained from public statements. The sole exceptions were Z.O.A. notables including Rabbi Silver, and Messrs. Redelheim, Goodman, Torczyner, who vainly asked Jews to vote for Mr. Nixon.

Cyprus 'Escape Route' Said Discovered

NICOSIA (Reuter). — An underground tunnel believed used as an escape route by Jewish refugees after World War II has been found during building work at the British base at Dekfelia.

The 300-yard long tunnel was brought to light by workers constructing a new telephone exchange at the base.

Thousands of Jewish refugees escaped from Cyprus after the war, but how they got away has remained a mystery.

PALESTINIANS ASK FOR U.N. HEARING

UNITED NATIONS (UPI).— Ten Arab delegations requested on Wednesday that a "Palestine Arab delegation" be heard by the U.N. Special Political Committee when it begins debate shortly on the Arab refugee problem.

Let's Go Back To Days of FDR —Khrushchev

MOSCOW (AP). — Premier Nikita Khrushchev last night sent a congratulatory cable to U.S. President-elect Kennedy, expressing the hope that relations between the Soviet Union and the U.S. "will again follow the line along which they were developing in Franklin Roosevelt's time."

The message said:

"Esteemed Mr. Kennedy, allow me to congratulate you on the occasion of your election to the high post of the President of the United States.

"We hope that while you are at this post the relations between our countries will again follow the line along which they were developing in Franklin Roosevelt's time, which would meet the basic interests not only of the peoples of the U.S.S.R. and the United States but of the whole of mankind, which is longing for deliverance from the threat of a new war.

"I think you will agree that the eyes of many people are fixed on the U.S. and the Soviet Union, because the destinies of world peace depend largely on the state of Soviet-American relations.

Ready for Peace

"We have declared and declare our respect for the peaceable and gifted people of the U.S. and we are ready to develop the most friendly relations between the Soviet and the American peoples, between the Governments of the U.S.S.R. and the United States.

"We are convinced that there are no insurmountable obstacles to the preservation and consolidation of peace. For the sake of this goal we are ready, for our part, to continue the efforts to solve such a pressing problem as disarmament, to settle the German issue through the earliest conclusion of a peace treaty, and to reach agreement on other questions whose solution would bring about the easing and improvement of the entire international situation.

"Any steps in this direction will always meet with the full understanding and support of the Soviet Government.

"I wish you fruitful activity in the responsible capacity of U.S. President and prosperity to the American people," Mr. Khrushchev's message said.

Five Mentioned For Secretary of State

WASHINGTON (Reuter). — One big question facing President-elect John Kennedy is his choice of Secretary of State, the top post in the Cabinet.

Among those most prominently mentioned for the job are:

Mr. Chester Bowles, former Governor of Connecticut, former Ambassador to India and former Congressman, who was Mr. Kennedy's foreign policy adviser during the election.

Mr. Adlai Stevenson, former Governor of Illinois, Democratic presidential candidate in 1952 and 1956, and one of the country's best-known foreign affairs spokesmen.

Mr. David K.E. Bruce, a former Under-Secretary of State, and, until comparatively recently, Ambassador to West Germany.

Senator William Fulbright, Chairman of the Senate Foreign Affairs Committee, a Rhodes scholar at Oxford University and keen student of foreign policy.

Mr. Eugene Black, President of the World Bank.

Names being mentioned for other key jobs in the Kennedy Administration are: Defence: Senator Stuart Symington, of Missouri, a former Secretary for Air.

Chief representative to the U.N.: Mr. Stevenson or Mr. Bowles.

Young men who have been prominent during the President-Elect's campaign and are thought likely to be named to high posts include:

Mr. Robert F. Kennedy, the President-Elect's brother and campaign manager, aged 34, is expected to be a key adviser in the White House.

Mr. Theodore C. Sorensen, Mr. Kennedy's chief speech writer and adviser, aged 32, is expected to become "Chief of Staff" — the job which Mr. Sherman Adams formerly occupied under President Eisenhower.

Mr. Lawrence O'Brien, 42, political organizer and campaign assistant, is expected to become a member of the new Administration team.

Paris Acts to Bar Officials' Revolt

PARIS (Reuter). — The Government yesterday acted swiftly to prevent a threatened spread of revolt amongst senior French officials in Algeria against General de Gaulle.

Its action followed Monday's declared "inability" by M. Andre Jacomet, the top civil servant in the Algerian administration, to carry out the declared policy of the President of the Republic.

Yesterday morning, the Cabinet, presided over by President de Gaulle, refused to consider M. Jacomet's resignation, instead, they summarily dismissed him from his post. They also suspended him from exercising his functions as a senior member of the Council of State, France's highest juridical body.

No Precedent

The penalty is without precedent, except in some cases immediately after the war arising out of collaboration with the enemy. By suspending him from exercising his functions as member of the Council of State, the Government has reduced M. Jacomet's income by about half. It has also, in effect, barred him from obtaining further high-level Government employment.

The Cabinet Ministers were unanimous in taking this decision which they considered was calculated to make anybody think twice who was contemplating imitating M. Jacomet in challenging the right of the Executive to define the policy of the country.

De Gaulle Position Seen Strengthened

By MAURICE CARR, Jerusalem Post Correspondent

PARIS. — Mr. Kennedy's victory has strengthened President de Gaulle's position, and by the same token caused consternation among Algérie Française crusaders. One of their spokesmen, Andre Morice, a former wartime collaborator and Defence Minister in the Fourth Republic, angrily described the U.S. election results as "a leap into the dark."

The anti-Gaullists are disappointed because they entertained hopes — possibly illusory ones — of pulling off a "deal" with Mr. Nixon, had he become President, whereby the U.S. would give Algérie Française champions a relatively free hand in North Africa in return for France's abandonment of her own atomic striking force, her full integration into NATO, and her renunciation of President de Gaulle's demand that France be treated as an equal partner with Britain in the Western alliance.

Observers believe that Mr. Kennedy, despite his reputed coolness towards France, will get on very well with President de Gaulle — and that not only because of certain personal affinities between them — their literacy, dynamism, and stubbornness. Possibly in their broad outlook on world affairs, but certainly where Algeria is concerned, President-Elect Kennedy sees eye to eye with President de Gaulle.

Canada's Nazi Party Announces Dissolution

MONTREAL (INA).—Andre Bellefeuille who created a furore in Canada 10 days ago by telling a national television audience that he heads a Canadian Nazi Party announced here yesterday that his "National Socialist Party is dissolved and dead."

NASSER TO SUDAN NEXT TUESDAY

KHARTOUM (UPI). — Abdul Nasser will pay a 10-day visit to the Sudan starting next Tuesday, it was announced here on Wednesday.

'Devoted to World Freedom'

HYANNIS PORT, Mass. (AP). — President-Elect John F. Kennedy, one hour after he received Vice-President Nixon's telegram conceding the Presidency, acknowledged his election victory yesterday and promised to devote himself to "the long-range interests of the U.S. and to the cause of freedom around the world."

He told the nation: "The next four years will be difficult and challenging. There is general agreement by all our citizens that a supreme national effort is needed to move this country to safety through the 1960's.

"We need your help. All our energies will be devoted to the interests of the U.S. and the cause of freedom around the world."

He closed on a lighter note: "My wife and I now prepare for a new Administration — and for a new baby."

His wife is expecting a child in about three weeks.

All Welcome New President

LONDON (Reuter). — Senator John Kennedy's win in the U.S. Presidential election was generally welcomed throughout the world yesterday — in the West, among the "uncommitted" countries and by the Communist bloc, with the exception of Peking.

PEKING Radio, in a broadcast last night, showed little enthusiasm for either Senator Kennedy or the beaten Vice-President Richard Nixon.

"On the eve of the elections, both Kennedy and Nixon stepped up talk about arms expansion and war preparations, also about a policy of strength," it said. "Kennedy pledged himself to strengthen the nuclear war potential and modernize the regular army, besides resorting to propagandist tactics aimed at subversion of the socialist countries."

The official Soviet news agency, Tass, said Senator Kennedy's victory showed that Americans were "tired of the cold war and the arms race." The electors had "voted for changes" — both of persons in the government and in official policy.

Radio stations and newspapers in other European Communist countries indicated their true feelings. BUDAPEST Radio, for example, describing the results as a crushing political defeat for the Eisenhower-Nixon Administration.

TUNISIAN Government officials expressed satisfaction at the result. A spokesman said: "We congratulate Mr. Kennedy on his success. While a Senator, he has already taken a position on the Algerian problem."

AN ALGERIAN rebel "government" spokesman said the positions taken by Senator Kennedy on the Algerian problem during his electoral campaign "were enigmatical if not contradictory. We are now waiting for him to adopt a policy. We will judge him by his acts."

YUGOSLAV officials said privately they favoured Mr. Kennedy as President because they believed he would be better able to keep down aggressive military circles in the Pentagon, whereas Mr. Nixon might have been influenced by the old administration. They thought the new development might contribute to a more conciliatory American policy and thereby to a relaxation of present world tension.

In the VATICAN CITY, the director of the newspaper "Osservatore Romano," said Mr. Kennedy's win "strengthens appreciation for the high democratic principles of freedom which guide American public life." He made no mention of Mr. Kennedy being a Catholic.

WEST GERMAN Chancellor Konrad Adenauer said: "The personality and political principles of the newly elected President are a guarantee that he will uphold the cause of peace and freedom with firmness and wisdom."

In LONDON diplomatic quarters, Prime Minister Ha-

Favourable Local Reaction

POST Diplomatic Correspondent

The election of Senator Kennedy was generally welcomed by diplomatic observers in Jerusalem. There was, however, no official comment until late last night. No formal greeting cables were sent to the new American President-Elect.

Senator Kennedy will become President on January 6 and before that date protocol does not permit President Ben-Zvi to react officially.

Premier Ben-Gurion met with Mr. Kennedy for the first time last March during his visit to Washington. The meeting took place at the home of the former Israel Minister in Washington, Mr. Ya'acov Herzog, and problems of the Middle East, Israel's aid to the new countries of Africa and Asia and other international issues were discussed. Little publicity was given to the meeting at the time.

Meanwhile political observers recall one of Mr. Kennedy's statements at the Z.O.A. convention in Washington on August 25, whose content no avow of particular significance. The Democratic Presidential candidate said at the time: "Three weeks ago I said in a public statement: Israel is here to stay. The next day I was attacked by Cairo radio, rebuking me for my faith in Israel and quoting this criticism from the Arab newspaper "Al-Ghoumeriya": 'As for the question of the existence and non-

---

KENNEDY WINS THE BIG STATES BUT POPULAR VOTE ALMOST EVEN

380,000 LEAD IN 64 MILLION VOTES

NEW YORK (Reuter). — Senator John Fitzgerald Kennedy, the boyish-looking, 43-year-old Democrat, last night won the U.S. Presidential election in one of the closest neck-and-neck races this century. He is the youngest man ever elected President and the first Roman Catholic. From early in the morning he was virtually assured of occupying the White House for the next four years, but a ding-dong battle in seven states held up the final announcement of victory — and his Republican opponent, Vice-President Richard Nixon, refused to concede until the issue was beyond any doubt.

Democrats Retain Control of House

WASHINGTON (UPI). — Democrats won continued top-heavy control of Congress on Wednesday, signalling an end of "divided government."

About as expected, the election returns made little change in the Senate lineup but indicated the big Democratic margin in the House would be shaved by perhaps 20 seats.

Democratic leaders, claiming an early presidential victory for Mr. John F. Kennedy, went ahead with plans to install Sen. Mike Mansfield of Montana as the new Senate leader to succeed Lyndon B. Johnson, the Vice-President-Elect.

There never had been any doubt that the Senate would stay under Democratic control in the 87th Congress which convenes on January 3.

Senate Democratic Leader Johnson won reelection to the Senate while also winning Washington for having exerted his power as Senate Majority Leader on behalf of Israel in a number of crisis situations.

His most memorable pro-Israel action took place in February, 1957, when the Administration threatened Israel with punitive sanctions. The White House was then exerting what Sen. Johnson considered "one-sided" pressure on Israel to withdraw from Sinai.

Sen. Johnson summoned his chauffeur and drove to the White House. A heated session ensued. Sen. Johnson bluntly informed President Eisenhower that the Senate would not approve economic sanctions against Israel.

An outspoken Texan, Mr. Johnson told the late Secretary of State. John Foster Dulles, that threats to impose sanctions on Israel were "unwise."

Sen. Johnson told the administration it had lost sight of the basic facts in the Israel-Arab dispute. He informed fellow Senators that "contrary to widespread assumptions in the U.N. and in Washington, the issue is not originally the result of Israel's armed invasion of Egypt. The issue was raised by Egypt's long-standing insistence of maintaining a 'state of war' with Israel and implementing it by both guerrilla raids and a double blockade in the Suez Canal and Strait of Tiran. It was Egypt's blockade maintenance of a 'state of war' and the exercise of belligerent rights ... that resulted in Israel's military counter-action."

Senator Kennedy was leading in California, Illinois, Minnesota and Alaska, and Mr. Nixon in New Mexico, Washington and Montana. Any one of the three states, California, Illinois or Minnesota, would have assured the Senator of victory as "counting went" through morning, for he was then only eight electoral votes short of the 269 he needed to be sure of a win.

Then came the announcement from the farm state of Minnesota had gone to the Senator, giving him all its 11 electoral votes and putting the Senator beyond any possible doubt. This gave Senator Kennedy 272 electoral college votes — three more than the minimum of 269 needed for victory.

Photo-Finish

It was one of the tense struggles ever — a real photo-finish. In the early stages, 47 - year - old Vice-President swept into the lead, but with two million votes counted Kennedy took over. But then on he kept the lead in some cases only by a narrow margin.

Nationwide returns at the night Israel time from the 533 of 166,167 voting units.

Kennedy 32,299,908 (50.3 cent).

Nixon 31,846,510 (49.7 cent).

Kennedy was definite in some in 22 States with electoral votes; Nixon in with 181. Two hundred and sixty nine are a majority.

Shortly after three o'clock in the morning (10 o'clock Israel Time), Vice-President Nixon, smiling bravely as tide went against him, issued a statement from his hotel in Los Angeles: "If the press trend continues, Mr. Kennedy will be the next President of the United States. I want Senator Kennedy to know, as all of you to know, that if this present trend does continue and he becomes the next President, all of us will wholeheartedly support him."

But his wife was in tears as she sorrowfully said: "guess I'll have to get a teaching again." Mr. Nixon and his wife then retired the night.

Three thousand miles away in Hyannis Port, Massachusetts, Senator Kennedy, spending the long, anxious hours home with his family, decided to go to bed immediately after he had heard the Vice-President's statement, press secretary, Mr. Pierre Salinger, said there would be no statement until Vice-President Nixon conceded victory.

Nixon Concedes

Mr. Nixon finally conceded much later in the day, sending a telegram to his rival saying he wanted to reiterate the congratulations and best wishes he had extended in his television statement in the early morning.

After his night of doubt the Bostonian Senator greeted the Presidential victory in the most powerful office the Western world — one of the narrowest popular vote majorities of any successful candidate in the 20th century.

Americans do not vote directly for President, but for Electoral College. Or the votes at stake in the Electoral (Continued on Page 5, Col.)

VICE-PRESIDENT-ELECT

Johnson Exerted Power for Israel

NEW YORK (INA). — Lyndon B. Johnson, the Vice-President-Elect nominee, is known in behind-the-scenes Washington for having exerted his power as Senate Majority Leader on behalf of Israel in a number of crisis situations.

Senate
(Necessary to control—51)

	Rep.	Dem.
Elected	21	27
Holdovers	13	44
New Senate	34	66
Present Senate	34	65

Governors — Elected. 15 Democrats. 13 Republicans; holdovers, 19 Democrats, 4 Republicans.

House
(Necessary to control—219)

	Rep.	Dem.
Elected	172	246
Leading	12	7
Indicated new House	184	253
(x) includes 3 Rep. and 3 Dem. vacancies.		
Present House (x)	154	283

The following are the elected Governors, with (x) denoting incumbent:

Arizona — Paul Fannin, R. (x). Arkansas — Orval E. Faubus, D (x). Delaware — Elbert N. Carvel D. Florida—Farris Bryant, D. Illinois — Otto Kerner, D. Indiana — Matthew E. Welsh, D. Iowa—Norman Erbe, R. Kansas — John Anderson, R. Maine — John H. Reed, R. (x). Massachusetts — John A. Volpe, R. Michigan — John B. Swainson, D. Minnesota — Elmer L. Adersen, R. Missouri — John M. Dalton, D. Montana—Donald R. Nutter, R. Nebraska — Frank B. Morrison, D. New Hampshire — Wesley Powell, R (x). New Mexico — Edwin L. Mechem, R. North Carolina — Terry Sanford, D. North Dakota — William L. Guy, D. Rhode Island — John A. Notte, Jr., D. South Dakota — Archie Gubbrud, R. Texas — Price Daniel, D (x). Utah — George D. Clyve, R (x). Vermont — F. Ray Keyser, Jr., R. Washington — Albert D. Rosellini, D (x.) West Virginia — William W. Barron, D. Wisconsin — Gaylord Nelson, D (x).

THE JERUSALEM POST

WEDNESDAY, FEBRUARY 1, 1961 • 15 Shvat, 5721 • 15 Sha'ban, 1380

POST
Published daily except on Saturday by The Palestine Post Ltd. Founded in 1932 by GERSHON AGRON
Registered at the G.P.O. Copyright of all material reserved; reproduction permitted only by arrangement.
Editor: TED R. LURIE
Head Office: 9 Rehov Havatzelet, Jerusalem. P.O.Box 81, Tel. 24233.
Tel Aviv: 52 Rehov Nahlat Binyamin, P.O. Box 1125, Tel. 64251/2.
Haifa: 34 Rehov Herzl. Tel. 4594/5.
Annual Subscription: IL 57.
Single Copy: 17 Agora.
Vol. XXXVII. No. 9948

Tunisia Lashes New UAR Radio Attack

Tunisia charged yesterday that the UAR has launched a new radio campaign of "insults and defamation" against her in the past 24 hours despite the decision to rejoin the Arab League.

"El Amal," official organ of the ruling Neo-Destour party in Tunis, said that Tunisia's decision to end the two-year boycott of the League by attending the meeting of Arab Foreign Ministers, which opened in Baghdad on Tuesday, was taken "because we believe the Arab League is not Cairo and does not depend on it... because we want the truth and for public opinion to know its hideous face."

A dispatch by the Tunisian press agency said that the decision to go to Baghdad "in no way prejudices the Tunisian Government's political differences with the UAR, which instead of replying to the goodwill gesture of Tunisia and to the wishes expressed by several Arab countries, intensifies its attacks against the Tunisian Republic."

The agency said that the UAR's radio attacks were even now being directed against both Tunisia and Libya, after having been previously aimed at Jordan, Iraq, the Lebanon and Saudi Arabia.

Session on Algeria

In Baghdad, the conference began yesterday with Algeria the first item on the agenda, and with the participation of the Tunisian Foreign Minister, Dr. Sadok Mokaddem.

When he arrived from Beirut, Mokaddem said that "without doubt" Tunisia's "rights would be guaranteed" at the parley — which observers interpreted to mean that the UAR must agree to discuss Tunisian grievances at the meeting.

The Algerian item was scheduled to be completed last night, after morning and afternoon sessions. The Algerian representative, Karim Belkacem, submitted a memorandum to the heads of the 10 delegations.

(Reuter, AP, Baghdad R.)

US Chimp Rides Space Rocket, Is Recovered Alive

CAPE CANAVERAL, Florida (AP). — A chimpanzee rode a rocket 155 miles into space and was recovered alive and in good condition. The little ape was recovered 420 miles down range in his space capsule.

The recovery of the chimp climaxed a dramatic adventure in which the booster rocket misfired and propelled the capsule higher and farther than intended.

Radio signals reported the pre-assigned behaviour tests during the flight without a hitch.

The one-ton capsule containing the chimpanzee was hauled onto the deck of the landing ship Donna at 2041 GMT.

Earlier, it was stated that should the flight prove successful, an American astronaut would be put into space in two months' time.

The error by the rocket could have meant only postponement in the launching of a manned capsule. Officials wanted a perfect performance before risking a human life.

Improper performance of the booster produced a higher than normal thrust that propelled the capsule to a peak speed of 5,000 miles an hour. The intended flight programme was to carry the one-ton capsule 135 miles up, 290 miles down range at 4,200 miles an hour.

Spaak Quits Nato; Back to Politics

PARIS (AP). — Paul Henri Spaak yesterday officially submitted his resignation as NATO Secretary-General, to return to Belgium and lead the Socialist Party in the forthcoming national elections.

The 62-year-old Belgian leader had been Secretary-General since 1957 when he succeeded Britain's Lord Ismay. He said he hoped to leave his post at the beginning of March.

He had been under Socialist pressure to return home following the month-long strike in Belgium which left the left-wing, and particularly the Socialists, squabbling and badly split.

M. Spaak, who headed Belgium's first Socialist Government in 1938, was generally regarded as the best Socialist hope of patching up their differences before the elections which may come as soon as April.

Mr. Dirk Stikker, Dutch Ambassador to NATO, is the most likely successor to M. Spaak.

SS Officer Held For Killing Polish Jews

SALZBURG (Reuter). — Austrian police yesterday arrested Hermann Hoefle, 49, a former Nazi S.S. officer, and charged him with murder in connection with the extermination of Jews in Poland, particularly in Warsaw and Lublin.

The Justice Ministry said the material for the charge was provided by the Central Office for the Investigation of Nazi Crimes, based in Ludwigsburg, West Germany.

Santa Maria Due At Recife Today

RECIFE, Brazil. — The rebel commander of the Portuguese liner Santa Maria yesterday promised to bring the ship's 620 passengers ashore here tomorrow.

This announcement was made by the local radio station, and was evidently based on word from Brazilian newsmen who had boarded the liner, cruising some 35 miles off the coast.

The report came after Rear-Admiral Allen Smith of the U.S. had sailed out for a conference with "Captain" Henrique Galvao of the Santa Maria aboard the American-chartered liner. The Admiral said, after spending about three hours in conference, that "the picture is not as definite as all concerned would like it to be."

Ad Smith had area — the conference with a view to discussing the disembarkation of the passengers, including "Americans, but from the tone of his statement it appeared some difficulties could have developed in the talks.

Mr. Kennedy yesterday called U.S. Ambassador Llewellyn Thompson back from Moscow for "consultation on all aspects of Soviet-American relations."

'Izvestia' Lauds Kennedy Message

MOSCOW (AP). — "Izvestia" last night commended President Kennedy's "most clearly expressed" concern about the State of the Union and promised him full support in seeking to ease international tension.

It added that this would take some time.

The comment, buried in a full page general news review, was the first public expression on the President's State of the Union message. An extended digest of this was published in morning papers, but without comment.

"Izvestia" noted that the world's political climate is determined by relations between the U.S. and the Soviet Union and added the usual claim that "it is not our fault that dark clouds are found there."

The Government newspaper agreed that it would "take time to eliminate all the debris burdening U.S.-Soviet relations," but added that the Soviet Union took one step by liberating the two RB47 fliers.

The passengers seemed connected with the stand to be taken on the future of the Santa Maria if she touches at a Brazil port by the new President, Mr. Janio Quadros, who assumed office in a ceremony in Brasilia yesterday from outgoing President Juscelino Kubitschek. The latter had threatened to turn the liner over to its Portuguese owners, and to intern Galvao and his 70-man band, at least for questioning.

The new President did not mention the Santa Maria during the inauguration ceremony, but he was earlier reported to favour granting Galvao and his crew political asylum.

(UP, AP)

Democrat Gain In Vital House C'ttee

WASHINGTON (AP). — The House of Representatives voted yesterday to enlarge its Rules Committee in an effort to curb the power of a conservative coalition.

The roll call vote was 217-212. Those who voted for were 195 Democrats and 22 Republicans. Against it were 64 Democrats and 148 Republicans.

The decision to boost the committee membership from 12 to 15 was a major victory for Speaker Sam Rayburn (Democrat, Texas), in a power struggle with Chairman Howard W. Smith (Democrat, Virginia) of the Rules Committee.

BEN-GURION RESIGNS OVER GOV'T CONCLUSIONS ON 'LAVON AFFAIR'

Knesset Marks 12th Birthday

The Knesset last night marked its twelfth birthday by holding its traditional Tu B'shvat reception.

Closing yesterday's session of the House, Speaker Kadish Luz said that in its brief history the Knesset had established a reputation for itself among world parliaments.

He noted that there were two facets to Knesset activity — the political rivalry on the one hand and cooperation in preparing legislation in the plenum and in committees. Mr. Luz also said that while the committees are overburdened with work, attendance in the House is often "quite slim."

B-G's Letter

The following is the text of Mr. Ben-Gurion's letter to President Ben-Zvi:

Mr. President,

I hereby have the honour to inform you that I am resigning from my membership in the Government.

I do so with profound regret. It may be that many citizens, not only members of my party, who have entrusted me with their confidence, will regard this step with concern. Nor is it easy for me to abandon endeavours which I consider important and in which I have been engaged for many years, and plans which I have yet to implement. My understanding of my obligation towards the State forbids me to bear the responsibility for the decision adopted by the Government on December 25, 1960, as this decision is incompatible with the fundamental principles of justice and the basic laws of the State, although I have no doubt that my colleagues adopted it in good faith and in what they believed was solely the interests of justice.

The law of collective responsibility obligates every member of the Government to bear the responsibility for its decisions and acts, even if he himself is opposed to them. It is true that on several occasions the members of the Government adopted decisions with which I did not agree, and I accepted the ruling of the majority and bore the responsibility. At this session, the Government adopted a decision which I cannot reconcile with my conscience, and I have no alternative but to resign.

(Continued on Page 3, — Col. 3)

CABINET CARRIES ON DURING TRANSITION

The outgoing Cabinet will continue as a transition Government until the formation of a new one. The law sets no limitations on the extent of this transition period.

The procedure for the establishment of a new Government is for the President to call on a Member of the Knesset — usually a member of the largest party — to undertake the formation of a new Cabinet.

Prime Minister David Ben-Gurion last night submitted his resignation, which automatically means the resignation of the Cabinet, to President Itzhak Ben-Zvi. The Premier, in his letter of resignation to the President, said his conscience forbade him to accept responsibility for the Cabinet's decision of December 25 last, which endorses the conclusions of the 7-man Ministerial Committee on the "Lavon Affair." The Prime Minister handed in his resignation to Mr. Ben-Zvi at 8.45 p.m. immediately after a ten-minute extraordinary Cabinet meeting at which he made a brief statement on his decision. It is not ruled out that Mr. Ben-Gurion may accept the leadership of a new Cabinet which is not bound by the decisions of the Ministerial Committee on the Lavon "Affair".

"The major cause of my resignation was that the Cabinet had turned itself into a court of law," Prime Minister Ben-Gurion told journalists last night upon emerging from Beit Hanassi. The Prime Minister tendered his resignation to President Ben-Zvi in a 35-minute meeting with the Head of State.

The Prime Minister went on to explain that two obstacles which had only recently been removed, had delayed the resignation he had intended submitting much earlier. One was the convening of the Zionist Congress which he had not wanted to disrupt by tendering his resignation in the midst of its sessions.

Although Mr. Ben-Gurion did not elaborate on the second "obstacle," it is understood that he was in all likelihood referring to the recent U.S. representations on the building of the second atomic reactor in the Negev. Tension between the two Governments over this question has recently been greatly alleviated following talks between the Israel Ambassador to Washington, Mr. Avraham Harman, and the former Secretary of State, Mr. Christian Herter, and the assumption of office of the new Kennedy Administration.

Not Conditional

Mr. Ben-Gurion was asked by reporters if his resignation was conditional. "There is no such thing as a conditional resignation," the Prime Minister replied.

In reply to another question, whether he would accept an invitation from the President to set up a new Cabinet, he said: "I prefer not to consider, at present, what the future may bring. I am still on leave and would like to complete my leave."

With a long and brisk stride, the Prime Minister shortly before 9 p.m. yesterday walked the several score metres from his office to Beit Hanassi to submit his resignation.

During his two-minute "resignation walk," along Ibn Gabirol and Alharizi streets, Mr. Ben-Gurion, accompanied by his secretary, Mr. Yitzhak Navon, was trailed by several dozen newsmen and photographers to the entrance of Beit Hanassi, where they waited outside while the Prime Minister was closeted with the President.

After about 15 minutes, a bottle of vermouth was sent into the room.

Mr. Ben-Gurion was still at the Galei Kinneret Hotel in Tiberias yesterday morning when the first intimation was received of his intention to submit his resignation. His Military Secretary, Aluf Mishne Haim Ben-David, called the Government Secretary, Mr. Katriel Katz, in the morning and conveyed the Prime Minister's request that the Cabinet convene in the

Dramatic Decision

POST Political Correspondent

Prime Minister Ben-Gurion's dramatic decision to resign is understood to have been brought about firstly by a detailed study of the entire material connected with the 1954 security mishap which has strengthened Mr. Ben-Gurion's conviction that there was a miscarriage of justice in the decision of the Ministerial Committee last month.

However, the immediate cause of his announcement should be sought in the form of the Knesset debate on Monday evening, and the statements made by members of Mapam, Ahdut Ha'avoda and the Progressives, all of them Coalition parties, attacking the Prime Minister and thus in effect supporting the no-confidence motion of the opposition parties.

This move is considered a logical outcome of his announcement two weeks ago that he had prepared a letter of resignation, the submission of which was held up at the last moment by Mapai Ministers.

It is expected that there will be a large majority in favour of the censure motion. Were Mr. Lavon to resign as Secretary-General of the Histadrut following such a decision, the situation might be somewhat eased, but this is by no means certain. If he does not resign, a number of Secretariat members, including some who had not put up to now taken a clear stand such as Mr. Aba Hushi, the mayor of Haifa, and Mr. Shaul Avigur, will press for a formal non-confidence motion in Mr. Lavon the passage of which could enforce his resignation.

Mr. Ben-Gurion might form would presumably exclude both Mapam and Ahdut Ha'avoda, the two parties which have attacked him most violently with respect to the "Affair" both within the Government and in the Histadrut. Negotiations for a new government may take some weeks at least, and this period would give Mapai a breathing space in which to complete its own internal discussions of the "Affair."

It is understood that the Prime Minister's letter of resignation is intended in the first place to dissociate him completely from the decision of the Ministerial Committee, but it does not actually ask for a further inquiry into the "Affair." On the other hand, it is understood that further study of the available material which has been made in progress during the past weeks has produced a line of reasoning that may shortly make a legal inquiry appear more fruitful than at present.

Any new government that

(Continued on Page 3, — Col. 3)

Reid Briefs Kennedy On Israel's Progress

WASHINGTON (INA). — President Kennedy received a detailed personal report yesterday on Israel achievements and Israel-American relations from ex-Ambassador Ogden Reid, who described the affinity of the two nations as "growing continuously closer."

Mr. Reid, who had tendered his resignation, met at the White House with President Kennedy and discussed Israel at length. White House sources described the new Chief Executive as interested in his first discussion of Israel since he was inaugurated.

Describing the importance of U.S.-Israel relations Mr. Reid, after talking with Mr. Kennedy, told newsmen of hopes that persistent quiet diplomacy "might bring greater tranquility to the area."

"The situation is quieter than before with "less tensions." He believed "the fruits of freedom will commend themselves to other countries in the area," and added there was "no alternative to peace."

Mr. Reid said he hoped progress could be made in translating armistice agreements into peace treaties.

He said Israel shares basic principles with America and that bonds were growing stronger. According to Mr. Reid, "Israel is a fascinating country. One can see the future grow before your eyes."

UN Setting Up Buffer Zone Between Rival Congo Armies

LEOPOLDVILLE (Reuter). — General Injerjit Rikhye, military adviser to Mr. Dag Hammarskjold on the U.N. Congo operation, said here yesterday the U.N. planned to set up a buffer zone of military posts along the explosive border between the Congo's Equateur and Orientale provinces.

Colonel Joseph Mobutu's troops and pro-Lumumba forces in Orientale are lined up facing each other along this frontier, and it is feared that a large-scale offensive by either side is possible.

There have already been reports in the past few days of clashes between Mobutu's forces and the pro-Lumumba troops deep in Orientale province.

Gen. Rikhye told a press conference here that an Ethiopian battalion was on its way to Basoko, where the latest clash was reported, to find out exactly what was happening.

Gen. Rikhye said the eventual withdrawal of more than 5,000 UAR, Guinea, Morocco and Indonesian troops would make the U.N. Congo force "largely ineffective."

The evacuation of these troops, decided on by their governments, was to start in U.S. Globemasters with the 500 UAR troops.

Guinea's approximately 500 men are to sail from the port of Matadi later this week and the 3,000 Moroccans will also be leaving shortly. The 1,100 Indonesians are due to withdraw later.

Gen. Rikhye told the press conference that the U.N. was "very seriously concerned" at the bombing of Manono, North Katanga area, by unidentified planes in the last 48 hours.

He said the U.N. had made "a very strong protest" to Premier Moise Tshombe of Katanga about the bombings.

He said the U.N. had no definite information of the bombing planes, but a U.N. officer at Albertville saw a plane with a Belgian crew load hand-grenades, take off and return 15 minutes later

Servatius Returns, With Assistant

Jerusalem Post Reporter

LYDDA AIRPORT. — Dr. Robert Servatius, Eichmann's lawyer, arrived here by El Al from Zurich shortly before midnight last night accompanied by his assistant, 29-year-old Dieter Wechtenbruch, and his attractive 32-year-old secretary, Miss Lisa Grude.

Dr. Servatius told reporters that he would now set up headquarters in Jerusalem. He expected to meet the Attorney-General today and would meet with Eichmann within the next two days. Conditions for meetings with Eichmann have not yet been finally decided.

The German advocate said he hoped it would be possible to start the trial on March 15, as scheduled. This would depend, however, on when he would submit the "very seriously concerned" and on other technicalities.

He said he would prefer to have the trial financed by the West German Government. If this could be arranged, he would not accept a fee from the Israel Government. On this occasion, he brought no message from Eichmann's family.

(Earlier story on Page 3)

HERUT AND G.Z. CALL FOR NEW ELECTIONS

The Knesset factions of both Herut and the General Zionists last night issued statements calling for new elections.

There was no formal reaction last night from the Coalition parties, whose central bodies are due to meet this week to decide on a course of action.

It is understood that the National Religious Party will not back the proposal, and with Mapai they command 63 votes. It is also probable that the six Progressive and three Poalei Aguda votes would go against the Herut and General Zionists proposal.

Reid to ECOSOC, Quitting Jewish Posts

WASHINGTON (INA). — The Senate Foreign Relations Committee yesterday confirmed the appointment of Mr. Philip M. Klutznick as Minister to the U.N. Economic and Social Council.

The Committee commended Mr. Klutznick for his views and achievements. The latter announced that to avoid any impression of partiality in his new diplomatic capacity he would resign as General Chairman of the United Jewish Appeal, as Chairman of the International Council of B'nai B'rith, as Honorary President of B'nai B'rith, and divest himself of his interests in the development of Ashdod in Israel.

Mr. Klutznick's statement that he was of the opinion assistance to underdeveloped nations should not be on a basis of religion drew the commendation of a number of members, and his background in Jewish fund-raising was characterized as an asset.

Objection to El Al Ad in Casablanca

CASABLANCA (INA). — A small demonstration took place on Boulevard Mohammed V here in front of a shop window which displayed an advertisement reading, "Travel by El Al."

The demonstration took place following publication of an article in the opposition paper "At-Tahrir" which demanded that the authorities take all necessary steps to ensure that the advertisement disappears as quickly as possible.

TREMOR IN CRIMEA

LONDON (Reuter). — A slight earth tremor shook the Crimea near Yalta at 1342 GMT (3.42 p.m. Israel time) Monday, Moscow Radio reported in a broadcast monitored here. The tremor made floors of houses in Yalta heave slightly, the report added

Mr. Ben-Gurion's resignation last night came as a surprise, for reports have been circulating that the Prime Minister was reconsidering his earlier statement that he wished to go. This hope was based on a misconception. Mr. Ben-Gurion, whose moves have often been described as "unpredictable," has in fact always been entirely clear as to his basic principles and aims. A careful reading of his published speeches invariably provides a reliable guide to his intentions, and to the underlying reasons for his actions.

Mr. Ben-Gurion has never tired of reminding the nation that it must evolve a practical political system which will place the rudder of the State in the hands of a responsible majority. By "responsible" he has always meant a body of leaders who consider carefully where their pronouncements will lead, and who, should they gain the voters' support, will be able in practice to implement their promises.

True to the circumstances in which the State was built, the political leadership of this country has been vested in pressure groups who can achieve action only by bargaining or compromise. This may have been unavoidable in the small, scattered community of pre-State days, but it does not work, in the present norm, in an independent and hard-pressed State. Mr. Ben-Gurion has endeavoured to impress on the political leaders the idea that a State must be run on the basis of law, not on that of agreements which can be disowned at any moment.

The Prime Minister has always adhered to the principle that the decision of the majority is binding on the minority. This is democratic principle that nobody will deny, except those who believe that a minority may, and even must, try to force its views on the majority until everybody agrees with it.

Considering Mr. Ben-Gurion's moves in the past one does not and any deviation from the basic principles he has been advocating. He offered to resign when the Cabinet voted to approve a decision by a group of insisters with which he was unable to agree. The leader of a party cannot consider himself a leader if his associates overrule him in the Cabinet in a major matter. Mr. Ben-Gurion implemented his announced intention when members of the Coalition parties withdrew its support in a vote of confidence — despite technically voting with the Government as they are required to do — then they were demanding Mr. Ben-Gurion's resignation. This is not likely, however, that he will again retire completely from political life, as he did in 1954. When he went to Sde Boker. He is more likely to remain to fight the issue to the end.

The struggle will be fought on several fronts. If the President asks Ben-Gurion, as the head of the largest party in the Knesset, to form a new government, Mr. Ben-Gurion will not have to obtain his Mapai support. In other words, the Lavon issue, which has plagued the Party for months, will have to be decided one way or another by the Party as a whole.

The other front is that between the members of the future coalition. The National Religious Party may be persuaded to join Mr. Ben-Gurion. If he is to form the government, he is not likely to include either Mapam or Ahdut Ha'avoda, the two left-wing labour groups, whom he has charged on numerous occasions with forming the opposition within the coalition. The Progressives, moreover, cannot join as long as they stand by the findings of the Committee of Seven which was chaired by the party's leader, Justice Minister Rosen — the very issue which caused the Prime Minister's resignation.

Whatever the solution, the nation's interests require that it be found quickly.

Published daily except
Saturday by The
Palestine Post Ltd. Founded in 1932 by
GERSHON AGRON
Registered at the G.P.O. Copyright of
all material reserved; reproduction
permitted only by arrangement.
Editor: TED L. LURIE
Head Office: 9 Rehov Havatzelet,
Jerusalem, P.O. Box 81, Tel. 24233.
Tel Aviv: 52 Rehov Nahlat Binyamin,
P.O.Box 1125, Tel. 64251.
Haifa: 34Rehov Herzl,Hadar Hacarmel,
P.O. Box 4810, Tel. 4594
Annual Subscription: IL 67.
SINGLE COPY: 20 AGORA.

Vol. XXXVII, No. 10316

THE JERUSALEM POST

SUNDAY, DECEMBER 17, 1961 • 10 Tevet, 5722 • 10 Rejab, 1381

IF your engine could talk it would ask for SONOL SPECIAL the year-round motor oil

---

KATANGA FIGHTING:

U Thant Supported On 'No Cease-Fire'

UNITED NATIONS (AP). — Acting Secretary-General U Thant won the backing of his Advisory Committee on the Congo yesterday in his stand that the U.N. should keep fighting in Katanga until it had achieved all its objectives.

Participants in a private meeting of the 18-nation Committee told reporters that all who spoke supported the Secretary-General and were against a cease-fire at this time.

The U.S. which has received a cease-fire plea from Katanga President Tshombe, was understood to fear that the Advisory Committee would rule out talks between Mr. Tshombe and Congo Central Premier Adoula that could bring Katanga 'back into the Congo and have Mr. Tshombe accept the role of Provincial President.

But a member of the Committee said after the meeting that the general opinion seemed to be that if progress is to be attained, the Tshombe-Adoula talks should be completely separated from the U.N. operation in Katanga, which should continue.

A decision on the loan has been held up for about two months while the U.S. re-studied the situation in the light of statements made by President Kwame Nkrumah at the conference of non-aligned countries in Belgrade and also because of internal developments in Ghana.

The U.S. through its agencies, the Development Loan Fund and the Export-Import Bank, will loan the $37m. to the Volta River Authority over a period of at least five years for the construction of a dam, power station and transmission grids.

The remaining funds in the $196m. project are to be provided by the International Bank for Reconstruction and Development, $47m. Britain $16m. and Ghana itself, which will provide $98m.

In addition to the dam project, the U.S. will extend loan assistance totalling $96m. as well as investment guarantees to a consortium of private American companies who will build and operate an aluminium smelter using power generated by the dam.

Tshombe Still In Elisabethville

BRUSSELS (AP). — A Katanga spokesman yesterday denied reports that President Moise Tshombe had fled Elisabethville for Kipushi, near the Rhodesian border.

The spokesman said the President had remained loyal to his pledge to stay among the Katangese population.

US to Back Ghana Dam

WASHINGTON (Reuter). — The U.S. has decided to release funds totalling $37 m. towards the financing of the Volta River project in Ghana, the State Department announced yesterday.

Meir: Drop Payment Offer If Refugee Custodian Named

By JESSE ZEL LURIE, Jerusalem Post Correspondent

UNITED NATIONS — If the General Assembly endorses the proposal to appoint a custodian for Arab property abandoned in Israel, "it would lead to the reconsideration on our part of our compensation offer," Mrs. Golda Meir warned the Special Political Committee on Friday afternoon.

In her 10-minute address, the Israel Foreign Minister added that there was not the slightest prospect of Israel permitting U.N. jurisdiction in this matter.

There is, in any case, little prospect of the Assembly endorsing the proposal, which the Arabs are trying to push through the back door by a two-nation amendment to the U.S. resolution.

Sponsored by three Moslem countries which usually front for the Arabs — Afghanistan, Pakistan and Indonesia — joined this time by Ghana, the amendment would enlarge the Palestine Conciliation Commission from three members to five and require the PCC to protect the property and interests of the Arab refugees, which would be a wedge for custodianship.

Mrs. Meir stated, "Every modern war creates a refugee problem. However, responsibility for the fact that Arabs ever became refugees (Continued on Page 4.)

Algerian Truce Next Month

By MAURICE CARR
Jerusalem Post Correspondent

PARIS. — A cease-fire in Algeria is predicted for the New Year or during January according to fresh press reports quoting officially inspired sources which last week forecast peace "before Christmas."

The existence of a secret Franco-FLN agreement is now generally acknowledged, but discussions are said to be still proceeding as to the manner of executing the agreement against the opposition of European settlers in Algeria.

A Jewish doctor, Louis Schwartz, Medical correspondent of the liberal evening paper "France Soir," was on Friday night the victim of an OAS plastic bomb which destroyed his home but caused no casualties. A similar fate befell Gaston Palewski, a Catholic of Jewish origin who is French Ambassador to the Vatican and who is reported to be serving as President de Gaulle's principal go-between with FLN emissaries in Rome.

These and other outrages occurred 24 hours after OAS commander Raul Salan addressed a letter to the French Socialist Party disclaiming responsibility for the recent murder of Algerian Socialist leader William Levy which he attributed to dissident "extreme right grouplets." Salan asserted he has given the OAS orders to cease attacks on politicians and journalists. Friday night's events indicate that he is either lying or is outflanked by Fascist fellow-travellers.

INDIAN TROOPS SAID IN NORTH

NEW DELHI (AFP). — Indian forces have moved into the northern territory which the Indian Government has previously stated has been held by the Communist Chinese, according to informed sources here yesterday.

EICHMANN IN DEATH CELL

Sentence of Death being pronounced by Justice Landau in the Jerusalem District Court on Friday morning. Judge Binyamin Halevi looks straight ahead of him while Judge Yitzhak Raveh cups his chin in his hands. Eichmann stares straight at the presiding judge. Below Judge Halevi is the court interpreter while the official court record is being compiled by the clerks sitting below Judge Raveh. The Attorney-General's head is just visible. Next to him are seen Dr. Robert Servatius and Mr. Dieter Wechtenbruch, defence attorneys.

Germans Agree with Penalty

BERLIN (Reuter). — Germans on both sides of the Iron Curtain expressed approval of the death sentence for Eichmann. A West German spokesman for Government spokesman said it could astound no one. The trial had stirred up the horrible events of the past, he said. There had never been any doubt the trial would succeed in proving Eichmann's "million-fold crimes."

A spokesman of the Free Democrats, which forms the government coalition with the Christian Democrats, commented: "The carrying out of this sentence will not even start to atone for the crimes which the henchmen of Himmler committed against the Jews of Europe two decades ago." The death sentence would probably be regarded as just even by the most convinced opponents of capital punishment.

Matthias Googen, a prominent parliamentary Deputy of Konrad Adenauer's Christian Democratic party, wrote in the Party newsletter that "We are convinced there are no longer and never will be, any more Eichmanns in Germany."

There was the dominant subject of West German newspaper commentators yesterday. Virtually all of them agreed with the Independent Hamburg newspaper "Die Welt," which said in an editorial: "The verdict is just."

The "New York Times" correspondent here reported: "Some observers here believe the trial and the coverage by press, television and radio provided for the Germans have been a more powerful educational factor than all the sermons preached and books and articles written on the Hitler era.

"There has been throughout the trial and there was again today considerable editorial comment warning the Germans that they could not hide their responsibility for what happened behind the man in the dock in Jerusalem."

The official East German Communist newspaper "Neues Deutschland," ran a large front-page cartoon showing the condemned Eichmann looking accusingly at a smiling photograph of Hans Globke, former official of Hitler's Interior Ministry who is now State Secretary in the Bonn Government.

An editorial in the paper charged that Eichmann was "a colleague of Schroeder, a tool of Globke and a co-worker of Heusinger."

(World Comment, Page 2)

Peking Barred from UN Seat

UNITED NATIONS. — The General Assembly on Friday climaxed a historic debate by refusing to give Nationalist China's seat to the Chinese Communists.

The vote on the Soviet proposal was 36 in favour, 48 against with 20 abstentions.

Israel abstained, together with 11 African states mostly belonging to the Brazzaville group.

The decision represented a substantial victory for the U.S. as the China issue received its first showdown test since the Communists took over the China mainland 12 years ago. The issue now goes over until next year when the Russians are expected to renew their demands.

The Assembly had virtually slammed the door on Communist China, minutes earlier in the afternoon when it decided that a two-thirds majority was needed to seat the Peking regime.

It was a tactical victory for the U.S. since it provided insurance that the hotly-contested move to seat the Chinese Communists would not scrape through by a narrow margin.

NATO FAVOURS TALKS ON BERLIN

LONDON (AP). — Foreign Secretary Lord Home said yesterday he hoped tension over Berlin would be relieved now that the Nato Council has approved the resumption of diplomatic contacts with the Soviet Union.

The Nato communique said the alliance must continue on its resolute course, combining strength and firmness of purpose with a readiness to seek solutions by peaceful means.

Counsellor in Moscow

Mr. Dov Sattath has been appointed Counsellor at the Israel Embassy in Moscow, the Foreign Ministry announced last night. Mr. Sattath, 45, is Deputy Director of the Ministry's East European Department. He has served in every Israel mission in Eastern Europe except Moscow and Bulgaria.

'Each Trainload to Auschwitz 1,000 Premeditated Murders'

By MACABEE DEAN, Jerusalem Post Reporter

Adolf Eichmann was transferred from Beit Ha'am in Jerusalem to his death cell at an undisclosed "central prison" on Friday, not long after he was sentenced at 9.25 in the morning by the Jerusalem District Court for the major role he played in murdering six million Jews.

According to Section 38 of the Criminal Code Ordinance, the sentence "will be carried out by hanging by the neck until dead."

The Court did not set any date for the execution. It only stipulated that Eichmann had the right to appeal against both the verdict and the sentence.

Eichmann was brought into the packed courtroom at 5.58 a.m. He brought no papers with him to his bullet-proof glass dock, nor were there any on his desk.

He nodded and smiled briefly at his defence counsel, Dr. Servatius, who was assisted by Mr. Dieter Wechtenbruch, and then sat down. He maintained his customary habit of ignoring the existence of the public. Immediately after he sat down, however, he slightly raised his right shoulder which paced the public, as if for protection. Then apparently realising what he was doing, he straightened up.

He had on the same suit and tie he wore when he was first brought into the Beit Ha'am courtroom more than eight months ago.

Seemingly Unmoved

He was composed, and apparently completely unmoved although now and then his mouth twitched. The three judges did not file into court until 9.16, and during this time Eichmann let his eyes wander over the prosecution and defence tables and the empty bench. Half-a-dozen times, for several seconds each time, he looked intently at the Menorah, emblem of the State, on the wall behind the judges' bench.

When the judges filed in, he scrambled to his feet as did everyone in the courtroom. He took his seat after the judges sat down.

Justice Landau, presiding, said, "I hereby open the 121st session of this trial. The court will now hand down its sentence. The accused will rise."

Eichmann jumped up swiftly and stood to a military attention facing the judges.

"Now, after reaching the end of the lengthy discussion in this trial, we must hand down sentence on the accused," Justice Landau continued. Although rather pale, he spoke in a firm, clear voice, reading from a sheaf of papers. On either side of him sitting rigidly still, were Judges Binyamin Halevi and Yitzhak Raveh.

"The Attorney-General has asked for the death sentence," Justice Landau continued, and then briefly analyzed the legal situation. (See Law Report on Page 2). Justice Landau noted that the court had decided that the "death sentence was not mandatory and that the matter of punishment is within the discretion of this court."

Eichmann, still standing stiffly erect, but supporting himself by the knuckles of both hands against the table, gulped several times. The expression on his face changed almost imperceptibly, as he could not believe what he had heard — although there had been nothing in Justice Landau's voice to indicate that he would hand down anything but the maximum penalty.

Heavy Responsibility

Justice Landau continued: "We have carefully weighed — fully conscious of the heavy responsibility placed upon us — the sentence we feel is proper to be imposed on the accused.

"We have arrived at the conclusion that in order to punish the accused, and serve as a warning to others, we must impose the maximum sentence provided by law.

"In our judgment we have described the crimes which the accused participated, and these crimes are so terrible that they have no parallel in their enormity and scope.

"The purpose of the crimes — of which the accused has been found guilty — was against the Jewish People aimed at the extermination of the Jewish People, aimed at the annihilation of an entire people from the face of the earth and it is this which distinguishes these crimes from those perpetrated against individuals.

"It may be said that such total crimes like these, also the crimes against humanity which are aimed at a group of people, are more grave than the sum total of the individual criminal acts against the individuals which form part of the group.

Unparalleled Suffering

"But at this stage of handing down sentence we can also consider, and perhaps also, the injuries inflicted on the victims as individuals, and the unparalleled sufferings which the accused and their families underwent as a result of those crimes.

"The dispatch by the accused of each train containing 1,000 persons to Auschwitz, or any other place of extermination, is the same as if he had committed one thousand premeditated murders.

"The measure of legal and moral responsibility for the acts of murder is not a jota less than the responsibility of the person who drove these persons with his own hands into the gas chambers.

"Even had we found the accused acted out of blind obedience, as he claimed, we would still say that a man who participated in crimes of such dimensions over a period of seven years must be punished by the severest punishment allowed by the law, and no order received could have served as a mitigating circumstance.

"But we found that the accused completely identified himself with the orders received and that he was motivated by an acute desire to achieve their evil purpose. It makes no difference to us, in handing down (Continued on Page 3, Col. 3)

Appeal to Be Lodged Today

Jerusalem Post Reporter

Notice of appeal against the judgment and sentence in the Eichmann trial is to be submitted today to the Jerusalem District Court by Mr. Dieter Wechtenbruch, assistant to Dr. Robert Servatius, who defended Eichmann.

Mr. Wechtenbruch said in Jerusalem on Friday he hoped that he would be able to draw up the reasons for his appeal within the specified period of 15 days and that he would not have to ask the President of the Supreme Court to extend the time limit.

It is believed that he will appeal on grounds that the court was not competent to try Eichmann, it erred in its judgment, and that the death sentence should be commuted.

Eichmann was formally transferred by the Ministry of Police to the Prison Service immediately after the trial ended on Friday.

He was taken the same day from Jerusalem to a prison, believed to be in Ramle. The handcuffs he wore en route were removed.

When he passed into the prison walls, Eichmann became a prisoner as any other accused sentenced by an Israel court. His clothes were taken from him and he was given prison dress from the store room. His guards were not specially chosen but were picked at random.

The light in his cell will be switched off at night — his previous places of detention were illuminated 24 hours a day. He will have no contact with other prisoners.

Eichmann's cell contains a bed, table, chair, and drinking water. The regular prison food will be brought to his cell from the central kitchen.

He will be allowed a daily walk in accordance with regulations applying to prisoners sentenced to death.

Counsel Says It's 10:1 on Execution

MUNICH (Reuter). — Adolf Eichmann's defence counsel, Dr. Robert Servatius, said here on Friday that an appeal against the verdict would be based on the question of the Jerusalem court's competence.

There were also some points of law which he thought could be contested, he said during a brief stop on his way home to Cologne.

He would raise the question of Eichmann's kidnapping and would ask the Argentine Government for a statement on it.

Dr. Servatius said the verdict of guilty was to be expected and that the trial had been a fair one. He said the odds were ten to one against the sentence not being carried out.

MOSCOW RELAY

Moscow Radio on Friday night broadcast a recorded excerpt of the reading of the judgment by Justice Landau. Following the translation from the Hebrew, the announcer praised the justice of the sentence. (Itim)

Son Sees 'Devilish Forces'

BUENOS AIRES (Reuter). — Klaus Eichmann, Adolf Eichmann's eldest son, has told reporters the family "will not ask for clemency on father's death sentence."

Asked if he considered his father guilty, Klaus replied: "If it is guilt having served the S.S. loyally, father is guilty." But those who feel responsible for German policy in Africa, should also be tried, he added.

"Neither my father nor I was anti-Jewish. If there was persecution, it was prompted by the war," he said.

In a written statement Klaus described his father as a "cornerstone of an ordinary family, endowed with love, morality, decency and constructive example, loyal to his folk and country.

"What devilish forces moved behind the Jerusalem trial?" his statement asked.

It went on to describe Adolf Eichmann as "typically German, spiritually and bodily prepared to obey... in order to build a strong, just and sovereign nation."

Commenting on the sentence, the statement said it "made inroads into another country's sovereignty, constituted a farce of justice, placed a soldier before a civil court, and was prompted by hatred while the judges were identical with the injured party."

The statement went on: "If this is justice, we fathers of growing generations shall never support armies which claim the defence of the civilised world."

In Linz, Austria, Otto Eichmann, Adolf's brother, who runs their father's wholesale electrical equipment business, told reporters: "We still believe Adolf will get away with his life."

AFTER he heard himself pronounced guilty and knew that he faced a death sentence, Adolf Eichmann said he had

EICHMANN'S only carried out his government's orders; he argued in mitigation that "obedience is considered a virtue."

SENTENCE

It is difficult to escape the impression that, at least at times, Eichmann is still trapped in the mental shackles of his period of office to be able to argue in his defence that if he did see horrors, they were government-ordered horrors which he was sworn to carry out, leaving him legally innocent of all crimes. Murder is everywhere reckoned a crime: if it were enough for a body of men to meet and make a formal decision to murder for this action to be no longer a crime, then we should be deprived of all common humanity, there would be no hope for anyone.

In their findings, the judges emphasized that while Eichmann was guilty of the formal crime of genocide, they also found him guilty of abetting the specific, concrete murder of untold numbers of people. Every train with a thousand victims despatched to a death camp made Eichmann party to the killing of a thousand persons, to a thousand murders. This is the essential argument. In the Nazi view, there was only an impersonal order shrouded in official double-talk, ordering a "final solution" for faceless masses. But the reality behind these pieces of paper were real people consciencelessly killing other people no less real and individual than themselves. This is the fact that has been made plain by the trial, and was its chief purpose.

There is on record no greater perversion of the powers of government than this "final solution," for the Jews, for the previous attempt of any nation to wipe out another was given this sordid semblance of legality.

To find Eichmann not guilty because his past part was to carry out orders which he himself now appears to recognize as criminal, would be to deny every man's humanity, to degrade all to the level of a robot. But whatever his crimes, we are bidden to see in Eichmann what his Nazi colleagues did not see in the Jews — a fellow human — with the same original rights as all other men. To allow him to claim he could not have done other than he did, would be to deny humanity. Together, trial and sentence must restore two, not one, human right: the right not to be wantonly killed, and the right not to obey an order to kill wantonly.

There is another issue. There was a good deal of criticism abroad of Eichmann's abduction, and opposition to the holding of the trial by an Israel court. One should not perhaps investigate the underlying assumptions of this criticism too deeply, or we may find that there are still some who are accustomed to the thought of Jews being killed but not yet reconciled to that of Jews seeking out one of the killers for punishment. Owing to the meticulous care with which the entire long procedure was carried out and particularly, perhaps, the way in which the trial itself was conducted, the criticism has been forgotten and the verdict fully recognized. In the same places voices have now been raised against the carrying out of the death penalty, on the grounds that it behoves Israel to show mercy. There are also a great many people in Israel today who are opposed to all killing, even that of Eichmann. They are entitled to their opinion in the matter, though it is one that will be decided by law, in a country that abolished the death penalty for murder, but retained it specifically for Genocide with only a single dissentient voice. But it is not for others to demand clemency. It was Jewish millions who were killed, Jews who risked life and liberty to bring Eichmann to Justice, and an Israel Government that risked its international reputation on its ability to carry out this difficult trial without flaw. If there is occasion for clemency, it can be granted only in Jerusalem, against whose spirit and people the crime was committed, and nowhere else.

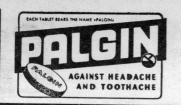

THE JERUSALEM POST Published daily except on Saturday by The ...lestine Post Ltd. Founded in 1932 by GERSHON AGRON
...gistered at the G.P.O. Copyright of material reserved; reproduction permitted only by arrangement.
Editor: TED R. LURIE
...ad Office: 9 Rehov Havatselet, ...rusalem, P.O.Box 81, Tel. 24233. ...l Aviv: 52 Rehov Nahlat Binyamin, P.O.Box 1125., Tel. 64251. ...ifa: 34 Rehov Herzl, Hadar Hacarmel, P.O.Box 4810, Tel. 4594
Annual Subscription: IL 76.
...OL. XXXVIII, No. 10449*

EACH TABLET BEARS THE NAME »PALGIN«
PALGIN
AGAINST HEADACHE AND TOOTHACHE

THE JERUSALEM POST

FRIDAY, JUNE 1, 1962 • 28 Iyar, 5722 • 28 Zai Alhaj, 1381
2.45 A.M.
TWELVE PAGES
PRICE: 45 AGORA

R. & S. BEN-ZUR (INSURANCE) LTD
Ben-Zur (London) Ltd.
Sicurconsult S.p.A Milan
Robert F. Marky—Zurich
Advice ★ Planning ★ Underwriting

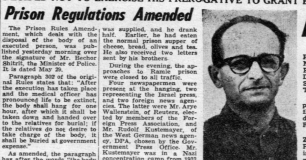

EICHMANN HANGED

ADOLF EICHMANN—TERMED BY THE SUPREME COURT A PRIME MOVER IN THE NAZI HOLOCAUST IN WHICH SIX MILLION JEWS WERE MURDERED—WAS HANGED LAST NIGHT. HE WAS INFORMED OF THE TIME OF HIS EXECUTION EARLIER IN THE DAY. SHORTLY BEFORE 11 O'CLOCK LAST NIGHT, IT WAS ANNOUNCED THAT PRESIDENT BEN-ZVI HAD DECIDED NOT TO EXERCISE HIS PREROGATIVE TO GRANT EICHMANN CLEMENCY.

Execution at 11.58 p.m.

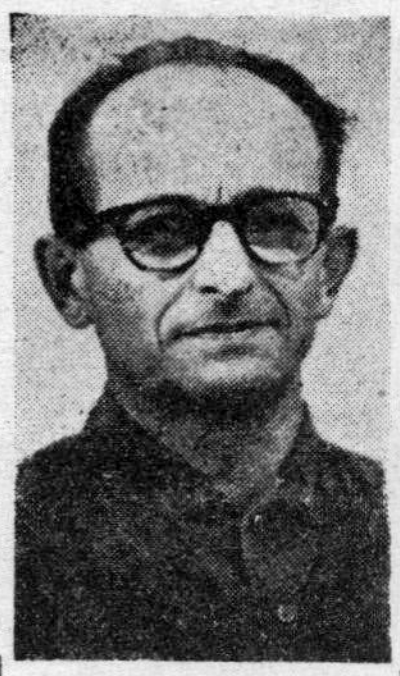

THE BODY WAS EXAMINED BY A GOVERNMENT PHYSICIAN, WHO PRONOUNCED LIFE TO BE EXTINCT AT TWO MINUTES BEFORE MIDNIGHT. THE EXECUTION WAS WITNESSED BY THE COMMISSIONER OF PRISONS, A GOVERNMENT PHYSICIAN, AN OFFICER OF THE TEL AVIV DISTRICT REPRESENTATIVE, TWO POLICE OFFICERS, WHO WERE PRESENT IN THE COURT WHEN THE DEATH SENTENCE WAS PRONOUNCED TO IDENTIFY THE PRISONER, AND A PROTESTANT CLERGYMAN.

The Justice Minister's written notification that the President had refused to pardon Eichmann, together with the judgment of the Court of Appeals, signed by the President of the Court, was tantamount to an order for Eichmann's immediate execution. A new regulation to this effect, amending the Mandatory Prison Regulations, was recently promulgated.

Early yesterday morning, the Minister of Justice submitted to President Ben-Zvi his advisory opinion that Eichmann should not be granted clemency. The President spent yesterday studying the relevant material in the case before reaching his decision. In addition to the Minister's recommendation, he also weighed many appeals from here and abroad, most of which opposed clemency.

Eyewitness reports of the execution were given at Beit Sokolow at 1.40 a.m., since, under the law, the body had to hang for one hour, and it took the reporters some time to reach Tel Aviv from Ramle.

Eichmann was brought into the execution chamber at 11.55 p.m., accompanied by three wardens and the Rev. William L. Hull, of Jerusalem. The death chamber, three by four metres, was 50 metres from his cell, with a trap door in the middle.

"When we came in, Eichmann was standing on the trap door, and no hangman was visible," the reporters said.

Eichmann was dressed in brown prison uniform, sandals and heavy woollen socks. First his ankles were strapped together, then his knees, and he complained that he could not stand up with his knees bound. The rope was then placed round his neck.

Eichmann was deathly quiet, but it was almost impossible to believe that this was a man about to die in a few seconds. He said "In a little while, gentlemen, we will all meet again. I have always lived as a man who believed in God" *(Ich war immer Gottglauebig)*, the phrase commonly used by the Nazis who rejected Christianity. The Rev. Hull had tried until the last moment to reconvert Eichmann to the Protestant faith, but he had not succeeded, Eichmann declaring that he no longer believed in Christ but had a faith of his own. Hull stood in front of him as the trap door fell open and tried to get Eichmann to say the word "Jesus," but instead, Eichmann said "Long live Germany, Austria and the Argentine." He also asked to be remembered to his wife, family and friends. His message to his wife was that he had "peace in his heart." He then said "I had to obey the laws of war and my flag."

As the rope was placed around his neck, two wardens standing out of sight, behind a blanket in the corner of the room, announced they were ready, and the Chief Warden said "Action."

The trap door opened and Eichmann fell some distance, remaining hanging a metre above the floor below, out of sight of the persons in the death chamber.

A reporter concluded, "The story has taken much longer to tell than it took to happen."

'Small Cog' to the End

In his appeal for clemency, Eichmann wrote that "only the leaders of the Nazi Party were responsible for the atrocities committed against the Jews. I was not a leader, and therefore I am innocent. The judges erred because they saw only part of the facts.

"I repeat, that I view with horror the heinous atrocities committed against the Jews. The criminals who implemented these crimes must be punished.

"But," Eichmann continued, "it is not correct that I personally was important and that I persecuted the Jews independently. The truth is that I did not have a high rank and that I only obeyed the order of my superiors."

Prison Regulations Amended

The Prison Rules Amendment, which deals with the disposal of the body of an executed person, was published yesterday morning over the signature of Mr. Bechor Shitrit, the Minister of Police. It is dated May 29.

Paragraph 302 of the original Rules states that: "After the execution has taken place and the medical officer has pronounced life to be extinct, the body shall hang for one hour, after which it shall be taken down and handed over to the relatives for burial; if the relatives do not desire to take charge of the body, it shall be buried at government expense."

As amended, the paragraph has after the words "the body shall hang for one hour" the following phrase: "after which it shall be taken down and *will be dealt with in such a manner as the Commissioner of Prisoners shall instruct.*"

(This paves the way for the Nuremberg precedent of cremating the bodies and scattering the ashes at sea.)

Other regulations of the Prison Rules, which are still in force, state that "The execution shall be carried out privately within the precincts of the prison not later than 8 o'clock in the forenoon," and "on the day prior to an execution, the gallows and apparatus shall be thoroughly tested by the superintendent and a representative of the Public Works Department."

A person condemned to death "shall be kept on such diet as the prison medical officer may direct, due consideration being given to his own requests in this matter."

A communique issued by the Government Press Office this morning at 1 o'clock, but dated May 31, said:

Adolf Eichmann was executed by hanging today in accordance with the death sentence passed by the Jerusalem District Court on December 15, 1961, the appeal having been dismissed by the Supreme Court on May 29, 1962, and the Minister of Justice having certified that the President had decided not to exercise his prerogative of clemency. The body was examined by a Government physician who pronounced life to be extinct at 23.58 hours.

Eichmann had been informed at eight o'clock in the evening of the President's refusal to extend clemency. When told that he would therefore die, he said: "Jawohl!" He asked for a bottle of wine, but had no other last request. A bottle of red, dry Carmel wine was supplied, and he drank half. Earlier, he had eaten the normal prison supper of cheese, bread, olives and tea. He also received two letters sent by his brothers.

During the evening, the approaches to Ramle prison were closed to all traffic.

Four newspapermen were present at the hanging, two representing the Israel press, and two foreign news agencies. The latter were Mr. Arye Wallenstein, of Reuters, elected by members of the Foreign Press Association, and Mr. Rudolf Kustemayer, of the West German news agency, DPA, chosen by the Government Press Office. Mr. Kustemayer was in a Nazi concentration camp from 1933 until the end of the war.

After the execution, the newspapermen were given an account of the 20 minutes preceding Eichmann's arrival at the execution chamber.

Eichmann was not wearing his glasses, which completely changed his appearance as it had been in the courtroom. He appeared calm, but pale, as he walked the 50 metres from his cell to the gallows supported by two warders. This is customary procedure in case the condemned man should faint or falter.

Rusk: No Headway In Talks with Russia

WASHINGTON (AP).—Secretary of State Dean Rusk said yesterday that his talks with the Soviet Union have not made any significant progress thus far, but they will be continued.

In his first press conference in more than a month, Mr. Rusk also sought to minimize difficulties between the U.S. and West Germany, calling them "hypothetical" because there has been no indication the Soviet Union would accept any Western proposals as a basis for a Berlin solution.

Mr. Rusk said that the Berlin problem does not turn around various details of a single proposal. He said the heart of the difference between the Soviet Union and the West is on key issues on which all of the Western powers are united.

At this point, Mr. Rusk said no progress has been made on the central issues at dispute with the Soviets.

He said he hoped to be able to visit Western Europe late next month but he could not say at this time what his specific schedule may be.

MAC AND DE GAULLE CONFER TOMORROW

LONDON. — Prime Minister Harold Macmillan is due to fly to Paris this week-end for private talks with President de Gaulle on a wide variety of topics, including European union and Nato.

At a press conference in Washington yesterday, Secretary of State Dean Rusk declared that sharing nuclear weapons with France would only make more difficult the eventual task of bringing nuclear weapons under international control.

Asked if he favoured Britain and France combining their nuclear forces, Mr. Rusk said no nation had made such a proposal but that the question of a nuclear force under Nato is under active discussion. *(AFP, AP)*

Wall Street Recoups In Avalanche of Buy Orders

NEW YORK (AP).—Buy orders from all over the world sent the Stock Market here substantially higher yesterday in another of Wall Street's biggest days.

The market was sharply higher at the start and continued to climb until around noon, when some profit-taking put many stocks below their best levels of the morning. The rise resumed in early afternoon trading. This attracted further profit-taking, but the market closed substantially higher.

The avalanche of buying put the high-speed ticker tape behind floor transactions from the start and the ticker tape was one hour and 45 minutes late at the close. This means it will be some hours before final figures and averages become available.

An hour before closing time, Standard and Poor's 500-stock index was ahead \$1.51 at \$59.59. This indicated the addition of some \$10,000m. to the quoted value of all stocks listed on the Stock Exchange at that time. The index closed at \$59.47 last Friday, so the latest reading showed it more than erased its huge loss on Monday and early Tuesday. The S & P 425 Industrials were up \$1.54 to \$62.67, also topping their \$62.58 close last Friday.

An informal compilation of the Dow Jones Industrial Average from prices believed to have been the final ones posted at the time the Stock Exchange closed showed the average to be up 9.45 points to 613.41.

In London Government securities, banks and insurance shares gained ground following the partial lifting of the squeeze on credit.

The announcement the Bank of England was releasing about £10m. worth of special deposits — which it was ordered to hold at the height of the credit squeeze last July — came mid-way through the day's trading on the Stock Exchange.

U.S. 'RETALIATION' TEST OVER PACIFIC

WASHINGTON (Reuter). — The U.S. plans to detonate a high-altitude nuclear explosion in the Pacific tomorrow, a spokesman for the Atomic Energy Commission said yesterday.

If all goes well, the shot is expected to take place shortly after darkness has settled on the Pacific Ocean. It will be the first of three or four designed to test the ability of the U.S. to retaliate after an enemy attack.

The Commission said that the tests might disrupt radio communications on certain bands for short periods.

The decision to go ahead with the high-altitude shots was taken after a group of scientists here disputed claims that the experiment would seriously interfere with the earth's belts of natural radiation, known as the Van Allen belts.

The U.S. wants to know whether such blasts can paralyse or destroy the radar system on which it relies to a great extent for advance warning of an enemy missile attack.

WORLD SOCCER CUP

SANTIAGO (AP).—Results in the second day's matches in the world soccer cup championships were:

Italy 0, West Germany 0. Russia 2, Yugoslavia 0. Hungary 2, England 1. Czechoslovakia 1 Spain 0.

INONU STAYS ON AS 'CARETAKER'

ANKARA (AP). — Turkey's President Cemal Gursel yesterday accepted the resignation of Premier Ismet Inonu's coalition government. The 78-year-old Premier was asked to remain in office until a new cabinet is formed.

Mr. Inonu's seven-month-old coalition cabinet, composed of his "People's Republican Party" and the "Justice Party," collapsed mainly over the issue of an amnesty for prisoners of executed Premier Adnan Menderes' regime.

The Justice Party, led by retired General Ragip Gumusapala, includes many diehard Menderes supporters.

Lebanese Plotters On Trial Today

A total of 310 persons accused of plotting to overthrow the Lebanese Government in a *coup* which failed last December 31, go on trial today, the Arab News Agency reported.

The Lebanese Parliament yesterday adopted a Government bill making it an offence, punishable by closure of up to five days, for a newspaper to publish material insulting the head of a foreign state.

350 Die in Worldwide Mishaps

Train and bus accidents throughout the world on Wednesday and yesterday killed at least 175 persons and injured more than 130 apart from a record death toll of 183 in the U.S. Memorial Day holiday.

In Northern Italy 62 persons were killed and 70 injured early yesterday when a speeding freight train crashed into a standing express crowded with holidaymakers.

In India, 69 persons died and 19 were injured on Wednesday when a bus plunged off a bridge into a river 850 kms. southwest of New Delhi.

The Philippine News Service said a bus went off a bridge into an 800-foot waterfall on Mindanao Island and 30 persons were feared dead.

Near Mexico City, a bus ran off a road on Wednesday night and fell into a 150-foot ravine, killing 14 passengers and injuring 43.

Three plane crashes which took 11 lives pushed to a record high America's Memorial Day toll of accidental deaths.

Road accidents killed 99 persons and 34 drownings were reported. Boating accidents took eight lives. Other accidents, not classified but including plane deaths, killed 42 *(AP)*

VOGHERA, North Italy (Reuter). — Police, firemen and soldiers yesterday recovered the bodies of 61 holidaymakers from the twisted rear coach of a stationary passenger train sliced in two by a goods train loaded with cement cylinders.

Infiltrator Killed

TEL AVIV. — An infiltrator from Sinai was killed and a second wounded and captured in a clash with an Army patrol in the Central Negev on Tuesday night. The Israel patrol suffered no casualties, the Army spokesman said.

Arms and ammunition were found on the infiltrators.

The U.N. Emergency Force has been informed.

Argaman Workers To Go Back Today

TEL AVIV. — The 425 employees of the Argaman dyeing and finishing plant are to resume work this morning. The 12-day-long dispute ended yesterday evening when the head of the Histadrut Trades Union Department, Mr. Yeroham Meshel, convinced the works committee, after all-day meetings, to press their workmates to go back to work.

A general lock-out of the textile industry, set for Sunday by the Manufacturers' Association, seems to be thus avoided. A general meeting of Argaman workers was to be held at 6 o'clock this morning and it was expected to accept the interim settlement.

The plant owner, Mr. Avraham Kalir, told *The Jerusalem Post* last night that he was satisfied with the settlement.

Both sides will meet in a month's time to thrash out such issues as payment for the period of the labour dispute.

...ICHMANN, whose name ... sent a shudder of fear ...rough the hearts of mil...ns of Jews as the great destroyer, has been executed after legal trial and appeal. He had ...de it his admitted busi...ss to root out Jews as ...ugh they were vermin, ...d his frenzied devotion ... this satanic aim sent ...lions to the death ...mps.

...t has been said that ...hmann's death will ...l no wounds. But in... ...ar as the history of his ...prehension, trial and ...cution help to restore ... feeling that justice may ... delayed, but that ul...ately evil will be pu...hed, it has helped to ...e out a little of the ...den regression into ...barousness brought in... ...our times by the Nazis. ...d it is certainly histo... justice that this task ...uld have been taken up ... completed by Israel, ...ose people were the ...ef sufferers of the Nazi ...rration.

...STICE

...ARELY has any dominant political party ... so much bedevilled ... trouble from within as Mapai in recent times. It is true, of course, that Mapai con... ... of a relatively large ...ber of people active ...esponsible positions in ... state and therefore ...e to develop an in...endent point of view. ... the same time their ...ccupation with party ...rs tends to lessen, and ... contacts with the ... and file are tenuous, ...ly for lack of time. ...o much cohesion and col...ve thinking is what has ... the two left-wing labour ...es, Ahdut Ha'avoda and ...am, appear rigid and of... ...even hypocritical, as they ...imously proclaim some ... of view that is clearly ...hared by all. But it is be...ng to look as though ...i will have to re-enunci... ...he goals and principles ...non to its members and ...re some sense of unity if ...eaders are not to find ...selves unable to carry on ... the tasks they have un...ken.

...KOL'S ...UTY

... the past Mr. Ben-Gurion ...een considered the worst ...der against what has be... known as the party ...rs' "lack of democracy." ...ately he always made ...wn decisions, and nobody ... have pretended for a ...ent that these were the ...ts of a vote taken in a caucus. Nor is this al... necessary: "democracy" ... consist either of collec... ...decisions, or of the will... ...elegation of power to one ...ore men by their suppor... Yet there have been ...y of occasions, from the ...nding of the Palmach on, ... a large proportion of the ... was actively opposed to ...decisions at the time, ...ch they may have come ...ppreciate their justness ...ubsequent years. Even ...avon "affair" was by no ...s the most serious of ... occasions, but merely ...which, for a variety of ...ons, was deliberately ... up into a crisis by op...nts.

... Eshkol, in his realm of ...e, has not been free of ...sm in the past, but ... to the specialized na... of his ministry, com... ... generally concerned ...olicies and not the fact ...they had not been ar... at democratically. But ...ly protests have veered ...is direction. There was ...ment that he should ... sprung his idea for a ...ng of the cost-of-living ...ance on the Manufac... ...' Association first, in... ... of the Party and the ...rut; there has been ...ly expressed resentment ...hat he should have ap...ed a Deputy Minister, ...Y. Korn, without con... ...g any official party fo... It appears that originally ...shkol may have wanted ...Korn as a personal as... ...t who would relieve ... a part of his intolerable ...n of work. When he ... there was no provision ...ch a post for a Knes... ...Member, he decided to ... through red tape by ...g he would make him ...deputy, which he is ...rized to do.

... appointment of a de... ... who will wield much ... certainly seems a mat... ...n which the party — ...oters — should have a ... When it is considered ... much of the criticism ...has always been aimed ...r. Shimon Peres derives ... the fact that he is ...ered a personal ap...ment of Mr. Ben... ...n's, Mr. Eshkol, usually ...ive to party atmosphere, ...d have thought twice ...e burdening his new ...y with so hostile a re... ...n by his party.

With deep sorrow we announce the untimely death of our dear daughter

CARMELLA HAFT

(nee Shitrit)

The funeral will take place on Sunday, June 3, 1962, at 11 a.m. from Rambam Hospital, Haifa.

The bereaved families
Shitrit
Haft

For Vacations
HOTEL MITZPOR
most modern hotel in
SAFAD
opening soon.
Limited number of places.
Tel. 147, Safad.

THE AMERICAN AMBASSADOR

CORDIALLY INVITES YOU TO MEET THE

U.S. Trade and Industrial Development Mission to Israel, June 3-27, 1962.

For appointments, visit Trade Mission Headquarters at the Tel Aviv-Jaffa Chamber of Commerce, Karlebach and Hachashmonaim Streets, Tel Aviv, Telephones 221137-8, or the U.S. Trade Information Center at the Near East International Fair, Pavilion 40C, Stand 960, Telephone 46236. In Haifa, telephone the Chamber of Commerce, Telephone 67469; in Jerusalem, the Chamber of Commerce, Telephone 81221; in Beersheba, the Mayor's Office, Telephone 2121.

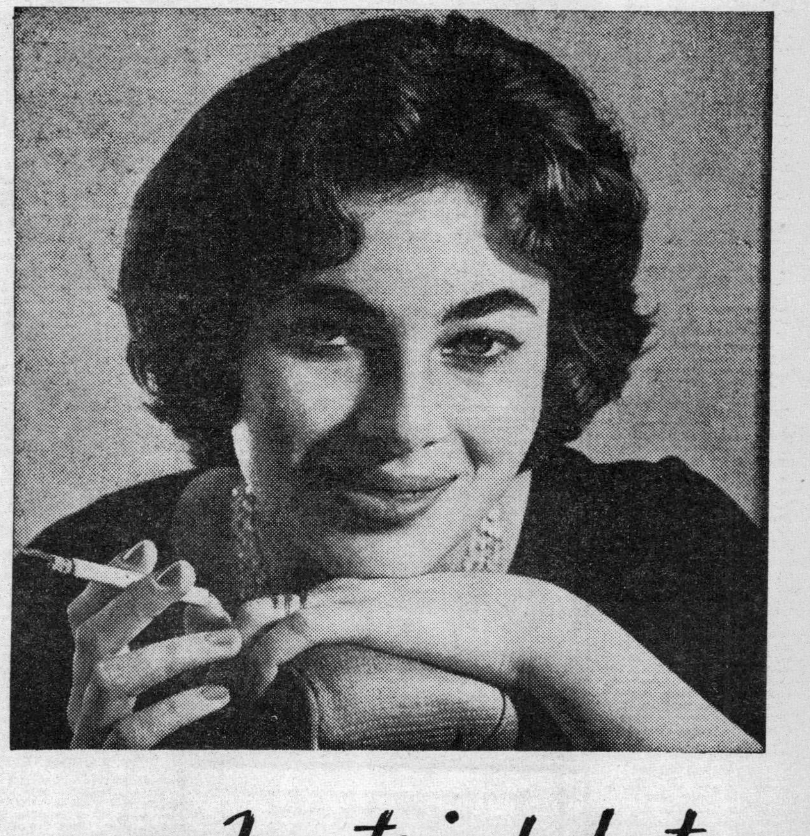

...yes, I've tried, but...
Ascot tastes better—
is better!

ASCOT — THE FILTER CIGARETTE THAT REALLY SATISFIES

THE JERUSALEM POST Published daily except on Saturday by The Palestine Post Ltd. Founded in 1932 by GERSHON AGRON
Registered at the G.P.O. Copyright of all material reserved; reproduction permitted only by arrangement.
Editor: TED R. LURIE
Head Office: 9 Rehov Havatzelet, Jerusalem, P.O.Box 81, Tel. 24293.
Tel Aviv: 52 Rehov Nahlat Binyamin, P.O.Box 1125., Tel. 64251.
Haifa: 34 Rehov Herzl, Hadar Hacarmel. P.O.Box 4810, Tel. 4594
Annual Subscription: IL. 76.
Vol. XXXVIII, No. 10570*

THE JERUSALEM POST

EIGHT PAGES
WEDNESDAY, OCTOBER 24, 1962 • 26 Tishri, 5723 • 25 Jamadi Awal, 1382 PRICE: 22 AGORA

U.S. FLEET POISED TO BLOCK ARMS TO CUBA; SOVIETS ISSUE WARNING

CUBAN CRISIS

THE hardening of Western opinion in support of President Kennedy's shattering demarche over the Soviet arms build-up in Cuba has been slow but perceptible. For weeks and months past, since the disastrous American venture in the Bay of Pigs, Western anxieties have centred mainly on the fact that American public opinion, always hysterically inflamed against the Communist world, might seek repair to its prestige, and could tempt or drive a President whose party is approaching an election into a rash move.

The photographic evidence of the missile bases in Cuba "where no Cubans are employed" appears to be solid: nor is it denied by the Soviet Union, which up to now has left Western critics of the American policy to produce the argument that there are also American missile bases in Western-aligned countries close to the Soviet Union. The situation in Cuba can thus be viewed as a Soviet attempt to achieve a balance of threats with regard to medium range missiles, and Soviet apologists will argue that this might favour peace in the long run, and that in any case the Soviets are no more likely to commit the lunacy of firing a missile at a target in the United States than the Americans are to fire one from a base in Europe or Asia.

This may be true. The struggle over the right to the placing of nuclear firing bases is more likely to be fought with conventional armaments, and even by such old-fashioned methods as blockades and the searching of suspect vessels on the high seas. And even this is not yet certain by any means. It is by no means impossible for the Security Council to devise some method of restoring the previous status to Cuba — one that is just barely tolerable for America, and does not require too much obvious yielding on the part of the Soviet Union.

The gradually swelling numbers of the United Nations now give it a certain flexibility even where the two major powers are locked in a flash-point struggle. The small nations cannot devise a solution and they certainly cannot impose one. But under certain circumstances they can make it possible for the powers to appear to yield to their pleas for restraint. In the 24 hours left before any actual confrontation by the American armada of a suspect Soviet vessel is expected some such formula can still be put forward.

In a country ringed by enemies such as this, there will be a measure of understanding for the American position. Whatever the strength of the Western defences in Europe, in Turkey and Persia, the dagger is now pointed also at the American heart itself. When a country feels its security threatened, it must act in its defence, or collapse internally even if the attack is never carried out. It has been profoundly instructive that even Mr. Nehru, a convinced pacifist with the true Oriental patience that can be so hard to understand as to seem automatically hypocritical to the Westerner, has been forced into active warfare by China, and that over a threat to a border area far removed from the vital life of India. It is not easy to see how the United States could ignore the establishment of a missile base in Cuba without any attempt to prevent such a development. That does not mean either that the base is not already operational, or that President Kennedy is anxious for a clash. It does mean that the West is not prepared at any point to permit itself to be consumed piecemeal by a slow Soviet advance. And as it can safely be assumed that the Soviet leaders are every ounce as determined to prevent a real clash as is the West, there are prospects that the excessive arming of Cuba may be dropped.

It will not be easy for either side to withdraw at this point. Mr. Diefenbaker as has become the Canadian tradition, has already sought to transfer the dispute to the noisy but less menacing forum of the United Nations. This is the place where it must go, if we are to breathe freely again.

WORKS COMMITTEE REPUDIATED

Wildcat Strike Ties Up Haifa Port

By YA'ACOV FRIEDLER, Jerusalem Post Reporter

HAIFA.—A general, wildcat strike of almost all of Haifa Port's 1,500 stevedores erupted yesterday morning. The strikers, who were in an ugly mood, repudiated the agreement reached on Monday night between their works committee, the Labour Council and Development Minister Yosef Almogi, who had intervened in his personal capacity.

A strike of this proportion is unprecedented at the Port. The Chamber of Shipping estimates the damage at a minimum of $50,000 a day. Labour Council sources maintain that Communist agitators had a decisive hand in bringing about the strike, directing their incitement at workers in the lower grades.

Teams of Port workers who are ready to go back to work will try to put the port into operation again this morning, the Haifa Labour Council spokesman said last night.

They will receive the necessary protection in case of trouble he added.

(Shortly before midnight Monday the Histadrut Executive repudiated the agreement, maintaining that it had not authorized the negotiators to make it. But works committee members insisted that Mr. Yeruham Meshel, Head of the Histadrut Trade Union Department, had given it Histadrut sanction when he met with them earlier in the afternoon. In any case, the strikers did not attribute their action to the earlier decision of the Histadrut Executive.)

The strikers practically paralyzed the harbour, tying up 26 of the 27 ships in port. The single working vessel was the s.s. T. Guilden, whose grain shipment was unloaded without incident at

(Continued on Page 3, Col. 4)

6 Ukrainian Jews Condemned to Die

MOSCOW (Reuter). — The Ukrainian Supreme Court has sentenced six persons including an 81-year-old man, to be shot for currency speculation, according to the newspaper "Ukranian Pravda" reaching here yesterday.

The six were among 15 persons — all with Jewish-sounding names —who stood trial in Chernovtsy, Western Ukraine. Alter Bronstein, 81, was described as the ring leader.

The sentences were reported in two paragraphs. The newspaper said that "other criminals were given different terms of imprisonment."

Mart to Probe Pact with Beirut

BRUSSELS (AP). — The Ministerial Council of the Common Market has instructed the European Economic Community Commission to open exploratory talks for a possible trade agreement between Lebanon and the Market, a spokesman for the council announced.

Lebanon is the first Arab state to have made such a request.

UK Diplomat Seeks Asylum in Russia

MOSCOW (Reuter). — A British official at the Australian Embassy here has asked the Soviet authorities for a permanent permit to stay in Russia, Tass said yesterday.

The Soviet news agency quoted the man, Gilbert Walker, as saying that for political reasons he did not want to return to capitalist countries, including Britain or any Commonwealth country. Soviet authorities were considering his request, Tass said.

Histadrut C'ttee May Meet Today

By MARK SEGAL
Jerusalem Post Reporter

TEL AVIV. — The Histadrut Central Committee is expected to hold an emergency meeting this morning to discuss measures for handling the Haifa Port strike.

This follows yesterday's meeting of *Sareinu*, the inner policy-making forum of Mapai leadership, on the subject. Complaints were believed to have been levelled at Development and Housing Minister Yosef Almogi for his independent activities in connection with the dockers.

Mr. Almogi, the former Haifa Labour Council Secretary, is believed to back the present Haifa Council leadership's view that "the Port issue should be left to Haifa to settle."

This attitude came under strong criticism at the *Sareinu* meeting, reflecting the previous night's renunciation by the Histadrut Executive of the settlement reached late Monday between the Haifa Council and the dockers.

A leading trade union official last night expressed the view that sufficient teams of men would be found to re-activate the port. "Our trouble is that we don't know who really speaks on behalf of the dockers any longer," he said.

Strong rumours in Tel Aviv last night that the Government may be considering as a final measure the application of labour mobilization orders could not be confirmed by official or semi-official sources in the trade union movement. However, these sources saw an intimation of such a possibility in yesterday's call to the dockers by the Transport Minister, Mr. Israel Bar-Yehuda, to return to work.

US ADMIRAL IN JORDAN

AMMAN (Reuter). — Admiral B.J. Semmes, Commander-in-Chief of the U.S. Naval Forces in the Middle East, arrived in Jordan yesterday on a five-day visit.

Chinese Widen Bridgehead In North-East India

NEW DELHI (Reuter). — Advancing Chinese troops threatening Tawang have widened their bridgehead in northeast India, the Defence Ministry stated here last night.

Its communique said Chinese forces had attacked positions in Bum La pass, 20 km. east of the Thag La ridge and advanced about 13 kms down the Nam Yang Valley.

Observers said it appeared the Chinese were trying to use a pincer movement to outflank Tawang—a Buddhist Monastery 80 km. south of the border where the Dalai Lama found refuge after fleeing Tibet. They added it appears the Chinese minimum aim is to occupy the Tawang area and control the Nam Yang River valley running southwest through Bhutan to Brahmaputra plains.

Chinese papers yesterday headlined the Government's declaration that its border forces "no longer need restrict themselves to the bounds of th illegal MacMahon Line" on the border between Tibet and north east India.

The declaration, in the form of a statement by a Defence Ministry Spokesman issued by the official New China News Agency early yesterday, said the Indian Government had "once and for all broken the bounds of this line."

Meanwhile, the British High Commissioner here, Sir Paul Gore-Booth, called on Mr. Nehru to convey the British Government's sympathy and assurance of support. U.S. Ambassador also called on Mr. Nehru. Russia, Egypt and Liberia are understood to be involved in mediation attempts.

The Soviet Union is understood to have suggested an immediate cease-fire and the opening of negotiations "without any preconditions, in a climate of mutual understanding."

Diplomatic circles here believe that in her present mood India is unlikely to agree to talks with the Chinese until they withdraw from Indian territory occupied by Chinese troops during the last three days' severe fighting.

A Defence Ministry spokesman said last night that further Chinese reinforcements had been observed at Longju, on the northeast frontier, and the attack on Kibitoo — at the eastern end of the frontier

(Continued on Page 2, Col. 2)

Bonn, Delhi Recognize Sallal

BONN.—West Germany has recognized the Republican regime in Yemen, the Foreign Ministry announced here yesterday. It was the first major Western nation to do so.

The Indian Government later announced it has also recognized the new regime.

Chancellor Adenauer's Government made it known over the weekend that recognition would be extended if Yemen promised not to establish diplomatic relations with East Germany.

From Aden, it was reported that the Yemeni Revolutionary Command yesterday broadcast a denial of reports that Yemeni planes bombed and strafed villages in the British-protected State of Beihan, in the Western Region of Aden, on Monday.

San'a Radio said the Yemeni Government believed that Britain was trying to justify her planned aggression against the Republic.

(British jet fighter patrols over Beihan have been increased and pilots ordered to destroy any planes committing hostile acts.)

British-officered troops of the South Arabian Federation, backed by artillery, moved into Beihan yesterday as a precautionary move following Monday's air attacks.

Riot police with clubs and shields moved into the main bazaar area at the Crater District of Aden as an angry mob waving Yemeni Republic banners shouted, "Down with colonial interference."

A crowd of about 500 strong shouted protests against the British Middle East Command announcement that troops and artillery had been dispatched to Beihan state.

Mecca Radio, quoting the Royal Yemenite Radio, said on Monday night that tribes loyal to the Imam Mohammed have inflicted heavy casualties of Egyptian troops.

San'a Radio earlier announced that 900 Saudi Arabian and 300 Jordanian troops were wiped out in air attacks by Yemeni planes as they moved to the Saudi-Yemeni frontier in a mass attack on San'a.

The Yemeni Republican Government yesterday renewed its request that the Arab League Council consider the "Saudi-Jordanian aggression against the Yemeni people and territory," a League spokesman announced in Cairo.

The Governor of Aden, Sir Charles Johnston, arrived in Aden from London yesterday after four days of talks with the Commonwealth and Colonial Secretary, Mr. Duncan Sandys. It is believed they discussed the draft treaty to merge the Colony of Aden with the South Arabian Federation, as well as internal security and the revolution in the Yemen.

(AP, Reuter)

'DEFEND CUBA' CALL AT U.S. EMBASSY

TEL AVIV. — Several dozen persons staged a demonstration late yesterday afternoon in front of the American Embassy here. They carried placards reading: "We Will Defend Cuba" and "We Will Defend Peace."

The demonstrators dispersed when a police patrol car arrived on the scene. They did not wait to be asked to move. No arrests were made.

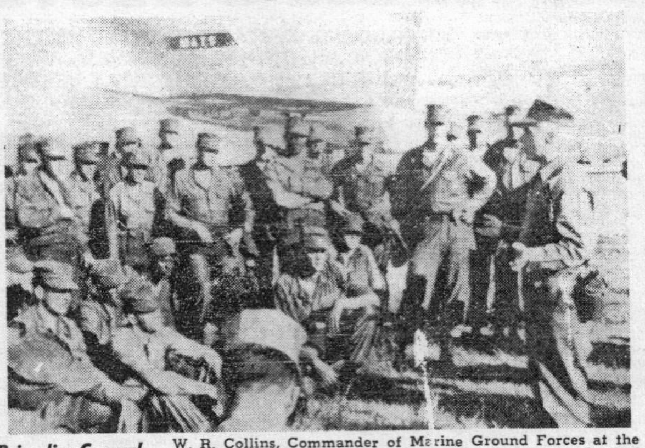

Brigadier-General W. R. Collins, Commander of Marine Ground Forces at the U.S. Naval base at Guantanamo Cuba, briefs a group of newly-arrived reinforcements after they were airlifted to the base on Sunday. (AP Radiophoto)

SOVIET BLOC STEPS UP COMBAT READINESS

MOSCOW (Reuter). — Russia yesterday stopped all leave for the forces, halted release of older age groups from strategic rocket, submarine and anti-aircraft forces and issued a "serious warning" to the U.S. on its Cuban policy.

Both the Soviet and Warsaw Pact higher commands ordered moves to increase the combat readiness and diligence of their forces.

Russia reaffirmed that Soviet arms deliveries to Dr. Fidel Castro were purely for Cuban defence.

No state which valued its independence could meet President Kennedy's demand "that military equipment which Cuba requires for self-defence should be removed from Cuban territory" a Government statement said.

A Tass statement said that the new instructions to the Soviet armed forces had been issued following a meeting of the Soviet Government attended by Marshal Rodion Malinovsky, the Defence Minister.

The Soviet Government called America's intended actions towards Cuba "an unheard-of violation of international law" and said it was requesting the Security Council to discuss "America's threat to peace."

It alleged American "imperialist circles" are "prepared to push the world into the abyss of a war catastrophe."

The 2,500 word Government statement did not mention or directly deny President Kennedy's charge that Soviet medium-range rocket sites were being prepared in Cuba. But it repeated the joint Soviet-Cuban statement of September 3 that Soviet arms and equipment sent to Cuba were "designed exclusively for defensive purposes."

It added: "The imperialist quarters of the U.S. seek to dictate to Cuba what policy she must carry through, what domestic order ought to be established, what weapons she should have for her defence."

It declared that the U.S. had "usurped the right... to engage in piracy."

The statement uttered a "serious warning to the U.S. Government, that, by taking the measures announced by President Kennedy, it assumes a grave responsibility for the destinies of peace."

It repeated the Soviet Union's earlier calls to America to normalize its relations with Cuba and renewed a pledge not to use nuclear weapons unless "an aggression is committed."

The statement added: "The U.S. Government arrogates to itself the right to demand that States report to it how they organize their defence, what they carry in their ships on the open sea. The Soviet Government resolutely rejects such claims."

Cuban Report Before B-G

POST Diplomatic Reporter

Foreign Minister Golda Meir yesterday evening reported to the Prime Minister on her recent discussions with U.S. Secretary of State Dean Rusk and other Foreign Ministers at the U.N.

It is assumed that Mr. Ben-Gurion and the Foreign Minister also discused the Cuban crisis.

Ambassador Avraham Harman was among the foreign envoys called to the State Department on Monday night for the emergency briefing just prior to President Kennedy's address. It is believed that Mr. Harman's evaluation of the Cuban situation was already before the Prime Minister last night. It is understood the Ambassadors were shown pictures of the missile bases in Cuba.

(The U.S. Embassy here were also in touch with the Foreign Ministry yesterday in connection with the situation.)

Mrs. Meir, it is understood, included in her report details of the present situation regarding the Arab refugee proposals of Dr. Joseph Johnson, the P.C.C. envoy, and the suggested resolution calling for direct Israel-Arab peace negotiations.

Paris Annoyed By Failure to Consult

By MAURICE CARR,
Jerusalem Post Correspondent

PARIS. — Extreme and undisguised displeasure were the initial French reaction to U.S. moves on Cuba. President de Gaulle is understood to be taking a dim view of the failure on Mr. Kennedy's part to consult his Allies before the fateful decision was taken to impose a quarantine on Premier Castro.

Washington's neglect to concert major policies with Paris as well as London has consistently been criticized by General de Gaulle as prejudicial to the Western alliance and has driven him to promote a European confederation as the third force between America and Russia.

Gen. de Gaulle was advised of Mr. Kennedy's intentions by Mr. Dean Acheson on Monday afternoon.

Dissatisfaction here is reflected in the omission of the French Government to hold an emergency meeting yesterday as did the British Cabinet; in the stress which a presidential Elysee Palace sources laid on the fact the Caribbean area lies outside NATO commitments, and in the silence of the Foreign Ministry whose spokesman at his weekly press conference yesterday refused to make any official statement and even avoided off the record comment.

MARKET PRICES DOWN

NEW YORK (AP).— As fear gathered concerning a head-on collision between the U.S. and Russia over Cuba, world markets registered confusion yesterday. Only Paris remained fairly steady. (Tel Aviv prices — Page 3.)

The New York stock market took what was apparently its worst loss in four months. It was transformed from a mixed affair—with defence related issues higher and consumer stocks lower — into a generally weak market.

An informal compilation of the Dow Jones industrial average, however, based on unofficial closing prices showed that indicator down 10.58 to 558.02. This was the worst loss since the end of June when the market was reaching its lows for the year.

Share prices plunged downward on the London Stock Exchange. Exactly the reverse condition prevailed in commodity markets.

UN Council In Emergency Session

UNITED NATIONS (Reuter). — The Security Council convened in emergency session on the Cuban crisis at ten o'clock Israel Time last night. The U.S., the Soviet Union and Cuba all requested the urgent meeting.

The U.S. was asking the 11-nation Council to endorse a draft resolution calling for "the immediate dismantling and withdrawal from Cuba of all missiles and other offensive weapons" under surveillance of a U.N. observer corps.

The Soviet Union formally requested the Council to examine the question of "violation of the Charter of the United Nations and threat to the peace on the part of the U.S."

Also before the Council was a letter from Cuba's chief U.N. delegate, Dr. Mario Garcia Inchaustegui, requesting consideration of "the act of war unilaterally committed by the U.S. Government in ordering the naval blockade of Cuba."

The Council chamber was full to overflowing. Experienced observers said the standing-room-only crowd of delegates far exceeded the numbers present for the 1956 Council sessions at the height of the Suez and Hungary crisis.

At the outset, Mr. Valerian Zorin, Soviet President of the Council, said that the reasons adduced by the U.S. for calling the meeting were "completely false."

It was a "clumsy attempt to cover up the unprecedented aggressive actions undertaken by the U.S. against Cuba, an attempt to cover up the arbitrary blockade of Cuba," he said.

Mr. Adlai Stevenson, chief U.S. delegate and the first speaker, said President Kennedy had ordered a quarantine on Cuba because — "the recent developments in Cuba — the importation of the cold war into the heart of the Americas — constitute a threat to the peace of this hemisphere and, indeed, to the peace of the world.

"The crucial fact is that Cuba has given the Soviet Union a bridgehead and staging area in this hemisphere — that it has invited an extra-continental, anti-democratic and expansionist power into the bosom of the American family — that it has made itself an accomplice in the Communist enterprise of world dominion," Mr. Stevenson declared.

Latin Americans Support US Stand

WASHINGTON (Reuter). — The Latin-American allies of the U.S. yesterday gave near unanimous support to President Kennedy's plans for a partial naval blockade to halt shipments of offensive weapons to Cuba.

Representatives of 19 Latin American states expressed their backing for the U.S. stand at an emergency session of the Council of the Organization of American States (O.A.S.).

They voted — with only Bolivia abstaining — for a U.S. resolution calling for joint action "including the use of armed force" to bar further shipments of offensive arms to Cuba.

SPAAK MAY CANCEL VISIT TO ISRAEL

BRUSSELS (AFP).— Foreign Minister Paul-Henri Spaak is likely to cancel his visit to Israel, scheduled for next Monday. Mr. Spaak said in a television interview last night that the tense situation in the Caribbean area would force him to remain in Belgium.

Troops Around World on Ale[rt]

America last night anxiously awaited a showdo[wn] with Russia as a massive armada deployed to halt la[rge] numbers of Soviet ships carrying offensive arms [to] Cuba, while the U.N. Security Council was holding [an] emergency session on the crisis.

America has said Soviet ships will be fired [on] should they run the blockade.

A fleet of more than 40 aircraft carriers, crui[sers] and destroyers sailed overnight from San Juan, Pu[erto] Rico, to join naval forces which left Southern Atla[ntic] seaboard bases on Monday.

The Soviet Union gave the U.S. a "serious wa[rn]ing," on her Cuban policy and ordered increased c[om]bat readiness in its forces.

Cuba had already been placed on war foo[ting] even before President Kennedy's blockade annou[nce]ment of last Monday night.

In Berlin, the British garrison was placed un[der] curfew as a "precautionary measure." About 4,000 [...] soldiers began a four-day "on guard" exercise in [the] Grunewald Forest.

The Japanese national news agency Kyodo yesterday quoted the director-general of the Soviet news agency, Tass, Mr. Dmitri Gotyunov, as saying that if the U.S. sank a Soviet ship there would surely be total war. In a report from Hiroshima Kyodo, also quoted Mr. Gotyunov, who is visiting Japan as head of a seven-member delegation of Soviet journalists, as saying if the U.S. attacked Cuba the Soviet Union would help Cuba.

A U.S. Defence Department spokesman said yesterday the U.S. armada of blockade ships is now on station ready to halt "large numbers" of Soviet vessels headed for Cuba.

The spokesman said there had been no contacts so far between navy ships and foreign vessels proceeding to Cuba, whether Soviet bloc, Allied or neutral.

The Defence Department indicated at a crowded press conference that interception of all Cuba-bound vessels, in accordance with the quarantine plan spelled out by President Kennedy on Monday night, would await a presidential proclamation expected later in the day.

But another authoritative Pentagon source said the orders had already gone to Admiral Robert Denison, U.S. Commander-in-Chief in the Atlantic, to prohibit entry into Cuba of selected list of weapons defined as "offensive."

The Defence Department spokesman said it was impossible for him to say at

BULLETIN: 1-15 a.[m.]

WASHINGTON (Reu[ter]) — President Kennedy [last] night signed a procla[ma]tion, effective today, or[der]ing a blockade against [the] delivery of offensive [wea]pons from the Soviet U[nion] to Cuba.

The White House [said] the proclamation w[ould] come into effect at 1[...] GMT (4 p.m. Israel tim[e])

that time when the "confrontation" betwee[n a] U.S. warship and a Ru[ssian] freighter would take [place] although other officials [said] it could come later in [the] day. Washington sources [said] the first Russian ship t[o be] intercepted might be the [Po]lotavia, apparently desi[gned] to carry missiles. The [Polo]tavia was said to be b[ound] for Cuba and the U.S. [Navy] was keeping a special w[atch] for her. Reconnaissance p[lanes] had taken photographs o[f the] vessel.

The Polotavia was u[nder]stood to have made trip[s to] Cuba every 10 days.

The White House [Press] Secretary, Mr. Pierre S[alin]ger, said that Soviet [me]dium-range ballistic mi[ssiles] were already in Cuba, i[n ad]dition to sites and faci[lities] to launch them.

The Defence Depart[ment] spokesman said that p[hoto]graphs taken over Cuba [had] shown a rapid buildu[p of] installations of mobile [me]dium-range ballistic mi[ssiles] within the past week.

State Department off[icials] disclosed that a letter [which] President Kennedy had sent to Mr. Nikita Kh[rush]chev along with a cop[y of] the President's televised [ad]dress.

Asked whether this [...] suggested a summit co[nfer]ence to discuss the grav[e si]tuation, the officials said [they] believed the President [had] made it clear that he h[oped] the Soviet Prime Mi[nister] might be prepared to r[eturn] to the path of "peacefu[l ne]gotiation." (Re[uter])

Khrushchev Smile[s]

MOSCOW (Reuter). — [A] smiling Mr. Khrushchev [last] night led the applause a[t the] Bolshoi Theatre after a [per]formance of Mussorg[sky's] opera "Boris Gudounov."

The Soviet Prime Mi[nister] went backstage and [per]sonally congratulated A[mer]ican singer Gerome H[ines] who took the leading r[ole].

UN Sceptical But Ineffectual

By JESSE ZEL LURIE,
Jerusalem Post Correspondent

UNITED NATIONS. — While the entire American press and the vast majority of the public lined up solidly behind President Kennedy, the assembly of world nations on the East River remained an island of doubt.

Britain and a few other allies have publicly supported the U.S. but most delegations said nothing publicly and many privately threw barbs at Mr. Kennedy's speech.

The Soviets may be ready now to admit they are providing medium-range missiles to Cuba since the lengthy Soviet statement issued here yesterday does not deny it.

But Russia's accusation that the U.S. blockade is contrary to international law and her call for abandonment of military bases in foreign countries found sympathetic agreement among many delegations who cannot distinguish between the legality of the Soviet base in Cuba and the American base in Turkey.

If, as expected, the Security Council debate ends in a veto deadlock and the matter is taken to the General Assembly, it is unlikely that a U.S. resolution would garner a two-thirds majority.

What Mr. Kennedy has done is to adopt as his own policy that enunciated by Israel in 1956: that defensive action must be taken not against a shooting aggression but against the increased threat of aggression—what the President calls "Upsetting the precarious status quo."

In 1956, the U.S. led a near-unanimous Assembly against Israel's arguments; it is unlikely that today the U.S. can lead two-thirds of the Assembly to the other side.

THE JERUSALEM POST Published daily except on Saturday by The alestine Post Ltd. Founded in 1932 by GERSHON AGRON
egistered at the G.P.O. Copyright of l material reserved; reproduction permitted only by arrangement.
Editor: TED R. LURIE
ead Office: 9 Rehov Havatzelet, rusalem, P.O. Box 81, Tel. 24233.
l Aviv: 52 Rehov Nahlat Binyamin, P.O.Box 1125,, Tel. 64251.
ifa: 34 Rehov Herzl, Hadar Hacarmel. P.O. Box 4810, Tel. 4594
Annual Subscription: IL 76.
SINGLE COPY: 22 AGORA.
ol. XXXIX, No. 10767*

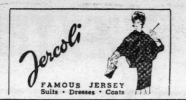

Jercoli
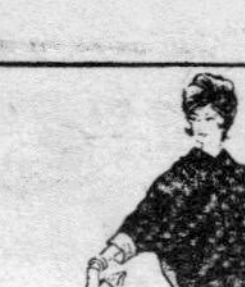
FAMOUS JERSEY
Suits • Dresses • Coats

THE JERUSALEM POST

MONDAY, JUNE 17, 1963 • 25 Sivan, 5723 • 25 Muharram, 1383

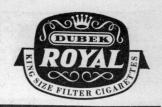

DUBEK ROYAL KING SIZE FILTER CIGARETTES

MR. Ben-Gurion has been Prime Minister, xcept for a brief period, nce the beginning of the State, and

EN-GURION'S ETIREMENT

his sudden decision to retire, not nown even to his intimates ntil yesterday morning, et almost with incredu- ty at first. In fact, he as long concentrated his nergies on two or three ajor problems, including curity, and withdrawn om most of the routine ork attaching to the rime Minister's Office. It thought likely that he ill now give his time enrely to specific problems - first among them the storation of a joint laour movement — the estion of relations with ws abroad, the closing the educational gap in rael between different ctions of the population. It is known that he had nsidered withdrawing om office earlier this ar, after the 15th Indendence Day, but hesitad to do so owing to crical relations with Jordan that time. Since then, e emergency has folwed another; if the situon is by no means calm w, there is also perhaps knowing when, in the ar future, it will be ich calmer. Only in a ajor danger or upheaval uld he be likely to ren to office once more.

Yet, inevitably, the quesn being asked is why Mr. n-Gurion should have cided to resign, and why this particular juncture. ere has been no specific ident. There has been no bridgeable rift: not over visit of Dr. Strauss, the mer German Defence nister; nor over the right proach to the German entists working in Egypt; over the resignation of Security Services chief; over his differences of nion with the Foreign nister, Mrs. Golda Meir, this respect; nor over Ben-Gurion's assault Herut in the Knesset a weeks ago; nor yet r differences that have gered on from the La "affair" in 1960-61. tainly all these together ve wearied both Mr. n-Gurion and his party ociates, who had been ustomed to yield to his gement in the recurrent ergencies of the past r decades. To the extent t the problems now arise hin Israel, rather than eatening us wholly from hout, it is proving more icult to achieve an agd solution.

f there has been a single nent in recent months t caused Mr. Benrion to feel that he was ng forced senselessly to tle windmills, it was at he considered the rant hypocrisy of party ders, who were fully inned at meetings of the eign Affairs Committee what precisely our relas with Germany inved, and were in agreent with these arrangents, but nevertheless in Knesset and the press ed as though these gs did not exist, in the venient certainty that rests of State made it ossible for Mapai to lish the details and exe their lack of honesty. Ve do not have to wait il the future to know Mr. Ben-Gurion has n a great Prime Minr, although the future no doubt remember wisdom more and his tankerousness less. The mate source of his imse, one might say ledary, prestige is his que capacity for seeing the future, for assesin advance problems have scarcely yet cast r shadows ahead. To extent, he has been, for , a prophet with honour is country.

) KURDS KILLED, AYS BAGHDAD

RUT (Reuter). — More 300 Kurdish rebels and munists were killed in ary operations in North- Iraq on Saturday, Bagh- Radio said yesterday. It ed a statement by the ctor of Military operas saying big quantities of d and supplies were d in caves in the area. any Kurdish deserters endered in response to ments by the Military rnor of the region, the said.

First Woman Orbiting To Space Rendezvous

SHIPS 12 SECONDS APART

MOSCOW (Reuter). — The first woman cosmonaut — pretty, smiling Valentina Tereshkova, 26, — blasted off into space yesterday to begin a joint flight programme with Cosmonaut Valery Bykovsky.

As their spaceships orbited close together in space, observers thought it possible they would attempt a rendezvous closer than the 6.5 km. of Andrian Nikolayev and Pavel Popovich.

"Seagull"—Valentina's call-sign — was launched at 12.30 p.m. (11.30 a.m. Israel time) to join "Hawk," the call-sign of Lieutenant-Colonel Bykovsky, who has completed 40 orbits since being launched three days ago.

Happy crowds in Red Square cheered this Soviet "first" while the well-built Valentina smiled hugely from her spacesuit in telecasts from the Cosmos.

A Tougher Bergman

The unmarried daughter of a tractor driver, she is considered by Western televiewers here to look not unlike Ingrid Bergman, although a little tougher.

According to official figures, the space pair are orbiting the earth with only 12 seconds difference in their timing — wih Valentina taking the longer orbit of 88.3 minutes.

There was no information on how long the flights would last. Unofficial reports have said the pair would probably land within a short interval of each other in two days.

Valentina's spaceship, Vostok Six, travelling at a distnce from earth of between 183 and 233 km. has the same angle of inclination to the equator — 65 degrees — as Bykovsky's Vostok Five.

They sent a joint report to the Communist Party and a message to Mr. Khrushchev. This said: "Have started carrying out joint space flight. Dependable communication been established between our ships.

'Feeling Fine'

Tass said she withstood well the boost period and the switch to the state of weightlessness and "feels fine."

Through interference, listeners in Moscow heard her excited — or delighted voice say: "This is Seagull . . . I see the earth . . . I feel excellent . . .the machine is working well . . ."

At about 2 p.m. (local time) Valentina's face, framed in a white space helmet, had flashed on the television screen from space. She was smiling and apparently talking to the Soviet ground control station.

Excitement reached a pitch not known here since the Soviet Union shook the world with the launching of the first spaceman, Yuri Gagarin, in April, 1961.

Official announcements began pouring out on Valentina, a former textile worker and an ace parachutist (see Page 2).

A linking of two spaceships while in orbit would be a step towards building large space laboratories in which people could live and work. Soviet experts said this is a high priority task.

TV Glimpse

During a television glimpse of Valentina lasting nearly three minutes a pencil floated weightlessly turning over and over in front of the smiling girl. Then Valentina faded away as her spaceship once again dipped below the horizon.

Moscow Radio had reported shortly after the space flight was announced that the spaceships had established two-way radio contact.

In a message, Mr. Khrushchev said: "Dear Valentina Vladimorovna and Valery Fyodorovich, cordial congratulations on the successful beginning of the joint space flight. I wish you good cheer, safe flight and successful landing."

Tass news agency said of Miss Tereshkova's launching:

"The flight is being made to continue the study of the effect of various space flight factors on the human organism, including a comparative analysis of the impact of these factors on the organism of a man and a woman, to carry out new medico-biological research and further improve and perfect the systems of piloted spaceships in conditions of simultaneous flight."

("Pravda" reported last night Miss Tereshkova had a woman "stand-in" for the space flight, who was equally talented, and had been "ready at any moment to replace her in the cabin of the spaceship.")

A Soviet psychologist, Mr. Alexei Lenotyev, quoted by Tass, said the orbiting was remarkable not only because a woman had been put into space. She was younger than the other cosmonauts, had less experience and lacked the training and the familiarity with danger of the pilots who became cosmonauts.

As her flight went on, Valentina sent greetings to the peoples of Africa and to the Near and Middle East.

Tass said the temperature in her cabin was 23.6 degrees Centigrade and relative humidity 33 per cent.

Col. Bykovsky — with a stubbly chin on his third day in space — was clearly seen on television at 5 p.m. He was eating and, when aware he was on the screen, waved a photograph of his baby son and wife before the camera.

(Cosmonette — Page 2)

Losing Height But Valentina Not Worried

MOSCOW (AP). — Lt.-Col. Valery Bykovsky had completed 40 revolutions around the earth by midnight (Israel time), but his ship was slowly losing altitude.

A report broadcast by Tass gave his minimum altitude as 168.5 km. compared to 173 when he started, and 203.3 km. maximum compared with 219 when he started out Friday.

Vostok Six, with Valentina Tereshkova aboard, has lost a trifle of altitude, about a kilometre on minimum and maximum, but she did not seem to worry about it. She ate early and went to sleep.

Mac to Get Vote But Likely to Quit Later

LONDON (Reuter). — Mr. Harold Macmillan is expected to survive as Britain's Prime Minister in today's parliamentary showdown on the Profumo scandal, but to quit his post when the political fever had time to die down, political sources said yesterday.

The sources forecast that on present form, his likely successor as head of the government would be either Mr. R.A. Butler, 60, now Deputy Prime Minister, or Viscount Hailsham, 55, Lord President of the Council and Science Minister.

They believed, however, that the closing of Cabinet ranks would ensure Mr. Macmillan of a solid vote of confidence from his party in today's debate, with his own future remaining a question for the weeks or even months ahead.

Big Majority Vital

In a vote of confidence such as is now involved, a Government majority which did not come reasonably near to its possible maximum would imply a loss confidence which might force Mr. Macmillan to tender his resignation.

The main task of the Prime Minister is to convince Parliament — and his own supporters in particular — that no reproach lies against him in relation to his handling of the crisis, which arose from revelations that his War Minister, John Profumo, was sharing the favours of Miss Christine Keeler, a call-girl, with the Soviet Naval Attache, Captain Eugene Ivanov.

Last night, the Soviet news agency, Tass, issued a statement declaring that Captain Ivanov was in no way involved in the "sex and security" scandal, and that the whole affair had been stirred up by political parties with an eye on the coming elections.

(UK Press reaction — Page 4)

US Inter-Race Violence Seen Spreading to North

JACKSON, Mississippi (Reuter). — The body of murdered integration leader Edgar Evers left this tense city yesterday for Washington for a military burial as racial turmoil continued to bubble throughout the Southern U.S.

There were warnings that it could boil over in Northern cities this week.

Jackson was recovering from the brief but violent riot which erupted on Saturday after a funeral march for the dead Negro leader, shot in the back last Wednesday. The riot left 14 policemen injured and 27 demonstrators in jail. Negro leaders toured the city later in a car with a loudspeaker appealing for non-violence.

Evers' body was taken yesterday morning in a hearse to Meridian to begin an overland train journey to Washington for burial with full military honours in Arlington National Cemetery on Wednesday.

Racial strife spread to the north in Cleveland, Ohio, where a 20-year-old white man was yesterday in critical condition with a bullet in the chest. He was shot during an argument with a group of Negroes after 300 Whites stoned Negro cars in retaliation for a brutal attack on a young White couple by six Negroes last Wednesday. Police arrested 40 persons.

Bonn Training 'Old Affair'

FRANKFURT. — Hans Merten, Socialist member of the Bundestag military aid committee, said yesterday that the West German Defence Ministry had been training two to four Israelis on "modern apparatus" for years. He said it is "a very old matter," when asked to comment on an interview he gave the "Neue Ruhr Zeitung" which quoted him on Saturday as saying Israel soldiers were being trained in Germany.

The modern apparatus, he said, includes electronic calculators.

UPI said yesterday that for some time it has been receiving private reports that a group of Israel soldiers was being trained in Rendsburg, in North Germany. The Israelis, the reports said, wear fatigue uniforms without insignia, both on and off duty. (AP, UPI)

NEW! another Olivetti Quality Product
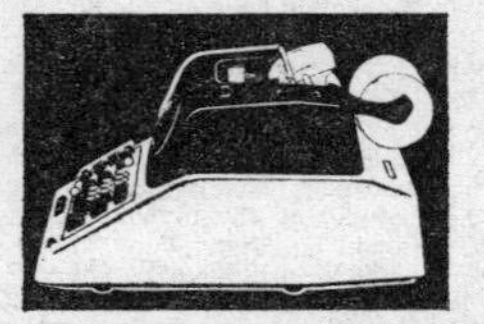
Olivetti Multisumma 24
Superautomatic printing multiplying machine with one register and a dynamic memory.
Sole distributors in Israel:
DELTA TRADING Co. Ltd.
Citrus House, Tel Aviv, P.O.B. 2938, Tel. 64484.
★ Exhibition Centre: 6 Rehov Ahuzat Bayit, Tel Aviv, Tel. 65418.
Sub Distributors:
★ Jerusalem, Hashichlul Ltd., 10 Rehov Luntz, Tel. 22363.
★ Haifa and the North: Yakir Fried Ltd., 7 Rehov Habankim, Tel. 54547.

BEN-GURION RESIGNS

Cabinet and Country Taken by Surprise

Eshkol Likely to Form Cabinet

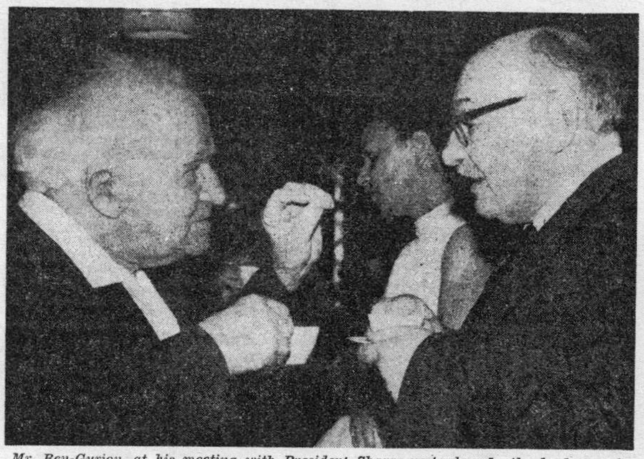

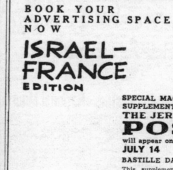

Mr. Ben-Gurion, at his meeting with President Shazar yesterday. In the background, the Government Secretary, Mrs. Yael Uzay. (Maor photo)

By ARI RATH, Jerusalem Post Political Reporter

The Prime Minister and Minister of Defence, Mr. David Ben-Gurion, yesterday submitted his resignation to President Shazar and, in what was taken as a sign of his final decision to withdraw entirely from public office, also submitted his resignation from the Knesset to Speaker Kadish Luz.

The Prime Minister's resignation is tantamount to the resignation of the entire Cabinet, and Finance Minister Levi Eshkol is now expected to be asked to form and head the new Cabinet of the same coalition partners — Mapai, Ahdut Ha'avoda, the National Religious Party and Poalei Agudat Yisrael.

The decision of the nation's 76-year-old leader to retire came as a shock to the nation and even his closest associates and friends were taken by surprise by the announcement to the Cabinet yesterday morning.

"I am not surprised only because he always made his mind up alone," said one spokesman close to the Prime Minister.

Personal Reasons

At the close of the Cabinet meeting, the Prime Minister announced that for personal reasons unconnected with any particular event, he was submitting his resignation to the President. He expressed his regrets that, with his resignation, the Cabinet is considered to have resigned. This was not his intention, he declared. He asked the Cabinet members to continue the present coalition and to submit the new Government to the Knesset no later than next week.

He thanked the members of the present Government, as well as the members of the different parties who had served in previous Governments since the establishment of the State, for their mutual trust and cooperation which had proved of such benefit to the country.

To Write History

Mr. Ben-Gurion's retirement from active Government service comes nine-and-a-half years after he retired for the first time to Sde Boker. Then he was away 14 months, but kept his Knesset seat. He expects to remain active, however, in the talks for labour unity and in matters concerning the development of the Negev, and also intends to write an historical study of Israel.

The first intimation of his resignation was given by Mr. Ben-Gurion yesterday morning, shortly before the Cabinet session, and only when the Cabinet agenda was completed did he tell the Ministers formally of his decision.

Mr. Ben-Gurion stressed that the resignation was prompted by personal motives, and had nothing to do with any actual political issue. When several Ministers asked what these motives were, Mr. Ben-Gurion declined to expand. He repeated that they were purely personal, and he could therefore not give any details.

The formal letter of resignation was submitted to the President at the end of a luncheon given by Mr. and Mrs. Shazar at Beit Hanassi for all the Ministers and their wives, the Knesset Speaker and Mrs. Luz, and the Government Secretary, Mrs. Yael Uzay. The luncheon had been planned last month as an opportunity for the new President to receive the entire Cabinet.

Calm and Cheerful

Mr. Ben-Gurion seemed calm and in a cheerful mood, and after dessert was served, he took Mr. Shazar outside and submitted the very brief letter of resignation, whose text has not been made public. The resignation of his seat was submitted to Mr. Luz shortly afterwards.

Unlike his first retirement and his resignation following the Lavon affair prior to the 1961 elections, Mr. Ben-Gurion this time did not issue any farewell message to the nation, nor has he given any detailed reason for his decision.

These are believed to be

(Continued on Page 2, Col. 6)

Moscow Says Reasons 'Not Only Personal'

LONDON (Reuter).—Moscow Radio yesterday said Mr. Ben-Gurion's resignation was not merely due to personal reasons caused by his age and fatigue. Commenting on the news of his resignation in its home service evening news bulletin, Moscow Radio said "his policy as Head of Government, and in particular his course of strengthening military and political links with the Bonn successors of Hitler, is meeting with ever increasing opposition, even inside the leadership of the ruling Mapai party."

PERES SEES MURVILLE

By MAURICE CARR, Jerusalem Post Correspondent

PARIS. — The Israel Deputy Defence Minister, Mr. Shimon Peres, accompanied by Ambassador Walter Eytan, called on Foreign Minister Maurice Couve de Murville here yesterday.

In the course of their 40 minute conversation, which is officially described as "cordial and interesting," the Israel visitors reviewed with the French Minister the international situation, with special reference to Middle East affairs.

HURRIES HOME

By ZE'EV SCHUL

LYDDA AIRPORT. — Deputy Defence Minister Shimon Peres cut short by one day his visit to the 25th International Air Salon in Paris to come back to Israel last night following the announcement of Prime Minister Ben Gurion's resignation.

Wearing a dark blue suit with the rosette of the French Legion of Honour in his lapel, Mr. Peres alighted here at 11.15 p.m. from an El Al plane. Aluf Ezer Weizman, O.C. Air Force, accompanied him on the flight back.

Mr. Peres' first action was to scan a copy of the late edition of "Ma'ariv," which already carried the news of the Prime Minister's resignation.

He declined to answer reporters' queries about Mr. Ben-Gurion's resignation, commenting: "I do not think the airport is the right place to discuss this issue."

Parties Hope for Speedy End to Cabinet Upset

By MARK SEGAL, Jerusalem Post Reporter

TEL AVIV. — All the political parties were last night strongly in favour of forming a new Cabinet as speedily as possible, while some hoped Mr. Ben-Gurion's resignation would lead to a widening of the coalition.

Mapai, however, still hoped to persuade Mr. Ben-Gurion to change his mind and withdraw his resignation, according to the party's Secretary-General, Reuven Barkatt. He admitted Mapai knew for some time of Mr. Ben-Gurion's intentions to drop out of public life, but had believed until the last moment that it would be possible to dissuade him from such a move. "It is hoped that by common efforts we will emerge from the present situation without undue difficulties," he said.

Ahdut Ha'avoda's political Secretary, Ze'ev Tsur, declared, "We have no choice but to respect Mr. Ben-Gurion's wish." The party's Central Committee is meeting Thursday and it is expected to be devoted largely to the new political situation. Ahdut Ha'avoda circles last night intimated that they may ask for another portfolio in the reformed Cabinet. They are known to be anxious to obtain the Defence portfolio and to oust Mr. Shimon Peres, now Deputy Minister.

The NRP Executive and Knesset faction will sit this morning in Jerusalem to formulate policy. NRP Secretary Moshe Kroneh last night said his party hoped the crisis will end quickly. NRP circles added they would welcome the widening of the coalition.

The Knesset faction and Executive of Poalei Agudat Israel will also meet today, as will those of the Liberals.

The Liberal head, Mr. Elimelech Rimalt, M.K., said the resignation did not come to him as a surprise. He thought that the move was made after Mr. Ben-Gurion became involved in difficulties with his own and other parties in the coalition. "If Mapai does not reinstate a stable government in the shortest possible period, then it will prove Mapai has lost the right to lead the country," Dr. Rimalt said. He sincerely hoped elections could be avoided. He stated, however, that the Liberals would not join the coalition at this stage.

Mapam 'Not Sorry'

Mapam's Knesset faction and Secretariat meet today, and the Political Committee Wednesday. Political Secretary Reuven Arzi declared that although Mapam was taken aback by the resignation, it was not sorry.

In reply to a question, Mr. Arzi said the question was never one of Mapam simply joining the coalition, but of its true participation in the Government. If, as Mr. Ben-Gurion wished, the same coalition was presented, then Mapam will continue to oppose it. However, if there were to be negotiations, then "Mapam has never refused to talk with anyone."

The Herut Knesset faction said in an official statement last night that if Mr. Ben-Gurion's resignation was a "real one and not just a form of exerting pressure," then "it means his retirement from public life."

"If so, and despite its having been long overdue, we regard this is a highly positive step for the nation's welfare," the Herut statement continued, adding, however, that Mr. Ben-Gurion's resignation provided no solution to the country's problems "which will only be saved by ousting the Mapai regime."

The statement was drawn up during the 60th birthday party of the Herut Executive's Chairman, Mr. Yosef Shofman.

Israel Protests Soviet Arrest of Israeli as 'Deserter'

Israel has protested to the Soviet Union over the forcible arrest in Kharkov of an Israel national for alleged desertion from the Soviet Army.

A statement issued in Jerusalem yesterday said:

A group of 37 tourists from Israel left for the Soviet Union on May 7, 1963.

It was learned on June 9 that one member of this group, Mr. Yehuda Cohen, had been arrested in the street in the city of Kharkov and forcibly taken into a car in the presence of another tourist belonging to the same group.

As soon as the Israel Foreign Ministry learned of this incident, the Director of the Consular Division invited the head of the Consular Section of the Soviet Embassy in Israel to see him and asked him to take vigorous steps to secure Mr. Cohen's release.

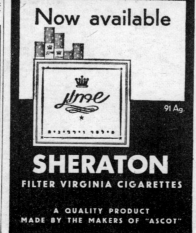

On the same day, the head of the Consular Section of the Israel Embassy in Moscow met the Deputy Director of the Near East Division of the Soviet Foreign Ministry, who promised to investigate the matter and inform him of what had happened to the tourist.

On June 11, the Deputy Director of the Near East Division of the Soviet Foreign Ministry told the head of the Consular Section of the

(Continued on Page 2, Col. 4)

Mapai Leaders Meet in Capital

President Shazar is to decide today on the order and timetable of the consultations with the various party delegations on the formation of a new Cabinet. The consultations are expected to be concluded this week.

All Mapai Ministers (except for Mr. Ben-Gurion) together with Messrs. M. Sharett, R. Barkatt, A. Becker, Z. Aranne, M. Namir, A. Govrin and M. Argov, met until late last night at Mrs. Meir's Jerusalem home to discuss the Party's future course. It was decided to convene the Party Secretariat today and the Central Committee tomorrow

The presence of Mr. Sharett was taken as an indication that he might be asked to join the new Cabinet.

The future of the Defence portfolio is believed to have been one of the main points of discussion at last night's meeting. Most likely, it will remain with the future Prime Minister, expected to be Mr. Eshkol.

Now available
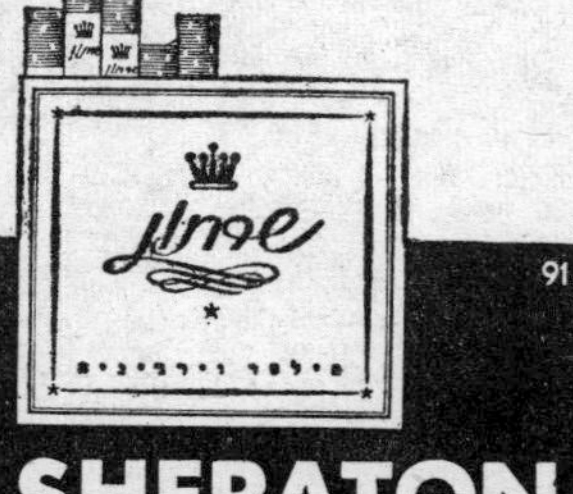
91 Ag.
SHERATON
FILTER VIRGINIA CIGARETTES
A QUALITY PRODUCT
MADE BY THE MAKERS OF "ASCOT"

BOOK YOUR ADVERTISING SPACE NOW
ISRAEL-FRANCE EDITION
SPECIAL MAGAZINE SUPPLEMENT OF THE JERUSALEM POST will appear on JULY 14
BASTILLE DAY
This supplement will emphasize the mutual cooperation and close ties between France and Israel, and will review the relationship between Israel and French Jewry.
An impressive array of outstanding writers and personalities in Israel and France will contribute to this issue.
ADVERTISEMENTS are accepted through all advertising agencies and at our offices in Jerusalem, Tel Aviv and Haifa.

EXTRA! THE JERUSALEM POST EXTRA!

SUNDAY, NOVEMBER 24, 1963 • 8 Kislev, 5724 • 8 Regeb, 1383

KENNEDY ASSASSINATED; SUSPECT HELD; JOHNSON TAKES OATH AS PRESIDENT

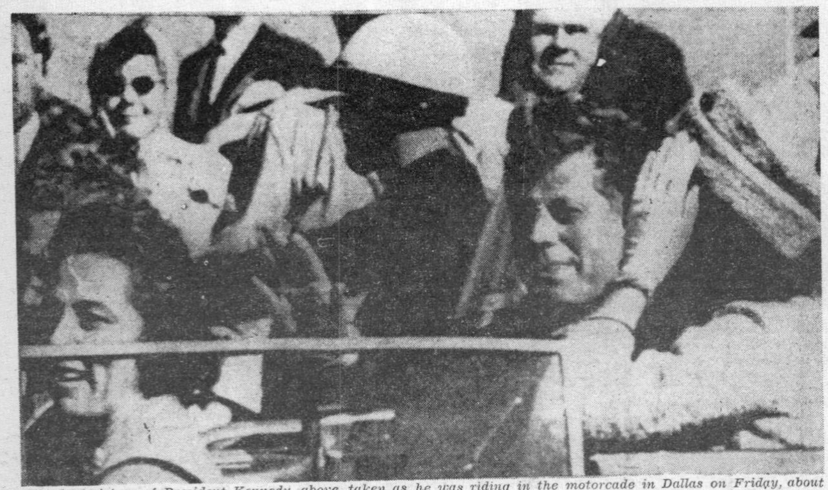

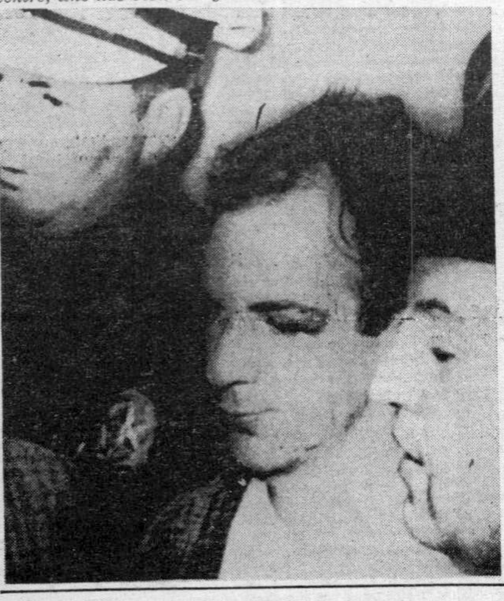

The last picture of President Kennedy, above, taken as he was riding in the motorcade in Dallas on Friday, about a minute before he was assassinated. Mrs. Kennedy is at his side, and seated in front of them are the Governor of Texas, Mr. John Connally, who was also shot, and Mrs. Connally, whose bullet-proof window was half-raised. Below: H. L. Oswald, 24, centre, who has been charged with the assassination, shown just after his arrest. (AP Radiophotos)

THREE RIFLE SHOTS FIRED

DALLAS, Texas. — A hidden gunman assassinated President Kennedy with a high-powered rifle on Friday. Three shots reverberated. Blood sprang from the President's face. He fell face downward in the back seat of his car.

His wife clutched his head and tried to lift it, crying, "Oh, no!" Half an hour later, John F. Kennedy, 46, was dead, and an hour later, Mr. Lyndon Johnson was sworn in as the 36th President of the United States.

Within the hour, police had arrested a 24-year-old man following the killing of a Dallas policeman. Homicide Captain Will Fritz said later that witnesses had identified the man as the slayer of the policeman, but he added that it had not been established that the man killed the President.

He is Harvey Lee Oswald, an American who four years ago said he was applying for Russian citizenship. He has a Russian wife. Oswald denied that he had shot anybody.

The assassination occurred just as the President's motorcade was leaving the Dallas business district at the end of a triumphal tour through the city's streets.

His special car — with the protective bubble down — was moving down an incline into an underpass that leads to a freeway route to the Dallas Trade Mart, where he was to speak.

Witnesses heard three shots. Two hit the President, one in the head and one in the neck.

The third shot wounded Governor John B. Connally of Texas in the side, but his condition was reported not critical.

The motorcade slowed down and then sped forward at high speed to Parkland Hospital near the Trade Mart.

Spectators, terrified at the sight and sound of the assassination, dived face forward for protection onto a grassy park at the entrance of the underpass, fearing more shots. Police swarmed onto the scene.

Holds Husband's Head

The First Lady cradled her dying husband's blood-smeared head in her arms as the presidential limousine raced to the hospital.

Lying wounded at the same hospital was Governor John Connally of Texas, who was cut down by the same fusillade that ended the life of the youngest man ever elected to the presidency. Mr. Connally and his wife had been riding with the President and Mrs. Kennedy.

Dr. Malcolm Perry, hospital surgeon who attended President Kennedy, said the President suffered a neck wound — a bullet hole in the lower part of the neck. There was a second wound in the President's head, but Dr. Perry was not certain whether it was inflicted by the same bullet.

President Kennedy lost consciousness as soon as he was hit and never recovered it.

Ballots and Bullets

He died without being able to deliver his last warning — that in today's world, freedom could be lost without a shot being fired, by ballots as well as by bullets. The warning was contained in the last speech he had prepared for delivery to a luncheon meeting in Dallas.

When the President was carried into the emergency room, Mrs. Kennedy walked behind — parts of her clothing drenched with blood. The U.S. First Lady remained composed but, inside the emergency room, clasped hands with the new President, Johnson, and his wife, Lady Bird, in a reflex display of deep anguish.

Shortly after Kennedy's death — "We never had any hope of saving his life," said one doctor — Mr. Johnson was driven to Dallas' airfield where he boarded the Presidential jet transport.

Before flying off to Washington to take up the reins of government, Mr. Johnson stood aboard the plane, his left hand on a Bible, and swore faithfully to execute the duties of President and defend the Constitution.

The oath was administered by U.S. District Judge Sarah T. Hughes, who became the first woman to swear in a Chief Executive. She was named to her post by Mr. Kennedy in October, 1961.

Also aboard the big silver, blue and white jet which Kennedy rode so often in life was the body of the assassinated Chief Executive. It was being taken home to the White House he occupied for 34 months to lie in state Sunday and Monday. *(AP, UPI)*

The 36th President

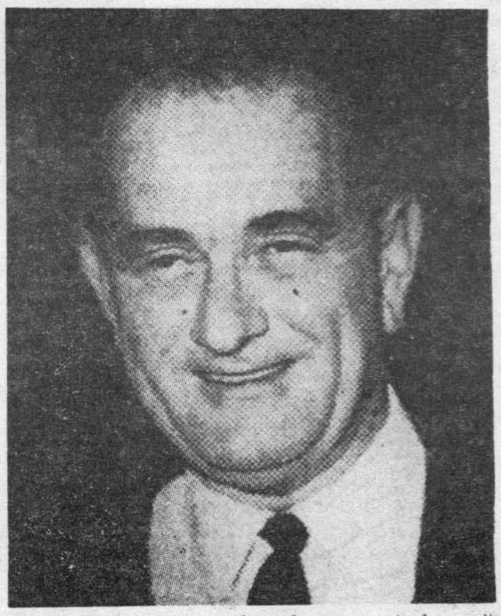

Lyndon Baines Johnson of Texas became the 36th President of the United States at 6.38 p.m. (Israel time) Friday. He took the oath of office in the hot, stuffy, Presidential compartment of an Air Force jet transport parked on the edge of Love Field, the Dallas Municipal Airport.

It was administered by an old friend of the Johnson family, U.S. District Court Judge Sarah T. Hughes, 67, the first woman ever to do so.

His wife, Lady Bird Johnson, was standing at his left as he repeated the Constitutional formula: "I do solemnly swear I will faithfully execute the office of the President of the United States to the best of my ability and to preserve, uphold and protect the Constitution of the United States, so help me God."

Delayed Ceremony

He turned and kissed his wife on the cheek, giving her shoulders a squeeze. Then he put his arm around Mrs. Kennedy, kissing her gently on her right cheek.

Mr. Johnson had deliberately delayed the ceremony to give the widow time to compose herself.

As members of the group of 27 persons jammed in the compartment started to shake his hand, the President seemed to back away.

"Now, let's get airborne," he said.

Immediately on his arrival in Washington, the President scheduled a late morning conference yesterday with Dwight D. Eisenhower, the 34th President, and with Secretary of State Dean Rusk. At mid-afternoon, he was to meet with his Cabinet.

After conferring with the Secretary of Defence at the White House, Mr. Johnson departed for his home in Washington, accompanied by swarms of secret service men and a massive motorcycle escort. The house was ringed with guards.

Funeral Monday

WASHINGTON (AP). — The body of John F. Kennedy lay in repose Saturday in the White House from which he governed the nation.

Through the day, his family, his close friends and high officials of the Government, including former President Dwight Eisenhower, were scheduled to view the body of the Chief Executive, assassinated Friday in Dallas.

Sunday it will be borne by solemn cortege to the Rotunda of the Capitol, where for 24 hours it will lie in state, to be seen by the public.

Funeral services will be held at 1700 GMT (7 p.m. Israel time) Monday at St. Matthew's Roman Catholic Cathedral with Richard Cardinal Cushing, Archbishop of Boston and a long-time friend of the Kennedy family, celebrating a Pontifical Requiem Mass.

Funeral Services

The final resting place has not yet been announced. One report, still unconfirmed, was that burial will be in the family plot in Brookline, Massachusetts.

In the early morning hours, the flag-draped casket of the fallen President was brought to the White House. Mrs. Jacqueline Kennedy rode alongside the casket. Her brother-in-law, Attorney-General Robert F. Kennedy, also rode in the ambulance.

As the ambulance pulled through the north-west entrance to the White House grounds, several hundred persons watched silently. Servicemen in dress uniforms carried the casket into the White House, followed by Mrs. Kennedy and the Attorney-General.

Sunday at 1800 GMT (8 p.m Israel time), members of the family, Supreme Court Justices, Members of the Congress and foreign diplomats were to accompany President Kennedy's body as it moved from the White House down Pennsylvania Avenue to the Capitol.

File Past

The public will be permitted to file past the bier in the Great Rotunda of the Capitol shortly after its arrival. At 1600 GMT (6 p.m. Israel time) Monday, the body will be taken to the Cathedral for the funeral services.

Cardinal Cushing, who will say the funeral mass, gave the invocation at Kennedy's inauguration, officiated at the President's marriage, baptized the two Kennedy children and said the funeral mass last August for the President's newborn son, Patrick Bouvier Kennedy.

The late President's family asked Friday night that no floral tributes be sent for his services. The White House issued the following announcement:

"The Kennedy family has expressed the desire that no flowers be sent to the White House or to the funeral. They asked that anyone wishing to do so donate an equivalent amount to charity."

Johnson Gets Clean Bill Of Health

NEW YORK (UPI). — Heart specialists predicted yesterday that President Lyndon B. Johnson would be a vigorously healthy Chief Executive despite the heart attack he suffered eight years ago.

They based their estimate upon the vigorous life Johnson has led since his months-long recuperation in 1955. He has been through "the political war," including the 1960 election, and "has even faced a mob," one specialist recalled. "You could have no better proof of his complete recovery," continued this professor of medicine, who for reasons of ethics spoke anonymously.

In the unanimous opinion of three specialists, a man who has had a complete recovery of years-long duration can face up to the most exacting tasks, including that of being President.

Suspected Killer is Ex-Marine, One-Time Defector to Russia

DALLAS. — Harvey Lee Oswald, 24-year-old ex-Marine who spent three years in Russia as a defector, was formally charged Saturday morning with the murder of President Kennedy.

Oswald is Chairman of an organization called the "Fair Play for Cuba Committee."

The charge of assassinating Mr. Kennedy by shooting him with a rifle was announced shortly before midnight local time and after about 10 hours of relentless questioning of Oswald by police and F.B.I. agents at Dallas police headquarters.

Earlier in the day, Oswald had been charged with the slaying of a Dallas policeman, shot shortly after Mr. Kennedy was assassinated.

Capt. Will Fritz, of the Dallas Homicide Squad, said that Oswald had not confessed and had made no statement.

The case will probably be presented to a grand jury before the middle of next week, the Dallas District Attorney, Mr. Henry Wade, said. If indicted, his trial will come up before a Texas State, not a Federal, Court.

Paraffin Test

In reply to questions by reporters whether fingerprints had been found on the murder weapon, described as a high-powered, 6.5 mm. rifle of Italian make with a telescopic sight, Mr. Wade said that at the present time he did not care to go into that. He said that paraffin tests had been made of Oswald's hands to see if he had recently fired a gun.

The District Attorney quoted Oswald's wife as saying that her husband had a rifle in his possession on Thursday night.

(Mrs. Oswald, who speaks only Russian, was in the police station with her two children.)

The rifle found in the warehouse from where the shots were fired was flown by jet plane to Washington for analysis by the F.B.I.

Oswald, handcuffed and held by two policemen, was brought before reporters shortly after midnight in the police line-up room. His cut and bruised face as white as chalk, his shoulders hunched, he said he had not killed the President or the policeman.

Police claim that Oswald, who qualified as a sharpshooter while in the Marines, was in the building from which the assassin fired the fatal bullet at Kennedy. But Oswald said it was not so, that he was in a movie theatre in nearby Oak Cliff.

Oswald was a stock clerk on the sixth floor in the Texas Schoolbook Depository, the building on Main Street from which the sniper fired the fatal shot. His employer is a private concern that stores schoolbooks.

Rifle Tucked Away

The bolt action rifle was found, tucked among books on the sixth floor. Near it were gnawed chicken bones and an empty soda bottle.

During the frantic search for the killer, police were posted at exits to the warehouse. Officials said a man, later identified as Oswald, walked through the door of the warehouse and was stopped by a policeman.

Oswald, they added, told the policeman "I work here." When another employee confirmed that he did, the policeman let Oswald walk away.

Kennedy was shot at 12.31 p.m. Mrs. R. C. Roberts, who works at Oswald's rooming house in Oak Cliff, said that Oswald rushed in "on the dead run" shortly afterwards. He ran to his room, came running back with a grey zipper bag and dashed out the door toward a bus stop.

Patrolling in Oak Cliff was Officer J. D. Tipplitt, a 39-year-old father of three. He was about five blocks from the Texas theatre where a double feature, "Cry Battle" and "War is Hell," was playing.

Policeman Shot

Tippitt fell to the street, shot twice by a 38-calibre pistol. It is not known how he accosted his slayer.

Then Mrs. Julie Postal, cashier at the Texas theatre, called police to say that a suspicious-looking man was in the theatre.

Three officers charged into the theater, and the house lights flared up.

Oswald, in the third row, centre section, leaped up and said: "This is it."

Some witnesses said he

(Continued on Page 4, Col. 6)

Israel Tributes

From President Shazar

To H.E. Lyndon B. Johnson, President of the U.S.

I am stunned with grief at the tragic blow which has afflicted the U.S. and all humanity. In my own name and that of my people, I express my profound condolences to the late President's family, to the American people and to the freedom-loving world.

ZALMAN SHAZAR
President of Israel

From Premier Eshkol

To President Johnson

The Government and people of Israel and I personally are shocked and deeply grieved by the tragic and dastardly assassination of President John F. Kennedy.

In his all-too-brief term of office he proved himself to be a great and dynamic President of the U.S. and a courageous leader of the free world.

He was, during his presidency as during his earlier career, a staunch friend of Israel and the Jewish people.

Please convey the deepest sympathy of the Government and people of Israel as well as my own sincere condolences to Mrs. Kennedy, her children and all the members of the late President's family as well as to the Government and people of the U.S. on their irreparable loss.

LEVI ESHKOL
Prime Minister

From David Ben-Burion

To U.S. Ambassador Walworth Barbour:

I can hardly tell how distressed and shocked I am at the terribly tragic loss of the great, courageous, wise and peace-loving President.

Not only Americans — the whole free world has lost a great leader and a true friend.

I am asking why? Why?

DAVID BEN-GURION

From Abba Eban

The Hon. Dean Rusk, Secretary of State:

In a mood of profound national and personal grief I send you my sincere condolences on the tragic death of President Kennedy. Nobody who knew him will ever lose the enduring impression of his personality and statesmanship.

ABBA EBAN,
Deputy Prime Minister and Acting Minister of Foreign Affairs

From Golda Meir

To the Hon. Dean Rusk, Secretary of State:

No words can adequately express my shock and sorrow over this tragedy. The U.S. has lost a great President and the world an ardent and determined fighter for peace.

The death of President Kennedy is a tragic loss to all men who want to live in freedom. The people and Government of Israel mourn this death together with all the world.

I shall never forget the impact of his personality when I was privileged to have a discussion with him last summer. Our first thoughts are those of profound sympathy for Mrs. Kennedy and the late President's family and for the people of the United States of America.

GOLDA MEIR
Minister of Foreign Affairs

Israel Proclaims National Mourning

National flags will be flown at half-mast today on all Government and local authority buildings as a sign of mourning on the death of President Kennedy, the Government announced Saturday.

Prime Minister Eshkol is expected to eulogize the late President at this morning's Cabinet session, and the Knesset will hold a special memorial session on Monday.

The first bulletin announcing the shooting of President Kennedy was received by Kol Yisrael from the Associated Press at 8.55 p.m. Friday, in time to be included in the 9 o'clock news. At 9.19, the Radio reported that two priests had been called to his bedside, and at 9.35 it interrupted the regular broadcast over the main wavelength to announce the death.

From then on, the switchboard was flooded with calls asking for information.

At 10.45, President Shazar telephoned his condolences to the U.S. Ambassador and shortly afterwards sent off his cable to Mr. Johnson.

The news broke into the quiet of a cool Sabbath evening, leaving whoever heard it stunned and unbelieving. Even after Kol Yisrael signed off, radios could be heard from almost every house tuned into the Voice of America.

What Can You Do for Your Country?

WASHINGTON (AP). — On his inauguration day, January 20, 1961, President Kennedy declared:

"My fellow Americans: Ask not what your country will do for you — ask what you can do for your country.

"My fellow citizens of the world: Ask not what America will do for you, but what together we can do for the freedom of man."

This, perhaps, is the most memorable statement Kennedy, then 43, made in his two years and 10 months in office.

CHILDREN NOT YET TOLD

WASHINGTON. — Grief-stricken Jacqueline Kennedy, tragically widowed at the age of 34, now faces the harrowing ordeal of breaking the news to the two Kennedy children.

Both children have birthdays next week — Caroline will be six on Wednesday and her brother John three on Monday.

Several hours after the shooting, they were taken quietly out of the White House to an unknown destination without being told of their father's death.

When she flew to Texas with the late President this week, it was Mrs. Kennedy's first formal trip since she recovered from the death of her premature baby in August.

The Kennedys were wed in 1953.

The White House flag was lowered to half-mast within moments of the news arriving.

Church bells in the neighbourhood began to toll, and people began drifting towards the White House to stand silently on the sidewalk, or in Lafayette Park across Pennsylvania Avenue, just to stare. Occasionally, a passer-by would ask a White House guard for news, then stand dumbly when told the President was dead.

Telephone service in America's capital collapsed temporarily. The sudden load of telephone calls swamped central stations and it was impossible to get a dial tone to make calls.

New York's newspapers told of President Kennedy's murder in huge, sombre headlines. The first to appear was the "New York Times" which, in a special early edition, printed three banner headlines over eight columns. The whole front page and 11 inside pages were devoted to stories and pictures on the assassination. *(Reuter, AP)*

McCormack Next in Line

WASHINGTON (Reuter). — The post of Vice-President now stands vacant, with the Speaker of the House of Representatives, Mr. John W. McCormack, of Massachusetts, first in line to succeed President Johnson.

The late President's brother, Attorney-General Robert Kennedy, is fifth in line.

The line of succession after Mr. McCormack, as established by law in 1947, is: The President *pro tempore* of the Senate, Senator Carl Hayden of Arizona; the Secretary of State, Mr. Dean Rusk; the Secretary of Defence, Mr. Robert McNamara; the Attorney-General; the Postmaster-General, Mr. John Gronouski; the Secretary of the Interior, Mr. Stewart Udall; the Secretary of Agriculture, Mr. Orville Freeman; the Secretary of Commerce, Mr. Luther H. Hodges; and the Secretary of Labour, Mr. Willard Wirtz.

THE JERUSALEM POST Published daily except on Saturday by The Palestine Post Ltd. Founded in 1932 by GERSHON AGRON
Registered at the G.P.O. Copyright of all material reserved; reproduction permitted only by arrangement.
Editor: TED R. LURIE
Head Office: 9, Rehov Havatzelet, Jerusalem, P.O.Box 81, Tel. 24233.
Tel Aviv: 52 Rehov Nahlat Binyamin, P.O.Box 1125, Tel. 64251.
Haifa: 34 Rehov Herzl, Hadar Hacarmel. P.O.Box 4810, Tel. 4594
Annual Subscription: IL 75.
SINGLE COPY: 22 AGORA.
VOL. XXXV, No. 10938

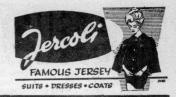

Develop Israel with Israel Bonds

THE JERUSALEM POST

MONDAY, JANUARY 6, 1964 • 21 Tevet, 5724 • 21 Sha'aban, 1383

EIGHT PAGES

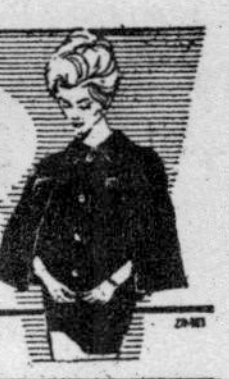
Jercoli
FAMOUS JERSEY
SUITS • DRESSES • COATS

POPE PAUL, RELAXED AND HAPPY, SPENDS 'UNFORGETTABLE DAY' AS PILGRIM IN ISRAEL

Pope Paul VI concluded a day-long visit to Israel at 9.07 p.m. last night, when he crossed the Mandel baum Gate into Jordan after a pilgrimage that ranged from Galilee to Judea. Before taking final leave of President Zalman Shazar in Jerusalem, the Pope expressed his full awareness of the freedom and equality enjoyed by the Catholic Church here. The Pontiff was replying to a farewell speech by the President, in which Mr. Shazar once again noted that Israel's hand "is stretched out in gesture of peace towards the neighbouring states, and our eyes lifted in search of true peace in the world . . . based on trust and respect among peoples."

THE Pope's whirlwind visit to the Christian sites in Israel has ended, and those who received him, or even caught a glimpse of his passage, could not fail to be impressed by the humanity and religious humility of this distinguished pilgrim, by his desire to share the experience of the millions who have trod this path before him and by his participation to give the pilgrimage a new symbolical value.

Yet his concern with the central mysteries of his faith did not prevent him from stopping to greet Arab villagers in Jordan when he passed by their homes or from lingering at Capernaum to examine the remnants of the ancient synagogue, or bestowing a blessing upon a supplicant.

Despite the solemnity of the moment at which the President of Israel received the Head of the Roman Church as an honoured guest to be welcomed and aided, an air of friendliness prevailed. The Pope referred to the links between the Jewish and Christian faiths, and emphasized the peace and concord which he seeks "for all peoples," for "the believing and the unbelieving." The mere fact that he ended his official address with "Shalom, shalom" would in itself have been taken by all as a gesture of friendship and concession to a Hebrew-speaking State of Israel.

This lack of formalism in his own approach gave the greater weight to his warm, almost anxious reference in his farewell speech in the evening to the oblique criticism that has been levelled recently at his predecessor, Pope Pius XII. Pope Paul pleaded ardently that this criticism, presumably in Hochhuth's much-debated play, "The Vicar," was unjust, that he knew from his own experience that Pope Pius had done all that was possible during the War for those in need of aid, without regard to religion. Whatever our own views in this matter may be, one could not fail to be moved by the courage and openness of the Pope's plea for understanding of this problem. We have been left with the image of a forward-looking spiritual leader not afraid to tread new roads.

* * *

It seems the more regrettable that Chief Rabbi Nissim should have chosen not to express the greetings of his own high office to the nation's guest. In most matters a Chief Rabbi must be his own authority, and had he declined to do so on some grounds of religious scruple it might be felt that this was a decision he must make for himself, but as what was involved was the place and form of the meeting, a mere question of prestige, his refusal was an unhappy one. As far as questions of staus and prestige are concerned, the Chief Rabbi might well have followed the lead of President Shazar, who found it possible to receive an unusual visitor in an unusual manner, without allowing points of protocol to mar the harmony of the visit.

By this withdrawal, Chief Rabbi Nissim has, in fact, placed a division between the religious and the lay representatives of the State. Such a division has in the past been more desired by the non-religious than the religious, who prefer to visualize the State as one body in which national and religious elements are too closely interwoven for religion to be excluded from any sphere. Usually, it was the religious authorities who protested whenever the civil authorities wished to go their own way. Rabbi Nissim has scarcely set the right example.

Saudia Agrees To Take Part In Arab 'Summit'

Saudi Arabia has agreed to attend the forthcoming Arab "summit" meeting, which opens in Cairo on January 13, Mecca Radio reported yesterday.

The radio said that the Saudi Arabian Kingdom had accepted the invitation to attend the talks on "Israel's conspiracy to divert the waters of the River Jordan," and was ready "to assume all its responsibilities together with its sister Arab States."

The radio did not say whether King Saud would head his country's delegation.

In Cairo Mr. Abdul Khalek Hassouna, the Arab League Secretary-General, yesterday met all the Arab envoys, except Jordan's, and said afterwards it had been agreed to form a committee, representing all Arab countries, which would meet on January 9 to discuss "the technical aspects of the diversion of the River Jordan."

Meeting with Nehru

A New Delhi message says that envoys of Egypt, Sudan, Syria, Jordan, Morocco, Lebanon, Iraq and Saudi Arabia jointly met Prime Minister Nehru and "conveyed their concern" over Israel's water plan.

According to an Indian spokesman, the Government sympathizes with the Arabs as it is against any "unilateral action" on international river waters by any country. *(Reuter, INA)*

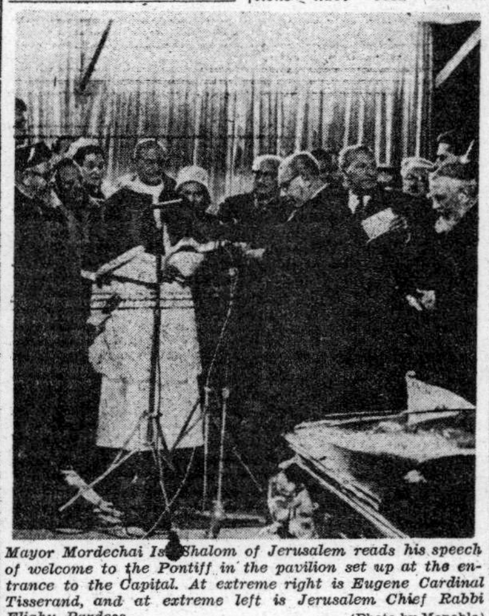

Mayor Mordechai Ish-Shalom of Jerusalem reads his speech of welcome to the Pontiff in the pavilion set up at the entrance to the Capital. At extreme right is Eugene Cardinal Tisserant, and at extreme left is Jerusalem Chief Rabbi Eliahu Pardess. (Photo by Manobla)

Terms 'Unjust' Charges Against Pius Twelfth

Pope Paul yesterday termed unjust allegations against the late Pope Pius that he did nothing to aid victims of the Nazis in World War II.

In reply to President Shazar's farewell statement at Mandelbaum Gate in Jerusalem before he ended his pilgrimage in Israel, the Pontiff said he had come in the spirit of the "Prince of Peace," whom he represents.

Speaking in French, he said that "we nurse only feelings of goodwill towards everybody, towards all men and towards all peoples. The Church loves them all equally."

Speaking of the spirit of peace he went on:

"Our great predecessor, Pius XII proved it forcefully and on several occasions. In the midst of the last World War everybody knows what he did for the defence and the rescue of all those who were caught in its tribulations, without distinction, and yet you know suspicions and even accusations have been levelled against the memory of this great Pontiff.

"We are happy to have the opportunity to state on this day and in this place that there is nothing more unjust than this slight against such a venerated memory. Those who intimately knew this admirable man know how far could go his sensibility, his compassion for human suffering, his courage, his delicate heart.

"Those who after the War came with tears in their eyes to thank him for their lives also knew it."

Follow Example

"Truly, following the example of he whom they represent here below, Popes desire nothing but the true well-being of all men."

The Pope said it was an unforgettable day for him. "We wish to express Our satisfaction with the visit and our gratitude for the welcome we have been accorded."

In conclusion he stated:

"We extend Our blessings and good wishes to you as We conclude our visit. It is with satisfaction that We consider that our Catholic children living in this country shall continue to enjoy the rights and liberty to which all men are today considered to be entitled. And wholeheartedly We lift Our eyes on high and pray that God's blessings may be lavished upon you, on Our Christian children round about Us here, and on everyone everywhere whose thoughts are of peace and reconciliation."

Shazar's Speech

President Shazar's farewell speech at Mandelbaum Gate follows:

This morning I had the honour and pleasure of welcoming our illustrious visitor upon his entry into our State. Having since journeyed through the land and met with his own flock, he has surely seen how the will and the hope of all that dwell in Zion are in consonance with the spirit of his own exalted words regarding the aspiration for justice and progress that are not only technical but also humane, and for peace that is not merely a precarious suspension of hostilities among peoples and social classes but that will at last make possible cooperation among men and nations in an atmosphere of mutual understanding.

As for us, our hand is stretched out in a gesture of peace towards the neighbouring states and our eyes are lifted in search of true peace in the world, peace firmly based on trust and respect among peoples.

Ancient Prophets

Today our illustrious guest spoke of our ancient prophets. It was they who in this land gave to us and to all the world our faith in the establishment of universal peace, more vital to humanity in our age than in any other. The prophets have shown us, too, the way to this longed-for goal. Micah, the man of Morasha, the very prophet who wrote of the day when men will beat their swords into "plough-shares and their spears into pruning hooks", wrote also: "Let every nation walk in the name of its God, and we in the name of the Lord our Gor, for ever."

We part from our great guest with the blessing: "May your departure be in peace."

From Jerusalem, city of David, city of peace, may he take with him our heart-felt blessing of peace.

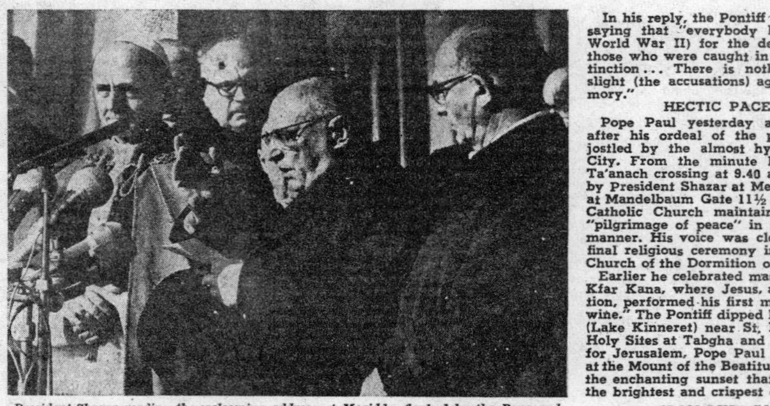

President Shazar reading the welcoming address at Megiddo, flanked by the Pope and Prime Minister Eshkol.

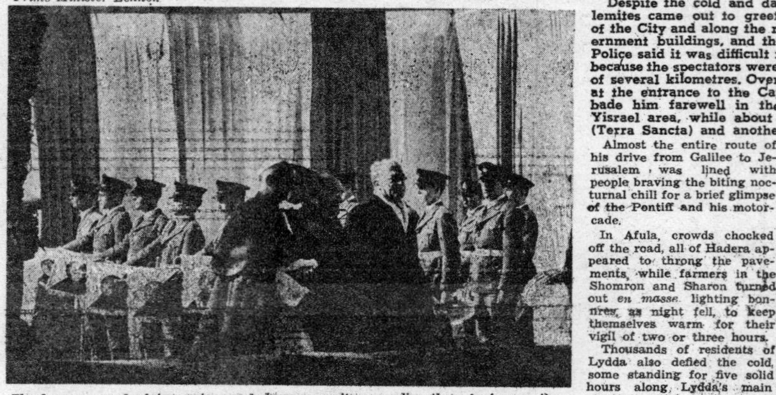

The honour guard of trumpeters and drummers, after sounding their fanfare as the Pope is escorted by President Shazar to the speakers' platform at Megiddo.

In his reply, the Pontiff also defended Pope Pius XII, saying that "everybody knows what he did (during World War II) for the defence and the rescue of all those who were caught in its tribulations, without distinction ... There is nothing more unjust than this slight (the accusations) against such a venerated memory."

HECTIC PACE OF LONG DAY

Pope Paul yesterday appeared relaxed and calm after his ordeal of the previous day, when he was jostled by the almost hysterical crowds in the Old City. From the minute he arrived in Israel at the Ta'anach crossing at 9.40 a.m. and the official welcome by President Shazar at Megiddo until the leave-taking at Mandelbaum Gate 11½ hours later, the head of the Catholic Church maintained the hectic pace of his "pilgrimage of peace" in the same quiet but dynamic manner. His voice was clear and strong when, in his final religious ceremony in Israel, he preached in the Church of the Dormition on Mt. Zion.

Earlier he celebrated mass in Nazareth, and drove by Kfar Kana, where Jesus, according to Christian tradition, performed his first miracle and water "was made wine." The Pontiff dipped his hand in the Sea of Galilee (Lake Kinneret) near St. Peter's rock, and visited the Holy Sites at Tabgha and Kfar Nahum. Before he left for Jerusalem, Pope Paul took refreshment and a rest at the Mount of the Beatitudes, and on Mount Tabor saw the enchanting sunset that marked the end of one of the brightest and crispest days of the winter.

25,000 LINE CAPITAL STREETS

Despite the cold and darkness, some 25,000 Jerusalemites came out to greet the Pope at the entrance of the City and along the roped-off route past the Government buildings, and through Rehavia to Mt. Zion. Police said it was difficult to set the number accurately because the spectators were streched out over a distance of several kilometres. Over 5,000 welcomed the Pontiff at the entrance to the Capital, and a similar number bade him farewell in the Mandelbaum Gate-Shivtei Yisrael area, while about 3,000 stood at Paris Square (Terra Sancta) and another 3,000 near Mount Zion.

Almost the entire route of his drive from Galilee to Jerusalem was lined with people braving the biting nocturnal chill for a brief glimpse of the Pontiff and his motorcade.

In Afula, crowds chocked off the road, all of Hadera appeared to throng the pavements, while farmers in the Shomron and Sharon turned out *en masse*, lighting bonfires as night fell, to keep themselves warm for their vigil of two or three hours.

Thousands of residents of Lydda also defied the cold, some standing for five solid hours along Lydda's main street to catch a glimpse of the Pope.

Meets Athenogoras Back in Old City

JERUSALEM, Jordan.—Pope Paul VI returne here last night, after spending the day in Israel, for the first of two meetings with the leader of 150 million members of the Eastern Orthodox Church, Patriarch Athenogoras.

The tall, bearded, 77-year-old Patriarch, had arrived here from Istanbul by plane yesterday accompanied by 12 Orthodoxx prelates and was welcomed at the airport by King Hussein. A crowd of about 1,000 greeted the Patriarch at the airport.

The Patriarch, who will also meet the Pope this morning, said he hoped his stay "will contribute to the unity of the Christian Church," Reuter reports.

First for Centuries

Last night's meeting, at the Apostolic delegation, was the first for five centuries between a Pope of Rome and a Patriarch of the Orthodox Church.

According to a text issued here, the Pope told the Patriarch that dubtless the roads which led to Christian unity might be long and sown with difficulties, but that these two paths converged on each other.

The Jordan, press yesterday morning omitted any reference to the incidents in the Old City on Saturday which hampered the progress of the Papal party on Saturday.

In an editorial, "Falastin" said that "when we inform the Pope today that we are preparing to regain our stolen right, we ask him to be on our side in this issue."

(Jordan Radio — Pg. 2, Col. 3)

Brilliant Scene at Leave-Taking

By SHALOM COHEN, Jerusalem Post Reporter

Pope Paul's departure from Israel was a brilliant occasion under the dazzling fluorescent lights installed at the Mandelbaum Gate crossing. The Pope, dressed in vivid crimson and white, and President Shazar, in black, arrived at the crossing to bugle fanfares as a Guard of Honour of officer cadets presented arms.

Brightly coloured standards carried by the khaki-clad guard, the long scarlet carpet, and profusion of flags all illuminated in the dark chilly night lent the scene larger-than-life, dream-like effect.

The high points of the ceremony were the brief speeches of President Shazar, followed by Pope Paul, and the repeated handshaking between the two. The Pope then raised his hands in blessing as he walked to and fro before entering his car and driving off into Jordan.

After his address, the Pope shook hands and exchanged greetings with members of the farewell party, which included Prime Minister Levi Eshkol; Deputy Prime Minister Abba Eban; Ministers Warhaftig and Shitrit, the Knesset Speaker; Mayor Ish Shalom; the Soviet, Italian, French, Belgian, and Netherlands Ambassadors; the O.C. Central Command.

Pope Paul's references to Pius the Twelfth sent a stir through the large body of some 250 newsmen. Like Mr. Shazar, the Pope delivered his farewell speech in firm, short phrases. The President spoke in Hebrew, and the Pope in French. (Texts in col. 4).

There were rolls of drums, more fanfares, presentation of arms and the incessant whir of TV cameras, and the Pope, the three Cardinals, and the Papal entourage, went into the dark night, away from Israel. Thousands stood quietly behind the police barriers in the Gate are

Last Farewell

In his last farewell, Pope Paul said to the Chief of Protocol, Mr. Avraham Gilboa, "I came to realize that the people who lived in this country are an energetic and forward looking people."

Pilgrim medallions in gold for the three Cardinals, and silver ones for the entourage, were presented on behalf of Dr. Wahrhaftig.

U.S. Cuts Order For 'Minutemen'

WASHINGTON (Reuter). — The U.S. will cut its purchases of Minutemen intercontinental ballistic missiles from 150 to 50 under the defence budget President Johnson will send to Congress in about two weeks, usually well-informed sources said today.

The reduction, the first since the U.S. entered the missile race against the Russians in the 1950s would bring the number of missiles in the Strategic Air Command to 1,000 during the fiscal year beginning July 1 — 100 short of the original target.

The President and Mr. Robert McNamara, Defence Secretary, were said to be planning an eventual arsenal of 1,200 Minutemen in the next few years instead of 1,850 as requested by the Air Force.

Mr. McNamara said after talks with Mr. Johnson last week that the defence budget would amount to $51,000m. — cut of $1,000m. from the current budget.

EGYPT-YEMEN

CAIRO, (Reuter). — A five-year trade and technical cooperation agreement was signed here yesterday between Egypt and Yemen.

Cardinal in Holocaust Chamber

By ERWIN FRENKEL, Jerusalem Post Reporter

The Dean of the College of Cardinals, Cardinal Eugene Tisserant, last night paid tribute to the memory of the six million Jews killed in the Holocaust with an unscheduled visit to the Chamber of Destruction on Mt. Zion.

Shortly after the Pope's arrival on Mt. Zion, Cardinal Tisserant left the papal entourage to descend into the Chamber.

Accompanied by the Minister for Religious Affairs, Dr. Zerah Warhaftig, Cardinal Tisserant lit six candles — symbolizing the six million killed — which flickered above black marble plaques, on which are inscribed the names of concentration camps.

The Cardinal stood silent a moment and said: "On behalf of the Pope, we express our sympathy and participation in the anguish and sorrow at the terrible destruction wrought upon the Hebrew People."

Cardinal Tisserant's agreement to visit the Chambre — considered an important Vatican gesture towards the Jewish people — became known shortly before the Pope arrived in Jerusalem.

Kneels on Stone Coenaculum Floor

By MOSHE KOHN, Jerusalem Post Reporter

Pope Paul VI yesterday evening knelt and prayed for about two minutes in the centre of the cold stone floor of the Coenaculum on Mt. Zion.

At about 8.12 p.m. the bells of the Dormition Abbey started pealing to announce the Pope's arrival on the Mount. About five minutes later, the Pope, his party, and their Israeli escorts entered the room which marks the site where Jesus ate his last supper with his disciples, and where, seven weeks later, on the Festival of Shavuot (Pentecost), his disciples gathered again, were visited by the Holy Sprit, and the miracle of "speaking in tongues" occurred.

The Pope quickly scanned the room, then strode to the centre of the floor and knelt facing the western wall, where a niche marks the "Seat of the Master" — in which Jesus sat at the Last Supper. The Pope ignored the carpet which had been spread before the low stone platform before the niche.

When he had finished praying, the Pope rose, spent about 30 seconds looking about the room and proceeded to the Dormition Abbey.

Only about 25 persons were admitted into the small room to witness the solemn scene.

The Pope stretched his arms out in blessing and strode briskly from the Coenaculum to the Dormition Abbey where Mary, mother of Jesus, is believed to have lain down in eternal sleep.

When the Pope appeared, members of the holy orders went from the altar bearing a huge cross and went outside the church to receive the Pontiff. Abbe Rudloff, the Father Superior, welcomed the Pope with a speech in Latin as he entered the rotunda. The Pope greeted the throng of about 300 with his arms outstretched in blessing.

There was enthusiastic applause as the Papal procession marched forward to the altar while the bells rang out. The Pope, followed by Cardinals Tisserant, Testa and Cicongnianni and members of the Dormition Church clergy, stepped down to the crypt where a life-size statue of Mary lies, as if in eternal sleep.

A few minutes later the Pontiff emerged to step behind the altar at the far end of the church and delivered a short address in French expressing his thanks for the welcome and his wishes for peace in the Holy City.

Lesser Job for Iraqi Deputy President

Brigadier Achmed Hassan el Bakr, former Iraqi Premier and present Deputy-President of the republic, has been appointed an Ambassador at the Foreign Ministry in Baghdad, Baghdad Radio reported yesterday. The post of vice-president has been abolished.

Record Berlin Crowd in Final Day's Crossing

BERLIN (Reuter). — A record 279,151 West Berliners poured into East Berlin yesterday to pay final calls on relatives before the gates at the wall were closed again at midnight.

As more and more people flooded in the centre of East Berlin) usually almost empty of cars and crowds, the sector resembled the bustling heart of the western part of the city.

A total of 1,238,918 visits have been made to East Berlin since the wall was opened on December 20 for the holiday period, the East German news agency, A.D.N., reported yesterday.

Yesterday morning cars on their way to East Berlin had to wait in queues up to two miles long for between one and two hours to be passed by the East German guards at the four crossing points.

To all who shared our grief on the passing away of our dear

Jacob Kopeliowitch

we want to express our heartfelt thanks.

Bluma Kopeliowitch,
Michael Kopeliowitch
and family

Notice
S.S. ZION
will arrive today
at 20.00 hours
and not at
10.00
as published.
ZIM
ISRAEL NAVIGATION COMPANY LTD

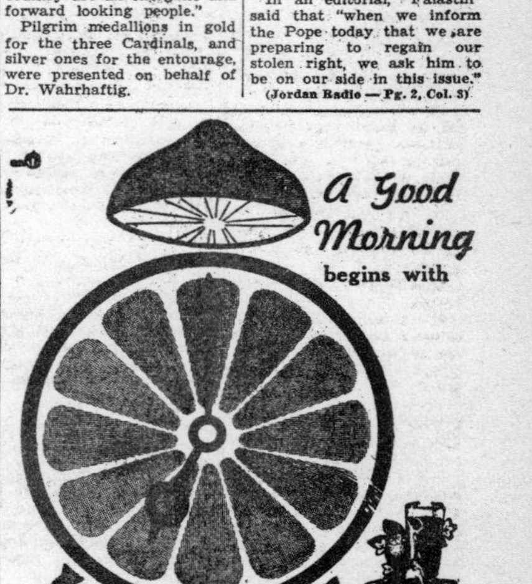
A Good Morning begins with
CITRUS FRUIT
Delicious and Nutritious
The Citrus Marketing Board

THE JERUSALEM POST Published in Jerusalem, Israel, daily except on Saturday by The Palestine Post Ltd. Founded in 1932 by Gershon AGRON. Registered at the G.P.O. Copyright of all material reserved; reproduction permitted only by arrangement.
Editor: TED R. LURIE

Editorial and Business Office: 9 Rehov Havatzelet, Jerusalem, Israel P.O.B. 81, Tel. 24233, 24321.
Tel Aviv: 52 Rehov Nahlat Binyamin, P. O. Box 1125, Tel 64251.
Haifa: 34 Rehov Herzl, Hadar Hacarmel, P.O.Box 4810, Tel. 64594.

Annual Subscription: IL 76.
SINGLE COPY: 22 AGORA.

VOL. XXXVI, No. 11190*

Rest on GUMAVIR KFAR-SABA -and be rested!

THE JERUSALEM POST

THURSDAY, NOVEMBER 5, 1964 • 30 Heshvan, 5725 • 1 Regev, 1384

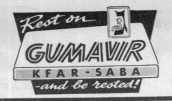

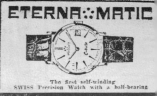

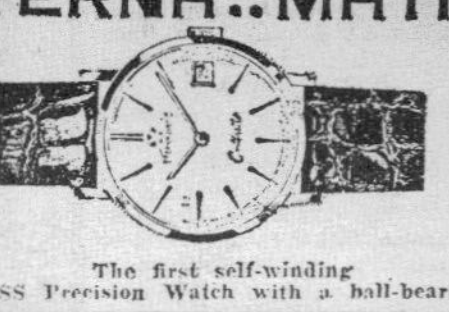
ETERNA·MATIC
The first self-winding SWISS Precision Watch with a ball-bearing

JOHNSON SWEEPS U.S. ELECTION BY GREATEST MARGIN IN HISTORY

MANDATE FOR SANITY

ISRAEL, together with the rest of the world, yesterday welcomed with relief the overwhelming victory of President Lyndon Johnson in the United States. It was, as Americans themselves understood, a victory for responsibility over a dangerous impetuosity in foreign policy, and for equality over discrimination in domestic policy.

Mr. Johnson's unprecedented triumph gives him a mandate in both areas, which he can be expected to pursue virgorously. For he has won the election not simply as the leader of the Democratic Party but as the standard-bearer of that middle-of-the-road American political stance which has dominated both parties in this century.

It was on this basis that he appealed to the American voter, and as the results show, the electorate understood and responded to the appeal. Traditionally Republican states in New England and the Middle West supported him, and liberal Republicans like Governor George Romney of Michigan, or like the defeated Senator Keating of New York, a staunch friend of Israel, who shunned Senator Goldwater were either elected or ran well ahead of their presidential candidate, indicating the voter's response to personality over party.

For the American Negro and other minority groups, who rightly viewed the election as a crucial test for the basis of American democracy, it was a vindication of faith. The much heralded "white backlash" in the north did not materialize, and even in most of the southern and border states the Republican appeal to white supremacy was rejected. Only in the five states of the Deep South, immersed in the racial crisis, did this appeal overshadow every other issue and interest.

The real issue therefore raised by President Johnson's massive victory is the future of the Republican Party. The radical right which, invigorated by the personal magnetism of Senator Goldwater, gained control of the party at San Francisco last summer, had long clamoured for a chance to bring its case to the American voter. That case has been emphatically rejected. But will the right accept the verdict and yield their leadership of the Party to the moderates who ruled it previously, or will they pursue their struggle on the grounds that they have only lost the first round? On this question may hang the future of American politics for many years to come.

For though the radical right this year benefited from the support it gained as a result of opposition to civil rights, this was not its only appeal. It rejected the pragmatism of the moderates for the vigorous pursuit of a simplistic image of an America which never was. That image of the past has always appealed to many Americans, as the more than 25 million people who voted for the Arizona Senator indicates. The Republican Party will have to decide whether this myth is to remain the sole property of its radicals, and whether it should continue to be associated with extremism and racialism.

President Johnson has presented Americans with a different dream; a "Great Society" in which there will no longer be any poor; where everyone will have a full opportunity to advance; a society aware of the complexities as well as the possibilities of the modern world, and above all concerned to maintain world peace by maintaining a strong defence, but also being ready to explore every avenue of peaceful coexistence.

It is this road which the mass of Americans have chosen to follow, and the attentive world is grateful.

DAYAN RESIGNS FROM CABINET

Jerusalem Post Political Reporter

TEL AVIV.—The Minister of Agriculture, Mr. Moshe Dayan, yesterday morning handed in his resignation from the Cabinet to Premier Levi Eshkol. Mr. Dayan had intended to resign from Mr. Eshkol's Cabinet on two previous occasions, but had reconsidered and remained at his post. This time he gave no previous notification of his intention, which took his associates by surprise, but he told Kol Yisrael last night that he had intimated to the Prime Minister his intention to resign some time ago and had had several talks with Mr. Eshkol on the subject.

The initial statement made by Mr. Dayan after handing Mr. Eshkol his resignation at 8 o'clock in the morning was: "To my regret I do not see my way to continue my membership in the Cabinet, in the absence of an identity of views which a Minister must have with the head of the Cabinet."

Mr. Eshkol's reaction was to express his regret at the absence of such an identity of views and at Mr. Dayan's resignation.

There was no indication yesterday that any other Cabinet minister intended to follow suit.

Policy differences

It was generally assumed that Mr. Dayan resigned in opposition to the alignment with Ahdut Ha'avoda, which is being engineered by Mr. Eshkol. Mr. Dayan is known to disagree with Ahdut Ha'avoda's view of total non-cooperation with Germany and with that party's economic policy. He is said to feel that under the alignment Ahdut Ha'avoda would achieve too much influence over Mapai's policy.

Mr. Dayan is also said to have felt unable to remain in the Cabinet at a time when it appeared that a rapprochement was being brought about by Mr. Eshkol with Mr. Pinhas Lavon and his group. It is understood he wished to be free of official responsibility in order to campaign within the Party for his views. The imminent assembly of the Mapai 10th Convention is considered to be an important factor in the timing of Mr. Dayan's resignation.

The timing of his resignation is understood to have been influenced, too, by his strong opposition to the economic programme of Finance Minister Pinhas Sapir, who is due to present his new programme to the Cabinet next Sunday.

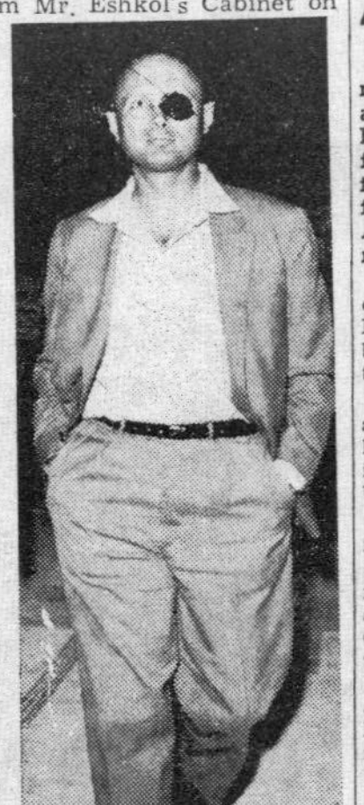
Mr. Moshe Dayan is seen leaving the Mapai Secretariat in Tel Aviv last week after the "alignment" issue was practically settled. (Photo by Berez)

Mr. Dayan out of office is expected to serve as a rallying force in the Party for a large segment of the opposition to the reinstatement of Mr. Lavon and the alignment with Ahdut Ha'avoda. Mr. Eshkol, meanwhile, has promised other Mapai leaders not to take any initiative in the direction of Mr. Lavon and his group before the "Min Hayesod" group's rally on Saturday.

Opposed to alignment, challenge to Eshkol

By YOSEF GOELL
Jerusalem Post Reporter

Mr. Dayan's resignation was interpreted in Jerusalem political circles yesterday as serving notice on Prime Minister Eshkol that his efforts to push through the alignment with Ahdut Ha'avoda would result in Mr. Dayan's placing himself at the head of a Mapai opposition centred on the "young guard."

It is believed that Mr. Dayan's resignation was prompted by two developments: the setting up of the "reconciliation faction" of officials close to Mr. Eshkol, which was interpreted as indicating his intention of placating the Lavonists, and Mr. Eshkol's refusal to postpone a decision on the alignment to permit a wider debate on the economic policies that it implied, and which Mr. Dayan opposes.

Mr. Dayan's step is seen as a direct challenge to Mr. Eshkol's leadership of the party, in reaction to the Prime Minister's firmness in insisting on conclusion of the alignment, regardless of the internal opposition in his party. Mr. Dayan's final decision was apparently taken on Tuesday night after several fruitless attempts to persuade Mr. Eshkol to agree to a thorough policy debate in Mapai bodies before a final decision on the alignment.

Didn't vote

Some Knesset observers noted yesterday that on the evening prior to his resignation Mr. Dayan, although present in the Knesset, did not take part in the vote on the no-confidence motions in the Government's German policy. It was also reported that earlier in the day he had walked out of a meeting of the Knesset Economic Committee after attacking some Mapai members of the Committee on their economic views.

Discussion of possible successors to Mr. Dayan in the Agriculture Ministry was purely speculative yesterday, but it was recalled that when Mr. Dayan had threatened to resign last year, the leading names that were mentioned as successors were Mr. Uzi Finerman, Secretary-General of the Moshav Movement, and Mr. Haim Gvati of Ihud Hakibbutzim, a former Director-General of the Ministry.

While these two candidates are still regarded as in the running, the name of Minister Akiva Govrin has also cropped up as providing the most convenient immediate solution to an unexpected crisis. It was felt that Mr. Govrin's appointment would avoid an internal party struggle between its moshav and kibbutz wings.

Mr. Eshkol has announced that he will make a statement to the Knesset next week on the resignation, and it is believed that he may name a new Minister of Agriculture in time for Sunday's Cabinet meeting.

Although there is no intention of having a full-fledged Knesset debate on Mr. Dayan's resignation, Herut leaders yesterday served notice that they would demand such a debate and would be ready to enlist the signatures of 40 Knesset Members that are required to force the issue.

Sources close to Mr. Dayan last night told *The Jerusalem Post* that his resignation was "a personal protest" against what they termed the Prime Minister's failure to act on issues of paramount national importance. Mr. Dayan was said to be troubled over "ineptitude in implementing" the party's economic policy, and that he was apprehensive that an alignment with Ahdut Ha'avoda would mean the adoption of an economic policy not in tune with the technological changes and modernization of the economy which he considers vital.

Speculation in the Knesset lobbies as to the causes of the resignation was further highlighted yesterday by Mr. Pinhas Lavon's appearance in the Knesset restaurant, where he huddled for a few minutes with Dr. Yohanan Bader, of Herut.

(Dayan hits — Page 6)

Peking to send Chou to Moscow

Communist Chinese Premier Chou En-lai will head a Peking delegation to Moscow to be on hand on for the 44th anniversary of the Bolshevik Revolution, the New China News Agency announced last night.

The official announcement confirmed reports in Eastern Europe that Peking's number one diplomat would make the trip to Moscow.

Such a trip would indicate a significant thawing of the long-time chilly relations existing between the Soviet Union and China.

The revolution celebrations in the Soviet capital begin Saturday but there was no indication in the brief announcement when Mr. Chou and his party planned to arrive in Moscow.

The Chinese did not send a delegation to the Moscow May Day celebrations six months ago, accusing the Kremlin of failing to invite them.

Moscow Radio announced yesterday that a Soviet delegation led by Railways Minister and Central Committee member B.P. Beschev had left by plane for Peking to attend ceremonies there for the Bolshevik revolution anniversary.

Mr. Chou will be making his first visit to Moscow since October, 1961, when he walked out of the Congress of the Soviet Communist Party. His walkout triggered a hectic name-calling era in the Sino-Soviet dispute which ceased, at least temporarily, when Mr. Khrushchev fell last month.

Tass said invitations from the Soviet Communist Party and Government to attend the week-end festivities were accepted by China, Bulgaria, Hungary, North Vietnam, East Germany, North Korea, China, Cuba, Mongolia, Poland, Rumania, Czechoslovakia and Yugoslavia — but not Albania.

No Israel ties now, Bonn says

BONN (UPI).—Under-secretary of State Karl Carstens said yesterday that the Bonn Government has no intention of establishing diplomatic relations with Israel at present.

Speaking in a parliamentary question period, Prof. Carstens termed the question of diplomatic ties with Israel "a very delicate and difficult complex in our foreign relations."

He declined to discuss the matter further, insisting that "all aspects of this issue cannot be said out in the open."

While "recognizing the feeling of moral obligation among the German people to normalize relations between our country and Israel," Prof. Carstens defended the Bonn Government's stand as "in the interests of all parties concerned."

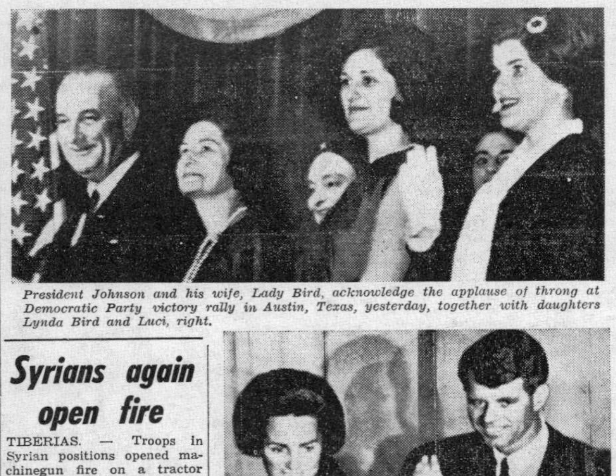
President Johnson and his wife, Lady Bird, acknowledge the applause of throng at Democratic Party victory rally in Austin, Texas, yesterday, together with daughters Lynda Bird and Luci, right.

Syrians again open fire

TIBERIAS. — Troops in Syrian positions opened machinegun fire on a tractor driver in the Jordan estuary, north of Lake Kinneret, yesterday afternoon.

An Israeli covering detachment returned the fire, and the exchange lasted for a few minutes.

No one was hurt and no damage was caused.

All was quiet yesterday in the Dan area, Upper Galilee, where heavy firing broke out on Tuesday. The Syrians had opened fire on a tractor working on a road east of the kibbutz. Work on the road continued without incident yesterday.

In the afternoon Syrian villagers who fled from their homes during the firing on Tuesday returned.

The wreckage of the Syrian tank damaged on Tuesday and the hits on some fortified positions could be seen clearly yesterday.

U.N. observers, accompanied by the Israel delegate to the Mixed Armistice commission, continued their investigation yesterday.

In Damascus a Syrian military spokesman said yesterday that one Syrian soldier and a civilian had been killed in the shooting earlier in the day, reports Reuter. He claimed that Israel had "incurred losses in lives and equipment."

Heavy French budget for nuclear arms

PARIS (Reuter). — France will spend more than 15,000m. francs (about £1,150m.) in the next five years to build up her nuclear strike force, including strategic thermo-nuclear weapons, Information Minister Alain Peyrefitte said here yesterday.

He told reporters that yesterday's Cabinet meeting approved France's second five-year military plan for 1965-1970 in which nuclear arms top the list of credits to be spent.

Bolivian president flees after revolt

LA PAZ, Bolivia (AP).—President Victor Paz Estenssoro was overthrown in a military revolt yesterday and fled the country. Gen. Alfredo Obando Candia, armed forces commander announced that he had taken over the government as head of a military junta.

He pledged to retain power as briefly as possible and to call new elections. He said Paz Estenssoro had brought trouble upon himself by fostering a constitutional amendment which permitted him to be elected to a third consecutive term. Paz Estenssoro resigned to avoid bloodshed, Gen. Obando said.

Paz Estenssoro arrived in Lima, Peru, last night.

The revolt was led by Vice-President Rene Barrientos, who broke with Paz Estenssoro last month after the President cracked down on anti-Government students and crushed a revolt of tin miners in the interior.

Led uprising

An Air Force General, Barrientos, led the uprising from Cochabamba. A military revolt broke out in La Paz on Tuesday and many units in various parts of the country rallied to the Vice-President.

As Paz Estenssoro fled, fighting broke out in the capital when his followers resisted efforts of the military junta to take over the Government.

Army planes bombed and strafed headquarters of Paz's National Revolutionary Movement.

SAPIR DENIES DEVALUATION

There is no foundation to the rumours of devaluation of the Israel pound, Finance Minister Pinhas Sapir said last night.

Speaking at a meeting of the economic institutions of the National Religious Party, Mr. Sapir explained: "Devaluation will not solve any problems, in the same way as the devaluation of 1962 did not solve the problems of the Israel economy."

The Government is preparing a new economic programme, designed to cure the economy of its present ills, and especially to reduce consumption, the Minister said. The proposed plan also aims at cutting down expenditure on public building.

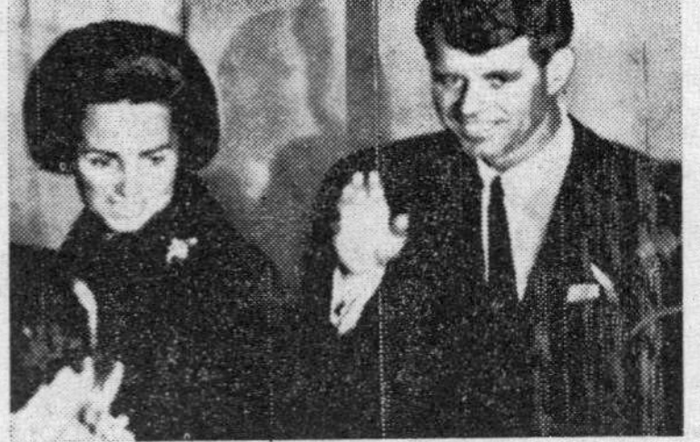
Robert F. Kennedy and his wife, Ethel, wave to crowd as they arrive at their hotel in New York on Tuesday, after he was elected U.S. Senator of New York. (AP Radiophotos)

Democrats score Congress gains

NEW YORK.—The Democrats swept into power aagin in Congress early yesterday on the wave of President Johnson's popularity.

They increased their majority in the House of Representatives and also gained an added seat in the Senate.

The final tally in the House was Democrats 294, Republicans 141, compared with 257 and 178 in the old House

The present Senate line-up is Democrats 67, Republicans 33, compared with 66-34.

The increase in House seats boosted President Johnson's prospects of pushing some of his more controversial measures through Congress. Among them are plans for health care for the aged and for more economic aid to depressed araes.

In the elections for Governors, the Democrats have gained one place. They now have 34 States and the Republicans 16.

Kennedy wins

The Senate race which captured most attention was in New York, where Robert Kennedy, former Attorney-General and brother of the late President, scored an upset victory by sweeping the Liberal Republican incumbent, Senator Kenneth Keating, out of office.

Senator Edward (Teddy) Kennedy, another brother of the late President, easily won his first full six-year term in his home State of Massachusetts.

"Bobby" Kennedy, 38, throughout the campaign had to fight off the "carpet-bagger" issue that he actually lived in Virginia, and had come into the Senate race solely to further presidential ambitions.

He was unable to cast a vote in his own contest.

It was the first Senate victory for a Democrat in New York since 1958. The other seat is held by Senator Jacob Javits, a liberal Republican who was re-elected in 1962.

Salinger defeated

In another key Senate contest, the Republican George Murphy, former Hollywood song and dance star, defeated the Democratic incumbent, Senator Pierre Salinger.

Representative William Miller, unsuccessful Republican vice-presidenital candidate, failed to carry his home county, Niagara. Mr. Miller has represented the county in the House of Representatives for 14 years.

Senator Mike Mansfield, 61-year-old Democratic majority leader, retained his seat in Montana.

State governors

In the 25 election contests for State Governors, one of the most significant was the re-election of Republican George Romney in Michigan.

He had pointedly refused to endorse Senator Goldwater's candidacy, and if the control of the Republican Party were to return to the moderates after the election he would be in the running for its leadership.

Governor Orval Faubus of Arkansas was re-elected for an unprecedented sixth term when he defeated Mr. Winthrop Rockefeller, brother of Governor Nelson Rockefeller of New York.

Texas Governor John Connally, injured by the bullets fired at the motorcade in Dallas last November, when President Kennedy was killed, was returned for another term. *(Reuter, UPI, AP)*

Friend of Israel is defeated

By JESSE ZEL LURIE,
Jerusalem Post Correspondent

NEW YORK. — Republican Kenneth Keating, who lost his Senate seat to Robert Kennedy, is the only friend of Israel to have been defeated in the election.

Supporters of Mr. Kennedy said yesterday that he would be in a position to assist Israel.

Republican Congressman Ogden Reid, a former Ambassador to Israel, retained his seat in White Plains, New York. The adjoining Westchester District elected a Democrat — Mr. Richard Ottinger, of Jewish descent — for the first time since 1921.

Jewish Congressmen Emmanuel Celler (Democrat, Brooklyn), Seymour Halperin (Republican, Forest Hills) and Charles Joelson (Democrat, Paterson, New Jersey) were all re-elected.

ANCIENT MAPS ON GREETING CARDS

We will be happy to show you our new samples. Please write or phone for an appointment.

The Universitas Booksellers

9 Rehov Shlomzion Hamalka, P.O.B. 1086, Jerusalem, Tel. 24050.

Barry intends to keep GOP reins

NEW YORK. — President Lyndon Johnson was swe[pt] back into the White House in triumph yesterday w[ith] the biggest popular vote in American history.

The President captured 44 States and the Distr[ict] of Columbia. Republican candidate Barry Goldwa[ter] gained five Southern States and Arizona, his nati[ve] territory.

Late last night, with votes from 97 per cent of t[he] precincts returned, Mr. Joh[n]son had won 41,214,171 (6[1] per cent) and Senator Gol[d]water 26,016,535 (38.7 per cen[t]).

The number of Electo[ral] College votes gained by [Mr.] Johnson was 486, and by [Se]nator Goldwater 52.

President Johnson's vict[ory] eclipsed even that of Fra[nk]lin D. Roosevelt's mass[ive] win over Governor Alf La[n]don in 1936.

The President will be f[ur]ther strengthened as leader [by] increased Democratic supp[ort] in Congress.

Early yesterday, with v[ic]tory assured, Mr. Johns[on] called on all Americans [to] bind our wounds and m[ake] this nation one people."

He told a rally of wi[ldly] cheering supporters at A[us]tin, Texas, near his ran[ch]: "There are many more thi[ngs] that unite us than divide [us]."

Tribute to Kennedy

His voice hoarse from [...] months of campaigning, [Mr.] Johnson added: "I know [that] this is more than a vict[ory] of party or person — it [is a] tribute to the programme [that] was begun by the late [be]loved President John Ke[nne]dy . . . a programme that [was] carried on until he was [ta]ken from us."

The election was a "m[an]date for unity, for a gov[ern]ment that represents no s[pe]cial interest — no busi[ness] government, no labour [go]vernment," he said.

Senator Barry Goldw[ater] made a formal declaratio[n of] defeat yesterday aftern[oon] and sent a message of c[on]gratulations to Mr. John[son]. At the same time he m[ade] clear that despite his o[ver]whelming defeat he inte[nds] to remain at the helm of [the] Republican Party.

Senator Goldwater sai[d in] his message, sent from h[is home] in Phoenix, Arizona, that [he] would help Mr. Johnson [in] any way he could to bui[ld a] "better America and se[cure] a dignified peace."

The Senator told repo[rters] that he had "no bitter[ness] and no rancour." He w[ill] now have plenty of tim[e to] devote to leading and str[eng]thening the party, he [said]. He did not think the con[ser]vative cause had been [...] His defeat was due part[ly to] the fact that some Rep[ubli]cans would not work for [him].

Asked about the next e[lec]tion, Senator Goldwater [said] he thought the Republi[cans] "would probably pick ano[ther] man to run."

(OTHER STORIES—Pg

Policy on M.E. static

WASHINGTON (UPI). — The election of President Johnson is not expected to spell any changes in U.S. policy in the Middle East, officials predicted yesterday.

U.S. officials feel chances of continued relative quiet in that area are good. The Middle East has not been an issue in the campaign.

However, the Democrats blueprinted their plans in a Near East platform plank approved at the Atlantic City convention in August.

They pledged to "work for the attainment of peace in the Near East as an urgent goal, using our best efforts to prevent a military unbalance, to encourage arms reductions and the use of national resources for internal development and to encourage the resettlement of Arab refugees in lands where there is room and opportunity for them. The problems of political adjustment between Israel and the Arab countries . . . must be peacefully resolved and the territorial integrity of every nation respected."

After his victory, President Johnson is expected to continue furnishing aid for the Near East countries. Aid to Israel, however, is expected to undergo a change in the years ahead with increasing prosperity in that country, officials pointed out.

Shazar, Eshkol send messages

President Shazar and Prime Minister Levy Eshkol sent messages of congratulations to President Johnson yesterday.

President Shazar said: "On behalf of the people of Israel and on my own behalf it gives me joy to send you and the American people our heartfelt congratulations on your historic victory. May it be given to you to achieve your great goals of democracy, equality and world peace. From Jerusalem, the city of peace, our blessings and our hopes go out to you."

Mr. Eshkol, extending congratulations on behalf of the Government and himself, said that President Johnson's "constructive leadership on behalf of peace, freedom and international fraternity has already given the world renewed hope for a better future. We are confident that your great talents and energy, supported by the dynamic efforts of the American people, will enable you to fulfil the high destiny to which you have been called."

Mr. Eshkol also sent a cable to Vice-President Hubert Humphrey, saying: "The Government of Israel and I send sincere wishes and heartfelt congratulations on your elevation to the Vice-Presidency. We know that the cause of peace and a better world will be advanced under the enlightened guidance of President Johnson and yourself."

Vietnam gets all-civilian Gov

SAIGON (Reuter). — S[outh] Vietnam's new Prime M[inis]ter, Mr. Tran Van Hu[ong] yesterday announced the [for]mation of an all-civilian [go]vernment, consisting ma[inly] of experienced technician[s ra]ther than politicians.

Mr. Huong kept for [him]self the key post of [De]fence Minister.

Major-General Ng[uyen] Khanh, the outgoing Pre[mier] will be Commander-in-C[hief] of the Armed Forces.

• *The State of Mapai*
• *Class war in economic policy*
• *Relations with Germany*

These are some of the matters of th[e] moment discussed in tomorrow's bump[er] 26-page edition of

THE JERUSALEM POST

which includes a special illustrated suppleme[nt] devoted to the new campus of the Tel Avi[v] University.

ORDER YOUR COPY TODAY.

JERUSALEM POST Published in Jerusalem, Israel, daily except on urday by The Palestine Post Ltd. unded in 1932 by Gershon AGRON. gistered at the G.P.O. Copyright of material reserved; reproduction permitted only by arrangement.
Editor: TED R. LURIE
torial and Business Office: 9 Rehov Havatzelet, Jerusalem, Israel P.O.B. 81, Tel. 24233, 24321.
Aviv: 52 Rehov Nahlat Binyamin, P.O.Box 1125, Tel. 50141.
fa: 34 Rehov Herzl, Hadar Hacarmel, P.O.Box 4810, Tel. 64594.
OL. XXXVI, No. 11356
PRICE : 28 AGORA

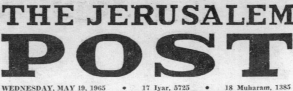

THE JERUSALEM POST

WEDNESDAY, MAY 19, 1965 • 17 Iyar, 5725 • 18 Muharam, 1385

ʼO hang a man in a public square and leave s body suspended for lf a day with the charge pinned on his chest is

LI COHEN

a demonstration, not an execuon. To order a man to be ecuted after passing a ecial "law" that he shall t be permitted legal aid r his defence, and to ep him incommunicado ter declaring that he has nfessed, is simple venance, and not a trial. The ay the Syrians dealt with i Cohen was barbarous en by Syrian standards justice, and these are t high.

Public executions are not e exception there, and bitrary arrest and the lling of political opponts are common enough. ıt there was a significant fference here, in the fact at Eli Cohen was not a rian. In many parts of e world — even Israel in rtime — a citizen who mmits treason against his n country is sentenced to ath. A man from another untry is not executed on political charge, however ave. If he is declared to ve been working for a reign power he is in some nse a soldier, and not a iminal. He may be imprined for long periods, but t infrequently he is in ne exchanged for some her person arrested unr similar circumstances.

Not long ago, the U.S. d the Soviet Union exanged two of their most nspicuous spies — Abel d U2 pilot Powers. Every nceivable effort was made Israel to have this view esented to Syria by interdiaries of high standing, d all the Syrians held in ael were offered in exange for Eli Cohen's life. happily the Syrians have little regard for their n citizens' lives to be inned to accept such an of-, and the relatives of ese men were unable to ake their voices heard.

Despite the tragic end- to this episode, the ople of Israel will rein warmly grateful to many distinguished d authoritative persons d organizations who atmpted to use their good ces to cause the Syrians reprieve their prisoner. is clear that these interlers felt strongly that s act of pseudo-legal rbarism was totally inceptable. They also derstood that while the nging might be due to ds among different secns of the Ba'th party in ria, its result would be increase immeasurably bitterness already felt in s country against the Syrs for their long series acts of cruelty against ividual Israelis. The tore of the border crossers l other minor offenders om they returned last r as broken men is one m on this list. Another the long and harsh detion of the Israeli mems of the boating party tured on the shores of ke Tiberias. In the long , between nations, such umanity counts as vily as political intranence, for it has no naal purpose to explain it.

t is small comfort to ept that Cohen had lt up something akin a public position for self. Obviously he had ome an embarrassment hin the Syrian ruling ue, where one group s only too anxious to ose mistakes made by ir rivals. Thus while side made sure that proper defence would denied lest Cohen reveal Ba'th party's weaks, the other side made e that he should not be wed to be exchanged spirited away without thing discreditable to associates being unered.

n the eyes of the world, Cohen remains a man rare courage, and no t of the Ba'th has erged with any credit at

U.S. air attacks on N. Vietnam resumed

WASHINGTON. — The U.S. resumed its air attacks on North Vietnam yesterday after a five-day lull.

Authoritative sources in Washington said that during the lull the Johnson Administration made a peace move to Hanoi through a third party. There was speculation that the third party was either Canada or India.

Meanwhile the North Vietnamese authorities yesterday rejected the reported U.S. attempt to start peace negotiations, according to Radio Hanoi.

U.S. air attacks on targets within South Vietnam continued unabated yesterday, with 150 missions flown.

About 2,000 South Vietnamese troops yesterday launched a massive assault on a key Vietcong supply base at Ba Long, 20 miles south of the North Vietnam frontier. *(Reuter, UPI)*

UN peace man in Dominica

SANTO DOMINGO (Reuter). — Rival Dominican factions continued block - by - block fighting yesterday in the northwest sector of Santo Domingo as the line of battle moved close to U.S. troop positions.

The fighting, in the fourth week of the civil war, continued as the special U.N. representative, Dr. Jose Antonio Mayorre, arrived to negotiate in an attempt to end the conflict.

At least one U.S. military officer was seen by reporters with the "reconstruction" forces of Brigadier-General Antonio Imbert Barreras.

U.S. military spokesmen declined to comment.

(Inter-American Force, Page 3)

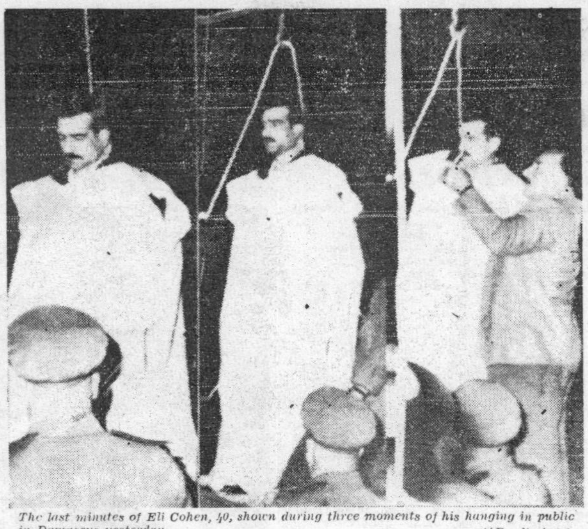

The last minutes of Eli Cohen, 40, shown during three moments of his hanging in public in Damascus yesterday. (AP radiophoto)

Syria hangs Eli Cohen in public square, as spy

ISRAELI DENIED DEFENCE

DAMASCUS (Reuter). — Eli Cohen, convicted of heading an Israeli spy ring in Syria, was executed by public hanging before dawn yesterday.

He was the first Israeli citizen to be executed in Syria.

The execution was attended by Lt.-Col. Salah al-Dilli, head of the special military court which sentenced Cohen to death on May 8, members of the court, newsmen and Rabbi Nissim Andbu, religious head of the Jewish community in Syria.

Earlier Cohen was driven in a heavily guarded military car from the Mazza prison down to police headquarters in the very heart of the city. The nearby Marja Square (Martyrs Square) looked like a battlefield with red-capped military police and troops throwing two parallel cordons around the gallows erected in the square garden.

In reply to questions by Col. Dilli, Cohen said, "I am sorry for what I have done and I confirm all my previous confessions." Questioned in the presence of Rabbi Andbu, Cohen said he had left no savings or debts.

Letter to wife

In a letter which he wrote in Arabic and French, Cohen asked his wife, Nadia, to remarry and not to leave their children fatherless. He appealed to her to look after the children, educate them and keep in constant touch with members of his family.

After writing the letter he repeated a prayer which the Rabbi read, and then walked for a distance of 30 metres to the gallows accompanied by Dilli and members of the special military court.

The executioner held Cohen's arm and helped him onto the platform of the gallows and fastened the rope around his neck. He died after 90 seconds.

The body, to which was attached the verdict of the court, remained hanging in public for six hours, and was later driven off in a small truck.

Its final disposition was not known.

Soldiers kept crowds from approaching too near.

The verdict said that Eliahu Ben Saul Cohen was sentenced to death in the name of the Arab people in Syria after being found guilty of entering a military place in disguise and of obtaining classified information and passing it to an enemy.

Cohen, who was 40, was arrested early this year. His trial began in February and lasted 40 days.

He came to Syria by way of Beirut in 1962, carrying the passport of a Lebanese emigrant in Argentina and assuming the name of Kamel Amin Thabet.

PRAISED BY FRIENDS

Eli Cohen's friends yesterday highly praised his personality.

"Intelligent and quick. He always kept his own counsel and was not talkative," a childhood friend recalled.

Cohen, born in Alexandria, Egypt in 1924, attended the elementary school of the Cairo Jewish community, transferred later to the Alexandria Lycee and completed his education at the Farouk University in Cairo (engineering).

He joined the Zionist Movement in 1941 and was a member of Hehalutz Hatzair from 1941 to 1946. He subsequently undertook various security assignments for Israel, even before the establishment of the State.

After reaching Israel he was immediately given special assignments which, according to his superiors, were all successfully carried out, with brilliance and persistence.

"Eli Cohen knew what he wanted and reached his goals," *The Jerusalem Post* was told in Tel Aviv yesterday. "He was always ready to take on new assignments — knowing that most of these put him in great personal danger."

"I see no reason why I should refuse. I am after all no better than anyone else," Cohen was accustomed to say.

A relative of Cohen, now serving in the Defence Forces, told Itim yesterday that the victim had been arrested by the Egyptian authorities in 1954 in connection

(Continued on Page 6, Col. 1)

Sense of shock and outrage in Jerusalem

The Foreign Ministry in Jerusalem yesterday expressed "shock and outrage at the fact that an Israeli citizen has been executed in Syria after a travesty of a trial, without any opportunity for legal defence, in defiance of the most elementary precepts of justice and in spite of the appeals by scores of personalities and organizations in enlightened countries asking the Syrian authorities to abide by the customary rules of justice and clemency."

The Ministry's statement added:

"Without entering into the details of the vague and unsubstantiated indictment, it is a fact that in no enlightened country is a foreign citizen executed in peace time on charges of espionage."

Eulogy in Knesset

POST Knesset Reporter

The first speaker in yesterday's foreign policy debate in the Knesset, Mr. Israel Galili of Ahdut Ha'avoda, prefaced his remarks by eulogizing Eli Cohen.

"Israel and the Jewish people will long remember this loyal son who sacrificed his life for the sake of the State of Israel, its existence and its independence," he said.

He described Syria's hanging of Eli Cohen as despicable barbarity, and said it was carried out after the accused had been denied legal counsel, and after all the appeals of leading world figures that his life be spared had been ignored.

Jordan rejects Eshkol offer

Jordan rejected yesterday the offer made by Israeli Premier Levi Eshkol on Monday to negotiate a peace settlement with the Arabs.

A Government spokesman said in Amman that Jordan rejected the proposals "because our firm policy rejects the Zionist presence itself in Palestine."

In Cairo, Mr. Eshkol's offer was front-paged by all Arabic newspapers, but there was no editorial comment or official reaction.

"Al Ahram" published the story under the headline, "Israel's official reply to Bourguiba's proposals," and "Al Gomhouriya" declared: "Eshkol offers peace terms to Bourguiba."

The Tunisian news agency, Tunis Afrique Presse, said that Israel's offer was "far from accepting the proposals of President Bourguiba."

The difference

President Bourguiba considered that the application of the U.N. resolutions should be a starting-point in "defreezing Arab-Israel relations," while Mr. Eshkol spoke "only of minor readjustments of the frontiers," reports Reuter.

A spokesman of the "Palestine Liberation Movement" said in Cairo that "the Palestine people have always rejected negotiations with the Zionist gang," the movement's radio, Saut Falastin, reported last night.

'Peace plan' aired as Eban meets Soviet envoy

The Deputy Prime Minister, Mr. Abba Eban, yesterday discussed Israel's peace plan outlined in the Knesset Monday by Prime Minister Eshkol, with the Soviet Ambassador, Mr. Dmitri Chuvakhin.

The meeting was requested by Mr. Chuvakhin.

General international problems were discussed and Mr. Eban took the opportunity to explain in greater detail the proposals for peace and cooperation in the Middle East made in the Knesset by Mr. Eshkol, a spokesman said.

QUEEN GETS BIG WELCOME IN BONN

BONN (Reuter). — Thousands of West Germans yesterday gave Queen Elizabeth of Britain an enthusiastic welcome on the first day of a state visit aimed at ending the bitterness of two world wars.

Crowds ten and 12 deep greeted the British monarch in this small capital city when she drove to call on President Luebke. They pitched flowers at her car, spilled into the roadway and delayed the royal procession of automobiles and outriders by about seven minutes.

(Radiophoto — Page 2)

Bonn envoy quits Syria

DAMASCUS (Reuter). — The West German Ambassador to Syria, Dr. Hans Mangold, left Damascus for Bonn yesterday.

Syria formally announced the severance of diplomatic relations with West Germany last Thursday after Bonn had agreed to establish diplomatic relations with Israel. France has since then been looking after West Germany's interests in Syria.

The West German Ambassador to Jordan will leave Amman tomorrow.

It was stated that officials in charge of consular, commercial and cultural affairs would remain in Amman to carry on their work.

The French Embassy in Amman has been looking after West German interests in Jordan since the diplomatic break.

Chief Chaplain joins family in mourning

The Chaplain of the Army, Aluf Shlomo Goren, accompanied the family of Eli Cohen yesterday evening in the ritual of tearing their clothes in mourning and reciting the *kaddish*.

Rabbi Goren was the first to enter on Tuesday the modest little flat in Bat Yam in which the Cohen family lives. During the course of the day, ever since the announcement of the execution came over the radio in the morning, neighbours and friends who had congregated outside were kept away by security officers.

After the visit of Aluf Goren, the doors were opened to all who wished to express their condolences to the mother, the widow, the five brothers and two sisters.

According to "Itim," Cohen's two daughters, Sofia, 4, and Irit, 2, had joined the family around the television set to follow the daily course of their father's trial.

Hafez offers Yemen military aid

DAMASCUS. — Lieutenant-General Amin Hafez, chairman of the Presidency Council, has announced that Syria is ready to offer "material and moral aid and support to the Yemeni revolution" in the political, military, economic, and social spheres.

General Hafez sent a cable to this effect to the Yemeni Prime Minister in reply to an appeal to the Arab heads of state for help to restore stability in Yemen.

Meanwhile the former Foreign Minister of the Yemen Republic, Abdul Qawae Hameen, said in Al Hauta, in the South Arabian Federation yesterday, that Yemen's Prime Minister, Ahmed Mohammed Noman had used "heavy weapons to destroy our homes, our town."

He told Reuter: "The Noman Government first attempted our arrest and assassination. When it failed, it sent a military force to overcome opposition elements."

The former Foreign Minister arrived in Al Hauta, about 20 miles north of Aden, on Monday.

Mameem said Prime Minister Noman wanted to establish a "one-man tribal system of rule, as in the past, whereas we opposition want a national, democratic, progressive system of government." *(Reuter, UPI)*

Damascus spurned countless appeals for fair trial

POST Diplomatic Reporter

Heads of state, the Vatican, world statesmen, and countless other people appealed to the Syrian authorities during the last few months to spare the life of Eli Cohen and to give him a fair trial. Throughout the trial the French lawyers engaged by Eli Cohen's wife, Nadia, were even refused permission to attend the hearing as observers.

To save Cohen's life, Israel offered, through intermediaries, to repatriate several Syrians in custody here, even if Cohen were to be imprisoned in Syria. For months Israel diplomatic missions abroad did their utmost to arouse public opinion.

News withheld

The news of the case was withheld in Israel because of a fear of prejudicing the efforts to save Cohen.

In January, when Cohen's arrest was announced, Syria passed a special decree which deprived Cohen of the elementary rights of counsel and appeal. The trial dragged on with continuous delays.

The Syrian insistence on taking Cohen's life, despite enlightened world opinion, is attributed partly to a desire to counter charges of "weakness" from the Nasserist press in Lebanon and particularly because of factional rivalries in the Syrian ruling junta.

The fight for Cohen's life was waged on a number of fronts. On the legal side, his wife obtained the services of two noted French lawyers, M. Jaques Mercier and Paul Arrighi, who appealed to Syrian President Hafez, the Supreme Court, and the Syrian Ambassador in Paris. Mercier even went to Damascus twice, once before the verdict and sentence — 10 days ago — and again after the sentence, on Sunday.

Promised interview

On Sunday, the Syrian military authorities promised him that he or his colleague would be received by Hafez before the sentence was approved by the Supreme Revolutionary Council. Returning to Paris the next day, Monday, Mercier told Mrs. Cohen's representatives that Hafez might receive him. At midnight the lawyer learnt from press reports that the sentence had been ratified, and shortly afterwards Cohen was executed.

The French lawyers were

(Continued on Page 6, Col. 2)

Syria claims Israel opens fire on border

DAMASCUS (Reuter). — Syrian and Israeli troops exchanged sporadic fire for more than two hours across the armistice line yesterday, a Syrian military spokesman said last night.

The spokesman accused Israeli forces of starting the firing and said the Syrians returned the fire.

There were no casualties among the Syrians and Syria had filed a complaint with the U.N.

With deep grief we announce the death of the head of our family

Bernard Oberlander

who died at the age of 81.

The funeral cortege will leave the Municipal Funeral Home, Rehov Daphna, Tel Aviv, at 12 noon and proceed to the Verbund-Sirkin plot in Herzliya.

The bereaved —
His wife Matilda;
His son David Oberlander;
His daughter Erna Rutenberg and family.

THE JERUSALEM POST

Published in Jerusalem, Israel, daily except on Saturday by The Palestine Post Ltd. Founded in 1932 by Gershon AGRON.
Registered at the G.P.O. Copyright of all material reserved; reproduction permitted only by arrangement. Editor: TED R. LURIE.

Jerusalem: 9 Rehov Havatzelet, P.O.B. 81, Tel Aviv: 81 Rehov Nahlat Binyamin, Haifa: 34 Rehov Herzl, Hadar Hacarmel,
Telephones 24233, 24321. P.O.Box 1125, Tel. 624215. P.O.Box 4810, Telephone 64564.

FRIDAY, OCTOBER 21, 1966 • HESHVAN 7, 5727 • RAGAB 7 1386 • VOL. XXXVI, No. 11787*

16 PAGES
Nobel Prize to Agnon, pages 1, 8 and 12, and to Nelly Sachs, page 3.
*
Paris Letter, page 7.

PRICE: 60 AGORA

Nobel Prize to Agnon and Sachs

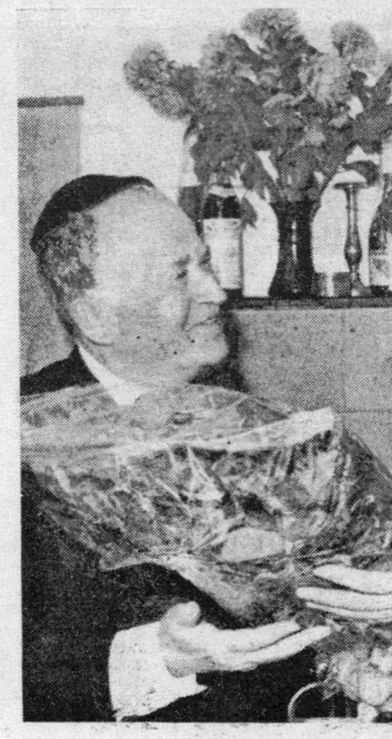

'Profound narrative art'

The Swedish Chargé d'Affaires, Mr. Carl-Erhard Lindahl, presents a bouquet of roses to Nobel Prize laureate S. Y. Agnon, upon arriving at the author's home in Jerusalem yesterday to inform him officially of the award decision.
(Photo by Meyerowitz)

STOCKHOLM (UPI). — The 1966 Nobel Prize for Literature was yesterday awarded to two Jewish writers, Shmuel Yosef Agnon of Israel and to Nelly Sachs, Berlin-born authoress who fled to Sweden in 1940.

Agnon was awarded the prize by the Royal Swedish Academy of Letters for his profoundly characteristic narrative art with motifs from the life of the Jewish people," the Permanent Secretary of the Academy, Dr. Karl Ragnar Gierow, said. Nelly Sachs received it for "her outstanding lyrical and dramatic writing, which interprets Israel's destiny with touching strength."

The Academy praised Agnon as "the foremost writer in modern Hebrew literature who has gradually penetrated linguistic barriers..." He is the first Hebrew writer to win the Literature Prize, and the first Israeli to receive a Nobel Prize.

The Academy said Agnon was a realist, "But there is always a mystical admixture which lends to even the greyest and grimmest scenes a golden outline of strange fairytale poetry."

INTENSE FEELING

On Nelly Sachs, it said: "With moving intensity of feeling she has given voice to the Jewish race's worldwide tragedy, which she expressed in lyrical laments of a painful beauty... Nelly Sachs' writing has become "the most intense artistic expression of the Jewish spirit's reaction to suffering in our time, and from that viewpoint, too, can indeed be said to fulfil the humane purpose underlying Alfred Nobel's will."

NELLY SACHS

The purpose of combining them as prizewinners "is to do justice to the individual achievement of each, and the sharing of the prize has its special justification to honour two writers who, although they write in different languages, are united in a spiritual kinship and, so to speak, complement each other in a splendid striving to present the cultural heritage of the Jewish people by the written word and from a common source of inspiration, which in them has proved to be a vital power," Dr. Anders Gesterding, of the Academy, later said in a broadcast speech.

This is only the second time in the history of the Literature Prize that it has been shared. The first was in 1917 when two Danes, Gjellerup and Pontoppidan, received the award.

The prize this year, worth 300,000 crowns (IL180,000), will be shared equally.

TO HELP FRIEND

Asked yesterday what she was going to do with the prize money, Miss Sachs "I'm going to help a very dear friend of mine." She did not elaborate. "In the spring I plan to travel to Israel," she said. "I have no further plans."

Members of Stockholm's Jewish Community, reporters and the cream of Sweden's cultural life flocked to Miss Sachs' tiny apartment yesterday. "I'm very, very happy and surprised. I'm also proud to share the prize with an author I have admired for many years, but whom I however never have had the pleasure to meet," she told the press. Red roses and cables streamed into the flat during her reception for the press.

Spanish writer Jose Maria Peman, often considered a possible candidate for the Nobel Literature Prize, called Agnon a "just writer." Peman said in a telephone interview from Cadiz that he "was happy that the divine country (Israel) was rewarded by the world academics." Peman explained that he recently visited Israel and was aware of "the effort of the country to conquer all."

In Barcelona, a sour note was struck by Spanish writer Jose Maria Gironella who confessed that he never heard of the Nobel Prize winners. Gironella said he hoped "the prize was given strictly for literary merit and not for political or racial reasons."

Agnon's Prize

AFTER two days of anxious doubts mixed with hesitant jubilation, it was formally announced yesterday that S. Y. Agnon, chronicler of Jewish life both in the fading Europe and in growing Israel, had received the Nobel Prize for Literature, together with a Jewish woman poet who once tended to the "Nordic" school in Germany, but, after barely escaping the Holocaust herself, has since written only of the destruction of the Jews.

While we might perhaps have wished that the most distinguished, the most original and the most human and perceptive of our writers should have enjoyed this great distinction on his own, it may be that the panel of judges in Stockholm felt that this division had a special significance. It has long been remarked that the Stockholm judges practise a certain rotation, selecting in advance groups of countries from which recommendations are invited each year, as they could scarcely expect to judge fairly on a world-wide basis every year.

If it had then been decided that the Jewish people should now be canvassed for their most significant writers, the judges may have felt, not so much that the whole of the prize should not go to Israel, but that it should represent both the Holocaust and destruction, and the Jewish revival. Nelly Sachs, the other prize winner, who is 75, is expected to visit Israel next year, and she will be certain of a warm and interested welcome.

But Agnon is another matter. He not only writes of life, the life of body and spirit, but he has also re-created this life as it grew and developed from its own sources and traditions and not as something created by outside pressures. Penetrating, often biting vision and a sharp sense of the dignity and indignities of life give these stories of happenings in and around the synagogues and their rabbis and communities a human appeal and significance that transcends their apparent themes and fills them with the universality of life. Now that several volumes have been successfully translated — not an easy task owing to the wealth of Talmudic allusions — readers abroad will also be able to judge their values.

The younger generation in Israel, which has little use for tales of life in the ghettos of Europe or the hardships suffered by their fathers' generation, not only read Agnon but also seek to imitate his manner and even the formal, deliberately archaic style, which yet has a simplicity which modern Hebrew does not always possess.

Agnon does not write the eulogies and lamentations that we so often the product of "Jewish" writers abroad. In Agnon's tales there is an old but vigorous life, changing and renewing itself endlessly, and bringing with it to Israel and the stories set here essentially the same manner and theme, of the vicissitudes of life reduced to their proper proportions by the constant consciousness that somewhere, perhaps in each man, perhaps in the people as a whole, there is also some older pattern and deeper understanding, some glimpse of eternity which draws its light from the beginnings of time and of history.

De Gaulle, Selassie air Somalia problem

PARIS (UPI). — Emperor Haile Selassie of Ethiopia conferred with President de Gaulle yesterday on the potentially explosive situation that may arise if French Somaliland becomes independent.

NEW YORK STOCK EXCHANGE

Closing Thursday, October 20, 1966
Dow Jones Industrial Average 783.68 -1.67

AmT&T	54⅜	IntT&T	65¼
Anacon	72¼	IntBusMch	318¼
BethStl	28½	Monsan	39¼
Boeing	44½	OlinMath	51¼
Chrysler	33⅝	PanAm	66⅜
Comsat	40⅜	ParkeDav	26¾
DowCh	59⅜	Polaroid	153
du Pont	149	PaRR	43½
EKodak	118¾	RCA	43
FairCam	111¾	SearsRoe	47¼
FordMot	42	SperRd	24
GenDynam	48½	StOnJ	67⅜
GenElec	92¾	USSteel	35½
GenMot	71¼	WestgEl	46¾
Homestk	38⅜	XeroxCo	260

Supplied by A. L. Stamm & Co., members N.Y. Stock Exchange, Albert Kaplan, rep. in Tel Aviv.

MAC fails to pin blame for Jerusalem explosions

Jerusalem Post Diplomatic Reporter

The Israel-Jordan Mixed Armistice Commission on Wednesday night failed to hold Jordan responsible for the October 7 mining of dwellings in Jerusalem, the U.N. Chairman abstaining on the Israel-sponsored resolution, leaving an equal vote between Israel and Jordan delegates. The U.N. official declared that he had abstained on the resolution as a whole because the investigation had been inconclusive. This, according to the MAC report issued in Jerusalem yesterday, referred to the tracking evidence.

The failure to adopt a condemnation, and the narrow "police investigation" system adhered to by the UNTSO, has met with strong criticism in official circles in Jerusalem. It was plain that the perpetrators had come from Jordan, they said. Referring to the MAC finding that tracks had been found some 500 metres from the scene of the incident leading to within a few metres of the frontier, official sources questioned, "Where could the perpetrators have come from, if not from Jordan?" As has happened before, in rocky terrain, tracks are often not continuous but are found in intermittent stretches, and it was illogical to invalidate the incriminating evidence because of almost inevitable blank patches it was pointed out.

It will be recalled that the question of the effectiveness of the UNTSO's system of operation was raised by Foreign Ministry officials 10 days ago with Gen. Odd Bull, UNTSO Chief of Staff.

The MAC report established that three demolition charges were exploded under two dwelling houses in the Romema quarter on the extreme northwestern outskirts on the Israel side of the Armistice Demarcation Line in Jerusalem. A fourth charge of six sticks marked "high explosive, dangerous, Hercules Powder Co.," which did not go off, was found under one of the buildings. The explosions damaged two dwelling houses, and Mrs. Myriam Canunyan, a tenant, was wounded at home. The scene of the incident was less than two km. from the Demarcation Line, as the crow flies.

(The U.N. Chairman, in his explanatory remarks, said that he had been ready to support the paragraphs summarised above, but not the others outlined below.)

In spite of the difficult nature of the terrain, it stated, footprints were found extending intermittently from a point some 560 metres from the scene of the incident to a point close to the anti-infiltration fence located five metres south of the Demarcation Line. These footprints, it stated, continued north of the fence on the Jordan side.

Tracking dogs (from Israel) linked up the intermittent footprints, and stopped close to the anti-infiltration fence. The Jordanian side operated their tracking dog on the alleged tracks pointed out by the Israel delegate at a location of about 45 metres on the Jordan side. Given the scent of the alleged footprints the dog (from Jordan) was given free reign. "The dog completed
(Continued on Page 8 — Col. 2)

Security Council resumes debate

UNITED NATIONS (Reuter). — The Security Council resumed its debate yesterday (9.25 p.m. Israel Time) on Israel complaints that armed gangs operating from Syria had committed acts of aggression against Israel. It was the Council's third session on the subject.

The first speaker was Mr. Jamil Baroody of Saudi Arabia who concluded a lengthy statement begun at the last meeting on Monday. Mr. Comay, the permanent Israel representative, was due to speak later.

As Mr. Baroody was speaking, a man in the public gallery began shouting. As guards hustled him out, Mr. Baroody said, "He is a poor man, don't hurt him," adding that the outburst was a result of Zionist brainwashing.

Other spectators in the gallery said the man shouted in English and Hebrew, "Long live the Jewish nation, long live Jabotinsky."
(Reuter, AP)

LBJ barnstorms in Australia

CANBERRA (Reuter). — President Johnson yesterday launched into his three-day Australian visit in Texas barnstorming style. There were roadside handshakes, schedule-breaking impromptu speeches to cheering crowds and "L.B.J." pens for overawed children and again there was caution over Vietnam peace prospects.

"I cannot say miracles will occur at Manila. I carry no magic wands." he warned on arrival by air from New Zealand.

RUSSIA LAUNCHES 2 SPUTNIKS FOR GUESTS

MOSCOW. — The Soviet Union yesterday launched two artificial earth satellites — one described as doing space research, the other for communications. Soviet bloc leaders were reported at the launching site in Central Asia.

The communications Sputnik called Molniya-1, which roared skywards from a secret launching pad, may be a major link in a new system linking Russia with its Communist allies. Earlier in the day, in what was believed to be a spectacular demonstration of Soviet rocket might for the visiting foreign leaders, the Russians fired the 130th in the four-year-old Cosmos series of research satellites.

NASSER AND TITO ARRIVE IN DELHI

NEW DELHI. — President Nasser of Egypt with an 80-man retinue, and President Tito of Yugoslavia, with a party of 30, flew into New Delhi yesterday for talks with the Indian Prime Minister, Mrs. Indira Gandhi, on current world problems.

Marauder gang said regulars of Syrian commando

TEL AVIV. — All evidence indicates that the four infiltrators — three of whom were killed and one wounded in a battle with border police Wednesday afternoon — were regular members of a Syrian commando unit and not el Fatah men.

All four men dressed and equipped identically with Karl Gustav sub-machineguns, hand grenades, water canteens and field rations, wore khaki uniforms, but none carried explosives — the hallmark of Fatah bands. They were evidently on an intelligence mission of gathering information, and had no intention of sabotage.

The fourth infiltrator, who has been identified as Mahmud el Hib, a member of the El Hib tribe which lives both in Syria and the Lebanon, was operated on Wednesday night at the hospital in Safed. He was gravely wounded in the stomach and is still on the critical list.

According to eye-witness accounts it was Mahmud el Hib who fatally wounded the Corporal Na'aman Rabakh, a Druse. Although el Hib was seriously wounded at the time, he managed to fire his submachinegun at Rabakh.

Surgeons at the hospital yesterday asked the investigators questioning him not to overtax their patient, who, if he survives, will probably be charged with murder, as well as infiltration.

El Hib was able to give his own name and that of his wife, Salima, to the constables who picked him up.

It is not yet clear whether the bodies of his three colleagues will be handed over to the Lebanon or Syria. U.N. observers continued their investigation of the incident yesterday, but did not complete them.

Cpl. Rabakh was laid to rest yesterday in his village of Sanieh, near Peki'in.

More than 1,000 persons attended, including the spiritual head of the Druse community, Sheikh Amin Tarif, and Mr. Jaber Mu'adi, M.K., who eulogized the deceased and dwelt on the part the Druse are playing in defending the country. Among the mourners were Mr. Pinhas Koppel, Inspector-General of the Police, and members of the border force.

EBAN CALLS ON ITALIAN PREMIER

ROME (UPI). — Israel Foreign Minister Abba Eban yesterday paid a courtesy call on Italian Premier Aldo Moro. Mr. Eban is here on a private visit to attend meetings of the Food and Agriculture Organization commission for the application of science and technology to development. He has also met unofficially with Italian Foreign Minister Amintore Fanfani and Treasury Minister Emilio Colombo.

The talks dealt chiefly with the Middle East situation and Israel's bid for association with the European Common Market.
(See E.E.C. to rule page 2)

Swedish envoy honours author

By MOSHE KOHN, Jerusalem Post Reporter

"Zeh li kavod gadol hayom — I am greatly honoured this day to congratulate you in the name of the Swedish Government and the Swedish people on the occasion of the sublime honour bestowed upon you on account of your life's work." The Swedish Chargé d'Affaires, Mr. Carl Erhard Lindahl, spoke these words, in a prepared statement, to S.Y. Agnon shortly after arriving at the Nobel Prize Laureate's home in the Talbieh quarter of Jerusalem accompanied by the State Comptroller, Dr. Yitzhak E. Nebenzahl, who acted as Hebrew-English interpreter in the impromptu conversation that followed between the two.

Mr. Agnon was quite beside himself with emotion in this climax to the more than 50 hours of tension following Kol Yisrael's premature announcement on Tuesday morning that he has been awarded the prize, and yesterday morning's report, also unofficial, that he was to share the prize with Miss Sachs. The first intimation he had of the official decision was a telephone call from the News Editor of The Jerusalem Post at 2.45, informing him that the Associated Press had just cabled the news, including the Royal Academy's citation, from Stockholm. At approximately the same time, Mr. Lindahl, who was having lunch with Dr. Nebenzahl at the King David Hotel's Regence Grill, was on the telephone to Stockholm receiving official notification.

RECITES BLESSING

When the official party arrived, Mr. Agnon and Dr. Nebenzahl embraced and kissed, and the author blurted to the Comptroller: "Tell him that when I heard the news I said the blessing: (Blessed art Thou oh God, our God, King of the Universe) Who is good and Who does good" (the traditional blessing recited upon receipt of good news).

Dr. Nebenzahl gently suggested that Mr. Agnon wait till the Chargé d'Affaires had made his statement. When Mr. Lindahl had done so, after first handing a bouquet of roses to Mr. Agnon, the author responded: "I have long admired the Swedish Academy, and as they have chosen me, I recited the blessing (aforementioned) today."

Mr. Agnon then proposed that they drink a toast. When the glasses had been filled, Mr. Agnon affectionately placed his left hand on Mr. Lindahl's and, raising his glass in his right hand, said:

Lichvod adon Hasar — To His Honour the Prince — after all, he is Sweden's Prince in our country."

Mr. Lindahl went on to say that it had been decided to award the prize to Mr. Agnon "for his deeply sensitive art of story-telling, with his motifs drawn from the art of the Jewish people."

Mr. Agnon: "I am very grateful. To God will grant me long life, they will yet see that they did not err in choosing me."

VISITED SWEDEN

Mr. Agnon went on to recall that he spent several months in Sweden in 1951, as guest of Chief Rabbi Wilhelm. He had been stricken with a heart condition and was confined for two months in the Serafinen (from the Hebrew "Seraphim") Hospital. "I was overwhelmed by the landscape, by the way of life, and by the good-heartedness of the people. Everybody — Dr. Christensen — he is no longer alive, unfortunately —and all the nurses were kind to me beyond words. I was only sorry that I did not have enough foreign currency to buy each of them a gift. If my doctor lets me go to Stockholm (for the award ceremony), I am going to buy a big cake to present to the hospital."

Mr. Lindahl replied that the Swedish
(Continued on Page 8 — Col. 3)

THE JERUSALEM POST

Published in Jerusalem, Israel, daily except on Saturday by The Palestine Post Ltd. Founded in 1932 by Gershon AGRON.
Registered at the G.P.O. Copyright of all material reserved; reproduction permitted only by arrangement. Editor: TED R. LURIE

Jerusalem: 9 Rehov Havatzelet, P.O.B. 81, Telephones 24233, 24321 · Tel Aviv: 81 Rehov Nahlat Binyamin, P.O.Box 1125, Tel. 624215 · Haifa: 34 Rehov Herzl, Hadar Hacarmel, P.O.Box 4810, Telephone 64594.

Border report & pictures, page 3

★

Jewish Scene, Letters, page 7

PRICE : 35 AGORA

SUNDAY, APRIL 9, 1967 • ADAR 'B 28, 5727 • ZI ALHAJ 29, 1386 • VOL. XXXVII, No. 11931

MIRAGES DESTROY SIX SYRIAN MIGS

By DAVID SLAV and ZE'EV SCHUL, Jerusalem Post Reporters

TIBERIAS. — Six Syrian Mig-21 planes were shot down over the eastern shore of Lake Kinneret on Friday in one of the most serious clashes on Israel's northern borders since the War of Independence. Jet fighters, tanks, guns, mortars and machineguns were used by both sides in the seven-hour battle. As a result of the mortar fire, a second lieutenant was fatally wounded. It is believed that the Syrians suffered some 30 to 40 casualties.

Three of the Syrian planes fell inside their own territory and the other three in Jordan. One Syrian tank was also knocked out. Israel Air Force fighter-bombers bombed out and silenced most of the Syrian forward and rear positions which had earlier fired on Tel Katzir, Ha'on and Ein Gev east of the Kinneret and on Gadot in the Hula Valley. Considerable damage was caused at Gadot. (Report in columns 2-3).

The clash began at 9.45 a.m. when Syrian positions at Amrat az-Din opened fire at an unarmoured tractor cultivating plot No. 52 near Kibbutz Ha'on. This machine was replaced by an armoured one and the shooting turned into a full-scale artillery war when the Syrians brought into action tank guns, and eventually heavy artillery from other positions, Israel forces returned fire. Syrian tanks at Khirbet Tawafik kept moving between the houses to avoid becoming sitting targets, and several houses were hit by Israel shells. One of the tanks was hit and four others withdrew hastily. Throughout the exchanges, the tractors continued ploughing, and when one of them was hit in the engine, it was replaced by another machine.

The Israel Air Force entered the fray at 1.35 p.m. after the Syrians had earlier ignored a cease-fire arranged by U.N. observers. The Israel planes silenced all the Syrian positions. While Mirage fighters provided an effective cover, the bombing units launched attacks against 12 separate artillery positions. At one stage of these attacks, bombing planes operated 28 consecutive minutes without encountering any resistance, apart from weak ground fire.

Within 10 minutes of the start of the air operations, Syrian Mig-21 appeared over the battle scene. They were engaged by Israel Mirages and after a brief air battle, two Migs were downed. A few minutes later a third was brought down. Later in the afternoon, Israel planes again silenced Syrian positions which had begun shelling Ein Gev and Gadot, further north.

Another three Migs turned up over the south-eastern Kinneret area and made contact with four Israel planes. Within a few seconds three Syrian planes were downed on the Jordanian side of the border. The pilots were clearly seen parachuting to safety.

At 5 o'clock, the Syrians called it a day, and another six tractors went out to plot 52 to complete the ploughing. The border area was quiet all day yesterday.

The development of the fighting, from what at first appeared to be a routine border incident to a major air battle, grew out of the Syrians' inability to use flat trajectory weapons in face of the accurate counter-fire of Israel armoured units. Six Syrian tanks, including Russian 34s, and one German Panzer of World War II vintage, resorted to hit-and-run tactics, rumbling out of trenches and from behind buildings to open generally inaccurate fire before retreating. The Syrians changed their tactics

(Continued on Page 8, Col. 3)

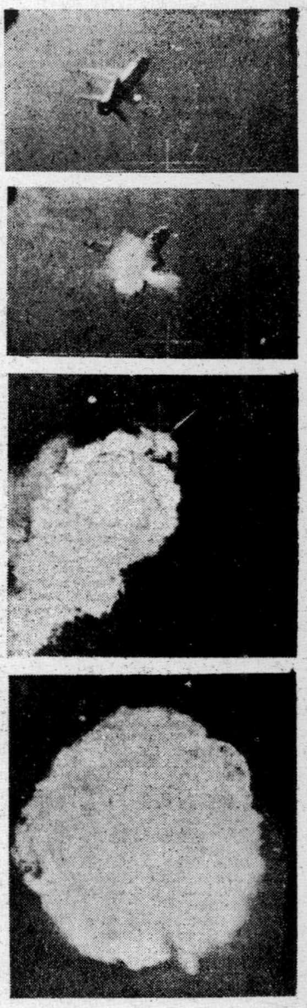

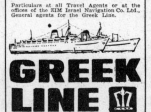

Top picture: A Mig is hit in the right wing.

Second picture: the right wing has disappeared.

Third picture: Both wings are missing, and the plane is afire.

Fourth picture: the plane is enveloped in a "fire ball" with the pilot in his escape capsule visible in the upper right hand corner.

Planes halted destruction, Eshkol says

Jerusalem Post Reporter

"Peace and the protection of our border settlements" were our main aim, the Prime Minister said in statements made over the week-end through Kol Yisrael. Mr. Eshkol said he had approved the use of Israel's Air Force against Syrian artillery positions in order to prevent the destruction of Israel border settlements. The Air Force action saved these settlements from catastrophe. Mr. Eshkol recalled Israel's declared position that there will be no restraint when the lives of peaceful citizens and the property of settlements along the borders are at stake.

The Prime Minister promised that at today's Cabinet session he would bring up their demands for improvements of defence against Syrian incursions and speedy reconstruction of the damaged settlements.

He stressed that work in Ha'on's fields was timed according to agricultural needs and that these areas had been worked by Israel farmers in the past years without any dispute.

Mr. Eshkol said Syria tried to exploit the deadlock in the recent discussions of the Israel-Syrian Mixed Armistice Commission over the question of borderland cultivation in order to increase incursions by shepherds and to create a new *fait accompli* in the Demilitarized Zone. These incursions had come in the wake of Syria's evasive attitude on continued participation at the M.A.C. sessions begun at the initiative of U.N. Secretary-General U Thant, the Prime Minister stated.

Mr. Eshkol at the same time urged Syria's rulers to respect Israel's sovereignty and to refrain from sabotage acts, "so that both countries could work their land on each side of the border in peace and tranquillity, even if there is no peace treaty yet." Quiet could be restored along the border once Syria would respect and comply with the General Armistice Agreement, he stated.

Mr. Eshkol said his "ledger could be closed any minute and a new one for pages of peace could be opened — peace with our neighbours, and even with Syria as both

(Continued on Page 8, Col. 4)

Shock for Syria

THE significant new departure in Friday's battle against the Syrians was the fact that the Israel planes had specific authority to pursue attackers as deeply into Syrian territory as they considered useful and that they were simultaneously sent out to "patrol" Syrian airspace as far as Damascus, in order to head off the planes before they reached Israel.

The policy paid off hand somely. First of all, the Migs were unable to interfere with the systematic destruction by Israel planes of the Syrian artillery positions in the hillside overlooking Lake Tiberias from which the settlements were shelled on this occasion and often before. Life on the border can be expected to be quieter, at least until this damage is made good, which it is estimated will take some time. Secondly, the Israel pilots had sufficient space to manoeuvre effectively and were thus able to score their extraordinary success. Israel's geographical dimensions were not designed for the jet age and it is not possible to deal with jet planes once they are over closely built-up areas.

There is another consideration more important than these, which are concerned directly with the battle fought on Friday. We seek respect for our borders in order to be able to live at peace within them, not because of the value of a particular field. Up to now we have not succeeded in convincing the Syrians, as the Egyptians were convinced, that this form of warfare endangers the prestige and even survival of their regime. On this occasion, the Syrians were surprised into a precipitate announcement that Israel planes had entered Syrian airspace, and later that Damascus had been bombed, and this warning can scarcely have been lost on the Syrian population even if it was not accurate. The average Syrian may never discover that it was not true that Israel planes were shot down in Syria as the Syrians claimed, but he will certainly know that one of their planes crashed near Damascus after an air battle.

It is the first time that the Syrian public has been made to feel that the hostilities against Israel could affect their own lives and not only ours. In the course of attacks and retaliatory actions over the years both Egypt and Jordan suffered a series of reprisal raids that took the battle back into the attacker's territory, culminating in the Sinai Campaign that effectively ended hostilities from Egypt, and all but border sniping from Jordanian forces. It has never been possible to apply this technique to Syria, which has all the topographical advantages over us, looking down on our border from a circle of hills and offering no targets vulnerable to counter-attack.

Syria's continued aggression derives in part from instability and continuous changes of government, as well as the increasing influence obtained there by outside powers which force intransige.nce upon her, but the almost complete immunity of the Syrians from punitive actions have made it easier for th^m to continue this policy. Rav Aluf Rabin, the Chief of Staff, observed that air-power was the only means of wiping out the Syrian's topographical advantage. On this occasion it was used with a minimum of casualties, even to the Syrians, and a maximum of political and military effect.

The Syrians will no doubt now set about rebuilding their gun emplacements and also, on^e must suppose, improve the training of their pilots, who did not fire back a single shot on Friday. Nevertheless, the battle may mark an important change in the long run.

U.N. Aden team angry at Britain

GENEVA (UPI). — The three-member U.N. mission on Aden yesterday renewed charges that it had received no cooperation from Britain and said that no decision had been taken on having discussions in London. But one member said his reported remark in Aden that Britain caused more bloodshed in the world than anyone else was "just a joke." The mission flew to Geneva from Rome to consider its report after breaking off its scheduled three-week stay in Aden after only five days.

The mission stopped over in Rome on Friday night to make an interim report to U.N. Secretary-General U Thant.

In the embattled colony yesterday, Arab terrorists gunned down a leading trade union official as he left his home. It was the second major political killing in one week. Abdul Khalit el-Teis, 43, vice-President of the Armed Forces Employees Union, is believed to have been assassinated by members of the National Liberation Front. Teis supported the rival Egyptian-backed Front for Liberation of Occupied South Yemen (Flosy). Earlier in the week, NLF gunmen killed Haidar Shamsher, a leading Flosy commando, as he stood on a street corner in Crater suburb talking with friends.

Yesterday's killing brought to 17 the number of persons who died, either by assassination or in clashes between rival nationalist factions and British troops, since the U.N. mission flew there last Sunday.

In a sudden move on Friday, British Foreign Secretary George Brown appointed Lord Shackleton, a Minister without Portfolio, as "overlord" in Aden. Lord Shackleton is expected to leave London for Aden in a few days and to remain there for some time. British officials have declined comment on the appointment.

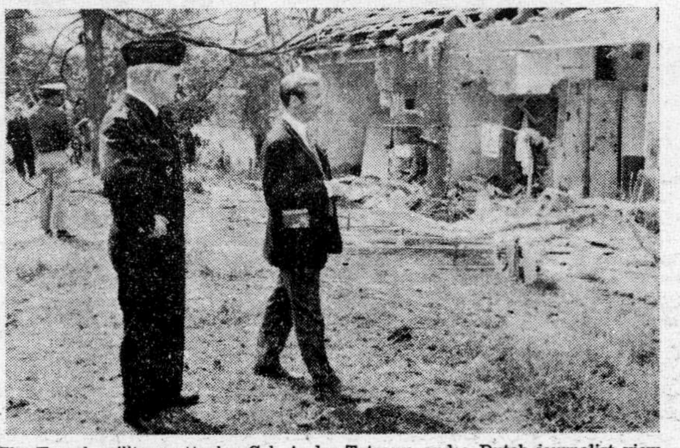

The French military attache, Col. Andre Tatraux, and a Dutch journalist view part of the wrecked homes at Gadot. (Photo by Sondervan)

Gadot suffers heaviest damage, hit by 200 shells

Jerusalem Post Staff

TIBERIAS. — Kibbutz Gadot, the village hardest hit by Syrian shellfire on Friday, was a shambles yesterday as settlers resumed repair work. More than 200 heavy mortar (122 mm.) shells were lobbed into the settlement during the attack, and not a single house escaped damage.

The roof of the communal dining hall was struck by a shell, and the cowshed and chicken runs suffered considerable damage. Oddly enough, not a single cow was injured, but dozens of chickens were killed.

The single human casualty was a Swiss guest, identified as Peter. He was struck in the leg by a piece of shrapnel while running for shelter. One family, which failed to reach the bomb shelters before the artillery barrage reached dangerous proportions, weathered the attack crouched on the floor of their stone house but luckily survived unscathed. Another group of persons was trapped in a communication trench but also emerged without a scratch.

Kibbutz Ha'on, lying closest to the point where the battle started, suffered least. Most of the Syrian shells landed in the fields. At Ein Gev, on the eastern shore of Lake Kinneret, a shell hit the cowsheds and killed eight cows. Other shells hit the Hebrew Ulpan, two homes and other buildings. At Tel Katzir, shells caused damage to two houses and the cow and poultry sheds. Two armoured tractors were also damaged.

Many shells fell into Lake Kinneret, exploded there and killed a large quantity of fish.

At Gadot, large groups of volunteers from neighbouring settlements began arriving on Friday evening bringing food, pressure lamps and other supplies. Repair crews temporarily restored water, telephone and electricity lines.

In spite of Friday's battle, the annual Kinneret March took place yesterday, with the participation of some 3,500 people, about 300 more than had originally registered. Would-be sightseers to the shelled settlements were turned away at roadblocks erected near the kibbutzim.

Israel note to Security Council

The head of the Israel delegation to the U.N. in New York, Mr. Michael Comay, on Friday submitted a formal warning to the President of the U.N. Security Council, calling the Council's attention to the "extreme seriousness with which the Israel Government views the recent developments which have menaced peace and tranquillity on the border with Syria."

The protest note also noted the lack of progress in the talks with the Syrians in the Mixed Armistice Commission due to "Syrian obstructions." The note draws the Council's attention to Syria's continued acts of aggression and provocation and to the belligerent threats of Syrian spokesmen.

On Friday night, the Director of the Foreign Ministry's Armistice Affairs Division, Mr. Moshe Sasson, received the acting Chief of Staff of the U.N. Truce Supervision Organization, Col. Floyd Johnson, and em-

(Continued on Page 8 — Col. 5)

No planes lost, Israel states

An Israel Army spokesman yesterday ridiculed the Syrian claims that Israel had lost five Mirage jets in Friday's air battles and that 70 Israelis were killed along the border.

He said that "all our planes returned safely to their bases."

Meanwhile, Amman Radio last night gave prominence to a news agency report from Beirut (see Page 3) on the fact that the "backbone of the Syrian Air Force" has been broken. A political commentator said: "The events of April 7 showed that the Ba'th youngsters wanted a chance to brag again, because they have been losing prestige, even though they knew it would cost the lives of Syrian pilots. They threw them into battle unprepared, knowing in advance the result to be expected. Three Migs were shot down over Jordan and God alone knows how many were shot down elsewhere."

Jack Maurice cables from Paris:

The French press yesterday described the border flare-up as a military, diplomatic and domestic setback for Syria which was not only defeated by Israel forces, but abandoned its Egyptian ally.

"Figaro's" Middle East expert Yves Cuau said: "The Egyptian Air Force, which had all the time it needed to intervene, avoided doing so, leaving the two antagonists face to face despite defensive agreements made between Damascus and Cairo."

"Le Monde" commented: "The Syrian Government's position is today even more delicate than ever, now that Friday's battle resulted in a stinging defeat for Syrian forces. Was it therefore indispensable for the Chief of the Israel General Staff to declare that the 'lesson' inflicted on Friday is still 'insufficient.'? It is not these bellicose declarations and bragging by both sides which will succeed in restoring peace to the Holy Land."

ROUGH NIGHT FOR HUMPHREY IN PARIS

BRUSSELS. — U.S. Vice-President Hubert Humphrey arrived in Belgium yesterday on the final stop of his two-week European tour and was assured by Premier Paul van den Boeynants of a friendly stay. But security measures for the 24-hour visit have been tightened following Friday's riots in Paris and previous demonstrations.

Mr. Humphrey was besieged in Paris on Friday night by about 5,000 angry Parisians screaming anti-American slogans to round off a day of wild street battles which marred his whirlwind visit.

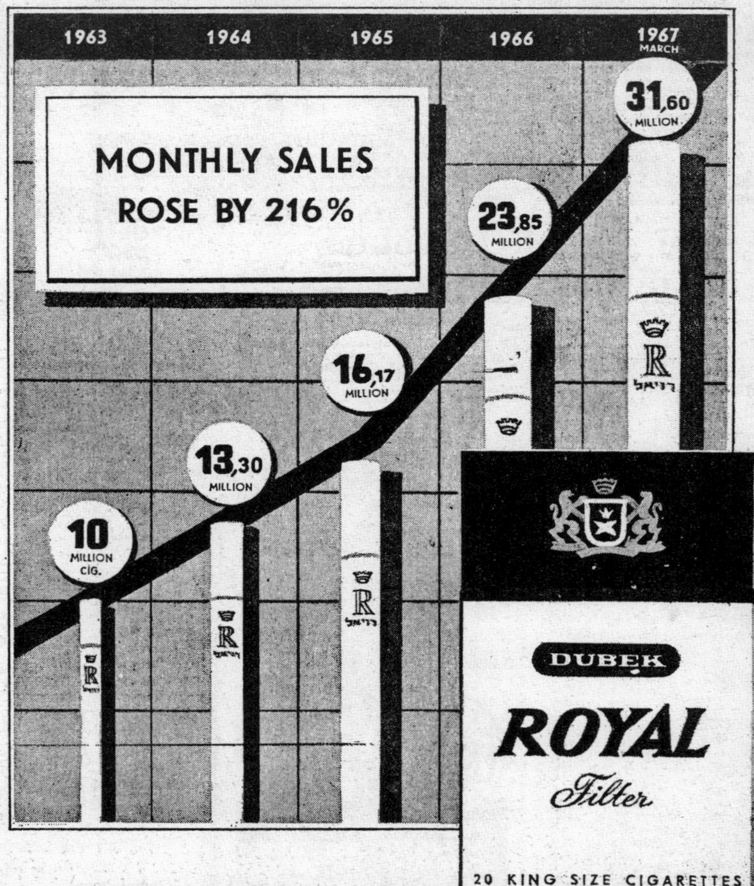

THE JERUSALEM POST

Published in Jerusalem, Israel, daily except on Saturday by The Palestine Post Ltd. Founded in 1932 by Gershon AGRON.
Registered at the G.P.O. Copyright of all material reserved; reproduction permitted only by arrangement. Editor: TED R. LURIE

Jerusalem: 9 Rehov Havatzelet, P.O.B. 81, Tel Aviv: 81 Rehov Nahlat Binyamin, Haifa: 34 Rehov Herzl, Hadar Hacarmel,
Telephones 24253, 24321   P.O.Box 1125, Tel. 624215   P.O.Box 4810, Telephone 64594.

FRIDAY, JUNE 2, 1967   •   IYAR 23, 5727   •   SAFAR 24, 1387   •   VOL. XXXVII, No. 11975

18 PAGES
including 12-page
Week-end Magazine
Rumania urges
Israel-Arab talks,
page 4
★
Tank forces
wait in Sinai,
page 3
★
Exercise aids
the nerves, page 5

PRICE: 80 AGORA

Dayan is Defence Minister as Gahal and Rafi join Gov't

By MARK SEGAL, Jerusalem Post Reporter

TEL AVIV. — A national emergency Government came into being last night, with Gahal and Rafi joining the coalition, and Mr. Moshe Dayan becoming Minister of Defence.

An official communique issued before midnight said: "The Gahal and Rafi parties yesterday evening agreed to the request of Prime Minister Eshkol to join a national unity Government. It was agreed that two Ministers of the Gahal party and one of Rafi would be co-opted to the Cabinet. Mr. Menahem Begin will serve as Minister without Portfolio on behalf of Gahal. The second Minister will be named today by his party.

"On behalf of Rafi, Rav-Aluf Moshe Dayan will serve as Minister of Defence.

"The proposed newly-constituted Cabinet met at a late hour last night. At this meeting Mr. Eshkol said: 'I greet the new members of the Cabinet who are assuming a supreme national responsibility. I am certain that the national unification will be received with sympathy throughout the nation in Zion and by the Diaspora, who have evinced a deep and historic sense of Jewish responsibility.'

"Earlier, the Cabinet met in its previous composition and discussed several current subjects. At this meeting the broadening of the coalition was approved. In the course of the meeting deep appreciation was expressed for Labour Minister Yigal Allon who dropped his candidacy as Minister of Defence.

"Premier Eshkol expressed certainty that a way would still be found for Mr. Allon to give of his experience and ability to security matters, in addition to his post as Labour Minister.

"The Ministers expressed appreciation of the Premier's success in broadening the coalition," the communique concluded.

MOSHE DAYAN

Defence Minister would have throughout the world, on the Arab countries, and, most important, on the home front.

It would also be in keeping with the declared intention to broaden the coalition.

Mr. Eshkol, in an extremely good mood, told the Secretariat of the course of the negotiations. He reported that the Alignment Cabinet Ministers, who supported Mr. Allon's appointment the previous day, unanimously endorsed the approach to Mr. Dayan after Mr. Allon withdrew his candidature. Mr. Allon said that these discussions must not weaken the nation's preparedness.

Mr. Allon expressed regret that "my candidature was exploited by political propagandists to attack the Alignment leaders and also for irresponsible opposition activity against the Government". He went on to say that the internal debates "are apt to distract the public from the war effort and to weaken its preparedness in this grave hour."

PREMIER APPLAUDED

Mr. Eshkol and other Ministers praised Mr. Allon's gesture as "an expression of profound national responsibility."

The Premier also reported that Mr. Begin's positive response to his approach, and termed him a "true patriot". Mr. Govrin praised the Premier, and Mr. Ariel Arieli led the Secretariat in applauding Mr. Eshkol, an unusual gesture in the Mapai Secretariat meetings.

A special session of the Independent Liberal Party executive last night heard of Mr. Eshkol's offer to Mr. Dayan. The party appealed to Rafi and Gahal to agree to join a national emergency Government.

The five-minister Committee, headed by Mr. Eshkol, informed the Rafi leadership at 7 p.m. that they wanted Mr. Dayan to become Defence Minister. The Rafi leaders then went into session at Mr. Ben-Gurion's home and returned later to the head offices in order to accept the Premier's proposal. Gahal also accepted, but did not decide last night on its second Minister, apparently because of the internal debate in the Liberal Party between the supporters of Mr. Sapir and Dr. Rimalt. They will decide today.

Mr. Ben-Gurion told the Rafi Knesset faction that although he has not changed his views on the present Government, he fully appreciated that in these grave and fateful days we must overcome the great problems facing the nation. This step was a very important one, and he was sure that the country would now have a wise, courageous national leadership.

(See Demonstration — Page 2)

New Defence Minister

A FIRST battle in the present struggle to re-establish the relative stability and security of the past ten years has been won in yesterday's agreement for a broader coalition.

The significant change is that Mr. Moshe Dayan will take his place in the new Cabinet as Defence Minister, by agreement with Prime Minister Eshkol, who appeared reluctant to accept this solution only a few days ago.

It is no chance appointment. It was Mr. Dayan's planning and what has been widely recognized — abroad as much as here — as his extraordinary military inventiveness, that freed the Straits of Tiran from Nasser's stranglehold ten years ago in the Sinai Campaign. His present return to the Government is as unpolitical an appointment as has been made in a long time, and derives from a widespread confidence that he is better qualified than any other man available to see ahead in the Tiran tangle, and to pursue Israel's policy aimed at nothing less than restoration of freedom in the Gulf.

The appointment had the support, not only of the opposition — Rafi itself and Gahal — but of two of the smaller coalition parties, the N.R.P. and the Independent Liberals, who in fact insisted on such a move. These groups together would not have been sufficiently strong to enforce the cooption of Mr. Dayan without the support of significant sections of Mapai, so that the move now represents a remarkably wide political spectrum. This corresponds to widespread public demand for Mr. Dayan's return, partly for his own sake, partly for his link with Mr. Ben-Gurion, whom a large part of the population would now, in a time of extreme tension, wish to see at least associated with the nation's councils, and no longer excluded from them.

Nobody can say today whether we are now headed for the crucial, final struggle with Nasser's Egypt or whether Nasser would still prefer to avoid such a conflict, as long as he can achieve the political prestige of having moved against Israel. In either case the struggle will be long, and the prime conditions for winning it are a government capable of rapid and flexible reaction to events, and public confidence.

Justified or not, there has been general feeling that Israel was taken by surprise by the U.N. forces' prompt evacuation of Sharm e-Sheikh and Nasser's re-occupation of the positions from which he was ousted by Israel forces in 1956. Whether a broader government, with a Cabinet increased to 21 members, will be able to keep one jump ahead of Nasser remains to be seen: perhaps an inner Cabinet, in the British style, will become necessary. Mrs. Golda Meir has declined to re-join the Government, as was also proposed. It is no secret at all that she has most vigorously opposed the present moves to broaden the Cabinet, in a deep conviction that the strengthening and unification of the Mapai-Ahdut Ha'avoda Alignment on which the present Government is based are of overwhelming importance for the future character of the nation and state. It is remarkable enough that at long last Herut, as part of Gahal, should have joined the Government which it has never been able to capture for itself. This deliberate putting aside of political differences could be a source of strength and create a new unity and sense of purpose. If the sense of purpose can assert itself and keep the conflicts at bay we may take new confidence from this double accretion of new strength.

U.S. aircraft carrier Intrepid is seen in the Suez Canal after leaving Port Said en route to the Red Sea, at dawn yesterday.
(AP Radiophoto)

U.S. effort in Mid-East crisis 'focussed on U.N.'

WASHINGTON. — "The focus of American effort to solve the Near East crisis without violence is in the U.N.," State Department Press Officer Robert McCloskey told newsmen yesterday. "We are doing everything in our power to seek a fair and just outcome to the crisis at that forum."

Mr. McCloskey said that the U.S. supports the British initiative to consult other maritime powers on their views on the international character of the Gulf of Akaba. He declined to answer further questions on the subject of negotiations. He said that he could not confirm reports that two ships bound for Israel had sailed into Eilat last night.

Talks here continue on many levels but there is no released information on their content. Secretary of State Dean Rusk briefed the Senate Committee on Foreign Relations in the morning and was due to brief the House Committee on Foreign Affairs yesterday afternoon.

SEEKS CAIRO ENVOY

Mr. Rusk saw Egyptian Ambassador Mustafa Kemal on Wednesday and Under-Secretary of State Eugene Rostow was scheduled to meet with Iraqi Foreign Minister Adnan Pachachi yesterday.

Secretary of State Dean Rusk yesterday described as speculative reports that the U.S. had proposed creation of an international naval force to test Egypt's blockade of the Gulf of Akaba. He said he could not confirm newspaper reports here suggesting that Britain, Holland and Portugal had pledged support for the concerted effort by maritime powers.

Mr. Yuri Tcherniakov, Soviet Chargé d'Affaires, conferred last night with Mr. Foy D. Kohler, Deputy Under-Secretary of State, presumably on Middle East developments, but no details were given.

LBJ-WILSON TALKS TODAY

President Johnson and British Prime Minister Harold Wilson, scheduled to confer here today on the Arab-Israeli crisis, will review the progress their diplomatic aides have made so far. Mr. Wilson left London for the U.S. yesterday.

The international declaration of free passage through the Gulf to Israel is the First step in an Anglo-American plan which, as a last resort, would involve multi-lateral naval action to guarantee free passage, but officials said it was hoped that this last resort would not have to be taken.

The second phase of the Anglo-American plan calls for those nations signing the international declaration on freedom of passage to work out cooperative measures to bring financial, economic and political pressures on President Nasser to get him to lift the blockade.   (UPI, Reuter)

AFTER MIDNIGHT

The Security Council members last night decided to postpone a meeting scheduled for today on the Middle East crisis until tomorrow, according to informed sources in New York quoted by Reuter.

Jordan unit fires at post in Jerusalem

A Jordanian Army position fired several bursts of small arms fire at an Israeli post on the Jerusalem border, it was announced in Jerusalem last night. The incident occurred at 3.05 o'clock in the afternoon. The Jordanian position is located about 400 metres north-east of Mandelbaum Gate.

An hour later another single shot was fired from the Jordanian position at the Israeli post. The bullet hit an Israeli house. There were no casualties. A complaint was lodged with the Mixed Armistice Commission.

Reuter reported from the Old City that the Jordanian authorities claimed that Jordanian forces opened fire on an Israeli helicopter which crossed the border into Jordanian territory in Jerusalem. The report said the helicopter flew back into Israel and that the Jordanians had complained to the M.A.C.

"Itim" reports that Mandelbaum Gate, which presented a bustling scene with tourists passing through, is now a quiet spot with only occasional persons coming through. Those coming from Jordan reported that there is tension in the Old City with heavy troop movements there.

Aluf Bar-Lev Deputy C-in-C

Jerusalem Post Military Correspondent

TEL AVIV. — Aluf Haim Bar-Lev, 42, has been appointed Deputy to the Commander-in-Chief of the Defence Forces.

Aluf Bar-Lev now becomes the second ranking officer in place of Aluf Ezer Weizmann, who had until now filled this post in addition to being Chief of the General Staff Branch.

ALUF BAR-LEV

Aluf Bar-Lev came to this country in 1939 and, like many other senior Army officers, is a graduate of the Mikve Israel Agricultural School. He finished a Palmach officers' training course in 1944 and was appointed company commander in 1945. The following year, 1946, he took part in various activities against the British. At the beginning of 1948, the War of Liberation, he was appointed Commander of the Eighth (Negev) Brigade of the Palmach.

During the Sinai campaign, he commanded an armoured brigade in the Rafa-Arish region, and penetrated as far as the Suez Canal. In 1957, he became C.O. of the Armoured Corps.

In 1961, he attended various refresher courses in the U.S., and became C.O. Northern Command in 1962.

In 1963, Aluf Bar-Lev was on extensive tours which took him to the Far East. On January 1, 1964, he was appointed Chief of the General Staff Branch. In May, 1966, he went to France for another study period.

He is married and the father of a son.

De Gaulle hears Syrian bid for his mediation

By JACQUES MAURICE
Jerusalem Post Correspondent

PARIS. — President de Gaulle conferred with Syria's Foreign Minister Ibrahim Makhous on the Mid-East crisis here last night as soon as he flew in from the Common Market summit talks in Rome.

Before driving to the Elysee Palace, Makhous said that Syria was "closely following de Gaulle's policy, which differs conspicuously from the aggressive attitude of the U.S.". Makhous, who was interviewed by the Communist daily "Humanite", added "We believe France could be an element contributing towards calming world tension, and this would enable the ferocious American attack to be smashed."

Makhous said peace could be restored to the Middle East if the U.N. forced Israel to respect its commitments and end "Israeli aggression" against Syria.

After his talks with Makhous, President de Gaulle will today discuss the Mid-East crisis with Saudi Arabia's King Feisal, who will be his lunch guest. The President's eagerness to avoid taking sides was confirmed again yesterday by the Government's diplomatic and parliamentary reactions to the situation. The Quai d'Orsay denied a London report that France was among some 20 leading maritime nations whom Britain has asked to sign a declaration upholding freedom of shipping through the Straits of Tiran.

The Government also turned down a request from all opposition parties, except the Communists, for an immediate debate on the Middle East.

FRENCH AMBASSADOR CALLS ON EBAN

The French Ambassador, M. Bertrand de la Sablière, yesterday called on Foreign Minister Abba Eban, at the latter's request, for a discussion of this week's developments in the Middle East, an official announcement said last night.

Iraqi jets off to bolster weak Jordan Air Force

BEIRUT (UPI). — An undisclosed number of Iraqi jet fighters flew from Baghdad yesterday, apparently headed for Jordanian bases. Baghdad Radio said the fighters left "to take their position at an advanced front with Israel." Jordanian Air Force Commander Col. Saleh el-Kordi was in Baghdad for official talks yesterday.

Baghdad newspapers hinted Iraq would reinforce Jordan's weak Air Force. Most of the Starfighters promised to Jordan by the U.S. last year still have not arrived, and most of Jordan's fighter pilots are training in the U.S.

President Abdul Rahman Aref of Iraq told his pilots they had "the chance of a lifetime to eliminate the shame of 1948" when the State of Israel was established. "I swear by Almighty God if I was not

in charge of the presidency I would be the first to go with you," Aref said. He also told them: "Au revoir in Tel Aviv and Haifa."

In another speech to troops leaving for Egypt by air, Aref said: "Remember, those of you who will fall will go straight to Paradise... don't kill women or children and don't uproot trees."

Meanwhile, Iraqi troops have arrived at a secret military air base in Sinai to take up their positions with Egyptian troops on the frontier. There were no details on the size of the Iraqi force which was flown in by Egyptian transport planes, AP reported from Cairo. Cairo Radio also announced the arrival of Kuwaiti Army
(Continued on Page 2, Col. 3)

NEW YORK STOCK EXCHANGE

Closing Thursday, June 1, 1967

Dow Jones Industrial Average 864.98 +12.42
Volume of shares traded 9,040,000

Admiral	22¾	Int'l T&T	89¾
Alcoa	89	Litton	98
AmT&T	56	McDon.-D	41⅜
Anacon	91	MinnMM	85¼
BethStl	34½	Monsan	46⅜
Boeing	94½	OlinMath	65¼
Burroughs	124½	ParkeDav	27¾
Chrysler	40⅜	PaRR	64¼
Comsat	64⅜	Polaroid	209¼
CrownCork	57¼	RCA	49⅜
DowCh	80⅛	ReynTob	37½
duPont	156½	SearsRoe	55⅛
EKodak	136⅜	SperRd	31⅛
FairCam	95⅛	StOnJ	61⅜
FordMot	50⅞	TransW.ir	70⅜
Gen.Elec	85⅞	USSteel	44⅜
GenMot	80⅝	WestgEl	50⅜
Homestke	43⅜	Woolworth	23
IntBusM	476	XeroxC.	277½
IntPap	29	Zenith Rad	60¼

Supplied by Albert Kaplan, Israel Representative
A.L. Stamm & Co., members N.Y. Stock Exch.

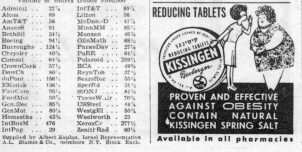

**48,000 km.
in 226 days
in a sailboat.**

In Plymouth, England, about half a million people gave an enthusiastic welcome to the British sailor who made this solitary ocean voyage.

You don't have to go to such lengths to get hold of Extra C. D. Oil by "Etz Hazaith". Although there has been a delay in supply in certain localities due to the present security situation, there is no need for concern or for hoarding. "Etz Hazaith" is taking all necessary steps to maintain the continuous production and supply of our superior oil.

Remember, it's worthwhile waiting a little for Extra Oil, because C.D. Oil is the oil for me.   (Advt.)

THE ORDER OF FREEMASONS in the State of Israel

All Freemasons are summoned to attend an

EMERGENCY ASSEMBLY

which will take place on Sunday, June 4, 1967, at 5 p.m. sharp at Beit Sokolow, 4 Rehov Kaplan, Tel Aviv.

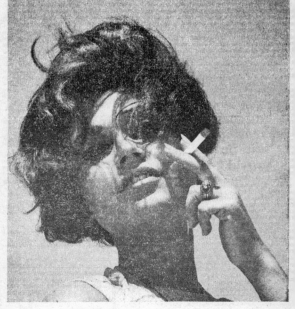
TO JUSTIFY TRUST

Mr. Dayan, wearing khaki but without his Rav-Aluf's insignia, said he was grateful for the trust put in him. He appreciated that he was assuming a heavy burden of responsibility and would do his best to justify the faith put in him.

It was learned that Mrs. Golda Meir had earlier declined a proposal that she serve as Minister without Portfolio.

Labour Minister Yigal Allon yesterday afternoon informed Mr. Eshkol that he withdrew his candidacy for the Defence portfolio, which the Prime Minister had offered him the previous day. Mr. Allon said his move was made to facilitate the formation of a national unity Cabinet. Mr. Allon added that he was willing to serve within or outside the Cabinet, in any capacity, civilian or military. The Prime Minister informed the Mapai Secretariat earlier in the evening that he had asked Mr. Dayan to assume the Defence portfolio in a personal capacity should the Rafi Party decline to join.

THIRD MEETING IN DAY

The Mapai meeting was the third in 24 hours, during which the pendulum of opinion swung among the party leaders oscillated between Mr. Dayan and Mr. Yigal Allon. Deliberations began in the Alignment Knesset faction two days ago.

Meanwhile, Mr. Eshkol had been told by the National Religious and Independent Liberal Parties that they would leave the coalition unless Mr. Dayan received the Defence portfolio. A special five-man Cabinet committee was formed comprising Messrs. Eshkol, Israel Galili, Moshe Haim Shapiro, Israel Barzilai and Moshe Kol. This committee proceeded to negotiate with Rafi and Gahal teams yesterday as the Mapai Secretariat held a second session, this time lasting for six hours, when the overwhelming majority held that the negotiations must cease forthwith in view of the increasing gravity of the nation's security, and because of the tremendous impact that the appointment of Mr. Dayan as

AIR FORCE WINS SUPREMACY AS ARMY DRIVES EGYPTIANS BACK INTO SINAI AND GAZA

THE JERUSALEM POST

Published in Jerusalem, Israel, daily except on Saturday by The Palestine Post Ltd. Founded in 1932 by Gershon AGRON.
Registered at the G.P.O. Copyright of all material reserved; reproduction permitted only by arrangement. Editors: TED R. LURIE.

Jerusalem: 2 Rehov Havatzelet, P.O.B. 81, Tel Aviv: 81 Rehov Nahlat Binyamin, Haifa: 34 Rehov Herzl, Hadar Hacarmel,
Telephone 24253, 24321.   P.O.Box 1125, Tel. 624215.   P.O.Box 4810, Telephone 64594.

PRICE : 35 AGORA

TUESDAY, JUNE 6, 1967   •   EYAR 27, 5727   •   SAFAR 28, 1387   •   VOL. XXXVII, No. 11978*

BULLETIN :
The army spokes-
man announced
that 374 enemy
planes were des-
troyed yesterday.
Nineteen Israeli
planes were lost.

Jordan shells Jerusalem; 10 dead, houses damaged

The Israel Defence Forces yesterday morning repelled an attempted Egyptian air and tank attack and smashed into Sinai as the Israel Air Force appeared to have won total supremacy.

Before nightfall an Israeli task force had captured the key town of Khan Yunis, thereby cutting off the Egyptian forces in the Gaza Strip.

(The British Broadcasting Corporation last night reported that Israel armour has sliced through the Gaza Strip to the Mediterranean and that Arab forces in the area "are no longer a fighting factor.")

At the same time, Jordanian positions yesterday morning began firing and shelling in Jerusalem and on Mt. Scopus — a battle which continued intermittently throughout the day. Effective Israel counter-action silenced most of the Jordanian positions by the end of the day. Ten civilians were killed and about a hundred wounded.

Three Syrian airplanes also went into action briefly yesterday morning, in the Megiddo area. Two were shot down.

ESHKOL: ARAB AIR FORCES DEFEATED

Jerusalem Post Reporter

Prime Minister Eshkol told the Knesset yesterday that the Egyptian Air Force was "heavily defeated." During the day the Syrian and Jordanian Air Forces also started to attack, and they also suffered heavy blows from our Air Force.

"Since morning our forces were compelled to beat back the enemy in order to rout the forces of the aggressive Egyptian dictator. The battle is still in full swing. Our army has not disappointed expectations — it is standing the test."

We had declared, Mr. Eshkol went on, that we would not attack unless others attack us. Nevertheless, the Syrians and the Jordanians opened fire on Israel territory and sent aircraft over our towns and villages. The Egyptian Army Commander issued an Order of the Day which was broadcast over Cairo Radio on June 3, stating that the Egyptian forces are launching an historic and holy war to retrieve the Arabs' "stolen" territory.

Nasser's troops were concentrated near Eilat in a bid to cut off the Southern Negev. When the Egyptian war machine started moving, we took action to protect our territory. The forces facing the Arab armies are Israeli in their entirety — and there are no others.

Mr. Eshkol's statement, to have been made at 7 p.m., was postponed while he conducted a short meeting of the Ministerial Security Committee. The Knesset was crowded with Members and foreign and local pressmen. Shortly after 8 o'clock, a bomb fell right by the building, shattering windows in the canteen. All present were shepherded into the shelter, where eminent personalities such as Mr. Kadish Luz, Mr. Ben-Gurion and Mrs. Golda Meir sat with senior officials, clerks, cleaning workers and a British TV technician clutching his tapes — all in high spirits and good humour.

As the Knesset session was announced, people streamed out of the shelter and neighbouring corridors, to find Mr. Eshkol, trapped by a British television interviewer, on his way to the Assembly Hall. He readily answered questions in English, such as: "Have you any territorial claims to make against the Arabs?" Answer: "None. All we want is security within our own frontiers."

He then announced the expansion of the Cabinet to include three new Ministers. Two of them came up to take oath of office — Mr. Menahem Begin, who put on a skull cap, and Mr. Yosef Saphir, both of Gahal. Mr. Moshe Dayan, of Rafi, co-opted as Minister of Defence, had come at the scheduled time of 7 p.m., but was compelled to leave before the delayed induction ceremony, to resume his duties.

MESSAGE FROM TEDDY KOLLEK, MAYOR OF JERUSALEM

Citizens of Jerusalem!

You, the inhabitants of our Holy City, were called upon to suffer the vicious onslaught of the enemy, while our determined airmen and soldiers were battling with him in the air and in the South. Your homes also became a battlefield.

In the course of the day I travelled throughout Jerusalem. I saw how its citizens, rich and poor, veteran and new immigrant alike, children and adults, stood steadfast. Nobody flinched; nobody failed. You remained cool, calm and confident, while the enemy launched his assault upon you.

You have proved worthy inhabitants of the city of David; You have proved worthy of the words of the Psalmist: If I forget thee, O Jerusalem, may my right hand forget its cunning. You will be remembered for your stand in the hour of danger.

Citizens have died for our city, and many have been wounded. We mourn our dead and will care for their families. We will tend our wounded.

The enemy inflicted much damage on houses and property. But we will repair the damage, and we will rebuild the City so that it will be more beautiful and more treasured than ever.

I pay special tribute to the police, Haga, the volunteers, and all those who contributed to the defence of the city.

Aid from Holland

THE HAGUE (AFP). — Israel Hercules transport planes took off from a Dutch Air Force base on Sunday loaded with military equipment. The material included radar and spare parts for anti-aircraft guns and aircraft. It was not known how many Israel transports took part in the airlift.

(map of Sinai / Mediterranean region)

Ruling the skies

By ZE'EV SCHUL, Jerusalem Post Military Reporter

TEL AVIV. — The Israel Air Force appears to have achieved almost complete supremacy in its counter-strikes against the Egyptian, Jordanian and Syrian air forces during the daylight hours. If this is confirmed, the Defence Forces will have solved one of its main, and most urgent, problems. The Egyptian supply lines will be at the mercy of Israel's Air Force and the Egyptians will have increasing difficulties in maintaining their already scanty water and food supplies.

The Egyptians were the first to be dealt with. According to Baghdad Radio at 8.50 a.m., the Israel Air Force swung out against bases in the Canal and Cairo area.

Syrians made a number of forays against Eilabun (Central Galilee), Megiddo, and Haifa Bay. Two out of three Mig-17s were shot down over Megiddo. Later another Syrian plane crashed over Tawafik, near Kibbutz Ein Gev, east of Lake Kinneret.

Not a single bomb fell on Tel Aviv or its vicinity throughout the day. The Jordanians sneaked across the 15 kms. to Netanya to bomb the southern outskirts of this seaside resort.

As far as the tactical situation of the advancing Armoured Corps and infantry units is concerned, the situation still appears rather vague, beyond the basic fact that the Defence Forces turned the Egyptian head-on assault. Egyptian reports say that the Israel forces were in action in the Kuntilla and other regions some 20-30 kms. inside Sinai.

By the early evening hours, it seemed that the Gaza Strip had been cut off at Khan Yunis.

As far as the Jordanian and Syrian frontiers are concerned, the Jordanians have put on a token show in Jerusalem, but shown no inclination for a massive entanglement with the Israel Defence Forces.

The Syrians, who started it all, have shown the least desire to fight Israel. Apart from sorties by their Air Force there has been no report of serious Syrian artillery engagements so far, and other Syrian units have stuck to their trenches — as of the early evening hours of yesterday. It is difficult to believe that the Syrians will remain passive, but there is every reason to believe that they will be more swiftly dealt with, and put on the defensive within hours if they venture into an open engagement.

Eban: took arms in self-defence

TEL AVIV. — Foreign Minister Abba Eban said yesterday that the events of the day culminated the pattern of aggression which had forced Israel to defend her territory and her integrity. "Never in history has there been a more righteous use of armed force," Mr. Eban told the press at Beit Sokolow.

Enumerating the main stages in the provocative actions against Israel, Mr. Eban pointed out the hundreds of tanks sent to the southern frontier of Israel; the large tank force opposite Eilat in a plan to sunder the Southern Negev from the rest of the country; the blockade of the Straits of Tiran; the threat of strangling encirclement, which resulted in the pact with Jordan; the placing of Iraqi troops in Jordan; the order of the day of the Egyptian Commander, General Mourtagi, calling on his troops in Sinai to wage a holy war against Israel. The acts of sabotage and terrorism from Syria and Sinai and, finally, yesterday morning, the movement of Egyptian regular troops against Israel, and the bombardment of the villages of Ramat Hakovesh and Nahal Oz, were also part of the pattern of aggression.

At noon, the Jordanians initiated an attack. Mr. Eban mentioned that he was discus- *(Continued on Page 6 — Col. 3)*

Gov't House taken

Israeli forces occupied Government House (the headquarters of the U.N. Truce Supervision Organization) in Jerusalem yesterday afternoon — 11 minutes after the compound had been occupied by Jordanians.

The Jordanian authorities had earlier demanded from Gen. Odd Bull that he leave the Headquarters. In it understood, Gen. Bull refused and cabled U.N. Secretary-General U Thant, who in turn appealed to King Hussein to refrain from attacking the Headquarters. But the Jordanians occupied the Headquarters.

Around 4 p.m. Israel forces got word to the U.N. personnel that they intended to recapture the compound. Eleven minutes later the fight was over. The U.N. personnel were safely ushered away, and in a long convoy were later seen leaving Jerusalem.

The U.N. personnel in residence were removed to safety and installed in the Eden and President Hotels last night. Some of them wanted to be allowed to cross into Jordan but their request was refused.

The U.N.T.S.O. Chief of Staff, Gen. Odd Bull, asked to have the building restored to U.N. control, but this was refused on the grounds that the U.N. was unable to hold it.

The Jordanians kept the Norwegian General and his staff virtual prisoners for almost three hours.

The building evidently was hit, heavily damaged, and showed signs of interior fires. The courtyard was strewn with the wreckage of U.N. and Jordanian vehicles.

Peace through war

ISRAEL has sought peace, and war has been forced upon her for the third time. The events of yesterday leave us in no doubt that those who wish to live in peace are indeed wise to prepare for war.

There is no full information yet from the three fronts on which the battle developed. Counter-attacks took the Israel forces deep into Egyptian territory, wreaked utter havoc with the Egyptian air force and their airfields; as the battle around Jerusalem developed Israel forces also struck into Jordan to silence the positions from which the attack had come, and those from which parts of the centre of the country were attacked. The Jordanian forces were under Egyptian command, and Nasser's plan provided for the placing of Egyptian forces in Jordan within the next few days, thus surrounding us and making effective defence infinitely more difficult and perilous — if not impossible.

In yesterday's battles Egypt's leadership was clearly discernible. It was they who sent orders to Jordan and Syria to begin attacking on their fronts because the Egyptian forces did not press forward quite as hard as they might have done, being superior in quality to Nasser's, if small in numbers by comparison, this may be because the Egyptian commander sent there did not seek too much prestige for Hussein's army, which might help to keep him on the throne. If they occupied the U.N. headquarters in the old Government House near Ramat Rachel in Jerusalem, it may have been as a result of Nasser's urgent appeal that they occupy some small corner of Israel territory for the sake of Arab prestige. It is also curious to note that the army which moved the least was that of Syria, although it was their persistent commando attacks which led to the present conflagration.

It was they who pressed for war against Israel, while Nasser counselled caution for a period.

One cannot foresee yet where the end of the battle will take us, but its purpose is the defence of Israel, the enforcement of our rights in the Straits of Tiran and elsewhere, and a stable and lasting peace, not territorial conquests. We have never sought more, and we will not accept less. Already, only a single day into this third battle for Israel, it is clearly discernible that the three are linked, continuations of Israel's effort in 1948 to implement the U.N. decision for the establishment of the Jewish State. The armies of seven Arab states attacked emerging Israel at that time in order to frustrate the decision, but what they brought about was the creation of more realistic and more defensible borders for Israel, and also the exodus of most of the Arab population of the country and the creation of the refugee problem. A truce and an armistice were negotiated with the aid of the U.N. — but they were disavowed in the shortest time, and the expected peace did not materialize.

Eight years later the pressure of marauders and other attacks from Egypt, and also from Jordan, had become so heavy that Israel's territorial integrity was threatened, and quiet was not restored on the southern front until the Sinai campaign ended infiltration and opened the Gulf of Akaba to Israel shipping. But here, again outside forces intervened, and Egypt was not obliged to recognize her defeat, or to negotiate with Israel either for the withdrawal of our forces from Sinai and the Gaza Strip, nor for the Israel withdrawal from Sharm e-Sheikh and thus was able to disregard both.

What began yesterday is the third battle in Israel's war of independence, but it also will not be the last unless this time we stand on our right, if all goes well, and force the Egyptians to the negotiating table. We shall not claim more than our freedom and independence and the cessation of hostilities; we are not fighting an ideological war; and we are not concerned with the internal affairs of neighbouring countries. But this time nothing less than full and open recognition of our existence and our rights will do if we are determined not to fight the battle over again in another decade.

1.30 a.m.

The Israel Defence Forces have occupied El Arrish after taking Rafiah and Sheikh Zuweid. Other towns taken were Khan Yunis, Der el-Balagh. At midnight we were engaged in a battle on the outskirts of Gaza.

In the central sector of the southern front, Auja el-Khafir was captured, and fighting was going on around the Um-Katef positions. Kuntilla also was captured.

Israel has taken a large number of prisoners as well as guns and tanks. The enemy suffered heavy casualties. Israel casualties are comparatively light.

On the Jordanian front, where shelling and bombing continued during the entire day, Israel forces counter-attacked, and Sur Baher, south of Jerusalem was captured. Also taken were Radar and Sheikh Aziz near Kibbutz Ma'ale Hamisha. A number of villages elsewhere, particularly in the north, were also captured. Israel forces are also sealing off Jenin.

"Our air force dealt a decisive blow to the enemy in an achievement without parallel," Rav Aluf Rabin announced in a broadcast at 1 a.m. this morning.

Aluf Mordechai Hod, O.C. Air Force said that Egypt lost 286 planes, of which almost all were destroyed on the ground and 20 were downed in aerial combat. The Syrians lost 52 planes, Jordan 27 and Iraq nine. There were also 34 probables.

Eight Israel pilots were killed, and eleven have been listed as missing.

U.N. move for cease-fire

UNITED NATIONS. — Brazil's chief U.N. delegate, Dr. Jose Sette Camara, sought support yesterday, in backstage consultations with other Security Council members, for an immediate call for a cease-fire in the Middle East. Informed sources said that the proposed Brazilian initiative countered a bid by India to have the Council call for the return of both sides to the positions they held before fighting began.

The Argentine was also reported to be backing the Brazilian move.

The council, which met in mid-morning, was still in recess in the afternoon, having heard brief opening statements at its opening session. Private talks were going on behind the scenes and in the Council chamber itself, which remained packed despite the official recess.

When the Council first assembled, at 3 p.m. Israel time, U Thant reported that Jordanian troops had captured Govern-ment House, the Jerusalem headquarters of the U.N. Truce Supervision Organization, and Israel forces had killed three Indian members of the deactivated U.N. Emergency Force at Rafah in the Gaza Strip area. India immediately asked condemnation of Israel for the air attack in which three of its nationals died.

Council President Hans Tabor, of Denmark, with support from the U.S. and Canada, wanted a resolution simply ordering an immediate cease-fire on all sides. Indian Ambassador Gopalaswami Parthasarathi wanted the measure to condemn Israel.

Soviet Ambassador Nikolai Fedorenko, with considerable support, wanted the cease-fire resolution to include an order to all forces to withdraw at once to positions they held on Sunday.

Mr. Tabor read to the Council the communications he had received from Israel, at 10.10 Israel time, and from Egypt, 20 minutes later.

Israel Ambassador Gideon Rafael told the 15-nation Council, "it is evident that in the early hours of this morning, Egyptian armoured columns moved in an offensive thrust against our border and at the same time Egyptian planes took off from air-fields in Sinai and struck out against Israel." He said Egyptian artillery shelled four Israel villages as the fighting began. Egyptian Ambassador Mohammed Awad *(Continued on Page 6, Col. 6)*

U.S. 'neutral' in conflict

Jerusalem Post — Near East Report I.

WASHINGTON. — President Johnson yesterday condemned the war engulfing the Middle East as "needless and destructive" and gave first priority to trying to end it through the U.N. Security Council. For the time being it appeared that the U.S. would not intervene directly to try to halt the fighting.

Mr. Johnson conferred with Secretary of State Dean Rusk and Secretary of Defence Robert McNamara. There was an unconfirmed report that he spoke to British Prime Minister Harold Wilson in London. Mr. Rusk and Mr. McNamara briefed Congressional leaders on the flare-up in a secret session.

Meanwhile, the U.S. yesterday officially declared itself "neutral in the Middle Eastern war. "Our position is neutral in thought, word and deed," said State Department Spokesman Robert J. McCloskey. He said all military and civilian aid programmes to countries in the immediate area or involved in the conflict "are urgently under review."

At 10.30 a.m., the Ambassadors of Iraq, Lebanon, Saudi Arabia, Egypt, Yemen, Tunisia, Libya, Algeria, Morocco and Sudan met Under-Secretary of State Eugene Rostow in a group; Earlier, Israeli Charge d'Affaires Ephraim Evron met Mr. Rostow for 30 minutes. The French and the British Ambassadors also met Mr. Rostow.

In London, British Foreign Secretary George Brown summoned the U.S., Soviet *(Continued on Page 6, Col. 2)*

Sabotage units

The Army spokesman said last night that a small unit of saboteurs penetrated from the Gaza Strip near Nir Am junction, opened fire on a private car, and also blew up a pipeline. At 11.15 an electric pylon near Heletz was sabotaged, and fire opened on an ambulance going from Nir Am to Yad Mordechai.

At 11.15 p.m. Jordanian artillery opened fire on Sde Eliyahu in the Beisan Valley.

Reports say airports of 3 Arab Capitals strafed

CAIRO. — An Egyptian Foreign Ministry statement said Israel planes attacked Egyptian airfields in the Cairo area and Suez Canal zone. Heavy gun and anti-aircraft fire could be heard on the desert outskirts of the city.

The wail of air raid sirens brought traffic in Cairo, a city of four million, to a halt shortly after 8 a.m. A few military trucks and cars, including taxis commandeered by officers, raced through the streets. Thousands of people braved the alert to throng the streets listening to first communiques over transistor radios. They wildly cheered and danced in the streets at the first announcement claiming 28 Israel planes had been destroyed. Later, Cairo Radio interspersed martial music with slogans, including a call: "All Arabs — we have a rendezvous in Tel Aviv."

There were three other air raid alerts in Cairo during the day. Cairo Radio alleged triumphantly that at least 86 Israeli planes had been brought down in an air raid on the El Arish airport.

But then, Cairo Radio went on to urge all citizens to observe restraint, remain quiet, and ignore evil rumours.

The Cairo authorities imposed censorship on all news out of Egypt.

The "joint Arab command" in Amman announced that Jordanian, Iraqi and Syrian air forces were conducting joint air operations against targets inside "Occupied Palestine." A Syrian military communique said "the Syrian Air Force is bombarding enemy airports and strategic targets. The *(Continued on Page 6, Col. 5)*

FRENCH SAID HALTING AID TO ISRAEL

PARIS (UPI). — France has suspended the delivery of all war materials to Israel and to all Arab countries involved in the Middle East conflict, informed sources said last night.

The sources said the decision was made following a meeting between Premier Georges Pompidou and Gen. Michel de Brebisson, Secretary-General of the National Defence Office which is in charge of sales and supplies of French war material to foreign countries.

SCOPUS ROAD OPENED, OLD CITY ENCIRCLED; 200 EGYPTIAN TANKS SMASHED; GAZA FALLS

THE JERUSALEM POST

Published in Jerusalem, Israel, daily except on Saturday by The Palestine Post Ltd. Founded in 1932 by Gershon AGRON. Registered at the G.P.O. Copyright of all material reserved; reproduction permitted only by arrangement. Editor: TED R. LURIE

Jerusalem: 9 Rehov Havatzelet, P.O.B. 81, Telephones 24255, 24321 · Tel Aviv: 81 Rehov Nahlat Binyamin, P.O.Box 1125, Tel. 624215 · Haifa: 34 Rehov Herzl, Hadar Hacarmel, P.O.Box 4810, Telephone 64504.

PRICE: 35 AGORA

WEDNESDAY, JUNE 7, 1967 • EYAR 28, 5727 • SAFAR 29, 1387 • VOL. XXXVII, No. 11979

OTHER WAR NEWS, pages 2, 3, 4

JERUSALEM

THE battle for Jerusalem has been won. Its brave, heroic, and weary citizens are unlikely to have to spend a third night in their hot and cramped shelters. The death toll in the fighting has not been low among civilians, though many of these deaths and injuries could have been avoided with more care.

It was a brief taste of the drawn-out trial of 1948, when the city remained on starvation rations and almost without water for many weeks. But there is a difference. In 1948 there was a deep fear that Jewish Jerusalem might fall — as the Jewish Quarter of the Old City had fallen after long and heroic resistance, when its ammunition gave out. There was no such fear this time and the aimless shelling was doubly resented as mere obedience to Nasser's order for a diversionary move that would cause Israel forces to be withdrawn from the Sinai front for the protection of their Capital.

But the current battles have a bitter logic, bitter for Nasser's strategy of domination of all Arab countries, and doubly bitter for his unwilling supporters, who have been dragged into a battle that is not of their own choosing. There were no indications during the past few years that Jordan's King Hussein had any intention of attacking Israel in force, or of making any move in Jerusalem. Presumably he knew himself that the result was likely to be disastrous for him, and likely to cost him his position in Jerusalem, if not his crown or his life.

Israel has had an account of its own with Jordan ever since 1948 for its failure to observe the Armistice Agreements. First of all, the free access to the Western Wall in the Old City, which was part of the Agreement, has never been implemented, and scarcely even debated. Access to the old Hadassah Hospital and Hebrew University buildings on Mount Scopus has not been free, but limited to fortnightly convoys for supplies and the exchange of the police guard in the buildings, and in times of tension the passage of the convoy has often been delayed or stopped. On Monday morning, when the battles in the South had begun, but the shooting in Jerusalem not yet started, security authorities were wondering whether this meant that the convoy, due today, would be held up, and whether perhaps the Jordanians would try out a lesser Tiran blockade themselves, and create new difficulties in contact with the Mount Scopus area.

The massed attack launched by Jordan upon Israel Jerusalem was unexpected, but its result could have been foreseen, despite the comparative strength of the Arab Legion forces, who are a very different body of men to Nasser's troops. There was no way of protecting Jerusalem against Jordanian shelling except by capturing the outlying positions from which this fire was directed, and some of them are deep in Jordanian territory. The Old City itself is a very much more delicate issue, for although some of the fire came from positions right inside the City, Israel was not prepared to shell this close-packed warren of old buildings containing some of the most treasured religious monuments of the three faiths, and so was severely hampered in dealing with the attack coming from this area. In a hard and costly fight, the City has been surrounded, and it is not expected to resist very long in this condition. The Jews of Israel will once more practise the ancient custom of visiting the Western Wall of the ancient Temple for prayer and remembrance.

Israel cannot permit itself to be locked out of the Old City again or to rely on the uncertain services of the U.N. for its right of access. The division of the city has been a painful and expensive anomaly for 20 years. Now it looks as though some entirely new solution to this problem will have to be found.

BULLETIN:

Israel planes over Cairo

CAIRO (Reuter). — Israeli planes flew over the centre of the city here last night.

Communications with Cairo broke down immediately after a Reuter correspondent sent this news.

NEW YORK STOCK EXCHANGE

Closing Tuesday, June 6, 1967

Dow Jones Industrial Average 862.71 +14.94

Volume of shares traded 9,230,000

Admiral	22⅛	IntT&T	91⅜
Alcoa	87¾	Litton	100⅛
AmT&T	56½	McDon.-D	41¼
Anacon	93⅝	MinnMM	83⅞
BethStl	34	Monsan	46¼
Boeing	97	OlinMath	67⅝
Burroughs	127¼	ParkeDav	26⅞
Chrysler	40⅝	PaRR	64⅞
Comsat	63¼	Polaroid	215
CrownCork	57½	RCA	51⅛
DowCh	80¾	ReynTob	37⅝
duPont	156⅜	SearsRoe	53⅞
EKodak	135	SperRd	31¼
FairCam	94¼	StONJ	61¼
FordMot	50⅝	TransW.Air	69¾
Gen.Elec	85¼	USSteel	43¾
GenMot	80	WestgEl	51¾
Homestke	45	Woolworth	23
IntBusM	477½	XeroxCo	283½
IntPap	29⅞	ZenithRad	58¼

Supplied by Albert Kaplan, Israel Representative A.L. Stamm & Co., members N.Y. Stock Exch.

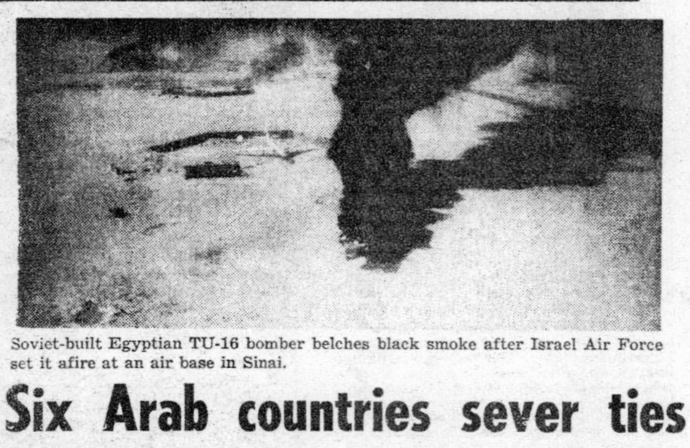

Soviet-built Egyptian TU-16 bomber belches black smoke after Israel Air Force set it afire at an air base in Sinai.

Six Arab countries sever ties with U.S.; Egypt closes Canal

Egypt, Syria and Algeria last night broke off diplomatic relations with the U.S., and Arab oil-producing states cut off supplies to both the U.S. and Britain after Arab charges that the two nations provided air cover to Israel during Monday's hostilities. They were followed by Yemen, Sudan and Iraq. Both the U.S. and Britain vigorously and angrilly denied the charges. Syria, Yemen, Sudan and Iraq also severed relations with Britain. Egypt and Algeria had done so earlier.

In addition, Egypt announced yesterday that it has decided to halt navigation in the Suez Canal so that the waterway will not be a target for Israeli air attack. Cairo Radio linked this decision with the allegations.

In Cairo, Alexandria, Damascus and Baghdad there were prolonged demonstrations in front of U.S. missions. Baghdad demonstrators set fire to the U.S. Information Service Library and the British Council. Mobs sacked and burned the U.S. Consulate in Alexandria. Another mob tried to force its way into the British Consulate. Demonstrators shouted "Down with Johnson, down with Wilson," outside the U.S. Embassy in Cairo.

In Beirut, Lebanese security forces dispersed a crowd of demonstrators outside the U.S. Embassy. Reports abroad that the U.S. Embassy was burned were denied as "not true."

In Amman, troops squashed anti-American and anti-British demonstrations. The troops headed off demonstrators marching on the embassies of the two countries.

In another development, British Prime Minister Harold Wilson announced the suspension of all British arms shipment to the Middle East for 24 hours pending reassessment of the situation. Mr. Wilson, addressing the Commons, urged the Arabs not to disrupt commercial arrangements on the basis of false statements.

The nations imposing a ban on oil shipments to the U.S. and Britain were Kuwait and Algeria. Iraq ordered a halt yesterday in the pumping of oil to British and U.S. customers. Iraq's pipelines cross Syria *en route* to the Mediterranean.

The U.S. State Department confirmed that Egypt had broken diplomatic relations and said it intended to make this action reciprocal. The new U.S. Ambassador to Cairo, Mr. Richard Nolte, was originally due to submit his credentials to President Nasser on Monday. *(Reuter, UPI, AP)*

U.S. and Soviets seek accord in U.N. Council

UNITED NATIONS (Reuter). — The U.S. and Soviet delegates discussed the Middle East crisis for almost an hour yesterday while the start of a scheduled meeting of the Security Council was delayed at least until midnight Israel time. Mr. Arthur Goldberg, the American representative, and his Soviet opposite number, Dr. Nikolai Fedorenko, met in the office of the Council President, Mr. Hans Tabor.

It was understood that they were trying to reconcile their differences on how the Council should go about calling for a ceasefire. Informed sources said Mr. Tabor was trying to obtain the agreement of the two super powers to a draft resolution which would enable the Security Council during the night to call for an immediate ceasefire.

Russia obstructed this bid all day Monday by insisting on adding other clauses to the simple appeal favoured by the U.S. and Britain. In particular the Russians want the Council to call for the withdrawal of Arab and Israel troops to the positions they occupied before fighting began on Monday. The Western powers objected to this because they said it would freeze the *status quo*, particularly Egypt's blockade of the Tiran Straits.

The Soviet Ambassador in London, Mr. Mikhail Smirnovsky, had a 10-minute meeting with Prime Minister Harold Wilson yesterday. No details were immediately available about the call, made at the envoy's own request shortly after Britain had denied Arab charges that British planes were involved in Arab-Israel fighting. Mr. Wilson has been in continuous contact with world leaders, including Soviet Prime Minister Alexei Kosygin, over the past few days as part of Britain's drive to get Russia to work with the Western Big Three to end the fighting.

Eshkol appeals to Kosygin

Mr. Eshkol has appealed to the Soviet Prime Minister a second time to show understanding for Israel's necessity to repel Nasser's "wicked aggression" and foil his declared and planned intention to destroy this country. In a letter to Mr. Kosygin, dated June 5, he also appealed to the Soviet Union to join an effort to pacify the Middle East. (Text of letter — Page 3.)

The Kremlin in a statement early yesterday, quoted by Reuter, demanded that Israel stop its "aggression" against Arab countries and withdraw its troops to behind the lines held before fighting broke out.

Prime Minister Kosygin yesterday held talks in Moscow with the Egyptian Ambassador, Mr. Mohammed Ghaleb. An official announcement by Tass said they had "a friendly conversation in which questions of mutual interest were discussed."

Tass breaks out with Israel version

MOSCOW (UPI). — Soviet news media reported for the first time last night that Israeli troops might be winning battles in the Middle East war. Tass broke into its solid string of Arab communiques to report Israeli claims of victories in Sinai and Jerusalem. The agency quoted a radio report by Israeli generals of Israeli advances in northern Sinai, its capture of three towns "on the road to the Suez Canal," its taking of Jenin, Gaza and the Old City of Jerusalem.

Syrian attacks repulsed

By DAVID SLAV
Jerusalem Post Reporter

TIBERIAS. — Syrian infantry and an armoured column tried to penetrate the Sh'ar Yashuv and Tel Dan areas yesterday, but were beaten back by Israel armour and the Air Force. During the 90-minute battle the Syrians shelled Dan, Daphne, Sh'ar Yashuv, Ma'ayan Baruch, Lehavot Habashan, Gadot and Yesud Hama'alah. They used long-range artillery against Rosh Pina and the frontier station at the Bnot Ya'acov Bridge. Shrapnel fell in Moshav Eliphelet.

In Rosh Pina, one resident was slightly wounded and 15 buildings hit. One house went up in flames, set alight by a brush fire. Telephone lines were cut. At Dan a resident was slightly wounded. In the southern sector, the Syrians attacked Ein Gev and Tel Katzir with artillery fire. One person at Ein Gev was killed and several wounded. The concert hall and other buildings were damaged. At Tel Katzir one building was hit.

SYRIANS BOMBED

Israel Air Force planes straffed and bombed the Syrian fortified emplacements on the slopes, silenced the guns and damaged most of them. At the same time, Israel artillery hit them from below. Tel Azaziat and Tel Hamra, old "acquaintances" of the settlers, were wrecked. All day and night, fire and smoke were seen rising from the Syrian positions. No Syrian planes were seen above the area all day.

At 3 p.m. the whole front was quiet. In all the settlements near the border, including Tiberias, people spent hours in shelters. They emerged in the afternoon to enjoy the cool air.

Syrian plane crashes on petrol station, kills nine

AFULA. — Nine were killed and a number were wounded when a Syrian Ilushin bomber was shot down by an Israeli fighter at 5.35 yesterday morning before it could drop any bombs.

The bomber was flying very low in a southerly direction over the rooftops of the buildings at Rehov Habanim and the Government housing quarter. Hit by the Israel plane, the bomber fell in flames near a petrol station on the outskirts of the town and exploded together with its load of bombs. Nine Israelis were killed instantly. The pilot and the co-pilot were also killed.

B.B.C. SEES JORDAN ARMY COLLAPSING

The British Broadcasting Corporation (B.B.C.) last night quoted "reliable sources" in Amman as saying that the Jordanian armed forces were "on the point of collapse." In a report by its diplomatic correspondent, the broadcast said Jordanian ground forces were "pinned down in isolated points" along the area bordering Israel. With "its air cover destroyed in the first hours of the attack, Jordan's forces must either stand their ground and be destroyed or pull out in a full-scale retreat across the river Jordan," the report said.

Only 36 hours after the start of fighting, Israel forces were deep in Sinai, had captured Gaza, made sweeping gains on the Jordan front, and had encircled the Old City of Jerusalem.

The Israel forces in Sinai destroyed 200 Egyptian tanks on Monday and yesterday, the Defence Establishment's spokesman told foreign correspondents last night. One hundred and fifty Egyptian tanks were destroyed yesterday and 50 the day before. The spokesman said that there were tank battles in Sinai yesterday as well as some air engagements. In general, the Egyptian forces were on the retreat.

Spearheads of Israel Armoured Corps units were last night reported to be well beyond El Arish, and engaged in large-scale tank battles along the Sinai coastal plain, with the Egyptians retreating westwards.

Israel Air Force units shot down eight Egyptian planes yesterday. The first six were brought down during the morning.

They were all of the Sokhoi-7 type, the most modern planes in use by the Egyptians. The other two were Mig-21s. A TU-16 of the Iraqi Air Force was shot down over Megiddo, after attempting a bombing run on Netanya. The bomber was brought down by anti-aircraft fire.

The mechanized units appeared to have advanced even faster than those during the Sinai Campaign, an Army spokesman said here yesterday. The Gaza Strip has been completely occupied; a sizeable part of the north-central section of Sinai was in Israel hands, and Israeli armour was engaging what seemed to be the last major Egyptian armoured unit still intact, southwards in the Kuntilla area.

KALKILYA, JENIN TAKEN

In Jordan, Israel units captured Kalkilya, Latrun and Jenin and reached the vicinity of the Samarian mountains in addition to its successes in Jerusalem. Jordanian units appeared to be retreating eastwards.

Reports of street fighting in the Old City were denied by the Army spokesman yesterday. However, with the conquest of Sheikh Jarah and the so-called French Hill, Israel has been able to relieve the defenders of Mt. Scopus, who had been besieged since the fighting started.

Some localities, like Abu Agheila, were yesterday captured by the Israel Defence Forces for the third time. Veteran commanders are also familiar with a good many of the others, notably Latrun and Jenin.

Yesterday's most significant development, however, was not any specific conquest but the noticeable westward movements of Egyptian units now abandoning the Kuntilla-Abu Agheila axis, the Egyptian "Maginot line" which had been reinforced by a crack armoured division. Observers here yesterday afternoon saw in the new Egyptian troop movements the first signs of a crack up and possible general retreat by the Egyptians to new positions further to the south.

LATRUN'S IMPORTANCE

Most important of yesterday's gains were the capture of Latrun and the artillery positions surrounding it, and seizure of Abu Agheila, the "impregnable" Egyptian position in Sinai. From Latrun the Jordanians had lobbed shells into Lydda. Artillery positions at Kalkiliya also fired some shells into central and northern Tel Aviv (suburbs).

In the Jerusalem area, Israeli troops last night outflanked the Jordanian held part of the city, taking Nebi Samuel in the North, with the fall of Ramallah considered to be only a matter of hours.

With the fall of the Old City, Ramallah and Latrun this entire front could be rolled back, possibly splitting the western half of Jordan by separating the Hebron and Nablus districts.

Israel units yesterday also stormed Kalkilya, one of the closest points on the Jordanian frontier to the Mediterranean. From there the Jordanians had shelled Tel Aviv. The troops were also reported to be consolidating their gains in the Jenin area, facing the Jezreel valley, despite a determined Jordanian counterattack at noon.

SYRIAN GUNS SILENCED

The Syrians' massive artillery bombardments of settlements along the entire length of the Upper Jordan Valley was countered by Air Force strafings and return fire. Israel continues to be on the defensive in Upper Galilee, with the Syrians once again gaining time, thanks primarily to their relative military insignificance.

The conflict with Jordan is primarily aimed against Jordanian artillery positions which continue to shell Jerusalem as well as settlements along the entire length of the central frontier — from Latrun northwards.

Armoured units succeeded in cutting off the Gaza Strip during the first few hours of hostilities, sweeping across the 14 kilometres separating Israel from the Mediterranean at this point. This was followed by the piecemeal whittling down of resistance, culminating with the surrender of Gaza at noon yesterday. Small pockets of resistance are expected to be mopped up within the next 24 hours.

Following the surrender of El Arish and Abu Agheila, the Egyptians are now withdrawing their remaining troops stationed in the Kuntilla area and are heading west. Much will now depend on the speed of the Israeli pursuit — whether this will give the Egyptians enough time to retrench.

EGYPTIAN COMMANDOS

The introduction of Egyptian commanders in the Jordanian army has unfortunately compelled Israel to take stronger measures than were initially anticipated. Prisoners taken at Latrun yesterday include a number of Egyptian commando officers and men. The highest ranking officer was a major who said that two commando battalions arrived in Jordan on June 3, immediately after the signing of the Egyptian-Jordanian military agreement. Their mission, they said, had been the sabotaging of airfields in Israel.

(Amman Radio broadcast the Jordanian Army's communique No. 36, which said heavy fighting is proceeding in the areas of Kalkilya, Bethlehem and Hebron. The communique said Israeli bombers raided Jordanian air installations, troop concentrations and reinforcement convoys, and alleged that napalm bombs and rockets were used.)

Observers here said yesterday that the fighting was entering a concluding phase on the Jordan front, and perhaps also on the Sinai.

Mt. Scopus relieved

By CHARLES WEISS, Jerusalem Post Reporter

After bitter fighting that lasted throughout Monday night and well into yesterday, all Jordanian Jerusalem outside the Old City Wall — including the "French Hill" adjacent to Mt. Scopus, Sheikh Jarrah and the road to Mt. Scopus — were in Israeli hands. The garrison on Scopus was relieved after a 24-hour siege.

In addition, the villages of Beit Iksa, Nebi Samuel and Shu'afat and the radar station above Ma'aleh Hahamisha to the north were captured. But snipers were still being mopped up in the Old City until last night.

As the troops being relieved drove out of Mandelbaum Gate into the Mea Shearim yesterday morning, they were greeted by large crowds of excited residents from the neighbourhood, clapping and cheering them on. The men were dog-tired; they just smiled.

Among the vehicles were a number bearing Jordanian licence numbers.

Mayor Teddy Kollek, in the company of the O.C. Central Command, made a quick tour of Jordanian Jerusalem outside the walls yesterday afternoon.

One soldier said to Mr. Kollek: "We've made your city bigger." His reply: "A bigger headache, you mean."

The Commander of the Southern District Police, Mr. Shaul Rosolio, showed up at 3 p.m. to ask about getting his border control police station at Mandelbaum Gate back. They told him he could have it at 14.00 hours today. Aside from the danger of sniper fire (still very real — a soldier was fatally wounded several minutes after Mayor Kollek reached the crossing point on his way out), there is the danger of looting, which must be prevented.

A party of three experts visited the Palestine Museum (known as the "Rockefeller") outside the Herod's Gate Quarter. They were the Government Director of Antiquities and Museums, Dr. A. Biran; the Director of the Hebrew University Archaeology Institute, Prof. Nahman Avigad; and the Secretary of the Israel Exploration Society, Mr. Yosef Aviram.

Walking a hundred metres past the control point on the Jordanian side of Mandelbaum Gate, we came across the body of a Jordanian soldier killed in the break-

(Continued on Page 2, Col. 6)

I would like to thank all of those who have expressed their good wishes on my appointment as Minister of Defence.

I would ask my friends to forgive me for not being able to reply to each one personally in view of the needs of the hour.

To all of Israel and to the Israel Defence Forces I extend my wishes for victory in our struggle.

GENERAL MOSHE DAYAN,
Minister of Defence

OLD CITY, MOST OF SINAI FALL, TIRAN OPENED

THE JERUSALEM POST

Published in Jerusalem, Israel, daily except on Saturday by The Palestine Post Ltd. Founded in 1932 by Gershon AGRON.
Registered at the G.P.O. Copyright of all material reserved; reproduction permitted only by arrangement. Editor: TED R. LURIE.

Jerusalem: 9 Rehov Havatzelet, P.O.B. 81,   Tel Aviv: 81 Rehov Nahlat Binyamin,   Haifa: 34 Rehov Herzl, Hadar Hacarmel,
Telephones 24233, 24321   P.O.Box 1125, Tel. 624215   P.O.Box 4810, Telephone 64594.

THURSDAY, JUNE 8, 1967 • EYAR 29, 5727 • RABIA AWAL 1, 1387
• VOL. XXXVII, No. 11980°   PRICE : 35 AGORA

Forces near Suez, West Bank taken

After 60 hours of battle Israel forces yesterday controlled most of the West Bank of Jordan, including the Old City of Jerusalem, Nablus, Ramallah, Jericho and Bethlehem; in Sinai they cut through to the approaches of the Suez Canal and captured Sharm e-Sheikh, the Chief of Staff, Rav Aluf Yitzhak Rabin, said yesterday.

The Defence Minister, Mr. Moshe Dayan, last night declared that Israel has achieved her main political aims in this campaign. Addressing an overflow press conference at Beit Sokolow, Mr. Dayan declared that from the very onset it was Israel's objective to ensure the free passage of shipping to Eilat.

Urged to describe the kind of peace Israel would offer the Arabs, the Minister said "Real peace." Asked further whether this depended on territorial negotiations, Mr. Dayan replied: "I am ready to give peace and take peace." He was sure that the Arab peoples were truly desirous of permanent peace.

He confirmed that he still supported the idea of a confederation of Israel and Jordan, adding "I also said that the real enemy of Jordan is Egypt. The only country that can protect Jordan is Israel."

Mr. Dayan declared that the Tiran Straits and the Suez Canal were two different issues, when asked whether Israel would now stand firm on the question of ensuring passage through the Suez Canal. He elaborated: "We could by now get to the Suez easily if we wanted to but it was not our aim to get there. Our problem was Sharm e-Sheikh, so why should we go right up to Suez. It was our business to settle the problem of free passage to Eilat and the concentration of Egyptian forces in Sinai... we were not fighting now to use Suez."

Mr. Dayan, during his visit to the Old City of Jerusalem yesterday, said:

"This morning, the Israel Defence Forces liberated Jerusalem. We have united Jerusalem, the divided capital of Israel. We have returned to the holiest of our holy places, never to part from it again.

"To our Arab neighbours we extend, also at this hour — our hand in peace. And to our Christian and Muslim fellow-citizens, we solemnly promise full religious freedom and rights. We did not come to Jerusalem for the sake of other peoples' holy places, and not to interfere with the adherents of other faiths, but in order to safeguard its entirety, and to live there together with others, in unity."

The Chief of Staff, at a press conference in Tel Aviv recalled that on the morning of June 6, the shelling of settlements started on the border as did troop movements and the movement of considerable air groups. We had to defend ourselves. Israel is too small a country to defend itself in any other but an active manner. Part of our mobilization preceded all these events, but the rest of our troops were mobilized by radio on the morning of June 5.

Since Egypt was the one to start the attack, and also because Egypt had the most powerful force numerically, most of our action was directed against the Egyptians. Our air reaction was, of course, immediate and our land forces entered the action a little later. We have never revealed, and I hope we never shall, what the size and numbers of the Israel defence forces are. I had occasion before the events of the recent days to be asked whether it was true that we had 600-800 tanks — and I can only say that whoever relied on this estimation was mistaken.

Our air force met the attackers and brought down some in the air and others on the ground. In air combat, as you will realise, there are no borders and no limitations. An Egyptian operational order fell into our hands at El Arish dated May 21. It detailed the action to be taken by the Egyptian air force against Israeli airfields.

ALONG SINAI AXES

Our land forces advanced along the main Sinai axes. We engaged in the main our armoured, mobile, mechanized, and infantry troops. The first stages of the battle were a break-through followed by the speedy advance of our forces which penetrated the enemy, who was entrenched in fortified positions which included artillery and armoured forces concentrations. The success of our action was due to the smoothly organized and coordinated direction of our commanders, and the actual fighting was the work of our well-trained highly-skilled men.

The Chief of Staff said that today we are actually witnessing the total destruction of the bulk of the Egyptian forces in Sinai. Although the rear actions are still in progress, it is a fact that the Egyptians are now attempting to withdraw their forces behind the Suez Canal in order to save whatever they still can.

Spearheads of the Israel Armoured Corps were last night reported to be within 20 kms. of the Suez Canal.

The Southern unit appeared to have by-passed Kuntilla in a head-on race southwards, covered an almost incredible distance within the past 24 hours.

The Tiran Straits are now in Israel's possession, taken by a parachutist unit which appears to have met little more than token resistance. Only one thing marred their day — the Israel Navy was there ahead of them.

Our forces are now on a line extending from Romani in the north through Bir Cafgata to the vicinity of the Mitla pass area, with the whole area behind this line under our control. The main efforts of the Egyptians are now devoted to extricating their forces towards the Suez Canal, Rav-Aluf Rabin declared.

He noted that the second stage, which started after the Egyptian action and Israel's immediate response to it, was the Jordanian shelling of Jerusalem and of settlements and towns all along the extended borders.

A few days previously, two Jordanian commando battalions had been transferred to Jordan and the Jordanian forces were in actual fact commanded by an Egyptian general. Their task was to tie down, hold and delay the Israel troops along the Jordan border while the Egyptian operation was in progress. I cannot say why Jordan started its side of the operation: the reasons are not known to me, and indeed it is not my job to engage in these speculations.

At a later stage shelling spread to the whole front and Tel Aviv received its share of fire as well. A look at the map will show what it means to have artillery fire directed at Israel from the Jordanian border.

NO CHOICE

Since it was Jordan who started, we had no choice but to react, and today the whole of the west bank of the Jordan is for all practical intents and purposes in our hands, including such ancient and famous places as the Old City, Nablus, Ramallah, Jericho and Bethlehem. A site of special significance to us, which was also taken, is the Etzion block, (between Bethlehem and Jordan), of which we have many memories from the days of the War of Independence.

The C-of-C. went on: "I cannot detail at present all the military moves that we made. It is as yet too early for this, and the battle is not over. I can mention only that this is a war we are fighting against Egypt, Jordan, Syria and Iraq. Despite all this, and in less than three days, we have succeeded in inflicting a devastating blow to their air forces and also to the Egyptian land forces. We have taken most of Sinai, including Sharm e-Sheikh, and we hold the territory west of the Jordan, where most of the Jordanian forces were broken, as was the Iraqi brigade which joined them in their action.

"Although it is not a military point, I would like to stress that all these actions were achieved by the Israel Defence Forces all alone and unaided. The battles were by no means easy. We have suffered casualties which, however, are comparatively small in view of the difficulty and complexity of the operation, the impetus, and the achievement to our credit.

"This war, which has not been at all like the Sinai campaign, was conducted on several fronts simultaneously. Of course every bereaved family cherishes beyond words the memory of its dead, and suffers with its wounded. I would like to say to them: Your sons, your fathers, fought like lions in the struggle that this war was thrust upon us. They knew — as did all of us — the full significance of this war and were aware of the supreme effort demanded of them. Words can never be enough. The bereaved families should endeavour to look at what was achieved by those who fell and by those of us who are still continuing the fight."

SIXTY HOURS

AT amazing, almost unbelievable, speed, the Israel Defence Forces have reached distant objectives. With the aid of a brilliant feint, they took Sharm e-Sheikh, where the crisis of the past weeks began when the U.N. forces suddenly pulled out, letting the Egyptians move in and blockade the Gulf of Akaba.

A heavy and perfectly disciplined and coordinated force of tanks and infantry rolled back the threatening Egyptian forces on the long border with the Sinai Peninsula, almost across to Suez, until the Egyptian forces are already beginning to withdraw into the security of the far side of the Suez Canal, while matchless, split-second flying destroyed most of the Egyptian air force before it could get off the ground, and much of what was left when it took to the air, silencing the threat to Israel cities and vital military installations. A total of 441 enemy planes were smashed in this time, wiping out the air forces of Egypt, Jordan and Syria. This is in itself an achievement. Jerusalem, ringed by series of well-entrenched Jordanian positions, and so much more seriously threatened than its inhabitants ever realized — suffered 36 hours of vicious bombardment, until each position in turn was painfully captured and neutralized. To make Jerusalem secure for the future the Israel forces occupied Ramallah, Jenin and Nablus, and stretched down as far as Jericho on the Dead Sea.

And yet there were still forces to spare to chase and bring down the Iraqi planes that raided Netanya, and to help villages on the Jordan and Syrian frontiers that suffered sudden raids. To crown all these varied military actions, they carried out the extremely difficult and sensitive task of occupying the Old City without destroying its sacred monuments, searching out and silencing enemy positions without being able to prepare the way by advance shelling, even though the Jordanians had been steadily plunging shells into the Israel half of Jerusalem. The encirclement and occupation of the Old City in the space of 48 hours is as impressive in itself as the destruction of Egyptian air power.

All this was the work of some 60 hours — half the time it took ten years ago to race to Suez and down to Sharm e-Sheikh, with the dubious aid of the British fleet standing by, but a sure promise of French air aid should it become needed. The Israel forces fought alone this time, without half-agreements and half-disappointments, without misunderstanding or recriminations. The Israel forces fought four Arab nations simultaneously and have defeated them, with, happily, only very moderate casualties, though that makes the loss of each individual soldier no less an agony to his family nor less of a blow to his small nation.

Let no one think that Zahal's fantastic array of simultaneous victories is due to luck or chance, the poor training and morale of the Egyptians, or even the profound consciousness of every soldier that he is fighting quite literally for his own survival and for that of his family and people. Their training and planning started with the watchmen of the "Shomer" — one of whose earliest theorists was Mr. Ben-Gurion — and it was continued in the difficult underground days of the Hagana, when defence against Arab hostility had to be prepared in secret for fear that British policemen would confiscate the small store of precious weapons. Utmost economy in the use of men and weapons, careful preparation for every possible emergency, the training of each man and woman as both an independent unit and as a disciplined subordinate, produced the prototype of today's superbly courageous army, with its eagerness to carry out plans that have always provided brilliantly unconventional solutions to every military problem.

However tough and even rough the discipline, officers and also men have been encouraged also to preserve their individuality, to retain a mind of their own, ability, to make a contribution to methods of training and planning. The result is an army with all the best qualities of the civilians of whom it is made up, fortified by devotion, loyalty and unity. They have proved victorious every time against armies whose officers were trained at some of the best European and American academies. The army was born out of need, not pride, and shaped by adversity, not privilege. It's face is the face of Israel, and the success of its youthful legions has marked the nation in gratitude, pride and a deep affection.

Moshe Dayan in the Old City.

BULLETIN:

The Israel forces have obtained their objectives in reaching the Hebron hills and the Jordan River, the Minister of Defence and the Chief of Staff told the Ministerial Security Committee yesterday.

They also reported that the Army was in control of the Sinai Peninsula as well.

The Committee decided to charge the Foreign Minister with informing the U.N. of Israel's agreement to its cease-fire resolution on condition that the other countries involved reciprocate.

U.N. Council's deadline for cease-fire

UNITED NATIONS (UPI).—The Security Council yesterday unanimously adopted a Soviet resolution calling for a complete cease-fire in the Middle East war at 10 p.m. last night (Israel time).

The move came as the Soviet Union issued a statement last night threatening to break diplomatic relations with Israel if it did not obey "immediately" the U.N. call for a cease-fire adopted on Tuesday. The Soviet statement made no such threat to the Arabs, although the Egypt and Iraq — but not Jordan — have refused to obey the cease-fire. The statement also threatened "other necessary measures" if Israel refuses to lay down its arms. These "measures" were not defined.

The Council yesterday acted at a session demanded by Russia on short notice as news circulated that Israel had seized command of the entrance to the Gulf of Akaba.

Soviet Ambassador Nikolai Fedorenko insisted on the resolution with the short time period for effectiveness of a cease-fire despite unanimous adoption of Tuesday's similar resolution, without a time-limit.

The Soviet resolution did not say what would happen if Israel and the Arabs did not stop fighting by the deadline.

In submitting the resolution, Mr. Fedorenko said: "Information reaching us clearly points to the fact that the aggressor forces continue to engage in military operations, paying no heed to the resolution of the Council."

Announcement was made here that Secretary-General U Thant has made arrangement for U.N. Observers "to observe implementation of the cease-fire." However, thus far, U Thant's office has declined to reveal the nature of those arrangements.

Mr. Eban told the Council unequivocally that the Israel Government had accepted the cease-fire approved by the Council on Tuesday night. He said neither Egypt nor Syria had accepted the cease-fire while Jordan which had, was not in a position to carry it out. The Israel Foreign Minister who did not directly announce acceptance of the earlier cease-fire when he spoke to the Council on Tuesday, said yesterday that "there is unilateral and so far unreciprocated acceptance of the cease-fire."

Resolution impractical

By JESSE ZEL LURIE

UNITED NATIONS.—The Security Council passed unanimously at 8.40 p.m. Israel time a resolution demanding a cease-fire at 10 p.m. Israel time last night. The resolution is completely impractical since, even had all parties accepted immediately, there would not be enough time to transmit the appropriate orders to the field commanders.

Observers here believe the Soviet Union's demand for an immediate deadline for the cease-fire was a desperate attempt to save Syria from the same military debacle that Egypt and Jordan have suffered. The Soviets fear that Israel will move troops from Sinai and Jordan, where all military objectives have been achieved, to Syria. Since the Arabs throughout this crisis have invariably done the opposite of what was expected of them, this view that Syria is in danger has been reinforced by yesterday's announcement from Damascus that Israel has attacked in force and is now on the road to Damascus. There is no confirmation of the Damascus announcement and none is expected.

AFTER MIDNIGHT

A heavy security guard was mounted last night at Rome's military airport where King Hussein was rumoured to be heading shortly.

Premier Eshkol accompanied by Aluf Uzzi Narkiss, O.C. Central Command, at the Western Wall yesterday.
(Photo Meyerowitz)

Premier, Chief Rabbis pray at Western Wall

By N. D. GROSS, Jerusalem Post Reporter

Mr. Levi Eshkol yesterday took part in afternoon prayers at the Western Wall. He was the first leader of a Jewish Government to visit the site of the Temple since its loss 1,897 years ago.

The Prime Minister, robustly cheered by the tired but elated boys and men who had freed the Holy City, was accompanied by the two Chief Rabbis. It was approaching dusk and, because the city's tortuous alleyways still possibly concealed last-ditch snipers, the official party's escort tried to speed their return to the newer city. But all still lingered, perhaps not fully realising that they have plenty of time to go again, and again.

Indeed a long file of prisoners was being led away across the splendid square of the Temple Mount, in front of the Dome of the Rock. When Rabbi Yitzhak Nissim approached, the file was broken to enable the Rishon Lezion, the First in Zion, to go by.

Earlier in the day, as soon as the road to the Wall was clear, the Chief Chaplain to the Forces, Aluf Shlomo Goren, came at an eager run, carrying a Sefer Tora. He recited the shehecheyanu blessing, congratulating himself and all Israel, both within the Land and without, on having the privilege of establishing the age-old hope — and without their right hand having lost its cunning.

Rabbi Goren sounded a vehement blast on the Shofar belonging to his father-in-law, "the Nazir." He stayed there several hours, reciting the Hallel psalms of praise for the delivery, and also the prayer for the souls of those who gave their lives for Israel's victory.

The Defence Minister, Rav-Aluf Moshe Dayan, came soon after and there he made his declaration: "We will not give up this place."

Other who made the pilgrimage included Dr. Yosef Burg, Dr. Zerah Warhaftig, Mr. Y.S. Shapiro, Dr. Ernst Nebenzahl, Mrs. Mrs. Rahel Ben-Zvi, Dr. Dov Joseph and Mr. David Shaltiel, respectively the military governor and commander of Jerusalem when its older section was cut off 19 years ago.

During the day streams of soldiers came to the Wall, some to pray, others just to stare. Many put petitions for the health of their dear ones in the spaces between the giant stones that Solomon had emplaced for the Glory of God. There were impromptu minyanim throughout the afternoon and even as dusk approached, some soldiers donned tefilin which they had not time to do at the normally proper morning hour. Then they were shooting their way in. Now they were still armed and still on watch, but they had a few minutes in which to voice their thanks to Him who had gone with them.

One chaplain brought to the wall a small sefer tora which had not seen action on several occasions. It had accompanied the advance troops into Gaza 11 years ago.

As it was being ceremonially taken out of its ark, the men sang the line from the Psalms traditional at that point in the service: Arise O Lord, let Thine enemies be scattered, let those that hate Thee be driven before Thee.

Around the corner, away from the Holy of Holies of the Wall itself, Yaffa Yarkoni was leading a sing-song. Again and again the boys went tirelessly through "Jerusalem of Gold," the song commissioned by the Mayor for the Independence Day Song Festival held 23 cents — or was it just days? — ago. "Caught in a sleep-like thrall / Jerusalem, world's loneliest city /, Within her Wall."

Israeli troops poured into the Old City yesterday morning through Saint Stephen's Gate at the north eastern corner of the wall and through Zion Gate at the southwest corner. The first columns were accompanied by Aluf Goren bearing a tora scroll, writes UPI correspondent Robert Musel. Tough Israeli troops covered with dust wept like small children at the sight.

Rabbi Shlomo Kook, grandson of the late Chief Rabbi of Israel, his voice vibrant with emotion, said, "This is the most (Continued on Page 4, Col. 6)

THE JERUSALEM POST

Published in Jerusalem, Israel, daily except on Saturday by The Palestine Post Ltd. Founded in 1932 by Gershon AGRON.
Registered at the G.P.O. Copyright of all material reserved; reproduction permitted only by arrangement. Editor: TED R. LURIE

Jerusalem: 9 Rehov Havatzelet, P.O.B. 81, Telephones 24233, 24321 Tel Aviv: 81 Rehov Nahlat Binyamin, P.O.Box 1125, Tel. 624215 Haifa: 34 Rehov Herzl, Hadar Hacarmel, P.O.Box 4810, Telephone 64594.

PRICE : 35 AGORA
45 FILS ON WEST BANK

SUNDAY, JUNE 11, 1967 • SIVAN 3, 5727 RABIA AWAL 4, 1387 • VOL. XXXVII, No. 11982*

Jerusalem stories pages 4 & 6
★
Battle pictures, war reports page 3

CEASE-FIRE IN FORCE; SYRIAN LINE BROKEN

By ZE'EV SCHUL, Jerusalem Post Military Reporter

MESUDAT YESHA, Upper Galilee. — Syrian defence lines east of the Upper reaches of the Jordan and Hula basin were cracked wide open on Friday when units of the defence forces closed in to deal with Syrian artillery positions which had been bombarding settlements in the border valleys almost incessantly for the previous five days. A number of positions, including such well-known names as Darbashiye, Ain Tina, Dardara and Jalabina, were taken in head-on assaults. There is a substantial number of prisoners.

The Army spokesman announced last night that Israel forces were holding the north-south line Massadeh-Kuneitra-Boutmiyeh, which is 20 kilometres east of the international frontier.

The Syrian Army, which has had almost 20 years to dig-in, had built a double line of positions running the entire length of the Gaulan mountains, starting at the foothills of Mount Hermon and ending near Lake Kinneret. The positions were planned, Russian style, as fortifications in depth, providing a maze of communication trenches and gun positions. The lower of these two lines, and the principal source of trouble for Israel, was held by units of the Syrian National Guard. The upper lines were held by regular army units.

Heavy fighting along the entire length of the Syrian frontier broke out at dawn on Friday after the Syrians, in complete disregard of the cease-fire they had agreed to the preceding day, stepped up their artillery fire. Heavy damage was caused all along the front. Gadot, east of Ayelet Hashahar, once again seems to have drawn most of the enemy fire, and is totally wrecked. Settlers in this area have been living in shelters for the past few days.

Actual contact with the Syrian units became unavoidable when it became clear that there was no other way of permanently silencing the Syrian artillery positions — all entrenched on heights well to the rear.

To enable Israel's forces to exploit topographical advantages, the units may have had to operate some kilometres east of the Jordan. At this stage there seems to be no intention of taking Kuneitra or any other Syrian areas beyond what is dictated by tactical need.

The Syrians are reported to have shown stiff resistance. They gave up only after intensive artillery and Air Force bombardments were followed up by a three-pronged drive of armoured units — operating along different elevations north to south, while other mechanized infantry units closed in from the South.

Fighting continued during the late hours of Friday afternoon. This time the stress was on silencing Syrian artillery positions east and south-east of Lake Kinneret.

The Defence Ministry spokesman, Mr. Moshe Pearlman, said that it is believed there are 600 to 700 Egyptian tanks still in Sinai, of which 200 may still be serviceable.

A revised evaluation of the number of Egyptian soldiers believed to have been in Sinai puts the figure at 150,000, and they are believed to have had between 900 and 1,000 tanks at their disposal. One hundred thousand men belonged to fighting units. They included four infantry divisions, and two armoured divisions, known as the Fourth and the Special Armoured Task Force. Thousands of Egyptian soldiers continued to struggle back on foot to Egypt yesterday, the Defence Forces making no attempt to stop them merely taking away their weapons. Six Egyptian generals have been captured.

Israel has taken possession of 70 of Hussein's 200 tanks. The 60 Pattons and 10 Centurions are in good condition. Of the remaining 130, quite a number have been put out of action.

Jerusalem Post Reporter

Announcement of a cease-fire agreement enforced at 6.30 p.m. yesterday between Israel and Syria was made in Tel Aviv by the Army spokesman and in New York at the U.N. Security Council. The spokesman said Israel will honour the agreement so long as it is observed by the Syrians.

The cease-fire was arranged between Defence Minister Moshe Dayan and the UNTSO Chief of Staff, Gen. Odd Bull, who received special authority to do so from Secretary-General U Thant. However, the armistice agreements on which the authority of the UNTSO had been based — except that with Lebanon — are considered to be null and void as a result of the acts of war.

Gen. Bull arrived at Mr. Dayan's office in the Kirya in Tel Aviv at 3 p.m., accompanied by a U.N. officer and Sgan-Aluf Shmuel Gatt, who was Israel's representative on the Israel-Syrian Mixed Armistice Commission. R/A Dayan offered Gen. Bull all the installations and equipment he might need in order to carry out his assignment in the Syrian border region.

UPI reported from U.N. Headquarters:— Council President Hans Tabor of Denmark adjourned the meeting, the 14th in two weeks on the Middle East crisis, with a caution to members to stand by for another emergency session if the truce breaks down.

It fell to Mr. Gideon Rafael, Israeli Ambassador, attacked by the Arabs and lambasted by the Soviet Union, to announce the cease-fire agreement to the Council.

Mr. Rafael told the Council: "General Dayan stated that Israel accepts any proposal made by General Bull for implementation of a cease-fire and supervision arrangements.

"General Bull asked what time and General Dayan said, 'right here and now'. General Dayan agreed that Israel will accept any hour which General Bull will fix and he could decide the hour on his own."

A few minutes later, Secretary-General U Thant advised the Council officially that Gen. Bull had fixed "16.30 hours Greenwich Mean Time" — (6.30 p.m. Israel time) for the cease-fire to become effective.

Gen. Bull asked Israel and Syria both to select observers to serve on their own sides of the truce line and to appoint liaison officers for duty across the line, presumably with U.N. personnel.

It was an unpredictable windup to a day that began with a 2 a.m. call from the Syrian delegation to advise Mr. Tabor that the situation was rapidly deteriorating, with Israeli planes menacing Damascus and armoured columns driving down the road to the capital through the key town of Kuneitra. This was denied by Israel.

Mr. Tabor consulted most of the 14 other members he could reach and convoked the Council on 4 a.m. The pre-dawn meeting got under way 33 minutes late, with Russia adding to the agenda a call for a cease-fire and withdrawal by Israeli troops from Arab territory.

Word was passed among the diplomats that Soviet Ambassador Nikolai Fedorenko was prepared to keep the Council in session until it voted on a resolution con-

(Continued on Page 6, Col. 4)

SOVIET BREAK WITH ISRAEL

SHARP regret will be felt among the general public as well as in official circles at yesterday's decision of the Soviet Union to break off its diplomatic ties with this country.

The Soviet Union was among the earliest sponsors of Israel at the time of its establishment, and this is a fact that is always remembered here; and of course perhaps also in the Arab world. It is one reason why we have always wished for closer and better relations with the Russians, quite apart from the fact that so large a proportion of the early settlers came here from Eastern Europe, and that their sympathy has always been with what they saw as a forward-looking government. Add to this the circumstance that one of the few remaining large Jewish communities lives in Russia, and it is clear that this link is particularly important to us and that we hope to see it restored in the not too distant future.

The other side of the coin is the Soviet Union's increasingly close relationship with both Egypt and, more recently, Syria. Some other powers have been sufficiently flexible in their diplomacy to be able to remain on excellent terms with both the Arab State and ourselves: the Soviet Union, on the other hand, allowed its relationship with Israel to shrink and wither almost from the time it began to develop its current relationship with Egypt.

Russia has given close political support to the Arab states, and particularly these two. and has not hesitated even to accept their open hostility towards Israel. This stand caused the Soviet Union to oppose and nullify many U.N. votes on numberless acts of Syrian aggression during the past few years and thereby no doubt tended to encourage such aggression and thereby indirectly also to contribute to the creation of the present conflict.

Israel was never successful in conveying the inherent danger of this attitude to the representatives of the Soviet Union. The far-reaching Soviet acquiescence in the closing of the Straits of Tiran to Israel shipping by Egypt some weeks ago appeared at the time the climax in this one-sided attitude, for the U.S.S.R. threatened military intervention against any outside power or group of powers that might take action to restore freedom of movement through the Straits. How much this attitude contributed to the subsequent explosion and the destruction of Egypt's forces is difficult to judge in retrospect, but it was certainly an important element.

Despite his success in obtaining a vote of public confidence by the simple ruse of a pretended resignation, Nasser is now at a critical point in his career, as a result of the destruction of so large a part of his military forces. He may himself harbour some doubts concerning the ultimate value of Soviet support for his ventures, which has ended in more disastrous defeat, and Israel's greatly increased strength. Perhaps, despite the Soviet Union's rough attitude to Israel, the day will come when the Arab countries will appreciate that the generous supplies of Soviet arms available to them are as dangerous to themselves as they are for us.

Russia cuts ties; sanctions threat

The Soviet Union yesterday announced its intention to break off relations with Israel, accusing this country of failing to observe the cease-fire on the Syrian border. A threat of sanctions was also made should military action not be halted. Israel has expressed the hope that relations will be restored when the Soviet Union shows more appreciation of Israel's problems.

The Foreign Ministry spokesman said in Jerusalem last night that the Soviet Ambassador, Mr. Dmitri Chuvakhin, that afternoon called on the Foreign Minister, Mr. Abba Eban, and presented a Note from his Government announcing its decision to break off diplomatic relations.

Mr. Eban expressed regret at the step taken by the Soviet Government and pointed out that Israel had always placed great importance and weight on relations with the Soviet Union. The Foreign Minister rejected the claim expressed in the Soviet Note that Israel maintained or continued to maintain an aggressive policy.

The Minister also expressed the hope that diplomatic and other relations will be maintained again with the Soviet Union on the basis of a more balanced understanding on the part of the Soviet Union of Israel's problems in the face of the aggressive policy adopted by the the Arab states.

The Foreign Minister stressed to the Ambassador that the struggle forced on Israel was a struggle for this country's very existence which enjoyed the support of progressive circles and friends of peace throughout the world.

Mr. Chuvakhin and a member of his staff drove to meet Mr. Eban in the Kirya here, escorted by a police car. The Ambassador looked grave. Soviet Embassy officials would give no information. However, informed sources said that the senior Embassy officials and remaining families would leave in the next few days.

(In Helsinki, the Foreign Ministry said the Soviet Union has asked the Finnish Government to look after its interests in Israel. A spokesman said Finland accepted the request.)

Czechoslovakia soon followed suit, while Hungary announced later that it would also break off relations if Israel did not implement the cease-fire.

In Moscow, the note informing Israel of the break was handed by First Deputy Foreign Minister Vasily Kuznetsov to Ambassador Katriel Katz at the Foreign Ministry. An Israeli spokesman, asked when the Israeli diplomatic staff would leave the Soviet Union, replied, "as soon as possible."

Tass said this was the note handed to the Israeli Ambassador:

"The news has just reached here that

(Continued on Page 2, Col. 4)

Calm view taken here of action

By FRANCIS OFNER
Jerusalem Post Diplomatic Reporter

Political quarters here last night took a comparatively calm view of the Soviet action, pointing out that it appears to be aimed at least as much at Arab ears as at Israel's.

Russia first severed relations with Israel in February 1953, at the time of Stalin's anti-Semitic "doctors' plot," — the pretext being the bomb that was exploded at the Soviet Embassy courtyard. It is recalled that relations were resumed a few months later at Soviet initiative.

Regarding the significance of yesterday's move with respect to the Arab world, it is pointed out here that severing and resuming diplomatic relations is a frequent procedure in the inter-state dialogue among the Arab states.

Concerning the Soviet threat of sanctions, it is pointed out here that Russia has in effect been practising economic sanctions against Israel since 1956, when they stopped buying Israel citrus and stopped selling us petrol.

FUTURE HOPE

Nevertheless, the hope is expressed here that Moscow will eventually adjust her Middle East policies to the realities of the region. It is considered that the emptiness of the reactionary, aggressive forces of Arab expansionism, as symbolized by Nasser has been exposed. The road is now seen open to a policy in which both the Arab states and Israel can live in peace and prosperity and enjoy the friendship of all major powers, including the Soviet Union.

Israel, it is noted, seeks neither an American nor a Soviet presence in this region, but would like to see the region as an area of cooperation of sovereign and equal states.

(See story on Page 2)

Soviets acting in frustration

By JACK MAURICE
Jerusalem Post Correspondent

PARIS. — The French Government feels the Soviet Union's decision to sever diplomatic relations with Israel confirms its inability to offer the Arabs anything more than verbal support after the setbacks to its diplomacy and military hardware during last week's lightning war. French officials were reluctant yesterday to comment on the fast-changing situation, but expressed the conviction that events fully justified President de Gaulle's refusal to side with either camp in readiness for the inevitable mediation and general Middle East settlement.

Despite the Moscow Communist summit, there is no fear in Paris of new military aid to Egypt since only massive intervention by the Soviet Air Force — unthinkable in the present context of East-West coexistence — could now reverse Israel's victory.

PARLIAMENT DEBATE

Premier Georges Pompidou is now trying to back Israel, in readiness for Thursday's full-dress Parliamentary debate on the Middle East. Jewish-born Maurice Schumann, Minister for Scientific Affairs, was on the verge of resignation in protest against President de Gaulle's policy, but M. Pompidou persuaded him to remain. There is also widespread indignation at the State radio's failure to condemn Egypt, in contrast with the French private networks whose coverage of the war's political and military aspects has been first class.

As peace seemed to be drawing nearer, France's Suez-time Premier, M. Guy Mollet, called on Israelis and Jews to "understand that nothing opposes them fundamentally. They must learn to live side by side and in the near future cooperate."

General Andre Beaufre, who commanded French land forces at Suez in 1956, said: "This 1967 campaign represents a model of military action aimed at creating an accomplished fact before international opinion can intervene. One cannot fail to admire the technical perfection of the campaign, the intelligence of its leaders and their skill in taking full advantage of circumstances as well as the energy and resolution of an entire people at arms roused to affirm its right to life."

Rumania for M.-E. negotiations

VIENNA (AP). — The Central Committee of the Rumanian Communist Party, in a statement devoid of any accusations against Israel, yesterday called for Israeli-Arab negotiations to ensure and consolidate peace in the Middle East.

The Rumanian statement made no mention of the East European summit meeting in Moscow on Friday nor of the declaration issued condemning Israel.

It said: "The course of events has demonstrated that the use of armed force cannot constitute a means of settlement of controversial problems between states and serves only the aims of imperialism with American imperialism at its head."

(Story — Page 2)

Nasser back as President

CAIRO (UPI). — Wild outbursts of jubilation in the National Assembly and the streets of Cairo greeted President Gamal Abdel Nasser's withdrawal of his resignation yesterday morning less than a day after he announced it.

Thousands of men and women wept joyfully in the streets, which were so packed Nasser could not drive to the Assembly to deliver his decision, when they heard that he was "submitting to the will of the people" by carrying on his leadership.

In an atmosphere changed from gloom to wild jubilation, groups ran through the streets shouting "Nasser, Nasser." Motorists sounded their horns in celebration.

In the National Assembly, one M.P. climbed on his desk and led the members in chanting "Nasser, Nasser, long live Nasser." Cairo Radio appealed to Egyptians to maintain order and not to harm foreigners or their property.

Similar demonstrations were reported from other Arab capitals, including Algiers, Beirut and Khartoum.

By 4 p.m. Cairo streets were returning to normal as hundreds of thousands of people went back to their homes and businesses. Traffic was able to move normally again.

It appeared that people were following the Government's appeal to stop the demonstration. Also they were undoubtedly exhausted after 20 hours of marching and shouting through the streets. Wailing Arabs roamed the streets during the night, urging Nasser to stay on.

Air raid sirens sounded and A.A. guns fired red flares into the sky. Reports circulated that the suburb of Heliopolis had been bombed, but later the police explained that the sirens had sounded and

(Continued on Page 2, Col. 1)

Mart commission votes for Israel

The European Common Market's Permanent Commission — the so-called Hallstein Committee — has recommended Israel's acceptance into the Market as an associate member.

Kol Yisrael's Paris correspondent, who quoted unofficial sources in Brussels for the report, added that the French delegate was the only one to oppose the recommendation. He said the decision was a political one and should have been taken by a higher body.

Our Paris Correspondent, Jack Maurice, writes that this was also the position of the Paris daily "Le Figaro," which yesterday questioned whether the commission had shown the necessary prudence in going beyond the drafting of a technical report "in as neutral terms as possible."

U.S. relieving oil shortage in Europe

WASHINGTON (Reuter). — American oil companies were yesterday authorized by the Government to step up oil shipments to Western Europe from the U.S. and the Caribbean to forestall shortages likely because of the Middle East war. The move was made possible by a decision, announced by the Department of the Interior, to treat the Western oil situation as an emergency.

The decision, sought by major U.S. companies for some days, enables them to pool resources and round up more ships to carry oil from the Americas to counter the stoppage of oil supplies from several Arab States, especially the key suppliers, Iraq and Kuwait.

Planes arriving here full

LYDDA AIRPORT.—Airplanes have started arriving here filled to capacity and returning largely empty — a complete reversal of the situation of the weeks preceding last Sunday.

Friday's arrivals included hundreds of Israelis, who immediately lined up at a special Army desk to receive their call-up notices on the spot.

The arrivals included a Belair charter flight, and flights of five foreign companies — Swissair, Alitalia, Sabena, BEA and KLM. All foreign airlines are expected to resume their flights today, with the possible exception of one unnamed airline.

With deep sorrow we announce the death of my husband

Engineer Eliahu Leszczynski ז"ל

The funeral will leave today, Sunday, June 11, 1967, at 3.15 p.m. from the Municipal Funeral Parlour in Rehov Dafna in Tel Aviv, for the Old Cemetery in Rehov Trumpeldor.

Mourned by his wife, Tania Lezczynski and his family, here and abroad.

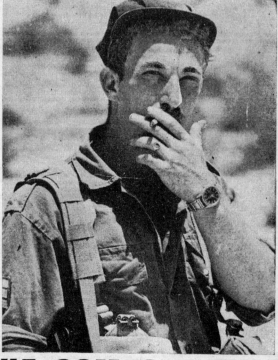

THE JERUSALEM POST

Published in Jerusalem, Israel, daily, except on Saturday by The Palestine Post Ltd. Founded in 1932 by Gershon AGRON. Registered at the G.P.O. Copyright of all material reserved; reproduction permitted only by arrangement. Editor: TED R. LURIE

Jerusalem: 9 Rehov Havatzelet, P.O.B. 81, Telephones 24233, 24321. Tel Aviv: 81 Rehov Nahlat Binyamin, P.O.Box 1125, Tel. 624213. Haifa: 34 Rehov Herzl, Hadar Hacarmel, P.O.Box 4810, Telephone 64594.

PRICE : 35 AGORA;
OR 45 FILS ON
WEST BANK

LBJ hints
Page 2
Patrick
O'Donovan
Page 3
Old City
functioning
Page 4

THURSDAY, JUNE 15, 1967 • SIVAN 7, 5727 • RABIA AWAL 8, 1387 • VOL. XXXVII, No. 11985*

200,000 at Western Wall in first pilgrimage since Dispersion

At the Western Wall — Some of the 200,000 Israelis who celebrated *Shavuot* at the wall of the Temple yesterday. (Goren photo)

ROAD TO THE WALL

For almost 20 years, since the War of Independence, the Jordan Government failed to honour its guarantee under the Armistice Agreement to permit the people of Israel access to the Western Wall in the Old City.

In the early years there were various arguments and excuses. In due course they realised that the U.N. force stationed at Government House and elsewhere, in which Israel had originally placed a good deal of confidence for the proper carrying out of the agreements, would not make any attempt to insist that they be carried out.

The Jordanians underestimated the deep resentment of this arbitrary attitude. Perhaps many Israelis, and even the citizens of Jerusalem, were only dimly aware of the fact that to be cut off from this ancient monument, from this physical link with the nation's past, gradually assumed the character of a new exile.

It is not chance that an almost life-size photographic reproduction of a section of the Wall occupies a place of honour in the new Knesset. The nation's historic link with its origin and history in this country is preserved chiefly in its writings — and foremost in the Bible, — in the nation's collective memory, and in archaeological finds. The Western Wall, and the living city of Jerusalem in which it stands, are the only visible, tangible survivors of a distant glory.

For centuries the Wall has been a place of pilgrimage to Jews, the religious first of all, but the non-religious as well. In the period of the British Mandate, people not only went to pray there, but annual pilgrimages, without any organization or appeal, mobilized practically every Jew whose feet would carry him there and back.

This tradition was renewed yesterday with an enthusiasm and fervour and in such numbers as must have astonished even those who were aware that these great blocks of stone that are said to date back to the Temple, recipients of the fervent prayers of so many generations, have acquired a national symbolism quite unmatched in Jewish life, which has dealt so largely in abstractions.

The two hundred thousand undertook the hot and laborious pilgrimage up Mount Zion and down again, down a long road that finally brought them face to face with the Wall, now strangely bare and exposed at the end of the large open space. Many more thousands may be expected in the coming days, and without doubt it will become the focus of every Jewish visitor's journey to Israel, and of that of many Gentiles as well.

Yesterday's pilgrims were the ordinary citizens, not the privileged who had already had a glimpse of the Wall since the capture of the Old City last week, and not those who will wait to visit it more conveniently. Old people made their way, and the lame, mothers with infants in carriages, and a multitude of children, and soldiers with a few hours of leave. They found that their city had served them well, in choosing a wide road, building the missing sections, providing an exit in a different direction to maintain one-way traffic, supplying police to control the crowds and soldiers to protect them, water to drink on the way, and in clearing the open space in front of the Wall to accommodate many thousands, and all in a surprisingly short time. In due course, no doubt, the great square created will be paved, and more trees planted to join the ancient fig tree fortunately preserved in the middle, and benches to rest on.

If there was anyone, here or elsewhere, who still had any shadow of doubt concerning the future of Jerusalem, yesterday's pilgrimage provided the answer: under no circumstances, whatever the pressures may be, will the citizens of Israel allow anyone to cut them off again from the Wall that stands at the centre of their city and is the essence and reason for its existence.

Egyptian troops, near collapse, arriving in Canal Zone

CAIRO. — Egyptian soldiers, many in a state of near collapse from thirst, hunger and fatigue, last night were arriving in the Suez Canal towns of Port Said, Ismailia and Suez after a gruelling trudge across Sinai.

Along the Suez Canal, more Egyptian soldiers were reported tramping home yesterday after the long walk across the forbidding desert.

The soldiers have been arriving in the three towns for the past two days, in pairs, singly and small groups. All were emaciated and covered with sand from head to foot. Many had congealed blood and sand over their arms and legs, and were covered with blisters.

Officials in Cairo said it was impossible to estimate the number of stragglers still plodding westward in 32-plus C. temperatures.

One officer who arrived in Port Said on Tuesday said he made it from El Arish — about 150 kms. — in four days. A private said he had to walk all the way from El Kuntilla, just across the international border from Israel, to Ismailia.

Informed sources said one of two international Red Cross officials who came to Cairo for relief was in Tel Aviv trying to
(Continued on Page 4, Col. 5)

Eban seen heading delegation to special U.N. Assembly

Jerusalem Post Diplomatic Reporter

Foreign Minister Abba Eban is likely to head a strengthened Israel delegation at the special U.N. General Assembly which is expected to meet on the Israel-Arab situation. Israel's Permanent Delegate, Mr. Gideon Rafael, is to return today to New York after two days of consultations here.

Should the Soviet Union at the Assembly table the resolution which was yesterday defeated in the Security Council — that Israel return to the 1949 armistice lines — observers estimate the motion would start off with about 40 to 50 assured votes from Soviet bloc, Arab, Moslem, and some neutralist countries. Adoption requires the votes of two-thirds of the 127-member Assembly.

At the Security Council, the U.N. came out clearly for direct Israel-Arab negotiations as a step towards permanent peace. The Soviet position against Israel is said to have hardened, but observers speculate that the possible attendance at the Assembly by Soviet Premier Kosygin might indicate talks between the Soviet leader and President Johnson.

WORLD PRESSURE

The significance of world pressures on Israel — now no longer the "underdog" — is that it could harden Arab resistance to a dialogue with Israel.

Another question is whether the Soviet Union failing at the Assembly would take unilateral action such as large-scale rearming of the Arabs.

It was not yet clear what stand the Latin American countries would take in the Assembly, as where differences of opinion arise between two countries, the Vatican's influence on these Catholic countries cannot be ruled out.

Official sources in Jerusalem, asked last night whether any Vatican representations have been received over Jerusalem, declined to comment. Yesterday, the Vatican weekly, "Osservatore Della Domenica," in an editorial said Israel started last week's fighting and that its recent declarations could make peace even more difficult.

It is understood that a Government statement on Holy Places is to be issued in Jerusalem today.

As regards the expected Assembly, observers predicted much lobbying and formulating of alternative draft resolutions.

Mrs. Golda Meir, now in the U.S. may participate in the Assembly session, it is understood.

Council rejects Soviet motion

UNITED NATIONS (UPI). — The Security Council yesterday rejected a Soviet resolution demanding condemnation of Israel and withdrawal of Israeli forces from Arab territory overrun in last week's war.

The Security Council then adjourned until 21.30 GMT (11.30 p.m. in Israel).

In separate votes, the Soviet Union, Bulgaria, Mali and India supported a call for Israel's condemnation, and these four countries were joined by Nigeria and Ethiopia in supporting a call for withdrawal of Israeli troops. The other 11 members are all abstained.

The Soviet Union had demanded a quick vote on its resolution to clear the decks for action on Foreign Minister Andrei Gromyko's demand for an emergency session of the General Assembly to take up anti-Israeli action in the Middle East crisis. The vote came at the end of a long morning meeting of the 15-nation Council, which planned to continue its own debate after a luncheon recess.

The second operative paragraph, demanding that Israel halt military activities and withdraw its forces behind the Armistice Lines, was defeated with six votes in favour, none against and nine abstentions.

With both operative sections defeated, the resolution as a whole was not put to the vote.

The Council has before it a U.S. resolution that calls for discussions among the parties directly concerned, on withdrawal of troops, renunciation of force, maintenance of vital international rights and establishment of a durable Middle Eastern peace.

THANT POLLS MEMBERS

Secretary-General U Thant began the poll of all U.N. members on the Soviet request for an emergency session of the General Assembly.

Before the vote, Britain called on the Council to consider appointment of a mediator to start peace talks between Israel and the Arabs. The French Ambassador, M. Roger Seydoux, told the Council the Soviet resolution either could "not be approved in the Assembly or, if approved, could not be enforced.

The Israeli delegate, Mr. Mordechai Kidron, denied any Israeli violation of the cease-fire and said any troop movements that have taken place were only behind Israeli lines. There was no advance on any front, he said.

Mr. Endalkachew Makonnen of Ethiopia told the Council an honourable peace in the Middle East must be based on an honourable foundation — "that is why we continue to insist on prompt withdrawal of Israeli forces." He said his Government was "dismayed" by recent statements by high-ranking Israeli officials expressing reluctance to accept a U.N. role in possible peace talks.

Prime Minister Levi Eshkol and Minister without Portfolio Menahem Begin visit troops in Sinai over the week-end.

Eshkol: To stay in Sinai till guarantees given

Israel went to war without any intention of territorial aggrandisement, but it will continue to hold the Sinai Peninsula until some permanent arrangement is made for freedom of sea passage through the Straits of Tiran and guarantees are given that Israel's security will not be threatened in the future.

This was stated on Tuesday by Prime Minister Levi Eshkol in a speech to a reserve unit encamped in the heart of the Sinai desert. The men, lined up in a brigade strength parade, were reviewed by the Prime Minister, accompanied by the Minister without Portfolio, Mr. Menahem Begin, and the commanding officers in the south — Aluf Yeshayahu Gavish, Aluf Ariel Sharon and Aluf Avraham Yoffe.

Mr. Eshkol stressed that the three weeks between the beginning of the Egyptian build-up and the outbreak of hostilities gave Cairo time to concentrate most of its forces in the Peninsula, and it became a death trap for Nasser's troops.

Israel regret at severance of ties

The Foreign Ministry spokesman on Tuesday said that the Israel Government has received with 'regret the decisions of Poland, Hungary and Yugoslavia to sever diplomatic relations with Israel. Israel holds the view that, even when differences of opinion arise between two countries, the severance of diplomatic ties does not serve to overcome the difficulties.

He noted that Israel was forced into a war by Egypt and her allies in order to defend her sovereignty against adversaries who aimed at her destruction. The Government of Israel is surprised that countries, which fought for their independence against the Nazi invaders, accepted at face value the declared intentions of the Arab states to annihilate Israel and showed no understanding for Israel's struggle.

Israel's aims have always been peaceful. Israel hopes that diplomatic relations will eventually be renewed and that these states will contribute towards assuring peace, stability and progress in this area, by adopting a more balanced attitude towards Israel.

Eban outlines policy to U.S. Ambassador

Jerusalem Post Diplomatic Reporter

Foreign Minister Eban met with U.S. Ambassador Walworth Barbour on Tuesday and set forth three main lines of thinking in Israel's policy. These were mutual observance of the cease-fire; direct negotiations with each of the neighbouring Arab Governments, and firm resolve to create a new situation in the Middle East in which Israel would have peace and security.

Mr. Eban, who initiated the 40-minute meeting in Jerusalem, did not go into further detail, authoritative sources said. Nor did the U.S. envoy define his Government's position.

SAPIR, PINCUS BACK FROM EMERGENCY TOUR

LYDDA AIRPORT. — The financial response of Western Jewry to Israel exceeded all expectations, Finance Minister Pinhas Sapir and the Jewish Agency Chairman, Mr. Arye Pincus, declared on their return here last night from an emergency fund-raising tour of the Americas and Europe.

Israel holds 5,499 Egyptian prisoners

TEL AVIV. — Israel holds 5,499 Egyptian prisoners of war, Aluf Shmuel Eyal, Adjutant-General, told reporters here yesterday. In addition, Israel prison camps hold 487 Jordanians and 33 Syrians. One hundred and seventy-nine wounded prisoners of various nationalities are in civilian hospitals.

Aluf Eyal categorically denied rumours that there were Russian prisoners in Israeli hands.

The Egyptian prisoners include 300 officers, among them nine generals and 10 colonels.

Sixteen Israeli soldiers are held captive by the Arabs. These eight and six seamen are in Egypt, two in Iraq, two in Syria, two in Jordan and one in Lebanon.

Aluf Eyal said he was discussing with an International Red Cross representative who arrived from Kantara yesterday, and with the permanent representative of the Red Cross in Israel, the possibility of an exchange of prisoners.

According to the Red Cross officer who arrived from Kantara, it seems that it was true that the Egyptians had lynched the Israeli pilot who had parachuted near Cairo.

MANY STILL WANDERING

Aluf Eyal said that many Egyptian soldiers are still wandering in the Sinai desert. Many of them have retained small arms, which they use against the Israelis. "We can only consider as prisoners those who give themselves up and enter prisoners' stockades." Water has been supplied by planes to some units in the Sinai. It was shared with the prisoners, when there were any in the units, Aluf Eyal said.

He revealed that yesterday an Israeli officer was shot in the stomach when he was addressing a group of Egyptians in Sinai over a loudspeaker, telling them to give themselves up as prisoners.

Meanwhile, Israel has allowed 6,000 prisoners to return to Egypt in the past two days without conducting any negotiations, it was announced here yesterday. Israel is also planning to work with the International Red Cross in a bid to find wounded Egyptian soldiers still stranded in Sinai. Defence Ministry spokesman Moshe Pearlman added.

He said that Israeli planes would fly over Sinai to search for Egyptians and that a Red Cross official would be allowed on each plane.

Mr. Pearlman said arrangements were concluded after Defence Minister Moshe Dayan met Mr. Marcel Boisard, a Swiss Red Cross representative, while touring the Suez Canal area yesterday. He brought Mr. Boisard with him to Tel Aviv and arrangements were then made. Mr. Boisard had crossed the Canal in a boat from the Egyptian side. (See also Col. 1 and 3)

3 killed by mine near Strip border

Three people were killed and two injured early on Monday morning when their jeep struck a mine in the Gaza border zone near Kibbutz Re'im. An Army ambulance coming to their aid blew up nearby. Both passengers, the driver and a doctor, were wounded. The casualties were removed by helicopter.

Local investigations suggest that the mine was laid after the cessation of hostilities.

Killed were Ya'acov Bulis, age 55, of the Jewish Agency, and two volunteers working in the settlement (because they were excused Army service); David Silberberg of Tel Aviv, and Yechiam Koloditsky of Holon.

Wounded in the jeep were kibbutz members Shlomo Banai and Eli Raz. The injured doctor is Aharon Zaretsky, of the Pediatrics Department in Ashkelon hospital.

On Tuesday morning, an explosive charge was discovered underneath a culvert on the road between Beersheba and Arad. The charge was dismantled.

SIX JEWS MURDERED

PARIS (UPI). — The American Jewish Committee yesterday stated that according to reports it had received from Tripoli, Libya, at least six Jews have been killed in recent anti-Israeli demonstrations.

TEL RESIGNS

AMMAN (Reuter). — Wasfi Tel, Minister of the Jordanian Royal Court, has offered his resignation which has been accepted by King Hussein, it was officially announced here last night.

The wedding celebration of David Ellman and Shaula Giladi has been cancelled. The *hupa* will take place as scheduled on Friday, June 16, at 2 p.m.

Kfar Hanassi

Jerusalem Municipality

NOTICE

Persons having property or other legal rights concerning real estate in the West Bank, Jerusalem district, are requested to submit full details concerning them as required by the questionnaire provided for this purpose, which is available at:

(A) Room No. 317, at the Municipality Secretariat, 22 Rehov Yafo;
(B) Municipal Information Bureau, 34 Rehov Yafo.

The completed questionnaire (two forms) should be sent to the office of the City Clerk, 22 Rehov Yafo, within two weeks of the publication of this notice. Note: It should be understood that handing in and receiving of the questionnaire by the Municipality is done for census purposes only.

TEDDY KOLLEK
Mayor

Jerusalem, June 13, 1967.

THE JERUSALEM POST

Published in Jerusalem, Israel, daily except on Saturday by The Palestine Post Ltd., Founded in 1932 by Gershon AGRON.
Registered at the G.P.O. Copyright of all material reserved; reproduction permitted only by arrangement. Editor: TED R. LURIE

Jerusalem: 9 Rehov Havatzelet, P.O.B. 81, Telephones 24233, 24321 — Tel Aviv: 81 Rehov Nahlat Binyamin, P.O.Box 1125, Tel. 624215 — Haifa: 34 Rehov Herzl, Hadar Hacarmel; P.O.Box 4810, Telephone 64594.

Keeping Posted, page 3
★
'Aliya' plans, page 4
★
Dinar called in, page 6

PRICE: 35 AGORA; OR 45 FILS ON WEST BANK

THURSDAY, JUNE 29, 1967 • SIVAN 21, 5727 • RABIA AWAL 22, 1387 • VOL. XXXVII, No. 11997*

OLD-NEW JERUSALEM BORDER IS ABOLISHED

FREE MOVEMENT FROM NOON TODAY

Jerusalem Post Reporter

The border between Old and New Jerusalem will be abolished today. The Municipality spokesman said last night that, as of noon today, access to all parts of the Capital will be open to all. The army will also relinquish control to the civilian police and the curfew in the Old City will be lifted.

All the laws of Israel and the ordinances of the Jerusalem Municipality will be put into effect and the city ordinance will be distributed in the old part of the city in Arabic, the spokesman said.

The city ordinances will bar all vehicular traffic within the walls of the Old City, except traffic for religious purposes. Establishment of bars and the sale of liquor within the walled city will also be prohibited.

In view of the greatly enlarged policing problem, the civilian police will be reinforced by border and military police units, the Police spokesman said last night. Jordanian constables of the Old City Force will be retained with the status of supernumeraries for the time being.

The new frontier between Jerusalem and the rest of the Western Bank will be guarded by the Army, and entry and exit will be by permit only.

All restrictions on buying and selling in the Old City will be lifted. However, business establishments will be required to obtain new licences.

CHARACTER OF SABBATH

The unification of Jerusalem will also alter the character of Sabbath observance in the city. According to Israel law all business premises must be closed one day of the week—the day depending on the owner's religious affiliation. Thus Moslem enterprises will be closed on Friday, Jewish enterprises on Saturday, and Christian enterprises on Sunday.

Municipal officials yesterday could not say what would happen on the question of public transport on Shabbat.

All former Old City municipal employees will be retained, but on a temporary basis. They may at a later stage, when the size of the new administration is determined, request permanent status by going through the regular procedures, the Municipal spokesman said.

The spokesman said that the Government has agreed to allocate all the funds necessary to cover the additional expenses incurred by the Municipality in order to extend its services to the new part of the city.

Access roads between the two parts of the City are also being improved. Mandelbaum Gate will be widened so as to straddle a major artery.

However, the Police appealed to the public last night not to rush to visit Jerusalem in the first few days, at least until some more passable entrances have been arranged. For the time being, the only entrances open to vehicles are Mandelbaum Gate and the dirt road through the Pagi quarter. Both are overtaxed with the heavily restricted traffic permitted till now.

Access on foot is possible through the Jaffa and Dung Gates or through Kafr Sur Bahir.

U.S. denies Israel claim to Jerusalem

WASHINGTON (UPI). — The U.S. yesterday protested Israel's claim to Jerusalem. State Department spokesman Robert McCloskey told newsmen that the "hasty administrative action taken today cannot be regarded as determining the future of the holy places or the status of Jerusalem in relation to them."

Mr. McCloskey added, "The U.S. has never recognized such unilateral action by any of the states in the area as governin the international status of Jerusalem." U.S. policy, he said, "will be governed by the President's statement of June 29 and the White House statement of this morning."

The statement urged Israel to avoid any quick annexation of the Old City of Jerusalem. "The President is confident that the wisdom and good judgment of those

(Continued on Page 6, Col. 6)

Moves will ensure no discrimination

The Foreign Ministry spokesman declared last night that the basic purpose of the ordinance concerning the fusion of the Jerusalem municipal areas is to provide full municipal and social services to all inhabitants of the city. The fusion of the municipal services will ensure that no social inequality and legal differences in respect of services, welfare and education enjoyed by all inhabitants of Jerusalem will exist. From now on all residents will be in a position to receive all the services normally extended by the municipality such as water, electricity, public health, welfare, education, etc.

As far as the protecting of the holy places is concerned, the spokesman continued, the law adopted by the Knesset on Tuesday guarantees the fullest protection of the holy places from any violation whatsoever and the free access to them. The law also calls for consultations between the competent Israel authorities and representatives of the various religions with a view to the implementation of this law. The law thus ensures for the first time in decades the respect and inviolability of the holy places of all three monotheistic religions, he said.

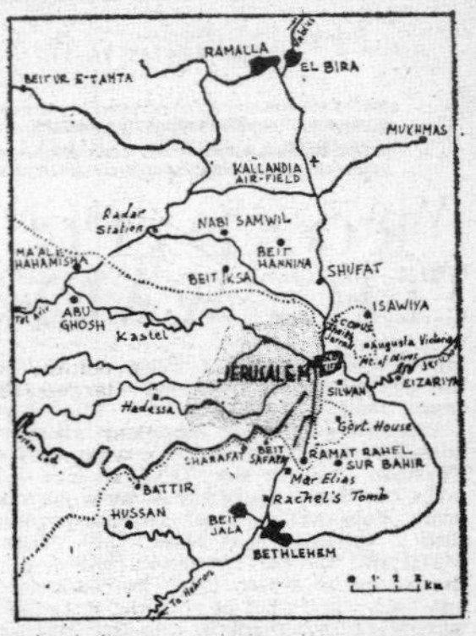

The new city limits of Jerusalem will run northwards between Beit Iksa and Beit Hanina to include Kalandia airfield. To the east the city will include Shufat and Isawiya, embrace Mt. Scopus and the Mt. of Olives, and run south, west of Eizariya to Sur Bahir and to a point just north of Rachel's Tomb, including Mar Elias and all of Beit Safafa.

Order unites Holy City

Jerusalem Post Reporter

"I am profoundly aware of the great historic responsibility which has devolved upon us," Mayor Teddy Kollek said yesterday morning after Interior Minister Moshe Shapiro handed him an administrative order enlarging the Capital city's limits to include the Old City. The order was contained in a specially printed copy of the official gazette, "Reshumot."

At the ceremony in Mr. Shapiro's office, the Minister recalled that "Jerusalem was never divided, even in the days of the Tribes. It was a *unicum*. I am certain that from today, for all time, it will be a united city."

To Mr. Kollek had fallen the privilege of presiding over a great, united Jerusalem, he went on. "Let us see to it that peace and mutual understanding shall prevail among all the city's residents. Let us see to it that all its residents shall enjoy all the great and sacred things which the city contains."

Mr. Kollek presented Mr. Shapiro with the emblem of Jerusalem, which contains the insignia of the last coin minted in Jerusalem when Bar-Kochba briefly ruled the city about 1,830 years ago.

Last night the Mayor told reporters: "I am certain that within a short time

(Continued on Page 2, Col. 4)

JERUSALEM UNITED

WEDNESDAY, 20th Sivan 5727 of the Jewish Calendar, 28th June 1967 of the Christian Era and 21st Rabia Awal 1387 of the Moslems, is a memorable date.

It is 23 days after Jordanian forces in the Old City, entrenched on the heights dominating Jewish Jerusalem, opened their artillery bombardment of the Israel Capital. It is 21 days after the Israel Defence Forces occupied the Old City and established Jewish administration there for the first time since the city was levelled by the Romans 1,897 years less three months ago.

It is the day on which the Jerusalem Declaration was officially published by the Minister of Interior of the sovereign State of Israel. It is the day on which this Declaration gave legal expression to the unification of the hitherto divided city of Jerusalem.

This capital city of the State of Israel has been the focal point of prayer and longing in the course of long tragedy-ridden centuries in the history of the Jewish people. Jerusalem suffered at the hands of nature and man. Earthquakes and invaders rocked or sacked the city time and again. Its population was killed or exiled. Its buildings and houses of prayer destroyed. Its fate packed with grief and sorrows. Undeterred by recurrent catastrophe, Jews throughout the world and throughout centuries stubbornly persisted in praying to return here and rebuild the city.

The foundation has now been laid for the replanning, repair and development of the united city. Prime Minister Eshkol as well as the Mayor of the city, Mr. Kollek, have shown a sense of the great historic responsibility arising out of the realization of this age-old dream. Their words and actions have indicated that they place their faith in inter-communal and inter-faith cooperation, so badly needed in this city and in the entire region.

The unprocedented gathering of 40 religious dignitaries of the world's three monotheistic religions in Mr. Eshkol's office Tuesday night, some of them men of great standing, has shown that the spirit of ecumenism, preached in Rome, is being implemented in Jerusalem. Three Patriarchs, two Chief Rabbis, the Mufti of Jerusalem, four Kadis, six Archbishops and a number of other spiritual leaders met in a spirit of goodwill and cooperation. Chief Rabbi Unterman, pointing out the great love for Jerusalem of all faiths represented here, invoked the words of the Prohpet Micah, according to which each religion should worship God according to its own faith.

The present harmony should not blind us to the magnitude of the challenges ahead. It may take time for Israel's friends to realize that the unification of Jerusalem, what they now term "Israel's unilateral action" is not in the interest of Israel alone. There is every reason to believe that it will prove a blessing for the City's whole population and for the genuine religious interests of the great religions.

Never before has any administration of this city paid so much attention to the universal character of Jerusalem as Israel is doing. Neither the Romans, nor the Byzantines, nor the Moslems and certainly not the Crusaders showed such concern for the rights and traditions of other religions. This also applies to the 19 years of Jordanian rule over the Old City—a period in which not only Jews but Israeli Moslems, were refused access to their holy places, and Christian pilgrims were admitted on sufferance on rare occasions. This has now been changed. The guarantee of freedom of worship contained in Israel's Declaration of Independence will pervade the place, as is befitting the City of Peace.

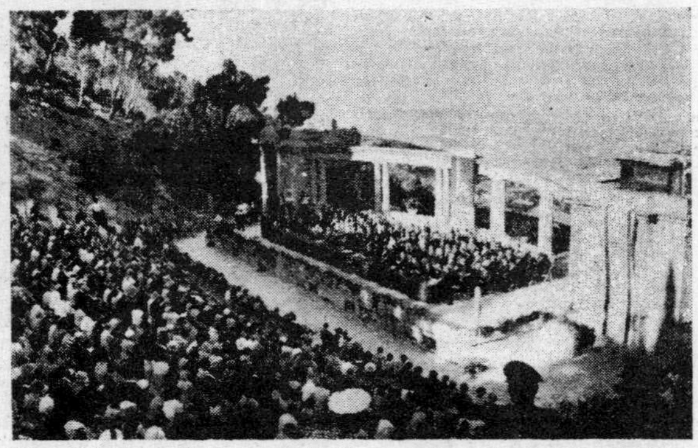

The crowded open-air theatre on Mt. Scopus during yesterday's award of honorary doctorates on the old Hebrew University campus. (Photo by Harris)

Shazar and Rabin head list of new honorary doctors

By ASHER WALLFISH
Jerusalem Post Reporter

The nation's first citizen, President Zalman Shazar, and its first soldier, Rav-Aluf Yitzhak Rabin, were awarded honorary doctorates by the Hebrew University of Jerusalem at its Mount Scopus amphitheatre yesterday afternoon. Six other personalities were also so honoured for their contribution to the advancement of the University and the country at large.

University President Eliahu Elath, who recalled that he had attended the opening of the University at the same spot 42 years ago, conferred honorary doctorates of philosophy on President Shazar, the Chief of Staff, Mr. Louis Boyar of Los Angeles, Bank of Israel Governor Mr. David Horowitz, Dr. Helen Kagan, Mr. Pinhas Rosen, M.K., Prof. Aryeh Dostrovsky and Prof. Moshe Zvi Segal. Prof. Reinhold Niebuhr, who is being honoured by the university with a doctorate but was prevented from attending by ill health, will receive his degree at a special ceremony.

Seated on the platform — against the background of the Dead Sea and the Wilderness of Judea — were the entire Senate of the University. In front of them, flanking Mr. Elath, were President Shazar, Premier Eshkol, Chief of Staff Rabin and the other recipients of the honorary degrees, Rector Rotenstreich, Faculty Deans, and other members of the Executive Council, and officers of the American, British and Canadian Friends of the University.

In the front row of the audience that filled the open air theatre were the Minister of Defence and almost all the Cabinet Ministers; Army *alufim;* the wives of the President, Premier and Chief of Staff; and the white-haired octogenarian father of Rav-Aluf Rabin.

Rav-Aluf Rabin stole the show, with his air of good-humoured embarrassment at finding himself in such unusual company and shaking his head at the pronouncement of his new title, "Doctor of Philosophy." In a compellingly sincere and unadorned speech he stressed that the honour bestowed on him was really a tribute to his comrades-in-arms.

The Chief of Staff, who was repeatedly

(Continued on Page 2, Col. 3)

'Compromise' motion at U.N.

UNITED NATIONS (Reuter). — A group of non-aligned states formally tabled a General Assembly resolution yesterday demanding the immediate unconditional withdrawal of Israeli troops from Arab lands, but omitting any condemnation clause.

Mr. Danilo Lekic, chief delegate of Yugoslavia, interrupted the general debate formally to introduce the new draft, which countered Soviet, American, and Albanian proposals, none of which was thought to have any chance of endorsement.

Mr. Lekic said the non-aligned countries had concerted their efforts to obtain agreement on the resolution, which would request that Israel withdraw its troops behind the old Armistice lines.

The resolution clashed with the U.S.-backed Israeli position that a precondition for withdrawal must be guarantees of Israel's right to exist and to freedom of innocent passage though the Gulf of Akaba and the Suez Canal.

Netherlands Foreign Minister J.M.A.H. Luns, came out flatly against the Soviet draft resolution and said an Israel withdrawal cannot "in itself bring about durable peace."

Dr. Luns said: "We have heard many times during this debate how intolerable a pressure has been created for the Arab States because of the military occupation by the armies of Israel of quite large Arab territories. I will not deny that this is an argument seriously to be considered, but I think it would be less than fair were I not to remind this Assembly of the equally intolerable pressure exercised upon Israel

(Continued on Page 6, Col. 2)

Hussein, Johnson fail to agree

WASHINGTON (Reuter). — President Johnson and King Hussein of Jordan conferred at the White House for two hours yesterday, but failed to reach an identity of views on means of restoring peace in the Middle East.

"Although there was not an identity of views, the exchange proved to be of definite value," a White House spokesman announced after the King's departure.

The President greeted Hussein with a long, firm handshake when the king arrived from the airport in a limousine flying the American and the royal Jordanian flags.

The two leaders had what the White House described as a "working lunch" together and were expected to continue their discusssions. Also at the White House and ready to participate in the talks were Defence Secretary Robert McNamara, Under-Secretary of State Nicholas Katzenbach, and other senior officials.

MARTIAL LAW IN RANGOON

RANGOON (AP). — General Ne Win, Chairman of Burma's Revolutionary Council, imposed martial law on parts of riot-torn Rangoon last night after a Chinese Embassy official was reported to have been stabbed to death by two Burmans. The Burma Broadcasting Service announced that two Burmans climbed over the Embassy's back wall and fatally stabbed a member of the staff, and wounded another. It said Embassy personnel captured one of the attackers and handed him over to the Burmese authorities. The other escaped.

Man blown up at LeninMausoleum

MOSCOW (UPI). — An unidentified elderly man haranguing a small crowd near Lenin's Tomb in Red Square was suddenly blown to bits by a crude home-made grenade in his coat pocket. Witnesses said the man, apparently in his eighties, was shabbily dressed and seemed to have come to Moscow from the country.

They said he approached Lenin's granite mausoleum and began shouting at passers-by about the situation in the Middle East. Suddenly he exploded.

Syrian Ba'th reveals anti-Nasser plot

The Secretary-General of the Syrian Trade Union movement, Khaled el-Jundi, has revealed at a conference of Syrian trade union leaders that, on June 9, following the Egyptian defeat, an attempt was made to "dispose" of Abdul Nasser. This was reported by the Syrian Ba'th journal, "A-Thawra," quoted yesterday by Kol Yisrael's Arabic service. Jundi did not specify who the plotters were, beyond describing them as the "fifth column."

NEW YORK STOCK EXCHANGE

Closing Wednesday, June 28, 1967

Dow Jones Industrial Average 868.85 — 0.52

Volume of shares traded 9,310,000

Admiral	23½	IntT&T	96⅛
Alcoa	83¾	Litton	104¼
AmT&T	58⅝	McDon.-D	46¼
Anacon	47⅜	MinnMM	82
BethStl	32½	Monsan	43¾
Boeing	106½	OlinMath	70⅛
Burroughs	137	ParkeDav	27
Chrysler	41	PaRR	68⅞
Comsat	72	Polaroid	208
CrownCork	59⅝	RCA	50¼
DowCh	80⅛	ReynTob	40
duPont	151½	SearsRoe	55⅛
EKodak	135	SperRd	35¼
FairCam	94½	StONJ	60¾
FordMot	51⅛	TransWAir	64⅛
GenElec	87¾	USSteel	43⅞
GenMot	78	WestgEl	54⅛
Homestke	44¾	Woolworth	28⅝
IntBusM	499	XeroxCp	283¾
IntPap	29⅝	ZenithRad	62½

Supplied by Albert Kaplan, Israel Representative A.L. Stamm & Co., members N.Y. Stock Exch.

See page 3 of this issue for Order for Men and Women to Report for Registration for Defence Service.

THE JERUSALEM POST

Published in Jerusalem, Israel, daily except on Saturday by The Palestine Post Ltd., Founded in 1932 by Gershon AGRON. Registered at the G.P.O. Copyright of all material reserved; reproduction permitted only by arrangement. Editor: TED R. LURIE

Jerusalem: 9 Rehov Havatzelet, P.O.B. 81, Telephones 24233, 24321 Tel Aviv: 81 Rehov Nahlat Binyamin, P.O.Box 1125, Tel. 624215 Haifa: 34 Rehov Herzl, Hadar Hacarmel; P.O.Box 4810, Telephone 64594.

SUNDAY, OCTOBER 22, 1967 • TISHRI 18, 5728 • REJAB 19, 1387 • VOL. XXXVII, No. 12092

PRICE: 35 AGORA

Sde Boker Opening page 2
★
I.C.C.Y.'s project page 5
★
Port strike page 6

Egypt missile sinks Israel destroyer

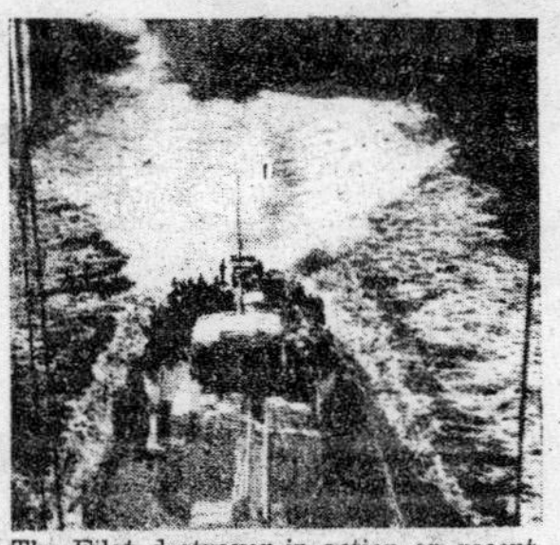

The Eilat destroyer in action on recent naval manoeuvres.

The destroyer Eilat sank last night after being hit by missiles from an Egyptian ship inside Port Said. The Eilat was 14 miles from Port Said in Israel territorial waters opposite a place called Romani in Sinai, the army spokesman announced.

A massive air-sea rescue operation was still underway at press time, and reports on survivors are expected only early this morning.

The attack came at 5.30 p.m. (Israel time) and the "abandon ship" order was given at 8. It sank shortly afterwards.

According to the Army spokesman, the ship reported in the late afternoon that it was under attack by Egyptian naval units and that it had been hit. Naval and air forces set out for the area to relieve the ship and to rescue survivors.

The U.N. was notified that the Israeli forces in the area were there solely for the purpose of rescuing survivors.

The missile is believed to have been fired by a Comar or Ossa missile-carrying craft with a range of up to 30 km.

The final message was received at 20.00 hours. It was: "They hit me and we are abandoning ship."

The evacuation was orderly in the ship's lifeboats and life rafts.

It is believed that only one missile struck the Eilat, but at a vulnerable spot.

The ship was hit at 5.30 and sank at 8 p.m.

The Central Negev Hospital in Beersheba was put on alert to handle wounded. The main hall was readied as a clearing station, the role it played during the Six Day War. Doctors were brought in from as far away as Tel Hashomer, as well as one staff physician flown back to Beersheba from Eilat.

The hospital authorities were told to be ready to handle burn cases.

The destroyer Eilat, one of the two largest warships in the Israel Navy, was acquired from Britain in 1956. It is of the Zambezi class and was commissioned in 1944. Its displacement is 2,500 tons, length 363 feet, width 36 feet and draft 16 feet. At the time it was taken over its registered speed was 31 knots.

Two destroyers of the same class were sold by Britain to Egypt about the same time.

The warships were welcomed with full naval pomp when they steamed into Haifa on June 20, 1956. Mr. David Ben-Gurion, then Prime Minister, was at the quayside with almost all members of the Government, and a squadron of jets flew over in greeting.

Egypt's version

CAIRO (Reuter). — Egyptian naval units sank an Israeli naval unit north of Port Said yesterday afternoon, Cairo Radio said last night.

The radio, quoting a spokesman of the Supreme Command of the Armed Forces, said that an Israeli naval unit approached the Egyptian coast north of Port Said at 1700 local time (1500 GMT) yesterday.

The spokesman added that the unit entered Egyptian territorial waters at 1730 local time. "Some of our naval units engaged and sank it," he said. All Egyptian naval units have returned safely to base, the spokesman said.

Further reports — officially unconfirmed — said fighting had erupted in Port Said between Egyptian and Israeli forces. An air raid siren sounded in Port Said at 6 p.m. following the naval engagement, reports said. These reports did not say whether it was an Israeli raid over the city.

WAR OR PEACE

THE full dimensions of yesterday's Egyptian attack on an Israel destroyer were still unclear last night at press time. The army's announcement of immediate rescue operations pointed to the grim possibility of large-scale casualties.

What appeared to be clear already, however, was that the ship was outside Egyptian waters and that it was attacked without provocation by what the army believes was a missile-carrying ship in or near Port Said.

Without doubt the attack was more than a grave violation of the cease-fire, but an act bordering on outright war. It is a further indication of Egypt's unrelenting belligerency, and the fragility of the present cease-fire. Cairo in past weeks has resumed her war-like operations throughout the Suez area, building fortifications and evacuating the civilian population.

These preparations together with yesterday's attack should make clear to all the continued inability of Nasser and his colleagues to think in other than military terms. Defeat in war appears to have altered nothing. Israel's policy after victory, on the other hand, was based on the possibility, however remote, of an ultimate peace settlement.

Israel will back any effort aimed at fostering peace. But it will resist all attempts at circumventing a real solution and surrendering Israel's hard-won advantages in return for ambiguous formulas. Those currently eager to bring forward proposals should be reminded that the only alternative to peace is war. Whoever encourages the Arab governments in their rejection of Israel's outstretched hand, is doing a disservice to the cause of peace. What is worse, such efforts may help lay the groundwork for a fourth war in this region.

As Foreign Minister Eban said before returning to the U.N., every proposal will be examined and judged on its merits. In the case of the possible appointment of a U.N. mediator for this region, as has been suggested, Israel would be prepared to receive him provided his task was clearly restricted to bringing the conflicting sides to the conference table.

Similarly, Israel will not object to reopening the Suez Canal. But this will only be made possible if Israeli ships will also pass unimpeded through the canal, and if the re-opening is not pursued at the price of a withdrawal of Israel troops from the Canal Zone without a peace settlement, as suggested by Moscow.

However, as long as the Arab states maintain their bellicose stand no peaceful solution to the area's problems will be found. What is needed is authentic moderation — a willingness to renounce war and belligerence. This will have to come from those who preach belligerence and not from those who advocate a peace settlement.

11 saboteurs surrender meekly in Gilboa area

By ZE'EV SCHUL,
Jerusalem Post Military Reporter

TEL AVIV. — Eleven men wearing the camouflage uniforms of the "Palestine Liberation Front" trooped sheepishly out of a little cave in the Gilboa region during the early afternoon hours of Monday last week. The saboteurs surrendered to a mixed unit of the Army and the Border Police. A few minutes earlier a grenade had been tossed into the cave opening after the gang members had failed to respond to an order to come out and surrender.

The gang was caught the same day it had forded the Jordan River. The military and police units started combing the area after receiving information from the Security Service. Some of the 11 men were suffering from light injuries caused by the grenade and all appeared to be dazed from its blast.

All are cooperating with their interrogators and have provided a mass of new information implicating Jordan in providing assistance and cooperating with the Fatah as well as P.L.F. gangs.

According to authoritative Military sources here on Friday, evidence gathered from the latest group and groups captured earlier points to a clear-cut division of tasks between the Syrians on the one hand and the Jordanians on the other. Assistance is also provided by the "Palestinian Commando" (or 421st Battalion) of the Iraqi Army units now stationed in Jordan.

The freely-talking 11 confirmed that the Syrians had trained them, provided them with arms and then put them over the border near Dar'a, some 40 kms. away from the Israel frontier. They had trained at the Duma camp, near Damascus. They also received their equipment there (including Chinese sub-machineguns) and were finally accompanied by a Syrian intelligence officer, a Captain Ahmed Jabril, to the Jordanian border.

After reaching Jordan territory the men contacted the Iraqi unit which provided them with Land-Rovers to bring them into the Jordan Valley (Jordanian side) near one of the river fords.

Military sources point out that the Jordanians did not interfere with the gang despite the fact that the Jordanians have officially and repeatedly repudiated all association with saboteurs. The Jordanians have not only desisted from interfering with the free movement of these gangs but seem to have adopted a policy supporting anything that might possibly weaken Israel's rule in the West Bank.

The Jordanians now merely "process" the saboteurs, taking pictures of them and then let them do very much as they please. It is now very much the fashion in Jordan to be seen in camouflage battle dress and with badges of the Assifah (Fatah) or P.L.F. units. It is also not unusual to see these men carrying their weapons. Since these are of either Russian

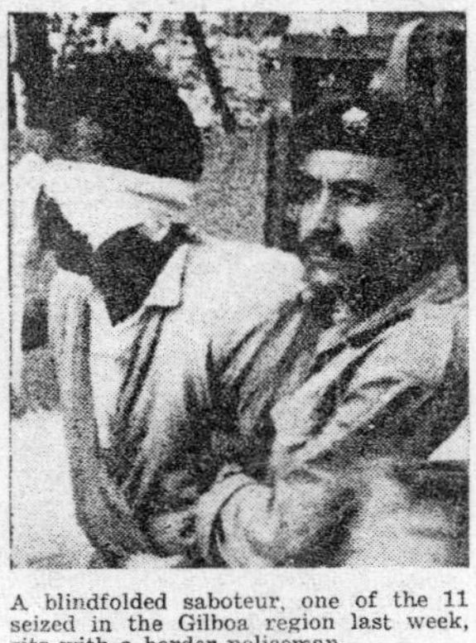

A blindfolded saboteur, one of the 11 seized in the Gilboa region last week, sits with a border policeman.
(Photo by Ippa)

or Chinese manufacture and differ from anything in use with the Jordanian forces there could be no mistaking them for anything but what they are, *The Jerusalem Post* was told.

In the case of the 11 men captured last week, the gang stayed for one week on the Jordan side, spending their time in coffee houses and "talking shop" with Jordanian Army officers. Other groups met with the chiefs of the Jordanian Intelligence and other high ranking officers. They, as well as other gangs which had passed through Jordan previously were briefed on what they, the Jordanians, knew about the positions of the Israel Defence Force units on the West Bank.

The gang forded the Jordan during the early morning hours of last Monday and was caught during the afternoon hours of the same day. Only two of the 11 are West Bank residents. One comes from a refugee camp in Lebanon and the rest are all former Palestinians, from the refugee camps near Damascus. All but the two West Bank men left the country in 1948. They are from 20 to 30 years old and are unemployed or apprentices who were tempted by the offer of a salary of 200 Syrian pounds per month plus "bonuses," and the vague promise that their families "would be taken care of" should anything happen to them.

Seren Avi, who was in charge of the unit which captured the 11 men on Friday, gave military reporters his personal account of the action.

"On Monday, I met a unit of the

(Continued on Page 6, Col. 6)

Protests on Vietnam sweep the world

WASHINGTON (UPI). — Anti-war demonstrators tried to storm the doors of the Pentagon yesterday, but were turned back by civilian U.S. marshals, backed up by soldiers with fixed bayonets.

The clash took place in front of the main hall entrance to the huge building, the nerve centre of the U.S. Defence Department.

Several demonstrators, including novelist Norman Mailer, were arrested.

Earlier thousands of demonstrators converged on the Pentagon in a massive protest demonstration against the Vietnam War. At the same time thousands of paratroopers and police stood by inside and outside the buildings.

Estimates of the total number of demonstrators varied, and leaders claimed that upwards of 150,000 were in the columns moving across the Potomac River towards the Pentagon. Police put the figure at much less, but other observers said about 60,000 to 70,000 people were taking part.

Anti-Vietnam war demonstrations swept major cities of Europe yesterday in a day of international solidarity with the Washington rally. Demonstrators marched in Paris, Dublin, Stockholm, Oslo, Amsterdam, Frankfurt, Moscow, Berlin and Munich. Smaller demonstrations were reported elsewhere in Europe and in other parts of the world.

The Washington rally, winding-up a week of anti-war protests, started off rowdily as counter-demonstrators clambered on a podium on the steps of the Lincoln Memorial, where a meeting was being held. In the Pentagon itself it was "business as usual." President Johnson was in the White House at the time.

The centre of Washington had a deserted village air with comparatively few shoppers. Tight security measures were imposed on the House of Representatives side, but the situation at the Senate wing was more relaxed. The demonstrators included large contingents of draft-age students from all over the country.

(Reuter, UPI, AP)

TEL AVIV PROTEST

TEL AVIV. — More than 50 persons demonstrated against "American aggression in Vietnam" outside the U.S. Embassy in Tel Aviv about noon yesterday. The protests was organized by Maki, the Israel Communist Party, and a number of overseas volunteers took part.

The demonstrators, who carried placards, stood outside the embassy for about 40 minutes and afterwards dispersed quietly.

(Itim)

South Vietnam votes today fo Lower House

SAIGON (Reuter). — South Vietnamese voters go to the polls again today to complete the final stage of the constitutional framework of their new Government.

Few observers here believe that anything like the 83 per cent of the country's 5.8 million registered voters who turned out for last month's presidential and Senate elections will be persuaded to vote.

They point out that the elections for a 137-seat Lower House is the fifth ballot the Vietnamese have been faced with in little over a year and many people show signs of apathy.

After the nine-year rule of President Ngo Dinh Diem, assassinated in 1963, a series of *coups* finally led to stabilization and last September's elections for a 117-member Constituent Assembly, which ends its work at the end of this month. It finally wrote a constitution and framed an electoral law for the current return to constitutional rule.

Eban sees Brown

LONDON (INA). — Foreign Minister Abba Eban spent one day in London on his way back to the U.N. Yesterday he met Foreign Secretary George Brown. He was accompanied by Israel Ambassador Aharon Remez.

They had a friendly exchange of views which did not result, however, in any shift of positions by either side, it is understood.

Mr. Eban left Israel on Friday after several days of consultations in Jerusalem.

Before leaving, Mr. Eban said that in view of the numerous proposals being considered, it was important for the Israel Government to clarify that it remains steadfast on its Middle East stand.

New motion on M. E.—Thant

UNITED NATIONS. — Secretary-General U Thant said yesterday that a new resolution had been drawn up for dealing with the Middle East crisis through Security Council action. But he said he did not know what the attitudes to it were on the part of Council members "individually or collectively."

U Thant told reporters he was "aware of the text of a resolution" — implying that he had been consulted about it. His disclosure followed persistent denials by many delegates close to the backstage talks that a specific formulation had been put on paper.

The backstage consultations yesterday entered a new, and reportedly somewhat more optimistic, phase, when Egyptian Foreign Minister Mahmoud Riad and U.S. Ambassador Arthur Goldberg again discussed the problem. Mr. Goldberg was understood to be planning a quick trip to Washington to report to the State Department on his talks. The American attitude, described by the Arabs as "inflexibly pro-Israeli," has been widely blamed for the slow progress of the negotiations.

Earlier, it was reported that the Security Council is expected to be called into session next Wednesday or Thursday to debate the Middle East situation. Six of the 10 non-permanent members of the 15-nation Council reached tentative agreement on Friday to call the Council into session to discuss a broad Latin American formula for a settlement. It was virtually a repeat of the Latin American resolution which failed to pass last summer's emergency session of the General Assembly. The six members are to meet again tomorrow. They include, Argentina, Brazil, Ethiopia, Mali, Nigeria and India.

But U Thant added that a meeting this week appears unlikely. He said General Assembly President Corneliu Manescu of Rumania doubts that agreement to meet can be achieved this week. *(Reuter, UPI)*

M. E. envoy — Page 2

YADIN REPORTS NEW QUMRAN SCROLL

The discovery of a new Qumran scroll was revealed by Professor Yigael Yadin in his lecture to the Israel Exploration Society annual conference at Binyenei Ha'ooma in Jerusalem last night. Prof. Yadin said it was too early to describe the circumstances of its acquisition and all that he would say was that the scroll was "kept illegally and under extremely bad conditions, which — in addition to the "natural" deterioration emanating from the lapse of 2,000 years — have further damaged its state of preservation."

He said he was calling the manuscript the "Temple Scroll" because of its detailed description of the Temple in Jerusalem.

The scroll is written on very fine parchment and its length (including all fragments and incomplete columns) comes to 8.6 metres, which makes it the longest scroll ever to have been found (the complete Isaiah scroll is 7.34 metres in length). In its present state, 66 columns — complete or fragmentary — are extant.

The unrolling of this scroll, which was difficult owing to its condition, lasted several months and was done by Mr. David Shenhav. Referring to his announcement as "Jerusalem of Parchment," Prof. Yadin said the scroll was unique in its contents, which deals with four groups of subjects:

1) Enumeration of the sacrifices according to the feasts; among them heretofore unknown feasts such as the "the feast of the wine" and "the feast of the oil," all celebrated by the special calendar of the Qumran Sect.

2) A large collection of halakhot (rules), dealing with varied subjects, amongst them ritual uncleanness and purification, in which the Pentateuch is often quoted with many interesting additions.

3) A description of the Temple: almost half the scroll deals with the plan of the Temple and details of the work therein. This part describes in detail the Temple and its courts, the Holy vessels etc., giving minutae of the measurements. The description is not identical with that in the known sources up to date, and it could be assumed that it refers to the Temple of times to come. The description abounds in terms and details which are particularly important to the understanding of the Temple plan and the teachings of the Sect. It is also full of details about the rules of cleanness appertaining to the Temple and its vicinity.

4) Some of the scroll's columns deal with the statutes of the King, in particular with unknown rules about the phases of preparedness and mobilization of the people of Israel when a war of extermination threatens them from an attacking foe. This description differs entirely from the description of the war in the scroll of, the "War of the Sons of Light against the Sons of Darkness," which concerns itself with an offensive war at the "end of the days."

One of the interesting, yet surprising things, said Prof. Yadin, is the style of the scroll, which is given as the word of God, and in most cases in the first person. The date of the copy, on paleographical grounds, is the Herodian period, that is the second half of the first century B.C.E. or the beginning of the first century C.E. and there is no doubt that the scroll was discovered in Qumran, he added.

Professor Yadin is still engaged in deciphering the scroll and he said he hopes to be able to publish more in due course. Meanwhile, *The Jerusalem Post* learns that a Bethlehem antique dealer has engaged an Israeli lawyer to recover what he calls his "lawful property." He points out that he was negotiating for the sale of the scroll which he says is worth "millions of pounds" to Israel (he declines to state through what channels) before the Six Day War.

Israeli authorities point out that the scroll had rightfully belonged to the Jordanian Government, under whose law all such antiquities are State property and that the jurisdiction invested in the Jordan Government had passed into the hands of the Israeli authorities in the occupied areas. They add that the antique dealer has recourse to the due process of law if he believes that he has been unjustly treated.

(Opening of the Conference — Page 6)

M.-E. desalting plan is an 'inducement to peace'

By CHARLES T. FENYVESI
POST—Near East Report Bureau

WASHINGTON. — Admiral Lewis L. Strauss — a head of the Atomic Energy Commission under the Eisenhower Administration — took issue yesterday with the State Department, which has described his proposal for the setting up of three giant nuclear desalting plants in the Middle East as "premature." Admiral Strauss, testifying at hearings in the Senate Committee on Foreign Relations, said the plan was "an inducement" to the establishment of peace in the region.

Two of the plants would be on Israel's Mediterranean coast and the third, a smaller one, at the north end of the Gulf of Akaba, in either Israel or Jordan. The plants would yield one billion gallons of fresh water and 1.4m. kilowatts of electricity a day.

Admiral Strauss referred to a letter to the committee, signed by Assistant Secretary of State William B. Macomber, Jr., which said: "Regional cooperation can advance the cause of peace, but we believe that effective economic cooperation between Israel and the Arab states will have to be founded on political understanding."

The plan was submitted to the Senate by Sen. Howard H. Baker, Jr., (R-Tenn.) and has 52 Republican and Democratic cosponsors. In his testimony yesterday Admiral Strauss expressed confidence that much of the estimated cost of $1 billion could be raised from private sources in the U.S. and Britain. He reiterated that the plan would help solve "the two fundamental problems" in the region: "water and displaced population." He suggested the setting up of a non-national corporation, in which the U.S. Government would subscribe one half of the stock, the balance to be offered for public subscription. The amount initially raised would be $200m., which would be used to begin the construction of the first plant.

The Committee on Foreign Relations is expected to recommend the adoption of the proposals. The committee's reservations centre around the financial burden the U.S. Government might have to bear.

The question remains what the Administration will decide to do with the plan. Specialists in the Department of Interior are strongly in favour of it. Some of Israel's friends here feel that the plants might help to provide a solution to refugee unemployment.

On the other hand, they question whether private financing could produce the low-cost money needed to make the plants feasible.

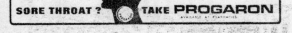

THE JERUSALEM POST

Published in Jerusalem, Israel, daily except on Saturday, by The Palestine Post Ltd. Founded in 1932 by Gershon AGRON.
Registered at the G.P.O. Copyright of all material reserved; reproduction permitted only by arrangement. Editor: TED R. LURIE

Jerusalem: 9 Rehov Hahavatzelet, P.O.B. 81, Telephone 28331 (8 lines) Tel Aviv: 44 Rehov Yehuda Halevi, P.O.Box 1125, Tel. 624215 Haifa: 34 Rehov Herzl, Hadar Hacarmel, P.O.Box 4810, Telephone 64594

32 PAGES
PRICE: 35 AGORA

THURSDAY, JUNE 6, 1968 • SIVAN 10, 5728 • RABI'A EL-AWAL 9, 1388 • VOL. XXXVIII, No. 12282*

JORDANIAN CHARGED WITH SHOOTING ROBERT KENNEDY

Robert Kennedy

YESTERDAY was again a day of horror and grief — not only in the U.S., but amongst all nations and peoples for whom America and democratic ideals are dear.

The attack on Senator Robert Kennedy, coming after the assassination of his brother the President, and the more recent killing of Martin Luther King, prompted profound disquiet about the very future of American society.

But for Israel this sense of shock last night turned into disbelief with the news that the assailant was a Jordanian who according to eye witnesses reportedly shouted that he sought to murder the Presidential candidate for "his country."

Such a grotesque conjunction of the tragedy of the Kennedy family, and the political conflict of our region—a conjunction which an Arab spokesman in the U.S. had the unbelievable termerity to justify—drains any words of comment of meaning.

At this hour, therefore, all that remains, is for us to join the Kennedy family, and the people of America in their fervent hopes and prayers that Robert Kennedy will survive, that he may once again rise to ignite the hopes and aspirations of the young and the downtrodden who esteem him so, that he may once again be able to pursue his goal of creating an America and a world in which the violent unreasoning passion which struck him down will breed no more.

Israel attacked by East bloc

MOSCOW. — "Pravda" charged yesterday that the Israel Government "is dominated by extreme right-wing bellicose elements. Israel rulers are actively preparing for a new armed clash with the Arab peoples in the hope of American arms shipments and American aid if they find themselves in a fix," commentator Yevgeny Primkaov wrote in the Soviet Communist Party newspaper.

East Germany accused Israel of blocking "steps for a peaceful settlement of the Middle East conflict" and of wanting to annex Arab territories. The charge was made by the East German Foreign Ministry in a statement referring to the first anniversary of the Six Day War.

In Belgrade the daily "Borba" said that "Israel is at the threshhold of international isolation, and with the exception of the U.S. there is no significant international power that approves Israel actions..."

The "Peking People's Daily" called on the Arab people to persist in their struggle against Israel until final victory. In an article marking the first anniversary of the war, the paper said that "the Chinese people have pledged firm support for the Arab people's just struggle."

(AP, UPI, Reuter)

Nasser says Arabs forces not yet ready for war

Rallies to mark the first anniversary of the outbreak of the Six Day War were held in Arab capitals yesterday, and President Nasser said in a speech in Cairo that "the forthcoming battle will decide the Arab fate for centuries to come." A fly-past of planes was staged over Cairo.

Nasser, whose 15-minute speech was broadcast over Cairo Radio, said that Egypt's armed forces were stronger today than ever before, *The Post's* Arab Affairs Monitor reports. But in spite of this and the "courageous stand" of the terrorists and opposition inside Palestine, this was not enough to provide victory at present. They constituted only "the beginning of the right way."

Israel had miscalculated, said Nasser, that Egypt would go down to its knees to beg for peace, that the masses would overthrow the regime and that the armed forces would never be able to regain their initial strength.

Nasser said that the Arab nation was "at the gates of victory" and Israel had begun to lose hope. Israel had lost the respect of world public opinion through its actions in Jerusalem and other occupied areas. Despite all its difficulties, Egypt was better off than a year ago.

Egypt was determined "to go the whole way until victory. This great nation is capable of patience."

King Hussein said that the Jordan Valley, which used to be a source of livelihood for thousands of people, had become "the theatre of Israel aggression. Israel wanted to starve all those whom it could not kill by bullets and napalm bombs." Last Tuesday Israel had shown world opinion its open defiance of U.N. decisions by "a barbarous onslaught on the town of Irbid."

Hussein said that "perhaps the Jews of Israel will soon turn against their statesmen, who have passed all limits by their aggression and obstinacy." He pledged full cooperation with the U.N. to conserve peace. The "U.N. must bring the issue to a just solution."

He greeted the Iraqi and Saudi Arabian

(Continued on Page 2, Col. 2)

June 5 strike partial; clash in Jerusalem

By ANAN SAFADI
Jerusalem Post Reporter

The strike called by residents of East Jerusalem and the Israel-held territories to mark the outbreak of the Six Day War was only partially observed. There was no response whatever to the strike call in the Gaza Strip, and most of the West Bank cities went about their usual business. On the other hand, a total strike was observed in East Jerusalem, Nablus, and Tulkarm, where tranport was the only sign of normal life.

In Jerusalem, 25 civilians, three police officers and one constable were wounded in 75 minutes of clashes in the Damascus Gate area, that apparently was touched off by a misunderstanding. Nineteen demonstrators were arrested, and a suspected ringleader was picked up later.

Buses were operating normally at dawn yesterday in Jerusalem. By 7 a.m., when shops in the Old City failed to start opening at the usual 6 a.m., it was obvious that there was going to be a total business strike. In the Old City's lanes, there was the usual flow of early shoppers, augmented by curious young residents.

At about the same time, only small trickles of children showed up at the schools, and soon after the school bells

(Continued on Page 8, Col. 3)

AFTER MIDNIGHT

The U.N. Security Council was called into session for midnight Israel time last night to consider Jordan and Israel charges arising out of Tuesday's clash across the Jordan River.

(Earlier report — Page 2)

Eshkol: Israel will win peace — or next war

PETAH TIKVA. — If war comes again, Israel will surely win again, "and it is just as certain that Israel will win the battle for peace," Prime Minister Eshkol said last night.

Speaking at a rally of 4,000 persons at the Oron Amphitheatre here, after a ceremony in which he was made a Freeman of Petah Tikva (earlier story page 8), the Prime Minister warned the Arab states that "reason does not abide the idea of a one-sided breach of peace, or of a privileged aggressor enjoying the fruits of his aggression."

Mr. Eshkol described Abdul Nasser as "a dictator seeking to buy victory (over Israel) cheaply for himself, on the furrowed backs of the Arabs of Israel, and incites them to terror."

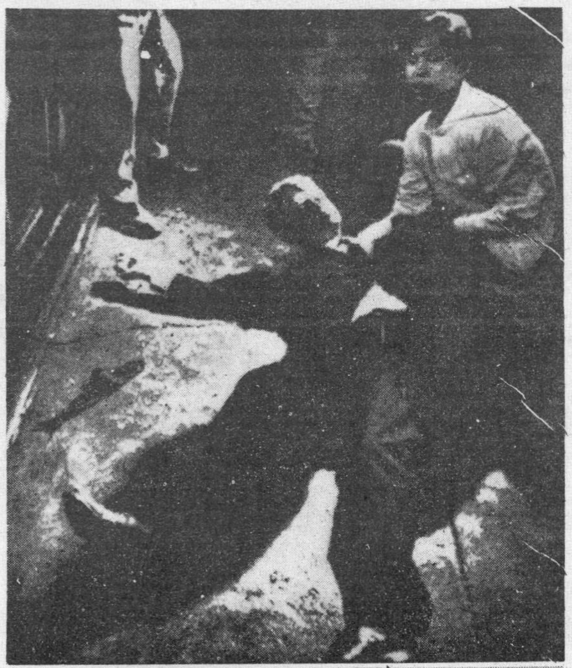

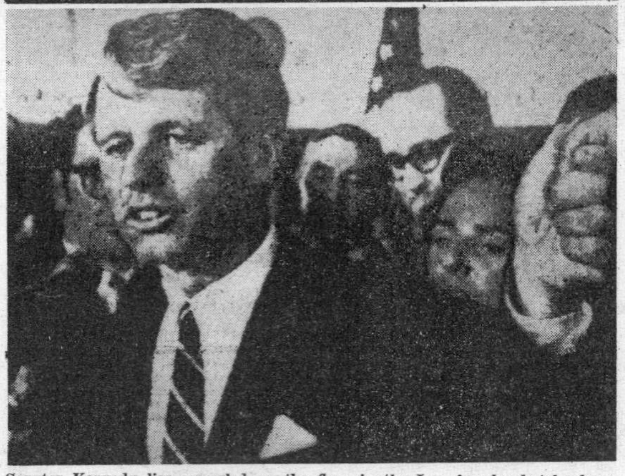

Senator Kennedy lies sprawled on the floor in the Los Angeles hotel where he was shot a few minutes after announcing, in lower picture, with his wife behind him, his victory in the primary. (AP radiophoto)

CRITICAL AFTER BRAIN OPERATION

LOS ANGELES (REUTER). — SENATOR ROBERT KENNEDY, WITH A MAJOR PRIMARY ELECTION VICTORY BEHIND HIM, WAS YESTERDAY CUT DOWN BY A GUNMAN WHO ONCE LIVED IN A VILLAGE NORTH OF JERUSALEM. WHILE SENATOR KENNEDY LAY IN HOSPITAL IN A CRITICAL CONDITION FROM SHOT WOUNDS IN THE HEAD AND NECK, THE LOS ANGELES AUTHORITIES CHARGED SIRHAN SIRHAN WITH ATTEMPTED MURDER.

Surgeons carried out a delicate, three-hour operation to remove one bullet which had penetrated the 42-year-old Senator's brain.

The medical team at the Catholic Good Samaritan Hospital reported in a bulletin that there had been impairment of the brain's blood supply governing many vital physical and mental functions.

Dr. Henry Cuneo, who assisted in the operation, said several major arteries were severed and Kennedy's brain suffered extensive loss of blood and oxygen as well as several blood clots. Cuneo said Kennedy also suffered injuries to the spinal cord.

The second bullet was apparently still lodged in Senator Kennedy's neck, but this was not regarded as a major problem.

The assassination attempt took place with stunning suddenness in the sumptuous Ambassador Hotel, where Senator Kennedy had only moments before delivered a victory oration. The gunman, a swarthy, dark-haired man, leapt from the shadows after the Senator had gone into the hotel kitchen, taking a short cut from the ballroom to the press room. He fired at point-blank range as Senator Kennedy was shaking hands with kitchen helpers.

Senator Kennedy, whose own brother, President Kennedy, was assassinated with a rifle four-and-a-half years ago, fell to the concrete floor, blood pouring from his wounds. The gunman emptied his eight-chamber revolver and wounded three other bystanders before he was overpowered and dragged away through hysterical, sobbing Kennedy supporters who clawed at him, shouting: "Kill him, Kill him."

Three other men were shot in the fusillade of bullets that felled Senator Kennedy. The men, standing near Kennedy in the ballroom of the Ambassador Hotel, were Bill Weizel, an associate producer of the American Broadcasting Company; Paul Schrade, an official of the United Auto Workers Union, and Ira Goldstein, a radio newsman.

Weizel, 30, hit in the abdomen, was in undetermined condition, as was Schrade, 43, with a scalp wound. Goldstein, 19, shot in the leg and back, was said to be in good condition in hospital.

Senator Kennedy's wife, Ethel, expecting her 11th child, rushed to her husband's side and nestled his head on her lap. It was a gesture like Mrs. Jacqueline Kennedy's after President Kennedy's murder in Dallas, Texas, on November 22, 1963.

The Senator was wheeled unconscious from the operating theatre to an intensive care unit while President Johnson ordered one of America's top brain surgeons, Dr. James L. Poppen, to make a 3,500-mile dash from Boston, Massachusetts, to give aid.

Ironically, Senator Kennedy was gunned down after vowing in his victory speech to put an end to violence if he were elected President.

Senator Kennedy received 46 per cent of the vote, Senator McCarthy 42 per cent, with 12 per cent for a local list supporting Vice-President Hubert Humphrey.

For the Republicans, Governor Ronald Reagan won as an unopposed "favourite son."

Sirhan family in U.S. 11 years

LOS ANGELES. — A 23-year-old man from a village near Jerusalem was charged here yesterday with the attempted murder of Senator Robert Kennedy. He is Sirhan Bishara Sirhan, and was charged on six counts of assault with intent to murder.

In Washington the authorities said that Sirhan was a Jordanian and came to the U.S. 11 years ago. The U.S. Immigration and Naturalization Service reported that Sirhan arrived in New York on January 12, 1957, as a permanent resident. They said he was born on March 19, 1944. He was not an American citizen.

In New York, the secretary-general of the Action Committee on American-Arab Relations said that Sirhan "may have been inflamed" by a statement made Saturday night during the Kennedy-McCarthy televised debate. Mohammed T. Mehdi said that while Kennedy was discussing Vietnam he said America should support Israel in the conflict in the Middle East. "It is this disrespect for the human Arab person which brings about this kind of violence," Mehdi said.

"We do not condone Mr. Sirhan's act and we are indeed appalled. However, his

(Continued on Page 2, Col. 4)

Fatah admits to 90% casualty rate

BEIRUT (UPI). — The Syrian-trained Fatah terrorist organization has been operating against Israel during the last year with a 90 per cent loss rate, a spokesman said yesterday.

But al-Fatah can draw on an almost unlimited supply of recruits, he added, all willing to die for the "Arab cause."

In the year since the Middle East war, the organization has increased its numbers, audacity and popularity, the spokesman said.

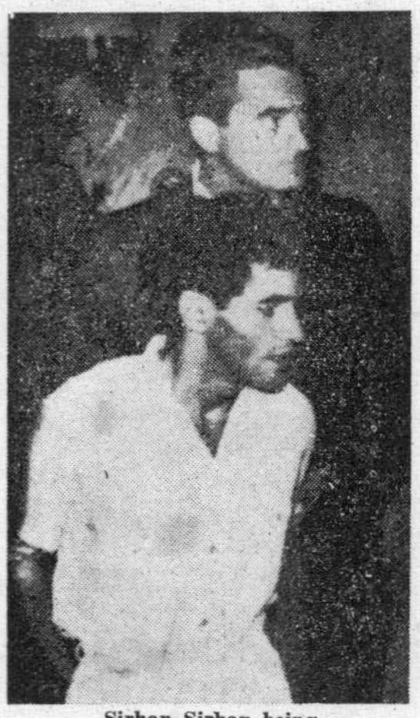

Sirhan Sirhan being taken into custody

MINE WOUNDS SOLDIER IN GAZA AREA

Jerusalem Post Reporter

GAZA. — A soldier was wounded when the half-track in which he was riding struck a mine near Kibbutz Nir Am at 8.30 yesterday morning.

NEW YORK STOCK EXCHANGE

Closing Wednesday, June 6, 1968

Dow Jones final averages 907.42 -9.21

Volume of shares traded 15,590,000

Admiral ..	20⅝	IntT&T ...	56
Alcoa	72½	Litton ...	82
AmT&T ...	48⅛	McDon.-D .	53⅞
Anacon ...	51½	MinnMM ..	114½
BethStl ...	31⅛	Monsan ...	41¼
Boeing	71¼	OlinMath ..	35¼
Burroughs	213	ParkeDav ..	31⅝
Chrysler ...	67⅝	PaRR	80⅜
Comsat ...	60½	Polaroid ...	120⅜
CrownCork .	67⅞	RCA	49¼
DowCh ...	79½	ReynTob ..	41⅞
duPont	158	SearsRoe ..	69¼
EKodak ...	84½	SperRd ...	55⅞
FairCam ...	72¼	StONJ	67¾
FordMot ..	58⅜	TransWAir .	38½
GenElec ...	89¼	USSteel ...	39¾
GenMot ...	81¾	WestgEl ...	72
Homestke ..	72½	Woolworth .	25
IntBusM ..	365	XeroxCo ...	306
IntPap	32¼	ZenithRad .	58¾

Supplied by Albert Kaplan, Israel Representative A.L. Stamm & Co., members N.Y. Stock Exch.

THE JERUSALEM POST

Published in Jerusalem, Israel, daily except on Saturday, by The Palestine Post Ltd. Founded in 1932 by Gershon AGRON.
Registered at the G.P.O. Copyright of all material reserved; reproduction permitted only by arrangement. Editor: TED R. LURIE

Jerusalem: 9 Rehov Hahavatzelet, P.O.B. 81, Telephone 28331 (8 lines) Tel Aviv: 44 Rehov Yehuda Halevi, P.O.Box 1125, Tel. 624215 Haifa: 34 Rehov Herzl, Hadar Hacarmel, P.O.Box 4810, Telephone 64594

CZECH REPORTS pages 2, 3, 7 & 8

PRICE: 35 AGORA

THURSDAY, AUGUST 22, 1968 • AV 28, 5728 • JAMAD AWAL 28, 1388 • VOL. XXXVIII, No. 12347*

FATE OF LEADERS UNKNOWN

PRAGUE. — The fate of party leader Alexander Dubcek and other reformists was uncertain last night. The Ceteka news agency reported that they were "under restriction" in the Central Committee building, where talks were going on with unidentified Soviet representatives on the future of the Government. But whether Mr. Dubcek had in fact been ousted or whether the Russians were trying to do a deal with him was not clear.

Another report said that Mr. Dubcek and other leaders had been taken to "an unknown place by Soviet troops."

Soviet tanks barred the way to the castle where President Ludvik Svoboda — his name means "freedom" — is a prisoner. A screen of anti-tank guns was also thrown round the castle.

Many other leading political figures were virtual prisoners inside public buildings sealed by tanks.

Soviet troops last night entered the National Assembly building in Prague as deputies were in session, the Czechoslovak new agency Ceteka reported. Ceteka said the deputies were continuing their meeting.

The Czechoslovak Foreign Ministry last night drew up a formal protest note addressed to the invaders and said the Government reserved the right to take "all necessary measures" if foreign troops were not withdrawn. In a note to the Soviet Union, East Germany, Poland, Hungary, and Bulgaria, the Foreign Ministry condemned the occupation as illegal and demanded the immediate withdrawal of foreign troops.

The note said that Czechoslovak citizens had been asked to remain calm and offer no resistance to the advancing soldiers in an effort to prevent "catastrophic consequences for Czechoslovakia's relations with the Soviet Union and a threat to international peace and security. For the same reason the army, security force and people's militia received no order to defend the country."

In Moscow, the Soviet new agency Tass said last night that reports that former President Novotny would be returned to the leadership of Czechoslovakia were "rumours."

(Reuter, UPI)

SOVIETS OCCUPY CZECHOSLOVAKIA

Soviet-occupied Czechoslovakia was plunged into turmoil last night, with its reformist leaders silenced, and a storm of anti-Russian protests sweeping the country. Four people were shot dead and 180 wounded in clashes with Soviet troops in Prague, and for a time the capital was on the brink of bloody strife. A total of 23 people are said to have been killed since troops from Russia, East Germany, Hungary, Poland and Bulgaria invaded the country on Tuesday night.

Youths hurled Molotov cocktails at Soviet tanks outside the radio station, and shooting flared in other parts of the city. For about two hours the dull thump of heavier weapons, probably mortars, was heard in the centre of the city, but the target was unknown. Violence also broke out in Bratislava, the Slovak capital, where two men died after being hit by Soviet bullets, and three others were wounded. In Kosice, Eastern Slovakia, one 17-year-old youth was killed and three people wounded in clashes with Soviet troops passing through the town.

The country's official news agency Ceteka late last night still seemed free from interference — free to report the latest developments and to refer to the Russians as "occupation forces." Then at 23.45 local time (22.45 GMT), the agency said: "At this moment the free news activity of Ceteka is ending." A last sentence, interrupted midway, said: "If further news is transmitted it will no longer be from the..." After that the Ceteka line went dead.

Before closing the agency put out an urgent message saying heavy firing from automatic weapons of the occupation troops was heard in Prague's central Wenceslas square. It gave no more details.

Single-sheet newspapers were tossed from taxi windows in Prague warning against collaborators. A clandestine radio operated from an unknown station.

Ceteka reported a mass rally in Bratislava of young people carrying Czechoslovak flags — one flag spattered with blood.

Ambulances raced across Prague last night, machinegun fire crackled in some areas and smoke billowed into the sky from several fires. But most of the shooting was by Soviet troops who fired over the heads of angry, menacing crowds or into the upper storeys of buildings. There was no sign of any organised armed resistance by the Czechs in face of the overwhelming Soviet strength, though there were isolated cases of retaliation.

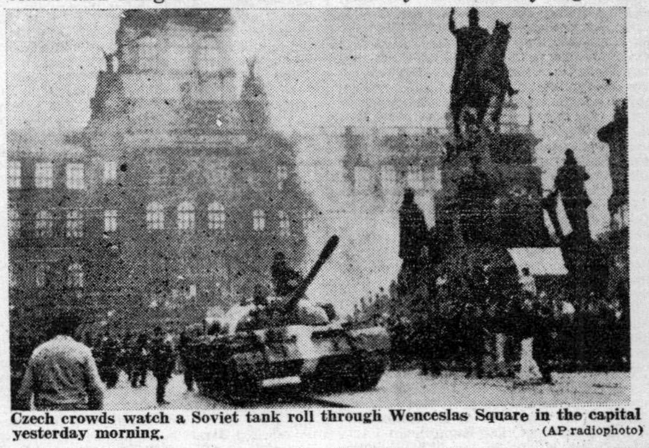

Czech crowds watch a Soviet tank roll through Wenceslas Square in the capital yesterday morning. (AP radiophoto)

Soviet tanks straddled the streets at every major intersection, and on all bridges over the Voltava river dividing the city. Rifle fire echoed over the river from a government building, known as the Premier's House. It sounded like a small-scale street battle.

Soviet troops opened up with heavy fire in Wenceslas Square last night. An artillery shell exploded in the area of the President's castle last night.

Czechoslovak youths sped across Wenceslas Square in motor-scooters, waving large national flags. They criss-crossed through a long column of Soviet tanks, yelling the names of their reform leaders, Dubcek and Svoboda. One confused Russian tank driver stopped at an intersection and rolled back without applying brakes. To the delight of the crowd, the tank crunched into a following tank.

Many of the Soviet troops appeared bewildered. Many more were nervously trigger-happy.

Crowds of Czechs, many of them students, roamed through the streets of the capital on foot or in lorries, chanting support for party leader Alexander Dubcek, who had given them new freedoms in defiance of the Kremlin, and hurling abuse at Soviet troops. Some people scrambled over Soviet tanks, arguing with the crews.

The general attitude of the Soviet troops suggested they were under strict orders to avoid bloodshed if possible.

The Soviet Union said yesterday its troops and those of its four closest East European allies had occupied Czechoslovakia to prevent a foreign-backed counter-revolution. It said it had done this at

(Continued on Page 8, Col. 4)

30 YEARS AFTER MUNICH

GERMAN troops have once again invaded Czechoslovakia — a mere 30 years after Munich. Once again, the Czech leaders have felt constrained to order their army not to resist and to appeal to their people to "remain calm." Once again, the Poles and the Hungarians are cooperating fully with the major aggressor. And the unfortunate Czechs and Slovaks, situated in what Goebbels called "that aircraft carrier in the heart of Europe," are once again paying the price of their geographical and political isolation and of their continued desire for a free and dignified existence.

Bitter — and instructive — though the parallel between Hitler's invasion of Czechoslovakia and that of Brezhnev may be, the intrinsic horror of the Red Army's brutal, unjustified and unjustifiable action yesterday is of another, and if anything, more bitter kind. The Nazis could have been stopped — even by the Czechoslovaks themselves, let alone by France and Britain. The Russians cannot be, short of courting the danger of a nuclear war for which no contemporary statesman is politically or psychologically prepared. The destruction of Czechoslovakia by Nazis was an element of their broad plan for the domination of Europe. It was in no sense essential to the security of Germany nor even to the security of their regime in Germany.

By contrast, there is certainly a sense in which the destruction of Mr. Dubcek's Czechoslovakia by the Russian Communists has come to be crucial, if not to the security of Russia as a state, at least to the maintenance of Communist rule in Russia in the sole form in which the Russians have known it: oligarchic, obscurantist and totalitarian. The Czechs' rejection of Novotny and all he stood for was rightly seen as, above all, a rejection of Russian-style Communism. The implications of this act for East Germany, Poland and Russia herself, through the irresistible processes of spin-off and spill-over, were profoundly (and rightly) feared.

The Soviet leaders could neither stomach the rise of Mr. Dubcek and the fresh winds of liberalism that carried him to power, nor — as it seemed at first — could they do anything about it. The Czechoslovaks stood firm while the vast machine of Soviet agitation and propaganda was brought to bear upon them. Perhaps the Russians hoped that if only they kept up the heat the Czechoslovaks, like Pavlov's dogs, would ultimately come to heel. But they did not: and Stalin's heirs struck out, unable to face yet another revolt and the prospect of new and ever more painful cracks in their system.

One conclusion that might profitably be drawn from this latest manifestation of the apparently ineradicable brutality and mendacity of Russia's rulers is that, as they become more frightened and confused by the changing world around them so they grow more dangerous. And the more dangerous they become the more important it is for other governments to assess Russian intentions and purposes in the clear light of day, rather than of their private hopes.

Clearly, the Russian leaders are on the defensive. Clearly, they are immensely concerned for their own future as individual politicians and, more generally, about the ability of their system to survive the long-term effects of more widespread education, greater familiarity with the outside world, and the effects of a technological society on the relationship between them and those they rule. Clearly, too, there can and will be no more than a very superficial stability in international affairs until the internal struggle for liberalism in Russia itself has been resolved one way or the other.

No one can nor should attempt to help the Russians find their way, at long last, out of Stalin's maze. They must do it themselves, even though the effect of failure will most assuredly extend far beyond Russia's borders. Meanwhile, there is no aspect of the Red Army's invasion of Czechoslovakia that we can find anything but disturbing.

Six want Council meeting

UNITED NATIONS — At the request of the U.S., Britain, France and three other Western countries the U.N. Security Council was summoned into emergency session last night to deal with the Soviet-led invasion of Czechoslovakia.

But Ambassador Joao Augusto de Araujo Castro of Brazil, Council President for August, made no immediate move to summon the Council into session.

The text of the request was not published immediately. It was expected that the signatories would present a resolution to condemn Soviet intervention in Czecoslovakia. But there appeared to be no prospect of meaningful Council action because Russia has the right of Veto.

The Security Council prepared for its emergency session as Secretary-General U Thant publicly denounced the Soviet move and called off a planned trip to Prague, Geneva and Vienna. He was due to leave for the Czechoslovak capital today.

In a strongly-worded criticism of Soviet action, U Thant said he deplored any resort to force to settle international problems.

U Thant saw Soviet Deputy Foreign Minister Malik and appealed for restraint by the Soviet Government and its Warsaw allies. The Secretary-General said he regarded the developments in Czechoslovakia as "yet another serious blow to the concept of international order and morality which form the basis of the U.N. Charter..."

Withdraw, says LBJ

WASHINGTON. — President Johnson called on the Soviet Union and other Communist forces yesterday to withdraw from Czechoslovakia, and said the U.S. was consulting urgently with its allies to consider steps in the U.N.

Mr. Johnson said in a statement that the "tragic news" of the invasion of Czechoslovakia by Communist forces "shocks the conscience of the world. In the name of mankind's hope for peace I call on the Soviet Union and its associates to withdraw their troops from Czechoslovakia."

Russia and its allies had "invaded a defenceless country to stamp out a resurgence of ordinary human freedom."

The President, whose statement was issued after he had held an emergency meeting of his National Security Council and later discussed the crisis with senior officials, branded the action of the Warsaw Pact countries as a "flat violation of the U.N. Charter."'

The Governments in London, Paris and Bonn was unanimous in deploring the Soviet takeover.

Prime Minister Wilson ended his vacation to order Parliament into session on Monday.

In Bonn demonstrators blocked the passage of the Soviet Ambassador's car, shouting "Murder" and "freedom for Czechoslovakia." In Paris the Government statement declared that Moscow's action had shown that the Soviets had not yet freed thmselves "from the policy of blocs... which is incompatible with the rights of people to dispose of themselves."

Tito, Rumanian support

BELGRADE. — President Tito yesterday condemned the invasion of Czechoslovakia as a "serious blow" to the Communist world. "The entering of foreign military units into Czechoslovakia without invitation or approval from a legal government has worried us deeply," the Yugoslav President said in a statement to the official news service Tanjug.

"The sovereignty of a socialist country was violated and trampled down and a serious blow was dealt to the socialist and progressive forces in the world," Tito said.

In Bucharest, Rumanian Communist Party Chief Nicolae Ceausescu said after a top-level meeting of Communist leaders yesterday that the invasion "constitutes a grave mistake and a serious danger to peace in Europe and socialism in the world." Addressing a crowd of tens of thousands gathered in front of the Party building, Mr. Ceausescu, said: "It is incomprehensible that one socialist state can encroach upon the freedom and sovereignty of another socialist state."

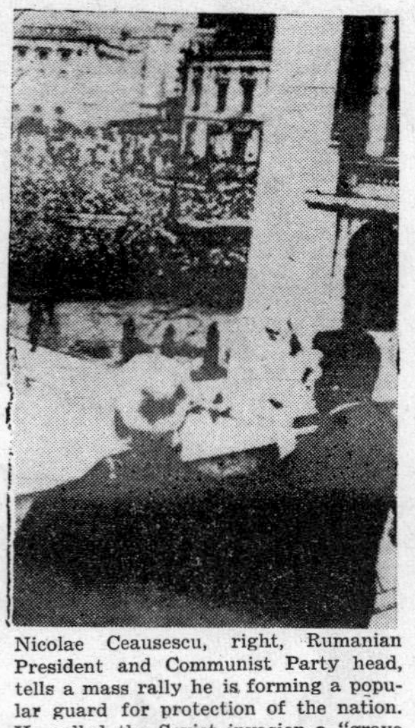

Nicolae Ceausescu, right, Rumanian President and Communist Party head, tells a mass rally he is forming a popular guard for protection of the nation. He called the Soviet invasion a "grave mistake," endangering the peace of Europe.

Firing across Jordan

Jordanian troops fired mortars at Israeli units in the Beit Yosef sector of the Beisan Valley at 9.10 last night. Fire was returned, and there were no casualties on our side. After a few minutes' exchange, the area became quiet again, the Israel Army spokesman reported.

New agency reports from Jordan said that one Jordanian soldier was killed, and a second wounded, in a clash in the morning across the Jordan near Manshiyeh village. They also reported an exchange of automatic fire in the Golan Heights area not far from Irbid.

AFTER MIDNIGHT

Czechoslovak President Svoboda said last night that the occupation was illegal and was undertaken without the consent of Czechoslovak authorities. Svoboda addressed the nation by radio.

Cabinet meets on Czech crisis

Jerusalem Post Staff

Premier Eshkol last night summoned an extraordinary Cabinet meeting at his vacation site to discuss the Russian invasion of Czechoslovakia.

A Government statement will be published today, it was announced officially in Jerusalem last night.

Information Minister Israel Galili said in Jerusalem that the developments were not confined to the relations between the two countries, but were an event of broad international significance which might also have an echo for the Middle East. Speaking to lecturers of the Central Office of Information, Mr. Galili said it was no wonder that Israelis, aroused at the news, had a profound understanding for the fate of any nation struggling for its independence, existence and freedom, in the face of violent intervention by neighbours many times bigger than itself, and in the face of the imposition of a regime and system of government from the outside.

The Israel Labour Party last night expressed the horror and shock of the people of Israel and all other free peoples at the armed invasion by the Soviet Union and its satellites of Czechoslovakia. The statement compared the act to the Nazi invasion of 1938.

Diplomatic observers in Jerusalem believed yesterday that the present victory of the "hard-liners" in Moscow was likely to create a feeling of fear among countries cooperating closely with the Soviet Union, in view of the danger of loss of independence. This applied particularly to pro-Soviet Arab countries, who were expected to treat the Soviet action with much circumspection, although not admitting their apprehension publicly. While a hard-line policy by the Kremlin may also increase Soviet threats in the Middle East, it would at the same time create more understanding for Israel's position in the region by the Western powers, it was held.

More immediate, the Russians were now likely to be forced onto the defensive at the forthcoming 23rd U.N. General Assembly which opens next month.

Maki and Mapam condemned the Soviet invasion of Czechoslovakia yesterday, while a Rakah spokesman justified the Russian action. The political bureau of Maki — the Israel Communist Party — yesterday registered its anger at the armed invasion. It appealed to Communist parties the world over to demand that the Soviet Union and its allies withdraw their forces from Czech soil. Maki is holding an open-air protest rally this evening in Dizengoff Circle.

The Rakah - New Communist Party political bureau has not yet published a statement. A party spokesman told *The Post* that "this does not indicate any confusion. Our stand is clear. The Warsaw Pact armies moved against counter-revolution at the request of Czech leaders... It was certainly no imperialist invasion, nor conquest."

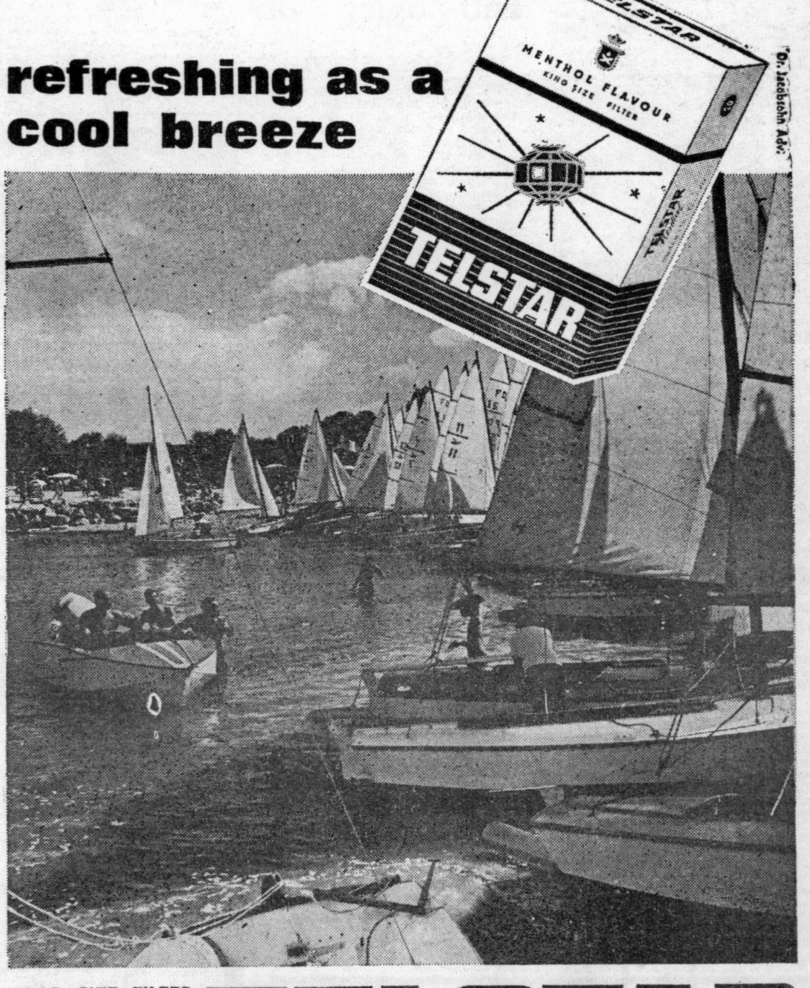
TELSTAR
MENTHOL FLAVOUR
KING SIZE FILTER
TELSTAR

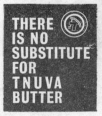

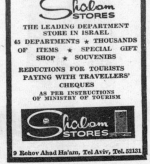

THE JERUSALEM POST

Vote table
page 3
★
Business
pages 4 & 5
★
Economic
Conference
page 8

Published in Jerusalem, Israel, daily except on Saturday, by The Palestine Post Ltd. Founded in 1932 by Gershon AGRON.
Registered at the G.P.O. Copyright of all material reserved; reproduction permitted only by arrangement. Editor: TED R. LURIE

Jerusalem: 9 Rehov Hahavatzelet, P.O.B. 81,   Tel Aviv: 44 Rehov Yehuda Halevi,   Haifa: 34 Rehov Herzl, Hadar Hacarmel,
Telephone 28331 (8 lines)   P.O.Box 1125, Tel. 624215   P.O.Box 4810, Telephone 64594

PRICE : 35 AGORA

THURSDAY, NOVEMBER 7, 1968 • HESHVAN 16, 5729 • SHAABAN 16, 1388, VOL. XXXVIII, No. 12408*

Nixon elected President, pledges to unite nation

Administration to include Democrats

NEW YORK. — Republican Richard M. Nixon was yesterday elected 37th President of the United States, after the most confused election the country has known. His Democrat opponent, Vice-President Hubert Humphrey, voice broken with emotion, told a nation-wide television audience he had congratulated Mr. Nixon on the triumph evidenced by unofficial results — which are still being re-checked.

In a see-saw battle in which the popular vote at no point separated the two men by a great margin, Mr. Nixon set the final seal on a remarkable comeback from narrow defeat at the hands of the late John F. Kennedy in the 1960 presidential polls. His triumph helped erase the more bitter memories of a 1962 drubbing in the California governorship race, which led him to announce he was quitting politics forever.

President-elect Nixon

Acknowledging his victory on television, Mr. Nixon said his administration would include Democrats, and he would unite the American people as well as "bridge the generation gap" and the gap between the races.

He promised to help President Johnson in efforts to bring peace to the world, and said Mr. Johnson had offered to help him prepare for his new Administration, which takes office on January 20.

Mr. Nixon's election followed a night of tension and confusion, with the verdict gradually swinging to him after the issue appeared to be sliding towards deadlock — and a possible constitutional crisis.

The big state of Illinois finally went narrowly into the Nixon column, to put him over the 270-vote majority needed for election by the 538-member electoral college.

The confusion was caused partly by delays in counting absentee ballots, and also by computer troubles afflicting the news election services (N.E.S.) system which produced the unofficial voting results.

The election was still a toss-up when N.E.S. announced it was initiating a complete re-check of all polls from big states, starting with those in states with narrow margins.

Compounding these uncertainties was a slowdown in vote-counting in Illinois itself. The tension built up until Illinois dramatically toppled to Nixon to give him victory.

A notable feature of the election — which contained several surprises between the two main contenders — was the failure by third party candidate George C. Wallace to siphon off enough votes to deadlock the election.

Mr. Wallace won his expected five southern states, but apart from New Jersey — where Mr. Humphrey's loss was attributed to a "white backlash" vote in Wallace's favour — did not influence the issue between the two major contenders.

The result in Maryland — home state of Vice-President-elect Spiro Agnew — was still undecided. Votes counted put it in the Humphrey bag by around 19,000, but there were enough uncounted votes to make this margin inconclusive.

Mr. Nixon planned to fly to Washington later in the day to confer with former President Dwight Eisenhower — whose grandson David is shortly to marry Mr. Nixon's daughter Julie. He then will take a short family holiday at the Florida Keys resort of Key Biscayne.

Through the long night after the polls had closed, the leading candidates were in a virtual deadlock — and they nearly tied in the popular vote. Mr. Nixon's edge at 19.30 G.M.T. (9.30 p.m. in Israel) was only 14,651 votes with more than 68 million votes cast. But in the electoral vote column, where presidencies are won, Mr. Nixon had 287, Mr. Humphrey 172 and Independent Party candidate, 45. Victory required 270 electoral votes.

TAKES CALIFORNIA, OHIO

Before the 55-year-old former Vice-President went over the top by capturing Illinois, he had reached the White House threshold by taking California's 40 and Ohio's 26 electoral votes.

Mr. Nixon paid tribute to "my wife, who has endured more of my speeches than even the members of the press" and his daughters, Tricia and Julie, "who ... gave us a tremendous lift all over the country."

Displaying an embroidered presidential seal, he said Julie had given it to him, and it was proof that "she never had any doubt at all."

Earlier, Mr. Herbert Klein, Mr. Nixon's chief spokesman, had acknowledged the election results were much closer than the G.O.P. camp had anticipated. He said the Vietnam bombing halt "did have a dramatic effect" on the voting.

Mr. Humphrey threw in the towel at noon in a somber, emotional speech at his Minneapolis hotel headquarters. (See column 4)
(Reuter, AP)

Humphrey offers total support and harmony

MINNEAPOLIS, Minnesota. — Hubert Humphrey yesterday conceded the presidential election to Richard Nixon and promised his total support to the new President-elect.

In a somewhat choked voice, Mr. Humphrey told a rally of his campaign workers that he had talked by telephone with Mr. Nixon shortly before making the concession statement, and had sent his opponent a telegram saying: "Please know you will have my support in unifying and leading the nation."

He added that he was "confident that with the constructive leadership of both parties we can go on building a better nation in the spirit of peace and harmony."

He would continue to dedicate himself, he told his supporters, "to public service and building a responsive, vital Democratic Party." He would also "continue my personal commitment" to the causes of civil rights, human justice and peace. Nevertheless, he said, "Now let's have some fun ... I haven't mown the lawn for some time, and there are still some things to do around home. I don't want you to think we're going to start campaigning right away."

President Johnson wired congratulations to Mr. Nixon and pledged, "I shall do everything in my power to make your burdens lighter."
(UPI, AP)

NEW YORK HEAVILY PRO-HUMPHREY

NEW YORK (AP). — New York City, with America's most concentrated Jewish vote, voted overwhelmingly for Mr. Hubert Humphrey, vote analysts said yesterday.

One television network said its computer showed that the Vice-President drew a larger percentage of Jewish votes than any candidate in recent history, including the late John Kennedy.

Jewish voters crossed party line, however, to give Republican Senator Jacob Javits a resounding victory.

Nixon and a new era

MR. Nixon, the favourite, has squeaked through. Mr. Humphrey, surprisingly, very nearly made it. Mr. Wallace, despite the Cassandras, with only five of the Deep South States supporting him, has done no more than nail his colours to the mast.

It has been an astonishing, often disturbing, and incomprehensible campaign that has been concluded. One of its surprises is that despite all its troubles and divisions the liberal wing of the Democratic Party showed it can still command vast support in the American public. That Mr. Humphrey should have done as well as he did in the face of the almost total loss of the traditionally Democratic South and the fact that he himself was the least desired of all the major candidates for the nomination in his own party is evidence of this persisting strength. This stream of opinion and interests, led by Roosevelt, Truman, Kennedy and Johnson, has dominated American political life. But the upsets of Vietnam and the Negro revolt have now all but obliterated its long-standing margin. Yet the movement, as this election showed, is still a potent force. In the years ahead the Democrats will therefore have to confront the tasks of reforming this potential behind a new leader.

If the Democrats, finally shorn of the southern white supremacists may now define themselves even more clearly than in the past as a fundamentally liberal movement, the Republican Party led by Mr. Nixon in the White House will face the challenge of keeping its often conflicting wings together. They range from New York liberals led by Governor Rockefeller and Senator Javits to Governor Reagan's conservative followers in California. Mr. Nixon, as the nominee of the centre of the party, is in a good position to achieve unity and this aim will undoubtedly express itself in his choice of Cabinet members.

In nominating him the party leaders rejected the pressure to choose a man like Wilkie, Dewey or Rockefeller and remembered the stunning loss suffered by their conservative candidate, Senator Goldwater in 1964. This time the party felt strong enough to finally choose a true-blue Republican, not a man of essentially independent views, like Hoover, or a fundamentally non-political soldier like Eisenhower.

But Mr. Nixon will now have to project this sturdy Republican support onto the canvas of a nation sorely divided by grievous domestic and foreign issues. Last night he gave clear indication of this aim when he announced that his would be an open administration, open to new ideas, new people and—significantly—of both parties.

Certainly Mr. Nixon will be a President well aware of the powers of his office and willing to use them. Thus while he will have come from the centre of his party, he can be counted upon to give his party a wholly new concept of executive action, forged by the experience of his predecessors in the White House and the problems, external and internal, facing the world's greatest power. In the exercise of his immense power Mr. Nixon will carry with him the hopes not only of his own countrymen, but of all men who look toward an open and free concept of democracy and the nations' right to peace and security.

Hussein: Israel 'may be' behind Amman battles

Has respect for terrorists

AMMAN (Reuter). — King Hussein said yesterday that Israel may have been behind the shooting incidents in Amman earlier this week which led to military action against a Palestinian guerrilla group.

The action was sparked off when an armed band attacked an army jeep containing an officer and two soldiers, he told a press conference.

King Hussein said at a press conference that it was possible that Israel might have been behind the troubles, "to create confusion and thus prepare an opportunity to strike. We are investigating the possibility." He said there was a strong chance that the men who started the trouble, whom he described on Monday as a "hired group," were acting on a plan not originating in any Arab State.

Questioned about a rumour that the troubles had been arranged by Syria and Egypt, the King said: "This is nonsense. Jordan has good relations with her sister Arab countries."

He denied that those arrested included members of terrorist organizations other than Kataeb al-Nasr (Phalanxes of Victory).

(The semi-official Syrian newspaper "Al-Thaawra" yesterday accused the U.S. Central Intelligence Agency of provoking the disturbances "to hit at Palestinian commando action" and liquidate the Palestine case.")

The King said the men had forced civilians, including women, at gunpoint into
(Continued on Page 8, Col. 2)

President-elect was in Israel just after 6 Day War

President-elect Nixon was in Israel on a two-day visit a fortnight after the Six Day War. On his arrival June 21, on this second visit here, he was reported as saying that, until a settlement with the Arabs is reached, Israel could not be expected to withdraw from territories which had been used as bases of aggression against her, adding: "There is no debate about who the aggressor was."

Before leaving Israel, he again told a press conference: "Israel should not withdraw under any circumstances from the areas it has acquired until there is a peace settlement."

Mr. Nixon made a similar declaration on his return to the U.S., noting that Israeli leaders had told him they were ready to assume a responsible role in solving the Arab refugee problem but that they could not do it alone.

The President-elect first visited Israel in 1966, together with his wife and two daughters. They arrived on August 1, Mr. Nixon spending about 36 hours here, during which he met Prime Minister Eshkol and Mr. Ben-Gurion, among others. His wife and daughters stayed on for a few days to tour holy places in Galilee.

Paris pleased; U.K. not so

PARIS.—Sources close to the French Government greeted Mr. Richard Nixon's election as a good omen for a continued improvement in Franco-American relations. Mr. Nixon had expressed very friendly views towards France and understanding of General de Gaulle's foreign policy in recent interviews which had been noted in Paris, the sources said.

Franco - American relations — often strained in the past — have been improving recently, and particularly since Washington and Hanoi agreed on Paris as the site for the Vietnam preliminary peace talks.

BRITAIN. — The Labour Government are reported to be disappointed. In a speech in London yesterday, former British Foreign Minister George Brown warned that America is likely to become more isolationist. "Bringing the boys back home" would not stop at Vietnam but would mean "the boys" would return from wherever they might be in the world, he said.

MOSCOW. — The Soviet mass media reported election results without comment. But all during the campaign Soviet newspapers stressed there was little choice between the tweedledum of Nixon and the tweedledee of Humphrey.

SAIGON. — Mr. Nixon's electoral success was welcomed by many South Vietnamese government officials who believed he would take a firmer line with Hanoi than Mr. Humphrey. News of the Republican's victory broke here in the early hours and there was no immediate official comment from the Government.

Anti-Soviet riot in Bratislava

PRAGUE (UPI). — Jeering students pulled down Soviet flags and burned them in Bratislava last night as they roamed the streets demonstrating against the Soviet occupation on the eve of the Russian Revolution anniversary. The police did not intervene.

In Prague, hundreds of police and Czechoslovak soldiers sealed off a 15-block area around the National Theatre in case of anti-Soviet demonstrations at a Russian ballet performance.

The student protest in Bratislava, the capital of the Slovak region of the country, began when an estimated 4,000 students gathered outside its National Theatre where the Soviet holiday was being celebrated by a performance of the opera "Romeo and Juliet."

DEMOCRATIC SENATE MARGIN SLIGHTLY CUT

WASHINGTON (AP). — Republicans cut into the heavy Democratic Senate majority in Tuesday's election but fell far short of achieving control. The lineup, with a tight race in Oregon still undecided, is 58 Democrats and 41 Republicans, a net gain of four Republican seats.

While winning six seats, the Democrats had held, the Republicans surrendered two of their own.
(Earlier report on page 3)

NEW YORK STOCK EXCHANGE

Closing Wednesday, November 6, 1968

Volume of shares traded 12,640,000
Dow Jones final averages   949.47 +3.24

Admiral	19¾	Int'T&T	57⅞
Alcoa	70¼	Litton	77¾
Am'T&T	54¾	McDon.-D	49½
Anacon	51	MinnMM	108¾
BethStl	31⅝	Monsan	56¼
Boeing	54⅝	OlinMath	39¾
Burroughs	225¼	ParkeDav	26⅞
Chrysler	67¾	Penn-Central	63
Comsat	52⅝	Polaroid	110¾
CrownCork	80¼	RCA	46¾
DowCh	80⅝	ReynTob	40⅜
duPont	171¼	SearsRoe	68½
EKodak	77¼	SperRd	42⅞
FairCam	80	StONJ	80¼
FordMot	58⅝	TransWAir	45
GenElec	94¾	USSteel	42
GenMot	88½	WestgEl	73¾
Homestke	36¾	Woolworth	31⅝
IntBusM	310	XeroxCo	264
IntPap	36	ZenithRad	58

Fidelity Capital (2 p.m. price) 14.71 15.99
Fidelity Trend (2 p.m. price) 31.83 34.60
Fidelity Fund (2 p.m. price) 20.86 22.55

Supplied by Albert Kaplan, Israel Representative
A. L. Stamm & Co., members N.Y. Stock Exch.

NEW ANTI-ISRAEL BLAST BY TASS

MOSCOW (UPI). — The Soviet Union last night "sharply denounced" Israel's policy toward the Arab states and warned that it "is fraught with the most serious complications."

A Tass statement said "Israel must not be allowed to profit from its aggressions and from the current armed provocations against the Arab states."

The Soviet blast appeared to have been triggered by the daring Israel commando raid deep into Egypt last week.

COUNCIL MEETING ON MID-EAST TOMORROW

UNITED NATIONS (UPI). — The Security Council yesterday postponed till tomorrow the meeting on the Middle East crisis scheduled for today.

The Council began meeting last Friday at the request of Egypt and Israel, which have charged each other with aggression across their cease-fire lines.

TREMOR IN NICOSIA

NICOSIA (AP). — A slight earth tremor shook Nicosia and other parts of Cyprus yesterday but no damage or casualties were reported.

AFTER MIDNIGHT

Al Fatah, the largest Arab sabotage organization, last night asked Jordan for guarantees so it may continue its operations against Israel. In a broadcast over its radio from Cairo, the organization demanded that the show of military force put up by Hussein in Amman during the past two days should not recur in future.

A number of shells were shot from the Jordanian side of the cease-fire lines at Israeli forces in the region of the Damia Bridge at 10.20 last night. Fire was returned and the exchange lasted for half an hour. Our forces suffered no casualties.

ARMSTRONG AND ALDRIN LAND SAFE ON MOON

THE JERUSALEM POST

Published in Jerusalem, Israel, daily except on Saturday, by The Palestine Post Ltd. Founded in 1932 by Gershon AGRON.
Registered at the G.P.O. Copyright of all material reserved; reproduction permitted only by arrangement. Editor: TED R. LURIE

Jerusalem: 9 Rehov Hahavatzelet, P.O.B. 81, Telephone 28331 (8 lines) Tel Aviv: 44 Rehov Yehuda Halevi, P.O.Box 1125, Tel. 624215 Haifa: 34 Rehov Herzl, Hadar Hacarmel, P.O.Box 4810, Telephone 64594

12 PAGES

MOON WALK WON'T BE A PICNIC page 3

★

'Times' on Russia's million prisoners page 9

PRICE : 35 AGORA

MONDAY, JULY 21, 1969 • AV 6, 5729 • JOMADA-ULA 7, 1389 • VOL. XXXIX, No. 12623*

ASTRONAUTS STEP ONTO LUNAR SURFACE THIS MORNING

HOUSTON SPACE CENTRE (AP). — Man landed on the moon yesterday — July 20, 1969. The American astronauts, Neil Armstrong and Edwin Aldrin Jr., settled down onto soil no man had ever touched before at 2018 GMT (10.18 p.m. in Israel). A dream of the ages had come true.

The two men etched their names beside the great explorers of the past as they brought their spaceship, the Eagle, down on the Moon's Sea of Tranquillity after a dangerous and difficult descent from the Apollo-11 command ship.

"The Eagle has landed," Mission Control has told the world.

"Tranquillity base here," said Armstrong, an Air Force colonel. "Eagle has landed."

Astronaut Michael Collins remained at the controls of the command vehicle, called Columbia, orbiting more than 96 km. overhead.

The drop to the surface in he four-legged moon lander took more than two hours and required the flawless meshing of men and machine to accomplish man's first visit to a planet other than earth.

LITTLE TIME FOR VIEW

Armstrong and Aldrin had little time to enjoy the view. They immediately began an extensive check of the landing vehicle for signs of any major problem, which would cause them to attempt an immediate blastoff to rejoin Collins.

The landing was the start of an epic exploration in which Armstrong and Aldrin are to walk the lunar surface, collecting precious bits of this new world, deploying scientific instruments and seeing what it is like for man to work in the moon's one-sixth gravity.

Armstrong is scheduled to take man's first step on another celestial body today at 0616 GMT (8.16 a.m.), followed about 20 minutes later by Aldrin.

Through world-wide television relays, millions were watching for glimpses of their excursion on the surface. Live pictures are to be relayed from a TV camera which the astronauts are to mount 9 metres from the landing craft.

Armstrong and Aldrin plan to explore outside their spaceship about 2½ hours. In all, they were to be on the lunar surface about 22 hours. In that time they will open the boundless frontier of space a little more and clear the way for future flights beyond present imagination.

The initial moments were for a decision to stay on the dusty surface. The spacecraft engine began kicking up dust from the moment it was 40 feet above on its descent.

TERSE APOLOGY

Commander Neil Armstrong took over manual control for the landing, the Space Centre was informed. His first description of the landing area was terse. He apologized for taking a little longer than planned in his landing.

"The auto-targeting was taking us right into a football field-sized crater," he said, "with a large number of big boulders and rocks—and it required us to fly manually over the rock field to find a reasonably good area."

As the landing was confirmed, the ground controller was heard to say: "We got a bunch of guys on the ground about to turn blue. We're breathing again."

The final touchdown on the lunar crust came after a tense 12 minutes as Eagle dropped swiftly from lunar orbit past the 40,000 feet and 20,000 feet marks, and slowed as it came through 1,500 feet. The astronauts' calm voices, matched by coolness and enthusiasm at Mission Control for the way the flight was going, ticked off the descent figures.

'TRANQUILLITY BASE'

At one point in the conversation shortly after landing, Mission Control referred to Eagle as "Tranquillity Base" — man's first space station on the moon's Sea of Tranquillity.

Ten minutes after landing Aldrin radioed: "We'll get to the details of what's around here. But it looks like a collection of every variety of shape, angularity, granularity. A collection of just about every kind of rock.

"Colour depends on what angle you're looking at . . . Rocks and boulders look as though they're going to have some interesting colours."

BULLETIN:

MOON WALK ADVANCED

HOUSTON SPACE CENTRE (AP). — The Apollo-11 moon landers requested permission to start their moon stroll at about 0100 GMT (3 a.m. today in Israel) and Mission Control said, "We'll support you any time." The original schedule called for the excursion at 0616 GMT.

LUNA-15 SWOOPS 10 km. OVER MOON

JODRELL BANK (AP). — The Soviet Luna-15 darted dramatically nearer the moon yesterday in a manoeuvre Jodrell Bank scientists said could only mean the unmanned probe was bent on reconnaissance during the Apollo-11 mission or was preparing to land.

Observatory director Sir Bernard Lovell said that after Luna-15 had carried out two course corrections, its mean altitude was 70 km.

In Moscow, Tass said Luna-15 was within 16 km. of the moon's surface at the lowest point of its new orbit, which soared up to 110 km. It added that the probe was functioning normally in its scientific exploration of lunar space.

The startling development left astronomers at Jodrell Bank, the West's main vantage point during Soviet space shots, uncertain immediately of its implications.

Hebrew broadcast

The radio's *Hayom Haze* programme, compered by Elimelech Ram, provided Israeli listeners with a live broadcast of the landing at 10.10 last night. Speaking in Hebrew from the Voice of America in New York, were Yigal Lossin and Ya'acov Reuel. As their voices intermingled with the sounds from the Control Centre in Houston and the voices of the astronauts themselves, it was possible to hear, "Altitude 1,600 feet . . . 1,000 feet, coming in beautiful . . ."

At 10.18 p.m. Israel time a voice came through clearly, "Man on the Moon." Eagle had landed at the south-western edge of the Sea of Tranquillity. Somebody in Houston laughed with relief.

5 Egyptian planes downed

Two Israeli aircraft lost, but pilots safe

TEL AVIV.—Israel jets yesterday afternoon for over four hours bombed Egyptian missile and artillery bases across the Suez Canal and shot down at least five Egyptian planes — delivering its expected counterblow to recent increased Egyptian shelling and commando raids. Israel lost two planes, but the pilots baled out safely in Israel territory.

The Israel air action followed by about 11 hours an overnight attack by Israel commandos who stormed Green Island, a fortress commanding the southern entrance to the Canal, in which scores of Egyptian soldiers were killed and wounded and anti-aircraft gun positions and other installations destroyed. Six Israelis were killed and nine wounded in that action. (See page eight.)

The two Israel operations were last night described by Israel sources as intended to give the Egyptian High Command second thoughts about its plans for an early attack on Israel. The Air Force planes blasted Egyptian military installations and commando bases along the length of the Canal from Ismailia to the Port Said area in the north. The Egyptians suffered heavy casualties in the air raids, it was stated.

The Egyptian aircraft appeared only a couple of hours after the Israel aerial bombardment began. The five Egyptian planes downed included two Sukhoi-7s, two Mig-17s and one Mig-21.

The Israel Army spokesman said the Egyptian air attacks wounded three Israel soldiers. Three other soldiers were wounded by Egyptian ground fire from across the Canal.

The Egyptian planes appeared over the regions of Romani in north-west Sinai, and at various points along the Canal from Kantara to points south of Port Tawfik in the south.

CEASE-FIRE PROPOSED

The U.N. observers proposed a cease-fire for 5 p.m. The Israel Army authorities agreed on condition that it be observed by the Egyptians. However, Egyptian fire continued. The observers then offered another cease-fire for 6.30 p.m.

The air action developed in the early afternoon, when Israeli aircraft attacked enemy positions along a wide area. Two batteries of SA-2 ground-to-air missiles were destroyed, as well as a number of field artillery and medium-range artillery batteries along the northern coast. The Israeli planes were unopposed in the air for two and three-quarter hours.

At about 4.45 p.m., the Egyptians threw in their aircraft to attack Israeli positions east of the Canal, particularly in the areas of Romani, Kantara, Ismailia and Port Tewafik. However, they caused little damage.

Israeli fighters intercepted the Egyptians, and in the resulting engagements knocked down five planes, all falling west of the Canal. At least two of the pilots were seen bailing out.

The Israelis lost one plane in a dog-fight, and another to anti-aircraft fire. It was the first time that the Egyptians downed an Israeli fighter in combat. Both pilots baled out safely in Israel territory.

POUNDING RESUMED

The Israeli air pounding was resumed after this for another hour, until 6.30 p.m. The artillery died down by 8 p.m.

It was the largest air operation along the Egyptian front since August, 1967, and, according to military sources, the most effective one.

The five Egyptian planes lost yesterday bring to 33 the number of Egyptian aircraft downed by Israel since the Six Day War. The breakdown comprises 20 Mig-21s, seven Mig-17s and six Sukhoi-7s.

Israeli plane losses in the same period now total five, including two fighter planes shot down on July 25, 1967 and December 1, 1967, and a Piper spotter plane shot down on March 9, 1969.

A high-ranking Israel Army officer stressed last night that yesterday's operations were aimed chiefly at halting the process of deterioration and escalation in the Suez Canal area. He hoped the Egyptians would understand the message conveyed by the two operations.

He said that Egypt now would have to reconsider its position, as it realizes that Israel can also hit heavily-fortified positions and is prepared to use aircraft in areas where the Air Force was not called into action before.

It was a choice between what Israel considers a very bad situation and a slightly better one as a result of yesterday's operations. He stressed that Israel was not interested in an all-out war or in any renewed war, for that matter, and held that Egypt also seemed not to be interested in such a development. If Israel would not hit the enemy everywhere it would be in a far worse position today.

The senior officer stressed that special measures and precautions had been taken so that U.N. observer posts in the Kantara — Port Said area would not be hit by Israel fire, and hoped that no U.N. personnel were injured. The Kantara-Port Said stretch of the Suez Canal was "quite well covered" by Israel's air force for well over four hours, after Egypt failed to take up two earlier cease-fire proposals by Israel.

Israel had been satisfied with the results achieved from 2 p.m. until 5 p.m., but the Egyptians apparently did not want the action to finish that way.

He denied "firmly and absolutely" that Israel's losses were any more than two planes, from which both pilots bailed out safely.

He said the Israel planes operated over the Kantara-Port Said area for over two hours without any interference, blasting a number of Egyptian artillery positions and two ground-to-air missile bases.

Regarding the Green Island raid, the senior officer stressed the operation was carried out almost without a hitch and if not for one unlucky blast of automatic fire and one grenade, Israeli casualties would have been far lower. The commando party finished its job without any interference by the enemy and the only reason the island installations were not completely blown up, was the time element: the Israel force had to withdraw before dawn,

(Continued on page 8, col. 3)

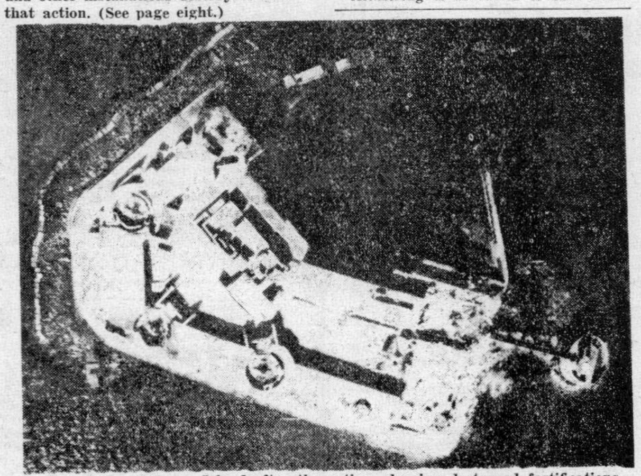

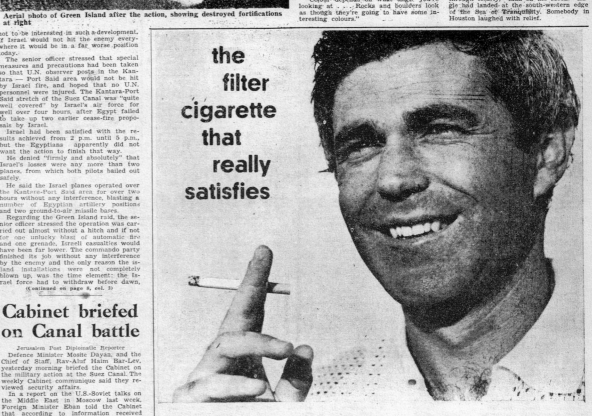

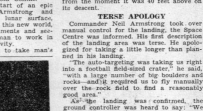

Aerial photo of Green Island after the action, showing destroyed fortifications at right

Man on the moon

IN an America troubled by racial, social and even psychological ills, the space programme has been an invaluable shot in the arm, a source of pride in achievement, a stimulus for individual and national effort. Much of the original decision to invest in the moon project was the late President Kennedy's, who saw in it an important part of his "New Frontier," and found the lively support of Lyndon Johnson.

There have been many protests that space research involves an unpardonable waste of funds in a largely hungry and ignorant world, but in fact the greatest part of the money has gone to subsidize basic and technical research at American institutions, and to create new techniques and advanced materials that may well create a new and greater American wealth in the next decade.

The first serious impetus for the space work came from the shocked realization that Russia must be well ahead to put its first Sputnik into orbit, and the early fears that satellites might be used for military purposes. If America had not struggled, successfully as it now proves, to close this gap, pre-emptive war would have remained at least a threat.

The Russians have learnt supremely well to keep their secrets, and it may be long before we know for certain what their moon-probe Luna-15 is doing up at the moon at this time, but it may be a fair guess even today that the Russians, who give so little information away themselves, want to have their own on-the-spot report on the progress of Apollo-11.

Not only the techniques are new, but also the men. It takes a supreme stoic courage to land a fragile little craft on the moon, and trust to the accuracy of the calculations, the perfection of the craftsmanship, to enable them to take off again 22 hours later. To pilot this machine to a safe landing-place in the full knowledge that a wrong choice will make it impossible to leave again is no small matter, and this thought has been with the space-men since they took off.

The greatest adventure of all, the walking on the moon's surface, is due only today, and after that the men will have to wait for long hours again before they finally discover whether the take-off goes smoothly as the touch-down did last night. This takes the quiet courage of the scientist and it takes away the breath of most of the earth-bound. Until the astronauts return safely, one can only wish them the satisfaction of success, and that their stupendous adventure may yield a rich harvest of discovery. But they have already made history in a new and spectacular form.

Egyptian version claims 17 planes

CAIRO. — Egypt claimed yesterday that its anti-aircraft guns and pilots had downed 17 Israel planes in battles over the Suez Canal and over Sinai. The Army communique, in declaring it was the "greatest Arab victory" since the Six Day War, made no mention of Egyptian losses.

The Egyptian communique said that after the Israel air attacks Egyptian aircraft retaliated with attacks on Israel positions in Sinai, destroying a ground-to-air missile base on the road to El Arish and three radar stations, and hitting artillery positions and ammunition dumps opposite Suez city and a column of tanks.

The Egyptians said that the Israelis attacked with 30 Skyhawk and Mirage jets in the northern section of the Canal at points in Port Said, Port Fuad and Kantara. They came in five flights of six planes each, it was added.

The Egyptians said 13 of the Israel planes were downed by ground fire and two in air battles.

Cairo Radio commentators last night said the Egyptian forces were now capable of achieving "victory over the enemy whether they were on the offensive or defensive." *(UPI, AP, Cairo Radio)*

Cabinet briefed on Canal battle

Jerusalem Post Diplomatic Reporter

Defence Minister Moshe Dayan, and the Chief of Staff, Rav-Aluf Haim Bar-Lev, yesterday morning briefed the Cabinet on the military action at the Suez Canal. The weekly Cabinet communique said they reviewed security affairs.

In a report on the U.S.-Soviet talks on the Middle East in Moscow last week, Foreign Minister Eban told the Cabinet that according to information received there was no change in the positions of the two powers and they remained divi-

(Continued on Page 2, Col. 6)

TOURISTS! Payment in foreign currency

30% REDUCTION!

DUTY & TAX FREE EXPORT SCHEME

Women's and Men's Suede and Leather Coats, Suits & Jackets

★

Men's Suede Jackets with knitted sections Special models $30-35

The Leader in Suede and Leather SALES ROOMS

I. Schneidman & Sons

25 Rehov Zamenhoff, Tel Aviv (corner 99 King George). Tel. 236665

EM museum

armenian museum opening today 4.30 p.m.

visiting hours daily 10 a.m.—5 p.m.

parking — outside jaffa gate

the filter cigarette that really satisfies

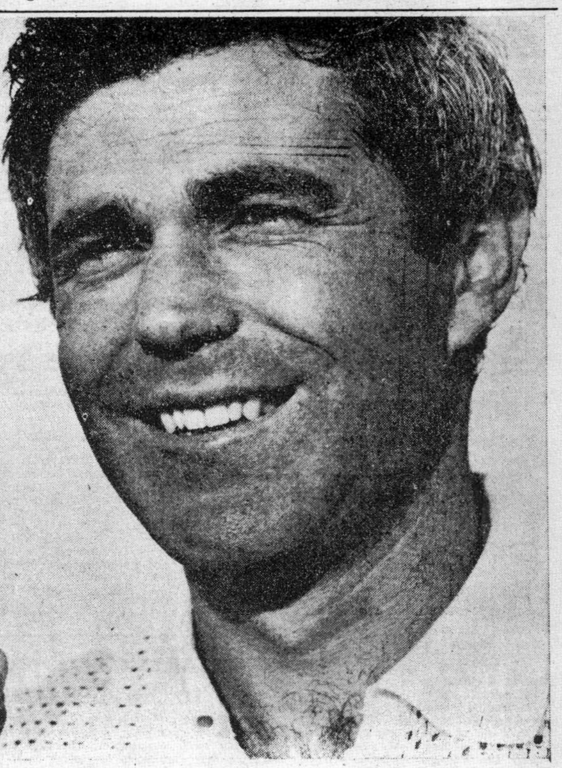

RICH NATURAL AROMA - PURE TOP-QUALITY TOBACCOS - NO ADDED ARTIFICIAL INGREDIENTS... THAT'S WHY

Ascot tastes better — is better!

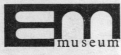

THE JERUSALEM POST

Published in Jerusalem, Israel, daily except on Saturday, by The Palestine Post Ltd. Founded in 1932 by Gershon AGRON. Registered at the G.P.O. Copyright of all material reserved; reproduction permitted only by arrangement. Editor: TED R. LURIE

Jerusalem: 9 Rehov Hahavatzelet, P.O.B. 81, Telephone 28331 (8 lines) Tel Aviv: 44 Rehov Yehuda Halevi, P.O.Box 1125, Tel. 624215 Haifa: 34 Rehov Herzl, Hadar Hacarmel, P.O.Box 4810, Telephone 64594

PRICE: 35 AGORA

SUNDAY, AUGUST 9, 1970 • AV, 7, 5730 • JAMAD TANI 7, 1390 • VOL. XL, No. 12946

Moscow-Bonn Page 2

★

Soviet arms and child Page 3

★

Life guards Page 8

QUIET ON SUEZ FRONT AS CEASE-FIRE STARTS

By ZE'EV SCHUL, Jerusalem Post Military Correspondent

There was total quiet along the entire leng th of the Suez Canal front yesterday, for the first time in almost three years. But the Egypti ans ushered in the cessation of hostilities with a particularly intensive five-hour artillery barrage on Friday night, and two Israeli soldiers were wounded in exchanges of fire around noon Friday.

Israeli warplanes, which have blasted Egyptian positions on the Suez Front almost daily in the past three months stayed at their bases yesterday. Their last blows were also struck on Friday, with heavy morning and afternoon attacks on Egyptian emplacements along most of the front.

The stillness on the Suez was contrasted with flurries of activity on the Lebanese and Jordanian fronts and in the Golan Heights, where the terrorists endeavoured to keep their promise to torpedo the cease-fire. Three Israeli soldiers were wounded when a patrol came under fire in the Golan yesterday morning, and there were numerous Katyusha and mortar bombardments — at Yardena and Menahamiya in the Beisan Valley on Friday night, on the Dead Sea Works at 3 a.m. yesterday morning, at Nahal Kalia in the southern Jordan valley last night, and in the Jabel Ross area of the Hermon on Friday and again yesterday. No casualties or damage were reported in any of the clashes.

Terrorists also opened fire with bazookas on an Israeli patrol on a road near Rosh Hanikra, on the Lebanese border, at 7 p.m. last night. Additional shells fell near the Dead Sea Work last night.

There was no supervision at all of the cease-fire yesterday. No Israeli or Egyptian planes were seen over the Canal Zone. The inspection apparently will be carried out by Israeli and Egyptian joint action with reconnaissance planes making the checks by flying along their own sides of the Canal. U.S. and Soviet satellites will provide a back-up to this procedure, and possibly also checks by U.N. observers.

What is also clear now is that the Egyptains will definitely not agree to Israeli planes in Egyptian airspace, contrary to earlier reports which suggested that both sides might agree to mutual inspection of each others front line zones.

One problem which will probably never be cleared up was whether Egypt's refusal to agree to mutual inspection was any

(Continued on Page 7, Col. 2)

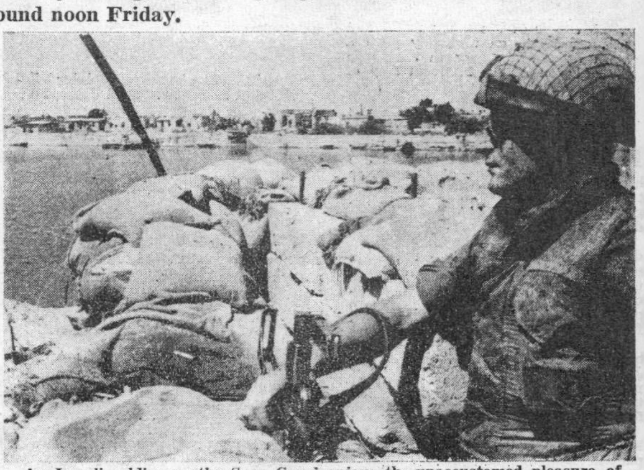

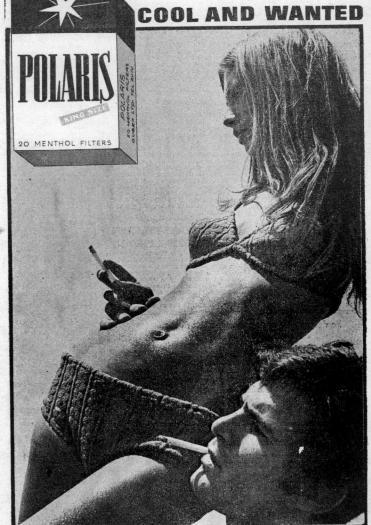

An Israeli soldier on the Suez Canal enjoys the unaccustomed pleasure of standing upright. In the background Kantara, on the West Bank. (Newsphot)

May be 'corridor to peace', Dayan says

Defence Minister Moshe Dayan said on Friday night the cease-fire agreement with Egypt was a "positive step" and that it may turn out to be a corridor leading to peace.

But he told television viewers during an interview he could not forecast the outcome of the forthcoming negotiations under the American initiative.

Mr. Dayan said that Israel agreed to an unconditional cease-fire and he was glad to hear from reports which he received from the U.S. that this cease-fire is in effect a freezing of the existing situation along the Egyptian frontline, with preservation of the *status quo*. In the framework of the cease-fire, no changes will be made and no fortifications built and no additional missiles brought in in addition to the ban on opening fire across the lines and on any advancement towards the lines.

This agreement commits both sides to refrain from military deployments on either side of the cease-fire line, the Defence Minister said.

Replying to a question on the means of supervision, he said that each side would see to it that its counterpart abided by the cease-fire, on the assumption that it will be possible to get the assistance in this of the U.N. observers posted along the cease-fire line. "If violations are committed against us, we shall have to decide in accordance with those violations whether to lodge a complaint about them or to tell the other side: if you shoot — we shall also do so," Mr. Dayan declared.

Asked whether the agreement was ap

(Continued on Page 7, Col. 5)

Bar Lev: Can't predict future

Jerusalem Post Reporter

Sixteen months of continuous military activity on the Suez Canal apparently convinced the Egyptians that they would not be able to attain their aims by force, and that it would be to their benefit to agree to a cease-fire, Chief of Staff Rav-Aluf Haim Bar-Lev said last night.

Interviewed on Galei Zahal, the Chief of Staff said that Israel's military activity "has always been aimed" at preveting war and "achieving a cease-fire," and would continue to do so. In this, he said, the military and political aims of Isdael were identical.

It is difficult, or impossible, at this stage, to estimate what the cease-fire would be like, R/A Bar-Lev said. He added that Israel's soldiers along all fronts understand that a cease-fire does not mean peace or that the war had or will end.

The Chief of Staff pointed out that the side breaking the cease-fire would be responsible for the cessation, and defined a breach as a violation of "any of the components includee in the cease-fire agreement — both the opening of fire and/or any significant alteration of the existing situation."

SILENCE ON THE CANAL

THE cease-fire is welcome because it means there will no shooting, or at least much less shooting, at least for a while, and therefore less likelihood of casualties. One will also perhaps agree with Deputy Premier Allon's phrase that progress towards peace is more likely during such a cease-fire than while a shooting war is in progress.

Families of soldiers will sleep more quietly; we shall all wait for the radio news bulletins less anxiously. Soldiers who have been living underground in bunkers on the Canal will be able to return to the upper world after a while, if the agreement is properly observed. According to the threats of the terrorist organizations in Amman, the children of the Beisan Valley wil have to go on sleeping underground.

The immediate benefits are obvious and undoubted. The long-term effects are still wholly uncertain and contain danger quite as much as hope.

According to the old theory, war is diplomacy continued by other means. Nasser and his mouthpiece Heikal speak as plainly as ever of the need for Egypt to "spearhead the pan-Arab struggle against Israel," but that they must be permitted to use political rather than military tactics if they see fit. They are, in fact, continuing war by diplomatic means. But diplomacy is the proper language between nations with a dispute to settle and it leaves behind no dead who cannot share the fruits of victory.

Even disguised as a curt command to Ambassador Jarring to work out a time-table for Israel withdrawal, Nasser's agreement to the American própsals spells negotiation over Israel's borders and what amounts to a rejection — a courageous rejection, possibly — of the "no peace, no negotiations, no recognition" formula of the Khartoum conference that followed the Six Day War.

There is no reason at present to suppose that Nasser has changed his ultimate objective, the destruction of Israel's independence and sovereignty, both in pursuit of the pan-Arab idea and of Egyptian leadership within this context. There is reason to see a change of method.

Last year, Nasser proclaimed his war of attrition against Israel and began to send commando teams across the Canal in the hope of causing serious damage to Israel's relatively thinly-spaced front line. These naval commandos in their rubber boats were better trained than any other men Egypt has put into the field. Nasser may have hoped for a first genuine victory, if in a limited field. The mission failed totally in disrupting Israel defences although the commandos repeatedly claimed casualties.

The 1967 U.N. Resolution and Rogers' proposals began to look more promising than a fruitless continued war, especially with Soviet-operated missiles and Soviet pilots to bolster his position and allow him to claim he is negotiating from strength and not weakness.

If Nasser has decided that war is not worth while, then the Israel army has won its most important battle. It will remain for the civilian negotiators to be as resourceful, as courageous and ultimately victorious as the army, if we are to see a secure and permanent peace.

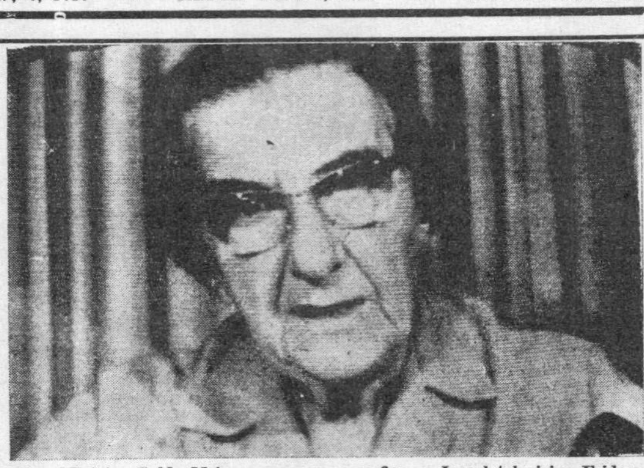

Prime Minister Golda Meir announces cease-fire on Israel television Friday night. (Emka photo)

Mrs. Meir informs nation of cease-fire

Text of Prime Minister Golda Meir's message to the nation, announcing the start of the cease-fire, broadcast on Israel radio at 8 p.m. Friday night and on television an hour later.

I am happy to announce to the people of Israel that a general cease-fire between ourselves and Egypt will come into effect today. This cease-fire, attained at the initiative of the U.S. Government, will commence at 24.00 hours, and will effect all forces on both sides of the cease-fire line.

In my address to the Knesset last Tuesday, I announced the Government's decision to reply affirmatively to the U.S. Government proposal concerning a cease-fire between ourselves and Egypt. Our affirmative reply to this proposal came after we had reached the conviction that the cease-fire would become effective on conditions which would prevent its being abused.

Israel was prepared to adhere strictly to the cease-fire arrangements as laid down at the end of the Six Day War, in accordance with the Security Council resolution of June, 1967. Egypt, however, to our great regret, consistently violated its undertaking, and even publicly declared that it no longer recognised its obligation to observe the cease-fire. Now the Government of Egypt has announced its agreement to a renewal of the cease-fire in accordance with the terms agreed upon between the governments concerned and the U.S. Government, and we welcome this announcement.

Israel, for her part, declares her complete readiness to maintain the cease-fire arrangements meticulously in all their provisions, on a basis of reciprocity.

Citizens of Israel: At the end of the Six Day War, we agreed to the U.N. cease-fire resolution, in the hope that it would not be long before negotiations would begin between Israel and her neighbours on a just and lasting peace. That hope has not yet been fulfilled, but the people and her government have never given up their readiness and their efforts to achieve this desired peace.

It is my hope that the cease-fire which begins today will be observed continuously by the other side, until peace is concluded between our countries. Israel, for her part, would like to regard the cease-fire as a natural stage to be observed on the road to a contractual peace established on defensible, agreed borders between us and Egypt. In the absence of peace, Israel will, of course, continue to maintain in full the situation as established at the time of the cease-fire, and will spare no effort needed to advance the development of the State, so that she should be able to face the trials awaiting her under all circumstances.

We have reached this stage due to our military steadfastness and our political struggle. Ahead of us still lie difficult trials, and what we need is great internal unity, founded on the assurance that our way is the right one.

With all our profound desire that the cease-fire — and not only on this front alone — should be a first step towards peace, we must remember that our road to peace is still a long and hard one.

On the threshold of the cease-fire between us and Egypt, the Government of Israel sends out its greeting to all the soldiers of Israel's defence army, on land, at sea and in the air. To our soldiers who are prisoners of war, and to all our front-line settlements, we send our blessing coupled with the deepest gratitude for the courage and resourcefulness they have shown, and are showing day by day. We bless them and send our love to each one of them, in the hope that, as in the past, so also in the future they will continue to fulfil their tasks successfully in defending the security, independence and prosperity of Israel at all times.

Jarring begins talks; Thant says he's hopeful

By YA'ACOV BEN-ISRAEL
Jerusalem Post Correspondent

UNITED NATIONS. — The U.N. envoy, Dr. Gunnar Jarring, began his newly reactivated peace mission by talking over procedural matters with Arab and Israeli delegates yesterday. He had successive appointments in his office here with Ambassadors Abdullah el-Erian of Egypt, Muhammad el-Farra of Jordan and Yosef Tekoah of Israel.

Secretary-General U Thant meanwhile told a reporter Dr. Jarring "is entering into intensive contacts and discussions" with the parties "on procedure — the site, the time and designation of their representatives for new peace talks." Another U.N. source said Dr. Jarring would be putting questions for the ambassadors to ask their governments on those points.

Later, on his way out, the Secretary-General was asked whether the consultations were going well. "Things have begun on a hopeful note," he said. He added that the Egyptian, Jordan and Israeli representatives would be contacting their governments over the site for the talks.

Before going to Dr. Jarring's 38th floor office Ambassador Tekoah pointed out that: "These are just preliminary discussions." He added: "At this stage we are going into various questions of procedure. Everything is open and this is really the situation at this hour."

U Thant informed the Security Council in a note Friday that Dr. Jarring had already begun work on the new peace effort, and quoted in full a letter he received from Dr. Jarring the same day.

Here is the text of U Thant's note "for the information of the Security Council:"

"I have been informed by the government of the United States that the peace proposal initiated by that government has been accepted by the governments of Israel, Jordan and the United Arab Republic. Subsequently, Ambassador Gunnar Jarring, my special representative to the Middle East, has been given confirmation of these acceptances by the permanent representatives to the U.N. of those three governments.

In accordance with that proposal and in the light of these acceptances, Ambassador Jarring has addressed to me on August 7th the following letter:

'The United Arab Republic, Jordan and Israel advise me that they agree:

(A) That having accepted and indi-

(Continued on Page 7, Col.4)

Jerusalem objects to Jarring text

Jerusalem Post Diplomatic Correspondent

Government circles in Jerusalem yesterday took exception to the fact that Dr. Gunnar Jarring in his letter to U Thant, announcing the acceptance by the parties of the U.S. initiative, adhered strictly to the original text of the Rogers plan and in effect ignored Israel's own letter of acceptance as announced last Tuesday in the Knesset by Premier Golda Meir. Israel's position was also not reflected in U Thant's report on Friday.

Ambassador Yitzhak Rabin arrived last night for urgent consultations in this connection. There is no question here that it was Washington, which, in effect, instructed Dr. Jarring and U Thant to employ the precise text of the Rogers plan in reporting the acceptances of the Governments of Israel, Egypt and Jordan.

Israel is now expected to demand further assurances from Washington that the U.S. understands and in fact accepts the conditions under which Israel is prepared to negotiate as outlined by Mr. Meir.

One of the main points in Israel's letter of acceptance of the U.S. initiative specifies the "withdrawal of Israeli armed forces from territories occupied in the 1967 conflict to secure, recognized and agreed boundaries to be determined in the peace agreements." This was one of the main points of the draft worked out by the special Ministerial committee

(Continued on Page 7, Col. 5)

Talks at F.M. level, Eban says

Jerusalem Post Reporter

TEL AVIV. — "The next political stage will be that the Foreign Ministers of all the sides involved will meet with mediator Jarring, who may come to the Middle East," Foreign Minister Abba Eban said in a television interview last night.

Mr. Eban said that Dr. Gunnar Jarring would come to the area in order to renew old contacts and to discuss the possibility of direct negotiations between the sides involved in the Middle East conflict. "I just want to remind the public that this stage will not be an easy one, not a smooth one," the Foreign Minister warned, "but serious and tricky," he said.

Mr. Eban added that he was convinced that Dr. Jarring would have to spend some time in the area. "In September-November the Foreign Ministers will be in New York for the U.N. General Assembly meeting, but if Dr. Jarring wants to establish real and serious contact with the Governments in the area, he had best pay a visit to, or establish a base near the Middle East," commented Mr. Eban.

"I am not sure exactly what steps Mr. Jarring will recommend," Mr. Eban said, "but I am almost positive that he will not be satisfied with doing the rounds of the area's capitals as in the past. I have reason to believe that he will set up his headquarters in a specified place and there come into contact with the sides.

"He has led us to understand, as have the initiators of the American peace plan, that meetings between the sides are to be on the Foreign Minister level."

Mr. Eban said that he personally believed that Nasser's acceptance was due to a number of reasons, "but I cannot exclude the possibility that a glimmer of a chance for peace may become apparent during the talks. I am not optimistic at this stage," Mr. Eban stated, "but I also cannot reject the hope that serious debate may develop."

THE JERUSALEM POST

Published in Jerusalem, Israel, daily except on Saturday, by The Palestine Post Ltd. Founded in 1932 by Gershon AGRON. Registered at the G.P.O. Copyright of all material reserved; reproduction permitted only by arrangement. Editor: TED R. LURIE

Jerusalem: 9 Rehov Hahavatselet, P.O.B. 81, Telephone 28331 (8 lines) Tel Aviv: 44 Rehov Yehuda Halevi, P.O.Box 1125, Tel. 624215 Haifa: 34 Rehov Herzl, Hadar Hacarmel, P.O.Box 4810, Telephone 64594

PRICE: 85 AGORA

FRIDAY, SEPTEMBER 18, 1970 • ELUL 17, 5730 • RAGAB 18, 1390 • VOL. XL, No. 12981

32-page magazine
★
Apple-picking soldiers page 7
★
Cholera cases page 8

SAVAGE BATTLES RAGE THROUGHOUT JORDAN

By ANAN SAFADI, Jerusalem Post Arab Affairs Reporter

Fierce fighting raged through Jordan yesterday after the new military government launched a wide-scale assault on terrorist positions. Five cities, including Amman, were hit by heavy artillery and rocket fighting. The new military governor-general, Field Marshal Habis el-Majali, clamped down a 24-hour curfew in Amman and Zarka, and ordered his troops to shoot to kill any violators. He asserted that he would continue with the government's task to restore law and order to Jordan during the night.

The Jordanian situation is believed to have been the main topic in a surprise meeting held last night between Egypt's President Nasser and Libya's head of state Mu'ammer el-Gaddafi, on the border of the two countries. Fatah leader Yasser Arafat had earlier appealed to Nasser to intervene. Following the meeting, Egyptian chief of staff Mohammed Ahmad Sadiq left for Amman with messages for Hussein and Arafat.

All communications were cut from Jordan yesterday, and the only word on the fighting came from Radio Amman, speaking for the government, and stations in Damascus and Baghdad broadcasting for the terrorists. The Jordanian government claimed that the Army was winning all battles, especially in the Amman area, but the terrorist radios contradicted this. They declared they had "liberated" all of northern Jordan. They further announced the appointment of three district governors in the area, two of whom serve in the posts under the Jordanian government. In a broadcast over Damascus Radio, the terrorists also named a military commander for the north and asked Jordanian troops to surrender their arms.

It appeared, however, that the Army did indeed have the upper hand, as terrorists called for help from "revolutionary" Arab countries in an emotional appeal which cried that Amman was burning. In code instructions to units in Jordan, the terrorist broadcasts stressed in all messages that "the situation is decisive" or "battles are fierce." Others told fighters to save ammunition and "exchange guards and have some rest."

RADIO WAR

Amman Radio, amid proclamations of victories, repeatedly quoted the Military Governor appealing to the terrorists to surrender their remaining strongpoints. The radio also listed captured men by name and the organization they belonged to, "to assure their families that they are safe and in good health."

Meanwhile, the Middle East News Agency reported last night that Amman has turned into a battlefield and that there were "thousands of casualties" in the streets. The agency added that many houses had been destroyed, and said that medical workers were unable to reach the wounded because of the continued fighting.

Playing it tough for the first time since the first terrorist crisis of November 1968, the Jordanian army yesterday announced it was prepared for a new proposed ceasefire on three conditions that seemed to be unacceptable to the terrorists. Replying to a proposal by an Arab League mediation committee, Amman Radio gave the conditions as an immediate end to terrorist shooting; the recognition of the constitutional right of the army to enter any Jordanian city; and the withdrawal of terrorists from all populated areas. The radio said the army was prepared to facilitate the terrorist withdrawal "to any point on the cease-fire line."

Meanwhile, the 14-nation Arab League met in emergency session.

Indications were that the terrorists were getting the worst of it in Amman,

(Continued on Page 8, Col. 4)

BULLETIN:

AMMAN (AP). — King Hussein's troops and armour blasted their way into Amman yesterday, fighting terrorists house by house for possession of the city, moving in behind an artillery barrage.

Heavy guns in fixed positions around Amman pumped salvo after salvo into this city of 600,000. Shells tore through white stone houses on the slopes of Amman's seven hills. People in refugee camps were mown down by the score.

Nests of terrorist machineguns kept up fire from rooftop points, as troops moved in behind armour to root out snipers.

SHOWDOWN IN JORDAN

FACED with the alternatives of abdication or a strong bid to reassert his authority, King Hussein opted for the latter and appointed a military government with a free hand to finally deal with the terrorists.

It had become increasingly clear during the past few months that the repeated agreements reached between the King and the terrorists (there were three in the past week alone) could not provide a solution to the increasing fragmentation of power in Jordan.

The airplane hijackings apparently brought the situation to a head. The Jordanian Government found itself impotent in the face of a flagrant violation of its sovereignty and the army felt its humiliation to be unbearable.

Fearing that a strong stand would lead to civil war and perhaps to the partition of Jordan between Syria in the north, Iraq in the east, Saudi Arabia in the south and Israel in the west, Hussein's first decision was to abdicate. Abdul Nasser persuaded him to change his mind.

The Egyptian President needs the Jordanian King. Hussein is Nasser's contact with the West, his line of communication to Washington and London. And Hussein is one of the few Arab heads of state supporting Egypt's acceptance — however nominal — of the American peace plan. His replacement by any of the terrorist leaders, including Yasser Arafat, who are opposed to the Jarring mission, would leave the Egyptian ruler almost completely isolated, without an escape hatch to the West, and more dependent upon Moscow than ever.

Russia is also interested in strengthening Hussein. The destruction of four "imperialist" aircraft was a victory for Peking, and Moscow, which has criticized the hijackings, wants to curtail the growing influence of the extremist Chinese-backed terrorists.

Declarations of support for the terrorists by Syria and Iraq have been revealed as little more than empty promises. The Syrians, despite their eagerness for a foothold in Jordan, have no troops to spare. The 12,000 Iraqis, whose presence on Jordanian soil Hussein has accepted, appear to be incapable of speedy action, and south of Amman they would come up against Saudi Arabian troops who will not remain inactive if the Iraqis attempt to aid the terrorists.

Should the civil war continue for any length of time, Nasser may try to persuade Hussein to compromise. The Egyptian leader was successful, last November, in persuading the Lebanese Government to back away from its showdown with the terrorists there, under an arrangement in which the terrorists were allowed a free hand in "Fatahland." Nasser may attempt to sell a new Cairo Agreement, under which the terrorists are granted complete freedom of action in a restricted area of Jordan — thus allowing Arafat to save face.

On the other hand, a speedy victory by the military government will strengthen Hussein's position not only vis-à-vis the terrorists but in his relations with Nasser as well. The Jordanian King could emerge from the struggle within his own country strong enough to escape from his subservience to Egypt. Such a posture of strength might make an all-important difference in the Jarring talks and in the future of the Middle East.

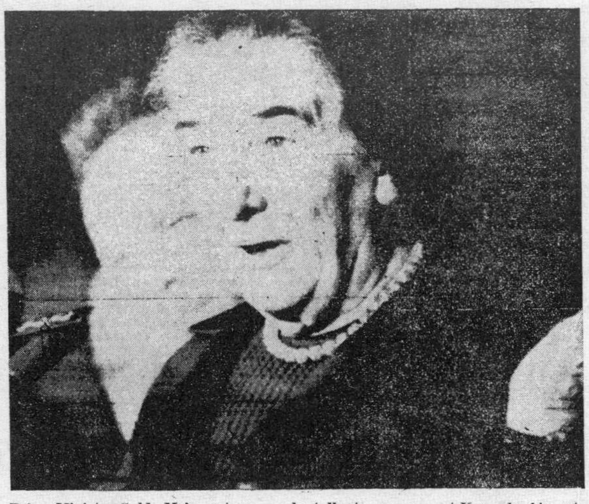

Prime Minister Golda Meir gestures as she talks to newsmen at Kennedy Airport in New York. Looking over her shoulder is Israeli Ambassador to the U.S. Yitzhak Rabin. (AP radiophoto)

NIXON, MEIR MEET THIS AFTERNOON

By ERWIN FRENKEL
Jerusalem Post Correspondent

WASHINGTON. — Prime Minister Golda Meir will meet with President Nixon here today amidst a heightened sense of crisis prompted by the fighting in Jordan. The events in Amman are expected to intrude upon the talks in a way not envisioned earlier.

Mrs. Meir, who before her meeting with the President (at 5 p.m. Israel time) will see Secretary of State William Rogers, is expected to focus strongly on the mounting Soviet military involvement in Egypt. Any more specific discussion of Israel's military needs will grow out of that point.

U.S. officials do not underestimate the military significance of the missile movements on the Suez front. They also claim understanding of Israel's anxiety and Jerusalem's decision not to restart the Jarring talks unless the missiles are moved back.

However, they do not believe that Israel's basic security posture has been impaired. They do not believe that Nasser is in any position to mount a large-scale attack or Canal crossing, and certainly not to sustain it.

One State Department official also rejected the idea that the Soviets would seek to provide air cover for any such attempt which would lead them to overfly Israeli-held territory. The Russians know that any such action could mean confrontation with the U.S., he said.

At least some State Department officials are prepared to concede that there have been a series of "misunderstandings" with Israel in recent weeks, for which the U.S. must claim part of the responsibility. But they stress that the U.S. has not been trying to play it cute. "We had to verify the missile violations from our own sources, precisely in order to maintain our unpartisan broker role," one official said.

They also protest the notion that the U.S. is being outmanoeuvred by the Soviets. The U.S. has no illusions about Soviet aims, they say, but it is a settlement rather than escalation of hostilities which alone can reduce the Soviet presence in Egypt, they believe.

HOW TO RECTIFY

It is for this reason that American leaders are expected to impress upon Mrs. Meir the need to find a way to resume the talks with Dr. Gunnar Jarring. But at the same time they are expected to agree that rectification of the missile movement is a necessary precondition. The open question is how that term is to be defined.

Little difficulty is expected on Israel's economic aid requests, for which precise details are not available. There is no confirmation to reports that the U.S. plans a $400m. to $500m. programme.

Mrs. Meir is scheduled to be back in New York on Sunday. But much of her Washington schedule after today's meetings remains flexible. Thus there remains the possibility that if necessary she may hold more than one meeting with the President. Her press conference here is scheduled at 11 p.m. Israel time today.

(See story Page 2)

Hussein seen able to beat terrorists

Israel Radio's senior military commentator, Aluf (Res.) Haim Herzog, said last night he could not imagine that Israel could stand by idly in case that Iraqi and Syrian troops would intervene in the fighting in Jordan. But at the moment any action by the Iraqis or the Syrians was unlikely, he stressed.

Transport Minister Shimon Peres said last night that in the event that Iraq, Syria and Saudia Arabia would annex parts of Jordan, this would put an end to any negotiations regarding the future of the West Bank. Speaking in an interview on Israel television, Mr. Peres said that should Jordan be occupied by its neighbours, even Israel's biggest opponents could not claim that the West Bank was occupied.

Mr. Peres stressed that whatever the outcome of the fighting in Jordan, King Hussein could not be a partner for peace negotiations with Israel because he had not effective rule over his country.

He predicted that the Palestinian element would come out much stronger in Jordan, once the fighting was over, because King Hussein would try to make a deal with those Palestinians who oppose the terrorists. He rejected any possibility that Israel should conduct secret negotiations with the Palestinian terrorists, because they were irresponsible outlaws. Even if Yasser Arafat or George Habash should gain the upper hand and head a Jordanian Government, they could not be partners for negotiations with Israel, he said.

Our military correspondent adds.

Military experts predicted the Army would win its all-out fight with the terror gangs. It was expected that King Hussein would order his army to get the unpleasant "job" over and done with as soon as possible — without necessarily liquidating the gangs but at least keeping them confined to the Jordan Rift facing Israel, where, he believes, the terrorists belong.

Egypt continues to hold a key position in the crisis but it has remained neutral in its reports on the situation. This was in turn interpreted here as an indication of Egypt's indirect support for the King. The Egyptians must know that the terrorists had little chance against Hussein's disciplined armour, artillery and infantry units.

Despite loud battle cries from Baghdad in support of the terrorists, there was also no indication that any of the Iraqi units in Jordan had gone to the aid of the hard-pressed gangs.

U.S. has no plans for military intervention

Jerusalem Post Correspondent

WASHINGTON. — Here The State Department spokesman said here yesterday that the U.S. has no plans for any military intervention in Jordan. However, Department officials stressed that the U.S. is watching the situation "minute-by-minute," and they do not rule out some kind of action if it becomes clear that the lives of the 54 hijack hostages, who include 38 American citizens, are endangered.

Last week the U.S. flew six military transport planes to Turkey to stand at the ready for the possible medical evacuation of the hostages.

(Defence Secretary Melvin Laird announced later that the U.S. is prepared to airlift Americans from areas of Jordan where there are clashes. He added that the U.S. would depend on the Jordanian Air Force to protect any airlift from the embattled area rather than use Navy aircraft from the U.S. Sixth Fleet.)

State Department Spokesman Robert McCloskey said that King Hussein has not requested any military aid from the U.S. He declined to comment on what the U.S. would do if such a request were made.

U.S. officials tend to believe that King Hussein's forces will be able to overcome the terrorists in the fighting that has broken out. But it is notable that State Department denials of any possible U.S. military action were less vigorous yesterday than on Wednesday.

The White House has set up a special top-level group to keep watch on Jordan developments and determine American responses. Contact continues with the U.S. Embassy in Amman, which has been damaged by small arms fire, but there are no reports of any harm to U.S. personnel, who have taken refuge in the inner rooms of the Embassy.

What worries U.S. officials is the lack of contact with the P.F.L.P., which holds the hostages. The last such contact was

(Continued on Page 8, Col. 5)

Terrorists 'protect' airline hostages

BEIRUT (Reuter). — The terrorists' Central Committee said last night all possible steps had been taken to protect the 54 hostages still held following the airliner hijackings last week.

Home of El Al manager broken into

ROME. — Thieves last night broke into the apartment of Mr. David Bar-Ness, the Director of El Al in Rome, while he and his wife were out. Mrs. Bar-Ness, the Israel Consul in Rome, is the former Lucy Sharon, who served as personal secretary to Mrs. Golda Meir when she was Foreign Minister.

Mine kills two Israelis

By H. BEN-ADI
Jerusalem Post Reporter

GAZA.—Two persons were killed and four injured in mine and grenade explosions in the Rafah area of the Gaza Strip yesterday. In Rafah, echoes of the terrorist campaign against King Hussein's forces led to a general curfew.

Two Kiryat Gat men were killed, and a third slightly injured, yesterday morning when their tractor struck a mine. The incident took place at about 5.40 a.m. one kilometre south of Kerem Shalom on the main road connecting Rafah and Sinai.

The dead men are 48-year-old Yitzhak Gertz and 23-year-old David Cohen.

The third man, Sylvester Gratzman, 23, a new immigrant, told "Itim" he and his two partners were on their way to soil reclamation work for a new agricultural settlement.

Gertz had lived in Kiryat Gat for many years. He originally came from Russia. He was married and the father of four daughters and a son. One of the daughters recently completed her army service.

Cohen, who immigrated from Morocco, was unmarried. He is survived by two brothers, both members of the Kiryat Gat police department. The funerals will be held today in Kiryat Gat.

In Rafah, three persons, including a three-year-old boy, were injured by a grenade explosion in the market at about six a.m. yesterday. They are 50-year-old Abdel Rahamim Hasnin, 50-year-old Lipiah Rahamim Hasnin, and three-year-old Jamil

(Continued on Page 7, Col. 4)

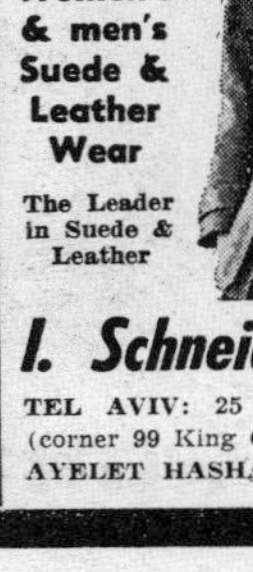

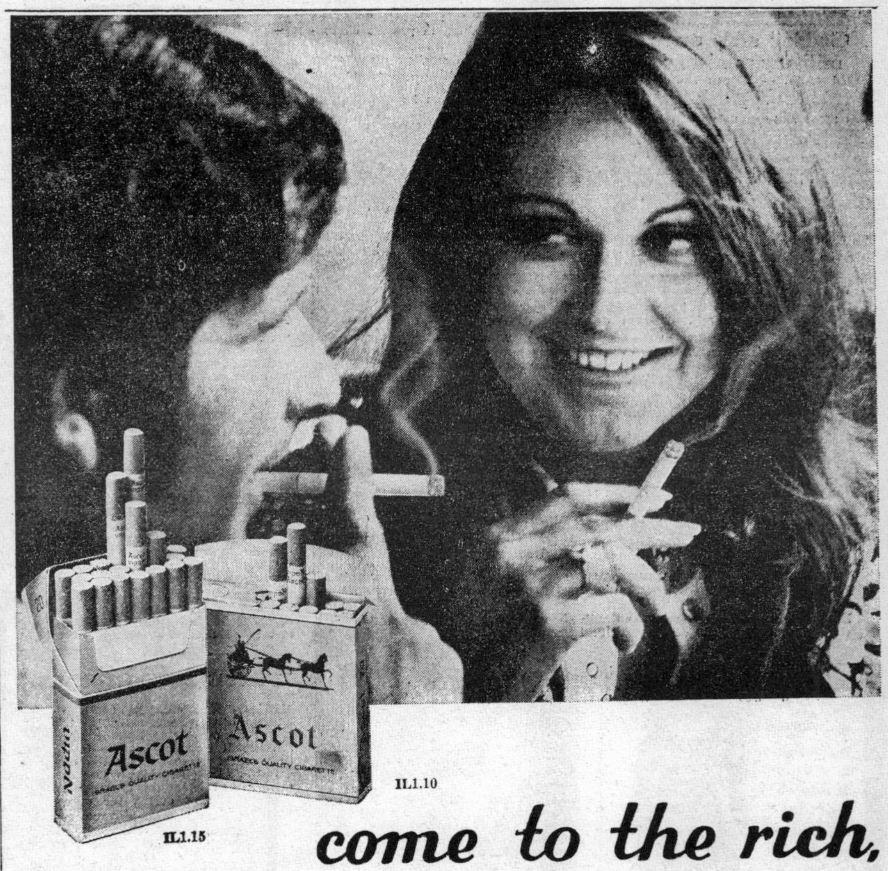

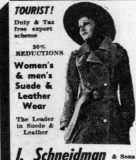

THE JERUSALEM POST

Published in Jerusalem, Israel, daily except on Saturday, by The Palestine Post Ltd. Founded in 1932 by Gershon AGRON.

Registered at the G.P.O. Copyright of all material reserved; reproduction permitted only by arrangement.
Editor: TED R. LURIE

Jerusalem: 9 Rehov Hahavatzelet, P.O.B. 81, Telephone 28331 (8 lines) Tel Aviv: 44 Rehov Yehuda Halevi, P.O.Box 1125, Tel. 624215 Haifa: 34 Rehov Herzl, Hadar Hacarmel, P.O.Box 4810, Telephone 64594

TUESDAY, SEPTEMBER 29, 1970 • ELUL 28, 5730 • RAGAB 29, 1390
PRICE: 40 AGORA VOL. XL, No. 12990*

NASSER DIES SUDDENLY OF MASSIVE HEART ATTACK

CAIRO (Reuter). — President Gamal Abdul Nasser of Egypt died last night, aged 52, of a sudden heart attack at his home on the outskirts of Cairo. Vice-President Anwar el Sadat announced Nasser's death over radio and television, his voice breaking with emotion, at 10.10 p.m. Cairo Radio and other broadcasts were interrupted for recitals from the Koran. The funeral will take place on Thursday at 11 a.m. Nasser had just accomplished another diplomatic success by bringing Jordan's King Hussein and terrorist leader Yasser Arafat together to sign a peace pact in Cairo on Sunday. His death came as a bombshell to the Egyptian people, and to the world at large.

In recent years, Nasser has had several spells of ill health, generally reported to be caused by faulty circulation in a leg. He twice underwent medical treatment in the Soviet Union, the second time last July just before he startled the world by accepting the American peace initiative for the Middle East. He had appeared to have recovered well after the treatment in Russia.

According to the provisions of the Egyptian constitution, Sadat — the only vice-president — takes over from Nasser. He said the Arab Socialist Union's Supreme Executive Committee held a joint session with the cabinet to discuss the situation arising from Nasser's death.

Mr. Sadat announced that the President had experienced the first symptoms of the attack at 3.15 p.m., as he was returning home from the ceremonies marking the end of the Arab summit talks on the Jordan crisis. He died in his suburban Cairo home at 6.15 p.m. of a "massive heart attack."

FUNERAL ON THURSDAY

The President's body was last night moved to the Kubbeih Republican Palace to await the funeral, which will take place at 11 a.m. on Thursday.

An official medical bulletin said that while Nasser was seeing off the Emir of Kuwait at Cairo airport yesterday morning, he suddenly complained of dizziness and weakness and began sweating heavily. The President drove to his home, at which his doctors were immediately called.

They found he had suffered a very severe heart attack as a result of coronary thrombosis.

All possible treatment was given including regulation of heart-beats.

Close to tears, the Vice-President told the people: "the U.A.R., the Arab nation, and the whole of humanity has lost one of its most precious, most courageous and sincerest of men."

Referring to Sunday's peace pact between King Hussein and the Palestinians, Sadat said Nasser had just devoted all his efforts to prevent a horrible tragedy from engulfing the Arab nation.

Egyptians wept openly in the streets of Cairo as the death was announced.

Nasser leaves a wife, Tahia Nasser, two daughters and three sons. He became a grandfather in 1967 when his daughter Mona gave birth to a baby boy.

A tall man with sparkling blue eyes and an infectious grin, Nasser was a civilian king in the hearts of most Egyptians.

Millions of Egyptian school children dutifully began their day by singing: "Nasser, We all love you, Nasser, We all cherish you, Nasser, We all follow you, Nasser, You are loved by all, Nasser."

At his death, he was graying at the temples and maintained an erect military bearing. He was as personally austere as he was politically flamboyant. A devout Moslem, he carefully obeyed Islam's rules of abstinence from alcohol, although he was a heavy smoker. He shunned the extravagant way of the Egyptian monarch he deposed — it was a strong reason for his immense personal popularity.

After a career of revolutionary and military activity, Nasser first came into the international limelight in the 1952 *coup* which deposed King Farouk and put General Mohammed Naguib in power. It soon became apparent Naguib was the figurehead and Nasser the main "backroom boy."

All through his early life he had been struggling. The son of a postal worker, he was born in Assiut province, January, 5, 1918. He found it difficult as young man to get into Cairo's military academy. He was finally admitted in 1937 after a year in law school and graduated as a second lieutenant to fight in Sudan and later in the 1948 war with Israel, in which he was taken prisoner in the Faluja pocket, along with an entire brigade.

After the 1952 *coup* Nasser held the post of Deputy Prime Minister and Minister of the Interior. In 1954 he became Prime Minister and Military Governor of Egypt.

ATTEMPTED ASSASSINATION

During this period the balance of power swung between Naguib, who supported a return to democratic government, and Nasser, who was backed by those who wanted to maintain the military regime. He escaped death by inches when five bullets were fired at him during a mass rally in Alexandria. The Sudanese Minister of Communications and an official standing near him were both injured.

The gunman was a member of the Moslem Brotherhood, then the government's biggest single opponent. On November 4, 1954, General Naguib was stripped of power because of allegations of being involved with the Brotherhood, and Nasser took over the duties of head of state, although the office of President remained vacant.

In 1955 he went to the Afro-Asian conference in Bandung, Indonesia, his firs trip outside Egypt except for a pilgrimag to Mecca, and also toured India, Burma Afghanistan and Pakistan to talk to thei leaders. He was, with then Presiden Nehru of India and President Tito o Yugoslavia, one of the three leaders o the "unaligned world."

He signed a pact with Czechoslovakia to exchange cotton, rice and other products for arms. An announcement that he had an offer of Russian aid to build the Aswan High Dam led Britain and the United States to make their own offers.

The year 1956 proved to be momentou — it saw Egypt's recognition of independent Sudan, a new constitution providing for a strong president and a plebiscite adopting Nasser as President an his nationalization of the Suez Canal or July 26 in retaliation for the West' withdrawal of offers to build the Aswan Dam.

In 1956, the U.S., Britain and the International Bank withdrew support for loan to start the Aswan High Dam. Nasse nationalized the Suez Canal and later received help from the Soviet Union fo construction of the dam.

The 1956 Suez debacle, in which h survived the joint attack by three countries, was perhaps his most spectacula political success. It was the event tha catapulted him to world prominence. Sue became a "symbol" and rallying poin for the "third world" emerging nation in their drive toward independence. I was also his first major move toward th Soviet Union.

In May 1967 he ordered U.N. troop stationed along the Israel-Egypt borde as a result of the 1956 war, to leav Egyptian territory, precipitating a nev Middle Eastern crisis. He moved Egyptia troops up to the Tiran Straits and declared a blockade of the Gulf of Aqaba cutting of Israel's port of Eilat. Fightin broke out on June 5 and ended withi a week with Israel victorious.

Nasser offered his resignation in broadcast on June 9, a day after acceptin the U.N. call for a cease-fire. The National Assembly rejected his resignatio and Nasser said he would bow to th wishes of the Arab peoples.

Then he channelled all his energies int rebuilding his country's demoralised arme forces. Soviet weapons and military experts poured into Egypt.

NASSER'S DEATH

THE death of Egypt's President, Gamal Abdul Nasser, has stunned Israel as well as the Arab world.

In the short run, the passing of Israel's chief enemy may perhaps bring a respite in the military movements at the Suez Canal and other war preparations against Israel, while Egypt adjusts to a new leadership, and the Soviets reassess their policy.

Despite his enmity, Nasser offered Israel a hope, however slight, which was afforded by no other Arab leader — that of a man strong enough to lead the Arab world to peace. This hope was strong in the early years of the Nasser-Naguib revolution, and never quite disappeared from Israeli thinking. Some even saw in Egypt's recent acceptance of the Jarring talks a move in this direction.

The future of Egypt and the Middle East is now, more than ever, wrapped in uncertainty. It will be a long time before another Egyptian or Arab leader attains the status achieved by Nasser.

In a situation of flux, the West may try to manoeuvre for a more favourable position with the new regime, and the Soviet Union may seize the opportunity to intensify even further its presence in Egypt. The new Egyptian leadership, for its part, may adopt a more extremist attitude.

Israel's hope for real peace remains in a stable Middle East. The death of President Nasser will not, unhappily, bring that goal closer to attainment.

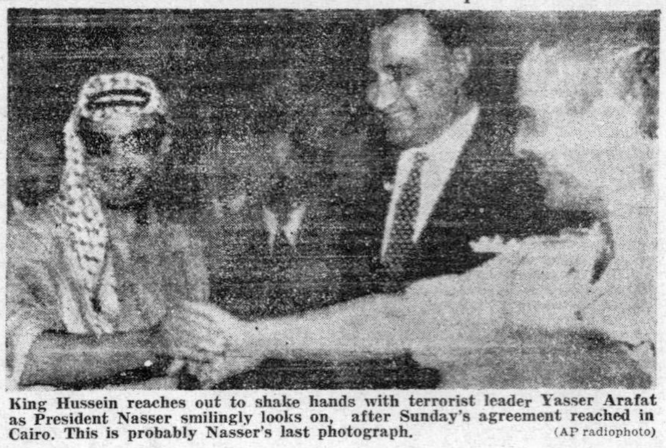

King Hussein reaches out to shake hands with terrorist leader Yasser Arafat as President Nasser smilingly looks on, after Sunday's agreement reached in Cairo. This is probably Nasser's last photograph. (AP radiophoto)

Israel hopes for new chapter, leading to peace

Jerusalem Post Staff

First official Israel reaction to President Nasser's death came last night from Minister Israel Galili, who recalled that in July 1952 the then Prime Minister, Mr. David Ben-Gurion, had welcomed the new regime in Egypt and expressed the hope that it would bring about new relations with Israel.

Mr. Galili, whose statement is understood to have been coordinated with Prime Minister Golda Meir, said that now with the forthcoming Government changes in Egypt, Israel is prepared once more to open a new chapter that will lead to peace on the basis of reciprocity.

Israelis were stunned to hear the news about 10.15 p.m. when the radio and TV interrupted their programmes for the announcement.

Nazareth residents who were up late enough to hear the news of Nasser's death from Cairo and other radio stations last night were shocked by the report. People went to each other's homes with the news and began discussing the implications.

Arab Knesset Member Abdul Azziz Zuabi told *The Post*, "I am sorry at his death. Nasser was the man who accepted the U.S. peace initiative which was the precondition for peace. It is hard to say who his successors will be. There is no doubt that he was the wisest man in the Arab world. I am concerned for my country, Israel, and I am therefore concerned as to who his successors will be. I sincerely hope that they will be as 'moderate' as he was among the Arabs," he said.

Tulkarm Mayor Hilmi Hanun, who met Nasser for the first time in 1958, told an Itim reporter that Nasser's death was a great loss to the entire Arab world especially at a time of travail for the Palestinian people.

Dr. Kadri Toukan, former Jordan Foreign Minister, who had met Nasser several times, said he was a "great Arab hero, a humanitarian, who was an example to all those who fought for their motherland. We feel this loss terribly and ask God to give us strength to bear this."

Hikmat al Masri, former Speaker of the Jordanian Parliament, said that Nasser's death was "a tragedy for the Arabs, the Moslems and for peace." Mr. Masri was overcome with emotion as he spoke. When Nablus Mayor Ma'azuz el Masri was informed of the news by Itim, he was stunned but managed to say, "Nasser was a great man and a great Arab leader."

Truce observers tour Amman; terrorists charge violations

AMMAN. — Arab cease-fire observers, driving in police cars with red lights flashing and green flags waving, yesterday began the dangerous and delicate task of defusing the explosive Amman situation.

After a night that, despite scattered bursts of fire, was the quietest since fighting on September 17, there was no sign up to 8 a.m. of either side beginning the military withdrawal from the capital required under Sunday night's Cairo agreement.

Terrorist sources said Jordan army units attacked three of their positions yesterday and warned they would "return fire" against army violations of the cease-fire.

(A Jordanian army officer yesterday claimed that 50 Syrians had been captured in his sector during the bitter Amman fighting. "We recognised them by their accents," said Captain Sayed Mohammed, a Beduin officer in the Fourth Armoured Division. "We were fighting against many Syrians as well as the *fedayeen*." During the height of the fighting, Jordan claimed that Syrian armoured forces had crossed the border, but this is the first time they were said to have moved as far south as Amman.)

The Damascus-based terrorist radio said Jordanian army units attacked the north Jordan town of Aljouni and opened heavy artillery fire on terrorist positions at Allan and Um el-Amat, south of the capital. The radio said the army used 106-mm. recoilless rifles, mortars and tanks in the actions.

There were no reports of fighting in Amman, where Military Governor Habis Majali announced a relaxation of the curfew for five hours in the morning in seven sectors and for four hours in the afternoon for seven other sectors. The

(Continued on Page 8, Col. 4)

Secure borders Israel's aim, Eban tells U.N.

UNITED NATIONS (Reuter). — Israel's Foreign Minister Abba Eban yesterday reaffirmed his government's readiness to resume peace talks under U.N. auspices "as soon as the violations" of the cease-fire standstill were rectified.

In a major address to the U.N. General Assembly, he submitted a map of the Suez Canal area marked to indicate the reported build-up of Soviet surface-to-air missile batteries since the standstill was initiated on August 7.

This showed a sharp increase in the number of batteries on a broader front and less than 20 km. from the Canal. On the cease-fire date they were more than 32 kms. further west and were fewer.

Mr. Eban said "not a single hour" passed after agreement to the 90-day cease-fire, before Egypt was moving up Russian-built missiles in the Suez Canal zone. Within a few days, he said, both Israel and the U.S. had verified this.

Mr. Eban told the General Assembly that Israel's aim in negotiation "will be the determination of new boundaries offering a firmer security than the old Armistice lines could ever provide."

"In short," Mr. Eban said in a major policy speech, "there are no solutions without peace — and there are no problems which peace cannot resolve."

New Israel protest on truce violations

TEL AVIV. — Additional ground-to-air missile batteries, both Sam-2 and Sam-3, have been advanced in the Suez Canal area, the Israel army spokesman announced yesterday. A further complaint was submitted yesterday to the cease-fire supervision authority concerning these grave violations by the United Arab Republic of the cease-fire and military standstill.

Moreover, construction work and other preparations for new sites intended for ground-to-air missiles are continuing within the same area.

Impact on all Arab states; problem of succession

By ANAN SAFADI
Jerusalem Post Arab Affairs Reporter

The news of Nasser's death had an immediate impact on all Arab states where radio stations interrupted their regular programmes for readings from the Koran. This included even Iraq where the ruling Ba'th party had voiced the sharpest attacks on Nasser until his last moments.

The Arab world will not easily find a substitute for Nasser among the existing rulers of the Arab states. He was the first to address the Arab man in the street outspokenly, and the first Arab to step on the stage of world politics.

The problem of replacement will be more evident in Egypt itself, where Nasser ran the country as a one-man show. He had eliminated his main rivals, and only two members remained of the 15-man military junta which, along with Nasser, overthrow King Farouk in 1952. These are Vice-President Sadat, 50, and Hussein e-Shafei, 52, a member of the nine-man Executive of the Arab Socialist Union, the country's only political party. Both are weak personalities.

STRONGMAN SABRI

There remains strongman Ali Sabri, who, while regarded as Moscow's creature, had climbed the ladder of power on occasion despite some attempts to suppress his image. It was feared last night that the massive Soviet presence in Egypt may eventually lead to Sabri's accession to power, but that for a time Sadat may be an interim President. But even if Sabri takes over power, Moscow will not find life in the Middle East as easy as it was during Nasser's lifetime.

Expressing the deep grief of Egyptian leaders, Sadat said in his broadcast last night that "the only way to do Nasser justice is for the entire Arab nation to stand fast, be patient, brave and capable until the achievement of victory for which Nasser had lived and died as a martyr."

"Peaceful spirit, return to your Lord, content. Enter my kingdom, and into my heaven," Sadat said quoting from the Koran.

TOURIST!
Duty & Tax free export scheme
30% REDUCTIONS
Women's & Men's Suede & Leather Wear
The Leader in Suede & Leather

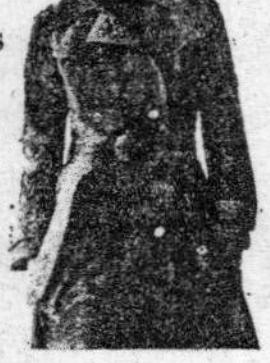

I. Schneidman & Sons
TEL AVIV: 25 Rehov Zamenhoff (corner 99 King George), Tel. 236665
AYELET HASHAHAR: Guesthouse

Develop Israel with Israel Bonds

TOURISTS!
Shalom STORES
THE LEADING DEPARTMENT STORE IN ISRAEL!
45 DEPARTMENTS
THOUSANDS OF ITEMS
GIFT SHOP — SOUVENIRS
*
ON INSTRUCTIONS OF THE MINISTRY OF TOURISM
REDUCTION FOR TOURISTS PAYING WITH TRAVELLERS CHEQUES
15% REDUCTION ON CLOTHING FOOTWEAR, SOUVENIRS, JEWELLERY, CARPETS AND FILMS
30% REDUCTIONS ON LEATHER COATS, SUITS, JACKETS, etc.
9 Rehov Ahad Ha'am, Tel Aviv, Tel. 52131
Shalom STORES
BEAUTY PARLOUR
HAIRDRESSING SALON FOR MEN AND WOMEN
EXPERT MANAGEMENT
POPULAR PRICES
(3rd floor)
Tonight open till 8 p.m.

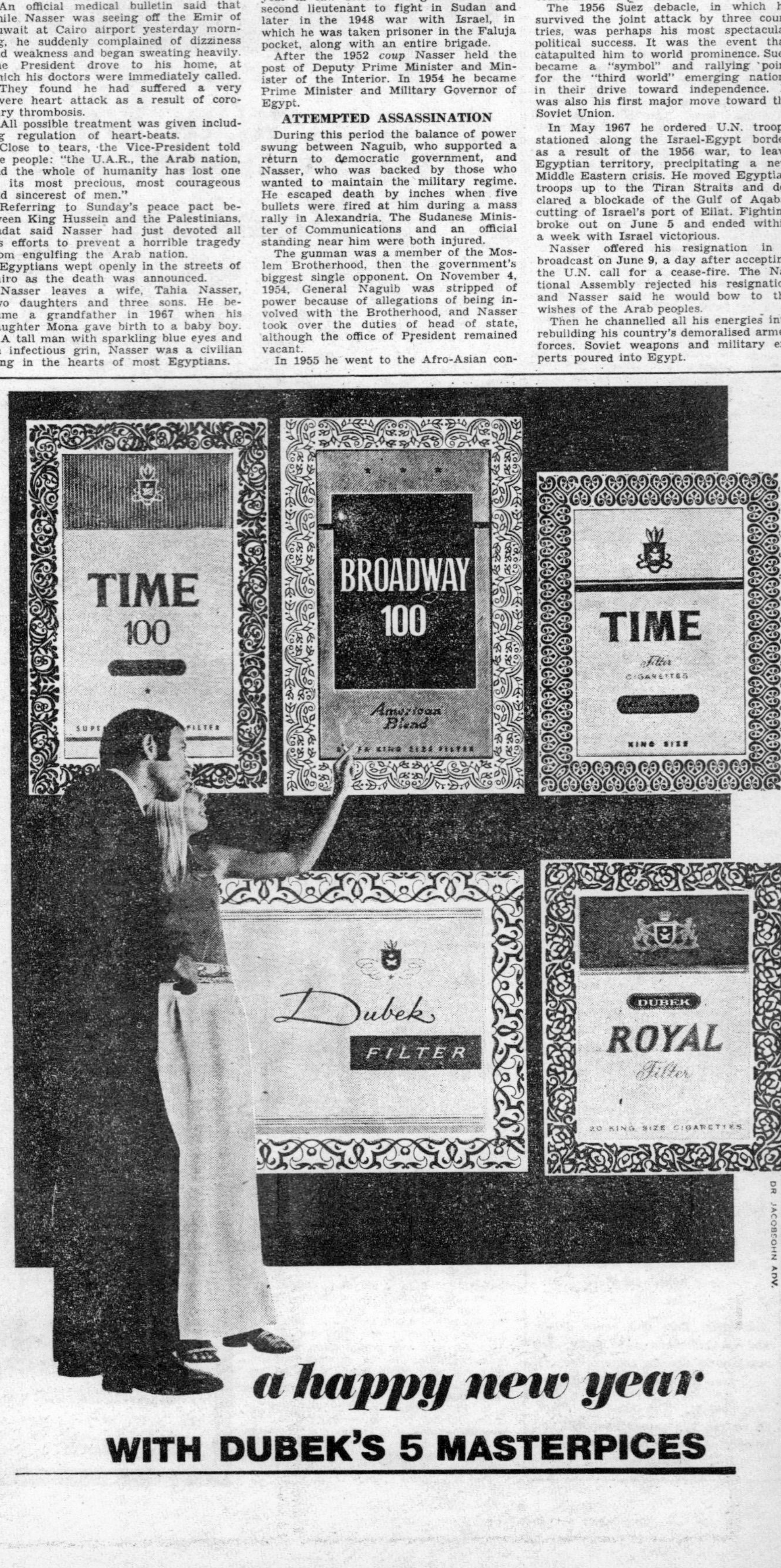

a happy new year
WITH DUBEK'S 5 MASTERPICES
DR JACOBSOHN ADV.

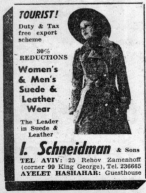

THE JERUSALEM POST

Published in Jerusalem, Israel, daily except Saturday by The Palestine Post Ltd. Founded in 1932 by GERSHON AGRON
Registered at the G.P.O. Copyright of all material reserved; reproduction permitted only by arrangement. Editor: TED R. LURIE
Editorial Offices and Administration: The Jerusalem Post Building, Romema, Jerusalem. Telephone 528181. P.O. Box 81 (91000)

Tel Aviv: 44 Rehov Yehuda Halevi, P.O.B. 1125 (61000). Tel. 624215 — Haifa: 34 Rehov Herzl, Hadar Hacarmel, P.O.B. 4810 (31040). Tel. 640794 — Jerusalem branch (adverts, subscriptions): 6 Rehov Aristobulus. Tel. 223966

Hijack Monday Page 3 ★ Computers Page 11 ☆ Yeshayahu Page 12

Price: 45 Ag.

WEDNESDAY, MAY 10, 1972 • IYAR 26, 5372 • RABI AWWAL 26, 1392 • VOL. XLII, No. 13480*

SABENA PLANE HOSTAGES FREED AS TWO TERRORISTS KILLED

By ZE'EV SCHUL and YITZHAK OKED, Jerusalem Post Reporters

LOD AIRPORT. — Israeli soldiers in the guise of white-overalled airport technicians stormed the hijacked Sabena airliner here yesterday afternoon, killing two of the four Arab terrorists after a brief exchange of shots and ending the 23-hour ordeal of the 90 passengers and 10 crew.

A sense of joy swept the country as Israel Radio broke into its regular programme at 4.45 p.m. yesterday with a bulletin announcing the rescue.

The Belgian Boeing-707, hijacked by four Arabs, two of them women, was liberated before the terrorists could carry out a threat to blow up the plane if terrorists imprisoned in Israel were not released.

The two terrorists shot dead were both men. One woman hijacker was seriously wounded. She had been sitting in a passenger seat, holding an explosive charge. A second woman terrorist was captured uninjured.

A woman passenger sitting next to the wounded woman terrorist was herself hurt seriously while another passenger was suffering from "medium" injuries. Three Israeli soldiers were slightly wounded in the operation.

The attacking soldiers, masquerading as El Al maintenance men in white overalls, examined all the aircraft wheels to replace those that had become deflated during the night, thus preventing takeoff by the airliner.

The men stormed the plane while sandwiches and cold drinks were being served on board — undoubtedly distracting the attention of the hijackers as well as that of their hostages.

LASTED FEW SECONDS

Passengers later told *The Post*, "They appeared everywhere ... we didn't see anything. All of us ducked under the seats." And mere seconds later, two of the terrorists were dead, while the woman hijacker, said to be the key figure in the affair, was wounded in her seat.

The only unwounded member of the terrorist quartet, a girl, was whisked away by the security forces. Passengers described the two male hijackers as European-looking and said they wore wigs. Both were killed in the first exchange of shots.

The fourth terrorist, described as a pretty girl and the "number two" of the unit, was still sitting in her seat, clutching a pushbutton device (which would have touched off the explosives) when the attack took place. She was seriously injured but

(Continued on page 12, Col. 3)

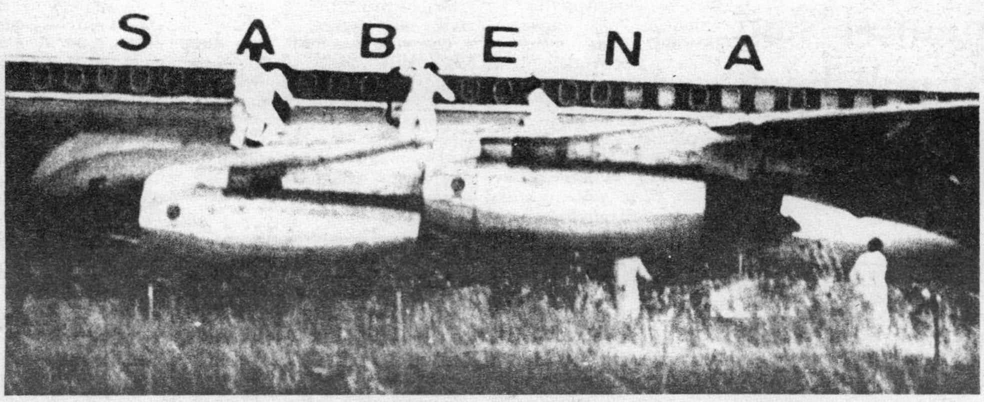

Soldiers masquerading as maintenance men seen at the moment they broke into the Sabena airliner in this long-shot photo taken by David Rubinger at Lod Airport yesterday.

RESCUE IS DESCRIBED

Photographer David Rubinger, picture editor of *The Post*, was taking pictures with a telephoto lens on the field about 700 metres from the plane when the rescue operation went into effect. Following is his report:

Shortly before 4 p.m., three Red Cross men drove up to the plane. They talked to the hijackers through the plane cockpit window for a few minutes. At about 4.10 p.m. two airport trolleys rolled up, carrying about 18 men dressed in white mechanics' overalls.

The "mechanics" then started looking over the plane, checking the wheels and other exterior parts of the plane.

"This went on for about five minutes and we photographers were taking shots," said Rubinger.

"Suddenly, apparently at a given signal, the 'mechanics' ran for the doors.

"We stood astounded for a few minutes. The next thing we saw was a woman passenger sliding down the wing."

HAPPY ENDING

IT took the Israel Army exactly two minutes to drive home the lesson that mightier nations have failed to grasp: surrender to blackmail only encourages more hijackings and endangers the lives of countless innocent passengers.

The Israel Government was faced yesterday with one of its most trying decisions. It had to implement what it had counselled other governments and airlines, for the past five years. Israel could not permit terrorist extortion, threatening one hundred lives and the air lines to the country, to succeed.

The government faced its grave responsibility with great determination buoyed by its faith in the resourcefulness of the army and the security branches.

The unprecedented, imaginative and bold operation which overcame the hijackers, will undoubtedly buoy the faith of passengers and airlines alike in civil aviation's capacity, if the will is there, to overcome the hijack nemesis.

Many people will be remembered for the part they played in the great Sabena drama. From the Ministers of Defence and Transport, the Chief of Staff and the unnamed soldiers who risked their lives, to the captain of the aircraft and his crew, the Red Cross officials and the passengers themselves.

There are many lessons to be drawn from this trying event. The first is that tight security measures must be instituted and applied everywhere. No country is immune from madmen or politically motivated fanatics. No airport can afford to be lax. El Al has taken the lead in security and would no doubt be happy to share its knowhow and experience with other airlines who have, up to now, scoffed at the security precautions, saying that a determined hijacker could not be stopped.

International civil aviation must be prepared now, more than at any other time, for possible reprisals by members of the Black September or other terrorist organizations. Israel has shown that a determined policy and tight security measures can prevent hijacking. If other nations would apply similar measures the international community could put an end to terror in the air.

Claim of trickery

FATAH THREAT TO BELGIUM

By ANAN SAFADI
Jerusalem Post Arab Affairs Reporter

The Fatah movement last night accused the Belgian government and the International Red Cross of deceiving the four terrorist hijackers. In a broadcast over Cairo-based radio, "Sawt al-Assifa" (Voice of the Storm), the Fatah said that the Belgian and the Red Cross representatives have helped "open a loophole" in their hijacking operation. The Fatah warned that the terrorists would be more careful "next time." The Fatah, in particular, threatened to take measures against Belgian interests.

The Fatah represented the hijacking operation as an achievement which demonstrated "a challenge on the land of confrontation." The Fatah said their victory was in dragging Moshe Dayan to the airport and keeping him there under difficult conditions for 20 hours, throughout all the 20 hours."

The Fatah gave its own version of the ending of the hijacking, claiming "several enemy soldiers were either killed or wounded."

The radio mentioned the death of two of the hijackers and the capture of two. It gave the names of the four as Major Ahmed Awad, Lt. Abdul-Aziz el-Atrash, Theresa Is'hak Khalsa and Rima Issa.

Other Arab stations, including Cairo's news agency, said the four hijackers were "deceived" by the Israeli troops, who were said to have approached the plane protected by a Red Cross flag.

Of all Arab radio reports only Amman's sounded different. Flashing the news of the army's capture of the plane barely an hour after it took place, the Jordanian state radio appeared to be satisfied with the defeat of hijackers belonging to the Fatah-affiliated "Black September" movement, whose first action was assassinating Jordan's Premier Wasfi e-Tel in Cairo last November.

The attack on the hijackers occurred shortly after Egyptian authorities announced they had placed

(Continued on page 12, Col. 3)

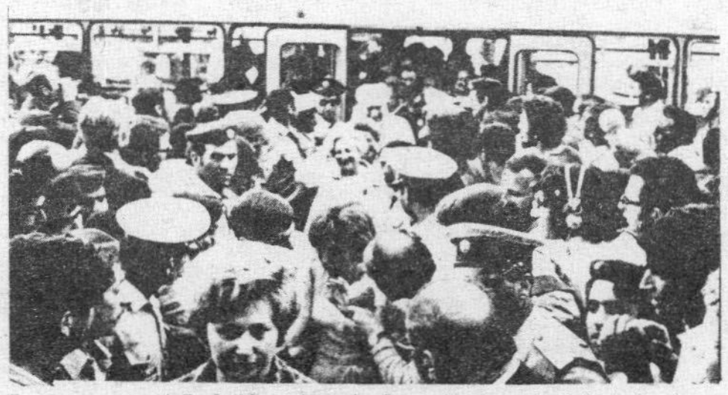

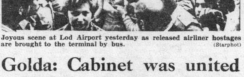

Joyous scene at Lod Airport yesterday as released airliner hostages are brought to the terminal by bus. (Starphot)

Golda: Cabinet was united against yielding to demands

Jerusalem Post Reporter

Prime Minister Golda Meir last night expressed the nation's gratitude to "our brave and intrepid boys" for having freed the captured Sabena plane.

Mrs. Meir, in a special statement on radio and television, stressed that the decision to go ahead with the operation to free the grounded airplane "was most definitely not taken with the assistance of any outside source, just as our soldiers, who performed the operation, were most certainly not helped by any foreign source."

The Prime Minister said: "The nightmare is over," explaining that the Government's deliberations were overshadowed by the knowledge that the plane was in danger of being blown up, and in the face of this, the Government had to weigh up, react and decide. She went on: "The Government had to take upon itself a tremendous responsibility and not to submit to blackmail and violence, and reject the demand to release hundreds of murderers from prison."

Mrs. Meir was gratified at the united stand of the Cabinet on this issue. "All of us were fully aware of the terrible significance of submission to the terrorists, and we had the fullest confidence and trust in our boys, in their bravery and their capabilities. Our decision was right and just, and the captured plane was indeed released."

Our Political Reporter adds:

The Cabinet met in emergency session at 10 a.m., following night-long top-level consultations between Prime Minister Golda Meir and Defence Minister Moshe Dayan, who remained at Lod Airport throughout. Transport Minister Shimon Peres arrived in Jerusalem by helicopter from Lod to report.

Condition of two passengers serious

Jerusalem Post Reporter

TEL AVIV. — The wounded woman terrorist underwent an operation and is now resting comfortably at the Sheba Government hospital. Doctors say that she is out of danger, the I.D.F.'s spokesman reports.

Sheba hospital doctors added that the condition of the passenger, Mr. Wildred Kordovski, continues to be serious and that he underwent a serious operation. They also said that the condition of the yet unidentified woman passenger is also serious.

Police hold priest, aide

By ZE'EV SCHUL

Airport police yesterday detained two of the passengers of the Sabena aircraft.

According to another passenger, Mr. Oskar Fischer of Antwerp, Belgium, the two, a senior Greek Orthodox priest and his secretary "embraced and kissed" the two male terrorists after the latter had announced their takeover of the aircraft.

Mr. Fischer, who was interviewed by *The Post* as he was passing through the customs, said:

"There is this one thing I want to check. There were two additional men on board the plane. I do not know whether they were actual members of the terrorist group or only friends. But after the terrorists thought they 'had won' the two men embraced and kissed them. They seemed to know each other quite well.

"I want to check up on this. I was told that we would all stay together as a group after our debarkation and I want to identify them."

This reporter took Mr. Fischer to the police and subsequently Mr. Fischer picked out an elderly frocked Greek Orthodox Priest and his young secretary, one of whose sleeves was smeared wtih blood.

Earlier, news agencies said the Greek Orthodox Metropolitan of Austria, Dr. Chrysostmos Tsiter, was among the passengers. He boarded the plane during the stopover in Vienna. He was invited to visit Israel by the Greek Orthodox Patriarch of Jerusalem, Benediktos, and was accompanied by his secretary, Michael Staikos.

Overflights claimed

Lebanon has complained to U.N. truce observers that Israeli Phantom jets twice flew over Lebanese territory Sunday and Israeli soldiers took up positions inside Lebanon for about two-and-a-half hours, according to a report last night from Reuter News Agency.

Reuter reported that the Chief of Staff of the U.N. observers, Major-General Ensio Siilasvuo, said one of the overflights and the troop penetration, up to a distance of 200 metres, had been confirmed by U.N. observers.

General Siilasvuo also reported a complaint from Israel that an armed Egyptian vessel approached the coast in the Suez Canal area, near the Israel-Egyptian cease-fire line, last Saturday. The complaint was not confirmed by U.N. observers.

U.S. STARTS MINING OF N. VIETNAM HARBOURS

SAIGON. — Hundreds of U.S. warplanes and a naval task force struck anew at North Vietnam yesterday after mining Haiphong and five other harbours in a concerted campaign aimed at strangling its supply lifelines.

The move was an unprecedented escalation of the war ordered by President Nixon.

The mines will not be activated until noon Israel time tomorrow so foreign ships will have a chance to leave the ports, ringed by an explosive network sown from the air in a move former President Lyndon Johnson never chose to make in four years of bombing North Vietnam.

No U.S. planes were lost in the mine-laying operation although a military spokesman said a North Vietnamese Mig fighter was shot down trying to stop the American aircraft.

Radio Hanoi reported that American destroyers shelled Haiphong yesterday. It also claimed that two U.S. destroyers shelling populated areas of Haiphong were hit and set on fire.

Peking Radio said China has lodged a strong protest with the U.S. against the bombing of Chinese ships by U.S. aircraft and warships in the coastal region of North Vietnam's Nghe An province. The radio, quoting a Foreign Ministry statement, said Chinese sailors were injured in the air and sea attacks on the Chinese ships Hung Chi 152 and Hung Chi 160 on May 6-8. It said the two vessels were severely damaged.

Shortly after President Nixon announced the drastic action, General Creighton Abrams of the U.S. Command Headquarters issued a statement saying: "U.S. Navy aircraft

(Continued on page 2, Col. 4)

Kissinger: Risk not unacceptable

WASHINGTON (Reuter). — White House adviser Henry Kissinger said yesterday President Nixon's order to mine North Vietnamese ports was a risk to U.S. relations with the Soviet Union and China, but did not involve an unacceptable risk.

Dr. Kissinger, speaking at a press conference, expressed the hope that the Russian leaders would understand why the President had decided to try to stop the supply of Soviet weapons to Hanoi and would go ahead with the planned summit with Mr. Nixon this month.

He stated flatly that the President had rejected a theory that the North Vietnamese offensive in the south was planned and conceived by the Russians as a deliberate attempt to humiliate the U.S. as Mr. Nixon prepared for summit talks due to begin in Moscow on May 22.

Dr. Kissinger said the White House had received no indication from the Soviet Union as to whether the summit would go ahead or be called off, and he thought it would be a day or two before any information was received here. "But we are proceeding with summit preparations and we see, at this moment, no reason to postpone the summit," he declared.

The State Department announced that Secretary of State William Rogers has cancelled the rest of his European visit because of the situation in South-East Asia.

Department Spokesman Robert McCloskey said Mr. Rogers' decision to cancel the remaining part of his trip, which was abruptly interrupted on Sunday when the Secretary was recalled to Washington, was made after consultations with President Nixon.

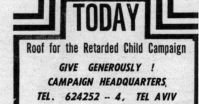

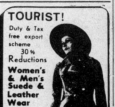

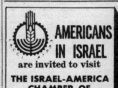

THE JERUSALEM POST

SECOND EDITION

★ U.S. sniper Page 4 ★ U.K. wins 2:1 Page 12

Published in Jerusalem, Israel, daily except Saturday by The Palestine Post Ltd. Founded in 1932 by GERSHON AGRON
Registered at the G.P.O. Copyright of all material reserved; reproduction permitted only by arrangement. Editor: TED R. LURIE
Editorial Offices and Administration: The Jerusalem Post Building, Romema, Jerusalem. Telephone 528181. P.O. Box 81 (91000)

Tel Aviv: 44 Rehov Yehuda Halevi, P.O.B. 1125 (61000). Tel. 624215 — Haifa: 34 Rehov Herzl, Hadar Hacarmel, P.O.B. 4810 (31040). Tel. 640794 — Jerusalem branch (adverts, subscriptions): 6 Rehov Aristobulus. Tel. 223966

Price: 45 Ag.

WEDNESDAY, MAY 31, 1972 • SIVAN 18, 5732 • RABI THANI 18, 1392 • VOL. XLII, No. 13497*

Twelve dead, 50 wounded in Lod terrorist shooting

Ten to 12 persons were killed and 45 to 48 persons wounded, 12-14 of them seriously, at Lod Airport last night when a gang of terrorists fired submachine guns and lobbed hand grenades into the crowded arrivals hall. The gang, numbering three or four persons, described by onlookers as "Japanese-looking" had alighted from an Air rFance plane, arriving from Paris and Rome at 10.30. Collecting their baggage at the conveyer belt in the customs hall, they suddenly produced Kalatchinikovs from their suitcases and bursts throughout the hall, interspersed with the lobbing of hand grenades.

As the passenger in the hall took cover, the terrorists ran towards the glass partition dividing the hall from the rest of the terminal building and started shooting at the crowd waiting for the arriving passengers.

The terminal hall was filled with smoke of the firing, which continued for a considerable time.

From there, the terrorists rushed through the gates onto the airfield, and threw grenades at a Scanair plane, damaging the engine.

One assailant was captured, one killed himself and a third was still at large, Israel Radio said last night.

Security forces rounded up the gang.

Defence Minister Moshe Dayan, Transport Minister Shimon Peres and senior army officers headed by O.C. Central Command, Aluf Rehavam Zeevi, were at the scene soon after the incident.

Dr. David Kreisler, deputy director of Tel Hashomer Hospital, said last night that all the operating rooms were working at capacity, 25 were the hospitals blood bank and other emergency equipment.

It is believed that Prof. Aharon Katzir, 58 of the Weizmann Institute was among the acsualties.

The Marxist Popular Front for the Liberation of Palestine (PFLP) last night claimed its guerrillas were responsible for the shooting.

Lod Airport was closed shortly after the 10.30 p.m. attack, and incoming planes were diverted to Nicosia, Cyprus, as maintenance crews worked feverishly to clear up the broken glass and ruined luggage in the blood-stained arrival hall.

Wheel spins faster

THE Bank of Israel Governor has again voiced his concern over the rising inflationary pressure. In the past ten weeks the means of payment have increased by 10 per cent, or twice as much as in the whole of 1970. The adverse effects of such overheating are already becoming noticeable in rising prices, in the slowing down of export expansion, in soaring imports, in the growing labour shortage and strike threats, in the rising demand for consumer durables and luxuries, and in the widening gap between the living standards of underprivileged groups and those at the top.

Mr. Sanbar said that the recommendations submitted by him three months ago, and as yet only partially carried out, were already outdated, as stronger measures were now required in view of the worsened situation. He no longer ruled out resort to fiscal policy, in particular to the Added Value Tax, notwithstanding the widespread misgivings expressed against this form of across-the-board taxation.

His words had a rather hollow ring, hovering somewhere between an authoritative statement of policies and mere good advice. The position of the central bank's Governor is complex. He is *ex officio* the government's economic adviser, but on the other hand he is obligated to carry out the government's economic policy even if he does not believe it to be right. The current issue concerns not the best way to fight inflation, but the basic approach to the problem. The administration has not yet made up its mind whether to call the bluff of vested interests opposing anything that might tend to end this apparently pleasant state of careless prosperity.

Everybody knows that this hesitancy is largely due to the unresolved tug-of-war between the government and the trade unions engaged in a massive repeat performance of their large wage-gain in 1965. One may hope that this time the disastrous consequences of acute inflation will be avoided, and a joint formula for action found before a slowdown overtakes us. But there are also ill effects to the current state of anxiety and lack of clear planning. It is not only that valuable time is being lost, and that the steps that will eventually have to be adopted will therefore have to be more radical and more painful to be effective. No less important is the loss of confidence in the democratic machinery that is inevitably generated by the sight of a government that is inactive and undecided, apparently fearful of the reaction of other power structures — that is, the Histadrut. Neither the incomes policy nor a possible, far-reaching tax reform should be decided by behind-the-scenes arrangements presented to the public as a *fait accompli*.

In order to be successful, a financial and fiscal policy must be based on the cooperation of the public and therefore on their participation in the process of policy making. Opinions may be divided on whether or not inflation should be permitted to continue at the speed of the past year. But a situation in which the government's actions do not coincide with officially announced policy is an insult to all the principles of democracy.

U.S. bombers hit Haiphong

North Vietnamese said beginning to pull back

SAIGON. — U.S. military authorities believe the North Vietnamese have begun to make their first withdrawals of troops from their two-month offensive in the South.

The sources said elements of two North Vietnamese divisions had pulled back from the besieged provincial capital of An Loc into Cambodia. They were identified as the 7th and 9th divisions and both were reportedly battered by hundreds of U.S. B-52 strikes.

The disclosure came as South Vietnam President Nguyen Van Thieu flew into Kontum city and declared his forces had "broken" the Communist siege of the major central highlands province capital. The President also visited Pleiku and the old imperial capital of Hue. There he promoted the marine commander.

U.S. sources in Kontum said that only mopping up operations remained to remove the Communist commandos from the city. Vietnamese officials said more than 1,000 Communist troops had been killed in the heavy fighting of the last five days.

At the same time the U.S. command announced in Saigon yesterday that U.S. fighter-bombers smashed one of North Vietnam's biggest railroad yards on the outskirts of Haiphong and wrecked 16 bridges across the country in a new series of air blows on Monday.

The strikes against the Uong Bi railroad yard 16 kms. northeast of Haiphong were the first on the installation since the resumption of the bombing of North Vietnam on April 6, and marked a further widening of the air war to new targets. *(AP, UPI)*

'Smart' bombs key to success

SAIGON (AP). — One of the principal reasons for the dramatic success of the resumption of full-scale bombing of North Vietnam has been the wide use of electronic "smart" bombs by U.S. Air Force fighter-bombers, American officials say.

Guided by laser light beams and television cameras to their targets, the bombs' almost pinpoint accuracy has accomplished more in two months against a certain type of target than the entire 1965-68 bombing campaign, these officials say.

"We've been able to cut most major bridges and roads from the defence lines north of Hue up to the Chinese border," says one official. "Both the north-east and north-west rail lines linking Hanoi with China have been cut."

Officials report there have been no signs of major movement of war materials from China southward either by rail or truck.

"The tactics of how to use the smart bombs under hostile conditions had not been really developed," says a source. But that was all changed by the North Vietnamese offensive and the tactics of successfully employing the electronic bombs began to bear fruit in April, the source adds.

Generally, a flight of two jets operate together in using the laser bombs. One is armed with a laser gun that throws out a light ray, much like that of a flashlight, on the target. But the ray is narrow, like a rope, and does not expand as would a flashlight fixed to the side of a barn.

The second jet drops the bomb, fitted with a mechanism in its nose, that homes in on the light ray. U.S. officials say the marking of error for a laser bomb is five feet or less. A "dumb" iron bomb dropped with normal trajectory has a margin of error of 150 feet.

The laser-guided bombs are generally 2,000 and 3,000 pound blockbusters.

Opec backs Iraq in oil fight

VIENNA (Reuter). — The 11-nation Organization of Petroleum Exporting Countries (OPEC) yesterday threw its support behind the Iraqi government which is threatening action against the Western-owned I.P.C., unless it increases oil output and meets other claims.

The general secretary of OPEC, Dr. Nadim Pachachi, said the organization was calling an extraordinary meeting and would announce a time and place shortly.

(Ultimatum — Page 3)

Hijackers hold plane for transom in Brazil

SAO PAULO (Reuter). — Two armed hijackers held 87 people aboard a Brazilian airliner at the city airport here yesterday demanding a ransom of one and a half million cruzeiros (about £200,000).

Military and air force police surrounded the plane, which was parked in front of a hangar with its engines still running, local radio reports said.

Sanbar urges tax to fight inflation

By DAVID KRIVINE
Jerusalem Post Economic Correspondent

The Governor of the Bank of Israel is to recommend imposition of an Added Value Tax this year as a way of increasing tax revenue, though he had recently stated that extra taxes should not be necessary.

The Governor, Mr. Moshe Sanbar, reminded newsmen yesterday that in his recent report on the means of payment, he had recommended a series of measures to counter inflation, and most of them have been adopted. But he had explicitly assumed then that the "framework agreement" signed by the Histadrut and the Manufacturers Association would determine the wage structure for the next two years.

"If that agreement is applied, new taxation should not be necessary; but the signs are that wage earners will get more." Asked what levy he recommends, he stated: "The Added Value Tax. It is the most intelligent tax, under present conditions."

Referring to the Bank's Annual Report for 1971, released to correspondents at his press conference yesterday, Mr. Sanbar showed that prices went up by one-quarter in 1970 and 1971 — "but that was a functional price rise. It was planned through taxes and the devaluation."

In the present year, prices are going up of their own accord — owing to excess demand, and not because the Government planned it that way. It is a cause for serious anxiety, the Governor said.

Since his last report on the means of payment (which has to be prepared whenever the money in circulation increases by more than 15 per cent in less than 12 months), the means of payment have shot up by 10.6 per cent — in 2½ months (March 1 to May 17).

"During the single month from

(Continued on page 2, col. 6)

Visit seen as 'show of flag'

Nixon discussing oil, Iraq rift with Shah

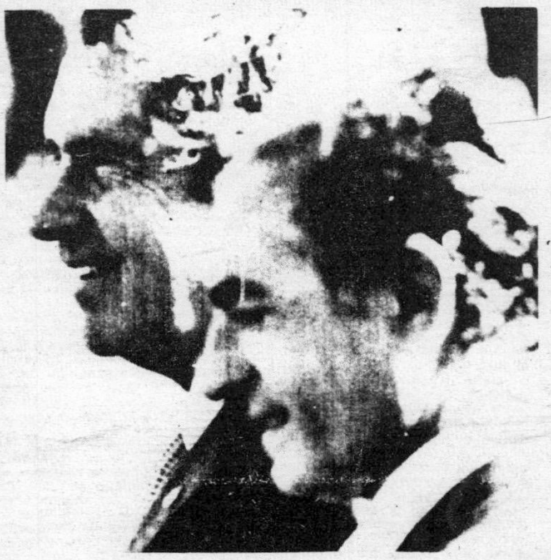

U.S. President Nixon with the Shah of Iran on his arrival in Teheran yesterday. (AP radiophoto)

TEHERAN. — President Nixon arrived here yesterday afternoon for a brief visit designed to "show the flag" in the critical Persian Gulf area and reassure the Shah of Iran of the continued interest of the U.S. in this region.

Two hours after arriving to a booming welcome at Mehrabad airport, Mr. Nixon was closeted with the Shah in a business session at Saadabad Palace, where President and Mrs. Nixon are staying during their 22-hour visit. Mr. Nixon was expected to assure the 52-year-old Shah, long considered one of America's firmest friends in this area, of continued U.S. concern for the stability of the area now that Britain has abandoned Aden and left the Trucial States.

Officials estimated at more than half a million the crowds that lined the 15-kilometre parade route from the airport to the Saadabad Palace. Among the cheering flag-waving throngs were school children, gymnast classes in colourful uniforms, boy and girl scouts and tens of thousands of ordinary citizens.

The President and the Shah rode in Mr. Nixon's bubble-top presidential limousine waving happily to the crowds who applauded them as they passed and shouted "welcome" in Persian.

Every few paces along the route, with the imposing snow-capped Alborz mountains in the background, were 10-foot long American flags and the same size green, white and red Iranian flags.

(Overnight, squads of municipal workers pasted little blue patches over some 5,000 American flags decorating Teheran. The flags had been given 51 stars and the patches corrected the error.)

Presidential adviser Henry Kissinger told newsmen aboard Mr. Nixon's plane that he expected talks with the Shah on general oil policy, the Middle East and South Asia, as well as on the new Soviet pact with Iraq, the neighbour with whom the Shah has occasional difficulties.

Mr. Kissinger said American military aid to Iran is proceeding in a routine fashion and no extended talk on that was necessary.

The Nixons were being honoured last night with a state dinner at Niavaran Palace. This morning Mr. Nixon will lay a wreath at the tomb of Reza Shah, the father of the present ruler, hold another meeting with the Shah at Saadabad Palace and then give a midday "dinner" honouring the Shah and Empress before leaving at 1.50 p.m. for Warsaw and another overnight stop before returning to Washington. *(UPI, Reuter)*

Briton charged as 'Israel spy' in Lebanon

BEIRUT. — The military public prosecutor here yesterday charged a middle-aged Briton and two Iraqis with spying for Israel, and referred them to the military investigating magistrate for further questioning, it was officially announced.

The three men — Robert Jackson, Issam Binyeh and Kassem Halim Kassem — were arrested on Friday.

Police are looking for an American, a Swiss and two Lebanese Jews.

The British Embassy is seeking consular access to Jackson, but this has not been granted.

Mr. Jackson, 52, worked for many years as an accountant in Iraq before coming to Lebanon in 1968, where he obtained a similar position with an international firm of accountants. He retired eight months ago to a villa he had bought in a small village north of Beirut.

According to "A-Nahar" newspaper, Jackson used to travel to Cyprus and then to Israel where he told intelligence agents about the movement of anti-Israel terrorists, submitted reports on the Lebanese economy, Arab airline companies, their budgets and assets. *(Reuter, AP, UPI)*

IRA GROUP SPURNS CEASE-FIRE BID

BELFAST (UPI). — The Provisional Wing of the Irish Republican Army yesterday answered the Official Wing's call for a cease-fire with bombs and bullets. In a flurry of attacks, gunmen killed two civilians, wounded a third and blew up a beer bottling plant and a laundry, a British Army spokesman said.

Other gunmen, believed to be Provisionals, fired at patrolling British troops more than 25 times, he said. The gunmen missed, but the soldiers said they shot at least four of their assailants.

In Londonderry, Roman Catholic housewives, supported by a men's committee, organized a "peace petition" in the Catholic Bogside and Creggan estates. Mrs. Mary Barr, one of the leaders, said they expected "many thousands" of Catholics to sign the document which rejects violence.

All three civilians were gunned down in pre-dawn shooting incidents and found later by troops, the spokesman said. A patrol found Leonard McAteer, 23, fatally shot, and his companion wounded in the eye in Ballynastreagh, a small town 50 kilometres south of Belfast. The bullet-riddled body of the third man, unidentified, was discovered in the gutter of a street dividing Catholic and Protestant districts in Belfast.

Bombs later heavily damaged Belfast's Morton's beer bottling plant and a laundry that catered to British troops in a nearby suburb, but injured no one.

Spokesmen said two armed men and two women forced their way into the bottling factory and planted four bombs. Two went off after the employees had time to flee, causing more than £100,000 worth of damage.

The bombings and shootings followed an indefinite cease-fire announced by the left-wing official wing of the IRA after weekend talks in Dublin. The official IRA said it had taken the decision "to avoid sectarian civil war which the Provisionals' bombing campaign is threatening to provoke."

In Belfast, a spokesman for the Provisional Wing described the cease-fire call as a "surrender."

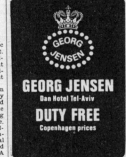

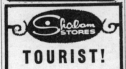

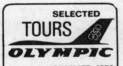

THE JERUSALEM POST

Published in Jerusalem, Israel, daily except Saturday by The Palestine Post Ltd. Founded in 1932 by GERSHON AGRON
Registered at the G.P.O. Copyright of all material reserved; reproduction permitted only by arrangement. Editor: TED R. LURIE
Editorial Offices and Administration: The Jerusalem Post Building, Romema, Jerusalem. Telephone 528181. P.O. Box 81 (91000)
Tel Aviv: 44 Rehov Yehuda Halevi, P.O.B. 1125 (61000). Tel. 624215 — Haifa: 34 Rehov Herzl, Hadar Hacarmel, P.O.B. 4810 (31040). Tel. 640794 — Jerusalem branch (adverts, subscriptions): 6 Rehov Aristobulus Tel. 222966

Price: 45 ag.

WEDNESDAY, JULY 19, 1972 • AV 8, 5732 • JAMADI THANI 8, 1392 • VOL. XLII, No. 13539*

Okamoto Page 3
★
Z.O.A. Page 9
★
Air Force Page 10

Egypt expels all Russian experts

Sadat vows battle • Bases taken over

By ANAN SAFADI, Arab Affairs Reporter

Egyptian President Anwar Sadat announced last night that he had asked all Soviet military experts and advisers to leave Egypt. He declared that the Egyptian government had from Monday taken over Soviet military installations and equipment and placed them under the control of his country's armed forces command. The bases and equipment would be considered Egyptian property.

In a dramatic statement broadcast over Cairo radio, Sadat called for a high-level Soviet-Egyptian meeting within the treaty of cooperation and friendship concluded with the Soviet Union for consultations on "future relations."

He announced that consultations were in progress to "determine a method of more effective cooperation in the future."

The Egyptian state radio said that Sadat announced his moves at yesterday's meeting with the Central Committee of the Arab Socialist Union, Egypt's sole political party. Earlier, "Al Ahram" had described the meeting as an "emergency one."

Sadat flatly stated that he had been at odds with the Soviets over the supply of sophisticated weapons which he said he needed for "the battle of liberation." He said that at one stage the Soviets had violated agreements he had reached with them during the four visits he had paid to Moscow since he took over power shortly after Nasser's death in September 1970.

(According to the Institute of Strategic Studies in London, the Soviet advisers operated Egypt's air defence consisting of anti-aircraft guns, 70 sites with six launchers each of SA2 surface-to-air missiles, a radar network and six squadrons of Mig-21 interceptors. Coordinated with this defence are up to 150-Mig-21J and an unspecified number of Mig-23 aircraft.

(The usually well-informed "U.S. Aviation Week" magazine said in June that 10 Soviet Air Force squadrons, most of them equipped with Mig-21 all-weather fighters, were operating with the Egyptian Air Force.)

REJECTS CONDITIONS

Sadat affirmed his rejection of any conditions on the use of weapons by Egypt. "The political decision in Egypt must remain the responsibility of the political leaders and the people of Egypt alone without permission from any party, whoever it is."

Sadat said: "The Soviet Union is a large state and has its international role which we cannot ignore and has its own special strategy. But as for us, a part of our land is occupied and our main aim on the Egyptian and Arab levels is the removal of the traces of this aggression. We believe this removal — considering Israeli stubbornness and American support for this stubbornness — can only be by battle."

The immediate dimensions of the move could not be estimated by late last night, but judging from the wording of Sadat's statement it appeared to mark an abrupt about-turn in Egyptian-Soviet relations — if not a beginning of the end of a long history of massive Soviet penetration that began in the mid-'fifties

(Continued on page 10, col. 2)

ISRAEL SEES 'NEW PATTERN' OF TIES

Jerusalem Post Military Correspondent

Observers here noted last night that the Egyptian move was not aimed at totally severing relations with the Soviet Union, but at establishing a new pattern of relations, in which Egyptian dependence on Russia would be greatly reduced.

In practical terms the move is likely to have an adverse effect on the operational capability of the Egyptian army. This depends, of course, on the extent of the estrangement, the observers add.

As to the possibility that the new situation would lead to a resumption of hostilities on the part of the Egyptians against Israel, this possibility always existed, the observers point out. In any case, no one can venture to predict what would be the extent and scope of hostilities, if they are renewed.

Post Diplomatic Correspondent David Landau reports that following top-level consultations in Jerusalem it was decided that Israel would withhold any immediate comment.

Sources in the capital believe that the U.S. was as much in the dark about the Egyptian moves as anyone else. They discount speculations that the U.S. was informed in advance by Sadat.

Furthermore, American-Egyptian relations have not shown any surface signs of improvement of late. Only recently Cairo asked the U.S. to reduce the number of its diplomats in Egypt.

If the Egyptian move does mean a halt in the supply of military hardware, it is difficult to see what alternative source Mr. Sadat is contemplating. France is quite incapable of supplying the quantity and quality of weapons which the Russians were giving Egypt; according to military experts China too is out of the reckoning, and the U.S. is really the only potential supplier. But it is considered highly unlikely that the Americans would wish to change their Middle East policy, especially before the Presidential elections.

SADAT'S SENSATION

PRESIDENT Sadat's demand that the Soviet Union withdraw all its military advisers from Egypt is only the beginning of wider developments whose full consequences cannot yet be assessed.

At first sight, however, the move would appear to be a serious setback for Moscow's Middle East policy. Russia has a tremendous political and economic stake in Egypt. It is estimated that the Soviets have poured some six or seven billion dollars in economic and military aid into Egypt. A setback of such dimensions in Egypt must affect Russia's overall power stance, with implications not only in the Middle East, but in the Indian Ocean as well. It is difficult to see how the Russians, for their own domestic as well as global reasons, can simply gloss over this.

Since Nasser's death the Russians anticipated the possibility of fickleness on the part of their Egyptian ally. They therefore tied Sadat to a 15-year Friendship Treaty which gave the Kremlin a good deal of control over Egypt's domestic and military policies. At the same time they sought insurance for their stake in the area, by seeking to spread their system of alignment to Iraq and Syria.

As a result Egypt no longer had the same singular importance for Moscow it once had. Yet it is difficult to see how a collapse of the Soviets' presence in Egypt could leave unaffected their hold in Iraq and Syria as well.

What Sadat expects to achieve is no less a speculative matter. He has, of course, been caught in the Russian vise of no peace and no war. Denied by the Russians what he considers essential war material, and lacking a fully capable army as well, even as he foreclosed the option of peace, Sadat has been sorely embarrassed at home by the very bear hug he thought could save him.

He has been smarting under charges that he is subservient to the Kremlin which has led Egypt in the path of Russian, but not Egyptian, interests. And there has been no secret about the growing friction between the Soviet advisers and Egyptian military personnel and politicians.

Freed of the Soviet embrace, Sadat would be freed of these embarrassments. Whether this will strengthen his shaky position at home remains to be seen.

To the degree that the Soviets, looking over their shoulder at the U.S., have restrained Egypt's war hawks, Soviet withdrawal could free the way for some Cairo military ventures. However, Sadat could equally seek to exploit his anti-Soviet ploy to elicit more Western political support against Israel.

Yet both in larger military and political terms, Soviet military withdrawal from Egypt must be considered a welcome development. For without active Soviet assistance, Cairo cannot easily think in terms of major war. Moreover, it is difficult to see how any Western nation or group of nations (even France and Britain together) would be willing or able to give Egypt the same kind of massive military and total political support as Moscow was prepared to supply.

Certainly one reason for yesterday's events is the firmness with which Israel, since 1967, has withstood the combined Egyptian-Soviet pressure. It is this resistance, with support from the U.S., which has led to this inevitable clash of interests in the Soviet-Egyptian alliance, thus opening an entirely new page in the region.

U.N. Council meets on officers held by Israel

UNITED NATIONS (Reuter). — The Security Council met last night to discuss Israel's refusal to agree to a Syrian demand to release six Arab officers captured inside Lebanon last month, as well as an Israeli request to consider proposals for a general exchange of prisoners of war among the Middle East belligerents.

The Israeli delegation requested the 15-nation Council to take up the issue, countering Monday's call by Syria and Lebanon for an urgent meeting to reopen debate on Israels capture of five Syrian officers and a Lebanese in southern Lebanon on June 21.

In a resolution adopted on June 26 the Council asked Israel to release the group and warned of further unspecified action if they were not freed.

The Foreign Ministry spokesman in Jerusalem said yesterday that Israel will not free a single prisoner without agreement on an overall exchange. He declined to comment on reports that a proposal for an overall exchange in stages was under consideration.

The spokesman said the convening of the Security Council seriously harmed negotiations being conducted through the International Red Cross and U.N. Secretary-General Waldheim on an exchange agreement. He recalled that the U.N. spokesman on Monday had declared that Dr. Waldheim was continuing his efforts.

It was thought here that Syria had called for the Council meeting because of internal reasons. Lebanon was opposed to the Syrian move but was drawn along.

Fischer—Spassky draw

REYKJAVIK (UPI). — Bobby Fischer and Boris Spassky last night agreed on a draw in the fourth game of the world chess championship after the 46th move.

Fischer, who won his first game from Spassky on Monday, opened with his king pawn and followed with an even attack against the Russian's Sicilian defence. Spassky played rapidly through the opening moves, taking only three minutes to complete the first 10. But the Russian world champion, whose loss to Fischer on Monday was his first defeat at the chess table in 12 years, sacrificed a pawn on the 15th move and took more than 30 minutes pondering the 19th move alone.

Spassky used a rare variation of the Sicilian defence — one which chess experts could never recall the Russian employing before. However, from the rapidity of his early play it appeared Spassky had a well-planned and thought-out defence and the Russian's seconds expressed confidence through the first 20 moves.

By the 33rd move, experts were already forecasting the eventual outcome.

The giant playing hall buzzed with noise as chess masters watched the game and discussed it. The huge "Silence" signs flashed almost continuously after a move and at one point arbiter Lothar Schmid asked that the doors to the hall be oiled to keep them from squeaking when people went in and out.

The Rev. William Lombardy, Fischer's second, said it was a brilliant game with either player in position to win. "It's a very difficult game to comment on," Lombardy said. 'It's one of those games one pawn will either lose or win and I wouldn't like to predict the outcome."

When told the Russian camp was optimistic, Lombardy gave a wry smile and said, "the Russians are always optimistic."

Neither Fischer nor Spassky were present when Arbiter Schmid started the American's clock. However, Fischer showed up within four minutes of the clock's starting and Spassky arrived a few minutes later.

The moves of the fourth game:

(FISCHER — white; SPASSKY — black)
1.P-K4 P-QB4; 2.Kt-KB3 P-Q3; 3.P-Q4 PxP; 4.KtxP Kt-KB3; 5.Kt-QB3 Kt-QB3; 6.B-QB4 P-K3; 7.B-QKt3 B-K2; 8.B-K3 0-0; 9.0-0 P-QR3; 10.P-KB4 KtxKt; 11. BxKt P-QKt4; 12.P-QR3 B-QKt2; 13.Q-Q3 P-QR4; 14.P-K5 PxP 15.PxP Kt-Q2; 16. KtxP Kt-QB4; 17.BxKt BxB ch; 18.K-R1 Q-Kt4; 19.Q-K2 QR-Q1; 20.QR-Q1 RxR; 21.RxR P-R4; 22.Kt-Q6 B-R1; 23.B-B4 P-R5; 24.P-R3 B-K6; 25.Q-Kt4 QxP; 26. QxRP P-Kt4; 27.Q-Kt4 B-B4; 28.Kt-Kt5 K-Kt2; 29.Kt-Q4 R-R1; 30.Kt-B3 BxKt; 31.QxB B-Q3; 32.Q-B3 QxQ; 33.PxQ B-K4.

'Israelis disguised as Americans'

KAMPALA (UPI). — President Idi Amin accused the United States yesterday of sending Israelis into Uganda disguised as U.S. citizens.

He warned U.S. Ambassador Clyde Ferguson that American-Uganda relations could suffer if the alleged practice was not stopped, U.S. officials said.

Israelis have been barred from Uganda since Amin broke diplomatic relations with Israel in April. But the President said he had "reliable information" Israelis were still coming in on false U.S. passports.

Nixon wants wide Soviet trade pact

SAN CLEMENTE, Calif. (UPI). — President Nixon has instructed Commerce Secretary Peter Peterson to try and reach a comprehensive new trade agreement with the Soviet Union before the end of the year.

Okamoto asks Japan retrial

By YITZHAK OKED
Jerusalem Post Reporter

TEL AVIV. — Kozo Okamoto, the Japanese terrorist who was sentenced on Monday to life imprisonment, has written a letter addressed to the Japanese Embassy in Israel. It is believed that Okamoto has requested a retrial in Japan.

The Japanese Embassy declined to confirm to *The Jerusalem Post* last night the receipt of such a letter. The Japanese Ambassador, Mr. Eiji Tokura, had told *The Jerusalem Post* on Monday night that he did not think that Japan would request Okamoto's extradition.

No decision has yet been taken on the prison where Okamoto will serve his sentence. It is possible though that he will remain in Ramle prison, the highest security jail in Israel.

Mr. Arieh Nir, Commissioner of Prisons, told *The Jerusalem Post* last night that it was still too early to talk about the conditions of Okamoto's imprisonment, whether he will be confined by himself or together with other prisoners in a cell. Mr. Nir said that he would have to consult the prison's psychiatrist. "It might be that we will have to do things in stages." There are still heavy guards around him, but already he is left unshackled for several hours in the day and they may be taken off his feet. Mr. Nir also commented that he has been very quiet in prison and that yesterday he acted the same as before his sentence, eating and sleeping as usual.

Mr. Nir added: "What I can say is that as of Monday night, Okamoto has ceased to be a V.I.P. and will now become a regular prisoner. The sooner he gets used to the routine of the prison, the better it will be fo. him.

Third Test drawn

NOTTINGHAM (AP). — England and Australia drew here yesterday in the third Test match of the five-match series. At close of play England, set a total of 451 to win in their second innings, had made 290 for four wickets. The series now stands level 1-1 with one draw.

Close study in U.S.

By SAM LIPSKI
Jerusalem Post Correspondent

WASHINGTON. — Defence Secretary Melvin Laird said at the Pentagon yesterday that the reports of Egypt's ouster of Russian military personnel were under close study, but he would go on no further.

At the State Department a spokesman said he would make no comment, interpretation, or other remarks on the reports, nor would he comment on the meeting between Joseph Greene, head of the U.S. mission in Cairo who was on Monday summoned to the Egyptian Foreign Ministry. Even officials normally prepared to offer background analysis were reluctant to discuss the development.

But one common line of reaction was that tension between President Sadat and the Soviets was not of recent vintage, that it had clearly increased since the Moscow Summit meeting in May, and that the abortive meeting between Premier Azziz Sidky and Soviet officials in Moscow earlier this week was almost certainly a precipitating factor.

These American sources, offering tentative appraisals, said it appeared the Soviets may have rejected Sidky's request for additional offensive weapons but that what probably angered Sadat even more was the probability that Moscow was lukewarm to Egyptian demands for renewed political pressure on Washington.

FINAL BID

It is believed in some circles here that the Sidky mission was a last attempt to mobilize Russian support for a new effort to get Washington to put pressure on Israel.

The Egyptians are said to have believed that President Nixon, facing re-election, would not want to endanger the accords reached in Moscow, and that he would even find his appeal enhanced if he could point to some diplomatic activity. But it now appears that it is the Soviets who do not want to risk the gains made at the summit — especially on such matters as the European security conference and trade agreements — and they have made this plain to Egypt.

Before American officials were willing to indicate what could now happen on the diplomatic front, they emphasized the need to know just how many Soviet advisers and personnel would be affected, the degree to which the Soviets themselves may have gone along with the move as a way of easing the tensions between Moscow and Cairo, and the impact of Sadat's political standing inside Egypt.

One experienced official cautioned against any conclusions that the Soviets would cut off all offensive weapon shipments to Egypt. The primary Soviet interest was in preserving a balance and they would continue to maintain Egypt's defensive capacity, as well as supplying those offensive weapons they considered necessary to maintain influence in Egypt.

The official saw no prospect of any early arms shipments to Egypt by other powers such as France or Britain and dismissed any suggestion that the U.S. might replace the Soviet Union in Egypt's favour as an arms supplier.

NATO sources: Russians weakened by ouster

BRUSSELS (UPI). — Egypt's expulsion of Soviet advisers weakens both the Russians and the Egyptians, Western analysts here said yesterday.

The news from Cairo caught Western diplomats here and the military men at NATO headquarters by surprise. All refused immediate comment — partially to await more facts and partially to avoid spoiling what looked like a boon for the West.

The Soviets are believed to have about 200 pilots stationed in Egypt. In recent months, these pilots have made daily sorties out over the Eastern Mediterranean and over Greece and Turkey, keeping an eye on Western military movements in the area.

This increase in Soviet airpower in the area had worried NATO strategists as much as the buildup in Russia's Mediterranean fleet. The analysts said Egypt's move might mean an end to the use of Egypt as one big Russian airfield.

In addition, Russia might lose the use of the Egyptian port of Alexandria for its ships. The analysts said this would be less serious,

(Continued on page 10, col. 5)

KREMLIN SILENT ON MOVE

MOSCOW (AP). — The Soviet Government yesterday withheld any immediate comment on President Sadat's request that Russia withdraw its military advisers from Egypt.

The Russians normally do not comment on foreign policy matters until they have been considered by the Kremlin leadership.

The government news agency, Tass, said only that a meeting of the ruling Arab Socialist Union's Central Committee opened in Cairo yesterday. "Egyptian newspapers point to the great significance of the meeting," the agency said.

Tass and the rest of the Soviet news media have made no reference to the withdrawal request.

Significantly, Moscow radio last night broadcast interviews with Soviet maintenance crews working at the Aswan dam in Egypt.

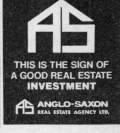

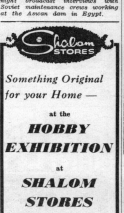

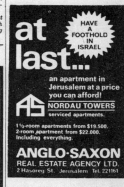

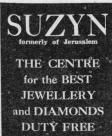

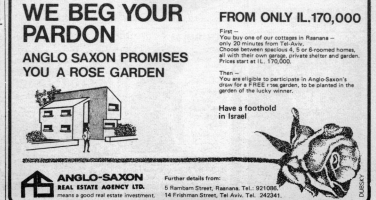

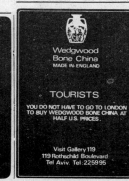

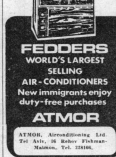

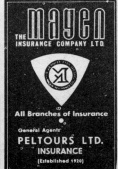

THE JERUSALEM POST

Murder in Munich
Pages 2, 3, 4, 5, 10

Price: 45 ag.

THURSDAY, SEPTEMBER 7, 1972 • ELUL 28, 5732 • RAJAB 29, 1392 • VOL. XLII, No. 13582

HOW HOSTAGES DIED REMAINS UNCLEAR

By BRIAN ARTHUR
Jerusalem Post Correspondent

BONN. — There was no complete reconstruction yet available of the gruesome and confused happenings at Fuerstenfeldbruck airbase near Munich, where the nine Israeli Olympic sportsmen were killed by eight Arab gunmen late Tuesday night.

Apart from the nine Israelis, four terrorists and one West German policeman were killed. Together with the two Israeli members of the Olympic delegation murdered at Olympic Village by the terrorists early Tuesday morning the death toll of the Munich massacre was 17.

According to available information, several Arabs left the helicopters after landing to inspect a waiting Boeing jet which they had demanded to fly them to an unnamed Arab country with their Israeli prisoners. At this point gunfire broke out. There was a dispute yesterday as to who had opened fire, but Mr. Manfred Schreiber, the Munich police chief, said later in the day he "believed" it was the police. Earlier, a Munich police spokesman insisted it was the terrorists.

Bonn government spokesman Conrad Ahlers told a press conference it had been the intention of the German police to try to gun down the Arabs under the relatively favourable conditions of the open airport grounds.

The Arabs immediately reacted by shooting up the airport tower and lights, plunging most of the area largely in darkness. They trained their machine guns on the helicopters and one helicopter went up in flames from an Arab grenade.

When German police finally gained control of the situation after killing at least four Arabs, they found the Israelis, still bound hand and foot, as they had been every since their capture on Tuesday morning, and riddled with bullets.

Heinrich von Mosch, Bavarian Interior Ministry spokesman, said bodies of the nine Israeli victims were found on the tarmac as well as in one of the helicopters. Previously, reports indicated all the Israelis were killed aboard a helicopter blown up by an Arab grenade.

The spokesman said the body of the police sergeant was found in the building of the military airfield. Arabs machinegunned the building.

He said a German-speaking Arab, who appeared to be the leader of the terrorists, was among those killed.

He said it also appeared certain that one or more of the Arab attackers had been employed in the Olympic Village.

The spokesman said there was no indication yet how and when the Arabs entered West Germany.

Asked about reports that Olympic authorities had received threats of possible terrorist action against the Israelis, von Mosch said, "in a very general form, yes, but nothing concrete."

He said a decisive element in the airfield tragedy was that the terrorists seized the helicopter pilots as hostages when they reached the airfield. This made it difficult for marksmen to pick out the terrorists in the floodlit darkness.

He said when the terrorists went to inspect the Lufthansa plane standing nearby, police feared they would spot policemen lurking in the vicinity.

He said there had been no possibility of trying to free the Israelis in the Olympic Village because they were bound hand and foot and the Arabs would have killed them.

The spokesman said the German negotiators originally tried to get the Arabs to agree to being transferred to the military airfield by daylight. But the Arabs refused. "We had to deal with people of unbelievable brutality."

Many foreigners from all over the world were taken on by Olympic officials for the duration of the Games, as cleaners, technicians, translators, shop and bar attendants, gardeners and hostesses. Yesterday, security men were going through their records with a tooth comb.

Mr. Dietrich Genscher, the West German Federal Interior Minister, told the press he had offered himself as hostage to the Arabs when he went to negotiate with them at the Israeli quarters at the Olympic Village on Tuesday. He said Mr. Merk, Munich police chief Schreiber and Hans Jochen Vogel, the former mayor of Munich who was responsible for bringing the Olympic games to this city, had also offered to take the place of the hostages.

Mr. Genscher said the Arabs allowed him into the room where the hostages were being held, and he found them all bound hand and foot. They were guarded by two Arabs with sub-machine guns.

"I was able to see for myself that it would be impossible to rescue them from the Olympic Village," the West German Interior Minister said.

He said when he entered the room with the hostages the terrorist told him they were ready to shoot one hostage every two hours. This made him realise the seriousness of the situation.

"They told me they were not afraid of a shoot-out because they had taken into account the possibility that they could all be killed, but they would kill all the hostages first," he added.

He said he had tried to extend the deadline by telling the terrorists he had talked with Egyptian authorities in Cairo — where they had demanded to be flown — and that the egyptians would probably not allow them to land in Cairo. The Arabs retorted that they would go ahead anyway and would negotiate with other Arab governments during the flight.

Mr. Merk said he was convinced the hostages would have faced certain death had they been flown to Cairo, because the Israeli government had refused to accept the terrorists demands to release prisoners.

Dr. Rene Burger, a physician for the Luxembourg delegation, said he withnessed the drama from his balcony across the street.

"I was a prisoner myself — of the police security," he said. I could not go out. I could not eat. I saw the Israelis through the window, blindfolded and hands tied.

"Once there was a chance the police could have wiped out the whole band of terrorists in five seconds — boom, boom, boom, just like that.

"The chief negotiator was outside the door. Another stood at a second floor window. A third looked down from the balcony on the third floor. Two were out in the open on the lower level.

"With sharpshooters all in position — and I saw them — the police could have done the whole job quickly and cleanly with five shots. It would have prevented the tragedy at the airport."

As the terrorists rejected all counter-proposals in daylong negotiations, German officials set up a trap of sharpshooters at Fuerstenfeldbruck Nato airbase 42 kms. west of Munich and prepared to snap it shut about 10 p.m.

At that hour the terrorists convinced they were being given safe passage — to Libya according to one report — left the Israeli apartment with their hostages and boarded three helicopters which had been flown into the Olympic village. They escorted their hostages, blindfolded and with hand bound, walking in single file and took off for the airport.

When the first helicopter landed in a floodlit area of the airbase the guerrillas made both pilots stand outside the aircraft. They opened both doors and trained machineguns on the hostages inside.

Police opened fire on one or two of the terrorists as they returned to one of the helicopters after inspectin ga jetliner.

ISRAEL CALLS ON WORLD TO HALT TERRORISTS

By DAVID LANDAU
Jerusalem Post Diplomatic Correspondent

Israel called on the nations of the world yesterday to take effective measures to wipe out Arab terrorism. A Government statement issued after a special Cabinet session following the Munich massacre said that the events of Munich should have shown the world the truly wicked nature of Arab terrorism.

The statement said that Israel herself would persevere in its struggle against the terrorist organizations, and would "not exempt those who aid them from responsibility for the acts of the terrorists." (See statement page 3.)

The Cabinet session adjourned at 11 a.m., after two hours, for the ministers to watch the memorial service broadcast live from Munich by Israel Television. Several ministers later professed themselves profoundly satisfied with the words of West German President Gustav Heinemann, who laid the blame for the massacre squarely at the doors of the Arab states which aid the terrorist organizations. (The ministers switched off the broadcast before the speech of Mr. Avery Brundage, and thus did not hear the Olympic President speak of the "two savage attacks" on the 1972 Games — the expulsion of Rhodesia and the murder of the Israeli sportsmen.)

Specially called into the Cabinet meeting were the Chief of Staff, Rav-Aluf David Elazar, and the Director-General of the Foreign Ministry, Mr. Mordechai Gazit. The Cabinet heard reports on the events of the previous night, and, apparently dissatisfied with the extent of its knowledge, ordered an inquiry into both German and Israeli security measures before and during the murder-kidnap drama. The Cabinet will hear the results of this inquiry at its next session, on Tuesday. Information will be gathered by the Prime Minister's office.

There have been reports that Israel asked the Olympic organizers before the games to be allowed to make its own security arrangements — but its request was turned down During the hours of the murder and kidnap drama Israeli and German security authorities are known to have been in close contact. A party of Israeli experts flew to Munich on Tuesday morning to be of assistance on the spot.

There have also been reports that the Israelis in Munich were not allowed to take an active part in the rescue operation.

Several ministers gave vent to their feelings of shock and revulsion before the Cabinet session. Foreign Minister Abba Eban told a radio reporter he would never forget how the sad news broke. In this he reflected the sentiments of a great many Israelis who went to sleep believing all was well and awoke to radio report of the true situation.

Interior Minister Yosef Burg spoke of a "Tisha Be'Av before Rosh Hashana".

Tourism Minister Moshe Kol expressed his conviction that Israel would finally overcome the terrorists "as we have overcome all our enemies".

Speaking at a memorial rally of Jerusalem schoolchildren later in the day, Dr. Burg criticized the decision reported from Germany to continue the Olympic Games. "People of goodwill are with us", he said. "But **they** don't decide on whether to continue the Olympic Games". The rally was organized by the Student Council to mourn the victims of the massacre. Several thousand of the Capital's school children attended.

Dr. Burg ordered all flags on public building to be flown at half-mast today until after the funeral ceremonies.

After the Cabinet meeting, Foreign Minister Abba Eban went into consultation with his senior staff to plan Israel's diplomatic and informational reaction to the Munich murders.

Israel's envoys abroad were instructed to stress that Israel holds the Arab states — and primarily Egypt — to blame for the terrorist attack.

Speculation on reprisal

The stern tones of the Government's statement caused some observers in Jerusalem to speculate on the possibility of Israeli action against the terrorist bases in neighbouring countries. The statement warned that "Israel will pursue its struggle against the terrorist organizations and will not absolve those who aid the terrorists of their responsibility for their actions."

Official ceremony at Lod today

Jerusalem Post Staff

The Cabinet decided yesterday to accord the eleven victims an official funeral. The ceremony will be held today after their coffins arrive at Lod Airport at 2 p.m. Then the coffin of each victim will be taken to his own home town for burial — and a Cabinet Minister will participate in each burial service.

A special El Al jet will leave Munich with the coffins at 8.45 a.m. (Israel time.)

Yesterday, the Chief Chaplain of the Army, Tat-Aluf Rabbi Mordechai Piron flew out to Munich at the head of a squad of army chaplains, to help the local rabbinate prepare the bodies for the flight home and burial.

The ceremony will begin at Lod Airport at 2 p.m. with a eulogy by Prime Minister Golda Meir. The bereaved families and other participants are requested to be at the airport by 1.30 p.m.

After the airport ceremony, the funeral corteges will leave for the appointed places of burial. The arrangements are as follows:

- The cortege of Yosef Gottfreud will arrive at the Har Hamenuhot Cemetery in Jerusalem at 4.15 p.m.
- The cortege of Zeev Friedman will arrive at the Haifa Cemetery at 5 p.m.
- The cortege of Yosef Romano will arrive at the Herzliya Cemetery at 4 p.m.
- The cortege of Yaakov Springer will arrive at the Holon Cemetery at 4 p.m.
- The cortege of Moshe Weinberg will arrive at the Petah Tikva Cemetery at 3.45 p.m.
- The corteges of Eliezer Halfin, Mark Slavin, Kehat Shorr, Andre Spitzer and Amitzur Shapira will arrive at the Kiryat Shaul Cemetery in Tel Aviv at 4.15 p.m.

Any changes in the arrangements will be announced over this morning's news broadcasts.

Arabs said leaving

MUNICH (Reuter). — Most of Egypt's and Syria's Olympic contingents left Munich by special flight yesterday and a spokesman for the Moroccans said a complete Arab withdrawal was possible. The Lebanese were remaining. A Tunisian spokesman said they had not yet decided whether to remain. The Kuwaits were reported about to leave.

The Moroccans were still in the village, but their spokesman, mentioning a possible Arab withdrawal, said they were considering leaving. Only a handful of Egyptian officials remained here, sources close to the squad said. The competitors had left "as a precaution," they explained.

The Egyptians and Syrians left the Village during the service in the stadium, to catch their plane. Most Arab delegations stayed away, save the Lebanese and Tunisians.

Israel wants U.S., Bonn to quit

By DAVID LANDAU
Jerusalem Post Diplomatic Correspondent

Israel has asked the U.S. and West Germany to withdraw their teams from the Olympic Games, it was authoritatively learned last night. The requests were transmitted yesterday evening.

The consensus of opinion at the Cabinet meeting earlier in the day was that the Games ought not to be resumed after the massacre. This view was not given expression, however, in the Cabinet statement issued yesterday — apparently since the ministers believed there was not much chance of the Games being called off.

Meanwhile, Reuter reported from Munich last night that four Dutchmen and 13 Norwegian athletes — almost a quarter of that country's squad — said they would leave the Games, disobeying their team's official line.

The Norwegian move came after news from the Philippines that President Ferdinand Marcos yesterday ordered the 77-member Philippines team home from the Olympics following what he termed the "violence and senseless death" of the Israeli hostages.

Bonn claims Israel rejected more security

Jerusalem Post Correspondent

BONN. — West German spokesman Conrad Ahlers said yesterday the German security forces in the Olympic Village had suggested additional protective measures to their Israeli counterparts following vague "warnings" of possible trouble. But he claimed the Israelis were satisfied with the existing situation and did not consider increased security necessary.

Mr. Ahlers also stressed several times that Israel had not been willing to release 200 Arab prisoners in Israeli jails in compliance with terrorist demands.

He implied there was no other choice for the German authorities but to take the risk of shooting to free the Israelis.

Mr. Ahlers was the subject of a hail of questions from journalists probing responsibility for the massacre.

The spokesman told a press conference that Israel, represented by Ambassador to Bonn Eliashiv Ben-Horin, was constantly consulted on the course of the negotiations and contingency planning.

He said the plan was to get the abductors and their prisoners out of the Israeli living quarters where they were holed up and into more favourable surroundings permitting police to take action with a chance of saving the Israelis.

Ahlers said there was no crew in the Boeing jet at the airport and that it was simply a decoy to lure the terrorists out into the open.

Games resume

MUNICH (Reuter). — The 1972 Olympic Games resumed here yesterday after the 24-hour suspension ordered because of the Arab terrorist attack on the Israeli team quarters.

The programme restarted with the handball match between world champions Rumania and Hungary. Events called off on Tuesday were being held yesterday evening and the remainder of the programme has been put back one day.

'Don't support terrorists'

BONN CALL TO ARAB STATES

By BRIAN ARTHUR
Jerusalem Post Correspondent

BONN. — West German political parties demanded yesterday that Arab Governments withdraw their support from the Palestine terrorist movement following the murder of the Israeli athletes.

The appeals by Chancellor Willy Brandt's Social Democrats, the minority coalition Free Democrats and Opposition Leader Rainer Barzel appeared to throw Bonn's improved relations with the Arab world back to a low-point.

The shift in political attitudes here was in effect adoption of the Israeli standpoint that Arab Governments are responsible for terrorists operating from their territory.

But the Bonn government itself, at a special Cabinet meeting yesterday, appeared to be moving more cautiously. Spokesman Conrad Ahlers said Bonn would "of course" discuss the problem with Arab governments, but he stressed that these states have only "slight influences" over terror groups.

Mr. Ahlers said security arrangements in the Olympic village where the athletes are living during the games, had been made in consultation with the Israeli authorities, who had turned down additional safety precautions offered by the West Germans.

During negotiations with the terrorists Brandt appealed personally by telephone to Egyptian Premier Sidky.

Generally reliable sources here said Mr. Brandt sought Egypt's aid in ensuring that the Israeli athletes being held hostage in the Olympic Village be treated in accordance with the Geneva Convention.

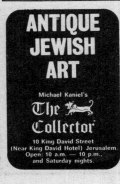

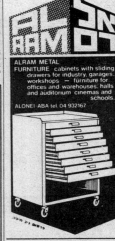

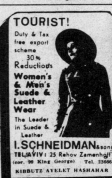

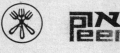

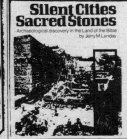

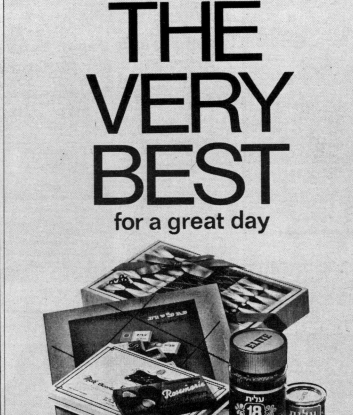

THE JERUSALEM POST

60 PAGES (including 48-page magazine)

Iron Curtain Page 5

Price: IL1.50

FRIDAY, SEPTEMBER 14, 1973 • ELUL 17, 5733 • SHA'ABAN 16, 1393 • VOL. XLIII, No. 13894*

Thirteen Syrian Mig 21s downed

Israeli jet lost, pilot is rescued

By HIRSH GOODMAN, Jerusalem Post Military Correspondent

Thirteen Syrian fighter planes were downed by Israel Air Force Phantoms and Mirages yesterday when they attempted to interfere with an IAF Mediterranean patrol, and with a subsequent rescue mission.

An Israel Mirage was hit but its pilot, who bailed out over the sea, was picked up safely by an Israel rescue helicopter. The same helicopter also picked up a Syrian pilot seen in the sea about a kilometre from the Israeli. The Syrian is now in hospital, having swallowed large quantities of sea water.

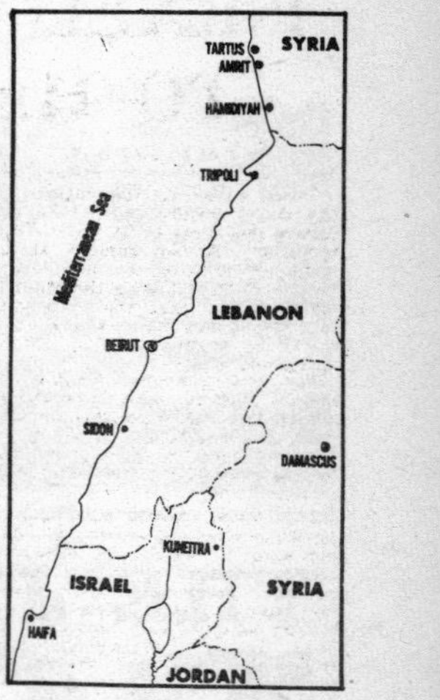

O.C. Air Force Aluf Binyamin Peled said last night that a group of 16 Syrian Mig 21s attacked an Israel patrol of four planes some 150 sea miles north of Haifa and 25 kilometres north-west of the Syrian port of Latakia. The Israelis were over international waters some 20 miles off the Syrian coast.

Within a few minutes, the patrol, assisted by an eight-plane covering force, had disposed of nine of the interceptors. The pilot of the Israeli plane that was hit managed to glide out to sea and ejected himself 10 miles from the scene of the dogfight. He spent two hours in the water before being picked up by a rescue helicopter.

Several Syrian Migs attempted to interfere with the rescue operation and four of them were shot down. This clash lasted four-five minutes. It took place at a medium height and between 10 and 20 miles out at sea.

The helicopter pilot related that he had considerable difficulty in rescuing the Syrian, who did not seem properly trained in sea rescue operations. The draft from the helicopter rotor capsized his rubber raft and two men had to get down into the water in order to pick him up.

The downed Israel pilot told reporters that he was not sure whether his craft had been hit by cannon fire or an air-to-air missile. "It happened after I shot down a Mig. I just knew I had been hit. I tried to fly on, but I soon saw that my engine was on fire and that I would have to abandon the plane. I glided out to sea for about 10 miles and then ejected at 10,000 feet."

He said that at no time did he have any doubt that he would be rescued. For the two hours he was in the water waiting for the helicopter, he did not come under Syrian attack.

The Syrian Air Force maintained a large force in the skies throughout.

Observers could point to no logical reason for the Syrians having attacked the IAF reconnaissance patrol. "All we know is that they fielded a huge number of planes," one source said.

"They seemed deliberately to pick a fight. They fielded a huge number of planes and made sure a dogfight was unavoidable."

Syria's loss of 13 aircraft all by cannon or air-to-air missiles is the largest in one day since the Six Day War. It brings to 60 the number of Syrian aircraft destroyed since the war. Six Migs were downed at no cost to Israel on January 8.

Arab reaction is low-keyed, shocked

Jerusalem Post Arab Affairs Reporter and agencies

Syria last night admitted losing eight MIG-21 jets, but claimed its air force has downed five Israeli planes.

The Syrians evidently downplayed the aerial combat, whose outcome appeared to have shocked Damascus. Other Arab capitals quoted the Damascus reaction to the action in a muted tone. Syria and neighbouring Lebanon closed down their air space throughout the combat.

'OVER COASTAL AREA'

Syrian comment was low-keyed in contrast to past encounters. They reported the fighting in a brief military communique saying that Syrian fighters took to the air after "large formations of enemy planes, totalling 64 in all, violated our air space over the coastal area."

Following a three-hour dogfight, the Syrians said eight of their planes were "hit," while claiming that five Israeli jetfighters were shot down.

Most of the Syrian planes which were hit crashed along the coastal area. One pilot was rescued at sea by the Israelis, while another was picked up in Lebanon by a Lebanese helicopter. The pilot was reportedly taken to a Beirut hospital, where he was visited last night by Lebanese Prime Minister Takieddin Solh.

Airliners taking off from Beirut as the battle began were told to change course to avoid Israeli jets over the Mediterranean, airport sources said. The airport was later shut down for two hours.

Several hours after the combat, Syria's Assistant Foreign Minister Mohammed Zakaria Ismail summoned all foreign ambassadors accredited to Damascus to warn them of the "grave consequences of Israel's latest aggression on Syria."

In Cairo, a government source said President Anwar Sadat followed closely the developments of the air fighting and received "successive and detailed reports on the situation. Urgent contacts were also held between the Egyptian and Syrian military commands, the source said.

He said despite the "Israeli provocative, sudden and premeditated aggression, Syrian pilots have shown complete alertness and great courage" in the fighting.

SYRIA'S AIR FORCE

Syria has 326 Soviet-built combat aircraft in its air force, according to the London-based Institute for Strategic Studies.

The air force includes 200 MIG-21 interceptors, 80 MIG-17 ground attack aircraft, 30 SU-7 fighter bombers and some Ilyushin light bombers, the Institute said in its report for this month.

There are believed to be many military depots around Tartous, Syria's second port after Latakia on the Mediterranean.

ATTEMPT TO MOLLIFY BEN-AHARON

Reiterates intention of resigning

Jerusalem Post Political Reporter

TEL AVIV. — The Labour Party leadership yesterday went out of its way to mollify Histadrut Secretary-General Yitzhak Ben-Aharon and reassure him that no one held him in any way personally responsible for the drop in Labour Alignment votes at the Histadrut elections.

This point was stressed by speakers at the post mortem on the Histadrut elections at the Labour Party Leadership Bureau's weekly meeting. Premier Golda Meir stressed that the losses were of the party and not of any individual and both she and Finance Minister Pinhas Sapir agreed that the election results must be analyzed in detail and necessary conclusions drawn for the Knesset election campaign. Mr. Sapir, for his part, was optimistic as far as the Knesset election forecast was concerned. They all resolved to get down to work immediately and put the Knesset election campaign machinery into top gear.

Ex-Ahdut Ha'avoda is already exerting its influence to try and counter pressure from ex-Mapai to remove Ben-Aharon from the Histadrut. The Kibbutz Hameuhad secretariat convened yesterday with Mr. Ben-Aharon to advise him against any hasty moves. Minister-without-Portfolio Israel Galili said the movement had the fullest confidence in Ben-Aharon as Secretary-

(Continued on page 2, col. 4)

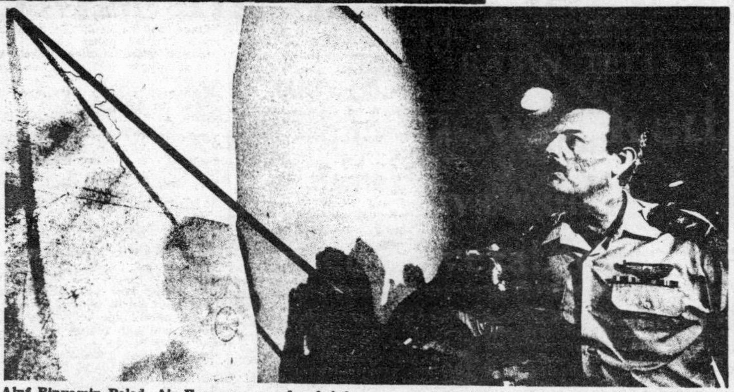

Aluf Binyamin Peled, Air Force commander, briefs newsmen in Tel Aviv yesterday on details of the air battle with the Syrians. (Bar-Tal)

Mrs. Meir to speak in Europe Assembly Oct. 1

STRASBOURG (UPI). — Prime Minister Golda Meir will address the 15-nation Council of Europe Consultative Assembly on October 1 to explain Israel's position on the Middle East crisis, Council officials said yesterday.

Mrs. Meir will take part in the general political debate at the House of Europe, seat of the Assembly, officials. The council invites for each session a foreign statesman to take part in the discussion of a particular problem. Last year the European legislators listened to an address by Tunisian Foreign Minister Mohamed Masmoudi.

Mrs. Meir is expected to arrive in a private plane on September 30 and return home on October 2.

JUNTA APPOINTS CHILE PRESIDENT, BREAKS CUBA TIES

SANTIAGO (AP). — The Chilean military junta named army chief General Augusto Pinochet Ugarte as President yesterday, formed a Cabinet and broke diplomatic relations with Cuba in a sharp reversal of the country's foreign policy.

A round-the-clock curfew, in effect since Tuesday, was lifted at noon for 6½ hours so civilians could leave their homes to purchase food and other necessities.

The curfew had been so strictly enforced in this city of three million — nearly a third of the national population — that civilians could not leave their homes even to borrow a cup of sugar from a next-door neighbour.

But a new flurry of shooting broke out downtown at noon and only a handful of pedestrians ventured into the streets there. Troops have been fighting for three days against snipers and other armed supporters of Salvador Allende, Chile's dead Marxist President.

A communique broadcast on the State radio network appealed to Chileans to go to medical centres during the 6½-hours of no curfew to donate blood "of whatever type."

The appeal followed unofficial reports that 500 to 1,000 people have died and many others have been wounded in fighting since Tuesday morning, when a coup toppled Allende's three-year-old government. The military authorities, in charge of the only radio network on the air, have not mentioned casualty figures.

Gen. Pinochet became President of the four-man junta and swore in a 15-member Cabinet composed mostly of military.

Rear-Admiral Ismael Huerta, the new Foreign Minister, advised the Cuban Ambassador, Mario Garcia Inchaustegui, that the junta in one of its first acts, broke diplomatic relations with Cuba. Inchaustegui and 160 members of his mission drove to Pudahuel international airport during the night and left for Havana in a Soviet airliner.

One of Allende's three daughters, Beatriz, left with the delegation, which includes her Cuban husband, Luis Fernandez Ona, the Embassy's first secretary.

Allende's widow, Hortensia, her two other married daughters and four grandchildren received asylum in the Mexican Embassy, the Mexican Government announced yesterday. They are to leave for Mexico City on Friday aboard a Mexican plane.

In Washington, the White House said yesterday that President Nixon had been receiving reports "for more than a year" relating to unrest in Chile, but that he had "no advance knowledge of any specific plans" for the coup that toppled Allende.

Deputy press secretary Gerald Warren thus turned aside reports that the U.S. Government had been told of the impending coup and did nothing to warn the Allende government. The presidential spokesman added that the U.S. Embassy in Santiago "was instructed to have nothing to do with persons approaching them in this regard, and those instructions were followed carefully."

The Post's Diplomatic Reporter adds:

Reports reaching Jerusalem say that all the Israelis in Chile are well, despite the recent convulsions in Santiago and the provincial towns.

The entire Israeli colony totals a few dozen souls, including diplomats and their families, experts sent by the Foreign Ministry's International Cooperation Department on technical and agricultural aid missions, and Jewish Agency emissaries.

In Tel Aviv, several dozen members of Mapam, joined later by members of Moked, yesterday held a demonstration to protest the Chilean coup. They stood at Kikar Malchei Israel, opposite City Hall, carrying placards condemning "Fascism" in Chile and the "murder of the socialists" there. They also presented a letter to the Cuban Embassy in Tel Aviv, protesting that country's severing of ties with Israel.

Syrian pilot in Haifa hospital

Jerusalem Post Reporter

HAIFA. — The Syrian pilot who was rescued by the Air Force from the Mediterranean was taken to the Rambam Government Hospital by helicopter at 5.15 yesterday afternoon. He was put into a room in the recovery ward on the second floor, under heavy guard.

He was reported last night to be in fairly good condition. Neither his name nor rank was revealed.

Newsmen and photographers who tried to get into the ward were stopped by an Army major in front of the entrance while several soldiers could be seen on guard inside the door. The major said no information would be issued until this morning.

Syria seen resuming Jordan ties

Jerusalem Post Arab Affairs Reporter

Syria was expected to announce the resumption of its relations with Jordan over the weekend, Damascus reports said yesterday. The Syrian move would follow a similar Egyptian step announced on Wednesday night.

The Egyptian and the Syrian decisions to resume their diplomatic relations followed Wednesday's conclusion of the summit held by Egyptian President Anwar Sadat, Syrian President Hafez Assad and Jordanian King Hussein in Cairo.

Meanwhile, Sadat was yesterday reported to have accepted the nomination of King Hussein's personal representative, Abdul-Mon'em Rifai, as Jordan's new ambassador to Cairo.

Rifai, a former Premier and a cousin of Jordan's present Prime Minister Zaid Rifai, has been credited with taking an active part in the reconciliation efforts with Egypt and Syria.

Glasgow Jewish bagpipers here

A Jewish bagpipe orchestra from Glasgow, probably the only one of its kind, arrived here aboard an El Al plane from London last night, to take part in the Three-Day March.

The orchestra, consisting of 18 men and girls, aged between 12 and 24, marched out of the passenger terminal to their bus playing their bagpipes to the sound of applause by the people present there.

(See story — page 3)

Arabs deny giving Rome terrorists Strela missiles

ROME (UPI). — Egypt, Syria and Iraq have denied supplying the Soviet-made Strela rocket launchers a group of Arabs planned to use to shoot down an Israeli airliner over Italy.

Delegates from the three countries, in a letter to officials of the current Assembly of the International Civil Aviation Organization in Rome on Wednesday, rejected accusations by Israel.

The Israel delegate in a letter earlier this week said Egypt, Syria and Iraq were the only Middle Eastern countries equipped with the sophisticated type of rocket launcher found in possession of five Arab arrested by Italian police eight days ago. Italian intelligence sources said the men had planned to use the weapons to shoot down an Israeli airliner on landing or takeoff from Rome's Leonardo da Vinci international airport.

The three Arab delegates said Israel produced no evidence to support its accusations against their governments. "We have received instructions from our governments to reject these accusatiois."

(See stories Page 4)

Plane-making go-ahead for Aircraft Industries

Jerusalem Post Aviation Correspondent

TEL AVIV. — Israel Aircraft Industries got the go-ahead yesterday to build additional series of Arava and West Wind aircraft. The decision by the Ministerial Economic Committee appears to have cleared the way for IAI's continued expansion.

The request for authorization of the new series came from Defence Minister Moshe Dayan, under whose office IAI nominally falls.

While no IAI spokesmen were prepared to comment officially on the decision, *The Jerusalem Post* learns that it comes just in time. It means that it can go on making the Arava and West Wind for the foreseeable future.

The company's entire production of the short-takeoff-and-landing, two-engined Arava has been spoken for the whole of next year. The 20 aircraft involved are all going to Mexico and Latin America. Later, local sales will probably include an initial two test planes for Arkia and possibly some for the Air Force, though the army has so far taken only one plane to try out, and reportedly has been dissatisfied with it.

The West Wind, a local stretch development of the Jet Commodore eight seater jet, retails for $900,000. It is currently undergoing trial flights with the U.S. Coast Guard after reaching the "finals" in a long series of elimination-tests against similar planes made by some of the world's leading aircraft manufacturers.

IAI has just completed setting up a network of retailers throughout the U.S. for this twin engined executive jet. While no figures of sales were available here yesterday, it is understood that the production line has long since past its economic break-even point because of the low initial development price (it was purchased airworthy from North American-Rockwell).

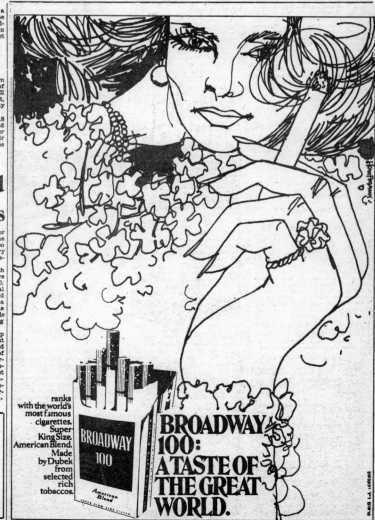

Egyptian-Syrian attacks held

Tanks battle as Syrians penetrate Golan line, Egyptians cross Canal, Israel planes maintain air supremacy

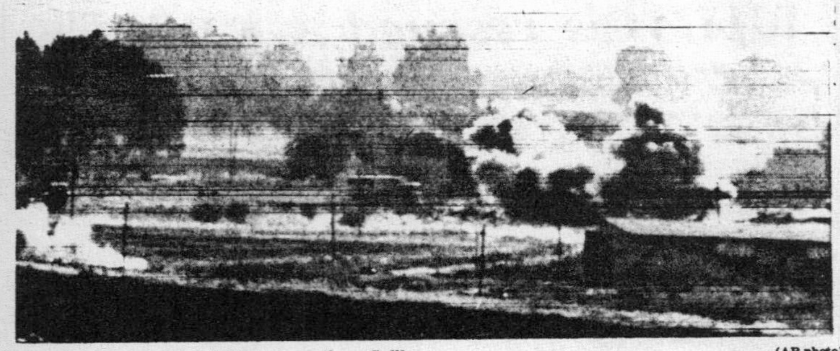

Syrian shells explode in a kibbutz in northern Galilee. (AP photo)

THE JERUSALEM POST

SECOND EDITION

Price: 65 Ag.

SUNDAY, OCTOBER 7, 1973 • TISHRE 11, 5734 • RAMADHAN 11, 1393 • VOL. XLIII, No. 13911*

By HIRSH GOODMAN, Jerusalem Post Military Correspondent

Israel forces yesterday contained invading Egyptian and Syrian units which crossed into Sinai and the Golan Heights under heavy artillery and air cover. The attack began shortly before 2 o'clock.

Two positions, one on the northern tip of the Canal and the other on Mount Hermon, which were taken by Arab forces in the late afternoon, were recaptured yesterday evening. No casualty figures were available last night, but Syrian and Egyptian losses were reported to be "heavy."

Israel will be fighting an estimated 350,000 troops on both fronts—250,000 of them along the Egyptian front alone. According to Defence Minister Moshe Dayan, the Egyptians have 2,000 tanks, 1,500 artillery pieces and 700 planes readied for the battle, while the Syrians have mobilized 800 tanks and 800 long-range and medium-range guns along the front.

Only limited Egyptian and Syrian forces managed to cross over the cease-fire lines as Israel maintained supremacy in the skies. The Egyptians crossed the Suez Canal at several points, attacking sparsely defended Israeli forward positions, while the Syrians brought troops by helicopter to positions on the Hermon and along the Golan Heights. The attacks were coordinated with massive artillery bombardments aimed at Israeli forces.

Throughout last night, Egyptian forces were attempting to build bridgeheads across the Canal, in an attempt to bolster commando and infantry units, which had taken positions on the Israeli side during the afternoon.

According to the army spokesman, an attempt by the Egyptians to transport troops by helicopter into Abu Rodeis in southern Sinai at 6 p.m. was fought off when Israeli Air Force planes destroyed eight (unconfirmed reports claim 10) of the helicopters in flight. Each helicopter carries an average of 30 men and their equipment.

Air raid sirens sounded off three times in Tel Aviv. According to Defence Minister Dayan, the sirens were in response to enemy planes flying in the direction of the city from the sea. Mr. Dayan said in reply to a question that the planes were equipped with missiles, but he would not elaborate.

Throughout the afternoon there was heavy aerial fighting both in the north and in Sinai. No losses for either Israeli or Arab planes were given. Mr. Dayan said last night there were no Israeli air raids on enemy positions beyond the battle front.

Up to last night Jordanian forces had remained out of the war, and in the administered territories, Mr. Dayan reported, life was normal. Mr. Dayan strongly advised the Jordanians not to enter the battle.

Israeli towns and settlements suffered in no significant way according to Mr. Dayan, who reported that there had been one fatality in the northern town of Kiryat Shmona.

No Israeli settlements had been evacuated, apart from the civilian oil town of Abu Rodeis in southern Sinai, where families were flown north yesterday morning before actual hostilities commenced.

There was no gauging last night how long the war was likely to last, or what it's scope would be. Israel is thought to have lost a certain advantage, observers point out, by not staging a pre-emptive attack. Defence Minister Dayan would not commit himself to a time limit last night, but stated the war would take neither months nor weeks.

The Syrians' air attack was directed in part against the Golan's Druse — several men and women were killed by strafing and 15 were injured, in the villages of Majdal Shams, Bukata and Mas'ade. The residents told an Israel Radio reporter the planes swooped on them while they were in the fields, strafing them mercilessly, then went on to spray fire at their homes.

Decision against pre-emptive attack

Jerusalem Post Reporter

The joint Egyptian-Syrian attack began just before 2 p.m. yesterday, timed deliberately for Yom Kippur. Israel learned earlier that the attack would take place. The Cabinet was called into extraordinary session, and Prime Minister Golda Meir informed U.S. Ambassador Kenneth Keating that the assault was imminent.

The Cabinet decided not to preempt the planned Arab assault, authoritative sources said. The decision was taken for political not military reasons to make it clear who was responsible for starting the war. The Israeli decision was taken deliberately, despite the military disadvantage involved, out of confidence that the situation of Israel's borders provided the additional security needed to make up for leaving the initiative to the enemy.

The attack was planned by Cairo and Damascus for some time, and was designed as a "maximum effort." The Egyptian aim, it is believed, is to regain parts of Sinai, especially the Mitla area, Sharm e-Sheikh and Abu Rodeis, while the Syrians apparently set their war aim as to retake all of the Golan Heights.

The Egyptians have amassed a huge tank force, said to number two thousand vehicles and have all of their airplanes estimated at about 500 in the air. Their aim yesterday was to establish beachheads west of Suez before nightfall and bolster them under cover of darkness.

Israel sources believe the Egyptians may also be seeking to attack Israel cities from the air.

The troop concentrations along the Syrian and Egyptian fronts were noted last week. However, it was first believed that the Arab forces were arrayed in a defensive alignment.

This changed into an offensive pattern at the end of the week. Even before that, however, Russian civilians in both Syria and Egypt began to be evacuated, indicating that an attack was in the wind.

5 Syrian ships sunk

Jerusalem Post Military Correspondent

Four Syrian missile boats and one torpedo boat were sunk in a naval battle between Israel and Syrian vessels near the Syrian port of Latakia yesterday evening. The Israeli naval unit suffered no losses.

The Syrian vessels, of the Soviet-built Comar and Ossa classes, were sunk with Israel-made Gabriel sea surface-to-surface missiles used in combat for the first time.

U.S. seeks cease-fire

NEW YORK. — Secretary of State Henry Kissinger, on instructions from President Nixon, yesterday sought an immediate cease-fire in the Middle East, the State Department spokesman said in New York.

The spokesman, Mr. Robert McCloskey, said that U.S. attempts to prevent the outbreak of war had failed, but Dr. Kissinger was under orders from the President to "make every effort to see that it is brought to a stop."

Kissinger flew back to Washington from New York — where he had been attending the U.N. session — after a series of urgent telephone consultations with the President.

Dr. Kissinger was to meet with a special task force set up within the State Department as soon as fighting broke out, McCloskey told newsmen.

One White House official said the President was "very, very concerned," and was giving direct guidance to Kissinger in their frequent telephone conversations.

At the direction of the President, he said, Kissinger immediately got in touch with the Foreign Ministers of Israel, Egypt and Syria and Soviet Ambassador Anatoly Dobrynin. The President ordered Kissinger to make a major diplomatic effort to prevent the fighting from spreading and to restore the cease-fire.

In each appeal, Dr. Kissinger had urged restraint and efforts to avoid escalation or continuation of the fighting.

McCloskey said although Kissinger spoke to U.N. Secretary-General Kurt Waldheim and the Security Council President, Sir Laurence McIntyre of Australia, there were no plans at the moment to call an emergency meeting. The U.S. would not oppose such a move.

McCloskey said that Kissinger

(Continued on page 2, col. 2)

Arabs claim success

By ANAN SAFADI
Jerusalem Post Arab Affairs Reporter

The Egyptians last night said they had poured reinforcements into the eastern bank of the Suez Canal, and claimed they had captured most of the Israeli-held side of the waterway.

The dispatch of reinforcements was announced shortly after an army spokesman in Cairo said the Egyptian forces had "succeeded in storming the Suez Canal all along the confrontation line and capturing most of the eastern bank of the waterway." The spokesman said the Egyptian flag had been hoisted over several positions captured during the afternoon.

Similar claims of success were made last night by the Syrians, who said they had "liberated" several positions across the cease-fire line on the Golan Heights. The Syrians said they succeeded in repelling an Israeli attack and moving into the offensive. They said fighting was being waged on the Israeli side of the cease-fire line late last night. The Syrians claimed to have "liberated" several positions, including one on Mount Hermon, and said three Israeli planes were shot down.

There were no reports of fighting at sea, although the Egyptians said late last night that their navy had gone into action. "Our naval forces also protected the flank of our forces on the Mediterranean coast, hitting important enemy targets on the northern shore of the Sinai Peninsula and scoring direct hits."

Both Egypt and Syria earlier warned all ships to stay out of their territorial waters. The two countries also closed off their air space.

As darkness fell, Cairo Radio repeated civil defence measures, including a complete blackout. A state of emergency has been declared throughout Syria.

Jordan's King Hussein ordered the commanders of his armed forces to keep in close touch with Egypt and Syria. He placed his forces under a state of alert.

There were no indications at this stage of Jordanian or Lebanese involvement, but Palestinian terrorist spokesmen claimed their own forces were "intercepting the enemy" along Lebanon's southeast border, which neighbours Syria's cease-fire line with Israel.

The war was first reported by Cairo, whose state-run radio interrupted its regular programme at 2.10 p.m., claiming an Israeli air and naval force had attacked two Egyptian positions on the western coast of the Suez Canal 40 minutes earlier. The two positions were named as Sokhneh and Za'afarana.

In a later broadcast, the Syrians announced their positions had been attacked at 2 p.m. Subsequent communiques reported the development of fierce clashes on land and in the air. Egypt said it had lost one plane and later amended the figure to ten, while claiming to have downed eleven Israel fighters.

Amid the broadcast of martial music, Cairo radio reported President Sadat has moved to military headquarters to personally supervise operations.

Syrian President Hafez Assad too was reported to have taken over the army headquarters. In a nationwide broadcast Assad accused Israel of launching a "blitzkreig" against Egypt and his country.

"We do not want to kill anyone, but we are repulsing those who want to kill us. We are fighting the battle of honour and dignity," Assad added.

Arab radio reported the progress of fighting with evident jubilation. Nevertheless, Cairo Radio later in the evening demonstrated caution, confining its reports to official statements. Cairo broadcast several code "appeals," the first of which urged "all our friends in beloved Sinai" to report to Cairo. "We are awaiting your news. God be with you and victory to all." Ten other messages addressed to different names said their messages had been "received."

STRONGER ARAB FORCES THAN '67

Russians flee scapegoat role

By ZEEV SCHUL
Jerusalem Post Reporter

TEL AVIV. — The total deployment of the Syrian and Egyptian armies — including mobilization of all of their reserve units — into the so-called front line offensive jumping-off platform was accomplished gradually during the past few weeks.

The total strength of the two armies by noon yesterday was believed to exceed the combined might of the Arab armies during the Six Day War by some 30 per cent. There was a similar increase in the number of guns, tanks and aircraft available to the two Arab countries.

The strongest indication of all that more than a mere jockeying for tactical positions was involved came when the Russian advisers started a wholesale exodus from both Syria and Egypt.

Russian civilian and military personnel, believed to number several thousand in Syria and a few hundred in Egypt, were evacuated with their families in an intensive airlift begun just over 40 hours ago and was expected to be completed by yesterday evening.

The reasons for the Russian departure are believed to have been their reluctance to become involved in another Arab fiasco, or even to be blamed for it by a vengeance-bent Arab population as the only available scapegoats. Then there was also the omnipresent threat of Israel Air Force counter bombings.

Finally a continued Soviet presence might also compel the Russians to intervene in the fighting at a certain stage in order to rescue their citizens.

Both the Syrian and Egyptian deployments were carried out during the past few weeks in accordance with Russian tactics, involving a multi-purpose deployment with medium-range tanks and artillery being brought forward.

When the total strength of the Syrian and Egyptian armies was poised and ready to strike, Israel Army H.Q. yesterday morning sent out its first mobilization orders. The Egyptians are understood to have advanced bridging equipment to the frontline and their attempt to cross the Canal took nobody by surprise here.

There was no plausible explanation for the timing of yesterday's two-pronged Arab strike. Commentators here pointed out that the Egyptian-Syrian attack could not be traced to any particular political pressure (internal or foreign) in either country. They apparently chose the Day of Atonement because they hoped to be able to achieve some measure of surprise on this most sacred day in the Jewish calendar.

The Observers pointed out the parallel of the period preceding the Six Day War, when at first nobody took the Egyptian war threats seriously — coming as they did when

(Continued on page 2, col. 3)

Meir: Israel first asked friendly quarters to act

Jerusalem Post Reporter

Prime Minister Golda Meir went on radio and television within a little more than four hours of the start of the Arab offensive, to voice full confidence in Israel's victory over the Egyptian and Syrian aggressors.

(The broadcast of Mrs. Meir's address — and of Mr. Dayan's, later in the evening — was, technically, in violation of the Broadcasting Authority's earlier decision to bar radio and television appearances by political leaders until after the Knesset elections. The technical rule was waived, however, in view of the unusual situation.)

Following is the text of Mrs. Meir's address:

Shortly before 2 p.m. today, the armies of Egypt and Syria started an offensive against Israel. They launched a series of air, armoured and artillery atacks in Sinai and on the Golan Heights. The IDF has entered the fight, and is beating back the offensive. The enemy has suffered grave losses.

The rulers of Egypt and Syria have long planned this violation of the cease-fire. Contemptibly, the aggressors are now spreading the lie that it was Israel which opened fire. But the responsibility for the renewal of the fighting and for the bloodshed lies with them alone.

Our enemies had hoped to catch the citizens of Israel by surprise on Yom Kippur, when so many of our people are fasting and praying in the synagogues. Our attackers thought that on Yom Kippur we would not be prepared to hit back at them. We were not caught by surprise.

For several days now, our intelligence services had been apprised that the armies of Egypt and Syria were lining up for a joint offensive. IDF patrols discovered that large armed forces were massing in offensive deployment in the vicinity of the Suez Canal and on the Golan Heights. The findings of the patrols checked with the reports already received. Our forces were duly arrayed to meet the danger.

We have no doubt that we shall

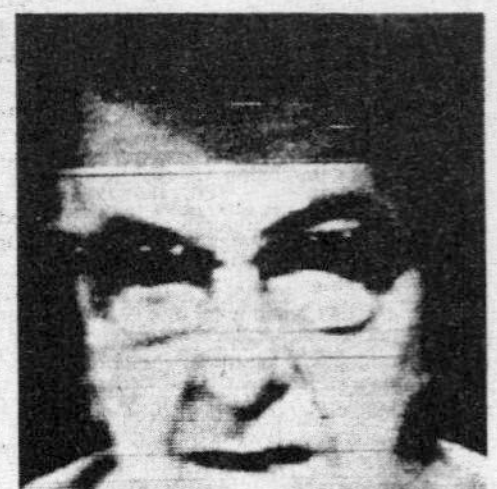

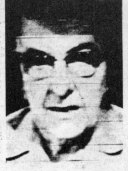

MEIR SPEAKING ON TV LAST NIGHT

be victorious. We are also convinced, however, that this renewal of Egyptian-Syrian aggression is an act of madness. It was our desire to prevent this outbreak. We appealed to a number of influential political quarters to intercede so as to frustrate the criminal initiative of the rulers of Egypt and Syria. While there was still time, we brought to the attention of friendly political quarters the information in our possession with regard to the plans for the launching of the offensive. We called upon them to act for the prevention of the war. For all that, the offensive has been launched.

As I said, the IDF is all set to repel the enemy's attack. Early this morning, a partial call-up of reserves was approved and begun.

Having regard to the gravity of the news, I was obliged to convene a meeting of the Cabinet on Yom Kippur. The offensive started

Continued on page 2, col. 1)

Blackout in force

Civil defence measures were ordered into effect yesterday evening. Residents were told to:

- Observe a total blackout;
- Fill all available containers with water;
- Remove all flammable materials from homes and shelters;
- Tape windows;
- Prepare first-aid kits and fire-fighting equipment for immediate use;
- Store mirrors and non-essential glass items;
- Avoid using cars and phones unless necessary;
- Be familiar with air-raid sirens: a rising and falling tone orders residents to go to the shelters and remain there until the all-clear, a steady, continuous blast lasting at least one minute.

For several hours after the sirens began sounding yesterday, phone service was disrupted, due to an overloading of the lines as relatives and friends called each other to exchange information.

Schools will be closed today and will remain closed until further notice, the Education Ministry announced at 11 o'clock last night, following a decision by the Government. The decision applies to all educational institutions, from kindergarten and elementary schools to high schools, with the exception of boarding schools, where studies will continue.

Parents are asked to keep their children off the streets and to tell them to listen to instructions by *Haga* men. Principals are to go to their schools and act in accordance with standing instructions.

Arabs fail to convene special Assembly session

UNITED NATIONS. — The Arab states yesterday unsuccessfully sought to convene a special weekend session of the General Assembly on the Middle East fighting but apparently avoided a Security Council meeting because of fear of another U.S. veto.

U.N. men confirm crossing of lines

UNITED NATIONS. — U.N. military observers on the spot confirmed that Egyptian troops had crossed the Suez Canal at five points yesterday and that Syrian forces crossed the Golan Heights cease-fire line at two places, a U.N. spokesman said.

The observers said they had not seen any attempt by Israeli forces to cross the cease-fire lines during Friday night, as alleged by the Arabs.

He said that none of the parties had laid any complaint of a violation of the cease-fire before the U.N. truce supervision organization, which controls obervers' operations.

(Reuter, AP)

Victory in few days: Dayan

Jerusalem Post Reporter

Defence Minister Moshe Dayan predicted last night that Israel would smite the Egyptians and Syrians "hip and thigh," but said it might take a few days.

In a television and radio address to the nation, Mr. Dayan said the Egyptians had inflicted some casualties on Israel forces on the eastern bank of the Canal, and had managed to capture a number of Israel strongholds, but the overall situation was somewhat better than had been expected under the circumstances.

In the Golan Heights the Syrians got a few of their tanks across the cease-fire lines, and broke through in several places, but scored no meaningful successes, and the situation there was fairly satisfactory.

The Defence Minister argued that the initial Arab advantage could only have been forestalled if Israel had resorted either to a huge per-

(Continued page 2, col. 1)

Israel takes offensive, bitter battles raging

Port Said military targets bombed

Jerusalem Post Arab Affairs Reporter

The Egyptians said last night that Port Said at the Mediterranean end of the Suez Canal was bombarded. The Cairo military command said this was the first time an Egyptian city had been bombarded, and warned that Israel "will have to bear the consequences of this operation."

Cairo Radio claimed that a number of houses and buildings were set on fire.

The Israel Army spokesman said last night that the Air Force went into action last night against military installations in the Port Said area.

Egypt's Foreign Minister, Mohammed Hassan Zayyat, interrupted the U.N. General Assembly's debate last night to charge that Port Said had been bombarded.

AFTER MIDNIGHT

An Egyptian De Castro-type minesweeper was hit by an Israel Navy vessel in the Gulf of Suez yesterday and went up in flames. The army spokesman said late last night that none of the Israeli vessels which participated in the battle was hit.

* * *

The spokesman said Israel planes during the day attacked missile batteries and other military installations in the Port Said region, rendering the batteries inoperative and badly damaging the installations.

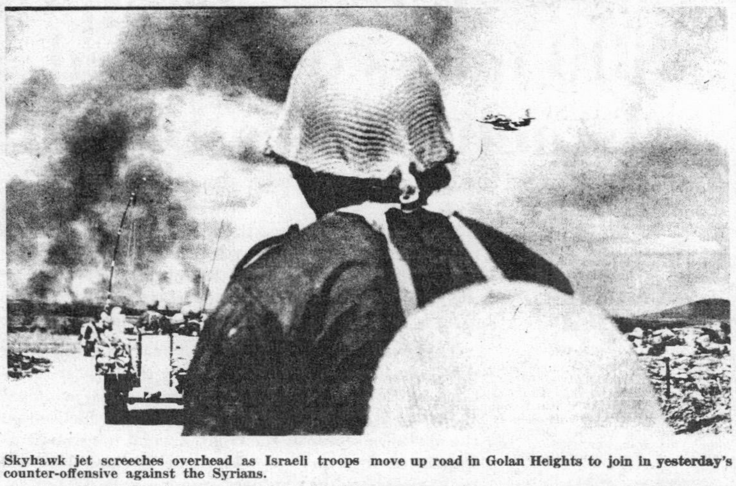

Skyhawk jet screeches overhead as Israeli troops move up road in Golan Heights to join in yesterday's counter-offensive against the Syrians.

THE JERUSALEM POST

SECOND EDITION

Price: 65 Ag.

TUESDAY, OCTOBER 9, 1973 • TISHRE 13, 5734 • RAMADHAN 13, 1393 • VOL. XLIII, No. 13913*

SYRIAN ARMOURED UNITS BID TO COUNTER-ATTACK

By ZEEV SCHUL and RONNIE HOPE, Post Military Reporters

TEL AVIV. — The Chief of Staff, Rav-Aluf David Elazar, last night confirmed that the tides of war had turned: that the Israel Defence Forces were now on the offensive on all fronts and that they "would continue to attack and destroy the enemy wherever and whenever he can be found..." Speaking to foreign and local military correspondents at Beit Sokolow, the Chief of Staff indicated that the army would not feel itself bound by any existing boundaries.

"The cease-fire line is not marked on the terrain where the fighting is taking place. We are now engaged in battle in that area and will fight wherever necessary in order to destroy the enemy." In reply to an earlier question as to whether he could confirm that Israeli troops had crossed the Suez Canal in pursuit of the Egyptians, the Chief of Staff replied with a laconic, "Not yet."

In his opening statement, the Chief of Staff lauded the outstanding fighting qualities of Israel's regular army which, he said, had blunted the advance of the two enemy armies. "All units fought in an exemplary manner. I think that the soldiers of 1973 are even better than those of 1967, who were better than those of 1956, who were better than those of 1948..." He added that reporters would yet "sing the praises of their exploits for a long time to come..."

R/A Elazar said that he could not, for the time being, disclose the number of Israeli casualties. "The quicker we advance and the stronger we attack, the fewer casualties we will suffer and the more the enemy will suffer."

Asked about the positions of the forces, the Chief of Staff remarked that fighting was still in progress. But he said that the Syrians had been completely ousted from the sector north of Kuneitra in the Golan. In the Hushniya region in central Golan, where the Syrians had made what he termed as a "very deep penetration," Israel had destroyed part of the invading force and ousted most of the others "although a few units may be a few hundred metres inside our lines." The same applied to the southern sector of the Heights where some Syrian units were still in the Rafid enclave region.

As to the Suez Canal, the Egyptians still held three bridgeheads (minus bridges) but are surrounded and they have retreated from some of the areas held by them earlier.

TO HIT OUT

General Elazar would not go into any details concerning operational plans but said: "Our aim is to hit out at the enemy — to cause them as many casualties as possible — to teach them a lesson and to win a decisive and significant victory — in short, to break all their bones."

Queried on an explanation for the belated mobilization orders given to reservists, the Chief of Staff remarked that the Premier and the Defence Minister had already explained the dominant considerations. But he stressed that the attack had not come as a surprise and that the frontline forces had been ready and braced for the onslaught and did everything within their means when it came.

Asked to compare the Arab and Israeli armies, the Chief of Staff remarked that the Arabs had more modern, better, and larger quantities of armour and other weapons than they had before. "But under actual battle conditions it was the Arabs who broke and were defeated, showing that the quality gap between the soldiers of the Israeli and Arab armies remained as wide as ever."

R/A Elazar said that "many hundreds" of Egyptian and Syrian tanks had been destroyed. He said he could not give the exact figure.

A foreign correspondent mentioned a remark attributed to R/A Yitzhak Rabin that he had "forgotten" to capture the triangle on the east bank of the canal north of Kantara, extending to Port Fuad. Elazar raised a laugh when he said he would ask Rabin what he had forgotten and would try to put it right.

Another correspondent mentioned that the press has begun calling the current hostilities the "Yom Kippur War" and asked the Chief of Staff what he would call it. His reply: "The War of the Day of Judgement."

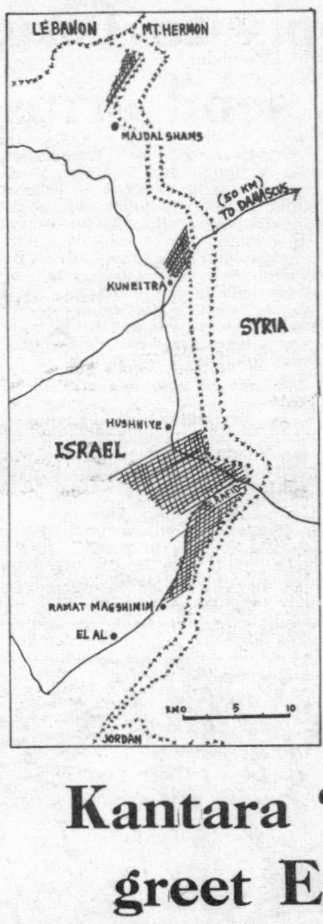

Jerusalem Post Military Correspondents

TEL AVIV. — Syrian armoured units late last night attempted a two-pronged counter-attack on the Golan Heights in a final attempt to regain some of the territory they had lost earlier in the day. One offensive was in the vicinity of the Hushniya-Rafid enclave and the other north of the Damascus-Kuneitra road. The attack started after sundown and was still in full swing last night.

The attacking units were apparently drawn from reserve Syrian units.

Informed sources said that the Syrians fiercely contested every inch of ground. Contradicting earlier reports, these sources said their armoured columns retreated in an orderly manner.

The Syrians lost tens of more aircraft yesterday, most of them in aerial combat. This number includes three new types of planes termed as Sukhoi 20's. The plane is claimed to be of a variable wing class but appears to be so new that it is not yet listed in the authoritative Observer's Book of Aircraft (1973 edition).

In the south, a three-pronged attack against the Egyptian spearheads included one IDF column sweeping on the road to Kantara, a second column on the Ismailiya-Bir Gafgafa axis and a third heading westwards to block the Mitla and Jidi passes.

While the Egyptians did not succeed in rebuilding their bridges, they are now operating a shuttle raft service across the waterway. Their dogged determination is shown by their continued shipment of reinforcements to the east bank of the Canal — and this in spite of having lost, like the Syrians, hundreds of tanks in battle during the course of the past three days.

Senior army officers stressed last night that in spite of favourable developments the Israel units still had a hard task ahead of them. More heavy fighting is expected today.

The Egyptians lost tens of planes yesterday, some of them in a second attempt to bomb the advancing Israeli columns.

Nixon to Brezhnev: Restore the peace

By DANIEL GOTTLIEB
Jerusalem Post Correspondent and Agencies

WASHINGTON. — President Nixon has appealed to Soviet Communist Party chief Leonid Brezhnev to join in a concerted big-power effort to restore peace to the Middle East, the White House disclosed yesterday. But presidential spokesman Ronald Ziegler would not reveal details of Mr. Nixon's message or of Mr. Brezhnev's response to the appeal made over the weekend.

Mr. Nixon told reporters the U.S. was seeking support for a position "which we hope and believe will be effective in stopping the fighting."

The White House declined to discuss Mr. Nixon's personal message to Mr. Brezhnev or the Soviet Party chief's response, which was received last night.

The President's appeal to Mr. Brezhnev was apparently an attempt to reach some measure of agreement with the Soviet Union in advance of the U.N. Security Council meeting.

Mr. Ziegler said the U.S. sought broad support from nations involved in the war and those with interests in the area to back Security Council efforts to halt the fighting.

Dr. Kissinger has kept in close touch with the Soviet Ambassador in Washington, Anatoly Dobrynin, and also consulted Israel and Egyptian diplomats, the White House said.

President Nixon, explaining to reporters the U.S. decision to take the Middle East crisis to the United Nations, said he had in mind "the importance of getting strong support for the position the United States will take."

At the State Department, spokesman Robert McCloskey told reporters the U.S. had not urged Israel to stop short of crossing the 1967 cease-fire line, although it had urged restraint on all parties to the fighting.

Mr. McCloskey said it was unfair to speculate that the U.S. did not want an immediate cease-fire in order to give Israel time to regain lost ground.

Informed sources said yesterday that Israel does not expect the U.S. to press for a cease-fire before Arab forces are pushed back to the 1967 cease-fire lines. This is regarded as the U.S. side of a secret understanding struck between Washington and Jerusalem. Israel, for its part, kept its side of the "agreement" by not launching pre-emptive strikes when it learnt that Arab forces were massing.

The U.S. is walking a tightrope in its handling of the latest Middle East crisis in order not to antagonize the Arabs. President Nixon's statement, explaining the U.S. call for yesterday's Security Council session, was significant in its vagueness.

"We are developing support for a position which we hope and believe will be effective in stopping the fighting," the President told reporters called into his office as he met with Secretary of State Henry Kissinger.

Israel would like the U.S. to hold off any cease-fire resolution in the U.N. for another 72 hours, the time it believes required for expelling the Egyptians from the east bank of the Canal and the Syrians from the Golan Heights line.

(See Brezhnev — page 5)

Israel seen attacking across cease-fire lines

By ASHER WALLFISH and DAVID LANDAU
Jerusalem Post Reporters

Israel is expected to extend the army's counter-attack into a full-blown punitive offensive across the cease-fire lines against the Egyptian and Syrian invaders. At the outset of the war, the decision in principle was taken to smash the enemy's armed might. Now, the military position on the ground and international political situation enable Israel to move from counter-attack to all-out offensive action.

Some foreign diplomats in Tel Aviv told *The Post* that Israel enjoyed "a reserve of sympathy" at the present stage of the conflict. The incontestable proof that Israel was the victim of premeditated aggression, and the consequent damage which it suffered, made it seem reasonable for Israeli forces to cross the cease-fire lines in hot pursuit of Syrian and Egyptian forces. As long as Israel did not occupy further territory, it need not lose this sympathy, the diplomats believed.

The Cabinet met at nine last night to hear reports from the battlefields and from the political arena at New York, where the Security Council was to convene.

There have been no approaches to Israel from any state to do anything or refrain from anything, one well-placed source told *The Jerusalem Post* in the early evening.

Constant contacts were being maintained with the U.S. But sources here were reluctant to divulge anything of their content.

"Our hands are not tied at this stage," the source told *The Post* "I think they (the Arabs) must be made to pay the price. We must hit them very hard for the dirty trick they pulled on us..."

At any rate, the source continued, Israel's immediate considerations at this stage were strategic, not political.

After the Cabinet meeting last night the following communique was issued:

"At the Cabinet's second meeting yesterday, the Chief of Staff reported on the situation on the war fronts.

The Minister of Finance reported on problems of financing the war effort and on the mobilization of the Jews of the world, especially in the U.S., Canada, Europe, Australia and South Africa.

He also reported on his meetings — to discuss the war effort — with the Histadrut Central Committee, the Manufacturers Association, the bank managers, the insurance companies, the Citrus Marketing Board and the artisans' representatives.

The Ministerial Economic Committee will meet today for a detailed discussion of the issue."

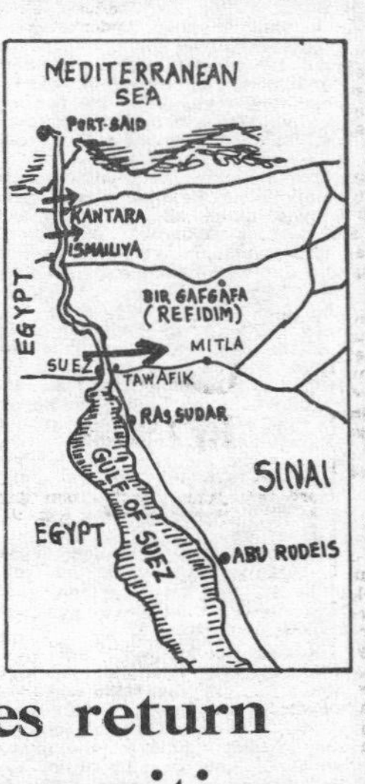

U.N. urges return to previous positions

UNITED NATIONS. — U.N. Ambassador John Scali told the Security Council after midnight last night that the U.S. wants the two sides to return to their positions which they held before the Middle East war broke out on Saturday.

He made the statement after the Council met following a postponement without explanation from a scheduled earlier meeting.

Shortly before the announcement of the postponement, U.S. Ambassador John Scali, who requested the special session, held intense private consultations with other key delegates.

Informed sources said they were trying to work out an agreed resolution calling for a cease-fire, but that disagreements which marked similar private talks over the weekend still persisted.

The informants said the U.S. favoured a cease-fire with withdrawal of Egyptian and Syrian troops to the October 5 lines along the Suez Canal and in the Golan Heights.

The Western European members — France, Britain and Austria — were said to want a simple cease-fire resolution with a provision that this should not prejudice the lines to be drawn between the opposing forces.

African and Asian members of the Council were reported to be ready to propose a cease-fire coupled with a call for Israeli forces to be wtihdrawn to the pre-June, 1967, lines.

3 Syrian Sukhois fall near Metulla

Jerusalem Post Reporter

METULLA. — Residents here yesterday watched three Syrian Sukhoi bombers crash in flames just to the south of their settlement after a brief dog-fight with Israeli jets.

The three Syrian planes came from the direction of Lebanon, one of the eyewitnesses told *The Post*, apparently intending to bomb Kiryat Shmona. Israeli fighters suddenly appeared overhead. They engaged the Syrian jets and, after a brief dog-fight lasting no more than a few seconds, three loud explosions were heard and the Sukhois fell in flames.

Showers start in the south

Heavy showers fell yesterday about 15 minutes in the southern coastal plain, from Khan Yunis to Rafah. Scattered drops also fell in other parts of central and southern Israel.

The weatherman said last night that the unusually low temperatures for this time of year would continue today.

EBAN TELLS U.N. ASSEMBLY:

'Secure borders saved Israel'

UNITED NATIONS. — Israeli Foreign Minister Abba Eban told the General Assembly yesterday that if Israel had performed "the folly" of going back to the previous armistice lines, then it might have been destroyed by the latest Arab attacks.

Mr. Eban told the Assembly, which interrupted its general debate to hear statements on the war situaion, that the Arab aggression proved Israel's insistence on "precise" negotiations for a peace settlement.

Egyptian Foreign Minister Mohamed Zayyat charged that Israel had launched a "decoy attack," and Egypt acted in self-defence. Zayyat took the floor after Syrian Foreign Minister Ismail Zakaria made the opening statement, accusing Israel of launching the aggression against his country and Egypt.

Mr. Eban said Israel had suffered a "tragic loss of life and blood." But he said Egypt and Syria have suffered much more "as a result of their leader's cynical aggression." He charged their attacks will go down in history "as one of the basest acts of which a government can have been responsible."

"There is not a single man or woman inside or outside of this hall who doesn't know in his heart" that Egypt and Syria started the war.

Mr. Eban said he had a telegram, from Israel last Saturday, six hours before hostilities began, saying that an attack was coming from the Arabs.

Having been forewarned, he said, Israel communicated assurances to the Arabs — presumably through a third party — that it would not take pre-emptive action.

He said the Arabs "invented the myth" of a ship crossing the Suez Canal silently in the darkness early on Yom Kippur.

"How idiotic would a man have to be to believe that on a day when there are no communications, with the vast majority of our soldiers in their homes or synagogues, when even forward posts are manned at their minimum level, that precisely on this day Israel would launch a war — on the day holiest to all those who cherish Jewish solidarities, in order to invite thousands of Egyptian and Syrian tanks to attack across a relatively undefended and totally quiescent line."

"The inconceivable mendacity of this allegation is fully exposed by the military facts and by the re-

(Continued on page 5, col. 5)

BAR OF GOLD

PARIS (UPI). — A Frenchman walked into the Israel Embassy yesterday, laid a bar of gold on a table and said, "I want to give this to you." Embassy officials said they have not decided yet what to do with the gold, worth 14,000 francs (about IL14,000).

Sirens in Haifa

HAIFA. — Air raid sirens ordered Haifa residents into their bomb shelters twice yesterday morning. No reason was given for the alerts, which occurred around 9 and 10 a.m. The all-clear was sounded 10 minutes after the first alert and 50 minutes after the second. *(Itim)*

Yariv adviser to Elazar

Aluf Aharon Yariv (Res.), the former Army Intelligence chief, has been appointed special adviser to the Chief of Staff.

Urgent messages now can reach soldiers

Civilians may now send urgent messages to members of their families serving in the armed forces — concerning births, weddings, *britot mila* and sickness — by dialling one of the following numbers: Jerusalem: 63111; Tel Aviv: 254122; and Haifa: 660961.

These numbers may be called, starting today, from 8 a.m. to 10 p.m. The service was made possible through the cooperation of the Civil Service Commission, the Ministry of Communications and the Army Radio.

Kantara 'residents' greet Egyptians

Jerusalem Post Arab Affairs Reporter

Egypt last night claimed it recaptured the ghost town of Kantara, east of the Suez Canal, alleging that the population in the completely deserted place have come out "in their masses" to greet the advancing Egyptian forces.

The Egyptians said they hoisted their flag over the town, and said "the Sinai district administration will be reinstated soon in Kantara," the region's former provincial capital.

The military communique said Egyptian troops had fought from street to street and building to building to force the Israeli occupying force to surrender. It said Egyptian forces had captured 30 Israelis "the only Israelis who survived in the city."

"The Egyptians still in the city were overjoyed and rushed to welcome brother Egyptians fighting for the honour of their country," the communique added.

The Egyptian claim was contained in "military communique number 16," which was the third issued yesterday. The previous two communiques, which came after 13 hours of silence, claimed the Egyptians were "in full control of the entire east bank of the Suez Canal," and said they were advancing deep into Sinai.

The Egyptian and Syrian claims of success came in the face of the decisive Israeli push.

The Syrians yesterday claimed they inflicted heavy losses to Israel's Air Force after constant air battles. The Syrians also claimed control of most of the central region in the Golan Heights, and said they were advancing deeper into the area.

The Cairo and the Damascus statements were made as their forces were hit by the Israeli counter-attack, which ended the Egyptian and Syrian offensives at mid-morning yesterday.

In a late communique, the Cairo military command claimed that Egyptian forces have carried out successful operations to deny Israel the use of oil wells at Bala'een on the western coast of Sinai. The Egyptians said that their forces raided the oil wells and left them in flames after clashing with Israeli troops and returning to their base "safely."

Other reports from Cairo said the Egyptian government ordered new emergency regulations, including rationing petrol for civilians and

(Continued on page 2, col. 6)

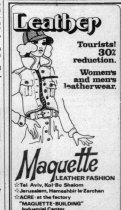

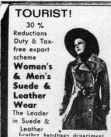

Israel drives 10 kms. towards Damascus

800 tanks destroyed, taken; Israeli planes blast targets

DAYAN: FINISH SYRIA SOON

Defence Minister Moshe Dayan last night predicted that the Syrian front would be "finished for all practical purposes" last night or during the night.

Mr. Dayan told a Shidurei Yisrael reporter: "I think the Syrians are practically broken. You can see their forces on this front withdrawing or running away. Those which remain have no military value on this front.

"We have to teach the Syrians a lesson — that the road fom Damascus to Eretz Yisrael, also leads from Eretz Yisrael to Damascus. Our forces are now moving on the road from Kuneitra to Damascus."

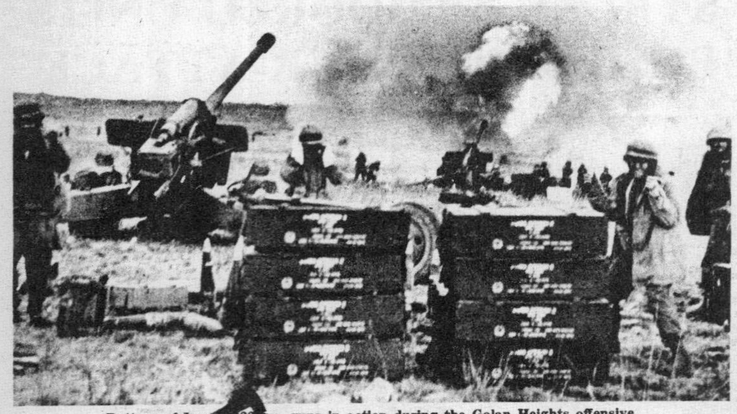

Battery of Isra[illegible]22mm. guns in action during the Golan Heights offensive.

THE JERUSALEM POST

SECOND EDITION

Price: IL1.50

FRIDAY, OCTOBER 12, 1973 • TISHRE 16, 5734 • RAMADHAN 16, 1393 • VOL. XLIII, No. 13915*

U.S. resupply to Israel reported as Soviets send arms to Arabs

By News Agencies

WASHINGTON. — The U.S. appears to be laying the groundwork for a major resupply effort for Israel, But knowledgeable officials stress that no decision has been made. They say the U.S. is concentrating on a diplomatic' drive to find a consensus with the Soviet Union and other powers for at least a cease-fire to end the fighting, and more preferably for a framework for a lasting negotiated settlement.

"We're in close and continuing contact with the Government of Israel," said Robert J. McCloskey, the State Department spokesman. At the same time, he said that a massive airlift of Soviet supplies to Egypt and Syria, reportedly under way, "would tend to put a new face on the situation" both for Israeli forces in the field and for the U.S.

But a highly placed Pentagon source said, "They've got scores of aircraft en route. It's not their normal shuttle to Cairo."

Witnesses reported, meanwhile, that a Boeing 707 transport plane bearing Israeli markings was loaded with Sparrow and Sidewinder air-to-air missiles at the Oceana Naval Air Station near Norfolk, Virginia. Officials described this as a resupply effort. Other observers said Israel undoubtedly already has asked Washington to speed up delivery of F-4 Phantom jets and other weapons promised in contracts for shipment this year and next.

McCloskey also pointed to a statement made on Monday by Secretary of State Henry Kissinger, that, "detente cannot survive irresponsibility in any area, including the Middle East." McCloskey said that "still stands."

A source at the Oceana Air Station told the Norfolk, Virginia, newspaper "Ledger-Star," another Boeing 707 with Israeli markings was loaded with arms last Saturday, the first day of the war.

The Pentagon's official spokesman declined to discuss anything to do with the resupply of Israel. But other officials said a moderate level of resupplies was continuing to flow.

The White House yesterday refused to respond to questions about whether the U.S. was resupplying Israel with arms. Presidential spokesman Gerald Warren also skirted a question on whether President Nixon had been in contact again with Soviet leader Leonid Brezhnev, saying instead that Dr. Kissinger "continues to be in direct contact" with major powers as well as the warring parties.

In Ramstein, West Germany, U.S. Air Force spokesmen yesterday, under orders to maintain silence, declined to comment on the report the Air Force was readying 48 F-4 Phantom jets in Germany to resupply the Israel Air Force. The spokesmen also declined to say whether

(Continued on Page 3, Col. 2)

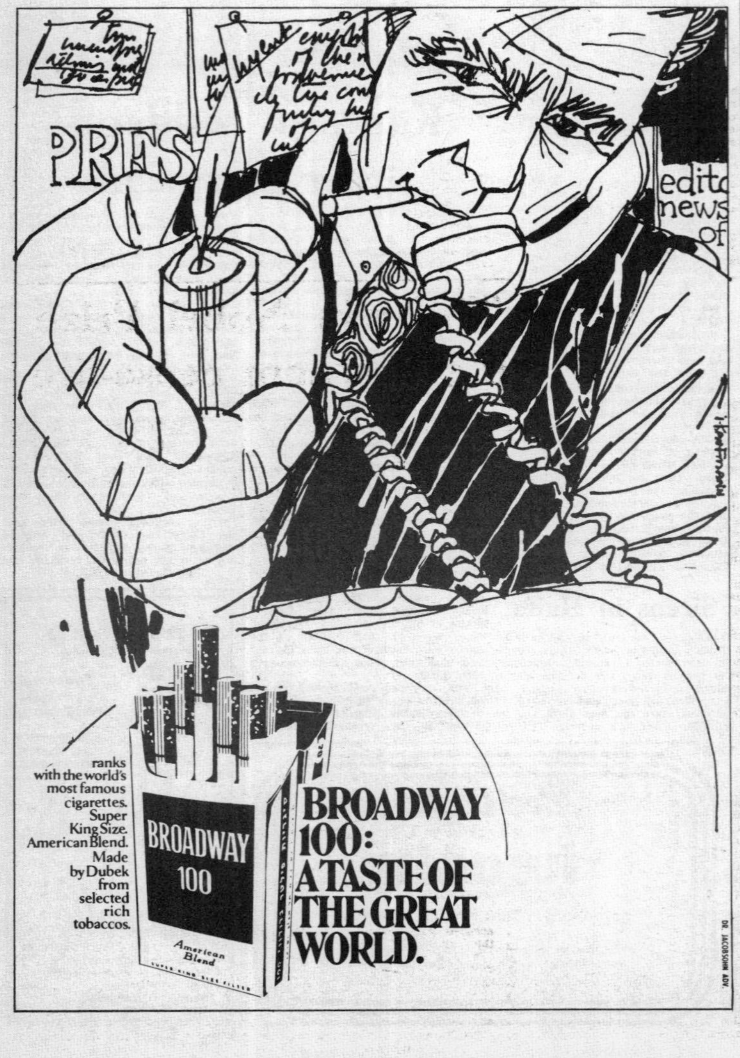

Attrition war in Sinai

Jerusalem Post Military Reporters

TEL AVIV. — Israeli forces continued their "war of attrition" against the massive Egyptian deployment along the Suez Canal during the past two days, keeping up a constant artillery bombardment, air force harassment and sniping at the enemy concentrations.

Informed sources said the steady pressure on the Egyptian concentrations at their Canal bridgeheads was beginning to show results. The Egyptians yesterday made no attempts to bring more reinforcements across the Canal, although some supplies may have been ferried across.

While the two main armies facing each other along the Canal front remained largely static, several minor engagements ended with Israeli victories on Tuesday and Wednesday.

Israeli commandos crossed the Canal and raided Egyptian supply lines and ordnance dumps on Wednesday night. The raid, in the southern sector, caused severe disruptions and heavy damage, informed sources said.

In another action, IDF forces on Wednesday broke through to an Israeli fortified position in the northern Canal sector on the Mediterranean coast. The men holding the position for five days had fought off Egyptian tank attacks under heavy artillery bombardment.

The relieving force pushed back an entrenched Egyptian force, armed with anti-tank missiles, which had blocked its advance.

The Egyptians left behind several of their dead on the battlefield. A later Egyptian attempt to capture the Israeli position was beaten off.

On Tuesday, an Egyptian drive towards Ras Sudar, south of the Canal, was blocked by Israeli infantry and armour. Then the Air Force was called in and the Egyptian force was wiped out. An Egyptian aircraft bombed Abu Rodeis, further south along the east coast of the Gulf of Suez on Tuesday night. There were some casualties and damage to buildings, but the oil installations were not hit.

Inside the Egyptian bridgeheads, the Egyptian units were reportedly still digging in, lining their approaches with anti-tank gun and missile emplacements.

Military correspondent Eli Landau, reporting from the southern sector on Wednesday, said the Egyptians were using infantry units armed with anti-tank missiles in their attempts to repel the Israeli armoured columns. He said the Egyptians were storming the tank formations in waves and were being literally mowed down. Their corpses were strewn over areas facing the Israeli lines for many kilometres.

Zayyat says 500 killed in Delta raids

UNITED NATIONS (Reuter). — Egyptian Foreign Minister Mohammed Hassan el-Zayyat told the General Assembly that he had word from Cairo yesterday that 500 people had been "murdered" in Israeli raids on the Nile Delta and the capital's suburbs. He spoke in the 135-nation body on the final day of its general policy debate.

"We still stand respectfully and bound by the charter, by U.N. resolutions and by its findings," he said. "We refuse, however, to be dictated to. We refuse, however, to be subjugated by long occupation and we simply refuse to stay occupied.

"We struggle, not because we guarantee success, but because we have no other option. It is our national duty. It is the only diktat we are obeying and are going to obey."

The Security Council, originally scheduled to meet on the war at 9.30 p.m. Israel time, postponed its session until 12.45 a.m. today. It was also supposed to hear a statement by Zayyat.

Earlier, Secretary-General Kurt Waldheim said in a written statement to the Council that the conflicting governments in the Middle East should "consider alternative courses before it is too late, so that fighting and bloodshed may cease."

Breaking the silence he had preserved since the war erupted last Saturday, he also urged the deadlocked Council members to make another effort to overcome "the obstacles to effective and peaceful action."

Lebanon: We downed an Israeli Phantom

BEIRUT (AFP). — The Defence Ministry here claimed yesterday that Lebanese anti-aircraft guns downed an Israeli Phantom jet at 3.10 in the afternoon and took its two-man crew prisoner.

The announcement said the plane crashed in Kafr Hiam, near Arkub, destroying several houses, killing one local man and injuring a number of children.

By RONNIE HOPE and ZE'EV SCHUL, Post Military Correspondents

TEL AVIV. — Israel armoured spearheads and infantry yesterday pierced through the Syrian defences beyond the Golan and by the evening had penetrated 10 kilometres inside enemy territory, advancing northeast along the Kuneitra-Damascus axis, the army spokesman announced here last night.

The two forces locked yesterday morning, following a 24-hour lull, in what was probably the largest single tank battle in this arena until now. The principal engagement, involving hundreds of tanks, focused on the northern sector of the front, around the Kuneitra-Damascus highway — where the Syrians lost 800 tanks destroyed or captured intact.

While capturing Damascus is one of the options open to the I.D.F., it is by no means certain that it will be taken up. Conquering the city and holding it would tie up large forces required elsewhere. It would also involve Israel in complex political problems.

Military circles said last night that Israel was close to reaching the turning point in the battle against Syria, in which Israel's aim is to break Syria's ability and will to fight. The importance of crushing Syrian resistance lies not only in that this will make it possible to put more pressure on Egypt, but also to deter Iraq and Jordan from active involvement in the war.

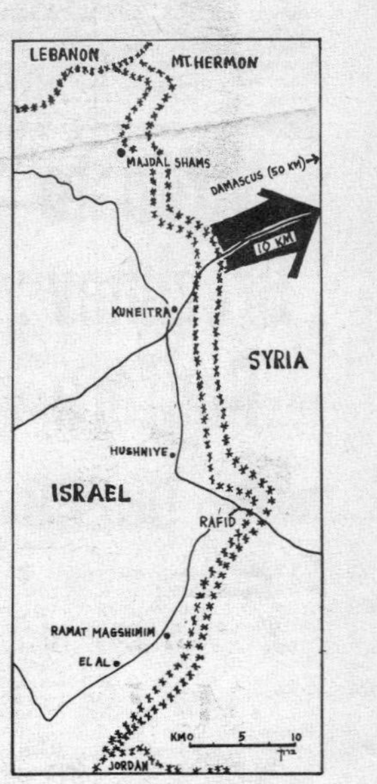

The air force, in addition to supporting the advance, devoted some efforts to bombing eight Syrian airfields, including Damascus International, which is now used only for military purposes. There was little interference. Altogether 11 enemy planes were shot down yesterday on both the Syrian and Egyptian fronts. The airfields bombed received "very basic and intensive treatment," a military source said. The aim was to prevent what is left of Syria's air force from interfering in the ground war.

The Israeli thrust was concentrated in the northern sector between Kuneitra and Mt. Hermon on a number of axes. Last night infantry units were clearing enemy pockets of resistance left behind by the rapidly advancing armour.

The break-through came after very heavy fighting. The Syrians had fallen back into their highly fortified line which they had build and held since the 1967 war. The ground offensive was preceded by heavy artillery and aerial softening up.

Well informed sources confirmed that the Rusians are flying arms into Syria, but said that this is of no great significance. The raids on airfields could disrupt this flow of supplies, it was pointed out.

Throughout the day, Syrian soldiers left behind by their retreating forces on the Israel side of the cease-fire line continued to surrender to IDF units. Roaming among the more than 800 destroyed and abandoned tanks left behind by the Syrian army, the Syrian infantry and tank men held out until noon Wednesday, in the hope that their units would be able to mount a counter-attack and reclaim some of the Heights they captured earlier in the week.

The Israeli spearheads, enjoying massive air support, were reported earlier in the day to be advancing on a wide front along the entire length of the Golan Heights.

Yesterday's counter-offensive was preceded by an intensive artillery barrage to soften the Syrian defences, during which Israeli gunners reportedly established new "records" in the swift pacing of their rounds. In addition to the artillery, the advancing columns also had a covering "airumbrella."

The continued pursuit of the Syrians across their home frontier arises from more than purely military considerations. The Chief of Staff's pledge on Sunday to pursue the Syrians whenever and wherever they could be found is now a reality. Politically, Israel will not be cowed into blind respect for the armistice lines.

Latest estimates of the Syrian line count a possible 2,000 tanks — five times the number they had in the Six Day War. Subtracting the estimated 800 tanks the Syrians lost this week, there is still a substantial number to account for. It may be assumed that a certain percentage consists of vintage armour and units that cannot be moved from where they are now stationed for internal-political reasons.

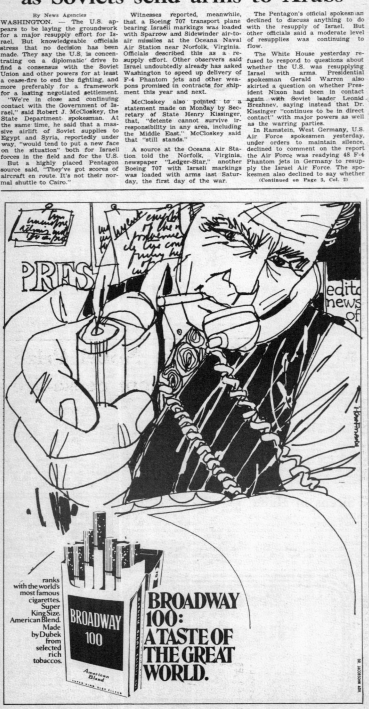

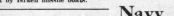

A Syrian T-62 tank captured intact in the Golan Heights, was shown yesterday to foreign correspondents in an Armoured Corps base. It is the first time that this tank, the most modern in the Soviet arsenal, has ever been seen outside the Soviet bloc and the Arab countries.

It is essentially similar to the T-54 and T-55 but carries a 115mm. instead of 105mm. gun and weighs 36.5 tons.

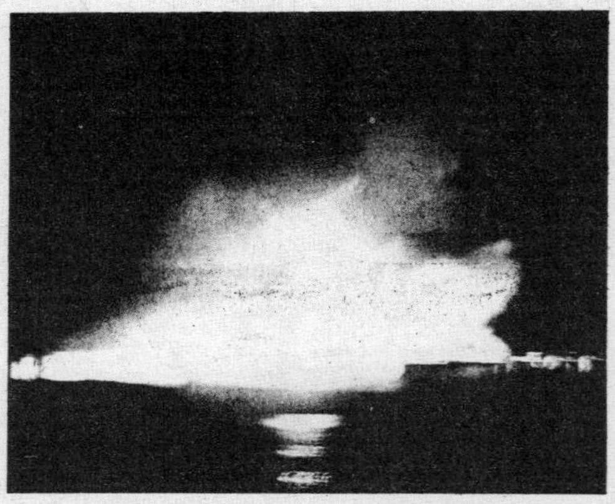

Tank farms in the Syrian port of Banias go up in flames after being hit by Israeli missile boats.

Navy bombs Syria ports, oil depots

Jerusalem Post Military Correspondent

TEL AVIV. — The Israel Navy bombed the Syrian coast on Wednesday night, setting fire to fuel installations and tank farms at Latakia, Banias and Tartus.

The Navy also suceeeded in sinking two more Soviet-built missile boats. All told, five Syrian-Soviet missile boats have been sunk in the war.

A military correspondent on one of the Israeli vessels described "the rather uncanny feeling" he had in seeing the Syrian missiles repeatedly zeroing in on the Israeli task force. In most cases the Israeli Gabriel missiles hit the Syrian ships first, sending the manually-controlled Styx missiles careening off course. Other Styx missiles were brought down by anti-aircraft fire.

Reuter reported from Banias that Syria has issued no casualty figures, but townspeople said the Israeli bombardment caused deaths and injuries. All along the coast, the normally bustling little towns and villages were sombre. Most of the shops were shuttered and blue blackout paint was splashed on windows and car lamps.

AFTER MIDNIGHT

CAIRO (UPI). — U.S. Phantoms from an aircraft carrier in the Mediterranean have joined in Israeli raids on Egyptian positions, the Middle East News Agency said yesterday, quoting "Arab diplomatic sources."

The claim of direct U.S. involvement in the Arab-Israeli fighting was reminiscent of similar claims made by the late President Abdul Nasser during the Six Day War.

Syrian refinery destroyed

By MALEK AL-HUSSEINI

HOMS. — Israeli aircraft destroyed a major power station and put a still-blazing oil refinery out of action for years to come during raids on this central Syrian town, officials said here yesterday.

I saw great pillars of black smoke and flames rising from the wrecked oil refinery more than 24 hours after the last Israeli bombing attack on Wednesday.

Experts said 80 per cent of the £20m. refinery was destroyed and it would not he in operation again for several years. Annual production at the refinery was estimated at one million tons.

The power station produced a fifth of Syria's electricity supplies. The director of the plant said at least 30 of his 450 workers were killed and about 100 injured.

Rescuers were unable to approach the inferno of flames and explosions that the oil refinery had become.

(Reuter)

Agnew resigns as Vice-President

WASHINGTON. — Spiro T. Agnew resigned abruptly as U.S. Vice-President on Wednesday "in the best interest of the nation," and pleaded no contest to a charge of income tax evasion. President Nixon began an 'immediate search for a successor.

A Federal court judge in Baltimore, Maryland, sentenced Agnew to a $10,000 fine and three years probation. The Justice Department at the same time dropped its criminal investigation of Agnew, but told the court it had evidence that Agnew was receiving cash payments from Maryland contractors as late as December, 1972, when he was Vice-President. He was the second Vice-President in U.S. history to resign.

Attorney-General Elliot Richardson said yesterday that the President had a key role in the plea arrangement — and thus in Agnew's resignation.

Richardson said on Wednesday that the corruption investigation involving Agnew had "established a pattern of substantial cash payments" to him by Maryland State contractors when he was Baltimore County Executive, Governor, and as Vice-President."

Agnew appeared yesterday morning at his office in the Executive Office Building adjacent to the White House to close out his affairs.

The White House said Nixon; who learned of the surprise decision, during a 40-minute meeting with Agnew on Tuesday, played "no direct role" in the legal arrangement for his Vice-President to resign and — in effect — plead guilty to a lesser charge. There was no explanation of the contradiction between the White House and Richardson statements. Nixon said Agnew had been subjected to "an

(Continued on page 5, col. 6)

Israel task force crosses Canal

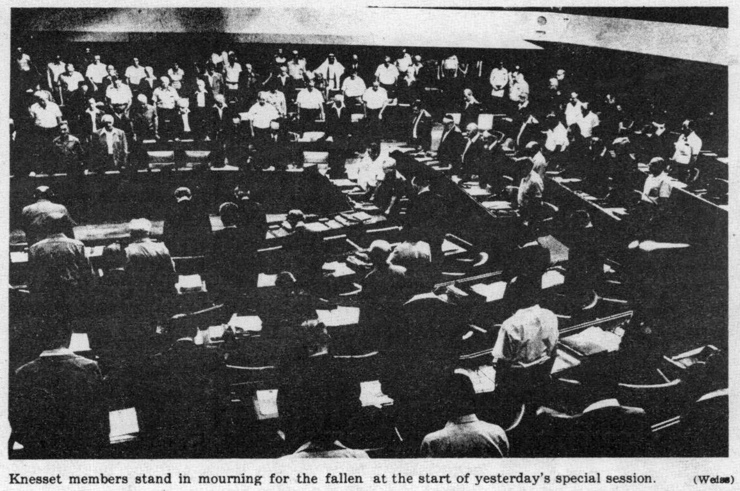

Knesset members stand in mourning for the fallen at the start of yesterday's special session. (Weiss)

THE JERUSALEM POST

SECOND EDITION

Price: 65 Ag.

WEDNESDAY, OCTOBER 17, 1973 • TISHRE 21, 5734 • RAMADHAN 21, 1393 • VOL. XLIII, No. 13919*

SYRIA LOSES 105 TANKS, 10 PLANES

POST Military Correspondents

TEL AVIV. — Israeli forces on the Syrian front yesterday morning destroyed 105 tanks and downed 10 aircraft as they repulsed three counter-attacks by enemy armour and commandos.

The enemy attacking forces included a number of Iraqi tanks, the remnants of the Iraqi division which was virtually wiped out on Monday.

The enemy left behind 40 knocked out tanks on the battlefield near Beit Jann, at the northern corner of the Israel--held bulge in Syrian territory, and some 65 tanks in the central sector of the enclave, near Tel Shams.

The Syrians also attacked Israeli forces from the air, and 10 enemy planes were shot down, mostly by small arms fire from the Israeli ground units.

The Israeli Air Force provided close support for the ground forces and also bombed military and strategic targets deep inside Syria, including two bridges near Tartous, missile bases, and radar installations.

Israeli forces in Syria are now concentrating on consolidating their positions in the area they now hold, an area which has a topographic advantage, making it relatively easy to defend.

The airlift of Soviet arms and ammunition into Syria continues, with some 12 to 15 Antonov transports landing there daily.

Some 800 Syrian and Iraqi tanks have been destroyed since the fighting began, according to a preliminary count. This is about 50 per cent of the total armoured strength used so far in combat by the enemy on the northern front.

An IDF spokesman said the northern front was quiet in the afternoon hours.

'Jordan in action on Syrian front'

AMMAN (Reuter). — Jordanian troops, sent to the Syrian front on Saturday, went into action there for the first time yesterday, the official Jordanian Radio said.

The reports said that the Jordanians repulsed Israeli forces at several places.

Anti-aircraft missile batteries destroyed

By ZE'EV SCHUL and RONNIE HOPE, Post Military Correspondents

TEL AVIV. — An Israeli task force crossed the Suez Canal in the central sector early yesterday to attack the Egyptians to the rear of their positions on the west bank of the Canal.

Its targets included surface-to-air missile sites, and artillery batteries.

Anti-aircraft missile batteries were reported to have been destroyed.

No details of the strength and further aims of the raiding force were available.

Ground operations in Sinai were limited yesterday to local artillery and tank duels.

The Air Force continued to give close support to the ground units. The Egyptians lost 12 planes in dogfights. With the Syrian loss of 10 yesterday, the total of enemy aircraft downed so far is 222.

Enemy interference with Air Force sorties is largely restricted to the missile systems. The Air Force is in turn concentrating on disrupting Egyptian and Syrian supply lines, the destruction of missile batteries and maintaining close ground support for the front line units.

Naval activity was limited to attempts by Egyptian missile boats to bombard Sharm e-Sheikh with a number of missile salvoes on Monday night. All missed their targets.

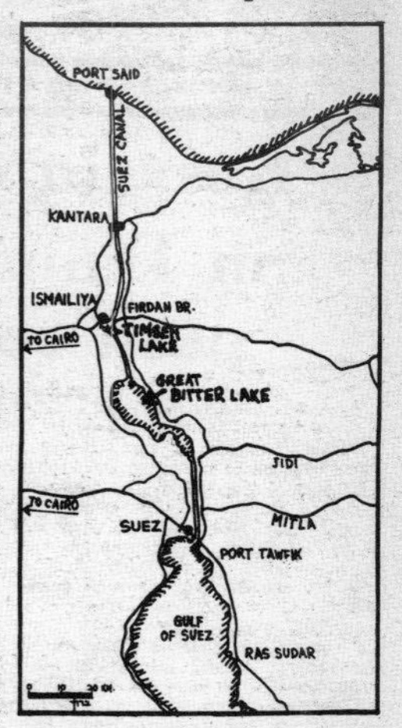

Cairo confirms

CAIRO (UPI). — The Egyptian military command yesterday confirmed Prime Minister Golda Meir's announcement that an Israeli force raided Egyptian positions west of the Suez Canal.

In a special communique issued at 9.50 p.m., it described this as "a desperate raid," which it said took place at 2.30 p.m.

It said Egyptian artillery destroyed three out of seven Israeli tanks which made a "desperate bid to raid some positions on the West Bank" of the Suez Canal.

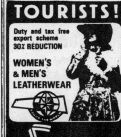

Hermon unit's fate unknown

KIRYAT SHMONA. — Following the official announcement of the fall of an IDF outpost on Mount Hermon in the first day of the war, the fate of the defenders is still unknown.

The men are still listed as missing because the Syrian authorities refuse to give details on the prisoners of war they have taken.

An Itim reporter who spoke with area Druse yesterday heard from them that three Syrian helicopters appeared there on Yom Kippur and circled above the outpost. After a while, one of the helicopters went up in flames.

It has also been learned that a Syrian helicopter pilot who fell into Zahal's hands told interrogators that a commando force had been flown in to take the outpost. He said the Israeli soldiers in the outpost fortified themselves as best they could.

But, the Itim reporter adds, there are doubts about the veracity of this account, and meanwhile the fate of the outpost's defenders remains unknown. *(Itim)*

AFTER MIDNIGHT

One person was slightly hurt and two houses and six cars were damaged as Katyusha rockets fired from Lebanese territory hit Kiryat Shmona at 11 o'clock last night. The occupants of the houses were in their shelters and none of them was hurt.

THE JERUSALEM POST will not appear tomorrow *Simhat Tora*. The next issue, on Friday, will contain a 16-page magazine including Lea Ben Dor's analysis of **Why We Didn't Know**, Philip Gillon on **Tending the Wounded**, Helga Dudman on the **Home Front**, Abraham Rabinovich following the **Golan war trail**, Hadassah Bat Haim's **Thoughts in the Queue**, reviews of books about the Dreyfus Case, Ellis Island, and others, art and theatre notes and broadcasting reviews.

'All the aid needed to repel our attackers'

MEIR THANKS THE U.S.

By ASHER WALLFISH
Jerusalem Post Knesset Reporter

Premier Golda Meir said yesterday that in the name of the Israeli nation she wished to thank the President and the people of the United States for acting in the American tradition of helping a State which was struggling to withstand aggression.

In a 40-minute statement to the Knesset on the conduct of the war — delivered at a special session convened during the recess — Premier Meir said she was convinced that the U.S. would do all that was necessary to deter dangerous trends in the policies and the actions of the Soviet Union and give Israel all the aid required to defend its existence and repel its attackers.

The U.S. was continuing to reply to Israel's requests for weapons and equipment in the quantities, categories and tempo dictated by the situation, she said. (Excerpts from Mrs. Meir's speech on page 2.)

She made these points:

- Israel does not want anybody else to fight in its place.
- The British and French arms embargo constitute cynical and immoral bias by enlightened states for selfish ends.
- She assumed that Soviet advisers and experts are arriving in Syria and Egypt with the airlift of weapons.
- Discussion of a cease-fire is pointless as the Arabs have made no proposals. They will be ready for a cease-fire only after they have been hit harder, it seems, and then they will have many friends to propose a truce.
- Any truce must include a full prisoner-of-war exchange.
- Israel's well-wishers must be made to realize that the Arab aim is to destroy the State of Israel.
- Israeli Arabs have offered aid for the war effort in many ways — which augers well for the future.
- Israel does not want to fight the Kingdom of Jordan.

Knesset Speaker Yisrael Yeshayahu opened the session, in the presence of President Ephraim Katzir, with a minute's silence for the nation's fallen, and expressed profound condolences to the next-of-kin and hopes for the speedy recovery of the wounded.

When the packed Chamber was seated once more, the Speaker expressed his wish that the prisoners-of-war return home soon.

Opposite the Speaker's dais, prominent in the Diplomats' Gallery, were the ambassadors of Britain, Finland, Denmark, Norway and Sweden.

Premier Meir spoke at first in a low and sombre tone and with firmness and confidence throughout.

Defence Minister Moshe Dayan was conspicuous by his absence — down in Sinai. Three or four M.K.s came in army uniform. From outside the Knesset building was blacked out.

Before the session ended Speaker Yeshayahu announced that the Knesset would convene again next week, in special session, for legislation to deal with the postponement of the elections (which were due to be held on October 30).

Gahal leader Menahem Begin, who opened the three-hour debate on the Prime Minister's statement, matched a bitter attack on Britain and France with warm praise for the U.S. and touched briefly on some of the lessons to be learned from the present war.

Gahal was firmly resolved to keep its questions about the events leading up to the war till after victory — "and there are questions," Mr. Begin said. All the Opposition, as well as the Alignment's two Coalition allies — the National Religious Party and the Independent Liberals — said that queries were inevitable but that now was not the time.

Mr. Begin said that Britain's violation of formal contracts in its refusal to send vital equipment to Israel threw a strange light on British Prime Minister Edward Heath's statement after his visit to Israel three years ago, that "now he understood Israel's security needs better." The Jewish People had paid with six million lives because Britain disowned the Balfour Declaration, and now the latter was denying vital equipment to a country facing an aggression supported by the Communist Empire.

Turning to France, Mr. Begin said that while it was sending weapons to Israel's enemies till the present day, it was denying this fact in a way that heaped obloquy upon itself.

Both Britain and France, he said, were trading their own destinies for immediate advantage and for a barrel of oil, for they were facilitating the Soviet Union's aims of breaking through the Suez Canal to link up its Mediterranean and Indian Ocean fleets, to dominate Aden and Somalia and to spread over the Persian Gulf.

The U.S., on the other hand, merited all possible gratitude for standing behind Israel.

Mr. Haim Zadok (Labour Alignment) said the Soviet Union had not committed such a massive act of deception since the Cuba missile affair in 1962. Today, when detente prevailed — and not the cold war of those days — the deception was all the graver.

Mr. Zadok said the solid support which Israel was receiving from the U.S. stemmed not only from friendship between the two peoples, but also from the profound aware-

(Continued on page 2, col. 2)

No U.S. troops but 'firm support' of Israel's arms needs

WASHINGTON. — The U.S. does not intend to send American military forces into the Middle East but will firmly support Israel's weapons needs, U.S. officials said yesterday. The statement followed a reported comment by Secretary of State Henry Kissinger at a White House dinner that if the Soviets introduced troops, the U.S. would follow suit.

Similarly, Melvin Laird, Domestic Adviser to President Nixon, was reported to have told a group of newsmen at a breakfast that the situation is becoming one of confrontation with the USSR.

U.S. Air Force C5A Galaxies, the world's largest military tranports, landed one after the other at an Israeli air base yesterday, carrying U.S. military supplies.

The Lockheed C5A Galaxy, according to "Janes World's Aircraft," is 75.5 m. long and 19.85 m. high, with an 11-ton payload. A typical load includes two M60 tanks or 16 three-quarter ton trucks or one M60 tank and two Bell Iroquois helicopters, five M113 personnel carriers, one M59 two-and-one-half ton trucks and a M151 quarter-ton truck.

At mid-afternoon, U.S. Ambassador Kenneth Keating drove onto the airfield.

"I'm just out here to take a look around," he told a reporter.

Washington officials yesterday said about 30 U.S. Air Force flights resupplied Israel with about 500 tons of war material during the first two days of the U.S. arms airlift.

They said the shipments amounted to about 10 per cent of the supplies the U.S.S.R. has flown to Egypt and Syria in the last six days.

The officials, who asked not to be identified, said the U.S. tonnages did not include aircraft the U.S. also is sending to Israel.

The U.S. resupply effort was launched on Sunday, the officials said, to keep the U.S.S.R. from upsetting the power balance in the Middle East.

In Norfolk, Virginia, the Israeli cargo ship Aben Dat prepared to sail yesterday to the Middle East with a load of U.S. bombs, jet fighters, and perhaps tanks, rushed aboard on Monday at the naval base here.

Witnesses reported seeing four holds of the ship packed with 250 and 500 pound bombs and three U.S. A4 Skyhawk jet fighters lashed to the ship's deck. All markings on the planes were obliterated.

Other sources said U.S. Air Force C5 and C141 jet transports are flying tanks and ammunition to Tel Aviv. In addition, they said F4 Phantom fighter bombers, withdrawn from U.S. units, also are being sold to Israel and delivered there.

Senator Henry Jackson on Monday challenged the State Department's announcement that the U.S. is resupplying Israel with weapons she has lost in the fighting thus far. "Some deliveries are being made, but certain crucial material is being withheld" from Israel, he said.

An aide to Senator Jackson said Phantoms are not going to Israel in the numbers needed to offset its losses in warplanes.

He also pointed out that although the State Department said the "massive" Soviet airlift has been going on since last Wednesday, Secretary of State Kissinger two days later spoke of it as being "moderate."

"The State Department," Jackson said, "has been five days late in beginning the U.S. resupply to Israel."

He was referring to the report by U.S. official that the American resupply operation began on Sunday.

U.S. air chief: 'We won't match Soviet airlift'

WASHINGTON (UPI). — U.S. Air Force Chief of Staff George S. Brown told a news conference the U.S. did not plan to match the Soviet airlift "ton for ton."

He estimated Israel was losing one plane for every two Arab fighters.

"The point is, Israel will run out of airplanes before the Arabs will," Brown said.

He said the U.S.S.R. has deployed its strongest-ever force in the Mediterranean — 60 combat ships.

Nixon meets four Arab foreign ministers today

WASHINGTON. — President Nixon will meet four Arab Foreign Ministers today to discuss the Middle East war, the White House announced yesterday.

Presidential spokesman Gerald Warren said the ministers — Abdelaziz Bouteflika of Algeria, Sheikh Sabah al-Ahmad al-Jaber al-Sabah of Kuwait, Ahmed Benhima of Morocco and Omar Sakkaf of Saudi Arabia — had requested the meeting.

Mr. Warren said that Dr. Kissinger, who discussed the Middle East crisis at an hour-long conference with President Nixon yesterday, would attend the meeting with the four Foreign Ministers.

Diplomatic sources said the Arab ministers intended to express their concern over the U.S. decision to send arms to Israel.

The announcement came amid reports that the envoys were carrying a message from King Feisal of Saudi Arabia, who has been under intense pressure from other Arab leaders to deny oil to the U.S.

It is understood that Nixon and Feisal have exchanged messages since the outbreak of the war. *(Reuter, AP)*

Belgian solidarity

BRUSSELS (INA). — A Belgian "Committee of solidarity with Israel" has been set up here under the presidency of former premier Gaston Eyskens. Several former ministers are among the many political figures who have joined the group.

Sadat: Cease-fire after Israel withdraws

Jerusalem Post Arab Affairs Reporter

Egyptian President Anwar Sadat yesterday said he would accept a cease-fire and subsequent peace talks only after Israel withdrew from all territories it captured in the 1967 war. Otherwise, Sadat said, he would go on fighting. Warning Israel against bombarding deep inside Egypt, he announced that Egyptian long-range ground-to-ground missiles were "ready to strike the very depths of Israel at any moment."

Sadat identified the ground-to-ground missile as the Zafer, the smallest of three Egyptian-made rockets which is said to have a range of 500 kilometres and be capable of carrying a 500-kilogram warhead. (Full story on page 2.)

"Our Egyptian Arab missiles of the Zafer type, which can cross Sinai, are now on their pads ready to be launched by a single order into the farthest depths of Israel," Sadat said. He warned Israel to remember what I have cautioned against in the past: an eye for an eye, a tooth for a tooth and a depth for a depth."

Sadat said that Egypt could have used these missiles "the very first minute" of the war, but "we are not advocates of extermination as the Israelis claim."

The Egyptian President said he began the war "for the sake of peace that is based on justice." He said Egypt had two aims: Israel's withdrawal from the occupied territories and the restoration of the Palestinian people's "legitimate rights."

Sadat said that once these two ends are guaranteed he would agree to a cease-fire and subsequent peace talks at "an international conference" where he would try to persuade other Arab leaders and Palestinian representatives to join him.

He made his "peace proposals" in the form of "an open letter" to U.S. President Richard Nixon. The letter contained five points expressing Egypt's position, the last of which stated Cairo's preparedness to reopen the Suez Canal. Sadat said he has already ordered the chairman of the Canal authority to make initial preparations in this direction.

Sadat offered nothing to indicate a change in his basic demands. What was new was that he appeared to feel that this time he was speaking from a position of strength.

The Egyptian President spoke at an extraordinary session of the National Assembly (parliament). His ceremonial address was broadcast over all Egyptian radio networks. Wearing a field marshal's uniform as supreme commander of the Egyptian armed forces, Sadat was received with wild applause. So was

(Continued on page 2, col. 1)

ISRAEL OBSERVERS: Sadat's aim: dismemberment of Israel

Jerusalem Post Diplomatic Correspondent

President Sadat's speech of yesterday was seen in Jerusalem as clearly revealing his ultimate aim: the dismemberment of the Jewish State. He spoke of two stages in Egyptian policy. First, to force a cease-fire with Israel undertaking to withdraw to the pre-'67 lines; and then to summon an international peace conference to discuss "restoring the rights of the Palestinians" — which is a euphemism for taking apart the State of Israel.

If the peace conference failed to materialize, observers in Jerusalem pointed out, Egypt could then launch an attack similar to the Yom Kippur attack — but this time from the pre-'67 lines — with imaginable results.

A top Israeli diplomat currently in New York referred to the Sadat speech as "the speech of a man who wants neither ceasefire nor peace."

Strengthening this assessment was the tone of the Egyptian leader's address. He simply did not relate to Israel as a possible partner in dialogue or negotiation. The tone was "one of dictation, not of negotiation," an observer said. There was "a boastfulness and arrogance born of an initial military advantage which is going to be meagre and transient," the Israeli observer said.

Kissinger, Tho win Nobel Prize for arranging Vietnam cease-fire

OSLO (UPI). — Henry Kissinger and North Vietnamese chief negotiator Le Duc Tho yesterday won the 1973 Nobel Peace Prize, the Norwegian Nobel Committee announced.

Kissinger, the new U.S. Secretary of State, and Le Duc Tho negotiated the Vietnam cease-fire during a series of secret meetings in Paris which stretched over several years. The agreement was finally signed in January of this year.

The decision came as a complete surprise here, since the two men had never been mentioned as possible candidates.

The committee said, "For more than three years they have used all their strength and good will to achieve a negotiated solution, a peaceful solution of the Vietnam war.

"Thereby, they have performed a feat which is in the best accordance with Alfred Nobel's thoughts, that conflicts should be solved through negotiations and not through war."

The Vietnam war was described as "the most gruesome and long conflict the world has experienced after the Second World War. It was a gruesome war that not only forced upon the Vietnam civilian population enormous sufferings but that also poisoned the atmosphere in and between other countries in the whole world.

"It is our hope that all parties in this conflict will feel the moral responsibility that the treaty on a cease-fire in Vietnam will lead to a lasting peace for Indochina's war-ravaged people," the statement said.

The South Vietnamese and Vietcong delegations stationed in Paris still have not made a political settlement as required under the cease-fire treaty. Both sides have accused each other of continuing the war.

At the State Department yesterday, Kissinger said the award gives him "more dedication to seek an end to hostilities in the Middle East and to move rapidly toward a just and lasting peace in the area."

"Nothing that has happened to me in public life has moved me more than this award," he said.

Kissinger and Tho will have to come to Oslo to receive the prize money of $130,000, a diploma and gold medal during the ceremony at Oslo University on December 10, marking the death of Alfred Nobel, the Swedish inventor of dynamite.

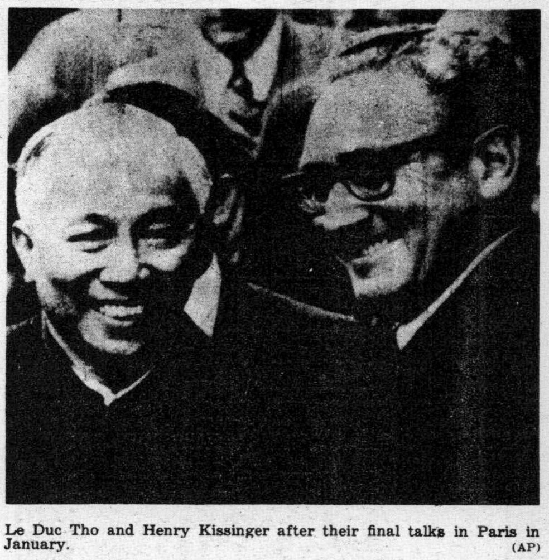

Le Duc Tho and Henry Kissinger after their final talks in Paris in January. (AP)

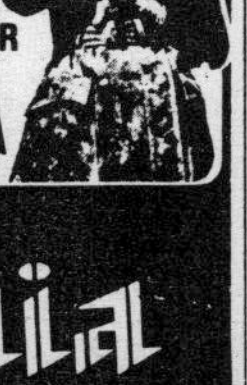

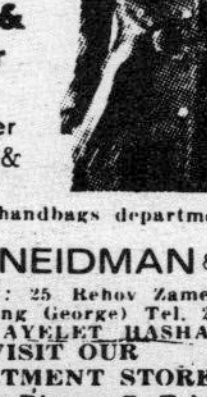

Shooting continues at Canal despite Israel-Egypt cease-fire

THE JERUSALEM POST
SECOND EDITION
Price: 65 Ag.
TUESDAY, OCTOBER 23, 1973 • TISHRE 27, 5734 • RAMADHAN 27, 1393 • VOL. XLIII, No. 13922*

A cease-fire was accepted by Israel and Egypt yesterday on the 17th day of the war as of 6.50 p.m., but shooting continued at the Suez Canal front.

Syria by late last night had still ignored the cease-fire which was initiated by the U.S. and Soviet Union.

In another sudden move, U.S. Secretary of State Dr. Henry Kissinger flew into Israel from Moscow at noon yesterday for talks with Prime Minister Golda Meir. Soviet Premier Kosygin flew to Cairo and Damascus. (See separate stories this page).

The lightning developments came on the heels of an American-Soviet agreement in Moscow in talks between Dr. Kissinger and Soviet leaders.

The cease-fire was promulgated in a Security Council resolution, that also called for immediate peace negotiations between the sides, and for implementation of the 1967 Security Council Resolution 242 "in all its parts."

Jordan also yesterday accepted the cease-fire, but said its expeditionary force in Syria would meanwhile remain under Syrian command. Iraq, which sent larger forces to Syria, rejected the cease-fire call.

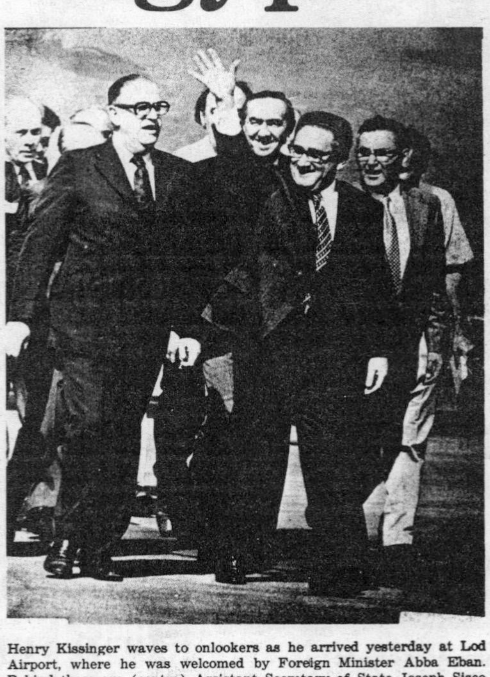

Henry Kissinger waves to onlookers as he arrived yesterday at Lod Airport, where he was welcomed by Foreign Minister Abba Eban. Behind them are (centre) Assistant Secretary of State Joseph Sisco and (extreme left) his deputy Alfred Atherton. (Werner Braun)

Kosygin expected in Damascus to push cease-fire

By ANAN SAFADI
Jerusalem Post Arab Affairs Reporter

Soviet Premier Alexei Kosygin was expected to arrive in Damascus last night, apparently to persuade Syria to accept the the cease-fire. Earlier, Mr. Kosygin was reported to be in Egypt, which announced its acceptance of the cease-fire in time for the Security Council deadline.

Jordan, which kept a low profile throughout the war, last night declared it would abide by the cease-fire. But it said its troops on the Syrian front were subject to instructions and decisions from Damascus.

Lebanon, the fourth Arab state neighbouring Israel, said it was withholding comment on the cease-fire pending Syria's decision. Lebanon, which was not a party in the latest war, had to deal with the Palestinian terrorist movement which is based in Beirut and which last night pledged to defy the cease-fire "and continue the armed struggle until the liberation of all Palestine."

Egypt's acceptance of the cease-fire was condemned by a number of Arab countries. Most outspoken were Iraq and Libya, which called for the continuation of the war. Saudi Arabia, Morocco, Algeria, Kuwait and Sudan, all of which had troops on either the Egyptian or the Syrian fronts, maintained silence and seemed to be waiting to hear Syria's attitude.

The Soviet Union appeared to be concentrating its efforts on Syria, the only country which is military relevant and which had not yet accepted the cease-fire.

The Syrians last night said they were still studying the cease-fire resolution. Their dilemma was that in accepting the resolution, they would also have to accept Security Council Resolution 242, to which they have never agreed before. In addition, a large Iraqi force, whose government has already rejected the cease-fire, is located inside Syria.

The Syrians ignored the cease-fire call most of the day yesterday. Damascus Radio reported it only late in the evening, along with Egypt's acceptance of it.

Egypt announced its acceptance at 2.30 p.m. in a broadcast statement attributed to the president's office. The statement said that President Anwar Sadat had instructed his army comand to observe the new cease-fire at the time set by the Security Council. Later Cairo Radio repeatedly broadcast a terse announcement stating, "Egypt has decided to observe a cease-fire at 6.52 p.m." last night.

The statement said the decision was

(Coninued on page 2, col. 7)

Nixon 'confident he can't be impeached'

WASHINGTON. — President Nixon is "quite confident" there are no grounds to impeach him, a White House spokesman said yesterday. Mr. Nixon, it was stated, was at his desk at 8.45 in the morning, and during the day consulted by cable with Secretary of State Kissinger and also worked on a statement to the nation on why he fired Watergate prosecutor Archibald Cox.

(Pressure for impeachment, page 5)

Mig 25s over Canal

TEL AVIV. — Two Mig 25s (Foxbat in the Nato code), flew over the Suez Canal area at a high altitude yesterday, apparently photographing the area. It is understood that the Egyptians do not fly the Mig 25, and it is assumed here that the pilots were Russians.

Likud will oppose cease-fire agreement

Says it will bring new war

By MARK SEGAL
Jerusalem Post Political Reporter

TEL AVIV. — The Likud executive yesterday came out strongly against the government's acceptance of the cease-fire resolution, charging it contained the seeds of a future war.

The Likud leadership also accused the government of "a serious failure" between Rosh Hashana and Yom Kippur by not taking deterrent measures against the concentration of enemy forces. They charged that "although the government had reliable information of enemy concentrations in the north and the south, it did not mobilize the country's forces nor transfer them in due time to the cease-fire lines in order to deter the enemy from its planned aggression or in order to smash them in their formative stages."

Accordingly the Likud will vote against the government in the Knesset. "Out of a sense of national responsibility we call on the people in this grave hour to strive for cancellation of this deplorable policy of the government and to effect the formulation of new policy for Israel leading to peace and security," the Likud statement said.

It added that despite Egyptian and Syrian agression in the bloody war against Israel, the government has undertaken, on the basis of yesterday's Security Council cease-fire resolution, to "commence immediate implementation" of Security Council resolution 242 of November 1967. The Likud executive contended this meant "the withdrawal of Israel in all areas and the partition anew of the Land of Israel."

The Opposition party said implementation of this resolution "will not bring peace but permanently jeopardize the security of Israel and her people." It was also noted that the Soviet Union continues to pour unlimited supplies of the latest arms and military equipment to the enemy arsenals "and experience has shown that Israel's enemies in their increasing effort to annihilate Israel, may well activate forces armed with the latest weapons to spring a sudden attack on Israel's forces in all the places they are deployed."

In the executive's discussion, many speakers felt that the government was entering a trap set by the Russians and in effect affording the Arabs and Russians a political victory.

Doubts among M.K.s

Jerusalem Post Political Reporter

TEL AVIV. — The Knesset Foreign Affairs and Security Committee's daily meeting ended an hour-and-a-half later than scheduled last night, reportedly because the Government found it necessary to explain at length its acceptance of the cease-fire agreement in the face of reservations — not only from Opposition but also from Alignment members.

The extra 90 minutes put in by Premier Meir and other Cabinet representatives in the Committee obliged the Cabinet to delay a meeting scheduled for last night. It will only be learned in the early hours of the morning, therefore, if and when a special Knesset session will be held to hear a statement from Mrs. Meir on the cease-fire decision.

It is also understood that, not only inside the Alignment, but also inside the National Religious Party, the second largest coalition faction, apprehensions exist that the cease-fire does not guarantee sufficient security measures for the future.

Some Knesset members wanted hard guarantees from the U.S. that there would not be a recurrence of the 1970 cease-fire which was exploited by the Egyptians to push forward missiles, which caused the loss of many lives in this war.

It is understood that the Government is concerned that a number of its own Knesset members may vote with the Opposition when the house decides on the issue.

BLACKOUT IS STILL IN FORCE

TEL AVIV. — The nationwide blackout is still in force, the Haga (Civil Defence) spokesman told The Jerusalem Post yesterday. He asked that the public listen to the radio and TV today for further instructions regarding potential changes in the blackout, due to the cease-fire.

Kissinger-Meir meet 3½ hours

No statement issued after talks

By DAVID LANDAU
Jerusalem Post Diplomatic Correspondent

TEL AVIV. — Premier Golda Meir and her senior Ministers met for over three hours yesterday with U.S. Secretary of State Henry Kissinger to discuss the cease-fire resolution, that he and Soviet leader Leonid Brezhnev had only the day before succeeded in bringing about.

Earlier in the morning, the Israel Cabinet had announced its unanimous decision to accept the cease-fire — provided the Arab side did so too.

Dr. Kissinger and an entourage of State Department Middle East experts flew into Lod airport from Moscow at noon — and left again en route to London before nightfall.

For three-and-a-half hours, the Premier and the Secretary of State conferred at a secret venue near Herzliya.

Dr. Kissinger and his party sped from the airport to the Herzliya site, where Premier Meir, Deputy Premier Allon, Defence Minister Dayan, and former Ambassador to the U.S. Yitzhak Rabin were awaiting them. They settled down to lunch together.

• Text of Israel Cabinet decision, page 6.

On the American side were Assistant Secretary Joseph Sisco, his assistant Alfred Atherton, and Ambassador Kenneth Keating.

At a closed session following the meal, Premier Meir and Defence Minister Dayan spoke with the Secretary alone for more than an hour.

Neither side made any statement to newsmen either before or after the meeting. Israeli sources said Dr. Kissinger had reported on the diplomatic contacts between him and the Soviets which had led to the cease-fire. The radio quoted Israeli sources as saying they were satisfied with the talks.

Dr. Kissinger was greeted by applause and cheers from newsmen and airport workers when his U.S. Air Force Boeing touched down just before one a.m. He emerged waving and smiling to the crowd, and exchanged friendly welcomes with Foreign Minister Abba Eban, U.S. Ambassador Kenneth Keating, and their respective staffs. The party of officials then left in a fleet of limousines bearing the U.S. and Israeli flags.

At the talks in the afternoon, Premier Meir was joined by Deputy Premier Yigal Allon, Defence Minister Moshe Dayan, Foreign Minister Abba Eban, and former Ambassador to the U.S. Yitzhak Rabin. The Chief of Staff, Rav-Aluf David Elazar, participated in the last hour of the talks, and Air Force Commander Binyamin Peled was also present for about 10 minutes.

Israel — both government and people — were as surprised by the sudden end of the war as by its sudden start. Neither the Cabinet nor the Foreign Ministry had any inkling until late Sunday night that things were moving so fast in Dr. Kissinger's talks in Moscow.

First word of the Moscow agreement is said to have reached Prime Minister Golda Meir between 9 and 10 p.m. Sunday. The Cabinet was called into a long night session, which ended yesterday morning at 4 a.m. The Cabinet approved the cease-fire resolution and gave appropriate instructions to the defence forces.

Israel believed until that time that while the Soviets were increasingly interested in obtaining a cease-fire (as the Arabs' military position de-

(Continued on page 2, col. 2)

The UN's cease-fire resolution

UNITED NATIONS (AP). — Following is the text of the U.S.-Soviet resolution approved by the Security Council at 6.50 a.m. Israel time yesterday (12.50 a.m. New York time):

Union of Soviet Socialist Republics and United States of America: Resolution.

The Security Council,

- Calls upon all parties to the present fighting to cease all firing and terminate all military activity immediately, no later than 12 hours after the moment of the adoption of this decision, in the positions they now occupy.
- Calls upon the parties concerned to start immediately after the cease-fire the implementation of Security Council Resolution 242 in all of its parts.
- Decides that immediately and concurrently with the cease-fire, negotiations start between the parties concerned under appropriate auspices aimed at establishing a just and durable peace in the Middle East.

No halt in U.S. airlift

WASHINGTON (AP). — The U.S. airlift to Israel is continuing despite the cease-fire arrangements, the U.S. Defence Department said yesterday. "We're doing what we were doing before," said Pentagon spokesman Jerry Friedheim.

The statement followed reports that the U.S. had told Israel that major shipments of arms would stop and that the Soviet Union was also stopping supplies to the Arabs.

Friedheim indicated that the Defence Department had not received any instructions to stop the airlift of weapons and supplies to Israel.

"We'll just have to see what our negotiators bring home," Friedheim said, referring to Secretary of State Henry Kissinger's talks in Moscow and Tel Aviv.

ISRAELI ASSESSMENT
Another few days would not have been decisive

By ERWIN FRENKEL
Jerusalem Post Reporter

Israel's assessment that another few hours or even days of war would not drastically change the military situation — already favourable — on the fronts, but would cost more Israeli casualties is understood to have weighed heavily in the decision early yesterday morning to accept the U.S.-Soviet sponsored cease-fire agreement.

This assessment was especially coloured by awareness of the continuing supply of Soviet arms to both Egypt and Syria enabling them to refurbish their armies and the limits — largely political — that would inevitably be placed upon the advance of Israeli forces in the direction of Cairo.

If continuing the war could not bring about total military capitulation of the enemy, then a cease-fire in place was a favourable option.

The government's decision, it was said was also affected by the contents of the cease-fire resolution, especially the third paragraph. This calls for immediate negotiations between the parties "under appropriate auspices aimed at establishing a just and durable peace in the Middle East."

This is interpreted as meaning talks under the auspices of the U.S. and the Soviet Union, divorced from the U.N. Security Council and the Jarring mission.

What could not be determined yesterday, however, was whether the U.S. and the Soviets had also reached agreement on the nature of the peace settlement that should be achieved. They were close to reaching such an agreement in 1969, when the Kremlin, spurred by Egypt, balked.

The narrow corridor of Egyptian forces on the east bank of the Canal do not enjoy a comfortable military position, with Israeli forces east and west of them.

Israel for its part, controlling a long stretch of the Canal from the west bank, would now be in a position of determining whether or not the Canal could again be opened, even more emphatically than when it controlled only the east bank, it was said.

At the same time, it was conceded that the present lines on the Egyptian front were not "logical" or given to permanency. However they would enable Israel to enter any forthcoming negotiations from a position of strength.

DAYAN: ISRAEL DID NOT ASK FOR CEASE-FIRE

Defence Minister Moshe Dayan said yesterday Israel did not ask for a cease-fire and had no need to ask for it: but once accepted, the cease-fire should be binding on all the belligerent parties. Mr. Dayan was replying to questions by foreign correspondents visiting troops fighting west of the Suez Canal.

Mr. Dayan said heavy losses were inflicted on the Syrian and Egyptian armies but they would be able to restore their strength due to the vast quantities of armaments and other equipment they were receiving from the Soviet Union and other states.

However, the important point, said the Defence Minister, was that "they have lost the battles and we are now here."

MILITARY POSITION FAVOURABLE IN BOTH SECTORS

By SRAYA SHAPIRO, Jerusalem Post Reporter

TEL AVIV. — All Israeli troops in the Suez Canal area were ordered to cease-fire at 6.50 p.m. yesterday, in conformity with the government decision to abide by the Security Council resolution of yesterday morning. But during the next hour, the Egyptians staged a massive artillery barrage on three targets — Israeli positions in the north, our Canal sector, the bridgehead north of the Bitter Lake and on units near the town of Ismailya. The Army spokesman said later the Egyptians were continuing to fire on Israeli positions "in many places."

The cease-fire found the Israeli forces in a favourable position west of the Canal about a mile from the Ismailya-Cairo road in the north and straddling the two roads and the railway leading to Cairo from Suez in the south.

Israeli units also broke through to a front of four kilometres at the Canal, south of the Little Bitter Lake. Three airfields in the area are also in Israeli hands, the Army spokesman said.

The area controlled by Israel west of the Canal is roughly 1,200 square kilometres, and its western-most perimeter is about 75 kilometres from Cairo, which can be reached over a slightly sloping plateau without natural barriers.

The Egyptians hold two bridgeheads on the eastern side of the Canal with largely decimated remains of five divisions and an estimated 400 tanks out of the 1,200 which they had massed for attack. The main Egyptian roads from the west side of the Canal are controlled by Israel, but the Egyptians still retain round-about approach routes.

There are still several Egyptian pockets in the Israel-held area west of the Canal, but it was too early yesterday to ascertain their importance.

On the Syrian front, Israeli troops now control some 600 square kilometres beyond the 1967 cease-fire line.

The northern front was quiet yesterday, a senior officer said. A bloody battle was waged all night Sunday to recapture the Israeli outpost on Mt. Hermon which fell to the Syrians on the first day of the war. The position was cleared yesterday morning. Two nearby Syrian outposts, some 150 metres above the former Israeli position were also captured. The posts command a clear view of the area to the east up to Damascus and beyond.

"Definitely a victory," the Army spokesman said about Israel's military position yesterday as the cease-fire was proclaimed. It could have been a more complete one had the fighting gone on for a few more days, he estimated. However, Israel's aim was not to gain territory, but to thwart the enemy offensive — and this was done. Another aim was to reduce to the utmost the war potential of the enemy, and this too was achieved.

Damascus is now about 40 kilometres from Israel's frontline, and Cairo less than eighty kilometres.

In the seventeen days of fighting, the Egyptians lost 240 aircraft, and about a thousand tanks. Some hundred tanks were knocked out yesterday, as well as eleven planes.

In Syria, 212 planes were shot down — seven of them yesterday — and about a thousand tanks including the losses of the Iraqi and Jordanian forces.

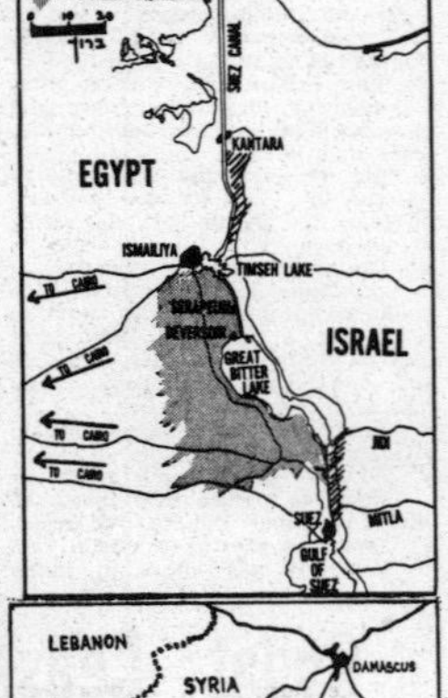

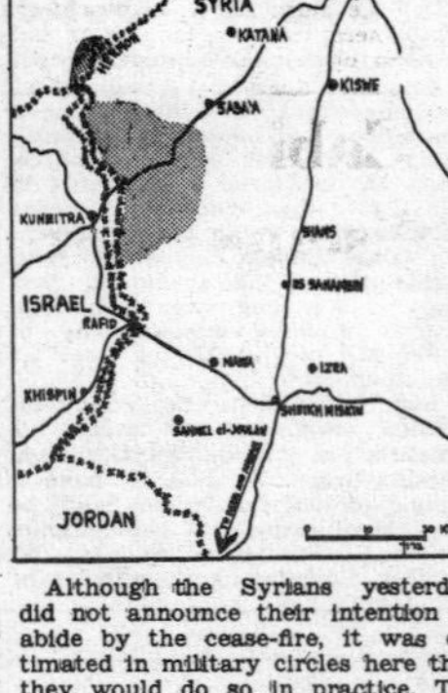

Although the Syrians yesterday did not announce their intention to abide by the cease-fire, it was estimated in military circles here that they would do so in practice. The Syrians also never acknowledged the cease-fire agreement in 1967.

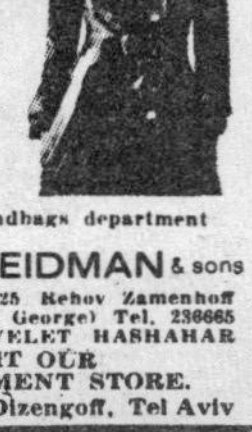

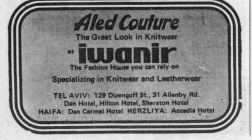

Israel, Egypt sign truce accord

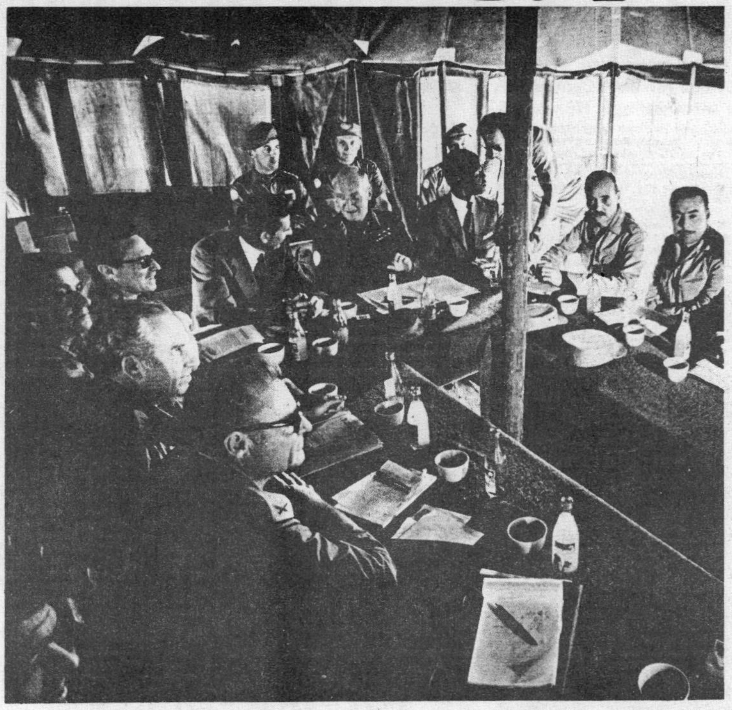

ACCORD SIGNED — Scene inside tent at Kilometre 101 of the Cairo-Suez road where the Israeli-Egyptian cease-fire agreement was signed yesterday. Israeli delegation on left shows Aluf Aharon Yariv, in dark glasses, who signed for Israel with his aides sitting beside him. At top of U-shaped table is UNEF commander, Finnish General Ensio Siilasvuo, flanked by two aides. Opposite Israelis are the Egyptians, with Egyptian Major-General Mohammed Gamazy who signed, at extreme left, sitting opposite Aluf Yariv. (David Rubinger)

Both sides 'correct' at brief ceremony

By CHARLES WEISS, Jerusalem Post Reporter

The American-inspired, six-point cease-fire agreement was signed by Egyptian and Israeli officers yesterday in a drab army tent pitched in the desert at Kilometre 101 on the Cairo-Suez road.

The principals arrived promptly at 3 p.m. They exchanged salutes — not handshakes — with each other. The Israeli delegation of six sat on the east side of the tent opposite the four Egyptians. At the head table sat three UN officers.

The Israelis were led by Aluf Aharon Yariv and the Egyptians by General Mohammed Gamazy. The UNEF commander, General Ensio Siilasvuo, sat at the head table, and called the proceedings to order. He said: "Gentlemen, let's sign," according to the spokesman of the UNEF, who came from Cairo for the ceremony.

He said it took place just a few minutes after the men took their seats. Each side signed three copies in English, handed them over to the others, and then signed their three. He described the mood in the tent as "correct."

Once signatures were affixed, the flaps of the tent were raised, and the several hundred journalists crowded behind barbed wire fences put up about 25 metres away on both sides — Egyptian and Israeli — could see, vaguely, what was going on.

Photographers and journalists were then given 35 minutes to peek inside from closer up. The generals glumly posed for pictures.

Then the press was shooed away and both sides settled down to work on details for putting the agreement into effect. After about half-an-hour, the officers took a ten-minute break. No details at all were released of these talks.

But in a statement made during the intermission, Aluf Yariv said that the agreement was the "first step on the long and difficult road that leads to settlement of the conflict and to peace."

(A United Nations spokesman in Cairo said last night that the second meeting between Egyptians and Israelis to discuss the implementation of the agreement would be held today at 10 a.m. again at kilometre 101.

(The spokesman, Rudolf Stadjuhar, said the two parties, after the signing, started discussion yesterday on modalities of the implementation of the agreement. He described the talks that followed the signing of the agreement as "useful and ocnstructive." Today's meeting will be attended by Gen. Gamazy and Aluf Yariv.)

It was learned later that the talks went on for several hours as the two sides tried to hammer out an acceptable interpretation of the text they had signed.

Most of the excitement and drama was provided by the press itself. Newsmen who came from Egypt broke ranks first. At one point, they tried to push their way by sheer muscle through the ranks of Egyptian military police and U.N. guards standing with fixed bayonets. That didn't work, and they were allowed close up by ones and twos.

Then the Israel-based newspapermen tried. Groups of six were permitted through the military police but the problem was in deciding which six. Everyone wanted to be among the first, and there were more than a hundred.

It kicked up a lot of dust, raised a lot of tempers and even had an effect on the negotiations inside the tent. When the scuffling became really wild, with shouting and curses, several of the officers in the tent turned to see what all the trouble about.

A number of observers noted that the day was November 11, the 55th anniversary of the 1918 armistice that ended "the war to end all wars."

General Yariv and Gamazy were applauded by Israeli and Egyptian soldiers respectively as they approached. An Israeli soldier shouted to Aluf Yariv: "Don't give in on the prisoners of war!"

No move yet, to meet today

By ARI RATH, Jerusalem Post Reporter

The signing of the cease-fire agreement between Israel and Egypt yesterday did not go much beyond the actual ceremony: both sides were sticking to their different interpretations of the six-point accord.

As a result there was a delay in the setting up of the U.N. check point at kilometre 101 on the Cairo-Suez road. This move would have signified that the cease-fire agreement was actually taking effect on the ground, and that the first Israeli prisoners of war were to be returned.

It is understood that both Aluf Yariv and General Gamazy agreed to sign first and argue later, rather than delay the signing pending agreement on outstanding points.

A main issue is understood to be Egypt's insistence that the supply route to the town of Suez and to the beleaguered Third Army along the Cairo-Suez road be put under full U.N. control, a point to which Israel is firmly opposed.

U.S. Secretary of State Kissinger's written interpretation, which was conveyed to the Israel government on Saturday from Peking, is understood to uphold the Israel understanding that the entire road is to remain under full Israel military control.

Talks between the Israel and Egyptian delegations on this and other points are to be resumed today.

First step to peace — Yariv

Here is the text of a prepared statement by Aluf Aharon Yariv, which he read out after signing the cease-fire agreement:

"By signing this agreement with Egypt, we have taken the first step on the long and difficult road that leads to a settlement of the conflict between us and our neighbours, and to peace with them.

"Let us not falter, let us not shy away. Let us see things as they are. Let us believe in our strength and put our trust in Zahal and the Jewish people in Israel and the Diaspora.

If there are doubts — if there is worry about our first step — let us say clearly that Zahal is standing fast and ready, and will remain standing fast and ready, to protect our interests on this front as on all other fronts.

"Zahal is our main insurance that we can proceed safely along the difficult road ahead of us."

BULLETIN

NICOSIA (UPI). — Two International Red Cross planes may fly to Tel Aviv and Cairo today to begin the first prisoner of war exchange between Israel and Egypt, a Red Cross spokesman said here last night.

THE JERUSALEM POST

SECOND EDITION

Price: 65 Ag.

MONDAY, NOVEMBER 12, 1973 • HESHVAN 17, 5734 • SHAWWAL 18, 1393 • VOL. XLIII, No. 13940*

ELAZAR SAYS ARMY'S PROBE TO BE 'UNFLINCHING'

Jerusalem Post Reporter

TEL AVIV. — The Chief of Staff, Rav-Aluf David Elazar, yesterday told newsmen the Israel Defence Forces would unflinchingly draw all the necessary conclusions from the internal army inquiry into reported shortcomings on the eve of the Yom Kippur War and the conduct of the war itself. He said the army inquiry, approved yesterday by the Cabinet, at his request, would in no way substitute for the investigation — by a legal or public body — planned by the Government.

The army would investigate four main areas: intelligence information and assessment on the eve of the war, the state of military preparedness when the war broke out, the actual conduct of the war, and fighting doctrines.

Rav-Aluf Elazar said that the entire army was put on full battle alert — the highest state of military preparedness by the regular army. A few hours later the first teams of reservists were called up, in preparation for the general mobilization.

At the same time, he was aware that there were some serious failures in observing the order for full battle alert at some of the lower echelons, the extent of which will have to be determined by the inquiry.

Had the reserves been called up 24 or 48 hours earlier, the war would undoubtedly have looked different and casualties would have been fewer, said R/A Elazar. The decision not to call up the reserves was taken at the highest military-political level on the basis of an assessment that despite all the signs of Egyptian and Syrian mass troop concentrations, there would be no war at that stage.

"We will never know whether the war would have broken out, had we called up the reserves, a move that might have caused the enemy to put off the attack for some time. But then we could have had a war a couple of weeks later, soon after the reserves were released," he said.

"This is in the very nature of things when a small regular army of a small nation has to face two huge regular armies, such as those of Egypt and Syria," he explained. "Although there is no hermetic defence, the chief task of the regular forces is to contain the enemy and then hit back and push back the enemy once the reserves move in, which is what actually happened in the October war," he said.

He realized there were some shortcomings in the way reserve units were equipped when they moved into the battle. But there were two sides to be heard on this point.

R/A Elazar said the alert of the Israel Defence Forces began 10 days before the war and reached its peak on Friday morning, as far as the regular army was concerned.

He recalled that last May the army had even more convincing intelligence data of stepped-up war preparations by the enemy. The government approved the assessment of the Chief of Staff and as a result some IL45m. were spent last May and June, in addition to the planned budget, to bolster the army's battle alert. In the event, war did not break out then.

The Chief of Staff took issue with "military experts" who seek to analyse the war in the press, exaggerating the significance of unimportant details. "It is a well-known fact that the individual commander cannot see the full picture of the battle and is concerned chiefly with his section of the front. But the final outcome of the battle is the result of the joint effort by different units and contingents. It may be less glamorous to fight for the holding of a bridgehead, rather than driving your tanks into Africa, but the holding of the bridgehead may be the crucial move of a particular battle," he said.

He cautioned against drawing hasty conclusions in connection with various phases of the war before a thorough investigation had been carried out.

NOT SURPRISED

There was also the enormous quantity of Egyptian troops — between 70,000 to 80,000 men in seven divisions, five infantry and two armoured — that attacked in the first wave.

Another surprise was the quantity of anti-tank personal missiles which the Egyptians used at fairly close range. But there was no question that both the Egyptian and Syrian soldier this time showed far more motivation, self-sacrifice and efficiency than in previous wars.

Even brigade commanders learned of the war only the day it broke out. Lower-ranking officers were told only at the outbreak of the fighting that this time it was the real thing.

(See also page 2)

Cabinet to discuss war inquiry

Jerusalem Post Reporter

The Cabinet is to discuss "the question of the investigation and examination of issues connected with the war which need investigation," an official communique announced yesterday. Premier Golda Meir has decided that such a discussion be held by the Cabinet as soon as she returns from London — and her decision was announced to the ministers at a Cabinet meeting yesterday by her Deputy, Yigal Allon.

The army, meanwhile, is going ahead with its own inquiries into the war. Chief of Staff David Elazar told the Cabinet that such inquiries were the accepted practice after a war, and indeed after every action in which Zahal was involved.

They would cover the preparations for the war, the army's state of preparedness, the battles themselves and the tactics employed, he said. The purpose of the inquiries, the Chief of Staff said, would be to ascertain facts and to facilitate the learning of lessons and the drawing of conclusions on the organizational and theoretical level.

Attorney-General Meir Shamgar also pointed out that the army's inquiries need not in any way prejudice or bar any investigation or inquiry that may be decided on by the Cabinet.

(Among the proposals which have been raised — and are due to be discussed by the Cabinet — are for a judicial inquiry to be established under a judge, or for an inquiry by a panel including non-political representatives of the public, non-political public figures.)

(Related stories on pages 2 and 8.)

Bourguiba message to Gaddafi

TUNIS (Reuter). — Tunisian Foreign Minister Mohammed Masmoudi returned home yesterday after visiting Tripoli to hand a message from President Habib Bourguiba to Libyan leader Muammer Gaddafi.

Mr. Masmoudi said on arrival here that Col. Gaddafi was not opposed to an Arab summit following yesterday's signature by Israel and Egypt of an American-sponsored document aimed at stabilising the Middle East cease-fire, but wanted Arabs to bide their time.

There have been reports that an Arab summit would be held in Algiers before any Israel-Arab peace conference took place.

WATERGATE

Nixon to meet all Congressmen

NEW YORK. — Senator Charles H. Percy (Republican-Illinois) said yesterday that every member of Congress has been invited to meet with President Nixon in six unusual sessions this week to discuss the Watergate case.

"At least nine hours will be spent by the President being interrogated by members of the Congress, explaining his position," Percy said on a TV programme.

Percy said he believes that to restore public confidence the President must make "total and complete disclosure" of the Watergate documents with "nothing held back."

There must be "direct access by the special prosecutor, without a court order, for all documentation he feels is relevant and necessary" including material related to political donations, the ITT case, operations of the plumber's unit and the President's personal finances, Percy said.

"Anything related to the possibility of criminal activity should and must be revealed," Percy said. "I think the President is prepared to do this now."

Meanwhile, Eugene J. McCarthy, the former U.S. Senator who sought the 1968 presidential nomination as a Democratic candidate, said yesterday he saw no need to remove the President from office.

(AP, UPI)

Golda: Europe stand 'Munich attitude'

By DAVID LENNON
Jerusalem Post Correspondent

LONDON. — Prime Minister Golda Meir shocked the delegates to the Socialist International Executive into stunned silence yesterday afternoon, with the force of her attack on their countries' "Munich attitude" towards Israel during the past month.

Delivering the opening address, Mrs. Meir said she understood Europe's worries about oil; but that did not excuse their refusal to let U.S. supply planes use European air bases.

She was also able to understand the behaviour of Chamberlain at Munich, she said, but pointed out that this had not helped in the long run. Neither will last Tuesday's resolution of the EEC Foreign Ministers help Europe in the long run, she declared.

During her 55-minute address, Mrs. Meir spoke of the tragic loss of life in Israel and pointed out that the number of Israelis killed was proportionately equal to two and a half times the U.S. losses in 10 years of the war in Vietnam.

Golda Meir said this was a war of the few against the many. "It is not good to be small and alone," she concluded.

Amid a stunned silence, conference chairman Bruno Pitterman of Austria asked who would like to speak next. There were no takers. Then the Prime Minister of Mauritius, Sir Seeaosagur Ramgoolam, said Israel was not the only small country present and that he could not understand the Israeli Premier's reference to Munich. However, no other delegate was ready to speak, so the meeting had an unscheduled 20-minute adjournment.

It became clear in the discussion after the recess that there would be little possibility of an agreed resolution emerging from the meeting. This was mainly because of the stand of Premier Dom Mintoff of Malta and the Mauritius Prime Minister, who both took what Harold Wilson described as "a line markedly different" from other participants.

The differences of opinion which emerged led the delegates to decide to carry discussions on during and after the official dinner, which had been intended to celebrate the conclusion of the session.

After the conference, it was clear that different interpretations regarding responsibility for the Middle East situation still separated the various speakers.

There was general agreement on the need for vigilance and care to turn the fragile cease-fire into a peace settlement. Many of the participants expressed the view that boundaries must be a subject for negotiation. This included the future of East Jerusalem. It was pointed out that U.N. Security Council resolution 338, which called for the implementation of 242, also calls for negotiations between Israel and her Arab neighbours.

The delegates expressed their full support for the principle of negotiation.

Discussion of the EEC resolution of last week found most of the EEC representatives trying to interpret it in its most favourable light for Israel, noting that it called for secure and recognized boundaries for Israel.

The highlight of Premier Meir's round of meetings in London today will be her meeting with Prime Minister Edward Heath at 10 Downing Street, scheduled for 2 p.m.

Shortly after her arrival on Saturday night, Mrs. Meir conferred on tactics with Labour Party leader Harold Wilson, who is host to the conference. During nearly two hours of talks they sought a way of neutralizing the danger presented by the anti-Israel bloc led by Dom Mintoff of Malta and Mauritius Premier Ramgoolam.

Austrian Premier Bruno Kreisky let it be known in discussions with journalists earlier that he did not think there was any real need for the emergency meeting. As there had already been a cease-fire, he said, the subject of the Middle East should be discussed in the framework of the European security conference.

The meeting was attended by 39 participants from 20 countries. With the exception of Denmark (in the midst of a constitutional crisis), all the Prime Ministers who had promised to come did arrive.

An unexpected visitor to the conference hotel yesterday morning was former U.S. Vice-President Hubert Humphrey. In London on private business, he insisted on meeting with his "friends," including Golda Meir.

The formal session yesterday afternoon was followed by a dinner at which the lobbying was expected to remain intense, with Mrs. Meir being anxious to use every moment available to persuade the Europeans that it is not in their interest to appease the Arabs.

Complaint to IRC on PoW murders

Jerusalem Post Diplomatic Correspondent

Israel submitted a formal complaint to the International Red Cross over the weekend concerning the cold-blooded killing of Israeli prisoners of war. The IRC — which does not itself investigate complaints — will pass on the complaint to Syria.

The complaint refers to 28 proven cases of the murder of prisoners. The 28 bodies were found in four separate places on the Golan, with their hands tied behind their backs.

Arabs want settlement in 4 weeks

Jerusalem Post Arab Affairs Reporter

The Egyptians expect their immediate outstanding problems with Israel to be settled within four weeks under the new truce agreement signed between the two sides yesterday. Egypt's government spokesman, Ahmed Anis, last night said that yesterday's accord was a "prelude" to a peace conference which the Cairo press expects to be held on the second week of December in Geneva.

Anis said that the agreement was the first move towards implementation of the U.N. Security Council Middle East resolutions aimed at settling the Israel-Arab conflict. He indicated that Egypt and Israel will now engage in intensive talks to solve immediate issues before the peace conference in which other Arab delegates will participate.

Anis stressed the question of Israel's withdrawal to the "October 22 cease-fire lines" as being one of the immediate outstanding issues. He made no mention of an exchange of prisoners. Anis said that yesterday's agreement was necessary in order "to determine the positions" especially on the western bank of the Suez Canal — where Israel has captured a bulge stretching from Ismailia to south of Suez. He said that the disengagement of the forces under the current truce would eventually lead to peace negotiations for the implementation of the Security Council resolutions "calling for an Israel withdrawal from all occupied Arab territories," which Israel captured in 1967.

Egyptian news media yesterday treated the truce agreement with evident scepticism. The Egyptian state radio networks and newspapers called for the maintenance of a high state of military preparedness.

Meanwhile, Beirut's "L'Orient Le Jour" yesterday claimed that Egypt has consolidated its military strength on the western bank of the Suez Canal by establishing a Fourth Army, which includes some 25,000 Algerian soldiers.

The paper attributed the report to a correspondent who accompanied Lebanon's Premier Takieddin Solh on his return home from a weekend vist to Cairo. The correspondent reported Solh as having quoted President Sadat as claiming that his armed forces, including the encircled Third Army, preserved their military strength "and would come out with surprises" should the fighting be renewed.

But Solh quoted Sadat as emphasizing that he was in favour of quick progress in the current peace efforts, although stressing that he had no intention of forming diplomatic relations with Israel. According to Solh, Sadat said that Security Council resolution 242 did not call upon Egypt to recognize Israel, but only its borders.

Seven incidents on both fronts

Jerusalem Post Military Correspondent

TEL AVIV. — A relatively quiet day was reported from the two fronts yesterday.

Five out of the total of seven incidents reported during the day took place along the Syrian lines — all of them in the Mazrat Beit Jann sector. At 7.50 a.m. there was a burst of machinegun fire directed at IDF outposts followed some two hours later by two salvoes of artillery fire. There were three more rounds at 11 a.m. and more machinegun fire bursts at noon and 2.10 p.m. IDF units did not return the fire.

In the south, a single shell was lobbed into the Israeli lines south-east of Kantara, at 11 a.m. A second incident occurred at 12.40 p.m. north-east of the Great Bitter Lake where a Third Army machinegunner fired a single burst into the Israeli lines. There were no casualties.

KLM refused ground service in Damascus

DAMASCUS (Reuter). — Damascus airport workers last night refused to provide ground services for a KLM Royal Dutch airlines plane because of Holland's alleged pro-Israeli attitude. The airliner which flew in from Beirut, returned to the Lebanese capital 40 minutes after landing.

Air transport workers said in a statement that the boycott was in accordance with resolutions voted by Syria's general workers federation and by a pan-Arab labour federation conference in Libya earlier this month. Under the conference resolutions, all Dutch and U.S. transport and goods were to be boycotted, the statement said.

Civilian air traffic here returned to normal only yesterday when the airport was reopened after being closed for 36 days because of the Middle East war.

Airport workers placed a large placard on the tarmac saying in French and English: "The air transport workers in Syria strongly condemn the imperialist-Zionist aggression against their Arab nation and condemn the American and Dutch aid to Israel."

THE JERUSALEM POST

Life of Ben-Gurion Pages 6-7

Price: 65 Ag.

SUNDAY, DECEMBER 2, 1973 • KISLEV 7, 5734 • ZIL-KI'ADA 8, 1393 • VOL. XLIII, No. 13957

BEN-GURION DIES AT 87, FUNERAL AT SDE BOKER

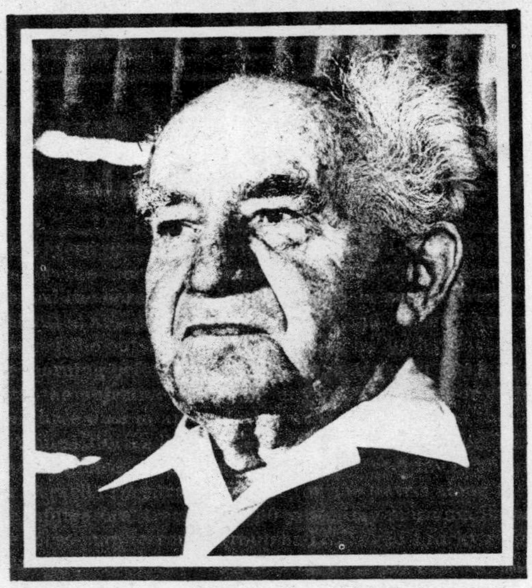

RAMAT GAN. — David Ben-Gurion died at 11.06 yesterday morning at the Sheba Medical Centre following a stroke he suffered a fortnight ago. He was 87.

During his last hours, his son, Amos, and his two daughters, Geula and Renana, were at his bedside, as were his personal physician, Dr. Boleslav Goldman, and members of the medical staff of the department.

David Ben-Gurion was taken to hospital suffering from a brain hemmorrhage on November 18. He was partially paralyzed, but remained conscious. A week ago his condition deteriorated and his consciousness became hazy. He took a sudden turn for the worse about ten o'clock yesterday morning, and passed away an hour later.

During his last illness he was visited by President Katzir, Prime Minister Golda Meir, other cabinet members, and the country's leaders. Visitors at his deathbed included Defence Minister Moshe Dayan, Transport Minister Shimon Peres, Mordechai Surkiss M.K. and Aluf Yona Efrat, Head of the Central Command.

Dr. Goldman said that on the whole Ben-Gurion's health had been good despite his age until his last illness. Although he was not always an "obedient patient," he was always reasonable.

Thus, some months ago, Dr. Goldman advised him that the time had come to end his Yoga practice of standing on his head, and Ben-Gurion reluctantly agreed. He continued his daily long walks until about two months ago.

Dr. Goldman said that, preceding him as Ben-Gurion's personal physician were Dr. Haim Sheba, who headed Tel Hashomer for years and in whose memory the hospital was renamed the Sheba Medical Centre, followed by Dr. Baruch Padeh, then Deputy Director-General of Tel Hashomer, and today Driector-General of the Ministry of Health.

Ben-Gurion will be buried beside his wife, Paula, at a site chosen by himself at the Sde Boker College, overlooking the rugged Biblical landscape of Nahal Zin.

On one of his early visits to the College, his favourite project, as a centre for educating youth in the pioneering tradition and studying desert reclamation — Ben-Gurion had spent a long hour gazing out over the valley and hills behind the College library. He later told his family that this was where he would like one day to be buried. In accordance with his own request, there will be no eulogies.

When his wife died five years ago, Ben-Gurion asked that she be buried on the spot he had chosen for his own burial place.

Owing to the emergency, there will be no formal funeral but the body will lie in state in the Knesset, from 10 a.m. today, throughout the night, and until 7.00 a.m. tomorrow, Monday, December 3. The public will be able to pay its last respects and file past the bier.

The funeral service will be held in the Knesset tomorrow, Monday, at 11.00 a.m. Both the funeral service and the final ceremony at Sde Boker will be broadcast on radio and television.

Presence at the funeral service in Jerusalem is by invitation only, and those invited to attend are asked to follow carefully the instructions attached to the invitation. The public will not be able to attend the funeral at Sde Boker and all roads leading to the kibbutz will be closed tomorrow, according to instructions which will be published.

Sirens will be sounded throughout the country at 11.00 a.m. tomorrow, at the start of the funeral service in Jerusalem, and a minute's silence will be observed. When the siren sounds, traffic will come to a halt and work will cease. The public is asked to rise in memory of David Ben-Gurion.

Cabinet holds special session

The Cabinet last night held a special mourning session in memory of David Ben-Gurion.

The meeting rose as, under a black-wreathed portrait of Ben-Gurion, Prime Minister Meir declared: "He was the chosen of the people, in the period of renaissance of the Jewish People, on its way to independence.

"What characterised Ben-Gurion was principally the power of leadership, thanks to which he led the nation to independence. He instinctively knew how to concentrate on essentials. We who worked alongside him, saw him in his full vigour, and also in his struggles within himself.

"He was privy to another secret: that we are a small nation, whose steadfastness continually grew to the measure of our unity and solidarity. He was a man who fought for his opinions — but he also knew there were things around which one had to unite.

He was a thinker, was interested in all human questions. Our world is made sadder, perhaps a little less secure, now that the giant of thought and action is no longer with us."

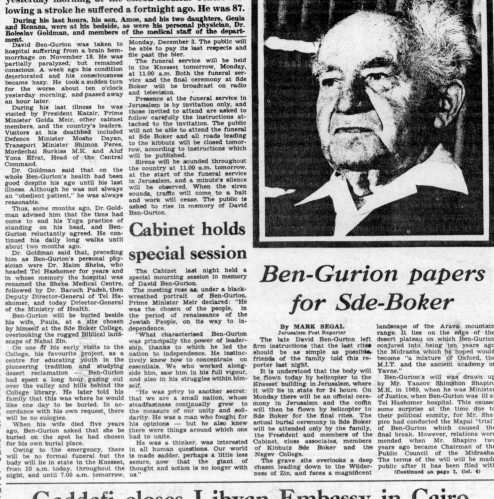

Ben-Gurion papers for Sde-Boker

By MARK SEGAL
Jerusalem Post Reporter

The late David Ben-Gurion left firm instructions that the last rites should be as simple as possible, friends of the family told this reporter last night.

It is understood that the body will be flown today by helicopter to the Knesset building in Jerusalem, where it will lie in state for 24 hours. On Monday there will be an official ceremony in Jerusalem and the coffin will then be flown by helicopter to Sde Boker for the final rites. The actual burial ceremony in Sde Boker will be attended only by the family, the President and members of the Cabinet, close associates, members of Kibbutz Sde Boker and the Negev College.

The grave site overlooks a deep chasm leading down to the Wilderness of Zin, and faces a magnificent landscape of the Arava mountain range. It lies on the edge of the desert plateau on which Ben-Gurion conjured into being ten years ago the Midrasha which he hoped would become "a mixture of Oxford, the M.I.T. and the ancient academy of Yavne."

Ben-Gurion's will was drawn up by Mr. Yaacov Shimshon Shapiro M.K. in 1969, when he was Minister of Justice, when Ben-Gurion was ill at Tel Hashomer hospital. This caused some surprise at the time due to their political enmity, for Mr. Shapiro had conducted the Mapai "trial" of Ben-Gurion which caused the final break. However, relations were mended when Mr. Shapiro two years ago became Chairman of the Public Council of the Midrasha. The terms of the will will be made public after it has been filed with

(Continued on page 2, Col. 4)

DAYAN, UNEF CHIEF MEET TODAY ON 101 DEADLOCK

By ANAN SAFADI
Jerusalem Post Arab Affairs Reporter

The commander of the U.N. Emergency Force in the Middle East, General Ensio Siilasvuo, is due to call on Defence Minister Moshe Dayan today in an effort to break the deadlock in the talks between Egypt and Israel at Kilometre 101 on the Cairo-Suez highway.

General Siilvasuo flew to Jerusalem from Cairo on Friday after conferring with the Egyptian Minister of War, General Ahmed Ismail Ali over Egypt's decision to break off the Kilometre 101 negotiations on the disengagement of forces at the Suez Canal front.

The U.N. commander's call on Dayan comes amid intensified international diplomatic activity aimed at maintaining the five-week old cease-fire.

At United Nations headquarters, Secretary-General Kurt Waldheim has had a series of unannounced meetings wtih the U.N. representatives of the U.S., the Soviet Union, Egypt and Israel, informed sources reported.

No details were disclosed, but observers assumed they were connected with the breakdown in the disengagement talks.

U.S. Secretary of State Henry Kissinger was in New York over the weekend, and discussed plans for the Middle East peace conference with top U.N. officials.

A U.N. spokesman said Kissinger was in telephone contact with Dr. Waldheim and also met with Bradford Morse, an American who is a U.N. Under-Secretary-General.

In Cairo, President Sadat met yesterday with the Soviet and American envoys to explain Egypt's decision to suspend the talks at Kilometre 101.

KISSINGER VISIT

In Cairo the authoritative newspaper "Al-Ahram" said that Kissinger has decided to visit the Middle East again because of the stalemate at 101. The paper said that Kissinger would clarify his government's views on the Middle East situation "especially as it has be come apparent during talks that the U.S. position is not clear enough to ensure implementation of the cease-fire agreement and the achievement of peace based on justice."

"Al-Ahram" indicated that Kissinger's planned visit to the Middle East became known through recent contacts between Egypt and certain "international quarters."

Discussing Egypt's differences with Israel over the question of the disengagement for forces, "Al-Ahram" said that Cairo had "irrevocably rejected" an Israeli proposal calling for Egyptian troops to withdraw from the eastern bank of the Canal in return for an Israeli pullback from the western bank, with the waterway as a "buffer zone."

The paper said that Cairo had also rejected an Israeli proposal to pull back to ten kilometres east of the Canal if the Egyptians thinned out their presence there.

"Al Ahram" reported that Israel had refused to agree to an Egyptian counter-offer calling for an Israeli withdrawal about 130 kilometres east of the Canal to a line stretching from El-Arish on the Mediterranean to Ras Mohammed on the Red Sea.

The paper added that the deadlock in the negotiations at kilometre 101 had cast a shadow over the plans to convene a peace conference in Geneva on December 18. There were no doubts about the prospects of holding the conference, said "Al Ahram."

Similar doubts were voiced also by Syria and Jordan — the two other Arab states invited to the peace talks with Israel although each for its own reasons.

In Damascus the official Syrian news agency said that Syria at present "sees no point in attending the conference since Israel has not started withdrawing from Arab territory as laid down in Security Council resolution 242" (of 1967).

In Amman, King Hussein said that he was withholding a decision on whether Jordan would take part in the peace talks pending clarifications from Arab states on their recent summit decision to consider the Palestine Liberation Organization (PLO) as sole representative of the Palestinian people. Speaking at the joint opening session of the two houses of the Jordanian parliament, Hussein said the decision was apparently intended to weaken Jordan's claim for the restoration of its sovereignty over the West Bank.

Reasserting his pledge to allow Palestinians on the West Bank "the right of self-determination through a free plebescite supervised by international quarters," Hussein said that Jordan, Syria and Egypt must coordinate an Arab strategy for peace negotiations. These countries were the most concerned in the conflict with Israel and must adopt a unified stand to prevent "partial solutions" to the Middle East crisis.

Meanwhile, Algerian President Houari Boumedienne stressed yesterday that the West Bank is Palestinian and does not belong to Jordan. The Algerian leader made his remarks in an interview with the Cairo paper "Al-Gomhouriya."

U.S. sends officers for truce force

WASHINGTON (AP). — The Pentagon said yesterday that 28 U.S. military officers have left for Middle East duty with the United Nation's Truce Supervision Organization.

Eight U.S. observers previously were assigned to the U.N. force. The additional manpower was requested by U.N. officials last month.

Meir: Breakdown at 101 shouldn't affect Geneva

Jerusalem Post Staff

Prime Minister Golda Meir said yesterday that the breakdown of the Israeli-Egyptian talks at Kilometre 101 should not prevent the opening of the peace conference in Geneva on December 18.

She said in a radio interview that she regretted the breakdown in the cease-fire negotiations between senior Israeli and Egyptian officers, calling the talks "useful contacts through which already something has been achieved." (The Egyptians announced last Thursday that they were discontinuing the talks when the two sides could not agree on a formula for the disengagement of their armies.)

The Premier said the talks with Egypt held out the possibility that the uncertain cease-fire could lead to peace and she hoped the talks would be resumed.

"The Arab preparedness to negotiate with us," she said, "points to a substantial change in the longstanding Arab position, which had ruled out any contacts with, and recognition of, Israel."

She said the breakdown of the talks "does not have to be a reason for not going (to Geneva). Without exaggeration, this was a point at which for the first time Israeli soldiers and Egyptian soldiers sat in tents and talked. And there is a certain value to personal contacts like simply shaking hands."

Text of interview on Page 9

The Premier said the change in Arab attitudes towards Israel was especially noticeable in comparison with the 1967 Arab summit meeting in Khartoum, which rejected any negotiations or recognition of Israel. "What happened at Algiers (the latest Arab summit last week) was that at least they did not repeat the nays of Khartoum."

In another radio interview yesterday, Aluf Aharon Yariv, Israel's negotiator at Kilometre 101, said that all the clauses of the cease-fire agreement had been realized, except the one on separation of forces. "And I think it is possible to go to the Geneva talks even so," he said.

Without mentioning the Egyptian blockade of the Bab el-Mandeb Straits specifically, Aluf Yariv said, "The cease-fire on sea appears to be maintained as well."

He said both sides had an interest in resuming the talks at Kilometre 101, "because two great armies are arrayed opposite each other and there are day-to-day problems which require continuation of the contact."

Aluf Yariv said Egypt broke off the talks when Israel rejected its proposals, which included a "deep Israeli withdrawal involving a pullback of many dozens of kilometres into Sinai." He said he preferred not to be more specific about the Egyptian proposals.

Israel, he said, had proposed a separation of forces at the Canal according to the principle of reciprocity in pullback, "a very important principle at this stage. They rejected our proposals and we rejected theirs."

Eban sees Keating on 101 talks

Jerusalem Post Diplomatic Correspondent

The U.S. ambassador and his top advisers met with Foreign Minister Abba Eban and Aluf Aharon Yariv yesterday to hear from them how and why the talks at Kilometre 101 had broken down. The meeting was at Mr. Eban's initiative and was held in his home in Herzliya.

Aluf Yariv told Ambassador Kenneth Keating of the Israeli stand on disengagement as it was put to Egypt's General Gamasy.

Mr. Eban stressed the delicate situation on the front lines, with daily Egyptian violations of the cease-fire.

Foreign Ministry officials said the meeting was not the result of any diplomatic intervention by Dr. Kissinger or the State Department aimed at breaking the deadlock at Kilometre 101. The officials said there had been no such intervention as yet — although action by Dr. Kissinger has been predicted by commentators in the U.S.

The Israeli officials seemed to feel that the disengagement issue would not be resolved until the peace talks themselves, due to open in Geneva on December 18. The possibility of Dr. Kissinger's visiting the Middle East before December 18 was not raised at the meeting yesterday, officials said.

A statement issued after the meeting said that Mr. Eban and the ambassador had also "discussed the preparations for the Geneva peace conference," but officials would not elaborate on this.

Oil crisis causes tension in EEC

LONDON (INA). — Differences in view on how to handle the oil crisis are leading to increasingly serious tensions inside the Common Market, just two weeks before an EEC summit conference in Copenhagen, the "Financial Times" reported yesterday from Brussels.

"The U.K. severely angered the Netherlands and the Brussels EEC commission yesterday, by vigorously opposing commission suggestions that it should come forward with new proposals to cope with the energy crisis. Britain quickly found support from France, and to a lesser degree from other countries. Britain argues that in the run-up to the Middle East peace conference, the Community should refrain from any action that might risk provoking reprisals from the Arab countries." (See "Dutch Reject," Page 5).

Gaddafi closes Libyan Embassy in Cairo

CAIRO (UPI). — The Libyan Government has closed its embassy in Cairo in a further escalation of its row with Egypt over Middle East policies, diplomatic sources said yesterday.

The embassy, officially called the "Relations with Egypt Bureau" since the conclusion of an agreement to merge the two countries into a single state, closed down on Thursday, the sources said.

The action came after all members of the staff were ordered to return home "for consultations," the sources said.

There was no official comment from Libyan diplomats or Egyptian Government officials.

The Libyan move sent Egyptian-Libyan relations plummeting to their lowest level since Libyan leader Col. Muammar Gaddafi came to power after a military coup on September 1969, the sources said.

It also seriously jeopardized the already shaky plans for union of the two countries, they said.

Gaddafi strongly criticized President Anwar Sadat's acceptance of the Middle East cease-fire. He aired his condemnation in speeches and newspaper interviews.

He also permitted Tripoli Radio and the Libyan News Agency to release the text of a message he had sent to Sadat taking issue with Sadat's postwar policies and saying that Egypt's agreement to have military disengagement talks with Israel at Kilometre 101 on the Cairo-Suez Road meant the loss of Arab dignity.

Gaddafi also boycotted the Arab Summit Conference held in Algiers last week, because of his opposition to Egyptian and Syrian policies of seeking a peaceful settlement of the Middle East crisis.

Shortly before the summit was held, Egypt recalled its Resident Minister in Libya, Dr. Mourad Ghaleb, for consultations, the sources said.

In view of Gaddafi's action in closing his embassy in Cairo, the sources said Ghaleb is not expected to return to Tripoli for the time being at least.

Sources said the Egyptian Embassy in Libya will be kept open.

Shooting incidents mar cease-fire on Canal front

By ZE'EV SCHUL
Jerusalem Post Military Correspondent

TEL AVIV. — The cease-fire on the Egyptian front was marred over the weekend by nine shooting incidents on Friday and an additional 10 yesterday. One soldier was injured. Two exchanges were reported from the Syrian front.

One Israeli soldier was killed on Thursday and three wounded in an exchange of small arms fire on the Cairo-Suez road near Kilometre 101.

The Egyptian-initiated fire over the weekend was seen here as an attempt to interfere with earthworks being thrown up by the IDF units in frontline positions.

On Friday the Egyptians attempted to advance some units south and east of the Small Bitter Lake on the Sinai side of the Canal along the northeastern tip of the Egyptian Second Army perimetre. They were stopped and forced to retreat by a mortar salvo, after earlier small arms fire failed to halt them. By noon the Egyptians had tried four times to advance their units. At noon a soldier was wounded by an Egyptian sniper at a point due east of Kantara. Israeli troops returned fire.

Two additional exchanges of fire came in the early afternoon in the Ismailiya area and two more in the late afternoon, one north of the Small Bitter Lake and one north of Suez.

Saturday's incidents induced exchanges at Kilometre 142 north of Suez and near Abu Sueir in the Ismailiya sector. Fire was also aimed at the Fayid sector and two exchanges occurred east of Lake Timsah, where outposts of the Egyptian Second Army were involved.

IDF units did not suffer any casualties in these exchangegs.

On the Syrian front two artillery salvoes were reported yesterday and one on Friday. All were aimed at the Kharteb sector near Maz-ra'at Beit Jann off the main Kuneitra-Damascus highway.

An army patrol also reported a single bazooka fired at it and missed yesterday morning in the Zar'it sector along the Lebanese border.

THE KNESSET

mourns the death of

DAVID BEN-GURION

Founder of Israel's Independence and First Prime Minister

The Government of Israel

mourns the death of

DAVID BEN-GURION

First Prime Minister and Minister of Defence

The World Zionist Organization

and

The Jewish Agency for Israel

deeply mourn the passing of

DAVID BEN-GURION

leader of the Zionist Movement and architect of the Jewish State.

The Workers of Israel

mourn the death of

DAVID BEN-GURION

founder of Israel's Independence,
Seer and builder of the restoration of Israel
builder of the Histadrut,
crown of the Labour Movement.

The Executive
General Federation of Labour in Israel
(Histadrut)

Moshe Dayan

mourns the death of

DAVID BEN-GURION

Accord on disengagement today

Elazar and Gamasy to sign document at Km. 101 with Unef chief present

THE JERUSALEM POST

32 PAGES (including 24-page magazine)

US foreign policy Page 8

Price: IL1.75

FRIDAY, JANUARY 18, 1974 • TEVET 24, 5734 • ZIL-HIJJA 25, 1393 • VOL. XLIV, No. 13998*

Jerusalem's YMCA tower serves as a striking backdrop to this snowy scene on King David Street. Police barricades are those used during Dr. Henry Kissinger's stay at the King David Hotel, on the opposite side of the street. (Rahamim Yisraeli)

By ARI RATH and SHALOM COHEN, Jerusalem Post Reporters

Israel and Egypt yesterday reached agreement on the disengagement and separation of their military forces at the Suez Canal front.

The agreement, which Israel Government leaders said definitely safeguarded Israel's vital security interests, culminates a week of hectic, dramatic and unprecedented diplomatic activity by U.S. Secretary of State Henry Kissinger.

It was reached as Dr. Kissinger completed his third round of shuttling between Aswan and Jerusalem, each time narrowing the gap between the Israeli and Egyptian disengagement proposals until the gap was finally bridged.

The military disengagement agreement is to be signed today at noon at the desert tent at kilometre 101 on the Suez-Cairo road by Israel's Chief of Staff, Rav-Aluf David Elazar, and Egypt's Chief of Staff, General Mohammed Gamasy, who also signed the six-point cease-fire agreement on November 11.

Details of the redeployment and limitation of forces along the newly agreed cease-fire and separation lines will be made known only today, once the three-page agreement is signed by the two Chiefs of Staff. Unef Commander General Ensio Siilasvuo, will be present.

The separation of forces is reported to involve Israel's evacuation of the west bank of the Suez Canal to a line east of the Mitle and Jidi passes, in return for a thinning out and reduction of Egyptian forces on the east bank of the waterway, with a buffer zone of Unef troops in between.

An NBC correspondent said last night Egyptian forces on the east bank of the Canal would be reduced to eight battalions and that the Unef buffer zone between Egyptian and Israel forces would be about 12 kilometres wide.

The fact that a military disengagement had been reached was announced simultaneously at 9 o'clock last night in Jerusalem, Cairo and Washington, with Foreign Minister Abba Eban making the announcement for the Israel Government at a press conference at the King David Hotel in Jerusalem.

After having read out the text of the agreed statement in both Hebrew and English, Mr. Eban said the accord marked a turning point from the cycle of wars in the Middle East and should be regarded as a first step towards permanent peace. In the immediate future, the separation of forces would strengthen the present cease-fire between Israel and Egypt, without which it would have been impossible to go on with the Geneva peace conference, he said.

Mr. Eban declined to divulge any details on the limitation of forces or their re-deployment.

In reply to a question whether there were also U.S. undertakings towards Israel, Mr. Eban said that not all the details will be included in the signed agreement with Egypt, declining to elaborate any further. He would also not be drawn into a question on whether any American guarantees were given to Israel.

Mr. Eban praised Secretary Kissinger's "exemplary role" and stressed there were never any American proposals. "Dr. Kissinger only explained to each side the views, anxieties, and aspirations of the other side throughout his intensive discussions both here and in Egypt."

The only point on which both Israel and Egypt accepted a proposal by the U.S. was on the limitation of forces, but the actual agreement on this issue was also bilateral, between Israel and Egypt.

Mr. Eban made it a point to stress Defence Minister Moshe Dayan's role in working out of the agreement.

Mr. Eban reiterated Israel's readiness to enter talks on military disengagement with Syria, which might be the next order on the agenda in Geneva.

The snow delayed the first working session yesterday by over an hour, as the Ministers Allon, Dayan and Eban and their aides were taken to the King David Hotel by a police jeep. The last outstanding, but substantive points were cleared up during that meeting, with Dr. Kissinger communicating several times with President Sadat in Aswan.

The Secretary then called on Premier Golda Meir for a 90-minute talk, after which the Cabinet met at Mrs. Meir's residence. It decided unanimously to empower the Prime Minister to give Dr. Kissinger Israel's positive reply to the disengagement proposals.

Mrs. Meir will make a statement to the Knesset next Tuesday on the disengagement agreement.

Soon after, the State Department's legal adviser, Carlyle Maw, was taken to Ben-Gurion airport in an army command car, bundled in blankets to be flown by an Israel Air Force plane to Cyprus and from there by an Egyptian air force plane to Aswan, to finalize all the points with Sadat.

Dr. Kissinger yesterday also called on President Katzir and had dinner last night with Mr. Eban and his aides. He is to call on the Prime Minister again this morning at 8 a.m. and will then fly directly to Aswan for another meeting with President Sadat. The Secretary is due to meet with King Hussein on Saturday at Akaba on the Red Sea and will visit Damascus for a few hours on Sunday before returning to Washington.

THE OFFICIAL ANNOUNCEMENT

In accordance with the decision of the Geneva Conference, the Governments of Israel and Egypt, with the assistance of the Government of the United States, have reached agreement on the disengagement and separation of their military forces.

The agreement is scheduled to be signed by the Chiefs of Staffs of Israel and Egypt at 1200 local time, Friday, January 18, at Kilometre 101 on the Cairo-Suez road. The Commander of the United Nations Emergency Force, General Siilasvuo, has been asked by the parties to witness the signing.

Nixon calls pact first step to Mid-East peace

WASHINGTON (AP). — President Nixon yesterday announced the Israel-Egyptian disengagement agreement along the Suez Canal, terming it a first step toward a permanent Middle East peace.

In a brief statement, the President said he was not underestimating the difficulties that lie ahead, but the agreement "is a very significant step reached directly as a result of negotiations between the two parties."

Nixon told reporters and a national radio-television audience that "This, I would say, is the first significant step toward a permanent peace in the Middle East."

He added that "I personally shall see that any negotiations, any efforts, that will lead to a permanent peace .. will have the full and complete support of the Government of the United States."

According to Nixon, the American people can be proud of the U.S. role in arranging the agreement, which he indicated has importance ranging beyond the Arab-Israeli conflict.

The Middle East is the area of the world where "the great powers can be brought into confrontation .. as recent events have shown," he said.

TERMS 'VERY GOOD,' ALLON SAYS ON TV

Jerusalem Post Reporter

Deputy Premier Yigal Allon told the nation last night that the disengagement agreement to be signed today contained "very good indeed — although perhaps not excellent — conditions" for Israel which would save human lives, provide security from sudden attack and open the path to talks for an overall settlement.

He said he was "very satisfied" with the terms of the agreement which did not provide either side with everything it had demanded, but at the same time served the interests of both sides.

Speaking over Israel TV, Mr. Allon said he could not yet give details or draw maps: but he assured the interviewer that the vital Mitla and Gidi mountain passes into Sinai proper would remain "in the rear" of the new Israeli defence line.

Neither side had imposed its demands on the other, nor had Secretary of State Henry Kissinger imposed his own views on either Egypt or Israel. Dr. Kissiger's role had been "indispensable" and he had shown himself a consummate diplomat. His efforts, and the agreement attained, faithfully served President Nixon's broad aim of ending the era of confrontation and beginning a new era of consultation, Mr. Allon added.

Apart from an early slip of the tongue when he referred to the east bank of the Canal as the west bank, the Deputy Premier made a confident, serious and satisfied impression. Interviewer Yoram Ronnen's questions were searching and provocative, and he clearly sought to put to the Deputy Premier all the doubts and confusions which have been voiced in the press and among the public during this hectic week of top-level, top-secret negotiations in Jerusalem and Aswan.

In his first question, Ronnen charged that the settlement was in fact a unilateral Israeli withdrawal. Mr. Allon conceded that in bald

(Continued on page 2, col. 2)

No more living PoWs in Egypt

Deputy Premier Allon revealed last night that none of the men listed as missing on the southern front are known to be alive in the captivity of Egypt or of any other Arab state. He said Israel had learned this yesterday from Dr. Kissinger who had, upon Israel's request, raised the subject with President Sadat.

'Commits Egypt to Syrian front'

By ANAN SAFADI

Jerusalem Post Arab Affairs Reporter

Egyptian Deputy Premier Abdul-Kader Hatem last night said that his country's agreement with Israel over the separation of forces "also commits Egypt in regard with the Syrian front." Hatem added that Egyptian President Anwar Sadat was in constant contact with Syrian President Hafez Assad for consultations on disengagement.

Hatem who functions as de facto Premier under President Sadat did not elaborate. Egypt and Syria fought the October war under a joint command.

Hatem's statement coincided with reports from Damascus that U.S. Secretary of State Henry Kissinger is expected to visit Syria tomorrow.

The Deputy Premier made his remarks in response to the disengagement agreement which he stressed was "a purely military and not political accord." He said that President Sadat was dispatching envoys to the various Arab states to explain the accord.

The Egyptian announcement on its agreement with Israel was identical to the official statement in Jerusalem.

SNOW PARALYSES LIFE IN CAPITAL

By ABRAHAM RABINOVICH

Jerusalem Post Reporter

Abba Eban, Yigal Allon and Moshe Dayan drove in a police jeep yesterday to their final talks with Dr. Kissinger but most other Jerusalemites with less pressing business stayed at home as the season's first snowstorm paralysed the capital and blocked off all roads to the outside world.

The snow began about 7 a.m. and fell throughout the day with intermittent breaks, leaving 20 cms. on the ground by nightfall. The storm was frequently accompanied by high winds, thunder and lightning.

As usual, the Municipality's plans to keep main roads cleared were frustrated by vehicles which skidded and broke down before the snowplows and salt spreaders could arrive. Two main arteries — Herzl Boulevard and Yermiahu Street — were impassable because of tieups involving scores of cars, buses and trucks. Eight young hassidim were seen attempting to dig out a car from a drift on Yermiahu with the points of their umbrellas. The driver of a bus stuck on Herzl Boulevard asked a passerby at 5 p.m. to tell the Egged main office to send sandwiches since he had eaten nothing but bread since leaving the garage at 7.30 a.m.

The road to Hadassah Hospital was blocked all day and by nightfall 400 employees were still stranded there.

Dr. Kissinger on his short-range forays from the King David Hotel to the President's and Prime Minister's residences was able to travel in his official limousine. Ten District Court judges cut off by the storm were transported home in a prison van, facing each other five in a row on the hard benches. The police also transported members of the Agranat committee which continued its investigation into the Yom Kippur War despite the snowstorm.

Another investigation — into the manner in which the Municipality coped with the snowstorm — was called for last night by newly elected Municipal Council Member Uri Huppert who said the Municipality was guilty of shortcomings in not dealing effectively with the snow despite at least two days' warning and a prior mobilization of manpower and resources.

Electricity failures blacked out sections of the city for hours at a

(Continued on page 2, col. 3)

Weather to improve

BEIT DAGON. — The weather is expected to improve over the weekend. There will be short breaks in the snow and rains today with longer intervals tomorrow, accompanied by a rise in temperature, the weatherman told The Jerusalem Post **yesterday.**

Danger to security, Likud charges

By MARK SEGAL

Jerusalem Post Reporter

TEL AVIV. — Reiterating their charge that the Government was endangering national security by a unilateral withdrawal into Sinai, the Likud leadership yesterday appealed to Mrs. Meir's administration to at least refrain from signing any agreement until the Eighth Knesset, opening on Monday, had an opportunity to debate and vote on this scheme.

The Likud leaders convened the local and foreign press in separate press conferences to explain their stand. The absence of Israel Television was highlighted by the presence of most foreign TV networks represented in Israel.

The Likud warned that this was a repeat of the Israeli withdrawal in 1957 which only brought another war and was bitterly regretted by its author, a previous Republican Secretary of State, John Foster Dulles. Spokesmen accused Dr. Kissinger of trying to restore his President's fortunes at Israel's expense.

The Chairman, Menahem Begin, charged that the Government was persisting in its continuous deception of the public since Yom Kippur, calling the withdrawal "disengagement." He criticised it for abandoning its own policies under which there would be no move unless Egypt ended its state of belligerency, and its insistence that Egyptian offensive weapons be withdrawn from the east bank of the Canal.

"The big question was where are we heading and where are we being led?" he said. Egypt had reaffirmed its intention of seeking the destruction of the Jewish State, and yet the Government was intent on lifting the encirclement of the Third Army and permitting heavily armed troops to remain in Sinai.

His fear of an Egyptian breach of the proposed agreement was based on Egypt's blatant disregard of the cease-fire agreements in 1967 and 1970 plus "the mini-war of attrition" which had so far cost the lives of 24 Israeli soldiers and left 90 wounded. Moreover, Israeli soldiers at the Mitla and Jiddi passes could be attacked by enemy artillery over the heads of the Unef buffer force.

Mr. Begin wanted to know why Israeli ministers agreed to being pushed into an agreement by "Kissinger's whirlwind nocturnal negotiations. Everyone knows that lack of sleep blurs the senses."

Again he questioned the caretaker Government's right to present the new Knesset with a *fait accompli* on such a fateful issue. There are now 40 new M.K.s, and "we the Likud comprise one-third of the House and represent nearly half a million voters, 100,000 of them in uniform."

He noted that the NRP and some Alignment MKs concurred with this Likud position, making up

(Continued on page 3, col. 3)

Disengagement to take a month

TEL AVIV. — Working out the technical details of the agreement in preparation for the actual beginning of disengagement is expected to take another 10 days, CBS correspondent Marvin Kalb reported yesterday in a broadcast to the U.S.

Kalb, who has accompanied Dr. Kissinger on his present visit, said that the process of disengagement and redeployment of forces, including a thinning out of the Egyptian units east of the Canal, would then probably take another three to four weeks.

From Aswan, UPI quoted informed sources as saying that Israel would withdraw to a line 32 kms. from the waterway within about six weeks.

The sources said Israeli troops also would hold some positions west of the two passes. The Unef would be deployed in a buffer zone between the Israelis and Egyptians.

There are expected to be Egyptian and Israeli "security zones" on either side of the Unef buffer zone, where heavy and long-range armaments would be prohibited as a mutual safeguard.

EGYPTIANS OPEN FIRE

Jerusalem Post Military Correspondent

TEL AVIV. — The Egyptians opened fire several times yesterday in the South. Israeli forces returned the fire and sustained no losses, the Army spokesman reported.

The spokesman said the Syrian front was quiet.

Labour backs Yeshayahu

Jerusalem Post Political Reporter

TEL AVIV. — The Labour Alignment Knesset faction yesterday reconfirmed Israel Yeshayahu as its candidate for the Knesset Speaker's post.

There were no other candidates and no dissenting votes were registered although there were a few abstentions.

We apologize for the snow

The Jerusalem Post apologizes to its readers for today's shortened "snow issue."

As a result of electricity and transportation breakdowns, we have been forced to curtail the number of pages and postpone publication of many advertisements.

We trust that our readers and advertisers will give us their understanding.

THE JERUSALEM POST

Seamen's strike Page 2
★
Soccer Page 3

Price: 80 Ag.

SUNDAY, JANUARY 27, 1974 • SHVAT 4, 5734 • MUHARRAM 5, 1394 • VOL. XLIV, No. 14005

Cabinet may accept Kissinger proposal on PoWs in Syria

By DAVID LANDAU, Jerusalem Post Diplomatic Correspondent

The Cabinet is expected today to give its approval, in part at least, to U.S. Secretary Henry Kissinger's efforts to bring about preliminary talks on Israel-Syria disengagement. The Cabinet is to consider proposals which the Secretary brought to Israel from Damascus last week.

Dr. Kissinger is understood to have raised with Syria and Israel the possibility of an agreed "middleman" — possibly the Red Cross — receiving from Syria the list of Israel PoWs.

Israel has said it would refuse to hold any negotiations with Syria until this list was furnished and until Syria allowed the Red Cross to visit the PoWs regularly, as the Geneva Convention stipulates.

The middleman arrangement could at once satisfy this Israeli demand and overcome Syria's reluctance to comply with it.

Observers here predicted that the Cabinet would approve the idea in principle — or at any rate not reject it out of hand.

These observers believe that some progress with Syria — preliminary to actual disengagement talks — will be achieved during the coming weeks. Dr. Kissinger himself has indicated that he is continuing his efforts, in Washington, to move the parties towards some preliminary agreement.

Well-paced sources in Jerusalem say Israel's offer to make over to the UNEF the two Syrian positions on the Hermon taken in the war, and to allow some 15,000 villagers who fled in the war to return to the newly-occupied Syrian territory, still stands and is at the centre of Dr. Kissinger's efforts. In return for these concessions, Israel demands a full exchange of prisoners. But there can be no discussion of this offer until a preliminary agreement is reached on the PoW list and regular, guaranteed Red Cross visits to the PoWs.

PAVE WAY

An agreement such as this could pave the way to substantive talks on disengagement, these sources say, just as the implementation by Israel and Egypt of five of the Six Points agreed upon on November 11 resulted in productive talks on the sixth point — disengagement of forces. As with Egypt so too with Syria a bout of Dr. Kissinger's personal diplomacy would probably be needed to bring about an actual disengagement accord. But the Secretary would only contemplate another visit to the region once a preliminary arrangement had been made which removed the PoW problem.

Dr. Kissinger is known to think that a substantive disengagement accord should involve Israel's withdrawal to the "lilac line" — the line held between 1967 and 1973. Syria would agree to a reduction of forces on its side of the line, with UNEF interposed in the vacated area.

Sources here say that there is far less external pressure and urgency on the Syrian disengagement issue than therew as before and during the negotiations with Egypt.

From a military viewpoint, too, Israel is much better placed in Syria than it was across the Suez Canal and there is no particular strategic advantage to be gained from disengagement.

The PoW issue, however, creates a sense of urgency and concern in Jerusalem — hence the obduracy which Syria is showing in exploiting the PoW question to gain maximal advantages. The pressure would be reduced to some extent if a preliminary arrangement were reached and Israel obtained the PoW list and was assured of Red Cross visits to them.

While hopeful that both a preliminary arrangement and an eventual disengagement accord can be reached, observers here stress the obstacles posed by Syria's internal and inter-Arab difficulties. Within the Syrian Ba'ath, in the Iraqi Ba'ath and among the hard-line Arab regimes such as Libya there is a good deal of suspicion over the Israel-Egypt disengagement accord and much wariness over possible Israel-Syria accomodations.

U.S.-SYRIA

Progress towards negotiations between Israel and Syria would probably lead to resumed diplomatic relations between Washington and Damascus. The London "Daily Telegraph" reported from Damascus yesterday that the resumption was "expected shortly."

The paper interpreted as "a good omen" the silence maintained by the Syrian government on the possibility of opening negotiations with Israel. "But obviously," it continued, President Assad will have to perform a delicate balancing act to obtain terms permitting Syria to take part in the Geneva conference, and this may turn on Israel's willingness to allow Syrian peasants to return to their homes in the war zone."

From Geneva, there were reports yesterday citing American diplomatic sources to the effect that nothing is expected to happen there until the Israel-Egypt disengagement is completed in early March. Observers in Jerusalem confirm this prediction. They assume that Israeli and Egyptian teams will return to Geneva in March to begin negotiating, in "working groups," the various aspects of an overall peace.

EGYPT

A key question is how far Egypt could go in these talks if there were no progress with Syria and/or with Jordan. To what extent is President Sadat influenced by the Arab hard-liners? Does he feel he has a commitment from the U.S. to tide him over, financially and politically, if he must weather a lean period in his relations with the oil states? Will he talk peace with Israel even if the Palestinians and/or the Syrians refuse to do so? These are unknowns which the coming weeks and months will answer.

Observers here discount a prediction in Lebanon's "An-Nahar" newspaper yesterday that disengagement with Jordan might precede disengagement wieh Syria. Although the idea of disengagement talks with Jordan, first mooted by Jordan itself at the Geneva conference opening, met with positive responses from Israeli ministers, observers here feel little will come of it in the forseeable future. They say there is no pressure from the U.S. to embark upon such talks with Jordan, though Washington is aware of Jordan's fear of being "left out" and would like some kind of token movement on the Israel-Jordan front too.

3 hurt by Syrian fire

Jerusalem Post Military Reporter

Three Israeli soldiers were wounded during three hours of intermittent Syrian artillery barrages in the central and southern sectors of the Golan Heights that began at one o'clock yesterday afternoon. Israel artillery returned fire, the army spokesman said.

The incidents occurred at three points on the Syrian front — the Kafr Nassej area, Kafr Ma'as, and the area south of the Rafid junction. They were the first exchanges of fire since January 18, when Israel and Egypt signed the disengagement agreement.

News agencies in Damascus quote a Syrian army spokesman as stating that Syrian artillery opened fire at Israeli units yesterday to prevent them from carrying out engineering work in the central and southern sectors of the front.

MOVING OUT. — Piled up on two trucks and a half-track are bed frames, mattresses, benches and kitchen equipment as this unit prepared to move out of Adabiya this weekend. (Rubinger photo)

SADAT ANXIOUS FOR EASING OF OIL EMBARGO

Feisal is key to future moves

By ANAN SAFADI
Jerusalem Post Arab Affairs Reporter

The political focus in the Middle East shifted to Saudi Arabia over the weekend as the disengageent of forces got under way on the west bank of the Suez Canal.

The immediate question appears to be whether Saudia will lift the oil embargo imposed on the West at the height of the October war. If King Feisal agrees to renew normal oil exports, both U.S. Secretary of State Henry Kissinger and Egyptian President Anwar Sadat will be able to claim diplomatic success. Kissinger will be able to argue that he helped restore oil supplies to the West by initiating the disengagement agreement, and Sadat will be in a position to say that his decision to negotiate with Israel has been accepted by Feisal, one of the major figures in the Arab world.

The Saudi Arabian stand on the oil embargo is bound to have an immediate affect on the oil-producing Arab states in the Persian Gulf.

So far neither Saudi Arabia nor any of the other Arab oil-producers appear to have acceded to Sadat's request that they ease the oil embargo, especially to the U.S. which, the Egyptian President has declared, has "changed its Middle East policy" in favour of the Arabs. If these states turn a dead ear to Sadat's appeal. Egypt might well become isolated — at least for a time — because of the disengagement agreement.

Saudi Arabia and other Arab oil-producing countries seem to be adopting a cautious attitude on the embargo pending a settlement on the Syrian front. Until recently, however, the oil-producing countries linked the lifting of oil restrictions to an Israeli undertaking to withdraw to the 1967 frontiers.

Libya over the weekend not only rejected Sadat's appeal, but demanded the suspension of Arab financial subsidies to Egypt in protest against the disengagement agreement.

The Libyan state radio charged that Cairo had violated the principles of the 1967 Khartoum summit conference at which Libya, Saudi Arabia and Kuwait undertook to provide Egypt, Syria and Jordan with financial aid on condition that there were no negotiations with Israel.

The Libyan call to suspend assistance to Egypt came after a surprise series of consultations between the Libyan and Saudi Arabian governments.

The Beirut newspaper "An Nahar" called on Saudi Arabia over the week-end to state its attitude. It said that Sadat was depending on Saudi Arabia in his latest political moves.

Meanwhile, the Egyptians yesterday presented the disengagement agreement as the climax of Egypt's "achievements" as a result of the October war. Referring to the Israeli disengagement moves, Egyptian state radio seid that the disengagement agreement has "washed the Arabs of the mud of defeat" suffered in 1967.

Dayan backs army command after attack by Sharon

Jerusalem Post Political Reporter

TEL AVIV. — Defence Minister Moshe Dayan last night reiterated his full confidence in the senior army command and stressed his faith in the high calibre of Israel's army commanders.

Mr. Dayan's comments were made in a statement released by the Defence Ministry Spokesman in response to harsh criticism of the army command levelled by Aluf (Res.) Ariel Sharon, M.K., in interviews published in "Ma'ariv" and "Yediot Aharonot" on Friday.

Mr. Sharon called for the dismissal of the Chief of Staff, Rav-Aluf David Elazar, charging him with the principal guilt for "the army's failings."

Mr. Sharon charged that he was a victim of political intrigues in the army which, he said, began when the present Minister of Commerce and Industry, Haim Bar-Lev, took over from Yitzhak Rabin as Chief of Staff. These intrigues had intensified since Elazar succeeded Bar-Lev.

Sharon claimed that promotions in the army now hinged on political considerations, and said he was prevented from becoming Chief of Staff for this reason.

Sharon said that when Rabin was C-o-S he did not allow political interference in the army. "Bar-Lev introduced factional appointments, and promoted his men. This system led talented commanders to walk out and thus Aluf Tal left his post in 1969. It was then that a particular wing of the Labour Party reasserted its control over the army's appointments. It was then that men got ahead not because of their talents but by political kowtowing.

"With Rabin it would never have happened. Bar-Lev and his successor... wanted little men around them, for whom they symbolized real authority."

Sharon charged that this was the direct cause of the disarray along the Suez Front when the war broke out.

He said that since Rabin left "a terrible thing happened and the IDF has ceased to be a brilliant army... The Defence Minister concurs with me that the army needs shaking up, as does our military thinking... We have lost our main weapon — the unique thinking of the I.D.F., which made it one of the best armies in the world, and not quantities of weapons and armour."

Asked if he had been offered the chance of staying in the army now and becoming O.C. Southern Command, would he have been prepared to give up politics, Sharon said that he would have done so. But "they did the very opposite: they got rid of me and cancelled my emergency appointment as Division commander because of neptoism."

Sharon said Dayan had told him that although he thought he should be Chief-of-Staff, the Alignment, as the dominant force in the Government, would never allow it because of his political views.

After mentiong that his relationship with Dayan "was rather complicated right now" and that they were now no longer as close as in the past, Sharon expressed the view that Dayan should remain Defence Minister in the next Government. "He is a very brave man and ah original thinker. He is certainly not to blame for the army's failings. But it's high time he changed his ways and started imposing his views on the Chief-of-Staff."

Sharon saw no need for an inquiry into the war's conduct believing that the army command's guitl was clear.

He recalled gratefully that Daayn used to visit the Southern Front lines day atfer day "he was the only man above the rank of division commander who came to that hell day atfer day during the most critical days. After the terrible fighting ended — the others began to appear. Sure, then all of them appeared. Bnt during the battles — only he came, because I think he is a very brave man."

Sharon thought Dayan's main failure was in giving too much leeway to the Chief-of-Staff and not using his ministerial power to interfere.

As to where the fault lay for the losses in the Yom Kippur war, Sharon expressed anger that aspersions were now being cast on the late Aluf Albert Mendel (killed in the war.) He said that on October 7, Mendel, who was O.C. Armoured Corps in Sinai, told him that he had received an order from above not to spread out his forces.

Sharon said Elazar was to blame because he did not bother to acquaint himself with the Southern Front, having been intimately involved in the Northern Front, where he had been O.C. previously.

Sharon claimed that the Army Command did not properly use the combined force of his division and tha tof 'Bren (Aluf Avraham Adan) which could have dislodged the Second Army from the Canal's East Bank.

He charged that the authorities failed to take the time factor into account. "I had a talk with Yigal Allon on the day before the cease-fire agreement on October 21. I warned Allon that we woud not have time to complete our mission. With a tremendous show of self-confidence he declared "I, as the one in charge of this subject in the Cabinet, can tell you that there in no problem of the time factor...

Sharon claimed that political officers from the Labour Party were installed in the Southern Command during the war. "It reminded me of

(Continued on page 2, col. 4)

White House denies Nixon to visit M.E.

WASHINGTON (UPI). — A White House spokesman yesterday denied reports President Nixon was considering a trip to the Middle East this spring.

White House Deputy Press Secretary Gerald L. Warren said, "the President has no such plans."

Cairo's "Al Ahram" newspaper, in a front-page report from its Washington correspondent, said Nixon was contemplating a tour and it was likely to take place next April. The correspondent quoted informed sources in Washington.

He said Nixon was considering visiting some of the countries that Secretary of State Henry A. Kissinger visited recently. Kissinger visited Egypt, Israel, Jordan and Syria.

Hussein to Rumania

AMMAN (UPI). — King Hussein will visit Rumania toward the end of this month for talks with President Nicolae Ceacescu, the royal court announced yesterday. The statement did not specify how long Hussein's visit will last.

Israel forces stream back across Canal

Jerusalem Post Staff

Huge convoys of trucks and armoured vehicles, carrying troops, weapons and equipment kept on streaming east over the weekend across the Suez Canal bridges, as Israel forces began the first phase of military disengagement with Egypt on Friday at noon.

The first stage of the troop pull-back is to be completed tomorrow at noon, when Israeli forces will have totally evacuated the area south of Suez city, including Adabiya port and Jebel Ataka and will hand over control of the Suez-Cairo road to UNEF troops. By tomorrow noon, Egypt is also to thin out part of its Second Army units on the east bank of the Canal's northern sector, moving them to the west bank of the waterway.

A UNEF Finnish batallion of some 600 men, bolstered by 300 Swedes and Indonesians, is to set up a temporary buffer zone in the areas on the west bank of the canal vacated by Israeli forces. After a "buffer time" of six hours, the UNEF troops will hand over these areas to the Egyptians. A U.N. spokesman said yesterday the "buffer time" could be more than six hours, but not less.

As the disengagement of Israeli and Egyptian troops continued, UNEF commander General Ensio Siilasvuo travelled to Suez City yesterday to brief Finnish officers watching over the troop separation.

UNEF officers were the only outside observers to witness the Israeli troop withdrawal from the west bank of the canal, as both Israel and Egyptian authorities barred newsmen from both sides from the area. All news agencies stressed that it was Defence Minister Moshe Dayan's personal decision to impose a news blackout on the first phase of the disengagement.

A UNEF officer, Colonel T. Kuosa, yesterday established a forward UNEF headquarters five kilometres west of Suez city, where he is to be joined tomorrow by an Israeli and an Egyptian officer to coordinate troop separation moves.

Israeli units were already seen redeploying and digging in along the new Israel defence line, west of the Mitle and Gidi passes, along the Baluza-Tassa-Ras Masala line to its southern end near the Gulf of Suez.

A senior UNEF officer said yesterday Israeli units were following scrupulously the Israel Chief-of-Staff's order not to damage any civilian installation and not to touch the concrete anti-aircraft missile launching sites.

Israel's withdrawal from the southern sector of its present lines on the west bank of the Canal will lift the three-month-long siege of the 20,000 men of Egypt's Third Army, marooned on the east bank of the waterway and of the some 15,000 citizens in the town of Suez. The Suez-Cairo road is to open for civilian traffic by Tuesday morning.

"The last force that will evacuate is is effect the southern 'plug' of our encirclement of the Third Army near the port of Adabiya, some 15 kilometres south of Suez city," an Israel operations officer told Israel radio ytsterday. "We are holding this spot opposite a sizable Egyptian force that was capable and could have connected up with the Third Army. When we pull out Monday morning the encirclement of the Third Army will be removed."

Removal of troops and equipment slowed down somewhat yesterday, because of the Sabbath, but the pace picked up again last night to meet Monday's deadline. Scores of soldiers from the northern sector of the west bank bulge were seen touring south, equipped with cameras, to have a last look of this part of Africa. An Israel officer told the radio yesterday that the sight of huge bonfires all over, with soldiers burning documents, private letters and anything else that could be of interest for the Egyptians reminded him of the Lag Ba'Omer feast. The meticulous cleaning-up campaign by all units also resembled the days before Passover.

There was also the continuous sound of heavy explosions, as Israeli army engineers and sappers blew up military equipment that cannot be moved across the canal. Despite strenuous efforts, a good part of the some 800,000 mines that were laid all over the west bank lines may have to be left behind for lack of time to dismantle them all.

Israel navy vessels also continued hauling equipment south, down the Gulf of Suez to Sharm e-Sheikh and Eilat.

LABOUR FIRM ON NRP DEMANDS

By MARK SEGAL
Jerusalem Post Political Reporter

TEL AVIV. — The Labour Party leadership is inclined to form a narrow coalition government rather than call new elections, according to authoritative party sources.

They indicated that the question was discussed at an informal meeting of the party leadership at the Jerusalem residence of Premier Golda Meir on Friday afternoon. The meeting, presided over by Mrs. Meir, lasted about four hours.

Labour Party Secretary-General Aharon Yadlin reported to his colleagues on the latest coalition discussions with the NRP and the ILP-Aloni bloc held in his office at party headquarters in Tel Aviv that morning. Mr. Yadlin told the Jerusalem meeting of the difficulties caused by the hard line of the National Religious Party on the "Who is a Jew?" issue, which is being equally strongly opposed by the ILP-Aloni bloc.

It is understod that Premier Meir led those who would prefer new elections to a narrow coalition in which the Labour Alignment would be held to ransom by one or other of the smaller parties. Finance Minister Pinhas Sapir reportedly inclined towards Mrs. Meir's view, but finally concurred with those who believed that the diplomatic situation warranted the early formation of a government, even a narrow-based one.

None of the participants entertained for a moment the formation of a broad national coalition with the Likud.

What served to persuade some participants against new elections, it was reported later, was the knowledge of a party-commissioned public opinion poll which did not indicate any improvement in the Labour Alignment's position if there were a vote in the near future.

As a result of Friday's meeting, the Alignment will now concentrate on seeking to find a formula for the "Who is a Jew?" issue that could satisfy both the NRP and the ILP-Aloni bloc.

THE JERUSALEM POST

J'lem traffic Page 3
★
North Sea Page 4

Price: 80 Ag.

WEDNESDAY, APRIL 3, 1974 ● NISAN 11, 5734 ● RABI AWWAL 12, 1394 ● VOL. XLIV, No. 14062

Agranat Commission blames Elazar, Gonen, Zeira, 3 others

Dayan cleared of negligence charge; Hofi is acting chief of staff; Cabinet defence machinery needed

Jerusalem Post Political Reporter

The Agranat Inquiry Commission on the Yom Kippur War has found the Chief of Staff, Rav-Aluf David Elazar, directly responsibility for the errors committed on the eve of the war, and recommends that he terminate his term of office. The commision bleared Defence Minister Moshe Dayan from any direct responsibility for the failures on the eve of the war, both with regard to the wrong assessment of intelligence information and the inadequate line-up of forces, particularly on the Egyptian front.

Rav-Aluf Elazar has protested against the findings of the commision, which he says has done him grave injustice, he states, however, that, under the circumstances, he can no longer continue in his post. The Cabinet, meeting in an extraordinary session until late last night, accepted Elazar's resignation "with regret" and approved the Defence Minister's announcement that Aluf Yitzhak Hofi, Head of the General Staff Branch, will be Acting Chief of Staff.

The Commission exonerates Prime Minister Golda Meir, commending her for the decision she took on the eve of the war, pointing out, however, that she should have informed the Cabinet two days before the war of the grave situation.

The Commission also recommended the dismissal of the Chief of Intelligence, Aluf Eliyahu Zeira, because of his "grave failures," pointing out, however, that he had served only one year in his post and that he found ready concepts of intelligence assessments.

It also recommended that Aluf Shmuel Gonen, the former O.C. of the Southern Command, should not hold any active post in the army until the inquiry into the war is completed, blaming him for the inadequate line-up of forces on the Egyptian front when the war broke out. The Commission also recommended that Tat Aluf Aryeh Shalev, Deputy Chief of Intelligence, and two other more junior intelligence officers should be dismissed.

These unanimous recommendations of the Agranat Commission were contained in a partial report that was submitted to the Prime Minister Sunday afternoon and were discussed last night for over four hours by the Cabinet.

The commission's interim report, which was Israel's political time-bomb, hit the country with total surprise, as it was expected that it would be published only at the end of the month, after Pessah and Independence Day.

Intelligence Chiefs

Members of the Commission had harsh words for the I.D.F., intelligence heads, O.C. Military Intelligence Aluf Eliyahu Zeira, his deputy, Tat-Aluf Arye Shalev, Sgan-Aluf Yona Bendman, head research, Egypt, and Sgan-Aluf David Gedalia, head of intelligence, Southern Command. The Commission unequivocally recommended that all four officers be removed from their posts forthwith.

The Commission found that the intelligence network, blinded by preconceptions and ignoring factual evidence, failed to give the defence forces adequate advance notice of the pending attack. This not only caused a lay in calling reserve forces up to the fron,t but also delayed the deploymentof forces positioned near the borders, so as to meet an enemy advance.

It was not until 4.30 a.m. on the day of the yar that the Army intelligence finally concluded that the Egyptians and Syrians were planning a coordinated attack, and even then they believed that the attack would not take place until 6.00 that evening.

The full responsibiliy for this mistaken assesment falls on O.C. Intelligence and his deputy in charge of research, who together constitute the heads of the only organization in the State dealing with intelligence research.

The Committee gives three main reasons for the intelligence network's failure:

- The first was blind belief in the preconception that the Egyptians would not go to war until they were able to stage deep air strike into Israel, particularly against Israel's major military airfield in order to neutralize Israel's air force, and a related belief that Syria would not go to war without Egypt. While this may have been true in the past, the Commission felt it was outdated, particularly in the light of new evidence which reached army intelligence with regard to new weapons purchased by the Arab States, "evidence which made the conception obsolecent."
- Secondly the Commission notes that O.C. Intelligence Aluf Zeira had made a firm undertaking to provide the IDF with adequate warning should a war become a certainty, an undertaking on which the IDF based its call-up procedures. The Commission ruled that Aluf Zeira was in no way entitled to make such a promise.
- Thirdly, in the days preceding the war, the Commission states, the Army Intelligence research department possessed a vast amount of deterrent information which had been supplied both by military field intelligence and other bodies. Because their refusal to budge from preconceived ideas, the Committee stated, O.C. Intelligence and the head of research did not appraise this information correctly, and claimed that the military build-up was of a defensive nature in Syria, and that Egyptian forces, amassed in the area of the Canal, were holding annual manoeuvres.

It was only on the morning of October 5 that the intelligence chiefs began to re-assess their previous conclusions, and that was only after very specific additional information reached their headquarters. Even then, they still claimed that the possibility of war was "extremely low," and it was only on the following morning, at 4.30 a.m., that they finally concluded that the enemy actually intended to attack — and this too was only after more information had been received.

The Commission pointedly blames army intelligence, and only army intelligence, for the mistaken conclusions, noting that only that body has the authority to assess, collate and disseminate the information conveyed by the State's various intelligence and counter-intelligence bodies.

While the Commission states that Army Intelligence's mistakes were not the only ones which led to the Israel Defence Forces being caught off guard, "First and foremost there was an unjustifiable delay in the deployment of reserves."

"We are convinced beyond a shadow of doubt that the Chief of Staff should have requested a call-up of reserves in the week preceding the outbreak of hostilities," they state, "to maintain a realistic balance between enemy forces in the field and Israel forces along the borders."

At the very least, the Chief of Staff should have ordered a call-up on the morning of October 5, "even if enemy intentions were not entirely clear." Furthermore, because of O.C. Intelligence Aluf Zeira's undertaking to provide the army with adequate warning, the IDF had no contingency arrangements for the defence of the State should war break out simultaneously on the southern and northern fronts, without mobilization of reserves.

The Commission also found that, despite the clear warnings of pending war on the morning of Yom Kippur, no steps were taken to deploy the armoured force in the vicinity of the Canal to block an Egyptian attack. Neither were any clear instructions given to O.C. Southern Command or to his subordinates on how to meet the pending attack. In the north too, clear instructions were lacking.

HEAD OF ARMY INTELLIGENCE ALUF ELIAHU ZEIRA

While the Commission found that O.C. Military Intelligence, Aluf Eliyahu Zeira, was a man of exceptionally high intellectual capabilities, who had vastly impressed both his superiors and his subordinate, and was highly regarded by the Government, he should not be allowed to continue in his position. The Commission notes that he took over just a year before the war, and had thus inherited many of the misconceptions of his predecessor — which, they carefully point out, may not have been misconceptions when his predecessor was in office. They take Aluf Zeira's self-confidence to task and claim this attitude left no margin to error.

The errors perpetrated by Aluf Zeira in understanding and assessing intelligence material on the eve of the October war left them no option, but to recommend that 'lAluf Zeira cannot continue in his post as Chief of Military Intelligence.'

TAT-ALUF ARYE SHALEV

The Commission found that the most serious shortcoming in the intelligence network was with regard to assessments of information — assessments which were the prime concern of Tat-Aluf Shalev in hi capa'city as Deputy Head of Intelligence and head of the research department. They note that he has held his post since September 1967 and had laid much of the groundwork for the body's operations. They accuse him of having been inelastic and plagued by preconceptions which prevented an objective study of material received on the eve of the war. They recommend that he shoud be removed from his post.

SGAN-ALUF YONA BENDMAN

Bendman directed the Egyptian desk at the Intelligence research department and the Commission considers him the focus of the body's incorrect assessment of Egyptian designs. It was here that we see the height of the misconception. On the morning of October 5, Bendman was presented with a long list of Egyptian preparations for war, but he nontheless concluded that there was no basic change in Egypt's outlook, and that the chances of war with that country were extremely low. As a result of S/A Bendman's incorrect assessment, the Commission recommends that he no longer be placed in a position to make intelligence estimates.

SGAN-ALUF DAVID GEDALIA

Gedalia was chief intelligence officer of Southern Command from 1971 until March 1974. He ignored evidence that the Egyptians were planning more than just an exercise, twice presented to him by a junior officer, even though this evidence was carefully documented and pointed clearly to Egyptian war preparations. Gedalia is further accused of not having brought the junior officer's conclusions to his superiors. Gedalia's offence is of particular gravity, and he should be relieved of all intelligence duties.

Defence Minister

Regarding the personal responsibility of the Defence Minister; we wish to point out that the interim report deals only with the intelligence and preparedness and the Minister's part in this. The central question is whether the Defence Minister was negligent in carrying out his duties on matters that were within his area of responsibility.

We weighed the following:

In assessing intelligence information the Minister has no special assessing mechanism of his own and is supplied by the assessments of the General Staff.

When the O.C. Northern Command warned the General Staff about the Golan Heights in the presence of the Defence Minister, the Minister was worried and took steps: he visited the Heights to see at first hand the condition of the settlements and demanded reinforcement of the force on the Golan. He also demanded and received an assessment from the Chief of Staff on October 3, in preparation for a meeting with the Prime Minister.

With regard to the Egyptian front, he relied upon the assessment of the General Staff with which no one in the General Staff took exception.

The Deputy Chief of Staff, Aluf Tal, on September 30 expressed serious reservations to the Chief of Staff and Chief of Intelligence on the Intelligence's soothing assessment, especially regarding the Syrian front. But he did not ask the Chief of Staff's permission to present his reservations to the Defence Minister and did not do so. According to him, he refrained from doing so for reasons of proper standards of behaviour toward his superior.

The Defence Minister was also influenced by the Intelligence Branch's ability to give advance warning of war in view of its correct assessment in April-May 1973, when the Minister differed with this assessment.

Although the Intelligence Branch was found to have been vindicated, after the fact, in its assessment in April-May, the Defence Minister was correct in issuing the following guidelines to the General Staff on May 21, 1973:

"I now speak as the representative of the Government and on the basis of information. We, the Government, say to the General Staff: Gentliemen, please prepare for war, as those who are threatening to begin war are Egypt and Syria.'

He prefaced this by saying, "A renewal of war in the second half of summer must be taken into account."

His confidence in the Intelligence Branch's "Defensive deployment in Syria, Multi-Branch Exercise in Egypt" grew after the Chief of Intelligence replied to his question on the morning of October 5 that he was utilizing every possible source of intelligence and warning. (This reply perhaps grew out of misunderstanding on the part of the Intelligence Chief, but objectively it was misleading.)

As to the state of alert on the Egyptian front, the Defence Minister was confident after he was told that a regular armoured force was there in accordance with plans.

From the General Staff discussions, he knew that this regular force, including the Air Force, was sufficient to stop even a massive invasion by the enemy until mobilization of the reserves. Operational details on the deployment of this force were not within his province but within that of the Chief of Staff.

He received no request or proposal to mobilize the reserves before October 6, or any proposal to replace the reserves in the strongholds along the Canal.

On the morning of Saturday, October 6, the Defence Minister agreed to the mobilization of everything needed for defence in accordance with the Chief of Staff's assessment. The additional reserve force was requested by the Chief of Staff for counter-attacks. The Minister wanted to delay the mobilization of this additional force so that no friendly country would be able to accuse Israel of causing hostilities through "escalation," since this could harm Israel in the matter of vital supplies.

This was unmistakably a political reason, with which one may or may not agree, but it certainly should not be dismissed out of hand.

In any case when the Prime Minister decided in favour of full mobilization of the reserves, the Defence Minister did not hold out for his view.

The problem which particularly occupied us was whether the Defence Minister, on Friday, October 5, should have reached an assessment different from that of the Chief of Intelligence and the Chief of Staff, and thus take such measures as full or partial mobilization of the reserves.

On that day, the Defence Minister suspected that the Egyptian exercise might be an attempt at attack. Should that not have compelled him to see even more clearly the possibility of coordination between the Syrian front (which caused him great concern) and the Egyptian front?

The next day, Yom Kippur, was in any case a critical day, because of the cessation of all regular activity. He saw the danger of war in the second half of 1973 as early as the spring of that year.

At the same time, in the view of the Chief of Staff and the Chief of Intelligence the probability of an enemy attack was still low on that

(Continued on page 12, col. 3)

Rav-Aluf David Elazar

Aluf Yitzhak Hofi

Elazar replies

Aluf Yitzhak Hofi, the Chief of Operations, is to act as Chief of Staff until further notice, it was announced last night. Rav-Aluf David Elazar made the announcement when he said that he could not continue in his post.

R/A Elazar yesterday appeared before the Cabinet in the early part of its meeting and read a letter in which he tendered his resignation while taking issue with many of the findings of the Agranat Commission.

His letter read in part:

"Mrs. Prime Minister, I am convinced an injustice has been done to me. I do not accept some of the main findings of the Commission against me. I shall bring several examples:

"The Commission found that according to information in his hands the Chief of Staff should have called for a partial mobilization of reserve land forces at the beginning of the week preceding the war, in order to maintain the proper balance between the enemy force deployed against us and between our forces. I submit that both during the time that I have been Chief of Staff and before then the Israel Defence Forces did not maintain the proper balance between enemy forces and ours because of a series of basic reasons which were well konwn to all the responsible parties concerned. Among these, there was a reliance of warning by our intelligence. This time, there was no such warning and the Commission has not established that the lack of such warning was my fault.

"I deny the finding of the Commission that a proper defence plan in detail was not prepared in case the regular forces would have to fight alone to stop the enemy simultaneously on the northern and Egyptian fronts. The truth is that there was such a plan both for the Northern and the Southern Commands. The plan was well known and rehearsed even by the lower command levels.

"I deny the finding that there was no clear instrutcion given that morning to the O.C. Southern Command. The truth is that in addition to the operational plans which had been prepared in advance, I gave instructions to both the Northern and Southern O.C.'s on the morning of October 6, and even ask them to meet with at noon, in order to ascertain they were ready to face battle. The Commission itself says nothing about the instructions given to the O.C. Northern Command, although the same instructions were given to both O.C's in the same manner.

"It is not the job of the Chief of Staff to enter into all tactical details, nor is he capable of it. I bear witness that while I was O.C. Northern Command, in 1967, I submitted to the Chief of Staff general plans, and did not get detailed instructions either for defence or for attack.

"I deny the finding of the Commission that the dispute between myself and the Defence Minister on the morning of October 6 1973, was about the forces needed for defences, while I supposedly demanded additional forces only for the purpose of counter-attacks. My demand to mobilize the entire force stemmed from my entire evaluation of the need for forces in case of war, for which purpose counter-attacks would be an integral part of an efficient defence.

This demand of mine proves that I did not have exaggerated confidence in the ability of the IDF to repel a total attack by the enemy on both fronts with the aid of the regular forces alone, as the finding of the Commission states. This is a totally unfounded contention. I never thought or said this, I have said just the opposite. I do not know on what the Commission based this assumption. My demand to mobilize a greater number of reserves, which was subsequently approved by the Prime Minister, proved to be correct, and was decisive in the result of the war, and were it not accepted, a certain disaster would have taken place, at least in the Northern front."

The Commission was ledastray by confusing the refinition of authorities of the Defence Minister and the Chief of Staff, added R/A Elazar. The Defence Minister, he said, had full operative authority, and all operative plans and decisions were brought to him prior to the war. It was only in time of fighting that the ball was entirely in the hands of the Chief of Staff, he told the Cabinet.

Heavy reinforcements to Golan Heights front

By HIRSH GOODMAN
Jerusalem Post Military Correspondent

Israel units on the Golan Heights have been heavily reinforced over the past few days to forestall any Syrian attempt to launch an attack. This step was taken after evidence continued to mount that Damascus was planning a major offensive.

Tension reached a peak on Monday when an additional Syrian armoured brigade was detected opposite the south-eastern corner of the Bulge taken in the October war, and when observers noticed the Syrians evacuating civilians from villages in the area. The Syrians have also deployed additional artillery batteries several kilometres from the front, and have bolstered their infantry units along the entire border.

The Syrians yesterday bombarded Israel positions on the Heights for the 22nd consecutive day. From 9.50 in the morning till after 6.00 p.m. the Syrians concentrated tank and artillery fire on positions in the southern sector of the Bulge, and at concentrations south of the Rafid junction, west of the pre-October frontier.

According to an announcement from the Army Spokesman no damage was caused and there were no Israeli casualties.

Yesterday was the first day since the firing began that Israeli positions in the northern sector of the Bulge — at Tel Shams and Mazret Beit Jann — were not shelled. Israel forces returned artillery fire, and, several times during the day, tanks were called in against forward targets.

David Slav reports from Tiberias:

A full-scale alert has been declared for Upper Galilee settlements in the wake of the tension on the Golan front. The security preparedness is not, however, interfering with normal life and work.

On the Golan itself, settlers are subject to a strict "defence regime." A Jordan Valley Regional Council delegation yesterday visited some of the settlements there to take stock of their needs. At Ramat Magshimim and Nob, in south Golan, the damage caused to the water and electricity networks by Syrian shelling earlier this week has already been repaired.

Yesterday's Syrian army communique said: "Today's fighting started at 9.50 a.m. when the Israeli forces tried to strengthen the frontline positions. It ended at 6.00 p.m.

A Syrian officer was killed and two soldiers wounded while "a number of Israel soldiers were killed or injured," the communique said.

Meanwhile, Israel delegate to the U.N., Yosef Tekoah, has been instructed to submit an urgent protest to Secretary-General Kurt Waldheim, against continuous Syrian aggression. The complaint singled out Syrian shelling of Israel settlements.

Meir: 'Not useful' to extend Israel law to Golan

Jerusalem Post Knesset Reporter

The Prime Minister told the Knesset yesterday that "the proposal to apply Israel Law to the Golan Heights does not appear to the Government to be useful at the present time."

Mrs. Meir was replying to a Knesset question at the start of yesterday's session, from Yitzhak Shamir (Likud-Gahal).

Asked by Zalman Shoval (Likud-State List) what truth there was in a television statement by settlement planner Ra'anan Weitz that Israel did not intend to annex the Gaza Strip, Mrs. Meir said that "the Government had not taken any decision of late which altered its previous decisions" regarding the Gaza Strip. Weitz was not authorised to express the Government's stand, she said.

But she did not say what the "previous decisions" were, nor did she react to a supplementary question as to whether the Gaza Strip was still regarded as "an integral part of the State," as Shoval put it, when he referred to a rough approximation of a statement made last year, by Minister-without-Portfolio Israel Galili.

The Premier also denied that any official proposal had been made on the Government's behalf to West Bank notables, regarding self-rule in the West Bank. Her questioner was Ehud Olmert (Likud-Free Centre).

A Private Members Bill calling for a national referendum on Judea and Samaria was submitted to the Knesset Presidium yesterday by a number of Likud members, including Menahem Begin and Elimelech Rimalt.

Under the bill a referendum would be held June 25 in which citizens would be asked to vote on the question: "Are you in favour of Israeli rule over Judea and Samaria?"

Mapam yesterday issued a statement opposing the holding of such a referendum.

New town for Golan

Jerusalem Post Reporter

Ground clearing for a new town in the central Golan Heights area will begin this week, it was learned last night. The site — approximately 17 kms. southwest of Kuneitra — will be developed for industry and as an urban centre serving the Golan villages.

Dayan: 'No crisis in north; U.S. trip satisfactory'

BEN-GURION AIRPORT. — Both the U.S. and Israel believe the firing at the Syrian front is not likely to take on "crisis proportions," Defence Minister Moshe Dayan told newsmen here yesterday as he returned from the U.S.

At the same time, Mr. Dayan added that he could not give a proper evaluation of the situation on the front until he receives a briefing at his office. He said he was heading there directly from the airport for this purpose.

The Defence Minister said his Washington visit was "satisfactory" since both Israel and Syria have now made clear their positions and, despite the wide gap between them, neither side insists the other must accept its position.

His talks with the U.S. Secretary of Defence, James Schlesinger, were also satisfactory, Mr. Dayan said, as "we have achieved more or less what we wanted concerning the continued supply of materiel."

The next step, Mr. Dayan explained, is for a Syrian representative to go to Washington to confer with Dr. Henry Kissinger, following which the U.S. Secretary of State will visit this region — probably at the end of April. If agreement with the Syrians is too long in coming, Mr. Dayan remarked, it may affect Israel's ability to make progress in talks with the Egyptians.

Mr. Dayan is due to answer five urgent motions for the agenda in the Knesset this morning — three about Egyptian violations of the weapons limitation clause in the disengagement agreement, and two about the Egyptian refusal to allow more searches for the bodies of missing Israeli soldiers near the Suez Canal.

The Likud, the NRP and the ILP will present motions about the Egyptian violations and the Likud and the Aguda will present motions about the cessation of the search for the missing.

Egypt said withdrawing excess guns

CAIRO (UPI). — Egypt is continuing to withdraw excess cannons from its Sinai positions, and by the end of this week its artillery strength will be down to the size prescribed in the disengagement agreement with Israel, diplomatic sources said yesterday.

"This issue is almost a closed book," a diplomat said. "The Egyptians have shown every intention of respecting the disengagement agreement."

Officers of the U.N. Emergency Force, which is now wedged in a buffer zone between Egyptian and Israeli lines in Sinai, yesterday carried out another inspection of the "limited forces and armaments areas" on both sides, according to a U.N. spokesman.

Israel complained last month that Egypt had in its Sinai positions double the 36 field guns it is allowed to have under the agreement.

Following the intervention of Unef Commander Lt. Gen. Ensio Siilasvuo, Egypt agreed to 'withdraw excess guns to the Canal's west bank, they said.

Some were pulled back last week, and the rest will be out of the area by next weekend, they said.

U.N. asked to free Syrian Jewry

UNITED NATIONS (Reuter). — Israel envoy Yosef Tekoah yesterday raised the plight of the Syrian Jewish community with Secretary-General Kurt Waldheim. He said the only solution was that proposed some time ago by U Thant, Secretary-General at the time. This was to permit the entire community to emigrate.

(Knesset debate — Page 3)

Cairo paper sees early pull-back

Jerusalem Post Arab Affairs Reporter

The semi-official Cairo daily, "Al-Gomhouriya," wrote yesterday that Israel and Syria were likely to separate their troops on the Golan front before "U.S. President Richard Nixon's forthcoming visit" to the Middle East "in the first half of May."

The paper said that a disengagement agreement between Syria and Israel was expected to be signed during U.S. Secretary of State Henry Kissinger's next visit to the Middle East later this month.

"Al-Gomhouriya" claimed that such an agreement could have been signed during Dr. Kissinger's last visit to Syria and Israel, but a number of "international and Arab factors" delayed the accord.

Egyptian President Anwar Sadat this evening delivers a nationally-broadcast speech, which the Cairo news media have been heralding as a "sensational revelation of the Soviet Union's intrigues in the Middle East."

The speech comes a few days after Sadat charged in a press interview that the Soviet Union sought to "deceive" Egypt into agreeing to a cease-fire at a very early stage of the October war. Sadat said the Soviets had told him then that Syria had agreed to a cease-fire. This was denied by Damascus when approached by Cairo for verification.

Beirut press reports unanimously agreed the situation in the Golan Heights was deteriorating.

One commentator, Fuad Mattar, of the newspaper "An-Nahar," expressed fears of an Israel counter-strike against Syria, and added "President Assad's regime cannot afford a major Israel strike now."

POMPIDOU DEAD

By JACK MAURICE
Jerusalem Post Correspondent

PARIS. — President Georges Pompidou died at 9 p.m. yesterday, the President's Office announced. A few hours earlier, the Office announced that Pompidou, 62, had cancelled all appointments because of an unstated illness. The cause of death was not immediately disclosed.

The official communique was issued at 10, signed by Prof. Jean Vignalou, the presidential physician. Pompidou died at his private residence. Immediately after the announcement, officials informed Alain Poher, 64, President of the Senate, that he would be the interim President under the constitution until the election of a new chief executive.

The large tricolour flag on the Elysee Palace has been hauled down. Rumours earlier yesterday swept Paris that Pompidou's resignation could come within weeks, as reports had spread that Pompidou was suffering from Kohler's disease, a form of bone marrow cancer. This is fatal in two years — and Pompidou was found to have it over one year ago.

Georges Pompidou

Pompidou has been in ill health since the beginning of 1972, three years after his election in June 1969 as the successor to Gen. Charles de Gaulle, founder of the Fifth Republic.

THE JERUSALEM POST

Soviet Jewry Page 3 * Nixon and France Page 8

Price: 80 Ag.

THURSDAY, APRIL 11, 1974 • NISAN 19, 5734 • RABI AWWAL 20, 1394 • VOL. XLIV, No. 14068*

Mrs. Meir resigns

Tells Labour Party meet, 'Five years are enough,' urges new elections

By ARI RATH, Jerusalem Post Political Correspondent

Prime Minister Golda Meir last night announced her decision to resign, bringing down her Government, and recommended that new elections be held without delay, with a younger member of the Labour Party heading the list. She told a hushed meeting of the Labour Party's Knesset faction and leadership bureau that her decision was "irrevocable."

"Five years are enough. I have come to the end of the road. It is beyond my strength to continue carrying the burden," she said. Her surprise decision was known only to few close associates before the party caucus opened its session at the Knesset. It brought to a sudden end the ongoing but unsuccessful efforts to find an agreed formula which would cope with demands that Moshe Dayan relinquish the Defence Ministry without causing a split in the party.

Despite Mrs. Meir's call for new elections, Labour Party leaders of the Mapai wing were talking last night of attempts to form a new Government based on the present coalition without going to the polls. Coalition executive chairman Moshe Baram told The Jerusalem Post last night he would make every effort in this direction, stating that in his view Finance Minister Pinhas Sapir would be the most suitable candidate for the Premiership under present circumstances.

Baram held that the Labour-Alignment's coalition partners, the National Religious Party and the Independent Liberals, were also not happy at the prospect of going to the polls again.

WAY OUT

Although Mrs. Meir emphasized that her decision to resign had nothing to do with the question of Ministerial responsibility that had arisen in the wake of the Agranat report with regard to Dayan, it was obvious last night that the party's Rafi wing, though regretting the Premier's resignation, held that the new situation could help in finding a way out of the impasse. The immediate result of the Government's resignation was that Dayan would not be singled out as the only Cabinet Minister who would have to quit because of the Yom Kippur War.

The Ahdut Ha'avoda wing of the party seemed somewhat taken aback by Mrs. Meir's decision, which in any case had put off any move concerning demands for Dayan's resignation from the Defence Ministry.

Commenting on the latest developments last night, Sapir expressed the hope that a split in the party could be averted. Before the meeting and the Premier's announcement, the Rafi leadership seemed pessimistic as to the prospects for an agreed solution. Had the Labour Party caucus adopted a decision last night that would have meant that Dayan alone would have to quit his post, Rafi may have voted against the Government in a Knesset vote, a leading Rafi member told *The Post*.

Addressing a Rafi caucus late last night, Dayan said the latest developments could lead to new political groupings. He said the Likud was trying to exercise pressure on Rafi in this direction.

CLEAR CONSCIENCE

Dayan said his conscience was clear. He had asked Mrs. Meir whether she wanted him to resign and she had replied that she wished first to consult the party. "As far as I am concerned, my party is Labour's Rafi wing which does not think I should be the only one to resign," he said.

The Labour Party Knesset caucus opened after an hour's delay, with secretary-general Aharon Yadlin wanting time to inform the NRP and the Independent Liberals of Mrs. Meir's expected announcement. The mood at the meeting was friendly, with no indication of the tensions between the three party factions.

Mrs. Meir came to the meeting relaxed and smiling — as if she had been relieved of a heavy burden.

Yadlin had learned of Mrs. Meir's decision earlier. He had met her at noon only to be told that there was no chance she would change her mind this time and coolly read out the proposals of a special six-man committee. He made clear that these were not agreed to by all the members, reflecting the impasse in the party.

At the Labour Party meeting in the Knesset yesterday. Front row, right to left, are Aharon Yariv, Yitzhak Rabin, Lyova Eliav, Shalom Levine, Nuzha Katzav, and Uri Feinerman. (Weiss)

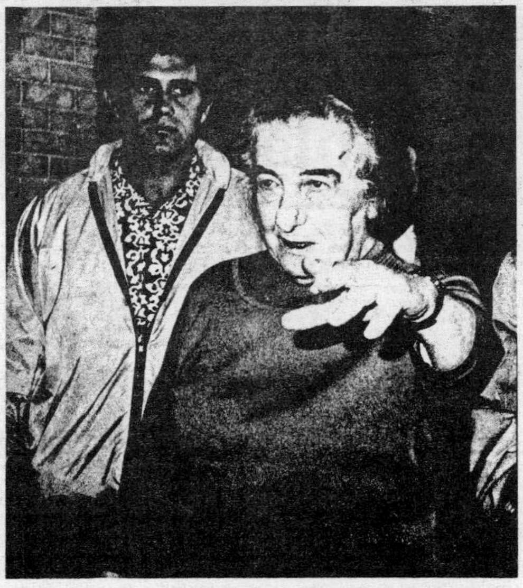

"You've taken enough pictures of me," calls out Prime Minister Golda Meir to news photographer Tova Weiss as she came out from the Labour Party meeting at the Knesset yesterday after announcing she would resign.

Golda's sealed letter: No eulogies, before or after

Golda Meir yesterday revealed the long-kept secret of a sealed letter she had deposited some time ago with Labour Party administrator Ya'acov Eini, which was to be opened only after her death.

After announcing her decision to resign, she told her Labour Party colleagues that her letter specified she did not want a word of eulogy after her death, nor did she want anything to be named after her.

"I also don't want any 'eulogies' in my lifetime, and definitely not afterwards, particularly since after a death people often say the opposite of what they really mean," she added.

NOT QUITTING OVER THE DAYAN ISSUE

Jerusalem Post Reporter

Premier Golda Meir said last night her decision to resign had no connection whatsoever with the question of whether Ministerial responsibility applied to Dayan or not. "Even had Dayan told me today that he was quitting his post, I would have resigned in any case."

She had given the matter a great deal of thought for some time and had reached the conclusion that she could no longer carry the burden of the Premiership. "I do not belong to any circle or faction. I had only a circle of one to consult — myself. This time it is final, irrevocable. I beg of you, please do not try to persuade me to change my mind. It will not help. I can no longer carry this burden to the best of my conscience. It is beyond my strength."

She said she did not feel herself responsible for anything, except that two or three times during the past months she had given in, against her better judgement, and had agreed to continue as Prime Minister.

She recalled that even last summer, before the Yom Kippur War, when the October elections were approaching, she thought she had had enough. But party colleagues kept on pleading with her, and "for me movement discipline is a sacred matter, not just lust for power, as some people claim. I was brought up that way all my life."

Although she thought that the present Government was a good one and had fine members, the fact could not be ignored that the "atmosphere created around the Government, without any justification, made it impossible for it to do its work properly and attend to the urgent issues that face us, even within the coming weeks."

It was a good thing that people thought their only problem was how to get rid of this Government. It is no coincidence that they do not criticize its policy, "because we do have a good policy."

Warning against any possible changes of the party's policy at its next convention, Mrs. Meir said in an obvious reference to calls for a much more dovish line from within the Labour Party, that she would regard such changes as a "calamity."

The former Government had much to its credit both in the spheres of economic development and defence, she stated. The Premier had special praise for the outstanding achievements of the army during the Yom Kippur War, since it was "properly equipped by the Government." The U.S. airlift during the war was also no small achievement.

Calling for new elections as the best way out of the present impasse, Mrs. Meir said what the public says could not be ignored although we only hear "the shouts against the Government and don't know the real views of the people." She was glad to hear that the Likud opposition also wanted elections, which should pave the way for an early poll.

Mrs. Meir had harsh words for the party's rebels without mentioning their names, although both Yitzhak Ben-Aharon and Lyova Eliav attended the meeting.

"Whoever throws stones today at the party leadership is considered as being young," she said, recalling that when Ahdut Ha'avoda split from Mapai in the 1940s its slogan was "if you are young — join us."

Assad to Moscow as Syrian group in Washington for talks

Jerusalem Post Arab Affairs Reporter

Syrian President Hafez Assad is scheduled to fly today to Moscow for talks with the Kremlin leaders.

Assad's trip follows a recent assertion by both Syria and the Soviet Union that the Russians must be incorporated in current Middle East activity as well as the U.S. This was made amid Russian expression of fear that Egypt was pushing Moscow away from the Middle East arena in favour of Washington.

The trip to the Soviet Union coincides with the arrival in Washington yesterday of a Syrian delegation for talks with Secretary of State Henry Kissinger for a military disengagement along the Golan front with Israel. The Syrian delegation, headed by Syria's army intelligence chief, Brig.-Gen. Hikmat Shihabi, was scheduled to begin substantial negotiations with Kissinger either late today or early tomorrow, Washington reports said.

Meanwhile, the Syrian leader's visit to Moscow was expected to touch on Damascus' quest for more Russian arms supplies. Recent Beirut reports said that Syria was seeking to obtain sophisticated weaponry including Mig-23 jets and Sam-7 ground-to-air missiles.

Assad may also mediate between Moscow and Cairo. The strained Egyptian-Soviet relations were aggravated recently with Cairo's charges that Moscow was withholding supplies for arms to Egypt.

With shooting on the Golan front continuing, the Syrian Government newspaper "Al Thawra" said yesterday the fighting "may get worse" unless Israel withdraws from all occupied Arab territory.

An official statement distributed by the Syrian News Agency said some Israeli shells landed yesterday within "tens of metres" of the Untso commander inspecting U.N. installations behind the Syrian lines. It said Maj.-Gen. Bengt Liljestrand and other U.N. observers accompanying him were not hurt.

Shooting for 30th day in the North

By HIRSH GOODMAN
Jerusalem Post Military Correspondent

The Syrians again bombarded Israeli positions on the Golan Heights yesterday. The Army Spokesman said there were no Israeli casualties.

Yesterday — the 30th consecutive day of fighting in the area — the Syrians concentrated their fire on positions in the southern and central sectors of the bulge captured in the October war, and against targets west of the pre-October cease-fire line near Tel Farris.

Several times the Syrians fired volleys of katyusha rockets at the Tel Mashara region, and Sagger anti-tank missiles at positions near Tel el Mal in the southeastern corner of the bulge.

Positions on the Hermon and in the northern sector of the bulge were not hit yesterday — presumably since the Syrians are unwilling to chance reciprocal fire against machines engaged in earth-moving projects on the slopes of the Hermon where they are fortifying Syrian positions there.

Over the past week Israeli gunners have concentrated their fire in the area, and according to spotters have scored good hits — seriously hampering Syrian efforts to break a road through to their positions on the Hermon range.

Israel has also concentrated fire against in-depth anti-aircraft positions along the entire perimeter of the bulge, apparently with good results.

France selling Libya six patrol boats

By JACK MAURICE
Jerusalem Post Correspondent

PARIS. — France hopes soon to conclude a deal for the sale of six high-speed naval patrol boats to Libya worth IL900m., "Le Monde" reported yesterday.

The influential newspaper's defence correspondent Jacques Isnard said Libya and India were the most likely customers for the PR-72 patrol boats, which are of entirely different design to those which Israel whisked away from Cherbourg at Christmas 1969.

The 475-ton boats have a top speed of 60 kph and can cover 4,000 kms. at an average speed of 30 kph with 37 persons aboard. In contrast with the Israeli gunboats which are equipped with missile launchers, the PR-72 carries automatically-fired cannon.

According to "Le Monde," negotiations with India are even further advanced than with Libya for the supply of patrol boats. Besides Libya a number of other Arab countries are discussing similar purchases with France. They include Morocco, Tunisia, Saudi Arabia, the United Arab Emirates, Iraq, Kuwait, Lebanon and Pakistan.

Begin sounds call for elections; Labour colleagues not surprised

By MARK SEGAL
Jerusalem Post Political Reporter

Reacting to Prime Minister Golda Meir's announcement that she will resign today, Likud leader Menahem Begin said last night that the Likud Knesset faction will initiate steps to form a caretaker government "of a different composition" to Mrs. Meir's fourth cabinet.

Without providing any details, Begin said, "It is possible. It requires a measure of political courageousness." Begin also spelled out the decision of the Likud Knesset faction and Executive adopted earlier in the day (before Mrs. Meir's announcement) when they urged the resignation of the government as a whole, claiming all of its members were responsible for the Yom Kippur failings, and the holding of new elections within 10 weeks.

Mr. Begin chose his words carefully in framing his reaction to Mrs. Meir's announcement, cautioning "it will only go into effect on being handed to the President. Don't forget we have already experienced a similar announcement, closely followed by a retraction in a matter of hours only a few weeks ago."

As to whether the likelihood now existed for forming a national unity coalition, Mr. Begin said: "All the ways are now open."

At the Herut Council session, Mr. Begin spelled out his view that not only Dayan but all cabinet ministers shared the responsibility for the army's unreadiness, especially the four ministers, members of the "kitchen cabinet" — Mrs. Meir, Allon, Galili and Dayan who made up the forum that decided not to mobilize the reserves on Yom Kippur eve.

Recalling the Gahal decision to leave the coalition in 1970, Begin said that "it was thereafter that decisions were made in the 'Cabinet kitchen,' and if the other ministers stayed on without protest, it means they complied and compliance means involvement in responsibility."

Mrs. Meir's step did not come as a surprise to her Mapai colleagues, to judge by their reactions. None of them spoke of striving to dissuade her. Labour Party secretary-general Aharon Yadlin in regretting the resignation said, "Perhaps there was no other way out," saying he could well appreciate her motivations. He did not rule out the prospect of new elections, though he did not think it good to have untimely polls.

Declining to name his candidate for the premiership, Yadlin stressed, "I do not despair about maintaining the party's unity." He declared that efforts would be made to this end and added, "Now it is up to us to crystallize our policy following Mrs. Meir's resignation announcement."

Police Minister Shlomo Hillel feared that Mrs. Meir's resignation was bad for the country but "perhaps there was no other way out of the impasse." Conceding that an

(Continued on page 2, col. 2)

The legal procedure
KNESSET TO MEET TODAY

Jerusalem Post Reporter

The Knesset is to meet this afternoon in special session, as scheduled, but instead of hearing a Government statement on the Agranat Commission's interim report, it will be informed by the Speaker that the Prime Minister has submitted a letter of resignation to the President, bringing down the entire Government.

The present Government will remain as a caretaker Cabinet until a new Government is formed or new elections are held.

In view of the Government's resignation, the Likud opposition can no longer submit its non-confidence motion, but has the right to demand a debate on the resignation, which it is expected to do.

Prime Minister Golda Meir is due to call on President Katzir after this morning's Cabinet session to submit her formal letter of resignation. She has first to inform the Cabinet of her decision to resign and her statement has to be entered formally in the Cabinet's official records.

The Cabinet was scheduled today to discuss the question of Ministerial responsibility in the wake of the Agranat report, on the basis of the legal opinion that was submitted yesterday by Justice Minister Haim Zadok to all Cabinet members (see story on Page 2).

Since no Minister can resign from a caretaker Government, and there is also no reshuffling of portfolios in such a Cabinet, it was difficult to predict last night how today's Cabinet discussion on the Agranat report would shape up.

The next move is for the President to open a new round of consultations with representatives of all Knesset factions to hear their proposals as to whom to entrust with the task of forming a new Government. Only if a number of factions representing a majority in the House advise the President that they intend passing a bill that would dissolve the Eighth Knesset, calling for new elections later this year, can the President refrain from inviting another Knesset member to form a new Cabinet.

Should the majority of the House agree to dissolve the Knesset and call for new elections, such a bill could be submitted only on May 6, at the end of the Passover recess, since no new draft bills can be submitted during the recess. This would mean that new elections could not be held before September as a 100-day period must be allowed for civil servants or army officers who want to run for office to resign before the new Knesset lists are submitted.

It seems doubtful at this stage whether the present Knesset will be able to approve in three readings the recently passed preliminary electoral reform bill in time for new elections later this year.

Japan denies arms aid to Egypt

TOKYO (Reuter). — The Japanese Foreign Ministry yesterday rejected as "nonsense" an Israeli newspaper report that Egypt has asked Japan for aid to set up a sophisticated military industry which would produce television-guided bombs.

A spokesman said: "Egypt has made no such request and Japan is not in a position to extend any military aid to any country."

U.S. says it's not arming Kurd rebels

WASHINGTON (AP). — State Department spokesman George Vest said yesterday the U.S. "absolutely denies" the shipment of any arms or aid to the Kurkish rebels in Iraq.

Iraqi Vice-President Saddam Hussein said made the charges in a news conference in Baghdad on Tuesday.

IRA STEPS UP ITS ATTACKS

BELFAST (UPI). — Irish Republican Army gunmen burst into a crowded primary school near the border yesterday and killed the school's principal in a deluge of gunfire, police said.

A police spokesman said the four gunmen caught their victim, a retired military officer, in the school's kitchen and riddled him with bullets as children attended classes in adjacent rooms.

The police identified the man killed as Lt.-Col. George Saunderson, who retired from Northern Ireland militia a year ago to become principal of the school.

In Belfast, the Ulster Defence Association (UDA), the largest militant Protestant organization in Northern Ireland, said it is polling its members to find out whether they should adopt an "aggressive" posture in the province.

Political sources said the UDA position amounted to a threat to start arming Protestants for attacks on the Catholic community.

Until now, the UDA — a legal organization — has restricted its vigilante-type activities to patrols in Protestant neighbourhoods.

Saunderson was the 992nd person killed in violence among the majority Protestants, minority Roman Catholics and the security forces in Northern Ireland since 1969.

Police said the attack occurred at Derrylin, a small County Fermanagh village about 2 km. from the border with the Irish Republic.

Rioting students earlier yesterday stoned British troops in Belfast's Catholic Andersontown district, where witnesses said soldiers shot and killed a social club manager by mistake on Tuesday night.

A British Army spokesman confirmed a British mobile patrol had come under attack from the club's direction and had fired back. He said the incident was being investigated.

Rome airport alert after letter threat

ROME (AP). — Rome's international airport was placed on alert yesterday after a letter received in Munich demanded 100,000 marks ($40,000) and threatened "serious reprisal against an Italian plane." The threat caused a Munich-to-Rome Alitalia flight to return to Munich 20 minutes after takeoff for a search.

A spokesman at Munich's airport confirmed a threat aimed at the Alitalia flight. Police thoroughly searched the plane and its passengers, but found nothing, the spokesman said.

A spokesman at Munich said the plane finally took off for Rome early yesterday afternoon.

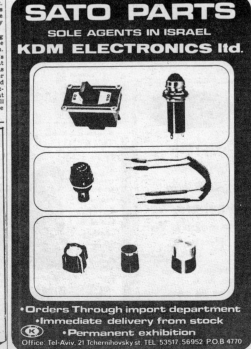

Eighteen murdered in Kiryat Shmona terror

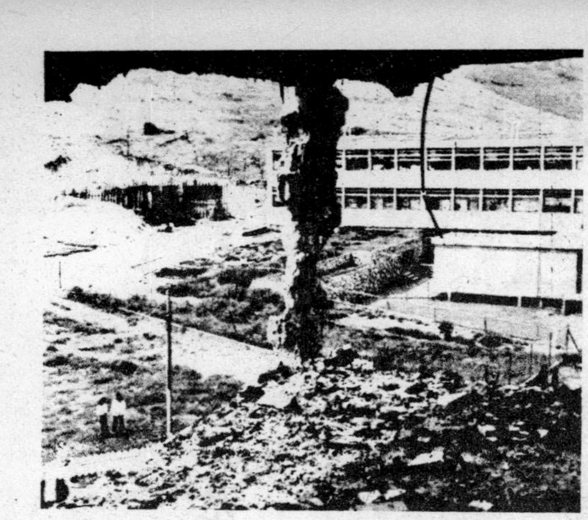

View from the room in the Kiryat Shmona building in which the three Arab terrorists were blown up yesterday. In background is school. On left, is the hill from which the murderers came. (AP)

Names of the victims

Shimon Biton, 30, his son Avi, five, and his two-and-a-half-year-old daughter; Ya'acov and Miriam Gueta, both 30; Esther Cohen, 40, her son David, 17, and her daughter Shula, 14; Fannie Shitrit, 30, and her children Yocheved, 11, Aharon, 8, and Motti, four; Hansa Stern, 47, and her daughter Rachel, eight; Shaul Ben-Eliahu, 30; Esther Wozana, 60; Acting Officer Mordechai Grady, 20, of Ramat Hasharon; Rav-Turai Suahil Abdak, 20 of Tarshiha.

Another 16 wounded were brought to Government Hospital in Safad, including one who was seriously wounded, Kamal Haboushi, 21, a Druse soldier from Julis.

Four had medium injuries. Mrs. Shoshana Biton, 27, fell off the balcony when she was shot at close range as she tried to get her three children out of their fourth floor flat. The others are Na'if Ma'arouf, 27, a Druse border policeman from Hurfeish; David Cohen, 29, a soldier, and Yosef Ben-Dror, 29, a border policeman, from Haifa.

Of the slightly injured, Albert Mishali, 19, a border policeman from Kiryat Tivon, was discharged. Those kept for treatment are Rani Moses, a five-year-boy from Tirat Carmel who was visiting relatives; Yoel Noel, 19, and Binyamin Sulimani, 22, both border policemen from Kiryat Shmona; Shlomo Rouif, 24, deputy commander of the Kiryat Shmona police; Eliyahu Ayesh, 43, of Kiryat Shmona; Yitzhak Hanukah, 27, of Kiryat Shmona; Hajaj Sinai, 41, of Kiryat Shmona; David Aboutbul, 24, a Kiryat Shmona soldier; Michael Meirowitz, 25, of Kiryat Bialik and David Zaguri, 26, of Kiryat Shmona.

THE JERUSALEM POST

40 PAGES including 28-Page MAGAZINE

OCTOBER ELECTION SEEN Page 2

Price: IL1.75

FRIDAY, APRIL 12, 1974 • NISAN 20, 5734 • RABI AWWAL 21, 1394 • VOL. XLIV, No. 14069*

Three Arabs butcher women and children, then die in blast

By HIRSH GOODMAN, Jerusalem Post Military Correspondent

Eighteen persons — mainly women and children — were massacred by terrorists in the northern Galilee town of Kiryat Shmona by three terrorists who crossed the border into Israel from Lebanon on Wednesday night. The three men infiltrated at a point between Metula and Misgav Am, and it is believed that they reached the outskirts of Kiryat Shmona under cover of darkness, waiting until the morning before "attacking" an apartment block on the perimeter of the town with the objective of killing any man, woman or child whom they found there. The three died in an explosion as troops stormed the building.

Ahmed Jibril's Popular Front for the Liberation of Palestine: General command claimed credit for the attack yesterday in an announcement from Damascus. Israeli army trackers on a routine patrol along the northern frontier noticed the infiltrators' tracks at 6.40 yesterday morning. It was quickly established that the three-man terrorist group had followed a rocky ridge running from the border near the vicinity of Misgav Am to a school on the outskirts of the town. According to the Acting Chief of Staff, Aluf Yitzhak Hofi, the army immediately notified regional defence authorities — including the Kiryat Shmona police — that terrorists had crossed the border, and that regional forces should be placed on maximum alert. The army also dispatched two limited units to the town to help the 20-man police force try and track down the terrorists.

Shortly before 8 a.m. the first evidence was uncovered that the terrorists had entered the town. A two-man police patrol was fired on from the entrance to a block of apartments about 200 metres from the school which, as far as can be ascertained, the terrorists never entered. The encounter with the police seems to have sparked off a massacre the proportions of which only became apparent later in the morning.

As soon as they left their night hiding places early in the morning, the terrorists entered two ground level flats and cold-bloodedly murdered five persons there. They then ran to the next building where they systematically entered each flat, killing almost every living soul in the four-storey building before coming to an empty apartment on the fourth floor. From there they began sniping at passers-by in the street below. By the time they had reached the apartment at approximately 8 a.m. the terrorists had killed 16 persons — including eight children, and wounded more than a dozen others. Two Israeli soldiers were killed later in the morning while trying to flush the terrorists out of the flat.

According to Aluf Hofi, Israel had no prior intelligence that the terrorists were planning any specific acts against Israeli population centres "or anything of that sort." He further told military correspondents that no unusual terrorist activity had been noticed on the Lebanese side of the border over the past few weeks.

The Acting Chief of Staff said that it was very difficult to prevent terrorist infiltration into Israel from Lebanon in that particular area because of the harsh topographical conditions and rocky terrain. He added that the short distance from the border to towns and villages in the area made track-

(Continued on page 2, Col. 1)

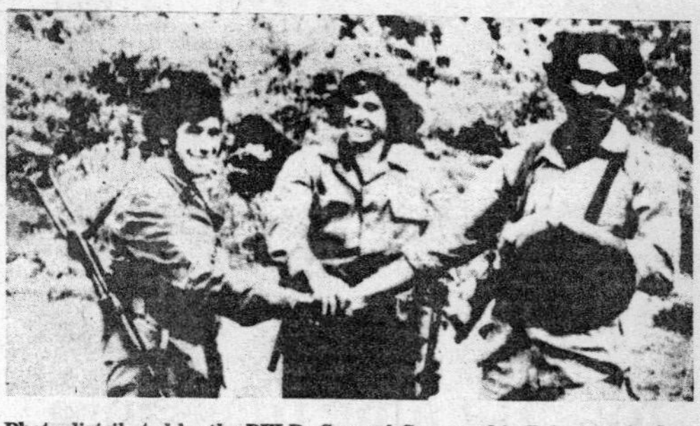

Photo distributed by the PFLP: General Command in Beirut yesterday showing the three terrorists who attacked Kiryat Shmona. Left to right, Monir Moghrabi, Ahmed e-Sheikh Mahmoud and Yassin Mousa el-Mouzani. (AP radiophoto)

'THERE IS MINISTERIAL RESPONSIBILITY'

Golda says she had to quit after public ire

Jerusalem Post Staff

Prime Minister Golda Meir briskly followed up her resignation announcement to the Knesset yesterday by noting that Israel has a fully functioning government pending formation of a new one and that the Cabinet would continue in its efforts to achieve peace.

On the internal political front, she noted that the Cabinet was dealing with the question of individual Ministerial responsibility in the wake of the interim Agranat report. She said that in resigning she could not ignore the public ferment.

As to the Agranat report, Mrs. Meir said that in her view there was no doubt that a Minister was responsible for the activities of his Ministry. "This principle is part of our constitutional concept of the reciprocal relations between the executive and the legislature. The matter is thus on the agenda of the Cabinet."

The Cabinet, she said, had also determined procedures for considering and acting upon the recommendations of the Agranat Committee in connection with arriving at a clear definition of authority in defence matters, setting up a Cabinet security committee, ensuring secrecy of Cabinet security discussions and ensuring effective operation of the intelligence community.

Mrs. Meir, wearing a blue suit and looking fit and well, read out her statement in a composed voice. The chamber was packed and in the VIP section sat the families of many Members, including the Prime Minister's son.

The six-hour debate that followed her statement was milder than had originally been expected when the special session was called during the Passover recess — at the request of both the Government and Likud — in connection with the Agranat report.

Explaining her resignation, Mrs. Meir said the public ferment could not be ignored: after much thought she had come to the conclusion that the public and its representatives should be given another chance to choose a new government.

But she added that the present Cabinet was vested with full authority until a new Government was chosen either by this Knesset or the next. "Our envoys abroad have been authorized to explain this. She added: "The Government will continue in political efforts to bring about peace between Israel and the Arabs."

(Statement text — page 12; Debate — page 2)

Yesterday morning, Mrs. Meir informed the Cabinet officially of her decision to resign. At noon she called on President Katzir to hand in her formal letter of resignation which said:

"In accordance with the provisions of section 23 of the Basic Law: The Government, and having informed the Cabinet of my intention, I herewith tender my resignation from the post of Prime Minister."

Mrs. Meir handed her resignation to the President exactly one month after she had presented to him her new Government on March 10. The forming of the short-lived Government was preceded by protracted coalition negotiations with the National Religious Party, which got bogged down several times over the question of "Who is a Jew."

The difficulties in the coalition talks were compounded by an earlier decision of Rafi leaders Moshe Dayan and Shimon Peres not to join the new Cabinet, in the wake of which Mrs. Meir had decided to return her mandate to the President, relenting afterwards to party pressure.

Following his half-hour-long talk with Mrs. Meir, the President made a public statement, formally announcing the Prime Minister's resig-

(Continued on page 2, Col. 1)

U.S. blasts massacre

WASHINGTON. — The State Department yesterday condemned the "brutal and senseless slaughter" in Kiryat Shmona, "particularly the murder of women and children, as we deplore all terrorist activity."

Spokesman George Vest added that "in this instance it is particularly regrettable" because the murders came "when the process of peace is already in motion. This attack underlines even more the urgent need for U.S. Secretary of State Henry Kissinger's continued efforts to bring peace to this region."

Vest said it is too early to say that the raid plus the political disruptions in Israel will delay Kissinger's planned trip to the Middle East later this month.

However, he said, "the events in the area are not slowing down his sense of urgency or efforts" to arrange a military disengagement between the Syrians and Israelis.

In that connection, Vest said a time has not yet been fixed for a meeting between Kissinger and the Syrian delegation to discuss disengagement. *(AP, JTA)*

Two hurt in North

Two Israeli soldiers were wounded by Syrian artillery fire yesterday.

The Syrians opened fire — for the 31st consecutive day — at 9 a.m. on Israeli positions in the southern sector of the bulge and on positions west of the pre-October cease-fire line. Positions in the area were shelled intermittently throughout the day, and by 8 last night, after several shells had fallen on the Israeli Hermon, quiet returned to the area.

MEIR PUTS BLAME ON LEBANON

By MALKA RABINOWITZ
Jerusalem Post Reporter

Prime Minister Golda Meir said yesterday Israel placed responsibility for yesterday's slaughter in Kiryat Shmona on the Lebanese Government and on inhabitants of that country who aided the terrorists.

Addressing a packed Knesset chamber after presiding over an extraordinary session of the Cabinet, Mrs. Meir said it was the nation's duty to defend and help the residents of that northern border town.

The 18 dead, she said, included eight children, five women, two soldiers and three male civilians.

It was not a movement of liberation that had perpetrated the attack but a movement of murder for the sake of murder. "This nation has suffered much through the generations," said Mrs. Meir. "And we are in an independent Jewish state capable of defending itself and its citizens."

A circular left behind by the terrorists in Kiryat Shmona was signed by the "Popular Front: General Command" and declared that the armed struggle would continue until Israel was destroyed and replaced by a "democratic Palestinian state of Jews and Arabs." To the surprise of the House, Mrs. Meir read out in full the text of the fairly lengthy terrorist outpouring, explaining — after Geula Cohen (Likud) called out, "Why are you reading that out?" — that it was to demonstrate the true nature of the terrorist movement.

The session opened with the House rising in tribute to the victims of the attack in Kiryat Shmona after Speaker Yisrael Yeshayahu condemned the "animal cruelty" of the murderers.

Mrs. Meir extended the condolences of the Government and the Knesset to the bereaved families.

Earlier, Foreign Minister Abba Eban issued the following statement:

"The full scope of the atrocity committed by Arab terrorists against men, women and children at Kiryat Shmona is still not fully clear, but it is already plain that an immense brutality has been perpetrated in violation of every law of civilization and humanity. Every civilized man and woman in the world must be asking to what lengths this peril will go.

"The lesson must be: implacable resistance to the terrorists and an end to the deplorable indulgence with which these organizations have been surrounded in many places."

EXTREME JIBRIL GROUP CULPRIT

By ANAN SAFADI
Jerusalem Post Arab Affairs Reporter

Responsibility for the Kiryat Shmona terrorist operation was claimed yesterday by Ahmed Jibril's Popular Front for the Liberation of Palestine-General Command which is a splinter group of George Habash's PFLP.

As three terrorists took over the building in Kiryat Shmona, the PFLP-General Command issued statements in Damascus and Beirut claiming that the operation was carried out by one of its "suicide squads." It said that the three men were holding hostages and that they were demanding the release of 100 terrorist prisoners within six hours, with 2 p.m. as the deadline.

The PFLP-General Command gave the following identifications and details on the three sabotuers:

Monir Moghrabi, 20, code-named Abu Khaled, a Palestinian born in Damascus. He joined the front shortly after graduating from a Syrian secondary school in 1971; Ahmed e-Sheikh Mahmoud, 20, code-named Abu Shaker, a Syrian who joined the front in 1972; Yassin Mousa el-Mouzani, 27, code-named Abu-Hadi, an Iraqi construction worker who served in the Iraqi army before joining the front in 1972.

The movement emphasized that they wanted Japanese terrorist Kozo Okamoto released among the 100 terrorists. Okamoto is serving a life sentence for his role in the May 1972 Lod airport massacre. The PFLP-General Command further demanded the release of all female terrorist prisoners.

The statement issued by it showed that the three saboteurs were instructed to take over a nearby school building which, however, was closed for the Pessah holiday.

But as the terrorist operation came to an end, it issued a communiquqe saying that its three men had set off explosive belts killing them with their hostages. The movement blamed the Israel authorities for "failing to heed warnings" against assaulting the building.

The PFLP-General Command claimed that the three belonged to a unit operating "inside the occupied territory." It denied that they had set out from Lebanon.

The terrorist attack came a few days after Fatah chief Yasser Arafat claimed to have instructed all terrorist members grouped in the Palestine Liberation Organization to avoid launching operations from Lebanese territory to prevent retaliation by Israel against Lebanon.

The Kiryat Shmona attack was viewed as part of operations planned by a number of terrorist groups

(Continued on Page 3, Col. 3)

AFTER MIDNIGHT

A car with Gaza licence plates blew up in Rishon Lezion at 11.30 last night. Two Arabs inside were seriously injured and were taken to Assaf Harofe Hospital. Police are investigating.

*

Likud leader Menahem Begin last night said his party has asked for a special Knesset session next week to debate the security arrangements in Kiryat Shmona.

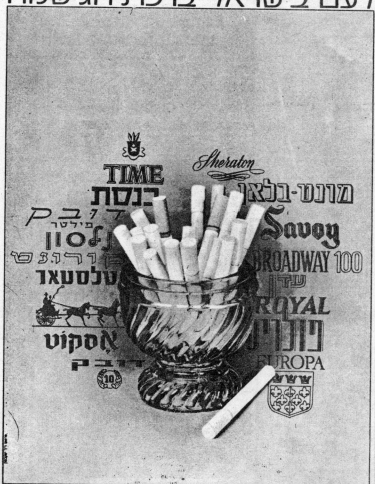

Three Arab terrorists die after butchering 20 in Galilee town

THE JERUSALEM POST

Ma'alot stories pictures Pages 2, 3, 10

Price: 80 Ag.

THURSDAY, MAY 16, 1974 ● IYAR 24, 5734 ● RABI TANI 25, 1394 ● VOL. XLII, No. 14096*

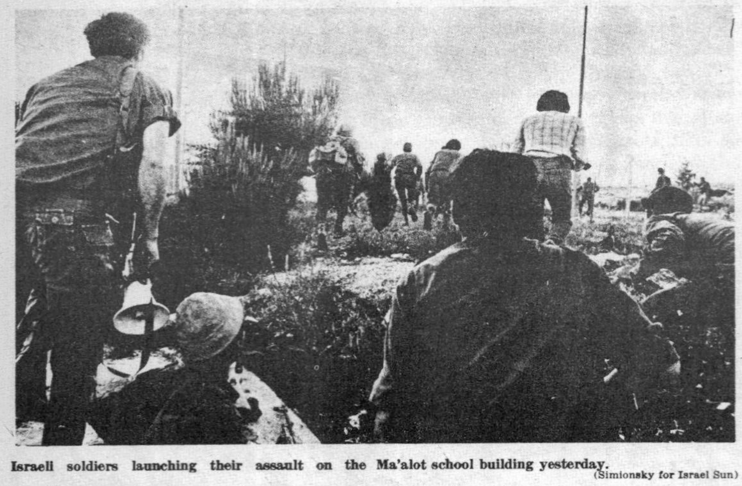

Israeli soldiers launching their assault on the Ma'alot school building yesterday. (Simionsky for Israel Sun)

Day-long drama ends with sixteen children murdered in school house

By YA'ACOV FRIEDLER, Jerusalem Post Reporter

MA'ALOT. — Israeli troops yesterday stormed the school building here where three Arab terrorists held 85 children hostage and killed the gunmen in a brief gunfight which left 20 persons, mostly children, dead and about 70 pupils wounded, nine seriously. The dead included 16 children, three members of a family killed early in the morning and a soldier who had been taking pictures from the nearby water tower.

The longest and bloodiest day of terror yet suffered by the country ended at the Netiv Meir School where the children had spent the night and where the terrorists had burst in before dawn — holding them hostage and demanding the release of 20 terrorists held in Israeli jails whom they wanted to be flown to Damascus.

Protracted negotiations were directed by the Defence Minister, the Chief of Staff and the O.C., Northern Command, who set up a forward command post near the school early in the morning. They were joined later by the French Ambassador at the terrorists' demand. An army unit assaulted the building to prevent the terrorists blowing it up with the 85 children they still held.

When the bloody day was over, it was still difficult to reconstruct events precisely. The three terrorists who had infiltrated from Lebanon, started their day of massacre at about midnight, when dressed in khaki and looking like soldiers, they attacked a van on its way home with women workers from the Ata Textile Plant near Haifa. Two women were killed and six others wounded, two seriously. (story — page 2).

The terrorists then made their way over the hills to Ma'alot and entered a dwelling block, number 134, which faces the Netiv Meir State Religious School building that dominates the city from a hillside. The terrorists went from door to door ordering tenants in Hebrew to open up, claiming to be police checking for terrorists. Most of the residents refused to open their doors and were saved, but the three men got into the second floor flat of the Cohen family, where they murdered three.

The father, Zion, 37, and the older son Eliyahu, 4, they shot dead, seriously injured the five-year-old girl, Miriam, and did not notice the deaf-mute 18-months-old baby Moshe. But they chased the seven-months-pregnant mother, Fortuna, who fled down the stairs screaming for help, and shot her dead, her blood staining the steps.

Then just before 4 a.m. the three terrorists crossed to the school, where one of them woke up a 50-year-old janitor, Ya'acov Kadosh. Wishing him "good morning" in Hebrew they asked whether there were any children inside. Kadosh, who felt no qualms about the 110 pupils who were sleeping, answered in the affirmative. Then the terrorists opened fire on him, wounding him in the shoulders.

They then entered the building, where the boys and girls, most of them from the Safad religious school and about 15 from Hatzor, were sleeping on separate floors, accompanied by a girl junior army officer, a teacher, a couple of instructors and two soldiers who had come along but had left their rifles outside in the excursion truck — apparently in line with instructions not to sleep with their guns.

In the confusion which ensued when the terrorists herded all the children into the first floor classroom, 17 of the children, the truck driver, a teacher, and an instructor managed to escape by jumping out of the windows.

Later in the morning, the terrorists released the girl officer, Narkis Mordechai, sending her out with an ultimatum, a list of the 20 top terrorists they wanted released. They named 11 in the list spelled out in Latin letters. They also gave her a leaflet in Arabic and English, setting out the aims of their organization and action. They demanded that three of the top terrorists choose the remaining nine to be released. They set 6 p.m. as the deadline, by which time they wanted the released terrorists to be in Damascus.

Early in the morning, Defence Minister Moshe Dayan arrived by helicopter and went into conference at the Local Council offices. On emerging at eight, the angry townpeople surrounded him, demanding security and had to have a way forced through the crowds into a waiting van by a group of soldiers and constables. The angry crowd banged their palms on the tender's tin roof until it drove off.

Mr. Dayan, joined by the Chief of Staff and the O.C. Northern Command, set up their advanced HQ near the school, and negotiations got under way with the terrorists who, through loud hailers, threatened to blow up the building at six if their demands were not met.

The terrorists used the hailers brought along by the pupils for the outing, and spoke in Arabic and Hebrew, demanding the presence of the French or Rumanian ambassador, with a secret code word that was to be broadcast by Radio Damascus, after the terrorist prisoners were released.

At about 11, the terrorists allowed two 15-year-old children who were ill, to leave the school. They were Rachel Laksiel and Biton Mahlouf. They gave Rachel a few notes with their demands to be forwarded by her, and she handed them personally to Mr. Dayan.

At the Mivtahim house, where all the children who had escaped were put up to wait for their parents who soon arrived, Rachel told reporters that at first all three had been very nervous, but as it became light they became calmer, especially one of the three who spoke fairly good Hebrew. (Narkis Mordechai claimed that she had recognized him from Safad, where she believed he worked, and could be seen in restaurants. This later proved a mistake, as the man in question was found in Safad.)

Rachel said he had been "quite nice" and encouraged the children, assuring them that everything would be over and they would be safe by six at night. The terrorists, who she said were heavily armed, and carried handgrenades, placed explosives, and allowed them to eat.

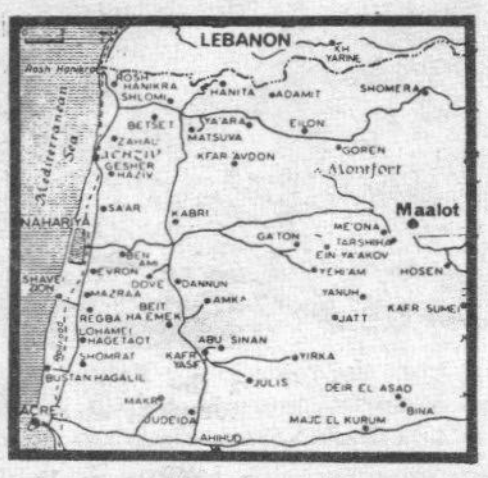

Location of Ma'alot in Western Galilee seen in map, some 10 kms. south of the Lebanese border, as the crow flies.

At first they forbade the children to play their transistor radios but after an argument, agreed, and then demanded to be told the contents of each news bulletin. "We were frightened, but one girl, Sara Mader, told jokes and cheered us up. The terrorists also told us that they had no intention to harm us and that everything would be all right."

Meanwhile, the terrorists fired occasional shots whenever anybody was spotted by them coming close to the building. At about 11, a Ma'alot soldier on leave, who had crept near to take photos, was shot and killed by them. At 12.30 a representative of the French Embassy arrived at Ma'alot and was escorted to the command post, carrying a small French flag and a sheet or cardboard with photos of terrorists on it. There was an uneasy quiet until the afternoon, when three terrorists from Israeli jails, one of them a girl, were helicoptered in, to name the additional terrorists to be returned. They were taken away again some time later.

Another lull ensued, with dozens of newsmen pressing against the barriers the police had put up, and protesting at the lack of official information. I met a Druse sergeant-major, 45-year-old Abu Sauhvagman, of Yarka village, who serves in the minority unit of the army, and had actually exchanged fire with the terrorists shortly after they entered the school at 4 a.m. He said that he had been in a jeep, and that when he passed the school, they had opened fire on him. He returned it and two exchanges took place, before he was ordered to stop, he said.

After noon, Police Minister Shlomo Hillel and the director of the Education Ministry, Elad Peled, arrived and met the released children and anxious parents at the guest house.

(Continued on page 2, col. 1)

'MODERATE' TERRORIST GROUP

PDFLP takes 'credit' for Ma'alot massacre

By ANAN SAFADI
Jerusalem Post Arab Affairs Reporter

The series of sabotage attacks topped by the Ma'alot school outrage was described by the Arab terrorist groups as a "protest gesture" on the 26th anniversary of the Declaration of the State of Israel. Other attacks included firing on Arab passengers from the Galilee village of Fassouta, arson at the Haifa Kishon seaside oil installation, and an abortive Katyusha bombing in the centre of Jerusalem.

The PDFLP identified the three terrorists who staged the Ma'alot attack as Aly Ahmed Hassan, 26, code named "Lino"; Ahmed Saleh Nayef, 20, code named "Harbi"; and Ziyad Abdul-Rahim, 22, code named Kamal Hassan.

Observers in the Arab capitals said the terrorist attacks were also a protest against U.S. Secretary of State Henry Kissinger's current mission.

Although the terrorists rejoiced over the casualties inflicted in the Ma'alot and the Fassouta attacks, they appeared to have received news of the outcome of the Ma'alot operation as a blow. The Popular Democratic Front for the Liberation of Palestine (PDFLP), which took responsibility for the attack last night, hurried to claim that its three-man squad had ended their mission by blowing themselves up, along with the school building, after having refused to extend the 6.00 p.m. deadline for the transfer of terrorist prisoners to Damascus.

The PDFLP is headed by Nayef Hawatmeh, whose "moderation" has recently been praised by several journalists abroad.

The main terrorist groups yesterday seemed to be in competition over each other's activities inside Israel, in an apparent bid to counter the heroic image of the PFLP-General Command, which took responsibility for the April 11 suicide attack in Kiryat Shmona.

While the Popular Democratic Front yesterday issued a flurry of "military communiques" on Ma'alot the Fatah-controlled overall terrorist command issued its own communiques, claiming responsibility for the Kishon fire and the abortive rocket attack in Jerusalem.

The Fatah-sponsored command admitted that "one batch of rockets were discovered and dismantled by the enemy," but claimed another batch "went off, hitting Musheirem (Mea Shearim) and Mascobia (the Russian Compound)."

The Beirut-based Fatah terrorist news agency, WAFA, later said that the Katyushas were aimed at vital targets, including the American consulate. Other terrorist sources said one rocket was aimed at the King David Hotel, where Secretary of State Kissinger was staying yesterday.

The Marxist PDFLP took credit for the Ma'alot attack in statements read to news agencies in Beirut. Titled "Military communique No. 1 of the command of the interior forces," the statement said the operation was carried out by "the

(Continued on page 5, col. 6)

Terrorists' movements unclear

By HIRSH GOODMAN
Jerusalem Post Military Correspondent

TEL AVIV. — It was not clear last night where the three Ma'alot terrorists entered Israel, or for how long they had been in the area. It was also not certain whether the three men were also responsible for the attack on the tender carrying workers to the village of Fasuta, some two kilometres from Ma'alot, three hours before the school was attacked.

Army trackers spent the whole day yesterday trying to ascertain where the border had been crossed, but failed to find any conclusive evidence. A senior military officer said it was not believed that the three were Israeli Arabs or inhabitants of the administered territories.

The Army has started an investigation into the entire attack, starting from how and why the terrorists managed to penetrate the town, and including the final assault on the school.

Observers raised serious questions about the defence arrangements in the region of the town, especially in light of the murder of 18 people in Kiryat Shmona by a terrorist group last month. They said it was blatantly obvious that security arrangements at the border village were inadequate. They pointed out that the three terrorists wandered around the village knocking on doors and shooting three members of one family, without being challenged at any stage.

This is especially serious in view of the fact that Israeli intelligence expected terrorist activity on May 15, and that for the past two days it had been known that infiltrators had crossed the border at Even Menahem, on the Lebanese border just a few kilometres from the town, and that they were in the area. There were no tracks leaving Israeli territory, and though trackers could not pick up the trail from the border crossing, it was suspected that the infiltrators were still in Israeli territory.

The incident on the road to Fasuta occured at 12.30 a.m. just three hours before the terrorists entered the village and attacked the school. The incident occurred only two kilometres from the town. The men responsible for the shooting had not been apprehended, and it was known that they were still prowling the area. There was no explanation last night of the fact that the village had not been alerted and no reinforcements sent to the area in case of further trouble.

Complaints about security in Ma'alot

Jerusalem Post Reporter

MA'ALOT. — Bitter complaints against slack security arrangements and almost total neglect by the Government of their town of 3,500 were voiced yesterday by the members of the Ma'alot Local Council, who met in special session with Police Minister Shlomo Hillel.

Council Chairman Eli Ben Ya'acov and his colleagues minced no words in attacking the Government for having forgotten Ma'alot almost since it was established over 20 years ago, and for not having heeded the warnings following last month's Kiryat Shmona massacre.

"You have made us step-children of Israel; is it because most of us are from Morocco? We don't even have our own police station. Our children have to travel some 40 kilometres every day to go to high school. There are not enough sources of livelihood in this town and not enough flats to accommodate our own children who grew up here and want to go on living here," were some of the charges voiced.

Some of the council members, who were on army reserve duty and had rushed home when they heard the news early in the morning, attended the meeting in their army uniforms.

They recalled their visit to Kiryat Shmona last month, when they realized that a similar attack could be made on their own town, only some five km. south of the Lebanese border.

Two soldiers killed

By HIRSH GOODMAN
Jerusalem Post Military Correspondent

Two soldiers were killed by artillery fire on Tuesday and five more wounded yesterday as fighting along the northern front continued.

The names of the dead are Segen Avraham Zussman, 21, from Hadera and Samal Reuven Breilenberg, 20, from Acre.

Yesterday, Israel Air Force planes were called in again against terrorist concentrations in Lebanon and on the southern Golan. The army spokesman said all the planes returned safely to base.

For the first time in three weeks, the Syrians yesterday fired several artillery salvoes at Nafah, some 10 kms. west of the cease-fire lines, after Israeli long-range guns earlier in the morning had shelled the Syrian army base at Katana, 15 kms. west of Damascus.

At noon, Israeli planes attacked Syrian military concentrations at Tel Kudne, on the southern Golan, for 15 minutes. In the afternoon a terrorist camp at Rashid-el-Fuhar in southern Lebanon was attacked from the air.

The heaviest shelling of the day was in the Tel Shams area, where nearly 150 shells fell in less than half-an-hour. Other places shelled included the Hermon and Mazrat Beit Jann areas in the northern sector, and near Tel Faris and Ramat Hamagshimim, both west of the pre-October cease-fire line on the Golan Heights.

Kissinger mission 'to go on'

Jerusalem Post Diplomatic Correspondent

U.S. Secretary of State Henry Kissinger and his wife Nancy visited Premier Golda Meir at her home last night to express to her their personal condolences on the Ma'alot deaths. The Secretary had followed the day's events from his hotel suite in Jerusalem.

After meeting Mrs. Meir Kissinger told reporters that despite the crime in Ma'alot he was determined to continue his activities in order to bring peace.

The Government had informed Dr. Kissinger early in the morning that it would have neither mind nor heart to pursue the disengagement talks until the tragedy at Ma'alot was played out. Dr. Kissinger decided to remain in Jerusalem and await developments.

He is to meet with Mrs. Meir and her negotiating team this morning for another examination of the disengagement problems before flying to Damascus and will return here tonight.

The Cabinet sat late into last night to prepare for this morning's meeting.

Earlier Dr. Kissinger expressed shock and outrage at the Ma'alot attack and said his government strongly condemned such actions. He called on all responsible governments to deal severely with such people.

In a statement issued to newsmen here he said:

"I was shocked and outraged to learn of the attack by fedayeen terrorists against a teenage campsite in Ma'alot early this morning and against other innocent civilians in the same area, our hearts go out to the families and all of Israel.

"The U.S. Government strongly condemns this mindless and irrational action and appeals to those holding innocent hostages to release them. Already there are reports that a father, mother and a five-year-old have been killed and others injured.

"Violence such as this will serve no cause but to undermine the prospects for peace in this area; further, we believe that it is time for all responsible governments to make clear that, whatever their political differences, such inhuman acts must be condemned and those who carry them out dealt with severely."

Asked whether the latest incident had caused second thoughts about the last U.S. vote at the UN. Security Council, U.S. spokesman Robert McCloskey said:

"It is always the intention and desire of the U.S. to vote on the merits and no one incident may be the same as the other. I would not want to anticipate a vote. I think the sense of outrage is reflected in the Secretary's statement."

Rabin gets another week to form his coalition gov't

Jerusalem Post Political Reporter

TEL AVIV. — President Ephraim Katzir yesterday granted Premier-designate Yitzhak Rabin an additional week in which to form a government. Mr. Rabin called on the President to request the extension because the Kissinger talks and other developments had delayed the coalition talks.

Mr. Rabin's deadline for forming a new Cabinet was to expire tomorrow. The new deadline is at midnight on Friday, May 24.

The events in Ma'alot caused the coalition negotiations to be suspended yesterday, and the Labour Party Central Committee meeting which was due to decide on the kind of coalition which Mr. Rabin is to form was postponed.

Labour Party circles were yesterday talking about the likelihood of a broad government and even a national coalition stretching from the Likud to the Civil Rights Movement. Authoritative sources in the Labour Party yesterday said the events at Ma'alot had rendered impossible the formation of a narrow government of 61. Labour politicians are alert to the growing sense of a deepening national emergency, it was said.

Agitation for as broad a coalition as possible began yesterday in the Knesset building, when members of the Independent Liberal Party and Labour's Ahdut Ha'avoda and Rafi wings came together at the initiative of Rafi's Mordechai Ben-Porat to campaign for as broad a coalition as possible.

Independent Liberal Secretary Yitzhak Barkai last night said his party would prefer a national coalition even as a temporary measure until the emergency has passed.

Zalman Shoval of the Likud's State List yesterday reiterated the need for a national coalition, reflecting his party's general feeling. Even in the National Religious Party there was a cautious response to this idea, and they await the return today of Chief Rabbi Shlomo Goren from France to obtain his advice on the matter.

Golda says terrorists will be thwarted

Mrs. Golda Meir assured the nation last night over Israel TV that any Government in Israel would do its utmost to thwart the terrorists.

"We shall lop off the hands reaching out to harm our young people and adults, everywhere, in country and town," she said. "I cannot promise that they will let us live in peace. But we must all do one thing — maintain our strength and our spirits unflaggingly."

She described Wednesday as a "bitter day, a day of horrors," detailing the developments at Ma'alot. The Government sat all day from nine a.m. to seven p.m. with a 90 minute break, she revealed.

"We were faced with the extremely grave question as to whether or not to free terrorists. Everyone in this country knows how grave that question is," she said.

"The Government decided that we will not wage wars over the bodies of children. So we decided to accept the terrorists' demands," she said, adding that the Defence Minister, the Police Minister and the Chief of Staff, who went up to Ma'alot, informed the three Arabs accordingly.

She said the French Ambassador (Jean Herly) got his government's permission to negotiate with the terrorists but they refused to talk to him, till he had the code password due to be sent to him and which he had not yet received.

She said that the two ambassadors on the spot, as well as the terrorists, had been told that the 20 terrorists had been assembled and would be ready to depart. The number was meanwhile increased from 20 to 23.

Mrs. Meir said that the Rumanian ambassador reported before 3 p.m. getting a message from Bucharest that the representative of the Hawatmeh group in Bucharest told his government that he would be the only ambassador with whom the terrorists would negotiate.

If Israel promised to release the terrorists from prison, the ambassador would get a code and a password from Bucharest, she said. But he had not got it by five o'clock.

At five the Rumanian ambassador arrived with the conditions of the terrorists, stipulating that the prisoners would have to be flown to Damascus or Nicosia. After they got there the Rumanian ambassador would receive a code acknowledgement. Then they would agree to free half the children, she said. The other half would have to be flown, together with the three terrorists, to some Arab country.

"The school was due to be blown up at six, and we knew we would not have enough time." She said that even if Israel had accepted the conditions it would have been physically impossible to effect all the transfers, and get the code confirmation back by six o'clock.

She agreed that certain aspects of security vigilance would have to be probed.

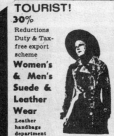

The nation and Government of Israel are outraged and grief-stricken at the shedding of the innocent blood of small children, pupils and adults at Ma'alot yesterday.

The Government of Israel mourns with the families whose loved ones fell at the hands of the inhuman terrorist murderers.

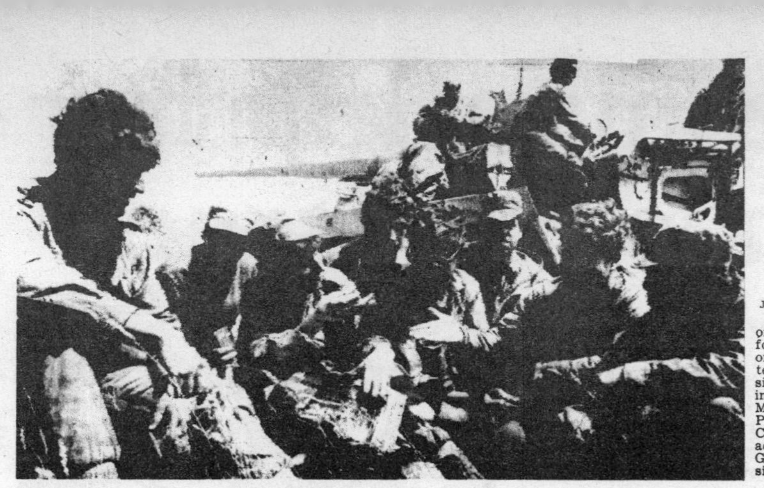

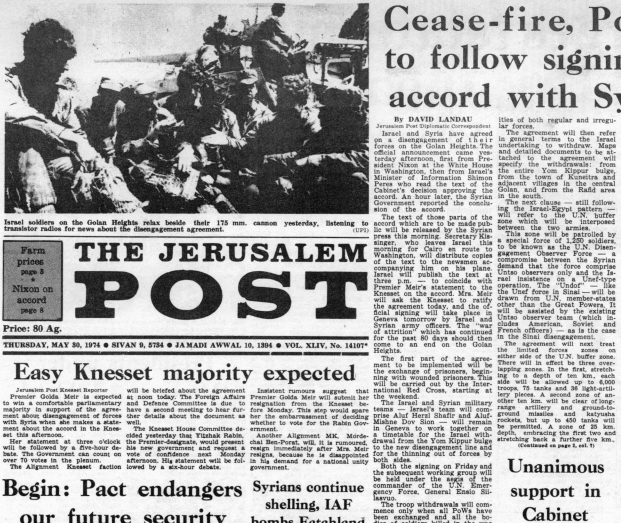

Israel soldiers on the Golan Heights relax beside their 175 mm. cannon yesterday, listening to transistor radios for news about the disengagement agreement. (UPI)

Farm prices page 3 * Nixon on accord page 8

THE JERUSALEM POST

Price: 80 Ag.

THURSDAY, MAY 30, 1974 ● SIVAN 9, 5734 ● JAMADI AWWAL 10, 1394 ● VOL. XLIV, No. 14107*

Cease-fire, PoW exchange to follow signing of pull-back accord with Syria tomorrow

By DAVID LANDAU
Jerusalem Post Diplomatic Correspondent

Israel and Syria have agreed on a disengagement of their forces on the Golan Heights. The official announcement came yesterday afternoon, first from President Nixon at the White House in Washington, then from Israel's Minister of Information Shimon Peres who read the text of the Cabinet's decision approving the accord. An hour later, the Syrian Government reported the conclusion of the accord.

The text of those parts of the accord which are to be made public will be released by the Syrian press this morning. Secretary Kissinger, who leaves Israel this morning for Cairo en route to Washington, will distribute copies of the text to the newsmen accompanying him on his plane. Israel will publish the text at three p.m. — to coincide with Premier Meir's statement to the Knesset on the accord. Mrs. Meir will ask the Knesset to ratify the agreement today, and the official signing will take place in Geneva tomorrow by Israel and Syrian army officers. The "war of attrition" which has continued for the past 80 days should then come to an end on the Golan Heights.

The first part of the agreement to be implemented will be the exchange of prisoners, beginning with wounded prisoners. This will be carried out by the International Red Cross, starting at the weekend.

The Israel and Syrian military teams — Israel's team will comprise Aluf Herzl Shafir and Aluf-Mishne Dov Sion — will remain in Geneva to work together on a timetable for the Israel withdrawal from the Yom Kippur bulge to the new disengagement line and for the thinning out of forces by both sides.

Both the signing on Friday and the subsequent working group will be held under the aegis of the commander of the U.N. Emergency Force, General Ensio Siilasvuo.

The troop withdrawals will commence only when all PoWs have been exchanged and all the bodies of soldiers killed in the war repatriated. The disengagement is expected to be completed within a month. Both U.S. and Israel officials indicated yesterday that, assuming the disengagement proceeds smoothly, they expect another session of the Geneva Conference to commence in July or the early autumn, with further Israel-Egypt talks probably the next item on the agenda.

The disengagement agreement contains a number of secret protocols which are designed to ensure that the accord is not destroyed by the actions of irregular ex-Palestinian forces. The nature of these is expected to leak out over the course of next week: all sides were anxious yesterday that they not be made public immediately.

The published accord to be signed tomorrow will open with an undertaking by both sides to cease all "hostile acts." This follows the pattern of the Israel-Egypt disengagement accord of last January, although there will be no express definition of "hostile acts" as embracing the activities of both regular and irregular forces.

The agreement will then refer in general terms to the Israel undertaking to withdraw. Maps and detailed documents to be attached to the agreement will specify the withdrawals: from the entire Yom Kippur bulge, from the town of Kuneitra and adjacent villages in the central Golan, and from the Rafid area in the south.

The next clause — still following the Israel-Egypt pattern — will refer to the U.N. buffer zone which will be interposed between the two armies.

This zone will be patrolled by a special force of 1,250 soldiers, to be known as the U.N. Disengagement Observer Force — a compromise between the Syrian demand that the force comprise Untso observers only and the Israel insistence on a Unef-type operation. The "Undof" — like the Unef force in Sinai — will be drawn from U.N. member-states other than the Great Powers. It will be assisted by the existing Untso observer team (which includes American, Soviet and French officers) — as is the case in the Sinai disengagement.

The agreement will next treat the limited forces zones on either side of the U.N. buffer zone. There will in effect be three overlapping zones. In the first, stretching to a depth of ten km., each side will be allowed up to 6,000 troops, 75 tanks and 36 light-artillery pieces. A second zone of another ten km. will be clear of long-range artillery and ground-to-ground missiles and katyusha rockets, but up to 450 tanks will be permitted. A zone of 25 km. depth, embracing the first two and stretching back a further five km.,

(Continued on page 2, col. 7)

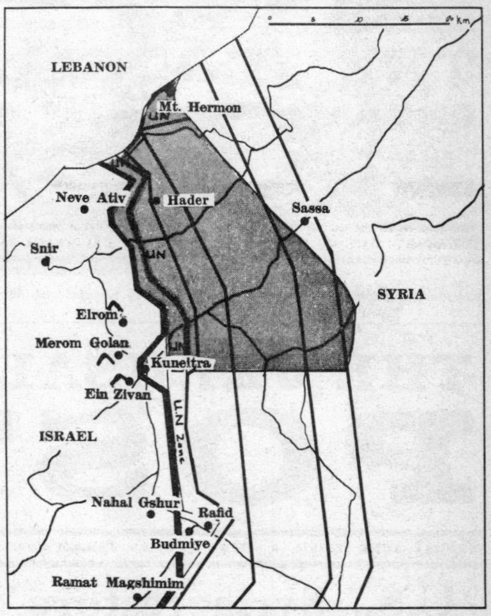

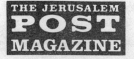

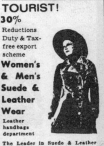

Map shows approximate disengagement lines according to the separation of forces agreement between Israel and Syria. The only changes in the 1967 cease-fire lines are in the Kuneitra and Rafid areas, where the town of Kuneitra and a number of villages, and Rafid and Budmiye, will be included in the U.N. controlled buffer zone. The three strategic hills west of Kuneitra, indicated by angular signs, remain in the Israel-held part of the Golan Heights. The U.N. buffer zone will be about 5-6 kms. wide in the bulge that was taken by Israel during the October war, but will narrow to about two kms. in the southern sector of the Golan Heights, where it will run parallel to the no-man's land between the 1967 cease-fire lines.

The first line to the left on the map marks the western border of the U.N. buffer zone and is known as the "blue" line. The second line from the left marks the eastern border of the U.N. buffer zone and is known as the "red" line. The third line from the left marks the 10-km. thinned-out forces zone. The fourth line from the left marks the 20-km. wide zone where neither side can keep any heavy artillery; and the fifth line from the left marks the 25-km. zone which has to be clear of Sam anti-aircraft missiles. Parallel lines will be drawn on the Israel side of the U.N. buffer zone.

The peak of the Hermon and the two Syrian positions on the Hermon that were taken by Israel in the October war will be handed over to U.N. control.

Easy Knesset majority expected

Jerusalem Post Knesset Reporter

Premier Golda Meir is expected to win a comfortable parliamentary majority in support of the agreement about disengagement of forces with Syria when she makes a statement about the accord in the Knesset this afternoon.

Her statement at three o'clock will be followed by a five-hour debate. The Government can count on over 70 votes in the plenum.

The Alignment Knesset faction will be briefed about the agreement at noon today. The Foreign Affairs and Defence Committee is due to have a second meeting to hear further details about the document as well.

The Knesset House Committee decided yesterday that Yitzhak Rabin, the Premier-designate, would present his new government and request a vote of confidence next Monday afternoon. His statement will be followed by a six-hour debate.

Insistent rumours suggest that Premier Golda Meir will submit her resignation from the Knesset before Monday. This step would spare her the embarrassment of deciding whether to vote for the Rabin Government.

Another Alignment MK, Mordechai Ben-Porat, will, it is rumoured, resign immediately after Mrs. Meir resigns, because he is disappointed in his demand for a national unity government.

Begin: Pact endangers our future security

By ASHER WALLFISH
Jerusalem Post Knesset Correspondent

Likud leader Menahem Begin has sharply attacked the agreement about disengagement of forces with Syria, warning that it contained a serious threat to the country's future security.

Begin told *The Jerusalem Post* last night that the agreement was faulty because it put the line of separation of forces west of the 1967 cease-fire line on the Golan Heights, instead of inside the enclave.

The agreement did nothing to ease the plight of the Jews of Syria, he charged. "They will be left in their ghettoes."

The Golan settlements, as well as the Israel units defending the Golan, will be within range of Syrian shelling. Begin said that thousands of terrorists would be coming into the evacuated areas along with the returning civilians, and these terrorists would have their hands free to strike against Israel without the agreement prohibiting them.

The return of civilians should have been limited too, he believed.

Disengagement brought no peace and promised no peace, he said.

The Syrian leaders had already hastened to repeat their demand — backed by the Soviet Union — for a total Israel evacuation of the Golan Heights. "This agreement offers us no protection because it is an arrangement whereby all Israel does is give, and all Syria does is take. We shall vote against it," Begin said.

The Likud discussed disengagement at a faction caucus last night but decided not to issue a statement in writing until a second caucus today.

Some elements in the Likud have suggested that the 39-man bloc should present its own resolution condemning the agreement at today's Knesset session, but should not vote against the Government resolution — abstaining instead. This will be settled today, as a tactical decision.

Shmuel Tamir, of the Likud's Free Centre wing, criticised the agreement still more vocally last night over Israel TV. He wrote Yitzhak Navon, chairman of the Knesset Foreign Affairs and Defence Committee, explaining that he was boycotting the Committee sessions on disengagement because the Government had kept the Committee in the dark for a whole week.

Most of the NRP faction in the Knesset will vote for the separation of forces agreement in the North, according to an explicit faction decision, but two or three of its 10 members will apparently be allowed to abstain when the Knesset debates the agreement this afternoon.

The NRP Ministers will vote for the agreement. The abstainers will be chosen to include representatives of the farming groups — and perhaps the Young Guard, according to reliable NRP sources. Nobody in the NRP will vote against.

One Young Guard leader told *The Jerusalem Post* that, by and large, everyone in the NRP took a positive view of disengagement in principle, while those who were dissatisfied were merely querying some of the details.

A statement issued by the five-member Aguda bloc yesterday said most of the faction supported the disengagement agreement. However, it had been decided to allow a free vote when the agreement comes before the Knesset.

Syrians continue shelling, IAF bombs Fatahland

Jerusalem Post Military Correspondent

The Syrian forces yesterday continued their assault on the Israel line despite the imminence of the disengagement agreement. There were no Israel casualties, according to an announcement from the Army Spokesman.

Also yesterday Israel Air Force planes bombed two terrorist concentrations in southern Lebanon for half an hour. Among the targets were bases at Ein Ata and Hatzbaya, in Fatahland.

Fighting along the northern front started before eight o'clock, with a Syrian bombardment of the Hermon. The region hardest hit was the central sector of the cease-fire lines. Fire was returned. During the morning the Syrians also used tanks against forward Israel positions along the southern sector of the pre-October cease-fire lines.

Artillery clashes continued intermittently until the early evening.

Bank Leumi floats IL 120m. in notes

Jerusalem Post Reporter

TEL AVIV. — Bank Leumi yesterday announced that it is floating a IL120m. mission of capital notes — which can be converted to Ordinary A shares. This is the largest capital emission ever floated in the country.

Of the IL120m., IL90m. is available to the general public, with IL30m. reserved for institutional investors. The subscription list will open next Thursday and close at midday the following day.

The capital notes bear 10 per cent interest: but if the purchaser decides not to convert them into shares, he will receive an additional six per cent interest, for a total of 16 per cent. The additional six per cent will be paid on July 1, 1977.

After this emission is taken up, the capital resources of Bank Leumi group will reach IL760m.

Unanimous support in Cabinet

Jerusalem Post Staff

The Cabinet last night unanimously approved the disengagement agreement with Syria and will bring it before the Knesset today for ratification, an official communique said.

The Cabinet statement expressed the Government's hope that "this agreement will constitute a further step towards pacifying the Middle East, channelling the national energy of all peoples of the region, to the benefit of its populations and promoting its economic, political and social progress.

"The Government of Israel expresses it deep appreciation to the U.S. Secretary of State," the statement went on, "for the great efforts he invested in securing the agreement, and thanks the President of the U.S. for his encouraging and positive stand."

Information Minister Shimon Peres said last night over Israel radio and television that "the agreement with Syria is a positive achievement, and we signed it in accordance with Israel's own interests and not by way of a capitulation to, or as a result of pressure from, any foreign interest."

Mr. Peres said the agreement would do much to calm down passions in the Middle East. "It augments the agreement with Egypt and establishes a precedent with Syria," he said.

The disengagement agreement has three important advantages for Israel, Mr. Peres noted: "For the first time Israeli-Syrian relations are based not on a transient cease-fire or a temporary cease-fire, but on demilitarized zones, a thinning-out of forces and on the actual existence of a treaty; secondly, in the sphere of Israel-U.S. relations, the agreement represents the further strengthening of a relationship that is very important to our country; and thirdly, the general picture in the Middle East as a whole after the agreement seems more conducive to peace and more in keeping with Israel's interests."

As for the Israel settlements in the area of disengagement, the Information Minister said that "we have been faithful to our basic stand — that is, not a single settlement has been affected, certainly not the settlement itself, and only in very few cases, have a few hundred dunams of agricultural land been affected.

Damascus delays report

By ANAN SAFADI
Jerusalem Post Arab Affairs Reporter

A cease-fire between Syria and Israel was expected to go into effect shortly after the two sides sign the disengagement agreement in Geneva tomorrow, Syrian Government sources said in Damascus last night.

Until a late hour last night the Syrians had not issued an official statement on the disengagement accord though their media reported President Nixon's announcement on the conclusion of the agreement.

President Assad yesterday summoned the Syrian National Front embracing the various political parties governing Syria with the ruling Ba'th party. He briefed them on details of the disengagement agreement. The details were to be published in the Damascus press today.

The conclusion of the agreement was reported by almost all Arab capitals.

The Cairo-based terrorist radio ignored the event, indicating its dissatisfaction with the agreement. Terrorist leaders have been expressing fears that the accord, which follows that between Egypt and Israel, would leave them out in the cold, struggling for their existence in Lebanon.

Meanwhile, the Palestinian National Council (parliament-in-exile) has been summoned for an extraordinary meeting in Cairo on Saturday to discuss the situation stemming from the Golan agreement. Despite terrorist voices opposing Middle East political settlements, a number of Palestinian leaders have urged jumping on the Egyptian and Syrian bandwagon and want to join the Geneva talks — mainly to contest Jordan's claim over the West Bank and wreck Amman's hopes for a political linkage with the Gaza Strip.

In Amman, government circles last night said that they hoped the Golan accord would pave the way for disengagement between Jordan and Israel in a prelude to a West Bank settlement. The Jordanians recalled that their future moves for a political settlement with Israel would depend on the attitude of Arab governments towards Amman's claim to the West Bank.

Soviets, Syria see pact as start to full withdrawal

DAMASCUS (UPI). — The Soviet Union and Syria said last night that the Syrian-Israel troop disengagement must be followed immediately by steps to get an Israel withdrawal from all "occupied Arab territory."

The call came in a joint communique issued at the end of Soviet Foreign Minister Andrei A. Gromyko's two-day visit to Damascus.

The communique described the troop disengagement agreement as "a first step and indivisible part of an overall settlement."

"A just settlement of the Middle East conflict cannot be achieved except on the basis of a complete Israel withdrawal from all occupied Arab lands and the safeguarding of the national rights of the Palestinian people," the joint communique said.

The communique also said Syria "reiterated its stand that the Soviet Union should participate in all phases of a settlement so as to establish a just and lasting settlement in the Middle East."

As Gromyko left for Moscow less than three hours before the announcement of the disengagement agreement, he said that in his talks with Syrian leaders, he had "exchanged views on the question of military disengagement. Contacts between the Soviet Union and Syria on this subject are of long standing, and we can say we share the same stand on the question," Gromyko said.

Egyptians say accord will lead to further withdrawal in Sinai

CAIRO (UPI). — The Israel-Syria military disengagement agreement clears the way for resumption of the Arab-Israel peace conference in Geneva with Syrian participation, government officials said yesterday.

It also opens up the possibility of negotiations on a further stage of Israel withdrawal on the Egyptian front in the Sinai peninsula, they said.

The agreement "boils down to another unilateral Israel pullback from some occupied Arab land and is, therefore, a gain and an added strength to the Arabs," one official said.

"But it is only a first step," he added. "It is, nonetheless, a major step that leads to Geneva."

The Geneva peace conference held its first round last December under U.N. auspices, with the U.S. and the Soviet Union acting as co-chairmen.

Egypt, Jordan and Israel attended; Syria boycotted the session saying it feared the conference would "lead us away from the path of drawing up a programme for a full withdrawal from the territories occupied in 1967."

The Egyptian official said that, with a disengagement agreement restoring to Syria all the land the Israelis seized in the Yom Kippur War, and a slice of the territory conquered in 1967 as a step towards a settlement, Syria now can be expected to join the Geneva talks.

Waldheim here next Wednesday

UNITED NATIONS (UPI). — An official U.N. spokesman said yesterday that Secretary General Kurt Waldheim would leave for Beirut next Sunday, and proceed from there to Damascus on Tuesday.

The following day he will probably visit Israel and from there to Jordan and Egypt.

8 killed in road accidents

Double hit-run driver kills three

Jerusalem Post Staff

Eight persons were killed and 11 seriously injured in road accidents over the last two days.

Three young persons were killed and five injured in two hit-and-run accidents involving the same car allegedly driven by a Nazareth man on the Haifa-Nazareth road on Tuesday night. The man was driving near Tel Hanan close to 2 o'clock, when he hit Moshe Ben Shalom Menahem, 17, killing him. He drove on, and in trying to overtake another car, collided head on with a commercial van driven by Yigal Amir, 24, of Kibbutz Ein Dor. Two women in Amir's car were killed: Galia Limor 22, of Merhavia and another woman whose name is being withheld for family reasons.

Seriously injured were Moshe Duvdevani, 40, his wife Pirha, 38, and their son Dani, 15, all of Ein Dor. The hit-and-run driver was also injured. Two men riding with him were unharmed. The driver, who was detained, is suspected of having taken the car without permission from a Haifa carpentry shop.

An elderly rabbi and three young people were killed and two persons injured late on Tuesday night when a car carrying Kfar Habad residents home from a wedding in Jerusalem suddenly swerved off the road near Shaar Hagai and overturned. Those killed were Rabbi Zalman Gorelik Shneor, 95, the rabbi of Kfar Habad and a Habad leader in Israel, Yehiel Goldberg, 23, Nehama Rozenberg, 19, and Yeshayahu Weiss, 34. Rabbi Melah Kaplan, 64, the rabbi of the Habad quarter in Lod, was seriously injured, and Yaacov Ofen, 20, of Ramat Gan, slightly injured. Both were yesterday discharged from hospital.

Rabbi Gorelik and the others killed with him were buried in Jerusalem yesterday.

Tzila Visoker, 51, of Beersheba, was killed and her husband Reuven seriously injured on Tuesday night when their car, which Mr. Visoker was driving hit a trailer-truck parked by the side of the Beersheba-Bet Kama road. The driver of the truck, Meir Damoul, was detained but released yesterday on IL5,000 bail by the Beersheba Magistrates.

A triple accident took place at the Nir Am crossroads near Ashkelon close to noon yesterday, seriously injuring four persons. Moshe Ran, 40, was injured in the head and taken to Tel Hashomer hospital in critical condition. The accident occurred when a pickup truck driven towards Sderot by Nadav Antikovsky, 34, of Kfar Menahem, collided with a car driven by Yaacov Adari, 21. Both vehicles crashed into a car parked at the crossroads, driven by Levi Shukri, 27, of Moshav Rehava. Antikovsky and Adari were injured, as was a passenger in the pickup truck, Ido Rosner, 58. The injured were taken to Ashkelon hospital.

A seven-year-old boy, Issa Tamim, of D'haishi refugee camp near Bethlehem, was seriously injured when he was hit by a car yesterday. The driver, Albert Buchwalter, was detained.

Pat Nixon looks forward to M.E. trip

WASHINGTON (UPI). — U.S. first lady Pat Nixon said yesterday she was looking forward to travelling to the Middle East with her husband next month.

As to the Syrian-Israel troop disengagement, she told reporters, "I've been praying for it for a long time. My prayers have been answered. It's such good news."

The President's wife discussed the forthcoming Middle East trip briefly with reporters after greeting 200 guests, representing eight international clubs from the Washington area, mostly diplomatic wives.

Mrs. Nixon said that she last visited Egypt in 1963 when her husband was out of office.

WOLF BLITZER, writing from Washington, examines the extent to which Dr. Kissinger's latest negotiating effort in the Middle East is dictated by President Nixon's need for a diplomatic success to offset his Watergate problems.

MICHAEL CHECHINSKI quotes chapter and verse to support his argument that the Soviet leadership views the existence of the State of Israel as incompatible with its interests.

YITZHAK DINUR, in a prizewinning essay, shows how Israel could use solar energy to replace the more conventional sources of power.

ZE'EV SCHUL takes a trip to Malawi and discovers the attractions for his compatriots of the only country in Africa that still maintains openly friendly relations with Israel.

In the Book Section, **DAN VOGEL** relates a free-verse cantata by Elie Wiesel to some recent studies of the Book of Job.

MENDEL KOHANSKY takes a look at the commercial theatre in Israel.

YOHANAN BOEHM talks to violinist Zvi Zeitlin.

IN THIS FRIDAY'S

THE JERUSALEM POST MAGAZINE

Nixon urges 'statesmanship for peace' by Israel

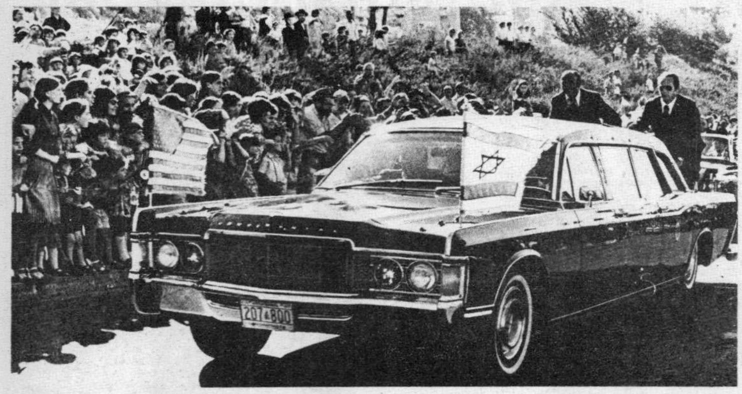

Presidential limousine driving through Jerusalem's streets with security agents perched at the back. (Rahamim Israeli)

THE JERUSALEM POST

SECOND EDITION

Price: 80 Ag.

MONDAY, JUNE 17, 1974 • SIVAN 27, 5734 • JAMADI AWWAL 28, 1394 • VOL. XLIV, No. 14122*

Atom pact seen announced today

By ASHER WALLFISH and DAVID LANDAU

U.S. President Richard Nixon last night called upon the leaders of Israel to choose the "right way" of statesmanship and recognise that "continuous war is not a solution for Israel's survival."

Mr. Nixon was replying to a toast by Prof. Ephraim Katzir at a state banquet given in his honour by the Israeli President at the Knesset's Chagall Hall.

The alternative was politically easier, said Mr. Nixon — adhering to the status quo and resisting initiatives. But initiatives might lead to negotiation.

He said the United States had been honoured to support Israel.

In his speech at the state dinner last night, the President assured Israel that the U.S. effort to seek "better relations" with the Arab states would "not mean" that American friendship and support for Israel would be "any less."

"We hope and trust that the great creative ability in this room will be used for works of peace in the same dedication as has been shown wherever war was concerned. I am confident that together we can find a way in this difficult area of the world," he said.

The way to build a permanent, just and durable Middle East would be more difficult than the U.S. opening to China, more difficult than ending the Vietnam war, and more difficult than continuing the dialogue between the two superpowers, he said.

"Here, where civilization began, we have the greatest challenge and the greatest opportunity to make sure that civilization continues. This is the cradle of civilization. We must make sure that it does not become its grave," he said. "Peace for Israel, peace for the Middle East, will mean that the whole world has a better chance for peace."

Mr. Nixon spoke after President Katzir reiterated sentiments of gratitude and appreciation expressed earlier in the day at B-G Airport.

The American President's support "contributed greatly to the strength of Israel to defend herself through her own efforts," said Prof. Katzir. He added: "A strong Israel is in itself a component of the peace and stability in our area to which your mission is dedicated." (Extracts from Katzir speech, Page 2.)

President Nixon sought yesterday to allay Israel's anxieties over the U.S.-Egypt nuclear cooperation agreement. In a first 90-minute working session shortly after his arrival with Premier Rabin, Defence Minister Peres and Foreign Minister Allon, the President explained the agreement with Egypt in the context of America's plans to promote economic development in the Middle East.

A start was also made at this session on a broad review of Israel's requests for long-term military and economic aid programmes — and this review will be concluded today, with Finance Minister Yehoshua Rabinowitz and Chief of Staff Mordechai Gur joining the Israeli side to contribute their detailed expertise.

Israel is hoping that the President will today approve multi-annual U.S. military and economic commitments to Israel — and that these commitments will find expression in the joint communique to be published at the visit's end today.

The communique is also expected to announce an American undertaking to supply Israel too with a nuclear power station and the enriched uranium required to fuel it. Israel had been negotiating with the U.S. for some time to receive a plant of this kind, but had not known — as Foreign Minister Allon admitted on Saturday — that Egypt was conducting parallel negotiations, and had certainly not expected to obtain the power station as part of a U.S. package with Egypt.

Peace took courage and entailed risks just as war did, said Mr. Nixon. The entire human race might have paid a great price without a dialogue between the U.S. and the Soviet Union. But the alternative to dialogue was a return to the cold war. "It is in this spirit that we go to Moscow again soon," he said.

In Moscow, however, the dialogue between the two strongest nations in the world would be continued "recognising that under no circumstances would there be negotiation at the expense of any other nation, large or small."

The U.S. did not consider it a simple task to bring an era of peace to the Middle East, nor was it certain the goal could be achieved. "But we do know we must try, that we must begin. There have been four wars in a little over a generation in this area. Unless we change the situation some way, somehow, there will be another war, terribly costly to the nations involved, and particularly to this nation, and also potentially very dangerous to the peace of the world."

"Under no circumstances does the fact that the U.S. is seeking better relations with some of Israel's neighbours mean the friendship of

(Continued on page 2, col. 5)

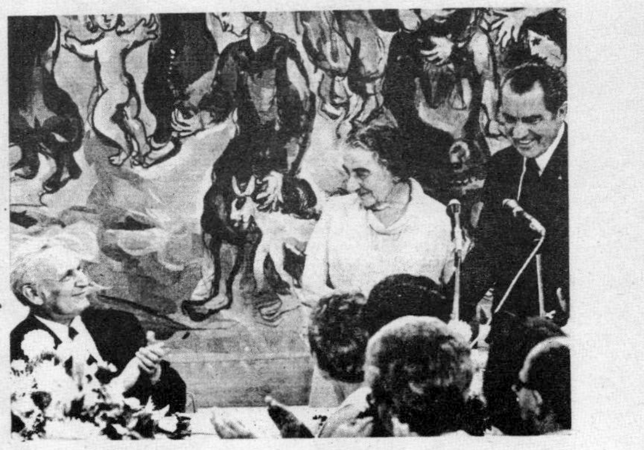

Mrs. Golda Meir thanks President Nixon for the special toast he raised in her honour at last night's State Banquet in the Knesset as President Katzir joins in the applause for her. The Chagall tapestry forms the backdrop to the dinner table. (Photo Emka)

Presidents under 'Moses and Tablets'

The Knesset banqueting hall was decorated lavishly with bouquets of flowers. The U.S. President and Mrs. Nixon sat at the long head table, with the President and Mrs. Katzir, seating 32 under the Chagall wall tapestry, where it displayed Moses holding the Tablets and King David, his harp. Other guests at the dinner sat at 36 smaller tables, each seating eight persons.

The President and Mrs. Nixon received the guests as they entered the banqueting hall—and exchanged greetings as they shook hands. Among those attending the glittering event were the Premiers and members of the present and previous governments, Members of Knesset, the Chief of Staff, the Chief Rabbis, members of the Supreme Court, the Mayor of Jerusalem, Diplomatic Corps, heads of national institutions, Moslem and Christian dignitaries, newspaper editors, and other civic leaders.

Entertainment was provided by the Bat-Sheva dance company, one of the world's great modern dance troupes founded nine years ago by Baroness Bathsheba de Rothschild with the artistic patronage of Martha Graham, and Israel's Kibbutz Choir.

The choir, made up of 70 men and women from kibbutzim, presented a carefully balanced programme beginning with Rossi's "Blessed be he who cometh in the name of the Lord" (words from Psalms, 118) continuing with a touch of local folklore in the "Sovevuni" hora, and concluding with, "There's a boat dat's leavin" from Gershwin's "Porgy and Bess."

The menu was:

Chilled Haogen melon; Dan river trout; Roast beef; Vegetable garni; chocolate mousse; coffee; petit fours.

Wines: White Avdat, Cabernet, President's Wine.

As it turned out, the local as well as the foreign press corps was effectively neutralized, from two-and-a-half hours before the banquet began.

The Foreign Ministry, which was in charge of press invitations, invited them all to the Knesset building to watch the banquet over closed circuit television, from a section of the Members dining room.

However, they were unable to get to a telephone, or a writing table, so that if any of the addresses at the banquet had departed from protocol, or anything untoward had happened, they would have been unable to report it.

Israeli officials noted with satisfaction the President's evident delight at the enthusiastic reception accorded him by the citizens of Jerusalem yesterday. The crowds who filled the capital's streets on his arrival — and who prompted him to stand spontaneously in his car to wave and smile — set a warm and relaxed tone for the afternoon and evening's events.

U.S., Syria restore diplomatic relations

DAMASCUS. — The hoisting of Syria's national flag in Washington and America's flag in Damascus will take place simultaneously today following the restoration of full diplomatic relations between the two countries yesterday.

A spokesman for the U.S. Embassy here said the American charge d'affaires would be hoisting the American flag over the Embassy after the Italian flag had been taken down following yesterday's announcement which ended a seven-year diplomatic break.

Italy has been looking after American interests in Syria, while Pakistan looked after Syrian interests in the U.S. since diplomatic relations were severed during the 1967 Middle East war.

The Syrian and American relations, broken because of U.S. aid to Israel, will be resumed at ambassadorial level, with ambassadors expected to be named within two weeks.

The announcement of resumption of relations ended President Nixon's 22-hour visit to Syria where he heard appeals for both U.S. economic aid and investment and for American help in persuading Israel to vacate the Golan Heights.

"President Nixon and I have agreed to consolidate dialogue and cooperation between our two countries for achieving a just and lasting peace," President Hafez Assad said outside his presidential palace as Nixon beamed.

Assad will visit America "soon" Nixon said, and the U.S. will take part in the Damascus trade fair next month. An unnamed "senior Syrian official" will visit Washington in the coming weeks, Nixon said.

A 21-gun salute greeted Nixon's arrival at the airport for his departure flight and he and Assad reviewed an honour guard. Also on the tarmac was a lineup of 1,500 teenage girls of the People's Militia who greeted Nixon on his arrival.

Nixon and Assad embraced each other before the President and his wife boarded the plane. Secretary of State Henry A. Kissinger, who visited Damascus 13 times during his successful mediation of Syrian-Israeli troop disengagement last month, also exchanged hugs with Syrian Government officials. *(Reuter, UPI)*

Our Arab Affairs Reporter adds: Reporting the departure of Nixon, Radio Damascus didn't mention Israel as the next stop of the American President in his Middle East tour. Radio Cairo and Amman reported almost fully the Nixon visit to Israel but neglected to mention Jerusalem as the site of the talks.

Nixon coverage

Visit to Yad Vashem

The U.S. President's day begins this morning with a visit to the Yad Vashem Holocaust Memorial Institute.

This visit is listed as private, without any press coverage — on the insistence of American security men. But last night the newsmen accompanying the President were appealing the privacy ruling

Presidential spokesman Ziegler has been heard remarking that security is too tight in Israel. Yesterday, the President was to have been welcomed at the entrance to Jerusalem by civic and religious dignitaries in a colourful ceremony — but this too was cancelled on security grounds.

Some observers here have suggested that the real grounds for this cancellation were political, with the President unwilling to be greeted in Jewish Jerusalem by Moslem religious dignitaries from East Jerusalem. Mr. Nixon is restricting himself to the western part of the Capital during his 24-hour stay, forbearing to visit the Holy Places in East Jerusalem — apparently also because of the political overtones which such a visit would carry.

Fahmy warns: Egypt would make A-bomb

CAIRO (UPI). — Foreign Minister Ismail Fahmy said yesterday nuclear cooperation between Egypt and the U.S. will serve merely peaceful purposes. But he warned Egypt would manufacture, or acquire, atomic arms if Israel did the same.

Addressing a news conference, Fahmy charged American Zionist circles of attempting to sabotage the recent Arab-American rapprochement.

"The Egyptian-American cooperation in the field of nuclear energy will serve peaceful purposes only," Fahmy said. He asserted Israel's failure so far to sign the nuclear non-proliferation treaty means that it is "planning to manufacture nuclear weapons.

"Although Egypt had signed the agreement, if Israel acquired or exploded a nuclear weapon, Egypt would be duty bound, in order not to expose its national security to danger, to manufacture or obtain a nuclear weapon," he said.

"Israel would be responsible then for introducing nuclear weapons to the region," he said.

He accused U.S. Zionist circles and "circles known for their total bias to Israel" of launching a "ferocious campaign" to prevent the improvement of relations between the U.S. and the Arab world, particularly Egypt.

Fahmy said the nuclear know-how which the U.S. will supply to Egypt "cannot be used for military purposes."

Nixon came via Jordan

The U.S. presidential plane yesterday crossed from the Syrian border into Jordan, and flew over Amman. It then turned west and entered Israeli air space via the West Bank. The plane cruised at 18,000 feet, averaging a speed of 450 mph.

This is the first time since 1947 that a flight from Syria to Israel has taken the inland route via Jordan rather than flying over Lebanon and out to sea, approaching Israel from the Mediterranean.

100,000 Jerusalemites cheer

By ABRAHAM RABINOVICH
Jerusalem Post Reporter

A sea of flags and cheering crowds greeted President Nixon upon his arrival in Jerusalem yesterday afternoon.

An estimated 100,000 persons — a third of the city's population — lined the seven-kilometre route from the city entrance to the King David Hotel. Although far from the welcome extended Mr. Nixon by two million Cairo residents last week, Jerusalem's reception was warm and *heimisch*. School children mostly dressed in blue and white, waved American and Israeli flags along the length of the route and cheered the presidential convoy, some of them chanting "Nixon, Nixon" and others singing.

"He helped us in the war when we needed him," said a sixth-grade boy from the Agron School, who was asked why he was cheering.

Adults along the route also appeared good humoured and many of them held up hand-made signs. These ranged from the hospitable ("Welcome to Jerusalem") to the affectionate ("Good Old Nixon") to the political ("Palestine is the Land of Israel"). The only visible reference to Mr. Nixon's domestic troubles was a sign held up by a smiling woman on Jabotinsky which read "Don't make us victims of Watergate." A placard which may have been worded less delicately was seen being held in tatters by a soldier on Herzl Boulevard. He was arguing with an American-looking youth.

Concern over the American agreement to furnish Egypt with a nuclear reactor was reflected in a Hebrew sign held up by two youths in the Valley of the Cross — "Nixon sells nuclear know-how to the Arabs and seeds to us." (In Hebrew, the words for nuclear and seed are identical.)

Onlookers along the first two-thirds of the route were disappointed at seeing the President sitting inside an enclosed vehicle which sped by at up to 60 k.p.h. Their disappointment was deepened by the knowledge that he had travelled in an open car with President Sadat. Opposite 40 Palmach Street, however, the presidential limousine stopped, its roof slid open and Presidents Nixon and Katzir stood as the procession continued.

Less than an hour before Mr. Nixon was due to arrive in the capital, the route to the hotel, which had been staked and roped to hold back the crowds, was empty except for some contingents of youngsters. "This is no joke," said a local journalist during a police press tour of the route. "If nobody shows up he won't give us a nuclear reactor." But as the radio reported that the President had left Ben-Gurion Airport and was speeding up to the capital, tens of thousands of people began to stream down to the route and to appear on balconies along the way. Along Tchernikowsky and Palmach, 500 American flags distributed by the Municipality the evening before were hung out on balconies by residents.

Chief Rabbi Ovadia Yosef issued a ruling last week that the blessing traditionally prounounced by observant Jews upon seeing kings applied to President Nixon in view of his far-reaching powers even though he was not a monarch. The blessing — "Blessed be He who shares his honour with blood and flesh" — presumably was uttered by some of the many Orthodox residents of the Givat Shaul quarter lining the entrance to the city.

The Jerusalem Municipality Youth Band at the entrance to town had a not dissimilar way of greeting the President — a rendition of "When the Saints Come Marching In."

Tight security precautions became evident by late morning when paratrooper detachments began to take up positions along the route. Jerusalem Police Chief Heinz Brietenfeld said last night that 2,000 police and soldiers were involved in keeping order in the capital. Every building along the route was searched and paratroopers could be seen on rooftops, some of them with their feet dangling over the edge as they watched the procession.

Police arrested two American youths for attempting to break through onto the procession route as the President approached near the Hebrew University and another two — an American and a Dutch youth — for attempting to demonstrate near the King David Hotel.

Many of the city's main roads were closed at 1.45 p.m. — two and a quarter hours before the President's arrival — and remained closed until midnight, causing extensive snarls. The same streets will be closed today from 8.45 a.m. until 4 p.m. These include Ruppin, Ben-Zvi, Tchernikowsky, Hapalmach, Jabotinsky, Keren Hayesod, Aza, Balfour and Ben-Maimon. Herzl will be closed for most of this time. The best way to get from north to south will be via Jaffa Gate and Hebron Road.

'What a beautiful house!'

Jerusalem Post Reporter

"Oh, what a beautiful house," Pat Nixon exclaimed on entering the presidential residence together with President Nixon, accompanied by Secretary of State Henry Kissinger and the American Ambassador to Israel and Mrs. Kenneth Keating.

In the reception hall President Katzir and his wife Nina had already been waiting for 15 minutes and extended a warm welcome. With them were Prime Minister and Mrs. Yitzhak Rabin, Israel's Ambassador to the U.S. and Mrs. Simha Dinitz, Gideon Shomron, director of the President's bureau, Chief of Protocol Avigdor Shoham, and the President's aide-de-camp, S/A Israel Yarkoni.

All the ladies wore afternoon dresses coming down to just below the knee: Mrs. Nixon — a red dress with pink-white-green fantasy flowers, Mrs. Katzir — a black dress with white jacket, Mrs. Rabin — a light blue dress, Mrs, Keating — a pink dress, and Mrs. Dinitz — a green dress.

The hosts sat down with their guests in a group of armchairs at the far end of the main hall, arranged in a half circle, with both Presidents in the middle. They conversed in low tones. No. details of the conversation were divulged to the press.

Orange juice was served, without any alcohol, as prescribed by the protocol people. The entire visit lasted exactly 15 minutes. At 6.30 p.m. the guests left Beit Hanassi, walking with their hosts along the red carpet under the concrete portico which leads from the entrance portals to the driveway. In front of his specially-built black Lincoln Continental, President Nixon shook hands warmly with President Katzir, waved to the host of photographers, newsmen and security men, and entered his car.

Mr. Nixon looked relaxed. As the American and Israeli security men jumped into their moving cars, the Presidential convoy briskly left the courtyard fo Beit Hanassi and headed for its next destination, the residence of Golda Meir.

Kissinger told to see Palestinians, report says

By VICTOR S. NAHMIAS
Jerusalem Post Arab Affairs Reporter

The Lebanese newspaper "Al-Hayat" said yesterday that on instructions from President Nixon Secretary of State Henry Kissinger will soon get in touch with Palestinian leaders. In a dispatch from its correspondent in Jedda, "Al-Hayat" said this will be the most important result of the talks that Nixon had with King Faisal of Saudi Arabia, since it appears that the Monarch succeeded in convincing the President of the necessity of this step.

The deputy Prime Minister of Saudi Arabia, Prince Fahd, who visited the U.S. recently, said in an interview with the Beirut weekly "Al-Hawades" that Kissinger had shown "complete understanding" concerning the rights of the Palestinian people.

Recently all news, mostly from Beirut, about official American-Palestinian contacts had been flatly denied by American sources. Palestinian leader Yasser Arafat left Cairo during the Nixon visit and remained in neighbouring Libya.

DAYAN WARNS AGAINST U.S.-EGYPT A-ACCORD

B-G AIRPORT. — Former Defence Minister Moshe Dayan yesterday described the U.S.-Egyptian nuclear cooperation agreement as a "complete surprise" to him, and warned that if Egypt is able to exploit this for non-peaceful purposes in the future, Mr. Nixon's visit will go down as "a fatal and historic mistake."

Speaking to newsmen on his return from a fund-raising visit to the U.S., Mr. Dayan noted that the agreement was not wholly negative in that it would increase American influence in the Arab world.

But at the same time, he said, the mere fact that the agreement provides for U.S. supervision indicates that the nuclear energy produced by the proposed plant could be used to produce nuclear weapons.

Mr. Dayan also expressed his concern that the U.S. might not always be in a position to exercise its control over the use Egypt makes of the nuclear plant. He cited the example of India as a country that received foreign aid to produce nuclear energy for peaceful purposes and has now managed to produce its own atomic device. He also noted that Egypt has no shortage of energy sources in view of recent oil strikes and the vast hydro-electric potential of the Aswan Dam which has not yet been fully exploited.

Haifa Mayor Yosef Almogi has also expressed his apprehension about the agreement, and scored Foreign Minister Yigal Allon's muted reaction to this on Saturday as "the utmost folly."

Speaking at the reception given yesterday by the Haifa Municipality for Aluf Raphael Eitan, OC, Northern Command, Mr. Almogi said that he was particularly incensed at Allon's attempt to compare the U.S. nuclear cooperation agreement with Egypt with that between the U.S. and Israel.

"To compare us with them is ridiculous," he said, "we have never thought of destroying Egypt, but Egypt has wanted to annihilate us and a nuclear power plant could well lead to the production of nuclear weapons that will one day be used against Israel." *(Itim)*

(Related stories — Pages 2 and 5)

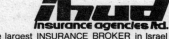

Nixon resigning today, Ford to be President immediately

WASHINGTON (AP). — Richard Nixon prepared to tell an expectant nation last night that he would resign as President. Word that the President had decided to leave office rather than undergo the trauma of impeachment came from sources in the White House and on Capitol Hill.

Amid an intensifying flurry of resignation reports, Mr. Nixon met for one hour and 10 minutes yesterday with Vice-President Gerald R. Ford who would become the 38th president of the U.S.

Shortly after Mr. Ford left the White House came an announcement that the President would address the nation on television and radio at 9 p.m. (4 a.m. Israel time).

Mr. Ford later summoned Secretary of State Henry Kissinger to a mid-afternoon meeting. Mr. Nixon also called Congressional leaders to the White House for an early evening meeting.

Congressional sources said the President's resignation — first in the 198-year history of the U.S. — would be effective at noon on Friday. Mr. Ford would become President immediately.

House Democratic Whip John McFall of California said he was told that Mr. Ford would take the oath of office this afternoon.

After his meeting with Mr. Nixon ended yesterday, Mr. Ford crossed the street to the Executive Office Building and conferred with his chief aide, Robert Hartman. A spokesman said he showed no strong emotion.

"He is a strong personality. He adjusts well to new situations," the aide said.

His presidency mortally wounded by the repeated blows of the Watergate disclosures, Mr. Nixon made his decision the same week he delivered the most devastating blow, the announcement on Monday that he had withheld damaging evidence from the prosecutors, Congress and his own lawyers.

A White House source said Dr. Kissinger was instrumental in persuading Mr. Nixon that the nation would be best served by his resignation. Dr. Kissinger and Mr. Nixon talked until nearly midnight Wednesday in the White House family quarters.

The source said Dr. Kissinger argued that the nation's foreign policy required that the uncertainty and the crisis of confidence plaguing the country come to an immediate end. Dr. Kissinger also went to the White House yesterday, but did not see Mr. Nixon.

As Secretary of State, Dr. Kissinger is the government official who would receive a formal letter of resignation.

As the Nixon presidency, launched with one of the most remarkable political comebacks in American history, ground to a close, Sen. Edward W. Brooke, Republican-Mass., introduced a resolution expressing the sense of Congress that Mr. Nixon should be immune from prosecution if he resigns.

One aide close to Mr. Nixon had suggested the chief executive would not resign until he had "all his ducks in a row" — an apparent reference to his intent to get his legal and financial affairs in order.

The official said Mr. Nixon's family — wife Pat and daughters Julie and Tricia — opposed resignation on grounds their husband and father was innocent of wrongdoing.

Speaking of the family, particularly the women, the aide said, "they just aren't looking at it realistically."

Among the three Nixon women, Julie Eisenhower was said to be especially adamant on the subject and wanted her father to fight even through a Senate impeachment trial.

By stepping down voluntarily, Mr. Nixon protects a lifetime presidential pension of $60,000 a year, $96,000 a year for office expenses, and an annual $20,000 pension for his wife, Pat, if she survives him.

But these funds could be jeopardised if Congressional leaders thought the President had not purged himself of taint in the Watergate scandal.

Thus as Senator Brooke introduced his resolution that Mr. Nixon should be immune from prosecution if he resigns, Democratic Senator Frank E. Moss of Utah said Congress should consider continuing impeachment proceedings against Nixon if he resigns without acknowledging guilt.

"If the President resigns still protesting his innocence, leaving the impression that he was forced out of office, then I think that Congress should consider going forward with the full proceedings," said Moss, Secretary of the Senate Democratic conference.

"We all feel that whatever abuses of power were committed ought somehow to be laid out on the public record," added assistant Senate Democratic Leader Robert C. Byrd of West Virginia.

Byrd indicated that the final filing of the report of the House Judiciary Committee, which has approved three articles of impeachment against Mr. Nixon, might serve that purpose.

Brooke's resolution would express the sense of Congress that Nixon should be immune from both federal and state prosecution if he resigns.

But last night Brooke said he would withdraw the resolution, or fail to press for its passage, if Mr. Nixon does not make a confession of guilt.

THE JERUSALEM POST

40 PAGES Including 28 page MAGAZINE

Price: IL2.-

FRIDAY, AUGUST 9, 1974 • AV 21, 5734 • RAJAB 22, 1394 • VOL. XLIV, No. 14168

Gloom and unreality in the White House

WASHINGTON (UPI). — Gloom, a sense of unreality and feverish activity filled the White House and the Executive Offices yesterday as President Nixon prepared for a nationwide television address that was to bring his resignation.

The White House staff struggled to maintain the appearance of "business as usual," a policy which Mr. Nixon had ordered during a Cabinet meeting on Tuesday. The press office issued a sheaf of routine "notices to the press" announcing a variety of presidential actions, messages and reports.

But the façade of normalcy failed to screen officials from the unprecedented process of transition under way.

Large crowds gathered at each of the black wrought iron gates to the White House, hoping to catch a glance of history in the making. White House sources said callers from across the nation jammed the White House switchboard, most of them imploring Mr. Nixon not to resign.

Volunteer telephone operators manned the switchboards and were instructed by one middle-level White House said to reassure the callers that the President was not stepping aside.

Deputy Press Secretary Gerald Warren tried to reinforce the impression of unshakable solidity by emphasizing that Mr. Nixon would be adressing the nation still as President of the United States. He rejected any suggestion that it might be the performance of a leader who had fallen from power.

In the press room, reporters from all over the world jostled with each other for strategic vantage places as they awaited an expected briefing. The break that the news media had waited anxiously for eventually came shortly after noon.

An obviously tense Ronald Ziegler, the presidential Press Secretary, making what might turn out to be his last announcement ever for Mr. Nixon, went grim-faced to the microphone to announce that the President would make his decision known to the American people in a television and radio address.

There was a break in Mr. Ziegler's voice as he stated the obvious that "this, of course, has been a difficult time."

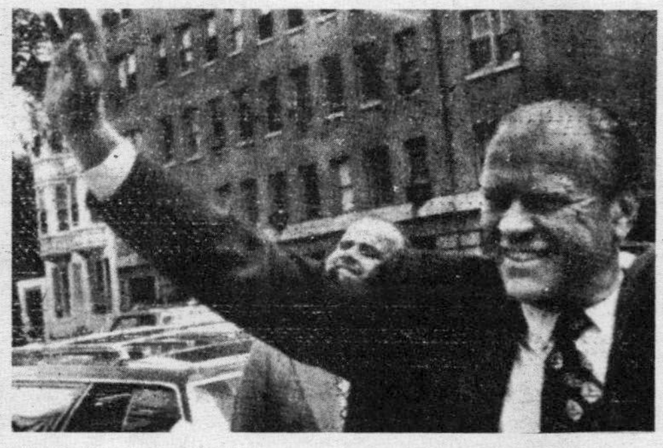

Vice-President Gerald Ford waves to tourists as he leaves Dirksen Senate office building in Washington on Wednesday. (AP radiophoto)

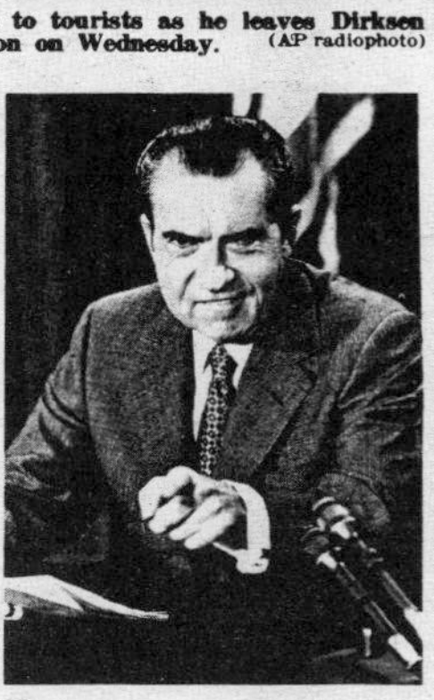

Confident and accusing — President Nixon, just before re-election for his second term in November, 1972. (Camera Press)

Ford will keep top Nixon men

WASHINGTON (AP). — As President, Gerald Ford will leave the current Cabinet intact and ask most top White House aides to stay on at least for the next few months, close associates of Mr. Ford said yesterday.

Although at least a dozen names are under consideration for Vice-President, a final choice is unlikely to be made for several days, the associates said.

One longtime friend of Mr. Ford said the emphasis over the next few days would be placed completely upon a smooth transition of power within the White House. "Jerry is by no means out to have any heads rolling," he said.

Among potential vice-presidents on a list drawn up by Mr. Ford's staff are former Attorney-General Elliott P. Richardson, former Secretary of Defence, Melvin R. Laird;

• Related stories on Pages 4 and 12

former New York Governor Nelson Rockefeller; Sens. Robert A. Taft of Ohio. Mark Hatfield of Oregon, Edward W. Brooke of Massachusetts, Robert Stafford of Vermont, Charles Percy of Illinois, Bill Brock of Tennessee, Gov. Ronald Reagan of California, former New York Sen. Charles Goodell, and Reps. Albert H. Quie of Minnesota and John B. Anderson of Illinois.

The Ford associate said only a few among those on the staff list are under serious consideration by Ford and he predicted extensive investigations would be made into the smaller list over the next few days.

The source said although a number of persons close to Mr. Ford have strongly urged that Rockefeller be the choice, Mr. Ford is unlikely to select the veteran millionaire politician.

Sometime following President Nixon's televised address, Mr. Ford will make a separate television appearance of his own. probably tonight. A final draft was being edited last night. Reportedly Mr. Ford will say "no one in the country could be sadder than I, but the country must go forward."

In conciliatory terms, Mr. Ford will generously praise the accomplishments of 6½ years of the Nixon presidency. In addition, a televised address to a joint session of Congress is under consideration.

Kissinger to notify Jerusalem

By ANAN SAFADI
POST Arab Affairs Correspondent

U.S. Secretary of State Henry Kissinger is due to communicate to Jerusalem over the weekend a Jordanian proposal for an Israeli pull-back some 10 to 12 kms. west of the Jordan River to a line stretching along the chain of mountains overlooking Jericho and the plain along both banks of the Jordan River.

The proposal was finalized yesterday by Jordanian Prime Minister Zaid Rifai at the end of his three-day talks in Washington.

The Jordanian plan for an Israeli "partial withdrawal" was posed as a precondition to Amman's participation in any future negotiations with Israel over a West Bank settlement, including the talks planned for Geneva. It omitted Jordan's long-time demand for a "military disengagement" with an undertaking to keep the evacuated areas demilitarized.

The Jordanian proposal reflected Amman's outright rejection to negotiate the reinstatement of its civil administration in the West Bank under Israeli military control. It left a number of options open towards negotiating "the restoration of parts" of the West Bank in the initial stage. It makes clear that Jordan would be prepared to negotiate an Israeli pull-back west of the Jordan river or from "parts" of the West Bank including Nablus,

(Continued on page 2, col. 3)

RIFAI TO KISSINGER

NO ACCORD TILL ISRAEL PULL-BACK

By WOLF BLITZER
Jerusalem Post Correspondent

WASHINGTON. — Jordanian Prime Minister Zaid Rifai is reported to have told Secretary of State Henry Kissinger during their two meetings at the State Department that there will be no disengagement agreement with Israel unless Israel agrees to a partial troop withdrawal from the West Bank. But Israeli officials here maintain that Israel will not withdraw its forces from the Jordan River in an interim agreement because this would require new Knesset elections.

In an overall peace agreement with Jordan — which would settle all outstanding issues — the Rabin-led coalition government would agree to withdraw some troops and to call for new elections, but not in an interim agreement, these officials told *The Jerusalem Post* yesterday.

This seems to be the first major stumbling block that Kissinger will have to bridge during the coming weeks if there is to be progress on a Jordanian front agreement.

Israeli officials here have indicated that in an interim agreement, the Rabin government would agree to allow the Jordanians to resume their administrative jurisdiction over parts of the West Bank. These officials maintain that such a step would not require new elections.

But Rifai is reported to have told the Secretary that his government will never agree to allow Jordanian administrations to be returned to parts of the West Bank while Israeli troops encircle those areas. He is also reported to have insisted that all Israeli settlers be evacuated during the implementation of a first stage agreement.

Rifai is believed to have told Kissinger that in an initial agreement, Israeli forces should be withdrawn 12 kms. from the river but he noted that the width of the withdrawal could be negotiated.

Rifai told three American newsmen after concluding his second meeting with Dr. Kissinger on Wednesday: "We believe that they should agree to new elections now." When one of the reporters noted that Likud leader Menahem Begin might win such an election, Rifai said: "Then there will be no peace in the Middle East."

It is believed here that King Hussein will arrive in Washington whether or not President Nixon remains in office. If Vice-President Gerald Ford becomes President, it is believed that King Hussein will be the first foreign dignitary to meet with the new President.

State Department officials have kept Israel Ambasador Simcha Dinitz informed about the contents of the Rifai-Kissinger talks. Dinitz had lunch with Under-Secretary of State Joseph Sisco on Wednesday, and at that time they scheduled a meeting for yesterday between Dinitz and Kissinger.

Five soldiers die in Sinai bus collisions

By H. BEN-ADI
Jerusalem Post Reporter

EL ARISH. — Five soldiers were killed in two road collisions in Sinai on Wednesday afternoon, it was announced yesterday. Both collisions involved buses.

In the first, at 3 o'clock, a bus carrying soldiers collided with a civilian truck near Jebel Libne. The truck crushed the left side of the bus, severely injuring eight soldiers. Four of them died while being taken by helicopter to the Soroka Medical Centre in Beersheba.

Half an hour later, at a point 50 kms. south on the same road, another bus collided with a command car, killing its driver and injuring two of his passengers.

The soldiers killed were Amram Ben-Simon, 29, of Sderot, Hagai Ben-Shmuel, 30, of Kibbutz Ruhama, Raymond Masoud, 27, of Moshav Yesha, Avinoam Cohen, 18, of Kfar Saba, and Ya'acov Lufton, whose age was not given, of Moshav Rinatya.

All the injured were yesterday reported to be out of danger.

Peres: won't affect U.S.-Israel amity

Jerusalem Post Political Reporter

TEL AVIV. — Defence Minister Shimon Peres said last night that support for Israel was so deeply rooted in America he did not think any Administration changes would affect it.

Mr. Peres, speaking at a seminar of the Israel Institute for Strategic Studies and Policy Analysis, was answering a question on whether the impending changes in the U.S. Presidency might not affect U.S.-Israel relations.

Naturally, he said, this kind of amity did not exclude differences of views from time to time. Mr. Peres noted that of all the partners of the U.S. on the world scene "Israel has not been the most expensive nor the worst friend." He noted that Israel had held its own without involving a single American soldier and "produced a situation in which the U.S. has become identified with peace and the Soviet Union with something else."

Rabin: Only readiness can deter Syria

Jerusalem Post Staff

Prime Minister Yitzhak Rabin said yesterday he was satisfied with the rate of the army's fortification and training preparations on the Golan. But this would have to be kept up to deter the Syrians from attacking.

Mr. Rabin made the statement at the end of an extensive tour of the fortifications. accompanied by Defence Minister Shimon Peres, Chief of Staff Mordechai Gur, O/C Northern Command Rafael Eytan and other senior officers.

Talking to soldiers at one of the many points he visited, Mr. Rabin said Israel was witnessing a tremendous effort by the Syrians to bolster their military strength through Soviet arms shipments, with declarations from Damascus that if their demands are not met they will renew the war.

The Prime Minister pointed out that there was limited room for manoeuvre in order to arrive at political solutions with the Syrians. The Golan Heights will remain an inseparable part of Israel; since the Syrians are unwilling to come to any agreement unless Israel withdraws from the Heights, they are preparing for war.

Reality had to be faced, Mr. Rabin told the soldiers, and Israel therefore had to get ready and to do so fast. Preparations on the Golan, he continued, were important for preserving the separation of forces. For Israel hereby hinted to the Syrians that, while keeping the agreement, it will not remain idle if they violate it.

In reply to soldiers' questions on settlement in Judea and Samaria, the Prime Minister said he believed in substantial settlement. "Our right to this land goes back to ancient times," he stressed.

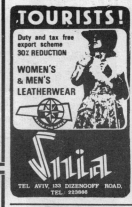

Phnom Penh's fall seen imminent

PHNOM PENH (UPI). — The Khmer Rouge rebel forces pushed through crumbling defence lines on the western edge of Phnom Penh yesterday and some were reported inside the city itself. The fall of the Cambodian capital appeared imminent.

Some reports said government artillerymen turned their guns toward the city and joined rebel forces in heavy shelling barrages as the end appeared near.

The insurgents cut the road between Phnom Penh and the airport and opened heavy artillery attacks on government defence positions and an army headquarters in the western part of the city.

(Detailed story on Page 4.)

THE JERUSALEM POST

YOM ATZMAUT SUPPLEMENT WITH THIS ISSUE

Price: IL2.50

TUESDAY, APRIL 15, 1975 • IYAR 4, 5735 • RABI THANI 4, 1395 • VOL. XLV, No. 13374

27th Independence fetes start this evening

By JUDY SIEGEL
Jerusalem Post Reporter

NIGHTFALL TODAY WILL bring to a close the solemnity of Remembrance Day for the Fallen and mark the onset of joyous celebration of the State's 27th birthday.

Reflecting this year's theme, "Volunteering and Personal Sacrifice," the 12 persons chosen to light beacons at the opening event on Jerusalem's Mt. Herzl are all volunteers who made special contributions to the country.

Places of entertainment which closed last night and re-opened this morning will fill up with Independence Day merrymakers as the holiday begins.

A central dance platform will vibrate with horas and music near Beit Agron in Jerusalem at 8 o'clock this evening and a similar programme is scheduled at the same time in the Vale of Rehavia. Dozens of *kumsitzim* will illuminate the nation's recreation areas at midnight.

The Capital will be left out of the customary fireworks displays this year, because of the sharp rise in the cost of imported fireworks. A few dozen localities which had some left from last year or who were given new displays by the Independence Day committee, will present heavenly extravaganzas.

Thanksgiving prayers tomorrow morning in most synagogues will give a religious touch to the celebrations. Chief Rabbi Ovadia Yosef has ruled that the hallel prayer be recited without a blessing; the Chief Rabbinate Council, headed by Rabbi Shlomo Goren, stand by last year's ruling to recite it with a blessing.

The Nature Reserves Authority will conduct tours of Jerusalem tomorrow morning. Following last year's success, a puppet theatre and entertainers will be presented in Sanhedria Park at 11 a.m.

The capital's Israel and Rockefeller museums will be open free to all comers between 10 a.m. and 5 p.m. tomorrow. (A special exhibition on the occasion of the Israel Museum's 10th birthday and Israel's 27th birthday will open at the Museum of Modern Art in the city of Paris. Initiated by Baroness Alix de Rothschild, the exhibition will give French children an opportunity to mould plasticine, make dolls and draw, as well as demonstrate to French teachers what the Israel Museum does with its 180,000 annual child visitors.)

Arthur Rubinstein will solo at a gala performance of the Jerusalem Symphony Orchestra tonight at its home base in the Jerusalem Theatre. The special evening was initiated by the Mayor of Jerusalem to benefit the musical education projects for the children of the city.

Post Offices will close at 1 p.m. (some at 4 p.m.) today, and not reopen until Thursday (except for the central Post Offices in Jerusalem, Tel Aviv and Haifa, which will accept telegrams).

President Ephraim Katzir will receive 100 outstanding soldiers at his residence tomorrow morning,

(Continued on page 2, col. 2)

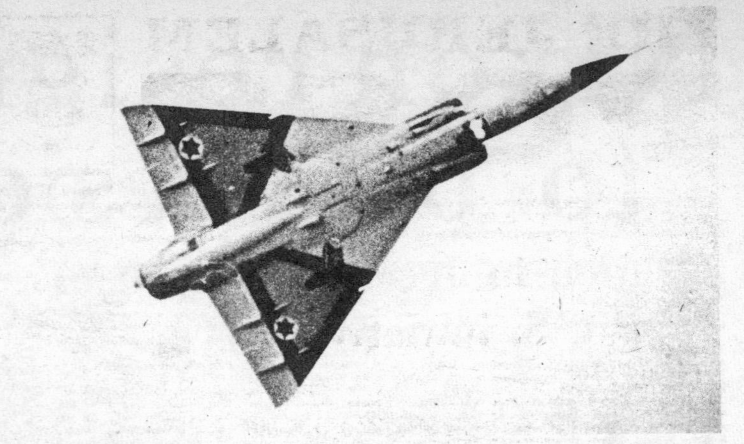

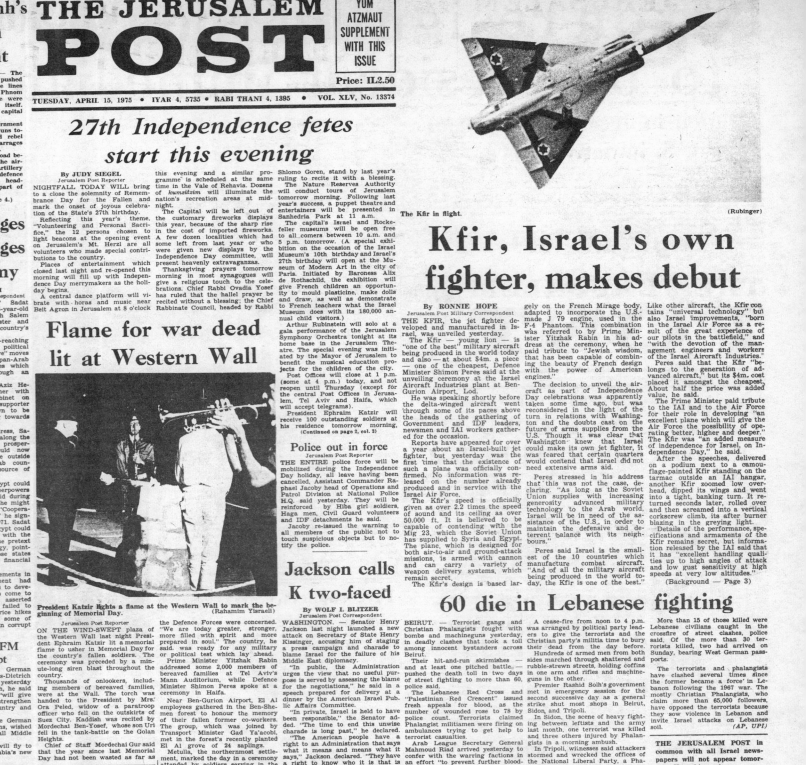

The Kfir in flight. (Rubinger)

Kfir, Israel's own fighter, makes debut

By RONNIE HOPE
Jerusalem Post Military Correspondent

THE KFIR, the jet fighter developed and manufactured in Israel, was unveiled yesterday.

The Kfir — young lion — is "one of the best" military aircraft being produced in the world today and also — at about $4m. a piece — one of the cheapest, Defence Minister Shimon Peres said at the unveiling ceremony at the Israel Aircraft Industries plant at Ben-Gurion Airport, Lod.

He was speaking shortly before the delta-winged aircraft went through some of its paces above the heads of the gathering of Government and IDF leaders, newsmen and IAI workers gathered for the occasion.

Reports have appeared for over a year about an Israel-built jet fighter, but yesterday was the first time that the existence of such a plane was officially confirmed. No information was released on the number already produced and in service with the Israel Air Force.

The Kfir's speed is officially given as over 2.2 times the speed of sound and its ceiling as over 50.000 ft. It is believed to be capable of contending with the Mig 23, which the Soviet Union has supplied to Syria and Egypt. The plane, which is designed for both air-to-air and ground-attack missions, is armed with cannon and can carry a variety of weapon delivery systems, which remain secret.

The Kfir's design is based largely on the French Mirage body, adapted to incorporate the U.S.-made J 79 engine, used in the F-4 Phantom. This combination was referred to by Prime Minister Yitzhak Rabin in his address at the ceremony, when he paid tribute to "Jewish wisdom, that has been capable of combining the beauty of French design with the power of American engines."

The decision to unveil the aircraft as part of Independence Day celebrations was apparently taken some time ago, but was reconsidered in the light of the turn in relations with Washington and the doubts cast on the future of arms supplies from the U.S. Though it was clear that Washington knew that Israel could make its own jet fighter, it was feared that certain quarters would contend that Israel did not need extensive arms aid.

Peres stressed in his address that this was not the case, declaring. "As long as the Soviet Union supplies with increasing generosity advanced military technology to the Arab world, Israel will be in need of the assistance of the U.S., in order to maintain the defensive and deterrent balance with its neighbours."

Peres said Israel is the smallest of the 10 countries which manufacture combat aircraft. "And of all the military aircraft being produced in the world today, the Kfir is one of the best."

Like other aircraft, the Kfir contains "universal technology" but also Israel improvements, "born in the Israel Air Force as a result of the great experience of our pilots in the battlefield," and "with the devotion of the management engineers and workers of the Israel Aircraft Industries."

Peres said that the Kfir "belongs to the generation of advanced aircraft," but its $4m. cost placed it amongst the cheapest. About half the price was added value, he said.

The Prime Minister paid tribute to the IAI and to the Air Force for their role in developing "an excellent plane which will give the Air Force the possibility of operating better, higher and deeper." The Kfir was "an added measure of independence for Israel, on Independence Day," he said.

After the speeches, delivered on a podium next to a camouflage-painted Kfir standing on the tarmac outside an IAI hangar, another Kfir zoomed low overhead, dipped its wings and went into a tight, banking turn. It returned seconds later, rolled over and then screamed into a vertical corkscrew climb, its after burner blazing in the greying light.

Details of the performance, specifications and armaments of the Kfir remains secret, but information released by the IAI said that it has "excellent handling qualities up to high angles of attack and low gust sensitivity at high speeds at very low altitudes."

(Background — Page 3)

Sadat pledges wide changes in economy

By ANAN SAFADI
POST Middle East Affairs Correspondent

EGYPTIAN PRESIDENT Sadat last night chose his 55-year-old Interior Minister Mamdouh Salem as the new Prime Minister and pledged to improve his country's economic situation.

Sadat promised far-reaching changes in the Egyptian political establishment with "creative" moves to meet international, pan-Arab and domestic circumstances which he said were going through an evolution.

Salem succeeds Abdel Aziz Hegazi, who resigned together with the entire Egyptian Cabinet on Sunday night. A staunch supporter of Sadat, Salem is known to be tough and uncompromising towards dissidents.

In a radio and TV address, Sadat vowed to take Egypt along the path of "productivity and prosperity." He stressed he would now open Egypt's doors to the outside world, especially the Arab countries which remain the source of production and defence.

Sadat asked whether Egypt could go on dealing with the superpowers under the detente, as it did during their cold war. He hinted he might still rescind the 15-year "Cooperation and Friendship treaty" he signed with the Russians in 1971. Sadat then questioned whether Egypt could have freezed its relations with the other Arab states under the pretext of its revolutionary ideology, pointing out that most of those states became Egypt's main financial backers.

Sadat said that some elements in the Egyptian establishment had failed to adjust themselves to developments which Egypt has come to face in recent years. He asserted that those elements also failed to cope with the dramatic price hikes in Egypt, indicating that some of them were even involved in corrupt practices.

West German FM visiting Egypt

CAIRO (UPI). — West German Foreign Minister Hans-Dietrich Genscher arrived in Cairo yesterday for a three-day visit which, he said in an arrival statement, "will give me the opportunity to strengthen the ties" between his country and Egypt.

Genscher added that the German people, and other Europeans, wished to contribute to an overall Middle East peace settlement.

From Cairo, Genscher will fly to Riyadh to meet Saudi Arabia's new King Khaled.

Flame for war dead lit at Western Wall

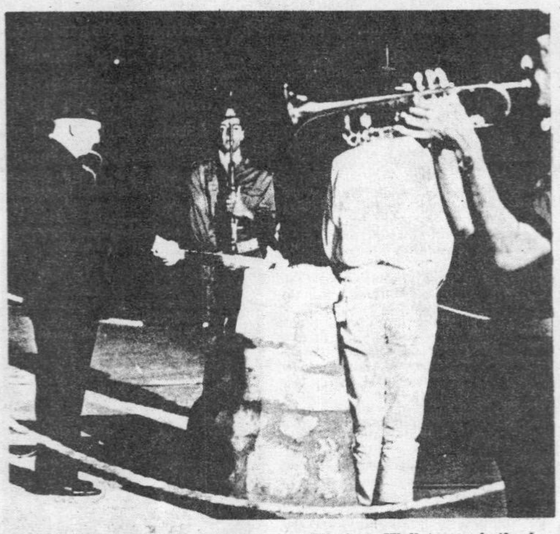

President Katzir lights a flame at the Western Wall to mark the beginning of Memorial Day. (Rahamim Yisraeli)

Jerusalem Post Reporter

ON THE WIND-SWEPT plaza of the Western Wall last night President Ephraim Katzir lit a memorial flame to usher in Memorial Day for the country's fallen soldiers. The ceremony was preceded by a minute-long siren blast throughout the country.

Thousands of onlookers, including members of bereaved families, were at the Wall. The torch was handed to the President by Mrs. Ora Peled, widow of a paratroop officer who fell on the outskirts of Suez City. Kaddish was recited by Mordechai Ben-Yosef, whose son Uri fell in the tank-battle on the Golan Heights.

Chief of Staff Mordechai Gur said that the year since last Memorial Day had not been wasted as far as the Defence Forces were concerned. "We are today greater, stronger, more filled with spirit and more prepared in soul." The country, he said. was ready for any military or political test which lay ahead.

Prime Minister Yitzhak Rabin addressed some 2,000 members of bereaved families at Tel Aviv's Mann Auditorium, while Defence Minister Shimon Peres spoke at a ceremony in Haifa.

Near Ben-Gurion Airport, El Al employees gathered in the Ben-Shemen forest to honour the memory of their fallen former co-workers. The group, which was joined by Transport Minister Gad Ya'acobi, met in the forest's recently planted El Al grove of 24 saplings.

Metulla, the northernmost settlement, marked the day in a ceremony attended by soldiers serving in the area. Kaddish for the fallen was said by a local man whose son was killed in a terrorist attack. At nearby Kiryat Shmona, scene of a murderous terrorist attack last year, kaddish was said both for fallen soldiers and for victims of the terror attacks.

At Acre, the day was marked at the war memorial at the eastern entrance to town, to which a procession of wreaths made its way from the Town Hall.

Typical of the hundreds of ceremonies throughout the country was that at Ramat Gan, where the 60 townsmen fallen in the country's wars were honoured at the local Yad Lebanim, with the bereaved families and the Mayor in attendance.

Services will be held this morning at all military cemeteries.

Memorial Day will end this evening simultaneously with the commencement of Independence Day festivities.

Police out in force

Jerusalem Post Reporter

THE ENTIRE police force will be mobilized during the Independence Day holiday, all leave having been cancelled, Assistant Commander Raphael Jacoby head of Operations and Patrol Division at National Police H.Q. said yesterday. They will be reinforced by Hiba girl soldiers, Haga men, Civil Guard volunteers and IDF detachments he said.

Jacoby re-issued the warning to all members of the public not to touch suspicious objects but to notify the police.

Jackson calls K two-faced

By WOLF I. BLITZER
Jerusalem Post Correspondent

WASHINGTON. — Senator Henry Jackson last night launched a new attack on Secretary of State Henry Kissinger, accusing him of staging a press campaign and charade to blame Israel for the failure of his Middle East diplomacy.

"In public, the Administration urges the view that no useful purpose is served by assessing the blame for the negotiations," he said in a speech prepared for delivery at a dinner by the American Israel Public Affairs Committee.

"In private, Israel is held to have been responsible," the Senator added. "The time to end this unwise charade is long past," he declared.

"The American people have a right to an Administration that says what it means and means what it says," Jackson declared. "They have a right to know who it is that is speaking in their name," he added.

Jackson was referring to Kissinger's "background" briefings for newsmen on the plane during his shuttle diplomacy.

Observers here noted that Jackson's attack against the Ford Administration in general — and Kissinger in particular—was one of the most bitter he has made regarding the Middle East.

(Knesset debate — Page 2)

AFTER MIDNIGHT

Soviet Premier Alexei Kosygin last night called on Arab nations to stand firm against partial settlements with Israel which "would legalize Israel occupation of Arab lands," and called for a speedy resumption of the Geneva conference.

60 die in Lebanese fighting

BEIRUT. — Terrorist gangs and Christian Phalangists fought with bombs and machineguns yesterday, in deadly clashes that took a toll among innocent bystanders across Beirut.

Their hit-and-run skirmishes — and at least one pitched battle — pushed the death toll in two days of street fighting to more than 60, police said.

The Lebanese Red Cross and "Palestinian Red Crescent" issued fresh appeals for blood, as the number of wounded rose to 78 by police count. Terrorists claimed Phalangist militiamen were firing on ambulances trying to get help to terrorist casualties.

Arab League Secretary General Mahmoud Riad arrived yesterday to confer with the warring factions in an effort "to prevent further bloodshed."

A cease-fire from noon to 4 p.m. was arranged by political party leaders to give the terrorists and the Christian party's militia time to bury their dead from the day before.

Hundreds of armed men from both sides marched through shattered and rubble-strewn streets, holding coffins in one arm and rifles and machineguns in the other.

Premier Rashid Solh's government met in emergency session for the second successive day as a general strike shut most shops in Beirut, Sidon, and Tripoli.

In Sidon, the scene of heavy fighting between leftists and the army last month, one terrorist was killed and three others injured by Phalangists in a morning ambush.

In Tripoli, witnesses said attackers stormed and wrecked the offices of the National Liberal Party, a Phalangist ally.

More than 15 of those killed were Lebanese civilians caught in the crossfire of street clashes, police said. Of the more than 30 terrorists killed, two had arrived on Sunday, bearing West German passports.

The terrorists and phalangists have clashed several times since the former became a force in Lebanon following the 1967 war. The mostly Christian Phalangists, who claim more than 65,000 followers, have opposed the terrorists because they sow violence in Lebanon and invite Israel attacks on Lebanese soil. *(AP, UPI)*

THE JERUSALEM POST in common with all Israel newspapers will not appear tomorrow, Yom Atzmaut.

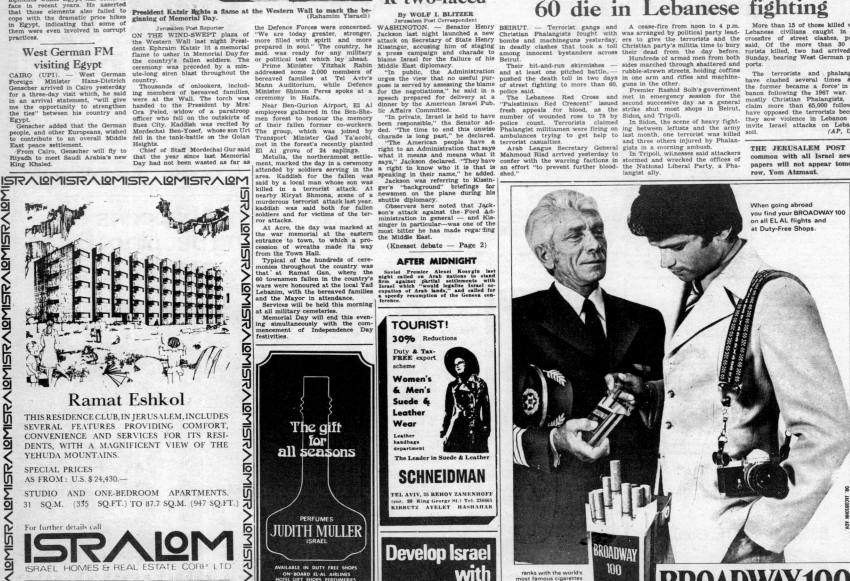

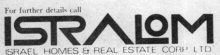

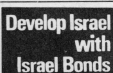

THE JERUSALEM POST

40 PAGES Including 28-page MAGAZINE

Price: IL2.50

FRIDAY, JUNE 6, 1975 • SIVAN 27, 5735 • JAMAD AWAL 27, 1395 • VOL. XLV, No. 13416*

SUEZ CANAL REOPENED AFTER EIGHT YEARS

Sadat: Would fight Israel for lands

PORT SAID. — President Sadat opened the Suez Canal yesterday after an eight-year closure and hailed it as "a contribution to peace" in the Middle East. But he indicated this would not deter Egypt from fighting Israel again if necessary to obtain its withdrawal from Arab lands and a solution to the Palestinian problem.

Resplendent in an admiral's white uniform, Sadat declared the Canal open to international shipping at 10.30 a.m. Following the speech he boarded the destroyer October the Sixth — the opening day of the Yom Kippur War — which broke through a thin chain strung 120 metres across the mouth of the Canal and nosed southward for a six-hour trip to Ismailia, 80 kms. away.

In his four-minute quayside speech, Sadat declared that "while making this initiative as a contribution to peace, Egypt reminds friendly nations that parts of its dear soil are still under foreign occupation and that an entire people (Palestinians) are still suffering the consequences of suppression and homelessness."

Egypt, he said, "reiterates its determination to do its holy duty towards its own and other Arab lands — in the Golan Heights, Sinai, and Palestine — and toward usurped Arab rights."

Later, speaking to Egyptian newsmen on the destroyer, Sadat described Israel's decision to thin forces in Sinai near the Canal as "a very important step." He said "this gesture means we start the process again. Let us hope it is not simply a tactical move by Israel."

Asked if there was sufficient momentum towards peace to renew the UN mandate in Sinai when it expires on July 24, Sadat said, "There is not yet sufficient momentum to renew the mandate." He added, "Let us be practical. The thinning out and withdrawal of some artillery by Israel must be followed by a main step. I am still hopeful and I am more hopeful since my talks with President Ford in Salzburg last weekend."

Sadat said there was no question of Israeli ships using the waterway. "We have been in a state of war for the past 27 years, therefore there will be no passage of Israeli ships through the Canal. But the passage of merchandise on other ships bound for Israel will depend on Israel's conduct."

Sadat said "the problem is not the passage of goods... but whether Israel will continue the process of peace, or return to its intransigent stand which led to the collapse of Kissinger's mission."

The foreign guest of honour at the ceremonies yesterday was the 14-year-old Crown Prince Reza Pahlevi, son of the Shah of Iran — who has pledged funds for developing the Canal zone. The prince was at Sadat's side and the President gave him an effusive welcome when they met. (See photo — Page 4)

The destroyer carrying Sadat led a convoy of five Egyptian ships that sailed majestically through a Pharaonic-style gate across the entrance to the Canal and on to its midway point of Ismailia, where celebrations continued late into the night. Two hours later, the first convoy of toll-paying ships entered the Canal on the way to the Red Sea. It consisted of five ships flying the Kuwaiti, Greek, Chinese, Soviet and Yugoslav flags.

The colour and pageantry at the ceremony at Port Said made it an occasion to compare with the original opening of the Canal, built by forced Egyptian labour more than a century ago. A 21-gun salute boomed a fanfare of trumpets when President Sadat arrived at Port Said.

Flotillas of small craft filled with dancing fishermen circled Egyptian destroyers and foreign merchant ships. Soviet-made Mig warplanes shrieked low overhead and loudspeakers on boats and trucks blared patriotic songs urging "a hundred claps for the hero of the Canal crossing... Sadat, you have made our hearts joyful."

Among the ships in the first convoy to ply the Canal's waters was the flagship of the U.S. Sixth Fleet. The cruiser Little Rock came at the invitation of the Egyptian Government, U.S. sources said, as a gesture of gratitude to the U.S. for the key role it played to help clear the waterway over the past 13 months.

Mashour Ahmed Mashour, the Canal Authority chairman who accompanied Sadat on the destroyer, called the first commercial convoy "purely symbolic, only half a dozen ships." But he said that beginning today two convoys a day would traverse the Canal, one northbound and one southbound.

"After 15 days or so, we will probably begin our old system of convoys night and day," Mashour said. "But it will be at least two months before we are handling anything like the volume of traffic that we handled before 1967."

Mashour said he now has 170 of the former pilots back at work and another 100 new ones, enough to meet the Canal's needs. Mashour's biggest worry now, he said, is insurance rates being charged for Canal shipping. "They plan to charge three times as much as the normal rate for war insurance," he said. "But happily some representatives of Lloyd's of London will be here for the Canal opening and we hope to persuade them this is not necessar ' *(UPI, Reuter, AP)*

Minister and newsmen scuffle with guards

PORT SAID (Reuter). — The opening ceremony — designed to give world-wide publicity to the Canal's reopening — almost misfired when over-zealous Egyptian security men refused admission to 200 reporters, photographers and television cameramen from around the world.

Minister of Information Kamal Abul-Magd intervened and got caught up in violent jostling between newsmen and security forces. No one was hurt in the ugly incident and the Information Minister eventually got the press in to cover the ceremony only minutes before President Sadat's arrival.

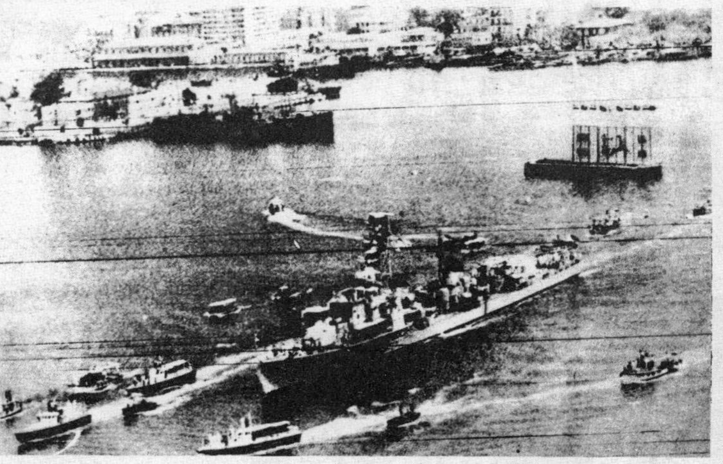

Surrounded by a swarm of small craft, the Egyptian Navy destroyer "October 6" with President Sadat aboard enters the Suez Canal at Port Said yesterday. At right the marker station for the entrance at the northern end of the Canal. In the background is Port Said harbour. (AP radiophoto)

Caution in Jerusalem on U.S. initiative

Jerusalem Post Diplomatic Correspondent

In Jerusalem, as in Washington (see below), officials declined to divulge details of the meeting on Wednesday between Secretary of State Kissinger and Ambassador Simcha Dinitz, but they thought to inject a note of caution into the near-euphoric optimism generated by leaks and reports from the Salzburg talks.

They indicated that Egyptian President Sadat's demand for progress on the Syrian front as well as on his own, and his efforts to concentrate Mr. Ford's attention on the problems of an overall settlement, could still raise obstacles in the way of an interim Israel-Egypt accord.

Observers here believe the chances of an Israel-Egypt accord — if it can be negotiated without the involvement of extraneous elements — have improved. They predict it would be based on a three to five year Unef mandate extension in a "non-use of force" agreement, with Israel withdrawing from the Mitla and Gidi passes and Abu Rodeis.

The observers were concerned at President Ford's apparent interest in the problems of an overall accord. They feel Washington's formulation of a final peace plan now might lead to arduous discussions on the Jerusalem-Washington axis which might head off the change of concluding an interim pact with Egypt.

In Tel Aviv last night, Prime Minister Rabin said deadlock in the Middle East was at an end and, in the newly created atmosphere, chances had improved for examining ways of moving toward a peace settlement. Rabin was addressing the national secretariat of the Labour Party's Young Guard.

Kissinger says Israel and Egypt 'even'

By WOLF BLITZER
Jerusalem Post Reporter

WASHINGTON. — Insisting that there has not been a U.S. "tilt" against Israel, Ambassador Simcha Dinitz said yesterday that his government is still very anxious to revive the U.S.-sponsored peace initiative in the Middle East.

He warned, however, that if "this turns out to be impossible, then we are prepared to go to Geneva under the original conditions and try to iron out our differences there."

In an interview with the "Washington Star-News," the Ambassador said the Geneva conference has been postponed over the past few months in order "to give a chance for bilateral diplomacy under the U.S. effort to revive an American initiative."

Warning that a Geneva conference could turn into a mini-United Nations, Dinitz noted that Israel would "rather believe and hope that there would be a possibility to have real negotiations and, if possible, under American initiative and American good offices."

Dinitz met late Wednesday afternoon with Secretary of State Henry Kissinger for about 90 minutes to hear about President Ford's meetings in Salzburg with Egyptian President Sadat. They also worked out details of Prime Minister Rabin's visit to Washington next week.

Kissinger reportedly told Dinitz that Israel's unilateral pullback of forces from the Suez Canal region was a helpful move, but that Egypt's decision to reopen the Canal — even though the talks had collapsed in March — was also a very helpful gesture.

The U.S., informed sources quoting Kissinger as having told Dinitz, believe Israel and Egypt are now "even" and it is up to both sides to continue the process at this time.

Kissinger said publicly earlier this week the Israeli gesture was not "decisive," but was a step in the right direction.

Israeli sources here said the meeting had been "factual and constructive and held in a friendly atmosphere." Embassy Minister Mordechai Shalev, Assistant Secretary of State Alfred Atherton and National Security Council Assistant Peter Rodman also participated.

After the meeting, Dinitz refused to give newsmen details of the conversation, merely noting that the Secretary had given him a "full report" of the Salzburg talks. Dinitz cabled a report on the meeting to the Israel Government on Wednesday evening.

American officials here believe that another Israel-Egyptian interim accord in Sinai is very much possible, based on the attitude adopted by Sadat last week. The Egyptian leader is said to be prepared to extend the Unef mandate for three years in exchange for an Israeli withdrawal from the Abu Rodeis oilfields and the Mitla and Gidi passes. The Egyptian leader is also reported to be prepared to implement other "elements of non-belligerency," although he adamantly refuses to end the state of war with Israel.

Kissinger is believed anxious to hear from Prime Minister Rabin next week that Israel will accept Egypt's terms, thus opening the way for a new pact.

State Department officials do not

(Continued on page 2, col. 4)

U.S. expects Egypt will allow Canal transit of Israel cargoes

Confirms Sadat gave secret assurances

Jerusalem Post Correspondent

WASHINGTON. — State Department officials here expect that Egypt will permit Israeli cargoes in third-country vessels to go through the Suez Canal, but are hopeful that Israel will not overly publicize it so as not to "embarrass" Egyptian President Sadat in the eyes of more radical Arabs.

The officials, who have privately confirmed that Egypt had assured the U.S. during the 1974 disengagement agreement to end its ban on Israeli cargoes once the Canal was reopened, are none the less concerned that this issue could become highly sensitive. Too much adverse reaction among the extremist Arabs could force Sadat to rescind his pledge, they warn.

At yesterday's State Department briefing, spokesman Robert Funseth declined to confirm that the Egyptians had secretly undertaken to allow Israeli cargoes through the Canal, but confirmed that secret assurances accompanied the 1974 pact.

In Jerusalem, Transport Minister Gad Ya'acobi said yesterday Egypt had made a written pledge to allow Israeli cargo through the Suez Canal, but an aide said a ship reportedly en route for the Canal with Israeli freight "does not exist."

A Liberian flagship was reported earlier to be steaming for the Canal with 9,000 tons of sugar for the Israeli government. Ya'acobi appeared to confirm this report in a radio interview.

Later an aide to Ya'acobi, Asher Ron, told a newsman that "to the best of our knowledge, the ship does not exist. And if it does, it is not headed for the Canal" with Israeli goods. He said the Ministry knew of no ship bearing Israeli cargo that was bound for the Canal.

It was reported last night that the State Department expressed its deep concern to the Israel Embassy in Washington on Ya'acobi's statement indicating the Liberian vessel was heading for the Suez Canal.

Terrorists rocket Kiryat Shmona

Grenade thrown in Jerusalem

By YORAM HAMIZRAHI
Jerusalem Post Reporter and Post Staff

KIRYAT SHMONA. — Arab terrorists staged a rocket attack on this northern town and threw a hand grenade at policemen in Jerusalem yesterday in an attempt to mark the eighth anniversary of the Six Day War.

The army spokesman said the rockets were fired from Lebanese territory at about 3 a.m. and hit in and around the town of Kiryat Shmona, three kms. from the frontier.

Residents said several rockets hit the area in the space of 25 minutes and damaged a kindergarten and set fire to a number of places in the town and on the surrounding mountain slopes. One resident was slightly wounded by flying glass from shattered windows. The fires were quickly brought under control by the Fire Brigade.

Prime Minister Rabin and the Chief of Staff, Rav-Aluf Mordechai Gur, flew to the town by helicopter in the early afternoon and toured the sites where the rockets hit. They were accompanied by Commerce Minister Haim Bar-Lev, who is chairman of the Government committee for development towns, and Aluf Rehavam Ze'evi, adviser on intelligence to the Prime Minister.

The Premier and his party talked to townspeople near the wrecked kindergarten and later met with the municipal council. Rabin said to newsmen: "I did not come here to make a political statement but to visit the site after the rocket attack which reminds us of the reality in which we live. I leave Kiryat Shmona encouraged by the determination and strength of the townspeople."

Power and phone lines cut by shrapnel had been repaired by early morning. Children who attend the destroyed kindergarten were sent to other kindergartens in the area.

Mayor Avraham Aloni said in the morning he had phoned the Premier to seek action on standing Government promises to build more shelters and reinforced security rooms in the town.

This was the third rocket attack on Kiryat Shmona since April 11 last year when three terrorists slipped into the town and killed 16 civilians and two soldiers in an apartment house before being killed by counter-attacking soldiers.

Wednesday night's attack sent local residents to shelters and security rooms or — in the absence of either — to stairwells and windowless entrance halls.

The rockets were fired from the Lebanese village of Markabe, about 5½ kms. northwest of Kiryat Shmona. Markabe is located in hilly bush-covered terrain.

The Katyushas are believed to have been of 182mm. calibre, a type rarely used until now by the terrorists. In operation, they are similar to mortars and can be mounted on vehicles. A fragment found near the kindergarten was inscribed with Russian Cyrillic lettering and the figure 182.

In Jerusalem, police said a grenade was thrown at a group of policemen and Haga Civil Defence guards engaged in setting up a road barrier near the District Court in East Jerusalem, part of the precautions taken on the anniversary of the war. One Haga man was slightly injured by flying grenade fragments.

The incident occurred at 7.30 a.m. at the corner of Saladin and St. George Streets.

The grenade was tossed from a height but it is not yet clear whether it was thrown from the solitary apartment house nearby or a passing bus. Police cordonned off the area and arrested eight persons.

The anniversary passed quietly in the administered area apart from minor incidents: in Beit Sahur near Jerusalem a crowd of pupils assembled in the morning and in nearby Beit Jallah anti-Israel slogans were scrawled on the walls.

(See photo page 2, leader, page 12)

3 Egyptians held in Sinai

Jerusalem Post Military Correspondent

An Egyptian officer and two soldiers were captured by an army patrol behind Israeli lines in Sinai on Tuesday night, the army spokesman announced yesterday. The Red Cross and the UN have been informed that the Egyptians, who were caught in the southern sector of the Suez Canal area, will be returned to Egypt "as soon as possible," the spokesman said.

The three men, commanded by a lieutenant, were probably on an intelligence mission. This is the first time since the disengagement agreement that Israel has reported capturing an Egyptian intelligence unit behind its lines. Footprints of such patrols have been found several times, but not reported in the press.

Peres, at air show, shows keen interest in F-16

By JACK MAURICE
Jerusalem Post Correspondent

PARIS. — The highlight of Defence Minister Shimon Peres' first day in France was a three-hour tour of Le Bourget air show where he displayed keen interest in the American F-16 warplane — to the evident distress of his escort, Serge Dassault, commissioner for the fair and son of aircraft builder Marcel Dassault.

He began his tour at the stand of the Israel Aircraft Industries which is presenting the Arava short-take-off-and-landing (Stol) aircraft, the Westwind 1124 executive jet, the Mark 11 Gabriel navy missile and other weapons.

Asked by a reporter whether his visit to the air fair was a retort to the United States, which is delaying deliveries of new military equipment to Israel, the Minister said, "Not at all. We are not dissatisfied with the Americans. This is all part of political life."

Peres' visit coincided with the last suspense-ridden hours in the contest between France's Dassault-Breguet Mirage F1-E and the American General Dynamics F-16 for an order from four Nato countries to replace F-104G Starfighters and other aging aircraft. The decision of Belgium is due tomorrow and it is expected to confirm those of Holland, Norway and Denmark to buy the F-16.

Peres stood beside Serge Dassault as they watched the F-16 perform aerobatics over Le Bourget followed by a French Air Force Mirage-F1 with eight 400-kilo bombs suspended from its wings. The Israeli minister commented: "It looks as if Europe will become completely American."

With Serge Dassault still at his side, Mr. Peres put probing questions about the American aircraft to its chief test pilot, Lt.-Col. Neil Anderson. (Earlier story — Page 4)

U.S.-Egyptian unit on investment

CAIRO (Reuter). — A joint Egyptian-American committee to promote and encourage investment in Egypt was formed yesterday.

'Yes' predicted in UK poll on Euromart

LONDON (AP). — Britons voted yesterday in their first referendum in history on whether to stay in the European Common Market. The latest public opinion polls predicted a massive "yes" vote by a 2-to-1 margin.

The question to which voters had to give a "yes" or "no" answer was, "Do you think the United Kingdom should stay in the European Community?"

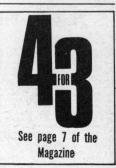

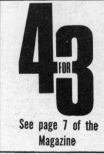

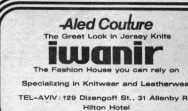

Joy at rescue of hostages

Jerusalem Post Staff

Israel was buoyed by relief ad joy yesterday as over 100 hostages, most of them Israelis, hijacked to Uganda last Sunday, were rescued and brought back 3,800 kms. following a spectacular night-time commando operation at Uganda's Entebbe airport. Three civilian hostages and an army officer were killed in the shootout with the terrorists and Ugandan troops. Another five civilians and four soldiers were wounded in the operation.

All seven terrorists and about 20 Ugandan troops were killed.

In a rare show of unity, Likud opposition leader Menahem Begin proclaimed "hats off" to Prime Minister Rabin at a special Knesset session yesterday afternoon.

Unqualified approval of the Israel raid came from U.S. President Ford and West German Chancellor Helmut Schmidt as Western reaction was generally favourable. For Jewish communities abroad, the news was an occasion for rejoicing. Arab reaction was generally low-key.

Government leaders stressed yesterday that Israel had acted alone and had consulted with no outside party before deciding on the rescue mission. Rabin told the Knesset the decision was taken only after it became clear that effective international action to free the hostages was not possible. He emphasized that last week's offer of an exchange for jailed terrorists had been genuine and not a tactic designed to gain time.

Few details were forthcoming from Israeli spokesmen on operational details. At a press conference in Tel Aviv, the mission commander, Tat-Aluf Dan Shomron, said surprise had been a key element and that the operation was "relatively" not difficult.

The effect of the successful raid on national morale was electric. Many compared it with the mood of gladness that followed the Six Day War and hailed it as a turning point. Prime Minister Rabin himself, in a television interview last night, said it had restored national confidence, and demonstrated the "latent power of this nation."

The terrorists, who hijacked an Air France airbus over Greece a week ago and brought it to Uganda, had thr atened to kill their remaining 104 hostages, mostly Israelis, unless 53 terrorists were released from jails in five countries.

Rabin accused Ugandan leader Idi Amin of "fully cooperating with the hijackers while putting on false pretences. The release of the non-Israelis exposed even more the evil plot being planned against the Israelis."

THE JERUSALEM POST

Price: IL2.15 (Including VAT)

MONDAY, JULY 5, 1976 • TAMMUZ 7, 5736 • RAJAB 8, 1396 • VOL. XLVI, No. 13747

The rescue. Also on pages 2, 3, 4

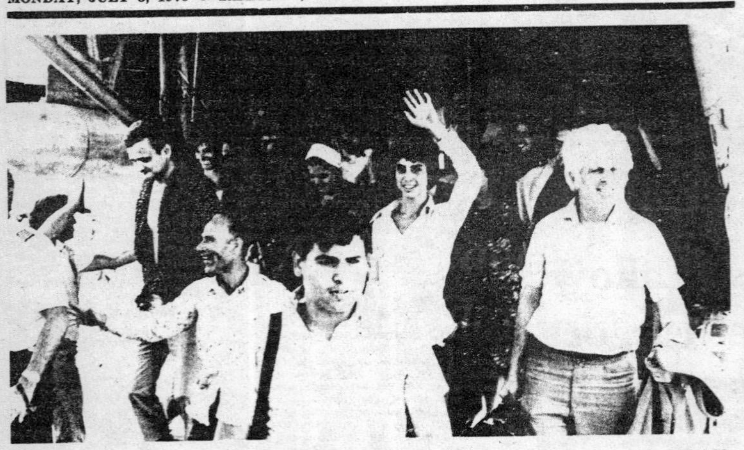

Hostages stream out of the IAF Hercules plane which brought them to Ben-Gurion Airport from Entebbe after their rescue by Israel commandos yesterday. Tall man at left dressed in polka-dot pyjama jacket is Air France navigator Lemoine. (Dekel)

Hostages back to jubilant Israel

Jerusalem Post Staff

BEN-GURION AIRPORT. — The hostages returned yesterday to scenes of national rejoicing reminiscent of the days following the Six Day War. They came home in three air force transport planes, two of which landed at Ben-Gurion Airport and the third at an air force base "somewhere in Israel."

Relatives were told to assemble outside the Yad Eliyahu stadium for transport to the base to be reunited with members of their families who had been freed.

First news of the successful raid on Entebbe airport was flashed over the army radio at three o'clock yesterday morning. The flash set off a wave of phone calls throughout Israel, and within an hour nearly every family with a member involved in the hijacking knew that the hostages had been freed and were on their way back home.

Relief was tempered with anxitey and apprehension, however, as news confirmed rumours that there were dead and wounded among the passengers.

By six o'clock yesterday morning, relatives of passengers had begun to gather outside Yad Eliyahu. An hour later a large crowd was present, which included a good number of onlookers and wellwishers.

Someone brought cakes, biscuits, and bottles of wine. He distributed the cakes, opened the wine, made a blessing and offered thanksgiving prayers.

At the scene of the reunion, the air force base, by eight o'clock soldiers were erecting a canopy from camouflage netting to provide shelter for the waiting families. They arrived from Yad Eliyahu in three buses, and by half past nine the canopied area was full. The air force provided soft drinks and biscuits, and the crowd's mood was, for the most part, festive.

People formed circles, danced and sang, over and over, "Am Yisrael Hai." A bearded old man, carrying a stick in one hand and a shofar in the other, was raised shoulder-high by the crowd. When he was set down he blew a triumphant "teruah" call on the shofar.

The process of reunification went on slowing during the late morning, and the crowd became quieter in the heat, reviving as the VIP's began to arrive. Prime Minister Rabin, Foreign Minister Allon, Opposition Leader Menahem Begin and Chief Rabbi Ovadia Yosef were acclaimed and even mobbed by the crowd, despite the efforts of military police to keep order.

Begin's reception was particularly enthusiastic. He was "chaired" by the crowd and throughout the compound there were chants of "Begin, Begin."

The first hostages entered the compound at 11.05. Tired, unshaven and dressed in crumpled and dirty clothes, they were embraced by weeping relatives, who accompanied them to a nearby building where they received food and drink.

Despite their tiredeness, the hostages, besieged by eager journalists and cameramen, replied patiently and articulately to questions.

One of the questions which has been exercising the whole of Israel during the past week, not out of idle curiosity but because of the vital bearing the answer could have had on the fate of the hostages, received varying responses from the passengers: How had Idi Amin behaved during the period of captivity in Entebbe?

Ahuva Zeitan, a nurse from Beersheba, was among those who had a good word for the Ugandan leader. "When Idi Amin came to the airport it calmed us down," she said. David Elerbaum, Haifa businessman based in Tokyo, told *The Post:* "Idi Amin tried to explain the Palestinian problem to us. He said that we Israelis have to try to understand them."

Ayache Sylver, a bookkeeper from Paris, was less impressed with Amin's behaviour, maintaining that hhe saw several indications of Amin's cooperation with the terrorists. "He would come to where we were staying — the old airport lounge — with about 12 guards. Amin and the guards were all armed — some with pistols, others with Uzi's. He seemed to be on good terms with the terrorists." According to Sylver, Amin consistently blamed the Israel government for the "delay" in releasing the passengers. He said that it was only the Israelis who were refusing to release the terrorists in accordance with the hijackers' demands.

Questioned about the most difficult moments during their eight days of almost unbelievable strain and tension, nearly all agreed that the worst spell was the hijacking itself. Ahuva Zeitan said her stomach contracted when, half-an-hour after take-off from Athens, the terrorists stood up and shouted to the passengers not to move. Aryeh Brodsky said he could hardly believe what was happening. His one thought was a hope that his two little girls would come safely out of whatever was going to happen.

According to Ayache Sylver, the Israeli passengers were far calmer than the other nationalities and much more restrained in the way they expressed their feelings of apprehension.

The terrorists "selections" which separated the Israelis from the other passengers were also bad moments, reminding Ahuva Zeitan, who was born in Tunisia, of waht she had learned about the Nazi "selection" of Jews for death in the camps in World War II. The presence of two Germans among the terrorists reinforced the parallel for her.

During the seven days of captivity, passengers got to know each other, exchanging life stories, playing cards, and even engaging the terrorists in conversation. Sarah Davidson, who kept a diary, talked on a number of occasions with one of the terrorists.

Many passengers said that the German girl was the cruellest of the terrorists and that her behaviour was irrational. She held a pistol in her hand almost throughout the period. But at night, when a blanket had fallen off a sleeping child, she would rearrange the bedclothes.

The male German was described as being more "humane," though he maintained a rigid distance from the passengers.

RABIN TELLS KNESSET SESSION:

Amin worked with gunmen

By ASHER WALLFISH
Jerusalem Post Knesset Reporter

Prime Minister Rabin said yesterday that all indications showed President Idi Amin to have worked hand in hand with the terrorists, despite his mask of guile and his pretence to be doing the contrary.

At an extraordinary Knesset session — rare parliamentary occasion on Sundays — Rabin said that Israel's announcement last Thursday about negotiating an exchange was not a stratagem to gain time. Had there been no alternative, Israel would have carried through that decision.

However, ever since the hijacking, ways had been sought to foil the terrorists directly, and the IDF as well as the "intelligence community" lost no time planning and preparing. When the time was ripe, the plan was put to the Cabinet which approved it unanimously.

Rabin described the rescue mission as "an exemplary victory in humanitarian and moral terms as well as military and operational aspects." The House rose to its feet and he expressed his condolesces to the families of the victims.

There had been no prior consultations with any other government. The decision on the rescue operation was Israel's sole responsibility. Israel would stand firm in the fight against terror, even if alone, although it would not release any government from the obligation to wipe terror out, Rabin said. The struggle was especially arduous in countries where Israel had no foothold because of hostility, absence of diplomatic ties, or cooperation between the government and the terrorists.

He stressed the close cooperation throughout between Coalition and Opposition, and the constant consulations with the Knesset's Foreign Affairs and Defence Committee. The Entebbe operation would not be an epilogue, Rabin said. New efforts and ever-newer techniques would be needed to cope with terrorists. He closed with warm praise for the IDF's achievement.

Likud leader Menahem Begin, in his turn, praised the unity of purpose between all factions and applauded Rabin with a *kol hakabod,* for his role as head of the team.

An unrelenting campaign should be mounted against the terrorists, Begin said — not a series of one-time reprisals. A big force of volunteers should be formed for this task, including veterans of the pre-1948 underground movements

(Continued on page 2, col. 7)

Gur says raiders used 'several tricks'

By JOSHUA BRILLIANT
Jerusalem Post Reporter

TEL AVIV. — About 80 Ugandan soldiers tried to resist the Israeli force in Entebbe, the Chief-of-Staff, Rav-Aluf Mordechai Gur, told a press conference here yesterday. The Ugandans were "intermingled" with the terrorists. Soldiers were stationed on the second floor, on the roof and around the old terminal building at the airport where the hostages were being held.

The Israeli force, commanded by the Chief Paratroop and Infantry Officer, Tat-Aluf Dan Shomron, flew out of Israel on Saturday afternoon.

Defence Minister Shimon Peres declined at the press conference to say what route the Hercules transport planes had taken on the flight. The planes evidently passed near Egypt, Sudan and Saudi Arabia. The radar operators in these countries might have picked up the Israeli aircraft, but evidently failed to realise the significance of the dots on their screens.

Rav-Aluf Gur said that the main problem facing the task force was how to surprise the terrorists. "We used several tricks to do that," and the surprise had indeed been complete. The Chief-of-Staff would not say what "tricks" were used.

The military authorities have not disclosed exactly where the force landed. According to foreign reports the troops attacked the airport building with machine-guns mounted on jeeps. Hercules planes are capable of carrying the vehicles, but Rav-Aluf Gur would not comment on the report.

Tat-Aluf Shomron told the press conference that the moment his men arrived at their destination they opened fire on the terrorists who were guarding the entrance to the old terminal building.

The commandos called to the hostages to lie down and not to move. However,one of the hostages got up and started running, and was killed. At least three more people were injured by shrapnel of a handgrenade.

Both Rav-Aluf Gur and Tat-Aluf Shomron said that as the hostages were in the unlit building where the battle was raging, it was impossible to say how each of the casualties had occurred.

Fighting spread to other areas of the airport. Fire was opened at the commandos from the area near the control tower, and this apparently caused the death of the officer commanding the attacking force.

The Chief-of-Staff said that in the course of the fighting, Ugandan soldiers moved near to a number of Mig planes. "We gave very strict instructions to our people that in case of shooting from that area they should hit the planes." Gur said he

(Continued on page 2, col. 5)

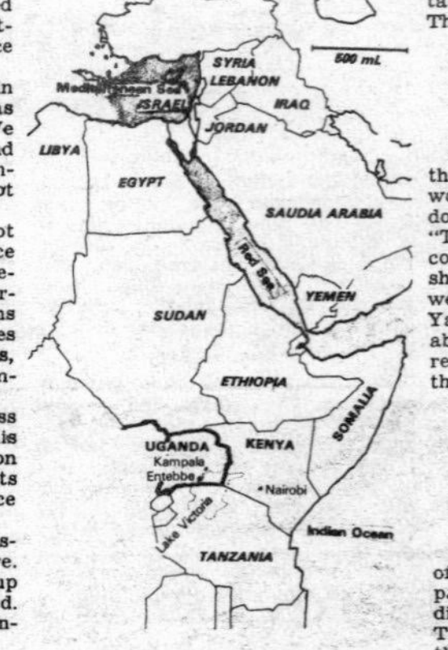

Rabin: Terror not uprooted

Jerusalem Post Reporter

Premier Rabin said last night that he hoped the Uganda action would stop Israelis from having doubts about almost everything. "The action should restore our self-confidence, reduce our cynicism and show us what a wonderful youth we have," he told TV interviewer Ya'acov Ahimeir, who had asked him about the possible effects of the rescue operation on the mood of the country.

Rabin warned that it would be over-optimistic to expect permanent change as a result of this one action by the army. "The operation proves that we're a people with great strength; we must only want to use it," he said.

The Premier said he thought the Entebbe action was a hard psychological blow for the terrorists and that it would also teach a lesson to those who play hosts to hijackers. "To my regret, I think that terror will continue; we haven't uprooted it yet," he added.

Four Israelis killed

Jerusalem Post Correspondent

Four Israelis — the commander of the rescue force and three of the passengers hijacked to Uganda — did not come back from Entebbe. Three of them were killed during the rescue operation, and one died of his injuries in a Nairobi hospital.

Sgan-Aluf Yonatan Netanyahu, who commanded the force which broke into the building at Entebbe airport, where the hostages were held, was one of the first casualties of the action. He was killed by a bullet in the back, fired from the control tower, apparently. The funeral will be held tomorrow at the Military Cemetery on Mount Herzl. Further details will be published.

Ida Borowicz, 56, of Bat Yam, immigrated to Israel from the USSR in 1969.

Jean-Jacques Maimoni, 19, of Netanya, immigrated to Israel with his parents and five elder sisters five years ago. His father, Victor, is employed by the French Consulate in Tel Aviv. Jean-Jacques was on his way to France to continue his studies, and was travelling in the company of the French Consul's son, his friend.

Few details were available last night about the third passenger killed, Pasco Cohen of Hadera. Pasco, his wife and their two children, aged 12 and six, were travelling to France on holiday. He was the secretary of Kupat Holim Meuhedet in Hadera, and his wife owns a haberdashery there. Pasco was the passenger taken to hospital in Nairobi, where efforts to save his life failed.

Hospitalized at Sheba Medical Centre in Tel Hashomer last night were nine wounded — five of the passengers and four soldiers.

Arabs shocked at rescue

POST Middle East Affairs Correspondent

Israel's daring rescue operation at Entebbe evidently had the Arab world in shock yesterday. In reporting the event, many Arab capitals stressed the alleged collusion between Israel and Kenya. This was seen as aimed at minimizing the great distance at which the operation was carried out — a distance which could set off alarm bells in several Arab states that have so far felt themselves too remote for Israeli retaliation.

Officially, most Arab governments yesterday declined to issue statements. They were devoting most of their attention -- or pretending to — to the current inter-Arab disarray, the Lebanese crisis, the weekend coup attempt in the Sudan, and the renewed rift between Algeria and the Morocco-Mauritania axis over the Sahara.

State-run Arab radios nevertheless reported the Israeli operation, with obvious distaste except in the case of Amman and the Christian-controlled stations, whose tone reflected satisfaction.

Cairo Radio, in a commentary on the Lebanese crisis, warned the Arabs that their disarray corresponded with a revival of morale in Israel.

Egypt yesterday denounced the Israel rescue as "an act of agression" against Uganda and the whole of Africa.

It called on the current African summit conference at Port Louis, Mauritius, to condemn the Israeli action.

Cairo Radio had earlier alleged that the Israelis succeeded in landing at Entebbe airport through claiming they were flying in with a number of the terrorists whose release the hijackers had demanded.

The Cairo version was adopted by the PLO organs, which added angrily that the Israelis had deceived both the hijackers and "good-hearted" Ugandan head of state Idi Amin Dada. "The Voice of Palestine," broadcasting from Damascus, warned that the PLO's "heroes" would teach Israel a lesson next time: they would take over an Israeli settlement and reject any protracted negotiations.

J'lem, areas Arabs go back to work

Jerusalem Post Reporter

In East Jerusalem and the West Bank, the spectacular Uganda rescue could be seen to have had a heavy impact yesterday. While keeping a low profile, the Arab population resumed normal business life after three days of political unrest which stemmed from protests against the imposition of Value Added Tax.

(Imposition of the tax, which went into effect on July 1 within the Green Line, has been postponed for another month on the West Bank).

Israelis in Nairobi hospital

By PETER PHILIPP
Special to Jerusalem Post

NAIROBI. — Between three to six Israelis wounded in the Entebbe airport operation are under treatment in hospital here, according to unconfirmed reports in the Kenyan capital.

Staff at the Kenyatta State Hospital said they were under strict orders not to give out any information. The Israelis are in the intensive care unit.

Kenyan authorities have imposed a news blackout on the circumstances of the Israeli commando rescue and especially on any aspect of Kenyan involvement. Although Prime Minister Rabin declared in the Knesset yesterday that the planes had flown directly to Uganda, observers here believe the Israeli aircraft may in fact have refuelled en route to Entebbe and that there is an official attempt to play down Kenya's role in the affair.

Between Kenya and Uganda there is a long simmering dispute and hardly a week goes by without a threat of war or invasion by Amin. Observers said that if it was true that 10 or so Ugandan Migs were destroyed in the Israel operation, then Amin had lost two-thirds of his Air Force.

AP reports from Nairobi:

Witnesses said the first sign of something unusual at Nairobi air-

(Continued on page 4, col. 4)

Ford hails rescue

WASHINGTON. — President Gerald Ford yesterday hailed Israel's daring rescue of the hijacked Air France passengers from Uganda in a message that seemed to indicate U.S. support for Israel in the political counterattack to come.

In a special message to Prime Minister Yitzhak Rabin, Ford said: "The American people join me in expressing our great satisfaction that the passengers of the Air France plane seized earlier this week have been saved and the senseless act of terrorism thwarted."

Observers in Washington saw in the President's message an American pledge of political support for Israel, particularly at the UN Security Council which will apparently be convened at Uganda's request.

Israel's bold rescue operation was welcomed by the Pentagon. "My God, you really can do something with military power," a Pentagon official said, obviously pleased that U.S. military equipment had been used in the action.

An American Jewish leader observed: "I feel great." And American Jews throughout the country echoed this sentiment as a groundswell of pride developed.

Bands, bunting, bells

WASHINGTON. — Amid muted strains of "America the Beautiful" and other patriotic music, President Ford led a group of distinguished Americans in a bicentennial salute on Saturday night.

Ford told an audience of about 2,000 at the John F. Kennedy Centre for the Performing Arts:

"Break out the flags, strike up the band, light up the sky and let the whole world know that the United States of America is about to have another happy birthday, still going strong at 200..."

Bands, bunting and bells heralded the Fourth of July independence day weekend throughout the country.

In New York, the tall ships of another era arrived in the harbour for one of the most flamboyant displays of sail since British square-riggers landed troops there in 1776.

Around the tall ships tens of thousands of private vessels, small and large, churned the waters.

In Philadelphia, people came in wheelchairs and baby carriages, in bikinis and tattered jeans, just to say "happy birthday, America" at the place where the nation was born 200 years ago.

They were all ages, colours and nationalities, and most were carrying cameras as they crowded, 200,000 of them, into the nation's most historic square mile. They visited Independence Hall, touched the Liberty Bell and saw the tiny house where Betsy Ross sewed the first flag.

But their number was far less than the 20 million which had been expected.

Crowds were also smaller than expected in Washington, where 500,000 people turned out Saturday for a parade of 50 bands, 60 floats and 90 marching units. About one million people were expected yesterday evening, as 33 tons of fireworks lit up the city.

Premier Rabin yesterday sent bicentennial greetings to President Ford.

The message said:

Dear Mr. President, On behalf of the people and government of Israel, I extend to you, and through you to the people of America, sincere expressions of friendship, tribute and respect on the occasion of the 200th anniversary of the Day of Independence of the United States of America. All Israel shares in this historic event, which is a celebration of democracy, decency and freedom everywhere. In gratitude and in brotherhood, we salute America—leader of the free world—as you enter into your third century of independence.

The national mood of elation over the Uganda rescue gave added zest to the American Ambassador's Fourth of July celebration here last night. Hundreds of leading Israelis, including almost the entire Cabinet, members of the Supreme Court, army officers, top officials and newspapermen, mingled with diplomats and American visitors on the lawn of Ambassador Toon's residence in Herzliya.

Premier Rabin, Ministers Peres and Allon and Chief of Staff Motta Gur were all warmly congratulated, hugged and kissed by the guests.

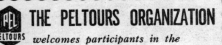

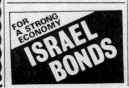

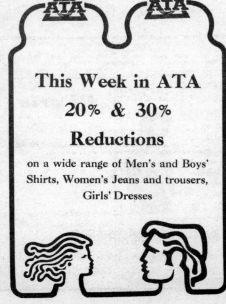

THE JERUSALEM POST

Sylvia Raphael weds her lawyer
Page 2

Price: IL2.75
(Including VAT)

TUESDAY, JANUARY 4, 1977 TEVET 14, 5737 • MUHARRAM 14, 1397 • VOL. XLVI, No. 13903

OFER KILLS HIMSELF

Depressed by rumours

By JOSHUA BRILLIANT, Jerusalem Post Reporter

Housing Minister Avraham Ofer shot himself to death yesterday. He was 55.

He left a note saying he lacked the strength to withstand allegations being spread that he had embezzled public funds before he became a minister.

Police were searching for him in the afternoon but he was discovered by a passerby who spied a body in a white Volvo sedan on the Tel Baruch beach north of Tel Aviv shortly before six o'clock. The passerby summoned police who later identified the Housing Minister.

They found a .22 calibre revolver and the suicide note by the body.

Ofer was alleged to have been involved in irregularities dating from the time when he headed Shikun Ovdim, the Histadrut housing corporation.

During the past few weeks a team of police investigators, headed by Nitsav-Mishne Reuven Minkowsky, head of the police investigations branch, had been examining complaints submitted by a Haolam Hazeh reporter, Yigal Laviv.

The minister was at his home in Jerusalem's Beit Hakerem Quarter yesterday morning. He spoke to two or three reporters who had been in steady contact with him, and then his driver took him to his home in Afeka, a suburb north of Tel Aviv. According to one report he told his driver that he would be contacting him.

Then Ofer left his home without explanation. He drove himself.

An aide who spoke to him over the phone yesterday morning said: "Such an act wasn't expected. He was in a bad mood because the investigation was taking 'another few days,' and 'another few days'."

The first signs that something was amiss were discerned in his bureau in Jerusalem in the morning. The new Austrian Ambassador, Dr. Ingo Mussi, arrived for a courtesy call and was told the minister had not arrived and no one knew his whereabouts.

Police declined to disclose details of what had happened. They referred reporters to the Prime Minister's Office. There they were told there was no comment apart from the official communique. This announced the minister's death in Tel Aviv, and expressed condolences to the family. The statement added that funeral arrangements would be announced later.

Whether there will be a State funeral will depend on the bereaved family. Government officials last night were examining the question.

The family's wishes were also to decide whether there would be a special Cabinet session today, and this too was being checked last night.

Prime Minister Rabin was informed of the suicide at about six o'clock. He was briefed in his Jerusalem office by Police Minister Shlomo Hillel, and Police Inspector-General Haim Tabori.

Aaron Sittner writes from the Knesset:

The news reached the Knesset about an hour after the session ended. Most MKs had left for home and the ushers were preparing to close the building. However, a few Members were still in the restaurant when the news arrived.

Amnon Linn (Likud), who was a close friend of the Housing Minister from the days when Linn was a member of Mapai, told *The Jerusalem Post:* "This should serve as a general alarm signal to us all — the Government side and the Opposition. It proves what the chase after publicity and self-aggrandizement can lead to. Ironically, some of the people who led the attack on Ofer had in years past gone to him for personal favours, such as obtaining housing for themselves or members of their families."

Linn said he had spoken with Ofer last Tuesday and asked him, "Avraham, what is the truth?" To this, Ofer replied "It is all one big lie."

Linn told *The Post:* "I still believe it's a big lie. Ofer told me he expected to be cleared of all suspicion tomorrow (Tuesday) when parliamentary questions connected with reported police interest in some of his past activities were to be answered."

The replies were to have been given by Police Minister Shlomo Hillel or, possibly, by Prime Minister Rabin.

Also in the Knesset restaurant late yesterday evening was Yitzhak Golan (ILP). He called Ofer's death "a tragedy not only for his family but for the nation too. The news media and politicians generally should reconsider their roles, and stop lynchings. It is definitely against the spirit of democracy to air all kinds of allegations against a person before he is indicted or brought to trial," Golan said.

(Obituary — Page 2)

Ofer's letter: 'My blood was spilled'

Here is a translation of the letter found by the police next to Ofer's body:

"For weeks and months I have been tortured, my blood has been spilled, I have been libelled and tormented. This time not even my sons and my family were spared. I have no doubt that the truth will emerge that I have not embezzled and I have not stolen and everything is slander and false accusations, but I do not have the strength to bear any more.

"I also see no point in carrying on. Even when I have been proven right, everything within me is in shreds.

"One thing puzzles me: Throughout my life, I only helped as much as I could and I wronged no one. Why did they persecute me all the time? I have done something with my life; I have worked, toiled, created. My life was not totally useless.

"I am grateful to all those who stood by me and brought me happiness and contentment. I ask forgiveness from all my friends and my loved ones, for leaving them like this. And to my beloved wife, my sons, my daughters-in-law and to all my family: I loved you all and will love you until the last moment. Please accept this act with understanding."

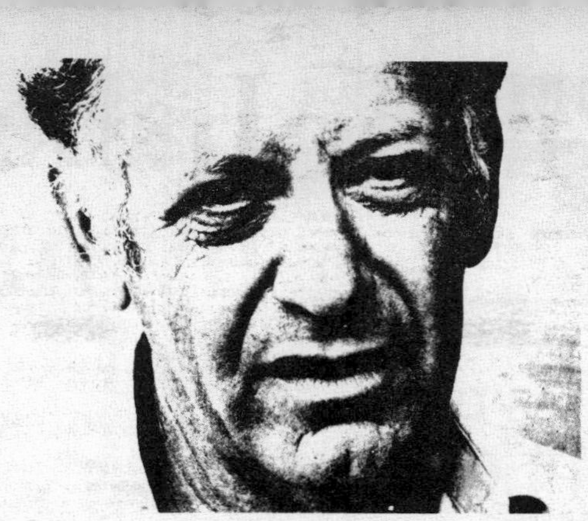

AVRAHAM OFER (Uzi Keren)

Rumours of scandal mushroomed this week

Jerusalem Post Staff

THE POSSIBLE involvement of Avraham Ofer in a financial scandal was transformed from a quietly pursued police investigation into the makings of a full-fledged public affair only in the last week. Last Wednesday MK Shmuel Tamir (Free Centre) submitted a parliamentary question to Police Minister Shlomo Hillel asking confirmation or denial of the reports of a police investigation of accusations against Ofer. MK Ehud Olmert (Likud) submitted a motion with similar intent.

The accusations concerned the purchase of 150 dunams of land from Arabs in the Neve Ya'acov area, northern Jerusalem, by the Histadrut's housing corporation, Shikun Ovdim, in 1970. At that time Ofer headed the company.

The original allegations against Ofer and Shikun Ovdim were made by Yigal Laviv, an investigative reporter for the "Haolam Hazeh" weekly. Recently, a lawyer who had worked with Shikun Ovdim on that sale, Haim Goshen, who is slated to appear as a prosecution witness in the Asher Yadlin bribery trial, was reported to have told police that the official payment recorded for the Neve Ya'acov land deal was fictitious. The price was reported to have been recorded at IL6m. but the sellers claimed they had only received IL3.5m.

Ofer, Goshen and Shikun Ovdim's treasurer were said to have been signatories to the deal. Reports have also appeared that Yadlin, at that time head of the Histadrut's holding company, Hevrat Ha'ovdim, had also been privy to the deal.

Police earlier yesterday refused to confirm or deny that they were investigating Ofer in connection with these charges. The national police spokesman said that "police were locking into numerous allegations" regarding the minister, and added

(Continued on page 2, col. 3)

Sought early end to probe

Jerusalem Post Political Reporter

Intimates of Avraham Ofer said yesterday he had been depressed during the last few days. He had however hoped, as late as Saturday, that the policy inquiry into allegations of malfeasance while head of Shikun Ovdim would be ended quickly.

After Sunday's Cabinet meeting, he met with Prime Minister Rabin and pressed him for an early end to the inquiry because of the mounting rumours about it. These rumours reached a climax after reports that Rabin had met on Saturday with the Ministers of Justice and Police and the Attorney-General to discuss the course of the inquiry.

The sources said that Ofer emerged from the meeting with the Prime Minister discouraged by the realization that the inquiry would drag on longer than for just a few days and no clear conclusion was quickly in the offing. These sources believed yesterday that it was the prospect of facing an indefinite period of uncertainty with rumours and mounting public suspicion against him, that drove the Housing Minister to take his life.

Other sources noted that Ofer was deeply hurt by the attitude of some of his Labour Party colleagues. He was by-passed in the choice for the party's campaign manager for the elections, and was affected as well by demands from some party quarters that he be dropped from the Labour Party Cabinet team in the election.

During the period before the arraignment of Asher Yadlin, Ofer had repeatedly sprung to his defence. He spoke out against the public lynching to which he said Yadlin was subject, asserting that Yadlin should be deemed innocent until proven guilty.

Rifai could head Jordan-PLO joint delegation to Geneva

By ANAN SAFADI
POST Middle East Affairs Correspondent

Cairo and Damascus have been conducting negotiations with Amman and the Palestine Liberation Organization on the possibility of sending a joint Jordanian-Palestinian delegation to a reconvened Middle East peace conference in Geneva, it was learned yesterday. Jordan's former prime minister, Abdul-Mon'em Rifai, who is now a senior political adviser to King Hussein, is mooted to head such a delegation. The 60-year-old Jordanian career diplomat is widely respected in Egyptian and Syrian political circles as well as the PLO leadership.

Cairo's semi-official "Al-Ahram" newspaper yesterday reported that the PLO was now studying a "formula of cooperation" with Jordan as a prelude to the Geneva conference, which the Arabs hope to reconvene early next spring.

The plan to incorporate Palestinian representatives in a joint delegation with Jordan is to be submitted for approval at the forthcoming meeting of the Palestine National Council (parliament) in Cairo. The idea is reportedly backed by Egypt for three main reasons: to restore Jordan's standing with regard to the West Bank; to forestall the controversy over the PLO's participation in Geneva as an independent party; and to relieve the PLO of the issue of accepting UN Security Council Resolutions 242 and 338, both of which govern the Geneva forum.

The proposed formation of the joint Jordanian-Palestinian representation is reported to have split the PLO leadership into three factions. The first favours the project, which they view as the opening of a new phase of Jordanian-Palestinian cooperation based on fresh links between the two sides as independent entities.

Another faction insists on representation independent of Jordan. This faction is believed to be the one whose representatives have met with Israel's political pacifists about the prospects of direct Israeli-Palestinian negotiations. (This despite official and persistent PLO denials of such feelers.)

The third faction, most militant of all, opposes any form of PLO involvement in any kind of political deliberations with Israel. This faction is best represented by the PLO official representative in Khartoum, Abu al-Khair, who yesterday said that the Palestinians should continue their armed struggle until they wipe out Israel.

In an interview with the Sudanese news agency, al-Khair said that, even if Israel withdrew to the pre-1967-war frontiers, "establishment of a Palestinian state in the West Bank and the Gaza Strip should constitute a material counterweight to the Zionist entity and could serve as a concrete base for continuing the Palestinian struggle for the creation of a Palestinian state in the whole of Palestine."

Al-Khair is known for his close association with the head of the PLO's political department, Farouk Kaddoumi — who, according to yesterday's Kuwaiti newspaper "Al-Qabas," is due to be dismissed in an imminent PLO reshuffle. The Kuwaiti paper said that Kaddoumi may be replaced by Khaled al-Hassan — a man favoured by Saudi Arabia, which has been pressing for a PLO reshuffle in its efforts to bolster the diplomatic drive being orchestrated by Egypt and Syria.

A PLO reshuffle would be aimed mainly at pacifying the movement's radical circles, which are rejecting the current Egyptian-Syrian notion for exploring an overall political settlement to the Israel-Arab conflict in the course of this year.

Kuwait's Minister of State Abdul-Aziz Hussein yesterday said that Arab foreign and defence ministers may meet in Saudi Arabia shortly to discuss the means of stepping up support for Arab front-line states.

(Leader — back page)

Paris PLO office denies signing pact with Peled

By JACK MAURICE
Jerusalem Post Correspondent

PARIS. — The Palestine Liberation Organization denied here yesterday it has signed a joint document with Israeli pacifists recognizing the existence of the State of Israel.

A statement from the PLO's Paris office said it would never countenance the "Zionist entity."

This statement counters the claim made in Tel Aviv on Sunday by Matti Peled, chairman of the Council for Israeli-Palestinian Peace, that he signed a document on these lines in Paris over the weekend. (A brief denial by the PLO was published in yesterday's *Post.*)

The PLO statement said: "We can confirm that no Palestinian leader acting on instructions from the PLO signed such a document. The PLO will not authorize any of its members to act in a way contrary to the aims of our people's struggle and the resolutions of the Palestinian National Council."

Former French Premier Pierre Mendes-France said yesterday: "I have nothing to say about the reports of this meeting. This is not the time to do so."

Mendes-France has been reported to have played the role of go-between in a series of meetings between Israeli pacifists and PLO representatives since he visited Israel last summer.

(Allon — page 3)

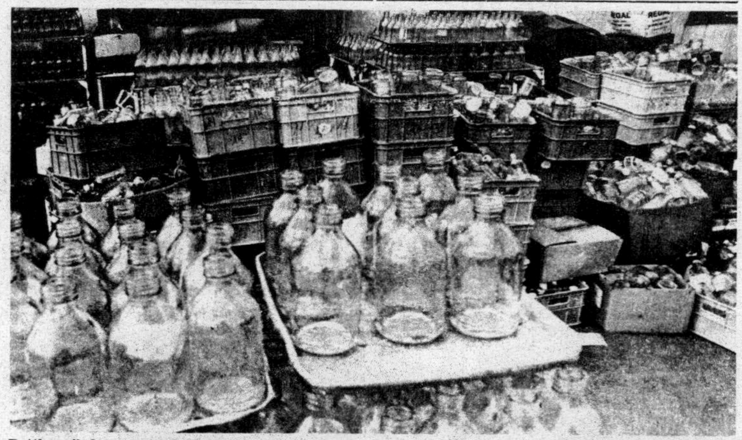

Bottles piled up yesterday outside the sterilization plant of Sheba Medical Centre, Tel Hashomer. There, as at other government hospitals, the non-medical staff walked out on Sunday. The strike is to continue today. (Lester Millman)

Danger of infection seen as hospital walkout continues

By SARAH HONIG
Jerusalem Post Reporter

TEL AVIV. — As doctors warned of the possible spread of infection among patients if the strike by 6,000 administrative and maintenance employees in 26 government hospitals is not immediately called off, the strikers yesterday decided to extend their walkout by at least one day.

By a vote of 33 to 14 the strikers' committee approved a compromise motion whereby they would stay away from their jobs for a third consecutive day, although they initially called only for a 48-hour walkout. The strike may end today, if agreement is reached in talks scheduled between the Minister of Health and the employees' representatives. Should the employees emerge unsatisfied, however, they have already announced that they will prolong their walkout.

Moderates among them proposed yesterday that the strike be called off as a gesture of good will before the talks, but the hard-liners urged an indefinite extension until their pay demands are fully met.

As the strike entered its second day yesterday the situation at the government hospitals continued to deteriorate. Doctors in a number of hospitals serving the Greater Tel Aviv area told *The Post* that, if normal work is not immediately restored, "there will be no avoiding harm to the patients. The wards are not filled with healthy people; and if people already in a weakened state of health are exposed to unhygienic conditions, there is no telling where it might end. They are very susceptible to infection, and the grossly unsanitary situation is surely conducive to infection."

One danger most doctors pointed to were the hospital dishes. While the strikers had made one exception — allowing kitchen staff to continue preparing meals — there is no one to wash the dishes.

In most wards the nurses volunteered to do the most urgent kitchen clean-ups, in addition to their regular duties. But being overburdened — as they already are — they could not always do a thorough job, could not do it frequently enough, and could not supervise general cleanliness.

Another source of danger are the lavatories and bathrooms, where conditions were described as appalling both by patients and by the medical staff. The shortage of clean bed linen was even more marked yesterday than on the first day of the strike, and bed-ridden and post-surgery patients continued to lie on soiled sheets which normally must be changed every few hours.

Only the most urgent surgery was performed for the second running day in most hospitals, and the processing of patients in emergency wards continued to be slow in view of the absence of the clerical staff. Even X-rays and various other tests had to be postponed if not urgent, because there were no employees to wheel stretchers.

Hospital switchboards were also out of operation, and telephone inquiries about patients' conditions could not be made.

The only improvement over the situation on Sunday was the fact that many of the nurses had made other arrangements to reach their hospitals, after the absence of the hospital bus drivers caused many nurses to reach work late on the first day of the walkout.

Elections set for May 17, but change still possible

Jerusalem Post Knesset Reporter

The Knesset Law Committee yesterday agreed on May 17 as the tentative date for the Knesset elections, but left the door open to switching the date after the first reading of the draft bill on the dissolution of the Knesset.

The May 17 date was a compromise between the Likud proposal for May 3 elections and the Alignment's proposal of May 31. The first reading of the bill has not yet been put on the Knesset calendar. Alternative suggestions of a May 12 date by Moked's Meir Pa'il and two Rakah members were rejected, as was an open proposal calling for elections 105 days after the adoption of the bill by the Knesset.

There are many objections to the tentative May 17 date. Mayor Teddy Kollek of Jerusalem is reported to have objected to holding elections on the morrow of the 10th anniversary of the Hebrew date of the reunification of Jerusalem in the Six Day War. He is said to have felt that this proximity would eclipse the festivities planned for Jerusalem Day.

On the other hand, the religious parties are uncomfortable at holding the elections so soon before Shavuot, with the possibility of having to process and transport ballot boxes from army outposts on the holiday. The compromise bill will thus be tabled for a first reading; but the various Knesset factions will continue considering an alternative date, which can still be set between the first and second readings of the framework bill.

The committee also approved an amendment to the Knesset Elections Law increasing the deposit required from each party contending in the elections from IL15,000 to IL40,000.

A meeting at which President Katzir was to have charged Prime Minister Rabin with the task of attempting to form a new government was abruptly postponed last night, presumably because of Housing Minister Ofer's death.

It was understood that Rabin was to have gone through the motions of trying to form a new government. These attempts would have gone on concurrently with the Knesset's processing of the dissolution bill calling for May elections. As soon as that bill is passed all attempts to form an alternative government will stop, and the current transition government will continue in office until the formation of a new one following the elections.

'You journalists killed him'

By DAVID LENNON
Jerusalem Post Reporter

TEL AVIV. — "You journalists killed him," one of Avraham Ofer's sons shouted as a reporter entered the family home last night. Other journalists were shooed away before they could reach the front door.

The single-storey house in the fashionable Afeka suburb of Tel Aviv was the target of a stream of visitors last night.

Ofer's wife and his three sons were gathered inside the house as neighbours, relatives and friends came to express their condolences.

The family only heard about the Housinm Minister's suicide note from the 9 p.m. television news. One visitor said that the family was startled by this revelation and angry with the police, who took the letter away with Ofer's body but did not inform the family of its existence.

Among the first of Ofer's political friends to visit the family was Dov Tzamir, head of the Information Department of the Labour Party.

The first of Ofer's Cabinet colleagues to arrive, at 9.30, was Defence Minister Shimon Peres. He was followed by Finance Minister Yehoshua Rabinowitz, one of Ofer's closest political allies.

By 9.45, Deputy Prime Minister Yigal Allon had joined those expressing their condolences.

Prime Minister Yitzhak Rabin, accompanied by his wife Lea, arrived at the Ofer house at 10 p.m.

17 reported dead in Beirut blast

BEIRUT. — A large bomb exploded outside the East Beirut headquarters of the Phalangist Party yesterday, leaving 17 persons dead in the most serious terrorist incident since Arab peace-keeping forces entered the city in mid-November, Phalangist sources said.

Initial reports said more than 50 persons had been wounded in the blast.

The explosion occurred near the barracks of the Phalangist security offices on Akkawi Street in the Ashrafiya section of East Beirut.

"There were bits of bodies all over the street. It was horrible," said Mrs. Sophia Anttreasian, a housewife whose apartment looks over the explosion site.

The Phalange spokesman said the explosion was a 155-mm. artillery shell. However witnesses said it appeared the blast came from charges planted in a car parked near the barracks entrance.

The Syrian peace-keeping forces in Lebanon yesterday ended their occupation of a number of newspapers as tough new censorship regulations came into effect.

The peace-keepers last month closed six daily newspapers and a weekly magazine.

The troops withdrew from newspapers including the French-language "L'Orient-le Jour" and the independent "An-Nahar." It was not clear whether these papers would now resume publication. (UPI, Reuter)

The Knesset mourns the death of

AVRAHAM OFER

Minister of Housing

and conveys its deepest condolences to the family.

The Government of Israel

announces with grief the death of

AVRAHAM OFER

Minister of Housing

and conveys its deepest condolences to the family.

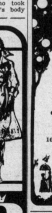

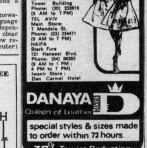

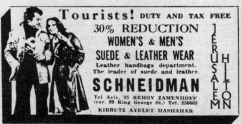

THE JERUSALEM POST

Late edition

Price: IL2.75 (Including VAT)

THURSDAY, FEBRUARY 24, 1977 • ADAR 6, 5737 • RABIA AWAL 6, 1397 • VOL. XLVII, NO. 13947★

Labour picks Rabin by narrow margin

Peres loses by 41 votes

TEL AVIV. — Prime Minister Yitzhak Rabin last night turned back the challenge of Shimon Peres and retained the mantle of Labour Party leadership by a slim margin of only 41 votes — 1,445 to 1,404. in the party convention. Some 2,810 delegates voted; 4 per cent of the listed delegates did not cast ballots.

The Convention, electrified by the Rabin-Peres contest, gave both Rabin and Peres rousing ovations after the final results were announced.

After the vote was announced, Rabin was nominated party leader by acclamation of the whole convention.

The 3,000 delegates and party officials who cast ballots last night had spent the tension-filled day in the Mann Auditorium here. Even while hearing speeches from Austrian Chancellor Bruno Kreisky and other foreign dignitaries, the convention remained focused on procedural jockeying for position between the two candidates.

The balloting finally started around 9 p.m., with a delay being caused by a last-minute check of credentials. Both Peres and Rabin appeared confident as they cast their ballots. The 24 booths on the second floor of Mann Auditorium closed at about 11.

An atmosphere of gloom settled over Peres headquarters upstairs in the Mann Auditorium even as the first results trickled in and the trend became clear. Peres sat with his chief party supporter, former Foreign Minister Abba Eban MK, and tried to keep up a brave front. But Eban, in a rare display of emotion, seemed fighting to hold back tears as it became clear that Peres would be the loser.

The voting was held alphabetically by the delegates' names, and the first ballot box to be counted, at about 11 p.m. was the letter Heh. The results: 37 for Rabin, 35 Peres. When he heard the totals, Peres said jovially, "So we've lost," which brought anxious smiles from the supporters gathered in the room.

While final voting was going on last night between 9.30 and 11.30, delegates gathered to hear greetings from socialist leaders.

Francois Mitterrand, Secretary-General of the French Socialist Party, received loud applause when he said, our problems are great, but you are an understanding people, and in the end we shall all accept whatever you decide about your own fate." He said that only the parties to the conflict themselves could solve their problems by direct talks.

Mitterrand did not refer to current French policy but said, "when you come to France, you shall hear my views."

The official results of the Labour vote were:
3,018-eligible voters
2,870-votes cast
2,865-votes approved
16-abstained
1,445-Rabin
1,404-Peres

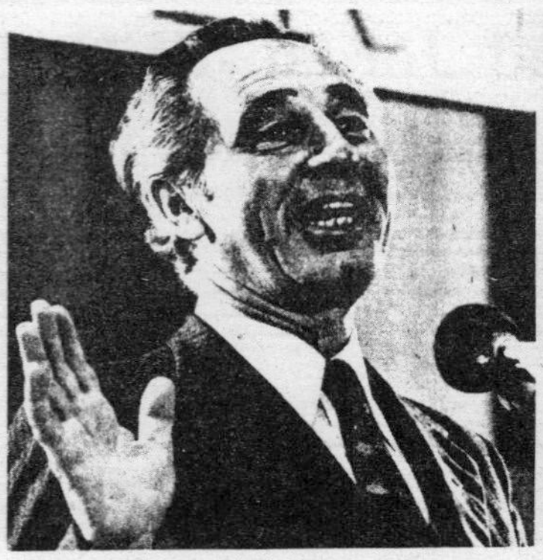

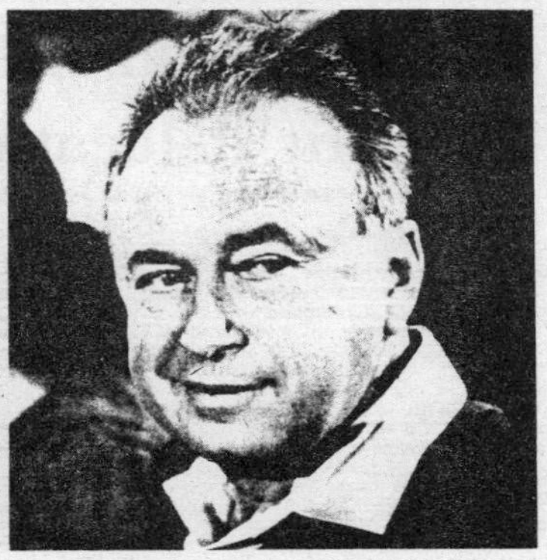

Defence Minister Shimon Peres on rostrum, Prime Minister Yitzhak Rabin in audience during yesterday evening's session of the Labour convention, when each man made his final plea for the delegates' votes. (Lester Millman)

Candidates, party leaders urge Labour Party to close its ranks

By JOSHUA BRILLIANT
Post Political Reporter

TEL AVIV. — Following the announcement of Prime Minister Yitzhak Rabin's victory, the two candidates and other party leaders called for Labour to close its ranks.

Thanking his supporters "who wanted to let me continue in my task," Rabin said Labour will win the Knesset elections if it keeps up its readiness and vigilance as it did during the leadership contest. He said Labour has the capability to continue leading the courtry.

Both Peres and Rabin called for party unity, and Peres shook the victor's hand. Peres thanked the thousands who supported his candidacy and who worked day and night with him during the campaign. Peres said that the style of the campaign had been honourable, and neither had to be sorry for having slighted his opponent.....

"I hoped this style will continue in the party life," Peres said.

He told the convention that he was not sorry for having run. "I believe this contributes to the party's revitalization," The Defence Minister wished Rabin "full success."

The 3,000 delegates rose to a standing ovations, clapping their hands above their heads, shouting "Rabin. Rabin" in unison.

"From this moment on, we are all united," Rabin said. "We have the strength, we have the ability, and the human resources, to lead this country to peace, security, economic development and social progress."

"All the best to you," he said, addressing the delegates, and then, "All the best to you, Shimon."

Former Defence Minister Moshe Dayan, a Peres supporter, sounded a more discordant note. "I regret the results and regret even more the consequences of the result," he told a reporter without elaborating.

Former Foreign Minister and Peres supporter Abba Eban told *The Jerusalem Post* after the results were made known that, in light of the large support the Defence Minister mustered, it was correct for Peres to have entered the race.

"It would have been artificial for half the party to find no expression in the vote" he said.

He stressed that they would abide by the decision of the party and support the party to the full... "However," he added, "the victorious camp must consider how it proposes to achieve party unity, and what steps it intends to take to give such a large minority a sense of solidarity."

The party cannot win on May 17, he said, by the efforts of only half of its members, but only but by bringing both the minority and majority together on a basis of mutual respect.

Transport Minister and Peres supporter Gad Ya'acobi claimed that since the vote was so close Peres deserved the number two position in the party and the next government.

As the result was announced, the Prime Minister stood and gave a weak smile. He did not seem overjoyed, with his majority and acknowledge the cheers of his supporters with nods of his head.

Peres, who had been in the hall previously, was not present when the Prime Minister entered to rhythmic shouts of "Rabin, Rabin," and took his seat at on the dais. When he did join the Prime Minister, Rabin did not rise, shook hands with him from a sitting position. This recalled the previous day's incident when Peres did not rise for Rabin's entrance into Binyenei Ha'ooma with former Prime Minster Golda Meir and Socialist International Presidency Willy Brandt.

Peres then sat down next to the Prime Minister. Although they sat with elbows almost touching, they men did not look at each other.

Analysts in the Peres camp seemed to agree that the swing to Rabin came only in the last few days, and that Peres had reached his high point too early. Had the vote been taken two weeks ago, they said, their candidate would have been the winner. Some compared the situation to the Ford-Carter campaign, in which Carter reached his peak several weeks before the election, and Ford began to close in on him in the last days.

Other Peres supporters noted that his speech to the convention had been too long and full of platitudes, and that Rabin had done better in the hot and poorly ventilated hall with his brief speech.

May appeal

Peres headquarters early this morning were said to be seriously considering appealing the election results. This followed claims from several ballot committee members that more than 100 extra votes had been added by padding the eligible voters lists prior to the vote. They claimed that that the figure of 3,018 eligible voters at the convention had never been memntioned earlier and was almost 100 votes higher than the expected number of delegates.

Vance struck by inter-Arab differences

By WOLF BLITZER
Jerusalem Post Correspondent

WASHINGTON. — Secretary of State Cyrus Vance returned from talks with Arab leaders surprised by the difference of views held in the Arab world regarding peace negotiations, the State Department informed Israel yesterday.

Vance reported on his trip to Israel and five Arab countries to President Carter during a morning meeting at the White House. He later went to Capitol Hill to brief — behind closed doors — the House Appropriations Committee.

Under-Secretary of State Philip Habib, who was on the trip with Vance, is reported to have told Israel Ambassador Simcha Dinitz that Vance was favourably impressed by the views he heard outlined in Jerusalem. The Carter Administration will work together with Jerusalem in the search for peace in the Middle East, Habib is supposed to have said.

Reporters here were told that the Habib-Dinitz meeting, which lasted an hour, was primarily concerned with the current situation in the Middle East and the Vance journey. Bilateral U.S.-Israel problems — such as Israel's request to export Kfir fighter bombers to Ecuador and the U.S. veto of concussion bomb sales to Israel — were probably not raised.

Vance has already indicated that he is prepared to return to the Middle East this summer, following the Knesset elections to work towards reviving a Geneva Conference during the second half of this year.

Earlier yesterday Israel sources here could neither confirm nor deny a report by syndicated columnists Rowland Evans and Robert Novak that Israel had acquiesced in State Department pressure to allow U.S. oil companies to drill for oil in the Gulf of Suez.

The columnists said that, following an appeal by the U.S. oil company to the State Department, and a subsequent U.S. message to Israel to stop hindering U.S. oil drilling in the region, Israel quietly dropped the matter and let the oil company continue its search for oil.

Carter: M-E tour great success

By WOLF BLITZER
Jerusalem Post Correspondent

WASHINGTON. — President Jimmy Carter said yesterday that after his meetings with Israel and Arab leaders before the end of May, the U.S. would determine its proper role in working towards an Arab-Israel settlement.

At a White House press conference, Carter said that he considers Secretary of State Cyrus Vance's just-concluded tour of the Middle East to have been "very successful."

Secretary Vance not only "probed" the Arab and Israel positions on all the key issues, Carter said, but also had a chance to compare their stands — where there was "harmony" and where there was "dispute."

Carter said that all the Arab leaders who were invited to meet him had accepted and "I look forward to meeting them."

Commenting on the deaths of Ugandan Anglican Archbishop Janani Luwum and two Cabinet Ministers, allegedly at the hands of Idi Amin himself, as well as reports of widespread killings in the country, Carter said that recent events in Uganda had "disgusted the entire civilized world." (Amin — Page 4)

Hussein flies to UK, rebuffing PLO team

Israel Arabs report warm welcome

Post Midcast Affairs Editor

Expectations of an early reconciliation between Jordan and the Palestine Liberation Organization seemed dashed last night when King Hussein flew unexpectedly to London — rebuffing a high-ranking PLO delegation which had come to Amman to negotiate a rapprochement. The Jordanian government said that Hussein was on a private visit which would last several days.

Reports from Amman said that Hussein was not eager for a reconciliation until the PLO reshuffled its overall leadership, and adopted the Middle East policy line of the confrontation governments — Jordan, Syria and Egypt. The Jordanians expect both issues to be raised by the Palestine National Council (parliament) at its session in Cairo next month.

Hussein nevertheless instructed his government to conduct exploratory talks with the visiting PLO delegation, headed by Khaled Fahoum, the PNC speaker. Fahoum, who is one of the chief advocates of a Jordanian-PLO rapprochement, last night met with Jordan's Prime Minister Mudar Badran for the second and last time in the two-day visit.

At the top of their agenda was Egyptian President Anwar Sadat's recent proposal that Hussein and the PLO declare "some sort" of a Jordanian-Palestinian confederation before the opening of new Middle East peace negotiations.

The two sides have had no relations since Hussein ousted the PLO from his kingdom in a bloody showdown in 1971 and 1972. The 1974 Arab summit in Rabat, which named the PLO, rather than Jordan, guardian of the West Bank, only widened the wedge between the two sides.

Their current dialogue, coming in a period of intensive diplomatic activity in the region, is thought likely to develop into a major event despite caution on both sides.

A joint Jordanian-PLO press release yesterday said that the two sides were studying ways of improving their relations, bolstering Arab solidarity and supporting Arabs in the "occupied land." This reportedly included the Israel Arabs too.

The first delegation of Israel Arabs ever to visit an Arab country returned yesterday from Amman after offering condolences to King Hussein on the death of Queen Alia.

Members of the delegation last night told *The Jerusalem Post* they received red carpet treatment in Amman. They were given an audience by Hussein and his brother, Crown Prince Hassan, and were entertained at government-initiated conferences with large groups of Jordan's leading politicians and thinkers during their five-day stay.

The meetings were reported to have focused on the prospects of lifting the ban on Israel Arabs' visits to neighbouring countries and ways of "restoring their relations with Arab kin and culture."

60,000 civil servants may strike on Monday

Jerusalem Post Reporter

Representatives of 60,000 civil servants yesterday said they would launch an all-out strike as of Monday unless a collective wage agreement is signed between them and the Civil Service Commissioner before then.

The civil servants last week gave notice of an imminent labour dispute, but ignored the customary 14-day cooling-off period in order to be able to beat the impending "package-deal" deadline which will freeze all wage agreements for at least four months. In doing so they followed the pattern set by workers at the radio and television, who also embarked on a short-notice strike to induce management to speed up negotiations.

The civil servants' claims came in the wake of wage agreements signed with the technicians, the non-graduate engineers and the academic workers. When these agreements were announced last week, Civil Servants Union head Chaim Bernstein announced that he would press for corresponding wage agreements for his union on a scale comparable with those given the other three groups.

Treasury, Civil Service Commission and Histadrut officials were all unavailable for comment yesterday as they were attending the Labour Party convention.

Broadcast journalists reach wage agreement

Radio and television journalists and production workers reached an agreement in principle with the Broadcasting Authority late last night on a wage agreement covering the period 1976-1978. The agreement, reached after 11 hours of continuous negotiations, followed the guidelines set down by Education and Culture Minister Aharon Yadlin, under the Broadcasting Authority law.

A four-hour strike by the journalists and production workers on Tuesday night halted television and radio broadcasts and prevented coverage of the opening of the Labour Party convention.

(Earlier stories — page 3)

Rabin-Peres duel gave life to a usually dull event

By YOSEF GOELL
Jerusalem Post Reporter

TEL AVIV. — The competition between Yitzhak Rabin and Shimon Peres for the Labour Party's candidacy for the premiership yesterday infused life into the first working sessions of the party's national convention.

National party conventions are usually dull affairs in which jaded party activists who have seen it all, and many times, spend more time gossiping, socializing and wheeling and dealing in the corridors than in the plenum. At yesterday's sessions at the Mann Auditorium, the plenum was full nearly throughout the day. The 3,000 delegates participated actively in the debates and in the voting on the procedural party matters which took up the bulk of the day, right through to the drama of the candidates' speeches in the evening and the voting which went into the night.

The explanation for the difference in mood was the unprecedented competition itself, with convention delegates being called upon for the first time to select the party's top leader, and the fact that so many of the convention delegates are people new to national politics.

This latter aspect dominated the mood of the convention throughout the day. It was especially noticeable in the few cases in which the establishment's proposals on party affairs were rejected by crushing majorities of rank-and-file members waving a sea of delegate cards.

One such vote was on a proposal for the constitution of the new Central Committee which is to be elected today and tomorrow. The preparatory committee's proposal was for a 601-member Central Committee. A minority proposal by Haifa region chairman Uri Agami for a 701-man committee, was voted in by an overwhelming majority.

A similar fate befell the preparatory committee's proposal for the institution of the principle of rotation in top political offices. The proposal called for changing party representatives in political posts after two terms in office with a third term to be conditional on the vote of an absolute majority. There was unanimity in regard to the rotation proposal.

The preparatory committee, however, proposed that the rotation principle be applied only gradually in reference to present office holders. This latter proposal was rejected by an overwhelming majority which opted vociferously for immediate application of the principle.

It is too early to say what effect this decision will actually have on the composition of the party's lists to various elective offices. The mood — that of a new spirit of populism in the party — was the important thing, and it was this mood which dominated the convention's business and spilled over into the applause for the contending candidates when they entered the hall to deliver their speeches towards evening.

Populism would be an understatement for with the entrance of the two, the mood changed to that of an arena acclaiming two gladiators scheduled to do battle. The picture resembled that of an American political convention, with organized cliques cheering for their candidate and the acclaim turning into cadenc-

(Continued on page 2, col. 3)

Nice guys speak last

Jerusalem Post Reporter

Nowhere was the sports competition aspect of the Rabin-Peres race so blatant as in the adamant insistence of the two contenders on speaking last at last night's convention. The assumption was that the last speaker would have the greater and more lasting impact on whatever undecided delegates remained an hour before the crucial vote.

The issue had been debated for the past week in the convention's preparatory committee and was submitted at the last moment to the decision of a three-man body: party secretary-general Meir Zarmi, steering committee chairman Aharon Becker, and convention chairman Shlomo Hillel.

The three decided that hearing substantive arguments so close to the event would be pointless and decided to settle the issue by rolling a pair of dice from a *shesh-besh* (backgammon) set. Peres won and became the man to speak last.

Convention chairman Hillel, with Haim Bar-Lev one of the two uncommitted Cabinet ministers, slipped up, however, in announcing the order to the convention. "The convention will now be addressed by Shimon Peres," he announced, and then immediately corrected himself, "I meant Yitzhak Rabin."

A cursory poll of some delegates after the speeches as to the validity of the "last speaker impact" theory, seemed to indicate that it held no water. Committed delegates did not change their mind; the uncommitted were still undecided and grappling with themselves.

Many gave Rabin points for taking only 20 minutes out of the allotted hour but noted that his speech was sincere but pale compared with Peres'. All agreed that Peres' speech, although impressive, was far too long.

Mine kills three near Dead Sea

BEERSHEBA. — Three residents of Arad were killed in a land mine explosion south of the Dead Sea Works yesterday, near Neot Hakikar.

The dead were identified as Shimshon Feier, 37, chief security officer of the works; Rami Shaham, 42, a sub-contractor for the works; and Amiram Katz, 45, proprietor of a petrol station at Neve Zohar and tourist guide for the area.

The three were travelling in a jeep near the southern dam of the company, off the field called Caledonia. It was learned that the area was an old marked minefield, and the jeep went some 130 metres into it before the mine, of IDF manufacture, exploded.

THE JERUSALEM POST

Officers to clog ports
page 3

Price: IL4.00
(Including VAT)

FRIDAY, APRIL 8, 1977 • NISSAN 20, 5737 • RABIA THANI 19, 1397 • VOL. XLVII, No. 13983★

RABIN QUITS

By DAVID LANDAU, Post Diplomatic Correspondent

Prime Minister Yitzhak Rabin has resigned. He will not lead the Labour Party into the elections, and intends to step down as Premier in the next few days. Rabin took his decision late last night in the wake of new revelations concerning the illegal bank account he and his wife Lea held in a US bank.

The account contained much more than Mr. and Mrs. Rabin at first admitted, and it was active, not dormant as they indicated, in the years since Rabin's term as ambassador to Washington.

Mr. Rabin told the nation in a brief broadcast close to midnight that he could not take upon himself the damage to his party which his personal lapse might cause. He termed the lapse "small in my view," but said "since I am Premier, and we are on the eve of elections, I have no option but to step down."

Mr. Rabin explained that his wife, Lea, would face prosecution. Attorney-General Aharon Barak, "to my regret," had not been prepared, Rabin explained, to make do with an administrative fine which Treasury officials had imposed on the couple and had indicated that Mrs. Rabin, at least, would have to stand trial.

"I have said before that I bear, jointly with my wife, formal and moral responsibility (for the account) and I am not ready for her to stand trial alone. I will not hide behind parliamentary immunity, and will face the issue together with her."

Speaking in sombre tones, the Premier said he had handed back to Party Secretary-General Meir Zarmi the mandate he had received from the Party Convention to lead it through the elections.

He said he knew there were constitutional difficulties in resigning from the office of Premier, because he headed an interim government. But he would "act to bring my term of office to a close as soon as possible." He would take advice on how precisely to achieve this in the days ahead.

(Legal observers note that the Premier can take "leave of absence," in which case his deputy, Yigal Allon, would take over.)

Rabin said that the account, held in a Washington bank, contained in March 1973, when he ended his tour as ambassador to the U.S., some $18,000.

Although by last month, when the account's existence was first revealed, there was only $2,000 left in it, there was "in fact $10,000 abroad in various forms," which was all returned to Israel after the initial publication.

Mr. Rabin sought to explain that the figure of $2,000 which was cited by his wife at that time represented the cash in the account when it was closed. "The rest of the money was en route to Israel in various forms."

In his interview on TV, Mr. Rabin said: "The responsibility for the accounts was morally and formally both my wife's and my own. The accounts were opened while we were in Washington during my tour as Ambassador. The money in the accounts came entirely from the period of my service there. I did not conceal the fact that the account existed. My wife travelled to the bank in a car belonging to the U.S. State Department bodyguards. There have been no deposits made since we left."

"At any rate, I am not oblivious of the fact that it was a mistake and an act of negligence that I did not close the account when I completed my tour of duty. Because we saw this as a mistake, we turned to the authorized authorities and asked them to arrange a composition.

"We presented all the material connected with the affair and the matter was discussed according to accepted procedures. The Treasury appointed a committee, which included police representatives. They recommended a monetary composition. To my great sorrow, during the past 24 hours the Attorney-General did not accept this recommendation, at least with respect to my wife, and in his opinion she is to stand trial and the file is to be passed on to the prosecution.

"I have announced in the past that we hold the responsibility jointly, and I am not prepared that she should stand trial alone, if that does in fact turn out to be the decision. I will stand with her, and I will not hide behind the immunity of a Knesset Member."

Asked if he himself withdrew anything from the account, Mr. Rabin said that this was irrelevant, as whatever his wife had done was acceptable to him, and there were no secrets between them.

Gidion Eshet adds:

The bank account of the Rabin family was revealed by "Haaretz" Washington correspondent Dan Margalit three weeks ago. The account had at the time $2,000. The Rabins also had about $8,000 in travellers checks, bringing the total to $10,000. When the Rabins left the U.S. in 1973, the account had about $18,000, and since then Lea Rabin had withdrawn some $8,000.

After the story was revealed by Margalit, the Rabins submitted to the Treasury all the relevant documents, including microfilms of all their bank transactions since they left the U.S. The investigation revealed that all the money in the account came in legally. Nevertheless it was evidently illegal not to bring all the money back to Israel.

The investigation also found that it was obvious that there was more than $5,000 in the account. It is a Treasury practice that in such cases if the sum is less than $5,000 a monetary "composition" (fine) is agreed upon. But above this sum other considerations enter.

According to Treasury sources, at this stage, the Attorney General informed the Finance Minister he, insisted that the investigation come under his direction.

After all the facts were cleared, the sources said, a dispute broke out between the Treasury and the Attorney General. (According to Defence Regulations 1941, the sole responsibility in such matters is with the Finance Minister or the Controller of Foreign Currency). The Treasury decided to agree to a monetary composition as proposed by the Rabins' lawyer, Shimon Alexandroni.

The Treasury based its decision on precedents. For that reason it appointed, together with the police, a committee which decided on Wednesday night on a fine of IL150,000.

The Attorney General strongly opposed this decision, insisting that the case of Lea Rabin, who made all the transactions, should be handled by the state attorney's office, and that in the case of Mr. Rabin himself, either nothing should be done, or that a small fine be agreed upon.

This was the situation yesterday morning, when the matter was brought to the attention of the Prime Minister himself. Mr. Rabin insisted that no distinction be made between himself and his wife. He said that he shared the responsibility with her and would not agree that only she undergo investigation by the State Attorney.

During yesterday morning, senior Cabinet members tried to persuade Mr. Rabin that the Treasury's position, which they agreed is the responsible authority was the right one.

But the Premier remained unconvinced and decided to announce his resignation.

During the day, Finance Minister Yehoshua Rabinowitz was reportedly considering taking the decision on the fine and thus thwarting the Attorney General's action. But with Rabin opposed, Rabinowitz did not take this step.

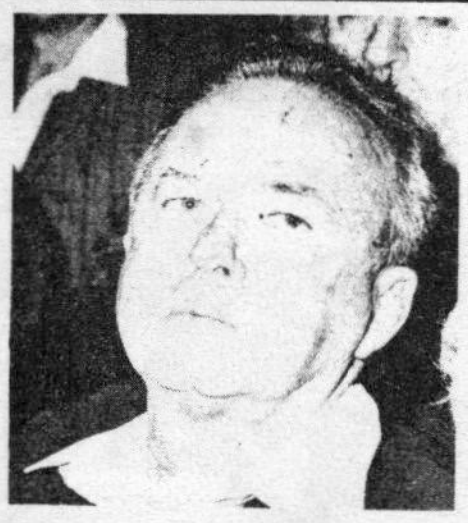

Prime Minister Rabin at the Labour Party Central Committee yesterday. (Gottfreund, IPPA)

Barak decided to prosecute

Attorney-General Aharon Barak said he takes "full and sole responsibility" for the legal decision that brought about Premier Rabin's resignation last night.

In a brief conversation after midnight last night, Prof. Barak indicated to *The Jerusalem Post* that he had not consulted with Justice Minister Zadok, nor indeed with anyone else, before reaching his decision that the issue be handed over to the police for possible prosecution.

Barak declined to say if he had met face-to-face with the Prime Minister yesterday.

Tel Aviv Maccabi win basketball crown 78:77

By STEVE KAPLAN
Jerusalem Post Sports Reporter

Tel Aviv Maccabi copped the European basketball championship last night in a thrilling 78-77 victory over Mobilgirgi of Varese, Italy.

Led by the sharp shooting of Jim Boatwright, who scored 28 points, Maccabi dominated the game throughout and fought off a late challenge by the Italians.

Maccabi started the game with a strong man-to-man defence which unnerved the Italian Five. Aulcie Perry controlled the boards, and Boatwright and Mickey Berkowitz led the early scoring, while the Italians repeatedly misfired.

The first half ended with Maccabi holding a firm 39-30 lead.

The Italians settled down in the second half as their star Bob Morse found the range. Maccabi's offence slowed down, and only Boatwright's shots from long range kept Maccabi in the game.

The Italians pulled to within four points of Maccabi, but the Tel Avivians kept fighting back now under the guidance of Tal Brody, who played only in the second half.

In the closing minutes, the Italians narrowed the gap to one point and then finally managed to tie at 61-61.

Boatwright again shone as the key player sinking three crucial shots in the last two minutes of play, each time boosting Maccabi's lead from one to three points.

In the last 90 seconds the Italians tried frantically to get at the ball, but Maccabi held them off.

For Israel the top scorers were Boatwright 28, Berkowitz 15, Perry 12. For Mobilgirgi: Morse 22, Menighin 19.

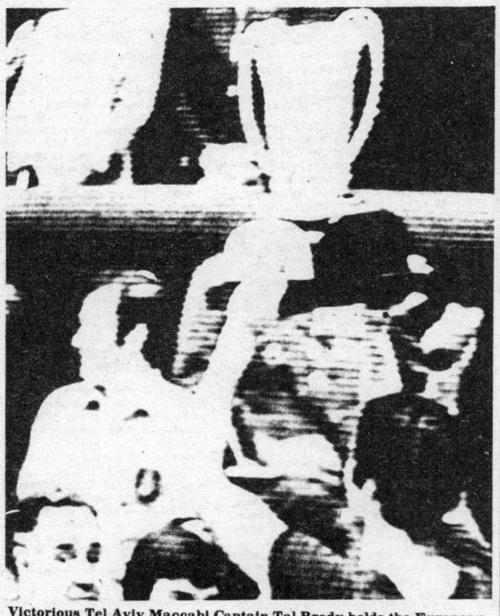

Victorious Tel Aviv Maccabi Captain Tal Brody holds the European Champions Cup aloft after last night's game. (Rahamim Yisraeli)

Vance to report on Sadat

By WOLF BLITZER
Jerusalem Post Correspondent

WASHINGTON. — Secretary of State Cyrus Vance has invited Israel Ambassador Simcha Dinitz to the State Department today to hear an official report on Egyptian President Anwar Sadat's meetings with President Jimmy Carter earlier this week.

The Dinitz-Vance meeting follows what appears to be a difference of opinion between American and Israeli officials here over the significance of Sadat's statements that Egypt is ready to normalize relations with Israel after the signing of a peace agreement in Geneva.

American and Israeli officials also apparently disagree on whether or not Sadat's visit was a success or failure from Egypt's standpoint.

Israeli officials, who have studied Sadat's public remarks in detail, have concluded that he has not changed Egypt's definition of peace "essentially." American officials, on the other hand, said they sense an important change in tone on Sadat's part.

After Sadat told a news conference on Wednesday that "everything will be normalized — that is what I am seeking," American officials quickly interpreted this statement as a significant step forward. But later Wednesday evening in an interview with ABC's Barbara Walters, the Egyptian leader, when pressed to spell out what he meant by normalization, said that he believes that this should include only an end to the state of belligerency between Israel and Egypt that has existed for 29 years.

He rejected Israel's definition of peace, insisting that Israel could not "impose" its will on the Arab states. Israel could not do it after its brilliant victory in 1967, and certainly not now, Sadat said.

Israeli officials regarded Sadat's remarks in the ABC interview as confirmation that Sadat is not really ready for "real peace" in this generation.

But American officials seemed to see things differently. They pointed out that "normalization" was an important "code-word" of the Arab-Israeli conflict and that it was important that Sadat was now using this term in public. In the past, Israel complained that the Arabs were not willing to normalize relations — even after a territorial withdrawal.

Israeli officials said yesterday that Sadat was unable to achieve many of his goals in his Washington visit. He was unable to win a U.S. commitment to sell arms, they said, adding that he did not receive Carter's pledge to support PLO participation at Geneva or the establishment of a separate Palestinian state on the West Bank and Gaza Strip.

Publicly, Sadat acknowledged differences on certain issues with the Americans, including the controversial matter of allowing Israel to retain defence lines beyond its legal borders — a proposal made by Carter last March 9.

But the Americans claimed yesterday that Sadat did not really believe these differences would be resolved during his first encounter with Carter. The more modest objectives of the trip were achieved, they said.

Despite the controversy over Sadat's comments, the Egyptian leader, as usual, scored some important propaganda points in America with his statements. Congressional leaders said they continue to be impressed by Sadat's "moderation" and his willingness to make peace with Israel.

Sadat revealed in a CBS news interview that he had asked the U.S. for $1B. in economic aid until 1980, when, he said, expected oil production in Egypt would rise to one million barrels a day and revenues would be increased. Presumably, the one million barrel a day figure would include oil from the eastern side of the Suez Gulf, currently controlled by Israel, but which Sadat is counting on being under Egyptian control before then.

PLO takes border village

By YORAM HAMIZRAHI
and Jerusalem Post Staff

Palestinian terrorists, backed by leftist forces, yesterday took by storm the southern Lebanese border township of Khiam in one of their most savage offensives. They promptly wiped out the largest local Moslem clan after accusing its heads of collaborating with Israel and the region's Christians.

The fate of the few hundred Christians living in the village, four kilometres north of Metulla, was not known by late last night. Christians who succeeded in fleeing from the township reported to Israelis at the border that the terrorists had "slaughtered" the Moslem Abdullah family, including the clan chieftain Sheikh Hussein Abdullah. The latter reportedly left his home to urge the terrorists not to harm Christians in his village.

Despite counter-claims from Christian circles in Beirut, the PLO terrorists appeared yesterday to be in firm control of Khiam. They occupied the village's secondary school and barracks after having ejected the small Christian militia force stationed there. The terrorists entrenched themselves in positions not far from a UN observation post in the township.

The terrorists were understood to have attacked Khiam from north and east. This was their closest assault to the border in the past week of attacks on the Christian-controlled enclave neighbouring Israel.

Christian villages reinforced their approaches as intermittent small arms and tank artillery fire continued through the night. Nine wounded Lebanese were brought for treatment in Israel across the Good

(Continued on page 2, col. 5)

Peres main candidate, Allon may challenge

Jerusalem Post Reporter

Defence Minister Shimon Peres, who lost to Rabin by 41 votes at the Labour Party convention six weeks ago, is now expected to be nominated as the party's candidate for the Premiership.

The decision is expected on Sunday, when the Central Committee will meet to pick the party's candidates for the forthcoming Knesset elections. The final deadline for submitting the lists of candidates is Tuesday evening, 35 days before the elections on May 17.

There were reports late last night that the Labour Party's Ahdut Avoda wing was trying to persuade Deputy Premier and Foreign Minister Yigal Allon to challenge Peres for the Premiership at Sunday's Central Committee meeting. But Allon was reported to be reluctant to take this step, since it might affect his position in the next Government which is likely to be headed by Peres, who has a much better chance to win.

Foreign Minister Yigal Allon said last night that if Labour Party members whose views he values propose him as a candidate for Prime Minister, "I will consider it in a positive light."

Senior Labour Party members pointed out last night that yesterday's elections of Knesset candidates by the party's central committee showed that the supporters of Peres had a clear majority in the party's major body. Yitzhak Navon, Peres, and Abba Eban each pulled more votes than Allon, while Ahdut Avoda veteran Yisrael Galili failed to be renominated.

Peres and Eban last night declined to comment on Rabin's decision to step down, but both seemed confident that they could easily master a challenge by Allon.

Mapam's leadership is to meet today to decide whether to remain in the Alignment with Labour following Rabin's resignation. The Alignment's left-wing partner had decided in February that Mapam would run on its own, should Peres win the nomination.

Baader-gang prosecutor gunned down while riding to work in German street

KARLSRUHE, WEST GERMANY. — Federal Prosecutor Siegfried Buback, one of the key figures in West Germany's prosecution of the Baader-Meinhof gang and other urban terrorists, was assassinated here yesterday morning while riding to his office.

Police said a motorcycle ridden by two leather-suited men wearing blue crash helmets pulled in front of Buback's official Mercedes limousine after it stopped at a red traffic light near the Karlsruhe Art Museum at 9.10 a.m. local time. When the light turned green the man riding pillion sprayed the car with at least 20 bullets from a submachinegun, according to witnesses.

The 57-year-old Buback and his driver, 29-year-old Wolfgang Goebbel, were killed instantly, and bodyguard Georg Wurler, 43, died soon after in hospital. The driver fell out of the car, and it rolled onto a sidewalk where passersby pulled Buback's body out. He had been shot several times in the chest and neck, severing the jugular vein, police said, and was pronounced dead upon arrival by helicopter at hospital.

The assassins fled. Their motorcycle, carrying a licence plate from Ludwigshafen, 50 km. down the Rhine, was found abandoned several hours later near the Karlsruhe-Frankfurt autobahn.

Police said later that there had probably been another two assassins, one apparently a woman, on a second motorcycle.

One person was taken into custody about five hours after the shooting, Baden-Wuerttemberg state interior minister Karl Schiess told a news conference in Stuttgart. But he warned: "We don't know whether this is a genuine suspect. We cannot give more information for fear of endangering the search."

Schiess said he didn't know if the assassins were connected with the Baader-Meinhof gang, three surviving members of which are on trial in Stuttgart in connection with bombings that killed four U.S. soldiers in 1972 and for the shooting death of a West German policeman.

Journalists at the scene of yester-

(Continued on page 3, col. 3)

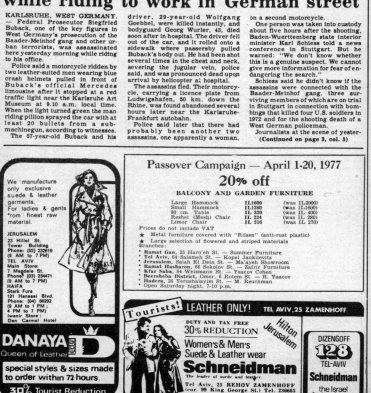

THE JERUSALEM POST

THIRD EDITION
3.00 a.m.

Price: IL3.00
(Including VAT)

WEDNESDAY, MAY 18, 1977 • SIVAN 1, 5737 • JAMADI AWWAL 29, 1397 • VOL. XLVII, No. 14015

Likud in first place; Labour loses heavily

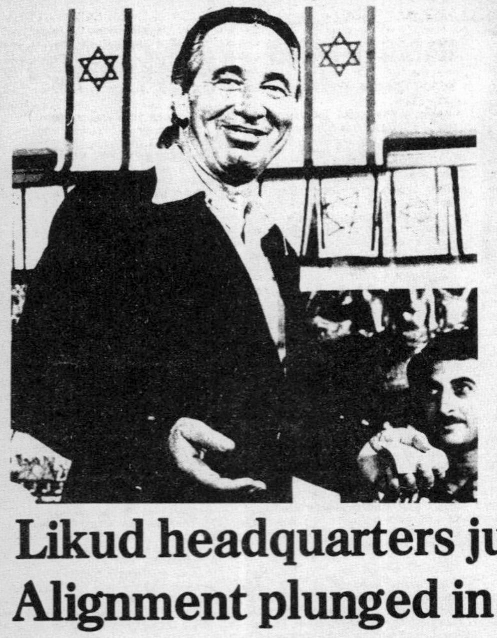

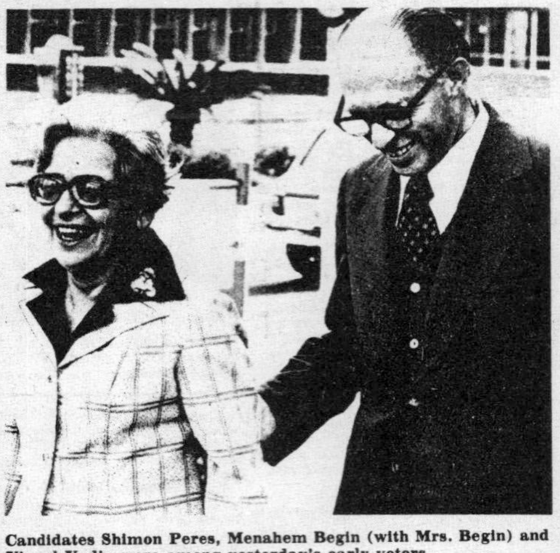

Candidates Shimon Peres, Menahem Begin (with Mrs. Begin) and Yigael Yadin were among yesterday's early voters.
(Millman (2), Sunphot)

DMC emerges as a major force

The prospects of a major Likud victory in yesterday's general election, projected by TV last night, stunned the nation and the parties.

Shortly after 11 p.m., Israel television projected that the Likud would have 44 Knesset seats and the Alignment would drop to 32, while the DMC would gain 16 seats and the NRP 11.

The TV projection, which was supported by election analyst Hanoch Smith, was based on more than 10,000 sample returns from special TV ballot boxes that were placed outside 25 polling stations throughout the country.

Early returns from regular polling stations appeared to verify the trend expressed in the TV projection, if not the precise distribution. In kibbutzim, for example, the Alignment vote was 10 per cent less than in the past elections and in the moshavim there was a drop of 11 per cent.

Analysts suggested that the Alignment's losses went mostly to DMC.

Dr. Dov Hevion of the Central Statistics Office pointed out that even with a small number of polling places reporting, the returns of these same stations in the 1973 elections showed a far higher return for the Alignment. However, he pointed out, if one combined the percentage of votes for the Alignment and the ILP in 1973, they were almost identical to the combined percentage voting for the DMC, the Alignment and the ILP in this election.

At 1 a.m. Alignment headquarters issued a forecast based on its own analysis of a sample of election returns. This projection showed that the Likud would win 40-41 Knesset seats; the Alignment 36-37; and DMC 17.

These figures, if borne out, would make it possible for the Alignment to form a coalition with the DMC and the NRP.

At 1 a.m. TV updated its prognosis to Likud-43, Labour-31, DMC-16, NRP-12, Rakah-4, Agudat Yisrael-3, United Arab List-3, Shlomzion-2, Shelli-2, Flatto-Sharon-2, Independent Liberals-1.

At 2:30, Smith announced his own projections, which he thought would sand up in the final tabulations:

This forecast gave the Likud 40-41 seats Alignment 31-32; DMC 15-16; NRP 11-12; Rakah 5; Agudat Yisrael 3; Poalei Aguda 2; United Arab List 2; Shelli 2; Flatto-Sharon 2; Shlomzion 2; Ind. Libs and CRM perhaps one each.

Peres: Suffered 'a heavy blow'

"There is no doubt we suffered a heavy blow," Shimon Peres said at 1:30 a.m,this morning.

Speaking on TV, Peres said the Labour Party would have to examine itself, in the light of the election results, but expressed confidence it would in the end be renewed.

"We didn't expect such a result," he said, adding that most of the Alignment losses went to the Democratic Movement for Change.

Peres said other reasons which led to Labour's losses were "international developments that made it difficult for us: a global inflation that affected us, a change of administration in the U. S., and the public was not exactly sure what we are up against in the United States."

Peres declined to lay responsibility for Labour's defeat at any person's feet. "It's a democratic fact and we've got to accept it gracefully, with courage and hope," he said.

Shortly after 2 p.m., Likud campaign chief Ezer Weizman said, "It looks like we might win and might lead the country for the next four years." Likud Leader Menahem Begin would not make any comment by 2.45 a.m.

Gloom hung over Alignment headquarters. Alignment leaders were not prepared at first to accept the TV projection as an accurate reflection of the state of affairs and declined to respond. However, it was clear that the trend of the election had been detected and, as the minutes wore on, Alignment leaders, while hopeful they would get more than 32 seats, began to reconcile themselves to the trend.

The blow-by-blow coverage which the radio devoted to the countrywide voting scene during the day left the impression that in no previous election had so many citizens complained about being denied the vote. Some of these gripes were due to the fact that the Voting Register was closed nearly nine months ago, and the Knesset decided not to have it updated. Some of the complaints stemmed from the fact that citizens had either failed to notify the Interior Ministry's population registry of changes of address, or had filed incorrect details which the computer could not digest.

The computer apparently ran amok in two cases, in Kiryat Motzkin and Kiryat Malachi, depriving hundreds of citizens of their vote at one fell swoop. Immigrants who spent their first period in absorption centres and moved around since, were the main victims among the 30,000-40,000 Israelis who were frustrated yesterday, but other citizens could find no logical reason for their disqualification and offered loud and sometimes violent protest.

One of the lessons of the experience was that awareness among voters of the need to actively check their presence on the register well before the elections is low, and should be encouraged systematically.

At the Knesset, special measures were taken — even in the parking lot — to expedite the tally of the soldiers' vote. By law, votes of men and women on active duty who vote on base are not counted there, but shipped direct to the Central Elections Committee for processing.

The first truck rolled in at nine p.m.

The beehive atmosphere at election headquarters — fifth floor of the Knesset building — dissipated for about quarter of an hour at eight p.m. It was time for the tradition of *haramat kosit* (proposing of a toast) to persons for a job well done. The host this time was, of course, Justice Eliyahu Manny, chairman of the Central Elections Committee. He saluted his director-general, Menahem Tarlo, and his assistants.

Among the guests were State Comptroller Yitzhak Nebenzahl, High Court Justices Haim Landau and Haim Kohn, Knesset Speaker Yisrael Yeshayahu, Minister of Police and Interior Shlomo Hillel, State Attorney Gavriel Bach and Mayor Teddy Kollek of Jerusalem.

(Continued on page 2, col. 6)

Likud headquarters jubilant; Alignment plunged in gloom

Jerusalem Post Staff

When the first television projections were broadcast, there were spontaneous cries of joy at Likud headquarters.

MK Yigal Horowitz said that Labour's apparent tremendous defeat had been "richly deserved." On the wall behind Horowitz were pictures of Herzl, Ben-Gurion, and Jabotinsky. "The people have endorsed the covenant between the disciples of Ben-Gurion and Jabotinsky," said Horowitz, who in 1965 followed B-G when the latter quit Mapai and formed Rafi.

At Alignment headquarters just before midnight, a grim-faced Shimon Peres declined to comment on the results available up to then. Abba Eban said the results were too tentative and fragmentary to provide a basis for comment. And Labour's campaign chief Haim Bar-Lev likewise preferred to wait before commenting on the "artificial" television prediction.

As the evening wore on, gloom settled over Alignment headquarters on Hayarkon Street as all the major leaders sat quietly around television sets watching commentators predict their downfall. Aides told the press they did not want to be disturbed.

Early scattered results were discounted as not representative, and the Alignment supporters gleaned hope from the first of its 100 sample districts, which showed the Alignment leading the Likud by three per cent.

Prof. Yigael Yadin, leader of the Democratic Movement for Change, expressed his "great, great joy." In just a few months, he said, his party had succeeded in becoming one of the Big Three.

Yadin expressed surprise at the decline of the Labour Party, and shook his head a number of times as the Labour Party's fall from power seemed to be confirmed with each succeeding result that came in.

Shmuel Tamir, who crossed from the Likud camp to join the DMC, said he was surprised at how well Likud did, but "will not feel uncomfortable" to sit with Likud in a governing coalition.

From the beginning, supreme confidence that the Likud would form the next government — for the first time in the history of the state — reigned in Mezudat Ze'ev in Tel Aviv.

Menahem Begin, MK, who recently recovered from a heart attack, was referred to on occasion as "prime minister." Yehezkel Flumin, MK, Likud's economic theoretician, even referred to Mezudat Ze'ev as "government house."

Ezer Weizman, who headed the Likud's campaign, interpreted the results as "a new page" for Israel. The Likud would now set out to "unite the people of Israel to face the problems ahead." The creation of the DMC played a major role in Labour's downfall, he said.

As results continued to pour in, indicating that the trend was continuing, the spectators at Likud headquarters here in Tel Aviv became drunk with joy. Attempts to clear the hall so that the results coming in co
d be properly tabulated were futile. The noise was impossible.

After the young ushers failed to evacuate the spectators, Ezer Weizman pleaded with "the future leaders of the country to set a personal example of responsibility. "One — two — three — four," he counted, "now get outside," but only a few responded to his plea.

Education Minister Aharon Yadlin was the first Alignment leader to react publicly to his party's losses as predicted by TV and borne out by early election returns. He said: "At this stage the results are not sympathetic to us."

Asked to give reasons for the Alignment's losses, Yadlin said it appeared "the DMC took votes only from us" without affecting the rise of the Likud-religious block.

Other reasons given by Yadlin for Labour's losses were internal squabbles in the Labour Party and weaker support from the U.S.

Envisioning his party in opposition, Yadlin said the party should spend its time renewing its morals and values until such a time as it would come to power again.

Moshe Dayan told *The Post* that the Likud victory was "an expression of the public feeling against territorial concessions in Judea and Samaria." He was happy about that, "although not operationally," he added cryptically.

He reckoned that the Likud could form a government even without the DMC, its partners being the NRP, Arik Sharon, and maybe Flatto-Sharon, "whatever he wants." Asked about the possibility of a Likud-Alignment coalition, he said "I don't know."

Ex-Prime Minister Golda Meir was up late following the election reports on television. A close associate told *The Post* that it was not Mrs. Meir's habit to comment before the final results were known, and suggested that the press "wait until tomorrow."

Yitzhak Rabin, formally Labour Prime Minister of the caretaker Government, flatly refused to make any comment on the predicted Likud victory last night. All his spokesman was ready to say was that Rabin would go to Labour Hq. in Hayarkon St. late last night, and that he would attend the Party's Central Committee's meeting scheduled for tomorrow. He was unable to say whether Rabin would show up at the next Cabinet meeting.

"War is at the gate" — was the prediction of Shulamit Aloni, head of the Citizens Rights Movement (which the television projection gave not a single Knesset seat). She saw in the good showing of the Likud, the NRP, and Flatto-Sharon a sign that the nation had become "less rational, more nationalistic, more mystical, less governed by common sense, and more influenced by money."

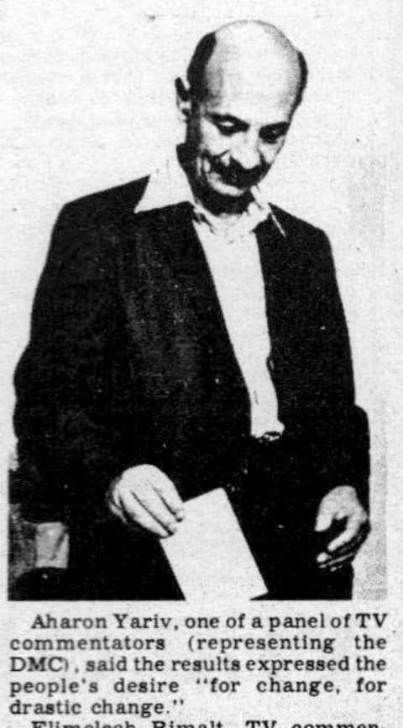

Aharon Yariv, one of a panel of TV commentators (representing the DMC), said the results expressed the people's desire "for change, for drastic change."

Elimelech Rimalt, TV commentator on behalf of the Likud, said that the people had been "sick of the present regime." They wanted a clear and unhesitating foreign policy. Domestic issues also played an important part in the campaign. Israel's democracy had begun working in full, he added.

Yitzhak Ben-Aharon, TV commentator representing the Alignment, saw his party's defeat as an expression of the people's "violent anger" over things that had been happening in the last few months. The sharp kick they had given the Alignment was not the product of "cool, rational thought," and the people would have reason "to cry long and hard over the decision they made today," he said.

Dr. Yitzhak Meir, TV commentator for the NRP, said that the Alignment's propaganda line, predicting disaster if the Likud was victorious, had boomeranged. The people had taken offence at this attempt to inhibit their democratic right to put the opposition in power.

Ben-Aharon added that a rightist government would pose "a very great danger for the state" in its present international situation. If such a government did not relinquish its principles it would soon "be booted out."

Rimalt, who until recently was chairman of the Liberal Party within the Likud, pledged that a Likud-led government would go to Geneva. He rejected the argument that Israel's lurch to the right would sour our

(Continued on page 2, Col. 1)

Speculation on coalition

Jerusalem Post Staff

Even before the official results of the election had emerged, party leaders last night engaged in coalition speculation.

Clearly, it appeared that President Katzir would ask Likud leader Menahem Begin first to try to form a government as the leader of the party with the most Knesset seats.

Former Liberal Party leader Elimelech Rimalt last night urged his own Likud bloc to opt for a coalition government that would include DMC in addition to the religious parties. His first preference was for a national unity government, but since this was unlikely, it was important, for reasons of what he termed tant, for reasons of what be termed "balance" that DMC join in a Likud Government.

At the same time, Rakah leader Meir Wilner said his party would do all in its power to prevent a Likud Government.

While stressing that results at 1 a.m. were not final, Alignment Education Minister Aharon Yadlin emphasized that he, personally, is against Labour joining a national unity government with the Likud. He said that if the Likud could for a coalition with the National Religious Party, "Labour will become a fighting opposition."

Talk of coalition, however, was very much in the air at DMC headquarters, and telephone calls between the three main parties had already been made, sounding out the various coalition possibilities.

"We will not join any government that does not accept our terms," Prof. Yigael Yadin, DMC leader, told *The Jerusalem Post* here at 1.30 this morning.

"And it will be very difficult to form any government without us.

"We will fight for our principles, even at the cost of not being in the government."

He said, "Our foreign policy will be a serious stumbling block for the Likud if they wish to form a coaliton with coalition with us."

DMC party feeling was that if new elections were to be held soon, the Likud could not expect to have yesterday's surprise result reaffirmed.

Dr. Yosef Burg, leader of the National Religious Party, told a television interviewer that he would prefer a national unity government to joining a coalition with the Likud (and the DMC).

Alignment leaders, including Shimon Peres, declined to speculate about an Alignment-led coalition, that would include the DMC and the NRP. From the electoral projections, this would be a mathematical possibility.

U.S. officials shocked by Likud's lead

By WOLF BLITZER
Jerusalem Post Correspondent

WASHINGTON. — State Department officials informed of the Israel Television pre-midnight prediction giving the Likud a large lead on the Alignment expressed shock and incredulity. They were reluctant to predict developments if the TV projection proved correct.

Before any results were known U.S. officials expressed hope that a new coalition government would be established quickly so that the U.S.-sponsored Middle East peace process could continue "on schedule."

During the past few weeks, American officials have been attempting to determine how long it might take to form a new government. President Carter told a press conference last Thursday that he would be inviting the next Israeli Prime Minister to Washington shortly after the elections.

The Americans are hoping that a visit to Washington by the next Israeli leader — whoever he may be — will be followed by another swing through the Middle East by Secretary of State Cyrus Vance, probably late in the summer. It is hoped here in Washington that Vance will successfully lay the groundwork for a reconvened Geneva conference toward the end of the year.

Assad said doubtful of West Bank state idea

By DAVID LANDAU
POST Diplomatic Correspondent

Syria's President Hafez Assad told U.S. President Jimmy Carter last week that he was frankly uncomfortable with the idea of an independent West Bank Palestinian state and did not see it as necessarily the best solution to the Palestinian problem. According to well-placed sources here, Carter has reported on this revelation by the Syrian leader to congressional leaders in Washington.

Israeli diplomats have apparently also been given similar reports of the Carter-Assad meeting at Geneva by their American counterparts.

Carter had also heard similar doubts about a third state solution expressed to him by Jordan's King Hussein.

Israeli intelligence analysts have long contended that Hussein is by no means alone among Arab leaders in harbouring these doubts, and that more radical leaders such as Assad do in fact share them. But the Geneva meeting was the first time that the Syrian leader actually chose to express them to the Americans, and Israeli sources consider this significant.

Assad reportedly acknowledged that he and other Arab leaders keep up a public front, favouring a third state solution, which in fact differs from their private feelings. He questioned the viability of that solution, wondering whether it would really solve the Palestinian problem, and cautioned that a third state might become a springboard for Libya's Muammer Gaddafi to launch military adventures in the area.

Assad did not suggest to Carter, as far as is known, any alternative approach to resolve the Palestinian problem.

Tunisia says it fears war with Libya

By DAVID LANDAU
POST Diplomatic Correspondent

Tunisia has told the U.S. and other Western countries that it fears attack by Libya because of a deadlocked dispute over oil drilling, Western diplomatic sources here revealed yesterday. Three weeks of talks between the foreign ministers of Tunisia and Libya broke down recently, and Tunisia's President Habib Bourguiba is afraid that Libya's Muammer Gadaffi may resort to war as Tunisia goes ahead with promising off-shore drilling in the Mediterranean.

The site of the drilling is in waters which Tunisia and Libya both claim as their own. (The two countries' coastlines are almost perpendicular to each other, and their claims to ocean-bed rights therefore run into each other.)

The legal rights and wrongs of the dispute are unclear, because the UN's Law of the Sea Conference, which has been trying for the past several years to draft a universally accepted code for the sea-bed, has yet to achieve its goal.

Tension between the two countries has been building up for several months. Libya rejected Tunisia's proposal for international arbitration, and, with the talks between the two foreign ministers now having ended in a standoff, Tunisia says it fears a turn for the worse.

Tunisia has no armed forces to speak of, while Libya has stockpiled impressive quantities of the latest planes and tanks, of both French and Russian origin.

In the event of actual attack Tunisia might well turn to Morocco for aid. The two states, though not contiguous, have cooperated closely in the past, and Morocco is at odds with Libya for having aided the Polisario guerrillas in the Spanish Sahara against Morocco.

Morocco recently demonstrated its martial prowess by sending a small but effective expeditionary force to Zaire to help the local army beat back an invasion of Katangan rebels aided by Cubans.

Libya has an on-off feud with Egypt on its eastern border, and usually maintains substantial forces there. But diplomatic observers have noted a cooling-off of late in the intensity of the Libya-Egypt quarrel.

Jerusalem voting habits as colourful as inhabitants

By ABRAHAM RABINOVICH
Jerusalem Post Reporter

The great rabbis of Geula came to do it in their Sabbath clothing flanked by clouds of Hassidim. The kibbutznikim at Ramat Rachel did it to the sound of a piano tinkling from the next room. The Arabs of Beit Safafa did it early and then relaxed in the shade of trees in the courtyard outside. New immigrants in Neve Ya'acov did it volubly in Russian.

No matter how they did it in Jerusalem yesterday, the spectre of the city's residents turning out in all their variety to choose the nation's leadership — each man aware that his vote was as good as anyone else's — was, to those moved by such things, very moving.

More than a quarter of the city's population — Arabs from East Jerusalem — were not eligible to vote since they have not chosen to take Israeli citizenship. But they were waiting for the results with almost as much interest as those who did vote.

"We're watching and the whole world's watching," said an Arab merchant.

"We think it would be better if Labour won. Begin just says no, no, no. With Labour, at least according to its platform, there's something to talk about."

Perhaps the best organized political machine in the city was that run by Rabbi Menahem Porush for Agudat Yisrael. Some 1,500 young men, most of them yeshiva students and all wearing crisp white shirts, were dispatched to sensitive neighbourhoods to canvass votes door to door, transport voters to polling places in a fleet of vehicles bearing the party's *gimmel* insignia, or simply stand outside polling places as a moral force.

In his headquarters off Strauss Street last night, ringed by a battery of telephones and aides and with hundreds of black-garbed workers rushing in and out, Rabbi Porush ran his operation with the crisp dispatch of a big-city American boss. He was up against the religious extremists of the Neturei Karta who last week raided his headquarters and whose posters calling for a boycott of the elections were posted all over Mea Shearim.

Likud, which in past Knesset elections has outdrawn the Alignment in Jerusalem, was particularly active in the Katamonim where much of its strength lies. A youth in French Hill who voted yesterday on his 18th birthday, indicated that Likud may also score this year with young voters. "I'm voting for the DMC but most of my friends are voting Likud," said Yigal. "They say it's time for a change."

Although a polling place had been set up in Yeshivat Hakotel in the Jewish Quarter of the Old City many residents of the quarter were assigned to a polling place in the Omariya School on the Via Dolorosa in the Moslem Quarter. Arabs with voting rights were also assigned to that polling place and another mixed one at the Rashadiya School opposite Herod's Gate. A late afternoon check at the latter polling place found that "only a few" Arabs had exercised their right to vote. It could not be determined yesterday how many East Jerusalem Arabs had chosen Israeli citizenship and were therefore eligible to vote.

However, there was a large turnout among Arabs from Beit Safafa in southern Jerusalem who had lived in the Israeli half of the divided village before the Six Day War. By mid-afternoon, more than half the approximately 50 eligible voters had cast their ballots. Some voters were being brought in rs and taxis provided by the Alignment to the polling station.

The most relaxed polling place visited in the Jerusalem area was the Kibbutz Ramat Rachel enclave where almost all the 81 eligible voters had cast their ballots early. The polling place secretary, a sun-burnt kibbutz veteran normally in charge of the orchards, was reading a newspaper flanked by a policeman and a Haga guard drinking coffee.

"Those who haven't voted are either dead or abroad," said the kibbutznik looking up from the paper. "You can report that thanks to the vigilance of the Israel police and Haga there were no explosions or other incidents at Ramat Rachel."

Hundreds of Jerusalemites utilized the work-free day to picnic in Sacher Park and other parks. Others washed their cars or crowded downtown cafes.

Attorney-General Aharon Barak, whose decision in the Lea Rabin Washington bank account case last month led to Premier Yitzhak Rabin's withdrawal from the race, was seen at dusk waiting patiently outside a bakery on Palmach Street while his wife bought something inside.

Forty of Jerusalem's 249 polling places opened with delays of up to an hour because personnel did not show up on time.

Marsha Pomerantz adds:

At a polling site in Jerusalem's Baka quarter voters were packed like sardines against the door, waiting to be let in one at a time. In their midst a woman turned to her aged mother, stooped under a black kerchief: "But you don't know how to read," she said loudly, as if it had just occurred to her. "How can you vote?"

After much discussion with the others, it was decided that the daughter would vote first, smuggle out the "right" ballot slip, and then her mother would go in to vote. The old woman glanced around at the surrounding faces, beaming her satisfaction with the arrangement.

Outside the same building, a little boy asked a local tough if he had voted yet. Yes. And whom did he vote for? "For Betar, of course," was the answer, referring to the football team supported by Herut.

Judy Siegel adds:

About the only people in Jerusalem's Sacher Park yesterday who said they hadn't voted or did not intend to vote were the children playing ball on the grass.

"We've been waiting for this chance for three years," said Ezra, a kiosk operator from the Nahlaot quarter. "All year long the parties take us for granted; now they're scared about what we have to say."

"We have to get the dirty politicians out," asserted Haim, his neighbour on the grass, which was so littered by papers and remains of lunch that it looked as if manna had fallen in the morning.

Hundreds of Jerusalem families and their relatives from Ramle, Lod, Ashdod and Tel Aviv took advantage of the fine weather and the work holiday to picnic. Many discussed politics as they listened to taped music, drank whisky toasts to their favourite candidates, played cards for money and barbecued their steaks.

In the crowded Katamonim quarters, the no-vote rate was higher. An elderly woman walking with her grandchildren said she didn't like any party. "They all promise the moon when they appear on TV," she noted bitterly, "but

(Continued on page 2, col. 6)

THE JERUSALEM POST

FRIDAY, MAY 20, 1977 • SIVAN 3, 5737 • JAMADI THANI 2, 1397 • VOL. XLVII, No. 14017 ★

Price: IL4.00 (Including VAT)

Somalia rejects Red Sea federation page 4

Peres offered defence post in unity coalition

By ASHER WALLFISH
Jerusalem Post Reporter

Shimon Peres would remain defence minister and also get the job of deputy premier if the Alignment came into the Likud-led coalition, Likud leaders are reliably reported to have told Alignment leaders after the election. They also offered to leave Haim Zadok in his current job as justice minister.

These offers, whose rejection disappointed the Likud, mirror that party's interest in broadening its projected coalition. The doyen of the Central Elections Committee, Yohanan Bader, told *The Post* proudly last night: "See, we can form a coalition with a majority, because we have 45 with Shlomzion, and the NRP will come in with the Aguda and bring us 16, and that makes 61. Anyway, Flatto Sharon will always vote with us."

When asked what assurance he had that the Aguda would join the coalition, Bader said: "If I could tell you what I know, you would not doubt that they are already in."

However, Bader said, many people in the Likud would not be happy about having to depend on the religious parties for their majority. "We need a counterweight. We need the Alignment and the DMC; but if you ask me, we need the Alignment more than the DMC."

Another Likud MK told *The Post*: "Don't get the idea that we want a broad coalition because we're apprehensive of going it alone. We can manage alone. But for national considerations it's obvious that the broader the base, the better."

The mood in Likud circles in Jerusalem was that they would not take the Alignment's "no" for an

(Continued on page 2, col. 2)

Latest estimate of Knesset lineup
(WITHOUT SOLDIERS' VOTES)

	Bader-Ofer	Seats
Likud and Shlomzion	3	45
Alignment and United Arabs	1	33
NRP and Aguda	1	16
Poalei Aguda		1
Democratic Front (Rakah)	1	6
DMC and ILP	1	16
Flatto		1
CRM		1
Shelli		1

Calculated privately for The Post by Dr. Yohanan Bader, veteran Likud representative in the Central Elections Committee.
Three parties may be affected by the results of the soldiers' votes. The Likud may gain a seat; the NRP and Democratic Front may each lose a seat.

Coalition expected in 2 weeks

By JOSHUA BRILLIANT
Post Political Reporter

TEL AVIV. — Likud leader Simha Ehrlich said yesterday that negotiations on forming the new coalition would begin after the Shavuot holiday.

The negotiations are expected to be concluded quickly. A source in the National Religious Party told *The Jerusalem Post* that NRP leader Yosef Burg and the Likud leadership had agreed to form at least a narrow coalition, commanding the support of 61 members of the 120-seat Knesset, within two weeks.

Meanwhile, the Likud's candidate for prime minister, Menahem Begin, will meet Acting Prime Minister Shimon Peres to receive a briefing on national affairs today. The meeting, which was arranged in a telephone call between the two leaders, will be held at Peres' office in the Defence Ministry at one o'clock.

The Likud's negotiators — Begin, Ehrlich and Yigal Horowitz — will also meet today. But negotiations with prospective partners have not begun yet, apparently because election results are not final. Any change in the figures because of soldiers' returns or surplus-votes agreements would affect the parties' bargaining position.

Begin, who was in Camp Kaddum yesterday, referred to the NRP and Shlomzion as if it was a foregone conclusion they would be in his cabinet.

Burg yesterday met Peres in an attempt to convince Labour to join a national unity government. Peres

(Continued on page 2, col.3)

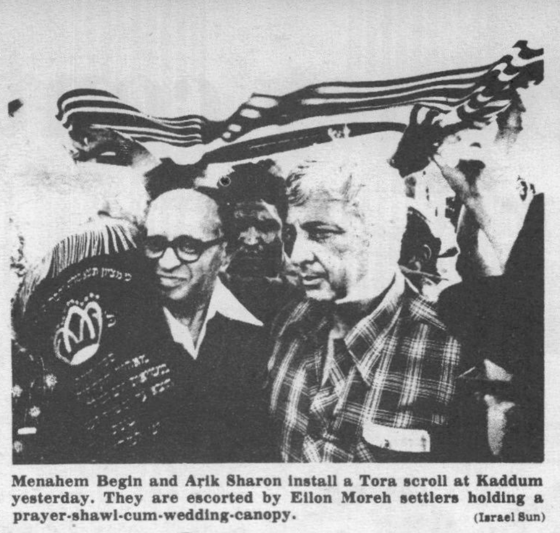

Menahem Begin and Arik Sharon install a Tora scroll at Kaddum yesterday. They are escorted by Eilon Moreh settlers holding a prayer-shawl-cum-wedding-canopy. (Israel Sun)

Vance, Gromyko agree to press Geneva talks

GENEVA (Reuter). — The U.S. and the Soviet Union yesterday agreed to press forward with plans to reconvene a Middle East peace conference this autumn, despite the Likud victory in Tuesday's Israel general election, a U.S. spokesman said.

Secretary of State Cyrus Vance and Soviet Foreign Minister Andrei Gromyko reached a consensus on this during a 105-minute meeting here devoted to the Middle East situation, the spokesman said.

Asked about a gloomy prognosis by UN Secretary-General Kurt Waldheim earlier yesterday that talks could not be held this year, the spokesman said Waldheim had made it clear he was speaking only for himself.

Gromyko told reporters as he left the hotel where his talks with Vance took place that it had been, "in general, a constructive conversation." He added that there were "elements of a business-like nature in the discussions."

Both sides agreed, he said, that the most expedient forum for considering the Middle East question was in the Geneva peace conference — which met briefly in 1973 under the co-chairmanship of the U.S. and Soviet Union.

The American spokesman could not say whether Gromyko had agreed to use Soviet influence in an effort to convince the Palestine Liberation Organization to recognize the existence of Israel.

This was one suggestion which U.S. officials said Vance planned to put to Gromyko, along with the proposal that the two countries hold regular consultations to help the search for peace.

Vance, asked whether the U.S. considered it dangerous now because of the Israeli election result, replied: "No, because it has continued to be dangerous for a long while."

State Department spokesman Hodding Carter said Gromyko's characterization of the danger of the Middle East situation was no different from previous Soviet expressions of concern.

He said there had been "no sudden

(Continued on page 2, col. 7)

Dismay in Washington

Begin: Settle Judea, Samaria

By JOSHUA BRILLIANT
Post Political Reporter

CAMP KADDUM. — Likud leader Menahem Begin indicated here yesterday that Jewish settlements will shortly rise throughout Judea and Samaria and Arab residents could get Israeli citizenship if they wanted it. But Arabs will not be evicted under a Likud-led government, he added. Begin avoided committing himself on whether Israel law would be introduced in the administered territories.

Begin's remarks were greeted with dismay in Washington. (See next column.)

Speaking at a ceremony marking the installation of a Tora scroll at the Kaddum synagogue, Begin referred to the fact that the Eilon Moreh group of settlers had moved into this military base on a "temporary basis," after squatting in Sebastia against army orders.

"In a few weeks or months there will be many Eilon Morehs; there will be no need for a Kaddum," he declared.

Begin chided a foreign correspondent for calling the area "occupied territory." "You've used this expression for 10 years, but since May 1977 I hope you'll start using the word 'liberated territories'," he said.

"A Jew has every right to settle in these liberated territories of the Jewish land," he added.

Aluf (Res.) Ariel Sharon, who took part in the ceremony, told reporters he believed "the new government's policy will bring about wide-scale settlement in Judea and Samaria."

When Sharon ended his statement, Begin commented, "very nice." But the Likud's candidate for prime minister also declared: "We don't want to evict anyone from his land. In this beautiful country, there is room for the Arabs who are working their lands and the Jews who will come to make the homeland bloom."

He criticized reporters for asking whether a Likud-led government would "annex" the administered territories. "We don't use the word annexation," he said. "You annex foreign land, not your own country."

"Will Israeli law be introduced in the West Bank — in Judea and Samaria?" another foreign correspondent asked.

"You use the word West Bank. Say Judea and Samaria," Begin replied. "Why is it so difficult for you to use

(Continued on page 2, col.4)

Washington: 'Worst fears coming true'

Jerusalem Post Correspondent

WASHINGTON. — U.S. officials were predictably angered yesterday following Likud leader Menahem Begin's assertion that he will establish more Jewish settlements in the heart of Judea-Samaria if he becomes prime minister.

"Our worst fears may be coming true," one U.S. source told *The Jerusalem Post*.

The U.S. government has since the Six Day War opposed establishment of Israeli settlements in the territories. Washington has maintained repeatedly and vocally that such settlements are "illegal" and block progress towards peace in the Middle East.

Begin's statements during the past 48 hours — including a highly publicized, comment that the West Bank and Gaza should be viewed as "liberated," not "occupied" — have concerned senior U.S. officials. They say they fear that President Carter's timetable for reconvening the Geneva Middle East conference may be upset now that it appears a Likud government will take over in Israel.

Publicly, U.S. officials continued yesterday to put forward a "business-as-usual" image, reiterating that the special relationship between Washington and Jerusalem was not a function of any particular elected leadership but rather in the best national interests of both countries. The White House made it clear once again that Carter will be inviting the next Israeli prime minister to Washington after a new government is formed.

But privately the Americans were making it clear that the U.S. would expect any elected Israeli government to cooperate in the "peace process" — to agree to negotiate far-reaching territorial concessions to the Arabs in exchange for peace.

U.S. officials have been hoping that the responsibilities of governing Israel would "moderate" Begin and the Likud. They have been telling reporters, however, that this may just be "wishful thinking."

In fact, Begin's visit to Kaddum in Samaria yesterday upset Washington. The Americans have been telling Israel for more than a year that the Kaddum settlement was an "obstacle" to peace and should be dismantled.

It was still too early to tell whether Begin's positions and statements, which the State Department clearly regards as "provocative," would affect his visit to Washington after a new government was formed.

Some officials were already suggesting privately that the U.S. should "snub" such a Likud-led

(Continued on page 2, col. 4)

DMC vows to stick to its principles

NRP aims to get Labour in coalition

Jerusalem Post Staff

The leadership of the National Religious Party decided yesterday to make a strong effort to persuade the Alignment to accept the Likud's invitation to join a national unity government.

This conclusion was reached at a brief meeting of the NRP's Knesset group, according to NRP secretary-general Zvi Bernstein. The prevailing view was that neither the Likud nor the NRP should take the Alignment's completely negative initial response to the invitation as its last word.

The Knesset group also endorsed the initiative taken by Zevulun Hammer to try to form a parliamentary bloc with Agudat Yisrael and Poalei Agudat Yisrael.

Such a bloc — consisting of 17 or 18 members — would be the third largest in the Knesset, topping the Democratic Movement for Change. This would strengthen the position of the religious parties in their demands for specific portfolios in the cabinet.

Agudat Yisrael's initial reaction to Hammer's proposal on Wednesday was negative, but that of Poalei Agudat Yisrael was favourable. His colleagues have now officially authorized him to persist in his efforts.

Interviewed on the radio newsreel yesterday morning, Hammer suggested that the Likud might persuade the DMC to enter the government if it were agreed that the coalition would adopt no basic principles. This would presumably enable the DMC to shelve its seven minimum conditions for entering any coalition — the most controversial of which is the one calling for new elections, under the constituency system, within two years.

The Democratic Movement for Change secretariat met in Tel Aviv yesterday to discuss the party's stance on coalition-making. After three hours of discussion it was clear that there would be no immediate compromise on the party's seven points.

Following the secretariat meeting DMC leader Yigael Yadin told the party's 120-member council that joining a coalition was not a question of "with whom we will form a government, but on what conditions."

DMC members told *The Post* that the critical issue for the Likud, in seeking DMC support, was the question of territorial concessions. If the Likud insisted on annexing the West Bank, then the DMC could not join them.

There appeared to be a little more room for manoeuvre on the question of electoral reform. The DMC has apparently decided to play a waiting game. It wants to see how the Likud will manage in its negotiations with the extreme religious parties first.

Aviad Yaffe dies of heart attack

Jewish Agency and World Zionist Organization director-general Aviad Yaffe died yesterday in Kfar Sava's Meir Hospital of a heart attack. He was 54.

Yaffe, generally known as "Adi," is survived by his wife Ora and daughters Dorit and Revital.

Born in Rehovot in 1923, Yaffe was brought up in Jerusalem, where his parents helped found the Beit Hakerem quarter. A member of the Hagana, he took part in the War of Independence, fighting around besieged Jerusalem and after the war entered the diplomatic service. From 1958 to 1962 he was consul-general in New York, and after a spell in the Foreign Ministry served as director of the Prime Minister's Bureau from 1965 to 1969. Entering the Knesset in 1972, he became deputy Alignment faction chief in 1974.

The funeral will leave Sunday morning from the Jewish Agency courtyard in Jerusalem for Har Hamenuhot.

Peres: Corruption hurt us the most

Jerusalem Post Reporter

TEL AVIV. — Defence Minister and Acting Prime Minister Shimon Peres attributed the Labour Party's defeat in Tuesday's elections to a number of domestic and international trends, but also cited the failure of demoralized party activists to push hard for victory.

Peres was addressing the first meeting of the Labour Party's Central Committee following Tuesday's electoral debacle. Beit Arlosoroff was packed with the 800-member committee, which decided by acclamation that Labour would under no circumstances join a Likud-led coalition.

Members in the hall tended to agree with Peres' somewhat detached analysis of Labour's failure but said, "so what can we possibly do about it."

All were clearly worried about the party's prospects of retaining its majority control of the Histadrut in its elections on June 21.

Peres attributed Tuesday's defeat to several factors: the party failed to explain its stands sufficiently; members held unreasonably high expectations — ("No other people in the world judges itself so harshly"); and there were accumulated failures and tensions deriving from the problems of absorbing the unrestricted immigration of Israel's first three decades.

Peres also cited the worldwide trend towards urbanization and its accompanying social ills and the inexorable world inflation, the party's failure to make inroads into the younger generation, and the fact that it was "too late with too little" in bringing about internal changes.

Corruption "hurt us the most," he said.

Peres also referred to two tactical mistakes: the fact that Histadrut elections were not held before the Knesset elections and thus were not exploited as a trial run for campaign tactics; and the fact that the elections were not held in conjunction with municipal elections.

Party secretary-general Meir Zarmi promised a full debate on Peres' analysis, and an opportunity for committee members to express their opinions on the reasons for the defeat, at an unspecified date. The impression was that this debate would not be held before the Histadrut vote, so that internal recriminations and the search for a scapegoat would not undermine party unity during the Histadrut election campaign.

Hussein: Why talk to Begin?

By RICHARD CARLETON
Special to The Jerusalem Post

The Israel election results "show a trend towards a more extreme attitude," according to Jordan's King Hussein.

The king told me in an interview in Amman on Wednesday that the election outcome portends a tougher attitude from the Israelis.

King Hussein said: "Sadly, I now take a pessimistic attitude towards the prospects for peace in the Middle East."

On the question of a meeting between Menahem Begin, Presidents Assad and Sadat and himself, King Hussein asked: "What would such a meeting be for?"

When I suggested that at least talk among the principals to the Middle East dispute would be a first step, the king interrupted to say bluntly: "Look, Begin has already said there is no such place as occupied Palestine, only liberated Israel. What point is there in talking to a man who takes that attitude?"

Hussein added: "There was a belief in the Arab world that the trend in Israel was towards a more moderate, conciliatory approach. The election results have disproved that theory."

Sadat and Assad in Saudi Arabia

AMMAN (Reuter). — Egyptian President Anwar Sadat arrived in Riyadh yesterday for summit talks with King Khaled of Saudi Arabia and President Hafez Assad of Syria, the Saudi state radio reported.

The tripartite conference will discuss the outcome of the recent meetings between the presidents of Egypt and Syria with U.S. President Jimmy Carter on peace prospects in the Middle East.

The mini-summit was also likely to discuss the victory of the right-wing Likud bloc in Israel and its impact on the Middle East peace talks.

The Egyptian and Syrian presidents will also exchange views with Crown Prince Fahd before his scheduled visit to Washington next week for talks with Carter.

The Saudi Radio, monitored in Amman, said Khaled yesterday called on Assad at the guest palace where he is staying.

Gur to get 'copter crash report today

Post Military Correspondent

The special committee set up to look into the cause of the military helicopter crash last week which left 54 dead will complete its deliberations today.

The committee, under the chairmanship of Aluf Avraham Orly, chief coordinator of activities in the administered territories, is expected to present its findings to Chief of Staff Mordechai Gur later today. The committee's conclusions will probably be released to the public early next week.

It can be assumed that the committee will have endeavoured to check four possible causes of the crash: pilot error, overloading, an on-board explosion, or mechanical failure.

Ten of those killed were Air Force personnel; the other 44 were paratroopers on brigade manoeuvres.

Meshel still Labour's choice

Jerusalem Post Reporter

TEL AVIV. — Histadrut Secretary-General Yeruham Meshel was yesterday overwhelmingly re-elected to head the Labour Party's list in the Histadrut — but not before facing a challenge and a vociferous debate.

Labour MK Jacques Amir, arguing that the choice should be postponed until next Tuesday, told a Labour Central Committee meeting here that the party's defeat in the Knesset elections should give everyone pause to consider the dangers that would follow from defeat in the coming Histadrut elections.

The Dimona MK did not argue against Meshel's candidacy. But he said there were other qualified candidates.

Tel Aviv Labour Council head Dov Ben-Meir, arguing for an immediate decision on Meshel, countered that it was too late to play around with the party's slate for the Histadrut. (The lists have to be submitted by the end of May for the June 21 election.)

Meshel was the only candidate offered by the party's Leadership Bureau. It seemed clear in the 800-member Central Committee that many were voting for Meshel only because there was not enough time for a full-scale consideration of the party's strategy in the crucial elections.

In his acceptance speech, Meshel said the party was preparing a list of candidates which would ensure that half the members of the Histadrut's governing body come from local labour councils and constituent unions.

Elsewhere in Tel Aviv, Mapam's political committee met yesterday on ways of seeing that the Histadrut elections do not produce a second Alignment fiasco. Mapam Knesset Member Aharon Efrat told them that in the Knesset election the Alignment's stalwarts in the Histadrut — especially labour council members — had declined to take an active part. "We must mobilize these forces immediately," Efrat, who was deputy Alignment Knesset campaign chief, said.

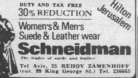

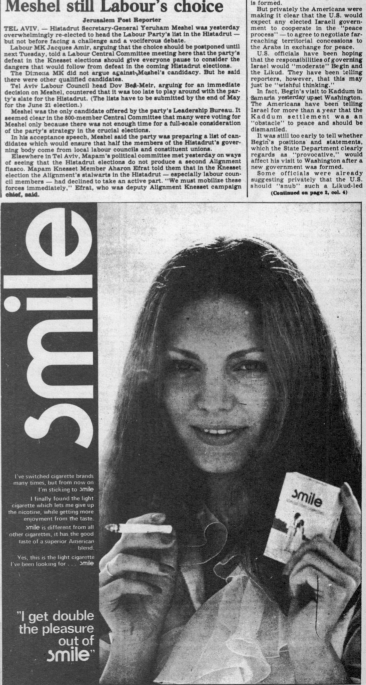

Era of currency control now ended

THE JERUSALEM POST

Social Betterment Page 3

Price: IL3.50 (Including VAT)

SUNDAY, OCTOBER 30, 1977 • HESHVAN 18, 5738 • ZIL-KI'ADAH 17, 1397 • VOL. XLVII, No. 14152

Now lawful to hold foreign currency

IL expected to settle at 15 to the $

10% overall price rise anticipated

Vat set at 12% but purchase tax off

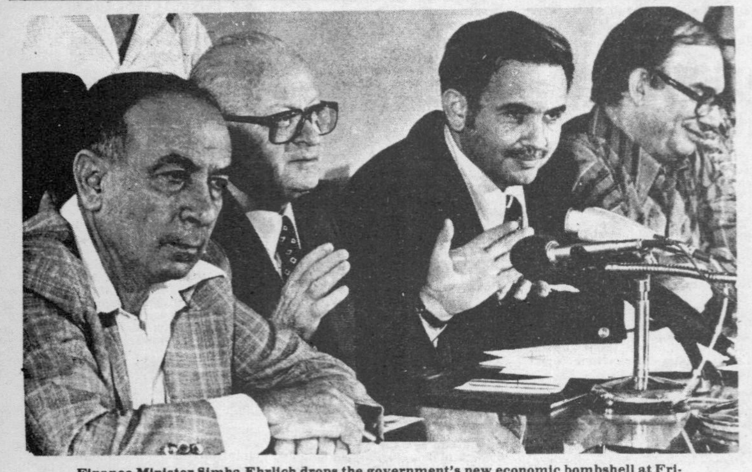

Finance Minister Simha Ehrlich drops the government's new economic bombshell at Friday afternoon's press conference. He is flanked by Minister of Industry, Commerce and Tourism Yigal Hurvitz (left) and by Deputy Finance Minister Yehezkel Flomin. On extreme right is Treasury Director-General Amiram Sivan. (Rahamim Yisraeli)

Ehrlich's bombshell is a 'risk' but 'it's necessary surgery'

By MEIR MERHAV, Jerusalem Post Economic Editor, and SHLOMO MAOZ, Jerusalem Post Economic Reporter

Some 38 years of currency control and fixed exchange rates came to an end Friday afternoon, with the Government's decision to make the Israel pound freely convertible and to abolish all controls on current foreign currency transactions.

The decision means that the Israel pound will be allowed to fall to about IL15 per U.S. dollar — a devaluation of about 44 per cent.

At the same time the 15 per cent defence duty on imports as well as export incentives have been eliminated. The entire policy package, of which many details have not yet been worked out, includes the following:

- From tomorrow, when the banks will re-open, the exchange rate of the Israel pound will no longer be fixed administratively, as it has been since the outbreak of World War II, when the British Mandatory Government introduced currency control. The value of the IL will be determined by supply and demand, and the Bank of Israel will apparently let it fall to about IL 15 per U.S. dollar.
- Export incentives, until now 30 per cent of the official exchange rate in the top category of domestic value added, will be abolished. So will the 15 per cent defence duty on imports.
- Customs duties will be slashed 20 per cent, if they are *ad valorem* — a duty of 50 per cent will now be 40 per cent, but specific duties will be raised 25 per cent, so that a duty of IL100 per unit will become IL125.
- Israeli citizens will be allowed to hold unlimited amounts of foreign currency accounts in Israeli banks, including foreign securities. They will be permitted to keep up to $3,000 in cash and another $3,000 per person in foreign bank accounts. They will also be allowed to take abroad Israeli currency to the equivalent of $3,000 per person.
- Israeli businesses will be free to keep accounts abroad and carry out current transactions without limitation.
- Foreigners will be completely free of any restrictions with regard to their transactions in foreign currency.
- The Value Added Tax has been raised from 8 per cent to 12 per cent as from November 1.
- Simultaneously, purchase taxes have been reduced and, on many products, abolished.
- There will be an impost, equivalent to the expected effective devaluation, on stocks of commodities and products. Tax inspectors will take inventories.
- The foreign travel tax has been abolished, but travel tickets will be subject to value added tax at the new rate of 12 per cent.
- The Bank of Israel has imposed stringent liquidity requirements on the commercial banks and, with the exception of credit for exports, the total volume of credits will be practically frozen for three months.
- The prices of subsidized products and services will immediately go up 15 per cent on the average. The cost of electric power will go up 25 per cent, as will that of water. Telephone and postal services will also cost more, the highest increase being for communication with other countries.
- Recipients of welfare payments will get an immediate increase of 12 per cent, to compensate for the expected price increases. Child allowances will also be raised by the same percentage. The immediate compensation will be absorbed in the April cost-of-living allowance, after price increases have become reflected in the consumer price index.
- Government departments will be required to absorb domestic cost increases, resulting from the devaluation, in their current budget. According to Treasury and Bank of Israel estimates, this may mean a 10 per cent real cut in their domestic expenditure up to the end of the year. The presentation of the budget for fiscal 1978 will be delayed to await the stabilization of the Israel pound and the repercussions of its new exchange rate on the size of the budget.
- The increase in the price of fuel announced Wednesday night — now disclosed to have been a preliminary to the sweeping reform of Friday — will remain unchanged.

The far-reaching economic reforms were announced at a dramatic press conference on Friday afternoon by Finance Minister

(Continued on page 2, col. 1)

Our Economic Editor explains:

Calculated risk or reckless gamble?

By MEIR MERHAV

Finance Minister Simha Ehrlich's sweeping reform goes far beyond the immediately visible steps of doing away with currency control, making the Israeli pound freely convertible at a floating exchange rate and the accompanying tight monetary policy. It is not far short of a revolution of the entire economic system as we have known it since 1939.

More than in most countries, the price system in Israel has been determined by the exchange rate of foreign currency. This has been because of the high import component of the nation's national product.

Until now, Israel has had a complex system of multiple effective exchange rates. As long as there are customs duties, effective exchange rates will remain multiple in Israel as they are everywhere else. But the abolition of the export incentives and the 15 per cent defence impost on imports, together with the floating of the pound, have gone a long way towards unifying the exchange rate.

One of the inevitable results of a price system geared to such a structure of administratively determined multiple exchange rates is that it misallocates resources.

In simple terms this means that enterprises which in reality are inefficient are artificially kept viable and others, which could expand and bring in foreign currency, are tethered to an unrealistic exchange rate.

Thus, for example, there are many exporters who got export incentives — and thereby a higher rate for their foreign currency — on the basis of an arbitrarily fixed content of domestic value added.

At the same time other industries got — again by administrative decision — less for their dollars. Examples are tourist services and, for many years, exporters of engineering services and other kinds of consultation work. Simultaneously, less than the real value in terms of pounds was paid for imports. By the same token, industries capable of producing import substitutes were held back from expanding.

The introduction of a floating exchange rate will do away with most of these effects.

The abolition of currency control is not a necessary component of a policy designed to give the pound its real competitive value. It represents, however, the ideological commitment of the government to the elimination, wherever possible, of government intervention.

But in addition, the government hopes that the abolition of currency control will stimulate foreign investment, in real assets and in financial assets alike, and will be a major incentive for the repatriation of foreign balances now illegally held abroad.

The critics of the lifting of currency control — first and foremost among them former Finance Minister Yehoshua Rabinowitz — argue that Israel's position, both political and economic, is too precarious to permit such a gamble.

There is the danger, they argue, that Israel's foreign currency reserves may become depleted to the danger point precisely when they are most needed, and that the freedom to hold foreign currency in Israeli banks will be no safeguard against much increased transfer of funds abroad.

To this the proponents of liberalism answer that the controls have also not prevented anyone who really wanted to smuggle currency abroad from doing so.

There is no doubt that the new risk is great — but only time will show who is right.

The new non-intervention by the government and the Bank of Israel is, however, apparently not quite what it seems to be. The biggest recipient of foreign currency is the government itself. It will therefore not simply let the Israeli Pound find its own level in the market, but will in reality refrain from intervention, through the Bank of Israel, when it "likes" the exchange rate which happens to be established by market forces.

That this is so was already revealed by Ehrlich's prediction that the pound on Monday, would settle at around IL15 per dollar.

Bank of Israel Governor Arnon Gafny went even a little further in his press conference last night and said that whenever the pound would fall, the central bank would not intervene as long as the fall was not caused by fortuitous factors or by intentional speculation.

Although Ehrlich expressed his hope that the new economic regime would make Israel into an important financial centre, it is unlikely that the hoped-for foreign deposits in our banks will be held in pounds. Nor is it likely that our foreign trade will be carried out in pounds. Apart from sudden sharp fluctuations, it is therefore not to be expected that the

(Continued on page 4, col. 1)

Geneva ball remains in Arab court

Post Mideast Affairs Editor

Qualified sources in Jerusalem last night said that there has been no breakthrough in the discussion of the Geneva working paper to warrant new decisions by Israel. "The ball remains in the Arab court," one authoritative source said.

The source was commenting on a meeting on Friday between Prime Minister Menahem Begin and U.S. Ambassador Samuel Lewis. The two men were reported to have reviewed a variety of regional topics, including the situation in southern Lebanon and the UN General Assembly resolution condemning the establishment of settlements in the administered territories.

The source said that deliberations on the working paper — which sets the procedural outlines for a reconvened Geneva peace conference — was a main topic discussed between Begin and Lewis. The source intimated that the Americans are trying to work out a draft that will compromise between the Arab views and the working paper concluded between the U.S. and Israel.

Lebanese army prepares for deployment

Jerusalem Post Staff and Agencies

Lebanese army liaison committees yesterday arrived in four areas of southern Lebanon to coordinate plans for the deployment of regular troops in those districts. This followed recent talks between Lebanese and Israeli liaison officers on firming up the shaky U.S.-mediated cease-fire in the region.

The deployment has been obstructed by the refusal of the Palestine Liberation Organization to pull back its forces which have been battling local Christian militias. Some 1,400 troops of a reconstructed Lebanese army have been standing by for some time for the takeover.

An IDF spokesman announced, meanwhile, that several anti-tank rockets were fired at an IDF patrol moving near the Lebanese border yesterday before dawn. The patrol, which was in the Zar'it area, returned the fire and suffered no casualties, the spokesman added.

This was the first shooting incident into Israel since October 5.

Meshel: Unions will strike

By JOSHUA BRILLIANT
Post Political Reporter

TEL AVIV. — The Histadrut will seek to organize strikes and demonstrations throughout the country against the government's new economic policy, Secretary-General Yeruham Meshel announced last night.

In some places there will be a full day strike, in some more and in others less, he said.

The labour federation will not repeat its abortive attempt at a country-wide strike. Emerging from a three-hour emergency meeting of the Central Committee (the Histadrut's cabinet), Meshel insisted the strikes and demonstrations must be "organized with the workers ... to give them a feeling that they are doing this, and not carrying out orders from above."

(A Histadrut call for a one-hour strike in protest against a subsidy cut earlier this year was a resounding failure as many workers claimed the call was an Alignment move against the Likud.)

The Central Committee last night demanded an increase in the cost-of-living allowance to be paid with January salaries, to compensate for the expected price rises.

Meshel complained that the government's measures put the entire economic burden on employees, especially those with low incomes. The 12 per cent compensation for the poor is nothing but "deceit" because it covers only payments for children and old-age pensions. It will not compensate for the family's overall expenditure, he said.

The Alignment Knesset faction held an urgent meeting last night, attended by former Bank of Israel governor Moshe Sanbar, and resolved to firmly oppose the government's new economic policy. The faction noted that the measures — following the economic doctrines of Prof. Milton Friedman — would

(Continued on page 2, col. 5)

Gafny: Reform will fail unless budget is slashed

Jerusalem Post Reporter

The new economic policy will fail unless the Government slashes the budget and stops pumping new money into the economy, Arnon Gafny, Governor of the Bank of Israel, said last night.

He told a press conference in Jerusalem that the brakes must be applied "or the Israel pound will decline very fast." He also said that he is opposed to wage increments that would increase the worker's take home pay.

Gafny said Israelis must pay a price — inflation — for the success of the new economic programme.

Deputy Governor Zvi Sussman said that while holders of foreign currency and bonds would gain immediately from the new economic moves, in the long run, all Israelis would benefit, since economic growth would resume and new job and business opportunities would be made available.

Gafny added that companies unable to endure real competition will be forced out of the market and be replaced by more stable firms.

He declined to confirm or deny reports that the Bank of Israel has arranged with overseas financial institutions to help out in case Israel's foreign currency reserves fall drastically as a result of a shift of foreign exchange out of the country.

But Gafny denied a report that the International Monetary Fund has promised Israel money in case this should happen. But he felt certain the IMF would come to Israel's aid "with hundreds of millions of dollars" if needed, as the organization usually assists countries trying to improve their economies in accordance with IMF recommendations.

Jerusalem calls UN vote 'unworthy of any comment'

Post Diplomatic Correspondent

Official Jerusalem has dismissed Friday's UN General Assembly resolution condemning the establishment of Israeli settlements in the administered territories as a "non-event" which did not warrant comment.

Authoritative sources said that the vote was not unexpected, and added that the American abstention came as no surprise. The U.S. decision was understood to have been conveyed in advance to Prime Minister Menahem Begin by Ambassador Samuel Lewis.

Begin had said earlier Friday that Israel would not consider itself bound by any UN resolution denouncing settlements in the areas.

"The attitude of the Israel Government towards the settlement issue has been made clear to everybody and nothing has changed," he said shortly after his meeting with Lewis.

Wolf Blitzer adds from Washington:

Israeli officials here were pleased that the U.S. has abstained. They said that they would have naturally preferred to see Washington join Jerusalem in voting against the resolution. But they acknowledged that this was unrealistic, given the State Department's long-standing opposition to Israel settlements.

Intensive diplomatic exchanges between the Israeli Embassy and the State Department last week were seen as crucial in convincing the administration not to join the anti-Israel majority in the world body.

(See story on Page 2)

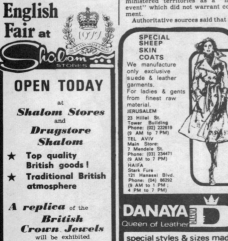

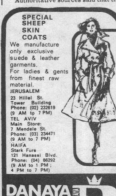

Tito tired, cancels planned Sadat visit

BELGRADE (AP). — Yugoslavia's 85-year-old President Tito is suffering from fatigue and has been told to curtail all activity for the next several weeks, Yugoslavia's official news agency reported on Friday. As part of this he has indefinitely postponed a visit by Egyptian president Anwar Sadat that was to have begun tomorrow. (Mme. Broz, P. 4)

Travel and lots of other things will cost more

Jerusalem Post Reporter

Foreign travel will become more expensive. Although the travel tax has been abolished, there will now be a 12 per cent value added tax on the ticket, in addition to the higher cost, in Israeli pounds, of the ticket itself. As a result, the longer the distance travelled, the greater will be the increase in the cost.

Until now, the fixed travel tax of IL1,000 per ticket, irrespective of distance, made short trips relatively more expensive, than longer journeys. The reform will make a one-way ticket to New York some 20 per cent dearer, but a one-way trip to Rome will go up only 7 per cent.

Electric power will cost 11 agora more per kilowatt/hour — a 25 per cent rise. The cost of water, which is largely determined by the cost of the electric power used to pump it, will go up 15 per cent.

Basic foodstuffs and public transport will become 15 per cent more expensive. Domestic air flights and railway fares will be revised to reflect the devaluation. Price-controlled products will be allowed to go up by 7 per cent without special permit from the Ministry of Industry, Commerce and Tourism.

The new price of a loaf of standard bread will be IL1.80 instead of IL1.55, soybean oil will cost IL10.25 (IL8.90) per 920 cc. bottle, margarine will be IL2.20 (IL1.90) per package, an average-sized egg will cost IL0.80 (0.70), milk will be IL3.40 per litre (IL2.95), frozen chicken will be priced at IL18.40 (IL16.00) per kilo. But not only the subsidized products have gone up — those which, like frozen meat, sugar or flour, are unsubsidized or even taxed have also been raised.

The Government also decided to impose a special impost on all stocks of imported products in order to mop up inflationary profits. This includes all imports not yet released from the customs. Past experience shows, however, that the Government has not been able to do this effectively and has been forced to accept importers' declarations on their inventories.

Dutch seek proof Baader gang abducted millionaire

AMSTERDAM (UPI). — Police staged a massive manhunt for kidnapped millionaire Maurits Caransa yesterday, seeking proof that the fanatic Baader-Meinhof terrorist gang was responsible for the abduction.

Armed units threw up roadblocks around the country, searched houseboats and holiday homes and sifted through telephone calls to newspapers claiming to know the whereabouts of the 61-year-old real-estate tycoon.

One caller said Caransa was being held in exchange for the freedom of Baader-Meinhof terrorist Kurt Folkerts, held on charges that he murdered a policeman.

An editor at the newspaper "De Telegraaf" said the caller demanded that Folkerts be released at midnight outside the Continental Club where several men abducted Caransa early Friday.

The call to "De Telegraaf" did not mention any threat to Caransa's life, the editor said, nor was there any demand for money. But other callers have demanded sums ranging from $1.25m. to $4m., the editor said. One person demanded the abdication of Queen Juliana.

One of the first calls after the kidnapping claimed Caransa was in the hands of the Red Army Faction, otherwise known as the Baader-Meinhof gang.

Pieter Bakker Schut, Folkerts' lawyer, said he doubted a connection between his client and the Caransa kidnapping.

Are black dollars now legal?

Jerusalem Post Reporter

The Bank of Israel will neither be obliged to buy foreign currency offered to it nor will it be required to sell it on demand. Nor will Israeli citizens have to sell foreign currency to the government — they will be allowed to keep it in Israeli banks, without limitation of amount, and will be permitted to buy and sell foreign securities and assets. Businesses will be free to convert their foreign currency receipts or not to convert them, as they see fit.

Any Israeli may take up to $3,000 out of the country and keep another $3,000, at any given time, in a foreign bank. No decision has yet been made with regard to past contraventions of the foreign currency regulations, but apparently there will be no prosecutions on that account.

Nor is it clear what will happen to Israelis who will repatriate money so far illicitly held abroad.

With the abolition of foreign currency control, however, the only remaining check on such transfers may be the periodic statement of assets required by the income tax authorities — but that, too, is likely to be of little importance, according to experienced observers.

Treasury reports every bank to set own rate

Jerusalem Post Staff

Starting tomorrow morning, every bank will set its own exchange rate for the dollar, and there will be no control on the spread between buying and selling rates, the Treasury's foreign currency controller, Dov Kantarovitz, said last night.

In a circular to all commercial banks, he suggests they post large signs in all branches, giving their exchange rates for various currencies. He predicted that in a very short time there would be a "standard" price for the dollar in all Israel banks — "a sort of monopoly that only the Bank of Israel would be able to break."

Moshe Merav, an official in the Bank of Israel's foreign currency division, said the central bank would place its worldwide data on foreign currency rates at the disposal of commercial banks, to assist them in setting their own exchange rates.

Every day at 4 p.m. the Bank of Israel will publish representative exchange rates as offered by the various banks.

Ernst I. Japhet, chairman of the board of directors of Bank Leumi, told *The Jerusalem Post* that plans are being made to have one branch correlate transactions for a number of branches in a given geographical area. The branch will centralize these transactions and transfer them to the main branch which serves as the main centre for all foreign currency dealings.

The first indication as to what the public can expect in terms of a new rate of exchange was visible at the Bank Leumi branch at Ben-Gurion Airport. Late evening travellers were advised last night that the buy and sell rates were IL15.18-IL15.33 for $1. For the time being, the limitation for foreigners leaving Israel was still a maximum of $30 which they could repurchase from local currency. Israelis, on the other hand, could purchase up to $700 at the IL15.33 rate.

Japhet, confirming the rate of IL15.18-IL15.33, said it was set in consultation with a number of bodies. But he claimed they are not indicative of what the rate may be tomorrow and was being used primarily as a temporary convenience for the tourist.

Daniel Recanati, managing director of the Israel Discount Bank, expressed the opinion that the rate of IL15.33 used by his bank's branch at Ben-Gurion will probably approximate the rate which will be in force when the banking system reopens tomorrow.

All special-class foreign currency bank accounts — such as Natad and others — except German reparations accounts, are formally abolished as of tomorrow morning and become Toshav (resident) accounts.

All Israelis may therefore from now on hold as much foreign currency in their Toshav accounts as they wish.

Dov Kantarovitz, foreign currency controller at the Treasury, said no

(Continued on page 6, col. 1)

Milton Friedman tells The Jerusalem Post what he thinks of the New Economic Plan — Back page.

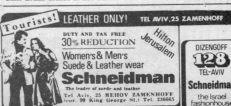

THE JERUSALEM POST

Tribute to B-G
Page 2

Price: IL4.00
(Including VAT)

WEDNESDAY, NOVEMBER 16, 1977 • KISLEV 6, 5738 • ZIL-HIJJA 4, 1397 • VOL. XLVII, No. 14167★

Israel official hints Sadat's response was favourable

Begin sends formal invitation to Sadat, gets immediate reply

Premier Menahem Begin yesterday sent Egyptian President Anwar Sadat a written invitation to come to Israel, and received a reply within a few hours. The letters were transmitted by the U.S. ambassadors in Tel Aviv and Cairo. A Begin aide hinted that Sadat's response was favourable. Begin reported on the invitation to the Knesset and discussed whether and how a foreign head of state might be permitted to speak there.

In Cairo, meanwhile, Sadat was telling U.S. congressmen he saw his proposed undertaking as a 'holy job' and an attempt to resolve psychological differences.

Observers in the U.S. looked on with pleasure and perplexity, as a message from Premier Begin was due to be given to President Carter.

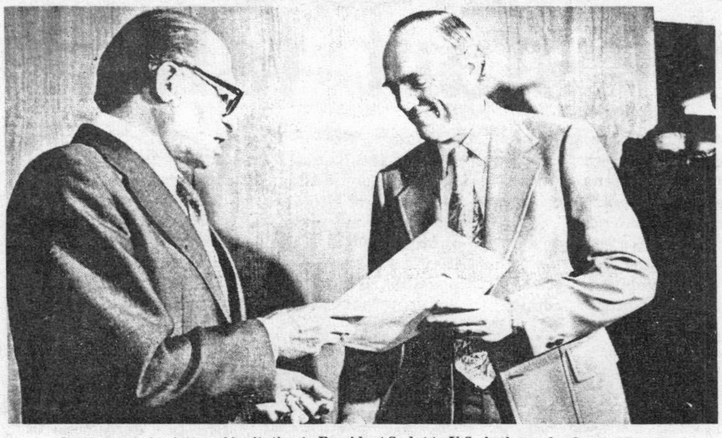

Begin hands his letter of invitation to President Sadat to U.S. Ambassador Samuel Lewis at the Knesset yesterday. (Eliahu Harati)

Weizman regrets Gur's suggestion that Sadat may be fooling Israel

Post Knesset Reporter

The Chief of Staff, Rav-Aluf Mordechai Gur, had "no need or justification" to suggest that President Anwar Sadat might be trying to pull the wool over Israel's eyes by declaring his desire to come to Jerusalem and discuss peace with Israel's leaders, Defence Minister Ezer Weizman told the Knesset yesterday.

Replying to four parliamentary questions on Gur's remarks, made in an interview published in yesterday's "Yediot Aharonot," Weizman said he himself "can only regret" those remarks, "which were made without my prior knowledge and without my approval." Weizman hoped that the remarks "will not have a harmful effect on the process now in motion in the direction of peace between us and our neighbours."

The defence minister said he had summoned the chief of staff home from his vacation "to clarify" the matter.

The Jerusalem Post learned that Weizman had drafted a reply in which he intended to say that, after his meeting with Gur he would "draw conclusions." But Likud MKs Geula Cohen, Hillel Seidel and Moshe Shamir interceded with him and with Prime Minister Menahem Begin, and that clause was deleted.

The questions had been submitted by one coalition member, the Likud's Avraham Sharir; a coalition supporter, Shmuel Flatto Sharon; and two members of the opposition, the Alignment's Yosef Sarid and Shelli's Meir Pa'il. In addition, the Likud's Pessah Grupper and the Alignment's Chaike Grosman submitted urgent motions for the agenda.

The questions and motions were all nearly identical; they asked what the minister thought about the chief of staff's speaking out on political matters, what he intended to do about it, and whether Gur's remarks might not have a harmful effect on current political developments.

Gur: Egypt at peak of war preparations

By HIRSH GOODMAN
Post Military Correspondent

Senior Defence Ministry officials and military sources expressed no surprise yesterday at Chief of Staff Mordechai Gur's statement that Egypt is currently at the height of preparing for war. But they questioned the timing of his remarks and his motives for possibly laying his career on the line.

An official source told *The Jerusalem Post* that Defence Minister Ezer Weizman was extremely upset by Gur's remarks in the "Yediot Aharonot" interview. Weizman himself said that the chief of staff had overstepped his authority when Gur said that "if (Sadat) has in mind another deception like that on the eve of the Yom Kippur War, his intentions are clear to us."

Gur's remarks, coming on the eve of an official invitation to Sadat to visit Israel, caused consternation among the country's diplomats. And the Prime Minister's Office made it clear that Prime Minister Menahem Begin was taken aback by Gur's statement. *The Post* learned that the chief of staff initiated the interview, giving it on Saturday night, several hours before leaving on vacation and before it was clear that Israel intended to invite Sadat. Sources close to Gur intimated that while Gur's remarks had been accurately reported, the chief of staff had not intended to undermine Begin's initiative. They claimed that the newspaper had linked what Gur said to developments that he was unaware of when he was interviewed.

Others in the defence establishment, however, are convinced that Gur's remarks were premeditated and intended to counteract the public

(Continued on page 2, col. 5)

Histadrut, manufacturers approve January cost-of-living increment

By LEA LEVAVI
Jerusalem Post Reporter

TEL AVIV. — The Histadrut and the Manufacturers Association agreed yesterday that the next cost-of-living increment should be paid in January to cover price increases until the end of the year resulting from the new economic policy.

It also was agreed that the C-o-L increment payable next April will cover the increases from January to March.

Another point agreed upon by the leaders of the Histadrut, headed by Secretary-General Yeruham Meshel, and the Manufacturers Association, headed by president Avraham Shavit, was that negotiations on a new work agreement should begin in January with hopes of completion by March 31.

The agreement reached at the meeting — described by Shavit as "one of the pleasantest meetings I've ever had" — is still subject to review and ratification by large bodies within both organizations.

In the joint communique issued after the meeting, it said that negotiations will begin in January because the economic situation is still too uncertain to permit a hasty beginning of talks. The communique also said that both organizations are concerned about possible pockets of unemployment and are seeking ways to avoid this, particularly through greater efficiency and higher production.

A committee of experts, representatives of the workers and employers, are to determine the C-o-L increments for January and April, using figures provided by the Central Bureau of Statistics.

Shavit told *The Jerusalem Post* after the meeting that "Meshel understood the position of the industrialists under the new economic policy, and we certainly understood the position of the workers."

He added, "It was no compromise. It was an agreement which met both our needs and, above all, helped to clear up some of the air of uncertainty facing both labour and industry as a result of the NEP."

If the feeling of "uncertainty" continued, Shavit felt, there might be industrial labour unrest.

Prices up 3.6 per cent in October

By SHLOMO MAOZ
Jerusalem Post Reporter

In October, the month before the economic reform, the consumer price index rose by 3.6 per cent to 146.1 points. The total price increase since January, not counting the last jolt given it two weeks ago, came to 25 per cent.

The last three days of October's price increases, following the NEP, contributed only one-third of a per cent to the increase.

The spokesman for the Central Bureau of Statistics, David Neuman, who released the data yesterday, said the bureau estimates that the recent measures taken by the government will cause prices to rise by another 7.5 per cent. This will be the immediate result of higher prices for basic foodstuffs, fuel, electric power, water and the increase in value added tax. It will not yet reflect the general okay given by the Ministry of Industry, Commerce and Tourism to raise prices by 7 per cent and more, where the import component is high.

These estimates should be taken with a grain of salt because the prices of electric power, mail, telephone and other services are to be increased this week or later this month.

The bureau is carrying out a price survey and will publish the prices of 1,300 products from the second week of November. The Social Betterment Committee of the Knesset is waiting for this data because it will serve as a first indicator of the price inflation that is to be expected as a result of the NEP.

The wholesale price index of manufactured products rose by 1.7 per cent in October, and by a total of 25.2 per cent since the beginning of the year.

Sadat:

Visit is a 'holy job'

CAIRO (AP). — Egyptian President Anwar Sadat said yesterday that his proposed trip to Israel is "a holy job" and that he will be ready to make it as soon as possible after receiving the official invitation.

Sadat said yesterday that his proposed trip to Israel is "a holy job" and that he will be ready to make it as soon as possible after receiving the official invitation.

But he emphasized he will be speaking for Egypt only and not for other Arabs when he addresses the Knesset, and the aim of the visit will be to explain his views and not to negotiate any agreement.

He told a 14-member delegation from the U.S. House of Representatives he views the visit as part of preparations for a reconvened Arab-Israeli peace conference at Geneva.

Sadat said, "We must do the impossible to break the vicious circle in which Arabs and Israelis have been moving for 30 years. This is for the sake of our future generations. Hence the holiness of the mission. If I do not try to break this vicious circle, God will bring me to account, and so will future generations."

Asked whether he would fear for his personal safety in Israel, Sadat snapped, "Never."

Sadat spoke in reply to a question by the delegation head, House majority leader James Wright, who said the proposed visit "may be a long-awaited breakthrough" towards Middle East peace.

Explaining the aim of the visit, Sadat said, "For me the Arab-Israeli conflict consists of 70 per cent psychological problems and 30 per cent substance. Let us overcome the psychological problems and go to the substance. For that I am going to the Knesset and if need be I shall open a discussion with its 120 deputies to give them the real facts in the area here — the other point of view — so that they can decide for themselves.

"I consider my visit to the Knesset part of the preparations for Geneva," the president said, reiterating his insistence that the Palestine Liberation Organization be represented there and that the negotiations should lead to establishment of a Palestinian state on the West Bank and in Gaza.

Pravda said yesterday that Israel's proposal to invite Egyptian President Anwar Sadat for peace talks was designed to divide the Arab camp.

The Communist Party daily said, "Despite many unclear points in the current Egyptian-Israeli dialogue, one can discern in it the attempts of Tel Aviv and the forces behind it to urge Egypt onto the road of separate negotiations and deals with Israel."

The "forces behind" Israel apparently was a reference to the U.S.

The Pravda statement signalled Soviet concern that Egypt may decide to go ahead with a new round of negotiations over Sinai if current efforts to reconvene the Geneva Middle East peace talks fail.

Pravda said the semi-official Egyptian press gave the impression Sadat was not serious but made his proposal out of exasperation with continued Israeli objection to a reconvened Geneva with Palestinian participation, a basic Arab demand.

Ghorbal sees Assad, Sadat accord on Geneva

Jerusalem Post Correspondent

WASHINGTON. — Egyptian Ambassador Ashraf Ghorbal yesterday predicted that Presidents Sadat and Assad would reach agreement today on a unified Arab position regarding the reconvening of the Geneva peace conference.

Meeting with reporters at a breakfast sponsored by "Foreign Policy" magazine, the ambassador also said that the unified Egyptian-Syrian position should pave the way for a reconvened Geneva peace conference before the end of this year. Sadat and Assad are due to meet today in Damascus.

Regarding the Sadat visit to Jerusalem, Ghorbal said that this was not an "off-the-cuff" idea. Sadat had been thinking about it for a long time so that he could dispel the belief in Israel that the Arabs want to destroy the Jewish state.

Klutznik going to Cairo

Philip Klutznik, the new president of the World Jewish Congress, will meet with Egyptian President Anwar Sadat in Cairo in mid-December, Dr. Nahum Goldmann, the former WJC president, told an Israel Radio reporter yesterday.

Begin:

Welcome with honour

By MOSHE KOHN
Post Knesset Reporter

Prime Minister Menahem Begin told the Knesset yesterday evening that he had handed American Ambassador Sam Lewis a letter officially inviting Egyptian President Anwar Sadat to Jerusalem.

Lewis was to transmit the invitation promptly to his counterpart, Hermann Eilts, in Cairo, who was to deliver it to Sadat. Lewis was in the Knesset, having arrived to take his seat in the VIP section during the 35-minute Ben-Gurion memorial session (see page 2).

Begin said he assumed Sadat would get the invitation only later last night, so, "as a matter of elementary courtesy," its full text would be published only this morning.

AP reported late last night that Begin received a reply from Sadat within hours. Yehiel Kadishai, head of the Prime Minister's Bureau, hinted that the response was favourable. It was also learned that the invitation was for Sadat to come on or after November 24.

The Prime Minister opened by giving his own brief tribute to Ben-Gurion. He said he had purposely asked the Knesset presidium to schedule this political discussion yesterday, for Ben-Gurion was the first of Israel's prime ministers to propose to the Arab leaders that they meet with Israel's leaders to discuss peace. Begin said he was only acting according to the precedent set by Ben-Gurion and followed by all his successors: Moshe Sharett, Levi Eshkol, Golda Meir and Yitzhak Rabin.

The Prime Minister was replying to six separate urgent motions for the agenda submitted by Kalman Kahana (Poalei Agudat Yisrael), Akiva Nof (Democratic Movement for Change), former foreign minister Yigal Allon (Alignment-Labour), Arye Eliav (Shelli), Avraham Melamed (National Religious Party), and Haim Corfu (Likud-Herut).

In Washington last night, Israel Ambassador Simcha Dinitz handed Secretary of State Cyrus Vance a personal message from Premier Begin to President Carter. The message, it was learned, was intended to update the President on recent developments regarding a possible visit to Jerusalem by President Sadat of Egypt, and other Middle East developments.

He went on to discuss a procedural question involving the Knesset itself. If Sadat accepts the invitation, he said, the House Committee will be asked to resolve that "the president of Egypt will be permitted to speak from the Knesset podium."

The Knesset, he noted, had a "general principle" according to which only MKs and cabinet Ministers could speak from the podium. Three foreigners had been granted the privilege: Malawi President Kamuzu Banda on May 27, 1968; UN General Assembly president Angie Brooks on April 6, 1970; and Costa Rican President Daniel Oduber on March 30, 1976. However, on those occasions only "greetings" had been involved, and the House Committee resolution under which they were invited to the podium explicitly limited the nature of their remarks accordingly. When Sadat comes, Begin said, there should be no limitations on what he is permitted to say. What is more, as Sadat has expressed a desire to meet all the MKs, the government agrees that all the Knesset factions, "without exception," shall be permitted to invite the Egyptian president to meet with them. Since Egypt is Israel's biggest and most powerful neighbour, Begin said, it was "only natural" that its leader should be the first of our neighbouring heads of state to come here. However, the government is also ready to welcome Syria's President Hafez el-Assad, Jordan's King Hussein, and Lebanon's President Elias Sarkis.

At this, the Democratic Front for Peace and Equality's Meir Wilner shouted: "And what about Yasser Arafat?"

From all sections of the House came cries: "Arafat isn't the head of any state."

And Begin himself said to Wilner, raising laughter all over the chamber and applause in the galleries: "Knesset Member Wilner, I hope you don't make any interjec-

(Continued on page 2, col. 4)

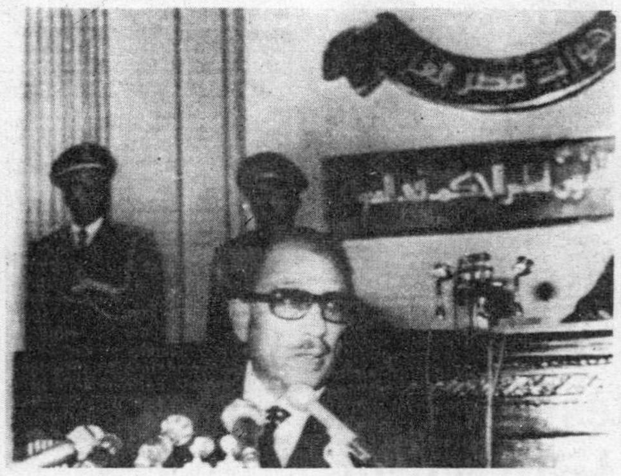

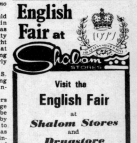

President Sadat during his speech in Cairo last Wednesday when he said he was ready to go to the Knesset to achieve peace. (AP radiophoto)

U.S. pleased, stunned by developments

By WOLF BLITZER
Jerusalem Post Correspondent

WASHINGTON. — The U.S. yesterday welcomed the possible visit to Jerusalem by President Sadat, calling it "a concrete contribution by the leaders involved towards moving forward negotiations for an overall settlement of the Middle East conflict."

In a prepared statement, the State Department's spokesman, Hodding Carter III, said that the U.S. believes "the recent exchange between the president of Egypt and the prime minister of Israel underlines their sincerity of purpose in seeking to put an end to three decades of strife."

Continuing, the spokesman said: "For our part we will do anything necessary to facilitate contacts, which we have always considered essential if the parties to the dispute are to settle their differences themselves at the Geneva conference."

It was clear here that the administration was welcoming the Sadat visit to Jerusalem but only in the sense that it might promote progress towards reconvening a Geneva conference. Officials at the State Department are refusing to comment on the possibility of separate Israeli-Egyptian negotiations outside the framework of the Geneva conference. The spokesman kept insisting yesterday that the U.S. supports all efforts aimed at reaching "a comprehensive settlement" of the Middle East dispute.

The Americans, stunned by Sadat's apparent decision to go to Jerusalem, possibly as soon as next week, were not informed in advance by the Egyptian leader of his willingness to make such a dramatic gesture. Although pleased by the move, the Americans are trying to make certain that the U.S. initiative aimed at achieving an overall settlement at Geneva is not derailed by separate Israeli-Egyptian negotiations.

The spokesman said that Secretary of State Cyrus Vance has not made any plans either to meet with Arab foreign ministers early next month during a visit to Europe or to resume some shuttle diplomacy in the Middle East. "There's nothing in the works," he maintained.

But other U.S. sources said that Vance is considering either one of these moves if the remaining procedural problems standing in the way of a conference are not removed shortly.

At this point, however, the administration has barely been able to keep up with the hectic developments of the past 48 hours, during which time Sadat told a nationwide CBS television audience in America that he was ready to address the Knesset next week. "I'm just waiting for the proper invitation," Sadat told CBS newsman Walter Cronkite. (See text on Page 4)

The State Department yesterday said that U.S. Ambassador Samuel Lewis received such an invitation from Begin in Jerusalem and was relaying it to U.S. Ambassador Herman Eilts in Cairo for transmission to Sadat.

The Americans are now waiting to see what develops in Damascus today during Sadat's scheduled round of talks with Syrian President Assad.

Analysts here believe that Sadat was, in part, motivated to take the initiative in visiting Jerusalem by his anger over the Syrian delay in responding to a set of procedures worked out by Israel and the U.S. for reconvening the Geneva conference. Egypt has accepted the procedures in principle and is said to be upset that the Syrians are still trying to dictate their own terms to Egypt.

It is believed here that Sadat may try to back out of the Jerusalem visit if Assad informs him today that Syria will go to the Geneva conference on the basis of the U.S.-Israeli "working paper."

Under such circumstances, Sadat could explain that he will be meeting with the Israeli leadership in Geneva and that there was, therefore, no need to go to Jerusalem.

But clearly such an excuse would damage Sadat's reputation in American public opinion, which has been captivated by the possibility that an Egyptian head of state might address the Knesset. The Sadat statement on CBS Monday evening was a banner headline in nearly every U.S. newspaper.

Israeli officials here and U.S. Jewish leaders are still pinching themselves over the Sadat announcement.

The U.S. spokesman told reporters that the U.S. believes an exchange between Sadat and Begin would be "helpful in the continuing efforts by all the parties to the conflict to reconvene that conference as soon as possible." He said that the Begin invitation to Sadat was being relayed by the U.S. "with the greatest of pleasure."

He also said that Vance has not been in direct contact with either Begin or Sadat, although the U.S. ambassadors there have communicated with the respective leaders.

Egypt informed the U.S. during this exchange, the spokesman said, that a Sadat visit to Jerusalem would not be a substitute for reconvening the Geneva conference, and that Egypt had no intention of moving away from the Geneva framework.

Regarding the just-concluded Arab foreign ministers' meeting in Tunis, the spokesman said that the U.S. welcomed the "flexible stance" taken there.

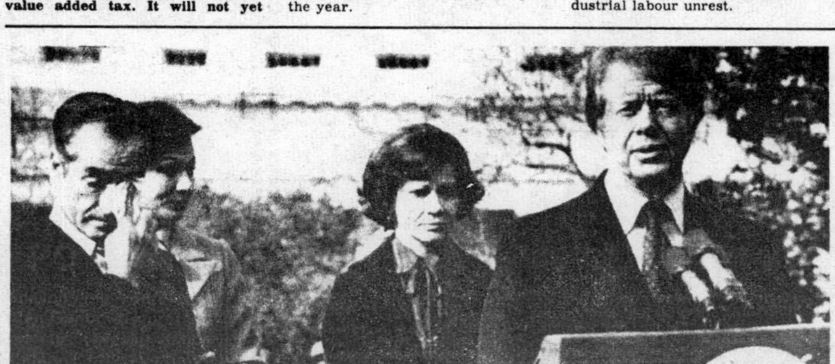

The Shah wipes his eyes from tear gas fumes as he is greeted by President Carter and the First Lady on the White House lawn yesterday. Anti-Shah protestors hurled tear gas at the police. (UPI telephoto)

Thousands protest against Shah in Washington

WASHINGTON (AP). — Police and competing forces of demonstrators clashed violently as the Shah and Empress of Iran arrived at the White House yesterday and tear gas wafted onto the lawn of the executive mansion during welcoming ceremonies by President Carter.

At least four police officers and eight other persons were hurt as pro- and anti-Shah forces rushed one another just as the Shah was arriving for his two-day state visit.

Mounted police charged into the crowds, on the Ellipse just south of the White House, and forced them back toward the Washington Monument, using sticks and tear gas.

Fighting between hooded protestors, mostly Iranian students, and supporters of the Shah continued in some areas of the monument grounds even after the Ellipse was cleared.

Carter proceeded with the ceremonies on schedule. Both he and the Shah dabbed their eyes, apparently irritated by the tear gas that drifted even into White House offices and those of the Treasury Department, two blocks away.

Police gave no official estimates, but it was clear that the demonstrators on both sides numbered well into the thousands.

Order appeared restored, except for a few isolated fistfights well away from the White House, within 30 minutes of the initial clash.

The eruption on the Ellipse occurred almost precisely the instant that the Shah was scheduled to greet the President after landing via helicopter nearby. The demonstrators threw rocks, cinder blocks, and wood from an unattended pile of lumber at the police. At that point, the mounted officers charged into the demonstrators.

THE JERUSALEM
POST

Includes special edition

Price: IL4.00
(Including VAT)

SUNDAY, NOVEMBER 20, 1977 • KISLEV 10, 5738 • ZIL-HIJJA 8, 1397 • VOL. XLVII, No. 14170★

اهلا وسهلا بالرئيس السادات

Ahlan wa Sahlan, Welcome to President Sadat, was a banner on the special edition of The Post distributed last night. That edition, in today's centrefold section, contains news on preparations for Sadat's visit, assessments of its meaning for the Mideast political scene, a profile of the President, a schedule of his visit and related features.

Smiling Sadat, Begin start talks

President Anwar Sadat and Prime Minister Menahem Begin started to talk last night, shortly after the Egyptian head of state exchanged warm greetings with Israeli leaders at an emotional arrival ceremony at Ben-Gurion Airport.

Begin emerged from a 30-minute session with Sadat at the King David Hotel last night hopeful that an "understanding" was developing between them, amid reports that the visit might produce diplomatic ties or a treaty. President Sadat addresses the Knesset at 4 p.m. today.

Well-informed Egyptian sources said that an exchange of diplomatic missions would be discussed during the talks; and Israel Radio, quoting Israel Foreign Ministry sources, said that an Israel-Egypt non-aggression pact was possible. But officials dismissed all reports that concrete accords would emerge.

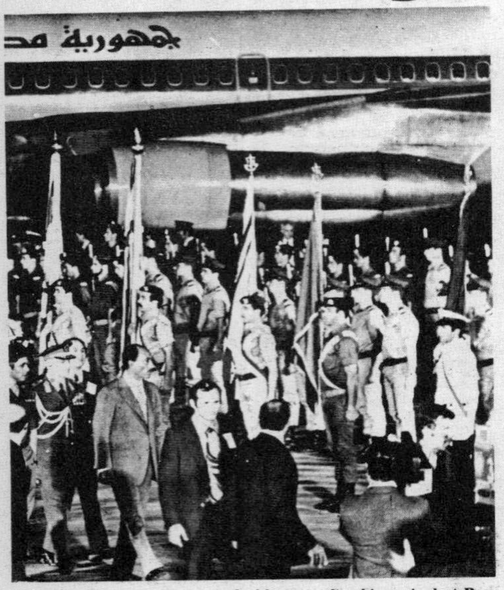

President Sadat reviews guard of honour after his arrival at Ben-Gurion airport last night. (Rahamim Yisraeli)

Airport welcome: Warmth is mutual

Jerusalem Post Staff

BEN-GURION AIRPORT. — Egyptian President Anwar Sadat exchanged smiles, quips and embraces with his Israeli hosts on arrival here last night. Recognizing persons he had never met and greeting with warmth, the smiling Sadat passed down a receiving line to meet past and present Israeli leaders as a large crowd applauded vigorously.

Operation "Gate 1977" — the code name for the security programme surrounding the Egyptian President's visit — almost fell apart at Ben-Gurion Airport when hordes of photographers and newsmen descended from Sadat's plane and swamped the historic first meeting between the leaders of Egypt and Israel.

The thousands of journalists, television crews and photographers who had arrived earlier were unable to see the first moment, and television viewers at home also saw more backs than faces before the national anthems were played.

At 7:55, Foreign Minister Moshe Dayan walked quietly along and singled out U.S. Ambassador Samuel Lewis, with whom he exchanged words briefly. At 7:58, a trumpet fanfare signalled the appearance of Prime Minister Menahem Begin and President Ephraim Katzir. The guard of honour dipped its flags and presented arms.

Suddenly, all heads turned as three white lights appeared to the left of the terminal building. The presidential Boeing had arrived. Slowly the plane taxied around and stopped in front of the red carpet.

El Al ramps were rolled up to the front and rear doors of the aircraft. The engines were shut down and the army band played another fanfare.

Protocol chief Amir was the first Israeli to enter the plane. He walked down the ramp with President Sadat and led him to the edge of the red carpet, where he introduced him to President Katzir and Prime Minister Begin.

The President of Egypt and the Prime Minister of Israel then walked together along the red carpet flanked by a line of waiting Cabinet members, the chief rabbis, ambassadors, the Chief of Staff and other state leaders. President Sadat shook hands with each in turn. When he shook hands with Ariel Sharon there was wild applause and laughter among the spectators.

According to Israel Television, President Sadat — even before alighting from his plane — asked Amir if Ariel Sharon was at the airport.

Sharon, now agriculture minister, was the army commander who led the Israeli counter-attack across the Suez Canal in the Yom Kippur War.

"I wanted to catch you there," said Sadat.

"I'm glad to have you here," Sharon replied.

A similarly warm response was evoked when he shook hands with Moshe Dayan. A warm embrace for Golda Meir brought further applause.

A person standing nearby reported that President Sadat told Dayan, "Don't worry, Moshe, it will be all right."

When President Sadat told Mrs. Meir he had been waiting a long time to see her, she replied, "Mr. President, I too have been waiting a long time to greet you."

To this, the President reportedly replied, "Well, here I am!"

(Continued on page 2, col. 2)

Begin says of Sadat:

'We understand each other'

By ANAN SAFADI
Post Mideast Affairs Editor

"I think we liked each other, honestly," Prime Minister Begin said as he emerged from a 30-minute meeting with President Sadat shortly after the Egyptian leader's arrival at the King David Hotel.

Begin described Sadat as "a charming man with a wonderful sense of humour.

"We understand each other very well and will understand each other better," he added.

Well-informed Egyptian sources said Sadat had come to discuss a "comprehensive settlement, including the exchange of diplomatic missions."

The cabinet will convene at nine o'clock this morning to hear a report from Premier Begin on his first round of talks with President Sadat.

Other participants in the meeting were Deputy Prime Minister Yigael Yadin, Foreign Minister Moshe Dayan and aides to President Sadat.

In answer to a question from the diplomatic editor of "Al-Ahram," Hamdi Fuad, the Prime Minister said he was looking forward to this afternoon's official talks with the Egyptian President. When Fuad asked him whether Israel was prepared to withdraw from territories the Arabs lost in the 1967 war, Begin said "Wait, wait. We're going to conduct talks with your President."

A close associate of President Sadat said that the Egyptian leader was far from being concerned with the Arab campaign against his visit here. The associate said that much of the violent reaction reported from Arab capitals is artificial. He said that reports received by the President indicate that the name of the game in the Arab capitals, especially those directly involved with the Middle East conflict, is "wait and see."

Prime Minister Begin said he told Sadat that he assumed the President had noticed how much he is appreciated by the Israelis. Begin stressed that the reaction to the distinguished guest was totally spontaneous.

In addition to members of the official Egyptian entourage (see page 1 of the Sadat visit special edition), the President was accompanied by a number of Egypt's foremost journalists.

NEWS ANALYSIS/David Landau

The unanswered question

President Sadat and Prime Minister Begin conferred last night at the Egyptian leader's suite in the King David Hotel — the first round of the political talks that will seal the success or failure of Sadat's visit here.

The key question, which last night still remained unanswered, is whether each of the two leaders is prepared to make the concessions that can open the path to negotiations and, ultimately, to peace.

Both men pledged over the weekend to present to the other detailed and specific peace proposals. Sadat said this was his intention in an interview aboard his plane to Israel with CBS correspondent Walter Cronkite. And Begin told his cabinet Friday that he, too, would be presenting an Israeli peace plan to his guest. (See Sadat visit special edition, page 1.)

But beyond the declared intention to talk substance, there was no clear commitment from either leader to shift from the positions that have barred the way to peace until now.

Premier Begin deliberately dodged a television newsman's questions on the cardinal issues of substance as he awaited Sadat's arrival at the airport last night.

The premier even declined to define what he would consider the success of the visit, saying only: "Give us a chance...When the visit ends in success, we shall all rejoice."

There seemed to be a distinct consciousness, however, within the Jerusalem political community — government as well as opposition — that this is the moment to produce whatever hitherto-unexpressed flex-

(Continued on page 2, col. 6)

Officials deny reports of separate peace

Foreign Ministry sources last night denied an Israel Radio report that President Sadat's visit would produce a non-belligerency agreement between Egypt and Israel.

The radio report said a separate peace with Egypt was possible within two or three months.

The officials dismissed as "speculation" all reports that any concrete accords would emerge from the current visit.

Violent protest erupts throughout Arab world

Jerusalem Post Staff and Agencies

A wave of violent protest surged through the Arab world and foreign cities over the weekend, at President Anwar Sadat's abandonment of its generation-long solidarity in anathemizing Israel.

As Arabs demonstrated angrily in several foreign capitals around the world, some Arab capitals issued official statements denouncing the Egyptian leader. According to Libyan envoys, Libya will sever diplomatic ties and dissolve an almost-forgotten federation with Egypt and Syria founded six years ago. (See earlier story, page 1 of the Sadat visit special edition.)

In Athens, an Arab student injured in the attack on the Egyptian Embassy Friday night, died yesterday.

Other demonstrations were reported from New Delhi, Madrid, London, Paris, Tunis, Dacca, Bucharest and Stockholm.

In Damascus, all work and traffic halted for five minutes yesterday to climax an official "day of mourning" for President Sadat's decision to visit Israel.

Demonstrations were also reported in Baghdad and in Libya, where a huge crowd set fire to the Egyptian Embassy after a march through Tripoli.

Workers in Syrian factories, government offices, ports and airports all took part in the stoppage, while the chanting of muezzins and tolling of church bells marked what Radio Damascus called "a black day in the history of the Arab nation."

Syrian President Hafez Assad and President Sadat publicly disagreed over the visit after two days of talks in Damascus last week. Since then the official Syrian press published increasingly bitter denunciations of Sadat's decision; and the National Front, which groups Syria's political organizations, called on the Arab

(Continued on page 2, col. 3)

Today's itinerary

President Sadat and his party are expected to leave the King David Hotel at 6.30 this morning, accompanied by Jerusalem Mayor Teddy Kollek, for prayers at al-Aksa Mosque. He will also visit the Dome of the Rock and the Church of the Holy Sepulchre.

At 11 o'clock, accompanied by Prime Minister Menahem Begin, Sadat will leave the King David for a visit to Yad Vashem. The two leaders will then return to the hotel for talks.

President Sadat will address a special session of the Knesset at four o'clock.

At 3.40 the Sadat party will leave the hotel and take the following route: King David, Keren Hayesod, Ramban, Ruppin. The government has called on the public to line the route and greet the guest.

Prime Minister Menahem Begin will give a working dinner for President Sadat at seven.

Carter: We pray with them

By WOLF BLITZER
Jerusalem Post Correspondent

WASHINGTON. — President Carter and the senior White House staff stayed at their television sets yesterday watching President Sadat arrive at Ben-Gurion airport. And so did the overwhelming majority of other Americans, as the three network television companies broadcast the arrival ceremony live via satellite.

In a statement issued by the White House, President Carter said "the hopes and prayers of all Americans" are with Begin and Sadat as they meet in Israel. He said, "The arrival of President Sadat in Israel is an historic occasion."

At the White House, aides nervously contemplated the outcome of the Sadat-Begin talks. No one here was willing to offer any speculation as to the outcome of this visit, which has aroused tremendous media and public interest in the U.S.

One White House secretary, clearly moved by the sight of Sadat shaking hands with leading Israeli personalities and the playing of the Israeli and Egyptian national anthems, broke down in tears.

Carter has sent messages to Jordan, Syria, Saudi Arabia and other Arab States urging them to support the Egyptian leader, whose popularity among the American public — especially within the Jewish community here — has skyrocketed. The Sadat visit is being compared with the landing of men on the moon a few years ago.

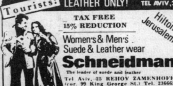

THE JERUSALEM POST

SECOND EDITION

IL4.00 (inc. Vat)

MONDAY, MARCH 13, 1978 • ADAR II 4, 5738 • RABI THANI 4, 1398 • VOL. XLVIII, No. 14267

THE BIGGEST dragnet in Israel's history was called off last night — and the first-ever curfew in a non-border area was lifted — when it was verified that none of the PLO terrorists who landed off the coast near Caesarea on Saturday afternoon and shed blood all along the coastal road until stopped just north of Tel Aviv, was at large. Nine terrorists were killed and two captured.

Their carnage was listed as 37 killed and 76 wounded. All of the dead were civilians.

The Prime Minister, who has postponed for at least a week his U.S. visit, due to start today, announced that the army and the police will be conducting inquiries into their handling of the terrorist landing and operation.

He is to make a statement to the Knesset today.

Reports from Lebanon voiced fear of Israel action in terrorist-held areas there.

Manhunt called off, terror toll now 37 dead, 76 wounded

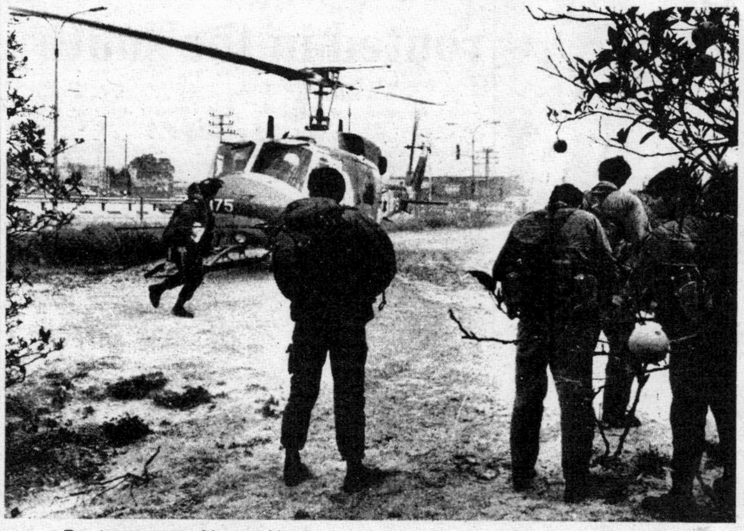

Paratroops engaged in searching for terrorists in orchards near Ramat Hasharon after alighting from a helicopter. (Lester Millman)

All terrorists accounted for

By HIRSH GOODMAN
POST Military Correspondent

The biggest manhunt in the history of the state was called off shortly before 9 p.m. last night after security authorities established beyond all doubt that all of the 11 terrorists who had landed at Ma'agan Michael on Saturday were either dead or in custody.

Simultaneously, the authorities lifted the curfew — the second in Israel's history — on the heavily populated region between the Yarkon River and Nahal Alexander. (The only other curfew in the history of the state was declared shortly after independence, when identification documents were issued.)

Last night it was believed that the final casualty toll was 37 killed and 76 wounded — several of them in critical condition.

Throughout the day thousands of police, soldiers, Border Police and Civil Guard volunteers combed hundreds of square kilometres of the area surrounding Saturday night's bus explosion just north of the Tel Aviv Country Club — an explosion which culminated an afternoon of indiscriminate terror which took the heaviest civilian death toll since statehood.

It has now become apparent that 11 terrorists, including one woman, landed at Ma'agan Michael in two Zodiac rubber commando boats on Saturday afternoon. They were let off near Israel's coast from a supply ship of undisclosed nationality in the early afternoon.

They were laden with Soviet missiles, rockets, machineguns and hand grenades.

Two of the gang are being held by the security authorities.

Until last night it was feared that three members of the terror squad were still at large, but this fear was allayed by the evidence given by the two captured terrorists which established beyond doubt that the three unaccounted-for members of the squad had died when the bus exploded. The bodies of six other terrorists were identified last night — four of them killed in a shootout with Border Police minutes before the bus exploded, and two others found in the brush around the bus later.

The fear that the three terrorists were still at large led to a government decision to declare a curfew in the area between the Yarkon River in the south, Nahal Alexander River in the North and the old Haifa road in the east. Over 300,000 Israelis — 10 per cent of the population — were affected by the curfew, coming out of their houses for only three short hours in the afternoon yesterday. Many businesses and shops in the Tel Aviv region remained closed all day because their owners live in the areas under curfew. The absence of thousands of workers from the administered territories, who were not allowed into the Tel Aviv area yesterday, caused stoppages in agriculture and construction as well as other businesses.

The Jordan bridges will reopen at 8 a.m. today.

Yesterday the army spokesman's office made public a copy of a letter found on the body of one of the terrorists — a letter which demand-

(Continued on page 2, col. 4)

Begin orders top-level probe after bus attack

By ASHER WALLFISH
Jerusalem Post Reporter

Premier Menahem Begin yesterday ordered the army and the police each to set up top-level inquiry teams, to probe in detail the sequence of events in the Saturday terror attack and the moves made by the army, the Border Police and the police in response to the actions of the terror gang.

Begin told the chief of staff, Rav-Aluf Mordechai Gur, and Police Inspector-General Haim Tavori to have a full report ready with all possible speed for his perusal.

The cabinet will meet this morning for a special session to be updated on developments connected with the terror attack, but the final reports of the two inquiry teams are not expected by this morning.

A number of Knesset members said yesterday in a closed forum that the reports made public so far on the terror raid left such an impression of confusion and poor coordination that a thorough probe was called for. However, they did not go so far as to suggest a formal commission of inquiry.

Reserves general to head army inquiry

By HIRSH GOODMAN
POST Military Correspondent

The army has established an internal inquiry commission to look into the implications of the attack. The inquiry is headed by a reserve general.

One of the major questions which are going to be asked at the inquiry is: How did the terrorists manage to infiltrate Israel's coastal defences? Millions have been spent on these defences, which were thought to have been improved to the point of invincibility after the "Marina incident" in 1976, in which several armed terrorists managed to land on Tel Aviv's main beach but decided to give themselves up, instead of carrying out their orders to attack a major hotel.

In March 1975 11 Israelis were killed and 11 others injured when eight terrorists who had infiltrated from the sea took over the Savoy Hotel in Tel Aviv.

Israel's naval defences are based on an interlocking radar system which allows shore patrols to spot not only vessels at sea, but also ob-

(Continued on page 4, col. 1)

Weizman holds Lebanon responsible for attack

Defence Minister Ezer Weizman yesterday held Lebanon responsible for Saturday's terrorist attack.

Speaking to newsmen at Ben-Gurion Airport on his return from the U.S., Weizman said: "I hold responsible for the operation any state which harbours the bases from which the terrorists set out." (The terrorists, who landed near Kibbutz Ma'agan Michael on the Mediterranean coast in two rubber dinghies, are believed to have set out on their raid from Lebanon.)

The defence minister, who was briefed on the situation by the chief of staff, Rav-Aluf Mordechai Gur, on the tarmac outside the terminal, went on to note that the outrage "illustrated once again the danger of uncontrolled Arab areas close to Israel's major population centres. We have warned of this for years now, long before this latest tragedy which proves the point once again."

In reply to a reporter's question, Weizman said he hoped the outrage would not affect the peace talks with Egypt — but noted that it would inevitably have some impact on the atmosphere surrounding those talks.

The defence minister said that although he had cut his visit to the U.S. short at the request of Prime Minister Menahem Begin, he fully agreed with the Prime Minister that he should be back in the country. At the same time, he said he hoped Begin's own visit to Washington would still take place, as several issues he had discussed concerning Israel's security requirements remained to be concluded.

Concerning his talks in the U.S., Weizman admitted that several differences existed between the two countries — "some more fundamental than others." He noted, however, that there was no reason why some of these differences should not be resolved. (Itim)

Don't retaliate, Young advises

By WOLF BLITZER
Jerusalem Post Correspondent

WASHINGTON. — U.S. Ambassador at the UN Andrew Young yesterday urged Israel not to retaliate militarily against the PLO's terrorist attack on Saturday.

While strongly deploring the PLO action, the UN ambassador said: "I would ask anybody to consider the consequences of violence, even retaliatory violence, however acceptable that may be in a situation, and not just have a knee-jerk reaction that when I'm struck, I want to strike back."

Asked whether Israel should now "turn the other cheek," Young replied that he would use that language if he were in Sunday Bible school. But he noted that since Israel and its citizens were facing "a life-and-death situation...I think they have got to make those decisions for themselves."

Young, who was interviewed on NBC's "Meet the Press," expressed the hope that Prime Minister Begin would visit Washington shortly so that peace negotiations could proceed. Israeli officials in Washington have begun contacts with the White House to reschedule Begin's visit. The Prime Minister was originally due here today but that trip has been put off by at least a week.

Efforts were being made here yesterday to schedule Begin's talks with President Carter sometime next week.

Earlier, in an ABC interview taped on Saturday evening, shortly before he returned to Israel, Defence Minister Ezer Weizman said that he hoped the terrorist action would not interfere in the peace negotiations. Asked specifically whether Israel will "will have to take action," but he refused to use the word "retaliate." The interview with Barbara Walters was televised yesterday on "Issues and Answers."

"This is not a light matter," he continued. "We know where it came from. We also know who is responsible. We have to make sure it does not happen again."

The terrorist attack has dominated the news in the U.S. It has dramatically brought Israel's security problems to the attention of the American public.

American officials recognize that the incident may make the negotiations more difficult, but they hope that the "cycle of violence" in the Middle East will not escalate.

Booby-trap suspects held in Jerusalem

Three young men suspected of planning to booby-trap a car in the centre of Jerusalem were yesterday ordered detained for 15 days by a Magistrate's Court judge.

A police spokesman said that the three suspects, Salman al-Farouk, Bassam Safdi and Khalil Hamdi, were arrested three weeks ago in their East Jerusalem home while they were preparing explosive devices with which to booby-trap the car.

The three are suspected of belonging to a hostile organization operating from Amman, of maintaining contact with its members and of receiving training in the preparation of improvised explosive devices. They admitted carrying out the offences attributed to them and the court ordered their detention. (Itim)

Eleven of the victims named

Jerusalem Post Staff and Itim

Saturday's terrorist rampage on the Tel Aviv-Haifa highway resulted in a reported death toll of 37, and 76 wounded.

Names of the dead that have been released for publication so far are: Amnon Drori (36 years old, of Kiryat Motzkin), Na'ama Hadani (5, of Haifa), Yosef Shoshinsky (58, of Ashdod) and his wife Katya Shoshinsky, Imri Tel-Oren (14, of Ramat Motza), Samal-Rishon Ya'acov Paz (23, of Bnei Brak), Yoav Mishkal (6, of Haifa), Yosef Elkana, a policeman, Ya'acov Segev (Kfar Sava), and Rina and Dov Boshkenitz (Haifa).

Yosef and Katya Shoshinsky will be buried this afternoon, the funeral leaving Tel Hashomer at 2:15 for the Ashdod cemetery. Other funerals taking place today are those of Amnon Drori, leaving Kiryat Motzkin at 1:30 for the Kfar Samir cemetery; Rina and Dov Boshkenitz, who will also be laid to rest in the Kfar Samir cemetery.

The army spokesman said yesterday that a final list of casualties would be released only when the difficult process of identification had been completed. At least five of the dead were terrorists; some of the unidentified bodies may have been terrorists as well.

Immediately after the end of the Sabbath, members of the IDF chaplaincy rushed to the scene of the carnage to collect the bodies and proceed with identifying them. Sometimes all the soldiers had to work with were charred remains. Identification of the children who died was especially difficult since

(Continued on page 4, col. 1)

Public takes curfew in stride

By HIRSH GOODMAN
and SARAH HONIG
Jerusalem Post Reporters

TEL AVIV. — The first curfew on any non-border area of Israel since the days of the British Mandate was imposed early yesterday to facilitate the hunt for any possible escaped terrorists. Some 300,000 people, including residents of Tel Aviv's north-of-the-Yarkon neighbourhoods and of Herzliya, Netanya, Petah Tikva and Ramat Hasharon, remained homebound but unpanicked for most of the day.

The curfew covered a nearly 200sq.km. area stretching from the north bank of the Yarkon northward to Nahal Alexander beyond Netanya and from the Mediterranean to the old Haifa-Tel Aviv road.

Police and security forces, aided by thousands of Civil Guard volunteers, manned roadblocks at every corner, making sure that people stayed put and did not interfere with one of the biggest manhunts in Israel's history. Dogs, helicopters, trained trackers and soldiers, policemen and Border Police units combed brush and beaches, orchards and abandoned buildings for the three or four terrorists who it was thought had managed to get away.

Schools in Ramat Hasharon, Herzliya, Hadar Yosef and other suburbs affected by the curfew were empty, playgrounds being used as makeshift headquarters where Civil Guard volunteers rested and dispensed coffee.

South of the curfew area, Tel Aviv itself was rainy and bleak yesterday — with many businesses closed, their owners being among the 300,000 unable to leave their homes. Passersby carried small transistor radios with them. Newspapers were quickly snapped up and people gathered around television sets in electrical-goods stores to watch the Prime Minister's press conference.

The failure of Arab workers from the administered areas to get to work was also felt.

Teachers were missing in schools in all parts of town. The schools were more heavily guarded than usual yesterday, even though they were outside of the curfew area.

The curfew was lifted for three

(Continued on page 4, col. 1)

S. Lebanese express sorrow at attack

Jerusalem Post Reporter

METULLA. — Residents of the southern Lebanese enclaves who visited the "Good Fence" here yesterday reacted with shock to news of the terrorist attack on Saturday afternoon, and many of them expressed deep sorrow and asked that their condolences be conveyed to the bereaved families.

The commander of the southern Lebanese forces, Major Sa'ad Hadad, said he had sent a letter of condolences to the Israel government. But many leaders said that the attack itself did not come as a surprise to them. They said they could not understand how Israel could tolerate a large terrorist presence close to its border — a presence which has lately been reinforced, they added.

Fatah braces for reprisal raid in South Lebanon

Jerusalem Post Staff

Palestinian terrorist leaders yesterday ordered their followers in southern Lebanon to take to their shelters in case of a massive Israeli retaliation for Saturday's terror rampage on the Haifa-Tel Aviv highway.

Foreign newsmen quoted a spokesman for Fatah, which took responsibility for the assault, as saying that all terrorist forces stationed in southern Lebanon had been put on the alert "in anticipation of a violent Israeli response."

Fatah was reported to have ordered civilians living close to terrorist bases to take refuge in shelters and other secure places until further notice. The order was said to have stirred panic, especially in the southern coastal town of Tyre and the neighbouring Burj el-Shamali and Rashidiya refugee camps.

Last November, more than 100 people were reported killed in an Israeli operation following a terrorist rocket attack on Nahariya, where three persons were killed.

The Fatah-controlled Palestine Liberation Organization (PLO) yesterday issued a statement making clear that one of the chief aims of Saturday's operation was to torpedo Egyptian President Anwar Sadat's peace initiative.

"It is a symbol for...the rejection of the capitulationist solution which some regimes are trying to enforce on our Arab nation and our Palestine people," the statement said.

Reports from Beirut yesterday claimed that Israel was moving reinforcements to the Lebanese border.

Premier Selim al-Hoss said last night that Lebanon had nothing to do with the Palestinian terrorist raid on Israel.

"It is very strange that Lebanon is mentioned in some statements attributed to Israeli leaders on Saturday's incident. Lebanon is not responsible for what happened and has nothing to do with it. Any attempt to involve Lebanon in the matter is pure calumny," he added.

It was reported from Metulla last night that tension is high in the southern Lebanese enclaves, and travellers arriving from the centre of the country said there is fear all over the south, especially in the port of Tyre, which is a terrorist base.

In the last few days there have been fewer exchanges of fire between the south Lebanese and the terrorists, but southern Lebanese spokesmen said that the terrorists are continuing to fortify on all fronts close to the Israeli border and also deeper inside the country.

Left up in French poll, but Gov't may survive

By JACK MAURICE
Jerusalem Post Correspondent

PARIS. — France's left-wing parties outdistanced the government coalition yesterday by at least 4 per cent in the first round of the general elections, according to computer predictions.

The outcome of the poll will not be known until next Sunday, when a runoff ballot decides party strengths in a new 491-seat National Assembly.

But early returns from polling stations all over the country indicated that the left-wing parties had won 50.6 per cent of the ballots cast, against 45 to 46.5 per cent for the supporters of President Valery Giscard d'Estaing's governing "Majority."

While votes were still being counted all over France and in overseas constituencies, it was already clear that the Socialist Party, with their 25 per cent share of the poll, had succeeded the Gaullists as France's biggest political party. The Socialists have not occupied this role since before World War II.

The Communist Party collected only 21 per cent, but many of their candidates are better placed than socialists to win next Sunday's runoff ballot. This is likely to make it easier for the communists to agree — with minimum loss of face after months of bickering — to conclude an electoral pact with the socialists.

The voting results however indicate that the opposition's lead over the government has narrowed substantially — from 6 to 4 per cent — since the last opinion poll was published a week ago.

This makes the second round of voting much more open than had been predicted and enhances the government's chances of maintaining their 20-year control of France.

The outcome of next Sunday's poll will depend in large measure on how the votes of minor parties, such as the Ecologists, who collected 4 per cent of yesterday's poll, are redistributed. Yesterday's 83.7 per cent poll was a record for France's Fifth Republic.

World leaders condemn terror attack

Jerusalem Post Staff

"An outrageous act of lawlessness and senseless brutality," was how President Carter described Saturday's terror attack in a condolence message to Premier Begin. "Criminal acts such as this advance no cause or political belief," the president wrote. "They inspire only revulsion at the lack of respect for innocent human life."

Secretary of State Cyrus Vance, in a separate message, declared that "the perpetrators should receive the punishment they deserve."

Messages also came in from UN Secretary-General Kurt Waldheim, British Premier James Callaghan and Foreign Secretary David Owen, and from German Foreign Minister Hans-Dietrich Genscher.

Owen wrote: "After my recent visit and with the memory of Israel so vivid in my mind, I was shattered to hear the news and saddened to think that this sort of thing can happen at a time when we are all working towards a peaceful settlement. These terrorists really have no wish to see peace; and their act will, I hope, be condemned by the whole world."

Austrian Foreign Minister Willibald Pahr was reported yesterday as saying at the end of a two-day visit to Kuwait that the terror attack was "linked to Israel's continued refusal to give the Palestinian people the right of self-determination," but added that terrorism would not solve the Middle East problem.

The French Foreign Ministry yesterday condemned the Palestinian terror raid and said it threatened to harm efforts to achieve a Middle East peace.

The ministry issued a communique which said: "The French government condemns blind acts of terrorism of this type which has caused many innocent victims. Such acts are bound to delay and handicap attempts to reach a peaceful settlement. On this sad occasion the French government expresses its sympathy to the bereaved relatives and to the people of Israel."

In a clear reference to Saturday's attack, Pope Paul VI yesterday told a crowd of 10,000 in Vatican City's St. Peter's Square that he could not remain insensible to "bitter and disappointing events" affecting public life.

In a message to *The Jerusalem Post*, the two Ulsterwomen who were recently awarded the Nobel Peace Prize for their reconciliation efforts in that province wrote: "We grieve with your people in their loss. We ask you to have the courage not to retaliate. The first people to break the cycle of terrorism and counter-terrorism will be the real peacemakers of the Middle East."

Arab governments justify massacre of Israel civilians

Jerusalem Post Staff

Saturday's terrorist rampage on the coastal road yesterday captured the headlines in almost all Arab capitals — many of which took pains to justify it.

Cairo, which only recently referred to a sabotage attack on Egyptians in Larnaca as a "terrorist assault," called the Country Club attack a "commando raid." So did all Arab capitals except for Amman, which termed it in news bulletins "the Tel Aviv incident."

Egyptian Minister of State for Foreign Affairs Butros Ghali yesterday claimed that Saturday's terrorist operation "underlined the importance" of giving the Palestinians the right of self-determination.

In a statement which contained no condemnation of the rampage, Ghali said that the latest terrorist violence "shows clearly the need to establish a homeland for the Palestinians."

Ghali expressed hope that Israel would not retaliate for the raid in a manner which could impede the current Middle East peace-seeking process begun by President Anwar Sadat.

"I hope that Israel will calculate its future steps before taking any action that may obstruct the peace efforts," Ghali said, adding that the new outburst of terrorist militancy demonstrated, above all, the need for achieving peace.

Saudi Arabia's state radio in Riyadh hailed the terrorist raid as a "courageous operation" which demonstrated the frailty of Israel's security. The radio said that Israel's "claim to security is impossible as long as the Palestinians are without a homeland." It said that Israel should realize that security cannot be attained by annexing territories and by denying the Palestinians the right to self-determination, but only through a peace settlement acceptable to all Arabs.

Jordan issued no official statement. Its state radio confined its reports on the rampage to dispatches from Israel.

Syria, too, failed to comment on the terrorist attack officially. The organ of the ruling Ba'ath Party, however, described the raid as "a daring one."

The chief spokesman of the Kuwaiti government, Abdul-Aziz Hussein, said yesterday that it was "natural that the Palestinian revolution should carry out actions to prove its presence and effectiveness." He said that Kuwait stood "by the revolution in its operations to realize the rights of the Palestinian people."

Libya's state radio said the raid "destroyed the myth of Zionist security and their military superiority."

Phone token doubles in price, to IL1

Jerusalem Post Reporter

The price of an *asimon* (telephone token) goes up by 100 per cent this morning — from 50 agorot to IL1. The increase was approved yesterday by the Knesset Finance Committee.

But the committee refused to approve other rate increases recommended by the Communications Ministry — such as for phone installations and for home phone calls.

The Communications Ministry wants to raise phone charges by an average 17 per cent, and postal fees by 40 per cent.

A committee source says these matters are to be discussed in a forthcoming price-freeze discussion between Finance Minister Simha Ehrlich and Histadrut Secretary-General Yeroham Meshel. Therefore, the committee will delay its action until it hears from Ehrlich.

Today, the committee will take up a request by the Transport Ministry for a hike in motor vehicle licensing fees.

Soviet Jews demonstrate against raid

MOSCOW (AP). — A group of Soviet Jews staged a demonstration yesterday in downtown Moscow to protest against Saturday's Arab terrorist attack.

The demonstrators also denounced the Soviet Union's support of the PLO headed by Yasser Arafat, who left Moscow three days ago following talks with Soviet President Leonid Brezhnev and other top Soviet officials.

After gathering across a main thoroughfare from the Soviet Union's "House of Friendship," the 27 protesters unrolled paper placards and chanted slogans including: "Shame to the murderers of children," and "Shame to those who protect murderers."

Initially, no uniformed Soviet police were on hand for the demonstration, which was called at short notice and apparently caught authorities off guard.

Later, however, persons in civilian clothes quickly rushed up and began ripping away the placards from the demonstrators, who were joined by Nobel Peace Prize laureate Andrei Sakharov and his wife.

Within a few minutes, about half a dozen uniformed policemen arrived and ordered the protesters to disperse. The police then set fire to the scraps of placards strewing the sidewalk. There were no arrests.

Sakharov's wife, Yelena Bonner, later told western correspondents that she believed the non-uniformed persons who ripped away the placards and shouted down the protesters were outraged ordinary Soviet citizens, rather than plainclothes security agents.

The handling of the demonstration contrasted with the authorities' more concerted efforts to foil and break up a protest staged last Wednesday by Soviet Jewish women seeking to leave the country.

More than 50 plainclothes security agents, plus uniformed police, were on hand there before any of the demonstrators even arrived at the protest site, on the steps of the Lenin Library.

Six of the women were seized on the spot, four others who had planned to take part were detained by police at their homes and driven away, and an additional 23 were not allowed to leave their apartments.

In connection with yesterday's demonstration, Sakharov, who is not Jewish, issued a statement on the terrorist attack, saying: "Our hearts are full of pain and sympathy for the victims of the crime and their families.

"The crime was committed two days after Yasser Arafat was received by the leadership of the USSR, in a situation when at last a possibility had appeared for settling the old opposition between Israel and the Arab countries."

FOR A STRONG ECONOMY
ISRAEL BONDS

THE JERUSALEM POST

Second Edition

IL4.00 (inc. Vat)

THURSDAY, MARCH 16, 1978 • ADAR II 7, 5738 • RABI THANI 7, 1398 • VOL. XLVIII, No. 14270

ISRAEL FORCES were digging in last night after seizing the entire southern Lebanese border area to a depth of 10 kilometres.

The military operation, designed to wipe out terrorist bases, began late Tuesday night. By 5 o'clock yesterday afternoon fighting was virtually over. Resistance to the land incursion was said to have been sporadic.

Prime Minister Begin said the Israel forces would remain in the area until an agreement is reached preventing the return of the terrorists to southern Lebanon.

The land attack in southern Lebanon was accompanied by raids on terrorist camps further north by the Israel Air Force and naval vessels.

The ground force stayed well south of the Litani River and Israeli spokesmen stressed that there was no intention of striking at Syrian troops, who are stationed north of the river.

IDF holding southern Lebanon

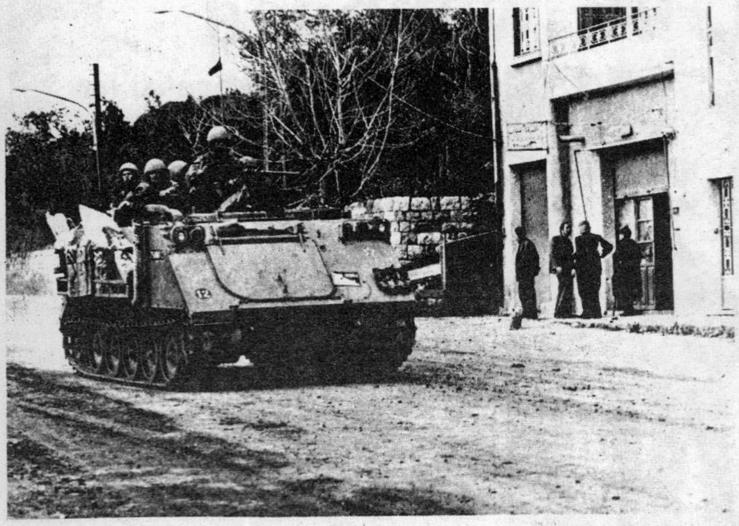

Israeli soldiers on an armoured personnel carrier drive through the street of a Lebanese village. (IDF photo)

Army digs in along 100-km. front

By HIRSH GOODMAN
Post Military Correspondent

WITH ISRAELI FORCES IN LEBANON. — The IDF dug in last night along a 100km. front 10 kms. inside Lebanon, after the largest military action ever staged against terrorist forces.

Israeli casualties were not announced but they are reported to be relatively light. One hundred terrorists were killed in close-in fighting and many more were killed by bombing, artillery and shelling from the sea. An undisclosed number of terrorist prisoners were brought into Israel.

Although all major targets were captured yesterday, ground action is expected to continue another day or two as Israeli troops straighten their lines and clean up pockets of terrorists not dealt with yesterday.

Terrorist reinforcements were also seen crossing the Litani river yesterday into southern Lebanon, and there is a possibility of contact with them.

Two thousand terrorists are normally located in the area struck yesterday, but most fled before the arrival of the Israeli troops. In some strongholds, however, there was stiff resistance. Difficult terrain, minefields and booby traps added to the hazards.

In a combined operation, Israeli infantry moved across the border on Tuesday night in a four-pronged attack from the Hermon to the sea, with armoured support and air cover. Naval ships also struck at targets along the coast.

Christian forces in southern Lebanon joined the Israeli attack, marking the first time in Israel's history that foreign troops have fought alongside its forces. (In the 1956 Sinai Campaign, French and British forces attacked Egypt while Israel was driving across the Sinai, but there was no cooperation between them.) Israeli troops passing through Christian villages were cheered and pelted with sweets and flowers.

The Israeli troops stopped well short of the Litani river to signal clearly to the Syrians deployed north of the river that Jerusalem had no desire to draw them into the battle. This message was amplified repeatedly at press conferences in Jerusalem and Tel Aviv by Prime Minister Menahem Begin and Defence Minister Ezer Weizman.

The troops were under strict instructions to avoid civilian casualties. They also moved cautiously to minimize their own casualties.

At a briefing to senior officers before the attack, Aluf Rafael Eitan, Chief of Operations, quoted a line from poet Chaim Nahman Bialik — "Revenge for the killing of a small child has not yet been invented by Satan." This reference to Saturday's massacre on the coastal road, in which many children died, was repeated by officers as they briefed the infantrymen gathered in groves behind the border and the armoured personnel beside their tanks.

In operation headquarters, identical briefings were conducted in adjoining rooms — one for the Israeli commanders in Hebrew and one for the Christian commanders in Arabic.

Despite the widespread anticipation of the action, the attack force attempted to achieve local surprise by sending infantrymen across the border before midnight to take up attack and blocking positions. At 1.40 a.m., planes dropped flares and artillery opened a massive barrage. Thousands of shells were dropped on El-Khiam, Taibeh, Rashaya el-Foukar, Nakar, Ras el-Maroun, Bint Jbail, and Ras el-Bayada. Tanks moved across the border to support the infantrymen.

The Lebanese Christians participated with their own Sherman tanks, artillery and troops. They also guided Israeli forces.

The commander of the Christian forces, Major Sa'ad Hadad, said "I've been waiting for this night a long time."

There was relatively strong resistance at Taibeh and Bint Jbail, but some Israeli officers expressed disappointment that many of the terrorist strongholds had been abandoned.

A major objective of the action was to break the tightening terrorist stranglehold around the Christian enclaves in the central and northern sectors of southern Lebanon.

Israeli planes struck at the port of Damour where the terrorists who committed Saturday's atrocity trained and from where they departed on their mission.

They also struck at the port of Tyre, the principal supply entry for terrorists in southern Lebanon, and at the Al-Uzai terrorist maritime base.

Chief of Staff Mordechai Gur denied at a press conference last night that targets in Beirut had been hit. Al-Uzai, about seven kilometres south of Beirut, was the closest target to the Lebanese capital, he said.

Meanwhile, Israeli naval craft intercepted with gunfire terrorist convoys attempting to reinforce and supply positions in the south along the coastal road.

The only Syrian reaction during the day was some firing at Israeli planes which observers thought more symbolic than practical. The possible reaction of Syria's 30,000 troops in Lebanon had been a major factor considered by Israeli planners.

(Photos — page 8)

Beirut says PLO is routed in the south

Jerusalem Post Staff
and Agencies

Lebanese government spokesmen last night said that the Israel Army had in effect taken control of an estimated 10 km.-wide strip in southern Lebanon stretching from the Mediterranean to the slopes of Mt. Hermon.

In contrast to statements from the Palestine Liberation Organization, Beirut radio quoted government officials as conceding that the entire southern border region had fallen to the Israelis and that the PLO had been ejected from all bases there.

The terrorists earlier had said that they were combating the massive offensive unleashed by Israel at midnight on Tuesday. Although the terrorists had been expecting the assault ever since Saturday's massacre north of Tel Aviv, they appeared to have been surprised by the intensity of the ground, sea and air drive.

"It's really a big operation. They mean to finish us off," one terrorist spokesman was quoted by foreign newsmen.

PLO officials said they estimated the number of Israeli troops in the campaign as "at least 25,000," operating on four major fronts.

The PLO spokesmen and their news media were initially quiet as terrorists were being pressed back from key positions by the Israel assault. It was only some 12 hours after the drive began that these spokesmen and the PLO's WAFA news agency and radio began to issue statements from Beirut and Damascus.

Suddenly there was a flurry of communiques, speaking of terrorist forces blocking Israeli advances and inflicting heavy losses. The communiques were ironically coupled with cries to Arab heads of state to help salvage "the Palestinian revolution and the Palestinian people" from an Israeli "liquidation" campaign.

PLO war communiques were often contradicted, if not ridiculed, by Lebanese officials who put out their own statements about Israel's thrusts deep across border positions. The officials spoke of a three-pronged tank assault coupled with a landing of seaborne troops.

The Lebanese officials had signalled as early as mid-morning yesterday the fall of several terrorist-held villages, including Bint Jbail, Maroun el-Ras, Yaroun, Taibeh, El-Khiam and others.

The same officials reported Israeli aircraft had penetrated as far as Beirut, where several terrorist strongholds in the area were bombarded. These included the coastal town of Damour, which the terrorists took over from Christians at the height of Lebanon's civil war two years ago. They said targets in the Beirut area also included the refugee camps of Murj el-Barajneh, Shatila and Sabra, where PLO chief Yasser Arafat is said to be marshalling his men from an underground bunker.

The Lebanese authorities closed Beirut International Airport for two hours, as Israel's warplanes swooped in the region.

Other targets hit by Israeli raids included several terrorist strongholds near the southern coastal town of Tyre, whose district was the scene of a similar bombardment last November.

Reports from Beirut said that the terrorists had deployed the bulk of their estimated 20,000 men in the south, although most of these were understood either to have fled or to have been redeployed away from the battleground, north of the Litani river.

Terrorists in Beirut and South Lebanon have been fighting Christian militias since Syrian troops ended the civil war elsewhere in Lebanon in November 1976.

There were no signs of Syrian military involvement in yesterday's fighting, except for one incident when Syrian troops fired on Israel's aircraft bombing Damour. The Syrian command in Damascus said yesterday it was providing its troops — referred to as an inter-Arab peacekeeping deterrent force — with anti-aircraft batteries.

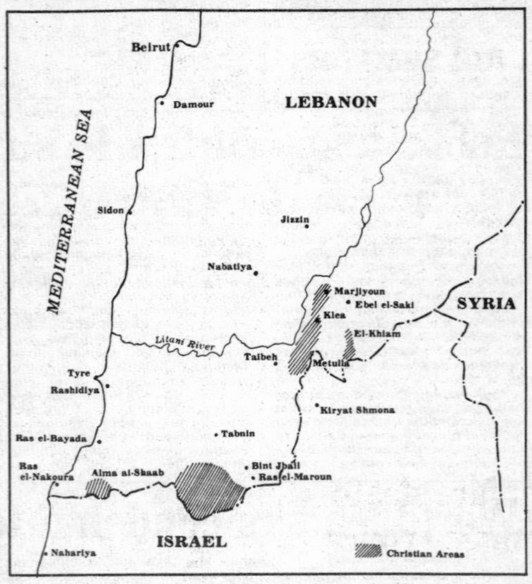

Begin wants accord on barring terrorists

By DAVID LANDAU
Post Diplomatic Correspondent

Israeli forces will remain in southern Lebanon until an agreement is reached ensuring that the area no longer serves as a base for terrorist attacks, Premier Menahem Begin said last night.

Begin said that "all relevant factors" (but not the PLO) would be "consulted" on this hoped-for agreement.

He indicated that Syria was among the "relevant factors," but was reluctant to elaborate, saying that diplomatic efforts to achieve the agreement had not yet begun.

Begin spoke at a press conference after a special cabinet meeting last night which had reviewed the day's fighting.

He announced that the military action had been effectively completed by sundown last night. It had been a day on which "Israelis, Jews the world over, and all men of goodwill, should say 'All honour to the Israel Defence Forces.'"

Chief of Staff Mordechai Gur said the terrorists had suffered some 100 dead in direct combat, and Defence Minister Ezer Weizman added that he assumed more had been killed in aerial and artillery bombardments.

Gur said there were usually some 2,000 terrorists in the area in question. Observers concluded from his report that most or many of the others had fled.

The IDF now controlled an area 10 kilometres in depth, across a 100-km. front, Gur said. He denied Lebanese reports that Israel was holding bridges on the Litani river, and added that some PLO reinforcements had apparently come south during the afternoon across those bridges.

Premier Begin said that the army had not been sent into Lebanon "to remain there permanently. We want peace with Lebanon and have no desire to rule any of its territory. But we will not acquiesce in a situation in which murderers come across from Lebanon to raid Israel... We expect an agreement or arrangement as a result of which the murderers do not return to all the places from which they have been ejected."

He expected the issue to be raised during his talks with President Carter next week. To date, he said, there had been no appeal from the U.S. that Israel end its incursion. The only message he had received from Carter and Secretary of State Vance were of condolences after Saturday's atrocity. (But see Wolf Blitzer's report.)

In his own letter to President Carter of Tuesday night, Begin said, he had explained that Israel was acting in southern Lebanon in the exercise of her "inherent right of self-defence."

The military action was not a "retribution or retaliation for the Saturday bloodshed — there can be no retaliation for the killing of innocent women and children," Begin said. It was an act of self-defence designed to thwart vaunted PLO threats to repeat such attacks as that of Saturday.

Lashing out at Russia's "sheer and shameful hypocrisy" in condemning the Israeli action, Begin exhibited a certificate, in Russian and Arabic, which had been awarded to a member of Ahmed Jibril's terror squad (an extremist PLO affiliate) upon completion of an officer training course inside Russia.

By Russia's own definition, moreover, in a draft international convention that Moscow had proposed, Lebanon qualified as an "aggressor" because it had harboured terrorists and failed to restrain them or deny them protection.

Jerusalem expects U.S. to promote agreement

By DAVID LANDAU
Post Diplomatic Correspondent

Israel is hoping that its seizure of southern Lebanon will spur Syria, Lebanon, Egypt and other Arabs to agree to impose new and stringent limitations on the PLO's freedom of movement in Lebanon. This, according to authoritative sources, is what Prime Minister Begin meant when he said last night that Israel would hold out for an "agreement or arrangement" involving "all relevant factors," before it pulled out of the area. Begin spoke at a press conference in Jerusalem (see above).

Other high sources said that Israel might be prepared for an agreement just between itself and the Lebanese government — provided that Syria gave its tacit consent too, giving the agreement significant added substance.

The sources all said they anticipated energetic American efforts in mediating such an agreement, with Israel keeping its own profile low. They did not expect that the "agreement" would necessarily be a formal document with signatures appended, but rather an understanding between governments.

All the Arab parties were obviously keenly interested in Israel's prompt withdrawal from the 1,000-odd sq. km. of Lebanese territory that it now holds, and hence, the sources said, there were good chances that the agreement Israel sought could be reached quickly.

Specifically, Israel will demand that the agreement provide that no PLO men be permitted to cross the Litani river southwards so as to pose a threat to the border areas.

The high sources denied an American report that President Carter has asked Begin to postpone his visit to Washington, scheduled for next week, until there is no significant Israeli presence remaining in south Lebanon.

The sources, who are close to the Premier, said they knew of no such message from Carter.

Other diplomatic sources said earlier in the day they had no reason to doubt that the visit would go ahead as planned.

After Israel's withdrawal, Jerusalem will expect the border area to be effectively policed against the PLO either by regular Lebanese Army units, or else by the Christian militiamen, whom Israel is apparently prepared to further aid and strengthen for this purpose.

(In this connection, observers noted Defence Minister Weizman's remark last night that "the Christians in the south have brothers in the north." Apparently Israel is expecting the Lebanese Christian establishment to assert itself and extend the government's authority throughout the country.)

Commenting on yesterday's action, a high source said Israel fully expected many of the terrorists to flee before the IDF could reach them. After all, the tense expectation of an Israeli incursion had been mounting in the area ever since Saturday's terror attack on the Haifa road.

The principal aim of the action, the source indicated, had thus not been to kill PLO men — though this had been an important subsidiary purpose — but to clear the border area of the terrorists — and hold onto it until effective measures were adopted by the Arabs themselves to ensure it remained clear.

With the troops pushing into Lebanon

By HIRSH GOODMAN
POST Military Correspondent

METULLA. — The troops had been waiting for three days. They had been waiting in mud and bitter cold to revenge Saturday's massacre on the coastal road. The command to move filtered down to the ranks at dusk on Tuesday and they were keen to move.

I joined a force charged with taking the biggest terrorist stronghold in the northern sector — El-Khiam. The soldiers slipped stealthily across the border in the late evening.

The task was to attack the village from two directions with another force and wipe out the terrorists expected to be there. Before they had reached the outskirts of the village, passing through what used to be a picturesque, almost postcard-like, hamlet in the Hermon foothills, thousands of artillery shells started to fall on the target. With the big guns still blazing, the night was illuminated by wave after wave of IDF planes dropping phosphorescent markers and incendiary bombs. At this time, an armoured force left Israel to make its way up to the village and rendezvous with the infantry.

It took us over seven hours to pick our way through three kilometres of minefields to the rendezvous. It was at 7.15 a.m. when the vehicle I was riding in hit a mine. (It was while I was listening to the radio news announcer explaining how smoothly the operation was going on.)

I picked myself up and moved to another vehicle. The rest of the journey to El-Khiam was terrifying. We could have hit another mine every second.

One of the things that struck me was the calm professionalism of the 18- and 19-year olds I was with. It was amazing how mature they were in a situation which tests one to the limits. After we had hit the mine, they calmly made sure there were no casualties, that nothing was burning, and that all their equipment was moved to other vehicles so that nothing would be left behind to aid the enemy.

Only after reaching El-Khiam and seeing it in ruins — this village having been the target of many Christian Lebanese shells in the past — did the dimensions of the South Lebanese war become apparent. Not a house, a streetlamp, a church or a mosque has remained unscathed. Destruction was apparent everywhere. A schoolroom desk, looking like a pile of firewood, stands deserted. Three mangy dogs sit in the sun trying to console a 90-year-old woman, unsure who has attacked her this time.

Israeli troops expected to find about 60 civilians in the town. They found fewer, but all those who had remained survived. It seemed almost unbelievable to me that despite the tons of explosives that had rained upon them, there had been no civilian casualties. It seemed as if the population — many of whom are elderly — has become indestructible.

The Israeli objective, however, was not El-Khiam, but a terrorist fortress on its outskirts. These fortifications had been bombarded, with the pillboxes and other defences razed to the ground. Unofficial estimates say 20 terrorists died there.

As we left El-Khiam in the early afternoon, we passed a column of Christian Lebanese forces moving in. They were jubilant. For them, El-Khiam had been a nightmare, with its terrorist-aimed guns making life in their centres of Marjayoun and Klea nearly impossible.

Cautious U.S. response to Israeli operation

By WOLF BLITZER
Jerusalem Post Correspondent

WASHINGTON. — The U.S. yesterday responded cautiously to the Israeli assault on terrorist bases in Lebanon, refusing to express in public either approval or disapproval. Privately, however, there were indications of tacit approval.

Officials here were taking a wait-and-see attitude as they sought to learn of the situation on the ground.

"We have not called for a halt" to the Israeli action, Secretary of State Cyrus Vance told reporters following a morning meeting with President Jimmy Carter and other senior U.S. officials.

Vance added that both the Israeli action and the terrorist attack on two Israeli buses over the weekend were "impediments" to the peace process. He said the U.S. did not know of the Israeli mission until it was actually under way.

The refusal by the U.S. government to complain publicly of the Israeli action was also accompanied by other indications of tacit U.S. approval.

At the State Department, spokesman Hodding Carter III told reporters that "it has been clear for some time that the presence of Palestinian military units in southern Lebanon posed a threat to Israeli security." He said these units have "not only declared open hostility toward Israel but have also launched terrorist attacks on that country, the most recent being the brutal act last Saturday."

The spokesman welcomed Defence Minister Ezer Weizman's statement that Israel's objective was neither to hold on to southern Lebanon nor to remain there. He said the U.S. hope is that the Lebanese central government will be able to extend its authority throughout the country — a reference to the fact that Palestinian terrorists, until now, have controlled large portions of southern Lebanon.

The U.S., he continued, would not initiate any action at the UN at this time to try to stop the fighting. But he refused to say what the U.S. position would be if other countries initiated a UN move. (Secretary Vance spoke by telephone with UN Secretary-General Kurt Waldheim on Tuesday evening, shortly after the IDF moved into Lebanon.)

Repeatedly, the spokesman stressed that the events of the past few days have underscored the need for a peaceful solution in the Middle East — "the only way to put an end

(continued on page 2, col. 6)

(Arabs condemn, p.2)

BULLETIN:

A top White House source told our Washington correspondent last night that the U.S. was "satisfied" with Mr. Begin's assurance that Israel has no intention of extending the IDF presence in Lebanon beyond the present depth of six to 10 kilometres.

Terror toll climbs to 33

Tuvia Rosner, who sustained critical injuries in his head during Saturday's terrorist attack on the coastal road, died on Tuesday night in Haifa's Rambam Hospital in Haifa, bringing the death toll to 33.

Rosner, an Egged employee, had been on the critical list since he was operated on in the Rambam Hospital on Saturday night. His funeral will leave the Rambam Hospital at 2.30 p.m. today for the Kfar Samir cemetery.

Two other victims of the terrorist attack to be buried at the Kfar Samir cemetery today are Yitzhak Alfandi and his son Erez. The funeral will leave the Rambam Hospital at 4.

Justice Minister Shmuel Tamir will eulogize Gail Rubin, the American photographer slain by the terrorists soon after they landed near Kibbutz Ma'agan Michael on Saturday, at Ben-Gurion airport this morning, before her coffin is placed on an El Al plane bound for New York.

(Funerals, p. 2)

Katyushas

KIRYAT SHMONA. — Two Katyusha shells fired from across the Lebanese border landed in Kiryat Shmona and Metulla at about noon yesterday. There were no casualties.

TO ALL OUR READERS

Owing to an increase in the price of printing materials, services and utilities, we are forced to increase the price of The Jerusalem Post Friday (weekend) edition to IL7.00. We are not however raising the price of the daily issue. Watch out in tomorrow's paper for a special subscription offer at the old price.

The Management

THE JERUSALEM POST

Kreisky protests
**
Page 2

IL5.30 (inc. Vat)

WEDNESDAY, SEPTEMBER 6, 1978 • ELUL 4, 5738 • SHAWWAL 4, 1398 • VOL. XLVIII, No. 14413

Begin and Sadat arrive at Camp David for M.E. summit

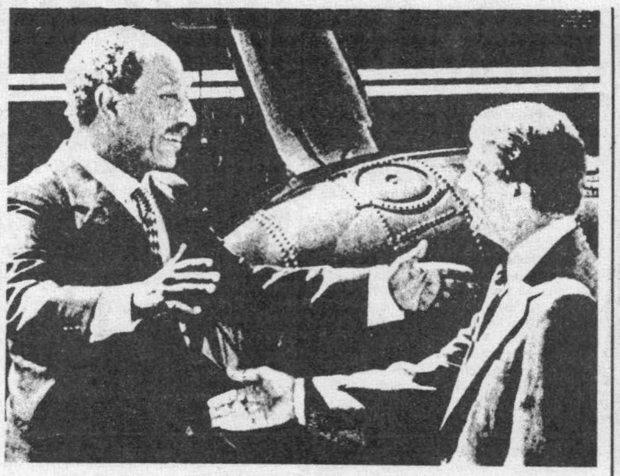

President Carter greets President Sadat on arrival at Camp David yesterday afternoon. (UPI telephoto)

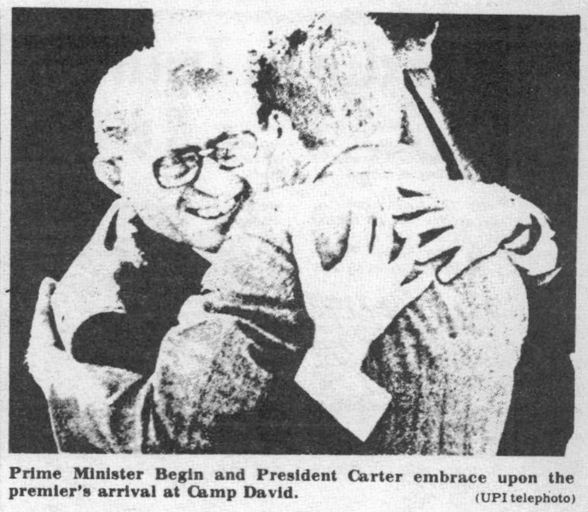

Prime Minister Begin and President Carter embrace upon the premier's arrival at Camp David. (UPI telephoto)

Two seriously injured in one of two bombings in Jerusalem

By DAVID RICHARDSON
Jerusalem Post Reporter

Two men, including a police bomb disposal expert, were seriously injured yesterday when one of two terrorist bombs exploded in Jerusalem. The sapper, Steve Hilmes, 31, was reported in critical condition last night.

Also seriously injured was Mordechai Baron, 48, of Jerusalem. No one was hurt in the second bombing explosion.

The explosions took place despite strict security procedures and a general security alert that has been ordered following fears of a stepped-up campaign by Palestinian terror organizations because of the Camp David summit.

In Beirut, a communique issued by the Palestine Liberation Organization claimed responsibility for both explosions and said that they were part of "stepping up the armed struggle" against the Jewish state.

Police detained some 15 suspects rounded up in the areas of the blasts.

The first explosion, in which the two men were injured, took place at 9.25 a.m. at a gas storage depot on Derech Beit Lehem in Jerusalem's Baka quarter. An Arab worker in the depot discovered a suspicious looking object under an old car door which formed part of the depot fence. Close to the door was a semi-trailer loaded with balloons of domestic cooking gas.

The worker immediately reported the object to the depot manager, Baron, who called the police. Baron warned police that should there be a blast, it might trigger a much larger explosion because of the gas tanks and an adjacent petrol station.

A police jeep arrived within eight minutes. Holmes accompanied Baron to the object which looked like a transistor radio wrapped in rags. As the two approached it, the bomb exploded, immediately — according to eye-witnesses — sheering off one of the sapper's legs and seriously damaging the other leg as well as an arm and an eye. Baron suffered burns and his condition at Hadassah Hospital last night was described as "serious but out of danger." The Arab worker who discovered the bomb was still being treated for shock late yesterday afternoon.

Police described the bomb as "not large, but a standard sabotage device — not homemade."

Hilmes, who is hospitalized at Shaare Zedek, was interviewed for a magazine article in last Friday's *Jerusalem Post*. The former American and Vietnam war veteran — where he was also wounded — came on aliya in early 1973 and volunteered for the bomb squad "because my basic urge is to help people and I'm perhaps better qualified for this job than others." Hilmes, who is apparently an orphan

(Continued on page 2, col. 5)

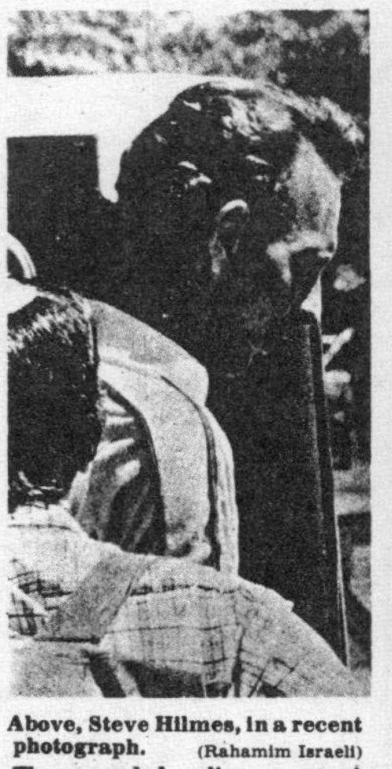

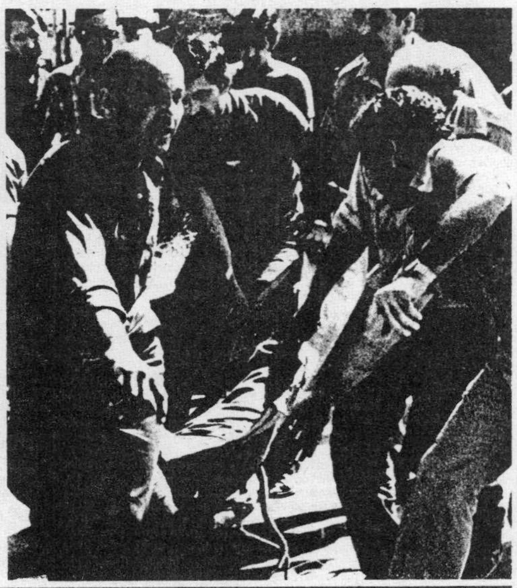

Above, Steve Hilmes, in a recent photograph. (Rahamim Israeli)
The wounded police sapper is evacuated from the site of yesterday's explosion in Derech Beit Lehem. (Hershkovits, Zoom 77)

Nkomo: We downed plane, didn't kill survivors

LUSAKA. — Guerrilla leader Joshua Nkomo said yesterday his forces had brought down a Rhodesian airliner with 56 people aboard and declared: "Smith has got to surrender."

Nkomo warned that the six-year-long bush war in Rhodesia would become increasingly bitter unless white minority Prime Minister Ian Smith capitulated and handed over power to the Patriotic Front nationalist guerrilla alliance.

But the guerrilla leader insisted his men did not massacre 10 of the 18 holidaymakers who survived the crash of the four-engined Air Rhodesia Viscount near the Zambian border on Sunday.

"We brought that plane down, but it is not true that we killed any survivors," Nkomo told Reuters.

The Rhodesian authorities said a guerrilla band herded survivors together beside the wrecked plane and shot dead 10 of them, including six women, at point-blank range.

In Salisbury, it was reported that security forces combed wild bush country yesterday in an air and ground search for guerrillas reported to have murdered the survivors of the crash.

Asked if the attack on the airliner meant bloodier confrontation, Nkomo said: "We have said that it is going to be intensified every day. We will make it much more bitter. This is war. Smith has got to surrender and just that."

Nkomo is co-leader of the Patriotic Front with Robert Mugabe, who is based in Mozambique. Nkomo's ZIPRA forces, believed to number at least 10,000 men, operate from Zambia.

In the past, Rhodesian helicopter-borne troops have struck across Lake Kariba, which forms part of the 720-km. Zambesi River frontier, to attack ZIPRA camps on the northern bank. Nkomo's ZIPRA army has expanded from 900 in the last four years, with Soviet and Cuban help.

Western intelligence sources said ZIPRA has been receiving increasingly sophisticated weapons from the Soviet Union, and was probably equipped with SAM-7 ground-to-air missiles.

Nkomo justified downing the civilian airliner, saying it was a military target, as Air Rhodesia Viscounts had been used to ferry Rhodesian troops and arms. ZIPRA had no interest in killing civilians, he added.

Air Rhodesia's general manager, Captain Pat Travers, rejected Nkomo's claim that the plane had been shot, affirming that "there is at present no evidence to suggest that the aircraft was brought down by hostile action."

Travers said the last message from the crew explicitly stated that the plane's two starboard engines were out of action.

"In our opinion, had the aircraft been hit by a missile or any other weapon, the crew's first reaction would have been to say so," he said.

Travers also denied that the airline was used for ferrying troops.

The incident touched off furious reactions from Rhodesian officials, including leading black politicians.

The Reverend Ndabaningi Sithole's ZANU party said: "The killing of innocent people is always horrifying, whether they are black or white, it is abominable."

Bishop Abel Muzorewa's United African National Council described the killing as a "senseless action."

Meanwhile, more deaths were reported in the six-year Rhodesian guerrilla war, with an official report of another 34 dead. The Rhodesian military command said they included 23 black civilians.

Also among the dead were three Rhodesian soldiers, two provincial officials, three guerrillas and three "terrorist collaborators," the military said. (Reuter, AP, UPI)

Four Soviet Jews face death sentence for economic crimes

By SRAYA SHAPIRO
Jerusalem Post Reporter

TEL AVIV. — Four Soviet Jews were sentenced to death in a mass trial which ended in the Donets regional court in the Ukraine on Monday, relatives of some of the convicted men learned here yesterday.

The men were allegedly involved in a 500,000 rouble ($750,000) racket of privately selling textiles produced in the factory where they worked near Baku, on the Caspian Sea.

Investigations into the case began five years ago, when most of the 50 people accused were arrested, but formal charges were brought only last year.

Most of the defendants, a great many of whom are believed to be Jews, admitted full or partial guilt, and received prison terms ranging between 10 and 15 years.

But the four men who denied any connection with the affair were sentenced to death. They are Gabriel Sapiashvili, 39, of Shukumi, Georgia, who is married and has three children; two others identified only as Adjashvili and Michailishvili, of Tbilisi, the Georgian capital; and a fourth man called Abassov.

An appeal against the death sentences has been filed, relatives of the condemned men were told in a telephone conversation yesterday with Russian lawyers.

The death penalty for "economic crimes" were frequent enough in the Soviet Union in the early 1960s when their obvious anti-Jewish bias caused an uproar in the West. A man was sentenced to death for similar crimes last year, but this was ultimately commuted to imprisonment.

Observers of Soviet affairs here refused to speculate yesterday as to whether the Donets sentence is an isolated case or an indication of a renewed anti-Semitic wave with economic crimes used as a pretext.

Syrians clash with militias in Beirut

BEIRUT. — Heavy-weapons duels erupted yesterday between Syrian peacekeeping troops and Christian rightist militiamen in suburban Beirut, shattering a 40-hour lull.

The flare-up, within sight of President Elias Sarkis' hilltop presidential palace, killed a young boy and injured three other civilians and two policemen, the Phalangist Party radio reported. No Syrian casualty figures were released.

It was reported, meanwhile, that Syria's forces in Lebanon had grown to 70,000, and that Syria intends to continue its role in the country.

President Hafez Assad, in addressing army units on Syria's front line with Israel, declared: "We shall continue to be an honest arbiter in Lebanon." He added that Syria would not be intimidated by threats,

(Continued on page 2, col. 7)

Sadat: Can't afford to fail at Camp David

By WOLF BLITZER
Jerusalem Post Correspondent

ANDREWS AIR FORCE BASE, Maryland. — Egyptian President Anwar Sadat arrived here from Paris yesterday declaring that the Camp David summit represented "the crucial crossroads" in the search for peace in the Middle East.

"We cannot afford to fail," Sadat said in an arrival statement. "No one has the right to block the road to peace. This is no time for manoeuvre and worn-out ideas. It is time for magnanimity and reason."

Sadat, who put on his glasses to read the prepared statement, was greeted by Vice-President Walter Mondale, Secretary of State Cyrus Vance and a large delegation of foreign ambassadors who stood along a red-carpeted receiving line.

The Egyptian president and his aides, joined by Mondale and Vance, boarded a U.S. military helicopter to fly to Camp David after the brief arrival ceremony. Mondale and Vance later returned here to meet Prime Minister Menahem Begin and the Israel delegation.

The vice-president was very brief in his welcoming remarks. "On behalf of President Carter and the people of the United States," Mondale said, "we welcome you again to the U.S. with a warm heart. The people of our country admire greatly your wisdom, your courage and your statesmanship. Welcome to the United States."

In reply, Sadat stressed America's key role in the peace negotiations. "All along we have held the view that this nation is the most qualified to be a full partner in the peace process," Sadat said. "Your heritage is unique and so is your global responsibility."

Sadat did not discuss specific issues in his arrival remarks, clearly determined to avoid any disruption of the pre-conference atmosphere. Similarly, both Carter and Begin have avoided public utterances on the controversial issues involved in the talks.

"I pray to God Almighty to guide us in this just endeavour and to enable us to achieve the noble goal which inspired President Carter to call for this conference," Sadat said. "This inspiration is and shall remain a brave and gallant act of statesmanship," he continued. "Together we shall proceed to build a viable structure for peace on the solid foundation of law and legitimacy. Together we shall realize the hopes of those who believe in the supremacy of right and justice and together we shall overcome."

The vice-president then approached Sadat, shook his hand warmly and said: "That's a good American line — "we shall overcome," a reference to the civil rights slogan of the 1960s.

Sadat's special "Egypt Air" plane touched down at 1:21 p.m. local time. Sadat stood between Mondale and Vance as a U.S. army band played the Egyptian and American national anthems. The two Americans placed their hands on their hearts as they stood to attention, while Sadat stood with his hands at his sides.

After shaking hands with the assembled dignitaries, Sadat walked over to a crowd of 200 Egyptian students who stood behind the airport gates chanting pro-Sadat slogans and singing patriotic Egyptian songs.

He wore a dashing black pin-striped suit, and a white shirt with a black and white spotted tie.

The entire arrival ceremony was broadcast live to Egypt by Egyptian radio, and was carried by the American TV networks.

In his statement, Sadat expressed appreciation to the U.S. for its friendship with Egypt. "The Egyptian people value very highly the ever-growing friendship and cooperation with the people and leadership of the United States," he said. "We are also gratified by the keen interest you are maintaining in the establishment of a comprehensive, just and lasting peace in the Middle East."

Sadat, who made an overnight stop in Paris to seek France's diplomatic support for his peace efforts, said before he left the French capital that he expected a down-to-earth encounter with Premier Begin. The talks would be just as important as his own historic visit to Jerusalem last November, the Egyptian president said.

"In Jerusalem, the initiative had a spiritual basis. At Camp David we are putting everything in its place and coming back to earth," he added.

Sadat had five hours of talks with French President Valery Giscard d'Estaing, and said they produced an identity of views both on Middle East and African affairs.

First round of talks between Carter, Begin

By DAVID LANDAU and WOLF BLITZER
Jerusalem Post Correspondents

CAMP DAVID, Maryland. — U.S. President Jimmy Carter and Prime Minister Menahem Begin were due to launch into a first round of talks yesterday evening, three hours after the premier helicoptered into the U.S. leader's mountain retreat here.

Carter has scheduled a first meeting with Egyptian President Anwar Sadat for this morning, and presumably will then be in a position to decide when to bring the two leaders together for their first face-to-face encounter since the abortive Ismailiya summit last Christmas.

Calling the Camp David summit "the most important, the most momentous" of his talks with Presidents Jimmy Carter and Anwar Sadat, Prime Minister Begin pledged upon arrival at Andrews Air Force Base to "make all endeavours possible to reach an agreement so that the peace process can continue and ultimately be crowned with peace treaties."

Begin spoke at an arrival ceremony here just two hours after the Egyptian leader was similarly welcomed by Vice-President Walter Mondale and Secretary of State Cyrus Vance.

Secretary of Defence Harold Brown also showed up in honour of the arrival of Defence Minister Ezer Weizman.

Begin, who flew here from New York in a special U.S. aircraft provided by President Carter, said in brief remarks: "Let us all hope that out of this unique political conclave a day will come when the nations of the world will say *habemus pacem* — we have peace."

Mondale, in welcoming the prime minister, said: "The American people deeply admire your leadership, its genius, its strength, its compassion. Above all we admire your profound commitment to peace so appreciated at this historic moment. Mr. Prime Minister, we welcome you with a warm heart."

Begin and his senior aides, like the Sadat party earlier, boarded a military helicopter which carried them to Camp David. The protocol for the arrival ceremony was slightly different for the two leaders because Sadat is Egypt's head of state while Begin is Israel's head of government.

Begin stood at attention with Mondale at his side as the military band played "Hatikvah" and the "Star-Spangled Banner" while a 19-gun salute was fired. Standing behind them were Foreign Minister Moshe Dayan, Defence Minister Weizman, Vance, Brown, Ambassador Samuel Lewis, Ambassador Simcha Dinitz and senior American and Israeli officials.

Begin walked over to a small crowd of local Jews who had driven to the air base to meet him as they sang "Hevenu Shalom Aleichem."

In his remarks, Begin praised President Carter and his hospitality in opening Camp David to the conference. Referring to his earlier talks with Sadat, Begin said they were held "in a spirit of understanding, in good will, in common striving for peace."

The prime minister did not refer specifically to any of the issues which will be on the summit's agenda.

U.S. officials were stressing as the summit opened that all arrangements — including its duration — were entirely "open ended" to foster the relaxed and unhurried atmosphere that Carter has set out to achieve.

The president's national security adviser Zbigniew Brzezinski sought to exude optimism and good cheer as he exchanged banter with newsmen at the camp's helipad, awaiting Begin's arrival from Andrews Air

(Continued on page 2, col. 5)

Hearty hug for Sadat

By DAVID LANDAU
Jerusalem Post Correspondent

CAMP DAVID, Maryland. — President Anwar Sadat of Egypt flung his arms wide in greeting as soon as he saw U.S. President Jimmy Carter from the steps of the helicopter that flew him here yesterday from Andrews Air Force Base near Washington.

The Egyptian leader, whose arrival for the summit conference preceded that of Prime Minister Menahem Begin by about two hours, descended quickly and threw himself into the president's hearty hug.

The phalanxes of newsmen, forbidden to question either of the leaders, faithfully measured the length of the Carter-Sadat embrace and the warmth of the kiss Sadat bestowed on the first lady, Rosalynn Carter.

The noise of the helicopter drowned out whatever was said by Sadat and his hosts; and the newsmen were, in any event, kept too far away to hear their conversation.

After the greeting, the Carters slowly escorted Sadat on foot along the winding, leafy path to the heart of the Camp David complex, out of the sight of the press corps for at least the next several days.

Secretary of State Cyrus Vance, who escorted Sadat on the 35-minute flight to Camp David, returned with the helicopter to Andrews Air Force Base to greet Premier Begin.

On hand at Camp David as a welcoming committee with the Carters were the president's national security adviser Zbigniew Brzezinski, assistant secretary of state for Near Eastern affairs Harold Saunders, and Carter's special Middle East envoy, Alfred Atherton.

Sadat invites pope to pray on Mount Sinai

CAIRO (AP). — Egyptian President Anwar Sadat has invited Pope John Paul I to pray on Mount Sinai where he hopes to build a church, synagogue and mosque when Israeli troops withdraw as part of a Middle East peace settlement, the press reported here yesterday.

The invitation to Mount Sinai and a visit to Egypt were made in a message delivered to the pope by Egyptian Minister of Culture and Information Abdel Moneim el-Sawy on Monday, the press said.

Togetherness under the trees planned by Camp David hosts

By DAVID LANDAU
Jerusalem Post Correspondent

CAMP DAVID, Maryland. — The Israeli and Egyptian delegations to the Camp David summit conference have been deliberately housed in alternate cabins to encourage chance, informal encounters.

To walk from one Israeli's cabin to another, an Israeli delegation member will have to walk past at least one Egyptian's cabin — and be prepared to exchange pleasantries with any passing Egyptian delegate.

There has been some good-natured wondering among the Israeli delegates about the criteria by which the rustically named cabins were allocated to the various conference participants.

Defence Minister Ezer Weizman is quartered in "Sycamore" and Foreign Minister Moshe Dayan in "Red Oak." Ambassador Simcha Dinitz has landed the most ominous name-plate — "Hemlock." Premier Begin's "Birch," Sadat's "Dogwood" and Carter's "Aspen" form a triangle in the centre of the complex.

President Sadat has asked for five breaks for prayers on Friday, the Moslem sabbath; so it is uncertain how much negotiating will be achieved on that day.

On Saturday there will be no formal talks at all, in deference to the Jewish sabbath. But all the main participants are expected to remain in the camp over the weekend — they have been expressly requested to do so by the American hosts. Therefore, a good deal of informal discussion is expected on various levels.

The White House, in its determination to keep the summit secluded, has turned down an Israeli proposal for some photo coverage today. Originally spokesman Jody Powell was inclined to agree to some pool photography of the three leaders strolling on the lawn this morning. But President Carter is understood to have vetoed the idea.

Terrorists call for summit protest strike

BEIRUT (UPI). — A Palestine Liberation Organization member group called for a general strike and protest demonstrations in Palestinian camps throughout Lebanon today to mark the start of the Camp David summit.

In a communique, the hard-line Democratic Front for the Liberation of Palestine called for "all the camps" to strike and stage meetings and demonstrations.

Itim reports that slogans denouncing the summit talks and calling for "death to collaborators with the Zionists" were painted on walls of houses in Atil village, in the Tulkarm district, on Monday night. The slogans were signed "Al-Fatah."

U.S. officials wrestle with Israel's military, settlement demands

By WOLF BLITZER
Jerusalem Post Correspondent

WASHINGTON. — As the Camp David summit opens, American officials continue to wrestle with the two "bottom line" conditions regarding the future of the West Bank and Gaza Strip laid down by the Israel government.

In recent days, the Americans have been informed by Israel that any ultimate solution will have to enable Israel to maintain an open-ended military presence in strategically important areas of Judea, Samaria and Gaza. An agreement would also have to grant Israeli citizens the right to purchase land and live there.

Any new formula devised at Camp David, the Americans have been told, will have to meet these two demands. As long as they are met, Prime Minister Begin and his team of advisers will be prepared to consider new, more flexible language.

But U.S. officials fear that they will not be able to come up with a joint Israeli-Egyptian statement of principles which fit within these limits. They sense that Egyptian President Sadat might go along with a prolonged Israeli military presence but is unlikely to accept permanent Israeli settlement in the West Bank and Gaza Strip.

In fact, the U.S. has never supported the establishment of Israeli settlements in the territories occupied during the 1967 war. The Americans have labelled such settlements as "illegal" under international law and "obstacles" to peace.

Officials here believe that it will be difficult enough to achieve a

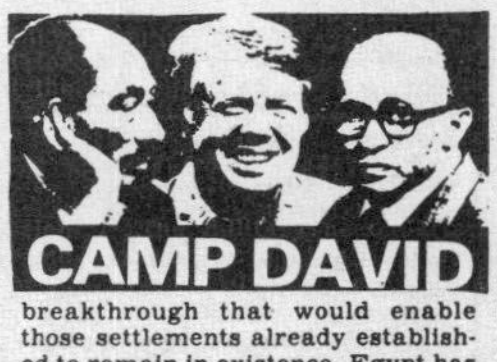

breakthrough that would enable those settlements already established to remain in existence. Egypt has been calling for the dismantling of these settlements.

It would be almost impossible to envisage an agreement allowing Israel to continue building new settlements and purchasing lands in Judea, Samaria and Gaza forever, according to the Americans. And this is exactly what the Israeli government is demanding.

Thus, this thorny question, involving firmly entrenched ideological commitments of the Likud government, appears to be developing as the major stumbling block to an agreement. According to well-placed sources here, it will probably be more difficult to resolve than the security-related issues involving a prolonged Israeli military presence.

Since it is unlikely that this settlement issue can be compromised successfully at the Camp David summit, the only way of avoiding a collapse over the talks on this issue will probably be for both sides to leave the matter ambiguous at this stage.

Israeli officials appear more likely to accept such a "solution" than their Egyptian counterparts. The Egyptians, according to their spokesmen who have already arrived here for the talks, are stressing that they will want a "specific" joint statement to emerge from the talks, one addressing this difficult question.

The Americans, for their part, have been preparing "dozens" of possible options to try to bridge the gaps on this issue as well as the myriad of others standing in the way of a settlement. But they say that President Carter will first want to hear what Sadat and Begin have to say in the early stage of the conference before submitting U.S. "suggestions."

U.S. officials do believe that it may be easier for Sadat and Begin to accept American proposals than to accept each others, partly because of facesaving.

THE JERUSALEM POST

Injunction in Samaria ★★ page 2

IL5.30 (inc. Vat)

MONDAY, SEPTEMBER 18, 1978 • ELUL 16, 5738 • HAWWAL 16, 1398 • VOL. XLVIII, No. 14423

Carter, Begin, Sadat due to make statement today

Camp David summit ends, outcome said favourable

By WOLF BLITZER and DAVID LANDAU
Jerusalem Post Correspondents

THURMONT, Maryland. — Jimmy Carter, Menahem Begin and Anwar Sadat were due to appear before dawn this morning in the East Room of the White House to make an announcement about the conclusion of the Camp David summit on Middle East peace. An American official said last night that today's announcement would "involve all three principals." It was set for 4:30 a.m. Israel time.

An Israeli conference source told *The Jerusalem Post* at 1 a.m. today that the summit had ended "favourably" but he said he was barred from providing substantive details. This would appear to indicate that at least Israel's minimum objective — continued peace negotiations — has been ensured.

Earlier yesterday, with the Camp David summit in its final hours, the summiteers were still battling, against each other and against the clock, in a last-ditch effort to put as much agreed substance as possible into the document that was to emerge from the 12 days of deliberations. American officials seemed pleased to be able to report "some movement" after lengthy meetings on Saturday between U.S. President Carter and Egyptian President Sadat (for four hours) and between Carter and Israel Premier Begin (four and one-half hours). Israeli sources too seemed almost certain that some measure of success for the summit had effectively been assured.

A high Egyptian summiteer, contacted late last night Israel time, was still being extremely circumspect. The meetings still in progress, he said, would determine the summit's outcome.

Observers here, wary now of the likely attempts by each of the parties to put as favourable (to themselves) gloss as possible on the summit's achievements, also preferred to withhold judgement until the concluding document (or documents) had been released.

Last night Carter closeted himself yet again with Sadat for nearly two hours. This followed the shortest yet Carter-Begin meeting — six minutes long, from 3:27 to 3:33 p.m. as recorded by the White House press department.

American sources said these closing meetings would still be crucial in formulating key phrases in the still-unfinalized document.

There was no official word, at this time of writing, as to whether Carter intended to convene with Sadat and Begin together, or to have the two of them meet alone before the summit ended.

The Israel cabinet yesterday heard a brief report on the last-minute deliberations at Camp David. The report was labelled "classified" since the cabinet held its discussion in its capacity as Ministerial Defence Committee.

The report was understood to have been made by Begin through his deputy, Acting Prime Minister Yigael Yadin.

In the morning, after attending church services at Camp David, the U.S. president met with Sadat for 45 minutes. A photograph of them released later by the White House showed Carter holding a document of several pages stapled together (and smiling), with Sadat holding some handwritten notes (and smiling too). An American spokesman confirmed that the paper in the president's hand was indeed "related to the summit negotiations."

On Saturday night Carter had sat with Begin from the moment the Sabbath ended, at about 8 p.m., until 12:25 a.m. in a marathon session at which, according to knowledgeable sources, the president had been "businesslike."

Carter was flanked by Secretary of State Cyrus Vance (who is a lawyer by training), and Begin had with him Foreign Minister Moshe Dayan and ex-Attorney-General Aharon Barak. Barak has played a major role for Israel in the final, drafting stages of the summit conference.

Simultaneously with the Carter-Begin meeting Saturday night, Defence Minister Ezer Weizman met alone with President Sadat.

American officials indicated that the moment the document was finalized it would be released — so as to ensure that the first impact was at least based on accurate facts rather than on tendentious leaks.

The officials said that the manner in which Carter would report on the summit to the American people —

(Continued on page 2, col. 4)

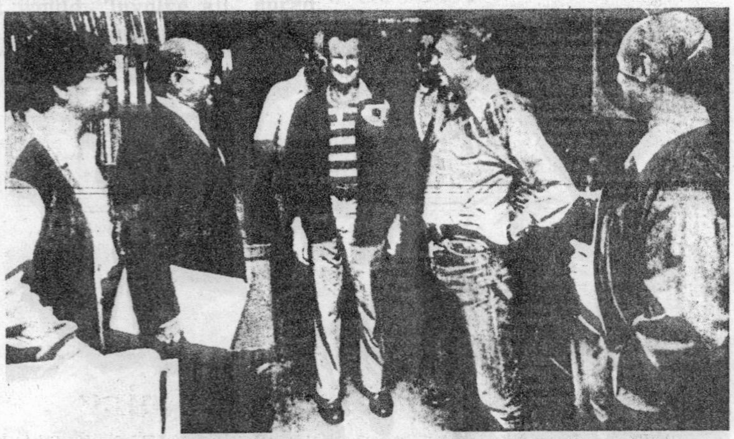

President Carter, accompanied by security adviser Zbigniew Brzezinski (in striped shirt), Secretary of State Cyrus Vance (behind him) and Vice-President Walter Mondale (behind Carter), prepares for a late Saturday meeting with Prime Minister Menahem Begin and Foreign Minister Moshe Dayan. At left, former Attorney-General Aaron Barak. (UPI)

Power sharing on West Bank

By JIM HOAGLAND
and EDWARD WALSH
The Washington Post

THURMONT, Maryland. — President Jimmy Carter has centred his intense but thus far unsuccessful efforts to build a Middle East peace agreement at Camp David on the concept of an interim sharing of power by Arabs and Israelis on the West Bank of the Jordan River, informed diplomatic sources here have reported.

But Carter's efforts for agreement have been stymied by the continuing fundamental differences between Sadat and Begin over the re-establishing of Arab sovereignty over not only the West Bank, but also the Sinai Peninsula and the former Egyptian-controlled territory of the Gaza Strip, the sources said.

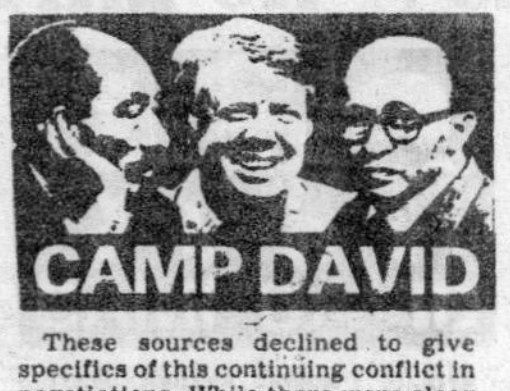

These sources declined to give specifics of this continuing conflict in negotiations. While there were clear indications that Egyptian and Israeli positions have significantly hardened over this point in recent days, the sources saw this as a natural part of the closing phase of such important negotiations rather than as a sign that agreement was impossible.

Diplomatic analysts assumed that Sadat is continuing to insist on a statement of broad principles that he could interpret as including an Israeli commitment now to return all of the territories occupied in the 1967 war to Arab sovereignty eventually.

Begin, who has previously insisted on Israel's right to retain at least part of the West Bank, is believed to be resisting making such a commitment. The conflict is reported to be obstructing efforts to make the three-way power-sharing a centrepiece for a final agreement for the conference.

It is unclear what reaction the idea will draw from Jordan's King Hussein, who ruled the West Bank before the Six Day War and whose par-

(Continued on page 2, col. 4)

15,000 die in Iranian 'quake

MASHAD, Iran (UPI). — About 15,000 persons died in an earthquake that demolished a major town and 40 villages in the remote salt desert of eastern Iran, officials reported last night.

"Only 2,000 of the 13,000 inhabitants of Tabas survived Saturday's earthquake, and all the buildings in the city were destroyed," the official news agency Pars said.

Earlier reports spoke of more than 18,000 killed and wounded in Tabas and surrounding villages in the epicentre of the world's strongest earthquake this year.

Reports from the scene said soldiers and survivors of the quake pulled bodies from under mounds of rubble and took them to the cemetery to be buried.

In addition to 40 villages destroyed, 60 more suffered serious damage, Pars said.

The Shah and Prime Minister Ja'afer Sharif-Eman Emami declared three days of national mourning and radio stations switched to classical music as a sign of grief.

Initial television footage from the scene in Mashad showed street after street of collapsed mud-walled houses, survivors wandering about and injured persons seeking shelter in broken structures.

The only things left standing were dozens of towering date palms.

The quake struck at 7:38 p.m. (6.38 p.m. in Israel) on Saturday. It swayed tall buildings in Teheran, 700 km. away.

"I was sitting in my house having the evening meal with my family," one survivor told the government radio. "Suddenly the whole building started shaking. We tried to get to the door and out, but it was shaking too much. Only my brother and I survived. The rest were buried under the rubble."

The devastated area, in Khorassan province, is near the Soviet and Afghan borders.

Dried-mud houses provide protection against the heat and cold of the desert, but are brittle and collapse easily during earthquakes.

Working together with the Iranian air force and army, relief authorities sent 20 giant hospital tents, 23,000 ordinary tents and 7,000 blankets for the tens of thousands left homeless.

The air force flew over the area and dropped lanterns, food and cooking utensils.

Pars news agency said that if help did not immediately reach many of those injured in Tabas and its environs, they would die, according to the city mayor. All the town's doctors were killed.

It was the deadliest earthquake to strike Iran — which straddles a world quake belt — since 1962. The 1962 disaster claimed 13,000 dead, also in Khorassan. (Reuter, AP, UPI)

Envoys to Costa Rica, Panama also recalled

Venezuela aiding rebels, says Nicaragua

MANAGUA. — Nicaragua yesterday charged that Venezuela had sent planes to strafe its territory in support of rebels opposed to President Anastasio Somoza.

A government communique said that the planes attacked early yesterday in support of a rebel column moving in from a sanctuary in a third Central American state — neighbouring Costa Rica. Costa Rica denied the charge. There was no official word from Venezuela yesterday.

The government reported this incursion while its troops were battling in the north — away from the Costa Rican frontier — against other rebel detachments fighting to end nearly 45 years of rule by the Somoza family.

The government claimed to have recaptured the city of Leon from rebels, and its national guard, using World War Two vintage Sherman tanks, was in action in nearby Estelí. Both cities are in the northern part of the country.

The invaders in the south, across the frontier of Costa Rica, enjoyed the complicity of that country, the government here said. They were Marxist-Leninists of various nationalities, it added.

Reports from Leon said that entire blocks of the city, Nicaragua's second largest, lay in ruins after national guards defeated rebels in a weeklong battle.

The air attack was at 4 a.m. (noon Israel time) near Penas Blancas on the frontier, it said, and a protest had been made to Costa Rica.

Informed sources said one Canberra jet bomber fired rockets and machineguns into Nicaraguan territory from Costa Rican air space. These sources spoke of only one plane in action.

Venezuela on Friday signed a mutual defence agreement with Costa Rica, which had complained of Nicaraguan incursions. It sent a squadron of military planes on what was described as a goodwill visit to Costa Rica, which has no army.

Nicaragua announced earlier that it had recalled its ambassadors to Costa Rica, Panama and Venezuela "for consultations" in view of their attitude to the rebellion.

The Foreign Ministry said the government had taken note through international news agency reports "of some attitudes by the governments of Costa Rica, Panama and Venezuela which can have serious repercussions in Nicaragua."

(Guerrillas who had seized the national palace in Managua on August 22, reportedly were granted refuge in Panama.) (Reuter, UPI,

(Israeli engineers — page 2)

School strike talks broken off

By LEA LEVAVI,
BENNY MORRIS
and SHLOMO MAOZ
Jerusalem Post Reporters

The teachers' strike enters its second week today, after negotiations between the government and the two striking unions — the Histadrut Teachers Union and the Secondary School Teachers Association — broke up after one hour in Tel Aviv last night. There are no plans for further negotiating sessions.

According to Shalom Levin, secretary-general of the Histadrut teachers' union, "The gap between our demands and the government's offer has grown wider and a settlement is further away than it was last week."

"Anyone who says there is only a difference of a few percentage points between what we want and what they are offering is either uninformed or deliberately misleading the public," Levin said.

Levin claimed that Civil Service Commissioner Avraham Friedman told the teachers at last night's negotiations that Finance Minister Simha Ehrlich and Education Minister Zevulun Hammer had decided not to participate in the talks themselves, as the teachers have requested.

Levin also asserted that Friedman claimed authority to negotiate only within the government's stated pay rise policy.

At yesterday's cabinet meeting, it was reported that the ministers had authorized its representatives to show "greater flexibility" in the negotiations, and that Friedman was probably empowered to offer the teachers a 22 to 23 per cent pay rise to settle the strike.

The strike has idled more than a million schoolchildren throughout the country, and the National Parents Association yesterday reportedly received President Yitzhak Navon's promise to look into the situation.

The parents, who threatened to "take action" if the strike continued into this week, also asked the Histadrut union to compromise in its negotiations.

A spokesman for the parents association said it was asked by the union to have patience for another day or two in the hope that the "war of nerves" will be won by the teachers.

The Histadrut Executive yesterday, after a stormy meeting, called on the government to speed up the neogtiations with the teachers to end the dispute.

At the start of the strike, the two unions demanded a 35 per cent pay rise and at least one month's salary advance immediately to continue the talks. The government stuck by its 15 per cent pay rise ceiling, arguing that any concession would result in a collapse of its pay policy.

Friedman, it was learned, was authorized by the cabinet to give special, favourable attention to the salaries of starting teachers. The unions complain that teachers in their first five years are comparatively the most underpaid in the profession.

In the cabinet discussion, all the ministers, with the exception of Yitzhak Moda'i, minister of energy and infrastructure, supported continuing the talks with the teachers. Moda'i argued that the talks should be suspended as long as the teachers continue to strike.

Education Minister Zevulun Hammer asserted that the cabinet had reached its limit of concessions. He said he opposed giving the teachers an increase of 10 per cent beyond the 15 per cent ceiling applying to all public sector workers.

The minister was apparently countering the charges that he favoured the teachers' position, which claims the extra 10 per cent is a minimum. Hammer added that what the cabinet is proposing will give the teachers an increase of 7½ to 8½ per cent above the 15 per cent ceiling.

In addition to Navon, the National Parents Association also called on Hammer and reportedly was told that his current offer to the teachers is as much as he can get out of the government and is only about 2½ per cent less than what the teachers are demanding.

Acting Prime Minister Yigael Yadin suggested at the cabinet meeting that a "long school day" be instituted and that teachers' wages be increased in this manner through overtime pay. Finance Minister Simha Ehrlich, at the end of the session, expressed satisfaction at the cabinet's rallying behind his pay policy.

A pre-kindergarten in Beersheba and three other nurseries in Haifa and Nahariya will reopen this morning under a court order, after parents complained that those running the schools had nothing to do with the central government or the striking teachers.

Meanwhile, the Engineers Union sent a letter to the civil service commissioner rejecting the government's 15 per cent wage offer as a basis for negotiations.

Judge: 'But this doesn't mean there wasn't corruption'

Yadlin's sister freed in bribe case

TEL AVIV (Itim). — The District Court yesterday freed Sara Hari, sister of former Kupat Holim head Asher Yadlin, from having to respond to the charge of being her brother's accomplice in the taking of a $30,000 bribe.

But Judge Menahem Ilan, in freeing Hari, quickly added: "I don't mean to say that an act of corruption hasn't been proved. All that my ruling says is that I do not have before me seeming proof that the accused (Hari) was a partner to the bribe and to the conspiracy to give it."

Following the ruling, which the judge said he would explain later, Hari moved from the dock to take her place among the spectators at the trial.

The ruling still leaves Yadlin himself — already serving a five-year prison term for bribe-taking and tax-evasion — on trial for allegedly soliciting through his sister a $30,000 bribe from his friend Mordechai Elison.

The prosecution charges that Elison, then head of the Ami overseas-operations subsidiary of the Histadrut's Solel Boneh building firm, gave Yadlin the money through his sister to get more contracts for Ami from Kupat Holim.

Elison, who said the money was never repaid, is a state's witness in the current trial.

Yadlin, who testified later in yesterday's session, contended that the money was to help out his sister, then in debt to her own insurance agency in Haifa.

Yadlin added yesterday that even before becoming Kupat Holim secretary he had tried to get Ami contracts from the Histadrut sick fund; after becoming its chief, "I could hardly ignore my previous promises," he said.

In announcing his ruling yesterday, Ilan said that evidence had been presented that Hari apparently knew she was receiving a benefit from Elison — one comprising money that didn't belong to him — and was getting it as a result of the friendship between Elison and her brother.

But, he added, "It's a long way from this to an assumption that she knew this was a bribe connected specifically with his position as chairman of the Kupat Holim central committee, especially as he held other positions and as his friendship with Elison predated his being made head of Kupat Holim."

The judge next turned to the charge by prosecutor Avraham Tal that Sara Hari and Yadlin had talked beforehand about bringing the money from Mexico. There was logic in this charge, the judge said; it seemed there had been discussions between the two before the money was received. But there was a great distance between such a claim and the existence of specific incriminating evidence which would require the accused to answer the charge, the judge said.

The last prosecution witness to testify yesterday was Yehoshua Eliaz, Hari's former partner in the Bituhim insurance agency in Haifa. The prosecution says that the $30,000 had been transferred to Yadlin, at Yadlin's request, from abroad camouflaged as a gift to Eliaz in Haifa from Eliaz's relatives in Mexico.

Eliaz yesterday affirmed that the transfer had been made from abroad and that IL100,000 worth was changed into pounds and withdrawn from Bituhim's bank account.

Asked by Yadlin's attorney, Shlomo Toussia-Cohen, why he had agreed to the deal, Eliaz said that Yadlin's standing in the Histadrut and Kupat Holim had made him feel nothing could be wrong.

At this point Judge Ilan interjected: "Is the cleanliness of a deal

(Continued on page 2, col. 4)

Carter improves in Israeli eyes

TEL AVIV (UPI). — The Camp David summit brought a marked increase in the number of Israelis who are satisfied with President Jimmy Carter's attitude towards Israel, a poll released yesterday said.

The Pori Institute poll published in "Ha'aretz" said 22.8 per cent of those questioned replied that they are satisfied with Carter's approach to Israel, compared with only 11 per cent who said so prior to the summit meeting.

The poll showed 37.2 per cent are dissatisfied with Carter's approach, versus the 52.8 per cent before the Camp David meeting.

Asked if they thought President Sadat wants a true peace with Israel, 52.9 per cent said yes, similar to the figure before the summit.

Hussein said planning to meet Sadat soon

BEIRUT (UPI). — King Hussein of Jordan will fly to Morocco in the next few days for post-Camp David talks with Egypt's President Anwar Sadat, Arab diplomatic sources said yesterday.

Hussein arrived in Spain on Friday on a private visit with his wife, Queen Nur, and planned to fly from there to the Moroccan capital of Rabat, the sources said.

Sadat was slated to fly to Morocco from his Camp David talks with President Carter and Prime Minister Begin, the sources said.

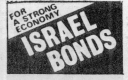

THE JERUSALEM POST

Knesset opens tomorrow
★★
page 3

IL6.00 (Inc. Vat)

SUNDAY, OCTOBER 29, 1978 • TISHRI 28, 5739 • ZIL-KI'ADAH 27, 1398 • VOL. XLVIII, No. 14453

'Real prize is peace itself,' laureates Begin, Sadat agree

Nobel peace Prize winners pleased as Washington talks resume

Jerusalem Post Staff

Prime Minister Menahem Begin and President Anwar Sadat of Egypt last night congratulated each other in a phone conversation for receiving the Nobel peace prize and agreed to immediately resume the peace treaty talks being held in Washington.

Earlier Sadat had responded to an appeal from U.S. President Jimmy Carter not to recall his delegation in Washington for consultations in Cairo. (See story — column one.) Begin learned of Sadat's decision during the phone conversation.

"Wonderful," the prime minister told Sadat in response, noting that they both agreed that "the real prize is peace itself."

Following the exchange Begin, flanked by his wife, five grandchildren and pianist Arthur Rubinstein, spoke to waiting reporters in the garden of his residence. (On Friday evening when the Nobel peace prize was announced, the prime minister declined to issue a statement for fear of desecrating the Sabbath.)

Begin, thanking the Nobel prize committee, declared that the award given to him "has, in fact, been given to the entire people of Israel, and I am nothing but the emissary through which the prize has been bestowed upon our people."

"As I have claimed all my life, no people yearn for peace as we do, and surely, no more than we do," he said.

Begin added that "although this is a day of joy, even greater joy will come when I can announce that the peace treaty has been concluded, signed and ratified."

Begin said he expects the negotiations in Washington to end successfully and that Carter will be invited to attend the ceremony of signing the peace agreement.

Meanwhile, congratulatory cables from Carter and other world leaders and Israeli political personalities poured into the prime minister's residence.

Begin told a television reporter that he had been aware of the possibility of the prize, but "never really entertained the idea of getting the prize."

In Cairo, Sadat was quoted as being "very happy" for winning the prize and not resenting having to share it with Begin.

"Why should he be disappointed?" Egyptian Prime Minister Mustafa Khalil said. "The president is honoured and this honour cannot be diminished if he shares it with some other person."

Khalil's statements to a news conference late Friday did not reflect the sentiment of the average Egyptian. Men-in-the-street, interviewed by UPI, said they were delighted because Sadat won but disappointed because it was split between him and Begin.

Khalil said he telephoned Sadat to congratulate him and the president was "very happy about it, and expressed appreciation for winning the prize."

Khalil said Sadat will donate the money value of the prize to his native Nile Delta village of Mit Abul Kom, about 64 km. north of Cairo, thus "giving another proof of his loyalty to Egypt's soil."

Sadat earlier this year donated revenue from his latest book, "Search for Identity," to the same village.

Khalil praised Sadat in glowing terms, declaring: "It was no coincidence that the greatest prize in the world was awarded this year to the greatest man, who contributed a great deal for the peace of this region."

Khalil said he did not know if Sadat planned to travel to Oslo to receive the prize on December 10. "If he has the time he will go," he said.

A quick sampling of the people's reaction showed most Egyptians believed Sadat should have got the prize alone.

"I cannot believe that Begin was awarded half the prize," said Ali Hamdi el-Gammal, editor of "Al Ahram." "What has Begin done to earn this, apart from placing obstacles in the way of peace?"

But this view was not shared by the influential "October" magazine which said that Begin deserved the prize. In pursuing peace he withstood opposition in Israel and even his own past, the magazine said.

Begin and Sadat talked to each other over the telephone yesterday

(Continued on page 2, col. 3)

A smiling Prime Minister Menahem Begin leaves his house after Shabbat accompanied by his grandchildren 24 hours after the announcement that he had been named co-winner of the Nobel peace prize with Egyptian President Anwar Sadat.
(Hershkovitz, Zoom 77)

Nobel laureate Sadat

Peace negotiations resume despite rift over settlements

By WOLF BLITZER
Jerusalem Post Correspondent

WASHINGTON. — President Jimmy Carter yesterday disclosed that he had talked Egyptian President Anwar Sadat out of recalling his delegation to Cairo from the Blair House peace treaty negotiations.

Speaking in Buffalo, New York, Carter told a political rally that he had telephoned Sadat on Friday evening. "I'll do what my friend Jimmy Carter told me," Carter quoted Sadat as having said.

And then Carter added: "They (the Egyptians) are going to stay there (in Washington) and negotiate."

Carter's remarks followed earlier indications from Cairo that the Egyptian delegation would return home for "consultations." There had been fears that the Egyptian move was designed partially to retaliate for Israel's decision to expand existing settlements in the West Bank and Gaza.

But Carter and other U.S. officials have been trying desperately to salvage the negotiations, which resumed on Friday with a series of separate meetings that Secretary of State Cyrus Vance held with the Israeli and Egyptian delegations.

Vance called off an earlier scheduled session between all three delegations, explaining that such a meeting would not be useful under the present circumstances.

Despite the uproar resulting from the unexpected Israeli decision on the settlements, Israeli, Egyptian and U.S. sources were still insisting that the negotiations on the draft peace treaty could continue.

Everyone — even Israeli sources — conceded that the Israeli move has complicated the talks. But they maintain that a treaty can still be hammered out if "goodwill" is demonstrated by all sides.

Foreign Minister Moshe Dayan and Defence Minister Ezer Weizman returned to Washington on Thursday evening. On Friday morning they met for 45 minutes with Vance at the State Department. Dayan later told reporters that the two sides continued to disagree on the settlements issue.

"I think the American position is very much against the Israeli cabinet decision," Dayan said.

Carter is still described by aides as furious with the Israeli government for issuing the settlement decision at this time.

Vance took the unusual step yesterday of issuing a statement in support of Assistant Secretary Harold Saunders, who has been sharply criticized in Israel for having reportedly made some controversial statements during a recent visit to the Middle East.

"I deplore the personal attacks on Assistant Secretary Harold H. Saunders in connection with his recent conversations in the Middle East," Vance said. "Mr. Saunders is an outstanding public servant who has had more than a decade of experience in dealing with the problem of the Middle East, and I have the utmost confidence in him."

State Department spokesman George Sherman said on Friday that Saunders' "mission was within the scope of the Camp David accords, and his discussions with Palestinians were within the scope of the Camp David accords."

Dayan and Weizman returned to the State Department late Friday afternoon for another 90-minute session with Vance. Later in the evening, the Egyptian delegation, headed by Defence Minister Hassan Ali and Foreign Minister Boutros Ghali, met with Vance.

Yesterday, being Shabbat, there were no formal sessions. But according to Reuter, Vance did drive to the Madison Hotel for talks with the two delegations, lasting about an hour each.

Asked afterwards about the settlements issue, Reuter quoted Vance as saying: "It has deterred progress in the talks." He added that it had not yet been resolved.

Cairo confirms: Talks continuing

CAIRO (UPI). — The Egyptian government yesterday reversed its earlier decision and has decided to keep its top negotiators in Washington for peace treaty talks with Israel.

The spokesman for the Egyptian delegation in Washington said Defence Minister Lt.-Gen. Kamal Hassan Ali and Acting Foreign Minister Butros Ghali will not be returning to Cairo for consultations with the government "for the time being."

In a dispatch from Washington, the Middle East News Agency quoted the spokesman as saying U.S. President Jimmy Carter had sent Egyptian President Anwar Sadat an "urgent message on the latest developments in the situation."

The spokesman said Defence Minister Ali had sent Sadat a "comprehensive report" on the progress of the negotiations following a meeting between Ali and Secretary of State Cyrus Vance on Friday night.

"In light of these developments, it was decided that Lt.-Gen. Ali and Dr. Ghali will not be going to Cairo for consultations with the government for the time being," the spokesman said.

"The Egyptian delegation will remain in close touch with the American secretary of state to continue assessing the situation," he said.

The spokesman's statement reversed an earlier decision, announced by Prime Minister Mustafa Khalil late Friday, that Ali and Ghali had been summoned home for consultations with Sadat.

Khalil denied that the recall was in protest against the Israeli cabinet's decision, but diplomatic sources said the Egyptian move was obviously an indication of displeasure.

But Carter's intervention changed all this, and barely six hours later, the government appeared to be wavering.

Mansour Hassan, spokesman of Sadat's National Democratic Party, told reporters the government has left it up to Ali, who heads the Egyptian team, "to decide whether it would be necessary for him to return home for consultations or to send one of his delegation members instead, or not to send anyone at all."

Hassan said Egypt had "no sense of a major crisis" in the negotiations, despite the cloud cast on them by the Israeli decision.

Asked whether Egypt was relying on the U.S. to deal with the controversial settlement issue directly with Jerusalem, Hassan said:

"The Egyptians always have been depending on themselves and they are also hoping for the cooperation of the U.S. as an effective party in the negotiations, and also hoping for the cooperation and understanding of the other party (Israel) too."

West hails award, Arabs and Soviets condemn it

U.S. President Jimmy Carter and other Western leaders praised the Nobel peace prize awards on Friday to Egyptian President Anwar Sadat and Prime Minister Menahem Begin, linking their congratulations to expressions of hope that the Egyptian-Israeli peace talks will succeed.

But the sparse Arab reaction was generally negative, as was the Soviet response — Soviet Foreign Minister Andrei Gromyko calling the award "a joke."

In Washington, U.S. President Jimmy Carter said the Norwegian committee "has ratified a decision already made by millions around the world."

In Bonn, Chancellor Helmut Schmidt sent separate messages to Begin and Sadat. In his cable to Sadat, he said, "Your courageous initiative of November 19 last year (when Sadat went to Jerusalem) opened an unequalled dialogue which always aimed at leading towards a just and lasting overall solution to the Middle East conflict."

Schmidt told Begin the award was "fitting recognition" and said he hoped "present efforts will contribute towards finding a comprehensive, just and therefore lasting solution bringing the long-desired peace to all peoples of your region, including the Israeli and Palestinian people."

Canadian Prime Minister Pierre Elliott Trudeau sent telegrams to both winners telling them although a peace treaty has not been reached "the beginning is of sufficient magnitude in itself to deserve the recognition of the world's highest honour."

Italian President Sandro Pertini cabled the two men that the award fuelled the hope that peace could return forever to peoples and lands which had been severely tested.

Particularly warm congratulations came from former U.S. Secretary of State Henry Kissinger, himself a Nobel peace laureate, who told an Israel Radio correspondent that both Begin and Anwar Sadat thoroughly deserved the joint honour. Their courageousness had brought their countries nearer to peace, demonstrating that the greatest victories of peoples should be measured by their rapprochement, he said.

In Paris, however, Soviet Foreign Minister Andrei Gromyko yesterday labelled the award "a joke" — but in good humour added that others did not share his opinion.

The Soviets' official Tass news agency was more serious saying the world had learned of the award with "undisguised bewilderment and indignation." Tass, however, made only passing reference itself, choosing instead to quote other publications that condemned the choice.

Hungary's official Communist party newspaper "Nepszabadsag" called the award "strange and unfair" and a "challenging insult" to the Palestinians.

In London, the "Times" and the "Guardian" praised the selection of Sadat but were less enthusiastic about Begin.

The "Times" said "No one can be surprised at the Nobel peace prize being awarded to President Sadat. But it is hard not to feel that by making Mr. Sadat share the award with Mr. Begin the Nobel committee have detracted a good deal from its value."

The newspaper noted that Begin had responded to the Sadat initiative with important concessions but said the Israeli premier was only pursuing a line of diplomacy well marked out by previous governments: "That of prying Egypt away from the Arab coalition facing Israel."

In an editorial condemning the reinforcement of Jewish settlements in Judea and Samaria, and in particular the timing of the announcement, the "Guardian" took a similar line. "Two rounds or even three of applause for co-prizewinner Sadat of Egypt; but only a muted ripple for Mr. Begin."

Talks on autonomy plan may start soon

By DAVID LANDAU
Post Diplomatic Correspondent

Israel and Egypt may well begin talks on the West Bank-Gaza autonomy scheme simultaneous to or immediately following the present treaty negotiations in Washington, according to well-placed observers in Jerusalem. Egypt could in this way demonstrate in a most practical and tangible form a "linkage" between its treaty with Israel and subsequent progress on the West Bank/Palestinian question.

Israel, the observers believe, would not — in effect could not — reject an Egyptian demand that the talks on the West Bank get under way immediately. After all, the underlying rationale of the two Camp David "frameworks" was that negotiations on the "Framework for Peace in the Middle East" would be conducted parallel with, or at least directly after, the negotiations over the "Framework for Peace between Israel and Egypt."

Meanwhile, in Jerusalem last night officials were expecting resumption of talks between Dayan and Weizman and the top-level Egyptian negotiators during the night (evening, U.S. time). This would be their first direct talks since the Israeli team was called home for consultations last weekend.

Rise in fuel prices expected to trigger 3.5% hike in all goods

By SHLOMO MAOZ
Jerusalem Post Reporter

Friday's rise in fuel and electricity prices will make all prices go up by an average of 3.5 per cent, economists in Israel predicted last night. The Histadrut has already demanded increased compensation for salaried workers against the expected wave of price hikes.

The government is also likely to raise the price of basic subsidized foodstuffs. The basic food prices will probably go up by much more than was originally planned because of the effects of spiralling inflation on the government's subsidies programme.

The ministerial economic committee is due to meet today and the decision to raise basic food prices may be taken at this meeting. It is expected that the new prices for most basic foods will be announced only after municipal elections on November 7.

Fuel prices went up by between 18 and 20 per cent, and electricity rates by 14 per cent. The first price rise to be triggered by higher fuel costs was that of cement, which went up by 17 per cent on Friday by authorization of the Ministry of Commerce, Industry and Tourism.

The next expected price rise is in transportation, both because of higher fuel costs and because of a government cut in subsidies to transport.

The ministry is also considering a request from the Dubek cigarette monopoly to raise its prices by about 20 per cent. The price of alcoholic beverages may also go up soon. Instant coffee manufacturers have apparently also asked for permission to raise their prices, although this was denied by the ministry spokesman.

Faced with the impending wave of price increases, the Histadrut is expected to demand a cost-of-living allowance for salaried workers every four months instead of semiannually. The Histadrut wants the c-o-l allowance to be linked by 100 per cent to rising prices (instead of by 70 per cent as at present) and is also expected to demand full linkage of income tax brackets to the cost-of-living index. The Histadrut Central Committee is due to meet today on this subject.

"The average man will feel the pinch almost immediately," Secretary General Yeroham Meshel said on Friday. "But he will feel it even more when other goods and services in which gas, electricity or water are important cost factors start going up in price. The producers and marketers don't absorb the rising costs, they pass them on to the consumer with compound interest."

The wave of price rises will also affect wage negotiations. The government has not managed to

(Continued on page 2, col. 3)

Dayan: Mutual concessions needed to conclude treaty

Jerusalem Post Staff

Both sides are going to have to make concessions in the Washington talks if a peace treaty is to be concluded, Israel's chief negotiator, Foreign Minister Moshe Dayan, told the nation in a weekend radio interview in Washington. "There is no choice," the minister declared. "Mutual concessions are the only way to close the gaps."

Dayan added that he himself believed the talks would succeed — if they continued "as they ought to continue, and as they began."

Defence Minister Ezer Weizman, Israel's second negotiator, agreed with this basically optimistic prognosis. He said the two sides' desire for peace was so strong, and their achievements on the road to peace so far were so impressive, that he could not imagine a regression at this late stage. Therefore, Weizman continued, the "present crisis" over Israel's decision to "thicken" the West Bank settlements would be overcome.

Both Dayan and Weizman said they were pleased, on the whole, that the dispute over the "thickening" had come out into the open at this stage — rather than later. "Before the first Israeli soldier is withdrawn, before an atmosphere of withdrawal descends on us, we must ensure a clear table'," Dayan explained. "For this reason, I do not regret the dispute over the 'thickening' at this time, nor other disputes."

In this context, Dayan spoke of "unrealistic" expectations "among some Israelis regarding Egypt's readiness to cut itself off from the broader Arab world."

By concluding peace with Israel, Egypt would be removing itself from the "war complex," Dayan said, but it would not give up its role in the Arab world. This appeared to be a reference to the current dispute between the two parties over the "linkage" of the projected peace treaty to the problem of the West Bank and Gaza.

Dayan said that both sides were proposing "tough amendments" to the draft text. "We Israelis certainly find the Egyptian proposals tough," he observed. And the Egyptians probably reacted in the same way to some of Israel's demands. "But if we want to bridge the gaps, there will be no option but to compromise."

Dayan said that he and Weizman had made it clear to U.S. Secretary of State Cyrus Vance at their meeting on Friday "that we want to negotiate over living together on the West Bank. Not over evacuation, or over limiting our presence there, or over freezing it. We do not want to rule the West Bank inhabitants; but nor do we intend to leave the area."

The two ministers made no bones of the wide divergence of view on this issue between Jerusalem and Washington.

Officer 'made deal' with Jewish terror suspect

By DAVID RICHARDSON
Jerusalem Post Reporter

An officer of the general security services involved in the interrogation of Yosef ("Jo-Jo") Nidam, the 31-year-old Bat Yam resident suspected of aiding terrorists, has been reportedly reprimanded for making promises to Nidam during the course of the investigation.

Nidam maintains that he cooperated with the investigators after being promised that a suspended sentence for drug offences would be forgotten as part of the verbal deal he concluded with the security agents. Nidam also claims that he was promised a passport and a ticket to the U.S. for himself and his wife.

The Jerusalem Post has learned from usually reliable sources that promises were indeed made to Nidam, and that he was feted by security agents and senior army officers who originally thought he was a "hero."

All of this took place against the advice and wishes of the police involved in the investigation, who considered Nidam's admitted smuggling of hundreds of kilos of drugs from Lebanon a very serious offence in itself.

Police have questioned at least two of Nidam's friends in Tiberias, who are also suspected of being involved in smuggling the explosives. "Nidam has reported that the police questioned these associates after realising that it was not possible for one man to carry such large quantities of material from the Lebanese border to the Bethlehem area.

The Post has also learned that Nidam will in all probability be tried by a military court, and will also be charged with drug smuggling in a civil court.

Nidam was arrested together with two East Jerusalemites, Ribhi Sharabati, 65, and his son shortly before they were allegedly to have placed a bomb in the heart of Jerusalem's cinema area on Thursday, October 5. The bomb, one of the largest ever encountered here, was defused by a police sapper 35 minutes before it was due to explode.

Nidam is also alleged to have smuggled explosives into the country from Lebanon, for the use of the terrorists. Police say he did this on four occasions, and that on the fourth, at least, he himself suspected that he was smuggling explosives — not just drugs, as he originally maintained.

THE JERUSALEM POST

Golda's life
**
Pages 4 and 5

IL6.00 (Inc. Vat)

SUNDAY, DECEMBER 10, 1978 • KISLEV 10, 5739 • MUHARRAM 10, 1399 • VOL. XLVIII, No. 14489

Nation mourns Golda, world pays tribute

State funeral set for Tuesday at Mount Herzl

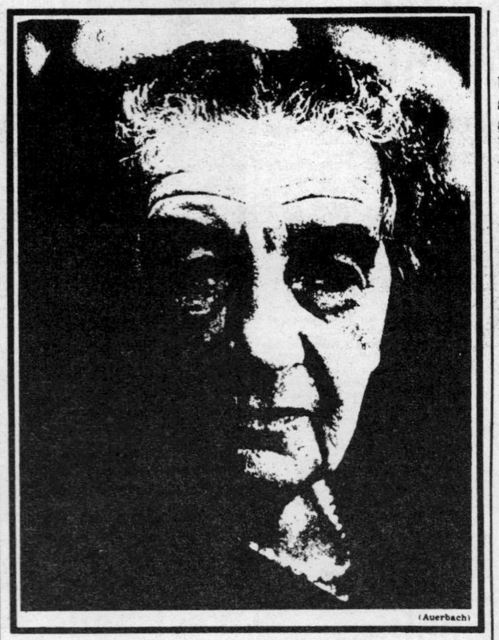

(Auerbach)

By ASHER WALLFISH
Jerusalem Post Reporter

Former prime minister Golda Meir will be buried in the Mount Herzl national cemetery in a state funeral on Tuesday, the cabinet decided in a special memorial session yesterday evening. Numerous foreign dignitaries are expected to attend the funeral for Mrs. Meir, who died on Friday afternoon at Hadassah Hospital.

Mrs. Meir will be buried in the plot next to that of the late premier Levi Eshkol, her colleague for some six decades in the Labour movement whom she succeeded in the high office.

The coffin will be placed in the Knesset tomorrow. Mourners will be allowed to pay their respects throughout the day and night, until shortly before the cortege sets out for Mount Herzl at 10 a.m.

The cabinet decided that while no period of national mourning will be declared, all national flags on government buildings, schools and army camps will be flown at half-mast during the funeral proceedings. The Magen David will also be flown at half-mast on Israeli missions abroad.

The cabinet decided yesterday, in accordance with Meir's last will and testament, that no eulogies will be delivered.

It turned down a proposal of former minister Yisrael Galili that funeral orations be delivered during the ceremony instead of eulogies. It also turned down his proposal that the bier be placed today in Tel Aviv at Histadrut headquarters for mourners to pay their respects there before it is brought to the Knesset.

At the cabinet session, the ministers stood in silence to pay their respects to the late premier. Acting premier Yigael Yadin, in a valedictory statement, compared Meir to the biblical prophetess Deborah in the period of the Judges.

The ministers then discussed the funeral arrangements as proposed by the cabinet committee on symbols and ceremonies. This is chaired by Energy Minister Yitzhak Moda'i, and includes the ministers of interior and religious affairs, as well as Minister without Portfolio Moshe Nissim.

At the committee meeting, which met beforehand, Education Minister Zevulun Hammer, who is acting interior minister, suggested that a precedent be set for the Meir obsequies, and for future funerals of former ministers, in that the flag be flown at half-mast. This was accepted.

National mourning is only declared when presidents, premiers and ministers die in office.

Moda'i reported on a meeting he held earlier with Galili at which Galili said the requests to have the coffin lie in state in Tel Aviv at Histadrut headquarters, and to allow farewell orations, had originated with "friends of Golda" and he was sure that the bereaved family "would also want this."

(The committee held its first preliminary session, to air tentative funeral arrangements, on November 16. It met two other times.)

The cabinet decided to turn down

(Continued on page 2, col. 4)

Death clouds Oslo awards

By MARK SEGAL
Jerusalem Post Correspondent

OSLO. — Prime Minister Menahem Begin and his family arrived here Friday for what was to have been the joyous occasion of his receiving the Nobel Peace Prize but now overshadowed by the death of former Premier Golda Meir.

King Olav has invited the Premier and Mrs. Begin to stay at the royal palace during his four-day visit to snowbound Oslo. The 75-year-old monarch is very much the father of the Norwegian nation and his hosting of the premier is regarded as a signal of honour here.

It is understood that the Court was taken aback at the refusal of President Sadat to come for the ceremony, which many Norwegians regard as an affront to their king, who had invited the co-laureates of the peace prize to stay at the palace.

Rumours as to Sadat's likely arrival continued to float around the press corps gathered from all parts of the world for today's award ceremony at Akershus Castle. But Sadat's emissary, Said Marei, told Norwegian TV that his president would definitely not be coming.

Begin was reportedly heartened by Marei's optimistic statement regarding Sadat's wish to pursue peace diplomacy and conclude a treaty with Israel.

Begin arrived Friday after an uneventful flight aboard a con-

The Nobel Prize award ceremony will be broadcast live from Oslo over Israel Television from 1:50 this afternoon.

verted 707 jet airliner bearing the insignia of the Israel Aviation Industries, and manned by an air and cabin crew of the Israel Air Force, with pretty first lieutenants serving as stewardesses. Contrary to expectations, he did not talk to the accompanying press party, kept at bay behind a dividing curtain.

The plane landed to extremely strict security arrangements; armed policemen and troops were in evidence around the airfield and on top of the terminal building. According to protocol, Begin's visit is a private one, and he and his party are in Oslo as guests of the Nobel Peace Institute and its committee. On hand as a reception committee were Nobel Peace Prize committee chairman Mrs. Aase Lionaes and other committee members, Norwegian foreign ministry chief of protocol, Israel Ambassador Hava Harel, and leaders of the Oslo Jewish community.

The premier's party was greeted on arrival at the royal palace by a Norwegian Air Force guard of honour, and during their stay at the royal residence are served by liveried footmen. The premier presented the king with a replica of a mosaic floor from a fifth century mikva excavated at Hulda, as well as a copy of his book "The Revolt," with a specially embossed silver cover.

The Norwegian press has ac-

(Continued on page 2, col. 1)

Begin says Golda fought for redemption of Jewish people

Jerusalem Post Reporter

"All her life she fought for the Jewish people, for its redemption and its future," Prime Minister Menahem Begin said of Golda Meir on television from Oslo last night. "She will be inscribed in the annals of our people for all the generations." Begin went on to describe Meir's role in the awakening of the Zionist spirit among Russian Jews when she served as Israel's first ambassador to the Soviet Union.

Begin read a telegram from U.S. President Jimmy Carter who described Meir as "one of us." Carter also called her "a true leader, idealistic, without illusions, with the wisdom to fight and the power to negotiate on behalf of her country."

Begin said: "She immigrated from the United States, and ascended the ladder of national responsibility, through hard work, with devotion, with faithfulness. All the years of her life she fought for the people of Israel, their redemption, their wellbeing, their future.

She was our first emissary to the Soviet Union and she brought the word of Zion to millions of Jews in those days, which are remembered by all, and tens of thousands of Jews came, with great love, to receive Israel's first ambassador. And she herself, as she once told me, said to them: "I thank you for having remained Jews."

She was Israel's spokesman to the nations of the world. And always addressed them with pride, with faith in the eternity of the Jewish people.

She was prime minister of the government of national unity and was prime minister in the days of the agony and the triumph of the Yom Kippur war.

She has historic achievements to her credit in the annals of the Jewish people, and her memory will be engraved in the hearts of our people throughout the generations.

May her memory be blessed."

A rare leader, Navon says

Jerusalem Post Reporter

President Yitzhak Navon, in a televised address to the nation last night, eulogized Golda Meir as "a rare leader, dedicated to the Jewish people" whose accomplishments are "not yet all known."

Meir, he said, identified with every Jewish community in the world and appeared before the world with "great courage and pride." In crises, he continued, "she stood firm with great faith, she practised what she preached to others." The president noted that "one could differ with her, but one always respected her."

In times of crisis, she stood like a firm cliff in the face of the threatening waves, Navon said. She identified completely with whatever task she undertook.

Sadat: Golda was great leader and honest adversary

Egyptian President Anwar Sadat described former premier Golda Meir on Friday as "a political leader of the first category" and "an honest adversary in the course of our confrontation, which we all hope has ended forever."

In messages of condolence addressed to President Yitzhak Navon, Prime Minister Menahem Begin and Meir's family, Sadat praised the late leader as a person worthy of a place in the annals of the Jewish people commensurate with the position she held at the helm of Israeli political life.

The text of Sadat's condolences, aired as an official presidential message, was carried in Cairo by the state broadcasting services as well as by the official Middle East News Agency. It was also featured on the front page of Cairo newspapers yesterday.

The message read as follows:

"I received with sorrow news of the death of Mrs. Golda Meir. As I offer you my heartfelt condolences I must note, for the sake of history, that she was an honest adversary in the circumstances of confrontation between us, which we all hope has ended forever.

"I credit her — as we pursue efforts to achieve an overall and lasting peace for the peoples of the region — for her undeniable role in the process of peace, when she signed with us the first Sinai disengagement accord. She proved herself always to be a political leader of the first category worthy of holding in your history a position commensurate with the position she held in your leadership.

"I repeat my condolences to you."

Special plane to fly 30 Americans

'Miz Lillian' expected to represent Carter at funeral

Jerusalem Post Correspondents

WASHINGTON. — Some 30 prominent Americans, including former secretary of state Henry Kissinger, Senator Abraham Ribicoff and Muriel Humphrey, will fly together to Jerusalem for the funeral of Golda Meir on a special plane.

Israel Ambassador Simcha Dinitz will accompany them.

Secretary of State Cyrus Vance, who will be coming from Cairo, will join the U.S. delegation to the funeral on Tuesday.

As of late last night (after midnight Israel time) the White House had not yet announced who will represent the president's family at the funeral, but there was widespread speculation that it would be either the president's mother, Lillian Carter, or his wife Rosalynn.

(Government sources in Israel said last night that Carter would be represented by "Miz Lillian."

The delegation will include leaders of Congress, trade unions, the American Jewish community and others.

The plane was scheduled to leave the U.S. tonight.

Carter and Vance on Friday called on everyone to rededicate themselves to the search for peace in the Middle East — in memory of Mrs. Meir.

The president issued a statement noting that Mrs. Meir embodied "the best of the Israeli spirit" and said he prayed that her dream of a Mideast peace "will soon be realized."

In his telegram of condolence to President Yitzhak Navon, Carter wrote that "Golda engaged the hearts of the American people as no other leader of a nation has ever done. Her warmth, spirit, and brave work for the cause of Israel drew our two people together...Golda's gift was extended beyond the bounds of her people. She spoke to all humanity."

U.S. Vice-President Walter Mondale, in his telegram to Navon, said, "I want to tell you how privileged I feel to have known Golda Meir...she had a universal conscience...humanity and leadership which has impressed us all — Israel and Americans alike. Golda will stand like a Judith in the chronicles of the modern era. Her career helped

(Continued on page 2, col. 2)

Doctors diagnosed Meir's lymphoma 15 years ago

By HAIM SHAPIRO
Jerusalem Post Reporter

Former prime minister Golda Meir died of lymphoma, a disease she was first diagnosed as having 15 years ago. But the illness did not affect her functioning until the last few months, doctors at Jerusalem's Hadassah Hospital, where she spent her last weeks, told a press conference last night.

Prof. Kalman Mann, director-general of Hadassah Medical Organization, described lymphoma as a neoplastic (tumorous) disease of the lymphatic tissues with low malignancy. Many of its victims live for many years, others for a few years, he said.

He said that when she entered the hospital about four months ago it was for back pains, the origin of which was uncertain. Later it became clear that the disease had affected her bones. Two weeks ago her liver became infected, resulting in jaundice.

Late Thursday night and early Friday morning her liver ceased functioning and she died at 4:30 Friday afternoon. During the time she was a patient, he said, she never mentioned her private struggle and showed the utmost kindness and sensitivity to the entire hospital staff, medical and non-medical.

He added that she knew of her condition in recent years, but was always optimistic. She fought her il-

(Continued on page 2, col. 3)

Carter now optimistic treaty 'soon be signed'

By WOLF BLITZER
Jerusalem Post Correspondent

WASHINGTON. — U.S. President Jimmy Carter, sounding an optimistic note on the Middle East, said on Friday evening that he was confident that an Israeli-Egyptian peace treaty "will soon be signed."

But the president, who was speaking in Memphis, Tennessee, before the Democratic Party's national mid-term convention, did not say whether the treaty would be signed before the December 17 deadline set at Camp David.

Carter's brief remarks on the Middle East took on a different tone than had his rather grim comments on the subject during a news conference on Thursday morning. At that time, Carter had warned of very serious

(Continued on page 2, col. 5)

Vance expected in Oslo today

Jerusalem Post Correspondent

OSLO. — U.S. Secretary of State Cyrus Vance will arrive here today, making a detour in his trip to the Middle East, to speak to Prime Minister Menahem Begin, according to usually well-informed sources here.

The aim of the surprise visit is to "galvanize" the peace negotiations with Egypt, the sources said.

Members of Begin's party declined to comment on the report.

At the same time, press rumours continued to circulate here last night that Egypt's President Sadat might still turn up for today's ceremony.

Vance flies to Cairo in attempt to break deadlock

Post Mideast Affairs Editor and Agencies.

U.S. Secretary of State Cyrus Vance flies to Cairo today for talks with President Anwar Sadat in an attempt to break the deadlock in the peace negotiations with Israel. He is scheduled to arrive in Jerusalem on Tuesday.

Vance said during a stopover in London yesterday that he would be willing to shuttle between Cairo and Jerusalem should the need arise in light of his talks with Sadat and Premier Menahem Begin.

Four main issues were expected to top Vance's agenda:

- Whether the Israel-Egyptian peace treaty, whose draft has already been endorsed by Jerusalem but not by Cairo, should be linked to a timetable defining the phased implementation of self-rule in the West Bank and Gaza.
- Whether the treaty overrides Egypt's mutual defence obligations to the Arab League states.
- Whether Israel is entitled to a fixed quota of crude oil from fields it

(Continued on page 2, col. 4)

Peace treaty still possible by Dec. 17 — Begin

OSLO (AP). — It is not too late to sign an Israel-Egypt peace agreement by the December 17 deadline set at Camp David, Prime Minister Menahem Begin said here last night.

"It shouldn't be impossible," Begin said in a Norwegian state television interview on the eve of receiving the 1978 Nobel Peace Prize, which he shares with Egypt's President Anwar Sadat.

"But of course no one can say surely that this deadline will be kept," he added. "If not by the deadline, maybe it will be signed on a different date.

"We, the Israelis, are prepared to sign the peace treaty as it is," he added. Asked whether that meant the next move was up to the Egyptians, he answered, "Yes, I think it is fair to say so."

In any case, Begin said, "We shall continue with our efforts until the good day comes — and I hope it will be soon — and we sign the peace treaty.

"We believe that agreements should be kept, and we want to keep the Camp David agreement completely, fully."

He said Israel's position regarding Palestinian Arabs "remains, autonomy for our neighbours and security for ourselves."

Khalil: Peace now depends on outcome of Vance mission

CAIRO (AP). — Egyptian Prime Minister Mustapha Khalil said yesterday that the future of the stalled Middle East peace talks depends on the outcome of U.S. Secretary of State Cyrus Vance's mission to Egypt and Israel.

In a telephone interview with the Associated Press after returning from a seven-nation European tour, Khalil also said a meeting with Israel Foreign Minister Moshe Dayan and Defence Minister Ezer Weizman never materialized because the Israelis never sought a get-together.

"I gave them my itinerary, but they never called me," the prime minister said.

Echoing the assessment of Egyptian President Anwar Sadat that the Vance mission is "very important," Khalil said, "They (the peace negotiations) depend on what happens tomorrow after Vance sees the president."

Vance arrives in Egypt today for a two-day stop before proceeding to Israel.

On whether a Vance shuttle or another summit was needed to break the logjam, Khalil said "It depends on what he (Vance) will bring up."

Police arrange funeral security

Senior police officers in the capital will meet today to make plans for the state funeral of Golda Meir on Tuesday.

The police will be involved in security arrangements, traffic direction and maintaining order. The IDF will also participate in the funeral arrangements, including security, and will supply a guard of honour both for the lying-in-state at the Knesset and for the funeral.

Dutch ex-premier here

Joop den Uyl, former prime minister of Holland and chairman of the Dutch Labour Party, arrived in Israel last night as the guest of the Israel Labour Party. He was received at Ben-Gurion Airport by Shimon Peres, chairman of the Labour Party. (Itim)

Teheran airport shut, fear of violence mounts before anti-shah procession

TEHERAN. — The Iranian government yesterday ordered Teheran airport sealed for 46 hours from this morning, creating near panic among the thousands of foreigners waiting for fog-delayed flights out of the riot-torn country.

In a move to placate the faithful during the holy Moslem mourning of Muharram, the government eased the martial law curfew by two hours, allowing people to remain on the streets until 11 p.m. The announcement said the relaxed curfew would be in effect for three days, beginning last night.

Thousands of frightened foreigners, many weeping, jammed fog-bound Teheran Airport in a desperate scramble to flee the country before an expected eruption of new violence.

Dozens of flights were diverted to Kuwait, Bahrain and Damascus, but as the fog lifted they began flying in to evacuate the foreigners. But airlines said there were too few seats for those who wanted to leave and it was sure that many would be left behind.

No reason was given for the airport's closure — from 10 a.m. (08.30 Israel time) today until 8 a.m. (06.30 Israel time) Tuesday.

The U.S. in a surprise move, yesterday flew military aircraft to Iran to evacuate most of the families of its military and civilian workers still there.

A Pentagon official said five C-141 transport jets were being used to fly 662 military dependents out of Teheran because of the difficulty bringing them out by commercial airliners.

Tanks rumbled back onto the streets of the capital yesterday on the eve of a mass protest march by opponents of Shah Mohammed Reza Pahlavi that organizers claim will "determine the future of Iran."

The military-led government, anxious to avoid sparking bloodshed, on Friday eased a martial law ban on processions to permit the march.

Military sources described the armour and heavily armed troops located at army bases in the city as a "precautionary measure."

Today's procession, organized by religious leaders opposed to the Shah's western-influenced reforms, is scheduled to parade along Shahreza Avenue — named after the monarch's father who founded the Pahlavi dynasty in 1923 — to Shahyad Square near the airport.

The National Front, the Shah's main political opponent, said in a statement yesterday the government's decision to allow the march "is certainly a victory... the government had no choice but to back off."

Moslem clergy spokesmen claimed troops opened fire on anti-shah demonstrators in the western city of Tabriz, killing at least 19 persons and wounding scores more, and said at least another 10 died in clashes in the southern holy city of Qom.

The Qom casualties included an army officer killed by a soldier who himself was shot dead by another member of the army in one clash, the spokesmen said.

Anti-shah demonstrators burned banks and other buildings in Isfahan, south Iran, causing heavy damage. Among the buildings destroyed was the Iranian headquarters of the Grumman Aircraft Corporation.

The four-storey building was virtually empty because of the Moslem weekend, but eight Americans in the office block escaped unhurt and took shelter from a screaming mob in the basement of a neighbouring building.

Troops moved in and shot dead at least four rioters, police said. That raised the death toll since Muharram began last Friday night to around 40, although the opposition claims the figure is far higher.

Informed sources reported the homes of several Americans in Tereran, including at least one U.S. embassy staffer, have been

(Continued on page 2, col. 2)

THE JERUSALEM POST

LATE EDITION 2.30 A.M.

IL7.00 (inc. Vat)

TUESDAY, MARCH 27, 1979 • ADAR 28, 5739 • RABI THANI 27, 1399 • VOL. XLIX, No. 14581

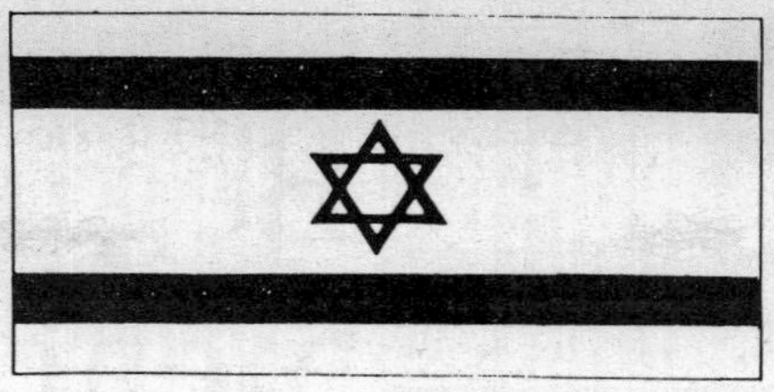

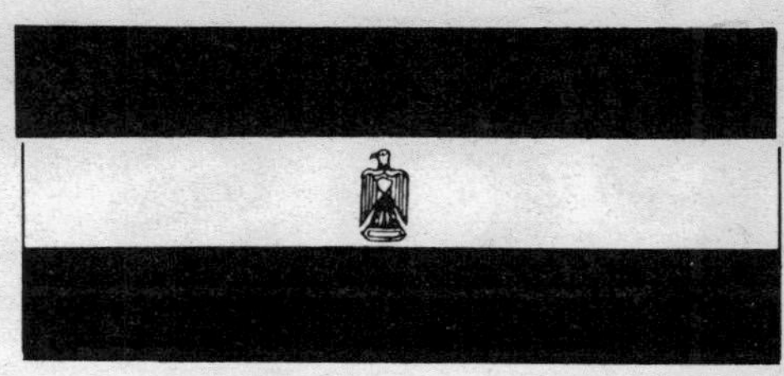

Israel and Egypt sign peace treaty declaring end to 30-year state of war

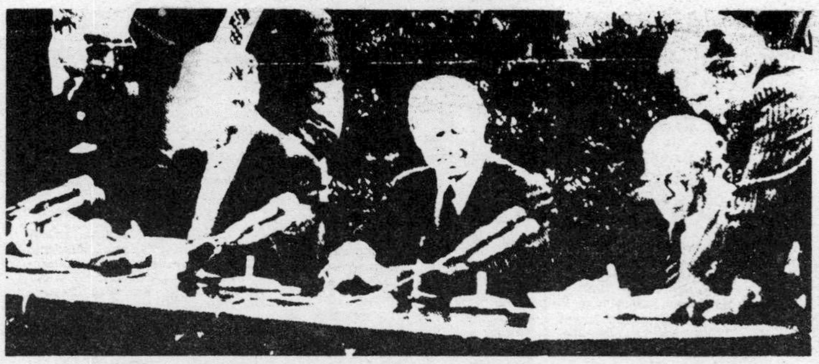

Prime Minister Begin and Egyptian President Sadat put their signatures to the Israel-Egyptian peace treaty in Washington yesterday. (UPI telephoto)

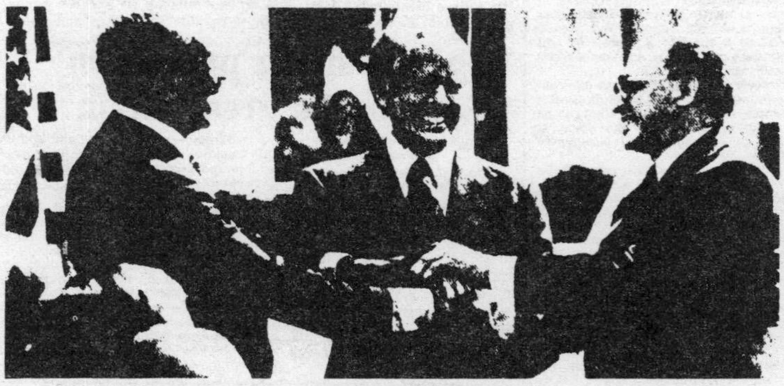

A triple clasp for peace unites an elated President Jimmy Carter, Prime Minister Menahem Begin and President Anwar Sadat following the signing of yesterday's treaty. (UPI telephoto)

Begin, Sadat and Carter pledge shalom, salaam at White House ceremony

By ARI RATH, WOLF BLITZER, DAVID LANDAU and MALKA RABINOWITZ

WASHINGTON. — President Anwar Sadat and Prime Minister Menahem Begin yesterday signed the Israeli-Egyptian peace treaty at a formal White House ceremony on the North Lawn. President Jimmy Carter, whose mediating was instrumental in achieving the agreement, signed as a witness.

It was Israel's first-ever peace treaty with a neighbouring Arab state.

The signing represented the dramatic culmination of 16 months of arduous negotiations beginning with Sadat's visit to Jerusalem in November 1977. All three men, during their remarks delivered at the simple but moving one-hour ceremony, stressed the significance of the occasion, but they also acknowledged the pitfalls on the road ahead.

"Today we celebrate a victory," president Carter declared, "not of a bloody military campaign, but of an inspiring peace campaign."

Only the night before, Carter had predicted that the signing of the treaty would eventually represent the most important achievement of his term in office.

Prime Minister Begin said it was the third "greatest day in my life," explaining that the establishment of the State of Israel on May 14, 1948, and the unification of Jerusalem during the 1967 Six Day War were the first and second greatest days of his life.

Sadat omitted at the last minute a powerful call for Palestinian rights from the text of his address at the White House ceremony. His speech as delivered made no specific reference to the Palestinians, although the prepared text distributed to newsmen earlier had contained a strong appeal to President Carter and the U.S. to support the Palestinians' aspirations for "self-determination and statehood" and to ensure the full implementation of the autonomy plan.

Two hours later the president's spokesman, Saad Zaghloul Nassar, said Sadat's omission had been inadvertent. He said two pages of the speech had been stuck together and the president had turned them both at once.

But some observers wondered whether Sadat's omission of the passage had nevertheless been a deliberate reaction to a noisy demonstration by Palestinian students and supporters, whose chorused slogans could be clearly heard during the ceremony. The demonstrators were kept by police about 300 metres away from the White House grounds.

While Sadat made no reference to Begin, but dwelt on President Carter's role in "performing the miracle," the Israeli leader paid generous tribute to Sadat as a man of "great civil courage" and referred to him as "our friend."

But Sadat did have praise for "the hundreds of thousands of Israelis who remained unwavering in their commitment to peace" — a clear reference to the "Peace Now" movement which, Sadat believes, had a major impact on Israeli policymaking.

President Carter's remarks were carefully uncontroversial. But he underscored "the obstacles that lie ahead" and added: "We must rededicate ourselves to the goal of a broader peace with justice for all who have lived in a state of conflict in the Middle East."

Carter called on other Arab states to join the peace process. "I am convinced," he said, "that other Arab people need and want peace; but some of their leaders are not yet willing to honour these needs and desires."

The omitted passage from Sadat's address asserted that "no one is more entitled to your support and backing than the Palestinian people. A grave injustice was inflicted upon them in the past. They need a reassurance that they will be able to take the first step on the road to self-determination and statehood. A dialogue between the U.S. and the representatives of the Palestinian people will be a very helpful development... We must be certain that the provisions of the Camp David framework... are carried out. There must be a genuine transfer of authority to the Palestinians in their land. Without that the problem will remain unsolved."

But Sadat did remind President Carter of his pledge that "the U.S. is committed without reservation to seeing the peace process through, until all parties to the Arab-Israeli conflict are at peace."

Begin's speech was in many ways the most moving — certainly the most personalized — of the three. He recalled his parents who had perished in the Holocaust, and his voice almost cracked as he declaimed in sonorous tones the words (in Hebrew) of Psalm 126.

Begin spoke of the peace treaty as "the cornerstone of cooperation and friendship" between Israel and Egypt. He, alone among the three leaders, did not dwell on the challenges and difficulties that still lie ahead, nor refer to their common pledge to reach a comprehensive settlement that would embrace Israel's other fronts.

There was, however, one common reference in all three addresses: Isaiah's immortal swords-into-ploughshares prophesy.

Begin raised the only laugh during the hour-long ceremony when he said he agreed with Sadat's praise of Carter as the "unknown soldier" — "but, as usual, with an amendment." Carter's efforts for the peace would be "remembered and recorded for generations to come," he said.

When the prime minister spoke of the day Israel took the Old City as the "second greatest day" of his life, there was applause only from a group of American Jewish leaders sitting together to the left of the signing dais. Most of the audience reacted in stolid silence. They seemed to feel that in making this remark Begin was uttering a pledge, on this most solemn occasion, that Jerusalem would remain reunited under Israel's rule at any cost.

The ceremony started exactly on schedule. Between 1,200 and 1,500 people gathered on the front lawn of the White House and heard the three leaders — "the president of the United States of America, the president of the Arab Republic of Egypt, and the prime minister of Israel" — introduced. There was steady applause as the three men walked together, Carter in the middle, to the heavy table and sat down behind three microphones. All three were smiling.

As a U.S. military band began to play the Egyptian national anthem, the three men, and later the rest of the assembled guests, stood at attention. Carter placed his hand across his heart. Afterwards the Israeli and U.S. anthems were played. Begin was seen singing along in Hebrew and later Carter in English. Sadat's lips did not move during the Egyptian anthem.

It was probably the last major occasion for the Egyptian anthem, since a new one has been commissioned by Sadat and is expected to be released shortly.

The U.S., Israeli and Egyptian flags flapped in the steady breeze behind the three men under partly sunny skies. It was chilly outside with temperatures hovering in the mid-50s (about 13 centigrade).

Throughout the ceremony the constant chanting of protestors, who had assembled across Pennsylvania Avenue, could be heard. They had interspersed themselves among the

(Continued on page 2, col. 5)

BEGIN, SADAT, CARTER SPEECHES ON BACK PAGE

Begin: Open border with Egypt in two months

Jerusalem Post Staff

Free border crossings between Israel and Egypt will start two months after the peace treaty is ratified and El-Arish is handed over to Egypt, Prime Minister Menahem Begin said yesterday. He was briefing the Israeli press in Washington four hours after signing the peace treaty.

Begin said it could take up to three weeks for the Egyptian Peoples Assembly (parliament) to ratify the treaty because of precedural complications. Israel, Begin said, could ratify the treaty within a day.

Begin said that in the last two days of talks wiith President Jimmy Carter and administration officials the U.S. had given Israel a firm commitment that it "won't tolerate violations of the treaty...It is clear that the reference was not to Israel but to other bodies."

Begin said the U.S. commitments included a promise to ensure arms supplies to Israel in the event of war, an assurance that the U.S. would "step up its presence, in the area" and take action to lift naval blockades, and that the U.S. would block attempts to subvert the treaty in the UN Security Council.

Negotiations with Egypt over the form of the autonomy to be granted to the West Bank and Gaza Strip will start within seven to eight weeks, Begin said. The talks will start after instruments of ratification are exchanged and after Israel's ministerial "committee of 11" prepares detailed proposals for autonomy as Israel envisages it.

Negotiations over West Bank and Gaza Strip autonomy will take place in El-Arish, Begin said.

Begin confirmed that he will fly to Cairo next Mondat for what he said would probably be a one-day visit. He said he had raised the proposal to Sadat in his meeting with him yesterday and Sadat had said 'for sure" to his idea.

Begin referred to a "gesture" by Israel following the signing, but said he preferred not to make this public now. It would not harm Israel's security one iota, he added.

Agreement was also reached on the supply of oil from wells off the Sinai shore which Israel is due to evacuate. Israel will withdraw from the Alma field seven months after the treaty ratified, and will immediately start to buy oil from the wells.Before Begin and Sadat's meeting the Egyptians had insisted on a seven-month gap between the evacuation of the field and the first shipments of Sinai oil to Israel, Begin said.

On the 15-year U.S. guarantee on oil supplies, he said "We are grateful, but would not want to activate it, in view of the U.S. own energy crisis. He would not like to hear it said in the U.S.one day that Americans freeze because we gave oil to Israelis — or to Jews."

He disclosed that British Premier James Callaghan told him at their recent meeting that Britain would take Israel into account with regard to North Sea oil next year.

Begin also declared he was against calling early general elections. It would not be right to exploit the peace move, he said, and anyway he

(Continued on page 2, col. 4)

Peres invited to Cairo

WASHINGTON (Itim). — Labour Party leader Shimon Peres has been invited by President Anwar Sadat to visit Egypt. The invitation was tendered yesterday when the two met for an informal chat at the Egyptian Embassy here, before the peace signing ceremony.

Crowds brave bad weather to mark peace

Jerusalem Post Staff

Israelis turned out in the thousands last night to participate in public peace celebrations which were held in most major cities. By far the biggest crowd — between 80,000 and 100,000 — gathered in Tel Aviv's Kikar Malchei Yisrael. Rather smaller crowds, estimated at about 2,000 people, attended ceremonies at the Western Wall in Jerusalem and in Haifa.

The Jerusalemites braved biting winds and unseasonably cold weather to participate in the celebrations. Children and adults joined in spontaneous dances, all for the benefit of the TV cameras that were covering the event for viewers throughout the world. About 100 high school pupils bearing flaming torches were interspersed among the crowd.

A discordant note was struck by some 200 anti-peace demonstrators, mostly Gush Emunim members and students at Jerusalem yeshivas, who held a pray-in at the wall. They said they were demonstrating not only against the signing of the treaty, but also against the "desecration of this holy place by holding a ceremony here."

Yehudi Menuhin topped the list of musicians who entertained the crowd in the plaza. The chief army chaplain, Aluf Gad Navon, recited a

(Continued on page 2, col. 3)

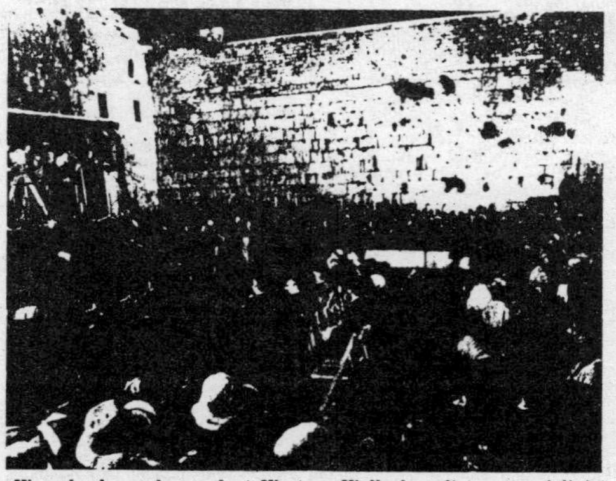

Warmly dressed crowd at Western Wall plaza listens to violinist Yehudi Menuhin serenade the Israel-Egypt peace treaty being signed in Washington. (Rahamim Israeli)

Nine hurt in Old City grenade attack

By DAVID RICHARDSON
Jerusalem Post Reporter

The restrained tone of yesterday's general strike in East Jerusalem was shattered when a grenade exploded in the centre of the Old City a few minutes before the peace treaty signing ceremony last night. Seven tourists and two Arabs were slightly injured.

Security forces already on high alert sealed off the area within minutes and arrested a number of people. This was the only serious incident reported yesterday.

Shortly before nine o'clock the grenade was hurled at a small Old City restaurant and hotel known as "Halil Rahman."

The wounded, among them tourists from the U.S. and Europe, were first taken to the Hospice Hospital in the Old City but were later moved to Shaare Zedek and Hadassah Hospitals.

Israel to move Gaza army headquarters out of town

By ASHER WALLFISH
Jerusalem Post Reporter

Israel has agreed to move the Gaza headquarters of the military government out of the town and into a relatively uninhabited part of the Gaza Strip, at Egypt's request.

Prime Minister Menahem Begin told Acting Prime Minister Zevulun Hammer of this and other gestures requested by Egypt through the medium of the U.S. — some of which were accepted in full or in part. Others were rejected.

After Israel received the original Egyptian request to shift the military government from Gaza over to Beersheba, Israel said "no." The compromise was to keep the headquarters inside the strip, but not in the town, whereupon Egypt sought a fixed date from Israel when the transfer would be carried out. Begin told Hammer that he had not agreed to set a date at this point since it was hard to estimate how long the construction would take. So the Israeli agreement had been given in principle.

Israel rejected an Egyptian request that the IDF stay away from urban areas entirely, but agreed that the presence of soldiers in town would be kept to the minimum level for ensuring law and order.

Israel had rejected an Egyptian request for absolute freedom of political expression, Begin told Hammer, but agreed to allow moderate local expression of a nature not calculated to cause incitement.

Begin said Israel had turned down

(Continued on page 2, col. 6)

Rebel tanks surround Amin in Entebbe

NAIROBI. — President Idi Amin was reported yesterday to be threatened by tanks or to have already fled from his residence near Entebbe airport in the face of advancing forces seeking to overthrow him.

A presidential aide, speaking by telephone from the Ugandan capital of Kampala, quoted the president as saying this morning that he could see 12 tanks from his house.

Ugandan exile sources said the tanks were Ugandan and were commanded by Minister of State for Defence Brig. Emilton Mondo, who had staged a coup against Field Marshal Amin.

But other exile sources said the president had fled Entebbe for the northwestern town of Arua which had been prepared for a final stand against the approaching Tanzanian and rebel Ugandan forces.

Travellers from Uganda said Entebbe was under shellfire from Tanzanian guns at the hill town of Mpigi.

The high ground at Mpigi, from which Tanzanian artillery can reach both the capital and the airport, was said to be the deepest advance of the Tanzanians in the five-month war. Fighting began in October when Ugandan soldiers occupied a large area of northwestern Tanzania and Amin claimed it for Uganda.

Other exiles said Amin offered his own resignation twice during the weekend to military advisers in his defence council, and it was rejected both times.

Despite the reports, Entebbe residents said there were no tanks and no fighting. They said the road from Entebbe to Kampala was open.

Exile leaders, meanwhile, wound up a meeting in Moshi, in northern Tanzania, and announced agreement on the structure of a provisional government after the possible defeat of Amin.

About 120 exiles travelled from the

(Continued on page 4, col. 7)

Anti-peace camp meets in Baghdad

Jerusalem Post Staff and Agencies

Arab opponents of the Israel-Egyptian peace treaty began gathering in Baghdad yesterday to take action against the government of Egyptian President Anwar Sadat.

Iraq, hosting today's anti-peace pact conference, called on Arab governments to take "concrete measures against Sadat on political, economic, informational and mass mobilization levels."

The conference of Arab League foreign and economic ministers took on expanded significance with the arrival in the Iraqi capital last night of Jordan's King Hussein, who is believed to be pushing for an alignment with Syria and Iraq. Hussein flew into Baghdad from Damascus after day-long consultations with Syrian leaders who had just wound up three days of talks with Soviet Foreign Minister Andrei Gromyko about renewed Moscow aid for the Arab eastern front against Israel.

In Moscow, a joint Soviet-Syrian communique yesterday condemned the peace treaty, charging it will only heighten tension in the Middle East. The seven-page statement was released by the official Tass news agency. Soviet Foreign Minister Andrei Gromyko returned from Syria yesterday.

"The main attention at the talks was devoted to the dangerous developments in the Middle East in connection with the conclusion of a separate treaty between Israel and Egypt with the active participation of the United States," the communique said. "The sides have resolutely condemned the treaty as one directed against the interests of the Arabs, including the Egyptian people."

Much of the credibility of the anti-Egyptian camp depends, however, on Saudi Arabia, whose position was swinging between maintaining economic ties with Egypt and joining other Arabs in imposing comprehensive sanctions against Cairo.

Syrian Foreign Minister Abdul-Halim Khaddam tried to dispel doubts in the rejection camp about the Saudi stand by telling Kuwait's "A Siyassa" daily that Damascus believed "Saudi Arabia will fulfil joint Arab resolutions."

Iraq's official newspaper "A-Thawra" yesterday warned that "those who continue supplying financial aid to Egypt are themselves traitors."

The government-inspired Saudi newspapers yesterday came out with surprisingly outspoken attacks on the peace treaty signed in Washington. "A-Riyadh" daily said that yesterday was a "black day for the White House."

The signing of the treaty was yesterday greeted by protest action including demonstrations and assaults on Egyptian embassies in a number of countries.

Yasser Arafat, whose Palestine Liberation Organization sponsored demonstrations and strikes in western Beirut, vowed to chop off the hands of Sadat and said his terrorist organization would chase the Egyptian leader as well as U.S. President Jimmy Carter and Premier Menahem Begin "out of the Middle East."

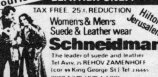

THE JERUSALEM POST

TUESDAY, APRIL 3, 1979 • NISAN 6, 5739 • JAMADI AWWAL 6, 1399 VOL. XLIX, No. 14587

IL8.00 (inc. Vat)

Taxmen after evaders

**

Page 3

Israel colours fly as Begin starts historic Cairo visit

Begin and Sadat toast 'peace and friendship'

Jerusalem Post Correspondent

"No more war — peace and friendship" was the toast proposed by both President Anwar Sadat and Prime Minister Menahem Begin at the state dinner last night at Kubbeh Palace in Cairo.

Prime Minister Begin's reception here, cool at first, became warm and friendly last night as crowds lined the route to the Kubbeh palace where President Sadat tendered the premier and his party a memorable official dinner. The dinner was held on the sumptuous grounds of the 19th century palace and the guest list included leading government personalities.

Sadat, welcoming the Israeli prime minister to his capital, said in a very brief speech that he would continue to fight for love and understanding, good neighbourliness and prosperity.

Begin, replying at greater length, said that the agreement signed in Washington last week was the first step in a comprehensive Middle East settlement. He appealed to the other Arab states, which he said had taken "negative attitudes" toward the negotiations. Begin also said that in his opinion there was no conflict of interests between Israel and Egypt. He foresaw the two working together for liberty and democracy and against totalitarianism and intolerance.

Welcoming Begin to Egypt, Sadat said: "We have started the peace process and have fought and are still fighting and will continue to fight for understanding, for love instead of hate, for good neighbourliness in all meanings of that word for coming generations, for prosperity of our nations, for peace between our nations and for the whole world. Ladies and gentlemen," Sadat concluded, "I ask you to raise your glasses, of our most precious Nile water, for Menahem and Mrs. Begin."

The two clasped hands and drank the toast with water, since alcohol is forbidden to Moslems.

Then it was Begin's turn.

"Today, Mr. President, I returned your visit to Jerusalem — after a short delay but, as the saying goes, 'better late than never.' When you agreed to accept my invitation and come to Jerusalem to address the Knesset, the Israeli people and the whole world, it was a turning point in the history of the two people and of the Middle East.

"We have negotiated for a peace agreement and pursued the aim of 'no more war.' We agreed to cease the state of war and make peace — the peace that we wished and prayed for.

"The negotiations were arduous. There were differences of opinion, but it is the results that are important. One week ago, before the eyes of millions, we signed a peace treaty — a treaty that our dear and great friend (U.S.) President (Jimmy) Carter, also signed. Yesterday the government of Israel ratified the agreement.

"A new dawn is breaking over the Middle East. The sun is rising and bringing the long darkness to an end. Let us thank God for this magnificent achievement. As we say in Hebrew, 'Hallelujah.'

"We know the sufferings of war. Several days ago I saw on our TV a young Egyptian in a wheelchair. I will never forget him. In our country, too, there are many young men in wheelchairs. We will never forget them, the Egyptians and the Israelis. There will be no more wheelchairs for our young men.

"In my opinion, Egypt and Israel never had conflicting interests. Now, we can develop common interests. In the struggle between liberty and totalitarianism, Egypt and Israel will be on the side of liberty. We will support democracy and oppose evil and intolerance.

"Our ancient civilizations can contribute to the values which make life worth living. The Middle East can be a shining example to the world. It was in this spirit that I came to Cairo.

"We hope that this treaty will be the first step towards a comprehensive settlement for all the states in the area and we all hope that it will last forever.

"I appeal to those states who have taken, or have been misled into taking negative attitudes, to abandon their militarism and their negativism and to join in the negotiations. I am convinced that, with the passing of days, this will come about.

"We wish you well, Mr. President, man of courage, man of peace. We wish the Egyptian nation well. Let us raise our glasses to the Egyptian people — to peace."

Begin concluded with a greeting in Arabic.

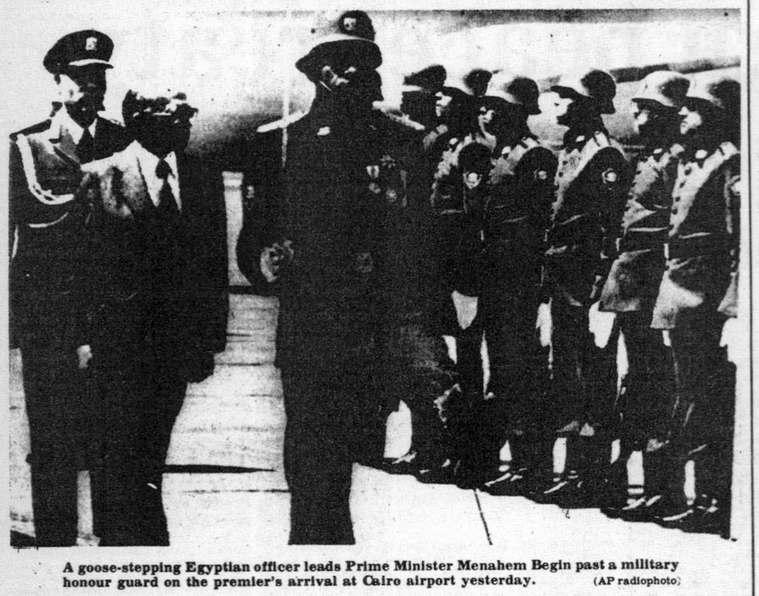

A goose-stepping Egyptian officer leads Prime Minister Menahem Begin past a military honour guard on the premier's arrival at Cairo airport yesterday. (AP radiophoto)

Correct reception for Begin

By ANAN SAFADI
Post Mideast Affairs Editor

CAIRO. — Prime Minister Menahem Begin was given a red-carpet reception marked by strict protocol when he landed in Cairo yesterday, the first Israeli premier to visit the Egyptian capital.

In marked contrast to the ebullient welcome given Egyptian President Anwar Sadat when he visited Jerusalem in November 1977, there were no cheering crowds or white doves when Begin stepped down from the Israel Air Force jet which had brought him here from Ben-Gurion Airport.

Greeted by Vice-President Hosni Mubarak at the head of a receiving line that included most of the city's top officials, Begin made no formal speech at the airport reception. While a lone Star of David flying over the airport building fluttered in a hot *hamsin* breeze, "Hatikva" was played for the first time at an official ceremony by an Arab military band.

One of the first things Begin saw as he stepped off the blue and white jet was an honour guard of goose-stepping officers at the head of a platoon of soldiers dressed in German World War II-type uniforms.

Although it was not a deliberate affront to Begin, who lost his entire family in the Nazi Holocaust, it seemed to underline the fact that Egyptian officialdom would much rather have had the premier come at a later date.

The receiving line waiting for Begin included Deputy Premier Fikry Makram Ebeid, Defence Minister Kamal Hassan Ali, Minister of State for Foreign Affairs Butros Ghali, and Chief of Staff Gen. Mohammed Ali Fahmy, as well as community leaders. Felix Iscaki, the 68-year-old leader of the tiny 500-strong Jewish community was also on hand to greet Begin.

Conspicuously absent was Prime Minister Mustapha Khalil.

Khalil's aides said his absence at the reception was due to a heavy schedule of engagements, but observers attributed Khalil's non-participation to the strained relations that reportedly erupted when the Israeli premier turned down a request by U.S. President Jimmy Carter to negotiate with the Egyptian premier.

Khalil's failure to appear at the airport climaxed two days of rumours about his imminent resignation over Sadat's refusal to postpone the Begin visit while the Arab world was isolating Egypt by withdrawing ambassadors from Cairo. Khalil was also reportedly upset over Sadat's reluctance to take issue with the U.S.-Israel memorandum of agreement, which the silver-haired Egyptian premier had vehemently opposed.

Official circles here denied the resignation rumours, although they told *The Jerusalem Post* that a cabinet reshuffle is expected soon. They declined to divulge the reasons for the expected reshuffle.

Begin reportedly told an Israel TV correspondent that Sadat plans to visit Jerusalem again soon, but that no date has yet been fixed.

Sitting in the VIP lounge at the airport, Begin told Mubarak that Hebrew and Arabic are similar, and the two men discussed the meaning of the word *hamsin*.

Begin theorized that the word referred to the 50 days of the year when the hot dry winds come out of the desert. The Egyptian official said it may refer to the five-day spells of hot weather that the *hamsin* usually brings.

With the Begin visit controversial in Cairo, the authorities appeared to take pains to subdue its impact.

Although it was broadcast live on television and radio, albeit during a late-morning hour when most Egyptians are going about their usual business, minimal efforts were made to feature the event.

During the Egyptian broadcast an announcer commenting on the occasion said "the road is still long on the way to peace in all of the Middle East." Speaking in matter-of-fact tones, the announcer went on: "It requires patience, more mutual faith, more self-confidence, more bridges of understanding and more removal of hatreds and old ambitions."

The Egyptian television crew filming the reception repeatedly aimed their camera at the Israeli flag during the ceremony.

But no sooner had Begin's motorcade sped away from the airport than several Egyptian security men hauled down the flag over the airport building and those outside the terminal. They appeared to pretend to be waving the flags to the long motorcade of Israeli officials, security and newsmen.

Few Egyptian citizens joined the hundreds of military policemen along the route to the Tahra Palace, where Begin and his entourage lunched and stayed the night. But despite the missing crowds, Begin's

(Continued on back page)

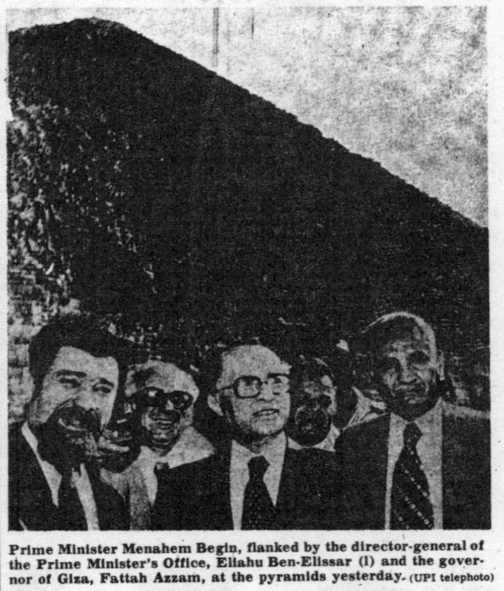

Prime Minister Menahem Begin, flanked by the director-general of the Prime Minister's Office, Eliahu Ben-Elissar (l) and the governor of Giza, Fattah Azzam, at the pyramids yesterday. (UPI telephoto)

Begin, visiting pyramids: 'M.E. can be great again'

Jerusalem Post Staff
and Agencies

Prime Minister Menahem Begin, describing himself as a "simple man," stood before the pyramids of Egypt yesterday and told reporters that the Middle East, the ancient cradle of civilization, could once again become a flourishing world centre.

The hub of a huge crowd of journalists, many of them Israeli, Begin recalled the part the pyramids had played in the history of the Jewish people. This was especially appropriate, he said, on the eve of Pessah.

Begin, wearing a neat suit and tie despite the blistering 42-degree temperature, told reporters, "I did not climb (the pyramid), I am too old for it."

He said the visit, which included a stop at the sphinx and a look at a pharaonic funeral boat, was one of his life-time dreams.

"It is one of the greatest experiences in my life. It makes an impression that cannot be actually expressed in human tongues because they are a unique phenomenon in the history of mankind."

Begin recalled Napoleon's

(Continued on page 2, col. 4)

Tanzanian planes raid second Uganda centre

NAIROBI — Tanzanian warplanes swept into Uganda yesterday for a second day of retaliatory air strikes, bombing a Libyan bank building in Jinja , the nation's second largest city, residents said.

In the besieged capital of Kampala, a huge fuel tank exploded earlier in the morning in the industrial area. One resident said that he saw warplanes flying over Kampala shortly after the explosion, but others said the tank was hit by artillery fire from encroaching Tanzanian ground forces.

Tanzanian warplanes joined the five-month-old war for the first time on Sunday by bombing and straffing President Idi Amin's strategic international airport at Entebbe, 35 km. south of the capital.

Yesterday's air strikes were directed against Jinja, 85 km east of Kampala and a major Ugandan industrial centre.

Residents said three warplanes roared over the town from Lake Victoria, attacking at tree-top level in an apparent effort to avoid detection. They dropped bombs on the Libyan Arab Development Bank and the barracks building of the two Ugandan army battalions based in the city.

The residents said the bombings did not cause any serious injuries, but caused considerable panic sending townspeople into the streets from their homes and offices.

Local news reports quoted other witnesses in Jinja as saying that President Amin arrived in the town shortly after the bombing and personally tried to prevent the widespread panic. These reports said that Amin stopped several people running away in the streets, ordering them to return to work.

Amin has not been seen in public for several days, though diplomatic sources in Kampala said he was definitely in the capital directing the war effort against the approaching Tanzanians.

In Tripoli yesterday, Libya said that it will not abandon Amin in his hour of difficulty. The senior Libyan who made the statement declined to comment on reports of active Libyan involvement in Uganda and said he had no news on the military situation in that country.

(Residents and diplomats in Kampala had reported that up to 2,000 Libyan soldiers were in and around the capital manning artillery brigades following what they called the virtual disintegration of the Ugandan army.)

In Moscoan Ugdan students yesterday staged their second demonstration in five days outside the Libyan embassy to protest against Libyan military support for Amin. (UPI, Reuter)

Rockets hit U.S. embassy in Beirut

BEIRUT (AP). — The U.S. Embassy in Beirut was hit by two rockets yesterday, but no one was injured, embassy and police officials reported.

Two unidentified men fired the rockets from approximately 135 metres away at the front of the embassy, and then escaped by car, the officials said. The rockets slammed into the first and fifth floors of the building. Two rooms were badly damaged.

The attack came in the wake of threats from Palestinian terrorists against "American interests" in the Middle East. But no one has claimed responsibility for the attack, officials said.

Israel is 'usurper,' Khomeini declares

QOM (UPI). — Revolutionary leader Ayatollah Ruhollah Khomeini condemned Israel as a "usurper" yesterday and called for the return of Jerusalem to the Arabs.

The 78-year-old Iranian leader spoke as he met Archbishop Hilarion Capucci and Palestinian leader Hani al-Hassan in his religious retreat in this holy Shia town 130 km. south of Teheran.

Heartfelt welcome for Begin at synagogue

By N.D. GROSS
Jerusalem Post Correspondent

CAIRO. — Many of the pitifully small remnant of this city's once-flourishing Jewish community assembled in the "Great Synagogue" in downtown Cairo yesterday afternoon for the *minha* service with Premier Menahem Begin.

The community now numbers 170 souls, mainly elderly. Their past glories were recalled by Begin in a two-minute address at the conclusion of the service.

He told the congregation, heavily outnumbered by the press corps, "Many of your sons are now gathered with us in Israel...We bring you greetings of peace."

Visibly excited, the premier then led the eager congregation in singing "Heveinu Shalom Aleichem." After beseeching the Almighty's blessing for peace on the entire House of Israel, Begin left amid ululations and loud applause. "Kaddish" at the conclusion of the service was recited by veteran JNF worker Cyrus Weiler of Jerusalem, whose two sons fell in wars with Egypt.

Amateur cantor Morad Gabai, who led the service, told me that the synagogue authorities had wanted to arrange a reception for Begin. But the Egyptian government vetoed this.

All signs of popular sympathy for the Israeli leader were forestalled by the security police who stopped passersby from collecting near the synagogue by stationing rifle-toting guards at three-metre intervals along the road leading to the synagogue and one-metre intervals in the immediate vicinity of the synagogue.

Only after strong persuasion by Israeli officials did local security officials, after a long delav, permit journalists beyond a minimal number to enter the synagogue.

As with other ceremonies, Israel flags, hoisted outside the synagogue barely minutes before the premier's arrival, were taken down immediately afterwards. This official semi-boycott contrasted strongly with the friendship shown by the populace whenever contact was established with visiting Israelis.

A gaily coloured canopy was erected outside the dignified 77-year-old stone building, with its 22-metre high cupola. But the canopy's design lacked all Jewish content, being the same Islamic art design as on triumphal arches honouring Sadat throughout this large city.

Older members of the community were moved to tears by the visit of Israel's premier, particularly one who helped bring peace between the country where they live and make a living and the country where many of their sons and almost all their hearts and souls live.

David Salam Sham, a withered ancient man, asked me with pathetic eagerness when former Egyptian Jews in Israel would be able to visit their birthplace again, and when he could go to Israel "at last."

Several people I spoke to said they were treated well by the authorities but yearned for contact with Israel.

However, one boy six months short of his Bar Mitzva, Michael Yosef Dana, seemed singularly unmoved by the occasion. He studies with all the community children at Lycee Babylon where he said they are taught Hebrew.

Dayan favours settlement— with consideration for Egypt

By ASHER WALLFISH
Post Diplomatic Correspondent

Foreign Minister Moshe Dayan said yesterday that while Israeli settlement in Judea and Samaria must and will go forward, it is up to Israel to show a degree of consideration for Egyptian sensitivities.

Briefing senior officials in his ministry, Dayan said that if Israel carries out a settlement programme circumspectly, there is no real risk of torpedoing its relations with Egypt.

Israel has six years at least to pursue its plans in Judea and Samaria, Dayan said — the current year, while autonomy is being negotiated, and the five years following, until new measures may possibly be taken. So settlement need not be a grab, he said.

The manpower available for settlements and the resources available to finance them are such that a faster tempo of settlement than at present is not very likely, he said.

Dayan warned that negotiations over the autonomy and the implementation of autonomy will present numerous obstacles. Egypt has to prove to itself and to the Arab world that it is gaining the maximum possible for the Palestinians, he noted. At the same time, the fact that the arrangements are treated as temporary, on a five-year basis, will enable both sides (Egypt and Israel) to reach a compromise, he believed. Both countries will always be able to reassure themselves that what is not attained now can always be fixed up later.

In the coming fortnight, Dayan said, the government will have to decide what principles to adopt, in advance of the autonomy negotiations, and who will conduct the negotiations on Israel's behalf.

In another development, some top men in the Foreign Ministry are said to resent the fact that Dr. Eliahu Ben-Elissar, director-general of the Prime Minister's Office, will keep complete control of all matters dealing with Israel-Egypt relations through the new committee of senior officials which he chairs. The committee was set up by the cabinet on Sunday.

These ministry men feel that their department is more qualified to handle the sphere of relations with Egypt than the Prime Minister's Office, especially on day-to-day matters which diplomatic and consular officials take care of as a matter of course — as distinct from major national decisions.

Also, they say, Ben-Elissar's maximalist approach, as reflected in the autonomy programme he drafted, may not make him the most flexible pilot for such a delicate task as guiding relations with Egypt.

Sea-launched terror attempt foiled; navy captures ship

By JOSHUA BRILLIANT
Jerusalem Post Reporter

The navy last week seized a cargo ship carrying six Fatah terrorists headed for a mission in Israel, the army spokesman reported yesterday.

The six terrorists were caught off Israel's Mediterranean coast on board the 500-ton Stefanie, the spokesman said. The vessel flew a Cypriot flag but was owned by the Fatah, he said.

A photograph the spokesman's office released suggested that terrorists had planned to leave the Stefanie at sea and cover the final stretch in a black rubber dinghy. But military sources would not say where they had planned to land. A senior military source said he believed they had wanted to force Israel to release prisoners.

The army spokesman merely reported that the terrorists had planned "a murderous attack" and that they had told their investigators that Abu Jihad, head of Fatah's military arm, had sent them.

The ship's five-man crew was captured along with the six terrorists.

The terrorists had been heavily armed with three LAW and RPG rocket launchers, three Kalachnikov assault rifles, an M-16 assault rifle, a Sterling sub-machinegun, and five pistols. They were also in possession of large quantities of explosives, detonators, and shells as well as leaflets in English, Hebrew and Arabic explaining their operation. The Fatah attempt came a few weeks after the navy intercepted the Cypriot Ginan which had carried terrorists. Earlier, at the end of September, Abu Jihad sent terrorists on board the Agios Dimitrios, which was intercepted near Eilat. Another squad was caught in a boat near Rosh Hanikra.

(See picture — Page 3)

Gas bubble at Harrisburg reactor decreases in size

HARRISBURG, Pennsylvania (AP). — A Nuclear Regulatory Commission official said yesterday that a dangerous gas bubble inside the disabled Three Mile Island nuclear reactor "is showing dramatic decreases in size." He also said the fuel temperature was dropping and releases of radiation were being confined.

"I think it's safer than yesterday," said Harold Denton, chief of operations for the NRC.

As area residents jammed local banks to withdraw money in the event of an evacuation, Denton briefed reporters on the bubble shrinkage and temperature decline, saying there is still some risk, but adding he did not believe evacuation was "warranted."

"I didn't expect such a rapid change," he said of the declining bubble measurements.

If the bubble kept growing inside the reactor vessel, it could expose the uranium core — a remote chance that could trigger the worst possible catastrophe, a melt-down. In a melt-down, the core melts, burns through the reactor vessel and sinks into the ground releasing much radioactivity. At its worst, a melt-down would contaminate thousands of square miles with radiation.

The bubble, made up of hydrogen and oxygen from chemical decomposition within the reactor core, was being "bled" by letting the gas dissolve in the constantly circulating cooling water and then allowing it to escape from the water outside the reactor. Denton said engineers would continue to follow this technique.

He confirmed a report by an official of Metropolitan Edison, which runs the facility, that the danger of an explosion caused by the bubble had been substantially reduced over the past 24 hours.

(Nuclear power — Page 4)

Cairo says it can survive Arabs' financial boycott

CAIRO. — The Minister in charge of economic cooperation yesterday downgraded the importance of Arab aid to Egypt's ailing economy and said Cairo will easily survive the boycott imposed at the Baghdad conference by Arab countries opposed to Egypt's peace treaty with Israel.

Gamal al-Nazer, the minister, said Arab aid to Egypt last year represented a mere 25 per cent of the total volume of financial assistance extended to the country.

He said that Egypt got $150m. as a grant and $600m. as a loan from Arab countries. On the other hand, loans extended by the U.S., Western European countries and international organizations exceeded $2b., he said.

The opposition Socialist Labour Party yesterday extended qualified welcome to the treaty, but warned it might have negative consequences for Egypt. The party, with 20 seats in a 360-seat parliament dominated by President Anwar Sadat's National Democratic Party, issued the statement after five meetings headed by party leader Ibrahim Shukri.

Meanwhile, the anti-Egypt action continued yesterday, with an official source in Amman announcing that Jordan has decided to sever political and diplomatic relations with Egypt. The announcement followed a cabinet meeting which reviewed the Baghdad decisions.

Jordan also blamed the U.S. for sponsoring a "separate peace" between Egypt and Israel. Prime Minister Mudar Badran told the 60-member consultative council that, before the treaty got under way, Jordan had submitted 12 questions to President Jimmy Carter's administration regarding the nature of the Middle East peace drive.

He said the U.S. answers were unsatisfactory, and "we realized from the start that a separate peace treaty was being arranged. (Reuter, AP)

THE JERUSALEM POST

Maccabi back in lead ★ Page 11

IL8.00 (inc. Vat)

SUNDAY, APRIL 22, 1979 • NISAN 25, 5739 • JAMADI AWWAL 25, 1399 • VOL. XLIX, No. 14601

Highest priority for Negev bases

By WOLF BLITZER
Jerusalem Post Correspondent

WASHINGTON. — President Jimmy Carter has requested that the highest priority — code-named "DX Brickbat" — be used by the U.S. Army Corps of Engineers in constructing two new Israeli airbases in the Negev.

This was disclosed by Maj.-Gen. James A. Johnson of the corps during a briefing in New York on Friday for more than 350 businessmen anxious to win contracts for the building of the bases.

"DX Brickbat," Johnson said, is a rarely used priority that gives the government the right to pre-empt materials from any production line or any means of transport. It is available only at the president's discretion to meet emergency situations.

The two bases have to be built during the next three years, about half the normal time required, Johnson said. This means that contracts will have to be concluded on an accelerated schedule. Proposals for the management assistance contract must be filed by Tuesday, for example, and the Corps of Engineers will then interview the top three candidates and award the contract by May 4.

"The Washington Post" reported yesterday that the corps requires proposals for the design and construction of the bases by May 1 and will interview the top five before making the award on May 15.

Johnson said that initially the Pentagon had thought of duplicating the Sinai bases in the Negev, but that because of new technological developments, a large part of the two bases will be newly designed.

Johnson said Israeli construction resources are fully committed elsewhere and only limited Israeli manpower will be available to the winning contractors.

According to "The Washington Post," Israel's ports will be prepared to expedite shipments of building materials. Johnson said the ports and available air bases are adequate to handle the shipments so that new ports will not have to be built — as they were in Saudi Arabia when it began a massive construction programme.

Johnson said the prime contractors for each base and for management assistance to the Corps of Engineers must be companies that are wholly American-owned, but that they may sub-contract with non-American companies as long as those companies are based in nations that have diplomatic relations with Israel.

Companies will not be barred simply because they are working in Arab countries, Johnson said, but their proposals will be carefully examined.

The construction of one of the bases will require moving about four million cubic metres of earth. About 1.5 million cubic metres will have to be moved at the other base, the general said. Each base will need about 330,000 cubic metres of gravel and other materials and about 100,000 cubic metres of both concrete and asphalt.

South Lebanon quiet but tense

Weizman: Haddad is a true patriot

Jerusalem Post Staff
and agencies

Defence Minister Ezer Weizman expressed unequivocal support on Friday for Major Sa'ad Haddad, Christian commander who last week declared an autonomous mini-state in southern Lebanon, and called upon the Lebanese government to take "several serious steps" to free Lebanon from the PLO terrorists.

Weizman was speaking as the situation in southern Lebanon, tense since armed clashes between UNIFIL, Haddad's forces and the terrorists towards the end of last week, began to return to normal. The fighting had started after a Lebanese battalion moved into southern Lebanon to join UNIFIL forces there.

Weizman, speaking in an interview on Army Radio, called Haddad a "true Lebanese patriot," like the Lebanese Christian militias in north Lebanon, who also object to the presence of Palestinian Arabs and terrorists in their country.

He said it is very possible that the Syrians (whose troops occupy most of Lebanon) have more influence on the actions of Lebanese President Elias Sarkis than Israel does on Haddad.

Israel is "still relatively restrained" in its reaction to recent terrorist attacks — all of which can be traced to Lebanon, the Defence Minister said. He advised the Lebanese government to cope with the problem.

UNIFIL forces, placed in a virtual state of siege since last Wednesday, received supplies yesterday when Haddad agreed to open roads in territory under his control to UNIFIL vehicles. A spokesman for Haddad said that the roads were opened permanently as a result of an agreement reached with UNIFIL, but UN spokesman Hugo Rocha said the roads were opened for only two hours and that there was no such agreement.

There was hardly any shooting in Southern Lebanon yesterday, but there was still much tension — a large part of it a result of the killing of a South Lebanese telephone technician last week.

Haddad says the man, who was laying a telephone line near UNIFIL headquarters at Nakura, had been killed by a Dutch soldier who opened fire at short range without any provocation. Rocha said the man, a Beduin, was found dead after a burst of fighting in the area, but added that UNIFIL could not confirm how he died.

Rocha also said that UNIFIL is in contact with UN headquarters in New York about a demand made by the man's relatives for compensation. He said the relatives had vowed to start a blood feud with the Dutch forces unless a *sulha* (reconciliation) with its ensuing compensation payment was arranged.

Another matter in dispute is the question of who bombarded the UNIFIL headquarters in Nakura after midnight on Wednesday. Sources in the area said that, in a meeting between Israel, UN liaison officers, UNIFIL representatives and Haddad, it was agreed that it was terrorists, and not Haddad's men, who attacked the UNIFIL camp.

But this was vehemently denied by Rocha, who told *The Jerusalem Post* that UNIFIL stands by its version that it was "the militias who opened fire."

Haddad met with UNIFIL officers and Israeli liaison officers twice last week: once before dawn on Thursday and again on Friday. Sources close to the meeting said that UNIFIL had agreed to publicly exonorate Haddad's forces of having fired at the UN troops.

But Rocha denied that any such commitment had been made and said the meetings were merely one of UNIFIL's attempts to keep peace in the area.

Haddad and the predominantly Christian leadership of the new "Free Lebanon" he declared last week are also incensed at a statement made by UN Secretary General Kurt Waldheim in New York on Friday. In a seven-page report to the Security Council, Waldheim accused the militiamen of harassing UNIFIL and using "forceful means" to impede the movement of the Lebanese army battalion to UNIFIL positions.

Travellers arriving from central Lebanon told residents of the Marjayoun area in Haddad's enclave that the units of the Lebanese battalion — split up between several UNIFIL positions — have been fired upon by terrorists. The passengers said the terrorists wish to prod the Lebanese battalion commander into moving into the Marjayoun area and up to the Israel border to the south.

Waldheim's statement also accused "armed elements" — a UN codeword for the PLO or Lebanese leftists — of having started an artillery duel with Israel by firing into Galilee.

In view of the strong support the PLO enjoys from the overwhelming majority of UN members, this derogatory mention was seen by UN observers to be highly unusual.

The Israeli view on UNIFIL's function in South Lebanon was expressed by Weizman in his interview. The minister said he is not against the deployment of UNIFIL in South Lebanon, and "does not belittle its value."

But at the same time he said: "I think one can manage without it, but we can also live with it. We didn't propose (its creation), and we didn't oppose it. There is no doubt that the UN force has contributed something, even a great contribution, and paid for it with casualties. But I see the UN force as a temporary arrangement, and eventually hope we will reach an understanding with Lebanon like the one reached with Egypt."

The spiritual leader of the Druse community in Israel, Sheikh Amin Tarif, on Friday asked the Israeli authorities to arrange a meeting between himself and Major Haddad. The 84-year-old sheikh wants to discuss ways of preventing the bombardment of the Druse town of Hasbaya in South Lebanon, where the Druses' most holy places are located.

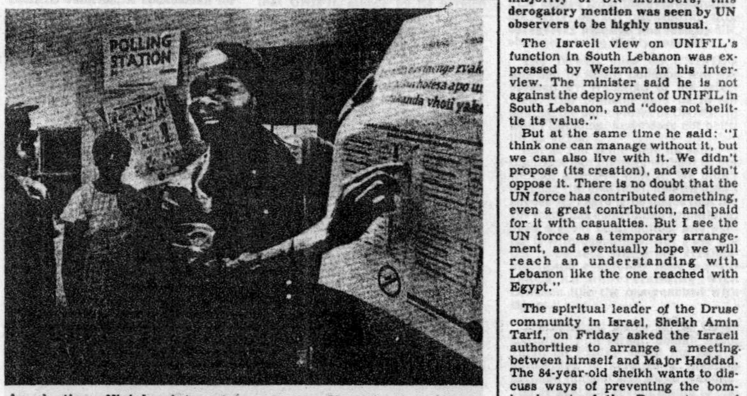

An election official points out to voters at Urungwe in northern Rhodesia how to mark their ballot paper with the aid of a poster designed to help black voters, many of whom are illiterate.
(UPI telephoto)

End of an era in Rhodesia

60% vote for majority black rule

SALISBURY. — A week that ended an era in Rhodesia closed last night with black buglers sounding a retreat in memory of receding white rule, as 60 per cent of all races voiced a massive vote of confidence in black majority rule.

Several hundred observers, mostly white, stood to attention in the grounds of the president's mansion in suburban Salisbury to hear the sounding of the retreat and watch the lowering of the green and white flag of white-run Rhodesia.

The ceremony was staged as results flowed in from the country's first one-man, one-vote election — which will install a black-dominated government after 88 years and seven months of white supremacy.

Election officials predicted that a last minute flurry of voters in the five-day parliamentary poll, which opened on Tuesday, would push the final turnout to 65 per cent or more of the electorate.

By the time the polls closed on Friday, they said, the figure had already reached 59.9 per cent, but the final result would not be known until later today.

Prime Minister Smith, speaking at a press conference on Friday said that the first black-majority rule elections constituted an endorsement that should produce diplomatic recognition from Britain and the U.S. "What more do you want?" said Smith, gesturing into a blinding mass of television camera lights and acknowledging that he will shortly hand over to a black prime minister.

As he spoke, the military announced that Rhodesian warplanes had streaked into neighbouring Mozambique to pound Communist-supplied guerrilla targets in Gaza province on the road to Maputo, the capital.

Last week the air force smashed up guerrilla bases in neighbouring Zambia on five separate missions. A brief war communique said all the aircraft returned safely to base, underlining Rhodesia's apparent freedom of the Southern African skies.

Mirroring the new defiant confidence in Salisbury, Smith said, "We'll continue knocking the living daylights out of these camps every day."

He said if the current changes did not yield international recognition, Rhodesia could hold the security situation indefinitely.

John Masunda, a guerrilla who surrendered to Rhodesian forces last week, said he thought the high voter turnout would have an effect on other guerrillas. "Some more will come home if the vote is big enough," he said.

Asked to go through the voting process slowly in order to allow pictures to be taken at each step, Masunda was kept holding his vote poised over the ballot box for ten minutes while photographers snapped away. He was the second guerrilla to surrender to security forces during the election week.

In Bulawayo on Thursday, more

(Continued on page 2, col. 4)

Kremlin seeking 'most-favoured nation' status

Surprise release for 5 Jews jailed as Prisoners of Zion

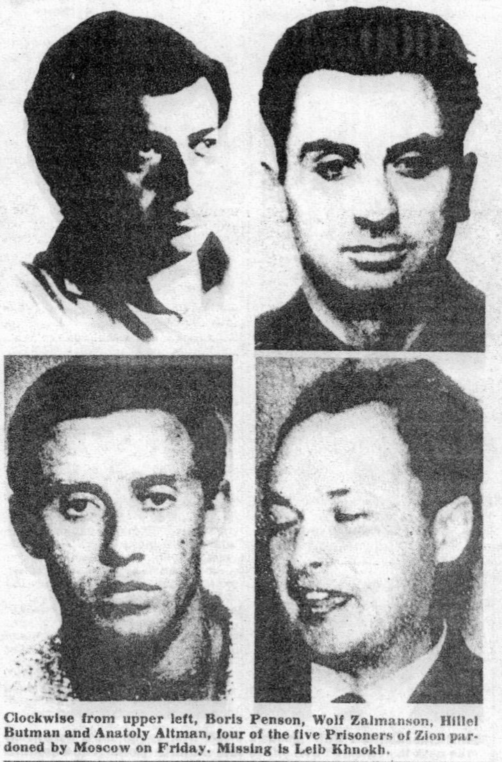

Clockwise from upper left, Boris Penson, Wolf Zalmanson, Hillel Butman and Anatoly Altman, four of the five Prisoners of Zion pardoned by Moscow on Friday. Missing is Leib Khnokh.

Jerusalem Post Staff and Agencies

MOSCOW. — Five Prisoners of Zion, convicted in 1970 of attempting to steal a Soviet plane in order to be able to emigrate to Israel, have been given surprise pardons and releases from Soviet jails by personal order of President Leonid Brezhnev.

In Israel, Prime Minister Menahem Begin told family members of the released men at a reception in his home that "there are grounds to believe the Soviet Union will release all the Prisoners of Zion and let them come to Israel."

Begin gave U.S. President Jimmy Carter a list of Prisoners of Zion while in Washington last month to sign the peace treaty with Egypt.

But Jewish activist circles in Moscow were cautious last night about expressing optimism that the five releases — plus a spate of exit visas issued to several other Prisoners of Zion — signalled a turnabout in Soviet policy on Jewish emigration.

Wolf Zalmanson, 39, brother of Sylva Zalmanson, said in a telephone call from Moscow to Riga, that he and Boris Penson, 33; Anatoly Altman, 36; Leib Khnokh, 35; and Hillel Butman, 46; were all surprised by their releases, which came late Thursday night and Friday morning.

Zalmanson, along with the other four and 21 other Jewish activists, was convicted for his role in an aborted airplane theft from Leningrad in 1970. He said he didn't know what prompted the sudden Kremlin move.

"Nobody expected them. Nobody asked for them," Zalmanson said about the pardons, which were personally signed by Brezhnev.

He said the authorities were "doing all they can to speed and ease the formalities" to issue the exit visas the Jews had sought so long.

Still in prison for the hijacking attempt are Zalmanson's brother-in-law Eduard Kuznetsov and Mark Dymshits, who were both originally sentenced to death but had their sentences commuted to 15 years. Also still jailed are Alexei Murzhenko, 14 years, and Iosif Medelvich and Yuri Fyodorov, 12 years each.

Begin praised the five men for their courage and promised a state reception to greet them when they arrived in Israel. "I shall personally go with you (the relatives) to greet them," Begin said.

Jewish activist circles in Moscow linked the releases to Moscow's desire to gain most-favoured-nation status in its trade dealings with the U.S. They said that there was also probably a connection between the releases and the current visit of a Congressional delegation to the Soviet Union.

The delegation includes Charles Vanik, the Ohio Democrat who wrote the Jackson-Vanik amendment that links U.S. trade benefits for the Soviet Union to Jewish emigration.

Asked to comment on the pardons, Vanik said that he was encouraged "by the developments that were taking place." He cited record emigration figures during the past months — including 4,418 Soviet Jews reaching Vienna last month from Moscow — and praised "cooperation" by government offices issuing visas.

U.S. officials said that emigration statistics for the first three months of 1979, showed that nearly 50,000 Jews may be allowed out of the Soviet Union this year. The previous annual record was about 35,000, in 1973.

Vanik said that he might be in favour of invoking a waiver in the amendment that would grant credits and favour tariff reductions in case of a freer Soviet emigration policy.

He said that such a waiver would amount to using the amendment instead of revoking it, but added that during a meeting last week with Premier Alexei Kosygin, the Soviet leader called the use of the waiver an "inadequate but constructive step."

He also indicated that a second look at U.S. trade policy with Moscow might be in order now that the U.S. has normalized ties with Peking.

"I just can't believe that human rights are better in the People's Republic of China than in the Soviet Union," he said.

Western observers in Moscow said the Kremlin has been trying to improve its relations with the U.S. while the two countries near agreement on a Strategic Arms Limitation Pact, and they linked the surprise Moscow moves to that impending agreement.

Activists meeting with the congressmen in Moscow said on Friday that they told the delegates not to be afraid to normalize relations with China while keeping restrictions on the Soviet Union.

Jewish sources who attended the Thursday night meeting told journalists that the congressmen showed concern that granting "most favoured nation status" to China might anger the Soviets, who have been seeking the same privileges from Washington.

The congressmen reportedly said they were concerned such Soviet anger might backlash into further crackdowns on Jewish dissidents in the Soviet Union.

In another surprise move, Leningrad activist Feliks Aronovick received permission to emigrate, the National Conference on Soviet Jewry announced on Friday in New York. Aronovick has been separated from his wife for over three years and has never seen his child.

And Leonid Slepak, the second son of exiled activist Vladimir Slepak, said he received an exit visa. Slepak, 19, said on Friday he had received the visa after avoiding the army for almost one year. His father, who has sought permission to leave the Soviet Union for nine years, was sent to Siberia last June for "malicious hooliganism." He had hung a banner from his balcony window announcing his desire to leave the country.

Wolf Zalmanson, who was the first

(Continued on page 2, col. 6)

U.S. and Israel sign trade agreement

Post Economic Reporter

A trade agreement between Israel and the U.S. was signed on Friday at the end of the two-day visit of the U.S. Trade Mission to Israel and Egypt headed by Special Ambassador Robert S. Strauss.

The agreement, two years in negotiation, provides for $325m. worth of Israeli exports to the U.S. It also commits the Americans to tariff reductions on Israeli goods averaging 70 per cent within the next decade.

Strauss told reporters on Friday that the mission he headed was no ordinary trade trip. President Jimmy Carter had decided on it immediately after Prime Minister Menahem Begin telephoned him to report on his visit to Cairo, he said.

Carter had asked Strauss to organize a high-level economic mission to Egypt and Israel in order to see what the U.S. could do to bring more than military hardware to the region. Both Israel and Egypt faced serious economic problems, and it was important to ensure their economic stability, Carter told him.

The delegation, which included Senators Abraham Ribicoff and David Durenberger, together with high-ranking U.S. government officials and businessmen, spent two days in both Egypt and Israel, "to get a first, intelligent impression of what the U.S. can do to encourage private investment in the two countries."

Replying to a question by *The Jerusalem Post*, Strauss said his mission had dealt with bilateral relations with each country and had not sought to establish economic ties between the two countries. The promotion of mutual commercial relations may be premature at this stage, Strauss said.

In reply to another question, Strauss said that the U.S. expects to benefit not only politically, but also economically, from the establishment of peace in the Middle East. The man in the street, he said, will judge the peace in terms of the concrete advantages that result.

Ribicoff was asked for his view of the American reaction to the huge amounts of additional U.S. aid for both countries that would stem from the treaty. He said that, while he could not speak for the other 99 U.S.

(Continued on page 2, col. 4)

Cairo picks diplomat for Sinai ceremony

CAIRO (AP). — Sa'ad Afra, an officer in the 1948 war with Israel and now a veteran diplomat, will head Egypt's delegation to the Sinai ceremony at which Egypt and Israel will exchange peace-treaty documents of ratification.

An Egyptian foreign ministry spokesman said that Afra, undersecretary of state at the ministry, was chosen after Israel announced the appointment of Eliahu Ben-Elissar, director-general of Prime Minister Menahem Begin's Office, to head the Israel side.

The ceremony is to be held on Wednesday at the U.S. early-warning station in the Sinai buffer zone separating Israeli and Egyptian troops. It will trigger a nine-month countdown for Israeli troop withdrawal from the western part of the Sinai.

Afra, in his mid-50s, was formerly Egypt's ambassador to Poland and then to Yugoslavia. He made his debut in political life in 1953 after participating in the army's "Free Officers" movement that toppled the monarchy in 1952.

He reportedly served for a while in the intelligence department before heading the press section of the Ministry of Information. He joined the Foreign Ministry in the early 1960s and was until recently head of the Arab Affairs Department.

Afra now heads the overall section for financial, administrative, consulate, emigration, press and cultural relations with the Eastern bloc.

Weizman and Eitan to Cairo today

By HIRSH GOODMAN
Post Military Correspondent

Defence Minister Ezer Weizman will be leaving for Cairo aboard an air force jet this morning for three days of talks with his Egyptian counterparts. The minister may also meet with Egyptian President Anwar Sadat.

Weizman, who will visit Alexandria tomorrow, is accompanied by Chief of Staff Rafael Eitan, O.C. Military Intelligence Yehoshua Saguy, and the chief of the Israel delegation to the joint Israeli-Egyptian military committee, Tat-Aluf Dov Sion. Weizman and Eitan are taking their wives with them.

The visit, which will also include several ceremonial acts, such as the laying of a wreath by Weizman at the grave of the Unknown Egyptian Soldier, will be devoted to discussions on matters of mutual security interest between the parties, including formalizing some aspects of the Israeli pullback from Sinai.

Arab gunmen face Belgian court

BRUSSELS (JTA). — The two Arab terrorists responsible for the Brussels airport attack last week, Khaled Dayek Dokh and Mahmud Hussein, were yesterday officially charged with attempted homicide.

The two men are due to be tried by the Brabant criminal court and, if found guilty, could face life sentences.

They have confessed to having carried out the April 16 attack at Brussels airport, which wounded 16 people, including a number of children.

Unconfirmed reports in the Belgian press say the two terrorists were guided during their stay in Brussels by the wife of an Arab diplomat. The papers did not report the country her husband represents.

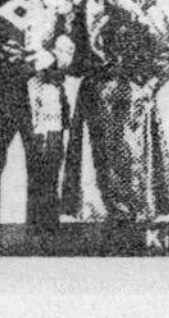

Egypt reports 99.9% vote for treaty, internal reform

CAIRO. — Egypt's Anwar Sadat yesterday issued a decree dissolving parliament as a result of a near-unanimous vote in favour of his domestic political reform programme.

The government reported that the referendum on Thursday also resulted in near-unanimous support — 99.5 per cent — for Egypt's peace treaty with Israel. Interior Minister Nabawi Ismail, who supervised the referendum, said 9,905,380 voters supported the treaty and 5,246 rejected it. Votes by 9,634 persons were voided for failing to comply with balloting rules.

Sadat's decree cleared the way for Egypt's first multi-party elections in more than a quarter-century. Elections are scheduled for June 7 and the 360 new members of parliament, 10 of whom will be appointed by Sadat, will convene on June 23.

The political reform programme, which starts with the dissolution of parliament, received a 99.9 per cent majority. Official final returns were 9,900,871 "yes" votes, 10,217 "no" votes and 9,772 voided ballots.

Ismail said the referendum turnout was about 90 per cent, with 9,920,260 persons voting out of an electorate of nearly 11 million.

"This magnificent result reflects the unanimous agreement of the Egyptian people to follow their leader on the path to peace, prosperity and democracy," Ismail said.

Officials said the outcome will strengthen Sadat's hand in dealing with his Arab detractors, who slapped political and economic sanctions on Egypt following the March 26 treaty signing with Israel in Washington. Syria, Iraq and the PLO branded Sadat a traitor, and some Arab terrorist leaders openly threatened violence against Egypt. (AP, UPI)

10,000 march in anti-Nazi protest

STRASBOURG, France (Reuter). — About 10,000 people paraded through the streets of this eastern French city to protest against attempts to end Nazi war-crimes trials.

The marchers carried banners in French and German opposing moves in the West German parliament to end the prosecution of former Nazis for offences committed during World War II.

Delegations from several countries, including a large group from West Germany, took part in the march. Other banners demanded the dissolution of clubs of former Nazis in West Germany.

Most of the demonstrators appeared to be young, although French war veterans and former concentration camp prisoners also joined the protest.

Two synagogues were vandalized in Strasbourg last weekend. Walls were daubed with swastikas and Jewish prayer books were destroyed.

(Nazi acquittal — Page 3)

Begin hails Sadat referendum triumph

Jerusalem Post Staff

Prime Minister Menahem Begin, upon learning of the results of the Egyptian national referendum on the peace treaty with Israel, telephoned President Anwar Sadat and congratulated him on his victory.

Begin described the vote — which was near-unanimous in supporting the treaty — as a victory for peace.

Sadat accepted the prime minister's congratulations warmly and said, "One cannot even begin to describe the tremendous feelings of the Egyptian people."

The two leaders agreed that following the treaty exchange ceremonies at El-Arish late in May, they would travel to Beersheba and address students at Ben-Gurion University of the Negev.

It also was agreed that they would fly in Sadat's plane along the Cairo-Ben-Gurion Airport route, thereby opening the Sinai corridor to tourism between the two countries.

THE JERUSALEM POST

Phones to Egypt ★ Page 2

IL8.00 (inc. Vat)

MONDAY, APRIL 23, 1979 • NISAN 26, 5739 • JAMADI AWWAL 26, 1399 • VOL. XLIX, No. 14602

Israeli gunboats shell PFLP headquarters in North Lebanon

By HIRSH GOODMAN
Post Military Correspondent
and agencies

Israeli gunboats yesterday afternoon shelled the headquarters of the Popular Front for the Liberation of Palestine near the Al-Barad River on the outskirts of Tripoli in northern Lebanon, in retaliation for yesterday morning's attack in Nahariya.

The buildings shelled, and apparently hit according to a senior military source, serve as a base of operations for George Habash, the man said by Israel to be responsible for yesterday's attack.

Israel's response, which was considered by observers here to be extremely mild, came at 5:35 p.m. The Israeli ships returned safely to port. Based on recent experience that Israeli attacks usually bring terrorist counter-attack in the form of indiscriminate bombardments of civilian settlements, a state of alert was declared in the North yesterday.

"This possibility has been taken into account," a senior source said. Meanwhile *The Jerusalem Post* has learned that the four terrorists who attacked Nahariya came in a French-made rubber dinghy — a "Slinger."

One of the terrorists was found to be wearing an explosive-laden belt, presumably to commit suicide rather than be captured if caught in a corner. The other three were not found to be in possession of similar belts, which have rarely been used by recently captured PLO terrorists.

All four were members of George Habash's Popular Front for the Liberation of Palestine — one of the more extreme rejectionist wings of the PLO, which among other acts of violence hijacked an Air France jet to Entebbe, Uganda, in 1976. The organization, according to authoritative sources, derives most of its finances and logistical support from Iraq and South Yemen.

In Beirut, a spokesman for the PFLP said the Israeli gunboats hit the refugee camp at Nahr Al-Barad, about 70 kms. north of Beirut. He denied Israeli statements that the gunboats struck a PFLP naval base, saying the target was a refugee camp for civilians.

"The bombardment resulted in the destruction of three civilian houses and wounding of 10 women and children," he said, adding that the gunboats approached the coast near Tripoli under an umbrella of Israeli warplanes.

He said the bombardment will not deter the PFLP, warning that "we will escalate our actions inside the occupied territories."

Terrorist organizations in southern Lebanon were last night reported to have gone on alert bracing for an Israeli retaliation. Scores of families were seen leaving Tyre and heading north, and three Israeli warplanes were reported to have flown low over the city, apparently on a reconnaissance mission.

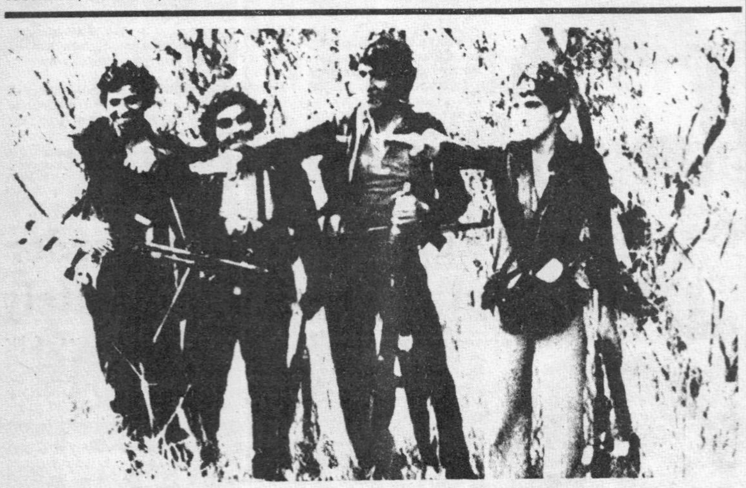

In this picture released in Beirut, the four terrorists who carried out the attack in Nahariya yesterday pose their right arms extended in what PLO officials said was an oath to go ahead with the raid. Left to right they were identified as Ahmed Bars (no age given), Samir Kintar, 18, Abdel Maguid, 24, and Muhanna Moayed, 19. (UPI telephoto)

Four die in seaborne attack on Nahariya; two terrorists killed, two others captured

By YOEL DAR
and YA'ACOV FRIEDLER
Jerusalem Post Reporters

NAHARIYA. — Four persons — a father and his two young daughters and a policeman — were killed early yesterday morning in an attack by four terrorists on this coastal resort community 10 km. from the Lebanese border.

Three other persons were wounded after the gang of terrorists slipped through the coastal defences and landed their rubber boat on the beach before dawn yesterday.

Two of the terrorists were killed, one of them by a recent immigrant from South Africa as they attempted to break into his flat. The other two terrorists were captured, with one of them wounded in the sharp exchange of gunfire with police and soldiers on the beach.

Killed were Danny Haran (Hirschorn) 32, and his daughters, Einat, 5, and Yael, 2, Nahariya residents, and police sergeant Eliyahu Shahar, 25, of Ma'alot.

Police sources said that Semadar Haran may have inadvertently smothered her younger child by covering her mouth with a cloth to stop her from screaming and revealing their hiding place in another room to the terrorists who broke into their flat.

It also was reported that Haran had pleaded with the terrorists to spare Einat's life, and that the terrorists were willing to leave her behind when they took him hostage at gunpoint, but that the little girl ran after them saying, "I want to be with Daddy."

The wounded are an officer, a civil guardsman and a soldier, whose names were not released by the authorities.

The Palestine Liberation Front (PLF), which is supported by Iraq, has claimed responsibility for the attack.

According to a reconstruction of the confused events, the gang of terrorists landed their rubber boat, equipped with an outboard motor, north of the city, between the city swimming pool and the palm beach, at about 2:30 a.m. The terrorists wore khaki uniforms and carried light arms, with backpacks crammed with various arms and ammunition.

On reaching the house of the Amnon Sela family, which stands alone and detached, the terrorists rang the bell, waking the family. Amnon called "who's there?" and was answered "company" in a bad English accent. The strange reply, repeated twice, aroused suspicion. Sela quickly got his gun while his wife went upstairs and saw the armed men through the window. She immediately phoned the police, saying she had seen men in khaki uniforms and wearing backpacks.

When the terrorists apparently realized they could not enter the fortress-like house, they ran along a dirt track to a four-storey apartment building some 100 metres away at 61 Rehov Jabotinsky. The iron safety door was open, enabling them to gain entry and walk up the stairs to the flat of the Haran family, where they gained entry by blowing the door open with a grenade. They overpowered Haran and took him and Einat as hostages, and then forced their way into another flat. There they kicked the flat owner in the groin and started forcing him and his daughter to go down towards the shelter, but the father and daughter managed to break loose and flee.

Another tenant, Charles Shapiro, 36, a new immigrant from Durban, was awakened by the noise and exploding grenades.

"I got out of bed and got hold of my little pistol and waited in the corridor," Shapiro said. "First they shot through my door and then they started knocking it down. I let the first terrrorist get in and then I shot him in the chest."

Shapiro said he saw two other terrorists in the apartment opposite his ground-floor flat. He held his fire fearing that he might hit his neighbour and his small daughter who were being held hostage.

When the injured terrorist cried out to alert his mates, Shapiro said that he fired again at close range at the terrorist, killing him.

Shapiro said that his killing one of the terrorists evidently rattled the others, and they shot through several other doors in the building and then ran back towards the beach, with their two hostages, Haran and his daughter Einat.

(Sitting among his tattered furniture and talking to newsmen afterwards, Shapiro, a diving instructor who came to Israel over a year ago, said he had bought the pistol for sport and had never expected it to save his life.)

As the terrorists made their way back to the beach with their two hostages, a border police jeep and a police patrol car drove up. In the car were Sergeant Shahar and civil guardman Shomron. The sergeant spotted the suspicious figures near the Sela house, and he fired two shots at them.

The terrorists fired back and threw a grenade at the police car, killing the sergeant outright and injuring Shomron.

Meanwhile, soldiers arrived, and in the exchange of fire that developed, another one of the terrorists was killed, as were Haran and his daughter.

Eye-witnesses claimed that the Harans were shouting not to fire, and it is not clear exactly how they were killed. There were reports that when the terrorists realized they were enclosed, they murdered the two hostages. Earlier reports said the two were killed when forced by the terrorists to stand up in the line of Israeli fire.

In the exchange, the third terrorist was wounded. The fourth terrorist had reportedly surrendered in the apartment house after he had been surrounded.

Just before 4 a.m., the chief of staff, Rav Aluf Rafael Eitan, and the O.C. Northern Command, Aluf Avigdor Ben-Gal, arrived in Nahariya. They were later joined by Defence Minister Ezer Weizman who arrived by helicopter. They received first-hand information on the events.

The wounded were taken to the local hospital, which had been placed on alert.

According to foreign reports, the gang had set out three hours earlier in their rubber boat from Tyre in Southern Lebanon, heading for the Israeli coast, in a stormy sea. They had been given specific orders to shoot indiscriminately to kill as many Jews as possible.

In Beirut, the PLO terrorist movement said that the Nahariya attack was carried out by one of its seaborne units. It added that the squad involved in the operation was named after the late Egyptian President Gamal Abdul-Nasser, whose policy

(Continued on page 2, col. 4)

Herut leaders to Begin: Fire Dayan

By SARAH HONIG
Post Political Reporter

TEL AVIV. — The Herut Executive and Knesset faction yesterday urged Prime Minister Menahem Begin to sack Foreign Minister Moshe Dayan.

This is an unprecedented decision in Herut, as it implies criticism of the government and is clearly a rebellious move that does not sit well with the party establishment. The decision is seen as an embarrassment to the prime minister because, although it is not binding, its impact cannot be ignored.

The decision was reached after a stormy session in which the resolution, proposed by Mattatyahu Drobles, joint chairman of the Jewish Agency Settlement Department, was put to the vote three times, narrowly passing each time.

Herut members have been angered at recent pronouncements by Dayan in which he suggested that the Golan Heights might be returned to Syria in return for a peace agreement, just as Sinai will be given back to Egypt. Such an arrangement could mean that settlements on the Golan might be dismantled. Dayan also has turned down a Likud Knesset faction request to appear before it to explain his statements.

Scathing criticism of Dayan came from nearly all the speakers, including those who voted against the resolution.

A satisfied MK Geula Cohen told *The Jerusalem Post* that "this is the first time I have seen such spirit in Herut." She told the meeting that "a demand for Dayan's dismissal is tantamount to a no confidence vote in the prime minister."

The party establishment, in an apparent attempt to force those present to face the seriousness of passing a resolution that could be seen as critical of the premier, insisted that the matter be put to the vote again and again. The resolution was passed narrowly, by 10 to eight. There were some 30 people present at the meeting, so about a third abstained.

Party executive chairman Avraham Schechterman, who opposed the resolution, told *The Post* that it was out of place.

Israel Radio last night quoted Dayan as saying that if Begin were to give the slightest hint that Dayan should resign, then he would do so immediately.

Begin moves to mollify Dayan in peace role

Post Diplomatic Correspondent

Foreign Minister Moshe Dayan is to be responsible for the evolution of normal relations between Israel and Egypt. An interministerial committee under Dr. Eliahu Ben-Elissar, the director-general of the Prime Minister's Office, which is already working on various aspects of this process, is to "present its decisions in the form of recommendations to the foreign minister."

This was announced to the cabinet by Premier Menahem Begin yesterday, and was subsequently incorporated in the official cabinet communique.

The move was seen as an effort on Begin's part to mollify Dayan's apparent anger and dismay at the role allotted to him in the coming stages of the peace process. Rumours had been circulated in the media to the effect that Dayan and his ministry were miffed at the creation of the Ben-Elissar committee, feeling that the unfolding of the normalization should come naturally within the purview of the Foreign Ministry.

Dayan's purported pique came on top of his failure to be named head of Israel's negotiating team in the autonomy talks with Egypt (Interior Minister Yosef Burg was last week elected to that post). Sources close to Dayan said he had turned down the job because he felt the negotiating authority would not be sufficiently broad. But sources close to Begin indicated that the premier did not actually offer it to him.

All of the sources lately have said that the reports of "tension" between the two men have been substantially exaggerated. Yet none of them denied that there has indeed been some resentment felt and expressed on both sides of late. Dayan's controversial statement on the future of the Golan Heights has fuelled the pressures upon Begin from within his own party to dismiss Dayan (see Herut story, this page).

Yesterday's cabinet decision, and Dayan's trip to the Far East which begins today and is to last three weeks, are expected to cool some of the heated criticism voiced against the foreign minister — and also to ease whatever tensions do exist between him and the premier.

Ben-Elissar told *The Jerusalem Post* last night that the premier's announcement to the cabinet has been fully coordinated with him in advance — and he felt no ill will whatever in regard to it.

He stressed that his committee had been established on a purely ad hoc basis, to prepare papers on the various aspects of the transitional period leading to full normalization. The intention had always been that the Foreign Ministry would steward relations between Israel and Egypt — as between Israel and all other countries — once full normalcy had been attained.

The committee had already done a good deal of work canvassing policy-opinions of the various relevant ministries and circulating position-papers on the economic and social, as well as political factors involved in the normalization process.

Ben-Elissar will represent Israel at the exchange of instruments of ratification due to take place at a brief ceremony at the U.S. Um Hashiba monitoring station on Wednesday.

Shamir to raise issue of death penalty

Knesset Speaker Yitzhak Shamir indicated yesterday that he would "speak to friends" about imposing the death penalty on convicted terrorists and murderers. Speaking at Ben-Gurion Airport on his departure for a four-day visit to France as guest of the president of the French Senate, Alain Poher, Shamir noted that he has expressed support in the past for implementing the death penalty.

Shamir warned that the terror organizations are carrying out their threat to intensify their actions against Israel, and called for heightened alertness to foil their attacks.

Brezhnev — Soviet man of letters

MOSCOW (Reuter). — President Leonid Brezhnev was yesterday elevated to the ranks of the Soviet Union's artistic elite with the award of the Lenin Literature Prize for his memoirs.

A citation on the front page of "Pravda" said that he was being given the prize, normally worth 10,000 rubles, for his three books of reminiscences and for his unflagging struggle for peace.

Weizman puts off Cairo trip after raid

By HIRSH GOODMAN
and DAVID LANDAU
Jerusalem Post Correspondents

Defence Minister Ezer Weizman's trip to Cairo was postponed on the recommendation of Premier Menahem Begin yesterday. According to a senior source, "It would have been totally incongruous for the defence minister of Israel to lay a wreath on the grave of the unknown Egyptian soldier while four terror victims were being buried in Israel."

Premier Begin used his "hot line" to President Sadat to inform the Egyptian leader of the decision to postpone Weizman's visit.

Israeli officials said Sadat had "shown full understanding" and had expressed his sympathy with the people of Israel in their grief over the victims of the terrorist attack.

Weizman himself later phoned his Egyptian counterpart, Kamal Ali, and explained the reasons for the postponement. Ali was also said to have been "extremely understanding."

Cairo radio networks reported Weizman's decision to put off his visit to Egypt at the top of their main afternoon news broadcasts. The networks said that Weizman had excused himself, explaining that Israel's "internal security" necessitated his stay in the country.

The Egyptian radio made no mention of the phone conversation Premier Begin had with President Sadat nor of the latter's expressions of condolences for the Nahariya victims.

The radios reported the Nahariya incident without commment, referring to the terrorist act as a "commando assault."

Weizman will now be going to Cairo, barring unforeseen circumstances, together with Chief of Staff Rafael Eitan on May 6.

This is the second time in two weeks that Weizman postponed his Cairo trip. He was initially supposed to have left on April 15, but for reasons believed to have been connected with the Egyptian decision to put off the exchange in the instruments of ratification, he put off his trip for a week.

Weizman's trip to Cairo was to have been for the most part ceremonial in nature. He was supposed to have had talks with Egyptian military personnel. Among other things he was slated to lay a wreath on the grave of the unknown Egyptian soldier, take a walk down the main streets of Cairo, and visit Alexandria. Both Weizman and Eitan were to have been accompanied by their wives.

Meanwhile, it was reported yesterday that Tat-Aluf Dov Sion, Israel's chief delegate to the joint Egyptian-Israeli military committee, will be leaving for Cairo this morning. He will be joining Aluf Avraham Tamir, head of the national planning department, in putting the final details together for Israel's pullback from El Arish and the rest of the Sinai over the next nine months. Both Tamir and Sion will be back in Israel within a few days.

Cabinet condemns Nahariya attack

Post Diplomatic Correspondent

The cabinet yesterday condemned the Nahariya terror attack, calling the terrorists "barbarous murderers" and expressing participation in the grief of the bereaved families.

During the cabinet session, Transport Minister Haim Landau briefed the ministers on last week's terror attempt in Brussels, and the cabinet statement praised the "Belgians and Israelis...who thwarted the designs of the terrorists."

Later in the day, Foreign Minister Moshe Dayan said that "no one can expect us to cooperate or try to understand, or have any dealings with an organization that perpetrates such attacks." Dayan was speaking to a gathering of "international publishers in Jerusalem for the book fair.

Experts seek answers to how terrorists landed unspotted

Post Military Correspondent

Military experts were yesterday examining how four terrorists penetrated Israel's considerable defences in the Nahariya area — the closest Israeli town to Lebanon along the coast.

Israel is known to have a highly complex series of defences in the area, including shore radar stations backed up by shore and sea patrols.

Experts yesterday did say that the sea was quite high, making it extremely difficult to pick up a small target such as a rubber dinghy.

But the IDF was at work yesterday checking whether it was human error that occurred in Nahariya, or whether there was a gap in the defences, which can be rectified.

Senior military sources reiterated yesterday that it is physically impossible to seal the maritime border completely, and that there is always a possibility of a successful penetration.

But this does not automatically preclude the possibility that yesterday's terrorist landing was not a result of an error or that somebody is going to be called upon to answer for it, they said.

The army is also checking with the police as to exactly what happened after the alarm was sounded. Initial reports seem to indicate a great deal of confusion, and anything but efficiency in dealing with the threat once it became apparent.

A senior military source last night denied that any of the Israeli dead had been hit by stray bullets fired by the security forces. While the facts are far from clear or final, it seems that two-year-old Yael Haran may have been smothered by her mother while her mother was trying to protect her from the terrorists.

Her father, Dan Haran, 28, was either knocked down and killed, or drowned by one of the surviving terrorists at the water's edge after he started to call for help. There is still no clear picture how four-year-old Einat Haran was killed.

Yadin loses cabinet battle against new settlements

By DAVID LANDAU
Post Diplomatic Correspondent

The cabinet yesterday endorsed a decision of the Ministerial Defence Committee to establish two settlements in Samaria, overriding an objection lodged by deputy premier and Democratic Movement chief Yigael Yadin.

Only Yadin's two DM colleagues, Shmuel Tamir and Israel Katz, voted with him in opposing the establishment of Shiloh and Eilon Moreh as two permanent civilian settlements in Samaria. Both settlements were pioneered by members of the Gush Emunim movement.

Yadin told newsmen later he opposed the two new settlements on two grounds:

- His longstanding dispute with the cabinet majority over the wisdom of planting Jewish settlements in the heart of the populated region of Samaria; and
- His feeling that the decision represented "a surrender to Gush Emunim, which had 'created its own facts'" and forced the government to recognize them.

The cabinet decision, while approving the two settlements, nevertheless asked the defence committee to rethink the siting of Eilon Moreh, after Foreign Minister Moshe Dayan pointed out that the site at Hawarra that the committee presently had in mind would involve the seizure of privately-owned lands. The government has always maintained that its programme for Jewish settlement on the West Bank would not require such confiscations.

Two Liberal ministers, Moshe Nissim and Gideon Patt, abstained in the vote on Shiloh — to express their disapproval of the way the Emunim settlers there had "put the government to shame" by pretending they had come on an archaeological dig while at the same time assuring the media that a permanent settlement would arise on the site.

Yadin revealed that the Ministerial Defence Committee, at its meeting last week which decided on the two new settlements, had also resolved that henceforth all settlement decisions would be announced publicly. This meant, Yadin said, that his party could carry its opposition to such settlements into the Knesset arena, no longer restricting itself to the ostensibly secret deliberations of the Knesset Foreign Affairs and Defence Committee to voice its protests.

The DM, said Yadin, would therefore convene to discuss how to pursue its case against the two new settlements by parliamentary means.

Rhodesian planes silence Zambia guns

SALISBURY (UPI). — Rhodesian warplanes yesterday bombed and strafed Zambian army positions to silence what the military command called "unprovoked rocket and mortar attacks."

It was the first time in the six-year-old war that Rhodesian air power was officially reported to have been used against Zambian positions, although clashes between Zambian soldiers and Rhodesian troops on their way to attack guerrilla bases in Zambia have been reported frequently.

The military headquarters communique reporting the action also announced that during the past 24 hours security forces fighting a bush war against the Patriotic Front guerrilla alliance had killed 12 insurgents and one collaborator.

The strike was launched as scores of reservists made for home in a gradual stand-down following a full mobilization in force during the five-day majority rule election that ended on Saturday.

(UPI, Reuter)

(Rhodesia — Page 4)

Nahariya terrorists planned to take hostages to Lebanon

By HIRSH GOODMAN
Post Military Correspondent

There are clear indications that the four terrorists who landed at Nahariya yesterday morning intended to take hostages back to Lebanon with them.

This may be the start of a new policy based on last month's success when in exchange for one Israeli held captive, Avraham Amram, the terrorists managed to secure the release of 76 of their men held in Israeli prisons.

In the past the terrorists have never managed to gain the freedom of a single of their number when taking hostages on Israeli soil.

Earlier reports said that the terrorists had taken to their dinghy Dan Harran and his daughter Inat — both of whom were killed on the beach — as human shields to effect their escape.

The decision to release the 76 terrorists in exchange for Amram, who fell into terrorist captivity during the Litani Operation, was taken by the defence minister in consultation with the prime minister and was severely criticized in and out of the defence establishment at the time.

There has also been some speculation that the last two terrorist actions, which were foiled in the Jordan Valley at Kibbutz Tirat Zvi and in the north, near Kibbutz Zarit earlier this month, may have been similarly intended.

Authorities who examined the bodies of the slain terrorists at the time were surprised that they were not found to be carrying a list of terrorists in Israeli prisons whose release they were assumed to be demanding.

Ghali advises U.S. to make direct contacts with PLO

CAIRO (UPI). — An Egyptian foreign policy-maker says the U.S. should establish "direct contact" with Yasser Arafat's Palestine Liberation Organization, because this will make the "voice of reason" prevail in the Middle East.

Butros Ghali, State Minister for Foreign Affairs, said yesterday in an interview published by the weekly magazine "October," that Egypt was aware of the difficult circumstances the PLO is facing as a result of "internal divisions and pressures."

"And yet, we hope the voice of reason will prevail," he said. "Naturally direct contacts between the PLO and the U.S. will help.

"We hope America will shed off the complex of refusing to have direct contact with the Palestinians," Ghali said. "We also hope the PLO will shed off the complex of rejecting everything and at all times."

These contacts, Ghali said, would dissuade the PLO from obstructing elections for the Palestinian autonomous councils in the West Bank and Gaza Strip.

Ghali rejected the Israeli contention that autonomy should apply only to the Palestinian inhabitants of the West Bank and Gaza, but not to the land on which they live.

"This is mere sophistry," he said, "because the people are tied to the land, and the land is the place where the people exercise their rights."

He said the "tempo" of normalizing Egyptian-Israeli relations "will be necessarily linked to progress in resolving the Palestinian problem."

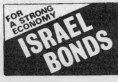

THE JERUSALEM POST

U.S. air crash ★★ Page 4

IL8.00 (inc. Vat)

SUNDAY, MAY 27, 1979 • SIVAN 1, 5739 • JAMADI THANI 29, 1399 • VOL. XLIX, No. 14630

• Sadat-Begin meet today in El-Arish, Beersheba
• Navon to welcome Sadat at City Hall
• Sadat to address Ben-Gurion University.

Flanked by the flags of their nations, the Israeli, Egyptian and U.S. delegations sit down on Friday in Beersheba to open talks on autonomy for the West Bank and Gaza Strip. (Nowitz)

Sadat in Beersheba today; to inaugurate air corridor

Vance closer to Egypt as autonomy talks open

By DAVID LANDAU and IAN BLACK
Jerusalem Post Reporters

BEERSHEBA. — The Israel-Egypt autonomy talks opened here on Friday with the two sides setting out their very divergent perceptions of the autonomy and U.S. Secretary of State Cyrus Vance stressing Israel's need for security but seeming closer to the Egyptian position on the political issues.

Interior Minister Yosef Burg, the chairman of Israel's negotiating team, called for an "a priori rejection" of "an independent Palestinian statehood." He referred to an "administrative council" that would run the problems of the Palestinians living in "Judea, Samaria and the Gaza district."

Egyptian Defence Minister Kamal Hassan Ali, standing in for Premier Mustapha Khalil who failed to appear, said the Palestinians' right of self-determination was "God-given." The task of the autonomy talks, he said, was to set a "self-governing authority," to arrange for "the transfer of authority from the Israeli Military Government to the Palestinian government."

Secretary Vance stressed the transitional nature of the autonomy, recalling that the Camp David accords envisioned it as a period during which all the broad and basic aspects of the Palestinian problem could be negotiated and resolved. Vance called for a "start to deal with the problems of the Palestinians living outside the West Bank and Gaza. They too, must know that an accepted and respected place exists for them in the international community." He also referred to Jordan's absence from the talks and to the hostility to them in the Arab world.

The opening session was marred by Premier Khalil's last-minute decision not to come. Defence Minister Ali opened his speech by explaining that "according to the instructions of President Sadat, Prime Minister Mustapha Khalil for procedural considerations was not able to participate in the opening session....He will be very pleased to welcome the delegations for our next meeting, on June 3, in Alexandria."

TEXT OF SPEECHES
Page 5

Apparently, Khalil felt slighted by the fact that his opposite number was given a face-lift for Sadat's historic visit. Streets along the motorcade route from the municipality to Ben-Gurion University have been freshly paved and painted, and the bulldozers have been busily at work clearing rubble from the town's main street, Derech Hanezi'im.

But Israeli officials were furious at Khalil's eleventh-hour snub, pointing out that he had known for the past month that Burg would head the Israeli side, but had not intimated that he would therefore boycott the opening session.

Some observers argued, however, that Israel was at fault for not arranging that Acting Premier Yigael Yadin (Premier Begin was airborne from London at the time) meet Khalil at Hatzerim airfield near Beersheba.

The next session of the talks will not be on June 3, as Ali announced, but on June 6. In a brief, closed-door coordinating session held after the three opening speeches, the Israeli side pointed out that they had a cabinet meeting to attend on June 3.

As to the venue of future meetings in Israel (the talks will alternate between Israel and Egypt), there is no decision yet, but one of the six Israeli ministers present on Friday suggested the Weizman Institute at Rehovot.

Plainly, Beersheba is not suitable — to judge by Friday's opening session. Local and foreign newsmen present commented adversely on the site, which was the entrance hall to the Negev University's administration building and which retained its entrance hall atmosphere despite

(Continued on page 2, col. 4)

Beersheba all set to cheer Sadat

By HARRY WALL
Special to The Jerusalem Post

BEERSHEBA. — "The city of Abraham welcomes President Sadat" proclaim the banners in Arabic that stretch across this town's streets, interspersed with the flags of Egypt, Israel and the city itself.

Earlier in the day, Cyrus Vance is due to arrive in El-Arish half an hour ahead of Premier Begin who will be accompanied by Defence Minister Ezer Weizman and Foreign Minister Moshe Dayan. A trilateral summit is scheduled, with discussion expected to centre on the autonomy negotiations and Israel's Sinai withdrawal plans.

The Negev's capital has been given a face-lift for Sadat's historic visit. Streets along the motorcade route from the municipality to Ben-Gurion University have been freshly paved and painted, and the bulldozers have been busily at work clearing rubble from the town's main street, Derech Hanezi'im.

The Egyptian president and his party, together with Premier Begin and U.S. Secretary of State Cyrus Vance, are due to arrive here by helicopter at 2 p.m. today when they will be welcomed by President Yitzhak Navon. After the playing of the national anthems and a formal gun-salute, the visitors will review an honour guard and will then be offered the traditional bread and salt welcome. Mayor Eliahu Nawi will greet the visitors and President Sadat will respond. He will also accept a key to the city.

After this public welcome, Israel's and Egypt's presidents are to meet on their own for a few minutes. At 3 p.m. the motorcade of Egyptian, U.S. and Israeli dignitaries leaves for a drive through Beersheba's streets to the campus where university president Yosef Tekoah will welcome them and introduce members of the faculty and others

(Continued on page 2, col. 2)

Egypt may open border at El-Arish immediately

By ANAN SAFADI
Post Mideast Affairs Editor

EL-ARISH. — Visiting Egyptian officials said yesterday that President Anwar Sadat was planning to respond to Premier Menahem Begin's appeals for a minimal normalization of relations between the two countries.

Sadat and Begin are scheduled to hold summit talks here today then fly together to Beersheba to deliver speeches at Ben-Gurion University.

Officials who accompanied Sadat yesterday for the celebration of this town's return to Egyptian sovereignty said that the Egyptian leader will respond positively to a number of normalization requests which Begin has been pressing recently. The officials did not elaborate, but indicated that the Egyptian leader will indeed acquiesce to Begin's appeals for the maintenance of open borders. Sadat, however, will limit the move to restricted traffic between Israel and the El-Arish area but not to mainland Egypt. Sadat insists on taking that step towards normalizing relations at the end of Israel's withdrawal from the bulk of Sinai in eight months time.

The officials said at the same time that Sadat would reject Begin's request to reconsider the question of evicting the Neot Sinai settlers from the vegetable field which Israel was supposed to relinquish together with El-Arish last Friday.

Initial signs here indicated that Sadat planned to focus on points of agreement with Begin rather than dramatize differences with him. The Egyptian leader, according to one reliable source, will take advantage of his meeting with Begin today to call on Arab leaders to join the peace negotiations with Israel in El-Arish.

The two leaders are due to inaugurate an air corridor between Egypt and Israel via the Sinai air-space today.

U.S. Secretary of State Cyrus Vance is scheduled to join the summit talks to lend momentum to the Sadat-Begin get-together.

Vance, who represented his government at the opening session of the West Bank and Gaza autonomy talks in Beersheba on Friday, is expected to play a major role in bridging the rift between Sadat and Begin over the essence of autonomy.

The autonomy negotiations will be resumed in Alexandria early next month.

Egyptian Defence Minister Kamal Hassan Ali, who led his country's delegation at the opening session over the weekend, described as "hardline" Israel's opening position, which was presented by Interior Minister Yosef Burg.

Speaking to reporters on his return to Cairo yesterday, Ali said that the negotiations are going to be difficult and arduous. However, he stressed Cairo's determination to continue efforts to overcome differences.

Sadat was also reported as maintaining that "the negotiations concerning the West Bank and Gaza will be very hard and very tiring." He was quoted as adding: "But we have no other choice than to succeed."

In a radio interview reported by Egyptian information officials, Sadat was quoted as reiterating that he saw no need for the participation of Palestinian representatives at this stage of negotiations on autonomy.

In the interview with Radio Monte Carlo, Sadat made the following points:

• The Palestine Liberation Organization is too unstable now to play a role in the peace process.

• The Arab world was being emotional in its opposition to Egypt's peace moves with Israel, and that Egypt will continue to deal with Jerusalem.

• The thorny problem of Jerusalem can be solved by granting the Arabs sovereignty over East Jerusalem, recognizing Israel's sovereignty over West Jerusalem, and establishing a joint Israel-Arab municipality to administer a united city.

Both sides restrained in talks

By DAVID LANDAU
Post Diplomatic Correspondent

Despite yawning gaps between Interior Minister Yosef Burg's speech and that of Egyptian Defence Minister Gen. Kamal Hassan Ali, observers noted that each man forbore from spelling out that demand which is most provocative and unpalatable to the other side. Thus, Ali did not urge that autonomy lead to the establishment of an independent Palestinian state, which Burg declared was anathema to Israel. And Burg for his part did not explicitly demand the right of continued free settlement and land expropriation for Israel (while Ali said that all previous settlement and expropriation is to be considered null and void).

Ali, by saying that the Palestinians' right to self-determination was "God-given" and that "we are not here to determine the future of the Palestinian people," underscored the transitional rationale of the autonomy and its aim of leaving the "permanent status" of the West Bank and Gaza Strip in abeyance pending future negotiations.

The most consistent divergence between the two ministers' addresses was in their characterization of the proposed autonomy. Both men cited the phrase "full autonomy"; but for Burg it was to mean an "administrative council," while for Ali it was to be a "self-governing authority." Both terms are used in the Camp David "framework," and his references to "Palestinians living outside the West Bank and Gaza... who identify with the people there" were received warily by Israeli observers. Israel sees the proposed autonomy as focusing on the West Bank and Gaza Strip, with the broader aspects of the Palestinian issue to await the "permanent status" negotiations.

The secretary seemed to have Israeli settlement activity in mind, at least in part, when he uttered a call for "maximum restraint and far-sightedness on the part of all.... The intentions of either side will be called into question if it attempts to pursue its own national objectives in a manner that conflicts with the purposes of these negotiations."

Significantly, U.S. Secretary of State Cyrus Vance echoed Ali's nomenclature. He too spoke of "self-governing authority" rather than "administrative council."

Vance also appeared to reject Israel's insistence that the "source of authority" for the autonomy must be the military government when he said: "In the U.S. we believe deeply in the proposition that governments derive their just powers from the consent of the governed. We believe that the Palestinian people must have the right for themselves and their descendants to live with dignity and freedom..."

The chasm between Burg and Ali was perhaps starkest in their references to Jerusalem. For Burg it was "the eternal capital of Israel." He pointedly mentioned it in a passage dealing with the Jewish nation's historic ties to "Eretz Israel," a passage in which he also spoke of Beersheba and Hebron.

For Ali, "Arab Jerusalem" was to be subject to the "principle of the 'inadmissibility of the acquisition of territory by war'" in Resolution 242, and all Israeli actions "which were taken to change the status of Arab Jerusalem are null and void."

Interestingly, though, Ali did not specifically demand that East Jerusalem be incorporated in the autonomy authority (a long-standing Egyptian position which Premier Menahem Begin firmly rejects). Ali said: "Arab Jerusalem will become a living testimony to the possibility of coexistence and cooperation between all peoples in the area."

the conflict. The negotiating history of that resolution leaves no doubt that this was the understanding of all parties..."

Vance's concern with the "broader aspects of the Palestinian problem" and his references to "Palestinians living outside the West Bank and Gaza... who identify with the people there" were received warily by Israeli observers. Israel sees the proposed autonomy as focusing on the West Bank and Gaza Strip, with the broader aspects of the Palestinian issue to await the "permanent status" negotiations.

Sadat raises the flag over El-Arish

By ANAN SAFADI
Post Mideast Affairs Editor

EL-ARISH. — Egyptian President Anwar Sadat yesterday hoisted his country's tricolour over this town in an emotional ceremony marking its return to Egyptian sovereignty.

Sadat, resplendent in the white uniform of an Egyptian navy admiral, arrived here almost exactly 24 hours after Israeli troops pulled out of El-Arish, ending Israel's 12-year occupation. To thunderous cheers, he signed a proclamation turning over control of the town from the military to the local civilian authorities.

In a day filled with symbolism, Sadat had knelt in thanksgiving upon arrival, placed a wreath of flowers on a monument commemorating Egyptian war dead, lit a peace torch that will be carried throughout Egypt, walked through a central square offering public figures a national flag he carried on his outstretched arms, and joined his guests at noon prayers in the local mosque.

Thousands of Egyptians, many of whom were driven in from Cairo, as well as El-Arishis thronged around Sadat as he officiated ceremonies or drove along the dusty streets of this Sinai town, which combines the depressing vistas of the desert with the majestic beauty of the sea.

Almost everywhere, the crowds hailed Sadat as "the hero of the crossing" (of the Suez Canal in the 1973 war) and of peace. Loudspeakers blared national songs, women ululated and Beduin played folk music and danced.

A massive show of Egyptian flags had overshadowed the appearance of Palestinian flags, presumably hoisted by Palestinian Arabs who have been living here since 1948. A sudden shift from praise of Sadat to slogans demanding "Arab Palestine" and that the "liberation of Jerusalem" be next was contained at one point by troops the Egyptians sent to the site.

Yesterday's main event was the flag-raising ceremony at the town's centre where some 2,000 guests from El-Arish and the rest of Egypt had gathered. Sadat stood at attention and saluted as the national anthem was played. Four officers representing different branches of the armed forces delivered the flag to him. After bowing to kiss it, Sadat carried the black, white and red flag on his

(Continued on page 2, col. 1)

Last Ramle prison escapee caught

HAIFA (Itim). — The last of the Ramle prison escapees was captured near here last night after eluding a police manhunt since January 8.

Gavriel Bozaglo, 24, who had been serving a 16-year sentence for armed robbery, broke out with seven other prisoners. Two were captured six days after the escape, three more a month later, and two in mid-March.

Bozaglo, who had grown a beard and changed his hairstyle, was first spotted last night in Kiryat Yam. Followed past Haifa, he was finally stopped at the Kiryat Ata intersection. He and three fellow passengers in a Chevrolet surrendered without resistance.

Hope for Prisoners of Zion in pre-Vienna Soviet thaw

MOSCOW. — Three leading Soviet Jewish activists yesterday released a statement saying they have been told the Soviet leadership has decided to take three steps – including the release of 12 prisoners – which would signal a marked improvement in emigration policies on the eve of the Vienna summit between U.S. President Jimmy Carter and Soviet President Leonid Brezhnev.

Jewish sources said the Soviet offer was relayed through a visiting Australian trade union leader, Bob Hawke, who spent the past six days in Moscow.

If the agreement goes through, the Soviets would release the following 12 persons: Anatoly Shcharansky, serving 13 years for treason; Iosip Mendelevich, serving 12 years for the Leningrad hijack plot; Alexei Murzhenko, serving 14 years for the Leningrad hijack plot; Yuri Federov, a non-Jew serving 15 years for the Leningrad hijack plot; Iosip Begun, serving three years in exile for violating passport rules; Ida Nudel, serving three years in exile for malicious hooliganism; Semyon Schnirman, serving two years for draft evasion; Vladimir Slepak, serving five years exile for malicious hooliganism; Boris Tsitionak and Mark Nashpitz, both serving five years exile for anti-Soviet slander; Amner Zavurov, serving three years in prison for parasitism and hooliganism; and Boris Kalendarev, serving two years in prison for draft evasion.

Scientists Alexander Lerner, Viktor Brylovsky and Vladimir Prestin telephoned the following statement to western journalists yesterday morning:

"We were told that the Soviet authorities have decided to release long-term applicants for departure, to release the 12 prisoners, and to limit the maximum term of waiting

(Continued on page 2, col. 1)

This set of State Peace Medals is to be presented today by the Prime Minister, Menahem Begin, to the President of Egypt, Anwar Sadat, during their meeting in Beersheba. The medals, which are issued by the Israel Government Coins and Medals Corporation, are of gold, silver and bronze. The olive wood presentation case is inscribed with a dedication in Arabic, which may be translated: State Peace Medals, gift of the Israel Government Coins and Medals Corporation, to President Anwar Sadat, May 27, 1979.

(Communicated)

THE JERUSALEM POST

Prisoners of Zion ★ Page 4

IL8.00 (inc. Vat)

MONDAY, MAY 28, 1979 • SIVAN 2, 5739 • RAJAB 1, 1399 • VOL. XLIX, No. 14631

Colourful and emotional ceremonies led by President Sadat and Prime Minister Begin in newly returned El-Arish, capital of Egyptian Sinai, and in Beersheba, capital of Israel's Negev, climaxed the symbolic first stage of the Israel-Egypt peace process.

In El-Arish, after meeting with war wounded from both nations, Begin announced agreement with Sadat on open borders.

In Beersheba nearly all the residents flocked to the streets to greet the Egyptian and Israeli leaders. At Ben-Gurion University a joint desert research project was unveiled.

Towards evening the two leaders inaugurated the Lod-Cairo air corridor.

Israel and Egypt proclaim open border; agree to accelerate peace 'momentum'

Begin, Sadat stress comprehensive pact

By HANAN SHER
Jeruslem Post Reporter

BEERSHEBA. — President Anwar Sadat and Prime Minister Menahem Begin reminded a Ben-Gurion University assembly here yesterday that their two nations have embarked on the first step towards a comprehensive Middle East peace — and not a separate pact between Israel and Egypt.

The steps, Sadat told a crowd of 3,000 — half of them BGU students — were "giant" ones, that are "meant to be followed up and completed." That "awesome task requires all the goodwill and cooperation we can muster," the Egyptian leader declared.

Noting that "the negativists, the enemies of peace" were claiming that Egypt and Israel had made a separate peace, Begin emphasized that the treaty was the first, "but indeed the decisive" step towards an over-all peace in the region.

The two leaders and their party arrived at the open plaza on the BGU campus about an hour behind schedule. During the interim, the crowds — which also included 50 to 60 university donors from around the world — was entertained first by the Kiryat Ono Youth Orchestra, and then by the Beersheba Orchestra under conductor Mendi Rodan, and by singer Shoshana Damari.

Escorted by Begin and a large number of Egyptian, Israeli and American officials, Sadat arrived just after Damari had finished singing the Yom Kippur War ballad, "The Last War." They were greeted by a prolonged standing ovation.

Opening the assembly first in Hebrew and then in English, BGU president Yosef Tekoah announced that the university had decided to establish a special $100 million Fund for Desert Development, in five to 10 years. Mutual research, development and settlement projects, he said, would make the desert become "a bond of friendship" in Israeli-Egyptian efforts "to give substance to peace." And he invited Egyptian scientists to take part in the project.

He presented a smiling Sadat with a Ya'acov Agam sculpture, "The Star of Peace," and then made a similar presentation to Premier Begin.

In his brief remarks, the Egyptian president said he had "no doubt" that Israel would demonstrate in the months ahead "a veritable willingness to live in peace with all its neighbours, including the Palestinian people."

The Egyptian leader reminded his Israeli audience that the challenge "is not of scoring a point here or there," but of building a "viable structure for peace." He added that the path was not through "fanaticism and self-righteousness" but with "tolerance, compassion and magnanimity."

Begin spoke of "practical steps" already taken in the process of normalization — "which is much more than the opposite of a state of war." He noted that Israeli ships had sailed through the Suez Canal, and would continue to do so; that El-Arish had been "peacefully and amicably" transferred to Egyptian sovereignty.

The prime minister said he was convinced that both countries "are determined to carry out faithfully all the commitments under the peace treaty" and "the establishment of completely normal and friendly relations."

Israel had done more than that, he said. It had begun autonomy negotiations with Egypt. Had it acted only in accordance with the letter of the Camp David Agreements, Begin said, Israel would have been obligated to negotiate "full autonomy" only if Jordan had agreed to enter the talks.

As the Prime Minister was speaking, two or three youths wearing "Peace Now" tee-shirts were stopped from unfurling a banner by ushers and security guards. A few moments after the speech, two of them were quietly escorted from the assembly plaza by the security men.

Nessim Gaon, chairman of the BGU board of governors delivered the closing remarks in Arabic, English and Hebrew. Then the official party walked to a raised area at the edge of the plaza, where President Sadat, Vice-President Hosni Mubarak and Prime Minister Mustapha Khalil, escorted by Begin, reviewed an IDF guard of honour.

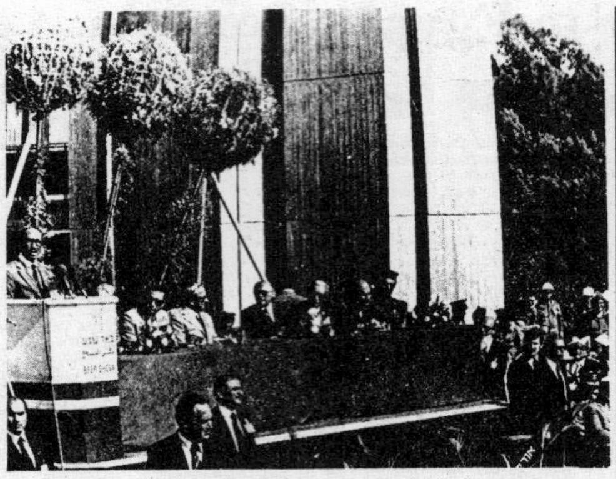

President Anwar Sadat delivers his address outside Beersheba City Hall. Seated on the dais from left to right are U.S. Secretary of State Cyrus Vance (hidden by the podium), Egyptian Vice-President Hosni Mubarak, President Navon, Prime Minister Begin, Egyptian Premier Mustapha Khalil, Deputy Premier Yigael Yadin, and OC Southern Command Dan Shomron. (Rahamim Israeli)

Navon and Sadat laud the bonds of peace

By IAN BLACK
Jerusalem Post Reporter

BEERSHEBA. — "Nation shall not lift up sword against nation, neither shall they learn war any more," proclaimed the huge banner strung across the plaza of the municipality of the Negev capital during yesterday's historic visit by Egyptian President Anwar Sadat.

This was the theme of a day of ceremonies and festivities that began with the meeting between Sadat and Prime Minister Menahem Begin in El-Arish and ended with the symbolic flight from the Hatzerim airbase to inaugurate the air corridor between Egypt and Israel and a new era in relations between the two countries.

The Beersheba part of the events began at 2.40 p.m. — almost one hour behind schedule — when President Yitzhak Navon was escorted into the municipality building by Mayor Eliahu Nawi, Deputy Premier Yigael Yadin and OC Southern Command Aluf Dan Shomron.

The crowd of some 2,000 — invited guests, dignitaries and hundreds of journalists — was restless after a long wait in the hot sun that was relieved only partially by the distribution of cardboard hats and tepid drinks by helpful schoolgirl volunteers.

As the loudspeakers blared out old and meaningful favourites like "Tomorrow" and "Song of Peace" the crowd applauded when Israeli and Egyptian ministers took their seats by the rostrum from which the speeches were to be made.

There was an amusing moment when Foreign Minister Moshe Dayan donned a hat (a *kova tembel*) for protection from the sun and tried to place one playfully on the head of his Egyptian counterpart Butros Ghali. Ghali, however, preferred the heat and folded the soft hat in his lap.

Sadat and Begin arrived with a heavy escort of motorcycle outriders at 2:50. As the Egyptian president inspected an IDF guard of honour and the army orchestra played the national anthems of Egypt and Israel a 21-gun salute boomed out in honour of the guest.

Sadat, in dark glasses and an elegant light-grey pinstripe suit appeared relaxed as he inspected the Israeli troops and went on to receive the keys to the city "to symbolize the opening of the gates of peace" and taste the traditional salt and bread and a glass of water — since he does not drink wine.

It was a colourful scene with the white, blue and olive of the IDF uniforms, the flags fluttering in a

(Continued on page 9, col. 4)

Transit limited to El-Arish front

By ANAN SAFADI
Post Mideast Affairs Editor

EL-ARISH. — Israel and Egypt yesterday proclaimed the border between the two countries open for visits by each other's citizens, thus marking another milestone in the peace treaty they signed last March.

The open border declaration was made by Prime Minister to an emotional gathering here of Egyptian and Israeli disabled war veterans. Some of the invalids burst into tears as Begin made his dramatic announcement.

Begin was joined on the visit by Egyptian President Anwar Sadat and U.S. Secretary of State Cyrus Vance.

Premier Begin did not go into details, leaving the practical interpretation of the proclamation uncertain. Reliable sources, while cautioning that specifics remain to be outlined, said that the open border at this stage would be limited to the El-Arish front and that transit would be restricted to selected groups.

"The president and I proclaim that the borders of Egypt and Israel are open," Begin said. "The people of Egypt will be able to visit Israel, and the people of Israel will be able to visit Egypt."

Begin indicated that arrangements for the implementation of the open border agreement will be discussed at a later stage, saying that he will be going to Alexandria for his next meeting with Sadat in the first week of July. He also noted that Foreign Minister Moshe Dayan will be holding talks with premier Mustapha Khalil early next month about the time the Israel and Egyptian delegations resume their talks on the West Bank and Gaza autonomy in Alexandria on June 6.

The open border announcement followed summit talks between Begin and Sadat at an improvised presidential beach resthouse that was renovated, painted and furnished within 24 hours from Israel's pullout from town last Friday at the end of a 12-year occupation.

The talks, in which Secretary Vance took part, touched on the divergent views between Sadat and Begin over the essence of the West Bank and Gaza autonomy. They also dealt with the controversial Neot Sinai vegetable patch. Sadat had insisted on the evacuation of the field within the framework of Israel's first-stage withdrawal from Northern Sinai.

Begin was accompanied here by Foreign Minister Moshe Dayan, Defence Minister Ezer Weizman and Interior Minister Yosef Burg.

In an action that was seen by observers as a gesture to Sadat, Premier Begin yesterday said that he planned to "take steps to free a number of prisoners whose release will not impair Israel's security." He did not elaborate, but was obviously referring to Sadat's request that West Bank and Gaza Strip political prisoners be set free parallel to the autonomy negotiations.

The total number of prisoners due to be freed in the Israeli gesture is expected to be around a score. They will include administrative detainees as well as convicted prisoners, and most of them presumably have affinity with the Gaza Strip or Egypt. The release will probably take another few days to arrange.

Both Sadat and Begin looked in good spirit when they emerged from their summit talks to meet with the disabled war veterans. So did Secretary Vance.

"You may rest assured that your great sacrifice did not go in vain. It paved the way for a new era of peace and security for all," Sadat told the war heroes gathering at the central cinema theatre.

"I seize this opportunity to greet Premier Begin, after we had our talks in which we have expressed our views to give every possible momentum for the peace process," Sadat said. He also greeted U.S. President Jimmy Carter "for sending his distinguished Secretary Vance to attend with Premier Begin and me the meeting of this great day."

Addressing the same group, Begin said:

"Five times we met on the battlefield...but from now no more war between us, no more wheelchairs for the young men of Egypt and Israel. No more bereavement, no more sorrow."

Begin was yesterday given a warm welcome here by the Egyptian hierarchy which had come to celebrate restoration of the Sinai capital to Egyptian sovereignty. El-Arishis curiously left the streets to the Sinai Beduin who chanted pro-Egyptian slogans including one assuring Sadat that they were "bloodthirsty enough to protect him" against his opponents.

Thousands of Egyptian soldiers patrolled the town until long after Begin, Sadat and Vance helicoptered off for their visit to Beersheba.

Egypt-Israel travel rules must still be worked out

By ASHER WALLFISH
Jerusalem Post Reporter

Administrative arrangements for travel between Israel and Egypt will have to await political decisions at a higher level, according to Yehudit Huebner, the deputy director-general of the Interior Ministry for special duties.

Before Moshe Dayan's trip to Cairo, the ministers of foreign affairs and of the interior will confer with their directors-general to formulate a set of proposals for these administrative arrangements. Their implementation will depend on what the Egyptian counterparts have in mind. Some negotiation is anticipated, which may not be concluded during Dayan's visit.

The arrangements will have to cover travellers arriving by air and sea, as well as land travellers crossing at borders such as Neot Sinai.

Until Egypt and Israel open consulates in each other's territory, a special system for processing visa applications will be set up. Police and health officials will be involved, as well as officials from the Foreign Affairs and Interior Ministries.

Joan Borsten adds from Cairo:
There has been no official confirmation that open borders means immediate tourism. But the news caused a sensation here in the office of an Egyptian travel agent yesterday.

The agent did not hear Prime Minister Begin's announcement on radio. Instead, he got word by telex from VIP Tours of Tel Aviv that the first group of bona fide Israeli tourists is due in Cairo on Thursday.

The two travel agents have been working together for at least a year, determined to be the first to bring Israelis to Cairo and Egyptians to Tel Aviv. But neither had really believed the borders would open before next December.

Suddenly there were preparations to be made. The telexes began to fly. "Please arrange for a bus to bring Israelis to Cairo from El-Arish," cabled the Israeli. "It will be air-conditioned," answered the Cairene. "Please contact civil aviation for a landing permit, as we are chartering a plane," cabled the Israeli. "Let's send a group of Egyptians back to Tel Aviv in it," suggested the Egyptian.

But the Egyptian travel agent says he can make no final plans until President Sadat or a member of the cabinet officially confirms Begin's open border announcement.

Terrorists in UN area of Lebanon fire at Christians

Jerusalem Post Reporter

METULLA. — A brief artillery duel took place yesterday afternoon between Palestinian terrorists and Major Sa'ad Haddad's militia forces in the coastal area of South Lebanon.

The exchange began when terrorists in the UNIFIL-controlled territory south of Tyre fired rounds from recoilless guns at a Christian fortification near the Shia village of Bayada, not far from the Hamra Bridge.

Haddad's spokesman told *The Jerusalem Post* that the French engineering corps of UNIFIL is dismantling the Haifa-Beirut rail line between Nakoura and the Hamra Bridge, and that they are using the materials to build UN fortifications.

The spokesman added that the terrorists are reinforcing their positions throughout the south, especially in the Arnoun Heights area, near Nabatiya and in the Tyre region. Today, he said, the terrorists have 15 permanent strongholds within UNIFIL territory.

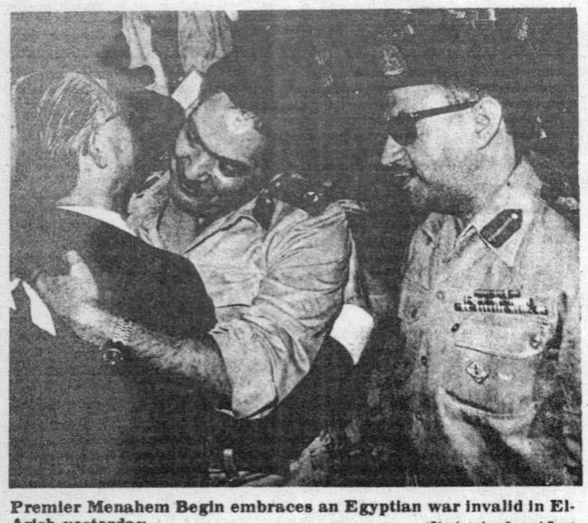

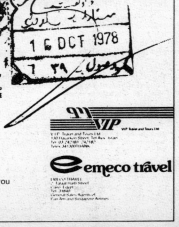

Premier Menahem Begin embraces an Egyptian war invalid in El-Arish yesterday. (Simionsky, Israel Sun)

Neot Sinai can't work vegetable field

By JOSHUA BRILLIANT
Jerusalem Post Reporter

EL-ARISH. — President Anwar Sadat yesterday rejected Prime Minister Menahem Begin's request to allow Neot Sinai settlers to continue working their vegetable field near here. The 2,000-dunam field was returned to Egyptian sovereignty on Friday.

Details of the Sadat-Begin tete-a-tete discussion on the matter were not revealed. But Begin told reporters later that he had been unable to convince Sadat to allow the settlers to work the vegetable field.

"President Sadat said it would be difficult (to allow the settlers across), and we must accept this announcement, to my regret," Begin said.

Sadat's refusal was not surprising. He had rejected an identical request when Begin was in Cairo two months ago. Minister of State for Foreign Affairs Butros Ghali last Wednesday turned down a second request relayed by Defence Minister Ezer Weizman and Justice Minister Shmuel Tamir.

Deputy Prime Minister Yigael Yadin on Thursday cautioned against renewing the request. He said Israel should not appear to be like a beggar. But the Neot Sinai settlers and supporters threatened violence unless the government yielded.

The field, near the local air base, was set on fire Friday. Melons, eggplants and tomatoes were destroyed.

Secretariat created to 'liberate Moslem land'

LONDON (AP). — A four-day international conference summoned to discuss the "liberation of Moslem lands" ended yesterday with a call to the world's 900 million Moslems not to give up their struggle until they have freed Palestine, Jerusalem and other "occupied" Moslem territories.

More than 100 delegates from 27 Moslem countries passed a resolution setting up an international secretariat for the liberation of Moslem lands and named Salem Azzam of Saudi Arabia as its first secretary-general. Its headquarters will be in London.

The resolution called on the new secretariat "to coordinate the activities of the various liberation and other movements and provide for the projection of their views."

Mauritania premier said killed in crash

DAKAR (Reuter). — Mauritanian Prime Minister Ahmed Ould Bouceif was believed to have died yesterday when his plane disappeared near the Senegalese capital of Dakar.

The Senegalese press agency reported that the plane crashed into the sea in bad weather north of Dakar airport and rescue workers said there was no hope of finding survivors. Eleven others were aboard.

The prime minister was on his way to an economic summit of West African states in Dakar.

War invalids get together in peace

By JOSHUA BRILLIANT
Jerusalem Post Reporter

EL-ARISH. — An Egyptian military surgeon who was part of the contingent of war invalids brought here yesterday by President Anwar Sadat to meet Israelis injured in war volunteered to treat the wounded Israelis. The Defence Ministry promptly accepted his offer.

A formal invitation will be sent shortly, Arye Fink, the director of the ministry's Department of Rehabilitation, told *The Jerusalem Post*.

The offer by Col. Hijazi Hussein Mohammed of the Hellemiya Military Hospital in Cairo, followed by Fink's invitation, reflected the mood at the meeting of 43 Israelis and 42 Egyptians who had faced each other in battle and now bear permanent scars.

In another move to increase contacts, Israel's organization of disabled war veterans gave Sadat a letter, addressed to his wife Jihan, which invited Egyptian war invalids to visit Israel and its rehabilitation institutions.

At first the mood was reserved when the Egyptians and Israelis met in the wood-panelled room which had served as the cinema hall of the military government headquarters here.

Most of the 43 Israelis suffered serious burns or required amputations. Some have artificial limbs. Nearly all the Egyptians were in uniform and most of the wounded interviewed by *The Post* were physicians. Three others arrived in wheelchairs. Two were blind.

There was a dramatic moment when an Egyptian battalion commander recognized Motti Ashkenazi, whom he had seen get hit in the central sector of the Suez Canal. The Egyptian recounted how Ashkenazi's tank was hit by a Sager anti-tank missile and the Israeli — badly burned — tried to flee. Ashkenazi confirmed it.

The ice began to melt when the Israelis handed bouquets of red and pink carnations to each Egyptian. It was "a touching gesture," according to Lt. Col. Mohammed Naguib, who suffered burns and impaired hearing following an Israeli air bombing at El-Shat, near Suez, on October 22, 1973.

The head of the Egyptian delegation, Brig. Gen. Dr. Mohammed Abu el-Ezz, identified an Israeli to whom

(Continued on page 9, col. 2)

THE JERUSALEM POST

Talk on
dropouts
★
Page 2

IL9.00 (inc. Vat)

THURSDAY, JUNE 28, 1979 • TAMUZ 3, 5739 • SHA'ABAN 2, 1399 • VOL. XLIX, No. 14653

F-15s engaged in first battle

5 Syrian Migs downed in dogfight over Lebanon

By HIRSH GOODMAN
Post Military Correspondent

Israel Air Force planes yesterday downed five Syrian Mig-21 fighters in a three-minute aerial battle over Southern Lebanon. There were no Israeli losses, according to an announcement from the IDF spokesman.

Two or three other Syrian aircraft were apparently hit but not destroyed during the dog-fights, which took place between Sidon and Beirut above the Mediterranean coast.

The incident took place at around 11 yesterday morning when between eight and 12 Syrian Mig fighters attempted to attack Israeli aircraft that were on a bombing mission over three terrorist targets in Southern Lebanon: Damour, Sidon and Tyre.

Israeli F-15 and Kfir interceptors, engaged the Syrian formation. During the two to three-minute air battle, according to O.C. Air Force Aluf David Ivri, the Israeli interceptors downed five Migs and damaged at least two others.

Immediately after the clash yesterday, the Egyptians were informed of the incident by a direct line. No immediate reaction was forthcoming, but the Egyptians condemned the raid later through the Egyptian Foreign Ministry. (See adjacent story).

This is the first time in history that the U.S.-built McDonnell Douglas F-15 has engaged in battle and destroyed an enemy aircraft in air-to-air combat.

At a meeting with military correspondents in Tel Aviv yesterday, Chief of Staff Rav-Aluf Rafael Eitan intimated that he was not surprised by yesterday's incident.

He said that for some time now Syrian fighters had been sent aloft while Israeli planes were carrying out the government's pre-emptive strike policy against the terrorist bases in Southern Lebanon. But Eitan noted that previously the Syrians had kept a respectable distance from the Israeli attackers.

Yesterday, however, the Syrian aircraft, which were grouped in two formations of four planes each, went through a series of manoeuvres that were highly indicative of hostile intent.

They did not fire the first shot, the chief of staff said, but when a plane advances at a rate of eight miles per minute, there is very little time for procrastination.

In line with traditional attempts to claim a role in dramatic regional events, the PLO alleged in a communique that it had downed two Israeli planes by shoulder-fired SAM-7 missiles. The PLO backed their claim by "eyewitness" testimonies channelled to foreign news agencies.

Even the Christian Phalangist radio quoted some of these eyewitnesses as claiming that an Israeli pilot and his co-pilot were seen bailing out of their plane and that they had been captured — in the area where the two surviving Syrian pilots were reported to have been recovered.

Syrians while on a bombing mission against the terrorists in Lebanon.

The clash yesterday was the first between Israeli and Syrian planes since April 1974, when four Migs were destroyed, and the first in the five years that the two sides have been bound by a disengagement agreement on the Golan Heights.

O.C. Military Intelligence, Aluf Yehoshua Saguy, who also attended yesterday's meeting with the press, said that it was "far from clear" what had motivated the Syrians to risk their aircraft and veer from the status quo which has existed in Lebanon for the past three years.

He indicated that it may have been an attempt by the Syrian leadership to divert attention from internal problems. The decision may also
(Continued on page 2, col. 7)

Knesset okays IL320b. budget; holds IL500m. in college funds

By ARYEH RUBINSTEIN
Post Knesset Reporter

By a vote of 47-3, the Knesset last night adopted a state budget of IL320b. for the fiscal year ending March 31, 1980. For the past three months government expenditures have been made on the strength of the interim budget passed by the Knesset in March.

The most significant vote of the day was on the allocation for higher education. Not unexpectedly, the House approved the Finance Committee's decision earlier this week, initiated by the Likud, to transfer IL500m. from grants to universities to a general reserve for higher education. (See related story)

The 67 votes in favour of the budget were cast by the coalition factions, and the three nays were cast by Gideon Hausner (Independent Liberals), and Moshe Shamir and Geula Cohen (Independents).

Members of the Alignment, Shai, the Communists, and the Citizens Rights Movement walked out of the chamber just before the vote. This was after Speaker Yitzhak Berman rejected a point of order by Amnon Rubinstein (Shai).

Oil off Ashdod

ASHDOD (Itim). — Drillers at the Ashdod V oil well off the coast yesterday brought their drills back up from a lower stratum and restruck a layer of oil that they had found in previous drilling.

There was no confirmation last night as to whether the well has commercial possibilities.

Rubinstein argued that the budget proposed by the government was illegal, since it was already clear that expenditures would be considerably higher than those set forth. Specifically, he said, the IL9b. allocated for subsidies on vital commodities was already unrealistic.

It was the second walk-out of the day — which started at 9 a.m. and ended at 8 p.m. In the course of the 11 hours, the Knesset rejected 150 opposition histagaymot (proposals disapproved by a majority of the Finance Committee and submitted to the plenum for final decision).

The first departure of opposition parties took place earlier in the day, when the Justice Ministry budget was about to be voted on. Deputy Speaker Pinhas Sheinman (NRP) had called for a vote, but a second later gave the floor to Justice Minister Shmuel Tamir.

Opposition members constituted a majority of the deputies in the chamber at the moment, and they suspected Sheinman and Tamir of having teamed up on a delaying tactic, in order to give the Likud whip time to round up a few of his colleagues. Sheinman insisted that Tamir had requested the floor earlier. But Moshe Shahal (Alignment) countered that, once the chairman had called for a vote, no one had the right to speak. When Sheinman overruled him, the entire opposition walked out.

The budget was presented for its second reading by Finance Committee chairman Shlomo Lorincz (Agudat Yisrael), who said that the big question was whether the budget was realistic. And his answer was:

no and yes.

No, if the question referred to the actual sums set forth, for there was no doubt that the year's expenditure would come to considerably more than IL320b. But yes, substantively speaking.

Lorincz explained that under Article 3 of the Budget Law — which he called "an unprecedented innovation" — if expenditure for existing programmes and activities increased because of inflation, such additional expenditure would be covered by the additional revenue that would be forthcoming as a result of changes in the exchange rate of foreign currencies and of higher tax receipts.

For example, Lorincz said, if the wages of government employees rose by more than the 42 per cent envisaged in the budget, government revenue from income tax, value added tax, and other taxes would also rise.

On the other hand, Lorincz said, if the government should decide to freeze the prices of basic commodities (which is precisely what it did last Sunday), the allocation for subsidies set forth in the budget would have to be increased, and a supplementary budget would be necessary.

He said that most members of the committee were opposed "on economic grounds" to the freezing of these prices. "But of course," Lorincz added, "the prime minister and the cabinet have the right to take non-economic considerations into account." Still, he said he hoped that
(Continued on page 8, Col. 3)

Dogfight marks change in Syria's Lebanon role

Jerusalem Post Staff
and Agencies

The Syrian involvement in yesterday's dogfight marked a change in Damascus' policy — a development that observers attribute to two factors:

The first is the quest by the Damascus authorities to shift attention from internal disturbances plaguing Syria since last week's assassination of over 40 artillery cadets in an anti-government raid on the military academy in Aleppo. Eighteen alleged members of the extremist Moslem Brotherhood were due to be hanged today for the assassinations.

Two cases of assassinations of Alawite Moslem intelligence officers serving President Hafez Assad's regime were also recently reported.

The second is the increasing intensity of Israel's punitive air raids against terrorist bases in Lebanon, where the Syrians claim hegemony. Yesterday's was the 11th Israeli air operation over Lebanon since the April 22 terrorist sea attack on Nahariya when four Israelis were killed. Damascus sources called yesterday a national alert in Syria covered anti-aircraft batteries, and part of its 400-plane air force.

Syria maintains some 25,000 troops in Lebanon, equipped with tanks, anti-aircraft artillery and, according to some persistent, but unconfirmed reports, a number of Soviet-made SAM-6 surface-to-air missiles. The Syrian force moved into Lebanon in June 1976 at the height of a civil war between Christians and an alliance that combined the Palestine Liberation Organization and Lebanese leftists.

Syria conceded yesterday that four of its jets were "hit" but claimed that two Israeli warplanes were

also shot down. A Syrian military spokesman issued a statement saying: "At 11.30 a.m., formations of hostile Israeli planes bombed civilian targets in the Damur area south of Beirut. They were intercepted by formations of Syrian fighters and were engaged in an air battle which resulted in the shooting of two hostile Israeli planes. Four Syrian planes were hit. All Syrian planes returned to base safely after they prevented the Israel enemy from accomplishing its mission."

The Beirut state radio said that two Syrian pilots who bailed out from downed Migs were picked up safely by residents of South Lebanon some three hours after the dogfight. But eyewitnesses at the scene said the Palestinian inhabitants had taken the Syrian pilots prisoner thinking them to be Israeli until the Syrians convinced them of their mistake.

Lebanese military sources said that one Syrian Mig-21 made a forced landing at the Lebanese air base with Israeli planes several hundred metres north of Riak in the eastern Bekaa province near the Syrian border, reportedly after running out of fuel.

U.S. claims Israel still selling arms to Nicaragua

By WOLF BLITZER
Jerusalem Post Correspondent

WASHINGTON. — Despite official Israeli denials, the U.S. claims to have evidence that Israel has continued to supply the Nicaraguan National Guard with military equipment, including Uzi submachineguns, Galil rifles and ammunition.

The matter has been the source of extensive diplomatic exchanges between Washington and Jerusalem. Israel has informed the U.S. that it stopped selling arms to Nicaragua last summer, following earlier U.S. protests. Since then, Israeli officials have maintained publicly that the arms embargo has been in effect.

But U.S. intelligence sources have reportedly come up with "strong evidence" that Israel has continued supplying arms and ammunition to Nicaragua. Israel has been confronted with the evidence, according to well-placed sources here, who said that Washington has registered a stiff protest over the issue.

U.S. officials believe that Prime Minister Menahem Begin, Foreign Minister Moshe Dayan and other senior Israeli officials may not be aware that lower-level Israeli of-

ficials were ignoring the official Israeli policy.

Other U.S. officials believe that Begin and Dayan may simply regard the matter as unimportant and therefore may be ignoring the violations of public policy. In any case, as the fighting in Nicaragua has intensified in recent weeks, the controversy has escalated in importance.

There have been numerous reports in the U.S. news media in recent days that Nicaraguan troops were armed largely with Israeli and South African military equipment — reports which have seriously embarrassed Israeli officials here as well as other pro-Israeli supporters.

This has been especially true in the wake of the Nicaraguan murder last week of ABC newsman Bill Stewart.

One U.S. newsman who returned from Nicaragua this past weekend said that he had personally met two Israeli "arms salesmen" in the Nicaraguan capital last week. He said the Israelis admitted being in Nicaragua in order to sell arms.

Publicly so far, the U.S. has taken a cautious position on the controversy even though privately key officials are very angry. (see story — Page 4)

Cairo: Air clash stresses danger to peace process

CAIRO (AP). — Egypt yesterday declared that the air battle between Syrian and Israeli jets underscored the grave dangers which could face the peace process because of Israeli attacks on Lebanon.

Cairo Radio broadcast only the Syrian account of the dogfights.

A statement attributed to a responsible source at the Foreign Ministry condemned the Israeli air raid on terrorist targets in Lebanon, but carefully refrained from assigning blame in the dogfight incident. Egyptian reaction would be limited to the statement, informed officials said.

The Palestinian problem should be speedily solved and peace should be established between Israel and its Arab neighbours to avert such dangers, the statement said.

'Even-handed' Washington had warned against fighting

By WOLF BLITZER
Jerusalem Post Correspondent

WASHINGTON. — Following the Israeli-Syrian aerial dogfight over Southern Lebanon yesterday, the U.S. registered a sharp diplomatic protest to Israel for supposedly provoking the Syrian aircraft to scramble against the Israeli planes.

Publicly, the U.S. did not explicitly accuse Israel of provocation, although this was strongly suggested in the official State Department reaction to the incident.

Reading from a written statement, acting spokesman Tom Reston said that some of the Israeli targets of recent weeks "have been extremely close to Syrian military positions."

Reston said the Syrians "have been scrambling aircraft from time to time in response to the Israeli actions. This dangerous combination of events culminated in the air battle today."

Washington was deliberately trying to take an even-handed position in public, refusing to cast blame. But privately officials let it be known that they thought Israel was largely the culprit for yesterday's incident.

According to informed sources here, the U.S. had repeatedly raised the matter of a possible Israeli-Syrian confrontation with Israeli of-
(Continued on Page 9, Col. 4)

OPEC meet may end in deadlock

GENEVA (Reuter). — A senior Iranian delegate to the OPEC meeting said last night Saudi Arabia was prepared to accept a price of $19 a barrel for oil.

But the delegate, Cyrus Ebrahimzadeh, said OPEC members had still not reached agreement on a new figure at their oil price-fixing conference in Geneva. And Saudi Oil Minister Ahmed Zaki Yamani said last night the OPEC gathering might end without an agreement on new prices.

Speaking during a short interval as OPEC ministers moved from their conference to a private room for further consultations, Yamani said: "We are not near an agreement but we may be near to a conclusion."

Asked whether they were concluding without agreement, he answered: "Yes, that is true."

One delegate said Yamani, who was trying single-handedly to block a substantial price increase, had told ministers before they adjourned that Saudi Arabia was prepared to leave its price at the current level of $14.50 a barrel. Others could then do what they wanted, the delegate quoted Yamani as saying.

(Earlier story — Page 4)

Cement workers strike may need gov't intervention

By MICHAL YUDELMAN
Post Labour Reporter

TEL AVIV. — The government may declare the Nesher cement company an essential industry so that it can serve back-to-work orders on workers, building industry sources told The Jerusalem Post yesterday. Sanctions by plant employees are causing a severe cement shortage.

Nesher's cement kiln in Ramle, which normally produces 670 tons of cement daily — a third of the national output — has been idle since June 10. The workers, who are demanding higher wages, are preventing the management from fixing a malfunction in the kiln, Nesher's personnel manager Simha Nir told The Post.

The continued cut in the production by Israel's only cement manufacturer will threaten the jobs of some 60,000 workers in the building trade, Nir said.

He explained that cement factories work around the clock, so "the amount of cement lost would be impossible to regain." Already the industry is suffering from a shortage which can only be made up by importing cement, Nir claimed.

In addition, one of the company's two works committees, which refused to accept the management's proposals, decided to "extort higher wages from the management under pressure," according to Nir.

The committee also began to impose further sanctions on Tuesday, he said, calling the workers' demands "far beyond the company's wage policy." Their new sanctions called for the reduction of the Ramle quarry's production by half.

The Post has learned that the Histadrut and local labour council have not approved the Nesher workers' sanctions, but so far all attempted negotiations have broken down.

NRP raps economic policies

By SHLOMO MAOZ
Post Economic Reporter

Prime Minister Menahem Begin yesterday told National Religious Party MKs that his price freeze on government-controlled basic commodities is not a final decision. But NRP ministers have been told to vote against freezing the price of imported beef when the matter comes up for the vote in next Sunday's cabinet meeting when, says Begin, final decisions on the price freeze policy will be taken.

The NRP does not want to be party to the economy's destruction, their Knesset faction told the premier yesterday. Protesting against the government's erratic economic policies, they pointed out that no sooner does the cabinet take an economic decision than it reverses it totally.

The premier agreed with his NRP coalition partners that a coalition committee should be set up to examine the entire issue of subsidies and the situation of the national economy.

The establishment of the proposed committee had been the brainchild of the party's Avraham Melamed, who had put it forward earlier as an ultimatum, threatening that if it was not set up, the NRP would not vote for the budget.

Another condition set for NRP support was the establishment of a committee to re-examine the budget which, the NRP claims, is "unrealistic."

A further NRP concession wrung from Begin was that the welfare budget would be subjected to special examination in view of what the party claims is a scatter-shot policy that entirely fails to hit any target.

The NRP would like to see help given to the poorer sections of the population through child allowances and the guaranteeing of a minimum wage, and not through the subsidized food which the entire population takes advantage of, irrespective of need.

The Ministerial Economic Committee must change its decision on price freezes, the NRP claims.

Lebanese report massive IDF damage to terror bases

Jerusalem Post Reporter

METULLA. — Lebanese villagers arriving here yesterday said the IDF bombing mission had caused great damage to terrorist-controlled areas. They told The Jerusalem Post that the terrorists had shot at Syrian planes flying over their positions during the dogfight.

Others coming from Dubin and Blat villages claimed to have seen a parachutist bail out and land north of Blat on the edge of a UN-controlled area, and a burning plane explode in the hilly section near Jezin.

Early yesterday there was an artillery duel between terrorists and Christian militia leader Major Sa'ad

Haddad's forces, after terrorists opened fire on militiamen near the Christian village of Debel.

Haddad's forces claim the terrorists came and retreated via a UNIFIL-held area without any interference from the Irish troops stationed there.

Haddad has sent a sharply worded protest to UNIFIL saying that if the terrorist attacks continue across UN-held territory his men will no longer respect UNIFIL suzerainty.

Heavy artillery exchanges in the eastern section north of Metulla yesterday set fire to fields throughout the area across the border in Lebanon.

Grants c'tee walks out over college budget cut

By SHLOMO MAOZ
Post Economic Reporter

The Planning and Grants Committee, the executive arm of the Council for Higher Education, has returned its mandate. The Council, meeting yesterday, expressed its understanding of the Committee's action and asked Minister Zevulun Hammer to seek a reversal of the Knesset Finance Committee's recommendation to chop IL500m. off the IL4.5b. budget for university

education. This was the upshot of an emergency meeting held yesterday by the council under Hammer's chairmanship.

The committee's members gave Hammer a fortnight to act.

Some committee members yesterday charged that the move announced this week is an attempt to politicize its work by making the universities' budget contingent on as yet unknown conditions. They stress
(Continued on page 2, col. 5)

STALIN'S LEGACY. Edward Crankshaw, in the first of two articles, explains why the Georgian dictator's imprint remains on the fabric of Soviet society.

GADDAFI'S GRANT. Nicholas Lemann looks into Arab investment in American universities and its information dividends.

GALILEE INHERITANCE. Ya'acov Ardon attends a seminar on northern problems.

All in tomorrow's Weekend edition of

U.S. congressmen demand Paraguay hand over Mengele

By JOSEPH POLAKOFF

WASHINGTON (JTA). — Both branches of Congress, using the power of publicity, yesterday moved to flush out Nazi criminal Josef Mengele from his hiding place in Paraguay and bring him to trial.

Mengele, a medical doctor, is accused of torturing and killing at least 400,000 inmates at Auschwitz, half of them children. He reportedly tried experiments on "physical change" on inmates who had no anesthesia.

Three congressmen asked Paraguayan Ambassador Mario Lopez Escobar at his embassy here to urge his government to at least revoke Mengele's citizenship so that he stands exposed as "the world's most wanted Nazi criminal." Mengele, now 67, is known as the "angel of death" of Auschwitz, where five million persons were killed by the Nazis.

Joining forces in the drive against Mengele,

who is wanted by the governments of West Germany, Poland and Israel, both the Senate and House are considering a joint resolution urging President Carter to "immediately call upon Paraguay to apprehend and extradite" Mengele to stand trial in West Germany.

Sen. Jesse Helms introduced a resolution in the Senate last week, and yesterday Rep. Robert Dornan presented an identical resolution in the House to help expedite U.S. governmental action. Liberals and conservatives from both parties are sponsoring the resolution.

In addition to their action against Mengele, Dornan, Rep. Jerry Lewis and congressmen from the Simon Wiesenthal Centre for Holocaust Studies at Yeshiva University in New York went to the Brazilian embassy here in the day to urge extradition of the Nazi war criminal Gustav Wagner. A Brazilian court last week refused to allow Wagner's extradition.

Dornan, Rep. Matthew McHugh and Rep. Christopher Dodd called on Escobar. With them were Rabbi Marvin Hier, dean of the Wiesenthal Centre; Rabbi Abraham Cooper, the centre's outreach programme director; and Wiesenthal's attorney, Martin Rosen of New York.

The ambassador was given a letter addressed to Gen. Alfredo Stroessner, Paraguay's president, signed by 40 congressmen.

The letter, which was authored by McHugh, said Mengele fled to Argentina from Germany after World War II and "later in an effort to elude authorities he entered Paraguay where he was naturalized as a citizen in 1959."

Asking Stroessner to help locate Mengele and "bring him to justice," the letter said Mengele has been "indicted for various crimes in several nations," and "stands accused of the torture, disfigurement and murder" of at least 100,000 children, and as many adults.

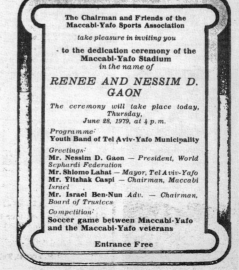

THE JERUSALEM POST

Sunday, February 24, 1980 VOL. L, No. 14854 IL15.00

Shekel makes debut today; Gov't takes steps to fight 'black money'

Finance Minister Yigael Hurvitz (fifth from left) faces the press at Friday afternoon's special news conference called to announce the currency change. In the foreground is a diagram explaining the changes. (Rahamim Israeli).

Sadat seeks to quell left, Moslem dissent

By ANAN SAFADI
Post Mideast Affairs Editor

CAIRO. — Obviously irritated over the unprecedented intensity of opposition activity, President Anwar Sadat ordered his ruling National Democratic Party over the weekend "to get to the masses" in an apparent attempt to dispel the impression that support for his regime is fading.

The underclared duel between Sadat and his opponents was mounted as Egypt and Israel prepared to exchange ambassadors on Tuesday — a step over which the opposition has pledged to fight the government in public.

The opposition comes mainly from the left-oriented Socialist Labour and Unionist Progressive Parties as well as the right-wing Moslem Brotherhood fundamentalist movement.

Israel's ambassador-designate Eliahu Ben-Elissar is due in Cairo today and his Egyptian counterpart, Sa'ad Murtada, arrives in Tel Aviv today. They will present their credentials to Presidents Sadat and Yitzhak Navon on Tuesday and take over the first embassies the two nations established last week in each other's country.

The Unionist Progressive Party, which has been flying twO flags of the Palestine Liberation Organization over its headquarters in the heart of Cairo since last week, had called on Cairenes to stage a march to the presidential palace on Tuesday to protest the exchange of ambassadors. The Socialist Labour Party, which has 30 seats in the 392-member parliament, urged Egyptians to hoist a million Palestinian flags to counter Israel's lone blue and white banner fluttering over the diplomatic mission in the Dokki suburb. The Moslem fundamen-

(Continued on page 2, col. 2)

More security in Cairo for Israelis, cooperating firms

Post Mideast Affairs Editor

CAIRO. — Authorities here have stepped up security measures for Israelis and a number of Egyptian firms after reported incitement of attacks against them.

The mass-circulation weekly, "Akhbar el-Yom," yesterday said that the opposition Progressive Party has circulated leaflets urging Egyptians to boycott some firms dealing with Israelis and sabotage others.

The paper said that among the target enterprises were a press distribution agency selling Israeli newspapers and a hotel with Israeli guests. The paper said that a number of Egyptian companies were now considering filing suit against the opposition party for "incitement to stir chaos" in the Egyptian capital. The weekly indicated that the legal action was being coordinated with the authorities.

Meanwhile, the massive security at Israel's embassy in the suburb of Dokki has been increased even further.

Shots were heard nearby on Friday. Minutes later, security forces arrested an attache at the Turkish embassy, Mustafa Sweilo, who allegedly shot another Turkish diplomat, Aziz Taner, for attacking his wife.

Ali due for urgent talks on Israel troop plans for areas

By ANAN SAFADI
Post Mideast Affairs Editor

CAIRO. — Defence Minister Kamal Hassan Ali has been instructed by President Anwar Sadat to hold urgent talks with his Israeli counterpart, Ezer Weizman, on the military presence which Jerusalem plans to maintain in the West Bank and Gaza Strip.

Ali is due in Israel tomorrow at the head of a high-powered delegation for a four-day visit at Weizman's invitation. He will be preceded by Egypt's first ambassador to Israel, Sa'ad Mortada, who is due today. Mortada will present his credentials to President Yitzhak Navon on Tuesday, when Israel's ambassador in Cairo, Eliahu Ben-Elissar, presents his to Sadat.

Informed Cairo sources say Ali will meet at least once with Premier Menahem Begin during his visit.

The sources said that Ali has been instructed by Sadat to negotiate the redeployment of Israeli forces in the territories with Weizman, with the aim of speeding their withdrawal from populated areas.

The sources said that Egypt is now giving priority to Israeli troop redeployment in the West Bank and Gaza, over its quest to get Israel to withdraw from the rest of Sinai sooner than 1982.

The Egyptians say they want an agreement on the redeployment by next May, which, they now insist, must be treated as a deadline rather than a target date for the completion of negotiations on West Bank autonomy.

(Hirsh Goodman adds in Jerusalem:

In their four days of talks Ali and Weizman are expected to conclude — in their shared capacity as the two ministers in charge of the normalization process — outstanding details on communications, travel and tourism agreements, drafts of which have been prepared by the various sub-committees.

They are also expected to finalize details for military attachés at the two countries' embassies in Tel Aviv and Cairo. There is an agreement in principle for military attachés. What has to be decided now is their rank, status and duties).

Sadat is to meet tomorrow with

(Continued on page 2, col. 5)

Cabinet no to Hurvitz on safe-deposit pry

By SHLOMO MAOZ
Post Economic Reporter

The cabinet on Friday rejected the one far-ranging idea that might have dealt a massive blow at the black money in the economy. Meeting to discuss the change over from Israeli pounds to the new shekels, Premier Menahem Begin, Deputy Premier Simha Ehrlich and Justice Minister Shmuel Tamir spiked a proposal that would have made the tax authorities, and possibly also the police, privy to the secrets people may be keeping in their bank safe-deposit boxes.

As the cabinet assembled, Begin asked sharply what the country's police chief, Inspector-General Herzl Shafir, was doing there. Who invited him, Begin wanted to know.

Begin remained firm that Shafir not join the meeting at which the police chief wanted to put forth the police view in support of the proposal that safe-deposit boxes be opened after a week's prior notice and then only in the presence of an income tax officer and possibly police, too.

Begin had been in on the secret of the currency change, but Finance Minister Yigael Hurvitz had kept from him his proposal on the safe-deposits. Begin immediately objected, supported by Ehrlich. But it was Tamir who spearheaded the opposition and ensured its defeat.

The basic opposition point was that Hurvitz's idea would constitute an infringement of privacy. But Education Minister Zevulun Hammer, Religious Affairs Minister Aharon Abuhatzeira, Housing and Absorption Minister David Levy, Agriculture Minister Ariel Sharon and Social Affairs Minister Israel Katz felt otherwise.

Katz praised Hurvitz's idea and suggested that a sample number of safe-deposits be opened compulsorily, claiming that since people's privacy was in any case invaded in other ways, this move — as part of the war against black money — was quite acceptable. It is estimated that there are between 20,000 to 30,000 safe-deposit boxes rented by the public in the country's banks.

Economic circles in Jerusalem yesterday said any such move would be bound to fail in a cabinet including the Liberal Party.

Friday's meeting was convened as a panic measure after Hurvitz and his director-general learned that a journalist had the news of the currency change and was about to publicize it. The cabinet session was thus moved forward to Friday, instead of being held today as planned.

The currency change, it was widely felt, will have no effect on inflation in either direction. There may be some minor problems in the next few days as people pay for goods and services in both the old and new currency, as for example in tendering bus fares and receiving change where speed is of the essence.

Until new cheque books are printed, cheques must be made out in Israel pounds.

Debts, both private and those owed by public bodies, should be divided by 10 and written as shekels, as will be done with salaries which, expressed in shekels, will be a tenth of the number of Israel pounds that they are today.

Yesterday, money changers in the Old City could be seen rehearsing the new rates of conversion, holding up IL500 notes and saying that these were now 50 shekels.

The introduction of the shekel was decided on in principle by the Knesset in June 1969. In November 1977, Bank of Israel Governor Arnon Gafny thought the time had come to make the switch to shekels. The decision by Begin and Ehrlich, who was then finance minister, came in May 1978. Thus the Menora Operation (its code name) was launched.

Hurvitz and Gafny finally put the operation into high gear in November 1979, when it was decided to keep everything a close secret for fear of causing public panic.

The decision to refrain from charging any tax as cash is changed is intended to avoid hitting at those who may quite innocently be holding large sums in cash. It is generally felt that many black money owners keep their wealth not in cash but in property, gold, foreign currency or diamonds.

Israel's new paper money. From top to bottom, the one shekel note, bearing a portrait of Sir Moses Montefiore (similar in design to its equivalent in old currency, IL10); the five shekel note, with a portrait of the first president of the state, Chaim Weizmann, (as in the old IL50 note); the 10 shekel note, depicting Theodor Herzl as in the old IL100 note; and the 50 schekel note, with a portrait of the first prime minister, David Ben-Gurion, as in the old IL500 note.

The new shekel coinage: (top to bottom) the new one agora coin (equivalent to 10 agorot in old currency); the new 5 agorot coin (equivalent to 50 agorot old style, or half a lira); the new 10 agorot coin, equivalent in value to one Israel pound (lira); and the new half-shekel coin, equivalent to the old IL5 piece.

Currency change effect only 'psychological'

By DAVID KRIVINE

The Knesset will be asked tomorrow to approve the Shekel Currency Bill, which substitutes one shekel in new currency for every 10 Israel pounds.

The announcement of the currency switch was made at a press conference convened at the Treasury on short notice on Friday by Finance Minister Yigael Hurvitz and the governor of the Bank of Israel, Arnon Gafny.

Two other bills will be tabled in the Knesset tomorrow. One requires that all sizeable transactions be registered, and the other that owners of capital report on all assets in their possession, within three months of the bill's passage into law.

The purpose of the currency reform is to substitute a stronger unit in place of the depreciated pound, Hurvitz said. The change will have only a psychological effect in the battle against inflation, he admitted.

The closer supervision of the flow of funds is aimed at wiping out black capital.

No new tax is envisaged at the moment — neither on the exchange of currencies, nor on the capital declared, according to Hurvitz.

There will probably be a rush today to convert pounds into shekels, though the pounds remain legal tender for three months, until they can be collected by the central bank.

The shekels, which were printed in great secrecy in Holland, have the same design as the old notes, but the denominations are divided by 10. On the new notes "shekalim" replaces "lirot." Because of the similarities, they will have to be scrutinized carefully in every exchange.

A new banknote of IS100 bearing the portrait of Ze'ev Jabotinsky will be released shortly.

Coins will also be replaced. The smaller ones, up to 25 agorot, are no longer valid currency and must be exchanged. The new pieces will be one agora (equal to 10 old ones), five agorot, 10 agorot (equal to a pound), and half-a-shekel (five pounds).

Asked whether this is not an opportunity to impose a one-time wealth tax, Gafny pointed out that wealth takes many forms, and the possession of cash is only one of them, so it would be unfair to tax cash alone.

The shekel was first used in Babylon five millennia ago, as a weight for measuring gold and silver. Its first Biblical mention is in Genesis, when Abraham buys the Cave of Machpela from Ephron the Hittite for "four hundred shekels of silver" to bury his wife Sarah.

Preparations for the demise of the pound began under Hurvitz's predecessor at the Treasury, Simha

(Continued on page 2, col. 2)

Tito has pneumonia

BELGRADE, Yugoslavia (AP). — Doctors for President Josip Broz Tito disclosed yesterday that the Yugoslav leader is being kept alive by a kidney machine, and is suffering from pneumonia.

The announcement shattered already faint hopes in some medical circles that the 87-year-old Tito is in a period of stabilization.

Doctors ban visitors from seeing Khomeini

TEHERAN (Reuter). — Doctors treating revolutionary leader Ayatollah Ruhollah Khomeini at a Teheran heart hospital last night banned all visitors until further notice, the official Pars news agency reported.

(UN commission, page 4)

Kabul under martial law; hundreds killed in fighting

KABUL. — The capital of Afghanistan was under martial law as fighting between anti-communist Moslem rebels and Soviet and Afghan troops continued for the second day yesterday on a reduced scale, after Friday clashes left hundreds of dead and several thousand injured, according to hospital sources.

A Western diplomat, who picked up an injured man in the street and took him to Joumouriet Hospital, counted more than 50 bodies lined up on the floor for burial. Another eye-witness saw six civilian dead lying in the street following renewed fighting yesterday morning.

The streets of Kabul were deserted, with Soviet and Afghan tanks and roadblocks seen in many parts of the city.

A general strike, which began on Thursday, was still in effect yesterday. Most merchants participated in the protest against the Soviet military presence by shuttering their shops.

Bitter fighting erupted simultaneously in different parts of the city shortly after midday Friday, suggesting that the uprising was carefully prepared.

One report from New Delhi quoted "reliable sources" as saying that 4,000 Afghan army troops turned guns on their Soviet commanders in Kabul on Friday, precipitating the martial law decree.

Diplomatic reports said the Soviet ambassador to Afghanistan and the commander-in-chief of the Afghan army met President Babrak Karmal Friday. A cabinet meeting followed and it was then announced that the 11th, 19th and 21st divisions of the Afghan army were "dismissed."

The heaviest shooting occurred near the Bala Hissar fortress, an Afghan army installation on the outskirts of the city, in neighbourhoods near the Soviet embassy and at a military area northwest of the city, where both

(Continued on page 3, col. 5)

Brezhnev hints at pullout

MOSCOW (AP). — Soviet President Leonid Brezhnev declared on Friday that the Soviet Union will pull its troops out of Afghanistan if the U.S. and Afghanistan's neighbours guarantee an end to "outside interference" in that backward Moslem nation.

Elsewhere in Friday's address, Brezhnev accused U.S. President Jimmy Carter of stirring up "anti-Soviet hysteria" to help him win the U.S. presidential election and as a pretext for expansion in Asia.

PLO-held Israeli woman exchanged for 2 terrorists

NICOSIA, Cyprus (AP). — A woman held by the Palestinian Liberation Organization for six years as an alleged Israeli spy was exchanged on Friday for two Palestinian terrorists serving life sentences in Israeli jails.

The exchange was carried out under strict secrecy and with tight security precautions at Cyprus' Larnaca airport. The two terrorists arrived in a jet which then took the woman away.

Both the Red Cross, who supervised the operation, and the Cypriot authorities refused to identify the three persons involved. But informed sources in Cyprus and Beirut said the woman was an Israeli who posed as an Arab while working as a psychologist in Beirut, where the PLO has its headquarters. She was arrested there in 1974.

The Israel army spokesman issued an announcement on Friday confirming that the exchange had taken place. He added that the two Palestinians "had almost completed their prison sentences" but refused to give any more details.

The Cypriot and Beirut sources said one of the exchanged terrorists was Willian Naguib Nassar, a Christian Palestinian, arrested in Jerusalem in 1968. Nassar, then a 22-year-old chemist, was one of the first operatives of Yasser Arafat Fatah terror group to be arrested. He was sentenced to life imprisonment for murder and sabotage. His release has been repeatedly demanded by Palestinian airline hijackers including those at Entebbe in 1976.

The sources identified the second only by his code name, Abu Ali, saying he was arrested in the Gaza Strip in 1971.

Car bomb in Beirut kills Jemayyel baby, 7 others

BEIRUT (AP). — Prospects of national entente in divided Lebanon slumped further yesterday when eight Christians, including the 18-month-old daughter of influential militia commander Beshir Jemayyel, were killed in a shattering blast in a mostly Christian sector of Beirut.

Apparently employing a remote control device, unknown assailants detonated a booby-trapped car near the passing limousine of Jemayyel, leader of the Phalange party militia, on a jammed street near the Foreign Ministry.

Jemayyel's daughter, Maya, and two escorts in the passing car were killed at once. Several others died within an hour, according to witnesses. Some 20 other people were injured. The 33-year-old Jemayel was not in the car.

The bomb attack coincided with a wave of kidnapping of Lebanese army soldiers by leftist gunmen of the breakaway Lebanese Arab Army in the Moslem-dominated west sector of the capital.

Weizman: Nuclear blast report—'nonsense'

By HIRSH GOODMAN
Post Military Correspondent

Defence Minister Ezer Weizman and other key Israeli defence officials have described as "absolute nonsense" a CBS News report aired on Thursday night that Israel exploded a nuclear device off the South African coast last September.

As in the past, they refused to make a direct comment on whether Israel possesses nuclear capability or not. But they went out of their way, both on and off the record, to ridicule the report on the U.S. television network which was based on previously-published — and publicly denied — data for a yet-to-be-published book by two Israeli journalists.

The reporter responsible for the story is Dan Raviv, the CBS radio stringer who works out of the Tel Aviv bureau. The manuscript is now at the military censor undergoing the mandatory examination. Raviv apparently got hold of a copy and decided it was worth smuggling to Rome, and thus evading censorship, to offer it to CBS TV news.

There is no evidence that Raviv tried to verify whether the claims by the two journalists, Ami Doron and Eli Teicher, were accurate.

Raviv also reportedly made no attempt to check the book's status at the censor and find out whether the "top secret" data quoted so dramatically by CBS would have been subject to his blue pencil — since everything put on the air by CBS had been published before.

It was not clear last night what action, if any, Israeli authorities might take against Raviv. The chief military censor, Tat-Aluf Yitzhak Shani, refused to comment to *The Jerusalem Post* on the consequences of Raviv's blatant evasion of censorship rules. In the past, the

(Continued on page 2, col. 5)

THE JERUSALEM POST

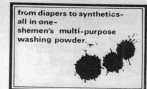

Wednesday, February 27, 1980 VOL. L, No. 14857 IL15.00

Budget debate

Meshel vows fight over wage pacts

Post Knesset Reporter

Histadrut Secretary-General Yeroham Meshel declared in the Knesset yesterday that cost-of-living increments were not a substitute for new wage agreements.

Clashing head-on with the government's determination to extend all existing wage agreeements until March 31, 1981, Meshel said the Histadrut had every intention of opening negotiations soon on all agreements that expire at the end of next month.

Meshel, Labour Alignment MK, spoke in the Knesset debate on the draft budget presented on Monday by Finance Minister Yigael Hurvitz.

Interest in the chamber was at something less than fever pitch. At 4:30 p.m., when Avraham Melamed (National Religious Party) was speaking, his audience consisted of Deputy Speaker Pinhas Scheinman, Hurvitz, one Likud deputy and 10 Alignment MKs.

Things were a little better at 5:50 p.m., when Avraham Sharir (Likud-Liberals) had the floor. In addition to the chairman and the minister, there were then 15 MKs present, representing five factions. Most of them were reading or engaged in conversation.

The House Committee allocated seven hours for the debate. But actually it will last longer — not only because the smaller factions are granted more than their arithmetical share of time, but also

(Continued on page 7, col. 3)

Stocks sink

Post Finance Reporter

TEL AVIV. — Announcement of the proposed 1980/81 budget precipitated what was described as an "unprecedented" decline in share prices on the stock market yesterday. While a total of 67 issues were listed as sellers only, with an automatic 5 per cent decrease in price, the prices of 55 other issues dropped by 10 per cent or more on extremely active trading.

Index-linked bond prices, a certain reflection of the public's expectations of future changes in the cost-of-living index, soared. Most bonds were marked up the maximum allowable 3 per cent.

Finance Minister Yigael Hurvitz attempted to reassure the public in the wake of the market's crash. Speaking on Israel Radio, he pledged that the government would support the stock market. He said all government bonds and other obligations, including those issued by previous governments, would be honoured.

How do you repay your dollar debts?

By SHLOMO MAOZ
Post Economic Reporter

Many Israelis are wondering what will become of their foreign currency debts or credits now that the Treasury has made transfers of non-Israeli money within the country illegal.

Affected are contracts written in dollars or other foreign coin, loans from abroad and other documents employing the practice, which has become common in the last several years as a safeguard against inflation.

The Bank of Israel's foreign exchange controller, Yosef Sarig, stressed yesterday that with the new regulation, there is no justification for debts to be repaid in non-Israeli money. According to legal opinion he has received, Paragraph 47 of the 1973 Contracts Law (general section) now applies: debts defined in currencies not allowed in Israel are to be paid in Israeli coin, according to the exchange rate on the day of payment.

But Sarig had no answer as to which figure would apply — the Bank of Israel's representative rate, a commercial bank's buying rate or its selling rate — or which commercial bank, if their rates differ. Ths question will almost certainly lead to disagreements and have to be resolved in court.

Israelis have one month, until March 26, to turn in to a bank whatever foreign cash they hold in excess of $500 in value. Beginning on March 27, possession of more

(Continued on page 2, col. 3)

Egyptian Ambassador Sa'ad Mortada and President Yitzhak Navon share a toast in Israeli orange juice, after ceremonies at Beit Hanassi during which Mortada officially presented his credentials as Egypt's first ambassador to Israel. (Rahamim Israeli)

Ambassador Eliahu Ben-Elissar shakes hands with Egyptian President Anwar Sadat after presenting his credentials in Cairo yesterday. (UPI telephoto)

Israel, Egypt linked by envoys

Sadat extols peace at Cairo ceremony

By ARI RATH
and ANAN SAFADI

CAIRO. — Israel's first ambassador to Egypt, Eliahu Ben-Elissar — the first permanent Israel envoy ever in an Arab capital — was accredited here yesterday as President Anwar Sadat broke all customary protocol to signify the historic occasion with a public statement hailing the peace. What is normally a brief, routine ceremony turned into a solemn, public reaffirmation and commitment by Sadat to the irreversible peace process, surprising even some of his aides.

The magnificent 100-year-old Abdin Palace in the heart of Cairo resounded twice to the sounds of Hatikva and the Egyptian national anthem played by the presidential guard's military band on Ben-Elissar's arrival and departure, and even tough-looking Egyptian security officials failed to hide their emotion.

Presenting his letter of credence, signed by President Yitzhak Navon and Prime Minister and acting Foreign Minister Menahem Begin, Ben-Elissar addressed Sadat in Arabic, "Sayid el-rais," Mr. President. Then came the big surprise. Sadat moved towards the battery of TV and press cameramen to show them the first Israel ambassador's credentials and make his prepared statement.

Visibly moved, he opened by saying, "This is a historic day. Today we are opening another new chapter in the history of our nations. It is a living symbol to our firm determination to live together in peace and harmony, and new evidence of our common belief in the oneness of the destiny of man.

"This step on the long road to peace does justice to our glorious heritage and great tradition of tolerance and fraternity. We are quite aware that, in order to rekindle the torch of hope in our hearts and minds, each and every one of us must lay a brick in the structure of peace. We are determined to do that.

"Let us vow to put an end to all suffering and misery. Let us vow, on this historic occasion, to complete our sacred mission and make the peace process irreversible. Let every one of us light a candle of understanding and compassion.

"With God's help we shall overcome."

Ben-Elissar, told earlier by the Egyptian chief of protocol that there would be no speeches at the ceremony, replied with a brief off-the-cuff address, praising Sadat's courage and vision which had made the peace "unavoidable." But he had prepared a reference, "appropriate for this historic moment," to the Jewish sage Maimonides, who lived in Egypt in the 12th century. Referring to him by his Arabic name, Mussa ibn Maimun, Ben-Elissar recalled and he used to open all his letters and speeches with the Arabic phrase *bism'illah — rab el-alamin*, (in the name of God — Lord of the universe). Sadat and Prime Minister Mustapha Khalil smiled and nodded in approval.

After reporters had left the richly-ornamented conference room, Ben-Elissar conferred for about twenty minutes with Sadat, Khalil and the head of the presidency, Hassan Kamel.

The forthcoming autonomy talks in The Hague are understood to have been mentioned at this first

(Continued on page 2, col. 6)

Egypt ambassador at Beit Hanassi

By DAVID LANDAU

President Yitzhak Navon and Egypt's ambassador, Sa'ad Mortada, both stressed their countries' "faithful adherence" to the letter and spirit of the peace treaty at the ceremony marking the envoy's presentation of credentials yesterday. "This meticulous fidelity," said Navon, "might well serve as an example to others."

Mortada pledged that Egypt would "continue to adhere to all her obligations in accordance with the letter and spirit of these agreements, with the aim of strengthening peace and establishing good neighbourly relations."

Navon spoke of "the problems we shall have to solve," and of the difficulty of achieving "further agreements with other countries in our region." But "many things that seemed impossible yesterday are now natural and self-evident," the president observed. "What seems hard to achieve today may be attainable tomorrow, if the open-mindedness and ardent desire for peace that animate President Sadat and our own Prime Minister Begin will also inspire the other leaders in the area."

Mortada sought "to reiterate the position of Egypt which derives from her Arab and Islamic responsibilities, as well as her commitment to the principles of the UN, non-alignment and African unity." He, too, spoke of "the difficulties that may lie in store," and he, too, invoked "constructive dialogue...mutual trust," as the means of eventually achieving "fully normal relations between our two countries."

Mortada referred to the peace treaty as "restoring peace and stability, and legitimate rights to all parties, first and foremost the right of the Palestinian people to a free and secure life.

"In this way," he continued, "we shall be able to set a good example of peaceful co-existence between the people of Israel and the Arab peoples of this region, removing the dangers that imperil their security and ensuring a comprehensive, just and lasting peace."

Navon opened his remarks with a pointed reference to "the presidential residence in Jerusalem." He called on "all peace-loving nations the world over...to express their practical support for our efforts to consolidate peace," and urged them not to take "any action that may injure this tender sapling that has just been planted in this bloodstained soil."

The president also made mention of the "hundreds of thousands of Arab citizens of Israel who...enjoy complete freedom and equality of rights. I hope they will be able to make an important contribution to the strengthening of the bridge of peace which has now been erected between our two countries."

The envoy spoke in Arabic and Navon in Hebrew, each address being translated into the other language.

The addresses were much longer and of greater political content than is usual on such occasions, and it was obvious that the two texts had been painstakingly prepared by the respective governments, with every phrase weighed for significance and nuance.

Mortada seemed nervous as he strode into the president's reception room, flanked by Chief-of-Protocol Ya'acov Aviad, and

(Continued on page 2 col. 4)

Begin's worry at U.S. arms for Egypt 'astonishes' Sadat

By ANAN SAFADI
Post Mid-East Affairs Editor

CAIRO. — President Anwar Sadat yesterday praised Israel's first ambassador to Egypt, Dr. Eliahu Ben-Elissar, as "the right man for the right position in the right moment."

Sadat's words were seen as an attempt to silence a Cairo press campaign attacking Ben-Elissar for defending the Israel government's settlements policy on the West Bank.

Sadat, speaking at a press conference for Israeli newsmen and Egyptian TV and radio, said, after Ben-Elissar presented his credentials, "I assured Eli that he was the right man for the right position in the right moment."

But he criticized Premier Menahem Begin for expressing Israel's concern over Egypt's quest for U.S. arms supplies, saying in answer to a question that he had been "astonished" to learn of the premier's position. "This attitude belongs to the past," when Egypt and Israel were still at war, Sadat said.

The Egyptian leader said that Israeli officials must see that they do not feed local opposition with bilateral conflicts on which to capitalize.

Sadat described the presentation of diplomatic credentials by the former head of Begin's office as a great event marking "the inauguration of an eternal monument for peace ... a great day ... a warm beginning of good neighbourly relations" between the two countries.

Sadat twice noted during the press conference that the establishment of diplomatic relations between the two countries was not subject to any restrictions. Since he made the remark out of context, it was difficult to tell whether he sought to assure reporters that Israel would enjoy the status of a friendly country, or to stress that there would be no connection between the newly-established diplomatic ties and the negotiations between the two countries on autonomy for the West Bank and Gaza Strip.

But Sadat did at one point urge Israel to cooperate in making further progress in the peace process. The two countries, he said, "must set an example" to encourage other Arab countries to join the negotiations for a settlement in the region.

"We should not stop half-way," Sadat said, leaving no doubt that he would like Israel to advance its 1982 withdrawal from the rest of Sinai, and to conclude an agreement on the proposed autonomy for the West Bank and Gaza.

Sadat indicated that a number of Arab governments were now awaiting a successful outcome of the autonomy negotiations to drop their opposition to the Israel-Egypt peace process.

He revealed that on Monday he had received an envoy of an Arab leader, with a message that the recent pan-Arab gathering in Tunis had resolved that combating Egypt's current autonomy moves "would harm the Arab cause."

Sadat did not identify the Arab leader concerned, but well-informed sources here on Monday told *The Jerusalem Post* that Jordan's King Hussein had informed Egypt he was suspending active opposition to the autonomy negotiations, though not dropping his reservations about the Camp

(Continued on page 2, col. 2)

Begin: Must be alert to Syria's moves in Lebanon

Jerusalem Post Staff

While calling for an explanation of Syrian moves in Lebanon, Prime Minister Menahem Begin yesterday again declared that Israel has never considered attacking Syria or anyone else.

The prime minister also reiterated Israel's desire for peace with Lebanon, and within Lebanon, while at the same time stressing Israel's moral commitment toward the Christian minority in that nation.

In a far-reaching interview on the army radio's evening newsreel, Begin questioned Syria's motives in Lebanon. He asked — do they intend to turn Lebanon into a Syrian protectorate, to establish a 'greater Syria?' Do they intend to attack the Christians? Or are they preparing an attack against Israel?

Because these questions are unanswered, Begin insisted that Israel must stand on guard in order not to be taken again by surprise. He rejected the suggestion of a "pre-emptive step," saying that "we must be careful."

The prime minister expressed regret that the months of quiet and tranquillity in Lebanon have ceased, citing the recent attack on the Beshir Jemayel family in Beirut in which eight people were killed. But, he said, this had no connection whatsoever with the peace treaty with Egypt.

Begin again expressed willingness to go to Beirut to conduct peace treaty negotiations, and he invited President Elias Sarkis to visit Israel. The prime minister emphasized that "we have no claims in Lebanon; we recognize its territorial integrity."

It was then that the prime minister referred to the Christian minority, saying that "we cannot conceive that a national or religious minority will be wiped out only because it is such a minority." He said that the Crhristian minority in Lebanon faced this danger in the past — of actual extermination — "but we prevented this by the steps we took."

'Egypt's autonomy position deviates from Camp David'

Post Diplomatic Correspondent

Prime Minister Menahem Begin yesterday termed Egypt's position in the autonomy talks a "wide deviation from the Camp David agreements." In a radio interview on the occasion of the exchange of ambassadors, Begin denied, though, that the autonomy talks were in "deadlock." The three parties, Israel, Egypt and the U.S., could still reach agreement by the May target date, he said, "if we all remain faithful to Camp David."

Begin said the Camp David agreements, painstakingly negotiated, advisedly defined the projected autonomous body as "an administrative council." For the Egyptian side, therefore, to propose a body with legislative and constitutional powers was "a decided deviation from Camp David." It was a proposal "which Israel cannot accept...we hope to persuade the Egyptians that they are raising difficulties for the negotiations by deviating from Camp David."

"Agreements," said the prime minister, "have got to be observed — just as we have both observed the peace treaty between us."

Begin said the government was "thinking about" the problem of the legal status of the Jewish settlements on the West Bank. It would soon publish its decisions — and these would not contradict the Camp David agreements.

The prime minister was moderate and circumspect on the question of American arms supplies to Egypt. "This is a problem of quantities and quality. It must be clarified in contacts between governments, not in public declarations."

To an army radio interviewer who tried to press him on this issue, Begin answered firmly: "I have said it is 'a problem. That is enough."

On the credentials ceremonies in Cairo and Jerusalem, Begin said, "This is a special day in the annals of the two nations and of the Middle East."

He continued: "Let us remember what passed between our two peoples in 31 years of hostility, five wars, bloodshed, widowhood, bereavement...

"This is a good day, a nice day — both for the Egyptians and for us Israelis."

Neutral Afghanistan mooted

WASHINGTON (AP). — President Jimmy Carter yesterday offered to support a neutral Afghanistan if the Soviet Union withdraws from that southwest Asian nation.

Carter's comments, in response to a letter from ailing Yugoslav President Josip Broz Tito asking for continued detente, followed an apparent offer by the Soviet Union to withdraw "as soon as all forms of outside interference directed against the government and people of Afghanistan are fully terminated."

An administration official said Carter "reaffirms that the U.S. did not interfere in the internal affairs of Afghanistan and that with the prompt withdrawal of all Soviet troops from that country, the U.S. would be willing to join in a guarantee of true neutrality and non-interference in Afghanistan's internal affairs."

The source said that a guarantee of neutrality would involve, in addition to the U.S., Afghanistan's neighbours — Iran, Pakistan, and the Soviet Union.

The Afghan government, meanwhile, announced yesterday that those responsible for rioting in the capital, Kabul, would be dealt with by process of law, Kabul Radio said.

Pakistan radio reported last night that Kabul was tense and under heavy military guard.

Authoritative sources in Islamabad said Afghan and Soviet troops were engaged in mopping-up operations on Monday and that they believed mass arrests were being made.

Tito sinking

BELGRADE (AP). — President Josip Broz Tito slipped closer to death yesterday, his doctors saying they had not been able to relieve his pneumonia and his heart had grown more erratic.

For the first time in the more than six weeks of Tito's hospitalization, a portrait photo of the 87-year-old leader was displayed on the Belgrade evening television news programme.

Electric Co. heads meet to discuss Amiad firing

The Electricity Corporation executive met last night to discuss the Board of Directors' decision to fire the Corporation's general manager, Ariel Amiad. The executive was reportedly shocked by the announcement, which its members heard only through the media. Amiad was not present at last night's meeting.

Key management workers in the corporation will meet in Haifa today to discuss the implications of the proposed sacking.

(Early story — page 2)

Carter seen ahead in first primary

MANCHESTER, New Hampshire. — New Hampshire voted yesterday in the first full-dress U.S. presidential primary of 1980, a contest that could cripple Democrat Edward Kennedy's White House ambitions and create a new Republican front-runner.

The skies were sunny, the temperature cold but bearable and election officials predicted a record turnout in the primary that traditionally gives Americans their first firm indication of how the political winds are blowing in the battle for the presidency.

Kennedy fielded an army of 1,600 young volunteers to bring his supporters to the polls and avoid a drubbing in his native New England at the hands of U.S. President Jimmy Carter. But the polls said Carter will win the Democratic primary by 25 percentage points.

The Jerusalem Post learns that Frank Lautenberg, the retiring president of the United Jewish Appeal, has been appointed a special assistant to Carter's national campaign chairman Robert Strauss.

Autonomy talks will resume today

THE HAGUE (UPI). — The U.S., Israel and Egypt today begin the second round of intensified negotiations on Palestinian autonomy with the participation of President Jimmy Carter's special representative for the Middle East, Sol Linowitz. Linowitz participated in similar talks in Israel nearly four weeks ago, at which little progress was reported.

The Israeli team is headed by Interior Minister Yosef Burg, while Premier Mustapha Khalil leads the Egyptian negotiators. The sessions will take place at a luxurious seafront hotel near here.

In Paris, meanwhile, Butros Ghali, Egypt's minister of state for foreign affairs, said that the talks should be halted if they failed to produce substantial results by the May 26 deadline date.

Ghali said that Egypt had respected the February 26 deadline set for the exchange of ambassadors.

"We hope that May 26, the other important date in the peace process, will make it possible to hold elections on the West Bank and in Gaza" to give birth to a Palestinian homeland.

TO OUR JERUSALEM READERS

From 10 a.m. Friday, February 29, the office of The Jerusalem Post at 6 Rehov Aristobolus will be closed.

It will re-open at The Jerusalem Post Head Office in Romema on Sunday, March 2, at 8 a.m.

Advertisements and messages for The Jerusalem Post may be left at The Book Stop shop, 6 Rehov Du Nuwas (almost opposite the old office).

THE JERUSALEM POST
Sunday, March 2, 1980
VOL. L, No. 14860 IL15.00
★★

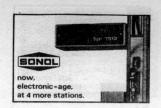

U.S. backs Security Council call to 'dismantle' settlements

Jerusalem Post Correspondent and agencies

WASHINGTON. — With the U.S. for the first time voting in favour, the UN Security Council yesterday called on Israel to "dismantle, all existing settlements in the occupied territories, including Jerusalem."

The council, by a unanimous 15-to-0 vote, deplored Israel's settlement policy as well as the Israeli decision to prohibit Hebron Mayor Fawd Kawasma from travelling to the UN to testify on the subject.

UN Ambassador Donald McHenry, just back from a tour of the Middle East including Israel and the territories, cast the U.S. vote, which clearly represented a major change in U.S. policy.

On earlier occasions, the U.S. always abstained on similar or even weaker language condemning the settlements.

Israeli officials at the UN and here in Washington were stunned by the U.S. vote. Although everyone recognized the administration's long-standing opposition to the settlements, few expected that the Americans would go along with such a sharply-worded resolution against Israel — especially during a presidential election year.

The U.S. action provoked immediate, and strong, condemnations by Israeli officials in Jerusalem, Washington, and at the UN in New York.

Before the vote, U.S. Secretary of State Cyrus Vance had met at the State Department in Washington with Israeli Ambassador Ephraim Evron and informed him of the U.S. decision. Evron's immediate reaction was sharply negative.

According to informed sources, the Israeli envoy predicted that the U.S., by calling for the dismantling of all settlements and suggesting that Jerusalem was "occupied territory,,, would seriously compromise its standing in the autonomy negotiations.

Vance insisted that the U.S. decision was "triggered" by Israel's announcement last month that Jews could resettle in Hebron.

Sources said that Vance had told Evron that without the Hebron decision the Security Council would not have raised the settlement issue at this time and the U.S. vote would not have occurred.

In earlier contacts, Israeli officials were led to believe that the U.S. would abstain on any such resolution calling for the dismantling of settlements as had always occurred in the past.

The resolution deplored the Israeli decisions to establish settlements in "the Palestinian and other Arab territories occupied since 1967." It expressed deep concern at the actions of Israeli authorities "in implementing that settlement policy in the occupied territories including Jerusalem and its consequence for the local Arab and Palestinian population."

The resolution, in its lengthy preamble, also pointed to the need "to consider measures for the impartial protection of the private and public land and property and water resources" in the territories.

It also called attention to the "special status of Jerusalem and in particular the need for protection and preservation of the unique spiritual and religious dimension of the holy places in the city."

The settlement policy, it added, had "grave consequences" in the efforts to reach a "comprehensive, just and lasting peace in the Middle East."

The resolution declared that all Israeli decisions involving settlements since 1967 — including in Jerusalem — have "no legal validity."

It called these Israeli decisions "flagrant violations" of the fourth Geneva Convention governing occupied territories and "serious obstructions" to a just peace.

Most dramatically, it called on Israel to "rescind" these measures, "to dismantle the existing settlements" and to "cease, on an urgent basis," the establishment of new settlements.

It also called on all states not to provide Israel with any aid to be used specifically in connection with settlements.

The UN Commission was asked to continue to examine the situation and report to the council by September 1.

Vance, during his meeting with Evron, said that the U.S. had managed to remove several even stronger sections in the resolution, including one threatening sanctions against Israel if it continued the settlement policy.

Informed sources here in Washington suggested that McHenry was the driving force in pressing for U.S. support of the resolution, but that Vance personally approved the U.S. vote.

It was unclear whether U.S. President Jimmy Carter had personally authorized the U.S. change in policy.

Sources said that special Middle East envoy Sol Linowitz, just back from talks in The Hague on autonomy, had recommended

(Continued on page 2, col. 6)

Snow-ploughs swing into action at the entrance to Jerusalem last night almost before the snow had begun to stick to the ground. (Rahamim Israeli)

Snow may continue for 48 hours

Jerusalem Post Staff

The weatherman was dreaming of a white Purim last night as snow fell in the mountains and below-freezing temperatures gripped much of the country.

More snow is expected throughout the day in Jerusalem, Hebron, the Galilee and Mount Hermon and could continue for the next 48 hours, the Meteorological Service said.

Accumulation in Jerusalem is not expected to exceed a few centimetres, and the weather service said it was unlikely that traffic would be disrupted.

Temperatures fell to minus 2 in the capital and were colder than normal for this time of year throughout the rest of the country, including Eilat.

The temperature is expected to reach 3 above zero in Jerusalem today, which should see the snow melting by afternoon, the weatherman said. But he said it was likely to start accumulating again in the evening.

He added that the cause of the harsh weather was a sudden influx of cold, unstable air which originated as a barometric low centred over Turkey. When the cold air mass reached Israel, it caused thundershowers and hail over most of the country.

A snow emergency headquarters was set up by the Jerusalem municipality yesterday evening. Several dozen men were standing by through the night in the event of serious snowfall. Salt spreaders and plows were kept on standby and contact was maintained with the army in the event its assistance was needed in clearing roads.

A municipal spokeswoman asked **drivers to leave their cars home today in the event of snow.**

Rain battered the capital virtually without letup through the weekend but the fire department reported no serious flooding of apartments.

The weather forecast did not bode well for the extensive Purim parades and outdoor festivities planned for today.

Elsewhere around the country, the bad weather was responsible for damage to beaches, flooding of homes and streets and a decline in burglaries.

Ashkelon and Ashdod beaches have been particularly badly hit this winter, sustaining hundreds of thousands of shekels' worth of damage. Rainfall in the south has been 120 to 159 per cent above the normal yearly average.

(See Purim, Page 2)

Police find 119 kilos of gold, hold seven E. J'lem suspects

Police early yesterday morning arrested seven East Jerusalem residents, including one woman, suspected of heading a gold smuggling ring linking the capital with Egypt. A search of one of the suspects' homes turned up 119 kilos of gold worth nearly IS12m.

Police, who began work on the case six months ago, think the smugglers were aided by UN personnel who brought gold, precious gems and foreign currency into the country hidden in their cars.

As police suspicions of the ring began to mount, a special team was set up, with staff drawn from National Police Headquarters and the local force.

The raid was led by Pakad Haviv Shviki. Those arrested are said to be well-respected members of East Jerusalem.

Orders to launch the raid were personally given by Inspector-General Herzl Shafir who has supervised the case from the outset.

The suspects will be brought to the Magistrate's Court this morning when police will ask for their remand in custody. (Itim)

IDF rescues trapped Scouts

Jerusalem Post Reporter

IDF patrols rescued about 50 Scouts trapped in the Judean Desert by flash floods yesterday evening, but an equal number of Scouts had to spend the night in the open.

A Jericho police spokesman told *The Jerusalem Post* last night that "for technical reasons the IDF could not extricate all the Scouts, but they posted patrols with them throughout the night." He added that the IDF would complete the evacuation today, weather permitting.

The Scouts had started out on their hike from Herodion at 6.30 a.m. yesterday. They had planned to reach the Dead Sea, but were trapped near Nahal Hatzatzon by raging floods.

Giscard begins 6-nation Arab tour

KUWAIT (Reuter). — French President Valery Giscard d'Estaing arrived in Kuwait yesterday at the start of an Arab tour to discuss oil, regional security, economic cooperation and international issues.

Giscard, who will discuss regional security in the light of the Middle East and Afghan crises, was originally due to make five stops — the Gulf States of Kuwait, Bahrain, Qatar, the United Arab Emirates (UAE), and Jordan.

But Paris announced on Friday night that he would go from Amman to Saudi Arabia for talks with King Khalid and Crown Prince Fahd on March 10. This reinforced speculation that the French leader and his Arab hosts might be working towards a new Middle East peace plan.

A newspaper in Qatar said last week Giscard was planning a European initiative to solve the Arab-Israeli crisis and would announce details after his 10-day tour.

NEWS ANALYSIS: Sarah Honig

Allon death leaves Peres unchallenged

During the last months of his life, Yigal Allon was embarked on an ambitious campaign to win the leadership of the Labour Party and its nomination for the premiership. These positions had in the past appeared to be just within his grasp only to elude him at the very last moment.

His sudden death left both friends and foes within Labour shocked, but the implications of the loss were immediately clear to party insiders. All agreed that, at least for the time being, Labour chairman Shimon Peres will not be challenged for the party leadership.

With Allon's passing, Labour has lost the one prominent figure capable of mounting such a challenge. It is now unlikely that a showdown of any sort over the party leadership will take place at Labour's July convention. The Likud, which looked forward to a weakening of the Labour opposition in prolonged internecine warfare, will now have to face a much more united antagonist.

The number of Peres' opponents in Labour has of course not been diminished by Allon's death. Those segments of the party which har-

(Continued on Page 4, Col. 4)

Bogota to negotiate on hostages' release

BOGOTA (Reuter). — The Colombian government will begin negotiations today with terrorists holding dozens of hostages in the Dominican Republic embassy, diplomatic sources said yesterday.

The Foreign Ministry told a meeting of diplomats accredited to Colombia that the talks would be held inside a Red Cross vehicle, the sources said.

On Friday the government said it had agreed to hold negotiations with the terrorists of the M-19 movement, whose hostages include 13 ambassadors, in a truck parked in front of the embassy. Israeli Ambassador Eliahu Barak is one of the hostages.

Government sources said the talks had been scheduled to start yesterday morning; no reason was given for the delay.

Earlier the terrorists spoke of killing two of the diplomatic prisoners, but withdrew the threat when the government agreed to negotiation, according to a Bogota radio station.

On Friday afternoon the terrorists freed the last five women hostages. The embassy invaders demand $50m. in ransom, freedom for 311 political prisoners, publication of an anti-government manifesto in foreign newspapers and safe passage out of the country.

In one, a woman terrorist who identified herself as "comandante numero cinco" — Commander No. 5 — said the diplomats to be killed had been selected but refused to identify them. She had answered a telephone call placed to the embassy by Radio Caracol, according to Yamid Amat, a Caracol director.

Israel won't advance withdrawal from Sinai

By JOSHUA BRILLIANT
Jerusalem Post Reporter

TEL AVIV. — Israel has flatly rejected an Egyptian request that the IDF withdraw to the international boundary in Sinai before April 1982.

Egypt's Defence Minister Kamal Hassan Ali had raised the matter in last week's talks with Defence Minister Ezer Weizman. But Weizman would not discuss it.

At Friday's press conference summarizing his trip to Israel, Ali said the Americans had explained to him that Israel did not want to advance its withdrawal because the two airbases being built in the Negev to replace ones in Sinai would not be ready before April 1982.

"Let us wait and hope they can be finished beforehand," Ali said. He also suggested "a withdrawal from the rest of Sinai before the two years are up. It is mentioned in the treaty that the final withdrawal will be from two to three years, so we don't always have to take the last date," the minister argued.

"Anyhow, I think the withdrawal has to start some time before the three years. It can't be within 24 hours. Do you agree?" he asked Weizman.

"I agree it's a very interesting point here," Weizman replied.

Weizman added that the withdrawal to the international boundary involved problems different from those Israel had encountered in retreating to the pre-

(Continued on page 2, col. 5)

Israel releases six political prisoners

CAIRO (Reuter). — Israel has released six Arab "political prisoners" during the past few days and has promised to free 34 more next week, Egyptian Defence Minister Kamel Hassan Ali said yesterday.

Ali told reporters on his return from a five-day visit to Israel the released prisoners were from the West Bank and the Gaza Strip.

Allon funeral at Ginossar

By SARAH HONIG
Post Political Reporter

TEL AVIV. — Yigal Allon, 61, Palmah commander, former deputy premier and foreign minister, and one of the leaders of the Labour Party, will be buried this afternoon with full military honours at Kibbutz Ginossar — his home since 1936.

Messages of condolences and tributes to Allon came over the weekend from both Israel and abroad, from friends and political adversaries alike.

President Yitzhak Navon mourned the loss of "a fixture of our native landscape." Prime Minister Menahem Begin called him a "hero of Israel." Labour party chairman Shimon Peres, Allon's sometimes rival, spoke of "one of the nation's great leaders."

Allon died on Friday morning in the Central Emek Hospital in Afula, after a massive heart attack.

He first felt ill on Thursday evening, about an hour after hosting visiting Egyptian Defence Minister Kamal Hassan Ali at his kibbutz. He was reported to have been in exceptionally high spirits throughout the visit, but soon after complained of severe chest pains. He arrived at the Afula hospital at 7:30 p.m., where a serious coronary thrombosis was diagnosed. He was admitted to the intensive care unit, where his condition was stabilized.

Early Friday morning, however, he suffered a second heart attack and lost consciousness. A pacemaker and several hours of efforts to resuscitate him were to no avail, and he died at 9:30 a.m.

His family, and former prime minister MK Yitzhak Rabin and long-time political associate Yitzhak Ben-Aharon were at his bedside. His last wish was that some of his colleagues be informed that he had been hospitalized. Doctors said he was in great pain when he reached the hospital, but that he tried to conceal it and assure his physicians that he was all right.

Allon is survived by his wife Ruth, son Yiftah and daughter Nurit.

The funeral cortege is to leave the Afula hospital this morning. The coffin will be placed in a military command car accompanied by six reserve generals. At noon it will arrive at Allon's birthplace in Kfar Tavor, and will stop at the village founders' house for a brief ceremony.

From there the cortege will proceed through the Golani junction to Tiberias and the shores of Lake Kinneret. At 1:30 p.m. the coffin will be placed at Gan Habanim in Kibbutz Ginossar, where mourners will be able to pass by the bier and pay their last respects. The funeral will be held in the kibbutz at 3.30 p.m.

Among those who will attend the funeral will be Lebanese Christian militia leader Major Sa'ad Haddad and his soldiers. Haddad called Allon "one of the architects of the Good Fence."

As soon as news of Allon's death became known, friends, colleagues, and former comrades-in-arms started flocking to Ginossar. Rabin, Peres and Labour Party secretary-general Haim Bar-Lev were there on Friday morning. Soon after kibbutz members started taking down Purim decorations, former Palmah fighters, Ahdut Ha'avoda veterans, Galilee Arabs and Druse leaders appeared. Many of the former Palmahniks kept a vigil on the kibbutz lawn throughout the rainy night.

Reactions of shock and grief at Allon's untimely death came from throughout the Israeli political spectrum.

President Navon said that "we have lost part of our homeland's landscape. Allon was an Independence War hero,

(Continued on Page 3, Col. 1)

Praise from world leaders

Jerusalem Post Staff and Agencies

Political leaders and other public figures from around the world poured out tributes and messages of condolence on the death of Yigal Allon.

Egyptian President Anwar Sadat sent the following message to President Yitzhak Navon:

"I received with great sorrow the news of the passing of Yigal Allon, the former foreign minister of Israel, and one of the Israeli leaders who contributed to the peace process through his sincere efforts that helped complete the first step towards peace, namely the agreement on the disengagement of troops (in Sinai) in 1974 and 1975.

"I send you and the family of the deceased and the Israeli people in my name and on behalf of the Egyptian people, our deepest condolences, praying that God will have mercy on his soul and grant you and his family solace."

The U.S. Department of State, on behalf of Secretary of State Cyrus Vance, sent the following:

"It is with sadness and a feeling of great loss that we note the death of Yigal Allon, one of Israel's great leaders. From the days of Israel's struggle for independence, Mr. Allon's devotion to his country has been exceeded only by his hope for a day when Israel could live in peace with all its neighbours. His counsel and leadership will be missed not only by his countrymen, but by all who support the cause of

(Continued on Page 3, Col. 3)

Anna Ticho dies at 86

By MEIR RONNEN
Post Art Editor

Anna Ticho, the veteran Jerusalem artist designated one of this year's Israel Prize winners, died at Bikur Holim Hospital in Jerusalem yesterday from a heart attack, at the age of 86.

A physically tiny but larger-than-life figure, the gallant little Ticho continually astonished the public and critics during the last few decades with her work improving from exhibition to exhibition. She was one of the leading Israeli artists of all time.

Although she painted flowers and still lifes and drew portraits, Ticho achieved immortality for her drawings of the Jerusalem hills. She began drawing Jerusalem and its surroundings in 1912, the year she arrived here from her native Austria as the bride of the late Dr. Avraham Ticho, an opthalmologist, who almost single-handedly wiped out trachoma in Palestine.

(This writer's father, who contracted trachoma here as a child, was among his first patients.)

The Ticho house, in a charming garden tucked away behind the old Egged bus station a stone's throw from Jaffa Rd., was a Mecca of sorts for Arabs from all over the Middle East.

Anna Ticho remained wedded to her art; and she went from strength to strength. By the Sixties she was creating studio landscapes entirely from memory...and imagination. They were a synthesis of hills, rocks and terraces, glimpses of tombs and Arab villages, bereft of man or *shikun*. They were the hills of her past, no particular spot but a synthesis of all of them. It was a tribute to her ability to grasp this essence that many people insisted that they themselves had stood "at that very spot," despite the fact that it existed only in her imagination, an archetypal figment of her mind's eye.

Ticho worked best in charcoal,

(Continued on Page 3, Col. 3)

THE JERUSALEM POST
Tuesday, June 9, 1981 VOL. LI, No. 15246 IS 5.50

Jets destroy Iraqi atomic site

(UPI telephoto)

Peres was not told exact date of strike

By SARAH HONIG
Post Political Reporter

TEL AVIV. — Labour Party chairman Shimon Peres last night confirmed that he had been informed of plans to destroy the Iraqi nuclear reactor from the air, but stressed that his knowledge was "general in nature only." He has not been informed of the exact date of the strike.

Earlier in the evening Prime Minister Menahem Begin disclosed that some three weeks ago Peres had written the premier saying he thought the air strike "is not desirable."

In Eilat last night Peres said that in the letter he had only expressed his opposition to staging the raid close to the French presidential elections on May 10. He declined comment on Begin's claim that he had termed the very idea of such a raid as undesirable.

Begin explained that he had let Peres in on the secret of the projected air action several months back. Begin went on: "Peres' approval here does not matter. We have the responsibility for running this country and not Peres."

Peres, who was campaigning in Eilat yesterday, said he would not express his opinion now of the political implications of the attack "so as not to make Israel's diplomatic battle more difficult."

Prof. Yuval Ne'eman, a nuclear physicist and leader of the nationalist Tehiya Party, praised the raid as a "most daring and vital action." He said that Iraq had already taken a number of steps to give the reactor a weapons-producing capacity. The Iraqis eliminated the safety mechanisms the French had introduced to ensure that it would be used for research only, he said.

Prof. Ne'eman also said that the Iraqis had bought natural uranium in Portugal and laboratories in Italy to produce plutonium from the uranium. The radiation danger from the strike, he claimed, "is very localized and extremely low at this point before the reactor is activated."

He estimated that if the core of the reactor has been destroyed, it will take the Iraqis at least three years to fix the damage.

Begin went out of his way yesterday to praise former prime minister Yitzhak Rabin's reaction to the operation. He lauded Rabin for "not engaging in carping criticism for its own sake."

Rabin praised the military execution of the mission, but said he would not comment on the timing until he received further information at today's session of the Knesset Foreign Affairs and Defence Committee.

The Labour candidate for defence minister, Haim Bar-Lev, said he cannot yet react "because the opposition was entirely left out of the picture, which is strange, considering that this was a very large-scale assault with complex ramifications."

Labour's candidate for foreign

(Continued on page 2, col. 4)

Bani-Sadr is warned not to oppose Islam

BEIRUT (AP). — Iran's revolutionary and religious patriarch, the Ayatollah Ruhollah Khomeini, stepped into the widening rift between supporters and opponents of President Abolhassan Bani-Sadr yesterday as a pro-Bani-Sadr demonstration closed Teheran's bazaar.

Threatening to "cut off the hands" of those who oppose Islam and foment civil strife, Khomeini warned that "any provocative speaker" would be arrested.

Although Khomeini did not mention Bani-Sadr by name in his speech, Iran-watchers here said the ayatollah's remarks clearly were aimed at Bani-Sadr, the secular-minded president who has been trying to ward off attacks by hardline Islamic fundamentalists allied with Prime Minister Mohammad Ali Rajai.

Khomeini's warning, made in a speech broadcast on Teheran Radio and monitored here, was his sharpest repudiation yet of Bani-Sadr.

Shortly before the speech was aired, shots reportedly were fired in Teheran's bazaar area as some merchants closed their shops in a show of support for Bani-Sadr.

A revolutionary spokesman contacted by telephone said there were verbal exchanges but no physical clashes when leftist groups and Bani-Sadr supporters were confronted by the "Hezbollahi," a colloquial phrase meaning "the Party of God," which is used to describe followers of clergy hardliner Ayatollah Mohammad Beheshti.

No injuries were reported.

Rail crash toll said 1,000

NEW DELHI (UPI). — More than 1,000 persons were feared killed on Saturday when seven packed passenger train cars plunged off a bridge into a swift moving river, an official said yesterday. The death toll would make it the deadliest recorded railway accident in history.

A district magistrate of Khagaria said that the disaster in Bihar state, about 1,100 kilometres southeast of New Delhi, was caused when the engineer slammed on the brakes to avoid hitting a cow on the tracks. Hindus consider cows sacred animals.

The magistrate said all nine cars of the train were packed with passengers and that hundreds more were riding on the roof.

"At least 1,000 people have died but we have pulled out only 97 bodies so far," Magistrate Krishna Saha said.

He said that the sudden halt of the train combined with heavy winds to derail seven of the cars which then plunged 50 metres off the bridge into the Bavmati river. Five cars were swept away by the current, officials said.

The previous deadliest rail accidents occurred in 1944, when 500 persons were killed in a tunnel wreck in Spain and 526 persons suffocated in a tunnel in Italy.

Begin says decision was made 'months ago'

By DAVID LANDAU
Post Diplomatic Correspondent

It was virtually "now or never," Prime Minister Menahem Begin said last night, explaining his decision to bomb the Iraqi nuclear reactor at this time.

By July, or at latest by September, the reactor would have been "hot already," Begin told a Kol Yisrael radio interviewer. A bombing attack then would have "endangered the lives of tens, perhaps hundreds of thousands of innocent people in nearby Baghdad," exposing them to radiation. "No Israeli government would have bombed under those conditions," he said.

Begin revealed that the decision to bomb the reactor had been taken "many months ago." But there had been "obstacles and problems" which repeatedly caused delays.

Government sources told *The Jerusalem Post* last night that the initial decision had been taken by the cabinet last October. A small committee of ministers was set up to decide on the timing and other operational details of the action.

This committee, the sources said, held "a great many deliberations" over recent months. Apparently it was this group that gave the green light on Sunday.

At 5 p.m. on Sunday, with the planes already on their way to Iraq, Begin convened the cabinet at his home and informed the ministers that the operation was under way.

In his interview last night, Begin brushed aside as "not credible" a French scientific report that the Iraqi reactor was being built solely for peaceful purposes. Israel's own hard intelligence information, Begin said, was that the reactor was intended to manufacture atom bombs of the Hiroshima-type for use against Israel. He indicated that the bombs would have been ready in four or five years.

Iraq's President Saddam Hussein, a "very cruel" ruler who had butchered his own closest colleagues, would have had "no hesitation" in dropping "three or four or five" of those bombs on Israel, Begin declared. They would have pulverized Israel's population centres, destroyed its industrial infrastructure, and decimated its army, he said.

Thus Sunday's Air Force action against the Iraqi reactor was "literally a life-saving operation."

"I've lived with this thing for two whole years," Begin continued, "and I wouldn't wish it on anyone." Sometimes, he said, when he would meet and chat with little children, "suddenly I would be struck by the thought: 'My God, what's going to happen to these children in a few years' time ... An atom bomb might fall on them.'"

Begin said Churchill's famous declaration after Dunkirk was apposite to express the Israeli nation's debt to its own air force ("those wonderful young men"): "Never have so many owed so much to so

(Continued on back page)

Prime Minister Menahem Begin welcomes U.S. Congressman Jack Kemp into his livingroom on Friday. Story on Page 3. (Rahamim Israeli)

France condemns the raid

PARIS. — French Premier Pierre Mauroy yesterday condemned Israel for destroying the French-built nuclear reactor, calling it an "unacceptable and grave act" and warning that the attack was likely to fuel the explosive situation in the Middle East.

But the Socialist leader dismissed any speculation that the attack may jeopardize President Francois Mitterrand's proposed visit to Israel. "For the time being there is no question of taking any measures other than this condemnation," Mauroy said.

The premier said the Iraqi nuclear site was "a research centre subjected to the control of the International Atomic Energy Agency." He said the Israeli planes had destroyed "the essential part of the centre."

Mauroy said that while France wanted to put some morality into arms sales, it also was determined to abide by contracts signed in France's name. He refused to say whether France would replace the destroyed equipment.

Before his election as president last month, Mitterrand was highly critical of the Osiris project. But the French government has said since the election that it will honour contracts signed under the previous administration.

The government of former president Giscard d'Estaing insisted, despite domestic and foreign criticism, that its involvement with Iraq was legitimate and that the "peaceful nature" of the project was covered by international guarantees.

"One has to combine economic wisdom with political morals," Mauroy said yesterday. We cannot convert our armament industries overnight."

The Italian Foreign Ministry expressed "serious concern" over the attack, a foreign ministry official said.

A spokesman said Italian Foreign Minister Emilio Colombo had discussed the attack with his French counterpart, Claude Cheysson, in their talks yesterday.

Two Italian companies, Snia-Techint and Snia-Viscosan, took part in a $50 million sale of a natural uranium fuel element in Iraq.

In other reaction, UN Secretary-General Kurt Waldheim described the destruction of the Iraqi reactor as a grave development that "could have far-reaching consequences."

The official Soviet news agency yesterday condemned the raid as a "barbarous attack." (AP, UPI)

U.S. insists attack came as surprise

By WOLF BLITZER
Jerusalem Post Correspondent

WASHINGTON. — The Reagan administration yesterday condemned Israel's attack against the Iraqi nuclear facility.

State Department spokesman Dean Fischer maintained that the U.S. did not have any advance information on the assault.

He told a packed news conference that the administration, as required under U.S. law, was investigating the possibility that Israel may have violated the terms of its arms contracts by using U.S.-supplied equipment during the raid.

The official determination on this sensitive issue, he said, would be relayed to the Congress "fairly quickly."

He did not rule out the possibility that Israel might face some military sanctions if the administration concludes that Israel used the weapons illegally.

Under the terms of those contracts, Israel can use U.S.-supplied arms only for its "legitimate self-defence," but not for offensive purposes.

The angry official U.S. reaction was clearly designed to try to distance Washington from the Israeli attack to allay concern in the Arab world.

Two hours before the official U.S. "condemnation," the State Department, in its initial reaction, merely expressed its "utmost concern" over the incident. Fischer said the escalation in the U.S. protest followed the arrival of "additional information" in Washington, but he declined to elaborate.

The U.S. statement, which Fischer said had been cleared at the highest level, called the Israel attack "unprecedented."

There were high-level meetings throughout the day at the White House, the Pentagon, the National Security Council and the State Department. Word of the raid dominated the news broadcasts all day.

The State Department spokesman, charged with speaking on behalf of the entire administration, expressed hope that the incident would not derail special U.S. envoy Philip Habib's Middle East mission. "That is our hope," Fischer said.

In the initial U.S. statement, Fischer said that "our initial estimate of potential radiation effects is that they would probably be minimal and limited to the immediate vicinity of the installation. This is based on preliminary information about the amount and quality of material in the facility at the time of the attack."

He said Washington was prepared "to respond to any requests for help in monitoring the extent of any nuclear effects and in dealing with any other related problems."

Regarding the Israeli assertion that the Iraqi nuclear development programme represented a threat to Israel, the spokesman said that the U.S. had "no evidence" that the Iraqis had violated their commitment to the nuclear non-proliferation treaty, which they have ratified.

The spokesman said that Iraq had accepted the "safeguards" of the International Atomic Energy Agency attached to the construc-

(Continued on back page)

Aliza Begin's condition improves

The condition of Aliza Begin, the prime minister's wife, continues to improve, although she will undergo further tests during the next few days. She was hospitalized at Hadassah Hospital in Ein Kerem last Thursday. (Itim)

Iraq's nuclear plans set back by three years

By HIRSH GOODMAN
Post Military Correspondent

The Israeli attack on the Iraqi nuclear complex on the outskirts of Baghdad Sunday afternoon has set back Iraq's march towards a nuclear weapons capability by at least three years, according to experts in Israel.

Military sources reported last night that the Tammuz 1 complex situated at Tuwaitha, 17 kilometres south of Baghdad, was destroyed totally. The main core building, housing a French-made Osiris reactor, was reduced to rubble, as were all the major outbuildings and laboratories servicing the site.

All Israeli planes returned safely. It was believed the first time Israeli forces have attacked Iraqi targets on Iraqi soil since the 1967 Six Day war, when Israeli planes bombed an Iraqi air base near the Jordanian border.

French radio stations last night reported that one French technician was killed. Israeli sources earlier claimed there were no casualties among the 150 to 200 French and Italian scientists and technicians at the complex.

A high-level government source said that the strike was a signal to Syria that Israel is ready to take action necessary for its defence, Israel radio reported.

Sunday's surprise attack was carried out by unspecified Israeli aircraft of American manufacture. Foreign reports claim that the reactor was bombed by nine phantom jets accompanied by F-16s.

The reactor is 980 kilometres from Israel, but experts here agree that the route to Iraq, surrounded by states hostile to Israel — was probably much longer. The raid was undoubtedly one of the most complex ever conducted by Israel, and the fact that it was carried out without Israeli losses was considered remarkable by local and foreign military analysts.

The Associated Press quotes intelligence sources in Washington as saying that the Israeli planes flew across the northern edge of Saudi Arabia on their way to Iraq. CBS News speculated that the planes were refuelled over Saudi Arabia on the way home.

UPI quoted U.S. sources in Washington as saying that the Israeli pilots identified themselves as Jordanians as they flew through Saudi Arabian airspace. Whether the ruse was used against Saudi Arabia or Iraq was not known.

The U.S., the AP report continues, has four highly sophisticated AWACS airborne warning and control aircraft in Saudi Arabia, but Pentagon sources said the planes were not in a position to detect the Israeli planes since they were oriented towards the Persian Gulf. The AWACS planes have a radar search range of 320 kms.

The route had to be planned in minute detail and all the necessary precaution taken to ensure total

(Continued on page 2, col. 2)

Reactor was 'worrisome'

LONDON (AP). — An independent research institute says nuclear developments in Iraq have been "worrisome."

As part of a recently published "strategic survey" report, the International Institute for Strategic Studies (IISS) said: "Suspicions about Iraq were intensified by her nuclear agreements with...Brazil (which had not signed the international nuclear non-proliferation treaty) for the exchange of information and with Italy for the purchase of 'hot-cell' facilities (used to shield technicians from radioactivity during the separation of plutonium from spent fuel)."

The report said that although Iraqi President Saddam Hussein has denied any intention to manufacture atomic weapons, "he alluded menacingly to improvements in Iraqi technology which would make his country 'a totally different' enemy in the near future."

IISS said that after the bombing attacks on the Tammuz site in the opening days of the war with Iran, Iraq refused to permit International Atomic Energy Agency (IAEA) inspections of the Osiris reactor and of a smaller French-built reactor while war conditions persisted.

"This was the first time a refusal had been issued on such grounds for such dangerous material, and it cast doubt on prior French and IAEA assurances that the weapons-grade uranium supplied to Iraq would be adequately safeguarded against military use," IISS said.

"These developments occasioned deep international concern, particularly in Israel, which moved in the United Nations to drop her long-standing objection to a nuclear-free zone in the Middle East."

Arab reactions show disunity unimpaired

By DAVID BERNSTEIN
Post Mideast Affairs Reporter and Agencies

Cairo yesterday joined other Arab capitals in condemning Israel's destruction of Iraq's nuclear reactor on Sunday, but the initial reactions seem to indicate that the basic divisions dividing the Arab world have not been bridged by the latest Israeli action.

Egyptian Foreign Minister Kamal Hassan Ali described the operation as an "irresponsible and unjustifiable crime," and said it represented "a sharp escalation of the explosive situation in the Middle East."

An official Egyptian statement carried by the official Middle East News Agency (MENA) and broadcast on Egyptian television later in the day said Israel's behaviour completely contradicted the "spirit of peace" which prevailed at last Thursday's summit meeting between President Anwar Sadat and Prime Minister Menahem Begin.

The statement noted that Egypt had no choice but to condemn the Israeli action "and express its deep sorrow that the Israeli government undertook such a step which is in direct opposition to all international agreements and the efforts for peace in the area"

Observers here explain the sharp Egyptian condemnation as reflecting Cairo's deep embarrassment that the raid came just three days after the Sadat-Begin summit, laying the Egyptian leader open to suspicion that he had been privy to details of the operation.

Prime Minister Begin, however, stressed last night in an interview on Israel Radio that the raid was a "highly classified military secret" which he could not, and did not, divulge to Sadat in Ophira last week.

It is yet to be seen how the raid will affect Israel-Egyptian relations, but judging from yesterday's initial reaction from Cairo it would seem that, despite the embarrassment which the raid has undoubtedly caused Sadat, it will not significantly affect the peace process with Israel.

Egypt stands to gain too much from the continuation of the peace process, the observers point out,

(Continued on page 2, col. 6)

Behind the French effort to build Iraq's nuclear machine

Post Staff and Agencies

In December 1974, Jacques Chirac, then premier of France, visited Baghdad to discuss the possibility of selling Iraq two reactors, one for power production, the other for research.

The Iraqis began by insisting on purchasing a 500-megawatt uranium graphite gas reactor developed by France.

When the French balked at the deal proposed by the Iraqis, the latter fell back on the suggestion that France should build them a 70-megawatt reactor, sell them six charges of 12 kilos of uranium enriched to 93 per cent, and help them to establish a nuclear research and training centre. The "Osiris" reactor to be built near Baghdad, costing a total of $275m., was to be ready by 1981.

The agreement signed in Paris by Chirac and Saddam Hussein in 1975 also committed Iraq to sell France 10m. tons of oil per annum and to purchase French armaments — warplanes, tanks, helicopters and missiles — to the tune of $1.6b.

THE DISCRETION and secrecy surrounding the Iraqi nuclear industry have been punctured by some violent and mysterious incidents.

• In July 1978, Palestinian terrorists attacked the Iraqi embassy in Paris. One French police officer was killed, another wounded.

• On April 5, 1979, saboteurs destroyed the core of an advanced 70-mgw research reactor — Tammuz 1 and Tammuz 2 (Tammuz was a god of ancient Babylonia) — lying in storage at Seyne-sur-Mer near Toulon awaiting shipment from Marseille to Baghdad. The two main speculations were that the saboteurs may have been Israeli agents or terrorists aided by French officials who opposed Iraq's nuclear programme.

• In June 1980 a senior Egyptian-born nuclear scientist, a key man in the Iraqi atomic programme, was killed in his Paris hotel, probably by Iranians, although the French police have not yet named a suspect.

• In August 1980 in Rome, bombs wrecked the offices of the SNIA Techint Company, which is supplying nuclear technology and equipment to Iraq. On the same day, there was an abortive bomb attempt on the life of the French scientist Jean-Jacques Graf, who had a project for supplying Iraq with a French atomic reactor. In both cases, the bombs were set by the "Committee for Safeguarding the Islamic Revolution" in Iran.

Following the sabotage at Seyne-sur-Mer, French Prime Minister Raymond Barre, during his official visit to Baghdad in July 1979, tried to convince the Iraqis to accept a different core design for the Osiris that would use low-grade uranium rather than weapon-grade fuel. France announced proudly that it had found such a fuel, which is called "Caramel," but the Iraqis adamantly demanded a duplicate of the destroyed core and the initial loading of 70 kg. of the enriched uranium.

President Hussein warned Barre that if he refused, he would risk an oil cut-off and the cancellation of French arms purchases. On his return to Paris, Barre had a meeting with President Giscard d'Estaing, the outcome being that the French government agreed to deliver a replica of Osiris and the enriched fuel to Iraq without conditions.

IN AN EFFORT to diversity their sources of nuclear material, the Iraqis followed up their French agreement with an accord with Italy, which imports more than a fifth of its oil from Iraq. Under the $50m. contract, Italy will give the Iraqis four research facilities, including a radiochemistry laboratory that could be used for reprocessing ir-

(Continued on back page)

THE JERUSALEM POST
Wednesday, October 7, 1981
VOL. LI, No. 15347 IS6.50
★★

Sadat assassinated

Mubarak pledges continuity on peace

Sadat salutes his troops yesterday only minutes before failling victim to an assassins' shots. (UPI telephoto)

Attackers shoot Sadat and aides at army parade

CAIRO. — The attack on President Anwar Sadat and his aides took place at about 12:40 p.m. yesterday when soldiers participating in a parade threw two hand-grenades and sprayed machinegun fire at the reviewing stand.

The Egyptian leader was hit in the chest and shoulder. He was rushed by helicopter from Nasr City, an eastern Cairo suburb, where the parade was being staged, to the Ma'adi armed forces hospital, south of Cairo, where he underwent emergency surgery.

The president later died of his wounds, officials and hospital sources said. He was 63. He is to be buried on Saturday.

The sources said the president died between 2:15 and 2:30 p.m.

Defence Minister Abdel Halil Abu Ghazalla also was hit, but Vice-President Hosni Mubarak, who was on the other side of Sadat in the reviewing stand, was unharmed, reports said.

The raiders were said to have killed nine persons besides Sadat, and 22 others were reported wounded.

Fawzi Abdel-Hafez, Sadat's personal secretary, was killed, an Egyptian official said. A number of foreign diplomats, who were in the reviewing stands with Sadat, also were reported hit.

An Israeli security man on the reviewing stand was wounded slightly, according to a high-ranking Israeli official accompanying Foreign Minister Yitzhak Shamir in New York. It was not made clear whether the security man was guarding the Israeli ambassador, who was not wounded.

A well-placed State Department source said late last night the U.S. had firm evidence that at least one of the assassins had been captured and had been identified as having ties with a Moslem fundamentalist group (related story below).

Reports said a group of men began firing at Sadat from a truck towing artillery as it passed the grandstand.

Two of the men jumped off the back of a truck and charged the reviewing stand.

"No one was sure it was real for a few seconds, then all hell broke loose," one witness said.

A brief but fierce gunbattle erupted between the blue-bereted soldiers and the guards around Sadat, and bullets sprayed into the grandstand behind the president.

Several people were seriously wounded, among them Belgian Ambassador Claude Ruelle and Australian Embassy First Secretary John Woods, as the crowd dived for cover among tumbling chairs, eyewitnesses said. Two Korean diplomats were reported wounded, as was Irish Defence Minister James Tully. Three U.S. military officers were also said to be injured, but an official report on exactly who was injured in the attack was not available as of late last night.

Spectators continued to flee in panic as the young soldiers in olive drab fatigues fired their weapons from the shoulder at the low platform. Many people lay bleeding on the stand. It was unclear if the assailants were caught.

Ambulances and security vehicles rushed to the stand and carried away the wounded, who included military men and Moslem and Christian leaders.

The soldiers charged at the same instant that six low-flying jetfighters

(Continued on Back Page)

Egyptian exile group claims it was behind the killing

BEIRUT (AP). — An exiled Egyptian opposition group claimed responsibility here yesterday for the assassination of Egyptian President Anwar Sadat.

An anonymous telephone caller identifying himself as the spokesman for the "Rejection Front for the Liberation of Arab Egypt" told the leftist Beirut newspaper *Al-Liwa* its secret "free officers" branch within the Egyptian armed forces staged the attack on Sadat.

The caller described the group as the military arm of a group formed by former Egyptian Army chief of staff Saad Eddin Shazli, known as the Egyptian "National Front." The caller spoke in Egyptian-accented Arabic. He gave no further details.

Shazli, who set up headquarters in Tripoli at the invitation of Muammar Gaddafi, Sadat's most implacable Arab foe, has branch offices in Syria, Lebanon and Algeria.

PLO sources said their latest information was that Shazli was in Algiers, capital of Algeria, although Libya's state-run Tripoli Radio said he would shortly make a statement on Sadat's assassination through the Libyan station.

The Libyan News agency JANA claimed yesterday that the assassination was part of an attempted military coup that was still under way. It said the rebels had killed many pro-Sadat officers.

The alleged coup attempt was apparently being led by a group called "the free officers," JANA said.

The agency said one of its correspondents near the Egyptian border picked up a radio broadcast by the group saying "the revolutionary forces in a number of military camps and bases had conducted large-scale liquidation operations against the Egyptian people's enemies from among high-ranking officers and commanders."

Shazli called on the Egyptian armed forces to act quickly to put an end to "treason and the alliance with Zionism and imperialism."

The Jerusalem Post, in common with all Israeli newspapers, will not appear tomorrow, Yom Kippur. Our next issue will appear on Friday, together with the regular Weekend Magazine.

Begin: Won't halt our drive for peace

By DAVID LANDAU
Post Diplomatic Correspondent

Israel will continue with its part of the peace process undeterred by the death of President Sadat, a source close to Premier Begin asserted last night.

The source said this resolve was the intended significance of the premier's statement, issued yesterday evening that "We hope that the peace process, despite the cruel act of its enemies, will continue — as we know President Sadat would wish with all his heart."

The premier's statement came at the end of a message of mourning and condolence that Begin read out in a hushed voice after the news of Sadat's death became official.

"I have lost today not only a partner in peace but also a friend," Begin lamented, saying that during their many meetings a real "personal friendship" had evolved between them.

The source close to Begin said there was no significance in the fact that the premier had couched his reference to the future of the peace process in terms of "hope" rather than making an outright pledge on Israel's part that the process will go forward.

Such a pledge was indeed made later in the evening by President Yitzhak Navon in a television tribute to Sadat (see story below). "We must continue the peace process and do everything possible to ensure its successful conclusion," Navon declared.

The source close to Begin said that while the president's words had not been specifically cleared with the premier, they reflected Begin's thinking precisely. The two men spoke by telephone immediately after Sadat's death was officially announced in Cairo, the source added.

The cabinet is to meet in special session this morning, and is expected to issue a fuller statement of Israel's reaction to Sadat's death.

Whatever the wording of cautious

(Continued on Page 2, Col. 2)

Navon: search for peace must go on

President Yitzhak Navon said last night that the factors that brought Anwar Sadat and the Egyptian leadership to strive for peace have not vanished with his death, and that Israel "must continue the peace process, doing whatever has to be done to bring it to a positive conclusion."

Speaking on Israel Television, Navon said that "we did not make peace with one man — however great — but with the Egyptian people, which on various occasions has expressed its support for peace."

The president said that it was difficult for him to speak of Sadat in the past tense, because ever since Sadat's historic visit to Jerusalem he has become "part of our lives." In their personal meetings, Navon added, they formed a warm, close relationship.

When he visited Egypt a year ago, Navon said, he met with the top leadership, including Vice-President Hosni Mubarak, and found that they fully supported Sadat's peace policy.

Egypt has lost a great leader who dedicated his life to his people's welfare, Navon said. On behalf of himself and his family, Navon sent his condolences to Jehan Sadat and her family, and expressed their deep shock at Sadat's tragic death. (Itim)

U.S. lauds Egyptian renewed peace pledge

By WOLF BLITZER
Jerusalem Post Correspondent
and agencies

WASHINGTON. — The U.S. yesterday welcomed what a White House spokesman said was Egypt's readiness to continue the Camp David peace process following President Anwar Sadat's assassination.

White House spokesman David Gergen told reporters: "We are pleased that the Egyptian government is pursuing its constitutional processes with regard to succession and are pleased by the continuity of Egyptian policy including the continued dedication of that nation to the Camp David accords."

Gergen, asked to explain how he could so confidently say that Egypt would continue Sadat's peace policies, replied that Secretary of State Alexander Haig had personally instructed him to issue the statement, based on the latest information reaching Washington from Cairo.

President Ronald Reagan, standing on the steps of the White House after assembling his major national security advisers for urgent meetings, said the assassination of President Anwar Sadat was "an act of infamy, cowardly infamy, that fills us with horror. America has lost a close friend. The world has lost a great statesman. Mankind has lost a champion of peace. In a world filled with hatred, he was a man of hope. He helped improve a world tormented by malice and pettiness. He was a humanitarian unafraid to make peace."

Spokesman Gergen, asked about the impact of Sadat's death on the administration's proposed Saudi AWACS sale, said the president remained convinced of its crucial importance. "The president views this tragedy as in no way lessening the urgency of the sale," he said. "Indeed, he views it more urgently." Reagan remains "dedicated to support the sale," he added. (See related story, page 4)

Several U.S. officials and former presidents Jimmy Carter and Gerald Ford warned of the consequences Sadat's death could have on America, the Middle East and the world.

Carter, who negotiated the peace accord with Sadat, said he thought Sadat had been "crucial to stability in the Middle East."

Former secretary of state Henry Kissinger said if there was an "indispensable man" in the Middle

(Continued on Page 2, Col. 6)

Arab capitals celebrate

Post Mideast Affairs Reporter
and agencies

There was jubilation in several Arab capitals yesterday following the news of President Anwar Sadat's assassination, with Syrians dancing in the streets of Damascus, militiamen in Beirut firing joyful salvoes into the air and crowds of people laughing and singing in the streets of Tripoli.

Only in the Sudan and Oman, Egypt's sole allies in the Arab world, was the news of Sadat's death received with sorrow.

Sadat's enemies in the Arab world, which generally condemned his peacemaking with Israel, began celebrating even before his death was officially confirmed.

When the news reached a rally staged by the ruling Baath Party of Syrian President Hafez Assad in Damascus, a speaker told the audience: "This is a victory, this is a victory."

The audience rose and applauded while the speaker added, "on this eventful day our comrades in the great Egyptian army, who fought with us the glorious October War of liberation have avenged us."

The official Libyan news agency JANA said in a statement telexed to Reuters that Sadat had trampled upon an Arab nation's honour and surrendered its rights.

The agency denounced what it called Sadat's "imperialist" policies and said that on the day that he paraded his military forces "the bullets turned towards him and his clique."

"On this occasion, while we congratulate all free Arab revolutionaries who opposed Israel, racism and the Camp David path, we warn that any president who follows such a path ... will meet the same fate as his predecessor," it said.

In Beirut, Palestinian and

(Continued on Page 2, Col. 4)

Hosni Mubarak

Mubarak a 'puzzle' in Egypt

Post Mideast Affairs Editor

The assassination of President Anwar Sadat yesterday has brought his deputy, Hosni Mubarak, to the forefront of the Egyptian leadership — at least temporarily.

Like his predecessor who took over following a stormy power struggle on the death of Gamal Abdul-Nasser in 1970, Mubarak is bound to face challenges for the presidency. These will either come from within the ruling hierarchy or army officers who see themselves as senior to the 53-year-old taciturn Soviet-trained airman.

Mubarak has been something of a puzzle, even to knowledgable Egyptians who differed over what an Egyptian administration controlled by Mubarak would be like. A majority, however, was virtually unanimous in the assessment that Mubarak would certainly bring

(Continued on page 3)

Vice-President now in control of Egypt

By DAVID BERNSTEIN
Post Mideast Affairs Reporter
and Agencies

Anwar Sadat's heir-apparent, Vice-President Hosni Mubarak, vowed last night that Egypt would remain committed to the dead president's goal of a comprehensive peace in the Middle East and would continue to honour "all international charters, treaties and commitments which Egypt has concluded."

Mubarak, who assumed effective control of the country soon after Sadat was gunned down while reviewing a military parade yesterday held to mark the anniversary of the 1973 Yom Kippur War, announced that, in accordance with the Egyptian constitution, Parliamentary Speaker Sufi Abu Taleb would be acting president for a maximum of two months, during which a new president must be elected.

Abu Taleb's first move as acting president was to declare a nationwide state of emergency, to remain in force for one year.

He also confirmed Mubarak in his post as vice-president and authorized him to act as commander-in-chief of the armed forces.

As such, Mubarak will continue to wield effective power until he is confirmed as president in a national referendum within two months.

Mubarak was being groomed by Sadat to be his successor, and few doubt that he will be the next president. The political bureau of the ruling National Democratic Party met late yesterday and decided unanimously to nominate him for the presidency, a nomination certain to be approved by a sweeping majority in the NDP-dominated parliament. The nationwide referendum will be held shortly afterwards to confirm his election.

In his address to the Egyptian people last night, Mubarak left no doubt in the mind of his listeners that although Sadat had departed, his regime remained intact and his policies would continue to be pursued.

"In the name of the great departed and the name of the people, its constitutional institutions and its armed forces," Mubarak said, "I declare that we will honour all international charters, treaties and commitments which Egypt has concluded.

"Our hands will not cease to push the wheel of peace in pursuance of the mission of the departed leader," he continued. "We will remember with pride when our banners are hoisted over the whole of Sinai (next April) and when a comprehensive peace is realized throughout the region."

He told a stunned nation that Sadat had been assassinated "by criminal and treacherous hands," noting that "God had willed that the leader should be martyred on the day that is his own symbol and among his soldiers and heroes."

It remained unknown last night who exactly was behind the assassination. The "Free Officers of the Opposition Front for the Liberation of Egypt," headed by exiled former chief of staff Sa'ad Eddin Shazli, who led the Egyptian forces in the

(Continued on Page 4)

Obituary — page 4
Related reports and pictures — pages 2 and 10

THE JERUSALEM POST
Sunday, October 18, 1981 Vol. LI, No. 15354 IS6.50

Police, extremists exchange fire

Mubarak moves to stamp out militants

CAIRO. — Moslem extremists exchanged fire with policemen in a Nile delta village yesterday, and President Hosni Mubarak moved firmly to stamp out religious militants, saying that they will not escape "the razor-sharp sword of the law."

Sources close to the government maintained that more than 1,500 people were arrested in the past 11 days, despite claims by government spokesmen that the number was much smaller.

Interior Minister Nabawi Ismail indicated that the nationwide security dragnet was still at work. He told reporters that police forces have been "raiding hideouts, making arrests and seizing arms. A small number of wanted persons is still at large."

Security sources said four extremists in two speeding cars opened fire on a group of policemen on guard at the village of Sandoub, 3 kilometres from Mansoura, the provincial centre of the Nile delta. Policemen returned fire and the assailants fled. There were no casualties among the police, the sources said.

Mubarak chaired several meetings with top aides for an appraisal of the security situation and economic and foreign policies, including peace moves with Israel. He first conferred with Foreign Minister Kamal Hassan Ali and later saw provincial governors and economic experts separately.

A government spokesman quoted Mubarak as telling the governors that public security was his "top priority."

In the state of emergency declared immediately after Anwar Sadat's assassination, a ban was imposed on training in the use of firearms, explosives and any form of violence without official authorization.

Offenders are liable to three years imprisonment, which would go up to at least five years if the training was intended to breach public security. People who know about such training and fail to report to authorities are liable to imprisonment from three to 12 months at least.

Government spokesman Mohammed Hakki said detainees held since Sadat died numbered "less than 100." Sources close to the government stuck to their estimate of more than 1,500 extremists and suspected trouble-makers.

Reliable sources said Mubarak's crackdown included a far-reaching purge of known fundamentalists from key positions in the armed forces and in government departments. (UPI, AP)

Chances improve for Saudi AWACS sale

By WOLF BLITZER
Jerusalem Post Correspondent

WASHINGTON. — President Ronald Reagan's chances of eventually winning Senate approval of his controversial sale of AWACS radar aircraft and other advanced weaponry to Saudi Arabia are clearly increasing with each day of intense White House lobbying.

The latest head count in the Senate still shows a slight majority opposed to the $8.5 billion sale.

But in recent days, the president's aggressive personal lobbying has proven remarkably successful in convincing opponents to switch.

The outcome, therefore, remains in doubt.

Reagan has even received some badly needed assistance from a handful of his Jewish supporters. Among those helping Reagan are U.S. Ambassador to Italy Maxwell Rabb, Ambassador to Austria Ted Cummings, and New York businessman Eli Jacobs — all active in Reagan's Jewish coalition during last year's presidential campaign.

But most of the American Jewish community, including Reagan's own leading supporters in the Republican Party, are strongly united against the sale.

Republican Senate leader Howard Baker of Tennessee has scheduled the final Senate vote for the last week of October, thereby offering Reagan more time to work on various senators.

Democratic minority leader Robert Byrd of West Virginia, who has remained undecided, is emerging as a potentially decisive element in the battle. If Byrd decides to support Reagan, he is expected to carry with him a few other undecided Democrats and perhaps even some who earlier opposed the transaction. West Virginia Democrat Jennings Randolph in fact announced yesterday he now favoured the sale.

In an interview with newspaper editors issued by the White House yesterday, the president said he was confident that the Senate would approve the sale. "If we don't, I believe we could lose all credibility," Reagan said.

Reagan also said Prime Minister Menachem Begin was not upset with the U.S. over the proposed AWACS sale, although he opposed it.

"As a matter of fact, when Mr. Begin left here after his visit (in September) and I told him what we were going to do, he told me he was going to maintain his position but he was not upset at all," Reagan said.

IRA car bomb in London wounds top British marine

LONDON (UPI). — A car bomb exploded and critically injured the head of Britain's Royal Marines Commando forces yesterday and wounded a woman, Scotland Yard said.

The Irish Republican Army later claimed responsibility for the attack.

Police said that 53-year-old Lt.-Gen. Sir Steuart Pringle, a veteran army officer who served two tours in Northern Ireland, had driven a few feet from his home in south London when the bomb went off.

The device was "similar to the one that killed Airey Neave," the close aide to Prime Minister Margaret Thatcher whose car blew up as he drove out of the Commons car park in March 1979.

Both the Irish Republican Army and the Irish National Liberation Army claimed responsibility for that attack.

Pringle, who is the 10th baronet in a 300-year-old line, was listed in "stable" condition at King's College Hospital where he underwent emergency surgery for "serious injuries," a hospital spokesman said. The woman, who was not seriously wounded, was not identified.

A hospital spokesman said that surgeons amputated Pringle's right leg below the knee, but hoped to save his left leg, also seriously injured. His condition was said to be stable.

The family's black Labrador which was in the car at the time of the explosion escaped unhurt.

Police had earlier reported that Pringle was killed in the blast, the second in a week to rock London's streets.

The IRA planted a bomb in a laundry van which blasted heavy nails into a passing troop bus on October 10, killing two persons and injuring 40 others.

Sudanese bolster defences

By Jerusalem Post Correspondent and Agencies

CAIRO. — Sudan said yesterday that it was taking "defensive measures" along its border with Libyan-occupied Chad, as internal security forces, in a clampdown on government opponents, arrested more than 1,300 persons.

The Middle East News agency, reporting from the Sudanese capital, said police had arrested 1,366 "suspects" at Omdurman, which is located opposite Khartoum, across the Nile.

In a separate dispatch, the agency quoted a Sudanese government spokesman as saying: "The defensive measures Sudan is taking at present along the border with Chad aim at preserving Sudan's independence and security. They do not aim at launching aggression on Libya or any other country."

This was the first official disclosure that Sudan was taking military precautions along its western border with Chad, which the Sudanese government has said was the target of daily Libyan aggressions."

Earlier, Sudanese president Jaafar Numeiri was quoted in the Cairo daily *Al-Ahram* as threatening to retaliate in kind and send saboteurs to Libya, which he accused of bombing Sudanese villages bordering Chad and of carrying out subversive activities in his country.

In an interview with *Al-Ahram*, Numeiri said Libyan agents, whom he described as "terrorists" and "murderers," have infiltrated his country and carried out unspecified subversive operations.

"We are seriously thinking of a defensive plan that could move such operations to the Libyan soil and I will ask our friends to assist. I will train a large number of what is called suicide army — commandos and infantrymen — to operate inside Libya," Numeiri said.

In Cairo yesterday there were signs of an easing of tension over Libya, following news of a secret cable Gaddafi sent to Washington in which he said he has no intention of starting a war with Egypt.

The report was received here with satisfaction by officials, who described a war with Libya as "redundant."

Government sources said yesterday that the tension in Egypt on the Libyan border was significantly decreased by the AWACS radar planes the U.S. sent to Egypt last week.

In Washington, a senior Pentagon official said yesterday that the U.S. plans to send more arms to Sudan before the end of the year to shore up its defences against a growing Libyan threat.

The official, who briefed reporters on condition that he was not named, said 20 M-60 tanks, 12 155-mm Howitzers and two F-5 fighters would be taken out of storage ready for shipment.

He said Libyan planes, mostly obsolete Italian-built aircraft, were making daily raids on the Sudanese who had no air defences.

Man slain in case of rape revenge

RAMLE (Itim). — Three hours after the police got a telephone call yesterday afternoon telling them, "I've got the man who raped my sister and I'll wipe him out, I've got two handgrenades," one man was dead, the caller was lightly wounded and an apartment completely destroyed.

Police who rushed to Rehov Hillel in Ramle tried unsuccessfully for more than two hours to convince the caller (whose name has not been released for publication) to hand over the grenades.

According to neighbours, the alleged killer suspected the dead man, Eli Uliel, 19, of raping his sister and photographing her in the nude.

They also said they heard shouts yesterday afternoon, "Let him give me the pictures and I'll leave."

Police say they had received a complaint about the alleged rape.

The apartment in Rehov Hillel belonged to Uliel's sister. The alleged killer broke into the flat and reportedly ordered the sister to leave. "When he saw the police trying to climb up to the apartment, he lowered the blinds, and then we heard the explosion," neighbours said.

Other flats were not damaged.

The hundreds of persons who congregated outside the apartment house saw flames burst out of the electric cables leading from the house, immediately after the explosion. The neighbours complained that an ambulance and fire engines were a long time in coming.

Reagan: Dayan earned the envy of the world

Jerusalem Post Correspondent

WASHINGTON. — Moshe Dayan, a popular figure in the U.S. for three decades, was warmly eulogized by President Ronald Reagan and other Americans.

Attorney-General William French Smith and a delegation of congressional leaders and others left to represent the U.S. at the funeral.

Israeli Ambassador Ephraim Evron, who worked closely with Dayan over the years, joined the special U.S. presidential aircraft carrying the delegation to Israel.

"We are deeply saddened to learn of the death of Moshe Dayan — a courageous soldier and a great Israeli statesman," said Reagan in a formal statement. "Dayan provided his nation with military leadership that was the envy of the world. His bold strategies brought him victory on the battlefield and respect from friend and foe alike."

The president continued: "His service as a statesman was no less distinguished. He demonstrated those inner qualities of good will and integrity that are essential for peace and security."

Former president Jimmy Carter said that Dayan's "dedicated and tireless efforts at Camp David helped to bring about a blueprint for peace between Israel and Egypt and all their neighbours."

Another former president, Gerald Ford, said: "An old friend and outstanding leader, Moshe Dayan will be badly missed as we move forward with the peace process in the Middle East.

Former president Richard Nixon paid tribute to Dayan as "a great military leader" who proved in his

(Continued on Back Page)

No eulogies or salvoes at funeral

Moshe Dayan will be given a State funeral today and will be buried at his request in his home village of Nahalal. Also at Dayan's request, no eulogies will be delivered and no salvoes will be fired, the IDF spokesman announced yesterday.

The coffin will be placed outside Nahalal's community centre at 1 p.m. and the public will be able to pay its respects to the deceased until 2.30 p.m. At 3 p.m., the funeral procession will leave for the Nahalal cemetery.

Entry into the Nahalal area will be permitted only to buses which will park at the entrance to the moshav.

Egyptians salute Dayan as diplomat

CAIRO (UPI). — President Hosni Mubarak yesterday praised the role played by Moshe Dayan in Egyptian-Israeli peace efforts and expressed confidence these efforts would bear fruit.

In a telegram to President Yitzhak Navon, Mubarak said he received news of Dayan's death with "deep sorrow."

"We remember with appreciation his positive role in the peace efforts which we trust will continue and bear the desired fruit," Mubarak said.

"Dayan played an important role in the negotiations between Egypt and Israel and made positive contributions that made the Egyptian-Israeli peace treaty possible," said Butros Ghali, minister of state for foreign affairs.

Foreign Minister Kamal Hassan Ali told reporters yesterday that "Dayan was an honest man. He fought for his country as a solider and then he fought for peace... he made constructive efforts during the negotiations."

Ali said that Ghali would represent Egypt at Dayan's funeral.

Dayan's death became a topic of conversation in Cairo's streets immediately after the Israel Radio an-

(Continued on Page 2, Col. 2)

Grenade wounds three in Old City

A mother and her two daughters were injured last night when a handgrenade was thrown at them in the Old City between the Jaffa and Zion gates. The three, Shoshana Goorji, 43, Ilanit, 14, and Lily, 10, of Tel Aviv, were rushed to Hadassah Hospital on Mount Scopus wounded in their arms and chests.

Ilan Goorji, 19, reportedly told the group of four families who were walking back to their cars from the Western Wall to throw themselves on the ground when he saw the grenade flying towards them. Their prompt response probably saved the party from more serious casualties.

Security forces combing the area detained seven suspects. (Itim)

State funeral for Dayan at Nahalal today

By DAVID LANDAU
Post Diplomatic Correspondent

Moshe Dayan, courageous soldier and brilliant statesman, succumbed to a massive heart attack in a Tel Aviv hospital on Friday night and will be buried today in a state funeral at the moshav of Nahalal where he grew up. He was 66.

At his bedside when he died were his wife Rahel, and his daughter, novelist Yael Dayan. They were joined later at his home in Zahala by his two sons, farmer Ehud and filmmaker Assaf, by former brother-in-law Ezer Weizman and his wife Reuma, and by Dayan's longtime political aides Mordechai Ben-Porat and Zalman Shuval.

Dayan took ill late on Thursday, but seemed to improve on Friday morning, sitting up in his hospital bed and reading the newspapers.

It was then that he reportedly asked his wife to ensure that there be no eulogies and no graveside volley at his funeral, should he die.

Among the foreign dignitaries attending the funeral today will be U.S. Attorney-General William French Smith, representing President Ronald Reagan, French Interior Minister Gaston Defferre will represent President Francois Mitterrand, and Dayan's longtime

(Continued on Page 2, Col. 6)

Obituary, photo tribute
Pages 6, 7

Navon, Begin mourn the soldier-statesman

Jerusalem Post Reporter

"For many long years Moshe Dayan symbolized, to this nation and to the world, the young generation of Israel fighting for its survival. In recent years, he was the untiring pursuer of peace," said President Yitzhak Navon last night in a broadcast to the nation.

"He was a man without fear — and therefore he could serve as an example to others," said Prime Minister Menachem Begin in his broadcast eulogy. "He was unequalled in our generation in fulfilment of the ancient Jewish heritage embodied in the command, 'After me'."

Navon, who knew Dayan well from the days when they both served under David Ben-Gurion, said:

"Moshe Dayan will be remembered for his great contribution in imbuing the spirit of fighting bravery into the IDF, and for his fruitful and original thinking in the field of foreign policy.

"At one and the same time he was a rough-edged sabra and a sensitive poet — and a brave and cunning.

(Continued on Page 2, Col. 2)

'Death never frightened me'

Jerusalem Post Staff

"I don't see death as something negative or threatening. In the end I will lie on the hill in Nahalal with my family and others," said Moshe Dayan 10 days before he died, in an interview with Israel Radio broadcast yesterday. "Why do you think death is a terrible thing? All through my life death passed close to me and it never frightened me," Dayan said in a weak and hoarse voice.

Dayan recalled his first brush with death on a mission for the British in Vichy-controlled Syria. A bullet shattered the binoculars he was holding, pushing glass deep into his left eye. "My friends wanted to give me to the French for treatment, but I said: No. If I die, okay, but I don't want to be a prisoner," he said. "I am not fatalistic. In combat if there is an artillery barrage I don't just walk into it saying nothing is going to hit me. That's nonsense. I will look to see where the shells are falling."

"Sooner or later death comes to everyone, and that is what will happen to me. I don't approach it with suspicion," Dayan said.

THE JERUSALEM POST

1932 50 1982

Friday, April 23, 1982 | Vol. L, No. 15511 | IS13.00

While some soldiers (left) spray foam on Yamit diehards ensconced on a rooftop, other troops clamber up ladders to apprehend them and carry them off. When the last demonstrator had been removed, bulldozers moved in. (IPPA)

Envoys recalled after Paris bombing

France and Syria at crisis point

By DAVID BERNSTEIN
Post Mideast Affairs Reporter and Agencies

French-Syrian relations plunged to a new low yesterday, when a Syrian-backed hit squad detonated a huge car bomb in the heart of Paris and Syrian soldiers serving with the occupation forces in Lebanon attacked the residence of the French ambassador in Beirut.

France responded to the car-bomb blast, which killed a woman and injured some 64 other persons on the crowded Champs Elysees, by expelling two Syrian diplomats and recalling its ambassador from Damascus.

Syria retaliated by expelling two French diplomats and recalling its own ambassador from Paris.

Syrian Foreign Minister Abdel-Halim Khaddam also cancelled a planned meeting in Paris today with his French opposite number, Claude Cheysson. He had been due to stop over in Paris on his way home from attending the UN Security Council in New York.

According to the Christian Phalange radio in Lebanon last night, a number of Syrian soldiers serving in Lebanon, led by a Syrian officer, launched an attack on the residence of the French ambassador in Beirut.

The radio said, however, that they were driven off by the detachment of French paratroopers charged with protecting the embassy. There was no report of casualties.

The target of the bomb blast in Paris earlier in the day — which shattered windows for three blocks

(Continued on Page 2, Col. 2)

All watch in awe as town turns to dust

By ABRAHAM RABINOVICH
Jerusalem Post Reporter

YAMIT. — The rumbling began shortly after first light and soon the bare tile floor on which I was lying began to shake. I had arrived in Yamit illegally in the dark a few hours before and was lying in the empty house to keep out of sight of soldiers, whose silhouettes I had been able to make out on the roofs of the one- and two-storey houses all around me.

The rumbling turned into angry growling and the sense that something terrible and implacable was approaching penetrated my drowsiness.

I ran out the rear door as four massive bulldozers rolled up and began lashing out at the neighbouring buildings. Their blades cut into the walls as if they were made of putty and in a few angry shakes and heaves the buildings were heaps of rubble. An officer ran into the building in which I had been hiding to check it out and a minute later it too was gone.

Soldiers sleeping in an adjoining house were roused by the officer and they hastily pulled on their boots. Paper party streamers left by the previous residents hung from the ceiling above them. A few moments later, the bulldozers had levelled the house.

Apocalypse had arrived in Yamit and in the dust and noise and destruction one could wander freely. Dozens of bulldozers and giant mobile air hammers were loose in the city like a pack of predatory beasts.

The air hammers, held aloft by crane-like devices, pecked at the upper stories of buildings like dinosaurs. The bulldozers took on the one-storey buildings, angling blows at the corners to topple the walls.

Shechunat Havatikim, the oldest section of Yamit, was already half gone two hours after sunrise. In the rear of a house still untouched stood a woman and a baby.

"My husband's getting the truck," said Esther Pinto. "We just wanted to see what it would be like at the end." She nodded at the ruins of her neighbours' houses all around her. "It's a pity we stayed."

As painful as it was to see the city die, however, she said it was preferable to turning it over intact to the Egyptians. "We received

(Continued on Page 2, Col. 2)

Bulldozers to complete razing of Yamit today

By JOSHUA BRILLIANT and MOTTI BEN-YANAI
Jerusalem Post Reporters

YAMIT.— Only some 50 persons remained here last night as this town went through its last hours before being reduced to rubble. Most of Yamit has already been demolished by dozens of IDF bulldozers.

IDF sappers are expected to blow up the town's bomb shelters and other structures too sturdy to be swept away by the bulldozers, and the obliteration of the town is expected to be completed by this afternoon.

By last night those remaining here were 10 disciples of Kach leader Meir Kahane, — still holding out inside a shelter "bunker" in which they barricaded themselves several days ago and threatened to commit suicide — and 20 university students barricaded in the 28-metre high war memorial, led by Tzahi Hanegbi. They and the one or two remaining families are to be evacuated today.

There is fierce competition between the Kach group and the students over who will be the last to leave.

The battle between about 200 helmeted soldiers and about 200 protesters who had barricaded themselves on the roofs of three long apartment buildings began at 7:45 a.m., shortly after an IDF helicopter hovered overhead.

The first unit approached the buildings from the north, placing ladders against the walls. The militants tried in vain to push the ladders away with long poles. At one point the protesters lowered a burning tire to try to deter the troops, but the soldiers quickly put the fire out and climbed the wall.

As the first soldier reached roof level, militants pushed down on his helmet, trying to force him back. His commanding officer, who was immediately behind him on the ladder, held him fast by the waist.

During the pushing and shoving, other soldiers climbed over an unguarded corner of the rooftop and engaged the militants from behind.

Resistance was stronger at the adjacent building, where the diehards stopped the soldiers from climbing onto the roof. The militants also emptied bags of sand on the troops below. Firemen then swept the rooftop with foam from hoses, drenching the militants and the soldiers as well.

OC Southern Command Aluf Haim Erez at one point opened fire with an M-16 assault rifle over the militants' heads, in an effort to drive them back from the roof edge. Some protesters raised their hands in response, but most did not and the fighting continued.

Some of the militants shouted at Erez, "Shame on you. It's with you that we'll have to go to the next war."

Only after the troops armed themselves with clubs and began fighting back was the battle decided. Eventually all the soldiers overcame attempts to push them back down and scaled the roofs.

A giant crane lifted a rust-coloured cage onto the roof, where the soldiers pushed two or three militants at a time inside. They were then lowered to the ground, to be

(Continued on Page 2, Col. 4)

Terrorists divided on response to air raids

BEIRUT (Reuter). — Strains appeared yesterday in the Palestine Liberation Organization amid reports of pressure on it from the Lebanese and U.S. governments not to retaliate after Wednesday's Israeli air raids south of Beirut.

First indications were that the bulk of the organization was against a military riposte for fear of provoking an Israeli invasion of South Lebanon. But several radical Palestinian factions called for vengeance.

Tension remained high in Lebanon as Israeli jets flew reconnaissance missions over Beirut and the south of the country, including areas bombed on Wednesday.

About 25 people were believed killed in Wednesday's two-hour air strike — during which two Syrian MiGs were downed by the Israelis in aerial combat — although estimates differed. The raids were concentrated around the Palestinian stronghold of Damour, 15 kms. south of Beirut.

Political sources said Prime Minister Shafik al-Wazzan Wednesday night contacted Salah Khalaf ("Abu Iyad"), a leading member of Yasser Arafat's Fatah, to urge restraint.

The state-run Beirut Radio said parliamentary speaker Kamel al-Assad was sending a message to Arafat calling on him to beware of the "trap" Israel was laying for his organization.

At the UN, a PLO central council member, Shafiq al-Hout, said the U.S. had appealed to the Palestinians through a third party not to retaliate for the air raids.

The PLO on Wednesday night

(Continued on back page)

Israeli officials flying to Cairo

Taba issue expected to be settled by Sunday

By DAVID LANDAU
Post Diplomatic Correspondent

Senior Israeli officials are flying to Cairo today for talks that is hoped will produce an agreed interim arrangement on the disputed Taba Beach, near Eilat. Well-placed sources in Jerusalem expressed optimism last night that the issue would be resolved tomorrow — enabling Israel to withdraw from Taba in the general withdrawal from Sinai on Sunday.

The cabinet had resolved on Wednesday not to withdraw from Taba unless the interim arrangement was worked out whereby Israeli civilian life can continue there pending a final settlement of the dispute by arbitration.

Two key points have been holding up agreement on an interim arrangement;

- Egypt wants a time-limit set for the duration of the arbitration. Cairo proposes that the parties agree in advance to limit the arbitration to a matter of months.
- Egypt is reluctant to allow work to continue on the nearly completed Israeli hotel in Taba during the interim period until the arbitrator's ruling is handed down.

Israel argues that to set a time-limit for the arbitration would be needlessly to court ithe danger of a new crisis if that time limit cannot be met. "Negotiations ought never to be limited in time," an Israeli source said last night.

As regards the hotel completion, Israeli sources say Egypt's position on this suddenly hardened a week ago. Before that the impression had been that Egypt would not object to

(Continued on Page 2, Col. 2)

Kiryat Shmona on alert, but life as normal

Jerusalem Post Reporter

KIRYAT SHMONA. — One day after the Israel Air Force's attack on terrorist bases in South Lebanon, life in Jewish settlements near the border returned to normal, although the state of readiness continued in the event of a terrorist attack.

UNIFIL sources reported that Israeli planes were seen flying over Lebanon on 40 different occasions yesterday.

Shops here were open and most children turned up at their schools. During the morning, the town's Thursday market was crowded with shoppers from all parts of Upper Galilee. Among those walking through the market was Economic Minister Ya'acov Meridor, who is also chairman of the ministerial committee on the Galilee. He chatted with shopkeepers and others about their problems.

Most residents of the town slept in shelters last night.

Pakistan bars EEC unit—it has a Jew

STRASBOURG. — The president of the European Parliament, Piet Dankert, on Wednesday accused Pakistan of religious and political discrimination for allegedly refusing entry to a parliamentary fact-finding mission.

He said the Pakistani authorities had refused a group of three deputies permission to enter the country and visit Afghan refugee camps in the north because one of them was Jewish.

The delegation will not leave, he said.

The delegation was to have been led by French Gaullist deputy Gerard Israel, but a Pakistani representative in Brussels had said that the government would not allow him in, for fear of alienating Arab allies, Dankert added.

"This is unqualified discrimination... because of political opinions and religious views," he told the European Parliament.

Dankert urged Belgian Foreign Minister Leo Tindemans to take the matter up with the Pakistani government.

Tindemans, current president of the European Economic Community's council of ministers, said he would discuss the matter with foreign ministers from the nine other EEC countries.

"This is certainly a very grave move indeed," he told deputies. "I'm sure we'll come to a common protest about this." (Reuter, AP)

Segen Eyal Tzur, mine victim, buried

RAMAT HASHARON (Itim). — Segen Eyal Tzur, 21, was buried yesterday in the Kiryat Shaul military cemetery. He was killed when his jeep went over a mine in South Lebanon on Wednesday.

Among the many mourners were Defence Minister Ariel Sharon; Chief of Staff Rav-Aluf Rafael Eitan and his deputy, Aluf Moshe Levy; the IDF chief chaplain Aluf Gad Navon; and Ramat Hasharon local council chairman Menahem Sherman.

Eyal's father, Aluf-Mishne Ya'acov Tzur, said *kaddish*. After the funeral ceremony, Sharon expressed his condolences to Aluf Tzur and his wife, Ziva.

Eyal Tzur was born in Netanya, but his family moved to Ramat Hasharon six years ago. The Tzurs have two other children, Carmit, 17, and Boaz, 11.

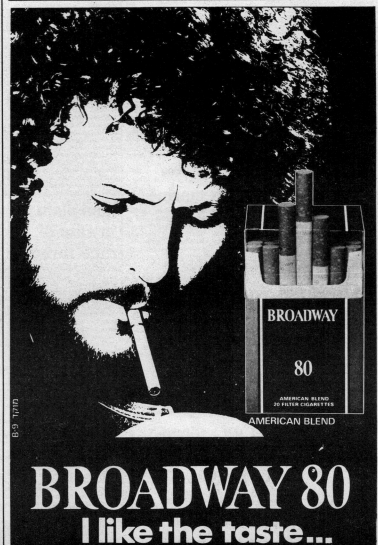

UK won't rule out force as fleet nears Falkland Islands

LONDON. — Prime Minister Margaret Thatcher yesterday told parliament her government is doing everything possible for a peaceful settlement of the Falkland Islands crisis. But she said force cannot be ruled out, in the dispute with Argentina.

"I cannot rule out the use of force. You have to be prepared to defend the things in which you believe and be prepared to use force if that is the only way to secure liberty and self-determination," she declared.

Thatcher defined the government's position as Foreign Secretary Francis Pym arrived in Washington carrying Britain's reply to Argentina's Falkland Islands package — something he has said falls short of British requirements "in certain important respects."

Before leaving London, Pym said the British plan would call for the withdrawal of Argentine troops, discuss an intermediate administration of the 149-year-old British Colony and propose a framework for negotiations on a permanent settlement. A summary was sent to Washington on Wednesday.

Meanwhile, lead elements of the British fleet steamed to within 500 kilometres of the islands yesterday and intelligence sources in Washington expect the British force first to recapture South Georgia and use it as a staging area for further operations.

The sources, who requested anonymity, said the carriers Hermes and Invincible were among the vessels forward deployed in a task force of about 40 combatant and support ships spread over hundreds of miles of the South Atlantic ocean.

About 10,000 Argentine troops were believed holding the Falklands which are blockaded by British submarines to prevent any sea-lift from Argentina for a resupply effort. The Argentines have been resupplied by air-lift.

THE JERUSALEM POST
1932 50 1982
Sunday, June 6, 1982
Vol. I, No. 15546 IS10.00

* *

IAF jets lash at Lebanon as rockets rain down on Galilee

Following the critical wounding of Israel's ambassador in London on Thursday night, Israel Air Force jets pounded targets in Beirut and other parts of Lebanon on Friday, striking at numerous terrorist concentrations. The terrorists retaliated by massive rocket and artillery barrages throughout the weekend in northern Israel. Israel replied with additional air strikes, artillery fire, and missiles from Naval patrol boats.

Top photograph shows the Beirut stadium which the PLO has used for the past several years as a training field and ammunition dump. Lower picture shows bomb craters following Israeli air strikes over the weekend. (IDF)

Habib may be back in Mideast today

By BENNY MORRIS
Post Diplomatic Reporter

U.S. special Middle East envoy Philip Habib may move forward his planned trip to the region and arrive today in Lebanon in an attempt to salvage the shattered cease-fire between Israel and the PLO, after consulting first with President Ronald Reagan in Paris.

According to Reuters, U.S. Secretary of State Alexander Haig said yesterday that Habib might fly to Versailles today to confer with Reagan on Israel's bombing attacks in Lebanon. Habib is now in London.

Haig told a news conference at the seven-nation economic summit that the bombing of the past two days was "a very serious turn of events."

Habib, who negotiated the Israeli-PLO cease-fire of July 1981, which has apparently collapsed, was due in the region to seek ways to shore up the cease-fire and perhaps to find a lasting solution to the Lebanon crisis. Habib will now have to work on the more basic task of reviving the cease-fire.

Israeli officials yesterday squarely attributed the attack Thursday night on Argov, which sparked the latest round of fighting on the Lebanese border, to the PLO.

The officials said that "all the strands, as usual, lead to Beirut (PLO headquarters) and that it is not of any great importance to which of the constituent bodies of the PLO the attackers belonged. We make no distinction between so-

(Continued on back page)

U.S. appeals for halt to acts of violence in Mideast

By WOLF BLITZER
Jerusalem Post Correspondent
and Agencies

WASHINGTON. — The U.S. is strongly appealing for "restraint" in responding to Thursday's assassination attempt on the Israeli ambassador in London.

The Americans are worried that Israel might undertake massive ground operations against the PLO in Lebanon — beyond the aerial strikes of Friday and yesterday.

The State Department called the ambassador's shooting "despicable."

In a statement released on Friday, the department noted that the shooting had triggered Israel's aerial strikes against Palestinian targets in Lebanon, calling it "a new spiral of violence in the Middle East."

Spokesman Alan Romberg said: "The U.S. is deeply and profoundly concerned over any loss of innocent life caused by this. We call on all parties in the strongest terms to refrain immediately from any further acts of violence."

While refusing to say whether the assassination attempt was a violation of the cease-fire, he said that Washington has urged all countries with influence on the combatants in the region to stop "the violence."

The Americans are fearful that the current fighting could easily tear apart the fragile 10-month cease-fire along the Israeli-Lebanese frontier.

In a letter to Prime Minister Menachem Begin, President Ronald Reagan registered his "deep sense of shock and outrage" over the shooting of Israel's ambassador to London and said he hopes

(Continued on Page 2, Col. 2)

Security Council calls for cease-fire

Jerusalem Post Correspondent

UNITED NATIONS. — The Security Council last night unanimously called for a cease-fire between Israel and the PLO, to go into effect at 6 a.m. Israel time today, Israel Radio reported at 1 a.m.

The resolution, drafted by Lebanon and modified by Japan, also calls on members of the council to "bring their influence to bear" on the parties to the conflict. The UN secretary-general is asked to make "all possible efforts" to implement the resolution and report to the council not more than 48 hours after its adoption.

The PLO deputy observer, Hassan Rahman, speaking at a press conference here, argued yesterday that his organization is "opposed to any act of violence that takes place outside of the occupied territories" including the attempted assassination of the Israeli ambassador in London.

"We categorically deny any connection to the assassination attempt in London," said Rahman. Rahman also said that the Israeli air-strikes should be regarded as "a breach of the cease-fire" arranged last July between Israel and the PLO and that his organization "still adheres to the cease-fire."

Israel's ambassador to the UN, Yehuda Blum, in a letter to the president of the Security Council, stressed that "the government of Israel for its part will take the necessary measures to protect the lives and ensure the safety of its citizens."

Air strikes spread panic in S. Lebanon

Post Mideast Affairs Reporter
and agencies

There was widespread panic in South Lebanon last night, following two days of Israeli air strikes and artillery barrages on PLO targets in Beirut and 15 other PLO centres between the capital and the border with Israel. Over 200 people were reported dead and hundreds more wounded, with the toll expected to continue rising.

Thousands of civilians reportedly jammed the main road leading northwards yesterday as Sidon and other towns and villages in the south were emptied of their inhabitants, apparently fearing that Israel was about to launch its long-expected land offensive against the PLO.

A spokesman for the Palestinian News Agency WAFA said that more than 130 people had been killed and 250 wounded in yesterday's strikes, which were concentrated on dozens of PLO targets in 15 PLO-controlled centres between Beirut and Sidon.

Official sources in Beirut were quoted as saying that Friday's air strikes on PLO targets in South Beirut left at least 70 dead, with the toll expected to rise as bodies were still being pulled out from under the ruins.

Lebanese police and PLO spokesmen are quoted as saying that many of the casualties have been civilians, including women and children. The Phalange-run Voice of Lebanon, however, reported that the Israeli planes had scored good hits on PLO military targets.

Among the casualties was Jean Lugot, a cameraman for the French television network TF-1, who was killed in Friday's air raid on PLO strongholds in Beirut.

Lugot, 51, was killed while he was

(Continued on Page 2, Col. 2)

'Hit list' said uncovered

Tight security for Jews after attack on Argov

By HYAM CORNEY
Jerusalem Post Correspondent
and Agencies

LONDON. — Police have thrown a security net around prominent Jews on an international "hit list" uncovered in raids following Thursday night's attempted assassination of Israeli Ambassador to Britain Shlomo Argov, an informed source said yesterday.

"We believe that we have frustrated a series of terrorist outrages," said Deputy Assistant Police Commissioner David Powis.

He refused to confirm or deny reports that a list of Jewish targets, living both in Britain and other European countries, had been turned up in raids following Argov's shooting.

But a source close to the investigation confirmed such a list exists and said detectives believe they have broken a terrrorist cell and are now only looking for fringe members who sympathize with various Middle East causes.

The assassination attempt on Argov was apparently carried out by an extremist faction of the PLO which received orders through the Syrian embassy in London, it was reported from reliable sources. Their action had been carefully prepared over several months.

The condition of Argov, meanwhile, continued to be critical with Norman Grant, a consultant neurosurgeon, saying he could not "state categorically" whether the 52-year-old ambassador would survive the attack.

Grant led an eight-man surgical team that performed a two-and-one-half hour operation at London's National Hospital for Nervous Disorders to remove bone

Shlomo Argov

fragments and a blood clot in Argov's brain. Doctors said a single bullet entered and exited the brain. The ambassador was still unconscious. (See story — page 3)

Five men, who reportedly entered England on false passports and are believed to have been in the country for some time, have been arrested in connection with the shooting.

The gunman, identified as a Jordanian, was discharged from Westminister Hospital after undergoing surgery for a wound caused by the bullet that lodged in his neck fired by Argov's bodyguard. Scotland Yard said he was being questioned by detectives with the Yard's anti-terrorist squad. No formal charges were expected to be filed until today.

The arrested accomplices inclu : another Jordanian and an Iraqi caught in a getaway car, a Syrian in a suburban house Friday and an Iranian in North London yesterday.

The Yard also uncovered a huge

(Continued on Page 2, Col. 6)

U.S. assures UK support over Falklands continues

UNITED NATIONS. — The U.S. assured shocked British officials yesterday that it still supports London's policies in the Falklands conflict with Argentina despite confusion over a UN vote on Friday night.

A White House spokesman told reporters at the Western summit in Versailles that the U.S. action in the Security Council — first backing Britain in vetoing a cease-fire call, then announcing it had intended to abstain — "does not indicate any change of position."

Reasons for the diplomatic mixup remained unclear, however.

Meanwhile, the commander of British land forces on the Falklands was quoted as saying preparations were on schedule for an attack on the Argentine garrison around the capital, Port Stanley.

Military sources in Buenos Aires predicted an imminent onslaught by British troops on the estimated 9,000 defenders of the key town. But the British commander, Major-General Jeremy Moore, was quoted

(Continued on Page 2, Col. 1)

Western leaders divided on major issues at Versailles

VERSAILLES (AP). — Leaders of the western world's industrialized nations, searching for unity at their summit here yesterday, found themselves divided on the Falklands crisis and strategy in their war on recession.

A heralded proposal by French President Francois Mitterrand to increase employment and spur economic growth through high technology received a cool reception from U.S. President Ronald Reagan and British Prime Minister Margaret Thatcher.

After the first session of their two-day meeting, Reagan's request for tough credit curbs against the Soviet Union was turned down by every other participant, French spokesman Michel Vauzelle said during lunch.

He said the opposition, led by Canadian Prime Minister Pierre Trudeau, was so "animated," the leaders postponed further discussion of the issue until later in the conference.

Britain was clearly upset over a belated U.S. decision to abstain in a

(Continued on Page 4)

BULLETIN—AP

Israel troops move into South Lebanon

Israel yesterday moved columns of tanks, artillery and other units into South Lebanon, primarily in the area which is under the control of UNIFIL, a UN spokesman said last night, AP reported from Beirut.

Shells fall all weekend

Jerusalem Post Reporter

KIRYAT SHMONA. — Between 500 and 700 terrorist rockets and artillery shells were fired at the northern border area between Friday night and late last night, claiming one Israeli life and indirectly causing the deaths by heart attacks of two more Israelis in bomb shelters.

Fifteen persons in settlements between Nahariya and Kiryat Shmona have been hospitalized with injuries. The fatality was caused when a motorist suffered a direct hit on his car.

There will be no schools in Upper and Western Galilee today and work in fields and factories will be carried out only on a limited scale, it was announced last night. Tourists have been advised to leave the area, and most reportedly had left by last night.

There has been heavy damage to property, buildings and utility poles, and many vehicles have caught fire.

The terrorist firing started at 5:11 p.m. Friday with Katyusha rockets falling on the Galilee panhandle. Rockets continued to fall Friday night and yesterday over the whole area, including Naharyia.

Inhabitants of the north spent all

(Continued on Page 2, Col. 6)

By JOSHUA BRILLIANT
Jerusalem Post Reporter

TEL AVIV. — The Israel Air Force, Navy and artillery yesterday continued to pound terrorist targets in Lebanon as hundreds of enemy shells throughout the weekend fell in Upper and Western Galilee and the Southern Lebanese enclave controlled by Maj. Sa'ad Haddad.

The two days of hostilities raised the possibility of an escalation and the cabinet met secretly on Friday to discuss the issue.

An invasion could lead to a clash with Syria, which has a division in Lebanon. But by last night the Syrians had not intervened, and a highly placed IDF source said definitely "no Syrians plane has approached our planes threateningly."

During the past two days one Israeli was killed when a shell hit his car, and several others were injured. Residents spent the Sabbath in shelters as some shells were fired at Haddad's enclave and Upper Galilee.

The IDF last night announced that the victim of the shell was Rav-Turai Uri Belansky, 20, of Ashkelon.

At 1 a.m., 40 Katyusha rockets were fired.

The enemy shelling resumed at 9:15 a.m. in the panhandle. Other shells fell on Marjayoun and Klea. A senior military source said yesterday's shelling was "unprovoked." Israeli gunners returned the fire and at 11 a.m. the air force was sent in.

The terrorist shelling spread to Western Galilee in the afternoon and a military source estimated last night that 150 to 200 shells fell. In one case a shell scored a direct hit on a house. A main road in a settlement was also hit.

Several cars were damaged, and sources said they included those of Economic Minister Ya'acov Meridor and an American diplomat. A spokesman at the U.S. Embassy declined to say to whom the car belonged.

Artillery gunners aimed at all the sites the enemy was shooting from, including the Nabatiyah heights, the Beaufort castle area, Tyre, Sidon and the Zaharani estuary. Enemy tank guns were sent into action.

The air force swooped on gun emplacements, terrorist camps in the field, and some targets the cabinet had set on Friday. These targets included a terrorist base, tanks, ammunition and bunkers dug into hills around Damour; several 130 mm. gun positions capable of reaching the panhandle and several caves where ammunition was stored in the Zaharani estuary; dug-out positions and 100 mm. and 130 mm. cannons and 85 mm. mortar emplacements on the Nabatiyah heights. An area further north — Sabra — was also hit, the army reported.

The Air Force did not attack the Beaufort Castle, a senior IDF source reported. He said he believed reporters watching the scene from Metulla mistook the target when they saw planes descend there to attack targets a few kilometres away.

The Air Force action continued until sundown. The Navy was involved as a missile boat shelled "sources of fire" near the Zaharani estuary, the army reported.

The fighting began on Friday, several hours after the cabinet ordered the army to attack 11 targets in Lebanon, including two in Beirut.

Israel has been waiting for a suitable opportunity to clobber the terrorists. While Jerusalem maintains the cease-fire reached with the PLO last July applies to all hostile activities, the PLO maintains the agreement applies to Lebanon only.

(Continued on Page 2, Col. 2)

More reports on the situation
Pages 2 and 3

THE JERUSALEM POST
1932 50 1982
Monday, June 7, 1982
Vol. L, No. 15547 IS10.00

Israeli forces advance 'on schedule' in massive thrust into South Lebanon

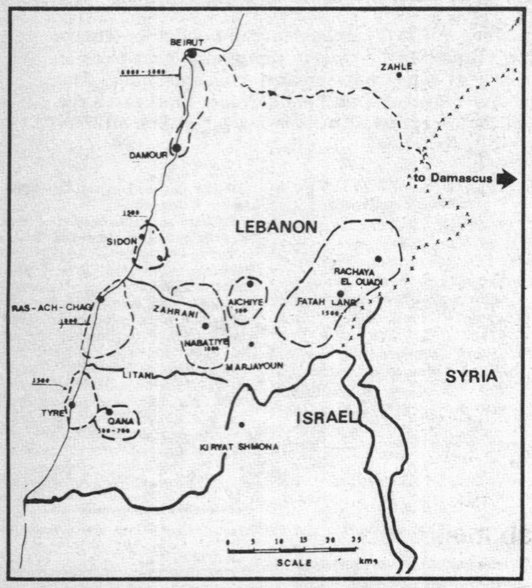

PLO concentrations in South Lebanon. The Zahrani River, south of Sidon, is approximately 40 kilometres north of the Israel-Lebanon border in Western Galilee. In his letter to U.S. President Reagan, Premier Begin writes that the army was instructed to push back the terrorists 40 kms.

Israel yesterday sent armoured columns and infantry deep into Southern Lebanon, in a massive thrust aimed at pushing PLO terrorist gunners back from the northern border. At midnight last night, UN spokesmen said that Israeli units had advanced to six kms. north of the Litani River, and had encountered stiff resistance on the coast near Tyre, and in the Arkoub region on the slopes of Mt. Hermon.

Reports from Israeli sources were still sketchy, but the Israel Defence Forces spokesman confirmed that two aircraft — an attack helicopter and a Skyhawk fighter-bomber — had been shot down over Lebanon.

Damascus said it had ordered its forces to "confront" the Israeli troops, and there were reports of "contact" at three locations.

'Peace for Galilee' move decided Saturday night

Jerusalem Post Reporter

The cabinet decided at a 3½-hour session on Saturday night to move into southern Lebanon. But it announced the decision at 4 p.m. yesterday, five hours after Israeli forces had launched a major multi-pronged push across the border.

The announcement by cabinet secretary Dan Meridor said that "Operation Peace for Galilee" had been launched "to place all the civilian population of the Galilee beyond the range of terrorist fire from Lebanon." It said that Israel will not attack the Syrian army "unless it attacks our forces," and that Israel "continues to aspire to the signing of a peace treaty with independent Lebanon."

A last minute attempt by Ambassador Samuel Lewis at 6 a.m. to forestall any Israeli action against the terrorists failed.

The government met tonight in a

(Continued on Page 7)

Peres, Rabin support government's action

Jerusalem Post Reporter

Labour Party leaders who yesterday were called to a meeting with Prime Minister Menachem Begin after operations in Lebanon had begun, later expressed support for measures taken by the government to defend the northern settlements from bombardment.

Labour Party chairman Shimon Peres and MK Yitzhak Rabin were among those at the meeting. Rabin later declared: "Now is the time for unity." (See fuller report, p. 3)

3 Arabs charged with shooting in court today

Jerusalem Post Correspondent

LONDON. — Three Arabs charged with the attempted murder of Israel Ambassador to Britain Shlomo Argov will appear in court here today, police said.

They are Ghassan Hasan Ahmed Said, 22, a Jordanian student, Marwan al-Banna, 21, also of Jordan, and Nowaf Nagib Miflih Rosan, 36, an Iraqi businessman. Said was also charged with the attempted murder of a policeman, co/in Simpson.

A Syrian was arrested in connection with the shooting on Friday but has since been released. An Iranian was still being held, but police said he was not likely to be charged.

Queen Elizabeth has sent a personal letter of sympathy to Hava Argov, the wife of the Israeli Ambassador, a Buckingham Palace spokesman told JTA last night.

(Argov's condition — page)

Begin to Reagan:

40km. push to end threat to Galilee

By BENNY MORRIS
Post Diplomatic Reporter

Prime Minister Menachem Begin yesterday informed U.S. President Ronald Reagan that the Israeli forces invading Lebanon will push back the PLO units "forty kilometres to the north."

"The army has been instructed to push back the terrorists to a distance of forty kilometres to the north so that all our civilians in the region of Galilee will be set free of the permanent threat to their lives," Begin wrote Reagan.

Observers noted that the terminology used by Begin is vague, probably deliberately so. The prime minister did not state from where the 40 kilometres begin — from the Israel-Lebanese border, from the Christian enclave-UNIFIL border, or from the UNIFIL-PLO- "state border."

Western sources in Israel last night said that during his recent visit to the U.S., Defence Minister Ariel Sharon said that Israel envisages a 72-hour campaign against the PLO in Lebanon, after which a reinforced UNIFIL, with an expanded zone, would keep the peace and secure Israel's northern border from long-range attack.

Meanwhile, in the major diplomatic initiative so far to halt the fighting, the U.S. is sending special Middle East envoy Philip Habib to Jerusalem in an effort to restore the cease-fire he helped negotiate in July, 1981 between Israel and the PLO. Habib is due to meet Begin and Foreign Minister Yitzhak Shamir this morning.

Habib yesterday met with and received instructions from U.S. Secretary of State Alexander Haig and President Reagan in Versailles, where the American leaders were attending the 7-nation summit of leaders of the major industrial Western states.

In his response yesterday to Reagan's messages of June 4, which urged "restraint" upon Israel, and of June 6, sent before the start of the ground invasion, Begin said that Reagan's "words of sympathy, friendship and understanding touched me deeply."

Begin went on to tell the American President that he had been in constant contact with the surgeon who operated on the wounded Israeli ambassador to Britain, Shlomo Argov, and gave Reagan a possible prognosis.

"I feel it is my duty...to describe to you the real situation," he went on. "For the last seventy-two hours, twenty-three Israeli settlements" in

(Continued on back page)

Heavy fighting reported

Post Mideast Affairs Reporter
and agencies

UN reports from Lebanon last night suggested that Israeli forces were running into stiff PLO resistance, mainly in the major PLO stronghold of Tyre but also near Nabatiyeh in the central sector of the battle-front.

UNIFIL spokesman Timur Goksel said in Naqoura last night that tank-led Israeli infantry had to by-pass Tyre, one of their main objectives, and press on for easier targets in the surrounding villages.

Earlier reports had spoken of heavy fighting along all three axes of Israel's advance into Lebanon.

For the first time since the latest round of hostilities began on Friday, there were indications last night that Syria had become involved in the fighting, with Damascus Radio confirming earlier reports that its forces had made contact with Israeli troops in the eastern sector.

Lebanon's state radio later said Syrian positions were pounding the advancing Israeli forces in the central sector of the invasion front with long-range heavy artillery, implying infantry or tank combat was involved.

A UN spokesman in Beirut, Samir Sanbar, yesterday provided what appears to th be the most detailed account of the Israeli offensive which followed more than 48-hours of intensive air and artillery bombardment of PLO positions in Beirut and some 15 other centres in South Lebanon.

Sanbar reported that at 11 a.m. yesterday, Israel launched a three-pronged offensive — up the Mediterranean coast, through the central sector, and from the southeast — apparently aiming for the major PLO strongholds of Tyre and Nabatiyeh.

UNIFIL spokesman Timur Goskel said in Naqoura last night that, by nightfall, it was estimated that three Israeli armoured brigades and one mechanized infantry brigade were in action. The PLO put the number of invading troops at 20,000.

Sanbar said an Israeli column of 100 tanks and 100 armoured personnel carriers had reached al-Bass on the coastal road opposite Tyre. He reported heavy clashes there between the PLO, aided by their leftist Lebanese allies, and the Israeli forces.

To reach Tyre, one of the main PLO bases in the region, the Israeli forces had to drive through a four-kilometre strip controlled by Dutch troops of the UN Interim Force in

(Continued on Page 2, Col. 2)

Syria orders army to 'confront' Israel

BEIRUT (AP). — Syria said last night it had ordered its army in Lebanon "to confront the Israeli forces," and claimed that "direct contact" had been made in three separate sectors of the central and eastern fronts.

A communique issued by Sana, the official Syrian news agency, did not say that there had been major fighting between elements of the 30,000-man Syrian force in Lebanon and the Israel force, estimated at 20,000 men, which moved across the border yesterday morning. But it did report contact at the Jarmak mountain range, in the central sector, and at Burghos and the Hasbaya intersection in the eastern Arkoub region, on the foothills of Mt. Hermon.

Industrial powers urge cease-fire

VERSAILLES (Reuter). — Leaders of the seven major Western industrial powers yesterday reached broad agreement on monetary stability and credits to the eastern bloc.

As the Versailles summit — he! in the shadow of crises in the Middle East and the Falklands — drew to a close, heads of state and government worked on the wording of their economic communique and issued a strong statement on the new outbreak of violence in Lebanon.

They called on both Israel and the Palestinians to "cease immediately and simultaneously all military activities."

Special U.S. Middle East envoy Philip Habib flew to Versailles to confer with President Ronald Reagan on the crisis and was expected to fly to Israel after the meeting.

The monetary accord, as European leaders have urged, is likely to commit the industrial countries to intervene, if necessary, on the exchange markets to counteract disorderly conditions.

But summit sources said the

(Continued on Page 4)

Israel loses plane, 'copter

By HIRSH GOODMAN
Post Military Correspondent

ON THE NORTHERN BORDER. — The Israeli advance into Lebanon was last night reported to be on schedule. But few details were available from Israeli sources.

The Israel Defence Forces spokesman declined to divulge casualty figures for the attack. He would confirm that Israel has lost one Skyhawk fighter and an attack helicopter, and that two helicopter pilots were missing, with the fighter pilot thought to be a captive of the PLO.

According to foreign sources, at 11 a.m. yesterday, Israeli forces entered Lebanon on three main axes.

The declared goal of the operation is to push back terrorist artillery and rockets from Israel's frontier. The government and the army made it clear that it is not the IDF's intention to engage the Syrians in any form of battle, and this message was also passed on to the Syrians by diplomatic means.

Judging from reports reaching Israel from the battlefield, it was clear last night that there are three major prongs in the Israeli attack. Mixed armoured, artillery and infantry forces were reported to be moving along the coastal highway and said to have reached the Tyre area, where fierce fighting was raging last night. A second force of similar mix entered via the central axis and was last night said to have encircled the town of Nabatiyeh.

A third force was moving in the Arkoub (Fatahland) area in the east.

By late last night there was no official Israeli confirmation of these reports. The government's policy is to refrain from any specific information being given out until the operation is completed.

There was also no official announcement on Israeli casualties other than the lost pilots.

Yesterday's attack was a combined land, air and sea operation, with Israel's armoured columns passing through territory being held by the Dutch, Norwegian and French UNIFIL detachments. In contradiction of UNIFIL spokesmen's reports, IDF officers deny that there were any exchanges of fire with UNIFIL during the day.

Army sources said that the air force flew many dozens of sorties against terrorists and all air strikes were directed against terrorist sources of fire. They pointed that the terrorists used hundreds of Strela missiles against the attacking aircraft.

Undoubtedly the most complicated part of yesterday's mission — again relying on reports from outside sources — was the battle in and around Tyre. This coastal city has a population of about 17,000, and military sources said last night

(Continued on back page)

Facing the enemy in southern Lebanon

By JOSHUA BRILLIANT
Jerusalem Post Reporter

TEL AVIV. — Implementation of the cabinet decision to "place all the civilian population beyond the range of terrorist fire from Lebanon" will require the clearing of a strip nearly 30 kilometres deep along Israel's border with Lebanon. The 130-millimetre cannon, longest-range weapons in the hands of terrorist forces in southern Lebanon, have a maximum range of 28 kms.

This will bring the Israel Defence Forces very close to a Syrian brigade at Meshki northeast of Metulla, and stretch a line at some points crossing the Zaharani River, east to somewhere between the Lebanese coastal cities of Tyre and Sidon.

Terrorist forces in southern Lebanon number 6,000 armed men, about half of the PLO's total strength in Lebanon. According to military sources, the terrorist concentrations include a string of heavily fortified positions, each housing a platoon-strength force.

It is believed that some areas are heavily mined, some with unmarked minefields, and that there are many booby-traps in the area as well.

Only a few of the terrorist positions are in villages, according to

(Continued on Page 7)

Israeli troops move across the border into Lebanon yesterday. (IPPA)

THE JERUSALEM POST
1932 50 1982
Wednesday, September 15, 1982
Vol. L, No. 15633 IS13.00

* *

El Al still grounded, stewards set to vote

By MICHAL YUDELMAN
Jerusalem Post Reporter

BEN-GURION AIRPORT. — El Al remained grounded yesterday, but all the airline's passengers, some 1,300 people, were flown out on chartered planes to Europe, and a chartered jumbo jet will be taking off today for the U.S. with El Al passengers.

An El Al spokesman said yesterday that all the airline's passengers are being notified of the changes in their flight schedules and so far the passenger flow is normal.

El Al's management met last night to discuss today's flight to Johannesburg. The airline's striking stewards announced that they are ready to interrupt their strike for the flight to South Africa, in the hope that this would better relations between the disputing sides and because of the importance of the route.

The El Al management announced at midnight last night that the stewards' offer came too late and was therefore impractical. The management expressed its regret that in the stewards' general meeting yesterday they did not decide to return to regular work. Management believes that all flights have to be carried out, not only the special ones.

Concerning the trip to Johannesburg, the management has yet to decide whether to use a chartered plane or not to operate the flight at all.

The cabin attendants (stewards and pursars) met for over six hours yesterday and decided to vote today on the Histadrut's suggestion to return to work and file court charges against the management for firing six stewards in violation of the work agreement.

Histadrut trade union chief Yisrael Kessar advised the stewards to return to work unconditionally, while negotiations begin between the workers and management. The Histadrut, in turn, will take legal action against management for firing the stewards.

But most of the cabin attendants are still demanding that management cancel the letters of dismissal as a pre-condition to returning to work. The secret vote on the Histadrut proposals will be held this morning at the air crews' headquarters here.

The cabin attendants, who refuse to board El Al planes due to the dismissal letters issued to several of them for not selling duty-free drinks and other items to passengers, say they are not on strike and are willing to return to work as soon as the dismissals are cancelled.

The stewards' works committee chairman, Jo Yehezkel, said that El Al manager Yitzhak Shander had promised them that if Sunday's three evening flights took off, management would cancel the dismissals. The three flights, to Bucharest, Athens and Cairo, which were due to leave between 7 and 8 p.m. Sunday, were delayed by the stewards, a number of whom were handed dismissal notices as soon as they landed on incoming flights that day.

But when the stewards agreed to let the three flights leave, somewhat after schedule, management refused to cancel the dismissals. As a result, the cabin attendants prevented Flight 001 taking off to New York that night.

Jemayel assassinated

By DAVID BERNSTEIN
Post Mideast Affairs Reporter
and agencies

Bashir Jemayel speaking to supporters last month.

Lebanese President-elect Bashir Jemayel was reported dead last night from injuries sustained when a massive bomb blast tore through his Phalange party's headquarters in downtown Beirut yesterday afternoon.

UPI and AP, in late bulletins from Beirut last night, cited government sources for news of Jemayel's death.

All earlier reports had carried eyewitness and Phalange accounts, according to which Jemayel had survived the blast with no more than minor injuries.

Government sources were quoted as saying that Jemayel's body was taken to the Hotel Dieu hospital in the Ashrafiyeh section of East Beirut, the same neighbourhood where he died. Some sources said that the body was later taken to the Jemayel home in the mountain village of Bikfiyeh.

For more than an hour after his body was dug from under the debris, official Beirut Radio played funeral music without interruption.

The Voice of Free Lebanon radio, operated by Jemayel, made no mention of his death, but issued statements telling members of the Phalangist-led Lebanese Forces militia not to venture out in uniform or carry guns without specific orders.

The sources said President Elias Sarkis informed Prime Minister Shafik Wazzan of Jemayel's death in the bombing of the party office at 4 p.m. local time.

Jemayel's body was found in the rubble of the building in Ashrafiyeh's main Sassine Square several hours after the explosion, the sources said.

The radio of Jemayel's Phalange party went off the air with no explanation a few hours after the explosion. The state radio began playing a dirge for a few minutes about 11 p.m. local time and then switched to classical music.

Jemayel, 34, was elected to succeed outgoing President Elias Sarkis in a controversial poll last month, boycotted by most Moslem delegates, and was due to take office later this month.

He had pledged himself to work for national reconciliation in an independent Lebanon freed from all foreign forces, and is reported to have made some encouraging contacts in recent days with the country's Moslem leaders — including elder statesman and former prime minister Sa'eb Salam.

But yesterday's blast may well have dealt a severe blow to these first tentative moves towards national reconciliation.

There is also the very real danger the assassination could spark off a new round of violence in Lebanon, with Jemayel's Phalange-led Lebanese Forces now the dominant militia in the country, following the demise of the PLO and its leftist allies.

Jemayel was about to address a weekly political meeting attended by some 400 party members when the blast occurred, entirely demolishing the back of the three-storey stucco building in East Beirut's Ashrifiye quarter and damaging other buildings in the vicinity.

Phalange sources suggested that Jemayel's predictable routine — he apparently attended a meeting at party headquarters every Tuesday at 4 p.m., about the time yesterday's bomb went off — was probably a factor in the blast. Jemayel had escaped two previous assassination attempts. On March 20, 1979, a car bomb aimed at him was defused, and on February 23, 1980, a car bomb exploded as his limousine passed nearvy. He was not in the car, but his 18-month-old daughter, Maya, was killed.

Jemayel's brother, Amin, and father, Pierre, have survived attempts on their lives.

Police sources estimated last night that the bomb which destroyed the Phalange building packed an explosive force equal to about 200 kilograms of TNT.

Earlier agency reports from the Lebanese capital quoted witnesses as saying that the 34-year-old Jemayel was dug out from under the rubble about an hour after the 4 p.m. explosion, and walked away unscathed.

"I'm safe. Thank God this inci-

(Continued on Page 2, Col. 1)

Jerusalem: Murder is blow to Arab moderates

By DAVID LANDAU
Post Diplomatic Correspondent

Officials in Jerusalem confirmed after midnight last night that their own information pointed to Bashir Jemayel being dead. But there was no complete confirmation of the agency report from Beirut.

Because of the unclarity, no Israel government statement was issued.

Unofficially, though, a highly placed source commented, "This is another proof, if proof were needed, of the fact that Lebanon has been ruled for years by PLO-type terror, and has lived under the fear of murder as a means of conducting politics. This is another demonstration of the need to restore freedom and democracy to Lebanon and to remove the terrorists and all foreign forces from that country. Otherwise, the violence will never end."

Non-government observers in Jerusalem noted sadly that Bashir Jemayel's murder would be used by Arab rejectionists to prove to moderates that Arab leaders who move towards peace with Israel come to a violent end — witness King Abdullah in 1951, President Sadat in 1981 and now President-elect Bashir Jemayel.

Princess Grace dies

MONTE CARLO, Monaco (UPI). — Princess Grace of Monaco, who abandoned the pinnacle of stardom in Hollywood for a real-life marriage to a handsome prince, died yesterday of injuries suffered in a fiery car crash last Monday, the royal palace said. She was 52.

The princess, the former film star Grace Kelly of Philadelphia died at 4.30 p.m., a palace spokesman said, adding she died of a broken right thighbone, collarbone and ribs when the car she was driving went out of control, plunged down a 45-foot embankment and burst into flames.

Iraq destroys Iran oil depot

NICOSIA, Cyprus (AP). — Iraqi Air Force jets yesterday bombed oil and other "vital installations" on the Iranian island of Kharg as ground fighting continued along the Iran-Iraq battlefront, an Iraqi military spokesman announced in Baghdad.

Iran said in a separate dispatch that Iraqi oil installations at Fao in southern Iraq sustained damage due to Iranian shelling which also killed or wounded 29 Iraqi troops. Twenty-five more Iraqis were killed or wounded by Iranian security forces in the same general area.

Draper opens talks in Jerusalem today

Post Diplomatic Correspondent

U.S. diplomat Morris Draper, newly elevated to the rank of roving ambassador, opens talks in Jerusalem with Foreign Minister Yitzhak Shamir this morning on the hoped-for withdrawal of all foreign forces from Lebanon.

Draper, who assisted peacemaker Philip Habib throughout the Beirut mediation effort, flew back to the region last night. He will be joined by Habib himself later in the month. The two men apparently plan to shuttle between Jerusalem, Damascus and Beirut for what could become a protracted negotiation.

Menahem Horowitz adds:

Shamir, speaking last night in Rosh Pina to mark the town's 100th anniversary, said he hoped that the talks will lead to a "withdrawal of all foreign troops from Lebanon without any additional delays or extensions."

He said that Monday's air strikes in the Bekaa Valley were meant to deter Syrian and PLO troops from committing any further cease-fire violations.

Page 3 — Cool Jerusalem reaction to King Hussein statement on recognition of Israel.

Bekaa now silent after air attack

Jerusalem Post Staff

JAB JENIN. — Following nearly a month-and-a-half of daily violations of the cease-fire by the Syrians and terrorists in the Bekaa Valley, the entire eastern Lebanese front was silent yesterday.

From time to time, reconnaissance flights by the Israel Air Force startled ground troops on both sides with sonic booms.

In the villages of Jab Jenin, Kamed al-Lus and Mansoura residents strolled in the markets and conducted their affairs without the tension that had prevailed since early August. Many villagers said they hoped that Monday's massive air strikes by the IAF have finally brought peace to the Bekaa.

But others said they expect the fighting to resume. Despite the calm, almost no farmers went off to work in fields located in the no-man's-land between the lines.

Syrian troops along the Beirut-Damascus highway in the central sector prevented Lebanese citizens from crossing from Israeli-held sectors to Syrian-held areas, for the first time in more than a month.

Syrian armoured forces appeared to have been thinned out on the mountain road where they were

(Continued on Page 2, Col. 3)

Eitan says air force destroyed Libyan SAMs

By BENNY MORRIS
Jerusalem Post Reporter

IDF Chief of Staff Rav Aluf Rafael Eitan yesterday revealed that the air force had destroyed a number of Libyan-manned SAM-8 and SAM-9 batteries during Monday's air assault on Syrian-held eastern Lebanon.

Speaking to the Knesset Defence and Foreign Affairs Committee, Eitan said that only IDF actions of this sort would curb Syrian and PLO attacks.

Eitan said that the Syrians do not want to evacuate their troops from Lebanon and that he anticipated a protracted negotiating process to secure their departure.

Committee chairman Eliahu Ben-Elissar asked if the IDF was properly equipped to face the harsh Lebanese winter. Eitan answered that it was, expressing the hope that there would be no "winter panic" among the public.

Eitan claimed that "not even a fingernail" of an IDF soldier had ever frozen during winter.

Eitan said that the Syrians had recently sent a brigade into northern Lebanon to reinforce their positions and that the IDF in Monday's raids had cut the Beirut-Damascus highway in two places.

According to Army Radio, Eitan also said that the IDF would keep contingents around Beirut so that the PLO would not again take hold in the Lebanese capital.

Sarid said that PLO Chairman Yasser Arafat had gained a political success from the evacuation of Beirut. Eitan countered that Arafat had "left on all fours," after being thoroughly defeated.

Tehiya MK Geula Cohen said the U.S. had, with its recent peace plan and announcements, encouraged Syrian belligerency. Cohen charged that after each war the U.S. always sows the seeds of the next.

Arens briefs Shultz on latest fighting

Jerusalem Post Correspondent

WASHINGTON. — Israel's ambassador to Washington Moshe Arens met here yesterday with U.S. Secretary of State George Shultz to inform him of the Israeli government's views on possible solutions to the Lebanese crisis and on negotiations for the withdrawal of all foreign forces from Lebanon.

Arens also explained the significance of Monday's military action in the Bekaa Valley and discussed the dangers of a renewal of full-scale war.

The meeting, which was requested by Arens, lasted about half an hour.

Pope John Paul is to receive Arafat today

VATICAN CITY (AP). — Pope John Paul II, despite sharp protests from Israeli officials and Jewish organizations, will go ahead today with a private meeting with PLO chief Yasser Arafat, Vatican sources said yesterday.

The audience will be low-key and probably short, held in the late afternoon after the pope's regular general audience in St. Peter's Square, the sources said.

Plans call for the pope to stop at the nearby Paul VI auditorium to meet Arafat in one of the small audience rooms before boarding a helicopter to return to his summer palace in Castel Gandolfo south of Rome, sources said.

The meeting in no way implies any kind of legal recognition of the Palestine Liberation Organization, said a Vatican official who asked that his name not be used. He said the PLO had sought the meeting and that the pope agreed to it in response to his "humanitarian concerns" for the Palestinian people.

Arafat is also due to meet, probably tomorrow, Italian President Sandro Pertini.

Both Premier Giovanni Spadolini and Foreign Minister Emilio Colombo have refused to meet Arafat after members of the governing Christian-Democratic coalition felt misgivings and said that such a meeting would weaken the western alliance and Italy's ties with Israel.

A number of Italian politicians, including several linked to the government majority, have said they plan to call on Arafat.

Extraordinary precautions are being taken to ensure the PLO's leader security during his expected two-day stay in Rome. 2,500 police have been mobilized for the visit.

Post Knesset Reporter Aryeh Rubinstein reports: Italian President Sandro Pertini was applauded at the festive opening session of the Inter-parliamentary Union conference yesterday when he expressed "our human solidarity" with the Palestinians.

"The Palestinians," he said, "are now compelled to the same tragic exodus which, for centuries, has been the destiny of the peoples of Israel. They too have had to aban-

(Continued on Page 2, Col. 6)

Renewal of UNIFIL mandate is in doubt

By BILL KRITZBERG
Jerusalem Post Reporter

HAIFA. — There are growing indications that UNIFIL's peace-keeping mandate in Southern Lebanon may not be renewed by the UN Security Council when it expires on October 19.

The war has brought into question the usefulness of the 7,000-man UN Interim Force in Lebanon. With a new Lebanese government taking office on September 24, the enhanced prospect of a restoration of strong Lebanese sovereignty in the south, and the removal of the terrorists from the area under UNIFIL control, it appears that the departure of UNIFIL forces is inevitable. The only question seems to lie with the timing of the withdrawal.

Israeli sources have expressed satisfaction that UNIFIL may leave. "We don't see any usefulness in an extension of the mandate," one source said. "We never wanted it to continue."

"UNIFIL's mandate was to remove *us* and it didn't succeed, so the mandate is inoperative," a senior IDF officer said. "We will solve the problem of the terrorists; the human problems don't require UNIFIL."

But Lieutenant-General William Callaghan, commander of UNIFIL, warned against expectations that the force might depart shortly. "Many people have predicted our demise before," he said.

"UNIFIL has outlived many such forecasts."

Callaghan said that the UNIFIL force has been quite successful, but "one thing was lacking in the mandate — the cooperation of the parties."

UNIFIL spokesman Timor Goksel was circumspect about the fate of the UN presence. "It's changing. It's difficult to predict," he said. Referring to the inhabitants of Southern Lebanon, he said, "they see the Lebanese government as we do, as the primary salvation of the country." Goksel noted that the countries contributing forces to UNIFIL "asked for a shorter renewal" of the mandate in August. These countries are beginning to "ask what it's for," he said. He expressed his own opinion, however, that UNIFIL is "indispensable."

Israeli and UNIFIL sources differed in their assessment of the local Lebanese attitudes towards a continued UN presence in the area. "The locals don't want them now," an IDF officer said.

Goksel observed, "There is a change for the better recently because the number of troublemakers has gone down since the Israeli invasion." He conceded, however, that "you don't need 7,000 men here for a humanitarian mandate."

Local residents in the area were divided on the issue. The Christians in Major Sa'ad Haddad's enclave said they would like to see UNIFIL leave, while Shi'ites living directly under UN control were more positive about its continued presence.

SPECIAL PRICES!!!
$13.50 bed and breakfast
$6.75 extra for single room
Naharia — Frank Hotel Tel. 04-920278
Netanya — Grinshtein Hotel Tel 053-22026
Herzliya — Eshel Hotel Tel 052-70208
Eilat — Adi Hotel Tel 059-76151/2/3/4
*Children up to age 12 in parents room — 50% off
Details and bookings: Sales Office 03-452111
At the hotels, and all Kopel branches
K HOTELS

THE JERUSALEM POST
1932 50 1982
Monday, September 20, 1982
Vol. L, No. 15636
NYT
IS13.00

At 5.30 p.m. tomorrow
and every Tuesday
SAA's SP 747
The finest way to Johannesburg.
Call 03-658388 or 657759.
Or your travel agent.
SAA SOUTH AFRICAN AIRWAYS
Share our world

Cabinet debates camp killings, U.S. demand to quit W. Beirut

By DAVID LANDAU
Post Diplomatic Correspondent

The cabinet convened in special session last night to consider the Beirut massacre and its aftermath. Prime Minister Menachem Begin and the ministers were confronted with a tough American demand that the IDF withdraw from West Beirut immediately.

The cabinet had also to grapple with the wave of worldwide condemnation which followed the massacre, and the unprecedentedly bitter criticism from opposition circles within Israel.

Before the cabinet met — at Begin's home after the end of Rosh Hashana — there were news media reports of deep shock and dismay among some of the ministers themselves over what had happened in Beirut and the IDF's imputed responsibility for it.

An outright confrontation seemed to be shaping up between Jerusalem and Washington over responsibility for the massacre. President Ronald Reagan, in a public statement, implicitly blamed Israel. (adjacent column)

Israeli government officials, including Chief of Staff Rafael Eitan, had earlier charged the U.S. with "blocking direct contacts" between the IDF and the Lebanese Army — thereby delaying the handing over of areas of West Beirut from Israeli to Lebanese control.

Eitan specifically accused U.S. special envoy Morris Draper of "refusing to establish direct contact" between Israel and the Lebanese Army. Eitan said the IDF had sought "for a week already" to

(Continued on page 2, col. 2)

BULLETIN

The Cabinet ended its special session after midnight last night with a declaration that charges of Israel responsibility for the Beirut massacre were a libel. The Cabinet authorised Foreign Minister Shamir and Defence Minister Sharon to continue contacts with U.S. envoy Morris Draper for the continued takeover by the Lebanese army of IDF-held parts of West Beirut.

Bodies of Palestinians lie among rubble in the Sabra refugee camp in Beirut yesterday. (UPI telephoto)

Hundreds brutally massacred in W. Beirut refugee camps

BEIRUT (AP). — Scores of bodies of men, women and children, most of them apparently shot in the head or back, were found inside the Sabra and Shatilla Palestinian refugee camps of West Beirut Saturday, and residents said they were killed by Christian militia forces.

Reporters said the number of bodies, littering the streets and seen inside the houses of the Palestinian shanty towns, may number in the hundreds. Correspondents reported seeing what appeared to be entire families shot to death inside their homes, and said it appeared men had been lined up against walls and shot, execution-style.

UN observers said yesterday that 1,000 Phalange militiamen had been seen near the airport area on Friday morning, when the massacre occurred. Their position indicated they came through Israeli lines at the airport, it was reported.

Israeli officers outside the camps maintained the killings had been done by the Phalangists, not the men of Israeli-backed Major Sa'ad Haddad. They said Israeli soldiers even shot one of Haddad's men who tried to go into the camps.

The Israeli officers admitted they allowed the Phalange militiamen to go into the camps but made clear the Phalangists were only to pick up weapons and fend off armed resistance. The officers said shooting was heard in the camps Friday but it was thought to be from armed resistance. It was not until Saturday morning that they realized a massacre occurred, the Israelis said.

The positioning of bodies in houses and against walls with bullet holes dug into the plaster behind them, made clear the victims did not die fighting.

Associated Press Reporter G.G. Labelle wrote on Saturday: "The first two bodies were distinguishable as those of human beings. They lay next to each other on the dusty main street of the Sabra Palestinian refugee camp.

"But then the bodies lay in piles.

(Continued on Page 2, Col. 1)

Outraged Reagan plans response to slaughter

By WOLF BLITZER
Jerusalem Post Correspondent

WASHINGTON. — An outraged President Ronald Reagan yesterday met with his top advisers to determine America's next steps in responding to the mass murder of Palestinians in Lebanon.

Even while those meetings were underway, however, Israel was coming under widespread condemnation for being at least indirectly responsible for the weekend massacre, which shocked the U.S. capital.

U.S. officials said there was strong evidence that Israel had permitted the killers — widely presumed here to have been Lebanese Christians allied to Israel — to enter the refugee camps on Friday night.

Israel officials were bracing for an enormous public outcry against Israel. Even George Will, the syndicated columnist well known for his strong support of Israel, called the tragedy Israel's "Babi Yar."

As he left one meeting in the early afternoon, Reagan refused to say whether he was planning to dispatch U.S. marines back to Lebanon. "There is nothing we can talk about now," he said. "We'll let you know when it's all been sorted out."

A White House spokesman, Mort Allen, said further high-level meetings were scheduled for later in the day. A decision on redeploying U.S. marines was not being ruled out.

Secretary of State George Shultz and Defence Secretary Caspar Weinberger left the White House insisting that no decisions had yet been taken by the administration on a specific new strategy for trying to avert further massacres.

Although it was the first day of

(Continued on page 7)

On Page 2
Attacks in Paris and Brussels
Hospital slaughter denied
On Page 3
Violent demonstrations

Lebanese army taking over

By JOSHUA BRILLIANT
Post Defence Reporter

TEL AVIV. — Lebanese Army troops yesterday entered several Palestinian refugee camps in West Beirut as the IDF handed over positions it had taken in the predominantly Moslem sector earlier last week.

The Lebanese soldiers began entering the Shatilla camp at 10:30 a.m. yesterday and arrived at the Sabra and Fakhani camps in the afternoon amid wild cheering by residents.

IDF officers said yesterday that Israel had advised the Lebanese army to enter some time ago. A senior IDF officer reported having raised the matter with the Lebanese Army's deputy chief-of-staff while expressing fears of Christian attack to avenge the assassination of president-elect Bashir Jemayel.

More formal contacts were established on Saturday evening and those, according to Chief-of-Staff Rav-Aluf Rafael Eitan, led to the Lebanese arrival in the camps yesterday.

Meanwhile, the IDF was thinning out its presence in West Beirut.

Election of Amin Jemayel now likely

By DAVID BERNSTEIN
Post Mideast Affairs Reporter
and agencies

This weekend's massacre of Palestinian refugees in Lebanon has had a dramatic effect on the Lebanese political scene, placing Amin Jemayel, brother of the late Phalange leader Bashir Jemayel, in an unexpectedly strong position to become Lebanon's next president later this week.

Lebanon's entire Moslem establishment — including Prime Minister Shafik Wazzan; former prime minister and Moslem elder statesman Sa'eb Salam; and Lebanon's Grand Mufti, Sheikh Hassan Khaled, all of whom called for the boycott of last month's election — are reported to have endorsed Amin's candidacy.

This now virtually assures a quorum when parliament is recalled, apparently tomorrow, to choose its candidate, and will also probably counterbalance the votes Jemayel was expected to concede to his two rivals in the election — the octogenarian leader of the overall Christian Lebanese Front, Camille Chamoun, and the moderate leader of Lebanon's National Bloc movement, Raymond Edde.

The Moslem move must place in some question the assumption that it was in fact the forces of Jemayel's Phalange Party that carried out the massacre to avenge his brother's death in last Tuesday's explosion. It is extremely unlikely that these staunch allies of the PLO would throw their weight behind the candidate of a party they believe responsible for the slaying of hundreds of innocent Palestinians.

The Phalange has itself denied all responsibility for the massacre, and both Wazzan and Salam are reported to have confirmed that they believe this to be the case.

Eyewitnesses in the camps themselves are reported to have said, however, that Phalange militiamen as well as members of Major Sa'ad Haddad's Israel-backed South Lebanese militia were involved in the slaughter.

If Amin Jemayel is elected with massive Moslem support, as now seems a distinct possibility, the stage could be set for the emergence of a united Lebanon that will stress its Arab character and will be looking to Syria rather than to Israel — as it had been hoped the late Bashir Jemayel would do.

Amin Jemayel is known to have close ties with the Syrians — who, significantly, did not blame the Phalange for the weekend massacre — and to be decidedly cool on the question of relations with Israel.

Labour Alignment calls on Begin and Sharon to resign

By MARK SEGAL
Post Political Correspondent

TEL AVIV. — The Labour Alignment last night called on Prime Minister Menachem Begin and Defence Minister Ariel Sharon to "draw personal conclusions" because of their ministerial responsibility for the Beirut atrocity and because they had ordered the Israel Defence Forces into West Beirut "in direct contradiction to their promises to the nation and the Knesset." At the same time, the main opposition party firmly rejected the levelling of false charges against the IDF. Appearing later on the TV Mabat programme, Labour Party chairman Shimon Peres said that Begin and Sharon were personally responsible, "as they knew what was liable to happen."

The Labour statement was issued after a caucus meeting of the Alignment members of the Knesset Foreign Affairs and Defence Committee, presided over by Peres. The Alignment resolved to request a special session of the Knesset this week to discuss "this grave failure." It is understood that the Knesset will be called into session on Wednesday.

After registering its "profound shock and anger" at the dreadful massacre in Beirut, which it held "was abhorrent to all Israelis," the Alignment called for the formation of a judicial inquiry commission to investigate how the atrocity happened. It also urged the government to pull out the IDF units from Beirut and to refrain from direct or indirect intervention in the internal affairs of Lebanon.

Condemning the terrorist attacks in Belgium and Paris, the Alignment urged the French and Belgian governments to punish their perpetrators.

Former premier Yitzhak Rabin

(Continued on page 2, col. 2)

Army Radio: 'Phalangists to clean-up camps'

Post Diplomatic Correspondent

Galei Zahal, the IDF radio station, reported at midnight on Thursday that the IDF had "decided to leave the cleansing out of the Sabra and Shatilla refugee camps to the Phalange forces."

The report, from Galei Zahal's correspondent in Beirut, came from IDF sources, it is reliably learned, and it was cleared by military censorship. It led off the station's midnight newsreel, and was broadcast at 1 a.m. and 2 a.m.

There was no "follow-up" the next day, however, either by Galei Zahal or by other Israeli media.

Eitan puts responsibility on Wazzan and Draper

By JOSHUA BRILLIANT
Post Defence Reporter

TEL AVIV. — Chief of Staff Rav-Aluf Rafael Eitan claimed yesterday that the bloodbath in the Sabra and Shatilla refugee camps came to the IDF's attention too late.

Eitan blamed Lebanese Prime Minister Shafik el-Wazzan and U.S. special envoy Morris Draper for developments. Had the Lebanese Army entered those camps when Israel advised it to, there "would have been no problem," he told reporters in Beirut yesterday.

It was quiet in the Burj el-Barajneh camp where the Lebanese Army had been deployed for the past 10 days, he noted.

But "all past efforts at direct coordination between Israel and Lebanese armies were blocked by the U.S. representative Draper who refused to help establish direct contact and also by Wazzan who didn't want any such contact.

"If the U.S. had pressed for such direct contact many of the problems that have come about in the past few days would have been avoided," Eitan charged.

A week before the massacre "we had been trying to coordinate with the Lebanese army to have it come in, but our efforts were in vain for all sorts of reasons, political and apparently not military," he added.

In one of the meetings a senior Israeli officer advised Lebanon's deputy chief of staff to assume responsibility for security there adding the IDF would not enter the camps — but the Lebanese Army did not, the officer said.

The massacre took place after the IDF appeared to have overcome the last active Mourabitoun, Amal, PLO and other armed groups, which have protected the Moslems in Beirut's western sector. Eitan said yesterday the "pockets of resistance" which were still evident on Friday "had ceased to exist everywhere."

The first Phalangist troops moved into West Beirut on Friday morning, captured some people but released them later in the day, an Israeli source told *The Jerusalem Post*.

An Israel radio reporter, who was in a Phalangist makeshift field operations room before the raid, said an operation officer was briefing men there. Shortly before the operation the Phalangists talked of going into Sabra and Shatilla "to kill terrorists," the radio reporter said.

Judging by Defence Minister Ariel Sharon and IDF sources past statements, the Phalangists had to cross IDF lines to reach the camps. Sharon said last week Israel "encircled" the camps.

But Eitan said yesterday the IDF was present only west of Shatilla.

Asked why the IDF let the Phalangists enter the camps, the chief of staff said, according to the Associated Press, "We don't give the Phalangists' orders and we're not responsible for them. The Phalangists are Lebanese and Lebanon is theirs and they act as they see fit. Whoever asks these questions doesn't understand what's going on in Lebanon."

According to Eitan, the soldiers

(Continued on page 7)

Warnings said 'ignored' by Begin, Sharon

By HIRSH GOODMAN
Post Defence Correspondent

Israel's intelligence services warned both the prime minister and the defence minister about the danger of massacres in West Beirut. But the warnings were said to have been ignored.

The government was warned that any attempt to disarm the Palestinian and leftist groups in Beirut without taking steps to protect them would leave these people open to the wrath of the Christians. They were warned also that allowing the Christian Lebanese Forces, as opposed to the Lebanese Army, to enter the refugee camps would be disastrous.

The army by last night still presented no clear account of Friday and Saturday's massacre in Beirut. It was not clear whether the Christian forces entered the camps with the approval of the IDF, whether they had done so despite the IDF, and whether any provisions were made to prevent contact between Palestinians who had given up their arms and the Christian forces.

The army's official explanation was that IDF forces were not deployed in the western zones of the city and were therefore powerless to prevent the massacre.

Whoever was responsible for the murders (and on this the Army is also mum) was, in some way, dependent on Israel. This raises the question why the IDF, knowing that massacres might occur, did not apply the influence it has with the Phalangists and Major Sa'ad Haddad's militiamen (one of whom was killed by the IDF in a clash in West Beirut) to pre-empt them.

Intelligence reports that massacres could occur were not a surprise. Christian desire for revenge against the Palestinians, especially after Bashir Jemayel's murder, was well known. Moreover, there were massacres after the Litani Operation in at least one town, el'Khiyam, where Haddad's men killed women and children until they were stopped by the IDF. There were revenge clashes between the Christians and the Druse in July this year after the IDF defeated the Syrians in the villages surrounding Beirut.

Three soldiers killed

Three IDF tank crewmen were killed during a clash in Beirut last Thursday, the IDF spokesman announced early this morning. The three had previously been thought to be missing.

Haddad denies role in massacre

Jerusalem Post Reporter

METULLA. — South Lebanon militia leader Major Sa'ad Haddad denied completely last night that soldiers under command had participated in the massacre in Beirut.

"The allegation that my soldiers had anything to do with that is a blood libel circulated by some of my opponents in Beirut," he said.

Haddad condemned the massacre as inhuman and shocking.

Egypt may consider recalling envoy

CAIRO (UPI). — Egypt is holding Israel responsible for the massacre of Palestinian refugees over the weekend in West Beirut and, should the situation escalate there, might consider recalling its ambassador to Israel.

This was stated by Foreign Minister Kamal Hassan Ali yesterday following a meeting with the U.S. ambassador in Cairo, Alfred Atherton.

"Egypt considers Israel responsible for the massacre," Ali told reporters after the meeting.

Asked why his country would consider such a move, Ali said: "Because the Israelis have said they entered West Beirut in order to control the situation, but the opposite happened there."

When pressed to elaborate Ali was quoted as saying: "We do not know what happened but we know that the Israeli forces were present when the massacre happened."

EIGHT PAGES
FROM SUNDAY'S
The New York Times
THE WEEK IN REVIEW
INSIDE TODAY

OUR MAN
IN LONDON

Attention all exporters and importers.
Now you have a friend in London,
to assist you.
Next time you're in London -
phone Moshe Meirav, and he'll be
happy to meet you.

MOSHE MEIRAV
U.K. REPRESENTATIVE
34 GROSVENOR SQUARE TEL. 01-629-9731
LONDON W1

Your other friends around the world are located in:
New York, Miami, Los Angeles, Nassau,
Cayman Islands, Buenos Aires, Sao Paulo,
Santiago de Chile, Punta del Este,
Rio de Janeiro, Montevideo, Toronto,
Montreal, Luxemburg, London.

ISRAEL DISCOUNT BANK
Wimmer Jacobsohn Tamir Adv.

THE JERUSALEM POST
1932 50 1982
Friday, November 12, 1982
Vol. L, No. 15681 IS20.00

* *

No word yet on Brezhnev's successor

MOSCOW (Reuter.) — The Soviet Communist Party's leadership pledged yesterday to continue the domestic and foreign policies of President Leonid Brezhnev following his death after 18 years in power.

Brezhnev, 75, died early Wednesday but the news was not made known to the Soviet people until 26½ hours later in simultaneous announcements on radio and television.

Extraordinary attempts by a team of doctors to revive the president at a hospital after he collapsed were fruitless. A well-placed Soviet source said the desperate medical efforts were largely responsible for the delay in announcing his death.

An autopsy report distributed by the Tass news agency cited a series of serious heart ailments and concluded simply, "Between 8 and 9 a.m. on November 10, 1982, a sudden stoppage of the heart occurred."

The government ordered a four-day period of national mourning leading up to Monday's funeral in Red Square, and the Communist Party vowed there would be no sudden changes of policy.

Brezhnev was only the fourth leader of the Soviet Communist Party since the 1917 revolution, but first signs were that his death left most Soviet citizens unmoved.

The Soviet capital went into official mourning with black flags hung outside public buildings, but the mood on the streets was calm.

There was no official word on who would take over Brezhnev's twin posts as party general secretary and head of state. But a possibly significant sign emerged with the naming of Yuri Andropov, 68, to chair a 25-member funeral committee.

The new general secretary will be chosen in secret by the Politburo and his appointment probably ratified at a plenary meeting of the party central committee in the next few days.

The Soviet political system lacks any firm procedure for changing leaders.

Analysts in Moscow said it might take several months for any shifts in foreign policy to become apparent.

Veteran Foreign Minister Andrei Gromyko is expected to retain his role as the Kremlin's chief negotiator.

Brezhnev's funeral will be held a day before a session of the Supreme Soviet which is due to approve the economic plan and budget for next year.

All sportng events have been cancelled for the next four days and schools will be closed on Monday.

Brezhnev is survived by his wife Viktoriya and by his son Yuri, who is first deputy minister of foreign trade, and daughter Galina, who is married to Yuri Churbanov, first deputy minister of internal affairs.

U.S. President Ronald Reagan was awakened in the middle of the night with news of the death.

At a Veterans Day ceremony in the state dining room seven hours after Brezhnev's death was announced from Moscow, Reagan read aloud a letter of condolence he wrote to the first deputy chairman of the Soviet presidium and then added:

"Now, I said for many years there are fundamental differences between the Soviet system and our own, but I believe our peoples for all our differences share a desire and a dedication to peace."

"As far as I see it, there is no change in the president's foreign policy whatsoever," said deputy White House press secretary Larry Speakes. (Related stories, pages 4 and 5)

Rescue workers search the debris for survivors of the explosion which destroyed the IDF headquarters in Tyre yesterday. (IDF photo)

Dozens killed, wounded in massive Tyre blast

By CHARLES HOFFMAN, JOSHUA BRILLIANT and Agencies

TYRE. — The Israel Defence Force spokesman announced last night that the bodies of 13 IDF members had so far been recovered from the debris of the IDF headquarters in Tyre, which was levelled yesterday morning by a massive explosion. At least 10 Palestinians, who were being held prisoner in the building, also died in the blast.

At least 25 persons were wounded in the blast. Of those, five were severely wounded, five received moderate wounds, six were lightly wounded and nine were discharged from hospital after treatment, the IDF said.

The families of all the fallen have been notified.

Of those killed in the explosion, five were IDF soldiers, six were Border Police and two were members of the General Security Services. The families of the fallen have been notified.

The building, which stood on the main road north to Sidon, housed the IDF aid unit in the area and units of the Border Police and Military Police.

Late last night, rescue teams were working in the lit-up area surrounding the debris, trying to reach dozens of trapped soldiers.

The casualities included an unknown number of Arab civilians and prisoners. An officer on the scene estimated that dozens of people were inside the building when the blast occurred at 7 a.m.

Hospitals in the north of Israel were put on a state of alert, with emergency wards ready to take a large numbers of wounded. Ambulances were standing by at the helicopter pads. A special IDF medical team with 10 doctors — five of them surgeons — was rushed to Tyre.

It was not clear last night how many people were missing. Itim reported that IDF commanders could not find the list of soldiers on leave and were asking the evacuated which men were still inside. However, some men were in a state of shock and could not provide the answers.

Two huge cranes were at the scene, carefully lifting pieces of masonry. Reports said the teams were working slowly, fearing another collapse.

Late yesterday, Defence Minister Ariel Sharon ordered Chief of Staff Rav-Aluf Rafael Eitan to appoint a commission of inquiry to "learn all the facts connected with the explosion." Eitan appointed Aluf (Res.) Meir Zorea, the defence establishment's controller, and asked him to present his findings and recommendations within a week.

Sharon called the blast "a disaster whose cause and circumstances we don't know yet, and in which many people were hurt."

The cabinet will meet at 10 a.m. this morning to discuss the explosion.

There were conflicting reports on what had caused the explosion. Some reports said that it was caused by a car-bomb parked outside the headquarters, which stood on the main road going north to Sidon. There were rumours on the scene of a gas explosion, and others of a suicide car-bomber, who drove straight into the heavily guarded main entrance of the building. This version was discounted by a representative of the IDF spokesman on the scene.

The IDF's official communique attributed the cause to a car bomb. However, a soldier who was interviewed in hospital said he believed explosives had been planted inside the building.

A Lebanese radio station suggested that IDF explosives had gone off in the building.

A previously unknown group called The Armed Struggle Organization claimed responsibility for the attack in a written message to the independent Beirut daily *An-Nahar*.

The Israel Defence Forces spokesman last night announced the times and locations of the funerals of six of the victims of yesterday's blast at Tyre:

The funeral of Hanan Ziv, a member of the General Security Services, will take place today, at 12.30 p.m. at Beit Yehoshua, his home moshav in the Sharon.

Shami Meir Ben-Moshe, also of the General Security Services, from Ramat Gan, will be laid to rest at 11 a.m. today at the military cemetery in Kiryat Shaul.

Rav-Turai Arye Mammo, of Tiberias, will be buried at 1 p.m. in his home town.

Turai-Rishon Amir Goffer, will be buried at his kibbutz, Gonen, in Upper Galilee.

The Druse village of Beit Jann will witness two funerals: Turai Dib Samir will be buried at 1 p.m., and an hour later Pakad Sa'ad Fuad will be laid to rest. Both men served in the Border Police.

The blast rocked the area at about 7 a.m. It was followed by several other explosions, possibly of IDF arms. Inside the building many soldiers were still in bed, while others were in the shower room when the blast occurred.

Sayed Sabag, of the border police, said he was in bed when the explosion covered him with debris. But iron rods had fallen around him, providing protection. He went to a comrade and dragged him out. They heard two reservists call for help from under the debris. "It was all covered with smoke and the smell of cordite was everywhere," Sabag said.

The force of the blast was almost entirely contained within the building. Only a few windows in a hospital less than 70 metres away were broken. The blast also failed to damage the concrete shell of a building 20 metres away. To some observers, this indicated that the explosion went off inside the building.

An officer who was asleep on a lower floor when the explosion occured said that the wall next to him remained standing for a short while, enabling him and several others to escape. He managed to find a radio and alerted a nearby IDF unit.

(Continued on Page 2, Col 6)

Habib returning as 'super envoy'

By WOLF BLITZER
Jerusalem Post Correspondent and Agencies

WASHINGTON. — President Ronald Reagan yesterday announced that his highly praised special Middle East envoy, Philip Habib, would return shortly to the region to try to remove all foreign forces from Lebanon.

Reagan told reporters that the Lebanon-related negotiations had always "worked better" when Habib was directly involved.

Habib will also expand his duties to take charge in renewed Palestinian autonomy negotiations.

Both Ambassador Morris Draper, who has been directly involved in the Lebanese negotiations, and Ambassador Richard Fairbanks, who has been waiting for the Egypt-Israel autonomy talks to get of the ground, will continue their responsibilities, although they will now report to Habib.

All three U.S. officials will participate in Reagan's meeting next Friday with visiting Prime Minister Menachem Begin. Habib will return to the region shortly thereafter, he said.

At a news conference, Habib denied that no progress had been made recently in removing all foreign forces from Lebanon.

He said the efforts, sponsored by the U.S., have been "ongoing — it is now going to be not only maintained but brought to a logical conclusion."

Officials said Habib would be given broad supervisory powers to seek solutions to a range of Arab-Israeli problems.

Draper returned to Beirut yesterday amid recurring Phalange-Druse clashes in the Shouf Mountains.

Government sources said Draper will brief Lebanese leaders on the outcome of his latest shuttle aimed at forging a Lebanese-Israeli agreement on the mechanics of planned

(Continued on page 2 col. 1)

Begin to U.S. for talks, Jewish, Christian meetings

Jerusalem Post Staff and Agencies

Prime Minister Menachem Begin arrived in the U.S. yesterday and said he expected an underlying friendliness in his meetings next week with U.S. President Ronald Reagan and Secretary of State George Shultz.

"I believe our talks will be imbued with the deep friendship between our two countries based on the community of interests between the United States and Israel," Begin said at Kennedy International Airport.

The prime minister said he first planned to meet with American Jewish leaders in New York and Los Angeles before his meetings next week in Washington.

Begin said that while en route from Israel he had heard the "horrible news about the new outrage perpetrated by enemies of mankind."

"I can only say that such an outrage will not deter us from doing our duty to insure peace and security to our people," he declared.

Los Angeles police said yesterday they are prepared for possible clashes between supporters and opponents of Prime Minister Begin when he visits the city.

Police and U.S. secret service officials were taking strict precautions to ensure Begin's safety.

BULLETIN

Radio broadcasts from Egypt's two powerful transmitters were weak between 8 and 9:30 p.m. last night, and went off the air entirely for seven minutes, Michael Gurdus, Kol Yisrael's radio monitor, reported. Gurdus said that such an occurrence was "strange," but would not attach any deeper significance to it.

Walesa to be set free soon

WARSAW (Reuter). — Lech Walesa, interned leader of the banned Solidarity free trade union, will be released in the next few days after asking for talks with the martial law authorities, a government spokesman said yesterday.

Spokesman Jerzy Urban told a press conference the decision to free Walesa was prompted by a letter Walesa sent on Monday to military leader Gen. Wojciech Jaruzelski and a subsequent meeting with the Interior Ministry.

He said there were no special conditions for the release of Walesa, who "no longer poses a threat to the internal security of the state."

The shipyard electrician who emerged as the leader of the first free trade union in Communist history has been a silent symbol of resistance since his internment under martial law last December 13.

The decision to free him was announced after the thin response to a call by Solidarity's underground activists for an eight-hour strike and demonstrations across the country on Wednesday to protest against the union's banning.

13 Birzeit faculty ordered to leave

Thirteen foreign faculty members at Birzeit University were ordered yesterday to leave the country within the next two months, as soon as their visitor's visas expire, for refusing to sign a pledge not to support the PLO.

The 13 — eight Americans, three British, one Frenchman and one Swede — were informed of the order after being summoned to the Ramallah military government headquarters, where they were immediately barred from teaching.

Testimony at Commission: Army heard of 300 dead Friday

By DAVID RICHARDSON
Jerusalem Post Reporter

Information that 300 people had been killed during the first few hours of the Phalange opearation in the Palestinian refugee camps outside Beirut reached army headquarters in Tel Aviv by at least 5.30 a.m. on Friday, September 17. This information had also been conveyed to Defence Minister Ariel Sharon's chief assistant, Avi Dudai, by midday that Friday, although Dudai vigorously denied this during his testimony before the Kahan commission last week.

This emerged during yesterday's open hearings of the commission investigating events surrounding the massacre of Palestinians at the Sabra and Shatilla refugee camps by Christian militiamen

Aluf Moshe Levi, (photo P.3) the deputy chief of staff testified later in the day reinforcing the general impression that the army's senior commanders were not especially aware of or apparently troubled about the conquences of sending the Phalange into the refugee camps.

Sgan-Aluf Moshe Hevroni, the bureau chief to the Head of Army Intelligence, said yesterday that Dudai "was not telling the truth" when he said that he did know of the reports which spoke of 300 killed in a refugee camp in Beirut.

Hevroni said that he first received such a report by telephone at his home at 5.30 a.m. on Friday morning. Later the same morning he saw the same report at his office and his assistant, Seren Moshe Sinai, had informed Sgan Aluf Reuven Gai, duty officer in the National Defence Unit attached to the Defence Minister's Bureau.

Gai, who also testified in open session yesterday, confirmed that Sinai had informed him about the killings, when they had met on the stairs outside the bureau of the chief of military intelligence; but said that he was given the information as "a story, as gossip" without being given a written report or being instructed to transmit it further.

Under further questioning, Gai who is an officer in the Situation Room of the National Defence Unit, explained that information his office received for transmission to the defence minister always originated in cables or specific telephone calls from the General Staff-Operations and not from the bureau of the chief of military intelligence. After speaking to Sinai he had contacted Operations and asked in general terms whether

(Continued on page 17)

PRICE CORRECTION

An error appeared in the HYPERSHUK advertisement on p. 2 of the Magazine of last Friday, November 5.

The correct prices are:

"Sunfrost" chopped spinach, 400 g.		"Shahaf" flaky pastry, 400 g.	
~~IS 50.—~~	IS 39.—	~~IS 28.40~~	IS 19.90

BAZAK
the most detailed,
practical and helpful
guide on Israel
Available everywhere

THE JERUSALEM POST

Wednesday, February 9, 1983

Vol. LI, No. 15757 IS20.00

THE JERUSALEM POST
INTERNATIONAL EDITION
The perfect gift for
your friends and relations
overseas

Kahan panel scores gov't, army leaders

By DAVID RICHARDSON
Jerusalem Post Reporter

The Kahan Commission, appointed by the government last October to investigate the events surrounding the massacre by Lebanese Christian Forces of Palestinians in two refugee camps in southern Beirut the month before, yesterday published its findings — a slim, buff-coloured book which has unleashed a political earthquake.

The commissiom found the Defence Minister Ariel Sharon, Chief-of-Staff Rav-Aluf Rafael Eitan, Director of Military Intelligence Aluf Yehoshua Saguy and the chief IDF Paratroop and Infantry officer Tat-Aluf Amos Yaron all bore individual responsibility for failing to prevent or to stop the massacres at Sabra and Shatilla.

Prime Minister Menachem Begin was found responsible for displaying indifference to the reports that the Phalange had entered the Palestinian refugee camps.

Foreign Minister Yitzhak Shamir was severely criticized for not verifying reports he had received of killings in the camps.

OC Northern Command Aluf Amir Drori was faulted for not continuing earlier steps to check the Phalange behaviour in the camps and to ensure the safety of the civilian population.

No specific recommendations were made regarding these three men.

The head of the Mossad, and Avi Dudai, personal aide to the defence minister, were cleared of responsibility.

The commission — Justice Yitzhak Kahan, the outgoing president of the Supreme Court, Justice Aharon Barak and Aluf (Res.) Yona Efrat — also unequivocally place direct responsibility for the massacres on the Lebanese Christian Phalange Forces and dismiss suggestions that IDF soldiers took part in the killings as "groundless...and baseless libel. Nor was there any indication of a conspiracy between anyone in the Israeli political or military echelon and the Phalange with regard to the camps, the report said..

At the same time, however, the commission bluntly rejects the government's assertion at the time, which was reflected in a cabinet statement on September 19, that Israel bears no responsibility for acts "perpetrated outside its borders by members of the Christian community against Palestinians in that same country..."

Maj. Sa'ad Haddad, the commander of the Southern. Lebanese militia, was also cleared of any involvement in the massacres.

The report makes a clear and basic distinction between the direct responsibility of the Phalange which is detailed in the first section of the report entitled "Description of Events," and between the indirect responsibility of the Israeli government, the IDF, the Mossad and other Israeli agencies or individuals.

The commission mentions that other institutions, too, might bear indirect responsibility. It singles out the Lebanese Army, the U.S. government and the governments of the contingents of the multi-national force in Beirut.

The structure of the commission's report leaves the impression that at least part of it was agreed upon before the warning letters to the nine persons were sent on November 24, and even before the final draft was ready. The commission stresses that it agreed on a standard by which it judged the major politicians and military officers, namely, their anticipation of Phalange behaviour towards the Palestinians.

"In our view, everyone who had anything to do with events in Lebanon should have felt apprehension about a massacre in the camps, if armed Phalangist forces were to be moved into them without the IDF exercising concrete and effective supervision and scrutiny of them."

The carefully worded and meticulously reasoned report focuses on the activities of the nine individuals warned last November, seven of whom were eventually singled out for severe criticism. But the report also emphasises the role of commissions of inquiry in the Israeli democratic system which "is obligated to consider not necessarily the legal aspects of the subject but also, and occasionally primarily, its public and moral aspects." The commission also recalls relevant principles of Jewish law and the lessons of Jewish suffering under exile or foreign rule.

In a short chapter entitled "Closing Remarks," the commission appears to set forth its credo about the maintenance of civilized values in the face of the brutalizing influence of war. "It seems to us that the IDF should continue to foster the (consciousness of) basic moral obligations which must be kept even in war conditions, without prejudicing the IDF's combat ability...But the end never justifies the means, and basic ethical and human values must be maintained in the use of arms."

"The main purpose of the inquiry...has importance from the perspective of Israel's moral fortitude and its functioning as a democratic state that scrupulously maintains the fundamental principles of the civilized world. We do not deceive ourselves that the results of this inquiry will convince or satisfy those who have prejudices or selective consciences, but this inquiry was not intended for such people."

The report's recapitulation of the events surrounding the massacres include new details of when information about the killings was first received by Israeli forces in Beirut or at the General Staff Headquarters in Tel Aviv.

There are also specific recommendations to re-examine decision-making and reporting procedures not only within the various sections of the army, but at cabinet level as well. Telephone discussions and conversations between the prime minister and his colleagues or senior officers are not sufficiently logged or recorded, it was found.

The commission's findings also expose long-suspected tensions between director of Military Intelligence Saguy, and Sharon and Eitan, and between military intelligence and the Mossad who strongly favoured close cooperation with the Phalange. There are also hints of tensions between Eitan and Drori.

Some of the commission's severest language is reserved for

(Continued on page 2, col. 4)

Sharon: 'U.S. hopes I'll be removed'

By MARK SEGAL
Post Political Reporter

TEL AVIV. — Taking the offensive, Defence Minister Ariel Sharon last night painted a picture of a U.S.-directed campaign to oust him and to impose on Israel a PLO state next door.

"It's immaterial whether the commission decided this or that way," he said to an audience of the Jabotinsky Lodge at the Plaza Hotel. "Israel would not submit to the Reagan Plan. Sharon added: "I hear that in Washington the administration's hopes have soared at the prospect of Sharon's removal so as to advance the Reagan Plan. I have been and will continue to stand along with others against whoever tries to impose a second Palestinian state alongside Israel, which would mean suicide for us."

Sharon took pains to identify his case with that of the entire army and particularly with the IDF commanders singled out by the commission's report.

Dwelling on the "political and military successes" of the Peace for Galilee campaign, Sharon remarked on the "unparalleled heroism of our soldiers and commanders." He singled out Chief of Staff Rav-Aluf Eitan, "a battle-proved soldier who brought our army through the last war to the greatest achievements in our annals."

"Raful brought honour to the IDF and to the Jewish people," Sharon said. Northern Command Aluf Amir Drori "bore all the burden of the northern battles on his shoulders," Chief of Army Intelligence Aluf Yehoshua Saguy "took a key role in all our wars," and Tat-Aluf Amos Yaron, "one of our bravest commanders," Sharon added.

When Sharon entered the hall, meeting chairman Eliyahu Galezer described him as "a great warrior who saved our country" and

(Continued on Page 2, Col. 2)

Defence Minister Ariel Sharon leaves the cabinet meeting in Jerusalem yesterday. (Rahamim Israeli)

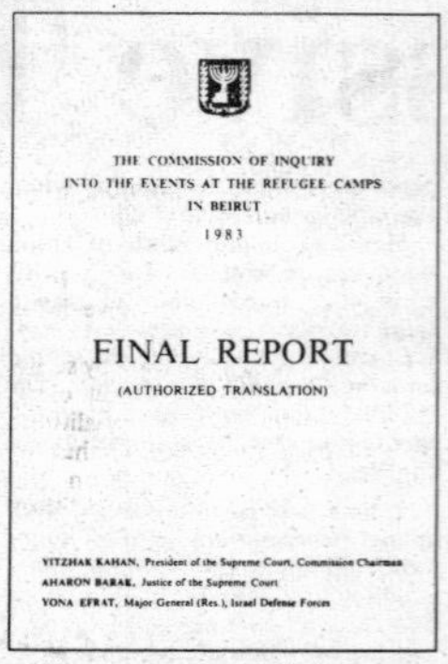

THE COMMISSION OF INQUIRY
INTO THE EVENTS AT THE REFUGEE CAMPS
IN BEIRUT
1983

FINAL REPORT
(AUTHORIZED TRANSLATION)

YITZHAK KAHAN, President of the Supreme Court, Commission Chairman
AHARON BARAK, Justice of the Supreme Court
YONA EFRAT, Major General (Res.), Israel Defense Forces

The complete official English translation of the Kahan Commission report is published as a special supplement enclosed without charge in today's *Jerusalem Post.*

The conclusions

Prime Minister Menachem Begin: A certain degree of responsibility; no penalty recommended.

Defence Minister Ariel Sharon: Bears personal responsibility; he should resign. Failing this, the prime minister should consider dismissing him.

Foreign Minister Yitzhak Shamir: Erred in not taking reports of killings seriously; no penalty recommended.

Chief of Staff Rafael Eitan: Dereliction of duty; no penalty recommended in view of the scheduled termination of his service in two months' time.

Chief of Military Intelligence Yehoshua Saguy: Breach of duty; should not continue in his post.

Head of the Mossad: Very limited responsibility because he was new in his position; no penalty recommended.

OC Northern Command Amir Drori: Breach of duty in failing to terminate the Phalangists' action; no penalty recommended.

Beirut divisional commander Amos Yaron: Misjudged the situation and failed to report adequately to his superiors; should not hold a field command for the next three years.

Cabinet seen adopting Kahan recommendations

Government may decide to resign if Arik Sharon refuses to quit

By ASHER WALLFISH
and DAVID LANDAU

The cabinet this afternoon is expected to approve by an overwhelming majority the implementation of all the recommendations of the Kahan Commission. This will mean, inter alia, that Defence Minister Ariel Sharon will have to quit his post.

At an extraordinary cabinet session yesterday, most ministers — including Sharon himself — made it plain that they favoured implementation of all the recommendations. Sharon, however, gave his colleagues the impression that he would prefer to be dismissed by the Prime Minister rather than to resign of his own accord.

The prime minister however said explicitly at the cabinet and at other meetings that he does not intend to sack Sharon.

In its recommendation regarding Sharon, the commission called on the defence minister to "draw the appropriate conclusions," and, failing that, called on the premier to "consider" dismissing him. The premier has the right to do so under a recently passed amendment to the Basic Law:Government, Paragraph 21(1).

The cabinet preferred not to complete its deliberations on the report and take its decision yesterday so as to enable Foreign Minister Yitzhak Shamir to return from Germany and have the floor, if he wishes. In addition, there are several other ministers who have not yet spoken.

But from the remarks of those who did speak yesterday, it was apparent that all of the coalition factions are unanimous in their readiness to implement the report.

Several ministers told *The Jerusalem Post* that they expect Sharon to dig in his heels in an attempt to remain in office. They said that if Sharon refuses to resign, and assuming that Begin remains reluctant to dismiss him, the premier would be willing to resign as an indirect way of achieving Sharon's ouster.

The resignation of a prime minister automatically means the resignation of the cabinet.

The Likud's coalition allies — the National Religious Party, Agudat Yisrael and Tami — have indicated that they would undertake to resist any Labour Alignment overtures and to join a new government under Begin.

The process could take many weeks. If the premier resigns, the heads of all the parties, in order of size, would call on the president and state who in their view is best able to form a coalition.

Since the Alignment would not be able to muster enough allies for a Knesset majority — providing the undertakings to Begin hold firm — Begin would be left as the cnly party leader capable of heading a coalition.

There was speculation last night that Sharon might end up as a minister without portfolio, either in the present cabinet or in a new one. This possibility is not strictly precluded by the letter of the commission's recommendations, but it is not considered a probability.

For one thing, Sharon might consider this an affront to his pride. Secondly, Begin would run up against criticism from the Opposition, and from legal circles, if this device were adopted.

The cabinet ministers were handed copies of the report early

(Continued on Page 2, Col. 5)

Tactical resignation of gov't is possible

By SARAH HONIG
Post Political Reporter

TEL AVIV. — Neither a portfolio switch within the cabinet nor early elections were ruled out yesterday. But in case neither option proves viable, a third way out of the crisis in which the Government found itself was proposed last night: the tactical resignation of the government, with prior agreement by all coalition partners to re-group in a new cabinet under Prime Minister Menachem Begin.

The major difficulty with this solution is that it would mean months in a state of political limbo while the country is beset by military problems and pressures from the U.S.

Once the government resigns without a Knesset vote for early elections, it becomes a transitional government. However, the President could first ask alignment leader Shimon Peres to form a coalition. Peres would have 21 days to do so and then another three weeks for a second try. It is possible that only after 42 tense days in which all sorts of political deals are attempted will Peres make way for Begin to reform his government.

But the supporters of the tactical resignation plan say it is unlikely the president would ask Peres to form an alternative government if all coalition factions immediately tell the president they support Begin.

This would automatically put Begin at the Head of a Knesset majority and allow him to form a new cabinet, without losing time.

This plan calls for keeping all the present coalition agreements intact to avoid a similar lengthy negotiation session as that which took place after the 1981 elections. In effect, nothing would be changed in the make up of the reconstituted cabinet, except Sharon's job.

Within the coalition, there were two contradictory tendencies — one, supported by Begin, preferred that the government as a whole resign and that the coalition ask for early elections so the voters can give their verdict. Begin is confident of being able to return to power.

But there was increasing clamour within the coalition, and even within Begin's own Herut Party, to avoid possible political pitfalls by

(Continued on Page 2, Col. 7)

Sharon must leave, Peres tells his faction

By SARAH HONIG
Post Political Reporter

TEL AVIV. — The Alignment will oppose any maneuver "to sidestep the recommendations of the Kahan Commission by switching cabinet portfolios and allowing Defence Minister Ariel Sharon to continue serving in any ministerial capacity," Labour chairman Shimon Peres yesterday told a closed meeting of the Alignnent Knesset faction.

The Alignment, whose members were cheered by the commission's findings, did not formulate any strategy yesterday. It will wait for the government's decision. However, the Peres declaration appears to be one policy line widely supported in the party.

Concurrently, the Alignment Knesset faction is gearing up for a battle which it hopes will leave it at the head of a coalition. Reports of a deal to set up a national unity government were strenuously denied by some Alignment sources yesterday, but energetically circulated by others.

Peres told his faction that he had not expected "so severe a report by the commission. This is far beyond what we could have imagined." He maintained that the report is so damning for the government, that it would be prudent for the opposition not to erupt into a chorus of criticism or jubilation now, so as not to damage itself and alienate any possible coalition partner. "For the time being, we should let the findings speak for themselves until we see what the government intends to do," Peres counselled.

In the first official statement on the Alignment's behalf yesterday, its Knesset faction chairman Moshe Shahal told a radio interviewer that the party's single demand at the moment is that Sharon be dismissed immediately.

Shahal said the party would not accept any other arrangement, including switching portfolios inside the cabinet. Shahal said all of the Kahan Commission's recommendations should "without exceptions or delay be immediately implemented."

He maintained that Labour was not considering any alternative coalitions or national unity governments. "These are not now on our

(Continued on Page 2, Col. 6)

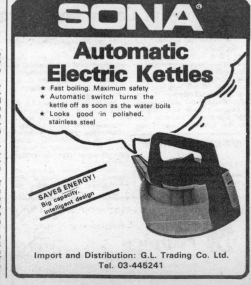

Changes likely in IDF command structure

By HIRSH GOODMAN
Post Defence Correspondent

"This is not a situation in which I can give you a convenient slogan for a headline like 'stunned' or 'shocked'," a member of the IDF general staff told *The Jerusalem Post* last night, when asked what impact the Kahan Commission's report had on the senior command of the IDF.

"We cannot say that some of the conclusions were unexpected. Ever since the nine warning letters were sent out we understood that the IDF would be affected by the findings," he continued.

Chief of Staff Rav-Aluf Rafael Eitan was unavailable for conment, and those close to him answered politely, but curtly yesterday, saying that any reaction from Eitan would come directly fron the chief of staff himself.

Eitan, who was perhaps treated more harshly by the Kahan Commission than any other person mentioned in the report, was rumoured yesterday to be considering resigning before his term expires in April. This rumour could not be confirmed in discussions with several senior officers yesterday, though one did say that "Raful is not one to accept charity."

The officer was referring to the

(Continued on Page 2, Col. 2)

Lebanese cautious

Post Mideast Affairs Reporter
and agencies

Lebanese leaders naintained a cautious silence yesterday on the outcome of the Beirut massacre inquiry, while PLO chairman Yasser Arafat criticized it for failing to lay the blame squarely on Prime Minister Menachen Begin as well as on Defence Minister Ariel Sharon.

In Egypt, senior editors of the state-guided press told the Associated Press that the report amounted to a call for the resignation of the entire Begin cabinet. *October* magazine's Anis Mansour called on Israel to "unseat Begin himself, the Khomeini of the Jewish people."

Some of the bitterest reactions to the findings came from Palestinian refugees in the Sabra and Shatilla camps.

"Sharon ought to be put on trial like the guy they brought from Bolivia to France," one 32-year-old

(Continued on page 2, col. 4)

'Satisfaction' in U.S. that Sharon may go

By WOLF BLITZER
Jerusalem Post Correspondent

WASHINGTON. — The Reagan administration yesterday reacted cautiously to the release of the Kahan Commission's recommendations.

White House and State Department officials made no public statements, believing they might be interpreted as interference in Israeli domestic affairs.

Privately, however, there was widespread satisfaction with the recommendation that Defence Minister Ariel Sharon resign. For some time, he has been viewed by the administration as the single most "anti-American" cabinet minister.

Sharon has also been largely blamed by the Americans for standing in the way of a speedy Israeli troop withdrawal in Lebanon.

The severity of the commission report on Sharon came as a surprise — albeit a welcome one — to several administration policy-makers. They were hoping yesterday that Sharon would eventually leave the Defence Ministry, thereby setting the stage for a more flexible Israeli negotiating position.

The administration is not especially eager for early Israeli elections because, they feel, this would further delay progress on the diplomatic front, and might in the end simply result in a stronger mandate for Prime Minister Menachem Begin.

At the State Department yesterday, spokesman Alan Romberg expressed the hope that the commission findings would not slow the negotiating effort in Lebanon.

"We don't see why the impact of this report — whatever that may be — should affect the Lebanese negotiations or the current Habib mission," he said, referring to special envoy Philip Habib, now in Jerusalem.

"Our view is clear," he said. "The issues being addressed are urgent and they must be resolved as soon as possible in the interests of Lebanese stability and sovereignty

(Continued on Page 2, Col. 1)

TIME
February 14, 1983
★★ REPORT ON KGB
★ BULGARIA
To Russia with love
★ NIGERIA
Exodus of the unwanted
★★ MIDDLE EAST
"Over my dead body"
Sole distributor:
BRONFMAN'S AGENCY LTD.

On the sixth anniversary of the passing of
our husband, brother, father and grandfather,

AVRAHAM FEITEL DICKENSTEIN ז"ל

son of Rabbi Benjamin

we will conduct a memorial service at the graveside
at the Kiryat Shaul cemetery, Tel Aviv at 11 a.m.
on Friday, February 11, 1983.
We will meet at the cemetery entrance.

The Family

SONA®
Automatic
Electric Kettles
★ Fast boiling. Maximum safety
★ Automatic switch turns the kettle off as soon as the water boils
★ Looks good in polished, stainless steel

Import and Distribution: G.L. Trading Co. Ltd.
Tel. 03-445241

THE JERUSALEM POST INTERNATIONAL EDITION
The perfect gift for your friends and relations overseas

THE JERUSALEM POST

Wednesday, March 23, 1983 Vol. LI, No. 15793 IS23.00

MKs ignore warning on discrimination

Yeshiva students will also receive large family grants

By AVI TEMKIN and CHARLES HOFFMAN
Jerusalem Post Reporters

The move to increase grants to large families overcame another obstacle yesterday when Finance Minister Yoram Aridor promised Knesset Finance Committee chairman Shlomo Lorincz (Agudat Yisrael) that IS34 million will be added to the Religious Affairs Ministry budget, enabling families of yeshiva students who do not serve in the army to receive the new benefits.

The problem arose when Lorincz realized that the IS820 a month boost proposed by the Treasury for each child, beginning with the fourth, will only apply to families with a member who served in the security forces. This excludes some 40,000 large Arab families and several thousand families of Orthodox Jews who are exempt from army service. The coalition MKs faced a sticky situation in trying to include the latter but not the former, while avoiding charges of discrimination.

National Insurance Institute figures show that about 120,000 families with four or more children receive regular child allowances, and 75,000 of them also qualify for additional grants, instituted in 1970, to families which include an army or police veteran. It is this item which the committee was asked to raise.

Following the 1970 provision, a way was found to extend the same benefits to yeshiva students, who have received the equivalent sums ever since through the Religious Affairs Ministry. Lorincz, before yesterday's committee session, apparently had either forgotten about the separate arrangement or assumed that the Treasury would automatically upgrade it along with the "soldiers' families" benefits. When it became clear that this was not the case, the MK objected, and Aridor promised the extra IS34m.

Attorney-General Yitzhak Zamir

(Continued on Page 2, Col. 4)

Begin undeterred by coalition debacle as Herzog elected president, 61 to 57

Posing in the Knesset yesterday after his election as the country's next president are Chaim Herzog and his wife Aura. Behind them, left to right, are their children Roni, Michael and Yitzhak. Son Yoel is abroad. (Rahamim Israeli)

By SARAH HONIG
Post Political Reporter

Prime Minister Menachem Begin intends to sweep yesterday's stinging coalition defeat in the presidential vote under the government's rug and to carry on as if nothing had happened. "The cornerstone to a Labour-led government has not been laid," he stressed, after opposition candidate Chaim Herzog received 61 votes to Supreme Court Justice Menahem Elon's 57. Two ballots in the Knesset vote were blank.

Begin told his aides that he does not regard what happened as a coalition crisis, will not consider resignation or any form of coalition shakeup and will not launch a "witch-hunt" to discover which seven coalition members prevented Elon's election.

At a two-hour meeting of the Likud faction last night, Begin urged colleagues not to cry over spilled milk. "These things happen," he said. "But now we have other work ahead of us."

Begin rejected proposals by some MKs for advancing Knesset elections or breaking up the coalition. He reminded his colleagues that he had withheld his decision on proposing Elon until all coalition parties had signed a written commitment to vote for him.

The faction's only decision was to send congratulations to Herzog.

But others in the Likud refused to let bygones be bygones. There were renewed calls for early elections, (now scheduled for mid-1985) and its Knesset faction chairman, Herut's Ronnie Milo, angrily resigned as deputy coalition executive chief.

Sources close to Begin said that the prime minister had "some very harsh things to say about those within the coalition who had betrayed it," but he thinks it futile and demeaning to try and discover their identities. This would only heighten antagonisms within the coalition and yield no constructive results, he feels.

Hammer calls for action: page 2
Elon's return: to court, Herzog's pledge: page 3
Coalition's dilemma
Soldier-statesman: Backpage

The sources stressed that Begin has "closed the presidential elections chapter" and will not again turn back to it or deal with the matter in any way. "What happened is in the past. We suffered a stinging blow, but there are more important issues before this nation, and there is no point in dwelling on what cannot be changed now. The Knesset's vote was a democratic verdict which we shall respect," Begin told those close to him.

Begin told his aides that he would very much like to see elections this year, since he believes he would be returned to power with an increased plurality and not have to depend on small and unreliable coalition partners. But Begin stressed that he would not precipitate an early vote without the agreement of his coalition partners.

The election result is no pretext for creating an upheaval in the coalition, Begin argued. He maintained that despite what top Likud whips have been saying for days, he never regarded the vote as a personal test or as a test for the coalition. He never threatened to resign if Elon were rejected, Begin's spokesmen stressed.

They quoted him as saying that what happened in the Knesset "is no reason for the coalition to sink into melancholy, nor for the Alignment to launch joyous celebrations. Everything must be viewed with a sense of proportion," Begin advised.

But the aftershocks in the coalition were severe. No one in its ranks would admit to being one of the seven "defectors," and coalition jokers were saying that "to judge from the declarations of coalition MKs, Elon must have been elected

(Continued on Page 2, Col. 2)

5 soldiers hurt by mines

Post Defence Correspondent

Five Israeli soldiers were wounded yesterday when they stepped on anti-personnel mines near the town of Nabrah in Lebanon's Shouf mountains. They were flown to Haifa's Rambam Hospital.

One of them was reported last night to be seriously wounded. Three were suffering from medium wounds in the legs and one was lightly wounded by splinters in his face.

The incident happened in the afternoon when a foot patrol entered the yard of a deserted house. Two soldiers simultaneously stepped on anti-personnel mines. A third soldier who tried to help them also stepped on a mine.

Reinforcements were sent in, but within a short time a fourth soldier stepped on another nine. The fifth soldier was injured from blast fragments.

Army officials said last night they do not believe the incident was a sabotage attempt directed against the IDF, but that the Christian owner of the house in question had placed the mines in order to protect his property from Druse neighbours. In the past, Druse in the village have plundered and burned homes left empty by Christian residents who have fled the area.

Habib sees Jemayel on withdrawal

BEIRUT (AP). — U.S. special Middle East envoy Philip Habib met Lebanese president Amin Jemayel yesterday to discuss the progress of negotiations on withdrawal of foreign forces from the country.

U.S. Ambassador Robert Dillon and Lebanese Foreign Minister Elie Salem also attended the meeting.

Informed sources said earlier that Habib had presented a conditional and unofficial agreement from Israel to drop its demand to keep a small force in Lebanon after it withdraws its troops.

Habib met later yesterday with the commander of the U.S. Marine peace-keeping contingent to discuss recent friction between the marines and the Israel Defence Forces on the southern outskirts of the capital.

Spokesmen for both Habib and Marine Colonel James Mead refused to give details of the meeting, which followed sharp criticism by Mead of the IDF.

Sharp EC condemnation of Israeli settlements

BRUSSELS (AP). — Government leaders of the 10 European Community nations said yesterday that Israeli settlements on the West Bank are "a growing and major obstacle" to peace in the Middle East.

They added they were "deeply disturbed" by the continued lack of progress towards a peace settlement.

They called on Israel and its Arab neighbours to remove all foreign troops from Lebanon and resume comprehensive peace negotiations.

In a statement at the end of a two-day summit meeting here, the EC prime ministers mentioned Israel by name.

"Above all the time has come for Israel to show that it stands ready for genuine negotiations...in the first place by refraining from enlarging existing settlements or creating new ones," the statement said.

It repeated the EC's position, agreed on at a 1980 summit meeting in Venice, that the Palestinian people, including the Palestine Liberation Organization, must be "associated with any Mideast peace plan."

But in the latest statement, the European leaders were more critical of Israel's settlements policy than three years ago.

The West Bank settlements "are contrary to international law and a major and growing obstacle to peace efforts," the statement added.

In the Venice declaration the settlements were only termed a "serious obstacle to peace," and "illegal under international law."

In their statement, the EC leaders termed "indispensible" American efforts to reach a comprehensive peace in the Middle East.

British Prime Minister Margaret Thatcher told reporters after the meeting that the EC leaders realized "that time is short if there are to be new negotiations."

She said "it is very necessary to make progress on pressing issues: securing the withdrawal of all foreign forces from Lebanon and "the underlying fundamental Palestinian" problem.

No lack of rumours about who defected

By ASHER WALLFISH
Post Knesset Correspondent

The fact that coalition candidate Supreme Court Justice Prof. Menahem Elon got seven votes less in yesterday's presidential election than the 64 the coalition commands in the Knesset set tongues wagging among MKs the moment that the vote was announced.

Labour's Uzi Baram, who headed the Alignment committee formed to drum up support for MK Chaim Herzog, had worked night and day for over a week with a handful of colleagues to make the Alignment's success possible. Apart from this committee, few are likely to know which coalition MKs promised to defect in favour of Herzog, and even the committee members cannot be sure that the promises they heard were kept.

It was generally assumed that the Alignment had been heartened by the influential role it played in getting the two new chief rabbis elected. Thus it strained every muscle to exploit potential defectors among the small coalition parties who proved to be weak links in the rabbinate elections.

MKs who volunteered to explain the bombshell result yesterday in some cases spread disinformation, just to sow more suspicions among the coalition partners.

Fear of defamation prevents publication of rumoured names.

One element of this propaganda was the allegation that a number of Alignment MKs did not vote for Herzog, which meant that more than seven coalition MKs had defected.

The pundits all claimed that the three-person Tehiya faction contained no defectors. They suggested that defectors had surfaced in the Likud, the National Religious Party, Agudat Yisrael and Tami, though the number of combinations suggested to make up the missing seven seemed endless.

Several factors were singled out as having produced the voting figures.

Most important of all were the personal grudges or calculations inside the coalition factions.

This factor merged with the reportedly overwhelming influence of millionaire Nessim Gaon of Geneva, (father-in-law of Herzog's son), over the Tami faction.

Labour's Jacques Amir told *The Jerusalem Post* he telephoned Gaon in Geneva and persuaded him to mobilize the three Tami votes, although Gaon at first seemed to be reluctant.

Agudat Yisrael was thought to be seeking an expression of its disappointment over the amendment to the Law of Return that failed on Monday. The National Religious Party was thought to be showing its appreciation to the Alignment for its help in getting Ashkenazi Avraham Shapiro and Sephardi Mordechai Eliahu elected chief rabbis.

The gossips talked about ministers who had a grouse against Prime Minister Menachem Begin and named three men in this context.

They talked about Likud MKs who did not understand why they themselves had not been proposed for president by the coalition; about Likud MKs who objected to voting for a relatively unknown judge; about coalition MKs long known to feel unhappy in the coalition for ideological reasons; about coalition MKs who felt unfairly treated by their colleagues in recent appointments; about Orthodox MKs who never miss an opportunity for a slight against the Supreme Court; and about defectors who felt sure their action would be blamed on other members of their faction.

Only one coalition MK was assumed for sure to have voted for Herzog — Tami Social Affairs Minister Aharon Uzan, who had made no secret of his intentions for several days.

On the other side, the four-man Democratic Front for Peace and Equality faction announced just before the session that it would vote for Herzog. The DFPE met with the Alignment leaders on Monday night, but both sides said there had been no horse-trading. However, the DFPE is said to have sought Alignment help when it raises issues concerning Arab land and slum clearance.

Tears, shock as result announced

By JUDY SIEGEL
Jerusalem Post Reporter

The first hint of the election result was the pallid face of Herut faction chairman Ronnie Milo, who had helped count the ballots and who had declared confidently on Monday that he would give IS1 million to the Israel Defence Fund if Chaim Herzog were elected.

After he, Labour Party MK Uzi Baram and National Religious Party MK Eliezer Avtabi had added up the totals yesterday, Milo slammed the desk with his hand and wordlessly left the rostrum. Baram, who had lobbied hard among coalition MKs on Herzog's behalf, had tears in his eyes.

Mispronouncing the name of Supreme Court Justice Menahem Elon as "Alon," Knesset Speaker Menachem Savidor announced the results: 61 votes for Herzog, 57 for Elon and two abstentions.

Prime Minister Menachem Begin and the rest of his cabinet seemed to freeze for a moment, in disbelief that the premier's personal choice for Beit Hanassi had been defeated.

The Alignment, also clearly stunned, revived quickly and left the Knesset chamber to shower congratulations on Herzog, who had left his seat after the voting had ended.

The dramatic end to the hour-long special Knesset session contrasted with the nonchalant beginning. When Knesset clerk Shmuel Jacobson started reading the names of the 120 MKs from Aharon Abuhatzeira to Dan Tichon, according to the Hebrew alphabet — the chamber was nearly half empty, as was the public gallery. MKs leafed through newspapers and chatted to their neighbours, inducing Savidor to berate them for their "annoying and unseemly" behaviour.

Herzog was fidgety in his seat before rising to cast his secret ballot, but returned looking calm. His wife, Aura, and three of their four children, as well as her sister Suzy Eban, wife of MK Abba Eban, looked down at Herzog during the voting. After announcing the

(Continued on Page 2, Col. 5)

Herzliya Municipality

To President Elect
Chaim Herzog

Heartfelt Good Wishes
to you, your wife Aura,
and to the members of your family
from all residents of your city, Herzliya.

Yosef Nevo, Mayor
and the members
of the Municipal Council

TIME
March 28, 1983
★★★ MIDDLE EAST
Angry marines, firm Israelis
★ ISRAELI ARMS FOR SALE
★ OPEC KNUCKLES UNDER
Sole distributor:
BRONFMAN'S AGENCY LTD.

Tourists
Foreign Currency Accounts
with Bank Leumi

Israel's first and largest banking group, with over US$20 billion in assets, welcomes you to our Foreign Resident and Tourist Centers. Visit us for all your banking needs.

- Exchange of travelers checks
- Cash advances in Israeli currency on your VISA credit card
- Redemption of State of Israel Bonds
- Unrestricted, tax-free foreign currency time deposits
- Expert financial counselling for the investment-minded
- Securities accounts
- Advisory and brokerage services for trading on the Tel Aviv and other international stock exchanges
- Money Desk for forward, spot and trade deals in foreign currencies and precious metals
- Trust and Property management programs
- Sole distributorship (in Israel) of Krugerrand gold coins

Foreign Resident and Tourist Centers
Tel Aviv
130 Ben Yehuda St.
Tel.(03)229231
Jerusalem
47 Jaffa Rd.
Tel.(02)227471/2
Haifa
123 Hanassi Blvd.
Tel.(04)86141

For further information please mail this coupon to:
The Manager
Foreign Resident and Tourist Center
130 Ben Yehuda St.
Tel Aviv 63401
or: The Manager
Foreign Resident and Tourist Center
47 Jaffa Rd.
Jerusalem 94221

Name ....
Address ....
....
Telephone ....
I am in Israel until (date) ....
Address in Israel ....
....
Telephone in Israel ....

Head Office: 24-32 Yehuda Halevi Street, Tel Aviv. Tel: (03) 632111
bank leumi בנק לאומי

THE JERUSALEM POST

Wednesday, August 31, 1983 — Vol. LI, No. 15411 — IS35

Begin resignation final; Shamir leads Herut succession hopefuls

Begin agrees to postponement to permit Likud coalition to pre-empt Labour try at government. • Herut ministers back Shamir, press for rapid decision • Levy isolated in ministers' forum, demands decision by Herut central committee • Possibles: Aridor or Levy — Foreign Minister; Moda'i — Finance; Arens to continue at Defence

Prime Minister Menachem Begin speaks yesterday to coalition leaders who tried to convince him to change his mind about resigning. (GPO)

Tough coalition talks look likely for Likud

By JOSHUA BRILLIANT
Jerusalem Post Reporter

TEL AVIV. — After the Likud chooses its candidate to succeed Menachem Begin as prime minister, it will probably face some tough negotiations with prospective coalition partners.

By last night, the Likud was still the faction with which the National Religious Party, Agudat Yisrael and Tami preferred to form a government, but none of these parties ruled out going with the Labour-Mapam Alignment.

Problems are expected over the question of division of portfolios and the policies the new government should implement.

Leaders of the potential coalition parties agreed it was the Likud's prerogative to nominate the prime minister. But that acquiesence did not extend to the division of portfolios — even those which would go to the Likud.

Some criticism was raised following reports that Yitzhak Moda'i was being spoken of as finance minister and Yoram Aridor as foreign minister. "The man is famous for his communicative qualities," one source said sarcastically about Aridor.

"Our deal was with Begin. If somebody replaces him and they want to change portfolios, there are partners who must express their views, he added.

In a similar vein, Education Minister Zevulun Hammer said yesterday the division of portfiolios must be discussed with his National Religious Party, although it was not demanding any more portfolios. "We haven't grown in size in the past month to be able to ask for more. I think we'll want to continue in the same roles," he said.

Problems are also expected over the joint platform. Tami leader MK Aharon Abuhatzeira said his party will demand changes in the cabinet's recent economic decisions. He recalled Tami was on the verge of quitting the present coalition because it believed the economic burden was not divided justly between the affluent and other sectors.

MK Menahem Porush of Agudat Yisrael said his party will demand that the candidate for the premiership sign an undertaking to implement all the commitments to the Aguda in the last coalition agreement.

Senior sources in Agudat Yisrael explained they wanted binding assurances because they did not expect Begin's successor to have as positive an attitude towards religious affairs as Begin had. "The Likud without Begin will be like the Alignment," one Aguda source said.

In an interview on Israel Television, Aguda MK Avraham Shapira said "Whatever happens, this will be a second government. If they really want to continue with the coalition, we must first know who will form it. We should know if we're taking the same path, with the same coalition agreement. A serious person does not sign any blank (papers)."

MK Abba Eban (Labour) smiled as he watched the live broadcast. It seemed as though Labour may have a chance of winning the ultra-Orthodox party's support for an alternative government.

But leaders of the small coalition parties said last night they believed talk of a coalition with Labour was "not realistic" and "not practical."

Abuhatzeira said he believed it was not realistic because he did not see where the Alignment would get the minimum 61 votes. Tami, he explained, would not join a coalition with the Rakah Communist list.

Meanwhile, The Council of Jewish Settlements in the territories yesterday decided to oppose the return of former defence minister Ezer Weizman to the cabinet.

By ASHER WALLFISH

The succession struggle within the Herut Party was on with a vengeance last night in the wake of Prime Minister Menachem Begin's announcement to his colleagues that his decision to resign was irrevocable.

Two and perhaps three Herut ministers emerged as likely candidates, and unless they can compromise on a shareout of the political spoils, the party seems headed for an upheaval which could threaten the coalition.

Begin acceded to his colleagues' plea to hold off his resignation letter to President Chaim Herzog for a few days, to enable his colleagues to approach Herzog with an agreed candidate to form a new coalition. Begin said he would probably tell his colleagues today how much time they had at their disposal.

Foreign Minister Yitzhak Shamir, deputy Prime Minister and Housing Minister David Levy — and possibly Minister without Portfolio Ariel Sharon — appeared to be in the running last night.

When the eight Herut ministers met yesterday afternoon and again in the evening to decide on the next step, Shamir emerged as the man with the most support. However, Levy insisted that he had as much right as anyone to run for the top job. He urged that the decision on a candidate not be taken by the eight Herut ministers, but be left to an open and democratic contest in the Herut Party central committee.

Between the afternoon and evening meetings of the eight ministers, when Sharon went to Shamir's bureau in the Foreign Ministry and conferred with him for an hour, speculation had it that Sharon was offering to support Shamir's candidacy against Levy provided Shamir paid him off. Sharon is reportedly seeking the post of chairman of the Ministerial Settlement Committee, a job held by the late deputy premier and agriculture minister Simha Ehrlich. Deputy Agriculture Minister Pessah Grupper has insisted on inheriting the chairmanship when he becomes minister.

At last night's meeting, Levy got no support from his colleagues for his proposal to leave the choice of candidate to the central committee. He dismissed his colleagues' apprehension that a contest would not be dignified and would create a vacuum in time as well as in leadership, which could be exploited by the Alignment to snatch power from Herut.

Shamir spoke little at the meeting. But he stressed that the candidate must be the man with most prospects of support in the coalition as a whole, and not only the man with backing inside Herut.

Sharon did not play a big role in the discussion. He said Herut had to remain in a position in which it could achieve its national goals and decide its candidate in that light. He said nothing to hint that he would stand against Levy if Levy ran in an open contest.

The ministers took no vote last night but decided to meet with their Liberal party and La'am faction colleagues this morning, to see which candidate and which procedure for naming the candidate they preferred.

The seven men who oppose Levy intend to use the Liberals' and La'am preference for Shamir as a weapon, either to deter Levy from going to the central committee, or to influence members of the central committee against Levy, should there be a contest.

By and large, the Liberals don't like Levy's social and economic policies. La'am finds him too dovish. So Levy's opponents in Herut are sure their partners will plump for Shamir.

The eight Herut ministers decided to meet again tonight and take a vote on the procedure for selecting the candidate: either by unanimous recommendation from themselves to the central committee or in open contest.

As of last night, Levy was adamant about an open contest.

Levy's supporters in the central committee were reported to be organizing for a contest, on the grounds that even if Levy lost, he

(Continued on Page 2, Col. 2)

Four French soldiers killed

Fighting intensifies in Beirut

BEIRUT. — The Lebanese Army mounted a navy-supported counter-attack against Shi'ite and Druse militiamen in mostly Moslem West Beirut yesterday, as U.S. Marines battled with rebel irregulars around the city's international airport.

Three French soldiers in the multinational peace keeping force in Lebanon and a para-military policeman at the French Embassy were killed in Beirut yesterday, the French Defence Ministry in Paris confirmed last night.

A ministry spokesman said two soldiers and the policeman were killed at the French embassy in a shelling attack that also injured several other people. Earlier yesterday, another French soldier was killed and two others injured at the Galerie Semaah crossing point between East and West Beirut.

There have now been 12 deaths among French soldiers since France sent 2,000 troops into Beirut last September.

State and privately owned radios said hundreds of troops landed by helicopters and boats at the Cadmos Hotel beach, just 400 metres from U.S. Marines protecting the six-storey building that now houses most U.S. Embassy personnel.

News agencies gave conflicting reports of the fighting. Reuter quoted U.S. marines at the scene as saying that American Embassy buildings on the Beirut seafront came under sustained attack by rocket-propelled grenades and

(Continued on Page 2, Col. 5)

Shouf postponement vexes IDF officers

By HIRSH GOODMAN
Post Defence Correspondent

ALEY. — The news that the redeployment of the Israel Defence Forces to the Awali line had been postponed once again yesterday, could not have been received by Israeli forces stationed in Lebanon.

Yesterday was the third postponement in recent days. For weeks now, forces on the front line have been living under harsh field conditions, waiting for the move. When the order finally comes, the move will be completed within a matter of hours — if there are no hitches.

The chances of a smooth redeployment are remote. Apart from the logistical problems involved in moving the army down the narrow and potholed axis leading down from the Shouf, the probability that the IDF may have to withdraw under fire is considered high.

The renewed fighting in Beirut, coupled with the sporadic shelling and exchanges between Druse and Phalangists in the Shouf, have brought tension in this area to a breaking point. Aley, and the roads leading to it, are deserted, sandbags covering shuttered windows.

The Christian quarter of the town has been boarded up; only very few of the Christian residents have dared to remain in this predominently Druse town strategically located on the Beirut-Damascus Highway.

Despite constant contacts with the Druse, including a meeting yesterday morning, Israeli officers in the Shouf have been unable to obtain any sort of guarantee that the Druse will hold their fire once the IDF starts pulling back. The Druse are determined to physically resist any attempt by the Lebanese army to deploy here, unless an ironclad political agreement has been

(Continued on Page 2, Col. 7)

Begin agrees to a further delay in Shouf pullback

Post Diplomatic Staff

Prime Minister Menachem Begin yesterday acceded to U.S. President Ronald Reagan's request that Israel once again delay its planned withdrawal from the Shouf Mountains of central Lebanon.

Begin met with U.S. special Middle East envoy Robert McFarlane just before telling the heads of the government coalition that he was firm in his resolve to resign. He agreed during the meeting to a limited postponement of the pullback.

Well-informed sources in Jerusalem said that Begin had agreed to a postponement of "a few more days," and that this postponement was the final one.

McFarlane returned to Beirut yesterday to renew his efforts to obtain an agreement between the rival Druse, Moslem and Christian factions before the partial Israeli pullback to the new Awali River line.

McFarlane handed Begin a personal message from Reagan asking for the postponement. The Americans, according to reliable sources, are convinced that the chances for achieving a Druse-Christian agreement in the Shouf have increased.

Such an agreement is vital, McFarlane reportedly told Begin, Foreign Minister Yitzhak Shamir and Defence Minister Moshe Arens at the meeting in Jerusalem. An Israeli pullback prior to the achievement of an agreement may well put paid to any chance of reaching such an agreement, he added.

The Americans, focusing their efforts on achieving agreement between the warring Lebanese factions, fear that the Israeli pullback from the Shouf will be followed by full-scale factional fighting and, possibly, a bloodbath, endangering the existence of President Amin Jemayel's government.

Arens has repeatedly said in the past that the achievement of an agreement between the warring Lebanese factions is not a precondition for the Israeli withdrawal.

Israeli officials have reportedly said that the IDF pullback from the Shouf will be completed by September 7, the eve of Rosh Hashana.

Opposition plays it cool

Alignment-led coalition is possible, Peres declares

Jerusalem Post Staff

TEL AVIV. — Labour Party chairman Shimon Peres believes it is possible to establish an Alignment-led government. In an interview on the Mabat television programme last night, Peres said that the Alignment, with its 50 members, is the Knesset's largest and most stable bloc and it is prepared to create as wide a coalition as possible to cope with the country's problems.

Asked about the basis of this conviction, Peres said: "The basis is need and possibility.

"I think that more and more Knesset factions are becoming convinced that this must be done quickly on as wide a foundation as possible, and there is no wide foundation without the Alignment."

The Likud government has collapsed and its successor must step into office as quickly as possible, Peres said. "I have confidence in the sense of responsibility of other Knesset members," he said.

Asked how he justifies his conviction that the Alignment can create a coalition when leaders of the National Religious Party, Tami and Agudat Yisrael have rejected the prospect, Peres answered: "Yesterday was yesterday, when a somewhat pathetic attempt was made to influence Begin. A different situation exists today and it will be different tomorrow. All parties must respond to the problems of today and tomorrow, and not to those of yesterday."

To a question whether the Alignment was maintaining formal contacts with party leaders, Peres said that informal talks were taking place and that they would continue.

Labour leaders would like to form a government — even if it is short-lived — until early Knesset elections are held. One party source explained that this would deny the Likud the ability to repeat election "stunts" such as it had pulled before the last elections when the price of colour TV sets was reduced and the Iraqi atomic reactor was bombed

Kohl visit off until situation becomes clear

Jerusalem Post Diplomatic Staff

West German Chancellor Helmut Kohl will put off his visit to Israel until the political constellation in this country becomes more stable, political sources said last night in Jerusalem. Kohl was supposed to arrive today.

Informed sources in Bonn said yesterday it was unlikely that Kohl would be able to travel to Israel before 1984, Associated Press reported.

Kohl's planned trip to Egypt, Jordan and Saudi Arabia in the second week of October will not be affected by the decision to scrap the trip to Israel, the sources said.

Although Bonn was bewildered by Begin's announcement of his intention to resign only days before the chancellor's planned visit, the decision to postpone was, nevertheless, greeted in Bonn with a sigh of relief. If Begin delayed resigning or changed his mind, there would have been no alternative to Kohl's visit taking place at a time of great political uncertainty in Israel.

Yesterday's statement by the prime minister's media adviser Uri Porat that Israel and the Federal Republic of Germany had mutually agreed to postpone the visit signalled a sharp change of direction. Until noon, everything was still uncertain. Preparations for the visit have been going forward in Bonn and Jerusalem for some time. Several days ago, diplomatic correspondents in the media were given details of the visit and black, yellow and red flags of the Federal Republic were hoisted into place in Jerusalem streets on Monday.

The first indication that Kohl might not after all visit Israel was the Government Press Office's announcement that German correspondents covering the visit had delayed their departure until the afternoon. Although the prime minister's [illegible]g with coalition leaders had not yet ended, reporters waiting outside the Prime Minister's Office where the meeting took place, concluded that the Bonn report meant that Begin had decided not to step back from his decision.

The decision to postpone the Kohl visit was taken during a number of telephone conversations between Foreign Minister Yitzhak Shamir and West German Foreign Minister Hans-Deitrich Genscher.

World population soars by 82 million

WASHINGTON (AP). — The world had its greatest one-year population growth in history over the past year, the U.S. Census Bureau reported last night.

The total of 4,721,881,000 (as of June 30) is an increase of 82,077,000 in 12 months.

THE JERUSALEM
POST

Monday, October 24, 1983

Vol. LI, No. 15451

NYT

IS45

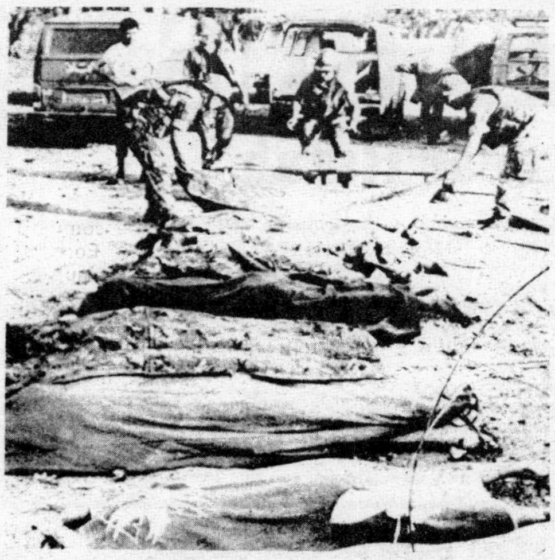

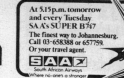

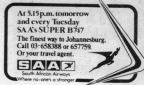

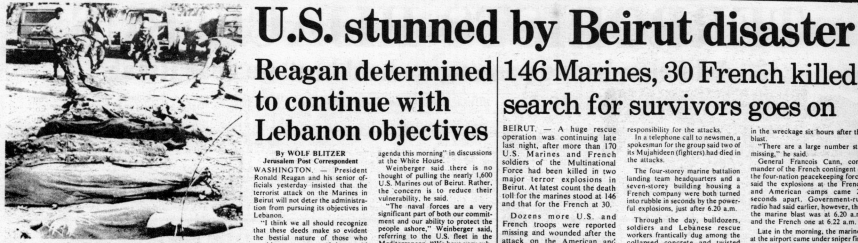

U.S. Marines cover the bodies of dead comrades after the bombing yesterday at Beirut Airport. (UPI telephoto).

U.S. stunned by Beirut disaster

Reagan determined to continue with Lebanon objectives

By WOLF BLITZER
Jerusalem Post Correspondent

WASHINGTON. — President Ronald Reagan and his senior officials yesterday insisted that the terrorist attack on the Marines in Beirut will not deter the administration from pursuing its objectives in Lebanon.

"I think we all should recognize that these deeds make so evident the bestial nature of those who would assume power, if they could have their way, and drive us out of that area," Reagan said. "But we must be more determined than ever that they cannot take over that vital and strategic area or for that matter any other part of the earth."

Defence Secretary Caspar Weinberger strongly suggested that Iranian troops, and their extremist Shi'ite supporters in Lebanon, were responsible for the attack.

Weinberger said it cannot be assumed that the U.S. will not retaliate. Reminded that Reagan said this country would not stand idly by while the marines were attacked, Weinberger said, "That certainly is true, and that is part of the agenda this morning" in discussions at the White House.

Weinberger said there is no thought of pulling the nearly 1,600 U.S. Marines out of Beirut. Rather, the concern is to reduce their vulnerability, he said.

"The naval forces are a very significant part of both our commitment and our ability to protect the people ashore," Weinberger said, referring to the U.S. fleet in the Mediterranean. "We have very substantial naval forces there now with the availability of a carrier and the battleship New Jersey which is one of the most powerful ships in the world, and with a number of other ships."

Fresh marine troops with morale said to be at a "fever-pitch high" boarded helicopters yesterday and left Camp Lejeune in North Carolina for Lebanon, where they will replace the marines killed and wounded in the bombing.

Shortly after Maj.-Gen. Al Gray ordered the marines to leave the camp, which is the home base for the marines killed in Lebanon,

(Continued on Page 2, Col. 4)

146 Marines, 30 French killed; search for survivors goes on

BEIRUT. — A huge rescue operation was continuing late last night, after more than 170 U.S. Marines and French soldiers of the Multinational Force had been killed in two major terror explosions in Beirut. At latest count the death toll for the marines stood at 146 and that for the French at 30.

Dozens more U.S. and French troops were reported missing and wounded after the attack on the American and French units' headquarters in southern Beirut.

While American spokesmen and Israeli observers speculated that the twin blasts were engineered by Syrian intelligence or Iranian Shi'ite fighters, who have long demanded the withdrawal of western troops from Lebanon, a new group called the "Free Islamic Revolutionary Movement" last night claimed responsibility for the attacks.

In a telephone call to newsmen, a spokesman for the group said two of its Mujahideen (fighters) had died in the attacks.

The four-storey marine battalion landing team headquarters and a seven-storey building housing a French company were both turned into rubble in seconds by the powerful explosions, just after 6.20 a.m.

Through the day, bulldozers, soldiers and Lebanese rescue workers frantically dug among the collapsed concrete and twisted metal in search of survivors. Work, facilitated by projectors, continued into the night.

"I haven't see such carnage since Vietnam," said marine spokesman Major Robert Jordan, 45, of Shenandoah, Georgia.

Colonel Timothy Geraghty, commander of the 1,600 marine force in Beirut told reporters that some of his soldiers were still trapped alive in the wreckage six hours after the blast.

"There are a large number still missing," he said.

General Francois Cann, commander of the French contingent of the four-nation peacekeeping force, said the explosions at the French and American camps came 20 seconds apart. Government-run radio had said earlier, however, that the marine blast was at 6.20 a.m. and the French one at 6.22 a.m.

Late in the morning, the marines at the airport came under sniper fire and were put on "condition one," their highest alert requiring them to wear flak jackets and helmets, carry their weapons, and remain in bunkers as much as possible.

Jordan said the terrorist bomb attack came while most marines were still asleep.

"A truck filled with explosives crashed through the gate, drove into the lobby... and detonated, collap-

(Continued on Page 2, Col. 6)

Treasury decides at what level to support market

By AVI TEMKIN
Post Economic Reporter

Prices of bank shares are due to be announced today at 9 a.m., based on the public's buying and selling orders, and on the degree of government intervention.

All orders for today's trading had to be in by last night to prevent an escalation of selling during the day which might have led to a collapse of the market.

Finance Minister Yigal Cohen-Orgad, Bank of Israel Governor Moshe Mandelbaum, and their senior aides last night were examining the computer data concerning the public's orders for today's trading. On the basis of the public behaviour, they will decide whether to intervene and, if so, by how much.

The government will buy bank shares to support the market; but nobody knows by how much. Economic observers were predicting that the shares would be allowed to fall by 10 to 15 per cent in shekel terms. If this speculation is correct, this will mean a fall of up to 30 per cent in dollar terms, taking into account the recent devaluation.

Although Treasury and Bank of Israel officials were not prepared to comment on today's expected developments, they did not disguise their satisfaction that a relatively small number of investors had given selling orders at the commercial banks up to last night.

One official described the atmosphere as one of "tense anticipation." Another remarked that it would be "the largest exercise of matching supply and demand that I have ever seen." A third official warned against exaggerated optimism. Although only a relatively small number of investors had placed selling orders, he noted, they might have placed some very large

(Continued on Page 2, Col. 1)

Orgad cites faith in banks

By ASHER WALLFISH
Jerusalem Post Reporter

Finance Minister Yigal Cohen-Orgad said yesterday that the government's action in closing the stock exchange and supporting bank shares boosted the confidence of foreign and local depositors, with some $20 billion in Israeli banks, here as well as abroad.

"They didn't take their dollars out," the new finance minister said in his maiden speech at the cabinet. "We'd proved to them they had every reason to feel confident. We showed them we were right behind the banks and right behind the economy."

One of the principal motives for the government's far-reaching support for the banks was concern for the way foreign depositors would behave, it has been revealed.

Cohen-Orgad said that since the 23 per cent devaluation, Israelis are showing themselves less eager for foreign-currency purchases. Though they still have lots of funds available, he said, they are looking not just to dollars. "Last Thursday alone they bought IS9b. worth of government development bonds," he said.

The minister said that the bank shares in the hands of the public (as opposed to the banks themselves) which had been worth $5b.-$4.5b. before the stock exchange closed, were today assessed roughly at $3b.

Project Renewal out of cash

By CHARLES HOFFMAN
Jerusalem Post Reporter

The Jewish Agency has recommended that work on $14.7 million worth of construction projects for its Project Renewal be halted because the Diaspora communities funding the projects have not raised enough cash.

A memorandum sent to the Project Renewal by the agency treasurer's office said that "cash-flow problems" concerning donations for nine renewal neighbourhoods make it necessary to stop work on 14 separate projects. These include day-care centres, youth clubs, sports facilities, community centres and day centres for the elderly.

The neighbourhood hardest hit by this decision is Givat Olga near Hadera, with $4.1 million worth of projects under construction. Givat Olga's Diaspora twin is Minneapolis-St. Paul.

A background paper prepared for this week's meeting of the Agency's board of governors notes that the gap between Diaspora donations and expenditures in the neighbourhoods has reached over $32m.

The paper warns that the deficit and cash-flow problems could delay a number of projects and lead to a "credibility crisis."

An agency document states that 13 Diaspora communities have a deficit of over $1m. each, stemming mainly from a gap that has emerged over the last several years between pledges and expenditures. The

(Continued on Page 2, Col. 2)

Terror attack seen as turning-point for U.S.

By DAVID LANDAU
Post Diplomatic Correspondent

Israel voiced shock and horror yesterday over the Beirut bomb blasts, as well as expressions of quiet admiration and relief at America's determination to stay put in Lebanon.

But there was also a pervasive feeling among many analysts that the blasts would mark a turning-point and that the situation in Beirut would not return to what it had been. The Reagan Administration, it was widely felt here, would act to reassert its prestige. There were differing assessments, however, of the nature of the American action.

A short-term effect of the disaster on Israeli policy-making could be on the Awali River line, where there has been pressure on the government for some time to seal off the bridges to traffic. Military and civilian officials who argue that the security risk of free traffic is too great will be powerfully supported by yesterday's bombings when the issue comes before the cabinet for decision shortly.

Israel's horror was expressed in a cabinet statement at midday which blamed the outrages on "forces that are interested in preventing a peaceful solution in Lebanon."

In a condolence message to President Reagan, Prime Minister Yitzhak Shamir wrote that "the unique role of the U.S. as leader of the free world, and the steadfastness of its forces in defence of freedom of liberty... (are) once again being tested by those who are determined to undermine stability and peace."

A senior official added that "the Americans seem determined not to cave in. From our standpoint — that is very positive."

At the same time, though, there was concern in some quarters here over a possible backlash against Israel building up within American public opinion. Said former premier Yitzhak Rabin: "Our problem is not with the administration: it is with the people."

The fear was that U.S. opinion would blame Israel for having dragged America into the Lebanon embroglio in the first place.

To ward off such putative attacks, cabinet sources noted pointedly after yesterday's session that "Israel has no (formal) position regarding the marines remaining in Lebanon. It was not Israel who asked them to come in, and they are not there to protect Israeli interests."

The sources sought in this way to steer clear of any impression that Israel was now urging the Americans to stay in Lebanon.

In fact, of course, as top officials readily admitted in private, the departure of the U.S. Marines would be a mortal blow to Israel's entire Lebanon policy as constructed under Begin and Sharon and scaled down under Shamir and Arens.

(Continued on Page 2, Col. 6)

3 Shi'ite villagers killed in riot in South Lebanon

By MENAHEM HOROWITZ
Jerusalem Post Reporter

METULLA. — Three Shi'ite residents of South Lebanon were killed and several more were wounded yesterday as Israel Defence Forces troops shot into the air to disperse an angry crowd in the village of Jibsit, near Sidon. Two IDF soldiers were slightly wounded in the incident.

An IDF unit entered the village yesterday to search the houses of several residents suspected of hiding weapons and explosives.

An angry mob surrounded one of the houses after the Israeli troops entered and began throwing rocks at the soldiers. A large force of reinforcements was called in to disperse the crowd. They fired several rounds into the air. The crowds continued to throw stones and also set several tires alight. The wounded Shi'ites were taken to a local hospital.

This is the second incident of violence in the past week between the IDF and the Shi'ites. Last week a mob attacked an IDF patrol in Nabatiya during a religious celebration.

Shi'ite leaders in Beirut have recently urged their co-religionists in the South not to cooperate with the IDF and to make every effort to harm Israeli soldiers.

Reconstruction of the bombings

Bloody dawn on a sleepy Sunday

By SCHEHEREZADE FARAMARZI
Associated Press Writer

BEIRUT (AP). — Most of the 1,600 U.S. Marines stationed at Beirut's International Airport were sleeping in yesterday morning, a slow day for the American peace-keepers. A few sentries stood guard duty, and at 6:20 a.m. the unit's cooks were just beginning to get up.

The sentry at the back gate of the compound noticed a large red truck pull into the airport parking lot, just outside the barbed wire, chainlink fence and barricades surrounding the marine area. He picked up his field telephone to the command centre to report it, when it suddenly accelerated, sped across the lot and smashed into the gate.

Crashing through two barricades and around a third, the truck hit the sandbagged entrance of a four-storey building where an estimated 200 marines were sleeping. As it came to halt in the lobby, the driver detonated an estimated 1,000 kilos of explosives in the back. The blast destroyed the building, hurling concrete and glass more than 100 metres. Doors and windows of nearby buildings were smashed, wounding more marines.

As the cries from men wounded and trapped in the wreckage began, a second massive explosion went off two kilometres away. Another suicide terrorist had repeated the attack on a 110-man unit of French soldiers.

This time, there were fewer barriers and no fence. Driving his explosive-laden truck into an underground garage, the attacker detonated a charge large enough to reduce the entire building to rubble.

It could not be determined whether either the marine sentry at the airport or the French soldiers guarding their company headquarters had fired at their attackers. There were few witnesses to either early morning attack.

Maj. Robert Jordan, of Shenendoah, Georgia, was sleeping at about 400 metres from the marine building when the first blast occurred.

"The door next to my rack (bed) blew off, (and) a rack that I have some of my belongings on fell down across the rabbi that was sleeping next to me, and glass imploded all over the area. All the doors were blown off their hinges."

As Jordan ran to the destroyed building, he saw marines staggering from the rubble, trying to help each other. Bodies could be seen in the wreckage.

Lebanese soldiers, civilian rescue workers, and British and Italian soldiers quickly arrived to help. The rescue workers included a number of men from the Shi'ite Amal militia from nearby neighbourhoods where gunmen had fired at and launched shelling attacks on the marines in recent weeks.

By late afternoon, grim-faced marines were still pulling out bodies and a few wounded survivors from the wreckage.

Sleeping bags, uniforms and personal belongings littered the ground along with rubble and glass shards. The wreckage of a jeep could be seen under the rubble. Other vehicles parked near by had been smashed. Bulldozers and cranes shifted the mess carefully.

"I cried, I cursed," said Staff Sgt. Alfonso Hernandez, 29, of Oceanside, California, trying to control tears and shaking voice.

(Eyewitness accounts from Beirut, Page 3)

France, Italy, UK to stay in Beirut

PARIS. — Premier Pierre Mauroy said yesterday that the 2,000-man French military contingent in Beirut would remain despite yesterday's devastating bombing attacks.

Withdrawal of the French troops from the multinational peace-keeping force "is a question that does not arise at the present time," the premier said.

Mauroy told a news conference that both Lebanese President Amin Jemayel and the main opposition leader, Walid Jumblatt, had expressed the desire that the French remain in Beirut.

Defence Minister Charles Hernu arrived in Beirut last night, where he was scheduled to fly by helicopter to French headquarters and then to visit the site of the explosion.

Hernu was accompanied by General Jeannou Lacaze, chief of staff of the French armed forces.

In Athens, French Foreign Minister Claude Cheysson, in Greece for an informal two-day meeting of European Economic Community foreign ministers, called yesterday's bombing "madness."

In London, Foreign Office Minister Richard Luce indicated Britain would make no quick decision about the future of its troops in Lebanon following the "gigantic tragedy."

The main opposition Labour Party, however, demanded that the Conservative government immediately reconsider its participation in the four-nation force in Beirut, where the 97-strong British contingent is the smallest.

In Rome, the government yesterday faced urgent calls for a review of its 2,000 troops in Beirut. But Prime Minister Bettino Craxi reaffirmed his country's commitment.

In Moscow, the Communist Party newspaper *Pravda* said that when the Marine contingent was first dispatched last fall it was to be there for a limited period to disengage "warring sides" and was to have no combat role.

But, said *Pravda*, the U.S. troops have been fighting, gunning and rocketing Lebanese towns.

"It appears that the Vietnam story begins to repeat itself," said *Pravda*. "The U.S.A. is getting drawn deeper and deeper into the fighting in the Lebanese mountains while generals get more and more freedom of action."

UN Secretary-General Javier Perez de Cuellar sent condolences to the presidents of the U.S. and France.

In Cairo yesterday, Canada's External Affairs Minister called the bombing "a senseless act of indiscriminate violence" and expressed sympathy for the U.S., France and Lebanon.

Allan MacEachen, deputy prime minister and secretary of state for external affairs, spoke to reporters after holding talks with President Hosni Mubarak and Foreign Minister Kamal Hassan Ali. (AP, Reuter)

Lebanese unity conference still on

Post Mideast Affairs Reporter
and agencies

Plans to hold the proposed Lebanese National reconciliation conference in Geneva moved ahead yesterday despite the massive bomb blasts in Beirut.

A Swiss Foreign Ministry spokesman confirmed in Bern yesterday that the conference will open at the end of this month in a Geneva hotel.

Druse leader Walid Jumblatt, one of the four main opposition leaders invited to attend the conference, indicated yesterday that he expects the conference to go ahead as planned.

"The only way of escaping from this hornets' nest," Jumblatt told reporters in Paris in response to events in Beirut, "is to find a stable political solution, and I hope that Geneva will provide such a result."

Jumblatt denounced "the two tragic attacks," and denied that his supporters had anything to do with them.

In Kuwait, Saudi Foreign Minister Prince Saud al-Faisal said he hoped "that bloodshed will not obliterate the optimistic picture that emanated from the recent cease-fire and the accord for convening the reconciliation conference."

In Cairo, Egyptian Foreign Minister Kamal Hassan Ali condemned "the ugly terrorist attack," describing it as an "action which is against peace and a solution for the problem in Lebanon... and the Middle East."

In Damascus, the PLO denied involvement, but an official spokesman said: "What has happened is not a surprise because he who comes into the bear's den must expect to get bitten."

While underlining that "the PLO has nothing to with the explosions," he said: "We hope the Marines and other multinational troops will leave at once and peacefully."

Mahmoud Labbadi, spokesman for Syrian-backed hardline rebels in Yasser Arafat's Fatah group, said: "The more dead Marines, the more American policy is unmasked — and the better for the Palestinian cause."

NEWS BACKGROUND

Likud expects losses in local poll tomorrow

By SARAH HONIG
Post Political Reporter

TEL AVIV. — The Likud is expecting considerable losses in tomorrow's municipal elections, while the Alignment is looking forward to gains, which it hopes will indicate a significant change in voting patterns in national politics as well.

The mood at Likud headquarters yesterday was far from optimistic with the general aim being to cut predicted losses. In Labour headquarters, spirits were buoyed by the expectation that the recent economic upheavals would result in a protest vote against the Likud, whose loss would be Labour's gain.

Labour candidates therefore have been striving hard for the past fortnight to link local politics and issues to the state of the national economy. Likud politicians, on the other hand, were hard at work arguing that local affairs and the Treasury's policy are separate and distinct questions.

The Labour line in recent days has been that any attempt to draw a line between local and national affairs is artificial. (See related story, page 2.) Some in the Alignment charged yesterday that the Likud is actively using its governmental powers to influence the vote. They allege that to prevent mass defections from the Likud by the many thousands of holders of bank shares for example, the Treasury intends to shore up their value and prevent a collapse in their prices when the stock market re-opens for full trading this morning.

One Labour mayoral candidate told *The Jerusalem Post* that this is a deliberate pre-election move to buy votes. This is hotly denied on the Likud side, where it is argued that "Labour must be afraid that it would fail in its tactics of getting residents to vote against a local council candidate because of the policies of the former finance minister. It would surely be in Labour's favour if holders of bank shares got an even worse beating."

According to Likud spokesmen, it is not even clear yet whether the government will have to step in at all when trading in bank shares resumes.

But even if the worst of the bank shares upheaval and the trauma of devaluation and the subsidies cuts is over, the Likud still expects to suffer from the public's resentment. Likud politicians do not expect this to affect the candidates for mayoral office, at least not the very popular ones.

(Continued on Page 2, Col. 2)

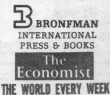

THE JERUSALEM POST

Friday, April 13, 1984

Vol. LII, No. 15578   IS140

TERRORISTS HIJACK BUS

33 Ashkelon-bound passengers held hostage near Rafah

By DAVID APPEL and DAVID FRIEDMAN
Itim Reporters

A No. 300 Egged bus carrying 41 passengers yesterday evening was hijacked by five terrorists while travelling from Tel Aviv to Ashkelon.

Pursuing soldiers shot out the bus's tires and brought it to a halt near Deir al-Balah in the Gaza District. An unknown number of passengers were reported wounded during the hijacking.

The terrorists, who were armed, forced the driver to head south toward the Gaza District. During the takeover, several passengers reportedly were wounded.

Near Deir al-Balah, soldiers manning a roadblock shot out the tires of the bus, bringing it to a halt. The IDF closed the area and hospitals in Ashkelon and Beersheba were alerted.

Eight persons escaped through the bus windows. One of them, a woman, was taken to hospital with light wounds.

The bus had crashed through several

BULLETIN: 1.30 a.m.

roadblocks between Ashkelon and Deir al-Balah, 15 kilometres south of Gaza on the road to El-Arish.

Another report said soldiers riding in a command car in pursuit of the hijacked bus shot out its tires. The bus swerved off the road and into a ditch, coming to rest leaning on its side.

A number of the remaining passengers in the bus were reported to be wounded,

although the number reported varied from three to eight. About 20 Magen David Adom ambulances had arrived near the scene by late evening.

Three Magen David Adom ambulances travelling to the scene reportedly were involved in a collision with an IDF vehicle.

Reinforced units of the IDF and police set up roadblocks throughout the Gaza District and the road south from Ashkelon was sealed. Many helicopters were observed flying south to the area of

the incident. Gaza District towns were reported to be unusually quiet, with hardly a person seen on the streets.

The bus hijacking was the first hostage-taking incident since March 1978, when a dozen Palestinian terrorists seized two buses of Israeli vacationers near Kibbutz Ma'agan Michael south of Haifa. The terrorists forced the passengers into a single bus and drove south towards Tel Aviv, where in a shootout that came to be known as the Coastal Road Massacre, 35 Israelis and nine terrorists were killed.

14 Labour MKs overcome election hurdle but two fail

By ROY ISACOWITZ
Jerusalem Post Reporter

TEL AVIV. — Fourteen of the Labour Party's veteran Knesset members last night got past the 60 per cent barrier, which makes them eligible for a place on the Alignment list to the July elections. But two party members, Tamar Eshel and Yehezkel Zakkai, will not appear on the list because they failed to get the backing of 60 per cent minimum of Labour's central committee.

Those who suceeded include former Prime Minister Yitzhak Rabin, who won the strongest backing — 88 per cent; Party secretary Haim Bar-Lev (84 per cent); former

minister Gad Ya'acobi (85 per cent); and former foreign minister Abba Eban (71 per cent).

Labour Party dove Yossi Sarid got 69 per cent.

Those who got through by a close vote were Tel Aviv branch chairman Eliahu Speiser (60.03 per cent), Jacques Amir (62 per cent) and Micha Harish (63 per cent).

Last night's balloting was held in accordance with a 1977 party rule that a Knesset member who has served two or more terms must win at least 60 per cent support in the central committee to be a candidate for inclusion on the party list.

About 90 per cent of the commit-

(Continued on Page 2, Col. 2)

Abu Jihad threatens more PLO attacks

AMMAN (AFP) — Yasser Arafat's deputy Khalil Wazir (Abu Jihad) said in an interview with the Jordanian newspaper *A-Doustour* that the PLO will take numerous actions in the near future against "the enemy, who understands only the language

of force."

Wazir also said that PLO chairman Arafat will visit Moscow soon, at the invitation of the Supreme Soviet. Wazir said relations between the PLO and the Soviet Union are good.

One killed, four wounded in South Lebanon ambush

By MENAHEM HOROWITZ
Jerusalem Post Reporter

METULLA. — A Lebanese civilian was killed and four Israeli soldiers were wounded in South Lebanon yesterday when a parked car exploded as an Israel Defence Forces patrol passed by. The ambush occurred near the village of Deir al-Kanoun, 10 kilometres east of Tyre.

The four soldiers were given first

aid on the spot and taken to Rambam Hospital in Haifa.

Yesterday's incident was the first time in several months that terrorists have used booby-trapped vehicles against IDF patrols in South Lebanon.

Light-weapons fire was opened yesterday morning at an IDF position near Sarafand, on the Lebanese coastal road. The Israelis returned fire.

A well-wisher greets Ariel Sharon at the ballot box yesterday evening. (IPPA)

Herut wants final say on Liberal candidates

By SARAH HONIG
Post Political Reporter

TEL AVIV. — Herut wants veto power over Liberal nominees for the Likud slate of Knesset candidates.

Liberal leaders will hear this from Herut representatives this morning when the two sides meet for the first time to discuss Herut's demand to amend the 1965 Gahal Agreement that determined the ratio of Herut to Liberal Knesset members. Herut will make it plain that veto power is their minimum demand.

The Liberals presidium will meet before the conference with Herut to formulate a common response to the Herut demands.

The Liberals did not react last night, but it is believed that at first they will put up "a brave fight" against Herut demands. They may, however, eventually settle for a face-saving formula to avoid Herut's tougher demands that Liberal representation on the list be reduced.

Herut's delegation will include

(Continued on Page 15)

Burg, Hammer to head NRP

By SARAH HONIG
Post Political Reporter

Ashkenazi Chief Rabbi Avraham Shapiro late last night brought about an agreement in the National Religious Party whereby Interior Minister Yosef Burg and Education and Culture Minister Zevulun Hammer will head the party's list in the coming Knesset elections.

Reporting this, Israel Television's midnight newscast said that former Tehiya Knesset member Hanan Porat, a leader of the Gush Emunim segment, had not decided what to do in the wake of the above development.

But there is still "almost no

hope" of unifying all splinters of the national-religious camp, according to sources in the NRP and its possible partners in Gush and Matzad.

The chances are that this sector will have at least two separate parties in July — the old NRP and the new Orot, composed of Knesset member Haim Druckman's Matzad and Gush Emunim.

The pessimistic outlook was heightened by a conference late yesterday between Druckman and Porat on one side and Rabbi Shapiro on the other side. Shapiro's proposals were reportedly totally unacceptable to Porat and Druckman.

Jan.-March trade gap drops

By AVI TEMKIN
Post Economic Reporter

A large increase in industrial exports during the first quarter of the year made possible a 10 per cent drop in the country's merchandise trade deficit compared with the same period last year. Imports increased slightly during the first quarter.

Figures released yesterday by the Central Bureau of Statistics showed that during the first three months of 1984, the deficit totalled $640 million, compared with $714m. in January-March 1983. Exports of goods totalled $1,396m., while imports totalled $2,036m.

Most of the decrease in the trade deficit took place in January. Since then there has been a slight increase in its level. Last month the deficit totalled $200m., compared with $195m. in March 1983.

The deficit increased last month despite a 8.5 per cent increase in exports, which totalled $542m. in March, compared with $500m. in the same month last year. Imports, on the other hand, increased from $693m. in March 1983 to $743m. last month.

Agricultural exports remained stable at $221m. in the first three months of 1984 ($218m. in January-March 1983). But citrus exports continued to fall, totalling $91m. last quarter, compared with $99m. in the same period last year.

Diamond exports rose from $265m. in January-March 1983 to $277m. this year, a 4 per cent increase.

Premier: It won't affect my plans for next cabinet

Sharon amasses 42% of Herut vote, Shamir 56

By JOSHUA BRILLIANT
Jerusalem Post Reporter

TEL AVIV. — Prime Minister Yitzhak Shamir last night won Herut's nomination for the premiership. But his rival, Minister-without-Portfolio Ariel Sharon, surprised nearly everyone by winning 42.7 per cent of the vote at the party's central committee meeting.

Shamir got 407 votes (56.14 per cent) out of 725 valid ballots. Sharon got 306, and attorney Arye Chertok got eight. Four votes were blank. The vote at the Fair Grounds

was perceived by many as setting Sharon firmly in a powerful party position. He has frequently complained of not being given enough responsibility in the government, and last night's vote apparently gives him a stronger argument for increased power within the Likud. But several senior party members told *The Jerusalem Post* the results do not mean Sharon is automatically No. 2 in Herut. They noted, for example, that Deputy Premier David Levy was not in the running yesterday. Deputy Agriculture Minister

Michael Dekel, a key Shamir supporter, insisted that the rating of members within the party will be made when the Knesset list is formed. This was confirmed when Shamir announced that Levy will head the party's campaign team for the elections.

When the vote was announced and Sharon walked in, surrounded by bodyguards, virtually all of the central committee members stood and cheered. Many climbed on their chairs and chanted: "Arik!

(Continued on Page 2, Col. 4)

NEWS ANALYSIS/Sarah Honig

Sharon success weakens PM

TEL AVIV. — Herut had cause to be shocked last night. Ariel Sharon's position in the party was considerably bolstered, while both Prime Minister Shamir and his deputy, David Levy, suffered serious setbacks.

Sharon's success proved that he is a force to be reckoned with and can now even vie with Levy for the No.2 position in the party hierarchy.

Despite the ardent wish of the rest of the party leadership to

banish him to a political corner, it will now be impossible to exclude Sharon from the leadership, much less to ignore him.

Since Sharon has proved popular with the party's grassroots but not with the leadership, Herut can expect Sharon to be a potential troublemaker during the election campaign if his ambitions in Herut continue to be frustrated.

Sharon is assumed to have received the vote of 10 per cent of

the committee members who belong to his Shlomzion grouping, as well as those of a variety of party malcontents, and some members of the Levy camp who are Sharon admirers and who felt safe voting for the former defence minister since there was no chance of a Shamir defeat.

Some members of the Herut Central Committee who defected to

(Continued on Page 15)

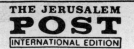

THE JERUSALEM POST
INTERNATIONAL EDITION
The perfect gift for your friends and relations overseas

THE JERUSALEM POST

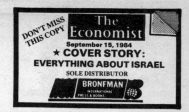

Vol. LII, No. 15711 Sunday, September 16, 1984 • Elul 19, 5744 • Zi al-Heja 20, 1404 IS200

DON'T MISS THIS COPY
The Economist
September 15, 1984
★ COVER STORY:
EVERYTHING ABOUT ISRAEL
SOLE DISTRIBUTOR
BRONFMAN
INTERNATIONAL PRESS & BOOKS

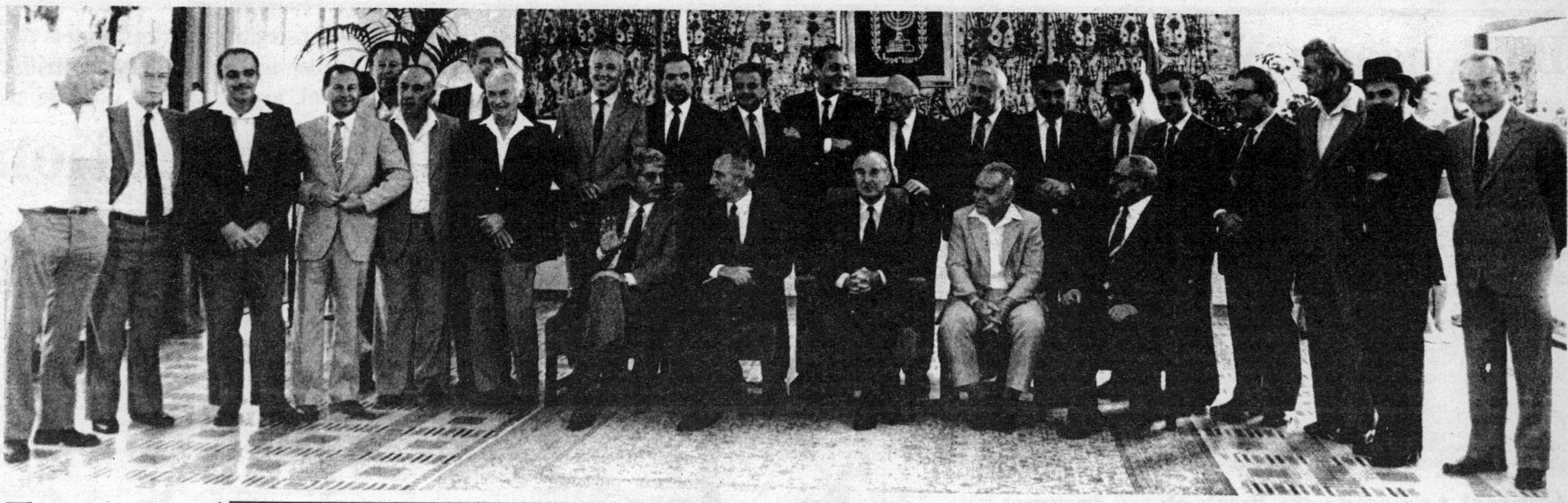

The cabinet

The national unity cabinet poses with President Chaim Herzog at Beit Hanassi on Friday, 10 hours after it received the Knesset's confidence by a vote of 89 to 18 with one abstention.

Standing from left to right are Arye Nehamkin, Yitzhak Rabin, Ya'acov Tzur, Amnon Rubinstein, Mordechai Gur, Yigael Hurvitz, Ezer Weizman, Haim Bar-Lev, Gad Ya'acobi, Gideon Patt, Avraham Sharir, Yitzhak Moda'i, Yosef Burg, Ariel Sharon, Moshe Nissim, Moshe Shahal, Moshe Katzav, Haim Corfu, Yosef Shapira, Yitzhak Peretz and Moshe Arens.

Seated with the president left to right are Vice-Premier David Levy, Prime Minister Shimon Peres, Deputy Prime Minister Yitzhak Shamir and Vice-Premier Yitzhak Navon. **(Story on page 3)** (Rahamim Israeli)

Peres plans contacts with heads of state

Jerusalem Post Reporter

Prime Minister Shimon Peres said on Friday he is planning to establish contacts with heads of state and governments in the Middle East and in Europe, apart from first tackling the urgent problems of the economy and withdrawal from Lebanon.

Asked in a brief television interview held for the first time with Peres in the Prime Minister's Office, how he felt in his new chair, Peres said it is not a question of where one sits, but of what one can do. We cannot waste time, there are many important and urgent matters to take care of, he said.

Earlier, at the handing-over ceremony Friday morning, at the Prime Minister's office Peres had warm words for his predecessor, Deputy Prime Minister and Foreign Minister Yitzhak Shamir, praising the good and friendly relations both of them developed during the long weeks of the coalition talks.

Following another ceremony at the president's residence, Shamir performed his first function as foreign minister by attending Costa Rica's Independence Day reception at the Jerusalem residence of Ambassador Eduardo Jenkins. (More items on ministerial changeovers, page 2.)

The man in charge

President Chaim Herzog leaves today for the Netherlands on a private visit (Story page 3). His place will be filled, as the law provides, by Knesset Speaker Shlomo Hillel.

There is an anomaly in this situation, in that the Knesset has not yet elected its deputy speakers. The next Knesset session is on Tuesday.

The election of the Knesset presidium has awaited the outcome of the government coalition negotiations. Hillel for the time being remains in sole control of a possibly turbulent house while acting as head of state.

THE ISRAEL EXPERIENCE
החוויה הישראלית
New Hit Multi Media Show in English
"...Moving and Touching!"
Old Jaffa Mall
At entrance to Old Jaffa
Open 7 Days a Week
Showtimes: 9 a.m., 12,2,5,6,8 and 9 p.m.

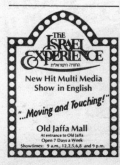

Shamir determined to ignore dissent

By DAVID LANDAU
Post Diplomatic Correspondent

Likud bloc chief and Deputy Premier Yitzhak Shamir intends to ignore the rumbling dissent against him within the Herut Knesset faction, confident that he has a solid majority of the party central committee behind him. Sources close to him said at the weekend that he would go ahead and appoint "whomever he thinks best" to the post of deputy defence minister, disregarding a petition signed by more than a dozen Herut MKs on Thursday asking that the choice be made by the party's Knesset faction.

Shamir is likely to appoint either his close confidant Michael Dekel, or else La'am's Ehud Olmert, to the deputy defence post.

The petitioners are seeking the appointment of Eliahu Ben-Elissar. They are supported by Industry Minister Ariel Sharon and by Deputy Premier David Levy, who both baulked earlier last week at Shamir's exclusion of Yoram Aridor from the unity cabinet.

The sources close to Shamir said he is determined not to flinch in the face of this continuing challenge to his leadership. They said that he feels strong enough to withstand even a joint assault by Levy and Sharon.

Lea Levavi adds:

Shamir told Israel Radio yesterday that he did not think anyone other than he is worthy of being the movement's leader. "If I thought otherwise, I might reach different conclusions personally. But I think the good of the Likud and of the state requires that I remain in my current position."

He said neither Sharon nor Levy has ever asked him to step down for their benefit, and in discussions both have expressed willingness to continue working with him. "There are no enemies in political parties; sometimes there are rivals, but the rivalry is always transitory," he said.

As for the statement by Sharon supporter MK David Magen that Shamir has finished his political career, Shamir said Sharon had dissociated himself from it completely. "They have been saying I finished my career since I was elected Speaker of the Knesset. It used to be thought that the Speaker's post was automatically the end of a political career, but I showed this is not necessarily true."

Ministry boycotted Herzog in Nazareth

Jerusalem Post Reporter

The Interior Ministry boycotted President Chaim Herzog's visit to Nazareth on Thursday, and no government representative was present at the various welcoming ceremonies for the president organized by Mayor Tawfik Zayyad, MK for the Communist-led Democratic Front for Peace and Equality.

Northern District representative Yisrael Koenig opposed the president's visit to Nazareth, claiming that it would be regarded as a political act, encouraging the town's Communist adminstration. At a meeting with Koenig prior to the visit, Herzog rejected these objections, stressing that he is the president of all of Israel's citizens. He demanded that proper arrangements be made for his reception in Nazareth.

The arrangements were indeed made, but primarily by the Nazereth municpality. According to Zayyad, the spontaneous and warm welcome for the president exceeded all expectations.

Herzog intends to pursue the matter, it is learned, and will write a letter to the interior minister – now Prime Minister Shimon Peres – demanding an explanation why the Northern District representative or his deputy was not present, at the visit.

Settlers' group leaves Nablus hotel

Jerusalem Post Reporter

Seven Jewish families who spent Friday night and yesterday in a small Nablus hotel returned to their homes last night as planned, having passed a quiet Sabbath in the West Bank city.

The families, members of a group calling itself the "Nablus nucleus" and planning to settle in the city, reserved places in the hotel in advance, fulfilling a plan they had made four months ago. The places were booked in the names of Japanese tourists. A spokesman for the families said they chose to spend this particular Sabbath in Nablus because the city, specifically Mt. Grizim, figures in yesterday's weekly Tora portion.

The spokesman said the families complied with an Israel Defence Forces request not to walk around the town, where tension was already mounting in anticipation of the anniversary of the Sabra and Shatilla massacre, which falls this week.

He said the families received cabled congratulations on their act from Knesset Members Haim Druckman (Morasha) and Geula Cohen (Tehiya).

Rafah mayor shot dead on way home after prayers

Jerusalem Post Staff
and Agencies

Rafah Mayor Abdul-Hamid Kishta was murdered on Friday night as he left a mosque after prayers in this Gaza Strip city's main street.

Kishta, 54, was shot in the head by a youth and died shortly afterwards at the government hospital in Khan Yunis.

An Israel Defence Forces spokesman said last night the assailant had not been identified and that a police investigation was under way. Reuter, however, reported that four local Arabs had been arrested. It gave no further details.

Kishta was walking from the Al-Awda Mosque to his home 200 metres away when the attack occurred. A youth approached his entourage, drew a pistol, and shot him in the back of the head from two metres.

Israel Radio last night quoted a statement broadcast on Damascus Radio, that "guerrillas killed him because he was a collaborator" with the Israeli military government in Gaza. Later, Damascus Radio reported that the PLO had claimed responsibility for the murder.

Kishta served two terms as mayor of Rafah, which lies at the southern end of the Gaza strip. Part of the city was returned to Egypt in April, 1982.

His family said last night that Kishta was a fair man, loved by his people, with no political stand and no enemies. They could not find a motive for his murder.

His funeral is to take place this morning, and security measures are being taken to ensure the maintainance of order in the city.

Unity terms ambiguous on settlement

By DAVID LANDAU
and ASHER WALLFISH
Jerusalem Post Correspondents

One of the first of the five to six new settlements to be erected this year by the unity government will go up in Samaria, close to the 1967 border. This has already been agreed informally between Likud and Labour, a high Likud source said last night.

Under the terms of the government's policy guidelines, five to six settlements out of the 28 approved by the previous government but not yet erected are to go up during the government's first year in office. Their location is to be decided upon "within one week of the government's taking office."

The Likud source said this decision would be made in informal

(Continued on Back Page)

Senior UN official due here today

Post Diplomatic Correspondent

The top political assistant to the UN Secretary-General, Brian Urqhart, is due in Jerusalem today and will meet with top government ministers and officials.

His visit, though not originally planned to coincide with the formation of the new government, is considered especially important in view of its timing. It wil enable Premier Shimon Peres and Defence Minister Yitzhak Rabin to discuss with the top UN official ideas for an enhanced Unifil role in South Lebanon which could help speed Israel's withdrawal from the area.

Towards the end of the Likud government, there were indications of a shift in attitude towards Unifil and its possible role, particularly on the part of former defence minister Moshe Arens. In the senior echelons of the army, it is understood, there is a willingness to see Unifil expand its operations and responsibilities in South Lebanon.

High Israeli sources stress, however, that Israel will not consider disbanding the South Lebenon Army under Gen. Antoine Lahad and rely solely on Unifil as a buffer between its border and PLO elements to the north.

Egypt to push for overall M.E. peace

CAIRO (AP). – Egypt said yesterday it is determined to seek a negotiated overall Arab-Israeli settlement, an Israeli troop withdrawal from Lebanon and an end to the Iran-Iraq war.

Prime Minister Kamal Hassan Ali outlined Egypt's principal foreign-policy objectives in a policy statement to parliament, is first since forming a new cabinet last July.

"Negotiation should replace confrontation and international dialogue should replace the use or threat of force," Ali told the 358-member parliament.

"An overall and just peace is not one of several available options but the only available alternative," Ali said.

He said his government will seek "to complete the peace march toward a just and comprehensive settlement of the Middle East problem, with the Palestinian question at its core, an Israeli withdrawal from South Lebanon and termination of the war between Iraq and Iran.

Ali said his government also will try to "expand the area of understanding with sister Arab states in the interest of Arab unity."

(Continued on Back Page)

Histadrut 'won't accept' C-o-L reduction

Budget cuts top agenda at first cabinet meeting

By AVI TEMKIN
Post Economic Reporter

The new government is today to hold the first in a series of discussions on how to cut $1 billion from its budget. The discussion will be followed immediately by a meeting between key ministers and Histadrut leaders in an attempt to persuade the Labour Federation to accept modification of the cost of living allowance system.

Histadrut Secretary-General Yisrael Kessar indicated on Friday that he will not agree to a reduction in C-o-L compensation. According to the economic plan drafted by former finance minister Yigal Cohen-Orgad, there would be a one-time, 10 per cent reduction in the allowance, within the framework of a wage-price freeze.

Finance Minister Yitzhak Moda'i, Economics Minister Gad Ya'acobi and Prime Minister Shimon Peres met on Friday, a few hours after Moda'i took over at the ministry. Various policy lines were discussed although the trio did not get down to details.

They decided that Moda'i would present to the cabinet his ideas on cutting $1b., and that a formal decision to trim the budget would be taken. Moda'i will meet the rest of the ministers and his ministry officials during the week to decide on the details of the cut.

According to sources close to the Treasury, today's cabinet meeting will not decide on operative measures; it will just be presented with Moda'i's general ideas regarding the budget and government expenditure.

According to economic observers in Jerusalem, the meeting between Peres, Moda'i and Ya'acobi may be the first in a regular series.

Although Moda'i has come up with some general ideas concerning the economy, he will need a few days to decide on specific measures, such as the introduction of new taxes, and the increase in value added tax to 17 per cent as proposed by the Cohen-Orgad plan, the observers said.

It has been learned that, within the new government's economic leadership, there are differences of opinion as to the benefits of introducing new taxes. Thus Moda'i has apparently decided to start cabinet-level talks with the measures to cut government spending, since this would show that the first priority is cutting the government's own "standard of living," before that of the public.

According to the plans prepared by the Treasury under Cohen-Orgad, the $1b. cut in the budget would be implemented via a $500 million cut in government operations – including some $150m. from the defence budget – and some $500m. from welfare allowances and subsidies on basic commodities. But it is not clear whether the new government will adopt this plan in its original, or in modified form.

The last few days have seen a continuation in the rapid devaluation of the shekel. On Friday the local currency lost 1.86 per cent of its value against the dollar, bringing the cumulative rate of devaluation since the beginning of the month to 11.1 per cent.

According to Bank of Israel sources, there are considerable differences of opinion within the central bank as to the benefits of speeding up the devaluation. Bank sources said that the Governor Moshe Mandelbaum has been upping the rate of devaluation to protect himself from any criticism about a further drop in the level of foreign currency reserves.

Sept. wages to include 13% C-o-L payment

By AVI TEMKIN

Wage earners will receive a 13.2 per cent cost-of-living compensation payment in their September salaries, following the 16.5 per cent rise in the consumer price index for August, the highest rise in consumer prices ever recorded for that month.

The increase in the net payments received by wage earners will be more than 13.2 per cent, however, since the Treasury will reimburse workers for the extra tax they paid in August due to the non-adjustment of income tax brackets. The ministry agreed with the Histadrut early this month to retroactively adjust the brackets.

Hikes in consumer prices over the last month brought the index to 5,746.9 points on a 1980-100 baseline. According to figures released by the Central Bureau of Statistics on Friday together with the CPI figures, an average family of four would need IS211,500 to buy the same basket of goods and services it purchased in 1980 with IS3,680.

According to economic observers, the rate of inflation for September may hit the 20 per cent mark, due to the influence of the High Holidays on prices and to the rapid devaluation of the shekel over the last weeks.

The observers added that since July, the rate of devaluation has been higher than the rate of inflation. Since wages have ever been lagging after prices, this means that there has been a relatively large erosion in real wages in the last two months.

Reacting to the inflation figures, the Treasury said that they reflect the urgent need to implement economic measures.

The ministry said that as of midnight, travel tax would be adjusted to IS32,800.

Since the beginning of the year prices have gone up by some 191.2 per cent, while in the last 12 months the cumulative rate of price hikes is 393.8 per cent.

The economy will therefore enter the traditionally inflationary autumn months with an average monthly rate of inflation of already some 15 per cent.

Prior to the CBS announcement, the Treasury calculated that the CPI had gone up by some 15 per cent. This deviation from the actual figures was apparently due to an unusually high rise in the prices of fruits and vegetables, by 19 per cent.

At the other end of the scale, end-of-season sales meant the prices of clothes and footwear went up by only 4.5 per cent in August (133.3 per cent since the beginning of the year).

Other items registering large price increases were food (18 per cent and 186.4 per cent since December); transportaton and communications (18.2 per cent and 187.3 per cent); education (17.4 per cent and (181.6 per cent); and housing (17.1 per cent and 228.4 per cent). It should be noted that the prices of food and housing have risen by 420.2 per cent and 425.3 per cent respectively in the last 12 months.

One of the main indicators as to future inflation was the large increase in wholesale prices. The wholesale price index of industrial output rose by 19.8 per cent.

The price index of input in residential building went up by 16.8 per cent, reaching 424.8 points on an October 1983-100 baseline. The price index of inputs in agriculture rose by 19.1 per cent.

Karameh blames Peres for 'attack'

BEIRUT (AP). – Lebanese Prime Minister Rashid Karameh yesterday held Israel responsible for a gunboat attack on mostly Moslem West Beirut, on Friday, calling it a "disturbing message" from Israel's new government.

The accusation came a day after the military command in Israel denied that any of its navy vessels had been involved in the shootout with Druse militias and West Beirut's Moslem Lebanese Army garrison.

Druse communiques and eyewitnesses said the attacking gunboat belonged to the Israeli-backed Lebanese Forces militia that controls East Beirut. A statement from the army's 6th Brigade in West Beirut blamed the hour-long shootout Friday that left a police major wounded on an "unidentified gunboat."

The Voice of Lebanon radio station of the Christian Phalange Party said the gunboat was Israeli, as did some Lebanese Army soldiers ashore.

A Lebanese Army corporal said the gunboat had aimed twice at the shore south of Beirut. Witnesses then reported that the vessel opened up toward the mostly Moslem sector's Avenue de Paris, panicking pedestrians and motorists along the seaside thoroughfare.

"The visit of the war vessel to Beirut's coast and its attack on the city is a disturbing message pointing to the hidden intentions behind the formation of the new government of Israel," Karameh said in a statement.

"We find no difference between the present and the past," the Syrian-backed premier said of the Labour-Likud coalition. "Prime Minister Peres has declared that his course of action to get out from the Lebanese quagmire and withdraw his army from the occupied south is conditional on the security of Galilee. This is the same slogan that the Likud government used to justify the occupation of South Lebanon."

The incident came shortly after a high-powered Syrian army delegation wound up talks with Lebanese Army commanders on field details and a timetable for the deployment of some 8,000 Lebanese troops in the embattled central mountains, at present controlled by Druse irregulars.

The Syrian delegation, led by Maj.-Gen. Ali Aslan, head of the Syrian Army operations, drove from Damascus on Friday morning, shortly after tank, artillery and mortar battles between Christian and Druse militiamen eased off in the hills just east of Beirut.

THE JERUSALEM POST

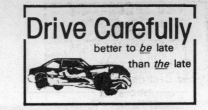

Vol. LIII, No. 15802 Friday, January 4, 1985 • Tevet 11, 5745 • Rabia Tani 11, 1405 IS500

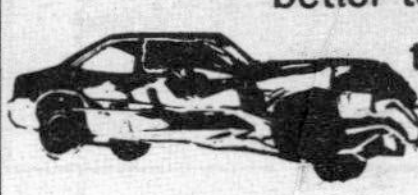

Bank heads: 'We won't quit'

By PINHAS LANDAU
Post Finance Reporter

TEL AVIV. – Bank Leumi Chairman Ernest Japhet, Bank Hapoalim management chairman Giora Gazit, Discount inner executive chairman Eli Cohen and Mizrahi general manager Aharon Meir yesterday squashed any talk of their possible resignations following the state comptroller's report on the 1983 bank share collapse.

In the first meetings the senior bankers have had with a reporter since the publication of the report, each of the senior executives told *The Jerusalem Post* that they have no intention whtsoever of resigning in response to the report's findings. Nor, they added, had they been asked to do so by their boards or major shareholders.

A press report yesterday of a proposal that these executives should assume management positions in their bank's operations abroad was met with incredulity and mirth. "This illustrates the press's imagination," one senior banker said.

Meanwhile, two distinct trends are emerging in the bank's thinking and actions in view of the almost certain establishment of an inquiry commission. First, they are gearing up for what is likely to be a protracted campaign to present their side of the bank shares story.

The initial shots in this campaign were fired on Wednesday evening when the two largest banks, Leumi and Hapoalim, reacted publicly for the first time since the report was issued on Monday. In essence the banks insist on the inquiry encompassing the political decision-makers, and the government policy that underlay the regulation of the shares.

At the same time the banks are acutely aware of the negative effect controversy may have on their recovery from losses they suffered in 1983, and are concerned for their image and contacts abroad. As a second tack, they are therefore plowing ahead with their operational planning for 1985 and beyond, and are keeping their foreign correspondent banks informed of developments here.

This "split-level" approach is not conducive to optimal management of the banks, particularly with the economy in such poor shape. The bankers, however, feel that they have no choice but to proceed with this "two-front war."

Yesterday was the fast of Tevet which commemorates the beginning of the siege of Jerusalem by the Romans. In Tel Aviv this week, the banks began withdrawing into their fortresses as they discerned a major attack forming against them. Their assumption is that the siege they are about to endure will be a long and unpleasant affair, and that the side with most stamina and endurance will be the victor.

Cabinet to decide on bank-share inquiry

By DAVID LANDAU
Post Diplomatic Correspondent

The cabinet is to decide on Sunday, probably without dissent, that a full-dress commission of inquiry must be set up to investigate the bank shares affair. A ministerial delegation will then be appointed to coordinate with the Knesset State Control Committee on the terms of reference of the commission.

This was the upshot of a top-level ministerial consultation yesterday under Premier Peres.

Neither Peres nor other key ministers, Likud or Labour, are enthusiastic at the prospect of a quasi-judicial commission laying bare the inner workings of Israel's leading banks. They believe this may weaken the banks' credibility at home and abroad – which in turn could gravely damage the national economy.

But Peres and the ministers recognized that there is no choice, since the heads of the banks are plainly not prepared to resign voluntarily despite the massive public pressure on them to do so.

The inquiry commission's meticulous investigation of the banks is not a matter of controversy among the politicians: they all acknowledge that this would be the commission's main task, since the state comptroller lacked the authority to investigate non-government institutions such as the banks and the stock exchange.

But there may well be controversy between Labour and Likud over the commission's other terms of reference – especially whether it is empowered to investigate and pass judgement on government policymaking.

The Likud would naturally be unhappy with a close examination of its economic policy, particularly if links were established between that policy and the banks' manipulation of their share prices in order to engender a false atmosphere of prosperity and wellbeing.

By the same token, Labour would benefit politically from the establishment of such links, but would be chary of the commission's close examination of possible links between the government and the banks in the early 1970s, when the share-manipulation began.

There have also been rumblings of a constitutional wrangle between the Knesset committee, or some of its members, and the cabinet over which of them is actually to set up the inquiry commisstion. By law either is empowered to do so.

State Comptroller Yitzhak Tunik has strongly urged that the Knesset committee, and not the cabinet, create the inquiry commission. He argues that it would be improper for the cabinet to set up a commission which is to inquire into the activities of various government agencies, and perhaps of the cabinet itself.

But the contrary argument was advanced yesterday with equal vigour by Justice Minister Moshe Nissim. He pointed out that commissions of inquiry set up by previous cabinets had been instructed to investigate government bodies, including the cabinet itself, and had done so without fear or favour.

The Agranat Commission and the Kahan Commission were two obvious examples, he said.

Moreover, Nissim added, it is not the cabinet or the Knesset committee which actually appoints an inquiry commission: this is the task of the president of the Supreme Court. The cabinet or the Knesset committee merely requests the court president to do so. The choice of commission members is his.

(Continued on Page 2, Col. 5)

Moda'i vows to tax self-employed

By ROY ISACOWITZ,
MICHAL YUDELMAN
and AVI TEMKIN
Jerusalem Post Reporters

TEL AVIV. – Finance Minister Moda'i yesterday undertook to impose a one-time tax on the self-employed by April. The government has so far failed to implement the tax, one of the components of the economic package deal.

Moda'i promised to collect the tax – at a rate of 4 per cent of average annual earnings – during a meeting with Histadrut Secretary-General Yisrael Kessar and other senior Histadrut officials after yesterday's meeting of the trilateral Economic Council. The tax is to be paid by all self-employed professionals, shopkeepers and merchants.

Government, Histadrut and manufacturers representatives yesterday decided to continue holding intensive, informal contacts, to reach a follow-up agreement to the package deal by the middle of this month. Histadrut participants said that they expect the sides to meet almost daily.

The council deferred a decision on a proposal by Kessar that the package deal remain in force as long as no follow-up agreement has been reached. Kessar said that the intention of the proposal is to prevent a wave of consumer spending in anticipation of post-package deal price rises.

Yesterday's session was limited to opening statements by the three sides, and the presentation of the reports of three sub-commnittee's dealing with unemployment and black capital.

Prime Minister Peres, speaking at the council, called on workers in public-sector services to accept a five-day workweek as an alternative to wide-spread dismissals. According to Peres's proposal, workers would be paid only for five days.

Peres said this would reduce workers' wages by 7 per cent.

Moda'i later said a second economic package deal will be formulated within a week or two, according to the schedule set by the government. He was speaking at a meeting of the Liberal Party's Central Committee.

Arrival in Israel seen as miracle by new olim • Absorption centres, hotels and army facilities mobilized to house thousands • Hospitals treat for malnutrition and unusual ailments • Newcomers, some barefoot, arrive without possessions

Wraps off massive operation to rescue Jews of Ethiopia

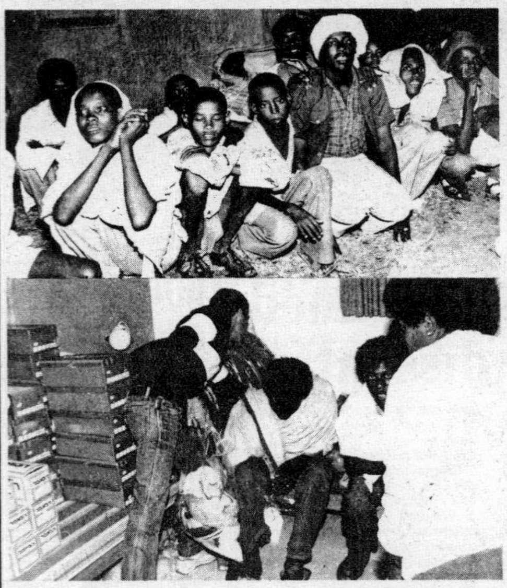

At top, a group of Ethiopian Jews a few hours after their "Magic Carpet" flight wait to be registered and get new clothing. At bottom, new arrivals shed sandals for tennis shoes. Many of the Ethiopian Jews arrived barefoot.
(Louis Rapoport)

By JUDY SIEGEL
and LOUIS RAPOPORT
Jerusalem Post Reporters

The official veil of secrecy on Israel's massive campaign to save the Jews of Ethiopia was lifted hurriedly yesterday, as government and Jewish Agency representatives told reporters in Jerusalem that "over 10,000" of them have arrived "in recent years."

A "press briefing on the absorption of Ethiopian immigrants" was held at Beit Agron, attended by local and foreign journalists. Officials disclosed some of the facts about the saving of Ethiopian Jews, which in the last two months has taken the form of a complex airlift, made more urgent by the recent drought and starvation in the African country.

The story of the rescue effort until now had been embargoed by voluntary agreement between the government and the Israel Editors' Committee so as not to jeopardize the operation. Only after news of the rescue dribbled out in the foreign and local press, and then became a flood in recent days, did authorities feel they had to make an official announcement.

The arrival of the immigrants – who come from an underdeveloped agrarian society and who arrive with their tattered rags as their only possessions – comes at a time of economic crisis. The estimated cost of the absorption of the Ethiopian Jews during the next two years is $300 million, some of which will be funded by the Jewish people abroad and some by U.S. refugee aid money.

The plan to rescue the most recent batch of Ethiopian Jews was taken by the Begin government and re-approved by the current government.

Yisrael Peleg, director of the Government Press Office, started the briefing by declaring that the Prime Minister's Office had asked the press office to provide reporters with details on the absorption of Ethiopian Jews. With him were acting Jewish Agency Executive chairman and permanent treasurer Akiva Lewinsky; Health Ministry Director-General Dan Michaeli; Deputy Director-General of the Absorption Ministry Shmuel Shenhar; and Moshe Gilboa, director of the World Jewish Affairs Division of the Foreign Ministry.

Lewinsky, filling in for executive chairman Arye Dulzin who is abroad on Agency business, said that "everyone in Israel feels the presence of Ethiopian Jews in the country." The big drama, he added, is their future absorption into Israeli society. "One day, a great deal will be written." Because of the Ethiopian Jews' background, their absorption will be much more difficult than those who came from the West, said Lewinsky. Aware of this, the interministerial committee, coordinated by the Absorption Ministry, which has directed the various authorities was determined "not to repeat mistakes" committed years ago with other groups of immigrants.

Related story — Page 3

A total of 1,500 Ethiopian children have been placed in Youth Aliya institutions – all of them religiously oriented because of the observant nature of the Ethiopian Jewish community.

Michaeli disclosed that 300 of the immigrants are now in local hospitals. Doctors have accumulated considerable experience in treating the unusual diseases and problems suffered by the Ethiopian Jews. He emphasized that there is no danger to the public from these ailments, and that modern treatment of malaria, tuberculosis and parasitic diseases are quicker and more efficient than in the past.

The newcomers, presented with immigrants' certificates on their arrival, are examined by medical specialists and those not requiring immediate treatment are sent to absorption centres and other facilities around the country.

(Continued on Page 14)

Premature publication

By JUDY SIEGEL
Jerusalem Post Reporter

Press leaks about the Ethiopian rescue forced the authorities to acknowledge the "open secret" yesterday rather than to present the whole saga after the operation was ended, as they had planned to do.

Yesterday's disclosure was precipitated by an interview with Yehuda Dominitz, director-general of the Jewish Agency's aliya department. Dominitz is a 35-year veteran of aliya and absorption work. The interview appeared in the January 4 issue of *Nekuda*, the bi-monthly journal of the Council of Jewish Settlements in Judea and Samaria.

Dominitz, who had been tight-lipped about the operation, told the writer – Balfour Hakkak of Mevasseret Zion – that the information was "not for publication." In the interview, Dominitz said that "the majority" of Ethiopian Jewry have already come to Israel.

The interview was purposely disregarded by most of the Israeli press, but *Ma'ariv* and *Yediot Aharonot* yesterday quoted from it on their front pages. As a result, the Associated Press picked up the story, embellishing it with reports that it had obtained from abroad. More international news agencies and Israel Radio followed.

It was officially announced that Dominitz had been told by Aharon, who is in London for Agency meetings, to "go on vacation." Domi-

(Continued on Page 2, Col. 4)

Three government hospitals about to close

By D'VORA BEN SHAUL
and DAVID RUDGE
Jerusalem Post Reporters

Three government hospitals, Rambam in Haifa, Hillel Yafe in Hadera and the government hospital in Nahariya are on the verge of closing. The hospital directors claim that they have no money to pay their bills and are running out of essential supplies.

The emergency ward of Rambam is to close its doors to the public today unless the Finance Ministry immediately transfers funds for urgently needed supplies. hospital director Yosef Brandes warned yesterday.

He said the hospital would reach the end of its oxygen reserves today. Food and medicines were also in short supply and there were was a danger of power cuts due to lack of fuel.

Brandes said Rambam owes about IS1 billion to its suppliers who are now demanding cash payments for any future deliveries, but the hospital did not have any funds.

Dr. Elitsur Hazani, director of the government hospital in Nahariya, said yesterday that the hospital which serves 250,000 residents of the Western Galilee owes IS150 million and has run out of some essential supplies. If there are no funds forthcoming by the first of the week, he said, the 350 patients now hospitalized will be sent to other hospitals, or if that is not possible, they will be sent home.

In Hadera, the Hillel Yaffe Hospital has enough fuel supplies to last only until tomorrow night, which will leave the hospital without heat or hot water for sterilizing equipment. It will also close if help is not forthcoming by Sunday, sources said.

Health Minister Mordechai Gur met early yesterday with Prime Minister Peres and Finance Minister Moda'i. Gur said that he could not do with less than IS5 billion at once, and a promise that the flow of budgeted funds will not be held up in the future.

But later in the day a Health Ministry source told *The Jerusalem Post* that Moda'i said he would transfer only the IS2 billion which was expected on January 1.

At Rambam Hospital in Haifa, after a lengthy telephone conversation with Moda'i, the contents of which are not known, Gur told reporters that "if anyone in the Treasury thinks he is going to take advantage of the general financial crisis in order to destroy the public health system, he'd better think twice."

With most government hospitals

(Continued on Page 2, Col. 2)

THE JERUSALEM POST
INTERNATIONAL EDITION
The perfect gift for your friends and relations overseas

THE JERUSALEM POST

Vol. LIII, No. 15839 Sunday, February 17, 1985 • Shvat 26, 5745 • Jomada Awal 26, 1405 IS335

Drive Carefully
better to *be* late
than *the* late

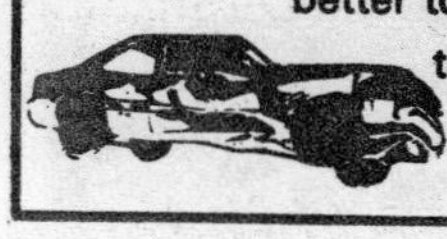

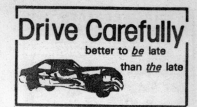

Inflation was 5.3% in Jan.

By AVI TEMKIN
Post Economic Reporter

The Consumer Price Index rose 5.3 per cent in January, the Central Bureau of Statistics announced on Friday, making January the second consecutive month of single digit inflation.

The increase in retail prices over the last month of the first package deal brought the CPI to 113.2 points on a 1980=1 baseline. From last month the CBS has divided the index, which was given until December on a 1980=100 baseline, by 100 to simplify calculations.

Since the cumulative inflation rate for December and January was just some 9 per cent, workers will not receive any cost-of-living compensation with their February pay. This allow ·ce is payable only after the inflation rate goes over 12 per cent. Thus, wage earners are certain to receive a C-o-L increment only in their March salaries, payable in April.

According to bureau officials, the CBS can already account for price increases of some 5 per cent in February. But the officials warned that to this figure should be added the price increases in the wake of the ending of the package deal – which were not recorded by them – and price rises in the coming two weeks.

The Treasury said on Friday that February's rate of inflation would be considerably higher than that of January and December. Unofficially, the ministry has estimated that February's inflation rate will be around 15 per cent.

January's rate was largely the result of hikes in government-controlled prices at the end of the first package deal. Most of the CPI items affected by controlled prices registered increases of 4 to 8 per cent.

Nevertheless, there were also non-controlled items which registered marked increases last month. Prices of fruit and vegetables went up in January by 10.2 per cent, above the seasonal increase, while housing prices went up 7.6 per cent.

Despite this relatively high rise in housing prices, CBS officials noted that over the last months of 1984 there was a steep fall in housing prices in dollar terms. According to the latest survey conducted by the bureau, prices of flats and houses owned by their occupants went down 6.2 per cent in the last quarter of 1984, and by 13 per cent in the second half of the year.

The large increase in the prices of fruit and vegetables has brought a Histadrut proposal to extend price controls to cover them. This proposal was raised by the labour federa-

(Continued on Page 2, Col. 1)

Herzog sees no new European initiative

No new Middle East initiative by the European nations should be expected, President Chaim Herzog told reporters on his return on Friday from an official trip to Europe.

He was met at Ben-Gurion Airport by Prime Minister Shimon Peres, Vice-Premier Yitzhak Shamir and Knesset Speaker Shlomo Hillel, whom he briefed concerning his five-day trip.

Herzog, whose visit took him to Luxembourg, Strasbourg and Brussels, said he presented to the European leaders he met Israel's position on its agricultural exports to Europe following the coming entry of Spain and Portugal into the EEC.

Taba talks may resume next week

Post Diplomatic Correspondent

Israel and Egypt are expected to resume talks next week concerning the entry of the Multinational Force and Observers (MFO) into the disputed Taba zone south of Eilat.

Egyptian President Hosni Mubarak has suggested that delegations from the two countries meet in Ismailiya. This was in the course of a verbal message delivered to Prime Minister Shimon Peres on Thursday by Mohammed Rassiouny, chargé d'affaires at the Egyptian Embassy in Tel Aviv.

A first round of talks concerning Taba, which was held in Beersheba last month, failed to resolve the controversy.

THE ISRAEL EXPERIENCE
New Hit Multi Media Show in English
"An Exciting Spectacular!"
Old Jaffa Mall
4 Pasteur St. at entrance to Old Jaffa
Open 7 Days a Week
Showtimes: 9 a.m., 12,2,5,6,8 and 9 p.m.

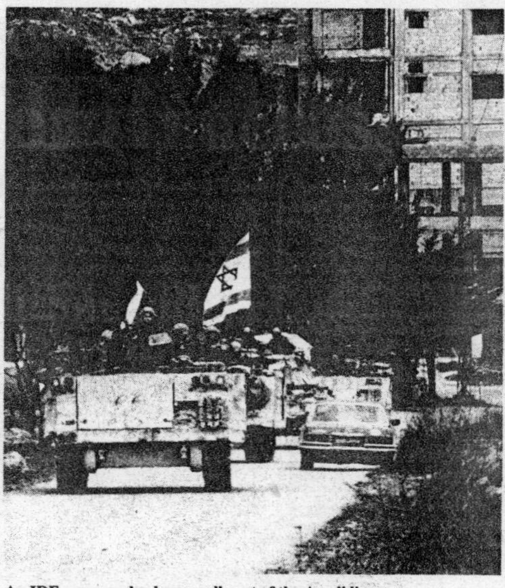

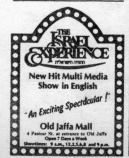

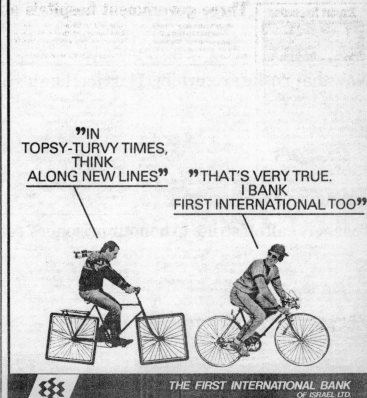

An IDF armoured column pulls out of the Awali line. (Andre Brutmann).

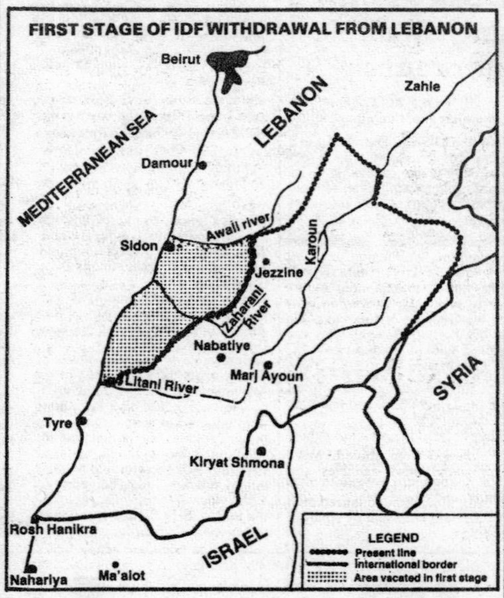
FIRST STAGE OF IDF WITHDRAWAL FROM LEBANON
Beirut
Zahle
LEBANON
MEDITERRANEAN SEA
Damour
Awali river
Sidon
Karoun
Jezzine
Zaharani River
Nabatiye
Marj Ayoun
Litani River
SYRIA
Tyre
Kiryat Shmona
Rosh Hanikra
ISRAEL
Nahariya
Ma'alot
LEGEND
Present line
International border
Area vacated in first stage

Troops redeploy along interim S. Lebanese line

IDF completes pullback I

By HIRSH GOODMAN
and JOSHUA BRILLIANT
Post Defence Reporters

The Israel Defence Forces yesterday afternoon completed without incident the first part of the three-staged pullback of Israeli forces from Lebanon. The pullback from Sidon started at 11:07 a.m. – 48 hours ahead of schedule – ending 32 months of Israeli military presence in the city.

By 12:30 p.m. there were no Israeli forces left in Sidon, along the Awali River or in the Shi'ite villages between the Zaharani and Litani Rivers.

Defence Minister Yitzhak Rabin, speaking to the press atop a hill overlooking Sidon yesterday morning, stressed that the withdrawal to the Litani River line was only the first stage of a plan for getting the IDF out of Lebanon and not an end in itself. He said the problem of terror from Lebanon had not been solved, and that stage one of the pullback was the first stage "of a plan for a new strategy against terror."

Chief of General Staff Rav-Aluf Moshe Levy said that he expected that the "major part of the pullback" would be completed within three months.

Yesterday's pullback was relatively uncomplicated and involved Golani infantrymen and tanks. All heavy logistical equipment and prefabricated buildings had been pulle dout of the area two weeks ago.

The main reason given for the trouble-free nature of the pullback, however, was the IDF's decision to advance the withdrawal by two days, thus creating an element of surprise. Another factor behind the absence of terrorist attacks during the withdrawal was that it took place on the Sabbath.

Early yesterday morning the two routes that the troops pulling back were to use – one running west to east through Jezzine to Metulla, and the other along the coastal road – were secured by paratroops and other specialized infantry. At 7 a.m. the Golani commander received orders that his men were to be prepared to pull back later that morning – orders that were greeted with jubilant cheers from the men. Minutes after the two Israeli tanks and several armoured personnel carriers guarding the Awali bridge on the northern outskirts of Sidon left their positions, the first Lebanese Army units, led by a jeep flying the Lebanese flag, moved into the city, (see adjacent story).

The small Israeli column headed east, and moved slowly toward Jezzine. It was joined by other units which pulled back from their positions one at a time. The army used bulldozers and graders to clear snow-covered roads around Jezzine. There was little tension along this 20 kilometre-long axis, however, since it is controlled by the Christians.

Israeli defence officials yesterday refused to say whether or not there had been cooordination with the Lebanese Army prior to the pullback. But Chief of General Staff Levy noted that "the fact is that minutes

(Continued on Page 2, Col. 4)

Roses greet Lebanese troops in Sidon

SIDON (AP). – The Lebanese Army yesterday moved rapidly to take over the Awali River crossings, the town of Sidon and its surroundings – all evacuated by the Israel Defence Forces in the first stage of its withdrawal from Lebanon.

According to reports from Sidon, there were no clashes, but according to Lebanese Radio, three alleged collaborators with Israel were executed there yesterday. There were no other indications of the disorder widely anticipated in the area after the Israeli troop withdrawal, and the entering Lebanese soldiers were showered with rice and roses by the cheering local population.

Thousands of Sidon residents danced in the streets. Sirens and horns blared and a new poster went up all over town heralding "my nation, my flag, my army – the generation of the future."

In a statement broadcast nationwide, Lebanese Prime Minister Rashid Karameh heralded "this historic day" and urged further efforts "to see that the withdrawal is complete and quick and without conditions."

Nabih Berri, leader of the Shi'ite Amal militia and state minister for South Lebanon in the Karameh government, called yesterday's activities "the first step toward liberation" of the nation from the Israelis, who have held the Shi'a-dominated South since their June 6, 1982, invasion.

Berri continued: "What we need from our citizens in Sidon and the rest of the South is to be prepared and to confirm to world opinion that we are ready to live together in peace."

Karameh also said he was "happy" to extend his congratulations to his fellow Lebanese and to "the national resistance especially" for forcing the Israeli withdrawal. "National resistance" is the phrase the Lebanese use for the almost daily terrorist attacks against Israeli forces.

A number of Israeli and Lebanese officials have warned that the withdrawal of the Israeli forces could spark sectarian warfare among the rival religious and political sects in South Lebanon.

But South Lebanese leaders yesterday reiterated their desire to keep the peace. Halim Fayyad, the governor of Sidon, urged residents to remain calm.

Fayyad also said in a statement broadcast nationwide: "We are all busy today in this blessed gift, which is to live through and witness moments of national pride... These are the movements of our enemies evacuating from our sacred ground."

The first word of the Israeli operation came shortly after 7 a.m. when Israel notified Unifil that it was abandoning the Awali front, and Unifil informed the Lebanese Army.

Timor Goksel, the Unifil spokesman, said there was no request from either side for any of the 5,200 Unifil troops or other UN forces to move into the area being vacated by the Israelis.

The actual pullback from the Awali River began shortly after Israeli soldiers lowered the Star of David flags that had marked the main river crossing into South Lebanon for the last 32 months.

Following several weeks of thinning-out operations, it took them only about two minutes starting at 11.07 a.m. to move their few remaining men and armoured vehicles out.

Israel army Chief of General Staff Moshe Levy arrived later by helicopter to inspect the scene.

He told reporters there had been "no problems" with the operation

(Continued on Page 2, Col. 6)

Lebanese minister says army to control South

BEIRUT (AP). – Lebanon's defence minister, Adel Osseiran, said in an interview with a French language magazine that PLO terrorists would not be allowed to operate against Israel from South Lebanon after the Israeli occupation ends.

Osseiran told *La Revue du Liban* that "The Lebanese in the South have come to realize that the nation and its interests are more important than any other personal interests, and that any regional problems cannot be solved at the expense of the South or of Lebanon."

He added, "That is why the Palestinians cannot act in any manner that would hurt the interests of the South."

Osserian insisted that when the Israelis leave "there will be no armed presence other than the legal army" of Lebanon.

Osseiran also reiterated the nation's stand on the more than 500,000 Arabs who have taken refuge in Lebanon since the 1948 creation of Israel.

He said that those who took refuge in Lebanon in 1948 were welcome to stay and enjoy "the full protection of the Lebanese government." He added, however, that the government still considered those who came later – such as the influx of families after the 1967 Arab-Israeli war – to be illegal residents.

Arafat seen accepting 'land for peace' formula

By DAVID BERNSTEIN
Post Mideast Affairs Reporter
and agencies

One of the PLO groups opposed to last week's Hussein-Arafat accord has distributed what purports to be the "official text" of the agreement. This confirms that, while Arafat did not accept UN Security Council Resolution 242, he did, for the first time, endorse the "territory for peace" formula at the heart of that resolution.

In Cairo, meanwhile, Egyptian President Hosni Mubarak once again confirmed over the weekend that he viewed the agreement as "a good step forward." He stressed that "of course, to start negotiations it needs many more steps forward."

Mubarak, who is due to visit Washington next month, was asked if he thought the accord was enough to persuade U.S. President Ronald Reagan to press forward with a new peace initiative. He replied: "I cannot promise – but I'm going to do my best."

Mubarak warned yesterday that Israel would commit a historic mistake if it rejected the Hussein-Arafat accord.

"If Israel failed to respond to this step and persisted in adhering to hollow slogans of rejection, it would commit a historic mistake for which it would be held responsible before

(Continued on Page 2, Col. 2)

'Nothing likely to come out of Soviet-U.S. talks on Mideast'

By WOLF BLITZER
Jerusalem Post Correspondent

WASHINGTON. – The Reagan administration has assured Israel and American Jewish leaders that nothing is likely to result from this week's meetings on the Middle East in Vienna between U.S. and Soviet officials.

The talks are scheduled to begin Tuesday. Richard Murphy, the assistant secretary of state for Near Eastern and South Asian affairs, is to represent the U.S. His Soviet counterpart is to be Vladimir Polyakov, a Foreign Ministry specialist on the Middle East. They will be joined by small staffs.

Secretary of State George Shultz assured a delegation from the American Jewish Congress on Friday that the U.S. had no intention of supporting a Soviet-proposed international conference on the Middle East.

The secretary and other officials described the sessions as aimed at exchanging views on several issues, including the Arab-Israeli conflict, the situation in Lebanon, the fighting between Iran and Iraq and the Soviet occupation of Afghanistan.

They sharply rejected the notion that the two superpowers would be

(Continued on Page 2, Col. 1)

Yosef expected to call for Ethiopian Jews' acceptance

By HAIM SHAPIRO
Jerusalem Post Reporter

Former Sephardi chief rabbi Ovadia Yosef, whose position regarding Ethiopian Jews was last week characterized as hardline, is today expected to call for their complete acceptance as Jews without preliminary conversion rites.

In a news report last week which was subsequently denied, Yosef reportedly told his protege, Interior Minister Yitzhak Peretz, not to register the Ethiopians as Jews until they had undergone a symbolic conversion ritual immersion ordered by the Chief Rabbinate.

But today he is expected to call for their complete and immediate acceptance "within the congregation of Israel" with no such rites.

Yosef is expected to make his remarks at a conference on Ethiopian Jewry organized by the Chief Rabbinate in Jerusalem. He is expected to argue that since the Karaites – who rejected Talmudic rule –

(Continued on Page 2, Col. 1)

Temperatures to rise after wet weekend

By YITZHAK OKED
Jerusalem Post Reporter

BEIT DAGAN. – A gradual return to spring weather is expected during the next two days. According to the duty weatherman at the weather forecasting centre here, today and tomorrow will be partly cloudy with a gradual rise in temperatures.

During the weekend weather was stormy throughout the country. Snow flurries were reported in the Hebron hills and Galilee.

Rainfall was spread across the country. Beersheba received about 25 millimetres, Mitzpe Ramon had 1.4mm and Eilat 0.1mm. From Friday morning to yesterday morning, the wettest spot was Hebron, with about 75mm of rain. Jerusalem was second with 53mm. Haifa had only 5mm and Tel Aviv 2mm.

On Friday afternoon heavy rain caused flooding and traffic jams in a number of places in Jerusalem. The capital's fire brigade received numerous calls about fallen trees and broken power lines. Firemen had to pump water from the basement of National Police Headquarters and from a telephone exchange in the neighbourhood of Talpiot, where some equipment was damaged.

Peres to have audience with pope

By ASHER WALLFISH
Post Diplomatic Reporter

Prime Minster Shimon Peres is to have an audience with Pope John Paul at the Vatican on Tuesday, the second and final day of his vist to Rome, it was learned in Jerusalem yesterday.

The late prime minister Golda Meir was granted a papal audience in 1973.

Peres leaves tomorrow for Rome at the invitation of Prime Minister Bettino Craxi, accompanied by Minister without Portfolio Ezer Weizman.

Peres and his party will fly from Rome to Bucharest for a one-day official visit at the invitation of Rumanian President Nicolae Ceaucescu.

All First International Bank personal current account holders (not just those on salaries) can now overdraw up to IS 50,000 at the prime interest rate.
Have you started banking at First International Bank?
Details in All Branches

Kesher Barel & Assoc.

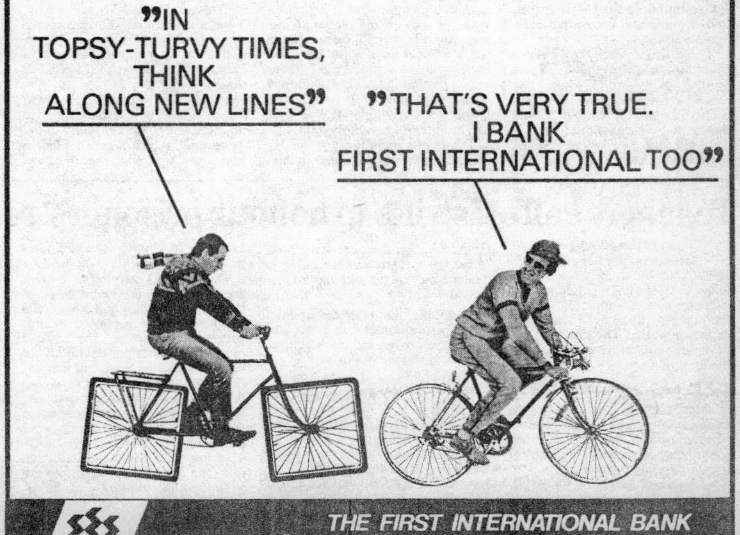
"IN TOPSY-TURVY TIMES, THINK ALONG NEW LINES"
"THAT'S VERY TRUE. I BANK FIRST INTERNATIONAL TOO"

THE FIRST INTERNATIONAL BANK OF ISRAEL LTD.

THE JERUSALEM POST
Vol. LIII, No. 15916 Tuesday, May 21, 1985 • Sivan 1, 5745 • Ramadan 1, 1405 IS430

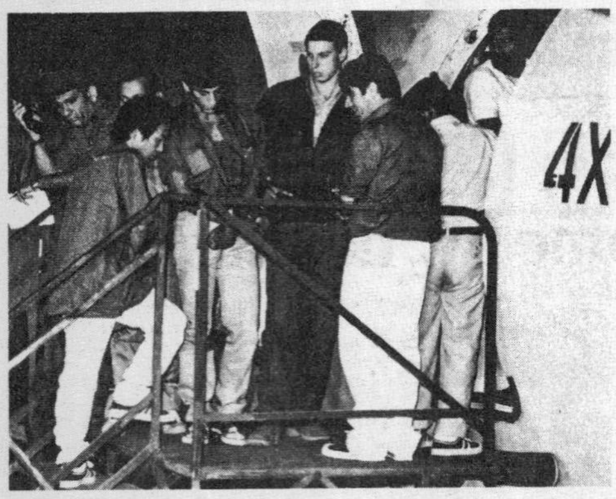
Terrorist Kozo Okamoto (climbing steps) and other released prisoners board a plane to fly them out of Israel last night. (IDF)

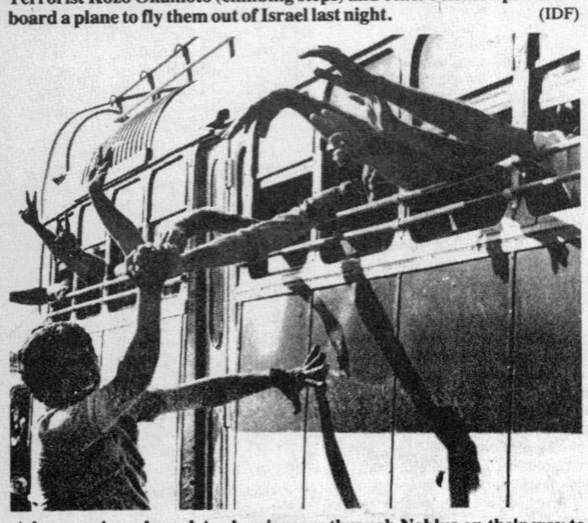
A bus carries released Arab prisoners through Nablus on their way to their homes in various parts of Judea/Samaria yesterday. (Andre Brutmann)

3 PoWs freed for 1,150 terrorists

Shamir said seeking release of Jewish ring

By DAVID LANDAU, SARAH HONIG and MARK SEGAL
Jerusalem Post Reporters

Vice Premier Yitzhak Shamir last night said that he would propose to the inner cabinet and to Prime Minister Peres that all accused and convicted members of the Jewish terror ring be pardoned and released from jail, according to a report broadcast by Kol Yisrael last night.

Sources at the Prime Minister's Office last night urged that "a matter of ransoming captives ought not to be mixed up with unrelated matters."

The sources declined further comment, but it was clear that on the Labour side of the national unity government there is no sympathy for the call to reprieve the Jewish terrorists.

The inner cabinet is understood to be split down the middle over the possible reprieve of members of the "Jewish underground" who would be willing to publicly express remorse for their crimes. But ministerial advocates of the reprieve, led by Yigael Hurwitz (Ometz) and Yosef Shapira (Morasha), believe they can win a majority in the full cabinet and they are urging that the decision be taken there.

Shapira said on television last night that he had been active on this issue for some considerable time. He was at pains to separate the matter from yesterday's release of PLO terrorists.

Shapira said the biblical adage "He who admits and desists is to be dealt with mercifully" (Proverbs 28:13) should apply to the members of the Jewish underground. He indicated that if reprieved they would not return to acts of criminal violence.

Shapira recalled that David Ben-Gurion had exercised mercy on similar occasions, and "his pupils" (a reference to Peres) should do likewise. This was apparently a reference to the decision in 1949 to free

(Continued on Page 2, Col. 4)

Groff says IDF men were treated well

GENEVA (AFP). – At times like this it is hard to express your feelings. I can't say that we made friends but we were treated well," said Yosef Groff, one of the three Israeli PoW's released yesterday.

The three, dressed in new suits given them by their captors, were answering journalists' questions before leaving Damascus for Geneva.

During the flight Groff said: "I played chess, and read the Bible which was given to me after I requested it from my guards. I was not given political books or even books dealing with the Palestinian problem.

"I kept a diary but I was forced to leave it with my guards. They promised to send it to me in another month through the Red Cross."

Shai, Groff and Salem due home this morning

By HIRSH GOODMAN
Post Defence Correspondent

Israel yesterday released 1,150 Palestinian and other terrorists – including mass murderers – in exchange for three Israeli soldiers who fell into terrorist hands in Lebanon in 1982.

The soldiers, Hezi Shai, 31, Nissim Salem, 21, and Yossef Groff, 24, were to be turned over to Israeli authorities in Geneva last night. There were due to arrive at Ben-Gurion Airport at 5 am today.

Under a complex plan arranged by the International Red Cross, Israel flew three planeloads of close to 400 terrorists to Geneva as the three Israelis were begin flown there from Damascus. In addition, more than 800 terrorists were freed from Israel jails and bused to their homes in the West Bank, Gaza and in Israel, and to Syria and Lebanon.

The prisoner exchange ended long months of secret negotiations with Ahmed Jibril's Syrian-backed Popular Front for the Liberation of Palestine-General Command who held the three Israelis.

Negotiations for the exchange took over 18 months, with final agreement reached in Geneva on April 22. The Israeli Inner Cabinet unanimously approved the terms of the agreement on April 1.

Senior government officials last night braced themselves for the political outcry they expect to follow news of the exchange. Among those released are several major terrorists – including Kozo Okamoto, the surviving member of the Japanese Red Army squad that killed 27 at Ben-Gurion in 1972.

One hundred and sixty-seven of the terrorists were convicted of involvement in terror attacks in which people were killed, and 116 others were involved in terrorists activities that left people maimed and injured.

About 600 of those released yesterday will be returning to their homes in Israel, Judea, Samaria and Gaza – including terrorists responsible for the 1978 Coastal Road massacre, the 1971 murder of the two Aroyo children in Gaza, the 1979 attack on Nahariya, in which Danny Haran and his two small daughters were killed, and members of the gang that murdered Aharon Gross in the Hebron market in July 1983.

Among those not released in the exchange was the killer of the Haran family in the attack on Nahariya, the killer of the Israeli couple in the Cremisan Monastery grounds, the killer of the yeshiva student-soldier Aharon Gross in Hebron and the killers of the soldier Avi Bromberg.

The three Israelis Yosef Groff, Nissim Salem and Hezi Shai, were originally due to land in Israel before midnight. But due to delays in both the arrival of the aircraft from Damascus, and in the complicated exchange process, they were not expected to be back in Israel before 5 a.m. today. By 11 o'clok last night only Salem and Groff had been handed over to Israeli officials at the Geneva Airport.

Without precedent – Page 5

At five minutes to midnight. Shai arrived at Geneva and handed to the Red Cross, completing the release of the Israelis.

Groff and Salem were captured by Jibril's organization on September 4, 1982, near Bahamadoun on the Beirut-Damascus highway. Shai, was captured on June 11, 1982 during the battle at Sultan Ya'acoub in the eastern sector of Lebanon.

Four more Israelis are still missing in action, Zvi Feldman, Zechariya Baumel and Yehuda Katz, who were last seen during the battle at Sultan Ya'acoub and Samir Assad, a Druse soldier who was captured in Lebanon in April, 1983.

Speaking to newsmen in Geneva yesterday, former justice minister Shmuel Tamir, Israel's chief negotiator in the exchange talks, insisted that Assad is still alive and being held by Nayef Hawatmeh's Democratic Front for the Liberation of Palestine.

"Hawatmeh is no longer repeating his claim that Assad was killed dur-

(Continued on Page 2, Col. 2)

Missing soldier's parents want American help

By WOLF BLITZER
Jerusalem Post Correspondent

WASHINGTON. – The parents of a missing Israeli soldier who is believed still to be captive in Syria yesterday appealed for international assistance in obtaining the release of their son.

Miriam and Yona Baumel said they came to Washington to try to meet with Secretary of State George Shultz and other influential Americans to seek their backing in winning the freedom of their son, 24-year-old Zachary Baumel, who was captured by the Syrians on June 11, 1982 in Lebanon.

The Buamels immigrated .o Israel from the U.S. in 1970 and maintain dual citizenship.

They decided to speak out publicly in the aftermath of yesterday's prisoner exchange with Syria.

The parents are convinced that Baumel and three other missing Israeli soldiers are being held captive in Syria.

Jewish protesters in Hebron decry prisoner exchange

By JOSHUA BRILLIANT
Jerusalem Post Reporter

HEBRON. – Scores of Jewish demonstrators yesterday sat in the middle of a busy square opposite the market here, listening to the blowing of a shofar and joining a prayer in protest against the release of hundreds of Arab terrorists in exchange for Israeli prisoners of war.

In Jerusalem, the wives of accused and convicted Jewish terrorists went on a hunger strike, demanding their husbands' parallel release; it is inconceivable, they argued, that Arabs with Jewish blood on their hands are set free while the Jews "prompted" by their attacks remain behind bars.

The settlers' leaders said they had had advance knowledge of the planned exchange and had tried to torpedo it. Shalom Wach, the head of the Kiryat Arba local council told the demonstrators that the settlers had raised the matter but realized the Knesset members were unanimous in supporting the exchange of prisoners or at least had decided not to oppose it.

Accordingly the settlers decided to make the best of the situation and press for the release of the accused and convicted Jewish terrorists. Shortly after 1 p.m., some of the wives of the men held in the Jewish terror case arrived at the lawn opposite the Knesset and unfurled placards reading: "The gentiles get freedom and the Jews – suffering."

Their only crime is that they defended themselves," Ze'ev Friedman's wife Rivka argued. "You can't have a situation in which the jails are emptied of Arabs, who will again walk free in the Hebron market, while the Jews remain behind bars."

Friedman was convicted on Sun-

(Continued on Page 2, Col. 6)

Amal militia storms Sabra and Shatilla

BEIRUT. – At least 32 people were killed and over 300 wounded as Shi'ite Amal militiamen fought their way into three Palestinian refugee camps here yesterday against heavy resistance from Palestinian fighters.

The militiamen, who surrounded the Sabra, Shatilla and Bourj Al-Barajneh camps after clashes erupted on Sunday night, appeared to have pushed forward on all fronts after more than 20 hours of bloody fighting that raged throughout the day.

There was no official casualty toll as the fighting continued at nightfall. But a survey of five hospitals indicated at least 52 dead and 325 injured, including 14 Shi'ite militiamen and 16 Palestinian fighters.

The battle closed Moslem-controlled West Beirut and cut the road to Beirut Airport, hampering its operations. Only a few airliners landed and took off during the day.

Amal has said it will not let the Palestinians regain the control of West Beirut and South Lebanon they enjoyed before Israel's 1982 invasion ousted the PLO.

An Amal official at the frontlines overlookign Sabra told Reuters that Shatilla fell to the militia at 3 p.m. after 12 hours of fighting, and that Amal was now fighting inside Sabra.

At Bourj al-Barajneh, Lebanese security sources said Amal pushed the Palestinians back into the camp from surrounding Shi'ite suburbs during the morning and was fighting inside the camp.

"The fighting began because the Palestinians want to be strong and regain the freedom of action they had before the Israeli invasion," an Amal commander at the frontlines said.

"Amal saw they were bringing in weapons and stopped it, and that's when the fighting began," he added.

The crackdown came as no surprise. Amal has vowed it will not allow the PLO to rebuild its power base in Lebanon to launch attacks against Israel.

Last month, Amal, aided by Druse militiamen ganged up on the Sunni Murabitoun movement, the PLO's main ally in Lebanon, and crushed them in two days of bloody fighting in West Beirut.

But PLO fighters have been slipping back into Beirut and other refugee camps in the South for some time. Those who made it to South Lebanon joined a three-week Moslem offensive in March that ousted Christians from their villages around Sidon.

Some officials said as many as 7,000 guerrillas were back and scattered across the country. That figure was probably exaggerated, but the Palestinian influence has been noticeably increasing in recent weeks. (Reuter, AP)

PFLP-GC are jubilant over 'heroic' exchange operation

DAMASCUS (AP). – The Popular Front for the Liberation of Palestine – General Command hailed the exchange of the Israeli soldiers for the 1,150 terrorists as "our heroic Galilee operation."

It said the negotiations with Israel, conducted primarily by former Austrian chancellor Bruno Kreisky, took more than two years, with 1,300 hours of secret talks.

PFLP – GC officials announced at a news conference in the Syrian capital that the three Israelis left Damascus on separate planes early yesterday for the handover in Geneva.

The PFLP – GC officials said the Palestinians to be freed include 121 men who originally were scheduled to be released November 24, 1983, but were held by the Israelis despite the International Red Cross protests.

Disclosing details of the sensitive negotiations for the first time, the PFLP – GC stressed: "We want in particular to thank Herbert Amory, who, acting on behalf of Kreisky, played the most important role in achieving the swap agreement."

Diplomatic sources said that Amory, Austria's ambassador in Athens, played a vital role in a secret diplomatic shuffle between Damascus and Jerusalem.

"We also want to express thanks and gratitude to the Austrian authorities, to the International Red Cross and the Swiss Federal Government for their help," the PFLP – GC added.

(Continued on Page 3)

'Now that Yoske's returning I just feel like it's a dream'

By MICHAL YUDELMAN
Jerusalem Post Reporter

The families of prisoners of war Nissim Salem, Yosef Groff and Hezi Shai yesterday awaited their arrival, excited, tense and somewhat incredulous.

"These three years have been a nightmare, hell. Now that he (Yosef Groff) is coming back I just feel like it's a dream, a good dream," Miriam Groff said when she learned that her son was on his way back to Israel.

For the first time in three years, she continues, she felt at peace. "All of a sudden I don't have to wake up in the morning thinking what can I do today, whom can I call to get Yoske back?

"I don't know what will happen when I see him. What I am sure about is that I'll be wearing a white dress. I want to be beautiful for myself, for Yoske. I want him to see his mother did not break down. I want to look like a bride because this is the greatest happiness I've ever had or ever will have," she said.

The Groffs spent most of the day watching and listening to Arab television and radio stations, which broadcast the announcement of the prisoner exchange several hours before it was released in Israel.

"There's Yoske! There's Hezi!" Yosef's father, Zvi Groff shouted when Jordanian Television broadcast a news conference held in Damascus just before the Israelis left there.

Miriam Groff was not in the flat at the time, and by the time a neighbour called her the broadcast of the news conference had ended. Miriam burst into tears, but her husband comforted her, "It's not so bad, just a few more hours. Patience."

The phone in the Groff's Holon apartment never stopped ringing yesterday, and the building swarmed with excited schoolchildren and neighbours. Coloured lights and yellow ribbons had been hung around the building, courtesy of the municipality, and a huge placard reading "Yossi is free" was tied to the balcony.

"It's been so long, we've been so tense, his poor mother," a beaming

(Continued on Page 2, Col. 6)

Teachers call off strike to honour prisoners' return

By LEA LEVAVI
Jerusalem Post Reporter

TEL AVIV. – The Histadrut Teachers Union last night decided to postpone a two-hour strike in the first grade that had been scheduled for this morning. The decision was made because of the return of the prisoners of war.

Negotiations between the union and the Education Ministry on how to safeguard teachers' jobs while cutting the education budget are expected to continue today. Disruptions of classes, as well a demonstration in Jerusalem by teachers who have received letters of dismissal, are threatened for tomorrow if there is no progress in the talks.

The ministry has sent dismissals to several thousand tenured and non-tenured teachers because of the need to cut the budget, and the union is demanding that the sackings be rescinded.

Yesterday the teachers opened kindergarten classes two hours late to protest against the ministry's refusal to cancel the dismissals.

Meanwhile, the threat to further disrupt matriculation exams has been lifted after the Secondary School Teachers Association and the Education Ministry reached an agreement at o'clock yesterday morning. The Finance Ministry, however, was not willing to sign the agreement, because the Education Ministry has not yet shown how it will make all reuired budget cuts. So the association had to settle for an exchange of letters with the Education Ministry.

The teachers agreed to a postponement of payment for some of the homeroom, duty and other hours which they were supposed to start getting in September. The number of teachers' hours per class is also to be cut by half an hour, but this will not reduce the amount of time children spend in the classroom. The teachers' hours to be cut are to come from ones slated for administrative purposes.

In return, a union spokeswoman said, the ministry has promised not to fire teaches "insofar as possible." A joint committee of union and ministry representatives is to deal wtih problems arising when individual teachers are not needed.

The agreement will prevent mass firings, the union spokeswoman said.

But leaders of the Histadrut Teachers Union, who have already seen copies of the letters exchanged between the rival union and the ministry, claim that a clause allowing "administrative dismissals" will in practice give the ministry latitude to fire thousands of teachers without the union having recourse.

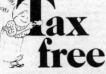

ARIDOR TESTIFIES IN BANK SHARES COLLAPSE INQUIRY
PAGE 7

THE JERUSALEM POST

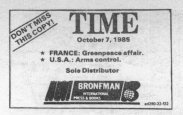

Vol. LIII, No. 16026 Wednesday, October 2, 1985 • Tishre 17, 5746 • Moharram 17, 1406 IS620

Air force hits PLO Tunis HQ

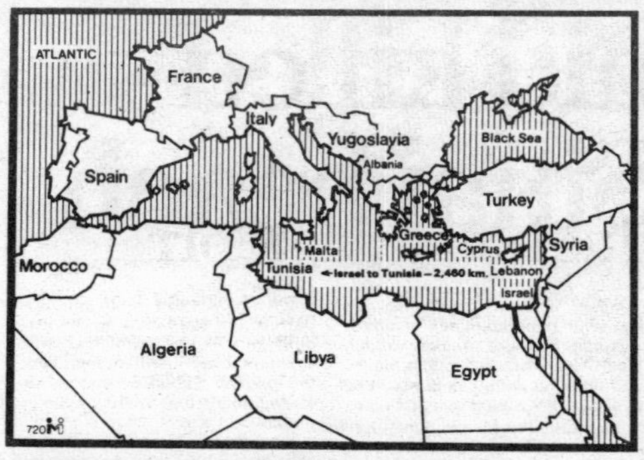

NEWS ANALYSIS/Hirsh Goodman

Raid's message: There's no hiding place for terrorists

The message behind yesterday's strike was two-fold: that the PLO is not immune to Israeli military reaction, no matter where it decides to locate its headquarters; and that the diplomatic process is not linked to Israel's on-going war against terror.

According to senior government officials, the fact that Jordan's King Hussein was in Washington at the time of the raid "did not hinder our planning, but actually enhanced it." The message, according to these sources, was that Israel would react with pin point accuracy against any terrorist threat, regardless of objective factors that would indicate that action by Israel is impossible.

"Our war against terror knows neither boundaries nor conventional restraints of diplomacy" *The Jerusalem Post* was told, "and that should now be crystal clear to those who thought otherwise."

The strike against the PLO headquarters in Tunisia was said to have been the brainchild of Defence Minister Yitzhak Rabin. One of the main problems facing military planners was the distance between Israel and Hammam Plage – a 4,800-kilometre round trip.

They had to take into account not only refuelling problems, and potential harassment from countries like Libya, but also technical difficulties with one or more of the aircraft involved.

According to foreign sources, Israel used F-16 single-engined fighters for the attack.

While the targets in yesterday's raid were further than the Iraqi nuclear reactor destroyed in 1981, military experts yesterday said that the operation against Arafat's Tunisian headquarters was less complicated.

Israel, again according to foreign sources, has had an aerial refuelling capability for several years, having converted Boeing 707 transport air-

(Continued on Page 2, Col. 6)

Peres to try to salvage peace moves in U.S.

By DAVID LANDAU
Post Diplomatic Correspondent

Prime Minister Shimon Peres will try during his visit to Washington later this month to repair the damage to peace prospects caused by yesterday's IAF raid on the PLO headquarters in Tunisia.

Highly-placed Israeli sources said last night they could hardly hope for Egypt to lift its suspension of the Taba talks in the fortnight before Peres's trip to Washington. Nor was there much likelihood of movement on King Hussein's initiative in the immediate aftermath of the bombing raid.

They said that Peres, in his talks in Washington, might be able to reinject into the diplomatic processes the momentum that yesterday's raid had inevitably reduced.

Some observers felt the impact of the raid, at home and abroad, might actually enhance premier Peres's ability to be forthcoming on peace issues, vis-a-vis both Egypt and Jordan. These observers argued that the IAF action would almost certainly improve the domestic standing of Peres, Defence Minister Yitzhak Rabin, and their Labour Party.

But there was real concern in some government circles in Jerusalem that the adverse fall-out from yesterday's raid might be heavier and more sustained than Peres and Rabin had anticipated. There were fears expressed that Egypt's suspension of the Taba talks might not be short-lived, and that King Hussein would be constrained to stand in even closer solidarity with PLO chief Yasser Arafat.

These concerns were expressed particularly by sources close to Ezer Weizman (Alignment-Yahad), the one minister who opposed the bombing raid when the 'inner cabinet' was asked to vote on it last Wednesday night.

Weizman agreed with his fellow-ministers that the murderous attack on the Israeli yacht in Larnaca harbour earlier that day was the 'last straw' in terms of Israel's capacity to suffer terror outrages without responding.

At a preliminary negotiation in Cairo on Thursday, it was decided to begin work on a document of arbitration – an advance which had long eluded Weizman and other Alignment ministers. Now this advance has been frozen – a development which, say the sources close to Weizman, will please only the Likud.

The Likud opposes arbitration on the Taba border dispute, and insists instead on the process of conciliation. The Cairo talks were to reexamine the possibility of conciliation, and also search for 'alternative solutions' to Taba.

In one immediate move to try and ease concern in Jordan following the IAF action, Peres made a point of distinguishing yesterday between Tunisia, which gave the PLO a free hand on its soil, and Jordan which, he said, prevented terrorist attacks from being launched from its territory. Peres spoke to high-schoolers in Sderot.

Earlier, Rabin had told a questioner that no PLO terrorist HQ

(Continued on Page 2, Col. 6)

60 said killed, 100 injured; Arafat's home hit, he escapes

By AVI HOFFMANN
Post Defence Reporter
and Agencies

Key buildings in the Palestine Liberation Organization headquarters in Tunisia were destroyed, and about 60 people were killed in the air raid mounted by the Israel Air Force yesterday. It was the furthest the IAF had ever flown on a bombing raid.

PLO chairman Yasser Arafat was not in his office as scheduled, and escaped injury. The damage and casualties were confirmed by a PLO spokesman.

Defence Minister Yitzhak Rabin said the air raid was in response to acts of terror by the PLO which were intended to undermine prospects for peace in the region. The raid follows an upsurge in PLO terror culminating in the murder last week of three Israelis vacationing in Cyprus.

The IDF spokesman said all the Israeli planes returned safely from the 4,800-kilometre round trip raid.

PLO sources in Tunis said eight IAF F-16s were employed, hitting the headquarters in a six-minute strike of surgical precision.

Jordan Television reported last night that the head of Force 17, Mohammed Natour (Abu Taef), and other top PLO men were killed in the raid.

A PLO spokesman said about 60 people, including "many" Tunisians, were killed in the raid on the beachside suburb of Hammam Plage, 20 kilometres south of Tunis. Another 100 were said to be injured.

The 10 a.m. raid destroyed Arafat's secret residence near the complex. He was not in the building but many of his guards, including Tunisians, were understood to have been killed there.

Other buildings razed included the PLO's political headquarters, administrative offices and surrounding homes, mostly residences of PLO officials. The only target which appeared to have been missed was the PLO's telecommunications headquarters, alongside which there was a large crater, according to an AP report.

Israel decided to hit the top-ranking planners and organizers of terrorist acts at Yasser Arafat's PLO headquarters, rather than strike at the perpetrators and low and middle-level echelons, Defence Minister Yitzhak Rabin told a press confeence in Tel Aviv following the raid.

"We have shown the terrorist groups and the world that there is no place where terrorist organizations can be immune to blows from our forces. The long arm of the IDF can reach wherever terrorist forces are deployed," said Rabin.

The defence minister noted that in the past six to eight months there has been an increased effort by the PLO, especially that part of the organization headed by Arafat, to carry out terror acts against Israeli targets, from the sea, in the territories under Israeli control, from the north and also against innocent Israelis travelling abroad, such as the recent cold-blooded murders in Larnaca.

"Israel will not tolerate," he said, "acts of terror by Arafat's PLO which are initiated to undermine the prospects for peace in the region."

Rabin dismissed as "total nonsense" suggestions that the attack was aimed at torpedoeing the peace process. "If there is one thing that damages the peace process it is the terrorist activities of the PLO under Arafat," he said.

"No one should assume that Israel will sit idly by while terror acts are perpetrated against its citizens," warned the minister. This was the only purpose of the attack against the PLO headquarters, said Rabin, stressing that Israel had nothing against Tunisia. But the PLO could not buy immunity by locating itself in

(Continued on Page 2, Col. 6)

U.S. calls air attack self-defence

By WOLF BLITZER
Post Washington Correspondent

WASHINGTON. – The Reagan administration yesterday appeared to condone Israel's aerial strike against PLO headquarters in Tunisia.

President Reagan said yesterday that Israel's strike was a justified retaliation against terrorists.

Asked whether that meant the Israelis had the right to retaliate by bombing a PLO headquarters in Tunisia when three Israelis were slain by terrorists in Cyprus, the president said the raid was justified "as long as you pick out the people responsible."

When asked whether the Israelis did in fact pick out the "right people," he said, "I've always had great faith in their intelligence."

A carefully drafted statement issued by the White House and the State Department said that, as "a matter of U.S. policy, retaliation against terrorist attacks is a legitimate response and an expression of self-defence."

The statement, first read to reporters by White House spokesman Larry Speakes, added: "From the preliminary reports available to us, this appears to be what was involved in this case."

But he added: "We are distressed by and deplore the cycle of violence in the Middle East, of which this latest incident is part. It underscores the urgent need to work for peace in the Middle East."

Speakes and other administration officials said the U.S. had not been notified by Israel in advance of the attack. The Pentagon flatly denied a Libyan report that the Israeli planes had refuelled aboard an American aircraft carrier in the Mediterranean.

State Department spokesman Charles Redman said: "We were not informed in advance and we're not involved in any way."

He said the U.S. understanding was that the Israeli attack "was not intended as an offensive act against Tunisia." It was instead "a retaliation against the PLO," he added.

Israel officials in Washington, af-

(Continued on Page 2, Col. 4)

EEC, Arabs and non-aligned express anger over raid

Anger and condemnation followed news of Israel's raid, with particularly strong comments coming from Arab capitals and the European Community.

Egyptian President Hosni Mubarak condemned the attack but said he would continue to support U.S.-backed efforts aimed at a lasting Arab-Israeli peace.

After a two-hour meeting with aides and ministers, he said Egypt condemned "any form of terrorism."

He expressed "deep sorrow that Israel, which talks about peace, actually goes to another country to kill Palestinians."

Earlier, the Foreign Ministry said Egypt would not meet Israeli officials as planned this week to discuss Taba.

But Mubarak's reaction indicated Egypt would not take tougher action. He said: "Does Israel truly want peace? We are serious about peace...we are still with peace."

Mubarak also said the raid indicated that Israel "is a state that does not really want peace. That is clear."

But when he was directly asked whether he contemplated any action other than condemning the air raid, Mubarak said:

"I don't convulse. I want to think logically, and I can't declare what I think about it. Let's leave that to circumstances."

A statement by Egyptian Foreign Minister Esmat Abdel-Meguid said Mubarak has sent a message to President Ronald Reagan "regarding the Israeli aggression."

Abdel-Meguid's statement said the action not only violated Tunisian sovereignty but also posed a "serious threat" to current Middle East peace efforts.

"In the face of this heinous criminal action, the Egyptian government will not receive the Israeli delegation that was scheduled to come to Cairo for talks on the problem of Taba – talks through which Egypt displayed its absolute keenness on peace," Abdel-Meguid said.

EEC foreign ministers meeting said the raid violates the sovereignty of a friendly, peaceful and moderate country and represents a further stage in the continuing violence and counter-violence in the Middle East."

The statement was endorsed by Spain and Portugal, who are due to enter the community next year.

It added that, "while condemning at the same time acts of terrorism committed against Israeli citizens, the ministers do not believe that they justify such action."

It said they hoped this new escalation of violence will not compromise efforts being made to achieve a peaceful solution to the Arab-Israeli conflict."

The French External Affairs Ministry issued a statement in Paris saying the government condemned the Israeli operation "on the territory of a sovereign state, a peaceful one and a friend of France." Such an

(Continued on Back Page)

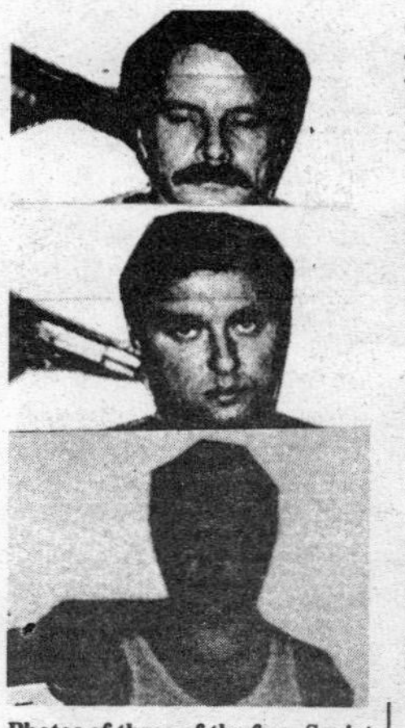

Photos of three of the four Soviet hostages delivered yesterday to a news agency in Beirut with pistols held to their heads. Top to bottom, commercial attache Valery Mirikov, embassy doctor Nikolai Svirsky, and attache Oleg Spirine. There was no picture of consular secretary Arkady Katkov. (Reuter).

2 Soviet hostages reported killed by Lebanese captors

BEIRUT (AP). – Two kidnapped Soviet Embassy personnel were reported killed by their captors yesterday in revenge for a bloody offensive by Syrian-backed militias against Moslem fundamentalists in Tripoli. But official Lebanese sources said they are still alive.

An anonymous caller purporting to represent the kidnappers, believed to be Moslem fundamentalists, claimed in a telephone call to a western news agency that two of four Soviets abducted Monday have been "executed."

However, no bodies have turned up. Hospitals that were checked said they had no bodies of foreigners in their morgues.

The caller, who said he spoke for the Shi'ite Moslem Islamic Jihad (Holy War), identified the pair as the commercial attache and embassy doctor.

When the Soviets were kidnapped by pistol-firing gunmen Monday, police identified the attache as Oleg Spirin and the physician as Nicolai Versky.

The caller said: "We have executed the Soviet commercial attache and the doctor. Our demands still stand. We are not going to execute any more today."

However, Lebanese intelligence sources said none of the Soviets has been killed.

The sources said Lebanese intelligence knows where the Soviets are being held in West Beirut.

They said two are held by the radical Shi'ite Hezbollah, or Party of God, and the other pair by Islamic

(Continued on Page 2, Col. 2)

BULLETIN

The Ethiopian Jews who have been protesting opposite the offices of the Chief Rabbinate for the past month are expected to end their demonstration today, according to peace activist Abie Nathan.

Speaking to *The Jerusalem Post* shortly before entering the residence of Prime Minister Shimon Peres close to midnight last night, Nathan said the decision to end the strike came after the Ethiopian leaders realized that a proposed hunger strike would have been impractical.

The Ethiopian leaders who accompanied Nathan to Peres's home refused to confirm or deny the report.

Gunmen kill three SLA soldiers

By MENAHEM HOROWITZ
Jerusalem Post Reporter

METULLA. – Three South Lebanese Army soldiers were killed yesterday when gunmen opened fire on them at Kafr Taibe on the northern edge of the Lebanon security zone.

The four gunmen, armed with automatic rifles and grenades, opened fire from a Mercedes car.

In the resulting gun battle, one of the attackers is believed to have been hit and a Unifil soldier was injured.

The gunmen escaped on foot. An RPG launcher was found in the blood-stained interior of the car.

Hope of a breakthrough in battle against Aids

By ILAN CHAIM
Jerusalem Post Reporter

Weizmann Institute researchers have isolated and synthesized a hormone they believe could yield a breakthrough in the treatment of Aids and other immunological diseases. But since Israel lacks a sufficient number of Aids victims, clinical testing will have to be done abroad.

The breakthrough discovery is a hormone found naturally in the thymus gland. Called THF (thymus humoral factor), its link with immunological processes was uncovered over the past 20 years at Weizmann by Prof. Natan Trainin, a cancer researcher in the cellular biology department. He was joined some seven years ago by Prof. Yigal Borstein, of the organic chemistry department, who synthesized THF half a year ago.

"It's too early to say how this revolutionary approach will develop," Borstein told *The Jerusalem Post* yesterday. "Since 1975, organic THF has been administered in about 100 cases in Israel, including two Aids (acquired immune deficiency syndrome) cases, with generally positive results. But no controlled study has been made."

With regard to the two Aids cases, Borstein noted that one victim, a 20-year-old male, had made a partial recovery of his immune defences, "the first such case known." The second victim, an older man in the later stages of the illness, showed some improvement but later died.

"The youth was in the early stages of Aids," said Borstein, "which he had acquired from blood received from abroad to treat hemophilia. He was given biologic THF, not the synthetic kind, and recovered sufficiently to leave (Beilinson) hospital. The older patient came back to Israel from the U.S., where he had acquired Aids, but was in the final stages of the disease. After treatment with biologic THF, his immune system improved slightly, but he died from complications."

THF seems to offer hope for an eventual cure for Aids. Borstein noted that "the youth's was the first Aids case stopped by external treatment."

Synthetic THF is the breakthrough that can now be tested, probably in the U.S. Borstein said negotiations are under way with

(Continued on Page 2, Col. 3)

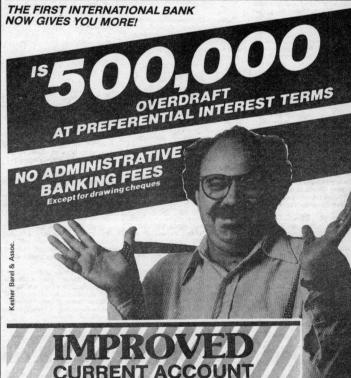

THE JERUSALEM POST
INTERNATIONAL EDITION
The perfect gift for your friends and relations overseas

THE JERUSALEM POST

Vol. LIII, No. 16029 Sunday, October 6, 1985 • Tishre 21, 5746 • Moharram 21, 1406 IS620

Tuesday at 4.45 p.m. & every Tuesday.
In super comfortable Jumbo 747's.
Johannesburg
The easy way
For details of our unique payment plan call your travel agent or 03-658388, 03-657759
WE MAKE THE DIFFERENCE SAA

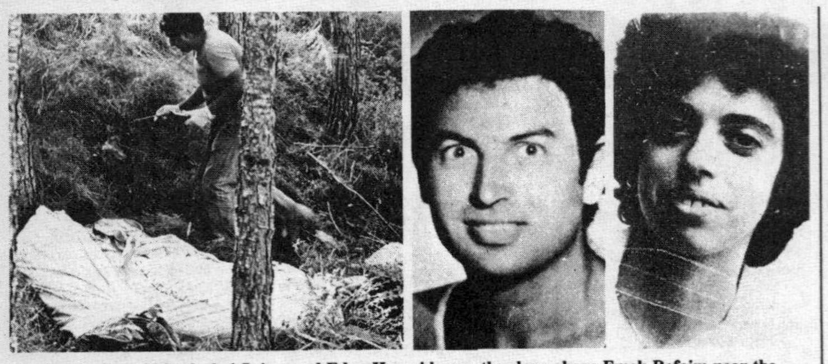

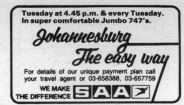

The bodies of Mordechai Suissa and Edna Harari lay on the slope above Emek Refaim near the capital, where they were murdered last Wednesday. Portraits of Suissa and Harari appear on the right. (Isaac Harari)

Six Israelis said killed in attack on Sinai beach

By ROBERT ROSENBERG, DAVID LANDAU and HIRSH GOODMAN
Jerusalem Post Reporters

Six Israelis were killed and an Egyptian officer gunned down yesterday afternoon when an Egyptian soldier or policeman sprayed the beach at Ras Burka, 40 kilometres south of Eilat, with gunfire. Late last night it was still unclear what had prompted the attack. The dead were four adults and two children.

Two Israeli children were lightly wounded in the attack and two other Israelis were reported wounded. According to reports reaching Jerusalem last night, one of the Israelis hit was Jerusalem judge Haman Shelah. His daughter was also reportedly hit. The total number of wounded and whether non-Israelis were included is not known.

The names of the dead had not been released for publication last night.

Egyptian President Hosni Mubarak sent a message to Prime Minister Peres expressing "deep sorrow" about the incident and Egyptian Foreign Minister Esmat Abdel-Meguid also called Israeli Ambassador Moshe Sasson in Cairo with condolences.

Egypt officially said that one Egyptian policeman was involved. Egyptian Defence Minister Abdel-Halil Abu Ghazallah called Sasson and said that the gunman would be punished to the full extent of the law.

In Cairo, the Middle East News Agency said the policeman, a member of the Central Security Forces which are deployed in Sinai, had been arrested and would stand trial.

According to Israeli sources, who still only had partial information last night, the incident occured at 4:20 p.m. when an Egyptian – either a policeman or soldier – fired at a group of Israeli tourists at the scenic viewpoint.

Fifteen minutes later, another burst of fire was heard. In this incident, an Egyptian officer who apparently had tried to apprehend the gunman was killed and an unknown number of soldiers were injured.

Last night, Egyptian and UN security forces were combing the area around Ras Burka, situated near Mitzpe Shaham, for two children who were in the group fired at but who ran away.

Egypt is forbidden by the 1979 peace treaty to have army troops in

(Continued on Page 2, Col. 3)

Hikers and rider killed in terrorist attacks

By ROBERT ROSENBERG
Jerusalem Post Reporter

The bullet-riddled bodies of a Jerusalem couple missing since last Wednesday were found yesterday near the Ein Kabu spring in Emek Refaim in the Judean Hills. They were killed by a terror group connected to some of the suspects in a similar killing near Beit Shemesh this summer.

A third Israeli was killed by terrorists near Kibbutz Sarid on Friday.

Security sources said that the couple, slain last Wednesday – apparently after the Israel Air Force raid on PLO headquarters in Tunis – were killed by a terror group.

According to security sources, the group that killed Edna Harari, 22, and Motti Suissa, 28, last Wednesday were also responsible for the recent shooting at an Egged bus in Halhoul, in which seven people were wounded.

The ambush of Migdal Ha'emek horseman Haim Falah, 30, in a Kibbutz Sarid field on Friday was probably not carried out by the same Judean Hills group, said the sources. They said that the Judean Hills group has apparently been living off the land.

Before last week's killings, eight people on outings in Israel and the West Bank had been killed by terrorists since 1979:

Uriel and Hadassah Barak, in the Hebron Hills, February 1979.

Ron Levy and Revital Seri, outside the Cremisan Monastery, October 1984.

Meir Ben-Yair and Michal Cohen, outside Beit Shemesh, June 1985.

Yosef Eliahu and Lea Elmakais, Mount Gilboa, July 1985.

In all except the Ben-Yair and Cohen case, the perpetrators have been caught. Several suspects remain at large in the Beit Shemesh case.

Acting Police Inspector-General Yehezkel Carthy told reporters who gathered at the scene where the bodies were found that the murders of Suissa, Harari and Falah "bore the marks of terrorism."

Southern District Commander Rahamim Comfort, conceding that "care must be taken" by hikers throughout the country, said that he doesn't think "the situation for hikers has gotten worse."

No arrests have been made in either of the murders.

Falah went riding on Friday afternoon, as he did every week. His body was discovered two hours later by a kibbutz member who was jogging through the field. The Migdal Ha'emek man's horse and pony returned home on their own a few hours later.

Suissa and Harari set out by car on Wednesday for the valley.

The girl's relatives reported her missing on Wednesday evening, and by midnight that night, police and

(Continued on Page 2, Col. 4)

U.S. fears Arab backlash, fails to veto UN swipe at Israel

By WOLF BLITZER and WALTER RUBY
Jerusalem Post Correspondents

WASHINGTON. – The Reagan administration refused to veto Friday night's UN Security Council resolution which sharply condemned Israel because it feared a veto would result in an anti-American backlash in the Arab world. Israel denounced the U.S. vote.

Authoritative U.S. officials acknowledged that the earlier U.S. statements condoning Israel's air strike against the PLO headquarters in Tunisia had already severely damaged the U.S. position throughout much of the Middle East. They were hoping that the U.S. abstention would weaken that anti American trend.

The U.S. ambassador to the UN, Vernon Walters, was instructed to work with the Tunisians and others at the Security Council to draft language which would result in an American abstention. The vote condemning Israel was 14-0 with the U.S. abstaining.

Foreign Minister Yitzhak Shamir, in New York, issued a strong statement denouncing the U.S. vote. He and other Israeli officials had been expecting an American veto, especially in the wake of the earlier U.S. statements defending the Israeli raid as an act of legitimate self-defence.

Shamir's spokesman, Avi Pazner, said that Shamir would raise the matter of the U.S. vote on Wednesday when he meets in Washington with Vice President George Bush and Secretary of State George Shultz.

Shamir said Friday that Israel "totally rejects" the Security Council resolution, and that he was "deeply disappointed" that it was not vetoed by the U.S.

The resolution said that the Israeli raid would have a serious effect on efforts to bring a comprehensive and lasting peace to the Middle East, and urgently requested all UN members to "take measures to dissuade Israel

(Continued on Page 2, Col. 3)

Reagan backs down from support for Tunis raid

By WOLF BLITZER
Jerusalem Post Correspondent

WASHINGTON. – President Reagan yesterday backed away from his earlier support for Israel's air strike against PLO headquarters in Tunisia.

In his weekly radio address, Reagan even appeared to equate the Palestinian murder of three Israelis at Larnaca and the subsequent retaliatory strike against the PLO.

"In shock and dismay," he said, "we've watched murderous attacks against Israeli civilians, and in response, an Israeli military raid on a PLO headquarters in a country that is an old friend of the United States."

Reagan did not say what he had suggested earlier in the week – namely, that Israel had responded in legitimate self-defense.

After referring to reports that a U.S. diplomat, William Buckley, held captive in Lebanon for many months, may have been killed and that a Soviet official was murdered in Lebanon last week, Reagan declared that "this return to violence is abhorent – all the more so because it is so useless."

The president said "armed struggle has solved nothing. There is no military option for resolving the difficult conflicts of the Middle East."

He went on to insist that "the only way to bring a lasting end to this dreadful cycle of violence is to deal with the circumstances that underlie it through negotiations – direct peace negotiations among the parties concerned.'

Reagan, whose brief comments did not address the U.S. refusal to veto Friday night's UN Security Council resolution which sharply condemned Israel, went out of his way to reassure Tunisian President Habib Bourguiba of continued U.S. support.

He praised a "gifted stateman whose country was affected by this week's violent events." He said Bourguiba "has been a true friend to America for decades.

"There is a particularly bitter irony about the events of the past week because President Bourguiba was one of the very first to urge a negotiated settlement of the Arab-Israeli conflict. Our hearts go out to him and to the innocent Tunisians swept up in this violence."

He concluded by saying: "In this horror, our hope lies in statesmen like President Bourguiba and King Hussein, President Mubarak and Prime Minister Peres. They are men of vision and peace."

Suissa's funeral set for noon today

Jerusalem Post Reporter

The fateful day-trip was to be their last. It was the first time Motti Suissa, 28, and Edna Harari, 22, had spent a day alone together since they met and fell in love three months ago, in the religious Young Israel movement.

The two, both from religious families, lived in Jerusalem. Edna lived at her mother's Romema apartment, and Suissa, a computer engineer who worked for Mateh Yehuda regional council, lived away from his Moshav Tirosh home in a rented flat in Givat Mordechai.

Relatives who spoke with *The Jerusalem Post* yesterday said that the two had not yet begun talking about marriage, explaining that until last week, they met only on chaperoned occasions.

The young woman, who worked as a lab technician at Hadassah Hospital in Ein Kerem, was known to fellow workers as "thoughtful, quiet and dedicated." Her father passed away several years ago, just after she completed her national service. Her funeral details were not known last night.

Suissa, who graduated from Ben-Gurion University, served in Nahal and went to the Kfar Haro'eh yeshiva high school. His funeral is scheduled for noon today at Moshav Tirosh.

Gorbachev may renew ties with Israel

PARIS (Reuter). – Soviet leader Mikhail Gorbachev said on Friday the Kremlin might re-establish diplomatic relations with Israel but only if there were moves towards an overall settlement of the Middle East conflict.

"As far as re-establishing relations is concerned, I think the faster the situation is normalized in the Middle East, the faster it will be possible to look at this question. For us there will be no obstacle," he said in reply to questions at a news conference in Paris. (See story page 4.)

Gorbachev, who returned to Moscow yesterday at the end of his four-day visit, said the Soviet Union had taken part in the foundation of the state of Israel and recognized its sovereignty, its rights and its security interests.

But he said there were big differences between how the Kremlin and the "ruling circles in Israel" understood the security question and called on Israel to rethink its ideas.

The Middle East was discussed by Gorbachev and his host President François Mitterrand, who agreed that both Moscow and Paris should take part in the search for a solution.

Gorbachev said efforts to find a Middle East settlement were complicated by U.S. insistence that American vital interests were at stake all around the world.

"What is left over for the other 200 countries in the world?" he said.

93 Jews left Soviet Union in September

Jerusalem Post Staff

Only 93 Jews left the Soviet Union last month, a spokesman for the Public Council for Soviet Jewry here said. He added that this was in spite of Soviet claims that emigration restrictions had been eased.

The spokesman also said that Prisoner of Zion Shimon Sheerman, serving out a three-year term, is expected to be released in three months.

Rubinstein calls for new look at punishments for terrorists

By SARAH HONIG
Post Political Reporter

TEL AVIV. – Shinui Communications Minister Amnon Rubinstein, who has until now adamantly refused to consider the death penalty, called last night for a reconsideration of punishments for serious terrorist crime.

Rubinstein said that the government must reopen its debate on the whole subject of security in the West Bank and punitive measures against terrorism.

High-ranking Likud sources told *The Jerusalem Post* last night that in the wake of the latest terrorist murders, the Likud plans to make sure that the battle against terrorism is placed on top of the national agenda and not allowed to be overshadowed by any other issue.

A leading Likud minister told *The Post* that terrorism in its latest form of murdering individuals in isolated places has become "public enemy No. 1. It should be combatted as would any other danger that takes such a toll in human lives. We are no longer dealing with isolated incidents but with an epidemic."

Trade and Industry Minister Ariel Sharon said that the nation now "faces two primary missions to which all our might should be devoted – the stabilization of the economy and the eradication of terrorism."

Herut MK Gideon Gadot told *The Post* that the "latest outrages will not intimidate us, but it is high time the nation's leaders decide on wiping out the PLO leadership. Only if Arafat and his cohorts are done away with, will the Arabs of Judea, Samaria and Gaza be shocked enough to lose their impudence."

Tehiya's Geula Cohen urged the government to launch a punitive attack on PLO headquarters in Jordan as well as to sentence terrorist murderers to death. "The fact that the murderers of the two Afula teachers are still alive and are not threatened by execution, encourages more murders, and those who oppose the death sentence cannot

(Continued on Page 2, Col. 6)

French researchers find way to speed diagnosis of Aids

PARIS (Reuter). – French medical researchers said yesterday they had found a way to identify cells under attack by the Aids virus, permitting earlier diagnosis of the fatal disease.

Professor Jean-Claude Chermann of the Pasteur Institute said this would allow doctors to pinpoint potential Aids victims long before symptoms developed.

"The disease has a long incubation period and the discovery of the cell that is under attack by the virus ...will enable us to detect a bad evolution, that is to say a bad prognosis for the future," Chermann said in a radio interview.

"As soon as the virus has been activated, as soon as the illness starts, it will be possible to see it. I think this is important and it represents a gain of two or three years."

The virus which causes Aids, or Acquired Immune Deficiency Syndrome, remains inactive in many carriers who do not develop the disease. But even when the virus is active, there is an incubation period of several years before symptoms appear.

"Among carriers who have no symptoms we will be able to see straight away those who are heading towards the illness and those who aren't."

There is no known cure for Aids.

State Dept. revokes Kahane's U.S. citizenship

By WOLF BLITZER
Jerusalem Post Correspondent

WASHINGTON. – Meir Kahane, leader of the Kach Party, is expected to appeal the State Department's decision on Friday revoking his U.S. citizenship.

The State Department announced that the U.S.-born politician was losing his American citizenship because he had effectively expatriated himself by becoming a member of a foreign parliament, the Knesset.

An announcement said that Kahane, who received Israeli citizenship under the Law of Return 14 years ago, would now have to apply for entry visas to the U.S. like all foreign citizens. His applications, the State Department said, would be studied on a case-by-case basis.

Since moving to Israel from New York, the founder of the militant Jewish Defence League had held joint U.S.-Israeli citizenship, like most Americans who have made aliya. But on Friday, the State Department said it had issued a "certificate of loss of nationality" because of his membership in the Knesset.

Kahane, during his recent visit to the U.S. said repeatedly that he would fight any effort to strip him of his U.S. citizenship. He expressed fear that the U.S. government would not allow him to return to the U.S. on his frequent speaking and fundraising trips.

In the past, the U.S. government has often prevented foreign nationals with criminal records from entering the U.S.

The Kach leader, for the same reason, said he would also strongly resist a parallel effort in the Knesset to force all members of that body to give up any foreign citizenships. There is pending legislation to this effect in the Knesset.

While in Washington in August, Kahane met with a prominent American Jewish attorney to explore possible avenues for appeal if he were forced to give up his U.S. citizenship in the aftermath of a new Knesset law. Kahane was advised that if he gave up his U.S. citizenship "under pressure," the U.S. government probably would still have to recognize him as an American national.

Kahane, at that time, was considerably more worried about the possible Knesset action than any negative decision by the State Department. For months, U.S. officials have been saying only that his case was extremely complex and that they were studying it. Friday's announcement, therefore, came as somewhat of a surprise.

But sources close to Kahane in Washington said that he was now likely to file an appeal.

In the present Knesset, there are two MKs who were raised in the U.S. and held American citizenship, although they were not born there: Moshe Arens (Likud) and Rabbi Eliezer Waldman (Tehiya). Arens gave up his U.S. citizenship when he was first elected to the Knesset in 1973. Waldman announced last year when he was elected that he was relinquishing his U.S. citizenship.

Former MK Yehuda Ben-Meir, who was born in the U.S. gave up his American citizenship in 1963 when he began his service in the IDF.

Ben-Meir and Arens told *The Jerusalem Post* last night that they never had any problems getting entry visas to the U.S. from the State Department.

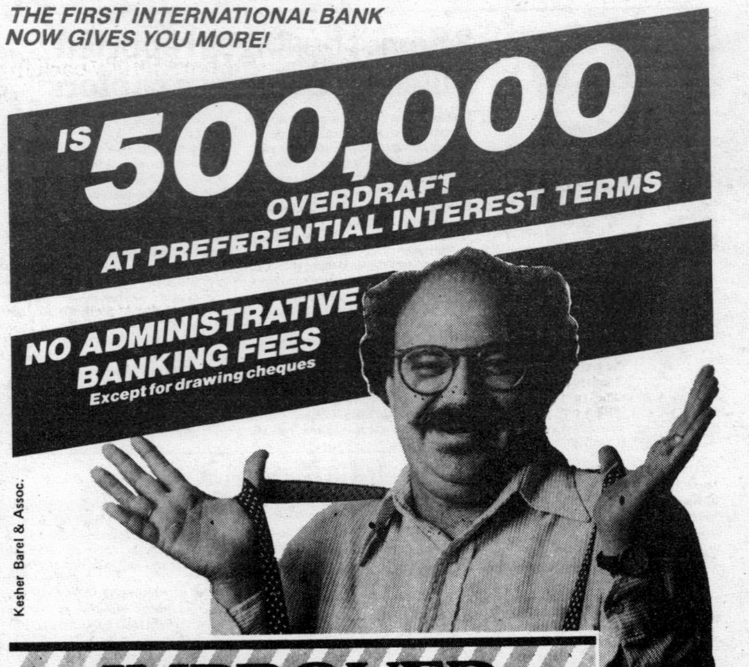

IMPROVED
CURRENT ACCOUNT
("OSH MESHUPAR")
for personal account holders

Another innovative first from First International Bank — this time for personal current account holders.
IMPROVED CURRENT ACCOUNT ("Osh Meshupar") — special benefits available exclusively to holders of personal accounts with First International Bank.
1. Overdraft drawing facilities increased to IS 500,000* at preferential interest terms.
2. Exemption from administrative banking fees — not including cheques drawn on the account or cash withdrawals from the teller. All other transactions — foreign currency, securities, short-term shekel deposits (Tafas and Pakam), cheque deposits, standing orders, automatic teller transactions, etc., etc. — are free.

If you don't yet have an account with the First International Bank, this is your chance. Now is the time to join all the other First International Bank customers who always benefit from bonuses and innovations in the fields of investment, savings and service. Today, in addition, they also benefit from the special bonuses of the Improved Current Account scheme.

* Granting of credit is conditional on appropriate securities.

THE FIRST INTERNATIONAL BANK OF ISRAEL LTD.

THE JERUSALEM POST

Vol. LIII, No. 16073 Wednesday, November 27, 1985 • Kislev 14, 5746 • Rabia Awal 14, 1406 IS620 (Eilat IS530)

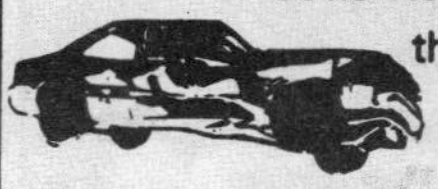

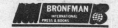

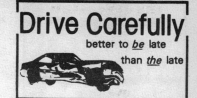

Defends rescue operation

Mubarak holds back from blaming Libya

CAIRO (Reuter). – President Hosni Mubarak said yesterday that the hijackers of the Egyptian plane taken to Malta this week, whom he identified as Palestinians "not from the PLO," were led by a man now in neighbouring Libya. But he ruled out a retaliatory war with Libya.

He said one of the hijackers' leaders was in Tripoli and even gave his hotel room number – 401 at the Grand Hotel.

But he refused to name the man or to disclose if Egypt had established that Libya was behind the Saturday night hijacking of an Egyptair Boeing 737 on an Athens-Cairo flight.

Asked if Libya was involved, Mubarak replied: "As a head of state, I cannot disclose this."

Forces in areas bordering Libya were placed on alert during the hijack. But Mubarak ruled out hostilities yesterday when reporters asked him if he had considered a "military option."

"We never call for war but we call for peace and if we ever have to go to war, it is because we want to bring peace," he replied.

Earlier Egyptian Defence Minister Field-Marshal Abdel-Halim Abu Ghazala told reporters Egypt had information Libya was responsible for the incident.

Libya was reported to have denied any involvement.

In other remarks after talks with Abu Ghazala, Mubarak said only six commandos took part in the rescue operation at Malta's Luqa airport.

The commandos fired only seven bullets, three of which hit a hijacker who was later "finished off" with a fire-axe by the plane's captain, Mubarak said. Some 60 people died in the hijacking, most of them during the rescue operation.

The president, responding to those who blamed Egypt for the deaths, said most were killed by shrapnel, phosphorous grenades thrown by the gunmen or smoke suffocation.

He said the commandos tried to save as many passengers as possible and 41 out of 97 passengers survived.

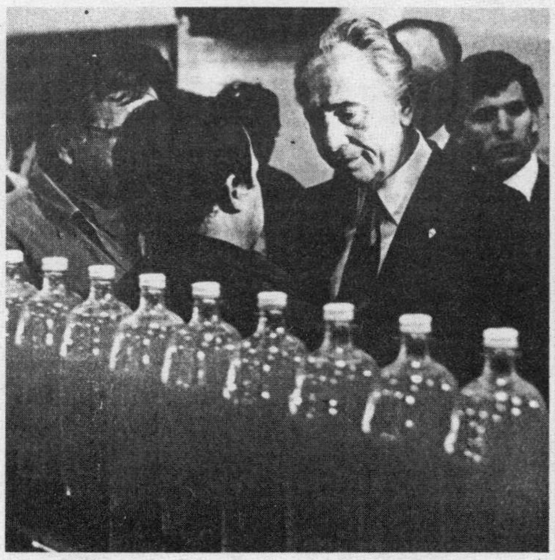

Prime Minister Peres tours the Crystal soft drink factory during his visit to Bat Yam yesterday. (Andre Brutmann)

Top official implicated in Pollard spy case

Post Defence Staff

A senior official has been implicated in the Jonathan Pollard spy case, *The Jerusalem Post* learned last night from authoritative sources.

An internal investigation has shown that the contact between the Israeli official and Pollard was unknown to top ministers and the Mossad.

Pollard, 31, a civilian intelligence analyst for the U.S. Navy, was arrested outside the Israel Embassy in Washington on Thursday on charges of giving secret documents to a foreign government.

Press reports yesterday based on an account in *The Washington Post,* identified the official implicated in the Pollard case as Rafael Eitan (no relation to the Tehiya MK and former chief of general staff). Eitan served as adviser to Begin and Shamir on terrorism.

Rafael (Rafi) Eitan, now in the limelight as a result of press reports linking him to the Pollard spy controversy, has spent most of his professional life in the shadowy world of the secret services. Reputedly the man who knocked out Adolf Eichmann in a Buenos Aires street when an Israeli team snatched the Nazi war criminal in Argentina in 1960, Eitan eventually became head of operations in the Mossad, Israel's senior security service.

Known as Rafi *Hamasriah* (Rafi the stinker) to distinguish him from the other Rafael Eitan (Raful). Eitan stayed on in the Mossad until the mid '70s, when Ariel Sharon became then prime minister Yitzhak Rabin's adviser on security affairs.

Sharon coopted Eitan as his assistant. But this honeymoon with the Labour government was shortlived and in March 1976, Sharon and Eitan left the Labour embrace.

Eitan went into private business and became a member of the Herut central committee.

He returned to security affairs when the Likud came to power and Menachem Begin named him adviser on terror in the Prime Minister's Office in July 1978, succeeding Amihai Paglin, who was killed in a car accident.

Begin did not concern himself much with anti-terror activities and gave his adviser much leeway. Eitan's status received a further boost when Sharon became defence minister in 1981.

A few months after the beginning of the Lebanon war, Eitan caused some controversy when he remarked

(Continued on Page 2, Col. 2)

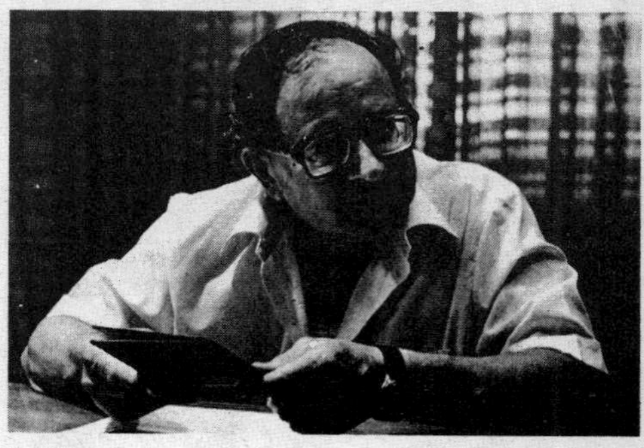

Rafi Eitan (David Rubinger)

Hassan disinvites Peres

RABAT (AP). – King Hassan II of Morocco yesterday said he did not anticipate having any "direct contacts" with Prime Minister Shimon Peres.

On Monday, Hassan had told reporters that Peres "sent word that he would like to see me. I replied that I would receive him with great pleasure, but told him 'you and I cannot be just tourists.'"

Peres publicly responded later that day that he would be happy to meet with Hassan. He reiterated his willingness yesterday.

But yesterday, the king told a group of French reporters at the royal palace that his comments should not have been interpreted as an invitation to face-to-face discussions, but rather a general offer intended only to demonstrate that the Arab side was open to discussions.

"If Mr. Peres has something concrete to propose, he can put it in an envelope addressed to the UN secretary general," Hassan told the reporters.

Hospitalized Tunisian said to be leader of hijack group

VALLETTA (Reuter). – Maltese authorities said yesterday that several people on board the Egyptair plane seized in flight over the weekend had named a Tunisian, now recovering from wounds in a Valletta hospital, as leader of the hijack group.

Government spokesman Paul Mifsud said the passengers identified the leader as Omar Marzouki, 20, from Tunisia. He said a magistrate had started questioning Marzouki about the hijacking, and if there was sufficient evidence against him he would be charged under Maltese law.

Mifsud, speaking at a news conference, also corrected the hijacking death toll so far from 60 to 59. He said the number of survivors was 39, making a total of 98 passengers and crew, including the five hijackers.

He said the figure of 60 dead which had been given yesterday had included a Canadian baby who had been counted twice.

In Tunis, Tunisian government sources said yesterday that the passport in Marzouki's name was false and that no passport in that name had been issued.

The official news agency TAP issued a similar denial three days ago in response to what it said were news agency reports stating that one of the hijackers had a Tunisian passport in the name of Omar Marzouki.

Maltese authorities said earlier that the wounded hijacker, one of a group of Arab extremists who seized the plane on a flight from Athens to Cairo on Saturday, was out of danger after surgery.

Pollard in court today on spy charge

By WOLF BLITZER
Jerusalem Post Correspondent

WASHINGTON. – Jonathan Jay Pollard is scheduled to appear today at a preliminary hearing in a U.S. District Court in Washington on charges of spying for Israel.

Federal prosecutors, at the court appearance, are expected to make public a considerable amount of specific information on Pollard's alleged espionage activities.

Reagan administration officials, hoping to limit the overall damage to American-Israeli relations, yesterday again expressed hope that the Israeli government would release the results of its own internal investigation in advance of today's hearing.

"We have requested the full and prompt cooperation of the government of Israel in determining all the facts concerning any Israeli involvement in this case and the Israelis have assured us that they will cooperate," State Department spokesman Charles Redman said.

The spokesman, responding to another question, said there clearly were "links" in the case to the Israeli Embassy in Washington. He did not elaborate.

U.S. officials are extremely upset over the incident, although they continued yesterday to try to ease the crisis somewhat. They do not want to see it overly weaken American-Israeli relations.

Thus, White House spokesman Larry Speakes said he did not expect the incident to permanently damage U.S.-Israeli relations.

Another U.S. official said Israel's image in America was deteriorating with every day of relative silence from Jerusalem.

"The U.S. has had a long and close relationship with Israel, and I would expect that relationship to continue," he said.

The Washington Post yesterday wrote that Pollard, after being con-

(Continued on Page 2, Col. 2)

Peres: Israel is willing to discuss Golan with Syria

By WOLF BLITZER
Jerusalem Post Correspondent

WASHINGTON. – Prime Minister Peres says he would be willing to discuss all issues in any peace negotiations with Syria, including the Golan Heights.

In an interview published yesterday in *The Washington Post,* Peres said he would welcome direct negotiations with Syria. But he said, "If you ask me, 'Are the Syrians ready?' to join the peace process, my answer is no."

The prime minister said that in his view, the Syrians have a "higher aim than peace in their political priorities. They feel that for them it is easier to lead the Arab world against Israel than for peace with Israel."

But, he continued, if Syria came to the conference table, Israel would be prepared to discuss all outstanding issues. This would include the Golan Heights.

"We have decided on the Golan Heights," he said. "We have a position. So, we would come with our position, and the Syrians are free to come with their position. I mean, don't expect us to come with the Syrian position."

Mendelson 'clinically dead'

VALLETTA (AP). – Nitzan Mendelson, 23, of Kibbutz Hulata, who was shot by the hijackers of the Egyptair jet, was pronounced clinically dead yesterday, Maltese authorities said.

She was in intensive care at St. Luke's Hospital, according to government spokesman Paul Mifsud.

She was one of five passengers – two Israelis and three Americans – shot execution style while the plane was parked on the airport tarmac on Sunday morning.

The other Israeli, Tamar Artzi, 24, of Kibbutz Revivim, was shot in the cheek and the thigh, and thrown onto the tarmac, where she lay in the rain for three hours before she was helped.

Artzi was quoted as saying the hijackers first freed 11 women of other nationalities and then asked any Israeli women to step forward.

"I thought they would allow us to get out of the plane, like the previous women, so I got up and identified myself as an Israeli and then they shot me and threw me out of the plane onto the runway," Artzi was quoted as saying on CBS-TV.

"I wanted to ask the hijackers not to kill me, but he shot me twice," Artzi was quoted as telling reporters. "The moment I saw that he was ready to press the trigger, I couldn't say anything and I turned around, perhaps from shock, perhaps by instinct."

Mendelson saw the hijackers shoot Artzi and did not get out of her seat, but the hijackers had her passport and found her by using the passport picture. They tied her hands and dragged her off kicking and screaming before shooting her in the head and dumping her on the runway.

The two women were traveling together on their way to East Asia. They met after Artzi placed an advertisement in a newspaper looking for a traveling companion.

Sharir finally back from travels

Tourism Minister Avraham Sharir arrived at Ben-Gurion Airport last night after a controversial three-week visit to the U.S. He met with an unexpectedly large reception from a press that had severely criticized his absence from the country while the major Skal tourism conference was taking place here.

Sharir justified his trip, saying it was essential to give a boost to flagging Jewish tourism from the U.S. He added that the Skal organizers had known of his plans weeks in advance.

Sharir's wife, Rivka, who had accompanied him, was pale and emotional: "It is no wonder people want to leave the country, if this is the way people behave," she told the waiting reporters. "Who wants to live in such a country?" (Itim)

Interest to drop 1 per cent on loans and overdrafts

Interest rates on loans and overdrafts are due to go down by 1 per cent next week. The Bank of Israel yesterday announced it was cutting the rate it charges commercial banks by that amount.

The central bank said it would be the sixth time since the launching of the economic plan that interest rates have been reduced.

The bank said that after the reduction the prime interest rate will be around 3 per cent a month and the average cost of commercial credit will amount to some 4 per cent a month.

The central bank added that it will reduce interest rates it pays banks for their deposits by half a per cent instead of 1 per cent to prevent too large a reduction in the interest rates the banks pay on shekel deposits.

Reagan approves delay of arms sale to Amman

WASHINGTON (AP). – President Reagan has signed legislation that formally postpones a $1.9 billion arms sale to Jordan until March 1 unless Jordan and Israel open meaningful peace talks before then.

Faced with overwhelming opposition in Congress to the sale, Reagan had been forced earlier to accept the delay of the sale of aircraft, missiles and other weapons. He signed the delay into law Monday.

Plan to build new coal port in south may be scrapped

By AVI TEMKIN
Post Economic Reporter

The Ports Authority and the Electric Corporation may be forced to scrap their plan to build a coal port to serve the Ashkelon power station now being constructed, and to transfer part of the $400 million accumulated for the project to the Treasury.

Senior economic sources who disclosed this yesterday added there is little sense in building the port, considering present budgetary constraints. The cabinet and the Ministerial Economic Committee have approved the project, but there has been a running debate about its location, with the Transport Minister favouring Ashdod and other ministers Eilat.

The cabinet will get a formal proposal to scrap the plans for the port, the sources said. "The Energy Ministry and the Ports Authority will have to find another way of feeding the station with coal," they said.

The cabinet is due to hold a special meeting today on the proposed budgetary framework for the coming fiscal year. The Finance Ministry's proposal totals $21.2 billion and takes into account a $600m. slash which the Treasury is demanding.

Finance Minister Yitzhak Moda'i boycotted Sunday's meeting in protest against what he called "sectoral and party campaigns against the budget." It is expected that he will attend today's meeting.

Economic observers in Jerusalem said yesterday they expect the cabinet to approve a slash of close to $500m.

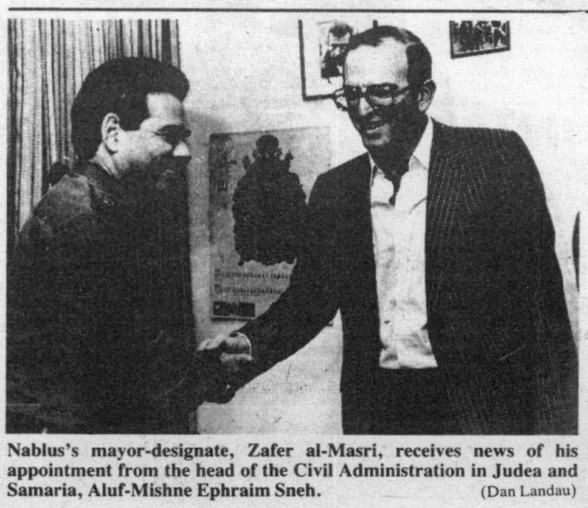

Nablus's mayor-designate, Zafer al-Masri, receives news of his appointment from the head of the Civil Administration in Judea and Samaria, Aluf-Mishne Ephraim Sneh. (Dan Landau)

Civilian mayor to take over in Nablus 'within weeks'

By JOSHUA BRILLIANT
Jerusalem Post Reporter

BEIT EL. – The military government in the West Bank announced yesterday it was planning to hand the administration of Nablus over to the local Chamber of Commerce within weeks and appoint its president, Zafer al-Masri, as mayor.

The move is expected to be the first of other local appointments in a drive to reintroduce a measure of local rule in several major West Bank cities which have been run by IDF officers since Israel clamped down on the Palestinian National Guidance Commettee three years ago.

The behind-the-scenes contacts with Nablus notables culminated on November 6 with a formal request by the Chamber of Commerce to assume the administration of the West Bank's most populous town. At a hurriedly-called meeting with the Chamber of Commerce leaders at his headquarters here yesterday, Aluf-Mishne Ephraim Sneh, the Civil Administrator, formally announced the authorities' approval.

Masri, 44, an uncle of Jordan's foreign minister, Taher al-Masri, was deputy mayor in 1982.

The mayor-designate, who views his appointment as a temporary one, pending elections in the town, told a reporter that as long as the area is under occupation, and the Arabs cannot terminate it, they should at least make life as bearable as possible.

THE JERUSALEM POST
INTERNATIONAL EDITION
The perfect gift for your friends and relations overseas

THE JERUSALEM POST

Vol. LIII, No. 16100 Sunday, December 29, 1985 • Tevet 17, 5746 • Rabia Tani 16, 1406 IS620 (Eilat IS530)

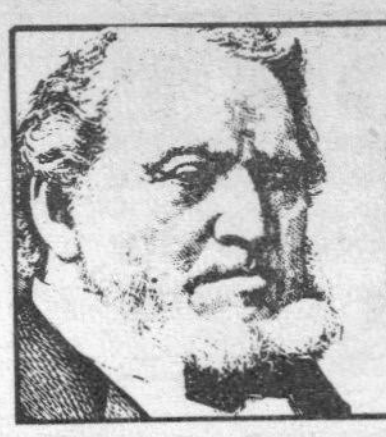

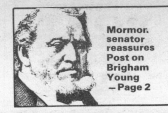

Mormon senator reassures Post on Brigham Young – Page 2

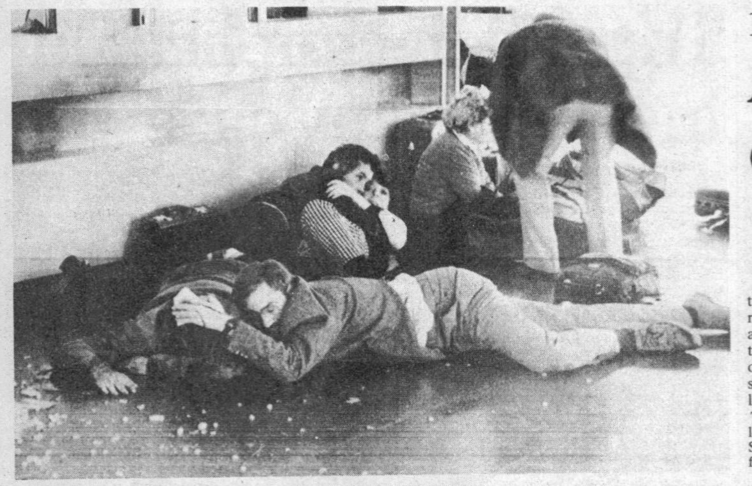

18 slain, 119 wounded in Rome and Vienna

Airport massacres blamed on Abu Nidal terror squad

Compiled from reports
by AVI HOFFMAN,
BENNY MORRIS,
LISA PALMIERI-BILLIG
and agencies

The renegade Abu Nidal faction of the PLO was probably responsible for the terrorist attacks at the El Al counters at the Rome and Vienna Airports on Friday, a senior military source told *The Jerusalem Post* last night.

The grenade and shooting attacks left 18 dead and 119 wounded. Several terrorists were among the fatalities.

A pamphlet found on one of the terrorists, claiming that the attacks were in response to the Israel bombing raid on PLO headquarters in Tunisia, tended to reinforce the Foreign Ministry's contention that the PLO was responsible.

But a telephone caller to a radio station in Spain, claiming to represent the Abu Nidal group, said the group was responsible. This is the usual way that Abu Nidal has claimed responsibility for attacks.

The military source said that following the severe blows to the PLO's "moderate" image suffered in the Larnaca and Achille Lauro episodes, it is logical to assume that the organization would be wary about again incurring the wrath of world public opinion. In addition, PLO chairman Yasser Arafat last month assured Egyptian President Mubarak that he was forswearing terror outside of Israel's borders.

The Abu Nidal group suffers from no such constraints and is quite capable of carrying out such an attack, the source said. This would serve the double purpose of hitting Israelis and westerners, and at the same time perhaps implicating the mainstream PLO.

The renegade PLO group is headed by Sabri El-Banna, known

(Continued on Page 2, Col. 2)

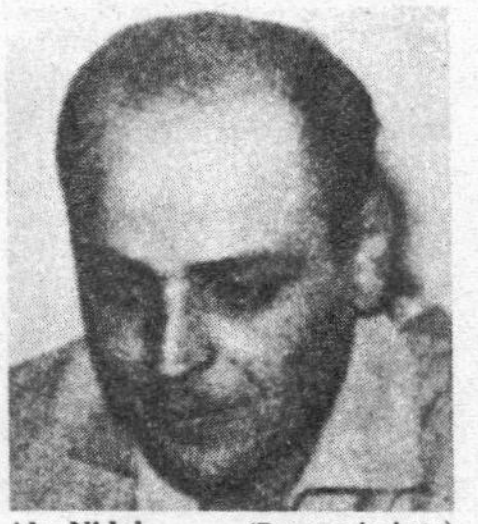

Abu Nidal (Reuter telephoto)

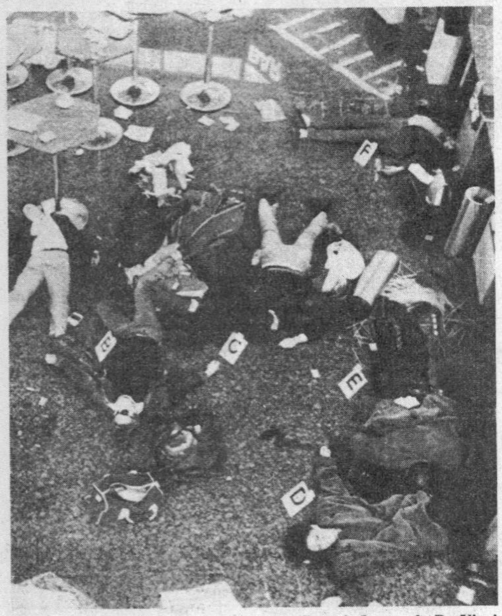

Injured passengers lie on the ground at Rome's Leonardo Da Vinci Airport during Friday's terror attack (top). Tagged bodies on the floor of the airport's international lounge after the massacre (above). (Reuter)

Israeli security men reacted swiftly

By ILONA HENRY in Vienna
and LIZA PALMIERI-BILLIG in Rome
Jerusalem Post Correspondents and Agencies

Fast action by Israeli security men prevented even worse bloodshed in Friday's airport massacres at Rome and Vienna, eyewitnesses said yesterday.

In Vienna, the Israelis immediately sprang into action as the terrorists hurled grenades and sprayed waiting airline passengers with automatic fire.

In Rome, witnesses told similar stories, praising the courage of an El Al security man who returned fire despite being wounded.

Eighteen people were killed and 119 wounded in the two attacks. The dead in Italy included three terrorists.

In Vienna the terrorists threw Soviet-made grenades at people waiting in line at the El Al check-in desk. Nearby were people checking in for an Austrian charter flight to Greece.

An Israeli woman, Eti Gana, threw herself on her nine-month-old son Michael, but her husband Eli was reportedly killed on the spot.

An Austrian tourist, bound for Israel, described how Israeli security men reacted swiftly to the attack. "They saved our lives.

"The terrorists were confused and started to run while shooting incessantly in all directions. Outside the building they managed to hijack a Mercedes car and tried to escape. The Austrian police managed to kill one of the terrorists and wounded two others."

Another eyewitness said the local security forces reacted slowly, and continued: "The slaughter would have been much worse if the two Israeli security men hadn't gone into action. The Israelis saved our lives."

At Leonardo Da Vinci Airport, Rome, El Al passenger Giuseppe Benenati, from Turin, told reporters he was shaking hands with one of the airline's officials when the man was hit in the shoulder by a bullet.

"The Israeli instantly pulled out a gun and managed to hit the terrorist despite his own injury," said Benenati. "He showed a lot of courage

(Continued on Page 2, Col. 5)

ISRAELI CASUALTIES

By YITZHAK OKED

Two of those killed in the attack on the Vienna airport Friday were El Al passengers – Israeli citizen Ali Gana and an Australian identified as M. Karner. Gana's wife Otti and son Michael were slightly injured, as were seven El Al passengers who are nationals of countries other than Israel.

In the Rome attack, seven El Al employees, all Israelis, were wounded. One of them, Nir Cohen, suffered serious injuries.

Five El Al passengers were also lightly injured in Rome. It was not known last night whether any of them were Israelis.

Late last night, 108 passengers from Rome arrived at Ben-Gurion airport, including three of those who had sustained light injuries.

U.S. urges Israeli restraint

By WOLF BLITZER
Jerusalem Post Correspondent

WASHINGTON. – The U.S. is cautioning Israel against military retaliation against the Palestinian terrorist groups which could overly upset the Arab-Israeli peace process.

In the aftermath of Friday's terrorist attacks at the Rome and Vienna airports, U.S. officials have stopped short of actually opposing any Israeli retaliation. Instead, they have simply asked Israel to consider the broader ramifications of any specific actions.

Clearly, the Americans do not want Israel to strike out randomly against some PLO groups, at least until the exact identity of those terrorists responsible for the attacks is determined.

The White House yesterday refused to comment on a press report that President Ronald Reagan had appealed directly to Prime Minister Shimon Peres to exercise caution.

But U.S. officials confirmed that the President, in private messages to various Middle Eastern leaders, has urged them not to abandon the peace process. Reagan reportedly expressed hope that the U.S.-

(Continued on Back Page)

Peres: Terror strikes those who justify it

Prime Minister Peres on Friday expressed deep shock at the attacks at the Rome and Vienna airports and said that "anyone who justifies terror must understand that terror will also strike back at him."

A statement released by Peres's office said: "The Israeli government will defend its citizens at home and throughout the world and will continue to use all means to fight the terrorists." Peres also called on the nations of the world to "organize against all forms of terror."

Transport Minister Haim Corfu said on Friday on Israel Radio that he will initiate an international conference of ministers responsible for civil aviation to decide how to combat terror attacks.

Progressive List for Peace Knesset Members Mohammed Miari and Mattityahu Peled sent a telegram to Peres yesterday condemning the attacks as "criminal, murderous actions" intended to destroy the slender chance for peace. The two called on Peres not to respond to "Abu Nidal's provocations."

The Israel Communist Party (Rakah) released a statement yesterday "condemning the murder of innocents" at the two airports. The party called on the government "to react with restraint...and not make the situation more serious."

At the other end of the political spectrum, Tehiya leader Yuval Ne'eman blamed the prime minister for promoting "an image of Israel as having given up" that "has led the terrorists, the Syrians and even the Egyptians to take more aggressive stands and actions." Tehiya MK Geula Cohen called on the government to cease all talks with Egypt until the PLO offices in Cairo are closed.

Ras Burka killer given life sentence

SUEZ (AP). – A military court yesterday convicted policeman Suleiman Khater of murdering seven Israeli tourists and sentenced him to life imprisonment at hard labour. The court found Khater had been in his right mind, but had not known his victims were Israelis when he fired.

Life imprisonment here generally means 25 years, with one-fourth of the sentence commuted for good conduct.

The sentence is subject to approval by military authorities, Khater's attorney said.

A senior police office in Suez said that the sentence would probably need approval from President Hosni Mubarak.

There is no appeal, except the possibility of a plea for clemency.

Khater was convicted of unpremeditated murder in the October 5 shooting death of four children, two women and a man, all Israelis, at Ras Burka in the Sinai where he was posted. He had given no plausible motive for his actions, the court said.

The killings caused serious political problems between Israel and Egypt. Israel charged that some victims had bled to death because Egyptian officers had refused to allow medical help on the spot to reach them for several hours.

Two minority opposition parties held rallies in support of Khater, and scores of people were arrested on Friday as they tried to hold a sit-in demonstration at Cairo's al-Azhar Mosque.

Last week there were five days of sometimes violent demonstrations at Zagazig University, where Khater is a third-year external law student.

While some opposition newspapers have portrayed Khater as a hero or a martyr, the state-owned press was silent until the last few days when they began attacking the opposition characterization.

Yesterday, Ibrahim Seda, editor of the state-owned weekly *Akhbar el-Yom,* admitted that the national press' reticence was wrong.

"We erred, and I am the first to have done so, in ignoring this case," he wrote in his weekly column.

"If the press had done its duty and given the case its due coverage, we would not have left the field open to people who have tried to distort it, fabricate details and inflame passions."

He gave examples of what he said were fabrications, including that the Israeli tourists tore up an Egyptian flag and spat on it and that the women among them were "almost nude," which would have been an extreme provocation to Moslem sensibilities.

Seda wrote that some opposition-ists had tried to use the case as ammunition against the peace treaty.

There have been few calls for abrogation, but most opposition parties including the Wafd, the only significant opposition in the People's Assembly, have demanded a freeze in normalization until an overall Middle East settlement is reached.

Although the charge against Khater, a 24-year-old sergeant, is punishable by no more than a life sentence, the prosecution asked for death under a legal technicality.

Handing down judgement, the court said it had taken into consideration his depressed psychological condition at the time of the crime, and also that the victims had been in a place that was not fit for tourism, Khater's attorney said.

The trial was in a military base near Suez.

The trial began in mid-November. Mubarak's referral of the case to a court-martial, where trials are generally much speedier than in civilian courts, indicated Egypt's concern over the possible ramifications in their already strained relations with Israel.

The Khater case has become something of a *cause celebre* for Egypt's opposition parties, based mainly on Mubarak's assigning it to a military court. The border police, to which Khater belonged, is a non-military force, posted on the Sinai border under terms of the 1979 Egyptian-Israeli peace treaty.

Officials, but not parents, satisfied with punishment

By BENNY MORRIS
and BARBARA AMOUYAL
Jerusalem Post Reporters

There was general satisfaction in Jerusalem with the life sentence with hard labour handed down yesterday to Suleiman Khater, the Egyptian security man convicted of murdering seven Israelis at Ras Burka on October 5.

But some relatives of the victims did not share in the general satisfaction, with at least one father calling the sentence "completely unacceptable."

Israeli Ambassador to Cairo Moshe Sasson said that Israel respects the Egyptian judicial system, and reportedly noted that in recent days the Egyptian press has begun to give details of what actually happened in Ras Burka.

Sasson and Foreign Ministry officials in Jerusalem said that Israel is still waiting for the official Egyptian report on the killings and their aftermath, when, according to eyewitnesses, the soldiers at Ras Burka failed to give the victims first aid and

(Continued on Page 2, Col. 2)

Syrian missiles diplomatic, not military threat

By HIRSH GOODMAN
Post Defence Correspondent

The Syrian SAM-6 and SAM-8 surface-to-air missiles recently deployed on Lebanese territory have been positioned very close to the Syrian-Lebanese border, and military experts here believe their primary function is to protect the SAM-2 missile sites the Syrians established on their border with Lebanon in recent weeks.

Though the missile batteries that have been placed in Lebanon do not pose a significant operational threat to Israel aircraft over and above that posed by the SAM-2s, they do constitute a sensitive diplomatic-political problem for Israel.

Defence Minister Yitzhak Rabin, who is interested in minimizing the tensions created by the new deployment, said Friday that all the Syrian batteries in Lebanon are north of the Beirut-Damascus highway – in other words, outside the zone of Lebanon that is of immediate interest to Israeli security needs along the northern frontier.

Rabin warned, however, that Israel would deal with the problem "in its own time and according to its own needs."

Now that the deployment of the missiles inside Lebanon has been made public – in a slip of the tongue by Prime Minister Peres while addressing the Israel Editors Committee on Thursday – Israel will have to deal with the problem. "How we do so is a political decision, not a military one," *The Jerusalem Post* was told by a senior military source last night.

While Israel may have not been pleased with Syria's decision in late November to deploy the long-range SAM-2s on its border with Lebanon, thus challenging Israel's freedom to patrol over eastern and northern Lebanon, no military action could be considered given that the SAM-2s were deployed on Syrian territory.

The situation with the SAM-6 and SAM-8 batteries, however, is different: "There is no doubt that the ball is now in our court," *The Post* was told by a senior Israeli government source. "Failing to react could be seen as a sign of weakness. But if we do act, very delicate diplomatic processes afoot in this region could be jeopardized," he said.

The source was referring to the American-sponsored peace initiative to bring Israel and Jordan together, and to King Hussein's planned summit with Syrian President Hafez Assad.

Experts here believe that the chances of the Syrians unilaterally moving the SAM batteries out of Lebanon are relatively small. According to these experts, the Syrians have nothing to lose by leaving them there (other than the missiles themselves) and a lot to gain, specifically in inter-Arab relations. By moving the missiles into Lebanon, these experts continue, Assad ostensibly moved to protect his SAM-2 batteries – but in fact posed a direct diplomatic challenge to Israel that is far wider than just Israel's ability to patrol the skies of Lebanon.

The Syrians, *The Post* was told, do not want war. But they also do not want movement on the peace front between Israel and Jordan, nor do they want the "idyllic situation" on Israel's northern border to continue unchallenged.

"We have to see Assad's decision to deploy these missiles in that context, not just the narrow one of protecting the SAM-2s, and we will have to act accordingly," a senior government source told *The Post.* "Assad has called all the moves until this point," he continued. "It is clear around the cabinet table here, that the time has come for Israel to take the initiative.

Syrians complain to UN Security Council

UNITED NATIONS (AP). – Syria said in a complaint to UN Secretary-General Javier Perez de Cuellar on Friday that Israel's air patrols over Lebanon posed a threat to the security of Syria.

ONLY ONE BANK OFFERS YOU
IS 1,000,000 OVERDRAFT
AT PREFERENTIAL INTEREST TERMS

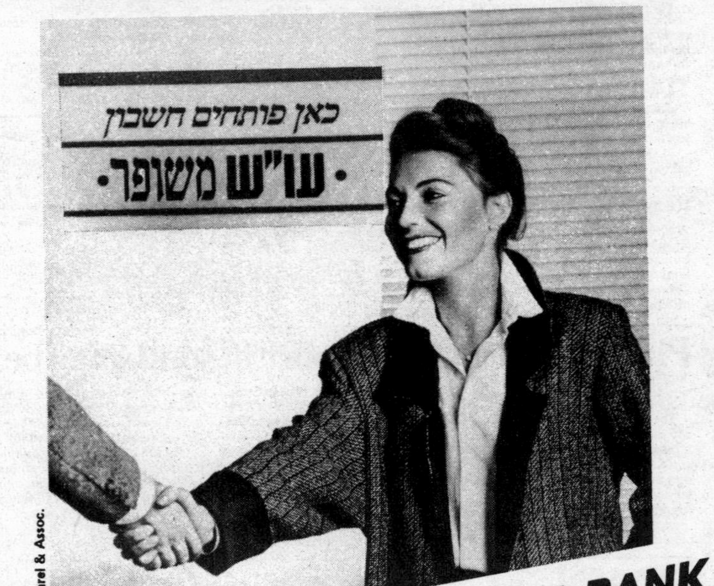

THE FIRST INTERNATIONAL BANK

The First International Bank is the only bank offering personal account holders a million shekel overdraft at preferential interest terms (subject to the appropriate securities).

If you've already opened an IMPROVED CURRENT ACCOUNT at First International Bank, then you're already reaping the benefits, if you haven't – then it's worth hurrying to open one.

In addition to the large overdraft, you'll also be exempt from administrative banking fees (except for drawing cheques). In fact, you're losing money every day that you delay in opening an IMPROVED CURRENT ACCOUNT.

Further details from any branch of First International Bank and Poalei Agudat Yisrael Bank.

* Granting of credit is conditional on appropriate securities.

THE FIRST INTERNATIONAL BANK OF ISRAEL LTD.

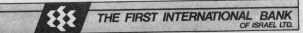

THE JERUSALEM POST

Vol. LIV, No. 16139 Wednesday, February 12, 1986 • Adar I 3, 5746 • Jomada Tani 3, 1406 NIS 0.62 (Eilat NIS 0.53)

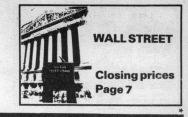

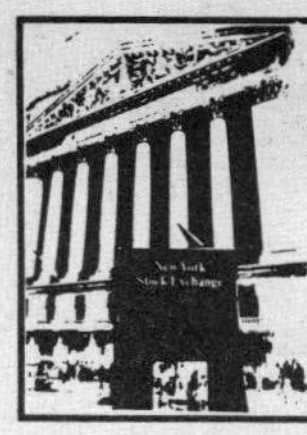
WALL STREET
Closing prices Page 7

Zamir quits as A-G; 3 mooted as possible successors

By DAVID HOROVITZ
Jerusalem Post Reporter

Three candidates last night emerged as likely successors to Attorney-General Yitzhak Zamir, who announced his resignation yesterday.

The three are Yoram Bar-Sela, deputy attorney-general; Prof. Daniel Friedman of Tel Aviv University, who was on the Bejski Commission investigating the bank shares collapse and is one of the country's leading law professors; and Meir Gabai, director-general of the Justice Ministry.

Sources in the legal establishment felt that the choice would finally be between Friedman and Gabai. Gabai is said to be acceptable to both major parties and has years of experience in the Justice Ministry. Plia Albeck, another senior Justice Ministry official, was also named as a possible candidate.

A political appointment was considered to be out of the question.

Zamir said yesterday that after seven-and-a-half years, he felt that "the time had come" to move on.

Justice Ministry sources said last night that Zamir's move had been prompted by growing criticism of his decisions by right wing MKs and groups, which had led him to fear that after the rotation of the premiership he would be relieved of his post and replaced by an attorney-general whose decisions would be more acceptable to the Likud and right-wing parties.

The sources said that by announcing his resignation now, Zamir was giving Premier Shimon Peres, rather than Yitzhak Shamir, the opportunity to appoint a replacement.

Zamir said yesterday that he would not play any part in selecting his successor.

The attorney-general is appointed by government approval of a recommendation by the justice minister. In

(Continued on Page 2, Col. 2)

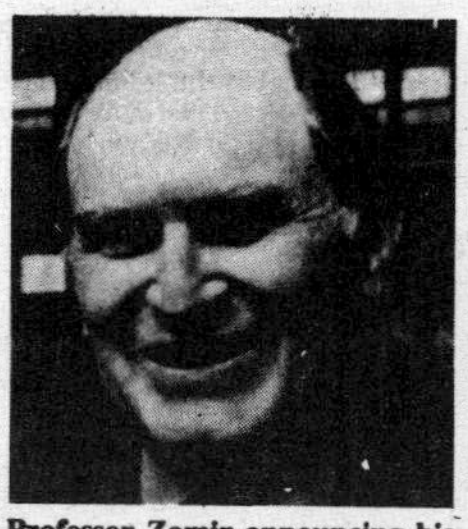
Professor Zamir announcing his resignation yesterday.
(Rahamim Israeli)

Hussein hopes Assad will join peace process

By YEHUDA LITANI and BENNY MORRIS
Jerusalem Post Correspondents

King Hussein of Jordan now hopes that Syria will join the peace process following his meeting with President Hafez Assad, planned for this month in Amman.

Diplomatic sources last night said the king hopes that if the Syrians do not agree to participate in the process, they will at least silently condone Jordan's participation, with or without the PLO.

According to these sources, the Jordanians had hoped the Amman meeting would take place in the next few days. But after Jordan premier Zaid a-Rifai's meeting with Syrian officials in Damascus this week, it seems likely that these will be a delay.

The Jordanians were now interested in Syrian participation in the process with or without the PLO, the sources said.

Special U.S. envoy Watt Cluvarius flew last night to Cairo to brief the Egyptians on the latest developments in the Jordanian and Israeli negotiating positions following the PLO's negative response to the latest American proposals.

The BBC Arabic service reported yesterday that U.S. Assistant Secretary of State Richard Murphy was expected to come to the Middle East soon to further intensive U.S. efforts in the peace process.

Murphy's trip to the Middle East will be finalized when the U.S. has received accurate information on Syria's attitude, the BBC said.

PLO chairman Yasser Arafat is expected in Cairo this month for talks on the peace process with Egyptian officials. According to Egyptian newspapers, the Egyptians will try to press Arafat to accept the American stand.

It had been expected that Arafat would meet President Hosni Mubarak and King Hussein together in Cairo. But, according to the Egyptian press, Arafat will meet Mubarak separately after the Egyptian president has met Hussein.

Diplomatic sources said last night that the peace process was not in "deep freeze" but rather, "fluid." Only if the Syrian government bluntly refused to enter the negotiations or condone Jordan's participation would peace efforts return to square one, they said.

Meanwhile, Israel has asked for "renewed reassurances" about America's basic positions on the PLO following the State Department spokesman's statement about the Palestinian problem on Monday.

Spokesman Charles Redman stressed that the U.S. believed that "the Palestinian problem is more than a refugee question."

Redman said there should be no confusion between [UN Security Council] Resolution 242 which

(Continued on Page 2, Col. 6)

Shcharansky home at last

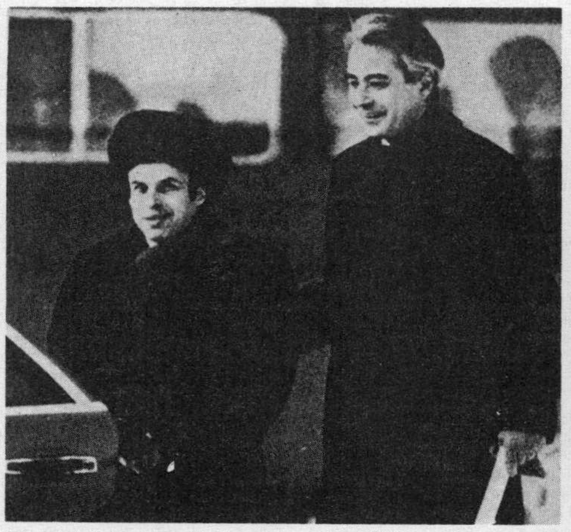
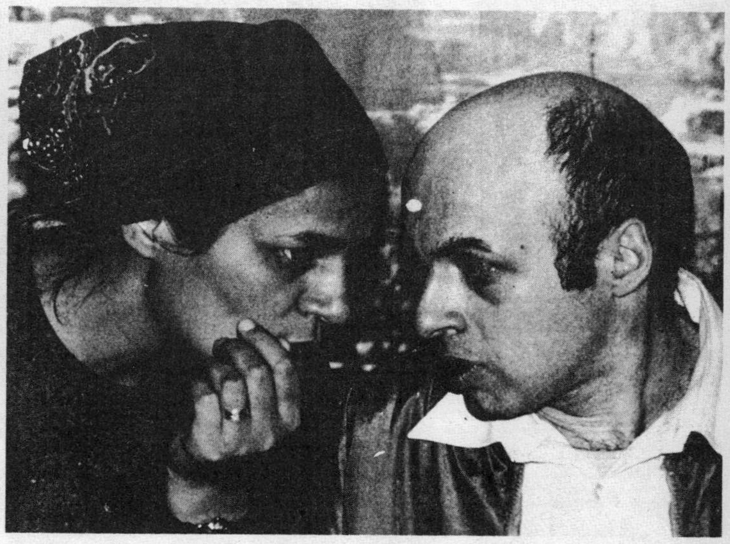

First steps to freedom. Shcharansky on the Glienicke Bridge between East and West Berlin. He is accompanied by the U.S. Ambassador to West Germany, Richard Burt. In picture on right Shcharansky with his wife Avital soon after landing at Ben-Gurion Airport yesterday evening.
(AFP, Brutmann)

After 12-year struggle, 'the happiest day'

By MICHAL YUDELMAN

BEN-GURION AIRPORT. – "This is the happiest day in our lives," Anatoly Shcharansky told thousands of well-wishers who greeted the released Prisoner of Zion and his wife, Avital, on their arrival in Israel last night.

Shcharansky was hugged and kissed by Prime Minister Peres and Vice-Premier Shamir moments after the Westwind plane that brought him from Frankfurt landed. Government ministers, the chief rabbis and Knesset members crowded around the Shcharanskys.

"How are you?" Peres asked.

"Everything's fine," Shcharansky answered in Hebrew.

As he passed the hundreds of journalists, photographers and television crewmen straining against the police barriers, Shcharansky waved a victory salute and smiled.

Inside the terminal building, Absorption Minister Ya'acov Tsur handed Shcharansky a new immigrant's card giving him all the rights and privileges of an Israeli citizen.

A large crowd of friends and activists for Soviet Jewry waiting inside the terminal burst into song with "Am Yisrael Hai" and "Hevenu Shalom Aleichem," applauding as Shcharansky walked in holding Avital by the hand, with Peres and the ministers.

Shcharansky said: "Brothers and sisters, the Israeli nation, during the years that I was in prison, there were very difficult days. I was in total isolation. For years I received no word from Israel. But there was not one day, not one moment, that I did not feel a bond with you all. And even when I was in a solitary cell, I sang an Israeli song."

Shcharansky, Avital and Peres spoke to U.S. President Reagan on the telephone, thanking him for his efforts in releasing Shcharansky. Peres said later that Reagan said he was "very much moved by this event."

Peres told the president: "I want to tell you how much our people, and I among them, feel in the face of this tremendous event. For us it is a historic and very emotional event.

"Thank you, in the name of the people and government of Israel, for your concern and your efforts that brought this very special man here, to his homeland, after 12 years in prison."

The prime minister told the president that the freeing of Shcharansky was a "great victory" for the human spirit and for freedom-loving people.

Avital told Reagan: "I just wanted to say thank you."

Speaking in English, Shcharansky told Reagan "Dear Mr. President, I am under strong stress now, sitting between our prime minister and my Avital. That's why don't be surprised if my speech wouldn't be smooth. But there are some things which I feel myself obliged to tell you. First of all, I know how great was your role in this greatest event of my and my wife's life...the fact that I could join my people today in Israel, and of course we are both very deeply grateful to you for this.

"Second, as you know very well, I was never an American spy. But I had wide contacts with many American politicians, journalists, lawyers and other public figures as a spokesman of (the) Jewish national movement and (the) Helsinki group movement And that's why I know very well how deeply the concern of all of your people and the problems of human rights all over the world.

"I know what a great role is played by your country in these problems. And I want to ask you to inform all your people about our deepest grati-

Further reports and background on the Shcharansky saga on pages 2 and 3.

tude to these people and this country for everything they do for the human rights in the world and for Jews who want to emigrate from Russia to Israel in particular. Thank you very much."

Peres later reported that Reagan had promised before the Geneva summit meeting that he would make all efforts to free the Prisoners of Zion, and he also mentioned the name of Anatoly Shcharansky, "and that's what he indeed did do."

Reagan also said that a major role in the release was played by West German Chancellor Helmut Kohl, "who also should be thanked."

Reagan said that he would continue his efforts to release other Prisoners of Zion. Then he said: "I wish you 'mazal tov', with all my heart," Peres reported.

Peres last night called both Shultz and Chancellor Kohl to thank them for their part in Shcharansky's release. Shcharansky himself also spoke to Shultz, who thanked the dissident for his work on behalf of freedom.

At the welcoming ceremony, Peres said: "It's very moving to see a man like Natan (Anatoly's Hebrew name) who for 12 years in solitude, and illness, without having anyone to turn to, stood like a rock with his Jewish pride and Zionist loyalty, against a giant power. This proves that you can imprison a body, but you cannot imprison the soul. You can shut in a man, but if his faith is strong, you cannot beat him."

"I have the same feeling about Avital Shcharansky," Peres continued. "She fought for years, without rest, without despair, leaving no stone unturned."

Peres listed the remaining Prisoners of Zion in Soviet jails and said the fight to release them would continue.

"Words are too poor to express this moment. Natan – welcome and may you be very happy among us."

Interviewed yesterday in the USSR, Shcharansky's mother Ida Milgrom, and his brother, said they would now apply for exit visas. Until now, they said, they refrained from doing so because they did not want to leave Anatoly behind.

Shamir said that Anatoly and Avital were symbols of the fight to release Prisoners of Zion, and that their victory would strengthen the Jews who remain in Russia, proving to them that their day of freedom would also come.

President Herzog, in a special address, described Shcharansky as "a symbol and a flag" for Soviet Jews wanting to emigrate.

In a message broadcast on Israel Army Radio, Herzog said the mathematician's struggle for human rights was "a source of identification, evidence of the flame of Jewish courage that cannot be suppressed."

Shcharansky, in remarks at the ceremony, denounced the KGB and said it had recently spoken of a "new conspiracy" of Jewish activists and Jewish journalists against the Soviet regime. He said he had always felt how great the KGB's hatred of Jewish activists was and how great was their desire that "this day" – the day of his coming to Israel would never arrive.

"Twelve years ago I said to Avital, on our parting: I'll see you soon in Jerusalem. But my way here became as long and as hard as the Galut (exile of the Jews). Because in these years the Pharaohs of our time decided to announce a new conspiracy of Jews, from Russia and other countries, against the regime. I know how

(Continued on back page)

Mandela won't be part of East-West prisoner swap

By ROY ISACOWITZ
Jerusalem Post Reporter
and Agencies

South Africa yesterday aborted the expected release of jailed black nationalist leader Nelson Mandela as part of the East-West prisoner swap, saying that Pretoria's conditions for freeing Mandela had not been met.

Israel was reportedly involved to some degree in the efforts to have Mandela included in the exchange of prisoners.

Justice Minister Kobie Coetzee said President P.W. Botha had set conditions under which he would have been prepared to free Mandela, including the release of Anatoly Shcharansky, Soviet dissident Andrei Sakharov and a South African soldier captured in Angola.

Nevertheless, a senior South African Foreign Ministry official was due to arrive in Israel yesterday in connection with Mandela, South African sources said.

South African Foreign Minister Roelofes "Pik" Botha was also reportedly due to fly to Geneva last night to organize the release. Unofficial sources said that Mandela, who has been in jail for 24 years, could be released as early as today.

It has been learned that the South African position was conveyed to the Kremlin via World Jewish Congress president Edgar Bronfman, who visited Moscow recently.

Only Monday did Shcharansky know

By WLADIMIR STRUMINSKI
Jerusalem Post Correspondent

WEST BERLIN. – Prisoner of Zion Anatoly Shcharansky became a free man at 10.55 yesterday morning, after spending nine years in Soviet prison. He was flown from the USSR to East Berlin on Monday. Yesterday, he was driven to the Glienicke bridge checkpoint between East Germany and West Berlin.

At the border, in the middle of the bridge, he was greeted by U.S. Ambassador to West Germany Richard Burt, the West German negotiator of the spy swap Ludwig Rehlinger, and East German lawyer Wolfgang Vogel, who negotiated the release on behalf of the Communists.

The West German government played a key role in obtaining Shcharansky's release.

As 200 newsmen watched from afar, Shcharansky, wearing a fur hat and an overcoat which appeared too large, was whisked away in a limousine to a waiting American plane. He was flown to a U.S. air base near Frankfurt, where he was reunited with his wife Avital for the first time since the day after their marriage in Moscow in July 1974.

German, American and Isaeli officials, including Ambassador Yitzhak Ben-Ari, greeted him at the Frankfurt air base, where Ben-Ari handed Shcharansky an Israeli passport. Avital and Anatoly then spent half an hour together in the VIP lounge before boarding the Arkia Westwind plane which brought them to Israel.

Shcharansky was examined on the special plane by an Israeli doctor, who said he was fit for the flight.

Shcharansky did not know he was to be exchanged until his arrival on Monday in East Berlin. He did not know where he was, thinking he might be in Scandinavia because of the heavy snow.

Shcharansky's release was part of an East-West trade which also included eight convicted or suspected spies. But at U.S. insistence he was set free a full half hour before the others, to underline Washington's view that he was not a western agent.

(See spies – Page 2)

Sources in Bonn told *The Jerusalem Post* that the release of East European spies by West Germany was the key element in obtaining the release.

Avital's prayer and Anatoly's promise

By ROBERT ROSENBERG
Jerusalem Post Reporter

BEN-GURION AIRPORT. – Avital uttered a public prayer for the Land of Israel and for aliya. Prime Minister Peres garnered boos and applause.

Scores of hora-dancing youngsters, the boys with skullcaps, the girls in skirts, sang *Am Yisrael Hai*. Former Prisoner of Zion Yosef Mendelevich warned that it shouldn't turn into a media event.

And Anatoly Natan Shcharansky, beaming and blinking into the lights and nodding to journalists remembered from Moscow when he was a leading spokesman of the Soviet dissident movement, spoke of "those still in jail, in their struggle for human rights."

The wife, who found strength during the 11½ years of separation in profound religious belief, clutched her husband's hand but backed off from his public kisses. She blushed when the prime minister called her a lioness, and she blushed when her husband put his arm around her.

Shcharansky arrived bareheaded, stepping out of an executive jet onto a tarmac lit by the world's media and into the arms of Peres and Yitzhak Shamir. Both spoke in the immigration hall, calling on the Soviets to free other Jews, and appealing to the world to keep up the struggle.

But it was Shcharansky, slight but not underweight, pale but not peaked, who commanded attention with his words.

Avital Shcharansky spoke only once to the public last night, saying "It is a day to give thanks to the Holy One, Blessed be His name, to pray that the Land of Israel be filled with immigrants, and that the land never be divided, never given up." The cheers of the crowd swept across the stage outside the Arkia offices.

The cheers grew when Avital pressed a blue and white skull cap onto her husband's head. He had flown bareheaded with her to Israel and met with the press and politicians without a skullcap, accepting it from her only in front of the thousands who cheered her for the gesture.

There were momentary surprises. *New York Times* reporter David Shipler somehow slipped through the crush to embrace Shcharansky. They had worked together in the years before prison, when Shcharansky spoke for the Helsinki Human Rights Movement, for Jews, for Pentecostalists, Seventh Day Adventists, dissidents of all religions and ethnic backgrounds.

(Continued on back page)

Fuel price likely to drop next week

By AARON SITTNER

Fuel prices will probably fall next week, in the wake of an agreement yesterday between Finance Minister Yitzhak Moda'i and Energy Minister Moshe Shahal.

The reductions will apparently range between 5 and 10 per cent for refined petroleum products, and will be followed by a cut in electricity rates.

As economists at the Fuel Administration in Tel Aviv forecast further cuts in world oil prices, Egypt yesterday announced a cut in its crude oil prices – to $15.50 per barrel for the heavy Ras Garib crude and $18 per barrel for the lighter Suez crude. (See also page 6.)

Egyptians here for talks

The Egyptian delegation to talks on normalization and Taba arrived here late last night.

The Egyptians are here for two days of talks in Herzliya.

Trading halts on Stock Exchange after 'Post' report on 'arrangement' shares

Bank of Israel admits inquiry into banking's main problems

Post Economic Staff

The Bank of Israel yesterday officially admitted that a professional team has been examining "the main problems of the Israeli banking system." This statement was a response to the report in yesterday's *Jerusalem Post* that the government was considering ways to reduce the cost of its obligation to redeem the "arrangement" bank shares in October, 1988.

The "arrangement" refers to the government's undertaking to guarantee the value of the shares, which collapsed abruptly in October, 1983, if the shareholders held them for a fixed period. Meeting this obligation will cost the Treasury an estimated $5 billion.

The Tel Aviv Stock Exchange management yesterday decided to halt trading in the shares, pending "clarifications" of *The Post* report that it had requested from the Treasury and the central Bank.

The Treasury officially stated that "the government will meet its obligations to the full." It added that "neither in the past nor at present have discussions taken place on this topic."

But senior Treasury officials told *The Jerusalem Post* that the subject was on the Treasury's agenda, and that efforts would have to be made to reduce the cost of implementing the "arrangement." Ideally this should be done within a formal honouring of the terms of the "arrangement."

If the options to be presented to shareholders by the Treasury for recycling the debt were not taken up voluntarily, compulsory measures would have to be taken.

The Bank of Israel quoted Examiner of Banks Galia Maor as saying that "the team that I led was not requested to consider, and did not consider in any manner, a change in the bankshare arrangement or a change in the government's obligations."

Should the government abide by the original terms of the "arrangement," it will purchase the bulk of the banks' equity in 1987 and 1988, and whether it wants to or not, may thereby end up nationalizing the banking system.

The Bank of Israel's statement yesterday, with its reference to "the main problem of the banking system," indicates that the real purpose of the "professional team" led by Maor is to examine ways to prevent this nationalization.

The team's broad composition – it includes senior bankers such as Baruch Yekutieli of Bank Leumi, Aviv Levin of Bank Hapoalim, and Avner Cassuto of Bank Discount, outgoing stock exchange chairman Meir Heth and Prof. Amir Barnea of Tel Aviv University – reflects this concern. An attempt has clearly been made to bring together the widest possible spectrum of views from both inside and outside the government.

The stock exchange trading halt was in line with the exchange's policy in cases such as these to protect investors from the possible consequences of panic responses. Following the Treasury and Bank of Israel statements, it was announced that trading would resume today.

Exchange sources said that no significant selling pressure had built up in the morning before the trading halt was called. One leading broker told *The Post* that there was plenty of buying interest waiting in the wings for the bank shares, should they fall.

Banking sources in Tel Aviv generally dismissed the idea that the government would fail to redeem the bank shares in full. In particular, the suggestion that the government might not repay the banks for the shares they themselves hold (known as the "nostro" position) was felt to be out of place.

The sources stressed that the government committee was only one of many forums in which ideas and alternatives for recycling the bankshare obligation were being discussed.

The Post story also sparked a response from members of the Knesset Finance Committee. MKs Haim Ramon (Alignment) and Dan Tichon (Likud) intend to table a bill which would give more voting strength to the regular shares in the "arrangement." If this were done, they claim, the value of the "arrangement" shares would rise and the amount the government would have to pay for their redemption would be reduced.

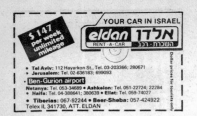

THE JERUSALEM POST

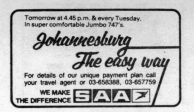

Vol. LIV, No. 16197 Monday, April 21, 1986 • Nisan 12, 5746 • Shaban 12, 1406 NIS 0.72 (Eilat NIS 0.63)

Bejski shocks financial system

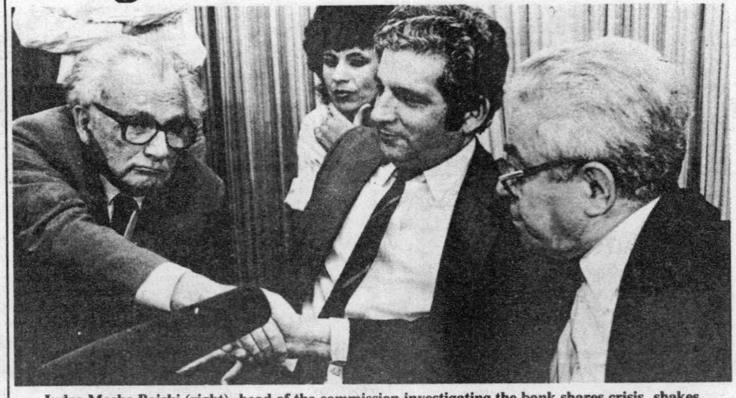

Judge Moshe Bejski (right), head of the commission investigating the bank shares crisis, shakes hands yesterday with State Comptroller Yitzhak Tunik, whose report led to the establishment of the commission. Between them is Prof. David Libai, chairman of the Knesset Control Committee, to whom the Bejski report was presented. (Isaac Harari)

Report insists top bankers must go

By PINHAS LANDAU
Post Finance Reporter

The Bejski Commission of Inquiry into the 1983 bank-shares scandal recommends a complete overhaul of Israel's financial markets. The commission also calls for the resignation or dismissal of the governor of the Bank of Israel, Moshe Mandelbaum, and the heads of the country's biggest commercial banks.

The commission recommends that the attorney-general pursue several areas of inquiry that the commission opened, with a view to bringing charges against those alleged in the report to have violated the law.

The theme of the report, stressed at length at the opening of the chapter on "conclusions and recommendations," is that the regulation of bank shares detailed in the report, represented far more than a business disaster for the banks but was a major blow to the country's economy as well.

"No less serious than the crisis itself," the report declares in stinging language, "is the lack of accountability of the senior personalities involved, which expressed itself in the blanket refusal of any of them to take responsibility for what happened."

Initial reactions last night from the banks were varied. Bank Hapoalim promised "co-operation" and said it would draw the necessary conclusions after studying the report. Bank Leumi complained that it had only received the report at 8:30 last night and had not received sufficient copies, and therefore would only

(Continued on Back Page)

Peres floats idea of Gaza-Jordan autonomy link

Jerusalem Post Staff

Prime Minister Peres said yesterday that Jordan is determined not to lose its stake in the Gaza Strip and that an autonomy solution for Gaza could be combined with the plans for autonomy on the West Bank.

In an interview for Pessah with *The Jerusalem Post*, to be published on Wednesday, Peres said that the idea of establishing an interim Israeli-Egyptian "condominium" in Gaza had come up against Egypt's "lack of political interest" in the region. Jordan, however, "has a political interest in not losing Gaza," he said.

Despite the difficulties, Peres acknowledged that "there are people in Gaza who would like to try their hand at the application of autonomy."

Peres said that he did not "suggest" the dismantling of Jewish settlements in Gaza – because "the scandals here would begin immediately" – but added emphatically that there was "no justification for taking more land" for Jewish settlements.

Gaza, he said, has almost doubled its population in the past 20 years, from 300,000 to 560,000, and the density in the area is "almost as bad as Hong Kong."

"I ask myself whether there is any justification for taking an extra 50,000 dunams, while the Negev, with 12 million dunams, is almost devoid of settlers," he said. He stressed that he was opposed to the allocation of any further land in Gaza for settlement.

Cabinet votes summer time from May 17 to September 6

By ASHER WALLFISH
Post Knesset Correspondent

The cabinet voted yesterday by 11 against six with one abstention to introduce summer time in Israel from May 17 to September 6, a decision which jolted Interior Minister Yitzhak Peretz out of his customary composure and moved him to hurl emotional accusations against the Alignment, which voted against him *en bloc*.

Peretz shouted at Energy Minister Moshe Shahal in the course of the debate, in which not a single Likud Minister took part: "You have been shedding my blood! You have been organizing a public lynch campaign against me! I would not be surprised if what you have done will lead to attempts on my life! You have been inciting against me and against all the Orthodox community!"

Peretz vainly tried to persuade the cabinet not to debate the issue until the High Court of Justice, which is considering a number of pleas against him, holds its next session today.

Interior Minister Yitzhak Peretz last night accepted the cabinet's recommendations on summer time, according to which the clocks will be moved forward one hour at midnight on May 17, the Saturday following Independence Day. Summer time will be in effect until September 6.

Attorney-General Yitzhak Zamir said that the High Court hearings on the summer time issue need not prevent the cabinet debating and taking decisions. He said later on in the debate that it would be inconceivable for a cabinet minister to act in contradiction of a cabinet decision by ignoring the principle of collective responsibility for cabinet action, to which they were all committed.

The emotion-charged debate followed a formal proposal by three ministers, Communications Minister Amnon Rubinstein, Energy Minister Moshe Shahal, and Economics Minister Gad Ya'acobi, to introduce summer time forthwith.

Peretz reminded the cabinet that the commission he appointed to study the problem did not advise the introduction of summer time this year. He quoted the findings of a German research project to the effect that road accidents would increase in the wake of summer time. He also quoted a French research project which held that summer time caused negative manifestations among the school population.

Shahal said in the debate that, if summer time were introduced forthwith, the country would save $5.6m. on energy. Orthodox Jews wanted summer time just as much as secular

(Continued on Page 2, Col. 4)

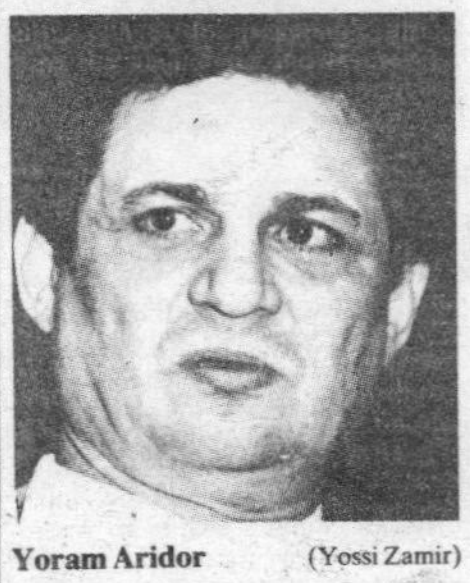

Yoram Aridor (Yossi Zamir)

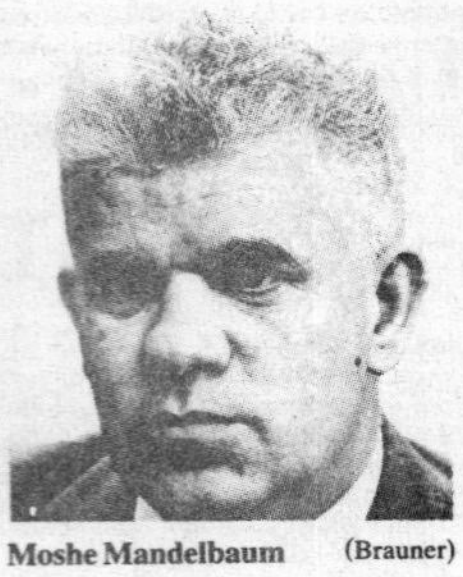

Moshe Mandelbaum (Brauner)

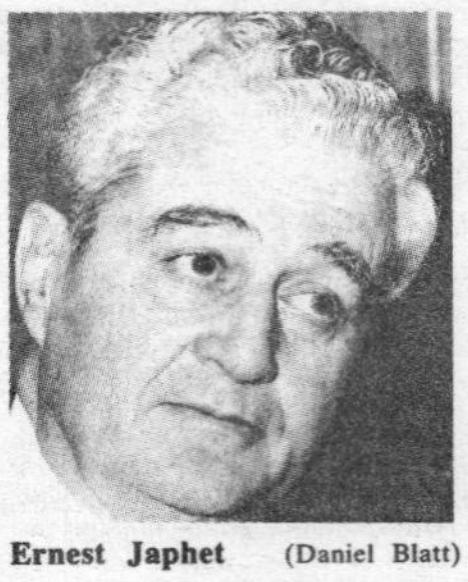

Ernest Japhet (Daniel Blatt)

The people and the price

The Bejski Commission called for the resignation within 30 days of six persons it found responsible for the bank shares crisis, and placed blame on nine others who have already left their posts. One person was found to bear some responsibility for the shares, but the panel did not call for her resignation.

• Persons who must resign within 30 days:

Dr. Moshe Mandelbaum, governor of the Bank of Israel
Ernest Japhet, general manager, Bank Leumi
Ephraim Reiner, chairman and president, Ampal, a subsidiary of Bank Hapoalim
Giora Gazit, managind director, Bank Hapoalim
Rafael Recanati, chairman and managing director, Discount Bank
Aaron Meir, managing director, Mizrahi Bank

• Persons who bear responsibility for the shares crisis but who have already left their positions:

David Shoham, formerly head of administration, Bank Clali
Ben Ami Zuckerman, former com-

(Continued on Page 2, Col. 1)

Duped woman in El Al case gets police protection

By JERRY LEWIS
Jerusalem Post Correspondent

Anne-Marie Murphy, the Irish woman arrested by Scotland Yard for trying to carry a bomb on to an El Al jet Thursday, was released late Saturday night but is being kept under police protection.

Meanwhile, Nezar Hindawi, the man accused of giving her the explosive device, told police he had been tricked by the leader of an Arab terrorist cell with which he was associated, police sources said. Hindawi said he was led to believe that the bag he had given Murphy contained drugs, not the five-kilogram bomb found by an El Al security

(Continued on Page 2, Col. 2)

Individual and collective blame

ANALYSIS
By MEIR MERHAV and SHLOMO MAOZ

The Bejski Commission Report, which last night hit the country with a shattering impact, will be discussed and debated for a long time. It is not only the first commission of inquiry to deal with a major economic problem; it has also interpreted its terms of reference in the widest possible way. Its analysis is therefore more far-reaching and its recommendations are more devastating than those of the Agranat and Kahan commissions, which dealt with the Yom Kippur War and the Sabra and Shatilla massacres respectively.

The report does not confine itself to the bank share crisis of October 1983 in its narrow sense, but ranges far beyond – to the very foundations of Israel's economy, with ramifications spreading far and wide.

In the process, the commission has blasted the accepted norms of business conduct, and has issued an unmistakably loud call for a new code of personal responsibility and accountability. In its recommendations – which call all those responsible for the crash to pay for their indifference, lax observance of the law, irresponsibility and even illegal actions – the commission states bluntly that none of those responsible should have waited for the commission's report. They should have realized that whoever has broken the law or failed in his duties, cannot continue in his job as if nothing has happened, let alone be kicked upstairs.

The commission has shown no mercy to any of those involved; it has censured those who are no longer in the public service and can therefore neither be fired nor otherwise punished.

The testimony of those directly involved made it appear that an air of collective guilt hung over the affair. The commission, however, dispelled this notion of collective guilt, and pinned individual responsibility on every one of those who made up "the system" from which all claimed they had no way out.

Refuge could have been taken, the commission says – in the law, even as it stands, or in a business ethic that seems to have been forgotten. Guilt and responsibility, the commission implies, are always individual, and the participation of others in the same culpable acts of

(Continued on Page 2, Col. 6)

Clash likely on governor's job

Jerusalem Post Staff

Prime Minister Peres said last night that the government would "fulfil all its commitments" to carry out the conclusions of the Bejski Commission's report.

"Israel is a democracy, and if a problem is discovered, there is no intention of hiding it. On the contrary, it will be set right," Peres said. He maintained that the report would have no effect on the government's economic programme, since the inquiry dealt with events that took place before the economic plan was instituted.

At the same time, the commission report has already set off maneuvering between the Alignment and the Likud over who will replace Moshe Mandelbaum as governor of the Bank of Israel. Peres wants to appoint Deputy Finance Minister Adiel Amorai to the position, but Likud ministers oppose giving the job to a Labour Party man.

However, the governorship has never yet been given to an active politician, so the appointment of Amorai, even if agreed to by Shamir, would constitute a precedent.

More on the Bejski report on pages 6, 7 and 9.

While Yitzhak Moda'i was still at the Treasury, he is known to have favoured the appointment of Meir Heth, former stock exchange head. The commission praised Heth in its findings, but also reprimanded him. But with Moda'i out of the Treasury, Heth's candidacy is obviously in doubt.

The Histadrut will implement all the Bejski Report recommenda-

(Continued on Page 2, Col. 1)

PM to discuss his 'Marshall Plan' in Paris

Prime Minister Peres said yesterday he intended to discuss his plan for Middle East economic development with French President Francois Mitterrand and Prime Minister Jacques Chirac during his 36-hour visit to Paris, which begins today.

Peres said he had already discussed the plan with U.S. Secretary of State George Shultz, West German Chancellor Helmut Kohl and Italian Prime Minister Bettino Craxi, and had approached British Prime Minister Margaret Thatcher. The reactions from the Europeans and the Americans had been "enthusiastic," he said.

In addition to discussing his Middle East Marshall Plan, as his programme has been dubbed, Peres is expected to discuss ways of halting terrorism. Tomorrow, he will explain Israel's stand on the issue before the Council of Europe in Strasbourg.

Britons moved from Moslem part of Beirut after two murders

BEIRUT. – A sad and weary group of 31 Britons were evacuated from Moslem West Beirut yesterday under armed escort after the killing of two British teachers and the abduction of a British television cameraman.

A Moslem group said it killed the kidnapped teachers in retaliation for Britain's support of the U.S. attack on Libya last Tuesday. Some evacuees, who included children and old people, spoke of living in daily fear of abduction since then.

Clutching suitcases and shopping bags, they arrived in Christian East Beirut after trundling across the Green Line battle-front dividing the city.

Meanwhile, a second group of Americans was evacuated from Sudan to Kenya overnight, bringing to nearly 300 the number of U.S. citizens airlifted from Khartoum, a U.S. Embassy spokesman said yesterday in Nairobi.

The Americans, mainly dependants of U.S. diplomats and non-essential embassy staff, were ordered to leave Khartoum by the State Department in Washington because of fears for the safety of U.S. citizens after an embassy communications officer was shot in the Sudanese capital on Wednesday.

Joining the airlift were a few private U.S. citizens who left the country voluntarily and about 20 nationals from Canada and Britain.

It was reported in Frankfurt that a special flight by a West German Lufthansa DC-10 yesterday brought 276 people out of Libya.

Many of those who arrived in Europe yesterday were West German women with children. They and some of the returning men, who were employed by West German firms in Libya, said they were relieved to be home but would return once the political situation stabilized.

In Bilbao, Spain police early yesterday defused a bomb planted on a window sill of a building where the Spanish-U.S. cultural association has its office.

Police said they received an anonymous telephone call from a person who said a bomb had been planted outside the "Aznar" building, in downtown Bilbao, and that it would explode in a few minutes.

Police said they rushed to the building, which was once used as an American consulate, and defused the bomb using a remotely controlled robot.

The Spanish-U.S. Cultural Association promotes cultural contacts between Spain and the U.S.

(See picture Page 2)

Israeli air experts going to U.S. to discuss cooperation

McDonnel Douglas interested in joining Lavi project

By AVI HOFFMANN
Post Defence Reporter

The giant U.S. aerospace corporation, McDonnell Douglas, is interested in joining the Israel Aircraft Industries' Lavi fighter project, *The Jerusalem Post* has learned.

IAI president Moshe Keret and the Lavi project director at the Defence Ministry, Tat-Aluf (Brig.-Gen.) Menahem Eini, are to travel to St. Louis next month to discuss, at the U.S. firm's request, McDonnell Douglas's participation in the Lavi programme.

IAI sources declined to confirm or deny any contacts with American companies, beyond noting that IAI officials go on routine business trips to the U.S.

It is unclear what kind of relationship McDonnell Douglas has in mind, but industry sources speculated that the company might be interested in co-production or building the plane under licence in the U.S. Such a partnership could be a giant step forward for Israel's next generation fighter, constantly under attack from various quarters for what is considered the intolerable burden it imposes on the country's economy. McDonnell Douglas manufactures the F-15, Phantom and Skyhawk warplanes in service with the Israel Air Force.

Defence Minister Yitzhak Rabin told *The Post* in an interview last year that Israel was actively seeking an American manufacturer to join IAI as an equal partner for the development and production of the Lavi.

The project, Israel's largest ever industrial endeavour, has cost $1 billion to develop so far and will cost another $1.2b. before production starts in 1990. The plane, due for its first flight this September, has been under constant review since its conception and counts among its critics the Pentagon, which objects to $250 million worth of U.S. military aid being spent on the plane annually, and the IDF chief of general staff, who would prefer cutting the Lavi budget rather than slashing Army funds.

If a major U.S manufacturer joins in producing the Lavi, then Israel's financial troubles with the plane are likely to be over. Apart from the direct financial and technological aid, the American partner could provide, a vast export market in the U.S. and elsewhere would open up. So far, the Lavi's only customer is the Israel Air Force. With U.S. participation other customers are likely to become interested, and instead of being an economic burden the Lavi might even start turning a profit.

Co-production with the Americans has always been a possibility and Israel, in the words of Rabin, has seen the Lavi as "a joint project between IAI and the aeronautical industry in the U.S." Over 120 American companies are involved, as sub-contractors, in the development of the plane. Major systems, such as the engine and parts of the fuselage and wings, are made in the U.S.

An industry source noted that the U.S. arsenal currently boasts several aircraft that were originally developed outside of the U.S. The British-designed Harrier and Hawk, as well as the French Dauphin helicopter are built in the U.S. and flown by various branches of the armed forces. IAI itself has supplied, on lease, two squadrons of Kfirs to the U.S. Navy's aggressor force.

The U.S. does not currently have a high-performance strike aircraft in development for the 1990s and the Lavi is therefore the front-runner to fit the bill, the industry source said, adding that several U.S. congressmen are lobbying for America to actively participate in Lavi production.

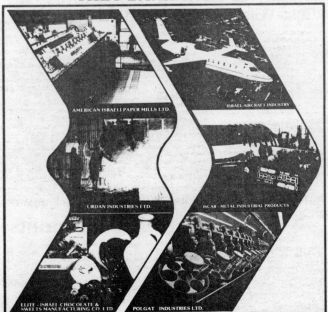

Shabbat Shalom FROM
YO SI PEKING
Chinese Restaurants
Glatt Kosher Exclusive

SHABBAT	BEGINS	END
Jerusalem	5:13 p.m.	6:26 p.m.
Tel Aviv	5:31 p.m.	6:28 p.m.
Haifa	5:24 p.m.	6:27 p.m.

Reservations:
Jerusalem: 5 Shimon Ben Shatah St., Tel. 02-226893
Tel Aviv: Naveh Avivim, 13 Oppenheimer St., Tel. 03-421888.

THE JERUSALEM POST

Vol. LIV, No. 16317 Friday, September 12, 1986 • Elul 8, 5746 • Moharram 9, 1407 NIS 1.40 (Eilat NIS 1.22)

Copies printed today:
50,600
THE JERUSALEM POST

SECOND EDITION

Three days of Sinai
Magazine, page 12

War on terror
Pages 6, 7

A laughing matter
Magazine, page B

Jurists up in arms –
Page 5

A living symbol: the case of Rudolf Hess
Magazine, page 6

Palestinian issue dominates summit

By YEHUDA LITANI, HIRSH GOODMAN and BENNY MORRIS in Alexandria

Prime Minister Shimon Peres, at the end of his first day of talks with Egyptian President Hosni Mubarak, told reporters late last night that Mubarak had not tried to press him to deviate from the national unity government guidelines on the Palestinian question.

Mubarak, speaking separately to newsmen after last night's talks, praised Israel for its flexibility on the Palestinian issue and criticized the PLO and the other Arab states for their intransigence.

"The Israeli position is improving a lot concerning the Palestinians," Mubarak told newsmen at the end of his three-hour meeting with Peres, which was dominated by the Palestinian issue. He did not elaborate, but referred newsmen to the joint communique planned for the end of the summit today. Israeli and Egyptian officials were still working hard last night to hammer out the communique.

Peres, however, said that for lack of time a joint communique might not be issued. But he stressed that in most matters of principle "understanding had been reached."

Mubarak was highly critical of the PLO and Arab states for their attitude. He told reporters that recent political actions by the PLO should be criticized, saying: "We mustn't ask Israel to make the effort (for peace) alone."

He slammed the PLO for freezing the Amman agreement, signed between King Hussein and PLO chairman Yasser Arafat on February 11, 1985, in which the PLO committed itself to coordinate its political line with the king. The freezing of this agreement "has put us in a difficult position while we are proceeding in our talks to solve the Palestinian question," Mubarak said.

He called on the Palestinian factions to reach agreement among themselves.

Asked about Jordan's participation in peace talks, he said only that Jordan is "an important partner in the peace process."

Neither Israel nor Egypt expects the summit to produce concrete results, it emerged from yesterday's talks. But further talks, possibly between working committees, are likely to continue, in an effort to achieve Jordanian-Palestinian participation in broader peace negotiations.

Mubarak said also that Egypt and Israel did not differ much over an international Middle East peace conference.

"There are no large differences concerning the international conference," a smiling Mubarak told reporters.

"The international conference is on the agenda but this should not negate the need for direct negotiations," the president said, citing the 1979 Israeli-Egyptian peace treaty as a product of direct negotiations.

Peres said that he and Mubarak agreed in principle on an international conference, but said that some "minor" differences existed on technical matters. Peres conceded that Mubarak still insists on the participation of the permanent members of the UN Security Council, including the Soviet Union.

While hopeful that an international conference would be convened in the foreseeable future, Peres said that one major component – the Palestinians – was still missing. The main problem was the basic difference in viewpoints between Jordan and the PLO. "The problem is not in Israeli policy-making, but in the Arab world," he said.

Peres emphasized that the international conference, which after an initial meeting would break up into regional committees, would not have the power to dictate conditions or a settlement.

On bilateral relations, Peres said that they had been "rusty" but now, during the summit, they were rehabilitated. "I had not imagined that there would be such hospitality and warmth," he said.

Peres said that he and Mubarak had "talked about everything – just about" including the Iraq-Iran war, and Libya's recent offer to China for union. He revealed this last piece of information with a smile on his face.

Peres revealed that on his trip to the U.S. next week he would not ask for greater American involvement in the Middle East peace process and said that he understood the American influence on this point. "There is wisdom in reserved involvement," he remarked.

(Continued on Page 2, Col. 2)

Europeans talk tough on terror

STRASBOURG, France (AP). – The European Parliament called Thursday on the governments of the 12 Common Market nations to set up a central anti-terrorist office and to strengthen extradition treaties.

In a resolution adopted by an overwhelming majority, the EC legislature reacted angrily to the recent wave of terrorism. But it also condemned the EC for failing to cooperate in combating terrorism.

The parliament appealed to Arab countries to "distance themselves unequivocally" from the terrorist attack of recent days and to "deprive terrorist organizations" of their logistical support.

The hijacking last Friday of a Pan Am jetliner in Karachi and the attack on a Jewish congregation at an Istanbul synagogue the following day and an explosion at a Paris post office last Tuesday claimed nearly 50 lives.

"Only a decisive action at the European level" can deal with terrorism, Derek Prag, a British Conservative, said in parliament.

The parliament's resolution said the Arab-Israeli conflict is at the root of the international terrorism and urged the EC foreign ministers to "initiate genuine community involvement" in the Middle East peace negotiations.

Only the Communist group voted against the emergency motion carried by 193 votes to 11 with one abstention, which regretted previous declarations by EC foreign ministers on the issue had not resulted in concrete action.

Poles set to free detainees

WARSAW. – Polish authorities will free 225 political prisoners under an act of clemency by next Monday state television reported yesterday.

The official PAP news agency also revealed that police questioned more than 3,000 people in an attempt to expose illegal groups and activities. Equipment was confiscated but no charges were pressed.

Interior Minister General Czeslaw Kiszczak was quoted as saying that those to be released would include Solidarity's underground leaders Zbigniew Bujak, Tadeusz Jedynak and Bogdan Borusewicz, who were all awaiting trial.

Wage talks break down

By ROY ISACOWITZ
Jerusalem Post Reporter

Histadrut Trade Union Department Chairman Haim Haberfeld has called an emergency meeting of union leaders this morning to discuss the breakdown last night of wage talks in the private sector.

The talks between the Histadrut and the Coordinating Bureau of Economic Organizations, representing the private-sector employers, were unable to resolve their differences over the level of the proposed minimum wage and the length of the agreement.

Dow plunges

The Dow Jones Industrial Average plunged 87 points yesterday – its sharpest one-day loss ever – as a wave of panic selling gripped the New York Stock Exchange.

The Dow, the most widely followed market indicator, ended trading yesterday at 1793, as the number of shares changing hands in the market approached a record high. Traders attributed the massive sell-off largely to concern over rising interest rates.

(Details on page 19)

Then the flags came out

By BENNY MORRIS
Jerusalem Post Diplomatic Correspondent

ALEXANDRIA. – The palms swayed gently in the Mediterranean breeze outside the ornate Ras A-Tin palace yesterday, but no Israeli flag rustled in the wind.

That was the scene as several hundred journalists waited for Prime Minister Peres and his entourage to arrive for his summit talks with President Mubarak.

Just one, barely discernible Israeli flag could be found: on Ambassador Moshe Sasson's limousine, parked in the courtyard.

Finally, as white-uniformed Egyptian sailors stood with their musical instruments, three large helicopters hovered into view over the palace's dome and crenellated walls, descending onto the grass amid the courtyard palms.

Still no Israeli flag was to be seen.

Israeli, western and Egyptian journalists fidgeted beside the main entrance, craning their necks to see who would emerge from each helicopter.

First emerged Peres's main guests – Knesset Foreign Affairs and Defence Committee chairman Abba Eban (who had been asked by Peres to be included in the entourage) and MK Dan Meridor, Peres's token Likud party representative. Then came Minister without Portfolio Ezer Weizman and the directors-general of the Prime Minister's Office and the Foreign Ministry, Avraham Tamir and David Kimche.

With a flourish of trumpets and a loud staccato of drums, Peres and his close aides emerged from the third helicopter.

As if by magic, two large flags suddenly rose above the walls over the main entrance to the palace, the Israeli and Egyptian national flags.

Ranks of naval cadets presented arms smartly and *Hatikva* was played by the brass band, followed by the Egyptian national anthem.

The palace has played an important role in Egyptian history. It was built in 1909 by Mohammed Ali, the Albanian-born officer who founded the Egyptian royal family.

It was from Ras a-Tin that the country's last monarch, King Farouk, sailed into exile aboard his private yacht in 1952 after a group of military officers led by General Naguib and Gamal Abdel-Nasser forced him to abdicate.

Peres. flanked by Egyptian Premier Ali Lutfi and led by a goose-stepping officer with a sword, inspected the guard and, turning sharply right, hailed the waiting Israeli journalists with a "shalom" and strode into the main building.

There Peres lunched with Lutfi, followed by talks between Peres and his entourage and the head of the Egyptian government – sans President Mubarak.

Despite the absence of flags and of Mubarak, the arrival of Peres, under a clear blue sky, in the courtyard of the imposing palace was a moving moment.

Jerusalem Post Reporter adds from Ben-Gurion Airport:

At the airport before leaving, Peres said: The government of Israel is determined to develop bilateral relations between our two countries and to make every effort to expand the circle of peace in our region while resolving the Palestinian problem."

(Continued on Page 2, Col. 6)

Prime Minister Peres receives a light from his Egyptian counterpart, Ali Lutfi, before going in for his meeting with President Hosni Mubarak in Alexandria yesterday. (Reuter)

Washington 'pleased'

By WOLF BLITZER
Jerusalem Post Correspondent

WASHINGTON. – The Reagan administration was very pleased by the Israeli-Egyptian summit, but cautioned against expecting any immediate breakthrough in broader Arab-Israeli peace efforts.

U.S. officials said that Secretary of State George Shultz has no plans to return to the Middle East in the near future. They said he is tied up with other commitments in Washington for the time being.

They noted, however, that if Israel and Egypt had managed to overcome their final Taba-related disputes a few days earlier, the secretary would have been prepared to participate in the Peres-Mubarak summit and to visit other countries in the region this week. "Now," an American official said, "it's too late."

Peres is scheduled to meet in Washington on Monday with Shultz, President Reagan and other senior U.S. officials. In the aftermath of the prime minister's summit yesterday, U.S. officials said, that visit to Washington has taken on greater importance.

The Americans are anxious to try to generate some momentum in peace efforts even in these final days of Peres's term in office.

U.S. may upgrade Israel status

Jerusalem Post Correspondent

WASHINGTON. – The Reagan Administration yesterday promised Defence Minister Yitzhak Rabin that it would seriously consider Israel's request for official recognition as "a major non-Nato ally."

Meeting with Israeli reporters following his sessions with Defence Secretary Caspar Weinberger and Secretary of State George Shultz, Rabin said that he was not offered any flat promise that Israel would eventually obtain this changed status in the relationship.

"But they promised to give it their full consideration," he said, noting that such a change would open the door to considerable economic and military benefits for Israel.

The need for Israel to obtain "equal treatment" with America's Nato allies in purchasing U.S. weapons and in winning U.S. defence contracts, Rabin said, was thoroughly discussed during his sessions at the Pentagon, the State Department and the White House.

Rabin also met yesterday with National Security Adviser John Poindexter and is due to meet today with Vice President George Bush.

The two leaders in conversation at the Ras a-Tin Palace in Alexandria yesterday. (GPO)

The long road to a Taba accord

By HIRSH GOODMAN
and YEHUDA LITANI
Jerusalem Post Correspondents

ALEXANDRIA. – The *compromis* agreement on the Taba issue signed yesterday in Cairo at 2:30 a.m. was made possible by the magic words "approximate locations" – two words that took Israeli and Egyptian negotiators 11 days to hammer out. The *compromis* document, which has not been released at Egyptian insistence, is eight pages long and comprises two sections: the questions the sides will place before the arbitrators and the replies of the two countries to those questions. Israeli and Egyptian officials yesterday said that the arbitration process could take as long as a year.

For the past five days, as the clock for the scheduled summit between Prime Minister Peres and President Mubarak was running out, negotiators spent 18 to 20 hours a day searching for a mutually acceptable formula that would answer Egypt's demand that Israel name a specific spot where it believes the Taba border should pass, and Israel's position that no specific spot be named since it is not sure where the 1906 border line is. It was not until 10 p.m. Wednesday night, after tremendous American pressure was placed on both sides, that the Egyptians agreed to the term "approximate locations" that finally resolved the issue. To narrow the term, Israel named two spots, 60 metres apart, where it believes border marker No. 91 should be.

Also under discussion in recent days was the question of who the arbitrators would be. On Tuesday morning, negotiators agreed to two international arbitrators, who have yet to be publicly named, and agreed that the two would select a third arbitrator. The selection will not be subject to either Israeli or Egyptian approval. In addition to the three international arbitrators, one Egyptian and one Israeli will participate in the arbitration. Israel's representative will be Ruth Lapidot, formerly the Foreign Ministry's legal adviser.

The signing ceremony at the Mena House Hotel was scheduled for 11:30 p.m., but was held up for three hours because the Egyptians had "forgotten" to type up the agreement. U.S. special envoy Richard Murphy, who played a crucial role in reaching the agreement, waited with delegates from both countries and about 40 journalists from around the world for the documents to arrive.

The delegates then sat at three separate tables – the Israelis on the left, the Americans in the centre and the Egyptians on the right. Avraham Tamir, Director-General of the Prime Minister's Office, made the speech on behalf of Israel, and not the Foreign Ministry's David Kimche, who had been Israel's chief negotiator.

Speaking later on Israel Radio, Kimche said: "It seems we got more or less what we wanted in these last talks. We had a certain conception, and we stick to that conception. The arbitrators are well-known personalities in their field, that is, we are speaking about legal experts who

(Continued on back page)

Two SLA men killed in clash with Shi'ites

Jerusalem Post Staff

Two Southern Lebanon Army soldiers were killed yesterday in the security zone when their hilltop position came under a pre-dawn attack by the Shi'ite Islamic Resistance militias, SLA sources said.

Five Nepalese Unifil soldiers were wounded in ensuing crossfire from an SLA reprisal launched shortly after the Shi'ites tried to overrun Hikban hill southeast of Tyre.

Three Shi'ites were also killed in the hilltop raid, Lebanese sources said. The Islamic Resistance includes members of Hizbollah and Amal militias.

The wounded Unifil soldiers were taken to Unifil's Nakoura hospital where all were reported to be out of danger, according to the UN spokesman.

Some of the more hazardous positions held by Unifil troops may be eliminated, said Marrack Goulding, UN Undersecretary-General, in an interview published in Beirut yesterday.

"We cannot allow our men to continue being fired on like rabbits," Goulding told the pro-Moslem paper *A-Safir*, referring to a series of recent attacks.

Bar-Lev clashes with comptroller on Suissa

By YORAM GAZIT
For The Jerusalem Post

A sharp difference of opinion emerged yesterday in the Knesset Interior Committee between the police minister and the police comptroller over the comptroller's report concerning allegations of misconduct by Prisons Service Commissioner Rafi Suissa.

Minister Haim Bar-Lev has insisted that Suissa remain in office. But Police Comptroller Avraham Adan told the committee yesterday: "The findings of the report were very serious. You had better read it."

The committee members have not yet seen the report.

In a tense, day-long meeting, Bar-Lev reviewed the misconduct allegations.

The first and most serious concerned criminal offences. Suissa was accused by three Prisons Service officials, who were transferred from their posts three months ago, of forgery, fraud and bribery. These allegations had been submitted to the police, who found no grounds for prosecution.

The second allegation concerned inaccurate and misleading information given by Suissa to the police minister. Suissa was said to have changed statistics concerning prison escapes and suicides, for example. Bar-Lev, Adan and Suissa, agreed, Bar-Lev said, that inaccurate and misleading information had been submitted to the police minister, but while Suissa said this was the result of negligence, Adan believed it was premeditated.

The third and fourth allegations concerned favouritism Suissa had shown to certain prisoners and hiring employees who were either relatives or friends of his. Bar-Lev said Suissa denied these allegations. Adan's report found that Suissa had hired persons who did not meet recruitment standards; they did not have the necessary educational background or had not served in the IDF. Suissa had explained that he had given these persons a chance to prove themselves and had fired those who were found unfit.

Suissa also admitted, said Bar-Lev, that he had allowed some prisoners and their relatives "freedom of movement." Some prisoners who were his relatives were sometimes allowed to go on leave and their relatives were allowed to visit them in violation of regulations.

Suissa, said Bar-Lev, justified what he had done on humanitarian grounds. The minister later told reporters: "His misconduct was the result of his soft heart."

The fifth allegation concerned Suissa's extra-marital relations. Bar-Lev rejected these allegations,

(Continued on back page)

NEXT FRIDAY

We'll be giving you all the information about our forthcoming **London Theatre Tours.** Experience and satisfied customers have made our tours the first choice for Jerusalem Post readers. First tour, **November 23 to 30th** inclusive.

Full details next Friday.

ZIONTOURS, 23 Hillel St., Jerusalem.
Tel: 02-233326/7/8

Commercial Real Estate
Requires
Super luxurious, big HOUSE
in Herzliya Pituah
or Kfar Shmaryahu
FOR AMBASSADOR.
Tel. 03-231616/03-492565
(24 hour professional service).
se057-16-f24

3 Lebanese Jews slain by Shi'ites

Page 2

THE JERUSALEM POST

Vol. LV, No. 16410 Thursday, January 1, 1987 • Kislev 30, 5747 • Jomada Awal 2, 1407 NIS 0.72 (Eilat NIS 0.63)

The cardinal's an easy target for controversy

Page 4

Disarray in prices predicted as new rules begin today

By MICHAL YUDELMAN and KEN SCHACHTER
Jerusalem Post Reporters

TEL AVIV. – Confusion is likely to reign today in appliance stores, new car showrooms and other shops, following a decision by the Ministry of Industry and Trade yesterday not to set maximum prices on the imported goods whose customs levies drop by 60 per cent today.

The only exceptions to the rule are new cars with engines of 1600cc or more, which will continue to be regulated, although ministry officials yielded to importers' demands and announced that profit margins on the sale of most such cars would be increased.

On private cars and taxis of 1601cc or more, controls will be lifted.

The car-pricing policy, signed by Finance Minister Moshe Nissim and Transport Minister Haim Corfu, will allow importers an 18 per cent profit margin on cars with 1600cc engines or smaller, widening the margin on many models and maintaining current levels on others.

On the whole, however, all cars of between 1301cc and 1600cc will be cheaper, while those smaller than 1301cc will be more expensive.

Aryeh Carasso, president of the Car Importers' Association, welcomed the lifting of price controls on some cars, but said that the profits of Israeli importers are still small compared with the 25-40 per cent earned by U.S. importers.

He acknowledged, however, that the new policy substantially boosts the 13 per cent markup importers have been allowed on cars up to 1300cc during the last two years.

A final list of car prices will be published by the government within the next few days. Included in the list of maximum prices will be commercial vehicles of up to 4.5 tons.

An initial government price list drew protest from car importers who said that their substantial investments required that they maintain an adequate profit margin.

For items other than cars each importer and merchant will have to calculate the price according to the customs reduction.

Consumers, too, will have to make their own calculations. They will face the difficulty, however, of being unfamiliar with the different reduction rates of each product and with the former prices as they figure out the new prices.

"Let consumers do some market research before they buy, and refrain from buying hastily," was the advice of Industry and Trade Ministry deputy-director general David Brodet.

He said the ministry had reached an understanding with the big marketing networks and the Federation of Chambers of Commerce, to ensure that the customs reductions benefit the consumer, instead of disappearing into middlemen's pockets.

The ministry decided not to set maximum prices, Brodet said, because thousands of items are involved. Theoretically, he explained, maximum prices do exist. These are the products' former prices, minus the tax reduction.

If the ministry finds that importers and merchants are abusing the tax reductions for their own profit, it will impose price controls and publish maximum prices for certain products, ministry sources said yesterday.

Asked how a consumer is to know the correct price of a product, Brodet replied: "And how did you know the correct price until now? These are products for which no maximum prices were set."

Asked why certain products will be reduced by a greater percentage than others, Brodet said that this was

(Continued on Page 2, Col. 4)

Lavi jet makes its maiden flight

The Lavi takes off on its maiden flight. (IAI)

Test a success, but funding still in doubt

By HIRSH GOODMAN
Post Defence Correspondent

The Lavi fighter yesterday made a 26-minute maiden flight during which the prototype, nearly seven years in development, "performed beyond expectations," according to chief test pilot Menahem Shmul.

After a morning of tense consutations against worsening weather conditions, the IAI, the Lavi's prime contractor, decided to give Shmul the go-ahead for take off at 1:31 p.m. – a mere ten-and-a-half hours before the expiration of an IAI promise to have the Lavi in the air in 1986.

The jubilation over the Lavi's maiden flight at the IAI yesterday was muted by the question marks about the future of the fighter on which $1.2 billion has already been spent. Dr. Dov Zakheim, the Pentagon official responsible for assessing the Lavi programme, is expected to arrive in Israel shortly with an alternate offer based on a modified F-16. One defence ministry official told *The Post* this week the offer "is going to be hard to refuse."

Pressures on the defence budget that have developed in recent months have also led to new questions in both the IDF and the defence establishment regarding the continued viability of the project that will cost another $4.5 billion before the Israeli air force receives its first Lavi in the next decade.

The uncertainty over the Lavi's future was accented at a post-maiden flight ceremony by Defence Minister Yitzhak Rabin yesterday. "Though this is a day of celebration, the Lavi's future is dependent on two governments: Israel and the U.S.," he told the hundreds of IAI workers, indicating in this way that the future of the plane was not entirely, or even primarily, in the hands of the government of Israel. (The U.S., by act of Congress, currently provides $300m. for the plane's development.)

Rabin was not present at the actual maiden flight yesterday, arriving after the completion of the flight. Chief of Staff General Moshe Levy was also absent. The flight was witnessed by O.C. Air Force Amos Lapidot and Minister Moshe Arens, a staunch supporter of the project, outside IAI officials.

Despite the questions, however, the satisfaction of the IAI yesterday when Shmul touched Lavi prototype # 2 down at Lod at 1:47 p.m., after reaching a maximum ceiling of 12,000 feet, was absolute. The cheering of hundreds of men and women involved in the project, and hundreds more who lined the roads surrounding Ben-Gurion Airport, greeted Shmul as he taxied up to his final position at the eastern end of the runway to be doused with fizz from dozens of bottles of champagne.

For the past two months many of those there to receive the plane had worked around the clock to witness this moment.

"Even if this is the end of the road, our achievement has been fantastic," one senior IAI executive said.

"We have taken a giant step forward," said IAI president Moshe Keret. "We are surer than ever before," he told a press conference last night. "that we can carry out the task we have been charged with on behalf of the Israeli Air Force."

Keret has been under extreme pressure since mid-September when the Lavi's maiden flight had been originally scheduled. The delay, caused primarily by a failure by the American Lear-Ziegler company to deliver the Lavi's flight-control system on time, played into the hands of the Lavi's critics.

Describing the flight yesterday Chief Test Pilot Shmul, a 41-year-old Israeli Air Force veteran with over 5,000 hours logged as a test pilot, said that he had taken off at 10 knots under the ground speed he had expected, indicating that the plane had excellent aerodynamic and thrust qualities. With the wheels down for the entire flight he first took the plane up to 5,500 feet, due to a low cloud ceiling at 6,000 feet, and then to 12,000 feet finding a "blue hole" through a cloud.

The main purpose of the flight, Shmul said, was to test the Lavi's responses. The plane responded beyond expectations, he said.

He explained that unlike other aircraft – "and I have flown most of them" – the Lavi's controls are not mechanically operated by the pilot and his stick, but by a "brain" in the centre of the aircraft that makes all the calculations. "It performed better than in simulation," he said. The next test flight, he said, would be within days, weather permitting.

Test pilot Menahem Shmul addresses a press conference after his flight yesterday. (Brutmann/Media)

'Won't lend my hand to fake conversions'

By DVORAH GETZLER
Post Knesset Reporter

In words that echoed Biblical wrath more than national political realities, Interior Minister Yitzhak Peretz told the Knesset yesterday that he had sent Premier Yitzhak Shamir a letter tendering his resignation from the cabinet. The letter by the leader of the ultra-Orthodox Sephardi Shas Party said: "I am doing this in order not to register Ms. Susan Miller as a Jew, which is what the High Court of Justice has asked of me.... I will never lend my hand to registering fake conversions."

Peretz wrote that a number of "solutions" to circumvent the problem had been suggested to him, but he thought it had to be confronted head-on. "Blessed is he who sanctifies the name of the Holy One in public.... Reform conversion is in no sense of the word a conversion, and has no meaning. It is an illusion."

In a Knesset term distinguished only by its desultoriness, an air of mounting drama dominated the business of the plenum prior to the mid-day announcement.

Peretz's wife sat in the VIP gallery, easily identifiable in a bright green kerchief, and surrounded by other modestly dressed women.

The plenum chamber filled slowly, with more than the usual comings, goings and whispered consultations.

Few MKs heeded the long list of written and oral parliamentary questions posed to Defence Minister Yitzhak Rabin and Deputy Finance Minister Adi Amorai. Everyone knew the real show was still to come.

As Amorai wound up the answer to his last questioner, Speaker Shlomo Hillel called on Citizens Rights Movement MK Shulamit Aloni to put her oral question to Peretz.

Aloni wanted to know what the minister intended to do about the High Court ruling in the Miller case

(Continued on Page 2, Col. 7)

Likud launches drive to persuade Peretz to retract resignation

By ASHER WALLFISH
Post Knesset Correspondent

The Likud yesterday began efforts to persuade Interior Minister Yitzhak Peretz, the Shas Party leader, to withdraw his resignation from the government.

Although Peretz announced his resignation from the Knesset yesterday, it will only take effect on Tuesday morning at the earliest.

The minister's move provoked a crisis in relations between the ultra-Orthodox Shas Party and its Likud mentor. But parliamentary observers emphasized that the move had not caused a coalition crisis.

Rabbi Arye Der'i, director-general of the Interior Ministry and Peretz's closest confidant, told *The Jerusalem Post*: "We haven't said anything about leaving the coalition. We're leaving [a decision on] that till next week."

After Peretz sent his letter of resignation to Prime Minister Shamir at 11 a.m. yesterday, Shamir sent urgent messages to Peretz, asking him to delay any announcement until a meeting could be arranged. Peretz declined.

Shas accused the Likud for the second day running of breaking its commitment to push a regulation through the Knesset Law Committee enabling the registration of a new category, "former nationality," on identity cards.

In Shas's view, this would have solved the problem of Shoshana Miller, who was converted to Judaism by a Reform rabbi in the U.S. and immigrated to Israel. The 30 days the High Court gave Peretz to register Miller as unqualifiedly Jewish expire next Monday. Shas had hoped the Law Committee would authorize a regulation whereby Miller would be registered as "Jewish, formerly Christian."

The Basic Law: The Government prescribes that a minister wishing to resign must notify the government of his intention to do so, then hand the prime minister his letter of resignation, from which time 48 hours must elapse before the resignation takes effect.

Peretz's announcement to the Knesset has no constitutional significance. He has to make the announcement at the next cabinet meeting, presumably on Sunday morning, and then count 48 hours.

At the same time, by jumping the gun and telling the Knesset before he told the government, Peretz has inadvertently drawn attention to a slight ambiguity in the law. He may

(Continued on Page 2, Col. 5)

Related stories on Page 4

Interior Minister Yitzhak Peretz in the Knesset yesterday. (Yaron Kaminsky)

Agreed budget cuts: NIS 230m.

By AVI TEMKIN
Post Economic Reporter

The economic inner cabinet has agreed on NIS 230 million in cuts from the state budget. But it is still at odds over the NIS 250m. in cuts that the Finance Ministry proposed making in the budgets of the Defence, Health and Education Ministries.

The Labour Party strongly opposes the additional cuts, and has even proposed in their stead a one-year extension of the levy on private cars and an increase in purchase taxes.

The economic inner cabinet – comprising Prime Minister Shamir, Vice Premier Shimon Peres, Finance Minister Moshe Nissim and Economics Minister Gad Ya'acobi – were empowered by the cabinet plenum to decide on all the cuts, and were to have reached final decisions by Tuesday. The lack of a comprehensive accord could force them to ask the cabinet plenum to decide on the still disputed cuts.

The economic inner cabinet may meet today to try to reach an accord on further cuts.

Solel Boneh sells its subsidiary for $90m.

By PINHAS LANDAU

In a dramatic year-end deal, Solel Boneh yesterday sold its Diyur subsidiary to Bank Hapoalim for $90m. It will use the proceeds to reduce its debt by that amount.

The troubled Histadrut construction concern will now be able to lower its debt by an estimated 20 per cent, improve its balance sheet, and meet the asset-sale targets imposed on it by agreements with the government and banks signed four months ago.

Hapoalim, for its part, has slashed its exposure to Solel Boneh by one-third, and aquired at today's low prices a portfolio of real-estate spread throughout the country. The bank intends to sell off this land, possible after improvements including residential building in some cases, over the next several years.

Both sides are thus understandably delighted at the deal, which one source described as "very complex, but brilliantly conceived and executed."

Solel Boneh was under pressure to sell a large chunk of its assets, which meant it would have received unrealistically low prices in a "firesale" atmosphere. The agreement with Hapoalim was based on valuations of the real estate owned by Diyur made by independent assessors, using "realistic estimates of realizable values based on market prices over the long term," according to a statement issued by Bank Hapoalim last night.

Jordan airline men here study reopening

Post Middle East Staff and agencies

A three-man delegation from Jordan's national airline is visiting Jerusalem to discuss the resumption of the airline's operations in the territories, Palestinian sources said yesterday.

Transport Minister Haim Corfu denied that Israeli officials had had any contact, formal or informal, with the delegation. But Palestinian sources said the group met with Israeli officials.

A West Bank Civil Administration official said he was unaware of the delegation's visit.

The delegation is particularly interested in arranging an air-shuttle from East Jerusalem to Jordan for passengers travelling to and from Amman airport, the Palestinians sources said.

The delegation, which reportedly includes Monib Towqan, manager of Amman airport, Adnan al-Mufti, director of the Jordanian Jet Autobus Co., and Osama Fada, a Jordanian businessman, is said to be staying in East Jerusalem.

The president of the Jordan's national airline, which has changed its name from Alia to Royal Jordanian, recently said he would like to see operations resume in the territories.

U.S. to present its five 'alternatives'

By WOLF BLITZER
Jerusalem Post Correspondent

WASHINGTON. – The U.S. Defence Department will next week present to Israel five "very attractive" alternatives to the production of the Lavi jet aircraft, U.S. officials said yesterday.

The five basic options, they added, will include an additional 19 possible "variations," all of which are designed to maximize employment levels in Israel and to save money in the process.

The package of alternatives, the officials said, included U.S. – Israeli co-production of F-16, F-18 or AV8 Harrier airframes specially fitted with "homegrown" Israeli-designed Lavi avionics.

The Americans believe that a co-produced alternative to the Lavi could begin service in the Israeli Air Force long before the first Lavi would be ready, and that Israel would also have a "proven" fighter, almost certainly superior to the Lavi,

(Continued on Page 2, Col. 1)

Sakharov meets Ida Nudel

MOSCOW (Reuter). – Soviet physicist Andrei Sakharov, released last month from internal exile, yesterday received two long-suffering Jewish would-be emigres in his Moscow flat. This was seen as a further indication that he intends to continue fighting for human rights.

The 65-year-old Nobel Peace Prize winner, who returned from the closed city of Gorky with his wife Yelena Bonner on December 23, chatted in his kitchen with his old friend Ida Nudel, and with Inna Meiman, the cancer-stricken wife of a colleague, whom he was meeting for the first time.

Nudel, 55, who is effectively exiled to the village of Bendery in the Soviet republic of Moldavia, flew here yesterday morning to meet Sakharov and spend New Year's Day in the capital.

Meiman, 54, who is dying from a tumour on the neck, wants to emigrate to the U.S. with her mathematician husband, Prof. Naum Meiman, 74, who with Sakharov monitored Soviet compliance with the Helsiniki accords during the 1970s.

The scene around the kitchen table, strewn with New Year's gifts of sweets and flowers from well-wishers, was reminiscent of the time before Sakharov was exiled in 1980, when he ran what amounted to a legal advice centre for dissidents.

Future of Israel science said in doubt

By BERNARD JOSEPHS
Jerusalem Post Reporter

A gloomy picture of Israel's scientific future, with droves of talented researchers abandoning the country for richer pastures overseas, was painted yesterday by the country's top scientist.

"We are facing a very serious situation which must be remedied at once," said Prof. Yehoshua Yortner, recently appointed president of the Academy of Sciences and Humanities.

He was speaking in Jerusalem a day after the academy's general meeting called for a big government boost in direct grants to scientists engaged in basic research.

An average American university spends around $90 million a year on basic research, he said. Last year, Israel invested $10m.

By failing to finance research, warned Yortner, the country was mortgaging its scientific future. "What is happening now will be reflected in 10 to 15 years. How we will fare scientifically in the year 2000 is being decided at this moment."

Israel's present scientific successes, seen in its electronics, aircraft and chemical industries, was the result of investment in basic research during the '50s and '60s, he said.

"Then we were pioneers in such things as computers and biotechnology. Now, I am sorry to say, the situation is very different."

Yortner complained that constant cutbacks in government support for the universities since the 1970s was already being reflected in the number of young, talented scientists who are conducting their research in the U.S. and Western Europe.

He described some of this as "hidden" emigration, and cited the case of a brilliant Technion inventor who is now teaching at the Haifa institution but conducting his research in the U.S.

This type of situation had resulted in a rich crop of potentially profitable Israeli-invented patents falling into the hands of foreign companies.

"We are losing a whole generation of talent," said Yortner. "We can't compete with the U.S. in terms of salaries and living standards, but we could give these people much improved conditions in which to carry out their research at home."

The academy, said the professor, was now calling on the government to set up a scientific research fund to provide grants of $20m. a year for the next three years, with the aim of halting the brain drain.

"We have done our homework and we believe that this is what is needed. We just hope the government will understand the importance of what is happening," he said.

But more than cash was required to turn the corner and return to the days when Israeli scientists were world leaders, he added.

"We also need a change in atmosphere. In Ben-Gurion's days he once ordered a cabinet meeting to be held at the site of an experiment in solar energy because he was so enthralled by the project. That is the kind of enthusiasm we need today."

THE JERUSALEM POST

Vol. LV, No. 16442 Sunday, February 8, 1987 • Shvat 9, 5747 • Jomada Tani 10, 1407 NIS 0.80 (Eilat NIS 0.70)

Soviets release 42 dissidents, one a Zionist

Jerusalem Post Staff and agencies

MOSCOW. – Soviet authorities have freed 42 dissidents and human-rights activists from labour camps, prisons and exile in the largest known release of political prisoners since thousands left Josef Stalin's camps 30 years ago, sources said yesterday.

One of the freed prisoners, Sergei Grigoryants, said late yesterday that the warden of Chistopol Prison, whom he identified as Maj. Akhmadeyev, showed him a list of 51 people earmarked for release. He did not know how many were actually freed.

"It's not really clear to me why I or anyone else on it [the list] is being freed," Grigoryants said.

Despite reports that "several" Jews were being released, apparently only one Prisoner of Zion, Roald (Alik) Zelichenok, has been freed. The list did not include other jailed Jewish activists, such as Yosef Begun, Yuli Edelshtein and Zachar Zunshein.

Roald (Alik) Zolichenok

Refusenik sources in Moscow reached by telephone last night said that they had no word that any Jewish prisoners of conscience other than Zelichenok were being released.

Some of the Jewish activists are upset at what they see as recent Soviet propaganda successes.

"The Western press is taking Soviet officials at their word when they state that 500 exit visas were granted last month, for example," said one activist. "But the real figures speak for themselves – 98 Jews arrived in the Vienna transit camp in January, and only 12 were refuseniks. At that rate, it will take 100 years to release all of the known refuseniks."

Zelichenok was one of 12 known

(Continued on Page 2, Col. 1)

An Israeli naval vessel confronts the merchant ship that attempted to land 50 Fatah members south of Beirut on Friday.

(Michael Giladi/IDF)

Boat intercepted

Israel Navy seizes 50 Fatah men

By JOSHUA BRILLIANT
Post Defence Reporter

TEL AVIV. – An Israel Navy force on Friday foiled a Fatah attempt to land 50 men on the Lebanese coast some 15 kilometres south of Beirut. The PLO men, who had boarded a small merchant vessel in Cyprus, were detained some 70 miles off the Lebanese coast, and taken to Israel.

The eight-man Egyptian crew was also brought here, OC Navy Aluf Avraham Ben-Shoshan said last night.

The interception was carried out by the crew of a missile boat, part of the force that routinely monitors the more than 100 ships that daily ply the route between Cyprus and Lebanon.

They spotted the 500-600 ton Maria R halfway between Larnaca and the Lebanese town of Khalde, and ordered its captain to stop.

The captain cooperated, and sailors inspected the vessel, which was sailing under a Honduran flag but is apparently owned by a Lebanese.

According to the missile boat's captain, the Egyptian skipper evaded questions until dawn, when he could see the Israeli vessel and realized that its guns were trained at his small boat.

Ben-Shoshan said suspicions arose when it transpired that the Maria R was carrying 50 men instead of the four normally found on board such a ship.

The passengers were ordered to move to the bow, where they sat, not offering any resistance.

The Israelis examined their passports and other papers and discovered that the passports, at least, were forged. More intensive questioning established that the passengers were members of Fatah. They were then transferred to another vessel and brought here.

Ben-Shoshan would not say how senior the men were. But he did say that they had been trained in various countries, and some of those countries were described as "very interesting." He declined to elaborate.

The eight-member crew was also taken in for questioning and their future was unclear. Ben-Shoshan said they would be released if they proved they had not known who they were carrying, but otherwise they would be tried along with the Fatah men.

No arms were found on board.

Fatah has been trying intensively to move commanders and organizers into the Palestinian refugee camps in Lebanon to reorganize its infrastructure there.

So far, several hundred Fatah organizers have reached Lebanon, using various routes. In some cases they sailed to the Christian part of Jounieh, and with the aid of the Christian-led Lebanese Forces reached Moslem-held West Beirut.

A Navy operation several weeks ago, in which two Cypriot ferries were stopped en route to Jounieh, highlighted the PLO's contacts with the Lebanese Forces. But Ben-Shoshan indicated that the Jounieh route is probably no longer in use.

The Maria R's destination, Khalde, suggested possible cooperation with the Druse who control that area. But Ben-Shoshan declined to point a finger at the Druse, saying it was not always clear who controls what in Lebanon.

But Friday's interception again pointed to Cyprus' role in the PLO return to Lebanon. Ben-Shoshan said that the PLO men change identities in Cyprus and that the island is a "major base" for PLO attempts to smuggle arms into Lebanon.

The PLO, he continued, uses passenger vessels, yachts, fishing and other vessels, and weapons are often concealed in shipping containers. Rocket-propelled grenades and machineguns had been found in food shipments, he said.

After 'Jerusalem Post' interview

Palestinian activist charged with incitement

By JOEL GREENBERG
Jerusalem Post Reporter

Charges have been brought against Palestinian activist Faisel Husseini for statements on the PLO made in an interview published in *The Jerusalem Post.*

A charge sheet was submitted to the Jerusalem Magistrates' Court, at the instruction of the Justice Ministry, a senior ministry source said.

The legal action came following a complaint filed by Kiryat Arba lawyer Eliakim Ha'etzni. He charged that statements made by Husseini in a January 23 interview in *The Post* magazine violated the Terror Prevention Act and the Penal law against sedition.

Ha'etzni's complaint cited the following:

□ Husseini said: "The PLO is the only legitimate representative of the Palestinian people."

□ Husseini compared the Palestinians under Israeli occupation to Europeans under German occupation in World War II, and drew an analogy between European and Palestinian resistance. "Once the PLO wins some victories on the outside and is perceived as strong, our morale here will also improve. We will be able to mount more resistance, non-violent or otherwise, and then the world will pay more attention."

□ According to Ha'etzni, Husseini identified with the PLO, in remarks he made on the development of the PLO's political power. "Today the PLO is in the first stage. But it's only a matter of time before we reach the second. For the time being I can't force any plan on you, but I can stop any plan from being carried out without me."

Husseini said last night that he believed the charges against him were the outcome of a campaign by Ha'etzni against expressions of opinion by Palestinians. Ha'etzni has recently filed complaints against the editors of the East Jerusalem *Al-Awdah* magazine for publishing an editorial stating that the PLO was the sole legitimate representative of the Palestinians. He has also made complaints against editors of the *Al-Fajr* newspaper for publishing an interview with Yasser Arafat.

Ha'etzni said his actions were meant to ensure enforcement of the law and to prevent "legitimization of the enemy," which, he said, would lead to Israel's "disintegration from within."

Alignment, Likud see budget row over soon

By MENACHEM SHALEV
and AVI TEMKIN
Jerusalem Post Reporters

Both the Likud and Labour believe that the present crisis over the state budget and approval of aid for the kibbutzim will be resolved soon, although the exact formula for breaking the deadlock remains unclear.

Prime Minister Yitzhak Shamir and Vice Premier Shimon Peres are expected to meet this morning to discuss the impasse. Ministers from both parties will hold consultations before today's cabinet meeting in order to consolidate their positions.

Finance Minister Moshe Nissim, who continues to insist that the NIS 266 million debt-rescheduling package for the United Kibbutz Movement be approved, told Likud members of the Knesset Committee that his office had already begun examining the financial demands of settlements in the West Bank and Gaza.

The Likud MKs have balked at approving aid for the kibbutzim, and are pressing also for budget allocations for the settlements and development towns.

Labour Knesset caucus chairman Rafi Edri said last night that his party rejects "trade-off" between the kibbutzim and the settlements. But Labour Party sources have said privately that they would not reject out of hand a Treasury-sponsored proposal for aid to the settlements.

Labour Party Chairman MK Uzi Baram also emphasized over the weekend Labour's support for aid to development towns.

MK Eliahu Matza (Likud), one of the sponsors of the Likud "revolt" in the finance committee against Nissim's proposals on the kibbutzim, told *The Jerusalem Post* last night he believes that ultimately NIS 100m. will be earmarked for both the kibbutzim and the settlements, thereby bringing the crisis to an end.

Matza, a supporter of Housing Minister David Levy, rejected Labour's contention that the crisis evolved from internal struggles within Herut. He said that Likud MKs "from all the camps" wished to tell Shamir and Nissim "that not everything goes."

MK Ariel Weinstein, who coordinates the Likud's finance committee members, called on Likud ministers not to take any decisions before informing Likud MKs. "We won't approve anything before we hear about the general framework of allocations for all the sectors," he said.

Berri wants swap involving Israelis

Jerusalem Post Staff

The head of Lebanon's Shi'ite Amal movement, Nabih Berri, yesterday proposed a three-way prisoner swap among his organization, Israel and at least one of the groups holding hostages in Lebanon.

Berri told reporters in Damascus that in the first stage of the exchange, Amal would release an Israeli airman captured last October when his plane was shot down over southern Lebanon in return for the release by Israel of about 400 Palestinians.

Sources in the Israeli defence establishment last night indicated that they would very much welcome an opportunity to negotiate the release of the airman and soldiers missing in Lebanon – but they wanted to do it discreetly.

Commenting on Berri's statement, they said their first priority was to take care of the soldiers missing in action – those who were kidnapped and the airman.

"Israel will not spare any effort to bring its soldier-sons back home," one source said. However, he added, Israel "would prefer" not to discuss these matters publicly.

Following Israel's release of 400 Palestinians, the Islamic Jihad for the Liberation of Palestine would then free four American teachers kidnapped at Beirut University on January 24.

Berri also expressed the conviction that missing Anglican envoy Terry Waite "will be released soon."

An anonymous telephone caller to a Beirut radio station said last night that Waite had been released in Beirut, but there was no immediate sign of the church envoy and no confirmation was available.

"I have spoken, I have worked and I have the feeling that he will be released soon," Berri said.

Berri said that Waite, who is feared held by the captors of American hostages with whom he had been negotiating, will be freed within 48 hours.

Waite disappeared in Moslem West Beirut on January 20 for secret negotiations with Shi'ite Moslem extremists.

(Continued on Page 2, Col. 3)

Iraqi planes bomb nine Iranian cities

NICOSIA (AP). – Iraqi warplanes yesterday bombed nine Iranian cities, including the holy city of Qom, seat of Iran's religious hierarchy, defying Iranian threats of massive missile retaliation. Iran claimed its gunners shot down two of the jets.

The official Iraqi news agency, monitored in Nicosia, said Iraqi fighter-bombers struck twice at Qom, 160 km south of Teheran, claiming that the targets were "reduced to rubble."

The Iraqi war report said a U.S.-made Hawk surface-to-air missile battery in Khorramshahr was destroyed in an air raid on that city in the oil-rich southwestern province of Khuzestan.

The agency said the air force flew 232 combat missions yesterday. Iraq's powerful air force, which outnumbers Iran's air strength by about 6-1, has long held supremacy of the skies in the 6-year-old Gulf War.

Iran's official Islamic Republic News Agency (Irna) said the cities of Tabriz, Isfahan, Boroujerd, Marivan, Arak, Andimeshk and Piranshahr were bombed, with many civilians killed or wounded. It did not give specific figures.

Palestinians meet EC group on aid for areas

By JOEL GREENBERG
Jerusalem Post Reporter

Palestinian businessmen and heads of chambers of commerce met over the weekend with a visiting delegation from the EC to discuss European aid to the territories and direct exports from the territories to European Community member countries, Palestinian sources said.

The EC delegation met last week with Israeli officials in an effort to follow up recent EC moves to grant preferential status to agricultural imports from the West Bank and Gaza Strip.

EC financial aid would be directed to various institutions in the territories, such as hospitals and schools, but not to private enterprises, the Palestinian sources said.

Discussions with Israeli officials have focused on allowing direct exports from the territories to EC nations. The move has been opposed by Israeli farmers concerned about competition. Israel has insisted that agricultural exports from the territories to Europe be coordinated through its agricultural cooperatives and the Agrexco marketing firm.

Husband jailed for $385,000 Baltimore swindle

U.S. Jewish woman leader not resigning

By WOLF BLITZER
Jerusalem Post Correspondent

WASHINGTON. – Shoshana Cardin, president of the Council of Jewish Federations (CJF) in the U.S., is not expected to step down from her position despite the sentencing of her husband, Jerome Cardin, to 15 years in prison for stealing $385,000 from a failed Baltimore financial institution of which he was part owner.

The CJF announced last week that it will hold its annual meeting in Jerusalem beginning on February 19. Shoshana Cardin, a devoted and highly-respected leader in the American Jewish community, is expected to chair the meeting. "She'll be in Jerusalem," a source close to her said.

Cardin was unavailable for comment, but her CJF associates and other leaders in the Jewish community said that they have received no indication from her that she plans to resign, adding that there has been no pressure on her to quit because of her husband's conviction.

"She's truly beloved," a source in the Baltimore Jewish community said. "She's remaining silent about her overall intentions."

In a recent editorial, *The Baltimore Sun* praised Cardin as an outstanding community leader in her own right and defended her decision to remain active in Jewish and non-Jewish philanthropic affairs.

The CJF is the major umbrella organization of more than 200 Jewish federations throughout the U.S. These federations are the backbone of Jewish fund-raising activities for both local and overseas needs, including programmes in Israel.

Jerome Cardin, a politically-influential and well-known Baltimore lawyer and businessman, was part owner of Old Court Savings and Loan, a local financial institution which went out of business nearly two years ago. Thousands of depositors lost money.

Its president and principal owner, Jeffrey Levitt, was convicted of stealing some $14 million from the institution and is currently serving a 30-year prison sentence. Legal action is pending against other owners of the financial institution.

Cardin, who has been active in Jewish and non-Jewish philanthropic activities in Baltimore for many years, is currently out of jail on $1 million bail. He is appealing his 15-year sentence.

The Washington Post has reported that he spent nearly $1 million on his legal defence but was still sentenced to the maximum 15-year prison term. His wife sat next to him throughout the many weeks of his highly-publicized trial in Baltimore. The judge had refused to consider his and his wife's direct appeals for compassion and a reduced sentence on the grounds of his record of philanthrophy and other services to the community.

The highly-publicized collapse of Old Court Savings and Loan resulted in a major "run" on many shaky financial institutions throughout Maryland. For weeks, thousands of depositors were seen on TV news programmes queueing day and night to make withdrawals. Several of these institutions were temporarily shut down, leaving depositors without money to pay bills, mortgages and other expenses.

The collapse of Old Court followed the failure of another Savings and Loan institution in Cincinnati, Ohio, controlled by Marvin Warner,

(Continued on page 4)

Porky politics

Page 4

THE JERUSALEM POST

Vol. LV, No. 16464 Thursday, March 5, 1987 • Adar 4, 5747 • Rajab 6, 1407 NIS 0.80 (Eilat NIS 0.70)

SECOND EDITION

Bruno warns of renewed inflation

Page 7

Months to repair damage

NIS 200 'loan' ends hospital strike

By JUDY SIEGEL
Post Science and Health Reporter

The Health Ministry estimates that it will take "months" to undo the damage and eliminate the backlog caused by the 10-day hospital workers' strike which ended yesterday.

The 11,000 cleaning workers and clerks at the 26 government hospitals returned to work yesterday afternoon, an hour or two after the signing of an accord with the Histadrut – but not with the Treasury.

Based on their interpretation of the agreement, the workers believe they will get a "standing loan" of NIS 200 per worker in their next pay slip and that the government's Padeh Committee – empowered to equalize government hospital workers' salaries with those of their counterparts at Kupat Holim Clalit hospitals – will resume its deliberations.

According to the Health Ministry sources the Treasury "did more than hint" that it would pay the NIS 200 standing loan (a grant given on condition that the workers stay on the job for the remainder of the month.) But the Treasury spokesman last night denied categorically that any hints or commitments have been made to the Histadrut, and declared that the NIS 200 payment would not be made.

Histadrut Trade Union chief Haim Haberfeld admitted last night that the Treasury had not in fact promised to pay the standing loan, but added that the Histadrut "would do all it could" to ensure that the Padeh Committee would raise the workers' salaries.

"We were all losers in this strike – patients, strikers and the government," said the Health Ministry spokesman. He claimed that the Treasury had erred seriously by resorting to the labour courts for injunctions against some of the strikers. "If they had left it up to us, it would have ended much sooner," he said.

Animosity between the Treasury and the Health Ministry was generated during the strike by the completely opposed philosophies and objectives of Health Minister Shoshana Arbeli-Almoslino and Finance Minister Moshe Nissim.

The Health Ministry plans to send a bill for some NIS 10 million to the Treasury for the catered meals purchased and the outside workers hired during the strike. Asked about this, the Treasury spokesman said that they would study the bill if they received one.

The returning strikers immediately went about cleaning up the garbage and restocking supplies.

Arbeli-Almoslino will bring to the cabinet either this Sunday or the next week her proposal to establish an independent panel to completely re-think the hospital system and make recommendations for its reform.

The Finance Ministry spokesman, however, commented that if the panel turned out to be a copy of the Etzioni Committee – which recommended higher salaries for teachers and was a "cause of endless trouble and expense" – Nissim would not support it.

Prosecution cites 'Post' interviews

Pollard gets life, wife 5 years

By WOLF BLITZER
Jerusalem Post Correspondent

WASHINGTON. – Confessed spy Jonathan Pollard was sentenced yesterday to life in prison for his espionage activities on behalf of Israel.

His wife, Ann Henderson Pollard, received a 5-year prison sentence for possessing classified documents.

Henderson-Pollard fell to the floor, weeping hysterically as U.S. District Court Judge Aubrey Robinson rejected the defendants' pleas for leniency.

The judge imposed a more severe sentence on the 32-year-old former naval intelligence officer than had been expected. As part of a plea-bargaining agreement last June, the government prosecutor had promised to ask for a "substantial" sentence, but not life.

In issuing his sentence, Robinson said that in all his years on the bench he had never received more "voluminous" submissions from the defence and prosecution.

Both the prosecutors and the judge appeared exceptionally bitter towards Pollard because of the large numbers of documents he had stolen.

In appealing for mercy, the Pollards expressed deep remorse over their criminal activities. They both insisted that they had been motivated by deep ideological commitment to Israel.

Pollard also expressed his deep regret over the injury he had caused his wife, his parents and his family, and went on to express deep regret over the damage done to U.S.-Israeli relations.

"I must admit that I wholly and unconditionally accept responsibility for my criminal culpability," he said. "I broke faith and took the law into my own hands."

Pollard emotionally appealed to the judge not to send his wife back to prison. He referred to his deep love for her, as she referred to her love for him during her tearful appeal for leniency.

Both Pollards were taken from the courtroom in custody, leaving relatives and defence lawyers stunned by the sentences. Because of Henderson-Pollard's stomach disorders, there had been speculation that she would receive a period of probation without actually having to return to prison.

But the judge accepted the position presented by Defence Secretary Caspar Weinberger in affidavits to the court that Pollard had severely damaged American national interests by transferring to Israel thousands of classified documents over an 18-month period.

Jonathan Pollard

But the U.S. prosecutor rejected the Pollards' arguments. One government prosecutor charged that Pollard continued to maintain a posture of "arrogance and deception." He urged the judge "not to swallow" Pollard's contention that his activities had caused no harm to America's national security because the material in the documents went to a friendly country.

"There was enormous damage done to our national security," the assistant U.S. attorney, Charles Leeper said.

Leeper said that Pollard had shown "utter contempt for the U.S. military and intelligence community." He accused Pollard of having a "warped" mentality that supported "Israel right or wrong."

The prosecutors referred to two interviews which Pollard had granted *The Jerusalem Post* and an interview his wife gave to CBS News last Sunday as evidence that they did not regret their crimes. They also accused Pollard of providing classified information to *The Jerusalem Post* – a contention rejected by Pollard's lawyer.

The prosecutors insisted that Pollard should have cleared his interviews in advance with the director of naval intelligence as had been determined in his earlier plea-bargaining agreement.

Yesterday's hearing lasted for more than three hours. It began as dozens of reporters and others scrambled for a limited number of seats. Pollard and his wife were escorted into the courtroom by federal marshals. Each had lost some 27 kilos since they were first arrested 16 months ago.

They sat across from each other at the defendants' table as their lawyers, Richard and James Hibey, presented lengthy arguments on their behalf to the judge.

First Pollard, and then his wife, approached the judge to make personal appeals. Henderson-Pollard repeatedly broke down and wept as she expressed her ever-lasting love for her husband. "I would never do anything to harm him," she said.

"I pray to God every day that I will be united with my husband. That's all I live for. He's the most wonderful man in the world."

The sentencing yesterday came a day after the U.S. indicted Israel Air Force officer Aviem Sella on espionage charges. The judge appeared influenced by this indictment, and seemed to ignore arguments made by the defendants' lawyers that testimony by Pollard and his wife before a federal grand jury had enabled the Justice Department to issue the indictment against Sella.

Republican Congressman Richard Cheney, a member of the House of Representatives Intelligence Committee, told reporters: "It is important that the Israeli government understand that some of us consider that was a totally inappropriate act by an ally to take.

Lebanese Army troops yesterday take up positions on the coastal road linking Beirut to Sidon. About 600 soldiers were deployed in a new bid to restore order under a Syrian-brokered plan. (Story – page 2)

Canada bars Aluf Yaron

OTTAWA (Reuter). – The Canadian government announced yesterday that it would not accept Aluf Amos Yaron as a military attache in Ottawa, apparently because of Yaron's involvement in the Sabra and Shatilla massacre following the 1982 Lebanon war.

A Foreign Ministry spokesman said yesterday that Canada would not look favourably on the appointment, but he declined to give a reason for this attitude.

Yaron, who is currently a military attache at the Israeli Embassy in Washington, was commander of the IDF forces in Beirut at the time of the massacre. He was subsequently reprimanded by the Kahan Commission for not preventing the Phalangists from slaughtering the Palestinians of Sabra and Shatilla.

Canadian Foreign Minister Joe Clark was quoted yesterday as acknowledging that the rejection of a nominated military attache was unusual.

In Israel, both the Defence Ministry and the Army yesterday declined comment on Canada's refusal to accept Yaron's credentials.

'Stupidest effort by Peres'

By BENNY MORRIS
Post Diplomatic Correspondent

Prime Minister Shamir believes that Foreign Minister Peres's efforts to convene an international conference for Middle East peace are the "stupidest" diplomatic move by an Israeli leader since the establishment of the state.

Shamir is understood to believe that there is no possibility of compromise between his utter rejection of the conference idea and Peres's propagation of it as the best avenue for progress in the peace process.

Shamir is understood to believe that Peres's activity on behalf of the international conference must cease forthwith.

Shamir is understood to have declared that the Likud, under the unity government, would never allow Israeli participation in such a conference and that he has consistently opposed the idea of such a conference since October 1985.

Shamir is understood to believe that Jordan so far has not presented Israel with any "concrete proposal" for peace or to start peace talks.

An international conference, Shamir believes, is the most convenient situation for the Arabs, and the Arabs' position will follow the most extreme common denominator. The Soviets are interested in the conference because it will enable them to impose terms and a solution. Shamir believes that Peres's activity on behalf of the conference has eliminated any chance that the Arabs would agree to direct negotiations with Israel.

Shamir is understood to be "sad" because of the present controversy with Labour and his foreign minister, but believes that there is no need for the sides to raise their voices or to make uncultured utterances in the process. He does not believe the disagreement over the conference should lead to a crisis or a break-up of the unity government.

Shamir believes that the confer-

(Continued on Page 2, Col. 3)

Coalition slanging in the Knesset

By DVORAH GETZLER
Post Knesset Reporter

The simmering row between the two major partners to the national unity government threatened to erupt in the Knesset plenum yesterday, but was kept in check by an uneasy compromise. Nevertheless, both Alignment and Likud MKs agreed that the storm over an international peace conference was far from over. It would burst forth again in the Foreign Affairs and Defence Committee, it was predicted.

At the heart of the storm stood an unruffled Foreign Minister Shimon Peres, aiming barbs of criticism at opponents to the left and right.

Peres's message was the need of this generation to prepare a war-free area for the next. That would only come about if this generation showed resourcefulness and understanding.

Until 1978, Israel had had only one course of action – "the security option." Since 1978, there also existed "the political option."

"The Camp David accords had wrought a dramatic change in Israel's status; the Egyptians not only flew the Israeli flag, they also invested their resources in agriculture, in road building. Only the blind could deny the dramatic nature of that change.

"It was Mr. Begin who made the peace!" interjected Deputy Minister Ronni Milo.

"But with our help! And where were you then? In which propaganda role were you serving? Why don't you show the people what you've done! You achieved a lot in Brazil [a reference to Milo's alleged arrangement over the adoption by Israelis of Brazilian babies], though the Brazilians deny it. When will you grow up?" Peres retorted.

"Watch out!" Milo warned.

"I have nothing to watch out for," Peres declared.

"I never returned a watch to anyone. I never received a watch, and never returned one!" sneered Milo in a reference to watch that Peres had received as a gift from financier David Balas, now on trial for fraud. (Peres returned the watch after Likud MKs publicized the gift.)

Peres's reply to that was to challenge Milo to compare what his income was – aside from what he earned "labouring for the public good" – and what he, Peres, earned. "Watch out! You won't pull the public along with you this way. You're not Begin!"

But that wasn't the end of the mud slinging.

It was Peres's version of the "Marshall plan" that would save Syria, Milo sarcastically suggested as Peres outlined his approach to the costs of war and peace.

What's happened to the Marshall plan, Milo persisted in baiting him.

"Nothing's happened – yet," said Peres, "But since you're such a budding statesman, we'll do it together."

Turning to Tehiya's Geula Cohen, author of one of the motions for the agenda (the others were tabled by the Citizens Rights Movement's Yossi Sarid, Mapam's Elazar Granot, and the Democratic Front for Peace and Equality's Meir Wilner), Peres insisted that it had been the Begin government of 1977 that had first floated the idea of an international peace conference – with the participation of the Soviets and a Pan-Arab delegation. "And that is something I would not accept," he said.

"An attack on the conference is first and foremost an attack on Begin," Peres baited Cohen.

Camp David, said Peres, had only negated the 1977 government resolution as it related to Egypt. But that decision still applied to the other Arab states, Peres insisted, over the repeated objections of the Likud's Ehud Olmert – "Even though you are a lawyer and you know how to give lots of advice," Peres taunted him.

(Continued on Back Page)

Cutting women's hair before the gassing

By ERNIE MEYER
Jerusalem Post Reporter

Gustav Boraks, an 86-year-old survivor of Treblinka, testified in Yiddish at the Demjanjuk war crimes trial yesterday. But he added little of substance to the testimony of earlier witnesses, except for his quiet dignity and evidence of what age can do to memory.

Expanding on the horrors that have emerged during the trial so far, Boraks tearfully told of an experience connected with his job in the camp. A barber by trade, he was allowed to live and put to work with another 15 men, cutting off women's hair before they were gassed.

"One day my sister-in-law with her two young children came into the shed we were worked," he said. "When she saw me, she almost fainted. She knew her husband had already been killed. She also knew she was going to her death and she implored me to save her children."

But Boraks was powerless to help.

Born in a small town near Lodz, Boraks had his own barber shop until the invading Germans took it away from him. With his wife and his two sons, Pinhas and Yosef, he moved to Krakow. One day the Gestapo arrested him for failing to wear the armband identifying him as a Jew. They beat him and threw him down three flights of stairs in prison. "But my wife had a fur coat," he said, "and when she brought it to the Gestapo, I was released."

Boraks did not remember the exact date in 1942 when he was taken to Treblinka, where his wife and children were killed on arrival.

The old man told his story in Yiddish, but there were continual difficulties with the translator. Finally, Judge Zvi Tal asked the witness a question directly in Yiddish, bypassing the translator. "Him I understand," said the witness, and Tal, with his rich Yiddish delivered in an authoritative tone, had a new job.

Led by prosecutor Michael Shaked, the witness told how Ivan the Terrible used a bayonet to prod the frightened women into the shed to have their hair cut. "They were wounded and whole chunks of flesh would hang from them. There was a lot of blood," he said.

When there was no hair to cut, the barbers had to sort clothing or do other work. "Anyone who did not work well was shot."

Boraks recalled how one day the deputy-commander of the camp, Kurt Franz, nicknamed Lalka, rode his horse to the entrance of the latrine and shot a man sitting in it. On another occasion, he said, Lalka had two boys, who were caught trying to escape, hung up by their feet in the freezing cold.

The prosecutor got Boraks to describe how he had identified photographs of Treblinka guards Fedor Federenko and Ivan the Terrible from a selection shown to him in 1976 by police inspector Miriam Radifker. "I recognized Ivan the Terrible, with his high forehead...eyes and full face. He used to spend much time in the barber shop," he said.

The photos had been sent to the Israel Police by the U.S. Justice Department, which at the time was holding denaturalization hearings against John Demjanjuk.

Boraks again identified the face of John Demjanjuk from photographs shown by the police here in 1981. In 1978, he flew with a group of other survivors to Ft. Lauderdale, Florida to testify in the proceedings against Federenko.

After the 11 a.m. recess, court president Dov Levin said that it was not convenient for Tal to carry the additional burden of translation, but he relented when defence counsel Mark O'Connor asked to continue with the arrangement.

With O'Connor now cross-examining the witness, the problem of translation really became daunt-

(Continued on Page 7)

Iran launches new offensive

Turkish jets hit Iraqi Kurdish camps

SIRNAK, Turkey. – Turkish Air Force jets bombed Kurdish rebel targets in Iraq yesterday, destroying their camps and ammunition depots in retaliation for recent attacks near this frontier town that killed 34 civilians, the government said.

Thirty jets bombed nine selected targets from 8 a.m. to 8:30 a.m. following reconnaissance flights over the area at daybreak. All aircraft returned safely to base, according to a General Staff statement.

It was not immediately known whether there were any casualties among the insurgents who wanted to establish an idependent Marxist state in Eastern Turkey. Unconfirmed reports, however, said 100 were killed.

Kurdish rebels raided a frontier village 10 days ago and killed 14 peasants, mostly women and children, bringing to 34 the number of villagers killed in the southeast region in the past month, authorities said.

In October 1984, Turkey and Iraq signed an agreement that allowed their armed forces to pursue Kurdish rebels into each other's territory, in an area extending 10km. from the border. Turkey and Iraq share a 320 km. border.

The Kurdish Labour Party is a Marxist-Leninist underground organization with headquarters in Syria. Its leaders say the group's aim is to set up an independent, Marxist Kurdistan in eastern Turkey that will be a member of the Warsaw Pact.

Intelligence sources estimate the strength of the party at a few thousand members. They accuse Syria of supplying the group with weapons.

In the Gulf War, Iran kept battlefront pressure on Iraq yesterday, launching a new offensive at Haj Omran in the north and claiming fresh victories on the Basra front in the south.

Iran's official news media said the Iranian forces attacked overnight along the Haj Omran-Rowenduz axis in Iraqi Kurdistan in order to open a new front in Iraq's northeast corner.

Iraq reported heavy fighting along the Basra front, but withheld comment on Iranian claims on its Haj Omran attack.

Soldiers violated orders in shooting Nablus youth

By JOEL GREENBERG
Jerusalem Post Reporter

A Military Police investigation has found that soldiers who shot and killed a Nablus youth this week violated IDF regulations concerning the apprehension of fleeing suspects, it was learned yesterday.

The IDF has delayed publication of the investigation's results, which reportedly show that soldiers did not completely follow orders which require troops to shout warnings and fire in the air before firing at the legs of fleeing suspects.

Eye-witnesses have said that the soldiers shouted but then immediately opened fire directly at three youths who fled a routine security check in downtown Nablus on Monday. One teenager was killed, another was wounded in the leg, and the third escaped.

In the Jelazoun refugee camp yesterday, soldiers sealed one house and rooms in three other homes belonging to persons suspected of planting a roadside charge last October north of Ramallah. The bomb exploded and caused damage, but there were no casualties.

Pending trial, Israelis can go home

NEW YORK (JTA). – The U.S. District Court in Manhattan has allowed the four Israelis indicted here for conspiracy to sell Iran American weapons to return to Israel until their trial, scheduled to begin May 18.

The permission of the court hinged on an assurance from the Israeli government that it would not prevent the defendants from returning to America for the trial. Although Israel refused initially, the court received a letter recently containing the necessary assurances.

Guri and Israel Eisenberg, Brig. Gen. Avraham Bar-Am and William Northrop were indicted last April along with 13 other defendants on charges of conspiracy to resell about $2 billion of American weapons to Iran.

polgat chain stores

THE THURSDAY DISCOUNT LINE

25% OFF KNITWEAR AT ALL POLGAT STORES

ONLY TODAY

ARIELY

Renting out your flat?

Hurry!
There are only a few hours left to place your classified ad for tomorrow's Luah Ma'ariv.
Just take your ad to any advertising agency, or to an office of Ma'ariv (or call 03-439439) and it will run in Hebrew in that paper.
Hand it in early enough to make sure it reaches the office of Luah Ma'ariv before 5 p.m. today and your ad will also appear in English in The Jerusalem Post.
Beat that deadline!

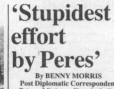

El Al's fatigued pilots

Page 4

THE JERUSALEM POST

Vol. LV, No. 16484 Sunday, March 29, 1987 • Adar 28, 5747 • Rajab 30, 1407 NIS 0.80 (Eilat NIS 0.70)

SECOND EDITION

Herut convention begins

Moment of truth for Premier Shamir

By MENACHEM SHALEV
Jerusalem Post Reporter

The best political show in town gets under way this morning as over 2,000 Herut activists, fervently hoping that last year's chaos will not be repeated, come to the Tel Aviv Fairgrounds for the Herut convention.

The convention is seen as a crucial test for Herut and its leader, Prime Minister Yitzhak Shamir. If the convention again degenerates into disorder, Shamir's hold over the party will be seriously undermined and, observers say, the lifespan of the National Unity Government drastically shortened.

A major stumbling block to a peaceful convention appeared to have been removed last night when Minister Moshe Katsav, chairman of the presidium, announced that he would not vie against Deputy Prime Minister David Levy for the post of deputy chairman.

Katsav, who has been under increasing fire from Levy and his supporters during the last few days, told *The Jerusalem Post* last night that his decision was "not a sign of weakness." Katsav said that he had received "hundreds of appeals" urging him to compete and although confident that he would win, he is more concerned about ensuring party unity and a peaceful convention.

MK and former finance minister Aridor, on the other hand, on Friday resisted Shamir's efforts to dissuade him from competing against Minister Moshe Arens for the post of chairman of the party secretariat. Aridor, the incumbent, is said to be disappointed at Herut leaders for excluding him from the cabinet and is in no mind to give up the powerful post without a fight.

The Arens-Aridor confrontation was, as of last night, the greatest source of concern for the Shamir/Arens camp. Aridor is likely to be supported by Levy backers against arch-rival Arens and he also commands the personal allegiance of members of the other camps. Arens's defeat would deal a serious blow to the Shamir camp and Arens's chances of succeeding Shamir.

Shamir, whose election as party chairman is assured, will call on the convention to elect the three ministers to the party posts in the interests of "party unity."

In a meeting in Tel Aviv last night, Arens lashed out sharply at Levy, saying that "the attempt to pit contenders against ministers was like playing Russian roulette with the future" of Herut.

Arens last night announced formally for the first time that he would seek the secretariat post. He had been under pressure from supporters to compete against Levy.

Late last night Katsav was still under heavy pressure to reverse his earlier position and to compete against Levy, who, Shamir supporters say, is the main instigator of the internal rivalries and yet faces no serious opposition himself. As of last night, Levy was opposed only by MK Meir Cohen-Avidov, a Sharon supporter. Shamir backers said last night that they would either vote against Levy or abstain, and one quipped that "we may yet wake up on Monday morning with Cohen-Avidov as our deputy chairman."

Minister Ariel Sharon, who will compete with Reuven Rivlin and MK Ovadia Ali for the chairmanship of the central committee, last night called on Shamir to assert his "leadership" and to ensure the election of the three ministers.

The convention is slated to open at 11 a.m., cutting short the customary Sunday cabinet meeting in Jerusalem. It will be under heavy security guard and is expected to be attended by several foreign diplomats, possibly including U.S. Ambassador Thomas Pickering. Leaders of other parties have not been invited, but Labour Secretary-General Uzi Baram said last night that

(Continued on Page 2, Col. 6)

Step towards int'l conference

China announces talk with Israel

Compiled from reports by DAVID LANDAU in Hongkong, WALTER RUBY at the UN, and agency dispatches.

China's official announcement yesterday that a high-level meeting had taken place between Chinese and Israeli officials was greeted in Hongkong as a significant development in the two countries' delicate relationship.

Diplomats and other China-watchers stressed that the Xinhua news agency report of the meeting was unprecedented. The meeting itself is believed not to be the first of its kind.

Xinhua reported, on its Chinese-language service, that Foreign Ministry Director-General Avraham Tamir met with the Chinese permanent representative to the UN, Li Luye, at UN headquarters in New York on Friday.

The Chinese agency and the Israeli spokesman at the UN said the talks focused on Middle East peace efforts and a possible international peace conference.

Avraham Tamir (IPPA)

"It was in a UN context rather than a bilateral context, and one of a series of meetings being held with members of the Security Council," Israeli UN spokesman Eyal Arad said.

The meeting was held at Israel's initiative and was arranged by the two countries' UN missions, he added.

Arad said although Israel was the seventh country to recognize the Peking government following the 1949 Communist revolution in China, the two countries had never established diplomatic relations.

Israel has shown growing interest in establishing diplomatic ties with China in recent years, and there have been reports of trade contracts through third countries.

Also taking part in Friday's meeting between Li and Tamir were Avi Primor, deputy director-general of the Foreign Ministry in charge of African and Asian affairs and Israeli UN ambassador Binyamin Netanyahu.

The Xinhau report said:

"Israel requested to meet with representatives of the permanent members of the Security Council, including China." The Chinese agency thus carefully set the encounter within a UN framework.

"Tamir and Li discussed the Middle East situation at UN headquarters. Li explained China's positions on the Middle East – that it supports an international peace conference on the Middle East under UN auspices and that the PLO is entitled to take part in such a conference."

The reference to an international conference must be especially gra-

(Continued on Back Page)

'U.S. spy in Israel' leak will be probed

WASHINGTON. – The U.S. Senate has opened an investigation into the accuracy and propriety of Republican Senator David Durenberger's suggestion that the U.S. recruited a senior Israeli army officer during the war in Lebanon in 1982.

The Minnesota lawmaker, the immediate past Chairman of the Senate Intelligence Committee, has been sharply criticized by U.S. national security officials for supposedly releasing sensitive and classified information.

Defence Secretary Caspar Weinberger has publicly denied Durenberger's allegation that the U.S. used an Israeli military officer as a spy. Israeli leaders have also firmly denied the senator's statements.

But *The Washington Post* and other U.S. sources in Washington have confirmed the thrust of his remarks, which were first reported in *The Jerusalem Post*. These sources said the mysterious officer worked for the U.S. from 1982 until 1984.

On March 15, Durenberger had told two Jewish groups in Palm Beach, Florida, that by authorizing the use of the Israeli officer to spy against Israel, CIA Director William Casey had "changed the rules of the game," possibly setting the stage for Israel's recruitment of former U.S. naval intelligence analyst Jonathan Jay Pollard in 1984.

"We changed the rules in the early 1980s," Durenberger is quoted as having said. "We recruited an Israeli to spy on Israel, and he got caught.... What I'm really saying to you is that this is not a one-way street. I can't justify Pollard, but I can understand it."

***The New York Times* said yesterday that the Senate Ethics Committee's preliminary investigation into**

(Continued on Back Page)

IDF clash with Amal reported

Jerusalem Post Staff

Israeli forces clashed with Shi'ite Amal militiamen yesterday evening during what was apparently an attack on terrorist strongholds in and around villages north of the security zone in Lebanon, news agencies in Beirut reported after midnight.

According to an Amal communiqué delivered to several Beirut newspapers, five Israeli soldiers were wounded in the clash.

Reuter news agency quoted Tyre police as saying that about 60 Israeli troops had landed from two helicopters at 7 p.m. in the village of Siddikin, just north of the security zone.

The Israelis fired assault rifles and heavy machine-guns during the operation to cut roads leading to the nearby Shi'ite villages of Yater, Kafra and Jibal al-Baten, the agency quoted police as saying.

Amal sources reported casualties on both side, Reuter said.

Carter wants PLO at international parley

By JOEL GREENBERG

Touring the West Bank yesterday, former U.S. president Jimmy Carter said the PLO should take part in an international Middle East peace conference.

In meetings with local Palestinians leaders on Friday, Carter said he would recommend to the U.S. administration that it push for an international conference and talk with PLO representatives, participants in the meetings reported.

Carter lunched yesterday in Bethlehem with mayor Elias Freij and the mayors of Jericho, Beit Sahur and Beit Jallah, after travelling to Hebron to visit the Cave of the Patriarchs. Settlers at the site shouted at him, "Israel is not for sale." He later told reporters: "There is a lot of animosity. The Holy places ae full of weapons, and it is obvious that they (the Palestinians) are living in very unpleasant circumstances."

(Continued on Page 2, Col. 3)

Former U.S. president Jimmy Carter gasps for air outside the Dung Gate on a morning jog around the Old City on Friday. (Rahamim Israeli)

Herzog's action on underground assailed by left, right

By JUDY SIEGEL, ASHER WALLFISH and BERNARD JOSEPHS
Jerusalem Post Reporters

President Herzog was under fire from the left – and facing pressure from the right – last night over his decision to set a maximum 24-year jail sentence for three members of the Jewish terrorist underground.

The three – Menahem Livni, Shaul Nir and Uzi Sharabas – are serving life sentences for murder. They were convicted of carrying out a machine-gun attack on the Islamic College in Hebron in which three students were killed.

They will now be entitled to home leave, probably as early as Pessah, and are likely to receive a one-third remission in their sentence for good behaviour.

The official announcement, on Friday, was apparently timed to come just before the weekend so as to limit the impact and reduce the amount of publicity.

Livni's wife Tsipora, whose husband has now been three years in jail, said she was pleased he would receive home leave. But she added, it was "shameful" that the president had not pardoned all three men.

Public opinion polls showed the vast majority of people thought a pardon should be granted, she claimed. Setting a 24-year maximum term had "pleased only the left and the enemies of Israel."

Voices on the right, including that of Likud Knesset faction chairman MK Haim Kaufman, welcomed the president's move but called for the men to be pardoned.

They were matched by those on the left who condemned Herzog's actions as an encouragement to terrorism.

Said Kaufman: "I hope that on Independence Day the president will grant all the members of the Jewish underground full pardons and wipe out their criminal records."

Another Likud MK Dov Shilansky, who is chairman of the House Interior Committee responsible for

(Continued on Back Page)

Pollard 'hurt U.S. spying' on Pretoria

By DAVID HOROVITZ
Jerusalem Post Correspondent

LONDON. – Jonathan Pollard, convicted Israeli spy in the U.S., gravely compromised American intelligence operations against South Africa, according to an affidavit prepared by U.S. Defence Secretary Caspar Weinberger, as reported in today's *Sunday Times* here.

The paper reports that Weinberger's 41-page sworn statement charges that Pollard fed Israel highly-secret American intelligence on South Africa and that Israel promptly passed it on to Pretoria.

Weinberger suggests that at least one American agent in South Africa was blown by Pollard in this way, and that others may have been similarly exposed, the paper reports.

Weinberger prepared his secret deposition for the Washington Federal Court in which Pollard was tried. According to the *Times* report, he noted that the U.S. maintains an intelligence-gathering effort against "friendly countries" and suggested that Pollard had done immense damage to this effort – particularly, in three countries: Israel, Saudi Arabia and South Africa.

The *Sunday Times* reports the CIA as being convinced "that much of the secret American material on South Africa was passed from Jerusalem to Pretoria. As a result, the South Africans were alerted not only to the fact that they were a target of America's intelligence gathering effort, but also to the extent of that effort and the way in which it was being conducted.

Much of the data on South Africa passed to Israel by Pollard was reportedly "raw intelligence," unedited reports from agents and monitoring stations which contained clues about when, where and by whom particular pieces of information were gathered; also assessments as to the reliability of informers, the report says.

The material was reportedly "more than sufficient" to give South African counter-intelligence agents evidence to track down the U.S. spies in their midst.

The *Sunday Times* suggests that this South African connection helps to explain the Reagan administration's dismay over the Pollard case, and Weinberger's insistence on demanding a life sentence.

Car-bomb in Beirut kills 7

BEIRUT. – Seven people were killed and 12 wounded yesterday morning when a car bomb exploded on a beachfront boulevard in Syrian-policed west Beirut. It was the first such bombing since the Syrians moved into Beirut last month.

Most of the casualties were civilians strolling or sitting along the seaside thoroughfare in the Ramlet al-Baida district.

A police spokesman said two people were killed in a Renault car parked next to the bomb car. The charge was estimated as 75kg. of "heavy explosives."

Angry Syrian troops brandishing assault rifles barred reporters from approaching the scene. Film was confiscated, four photographers were beaten up and one, struck by a rifle, had his mouth cut open.

Soviets allow refusenik protest

By WALTER RUBY
and Agencies

Some 30 refuseniks staged a demonstration in the Soviet capital on Friday, but unlike last month's protests, police did not intervene.

At the same time, several Soviet Jews in Moscow and abroad have started hunger strikes.

The demonstrators gathered at a central Moscow park Friday, bearing signs demanding visas to Israel or reunion with family members abroad. The protest lasted about 45 minutes.

Yosef Begun and his son, Boris, participated. Some of the refuseniks said they had been called at home the previous night by local government officials and told they should not participate in the protest because their safety could not be guaranteed. But unlike the Jews who demonstrated on the Arbat last month and who were beaten and detained, Friday's protesters were not disturbed by police.

The Public Council for Soviet Jewry said in Tel Aviv last night that the demonstrators had presented a list of demands to the nearby Ovir office which handles exit visas and that they planned to demonstrate for another two days.

Begun told reporters that British Premier Margaret Thatcher, who arrived in Moscow yesterday, had invited him to a British embassy breakfast on Wednesday.

Thatcher plans to discuss human rights and nuclear arms issues in her talks with Kremlin leader Mikhail Gorbachev.

Thatcher's decision to breakfast

(Continued on Page 3)

'Heavengate' titillates America

By SIMON HOGGART

WASHINGTON. – Most Americans aren't born-again Christians, and so have been following the "Holy Wars" here with ribaldry and glee. Another delightful coincidence has come along: a new book called *Christian Wives*, on how to stay happily married while true to God, is almost out. The author is Tammy Faye Bakker, wronged wife of the TV evangelist Jim Bakker, and a central character in what is probably the biggest religious scandal of the century.

Mrs. Bakker takes an old-fashioned view of marriage and believes that a man should always be head of the house. "I love being under submission to my husband," she wrote, adding that a wife should always "dress sexy and keep herself exciting." She reveals that she never takes off her make-up, not even in bed.

This must be why her face looks thickly encrusted with geological eons of gunk. Some people who've seen the "Jim and Tammy Show" suspect that it may be too late ever to remove it. Goodness knows what her pillows look like.

The Holy Wars, or "Heavengate" as some papers call it, has held America transfixed for a week. It has also delighted "People for the American Way," a growing liberal lobby group in Washington which has been hammering at the TV preachers for years, hoping to expose their methods, their far-right politics and their stupendous wealth. Now it suddenly looks as if the preachers are doing the job for them.

Before his dalliance with a 21-year-old secretary, Bakker had what was the fastest growing TV ministry, with some 14 million people reckoning to watch the daily show at least some of the time. More valuable, he has half a million "members" who send in $15 a month. With other contributions, solicited during each show, the annual income is well over $100 million.

Much of this has gone to building a vast theme park in South Carolina called "Heritage USA," the third most popular in the country after Disneyland and Disney World. That cost around $160 million, and Bakker had been planning a full-size replica of the Crystal Palace for a further $75 million. In spite of its massive income, Bakker's

(Continued on Page 3)

EIGHT PAGES FROM SUNDAY'S
The New York Times
WEEKLY REVIEW
INSIDE TODAY

THE JERUSALEM POST

Vol. LV, No. 16613 Monday, August 31, 1987 • Elul 6, 5747 • Moharram 8, 1408 NIS 0.95 (Eilat NIS 0.85)

VENTILATION MEANS...
Venta
CEILING FANS
TWO DIRECTIONAL
RAMAT-GAN: 03-7513251
HAIFA: 04-722611 JERUSALEM: 02-222550

Single vote dooms the Lavi

Jerusalem Post Staff

The cabinet yesterday decided to scrap the Lavi warplane project, after seven years and nearly $1.5b., mostly in U.S. funds, had been devoted to its development.

The ministers cast the die by the narrowest of narrow majorities, 12 votes against 11, with one abstention, following irresistible pressure against certain ministers.

The vote largely represented a confrontation between the Likud (which wanted the Lavi project to continue) and the Alignment (which wanted to halt it).

After the vote, Minister-without-Portfolio Moshe Arens, one of the fathers of the Lavi project, announced his intention to resign rather than accept responsibility for "the tragic decision." The Alignment minister who tipped the scales yesterday, Health Minister Shoshana Arbeli-Almoslino, who abstained when all her party colleagues ganged up against her, said she still favoured the project, even though her vote had ensured its cancellation.

The decision sent tremors throughout the political system, giving rise to a wave of accusations and counter-accusations last night. Despite some calls on the right for early elections or the establishment of a Likud-led narrow coalition which would reverse yesterday's decision, observers were united in the view that the decision would have no effect on the immediate future of the national unity government.

Generally, the Labour Party and the left reacted favourably while the right responded angrily, describing the step in terms of "a national disgrace" and "capitulation to American pressure."

Actual political fallout is expected only in the Likud, with doubts over the immediate political fate of Moshe Arens and the medium-range future of Finance Minister Moshe Nissim.

The U.S. expressed great satisfaction with the cabinet vote.

"We welcome Israel's cabinet decision to terminate the Lavi. We recognize this was a difficult decision, but it is one that we believe will best serve Israel's interest," the Pentagon spokesman, Lt. Commander John Carman, said.

A State Department spokesman commented: "We are very happy with the decision. As we told Israeli Defence Minister Yitzhak Rabin last month during his visit here, the U.S. will be very helpful in getting Israel over this difficult period.

Informed observers believe that the cabinet decision will work in Israel's favour to break a logjam that existed rearding some pending military contracts with the Pentagon.

The staff of Israel Aircraft Industries have reacted furiously to the cancellation. The Treasury and the Defence Ministry will today begin a frantic effort to minimize the number of dismissals at IAI and at other plants connected with the Lavi project. The Treasury's problem will be how to bridge the short term problem, when an undetermined number of workers could be dismissed, and the more distant difficulties when the defence industries will be working on new projects for the Defence Ministry.

Senior military sources expressed relief at the cabinet decision, arguing that by scrapping the Lavi, the government had accepted the IDF's presentation of its needs for a future war.

Long-term planning in the IDF had virtually come to a halt as the Lavi issue dragged on and on. Yesterday, immediately following the cabinet's decision, Chief of General Staff Rav-Aluf Dan Shomron, his deputy, Aluf Ehud Barak, the head of the IDF's Planning Branch, Aluf Danny Yatom, and the Air Force's next commander, Aluf Avihu Bin-Nun held a meeting about the immediate implications.

Shomron described the cabinet decision as "difficult and painful for everyone. But given the limits on our ability and our needs this is the least undesirable choice."

While the senior command was happy with the decision it was careful not to appear too elated in public, especially as the issue had become so politicized over the weekend. The IDF clearly did not want to create an impression that it was ranged against the Likud.

Vanunu goes on trial

By MENACHEM SHALEV
Jerusalem Post Reporter

The trial of Mordechai Vanunu, who is accused of revealing Israel's alleged nuclear secrets to the London *Sunday Times*, got off to a quick start in Jerusalem yesterday as four witnesses for the prosecution took the stand to testify against the former Dimona nuclear technician.

Tat-Nitzav Shimon Savir, head of the police general investigation unit, was the first to testify. He presented the court with the confessions extracted from Vanunu after he arrived in Israel last October. Savir was followed on the witness stand by three Shin Bet operatives who were involved in Vanunu's interrogation. Other Shin Bet operatives are expected to testify today.

Defence attorney Avigdor Feldman and prosecutor Uzi Hasson accepted the court's suggestion to combine the presentation of the State's case against Vanunu with the "mini-trial" hearing which is meant to establish the admissibility of Vanunu's confessions.

Feldman contends that the "circumstances under which Vanunu was brought to Israel" negate the admissibility of the confessions as well as the court's jurisdiction in the case. Thus the confessions presented yesterday were admitted as evidence on condition that the court would eventually reject Feldman's argument.

Vanunu was brought to the court under tight security procedures at 7.20 a.m. He again succeeded in throwing off the helmet which police forced him to wear. "He has become quite adept at removing the helmet without the use of his hands, which were handcuffed," quipped Feldman.

Vanunu has pledged not to reveal any secrets if the police agree to treat him "like any other prisoner." On the basis of this commitment, Feldman has appealed to the security authorities to discontinue the tight security; he expressed the hope yesterday that they would do so "informally." At the same time, he has also appealed to the court to order the police to do so.

Feldman described the State's attitude towards Vanunu as "paranoid."

Some 40 local and foreign journalists waited outside the courtroom in the hope that district court judges Eliahu Noam, Zvi Tal and Shalom Brenner would reach a quick decision to open the proceedings to the public. In the absence of such a decision, the reporters spent the morning repeatedly interviewing Vanunu's brother, Asher, *Sunday Times* journalist Peter Hounam (who has been covering Vanunu since his days in Australia), and each other. Vanunu's family were not allowed to be present in the courtroom.

Feldman, who has asked the court to open parts of the proceedings to the public, said that the court had taken note of the immense interest the trial had aroused in Israel and around the world and that yesterday's decision by the judges to release some details for publication gave him cause for optimism that his request would be granted. The sessions most likely to be open to the public, it is believed, will be those when the defence calls experts from abroad to testify on the general dangers and alleged illegality of nuclear weapons.

The current proceedings, which will be held in camera in any case, are expected to end before next Sunday. Further dates for the trial have yet to be set.

Ministers at the heart of the drama

By ASHER WALLFISH

The cabinet decision yesterday to close down the Lavi warplane project, by a vote of 12 to 11, with one abstention, highlighted the role played in the drama by Minister-without-Portfolio Moshe Arens, Health Minister Shoshana Arbeli-Almoslino (who abstained) and Tourism and Justice Minister Avraham Sharir, who exercised his proxy vote from abroad.

The 12 "nays" included nine from the Alignment, as well as Finance Minister Moshe Nissim (Likud-Liberals), Religious Affairs Minister Zevulun Hammer (National Religious Party), and Minister-without-Portfolio Yitzhak Peretz (Shas). The 11 "ayes" included 10 from the Likud as well as Minister-without-Portfolio Yigael Hurvitz (Ometz) and Minister-without-Portfolio Yosef Shapira (NRP).

Several ministers told *The Jerusalem Post* that a mood of gloom had prevailed before and during the vote, with both sides grasping the traumatic implications of scrapping such a prestige project, in which so much money and goodwill had been invested.

Prime Minister Shamir opened the meeting by recalling that he had hoped to avoid a decision by a narrow majority. He then asked Defence Minister Rabin and Nissim if they wished to put to the vote their original proposal, which simply called for a halt to the project. They said that the motion tabled by Foreign Minister Peres should be voted on first.

But at this point Peres asked Sha-

(Continued on Page 2, Col. 2)

The two ministers at the centre of yesterday's cabinet drama, Shoshana Arbeli-Almoslino and Moshe Arens, face the press. (Harari, Harati)

Labour, Likud tension rises

By MENACHEM SHALEV
Post Political Reporter

The decision to scrap the Lavi has further exacerbated the strained relations between the two major coalition partners. Its effects were felt immediately in the Likud, where relations between Herut and the Liberals deteriorated and politicians went scrambling in the wake of Minister-without-Portfolio Moshe Arens's decision to resign. Labour was more reserved, apprehensive about the immediate turbulence within the Israel Aircraft Industries and the anticipated negative reaction of public opinion.

From a political point of view yesterday's decision was taken as a double edged sword for both parties: Labour, led by Foreign Minister Peres, won a victory but may have lost some votes. It gave the Likud an excellent elections slogan in "Labour shot down the Lavi." The Likud was thrown into disarray and Prime Minister Shamir's newly-perceived leadership was tarnished.

•The Likud - confidantes of Arens's and sources in the Prime Minister's Office said last night that despite the pressures reportedly exerted on him, they believe that Arens will indeed resign. Talk of possible successors, however, appeared premature as Shamir made clear yesterday that he would not appoint a replacement if Arens re-

(Continued on Page 7)

A dejected worker contemplates the Lavi in its hangar at Israel Aircraft Industries yesterday. (Hanoch Guthmann)

IAI workers up in arms; plan to fight decision

By JOSHUA BRILLIANT
Post Defence Reporter

BEN- GURION AIRPORT.- The Israel Aircraft Industries will tomorrow start folding up one of the country's most ambitious projects - in which it developed a fighter aircraft believed to be on a par with the best in the world.

But workers were planning drastic action in a desperate attempt to force the government to reverse its decision and save the jobs of thousands of top- notch engineers who may now find themselves jobless.

One of the measures considered for today calls for blocking the airport's runways thereby cutting off Israel's air links with the outside world.

Defence Minister Yitzhak Rabin has appointed the Ministry's Director- General, Aluf (res.) David Ivri, to take care of the closure details and try to minimize their impact. Ivri had been the Chairman of the IAI's Board of Directors and was one of the Lavi's staunchest supporters.

The government will pay the IAI the entire $209m. allocated for the Lavi for the current fiscal year. Projects not connected with the Lavi will not be affected and efforts will be made to find alternative jobs for the workers engaged in the Lavi programme

All the Defence Ministry's efforts are designed to minimize the damage to the project and to its workers,' a ministry statement said yesterday.

Thus test flights on the gleaming white Lavi prototype are to continue

(Continued on Page 2, Col. 6)

An end to 20 years of euphoria

Yesterday was a historic day for Israel. It brings to a close the 20 years of euphoria that started with the victory in the Six Day War.For the first time, it has been admitted that Israel is not a superpower as some politicians would have had us believe.

The decision to halt the Lavi is in effect an admission that Israel can no longer hold to the course embarked on after France's President Charles de Gaulle imposed an embargo on the shipment of arms to Israel, and especially of fighter planes.

Yesterday's decision was a tacit admission that Israel cannot keep advancing towards higher and higher standards of living, while maintaining the world's highest defence budget. It is also an admission that we cannot produce every kind of weapon – jet fighters, tanks, missile boats and every type of sophisticated electronic device, the kind of projects which even Europe's richest countries cannot afford unless they do so jointly.

The decision also amounts to an admission that like most of the western world we, too, are subordinate to the hegemonic power of the U.S. It is a realization that we have to obey the Americans' orders just

COMMENT
SHLOMO MAOZ

as do the Japanese, the Germans and the British, not to mention other lesser powers.

It is an admission that, having failed to convince many of the young generation to remain in Israel with its lower standards of living simply by appealing to basic Zionist principles, the Lavi project must be scrapped so as to make possible a low tax burden on the general public and to aim for real growth of our economy.

This is is a climb down towards becoming a more normal nation. It has been done with a lot of pain, but that was the only way to stabilize our economy for the long run and create hope for changes for the better for the next generation in Israel.

The unity government's decision on the Lavi has given it a new record of achievement, since it was unexpected.The Lavi decision may be the last blow to an ego trip and the puncturing of a dream of becoming a mini-empire. But it is a vital beginning, the start of a struggle against vested interests in agriculture, industry and social welfare.

Beyond that the Treasury will have in the near future to re-open

(Continued on Page 7)

Ben Johnson sprints to new 100m. record

ROME (Reuter). – Ben Johnson of Canada broke the men's world 100 metres record when he clocked 9.83 seconds at the World Athletics Championships here last night. The previous record of 9.93 was set by American Calvin Smith in Colorado Springs, U.S. on July 3, 1983.

Sicke Gladische is the top woman sprinter, winning in 10.83 seconds.

There was another world record when Bulgaria's Stefka Kostadinova broke her own high jump record by 1cm., clearing 2.09m. (See Sports p. 5)

FUND FOR THE VICTIMS OF THE EARTHQUAKE IN MEXICO

The Central Institute for Cultural Relations Israel-Latin America, Spain and Portugal, at the request of the Foreign Office of Israel, and in cooperation with the Literary Fund "Rosario Castellanos," the Chamber of Commerce Israel-Latin America, Spain and Portugal, and the Friendship Association Israel-Mexico (Tel Aviv); and with the support of H.E., the Ambassador of Mexico in Israel and the Ambassador of Israel in Mexico, organized the Solidarity Fund with the Mexican People, dedicated to help the victims of the earthquake which devastated parts of Mexico City and other places in that country in 1985.

The contributions were used entirely to buy electronic medical equipment, made in Israel, which was donated to the Juarez Hospital and to The National Institute of Cancerology in Mexico City in April, 1987.

Its mission concluded, the Fund expresses its sincere thanks to all the institutions, both public and private, and to all the persons who participated in this noble enterprise.

Dr. Moshe Liba, Director General — Sr. Aaron Eisen, Treasurer — Dr. Netanel Lorch, President

NOTICE TO SUBSCRIBERS

Please note the following new telephone numbers of our Subscription Offices in Jerusalem.

The Jerusalem Post (Daily) 02-551615, 551617

The Jerusalem Post (International Edition) 02-551614

Effective September 1, 1987

1987 Edinburgh Festival Production in English
Joseph Mundy's critically acclaimed hit satire
"IT TURNS, IT BURNS"
Written and directed by **Joseph Mundy**
with
Israel Biderman (Habimah), **Gideon Shemer** (Cameri), **Ruth Harlap**
Sept. 13 – Tzavta, Tel Aviv; Sept. 15 – Hechal Tarbut, Carmiel; Sept. 16 – Kfar Sava, Auditorium; Sept. 19 – Jerusalem Theatre; Sept. 26 – Moadon Haifa Theatre. Tickets: Le'an, Kla'im, theatre box offices. Production office: 03-5463299, 03-452876 (for group bookings)

MANY WAYS TO MAKE A WISH.
ONE WAY TO MAKE
A WISH COME TRUE

Israel Discount Bank's Tax-Free Foreign Currency Accounts*

No matter what your reasons for wishing to save, you'll discover many benefits to placing your foreign currency in a tax-free deposit account at Israel Discount Bank.

For your part, you pay absolutely no account charges whatever. For ours, we offer extremely competitive interest, at the best prevailing rates, which is free of all taxes in Israel.

You enjoy access to your funds whenever you wish, and may transfer them almost anywhere worldwide.

Tax-Free Foreign Currency Accounts, at Israel Discount Bank, are conducted with the utmost confidentiality. So, all in all, it's no wonder they've become so popular.

To obtain further details, make sure to visit one of our Tourist Centers or branches today.

* For foreign residents, tourists, Israelis residing abroad, new immigrants, temporary and returning residents.

Over 250 offices and branches in Israel and abroad.

Total Assets exceed US$10 billion.

SOUVENIR GIFT for Account Openers for a Limited Period Only.

Our main tourist centers in Israel: Tel-Aviv, 16 Mapu St., Tel. (03)247276, Jerusalem, 62 King George St., Tel. (02)637902/3, Netanya, 14 Kikar Atzmaut, Tel. (053)43255, Haifa, 47 Atzmaut Road, Tel. (04)546111
Head Office: 27 Yehuda Halevi Street, Tel Aviv, Israel. Tel. (03)637111
U.S. SUBSIDIARY: ISRAEL DISCOUNT BANK OF NEW YORK Main Office: 511 Fifth Avenue, Tel. (212)511-8500. Other subsidiary banks and offices: Buenos Aires / Cayman / Curaçao / London / Los Angeles / Mexico Miami (2) / Montevideo (2) / Montreal / Nassau / Punta del Este / Rio de Janeiro / Santiago de Chile / São Paulo / Toronto

ISRAEL DISCOUNT BANK
DAHAF

Epilepsy and religion
Page 4

THE JERUSALEM
POST
Vol. LV, No. 16620 Tuesday, September 8, 1987 • Elul 14, 5747 • Moharram 15, 1408 NIS 0.95 (Eilat NIS 0.85)

Mizrahi plans dollar contracts
Page 7

Honecker starts historic visit to Bonn

BONN. – German leader Erich Honecker began a landmark visit to West Germany yesterday and was immediately urged by Chancellor Helmut Kohl to end shooting at the border and dismantle the Berlin Wall.

The start of Honecker's historic five-day visit brimmed with symbolism pointing to the four decades of German division. At the chancellery, an army band played the two national anthems, and the two states' near-identical flags flew side by side.

"We want peace in Germany, and this means that weapons must be silenced along the frontier. Violence that hits innocent people hurts peace," Kohl said in a dinner speech.

"Germans suffer under the division. They suffer because of a wall that is literally in their way and repels them," he added. "In dismantling what divides people we would heed demands from the Germans, demands that cannot be ignored."

Honecker did not reply directly to Kohl's demand to scrap the shooting order and tear down the wall built by East Berlin in 1961 to stop a flood of refugees.

The Communist leader said his first contacts in Bonn had shown that East and West Germany were separated in two opposite camps and could not be united.

"Socialism and capitalism are like fire and water," said Honecker, changing his prepared speech text in apparent reaction to Kohl's strong plea for concrete steps towards a united Germany.

Outside the Redoute Castle where the dinner was held, human rights activists monitoring alleged abuses in Eastern Europe protested at the visit, shouting "Honecker out."

Honecker, 75, and Kohl, 57, looked stiff and uneasy during their public appearances at the start of the first visit to West Germany by an East German leader.

Previously, the two men had only met at funerals – twice in

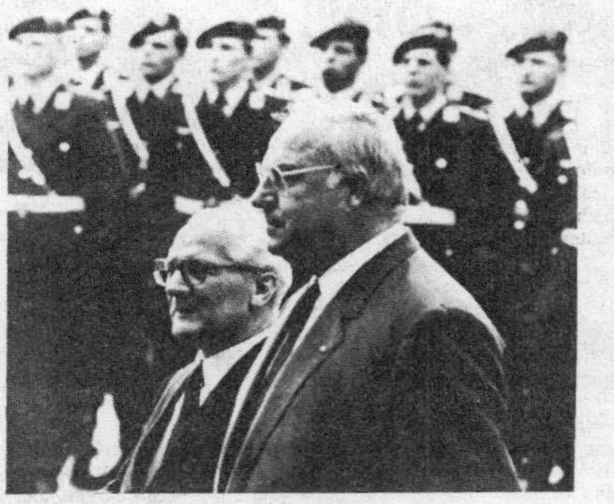

East German leader Erich Honecker (left) and West German Chancellor Helmut Kohl review a honor guard in Bonn yesterday. (AFP)

Moscow at the burials of Soviet leaders Yuri Andropov and Konstantin Chernenko, and last year at the interment of assassinated Swedish Premier Olof Palme in Stockholm.

In East Berlin, East Germans polled by correspondents near the Berlin Wall said they hoped the visit would bring more chances to travel to West Germany.

Relaxation of East Berlin travel restrictions has led to expectations that more than 2.5 million East Germans will visit West Germany this year, among them more than one million of working age.

"I've got an aunt over there," said Mario, a 17-year-old apprentice from the provincial town of Magdeburg. "If I have to wait until I'm 65 to visit her, she will long be dead."

Honecker, who began his political career in the Saar which is now part of West Germany and was jailed by Hitler for 10 years, will tour major industrial centres and his hometown of Wiebelskirchen after his two days of talks in Bonn.

Since the Berlin Wall was erected and the border fortified, 188 East Germans have been shot dead in escape attempts, three along the wall in the last 12 months alone.

But diplomats said the shoot-to-kill order had been suspended temporarily and replaced by increased electronic surveillance. In the week before Honecker's trip, nine East Germans managed to escape unhurt.

Honecker also met President Richard von Weizsaecker, who accepted his invitation for a return visit to East Germany.

Weizsaecker said the German nation was a cultural entity, not confined to the physical borders of the country united by Otto Bismarck in 1871 by grouping the small German states.

"The people in both German states belong to the same nation, a nation that wasn't born with Bismarck nor destroyed with Hitler," Weizsaecker said.

West German police kept security tight around Honecker, who was flown by helicopter to the guest residence of Gymnich Castle after his talks, despite his deep dislike of flying.

Right-wing youths protesting at the division of Germany held up a banner quoting a line from a banned verse of the East German anthem – "Germany, United Fatherland." The verse was dropped in the 1950s, after the Communist authorities abandoned ideas to reunite with West Germany. (Reuter)

Other refuseniks also

Yosef Begun gets exit visa

By SARAH HONIG
and Agencies

Emerging triumphant from a 16-year struggle, Soviet refusenik Yosef Begun yesterday said he was the happiest person in the world after learning that Soviet authorities had issued him and several other prominent refuseniks exit visas. The 54-year-old Hebrew teacher told correspondents that he did not know when he, his wife Inna and her mother, Vera, would leave the country for Israel, "my homeland," but he thought it would be very soon.

Other long-term refuseniks to be released included Viktor Brailovsky and his family, Semyon Yaniovski, Lev and Ella Sud and Dr. Vladimir Lifshitz.

News of their release was greeted with unbridled joy in Israel with Prime Minister Shamir, Foreign Minister Peres and other leaders expressing hope that they would arrive shortly.

"I am very glad and I hope to see them in Israel soon, as well as other Soviet Jews," Shamir said.

But Begun said in a telephone conversation with Soviet Jewish activists here that the visas do not represent a major shift in Soviet policy and that the activists should continue their struggle for the release of Soviet Jews.

Activists predicted last night that the welcome celebrations held thus far for Prisoners of Zion at Ben-Gurion airport would pale in comparison to what awaits Begun and Brailovsky.

Kibbutzim and settlements that had adopted the two were already preparing apartments for them in the hopes that the activists and their families would come to live with

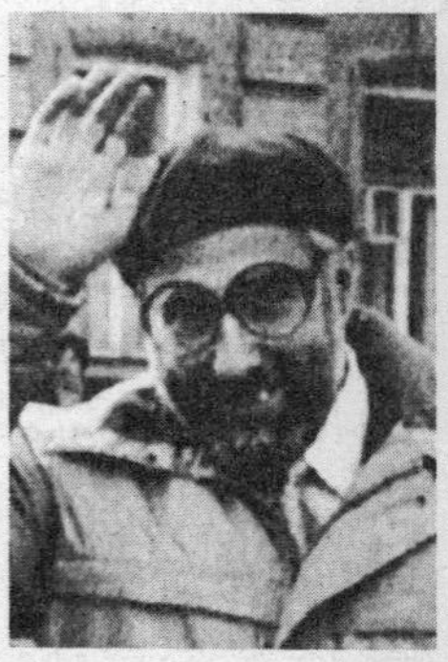

Yosef Begun in Moscow earlier this year (AFP)

them. Hadasha in the Shomron and Magan Michael on the coast both adopted Begun and are vying to become his home. Kibbutz Yiftah in the Galilee adopted Brailovsky, a 52-year-old cyberneticist who has waited 15 years to come here, and expressed hope that he would accept its invitation.

Brailovsky told friends that he felt "a little crazy" after receiving his visa. He said he hoped to work in Israel in his field. Leaving with him are his wife, Irina; his daughter, Daliya, 13; his son, Leonid, 26; and Leonid's wife and baby boy. He said he hoped to be reunited with his father and brother who live in Israel within the next two months. Asked whether he would be ready to leave the Soviet Union on short notice, he

(Continued on Page 9)

Lebanese free German hostage

BONN (Reuter). – West German hostage Alfred Schmidt was freed yesterday to the custody of the West German embassy in Damascus. Bonn said it made no concessions to the kidnappers who held him for eight months. Schmidt was released by Shi'ite Moslem kidnappers in Beirut and was taken by Syrian army officers to Damascus where he said: "It's wonderful to be a free man again."

Looking tired out in good shape, Schmidt said: "They didn't mistreat me. The treatment was all right."

Asked how felt, Schmidt, 47, replied: "I'm okay – 50-50."

As for his plans, Schmidt said: "I want to see my family and friends. I've missed them."

Security men then whisked him

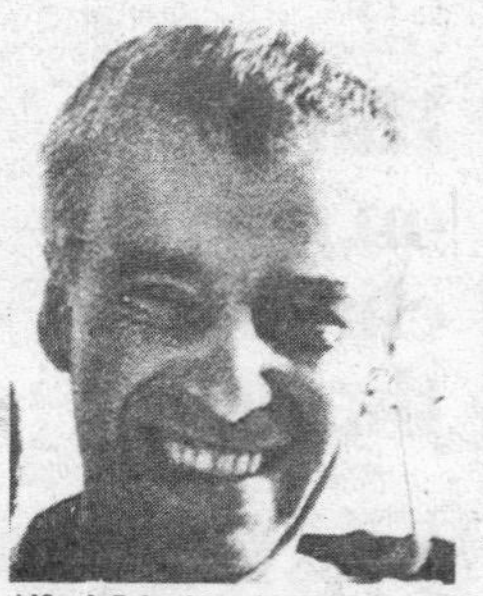

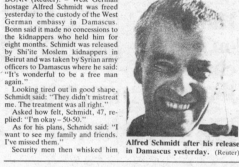

Alfred Schmidt after his release in Damascus yesterday. (Reuter)

away, apparently heading for Damascus Airport. Informed sources said a special aircraft carrying a senior West German security official had earlier landed to fly him to Bonn. It was not immediately known when it would take off.

Schmidt was released in South Beirut, a Shi'ite stronghold, early in the morning under what his captors indicated was a Syrian-brokered agreement.

In Bonn, a government spokesman said: "Iran and Syria both helped win [Schmidt's] release. They both said they would help us and they did."

But spokesman Friedhelm Ost told a news conference that reports of Bonn agreeing to free a suspected

(Continued on back page)

Starts Bonn visit

Rabin expects better ties with defence industries

Jerusalem Post Staff

BONN. -- Relations between the Israeli and German defence industries are expected to improve in the future, Defence Minister Rabin said yesterday at the end of the first day of his visit to West Germany.

Rabin met with his German counterpart Manfred Woerner for a first round of talks and during a formal reception yesterday on the first day of his official visit.

He is scheduled to visit the former Nazi concentration camp at Dachau in Bavaria today.

Rabin, who made history in 1975 as the first Israeli prime minister to visit Bonn, is the first Israeli defence minister to visit Germany. Diplomatic sources said a visit by Woerner to Israel in April last year had paved the way for Rabin's second visit, but stressed that no arms deal was expected.

The visit was overshadowed by the meeting between the leaders of the two Germanys, Helmut Kohl and Erich Honecker, but this only highlighted the business-like character of Rabin's trip.

Prior to his departure, Rabin said

(Continued on Back Page)

'Used to hearing Arafat speak with two voices'

Arafat acceptance of 242, 338 dismissed here

By BENNY MORRIS
and agencies

Israeli officials unanimously dismissed PLO chairman Yasser Arafat's reported acceptance in his speech yesterday in Geneva of UN Security Council resolutions 242 and 338, which imply recognition of Israel's right to exist.

Sources in both the Prime Minister's Office and in the Foreign Ministry said that Israel is "used to hearing Arafat speak with two voices. He has no credibility."

The Foreign Ministry sources said that often in the past Arafat has spoken "with one voice to Europeans and with another voice to his (Arab) constituency. His declarations (of acceptance of 242 and 338) are not to be taken seriously."

The sources in the Prime Minister's Office said that Arafat has often said things "to please his hearers," only to retract or qualify them immediately afterwards.

Four Knesset members hugged and kissed Arafat in Geneva, one of the Israelis said. "Arafat kissed me and shook my hand, and told me 'Here we have one of the best fighters for justice and peace.' " MK Charlie Biton told Reuters. They met at a reception Arafat gave at a luxury hotel for delegates to the UN conference of non-governmental organizations on the "Palestine" question.

Biton described mutual embraces and kisses between Arafat and Matti Peled and Mohammed Miari of the Progressive List for Peace and Tewfik Zayyad and himself of the Democratic Front for Peace.

Arafat yesterday urged the convocation of an international conference on the Middle East and charged that the "fundamental obstacle" to peace in the region is "the American-Israeli stumbling block." Arafat said the PLO supported a conference under UN auspices "on the basis of international legality as well as the international resolutions approved by the UN relevant to the Palestinian cause and the Middle East crisis, including resolutions 242 and 338." The PLO leader said the proposed conference should be held in order "to put an end to the Israeli occupation in Lebanon, Syria and other occupied Arab territories."

U.S. envoy warns of Jew hatred in Austria

VIENNA (AP).- Departing U.S. Ambassador Ronald Lauder said in an interview published yesterday that anti-Semitism in Austria will grow if Austrians do not publicly condemn it.

In an interview with the weekly Profil news magazine, Lauder, who is Jewish, illustrated anti-Jewish sentiment among some Austrians with a personal anecdote. He said a Viennese shopkeeper told his wife and daughter that Jews were behind the controversy surrounding President Kurt Waldheim's wartime past, and "practically" told them they were not welcome in his shop.

He told Profil the incident happened in June 1986.

Waldheim was elected president that month by a 54 per cent majority following a campaign overshadowed by allegations that he was involved in Nazi atrocities in the Balkans as a soldier in the German

(Continued on Page 2, Col. 2)

Strategic expert lauds decision to scrap Lavi

Yariv: Arab armies stronger

By JOSHUA BRILLIANT
Post Defence Reporter

TEL AVIV.- The cabinet was wise to scrap the Lavi in favour of alternate weapon systems because the Arab armies have become bigger and faster than ever before while the IDF has reached the limits of its ability to grow, Aluf (res.) Aharon Yariv, head of the Tel Aviv University's Jaffe Centre for Strategic Studies, said yesterday.

Speaking at a press conference here to mark the release of the centre's Middle East Military Balance report, Yariv said the Arab armies are bigger, faster, better equipped, more strongly fortified and in possession of greater fire power than in the past. Under these conditions, it would be difficult for Israel to quickly decide the outcome of a war by advancing into enemy territory.

On the other hand there have been some positive developments for Israel. The Arabs are short of money and skilled manpower, partly because of the drop in oil prices. The Iraq-Iran war has divided the Arab world, leaving no anti-Israel coalition at present, and there is peace -- albeit cold -- with Egypt.

Therefore, Yariv argued, Israel should take advantage of the situation to advance the peace process. Israel is now in a position of strength and no one is threatening it but Israel's strategic position cannot improve, he said. "It can only worsen."

His gloomy prediction was based in part on the centre's 462-page report, published in cooperation with *The Jerusalem Post*.

The centre's figures show that the number of tanks in Egypt, Jordan and Syria grew from 4,500 in 1973 to 7,300 last year. In Israel the number rose from 2,000 to some 4,000.

Egypt, Jordan and Syria had 750 combat planes in 1973 compared with Israel's 300. Israel now has some 630 planes -- but its three neighbours have 1,400. The balance sheet would have appeared much worse if Iraq would have ended the war with Iran and turned its attention westward.

The Arab armies are also qualitatively better. They have acquired modern, first-rate, weapons like F-15s, F-16s, MiG-29s and Tornado fighters. Jordan has Chieftain tanks, Egypt has the American M-60A3 and Syria has some 1,000 T-72s. These countries also have missiles enabling them to hit major Israeli cities.

In spite of efforts to recruit better-educated soldiers, the Arabs suffer from a shortage of proper technical personnel.

But on the whole the qualitative gap is narrowing, said Yariv, a former chief of military intelligence. He warned that if this process continued the Arabs might try to settle the dispute by military means.

Part of the centre's study concerns the unconventional balance of power. No information is available about the Arabs' biological warfare capabilities, the authors said. But Tat-Aluf (res.) Aharon Levran, who compiled much of the study, noted that Egypt has had chemical weapons for years, Syria has transferred material to Iran and is advancing towards development of chemical warheads for its own missiles.

Moreover, the taboo on the use of gas was broken by Iraq in the Gulf War.

The report said the principal Arab

(Continued on Page 4)

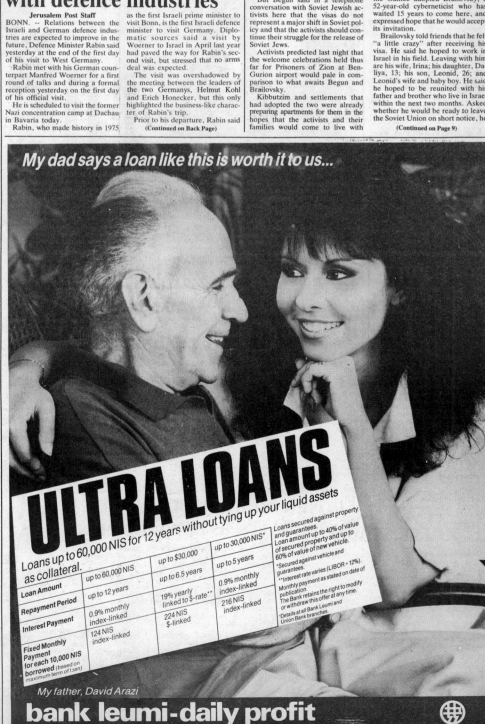

SHABBAT	BEGINS	ENDS
Jerusalem	4:30 p.m.	5:41 p.m.
Tel Aviv	4:48 p.m.	5:43 p.m.
Haifa	4:39 p.m.	5:41 p.m.

THE JERUSALEM POST

Vol. LV, No. 16649 Friday, October 16, 1987 • Tishrei 23, 5748 • Safar 24, 1408 NIS 1.80 (Eilat NIS 1.55)

SECOND EDITION

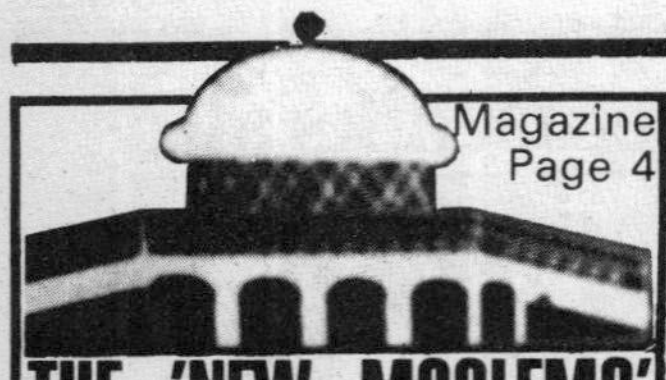

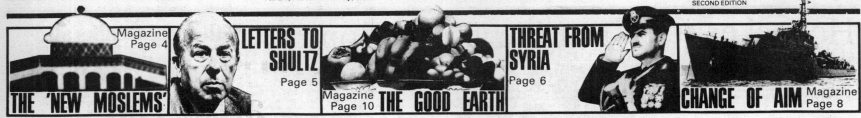

THE 'NEW MOSLEMS' Magazine Page 4

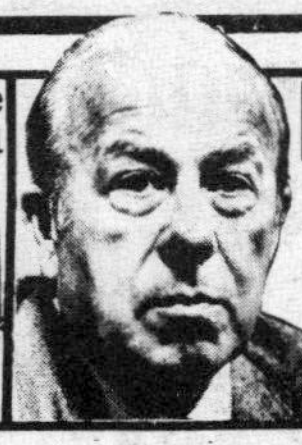

LETTERS TO SHULTZ Page 5

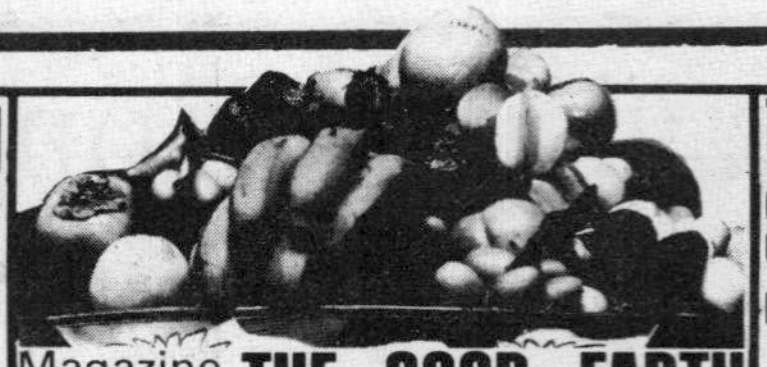

THE GOOD EARTH Magazine Page 10

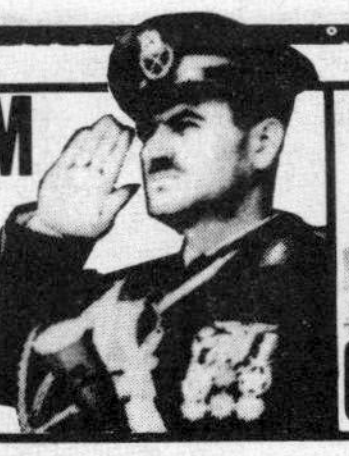

THREAT FROM SYRIA Page 6

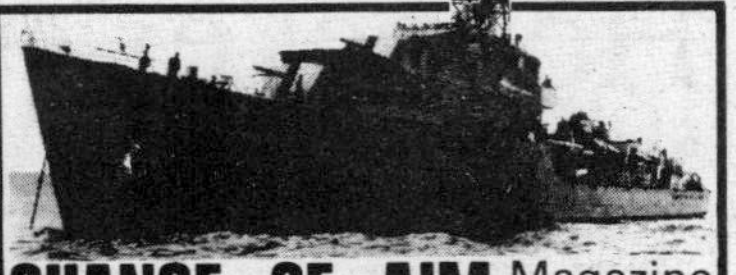

CHANGE OF AIM Magazine Page 8

Ida Nudel, in tears, arrives to tumultuous welcome

'It's the moment of my life'

By BERNARD JOSEPHS and HAIM SHAPIRO

Ida Nudel, the prisoner of Zion, whose 16 year struggle for freedom inspired millions around the world, arrived in Israel last night to a tumultuous welcome.

"It is the moment of my life. I am home at the soul of my Jewish People. I am a free person among my own people," said the diminutive 56-year-old freedom fighter at a press conference just a few moments after arriving on the first direct flight from Moscow to Tel Aviv for years.

Nudel, pale, bespectacled, and with her greying hair tied in a ponytail was in tears as she answered questions at a packed press conference. Earlier she had landed at Ben-Gurion Airport aboard a private Boeing jet owned by American oil billionaire Armand Hammer. The first to see her was her sister, Elena Fridman, who boarded the aircraft while Prime Minister Shamir, Vice Premier Peres and a host of other VIPs, including film star Jane Fonda, waited for her to alight.

The pair had not seen each other for 16 years and embraced emotionally.

Ida, who smiled and waved but whose eyes were filled with tears said, "Some hours ago I was almost a slave in Moscow. Now I'm a free person in my own country."

But she said that, despite her joy, her feelings were mixed. Before leaving Russia she held a party for all the refuseniks.

"They were happy for me but they were also a little sad about my leaving because they were a bit disappointed that it wasn't their turn. I promised them that their moment will come and I will put all my strength into winning their freedom. I will try in every way I can."

Nudel first sought an exit visa in 1970, telling friends that she could not stand the discrimination against Jews in the Soviet Union. Her sister, Elena, her only living relative, received permission the following year to leave Moscow with her husband and son.

But the authorities would not let Ida Nudel leave because they said she possessed state secrets due to her job at the Moscow Institute of Planning and Production, where she checked hygiene at food stores.

In 1978, after hanging a sign reading, "KGB, give me my visa" from the balcony of her flat, she was sentenced to four years exile in Siberia. After that she was granted a permit that banned her from living in Moscow and forced her to live in the remote town of Bendery in Moldavia.

"They were hard times. Sometimes they were too tough for human beings to stand," she said last night.

Asked how she felt at seeing her sister she went on, "There are not enough words do describe how I feel. I am overcome with emotion. Of course she is older but her eyes are the same. They are the eyes of my little sister."

Nudel sometimes stumbling over her words which she spoke in English thanked the "Israeli people and the Israeli government for their trust and sympathy."

She went on to thank the American, British, French, German, Australian and Swedish governments for their aid.

"I thank all of them personally. I hope that now there will be a change, a little change in the Soviet Union and that all who want will come to Israel and live as a free people.

"I thank every boy and girl and every man and woman who want to live in dignity in a peaceful way."

Addressing campaigners for Soviet Jewry she said, "Never feel your struggle is in vain. All those years I felt the sympathy from thousands of people, Jews and non-Jews alike. You must continue the struggle. There is no choice but to make the Soviets let our people go."

(Continued on back page)

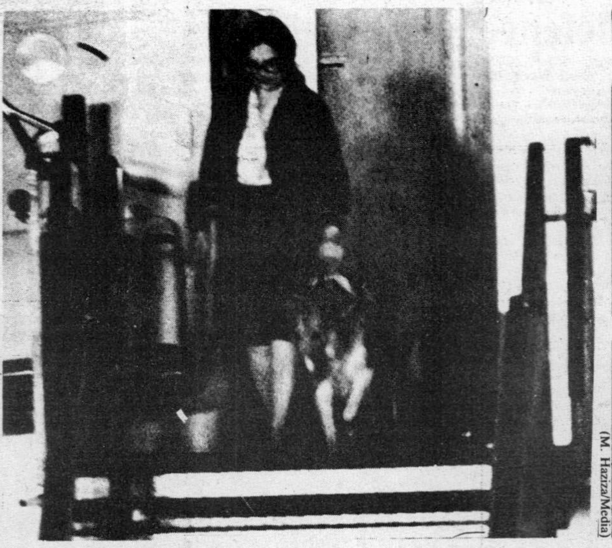

(M. Hazza/Media)

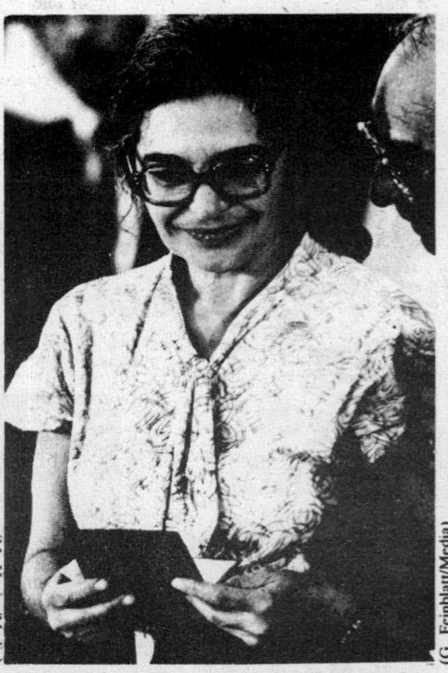

(G. Feinblatt/Media)

Hammer on how he clinched the deal

Oil billionaire Armand Hammer revealed last night that he clinched the release of Ida Nudel as part of a deal in which he pledged to help the Russians get their army out of Afghanistan.

Speaking at the press conference after Nudel's arrival, Hammer, who has for some time acted as go-between in negotiations between Moscow and Jerusalem, said that three weeks ago he was asked by Soviet Foreign Minister Eduard Shevardnadze to go to Afghanistan in a bid to settle the problem by negotiating with both sides.

"I said I'll go but you must give me Ida Nudel in return."

The Soviet minister immediately replied, "I promise to," said Hammer. The owner of the Occidental oil company said that he then went to Kabul, the Afghanistan capital.

(Continued on back page)

6 per cent more in next pay packet

By AVI TEMKIN
Post Economic Reporter

Wage earners will receive increases of 5.5 to 6.5 per cent in their October salaries. The increase includes payment of a 5.5 per cent Cost of Living allowance and the adjustment by 7.8 per cent of the income tax brackets. The wage rise will be some 7 per cent for those at the higher end of the wage-scale, those earning NIS 4000 a month or more.

To offset the effects of the payment of the allowance on prices and exporters' profitability the Treasury is planning a new round of reductions in the employers' contributions to the National Insurance Institute. This month the Treasury transferred over NIS 300 million to the NII on behalf of the employers, as part of the package deal of last January, in which it pledged to pay part of the employers' NII fees. Treasury officials said the ministry is planning to make a further reduction in these fees. This, the Treasury hopes, will obviate the need to devalue the shekel, a move the ministry staunchly opposes.

(Continued on Page 17)

Fifty held in Gaza crackdown

By JOEL GREENBERG and Agencies

Security forces have broken up an Islamic Jihad terror cell in the Gaza Strip, arresting at least 50 suspected members and uncovering a large underground arms cache, security sources said.

The arsenal was found in Gaza's Shaja'iya neighbourhood, the site of a shootout last week in which four Islamic Jihad gunmen and a Shin Bet agent were killed.

Security forces have been carrying out intensive searches of Shaja'iya since the shootout and have arrested dozens of Gaza residents.

Two of the gunmen killed escaped in May with four other security prisoners from the Gaza jail. One prisoner was captured and another was killed by IDF troops when they fatally shot three men who ran a roadblock in the Gaza Strip a week ago.

Chief of General Staff Dan Shomron said this week that the escaped prisoners had been involved in the murder of Israelis in Gaza since the jailbreak.

The unrest in the territories appears to be waning. In the West Bank, a petrol bomb was thrown Wednesday night at an Israeli car near Rachel's Tomb in Bethlehem, but caused no casualties or damage. The neighbouring Dehaishe refugee camp remained under a curfew imposed Tuesday night after an Israeli boy was injured by a stone hurled from the camp at a car.

(Continued on Page 17)

Woman of 68 raped and murdered

By JONATHAN KARP
For The Jerusalem Post

TEL AVIV. -- A 68-year-old woman was sexually assaulted and murdered in her succa in a courtyard next to 194 Rehov Arlosoroff on Wednesday night.

Dr. Miriam Vilamovsky's body was found in the succa early yesterday morning by a neighbour, Uri Mana'im, who immediately notified the police. Officers who arrived at the site said they recognized the obvious signs of struggle: overturned objects in the succa and marks on Vilamovsky's throat.

Police yesterday afternoon arrested one suspect, a 46-year-old man from a village near Afula, and today will bring him before a court for his formal remand hearing, a spokeswoman said.

The attack occurred around midnight on Wednesday, police said. Vilamovsky was cleaning up her apartment after hosting family members and friends at dinner in the succa. When she left the building to dump the garbage, a man grabbed her from behind and threw her down on the grass, where he tried to rape her.

Detectives found Vilamovsky's

(Continued on Page 17)

Trade deficit hits dollar and stocks

LONDON (AFP). -- The announcement on Wednesday of a hefty U.S. trade deficit of $15.7 billion in August depressed the dollar yesterday, as it fell to lows of 1.7955 Deutschmarks and 141.55 yen before a very slight recovery in late afternoon.

Fear of U.S. Federal Reserve intervention and operations by European investors brought the greenback up to almost DM1.80 at the end of the trading session.

Wall Street stocks had plummeted on Wednesday at a dizzy rate on receipt of the news of the higher-than-expected trade deficit. The Dow Jones Industrial average dropped by more than 80 points, one of its sharpest declines ever in a single session, before recovering by about 15 points to 2,441 during early

(Continued on Page 2, Col. 1)

Golan wine wins gold at world contest

By DAVID HOROVITZ
Jerusalem Post Correspondent

LONDON. -- The Golan Heights Winery has won Israel's first ever gold medal in the prestigious International Wine and Spirits Competition, beating hundreds of entries world-wide to take the award for the best Cabernet Sauvignon.

At the awards ceremony, held at the House of Commons last night, Golan Heights also won three silver and two bronze medals.

Set up in 1983 with a staff of two, Golan Heights now produces 130,000 cases of wine a year, half of which is exported. Already the only Israeli winemaker with products on the shelves of Harrods, London's most prestigious store, Golan Heights wines sell well in the U.S., Germany and Holland, and it is even hoping to export to France, albeit mainly for the kosher market.

Ninety per cent of the company's vineyards are on the Golan Heights -- including 400 acres in the "Valley of Tears" from which 250 burnt-out tanks, the legacy of the Yom Kippur War, had to be removed before planting could begin. The other 10 per cent are in the Upper Galilee.

Shimshon Welner, general-manager and founder of the winery, which produces 18 different wines under the Yarden and Gamla labels, said that not only was he astonished to receive the gold award, but his competitors were also amazed at his success.

"Apparently several of them rang the organizers to ask whether there had been some mistake. They were very pleasant about it, but they were certainly surprised."

'Defiant' Iranians hit U.S. tanker

MANAMA, Bahrain (AP). -- An Iranian missile yesterday hit and set ablaze an American owned supertanker moored off Kuwait's main oil terminal, in what diplomats called a show of Iranian defiance after two recent debacles at the hands of the U.S. Navy in the gulf.

Kuwaiti firefighters and the ship's crew brought under control the fire aboard the 275,937-ton *Sungar* after five hours. No casualties were reported. Iraqi warplanes hit an Iranian-chartered supertanker, which was reported to be still on fire some 12 hours later, near Iran's big Kharg Island terminal.

It was the 13th ship reported hit along Iran's coast in the last 10 days, in what Baghdad says is a campaign to destroy Iran's war-making potential.

Meanwhile, a West German navy flotilla of three ships set out for the Mediterranean to assist U.S. forces in the Gulf.

Italian airliner missing

ROME (AP). -- An Italian airliner with 37 people aboard disappeared from radar screens while flying over northern Italy last night, officials said. Italian news agencies said the plane had crashed. The plane was flying from Milan to West Germany.

Mansdorf challenge

Israel tennis champion Amos Mansdorf will be up against it this afternoon in the $105,000 Riklis Israel Tenis Centre Classic Grand Prix tournament in Ramat Hasharon. He faces the great Jimmy Connors in an intriguing semi-final clash of this Nabisco Grand Prix tourney. Their match will be preceded earlier by the other semi-final between the second and third seeds respectively, Brad Gilbert of the U.S. and Peter Lundgren of Sweden at 2 p.m.

Slepak to get visa at last

Vladimir Slepak, who first sought to leave the Soviet Union more than 17 years ago and spent five years in internal exile, will finally be permitted to emigrate, he said on Wednesday.

Slepak said he was invited to Ovir, the Soviet visa office Wednesday afternoon and informed that his application would be approved. He said no reason was given.

"It is like it is happening to somebody else, and I am watching from a distance," Slepak said when asked how he felt.

Asked where he would go, the 59-year-old refusenik said, "Israel, of course." He and his wife, Maria, both received permission to leave.

Asked when he would leave, Slepak said, "As soon as I can sell the car to buy plane tickets."

Shultz due today on 'real' business

By MENACHEM SHALEV and WOLF BLITZER

U.S. Secretary of State George Shultz and a host of top State Department officials are scheduled to arrive here today for three days of intensive talks on the peace process, U.S.-Israel relations and the Middle East situation in general.

Foreign Minister Shimon Peres told Labour party ministers in a meeting on Wednesday morning that he expects Shultz to hold "real and discreet" meetings here, which will not be merely "ceremonial." Energy Minister Moshe Shahal told the ministers that he believes that Shultz is carrying concrete proposals of "guarantees," meant to budge Prime Minister Yitzhak Shamir from his opposition to the international conference.

But sources close to the prime minister insist that that "indications" from Washington reveal that the international conference will not be a major point on Shultz's agenda. They say that Shultz does plan to engage in discussion concerning the "substance" of the peace process, and to raise new ideas concerning the Camp David autonomy proposals, which might subsequently be conveyed to Jordan's King Hussein.

But both sides acknowledge that Hussein is not likely to change his position concerning the need for an international conference and that, thus, no dramatic progress can be expected from Shultz's talks here.

Shultz said yesterday that he hoped to meet with a group of Palestinian leaders from the West Bank and Gaza during his upcoming visit. The Secretary noted that he had "a good session" at the State Department earlier this week with the visiting mayor of Bethlehem, Elias Freij.

At a State Department news conference, Shultz once again appealed to Palestinian leaders -- without referring by name to the PLO -- to accept America's minimal conditions for U.S. recognition leading to their participation in the peace process with Israel.

He said the Palestinians have "legitimate rights and concerns." He also said that "Palestinians must be involved in the peace process if it's to mean anything. And there isn't any question about that.

"But it's also true that there isn't a role in the peace process for people whose tactics are violence and who refuse to renounce violence, who refuse to recognize that Israel is there as a state and are ready to talk and try to make peace."

Shultz was cautious in discussing his general objectives during his Middle East visit. "I don't go there with any particular new thing," he said. "I hope, perhaps, some others will have something new to say." Other State Department officials said the Secretary hoped to narrow procedural differences leading to the start of direct peace negotiations, perhaps at an international conference. But they were not very optimistic.

(Continued on back page)

Foreign Ministry row as stage is set for top overseas appointments

By MENACHEM SHALEV
Jerusalem Post Reporter

A fierce row broke out this week between the Foreign Ministry's twin directors-general: Avraham Tamir and Yossi Beilin. Ignoring Beilin's strenuous objections, Tamir convened the "third appointments committee" which he heads, and proceeded to name the Israeli ambassador to Washington's next bureau chief.

The heated contest over the relatively junior post is considered a harbinger of bigger things to come. A bumper crop of appointments abroad -- nearly a third of all the ministry's foreign postings -- is expected this summer. These include the cream of the crop, with six of the ministry's seven top posts up for grabs: ambassadorships to the UN, London, Paris, Bonn and Tokyo and the post of consul-general in New York.

Meetings of the "second" and "supreme" appointments committee, which appoint middle-level and top-level diplomats respectively, had been scheduled for this coming Sunday, but have been postponed because of the visit of U.S. Secretary of State George Shultz.

Foreign Ministry personnel, in a perpetual buzz over appointments that affect their personal fortunes, will thus have a few more days to worry, but will also have more time to cajole, lobby and influence to get the posting of their choice.

The "third" committee, entrusted with appointments up to the level of first secretary, convened on Wednesday and appointed Yossi Amrani as bureau chief in Washington, much to the chagrin of Beilin, who claimed that appointments in Washington were within his purview and who had his own candidate for the job, Yuval Frenkel, an aide to Peres's political adviser Nimrod Novik.

The Foreign Ministry is rife with gossip and guesses about the expected appointments. Foreign Minister Peres has yet to intervene but is said to be eager to make all the appointments coming due before the next elections.

The "second" and "supreme" appointments committees are the same. They have seven members: the two directors-general, deputy director-general Yeshayahu Anug, Peres's bureau chief Uri Savir, deputy director-general for administration Yitzhak Shelef, controller Benny Navon, and the head of the employees union, Victor Harel.

Coalitions and counter-coalitions abound in the committees. For example, there is the so-called "Peres mafia," composed of Beilin, Savir, Navon and sometimes Shelef. Savir and Shelef, as well as Anug, also belong to what is termed the "Canadian mafia," having served together in Ottawa in the early 1980s. The workers' representatives usually side with Tamir.

But sources in the seven-man committee say that contrary to the impressions created by this week's row, Beilin and Tamir usually agree on 80 per cent of the appointments.

(Continued on Page 2, Col. 2)

BETH DAVID BREAKS GROUND

The Beth David Institute took a major step forward during Hol Hamoed Succot in its plan to establish a modern facility for the handicapped in the Judean Hills.

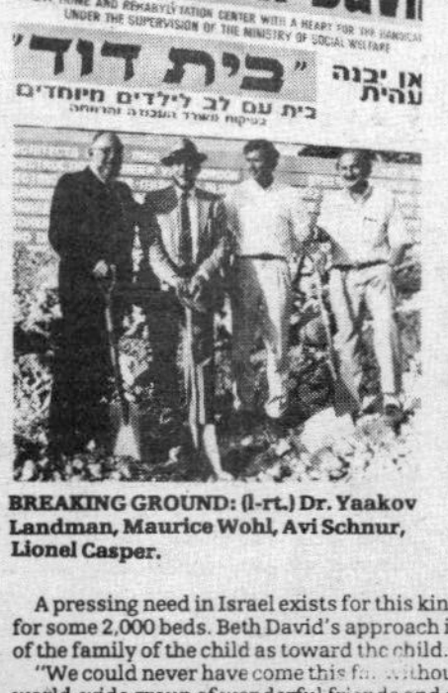

BREAKING GROUND: (l-rt.) Dr. Yaakov Landman, Maurice Wohl, Avi Schnur, Lionel Casper.

In a two-step programme, an afternoon groundbreaking ceremony was attended by Jerusalem Chief Rabbi Yitzhak Kolitz, government officials and prominent supporters at the construction site off the Tel Aviv-Jerusalem highway near Kiryat Telshe Stone.

That same evening, a gala dinner featuring Rabbi Shlomo Riskin as guest speaker, took place at the Succa of the Ramada Renaissance Hotel. Among the noted honorees were: Mr. and Mrs. Maurice Wohl, Mr. and Mrs. Avi Schnur, Mr. and Mrs. Lionel Casper, and Mr. and Mrs. Barry Liberman. Top rabbinic and public figures participated.

"After seven years of operating from woefully inadequate quarters of a temporary nature in Maoz Zion, we have managed to make the 'great leap' forward," stated Beth David Institute founder and director Rabbi Dr. Yaakov Landman, "And when we will open our doors, G-d willing, in another two years, we will assume a pre-eminent role as Israel's leading residential centre for the handicapped."

A pressing need in Israel exists for this kind of centre, with an overall national need for some 2,000 beds. Beth David's approach is geared as much toward the special needs of the family of the child as toward the child.

"We could never have come this far without the consistent, generous support of a world-wide group of wonderful friends and supporters," Rabbi Kolitz told the groundbreaking event participants.

(Communicated)

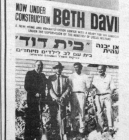

Demjanjuk son-in-law
Page 2

THE JERUSALEM POST

Vol. LV, No. 16684 Thursday, November 26, 1987 • Kislev 5, 5748 • Rabia Tani 6, 1408 NIS 1.05 (Eilat NIS 0.90)

SECOND EDITION

Babies pile up in Negev
Page 4

Harsh words for 'Mossad misinformation' and Israel's desire 'to dominate'

Iraqi envoy sees no sign of Israeli sympathy

By DAVID HOROVITZ
Jerusalem Post Correspondent

LONDON. -- The Iraqi ambassador here yesterday slammed reports of a growing rapprochement between Israel and Iraq as "Mossad disinformation," adding that there was no prospect of any warming of relations "as long as Israel continues to arm Iran to the teeth."

Ambassador Mohammed Sadiq al-Mashat told *The Jerusalem Post* that he paid scant heed to Foreign Minister Peres's recent statements condemning the Khomeini regime and praising Iraq for confronting fundamentalism.

"I hear the words, but where is the action?" he asked, charging that Israel has been sending arms to Iran from the start of the conflict, and that the entire Iraq-Iran war was sparked by Israel's desire to "cripple and divide Iraq" and to "dominate and expand their reign in the whole area."

Al-Mashat dismissed out of hand suggestions that Israeli arms are being sold to Iraq or might be in the future. "Unlike Khomeini, we buy our arms openly," he said, naming the Soviet Union and France as major suppliers. "We have purchased not a single bullet on the black market."

Al-Mashat, who spoke to *The Post* after addressing a luncheon of the British Diplomatic and Commonwealth Writers Association, asserted that "Israel does not want peace." He agreed that some sections of the Israeli public support a withdrawal from the West Bank and Gaza, but believed that they were "only a small slice of the pie."

The ambassador claimed that the Khomeini regime had been installed in Teheran as part of a Western effort "to use religion to fight communism. That was the plan, but Israeli intelligence turned the Iranian tide against Iraq, to stop, divide and finish Iraq." Israel, he added, was the only beneficiary of the continued fighting.

Al-Mashat claimed that the "Mossad disinformation" concerning Israeli-Iraqi ties was actually designed for the Ayatollah's benefit. "The war is very unpopular within Iran," he explained, apparently suggesting that the notion of Israeli-Iraqi alliance would spur Iranian enthusiasm for continued conflict.

Six soldiers killed

Terrorists on gliders strike army camp

A terror gang which arrived by glider from Lebanon last night attacked an army camp next to the Gibor junction near Kiryat Shmona, according to an AFP report.

The report said the terrorists landed at about 10 p.m. at the camp and immediately opened fire.

Six IDF soldiers were killed in the attack, according to informed sources quoted by the news agency. It said the IDF reported "many casualties", and gave no further details, though it said the exchange of fire continued late into the night.

AFP said it was not immediately known last night how many terrorists took part in the attack and to which group they belonged.

The area was completely closed off by the IDF and helicopters and troop reinforcements were rushed to the scene, AFP said.

Several years ago a Palestinian terrorist flew a glider into Israel near the Lebanese border. He immediately gave himself up to the IDF.

In April 1981, terrorists tried a similar infiltration using a hot air balloon in the northeast of the Galilee. The balloon was shot down several dozen metres from the border and its crew of two were killed.

Fatal stabbings in Jerusalem

Jerusalem Post Staff

Two Jewish supermarket employees were murdered late last night in a parking lot underneath the Mi Vami restaurant near the Hamashbir building in downtown Jerusalem.

Sources at the scene said supermarket manager Rafi Weitzman and the store's security guard, Zechariya Maimoni, had been stabbed, though police were still investigating how the murders took place.

The employees worked in the supermarket on the basement floor of the Hamashbir building. The motive for the attack was not immediately known.

Hussein in Damascus to work on Assad's *sulha* with Baghdad rival

AMMAN (Reuter). -- Jordan's King Hussein flew to Damascus yesterday to try to speed up a reconciliation between presidents Hafez Assad of Syria and Saddam Hussein of Iraq.

The official news agency Petra said the king would discuss implementation of decisions taken at the Arab summit in Amman two weeks ago, where the Jordanian leader arranged a meeting to break the ice between the Syrian and Iraqi leaders.

Diplomats said the king, who opened talks with Assad shortly after his arrival, was expected to push for an early resumption of diplomatic ties between the two neighbouring Arab countries, broken since Syria backed non-Arab Iran in the Gulf war.

Syria's backing for Iran since 1980 was a main obstacle in earlier Jordanian attempts to bridge the gap between the two men who have been at personal and ideological loggerheads for almost 20 years.

King Hussein sees a reconciliation between Damascus and Baghdad, ruled by rival wings of the pan-Arab Baath party, as a precondition for ending the seven-year-old Gulf war.

Assad appeared to open the door for better relations by aquiescing in summit resolutions which condemned Iran for not heeding a UN-ordered truce and expressed solidarity with Iraq.

Syrian Foreign Minister Farouq al-Shara said in Damascus last week Syria would continue its efforts to end the Gulf war which has started spilling over into neighbouring Arab states.

Since the Arab League meeting, news media in Damascus and Baghdad have quenched their normal torrent of mutual abuse and a group of top Syrian businessmen flew to Iraq on Saturday for talks they said would include possible resumption of trade ties.

Diplomats in Damascus said the trade team went to Baghdad despite a formal ban on travel to Iraq.

Foreign Minister Taher al-Masri was reported on Monday as saying King Hussein would also travel to Baghdad to encourage Syria and Iraq to hold bilateral talks on normalizing relations.

Masri told the Paris-based news magazine *Al-Mostakbal* that an early resumption of diplomatic relations was expected.

Asked about reports that ties may be resumed within two weeks, he said: "Yes. The convention is to restore diplomatic ties as a first step in normalizing relations between two countries."

IBA staffers charge Porat foiled return of broadcasts

By JEFF BLACK
For The Jerusalem Post

Furious Broadcasting Authority journalists stormed out of a meeting late last night with the IBA management after an acrimonious day of accusations and counter-accusations whose result was the continuation of the seven-week shut-down of Israel Television and Radio.

The journalists' walkout came in the middle of IBA director-general Uri Porat's explanation of new plans for television and radio. These plans, which were leaked to some Hebrew papers yesterday by an IBA official, led to the journalists refusing to approve the agreement reached Tuesday night which would have ended the strike.

According to the journalists, the plans will change the structure and content of television and radio programmes and create an impression of overstaffing. The journalists argued that it was impossible to negotiate an agreement to go to arbitration one minute, and then, seconds later, introduce new conditions to take effect during the arbitration period.

(Continued on Page 2, Col. 7)

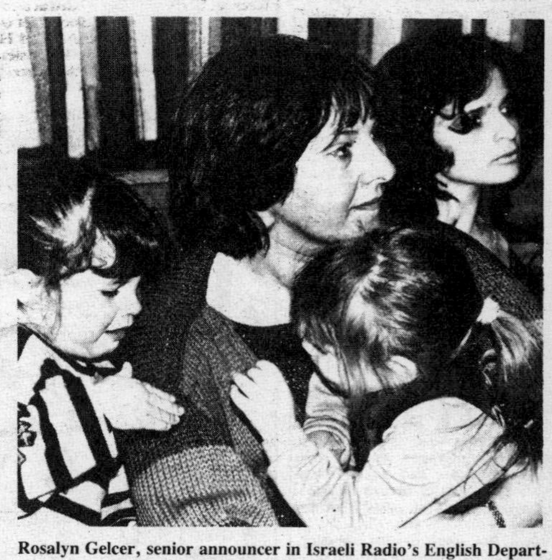

Rosalyn Gelcer, senior announcer in Israeli Radio's English Department, is tugged by her impatient daughters as she listens intently to developments yesterday at strike headquarters for IBA staffers at Jerusalem's Beit Agron. (P. Tiktiner/Media)

Progress in KH talks but outpatient clinics closed

Kupat Holim Clalit hospital doctors will today keep all outpatient clinics closed, as they were yesterday, as part of continuing sanctions against the health fund's management.

The doctors decided last night to proceed with the sanctions despite "progress" in negotiations with management late last night. However, all operating rooms will function as normal. There was no non-emergency surgery two days this week.

Negotiations were in progress last night between the doctors' representatives and management in an effort to end the sanctions, now in their seventh week. The physicians have been demanding the right to decide how a second shift will be instituted in the hospitals' operating rooms and clinics.

Israeli role alleged in smuggling of tank technology out of U.S.

By WOLF BLITZER
Jerusalem Post Correspondent

WASHINGTON. -- The U.S. Justice Department has accused Israel of participating in a conspiracy to smuggle restricted technology for the manufacture of tank cannon barrels out of the U.S.

The Israeli Embassy in Washington has flatly denied the allegation. "We are confident that any review will establish that Israel Military Industries (IMI) and the government of Israel and its employees had acted in full compliance with U.S. laws and regulations," embassy spokesman Yossi Gal said.

The Pentagon, as of late yesterday afternoon, had not yet issued any formal statement on the dispute, which resurfaced on Tuesday when the Justice Department announced that a Connecticut company, Napco Inc., had agreed to pay $750,000 in fines for violating U.S. export law by smuggling equipment and technology to Israel for manufacture of the 120 mm. tank barrel cannons.

The guilty plea followed a two-year investigation by the Justice Department, the Customs Service and other U.S. law-enforcement agencies.

The new technology enables the tank barrels to be produced faster, and at less cost, than older processes. In addition, the court papers said, the process results in a cannon "with greater range, more accuracy, and a life expectancy of 800-1,500 rounds," as opposed to the older version's only 200 rounds.

"As known to Napco," the court

(Continued on Back Page)

Spy chiefs gather to honour Israel's former friend in CIA

By ANDY COURT
For The Jerusalem Post

It looked like an ordinary tree-planting ceremony, except that the well-dressed, middle-aged men, some of whom arrived in Volvos and Peugeots with special antennas, seemed to know one another particularly well.

Some of the cars had diplomatic plates. Some of the young men on the periphery had plugs in their ears. Border Policemen surrounded the area, one of them walking a dog through the upturned field.

The defence minister and the American ambassador were there. Newspaper photographers were not. It seemed to be the wrong place to ask an obvious question.

"What is he doing now?" one attempted.

"I don't want to know," someone replied.

The past and present heads of Israel's security services gathered yesterday on a hill near Mevasseret Zion, in the Jerusalem corridor, to pay tribute to James Jesus ("Jim") Angleton, the CIA's former chief of counter-intelligence, who developed a special relationship with Israel when relations between Washington and Jerusalem were at their lowest ebb. The purpose of the unusual gathering was to dedicate a memorial forest in his name. He died eight months ago at the age of 69, having left the CIA 10 years earlier.

Angleton played a key role in strengthening relations between the CIA and Israel's fledgling intelligence services from the 1950s on, former intelligence officials say. He was an important ally in the highest echelons of the American administration at a time when almost all other channels in Washington were unreceptive to Israel. He was the right-hand man of CIA chief Allen Dulles, the brother of John Foster Dulles, the U.S. secretary of state at the time who never forgave Israel for its collusion with France and Britain during the 1956 Suez campaign, behind Washington's back.

The list of those attending yesterday's ceremony would make up a "Who's Who" of the Israeli secret services: former Mossad chiefs Meir Amit, Zvi Zamir, and Yitzhak Hofi; former military intelligence chiefs Aharon Yariv, Shlomo Gazit, and Binyamin Gibli; former GSS heads Avraham Ahituv and Amos Manor.

Angleton "was a friend you could trust on a personal basis," Defence Minister Rabin said at the ceremony. Rabin knew Angleton from the days when he was Israel's ambassador to the U. S. in 1968-73.

The current heads of the security services were there, too, but no one was inclined to mention their names.

The American guests at the assembly included U.S. Ambassador Thomas Pickering and Angleton's wife, Cicely. One of Angleton's daughters -- Guru Sangat Kaur -- is an American Sikh, whose all-white outfit added to the intrigue of the event. Angleton's granddaughter -- Guru Sadhana Kaur --was dressed just like her mother.

Guests at the ceremony talked about Angleton's love of orchids, and of the unusual jewlery he had hand-made for his friends. There was less talk about the business side

(Continued on Back Page)

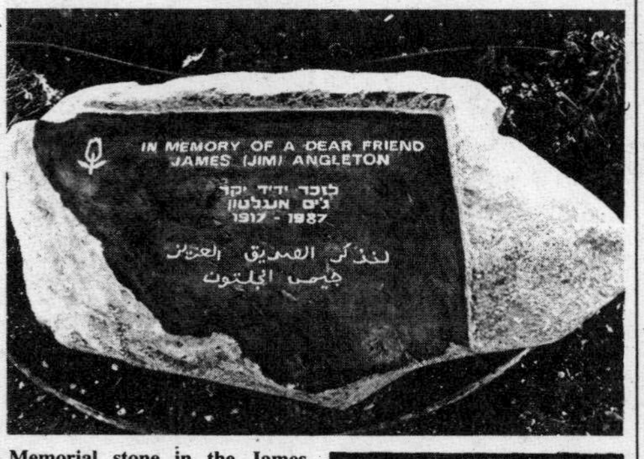

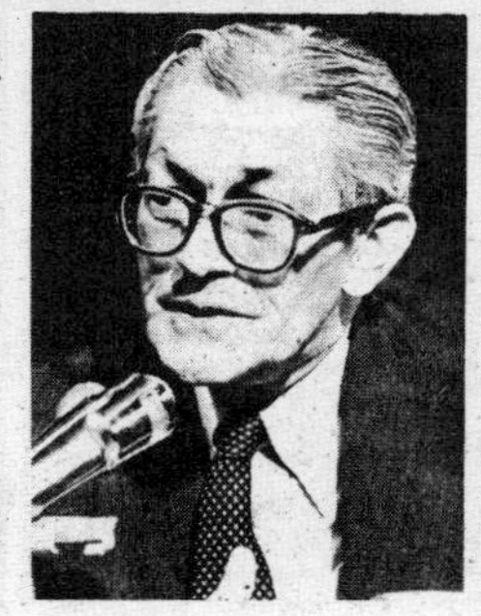

Memorial stone in the James Angleton Garden dedicated in Jerusalem yesterday in honour of the former CIA chief of counter-intelligence (right) (Media)

Nissim won't loosen his purse strings until Arab local councils end strike

By ELAINE RUTH FLETCHER
Jerusalem Post Reporter

Finance Minister Moshe Nissim won't release any funds to Arab municipalities until they end their strike, officials said yesterday.

The decision followed a demonstration by about 130 Arab municipal officials at the Interior Ministry yesterday, the fourth day of the strike. The officials drove to Jerusalem from towns and villages in the Triangle and Galilee in a convoy of some 50 cars and turned in their municipal office keys to the Interior Ministry. Arab municipal leaders also called yesterday on students to stay away from school for the rest of the week.

However, two small villages in Galilee, Kfar Bani and Sha'ab, said they would respond to the government's call to end the strike.

At the demonstration in front of the Interior Ministry, a dozen MKs from Mapam, Rakah, and the Citizens Rights Movement appeared to give support to the strikers.

When police barred the demonstrators from entering the ministry, Alignment Minister-without-Portfolio Ezer Weizman, formerly in charge of Arab affairs, strode through the crowd into the building. He soon emerged with an announcement that the ministry's director-general, Aryeh Deri, would meet with the municipal leaders.

Deri told the municipal officials that some allocations were to have been distributed yesterday, but had been delayed by bureaucratic snags in the Finance Ministry.

Deri said that some NIS 2.5 million had been added to this year's development budget of NIS 7.5 million. The government was ready to begin audits and to cover the entire deficit in the most deeply troubled 22 municipalities, he said.

But Arab council heads continued to insist that the Interior Ministry deal with the deficits of all 48 local councils at the same time. The leaders also said that Deri's remarks did not respond to their more fundamental complaint -- that their councils receive only 25 per cent of the local budget allocations that Jewish local councils of comparable size receive.

Because of the inequities, councils can't live within their budgets, and some haven't paid salaries since September, they said.

At the close of the meeting, Mohammed Ghanaim, council head of Sakhnin, handed Deri an envelope containing the keys to their municipal buildings. Deri rose and walked out of the room, leaving the keys on the table.

The strike is scheduled to end on Friday.

Labour pressured on WZO candidate

By CHARLES HOFFMAN
Jerusalem Post Reporter

Labour Party leaders were meeting late last night to decide the political fate of Akiva Lewinsky, amid mounting pressure from several groups in the party that he withdraw as a candidate for chairman of the

(Continued on Page 2, Col. 1)

Jakobovits: Tora scholars reject 'uniqueness' of Holocaust

By HAIM SHAPIRO
Jerusalem Post Reporter

Despite widespread acceptance of the Holocaust as a tragedy unique in Jewish history, leading Tora scholars are "unanimous" in "denying the uniqueness of the Holocaust as an event different ... from any previous national catastrophe," according to British Chief Rabbi Sir Immanuel Jakobovits.

The British chief rabbi noted that this was the case, despite the existence of what he described as "an entire industry, with handsome profits for writers, researchers, filmmakers, monument builders, museum planners and even politicians." **He added that some rabbis and theologians were "partners in this big business."**

The theme of Jakobovits's "B'nai B'rith Jerusalem Address" last night was "Religious Response to the Holocaust: Retrospect and Prospect." For him, rebuilding is far more important than remembering. The survivors, he said, could only overcome the past and focus on the future by "recognizing in the Holocaust a replication of Jewish history's cycle of appalling catastrophes followed by survival and regeneration."

Referring to that section of Tora leadership which was "hardest hit" by the catastrophe of European Jewry, the hassidic and yeshiva worlds, **he said that it was rabbis from those sectors who were least concerned about commemorating the catastrophe with special prayers or fast days.** The hundreds, if not thousands, of Tora luminaries who perished are "seemingly unremembered."

This follows, he noted, the halachic response of two of the greatest sages of the period, the Rabbi of Brisk (Rabbi Velvl Soloveitchik) and the Hazon Ish (Rabbi Avraham Karelitz), who opposed any commemoration other than that already observed on Tisha be'Av.

Jakobovits speculated that the Hazon Ish objected to establishing a special anniversary for remembering the Holocaust because he feared **that the day would be "appropriated in a secular format." If so, he added, this is indeed what has happened.**

To be sure, the British chief rabbi said, there were Tora scholars who searched for reasons for this catastrophe. One such scholar, formerly a bitter opponent of Zionism, concluded that anti-Zionism was the source of the evil. Another argued that the visit of the Mufti to Germany in 1942, in his frenzied efforts to prevent Jewish immigration to Palestine, set in motion the extermination.

More than one scholar saw assimilation, emancipation, religious reform and lack of faith as the cause of the tragedy. As for the results of the Holocaust, **Jakobovits expressed his own conviction that the State of Israel would not have come into being had it not been for this tragedy.**

As for the future, he warned against a view of Judaism in which the Holocaust assumed a central role.

"Would it not be a catastrophic perversion of the Jewish spirit if brooding over the Holocaust were to become a substantial element in the Jewish purpose, and if the anxiety to prevent another Holocaust were to be relied upon as an essential incentive for Jewish activity?"

He called for a shift in emphasis from "the survival of Jews to the survival of Judaism. **For without Judaism, Jewish survival is both questionable and meaningless."**

EIGHT PAGES FROM SUNDAY'S
The New York Times
WEEKLY REVIEW
INSIDE TODAY

THE JERUSALEM POST

Vol. LVI, No. 16772 Tuesday, March 8, 1988 • Adar 19, 5748 • Rajab 21, 1408 NIS 1.15 (Eilat NIS 1.00)

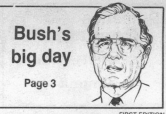

Bush's big day
Page 3

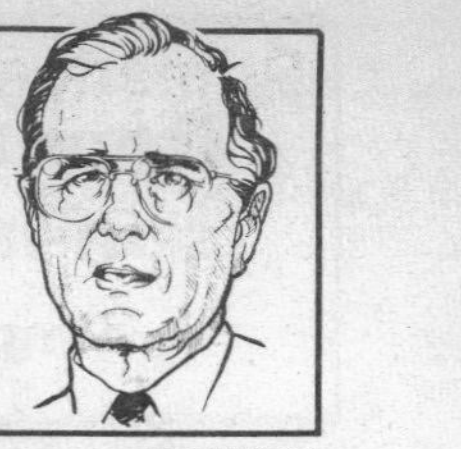

FIRST EDITION

Grenade attack on police jeep

By JOEL GREENBERG
Jerusalem Post Reporter

A border policeman was lightly wounded yesterday by a grenade tossed at his jeep in the West Bank village of Idna, west of Hebron, when troops arriving to make arrests were met with a barrage of rocks, petrol bombs and metal debris, military sources said.

Troops returned fire and wounded seven villagers, one seriously. Soldiers at the scene said they had detected flashes of gunfire directed at them and pointed to a pock-marked wall that they said had been hit by the bullets.

The incident was the first grenade attack on troops since the start of the uprising in the territories, and raised concerns in the IDF that Palestinian rioters could start attacking troops with live ammunition and explosives.

The IDF is investigating reports by soldiers that they were fired on by rioters at the Askar refugee camp near Nablus on Sunday. A makeshift bomb injured four soldiers in the Gaza Strip on Friday, and a bomb was set off and shots fired at an army vehicle in Gaza last month.

Though Palestinian activists in the territories are known to have a small supply of weapons and explosives, the PLO has forbidden armed attacks by rioters, to maintain the image of an unarmed popular revolt.

Security sources gave the following details of the incident:

Troops arrived at the village at 3 a.m. and imposed a curfew prior to a sweep aimed at netting suspected riot leaders. The sweep was the latest in a series of IDF raids on West Bank villages in response to riots and attempts by residents to close off their villages with rock barricades.

The troops were confronted by villagers who waited for them behind barricades and pelted them with rocks, petrol bombs and the grenade. Several suspects were arrested in searches after the grenade attack, but others evaded arrest by fleeing to surrounding valleys.

(Continued on Page Three)

Rabin, after three hostages, three terrorists die in Negev bus hijacking:

'Attack was PLO bid to get back in picture'

The terror attack in the Negev yesterday was part of a PLO attempt to "get back into the picture," after being pushed to the sidelines by the Shultz peace initiative, Defence Minister Rabin said last night.

Rabin said that the purpose of the attack was to carry out murders pure and simple, and to engage in negotiations for the release of hostages in order to achieve maximum publicity.

With the U.S. Secretary of State George Shultz's initiative now on the table, the PLO has been shunted aside – "they simply cannot accept the terms for possible political movement as spelled out in the American plan," the defence minister stressed in an interview with *The Jerusalem Post* editorial staff.

The PLO aims to do everything possible to stop the Shultz plan from succeeding, Rabin noted. The recent upsurge in terror activity could thus be construed as part of the PLO bid to re-establish itself as a factor in the situation, "to show that they exist," he said.

"In the 22 years of their existence the PLO has made 'armed struggle,' that is, terror, its primary purpose. That has failed them, whereas events in the territories over the past three months have achieved much more.

Compiled from reports by Yoram Kessel, Hirsh Goodman and Menachem Shalev

On the one hand they have thus tried to jump on the bandwagon of the events; but on the other they also cannot give up their terror," Rabin said.

He said this explained the recent spate of terror actions, which included five attempted attacks from Lebanon, and which climaxed in yesterday's attack.

Prime Minister Shamir said yesterday that the terrorists who had carried out the attack "were the same people who are igniting the disturbances in the territories."

But, Shamir added, "nothing will ever be achieved by violence and murder." Israel "will never tire from the combat" against the terrorists, he said.

Shamir said that the terrorists are maintaining a daily effort to inflict losses on Israel, adding that "only yesterday six terrorists who had tried to infiltrate from Lebanon were killed."

Foreign Minister Peres said that the Dimona attack was "an example of the PLO's criminal attitude."

Peres said that Israel would conduct an uncompromising battle against terrorists. "We will continue to hit them anywhere they are found," he said.

Both Peres and Shamir expressed their appreciation for the actions of the security forces in stopping the terrorists, singling out for praise the police anti-terror unit. Both, in the Knesset yesterday and in the *Post* interview, stressed the role of the PLO, blaming it not only for yesterday's bus hijacking but also for other infiltration attempts and Katyusha attacks in recent weeks.

Despite a clear escalation in the PLO's military activities since February 20, Israel has refrained until now from military retaliation against the PLO. It was believed that to retaliate now, given the political climate, would have been misinterpreted by the world as an Israeli attempt to keep the PLO out of the political process by force.

The minister's words, taken in the context of yesterday's incident, developments on the Lebanese border, the attempted car bombing in Jerusalem last week and the use of a grenade against Israeli forces in Idna

(Continued on Page 2, Col. 5)

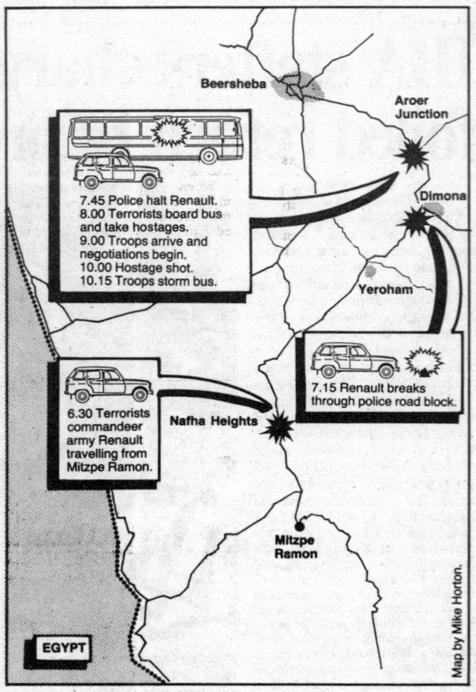
Beersheba
Aroer Junction
Dimona
7.45 Police halt Renault.
8.00 Terrorists board bus and take hostages.
9.00 Troops arrive and negotiations begin.
10.00 Hostage shot.
10.15 Troops storm bus.
Yeroham
7.15 Renault breaks through police road block.
6.30 Terrorists commandeer army Renault travelling from Mitzpe Ramon.
Nafha Heights
Mitzpe Ramon
EGYPT
Map by Mike Horton.

Bus stormed in less than a minute

By KENNETH KAPLAN and BRADLEY BURSTON
Jerusalem Post Reporters

Three Israelis, a man and two women, were killed and eight wounded when three Fatah terrorists who had infiltrated from Egypt took hostages on a bus early yesterday morning on the Beersheba-Dimona highway. An anti-terror Border Police force stormed the bus when the terrorists began shooting the hostages.

All three terrorists were killed in the police unit's assault.

The terrorists boarded the bus on a desolate stretch of road near the Aroer junction after the driver and all but six of the passengers managed to escape. The bus was carrying workers from Beersheba to the nuclear research facility at Dimona.

The terrorists identified themselves as members of Fatah during negotiations with the IDF and Negev police force which sped to the site. The terrorists demanded the release of Palestinians arrested during the last three months of unrest in the West Bank and Gaza Strip, and threated to kill one hostage every half-hour until their demands were met. They also demanded to speak to the Red Cross.

OC Southern Command Yitzhak Mordechai, who commanded the combined force which assembled on a hill overlooking the road, initially agreed to the terrorists' demand to negotiate "in an effort to spare lives."

However, when the terrorists executed the first of their hostages, approximately one hour after negotiations began, Mordechai gave the go-ahead to storm the bus.

According to a preliminary investigation conducted by the IDF at the Southern Command yesterday afternoon, the terrorists shot and mortally wounded two more hostages, both women, when the Border Police unit began its assault. One woman died shortly after the rescue operation, which took less than 40 seconds. The second was declared dead on arrival at Soroka Hospital in Beersheba.

Killed in the incident were Victor Ram, 39, a widower and father of three and an engineer at the Dimona facility; Miriam Ben-Yair, 46, a mother of four; and Rina Shiratsky, 31, a mother of two.

Six of the eight wounded, all of them women, were treated at Soroka Hospital for light injuries resulting from grenade fragments, and were released later in the day.

Two other women were hospitalized for gunshot and shrapnel wounds. Their injuries described as moderate.

It was still not clear last night when and where the eight were wounded. All of the killed and wounded were Beershebans.

The incident began at around 6:40 yesterday morning, when the three terrorists attacked an IDF Renault 4 sedan near the isolated Nafha Prison north of Mitzpe Ramon. The car's occupants, four officers from the IDF's officer training school, were en route to an athletic competition and were out of uniform and unarmed. When the terrorists opened fire with automatic weapons, the soldiers fled the scene, uninjured.

The four ran toward the prison where they alerted the police, who quickly set up roadblocks as far away as Ashdod.

The terrorists, meanwhile, took the car and drove northward toward Beersheba. Approximately a half-hour later, the car was sighted by police who had just set up a roadblock at the Dimona-Yeroham junction. Police opened fire on the car and chased it. During the chase, the terrorists fired on passing vehicles.

Half-an-hour later, at around 7:45, the police succeeded in puncturing one of the Renault's tyres near the Beduin village of Aroer, some 20 kilometres from Beersheba.

The terrorists got out of the Re-

(Continued on Page 2, Col. 3)

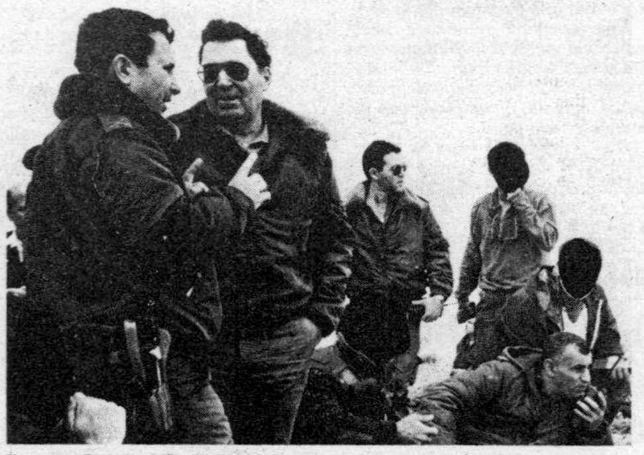

Deputy Chief of Staff Ehud Barak (left) confers with his chief, Dan Shomron, while O/C Southern Command, Major-General Yitzhak Mordechai (extreme right), controls the rescue operation. (IDF)

Return to terror undercuts 'uprising'

Fatah radio claimed last night that the Dimona bus operation was a reprisal for the Limassol car bombing in which three senior Fatah officers were killed. According to Defence Minister Yitzhak Rabin, the PLO's intention was to undermine the Shultz peace initiative.

But even firm supporters of the PLO in the territories felt last night that this operation could undermine the *intifada* – the uprising in the territories that started three months ago. They know that as long as the rioters limit their arsenal to stones, crowbars and even petrol bombs, they can maintain the image of the underdog, the occupied, the David who rises up against the Israeli Goliath.

But when atrocities start, the Palestinians may reassume the old terrorist image and rapidly lose the support they have won all over the world. The PLO leaders seem unable to resist intoxication with the successes of an uprising which they did not start, but which developed within the territories out of genuine despair.

ANALYSIS
Yehuda Litani

The Palestinians' use of terror automatically turns the Israelis from aggressors to victims. Many Palestinians in the territories are aware of that and for that reason have chosen different tactics during the last three months. But the extremists in Israel knew they could always count on their counterparts among the Palestinians in the attempt to undermine any peace initiative.

The Dimona operation might be regarded as a military success by some Palestinians, but it did not have the same impact as the hang glider operation in November when an army base was attacked, since its targets were civilians and not soldiers.

The terrorist action in Aroer yesterday and other attempted attacks by the PLO during the last two weeks – in addition to the apparent use of guns and the use of hand grenades against the IDF by Palestinians in the territories – are clear deviations from the path the uprising has been taking since last December. A deviation that could cause it to fail and dash the hopes of the Palestinians for the foreseeable future.

Shultz sees senators' letter as 'boost'

By WOLF BLITZER
Jerusalem Post Correspondent

WASHINGTON – Secretary of State George Shultz and his top aides believe that their reactivated Arab-Israeli peace initiative has been significantly bolstered by the unprecedented letter signed by 30 U.S. senators urging Prime Minister Yitzhak Shamir to accept the principle of exchanging land for peace.

But well-informed administration and congressional sources flatly denied that Shultz or anyone else in the Reagan administration had anything to do with encouraging the senators to write the letter.

Indeed, the major organizer was Democratic Senator Carl Levin (Michigan) who has been described as deeply worried about Shamir's position on the peace process. Levin, in turn, asked Republican Senator Rudy Boscwitz (Minnesota) to co-sponsor it. Both senators are Jewish and among the most active supporters of Israel in Washington.

They also have great respect for Shultz as someone who is very pro-Israeli.

Levin, after drafting the letter earlier last week, showed it on Wednesday evening, March 2, to Tom Dine, executive director of the American Israel Public Affairs Committee (Aipac), the official pro-Israeli lobbying organization on Capitol Hill. Dine, according to informed sources, tried unsuccessfully to convince Levin to delete the section in the letter calling on Shamir to accept the principle of land for peace.

Levin, according to the sources, refused, insisting that that was the heart of the peace process. He said he was angry that Shamir had been quoted in the February 26 issue of *The New York Times* as saying that "this expression of territory for peace is not accepted by me."

But neither Dine nor anyone else, the sources said, strongly pressed Levin to kill the letter. Levin, the next morning, began circulating the letter among his colleagues for signatures.

Israel Embassy officials quickly

(Continued on Page Four)

'We're going to die, and we're going to blow you up with us'

Hostages recall their ordeal

By BRADLEY BURSTON
Jerusalem Post Reporter

BEERSHEBA – "I lay on the floor and thought to myself: 'That's it. We're dead. All of us,'" recalled Stella Bechar, a 46-year-old mother of four, hours after her rescue from the terrorist attack in which three of her co-workers were killed.

Bechar, hospitalized in Soroka Hospital's orthopedic ward, suffered multiple shrapnel and gunshot wounds in the attack.

"They were all very young," she said, speaking of the terrorists, "their faces were uncovered, one of them had a moustache. Each has a gun, a Kalashnikov, ready to shoot."

During the negotiations between their captors and police officials, "we talked among ourselves, we tried to create a calm atmosphere. I asked one of [the terrorists] if he wanted some milk because he said he was thirsty. We even tried to joke with each other, and we told each other that there is a God, that we would get out of this alive.

"It wasn't that we were not frightened," she added. "We were terrified."

At first, the terrorists seemed fairly relaxed. "They told us, in Arabic, they would do nothing to us if we sat quietly. 'We only want the Red Cross to come,' they said. But as it went on, we were in true distress. Some of the women, some of the mothers, managed to escape."

According to fellow hostage Daisy Sorek, only the women in the front and centre sections of the bus were able to escape.

"There wasn't enough time to get off. We tried to talk to them. I asked them in Arabic what they wanted, but they wouldn't say. They just said they wanted the Red Cross."

"The terrorists were getting more and more impatient," said Bechar. They began opening our purses to see what was in them." In the main, Bechar continued, what they found was knitting.

"What could they find? Make-up, knitting," she laughed quietly. "We knit every day."

As negotiations continued, the terrorists became angry. "They got mad, because there were voices from outside and they could not hear them well. At some point, he [one of the terrorists] got a megaphone and became very, very agitated. He said, over and over, in Arabic, 'Every half-hour, one.'

The leader of the terror gang then called Victor Ram and ordered him to stand at the front of the bus, Bechar continued. "Then they shot him, they shot him in the chest, and he just fell, immediately. And then we knew: we're not getting out of this alive."

"They seemed very confused," said Sorek. "After they shot [Ram] the commander's gun didn't work any more. Something was wrong with it."

At that point, Rahel Matza – now recovering from surgery following gunshot and shrapnel injuries – assumed the role of spokeswoman for the hostages. "I told them, 'It's such a shame, you're so young. You don't have to do this.' But they said 'No, we're going to die, and we're going to blow you up with us.' Then they asked us if any of us knew how to drive. We all do, but we said no. We felt we were dead women, that we were dead already."

"We sat there," said Sorek, "and we could see from the windows that the soldiers were arriving by helicopter. But I thought, to be honest, that we were finished. They killed one, then they shot another, and we thought 'Here, they'll get us all, one by one.'

"There were 11 of us, all sitting next to each other. And the one behind me was shot, and the one sitting in front of me was killed."

Bechar can remember nothing of the subsequent rescue operation. "I remember that there was a pile of purses next to me and I lay down next to them. I remembered that on the television they always say it's a good idea to lie down. All of us lay

(Continued on Page Three)

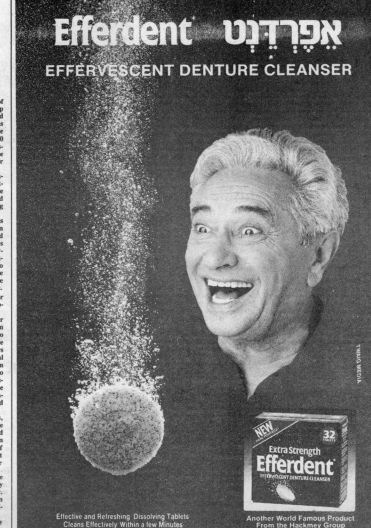

Primaries status report

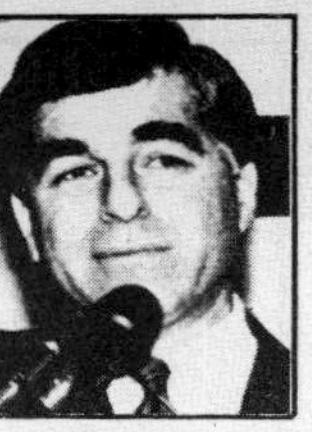

Page 3

THE JERUSALEM POST

Vol. LVI, No. 16792 Thursday, March 31, 1988 • Nisan 13, 5748 • Shaban 14, 1408 NIS 1.15 (Eilat NIS 1.00)

SECOND EDITION

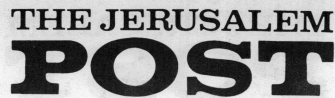

Journey to a closed city

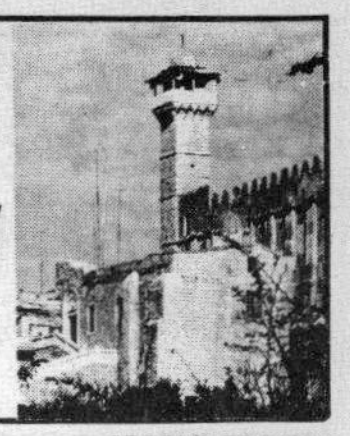

Page 4

U.S. ready only for 'restricted' int'l parley

By WOLF BLITZER
Jerusalem Post Correspondent

WASHINGTON – Secretary of State George Shultz yesterday said that he would ask the UN secretary-general to extend formal invitations to an international peace conference on the Arab-Israeli conflict only if it becomes clear in the coming days that the parties themselves have accepted the kind of "restricted" international meeting that the U.S. has proposed.

Meeting for 30 minutes with seven Washington-based Israeli correspondents, the secretary appeared surprisingly hopeful that he could still succeed in achieving a procedural breakthrough in arranging Arab-Israeli peace negotiations during his visit to the region next week. "We'll keep working at it," he said. Later in the day, Shultz met with Arab journalists in Washington.

He pointedly sought to reassure Israel that his peace proposals were fair and balanced. In the process, he again denied that his meeting last Saturday with two Palestinian American citizens, Professors Edward Said and Ibrahim Abu-Lughod, who are members of the Palestine National Council (PNC) represented any change in U.S. policy towards the PLO.

"In this case," he said, "we felt that there is a difference between the two [Palestinian] units." Moreover, he added, it was "beyond the pale as far as I am concerned" to prohibit the secretary of state from meeting with two prominent American citizens, professors at distinguished universities.

The secretary rejected any negotiations with the PLO because it has "promoted terrorism" and "in its essence, doesn't seem to be able to recognize" Israel's right to exist.

Asked whether he was planning to meet with Palestinians next week, Shultz replied that any such meeting would be the result of fresh Arab initiatives – not his own. He recalled that West Bank and Gaza Palestinians, intimidated by extremists, had refused to meet with him during his October and early-March visits to the region.

Shultz said his willingness to meet with the Palestinians at the American Colony Hotel in East Jerusalem had represented a change in the earlier U.S. pattern of having a visiting secretary of state meet with Palestinians only at the U.S. consulate in West Jerusalem. But the Palestinians did not attend.

"I don't have any plan to organize another meeting," he said. But if "some interested parties" – he cited Egypt and Jordan – organized a session with "legitimate Palestinians who are not PLO," he would be prepared to meet with them, he said.

Other U.S. officials later in the day said that Shultz would be pleased to meet with a delegation of West Bank and Gaza Palestinians but that the meeting would have to be initiated by the Palestinians.

"We aren't taking any steps," spokesman Charles Redman said, but added, "talking with Palestinians is an important part of this process, so it would certainly be a positive development if such a meeting should emerge during the course of this visit."

Shultz, answering questions, expressed confidence that both Prime Minister Shamir and Foreign Minister Peres would themselves eventually be successful in negotiating transitional and final peace arrangements with their Arab counterparts once actual talks got off the ground.

Shultz said that both Syria and the Soviet Union were still demanding that the conference have "plenary" powers – a position rejected by Washington. After Shultz met with the Israeli reporters, he had a separate session later in the day with Washington-based Arab journalists. During that second meeting, the secretary said that he would continue to differentiate between the PLO and the PNC.

Asked whether the UN secretary-general would be asked to extend invitations to an international conference, Shultz replied that there was "no point" in making any such request "until I know what people are ready to do, and if enough of the right people are prepared to go to a conference, which is of the type that we have in mind and are willing to sign up to that. Then it's worthwhile for him to issue the invitations."

Regarding his meeting with professors Said and Abu-Lughod, Shultz made a point of noting that "they don't expect Israel to go away. I felt that [the meeting] was a good thing," he said, but added that it did not change the long-standing U.S. policy of refusing to deal with the PLO.

If the PLO wants to come to the negotiating table, he said, it should accept UN resolutions 242 and 338 and Israel's right to exist.

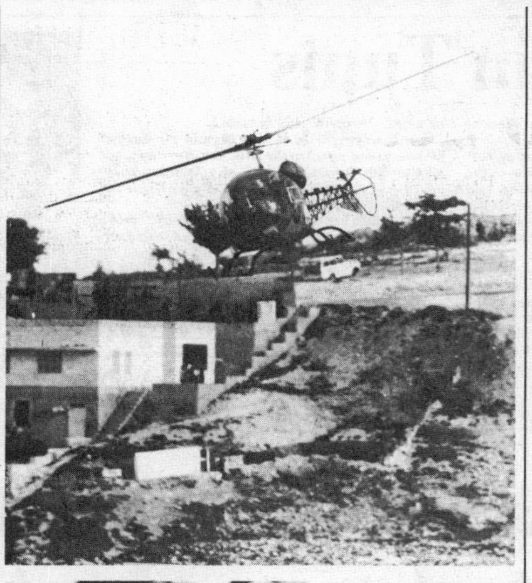

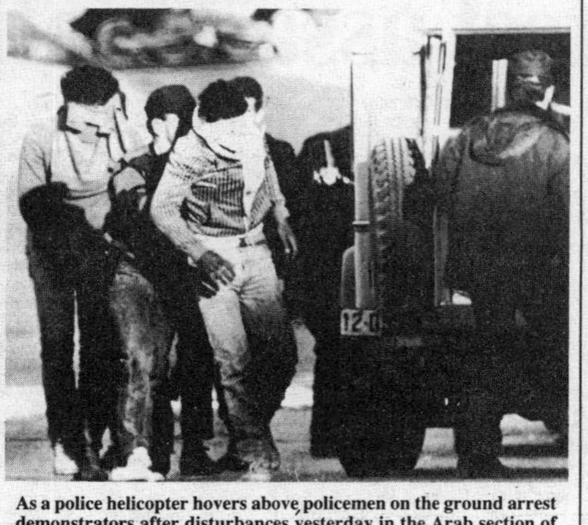

As a police helicopter hovers above, policemen on the ground arrest demonstrators after disturbances yesterday in the Arab section of Jerusalem's Abu Tor quarter. (Yitzhak Elharar / Scoop 80)

Some of the worst clashes since the beginning of the uprising

4 killed, 50 wounded in W. Bank Land Day

By JOEL GREENBERG
Jerusalem Post Reporter

In one of the bloodiest days since the start of the uprising in the territories, troops shot and killed four Palestinians and wounded more than 50 in clashes with rioters in the West Bank. Six Israelis were hurt.

The Land Day protests erupted in dozens of villages, despite an unprecedented security crackdown and media ban in the area.

"The high number of casualties is an indicator of the forceful and immediate reponse of [IDF] forces in places where there were disturbances and violence," said OC Central Command Amram Mitzna.

He said troops had carried out orders to respond quickly and aggressively to rioting, and that "some of these [incidents] would not have occurred had we not, at our own initiative, gone into villages and patrolled."

Mitzna noted that while towns had remained calm, protests had erupted in villages. He said most of the injuries were caused by gunfire, while others by beatings and tear-gas.

A general strike paralyzed the West Bank, and barricades of rocks and burning tyres littered the roads.

Most of the information on yesterday's events came from military and Palestinian sources, and could not be independently confirmed because of the ban on free media coverage in the territories.

The most serious incident occurred at the village of Deir Abu Mash'al near Ramallah, where a 50-year-old woman, Wajiha Rabia, was fatally shot and three members of her family were wounded.

Officers at the scene said that at 3 a.m. yesterday an army jeep on patrol encountered a barricade of rocks and burning tyres near the village. The road was covered with nails, which earlier punctured three tyres of a car driven by a settler from neighbouring Neve Tzuf.

When the soldiers got out of their jeep to check the area, four pistol shots were fired at them from olive groves by the roadside. The soldiers returned fire and began searching the area.

Tracks in the olive grove led to Deir Abu Mash'al. An IDF force that entered the village at about 8 a.m. to apprehend suspects was met with a barrage of rocks and bottles hurled from rooftops.

During the search, troops spotted a man fleeing into a house. As the soldiers tried to arrest him, villagers attacked them with sticks, pitchforks, axes, metal rods and pickaxes. One of the suspect's brothers hit a soldier in the head with a pickaxe, knocking him unconscious.

When villagers continued assaulting the soldiers and tried to block them from evacuating their wounded comrade, the troops opened fire, injuring two of the suspect's brothers and his father.

The suspect's mother was shot in the leg by a soldier whom she tried to attack with a rake. She was hit in a major artery, and later died from loss of blood, despite treatment by a local doctor and army medics.

Sources in Ramallah Hospital said Rabia had been shot in the head. They quoted the woman's daughter as saying that troops had burst into the house looking for suspects, and opened fire when one of her brothers fled and family members lunged at them.

At Shuyukh near Hebron, troops shot and killed Abdel Karim Halaike, 25, and wounded six villagers, including a young boy, a teenage girl and a 55-year-old man in a clash with rioters who pelted them with rocks. Four others were wounded by rubber bullets.

A local teacher, Issa Warasneh, reported that troops who had arrived by helicopter fired tear-gas, rubber bullets and live ammunition while pursuing the protesters into the village. Villagers said some 20 persons had been wounded.

At Burka, north of Nablus, troops shot and killed Khaled Aref Kassem, 22, and wounded two villagers in a clash with rioters, Palestinian and military sources said.

Shaker al-Malasa, 20, was fatally shot in a riot at Deir Ibzia near Ramallah.

At Yamoun village near Jenin, troops shot and wounded seven villagers, one critically, in a clash with rioters who pelted them with rocks and a petrol bomb, military sources said. Palestinian sources said troops stormed the village after marching protesters raised Palestinan flags. They said two villagers were seriously wounded.

At Beit Omar rioters clashed with troops in defiance of a curfew, and one was shot and wounded.

At the Nur Shams refugee camp near Tulkarm, troops clashed with rioters who toppled part of the fence in front of the camp. Five residents and one soldier were wounded.

At Sawiya, midway between Ramallah and Nablus, a soldier was injured when he was struck in the eye by a stone. Three Israeli motorists were hurt in other locations when their vehicles were stoned.

Military sources said 17 Palestinians were wounded by gunfire in 11 other locations.

Relative quiet in Israel

Compiled from reports by Elaine Ruth Fletcher, David Rudge, Jonathan Karp, Ken Schachter, Bradley Burston and Andy Court.

Land Day passed peacefully inside Israeli Arab communities yesterday, providing a striking contrast to the violence seen on the West Bank.

Local Arab leaders policed a general strike in over 60 towns and villages and maintained order in four demonstration sites in the Triangle, Galilee and Negev. Police and some soldiers, meanwhile, avoided entering Arab villages, although main roads were constantly patrolled by over 4,000 officers and troops.

Police said that 7,000 people demonstrated in Sakhnin, 5,000 in Taiba, 1,000 in Kafr Kanna and 250 in Rahat. Busloads of Jewish sympathisers joined the demonstrations, some wearing kaffiyes and T-shirts with Hebrew slogans like "We want peace."

Alignment MK Mohammed Wattad told Army Radio that today, "Israeli Arabs will be seen as much more complete citizens than they were yesterday."

Police Minister Haim Bar-Lev said that Israeli Arabs had learned the lesson of previous disturbances, and praised both police and Arab leaders for maintaining the calm.

"Today we created a situation that allowed Israeli Arab residents to express their political views in legal ways," said Bar-Lev.

The picture was not entirely idyllic. A Haifa youth was lightly injured by a stone. In all, police reported 72 illegal incidents in Israel and Arab East Jerusalem, including 15 incidents of vehicles being stoned and barricades being erected, as well as a number of PLO flag-raisings.

An East Jerusalem Arab was wounded when police broke up a demonstration in the city. Police arrested 20 people around the country on Land Day, including suspects in a petrol-bomb attack on Sha'ar Ha'amakim, Tuesday night.

But Israeli Arabs also acted quickly and decisively to defuse many potential trouble spots.

In divided Barta'a, a mixed Jewish-Arab peace group patrolling the Wadi Ara highway prevented a violent clash between residents of the West Bank portion of the village and Border Police. The peace group arrived as Border Police were firing tear gas at villagers who tried to cross to the Israeli side of the village to demonstrate. The peace activists positioned themselves between the Border Police and stone-throwing villagers, then negotiated with the villagers to disperse.

Local council members and strike committees took extraordinary pains to avoid incidents that might have led to violence.

In every village of the Triangle and Galilee, well-organized crews of local Arabs patrolled streets from dawn to dusk. Strike marshals also stationed themselves at entrances to towns to make sure youths didn't spill out onto the main highways. And some were equipped with municipal jeeps and walkie-talkies to respond quickly to trouble spots.

In Taiba, local council leaders cut short a rally after fist-fights broke out between rival youths from Rakah and the Islamic movement.

And in Baka al-Gharbiya, local council leader Samir Darwish spent

(Continued on Page 2, Col. 5)

Gorbachev ready for Israel ties

MOSCOW (Reuter) – Soviet leader Mikhail Gorbachev has said again that Moscow is willing to find a way to restore diplomatic relations with Israel, broken off after the Six-Day War in 1967, *Pravda* said yesterday.

The issue came up during talks on Tuesday between Gorbachev and the visiting Italian Communist party leader Alessandro Natta.

"Within the framework of preparations for carrying out an international conference (on the Middle East) a way will also be found to restore normal relations between the USSR and Israel," the Communist party newspaper quoted Gorbachev as saying.

The Soviet news agency Tass said yesterday that a special bone clinic in Kurgan, Siberia, was preparing to receive a group of Palestinian patients injured in anti-Israeli demonstrations.

Sharon lashes out at Shamir

Post Diplomatic Correspondent

Industry and Trade Minister Ariel Sharon yesterday bitterly accused Prime Minister Yitzhak Shamir of "preferring petty political interests" over the national good.

Sharon's outburst at the weekly inner cabinet meeting came after Shamir again refused to submit Sharon's proposals for dealing with the riots in the territories to a vote.

Sharon has repeatedly criticized Defence Minister Yitzhak Rabin's handling of the disturbances. He has made numerous proposals.

Sources close to Shamir said last night that the prime minister was actually saving Sharon from a "disgrace," since his proposals were bound to be defeated by a nine to one vote in the 10-member inner cabinet.

Gavish quits as head of Koor

By JUDY MALTZ

In a surprise move, Koor's managing director Yeshayahu Gavish yesterday announced his resignation, saying that all his efforts to bring about the recovery of the concern were being undermined by the Histadrut, which owns the giant company.

Gavish denied that his resignation was connected to the unprecedented losses of $100 million which Koor is expected to show in its 1987 financial statements, due to be published in June.

In a letter submitted to Histadrut Secretary-General Yisrael Kessar

(Continued on Page 7)

IDF closes East Jerusalem news agency

By ANDY COURT
Jerusalem Post Reporter

OC Central Command Amram Mitzna yesterday ordered the Palestine Press Service closed for six months. The agency, situated in East Jerusalem, is one of the foreign press's main sources of Arab reports from the territories.

The High Court of Justice, meanwhile, rejected the Foreign Press Association's petition for a temporary injunction against the IDF's ban, ending on Friday, on free press coverage in the West Bank and Gaza Strip.

The court, however, issued an order nisi, requiring the government, the defence minister, and the IDF commanders in the areas to explain within 30 days why such restrictions were necessary.

With its network of stringers throughout the territories, the Palestine Press Service gained prominence during the past four months of the uprising.

The agency has been heavily quoted by foreign news agencies and newspapers. There has been even greater interest in its reports since the army temporarily decided to allow only a limited number of Israeli and foreign reporters into the territories and then only under escort by IDF spokesmen and with the obligation of sharing their reports with their colleagues, under a pool system.

The restrictions have been in effect since Wednesday and are scheduled to continue until tomorrow, but the army said it may extend them if the situation so warrants.

The PPS was closed according to Article 129 (1)(b) of the Mandatory 1945 emergency regulations, which were incorporated in Israeli law. "I believe that the order is necessary for maintaining public safety and public order," Mitzna said in his order closing the agency. He provided no further explanation.

Security sources, who refused to be named, charged that the PPS is the PLO's major information network in the territories. One source even charged that the PPS had provided a PLO radio station abroad with the names of Arabs accused of co-operating with Israeli authorities so that the station could broadcast the names along with a call for stopping their activities.

Ibrahim Karaeen, co-owner of the PPS, said the charges were groundless and that the authorities had closed his operation because it was keeping foreign journalists too well-informed about events in the territories.

(Continued on Page 2, Col. 2)

Official concern over Christian politicization

By HAIM SHAPIRO
Jerusalem Post Reporter

Government circles expressed concern yesterday over what they called the growing politicization of the heads of the Christian communities, following a highly critical interview by Latin Patriarch Michael Sabbah in two Italian papers.

The interview, which appeared yesterday in *La Repubblica* and *Il Messaggero,* quoted the patriarch as saying that the Palestinian uprising was a natural reaction to the occupation.

The comments constituted a marked shift for Sabbah, the first Arab to be appointed Latin patriarch, who has until now insisted that his concerns were primarily religious.

"It is normal for the people to rebel and say 'enough' after 20 years of occupation," Sabbah was quoted as saying. "I hope all this suffering will not be in vain, that this clear expression against such a long military occupation will make people understand it has to end."

As for Israeli claims that there was no one with whom to speak, he said: "It is so simple, ask the Palestinians, call for a referendum.... If the people say the PLO then it's the PLO."

Asked to comment on the interview, Uri Mor, acting head of the department of Christian communities in the Religious Affairs Ministry, would only say that the patriarch was free to speak as he saw fit and that the government would not interfere in the internal affairs of the churches.

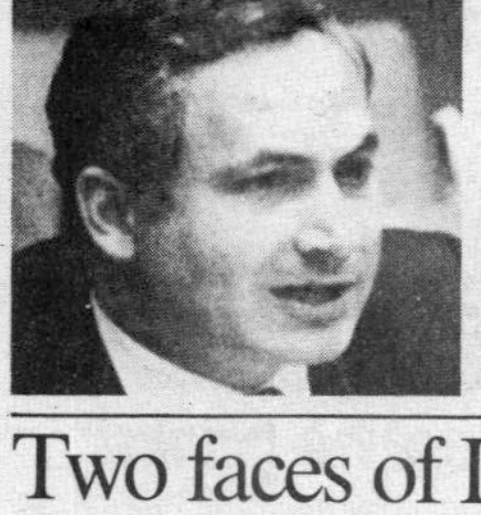

Netanyahu resigns, opts for Likud, blasts U.S.

By MENACHEM SHALEV
Post Diplomatic Correspondent

Only a few hours after submitting his immediate resignation yesterday, Israel's ambassador to the UN, Binyamin Netanyahu, launched a blistering and undiplomatic attack against the U.S. administration, which, he said, was "actively engaged in direct negotiations with the PLO."

Appearing on Israel Television, Netanyahu said that U.S. Secretary of State George Shultz had "crossed the Rubicon" in his peace plan and his meeting on Saturday with members of the Palestinian National Council.

Netanyahu, who is considered to be close to Shultz personally and extremely popular among conservative supporters of the administration, said that Shultz's peace plan was "very dangerous" and that the secretary had been "influenced" by "all sorts of Arabist officials" in the State Department.

"Who is the adminstration?" Netanyahu asked sarcastically, maintaining that the U.S. government must contend with "the greatest columnists, senators and Jewish might." (Continued on Page 2, Col. 2)

Two faces of Land Day – in Israel and the West Bank

ANALYSIS
Yehuda Litani

There was a real difference between the Land Day events held yesterday by Israeli Arabs and those held by the Palestinians in the territories. While self-restraint by activists made for a relatively quiet day in the Israeli-Arab sector, the West Bank had one of its most violent days since the uprising began last December.

The inhabitants of the territories do not have to maintain a delicate balance, like the Israeli Arabs, between their loyalty to the state and their Palestinian identity. The bulk of them feel now, after more than three-and-a-half months of continuous rioting, that it is an all-out struggle against the Israelis – and that is also how the IDF is treating it.

That explains, in a way, the large number of casualties in the West Bank yesterday. Unlike inside Israel, in the West Bank neither side exercises self-restraint; the goal of each is to hit the other hard.

The clashes in the West Bank yesterday were mainly in villages, most of them remote. Now, after more than 110 days of the uprising, the resistance is mainly in the rural areas and the refugee camps of the West Bank, since it is easier to endure longer periods of strife there.

In contrast to the West Bank, in Israel proper, the delicate balance that Israeli Arabs have to maintain between their loyalty to the state and their identification with their Palestinian brethren in the territories was well kept yesterday.

The message sent by the Israeli Arabs was clear: while showing our feelings for, and identification with, our brothers in the territories, we are still Israelis, and that is why we are trying to keep law and order.

The self-restraint demonstrated yesterday in Israel showed how well organized the Israeli Arabs are. It also showed the growing strength among Israeli Arabs of the Rakah party, which was the main force behind the day's events.

The massive police presence in every town and village where demonstrations were planned also helped calm the atmosphere. The acceptance by police of the request by Israeli Arab leaders not to enter their villages and towns, but stay on the outskirts, may have prevented violent clashes.

While the Israeli Arabs will demonstrate only on dates agreed upon by their leadership and try to prevent violence as much as possible, the territories' inhabitants will continue their uprising for as long as they can.

Index soars
Page 6

THE JERUSALEM POST

Vol. LVI, No. 16805 Sunday, April 17, 1988 • Nisan 30, 5748 • Ramadan 2, 1408 NIS 1.20 (Eilat NIS 1.05)

SECOND EDITION

Betar bite the dust
Page 7

PLO's Abu Jihad gunned down in Tunis

TUNIS – Tunisian police last night were examining three rented vehicles found at the beach after an eight-member assassination squad had shot its way into the home of Khalil al-Wazir, military commander of the PLO, killing him in a hail of machinegun fire as he emerged from his study.

The terrorist organization immediately blamed Israel for the killing, saying it was the second strike at the PLO on Tunisian territory since the movement moved its headquarters to suburban La Marsa after it was driven from Lebanon by the Israeli army in 1982.

The PLO said Wazir, also known as Abu Jihad, was riddled with more than 100 bullets by the assassination team, which included a woman. No arrests have been made, but Tunisian sources reported that three vehicles, two Volkswagen minibuses and a Peugeot 305, possibly used in the 1:15 a.m. attack were found on a beach about 40 kilometres north of Tunis. The assassins had rented the vehicles, reporters at the scene said, leading to speculation that the assassins may have fled the country by sea.

Wazir was the most senior Palestinian official to be assassinated since the founding of Fatah, the largest group in the PLO, in 1964. He was PLO Chairman Yasser Arafat's closest aide, a member of the PLO Executive Committee, No. 2 man in Fatah, and was in charge of military operations inside the occupied territories.

Arafat, who was in Bahrain, broke off his tour of the Gulf states to return to Tunis. A PLO source on Bahrain said the PLO leader was "quite shocked and angered."

PLO officials vowed to intensify the war against Israel and step up the uprising of Palestinians in the West Bank and Gaza. A spokesman in Tunis said the attack was carried out by the "Israeli terrorists of Mossad (the secret service) and their American backers who are determined to liquidate our people."

Wazir's wife Intisar was quoted as saying that an eight-man commando and a woman in camouflage clothes and hoods covering their faces, entered the villa in the dead of night. His wife, daughter Hanan, 14, and son Nidal, 2, the youngest of his five children, were in the house at the time but were unhurt. Mrs Wazir said she was woken by Nidal, who said he heard "boom-boom" outside.

Wazir was reported to have been in the study of his house reading when the attackers drove up to the villa at Sidi Bousaid, and killed a Tunisian bodyguard in a car outside, then burst into the house and killed the two other bodyguards.

"They then broke into Abu Jihad's study," said a PLO spokesman. "Everything happened within seconds. He had drawn his pistol to defend himself but they mowed him down with literally hundreds of sub-machine gun bullets."

Wazir died on his way to hospital, the official Tunisian news agency TAP said. The telephone lines to the villa was reported to have been cut half an hour before the dawn attack.

(Continued on Back Page)

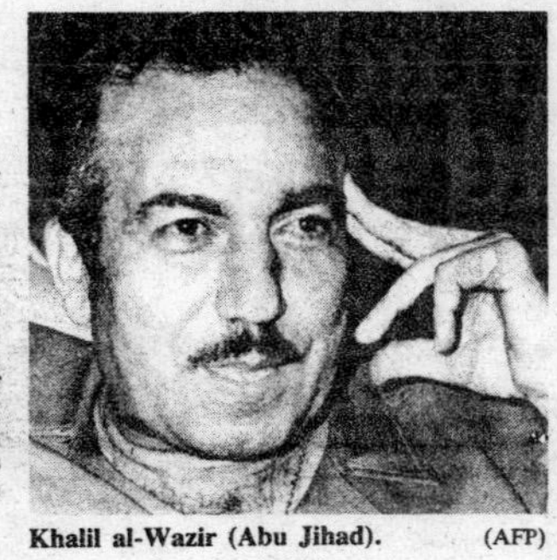

Khalil al-Wazir (Abu Jihad). (AFP)

Jerusalem: 'No comment'

By MENACHEM SHALEV
Post Diplomatic Correspondent

Israel officials last night declined to comment on the killing of Abu Jihad. Many government officials expect that in the short term it will result in a new wave of terror and in increased turbulence in the territories.

There were conflicting views, however, on the effect the killing would have on a Middle East peace process. Sources in Jerusalem said that the PLO and the inhabitants of the territories would likely adopt a harder line toward the peace process.

Abu Jihad's death, the sources said, might result in some loss of prestige for the PLO but it would also increase Jordan's reluctance to proceed with the peace process without the organization's acquiescence.

Intelligence experts said that the operational capabilities and morale of the PLO had suffered a serious setback with the killing.

"Abu Jihad was the main source of the PLO's wishful thinking that the 'armed struggle' will actually achieve its aims," one official said.

The official added that the killing was likely to spark a wave of anti-Israeli terror, inside Israel and abroad, intended to regain the lost prestige. He added that the killing would spark a new wave of riots in the territories.

Another senior government official, however, said that in the longer term, Abu Jihad's killing would allow Yasser Arafat more room for political maneuvering within the context of Soviet and American Middle East peace efforts.

The official said that the killing was a "gift" to both Arafat and to Jordan's King Hussein, who expelled Abu Jihad from Amman two years ago. It would allow Arafat to "bow" to Soviet pressure, which is presumably aimed at forcing the PLO to accept Hussein's terms for participation in a Jordanian-Palestinian delegation to peace talks by accepting UN Security Council Resolution 242.

The official said that Abu Jihad was the main source of opposition to Arafat's diplomatic maneuvers within "the PLO chairman's close circle."

But another official claimed that of the PLO "triumvirate," which includes Arafat, Abu Jihad and Abu Iyad, Abu Iyad was the more critical of Arafat's policies.

Most officials agreed that the killing of Abu Jihad, who was more popular than Arafat himself in many Palestinian circles, would make it nearly impossible for a peace process to proceed without the PLO. And since the killing was likely to result in at least a temporary hardening of the organization's positions, it would most likely hinder

(Continued on Page 2, Col. 2)

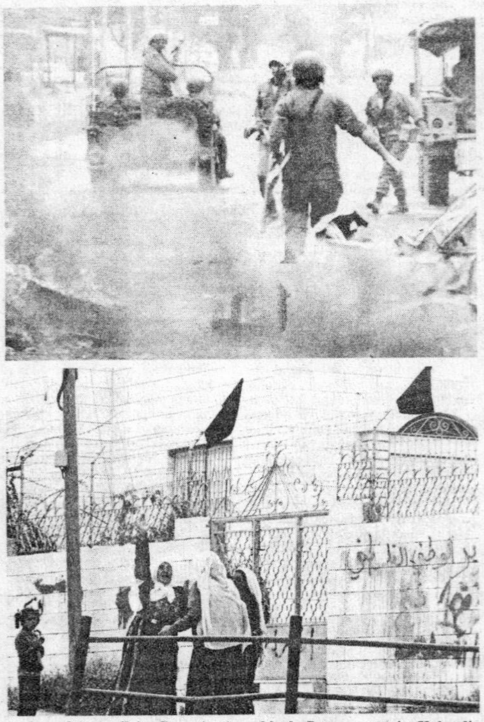

A day of turmoil in Gaza (top) as black flags go out in Kalandia refugee camp yesterday to mourn the death of Abu Jihad. (AFP/Media)

At least 12 killed in worst single-day toll

Riots erupt in territories to protest assassination

By JOEL GREENBERG
and BRADELY BURSTON
Jerusalem Post Reporters

Troops shot and killed at least 12 Palestinians and wounded scores in the West Bank and Gaza Strip yesterday as protests erupted throughout the territories in response to the killing of PLO military chief Khalil al-Wazir, alias Abu Jihad.

The death toll was the highest in a single day since the start of the Palestinian uprising on December 9. More than 150 Palestinians have been killed in the unrest.

News of Wazir's death brought instant expressions of shock and grief in towns and many villages. Black banners and Palestinian flags were flown from buildings, Koran verses were read over mosque loudspeakers, and hundreds participated in mock funerals and marches.

Youths built roadblocks of burning tyres and rocks, and hurled stones at troops. Palls of smoke hung over Gaza city and parts of Nablus, which was declared closed to the media.

Ten refugee camps in the West Bank and Gaza Strip were under curfew last night.

The Supreme Moslem Council and nationalist groups declared three days of mourning and a general strike in the territories.

Mourners paid condolence calls at the homes of Wazir's cousins in Gaza and Nablus. Troops used tear-gas to disperse youths who pelted them with rocks near the Gaza home of Ahmad Wazir, but later withdrew.

Leading PLO-backers in the territories blamed Israel for the killing and predicted that it would fan the flames of the Palestinian uprising.

Gaza lawyer Fayez Abu Rahme, a cousin of Wazir, called the killing a tragedy for the Palestinian people, and said it would "increase the emotion of the *intifada*."

Al-Fajr editor Hanna Siniora said the assassination was "an exact replica" of the April 1973 Israeli commando killing of three Palestinian leaders in Beirut. "The policy of eliminating people is a boomerang that only strikes at the people who use it," he said.

"Instead of trying to send a political message to the Palestinian people, the Israeli government is sending a message both inside and outside the occupied territories that it wants to continue the occupation. It's only showing the stick, and its actions silence the voices of the moderates."

Deposed Hebron mayor Mustafa Natshe charged that the killing was designed to thwart current Middle East peace initiatives and to win popular support at home for the government.

In Gaza, where Wazir was raised, violent disturbances and mass marches began almost immediately following reports on Israel Radio and Radio Monte Carlo that he had been killed.

According to Palestinian sources, eight Gazans were shot to death in the violence and more than one hundred wounded. Military sources confirmed seven dead.

In urban centres, refugee camps, and villages the length of the strip, black banners and Palestinian flags were affixed to rooftops, and verses from the Koran were broadcast via mosque loudspeakers.

Hospitals and clinics quickly overflowed with wounded, with ambulances and private cars arriving every few minutes with new cases. Doctors in the strip's three major hospitals listed over 140 cases of gunshot wounds yesterday.

IDF officials said last night that official casuality figures have yet to be determined, and that the fact that the families of the dead spirited their bodies away for burial has made confirmation of the circumstances of the deaths all but impossible.

Military sources in Gaza added that the large number of deaths was mostly due to a wave of petrol bomb attacks yesterday on IDF troops. Soldiers are under orders to shoot back at persons hurling petrol bombs.

The sources said that 15 petrol bombs and an old-style Miles British hand-grenade were thrown at troops in A basan alone. Another four petrol bombs were hurled at troops in Rafiah.

Wazir's family received condolence calls near the Gaza Turkish bath they have operated for years. Islamic fundamentalist organizations and the outlawed Fatah-affiliated Shabiba youth organization sent wreaths.

The widespread violence attracted many representatives of the media, who had been absent during the relative quiet of recent weeks. The American CBS television network sent three crews to film the disturbances.

(Continued on Back Page)

PLO leaders planning 'reprisals' against Israel

Jerusalem Post Staff
and Agencies

PLO leaders were last night reported to be considering attacks on Israeli targets worldwide in reprisal for the murder of Khalil Wazir, alias Abu Jihad.

According to press reports in London, Fatah's Central Committee is to take a decision on reprisals after Wazir is buried today. PLO leaders were quoted as saying that "fascist and racist leaders in Israel" were responsible for the killing. And a PLO spokesman was reported to have declared that "his martyrdom will not go unpunished."

Among the options reportedly under consideration were reprisals in Israel or attacks abroad, in breach of the so-called 1985 Cairo accords which limited operations to inside Israel.

PLO chief Yasser Arafat, who returned last night to Tunis from the Gulf, told Radio Monte Carlo that Israel was wrong if it believed it could choke off the Palestinian uprising by killing Wazir. Wazir and the Palestinians killed in the uprising were "beacons lighting the road to Jerusalem," he said.

"It was Mossad," said the official PLO spokesman, Ahmed Abdel Rahman, in Tunis. "Shamir, Peres and Rabin. They're all responsible. The Palestinians will take revenge."

In Cairo, Tunisian Prime Minister Hedi Baccouche yesterday condemned the assassination of Wazir and pledged all-out efforts to lay hands on the culprits.

Baccouche made the statement upon arrival here from the Sudanese capital Khartoum on a three-day official visit and talks with Egyptian President Hosni Mubarak.

"We received the news of Wazir's death in Tunisia with great sorrow because Abu Jihad was one of the reliable leaders and because his death has harmed the Palestinian cause," Baccouche told newsmen at Cairo Airport.

He vowed that Tunisia would use "all its means to arrest the culprits."

An official of the Democratic Front for the Liberation of Palestine said they had learned of a plan by Mossad agents to kill PLO leaders overseas after failing to crush the uprising.

(Continued on Page 2, Col. 6)

'Severe blow to Fatah terror'

Jerusalem Post Staff

The elimination of Abu Jihad is "operationally a very severe blow to Fatah terrorist activity," Dr. Ariel Merari of the Jaffee Centre for Strategic Studies at Tel Aviv university told Israel Radio yesterday.

"This is one of those rare cases in which the departure of one person has a direct effect on the quality of operations," he said. "Not that (terror) will stop of course, but I think it will take them a long time to find somebody of that calibre."

Merari said that although "Israel had all the reasons to eliminate Abu Jihad", the killing was probably at the behest of PLO chairman Yasser Arafat, who had fallen out with his top deputy during recent years.

Merari recalled that due to a growing rift between the two, there had been fighting between PLO factions in southern Lebanon, especially in Sidon. Several terrorist commanders sent by Arafat to the Ein Hilwe camp in Sidon were killed by Abu Jihad's men, who actually controlled the area.

Therefore, said Merari, although "I don't know who was behind the killing, if I had to venture a guess, I

(Continued on Page 2, Col. 5)

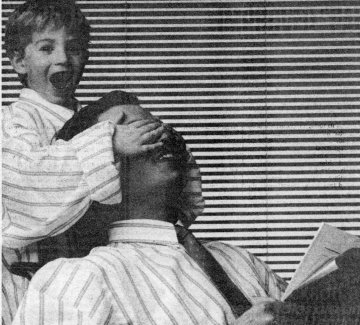

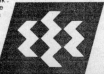

Hijackers threaten 'massacre'

ALGIERS (AP) - Shiite Moslem hijackers of the Kuwaiti jumbo jet threatened last night to fly the plane to another country where they would "massacre" all their hostages – but set no deadline.

"We are working to blow up this plane, killing all the Kuwaiti citizens aboard if the Kuwait government does not give freedom to our 17 brothers," said a hooded hijacker, reading a statement in Arabic to three reporters atop the gangway leading to the plane.

Three hijackers, all wearing light blue hoods, were present for the 15-minute encounter with reporters representing *The New York Times*, the French news agency and the Algerian government News Agency.

"In view of the Kuwaiti intransigence, we are asking our Algerian brothers to refuel the plane so that we can take off because we intend to settle our score with Kuwait somewhere else," the statement said.

(Earlier report on Page 3)

Jackson accuses Israel of taking part in South African raids on Angola

By WALTER RUBY
Jerusalem Post Correspondent

NEW YORK – Jesse Jackson has accused Israel of participating in a recent South African incursion into Angola and has apologized for calling Jews "Hymies."

In an interview published yesterday in *The New York Times*, Jackson also indicated he would consider cutting aid to Israel if he becomes president and Israel continues to refuse to withdraw from the occupied territories. In contrast to remarks last week in which he said he would not negotiate directly with PLO chief Yasser Arafat, Jackson told the *Times* that the U.S. must talk with the PLO "sooner or later." Jackson also said he supports the principle of a Palestinian state.

Jackson's tough language on a number of sensitive issues touching Israel and black-Jewish relations seemed in striking contrast to the more moderate language he has employed in recent weeks.

On Israeli-South African collaboration, Jackson said, "I guess it was two months ago – when South Africa invaded Angola – and it was really a South African and Israeli joint project." Jackson did not make clear which South African military action he was referring to, and offered no corroboration for his charge of Israeli involvement.

Jackson said that in the delicate and troubled relationship between blacks and American Jews, "The level of relationship and trade and military relationship between Israel and South Africa is a source of pain."

On Middle East issues, Jackson said that as president he would use "diplomatic clout" to push the peace process forward, pressing Arab-Americans to try to get the Palestinians to recognize Israel, and seeking "to get Israel to recognize that the present posture is an untenable one..the present pain being heaped on the Palestinian people – the killings, the beatings, and the expulsions – is wrong."

Pressed if he would cut off aid if Israel proved intransigent, Jackson replied, "Well, your approach should not be one of threat. But you must finally use your leverage in order to protect our vital interests in the region."

Jackson said, however, that he hesitated to make the point explicit because, "You don't solve something this delicate by offering threat as a lever... Carter didn't threaten to cut off aid. He offered aid as an encouragement. He did not threaten to make Israel hurt. He offered to make Israel more secure...and that would be my approach."

Seeming to back away from last week's pledge not to talk to Arafat, Jackson said, "As a matter of principle, I support the Palestinian state. As a matter of fact, the PLO is by far the most representative organization of the Palestinian people, and...we must bring Israel security by convincing its adversary to cease being its adversary."

(Continued on Page Four)

'War of ads' in American press

Page 4

THE JERUSALEM POST

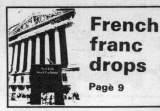

Vol. LVI, No. 16812 Tuesday, April 26, 1988 • Iyar 9, 5748 • Ramadan 11, 1408 NIS 1.20 (Eilat NIS 1.05)

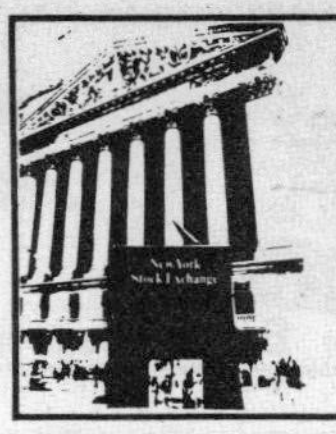

French franc drops

Pagè 9

FIRST EDITION

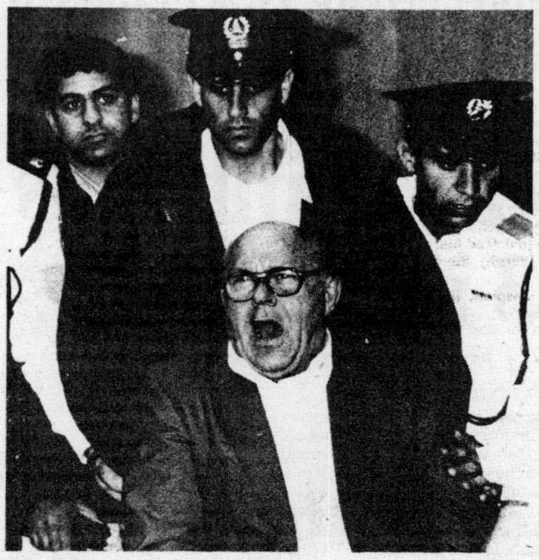

John Demjanjuk leaves the courtroom yesterday in a wheelchair after being sentenced to death. (Eliahu Harati)

Death for 'Ivan the Terrible'

By ERNIE MEYER
Jerusalem Post Reporter

John Demjanjuk, "Ivan the Terrible" of Treblinka, was sentenced to death yesterday afternoon for war crimes and crimes against the Jewish people and against humanity. Sentence was pronounced by Judge Zvi Tal, speaking for the special court composed of Justice Dov Levin, Judge Dalia Dorner and himself. Shortly before the session opened to a packed courtroom, Demjanjuk was brought in sitting in a wheelchair. Defence counsel John Gill explained that his client was suffering from back pains and could not stand up when the judges walked in.

Gill started his pleading with a complaint about the defence not receiving an adequate translation of the verdict. But Judge Tal cut him short by reminding him that he had received the full record of the simultaneous translation plus a translation of the sections not read out in court.

State Attorney Yona Blatman started his pleading for the prosecution by denying that Demjanjuk had been merely a small cog in the Nazi machinery of extermination. "Demjanjuk stood at the entrance of hell and was zealous in the extreme. He was one of the greatest oppressors the Jewish people has ever had. With every fresh transport, Demjanjuk committed premeditated murder a thousand times over."

Blatman said that death was the only punishment for Demjanjuk's crimes. He insisted that the death penalty was mandatory in such cases and that the legislators had meant to make it so, rather than making death the maximum penalty.

Justice Levin disagreed and said that the law gave the courts discretion regarding the penalty. Blatman admitted that this was so in the case of treason, for instance, but insisted that in the present case the judges had no choice.

"There can be no doubt that the law covering Nazi crimes is in a special category and not open to regular interpretation," he said. "The court must impose the death penalty, that is the correct reading of the law."

Demjanjuk was seen shaking his head and repeatedly crossing himself during the discussion between Blatman and the bench.

Blatman went on to say that by his actions Demjanjuk had excluded himself from human society. "There is no statute of limitations for his crimes. Just as there is no word to describe these crimes, no death is sufficient to atone for them. We demand the death penalty."

At this stage, Gill asked for a recess, but Justice Levin instructed him to carry on with his pleading. Gill then said that eyewitness testimony had been the cornerstone of the court's verdict, and that a large percentage of the known cases of wrongful executions had been based on such testimony. He mentioned the Frank Walus war crimes case in the U.S., where 11 witness identifications were later found to be mistaken. "We are in any case opposed to the death penalty, and the tendency in enlightened countries has been away from it," he said.

Gill cited the famous Lindbergh child-kidnapping case and the Sacco and Vanzetti case, in which suspects were wrongly executed. He even quoted Charles Dickens, who had deplored that "the irrevocable death penalty is imposed by fallible men." Finally, Gill cited an article in the Stanford University Law Review, which surveyed 350 cases of people being wrongly sentenced to death.

Levin: "We get your point. You don't have to elaborate. You said you are going to appeal and may even offer new testimony, but we now have to decide on a sentence."

Gill: "Don't commit a second horrendous crime."

Levin: "Crime is not a felicitous choice of word."

Gill: "The taking of any innocent human life is a Holocaust."

In his final plea to the court, Gill spoke of the new legal standard he said was emerging in the U.S., which required proof beyond the shadow of doubt, rather than merely beyond reasonable doubt. "I humbly and respectfully ask the court not to impose the death penalty," Gill concluded.

Defence counsel Yoram Sheftel restricted himself to saying that since the defence would appeal in any case, it was not pleading mitigating circumstances for its client.

Levin then announced: "The convicted man has the last word."

At 10:45 a.m., seated in his wheelchair, Demjanjuk started speaking in Ukrainian in a loud and clear voice.

"It has been very painful to me to listen to reports of the tragedy that befell your people during the Nazi period. Six million died a terrible death and I hope that they

(Continued on Back Page)

Le Pen taps well of anti-Arab feelings in French vote

PARIS (Reuter) – Extreme right-wing leader Jean-Marie Le Pen, who rocked the political establishment by winning over 14 per cent of the vote in presidential elections on Sunday, has tapped a deep well of fear of and anger at the more than 1.5 million North African Arabs living in France.

"Why did I vote for Le Pen? Because of the immigrants, that's why," said an elderly man in the street. His reply was echoed on television screens and radio stations around the country.

Almost 4.5 million voters opted for Le Pen's no-nonsense anti-immigration and anti-tax policies, but the 59-year-old former paratrooper did not make it through to the second voting round. **(Photo Page 3)**

Socialist President Francois Mitterrand and conservative Prime Minister Jacques Chirac topped Sunday's first round of voting and face each other in a runoff for the presidency on May 8.

Anti-racist groups who have battled the immigration policies of Le Pen's National Front were downcast at his strong showing.

Abder Dahmane, president of Generation 2001, a Franco-Arab friendship society, said all Western European nations should be on the alert to prevent Le Pen's policies spreading.

He accused Le Pen of being a "closet Nazi" and said: "If this phenomenon crosses borders, it will be a European catastrophe with fascist forces at work."

Newspapers said yesterday that

(Continued on Page Seven)

Final results

PARIS (Reuter) – Final results in Sunday's first round of the French presidential election, announced by the Interior Ministry yesterday, confirmed that President Francois Mitterrand and Prime Minister Jacques Chirac will face each other in a second round run-off ballot on May 8.

The results were: Mitterrand, Socialist, 34.11 per cent; Chirac, Neo-Gaullist, 19.95 per cent;, Raymond Barre, centre-right, 16.53 ; Jean-Marie Le Pen, extreme-right, 14.38 ; Andre Lajoinie, Communist, 7.6 per cent; Antoine Waechter, Greens, 3.77 ; Pierre Juquin, Dissident Communist, 2.09 ; Arlette Laquiller, Workers' Struggle, 1.99 and Pierre Boussel, Trotskyite, 0.38.

The ministry said 30,370,420 votes were valid of the 30,995,161 cast in France, its foreign territories and by absentee ballot from citizens living abroad. It said 38,086,857 citizens had registered to vote and that participation was 81.38 per cent.

A television poll carried out immediately after the first votes in the preliminary round were counted indicated that voting intentions in the second round on May 8 will produce a 55 per cent vote for Mitterrand and 45 per cent for Chirac.

14 E. J'lem merchants jailed for violating IDF's order on hours

By ANDY COURT
Jerusalem Post Reporter

Fourteen East Jerusalem merchants who yesterday followed the business hours of the Arab uprising, rather than those ordered by the army, spent last night in jail cells in the Russian Compound.

The shopkeepers, most of them middle-aged men, were arrested shortly after they opened their stores for business at 2 p.m., in violation of an order issued Sunday by OC Central Command Aluf Amram Mitzna.

As a large crowd of East Jerusalemites gathered in front of the stores on Rehov Hanevi'im, across from the Damascus Gate, the police moved in.

Armoured cars and a water cannon blocked both sides of the street. Mounted police chased away bystanders and potential customers. One by one, the merchants were forced to lock up their shops. They were then led to a pale grey bus which transported them to the police station.

The 14 are being detained and investigated on charges of violating Mitzna's order, which is based on Emergency Regulations carried over from British Mandatory times.

Asked why these merchants were singled out for prosecution, Avi Cohen, head of the Jerusalem police's investigations branch, replied, "You have to start somewhere."

Neither Police Minister Haim Bar-Lev nor Jerusalem police officials would say yesterday whether more orders will be issued to East Jerusalem merchants.

"Here in Jerusalem, we didn't get involved over the course of three months, but we don't think it is a subject that we can ignore," Bar-Lev told a delegation from the Sadat

(Continued on Page Nine)

New measures may restrict thousands to Gaza Strip

By BRADLEY BURSTON
Jerusalem Post Reporter

GAZA CITY – Tens of thousands of residents of Gaza refugee camps may be legally restricted to the confines of the Gaza Strip, under new Civil Adminstration measures aimed at "taking the initiative" in the area, *The Jerusalem Post* has learned.

Sources close to the Civil Administration said the recent IDF operation to confiscate the identity cards of adult males in the Shatti and Deir el-Balah refugee camps was the first stage of the plan, now extended to include residents of Jebalya, the largest camp in the territories.

Gazans whose ID cards were confiscated were given papers restricting them to the Strip until they fulfilled the requirements of a separate document available for NIS 5 at the Gaza Interior Ministry offices.

The form contains four spaces which must be stamped by officials of other offices.

To secure the return of their ID cards, residents must undergo separate checks at the income tax, customs and VAT offices to ascertain that they have paid their taxes in full. Then the police must stamp a section stating that the bearer has no outstanding traffic or other violations. Receipts must also be obtained from the municipality to show that water and electricity bills have been settled. A final section is to be filled in only if the bearer is wanted for interrogation by the security forces.

Yesterday, residents of Deir el-Balah and some areas of Shatti said they intended to protest against the measures by leaving their cards in the hands of the authorities.

The hundreds of Gazans who attempted to recover their cards yesterday had to stand in long lines at the various offices. Police and tax offices have been operating with skeleton staffs of Israeli clerks since early last month, when local employees resigned *en masse*.

Restraining orders were issued yesterday against scores of Gazans

(Continued on Page Seven)

Terrorist boat sunk off Lebanon coast

Jerusalem Post Staff

The Israel Navy sank a terrorist boat off the South Lebanese coast on Sunday night, the IDF spokesman reported yesterday.

"A navy boat on a routine patrol off the South Lebanon coast last night identified a small, suspicious terrorist boat," the spokesman said. "The navy boat opened fire and sank the terrorist boat."

Military sources said the Israeli boat had come under fire when it approached the small craft. The Israelis returned fire, destroying the boat.

According to unconfirmed reports, one terrorist was on the boat, and he drowned. There were no Israeli casualties.

The navy patrols the Lebanese coast to prevent terrorists from entering Israel by sea. According to regulations, boats must fire warning shots before attacking suspicious vessels.

Six months ago, an Israeli naval commander was killed after his patrol boat identified itself to a terrorist boat and issued a warning.

Reunion of Arafat and Assad called 'gift to the *intifada*'

Post Arab Affairs Reporter
and Agencies

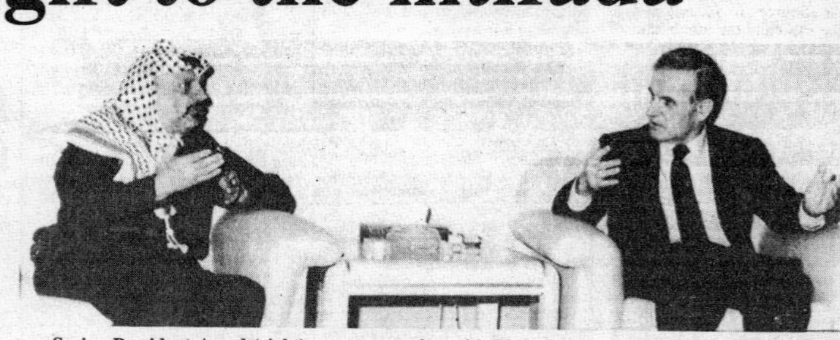

Syrian President Assad (right) meets yesterday with PLO chairman Arafat at the presidential palace in Damascus. (Reuter)

DAMASCUS (AP) – President Hafez Assad of Syria and PLO Chairman Yasser Arafat met yesterday, seeking to bury the hatchet after five years of bloody rivalry, and to revive a hardline alliance against Israel and U.S. Middle East peace plans.

The Assad-Arafat meeting lasted three and a half hours, according to presidential spokesman Jibran Kourieh.

"Talks were about the Arab and Palestinian situations, in particular about the popular uprising against the Israeli occupation of Arab territories and the necessity of supporting the uprising" Kourieh said.

"This meeting, this reconciliation is a gift to the *intifada*," declared Nayef Hawatmeh, leader of the pro-Moscow Democratic Front for the Liberation of Palestine earlier.

"We all agreed that this is a rare opportunity ... that would lead to the restoration of warm relations between Syria and the PLO," he added.

It was only the second time that Arafat and Assad have talked face-to-face since the Syrian president threw the PLO leader out of Syria in June, 1983.

They met briefly at the Arab summit in Amman, Jordan, last November.

If their talks are successful, it will mean the end of a rift that has bedevilled the Arab world and seriously hampered the Arab quest for unity to confront Israel.

Syria's Foreign Minister, Farouk al-Sharaa and seven of Arafat's senior aides attended the meeting in the heavily guarded palace, the spokesman said.

Like Arafat, most of them, all members of the ruling central committee of Fatah, the main PLO group, had not visited Damascus since Arafat was expelled at the height of a Syrian-backed mutiny in the PLO.

They arrived in Damascus last week for the funeral of the PLO's military commander, Khalil al-Wazir, assassinated in Tunis on April 16.

The aides included Salah Khalaf, one of Arafat's closest advisers and like Arafat and Wazir, a founder of Fatah, and Farouk Kaddoumi, head of the PLO's political department and "foreign minister."

Prior to the Arafat-Assad meeting, the Fatah delegation held preparatory talks with Syrian Vice-President Abdul-Halim Khaddam.

Palestinian officials said all the Syrian-based anti-Arafat groups, except Abu Musa's, also held talks with the PLO leader's Fatah delegation. A firm PLO-Syrian *rapprochement* could lead to a merger of the majority of PLO factions, they said.

The Arafat-Assad meeting also followed a crucial preparatory session between Assad and a ranking Libyan envoy, Lt. Col. Mustafa Kharroubi, who accompanied Arafat from Tripoli to Damascus Sunday to cap a mediation effort by Col. Muammar Gaddafi and Algerian President Chadli Benjedid.

Hawatmeh said the top priorities in the Assad-Arafat meeting were the four-month-old Palestinian uprising against Israeli occupation in the West Bank and Gaza Strip and the latest American Middle East peace plan, presented to the region's leaders last month by Secretary of State George Shultz.

"These are two very important developments, how to bolster the uprising and foil Shultz's plan," Hawatmeh said.

Hawatmeh said the third major issue is to prepare a joint working paper to be presented at an extraordinary Arab summit. The summit is tentatively scheduled for early June in Algiers, but Arab diplomats said moves were afoot to switch the site to Damascus as a signal of Arab backing for the Syria-PLO *rapprochement*.

Asked if it was not too early to talk of an alliance when Arafat had been in Damascus only 24 hours, Hawatmeh declared: "The fact that he's here means the feud is over.

"The martyrdom of Abu Jihad certainly pushed the reconciliation forward," Bassam Abu Sharif, Arafat's adviser, told reporters in Nicosia in a telephone interview from Tunis on Sunday.

"Joining hands with our Syrian brothers is the response for Israel's crime. Abu Jihad's blood is the bridge of unity for the forces fighting the Zionist occupation of Arab land," he said.

Commenting on the timing of the PLO-Syrian reconciliation, a Western diplomat said: "They should thank the Mossad."

A PLO-Syrian *rapprochement* is sure to strain Egypt's ties to other Arab states. And Egyptian President Hosni Mubarak had harsh words for the PLO yesterday in the wake of Arafat's visit to Damascus.

Mubarak said he was "astonished" at the PLO's behaviour after Egypt had sacrificed so much for the Palestinian cause.

U.S. abstains

UN condemns slaying of Abu Jihad

UNITED NATIONS (AF) – The Security Council voted 14-0 yesterday to condemn the assassination of PLO miliary commander Walid al-Wazir (Abu Jihad), which has been widely blamed on Israel. The U.S. abstained from voting on the resolution.

Tunisian officials and Israeli sources say Israeli commandos gunned down al-Wazir at his home in suburban Tunis on Saturday last week.

Officially, Israel has neither confirmed nor denied the allegations.

The resolution condemns the slaying, but does not explicitly con-

(Continued on Back Page)

Reconciliation to derail peace process

ANALYSIS
Menachem Shalev

A possible reconciliation between PLO Chairman Yasser Arafat and Syrian President Hafez Assad would promote Arab extremism and put off any hope of progress in the peace process, Israeli officials said yesterday.

Prime Minister Yitzhak Shamir said that "more and more Arab elements in the region are attracted to Syria, the most extreme state, and it seems that Arab extremism is valid currency nowadays in the Middle East."

But, Shamir added:"We are not particularly concerned" by the development.

A senior government official told *The Jerusalem Post* that despite their meeting in Damascus yesterday, both Assad and Arafat appeared to be clinging to their previously-held positions.

But, the official warned, a genuine rapprochement between Syria and the PLO would have grave consequences for the positions of Egypt and Jordan in the Arab world, create a crisis between the "confrontation states" and moderate Arab states, and, ultimately, deal a death blow to the already-crippled peace process.

Assad's precondition to a reconciliation is that the PLO gradually disengage from its ties with Egypt, the official said. Such a development would constitute a serious blow to Egyptian prestige and would mark a Syrian victory in the ongoing debate in the Arab world on the Egyptian "treachery" of signing a peace treaty with Israel.

As a result, and in order to hold on to its recent diplomatic gains in the Arab world, Egypt would probably find it necessary to distance itself even further from Israel – a process already begun in the wake of the disturbances in the territories.

A Syrian-PLO convergence would also force Jordan's King Hussein to renounce the terms of the April, 1987 London agreement on the peace process, the official said.

The PLO was frustrated by the failure of the uprising in the territories to yield any tangible political gains and its prestige was damaged by the killing of Abu Jihad, thus adding to its motivation to effect a significant change in its alignment in the Arab world.

Perhaps alluding to such a development, Hussein, in an interview with NBC's *Sunday Today*, said that

(Continued on Page Seven)

Soviets, Saudis likely to resume ties after 50-year break

BAHRAIN (Reuters) – The Soviet troop withdrawal from Afghanistan is expected to set the stage for a resumption of formal relations between Moscow and staunchly anti-communist Saudi Arabia after a 50-year break, diplomats and political analysts say.

They said that by putting an ambassador in the kingdom, long a bastion of American influence, the Soviet Union would score a major coup that might be quickly followed in Bahrain and Qatar, the only two other Arab countries that still have no ties with Moscow.

"The Saudis have made Afghanistan a condition for so long it would be hard for them to back down now," said one diplomat.

According to an agreement signed in Geneva on April 15, the Soviet Union on May 15 will begin a nine-month withdrawal from Afghanistan of an estimated 115,000 troops, ending nine years of occupation.

In 1927, the Soviet Union was the first country to recognize the new Saudi kingdom, but there have been no formal ties since 1938 when the last Soviet ambassador was asked to leave.

The intensely-religious kingdom, home to Islam's two holiest sites, has long been opposed to what it describes as atheist communism and is a major backer of Afghan Moslem guerrillas. It now maintains no formal ties with any eastern bloc country or with Communist China.

But diplomats and analysts say the Saudis have been driven more by suspicion of Soviet motives in the Middle East than by religious zeal.

Mark Katz, a Washington-based analyst of Soviet-Arab relations, told Reuters the Saudis are impressed with the liberalism introduced by Soviet leader Mikhail Gorbachev.

They also feel Moscow is now less interested in supporting radical leftist movements than a decade or two ago.

Diplomats said a Soviet flag in Riyadh's new diplomatic quarter would make the Americans stand up and take notice of one of their major allies that feels it is ignored.

Relations between Riyadh and Washington have increasingly been strained by Congress's refusal to approve weapon sales to the kingdom and by U.S. support for Israel.

Turned away by their traditional arms supplier, the Saudis have turned more and more to other countries for their defence needs.

One recent country to fill the void was China, which sold the Saudis medium-range missiles. When the Americans protested, the Saudis made it clear the U.S. ambassador was no longer welcome in Riyadh, diplomatic sources said.

The ambassador returned to Washington and a new one was named.

Diplomats say Moscow stands to gain from the Saudi disenchantment with the U.S. They want the Saudis to persuade the Afghan guerrillas to allow a smooth withdrawal of Soviet troops from Afghanistan.

Moscow would like port facilities for its Gulf fleet, and the respectability conferred by having relations with Saudi Arabia might convince a country like the United Arab Emirates to accept Soviet ships, diplomats say.

Mubarak avoids criticizing Israel

Egypt to go all out for peace

Jerusalem Post Staff

Egypt won't spare any effort to bring peace to the region, President Hosni Mubarak said in a speech in Cairo yesterday to mark the sixth anniversary of the completion of Israel's withdrawal from Sinai.

Mubarak avoided any criticism of Israel and instead called on regional leaders to assume the "responsibility" of making peace, Israel Radio reported.

"We never entered war for the sake of war," said Mubarak in remarks broadcast from the Egyptian capital. "Our heroes in the armed forces entered battle with bared breasts, ready for battle only in order to achieve peace.

"We won't spare any effort in the national and international arena in order to bring the peoples of the region to this supreme goal, to channel all efforts to construction and development.

"The responsibility of peace is not any lighter than the yoke of war," Mubarak added. "The responsibility of peace ... obliges us not to waste our energy on things that have no benefit, or on political arguments that do nothing but harm the national consensus."

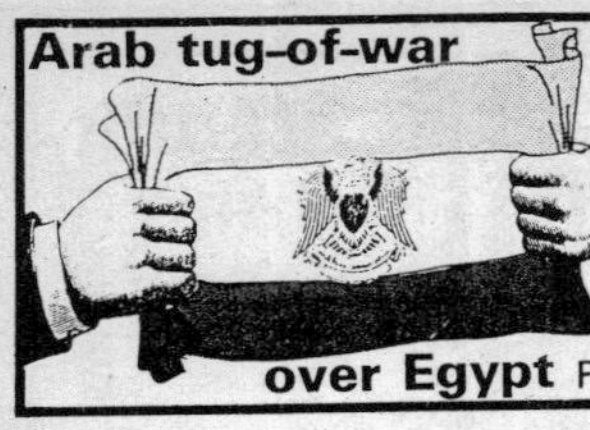

THE JERUSALEM POST

Vol. LVI, No. 16825 Thursday, May 12, 1988 • Iyar 25, 5748 • Ramadan 27, 1408 NIS 1.20 (Eilat NIS 1.05)

SECOND EDITION

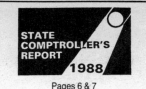

STATE COMPTROLLER'S REPORT 1988

Pages 6 & 7

Syria poised to intervene in Beirut

By DAVID RUDGE
Jerusalem Post Reporter

ROSH HANIKRA – Syria was last night reported once more to be on the verge of sending its troops into battle-ravaged South Beirut to quell the fighting between rival pro-Syrian Amal and Iranian-backed Hizbullah Shi'ite militias.

Brig.-Gen. Ghazi Kana'an, head of Syrian military intelligence in Lebanon, reportedly returned to Damascus from the Lebanese capital last night to brief Syrian President Hafez Assad on the latest situation.

Earlier in the day, Beirut Radio broke into its programmes to broadcast a statement by Kana'an indicating that Syria was prepared to deploy troops in the southern slum suburb of the city.

"If the fighting continues, we will have no other option but to respond to the pleas of the population to end their ordeal," Kana'an was quoted as saying.

He reportedly compared the fighting in South Beirut to the situation that existed in Moslem West Beirut before Syrian troops moved in last February to end vicious street battles between Amal militiamen and left-wing Lebanese factions.

News agencies reported that over 20 people were killed and nearly 70 wounded in fierce fighting in South Beirut yesterday morning before yet another Syrian- and Iranian-brokered ceasefire came into effect.

This brought the casualty toll to over 150 killed and nearly 600 wounded since the internecine battles started on Friday.

The resurgence of fighting, following an overnight truce on Tuesday, began shortly before dawn. Reports from Lebanon said Amal militiamen, under cover of tank, artillery, mortar and heavy machine-gun fire, launched a major offensive to recapture positions taken by the Islamic fundamentalists in previous days.

But the reports said the Hizbullah counter-attacked and took over even more districts previously held by Amal. Observers thought it highly unlikely that the truce – the fifth since the fighting started – would last.

The rival militias were reported to be fortifying their positions in preparation for another round of fighting.

Some 18 foreign hostages kidnapped by Shi'ite

(Continued on Page 2, Col. 4)

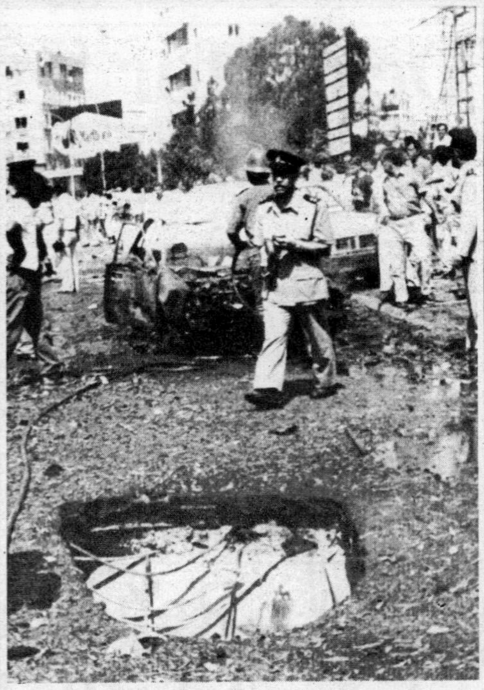

Remains of the booby-trapped car which blew up near the Israel Embassy in Nicosia yesterday. Three people were killed in the blast which blew a hole in the road. (AFP)

Intended for Israel Embassy

Arab held as car bomb kills 3 in Nicosia

Jerusalem Post Staff
and agencies

NICOSIA – Cyprus police yesterday announced that they were holding a 28-year-old Lebanese Arab suspected of involvement in the powerful car bomb intended for the Israel Embassy in Nicosia. The bomb killed three people and injured 19 as it blew up on a busy avenue in the Cypriot capital.

Dead were the driver of the car bomb, a four-wheel-drive Mitsubishi Pajero; a Cypriot woman in the car behind; and a pedestrian, 64-year-old Andreas Frangos, a retired Cypriot diplomat, who died at hospital. Nine of the injured were in serious condition, police said.

An anonymous caller telephoned NBC-TV in New York to say Palestinian terrorist Abu Nidal claims responsibility for the explosion.

The caller gave no other details.

Ambassador Aharon Lopez said the embassy had not received any threat or warning of the attack.

"At about 10:15 a.m. we heard a powerful explosion," Lopez said in a telephone interview from Nicosia yesterday.

"All embassy officials as well as members of their families are safe," Lopez noted, adding that he had stayed in the embassy building after the explosion was heard. "We saw a crowd gathering, ambulances, police vehicles."

Last night the embassy staff were meeting at the ambassador's home to express collective relief at the lucky escape, he said.

Police said a man seen running away across wasteland as the jeep exploded dropped a bag containing a remote-control device and was later arrested.

He was identified as Omar Ahmad Hawillo, 28, a student at a Nicosia college who had arrived on March 21. He will appear in court today.

Police said Hawillo had not been charged yet, adding "if we can find evidence against him, he will be prosecuted."

Charred remains of the driver were found 400 metres from the bridge.

Pieces of flesh and charred, twisted metal were scattered over a wide area. Windows were broken up to a kilometre from the blast, which went off 150 metres from the embassy building.

Ambassador Lopez said that Cypriot police guards stationed outside the embassy twice prevented the Mitsubishi from parking outside the building. On the second occasion it sped off towards central Nicosia.

It exploded minutes later on a bridge over the dried-up Pedhieos river, turning Grivas Dhigenis Avenue into a maelstrom of shrapnel, blazing cars, burned flesh, broken glass and blood.

"I had just bent down to change radio stations before the lights changed," said neurologist Adonis Tselonis. "When I looked up, I saw the third vehicle in front of me exploding into pieces. My car jumped up in the air and I saw people on the pavement being knocked down by the boom. It could have been me."

The blast tore a metre-wide hole in the bridge, tossed two blazing cars in the air, toppled a lamp post and iron railings and smashed hundreds of windows along the avenue.

A man in his 50s – hair singed, body blackened and clothes shredded – was helped on to a makeshift stretcher at the roadside. He seemed too shocked to realize his left leg had almost been severed.

A hand, torn off at the wrist, lay on the road about 75 metres from the blast site. Pieces of flesh littered the area.

The main tank of a blue sewage truck ahead of the Mitsubishi was holed by shrapnel, sending its contents pouring into the street.

A shopkeeper clearing broken glass from his shop overlooking the bridge said a ringing telephone made him move away from the display windows just before the explosion.

"I was sitting at my desk when it went off. The force from the explosion threw me against the wall. I was lucky," he said.

A security source said the bomb appeared to have gone off accidentally.

President George Vassiliou visited the scene and told reporters: "It is tragic that so many innocent people have had their lives cut short for

(Continued on Back Page)

Fears that anniversaries will spark fierce unrest

By JOEL GREENBERG
Jerusalem Post Reporter

Security officials are bracing for possible heavy unrest in the territories next week during the Id al-Fitr feast marking the end of the Ramadan holiday, and on May 15, the anniversary of Israel's independence according to the Gregorian calendar.

Leaflet No. 16 of the "Unified National Leadership of the Uprising" was issued yesterday in the territories, but the military authorities banned publication of its contents in the press.

Meanwhile, three editors from the East Jerusalem *Al-Fajr* newspaper and one from the banned *Al-Awdah* magazine were arrested Tuesday night and put in administrative detention. They were identified as Talal Abu Afifeh, Riad Jubran, Musa Jaradat and Hassan Abed Rabo. More than 20 Palestinian journalists have been arrested during the uprising for alleged security offences. Four Israelis, editors of the extreme left-wing *Derech Hanitzotz* newspaper, are also being held.

Khaled Abu Toameh, an editor on Israel Television's Arabic service and a freelance journalist, said police entered his East Jerusalem home Tuesday and confiscated his personal telephone book and documents.

In the Nablus military court, the trial of 95 villagers from Kabatiya charged with lynching a suspected "collaborator" on February 24 began. Mohammed Ayad, who villagers suspected of working with the Shin Bet, was killed after he opened fire at a mob that stoned his home, killing a four-year-old boy and wounding 14 persons.

A total of 47 villagers were brought into the Nablus courtroom in groups of five to hear the charges against them, and most pleaded not guilty. The trial of 48 others will begin on Thursday. Five are accused of breaking into Ayad's home, hitting him with an axe, stabbing him, and hanging him to death on an electricity pylon.

In the Gaza Strip, the Civil Administration completed issuing new ID cards to residents of the Rimal neighborhood in Gaza. Some 6,170 cards were distributed.

The issuing of the new cards is apparently designed to tighten controls and computerize data on Gaza Strip residents, including information on security offences and non-payment of taxes. An Interior Ministry official overseeing the operation denied that the new identification cards would bear markings indicating the holders' security records.

Military sources said the IDF was considering closing the Gaza Strip to the press tomorrow, when large crowds are expected in mosques to mark the last Friday of Ramadan.

In an interview with the army's *Bamahane* journal, IDF Judge Advocate-General Amnon Strashnov said close to half of the 5,000 Palestinians imprisoned in the territories have been formally charged. He said 1,700 were being held in administrative detention, and that half of those charged had already been tried.

Strashnov said that since the start of the uprising 10 soldiers had been courtmartialled for excesses, including unjustified firing at rioters.

In a meeting with the Israel Bar, Strashnov said he would favourably consider their proposal to allow administrative detainees to appeal their imprisonment to a military judge. Recently introduced military legislation cancelled the requirement that administrative detainees be brought before a judge within 96 hours of their arrest.

Saguy: Uprising harms training

Post Defence Reporter

The IDF's extended deployment in the West Bank and Gaza has "seriously harmed the soldiers' basic level of training," Ground Forces Commander Aluf Uri Saguy said last week.

Saguy's remarks, made before a forum of senior officers in the command, appear in the latest issue of the IDF's weekly Bamahane.

"Only if the uprising in the territories tapers off with the coming of summer will we be able to stabilize the training process for the regular army," Saguy continued.

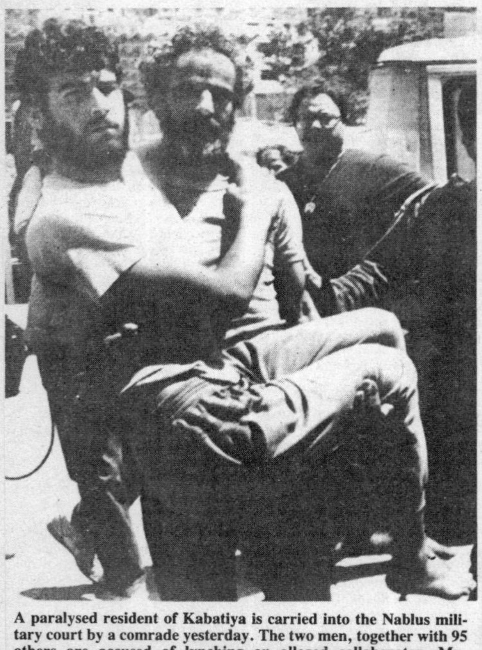

A paralysed resident of Kabatiya is carried into the Nablus military court by a comrade yesterday. The two men, together with 95 others are accused of lynching an alleged collaborator, Muhammed Ayad in February. Before he was killed Ayad managed to open fire on the mob, killing a child and wounding 14 people, including the man above. (Reuter)

SLA accuses Unifil of protecting terrorists

By DAVID RUDGE

ROSH HANIKRA – The South Lebanese Army yesterday accused Irish Unifil troops of continuing to cooperate with terrorists engaged in hostile acts against SLA and IDF troops inside the security zone in South Lebanon.

Senior SLA sources said they had proof that Irish troops deployed in the central sector of the zone, near the village of Barashit, had given protection to two gunmen wounded in a clash with IDF troops near the border of the zone in the early hours of Tuesday morning. The allegations were categorically denied by Unifil.

The sources alleged that it was not the first time Irish Unifil troops in that region had assisted terrorists to escape beyond the northern border of the zone.

Unifil spokesman Timur Goksel stressed that on Tuesday, nobody had approached a Unifil position or troops in the area for assistance.

Unifil sources, however, noted that Irish troops in the same area had given medical assistance to an SLA soldier who was wounded on Saturday in a roadside bomb blast that claimed the lives of two other SLA soldiers.

The sources said Unifil was aware that certain SLA officers were obsessed with the (mistaken) belief that Unifil troops were helping gunmen to escape from the zone. "This matter has been raised frequently and we are getting tired of these baseless allegations," said a source.

U.S. and Soviets try to unblock arms ban log-jam

GENEVA (AP) – The U.S. and Soviet Union began a diplomatic effort yesterday to clear up a dispute over anti-cheating measures in their nuclear missile-ban treaty that threatens U.S. Senate ratification of the pact.

U.S. Secretary of State George Shultz and a Soviet spokesman expressed optimism the dispute could be resolved during two days of talks between Shultz and Soviet Foreign Minister Eduard Shevardnadze.

But Shultz acknowledged he could not guarantee Senate approval of the treaty before President Reagan holds a fourth summit meeting in Moscow with Kremlin leader Mikhail Gorbachev later this month.

The Senate has indefinitely postponed debate on the treaty, which had been scheduled to begin yesterday.

Egypt presents new plan to break Taba deadlock

MADRID – A senior Egyptian official, Mustafa Khalil, yesterday presented new proposals in an attempt to break the deadlock in the dispute with Israel over the Taba issue.

In a meeting with Foreign Minister Shimon Peres, who is here for the Socialist International Council, Khalil said that the proposals were a further attempt at reaching a compromise solution. Khalil, vice president of the ruling party in Egypt, brought the proposals in the name of Egyptian President Hosni Mubarak.

Peres replied that the Israel government would study the proposals carefully. The contents of the new Egyptian offer have been cabled to the Prime Minister's Office in Jerusalem.

Israeli officials here said that the new Egyptian proposals were similar to ideas raised earlier in the negotiations, calling for Egyptian sovereignty over Taba and a right for Israel to use the tourist facilities in the disputed strip of land. They said that the proposals represented an attempt by Egypt to show more flexibility.

Peres met here yesterday for a second time with Alexander Zotov, a Soviet observer at the Socialist International Council meeting. Both Peres and Zotov said after the meeting that the contacts between the two governments would continue.

In a speech before the council meeting, Peres reported on the meetings with Zotov and said that the Soviets were showing some but not enough flexibility. Zotov, who attended the meeting, shook his head, apparently signalling his disagreement, but he did not elaborate.

Peres said yesterday that Soviet officials had told him Moscow could discuss re-establishing diplomatic relations with Israel following an agreement on a Middle East peace conference.

A draft resolution on the Middle East is expected to be agreed upon at the Council meeting today or tomorrow. The document states that the Palestinian uprising had been caused by frustration and was also the result of unbearable conditions in the Israeli-occupied territories.

It further calls for an International Peace Conference based on Security Council Resolution 242, the security of the existing states in the region and the rights of the Palestinians to self determination.

Peres, facing sharp criticism from fellow socialists over Israel's handling of the five-month uprising in the territories, said the two key issues for peace were the rights of the Palestinians and Israel's right to security.

"Do not forget one of the two if you are ready to extend a helping hand," he told the leaders at the meeting. "Palestinians, and you must understand that there is a big security problem concerning Israel. It is not an invention or a pretext."

Conference sources said there had been sharp discussions behind closed doors as the Socialist International's Middle East committee, which includes Palestinians, tried to draft a resolution on the situation in the region. Former Italian Prime Minister Bettino Craxi told the meeting that Israel could not occupy Arab territories with impunity.

"Sooner or later the rebellion comes ... detention or execution of its chiefs are useless against a popular uprising." (Reuter, AP, JTA)

Soviet spy Kim Philby dies in Moscow

LONDON (AFP) – Former spy Kim Philby, who passed secrets to the Soviet Union while working for the British intelligence services, has died in Moscow, the British Broadcasting Corporation reported yesterday. Philby was 76.

The BBC cited diplomatic sources in London in reporting the death of Philby, who escaped to the Soviet Union in 1963 and has lived there ever since.

Basketball fever hits Tel Aviv

By DANNY BEN-TAL
For The Jerusalem Post

TEL AVIV – There's basketball fever in Tel Aviv and the only cure is a high-priced ticket for tonight's national championship final play-off between perennial rivals Maccabi and Hapoel Tel Aviv.

Each side has won a play-off game, and each time by a single point in the dying seconds. For the first time in years there seems to be a real possibility that Maccabi may be ousted as national champions. No wonder this sporting event has captured the public imagination.

All 9,300 tickets for the game at the Yad Eliyahu stadium were sold out within hours of going on sale.

Since then the phones at the Hadran ticket agency have been ringing non-stop with inquiries from as far away as Eilat.

"All of a sudden I'm everybody's best friend," agency manager Avi Albeck told *The Post*.

On the blackmarket NIS 15 tickets start at NIS 100. Touts patrolled the street outside the Hadran offices yesterday, pouncing on anybody naive enough to look for last-minute cancellations.

The Maccabi and Hapoel unions have also been besieged for tickets. Hapoel players have received an allocation of just one ticket each and even Maccabi chairman Eldad Bukspan is desperately seeking 150 tickets for his union's functionaries. (See game preview, page 5.)

Anne Pollard sent to Mayo Clinic for tests

WASHINGTON (AP) – The jailed wife of convicted spy Jonathan Pollard has been moved to the Mayo Clinic for tests to determine whether her health is deteriorating, officials and family friends said yesterday.

Anne Henderson-Pollard, who was sentenced in April 1987 to five years' imprisonment as an accessory in her husband's spying for Israel, was flown May 9 from Lexington, Kentucky, to a Rochester, Minnesota, prison medical facility, said Kathy Morse, spokeswoman for the Bureau of Prisons.

Anne Pollard, who suffers from a degenerative stomach disease, will undergo tests at the nearby Mayo Clinic by her former surgeon Bernard Goldberg, said David Turner, who heads a group called "Justice for the Pollards." He said that for the first time since the Pollards' imprisonment, a friend from Israel was allowed to visit the couple.

The friend, Amnon Dror, wrote a letter to the White House saying he was shocked by Anne Pollard's condition. He said she was so thin her bones showed through her skin, her skin color was yellowish and she clutched her stomach in pain throughout the 11-hour visit.

Jerusalem residents urged to conserve water

By ANDY COURT

Jerusalem municipality officials yesterday urged the public to conserve water during the next two weeks, following breakdowns in the pipeline that supplies water to the capital.

The breakdowns come only days after the State Comptroller's report criticized the reliability of the pipeline that supplies almost all of the capital's water. In case of accidents and emergencies, the pipeline cannot supply sufficient water, the Comptroller said. He noted that work on strengthening the system is three years behind schedule. (See story – Page 6.)

Two of the water lines which run from wells in the coastal plain to Jerusalem burst on Tuesday night, according to Yehezkiel Zakai, director of the Mekorot Water Company. Two major wells that normally supply water to the city are also out of order. One of them collapsed from old age a month and a half ago, and will take a week to 10 days to repair. The other is down for a day or two for yearly maintenance.

Nelu Rubin, director of the city's Water Department, said that Jerusalem is to receive about 15 per cent less water than it uses daily. The municipality's water-storage pools will be able to make up the difference. But the pools are already 30 per cent depleted because of disruptions to the water supply two weeks ago, when a water main burst and the electricity supplied to the pumping station failed.

The intifada and the national psyche

Page 4

THE JERUSALEM POST

Vol. LVI, No. 16850 Sunday, June 12, 1988 • Sivan 27, 5748 • Shawal 28, 1408 NIS 1.20 (Eilat NIS 1.05)

Europe's soccerfest kicks off

Page 7

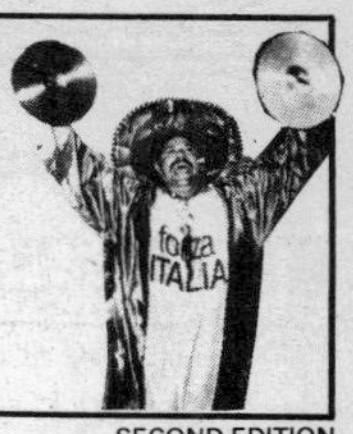

SECOND EDITION

Arson suspected as fires ravage forests

By ANDY COURT
Jerusalem Post Reporter

Fire and forestry officials suspect that arsonists ignited a significant number of the fires that devastated thousands of dunams throughout the country yesterday.

Fires were still raging last night between Givat Nili and Kibbutz Regavim in the Menashe Hills. The fire reportedly broke out in 10 different places at the same time, which led fire officials to conclude that it was the work of arsonists.

Two youths from the nearby village of Jisr e-Zarka were arrested on suspicion of starting a previous fire near Kibbutz Ma'agan Michael.

Two Arab youths were also arrested yesterday afternoon for allegedly starting a fire near Kibbutz Ma'ale Hahamisha in the Jerusalem corridor. The two were spotted by the crew of a helicopter which hovered over the burning area.

Over 100,000 dunams of land has been burned since the beginning of May – more than five times the average damage for an entire summer season, according to Jewish National Fund spokesman David Angel.

More than 50 per cent of the pasture land on the Golan Heights has already gone up in smoke, causing serious economic damage to the kibbutzim and moshavim in the area, he said.

Angel attributed "more than 50 per cent" of this season's damage to arsonists.

Throughout the country yesterday, members of the police, the fire department, the Jewish National Fund, the Nature Reserves Authority and various volunteers fought the advancing flames.

One of the worst of the blazes yesterday burned down mature oaks, pistachio, and terebinth trees in the nature reserve near Moshav Bar Giora in the Jerusalem corridor. Between 6,000 to 8,000 dunams in that area, including a large swathe of pasture land, was turned into a charred, black zone.

The fire began not only near Bar Giora, but also Nahal Refa'im and Nahal Hama'arat-Ein Koby, not far from Betar and Batir.

Flames threatened the gas tanks of Moshav Nes Harim, as well as the chicken coops and homes of Moshav Bar Giora and Moshav Mata.

Eight fire trucks worked in the area, and four planes dumped water from above.

Eli Peretz, fire chief for the Beit Shemesh area, said that an investi-

(Continued on Back Page)

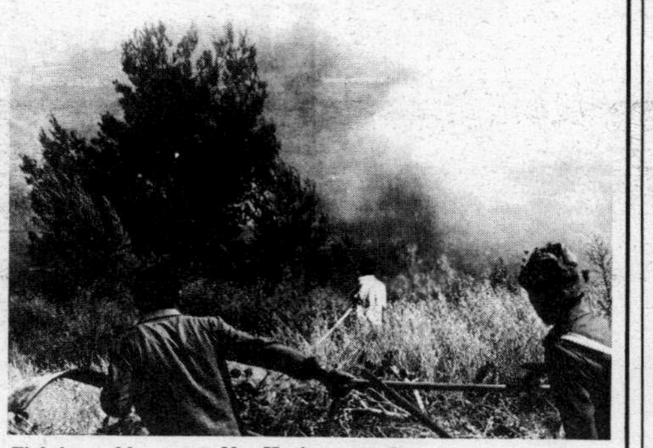
Fighting a blaze near Nes Harim yesterday. (Scoop 80)

Shevardnadze warns:

Understandings on Middle East are serious

By MENACHEM SHALEV
Post Diplomatic Correspondent

The superpower understandings on the Middle East reached during the Moscow summit should definitely be heeded, Soviet Foreign Minister Eduard Shevardnadze told Prime Minister Shamir in their meeting on Thursday. Shevardnadze referred several times to the "understandings," and advised Shamir to "think this matter over," informed sources said here last night.

Many Israeli experts have concluded in recent days that a joint U.S.-Soviet Middle East peace plan is likely to be formulated by the beginning of 1989, after a new U.S. administration comes to power.

Reports from Algiers indicate that the reports of the superpower understandings also figured prominently at the Arab summit last week, and Middle East experts ascribe some of the "moderate" decisions of the summit to the presence there of Soviet Deputy Foreign Minister Yuli Vorontsov.

Shamir said on Friday that the summit resolutions were unimportant and "not surprising" while Foreign Minister Shimon Peres declared that despite the resolutions, "the Jordanian option is not dead."

The summit boosted the position of the PLO and diminished the stature of Jordan's King Hussein – but did not shut the door on the peace process, Foreign Ministry experts said over the weekend.

Despite the generally hostile and negative tone of the resolutions, the experts noted several "moderate" aspects: There was no clear-cut statement that the PLO should be represented independently in an international conference; the resolutions did not specify a conference with "full powers," or explicitly rule out the possibility of a future Palestinian-Jordanian confederation.

Middle East experts noted that the summit undercut UN Security Council Resolution 242 as the basis for an international conference. But the summit did not reject the Shultz peace initiative, although it criticized it.

Shamir is expected to report to the cabinet today on his Thursday meeting with Shevardnadze.

Foreign Ministry officials said last night that they would extend the

(Continued on Page 2, Col. 6)

Pollard moved to tough new prison

By WOLF BLITZER

WASHINGTON – Convicted spy for Israel Jonathan Jay Pollard has been moved from the federal prison in Springfield, Missouri, to the maximum security facility in Marion, Illinois.

His father, Dr. Morris Pollard expressed deep concern over the transfer, given the "notorious" reputation of the Marion prison.

In a telephone interview with *The Jerusalem Post*, he recalled that Amnesty International, the London-based human rights organization, has been very critical of the Marion prison, where hardened criminals are held.

Dr. Pollard said he had been informed by prison authorities that his son, for his own protection, would remain in isolation at Marion. There have been repeated threats against his life made in recent years by neo-Nazi and Black Muslim prisoners.

Pollard, 34, has been kept in isolation since his initial arrest in 1986.

Stabbing suspect held, home demolished after confession

By JOEL GREENBERG
Jerusalem Post Reporter

Security forces arrested a suspect in Tuesday's stabbing of el-Bireh Mayor Hassan Tawil, and demolished his house at the Jalazoun refugee camp on Friday. The suspect has confessed to carrying out the attack, security sources said.

The quick arrest was apparently facilitated by an identification of the attacker made by Tawil. Tawil, who is recovering at Hadassah Hospital in Ein Kerem from wounds in the heart and stomach, told Israel Television last week that the attacker was not from el-Bireh, and had asked to apply for a passport before stabbing him.

The suspect, Hamis Jodeh Faraj, 26, was arrested at his home on Thursday night in a special operation of the IDF and the Shin Bet, a military spokesman said.

Faraj is suspected of "following Tawil's movements with the intention of assassinating him, and attempting an attack in the past without success," the spokesman said. Faraj attacked Tawil out of nationalist motives, and has been jailed several times in the past for participating in disturbances, according to the spokesman.

At about 1:30 p.m. Friday, the IDF demolished the three-room house where Faraj lived with his 60-year-old mother at the refugee camp, north of el-Bireh. A curfew was clamped on the camp during the operation, and residents said electricity was cut off.

Reporters saw a dozen army vehicles and two bulldozers enter Jalazoun, and saw troops remove belongings from the house and scan political literature they found in drawers. One of the bulldozers worked for half an hour to raze the one-storey structure, as Faraj's mother watched from a neighbouring home.

"I don't know why they are destroying my house," she told reporters.

The IDF commander in the West Bank, Tat Aluf Gabi Ofir, said the demolition was meant to demonstrate to Arab public servants that "we stand behind them all the time, and will not allow them to be harmed."

The clandestine leadership of the uprising in the territories has issued threats against Israeli-appointed Arab mayors and Civil Administration employees in an effort to engineer their resignation.

In other developments, sources in Nablus said troops took about 70 men out of their homes on Arba wa Ashreen Street Friday night, and beat them on the head and other parts of their bodies, following stone-throwing at troops in the area earlier in the evening. The soldiers cursed the men and warned them that if unrest continues, they would return to beat them and vandalize their homes, the sources said. They added that 16 persons were taken to the Ittihad Nisai Hospital for treatment, but none could be admitted for lack of room.

A military spokeswoman said she knew nothing of such an incident, but ten persons had been injured by troops who used force to subdue them when they resisted arrest after clashes in the old city of Nablus. She said soldiers shot and wounded three rioters in the legs while breaking up the protest. Local sources said four persons were wounded, including two girls aged 10 and 11, who were shot in the shoulder. Others were wounded by rubber bullets and beating, according to the sources. (Continued on Page 2, Col. 6)

Shultz warns:

'Don't move embassy to Jerusalem'

By WOLF BLITZER
Jerusalem Post Correspondent, and agencies

WASHINGTON – Secretary of State George Shultz has warned that any unilateral transfer of the U.S. Embassy from Tel Aviv to Jerusalem would "ruin" the U.S.-sponsored Arab-Israel peace process.

He was referring to recent statements by Democratic presidential candidate Michael Dukakis, pledging to recognize Jerusalem as Israel's capital if elected to the White House in November.

"It would be a gigantic mistake," Shultz said on Friday in an interview with NBC News. He described Jerusalem as "occupied" territory, subject to negotiations, the same as the West Bank, the Gaza Strip and the Golan Heights.

Jerusalem Mayor Teddy Kollek yesterday called the argument "futile," saying issues such as American tourism and investment were much more important to the holy city than the transfer of embassies. "These are useless discussions since pressure

(Continued on Page 2, Col. 3)

Areas pleased with Arab summit

Palestinian leaders in the administered territories have welcomed the outcome of the Algiers summit.

The summit, according to Fayez abu Rahmeh, head of the Palestinian Lawyers' Association in the Gaza Strip, "conformed to the wishes of Palestinians in the occupied territories." By declaring their support for an independent state and the rights of the PLO to take part in peace negotiations, Arab leaders clarified the PLO relationship with both Jordan and Syria, he said.

For Bassam Shaka'a, former mayor of Nablus, the summit was significant in the support it expressed for the *intifada* and its "condemnation of the policy of the U.S." Mayor Elias Freij of Bethlehem – generally considered a moderate – said he was pleased that the summit had confirmed the presence of the PLO at an international peace conference.

PLO Chairman Yasser Arafat hailed the summit as a triumph for the *intifada*.

"It's a victory for our people inside ... It shows the Arab world stands behind the Palestinian uprising. The children who throw stones in Palestine say we will fight on," a jubilant Arafat told a news conference after the closing session.

The PLO will receive $43 million a month to support the uprising in the West Bank and Gaza Strip, the summit agreed. (AFP, Reuter)

Freed Russian priest tells of 36 years of hell

MOSCOW (Reuter) – Russian Orthodox priest Vasily Shipilov, who spent 36 years in Soviet labour camps and psychiatric hospitals, described yesterday how he was beaten every time he crossed himself.

"It's impossible to say how many times I was beaten over all those years but I forgive the people who beat me," said Shipilov, 60, trembling and confused after being released from a Moscow clinic on Friday.

A British Anglican vicar who campaigned for Shipilov's release by fasting in a cage in a London church throughout Lent, told reporters the priest must have been beaten hundreds of times as he crossed himself every time he stood up or sat down.

Shipilov said that as a result of one beating, he suffered a fractured skull and recently orderlies broke his leg after accusing him of trying to escape.

"What kind of hospital is it where they beat people? Listen to me, listen to me," he shouted.

Shipilov appeared shocked to meet the western press at the Moscow flat of Christian dissidents after 34 years of isolation so complete that he said he had not heard of Kremlin leader Mikhail Gorbachev.

He seemed unsure of the order of events in his blighted life, but he said he was arrested for the first time in 1949 for breaking passport

(Continued on Back Page)

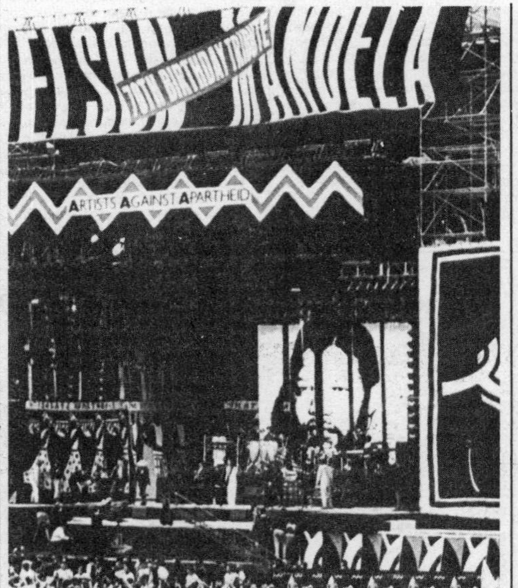

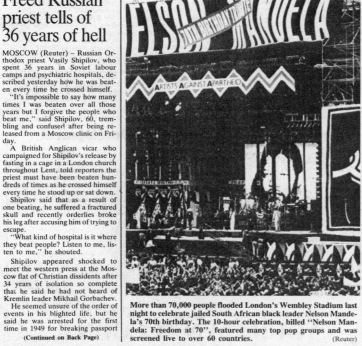

More than 70,000 people flooded London's Wembley Stadium last night to celebrate jailed South African black leader Nelson Mandela's 70th birthday. The 10-hour celebration, billed "Nelson Mandela: Freedom at 70", featured many top pop groups and was screened live to over 60 countries. (Reuter)

PLO rivals battle in West Beirut

BEIRUT, (AP) – PLO leader Yasser Arafat's loyalists and Syrian-backed dissidents battled with mortars and rockets Saturday at two devastated refugee camps in west Beirut. Police said nine people were killed and 35 wounded.

That upped the casualties to 19 dead and 95 wounded since the new round of inter-Palestinian clashes broke out in Shatilla and nearby Bourj el-Barajneh camps last Wednesday.

The fighting, which raged into the afternoon Saturday, pitted Arafat's mainline Fatah guerrillas against the Syrian-supported breakaway Fatah-Uprising faction of Said Abu Mousa.

Shell blasts and staccato bursts of gunfire shook Beirut as Palestinian antagonists in the city hammered each other's positions with 82-mm mortars, 106-mm recoilless cannons, rocket-propelled grenades and heavy machine guns, police said.

They said Mousa's gunners, stationed in Syrian-controlled hills in Lebanon's central mountains overlooking Beirut, pounded both camps with 155-mm howitzers and 130-mm and 160-mm mortars.

The heavy clashes continued during the day despite several cease-fire calls by a security committee made up of representatives of various Palestinian groups.

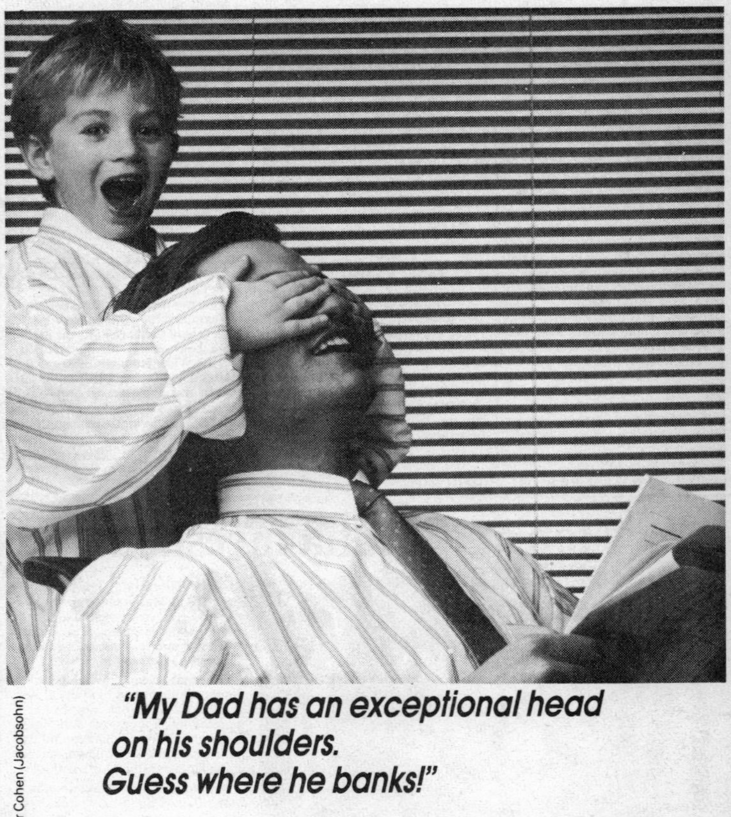
Tamir Cohen (Jacobsohn)

"My Dad has an exceptional head on his shoulders. Guess where he banks!"

People with exceptional ideas need a bank that can offer exceptional solutions. They know that it's worth their while working with a bank that thinks creatively and is willing to consider unconventional ways of matching clients' special needs. In today's business world, a routine approach is no guarantee of success. Today's businessmen demand that those they work with, including their bankers, match their own creative, innovative and individual style of doing things.

This is their philosophy, and this is the recipe of their success. It is also the secret of the First International Bank's success. People with an exceptional head on their shoulders work with a bank that works overtime for them and that is open when other banks are closed. They prefer a bank that offers them more: Improved Checking Accounts, Refund of banking fees on Improved Business Accounts, Special benefits on savings and deposit accounts, and an improved standard of service and technology. Our banking principle is well known: to be exceptional.

Join First International Bank, and you can be exceptional too.

THE EVER EXCEPTIONAL. THE FIRST INTERNATIONAL BANK.

Moscow cancels history exams in major reform

MOSCOW (Reuter) – The Soviet Union has cancelled end-of-term history tests in a major reform move lauded by the government newspaper *Izvestia*, which denounced the country's history classes as lies passed on from generation to generation.

Praising the move, which affects pupils aged 6-16, as a bold, honourable decision, *Izvestia* called for the urgent preparation of new history texts during the summer break.

It suggested that if full textbooks could not be prepared by September, intellectuals whose recent writings had broken with the previous official version of Soviet history should compile collections of articles and documents for classroom use.

The report did not specify who had ordered the cancellation of the exams and social studies tests, but analysts said a move of such broad dimensions could only have been decided at the top.

"Huge, unmeasurable is the guilt of those who deluded generation after generation, poisoning their minds and souls with lies," *Izvestia* declared in unusually strong language.

"Cancelling the exams was the only possible sober and honourable decision," it said. "Only yesterday it was impossible to imagine that such a decision could be taken.

"Everyone – teachers, parents, students – can feel only relief and thanks toward those who had the boldness to say that these exams would not take place."

Knowledge of the truth about the Soviet past is a potent weapon in the reform drive of Kremlin leader Mikhail Gorbachev, who is facing a mounting tide of conservative opposition.

Although Gorbachev said early last year that there must be no "blank spots" in Soviet history, only in recent months have progressive historians been able to publish critical accounts of the most sensitive periods of the country's past.

The increasingly bold articles on the repressions of dictator Josef Stalin and the corruption which flourished under his successors are giving Soviet citizens their first inkling of how badly power has been abused in their country.

With the approach of a major Communist Party conference on political reform later this month, the information drive has been picking up steam. One article this week notably described the late Soviet leader Leonid Brezhnev as a "neo-Stalinist".

Analysts view the upsurge of the revision of Soviet history as part of Gorbachev's drive to make his reforms irreversible by impressing on his citizens that the huge problems faced at present are the legacy of a past which must not be repeated.

Behind the campaign they see the hand of Politburo member Alexander Yakovlev, one of Gorbachev's closest aides and the man who, according to well-informed Soviet sources, has taken over control of the media from his colleague Yegor Ligachev.

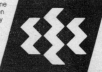

EIGHT PAGES FROM SUNDAY'S
The New York Times
WEEKLY REVIEW INSIDE TODAY

THE JERUSALEM POST

Vol. LVI, No. 16893 Monday, August 1, 1988 • Av 18, 5748 • Zul Hijja 19, 1408 NIS 1.20 (Eilat NIS 1.05)

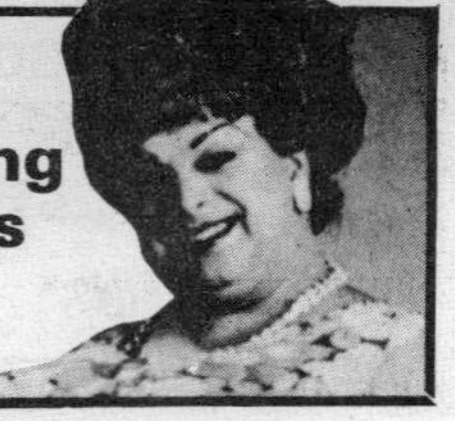

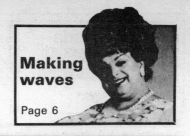

Making waves
Page 6

E. Jerusalem activist in jail again

By ANDY COURT
Jerusalem Post Reporter

Less than two months after his release from administrative detention, Palestinian activist Faisal Husseini was back in jail last night – and 'is Arab Studies Society in East Je- usalem was closed down for one ear.

For Husseini – a leading PLO representative in the territories and the n of Abdel Kader Husseini, the ommander of Arab forces in Jeru- lem during the 1948 – this is the ird time in 18 months that he has en jailed without trial. He has nt 12 of the past 16 months in ministrative detention and his ovements were restricted during rt of the time that he was free.

A statement released yesterday y Jerusalem police spokesman Rafi

(Continued on Back Page)

Kessar attacks Labour Party

By JEFF BLACK
Post Labour Reporter

TEL AVIV – Histadrut Secretary-General Yisrael Kessar yesterday attacked the Labour Party's leadership, accusing it of "turning the party into an elections-only party." This change, he said, "will destroy the labour movement."

Summing up a marathon 10-hour discussion on Hevrat Ha'ovdim's future at the labour federation's weekly central committee meeting here, Kessar attacked Labour Party tacticians who want to diminish the Histadrut's role in the general elections, because of the current crisis within Hevrat Ha'ovdim.

Kessar won the support of the central committee for his reorganization plan for the giant Histadrut holding company. The plan, as reported last week, calls for greater centralization and for top officials to be made directly responsible for the company's future.

During the meeting, a number of committee members called for Hevrat Ha'ovdim Secretary-General Danny Rosolio's resignation, because of the crisis rocking the holding company. Rosolio hit back, charging that "some members have been after my head for some time."

Na'amat head Masha Lubelsky was the first to raise the Rosolio problem, without directly demanding replacement. She reminded the committee that Hevrat Ha'ovdim belongs to the country's workers and not the United Kibbutz Movement, to which Rosolio is affiliated. She said the UKM must remember that Kessar has the authority to fire Rosolio whenever he wants and added that "if Kessar chooses to replace him, then the central committee will support his decision." Lubelsky said that Hevrat Ha'ovdim had debts of more than $1.5 billion.

Other committee members, such as Pinhas Shomer and Raya Ratig, called for the replacement of Hevrat Ha'ovdim's entire senior echelon, "from Rosolio downwards."

Rosolio, in reply, claimed that Hevrat Ha'ovdim's losses were less than the alleged $1.5 b., and insisted that Kessar had been a full partner in all the decisions taken concerning the company's activities. Ya'acov Avimor, head of the Afula Labour Council, said that whoever attacks Rosolio is attacking Kessar as well.

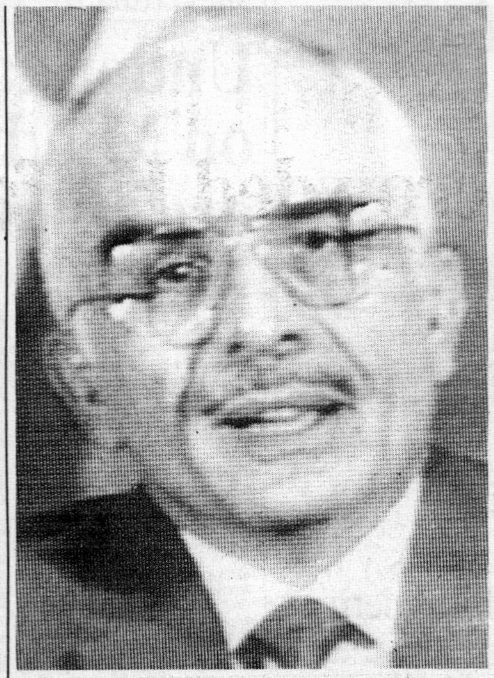

King Hussein speaks last night on Jordanian Television. (Isaac Harari)

'Legal and administrative ties to be cut'

Hussein drops Jordan's claim to the West Bank

By YEHUDA LITANI
ELAINE FLETCHER
and Jerusalem Post Staff

In a landmark speech, King Hussein said yesterday he was cutting legal and administrative ties with the West Bank to clear the way for the PLO to "secede" from Jordan and set up an independent Palestinian state.

The king failed to say whether he would cease Jordanian payments to 20,000 West Bank civil servants, eliminate all West Bank participation in the Jordanian government, or revoke West Bankers' Jordanian passports – leaving intense speculation over the meaning of his latest moves.

But Israeli officials and many West Bank Palestinians said it seemed that the policy changes – which had already resulted in the dissolution of parliament – could be more significant than what they previously assumed.

"We have underestimated Hussein's intentions in the last few days. It seems he's really serious, and he means business," said a top government official. "The unity of the two banks is dead," observed a prominent Palestinian newspaper editor, while a leading pro-Jordanian said, "We are stateless."

Hussein appeared to be waiting to work out the details of his new West Bank policy with PLO chief Yasser Arafat who is expected to visit Amman this week, added Dr. Matti Steinberg, a senior lecturer at the Hebrew University.

The monarch's speech opens the door for a new dialogue among Jordan, Arafat and even more radical PLO elements, other analysts said. But it also challenges the PLO to fill the vacuum that could be left by Jordan's political and economic retreat from the territories.

In his 30-minute televised speech, Hussein said the era of East and West Bank unity had come to an end. He appeared before the cameras in front of a giant portrait of his grandfather, King Abdallah, who united the East and West banks in 1950.

"We had never imagined that the preservation of the legal and administrative links between the two banks could constitute an obstacle to the liberation of the occupied Palestinian land," the king said in the address.

But, he added, "we respect the wish of the Palestine Liberation Organization, the sole legitimate representative of the Palestinian people, to secede from us in an independent Palestinian state."

He said Jordan's institutional ties with the West Bank were perceived as contrary to a "general Palestinian and Arab orientation towards stressing the Palestinian identity.

"...since there is a general conviction that the struggle for occupied land could be enhanced by dismantling legal and administrative links we have to fulfill our duty."

Jordan last week halted its $1.3 billion development plan for the West Bank and dissolved the lower house of parliament, in which West

(Continued on Back Page)

The "West Bank" – those parts of central Mandatory Palestine not held by the Israel Defence Forces at the end of the fighting in the 1948 War of Independence – were annexed to the Hashemite Kingdom of Transjordan by King Abdallah (King Hussein's grandfather) following the December 1, 1948 Jericho Congress of Palestinian Arabs.

That congress, which was attended by 2,000 local Palestinian dignitaries, unanimouslty asked Abdallah to unite Transjordan with Arab Palestine in a single monarchy to be headed by him.

On April 11, 1949, elections to a chamber of deputies were held throughout the two parts of the kingdom. Over half of the electorate of 300,000 were from the West Bank, and half of the members of the parliament subsequently came from that part of the united kingdom.

The other Arab countries which had participated in the war against Israel – Egypt and Syria and the rump "Palestine government in Gaza" – as well as the Arab League, all rejected that annexation of Arab Palestine.

Shultz: The king is still a partner for peace talks

By WOLF BLITZER
Jerusalem Post Correspondent

WASHINGTON – Secretary of State George Shultz said yesterday that Jordan's King Hussein must remain a partner in peace negotiations with Israel.

"He has to be a partner, and everybody recognizes that, because Jordan has the longest border with Israel of any Arab state," Shultz said. "So if there is going to be peace between Israel and its neighbours, then Jordan is involved."

Interviewed on the CBS News' *Face the Nation,* Shultz suggested that Hussein's most recent statements were designed to register "the fact that the Palestinians living on the West Bank and Gaza have asserted themselves as wanting to speak for themselves."

But how all of this will play itself out in the end, Shultz added, "remains to be seen."

He rejected the notion that Hussein's actions were designed to force Israel to deal with the PLO. "I think the PLO, if it wants to be a partner in the peace process, has to change its ways," Shultz said.

The secretary sharply denied that there has been any change in the long- standing U.S. position toward the PLO. He rejected a suggestion by Egyptian President Hosni Mubarak last week that the U.S. was now prepared to meet with low-level PLO members.

Shultz said the U.S. remains prepared to meet only with "credible" Palestinians who are not members of the PLO..

"It is also true that we need to keep the pressure on the PLO to recognize that Israel is there, [that] Israel is going to stay there," he said. "It's a fact of life and they might as well accept that fact. They ought to stop the terrorism and recognize that [UN Resolutions] 242 and 338 are the roads to peace."

Shultz said that as long the PLO continues its long-standing approach, which "basically calls for the elimination of Israel as a state and uses terrorist tactics, they are not a suitable peace partner."

It was announced in Washington that Undersecretary of State Richard Murphy is due to arrive in Amman towards the end of the week. He is expected to warn King Hussein that his recent steps, cutting out Jordanian involvement in the West Bank, were potentially dangerous to his own position.

Move takes Israeli officials by surprise

By MENACHEM SHALEV
Post Diplomatic Correspondent

The country's leaders stuck to their political guns in reacting to King Hussein's speech last night, but officials confessed their surprise at the king's apparent resoluteness in carrying out his threats to separate Jordan from the West Bank.

Prime Minister Shamir said that "Hussein has shattered the illusion that he is a partner in territorial compromise," while Foreign Minister Peres maintained that the king's statement was "more declarative than practical."

Government analysts, however, said that the king's statement was more sweeping than they had expected. Although it remains to be seen what practical form will be given to Hussein's intention to sever "legal and administrative links" with the West Bank, Hussein appears to be fulfilling their "worst-case scenario."

Shamir said that Hussein had given up his aim of achieving an Israeli withdrawal to the 1967 borders – "and there is no reason to be sorry about this." He said that there is no reason to change Israel's policies, and that peace with Jordan should still be sought "since Jordan has the longest border with Israel."

"As to the Arabs of Eretz Yisrael," Shamir continued, "the importance of the Camp David autonomy agreements is only strengthened" in the wake of Hussein's speech.

Peres said that Hussein is challenging the Palestinians to "get along by themselves." He added that the speech is a "result of the diplomatic freeze," which can only be resolved by a decision in Israel. "You can't carry out policy on the basis of what others say," he said.

But the foreign minister also appeared to be taking up Hussein's challenge by saying : "We are ready to negotiate with Jordan on peace with Jordan, ready to negotiate with the Palestinians on the solution to the Palestinian problem, ready to negotiate with both on the border of peace with Jordan and on the solution to the problem."

A Foreign Ministry official said that after Hussein's speech "the November elections will mean that the Israeli people have to decide whether they prefer to speak to Jordan – and vote Labour – or to the PLO –

(Continued on Back Page)

Pro-Jordanians in areas meet amid confusion

Jerusalem Post Reporter

Palestinian supporters of Jordan in the West Bank held intensive consultations last night amid confusion over the scope of the measures contemplated in Amman.

Few were willing to comment publicly on King Hussein's speech, though private assessments ranged from gloomy predictions of an end to Jordan's ties with the West Bank, to confident declarations that little would change on the ground.

Some pro-Jordanians seemed genuinely shaken and suprised by the king's move, and spoke of imminent isolation from the Hashemite monarchy, and possible legal and administrative changes which could have a decisive effect on Palestinian daily life in the territories.

Others, however, seemed less alarmed. "It's not a bad speech," said Amin Majaj , a Jordanian member of parliament from Jerusalem. "I don't think the situation is serious, I'm an optimist. The economic and social connections between the East and West Bank are such that they can't be severed. I don't believe it will happen."

Musa Abu Ghosh, a member of parliament from Ramallah, said prior to the king's address that a severance of ties between the two banks of the Jordan would be "a catastrophe and a new burden on the people's shoulders." He expressed confidence that despite the Jordanian moves, forthcoming talks between Hussein and PLO chief Yasser Arafat would produce "a solution to the benefit of the people."

Immediate reactions in the Gaza Strip were mixed last night. Some residents seemed to welcome the king's disclaimer. Khaidar Abdel Shafi, a left-wing former member of the PLO's Executive Committee, told *The Jerusalem Post* that recognition of the PLO as the sole legitimate representative of the Palestinian people, and an admission that the Palestinian issue stands " by itself" and is not affected by any considerations pertaining to any Arab country "is in line with the Palestinian demands."

But Rashad a-Shaawa, long considered a "Jordanian consul" in the Strip, said it was too early to assess the significance of the speech. Several weeks must pass before one can come to conclusions, he said. Only then will it become clear what concrete steps the king has in mind.

Shaawa, who has issued travel documents enabling Gazans to visit Jordan, said he did not believe that that practice would stop.

Rival Russian churches take step to harmony

By HAIM SHAPIRO
Jerusalem Post Reporter

The visit of Metropolitan Filaret, a senior official of the Russian Orthodox Church and overseer of its foreign relations, took a historic turn last week when the churchman took the unprecedented step of calling on White Russian clergy in Jerusalem.

The two churches, one based in Moscow and the other in New York, both regard themselves as the legitimate heir of the Russian church. But the White Russians, in the U.S., claimed that the Moscow-based church was a puppet of the Soviet regime, while the Red Russians considered the American church a breakaway.

Before 1967, Israel had recognized the legitimacy of the Moscow church, while Jordan had recognized the White Russian hierarchy.

During his visit, Filaret, who left the country last night, paid an official call at the White Russian convent in Gethsemane, where he discussed the policies of glasnost and perestroika with the White Russians.

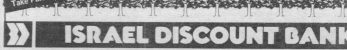

Crisis in battle against syndicate

Italy's top anti-Mafia investigator asks to quit

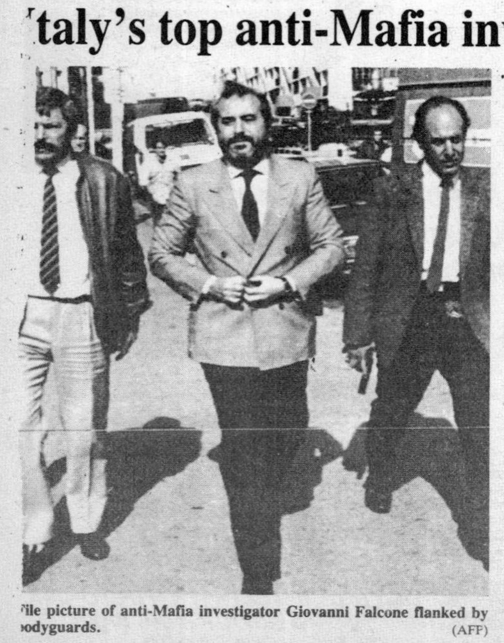

File picture of anti-Mafia investigator Giovanni Falcone flanked by bodyguards. (AFP)

ROME (Reuter) – Italy's best-known anti-Mafia investigator has asked to quit, citing obstruction and discord with his superior, in a crisis over the conduct of the fight against the crime syndicate.

Giovanni Falcone, architect of an unprecedented mass Mafia trial last year and the most experienced member of a pool of anti-Mafia magistrates in the Sicilian capital Palermo, said in a letter he wanted an immediate transfer to other duties.

His move heightens a crisis which broke 10 days ago with charges by a senior magistrate, backed by Falcone, that incompetence and misguided policies were crippling operations.

Falcone's letter was released on Saturday as the Supreme Council of Magistrates, the judiciary's governing body, met on the orders of President Francesco Cossiga to investigate the allegations. The charges were levelled in a newspaper interview by Paolo Borsellino, a former member of the pool and now public prosecutor in the Sicilian town of Marsala.

Borsellino alleged Falcone had been taken off Mafia cases, that senior officials were trying to dismantle the pool and that police had lost track of Mafia operations since the mass trial ended in December with nearly 340 convictions. "We risk creating a dangerous vacuum, we are going backwards, like 10, 20 years ago," Borsellino said.

Falcone said he had radical differences with Palermo's chief investigating magistrate, Antonino Meli, who had put himself in charge of all Mafia inquiries in Palermo.

Meli, a former appeal court judge, was made head of all Palermo's investigating magistrates last January in a straight race against Falcone on the grounds of seniority rather than experience in Mafia crime-busting.

He has dimissed Borsellino's allegations as unfounded but has said pool magistrates must spend time on other crimes.

The pool was set up five years ago after one of Meli's predecessors, Rocco Chinnici, was blown up by a car bomb. Falcone has been with the pool throughout. He struck the mafia its biggest blow by "confessing" Tommaso Buscetta, the first big boss to break the Mafia's code of "omerta" or silence on a large scale.

Buscetta's evidence was instrumental in the mass Mafia trial, which has been followed by a fresh battle for supremacy among rival clans in and around Palermo. Victims of mafia killers since the verdict include a former mayor, an undercover policeman, and six defendants released from jail after the trial.

THE JERUSALEM POST

Vol. LVI, No. 16910 Sunday, August 21, 1988 • Elul 8, 5748 • Moharram 10, 1408 NIS 1.20 (Eilat NIS 1.05)

FIRST EDITION

First violation of ceasefire

Shooting stops in Gulf War

NICOSIA (Reuter) – Iran and Iraq yesterday implemented a UN ceasefire, silencing the guns along their 1200-km war front after almost eight years of fighting that killed up to a million people.

But within hours there were reports of ceasefire violations, as Iraq accused Iran of killing one of its soldiers and harassing a ship in the Gulf yesterday.

The Iraqi news agency INA said the soldier was shot by a sniper at Saif Saad on the central war front more than three hours after yesterday's ceasefire deadline.

Iran sent boatloads of troops onto the Shatt al-Arab waterway, scene of some of the bitterest fighting in its war with Iraq, in a show of strength shortly after the ceasefire went into effect.

Teheran Radio reported calm on both banks of the disputed border waterway when its troops set out in boats flying the green-white-and-red Iranian flag, watched by unarmed UN military observers.

A 350-man force of blue-helmeted UN officers from 24 countries took up positions along the border to monitor the ceasefire.

Iran, which stalled for a year in accepting the UN ceasefire resolution, hailed the event but cautioned it did not mean a final end to the war.

In the Iraqi capital Baghdad, motorists sped through the streets honking horns, spraying water and banging tambourines.

In each province of Iraq, a 101-gun salute boomed out calling the Moslem faithful to dawn prayers.

Radio Baghdad announced at 7 a.m. that the ceasefire had gone into effect then played patriotic songs.

Before the cessation of hostilities, Iraq pledged to abide by the ceasefire but warned Iran it would not drop its defences.

But Iranian leaders said work still had to be done to achieve peace and hinted at hard bargaining when they meet the Iraqis at the conference table in Geneva on Thursday.

"There should be no violation on the fronts and, God forbid, not one unauthorized bullet should be fired," Iran's military chief, Ali Akbar Hashemi Rafsanjani, told Teheran Radio, monitored in Nicosia.

"We will abide by the ceasefire completely and there will be no shooting," President Ali Khamenei told troops on the southern front.

He said Iran would cooperate sincerely with the observers in the field and with UN Secretary-General Javier Perez de Cuellar in implementing Security Council resolution 598.

In a series of actions and announcements, Teheran made clear that it intended to press ahead as quickly as possible with the immense job of rebuilding the Iranian economy.

Teheran Radio quoted an official as saying that Kharg Terminal in the northern Gulf, Iran's main oil export outlet battered by scores of Iraqi air raids, resumed normal operations yesterday.

The official also said Iran Air flights to Europe reverted to their old route over Turkey, abandoned for years because it was too close to the dangerous skies near the war front.

Oil Minister Gholamreza Aqazadeh said the ceasefire improved prospects for unity in the Organization of Petroleum Exporting Countries (Opec), rent by the Iran-Iraq conflict.

(Continued on Back Page)

Inmates charge:

'Ketziot prisoner deliberately shot by senior IDF officer'

By JOEL GREENBERG
Jerusalem Post Reporter

A Palestinian prisoner killed during a riot at the Ketziot detention camp last week was deliberately shot at close range by a top officer of the facility, and his evacuation was delayed, according to inmates who spoke to visitors at the camp over the weekend.

Troops opened fire with live ammunition after they ran out of teargas and their rubber-bullet canisters jammed, officers told the visitors.

The IDF Southern Command spokesman declined to comment last night on details of the accounts. He said that an officer appointed by OC Southern Command Yitzhak Mordechai was investigating the incident "in detail, from every angle," and that the results of his inquiry would be submitted to Mordechai early this week.

After making an initial inquiry at Ketziot last week, Mordechai said that the troops had acted properly. Two prisoners were killed and at least one wounded during the August 16 riot at Ketziot. Located in the Negev near the Egyptian border, the camp holds at least 2,500 administrative detainees.

Inmates at the camp's "A" compound began an open-ended hunger strike on Wednesday last week, and detainees in compound "B," where the killing took place, were on a hunger strike until Thursday last week, prisoners reported.

Following is a composite account of events at Ketziot, as reported to independent interviewers by three sources: prisoners held near the section where the shooting took place, who learned of the events from their fellow inmates; a released prisoner from the Hebron area who witnessed the riot; soldiers at Ketziot:

On the morning of August 16, several detainees who were taken from section B-3 to clean soldiers' quarters refused to carry out the work, saying the Geneva Convention forbids labour by administrative detainees. As punishment, all

(Continued on Back Page)

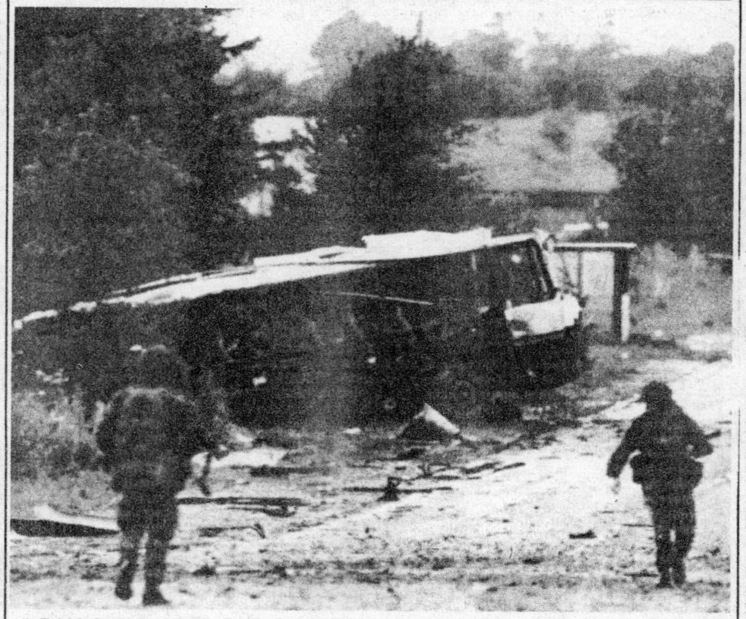

A British foot patrol passes by the wreckage of the bus early yesterday morning. (AFP)

Eight British soldiers die when IRA landmine rips through bus

OMAGH (Reuter) – Eight British soldiers were killed and 27 wounded yesterday in the bloodiest attack on British forces in Northern Ireland for nearly a decade. The IRA in a statement to Irish news media claiming responsibility for the explosion vowed: "We will not lay down our arms until the peace of a British disengagement from Ireland is granted to our nation."

A police spokesman said the soldiers died just after midnight when a huge landmine wrecked an unmarked bus carrying 39 of them back to their barracks in Omagh, County Tyrone, after leave in England. The explosion left a 2-metre-deep crater in the roadway.

"The bus was a mess of mangled wreckage. It was a miracle anyone got out alive," said Paddy Bogan, president of Northern Ireland's Alliance Party, who lives near the scene of the blast.

"Mutilated bodies were strewn over a radius of 50 to 100 yards. I saw seven bodies. The faces of the wounded were terribly cut and injured," he said.

Rescue work was hindered by fears that another booby-trap bomb may have been left in the area – a ploy frequently used by the IRA.

The blast, likely detonated by remote control, raised serious security questions for Britain. The soldiers had been carried in an unmarked bus late at night to reduce any danger of identification as a target.

A government spokesman said Prime Minister Margaret Thatcher, who has forged links with Dublin to combat cross-border guerrilla activity, was "deeply shocked and distressed" by the attack.

British minister for Northern Ireland Tom King acknowledged after recent talks with Dublin officials that the province faced a crucial time as the IRA stepped up its guerrilla campaign.

Attempts to develop a form of power-sharing government involving both Protestants and minority Catholics in governing the province have met with little success. At the same time, resistance by paramilitary groups has grown.

Two other bombs exploded early Friday. One injured three police officers in Lisnaskea and the other damaged the Mourne Country Hotel in Newry, Northern Ireland's newest luxury hotel.

An IRA message to a Belfast radio station said the hotel, near the border with the Irish Republic, is "a meeting place for members of the security forces and informers." The IRA claimed responsibility for that bombing and the one in Lisnaskea, west of Belfast.

Also on Friday, funerals were held for a British soldier whom IRA guerrillas killed last week in Belgium, and for a Protestant grocer shot to death in his Belfast store.

Two other bombs exploded early Friday. One injured three police officers in Lisnaskea and the other damaged the Mourne Country Hotel in Newry, Northern Ireland's newest luxury hotel.

Also on Friday, funerals were held for a British soldier whom IRA guerrillas killed last week in Belgium, and for a Protestant grocer shot to death Wednesday in his Belfast store.

Eight-year-old loses both legs

25 hurt in blast on crowded Haifa mall

By YA'ACOV FRIEDLER
Jerusalem Post Reporter

HAIFA – An eight year-old boy lost both his legs, when a small bomb exploded in the crowded Nordau Street pedestrian mall here at about 9 p.m. last night, injuring 25 people. Jonathan Meir lost both his legs, his 18-month-old brother was seriously wounded, and five other members of the same family were among those injured.

The explosion sparked fears amongst civic leaders that it would harm the good relations between Jews and Arabs in this mixed city which had so far not been disturbed by any locally-perpetrated terror acts.

The police immediately carried out arrests in the mall, taking in "several dozen" Arabs for questioning, most of them from out of town. Three of the arrested men were reportedly seen running away from the scene of the explosion, police spokeswoman pakad Ahuva Tomer told *The Jerusalem Post*. "Every possible motive" including criminal intent were being investigated. It appeared most likley that the bomb was a terror outrage, she said.

The bomb had been placed at the base of a tree outside the Eretz Pla'im toy shop at 11 Nordau. The Kapulsky Cafe next door was crowded inside and out, as was the entire mall by the usual Saturday night strollers.

The toy shop window was smashed, and tables and chairs outside the cafe were also damaged. The pavement was stained with pools of blood and littered with blood-soaked serviettes which had been used by the injured. *The Jerusalem Post* office is situated close by, on the other side of the road.

Police cleared the area and cordoned it off. The wounded were evacuated to the Rothschild and Rambam hospitals, while some of the lightly hurt went on their own for treatment. There were no reports of any anti-Arab outbreaks.

Mayor Arye Gurel, who is in Duesseldorf, West Germany, Haifa's twin city, was informed of the incident by phone. He called on residents to remain calm and keep the peace. Nothing should be done to harm Jewish-Arab relations in the city, which had been so carefully nurtured, he said.

MK Amnon Linn of Haifa, an expert on Arab affairs, told *The Post* at the scene of the explosion that as serious as it was, he hoped no Haifa Arabs were involved because that would be a very grave change in the situation.

There have been several cases of arson in the mall since it was opened over a year ago, but which were proven to have been committed by criminal elements, motivated by commercial competition between shops. The bombed shop moved into the premises from across the road only a few weeks ago.

By press time, police were still searching courtyards and concealed places for possible further explosives.

PFLP: Target was Moshav Avivim

IDF kills terrorists near Lebanon border

By KENNETH KAPLAN

Three Palestinian terrorists were killed late Friday night when they were intercepted by an IDF patrol just north of the Lebanese border in the central district of the security zone. There were no Israeli casualties in the clash.

Military sources said the three, armed with rifles, explosives and grenades, were "apparently on their way to carry out an attack inside Israeli territory."

In two other unrelated incidents in southern Lebanon, three Israeli soldiers were lightly wounded Friday afternoon in an explosion near Marjayoun, and a terrorist was killed yesterday in an attack on a South Lebanese Army outpost.

In Sidon, George Habash's Popular Front for the Liberation of Palestine claimed responsibility for Friday night's infiltration attempt, but said the three had carried out a raid on Moshav Avivim.

A PFLP statement said the terrorist squad "killed or wounded several Zionist enemy soldiers" in a four-hour battle "before they were martyred on the land of Palestine."

Military sources said the claim was "nonsense."

The incident occurred at about midnight on Friday night when an IDF patrol spotted the three moving south of the Lebanese village of Maroun a-Ras, some two kilometres north of Avivim.

The troops opened fire, killing the three. There were no Israeli casualties in the exchange.

On Friday, three IDF soldiers were lightly wounded by shrapnel when a car exploded some 40 metres from their jeep. The driver of the car and a passenger were killed in the blast.

Military sources said last night it was still not clear whether the incident was a suicide car-bomb attack or whether the Lebanese car had hit a mine.

The three soldiers were given first aid in Kiryat Shmona before being taken to hospital in Haifa.

In Beirut, an anonymous caller phoned a news agency and said the attack was carried out by the Shi'ite Islamic Resistance group.

IDF only interested in central figures in strike squads

No mass arrests of 'popular committees'

By YEHUDA LITANI
and JOSHUA BRILLIANT
Jerusalem Post Reporters

Despite the outlawing of the "popular committees" of the intifada last week by the Ministry of Defence, the IDF and police will arrest only central figures in the "strike forces" of the intifada who are linked to the PLO, reliable security sources disclosed last night.

The sources added that "there will not be mass arrests, we do not intend to arrest popular committee members whose only activity is community service like aid to needy families or blood donations."

The security source denied reports about the expected deportation of another 15 Palestinian activists – 25 were deported last week – but he said, "We will no doubt continue the deportation policy as we have during the last nine months of the intifada."

The security source added that "the new steps, the outlawing of the committees and the expulsions, will slow the intifada but will not stop it completely. It is too late to stop it now, despite the political echelon's wish. The intifada will continue whether we want it or not."

In incidents reported on the weekend, two Gaza Strip residents were shot and wounded and at least 20 people, including an 85-year-old woman, were reportedly treated for injuries sustained by beatings and tear gas as residents clashed with soldiers throughout the Strip.

The curfew that had been imposed on all the Gaza Strip on Sunday night was lifted from the cities and a few refugee camps on Wednesday and this morning only the curfew on the refugee camp of Nusseirat was in effect.

The two Palestinians shot were identified as Ramadan al-Sueer, 67, injured during a violent demonstration in Gaza City, and Mohammed Mussa Hamdan, 18, from Rafah.

Amna Mansour, 85, of the Sajahiya neighbourhood in Gaza reportedly sustained fractures in both legs and was taken to Shifa Hospital.

The deepest impact was created by thousands of Gazans chanting "Allah Akbar" from midnight to 4 a.m. throughout town, chants that were also broadcast over mosque loudspeakers. "It was the first time anything like this happened here," a resident said.

Joel Greenberg adds:

A Palestinian wounded in a clash with troops last week died in an Israeli hospital, and several others were wounded over the weekend in violent confrontations in the West Bank.

Sa'ud Abdallah, 22, died after being shot in the stomach during a clash Thursday at the village of Tamun, near Jenin.

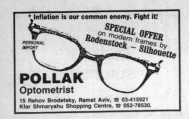

THE JERUSALEM POST

Vol. LVI, No. 16934 Tuesday, September 20, 1988 • Tishrei 9, 5749 • Safar 9, 1409 NIS 1.20 (Eilat NIS 1.05)

FIRST EDITION

Mass polio vaccination in Hadera

By LEA LEVAVI
Jerusalem Post Reporter

TEL AVIV – Residents of Hadera and the surrounding areas, who are 35 years old and younger will be vaccinated against polio, after the polio virus was found in sewage in the area, Health Minister Shoshana Arbeli-Almoslino announced at a press conference here last night.

The press conference was held the day after the sixth and seventh cases of polio were confirmed. Most of the victims have mild or relatively mild cases, but the first two victims remain in very serious condition. She said the vaccination campaign will begin this morning when 1,000 babies who have not yet been vaccinated will be summoned to receive the Salk vaccine.

On Thursday, 50,000 schoolchildren will receive the oral Sabin vaccine. If necessary, the schools will be kept open later or the vaccinations will continue on Friday.

Starting on Sunday approximately 70,000 adults and preschool children will receive the Sabin vaccine. Most of the vaccinations will be done at schools but pregnant women will receive the Salk vaccine at family health clinics.

Arbeli-Almoslino said samples of sewage and water from all over the country are now being examined and additional steps will be taken if necessary.

She stressed, however, that the current vaccination campaign is largely preventive because over 97 per cent of the population has either natural or acquired immunity to the virus. The difficulty in finding those that are not immune, prompted the health authorities to vaccinate everyone.

She said that the campaign will cost $110,000 and that vaccinating the entire population, which she hopes will not be necessary, would cost over $1,500,000.

150 reported dead

Burmese troops fire on protesters

RANGOON (AP) – Army troops under orders to halt all demonstrations fired on crowds of defiant students, Buddhist monks and other protesters yesterday in downtown Rangoon, one day after a military coup overthrew President Maung Maung.

The troops also stopped crowds armed with spears and other primitive weapons from entering the city from outlying areas to reinforce the demonstrators, diplomats and eyewitnesses said.

Unofficial estimates put the number of dead in Rangoon since the violence erupted on Sunday night at about 150, including 17 soldiers, with an unknown number of wounded.

The military said soldiers fired on "violent and unruly mobs" in the capital and elsewhere yesterday, killing 23 people and wounding 23. It said its figures were incomplete.

The suppression was triggered by troops enforcing decrees announced on Sunday night after Defence Minister Gen. Saw Maung and 18 other senior military officers seized power. The ousted civilian leader Maung Maung had promised multiparty elections to end 26 years of military-dominated, one-party rule in Burma. Saw Maung promised multi-party elections but did not set a time.

Three key opposition leaders, reacting to the killings by troops, vowed to "continue our struggle for democracy by various means until the goal is achieved." The statement was issued by former military officers Aung Gyi and Tin Oo and Aung San Suu Kyi, the daughter of deceased national hero Aung San. Former prime minster Nu, another opposition figure, deplored the killing of peaceful demonstrators yesterday in Rangoon.

Israeli satellite soars into space

By JUDY MALTZ
Jerusalem Post Reporter

Israel yesterday entered the space age, with the successful launching of its first satellite, the Offeq-I.

The country becomes the eighth space power in the world and the first in the Middle East, with the capacity to independently gather intelligence on its Arab neighbours.

The dramatic lift-off of what was described as an "experimental" satellite took place at 11:33 yesterday morning and was observed by scores of bathers on Palmahim beach south of Rishon Lezion, along with hordes of reporters and photographers, who had been awaiting the launch for 48 hours. The launch was delayed for fifteen minutes to avoid detection by a satellite passing above, according to Prof. Dror Sadeh of the Israel Space Agency (ISA). The most enthusiastic spectators at the launching site were its promoter, ISA, and its main contractor, Israel Aircraft Industries (IAI).

Foreign press reports in recent weeks had said that Israel was soon to launch a military spy satellite, but officials at IAI denied that the Offeq-I would serve this purpose.

The Offeq – "horizon" – was placed in orbit by a Shavit satellite launcher, which Sadeh described as "far more complex" than an ordinary missile. According to foreign sources, the Shavit is based on the Jericho-III solid-fuel rocket, developed by Rafael, the Weapons Development Authority.

"This is an extraordinary technological success," Moshe Keret, IAI's managing director, told Army Radio. "I think this is a great day for all of us."

The declared purpose of the launch, according to IAI, is "to demonstrate a capability to orbit a satellite and to check the functional ability of its subsystems in a space environment." This, the company said, entailed collecting data on space environment conditions and the earth's magnetic field, generating solar power, and testing the quality of transmission from space and its ability to withstand vacuum and wightless conditions.

Observers at home and abroad, however, believe this test launch will pave the way for Israel to send its own military spy satellite into space. Until now, the country has relied on the U.S. for satellite information on other countries, but some Israeli officials have charged that the U.S. has not always been reliable.

An analyst attached to *Jane's Defence Weekly*, the London-based defence magazine, maintained yesterday that the Israeli satellite was believed to be carrying a 3-kilogram payload for surveillance purposes, using U.S. optical equipment, apparently for monitoring activity in Arab countries.

Last month, IAI signed an agreement with the French space firm Arianne to launch a communications satellite, the Amos, into orbit in 1993. The Amos, which is much bigger than the Offeq, must be put into a higher orbit, and has the specific function of communications, according to Dr. Gerald Steinberg, a senior lecturer at Bar-Ilan University and an expert on space technology.

Minister of Science and Technology Gideon Patt said yesterday that the Offeq is the only satellite in the world to be launched westwards. The reason is to avoid heavily-populated areas, in case of failure.

(Continued on Back Page)

Washington: We didn't contribute to launch

By WOLF BLITZER
Jerusalem Post Correspondent

WASHINGTON – The U.S. yesterday dissociated itself from Israel's launching of a satellite in space.

"We were not in any way involved nor did we assist in this launch," the State Department said.

Spokesman Charles Redman, asked to react to the dramatic development, insisted that the U.S. did not have "any details on the launch beyond what has already been reported by the Israelis."

But in an obvious effort to reassure the Arabs about Israel's intentions, he pointedly added: "I would only note that Israel's leaders have stressed that the goal of the satellite launch is for peaceful purposes of space research and technological advancement."

Underlining the potential sensitivity of the subject, Redman refused to say whether the U.S. was seeking to obtain further details of the satellite from Israel.

U.S. officials yesterday predicted that the Arab states would now intensify their own efforts to launch satellites to spy on Israel.

In recent years, according to newspaper reports here, the U.S. has on a limited basis shared with Israel some of its own satellite reconnaissance photography but not on a "live-time" basis.

Israeli officials often complained, but to no avail. This apparently resulted in Israel's decision to go ahead with its own satellite programme.

Bob Woodward of *The Washington Post* wrote in his book on the late CIA Director William Casey, *Veil*, that after Israel's 1981 bombing of the Iraqi nuclear reactor, the U.S. withdrew much of its satellite photography cooperation with Israel.

"Israeli access would be restricted to photos of those countries that posed an immediate threat or are on Israel's border," Woodward said.

But Israel was not authorized to receive "real-time transmissions from the advanced KH-11 satellite, nor was any block of time allocated to Israel on the U.S. satellites as had been requested," Woodward added.

An independent reconnaissance capability by Israel would of course reduce Israel's dependence on the U.S. for this kind of information.

As a result, the Americans were not exactly pleased by this latest development. With the U.S. sharing its photography with Israel, it could also effectively control the kind of intelligence Israel was receiving.

U.S. analysts said that Israel was probably motivated to accelerate its satellite capability by the proliferation of ballistic missiles in Syria, Iraq and elsewhere in the region. In advance of the development of the Arrow anti-tactical ballistic missile, Israel would have to undertake a pre-emptive strike to deal with the problem most effectively. But that, according to authoritative sources here, required a much greater satellite intelligence capability than was available to Israel. Israel's own satellites, if successful, should help.

The shot heard round the beach

By MICHAEL ROTEM
For The Jerusalem Post

Bathers on a beach south of Tel Aviv, more accustomed to such hazards as jellyfish and broken glass, got the shock of their lives yesterday as Offeq-I roared out from behind a sand dune close to where they had spread their towels, and out into space.

"At first we thought it would fall into the sea, but then it disapeared among the clouds," said the surprised bathers, who by chance witnessed the historic launch of Israel's first satellite just before noon from a spot next to the beach.

A deafening roar accompanied by a cloud of smoke and spewing flames heralded the coming of age of Israel's space programme. Offeq-I climbed westward in a curve. It's first stage fell, as the second stage ignited and disappeared into the blue yonder leaving only the distant dying roar and the spontaneous applause of journalists.

And on the beach, bathers lolled under the late-morning sun, oblivious to the fact that they would soon witness the shot that launched Israel into the space age.

Offeq-I orbits in opposite direction from all other satellites

'It's our calling card to the space age'

By JUDY SIEGEL
Post Science and Health Reporter

"Offeq-I is our calling card to the space age. Instead of our children and grandchildren sitting by and watching what other countries do in space, Israel will be part of the technological future," said a jubilant Prof. Yuval Ne'eman, chairman of the Israel Space Agency.

In an interview with *The Jerusalem Post*, Ne'eman said the successful launching of the 150 kilo experimental satellite, boosted into space by some 20 tons of rockets in two stages, will add great international prestige to Israel's standing in scientific and technological fields. "It was a project in which millions of different parts all had to work tip-top, and they did. A number of Europe's Arianne satellites had to be blown up because of faults in them."

The Arab countries have purchased technology from other countries, including China and the Soviet Union but "it will be many years" before they get to the level that Israel has reached with Offeq-I, said Ne'eman.

Commenting on the pre-launch "leak" that put the story in *Time* magazine and Britain's *Flight* magazine, he said that he favoured putting the informants behind bars, "although that is up to the government."

The space agency linked up with the Israel Aircraft Industries (IAI), which hired a number of subcontractors.

Such a level of planning, building and launching have been accomplished so far only by the Soviet Union (which was first in 1957 with the Sputnik), followed by the U.S. (in 1961), Canada, France, Japan and Britain, with Brazil and India about to join the elite group.

Ne'eman said that Offeq-I is strictly a civilian project and has nothing to do with surveillance. It will last for a bit less than a month, burning up after Israeli scientists glean all the information they need from the satellite. This includes data on how it uses energy from its solar collectors and how it withstands the vacuum and low temperatures of space. It is revolving around the earth every 90 minutes, able to see a swath of the planet from 36 degrees south to 36 degrees north, "including the Olympic Games in Seoul."

Offeq-I revolves in the opposite direction of every other satellite in the world, going east to west. Its orbit ranges in height from some 250

(Continued on Back Page)

Swedish satellite reveals Saudi missiles

STOCKHOLM (Reuter) – Swedish space researchers released satellite pictures yesterday which they said showed secret Saudi Arabian installations of Chinese-made ballistic missiles capable of reaching most targets in the Middle East.

They said the pictures of the base area around the Sulayyil oasis some 475km. south-west of Riyadh show deployment sites, assembly and storage buildings, training sites, barracks and bunkers.

"The operational area probably contains between eight and 12 launchers served by two or three army battalions," said Christer Larsson, arms expert with Stockholm-based Space Media Network (SMN), a private firm.

Saudi Arabia confirmed last March it had bought a number of Chinese CSS-2 intermediate-range ballistic missiles with a 3,200km. range, a move which upset both the U.S. and Israel.

Rabin:

Plastic bullets will end riots

By JOEL GREENBERG
and Post Defense Staff

Defense Minister Yitzhak Rabin said yesterday that the IDF's use of plastic bullets in the territories had contributed to the high number of Palestinian casualties during clashes between troops and rioters in recent days.

Some 50 Palestinians have been wounded and two killed in the territories since Saturday, when the West Bank erupted in violence on the anniversary of the 1982 Sabra and Shatilla massacres.

According to military sources, soldiers are permitted to fire plastic bullets freely at stone-throwers, even in situations which are not life-threatening. Plastic bullets are considered non-lethal at ranges of above 70 metres.

Rabin has changed orders on firing plastic bullets, cancelling an earlier restriction which limited use of the bullets to specially trained officers. Now most soldiers in the territories may carry plastic bullets, after being instructed in their range and effectiveness.

"Whoever wants to disturb the peace will have to understand that the number of injuries will in-

(Continued on Back Page)

Egypt: Attack was trap for drug-runners

Jerusalem Post Reporter
and agencies

Egypt informed Israel yesterday that it had advance information that Turkish drug runners were planning to transfer a large shipment of hashish to boats from the Gaza Strip and had laid a trap for them.

The information was in explanation of the Egyptian coast guard action on Sunday in which one boat was sunk off El-Arish and some Gaza boatmen wounded. The Egyptians say they hauled in five tons of hashish in the action.

Israeli Foreign Ministry sources say they believe the Egyptian explanation and add that this was not the first occasion in which foreign ships, including those under the Turkish flag, have been involved in drug-running in the area.

An Egyptian Foreign Ministry official yesterday said that Egyptian coast guard units had repelled a large vessel and eight small launches 15 kms off El-Arish that had entered its territorial waters off Sinai with large quantities of drugs.

The ministry statement came a day after Israel Radio reported an Egyptian helicopter fired on three fishing boats Sunday, wounding two fishermen from the Israeli-occupied Gaza strip. One of the boats was set ablaze and sunk, and the whereabouts of its crew was unknown, the radio said.

The wounded fishermen, brothers Azzam and Hossem Bachar, were pulled from the water by crewmen in another boat and taken to a hospital in Gaza.

On September 9, the Egyptian navy seized an Israeli fishing boat and a tour boat in the Red Sea for straying into Egyptian waters. The tour boat was released after about five hours, but the fishing boat and its crew remain in detention.

Resolution near in Leumi crisis

By PINHAS LANDAU

The Bank Leumi boardroom crisis seems headed toward resolution after the Council of Otsar Hityashvut Hayehudim demanded in a meeting last night that Leumi's directors "terminate their period in office." In a statement issued after the meeting, the Council made clear its intention to remove any directors not acting on its instructions within two weeks.

But outside director Shimon Shetreet, whose public status puts him beyond OHH's control, toid the Council only that he would "consider" their demand.

Shetreet was one of several directors to appear before the Council at yesterday's meeting. His colleagues Elisha Shahmoon, Mordechai Yonah, Yehoshua Forer and the other outside director, Menahem

(Continued on Page Ten)

OFFEQ – 1
Specifications

Shape	Octagonal
Height	2.3 meters
Lower base diameter	1.2 meters
Upper base diameter	0.7 meters
Weight	156 kg
Solar power supplied	246 watts
Average power consumption	53 watts
Voltage, unregulated	25-42 volts
Communication	S band
Telemetry rate	2.5 kbits/second
On-board memory	128 kbytes

The Space Club

U.S.S.R.	1957
U.S.	1958
Japan	1964
France	1965
China	1970
U.K.	1971
India	1982

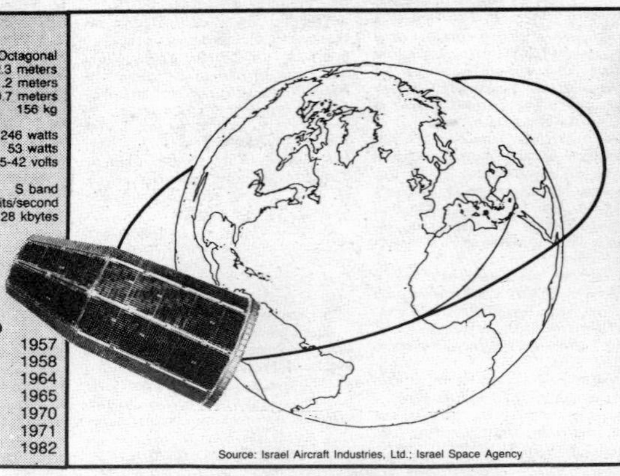

"Offeq-1" was launched westwards over the Mediterranean into a low, eliptical orbit with its perigree (point at which it is closest to earth) at 250 kms over the Middle East and its high point at 1,000 kms. The satellite orbits east to west every 90 minutes repeating the flight path every 7 revolutions of the globe. The satellite rotates on its axis once every second ensuring inertial stability so that the body-mounted solar panels face the sun in order to generate electricity required by its systems. Offeq-1 will have a life-span of about one month and will burn up as it re-enters the atmoshphere.

The launch vehicle was a "Shavit" three-stage rocket. The first stages crashed into the sea.

Source: Israel Aircraft Industries, Ltd.; Israel Space Agency

Graphic: Ruth Kovel

Seoul '88

Arab and Asian countries protested to the Seoul Olympics organizers yesterday over the identification of Jerusalem as Israel's capital during Saturday's opening ceremony.

Sheikh Fahed al-Sabah of Kuwait, president of the Olympic Council of Asia, said he had objected on behalf of the 36-member organization that Israel's capital was named as Jerusalem, in a listing of facts about the country flashed on a screen as the Israeli team walked into the stadium.

In the games themselves, an unheralded Australian Duncan Armstrong flashed past three world record-holders to snatch the gold medal in the Olympic swimming competition's first world record. There was a scare when world champion Greg Louganis cracked his head on the diving board but came up smiling and continued despite taking three stitches in his scalp.

(Full Olympics Coverage pages 10 and 11).

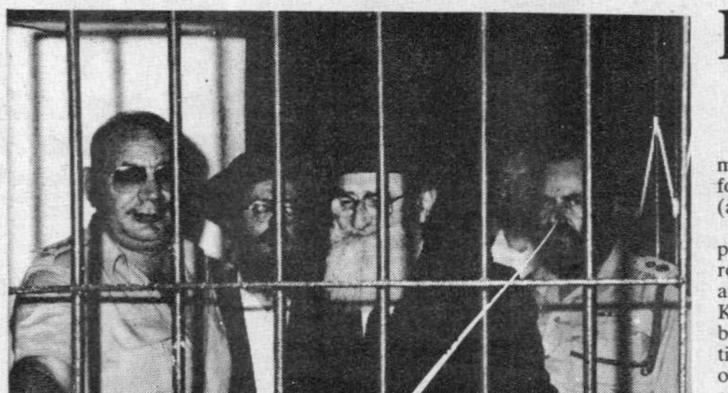

Jerusalem Chief Rabbi Yitzhak Kulitz (centre) visits Maasiyahu Prison to deliver a message of spiritual reawakening to the inmates in preparation for Yom Kippur.

Kapparot: A sacred rite or an embarrassment?

By HAIM SHAPIRO
Jerusalem Post Reporter

For some Jews, it is one of the most sacred rites of the Jewish year, for others, it is an embarrassing or (at best) a tolerated custom.

The practice of *kapparot*, in which penitent Jews swing a live chicken (a rooster for a man, a hen for a woman) around their heads before Yom Kippur – the day of penitence – has been hallowed by centuries of tradition. But some of the greatest rabbis over the ages have condemned it, and some communities, which were the most scrupulous in their observance, did not practice it at all.

For many Sephardim, it is the central aspect of preparation for Yom Kippur.

Naomi, a Jerusalem housewife, who does not light Shabbat candles, nevertheless gets up early on Erev Yom Kippur and takes her three children to the market, where they all perform the rite.

But former Ashkenazi Chief Rabbi Shlomo Goren does not practice *kapparot* at all.

"I'm a vegetarian. What do I have to do with chickens?" he said, but then he added that although he distributes large sums of charity before Yom Kippur, he does not even carry out the ritual, as many do, with money which is later given to charity, substituting for the chicken.

Goren told *The Jerusalem Post* that *kapparot* is a custom which can be traced to the 10th century, when the *gaonim* would sow wheat or barley in special pots before Rosh Hashana and then perform the ritual with the sprouts before Yom Kippur. Later, he said, the custom arose of using animals, such as lambs, which were given to the poor.

Rashi, who reported the custom of growing sprouts, attributed it to the Talmudic period, making it as early as the fifth century.

But Rabbi Yosef Karo, the edditor and compiler of the Shulchan Aruch, which is the normative guide to religious practice for Orthodox Jews, was scornful of the practice.

"It is a foolish custom and it must be eliminated," Karo wrote in the first edition of the Shulhan Aruch, printed in his own lifetime.

"Later, this sentence was censored out by the rabbis who came after him," Goren said.

Rabbi Moshe Isserles, who edited the Shulhan Aruch version for Ashkenazim, described it as a custom which had become sanctified by tradition and could not be changed.

The Gaon of Vilna in the 18th century also considered it very important and wrote at length as to whether a pregnant woman should carry out *kapparot* with three chickens, a hen for herself and another hen and a rooster, to cover the possibility that the child would be a girl or a boy.

Today, among Ashkenazim, it is Hassidim who maintain the practice of using a chicken. According to Rabbi Natan Maimon, leader of the Bratzlav Hassidim of the Har Nof quarter of Jerusalem, the custom is growing in popularity.

"Tens of thousands of Ashkenazim and Sephardim practice it," he said, adding that it is carried out early in the morning on the eve of Yom Kippur, before the *shaharit* prayer. Like a sacrifice, it is a surrogate for the person, who in sinning, deserves death, as one who rebels against a king. Either the chicken or the money is given to charity.

"You can't give a gift to *Hashem*," he said, "but the poor are His representatives."

Among those who condemned the practice altogether were the medieval sages the Ramban (Nachmanides) and the Rashba (Rabbi Moshe Ben-Aderet).

The country will come to a halt tonight as the Jews of Israel join their brethren throughout the world in observing Yom Kippur.

Bus services will end early this afternoon and banks, post offices and shops will also close early to prepare for the fast. No traffic will be allowed to or from the administered territories.

According to the Jerusalem Religious Council, the fast begins at 4:57 tonight and ends at 6:14 tomorrow night. Synagogue services, for the most part, are scheduled to begin at 5:30.

In their Yom Kippur message, the chief rabbis, Avraham Shapiro and Mordechai Eliahu, this year dwelt upon the tragedy of traffic accidents.

Massacre and mayhem in Pakistan
– Page 3

THE JERUSALEM POST
Vol. LVI, No. 16942 Sunday, October 2, 1988 • Tishrei 21, 5749 • Safar 21, 1409 NIS 1.20 (Eilat NIS 1.05)
SECOND EDITION

Police probe death of Hebron man after stoning of Levinger

Jerusalem Post Staff

The military and the police are investigating the death of an Arab merchant who was shot on Friday in Hebron in the uproar that followed a stoning attack on a car carrying Rabbi Moshe Levinger in the centre of town. Another Palestinian was shot and killed on Friday during a clash with an IDF patrol in Hebron.

Four Hebron residents were injured in the disturbances that followed the stoning of Levinger's car, one of whom fell off a roof while running away.

The town is still under curfew, and journalists have been barred from the area. Local merchants yesterday declared three days of mourning, including a commercial strike, for their slain colleague, Kayed Salah, 42, who owned a shoe store.

Thirty people were wounded by gunfire over the weekend in other clashes in the territories with the security forces. A general strike of trade and transportation has been called for today in the latest leaflet issued by the Unified Leadership of the Uprising.

The strike was called to protest against the closing of West Bank schools and universities until November 15, a step announced Friday by the civil administration. A senior defence source said that the schools would be kept closed to try to prevent an expected upsurge in violence by student activists.

The IDF on Friday extended the closure of the Palestine Press Service for an additional year, the Defence Ministry said. The service, run by Raymonda Tawil and Ibrahim Kara'in and closed in March for allegedly inciting violence, monitored events in the occupied territories and was a key source for foreign reporters.

The disturbances in Hebron began on Friday when a car carrying Levinger, his two sons, a daughter and grand-daughter was attacked. His son Menashe, who was behind the wheel, said that as they were driving to Jerusalem their way was blocked by Arabs, who threw stones at the front and rear windshields. The passengers were lightly injured from broken glass.

Menashe said that when they reached a military roadblock and told the soldiers there what had happened, more rocks rained down on the car from the roadside and nearby rooftops. More troops were called in and the soldiers fired rubber bullets and tear gas at the attackers, he said.

(Continued on Back Page)

'Plastic bullets tested on dummies'

By DAVID HOROVITZ
Jerusalem Post Correspondent

LONDON – The IDF first tested its plastic bullets on dummies built to simulate the human body, according to Israeli military sources quoted in today's *Sunday Times* here.

Thus, the *Times* reports, Israel knew exactly the kinds of injuries the bullets could inflict. The sources said that it had been decided to use the plastic bullets after Israel experimented with other new methods of riot control.

The plastic bullets were first bought from France, but they have since been manufactured in Israel, the paper reports.

Post Military Reporter adds:

Many of the soldiers serving in the territories have been issued clips of plastic bullets for their personal weapons, following a short course in which they were trained how to use the bullets.

This contradicts the impression created recently by official spokesman, that plastic bullets were issued only to sharpshooters and officers. This was indeed the case two months ago when the bullets were first introduced, but it has been learned that new orders were issued two weeks ago by Defence Minister Rabin.

At that time he introduced a tougher policy aimed at inflicting bodily harm on rioters while keeping fatalities down to a minimum. Plastic bullets were issued to a large number of troops, along with strict instructions on the circumstances warranting their use and the ranges in which they were permitted to be used.

Soviet leader shifts opponents to clear decks for radical reforms

Gorbachev transforms the Kremlin

MOSCOW – In an impressive display of his political power, Mikhail Gorbachev has cleared the Kremlin decks for a radicalization of his reform programme.

With imposing sweep, in the course of a one-hour meeting of the country's top Communists on Friday, he achieved a total reshaping of the Soviet Union's top power structure.

Then yesterday, in a second phase of his dramatic weekend activity, Gorbachev was unanimously elected president by the 1,500-member Supreme Soviet to replace Andrei Gromyko, increasing the Soviet leader's power by unifying the top party and government jobs.

Gorbachev used his first speech as Soviet president to demand that there be no delay in pressing ahead with his radical reform programme.

Within minutes of his election as head-of-state he unveiled a plan for local self-government across the Soviet Union.

"We need practical movement ahead," he told the delegates to the Supreme Soviet in a short acceptance speech. "People see and understand our problems and difficulties, but they demand more decisive and energetic steps. Nothing can be put off till a later date."

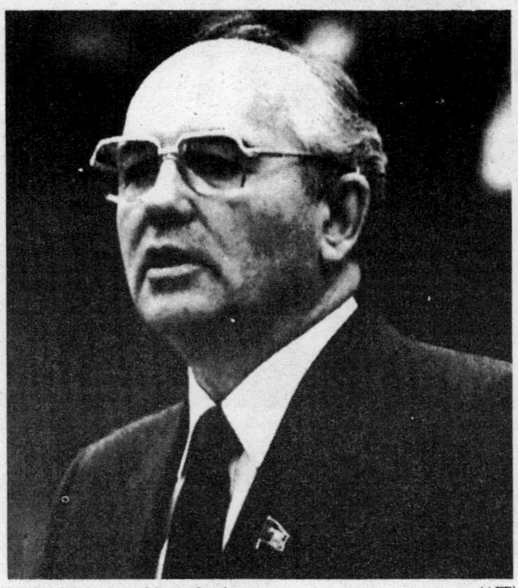
Gorbachev exerts his authority. (AFP)

The 57-year-old Gorbachev clearly pitched the 10-minute address to set the tone for his twin occupation of the presidency and the Communist Party leadership.

His election as head-of-state replacing Gromyko, 79, emerged from urgently-summoned sessions of the party's policy-setting central committee and the Supreme Soviet.

Both were called at unprecedentedly short notice – as a result of a decision by Gorbachev himself last Wednesday, according to reliable Soviet sources.

There has been no explanation for the urgency, which sparked widespread speculation in the outside world of a crisis in the Kremlin and a possible challenge to Gorbachev.

But the smoothly-oiled proceedings on Friday and yesterday in an atmosphere of complete serenity in Moscow left no doubt he had been total master of the situation.

In his address, Gorbachev indicated that he saw a planned decentralization of power and its delegation to local government bodies or Soviets in more dramatic terms than had been earlier envisaged.

He said the Soviets "must become the real and supreme masters on their own territory and correct the abnormal situation that has arisen in many places as a result of dictatorship by central ministries.

"The principles of self-financing, self-support and self-management must be introduced everywhere," he declared.

Gorbachev told the deputies that it was time for local government bodies to take on more responsibility.

"The Soviets will take on their shoulders the major burden of state work," he said. "As the situation changes, we must change accordingly."

In Friday's extraordinary meeting of the Communist Party Central Committee Gorbachev dramatically streamlined the party apparatus and rammed through the biggest personnel changes in his 3½ years in power.

First, he had the session approve the retirement of five senior officials, including Gromyko, linked to the now discredited rule of former leader Leonid Brezhnev.

Second, he effectively neutralized the power of the two members of the ruling politburo – Yegor Ligachev and Viktor Chebrikov – who have been sniping at his perestroika reforms.

Third, he moved energetic supporters into positions that will ensure him control over the key areas of ideology, international relations and probably state security.

Fourth, he achieved clearance from the 300 members of the Communist Party central committee, many of them conservatives, for a drastic shakeup of its ossified bureaucratic apparatus.

Asked at a news conference whether all this meant a strengthen-

(Continued on Back Page)

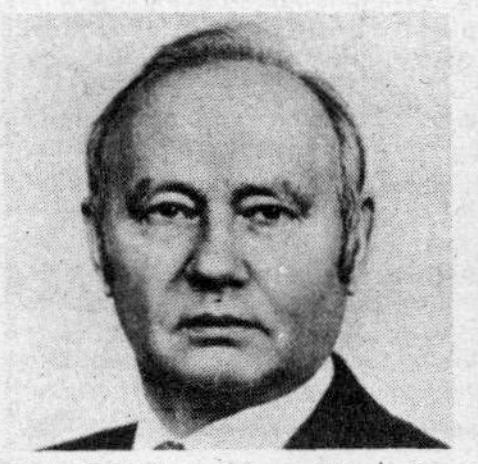
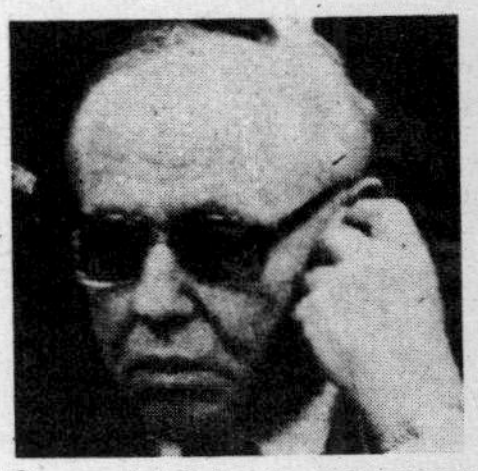
Gen. Vladimir Kryuchkov, 64, left, appointed head of the KGB yesterday. At right, the man he replaced, Victor Chebrikov. (Reuter)

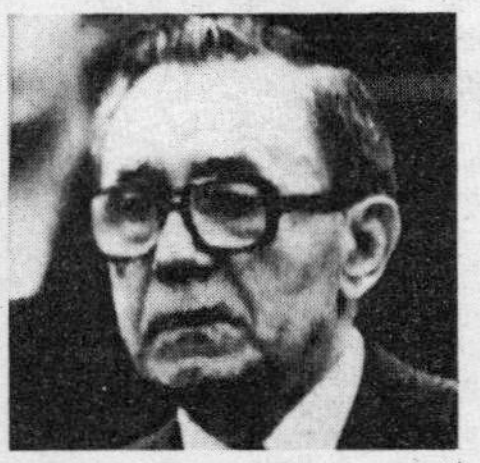
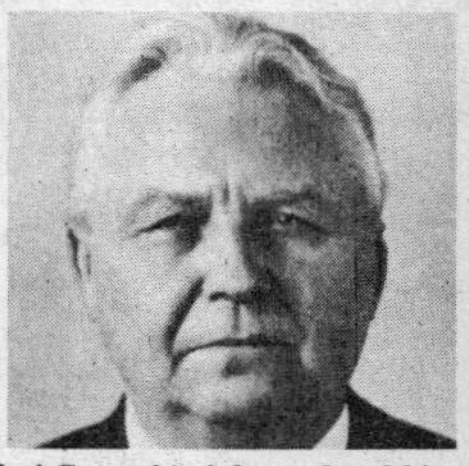
Out of a job: State President Andrei Gromyko, left, tendered his resignation yesterday to the Supreme Soviet. Also displaced, the man considered No. 2 at the Kremlin, Yegor Ligachev, right. (AFP)

How Shultz sees the shakeup

UNITED NATIONS (Reuter) – U.S. Secretary of State George Shultz said the radical Kremlin power shakeup shows Soviet leader Mikhail Gorbachev is determined to pursue his reform programme.

Calling Gorbachev a "strong and determined person," Shultz said that "if there is any message from this, it's that he intends to pursue that (reform) programme."

Asked if the shakeup would leave Gorbachev and Foreign Minister Eduard Shevardnadze more firmly in control of foreign policy, Shultz told reporters at a press conference: "I have never had any question in my mind that Mr. Gorbachev and Mr. Shevardnadze are in firm control of their foreign policy."

"They're not shrinking violets," he said, adding: "They are strong individuals. They do their homework and they're ready to deal with you."

'Hearty congratulations' from Herzog

President Chaim Herzog last night sent a telegram to Soviet leader Mikhail Gorbachev, offering "heartiest congratulations" on his election as president of the Soviet Union.

Herzog added: "I trust that the period of your presidency will see the advance of world peace, the opening of a new page in the development of relations between our two countries and the removal of barriers existing between Israel and the Jewish people on the one hand, and our brothers and sisters in the Soviet Union."

Kurds want Israel to take more children

By YEHUDA LITANI
Post Middle East Editor

DIARBAKIR, Turkey – Leaders of the Kurdish refugees in the Diarbakir camp have asked Israel to take in many more than the 200 refugee children it has offered to accept.

Speaking in this camp near the Syrian border, the refugee leaders say that Israel's offer is marginal. "What is 200 children compared to the vast number of the homeless refugees here?" they said "we expect from the Israelis to do much more after the long history of cooperation between us."

The leaders said that "we shall never forget your assistance to us in the times of Mula Mustafa Barazani but now its bad times again for us, maybe even worse than ever. The Iraqis are trying to annihilate us. Even if the Iranians will allow our entry there, we very much hesitate whether to go mainly because of the bad economic situation in Iran. We are here living in tents and the winter is about to come. We expect a

(Continued on Back Page)

Seoul '88

SEOUL (Reuter) – Front-running Kenyans handed out a lesson in longer distance racing at the Olympic Games yesterday and stern Steffi Graf sobbed in delight at winning the first golden slam of tennis.

Florence Griffith Joyner found 400 metres a lap too far in her quest for a historic fourth gold medal and the Soviet Union trod on the toes of Brazil's samba-style soccer stars to win the Olympic title after extra time. This culminated a splendid weekend for the Soviets who won all three ball sport finals on offer – in basketball and handball as welll as the soccer.

In a low-key but emotional ceremony in an office beneath the Olympic stadium, Carl Lewis was handed Ben Johnson's 100 metres gold medal and said: "I don't believe it is tainted."

Full Seoul Coverage pages 9 and 11.

Final talks on Taba ruling 'only after elections'

By MENACHEM SHALEV
Post Diplomatic Correspondent

The inner cabinet is expected to ratify last week's international arbitrator's award of Taba to Egypt at a meeting on Wednesday and to authorize U.S.-Israeli-Egyptian talks on its implementation, informed sources in Jerusalem said last night.

The sources added, however, that all three countries appear to agree that the substantive part of the implementation talks will be held only after the upcoming November 1 elections, although technical talks may take place before then.

U.S. State Department legal adviser Abraham Sofaer has asked the governments of both countries to pass on to the U.S. their views on the implementation, including the issues of arrangements for the installations in Taba and the delineation of the final border from pillar 91, which the arbitrators found was located at the position advanced by Egypt, and the sea.

Informed sources confirmed last night that it is inevitable that the final border will run from pillar 91 to the so-called Parker pillar on the shore.

Egypt has already signalled its willingness to consider special arrangements for the management of the Sonesta Hotel in Taba and for special entry procedures for Israelis to the area. But officials in Jerusalem expect the Egyptians to be far less forthcoming than they were in the compromise efforts which preceded the arbitration award.

In May of this year, the Egyptians agreed to Israeli management of the Sonesta hotel; appeared willing to waive their demand that 90 per cent of the hotel employees be Egyptian; agreed to an Israeli internal hotel security force; agreed not to prosecute Israelis for offences committed in Taba except in very special circumstances; and agreed to allow Israelis unrestricted access to the site – all in return for a declaration of Egyptian sovereignty over Taba.

These proposals were rejected at the time by Prime Minister Yitzhak Shamir. At this juncture, the Egyptian concessions are expected to be

(Continued on Back Page)

A plague on both their houses, is the view as deadlock continues

Lebanese vent anger on politicians

BEIRUT (AP) – "Do you have a car, girl?" asked Abu Mohammed, a middle-aged coffee vendor whose temper boiled as he watched Syria's Lebanese allies meet in the Bristol Hotel to discuss Lebanon's dual government.

"Then don't lose this precious opportunity. Pack it with explosives and crash it into the hotel where all those leaders are meeting. Let's get a new set," he said, balancing the glasses and coffee cups rattling on his tray.

Fatima, a Sunni Moslem, was more explicit. "I wish the leaders from both sides could be heaped together and set on fire. Those hypocrites have been sucking our blood for 13 years and now they give us this – partition.

"I want the whole world to know we don't want partition. We want to coexist with the Christians," the incensed housewife added.

George, a bank clerk in Christian east Beirut, suggested the government take a trip: "I have just one piece of advice for all politicians and militias – go to hell."

Those angry comments sum up the disgust that many Lebanese, Moslems and Christians alike, feel at the political deadlock triggered on September 23 when Parliament failed to elect a successor to President Amin Gemayel.

Five minutes before his term ended, Gemayel appointed his Christian army commander, Gen. Michel Aoun, to head a six-man military cabinet to fill the vacuum until a new president is elected.

But the incumbent Syrian-backed cabinet of acting Prime Minister Salim Hoss, a Sunni, rejected Aoun's cabinet. Both governments have since been vying for legitimacy and recognition. This has nudged Lebanon further down the road to formalizing the partition of a country already splintered into sectarian cantons by a 13-year-old civil war.

The crisis is bizarre, even by the chaotic standards of a country plagued with street battles, car bombings, kidnappings, assassinations and bank robberies since the war started.

The impasse gives fresh meaning to the words of Lebanese poet Kahlil Gibran, who wrote in *The Garden of the Prophet* in 1934: "Pity the nation divided into fragments, each fragment deeming itself a nation."

Despite the violence, in which more than 130,000 people have been killed, most Lebanese have tried to cling to the symbols of legitimate authority: the presidency, the government, parliament and the army.

But now these last vestiges are disintegrating. The writ of the president barely extends beyond the state palace atop a hill southeast of Beirut.

Real power is in the hands of the rival warlords, all of them dependent to one degree or another on outside powers such as Syria and Israel.

The government, before it was cleaved in two, had been crippled by inertia and had not even met in full session for years because of sectarian differences.

The 42,000-man army has split four ways, some units with Aoun, others with Moslem or Christian militias. Some just sit on the sidelines.

Government departments, which somehow have continued function-

(Continued on Back Page)

Stalin's last laugh

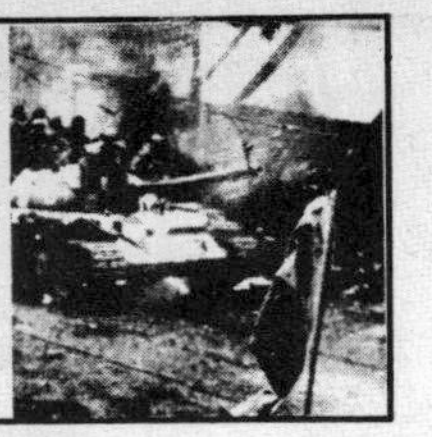

Page 5

THE JERUSALEM POST

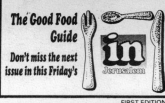

Vol. LVI, No. 17011 Thursday, December 22, 1988 • Tevet 14, 5749 • Jomada Awal 12, 1409 NIS 1.30 (Eilat NIS 1.15)

FIRST EDITION

Jumbo crashes in UK

LONDON (Reuter) – A Pan American Boeing 747 jumbo jet carrying up to 258 passengers crashed near the Scottish border village of Lockerbie last night. The aircraft, Flight 103, had left London's Heathrow Airport for New York.

There was no immediate word on survivors

A witness told the British Broadcasting Corporation that there was practically no chance that there were any survivors from the jumbo jet, which went down in a gigantic fireball on a filling station near Lockerbie in Dumfriesshire, near the English border.

Nearby houses were set ablaze, witnesses said, and inhabitants seriously injured. Eyewitnesses said the main highway between Scotland and the English border had been cut and that several cars appeared to have been set alight.

Three children were aboard the jumbo which took off from London's Heathrow Airport at 18.00 GMT and crashed around an hour later, the RAF base at Pitreavie said. It disappeared from radar screens seconds before the crash, the spokesman added.

Pat Coffey, an RAF spokesman in Edinburgh, the Scottish capital, said five rescue helicopters had been sent to the scene.

New leaflet rejects elections in areas

By JOEL GREENBERG
Jerusalem Post Reporter

Leaflet No. 31 of the Unified National Leadership of the Uprising, distributed yesterday, rejects proposals for elections and unilateral autonomy in the territories and welcomes the U.S. decision to talk to the PLO as an "achievement of the uprising."

In the West Bank, a Palestinian critically wounded in Nablus last Friday died of his wounds at Ramallah hospital. Abdel Rahman Kaddura, 20, had been shot in the chest during the bloodiest clashes in the city since the start of the uprising. He was the sixth Palestinian killed in Friday's violence, and the eighth from die in Nablus in the past week.

In West Bank clashes yesterday, nine Palestinians were wounded by gunfire as the territories were paralyzed by a general strike called to mark the anniversary of last year's "Peace Day" protests by Israeli Arabs.

Troops raided several villages to make arrests and compel residents to paint over nationalist graffiti and remove flags, Palestinian sources said. In Nablus, which has been under curfew for a week, residents reported that they were forced to remove black flags hung in mourning for the Palestinians killed on Friday.

The latest leaflet, entitled "The Palestinian Call for Peace and Legitimate Rights," says the U.S. decision to begin a dialogue with the PLO is "one of the achievemments of the intifada, and a victory for the justice of our cause." It calls on the U.S. administration "to develop its political position, confirm our people's rights to self-determination, recognize the Palestinian state and reopen the PLO office in Washington."

The handbill appeals to European governments to recognize the Palestinian state, raise the level of PLO diplomatic representation in their capitals, and increase their economic and political pressure on Israel "to comply with the international will." It also calls on the "democratic forces" in Israel to pressure their government to change its position and agree to a UN-sponsored international conference that will safeguard Palestinian rights.

Arab states are called upon to open Palestinian embassies in their capitals, to pressure the U.S. to recognize the Palestinian state, and to support the uprising "materially and morally."

Proposals by Israeli politicians for elections and unilateral autonomy in the territories are only aimed at "creating an alternative [Palestinian] leadership," the leaflet says. Proposals to participate in municipal elections in Jerusalem are condemned as "splintering the national position and...isolating its inhabitants from the rest of our people under occupation." In its schedule of protest activities, the leaflet calls for special prayers and the ringing of church-bells on Christmas Day and on January 7, the Greek Orthodox Christmas, to protest against the "repression and tyranny of the occupation." It designates December 24 and January 6 as "days of national mourning" for Palestinians killed in the uprising, "to express rejection of the occupation and any Israeli participation in Christmas celebrations." Palestinians are urged to visit the families of the "martyrs."

(Continued on Back Page)

U.S. offers huge rewards for anti-terror leads

By WOLF BLITZER
Jerusalem Post Correspondent

WASHINGTON – The U.S. yesterday announced that it will pay as much as $500,000 for information leading to "the prevention, frustration or favourable resolution of terrorist acts against U.S. persons or property overseas."

Since 1984, the U.S. has offered large financial rewards to anyone with information leading "to the arrest and conviction of the perpetrators of specific terrorist acts."

Yesterday's announcement, made at the State Department, would dramatically expand the earlier programme. "We will continue to pursue all the possible means of combatting terrorism," said spokeswoman Phyllis Oakley in making the announcement.

In order to publicize the expanded programme, she said, the State Department is distributing posters advertising payment of up to $500,000 for information that aids in the prevention of terrorist acts or leads to the arrest or conviction of individuals who have committed such acts.

The posters, she said, will be printed in English, French, German, Spanish and Arabic, and will be sent to all U.S. diplomatic posts overseas.

She said the selection of these five languages was the result of "efficiency – we want to hit the areas where we think that we're going to have the most impact based on experience from terrorist incidents.

She described the rewards programme as "one of the tools that we have to prevent and investigate incidents of terrorism."

Shamir to present gov't today

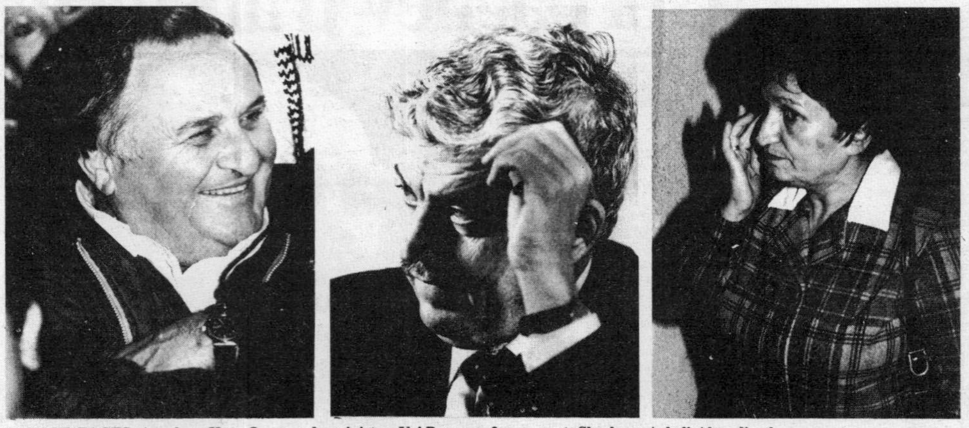

LABOUR FACES: Avraham Katz-Oz named a minister; Uzi Baram refuses a post; Shoshana Arbeli-Almoslino loses a post. (Hanoch Guthmann)

Oscar Franklin

Likud leader Yitzhak Shamir will present his new broad-based government to President Herzog this morning, 51 days after the general elections.

The coalition consists of the two major parties, and two or three religious parties – Shas, the National Religious Party and possibly Agudat Yisrael, which was undecided late last night.

This morning's lengthy agenda starts with the signing of the coalition agreement between the Likud and Labour, finalized last night by Dan Meridor and Moshe Shahal. The agreement has been approved by the parties' central committees. (See Labour story below).

At 9:30, the new cabinet is scheduled to convene for its first meeting. The Knesset will hold an extraordinary session half an hour later, when the new ministers will declare allegiance to the Knesset and its laws. Shamir will detail the new coalition guidelines, which do not deviate markedly from those of the outgoing national unity government.

Last night, the religious parties – which were at the centre of the elaborate coalition negotiations for six weeks and whose spokesmen only 24 hours earlier had branded Shamir and the Likud as "liars" and "traitors" for reneging on earlier accords – declared their readiness to join the coaltion.

Inevitably, their positions have been whittled down: the three parties – Shas, the NRP and, if it joins, Agudat Yisrael – will have only four ministers (instead of six to eight) and command only relatively minor portfolios.

The new government will be the biggest ever, with 26 ministers – 11 from each of the two major parties, two from the NRP and two from Shas. The Aguda is expected to have control over the Ministry of Labour and Social Welfare but, as in the past, will not assume a full ministerial post.

The appearance of the new government bears a remarkable resemblance to the outgoing national unity government. But there are some deviations.

Shamir is slated to remain prime minister for the entire four years rather than rotating with Peres, and the Labour leader will transfer from the Foreign Ministry to the Treasury.

Unlike the previous national unity government, in which there was complete parity between the two major blocs, this time there will be parity between the two major parties, Likud and Labour, with the religious parties formally unaligned to either.

THE CABINET

Prime Minister - Yitzhak Shamir (Likud)

Vice Premier and Finance Minister - Shimon Peres (Labour)

Foreign Minister - Moshe Arens (Likud)

Defence Minister - Yitzhak Rabin (Labour)

Deputy Premier and Housing Minister - David Levy (Likud)

Deputy Premier and Education Minister - Yitzhak Navon (Labour)

Industry and Trade Minister - Ariel Sharon (Likud)

Energy Minister - Moshe Shahal (Labour)

Justice Minister - Dan Meridor (Likud)

Police Minister - Haim Bar-Lev (Labour)

Economics and Planning Minister - Yitzhak Moda'i (Likud)*

Health Minister - Ya'acov Tsur (Labour)

Tourism Minister - Ronni Milo (Likud)

Agriculture Minster - Avraham Katz-Oz (Labour)

Science and Development Minister - Gideon Patt (Likud)

Communications Minister - Gad Ya'acobi (Labour)

Transport Minister - Moshe Katsav (Likud)

Religious Affairs Minister - Avner Shaki, Zevulun Hammer or Yosef Shapira (NRP)

Absorption Minister - Yitzhak Peretz (Shas)

Interior Minister - Arie Der'i (Shas)

Welfare and Labour Ministry (Agudat Yisrael)**

Minister without Portfolio in charge of the Arab Sector - Ehud

(Continued on Back Page)

Religious parties stampeding in

By HAIM SHAPIRO
Jerusalem Post Reporter

Shas and the National Religious Party last night stampeded into the new Likud-Labour coalition, though still smarting from the way Premier Shamir reneged on his coalition promises. Agudat Yisrael was apparently close on their heels.

The only religious party left out in the cold is Degel Hatora, which has asked for a court order to stop Shamir from presenting his cabinet until the prime minister agrees to carry out the promises made to the small ultra-Orthodox party.

The Jerusalem District Court yesterday rejected the Degel Hatora request for a temporary injunction, but will hear the case today.

In fact, Degel had decided not to be part of the coalition before Shamir presented the religious parties with the fait accompli of the expanded coalition and narrowed benefits, but it insists that the two parties have a legal commitment to provide "equal terms" for the ultra-Orthodox community as promised.

The first religious party to capitulate was Shas, which called a meeting of its Council of Tora Sages. They approved the recommendation brought forward by party leader Yitzhak Peretz, to participate in the government "in view of the country's spiritual and diplomatic situation."

The decision provided a solution for the embarrassing situation in which party strongman Arye Der'i found himself. Der'i, who did not run for the Knesset but nevertheless resigned as Interior Ministry director-general in order to participate in the election campaign, would have found himself without an official position had Shas not entered the coalition.

Although Shas is to receive the Interior Ministry, Peretz is unwilling to become interior minister because he would have to register non-Orthodox converts as Jews under the existing law. The Council ruled that Der'i should serve as interior minister and Peretz as absorption minister for two years, after which the two are to rotate their positions.

(Continued on Page Ten)

Labour storm over lack of female ministers

By DAN PETREANU
Post Political Reporter

Labour's central committee meeting degenerated into near pandemonium yesterday when Shimon Peres, in presenting his list of ministers, failed to include a woman.

Earlier, the committee overwhelmingly endorsed Peres's proposal to join the Likud-led coalition, after a short and very quiet discussion highlighted only by MK Haim Ramon's angry denunciation of the unity scheme.

But bedlam erupted in the crowded Givatayim cinema when it was learned that Peres's proposed cabinet list included men only. After a vigorous debate, the list was approved by a two-thirds majority, with almost half of those present abstaining.

It remains unclear whether Secretary-General Uzi Baram – who initially agreed to his inclusion in the list of 11 ministers presented by Peres – would actually join the cabinet.

Baram had pledged earlier in the day that he would not join the government unless Peres included at least three new faces in the list of ministers. Last night, he said again that he would not join the government – enabling Rafi Edri to join in his place.

Baram had harsh words for Peres, who "could not make the courageous decision to replace a few ministers." Baram said this was particularly ironic in light of the fact that the normally "non-initiating" Shamir had included three new ministers in his list.

Peres added Avraham Katz-Oz to the cabinet, and placed Rafi Edri in the 12th position – in case the large parties increased their representation as a result of religious parties' not joining. The other ministers proposed by Peres are Yitzhak Rabin, Yitzhak Navon, Moshe Shahal, Ezer Weizman, Mordechai Gur, Ya'acov Tsur, Gad Ya'acobi and Moshe Shahal. Outgoing ministers Shoshana Arbeli-Almoslino and Arik Nehamkim (who voluntarily withdrew) do not appear on the new list.

(Continued on Back Page)

Shamir and Peres will not be moving anywhere very fast

ANALYSIS
Asher Wallfish

The accords of various kinds between the Likud and the Alignment which have emerged from the final few days of frantic negotiations between them mean that Prime Minister Yitzhak Shamir and his finance minister-to-be, Shimon Peres, will not be moving anywhere very fast, policy-wise.

This morning, before the Knesset meets in special session to give the new coalition a vote of confidence following Shamir's presentation of his government, the t's will be crossed and the i's dotted on these accords. But their content was known last night, in virtually complete detail.

Unless they both happen to be exactly on the same wavelength to start with, they will go forward like two convicts in leg-irons, hobbling painfully. And if hobbling proves too painful, they will just stand still.

The secret memorandum of understanding between them requiring the consent of both men to "decisions of prime significance on diplomatic and security issues, secret as well as public," could mean for instance that the prime minister will be sharing responsibility with Peres for major operations of the domestic as well as overseas intelligence services.

It means that when some foreign go-between puts serious proposals regarding the peace process to Shamir or Peres, each will be forbidden to keep the proposals from the other, and neither will be authorized to approve or reject them without consulting the other.

The basic policy guidelines appear to keep the Alignment on a short leash where the future of the peace process is concerned, since they spell out Camp David as the basis for it. The guidelines talk of renewing negotiations for full autonomy for the Arab residents of Judea, Samaria and Gaza, with their active participation.

The only potential leeway, inserted at Peres's demand, may reside in the clause referring to the government discussing "proposals for negotiations" with Jordan.

Israel rejects a Palestinian state, or talks with the PLO, the guidelines say. They add a commitment to rule out all change in sovereignty over Judea, Samaria and Gaza during the government's term, without agreement between the Likud and the Alignment, thus effectively blocking moves for constitutional annexation, as demanded by Tehiya and a few Likud hard-liners.

Within a year, according to the guidelines, between five and eight new settlements will be set up. A list has already been drawn up by the two parties.

Towards the end of the coalition's first year, Shamir and Peres will meet to decide on the timing of further settlement, by mutual consent, according to a list already drafted.

While both men will continue to enjoy their former veto on proposals brought to the inner cabinet, the working of that exclusive body could become more efficient thanks to a clause in the secret memorandum. This is because Shamir and Peres will now prepare the issues brought up in the inner cabinet in full consultation.

The fact that the flow of classified information reaching Shamir in writing will also go to Peres will make it easier for both men to read each other's mind. The memoran-

(Continued on Page Ten)

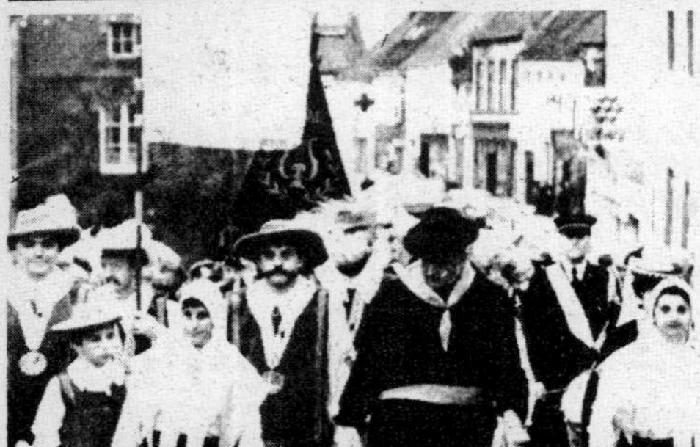

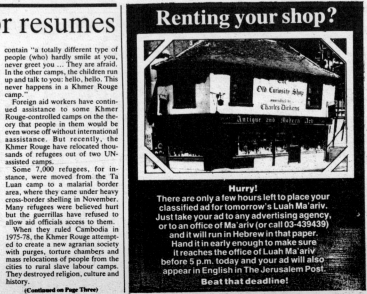

Members of the Turkey Breeders Brotherhood walk in the streets of Licques, northern France, during their annual parade this week. The brotherhood hopes to sell 35,000 turkeys for Christmas. (Reuter)

Khmer Rouge horror resumes

Peter Eng

SITE B, Thailand – Mom Sokhon escaped to a refugee camp in Thailand after surviving four years under a Khmer Rouge government that had slaughtered six of her relatives and hundreds of thousands of other people in Cambodia. But in Thailand, she wound up in the Khmer Rouge guerrilla-controlled camp of Huay Chan. There, she said, the horror began again.

The guerrillas forced the girl, then 15, to toil all day making punji, bamboo spears for impaling enemy soldiers. She said she had to make regular treks through heavily mined mountain passes from the camp to Khmer Rouge bases inside Cambodia, hauling punji, rice and B-67 anti-tank rounds.

On each journey, at times a month long, mines blew off the legs of two or three women in the unit, she said. Sometimes, Vietnamese soldiers would open fire and kill unit members.

"If anyone refused to join the transport team, she would be punished with no food and sent to an underground prison," she said.

After five years at Huay Chan, Mom Sokhon fled in November to this refugee camp in eastern Surin province controlled by the non-Communist guerrillas of Prince Nodorom Sihanouk. She fears the Khmer Rouge will hunt her down.

International aid officials say tens of thousands of Cambodian refugees remain virtual prisoners in camps in Thailand where the Khmer Rouge force people to serve their war machine bent on re-seizing Cambodia following the 1978 Vietnamese invasion.

A senior official experienced with rebel movements in Africa and the Middle East said that even in the ruthless world of guerrilla warfare, it is unusual to use children, sometimes seven years old, as military porters.

"The disregard for the sick and the disabled is extreme," he said. Aid officials said hundreds, perhaps thousands, of refugees have died of malaria, tuberculosis and other diseases because the Khmer Rouge refused to treat them properly or would not allow them to see foreign doctors.

Another official said these camps contain "a totally different type of people (who) hardly smile at you, never greet you ... They are afraid. In the other camps, the children run up and talk to you: hello, hello. This never happens in a Khmer Rouge camp."

Foreign aid workers have continued assistance to some Khmer Rouge-controlled camps on the theory that people in them would be even worse off without international aassistance. But recently, the Khmer Rouge have relocated thousands of refugees out of two UN-assisted camps.

Some 7,000 refugees, for instance, were moved from the Ta Luan camp to a malarial border area, where they came under heavy cross-border shelling in November. Many refugees were believed hurt but the guerrillas have refused to allow aid officials access to them.

When they ruled Cambodia in 1975-78, the Khmer Rouge attempted to create a new agrarian society with purges, torture chambers and mass relocations of people from the cities to rural slave labour camps. They destroyed religion, culture and history.

(Continued on Page Three)

Power of the word

Page 5

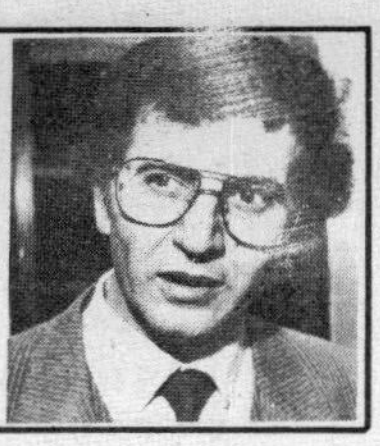

THE JERUSALEM POST

Vol. LVII, No. 17053 Thursday, February 9, 1989 • Adar I 4, 5749 • Rajab 3, 1409 NIS 1.40 (Eilat NIS 1.20)

SECOND EDITION

Text of State Department report on areas

Page 7

Suspect German firm had Zyklon B role

By DAN IZENBERG and ERNIE MEYER

Degussa, the West German company suspected of selling chemicals to Libya for the production of poison gas, owned a large share of the firm which marketed Zyklon B, used by the Nazis to exterminate millions of Jews and others in World War II.

According to U.S. historian Raul Hilberg, author of *The Destruction of the European Jews,* Degussa owned 42.5 per cent of the shares in the Degesch Company (the German Vermin-Extermination Company) which manufactured Zyklon B and sold it to the German army and the S.S.

The other owners of Degesch were I.G. Farben, a pre-war industrial giant which played a critical role in the German war effort and was split up by the Allies after the war, and the Theo Goldschmidt Co.

Hilberg records that a Degussa executive was convicted of Nazi war crimes and sentenced to five years in jail by the Nuremberg Military Tribunal.

Earlier this week, *The Jerusalem Post* reported that Degussa knowingly bought gold, silver and precious metals stolen from Jews by the German military authorities in the Lodz and Pabianice ghettos in Poland.

A spokesman for Degussa yesterday denied the company had been involved in the production of Zyklon B.

"It cannot be said Degussa ever delivered Zyklon B," the spokesman said on condition of anonymity in a telephone interview from Frankfurt. "It was only part owner of Degesch and two of its board members were acquitted of war crimes."

The spokesman also said Degesch officials did not realize the gas they were producing was being used to kill human beings. "The SS had camps where pesticides were used," he said. "There were huge prisoner-of-war camps which also had to be treated with pesticides. So no one knew what the Zyklon B was being used for. It was misused by the Nazis."

He admitted, however, that the authorities had ordered the company to make changes in some of the gas shipments by omitting a tear-gas-like compound which caused humans to choke and forced them to escape from the gas.

(Continued on Back Page)

Settlers up in arms as motorist dies in blaze

By JOSHUA BRILLIANT and JOEL GREENBERG
Jeruslem Post Reporters

ALFEI MENASHE – A resident of Alfei Menashe in the West Bank was killed last night when his van caught fire, but it was not immediately clear whether he was the target of a petrol bomb attack.

The incident set off a rampage by settlers from Ariel who tried to enter an Arab village and stoned Arab cars, injuring at least three motorists. Troops surrounded other settlements and neighbouring villages to prevent further reprisals

The settler killed was identified as Albert Jerassi, 38, a father of three. He was on his way home in a Peugeot van when it caught fire shortly before 7:00 p.m.

Initial reports said the vehicle had been hit by a petrol bomb, but police investigators were unable last night to establish the source of the blaze. The drivers' window was open when the vehicle caught fire, but initial examinations failed to find glass fragments or other remnants of a petrol bomb, nor did they reveal a single focus for the blaze. One possibility being checked is that an unidentified object exploded in the car.

A man who rescued Jerassi from the vehicle said he found him gagging in thick smoke that enveloped the cabin. Jersassi was rushed to Meir Hospital in Kfar Sava, where doctors pronounced him dead.

The incident occurred near the entrance to Alfei Menashe, at a spot where the road to the settlement cuts through steep cliffs in the area of previous petrol-bomb attacks on cars from the town. The scene of the incident is minutes away from a permanent IDF checkpoint, which monitors all traffic on the road.

Troops rushed to the scene, closed off the area and declared it a closed military zone, preventing Alfei Menashe residents from leaving the town, and blocking attempts by settlers to enter neighbouring Arab villages. Kalkilya was also declared a closed zone to prevent reprisals.

Curfews were reported in the neighbouring villages of Hable, Ras Atiya and Ras a-Tira, as troops searched for suspects.

OC Central Command Amram Mitzna arrived on the scene to oversee the army's operations and meet with settlers. Residents of Alfei Menashe held an emergency meeting to discuss retaliatory and protest action, and in a confrontation with Mitzna, charged that the army had failed to ensure their security.

Meanwhile, settlers from Ariel on the Trans-Samaria highway tried to enter the neighbouring village of Bidya, charging that their cars were stoned on the highway, but they were blocked by troops.

At the Haris junction near Ariel, settlers stoned Arab cars, injuring at least three passengers in one vehicle. The car's windows were smashed, and one passenger had blood streaming from a wound near his eye. Passengers said they were attacked as they were returning from a visit with Jewish friends in Jaffa, and that they could have been killed if it were not for the intervention of Border Police. Troops barred Ariel residents from leaving the town to prevent further reprisals.

Jerassi is the third Alfei Menashe resident to be killed on the road to the settlement. In late 1987 Ofra Moses and her son Tal were killed, and several months later Edna and Moshe Regev were fire-bombed and injured on their way to the airport.

Reacting to the incident, Prime Minister Shamir said last night that it placed the "unbalanced" U.S. State Department report on Israeli human rights violations in the territories "in a very special light."

Speaking to reporters in Jerusalem, Shamir said: "This is very grave incident, an attack that has again taken life at the very same place. It puts a very special light on the human rights report which the U.S. has published, and proves once again the lack of balance between this report and reality."

Shamir said that Israel would respond to the report by "explaining our positions and the reasons for the violence. We regret the suffering and loss of life of the Palestinians, but we shall also point to the sufferings of the Jews."

Million to strike on Sunday

By ANDY GOLDBERG

TEL AVIV – A million workers will participate in the open-ended general strike due to start Sunday unless a last minute agreement is reached with the Finance Ministry, trade union officials told a press conference yesterday.

The officials said they were pessimistic about the chances for reaching agreement.

But in an attempt to avert the stoppage, the Histadrut and the private employers, with Finance Minister Shimon Peres, were locked in talks late last night over a new cost-of-living accord, one of the Histadrut's main conditions for calling off the strike.

The talks began early in the evening at Histadrut Trade Union Department head Haim Haberfeld's office here before moving later to Peres's bureau. The gap dividing the two sides still remains the Treasury's and employer's insistence that salaried employees waive most of the compensation due them following the price rises caused by the devaluation and recent subsidy cuts. At press time, the talks were continuing.

On one issue, the Treasury has gone toward the Histadrut. Peres said yesterday he would increase the tax rate on top incomes from 48 per cent to 51 percent for a period of one year. Peres made this statement to Likud members at the Knesset finance commitee. The Histadrut had demanded this move which will effect around 35,000 people as a way to spread the burden of the new econimic programme.

Haberfeld denied allegations yesterday morning that the strike was called by union leaders against the wishes of their members, stating that he was "astounded at the willingness of the public to join the strike." Isolated stoppages at a number of big firms will start today as union officials call mass meetings to explain the strike's aims.

Haberfeld, who would not say how long the strike would continue, maintained that decisions on the duration and breadth of the strike would be taken on Sunday, "according to developments."

Aside from the need for a new c-o-l accord, the Histadrut would only agree to abort the strike if the Treasury increases price supervision, introduces a special NIS 200 million fund to reduce unemployment, and makes a commitment not to charge patients for hospitalization or to change the minimum wage law unilaterally, Haberfeld insisted.

Other demands presented by the Histadrut include the imposition of a 3 per cent surtax on high earners, an arrangement that would give workers tax rebates on 10 per cent of their income in order to buy shares in their companies, and tax rebates for both workers and firms on profits arising from increased productivity.

"The central question is how the economy will look in two years' time," Haberfeld said, adding that the Treasury had not yet replied to any of the requests and had simply requested clarifications.

The strike, expected to start officially at 6 a.m. Sunday, will lead to widespread disruption of the economy. Public employees, including those of government companies, will strike, though government workers in the territories will be exempt. Television and radio programmes

(Continued on Page Ten)

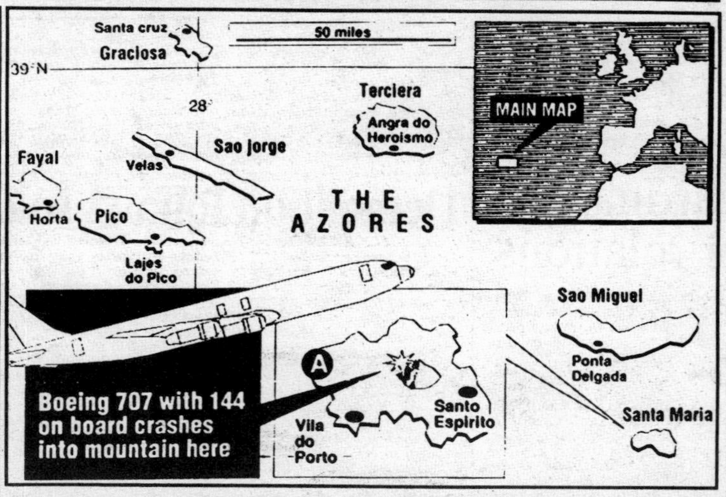
Santa cruz
Graciosa
50 miles
39°N
28°
Terciera
Angra do Heroismo
MAIN MAP
Fayal
Velas
Sao Jorge
THE AZORES
Horta
Pico
Lajes do Pico
Sao Miguel
Ponta Delgada
A
Boeing 707 with 144 on board crashes into mountain here
Vila do Porto
Santo Espirito
Santa Maria

An American charter airliner crashed into a mountainside yesterday on the island of Santa Maria in the Azores. All 144 people on board were feared dead. (Story below) (Reuter)

U.S. downplays human rights report

By WOLF BLITZER
Jerusalem Post Correspondent

WASHINGTON – The State Department yesterday sought to soften the widespread criticism in the American news media of Israel's human rights record on the West Bank and Gaza Strip.

Assistant Secretary for Human Rights and Humanitarian Affairs Richard Schifter told reporters at a briefing that the situation in the territories was unique. "It is not the typical setting for gross human rights violations – as would be mass killings or total repression," he said.

He suggested that much worse human rights violations were documented in the more than 1,600 pages contained in this year's worldwide report on 171 countris and areas.

But over the past 24 hours, the U.S. news media have focused attention almost exclusively on the 12 pages describing Israel's alleged human rights violations in the territories – a point sharply criticized by Schifter and other U.S. officials.

It was also condemned in an editorial yesterday in *The Washington Post.*

Schifter said: "It is not my job to determine which of our country reports is the most newsworthy, but it is my job to form a judgement as to the rank order of the problems we face in the field of human rights worldwide."

The situation in the West Bank and Gaza, he said, was by no means among the worst violations.

"It is a situation in which an occupying army responds to serious civil disorder by using what in our judgement is excessive force or by imposing excessive punishment," he said. "That is the human rights problem with which we're dealing in the occupied territories."

Israel rejects U.S. report on areas

By MENACHEM SHALEV
Post Diplomatic Correspondent

Israel yesterday politely deflected the State Department's criticism of IDF human rights violations in the territories, rebuffing the essence of the annual U.S. report but taking care, at the same time, not to offend its authors.

Prime Minister Yitzhak Shamir told a delegation of the Conference of Presidents of Major Jewish Organizations in Jerusalem that the IDF is carrying out its tasks in the territories in an "exemplary and humanitarian way."

Foreign Minister Arens, in an interview to be published tomorrow in *The Jerusalem Post*, said that "when you have to contend with violence on a scale and in a scope of the kind that we have to deal with, it probably is impossible to maintain a standard of respect for human rights that you do ordinarily in any democratic society, and that we do in Israel in day-to-day life."

Sources in Jerusalem last night expressed concern that the negative impact of the Israeli chapter in the State Department reports would probably make upcoming battles against arms sales to Arab countries much tougher, and might also set back efforts to end the U.S.-PLO dialogue.

Arens said that he had yet to read the report, and that Israel's authoritative reply will be forthcoming from the Defence Ministry. He added, however: "I know Mr. Shifter, and he's a very fine man. So my initial response on being told that he's said something or other would be to treat it with considerable respect.

"When you have people getting burned alive by Molotov cocktails which get thrown into buses, it's not easy, and maybe impossible" to maintain respect for human rights.

Shomron: Report ignores circumstances

By KENNETH KAPLAN
Post Defence Reporter

The U.S. State Department report on alleged human rights violations by Israel in the fight against the Palestinian uprising does not take into account the circumstances surrounding the IDF's actions in the territories, Chief of General Staff Dan Shomron told Israel TV last night in Washington.

"Palestinian civilians have chosen violence as the means to push Israel out of the territories. The report shows that when there is an increase in the number of violent incidents – and the reaction by the army involves, by necessity, the use of force – then there are more people hurt," Shomron said.

In Israel, the IDF Spokesman's Office released an official nine-point statement yesterday addressing some of the major points made in the report, while Defence Ministry sources said last night the report had been received, and the defence establishment would respond once it had been studied.

Following is the complete text of the IDF statement:

Israel is a democratic country which places human rights as a fundamental principle guiding its behaviour. We have no interest in squabbling with the report's authors. The report examines the acts of state and not the circumstances surrounding the riots by local residents.

□ **Deaths of local residents:** Every fatality involving a resident of the territories and resulting from IDF activities is investigated by the Military Police. Every such file is then passed on to the office of the judge advocate-general. In every instance where evidence exists of violations, legal steps are taken.

□ **Trial of Palestinian rioters:** The trials are carried out openly according to the rules of evidence accepted

(Continued on Back Page)

Three Palestinians killed in areas

By JOEL GREENBERG and MICHAL SELA

Two Palestinians were killed in the West Bank and a Gaza Strip youth died of his wounds yesterday as the territories were paralyzed by a 48-hour general strike called to mark the end of the 14th month of the uprising.

In a violent confrontation at Kabatiya, near Jenin, troops shot and killed 18-year-old Kamal Zakarneh.

According to reports from the town, Zakarneh was shot in the abdomen and died instantly. Additional clashes erupted after he was killed, and two other persons were wounded in the hands, the reports said.

Zakarneh was buried in a mass funeral attended by thousands of mourners who carried Palestinian flags and chanted nationalist slogans. Troops imposed a curfew on the town after the procession, but clashes continued in defiance of the ban, according to the reports. Several other people were reported wounded.

At a-Silah al-Harthiya, near Jenin, Ghanam Jaradat, 17, was critically wounded in the abdomen and died later at the Jenin hospital. Another villager was wounded.

Palestinians said Jaradat was shot during a clash with troops, but military sources said the circumstances of the shooting were unclear. According to the IDF, Border Police entered the village after shots were heard, and the casualties were reported later. The army is investigating.

Meanwhile, Akram Abu Nahla, 20, from Rafah, died yesterday morning in Sheba Hospital at Tel Hashomer from bullet wounds to the head received on Tuesday evening. He was hit during a violent demonstration in Rafah which troops dispersed with plastic bullets at about 7 p.m. He received first aid at the Nasr Hospital in Khan Yunis before being taken to Tel Hashomer.

Andy Court adds:

A petrol bomb thrown near Herod's Gate of Jerusalem's Old City ignited but caused no damage at about 2 p.m. yesterday, the police said.

Inmate killed as Palestinian prisoners riot

Jerusalem Post Reporter

MEGIDDO – Guards at the IDF prison here opened fire, killing an inmate, after 1,300 Arab prisoners rioted, hurling stones and iron bars at guard towers and climbing the prison fences.

Nineteen other inmates and one soldier serving as a guard were injured. The detainee who was killed was from Tulkarm.

About 350 visitors from the Tulkarm area took part in the riot. Fifty-five were arrested.

Most of the 1,700 prisoners in Megiddo facility are awaiting trial on charges of disturbing the peace in the West Bank during the intifada.

The riot began just before noon, following a decision by the prison commander to cut short visitors' day at the prison. The commander decided on the move after a guard spotted a visitor waving a Palestinian flag and other visitors tore licence plates off Israeli cars parked nearby.

When a prisoners' representative relayed the comander's decision to the detainees, some responded by singing nationalist songs and chanting slogans.

The mood turned into what one guard later called a "contagious craze." Prisoners began throwing stones, wood and iron bars at the guard-towers, breaking the special security glass windows and injuring one guard with a stone.

A few hundred prisoners charged towards the prison fences, shook them, and began climbing them. The guards shot into the air, fired dozens of teargas grenades and shot rubber bullets, but to no avail.

The prison commander decided that the guards' lives were in danger and ordered to shoot at the rioters. After several rounds were fired, 20 prisoners fell to the ground, and the guards seized the moment of shock to storm the rioters and regain control.

One prisoner was hit by a bullet in the lower back and killed. Five others sustained bullet wounds in the back and stomach, and were transferred to the Afula hospital. Fourteen other prisoners were wounded. The 350 visitors who witnessed the clash responded with their own riot – smashing windows of cars parked in the area and blocking the main Hadera-Afula road. A large contingent of police and military police came to the area and used teargas to end the disturbance.

Fifty-five West Bank residents were arrested and questioned by the Afula police. Another 250, mainly women and children, were held by police for four hours.

U.S. jet crashes in Azores; 144 feared dead

LISBON, Portugal (AP) – A U.S. charter jet filled with Italian tourists slammed into a fog-covered mountain in the Azores and exploded in flames yesterday, and all 144 people on board were feared dead, officials and news reports said.

Maria della Versesi, a spokeswoman at the Italian Embassy in Lisbon, said all 137 passengers were Italian and the seven crew members were American.

The aircraft belonged to the U.S. airline Independent Air Corp., based in Tennessee. The flight originated in Bergamo, Italy, and was to have proceeded to Puerto Plata in the Dominican Republic and Montego Bay in Jamaica after refueling in the Azores.

The Portuguese news agency Lusa quoted an official from the Azores Civil Protection Service as saying about 50 bodies had been recovered and it appeared all on board had died.

Afonso Pimentel, a Lusa reporter based in the Azores, said the Boeing 707 was preparing to land at Santa Maria airport when it crashed into Pico Alto, a fog-covered 574-metre mountain.

A.L. Pittman, president of Independent Air Corp., said in an interview in that the 15-year-old company makes 400 to 500 charter flights a year, mostly in the Caribbean and Europe. Pittman said the 20-year-old jetliner that crashed had a relatively low number of flight hours and no history of trouble.

The Azores is a chain of 10 islands in the mid-Atlantic. Santa Maria is 1,200 km. west of Portugal.

If all 144 aboard the aircraft perished, the crash would be the worst air disaster in the history of Portuguese civil aviation.

Israel, China to talk at UN

By MENACHEM SHALEV

Implementing the agreement of their respective foreign ministers in Paris last month, the Israeli and Chinese representatives at the UN have scheduled a meeting in the next few days to discuss bilateral issues, sources in Jerusalem said last night.

Foreign Minister Moshe Arens and Chinese Foreign Minister Qian Qichen agreed in Paris last month that the UN representations of both countries would serve as a regular channel of contact between the two countries. The two ambassadors are expected to discuss previous plans, currently in abeyance, for Israel to open an academic centre in Peking.

Israel wants UN officer dumped

By MENACHEM SHALEV

The Foreign Ministry yesterday demanded that Unifil depose the commander of its Norwegian contingent, after the officer repeated his comparisons between the IDF and the Nazis, and said that he was "overjoyed" by the impact his words have had.

Foreign Ministry spokesman Alon Liel said last night that "in light of the fact that the battalion commander is repeatedly uttering his despicable opinions, Israel expects the Unifil command to draw the proper conclusions regarding the officer, as warranted by our mutual desire for cooperation."

Norwegian Colonel Jan Erik Carlsson, who last week said that the IDF was behaving in South Lebanon "just like the Nazis," said in a later interview with an Oslo newspaper that his statements had "helped me turn the spotlight on the expulsion of innocent inhabitants of South Lebanese villages."

Liel noted that the Norwegian government had expressed reservations about the officer's remarks, and that Deputy UN Undersecretary General Marrack Goulding had apologized to Israel's representative at the UN, Yohanan Bein.

The battle of the sick funds

Page 8

THE JERUSALEM POST

Vol. LVII, No. 17068 Monday, February 27, 1989 • Adar I 22, 5749 • Rajab 21, 1409 NIS 1.40 (Eilat NIS 1.20)

SECOND EDITION

EIGHT PAGES FROM SUNDAY'S The New York Times WEEKLY REVIEW INSIDE TODAY

Man shot dead as stones fly in Gaza

By JOEL GREENBERG and MICHAL SELA

Soldiers escorting tax collectors in Gaza shot and killed a man yesterday when they came under a hail of stones, and another Palestinian was shot and wounded, apparently by Arab assailants believing him to be a "collaborator".

Meanwhile, new intifada leaflets are calling for a strike in the territories tomorrow, and expressed support for recent meetings between Palestinians and Israeli politicians.

In Gaza, the Sheikh Radwan quarter turned violent when tax collectors escorted by soldiers came in the morning to collect debts from the Sukkar family. Soldiers killed Ahmad Abdul-Muharram, 20, and wounded another man, according to both IDF and Palestinian sources.

Angry neighbours set tyres alight and blocked the roads until the army imposed a curfew on the quarter.

Almost at the same time, Shifa Hospital deputy director Abd al-Ra'uf Khiles was shot and wounded in the head and shoulder. After receiving first aid he was referred to Barzilai Hospital in Ashkelon.

Graffiti on the hospital walls has recently been accusing Khiles of collaborating with the authorities. Last Wednesday a woman in a Gaza pediatric hospital was murdered in similar circumstances.

Also in Gaza, curfew was imposed on Rafah and Beit Hanun, and five people were sentenced by the Gaza military court to from seven to nine months imprisonment and fines ranging from NIS 750 to 1,200 "for throwing objects." The new leaflets, by the "Unified National Leadership of the Uprising" and the Islamic Resistance Movement (Hamas), have called a general strike in the territories tomorrow, municipal election day.

Leaflet 35 of the PLO-backed "Unified Leadership" urges "the masses of our people in Jerusalem, the capital of our state, to boycott the elections to Teddy Kollek's municipality, during which the 'strike groups' will paralyze public and private transportation."

Hamas leaflet 36 also calls a strike on election day, but says the shutdown is to commemorate Palestinians killed in the uprising.

The leaflet of the "Unified Leadership" expresses support for recent meetings between prominent Pales-

(Continued on Back Page)

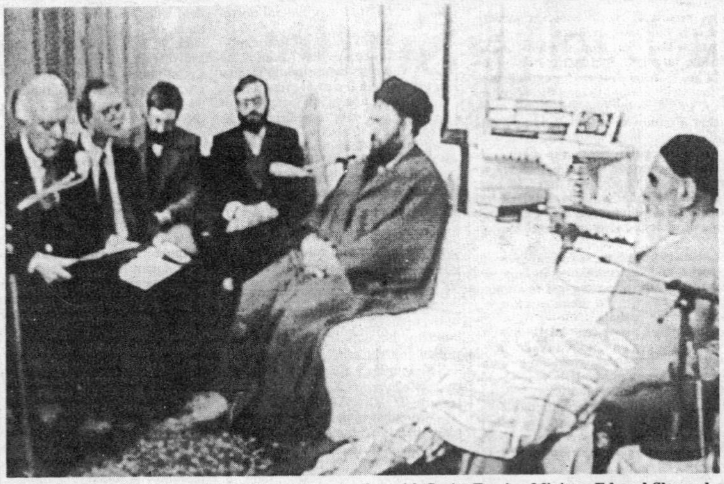

Ayatollah Ruhollah Khomeini, right, meets yesterday with Soviet Foreign Minister Eduard Shevardnadze, left, while Khomeini's son Ahmad, centre, looks on. The Iranian news agency released the photograph of the meeting screened on Iran TV. (AFP)

Khomeini meets Shevardnadze, gives blessing to better relations

NICOSIA (Reuter) – Iranian spiritual leader Ayatollah Ruhollah Khomeini gave his blessing to better relations with Moscow yesterday and pressed Soviet leader Mikhail Gorbachev to contemplate eternity.

Teheran Radio said that in a meeting with Soviet Foreign Minister Eduard Shevardnadze, believed to be the ayatollah's first one-to-one meeting with a visiting foreign minister, Khomeini delivered a short sermon for Gorbachev.

Khomeini sparked a crisis in relations with the West earlier this month when he called on Moslems to kill British author Salman Rushdie for alleged blasphemy in his book *The Satanic Verses*. The Iranian parliament will tomorrow debate a bill to break diplomatic ties with Britain, which closed its Teheran embassy over the Rushdie affair. (Related report – Page 3)

There was no indication whether Shevardnadze raised the Rushdie issue during the meeting, as Britain had asked him to do.

Teheran Radio, monitored here, broadcast 22 minutes of the meeting at Khomeini's home in north Teheran in which Shevardnadze, speaking through an interpreter, relayed a message from Gorbachev to Khomeini.

Shevardnadze quoted Gorbachev as saying Moscow respected freedom of choice for nations and, while backing Iran's 1979 Islamic Revolution, defended the Soviet system as the right choice for its own people despite "gross errors" in the past.

Teheran Radio said Khomeini welcomed the Soviet troop pullout from Afghanistan. He stressed the need for cooperation with Moscow against "devilish acts of the West" and for the withdrawal of foreign forces from the Gulf.

Gorbachev said in his message that Moscow was also ready to expand cultural and social exchanges with Iran. He said Teheran and Moscow could cooperate for a settlement in Afghanistan. "Let the Afghan people decide their destiny without outside interference."

Search scaled down

ASHKELON (Itim) – The search effort for missing soldier Avi Sasportas was scaled down yesterday after 10 days.

Police sources said that the searches had been unprecedented, both in the extent of the area covered and the number of people taking part. Some 500 square kilometres had been searched, including wells, orchards and ditches. Of the 22,500 persons who had participated, 14,362 were volunteers, 7,500 soldiers, and about 750 members of the Green Patrol and the Border Police.

Yesterday some 150 volunteers showed up, compared with 5,000 on Shabbat. The special police intelligence unit set up to continue the search includes 32 investigators. The unit is provided with an IDF helicopter, dogs, and General Security Services liaison.

Polling day is holiday

Jerusalem Post Staff

Municipal election day tomorrow will be an official holiday, after Interior Minister Arye Der'i, who wanted it cancelled on grounds of lost productivity, announced that he had given up.

Der'i (Shas) complained that the head of the Interior Committee of the Knesset, MK Yehoshua Matza (Likud) had put party over national interests by delaying discussion of the holiday, thus ensuring that it could not be cancelled in time. Der'i said under these circumstances he was approving the holiday and called on MKs in the committee to cease their deliberations.

He also said that right after the elections, he would present a draft law to cancel election day holidays, thus putting Israel in line with other western democracies.

Chief Egyptian negotiator declares:

'The Taba dispute is behind us now'

By MENACHEM SHALEV and ASHER WALLFISH

TABA – "The Taba dispute is over, it is behind us now," declared chief Egyptian negotiator Nabil el-Arabi last night shortly after Israel and Egypt signed a series of agreements settling the seven-year Taba dispute.

According to the agreement Israel will withdraw from the 1.2 sq. km. enclave "on or before noon of March 15, 1989".

Egypt has undertaken to pay the owners of the Sonesta hotel and the Rafi Nelson resort village the compensation agreed on yesterday before the March 15 withdrawal date.

The haggling over the final border line continued until the very last minute yesterday and held up the signing ceremony for over 25 minutes. The final dispute, over just 4.68 metres of border, was settled by the Americans who cut a line down the middle between the points

Taba text – Page 2

contended by the sides. The new border cuts through a prefabricated hut of the IDF liaison unit at the Taba border crossing.

"We have finalized the Taba process," said the head of the Israeli delegation, Foreign Ministry director-general Reuven Merhav. "Despite its small size, it has become a symbol of complex negotiations. But it must be turned into a cornerstone for cooperation in the best spirit of our peace treaty and a springboard for the strengthening of mutual confidence between us,"

In his statement, Arabi described the signing as "a happy moment for Egypt." He said that the completion of negotiations was a "credit to both Egypt and Israel. Egypt and Israel have succeeded with patience, perseverance and goodwill in overcoming obstacles which on several occasions seemed insurmountable."

Arabi said that Egypt would endeavour to make Taba a "meeting place for tourists from all over the world."

U.S. State Department legal ad-

(Continued on Back Page)

Demolition follows soldier's death

By JOEL GREENBERG
Jerusalem Post Reporter

The IDF yesterday blew up the upper floor of a building in the Nablus casbah, from where assailants dropped the rock slab that killed Staff Sgt. Binyamin Meisner on Friday.

Windows of homes overlooking the alley where Meisner was killed were bricked up, and the gate to the alley was removed in preparation for sealing the area off.

The building partially demolished belonged to the Touqan family, a leading clan in Nablus. The floor destroyed was unoccupied. Former mayor Hafez Touqan said the structure was more than 400 years old, and its demolition was "a destruction of civilisation, history and culture. This has no deterrent effect whatsoever."

Casbah residents said two charges were detonated in the building, and the explosion destroyed two neighbouring apartments whose ceilings collapsed, leaving 17 persons homeless. An IDF spokeswoman declined to comment on the allegations.

Windows of neighbouring homes were shattered by the blasts, and the roof of another building was damaged, residents said. The second explosion was followed by a chorus of whistles and shouts of "Allahu Akbar" from adjacent buildings, according to reports from the scene.

Most of Nablus remained under curfew as security forces continued intensive searches in the casbah, arresting and interrogating suspects. Palestinians reported at least 40 people detained.

Special efforts were made by troops to remove rocks from rooftops. Casbah residents reported that soldiers moved from roof to roof, ordering residents to throw down rocks and debris found on top of buildings.

At the Cairo-Amman Bank, stone blocks piled on the roof for construction of a second storey were carted off by an army truck, Touqan said.

(Meisner was killed by a slab of Jerusalem stone weighing about 15 kilograms, and dropped from a height of about 12 metres.)

In other parts of the city Palestinians reported that troops enforcing the curfew pointed guns at windows and fired at homes to chase occupants off porches and roofs.

One indication that the curfew could be prolonged was a visit to the city by the head of the Judea and Samaria Civil Administartion, Tat-Aluf Shaike Erez. Erez met with local community leaders to discuss logistic arrangements and public services during the curfew.

Victim of Nablus ambush buried

KIRYAT TIVON – "The country relies on boys like Benny in the IDF for its security," OC Central Command Amram Mitzna told the thousands of mourners who gathered to pay their last respects yesterday to Samal-Rishon Binyamin Meisner, the reserve paratrooper killed in an ambush in Nablus on Friday. Meisner was struck on the head by a building block while on patrol in the casbah.

The funeral cortege left from Meisner's parents' home in Rehov Deganiot in Tivon for the local military cemetery. The flag-draped coffin was borne by six members of the elite unit in which Meisner, 25, had served during his regular and reserve military duty. The mourners from all over the country included comrades-in-arms, sportsmen, and members of the Society for the Protection of Nature. Meisner recently began working at the society's field school in Eilat.

In his eulogy, Kiryat Tivon council head Amihai Ben-Dror noted how much Meisner had loved his home-town and the entire country. He had been an outstanding sportsman, a member of the national water polo team who had been a credit to all of Tivon and was greatly admired by its residents, Ben-Dror said.

The country's leaders should consider the lost potential of boys like Benny when making vital strategic decisions, Ben-Dror added. (Itim)

No need for peace stopwatch, insists Shamir

By ASHER WALLFISH
Jerusalem Post Reporter

Prime Minister Shamir poured cold water yesterday on calls in the cabinet to draw up a fresh set of proposals for expediting negotiations on the Middle East dispute.

"There is no need for us to hurry," he told Alignment ministers. "Meanwhile the Arab residents in Judea, Samaria and Gaza are exerting pressure on the PLO leadership to show more flexibility."

Some cabinet members understood him to mean that the Palestinians were urging the PLO leadership to shift closer to the Israeli position. Others understood the Palestinians were urging the PLO leadership not to make them bear the brunt of the uprising which had not produced substantial political results.

Shamir urged his colleagues not to "stand by with a stop-watch, and count how long it is taking" for the new national unity coalition to reach the negotiating phase. "You cannot expect instant results in our situation," he said.

In any case, he reminded his colleagues, if he had any package of proposals on which to consult and seek endorsement, he would present it to the inner cabinet and not the full cabinet.

Communications Minister Gad Ya'acobi urged that before Shamir goes to Washington, the cabinet should formally reiterate its commitment under Security Council resolution 242, to the principle of "territory for peace."

Ya'acobi said Israel ought not to pose any prior conditions for elections in the territories.

He said that whatever ideas Shamir presented in Washington should have cabinet endorsement before he left.

Shahal argued that the prime minister evidently accorded the PLO a role in the pattern of relations since he admitted it was setting the tone in the territories.

After the meeting, Transport Minister Moshe Katsav told reporters that Shahal was construing the prime minister's words inaccurately since there could be no question of Israel recognising any political status for the PLO or talking to the PLO.

Apart from hearing Shamir's report on his meetings in Paris last week with French President Mitterrand, the cabinet also heard Foreign Minister Moshe Arens's report on his meetings with President Mubarak and his ministers, and with Soviet Foreign Minister Eduard Shevardnadze, in Cairo last week.

Prospects of relations with Moscow said receding

By MENACHEM SHALEV
Post Diplomatic Correspondent

Close scrutiny of Soviet Foreign Minister Eduard Shevardnadze's speech in Cairo last Thursday reveals that prospects for a near resumption of relations with Moscow have suffered a serious setback, officials in Jerusalem believe.

The Kremlin, it seems, has added a new and seemingly insurmountable precondition, with Shevardnadze's assertion that Jerusalem must agree to talks with the PLO before ties are reestablished.

At the same time, the Soviet minister reconfirmed that relations would be resumed only at the starting point of an international conference. According to officials here, the public utterance of this explicit timetable contradicts recent private statements of Soviet officials who have said that Moscow expects only a general positive movement on the peace process from Jerusalem before resuming relations.

The Soviet stipulations took officials in Jerusalem by surprise. "The Soviets were on a high tree even before the speech," one senior official said. "Now they have climbed to a point from which it seems impossible to step down."

Shevardnadze stated: "We would like the government of Israel to know that once it opts for the conference and agrees to a dialogue with the PLO, our two countries could take yet another step toward reestablishing full diplomatic relations, and the beginning of the conference would be a starting point for resumed relations."

Although the Shevardnadze-Arens meeting was characterized by almost total disagreement on all the major issues, officials in Jerusalem maintain the Shevardnadze statement could not have been formulated in Cairo but must have been worked out well in advance, before the start of the trip.

Government analysts say that the injection of a dialogue with the PLO as a prerequisite to relations conforms with the general tactical thrust of Shevardnadze's visit, which has placed the PLO at the centre of Soviet Middle East strategy.

The wisdom of this strategy for the Soviets is being seriously questioned here. A dialogue with the PLO is an absolute non-starter as far as the current government in Jerusalem is concerned and, despite their public statements, Amman, Cairo and Damascus are also believed here to be less than enamoured with the Palestinian organization.

Soviet attempts to bring about a reconciliation between Syrian President Assad and PLO chairman Arafat appear to be part of the Soviet strategy to bring together the two chief Soviet-influenced parties to the conflict.

But the PLO, analysts say, is looking to Washington, and not to Moscow, to further its position in the peace process jigsaw-puzzle. Assad, too, is increasingly wary of the Kremlin in the wake of its refusal to supply Damascus with all the sophisticated weapons which it desires and its warning to Assad that it would not support further belligerency against Israel.

Statements made by U.S. President Bush and by Secretary of State Baker in reaction to Shevardnadze's highly visible tour of the region indicate that the new Administration is not keen to facilitate a Soviet entry into the peace process.

Moscow doesn't insist

The Soviet Union does not absolutely insist that an international conference precede the resumption of diplomatic ties with Israel, Prof. Rodimir Bogdanov said in Tel Aviv yesterday. Bogdanov, deputy head of the Soviets' U.S. and Canada Institute and president of its Peace Committee, is in Israel for a series of lectures. He said the Soviet position favouring a conference was a proposal rather than a pre-condition for diplomatic relations with Israel.

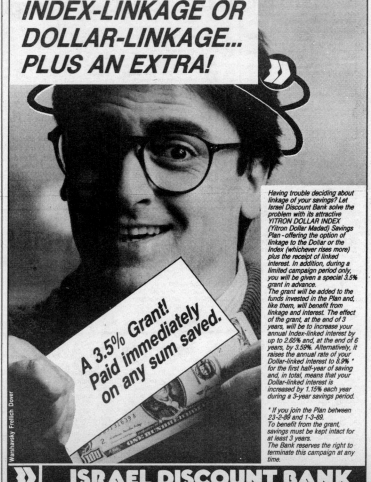

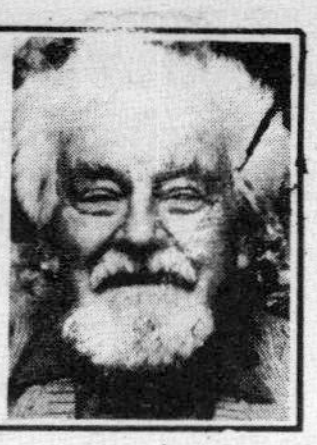

Death of the man who understood animals

Page 3

THE JERUSALEM POST

Vol. LVII, No. 17070 Wednesday, March 1, 1989 • Adar I 24, 5749 • Rajab 23, 1409 NIS 1.40 (Eilat NIS 1.20)

SECOND EDITION

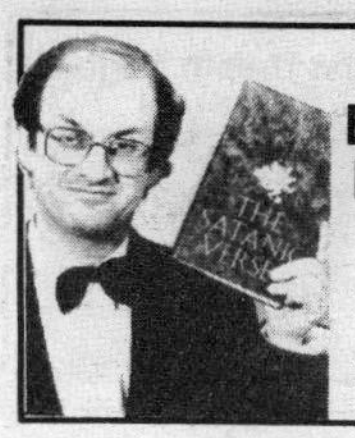

Edward Said: Rushdie and the whale

Page7

Plan on NIS 4 billion kibbutz debt approved

By JUDY MALTZ
Jerusalem Post Reporter

The government and the banks yesterday finally came to the rescue of the country's kibbutzim, agreeing to write off and reschedule NIS 4 billion worth of their debts, as part of a wide-ranging recovery programme.

Under the terms of the agreement, the government will reschedule NIS 3 billion worth of the debt over a period of 25 years at the relatively low interest rate of 4.5 per cent. It will also inject a total of NIS 650 million in funds into the kibbutzim over the next six years. The banks, mainly Hapoalim and Leumi, will write off another NIS 1 billion within the next five years.

The total amount of the kibbutz debts has been estimated at NIS 6.75 billion.

About two-thirds of this sum is owed by the United Kibbutz Movement (UKM) and the rest by the Kibbutz Artzi. In recent weeks, a fierce row had erupted between the government and the banks over who should bear the brunt of the debt write-offs.

The kibbutzim, for their part, have agreed to reduce their standard of living over the next few years by 5 per cent and to cut back their new investments by the same percentage. They will be left with NIS 1.7 billion in long-term debts to repay. As part of their recovery programme, the kibbutzim have agreed to raise NIS 500 million on their own, mainly through the sale of assets.

"Today we can say with certainty that this programme will be successful," said Aharon Yadlin, secretary-general of the UKM, following the signing of the agreement. (See also page 8)

Anonymous call to Israel Radio

Threat to kill Sasportas unless Palestinians freed

By JOEL GREENBERG
and MICHAEL ROTEM

An anonymous caller to Israel Radio warned yesterday that missing soldier Avi Sasportas would be killed if Israel did not release 1,500 imprisoned Palestinians.

The caller, who spoke Hebrew with an Arabic accent, promised to deliver a cassette showing Sasportas, but did not claim to speak for any group.

On Monday, a man speaking for the "Arab Palestinian Army" called the Jerusalem bureau of Agence France Presse and said the group was holding Sasportas in the territories, would soon publish a series of demands, and would by this afternoon release a video film of him.

Yesterday's call was made to Israel Radio's newsroom, and was received by duty editor Yuri Wasserman.

The quality of the line indicated that the call had come from Jerusalem or the surrounding area, Wasserman said. He added that the caller spoke in a deep voice, sounded decisive, and could have been between 35 and 45 years old.

Police investigators later questioned Wasserman about the call.

OC Central Command Amram Mitzna sought to play down the anonymous messages. "I don't know anything about the 'Arab Palestinian Army'group," he told reporters at Jerusalem's Hadassah Hospital, where he was visiting a Border Policeman stabbed Monday in Ramallah. "Every so often groups calling themselves different names pop up. Information arrives all the time, much of it has turned out to be nonsense, at least until now. As time goes by, all kinds of organizations or individuals engage in the sport of putting out such information.

"But every bit of information is examined and checked thoroughly," Mitzna said.

On Monday night, Ashdod police arrested a 21-year-old man who allegedly harassed the missing soldier's family over the telephone. The suspect is said to have called the family and played them news items he had recorded from Arab radio stations. The man has been tried for similar offences in the past.

U.S. insists PLO stop all attacks against Israel

By WOLF BLITZER
Jerusalem Post Reporter

WASHINGTON – The United States yesterday informed the PLO that it must cease all attacks against Israeli targets.

State Department spokesman Charles Redman said that the PLO was informed in Tunis that "attacks against Israeli civilian and military targets inside or outside of Israel are contrary to the peaceful objectives of the dialogue."

Redman said that the message had been conveyed directly to the PLO by the U.S. ambassador to Tunisia, Robert Pelletreau, during a meeting with the PLO's representative in Tunis, Hakam Ballaoui.

Redman added that the meeting had originally been requested by Ballaoui, but because of last week's unsuccessful attempt by a PLO-affiliated splinter group to infiltrate into northern Israel from Lebanon, "we felt it was important to get our views across on that particiular incident to the PLO."

The attempted infiltration had been organized by the Democratic Front for the Liberation of Palestine, which is affiliated with the PLO.

Redman declined to discuss other substantive details of the U.S.–PLO meeting, the fifth since the direct dialogue was initiated.

While warning the PLO to stop all military operations against Israel, the State Department also appealed to Israel for restraint in its military operations in Lebanon.

Referring to yesterday's Israel Air Force strike against DFLP targets near Beirut, the spokesman said: "This latest sequence of actions and reactions in South Lebanon underscores once again the need for agreed-on security arrangements that could ensure stability in the region and security for the peoples of South Lebanon and northern Israel. As I've said previously, we deplore the loss of life and needless suffering of innocent people on both sides, Lebanese and Israeli alike."

37 killed, 1,000 arrested in Venezuela price-rise riots

CARACAS (AFP) - Venezuela's President Carlos Andres Perez announced yesterday that his government was suspending civil liberties in the face of two days of rioting against austerity measures that have reportedly left at least 37 people dead.

Perez said he was suspending constitutional guarantees, including those protecting free association, public demonstration, and freedom of speech as well as the prohibition against detention without trial.

The widespread violence and looting was sparked by price increases for petrol and bus fares, a police spokesman said yesterday. Andres Perez called out troops early yesterday to restore order, said the police spokesman. He reported that more than 1,000 people were under arrest, mostly for looting stores.

He said armed looters were responsible for most of the deaths. One police commander, Rafael Mesa Esturis was shot dead during the disturbances and 11 policemen were injured.

Police agents said at least 11 Caracas neighbourhoods were raided by looters who began their rampage after a bus fare increase of 30 per cent went into effect on Monday, the day after a 90 per cent rise in the price of petrol.

Residents said the violence was the worst in Caracas since a popular insurrection toppled Venezuelan dictator Marcos Perez Jiminez in January 1958 and led to the establishment of democracy in the country.

Perez, who took office on February 2, has introduced an austerity programme to conform with International Monetary Fund (IMF) loan guidelines. Witnesses said most shops were closed in Caracas, a city of four million people, following the violence which began on Monday morning and continued sporadically overnight until yesterday morning.

Buses were not running, forcing thousands of people to walk through streets littered with debris.

Egyptian FM lauds Taba pact, but raises areas issue

The Jerusalem Post's Elaine Ruth Fletcher interviews Ismed Abdul Maguid

CAIRO – The resolution of the Taba border dispute is an "incentive" for normalizing relations between Egypt and Israel, which "has to be taken very seriously and encouraged," Egyptian Foreign Minister Esmat Abdel Maguid said in his first interview with an Israeli newspaper since the signing of Sunday's agreement. Abdel Maguid said Israelis and Egyptians should try to bolster relations based on their common sense of "human brotherhood."

But that same human sensibility leads Egypt to oppose Israeli actions in the occupied territories, Abdel Maguid said.

"There are things we don't like in Israel. We do not agree with what Israel is doing in the occupied territories. But many Israelis also are opposed [to Israeli policy]; I know it and I feel it."

Abdel Maguid spoke on the same day the leftist "Tugama" opposition party condemned the Taba agreement. The party newspaper, *Al-Ahali*, said Tourism Minister Fouad Sultan had been "blackmailed" by the Israelis in negotiations over the control and management of the Sonesta Hotel.

Abdel Maguid said that opposition to the peace treaty with Israel, still strong among intellectuals and the opposition, is a "part of the legacy of the past" to be gradually overcome.

Abdel Maguid maintains that the peaceful resolution of the Taba issue had touched a positive nerve in Egyptian public opinion here.

He stressed that he was speaking "as an average Egyptian."

The average Egyptian is a "peaceloving one," Abdel Maguid said. "But there also are things you cannot pressure him on. He has seen the fruits of peace, the benefits, but also the problems. Still these problems are minimal in comparison to going to war."

Abdel Maguid said that Egypt is "satisfied" with the peace between Israel and Egypt. "But we think it should be made into a comprehensive peace," he said, referring to calls for an international peace conference.

He said that Egypt had tried repeatedly to convey its desire for a comprehensive peace, a genuine peace and a peace conference both to the Israeli public and to its government.

If Israel remains unconvinced then "what more can Egypt do?"

But Abdel Maguid said he remained optimistic that public opinion in Israel was moving in the right direction. And he pointed to recent Israeli polls indicating that 50 per cent of the public is ready to talk to the PLO as a "very encouraging trend." Speaking just a month before the 10th anniversary of the signing of the Israeli-Egyptian peace treaty, Abdel Maguid said he affirmed that the course the late president Anwar Sadat had chosen was a "great" one.

Despite the current differences, Israel and Egypt must strive to understand each other's points of view.

Takeover in Petah Tikva, Beersheba, Ashdod; leading in Ramat Gan and Holon; Kollek's list loses absolute majority; Gurel clinging to narrow lead in Haifa

Landslide for Likud

Compiled from reports by Michal Yudelman, Andy Goldberg, Andy Court, Dan Izenberg and Haim Shapiro

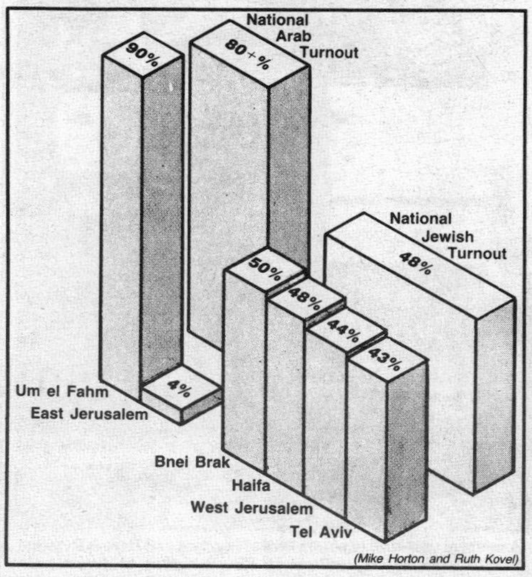

(Mike Horton and Ruth Kovel)

More election reports and comment on pages 2 and 12.

The Likud yesterday consolidated the trend it had set in the Knesset elections, with a dramatic sweep of the local elections.

In a swing which gained momentum as counting continued through the night, Likud took Beersheba, Petah Tikva, Ashdod and Ramat Gan by storm, was threatening to capture the perennial Labour stronghold Holon, and strengthened its position in several other local authorities. The Likud increased its power in Tel Aviv, and its incumbents in Herzliya and Kiryat Shmona won resounding new votes of confidence.

The Likud's Shlomo Lahat consolidated his hold in Tel Aviv, with his party also increasing its power in the council.

In Jerusalem, although Teddy Kollek again won a massive personal majority (around 64 per cent), his One Jersusalem list fared badly. It fell away from its previous overall majority of 17 seats in the 31-seat council to a projected 14 or less. This decline was caused in part by a strong showing of the new combined Citizens Rights Movement-Shinui list. The Likud declined but there were massive gains in Jerusalem for the religious parties, who more than doubled their strength in the council, a trend also seen in Tel Aviv.

The sole bright spots for Labour were in Haifa and Rehovot.

It was a night described by Labour Secretary-General Uzi Baram as "very hard to take – this is a national trend." Labour's incumbent in Haifa, Arye Gurel, just managed to stave off the challenge of the Likud's Tat Aluf (res.) Rami Dotan.

But after midnight, Prof. Yehudit Naot, the CRM-Shinui candidate, formally complained to the police about irregularites in the election and pressed for a new poll.

As Labour's gloom deepened, the fact that Michael (Mish) Lapidot forged ahead to take Rehovot was small consolation.

Cautious celebrations began late last night in Likud headquarters in Tel Aviv as projections showed the party achieving many of the aims it set up for itself on its way to achieving "Israel's second political revolution." Likud's Moshe Arens told *The Jerusalem Post* that "if the projections are true, then it's certainly a big success. It looks like we've taken Beersheba, Petah Tikva, Ashdod, other major cities; of course I'm satisfied."

Arens was surrounded by Minister Ronni Milo and several Likud campaigners and activists, many of whom were much less cautious in their reactions and effusively predicted Likud victories in major towns, even in Haifa despite the late TV projection that Arie Gurel would barely retain his position.

Across town, in sullen Labour headquarters watching the returns come in, were Shimon Peres, Micha Harish, Michael Bar Zohar, campaign head Yitzhak Peretz and several others, who watched with increasing dismay as Labour appeared to have been hit in nearly every major locality. Peres, at several points tried to break the tension by making jokes about Um el Fahm. "At last, at last" said Peres when hearing about the Islamic Front victory, in the largest Arab municipality.

Likud's fears that the low voter turnout (48 per cent in the Jewish sector) would damage its election chances proved groundless. As soon as returns began to flow in, smiles returned to the faces of Likud activists.

Running counter to the overall low perecentage poll, religious voters turned out in strength and in Jerusalem it paid off handsomely. Combined, Aguda and Shas almost doubled their percentage of the vote and the new women's religious list Emuna was expected to garner two of the 31 seats.

Shas fared well in all locations.

Israeli Arabs responded dramaticaly to the challenge presented by the Islamic fundamentalists and the left-wing lists. In Um el-Fahm, where more than 90 per cent voted, the fundamentalists scored a resounding triumph, capturing a projected 12 of the 15 council seats.

In several Arab villages, turnout exceeded 95 per cent.

The elections were marked by an exceptionally low turnout, which observers attributed to the balmy weather.

Beaches, parks and cafes were crowded, but voters kept away from the polls, where only 48 per cent of the eligible voters turned up.

Interviewed immediately after the early returns indicated a drastic falloff for his One jerusalem list, Teddy Kollek vowed that he would not resign in frustration at having to form a coalition with his religious and na-

(Continued on page 10)

Threats lead to mass E. Jerusalem stayaway

By ANDY COURT
Jerusalem Post Reporter

A smaller proportion of East Jerusalem's Arabs voted yesterday than in any previous Jerusalem municipal election in their 21 years under Israeli rule, acccording to preliminary statistics released by Jerusalem's election committee last night.

By 8 p.m., 2,500, or 3.1 per cent of the city's 80,000 non-Jewish residents had voted. In 1983, 18 per cent had voted. In 1973 the figure was 8.6 per cent.

Jerusalem has a total of 320,000 eligible voters, according to the municipality spokesman.

Officials in Mayor Teddy Kollek's campaign had expected an even lower turnout of Arab voters – about 1,500 – because of threats by the intifada leadership. They thus regarded the vote as an achievement.

During three-and-a-half hours yesterday morning, only six out of 5,300 eligible Wadi Joz residents showed up at the local fire station to vote, according to poll chairman Ya'acov Hof.

"Maybe they'll come when it gets dark and no one can see them," one of Hof's aides said.

A trickle of Arab voters could be observed in East Jerusalem's commercial district, the Christian Quarter of the Old City, and Beit Safafa village. A number of those voting said they were municipal or government workers, or relatives of those workers.

"I heard that they said they'd kill people who vote," said one Arab resident from the Christian quarter, "but I'm not afraid of anybody. I voted for Teddy, because he's good for us."

The main benefactors of the Arab vote are likely to be Kollek's One Jerusalem party and the Citizens Rights Movement-Shinui party.

"If we receive 5,000 Arab votes [roughly one city council mandate], I'll say 'thank God,' " said Maurice Zilka, One Jerusalem's co-ordinator in the Arab sector.

In 1983, about 12,500 East Jerusa-

(Continued on page 10)

2 am: Latest projections

Jerusalem: Teddy Kollek wins with 64 percent but loses majority in council. Religious parties double vote.

Tel Aviv: Shlomo Lahat an easy winner. Likud council strength consolidated.

Haifa: Labour's Arye Gurel barely clings to power.

Other major Likud gains: Petah Tikva, Ramat Gan, Beersheba, Ashdod

Labour gain: Rehovot

Um el-Fahm: Sweeping victory for Islamic fundamentalists

Teddy stays put but ...

Mayor Teddy Kollek maintained his popularity in the capital yesterday but the fortunes of his party, One Jerusalem, plummeted – from 17 seats in the outgoing council to 14 or less in the new one.

Kollek said he would seek "new arrangements" enabling him to govern without coalition partners. He specifically ruled out as a coalition partner the Citizens Rights Movement, which took up to four seats, saying it was "divisive and did not speak the truth."

The religious parties, led by Shas, doubled their strength in the council. Speaking above the din of rejoicing supporters who sang and danced at party headquarters, Shas Party leader Rabbi Nissim Ze'ev said he would join a coalition with Kollek only if movie theatres were closed on Friday nights and the status quo on religious observance was rolled back to the state of affairs two years ago.

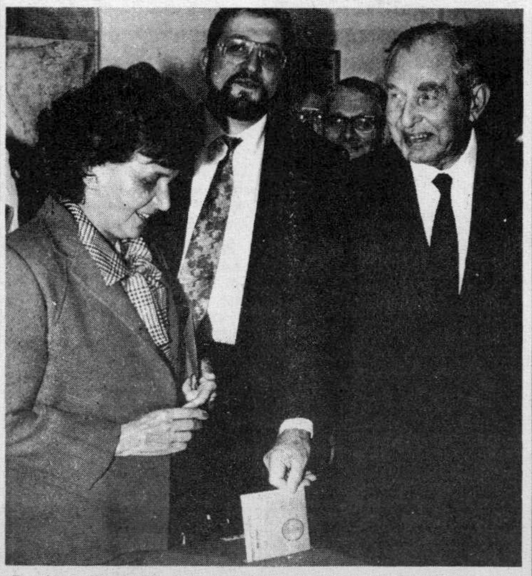

President Chaim Herzog casts his ballot in Jerusalem as his wife Aura and Interior Minister Arye Der'i look on. (Harari)

Fundamentalists win in key Arab town

By YEHUDA LITANI
and MARDA DUNSKY

The Islamic movement yesterday scored a sweeping victory in Umm el-Fahm, Israel's second-largest Arab city, taking control of the mayoralty and 12 of the 15 seats on the city council.

More than 90 per cent of the city's 12,000 eligible voters cast their ballots in the most dramatic contest in Arab sector voting, a race that ended with the ouster of Hadash incumbent Hashem Mahamid, who is also No. 5 on the party's national slate for the Knesset.

Throughout the country, Arab voters turned out in record numbers – an estimated 85 to 90 per cent, compared with 50 per cent for the Jewish sector.

Initial reaction to the Umm el-Fahm race was mixed. Former Labour Party secretary-general Uzi Baram characterized the Islamic movement in general as "dangerous," and Interior Minister Arye Der'i speculated that the success of the Islamic list in Umm el-Fahm could result in a national Arab religious list in the next elections.

Arab observers, however, declined to attach such sweeping political significance to the results, viewing it instead as largely a reaction to conditions in Umm el-Fahm itself.

Sheikh Hashem Mahajneh, spokesman for the Islamic Bloc, called the vote "a local matter" and said residents voted "according to what they saw in the area."

Majd al-Hajj of Haifa University said that the vote was not an indication of polarization among the Arab electorate, and that the results should be viewed "against a local background." He added that the Islamic movement in Umm el-Fahm is itself not a new phenomenon, but has been active there since 1978.

The participation of the Islamic lists was indicative of a new trend within the Arab sector in which the traditional struggle between Zionist and non-Zionist parties has been superseded by a contest between the fundamentalists and the non-Zionist left wing.

Soviet Jews to get home-made matza this year

Jerusalem Post Reporter

Soviet Jews will be eating ultra-kosher matzot this Pessah – with the import of the flour and the baking of the matzot supervised both by Orthodox rabbis and by the Soviet authorities.

The Soviet minister of religions, Konstantin Kharchev, joined with New York Soviet Jewry activist Noah Dear in Moscow yesterday to formally launch the matza-baking activities in the capital and in three other cities, Leningrad, Minsk and Kiev.

Dear, a New York City councillor representing an Orthodox district of Brooklyn, has imported to Russia 150 tons of rabbinically supervised flour from Strasbourg, France at a cost of $200,000.

Dear told *The Jerusalem Post* that he has arranged, with Kharchev's consent, that Habad rabbis from Moscow's Marina Roscha synagogue, who are not supervised by the minister, join with Rabbi Avraham Adolph Shayevitch of the main synagogue there in supervising the matza baking.

Death of a Socialist dream Page 5

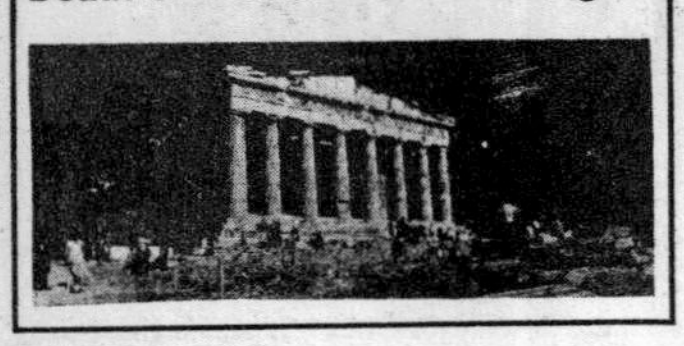

THE JERUSALEM POST

Vol. LVII, No. 17121 Wednesday, May 3, 1989 • Nissan 28, 5749 • Ramadan 27, 1409 NIS 1.50 (Eilat NIS 1.30)

FIRST EDITION

Beirut's nightmare: an envoy's testimony

Page 7

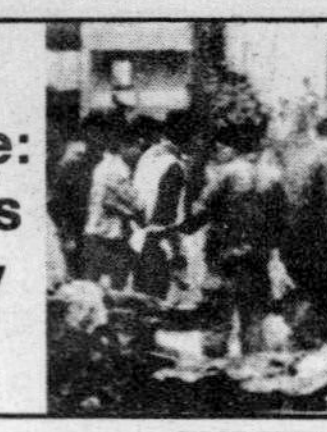

Body found in Jaffa – believed to be missing boy

By MICHAEL ROTEM

TEL AVIV – Police are almost certain that a badly decomposed body found yesterday in Jaffa is that of Oren Brahami, 13, who has been missing for 10 days.

A police source said that the boy was apparently murdered shortly after his disappearance from his Bat Yam home.

The body was found shortly late yesterday morning by a group of Civil Guard teenage volunteers, in an abandoned wing of the Armenian monastery near the Jaffa harbour.

The body was hidden under a pile of garbage. It was in such bad condition that police at first issued a statement that it was the body of a young woman who had been murdered.

Only after the body was taken to the Abu Kabir forensic institute for autopsy was it discovered, according to police, that it was probably that of the missing boy. The sources added that apparent signs of violence were found on the body, and that the boy was probably sexually molested before being murdered.

The monastery where the body was found is unused most of the year. Its doors are locked, but there are windows leading into the complex of chambers and staircases. The body was found in a small room on the upper floor.

The Pisgah park which surrounds the monastery is known as a trysting place for lovers. A number of violent crimes have been carried out there.

A special investigation team will have to determine whether the body is indeed that of the missing boy. The murderer is thought to know the area of the crime well and was familiar with the small gap in the park fence which enabled him to enter the monastery.

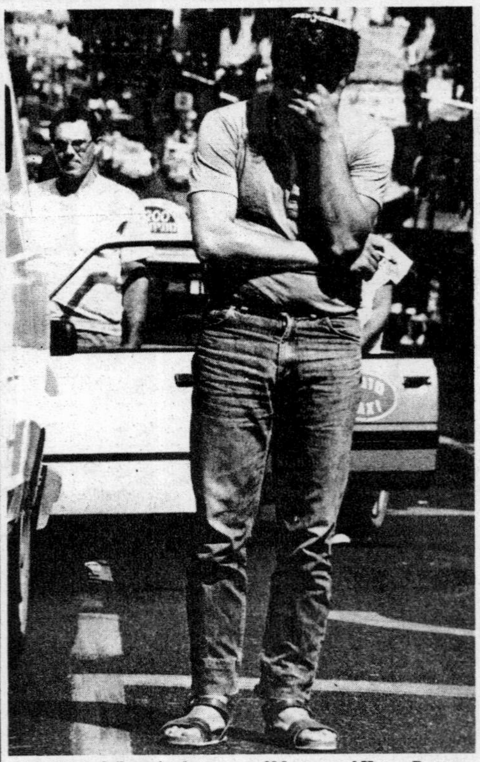

A moment of silence in observance of Martyrs and Heroes Remembrance Day stopped traffic at 10 a.m. yesterday on Jerusalem's Jaffa Road. (See stories – page 2, back page) (Sammy Avinisan)

E. German Jews allowed to commemorate Holocaust

The Post's Charles Hoffman reports from East Berlin

The Jewish community here yesterday for the first time joined Jews in Israel and around the world in commemorating Martyrs and Heroes Remembrance Day.

In previous years no Jewish ceremony commemorating the Holocaust was permitted. Instead, Jews observed a day set aside by the government for all "victims of fascism" every year in September.

The president of the Jewish community, Dr. Peter Kirchner, said yesterday that this change was part of a general shift of government policy towards Israel which began last year. "Previously," he said, "marking holidays or other events connected with Israel was not desirable."

He said that East German leader Erich Honecker had agreed to allow a separate Jewish ceremony after the community requested this during a meeting last summer. Kirchner added that Honecker had also been responsive to Jewish concerns that anti-Israel propaganda in the press might arouse anti-Semitism, especially among young people who don't distinguish between Israel and Jews.

Kirchner met yesterday with a delegation of Israeli journalists here for a week to learn about the Jews of the German Democratic Republic. The delegation was invited by the secretary of state for religious affairs, Kurt Loeffler, and the trip was arranged through the World Jewish Congress.

(Continued on page 2)

Arafat: PLO Covenant is now 'null and void'

Scepticism in Jerusalem

By MENACHEM SHALEV and DAN PETREANU
Jerusalem Post Correspondents

Official Jerusalem reacted to Arafat's statement last night with public disdain and scepticism, but senior officials admitted privately that they were surprised by the explicitness of his rejection of the Palestinian Covenant.

Avi Pazner, the Prime Minister's media adviser, said that the PLO chairman was "continuing with his same old lies." Arafat, Pazner claimed, is "characteristically" lying when he claims that he was elected on a platform of a two-state solution: "Arafat was elected on the basis of the Covenant – and nothing else."

"There is no reason to take Arafat seriously," Pazner said. "Talk is very cheap for him. He feels the need to repay President Mitterand for the meeting. In a week, he will find some explanation of why the Covenant has not, in fact, lapsed, just like he has 'explained' that incursions from Lebanon and the intifada are not terror."

Foreign Minister Moshe Arens's spokesman, Danny Naveh, reacted similarly, saying that Arafat's statement is "part of his web of lies."

Naveh said that for months, Arafat has been claiming that the Covenant, or parts of it, do not exist, and that the Algiers PNC decisions have superseded the Covenant. "In practice, however, Arafat has done nothing to change or cancel even one letter in the Covenant."

Privately, however, Foreign Ministry officials conceded that in Paris, Arafat had "probably scored another public relations coup." They expressed concern that his statement on the Covenant might undermine what they term "a new and gradually growing disenchantment with the PLO."

Senior government analysts admit that Arafat's forthright statement had not been expected. They said that there had been indications that he would express reservations about the Covenant, but not that he would declare it *"caduque."*

It was clear from comments made last night that the French word *caduque*, used by Arafat to describe the status of the Covenant, will be the subject of a linguistic-legal debate.

Pazner, for example, cited the word as it is used in French commercial law, in which the word means "lapsed" and is used in reference to contracts which no longer have legal validity. In the French law of inheritance, however, the word is more unequivocal, meaning "null and void."

Labour Party doves, meanwhile, welcomed Arafat's statement, saying that it may now be time to call for talks with the PLO. Labour Knesset faction chairman Haim Ramon told *The Jerusalem Post* that Arafat's statement was "a great step forward."

"The Labour Party platform conditions the acceptability of the PLO as a negotiating partner on the organization being based on the charter," he said.

Referring to the assertion by the Prime Minister's Office that the statement was "a lie," Ramon said: "there were those who in 1977 said Sadat was lying as well. Now is the time to put his words to the test. If

(Continued on Back Page)

Mitterrand called for move

By MICHEL ZLOTOWSKI
JP Correspondent

PARIS – French President Francois Mitterrand, specifically referring to the Palestinian Covenant, yesterday asked PLO chairman Yasser Arafat to "clear up contradictions" in the Palestinian position on Israel. A few hours later, on the French TV Channel TF1, Arafat declared the covenant "null and void."

The Palestinian leader, speaking Arabic, used the French word "caduque," which, in commercial law, is used to describe contracts which have lapsed. Another translation, in the law of inheritance, is "null and void."

Article 15 of the covenant, adopted in 1964 and endorsed in 1968, says: "The liberation of Palestine, from an Arab viewpoint, is a national duty and it attempts to repel the Zionist and imperialist aggression against the Arab homeland, and aims at the elimination of Zionism in Palestine."

Arafat had been pressed by Mitterrand to clear up contradictions between the covenant and the PLO's decision six months ago to recognize Israel's right to exist.

"I was elected on a political programme founded on the basis of two states," Arafat told French television. "As for the covenant, I believe there's an expression in French, 'C'est caduque.'"

Presidential spokesman Hubert Vedrine read an official statement that implied Mitterrand had urged Arafat to drop the article of the covenant that calls for the destruction of Israel.

"During the meeting, Mr. Francois Mitterrand noted that the continuation in force of the covenant of the PLO, adopted in 1964, was contrary to important points of the political programme adopted by the Palestine National Council in Algiers on Nov. 15, 1988, and he believed things should be made clear," the statement said.

A senior French official said Arafat's declaration was "very important. ...This is the first time he has said clearly that the covenant is obsolete."

Arafat earlier emerged from the one-hour-and-a-half meeting with Mitterrand wearing a bright smile. Costumed in his usual black-and-white checkered keffiyeh and his green army fatigues, he approached the crowd of reporters and said in Arabic, then in English, "It was a very successful, fruitful meeting. It was a very important meeting to push forward the peace process in the Middle East."

Arafat then entered his armoured limousine flying the Palestinian colours and left grounds of the presidential palace.

A few minutes later, spokesman Vedrine called in the reporters and read a statement explaining that Arafat's declarations in Algiers and Geneva last year had made possible the meeting between the Palestinian leader and the French president.

"France linked this meeting to the adoption by the PLO of the UN resolutions involving the recognition of the State of Israel and of her rights, and to the renunciation by the PLO of all forms of terrorism," he said. "These declarations must

(Continued on page 10)

Olmert: 'Very interesting indeed'

By MENACHEM SHALEV
Post Diplomatic Correspondent

Minister Ehud Olmert, Prime Minister Yitzhak Shamir's candidate for the post of ambassador to the U.S., expressed surprise that Yasser Arafat had declared the PLO charter null and void, and told *The Jerusalem Post* the statement was "very interesting indeed."

Senior Likud sources, meanwhile, say that a top private lawyer has submitted an expert opinion which states that there is no legal barrier to Olmert retaining his post as minister while serving in Washington as ambassador.

The opinion states that while the law forbids a minister to serve as a "civil servant," there is no legal obligation to define an ambassador as a civil servant. The sources expressed confidence that Attorney General Yosef Harish would reach the same conclusion.

Olmert's proposed appointment would require the approval of Finance Minister Shimon Peres. Peres is expected to demand, in return, that the post of UN ambassador be earmarked for the candidate of his choice.

Sources in Foreign Minister Moshe Arens's bureau, however, claim that Uri Savir, Peres's former bureau chief, should be viewed as a political appointee, although he is a ministry employee.

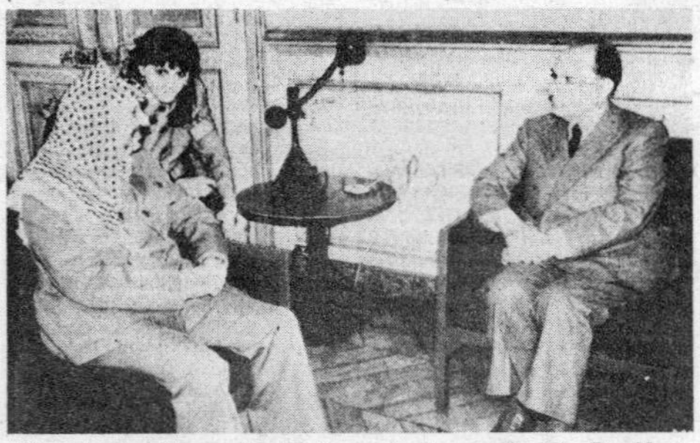

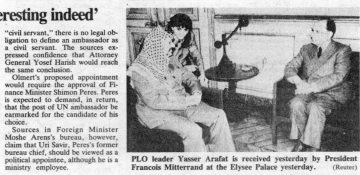

PLO leader Yasser Arafat is received yesterday by President Francois Mitterrand at the Elysee Palace yesterday. (Reuter)

Shamir reads names of his slain family

Jerusalem Post Staff

Prime Minister Shamir read aloud the names of his slain father and mother yesterday, joining thousands of Israelis who read aloud names of the six million.

Shamir, 73, joined the programme outside the Knesset, where six torches flickered in the wind. He lost his parents, two sisters, their husbands and their children.

"My father, Shlomo Ysernitzky, who escaped before the train left for a death camp and while seeking shelter among friends in the village where he grew up, they, his friends from childhood, killed him," Shamir said, his voice quivering.

He paused, then named as other Nazi victims his mother, Pearl; his sisters, Miriam and Rivka; their husbands, Mordechai and Ya'acov, and their children.

Shamir has never disclosed details about how his family perished, but they are believed to have died in death camps, said his aide, Yossi Ahimeir.

The prime minister also read out the names of 30 other victims before other cabinet members continued the listing.

Shamir, born in Ruzinoy, Poland, came here alone in 1935.

Top Arafat aide gunned down in Sidon

Post Arab Affairs Reporter and news agencies

The personal representative in Lebanon of PLO chairman Yasser Arafat was gunned down in Sidon yesterday, and last night was in critical condition hovering on the edge of death.

PLO chief Yasser Arafat, on a visit to France, said that Issam Salem al-Louh was "in a coma and receiving emergency treatment" after the shooting.

"Salem is wounded in the head. He is undergoing surgery, but his chances of survival are very slim," said a police spokesman in Lebanon. Earlier reports from Lebanon had said that al-Louh had already died.

Witnesses in Sidon had said that al-Louh, 44, was shot in the head at point-blank range by a man wearing a carnival mask. The killer then escaped after firing in the air. Security sources reported earlier that Salem had been machine-gunned to death in a Sidon gift shop.

No group claimed responsibility for the attack. But there was specu-

(Continued on Back Page)

Intifada violence could blur the Green Line

ANALYSIS
Yehuda Litani

The intifada is threatening to cross the Green Line.

Recently, there have been a stream of reports about stoning incidents in the Triangle area, and stone barriers on roads near Beduin settlements in the Negev.

Last week it was reported that an Israeli Arab from the Triangle took an active role in disturbances on the West Bank.

MK Ra'anan Cohen (Labour), said at a press conference yesterday that, since the beginning of 1987, there have been 600 intifada-related incidents in the Israeli Arab sector.

There are two aspects to this phenomenon: the Popular Front for the Liberation of Palestine is trying to mobilize Israeli Arabs to join the intifada, while one of Fatah's military arms, Force 17, is trying to motivate the residents of the territories to step up terrorist activity within the Green Line.

According to reliable Israeli sources, Fatah has stopped all its military activities from Lebanon. The present goal of the military wing of the organization, and especially Force 17, is to mobilize Fatah cells in the territories to embark on terrorist actions in the population centres of Israel proper. By doing this, the organization expects to broaden, as much as possible, the definition of "intifada" acceptable in international and U.S. eyes.

Fatah's leadership seems unable or unwilling to rein in Force 17's new activities. Nevertheless, Fatah remains opposed to the participation of Israeli Arabs in such intifada activities as throwing stones and petrol bombs. This stems from Fatah's recent acceptance of a two-state solution to the Arab-Israeli conflict. Thus, Israeli Arabs should operate, within the framework of Israeli democracy, in the struggle for equal rights with Israel's Jewish population.

Since one can assume that Force 17 cannot operate without Yasser Arafat's approval, it is a safe bet that Arafat wants it both ways.

The PFLP, according to the sources, supports the idea that Israeli Arabs should play an active role in the intifada. The PFLP is thus encouraging its main supporter among Israeli Arabs, the Abna el-Balad (Sons of the Village) organization, to share the burden of the

(Continued on page 2)

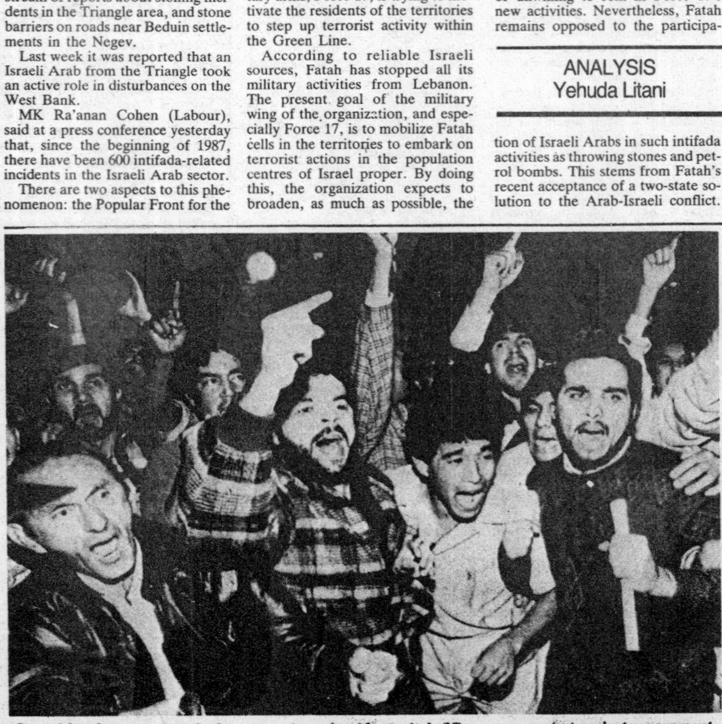

Opposition demonstrators in downtown Asuncion, the capital of Paraguay, protest against government supporters Monday night after national elections. General Andres Rodriguez won a landslide victory amid allegations of voting fraud. (See story – page 3) (Reuter)

Broadcasting chief to be elected today

By GREER FAY CASHMAN
Jerusalem Post Reporter

Broadcasting Authority chairman Aharon Harel has convened a meeting today of the 31-member IBA plenum to vote on the authority's new director-general.

As of last night there appeared to be only one nominee, Arye Mekel, a political adviser to the prime minister whose candidacy has been jointly endorsed by Prime Minister Shamir and Education and Culture Minister Yitzhak Navon.

The legal procedure requires that the plenum signify its approval by a majority vote. The name of any other candidate who gains nine or more votes must also be conveyed to Navon, who is the minister with parliamentary responsibility for the Broadcasting Authority and he in turn must bring the matter before the cabinet.

(Analysis – page 2)

Baker leading fight against PLO admission to WHO

By WOLF BLITZER
Jerusalem Post Correspondent

WASHINGTON – Secretary of State James Baker was yesterday described as personally leading the drive against the PLO being admitted as a full member of the World Health Organization.

The secretary has in recent days ordered U.S. embassies around the world to issue strong warnings that U.S. funding for the WHO and any other international organization that accepts "Palestine" as a full member will be suspended.

On Monday, Baker issued a sharply worded public statement outlining this threat. His warning followed a meeting over the weekend with President George Bush, who approved it.

According to well-informed sources, many high-ranking State Department officials were surprised by Baker's statement, which did not result from extensive internal consultations. "Baker feels very strongly about this issue," one source said.

The WHO's director-general, Dr. Hiroshi Nakajima, met yesterday in Washington with the acting assistant secretary of state for international organizations, N. Charles Smith. There was no official word on the substance of that discussion.

But privately U.S. officials said that Smith had again underscored the seriousness with which the administration considers the PLO application for full membership in the WHO. He urged Nakajima to derail any formal vote on the matter.

The PLO currently has observer status at the WHO.

Since more than 90 UN member states have already recognized the PLO's declared state of Palestine, a formal roll call at the WHO would probably result in the PLO's admission as a full member.

State Department spokeswoman Margaret Tutwiler yesterday publicly reiterated Monday's blunt threat to cut off U.S. funding to the WHO and other UN-affiliated agencies.

(Continued on Back Page)

Prague Jews blast leaders
Page 7

THE JERUSALEM
POST
Vol. LVII, No. 17137 Tuesday, May 23, 1989 • Iyar 18, 5749 • Shawal 17, 1409 NIS 1.50 (Eilat NIS 1.30)
SECOND EDITION

Bush's $ worries
Page 8

Chinese troops break through blockades, beat up protesters

BEIJING (AP) – Violence broke out late last night between Chinese troops and civilians for the first time since students launched their campaign for democracy here ten days ago.

Chinese soldiers burst through blockades set up by residents in the early hours of Tuesday local time and beat people as they headed toward Tiananmen Square, still controlled by tens of thousands of students and sympathizers.

According to one report, 15 residents were injured in one clash that occurred about 24 kilometres southwest of the square.

The Beijing city government announced late last night that the "marked influx" of people from other cities had made it harder to restore order and it was hoped they would leave Beijing immediately.

But the mobilization of hundreds of thousands of citizens for the second straight night, setting up roadblocks to protect the students in the square from advancing troops, was a severe setback for the government of Premier Li Peng, which has failed to end the protests despite declaring martial law on Saturday.

A Chinese journalist said 80 truckloads of soldiers moved through blockades at Fengtai in southwest Beijing and had already reached Changan Avenue – the city's main boulevard and a major route for the huge marches that have been held in recent weeks – shortly after 1 a.m. He reported that the estimated 2,000 soldiers, armed with Chinese-made AK-47 semi-automatic weapons were hitting citizens with bricks and sticks. They had, however, not opened fire. He said the soldiers had picked up bricks from construction sites and were using them to fight citizens.

Other reports, however, claimed the soldiers had not succeeded in reaching Changan.

Further out from the centre of the Chinese capital, soldiers clashed with crowds in a southwest suburb but here they apparently failed to break through blockades erected by civilians to keep the army out of central Beijing.

Witnesses said soldiers hit people with sticks and belts, but again did not open fire. They said some soldiers, who were also armed with AK-47s, pushed through throngs of residents trying to block their way, but that military vehicles did not advance.

Witnesses said the clash ended by 1 a.m. and that basically the standoff with Beijing residents at blockades throughout the city continued.

As the crisis on the streets deepened, diplomats estimated that China's leaders were locked in a fierce power struggle, as reformist and hardline factions were wrestling for control of the country. The reform-minded Communist Party leader Zhao Ziyang – who returned to his office this week after three days' "sick leave" – is believed to have succeeded in fighting back against Li but Li was not yet beaten.

A party spokesman could only say: "I cannot tell you whether Zhao Ziyang is or is not general-secretary of the Communist Party."

In what was seen as a blow to Li's authority, more than 100 top military officers signed a letter yesterday opposing martial law in Beijing and saying the People's Liberation Army "will never shoot the people." The letter, sent to the People's Daily, the mouthpiece of the ruling Communist Party, was also signed by former defence minister Zhang Aiping and former chief of staff Yang Dezhi.

Members of the National People's Congress, China's legislature, also began gathering signatures needed to open a special session on the legality of martial law, sources said.

The state-run television news quoted an officer as saying he had been told to pull back his troops because of widespread popular opposition to martial law.

A strong statement of support for the students came from National People's Congress chairman Wan Li, known as a leader in the reformist camp, who was quoted as saying: "We will firmly protect the patriotic enthusiasm of the young people in China."

Palestinian killed by rock thrown at car; gunshots fired at soldiers and policemen

By MICHAL SELA
JOEL GREENBERG
and Post Defence Staff

Jewish-Arab violence took a new turn yesterday when a Palestinian was killed by a rock thrown at his car near Kiryat Gat.

A soldier was wounded in the head by a rock thrown at him near Hebron, and an Arab labourer was injured by a rock in Jerusalem. Shots were fired at soldiers in the Negev and at policemen in Bethlehem. An arson attack blamed on Arabs was reported in southern Israel, and Palestinians said settlers had set their fields alight in the West Bank.

A villager from the Hebron area was killed when a rock hit him as he drove on the Kiryat Gat-Hebron road. The attack occurred at about 4 p.m., when the stone was thrown from a moving white GMC transit headed westward on the road, six kilometres east of Kiryat Gat. The stone broke the window and hit the driver, Abd al-Aziz Zabadi, in the head. The passenger sitting next to him took control of the wheel and stopped the car. With the help of passing cars, he called an ambulance who took the two of them to Barzilai Hospital in Ashkelon, where doctors confirmed the driver's death.

Zabadi, 42, was a wheat dealer from Hartha, a small village near Dura, not far from Hebron. The police are checking all the GMC cars that fit the description of the vehicle as given by the passenger, said Assistant Commander Tuvia Golan said. "I consider this very serious," he told *The Jerusalem Post* "and we will do our utmost to find the car and the stone-throwers."

The spokesman of the West Bank Civil Administration told *The Post* that no compensation is paid to Palestinians who are injured or for property damaged inside Israel.

At Yatta, south of Hebron, a soldier was wounded in the head by a rock during clashes with villagers. The soldier was evacuated to Hadassah Hospital in Ein Kerem, where he was reported to have suffered light injuries.

Near Moshav Nevatim in the Negev, three air force men said they were shot at while they stood at a soldiers' hitchhiking station. They told police that a van stopped near them, a man got out and began shooting at them with an automatic weapon. The airmen, who were unarmed, began running away and the gunman then returned to the car, which drove off. Roadblocks were put up over a wide area and police began a search for the car and gunman. There are no reports of either being found. The roadblocks were dismantled after several hours.

Negev police spokesman told *The Post* that the settlements in the area were put on alert for several hours and policemen at roadblocks checked suspicious cars. The police crime laboratory has been checking around the incident site and a special investigation team was established to follow it.

In Bethlehem, shots were fired at a police van near police headquarters in Manger Square, but there were no casualties, a police spokesman said. Policemen in the vehicle reported that at least three shots were fired, one of which hit a wheel. Troops were rushed to the scene and searched the area, and neighbouring shops were ordered shut.

Three Palestinian-owned cars parked near the Ashkelon power station were set on fire yesterday. Two cars were totally burnt and the

(Continued on Back Page)

PLO denies calling for revenge

TUNIS (AFP) – A senior PLO official yesterday distanced the organization from a new leaflet issued in the territories calling for revenge killings of soldiers and settlers.

PLO spokesman Ahmed Abderrahman asserted that the official text of leaflet number 40, which has not yet been released at PLO headquarters here, contains "absolutely no appeal for the execution of a soldier or settler for each Palestinian martyr" killed in the uprising.

He said that the text obtained by correspondents in Jerusalem on Sunday may have been a rough draft.

Blunt statement of U.S. policy

Baker tells Israel: 'time to be realistic'

By WOLF BLITZER

WASHINGTON – In a hard-hitting speech before a pro-Israeli lobbying organization, Secretary of State James Baker yesterday called on Israel to "forswear annexation" of the West Bank and Gaza and to "stop settlement activity" there.

"For Israel," he declared, "now is the time to lay aside, once and for all, the unrealistic vision of a Greater Israel. Israeli interests in the West Bank and Gaza – security and otherwise – can be accommodated in a settlement based on Resolution 242."

The secretary, addressing more than 1,000 people attending the annual policy conference of the American Israel Public Affairs Committee, also called on Israel to "allow schools to reopen" in the territories.

"Reach out to the Palestinians as neighbours who deserve political rights," he said.

Baker's unusually blunt speech, which clearly took Israeli officials and other observers in Washington by surprise, was the most far-reaching and authoritative Middle East policy statement of the Bush administration to date. His aides said the speech had gone through several very careful drafts.

The secretary, who spoke just before receiving Defence Minister Yitzhak Rabin at the State Department, was warmly received by the Aipac activists at the Sheraton Washington luncheon. He was repeatedly interrupted by applause when he reaffirmed U.S. support for Israel.

"I was proud to work in the Reagan administration that recognized the importance of U.S.–Israeli strategic cooperation and gave fibre and sinew to our strategic partnership," he said.

But his message to Israel to renounce annexation and settlements and to reach out to the Palestinians was met by silence.

Rabin, following a meeting with Baker yesterday afternoon, cautiously expressed his disappointment over the Secretary's speech before AIPAC.

"If I had written the speech," Rabin told Israeli reporters in his hotel suite, "I would have written it totally differently. I would have addressed the Palestinians more and Israel less."

(Continued on page 10)

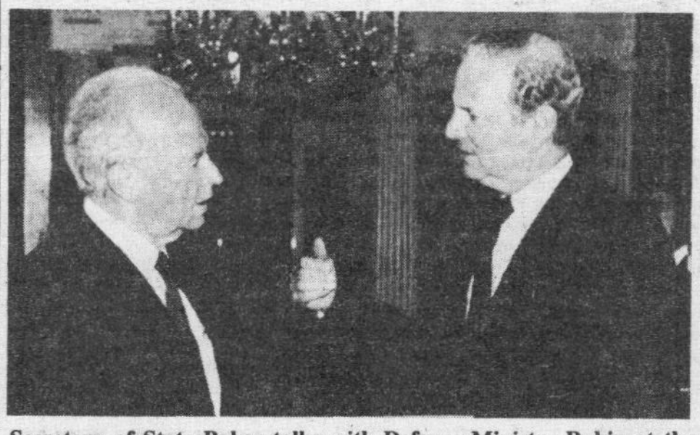

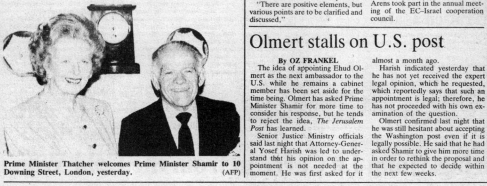

Secretary of State Baker talks with Defence Minister Rabin at the State Department in Washington yesterday. (AFP)

Herzog lashes out at 'taking law into one's own hands'

By GREER FAY CASHMAN
Jerusalem Post Reporter

President Herzog yesterday warning that if "the practice of taking the law into one's own hands" continues unchecked, it will lead to anarchy and chaos. Speaking at Beit Hanassi, at the the swearing-in ceremony of eight judges, Herzog called for the curtailment of the trend.

At a time when the public finds itself pressured by current events, said Herzog, there is a tendency "to forget the principles of law and justice which are part of our heritage, and the values on which our legal system is founded: that a person, regardless of race or religion, is presumed innocent until found guilty in court."

Israeli society cannot be true to itself nor to its traditions if it fails to protect the status of the law, he said.

Supreme Court President Meir Shamgar and Justice Minister Dan Meridor spoke in a similar vein. Stressing the duty of a judge to uphold law and justice, Shamgar also mentioned the need for tolerance, and stated that the judges should set for themselves standards exceeding even what the public expects of them.

Mindful of the backlog in cases due to come before the courts, Meridor was optimistic that with the appointment in recent weeks of a total of 20 judges – with more such appointments anticipated in the near future – the meting out of justice would move at a faster pace.

As for those who take the law into their hands, he said: "We change laws when it becomes impossible to live by them, but while a law re-

(Continued on page 2)

Thatcher stops short of support for Shamir plan

By DAVID HOROVITZ
Jerusalem Post Correspondent

LONDON – Prime Minister Thatcher yesterday expressed understanding but not support for Premier Shamir's proposals for elections in the territories, after three hours of what she described as "full and friendly" discussions. A statement released by her office later spoke of the need for a solution based on land for peace.

As she emerged smiling from 10, Downing Street beside Shamir in the late evening, Thatcher said that the talks had not reached "any magic conclusion. I don't think there is one."

Asked by *The Jerusalem Post* whether she had suggested refinements or clarifications to the Shamir proposals, she replied only that there had been "a very thorough discussion" and that the two had reached "great understanding."

Thatcher told Shamir that there could be no peace unless Israel was prepared to compromise on territory.

Later, a Downing Street statement described Shamir's plan as "a useful step forward", but stressed the need for progress towards talks on a solution "based on territory for peace."

Briefing Israeli journalists after the talks late last night, a relaxed Shamir said that while he had explained his proposals in considerable detail, Thatcher had not presented a similarly detailed response. She had stated that many elements still remained to be fully formulated.

Earlier yesterday, at a briefing for leading British media figures, Shamir said he was sure Britain and Europe would demonstrate support and understanding for his election plan, and would not confine themselves to what he termed useless meetings with PLO officials. Since they were interested in a quiet, sta-

(Continued on page 10)

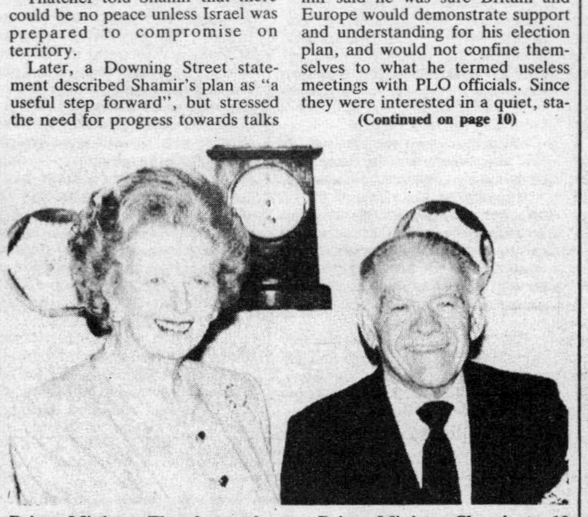

Prime Minister Thatcher welcomes Prime Minister Shamir to 10 Downing Street, London, yesterday. (AFP)

EC: Process must include PLO

By YOSSI LEMPKOWICZ

BRUSSELS – The European Community's Middle East position has not changed, and "we are still saying that the peace process and a global solution in the Middle East must include the PLO," the Spanish president of the EC council of ministers, Francisco Fernandez Ordonez, said here last night.

He was speaking just minutes before an informal dinner with Foreign Minister Moshe Arens, at which the Shamir plan for elections in the territories would be discussed.

Ordonez hinted that the 12 EC foreign ministers would ask Arens for clarifications on several points.

"There are positive elements, but various points are to be clarified and discussed,"

"These clarifications concern in particular the timetable of the plan, the issue of the participation of Palestinians in East Jerusalem, and the question of guarantees that Israel will give concerning the electoral process" – an obvious reference to the question of international supervision.

For his part, Arens asserted that Israel's initiative has "great merits," and said he hoped he would win European support. "Our plan is not only the best way but also the most efficient way of advancing the peace process," he said.

Before speaking to journalists, Arens took part in the annual meeting of the EC–Israel cooperation council.

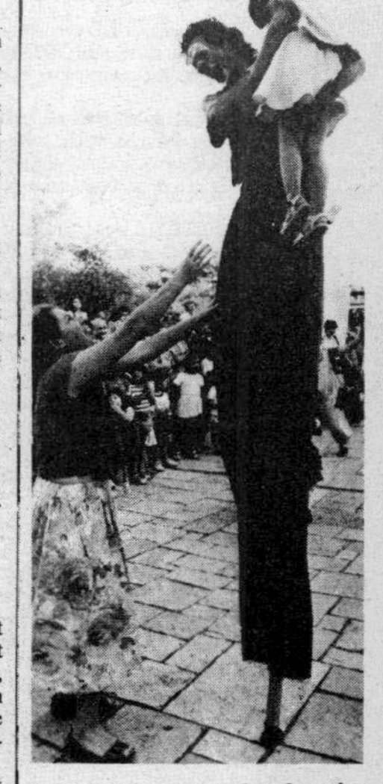

'Give me back my daughter,' a mother laughs to a high-stilter performer yesterday outside the Jerusalem Theatre as a crowd enjoys one of the Israel Festival's street theatre productions. (G. Feinblatt/Media)

An uglier intifada

ANALYSIS
Joel Greenberg

Yesterday's shootings at soldiers in the Negev and at policemen in Bethlehem give added urgency to the question of whether the Palestinian uprising is becoming an armed revolt.

The attacks came two days after a leaflet of the uprising leadership urged Palestinians to kill a soldier or settler for every "martyr" killed in the intifada.

The shootings followed last week's firefight between soldiers and Palestinian gunmen near Hebron, the first armed clash since the start of the uprising.

The developments indicate a new escalation in the level of violence in the territories, but hardly signal a transformation of the Palestinians' popular uprising into a war of guns and armed militias.

Shootings at soldiers and policemen occurred before the intifada and are not a new phenomenon. But within the context of the uprising, every attack is magnified and subjected to speculation on the general course of the revolt.

A shootout similar to the Hebron firefight occurred with Islamic Jihad gunmen in Gaza seven weeks prior to the outbreak of the uprising.

More important, the incident near Hebron was not a planned attack by the Palestinians, who over the past year attacked fellow Arabs, not soldiers. According to OC Central Command Amram Mitzna, their targets were Palestinians who cooperated with the authorities,

(Continued on page 10)

Olmert stalls on U.S. post

By OZ FRANKEL

The idea of appointing Ehud Olmert as the next ambassador to the U.S. while he remains a cabinet member has been set aside for the time being. Olmert has asked Prime Minister Shamir for more time to consider his response, but he tends to reject the idea, *The Jerusalem Post* has learned.

Senior Justice Ministry officials said last night that Attorney-General Yosef Harish was led to understand that his opinion on the appointment is not needed at the moment. He was first asked for it almost a month ago.

Harish indicated yesterday that he has not yet received the expert legal opinion, which he requested, which reportedly says that such an appointment is legal; therefore, he has not proceeded with his own examination of the question.

Olmert confirmed last night that he was still hesitant about accepting the Washington post even if it is legally possible. He said that he has asked Shamir to give him more time in order to rethink the proposal and that he expected to decide within the next few weeks.

Syria, Libya threaten to oppose PLO at Casablanca

Post Arab Affairs Reporter
and news agencies

Syria and Libya threatened to derail efforts to rally an emergency meeting of the Arab League around the PLO's Middle East peace strategy yesterday, upstaging Egyptian President Hosni Mubarak's arrival in Casablanca for Egypt's first Arab summit in 15 years.

Gaddafi said he would attend only if the summit does not recognize Israel, the Libyan news agency Jana reported late yesterday. "We will not accept any deviation or concession," he was quoted as saying about an agreement reached with Syrian President Hafez Assad, Algerian President Chedli Benjedid and Tunisian President Zine al-Abdine ben Ali in Tripoli to facilitate his attendance. All three leaders visited him within a 48-hour span on the eve of the summit in a bid to persuade him to attend.

Gaddafi said late last night over Libyan Television that he and the three leaders also had agreed to withdraw from the proceedings should there be any hint of concessions to Israel.

"We recognize only one state of Palestine," Gaddafi said in an interview with French Television. He earlier said he would boycott the meeting because of Mubarak's presence.

Morocco's King Hassan II, flanked by his eldest son, Crown Prince Mohammed, and his younger son, Prince Rashid, met Mubarak as he landed in Casablanca in a presidential jet. Hassan, in a white cloak and a fez, and Mubarak in a dark suit, embraced as gunners fired a 21-gun salute.

Egypt last attended an Arab summit in 1976. Then-president Anwar Sadat went to Jerusalem the following year.

As Hassan welcomed Mubarak and other guests at the airport, foreign ministers gathered in a downtown hotel trying to reconcile views on Syria and the Lebanese crisis.

But delegates at a pre-summit foreign ministers meeting said Syria was sticking firmly to radical positions, rejecting the Palestine National Council's declaration of a state last November, saying the terms amounted to unacceptable recognition of Israel.

Foreign ministers also haggled over who would represent Lebanon at the summit, but apparently compromised by agreeing to invite both the feuding Christian and Moslem prime ministers.

Hamas: No compromise

NICOSIA (Reuter) – *Hamas* called on Arab leaders starting an emergency summit in Casablanca to open their borders "to those who want to carry on a *jihad* [holy war]...against Zionist occupation."

Reject "compromises regarding any part of Palestine and affirm the right of the Palestinians to all their land," *Hamas* said.

Hyperinflation woes

Page 8

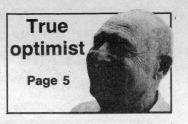

THE JERUSALEM POST

Vol. LVII, No. 17145 Thursday, June 1, 1989 • Iyar 27, 5749 • Shawal 26, 1409 NIS 1.50 (Eilat NIS 1.30)

True optimist

Page 5

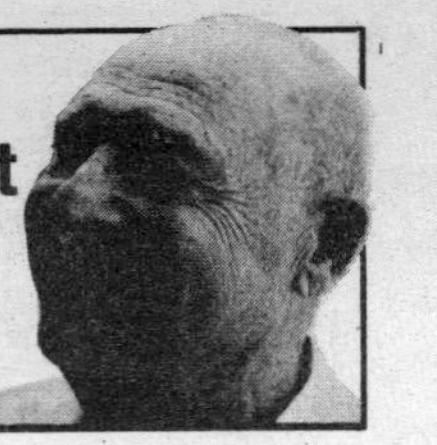

Bush to Soviets: End division of Europe

MAINZ (AP) – U.S. President George Bush yesterday challenged the Soviet Union to bury the Cold War by ending the "tragic division" of Europe, starting by tearing down the Berlin Wall.

He also called for freedom and democracy across the continent, saying Communism has failed to live up to its goals.

Fresh from his debut at the Nato summit, Bush made his comments in a half-hour speech in the Rhine city of Mainz.

Bush clearly intended his message not only for the audience here – which interrupted him numerous times with applause – but also for Soviet President Mikhail Gorbachev.

"In the East, brave men and

(Continued on Page Ten)

U.S. Speaker Wright quits in scandal

WASHINGTON (AFP) – Jim Wright, the speaker of the U.S. House of Representatives and one of the most powerful men in U.S. government, resigned yesterday under a cloud of alleged ethics violations that left his 34-year career in shambles.

The 66-year-old Texan, leader of the majority opposition and second in the line of presidential succession, preceded his expected resignation with a rambling, point-by-point defence against the ethics charges.

"All of us are prone to human error," he said in an emotional speech to a packed chamber. "I'm convinced I'm right – maybe I'm wrong."

Wright had been the subject of a year-long investigation that culminated in a televised review of allegations that he improperly accepted gifts from a developer friend and that he circumvented House limits on outside income.

Air Force raids bases

IDF kills Hizbullah men near border

Jerusalem Post Staff

MANARA – Three Hizbullah infiltrators were killed early yesterday by an IDF unit in the South Lebanon security zone and another captured by a South Lebanese Army unit. The Air Force meanwhile attacked Palestinian and Shi'ite bases in South Lebanon.

The clash with the Hizbullah force occurred at 4 a.m. when an IDF unit spotted the gang between the villages of Hulla and Shakra, just north of the security zone, four kilometres from Kibbutz Manara on the Israeli border.

The infiltrators were wounded before they had a chance to return fire. Hizbullah later acknowledged that the men were theirs. They carried 60 kilos of explosives as well as rifles and an abundance of ammunition. On their foreheads were red ribbons inscribed with excerpts from the Koran.

Yesterday afternoon SLA soldiers wounded and captured another terrorist in the same region.

It was the third consecutive night in which IDF and SLA units clashed with armed bands on the way to attack either the Israeli border or the security zone.

Six terrorist were killed in those incidents and two captured.

"Let there be no illusions that we have reached a state of quiet on the northern border," said Aluf Yossi Peled, head of the Northern Command.

In the security zone, an extensive investigation is still under way to find out whether the gang that tried to attack Metulla on Sunday and fired the Katyusha rockets at the town had the collaboration of residents of the security zone. Dozens of Shi'ites were arrested in the zone.

In yesterday's air force strike, the planes hit a base belonging to the Abu Nidal organization near Sidon and a Hizbullah base east of Mashara, not far from Lake Karoun.

The targets were described as command centres and ammunition dumps and were said to have also been used for planning terrorist attacks into the security zone.

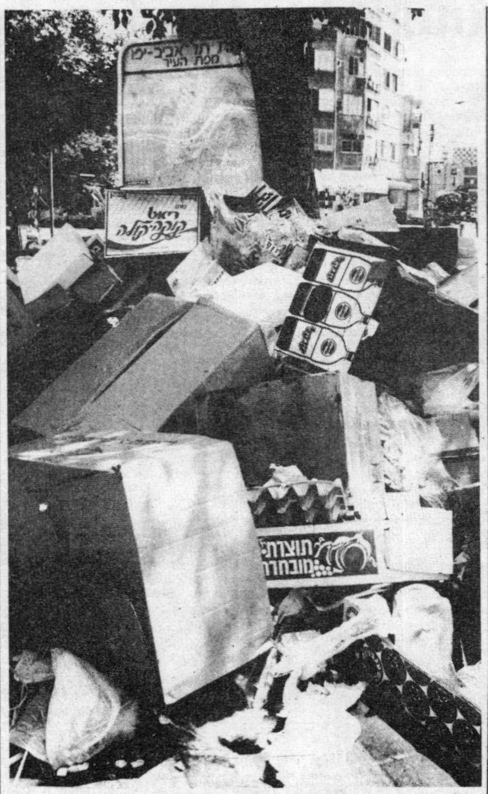

In Tel Aviv, emergency cleanup crews that tried yesterday to clear piles of garbage such as this one on Dizengoff Street were confronted by violence from municipal sanitation workers staging a work slowdown. Meanwhile, city residents say, the heaps – and the odour – are growing worse every day (Story – Back page). (Andre Brutmann)

Central bank: Incalculable losses

Intifada cost Israel $650m. in lost exports

By SHLOMO MAOZ and AVI TEMKIN
Post Economics Staff

The Bank of Israel reported yesterday that the intifada cost Israel $650 million last year in export losses, and caused further, incalculable losses by creating a climate of uncertainty that deterred investors and consumers – both foreign and Israeli – from putting money into the economy.

Together, these ill effects were holding back economic growth, Bank of Israel Governor Michael Bruno said in a news conference marking the submission of the bank's annual report.

The intifada reduced the business sector's production by 1.5%, but this was less than was previously feared, Bruno said.

The $650 million losses in exports included $280 million in tourist dollars that the intifada kept out of the country. Exports fell by 4.2% and tourism by 15% in 1988, the report said.

Israeli exports to the territories fell by about 40%, while imports from the territories dropped by 48%. Israel's "trade surplus" with the West Bank and Gaza decreased by 76% to a total of $42 million.

Although the number of Palestinians working in Israel rose last year to 109,000 compared to an average of 103,000 in the previous two years,

Trade with territories

	% change 1986	1987	1988
Imports			
Goods	26.2	5.7	-48.4
Services (Mainly wages)	-0.7	14.4	-23.6
Total	9.4	11.1	-31.4
Exports			
Goods	15.6	5.0	-40.2
Services (Mainly wages)	8.5	14.7	-14.2
Total	14.3	6.7	-35.2

absenteeism increased markedly. The Palestinians' sporadic strikes caused a 25% decrease in the effective supply of workers from the territories. A full-time strike could not be accomplished because there was not enough alternate employment in the territories, the report stated.

However, the brief and frequent strikes had little effect on the Israeli economy, as employers, especially in the building sector, adapted quickly to the loss of workers. The depleted workforce was called on to work harder, and their increased productivity made up for the loss of the Palestinian employees, the report said. The shrinking of the labour supply also resulted in a 10% salary rise for Arab workers who remained on the job.

The bank said this rise in wages had a "negative effect" on the economy. Before the intifada, economic integration of the territories with Israel had been proceeding rapidly. Employment of Palestinians in Israel rose by 30% between 1982 and 1987, compared to an 8% increase in Israeli workers. On the eve of the intifada, workers from the West Bank and Gaza represented 11% of all those employed in the business sector. Two-thirds of these workers were unskilled, and a number of industries were highly dependent on them.

To prevent further damage to the economy, the Bank recommended greater mechanization of industry, the shutting down of production lines that rely heavily on unskilled workers, and the limited import of unskilled foreign workers.

Despite free-trade pacts with U.S. and EC

Customs Authority to up exchange rate for imports

By SHLOMO MAOZ

Contrary to the intention of Israel's free-trade agreements with the U.S. and European Community, the Customs Authority will impose a 0.5% hike in the exchange rate for imports beginning next Tuesday, thus increasing income from purchase taxes and duties on these goods, *The Jerusalem Post* has learned.

The Customs Authority is taking this step unilaterally, without consulting with the Bank of Israel, which determines exchange rates for tax and duty evaluations. Central bank officials expressed surprised yesterday when they learned of the move, which is tantamount to a selective devaluation of the shekel.

At a news conference in Jerusalem, Bank of Israel Governor Michael Bruno lashed out at import barriers, saying that overprotection of Israeli-made goods could not be sustained in the coming years.

Sources said the Customs Authority is also strengthening a number of non-tariff barriers to imports, such as requiring additional licences for EC imports, and increasing the Israel Standards Institute's control over foreign goods.

Such bureaucratic delays are forcing importers to store their goods for longer periods. Longer storage adds to the importer's cost, and the increase is passed on to Israeli consumers. It is mainly importers of shoes, and of bathroom and plumbing fixtures, who have been affected by these delays, sources said.

These import barriers come against a background of Israel's $3.7 billion trade deficit with the EC last year – larger than Israel's deficit with the rest of the world, which came to $3.17 billion.

Levy may agree to postpone showdown

Shamir: Opponents of plan aim to undermine gov't

By DAN PETREANU
Post Political Reporter

Prime Minister Shamir last night said the Likud members opposed to his diplomatic initiative aim to undermine the national unity government, which he said must be preserved "even at the cost of great sacrifices."

Speaking at a ceremony in Jerusalem commemorating the merger of the local Herut and Liberal party branches, Shamir asserted that "it is absolutely forbidden to impair the unity of the Likud, the unity of the government, and the unity of the state."

Earlier in the evening, the prime minister met in his office for an hour with Housing Minister David Levy – a key opponent of his plan – and managed to extract from him an agreement that could mean postponement of a party central committee meeting. The two agreed in principle that the "date and agenda" of the meeting – at which the internal opposition, led by committee chairman Minister Ariel Sharon, plans to challenge Shamir – "should be discussed and determined together."

Shamir's aides said this represented an agreement by Levy that the "the committee need not necessarily be convened in June, at the beck and call of Sharon."

They told *The Jerusalem Post* that Levy was not expected to renounce his opposition to the plan after his hard-line public condemnation of it. Indeed, after the meeting Levy told reporters that his opposition remained firm.

Yesterday morning, aides to the three Likud ministers who oppose the plan – Levy, Sharon and Yitzhak Moda'i – met and continued discussing coordination of their efforts to fight the plan.

The Prime Minister's office, however, issued a statement yesterday asserting that the differences of opinion in the Likud were not ideological but "procedural and tactical."

Such differences over "details," Shamir said in his speech, must not be allowed to undermine either the Likud or the government "as long as there is no Arab partner that has accepted the initiative."

Crediting the initiative with "already doing us much service" – especially improving Israel's international standing – Shamir said it was "a clear result of the unity government."

Repeating a point he raised in the Likud ministers' meeting yesterday, Shamir credited the unity government with "unprecedented strengthening" of world Jewish support for Israel. "The day they hear that, God forbid, the unity government has broken up will be a day of mourning in the Diaspora."

"And those who want to weaken this government are the same ones attacking the initiative," he charged.

Alluding to the demand by his opponents within Likud that East Jerusalem Arabs not be permitted to vote in elections in the territories, Shamir said: "On anything having to do with Jerusalem there must be not even a shadow of a doubt: it is all ours."

But then he added: "To the outside, Israel must be tough and unyielding – but amongst ourselves, compromises are sometimes necessary and even desirable."

'Arafat is building an army in Lebanon for Palestinian state'

LONDON (Reuter) – PLO chairman Yasser Arafat is building an army for a future Palestinian state and 200 fighters have completed basic training in South Lebanon for the new force, *Jane's Defence Weekly* reported yesterday.

The magazine, published in London, said Arafat wanted the force to replace existing militias within the PLO.

Senior officers of Arafat's Fatah faction, the largest group in the PLO, are running training courses near the Mieh Mieh camp east of Sidon, *Jane's* said.

It said the officers were graduates of Indian, Pakistani and East Bloc military academies and also included veterans of the Jordanian army.

Two weeks ago, some 200 Palestinians completed basic training for the Palestine army at the Rashidiyeh refugee camp south of Tyre.

Jane's said the army had been re-equipped with new Kalashnikov assault rifles and rocket-propelled grenades and had shoulder-held SA-7 surface-to-air missiles, anti-aircraft guns and mortars in its arsenal. "Today, Arafat controls about 2,000 full-time trained fighters led by hand-picked officers and about 7,500 part-time militiamen in South Lebanon," the report said.

Electricity rates raised again

By LARRY DERFNER
For The Jerusalem Post

Electricity rates go up 10 per cent today, marking the third rate hike since January and bringing the cumulative increase for the year to 35.5 per cent.

Petrol prices remain unchanged, however, while fuel costs for industry increase 2.5 to 7 per cent, Energy Minister Moshe Shahal said yesterday.

The steep increase in electricity rates was ordered because the Israel Electric Corp. now pays considerably more for fuel to run its power stations and because the utility's operating expenses are growing, said David Uzan, head of the Energy Ministry's electricity economics section.

Despite rising rates, the IEC maintains that electricity in Israel is still cheaper than in Europe.

Troops kill Gazan, 2 die of wounds

By JOEL GREENBERG
Jerusalem Post Reporter

Troops shot and killed a Palestinian in the Gaza Strip, and two others from the area died of their wounds yesterday, during a general strike in the territories called by the Islamic Resistance Movement (Hamas).

At least 29 Palestinians were reported wounded in clashes with troops, and a settler was injured by a rock in the Gaza Strip.

An eight-month-old baby wounded in the head by a plastic bullet in Tulkarm on Tuesday was reported in stable but very serious condition at Makassed Hospital in East Jerusalem. His mother said she had been walking home when troops firing at demonstrators wounded her son.

Hamas called yesterday's strike to protest what it said were blasphemous remarks about the prophet Mohammed made by Prime Minister Shamir in an Independence Day interview to *The Jerusalem Post*. The strike was observed throughout the territories, the second time in a month Hamas has succeeded in enforcing a general strike on a different date than that set by the PLO-backed uprising leadership.

At the Khan Yunis refugee camp, troops shot and killed Ahmad Abu Khatab, 20, when they clashed with a crowd protesting the death of a local teenager who died during the night at Tel Hashomer Hospital. Mohammed al-Farjani, 16, had been shot in the head in a clash with troops on May 14. Palestinians said Abu Khatab, a Hamas activist who had been arrested previously, was shot in the chest.

Nawaf Salah, 20, of the Nusseirat camp, died early yesterday at Tel Hashomer after being shot in the head and critically wounded Tuesday by a plastic bullet during a clash with soldiers.

Another 25 Palestinians were wounded in other Gaza Strip clashes, according to hospital reports. The IDF confirmed three wounded.

A settler from Netzer Hazani, Moshe Elkayam, was slightly injured yesterday when a stone smashed the window of his car near Elei Sinai, in the northern Gaza Strip. Elkayam, 41, was treated at the Barzilai Hospital in Ashkelon and released.

At Makassed Hospital in East Jerusalem, eight-month-old Mohammed Hamdan of Tulkarm remained unconscious and partially paralyzed at the hospital's intensive care unit. Doctors said the plastic bullet had not lodged deeply in the child's brain, and it was unclear how extensive or permanent the paralysis would be.

The baby's mother, Samira Hamdan, said she had been walking home from her parents' house, carrying her infant and holding the hand of her three-year-old daughter, when she passed by marching demonstrators who confronted troops. (Sources in Tulkarm said hundreds had participated in the march.) She told reporters: "I arrived home and opened the door, and then the soldiers opened fire. A bullet hit the baby's head, and I saw it bleeding."

Elsewhere in the West Bank, troops shot and wounded a 15-year-old in the chest during stone-throwing clashes sparked by a raid on Kafr Labad, near Tulkarm. The teenager was reported in fair condition at Ittihad Nisa'i Hospital in Nablus. In Hebron, soldiers shot and wounded three masked youths who pelted them with stones, military sources said.

Defence Minister Rabin has apologized for an incident in which troops used pages of the Koran as toilet paper at the West Bank village of Deir Ballut. Rabin's apology came after the Supreme Moslem Council in East Jerusalem sent him a letter protesting the incident.

Sources in Nablus said troops searching a graveyard in the Rafidiya neighbourhood found a cache of hatchets and iron bars used by members of the "popular army" operating in the city.

New novel hits West's fossilized anti-Communism

Glasnost brings John Le Carre in from the Cold War

By MARK TREVELYAN

LONDON (Reuter) – John Le Carre's cold war days are over, but the master spy novelist doesn't mourn their passing.

For more than two decades, the icy confrontation between superpowers caught in the grip of the arms race gave Le Carre the perfect backcloth for his taut, suspense-filled tales of duelling Western and Soviet agents.

Relations have thawed in the four years since Mikhail Gorbachev took power in the Kremlin. But Le Carre, whose new book *The Russia House* comes out next month, says the political ferment whipped up by the new leader poses challenges for spies and spy writers alike.

"You don't know where the real sources of power are, you don't know where the real alignments and conflicts are. Paradoxically, this is of course a very strong case for spying the hell out of them," he said.

The Russia House, copies of which adorn the mantelpiece of Le Carre's elegant North London home, is the fruit of two visits he made to the Soviet Union in 1987. They were eye-opening trips for the man Moscow once called a cold war provocateur.

Le Carre found Soviet citizens familiar with his work through clandestine translations, with fans reputed to include Raisa Gorbachev, the Soviet leader's wife. "I very quickly discovered that I was a naughty and slightly dangerous, bemusing name for them to play with," he said.

Soon to be serialized in the glasnost flagship *Ogonyok*, *The Russia House* is the story of Barley, a genial, boozy English publisher selected as an unwilling agent by Western spymasters investigating leaked Soviet defence secrets, and is set in a Moscow abuzz with Gorbachev's reforms. It moves away from the traditional Le Carre suspense formula towards a subtler blend of romance, intrigue and ideas.

But the theme of espionage remains central, with Barley's British and American controllers portrayed as unyielding cold warriors whose thinking on Soviet Russia remains rooted deep in the past.

Le Carre is scathing about what he sees as the persistence of calcified anti-Communism in the West. He sees secret services, resistant to change, as the last refuge of national inhibitions, chauvinism and mistrust.

"The cold war has produced a situation where we fantasize about one another and where we have done so for so long that the fantasies have become reality," he said.

At 57, Le Carre, whose real name is David Cornwell, can look back on a quarter of a century of best-selling novels. Earlier he taught for several years at Eton, England's foremost public school, and worked in the diplomatic corps and in intelligence – a period on which he gives nothing away.

On the other hand, Le Carre believes *Spycatcher* – the memoirs of retired MI5 agent Peter Wright which the government fought unsuccessfully to suppress – served a useful purpose in describing "a secret organization that went rotten inside."

But he pours scorn on the infamous Cambridge spy ring of intellectuals and aristocrats whose best-known members were Kim Philby and Anthony Blunt.

"The Western traitors and the Western defectors had available to them, however faulty, the ordinary instruments of a very fair democracy. They could have gone public. They chose to enjoy the benefits of our society and go secret.

"Those guys were very sneaky and the other option was always available to them. Now the reverse is not true in the Soviet Union and therefore one can understand, in a curious way, a conspirator emerging from a closed society much more easily..."

Le Carre sees his new novel as carrying his work into a brighter future and reflecting the possible dawn of an era of superpower cooperation. "It seems to me genuinely possible that a political dream could be realized where the cold war could end and the real enemies could be identified...the ecological problems, starvation, terrorism, Islamic extremism, greed..." he said.

Yeltsin: Reforms have failed, Gorbachev is too powerful

MOSCOW (AP) – Mikhail Gorbachev's reforms have failed to improve Soviets' lives, and the president has accumulated so much power there is danger of a "new dictatorship," outspoken Communist reformer Boris Yeltsin said yesterday.

Yeltsin, in his first nationally televised address as a member of the new competitively-elected Congress, said the 2,250-member body should wrest power from the 20-million-member Communist Party that has ruled the Soviet Union since 1917.

His proposals to radically alter the Soviet power structure, making the party subservient to the Congress of People's Deputies, would require the president to submit to an annual, nationwide referendum on his performance.

"The promised programme and the promises of the past four years have not been fulfilled," Yeltsin told the Congress. "People have begun to live worse."

The one-time Gorbachev protege who was fired from his powerful party posts said the president, who is also Communist Party general-secretary, had been given "extraordinary powers" in the political overhaul that created the Congress. He suggested Gorbachev might be tempted, like past Kremlin chiefs, to abuse power.

THE JERUSALEM POST

Vol. LVII, No. 17175 • Friday, July 7, 1989 • Tammuz 4, 5749 • Thu Al-Hijjah 3, 1409 NIS 2.80 (Eilat NIS 2.45)

SECOND EDITION

Trapped passengers burned alive:

14 die as terrorist steers J'lem-bound bus into abyss

AT THE SCENE:

Volunteers join fight to save lives

By JOEL REBIBO
Jerusalem Post Reporter

Yishai Peretz was sitting in a Talmud class in the Imrei Baruch Yeshiva in Telshe-Stone when he noticed smoke rising from the ravine across the Tel Aviv–Jerusalem highway.

He ran out of his classroom without a word of explanation and spent the next two hours helping police, army, and Border Police evacuate bodies.

"When I arrived, the bus was on fire, and there were about 10 people who had been thrown out of it as it tumbled down the hill.

"Some were dead," said the youth, his white shirt deeply stained with blood. "I tried to comfort a man whose leg was almost completely severed."

Shimon from Ashkelon (he wouldn't give his last name) was driving to Jerusalem when he saw a small crowd standing along the highway. He got out and saw the bus below. "The bystanders were frozen in place, in shock. I shouted 'Hevre, let's get down there.'

"We saw people along the hill who had been thrown out of the bus, so we helped them. I helped a little girl named Haya. I made sure that she didn't move and that no one gave her water.

"The fire was just starting when we got down the hillside. We tried to approach the bus and calm the people down. But they were screaming and couldn't hear us. And then it blew up.

"That's what eats us up, we
(Continued on Page Two)

A bearded Palestinian man shouting "Allahu Akbar" seized the steering wheel of a No. 405 Jerusalem-bound Egged bus from Tel Aviv yesterday and sent it crashing over a steep precipice, killing 14 passengers and injuring at least 27, seven of them seriously.

Among the dead were several who were trapped inside the bus and burned alive when it exploded in flames at the bottom of the ravine.

Forensic experts at Abu Kabir were last night still trying to identify some of the dead who had been burned beyond recognition. Names of the dead were not released by press time.

Senior police officers said the attack had been planned, and that this would make it the most deadly terrorist incident in Israel since the Coastal Road massacre in 1978, when 37 people were killed and 76 were wounded.

Police Inspector-General David Kraus said last night that the police had been placed on high alert, especially in the Jerusalem area, to prevent reprisal attacks against Arabs.

The terror suspect, 28, was a

The alert was announced after the Kach movement distributed leaflets calling for attacks on Arabs.

Kraus's assessment that the attack had been planned was apparently based on the preliminary interrogation of the suspect's father, who was reportedly among the passengers on the bus and was arrested yesterday afternoon.

Police and General Security Ser-

**Compiled from reports by
Kenneth Kaplan, Ben
Lynfield, David Makovsky,
Abraham Rabinovich,
Michael Rotem
and Jon Immanuel**

vice officers were interrogating the suspect, under guard at Hadassah Hospital in Ein Kerem, where he is being treated for "moderate injuries." Police reported that the suspect had begun speaking to his interrogators after hours of not cooperating. They said his identity was known. Kraus said that the suspect's father, who had also been on the bus, was also under arrest.

worker in Tel Aviv's Carmel market, and had not been in Gaza in weeks. Arab sources say that the man was a member of the Islamic Jihad.

Israel Radio reported at midnight that the suspect told interrogators that he acted out of revenge, saying his family members were beaten by the IDF.

Investigators moved from bed to bed in the two Jerusalem Hadassah hospitals and Shaare Zedek, as well as Sheba Hospital, Tel Hashomer, taking statements from the injured as they recovered sufficiently to speak. Many of them had been asleep at the time of the attack, or had not seen what occurred at the front of the bus.

Medical staff at Hadassah Ein Kerem, where 14 of the wounded were taken, worked feverishly in the emergency ward for hours after the crash. The most serious cases were rushed into surgery shortly after their arrival, while others, bandaged but still covered with drying blood,

(Continued on Page Eight)

Further reports,
photographs – Page 2

DISASTER'S AFTERMATH: Soldiers and yeshiva students stand by the body of one of the victims of yesterday's terror attack on the Tel Aviv-Jerusalem bus. The burned-out skeleton of the bus, upper right, is being winched up to the main road. (G. Feinblatt / Media)

Jews, Arabs condemn attack as madness

**Jerusalem Post Staff
and news agencies**

"This tragic incident comes to remind us that the fight against terror in our country has not ended," said President Chaim Herzog, expressing the widespread revulsion at the bus attack in which 14 were killed and 27 injured.

"We will unite as a people and as one family in these difficult moments," Herzog said. "Our hearts are with the families who have lost their loved ones."

Prime Minister Yitzhak Shamir described the attack as "a new peak of madness which stems from hatred

fed by constant incitement." He called it "an awful catastrophe, the fruit of a brain consumed with hate. We will find a way to deal with acts like this, to prevent them wherever possible."

U.S. Ambassador William Brown called it "a loathsome action and we are sickened by it. We offer our deepest condolences to the families of all the victims of this terrible tragedy."

Vice Premier Shimon Peres said: "From every incident we have to draw conclusions. I have no doubt that there are ways to prevent acts like this in the future."

The Citizens Rights Movement called it "one of the worst attacks we have witnessed, from which every soul recoils in revulsion. It shows that when the gates of peace are locked, the gate of fanaticism and hate opens."

Mapam issued a statement expressing "pain and anger." It said: "Only a demented extremist could have perpetrated such an act against innocent persons."

The future of Arab-Jewish relations has been placed in jeopardy, Mapam noted, adding that the PLO's stated determination to re-
(Continued on Page Four)

Despite Likud central committee decision:

Shamir says his peace plan has not changed

**By MENACHEM SHALEV
Diplomatic Correspondent**

Prime Minister Shamir and Foreign Minister Arens sought yesterday to downplay the significance of Wednesday's Likud Central Committee decisions, telling the U.S., Europe and Egypt that nothing had changed in the government's peace initiative.

Arens sent an oral message to this effect to Egyptian President Hosni Mubarak, and both he and Shamir also met with U.S. Ambassador William Brown. A spokesman for the prime minister quoted Brown as saying that as far as Washington was concerned, the initiative remains unchanged as long as the government does not decide otherwise. [See US Reaction Pg 18].

Shamir said yesterday that the initiative "will continue to exist." The U.S. knows, Shamir said, that "the conflict cannot be settled without serious involvement of the Likud."

In an interpretation of the central committee action which clearly contradicts the intentions of their opponents, Shamir and Arens claimed that the clause which advocates "the eradication of terror and violence before the start of negotiations with the Arabs" refers to the negotiations which are to be conducted *after* elections in the territories are held.

Foreign Ministry sources explained that the term "negotiations" is used in the initiative only in the context of post-elections talks, while talks before the elections are termed "dialogue." Avi Pazner, Shamir's

media adviser, said that the violence and terror must stop before the start of "formal" negotiations, and does not prohibit "any or all" contacts with residents of the territories.

Arens also told Brown that the decision by which East Jerusalem residents would not be permitted to participate in the elections had no bearing on the government's initiative, since, in the Likud's view, East Jerusalem had never been included in the initiative in the first place.

In his message to Mubarak, conveyed through Egyptian Ambassador Mohammed Bassiouni, Arens claimed that the Likud meeting had actually strengthened the initiative. He repeated the message in a meeting with the ambassadors of the seven industrialized nations, to whom he also appealed for support for the government's plan to rehabilitate residents of the Gaza Strip refugee camps.

Defence Minister Rabin yesterday rejected the Likud's "explanation" of the decisions, offered by several Likud ministers in phone conversations. Rabin said that as defence minister, all the contacts which he maintains are "formal," and thus prohibited according to the Likud's view.

Authoritative Labour Party sources greeted the explanations offered by Shamir and Arens with disdain, terming them "pathetic." The sources said that Shamir and Arens had "capitulated to the diktat of Ariel Sharon. They should avoid spreading false and childish explanations."
(Continued on Page Four)

Gorbachev calls for 'common European home'

STRASBOURG, (AFP) – The Soviet Union is prepared to offer unilateral cuts in its short-range nuclear weapons in Europe provided Nato agreed to open talks on the weapons, Mikhail Gorbachev said here yesterday. The Soviet president made the proposal in an address to the Council of Europe at the end of a three-day official visit to France.

In addition to unveiling new proposals on arms reductions, including a call for the post-war nuclear doctrine of deterrence to be replaced with one of "moderation," the 58-year-old Soviet leader outlined in greater depth his plans for a "common European home."

He said the Soviet Union was prepared to adhere to Council of Europe international conventions on the environment, culture, education and the media and suggested the creation of "a European institute" to be used as a forum for comparison of human rights laws in east and west Europe.

French Foreign Minister Roland Dumas, who was present, called Gorbachev's remarks "important" and said they marked a "big step forward toward Western Europe." The Soviet leader had set out objectives for closer relations between East and West Europe "which we can subscribe to," Dumas added.

Gorbachev's address, the first by a Soviet leader to the Council, linked the arms reductions proposals with moves toward overcoming the post-war division of the European continent.

But Nato heads of state said at a meeting in May that they would not open any talks on reducing short-range nuclear weapons in Europe until a agreement on conventional arms cuts had been implemented.

Gorbachev called for the establishment of a joint European Economic Community-UN working group to study ways to put military industries to use in the civilian sector and said he favoured the withdrawal of all foreign troops from European countries. But "I don't pretend to have a ready-made plan in my pocket" for how the European home could be built, he said.

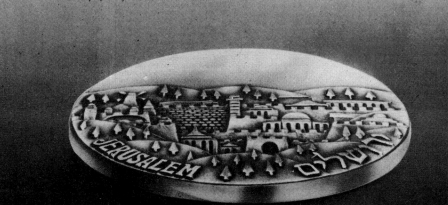

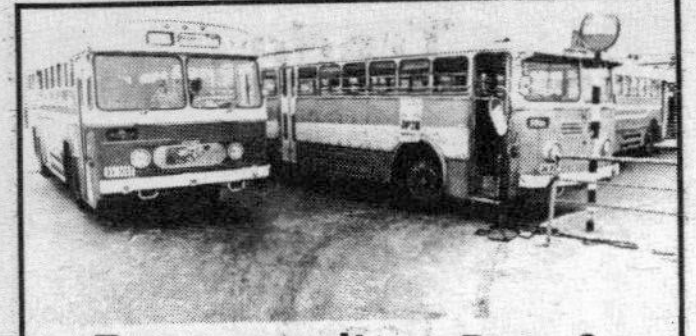

Bus security – Page 2

THE JERUSALEM POST

Vol. LVII, No. 17194 Sunday, July 30, 1989 • Tammuz 27, 5749• Thu Al-Hijjah 26, 1409 NIS 1.60 (Eilat NIS 1.40)

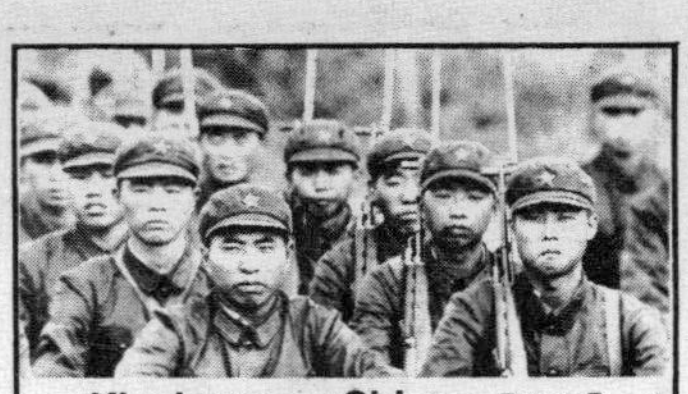

Kissinger on China – Page 5

U.S. officials, Congressmen privately express admiration

Bush and U.K. deplore the abduction

By WOLF BLITZER in Washington
DAVID HOROVITZ in London
and MENACHEM SHALEV in Jerusalem

WASHINGTON – President George Bush has indirectly criticized Israel's commando operation that resulted in the taking of a Hizbullah militia leader in south Lebanon.

"I don't think kidnapping and violence helps the cause of peace," the president said tersely Friday.

Israel's ambassador to Washington, Moshe Arad, expressed displeasure at the president's statement. He told a State Department official that the action was part of the ongoing fight against terrorism.

The Prime Minister's media adviser, Avi Pazner, last night sharply criticized the condemnation of the kidnapping, saying that "many countries are displayirg a total lack of understanding of Israel's anti-terrorist activities."

"I don't remember that these countries expressed such indignation when Sheikh Obeid sent people to murder and kill. We didn't hear such condemnations then," Pazner said.

He said the criticism against Israel was "absurd" as it comes at a time when "the world sees daily television reports about the Syrian artillery decimation of Beirut, in which dozens of people are being killed daily." To this, Pazner said, the world reacts with "total silence."

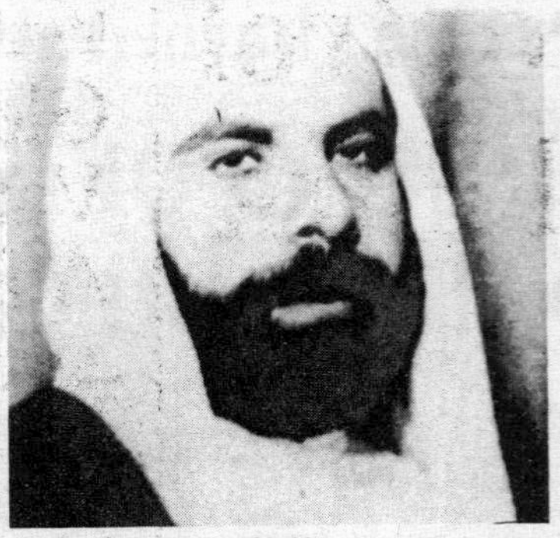

Sheikh Abdel Karim Obeid (Reuter)

He added that Israeli action was "absolutely legitimate" and that criticism would not deter similar actions in the future. "Countries which are not threatened by terrorism find it hard to grasp the situation, perhaps," he added.

The Foreign Ministry last night refused to comment specifically on the kidnapping. Danny Naveh, the foreign minister's media adviser, said only that "Israel has never ceased its struggle against terrrorism and will not refrain from future activity to prevent terrorist attacks."

But Minister Ehud Olmert deflected U.S. criticism of the action, saying: "I am sure that most Americans would have been proud had their government been able or willing to take similar measures against the kidnappers of Americans."

"This operation is one of those things which you have to criticize for the record but deep in your heart you

(Continued on Back Page)

Sheikh 'played major role' in planning attacks against Israel

Hizbullah turns to UN after IDF kidnap in Lebanon

By DAVID RUDGE
Jerusalem Post Reporter

METULLA – The Hizbullah yesterday called on the UN to intervene and secure the release of Sheikh Abdel Karim Obeid, now being held in Israel after being snatched from his south Lebanon home by IDF commandos.

The supreme Shi'ite council in Lebanon and the more moderate Amal Shi'ite movement joined in the call and in denouncing Israel's "latest act of aggression".

Radical heads of the Hizbullah threatened widespread retaliation if Israel does not release Obeid and his two aides, who were taken at the same time.

Hizbullah chief Sheikh Abass Musaweh declared in Beirut that the organization would not consider exchanging Israeli soldiers, believed held by the Hizbullah, for Obeid and other Islamic fundamentalists in Israeli hands.

He accused Israel of violating the "sacred immunity of Moslems" and warned this would lead Moslems to attack Jewish religious leaders.

Obeid and his two aides, Ahmed Obeid and Hashem Fahes, were snatched in the early hours of Friday morning during a daring raid that was described by senior IDF officers as an operation performed with surgical precision.

Obeid, 36, is reportedly a central figure in the Iran-backed Hizbullah. According to the IDF, he was head of the Hizbullah in south Lebanon and took an active role in planning and authorizing attacks against IDF targets in the security zone, and katyusha rocket attacks on the zone and into Israel.

Obeid, educated and trained in Iran, has also been linked to various kidnappings in south Lebanon, including the abduction last year of American Colonel William Higgins, who was serving with the UN peacekeeping troops.

The IDF raid was carried out between 1 a.m. and 2 a.m. Friday while Obeid, his wife, five children and relatives were asleep in their home in Jibchit village, 3 kms southwest of Nabatiyeh and a few kilometres from the northern border of the security zone.

Jibchit has long been a centre of Hizbullah activity, although the region has been controlled by Amal since the fighting between the rival Shi'ite factions last year.

A helicopter landed the raiding party, reportedly composed of 25 IDF commandos, in a wadi near the village. Some of the party was detailed to guard the escape route and the landing point, while the rest made their way on foot to the village.

The commandos, reportedly dressed in dark clothes and armed with silenced pistols, stealthily negotiated the streets of the village to Obeid's house. A small explosive device was used to blast open the front door and the raiding party burst in.

According to an IDF source, the commandos overcame Obeid's bodyguards after a short gunbattle and quickly searched the rooms for the sheikh himself.

Obeid's wife and five children were tied up and gagged, but were unharmed. The commandos grabbed Obeid and two assistants and took them back to the waiting helicopter. Helicopter• gunships were brought up to support the commandos.

The British newspaper *The Daily Telegraph* said the operation was the work of 25 commandos from the IDF's "most secretive special forces unit." The paper said the unit, which is answerable only to the chief of military intelligence, serves as "heavyweight back-up for Mossad operations when military might is needed."

It said the unit was 200-men

(Continued on Back Page)

Massive win for Rafsanjani

NICOSIA (Reuter) – Iranians voted overwhelmingly for Parliament Speaker Ali Akbar Hashemi Rafsanjani as president with enhanced powers, according to the first returns of yesterday's election and constitutional referendum.

An election official said on Teheran Radio that Rafsanjani won 13,468,355 of the 14,192,802 votes counted so far in Friday's poll. The Parliament Speaker, regarded as a pragmatist, had won more than half of the 24 million possible votes, and about 95 per cent of those counted so far.

The radio said that an overwhelming majority of the referendum votes counted, or 96.4 per cent, favoured proposals including the abolition of the post of prime minister and the transfer of the premier's powers to the president.

The voting trend indicates that Rafsanjani, a 54-year-old clergyman, will become Iran's most powerful top executive since the 1979 Islamic revolution. Some 24 million people were eligible to vote in Friday's election, which followed the death last month of Iran's supreme leader, Ayatollah Ruhollah Khomeini.

Officials said the turnout was massive. The final count may be announced in one or two days. Official results, after any complaints of voting irregularities have been investigated, are expected within a week.

Rafsanjani will take over from incumbent President Ali Khamenei, who was chosen to succeed Khomeini as Iran's spiritual leader, and, acting in that capacity, will have to ratify Rafsanjani's election victory.

"Although the Speaker was expected to win against the Majlis

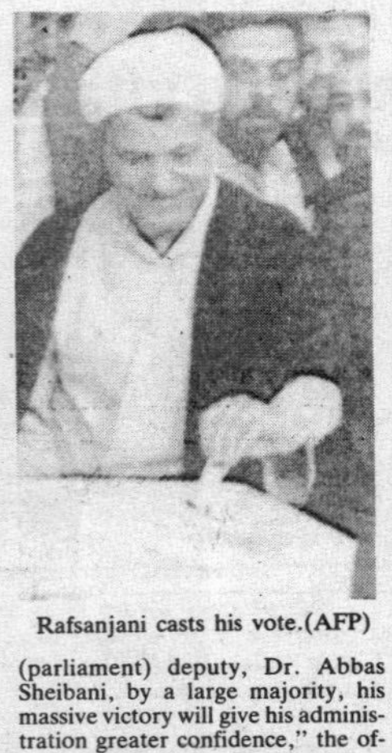

Rafsanjani casts his vote.(AFP)

(parliament) deputy, Dr. Abbas Sheibani, by a large majority, his massive victory will give his administration greater confidence," the official news agency, Irna, said in a report received in Nicosia.

Sheibani, 58, Rafsanjani's sole challenger, is a former agriculture minister who spent 13 years in jail prior to the 1979 revolution for opposing the Shah's pro-Western monarchy.

Rafsanjani has pledged to rebuild the economy, increase the role of the private sector and improve foreign relations.

He has pledged to cooperate with various groups and not to exclude competent people because of their political affiliations.

Assistant Secretary of State due here this week

U.S. official to press Palestinians on election

By MENACHEM SHALEV,
YEHUDA LITANI and
JOEL GREENBERG

U.S. Assistant Secretary of State John Kelly will try to persuade Palestinians here to accept the government's elections proposal and to agree to the formation of a delegation which would negotiate the modalities of the elections, Israeli officials and Palestinian sources said last night.

Kelly, who is due here Wednesday for a 48-hour visit together with Deputy Assistant Secretary Dan Kurzer, will meet with 12 prominent Palestinians on Thursday afternoon in East Jerusalem. Sources expect Kelly to brief the Palestinians on the developments in the U.S.-PLO dialogue.

American diplomats have said in recent days that they accept the 10 Egyptian conditions for the holding of elections in the territories, which, they added, were conveyed to Jerusalem after Egyptian coordination with the PLO.

Officials in Jerusalem said that Washington may agree eventually to sign a joint memorandum with the PLO expressing its support for the conditions, but at the same time is

(Continued on Back Page)

A language Hizbullah understands

By KENNETH KAPLAN

While the IDF had several good reasons to attack Sheikh Abdel Karim Obeid, the Iranian-educated leader of the Hizbullah in southern Lebanon, the decision to abduct him indicates the IDF's readiness to play hardball with the extremist Shi'ite organization which is believed to be holding at least two IDF soldiers captive.

Hizbullah has become a difficult enemy for the IDF to combat. Its members do not wear uniforms and fade easily into the Shi'ite population. Unlike the Palestinian terrorist organizations, it does not have many concentrated training areas or headquarters in the south. Its power base is in the Syrian-controlled Bekaa Valley, where the IAF is less apt to strike.

Recently the Hizbullah, has joined forces with Palestinian organizations in attempts to infiltrate Israel. Forecasts for the coming year see them entrenching themselves in a number of areas in the south.

The IDF, meanwhile, appears to have a high appreciation of the importance of individual leaders among the Shi'ite community in the south. Ever since Daoud Daoud, the commander of the Amal militia in the south, was assassinated last September, his organization has been weakened. Among the outward signs of this are pacts that have been concluded with the Palestinian organizations, and even a modus vivendi with Hizbullah which Amal defeated last winter.

Sources in Lebanon have offered another motive for an attack on Obeid, suggesting the IDF is aiming to torpedo the emerging rapprochement between Amal and Hizbullah which has given Hizbullah limited freedom of action.

For these reasons, a surgical attack against a single regional leader could be considered both practical and effective. The IDF is convinced that Obeid is the key man for Hizbullah in the south. But instead of killing Obeid, the IDF abducted him.

Hizbullah is believed to be holding Rahamim Alsheikh and Yossi Fink, two Nahal soldiers captured in February 1986 when their patrol was ambushed in the security zone. The navigator of an IAF Phantom jet downed over Lebanon in October of that year, Ron Arad, was last

(Continued on Back Page)

Jaruzelski quits as party chief to handle president's job

WARSAW (Reuter) – President Wojciech Jaruzelski resigned yesterday as leader of the Polish Communist Party, the official news agency Pap said.

He was replaced as party chief by 62-year-old Prime Minister Mieczyslaw Rakowski, the news agency reported. The vote was 171 to 41 in the Central Committee immediately after General Jaruzelski stepped down to concentrate on his new post of president.

The leadership change ended nearly eight years of rule by Jaruzelski who became the party's First Secretary on October 18, 1981, and led Poland through one of its most turbulent postwar decades. The 230-member body accepted the resignation with one abstention, it added.

The departure of the 66-year-old general closed a turbulent eight-year period in the party's history which began when he took over as first secretary on October 18, 1981.

Jaruzelski stepped down from the party leadership just 11 days after he was elected to the powerful new post of President of Poland.

Sources close to Jaruzelski said he was leaving all his party posts to concentrate on his new job.

Rabbinical courts sometimes invalidate Reform marriages performed abroad

HAIM SHAPIRO
Jerusalem Post Reporter

Although the High Court of Justice decision rejecting the petition of Reform rabbis to perform marriages is apparently only valid for Israel, the rabbinical courts in Israel have not infrequently invalidated Reform marriages performed abroad, ruling that the two parties were not married to each other and that they were therefore free to remarry.

According to Rabbi Simcha Miron, the former director of the rabbinical courts administration, this form of annulment is resorted to in dozens of the hundreds of Reform marriages with which the rabbinical courts deal each year.

Noting that the option is based upon the ruling of the late U.S. rabbinical authority, Rabbi Moshe Feinstein, according to which Reform marriages are not halachically valid marriages, Miron said that the rabbinical courts did not use this option blindly. They only resorted to it when there were extenuating circumstances, such as a recalcitrant – or missing – husband, or when the wife already had children from a subsequent marriage, who would otherwise be considered mamzerim. But the fact that the rabbinical courts resort to this option, is not widely known, not even among those closely familiar with the subject. A leading jurist, whose field is not family law, expressed his disbelief when he first heard of such rulings, only to concur that they were indeed within the law, after conferring with his colleagues.

Rabbi Richard Hirsch, director of the World Union for Progressive Judaism, told "The Jerusalem Post" that he had been unaware of such rabbinical court decisions and said that he would have to know the specific circumstances before commenting on any particular case.

But he did add that "the concern of the rabbinical courts, is often to protect halacha, which takes precedence over compassion. Halacha becomes a retrogressive force to prevent the resolution of inter-personal problems," Hirsch said.

However, Prof. Dov Frimer, who lectures on family law at the Hebrew University, said it was sometimes difficult to tell who was being strict and who lenient, who was acting harshly and who humanely. Feinstein represented one extreme, the other being identified with Rabbi Eliahu Yosef Henkin, who recognized Reform marriages as valid.

Feinstein had acted out of concern for those who might otherwise be considered "mamzerim," Frimer said, while Henkin had not wanted to write the Reform stream out of Judaism. Ever since the Reform decision to recognize patrilinear descent, Frimer added, he had the impression that the view of Reform marriages as invalid was gaining adherents among the rabbinical judges.

Frimer also stressed that even Feinstein had favoured "gittin" (religious divorces) in dissolving Reform marriages, whenever possible. On the other hand, even those who recognized Reform marriages did not consider the Reform marriage ceremony itself as binding, but viewed other factors, such as cohabitation and the desire to live together as a married couple to be the determining elements.

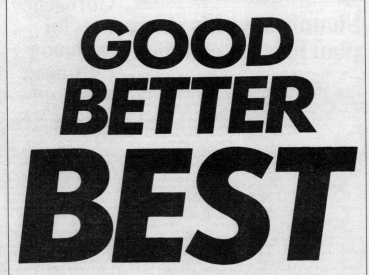

Hugo heads for U.S. mainland
Page 3

THE JERUSALEM POST

Vol. LVII, No. 17239 Wednesday, September 20, 1989 • Elul 20, 5749 • Safar 19, 1409 NIS 1.60 (Eilat NIS 1.40)

Trade barriers going up
Page 8

Huge blaze raging out of control in Mount Carmel National Park

5 fires set deliberately; 8,000 dunams destroyed near Haifa

By DAVID RUDGE
Jerusalem Post Reporter

HAIFA – A huge blaze that destroyed 8,000 dunams of forest and brushland in the Mount Carmel National Park here continued to rage out of control last night despite the efforts of hundreds of fire fighters.

Late last night, the authorities were considering the evacuation of Kibbutz Beit Oren, on the Carmel south of the city. The fire was spreading towards the kibbutz, which has stockpiles of poisons and two large gas containers.

Police said the fire, which broke out in five separate places around midday, was started deliberately.

Ten suspects were detained for questioning in connection with the arson, which a senior police officer said was "most likely nationalistically motivated."

An anonymous caller told Israel Television's Arabic service that a group called Direct Revenge had set the fire.

Eleven people, including six Druse youngsters from the village of Usfiya who had been hiking in the area, were injured and taken to the Carmel Hospital. Most of those admitted, among them a policeman, two firemen and a Nature Reserves Authority ranger, were treated for smoke inhalation.

Dozens of rare animals in the Mount Carmel Hai Bar (Animal Sanctuary) were burned alive. NRA wardens saved scores of others by herding them into enclosures away from the flames.

Haifa University was evacuated early in the afternoon, and later 80 children and 40 adults were moved from Kibbutz Beit Oren to the safety of Kibbutz Ein Hacarmel.

At one stage, it was feared that the blaze would spread to Tirat Carmel and Haifa's Denya quarter. Emergency plans were prepared for a mass evacuation, which was made unnecessary by a sudden shift in the wind that whipped the flames towards Beit Oren.

The kibbutz was the scene of intensive fire fighting last night when a renewed outbreak threatened the settlement. Reinforcements of fire fighters were rushed to the scene. Haifa district fire brigade commander Moshe Vardi told *The Jerusalem Post* that the blaze was still burning out of control in several areas late last night.

"We are prepared to deal with the fire throughout the night and we expect intensive fire fighting to continue in the morning, and probably later," said Vardi.

More than 80 firemen with 20 trucks, many of them brought in from surrounding regions and the Tel Aviv district, fought the blaze throughout the day and night. The firemen were aided by over 300 police and Border Police, 130 civil guards, more than 200 soldiers and hundreds of volonteers, JNF workers and NRA wardens.

Air force helicopters and crop-spraying planes flew scores of sorties, dumping tons of water on the inferno where the difficult terrain made access for fire engines impossible.

The aerial operations ceased as darkness fell.

OC Northern Command Aluf Yossi Peled and Police Minister Haim Bar-Lev visited the scene and were briefed by Vardi and Northern District Police Commander Albert Musafia.

The fire erupted on both sides of the main road running along Mount Carmel from Denya to Usfiya. The road was closed to traffic throughout the day and night with only emergency and fire fighting teams allowed through.

NRA deputy director-general Dan Peri, who surveyed the devastation from the air, said it was the worst fire on the Carmel and one of the worst in the country since the establishment of the authority in 1964. The damage, he said, would take dozens of years to repair.

Haifa Mayor Arieh Gurel, who also visited the scene, said the arsonists had "no feelings and no sense."

The fire destroyed natural beauty

(Continued on Back Page)

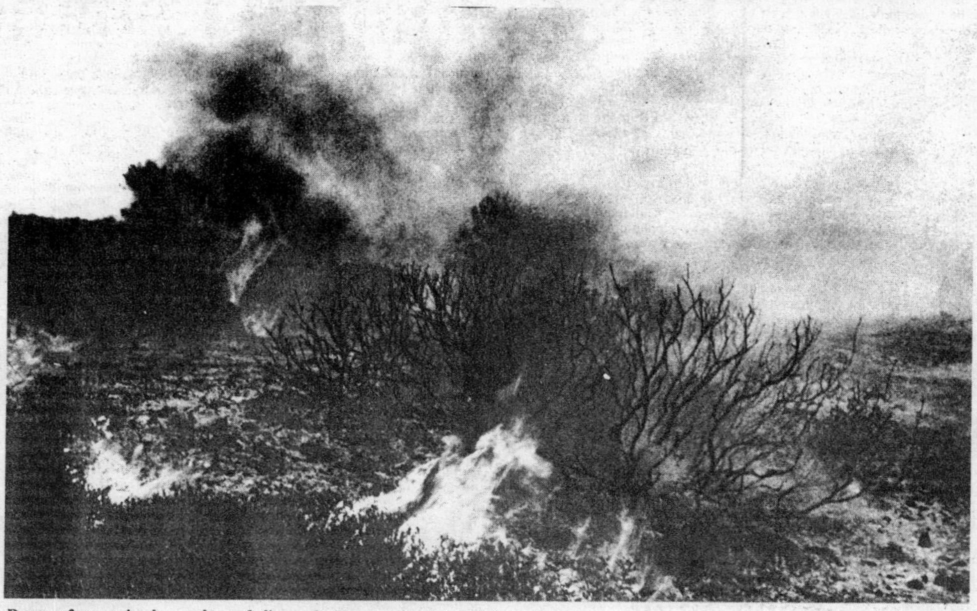

Dozens of rare animals were burned alive as the blaze ravaged the Hai Bar sanctuary. (Israel Sun)

'It looks like the morning after the bomb'

By DAVID RUDGE
Jerusalem Post Reporter

HAIFA – The blackened, fire-ravaged trees stood out starkly amid the piles of ashen debris on the part of Mt. Carmel known as Little Switzerland.

"It's like the morning after the bomb," said Igor, a member of Kibbutz Beit Oren and one of the hundreds of volunteers who battled desperately yesterday against the huge blaze that swept large tracts of this area of natural beauty.

Igor, 34, had earlier tried to tackle flames that were spreading close to his kibbutz, but the area proved inaccessible.

"We used beaters but to little effect. The flames were too fierce," he said.

At about 1:30 p.m. the kibbutz was instructed to evacuate a number of its residents. Some 80 children and 40 adults, mainly women, were taken in private vehicles to Kibbutz Ein Hacarmel.

The remainder chose to stay behind to do what they could to protect the settlement from the encroaching fire.

Earlier, in the morning, two other members, teenagers Reuben Bar-Hai and Boaz Ben-Haim, had taken out the kibbutz fire-fighting equipment – consisting of a tractor and water container – to try to deal with one outbreak of fire in a wadi near the kibbutz. The teenagers were lucky to escape with their lives. The tractor and container were destroyed.

"We got to the place and within seconds we found ourselves surrounded by flames," said Boaz.

"We didn't know which way to turn because we couldn't predict the movement of the fire," he said.

In the end they decided to abandon the tractor and flee.

"We were just very lucky that the way we chose was not the way the fire was moving," said Boaz, who was covered with cuts and scratches.

"It was terrifying. I really thought it was the end," he added.

In another area, Nature Reserves Authority wardens battled, at times with their bare hands, to save the lives of rare animals in the Hai Bar sanctuary.

An estimated 5,000 of the reserve's 7,000 dunams were destroyed, and despite the efforts of the NRA dozens of animals were burned alive, including Cypriot wild sheep, roe and fallow deer and gazelles.

One of the NRA rangers, Avi Tzariri, managed to save an eagle's nest in addition to herding 80 animals into a safe enclosure away from the flames.

The authority's director-general, Dan Perry, said that the animals in the sanctuary included rare species mentioned in the Bible.

He added that the authority would have to provide food for the animals as their own natural resources had been wiped out.

Salman Abu Rukun, an authority ranger for the past 13 years, said it was one of the worst fires and certainly the most dangerous he had ever seen.

"This area is surrounded by residential areas, and the fire could easily have caused loss of life and property. As it is, thousands of dunams of some of the most beautiful scenery in the country has been destroyed, and along with it the entire ecosystem," he said.

Baker wants 3-way talks with Arens, Egyptian FM

By WOLF BLITZER
Jerusalem Post Correspondent

WASHINGTON – Secretary of State James Baker yesterday said he hopes to host a three-way meeting at the UN next week with Foreign Minister Moshe Arens and Egypt's Foreign Minister Esmat Abdel Meguid.

At a State Department news conference, Baker said such a meeting will help to implement Israel's proposal for Palestinian elections in the West Bank and the Gaza Strip.

Baker said he was "encouraged by the recent diplomatic activity." The U.S. intends "to remain actively involved and engaged with the parties," he added.

"Let me say that we strongly support the government of Israel's elections initiative," Baker said. "We see Egypt's 10 points not as an alternative to the Israeli government's proposal. On the contrary, we think they represent Egypt's acceptance of the Israeli proposal and their views – Egypt's views – on how to get to elections and make it work – how to get a dialogue."

Meanwhile, the State Department's ranking Middle Eastern specialist yesterday singled out Egyptian President Hosni Mubarak for praise for his role in trying to promote an Israeli-Palestinian dialogue.

"President Mubarak has been particularly helpful and energetic in seeking ways to advance the process," Assistant Secretary for Near Eastern and South Asian Affairs John Kelly said.

Testifying before the House Foreign Affairs Subcommittee on Europe and the Middle East, Kelly said that Egypt's 10-point proposal constitutes "a constructive and valuable

(Continued on Back Page)

Meeting fails to bridge coalition gap

Shamir rejects key points of Mubarak's peace proposals

Compiled from reports by David Makovsky, Menachem Shalev, Dan Petreanu, Michal Yudelman and Tom Tugend

Prime Minister Shamir last night sharply rejected key points of Egyptian President Hosni Mubarak's peace proposals, among them the participation in negotiations with Israel of Palestinians who do not live in the territories.

Yesterday morning's meeting between Shamir and Defence Minister Rabin, in which Rabin reported on his Cairo talks with Mubarak on Monday, apparently failed to bridge the gap between the two regarding the proposals.

But a full-blown coalition crisis has been forestalled for at least several weeks, until Vice Premier Shimon Peres and Foreign Minister Moshe Arens return from the U.S. and a decisive inner cabinet meeting is held.

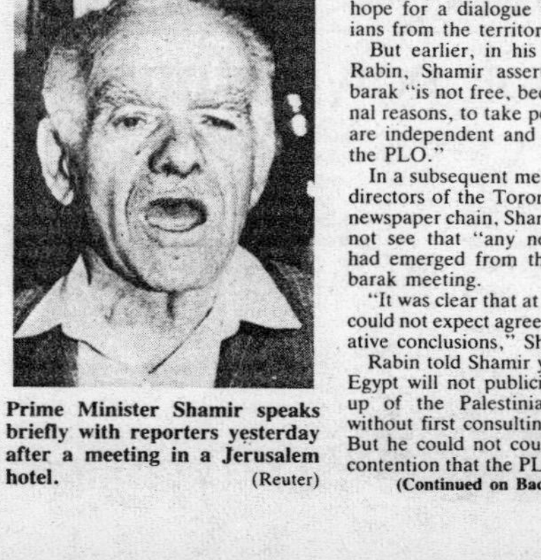

Prime Minister Shamir speaks briefly with reporters yesterday after a meeting in a Jerusalem hotel. (Reuter)

Addressing members of the Israel Bar yesterday, Shamir said: "I want to emphasize that our hands are extended towards peace, and we will not tire in our efforts, but we will not change our initiative due to the fact that we have yet to find partners."

Shamir explicitly rejected two other points in the Mubarak plan – the acceptance of the "territories-for-peace" formula, and the right of East Jerusalem Arabs to vote in the proposed elections in the territories.

The premier called on Egypt to persuade Palestinians to accept the Israeli proposal, and expressed hope for a dialogue with Palestinians from the territories.

But earlier, in his meeting with Rabin, Shamir asserted that Mubarak "is not free, because of internal reasons, to take positions which are independent and not linked to the PLO."

In a subsequent meeting with the directors of the Toronto-based *Sun* newspaper chain, Shamir said he did not see that "any new elements" had emerged from the Rabin-Mubarak meeting.

"It was clear that at this stage one could not expect agreement or operative conclusions," Shamir said.

Rabin told Shamir yesterday that Egypt will not publicize the make-up of the Palestinian delegation without first consulting with Israel. But he could not counter Shamir's contention that the PLO would play

(Continued on Back Page)

Has Arafat asked for visa - or hasn't he?

By WALTER RUBY
Jerusalem Post Correspondent

UNITED NATIONS – Secretary-General Javier Perez de Cuellar said yesterday he believes the PLO has asked the Bush administration for a visa for Yasser Arafat to address the UN.

Perez de Cuellar's remarks appear to fly in the face of comments yesterday by John Kelly, the U.S. assistant secretary of state for Near Eastern and South Asian affairs, who said that the Administration has received no request from the PLO for a visa for Arafat, and that no decision has been reached on whether to grant such a request.

In comments to *The Jerusalem Post* after a press conference marking the opening of the 44th General Assembly, Perez de Cuellar said of the PLO: "I know of their interest [in receiving a visa] and I think they have asked. But the Americans have not told me whether or not they have received a request for a visa. As I have said before, Mr. Arafat should be granted a visa."

During the press conference, the secretary-general touched only briefly on the Israeli-Palestinian conflict, saying that one of the "permanent frustrations" in his job is that he "cannot do enough to facilitate a solution."

Asserting that the Egyptian 10-point plan contains "very interesting ideas," Perez de Cuellar said he intends to explore the plan with President Hosni Mubarak when the Egyptian leader speaks here later this month "and then see what we can do to help."

Perez de Cuellar repeated his support for the convening of an international conference on Middle East peace, calling it "the best forum for solution of the Middle East crisis."

In exclusive interview with *The Post*

Glemp rejects new Vatican stand on Auschwitz convent

By DAVID HOROVITZ
Jerusalem Post Correspondent

BRISTOL – The crisis in the Catholic church over the Carmelite convent at Auschwitz deepened yesterday as Polish primate Cardinal Jozef Glemp told *The Jerusalem Post* that he did not support a Vatican call for the convent's relocation.

In a statement released yesterday by its Commission for Religious Relations with Jews, the Vatican said the Carmelite nuns should be moved to another site and offered to provide funding for an alternative prayer centre.

The unprecedented statement was the first time that the Vatican had commented officially on the controversy.

But Glemp, on a 24-hour visit to England, told *The Post* that to comply with the Vatican statement would be to deny the nuns at the convent their rights.

The Vatican, he said, was seeking the "administrative enforcement" of the 1987 Geneva agreement under which the Church committed itself to relocating the convent by last February. But in concluding that agreement, the Catholic cardinals involved had failed to "consult with Polish society on whether to move the Carmelite sisters," Glemp said. There were also certain "material and administrative problems" that were not foreseen when the agreement was negotiated.

In short, the agreement – or "declaration of intent" as Glemp called it – had proved to be nothing more than "wishful thinking." Its enforcement was "unacceptable."

In Bristol to consecrate a church, the 60-year-old primate told a press conference that Jewish protesters who have called for the nuns' transfer were infringing on the dignity of "women who devote their whole lives to God."

The nuns wanted nothing more than to "close themselves from the world and devote their whole lives to asking God to forgive humanity for the crimes that were committed in the camp," he said. They came "with the best of intentions-...without any wish to offend anybody."

Those Jews opposed to their presence should remember that it was not only Jews who died at Auschwitz, he declared. "Polish people were also exterminated."

(Continued on Back Page)

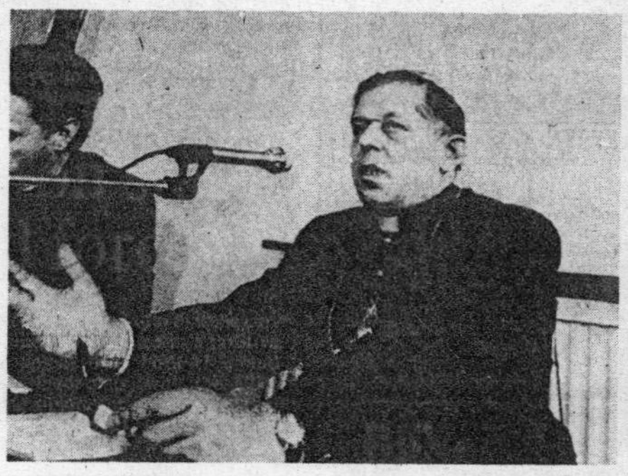

Cardinal Jozef Glemp expresses his views Monday about the convent at a press conference in Bristol, England. Glemp was on a 24-hour visit to Bristol to consecrate a Polish church. (AFP)

Gorbachev: Sweeping changes needed in party's leadership

MOSCOW (AFP) – President Mikhail Gorbachev yesterday called for sweeping changes in the leadership of the Communist Party to tackle what he said was a "watershed stage" for his programme of reforms.

"The country has made a breakthrough to democracy, freedom and glasnost. Obsolete theoretical notions are being decisively updated and society is undergoing revolutionary renovation," Gorbachev told a special plenum of the Central Committee.

The plenum was called to discuss the nationalities problem against a background of increasing ethnic tension.

The plenum's decision yesterday to convene the next party congress, its supreme organ, six months early, in October 1990, will "inject fresh blood into party bodies at all levels," including those of the ruling Central Committee and Politburo, said Gorbachev.

The president, who currently faces a mostly conservative Central Committee, hopes that the elections will bring to the fore "people who are capable of advancing the cause of perestroika."

The congress will also redraw the party rules and draft a new political programme to take account of the deep changes in Soviet society, he said.

"Real life and perestroika have been proceeding at such a pace that we have often lagged behind. Much of what previously seemed correct no longer satisfies us. We now need to go even further and look for new approaches and solutions.

"Perestroika, launched by the April 1985 party Central Committee plenum and the 27th Party Congress, is today living through a crucial, I would say a watershed, stage," Gorbachev told the committee members.

Only a congress can formally elect new Central Committee members. Some of the more than 300 members making up a radical faction in parliament have called for an earlier meeting to bring more reformers into senior positions.

The position of the most prominent member of the radical group, former Moscow party boss Boris Yeltsin, is also likely to be discussed at the plenum – six months after a commission was set up to investigate his public pronouncements.

Yeltsin, who has just completed a highly publicized trip to the U.S., is alleged to have deviated from official party policy.

He was publicly humiliated on Monday by the party daily *Pravda*, which reprinted an article from the Italian newspaper *La Repubblica* portraying him as constantly drunk during his U.S. tour.

The article also suggested that he spent on himself most of the money he had raised at various functions held in support of Soviet Aids victims.

Meanwhile, Tass reported yesterday that two militiamen were killed and two seriously injured on Monday by a mob of 200 to 300 in a village near Nagorny-Karabakh, in the southern Soviet republic of Azerbaijan.

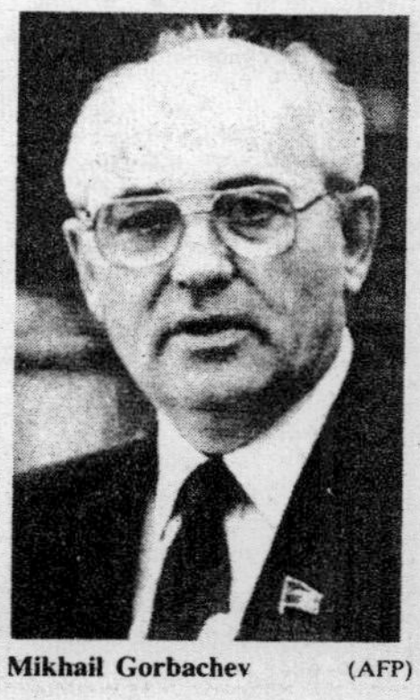

Mikhail Gorbachev (AFP)

SHABBAT	BEGINS	ENDS
Jerusalem	4:07 p.m.	5:19 p.m.
Tel Aviv	4:25 p.m.	5:21 p.m.
Haifa	4:15 p.m.	5:18 p.m.

THE JERUSALEM POST

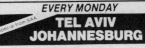

Vol. LVII, No. 17281 Friday, November 10, 1989 • Heshvan 12, 5750 • Rabia II 11, 1410 NIS 2.80 (Eilat NIS 2.45)

SECOND EDITION

E. Germany demolishes 'Iron Curtain'

BERLIN – After decades of keeping its citizens penned in behind a barrier of guns, barbed wire and minefields, East Germany yesterday opened its borders, including the Berlin Wall, in an unprecedented bid to stem mounting agitation for democratic reforms.

The historic reversal, which follows the failure of the ailing Communist regime to prevent mass flight to the West, was announced after the Politburo was overhauled, a move which brought in advocates of reform and tossed out longtime hardliners.

Guenter Schabowski, a Politburo member and party media chief, told a news conference in East Berlin that East Germans who want to emigrate can go to West Germany directly. He said the decision means all East Germans "can travel over all East German border checkpoints," including the 28-year-old Berlin Wall.

Schabowski said that those who want only to visit the West need exit visas, which

Soviets – Page 3
Berlin Wall – See below

would be issued as quickly as possible. He mentioned no limits on the length of stay abroad.

The German Federal Republic said it is prepared to take all East Germans who flood across the newly-opened border. An Interior Ministry source said, "No one will be turned back."

In Washington, the White House said it was surprised and pleased by East Germany's decision to open its borders. "We applaud the decision by the East German government to allow its citizens to travel freely," White House spokesman Marlin Fitzwater said.

"We have always called for and supported freedom of movement. The East German decision would be an important step in the direction of peaceful and evolutionary democratic reform," the spokesman added.

Schabowski said the free travel measure, approved by the central committee yesterday, would stay in force until a new travel law was passed.

East German border police at the Berlin Wall's Checkpoint Charlie crossing point were stunned yesterday to learn that citizens could now travel through to the West freely.

After reading a news dispatch about the open borders, a young guard, shaken out of his normally severe bearing, said animatedly, "People are going to read this and say 'there must be some mistake.'"

"It's not good," another guard said an hour after the decision was announced. "We will lose our jobs."

Tens of thousands of East Germans have fled West since the spring in legal and illegal waves, turning their back on the Communist system. Hundreds of thousands have taken part in protests throughout the country calling for democratic reforms, including free travel and free elections.

Less than a week ago, East German officials announced that East Germans who wanted to emigrate to West Germany could do so over the Czechoslovak frontier, which has resulted in a surge of more than 50,000 new refugees since Saturday.

Earlier yesterday, in a bid to save its political life, East Germany's Communist elite called an emergency party conference and a parliamentary session to tackle the deepest crisis in the country's 40-year history.

The Communist Party's central committee set a party conference for December 15-17. A party conference, a forum for making major policy changes, was last held in 1956. The official ADN news agency said the conference would discuss personnel changes in the 163-member central committee.

About 40,000 people demonstrated Wednesday night in Neubrandenburg and near Karl Marx Stadt for free elections and an end to authoritarian one-party rule, the state news agency ADN said.

Communist Party chief Egon Krenz called for a law ensuring free and democratic elections in a speech to the central committee published yesterday. He called for a "new election law that ensures free, democratic general elections with a secret ballot." He proposed "public supervision in every stage of the balloting."

Krenz did not say whether he was urging a true multiparty system in East Germany. Officials already say elections are democratic, even though the system guarantees the Communists virtually unanimous approval.

Krenz also promised new laws on freedom of assembly, association and the press, but gave no details. He said independent groups might have a role in the nation's politics.

Besides the party conference, the Communist-dominated parliament, a former rubber stamp now winning more attention thanks to promises of free elections, will meet next Monday to elect a new prime minister and openly debate on the crisis.

(Continued on Page 14)

Poll shows U.S. Jewish leaders hold dovish opinions

By WOLF BLITZER
in Washington
and MENACHEM SHALEV
in Jerusalem

A major new poll has found that the American Jewish leadership holds surprisingly dovish positions on the Arab-Israeli conflict. The poll has yet to be made public and is likely to arouse a storm both in Israel and in the American Jewish community.

The poll, commissioned by the Israel-Diaspora Institute at Tel Aviv University, partially funded by the American Jewish Committee and carried out by Professor Steven M. Cohen of Queens College in New York, surveyed hundreds of professional and lay leaders of all major American Jewish groups on issues such as exchanging land for peace, accepting a Palestinian state and dealing with the PLO.

According to sources in Jerusalem, the findings of the politically explosive poll have been suppressed so as not to embarrass Prime Minister Shamir before his trip to the U.S. next week.

But Cohen and Ira Silverman, who is executive vice president of the Committee, flatly deny these charges, saying that the poll's findings are preliminary, that they have to be "checked and analyzed" and that many questionnaires are still outstanding.

While the Jewish leadership, according to the preliminary findings, is generally reluctant to intervene publicly on security issues facing Israel, it reportedly still has expressed views that would be regarded as even more dovish than those associated with the mainstream of the Labour Party.

Likud leaders and their supporters in the American Jewish community are likely to be deeply angered by the poll's conclusions.

One Jewish political activist in Washington who received a questionnaire and is regarded as a political hard-liner charged yesterday that the questions were phrased in a biased way to elicit dovish responses. He asked not to be identified.

But many others denied that charge, insisting that the poll was fair and thorough.

Already, there has been considerable advance discussion of the poll in the American Jewish community and in Israel.

The poll is not a national survey of rank-and-file American Jewish public opinion – only the leaders and opinion-shapers.

Still, its results could have a significant political impact in influencing attitudes in the Bush administration and Congress, which carefully monitor American Jewish opinion toward Israel.

The poll includes a lengthy and very detailed set of questions on a variety of issues related to the peace process.

Cohen confirmed that he had been asked whether it was possible to release the poll before Shamir's arrival. "But I personally decided that I did not yet have enough results to begin my analysis," he said.

He denied that any pressure was exerted on him either to accelerate the release of the poll or to suppress its results.

Austerity looms after Histadrut poll

By AVI TEMKIN
Post Economics Correspondent

The Treasury is to launch a package of new austerity measures immediately after the Histadrut elections, which will include price hikes, cuts in allowances and dismissals in the public sector.

According to government officials, bus fares are expected to go up by about 20 per cent almost immediately after the elections. The officials said electricity rates, which the Energy Ministry wants to raise by 15 per cent, could also go up after the elections.

The Treasury is already working on a package of budget cuts for fiscal 1990-91. This would be based on cuts in National Insurance Institute payments, with old-age allowances a prime target for the proposed slashes. The ministry also wants to reduce half a tax credit point from the credit points of married working women. Plans for a reduction in the income tax imposed on middle-income groups have been shelved for the time being.

The package will also call for cuts in the budget grants for local authorities and for a new round of manpower cuts in the public sector.

(Report – Page 13)

White House exasperated, but Shamir gets his invitation

By WOLF BLITZER,
MENACHEM SHALEV
and DAN PETREANU

U.S. President George Bush last night finally invited Prime Minister Yitzhak Shamir to the White House next Wednesday.

The long-delayed invitation was conveyed in a telephone call from National Security Adviser Brent Scowcroft to Israeli Ambassador Moshe Arad.

The decision to extend the invitation was made at a high-level meeting earlier in the day that Bush had with Scowcroft, Secretary of State James Baker, and other senior U.S. officials.

A formal White House press announcement was expected late last night, but might be delayed until this morning.

The administration, by all accounts, delayed sending the invitation to underscore its deep disappointment with Shamir and his hardline attitude towards Baker's five-point framework proposal.

Earlier in the day, Israeli officials expressed their own irritation over the highly publicized and embarrassing delay, which clearly has already marred Shamir's U.S. visit.

The prime minister is now likely to also meet separately with Baker while in Washington.

Shamir is due to speak before a national Jewish convention in Cincinnati next Thursday. From Cincinnati the prime minister will go to New York for additional meetings with Jewish leaders.

During their meeting at the White House, Bush and Baker reportedly expressed exasperation with the set of conditions attached by the Israeli cabinet last Sunday to Baker's proposal for achieving Israeli-Palestinian talks.

For the past month the Americans have been pointedly using the prospect of a Bush-Shamir summit as a way to signal their differences with the prime minister.

What had so angered Bush and Baker, according to informed sources, was that the assurances the cabinet demanded concerned points that the U.S. had for weeks repeatedly dismissed as likely to undermine the overall peace process.

On Wednesday, for example, Baker told reporters that any preliminary Israeli-Palestinian talks in Cairo should focus primarily on the arrangements for elections in the West Bank and Gaza, but "the negotiating process" should also be addressed.

Israel has demanded that any dialogue revolve strictly around the elections and nothing else.

The U.S., in addition, still refuses to accept the Israeli request that only Palestinian residents of the West Bank and Gaza be eligible to participate in a Palestinian delegation to talks. American officials have long felt that a few "outside" Palestinians will also have to participate.

In what was viewed as a sign of displeasure with the White House's wavering on whether a meeting would be held, Shamir said earlier yesterday that while "every meeting

(Continued on Page 14)

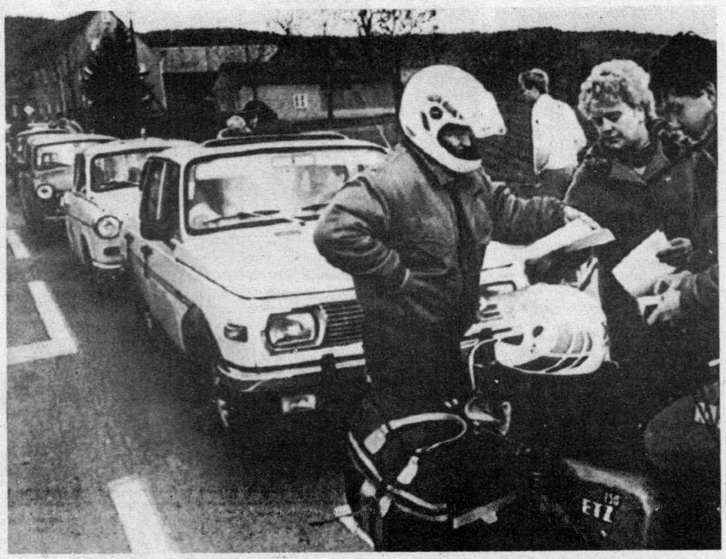

Members of the East German 'Democratic Uprise' group hand out leaflets at the Schoeneberg border point yesterday to citizens wishing to leave the country urging them to stay and fight for reform. (AFP)

IDF smashes 'Red Eagle' terror gang in Nablus

By JOEL GREENBERG
and MICHAL SELA

Crack troops yesterday burst into a house near Nablus, shot and killed a Palestinian and caught five others belonging to the "Red Eagle" gang that was responsible for slaying nine local residents, assaulting others and attacking soldiers, military sources said.

In riots that broke out in Nablus after the incident, troops shot and killed a local youth and wounded four others. A Border Policeman was wounded by a rock.

A curfew was clamped on the city and surrounding refugee camps.

The Red Eagle gang, affiliated with the Popular Front for the Liberation of Palestine, was considered one of the most dangerous in the territories and had been sought for months by the security services. Townspeople reported that it had imposed a reign of terror on Nablus along with another gang, "The Black Panther," nominally affiliated with Fatah and still at large. Residents described the groups as "out of control," defying appeals by PLO chief Yasser Arafat to halt their unbridled killings.

The groups are believed to have perpetrated a series of slayings of men and women thought to be cooperating with the authorities, or accused of immoral behaviour, such as drug-use and prostitution. Gang members took their victims from their homes, bound their hands, hacked and stabbed them to death and dumped their bodies in the alleys of the casbah. Others were kidnapped and violently interrogated. The gangs are also believed to have hurled petrol bombs at soldiers.

The seizure of the Red Eagle members is seen as a major success of the security services and the IDF. The Shin Bet chief arrived at the site of the capture, along with IDF Chief of General Staff Dan Shomron and OC Central Command Yithzhak Mordechai.

Shomron said he hoped the arrest of the gang would influence the atmosphere in Nablus and the surrounding area. Mordechai vowed to continue the campaign to catch wanted youths and combat groups of fugitive gunmen.

According to the IDF, yesterday's incident began when soldiers and Border Police were combing the village of Jneid, outside Nablus, and saw suspicious movement on a rooftop.

Soldiers surrounded the house, and called the occupants to come out, according to Mordechai. When the calls were ignored, the troops burst in, and a soldier spotted the leader of the gang opposite the doorway, drawing a pistol. The soldier shot and killed the leader, 23-year-old Aiman Ruzeh, and another five gang members surrendered and were caught. Two had been on the roof, others on their way up, or in the kitchen preparing breakfast. One of those arrested was identified as Jaber Hawash, 17.

The group was found in possession

(Continued on Page 14)

2 soldiers hurt by S. Lebanon roadside bomb

By KENNETH KAPLAN
Post Defence Reporter
and news agencies

Two IDF soldiers were wounded in south Lebanon yesterday morning when a roadside bomb exploded near the village of Kaukabe in the eastern district of the security zone. The soldiers were evacuated by helicopter to Rambam Hospital in Haifa.

One soldier, a lieutenant in Nahal, was lightly wounded, while the second, a tracker, sustained moderate shrapnel wounds in the arm and stomach. A doctor at Rambam said the tracker underwent a complicated operation to repair a fracture in his arm caused by the shrapnel.

Also yesterday, several Katyusha rockets were fired in two salvos from outside the security zone toward Israel and the security zone. The IDF said one landed in the Galilee panhandle, while sources in Lebanon said a dozen fell just over the border, not far from Metulla.

A Lebanese civilian was slightly hurt in the barrage, launched from the Bekaa valley at about 10:30 a.m.

Residents of Metulla and nearby settlements heard the explosions clearly and went on alert for a short while.

Half an hour earlier, a salvo of three rockets fired from orange groves outside the Rashidiyeh refugee camp near Tyre fell in Western Galilee. The rockets caused no damage or casualties.

South Lebanese Army forces in

(Continued on Page 14)

Moslem fundamentalists emerge big winners in Jordanian poll

By RUTH GINSBERG
and news agencies

Moslem fundamentalists were the big winners in Jordan's first parliamentary election in 22 years, doing especially well in the Palestinian refugee camps of Amman.

None of the 12 women among the 647 candidates won a seat in the first national election in which women could vote and seek office, and several former government ministers were defeated.

With most votes counted yesterday from Wednesday's poll, the Moslem Brotherhood and affiliated Islamic groups had won 34 of 80 lower-house seats, prompting one West Bank observer to comment that "If really free elections were held in the territories, the fundamentalists would win more seats than the PLO."

West Bank political observers said the Moslem groups are likely to be accorded several seats in the cabinet as a result of their strong showing.

Formal announcement of national results of the poll were withheld pending a recount begun late yesterday in the southern town of Kerak.

Government sources in Amman conceded last night that leftists had also done better than expected, with at least 11 Marxists or left-leaning Arab nationalists among the winners. But in many outlying districts, clan support remained a more important factor than political platforms.

Officials clearly were taken aback at the nationwide strength of the fundamentalist and leftist vote, which may allow radical deputies to achieve a parliamentary majority on some issues.

"We're drinking vinegar," an official said. "Our projections on the power balance were upset. The only hope is that tribal leaders, liberals and reformists will organize themselves as a moderate force in the new parliament."

Fundamentalist candidates swept all three seats in the heavily Palestinian 2nd district of Amman, which includes the Wahdat refugee camp. In that district, Brotherhood leaders Abdul-Munim Abu Zant, a fiery imam, and Ali Hawamdeh won two to three times as many votes as any other candidate. Yakub Karash, an independent fundamentalist whose platform was more liberal, came in third.

In Amman's 1st district, another heavily Palestinian area, Brotherhood candidates Ali Al-Fakhir and Majed Khalifeh won seats.

Laith Shbeilat, a U.S.-trained engineer and an Islamic deputy in the previous parliament who gained prominence as an outspoken and articulate critic of former prime minister Zeid a-Rifai, topped the polls in Amman's 3rd district, a prosperous middle-class area where 55 candidates competed for five seats.

Shbeilat and leftist lawyer Faris Nabulsi pushed former foreign minister Taher al-Masri, who represented Nablus in the old parliament, into third place.

The Brotherhood, campaigning on the slogan "Islam is the Solution" and calling for "liberating Palestine from the [Jordan] river to the sea," attracted the largest crowds during the three-week campaign.

A Jordanian political source said the Brotherhood and its leftist rivals had benefited from a low voter turnout. Despite the excitement of the unusually open campaign, only 540,000 people voted, 53 per cent of the 1.02 million registered voters.

The fact that the Brotherhood has the status of a charitable organization also allowed it to run a better-organized campaign than other political parties, which technically remain banned.

Among the left-wing victors was Mansour Murad, a Circassian candidate in Amman's 3rd district who edged out a member of the Moslem Brotherhood. Murad was convicted in Greece of participating in a 1969 hand-grenade attack by Palestinian terrorists against the El Al office in Athens. A child was killed and 14 people were wounded in the blast. Greece freed him in 1970 in order to win the release of 55 hostages aboard a hijacked Olympic Airways jetliner.

None of the 12 women running for the first time since women won electoral rights in 1974 came close to victory. Women's rights activist Toujan Faisal, accused by fundamentalists of apostasy, was trounced by a 4-1 margin by a Moslem Brotherhood candidate in her Amman district.

Berlin Wall, Cold War symbol, now redundant

By MARTIN NESIRKY

EAST BERLIN – (Reuter) – The Berlin Wall, for 28 years the most potent symbol of a divided Europe, lost its meaning last night when East Germany threw open its heavily-guarded borders with the West.

"Today, the decision was taken that makes it possible for all citizens to leave the country through East German crossing points," was the way Communist Party media chief Guenter Schabowski announced the news at his dramatic news conference.

The decision effectively dismantles the "Iron Curtain" along the border to West Germany and makes the Berlin Wall redundant.

The Wall has tormented divided Berliners and exasperated the West since the Communists erected fences and concrete barriers on August 13, 1961 to stem a westward flow of emigrants.

East Germany called the Wall an "Anti-Fascist Protection Barrier". It was ostensibly built to protect East Germans from Western fascism.

In reality it plugged a hole in the Iron Curtain through which 2.3 million East Germans had fled in the 12 years after the founding of the Soviet-backed Communist state in 1949.

More than 100 East Germans have been shot dead trying to climb the four-metre high wall.

East German hardline leader Erich Honecker, who built the Wall, said early this year it would stand for a hundred years.

But his words rang hollow as thousands of East Germans began fleeing to the West again. To date, 225,000 of them have left.

Honecker, who refused to accept the reforms sweeping most of Eastern Europe, was ousted from the leadership on October 18 and replaced by the more reform-minded Egon Krenz.

The removal of the Wall was one of the key demands heard in the mass demonstrations that have swept East German cities in recent weeks.

The Wall may remain, snaking 160 km around West Berlin, an enclave city deep in East Germany. But if East Germans can pass through almost at will, then the Wall will rapidly lose its significance and will gradually gather dust as a powerful symbol of a failed attempt to keep a country behind bars.

"The Wall? It belongs in a museum," rejoiced one young East German woman when told about the decision to liberalise travel.

"This is in effect the end of the Wall and the barbed wire," said Otto Lambsdorff, chairman of West Germany's Free Democratic Party.

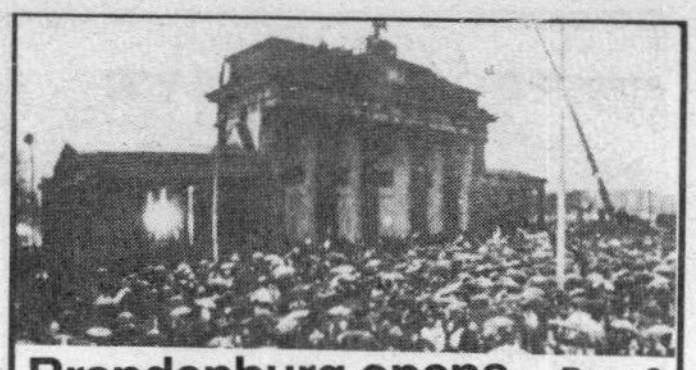
Brandenburg opens – Page 2

THE JERUSALEM
POST
Vol. LVII, No. 17318 Sunday, December 24, 1989 • Kislev 26, 5750• Jamad I 26, 1410 NIS 1.80 (Eilat NIS 1.55)

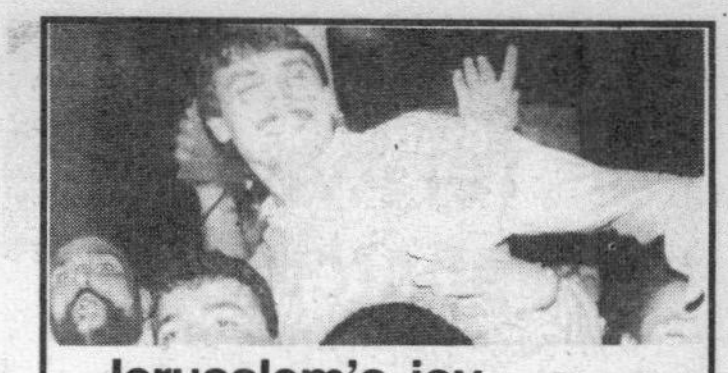
Jerusalem's joy – Page 7

Ceausescu overthrown, fighting rages on

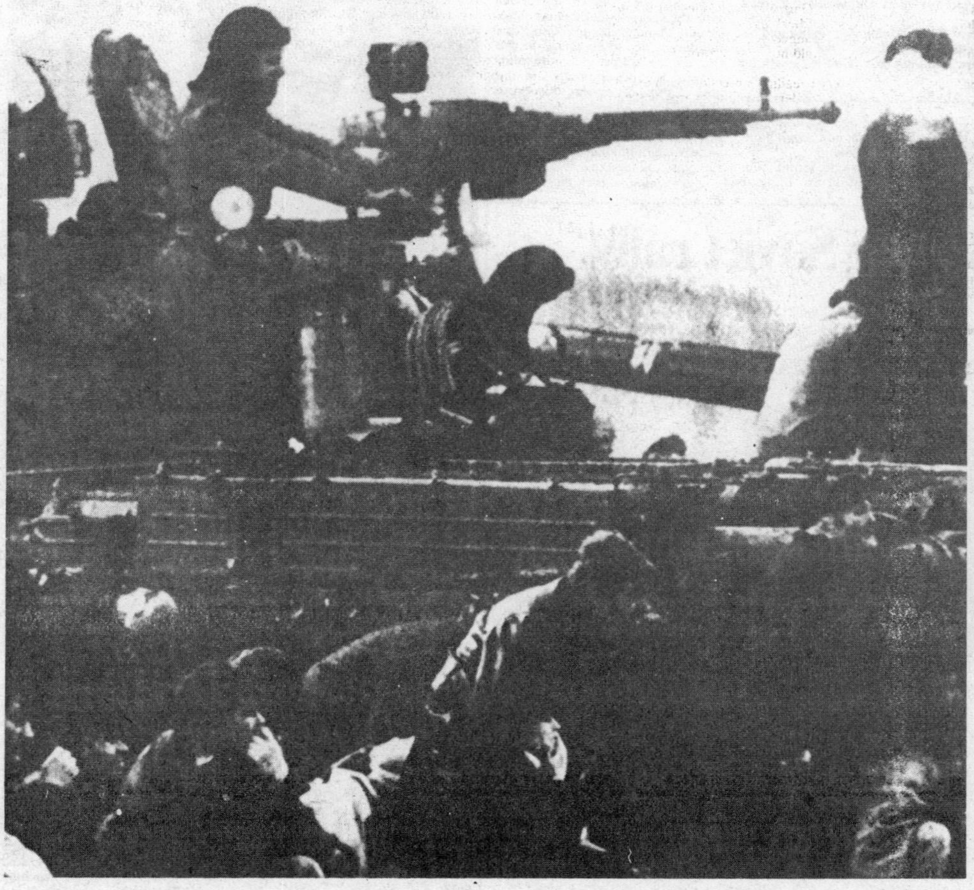
An army tank attacks pro-Ceausescu troops while Bucharest citizens try to protect themselves during heavy fighting yesterday. (Reuter)

Romanian rebels tighten grip

BUCHAREST (Reuter) – Fierce battles raged through the Romanian capital last night as the last remnants of ousted leader Nicolae Ceausescu's Securitate police defied calls to surrender.

The pro-democracy National Salvation Front, which is promising that free elections will soon be staged and single party rule ended, said Ceausescu, his wife Elena and members of his family had been captured by the army and would be put on trial.

In a reference to continued bloodletting in the streets, Front spokesman Ion Iliescu said that he hoped the "viper's dying screams will soon cease."

The country-wide death toll after three days of virtual civil war remains unclear. Hundreds have definitely died in the capital but the overall death toll throughout the country may be in the thousands.

Correspondents saw bodies littering the streets of Bucharest and truckloads of coffins were taken to special mortuaries. The Yugoslav news agency Tanjug said 12,000 people had been killed this week in the city of Timisoara, where the rebellion began.

Soviet television reported late last night that security forces loyal to Ceausescu had been parachuted into Timisoara and fighting was still going on.

"Armed clashes continue as you are watching this programme," the Moscow report added. "Again there are dead on the streets, again blood is flowing."

The Soviet television comments came at the end of a report, recorded earlier in the evening, showing jubilant, cheering crowds in the city celebrating the fall of Ceausescu and chanting "perestroika, perestroika".

More reports – Page 3 & 5

A key factor in the outcome of the battle could be the attitude of the other Soviet bloc states. Foreign embassies, including the Soviet mission, were damaged in the fighting. Foreign ministers of the Warsaw Pact were being convened, possibly as early as today, to discuss the situation.

In Moscow, Soviet leader Mikhail Gorbachev told parliament: "We have set up contacts with Warsaw Pact countries to coordinate our mutual actions in order to extend our support to the Romanian people." But Soviet Prime Minister Nikolai Ryzhkov said it would be wrong to send in Soviet troops.

Later, Tass issued a government declaration that said "the Soviet Union is ready to render rapid and effective humanitarian aid to the Romanian people and the new leadership of the country to liquidate the consequences of the tragic events of recent days."

Iliescu, who has announced a programme of democratic reform for the country, said on Romanian television that the "dictatorial family, Nicolae and Elena Ceausescu, was captured."

Referring to Ceausescu as a "poison hyena," he said the former president, who had ruled since 1965, and his wife, the second most powerful person in the country under the old regime, would be tried.

Also captured were Emil Bobu, the third most powerful person in the country who assumed command when the Ceausescus were traveling abroad, and Ceausescu's brother, Ilie, formerly a deputy defense minister, Iliescu said.

Yesterday's announcement was the first definite word from the opposition that Ceausescu was in their hands. They gave no details on how or where the 71-year-old ex-leader was caught, or where he was being held.

Two of Ceausescu's top aides and his son Nicu also were arrested.

Romanian television announced that Ceausescu would not be brought before the cameras at the

(Continued on Page 4)

Israel cabinet to discuss recognition

By MENACHEM SHALEV, JUDY SIEGEL and DAN PETREANU

Several ministers, led by Communications Minister Gad Ya'acobi, are expected to demand at this morning's cabinet meeting, when the Romanian situation is likely to be discussed, that Israel recognize the new Romanian National Salvation Committee.

The Foreign Ministry refrained throughout the weekend from commenting officially on the overthrow of President Nicolae Ceausescu. Sources in Jerusalem said that the government was waiting for the situation in Bucharest to stabilize before making any public comment. (Continued on Back Page)

Tel Aviv embassy supports revolt

By ANDY GOLDBERG, Jerusalem Post Reporter

TEL AVIV – The Romanian Embassy yesterday afternoon declared its support for the National Salvation Committee and the provisional government in Bucharest, and called the overthrow of Nicolae Ceausescu "a revolution of historic proportions for the Romanian people."

Earlier in the day a number of embassy employees took down the gate with its sign stating "The Embassy of the Socialist Republic of Romania." As it smashed to the ground, clapping and cheering broke out among

(Continued on Back Page)

Noriega fights back against U.S.

PANAMA CITY – The U.S. sent 2,000 more troops into Panama yesterday to help 23,000 soldiers already there battle against stubborn and growing resistance apparently directed by fugitive General Manuel Antonio Noriega.

Despite American hopes that Panama would quickly fall under the control of its new, U.S.-installed government, fighting picked up on the fourth day of the invasion, with a U.S. embassy official saying there was considerable gunfire near the embassy.

Some 300 U.S. troops swept through Panama City's main avenue yesterday to recover arms and strategic positions held by snipers loyal to the ousted regime of Noriega.

Sniper fire and looting of stores in the city's centre ended, but skirmishes between invading U.S. forces and Noriega loyalists continued in the populous San Miguelito district.

Defence Department officials said there was increased action by Noriega's paramilitary Dignity Battalions, who fired small arms at U.S. troops and continued looting overnight in defiance of a curfew. American helicopter gunships were in the air much of the night.

More reports – Page 2 & 8

General Maxwell Thurman, the commander of U.S. forces, said opposition to the American invaders was "organized, not disorganized" and that Noriega was the "guiding hand" of the resistance.

There were growing casualties from the U.S.'s biggest military operation overseas since the Vietnam War. Pentagon officials said 21 American servicemen and two U.S. dependents had been killed since the fighting began early on Wednesday. Another 222 were wounded and two were missing.

The officials put at 139 the number of Noriega loyalists in the Panama Defence Force killed, with 95 wounded and 1,880 captured.

The two main hospitals in Panama City reported a total of 51 Panamanian civilians killed and 835 wounded, but the toll was believed to be much higher.

Noriega's representative to the United Nations said there had been as many as 7,000 deaths.

The additional U.S. troops, from the Army's 7th Light Infantry Division, were airlifted throughout the day from Fort Ord, California, as U.S. commanders in Panama reported growing concern over the harassing attacks – and weapons supplies – of Noriega's "Dignity Battalions."

"It's simply a difficult operation. .... There are a lot of places to hide," said Lt. Gen. Tom Kelly, director of operations for the Joint Chiefs of Staff, as Noriega continued to defy capture.

On Thursday, President Bush had said that "Operation Just Cause"

(Continued on Page Two)

Determined to avoid a crisis atmosphere despite continued fighting in Panama, President Bush enjoyed the beginning of the Christmas weekend at his Camp David retreat yesterday and planned to go fishing and hunting next week.

Some Americans were certain to question the propriety of a jolly family Christmas – Bush and his wife Barbara were to be joined by their five children and 11 grandchildren – at a time when American soldiers were dying in Central America.

White House spokesman Marlin Fitzwater said Bush would receive his regular intelligence briefings daily throughout the holiday and was prepared to alter his plans immediately if necessary.

Seven W. Bankers killed in weekend violence

By JOEL GREENBERG and MICHAL SELA
Jerusalem Post Reporters

Seven Palestinians died in weekend violence including five shot by troops, a sixth who died of wounds sustained in an earlier clash and a Nablus woman hacked to death by Arab assailants.

Soldiers shot and wounded 59 Palestinians in the Gaza Strip and at least nine more in the West Bank over the weekend, according to Palestinian sources. The army confirmed 14 wounded in the Gaza Strip and seven in the West Bank.

The most violent incident was in Jaba', near Jenin, where soldiers shot and killed a teenage boy and girl and wounded at least seven others. Military and Palestinian accounts of the incident differed.

According to military sources, troops arrived at Jaba' to arrest wanted youths and encountered resistance when they tried to enter the home of a man suspected of involvement in terrorist attacks. A teenage girl stabbed an officer in the stomach, wounding him lightly, and he fired back, killing her. The wanted man was shot when he resisted arrest. He was taken to hospital. Jaba' was closed off.

According to reports from the village, soldiers had been hiding in a building near the home of Muhammad Alawneh, 22, wanted since August 1988. After Alawneh arrived at the house, the troops tried to enter, but were blocked by family members who pushed a refrigerator and furniture against the front door.

According to these accounts, soldiers fired into the house through the windows, killing Alawneh's 15-year-old sister, Shifa, seriously wounding his six-year-old brother, Adham, in the chest, and wounding another sister, Asmahan, 19, who was later arrested. Family members tried to barricade the windows against the gunfire, but failed.

Finally, Alawneh came out the front door and stabbed an officer in

(Continued on Back Page)

Mubarak and Assad to talk about renewing ties

CAIRO (AFP) – Syrian Vice President Abdel Halim Khaddam announced here yesterday that Syrian President Hafez Assad and his Egyptian counterpart Hosni Mubarak will hold a summit expected to lead to a renewal of diplomatic relations between the two states.

The date and venue for the meeting is to be fixed later, said Khaddam, the highest-ranking Syrian official to visit Cairo since ties were severed in 1977.

He told reporters that the summit, which was "closer than we think," would have "practical and concrete results aimed at correcting the course of relations between the two countries."

Khaddam, whose arrival yesterday was unexpected, met for two hours with Mubarak and was Premier Atef Sedki's guest at a luncheon attended by top officials including Osama el-Baz, the president's political adviser.

The meeting focused on relations between Syria and Egypt, which the Syrian vice president said had "historic links which will be pursued into the future." He delivered what he called a "cordial" message from Assad.

Relations between the two countries were severed after the November 1977 visit to Jerusalem by then-Egyptian president Anwar Sadat.

Last week, Egypt and Syria restored air links after a 12-year break while the Egyptian president travelled to Libya for talks with Libyan leader Col. Muammar Gaddafi.

In another diplomatic development, el-Baz held talks here yesterday with a high-ranking PLO delegation that included two executive committee members, Mahmoud Abbas and Abdallah Hourani.

The talks were part of efforts to advance the Middle East peace process, the president's political adviser said.

Reliable Palestinian sources said that PLO chief Yasser Arafat was also expected to visit the Egyptian capital shortly.

Big drop in
Tel Aviv
shares
Page 5-6

THE JERUSALEM
POST

Vol. LVIII, No. 17354 Monday, February 5, 1990 • Shvat 10, 5750 • Rajab 10, 1410 NIS 1.90 (Eilat NIS 1.65)

FROM SUNDAY'S
The New York Times
WEEKLY REVIEW
INSIDE TODAY

SECOND EDITION

15 slain as terrorists hit Israeli tour in Egypt

By DAVID MAKOVSKY
Jerusalem Post Reporter

Masked terrorists, firing semi-automatic weapons and hurling hand grenades, killed, according to unofficial reports, as many as 15 passengers, at least eight of them Israelis, on an Egyptian tour bus, 50 to 60 kms. east of Cairo, at 4:30 o'clock yesterday afternoon.

Cairo Radio said that at least three of those killed were women. Nearly all of the 31 passengers who were not killed were wounded.

Unknown Egyptian group claims responsibility

CAIRO (Reuter) – A hitherto unknown Egyptian group claimed responsibility for the attack. An anonymous caller told an international news organisation in Cairo that The Organization for the Defence of the Oppressed in Egypt's Prisons mounted the attack.

"The organisation launched the attack on the Jewish bus to discipline (President Hosni) Mubarak's regime and his (new) Interior Minister who started his term with savage torture of prisoners in Torrah prison," the caller said.

He spoke classical Arabic with an Egyptian accent, and muttered the phrase Allah-o-Akbar (God is Great), an indication that he represented an outlawed Moslem fundamentalist faction.

A hitherto unknown Egyptian guerrilla group claimed responsibility for the attack.

At least two assailants and possibly three or four, driving in a white Peugeot 505, overtook the tourist bus and began firing from their car. They boarded the bus, continued firing and threw grenades. When the Egyptian Interior Police arrived at the scene they immediately cordoned off the area, and began hunting for the terrorists.

Egyptian President Hosni Mubarak telephoned Prime Minister Yitzhak Shamir late last night to convey his regret at the murderous attack. Middle East News Agency published a statement by the office of President Hosni Mubarak saying: "The Arab Republic of Egypt regrets the savage attack against some Israeli tourists. It considers this murderous act to be aimed in the first degree against efforts to push forward the peace process in the area. Egypt denounces this brute attack."

Of the 31 mostly middle-aged Israelis on board the bus, at least nine were brought to Heliopolis Hospital last night. At least two of them were

(Continued on Back Page)

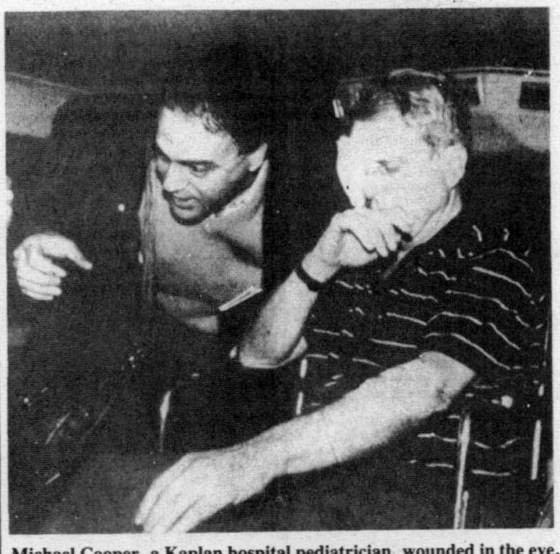

Michael Cooper, a Kaplan hospital pediatrician, wounded in the eye, waits in an ambulance outside a Cairo hospital before being flown home. (Reuter)

Cries of 'Down with the party' at huge Soviet rally

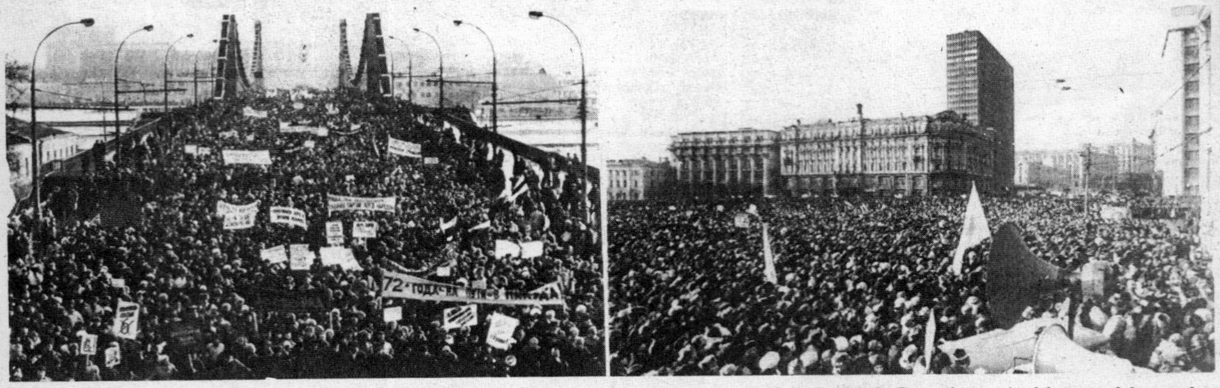

Hundreds of thousands of demonstrators cross the Moskva River on Krimsky Bridge yesterday on the eve of the Communist Party plenum. At right, part of the crowd assembles in a square near the Kremlin to show support for glasnost and perestroika. (Reuter)

MOSCOW (Reuter) – Hundreds of thousands of people massed beside the Kremlin walls yesterday, demanding radical reforms in the Soviet system in the biggest unofficial demonstration Moscow has seen since the 1920s.

The march and rally, organized by reformist and national groups, piled pressure on the Communist Party leadership as it prepared for a critical Central Committee meeting today and tomorrow that could spell the end of its stranglehold on power.

"It is necessary to restructure the Communist Party. There must not be a party monopoly on power," radical leader Boris Yeltsin, a former member of the ruling Politburo, told the crowds.

In an initial report, Soviet television said this was the biggest "democratic" demonstration ever held here, but later suggested that a number of extremist groups had sought to use the demonstration for their own purposes.

The Tass news agency was even more critical, saying the demonstration was organized by "so-called democratic forces" who sought to put pressure on the authorities.

Many people turned up thinking the demonstration would be a show of support for perestroika, but later left when they realized extremists sought to put forward "ultra-radical" demands which could "destabilize" the situation, Tass said.

Demonstrators swarmed into central Moscow from the city ring-road, waving banners reading "Down with Article Six" – the clause in the Soviet constitution which guarantees the party's "leading role" in society.

Other placards said "No to Fascism in the USSR" and called for freedom for the Soviet Baltic republics. Some marchers chanted slogans against the KGB and called for the retirement of Yegor Ligachev, the Politburo's leading conservative.

The demonstration came as the 20-million-strong Communist Party, which has ruled since the 1917 Bolshevik Revolution, appeared to face a turning point in its history.

"The party is going through its most difficult time, perhaps the most difficult in its entire history," the government daily *Izvestia* said yesterday.

The policy-setting Central Committee is meeting to debate proposals that include giving up its constitutional right to power, changing its structure and increasing accountability to the people.

Police estimated the crowd at yesterday's demonstration at 200,000. So many people took part that the venue was shifted to the huge Manezh Square facing the Kremlin from the original site in a smaller square about two km. away.

Many marchers waved the once-banned flags of the powerful Baltic Popular Fronts, which are pressing for independence in the republics of Latvia, Lithuania and Estonia.

Police closed off some streets and underground railway stations in the vicinity and marshalled the crowds, but made no attempt to stop the demonstration, whose organizers included the Democratic Platform, a reformist group within the party.

One speaker, historian and archivist Yuri Afanasyev, said: "I end with a call: hail the powerful non-violent 1990 all-union revolution." He called for further mass rallies across the Soviet Union in three weeks time.

A moment of silence was observed for hundreds of people who have died in ethnic clashes in the south of the country.

The clashes between Armenians and Azerbaijanis, the separatist threat from the Baltic republics and economic stagnation that refuses to yield to reforms have faced Soviet leader Mikhail Gorbachev with an unprecedented crisis.

(Continued on Back Page)

Bus attack recalls Ras Burka deaths

By GREER FAY CASHMAN
Jerusalem Post Reporter

Yesterday's attack on the tour bus was the latest in a string of attacks on Israeli targets in Egypt in the last six years.

The most notorious was the attack in October 1985 on a group of Israeli vacationers on the Sinai coast at Ras Burka. In that attack, seven Israelis – two of them children – were gunned down by an Egyptian soldier.

Following the Ras Burka incident, the Egyptian government dragged its feet. Initially, President Hosni Mubarak downplayed the severity of the incident. There followed claims that the Egyptian soldier was demented, and the Egyptian government delayed its response to the claims for compensation by the victims' families until last year.

By contrast, last night the Egyptian Ministry of Interior strongly condemned what it called the savage attack.

In June, 1984, Israeli diplomat Zvi Kedar was shot from a passing car as he was about to leave his home in the Ma'adi Quarter of Cairo. He was not seriously wounded.

In May, 1985, Egyptian soldiers fired on an Israeli diver's boat in the Gulf of Eilat, causing damage but no loss of life.

Israeli diplomat Albert Atrakchi was gunned down by members of ling to Cairo from Rafah. Tens of thousands of Israelis have visited Egypt each year since the 1979 peace treaty, although the numbers dropped precipitously after the 1985 Ras Burka terror attack, but has recently picked up.

An Egyptian interior ministry statement, released by the Middle East News Agency (MENA), said the attackers used two sub-machine guns and hurled four grenades at the bus. Two of the grenades exploded, MENA said.

'The interior ministry deeply regrets this savage incident which led to the death or injury of innocent people," it said.

Egypt's new security head, Interior Minister Mohammed Moussa, rushed to the scene and directed the manhunt himself.

Rabbi okays sabbath flights for Soviet Jews

By HAIM SHAPIRO
Jerusalem Post Reporter

Sephardi Chief Rabbi Mordechai Eliahu has ruled that it is permissible to bring immigrants from places of possible danger in the Soviet Union on the Sabbath.

According to those active in the immigration of Soviet Jews, thousands of potential immigrants now have exit visas, but there are no places to be had on suitable flights out of the Soviet Union. Religious Affairs Minister Zevulun Hammer, who returned last week from a visit to the Soviet Union, said that Jews had told him that they feared a growing wave of anti-Semitism would lead to an outbreak of physical violence.

Some Jews had related, according to Hammer, that buildings in which Jews lived were being marked in preparation for a pogrom, which is being planned for May 5.

Eliahu's ruling, made public by the chief rabbi's office yesterday, is based upon the principle that *pikuah nefesh*, the saving of life, supercedes the observance of the Sabbath. Even if there was only a possibility of danger, he said, the principle applied.

Nor was it necessary to rely on planes flown by non-Jewish crews. In such a situation, he said, Jews were even commanded to fly the planes.

When asked if he concurred with the ruling, Ashkenazi Chief Rabbi Avraham Shapiro said that there was no question that *pikuah nefesh* took precendence over the Sabbath. But there was still a question, he said, as to what actually constituted *pikuah nefesh* in connection with the immigration of Soviet Jews.

Big gun duels hush bells tolling for Beirut's dead

BEIRUT (Reuter) – The thunder of exploding shells and rockets yesterday drowned out the sound of church bells tolling for nearly 200 people killed so far in Beirut's current Christian war.

For 70 heart-stopping minutes, shells, rockets and mortar bombs crashed into the city's battered streets at a rate of one a second.

Salvoes of rockets screamed out of their multi-barrelled launchers as Gen. Michel Aoun's 15,000-strong army and his foes in the Lebanese Forces (LF) militia battled from street-to-street for control of rubble-covered ruins.

At East Beirut hospitals, the moans and screams of the wounded and the cries of bereaved relatives filled wards, as doctors and nurses scrambled frantically to save those they could.

At least 195 people have been killed and more than 1,000 wounded since the fighting erupted last Wednesday when Aoun ordered the LF to surrender its arms in a bid to take control of Lebanon's 800 sq. km. Christian enclave.

Militia leader Samir Geagea said he had agreed to a 12:30 p.m. ceasefire – the seventh in four days – but nearly an hour later there was no sign of a let-up in the battles.

Aoun's troops were advancing under heavy tank, artillery and rocket barrages towards the LF's main stronghold in the area of Geagea's headquarters at Karantina, where he was believed to be directing the battles from an underground bunker.

The LF said its fighters repelled several attacks, but Aoun's radio station said its troops were slowly advancing.

Fires blazed out of control for the second day at the Dora oil depot – Lebanon's largest – sending flames shooting into the sky while huge clouds of dense black smoke hung above the burning city.

Beirut Bishop Abou Nader said the bells were tolling "in grief for the innocents who died, and those who are being killed, humiliated and terrorised."

Doctors, exhausted and operating under fire around the clock, said the fighting was among the worst they had seen in Lebanon's 14 years of sporadic civil war.

Several hospitals were turning the wounded away. Blood-washed wards were choked with the dying, while mortuaries were packed with mutilated and charred corpses.

Appeals were made for doctors and blood donors and there was a critical shortage of medical supplies.

"Hospitals are exchanging medicine with each other because of the shortage. Our operating room was hit. We are turning away critical cases," Dr. Sami Abboud told Reuter by telephone from one East Beirut hospital.

Thousands of Beirut residents sheltered in basements and corridors on the edges of the frontlines, where tanks and armoured personnel carriers raked the streets with gunfire.

Several stray shells tore into Moslem West Beirut killing two people and wounding 10. The Moslem sector has been partially paralysed for fear of a spillover in the fighting since the Christian war erupted.

Most passengers from Jerusalem area, Rehovot

Jerusalem Post Staff

The bulk of the passengers on the bus apparently consisted of a group of friends, some of whom worked at the Weizmann Institute and Kaplan Hospital in Rehovot and others at institutions in Jerusalem. The Foreign Ministry last night was in touch with the families.

Following is a list of the bus passengers supplied by the Ofakim Travel Agency of Tel Aviv:

Mrs. Edna Barak and Prof. Yigal Barak of Rehovot, Mrs. Lea Bebe Bardicef and Uri Bardicef (no address given), Isachar Benjamini and Judith Benjamini of Tel Aviv, Ruhama Berliner of Mevasseret Yerushalayim, Eliezer Betser and Mrs. Rivka Betser of Rehovot, Mrs. Orna Bukai of Tel Aviv, Mrs. Miriam Cohen of Ramat Gan, Michael Cooper and Mrs. Rina Cooper of Rehovot, Hersh Dank of Herzliya, Pinchas First of Tel Aviv, Ms. Nahada Gafni of Jerusalem, Mrs. Hannah Horowitz and Shmuel Horowitz of Har Adar, Mrs. Marion Kadmon of Jerusalem, Mrs. Bronislava Koblenz of Bat Yam, Mrs. Hana Lahav and Noam Lahav of Mevessaret Yerushalayim, Mrs. Anat Lederman of Givat Shmuel, Mrs. Lea Luvshis of Holon, Mrs. Aya Meiri of Tel Aviv, Eli Edward Miron (no address given), Mrs. Zvia Schumert of Jerusalem, Mrs. Judith Shiftan and Zeev Shiftan of Jerusalem, Mrs. Eugenia Kasjebard of Tel Aviv and Mr. Aronewitch of Sweden.

Mubarak: Don't put Soviet Jews in territories

CAIRO (AP) – President Hosni Mubarak warned yesterday that permitting Soviet Jews to settle in the territories would have grave consequences for the peace process and Middle East stability.

Thus, Mubarak joined other Arab spokesmen who have been protesting against the mass immigration of Soviet Jews to Israel,

The state-owned Middle East News Agency said the warning came in protest messages to Presidents George Bush and Mikhail Gorbachev, which were delivered to diplomatic envoys yesterday.

Egyptian Foreign Minister Esmat Abdel-Meguid sent a similar message to Foreign Minister Moshe Arens on Saturday, the agency said.

The three messages, the agency said, dealt with "the grave negative consequences" on the peace process and the region's security and stability that would result from permitting Soviet Jews to settle in the West Bank and the Gaza Strip.

Palestinians 'ready to accept U.S. positions'

Egypt official: Talks could start Sunday

By DAVID MAKOVSKY

The long awaited trilateral meeting between the foreign ministers of the U.S., Egypt, and Israel could convene next Sunday in Geneva to iron out remaining obstacles to an Israeli-Palestinian dialogue, a senior Egyptian said yesterday.

The Palestinians are prepared to agree with U.S. positions on all outstanding issues blocking commencement of the talks, the official said in a lengthy interview with *The Jerusalem Post* conducted before the terrorist attack on the Israeli tourist bus in Egypt.

Egyptian President Hosni Mubarak would be willing to meet Prime Minister Yitzhak Shamir for a summit meeting, the official said, if Israel is prepared to resolve the last issues dividing both sides. If Shamir is ready to deal, he said, Egypt would provide him with a "red carpet welcome."

"The moment we are invited, we will come," diplomatic sources in Jerusalem responded last night.

The senior Egyptian official predicted that by end of the trilateral meeting the PLO will be ready to either concede the right to announce the Palestinian delegation to Egypt or to have one delegation member spontaneously announce the other members.

According to the official, the following picture emerges:

• Egypt would like a trilateral meeting next week, even if the inner cabinet does not approve plans to resolve the remaining issues in advance, but views the talks as "exploratory" before a final Israeli decision. The U.S., however, has been adamant that a trilateral meeting should be the last word before an Israeli-Palestinian dialogue commences.

• The PLO has already accepted the suggestions of the U.S., Vice Premier Shimon Peres and Defence Minister Yitzhak Rabin that two of the Palestinian delegates hold dual residency, with homes in both East Jerusalem and in the West Bank. Included on the list would be two deportees who are still listed on the current West Bank population registry and who do not hold positions in the PLO or engage in terrorist activity.

• Egypt will present a list of Palestinian candidates to the Israeli delegation during the meeting and Israel, having accepted the above criteria for eligibility, will have the right to veto names on the list. "The principle is important," the official said. "Once we have the principles accepted, the exact names can be worked out. The Palestinians choose the list, and you have the veto. We know Israel will not come [to the Cairo talks] unless there is an acceptable list."

• The Soviets could join the U.S. and "supervise" or observe the Israeli-Palestinian dialogue in Cairo, but first it should work out with Israel a timetable for resuming full diplomatic relations between the two countries.

Prime Minister Yitzhak Shamir has so far refused to accept the positions of Peres, Rabin, and the U.S. and compromise on the composition of the Palestinian delegation. The senior Egyptian official was hopeful that Shamir –no longer paralyzed by hardliners after Wednesday's Likud Central Committee meeting – would convene the inner cabinet on Thursday and agree to the compromise outlined above.

The official said he did not think Foreign Minister Moshe Arens' departure for Europe on Thursday should delay such a meeting, as Arens could vote by proxy.

According to the scenario, Arens will arrive in Geneva after visiting Prague to inaugurate the renewal of diplomatic relations with that country. Secretary of State James Baker would arrive in Geneva after talks in Moscow with his Soviet counterpart, Eduard Shevardnadze.

Hizbullah arms German fascists

LONDON – President Bush's key intelligence advisers in Washington are warning foreign governments that overwhelming evidence exists of links between the Lebanese-based Arab terror group Hizbullah and German right-wing extremist groups, according to a *Sunday Telegraph* report.

They say the unlikely alignment may result in attacks by newly-armed German groups on U.S. military and diplomatic targets.

The Central Intelligence Agency is convinced that some of the large quantity of weapons and explosives smuggled into southern Europe by Hizbullah in the past nine months have been passed to West German nationalist groups for use against U.S. targets.

The warning comes less than a week after West Germany's own internal security service, the BKD, produced a secret report recommending that the extreme right-wing Republican Party should be kept under surveillance for "anti-constitutional activities."

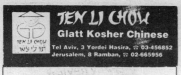

SHABBAT	BEGINS	ENDS
Jerusalem	5:09 p.m.	6:24 p.m.
Tel Aviv	5:27 p.m.	6:26 p.m.
Haifa	5:19 p.m.	6:25 p.m.

THE JERUSALEM POST

Vol. LVIII, No. 17388 Friday, March 16, 1990 • Adar 19, 5750 • Shaaban 19, 1410 NIS 3.00 (Eilat NIS 2.60)

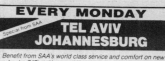

Shas tipped the scales against Shamir

By DAVID MAKOVSKY
Post Diplomatic Correspondent

Shas proved to be the pivotal force in toppling the government last night, after Prime Minister Yitzhak Shamir refused to accept the mediation plan of Sephardi leader Rabbi Ovadia Yosef that would enable Israel to respond favourably to a U.S.-brokered formula to advance an Israeli-Palestinian dialogue.

As a result of Shamir's rejection, Yosef instructed Shas parliamentarians not to support the government in the Knesset's no-confidence vote. All the Shas MKs left the building before the vote, except Absorption Minister Yitzhak Peretz, who was given a special dispensation to vote for the government.

For over an hour, Shamir, later joined by former vice premier Shimon Peres and former defence minister Yitzhak Rabin, took the highly unusual step of arguing their respective party cases before Yosef at his Talbiyeh home.

Yosef presented a document that reportedly called on both parties to agree within a week to U.S. Secretary of State James Baker's proposal on the composition of a Palestinian delegation to a dialogue.

The document also reportedly stipulated that Jerusalem would be outside of any autonomy arrangement, that the PLO would not be allowed to take control of the Palestinian delegation in Cairo, and that the inner cabinet would decide on guidelines for negotiations. The document also stated that all Labour ministers would be returned to the government. Peres signed, but Shamir refused.

Shamir reportedly only agreed to reach a decision on the Baker formula within two weeks, but would not commit himself to a decision.

Yosef made it clear to both sides that Shas would side with the party that signed the compromise. Peretz later told *The Jerusalem Post* that after Shamir refused, Yosef said that "he would now instruct his delegates not to vote in favour of the government."

The five Shas MKs preferred to topple the government by being absent from the plenum rather than vote against Shamir. Observers be-

(Continued on Page 13)

Historic vote fells government

By ASHER WALLFISH
Post Knesset Correspondent

Prime Minister Yitzhak Shamir's narrow coalition fell last night in a historic no-confidence vote of 60 against 55, some 11 hours after the resignations of the Labour Party ministers took effect. Shamir now heads a caretaker government for an indeterminate period.

Shamir was brought down by the ultra-Orthodox Shas faction on the orders of its mentor, former chief rabbi Ovadia Yosef, because he refused to show flexibility in the negotiating process for elections in the territories and accept a compromise agreed to by Labour.

Last night it appeared likely that Labour will manage to form a new government more easily than the Likud.

Shamir became the first Israeli premier to be felled in a no-confidence vote. Although he knew over an hour and a half before the fateful vote that he was bound to lose, he showed no inclination of going to the president to tender his resignation, thus sparing himself indignity.

The 60 votes which put an end to Shamir's 15-month-old government came from the Alignment, Agudat Yisrael, the Citizens Rights Movement, Shinui, Mapam, the Democratic Front for Peace and Equality, the Arab Democratic and the Progressive Peace List.

Supporting Shamir were, apart from his Likud bloc, the National Religious Party, Degel Hatora, Tehiya, Moledet, Tsomet and a lone Shas member, Rabbi Peretz.

But the other five Shas MKs, by staying out of the chamber and voting with their feet on Rabbi Yosef's orders, sealed Shamir's political fate at this stage. Thus, 115 of the 120 Knesset members took part in the vote, but the five who did not participate tipped the balance.

Knesset Clerk Shmuel Jacobson called the roll of names and each MK announced his vote. Before Speaker Dov Shilansky announced the count, Jacobson asked: "Is there any MK present whose name was not called ?" A wit in the chamber shouted "Rabbi Ovadia Yosef," setting off a wave of laughter.

(Continued on Page 15)

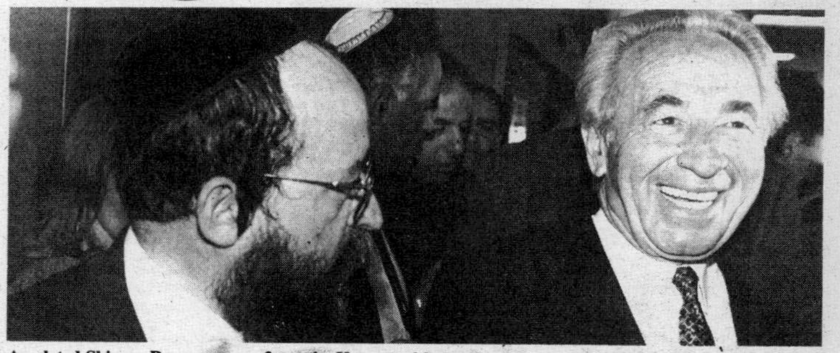

An elated Shimon Peres emerges from the Knesset with Agudat Yisrael MK Moshe Feldman. (G.Feinblatt)

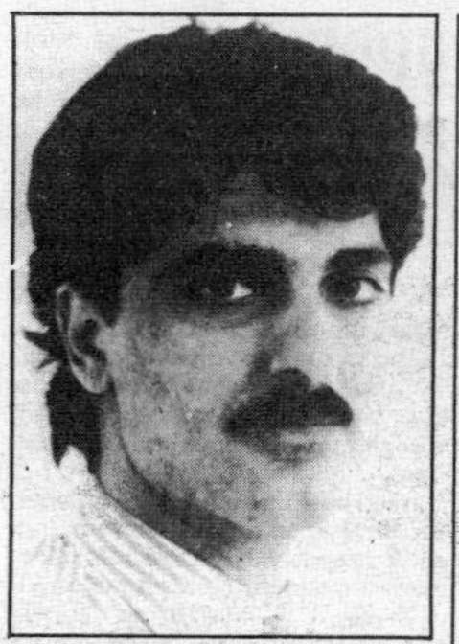

Farzad Bazoft

UK hits Iraq for executing journalist

LONDON (AFP) – Foreign Secretary Douglas Hurd announced yesterday that Britain was recalling its ambassador in Iraq, just hours after the execution in Baghdad of Farzad Bazoft, a journalist with the British newspaper *The Observer*.

Hurd also told the House of Commons that all Iraqi nationals studying in Britain were being sent home, training courses in Britain for Iraqi soldiers were being cancelled and that all ministerial visits to Iraq were suspended.

The announcement came shortly after Prime Minister Margaret Thatcher had told the Commons that the "Iraqi action is an act of barbarism deeply repugnant to all civilised people."

(Full story, page 15)

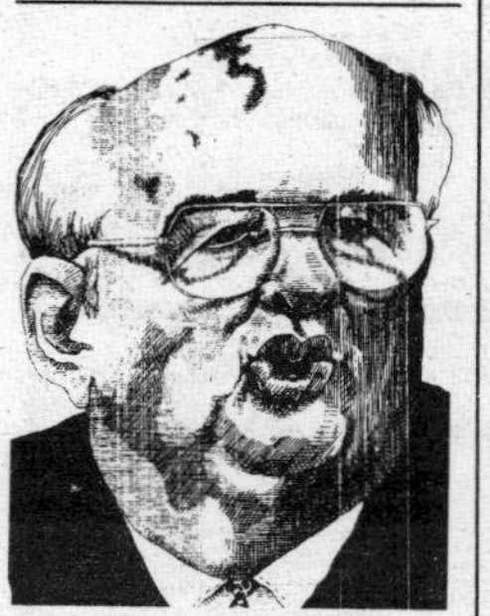

Gorbachev grows stronger, Page 3.

'Heavy damage' to Libyan plant

Jerusalem Post Staff

The Libyan plant which the U.S. claims produces chemical weapons was heavily damaged by a fire which broke out on Wednesday, White House spokesman Marlin Fitzwater said yesterday.

An Israeli expert said yesterday the blaze could have been ignited by a single person or – as an analysis for *The Jerusalem Post* by Giora Shamis points out – it may simply have been an accident. **(Stories, page 15.)**

Ethiopians

While Israel focuses its attention on Soviet Jewish immigrants, Ethiopian olim are languishing in absorption centres, complaining that they have been forgotten.

The Jewish Agency contends that the Ethiopians are being taken care of and that they are being given the means to lead independent lives.

(See page 7).

Herzog to start consultations

By GREER FAY CASHMAN
Jerusalem Post Reporter

President Herzog intends to consult with heads of Knesset factions as soon as possible. His office will today begin making appointments for Sunday.

By law, Herzog must meet with all the faction heads in order to decide whom to charge with the responsibility of forming the next government.

The president was formally notified last night by Knesset Speaker Dov Shilansky of the results of the Knesset's no-confidence vote.

Spotlight turns to president

By ASHER WALLFISH

The coalition crisis has come to a head and Prime Minister Yitzhak Shamir now leads a caretaker government following his defeat in the no-confidence motions.

What does the new situation mean?

It is now up to the president to summon the parliamentary factions and consult with them on the formation of a new government.

What happens to the election process for the Palestinians in the territories?

It stands still, pending the installation of the new government.

How much time does the law allot for the formation of the new government?

There is no time limit.

How does the president direct the government-forming process?

He gives the task of forming the new government to the MK who says he can muster a majority for that government in a parliamentary vote of confidence, and who presents the signatures of the supporting factions.

Since the Alignment managed to defeat Shamir in the no-confidence vote, does that mean it will have no problem wrapping up a narrow coalition soon?

The factions that withdrew their confidence from Shamir last night may take other calculations into consideration when deciding whether or not to support Alignment leader Shimon Peres. A delicate balancing act would be required to keep factions like Mapam happy inside a narrow coalition together with a faction like Agudat Yisrael, although both parties were eager to defeat Shamir. A faction like the Democratic Front for Peace and Equality, which might lend Peres support on the initial vote of confidence, would not be a member of Peres's coalition and any dispute with the Alignment about economic issues or events in the territories could sour its relations with the Alignment totally.

What tactics can we expect Prime Minister Shamir to adopt in the government-formation stage?

Shamir will operate in a blocking mode. His target will be the religious parties. If, for instance, only Agudat Yisrael backs Peres, the Alignment will not have a meaningful majority, and will remain perilously dependent on the six votes of the Communists and the Arabs. So Shamir will aim to prevent the other three religious factions from teaming up with Peres.

What other scenarios are possible?

A bid to create yet another national unity coalition which the religious factions will certainly press for, and a bid for early elections, which would require that a majority of the House pass a special law.

U.S. hopes Labour can form gov't

By WOLF BLITZER
Jerusalem Post Correspondent

WASHINGTON – Senior administration officials are hoping that Shimon Peres can form a narrow Labour-led coalition government in the coming days.

Such a government, they assume, would be prepared to cooperate with Secretary of State James Baker's proposal for organizing an Israeli-Palestinian dialogue.

The officials are refusing to comment publicly on yesterday's vote of no-confidence, insisting that any open statement could be interpreted as improper interference in domestic Israeli politics. Privately, however, they have been encouraged by the prospect of Labour's forming a coalition with the smaller parties on the left and some of the Orthodox parties.

Until now, the Bush administration had assumed that the likelihood of Labour forming a government was remote, but that has now apparently changed.

Still, the Americans sense that the political situation in Jerusalem remains uncertain. They recognize that Labour's efforts, while promising, might yet collapse. They thus want to take a low public profile and let the political situation clarify itself.

The collapse of the government was a source of considerable interest in the U.S. news media. There was widespread speculation that President Bush's recent comments on

(Continued on Page 13)

Shas stance promises uphill battle for Likud

ANALYSIS/Sarah Honig

Political observers say that last night's no-confidence vote – which for the first time in Israel's history felled a government – bodes ill for the Likud in any efforts to set up a narrow coalition, because the party that sealed the government's fate was a member of the national unity coalition.

Some in the Likud went as far as to predict that the alliance which existed for over a dozen years between the Likud and the religious parties has come to an end, at least for the remainder of this Knesset's term.

While the religious electorate is still judged as more right-leaning, the religious parties may in the immediate future jump on the bandwagon of a narrow Labour coalition.

There may be stormy reverberations in the Likud, with the "constraints" faction now seeking to topple Prime Minister Yitzhak Shamir from the party leadership. Some have already suggested that he resign.

According to a senior Likud minister, the fact that Shas, a coalition partner, brought about its downfall

(Continued on Back Page)

By the 29th name, the suspense was over

By DAN IZENBERG
Jerusalem Post Reporter

It wasn't until Knesset Clerk Shmuel Jacobson came to the 29th name on the list of 120 MKs that it finally became clear that the government of Prime Minister Yitzhak Shamir had fallen.

There was no reply when Jacobson called out the name of MK Arye Gamliel (Shas), one of the less prominent members of the 12th Knesset, but one of those upon whom Shamir's fate depended.

After a pause, Jacobson called out: "Not present."

In the following moments, four other members of Shas failed to reply when their names were called out.

The gravity of the hour was lightened for a moment when Degel Hatora MK Avraham Ravitz announced that "with great sorrow," he was casting his vote against the no-confidence motion.

When it was over, Labour MKs Haim Ramon and Uzi Baram, two of the most vociferous opponenets of the national unity government and architects of its fall, hugged each other. The moment belonged partly to them.

According to Israel Radio, Ramon had been harshly attacked only a few hours earlier by Yitzhak Rabin in a closed faction meeting. Rabin had accused Ramon of making promises, but of failing to deliver

(Continued on Page 13)

INSIDE

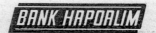

Five ministries too many

Page 2

THE JERUSALEM POST

Vol. LVIII, No. 17403 Tuesday, April 3, 1990 • Nisan 8, 5750 • Ramadan 8, 1410 NIS 2.00 (Eilat NIS 1.70)

Jordanian soldier captured

Page 10

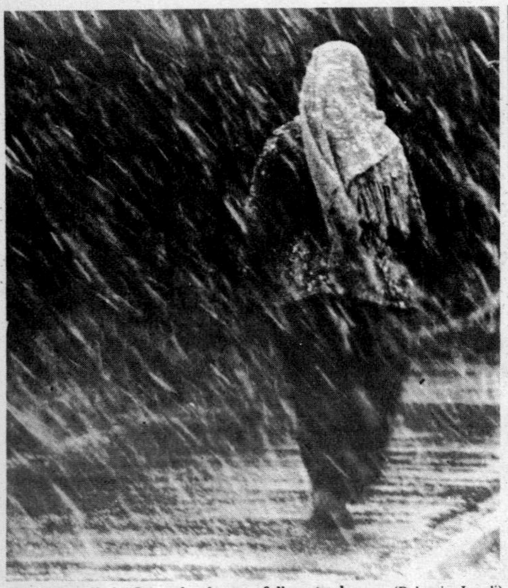

Solitary walk in Jerusalem's snowfall yesterday. (Rahamim Israeli)

Saddam Hussein boasts of Baghdad's power to use chemical weapons

Iraq threatens to scorch Israel

By BEN LYNFIELD
Jerusalem Post Reporter
and news agencies

Iraqi President Saddam Hussein yesterday threatened to incinerate half of Israel with advanced chemical weapons if it joined what he called a big power conspiracy against Iraq.

"I swear to God we will let our fire eat half of Israel if it tries to wage anything against Iraq," he said in his first major reaction to charges that Iraq had tried to obtain triggers for nuclear weapons.

The remarks came amid mounting tensions between Iraq and the West, fuelled by the London arrest last Wednesday of five people allegedly involved in trying to smuggle triggers for nuclear weapons to Baghdad.

Saddam said in a radio broadcast that Iraq had no need of nuclear arms because it had become the only nation besides the U.S. and the Soviet Union to possess binary chemical weapons, composed of two components that, when combined, produce a deadly nerve agent.

"Do they think the $10,500 worth of triggers were enough to produce atomic bombs?" the Iraqi leader asked. "What nonsense! We don't need an atomic bomb because we have binary chemicals."

Avi Pazner, a senior adviser to Prime Minister Yitzhak Shamir, said last night that "Israel has no aggressive intentions against anyone, but has sufficiently proven in the past that it is able to defend itself and will not be blackmailed by threats like that."

Iraq's possession of binary chemical weapons has been known to Israel since 1988, Dr. Gerald Steinberg, an arms control specialist at Bar-Ilan University, noted yesterday. He doubted that Saddam is actually capable of carrying out his boast of destroying half of Israel, given the inaccuracy of Iraqi missiles during the Gulf War and the failure of its recent efforts to launch a satellite.

"They could probably get a few missiles through to Tel Aviv, but they'll also hit Damascus, Cairo and Beirut in the process," Steinberg said.

During his speech, Saddam also criticized the West for its outcry over Iraq's execution last month of London-based journalist Farzad Bazoft on espionage charges. Iraq, he claimed, is facing a major conspiracy.

"The big powers seem to have decided to play the game themselves and directly," he said. "Let the one who wants to try his luck [against Iraq], let him try."

Saddam asserted that Bazoft had given Israel information which could have led to the bombing of a plant where up to 300 Iraqis worked.

He said Iraq did not intend to attack anyone, but "if a wasp tries to advance towards Iraq or wage aggression against it, we will cut its tail from the back, its head from the front and leave only its middle.

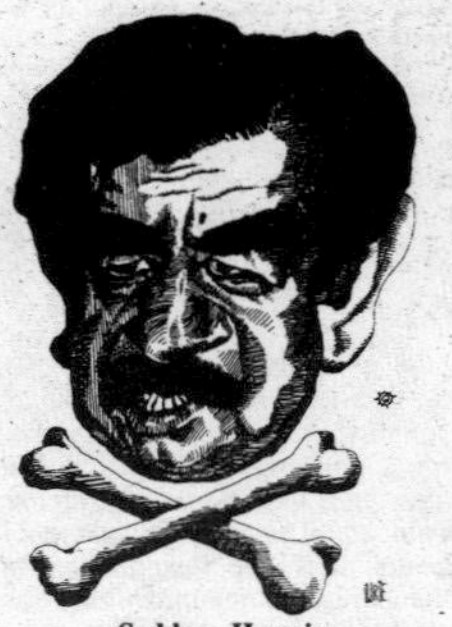

Saddam Hussein

"He who threatens us with an atomic bomb, will be annihilated by binary chemicals," he said.

The Iraqi president said his country acquired binary weapons in the final days of the eight-year Gulf War, but had not used them against Iran.

Iraq has admitted using other chemical weapons against Iran, but denied reports that it used them on its own dissident Kurdish minority.

Israeli, U.S. and British agents had tried to sell enriched uranium to Iraq to try to prove that it was making a nuclear bomb, Saddam charged.

He also complained about the killing in Brussels 10 days ago of international arms dealer George Bull, who was shot dead by unknown assailants. Hussein said Bull had recently visited Iraq.

Meanwhile, the Iraqi Foreign Ministry issued a separate statement yesterday saying the U.S. and Britain had cooperated in the nuclear trigger affair in a bid to damage

(Continued on Back Page)

Freak April snow

Compiled from reports by Larry Derfner, David Rudge and Matthew Seriphs

Jerusalem early yesterday morning had its third recorded April snowfall in 120 years – the others were in 1870 and 1949 – and the fourth may occur today, weather forecasters said.

Rain was plentiful throughout the country, especially in the Golan region, where reservoirs are sorely in need of water.

Showers are due to continue until late tomorrow afternoon, when skies should clear and temperatures climb gradually back to normal, the Meteorological Service's forecasting unit reported.

Safed was the coldest place in the country yesterday, with the mercury dipping to near zero.

As the temperature in Jerusalem dropped to two degrees, snow fell for about an hour, reaching a depth of one centimetre. Roughly the same amount fell on Hebron and Mt. Meron in the Galilee, while heavy snows fell on Mt. Hermon.

In the south, the meteorological centre reported, some 56mm. of rain fell in the 48 hours up to yesterday morning. Eilat received 4mm. of rain. In the Negev, where the Electric Corporation reported brief power outages, a number of low-lying roads were closed to traffic.

(Continued on Back Page)

State Dept. blasts Iraq

WASHINGTON (Reuter) – The U.S. said yesterday that Iraqi President Saddam Hussein's threat to retaliate for an Israeli attack by destroying half of Israel with chemical weapons was "inflammatory, irresponsible and outrageous."

"In a region which is already volatile enough, no one should be trumpeting chemical weapons," State Department spokeswoman Margaret Tutwiler said. "We should be trumpeting their destruction."

Saddam made the threat in a radio broadcast that was his first major reaction to charges that Iraq had tried to obtain triggers for nuclear weapons.

Shamir lashes back at Baghdad's threat

By ASHER WALLFISH
and BEN LYNFIELD
Jerusalem Post Reporters

Prime Minister Yitzhak Shamir lashed out sharply against Iraqi President Saddam Hussein's chemical warfare threats in an official statement issued last night, warning him that Israel would find the way to foil the villainous intentions of its enemies.

Jerusalem has also issued a call to the industrialized world to impose an embargo on the supply of materials and know-how that help Iraq produce non-conventional, and especially chemical weapons.

In a personal statement released through his bureau, Shamir said Saddam's declaration "once more lays bare the fundamental truth which lies at the basis of the Middle East situation: the extreme hostility towards Israel and the ongoing aspiration to destroy it."

Shamir stressed the "brutality at home and abroad for which the Iraqi regime is notorious."

He said that "the winds of peace blow around the world and everyone talks about a new world of co-

(Continued on Back Page)

Signals of Israeli capability

By ABRAHAM RABINOVICH/Jerusalem Post Reporter

Veiled hints of possible Israeli efforts to interfere with the Iraqi nuclear effort have been made periodically over the past year.

A year ago, Israeli authorities, in a briefing to reporters, warned that Iraq was attempting to build a nuclear warhead for ground-to-ground missiles. They said that the first test of such a warhead was planned for mid-1991. Iraq still possessed 12.5 kilograms of enriched uranium, they said, which had survived the Israeli Air Force attack on the Iraqi nuclear plant in 1981 and was sufficient for two "small" bombs.

Three months ago, then-defence minister Yitzhak Rabin told the Knesset that Israel was closely following Iraqi weapons development, "in order to permit the security establishment to take the necessary steps." This Sunday, a former Israeli Air Force intelligence officer said that Israel was capable of reacting to Iraq's nuclear threat "where and when we want."

According to foreign press accounts, Iraq has constructed five or six well-protected underground facilities to house nuclear laboratories and workshops.

In the latter stages of the Iran-Iraq War, Iraq unleashed close to 200 conventionally-armed missiles at Iranian cities, with devastating effect. Iran, however, had virtually no air force or other strategic means of retaliation.

Fatah terrorist cell uncovered in capital

By RON KAMPEAS

The exposure of a Jerusalem-based, Fatah-affiliated terrorist cell by security forces was a "major blow" to the intifada in Jerusalem, police said yesterday.

Police spokesman Uzi Sandori said the cell was responsible for at least one murder, and possessed a small arsenal of stolen weapons. He said eight suspects, all from the Jerusalem area, have been arrested since Friday and are cooperating with police. All were linked to Fatah, Yasser Arafat's mainstream faction of the PLO, Sandori said. More arrests are expected in coming days.

He said the investigation, which lasted several weeks, was a cooperative effort between security forces and the minorities department of the Jerusalem District police.

The cell was responsible for 15 intifada-related attacks in the Jerusalem area since late 1988, Sandori said. They included the stabbing to death of a so-called "collaborator" in the village of Sawahra a-Sharkiya on March 18; the serious injury of Keidar's security officer on February 23 as a result of a booby-trapped water meter; the serious injury of a local Arab who was forced by the army to clear a booby-trapped roadblock on the Keidar road on December 30; and concealing an explosive device in a paint can left next to the Nava coffee shop on Jaffa Road on April 24, 1989.

Other incidents included stoning attacks on Border Police patrolling the area around Jebel Mukaber, bordering the Jewish neighbourhood of East Talpiot, Sandori said.

"This capture is at least as important as the March 1989 exposure of a terrorist cell affiliated with Ahmed Jibril's Popular Front for the Liberation of Palestine-General Command," Sandori said.

Sandori added that a small arsenal of stolen weapons, including a pistol, an Uzi submachine-gun, a Browning machine-gun, dynamite and several home-made explosive devices, was discovered during the investigation leading up to the arrests.

Likud scouts Rabin

By SARAH HONIG
and MICHAL YUDELMAN
Post Political Correspondents

The Likud may invite Yitzhak Rabin to join a coalition if Labour fails to put a government together, *The Jerusalem Post* was told last night.

Labour Party leader Shimon Peres is said to be seriously considering going to the president on Thursday to ask for an extension of his mandate to form a government, according to senior sources.

Labour's leaders, who yesterday postponed a decision on whether to present a narrow government or wait for another party to join the coalition, did little yesterday but watch the action in the Likud court, where efforts were being made to prevent defections from its block of 60 and to begin work towards forming a coalition.

Some in the Likud believe that the real impediment to the recent national unity coalition was Labour Party chairman Shimon Peres, "his personal ambitions and those of his close entourage." Rabin is believed to share this assessment and according to many in the Likud, "there is more than a possibility of cooperation with Rabin."

But the main question is whether Rabin can bring the rest or most of Labour with him into a national uni-

(Continued on Back Page)

Unemployment and aliya to top agenda at Histadrut convention

By JACOB WIRTSCHAFTER
Jerusalem Post Reporter

Despite the Histadrut's waning political power, problems at its plants, and increasing unemployment, the labour federation opens its 16th national convention in Jerusalem tonight on an upbeat note over the renewal of international ties.

According to Histadrut spokesman Shmuel Solar, unemployment and immigration will be the dominant issues at the convention.

Of the 150 foreign guests expected at the convention, half hail from the Eastern Bloc, including the Soviet Union. Also attending are delegates from Africa, Asia, and Latin America, and a substantial Egyptian delegation, including five union leaders. Representatives from Communist Party-affiliated French and Italian unions will be present for the first time.

In his opening address to the 1,500 delegates tonight, Secretary-General Yisrael Kessar was expected to demand that the absorption of Soviet immigrants be included in an overall plan for creating jobs for the population as a whole.

At a Tel Aviv press conference yesterday, organizers said the convention would not be a nostalgic celebration of the union's accomplishments, but rather a forward-looking event where the membership will take on the challenges of the current political and economic situation.

The union places the blame for most of the present economic difficulties on the government.

"The Histadrut will never accept the notion that we should get used to high unemployment," said Tel Aviv University Professor Efraim Sadka, a member of the convention's organizing committee.

The government has been getting a free ride from the Histadrut, Sadka said, citing the trade union's role in providing universal health services and child care thoughout the country.

Today, the foreign guests will be present at the opening of the federation's new East Jerusalem office, which is charged with organizing Arab workers.

Earlier this week, Arab delegates in the Labour Party's Histadrut faction threatened to boycott the convention because their representation to the body was cut by half.

03849317

Hospital staffers to strike today

By JUDY SIEGEL
Post Science and Health Reporter

A 24-hour strike by 2,600 doctors in all government and municipal hospitals ends at 7 this morning, but the fight for equalization of pay with Kupat Holim Clalit counterparts will be taken up by 10,000 state hospital cleaning workers and clerks.

The administrative and maintenance personnel say their strike, beginning at 7 a.m. today, will be open-ended. Laundries, kitchens, and supply warehouses will provide only minimal services, Pessah preparations will be halted, and admittance procedures will be disrupted.

After seven hours of unsuccessful negotiating, the Health Ministry said last night that it would apply this morning to the Jerusalem District Labour Court for restraining orders against the strikers.

But it is not certain whether these will be granted since the same court refused to grant similar orders against the doctors.

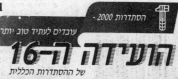

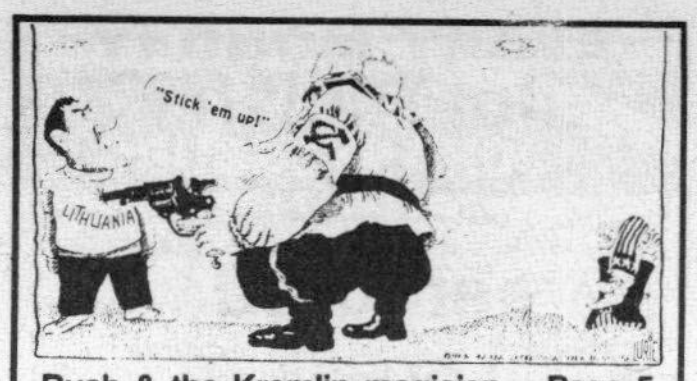

Bush & the Kremlin magician – Page 5

THE JERUSALEM
POST

Vol. LVIII, No. 17405 Thursday, April 5, 1990 • Nisan 10, 5750 • Ramadan 10, 1410 NIS 2.00 (Eilat NIS 1.70)

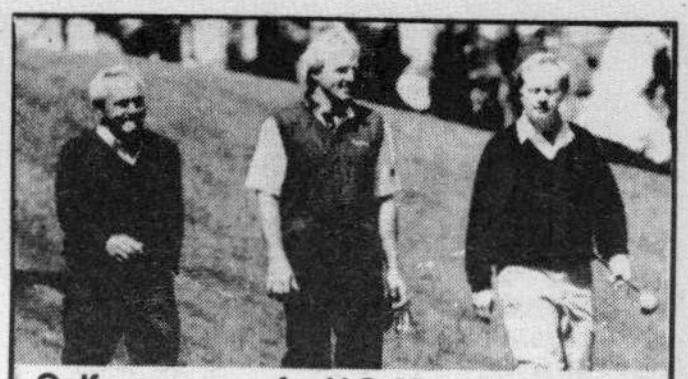

Golfers prepare for U.S. Masters – Page 9

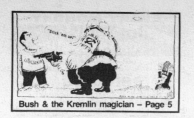

Baghdad gets Arab backing against 'West's campaign'

BEN LYNFIELD
Jerusalem Post Reporter
and news agencies

Baghdad yesterday continued its war of words against Israel and the West, while the Arab states backed President Saddam Hussein's threat Monday to "incinerate half of Israel," if it moved against Iraq.

Iraqi Foreign Minister Tarik Aziz, arriving in Amman for an emergency meeting of the Arab Cooperation Council (ACC), claimed that Israel was planning a new attack against Iraq, to follow up its 1981 strike on the Osirak nuclear reactor.

"Israel wants to attack the Iraqi industrial and scientific sites to maintain the balance of power, which has changed," he claimed.

Pointing to Israel's satellite launch Tuesday, Aziz rebuked the West for criticizing the technological strides of Arab states but not those of Israel.

"When an Arab country achieves a similar achievement then the whole fuss comes, the comments, suspicions and attempts to discredit the image of [that] Arab country," he said, in an apparent reference to criticism of Iraq after the arrests in London last week of five people who allegedly attempted to smuggle nuclear triggers to Baghdad.

The ACC, formed last year, is an economic alliance, which includes Iraq, Jordan, Egypt and North Yemen. Yesterday's session, its first-ever emergency political meeting, was requested by Jordan, which has strongly backed Iraqi allegations of a "Western campaign" against Baghdad.

Egypt's Foreign Minister, Dr. Esmat Abdel-Maguid, arriving in Amman for the meeting, said that the ACC session would reaffirm Arab solidarity with Iraq against what he called a malicious campaign waged by Israel, the U.S. and Britain.

But in Cairo, an Egyptian official who asked not to be identifed said that in fact, Abdel-Meguid will "whisper into Iraq's ear to cool it."

He added: "I think Egypt will also tell Iraq there is no need for such heated words while Cairo pushes for direct peace talks between the PLO and Israel."

Meanwhile, newspapers in Syria yesterday urged Arab states to unite against what it termed an Israeli campaign to destroy their power. Syria, worried over a slackening of Soviet support, and its exclusion from regional alliances, sought a reconcilation with arch-rival Iraq in February but was rebuffed by Saddam.

"In a battle like this, personal tensions and [minor] disputes should be abandoned, so that all unite against the Zionist danger which is threatening our presence and future," the official daily *Tishreen* said.

In Teheran, Iranian newspapers advised readers not to take seriously Saddam's threat against Israel. The daily, *Kayhan International*, termed Saddam's threat a "childish prank," and said Israel should not be alarmed because Saddam is "nothing more than a stooge of the West."

Peres claims 60-plus MKs, but Likud says it's a bluff

By SARAH HONIG
and MICHAL YUDELMAN
Post Political Correspondents

Labour leader Shimon Peres reported yesterday to the President that he had the support of a majority of the Knesset to form the next government, but the Likud continued to insist last night that he was bluffing.

Peres phoned President Chaim Herzog at approximately 5:30 in the evening to notify him that he could now form a government, and that he had asked Knesset Speaker Dov Shilansky to convene the Knesset as soon as possible for a vote of confidence. Just before 7:00 p.m., a messenger arrived at Beit Hanassi with a letter from Peres to Herzog confirming the details of their telephone conversation.

The identity of the MK who supposedly put Labour over the top, however, remained a closely held secret. Suspicion immediately centred on breakaway Liberals Yitzhak Moda'i and Avraham Sharir.

MK Benny Begin warned last night that the five breakaway Liberals are deluding themselves if they think "that bank guarantees will assure them of seats in the next Knesset and of lucrative portfolios. Any agreement they now sign will not hold water unless deliberated and approved by the Likud Central Committee. Otherwise, nothing is binding on any of the Likud Knesset members. Neither I nor my colleagues are obligated by whatever deal they come up with."

As the day progressed, Moda'i moved towards the Likud, thereby focussing speculation on Sharir, the prime Likud malcontent. Late last night, Moda'i visited Sharir in his Ramat Aviv home, in an attempt to persuade him to join an agreement being finalized between the breakaways and the Likud.

While his colleagues in the Moda'i-led Liberal Five were hard at work extracting benefits and assurances from the Likud, Sharir upstaged them all.

Sharir, it was thought, was the secret weapon Labour strategists had been boasting about since the unity government fell.

"For some time now, there has been an unsigned agreement between us and Sharir," a high-ranking Labour source said. "The agreement, however, hinged on Moda'i's crossing the line as well. Sharir made it clear to us that he wouldn't move without Moda'i."

The source surmised last night that Peres may have acted before Sharir actually affixed his signature to the deal, and while Modai's position was still unclear.

Peres's move, he said, came in order to create a political *fait accompli* and in the hope that it would entice other parties to join his coalition.

"We'll blow Sharir sky high!" "We'll force him to resign," and "He will never hear the end of this; it's the end of him," were the spontaneous reactions of sources in the Prime Minister's Office to Peres's

(Continued on Back Page)

Speaker to decide

By ASHER WALLFISH

Knesset Speaker Dov Shilansky said last night he would decide today when to convene the Knesset to hear Peres present his new government.

After hurrying back from an official trip abroad earlier than intended, because of the rapid pace of developments, Shilansky conferred last night with Likud deputy speaker Dan Tichon whom he had left in charge.

Yesterday morning, before Shilansky got back, Tichon said the Knesset would probably be convened only next Wednesday, in order to make sure that various MKs who were abroad could return in time.

In a radio interview, Shilansky said he would certainly summon the Knesset "soon" for a special session during the recess, on the strength of the 20 Labour signatures that had been presented to him along with a formal letter from Peres.

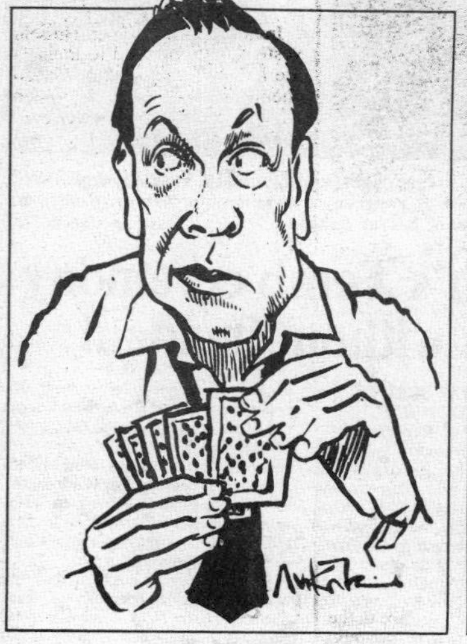

Yitzhak Moda'i

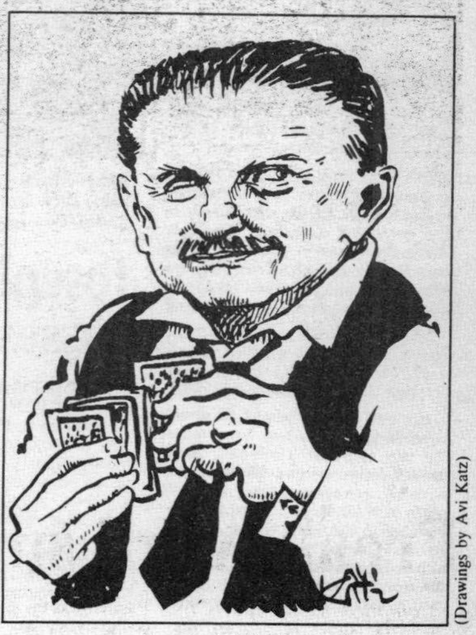

Avraham Sharir

(Drawings by Avi Katz)

Sharir: Man behind the mystery

By CALEV BEN-DAVID
Jerusalem Post Reporter

A government led by Shimon Peres would be a "disaster," said Avraham Sharir in 1982 when he was serving as Tourism Minister in the Likud government.

Late last night, he was reportedly about to join up with Peres as Knesset Member No. 61 in a Labour-led coalition. Yitzhak Moda'i was reportedly trying to tug him back to the Likud fold.

The subject of the controversy, meanwhile, was in hiding.

Sharir's sudden emergence into the political spotlight reflects a drastic drop in his own political stock more than an improvement in his opinion of Peres. For Sharir, a deal with Peres may be his best hope to extend a political career.

Born in 1933, Sharir was active in the General Zionist youth and student movements. After serving in the Air Force and graduating from the Hebrew University Law School, he became involved in Liberal Party politics and was appointed party secretary-general in 1974.

In 1977 he was elected to the Knesset on the Likud ticket, and four years later handed the Tourism portfolio. He was immediately criticized for appointing unqualified relatives and cronies to key Tourism Ministry posts. His alleged abuse of ministry perks – including using his official car and driver to pick up dog food for the family pet – become the subject of media and public ridicule. Particularly satirized was his excessive penchant for foreign travel; when Ofek-1 was launched, comic Meni Pe'er quipped, "I don't know why Israel needs a satellite when we have Sharir up there circling the globe 24 hours a day."

More serious attacks on Sharir came when he was also awarded the Justice Ministry portfolio in 1986, after fellow Liberal Moda'i resigned from the post under pressure from then-prime minister Peres. Sharir was accused of neglect and incompetence in his running of the ministry. When he made a controversial attempt to block the extradition of murderer William Nakash to France, he was overruled by the High Court of Justice.

(Continued on Back Page)

U.S. experts say Iraqi threat does pose danger to Israel

WASHINGTON – With the largest arsenal of poison gas in the Third World and an array of mid-range rockets to deliver it, Iraq is in a position to cause widespread fatalities in Israel, according to U.S. experts.

Whether Iraq would be willing to run the risk of nuclear annihilation by Israel as a result of a massive poison gas attack is much less certain, the experts said. U.S. specialists believe that Israel has a nuclear arsenal of at least 100 weapons.

Iraq has been producing mustard gas and two nerve agents, Tabun and Sarin, at a chemical weapons plant under the supervision of a ministry headed by the president's son-in-law, Hussein Kamil. Iraq may also be producing phosgene and compounds of arsenic and cyanide.

The U.S. intelligence community estimates that Iraq has an annual poison gas production capacity of up to 13,200 tons.

During the Gulf War, Iraq used chemical weapons extensively against Iran, killing or injuring as many as 50,000 people, according to Iranian claims. Saddam also employed poison gas at home against rebellious Kurds.

The gas was in artillery shells, surface-to-surface rockets and gravity bombs dropped from planes.

Iraq has Soviet-made Scud B surface-to-surface missiles with a range of 300 km., more than enough to reach Israeli cities from western parts of Iraq. In addition, the Iraqis have deployed a modified version of the Scud B, called the Hussein, with a range of 600 km. and they have made limited deployments of another model, called the Abbas, with a range of 900 km.

None of them has pinpoint accuracy, but with poison gas, accuracy is less of a consideration than with conventional explosives; a near-miss can be quite lethal.

(The Baltimore Sun)

Bush hails exodus, pledges support for direct flights from Moscow

By WOLF BLITZER

WASHINGTON – President George Bush yesterday pledged to continue his efforts to persuade the Soviet Union to allow direct flights from Moscow to Tel Aviv.

At a White House ceremony before the Pessah holiday, Bush hailed the increased emigration of Soviet Jews to Israel, noting that more than 15,000 have arrived so far this year.

"The modern exodus is a great event for all those who delight in human freedom," he said.

"The United States has worked hard to open up this lifeline," he continued. "And we will continue to do everything necessary to make it possible for Soviet Jews to get to Israel, including continuing to press for direct and indirect flights."

The U.S., he said, is "glad that so many will celebrate the seder in Israel and we're going to keep working so that many more can join them."

Bush was joined at the ceremony by several American Jewish leaders as well as some long-time refuseniks recently permitted to leave the Soviet Union. Among them were Zev and Carmella Rais and Natasha and Leonid Stonov.

Addressing the Rais family, Bush said: "May you and your children enjoy many years of happiness together in your new home in Israel. For nearly two decades, you've been a brave symbol for all refuseniks."

Bush applauded what he described as "the dramatic changes that have taken place in the Soviet Union making possible the emigration of many who have long sought to leave." He pledged not to forget "those who are left behind."

The president made no mention of the $400 million in U.S. housing guarantees sought by the Israeli government for Soviet Jewish resettlement.

On Tuesday, the House of Representatives took an initial step toward approving the $400m request. But the legislation still has to work its way through the Senate and needs to be signed into law by Bush before it takes effect.

Congressional sources said yesterday the Bush administration could be expected to eventually reach agreement with the Israeli government preventing any of the $400 million to be used beyond the Green Line.

'Threat alters the balance'

By DOUGLAS DAVIS

LONDON – Observers here who closely monitor the Arab world believe the military equation in the Middle East has been radically altered by Iraqi President Saddam Hussein's recent announcement that he possesses chemical weapons and would use them against Israel.

"Saddam's declaration will be a source of confidence and pride to other Arab leaders," one senior source told *The Jerusalem Post* yesterday. "For the first time, they will feel they can confront Israel on an equal footing and cause real damage.

"I think Saddam means what he says when he warns Israel not to attack," he added. "On the other hand, it is difficult to imagine the Israelis sitting on their hands while he makes a nuclear bomb."

Meanwhile, an editorial in the *London Times* yesterday accused Saddam of raising the stakes in the "war of terror."

The newspaper noted that Iraqi attacks involving chemical weapons had been meticulously documented by the UN but had been met with near-silence by the international community.

"If Iraq is not challenged this time, the world can give up any hope of enforcing the Chemical Weapons Convention, which is entering the final negotiating stages in Geneva. Iraq's threat, while directed against Israel, has global implications," the paper said.

Intervention to ensure Iraqi compliance with international law, according to the paper, would be completely justified, "including preemptive strikes, on the lines of Israel's destruction of the Osirak nuclear reactor in 1981."

Aliya crush may bring temporary absorption centres

By HERB KEINON
Jerusalem Post Reporter

With Soviet immigrants arriving at a dizzying pace, the Jewish Agency is considering setting up temporary absorption centres in various development towns because of the housing crunch in the centre of the country.

"The idea is to take hundreds of empty flats in a place like Dimona, put up a sign that it is an absorption centre, and provide absorption services for a while," said Jewish Agency spokesman Gad Ben-Ari. Then, at a stage as yet undetermined, the Agency will "fold up" its services, such as Hebrew classes and social workers.

Ben-Ari said Agency staff hope the temporary absorption centres in outlying areas will provide incentive for newcomers to remain there rather than undertake the difficult search for flats in the centre of the country.

Ben-Ari denied that the temporary centres represent a retreat from the direct absorption concept, whereby immigrants go straight into the private housing market. Rather, it is an attempt to introduce the immigrants to areas they might not otherwise choose.

The Agency is also developing an emergency plan to provide temporary housing for 60,000 immigrants in various guest houses, kibbutzim and hotels.

Innocent deed, says Teddy Kollek of his Chagall-filled suitcases

By MEIR RONNEN
Post Art Editor

A report on Paris Radio yesterday claiming that Mayor Teddy Kollek had smuggled the Ida Chagall gift to the Israel Museum out of France without obtaining the necessary permits brought a muted response from the Jerusalem mayor yesterday.

Kollek, who is chairman of the Board of the Israel Museum, brought the 103 works by Marc Chagall to the museum from France last weekend, carrying them in five suitcases packed for him by the Chagall family in Paris. He told *The Post* last night that he had no idea that he was required to obtain permits from the French National Museum and French customs.

The mayor was endeavouring to contact Ida Chagall in Paris last night.

A spokesman for Kollek said that, as of late last night, the mayor had received no complaint about the episode, official or otherwise. He said Kollek had been amazed by the report, and said that if an official complaint was lodged, he would respond.

Worst intra-Arab strife since intifada began

By JOEL GREENBERG

Fresh reports from Awarta, south of Nablus, indicate that six homes of Fatah activists and two of their cars were torched in the village on Tuesday by backers of the Popular Front for the Liberation of Palestine.

Local sources said the arson attacks climaxed a week of clashes between supporters of the two groups, and were the most extensive incident of inter-Palestinian strife since the start of the uprising. PFLP backers are a majority in Awarta.

Earlier this week, PFLP supporters in the village kidnapped a Fatah backer, Najih Shurab, and, according to some accounts, forced him to confess at the local mosque to "collaboration" with Israel. Members of Shurab's family responded by stoning PFLP backers, some reports said.

On Tuesday evening, masked PFLP activists set fire to six homes and two cars of Fatah backers, and prevented firemen from approaching the homes, claiming they belonged to "collaborators." Occupants of the houses were evicted before the buildings were torched. In subsequent clashes between Fatah and PFLP activists, two persons were reported wounded.

In another incident of internecine violence, masked youths this week broke into the house of former Beit Jalla mayor Jabara Hamis after he refused to comply with their demands for contributions, ostensibly for Palestinians wounded in the intifada, Itim reported. According to the report, the intruders left a threatening note and fired a shot inside the house. Hamis's wife was cut by glass fragments.

In clashes with troops yesterday at the Tulkarm refugee camp, three boys aged 8, 9 and 10 were injured by rubber bullets, Palestinians said. A 13-year-old was wounded by rubber bullets at the Balata refugee camp near Nablus, and a 15-year-old was treated for beating injuries, local sources said. The IDF had no reports of the incidents.

Carter meets Arafat and Mitterrand

PARIS (AP) – PLO Chairman Yasser Arafat, President Francois Mitterrand of France and former U.S. President Jimmy Carter met yesterday to discuss how to rejuvenate the Mideast peace process, Carter said, adding that some leaders did not represent the region's yearnings for peace.

"I think that peace is necessary in the Middle East. I think that peace is inevitable in the Middle East," Carter said after the three-way meeting at the presidential Elysee Palace.

"The problem is among the leaders who don't adequately represent the yearnings of the people [for peace], in Israel, among the Palestinians, the Syrians, the Jordanians, the Lebanese."

Arafat, who was to hold a news conference later, said the United States, France and the major powers have a "fundamental role" in the peace process.

Jewish leaders objected to Arafat's meetings in Paris.

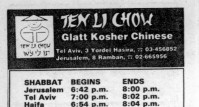

SHABBAT	BEGINS	ENDS
Jerusalem	6:42 p.m.	8:00 p.m.
Tel Aviv	7:00 p.m.	8:02 p.m.
Haifa	6:54 p.m.	8:04 p.m.

THE JERUSALEM POST

Vol. LVIII, No. 17432 Friday, May 4, 1990 • Iyar 9, 5750 • Shawal 9, 1410 NIS 3.00 (Eilat NIS 2.60)

Soldiers in Jabalya faced a 'black sea'

By ABRAHAM RABINOVICH
Jerusalem Post Reporter

JABALYA, GAZA STRIP – The angry sound of prayer from the nearby mosque made Lt. Itamar uneasy in the pre-dawn darkness. Whatever the imam was saying from the pulpit was clearly not about turning the other cheek and there was an unruly edge to the congregation's responses.

"I didn't like the sound of it," the young Nahal officer recalled yesterday. "I said to myself I want to get us through this day without injuries."

His own prayer would go unanswered. Less than two hours after the sun rose last Thursday, three dead Palestinians and 150 wounded were being evacuated from the small plaza in front of the outpost he commanded in the heart of the Jabalya Refugee Camp. Twelve soldiers were also being treated for injuries. It was the worst clash in the territories in months and Arab sources termed it a massacre.

During the first visit by a journalist to the outpost since the clash eight days ago and the imposition of a curfew on the camp, soldiers and officers yesterday said the incident reflected an uncommon measure of

(Continued on Back Page)

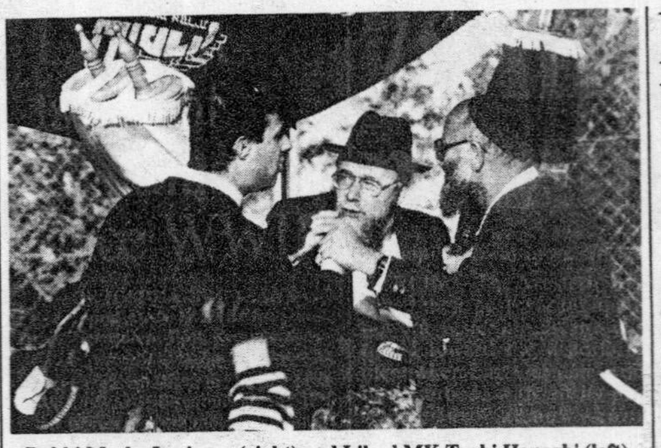

Rabbi Moshe Levinger (right) and Likud MK Tzahi Hanegbi (left) hold Tora scrolls at yesterday's ceremony in Nablus. Centre is Rabbi Dov Lior of Kiryat Arba. (Yoav Lemer/Zoom 77)

Joseph's Tomb ceremony passes without incident

By MATTHEW SERIPHS
and DAN IZENBERG
Jerusalem Post Reporters

A religious ceremony billed as "non-political" by its organizers passed peacefully yesterday evening in Nablus, as settlers and MKs from Israel's far right attended what was to have been a celebration involving 5,000 people.

Fewer than 150 guests, including Knesset Speaker Dov Shilanski, Tehiya MK Geula Cohen, Moledet MK Rehavam Ze'evi, and Likud MK Tzahi Hanegbi; protesters, including CRM MK Yossi Sarid; and newspersons were allowed access, in an IDF bid to limit potential targets for violence.

The IDF brought life to a standstill yesterday in Nablus and surrounding refugee camps, as it imposed a curfew to allow the students to hold a Tora dedication ceremony, at the Od Yosef Hai Yeshiva, at Joseph's Tomb, a site sacred to both Jews and Moslems. On Wednesday, Islamic Resistance Movement (Hamas) activists distributed leaflets calling on Palestinians to attack ceremony participants.

Heavy security ensured that the occasion passed without incident. Twenty Peace Now demonstrators, however, exchanged heated words with ceremony guests, some of whom lifted Rabbi Moshe Levinger to their shoulders, only days after he was convicted of the death by negligence of a Hebron Arab.

Peace Now had obtained permis-

(Continued on Back Page)

Mubarak blasts Shamir

By BEN LYNFIELD
Jerusalem Post Reporter
and news agencies

Egyptian President Hosni Mubarak, at the close of what he called "a historic visit" to Damascus yesterday, sharply attacked Prime Minister Yitzhak Shamir for "putting aside all peaceful solutions" to the Middle East conflict.

It was his second attack on Shamir since the premier said on Independence Day that a new government does not need to enter into a dialogue with Palestinians in the near future and that Cairo need not be the venue for such talks.

Mubarak, following intense talks with Syrian President Hafez Assad, said that Shamir's remarks had "depressed" him. "He [Shamir] did not

(Continued on Page 11)

Bush assures Kollek on Jewish rights in J'lem

By LARRY COHLER
Jerusalem Post Correspondent

WASHINGTON – Jerusalem Mayor Teddy Kollek emerged from a meeting with President George Bush yesterday saying that he had "no doubt that the president has no objection to Jews settling all over Jerusalem."

Kollek said that the president had specifically endorsed a letter written by Secretary of State James Baker, affirming the right of Jews to "live where they want – east or west" in Jerusalem. A separate letter written by Bush to Senator Rudy Boschwitz failed to specifically affirm this right.

Kollek said that he had told the president that the move of Jewish settlers into St. John's Hospice in the Old City's Christian Quarter was "an unfortunate incident." (St. John's – Page 2)

But Kollek said he also told the president that "freedom of access, freedom of worship and freedom of expression have not been affected at all." He noted that the Christians in Jerusalem had experienced a "quiet and peaceful" Easter.

Kollek said he discussed with the president the current situation regarding Soviet Jewish immigrants coming to Jerusalem. He told Bush that the Arab population had doubled since 1967 and the Jewish population had risen by 85 per cent. Even with the new immigrants coming in, Kollek told the president, "we plan to keep about the same ratio.

"I told him we hope to get a good number of the Soviet Jews and also Ethiopians, Argentinians and others coming to Israel."

Kollek said he expected to get between 10 and 12 per cent of the Soviet Jews now flooding Israel if economics permitted, since that is approximately Jerusalem's share of Israel's population at this time. He said he carried no message from Bush to the Israeli government. "I only wish Shamir's government would leave me alone," he said when pressed about whether he was acting in any capacity as a messenger.

Also present at the 25-minute meeting were National Security Chief Brent Scowcroft, Assistant Secretary of State Lawrence Eagleburger and CIA head Robert Gates.

Rabin to challenge Peres

By MICHAL YUDELMAN
Post Political Correspondent

Former defence minister Yitzhak Rabin yesterday announced his candidacy for the Labour Party leadership and raised the possibility he would lead the party into a national unity government under Prime Minister Yitzhak Shamir.

If the Likud forms a narrow government and Labour goes into opposition, Rabin told a meeting of former Labour ministers, the party will act to advance the next Knesset elections. This would be preceded by a contest for the party leadership in a democratic "primaries" process.

Former ministers Moshe Shahal and Mordechai Gur have also announced their candidacy for party chairman in the next party elections.

Rabin said that if the Likud encounters difficulties in forming a narrow government, and the possibility arises of setting up another national unity government, he has no intention of crawling to it, as some Labour sources have claimed. Such a government's only justifica-

(Continued on Page 11)

NRP delays Shamir gov't

By SARAH HONIG
Post Political Correspondent

The Likud now expects to have its government formed in the third week of Prime Minister Yitzhak Shamir's 21-day mandate, which began on April 27.

The delay stems from the National Religious Party's insistence, during the first round of talks with the Likud, on spending a week "exploring the national unity option."

The NRP envisions a national unity coalition under Shamir that no longer has parity between the major partners in the inner cabinet and would not say yes to U.S. Secretary of State James Baker's proposal. Should this prove unfeasible, the NRP would inquire with both parties about early elections.

The NRP leaders who attended the meeting with the Likud yesterday quite clearly indicated that should these options be unworkable, the party would come back to the Likud and join its narrow coalition.

Shamir told the NRP representatives that what they are doing is "tantamount to asking for a time-out when what we don't have is

(Continued on page 14)

Public alarmed over shortage of Gamma Globulin

By JUDY SIEGEL
Post Science and Health Reporter

A shortage of the vital serum Gamma Globulin (GG), caused by the Health Ministry, has aroused panic among people who have been in contact with Hepatitis A patients and are in danger of contracting the disease, *The Jerusalem Post* has learned. Some doctors have brought GG into the country illegally and sold injections of the serum, even though it had not been ministry-tested for Aids, and may not have been properly refrigerated.

The only statement that Health Ministry Director-General Dr. Moshe Mashiah would make through his spokesman was: "The previous health minister started dealing with the problem. You'll have to wait until there is a new minister." The ministry's pharmaceutical division admitted yesterday that it was "unaware" of the shortage, but after checking *The Post's* information, admitted that supplies of GG had run very low. Officials said they hoped a new shipment would arrive next week.

The ministry has forbidden Magen David Adom to produce GG, leaving Israel dependent on a foreign supply made erratic by a world shortage. Private pharmacies around the country ran out of locally made GG months ago, and only a few have small amounts of imported

(Continued on Page 7)

Cuts for absorption

Jerusalem Post Reporter

The Finance Ministry is to seek a NIS 400 million cut from the 1990/91 state budget in order to finance immigrant absorption, according to a new economic plan to be submitted to the cabinet within two weeks.

The document says the government will have to spend NIS 3.2 billion on absorption this fiscal year, anticipating 150,000 immigrants. (Full story, page 14.)

Stalled peace moves hamper Israel at EC

By DAVID MAKOVSKY
Post Diplomatic Correspondent

Western Europe, Israel's largest trading partner, is refusing to negotiate the new pacts that Israel will need to compete in the post-1992 European Community. The current impasse on peace is the reason, senior Israeli and European officials have told *The Jerusalem Post.*

"Israel has been put on hold," Gwyn Morgan, EC Ambassador to Israel. "Recent events do not facilitate Israel's chances of taking advantage of those benefits that would accrue to the European Community (EC) in 1992. There is no doubt that should Israel look serious about the peace process, this would certainly positively impact upon the EC's current reticence in dealing with Israel."

Morgan cited the intifada and the recently initiated settlements in the territories as factors that have tarnished Israel's image in Brussels.

Avi Primor, Israel's ambassador to the European Community and Belgium, said that "Europe is angry with us. They are not anti-Semites, but they think of Israel as part of the rejectionist front on peace. The problem is fundamental. The Europeans want to see some political movement."

He continued: "Not all decisions made by the EC are based on hard

(Continued on Page 11)

Both Iran, Iraq chemicals used in Kurdish massacre

By PATRICK TYLER

WASHINGTON – A Defence Department reconstruction of the final stages of the Iran-Iraq War has assembled what analysts say is conclusive intelligence that one of the worst civilian massacres of the war in the Iraqi Kurdish city of Halabja was caused by repeated chemical bombardments from both belligerent armies.

The finding does not alter U.S. concern about the proliferation of chemical weapons, especially in Iraq's larger and more sophisticated chemical arsenal.

But it calls into question the widely reported assertion of human rights organizations and Kurdish groups that Iraq bore the greater responsibility for the deaths of hundreds of Iraqi Kurds – women, infants and elderly – who died at Halabja in what has been described as a vindictive chemical strike ordered from Baghdad in mid-March 1988 for Kurdish assistance to Iranian forces.

Iran has insisted that Iraq was responsible, and while Iraq asserted at the time that Iran also had used chemical weapons in the battle, international condemnation has focused largely on Baghdad.

The Halabja massacre became the most horrifying symbol of Iraqi chemical warfare. Iran's religious leadership exploited the episode by helicoptering hundreds of foreign journalists into the city, 240 kms. north of Baghdad and just inside Iraqi territory, to see and photograph the piles of civilian corpses.

At the time, some Defence Department officials asserted in Wash-

(Continued on Page 11)

We are happy to announce the birth of our son,
YAIR
Brother to *Yael, Yochanan, Naomi*
Grandson to *Nina and Ari Golad*
and *Karl Israel*
Great-grandson to *Amalia Lothringer*
Margreeth and Adi Golad 18 Nissan, 5750
Hattem, The Netherlands 13 April, 1990

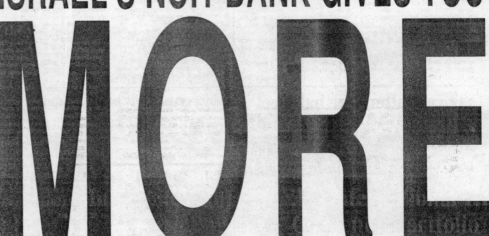

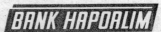

'King of Jerusalem' honoured
Page 2

THE JERUSALEM POST
Vol. LVIII, No. 17454 Thursday, May 31, 1990 • Sivan 7, 5750 • Thu al-Qadah 7, 1410 NIS 2.00 (Eilat NIS 1.70)

Making the most of your kitchen
Page 7

IDF thwarts attack by terrorists from Libya

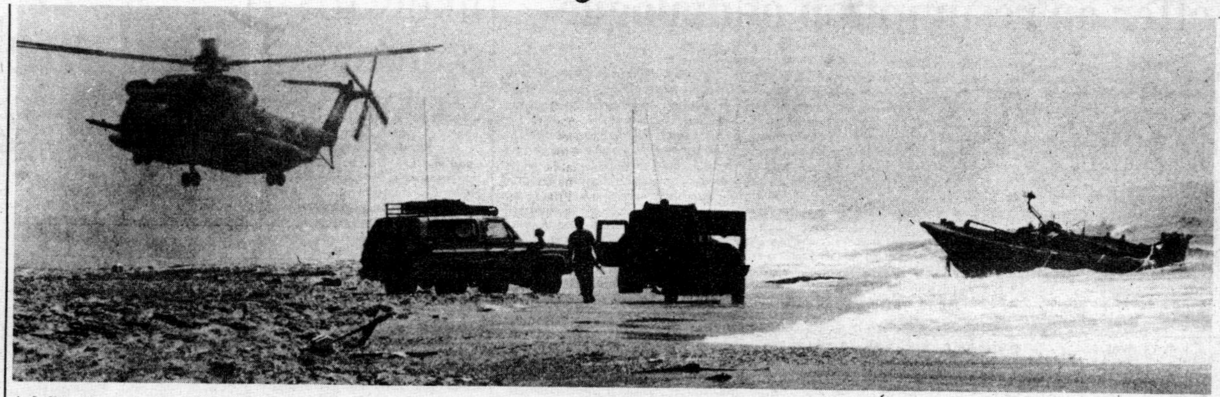

A helicopter arrives at Nitzanim Beach yesterday to evacuate the bodies of four terrorists killed in the attack. (Andre Brutmann)

By JOSHUA BRILLIANT
Jerusalem Post Reporter

TEL AVIV – Navy boats, spotter planes, assault helicopters and troops brought in by helicopter yesterday foiled a terrorist attempt to land on the coast and carry out attacks.

The terrorists originally hoped to reach Tel Aviv's beachfront hotels. But four of them were killed shortly after landing in an IDF training zone at Nitzanim, and seven more surrendered there. Five more surrendered at sea, off the coast of Kibbutz Ga'ash, north of Herzliya. There were no Israeli casualties.

The raid, planned and organized in Libya, was carried out by the Palestine Liberation Front, headed by Mohammed Abbas (Abul Abbas), which was also responsible for the October 1985 attack on the Italian cruise ship Achille Lauro. The attack came as Arab heads of state were winding up a three-day summit conference in Baghdad, but Chief of General Staff Dan Shomron and Chief of Military Intelligence Amnon Shahak doubted the coincidence was intentional.

Some five months ago, sources said, Israel had received indications that such an attack was being planned, but the warnings were not specific.

The terrorists set out from the Libyan port of Benghazi the sources said. Their mother ship, whose name is not known here, carried six aluminum speedboats which had been designed in Cyprus, but built in Libya.

One speedboat served as a mini-tanker, so that the others could leave the mother ship far from Israel's coast and be refueled on their way to shore, the sources said. The terrorists were equipped with a cannon, katyusha launchers, Strella anti-aircraft missiles, grenades, machine guns, automatic rifles and silenced pistols. One of the maps they carried, photocopies of which were released to reporters, was a tourist map of Tel Aviv with the town hall and other area circled.

The terrorists are believed to have left their mother ship on Tuesday at 5:00 or 6:00 p.m. Navy commander Micha Ram said this probably took place some 200 km. from the coast.

One boat sank while being lowered into the sea, and the mother ship apparently turned towards Port Said in Egypt.

Later on, two of the remaining five vessels broke down and the terrorists moved to the two attack boats that were left and refueled. The tanker speedboat turned towards Port Said as well, and the attack vessels split up.

Navy personnel spotted the first vessel at 6:45 a.m., some 40 km. off

(Continued on Back Page)

More pictures, Page 2

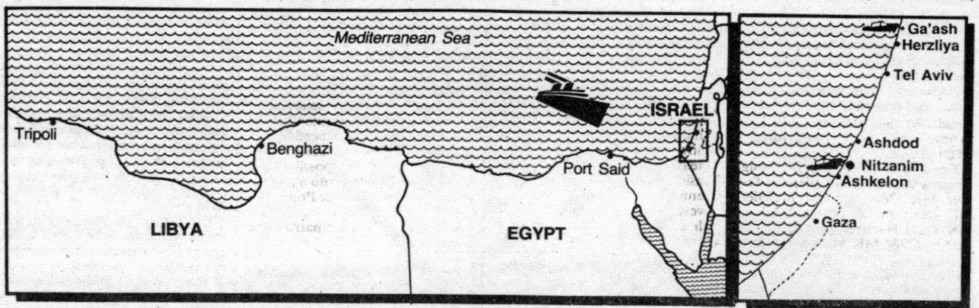

(Ruth Kovel)

Arens says U.S. should stop talks with PLO

By DAVID MAKOVSKY
Post Diplomatic Correspondent

The U.S. should terminate its dialogue with the PLO in the aftermath of the failed terror attack, Foreign Minister Moshe Arens said yesterday. He said its perpetrator, the Palestine Liberation Front headed by Mohammed Abbas, is a constituent member of the PLO and Abul Abbas himself sits on the PLO Executive Committee.

Prime Minister Yitzhak Shamir avoided responding when asked last night if Israel would take any retaliatory measures against Libya for its alleged role in launching the attack.

Arens, who has previously called upon the U.S. administration to break off its talks with the PLO, indicated that America will not be able to refute PLO involvement in terrorism after yesterday's attack.

"The U.S. holds talks with the PLO on the assumption that the PLO has ceased terrorism," he said, "and now we have additional proof that the PLO in fact continues terrorism. Last week at a congressional hearing, congressmen charged that the State Department was ignoring the role of the PLO in terrorism. I hope that this event will convince the U.S. administration of the real situation."

Ambassador Moshe Arad, upon Arens' orders, has begun pressing this issue with the administration. Yesterday, Arad asked Assistant Secretary of State for Near Eastern Affairs John Kelly and other administration officials to terminate the dialogue with the PLO, a Foreign Ministry source said last night.

According to the rules set by the U.S. in December 1988, it will end the dialogue if the PLO deviates from Yasser Arafat's promise to cease engaging in terrorism. Until now, the administration has consistently disregarded reports implicating the PLO in cross-border attacks from Egypt, Lebanon, and Jordan. U.S. Secretary of State James Baker's statement that the PLO is adhering to its promise not to engage in terrorism, made at congressional hearings a few months ago, also angered Israel.

State Department spokeswoman Margaret Tutwiler's swift condemnation of the foiled attack, however, was appreciated here. Last summer, it took the administration two days to fully condemn the attack on the 405 bus on the Jerusalem-Tel Aviv highway.

U.S. hits attack, silent on PLO talks

By LARRY COHLER
Jerusalem Post Correspondent

WASHINGTON – The U.S. State Department said while it was "horrified" by yesterday's terrorist attack, it was too early to say what action, if any, the administration would take concerning its dialogue with the PLO in Tunis.

The Conference of Presidents of Major American Jewish Organizations also shrank from urging an outright halt to the dialogue, and called instead for a reassessment of the U.S. policy of talks with the PLO.

"We are horrified by this terrorist attack," said State Department spokeswoman Margaret Tutwiler. "The United States government is going to, and wants a full review of this. We could not be taking it any more seriously than we are."

Unlike other cases in which the U.S. doubted whether civilians were the target of attempted Palestinian attacks, Tutwiler said of this latest try, "We have enough information to know that this was pure and simple terrorism."

She also said the U.S. considered Abul-Abbas's group, the Palestine Liberation Front, to be a part of the PLO. But Tutwiler stated that the U.S would not declare an immediate end to its Tunis talks, even though Abbas had claimed responsibility for the attack, and that further in-

(Continued on Back Page)

Arafat refused to break Abul Abbas ties

By BILL HUTMAN
and DAVID RUDGE
Jerusalem Post Reporters

Mohammed Abbas (Abul Abbas), whose Palestine Liberation Front group claimed responsiblity for yesterday's attack, is considered a close associate of PLO head Yasser Arafat.

Following Arafat's renunciation of terrorism, the U.S. called on Arafat to break his ties with Abbas in order to show that the PLO had changed its ways, said Anat Kurz, director of the Jaffee Centre's Project on Terrorism and Low-Intensity Warfare at Tel Aviv University. But Arafat never complied with the U.S. demand, she said.

The aborted infiltration attempt provided "irrefutable proof" that Arafat is still committed to terrorism "in the most brutal and vicious way," said Dr. Yossi Olmert, director of the Government Press Office.

"At a time when Arafat is continuing to claim that he has renounced terrorism, his subordinates, who are full-fledged members of the PLO, are actively engaged in preparing and implementing terrorist acts," said Olmert.

Abbas's pro-Iraqi PLF group has specialized over the years in naval operations, such as the infamous 1979 attack on Nahariya in which four people were killed, as well as the 1985 hijacking of the ship Achille Lauro.

Abbas, a member of the PLO's

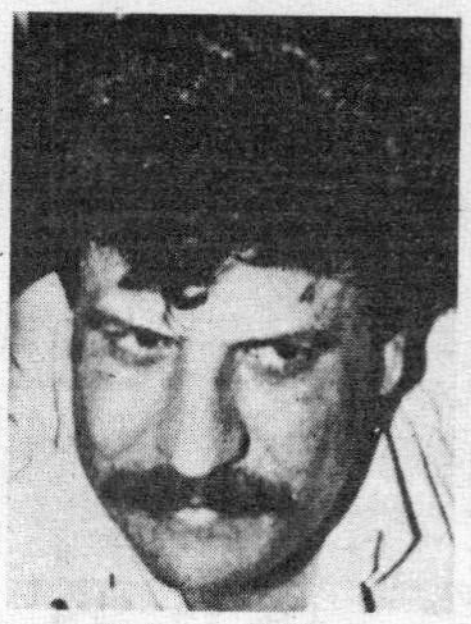

Mohammed Abbas

executive committee, was sentenced in absentia to life in prison by an Italian court for masterminding the hijacking. The Italian government, which sentenced two other PLF members to life sentences, allowed Abbas to leave the country because he helped negotiate an end to the hijacking.

After the seizure, in which an elderly American passenger, Leon Klinghoffer, was shot at close range and then thrown into the Mediterranean in his wheelchair, Abbas said that he would continue to use terrorism as a weapon against Israel.

"In the struggle against the Israeli enemy, people who are not involved can become victims of the situation, and when such things happen we feel sorry about it. But we are not sorry for the action, because the action was directed against Israel," said Abbas, at the Palestine National Council meeting in November, 1988.

Several weeks ago, the U.S. government rescinded the warrant it had issued for Abbas's arrest in the wake of the Achille Lauro incident.

A heavy-set, mustached cigarette-smoker, Abul Abbas, 42, was associated with Ahmed Jibril's Popular Front for the Liberation of Palestine-General Command until the early 1970s. He broke off from Jibril's group and formed the PLF because of his dissatisfaction with Jibril's growing connections with Syria.

The PLF was one of the first terrorist groups to employ hang-gliders in their attacks on targets within Israel. In 1981 the group attempted two such attacks, both of which were foiled by security forces.

In 1987, three PLF terrorists successfully infiltrated into the Beit She'an Valley, but were captured by IDF soldiers before they had succeeded in carrying out an attack.

Following the assassination of Abu Jihad in 1988, Abbas was reportedly named Fatah coordinator for activities in the occupied territories.

The PLF has bases in Lebanon and Iraq, and coordinates some of its activity in Libya, said Kurz.

PLF: Teach the enemy a lesson

SIDON (Reuter) – The Palestine Liberation Front, in a statement issued in Baghdad, said that its operation, months in the planning, was carried out "in response to the tears of mothers and the screams of children and the wounded and in retaliation for the Zionist massacre against our workers.

"Our elite naval units," the statement continued, "moved to teach the enemy a lesson of combat on the coast of Palestine." The PLF said the attack was "to draw up new features for armed struggle against the Zionist enemy, to liberate Palestine and achieve the freedom of our struggling people."

IDF kills terrorist in security zone

By DAVID RUDGE
Jerusalem Post Reporter

A member of the Palestine Liberation Front of Talat Yacoub was killed in a clash on Monday with IDF troops along the northern border of the security zone in south Lebanon.

Arab summit blasts Soviet immigration

Post Middle East Staff
and news agencies

Arab leaders, closing an emergency summit in Baghdad yesterday, sharply criticized what they termed the "transfer of Soviet and other Jews to Palestine and other occupied Arab territories" and blasted the U.S. for its backing of Israel.

A 20-page final communique, climaxing a three-day Arab summit, also called for political and economic punishment of any country that recognizes Jerusalem as Israel's capital.

The statement appeared to mark a setback for Egypt and Saudi Arabia, whose leaders had struggled for resolutions that steered clear of emotional rhetoric.

Still, at Egyptian urging, some last-minute changes were made in the draft text, tempering an outright threat of economic sanctions, and possibly an oil embargo, against states that encourage Jewish emigration to Israel.

Instead, the leaders instructed the economic, financial and foreign ministers of the 21 Arab League countries to meet within two months to re-evaluate relations and recommend to the next summit, slated for Cairo in November, possible sanctions against states that facilitate emigration to Israel.

Egyptian President Hosni Mubarak flew to Damascus after the summit for talks with Syrian President Hafez Assad, who had boycott-

(Continued on Back Page)

Palestinians see attempted raid as mistimed

By JOEL GREENBERG

Palestinian activist Faisal Husseini declined to condemn yesterday's attempted raid on the Israeli coast, but said he would not have ordered such an attack.

Other Palestinian activists on a hunger strike with Husseini in East Jerusalem privately criticized the attempted raid as a damaging blow to their cause at a time when they are waging a campaign to win international support in the wake of the Rishon Lezion massacre.

"I don't know what pushed Abul Abbas to action, but I would not have taken this decision [to launch the raid]," Husseini said.

U.S. sending Soviet Union mixed signals on trade

The Washington Post and Reuters

WASHINGTON – American officials are sending mixed signals on whether trade agreements will be signed during the U.S.-Soviet summit that opens today – possibly letting the decision hinge on last-minute Soviet political concessions.

U.S.-Soviet agreements on overall trade, grain and soy products sales, air services and maritime shipping are ready to be signed by presidents George Bush and Mikhail Gorbachev at their four-day meeting here.

But even as Gorbachev was heading to Washington from Canada yesterday afternoon, there was no single Bush administration voice on whether any of the trade pacts will actually be signed.

The main topic at the summit, however, is expected to be Germany.

Bush is prepared to offer Gorbachev assurances about the future of Germany as part of an effort to help him stabilize an internal situation that appears increasingly desperate, a senior administration official said.

Chief among the assurances is likely to be a proposal for future negotiations to limit the military forces of a united Germany, which U.S. sources described as a volatile political problem for Gorbachev, adding to his growing economic and ethnic woes.

31050319

Earthquake in Central Europe leaves 9 dead, hundreds injured

BUCHAREST (Reuter) – At least nine people died yesterday as a powerful earthquake rocked central Europe from the Baltic to the Black Sea and as far south as Yugoslavia.

The size of the quake has been reported as ranging from 6.5 to 7.5 on the Richter Scale.

Romanian television said eight were killed and 260 injured in Bucharest and in towns to the north and east of the capital.

Bulgarian television reported that a woman died of shock in a town on the Danube River, which divides Bulgaria from Romania.

The Soviet news agency Tass quoted a member of parliament, Ilmar Bisher, as saying the quake caused serious damage in the Soviet republic of Moldavia bordering on Romania.

"According to first reports, there was not only destruction but dead and wounded," he said.

Bucharest radio and television reports said the Romanian toll was expected to rise. A witness reported seeing three people who had been killed by falling rubble in a Bucharest street.

Bucharest police and rescue workers said many of the casualties were among people who leapt in panic from the balconies of high-rise flats. Thousands more fled from offices and homes as tiles and masonry tumbled from rooftops.

"For a few seconds, I thought I could see death; then I ran for my life," said office worker Dana Niculescu.

Strong shocks were felt for thousands of miles across the Soviet Union, Bulgaria, Yugoslavia and Turkey.

Romanian television said the quake was centred in the hilly and sparsely populated Vrancea region northeast of Bucharest.

The area was last hit by a major earthquake in 1977, when a tremor measuring 7.2 killed more than 1,000 people and devastated much of Bucharest, now a city of 2.3 million people.

Romanians, still dizzy from the bloody revolution which brought communist rule to an end in December, were in panic.

Schools were evacuated and children sat in playgrounds still trembling from aftershocks 30 minutes after the main tremor.

The earthquake is unlikely to have caused an accident at any nuclear power plants in the region, the International Atomic Energy Agency said in Vienna.

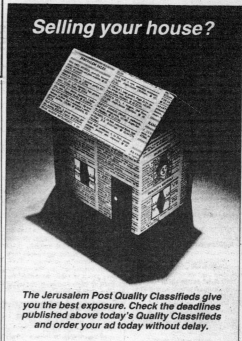

Albania to let the 'embassy refugees' go
Page 3

THE JERUSALEM POST

Vol. LVIII, No. 17486 Sunday, July 8, 1990 • Tamuz 15, 5750 • Thu al-Hijjah 15, 1410 NIS 2.20 (Eilat NIS 1.90)

Martina wins record ninth Wimbledon title
Sport / Page 7

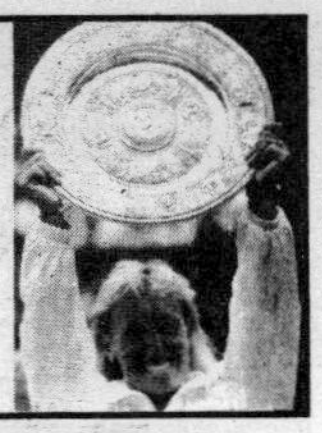

Jibril vows more terror after IAF hits bases

By JOSHUA BRILLIANT
Jerusalem Post Reporter
and news agencies

A Palestinian extremist group yesterday vowed to pursue its armed struggle against Israel after Israeli jets attacked two of its bases in Lebanon, blasting an ammunition dump and wounding 11 people. Other reports said that eight people were wounded.

Ahmed Jibril's Popular Front for the Liberation of Palestine-General Command (PFLP-GC), in a statement issued here, also called on Palestinians to reject the "cowardly" policies of Yasser Arafat's PLO.

Israel Air Force jets on Friday morning attacked two PFLP-GC bases in Syrian-controlled areas in Lebanon, but an Israeli military source said last night that the Syrians did not intervene.

The IDF spokesman described the targets as bases for organization and departure for attacks on Israel.

The raids began at 7:30 a.m. when four jets appeared over Sultan Yaakub, in the Bekaa, some 40 kilometres north of Israel. The planes hit an ammunition dump, setting it ablaze and generating a chain of explosions. A Lebanese police source told AP that the jets also attacked a training camp and a communications centre and inflicted severe damage.

They also dropped three delayed-action bombs and the last one exploded at 10:30 a.m. but no one was hurt then, the report from Lebanon said.

Five minutes after the planes appeared over Sultan Yaakub, four other jets attacked a PFLP-GC's base at Khan Hayat, north of Tripoli, some 160 kilometres from Israel's border. According to the IDF spokesman the targets there were also hit.

The attacks were reportedly launched after night-long patrols by three warplanes which, according to Lebanese sources, dropped 1,300 flares in the south.

PFLP-GC men reportedly fired twin-barrelled 23mm. anti-aircraft

(Continued on Back Page)

PLO says nothing new in Bush's offer on resumption of dialogue

LONDON (Reuter) – U.S. President George Bush said on Friday he would resume talks with the PLO if it condemned May's aborted Tel Aviv beach raid and punished the plot's mastermind, but the PLO apparently rejected Bush's offer, saying it was nothing new.

Declaring he wanted to revive Middle East peace efforts, Bush said that if the PLO responded, he would urgently consider renewing their dialogue, which had been useful.

"What I want to see is the peace process go forward," Bush told a news conference at the end of a two-day Nato summit in London.

Bush told reporters: "I would like to think that Mr. Arafat could some way bring his council not only to denounce that particular terrorist act but also to take some action against the person who perpetrated it.

"Then I think we would certainly give rapid consideration to renewal of the dialogue," he said. "I happen to think the dialogue has been useful.

"I don't think Mr. Arafat particularly agrees with that, and I'd be quite confident that Mr. Shamir doesn't, but nevertheless, that's the view of the United States."

PLO officials in Tunis said on Friday they saw nothing new in Bush's restatement of conditions for resuming talks.

The officials said the conditions appeared to be exactly the same as those set by Washington in the weeks leading up to the suspension of the 18-month dialogue on June 20.

"It doesn't seem new but I'd like to see the whole text," said Bassam Abu Sharif, adviser to PLO chairman Yasser Arafat.

The *Washington Post* said on Friday the U.S. was trying to devise a formula allowing Arafat to show he was serious about renouncing "terrorism" without upsetting other PLO leaders.

But Washington still wanted Mohammed Abbas, the leader of the Palestine Liberation Front which carried out the raid, to be disciplined, it added.

The PLO has said that only the Palestine National Council (PNC), the Palestinian parliament-in-exile, can act against Abbas.

Salah Khalaf, a chief aide to Arafat, told Agence France-Presse yesterday that the PLO's central council is to meet on July 18 in Baghdad to discuss the suspension of talks.

The central council acts as a steering group when the PNC is not in session.

Khalaf, better known by his nom-de-guerre Abu Iyad, criticized the latest call by Bush for the PLO to condemn the failed beach attack.

Accusing Bush of "not wanting to settle the problem," Khalaf voiced surprise and said, "we had heard a different song from the Egyptian and Swedish mediators" trying to restore the dialogue.

Meanwhile, Libya yesterday appeared to urge the PLO to resume terrorist attacks against Israel and said it should not worry that the U.S. had suspended a dialogue with it.

"He who lays down his arms and goes for dialogue has already sentenced himself to be the weak party, pleading for what could be extracted by fighting," the official news agency Jana said in a commentary.

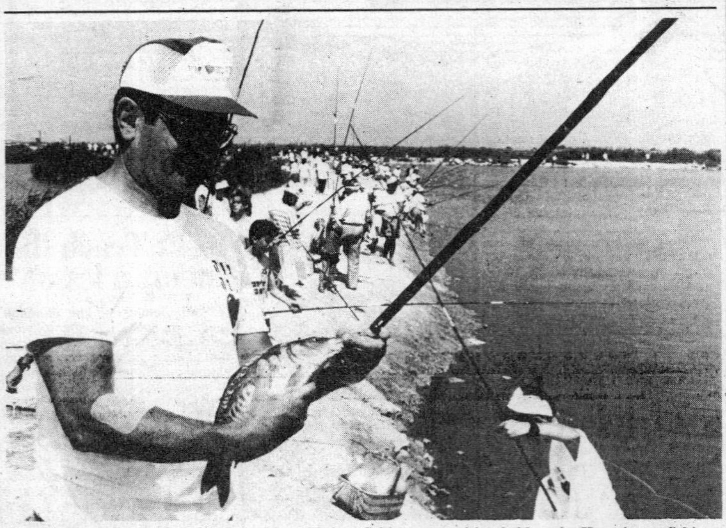

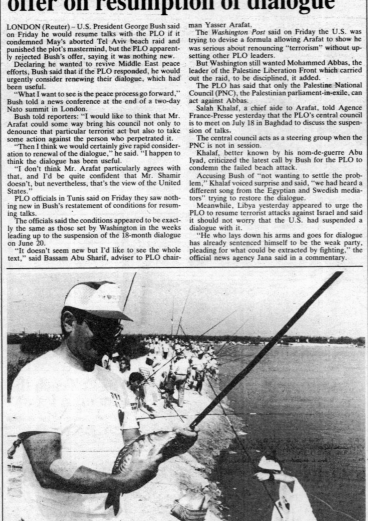

Angler Shabtai Angel contemplates his catch in a fishing competition held at the Hama'ayan fishing park near Rishon Lezion. (Michael Freidin)

Doctors likely to continue strike

By JUDY SIEGEL
and JACOB WIRTSCHAFTER
Jerusalem Post Reporters

Despite yet another round of talks last night between government, Kupat Holim Clalit and Israel Medical Association (IMA) officials, regional strikes by thousands of doctors will apparently continue into their second week today.

No progress was made at Friday's marathon meetings that ended shortly before Shabbat and included Finance Minister Yitzhak Moda'i, Health Minister Ehud Olmert, Histadrut Secretary-General Yisrael Kessar and IMA doctors. The government has so far rejected the IMA's ultimatum to rescind court orders that cancelled Clalit hospital doctors' second shift, and to let the second-shift scheme continue beyond the end of July.

If no solution is found, all government, Clalit and other public hospitals in the North, Tel Aviv, the Dan Region, the Coastal Plain and the South (excluding Jerusalem) will run on a reduced Shabbat schedule today. This means no non-emergency operations, no outpatient clinics and only a minimum of physicians on the ward.

In addition, the clinics of all four health funds are to be closed today, except for the treatment of emergency cases by no more than 30 per cent of their doctors. Independent doctors who receive patients at home or at office clinics have been told not to receive more than 30 per cent of their regular complement of patients, though this will be difficult for the IMA to enforce.

Meanwhile, IMA chairman Dr. Miriam Tzangen sent a letter on Friday to President Chaim Herzog in response to his criticism of doctors in his Israel Radio talk in the afternoon. Tzangen wrote that if Herzog had proposals on how the doctors could resolve the crisis without striking, after the Treasury had "disrupted" negotiations by applying for court orders against Clalit, "we'd like to hear them."

She continued: "The doctors, unlike ministers or politicians who get

(Continued on Back Page)

'Mengistu flew to Israel for secret talks'

By DAVID MAKOVSKY
Post Diplomatic Correspondent

Ethiopian leader Mengistu Haile Mariam flew to Israel in secrecy last week, according to Italian newspaper reports.

The daily *Il Messaggero* said the Ethiopian leader met with Israeli and U.S. officials in Tel Aviv.

Mengistu's regime is in mortal danger, with rebel forces chalking up victory after victory in Eritrea and the key northern province of Tigre. The Eritreans have captured both of Ethiopia's Red Sea ports, Massawa and Asab, and have surrounded the provincial capital of Asmara, Ethiopia's second biggest city.

Mengistu, who lost a great deal of Soviet military support recently as Mikhail Gorbachev cut back on Soviet aid to Third World allies, is losing the long-running war against Eritrean and Tigrean rebels, with some insurgent forces now reportedly within artillery range of the capital, Addis Ababa.

Ethiopia resumed diplomatic relations with Israel last November

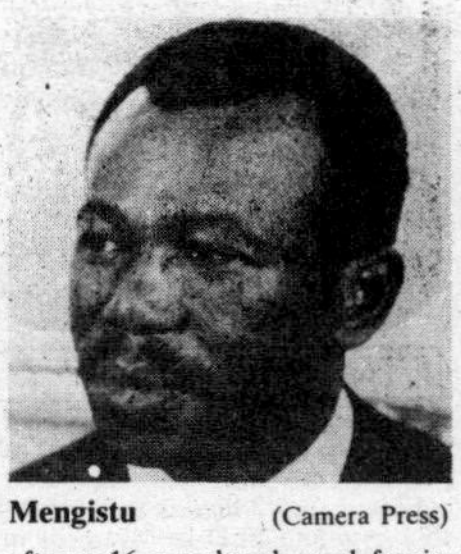

Mengistu (Camera Press)

after a 16-year break, and foreign reports claimed that Israel was providing military assistance to Mengistu.

According to the Italian newspaper *Il Messaggero*, Mengistu also secretly travelled to Rome on June 17 and spoke for three hours with Premier Giulio Andreotti at Ciampino Airport. He then went to an unknown location in the Via Veneto area, the newspaper said. The U.S. Embassy is located in that neighbourhood.

Mubarak meets with Arafat

Post Middle East Staff

Egyptian President Hosni Mubarak, who is striving for a resumption of the dialogue between Washington and the PLO, met PLO Chairman Yasser Arafat in Taiz, Yemen yesterday.

It was their first meeting since the U.S. suspended its dialogue with the PLO last month after Arafat failed to condemn the Palestine Liberation Front's abortive attack on Israeli beaches.

The Egyptian leader's visit to Yemen was announced only on Friday. It follows a report in *The Washington Post* last Thursday that the U.S. and Egypt had agreed on a plan for restoration of the dialogue during a visit to Washington early last week by Egyptian Foreign Minister Esmat Abdel-Meguid.

According to the reported plan, the U.S. would resume the dialogue if the PLO drops PLF leader Abul Abbas from the PLO Executive Committee, condemns the PLF for carrying out the raid, and reduces the PLF's status within the PLO.

The Yemeni news agency Saba reported only that Mubarak, Arafat, and Yemeni President Ali Abdullah Saleh discussed Palestinian and other Arab developments at the meeting, but gave no details.

The London-based *A-Sharq al-Awsat* newspaper asserted yesterday that Arafat and Syrian President Hafez Assad would meet in Cairo this month to end their long rift.

Reshuffle in Albania

VIENNA (Reuter) – Albania's ruling Communist Party, rocked by unprecedented public dissent, carried out a reshuffle of top party and government officials yesterday.

The official news agency ATA said changes included the replacement of Interior Minister Simon Stefani with Central Committee secretary Hekuran Isai. Stefani would also relinquish his role as deputy prime minister. (See page 3)

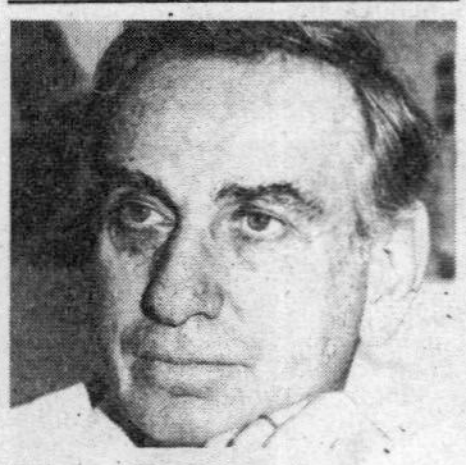

Zalman Shoval (Israel Sun)

MK Shoval likely to be appointed envoy to the U.S.

By DAVID MAKOVSKY
Post Diplomatic Correspondent

MK Zalman Shoval (Likud) will be officially appointed Israel's next ambassador to the U.S., probably as soon as next week's cabinet session, Foreign Ministry sources say.

A protege of Moshe Dayan when he was foreign minister, Shoval, 60, will be replacing Moshe Arad, who is completing a three-year stint.

Shoval, who left a lucrative career in banking to become a Knesset member, is expected to depart for Washington in August, but has already begun meeting visiting congressmen and other U.S. officials.

He is a fluent English speaker and did his doctoral work in international affairs at the University of California at Berkeley.

Other ambassadorial appointments expected to be filled in the coming month are postings to France and Egypt. The latter was vacated with Shimon Shamir's sudden resignation last week.

Perestroika in danger as rival groups vie for power at Soviet congress

By WALTER RUBY
Jerusalem Post Correspondent

MOSCOW – The future of perestroika hung in the balance yesterday as conservatives, moderates and progressives struggled for positions of power at the 28th Congress of the Communist Party of the Soviet Union.

After intense wrangling, the Congress put off until tomorrow a vote on the next general secretary of the Communist Party. Mikhail Gorbachev has given notice he will fight to retain the post, and most observers here believe he will prevail.

But there are many delegates – on both the conservative and liberal sides – who feel that Gorbachev ought to step down from his party position and concentrate all of his energies on serving as president of the Soviet Union.

There appears to be a good chance that alternative candidates to Gorbachev will be nominated for the position of general secretary. There is also a good chance that a new deputy general secretary position will be created, with the idea that the deputy would effectively run the party, while Gorbachev would continue in a symbolic role, devoting most of his energies to the presidency.

Conservatives seem likely to push Yegor Ligachev for the new position, but it is not clear whether they have the votes to prevail.

After some cajoling by Gorbachev, the Congress yesterday reversed an earlier position and voted to consider the performances of the present members of the Politburo on a collective, and not on a person-by-person, basis.

Several members of the Politburo, including Gorbachev allies Vadim Medvedev, Alexander Yakovlev, and Prime Minister Nikolai Rhyzkov have been harshly criticized from the floor of the Congress, and there was some doubt here as to whether they would survive votes of no confidence.

Even without the person-by-person votes, it seems likely that one or more members of the Politburo will be dropped. At this point, it appears that Medvedev, who is in charge of party ideology, is the most likely sacrificial lamb.

On Friday, a group of leaders of the Democratic Platform, the left wing of the Communist Party, said they are likely to walk out of the party at the end of the Congress. Boris Yeltsin, the unofficial leader of the Democratic Platform, has continued to make similar threats.

But many observers here feel that unless there is a total conservative victory in the Congress – such as the election of Ligachev to the assistant general secretary post – most of the Democratic Platform leaders, including Yeltsin, will find a reason to stay within the party for the time being.

The Democratic Platform people may reason that to cut themselves off from the institutional and financial power of the party would be too

(Continued on Back Page)

Finnish Unifil troops step up security after threat by PLO

By DAVID RUDGE
Jerusalem Post Reporter

ROSH HANIKRA – Security precautions have been stepped up for Finnish troops serving with Unifil in South Lebanon following threats issued by the PLO over the Finnish government's decision to allow Soviet Jews to fly directly to Israel via Finland, *The Jerusalem Post* learned yesterday.

Soldiers of the 520-man Finnish contingent are continuing regular operations, including patrols and checkpoint duty, but with stricter security measures in force, according to reports from the region.

Finland is one of nine countries which contribute troops to the UN's peacekeeping force in Lebanon. Its troops are deployed in the central sector of South Lebanon up to the Litani River, an area of operations which partly overlaps the security zone in South Lebanon.

'West Germans built Iraqi supergun plant'

BONN (Reuter) – Leading West German firms helped to build a weapons factory where Iraq's "supergun" was to be made, *Der Spiegel* news magazine said yesterday.

The Hamburg-based weekly said "confiscated documents" showed that the factory near Baghdad was designed to produce guns, and experts feared it was also where a cannon some 150 metres long with a range of 1,000 km. was to be built.

Britain and other West European countries have confiscated shipments suspected of being parts of an Iraqi supergun that could hit Israel.

***Der Spiegel*, in a report to be released in tomorrow's edition, said prosecutors had clear evidence that several leading West German steel and construction firms helped to build the plant.**

The magazine named several companies it said were involved.

Grenade thrown at police patrol

By RON KAMPEAS

A grenade was tossed at a police patrol on Sultan Suleiman Street outside the Old City's Damascus Gate in Jerusalem yesterday.

The grenade, which dated back to the Mandate, did not go off. Police sappers removed it within minutes.

"I was standing on the sidewalk when I heard something fall nearby," one policeman said. "I looked up, and saw the grenade coming from above. I think the grenade was tossed from the Old City walls."

Several dozen Palestinians were detained, and released a short while later.

On Friday, there was a beefed-up police presence in the Old City because thousands of Moslems were attending prayers at the Al-Aksa Mosque. Thursday night marked the end of the Moslem feast of the sacrifice, Id al-Adha.

The right bank for people with rights!

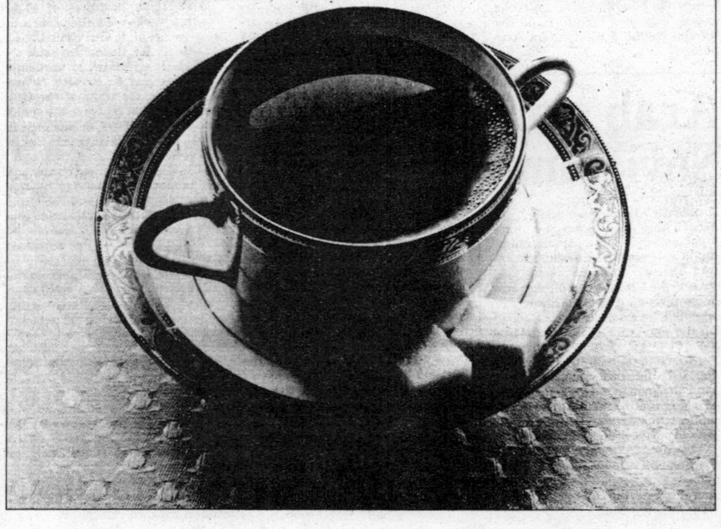

Make the most of your right to hold a tax-free foreign currency account. The smart money goes to First International – the unconventional, competitive bank that offers you high interest plus all the right choices:

The right currencies: $, £, DM, SF, Y, etc. – in any combination.

The right terms: a broad range of amounts and maturities, at fixed or floating interest rates, with automatic renewals.

The right hours: most of our 78 branches are open until 2 p.m. daily* and from 4 to 7 p.m. on Mondays and Wednesdays.

Get **the right answers** to your questions about confidential, tax-free foreign currency accounts for tourists, foreign residents, new immigrants, temporary residents and returning residents.

Come into any of our friendly branches. We're looking forward to welcoming you – right away.

Main Branches:
Jerusalem - 10, Hillel st.
Tel Aviv - 9, Ahad Ha'am st.
Haifa - 3, Habankim st.

* 12 noon on Friday and eves of holidays.

Tamir Cohen (Jacobsohn)

THE EVER EXCEPTIONAL THE FIRST INTERNATIONAL BANK.

98979319

TEN LI CHOW
Glatt Kosher Chinese
Tel Aviv, 3 Yordei Hasira, ☎ 03-456852
Jerusalem, 8 Ramban, ☎ 02-665956

SHABBAT	BEGINS	ENDS
Jerusalem	6:57 p.m.	8:14 p.m.
Tel Aviv	7:15 p.m.	8:16 p.m.
Haifa	7:08 p.m.	8:17 p.m.

THE JERUSALEM
POST
Vol. LVIII, No. 17509 Friday, August 3, 1990 • Menahem Av 12, 5750 • Moharram 12, 1411 NIS 3.30 (Eilat NIS 2.85)

Every Monday & Wednesday
Special from SAA
TEL AVIV
JOHANNESBURG
Benefit from SAA's world class service and comfort on new Jumbo 747's with convenient departure and arrival times.
We didn't invent flying. We just perfected it.
For details call your travel agent or: SAA, 03-5102828 Jerusalem, 02-233137/8 Haifa, 04-670094
SAA
SOUTH AFRICAN AIRWAYS

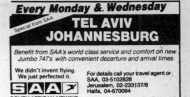

Big powers lash Iraq for its blitzkrieg

Kuwait falls to Saddam

Jerusalem Post Staff and news agencies

Iraqi tanks thundered across the desert border into Kuwait in the dark hours of yesterday morning at the head of a blitzkreig invasion that overwhelmed the tiny emirate, ousted the most stable royal family in the Gulf, sent world oil prices soaring, and put fabulous wealth in the grasp of Saddam Hussein, under the stunned and horrified gaze of his Arab neighbours.

"The Iraqis have occupied all of Kuwait," one government official shouted down a telephone and initial reports put the number of dead or wounded at up to 200. One of those killed was a member of the royal family.

A Dutch woman journalist at the Hilton International Hotel told *The Jerusalem Post* through an intermediary in Cyprus: "The hotel is taken, the hotel is taken. We are cut off." The conversation ended abruptly.

Informed Israeli sources warned last night that this country is likely to be Saddam Hussein's next target.

The emir, Sheikh Jaber al-Ahmed a-Sabah, fled to Saudi Arabia as Baghdad's elite Republican Guards swept through Kuwait City to seize the palace and key installations – including the Central Bank holding the gold reserves of one of the world's richest countries.

Kuwait has vast oil reserves and a population of only two million – two-thirds of them foreigners, including 300,000 Palestinians.

Some 350 Iraqi tanks swept into the capital a few hours after crossing the border 40 kilometers away.

The American aircraft carrier Independence and six escort ships in the Indian Ocean headed toward the Gulf area, but their intentions were not immediately clear.

In a warning clearly aimed at Washington, Baghdad threatened to turn Kuwait into a graveyard if any outside power intervened.

A young Kuwaiti woman in London told *The Jerusalem Post*, "Let Israel hit Iraq." She said she had spoken to her father and brother at their home in the exclusive Abdulla a-Salem neighborhood of Kuwait City: "People have emptied grocery stores of food and we've also heard that several thousand people have been shot."

"Iraqi tanks are patrolling the main roads and we hear the troops are moving south to the Saudi border."

"My father is very pessimistic about the situation. We are a peaceful country and look at what has happened to us!"

Yesterday evening Kuwaiti forces were reported still fighting fiercely in pockets outside the capital. Some radio and television transmitters were broadcasting passionate calls for resistance and appeals for help.

Kuwaiti Crown Prince Sheikh Saad al-Abdulla a-Sabah, in a clandestine broadcast to the nation, vowed to fight Iraq's invading troops "until we clean their treachery from our land."

The invading troops set up roadblocks at major intersections in the capital.

Witnesses said the bombardment of ports and military airports by artillery and the air force was vicious.

The invaders surrounded the palace of the ruler, and residents in the vicinity said that it was seized after two hours of heavy artillery barrages. Explosions and gunfire reverberated around the city of steel and glass skyscrapers.

All oil export terminals closed, choking off shipments which, under an Opec agreement negotiated last month, were being reduced to a quota of 1.5 million barrels a day.

It was not immediately clear if the invasion would interrupt oil production or the free movement of tankers through the northern Gulf.

A statement from the ruling Revolution Command Council in Baghdad said Iraq would withdraw "as soon as things settle and when the free provisional government asks us to do so." Iraq used what U.S. officials dubbed a trumped-up coup in Kuwait led by revolutionaries as a pretext for its invasion.

The "free government" broadcast its first communique from Kuwait saying it had dismissed the National

(Continued on Back Page)

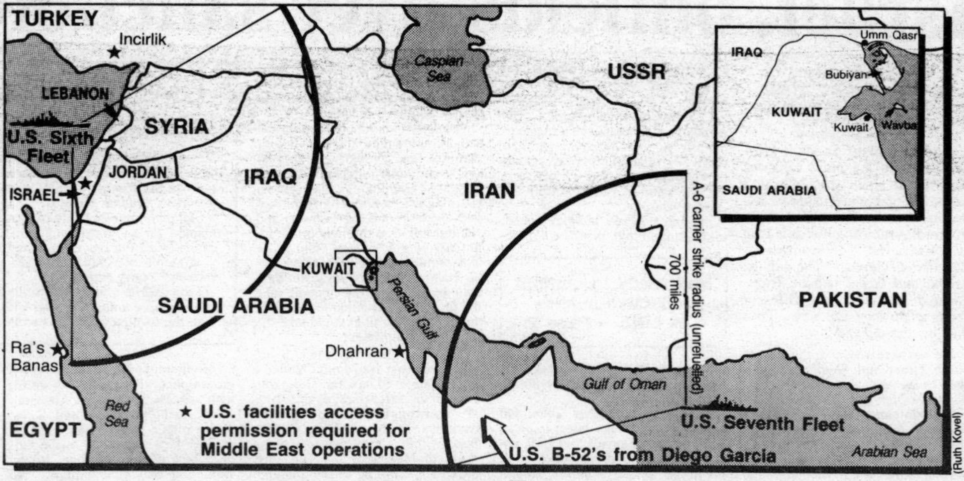
TURKEY
Incirlik
LEBANON
U.S. Sixth Fleet
SYRIA
ISRAEL
JORDAN
IRAQ
Caspian Sea
USSR
IRAN
KUWAIT
SAUDI ARABIA
Persian Gulf
Dhahran
Ra's Banas
EGYPT
Red Sea
★ U.S. facilities access permission required for Middle East operations
A-6 carrier strike radius (unrefueled) 700 miles
PAKISTAN
Gulf of Oman
U.S. Seventh Fleet
U.S. B-52's from Diego Garcia
Arabian Sea
IRAQ
Umm Qasr
Bubiyan
KUWAIT
Kuwait
Wavba
SAUDI ARABIA

(Ruth Kovel)

Bush seeking total ban on Iraqi oil deals

Compiled by Jerusalem Post Staff

U.S. President George Bush condemned Iraq's invasion of Kuwait yesterday as "naked aggression," banned the imports of oil and other goods from the Baghdad and froze control of Iraqi assets in the United States.

Bush asked Nato countries "to cripple Iraq totally" by refusing to buy any of their oil, according to a Nato source in Brussels.

He demanded Iraq's withdrawal from Kuwait, but said he and his advisers "were not discussing" the use of military force.

Cutting short a trip to Mongolia, Secretary of State James Baker flies to Moscow today in order to issue a joint statement with his Soviet counterpart, condemning the invasion and calling for an immediate Iraqi retreat.

The Soviet Union meanwhile suspended deliveries of arms and other military equipment to Iraq, the official Tass news agency said.

The Soviet Union, for years Iraq's main arms supplier, called on Baghdad to withdraw its forces from Kuwait speedily. Moscow also has good relations with Kuwait.

Arab foreign ministers meeting in Cairo late last night agreed to hold an emergency summit to discuss the crisis. Syria was the first Arab country to react strongly, by putting its armed forces on full alert.

(Continued on Back Page)

U.S. foreign policy gave Iraq room to expand

By DORE GOLD
Special to The Jerusalem Post

The Iraqi conquest of Kuwait represents a major foreign policy failure for the Bush administration. The invasion came after a year in which the general policy of the administration toward Iraqi President Saddam Hussein was one of accommodation. Baghdad's intentions were repeatedly misread. Even during the past weeks, since the crisis began on July 17, the administration failed to deter Iraqi expansionism, holding only a small joint naval exercise with the United Arab Emirates at the latter's request

No mass evacuation of U.S. citizens was conducted even after the Iraqi troop concentrations were apparent. The general expectation in Washington was that the entire crisis would blow over quickly, with Egyptian and Saudi mediation. Clearly, now that Kuwait has been attacked and occupied, some of the basic assumptions that have driven the administration's Middle Eastern policy will have to undergo considerable revision.

Increasing Iraqi military activism throughout the Middle East was already evident by mid-1989. In March 1990, Iraqi attempts to smuggle U.S.-made capacitors for nuclear weapons were uncovered. But even with the growing evidence of the Iraqi military challenge, many U.S. experts argued that it was dangerous to isolate or confront Iraq.

The administration appeared to follow this wisdom when it opposed congressional efforts to impose sanctions on Baghdad; Iraq's commercial importance to the U.S. was stressed by some administration spokesmen like Deputy Assistant

Continued on Page 15

Invasion justifies 'Mideast Hitler' fears – Shamir aide

By DAN IZENBERG
Jerusalem Post Reporter

Iraqi President Saddam Hussein's invasion of Kuwait is proof that his threats against Israel must be taken seriously, Aviezer Pazner, Prime Minister Yitzhak Shamir's spokesman, said yesterday.

"We need to call on the international arena to open its eyes and see what is happening and to understand that we need to take Saddam Hussein seriously, that he threatens and then carries out," said Pazner.

He said there is no need for Israel to take action at this point, but that officials are closely monitoring events in Kuwait. "The prime minister has been briefed fully on all developments in the situation since early in the morning," said Pazner.

During a break in yesterday's marathon cabinet session on the budget, senior army officials briefed Shamir, Foreign Minister David Levy, and Defense Minister Moshe Arens on the developments in Kuwait. In the evening, the three ministers and Deputy Foreign Minister Binyamin Netanyahu met again to discuss Levy and Netanyahu's upcoming trip to Washington, where they are to meet Secretary of State James Baker. The talks there, which were to have focused on the peace process, are now likely to include the Iraq-Kuwait crisis, too.

In a strongly worded statement, the Foreign Ministry condemned the invasion, branding it "unbridled aggression, demonstrating the true nature of the Iraqi regime ... Iraq's action proves where the true threat to peace in the region comes from."

Arens warned that Hussein has the same expansionist aims as Nazi leader Adolf Hitler. "First he wages

(Continued on Back Page)

Kuwait suffers effects of 'the kiss of death'

By THOMAS O'DWYER

The writer, now on the staff of The Jerusalem Post, *was in Bahrain and Dubai in 1988-89 covering the Iran-Iraq war* for *Reuters.*

A kiss is just a kiss in the Arab world, where everyone embraces everyone else. But now Kuwait has experienced the kiss of death.

Two years ago a similar thought came to my mind when the phone summoned us reporters from a dawn sleep to board the press helicopter and head out into the gray light to meet a blazing oil tanker limping in from the Gulf.

The night before I had watched Saddam Hussein on a TV bulletin in Dubai as he embraced and kissed his great comrade and ally Sheikh Jaber al-Jaber a-Saleh of Kuwait. Now we were flying out to see a tanker outbound from Kuwait, the Danish Kate Maersk, whose radio room (and its officer) had been blown away by a Chinese C601 missile fired from an Iraqi Tu-16 bomber.

In the dying two years of the eight-year Gulf War, Iran had been the enemy the world loved to hate. Its gunboats attacked Western tankers and fired on American helicopters.

Iran will see the invasion of Kuwait as vindication of its claims during the Gulf War that Iraq was a ruthless aggressor. As one young

(Continued from Page Five)

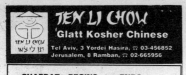

Inside

RELATED STORIES:

- Only non-conventional arms can stop Saddam Hussein, Yitzhak Rabin warns. The international community can do little; Israel must draw the necessary conclusions. Asher Wallfish interviews the former defense minister. **Page 2.**
- Iraq is holding nearly two million people hostage in Kuwait to prevent any counter-attack against its invasion force, notes a Haifa University expert on Iraq. "It's a classic case of hijacking," Dr. Amatzia Barak tells David Rudge. **Page 2.**
- Saudi Arabia and the other Gulf states are likely to seek superpower protection. Egypt and Syria, on the other hand, may draw closer together. In the short run, the Israeli-Palestinian question could be put on a back burner, according to analysts speaking to defense reporter Joshua Brilliant. **Page 5.**
- Soaring oil prices and fears of resultant inflation pushed down shares on Tel Aviv's stock market yesterday. Galit Lipkis reports from the bourse. **Page 5.**
- The Arab world's reactions to the takeover of Kuwait were generally muted. **Page 5.**

Outnumbered 50 to 1, Kuwait had no chance

By DOUGLAS DAVIS
Jerusalem Post Correspondent

LONDON – It was always clear that Kuwait would provide no match for Iraq's overwhelming military might, and its immediate collapse in the face of Saddam Hussein's "mugging" surprised few political or military observers.

According to *Jane's Defence Weekly*, Kuwait's air defenses consisted of an integrated system built around six batteries of 1-Hawk SAMs and could deploy an armed force numbering some 20,300 men against Iraq's 5,000 motor torpedo boats, 600 fighter aircraft and one million battle-hardened troops.

It is considered highly unlikely that the six-nation Gulf Cooperation Council (GCC), which consists of Saudi Arabia, Bahrain, Qatar, Oman, the United Arab Emirates and Kuwait, will spring to the defense of its embattled member-state.

Despite the ambitious plans, announced shortly after the GCC was established in 1981, to create a 10,000-man "peninsula shield" for mutual defense, little headway has been made in creating a credible deterrent.

Joint exercises have been held each year since 1983, but not all of the member-states have participated.

Despite its access to sophisticated weaponry and intelligence, including Saudi Arabia's U.S.-supplied Awacs surveillance planes, the GCC has neither the muscle nor the guts to stand up to the Iraqi steam-roller.

BIG BUSINESS OPPORTUNITIES!
Let Us Show You How To Start or Run a PROFITABLE Import/Export Business!
★ **Work in your spare or full time** and become an international trader ★ **No experience or capital investment needed**
★ **WADE WORLD TRADE COMPANY,** with 42 years' experience in 120 countries, will provide you with hundreds of import/export business addresses, plus all the necessary techniques and procedures for success.
★ **Step by Step,** you will be instructed on how to trade internationally, what attractive products to choose, and how to market them successfully.
★ **If you want to start your own business or extend an existing one and enjoy greater profits,** contact us now for a free booklet:
Tel. 052-583218, 581386, ELECTIVE LTD.
2 Hadar St. P.O.Box 5511, Herzliya 46154

T O U R I S T
ONLY ISRAEL'S No. 1 BANK OFFERS YOU A
SUPER Summer SPECIAL
Bank Hapoalim offers:
■ Higher Interest
■ Free Tourist Bonus Book
■ New Profitable Products
and more
Higher Interest and Confidentiality
Bank Hapoalim's VIP Free Foreign Currency Account offers you fully confidential, tax-free deposits, and for a limited time only, pays you a higher than usual interest rate.
Special Tourist Bonus Book
Now when you open a VIP account we'll give you a special coupon book of discounts on tourist services, including museums, tours, car rentals, and more.
New Products
We now offer you uniquely profitable foreign currency investment opportunities: Zero Coupon deposits, Currency-Mix accounts, guaranteed monthly income and Moriah and Ankor mutual funds.
International Private Banking
We offer expert, confidential private banking with the experience and know how to preserve and increase your assets in Israel and around the world.
Security and Expertise
As Israel's largest bank, with assets of over $33 billion, we offer you security and stability. As a major international financial group, Bank Hapoalim has the expertise to assist you in your special financial needs in Israel and worldwide.
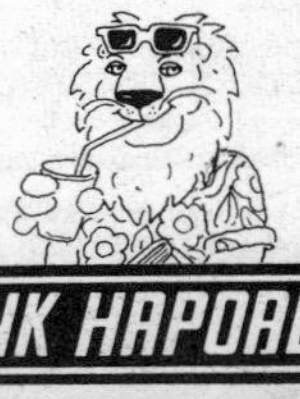
BANK HAPOALIM
Tourist, Foreign Resident and Olim Centers: Tel Aviv - Central Branch, 50 Rothschild Blvd., Tel: (03)673333 - 104 Hayarkon St., Tel: (03)243311. Jerusalem - 16 King George St., Tel: (02)207628. Haifa - 105 Hanassi Blvd., Tel:(04)353311. Netanya - 14 Kikar Ha'atzmaut, Tel: (053)339741 And 315 branches of the group in Israel.
KESHER BAREL

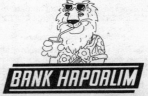

Poor kids fail to make the grade
Page 2

THE JERUSALEM POST

Vol. LVIII, No. 17551 Monday, September 24, 1990 • Tishrei 5, 5751 • Rabia I 5, 1411 NIS 2.20 (Eilat NIS 1.90)

EIGHT PAGES FROM SUNDAY'S The New York Times WEEKLY REVIEW INSIDE TODAY

Saddam threatens 'deluge' against Israel, oilfields over sanctions

By DAN IZENBERG, JONATHAN SCHACHTER, JOSHUA BRILLIANT, JON IMMANUEL, and news agencies

Iraqi President Saddam Hussein, issuing his most ominous war threat since the August 2 takeover of Kuwait, threatened yesterday to strike at Israel and at Saudi Arabian oilfields if Iraq is "strangled" economically. Saddam declared: "The oil, its areas, and Israel will be transformed into something different from what they are now. Thus will be the deluge."

He has threatened in the past to strike Israel and Saudi Arabia if war broke out, but insisted Iraq would not fire the first shot.

The statement was broadcast by Baghdad Radio after a meeting of the Iraqi leadership. Saddam accused the U.S. and its allies of resorting to the "law of the jungle" by pushing for tighter sanctions to force Iraq out of Kuwait.

"It is those who create this deluge who will be strangled," Saddam said. "The oil lands in Saudi Arabia and other countries will be unable to meet the requirements of the occupation forces."

He also vowed that Iraq's annexation of Kuwait was "eternal and irreversible under any circumstances."

The statement continued: "The major issue concerns the struggle of the Arabs and Moslems in their righteous jihad [holy war] against falsehood. The prime objective is the liberation of Palestine from the Zionist usurpers."

A senior Israeli military source said last night that "Saddam's rhetoric repeats itself, but we take his words seriously and are preparing for any eventuality."

Iraq ready to commit 'collective suicide' ON LINE – Page 2

Saddam's statement coincided with a report in the latest issue of *Time* magazine saying that U.S. analysts believe he would launch a major missile attack on Israel, accompanied by an aircraft attack, if he believed that his country was about to be strangled by the UN sanctions arrayed against him.

In describing what it termed a "three-part scenario for victory" being prepared by Saddam, *Time* reported that American analysts were predicting that, if the Iraqi president felt backed into a corner, he would "immediately" lash out against the West by launching missile attacks against Saudi oil facilities.

Those missiles would be equipped with a combination of conventional, chemical, and biological warheads, and would wipe out Saudi oil production capability, in the process touching off "a crippling recession, with widespread joblessness, and ruinous inflation throughout the industrial world," *Time* said. The U.S. would respond with a devastating bombardment of Iraq, but Saddam would be betting he could take the physical destruction longer than the U.S. and its allies could take the economic punishment.

Secondly, *Time* said, the U.S. analysts fear that Iraq would launch a salvo of up to 60 missiles, along with a major aircraft attack, against Israel. Americans have already detected the movement of missiles to western Iraq, within a five-minute striking range of Jerusalem and Tel Aviv. Saddam, according to the analysts, would "try to make it appear that the U.S. and Israel had provoked the attack, possibly by having an Iraqi aircraft drop a bomb on Baghdad," *Time* reported.

In response, one analyst said that "the Israelis would wipe out Baghdad," assuming that the U.S. did not beat them to it. However, Israeli involvement would cause "an enormous upheaval" in the Arab world, with Saddam betting that American allies, such as Egypt and Syria, would either switch sides or their regimes face overthrow in the face of intense popular outrage. In any case, said one U.S. official, "No American would be safe anywhere in the region."

The third component in Saddam's strategy, according to *Time*, is the activation of an Iraqi terrorist network, which would strike at targets in Europe, Japan, and the U.S., probably using tactics of biological warfare. "People are moving, gear is under way," one source told *Time*.

Secretary of State James Baker said yesterday on the U.S. TV program Meet the Press that bringing Israel into the Gulf conflict would not necessarily unify the Arab countries against the U.S. and its allies. Referring to Saddam's threat to widen the Gulf conflict to include Israel, Baker said: "One more case of unprovoked aggression I don't think is going to lead to uniting the Arab countries, the majority of which are strongly united in support of the

(Continued on Page 7)

Levy: We won't give Saddam alibis

By JONATHAN SCHACHTER, Jerusalem Post Correspondent

NEW YORK – Arriving here last night for the meeting of the UN General Assembly, Foreign Minister David Levy responded immediately to the threats voiced earlier in the day against Israel by Iraqi president Saddam Hussein.

"Israel is behaving very cautiously so as not to create an alibi or be blamed for an explosion," said Levy, "but we are following very carefully all the movements and actions in the field.

"Caution does not mean that we have to accept a danger to our security," Levy added.

Levy said he would continue to present Israel's position on the Gulf crisis in his coming meetings with administration officials as well as with the foreign ministers he intends to meet this week at the UN.

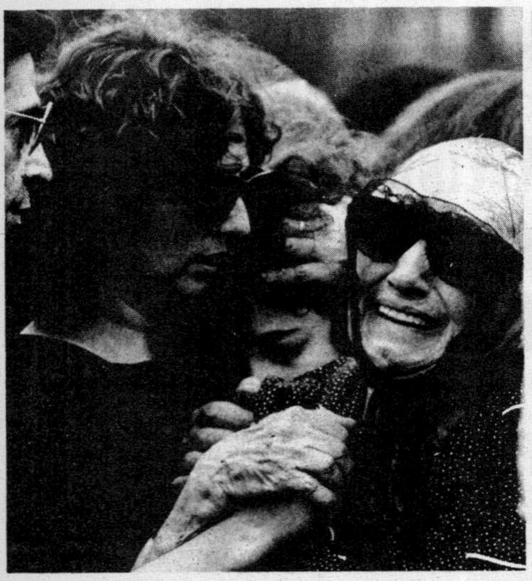

The mother, Zipporah, and sister Ruti (left), of reserve soldier Amnon Pomerantz, who was buried yesterday in Moshav Avihayil. Pomerantz was killed on Thursday in the Bureij refugee camp in the Gaza Strip, when a mob stoned and burned his car after he mistakenly entered the camp on his way back to his unit, which was stationed south of the camp. At Pomerantz's funeral, attended by OC Southern Command, Aluf Matan Vilna'i, and OC Air Force, Aluf Avihu Bin-Nun, and Moledet MK Rehavam Ze'evi, the deceased's battalion commander said: "We will remember you as a good soldier and friend, always ready to help..." (Danny Lev/IPPA)

IDF to demolish homes, will widen Bureij road

By JOSHUA BRILLIANT, DAN IZENBERG, and MATTHEW SERIPHS
Jerusalem Post Reporters

The IDF is planning to demolish the homes of the rioters directly involved in slaying reservist Amnon Pomerantz and will probably seal houses and widen the road at the site of the Rosh Hashana murder in the Gaza Strip's el-Bureij refugee camp, a senior military source in the Southern Command said yesterday.

The IDF source sought to dispel Palestinian fears that wide-ranging punitive measures will be taken throughout the strip. These fears have already caused anxiety there, but Southern Command did not plan any policy changes nor did the government seem to have ordered any following yesterday's cabinet meeting.

Pomerantz, an engineer, was buried yesterday afternoon in Moshav Avihayil beside the grave of his father, who died seven years ago.

Defense Minister Moshe Arens and Army Chief of General Staff Rav-Aluf Dan Shomron briefed the ministers on Thursday's events in the el-Bureij refugee camp. The discussion was held in the framework of the ministerial defense committee, whose deliberations are confidential.

A well-informed source said afterwards that the army was investigating whether Pomerantz, who entered the camp by mistake, had received proper instructions on how to reach his base, and why the army lookout at the entry to the refugee camp had not noticed Pomerantz's car.

The 46-year-old reservist was killed when he made a wrong turn and drove into el-Bureij instead of a nearby army base. He had been giv-

(Continued on Back Page)

War goods reaching Iraq via Akaba: U.S. experts

DHAHRAN, Saudi Arabia (AP) – Despite the UN-imposed economic sanctions on Iraq, sizeable amounts of military equipment and material with war potential are continuing to slip through the naval blockade, U.S. officers said yesterday.

Many cargoes marked for delivery to the Jordanian port of Akaba are actually being transshipped overland to Iraq, they said.

The extent of the leakage through Akaba, and what kinds of material are involved, are classified. But officers familiar with the situation indicated in interviews in recent days that it was fairly extensive, notwithstanding a concentration of effort in the Red Sea against such shipments.

One cargo vessel, intercepted by the U.S. Navy within the last week, had a deck cargo of British-made Land Rovers painted in military camouflage colors, they said.

Another ship was carrying a load of scrap metal, aluminum, silica and other materials that are "basic components in the manufacture of explosives," one officer said.

In both cases, the cargoes were listed on the ships' manifests as bound for Akaba, and there was no way for American boarding parties to determine whether they were ultimately destined for Iraq, the officers said.

"We suspect that's where some of the stuff labeled for Akaba is going, but we don't have proof," said Capt. Paul Prokop, commander of U.S. Coast Guard teams taking part in

(Continued on Page 7)

Antisemitism growing, cabinet told

By DAN IZENBERG
Jerusalem Post Reporter

Antisemitism is on the rise throughout the world despite efforts by Israel, Jewish diaspora communities and some governments to stamp it out, according to a report presented to the cabinet yesterday.

The report, drafted by a committee headed by Cabinet Secretary Elyakim Rubenstein, was the third submitted to the government since the committee was founded in 1988 to monitor international antisemitism. The previous report was completed in February, 1990.

Over the past seven months, antisemitism has been expressed in the desecration of Jewish cemeteries – most notably, by the vandalism in the French town of Carpentras last May.

There have also been increasing incidents of violence against Jews, including 10 incidents in South America, three in Western Europe, two in the U.S., two in South Africa and one in New Zealand.

The committee pointed to the following developments in the rise in antisemitism:

☐ Increasing incidents in eastern Europe, including Hungary, Poland, Romania, East Germany and Bulgaria, as a result of the collapse of Communism.

☐ The desecration of Jewish cemeteries, which began in Carpentras but then spread to other countries, including England, East and West Germany, Switzerland, Italy and Sweden.

☐ The increasing strength of right-wing parties in Western Europe – including France, Italy, Belgium, Denmark and Germany – and South America. The committee found that France has experienced a wave of political antisemitism unprecedented since World War II.

☐ Christian and Moslem-inspired antisemitism is on the rise. In some cases, extremists from both religions cooperated to disseminate antisemitic literature.

☐ The Soviet immigration to Israel has galvanized the Arab world into fierce opposition, including antisemitic attacks.

The committee warned that popular antisemitism in the Soviet Union, led by the Pamyat organization, is becoming increasingly dangerous. The Soviet government, while aware of the growing hatred, has not been able to effectively fight it, the committee indicated.

"In day-to-day life, these tendencies express themselves in antisemitic slogans, acts of vandalism, attacks and threats of pogroms which create an atmosphere of anxiety among Jews," the committee wrote.

It singled out the pronouncements of Ivan Polozhkov, a member of the Soviet Politbureau and Communist representative in the Russian Republic, who said recently, "The [Communist Party] must protect the interests of the wage-earners while the Pharisees, the money changers and the merchants who were thrown out of the Temple by Jesus will find protection in other parties." The committee found in such expressions, examples of "classic, Christian antisemitism."

The committee also found increasing instances of antisemitism in the U.S. It referred to expressions of antisemitism in black-Jewish relations in New York and Los Angeles, including the public appearances of black activist Louis Farrakhan. It also referred to a recent film released

(Continued on Page 7)

Levinger ruling rejected; court finds him guilty

By DAN IZENBERG
Jerusalem Post Reporter

The Jerusalem District Court yesterday overturned a lower court decision and found Rabbi Moshe Levinger guilty of assaulting an Arab family in Hebron, trespassing and insulting an Israeli soldier, court spokeswoman Etty Eshed said.

The file – concerning an incident that occurred on May 28, 1988 – has been returned to the Jerusalem Magistrate's Court for sentencing, Eshed informed reporters in a written communique.

According to the indictment, Levinger entered the home of the Samooch family in Hebron after his daughter complained that she had been harassed by Palestinian children. He attacked the mother of the household and her son, and tried to attack a daughter, aged seven. When a soldier ordered him to leave the house, Levinger refused and called him a "PLO agent."

The trial was originally heard by Magistrate's Court Judge Yoel Tsur, who rejected the testimony of the Samooch family and found Levinger innocent.

Judges Eliyahu Noam, Arye Hager and Ya'acov Zemah sharply criticized Tsur, saying he had erred "by focusing excessively on the details – not necessarily the important or substantial ones – without looking at the whole story."

The judges concluded that "the decision to exonerate [Levinger] reached by Magistrate's Court Judge Tsur ignores and contradicts the evidence, has nothing to do with the natural course of events, and is illogical."

Eshed pointed out that it was rare for an appeals court to intervene on questions of fact or in determining the credibility of witnesses following a lower court decision, as happened here.

Cinema manager slain in attempted robbery

By LARRY DERFNER
Jerusalem Post Reporter

TEL AVIV – The manager of the Rav Chen cinema in Dizengoff Square, Haim Salman, was shot to death yesterday morning as he fought with a man who was trying to steal a bag containing some NIS 70,000 which he was about to deposit in a bank.

The bag, with the cinema's receipts for the end of last week, was still in Salman's possession when he arrived at Ichilov Hospital, where he died about an hour-and-a-half later from gunshot wounds in the head, chest and stomach.

Salman, 56, of Tel Kabir, leaves a wife and three children.

The robber escaped on a white Vespa motorscooter, which police found abandoned on Rehov Zvi Bruck, which is near the cinema. The Vespa had been stolen from the municipality in June, police said.

The killing took place just before 8:30 a.m. The head of maintenance at the five-theater complex, who identified himself only as Yossi, was upstairs in the building at the time. He told Israel Radio:

"[Salman] yelled, 'Yossi, Yossi.' He always yelled when he wanted me, so I answered, 'One moment, I'll be right down.'

"Then I heard two shots, and I went down and opened the side door. I went outside and saw him lying on the ground," Yossi said. He did not see the robber.

An employee at the Bank Hapoalim branch three doors from the cinema told *The Jerusalem Post* that a passerby heard the shots and saw Salman lying in front of the theater. The employee let the witness in to call police, and the first squad cars arrived a minute later.

An attendant at a gas station across the street said, "I heard two shots and some yelling, but I hear noise all the time. I was busy, so I didn't get involved."

A few people who saw the murderer drive off told police he was wearing a black motorcycle helmet.

Police, however, said they did not have a good description of the killer nor any other good leads.

Mooky Greidinger, manager of Israel Theaters Ltd., the chain that owns the Rav Chen, said Salman's struggle with the murderer and refusal – even unarmed – to give up the money was "in character."

"That was Haim. He was a strong, husky man, and he ran the cinema like it was a part of himself," Greidinger said.

Salman took over the management of the Rav Chen early last year. Prior to that he managed the Esther Cinema in Tel Aviv for about 2½ years, and worked at the city's Gat Cinema for two years.

Griedinger said the chain will review its security regulations, and might require armed escorts.

Shas MK threatens coalition

By SARAH HONIG and MICHAL YUDELMAN
Post Political Correspondents

Shas MK Arye Gamliel yesterday threatened to "bring down the coalition" if Eli Tsuberi, his parliamentary aide, is not freed from jail "at once." Tsuberi has been in custody for the past three weeks, suspected of bugging the phone of *Yediot Ahronot* investigative reporter Mordechai Gilat, who broke the story of corruption charges against Interior Minister Aryeh Deri.

The bugging was allegedly ordered by either Deri or other Shas higher-ups.

Shas is accusing the police of keeping Tsuberi in custody in order to get him to testify against whomever employed him.

"I'm still giving the police a chance to open their eyes and do what is just, but if they turn into an unjust and wicked police, I will not be able to remain in the coalition," Gamliel said in a radio interview.

Kibbutz Shomrat rape suspects to face charges

The state attorney has decided to try seven persons suspected of gang-raping a 14-year-old girl in Kibbutz Shomrat two years ago.

The decision was reached after a psychologist decided that the victim is now capable of testifying.

Two years ago, the Haifa District Attorney's Office decided to close the case after a psychologist ruled that testifying might hamper the girl's recovery. The change in the same psychologist's evaluation has now led to the decision to prosecute. (Itim)

Behind the
Four Species
of Succot
Page 6

Saddam's
Trojan
horses
Middle East / Page 8

THE JERUSALEM POST

Vol. LVIII, No. 17559 Wednesday, October 3, 1990 • Tishrei 14, 5751 • Rabia I 14, 1411 NIS 3.30 (Eilat NIS 2.85)

Largest issue of gas masks since WWII

By JOSHUA BRILLIANT
and DAN IZENBERG
Jerusalem Post Reporters

As the entire nation readies to receive gas masks in the largest post-World War II distribution, the IDF has begun moving millions of masks from its warehouses to schools and other distribution points. It has also placed orders for additional gas masks earmarked for West Bank and Gaza Strip Palestinians, military sources said yesterday. (See story page 2).

"Pilot plan" distributions to the 30,000 residents of Yokneam, Kfar Yona and Ofakim will begin on Sunday. Distribution in the urban centers will start the following week. Civil Defense reservists will be called up to assist in the distribution.

Kfar Yona readies for gas masks

By LARRY DERFNER
Jerusalem Post Reporter

KFAR YONA - This town of 15,000 people, squeezed midway between Netanya and Tulkarm in the narrow "bottleneck" of Israel, is to have its day in the sun next Sunday. A flood of national and international media representatives, along with high-level IDF observers, are to converge here, one of three towns - the others are Ofakim and Yokne'am - chosen as test sites for the nationwide distribution of gas masks.

"Nobody's panicky or hysterical; we're all taking it calmly," local council head Ephraim Deri told The Jerusalem Post.

Deri said a retired colonel on the council told him of the IDF's choice

(Continued on Page Two)

A warm Succot expected

By HAIM SHAPIRO
and LEA LEVAVI
Jerusalem Post Reporters

Despite the cool snap and occasional flurries of rain of the last few days, the country is expected to enjoy warm, dry weather over the Succot holiday which starts tonight.

According to the Meteorological Service, the temperatures are due to rise today and will stay high throughout the holiday. This is particularly important for families who have erected the traditional succot, or booths, in which Jews are commanded to eat and sleep throughout the festival, as well as for those who have planned picnics and hikes.

Markets throughout the country have been crowded with people buying the traditional four species, lulav (palm), etrog (citron), hadas (myrtle) and arava (willow). In the large cities, special markets have been set up to sell the four species and succot decorations.

In an effort to keep the public from wantonly cutting trees to provide s'chach (greenery) for succa roofs, municipalities have been distributing branches from tree prunings.

During Succot, the Kurdish Jewish community here will celebrate the annual Saharana festival featuring traditional rituals and folklore. The gathering, on Monday and Tuesday, is to be held at Ma'ayan Harod, near Afula.

(Continued on Page Two)

78 million Germans hail new and united beginning

Compiled from news services

BERLIN - The Western Allies ceded their post-war occupation powers yesterday as the clock ticked toward the historic moment when East Germany would be absorbed, with all its problems, into a new united Germany.

As midnight approached, a vast party across the land of 78 million people was under way, with fireworks and ceremonies to last through today. Yesterday, October 2, was declared a national holiday. A spate of marriages was scheduled by couples planning to join their lives as the two Germanys united, according to press reports.

Police were gearing up for trouble from rightist and leftist radicals planning counter-demonstrations where the Berlin Wall used to stand. Hundreds of riot police assembled in alleys behind Leipziger Street in East Berlin, a march route for radicals from the west.

City authorities banned demonstrations near the Brandenburg Gate, the 200-year-old monument that was a major focus of celebrations that started at the nearby Reichstag, the old German parliament building, at midnight (1 a.m. Israel time).

Chancellor Helmut Kohl told the Frankfurter Allgemeine newspaper that the new Germany would help stabilize Europe. He said it would not be a "restless Reich" like Nazi Germany.

Instead, the unification of Germany is a "European, indeed a world event of historic rank," Kohl said.

Several German newspapers published the approved verse of the national anthem to be sung in unified Germany - not the old Deutschland

Ueber Alles verse - but the third verse, which starts: "Unity and justice and freedom for the German fatherland." The verse admonishes Germany to "bloom," not to be "above all," the old mission that still frightens some Europeans.

A year ago, the rush toward unity was barely starting. East Germans were demonstrating for political freedoms and the right to leave their country. The Communist government opened the Berlin Wall on November 9, but was soon swept away in a peaceful popular revolution.

East Germans began to demonstrate for unification. The cause was taken up by Kohl and his government and eventually approved by Moscow and the Western allies.

The Soviets agreed to let united Germany remain in Nato, and pledged to remove their troops from East Germany by the end of 1994. West Germany is paying Moscow $9.5 billion to finance the withdrawal, and the Allies will keep troops in West Berlin until the pullout.

The last formal steps clearing the way for unity were taken mostly by the four powers who defeated Nazi Germany and retained legal powers as occupiers in Berlin.

In New York on Monday, U.S. President George Bush and Soviet Foreign Minister Eduard Shevard-

(Continued on Back Page)

Willy Brandt talks to Jerusalem Post:
'Curb German arms exports'

By HENRYK BRODER
Jerusalem Post Correspondent

BERLIN - "This is the right moment to restrict the export of German arms and military supplies," former German chancellor Willy Brandt told The Jerusalem Post on the eve of German unification, which went into effect at 1 a.m. today. (Text of interview on Page 5.)

Brandt said he could understand the concern of Germany's neighbors with the influence and power of a greater Germany, but insisted there was "no reason" for it.

"The German army will be reduced by half, foreign troops will leave Germany, and we renounce atomic, biological, and chemical weapons. Germany will be part of the new European peace order and this can only be in the interest of our neighbors."

He predicted that the process of social and cultural unification would require "four to five years," and that "the part of Germany which was called the GDR will become particularly advanced and developed."

Germany should not assume responsibility for the economic rehabilitation of other Eastern European countries, Brandt said, because "it is more than we could handle and it would be misunderstood politically – as if we...were striving for supremacy."

An air balloon, with a peace dove logo, appears to sit on top of Berlin's Brandenburg Gate yesterday. (inset) Young people march through the gate waving the German flag. (Reuter)

Iraq told to pull out 'for the sake of Palestine'

News agencies

Saudi Arabian Foreign Minister Prince Saud Al-Faisal yesterday appealed to Iraq to withdraw from Kuwait so that international attention could be shifted to the Palestinian issue.

In a speech to the UN General Assembly in New York, he said the "adventure of the Iraqi regime" in invading Kuwait should not be allowed to veil the cause of Palestinians.

"It is for Palestine that Iraq should withdraw from Kuwait and adhere to international legitimacy, so that we can mobilize international legality to realize for the people of Palestine what will be realized for the people of Kuwait," he said.

"The Iraqi regime, which claims a monopoly over the salvation of Palestine, is following the same Israeli method of occupying the land, dispersing the people and refusing withdrawal," he claimed.

President George Bush, meanwhile, held one-on-one talks with nearly two dozen world leaders and renewed his Monday General Assembly indictment of Iraq that held out the possibility of "opportunities" for settling Saddam's quarrels

with Kuwait once Iraq withdraws unconditionally.

Heartened by unbroken support he heard from the world leaders for standing up to Saddam, Bush said he hopes the Iraqi leader will reverse course and withdraw.

Bush met yesterday with the Soviet Union's chief of staff, Gen. Mikhail Moiseyev, who told him, "We cherish what is uniting our two nations today, and we fully understand the contribution you both made to the improvement of our ties."

The Saudi minister did not refer to the U.S. by name when he ex-

(Continued on Back Page)

Accord on U.S. housing guarantees

By DAVID MAKOVSKY
Post Diplomatic Correspondent

NEW YORK – After months of negotiations, the Bush administration and Foreign Minister David Levy yesterday agreed on the terms for $400 million in U.S. government-backed housing guarantees for Soviet Jewish absorption.

Israel, however, has accepted the U.S. condition that it provide periodic written reports on how much it spends on settlement activity in the territories, senior Israeli officials said.

It is believed that this condition was demanded by President

George Bush, and not his aides. U.S. officials have privately expressed frustration that settlement funding has been tucked away in a variety of undisclosed budgets, beyond the unconfirmed $80 million in the official government budget.

U.S. officials fear that the wave of Soviet Jewish immigration will lead to soaring housing prices, and cause immigrants or squeezed Israelis to move to the territories out of economic necessity, resulting in the expansion of existing settlements.

It is believed that the reporting requirement does not require figures on East Jerusalem, as Israeli officials

said the topic of East Jerusalem was never raised. (Earlier this year Bush termed the new Jewish neighborhoods over the old border as "settlements." He appears to have dropped the subject because of protests Israel and American Jewish leaders.)

Originally, the administration wanted Israel to disclose settlement plans and projected expenditures in advance, but dropped the demand after Levy insisted it would represent an infringement on Israel's sovereignty.

Israeli officials claimed the agreement marks a softening of earlier

(Continued on Back Page)

Nobel Prize for transplant pioneers
Page 3

THE JERUSALEM POST

Vol. LVIII, No. 17563 Tuesday, October 9, 1990 • Tishrei 20, 5751 • Rabia I 20, 1411 NIS 2.20 (Eilat NIS 1.90)

The world's first kosher circus
Jewish World / Page 8

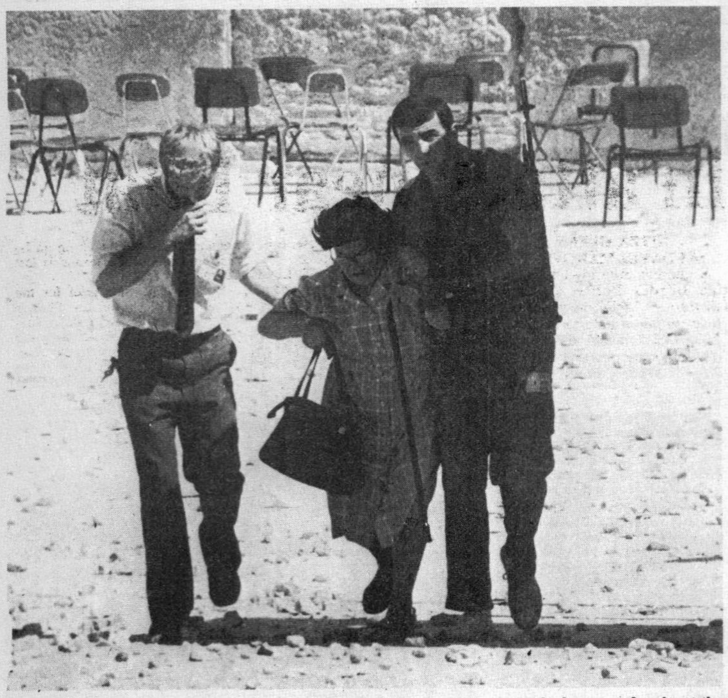

A visiting Christian pilgrim and a Border Policeman help a woman escape the barrage of rocks at the Western Wall. More photos on Page 2. (Photo by Zeev Ackerman)

21 Arabs die as the police quell Temple Mount riot

125 Arabs injured; 19 Israelis hurt as Moslems pelt Succot worshippers at Western Wall; attack seen as bid to help Baghdad

By RON KAMPEAS
Jerusalem Post Reporter

Police yesterday shot dead 21 Arab rioters on Jerusalem's Temple Mount, in the worst disturbances in the city since 1967. At least 125 of the vast mob of rioters were wounded in the violence, which began with a barrage of stones from the Temple Mount.

Eleven Israeli worshippers and eight policemen were wounded at the Western Wall by a hail of stones hurled from the area adjacent to Al-Aksa Mosque. The violent clashes lasted some 45 minutes.

One of the Arabs killed on the Mount was an Israeli from Tamra.

Many of the 125 Arab injured brought to Makassed and Augusta Victoria Hospitals were said to be in critical condition last night by hospital officials.

Hundreds of Arabs, including prominent East Jerusalem activist Faisal Husseini, were arrested. Most were released last night, but Husseini was placed in detention for 48 hours. He had arrived on the Temple Mount less than an hour before the riot broke out, according to police.

Palestinian sources say the riot was triggered by the announcement of the Temple Mount Faithful, an Israeli right-wing group, that it would attempt to enter the Temple Mount and lay a cornerstone for the Third Temple. A police ban on such a move was upheld this week by the High Court of Justice.

Some 5,000 Arabs were waiting on the Temple Mount for the Faithful group and had amassed an arsenal of rocks. Husseini's supporters said he had gone to help protect the Mount against the anticipated incursion.

The Faithful make a demonstrative attempt to enter the Mount every pilgrimage holiday in an attempt to assert Israeli sovereignty on the site of the ancient Temple. This time, however, the group did not attempt to pass by the policemen barring their way at the Moghrabi Gate entrance to the Temple Mount.

After a brief demonstration outside the gate by 40 of its members, the group marched out of the Old City through the Dung Gate towards the Shiloah Pool in Silwan.

At that moment, according to police, a Moslem official began crying "Allahu Akhbar (God is great)" from a mosque loudspeaker. The cry was heard on the Temple Mount, and the rioting started.

The rioters were urged on by repeated cries of "jihad" from mosque loudspeakers, as they hurled stones

(Continued on Back Page)

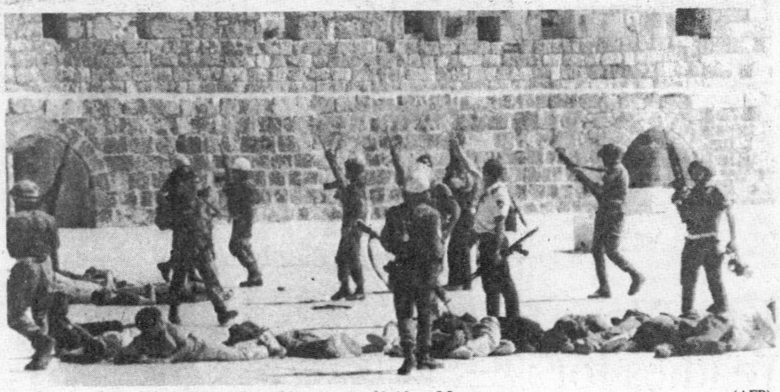

Police guard captured Palestinian rioters near Al-Aksa Mosque. (AFP)

Riot was fed by 'hysteria' from Baghdad, says Shamir

By DAVID MAKOVSKY
Post Diplomatic Reporter

EIN HAROD – Yesterday's Temple Mount riot was planned and not spontaneous, Prime Minister Yitzhak Shamir charged last night. It was fueled by "fanatical hysteria" whipped up by Baghdad, he said.

Speaking at a festival here in honor of Kurdish Jews, the prime minister stopped short of saying the disturbance was planned in Baghdad.

"Somebody tried to exploit the fundamentalist, fanatical hysteria being broadcast from Baghdad and ignite an unholy fire in Jerusalem. The conspiracy did not succeed," Shamir declared.

The prime minister defended police and Border Police against charges of brutality in the death of the 21 rioters.

"Our security forces were vigilant and performed their duty," he stated, adding that Israel regrets the loss of all life.

Shamir sharply rejected criticism of Jerusalem Mayor Teddy Kollek, who suggested that the rioting may have been inspired by a statement by Shamir earlier this week calling for the construction of a new Jewish neighborhood near Augusta Victoria Hospital on Mt. Scopus.

During his speech yesterday, Shamir called on Jews not to stay away from East Jerusalem.

"The Jewish people will keep coming to Jerusalem and the Western Wall. The Jewish people will keep coming in masses to the eastern part of Jerusalem. They (the rioters) will not deter us. They will not frighten us."

Shamir denied any connection between the riot and a demonstration by the Temple Mount Faithful, which was held a kilometer away after police denied them permission to lay the cornerstone for a Third Temple on the Temple Mount.

The cabinet is expected to devote part of its Sunday session to yesterday's rioting.

Greer Fay Cashman adds:

In a statement released last night, President Chaim Herzog said that the tragic events on the Temple Mount emphasised how fragile the situation was in this holy place where the Israeli government, has, over the years, established the required balance for freedom of worship. This delicate balance, he said, has been upset by a premeditated attempt by Moslem extemists to harm Jewish freedom of worship.

He expressed regret at the loss of life and declared that public figures on both sides would have to make a supreme effort to restore calm.

Chief of General Staff Lt.-Gen. Dan Shomron warned West Bank and Gaza Strip residents against rioting.

In a statement issued in Tel Aviv, he said that "under no circumstances" would the IDF let residents of the territories "exploit the events to disturb order in those areas," and urged residents not to heed "incitement from within and from abroad."

UN members decry police 'atrocity' in Jerusalem riot

By JONATHAN SCHACHTER
Jerusalem Post Correspondent

NEW YORK – Members of the UN Security Council last night condemned Israeli police handling of the riots in Jerusalem as a "shocking atrocity" and a "flagrant violation of international law."

PLO observer Zuhdi Terzi described a "planned action of aggression" by a group of zealots who, "protected by the Israeli Army," attempted to lay the foundation of a new Temple.

Israel's Ambassador Yohanan Bein called the actions by the Palestinian stone-throwers an attempt by the PLO to divert attention in the Arab world "from its despicable cooperation and collusion in the aggression of Saddam Hussein against a fellow Arab State and Israel."

Among the countries that vociferously condemned the police response was the Soviet Union, whose ambassador, Yuli Vorontsov, called it "a new flagrant violation by Israel of international legal norms," that "should be unconditionally condemned by the Security Council."

Other members of the Council called for the establishment of a linkage between the situation in the territories and the Gulf crisis, and the convening of an international peace conference to deal with the Palestinian situation.

Speaking to reporters before the meeting, U.S. Ambassador Thomas Pickering said he did not think such a linkage would be accomplished during the session.

Iraq threatens retaliation for Temple Mount dead

BAGHDAD (AP) – Iraq threatened to retaliate for the yesterday's killing of Palestinians on the Temple Mount and predicted the "crime" would lead Arabs to "the liberation of Jerusalem and all other holy places."

The term "holy places" referred to Saudi Arabia, which Iraq has condemned for allowing foreign military forces on its soil. Many Moslems claim that is a desecration of Islam's holiest shrines at Mecca and Medina in Saudia Arabia.

"This vicious crime will not go without retaliation, and the Arab nation is certainly capable to retaliate and it will," said *Al-Thawra*, the newspaper of the Arab Baath Socialist Party.

In an editorial for today's paper, obtained by the Associated Press yesterday, *Al-Thawra* described the killing as "a massacre which has been made possible with American aid and support to Israel."

"What happened in occupied Palestine is a crime...and will cause a widescale indignation in the Arab and Islamic world," the newspaper said.

"It would not have been possible without the support of the American imperialism, which provides the Zionist entitity with all necessary weapons and political protection.

"It will turn into a massive wave of indignation, which will take the pan-Arab struggle into a step towards the liberation of Jerusalem and all other holy places and reclaim the Arab homeland from treachery and occupation," the editorial said.

Iraqi chemical threat 'limited'

By JOSHUA BRILLIANT
Jerusalem Post Reporter

TEL AVIV – Iraq has only "limited" ability to launch a chemical attack and Israel's prospects of foiling it are "not bad," Defense Minister Moshe Arens said in an interview published in the latest issue of the *Air Force Magazine*.

While Arens did not say how "limited" the Iraqi chemical capability is, he said that "our chances of foiling the attack are not bad. Our prospects of deterring [Iraqi ruler] Saddam from acting are also not bad.

"They know how we will retaliate if they try something. But despite all this, the probability of an Iraqi attack against us is not nil."

Intifada had been 'buried' too soon

ANALYSIS / Jon Immanuel

Yesterday's events on the Temple Mount underlined a common misreading of the past few months' lull in the intifada. The uprising had not disappeared, as many here had thought; the Palestinians were just waiting for a spark to re-ignite it.

On September 23, Hamas Islamic fundamentalists and local Fatah activists agreed to play down their differences, and to aim for closer coordination of intifada strategy.

After the brutal killing of reservist Amnon Pomerantz in Gaza's el-Bureij refugee camp on September 20, which showed that the embers were still burning under the surface, Fatah called for an escalation of the intifada.

Over the past two weeks, more Palestinians have been killed by Israeli troops than in the previous three months. However, OC Central Command Yitzhak Mordechai insisted that the killings were isolated incidents and did not indicate a renewal of the intifada or a relaxation of orders on opening fire. But logic dictates that if troops were not violating open-fire orders, then Palestinians had regained some of their old boldness in confronting the IDF. Facts say that the increased activity was connected to the el-Bureij killing and its aftermath.

Despite the feeling that the Palestinians had shot themselves in the foot by supporting Iraq, the entire thrust of local Palestinians' support for Iraq came down to the feeling that they had nothing to lose.

By taking a stand against the policy of the Western world which alone is in a position to help them achieve their aims, local Palestinians made it clear that sooner or later they would again use force to back up their demands.

Israeli leaders missed the point that the intifada exploded in the first place only because a sufficiently critical mass of Palestinians in the West Bank and Gaza Strip felt they had nothing to lose.

IDF is reinforcing territories

By DAVID RUDGE,
MATTHEW SERIPHS
and JON IMMANUEL
Jerusalem Post Reporters

The IDF is sending reinforcements to the West Bank and Gaza Strip to prevent an upsurge of violence in the wake of the Temple Mount killings, IDF spokesman Brig.-Gen. Nahman Shai said last night.

Curfews had been imposed across almost the whole of the Gaza Strip and much of the West Bank.

"We are alert to the possibility that the situation might be used by various elements to stir up the population and break the relative quiet that has existed in the territories in the past few months," Shai told *The Jerusalem Post*. "We are all sorry about what happened on the Temple Mount, but we cannot allow the

(Continued on Back Page)

Deri sheds moderate image, threatens Likud coalition

By SARAH HONIG,
MICHAL YUDELMAN
and MICHAEL ROTEM
Jerusalem Post Reporters

Interior Minister Aryeh Deri yesterday warned that "if the police continue to hound Shas, if they continue to arrest Shas members and put them through grueling interrogations, I will find it increasingly difficult to control the party rank and file and prevent them from taking political countermeasures."

Though Deri did not elaborate, his warning was seen as his most extreme to date. Until now, he has let other Shas leaders issue the threats, while he attempted to appear moderate. Thus Deri's remarks to supporters in Jerusalem was seen as an indication of Shas's increasing militancy.

Meanwhile, Deputy Finance Minister Yosef Azran, and lawyer David Glass were questioned in Tel Aviv yesterday about their alleged involvement in the bugging of telephones of public figures.

As they left the interrogation room, Glass told *The Jerusalem Post* that he strongly denied any connection with the bugging. Glass is a partner in the law firm which employs lawyer Shlomo Deri, the minister's brother.

Azran said : "All I was questioned about was my meeting with private investigators in the Ramada Hotel."

Azran told his interrogators that all he had ordered from the investigators was to find out who in the National Religious Party was responsible for "vicious rumors" reportedly leaked to the press.

As for Deri, Shas insiders told the *Post* that Deri has been appearing relaxed and "is convinced that the police will be unable to put together a case against him that will hold up in court, and will probably not even prosecute him." The sources also said that "the pressure is off him personally," as the police investigation concentrates more and more on the party, "rather than on Deri's behavior."

It is precisely this focusing on other Shas figures that has drawn more moderates into the militant circle, which is threatening the Likud with a political vendetta unless it calls off the police investigation.

Shas on Sunday issued a warning to the Likud that "it must restrain the police and call off the persecution of Shas leaders."

(Continued on Back Page)

Jewish family saved by Arab villagers

Jerusalem Post Staff

A six-member Jewish family was saved from stonethrowers yesterday by an Arab family in the village of Sur Baher, southeast of Jerusalem, Israel Radio reported last night. When the family's car entered the village by mistake, it was pelted with rocks and overturned by rioters.

The passengers managed to escape from the car, and a local family took them into their house until police arrived to escort them from the village. In the meantime, the rioters set the empty car alight.

Arab strike to protest 'massacre'

By DAVID RUDGE
Jerusalem Post Reporter

SHFARAM – Israeli Arab leaders have declared a two-day general strike of the entire Arab community starting this morning to protest the "government-inspired" Temple Mount "massacre."

They also called for a demonstration later today in the normally peaceful Galilee village of Tamra to coincide with the funeral of resident Adnan J'naideh, who was killed in the rioting. J'naideh, 28, is to be buried in his home village at midday. His body was removed from the Makassed Hospital on the Mount of Olives by his family, covered with a white sheet and brought to the village by car.

"My son's fate took him there to die, and that was his end," J'naideh's father, Halef, said last night. Friends and relatives described the young grocery shop owner as a quiet, polite and deeply religious person who went to Jerusalem to pray at the mosque every week.

"He was not one of the rioters. He went to pray, and as such should not have been among those hurt,

(Continued on Back Page)

U.S. gov't revived by new budget proposal

WASHINGTON (AFP) – The United States yesterday appeared to be climbing out of a budget-deficit quagmire that threatened widespread chaos. Federal employees return today from a long holiday weekend.

The House of Representatives, whose rejection of a politically explosive budget deal Friday prompted President George Bush to shut down major portions of the government, overwhelmingly passed a new budget resolution it hopes will gain Senate and White House approval.

The new budget is essentially a retread of the rejected version, but softens proposed cuts in medical care for the elderly by one-third. It also defers the issue of new taxes for congressional committees to decide. (Story page 6)

89109312

Soviet chaos reigns as food runs out
Page 3

THE JERUSALEM
POST

Vol. LVIII, No. 17603 Monday, November 26, 1990 • Kislev 9, 5751 • Jamad I 9, 1411 NIS 2.20 (Eilat NIS 1.90)

EIGHT PAGES FROM SUNDAY'S The New York Times WEEKLY REVIEW INSIDE TODAY

Barak named new IDF chief of staff after Dan Shomron

BRADLEY BURSTON
Jerusalem Post Reporter

In a step that caught nearly the entire cabinet off guard late yesterday, Defense Minister Moshe Arens and Prime Minister Yitzhak Shamir announced their decision on the successor to Chief of General Staff Dan Shomron – Shomron's deputy, Maj.-General Ehud Barak.

Moments before, Barak had briefed the ministers on yesterday's Egyptian border terror attack. Barak and his aides were then asked to leave the meeting and the announcement was made, to the surprise of many. Though the Barak nomination was met with nearly unanimous support, Agriculture Minister Rafael Eitan (Tsomet), himself a former chief of general staff, was vocal in his dissent.

"You have to look at the record," Eitan said. "In my view [OC Northern Command Maj.-General] Yossi Peled is ten times better for the post." None of the other ministers supported Eitan.

(Profile Page 10)

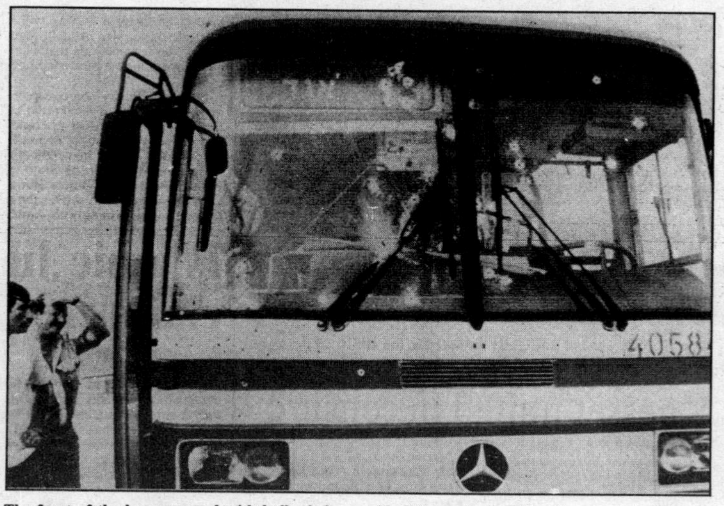

The front of the bus peppered with bullet holes outside Eilat yesterday after it was attacked by the terrorist who crossed the border. (Reuter)

Stop further border incursions, Levy tells Egypt
4 killed, 26 wounded in attack near Eilat

NITZA GEFEN and DAVID MAKOVSKY

A gunman wearing an Egyptian Border Police uniform killed four Israelis and wounded 26 yesterday in an attack on Israeli vehicles travelling along the Israeli-Egyptian border. The attack occurred at 6:30 a.m. at 'border point 81,' 21 kilometers north of Eilat.

The dead, all Eilat residents, are IDF Sgts.-Maj. Michael Tzuberi, 34, Avi Serlin, 38, and Haim Ashkenazi, 32, and Egged bus driver Ziko Wahaba. Two of the injured are in serious condition and 18 were released after treatment for superficial wounds.

The terrorist was apparently wounded by a security guard on the bus, but managed to escape back across the border. He was later captured by the Egyptian police.

Foreign Minister David Levy summoned Egyptian Ambassador Mohammed Bassiouny to his office and told him that "Israel cannot accept repeated attacks against its citizens on the border with Egypt or in Egyptian territory." He demanded that Egypt prevent further incursions.

At the same time, Levy expressed satisfaction that senior Egyptian officials were quick to condemn the attack.

Levy said he agreed with Bassiouny, whom he cited as saying: "We cannot allow the enemies of peace to destroy the peace between Egypt and Israel."

Levy asked Bassiouny to provide Israel with an update on its investigation of the assailant. It is believed that he also asked for information about the investigation of those apprehended for the attack on an Israeli tour bus near Alexandria last February.

Besides expressing grief for the victims, Prime Minister Shamir called on Egypt to bring the perpetrators "to justice without delay and to give them the severest punishment possible under law." There is no extradition treaty between Egypt and Israel.

Yesterday's attack followed recent infiltration attempts from Jordan and Lebanon.

In an interview with *The Jerusalem Post*, Levy said: "Saddam Hussein has created an agitated climate in the region. He has appropriated the fundamentalist cause and the infiltrations should be seen in this light."

IDF Chief of General Staff Dan Shomron briefed the cabinet on the incident after returning from the site.

(Continued on Back Page)

U.S. wants UN Thursday meet on war move

News agencies

The U.S. is calling a UN Security Council meeting for Thursday to discuss authorizing a deadline for a possible war against Iraq, it announced yesterday.

U.S. Secretary of Defense Richard Cheney, meanwhile, warned that Saddam Hussein could have nuclear capability in a year or less.

"There are a lot of estimates," Cheney said. "They range from worst case assumption a matter of a year or less to having some kind of crude device – to one [estimate] of five to 10 years of having a deliverable weapon."

Speaking about American plans, Secretary of State James Baker said, "I think the council will want to explore a resolution that would make it very clear that members could utilize all necessary means after a certain date to implement the prior resolutions. We're talking about a resolution that would lay the political foundation for a possible use of force."

Washington, which holds the rotating chairmanship of the Security Council until Yemen, a backer of Iraq, takes over on December 1, believes Saddam must be convinced that the U.S. and its allies in the Gulf will go to war and are doing more than "rattling sabres."

Baker was speaking after a grueling trip halfway around the world in which he lobbied 13 Security Council members and won qualified support for war against Iraq.

Canada, however, doubts that a UN deadline will help get Iraq out of Kuwait, but will not oppose an American-backed ultimatum in the Security Council, Foreign Minister Joe Clark said in Cairo yesterday.

"Our preference would be for a resolution that would be more straightforward, that simply stated the goal of authorizing the enforce-

(Continued on Back Page)

Close-knit Eilat stunned by the terror that struck from the dunes

NITZA GEFEN
Special to The Jerusalem Post

EILAT – The first wounded arrived at Josephthal Hospital at about 7:30 yesterday morning. At first, there was confusion about the number and condition of the casualties. Worried relatives milled about, trying to learn something about the victims.

But the hospital quickly organized itself, and within minutes of the alarm three operating theaters were fully staffed.

Five of the seriously injured underwent surgery and by yesterday evening were reported in good condition. One soldier, with a serious head injury, was helicoptered to Soroka Hospital in Beersheba.

Among the injured was a girl with light shrapnel wounds on her forehead. Yesterday was her 12th birthday, and she was on her way to a day of fun in Tel Aviv. Her mother sat beside her, hugging her, both of them pale. "We need to say a prayer of thanks," said her father, David Golan, 52, a civilian employee at the Air Force base in Uvda. "We were on our way to the base to catch a plane north."

Pnina Buhana, the wife of the Egged guard who drove off the terrorist, was not particularly upset when a friend told her that her husband had been slightly injured in a traffic accident. "Nothing serious, don't worry," she was told.

"I didn't think anything really bad had happened," she said. "This isn't the first time there has been an accident in the area. I sent the children to school and then drove to the hospital. He's now being operated on. I didn't manage to speak to him."

Aharon Shemesh, 61, a construction worker at Uvda, was waiting to go into the operating theater. He described how he was hit:

"I was sitting behind the driver. I always sit there. A military bus passed us. Then, two kilometers on, the military bus was standing across the road. Next to it stood a military van. A man in white sports shoes was standing there. A soldier in uniform was lying in the road. The man in the sneakers held a Kalashnikov and I began to shout: 'It's terrorists.'

"Exactly at that moment, he opened fire. I thought I saw another guy hiding behind the van, also shooting. They fired from a distance and didn't close in on our bus. Ziko Wahaba, the driver, shouted at us: 'Shoot him,' and then he was hit by a burst, and I was hit by two bullets in the hand. I saw how two of my fingers were blown off. I immediately hit the floor. Everyone lay on the floor. There were screams of pain all over."

Micha Zino, another civilian IDF employee on the bus, also recalled the attack. "There were shots. The driver was hit. I shouted to the guard to shoot so that the terrorist would know that we were armed too. He fired into the air and then in the direction of the terrorist. But his magazine ran out and he was hit. Another worker got off the bus with an Uzi. I also got off, crawling. There was a van there, and a soldier lying in the road. I grabbed his gun and ran after the terrorist who had begun to run towards the border."

As the injured are wheeled into the operating theater, one after another, the bus driver's wife sits there, stunned. We are asked by a hospital security man, gently, not to approach her.

Word of the driver's death spreads quickly around town. One of the driver's two daughters is told what happened by her teacher. The class is in shock. The teacher knew the driver. Eilat is a small place, everyone knows everyone.

Residents are stunned. "This was all that we need," said one. "The Gulf crisis harmed our tourism, there are no foreign tourists. Now this. Those who still thought of coming here will stay home." Behind a hill near the border, a UN helicopter is in the air and soldiers can be seen searching among the dunes.

Meanwhile, Simi Amer, whose husband and older son were both on the bus, waits at the hospital. Another son calls and tells her that both were injured. "When I saw that my son was only scratched, I breathed a sigh of relief. But my husband is still being operated on. I hope he will be okay."

Intensive contacts between Israeli-Egyptian military

BRADLEY BURSTON
Jerusalem Post Reporter

TEL AVIV – The dawn terror attack yesterday north of Eilat that left four Israelis dead and 26 wounded has sparked intensive contacts between senior IDF officers and the Egyptian Army, military sources said last night.

The contacts are aimed at resolving questions stemming from the terror spree of the lone gunman, wearing an Egyptian Border Police uniform, who was captured by a large detachment of Egyptian troops after recrossing the border in rough desert terrain.

Under discussion, the sources said, is the behavior of other Egyptian border patrolmen in the area, in particular the guards manning an observation tower in the vicinity of the attack.

The IDF will also request all possible information gained in the interrogation of the captured patrolman, underway since noon yesterday, and will move toward improved coordination between Egyptian and Israeli border security arrangements.

But Egyptian authorities have already refused a request that Israelis be permitted to participate in the investigation .

The Amman-based Sheikh Tamimi faction of the Islamic Jihad organization has claimed responsibility for the incident, stating that the attack was dedicated to the memory of Suleiman Khater, the Egyptian border policeman who killed seven Israeli vacationers at Ras Burka four years ago. Khater was subsequently arrested, tried and committed suicide in an Egyptian prison.

Last night IDF Chief of General Staff Dan Shomron strongly warned against "making the mistake of relating to the Egyptian Border as one would, for example, to the northern border."

The Egyptian border remains a border of peace, Shomron emphasized, and, while IDF soldiers there are armed and observe security regulations, their behavior is that of troops serving on a border of peace.

But former defense minister Yitzhak Rabin took issue with Egyptian handling of border security.

"The Egyptian government and its security and intelligence arms can do a great deal more, can institute much more serious measures to prevent terrible acts such as this. And this must be vigorously demanded of Egypt."

Rabin conceded that Egypt must contend with internal terrorism, citing the recent assassination of their speaker of parliament. "But that took place in a densely populated area. In Sinai, and certainly along the border with Israel, and in daylight hours, it is possible to track the movements of every single individual."

'Human bomb' wounds three

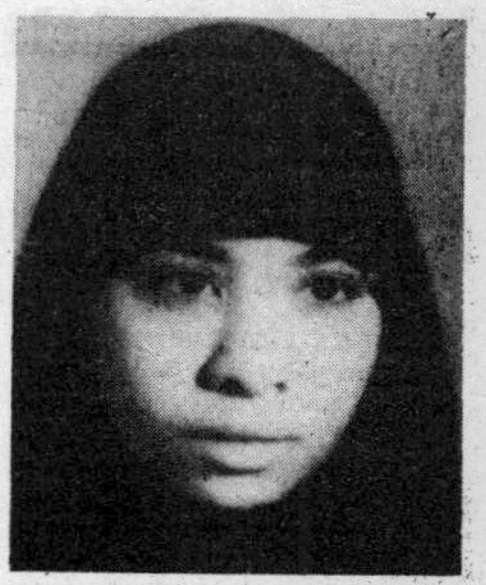

Suicide attacker Fadwa Hassan Ghanem, 19. (AFP)

DAVID RUDGE
Jerusalem Post Reporter

METULLA – Two IDF soldiers, an officer and a sergeant, were lightly wounded in a suicide bomb attack by a lone woman terrorist inside the security zone in South Lebanon yesterday.

The woman, with explosives apparently strapped to her body, blew herself up when she was three meters from an IDF foot patrol of Givati Brigade soldiers.

She was killed outright in the blast, which slightly injured two members of the patrol and a young Lebanese civilian nearby.

The two soldiers, Lieutenant Ami

(Continued on Back Page)

Draft budget brings down capital markets

ALISA ODENHEIMER
Jerusalem Post Reporter

The country's capital markets reacted unfavorably yesterday, as news of the 1991 state budget proposal – along with its enormous deficit and the planned funding – brought on expectations of skyrocketing interest rates.

Bond prices dropped sharply yesterday, as the cabinet began its marathon discussion of the NIS 79 billion budget, with its accompanying NIS 12.6b. deficit. A considerable part of the deficit, NIS 5.2b., will be financed by borrowing on the domestic market, according to the budget proposal. Yesterday's cabinet session on the budget proved to be little more than a warm-up for what may be fireworks tomorrow, when the cabinet will be asked to vote on the proposal. (See Page 6)

Finance Minister Yitzhak Moda'i is seeking cabinet approval of NIS 1b. in proposed cuts, and NIS 2b. in additional taxation.

Sources in the Treasury's budget division said that the lion's share of the proposed cuts would come from a NIS 2,500 reduction in the absorption basket for new immigrants. Cuts in milk, frozen poultry and transportation subsidies, a reduction in the number of those entitled to second-child allowances, an across-the-board cut in government spending, and a reduction in the defense budget make up the remainder of the proposed cuts.

Finance Ministry officials claimed last night that Prime Minister Shamir had hinted during yesterday's meeting that he was sympathetic to Moda'i's attempts to cut the defense budget. Moda'i enjoyed unexpected support on the issue from Housing Minister Ariel Sharon, who said that the U.S. presence in the Gulf made it possible for Israel to cut defense spending.

Sources in the Finance Ministry said that negotiations with the Defense Ministry were proceeding smoothly, and that they expected to find a compromise solution.

Meanwhile, Modai's economic plan, approved by the cabinet in September, is due to be presented to the Knesset this afternoon.

Farm water may be cut if no rain

DAVID RUDGE
Jerusalem Post Reporter

Water rationing for agriculture may have to be introduced soon if there is no rain in the foreseeable future, Martin Sherman, an adviser to Agriculture Minister Rafael Eitan, told *The Jerusalem Post* yesterday.

Rationing might have to be followed by cutbacks in the supply of drinking water in homes if there is no improvement, said Sherman.

He stressed, however, that rationing was only a short-term solution to the present crisis.

"In the long run, we have to increase the country's water resources in such a way that we are no longer dependent on rainfall," said Sherman.

"The only possible solutions at this stage are to import water or construct more desalination plants.

"Importing water involves political and technical problems, not least the need for building unloading facilities, which would have to be at least 3 kms offshore to cope with the size of tankers needed to transport the water. Even then, we would only be

(Continued on Back Page)

26110318

Israel reviewing ties with South Africa

DAVID MAKOVSKY

Israel is "reexamining its ties with South Africa as a result of the changes taking place in that country," Deputy Foreign Minister Binyamin Netanyahu said yesterday after meeting with a senior South African diplomat. No further details were available.

The meeting between Netanyahu and Assistant Secretary John Ferguson, who is in charge of Middle Eastern and Far Eastern affairs, was the most senior official encounter with a South African official since Israel formulated new rules concerning ties with South Africa more than three years ago.

Netanyahu expressed the government's appreciation of the South African government's decision to begin negotiations with blacks and change its apartheid system.

In March 1987, the government pledged to downgrade its relationship with South Africa, because of apartheid. Nonetheless, foreign sources have reported on ongoing military ties with Pretoria.

Netanyahu, who is leaving today for a conference in Washington of Israeli consuls general, was not available for comment.

KGB fears bloodshed
Page 3

THE JERUSALEM POST

Vol. LVIII, No. 17626 Sunday, December 23, 1990 • Tevet 6, 5751 • Jamad II 6, 1411 NIS 2.20 (Eilat NIS 1.90)

Paul Nitze on the nuclear card
Page 4

Added flights to continue as crisis in USSR worsens

Record 7,000 Soviet immigrants are flown in over the weekend

BILL HUTMAN, Post Reporter and Agencies

An unprecedented number of Soviet immigrants were airlifted here over the weekend, as efforts intensified to rush Soviet Jews to Israel from a country rapidly descending into chaos.

Some 7,000 immigrants arrived between Thursday night and early this morning, at a rate of about 100 an hour.

From late Thursday to Friday afternoon, planes carrying the immigrants landed at Ben-Gurion Airport hourly from Eastern European transit points, primarily Warsaw and Budapest. More flights arrived during Shabbat.

Twelve more flights, carrying some 2,000, were expected to arrive between last night and this morning, Jewish Agency officials said.

Permission was obtained to increase the number of flights from the transit points earlier last week, the officials said. The agency wants to bring the immigrants here quickly given the increased tension in the USSR, they added.

Since last Wednesday, over 1,000 Soviet immigrants began arriving daily. Agency chairman Simcha Dinitz announced yesterday that "from now on, between 1,200 and 1,500 Soviet immigrants will arrive daily." Less than a thousand had been arriving before the extra flights were added.

Over 30,000 immigrants arriving in December, and 40,000 in January, according to agency estimates.

The government must reappraise its absorption plans given the sudden increase in the pace of immigration, Dinitz said.

El Al made extra planes available over the weekend to transport the immigrants, while the Polish airlines, Lot, and the Hungarian airlines, Malav, also added Tel Aviv-bound flights to their normal schedules.

El Al was forced to send planes to Bucharest because a national strike in Romania had left Soviet immigrants stranded in the capital.

Though the Ministry of Transport obtained an order allowing flights to land on Shabbat, the absence of Absorption Ministry officials at the airport forced the arriving immigrants to be transferred to hotels. Last night, they were bused back to airport to be processed by ministry officials.

Absorption Minister Yitzhak Peretz is scheduled to report to the cabinet today on the recent upswing in immigration. Barring unexpected developments, he will not attend the aliya cabinet – which he is boycotting – in the evening.

Asher Wallfish adds:

Deputy president of the Soviet Academy of Sciences, Yuri Usipian, told visiting Knesset Speaker Dov Shilansky Friday that "there will be no change in Soviet foreign policy vis-a-vis Israel, and I believe that our emigration policy will not change either."

Usipian, a member of the Supreme Soviet, is considered by Israeli diplomats in Moscow as being close to President Gorbachev. He gave a dinner at the academy in honor of Shilansky and Labor MK Arye Eliav, which was also attended by ambassador Arye Levin. The prospects for Israel-Soviet cooperation in economic, cultural and scientific fields were discussed.

The Israeli guests walked through thick snow to the academy and back – eight kilometers each way – in order not to violate the Shabbat, Shilansky's media adviser Yair Amikam reported by phone from Moscow last night.

Coming into the warmth

BATSHEVA TSUR
Jerusalem Post Reporter

It had none of the exhilaration of a history-making moment. There appeared to be no kissing of the holy soil, as the 200 or so new arrivals disembarked from Flight 3574 from Bucharest – one of five which brought some 1,200 Soviet immigrants from three East European capitals in a 24-hour span – arriving at Ben-Gurion Airport after midnight Friday.

Rather, the newcomers had the dazed and bewildered look of refugees who had been through an arduous trek and as yet had no idea where they were going.

They were 8½ hours late. Their flight had been held up in Romania, but received a special dispensation to land on Shabbat.

In the arrivals hall, five young, Russian-speaking absorption officials were on hand.

The stairs leading up to the Absorption Ministry office, where newcomers usually wait on orange plastic chairs to be processed and receive their immigration papers, was blocked by row upon row of baggage carts. They were stacked with what, for many, must have been the last tangible remains of the homes they had left behind.

A box with some 20 pairs of new shoes, which had burst open, lay unclaimed in a corner, together with two unmarked suitcases which seemed to have gone astray.

Last night, the Shabbat arrivals were to return to the airport, go through the immigration process and claim their baggage.

Now all the new arrivals had arrived in the hall. There were no dignitaries on hand, no fanfare, none of the traditional orange juice.

As a young absorption official explained the procedure, someone remembered that the lights had not yet been turned on. The airport lights are dimmed between flights to save energy.

Almost all of the immigrants were wearing the familiar fur hats. Some also wore fur overcoats, but these soon came off as the temperature difference between the Romanian capital and Lod became evident, to reveal the western-style jeans most were wearing.

Many seemed to have traveled in large families – young parents with children, or babies in arms, accompanied by grandparents and other relatives.

Anatoly Churgin from Chernovtsy in the Ukraine, an electrical engineer, was typical. He, his wife, baby, parents and sister had traveled a day and a night by train

(Continued on Page 2)

Israel ferry capsizes in heavy seas 30 meters from American carrier

19 U.S. sailors drown off Haifa

DAVID RUDGE
Jerusalem Post Reporter

HAIFA – Three inquiries are being held into Friday night's ferry boat disaster in Haifa bay which claimed the lives of 19 American sailors.

The head of the Transport Ministry's shipping division, Shabtai Levy, appointed a three-man team to discover why the ferry Al Tuvia capsized and sank within 15 seconds.

Sabotage has virtually been ruled out, following an extensive examination by Israeli Navy divers of the wreck, now lying on the seabed 20 meters below the surface.

The divers, who photographed the boat from several angles after first recovering the remaining bodies from inside, reportedly found no signs of damage.

Meanwhile, U.S. Ambassador William Brown told a press conference here: "It is on such occasions, painful and bitter as they are, that you find out who your true friends are. We know and deeply appreciate the fact that even as we meet here with you, there are those who under very difficult circumstances, as they have through the night, have been working even at risk to themselves to save people. We profoundly appreciate Israel's assistance."

President Herzog and Prime Minister Shamir both expressed their condolences to President Bush and the American people over the tragedy.

"Our military and civilian authorities made every effort and worked to save as many lives as possible, and we were gratified that most of the people involved in the accident were saved" Shamir said. "Together with you, the bereaved families and the American people, we mourn the dead and wish the wounded a speedy recovery."

The inquiry team, composed of chief engineer Dr. Paul Mink, retired coastal police officer Deputy Commander Michael Baram, and headed by Capt. Haim Harari, began gathering evidence from eyewitnesses and experts yesterday.

Levy has requested that they submit an interim report today.

(Continued on Page 6)

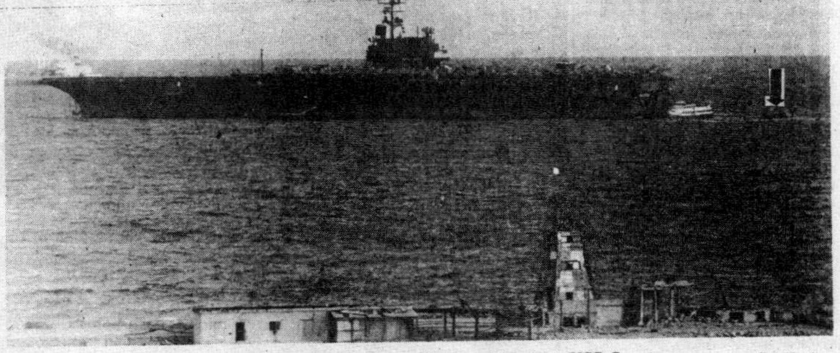

Arrow shows spot where the ferry sank, a short distance from the USS Saratoga. (Melling).

'There was panic as the boat sank'

DAVID RUDGE

A welcome shore leave after four months at sea ended in tragedy for scores of American sailors being ferried back to the aircraft carrier USS Saratoga from the Haifa port late Friday night.

Disaster struck around midnight when the Israeli-owned launch Al Tuvia was waiting just 30 meters from the carrier while sailors aboard another, larger, ferry disembarked onto the ship.

Suddenly, for reasons still not clear, the smaller craft capsized.

Shocked crew members aboard the Saratoga watched in horror as dozens of their comrades were hurled into the cold winter waters of the Mediterranean, over one nautical mile from shore.

In the space of 15 – 20 seconds, the Al Tuvia sank, taking with it many more sailors who had been trapped on the lower deck.

"More and more water came aboard and then, all of a sudden, tons of water rushed in. The boat started sinking and there was panic," said one of the survivors. "Everybody started trying to get out through the windows. There were five or ten people trying to crawl out through one tiny window.

"I made it, thank God, but when I looked up all I could see was dark water above me. I paddled my way up and grabbed onto the somebody's leg and he pulled me up," the young sailor told reporters as he recuperated at Haifa's Rambam Hospital.

The skipper and crew of the larger ferry, the Carmelit, watched helplessly as the Al Tuvia began to ship water and suddenly "turned turtle." The Carmelit's skipper radioed an SOS to the harbor and immediately began searching for survivors.

One of the rescued American sailors swam underneath the overturned Al Tuvia to reach the surface, where he and another sailor clung to a liferaft and waited to be picked up.

"The first (rescue) boat went straight over our float, but after that he came back and took us ashore," he said.

"I thought I was going to die," said another survivor after receiving treatment, warm drinks and clothing at Rambam. He said he had spent nearly an hour in the water, waiting and hoping to be rescued.

Within nine minutes of the alarm being raised, the Israel Navy, Air Force, harbor authorities and emergency services swung into action, aided by helicopters and rescue boats from the Saratoga.

An IAF plane flew dozens of sorties, dropping flares over the scene, lighting up the night sky.

Helicopters buzzed overhead, their searchlights stabbing the water as Israel Navy ships and rubber dinghies, coastal police boats and tugs from the Saratoga, crisscrossed the area.

Israel Navy commander Rear Admiral Micha Ram said that more than 500 Navy and Air Force personnel were involved in the rescue operations, as well as scores of police, harbor workers, volunteers and Magen David Adom workers.

Dozens of sailors were plucked from the water. Some were taken directly back to the Saratoga, although most were brought ashore where a fleet of MDA ambulances waited on the jetty to take them to Rambam, Rothschild and Carmel hospitals.

The ambulance crews worked tirelessly as boats continued to bring cold, soaked and shocked survivors to shore, as long as three hours after the disaster.

One of the last to come ashore was a young sailor, his sodden civilian clothes clinging to him. He gave the first inkling as to the possible cause of the tragedy.

"There were too many people

(Continued on Back Page)

Soviet 'democrats' urged to resist

WALTER RUBY
Jerusalem Post Correspondent

MOSCOW – In the political salons of central Moscow following last Thursday's stunning resignation of Foreign Minister Eduard Shevardnadze, concern was focused on his clarion call to the nation's democratic forces to resist the imminent imposition of dictatorship.

The Inter-regional Group of Deputies issued a statement urging the "various [democratic] parties, movements, and groups" to join forces under the leadership of president Boris Yeltsin and the pro-democratic deputies in the Supreme Soviet of the Russian Republic to thwart the expected attempt to reimpose hard-line rule.

President Gorbachev yesterday threatened to use the full force of his powers unless leaders in Moldova and minority groups there act within 10 days to end ethnic conflict. He ordered the dissolution of two self-styled republics set up earlier this year by the republic's Turkish and Russian minorities. (See page 3)

Members of the group muttered dark fears about their former ally, President Gorbachev, theorizing that he has made an alliance with the army, KGB and orthodox Communists to crack down on democracy in return for being allowed to continue in power. As evidence, they pointed to Gorbachev's demand for vastly increased presidential powers and his threat to impose states of emergency on republics and autonomous areas that refused to sign the proposed Union Treaty.

Alexander Yakovlev, long Gor-

(Continued on Back Page)

Israel missile test alarms Gulf force

ALLISON KAPLAN
in Washington
BRADLEY BURSTON
in Tel Aviv
and agencies

U.S. forces in the Persian Gulf went on "Condition Red" alert for about 15 minutes Friday morning when U.S. intelligence initially interpreted the test-firing of an Israeli missile into the eastern Mediterranean as a possible pre-emptive strike against Iraq.

The alert took place just four hours before Secretary of Defense Dick Cheney and Joint Chiefs of Staff Chairman Gen. Colin Powell arrived in Saudi Arabia to meet with more than 15,000 U.S. military personnel, according to U.S. media reports.

Sirens rang out and personnel immediately leapt into bunkers and put on gas masks and rubber gloves

(Continued on Back Page)

Israel promises to share information with Washington

U.S. may widen its Dotan probe

ALLISON KAPLAN
Jerusalem Post Correspondent

WASHINGTON – U.S. and Israeli officials here expect the American investigation into the Rami Dotan bribery affair will extend into a long-term, full-scale probe encompassing the Departments of State, Defense and Justice.

Inquiries have been made at the Israeli embassy by these agencies, and the American officials have been assured that as details emerge in Israel on the former IAF arms procurement chief and his accomplices they will be shared with U.S. authorities.

A probe by the Federal Bureau of Investigations is already under way to determine whether employees of American companies that did business with Dotan were engaged in his illegal activities.

The FBI is cooperating with General Electric, which is conducting its own internal investigation and has already suspended one employee over the matter. The FBI has contacted Israeli authorities and they are working together on the investigation.

In Israel meanwhile, former defense minister Yitzhak Rabin defended himself against charges that he made a serious error in promoting Dotan to Brigadier General and making him head of arms procurements even though allegations had already been raised and Dotan was under suspicion.

"I don't and didn't know Dotan," Rabin said in an interview on Army Radio. "The allegations sent me were studied and shown to have no basis at the time. I gave Dotan the post and rank recommended by the Chief of General Staff and Air Force commander, and let the investigation which was in progress know of the suspicions regarding Dotan which remained unanswered."

Rabin said he did not believe the affair would damage Israeli-U.S. re-

(Continued on Back Page)

Bush expects Soviets to stand firm on Gulf

CAMP DAVID, Maryland (Reuter) – President Bush expects the Soviet Union to stand by the U.S. against Iraq's occupation of Kuwait despite the resignation of Soviet Foreign Minister Eduard Shevardnadze, he said yesterday.

"I am convinced from what we have received so far from the Soviet Union that the policy on the Gulf will continue," Bush said in a news conference with British Prime Minister John Major at his presidential retreat here.

"We had a very close relationship with Eduard Shevardnadze ... but life goes on and we will pursue the policies in the Gulf confident that the Soviet Union will continue on its path," Bush said in his first comment on the resignation.

Meanwhile, an unbending Iraq said yesterday it would use chemical weapons to fight any attack by the U.S.-led military alliance seeking to drive its troops from Kuwait.

U.S. Defence Secretary Dick Cheney, in Saudi Arabia, warned Saddam Hussein against deploying chemical arms. "I think he knows our response would be overwhelming," he said.

Gunboat intercepts Lebanese ferry, detains passengers

IDF force kills terrorist on Jordanian border

BRADLEY BURSTON
Jerusalem Post Reporter
and news agencies

IDF forces patrolling the Jordanian border yesterday tracked down and killed a lone terrorist as he attempted to breach the security fence. On Friday night, a Navy gunboat intercepted a Lebanese ferry en route to Cyprus and detained eight Lebanese and Palestinian passengers.

There were no IDF casualties in either incident.

Military sources said last night that the infiltrator, found to have been carrying a petrol bomb and two copies of the Koran, intended to carry out a terror action within Israel.

The incident, the eighth penetration of the Jordanian border this year, occurred near the small settlement of Argaman.

According to military sources, IDF troops discovered fresh footprints beside the border, and, coming upon the infiltrator after a brief pursuit, opened fire when he refused commands to halt.

Residents of nearby Argaman said yesterday that they were alerted to the possibility of an infiltration by the arrival of a low-flying IDF helicopter early yesterday.

Argaman resident Meir Ahiam expressed surprise that the infiltrator was armed only with a petrol bomb. "To arrive here without weapons other than a petrol bomb," Ahiam told reporters, "this must have been someone very seriously fanatical."

Military sources last night credited higher levels of alertness both among IDF troops and residents of the region for the swift conclusion of the incident.

23129316

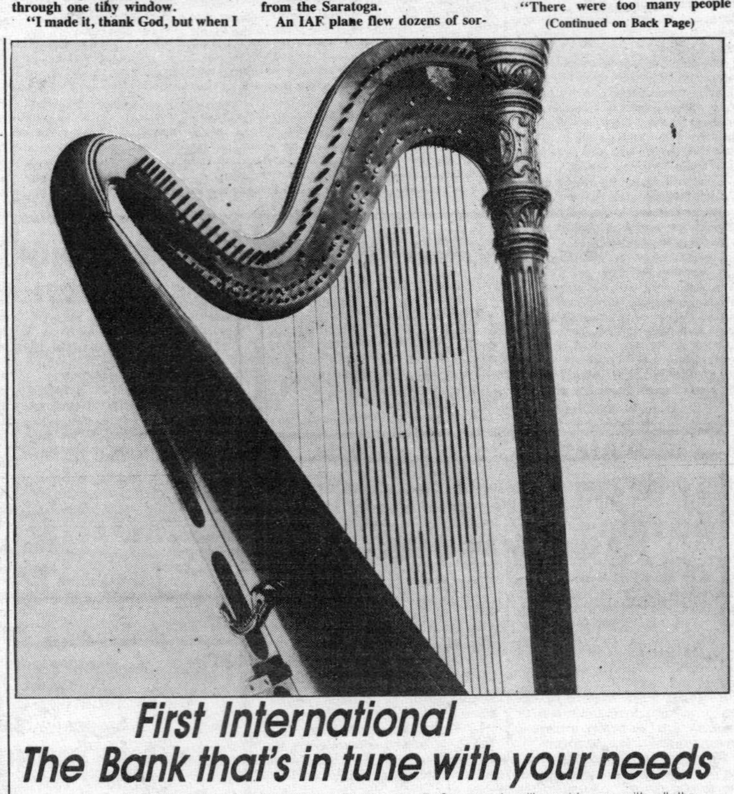

First International
The Bank that's in tune with your needs

The First International Bank has consistently pioneered unconventional and competitive personal banking services. At First International, it's the customer who calls the tune.

If you are a foreign resident, tourist, new immigrant or temporary resident – you have the right to hold a tax-free foreign currency account. Go where the smart money goes. Go First International.

■ High interest rates
■ Any combination of currencies: $, DM, SF, Y, etc.
■ Flexible terms: A broad range of amounts and maturities at fixed or floating interest rates, with automatic renewals.
■ Convenient opening hours: Most branches are open daily until 2 p.m. (till 12:00 on Fridays and holiday eves) and from 4 – 7 p.m. on Mondays and Wednesdays.

■ Our experts will provide you with all the information about our confidential tax-free foreign currency accounts.

Come to the bank that's in tune with your needs. Stop into any of the 78 friendly First International branches – a warm welcome awaits you.

Main Branches:
Jerusalem – 10, Hillel St.
Tel Aviv – 9, Ahad Ha'am St.
Haifa – 3, Habankim St.

Tamir Cohen (Jacobsohn)

THE EVER EXCEPTIONAL
THE FIRST INTERNATIONAL BANK OF ISRAEL.

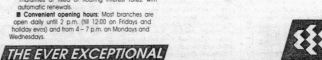

Your child and the gas mask

Page 2

THE JERUSALEM POST

Vol. LIX, No. 17650 Sunday, January 20, 1991 • Shevat 5, 5751 • Rajab 5, 1411 NIS 2.40 (Eilat NIS 2.00)

Gorbachev drops top liberal aides

Page 3

Seventeen are lightly injured as around 10 Scuds carrying conventional warheads hit Tel Aviv and Haifa areas

Iraqi missile attack is calmly absorbed

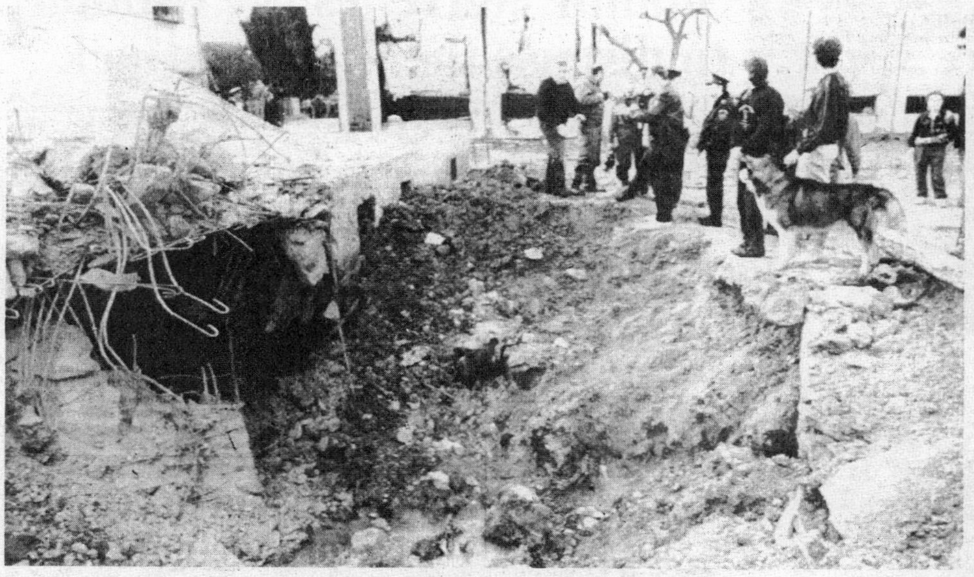

Police and rescue workers at the crater left by one of the missiles that hit the Tel Aviv area yesterday. (AFP)

Jerusalem Post Staff

Iraqi missiles struck Israel for the second time early yesterday, a day after a first salvo of Scuds before dawn on Friday abruptly brought Israel into the Gulf war.

Despite strong statements by Israeli leaders that this country would retaliate if attacked, senior government officials last night said Israel would give the U.S., "a little more time" before taking any action. (See 'Won't retaliate,' below.)

The U.S. meanwhile has sent Israel at least two additional batteries of Patriot anti-missile systems, along with American military personnel to operate them, as a part of the intensified U.S. effort to help Israel defend itself against further Iraqi missile attacks. The U.S. offer of additional Patriots was made on Friday after the first volley of missiles hurled by Iraq onto Israel's coastal plain.

The decision by Israeli leaders to accept weapons in Israel which will be manned by U.S. soldiers sets "quite a precedent," a Washington official said. (See story below.)

Although at least 10 missiles struck the Tel Aviv and Haifa areas over the weekend, only 17 persons were directly hurt by the blasts, all of them slightly, according to Haga (civil defense) officials. The lightness of casualties astonished Haga officials.

All the missiles carried conventional warheads.

Operating on a worst-case possibility that the missiles might contain chemical warheads, Haga officials directed residents to take shelter in sealed rooms in their apartments, rather than descend to basement shelters appropriate for defense against high explosives.

False alarms, some local and some national, sent residents to shelters several times over the past three nights. Civil defense officials praised the discipline showed by the public.

Some Scuds caused heavy damage to buildings, including private apartments. In a number of cases, residents were spared certain death by having taken shelter in another part of the house. One missile tore through the reinforced concrete roof a public shelter which was empty because nearby residents were in their own sealed rooms. The shelter could hold 50 persons. Injuries were mainly from blast and splinters. Heavy smoke was seen to rise from one Scud blast in Tel Aviv. A crater outside one building was 2.5 meters deep and seven meters across. Army officials said the missile carried more than 200 kilograms of explosives.

Despite suggestions that the public be directed to take shelter in basement shelters henceforth, in view of the fact that the Iraqis had fired only explosive warheads, civil defense officials insisted that the public continue to guard themselves against a possible chemical attack. Military officials said it was clear that not all the Iraqi mobile launchers had been destroyed and that more attacks could be anticipated.

After each missile hit, Haga experts were sent to the site in protective clothing to determine whether the payload was conventional or not. In every case, it was. Residents were asked to remain in their sealed rooms and to listen to the radio until this could be clarified. Sirens sounding the all-clear and announcements on the radio signalled when they could remove their masks and leave their sealed rooms.

The missile impact yesterday came almost an hour after dawn, indicating an Iraqi willingness to fire in daylight despite the risk of observation of the launching site from the air. Army spokesman Nahman Shai said "three or four" missiles had landed. In later broadcasts, members of the public who had scavenged parts of the shattered missiles were asked to turn them over to the authorities. In at least one such announcement, the public was asked to report any sighting of "parts of a missile."

Bush on Scuds: 'Darndest search and destroy operation'

Aerial attacks on Iraqi strategic targets continue without respite

ALLISON KAPLAN in Washington and news agencies

The around-the-clock air assault on Iraq by international forces, known as Operation Desert Storm, has continued ceaselessly, with Pentagon officials indicating that the air bombardments of strategic Iraqi targets would continue well into next month before any full-scale ground attacks would be launched.

The first Iraqi prisoners of war were taken yesterday when U.S. ships and helicopters, together with a Kuwaiti patrol boat, engaged Iraqi forces occupying nine Kuwaiti oil platforms in the northern Arabian Gulf. [Story – Page 3]

Military officials said that the Iraqi forces had been firing on allied aircraft with anti-aircraft artillery and shoulder-fired surface-to-air missiles.

General Colin Powell, chairman of the Joint Chiefs of Staff, yesterday told reporters that military targets around Iraq's capital as well as airfields and air defenses had been "the first set of targets" for some 4,000 air raids in the first two days of the war.

But the air strikes "will now begin concentrating on the Saddam's Republican Guards and some of the forces in the theater" of southern Iraq and Kuwait, he added.

Asked if that would bring the some 700,000 U.S. and allied forces in the Gulf closer to a ground war with the over 500,000 Iraqi troops facing them in occupied Kuwait and southern Iraq, Powell declined to comment.

An Iraqi diplomat was called to the State Department unexpectedly yesterday, and U.S. officials said one purpose was to discuss prisoners of war, AP reported.

The Iraqi diplomat was told that his government, like all others, is obligated to provide "humane treatment" to prisoners of war.

A man who answered the telephone at the Iraqi Embassy confirmed that the deputy chief of mission went to the State Department.

Cable News Network reported a meeting with the diplomat, Khalid Al-Shewayish, during which he was given a letter reminding Iraq that it is a signatory of the 49th Geneva Convention regarding treatment of prisoners of war.

The obvious desire by the Bush administration to keep Israel out the Gulf war has been impressed on the leaders of the military operations in the Gulf. Administration officials feared that any Israeli involvement in the conflict would gravely weaken their international coalition. When Bush urged the Israelis not to retaliate against the Scud missiles Iraq hurled Friday and Saturday mornings, he coupled it with a pledge to launch "the darndest search and destroy mission that's ever been undertaken" against the Scud platforms. Yesterday, he called Prime Minister Shamir twice to assure him of the efforts, and there was widespread praise and a great deal of surprise at Israel's decision not to retaliate.

With the knowledge that the elimination of Iraq's mobile Scud launchers was crucial to preserve Israeli restraint, the search for them was redoubled, according to military officials.

On Friday, General Norman Schwarzkopf, chief of U.S. forces in the Gulf, compared locating the mobile Scuds to "finding a needle in a haystack."

Senior U.S. military officials said 11 previously undetected mobile launchers had been hit on Friday. British officials announced late yesterday that their Tornado reconnaissance planes had located additional Scud sites.

"Each one that we find will be destroyed, and that will progressively eliminate that particularly nasty menace," said Tom King, British Secretary of State for Defense, at a press conference in London.

As the allied bombardment against Baghdad intensified, concern grew over possible international terrorist activity. Threats were made to American, Israel, British and Australian instalations in Thailand. U.S. citizens were instructed to use caution in visiting there.

The U.S. and its allies have also begun shifting their massive bombing raids from Baghdad and military complexes to Iraqi troop concentrations, America's top military officer said yesterday.

Pentagon officials, who asked not to be identified, said on Friday that giant U.S. B-52 bombers had begun heavy strikes against the elite Republican Guards based near the Iraq-Kuwaiti border.

Air strikes by U.S., British, French, Italian, Canadian, Saudi Arabian and Kuwaiti warplanes have thus far

(Continued on Back Page)

Emergency airlift of Patriots now being deployed

BRADLEY BURSTON and ALLISON KAPLAN
Jerusalem Post Correspondents

U.S. and Israeli technical crews worked through the night deploying an emergency shipment of Patriot anti-missile missles airlifted by the Bush administration yesterday after a dozen Iraqi Scud missiles crashed into Israel over the weekend.

The shipment of the Patriots, said to be the largest single airlift of U.S. military hardware to Israel since the 1973 Yom Kippur War, was set in motion on Friday after telephone consultations between President Bush and Prime Minister Shamir.

Pentagon spokesman Pete Williams said American crews were being brought in from U.S. military instalations in Europe to man the Patriots "on a temporary basis."

The first two batteries of Patriots are expected to be operational by this morning, Defense Ministry officials indicated last night.

But military experts warned against exaggerated expectations of the Patriot's ability to counter the missile threat.

California weapons analyst James Hackett told *The Jerusalem Post* last night that while the Patriot's software has been expanded to widen the area protected by the missile, it cannot solve Israel's missle-defense needs by itself.

Western sources agreed that only an effort combining Israel-based Patriots with intensive U.S. search-and-destroy missions against missile launchers in western Iraq would bring the threat to an end.

In a military briefing in Saudi Arabia yesterday, Marines Gen. Robert Johnston said that Iraq still possessed some thirty stationary and 20 mobile missile launchers.

He noted that the decrease by half to four Scuds fired on Saturday compared to Friday may indicate the measure of damage done to the Iraqi missile capability.

Meanwhile, IDF officials reacted sharply yesterday to a U.S. network news dispatch in which a correspondents pinpointed missile craters on a map.

In condemning this and other detailed reports of the missile attack, IDF Spokeman Brig.-Gen. Nachman Shai told foreign correspondents that the information could be used by the Iraqi military in calibrating future assaults.

Shai told the reporters that if they "want to commit suicide," they should do so elsewhere.

THE JERUSALEM POST regrets that the missile attack on central Israel prevented delivery of the paper on Friday to readers living north of Netanya and caused disruption of delivery in other parts of the country.

'Israel promises U.S. it won't hit back at Iraq for the moment'

DAVID MAKOVSKY
Post Diplomatic Correspondent

Despite pledges of retaliation for two Iraqi missile attacks over the weekend, Israel will delay such an attack for now, a senior Israeli official told *The Jerusalem Post* last night.

A senior Bush administration official said Israel has already pledged to the U.S. that it will not retaliate, Reuters said.

Israel is hoping that the arrival of at least several Patriot anti-missile missile batteries airlifted from the U.S. will help prevent future attacks.

"Saddam Hussein is trying to drag us into this war, and we don't have to play into his hands," a senior Israeli official said last night. The Americans are working hard to get rid of the missiles, and therefore "Israel wants to give the U.S. a little more time," the official said.

This does not mean that Israel disavows the right to retaliate. In a phone discussion with President Bush yesterday morning, Prime Minister Shamir said, "we appreciate the U.S. efforts, but the firing of missiles has not stopped and Israel reserves the right to protect itself."

U.S. has secured a pledge from Jerusalem that it will definitely not retaliate for the two recent attacks, but enable the U.S. to continue its search and destroy missions in western Iraq for mobile and fixed surface-to-surface Scud launchers aimed at Israel, Reuters reported.

"We are very happy with their decision," a senior Bush administration reportedly said yesterday.

The Israeli position will change if it is hit with a gas attack, according to Reuters. "If he thinks either Israel or the coalition will sit idly by if there's a gas attack, he's very much mistaken. The consequences would be 'extremely severe,'" the official said.

Defense Ministry Director-General David Ivri said last night on Israel Television that Israeli reluctance to retaliate immediately stems from its concern that such a retaliation could seriously complicate the war aims of the anti-Iraq coalition.

The U.S. and its allies are removing the Iraqi threat to Israel by flattening their war machine, and the feeling for now among Israeli offficials is that Israel sould not risk compromisng this vital objective.

While Arab officials in Egypt and Syria have publicly said they would understand an Israeli retaliation,

(Continued on Back Page)

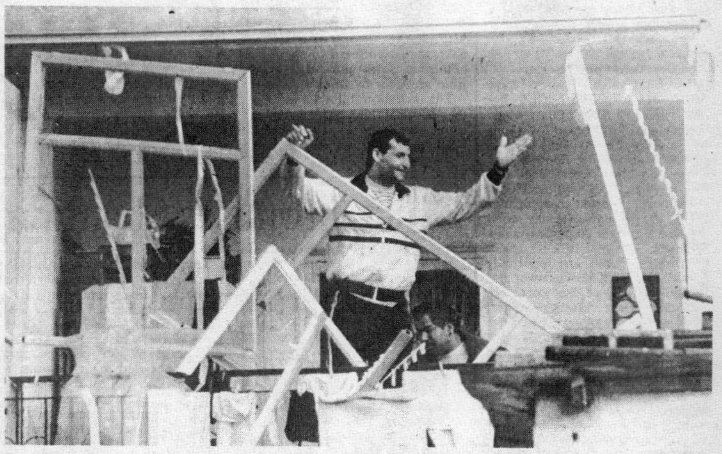

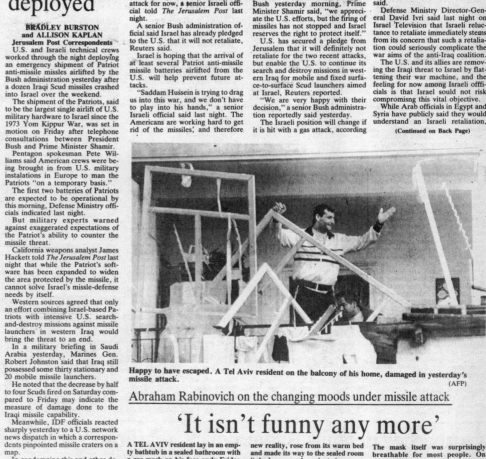

Happy to have escaped. A Tel Aviv resident on the balcony of his home, damaged in yesterday's missile attack. (AFP)

U.S. prepares for possibility of long war; supplies to Gulf stepped up

WASHINGTON (Reuter) – The U.S. is stepping up the flow of military supplies to the Gulf, preparing for the possibility of a long war despite the early success of air attacks on Iraqi forces, defense officials said yesterday.

"The Iraqis are taking a hell of a pounding from allied air [attacks]. We are increasing the pressure in both Iraq and Kuwait, but we have made clear that this could go on for some time," said one Pentagon official.

He and other officials, who asked not to be identified, said the military was not running short of bombs and rockets, despite over 4,000 allied air missions by late yesterday, but that ammunition and supplies were being used at a high rate and it was necessary to prepare for re-supply shipments.

In Saudi Arabia yesterday, U.S. Marine Maj.-Gen. Robert Johnston told reporters there was no way to tell how long it would take to get Iraqi forces out of occupied Kuwait.

"This could be a long campaign. It will be done with great caution...," Johnston said.

Defense Secretary Dick Cheney Friday night authorized the armed forces to lease up to 181 commercial airliners to carry troops, ammunition and supplies to the region.

Yesterday, the Pentagon asked families and friends of over 450,000 U.S. troops in the Gulf to limit shipments of personal items to letters and audio cassettes to help save cargo space for "what is necessary for sustainment."

"We anticipate this mail restriction may be necessary for the next two to three weeks. However, this will be reviewed as the situation changes," the department said in a statement.

Defense officials declined to say what military cargo would take priority on ships and aircraft. But one noted that fighters, attack jets and bombers in the Gulf were using bombs and rockets at an almost unprecedented rate.

Large stockpiles of food, ammunition and supplies were built up in Saudi Arabia and other areas of the Gulf during the five-month U.S. buildup, but supplies are used much more quickly in a war situation, said one official.

"This war could end next month," he said. "Or, it could go on longer depending on what kind of punishment the Iraqis are willing to take."

Cheney himself cautioned reporters after the initial U.S. and allied aircraft attacks against Iraqi forces that the war could go on for a "considerable time."

In London yesterday, British Prime Minister John Major told a news conference he had never been caught up in euphoria over the early success of allied air attacks. He said it was possible that the morale of Iraqi forces might crack quickly.

"But on the understanding that that doesn't happen, then it may be a considerable time before the matter is satisfactorily concluded," he added.

Abraham Rabinovich on the changing moods under missile attack

'It isn't funny any more'

A TEL AVIV resident lay in an empty bathtub in a sealed bathroom with a gas mask on his face early Friday morning and found it hard to control himself.

"I couldn't stop laughing," he told a radio interviewer.

There were few Israelis who chose to see absurdity rather than terror as war came again to Israel over the weekend – a strange war in which the troops on the line facing hostile fire are families huddling in sealed rooms wearing gas masks.

Many tried to dismiss the wail that wakened them early Friday as a false alarm – the Americans, after all, had blitzed Iraq on the opening day of the war and it was unthinkable that the Iraqis could or would fire missiles at Israel. The persistent wail, however, would not be ignored and the nation, forcing itself to face a new reality, rose from its warm bed and made its way to the sealed room it had prepared against Armeggedon.

The act of slamming the door shut, taping its edges, covering its foot with wet towels and putting on the gas mask was an acknowledgment of mortality, possibly imminent. It was a situation that filled most with fear, some with terror, none more than the parents of young children who panicked at the sight of the masks and refused to put them on. The notion of missiles falling out of the sky from far away was particularly frightening for some.

BY THE second night, the mood was easier. With the sound of the alarm, one stumbled to the sealed room, half asleep, as in a drill and no longer felt slightly silly putting on the mask.

The mask itself was surprisingly breathable for most people. On French Hill, two teenaged boys and a girl friend played guitar and sang through their masks, trying to cheer up their anxious elders. In Jerusalem's Rehavia Quarter, a resident answering the phone in his sealed room found himself giving an interview to a newspaper in the United States through his gas mask for a quarter hour.

After the second shelling, many people who had opposed an Israeli attack on Iraq changed their mind. "It's not funny any more," said a Jerusalem teacher. "If we don't do something this could become a habit. I opposed an attack by us because that's exactly what Saddam Hussein wants. Well, I think we should let him have what he wants."

Foreign clients remain loyal

Business / Page 7

THE JERUSALEM POST

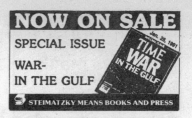

Vol. LIX, No. 17653 Wednesday, January 23, 1991 • Shevat 8, 5751 • Rajab 8, 1411 NIS 2.40 (Eilat NIS 2.00)

3 die, 73 hurt as Iraq strikes at Tel Aviv

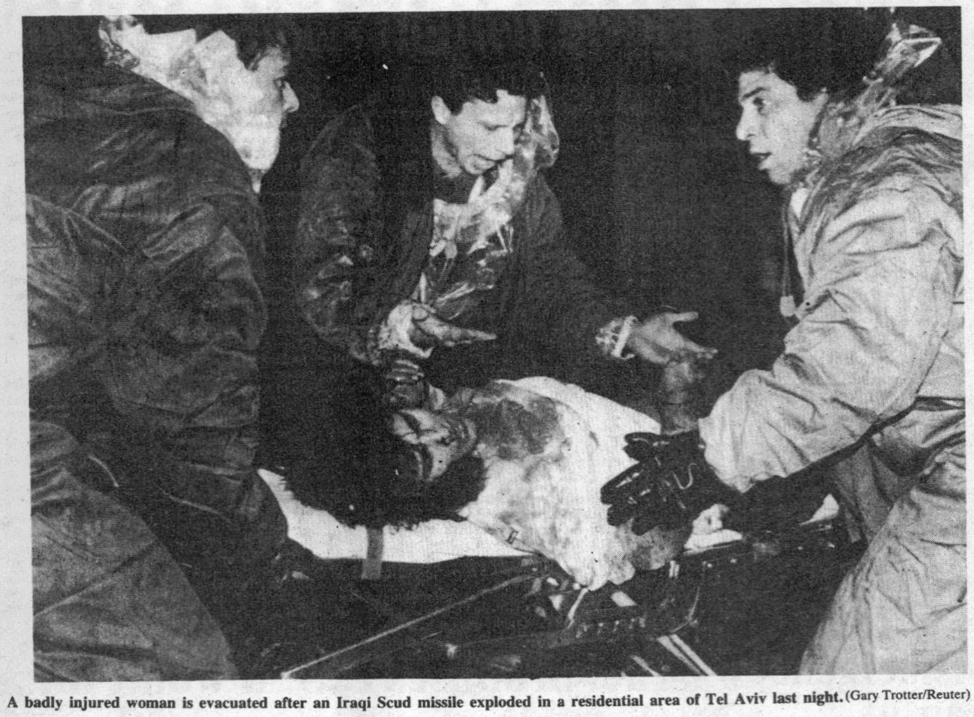

A badly injured woman is evacuated after an Iraqi Scud missile exploded in a residential area of Tel Aviv last night. (Gary Trotter/Reuter)

Shamir convenes the cabinet to discuss the missile attack

BRADLEY BURSTON, DAVID MAKOVSKY and PAUL KOHN
Jerusalem Post Reporters

TEL AVIV – Three people were killed and at least 73 wounded yesterday evening, several seriously, as an Iraqi Scud missile hit the Tel Aviv area for the third time in five days.

Prime Minister Shamir is to convene the cabinet this morning to discuss the attack. Late last night an official in the Prime Minister's Office said: "This is another murderous act of Saddam Hussein. He will have to pay."

Last night, Shamir heard reports from Defense Minister Moshe Arens and other officials about the extent of the damage, but officials stressed its full extent was still unknown.

Officials in the Prime Minister's Office refused to confirm that there had been consultations between Shamir and Deputy Secretary of State Lawrence Eagleburger, but did not rule this out. Shamir is to meet Eagleburger this morning.

Health Minister Ehud Olmert said Israel would strike back and ensure its retaliation was effective.

"It is not a question of whether Israel will retaliate, but when and how. I think that this policy has not changed in spite of tonight's events," he told BBC television.

Deputy Foreign Minister Binyamin Netanyahu also said that Israel would retaliate.

"We will act in due time and in due measure to neutralize him," he told CNN. "The important thing is not to act with our hearts ... The people of Israel expect us to act with our heads, not with our hearts.

"I am sure," he added, "that the missiles are falling exactly where Saddam Hussein wants them to. He's a master terrorist and this is classic terrorism."

Blast damage ranged over a wide area, with a score of buildings within a kilometer of the impact affected. The two-story building directly hit by the missile's explosive warhead collapsed, trapping a number of residents.

Three hours after the explosion, rescue crews in yellow helmets and military personnel were working frantically to find and free those trapped in their homes.

Zehava, a mother of five who lives across the street from the house that suffered a direct hit, told *The Jerusalem Post* that the blast came only seconds after the sirens had sounded. She and her husband Yehuda had just managed to reach their sealed room, and had not had time to put on their gas masks when "a tremendous blast" threw them against the walls of their room.

"The whole building swayed as if we had been hit by an earthquake," she said. "Luckily my phone was still working, and I had the presence of mind to call my brother-in-law who immediately picked up my five children, ages one to 12.

"Now that the children are safely away, my biggest worry is that I have no insurance against war damage and I do not know what will happen to us."

She and other shell-shocked neighbors said that police, ambulances and army vehicles arrived within three minutes of the blast. They immediately evacuated the injured, including many children.

Prof. Dan Michaeli, director of Ichilov Hospital, said shortly before midnight that almost none of the injured were in serious condition. Of the 50 who had been admitted, 20 had been released by midnight. Most suffered cuts from glass splinters and shock.

Shortly after the attack, hundreds of onlookers began to gather at the site, as a large force of police sealed off the area. The crowd, plus a power failure in the area, hampered efforts by more than 30 Magen David Adom ambulance and mobile care teams to evacuate the injured to Ichilov and Tel Hashomer hospitals.

The strike came less than 48 hours after Patriot batteries were put into operation by U.S. and Israeli anti-aircraft personnel. At least two Scuds were reportedly downed by the Patriots.

Asked if the IDF planned to retaliate, IDF spokesman Brig.-Gen. Nahman Shai declined to respond directly. "The blow was grave, very grave," he said. "We have said in the past, to all the nations of the region, that Israel is not prepared to accept attacks such as this without reacting.

"I have not yet been in the room where the defense minister, the chief of general staff and others are now holding consultations, and I would certainly not reveal at this time a change in policy, if any. But this is certainly a blow that will cause soul-searching, there is no doubt about it."

Despite the attack, the IDF announced last night that work would resume all over the country this morning. Schools will remain closed.

(Continued on Back Page)

Iraq burns oil fields

ALLISON KAPLAN
Jerusalem Post Correspondent and news agencies

WASHINGTON – Iraqi forces began setting fire to Kuwaiti oil installations yesterday, but their military resistance to the unrelenting air bombardment of their country remained limited to the launching of Scud missiles.

"He's doing little or nothing at the moment but launching the Scuds, which is a terror weapon more than anything else," said Lt.-General Thomas Kelly at a Pentagon briefing yesterday.

Kelly said that Iraqi aircraft were in the air, but were "electing not to fight" and were flying to bases in the northern part of the country.

The oil field fires in Kuwait, he said, were having "no effect on U.S. military operations."

U.S. military spokesmen have said that Iraqi leader Saddam Hussein may be marshalling his air defenses for the expected ground war when allied troops try to push Iraqi forces out of Kuwait.

It was unclear yesterday whether the purpose of the oil fires was to create smoke thereby clouding the allied view from the air of Kuwait, or to destroy Kuwait's resources.

Military sources in London said yesterday that Iraq was making wide use of fake buildings and weapons systems in an attempt to deceive allied bombers.

The tactic was first disclosed by British Armed Forces Minister Archie Hamilton, who said planes hunting mobile Iraqi Scud missile launchers might be attacking cardboard and plywood decoys.

The military sources said the Iraqis were making wide use of the tactic, borrowed from the Soviet Union.

They had produced a wide range of decoys including dummy missile launchers, both fixed and mobile, communications centers, factories and storage bunkers at chemical weapons plants, the sources said.

The Iraqis, who have learned much of their military doctrine from Moscow, were also thought to have built dummy aircraft shelters, planes and artillery.

The decoys were said to work better in bad weather when visibility was poor.

In Amman, a Jordanian security source said Iraq was deploying dummy plastic missiles around two air bases in the west of the country. The decoys were accompanied by equipment emitting electronic signals to fool attacking planes, the source said.

The success of Patriot anti-missile systems in Saudi Arabia continued to earn their laurels early yesterday morning, when Iraq launched six Scud missiles at the cities of Dhahran and Riyadh.

The U.S. military reported that the missiles were either intercepted and destroyed by Patriots or fell harmlessly in unpopulated areas, causing no injuries. At the same time, the military was investigating why a Patriot was fired accidentally yesterday in southern Turkey.

An American pilot downed by Iraqi anti-aircraft fire Monday was dramatically rescued on enemy soil after being spotted by two U.S. A-10 Thunderbolt attack planes. The aircraft flew an eight-hour mission, refueling four times in the air, to search for the pilot, with whom they had radio contact.

The pilot was picked up by a helicopter which fired at and destroyed an Iraqi truck heading for the rescue site.

"It was a rather indescribable feeling to know that he was now on the helicopter and we were coming out of enemy territory," Capt. Paul Johnson, the pilot who led the rescue mission told the *Washington Post*.

In a skirmish yesterday off the Kuwaiti coast, American A-6 planes attacked an Iraqi warship laying mines in the Gulf.

The Iraqi ship was left "dead in the water" and appeared to be sinking, according to Lt.-Col. Greg Pepin at the daily news briefing at U.S. Central Command in Saudi Arabia. U.S. forces attacked three additional ships in the area, he said.

Eagleburger talks lead to improved but incomplete U.S.-Israeli understanding

DAVID MAKOVSKY and ASHER WALLFISH
Jerusalem Post Reporters

U.S.-Israeli cooperation has "improved," but after two days of talks with U.S. Deputy Secretary of State Lawrence Eagleburger there is still not a full understanding, Foreign Ministry sources said last night.

Eagleburger was expected to have a phone conversation with President Bush, who will decide whether to give his approval to those issues agreed upon with his Israeli interlocutors.

Eagleburger held "substantive" talks for two hours yesterday with the forum of the three top senior Israeli officials – Prime Minister Shamir, Foreign Minister David Levy, and Defense Minister Moshe Arens – sources say. While the Prime Minister's Office termed the talks "friendly," other Israeli sources characterized it as "frank," a diplomatic buzzword suggesting differences. The Prime Minister's Office said the talks focused on security and economic issues, but refused to divulge details.

Meanwhile, Levy told the Knesset's foreign affairs and defense committee that "Israel and the U.S. will now maintain contact to coordinate with each other and keep each other fully up-to-date."

Levy attributed the U.S. decision to Israel's insistence on its right to react after the missile attacks.

The U.S. has been withholding electronic identification codes from Israel, making it impossible for the IAF to retaliate unless it wished to risk an accident with allied forces flying over Iraq, the *Los Angeles Times* reported from Washington yesterday.

The *Times* also said that the U.S. and Israel have also apparently worked out an air corridor, should additional missile attacks cause serious casualties or deaths.

The report said that Israel could not respond to last week's attack, because the U.S. withheld from Israel the proper air codes, known as "IFF" (Identification Friend or Foe). Lacking such codes, Israeli aircraft could be mistaken as an enemy aircraft during any raid. The report said that the withholding of IFF suggests that it was more than simple U.S. persuasion that prevented Israel from retaliating for missile attacks on Tel Aviv.

According to the report, if another Iraqi missile attack triggers retaliation, Israel is to first notify the U.S. air attache in Tel Aviv, who would then relay Israel's intention to the U.S. command in Riyadh. The information then would be sent to the U.S. Airborne Warning and Control System (Awacs), which would clear the necessary air space.

The article says that Sen. Arlen Specter was a key interlocutor with the White House in cementing the U.S.-Israel understanding.

Levy told the foreign affairs and defense committee that "during the deputy secretary's first visit before fighting broke out, we advised Eagleburger that we could give no commitment to refrain from retaliation. "Eagleburger left, and within hours – but before the hostilities started – we were assured from Washington that a joint coordinating apparatus would be set up. After hostilities began, Washington confirmed several times that it recognized the need to block the Iraqi threat against us, and so it would concentrate on destroying the missile launchers."

"Eagleburger has full authority from the president to take decisions. He doesn't need to go through channels," Levy said.

"The Americans would not have sent us the supplies they did, and agreed to coordinate with us in the most sensitive spheres, had they felt we were not serious about respond-

(Continued on Back Page)

Arens warned of continuing threat

Military Pool Reporter

REHOVOT – Defense Minister Moshe Arens said yesterday, before last night's missile attack, that Iraq still has a significant military capability and is able to fire missiles at Israel.

He indicated that work resumed throughout the country yesterday, despite the continued Iraqi threat, because the government wanted to demonstrate Israel's ability to withstand a prolonged conflict.

Arens, who spoke to reporters during a visit to an F-15 squadron south of here, said he had no doubt the U.S. and its allies had destroyed Iraqi missile launchers. Iraq's ability to attack Israel "may now be smaller than it used to be," but Saddam Hussein "still has the ability to [attack us] again," he cautioned.

Chief of General Staff Dan Shomron, speaking at the Knesset foreign affairs and defense committee yesterday morning, also warned that the Iraqi missile threat had not disappeared.

Arens quashed hopes for a quick allied victory and an end to the threat of Iraqi missiles and aircraft. "It's really not likely the [hostilities] are going to be over in a few days," he stated.

Asked whether the decision to resume work in Israel was a calculated risk, the minister said "it's simply a demonstration that the people are ready for any kind of confrontation or crisis that may be over an extended period of time. Our defense forces will do what they need to do, and our civilian population will do what they need to do – which means go to work."

He declined to say how Israel will respond to a third Iraqi attack. But the meeting with reporters was held in an F-15 hangar. The silver-colored interceptor flanking him carried Python and Sidewinder missiles and three fuel tanks, which made it possible to fly the aircraft to Iraq and back.

Israel asks U.S. for $3b. war aid, $10b. for absorption

ALISA ODENHEIMER
Jerusalem Post Reporter

The government yesterday presented the U.S. with a $3 billion tab for the costs directly and indirectly incurred as a result of the Gulf war.

In a meeting with Deputy Secretary of State Lawrence Eagleburger in Jerusalem yesterday, Finance Minister Yitzhak Moda'i said Israel had suffered losses and had incurred expenses ranging from a dearth of tourism to extra defense costs.

He also told Eagleburger that Israel will ask the U.S. for an additional $10 billion in special aid during the next four or five years to help finance immigrant absorption.

Speaking to reporters following the meeting, Moda'i denied the U.S. and Israel had struck a deal in which Israel would refrain from retaliating for the Iraqi missile attacks in exchange for foreign aid. He added, however, that Israel's decision to act as it has is based on "wide-ranging considerations."

"The aid is not in payment for anything," he said. "Other countries are receiving aid, and there is no reason that we should not receive aid for our costs in this war, which is not being fought on our behalf at the moment, and from which we are only getting hurt."

Moda'i also said that the U.S. envoy had not spoken of any political pre-conditions for granting the aid requests. "I think that our guest understood very well that this is not the time to play around with political conditions or red tape, and that he will arrange for the aid to be granted in full, and not in several payments."

(Continued on Back Page)

Schools to stay shut for now; high schools may reopen soon

BILL HUTMAN
Jerusalem Post Reporter

Schools will remain closed today. Education Ministry officials predicted that while secondary schools may open in the coming days, elementary schools will stay shut at least until next week.

Education Minister Zevulun Hammer and Defense Minister Moshe Arens agreed that for pupils' safety, schools should not reopen today, Education Ministry spokesman Yitzhak Rath said yesterday.

The decision was made just minutes before last night's Scud missile attack, he said.

"The only consideration for opening schools is the safety of the children," Rath said.

The ministry had planned to open secondary schools today, despite a warning early yesterday from the National Parents Association that parents would not send their children back to school out of concern for their safety.

Hammer, in expectation of a school reopening, had prepared a statement for parents in which he admitted: "We are taking a certain risk, but we believe we have no choice."

Hammer has a say on the issue butthe Defense Ministry has final approval in the matter.

This evening, the ministry will announce whether any part of the school system will reopen tomorrow.

In the meantime, plans are being drawn up to lessen the damage caused by the loss of at least one week of studies, ministry adviser Yisrael Cohen said.

There is concern for 11th- and 12th-graders who have lost time they need to prepare for matriculation examinations, Cohen said.

The ministry wants high school pupils to return as soon as possible; it is less concerned with the effects the break will have on elementary and junior high pupils, he added.

Gorbachev defends Baltic policy, reaffirms glasnost

WALTER RUBY
Jerusalem Post Correspondent

MOSCOW – Declaring his commitment to glasnost and perestroika, President Gorbachev said yesterday he has no intention of declaring presidential rule in the Baltic republics.

But in a statement to foreign journalists, Gorbachev defended the main points of his Baltic policy, said that a proposal by Russian Republic President Boris Yeltsin for a Russian army is "fraught with serious danger."

"I believe every sensible person can understand what this can lead to," Gorbachev said.

In brief comments on the Gulf war, he said the international community "must do its utmost to prevent the conflict from spreading," adding that he is in close touch with the U.S. and Arab governments.

The 15-minute statement clearly designed to reassure Western political leaders and public opinion that Gorbachev intends to continue his reformist course despite the recent crackdown in the Baltics. "The events in the Baltics in no way constitute expression of the line of presidential rule," a term used here to describe the suspension of democratic rights and the institution of a state similar to martial law, he stressed. "Neither our internal nor external policy has been altered ... The achievements of glasnost and perestroika remain ..."

Gorbachev also appeared to divorce himself from pro-Communist groups in Lithuania and Latvia, both called the "Committee for National Salvation," which have demanded the dissolution of pro-independence parliaments and the institution of presidential rule.

Seeming to imply that he blames the so-called "Black Beret" special forces in Latvia for precipitating the shooting in Riga Sunday night that left several dead, Gorbachev said, "No arbitrary actions on the part of the army are allowed, and the army should act only in accordance with orders..." The Black Berets are under the nominal control of the Interior Ministry, but have operated almost independently.

But Gorbachev pinned the main blame for the shootings in Vilnius and Riga on the pro-independence leadership.

He said that "unconstitutional laws" passed by the parliaments of the republics "will have to be abandoned.."

He also said that the Baltic republics can leave the Soviet Union "only through referendums and and the expressed will of the entire population according to law."

After meeting Gorbachev here earlier in the day, Latvian President Anatolijs Gorbunovs said that Gorbachev did not threaten direct presidential rule.

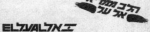

Back from the brink in Yugoslavia
Page 3

THE JERUSALEM POST

Vol. LIX, No. 17656 Sunday, January 27, 1991 • Shevat 12, 5751 • Rajab 12, 1411 NIS 2.40 (Eilat NIS 2.00)

The gentle art of bird watching
Page 7

Giant oil slick set ablaze; moving towards allied fleet

Compiled by The Jerusalem Post staff from news agency reports

DHAHRAN, Saudi Arabia – A 50-kms-long oil slick, part of it ablaze and being fed by more crude released by Iraqis, moved down the Gulf waterway crowded with allied warships, Western military sources said yesterday.

A Saudi official said the sea of oil, being fed from several sources, contained at least six million barrels and more - probably eight million - the equivalent of three supertanker loads, making it one of the biggest slicks in history.

Washington and Baghdad blame each other for the black mass now threatening the region's drinking water, bird and marine life.

Saudi officials said the oil was moving at a rate of 20 kms a day, and U.S. Air Force spokesman Lt Col Mike Scott told reporters in Riyadh it stretched for 50 kms and was 12 kms wide.

It would not affect military operations of the allied forces in the Gulf aimed at forcing Saddam Hussein's occupation army from Kuwait, he said.

A senior engineer on a British navy support ship said, however, the slick could disrupt operations. It could affect cooling systems on warships and onboard fresh water, produced by evaporation of clean sea water, which could not easily be replaced.

Western military experts have speculated that Baghdad hoped to hamper any amphibious assault by allied troops against Iraqi positions in Kuwait.

U.S. military officials said drinking water for the hundreds of thousands of troops deployed in the kingdom for Operation Desert Storm against Iraq would not be affected.

As the thick black mass grew, officials said it threatened drinking water to coastal nations dependent on desalination plants. Booms were being put round some plant seawater intakes.

Washington has said Iraq was

(Continued on Back Page)

No casualties after Patriot crews score bullseyes on Scuds with conventional heads

Scuds downed over Tel Aviv, Haifa

BRADLEY BURSTON
Jerusalem Post Defense Reporter

Iraq once again launched Scud missiles against Israel last night – one at Tel Aviv and three at Haifa – but Patriot missiles successfully intercepted and downed the terror weapons. The Iraqis also sent another Scud toward the Saudi capital of Riyadh, which U.S. forces also downed with Patriot missiles.

No injuries were reported in the Israeli attacks, which took place around 10 p.m. The Scuds were equipped with conventional warheads. It was the sixth Iraqi attack on Israel in nine days.

Minutes before the attack, Defense Minister Moshe Arens said that Patriot crews are in the midst of improving the operation of the missiles, and of studying the particular problems involved in intercepting the Scuds.

"We are looking forward to better results," Arens told Israel Television, adding that even with maximal performance, the system cannot provide "100 percent immunity" against Iraqi Scuds.

Last night the IDF announced that the Air Force had already incorporated improvements in the Patriot's system as a result of analysis of the attack Friday night, in which one person was killed and 69 injured. The attack on Friday, soon after Shabbat, was a multiple strike against central and northern

Toll in Friday night's attack was one killed and 69 injured

Israel, which, in addition to the human toll, also caused widespread destruction of homes and property.

Yesterday, two additional Patriot batteries were rushed into operation, making a total of six batteries delivered and deployed in the course of the week.

The emergency deployment of four Patriot batteries was completed on Friday, just as the two additional batteries were airlifted to Israel.

Responding to concerns over the safety of downing Scuds over Israeli territory, Israeli experts said last night that the limited range of the Patriot made interceptions in urban areas all but inevitable.

Analysts also suggested that U.S. press reports of a shortage of Patriots relative to Iraqi Scud stockpiles are misleading. "The true limiting factor for the Iraqis is the number of launchers, not the number of Scuds," one analyst told *The Jerusalem Post*. "If the number of launchers is substantially reduced, the Scud inventory will become irrelevant," the analyst said, noting that while as many as 1,000 Scuds may be stockpiled in Iraq, only a small fraction have the range to reach Israel.

Though IDF experts now believe that Patriot missiles hit all seven Scuds fired on Friday, destroying five and deflecting two, explosive warheads and missile fragments damaged as many as 1,000 apartments, swelling local hotels with families evacuated from the ruins. The total number of evacuees since the missile attacks began is now 4,000, the IDF said last night.

Tel Aviv Mayor Shlomo Lahat yesterday called on all Tel Aviv residents who had fled the city to return, reportedly terming them "deserters."

But Minister Arens took issue with the characterization, declaring that "It is difficult to find another example in the world of the behavior (of Israel's public) under conditions that no one could have foreseen a few months ago, and for which no one could prepare."

Killed in the Friday night attack was Eitan Grundland, 55, of Ramat Gan. Grundlan was killed when a portion of his home collapsed. Grundland, a plastics factory owner, will be buried later today. Grundlan's wife was injured in the incident, but is listed in good condition.

Over half of the 204 Israelis injured in the five Iraqi missile attacks to date were over the age of 65, IDF Chief Medical Officer Brig.-Gen. Yehuda Danon disclosed yesterday.

Nearly one out of every six injured were children, Danon added.

All of the casualties were residents of urban areas, and the only soldier injured was at home on a short leave when the missile struck.

Danon also stated that chemical-warfare examination crews have been able to rule out the presence of chemical weapons within minutes of their arrival at the scene of a missile crash.

Cleanup efforts continued late yesterday at the sites of missile damage. In the Tel Aviv area, one missile struck in a residential area, injuring over 500 apartments.

Volunteers assisted city workers in sealing damaged apartments, and reinforced police patrols were stationed to guard against looting.

Earlier in the day, a special IDF canine unit was employed to determine if residents were still trapped under debris.

Other large fragments landed in the center of a street, forming a large crater, and in the yard of a government building, damaging adjacent offices.

EC turnabout; bigger Israeli role envisaged in the new Europe

DAVID MAKOVSKY
Post Diplomatic Correspondent

The European Community, in a major turnabout reflecting Israel's gains due to its Gulf restraint policy, has decided to negotiate an enhanced role for Israel in the economically integrated Europe of 1992. The Brussels-based European Community Commission has informally jettisoned its old policy of linking ties with Israel to a Palestinian settlement, European officials said.

The diplomats also confirmed a Foreign Ministry statement that the EC Commissioner for Middle Eastern affairs, Abel Matutas, had agreed to drop science-related sanctions imposed on Israel last year.

According to Reuters, an EC meeting in Brussels on Thursday discussed providing Israel with $210 million in aid to compensate for Gulf war costs. Egypt, Jordan and Turkey, the so-called "front-line" states, are due to receive $700 million in EC aid.

One European diplomat said, "we now want to talk with Israel and see how Israeli companies can get a foothold in the new Europe. We now want to discuss things as friends, and we want normalization."

Another European diplomat said, "an Exocet missile has just been shot through the old policy." Officials say that the previous policy was pressed by Italian Foreign Minister Gianni DeMichelis, who last month completed his six-month rotation as EC chair, and has now been replaced by Luxembourg Foreign Minister Jacques Poos.

In a prepared statement, Foreign Ministry spokesman Yosef Amihud said the Commission's decision were "taken due its appreciation and understanding of Israel's position, and as a result of Iraq's aggression against it."

Until now, the EC has linked the vital issue of economic ties to Israel with progress on a Palestinian settlement. Europe is Israel's largest trade partner, with an annual volume of over $7 billion.

Israel would also like to see the EC liberalize its policy on rules of origin – lowering the percentage of Israeli products that has to manufactured in Israel to qualify for lower

(Continued on Page 6)

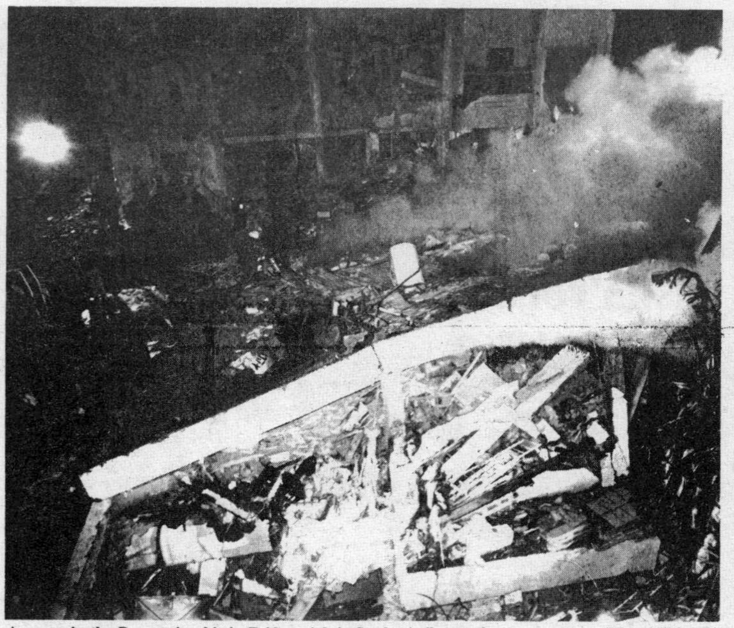

An area in the Dan region hit in Friday night's Scud missile attack. (Michael Weinraub)

The dilemma of Israeli decision-makers

'U.S. offered to send crews for Patriots on January 11'

ALLISON KAPLAN
Jerusalem Post Correspondent

WASHINGTON – The U.S. offered to send army crews together with the final elements of two Patriot batteries that arrived in Israel on January 11, Israeli officials here confirmed to *The Jerusalem Post* at the weekend.

Israel refused the offer, apparently deciding that taking the risk of standing unprotected by the Patriots on the January 15 UN deadline for the use of force against Iraq was preferable to setting the disturbing precedent of allowing American soldiers to defend Israeli territory.

Israeli decision-makers had hoped that by the time the country would be directly threatened by Iraqi missiles, Israeli crews would be prepared to man the Patriots.

Israeli soldiers, who last November began Patriot training in Texas, were expected to return to Israel by the end of January.

"It didn't make much sense on January 11, four days before the deadline...when our people were almost finished with their training, to break with our long-standing policy of not accepting American soldiers," an Israeli official said.

Officials stressed, however, that in their view, the offer of the American crews came virtually at the last minute, and that a series of bureaucratic tie-ups by the U.S. also played a role in delaying the deployment of Patriots in Israel until the first two weeks of January.

The delays stemmed from drawn-out negotiations over the operation and maintenance costs of the Patriots, and the costs of training the Israeli crews, which the U.S. wanted Israel to cover. There was also last-minute disagreement over whether Israel would receive the advanced model of the Patriot, which has proven successful in Saudi Arabia and Israel at intercepting ballistic missiles, or a less-advanced version, which was developed to shoot down aircraft and which the IDF had determined was ineffective against a missile threat.

Yesterday the families didn't go to Dizengoff

MARTHA MEISELS
Jerusalem Post Reporter

TEL AVIV – Dizengoff Street was dark and deserted last night with none of the bumper-to-bumper traffic of a usual Saturday night, when out-of-towners flock to the big city. Buses and taxis seemed to be the only vehicles plying the route, and even these, were few and far between.

At the hotel strip along the sea front, lights were ablaze in windows of the Hilton and Sheraton, where many of the foreign journalists and visiting celebrities are staying. Most of the other hotels along the strip, however, are almost entirely in darkness.

During the mid-morning hours, it was hard to tell whether the rain or the state of emergency was keeping the crowds away from Dizengoff. When the sun came out around noon, the sidewalk cafes and restaurants began to fill up, but with an older-than-usual crowd.

Noticeably missing were families with young children, who usually come to Dizengoff on Saturday morning from the outlying suburban communities.

Many area residents spent the mornings in the comfort of their homes, telephoning to check up on friends and relatives who may have been close to Friday night's missile fallout.

MDA says 476 were aided on Friday

JUDY SIEGEL
Jerusalem Post Reporter

Magen David Adom evacuated 476 people suffering from heart attacks or hysteria, or who mistakenly injected themselves with nerve-gas antidote between 6 and 10 p.m. on Friday.

MDA was too busy last night to provide a breakdown of the figures, except to say that 274 of the victims were in the Dan region and the rest throughout the country.

In addition, 26 ambulances evacuated people hurt in Friday night's missile attack.

Teheran says pilots won't be allowed to leave; three Iraqi Migs shot down in dogfights

Twenty-four Iraqi planes 'take refuge' in Iran

ALLISON KAPLAN
Jerusalem Post Correspondent and news agencies

WASHINGTON – U.S. military officials confirmed yesterday that at least 24 Iraqi aircraft have left Iraqi air space and landed in Iran since the beginning of Operation Desert Storm.

Also, a U.S. F-15 jet shot down three Iraqi aircraft, which were reported to be Soviet-made MiG 23s, and U.S. Marines near the border fired the heaviest artillery barrage of the war, shelling Iraqi positions inside occupied Kuwait.

Navy Rear Admiral Michael McConnell said at the Pentagon yesterday that about a dozen of the Iraqi planes that had gone to Iran were combat aircraft, and the others were transport or passenger carriers. It was unclear, he said, whether the landings were emergencies made to refuel or to avoid enemy aircraft, or whether the Iraqi pilots were defecting.

McConnell left open the possibility that the Iraqis were directing the planes to Iran as a strategic move, to temporarily protect them from destruction by the allied forces in Saudi Arabia, in order to bring them into the conflict later.

Meanwhile, the Soviet Union has handed over valuable intelligence information that may have helped the allies hold down expected casualties in the air war with Iraq, a U.S. military source said.

The senior military source, speaking on condition of anonymity, said the U.S has been "very pleased" with details the Soviets have provided about Iraq's arsenal, including its weapons and its air defense system.

An Iranian diplomat affirmed that his country would remain neutral and that the Iraqi pilots would not be allowed to leave Iran and rejoin the effort against allied forces in Saudi Arabia.

Iran's ambassador to the UN, Kamal Kharrazi, confirmed yesterday in an interview on the Cable News Network that at least seven Iraqi planes had made what he termed "emergency landings" in Iran.

Iran also announced that one of the aircraft blew up as it was touching down.

Kharrazi said that in accordance with the Geneva conventions, the pilots would be held in Iran until the end of hostilities, and would not be permitted to return to Iraq.

Kharrazi declared that Iran would remain neutral in the Gulf conflict and would "seize any plane from any side," which entered Iranian air space.

Three Marines were reported killed in a vehicle accident related to the operation.

U.S. forces in Saudi Arabia reported that while they have virtually shut down Iraq's ability to produce chemical and biological weapons, U.S. official said that a great deal of

(Continued on Back Page)

Rain in most areas, snow in some

JUDY SIEGEL
Post Science Reporter

The last two days brought much-needed rain to most of the country, and even light snow on the Golan Heights, Upper Galilee, and Samarian and Negev hill country.

Uri Batz, the duty forecaster, said that 26mm. of rain fell in the Jerusalem area over the past 48 hours, out of a total of only 113mm. for the entire winter; in Tel Aviv, 20mm. fell, of a total of 168 mm., and in Haifa nine millimeters out of 137 mm.

The Meteorological Services are not providing forecasts for security reasons. "When the war is over, we will be happy to tell the country again what the weather will be," Batz said.

27011317

Made in Germany – Iraq's deadly arsenal

JOHN KAMPFNER
Sunday Telegraph

BERLIN – How can a people who thought they had finally been readmitted into the community of moral nations be both pacifists and merchants of death? That is the question Germans have been forced to confront since the start of the Gulf war.

For a country that had become used to having others decide for it and defend it, the outbreak of hostilities in the Gulf has shattered the hope that a united Germany could, for the moment at least, take a leading role in Western collective responsibility.

While young people march for what Helmut Schmidt, the former Social Democrat Chancellor, has called "pretend pacifism," a small band of middle-aged businessmen enjoy riches accrued by helping Saddam Hussein build weapons of mass destruction.

Evidence that more than 100 German firms may have broken the UN embargo on Iraq (a total second only to Jordan's, which depended heavily on its neighbor), follows years of half-hearted investigations into German corporate involvement in Iraq's military build-up. Such allegations are anything but new. Two years ago the Americans handed the Bonn government intelligence reports of large-scale participation by German firms in a poison gas factory in the Libyan desert at Rabta.

It was only after a howl of protest in the United States – petulantly dismissed at the start as "German-bashing" – that Chancellor Helmut Kohl ordered action. His Economics Ministry countered then that its export controls were strong enough. Soon afterwards, it strengthened them.

After the invasion of Kuwait on August 2 and the imposition of sanctions, the Germans boasted that their laws preventing the sale of sensitive equipment to areas of conflict were among the most stringent.

U.S. and British intelligence services, however, have provided Bonn with a detailed blacklist of German firms, compiled largely through telephone taps. According to the Consumers' Initiative in Bonn, a small self-funding group, 87 German companies have helped arm Iraq in one way or other. For months, the magazine *Der Spiegel* has revealed names of companies indulging in dubious practices with Iraq. The response of the Government was ostrich-like as usual.

Only nine firms are being formally investigated and seven businessman have been detained. One is from the Hamburg-based firm WET, another from a company near Frankfurt, Pilot Plant. Both firms are alleged to have delivered chemical equipment for military purposes.

One company based near Munich is said to have provided mycotoxins, ostensibly for medical research, but which experts say can be developed into a bacterial fungus that causes respiratory problems and has one of the highest fatality rates of known biological weapons.

Numerous German technicians are reported to have worked at two plants in Samarra, which produced 900 lb of chemical gas ingredients a day. According to *Spiegel*, the Germans were helping the Iraqis produce hydrogen cyanide, or "dusty mustard," which can penetrate some gas masks.

If the allies fail to dispose of Saddam himself, they may have the Germans to thank. The Augsburg-based construction firm Walter-Thosti-Boswau admitted last week it had built a huge nuclear- and chemical-proof luxury bunker for the Iraqi leader, with a conference room, swimming pool and chandeliers, at a cost of £35 million.

Among the better-known companies implicated is Messerschmidt-Bolkow-Blohm.

Top three grades back to school from 9 o'clock this morning

BILL HUTMAN

Tenth, eleventh and twelfth grade high school classes are scheduled to reopen at nine o'clock this morning, nearly two weeks after the school system was closed down because of the danger from missile attacks. The only exception is Ramat Gan, where the opening will be delayed a day.

Pupils should bring their gas masks with them to classes, and in the event sirens go off on their way to or from school should don the masks and enter the nearest building, according to guidelines released by the Education Ministry.

However, the situation is "day to day, and even hour to hour," so parents should listen to the radio or call the ministry for up-to-date information on school openings, including today's, said ministry spokesman Yitzhak Rath.

If all goes well on the high school pupils' first few days back at school, seventh through ninth grade classes will also be reopened, he added.

Classes today are scheduled to start at 9 a.m., except at boarding schools where they will open at 11 a.m. to give pupils time to arrive.

Parents and pupils with questions about school openings can call the ministry in Jerusalem from 7 a.m. at 292890-7.

Pupils will spend much of today helping to seal classrooms and holding discussions with their teachers on the war in the Gulf and the missile attacks, Rath said.

The ministry is aware that some high school pupils will not return to school today because their parents believe it is safer for them to be at home, or want them to look after younger siblings, he added.

But while the ministry wants parents to send their children back to school, no action will be taken against those who don't, Rath said.

Some elementary school principals and teachers have been asked to return to school today to begin to pepare material in the event the ministry is forced to adopt a home-study program for the lower grades.

A ministry team since late last week has been working out the details of the program, which it is supposed to present to Education Minister Zevulun Hammer this afternoon.

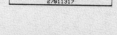

THE JERUSALEM POST
Vol. LIX, No. 17666 Thursday, February 7, 1991 • Shevat 23, 5751 • Rajab 23, 1411 NIS 2.40 (Eilat NIS 2.00)

Benazir Bhutto on 'an Islamic initiative'
Page 5

Baker's post-war vision

ALLISON KAPLAN
Jerusalem Post Correspondent and news agencies

WASHINGTON – Secretary of State James Baker told a congressional panel yesterday that reconstruction of post-war Iraq would be aided by the American-led coalition. He also suggested that there would be a role for Iraq in Middle East peace-making efforts once the war over Kuwait ends.

While acknowledging the Gulf crisis has "stirred emotions among Israelis and Palestinians that will not yield easily to conciliation," Baker said there may still be opportunities to bring an end to the conflict and reiterated that the U.S. was intent on pursuing that goal.

On Iraq, Baker said: "The time of reconstruction and recovery should not be the occasion for vengeful actions against a nation forced to war by a dictator's ambition. The secure and prosperous future everyone hopes to see in the Gulf must include Iraq."

Baker's suggestions for the post-war era came as Iran was discussing ways to end the Gulf War with Soviet and Turkish ministers, despite Washington's rebuff of its offer to mediate in the conflict. Iranian officials said yesterday that Foreign Minister Ali Akbar Velayati was due to meet Soviet Deputy Foreign Minister Alexander Belonogov. Turkish Foreign Minister Ahmet Kurtcebe Alptemocin was expected in Teheran yesterday.

Iran has disclosed no specifics about its initiative announced by President Ali Akbar Hashemi Rafsanjani on Monday. But Rafsanjani, who has kept Iran neutral in the war over Kuwait, said peace should be based on withdrawal of Iraq's troops from the emirate and of U.S.-led allied forces from the region.

The Iranian mediation offer was brushed aside by President Bush on Tuesday. "There's nothing to negotiate about," he told reporters, because Iraq refused to observe U.N.

(Continued on Back Page)

'U.S. bombing us out of the 20th century'

Relentless blitz pulverizing Iraq

Compiled from reports by Allison Kaplan, Jonathan Freedland, Thomas O'Dwyer and news agencies

The massive air blitz against Iraq and occupied Kuwait continued to intensify yesterday, as the U.S. reportedly prepared to unleash the fiercest concentration of bombing ever directed against any army.

Allied forces rained bombs and missiles on Iraqi troops and cities, knocking out a key bridge across the Tigris in one strike at the heart of Baghdad. (Story, page 3)

Iraq accused the U.S.-led allies of trying to blow it out of the 20th century and said it was cutting diplomatic ties with Washington and its major allies in the Gulf War: Britain, France, Egypt, Italy and Saudi Arabia.

In the estimated 2,000 sorties yesterday U.S. F-15 fighters shot down two Iraqi Su-25 bombers and may have downed two Iraqi MiG-21s ground-attack planes, a U.S. military spokesman said. Another three fleeing planes landed safely in Iran, a Saudi spokesman said.

The heavy firepower of the U.S. war machine, B-52 bombers and the 16-inch guns of the battleship Missouri, pounded Iraqi defences and troop positions.

U.S. B-52 bombers are to start bombing Iraqi front-line troops dug in along the Kuwait-Saudi border, military sources said yesterday.

They said this marked a switch of emphasis from the use of B-52s against Iraq's elite Republican Guard, which is held in reserve on the Iraq-Kuwait border. However, the Republican Guard would continue to be the main target of precision bombing from other allied strike aircraft.

The sources have described saturation bombing that will last around the clock for three or four days and be carried out by more than 2,000 planes, ranging from high-level, eight-engine B-52 bombers to two-seat F-15E Eagles capable of performing at Mach 2.

Allied planes already have flown more missions over Iraq and Kuwait than were carried out against Japan in the last 14 months of World War II. In the three weeks since the Gulf conflict began, they have dropped more high-explosive tonnage than did the combined allied forces during all of history's biggest war, according to a British defense consultant. But that initial air campaign, military officials said, has not been as intense as the one awaiting the dug-in Iraqis in Kuwait and southern Iraq.

Britain has denied that its aerial bombing of Iraq has reached its most intensive level since the war began. The Ministry of Defense said last night that the targeting of Iraqi military positions was merely "continuing."

A spokesman said it was impossible to talk of a stepping up of the British part of the air campaign – thought to amount to 3,500 British sorties in the last to weeks – since "one cannot compare a Jaguar sortie with a Tornado sortie."

Leading defense analysts told *The Jerusalem Post*, however, that there has been a marked change: a shift in quality rather than quantity.

According to Neil Cook, aviation editor of the respected *Janes' Defence Weekly*, "the sortie rate has not gone up dramatically, but there has been a switch in tactics by the Royal Air Force."

"The priorities have changed," said Mr Cook. "Now the targets are no longer Iraq's airfields – now seen as irrelevant – but so-called "point targets," such as supply lines, briudges, command and control centers and ammunition dumps."

U.S. military officials contend that relentless strikes by allied bombers are "clearly" sapping Iraq's ability to resist a ground assault.

The chief of French forces in the Gulf said about 30 per cent of Saddam's Republican Guard had been neutralized by more than two weeks of saturation bombing.

It was the first time an allied commander had put a figure on damage to the 150,000-strong armored force, Iraq's main line of defense against a ground offensive.

The fighting capability of the Republican Guard is likely to be a key factor in any decision by U.S. President George Bush for a ground war, risking high allied casualties and an erosion of political support.

There were conflicting reports of the punishment taken by Saddam's elite troops entrenched in northern Kuwait and southern Iraq.

The *New York Times* quoted Pentagon officials as saying bombing had been largely ineffective with 10 Republican Guard divisions still substantially intact. Military sources in London said one of three armored divisions had lost up to 150 of its 200-300 tanks.

French General Michel Roquejeoffre told a news briefing in Riyadh: "You can reckon that the Republican Guard has been diminished by at least 30 per cent."

But that may seem academic in the coming few days, as the saturation bombing continues to accelerate.

When asked last week about Iraq's ability to withstand the allies' opening air attacks, the U.S. commander, Gen. Norman Schwarzkopf, said, in apparent reference to the planned new campaign. "The best is yet to come."

(Continued on Back Page)

Three F-16 Fighting Falcons from the 87th Tactical Fighter Wing, with a KC-135 refuelling tanker before their bombing mission yesterday. They carry 2,000-pound bombs. (Reuter)

Baker: U.S. will consider additional aid

ALISA ODENHEIMER
ALLISON KAPLAN
DAVID MAKOVSKY
Jerusalem Post Reporters

WASHINGTON – Secretary of State James Baker said yesterday that since Israel has made "no formal request" for immediate economic and military aid, he does not expect such aid to be included in a special supplemental 1991 package designed to finance Operation Desert Storm.

He added however, that the U.S. would "consider" any such request, and that it was encouraging its European allies to assist Israel.

"I think there will be contributions coming from other than the U.S. to help defray some of those costs that Israel is incurring," Baker said.

In recent days, the Bush administration has sent strong signals to the Israeli government and to the American Jewish community that it does not want aid to Israel or other countries combined with the U.S. war costs included in legislation.

As a result, Israeli sources have said that when a formal request for assistance is made, it will either be

(Continued on Back Page)

IAF strikes hard at Fatah again to halt Katyusha rocket attacks

DAVID RUDGE
Jerusalem Post Reporter

ROSH HANIKRA – IAF helicopter gunships blasted Fatah targets in the Iklim al-Toufah region north of the security zone in South Lebanon yesterday afternoon.

At least one gunman was reported killed and two others wounded when their truck took a direct hit from rockets fired from the helicopters.

The helicopter strike occurred while Lebanese army troops, in trucks and armored personnel carriers, deployed in South Lebanon for the first time since the beginning of Lebanon's civil war nearly 16 years ago.

The IDF spokesman said the vehicle was hit and destroyed. It was apparently one of the vehicles mounted with launchers used to fire Katyushas towards the security zone and the Israeli border in the past few days.

Fatah outposts in the villages of Houmine and Sarba, in Ikilm al-Toufah, were also hit, according to reports from Lebanon.

According to reports from Lebanon, some 2,500 Lebanese army soldiers took up positions south-east of the South Lebanese market town of Nabatiya, a few kilometers from the northern perimeter of the security zone.

The Lebanese army troops also moved down the coastal road from Sidon towards the port town of Tyre, where they are scheduled to deploy later today.

There were no reported attempts by the Lebanese troops, however, to move into the Iklim al-Toufah area itself – the scene of heavy fighting a year ago between rival Amal and Hizbullah Shi'ite organizations.

On Tuesday, IAF warplanes blasted other Fatah positions in the area and on the outskirts of Palestinian refugee camps, east of Sidon.

(Continued on Back Page)

Jordan heightens the alert status of its troops near the Iraqi border

BRADLEY BURSTON

Jordanian troops near the border with Iraq appear to have been placed on heightened alert status.

The heightened alert may be a signal to allied forces that Jordan intends to honor its assurances that Iraqi military hardware will not be allowed across the border.

However, in an impassioned television address last night, King Hussein made no reference to his often-underscored policy of forbidding the entry of all foreign military elements to Jordanian territory and airspace.

The Jordan-Iraq border has been closely watched by allied airborne intelligence. During the first weeks of the Iran-Iraq War, Iraq used Jordan as a "safe harbor" for warplanes considered vulnerable to Iranian shelling.

The unusually agitated manner of the king last night was seen by observers as a token of the protracted frustration and extreme tension that characterized the position of since the invasion of Kuwait.

The speech may also have been intended to head off mounting militancy and popular demands to send forces to fight in support of Saddam Hussein.

His voice rising, Hussein said that he had called for a cease-fire for weeks on end, but that no one had heeded his plea.

In a reference to statements earlier in the evening by U.S. Secretary of State James Baker, Hussein attacked the "new world order" as worse than the World War I-era Sykes-Picot Agreement, a British-French proposal to carve up areas in the Middle East after the war.

"We, the Arabs and Moslems, are facing a new imperialism," Hussein said, "Western hegemony, French, American, British hegemony, and Israeli hegemony that will rule over us."

Meanwhile, Jordanian security forces near the Syrian border used tear gas to control a crowd of hundreds of Jordanians, after the crowd stormed and unloaded a convoy of food trucks bound for Saudi Arabia.

The crowd reportedly demanded that the food be re-routed "for the starving people of Iraq."

Treasury pushes economy back to peacetime

ALISA ODENHEIMER
Jerusalem Post Reporter

Finance Minister Yitzhak Moda'i yesterday convened an emergency meeting of the ministerial economic committee, hoping to push the economy out of its war-induced stupor.

"Production is down by 25 percent right now, and the minute it gets dark, everything closes," Moda'i told Israel Television last night. "I don't see that the economy is back to normal yet."

The committee approved a list of 10 decisions, entitled "Returning the economy to normal activity." It said that all schools and day-care centers would be opened by Tuesday and, as of today, hospitals and clinics would return to their normal level of activity. The only exceptions are Tel Hashomer, Beilinson, and Rambam hospitals, which will return to 65 percent of their regular activity.

The decision also calls for the gradual return of employees from the territories to their jobs in Israel, with preference given to those in farming, building and export industries.

The IDF will also provide soldiers to help pick fruit, and to give assistance in the schools.

Other points include:

☐ Special arrangements for payment of taxes. The deadline for property tax payments and outstanding income tax payments for 1990 will be postponed from the end of January until the end of February, without interest.

Requests for deferment of VAT, purchase tax, or other taxes will be dealt with on an individual basis.

☐ Changes in the rules governing

(Continued on Back Page)

Experts differ on state of Iraqi armed forces

Israeli leaders and analysts have been voicing conflicting estimates of the current state of the Iraqi military.

Despite the relentless allied air assault, the ranks of the Iraqi armed forces have yet to exhibit evidence of having reached the "breaking point," Defense Minister Moshe Arens indicated yesterday on Israel Radio.

But former IDF chief of staff Mordechai Gur said yesterday that the allies may be overestimating the ability of Iraqi ground troops to stand up the the allied air onslaught.

"I felt from the start that the West has very, very greatly exaggerated the strength of Iraqi ground forces, and when they are attacked, it will be possible to overcome them relatively quickly," Labor MK Gur said. "My assessment has not changed."

Once a coordinated ground, sea and air action finally gets underway, Gur envisions the early surrender of many Iraqi forces in the face of far superior firepower.

Gur told Israel Radio that the current allied air assault was a positive development from both U.S. and Israeli standpoints, with the allies causing significant damage to Iraqi long-term strength.

Yet another view was expressed by military historian and former IDF staff college commander Meir Pa'il. He was dissatisfied with the allied war effort so far, saying that the Americans were conducting "a very interesting, clumsy war."

Reserve colonel and former MK Pa'il said that although some successes had been achieved, the U.S. was "basically wasting time" and only fragments of key Iraqi forces had sustained damage.

Pa'il opposed repeated calls by Gur and others to drop the policy of restraint. "We should do whatever we can to deprive ourselves of being involved in the war," he said.

According to Pa'il, the policy of restraint has gained Israel a higher level of world support than it even had around 1948.

Germany – Data from Israel 'not enough' to act on

HERB KEINON
Jerusalem Post Reporter and news agencies

Israel and German security agencies have for years traded information regarding the transfer of arms and technology to Iraq, but this hasn't been enough for Bonn to prosecute firms doing business with Saddam Hussein, the German ambassador to Israel said yesterday.

Otto von der Gablentz, speaking at the B'nai B'rith World Center in Jerusalem, said, "In the last couple of years, we have asked the Israeli government and government agencies to provide us with information and proof to prepare legal proceedings against these firms." He said, however, that it was "very possible" that the information Israel provided was insufficient to prosecute lawbreakers.

The ambassador said that only 0.2 percent of the arms in the hands of the Iraqis is due to legal German transfers, but admitted that Germany has not done enough to stem the illegal flow of weapons. Germany has come under a barrage of criticism for not stopping German firms from selling chemicals and technology to Iraq.

■ An article by an American investigator which appears in the Tel-Aviv based magazine *Monitin* asserts that Germany has a nuclear bomb and tactical nuclear weapons, and may have supplied some supplementary technology to Iraq. [Story – Page 10]

In Bonn yesterday, the government cracked down on companies violating export laws as more reports surfaced of German involvement in helping Iraq develop its chemical and biological weaponry.

Chancellor Helmut Kohl's cabinet agreed on a package of proposals that would tighten penalties for violations of German export law or UN sanctions, allow domestic intelligence officials to eavesdrop on mail and telephone conversations of suspected companies, and beef up customs agencies.

Parliament must approve the package, which requires several changes in existing law, but that was expected given the widespread outrage over the Iraq scandal and what Foreign Minister Hans-Dietrich Genscher has called Germany's "merchants of death."

The government took its action as a leading news magazine implicated yet another German firm in Iraq's weapons buildup.

***Stern* magazine reported yesterday that a subsidiary of one of Germany's largest companies helped Iraq build a secret research and testing facility for chemical and bacteriological weapons, and promised to exclude Israel from its production.**

***Stern* said that Thyssen Rheinstahl Technik of Dusseldorf, a subsidiary of steel and engineering giant Thyssen AG, and at least eight German subcontractors had helped build the secret facility in the small Iraqi town of Salman Pak.**

The magazine said the project began "harmlessly" with a contract in 1980 between the subsidiary and an Iraqi-owned construction company to help set up a chemicals laboratory, a guest house and a theater.

The company denied delivering any laboratory equipment or chemicals to Iraq and said it had no indications that the construction it did for Iraq would be used later for a poison gas factory, *Stern* said.

Thyssen AG, the parent company, reportedly plans to sue the magazine over the report.

Thyssen officials last week acknowledged the company had sold pumps to Iraq, but denied doing any weapons business either before or after the UN trade embargo began last August. The pumps were meant for use in oil refineries and had been sold to Iraq for years, said Werner Bartels, a board member of Thyssen AG.

"It couldn't be known that they could have a military use," he said, adding the pumps were sold to Iraq with the approval of the German government.

Recent news reports have alleged the equipment was used to pump fuel into the motor of Iraq's Scud-B missiles.

According to *Stern*, the contract between the Thyssen subsidiary and Iraq was worth about 21.5 million marks ($14m.) and included an "Israel clause." Through that, the company guaranteed it would boycott Israel and deny it "advice or expertise," the magazine said.

In another report yesterday, *Quick* magazine said German firms had built 1,000 camouflaged steel bunkers now being used by Iraq to hide missiles and tanks from attacks by the allied forces. It published plans and photographs of the bunkers.

07021312

What now? Rubinstein, Brzezinski, Dore Gold
Pages 5, 6, 7

THE JERUSALEM POST

Vol. LIX, No. 17685 Friday, March 1, 1991 • Adar 15, 5751 • Shaban 15, 1411 NIS 3.50 (Eilat NIS 3.00)

David Kushner on The brave new Turkey
Page 6

VICTORY IN 100 HOURS!

Allied, Iraqi military chiefs to discuss truce

Baker to make first visit here

DAVID MAKOVSKY and ALLISON KAPLAN
Jerusalem Post Correspondents

U.S. Secretary of State James Baker is to arrive here within two weeks for his first ever visit, during a high-profile swing through the Middle East aimed at demonstrating that the U.S., after defeating Iraq in battle, will maintain momentum in the search for comprehensive Middle East peace and security.

Baker, whose timetable has not been finalized, will not bring any comprehensive U.S. blueprints for solving the so-far intractable Arab-Israeli conflict, Western diplomats say. Any such plans have not been fully developed.

At the top of his agenda will not be Arab-Israeli issues, but the mechanics of moving from the war to three other crucial areas of discussion – Gulf security arrangements, post-war reconstruction, and regional arms control.

Baker's spokesman, Margaret Tutwiler, laying out a preliminary schedule for his trip, said he is fully aware of the magnitude of the task he faces.

"The secretary and the president do not underestimate the difficulty

(Continued on Page 13)

Soviets hail truce; call for peace conference

WALTER RUBY
Jerusalem Post Correspondent

MOSCOW – Soviet Foreign Minister Alexander Bessmertnykh yesterday hailed the allied victory in the Gulf war and called for an international conference on the Middle East as a follow-up. Meanwhile, Soviet Jews expressed joy at the Gulf news and predicted an upsurge in aliya.

The denouement of the war, Bessmertnykh said, was "the first time in world history that combined forces repelled aggression." The cease-fire and Iraq's acceptance of all Security Council resolutions amounted to "a victory for a sense of realism ... (and) for the political line of Gorbachev."

The Soviet Union "will spare no further effort to find a Middle East settlement acceptable to all sides," Bessmertnykh said, and called for early resumption of talks in the UN Security Council to pin down a final settlement.

The warm line by Bessmertnykh toward the allies represented something of a turnabout. Only two days ago, Deputy Foreign Minister Alexander Belonogov was strongly critical of the U.S. and the other members of the international coalition

(Continued on Page 13)

War's end is turning point for Arab world

ANALYSIS / Barry Rubin

The Jordan Television reporter almost broke into tears when he could no longer keep Iraq's defeat from himself or his viewers. At the same time, Kuwaitis were celebrating their country's liberation. Which way will the Arab world go: cheering Saddam's debacle or mourning Iraq's humiliation?

The first issue is whether Arabs will believe that Saddam lost the war, especially if his regime survives. Among Jordanians, Palestinians, and those in North Africa and Yemen, there are convoluted explanations of Saddam's brilliant strategy in forcing the allies to cease fir-

(Continued on Page 13)

Top priority to return of POWs

ALLISON KAPLAN
Jerusalem Post Correspondent and news agencies

A smiling President George Bush, at his desk in the Oval Office of the White House, announces last night that a meeting to settle terms of the truce will be held. (Reuter)

The allies completed their stunning victory in the Gulf war yesterday, halting a six-week air and naval bombardment which was capped by a 100-hour blitzkrieg that broke Iraq's military back.

U.S. President George Bush, who had announced a cease-fire from 05:00 GMT (7 a.m. in Israel) after the routed Iraqis accepted all 12 UN Security Council resolutions on Kuwait, said last night that Baghdad had agreed on the first meeting between the military commanders of the two sides to settle the truce terms.

Bush announced the plans for such a parley, set to take place "very soon," during a meeting with Kuwait's ambassador to the U.S., Saud Nasir al-Sabah.

In an emotional speech before the television cameras, the Kuwaiti official told Bush that "you will go down in history as the great liberator of my country."

Bush, welcoming the meeting of the commanders, said that the return of allied prisoners of war would be a top priority in the discussions with the Iraqi military.

"We are going to get back our PoWs and we're going to do it fast," Bush said.

Earlier in the day, State Department spokesman Margaret Tutwiler said that efforts to set up the meeting had been made through the Soviet Union. In a telephone call to Soviet Foreign Minister Alexander Bessmertnykh, Secretary of State James Baker asked him "to encourage the Iraqis to designate a military representative to meet with our coalition representatives in order to deal with the military issues of a cease-fire," according to Tutwiler.

In his speech late Wednesday night, Bush declared a "quick, decisive and just" victory after the U.S.-led allied forces had crumbled Saddam Hussein's military machine like so many toy soldiers and tanks.

Military sources in London said the allies took 175,000 Iraqis prisoner. Thousands of Iraqis were killed in the land push and the 38-day bombing campaign that preceded it.

As the allied focus switched to the post-war era, Britain said Iraq must destroy its missiles and weapons of mass destruction. Prime Minister John Major said Iraq should be treated as an international pariah as long as Saddam remains in power.

Washington said an arms embargo must continue for as long as Saddam rules Iraq.

The fighting peaked on Wednesday, when allied armies claimed control of Kuwait City and devastated Iraq's best forces in the biggest tank battle since World War II.

Iraq's 42 army divisions were crushed, the Pentagon announced last night.

In the war, 4,000 of Iraq's 4,200 tanks were destroyed as were 2,140 of 3,500 artillery pieces.

At least 126 allied troops were killed in the fighting. Iraqi casualties were far, far higher. The Saudi ambassador to Washington, Prince Bandar bin Sultan, quoted Saudi military sources as estimating 85,000 to 100,000 Iraqi soldiers killed or wounded.

Allied commanders have refused to provide any count of Iraqi dead, and Baghdad has been silent on the issue.

A French military expert, retired Colonel Jean-Louis Dufour, estimated up to 150,000 Iraqis may have died.

Allied commander General Norman Schwarzkopf said "a very, very large number" of Iraqis had been killed.

U.S. military officials in Saudi Arabia said last evening that they had received word of some sporadic Iraqi artillery fire after Bush's deadline, but "we think it's from units that just haven't gotten the word," said Lt.-Col. Mike Gallagher.

Later, U.S. military spokesman Brig.-Gen. Richard Neal said Iraqi

(Continued on Page 13)

Yeshiva student found murdered in Jerusalem

ARYEH DEAN COHEN
Jerusalem Post Reporter

A yeshiva student missing since Wednesday night was found stabbed to death with multiple wounds yesterday in the Moslem Quarter of Jerusalem's Old City.

Police found the body of Elhanan Atali, 25, in an abandoned storeroom at the corner of Hagai Street and the Street of the Chains, only half a block from the Ateret Cohanim yeshiva where he studied. His throat had been slit and he had been stabbed the back.

Several suspects were detained for questioning and police immediately increased patrols in the Old City to prevent further violence. Police sources attributed the murder to nationalistic motives.

Atali, whose family lives in the Old City, was found after a fellow student discovered his glasses and a large bloodstain near the apparent scene of the crime, and alerted police.

According to Jerusalem Police Commander Haim Albaldes, Atali disappeared Wednesday night after trying to find a ride to a Purim party in Hebron.

"He promised to find a friend with a car; they were all supposed to meet at about 10:30 p.m.," Albaldes told Israel Radio. He said that contact was lost with Atali shortly afterwards, and friends searched for him until shortly after midnight. His body was discovered early yesterday morning.

Interviewed later on Educational Television's evening news program, Albaldes said police believe the murder occurred between midnight and 1 a.m. He said "a number" of suspects are being held for questioning and a special investigative unit is looking into the murder.

Atali was buried on the Mt. of Olives yesterday afternoon. The funeral took place without disruptions or violent demonstrations, with police taking up positions along the route to prevent any such outbreaks.

Albaldes said he does not believe the timing of the incident indicated it was an attempt to breathe new life into the intifada in Jerusalem. He noted that there had been no organized intifada-related incidents in the city over the past one-and-a-half months.

The city is safe, he added. "Everyone can move about the city freely, but it is impossible to secure every corner and intersection."

Yesterday morning, yeshiva students stood in clusters near the scene of the murder, most of them too upset to speak to reporters.

"It's a very difficult thing for us," one student who asked not to be identified said. "We won't do anything illegal, and the entire direction taught at the yeshiva is to obey the law, but we will insist that the police and other security forces do everything they can to insure our safety."

The student said there had been no incidents in recent weeks, although he noted that some of the yeshiva's Arab neighbors took to

(Continued on Page 13)

Beduin woman, 3 children discovered burned to death

BEIT SHE'AN – A Beduin woman and her three children – a 2-year-old son, and 4- and 6-year-old daughters – were found burned to death near here yesterday. Police have arrested her husband and four others on suspicion of murder.

The tragedy occurred at an encampment near the settlement of Menahemiya in the Jordan Valley. Kerosene had been poured over the bodies and set alight.

Magen David Adom units that arrived on the scene, including a doctor from Tiberias, could do nothing but declare the victims dead.

At first it had been that the woman, about 35 years old, had apparently decided to take her children's lives along with her own, Israel Radio reported last night.

SHABBAT	BEGINS	ENDS
Jerusalem	4:59	6:12
Tel Aviv	5:17	6:14
Haifa	5:08	6:13
Beersheba	5:15	6:12
Eilat	5:17	6:15

IN SUNDAY'S JERUSALEM POST
Martin van Creveld on Wargames

State of emergency is declared over

Unseal rooms and put away your gas masks

MICHAEL ROTEM
Jerusalem Post Reporter

TEL AVIV – The state of emergency in Israel is over, IDF spokesman Nahman Shai announced yesterday morning. All residents should store their gas masks inside the original cardboard boxes in a dry and safe place.

Sealed rooms in homes and public buildings may be opened. The public is asked not to throw the plastic sheeting and masking tape into the garbage, but to bring or send them with children to the special collecting stations that will be opened in schools, so they may be recylced.

Haga has requested that public disconnect the filters from their gas-masks, wrap each piece in a plastic bag and seal the bag firmly, Israel Radio reported last night. Air pumps and *mamats* should also be sealed in plastic bags. Air pumps must be switched off before sealing, but the batteries must not be taken out. Mask components must not be rinsed or washed, only wiped with a dry cloth.

All restrictions imposed on public gatherings and other emergency orders concerniing civilians are canceled, the spokesman said.

The IDF, however, remains in a state of alert, the spokesman stressed. If another emergency occurs, the public will be notified by broadcasts on the radio.

End of an episode. Two Jerusalem youngsters lose no time yesterday in taking down the plastic protective sheets and opening up their family's formerly sealed room. (Avi Hazon)

Lufthansa leads airlines return

EVELYN GORDON

Germany's Lufthansa airline is to fly here today in a pointed attempt to be the first foreign airline to return among those which halted flights during the Gulf war.

With the cease-fire apparently holding, the German flag-carrier's resumption of services is to be followed by Air France on Sunday and by British Airways, Swissair, Alitalia, Austrian Airways, and Olympic Airways during the week.

Tower Air was the only foreign carrier to keep flying to Israel during the war.

Lufthansa will run three flights a week – on Wednesday, Friday and Saturday – for the next few weeks. It hopes to return to a normal seven flights a week by the end of March.

'Technically, the threat still exists'

Arens says Iraq must pay for Scud damage

BRADLEY BURSTON
Post Defense Reporter

Israel will demand that Iraq pay for the damage its Scud missiles caused, Defense Minister Moshe Arens said yesterday.

Technically, the missile threat still exists, he said, but insisted the decision to rescind emergency regulations was not made with undue haste.

In present circumstances, Iraq would not fire at Israel for fear of an immediate resumption of the war, Arens said in broadcast interviews.

"We are storing away the gas mask kits, dismantling the sealed rooms and returning to routine life. Nonetheless, in the Middle East there's always room for apprehension," he said.

Arens described the U.S. victory over Iraq as "an excellent effort that has surely earned the admiration of the entire world – because it brought Saddam Hussein from the 'mother of all battles' to the 'mother of all defeats.'"

Arens said Israel has every right to claim reparations for the millions of dollars worth of damage the Scud missile strikes caused to homes and property – and he assumes the government would act to demand such compensation from Iraq.

He said yesterday's decision to lift emergency regulations was made partly because of the "social and economic price we have paid for those measures of caution in effect for the last six weeks.

"After several days in which Saddam Hussein has actively searched for a way to end the fighting, and finally found it in President Bush's speech last night, the chance is extremely slim that he would make a move that would immediately result in renewed warfare."

The Iraqi people will decide ultimately who rules Iraq and must now prove they want peace, he said.

Arens aide Danny Naveh had earlier announced on Army Radio the decision to lift the emergency.

"Yes," said Naveh, "this is the moment we've been waiting for, for several weeks now. The moment we can begin to breathe easily."

The timing was also fortuitous, Naveh said.

"Here on Purim we have an additional cause for joy that we can return to routine."

Most reserve troops mobilized because of war will be discharged shortly, IDF sources said last night.

Purim peace brings people out in Tel Aviv

HELEN KAYE and MICHAEL ROTEM
Jerusalem Post Reporter

After 43 nights of silent streets and empty sidewalks, Tel Aviv became a city of people again last night.

Happy people with smiling faces poured into "the city that never stops" to celebrate Purim, the cease-fire in the Gulf, and most of all their release from gas masks and sealed rooms.

They thronged the streets, the sidewalk cafes, the movie theaters and the restaurants. Some were costumed or masked, but most were not. Balloons floated in the air. Sidewalk vendors of foam spray, masks, and noisemakers traded briskly. Children ran, shouting and strollers were almost a pedestrian hazard. **(Pictures – Pages 2, 18; Purim in Jerusalem – Page 2)**

Just about everybody seemed in high spirits, relieved that it was all over, that they could walk freely without part of their minds listening for the air raid siren.

"It's the first time that we've been out at night since the war started," said Meira Behar, a Ramat Gan teacher out with her husband and their two small children. "We were here during the day, but came back again now, just to be out. It's wonderful not having to worry."

Mazal Mizrahi, out for the first time at night with her 10-month-old baby Dina and older daughter Ravit, said that she wouldn't have come out with the children if the emergency hadn't been lifted. "We're going back to living normally," she said thankfully.

About 5,000 celebrants, many of them children in colorful costumes, crowded Dizengoff Square. Police had to set up roadblocks in order to prevent huge traffic jams from forming in the area.

Down on the beach, an almost full moon shone on children playing in the sand, while family dogs pranced along the shore. While it seemed a little chilly for night strolls along the Tayelet promenade, here, too, whole families walked. Elderly residents who hadn't dared venture out for weeks were sitting on the plastic chairs facing the ocean and looking out over the moon-tipped waves.

A popular beachside restaurant opened last night for the first time since January 17, and although the place was nearly empty at around 7 p.m., manager Ephraim Raber expected a large crowd. "People have been sitting at home for weeks and now they want to go out," he said. "They'll start coming in at around 9:30 or so."

The restaurants in Little Tel Aviv around the old port and those in Old Jaffa reported a flood of reservations. Many of them planned to serve champagne on the house in honor of Purim and peace.

The municipal sanitation department will work overtime for the next couple of days picking up holiday litter, yet another sign of "back to normal."

Schools back to normal Sunday

Jerusalem Post Reporter

Schools return to normal schedules Sunday, as do most pre- and after-school programs that had been canceled because of the war.

Parents no longer have to help out in kindergartens and the lower grades, now that Haga (Civil Defense) regulations have been lifted, the Education Ministry spokesman said.

The ministry and the Histadrut's teachers union are considering a plan to have kindergarten teachers make up days lost during the war by keeping kindergartens open on Fridays. A decision is expected next week, the ministry spokesman said.

Package deal is signed
Page 7

THE JERUSALEM POST

Vol. LIX, No. 17755 Sunday, May 26, 1991 • Sivan 13, 5751 • Zul Kida 13, 1411 NIS 2.50 (Eilat NIS 2.10)

Homecoming; The aliya of Ethiopian Jewry
Pages 11 - 16

Ethiopian Jewry rescued

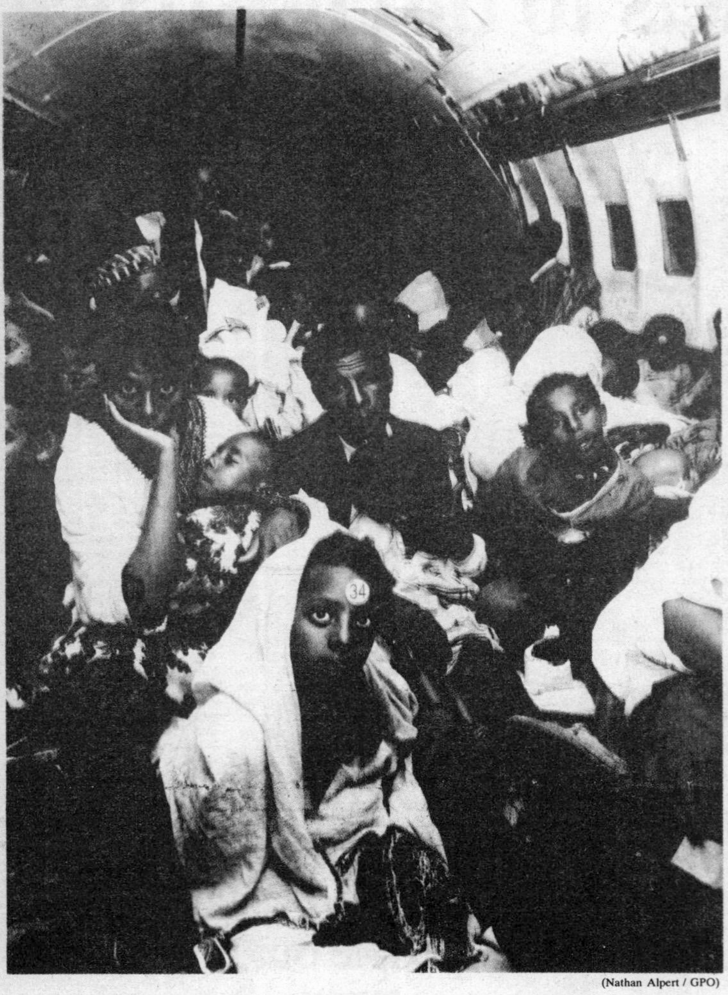

(Nathan Alpert / GPO)

On the way as the long wait ends

(Louis Rapoport)

14,400 are flown here in a 24-hour airlift

LOUIS RAPOPORT
Special Correspondent

Israel made history yesterday, completing a massive, lightning airlift that carried some 14,400 beleaguered Ethiopian Jews from Addis Ababa to their ancestral homeland in a breathtaking 24 hours.

"Operation Solomon," conducted by the IDF in coordination with the Jewish Agency, the Foreign Ministry, and other bodies, as well as the Ethiopian government, brought tears to the eyes of many of the thousands of Israelis who took part in the reunification of Ethiopian Jews with their 20,000 family members already in Israel.

"This is the reason why Israel exists," said one El Al ground-crew worker,as he helped an enfeebled old woman onto one of the hundreds of buses that transported new arrivals to 46 absorption centers and hotels around the country.

President Bush, who as vice president played a major role in the 1984-85 Operation Moses airlift of some 8,500 Ethiopian Jews from pestilential Sudanese refugee camps, made a personal and successful appeal to the Ethiopian government to fully support Israel's reunification effort.

The complex operation involved a total of 40 sorties of IAF and El Al planes of various sizes – including a reported world record 1,080 passengers on one Jumbo cargo flight – and at least one flight by Ethiopian Airlines.

There were no seats in the jumbos, and the new immigrants sat packed together in what seemed like a "human carpet." One army bus driver, commenting on the new world record, said: "You could never do it with pudgy Russians and Israelis, with five suitcases in each hand. They are thin, these Ethiopians."

The new immigrants were not allowed to bring anything more than a small bag of belongings, in order to maximize space and passenger capacity.

Leaders of the Ethiopian Jewish community reacted to the giant rescue operation joyfully, calling it "our biggest day." They offered prayers and thanks for the successful outcome of the operation, which was sanctioned by rabbinical authorities in the name of *pikuah nefesh*, the religious imperative that allows for violations of the Sabbath in order to save Jewish lives.

"We dreamed, we fought, we waited for this day to arrive," said Rahamim Elazar, a longtime community activist and director of Israel Radio's Amharic broadcasts. "I always believed Israel would save them, and it did. We applaud this country for its great heart."

Although planning for a rescue operation began over a year ago, when thousands of Ethiopian Jews from the strife-torn north flocked to the compound of the Israeli Embassy in Addis, Prime Minister Shamir did not give the final go-ahead for the Friday-Saturday operation until Tuesday, after Ethiopian dictator Mengistu Haile Mariam fled his country as rebels closed in on the capital, an informed source said.

The prime minister stood at the ramp of the first plane, an unmarked IAF Boeing 707, which arrived at 4.45 pm on Friday, and said: "I am happy. I have the feeling that we achieved our goal. We waited for many years. Now the whole Jewish community is coming. They are the remnant of a Jewish community that lasted for thousands of years, who are now coming back to their country...They have come back to their homeland."

Shamir, Defense Minister Moshe Arens, Foreign Minister David Levy, Housing Minister and Aliya Cabinet head Ariel Sharon, Chief of General Staff Lt.-Gen. Ehud Barak and other Israeli leaders warmly welcomed the first arrivals – many of whom were clad in traditional white *shamma* robes – as they descended shakily down the ramp.

Chief of General Staff Lt.-Gen. Ehud Barak briefs Prime Minister Shamir on Friday afternoon after greeting the first Ethiopian arrivals at Ben-Gurion Airport. (André Brutmann)

The Ethiopians descended into a forest of microphones and cameras, and a jostling crowd of smiling, almost-hysterical people, all of whom seemed to be carrying cellular telephones and walkie-talkies. The Ethiopians, in contrast, seemed stunned by the scope of events and even more quiet than usual.

The prime minister was briefed by Barak as they walked from the ramp. In whispered tones, Barak told him: "In half an hour, another plane will land, then 2,000 are coming, then another 5,000 from the embassy towards 7 [p.m.]. There's a curfew [in Addis] at seven, and our people are in talks in order to get around the curfew. If it's yes, then the airlift will continue all through the night, every half hour."

Barak told the prime minister that the reason the operation was delayed for at least two hours earlier in the day was that "thousands of others – non-Jews – want to come, and it has created difficulties."

Shamir asked, "is it possible to finish by morning?" Barak replied, "It's possible, but mistakes can happen."

The excitement was palpable among the hundreds of Agency workers, military personnel, dignitaries and airport workers – including dozens of veteran Ethiopian immigrants – who greeted the first plane with applause.

But as each subsequent flight came in – especially the four El Al jumbos crammed with their precious cargo, including several babies born either on the way to the planes or during the flights (**see separate story**) – elation, wonderment and waves of emotion swept through the crowds. "I have to keep pinching myself," said one escort from the Army Spokesman's Office. "It's like watching a scene from the Bible."

Air Force chief Avihu Bin-Nun, watching the newcomers disembark from the first flight, told a reporter: "We hope to keep the operation quiet because if the story breaks it could hurt. We have more planes ready than we need according to the rate they are coming out." Two hours later, the BBC broke the story of Israel's airlift, but censorship in Israei was not lifted until the operation was completed.

Former Knesset Speaker Shlomo Hillel, who for years worked assiduously on behalf of Ethiopian Jewry's aliya, said in a voice trembling with emotion: "I'm very excited. I had worried about their fate. Today is one of the biggest days for the Jews of the world and for Israel. It is what Israel is all about. We won't abandon Jews."

MK Geula Cohen, who was also among the crowd greeting the first arrivals, termed the aliya of Ethiopian Jewry "miraculous" and a sign that the Age of Redemption is at hand.

Throughout the next 24 hours, the emotional scenes were repeated over and over again. At one point, around 8.30 a.m. yesterday, three planes landed within five minutes of each other.

An hour after the operation ended yesterday, Israel Television interrupted regular programming with a television special, breaking the news in Israel of the airlift for the first time.

Arens said that both the Ethiopian and American governments had contributed to the "happy ending." Barak, hoarse and exhausted, smiled broadly and pronounced the effort "a great success."

In Ethiopia, the operation ran smoothly despite the holdup caused by thousands of non-Jewish Ethiopians who besieged the large embassy compound trying to "hitch a ride" out of the war-torn country.

Zimne Berhane, an Ethiopian-born Jewish Agency official who was the main organizer of the Ethiopian Jews living in the compound, said later that "all of Addis was there," and that the scene was reminiscent of Saigon in the days before its fall to the Communists. (**See separate story**)

Operations in Ethiopia were headed by Deputy Chief of Staff Amnon Shahak, who shuttled between the Israeli Embassy, which was reopened in Addis in 1989, and the airport some 8 km away. The scene at the Addis airport contrasted sharply with the scenes at Ben-Gurion Airport and at an air base somewhere in central Israel, where the IAF planes landed.

At the Addis airfield, whose outer perimeter was guarded by Ethiopian government troops, hundreds of Israeli personnel could be seen around the landing strips, where groups of Jews numbering from 400 to over 1,000 huddled on the tarmac to wait for their flight.

There was no panic whatsoever, in contrast to some of the scenes during Operation Moses. The Israelis in attendance, carrying blue-neon torches after dark fell, maintained order throughout the night. This reporter saw no Ethiopian soldiers around the Israeli planes.

None of the reporters who were allowed to fly to Ethiopia in order to accompany the immigrants reported hearing any shooting, despite the fact that rebel forces were within 18 km of the capital.

Reporters on the flights joined crew members, medical teams and others in handing out bottles of mineral water and a light meal to the Ethiopian Jews, many of whom asked for help in opening the bottles.

Former Prisoner of Zion Natan Sharansky, one of the reporters on a flight, was asked by a Ha'aretz reporter later if he had been recognized. Sharansky replied, "They recognized me as one of the people who handed out bottles of water – one of the crew."

One seasoned reporter, who couldn't help periodically bursting out in tears, said later that he had never seen such warmth and fraternity among the hundreds of sabras involved in the operation. "The singing and clapping and pure joy was the kind of thing that makes you forget about all the trials of living in this country," he said.

Israelis of Yemenite extraction seemed to have a particular affinity for the new immigrants, harking back to the traditional close links between Ethiopia and Yemen, a few kilometers across the Gate of Tears at the mouth of the Red Sea.

"My grandparents and parents always talked about 1950 and the Magic Carpet," said one woman soldier, Hila Ben-Shalom, referring to the airlift of Yemenite Jewry to Israel. "Now I know what they were feeling. I am absolutely overwhelmed."

Another constant refrain, heard from many quarters, was that we were watching the wheels of history, turning very fast, right before our eyes. "History," exclaimed Lt.-Col. Ra'anan Gissin. "You see the greatness of Israel."

Toward the end of what turned out to be a transcendental day for thousands of Israelis and new Israelis, two veteran Ethiopian immigrants, young women who were among the hundreds of volunteers lending a hand, sat on the curb of a street a few hundred meters from the IAF airfield. "Thank God," said Pennina Oshuter. "We thank God," said Desta Usef. "We thank God for Israel."

Foreign Minister David Levy said last night that between 1,500 and 2,000 Jews still remain in Ethiopia, and said that Israel would persist until all had been brought to Israel.

The plan was devised months ago

BRADLEY BURSTON, Post Defense Reporter

The Air Force plan for evacuating the Ethiopian Jewry was outlined months ago, IAF commanders revealed last night, adding that changes and improvisations were executed throughout the mission.

In a meeting with military correspondents, overall mission commander Deputy Chief of General Staff Maj.-Gen. Amnon Shahak disclosed that as late as the day before the airlift began, planners had yet to receive answers to such critical questions as whether olim would be allowed to travel the streets of Addis Ababa despite the nightly curfew, or the extent to which Israeli planes could use the small airport's single take-off runway. (Full report, Page 12)

Shamir thanks Bush for help; U.S. requests 'no settling in the areas'

ALLISON KAPLAN
Jerusalem Post Correspondent

WASHINGTON – Prime Minister Shamir telephoned President Bush Friday morning to thank him for his role in persuading the Ethiopian government to permit the Jews to leave, White House officials said Friday as they publicly announced the start of the airlift, only hours after it had begun.

State Department officials meanwhile confirmed that Israel had been asked not to settle the new arrivals over the Green Line.

White House spokesman Marlin Fitzwater said that that the U.S. was "delighted" with the airlift, and expressed appreciation towards acting president Tesfaye Gebre-Kidan for allowing the exodus to take place.

"We understand that the Ethiopian decision to allow the Falashas to depart the country was taken in response to a letter from President Bush on May 22," Fitzwater said.

The Bush letter, asking the new president of Ethiopia to allow the massive airlift to take place, is viewed by American and Israeli officials as the key element in moving the operation forward.

It was a follow-up letter to the message that Bush had sent to former President Mengistu Haile Mariam at the end of April, which had been delivered by former Minnesota Senator Rudy Boschwitz.

Boschwitz traveled to Ethiopia on April 26 as an emissary from Bush, to press Mengistu to allow the Jews to emigrate, and to offer U.S. mediation between the government and the rebels.

White House officials said that Shamir telephoned Bush on Friday to thank him for his role in pushing the Ethiopian government to permit the Jews to leave. Shamir spoke with the president while he was on board his airplane heading for his vacation home in Kennebunkport, Maine.

"The prime minister and the president also discussed the Mideast peace process. The prime minister expressed his appreciation for Secretary Baker's efforts in the Mideast and said he hoped the peace process

(Continued on Back Page)

'Magnificent example of Zionism in action'

Jerusalem Post Reporter

President Herzog yesterday said that Israel had used the best resources at its disposal to bring the remnants of the Ethiopian Jewish community to the Promised Land.

The operation, he said, was a magnificent example of Zionism in action, demonstrating the principles for which the state was created.

Cliffhanger countdown that ended at dawn

ABRAHAM RABINOVICH

The countdown for the evacuation began in Addis Ababa at 7 p.m. Thursday, when members of "the committee" were assembled in the Israeli embassy to be told that after years of waiting the operation would begin at dawn.

The committee consisted of local Ethiopian Jews who each served as liaison with 30 families. They were to keep the secret through the night and at 5:30 a.m. begin making their rounds. The Jews were to be told to leave all their possessions and make for the embassy with only the clothes on their backs.

Final agreement on the evacuation had been received from the Ethiopian government at noon Thursay, and Israeli and Ethiopian officials met through the afternoon to work out details, including procedures for the Israeli planes to land.

On Friday morning, Zimna Berhane, a veteran Ethiopian immigrant serving as a senior coordinator for the Israeli effort in Addis Ababa, was at the gate to the embassy compound when the Jews began to arrive. The initial trickle quickly became a flood, as Jews streamed in from the four neighborhoods in which they had been living in rented quarters.

"It looked like the exodus from Egypt," said Berhane yesterday in his Jerusalem home.

Unlike that exodus, however, it soon became apparent that the local population was eager to join this one. Non-Jewish Ethiopians, through whose neighborhoods the Jews passed, joined them en masse in the hope that they too could escape.

"They are all afraid of terrible massacres,"- said Berhane. "Not from the rebels, but from the bloodletting that would come with general chaos. There are robbers and general rabble. The non-Jews just want to get out, and they don't care if it's Israel or anywhere else."

The guards at the embassy gate, including local policemen, were periodically overwhelmed by the mass of people struggling to get in, and the gate had to be shut from time to time.

Jews were permitted entry into the compound when the head of the household flashed an identity card which also listed other members of his family. Only a cursory glance could be devoted by the guards at the main gate, but those people permitted in were examined more closely at check points inside the compound. "We found dozens of non-Jewish infiltrators and we ejected them."

(Continued on Back Page)

26951314

Yuppie truckies
Motoring / Page 5

THE JERUSALEM POST
Vol. LIX, No. 17775 Tuesday, June 18, 1991 • Tamuz 6, 5751 • Zul Hijja 6, 1411 NIS 2.50 (Eilat NIS 2.10)

The vanishing 'White Jews' of Cochin
Jewish World / Page 8

Eight no-confidence moves beaten

Chaos in Knesset as Peretz again blasts kibbutzim

DAN IZENBERG

The government easily survived eight opposition no-confidence motions yesterday, during a four-and-a-half hour debate which erupted into pandemonium during a speech by Absorption Minister Yitzhak Peretz.

The motions, which were all defeated by 59 votes to 49, included criticism of the government for its alleged failure to advance the peace process and the administrative flaws revealed in the state comptroller's report.

But these issues were overshadowed by an attack on Peretz for his comments during a televised debate last week in which he accused the kibbutzim of tearing Sephardi immigrants away from their faith during the mass aliya of the 1950s.

During an emotional address to the plenum, which began on a mildly conciliatory note, but drew loud shouts of anger and some ridicule from the opposition benches, Peretz, beads of sweat appearing on his forehead, suddenly pointed his finger at the Labor Party benches and shouted: "For the last half hour they have been trying to shut me up. They talk high and mightily about democracy but act like dictators. All day long you say nasty things about the religious."

Then, in a voice which cracked with emotion, he shouted: "We will not be intimidated by you. The kibbutzim did carry out a campaign of *shmad*." Peretz explained that the word originated in the Talmud and "does not mean conversion to another faith; it means tearing out the Tora and mitzvot from a Jew."

Peretz became so upset that Communications Minister Rafael Pinhasi (Shas) went up to the podium to calm him down.

Peretz said his opposition to sending immigrants from Ethiopia to secular kibbutzim stemmed from his own experiences 30 years ago when he visited Sephardi Jews who had been sent to such kibbutzim. "I saw their tears and pain," he said. "I heard things that broke my heart. Young girls told me, with eyes red from crying, how they had been forced to wear very short shorts and sleeveless blouses. There was nothing I could do."

At this point, opposition members, who had earlier shouted angrily at Peretz, broke out in laughter and the minister became increasingly agitated.

The shouting on both sides continued until Speaker Shevah Weiss called a five-minute recess. The break did little good, however, and

(Continued on Back Page)

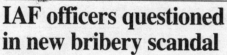

Finance Minister Yitzhak Moda'i (center) with traffic model at Ramle District Police headquarters yesterday after announcing a new traffic police corps. Moda'i and Police Inspector-General Ya'acov Terner (left) agreed to the hiring of 150 patrolmen for the force – to operate as an experiment for 21 months – and to bolster the existing traffic branch with an additional 28 patrolcars, nine motorcycles and two helicopters. The program will cost about NIS 39 million. 'Aim of the new traffic police is not to fight road accidents but to prevent them,' Moda'i said. At right is Otniel Schneller, head of the Transport Ministry's road safety administration. (Text: Michael Rotem; photo: Israel Sun)

South Africa buries apartheid after 41 years

Compiled from News Agencies

CAPE TOWN – South Africa's Parliament yesterday abolished the last major apartheid law in an overwhelming vote that ends the racial classification of that country's citizens.

The repeal of the Population Registration Act was a milestone in the dismantling of apartheid. But the action did not address the biggest race reform still confronting South Africa: negotiating a new constitution that will give Blacks the vote. **(Related story on Page 3)**

The Population Registration Act of 1950 classified citizens as Black, White, Colored (mixed-race) or Asian and served as the foundation of virtually all apartheid measures.

"It was an act of racial bigotry and caused untold suffering and humiliation," said Barney Desai, spokesman for the Pan African Congress, a militant anti-apartheid group. "I'm not going to say, 'Hooray.' But in essence, one is saying goodbye to a bad dream."

Racial classification determined where a person could live, which schools one could attend, which public toilets one could use and which cemeteries one was buried in.

Many racial restrictions already have been removed by President F.W. de Klerk, but the lives of most Blacks have not been radically changed by his reforms.

Of the 308 members in the three-chamber Parliament, only the 38 members of the pro-apartheid Conservative Party voted against scrapping the Population Registration Act.

Parliament approved a replacement measure that ends all new race classifications and removes race references that remained in other laws. But people already racially classified will remain so until a new non-racial constitution is negotiated.

Since coming to power in 1989, de Klerk has moved swiftly to end statutory discrimination. Neighborhoods, hospitals, property ownership, parks, beaches and many other facilities have been legally desegregated.

Critics note that some reforms have loopholes allowing Whites to retain segregation if they wish. For example, White public schools may now be integrated, but only if 72 percent of White parents at a school vote in favor of accepting children of other races. About 100 schools in Johannesburg, Cape Town and Durban – including the country's Jewish day schools – have began accepting Black students, but the vast majority remain segregated.

The repeal of the Population Registration Act is likely to bring a further easing of foreign sanctions, which have been steadily crumbling over the past year in response to de Klerk's reforms.

De Klerk says he is ready to begin Black-White talks on a new constitution that will give the 30 million Blacks equal voting rights.

But the African National Congress and other anti-apartheid groups say the government must first free all political prisoners and do more to end violence in Black townships. About 4,000 Blacks have been killed in violence during the last year and a half. The ANC has repeatedly claimed de Klerk has not done enough to end the violence, mainly between supporters of the ANC and the Zulu-based Inkatha Freedom Party.

Only last week, Parliament member Jac Rabie told the mixed-race chamber of Parliament that nearly everyone in his family was classified differently. Rabie himself was once classified Asian, but is now officially Colored.

The new law "means my white uncles and I are now the same," he said yesterday.

Parliament has separate chambers for whites, Coloreds and Asians while Blacks, who are a majority of the population, are excluded.

Pro-apartheid Conservative Willem Botha said the Population Registration Act was one of the country's best laws and was repealed because the governing National Party "has become ashamed to be White."

But Tony Leon of the anti-apartheid Democratic Party said, "Those of us who were never part of that humiliation can only say thank God it's coming to an end."

The United States is pleased with South Africa's repeal of the last legal pillar of apartheid but is still not ready to lift its economic sanctions against Pretoria, administration officials said on Monday.

Officials said South Africa had now satisfied four of the five conditions laid down by Congress in 1986 legislation for the lifting of sanctions.

South Africa's white-dominated parliament voted in Cape Town earlier on Monday to end race classification, the legal foundation of apartheid since 1950.

The officials said the Bush administration was still studying South Africa's claim to have fulfilled Con-

(Continued on Back Page)

(AFP)

De Klerk clutches his speech on his way to Parliament yesterday.

Interview with Nelson Mandela on Page 5

IAF officers questioned in new bribery scandal

BRADLEY BURSTON and MICHAEL ROTEM

Air Force procurement procedures, already tightened in the wake of the Dotan affair, are to become even more stringent following revelations of a new bribery scandal, military sources indicated yesterday.

Military Police detectives have questioned an IAF colonel and a lieutenant-colonel on suspicion of accepting bribes from importers of defense hardware, the sources said. They were released on bail, a police spokesman said.

Because the case has no apparent tie to the multi-million dollar Dotan bribery and embezzlement scandal, it has raised fears that additional financial irregularities may be found in the procurement apparatus.

The affair is not connected with the Rami Dotan affair – in which the former IAF procurement chief was convicted of running a massive procurement fraud and bribery scheme – but was discovered during Dotan's interrogation, police sources said yesterday.

The main suspect is an Israeli agent of a U.S. firm which sells spare parts for fighter planes. The suspects gave bribes, described by police as "relatively small," to IAF officers and a Defense Ministry official to encourage them to buy spare parts from them, and gained an unfair advantage in the public tenders for the supplying parts to the IAF.

"This new affair is not as big as the Dotan affair, but digging into the Dotan case was like opening a Pandora's box," a police source participating in the new investigation said in an interview yesterday. "These suspects [may have given] small sums and petty objects as bribes. But what bothers us [most] is the fact that the Dotan affair was not an isolated incident in the IAF as we'd wanted to believe."

Already under strong pressure from Chief of General Staff Lt.-Gen. Ehud Barak, Air Force Commander Maj.-Gen Avihu Bin-Nun has issued strict orders to uncover and root out other suspicious procurement-related activities.

Longstanding policies of according IAF arms procurement specialists wide latitude in decision-making, minimal supervision and tacit backing by the defense apparatus have been blamed by General Staff

(Continued on Back Page)

Comptroller asked to probe war compensation funds

ASHER WALLFISH

The State Audit Committee asked the state comptroller yesterday to probe allegedly chaotic and arbitrary mismanagement of funds set up during the Gulf war to compensate victims of Scud missile attacks.

The Savyon Local Council was the only municipal body of the six involved which had complied with a May 8 request by committee chairman David Libai to submit a written statement listing donors, contributions and expenditures, Libai complained in a committee meeting.

"Millions of dollars are still lying untouched in the funds' bank accounts, while the Scud victims are struggling vainly to win their rightful compensation," Libai said.

Dov Staub, director of the Treasury's property tax and compensation fund, revealed that his fund was cleaned out as a result of war damage payments, was deep in the red and had to take a loan from the Treasury.

"We paid the compensation," Staub said. "Since the funds managed by the local councils have money which they don't know what to do with, they should replenish the property tax and compensation fund."

Most of the $9.5 million contributed to the Tel Aviv Foundation – an all-purpose independent philanthropic organization – is to be spent on improving the Ezra and Hatikva quarters, the hardest hit in Tel Aviv, a local official told the committee.

"We spent $300,000 [of the contributions] on compensating Scud victims. The fate of the rest of the money will be determined by a subcommittee of the city council," foundation director Hanan Ben-Yehuda said.

Committee members reacted negatively to Ben-Yehuda's statement, but were assured by deputy city manager Meir Doron that most of the donations would go to reconstruct Ezra and Hatikva, by making up the difference between what the Treasury's fund paid out and costs.

Ramat Gan spent NIS 3.5m. of the NIS 4.5m. contributed for repairs and compensation to bombed out residents, mayor Zvi Bar reported.

Representatives from Haifa and Petah Tikva reported that they had gotten minor donations. A representative from the Azor City Council said there was missile damage in his town, but no donations came in.

Ramat Gan treasurer Yigal Sa'adya, warned that fund donors would never give another penny if their names were made public, because they feared being swamped with additional requests. Libai retorted that all he need do was send their names and other details confidentially to

(Continued on Back Page)

'Understandings' on Palestinians

JONATHAN SCHACHTER

NEW YORK – Foreign Minister David Levy has arrived at "understandings" with Secretary of State James Baker on the status of a Palestinian delegation to a regional peace conference, *The Jerusalem Post* has learned.

"There are understandings between the U.S. and Israel that would help overcome this obstacle," an aide to Levy said. However, the aide added, no details could be disclosed.

While nothing has been finalized, the aide said, Levy would bring the ideas back to Jerusalem for discussion by the government when he returns this afternoon.

Baker and Prime Minister Shamir had reportedly reached a compromise on the composition of the Palestinian delegation to the talks during Baker's last visit to Jerusalem, but in a letter to President Bush two weeks ago, Shamir wrote that Israel would have to be allowed veto power on the composition of the delegation.

The issue became a source of tension between the administration and Israel in subsequent days, and formed the basis of the frustrations

(Continued on Back Page)

Hussein picks Masri as PM

AMMAN (Reuter) – King Hussein yesterday asked Foreign Minister Taher Masri to form a new government, and accepted the resignation of Prime Minister Mudar Badran, official sources said.

Political sources said that by appointing a moderate of Palestinian origin, Hussein was signalling his commitment to the U.S.-led Middle East peace initiative and to leading the country towards greater democracy.

Masri has been foreign minister for more than five years in three different governments. Badran took office in December 1990, a month after Jordan's first general election in more than two decades.

Masri, who will be the first prime minister of Palestinian origin in 20 years, comes from a wealthy and politically-powerful family from Nablus, where he was born in 1942.

His appointment comes a week after King Hussein endorsed a national charter which paves the way for multi-party democracy after more than three decades of autocratic rule.

The peace process, in which Jordan is a key player, also made the change of government necessary, analysts said.

Desperate Syrian Jews 'fear for their lives'

BILL HUTMAN

Syrian Jews are living in "fear for their lives," and are desperate to leave the country, according to reliable reports by Syrian immigrant leaders yesterday.

The reports were released after the immigrant leaders met with Prime Minister Yitzhak Shamir, and received approval for going public with the story they said they have been forced to keep under wraps for years.

"We have decided to be silent no longer and make our voice heard so the entire world will know the shocking story of what is happening to the Jews of Syria," said Yosef Kalash, chairman of the Organization of Syrian Immigrants.

Some 3,000 of the 4,000 Syrian Jews live in a small Damascus "ghetto," where the Syrian authorities maintain a rule of terror, Kalash said.

Their situation, while never good, has deteriorated recently, with reports of kidnappings, torture, and destruction of property, Kalash told reporters in the office of Jewish Agency Absorption Department head Uri Gordon.

In order to ensure the Jews do not try to escape, the authorities have taken over apartments in the quarter and given them to non-Jews, in particular Palestinians, who keep a close watch on the Jews.

"We must not keep quiet anymore about what is going on, because when we are quiet it only make the Syrians think they can do what they want," Kalash said.

He maintained that the recent video footage from Damascus shown on Israel Television was staged, and hid the truth about how the Jews of Syria lived.

"The time has come to begin the public struggle for the release of the 4,000 Jews remaining in Syria," Gordon said. He called on U.S. to use its influence on Syria to secure the Jews release, and added that a UN delegation should be sent to investigate the situation.

Foreign Minister David Levy reportedly raised the issue of Syrian Jewry during his recent talks in Washington with Secretary of State James Baker.

Some 13 Jews are presently being held in Syrian jails for trying to flee the country, Kalash said. Jews who have been jailed before for trying to escape have been released, but only after having been beaten and in at least one case permanently disabled, he added.

One of the Jewish quarter's main synagogues was destroyed recently by the Syrian authorities, according to Kalash.

The authorities have also built a headquarters in the quarter to keep a close watch on the Jews living there, and in other parts of the country. Jews who have been brought into the headquarters for questioning have been beaten and tortured, according to Kalash. He accused the recently appointed official who is in charge of the Jews, Amid Isa el-Asad – reportedly a general in the Syrian army – of being more brutal then any of his predecessors.

With the prime minister's approval, the Organization of Syrian Immigrants plans to send a delegation to the U.S. to raise interest there in the fate of the Jews remaining in Syria, Kalash said.

18661314

$
DM
£
Tamir Cohen (Jacobsohn)

AT THE FIRST INTERNATIONAL
YOU CALL THE TUNE – WE PROVIDE THE HARMONY!

The First International Bank has consistently pioneered unconventional and competitive personal banking services. At First International, it's the customer who calls the tune.

If you are a foreign resident, tourist, new immigrant or temporary resident – you have the right to hold a tax-free foreign currency account. Go where the smart money goes. Go First International.

■ Best interest rates
■ Any combination of currencies: $, DM, SF, Y, etc.
■ Flexible terms: A broad range of amounts and maturities at fixed or floating interest rates, with automatic renewals.

■ Convenient opening hours: Most branches are open daily until 2 p.m. (till 12:00 on Fridays and holiday eves) and from 4-7 p.m. on Mondays and Wednesdays.
■ Our experts will provide you with all the information about our confidential tax-free foreign currency accounts.

When you come to the First International, you call the tune and we provide the harmony.
Stop into any of our 84 friendly branches – a warm welcome awaits you.

Main Branches:
Jerusalem – 10, Hillel St.
Tel Aviv – 9, Ahad Ha'am St.
Haifa – 3, Habankim St.

THE EVER EXCEPTIONAL THE FIRST INTERNATIONAL BANK.

'Go Galilee' is new tourist cry
Page 5

THE JERUSALEM POST

U.S. Indians will picket World Series
Sport/Page 9

Vol. LIX, No. 17876 Sunday, October 20, 1991 • Heshvan 12, 5752 • Rabi Tani 12, 1412 NIS 2.70 (Eilat NIS 2.30)

Moscow restores ties with Jerusalem

DAVID MAKOVSKY

The Soviet Union have formally restored full diplomatic relations 24 years after severing them, thereby ending an era of bitter enmity between the two countries.

The brief signing ceremony at the Foreign Ministry in Jerusalem Friday came just an hour before Foreign Minister Boris Pankin joined Secretary of State James Baker in formally issuing invitations to the Middle East peace conference. The two had met earlier in the day.

After the invitations were issued, Pankin spoke of a more evenhanded Soviet approach to the Middle East at a joint press conference with Baker. "In the past, the Soviet Union tended to sort of side with the Palestinians and the Arab states, while the U.S. sided with Israel, and this did not bring any tangible fruit.

"The new approach now is certainly not to have any proteges and support their positions no matter what they say and no matter how legitimate they may be."

Foreign Minister David Levy hailed the restoration of ties. "Clearly, this ... brings us to a more open dialog, so that they hear Israeli positions directly, face-to-face."

He called the prolonged rupture an "historic mistake" by the Soviets.

The restoration of relations fulfilled Israel's condition that Moscow take such a step before assuming the conference co-chairmanship. It was also the first diplomatic payoff for Prime Minister Shamir's agreement to attend the conference.

Israeli sources said the two-hour delay in holding the ceremony was due to Pankin's wish to confer with Baker to make sure Israel had agreed to attend the conference. The Soviets had indicated that they would not renew ties unless Israel did so.

According to the formal statement, the two countries "have decided to restore their diplomatic relations as of the day of issuance of this joint statement." They will exchange ambassadors and conduct relations "on the basis of equality, mutual respect for sovereignty and non-interference in each other's domestic affairs."

Such a resumption "fully serves the interests of a comprehensive settlement in the Middle East, the establishment of a lasting peace and stability in this region, and further development of international cooperation."

Aryeh Levin, now consul-general in Moscow, will become Israel's new ambassador. Levy noted that the two countries had established a joint committee on economic cooperation that would meet soon in Moscow and Jerusalem.

Foreign Ministry assistant director-general for Eastern Europe, Yosef Govrin, who was assigned to the Israeli embassy in Moscow when the Israeli flag was lowered in 1967, attended the signing ceremony.

While here, Pankin held two rounds of talks with Palestinians. On Thursday night, he met with three Palestinian activists in an East Jerusalem hotel. The Palestinians told reporters after the two-hour meeting they had discussed the composition of a Palestinian delegation to the peace talks. Pankin said they talked about preparations for the conference.

On Friday, Pankin met with an expanded delegation, including hard-liners who oppose the peace process, and also held two rounds of talks with Baker, one unscheduled.

After jointly announcing the peace conference with Baker, Pankin left to continue a six-day regional tour. Levy said that he hoped that during his trip to Damascus, Pankin would convince Syria to reverse its opposition to joining multilateral talks on such regional issues as arms control and water. Pankin is also visiting Amman and Cairo.

Following is the text of the joint statement issued by Pankin and Levy:

In the interest of the two nations, the Union of Soviet Socialist Republics and the State of Israel have decided to restore their diplomatic relations as of the day of the issuance of this joint statement and exchange diplomatic representations at the level of embassies.

The two sides state their readiness to maintain their bilateral relations in accordance with the United Nations charter, the rules of international law, and on the basis of according mutual respect for sovereignty and noninterference in each other's domestic affairs.

The two sides firmly believe that the reestablishment of full diplomatic relations between the USSR and the State of Israel fully serves the interests of a comprehensive settlement in the Middle East, the establishment of a lasting peace and stability in this region and a further development of international cooperation.

Jerusalem, October 18, 1991.

Foreign Minister David Levy toasts the restoration of ties between Israel and Moscow with Soviet Foreign Minister Boris Pankin on Friday following a signing ceremony at the Foreign Ministry in Jerusalem. (Isaac Harari)

Shamir expected to win vote for talks with Arabs

Bush, Gorbachev to open parley in Madrid, Oct. 30

DAVID MAKOVSKY

The cabinet is expected to begin a two-part session on Israel's attendance at the Middle East peace conference today. It is expected to back Prime Minister Shamir's recommendation to attend the conference at the Royal Palace in Madrid on October 30.

In an historic Friday afternoon joint statement here, Secretary of State James Baker and Soviet Foreign Minister Boris Pankin, whose countries are co-chairing the conference, formally announced the convening.

At the White House, a spokesman announced that Presidents Bush and Gorbachev would give greetings at the conference opening.

Arriving in Madrid from Israel, Baker told a press conference that "we are hopeful there will indeed be this conference in Madrid, but we do not take anything for granted and are not making any assumptions."

Asked why Madrid had been chosen for the conference, Baker said Spain had good relations with all the countries invited and extensive connections throughout the Middle East.

"We could not have found anywhere a more cooperative spirit and a more willing attitude," Baker said, thanking Prime Minister Felipe Gonzalez for taking on "this rather large responsibility."

In Jerusalem, an official in the Prime Minister's Office said last night that "we don't expect the debate on the conference to end at the regular Sunday cabinet meeting. The prime minister wants every cabinet minister to be able to voice his opinion and this takes time. So a special cabinet session will be held on Wednesday, and then we definitely expect a majority to approve Shamir's recommendation to attend the conference."

The second cabinet session is set for Wednesday because Shamir will be leaving tomorrow for a 24-hour visit to Strasbourg, France, where he has long been scheduled to address the European Parliament.

All parties are expected to give their formal reply to the conference invitations by midnight on Wednesday. Israel received its invitation from U.S. Ambassador William Brown, and U.S. Consul-General Molly Williamson delivered the Palestinian invitation to Faisal Husseini's home in East Jerusalem yesterday.

The opening ceremony is expected to take up to three days. The European Community will send a delegate, and both the UN and the Gulf Cooperation Council will send observers.

Thereafter, direct bilateral talks will begin between Israel and Syria, Israel and the joint Jordanian/Palestinian delegation, and Israel and Lebanon.

Multilateral talks dealing with regional issues such as water and arms control, which are to include Gulf states, are to commence within two weeks of the opening ceremony. Syria, however, has yet to say it will attend these discussions.

The issuance of invitations culminated eight months of post-Gulf war diplomacy and eight trips to the region by Baker.

At his joint news conference with Pankin, Baker said:

"The negotiating process that we are seeking to launch with this invitation holds the hope of a new era in the Middle East: The hope of an era marked by acceptance and not by rejection, the hope of an era marked by dialog and not by violence, the hope of an era marked by cooperation and not by conflict, and the hope of an era marked by hope itself, and not despair."

"The road to peace will not be simple. To the contrary, it will be extremely difficult, with many problems, many hitches and probably many interruptions along the way. Old suspicions will not disappear quickly; the gaps are real, and the gaps will not be easily overcome."

Asked if he would call on Israel to freeze settlements while the conference is meeting, Baker replied: "... we have never made that request of the Israeli government. We have suggested a suspension of settlement activity in exchange for a

(Continued on Page 2)

Palestinians stay mum on list of 14 delegates

DAN IZENBERG

Faisal Husseini yesterday delivered the final list of 14 proposed Palestinian delegates to the regional peace conference to the U.S. consul-general in Jerusalem.

Husseini received an invitation on behalf of the Palestinians to join the conference and a letter of assurance on issues relating to the talks, Palestinian and American sources said yesterday.

Palestinian leaders met yesterday to draft the final list of delegates, but refused to divulge the identities of the 14 – seven delegates and seven alternates – who will form the Palestinian portion of the joint delegation with Jordan.

The Associated Press, quoting a source close to the talks, said the delegation would be headed by 71-year-old Dr. Haider Abdul-Shafi, a Gaza Strip physician. Abdul-Shafi is regarded as a supporter of the PLO's mainstream Fatah faction headed by Yasser Arafat. He was a member of the PLO's first executive committee in 1964 and was expelled to Sinai by Israel in 1967, but later allowed to return.

A Palestinian reporter from Gaza who spoke to Abdul-Shafi yesterday evening quoted him as saying "it is very possible" he would head the delegation.

Israel Radio, meanwhile, named Radwan Abu Ayash, former head of the Arab Journalists' Association, and Samich Kanaan of Nablus, one of the prisoners released in exchange for three Israeli POWs in

(Continued on Page 2)

Shamir expects to overcome opposition of Sharon, right-wing

No immediate threat to cabinet

MICHAL YUDELMAN

The government is bracing itself for fierce opposition to the peace conference from Housing Minister Ariel Sharon and the right-wing parties at the cabinet meeting today, where Prime Minister Shamir intends to recommend that Israel go to Madrid.

Most ministers, however, are expected to support Shamir, and there is no immediate threat to the coalition's integrity.

Despite their increasing protests against the conference, Tzomet and Moledet do not intend to withdraw from the government at this stage. If Tehiya – which is torn between those in favor of immediate withdrawal and those who support remaining in the government – quits alone, the coalition will still have a majority.

A coalition crisis which might topple the government is only expected after the opening of the conference, when the negotiations over territorial concessions begin.

Science Minister Yuval Ne'eman (Tehiya), Moledet's Minister Rehavam Ze'evi and Agriculture Minister Rafael Eitan (Tzomet) met Shamir on Friday and expressed their objection to the conference.

Ze'evi said after the meeting that "I pray we will not get to this conference, which is a trap posing many dangers to our very existence in the land of our fathers." However, the three ministers were united in their decision to remain in the government until it begins negotiating on territorial issues or on autonomy.

Shamir does not intend to react to Sharon's demand yesterday that the prime minister resign. Sources close to Shamir told *The Jerusalem Post* that this is not the first time that Sharon has attacked Shamir, who is not expected to dismiss the errant minister so as not to aggravate the looming crisis.

An internal rift, meanwhile, is threatening Tehiya, whose central committee is to convene in an atmosphere of crisis this afternoon to decide on the date of the party's withdrawal from the government. The opposing forces backing the two sides – deputy minister Geula Cohen and party chairman Ne'eman – appear almost balanced at this point, and the final decision will depend on no more than a few votes, Tehiya sources said.

Cohen, spearheading those demanding to bolt the government immediately, charged Shamir and Foreign Minister David Levy with "selling us to the PLO" and threatened to wage a "world war" to save the territories.

"Baker drove Levy to submission, Levy defeated Shamir and Israel has fallen into the conference-trap, which will turn into the sacrificial altar to which we will all be bound. But the responsibility will not rest only with Shamir and Levy, who sold us to the PLO, but with Tehiya, Moledet and Tzomet unless they quit the government immediately. Judea, Samaria and Gaza are not Sinai, Jerusalem is not Yamit, and we, the trustees of Eretz Yisrael, will wage a world war on them," Cohen said.

Cohen is supported by MK Elyakim Ha'etzni, party secretary-general Danny Dayan, Benny Katsover and Daniela Weiss.

Ne'eman will insist at the meeting

(Continued on Page 2)

Bush hails potential for 'true peace'

ALLISON KAPLAN

WASHINGTON – President Bush personally welcomed the issuance of peace conference invitations, saying that the "historic gathering" that he and President Gorbachev are opening will have "the potential to bring true peace and security to the peoples of the area."

"As the invitation makes clear, the objective of the effort is nothing less than a just, lasting and comprehensive settlement of the Arab-Israeli conflict," Bush said in a statement released on Friday, shortly after Secretary of State James Baker and Soviet Foreign Minister Boris Pankin announced that the invitations were being sent out.

Although Bush's personal stake in the success of the conference is significant, his presence will be extremely brief, according to White House officials. After Bush and Gorbachev arrive in Madrid on Oct. 29, they will meet to discuss nuclear disarmament and other bilateral topics, including American aid to the Soviet Union, before opening the ceremonial phase of the talks on Oct. 30.

Bush is set to return to the U.S. later on the same day in order to help kick off his 1992 re-election campaign with a massive fund-raiser set the following day in Houston.

Administration officials described the so-called "mini-summit" as "informal," though it will be their first meeting since the attempted coup against Gorbachev. The administration is playing down the meeting, not wanting it to overshadow the peace conference.

Bush has reportedly been planning for a long time to personally participate in the opening, despite the political risks he faces if he is identified with a failure. As one administration official told the *Washington Post,* even if the conference

(Continued on Page 2)

Baker, Pankin optimistic about talks, but warn of difficult path

ASHER WALLFISH

U.S. Secretary of State James Baker said Friday that the joint U.S.-Soviet invitation to the peace conference "offers the peoples in this region a pathway to ending an era of confrontation and it offers a basis for a new future."

At a joint news conference with Soviet Foreign Minister Boris Pankin at the King David Hotel in the late afternoon, his face often breaking into a satisfied smile, Baker said "the road to peace ... will not be simple. To the contrary, it will be extremely difficult with many problems, many hitches and probably many interruptions along the way.

"Old suspicions will not disappear quickly," he continued. "The gaps are real and ... will not be easily overcome ... We will be taking one more step forward toward achieving the peace and security that the peoples of the Middle East have so long been denied.

"I hope and believe that the government of Israel, when the matter is presented to them, will decide to continue on their current course and move forward for peace, the peace Israel deserves so much.

"Today is an important day and I think this is an important moment. An American secretary of state and a Soviet foreign minister are together in Jerusalem for the first time in history. What's more, the Soviet Union has restored full relations with Israel after a break of 24 years."

The conference in Madrid, he stressed, is to be followed dy direct negotiations designed to achieve real peace.

Baker said: "We have witnessed new beginnings in other parts of the world. The negotiating process that we are seeking to launch with this invitation holds the hope of a new era in the Middle East. The hope of an era marked by dialog and not by violence, the hope of an era marked by cooperation and not by conflict, and the hope of an era marked by hope itself and not despair."

Pankin, presenting a dour expression, said, "The stage that we have now come to represents a very important turning point for the entire situation in the Middle East. We made an important contribution to the convening of this conference in our capacity as future co-chairmen.

"We are convinced that history is now holding out an opportunity that we must not pass up."

Referring to the restoration of full diplomatic relations, Pankin said, "This is a logical and natural step which is fully consistent with current reality. This step does not represent a present that we are making to each other, or a new challenge."

When Baker and Pankin met Friday morning, they and their aides revealed nothing of the conversation.

Upbeat Arab reaction to invitations

AMMAN (AP) – Most Arab governments reacted positively to the joint U.S.-Soviet invitation to a Middle East peace conference.

Jordan, Friday, accepted the invitation to the peace conference it had received from Presidents Bush and Gorbachev.

In Cairo, President Hosni Mubarak, who also accepted his invitation, said yesterday the Egyptian delegation would be no more than an observer.

The comment contradicted the previous Egyptian position that it would attend as a participant.

The more radical Palestinian groups, along with Iran, Iraq and Libya, branded the conference a sell-out, but PLO leader Yasser Arafat began a regional tour to try to build Palestinian union and repair his own image, damaged by support for Saddam Hussein in the Gulf war.

Syrian President Hafez Assad urged all parties involved to work hard for regional peace.

Spokesman Jibran Kourieh said Assad had stressed in a meeting with Soviet Foreign Minister Boris Pankin that Syria "is keen to see a just and comprehensive peace prevailing in the region based on UN Security Council resolutions 242 and 338."

The Libyan news agency Jana said Moammar Gadaffi had accused Arab governments of treating their masses like sheep. "Arabs are not to pay for the errors of Hitler," he said, adding that Libya would never recognize Israel.

(Continued on Page 2)

Arafat meets with Assad to discuss parley strategy

DAMASCUS (AP) – PLO Chairman Yasser Arafat, on his first official visit to Damascus since being expelled eight years ago, met with Syrian President Hafez Assad yesterday to mend fences and discuss a strategy for the peace conference.

Arafat also was expected to try to placate Palestinians who are still opposed to negotiations with Israel, but he had a tough job ahead of him. Many Palestinians, both here and in other lands, consider acceptance of the conference conditions a sellout.

Arafat was last in Syria in 1988, but only for a few hours to attend the funeral of Abu Jihad, who was killed in Tunis.

He was expelled in 1983 during a struggle for control of the PLO that developed in the wake of Israel's 1982 invasion of Lebanon, which drove Arafat from Beirut.

Soviet Foreign Minister Boris Pankin traveled to Damascus from Israel and was expected to meet with Arafat before leaving today. The Soviet envoy was received by Assad yesterday.

Arafat has not made a public statement about the conference announcement, but started a regional tour expected to take him to Jordan and Egypt. He has been ostracized for backing Iraq during its invasion of Kuwait.

Arafat was met at the airport by Vice President Abdul-Halim Khaddam. It was the first time the PLO leader has been greeted here at such a high level.

Hamas activists arrested in Gaza

ALON PINKAS

Several dozens Hamas activists were arrested in the Gaza area last week in a joint IDF and General Security Service operation, according to the IDF.

The operation, coming soon after the arrests of 460 Popular Front for the Liberation of Palestine activists, is considered by officials as a setback to the Hamas movement, which is increasingly strong in Gaza.

Asked if the timing of the operation is connected to the peace conference, scheduled for the end of the month, a military source said: "It was not planned that way, but obviously we are strengthening the moderates that way."

Asked whether these moderates are, ironically, Fatah members, the source replied, "The government won't care to admit it, but yes, when it comes to the group composition of the Palestinians, Fatah, compared to Hamas, are the moderates."

IDF MiA, Yossi Fink, pronounced dead

ALON PINKAS

The IDF last night confirmed the death of missing soldier Yossi Fink, based on information supplied by UN officials.

"In the framework of the UN Secretary General [Javiar Perez de Cuellar's] effort to advance a solution to the matter of Israeli prisoners and missing in action, findings were transferred to Jerusalem concerning the fate of missing soldier Yosef Fink," the Defense Ministry statement said.

"This came after the findings that were given to Israel previously did not make it possible to determine his fate unequivocally," it said.

Information provided last September, apparently by Syrian officials, on both Fink and Rahamim Alsheikh, who disappeared together in February 1986, was insufficient to conclusively prove Fink's identity.

Yossi Fink.

The additional information provided the missing details needed to conclude that the corpse held by Hizbullah is Fink's .

The bodies of both Alsheikh and Fink are still held by Hizbullah, but Israel expects to receive them.

The official statement, issued jointly by the IDF and the Ministry of Defense, expresses hope that further information on the remaining four MiA's will be forwarded soon.

In May 1986, Hizbullah leader Abbas Musawi acknowledged that his organization was in fact holding two Israeli soldiers. Since then, and until last September, no information was forthcoming.

28191312

Japanese are tops at Rummikub	THE JERUSALEM POST	U.S. budget deficit is its biggest ever
Entertainment / Page 7		Finance / Page 11

Vol. LIX, No. 17886 Thursday, October 31, 1991 ● Heshvan 23, 5752 ● Rabi Tani 23, 1412 NIS 2.70 (Eilat NIS 2.30)

Bush: Peace need not be a dream

Spanish Premier Felipe Gonzalez opens the peace conference yesterday in Madrid.

(AFP)

Bush speech puts Israel at ease over U.S. role as honest broker

ANALYSIS
David Makovsky

President Bush's conciliatory speech yesterday seemed to quiet Israeli concerns about the U.S. role as honest broker in the peace process, at least judging by Prime Minister Shamir's reaction.

Shamir praised the speech as "very good" and "well measured" at a briefing to Israeli reporters.

"The speech set the guidelines for the process which the U.S. is initiating," Shamir said. "It has no need to [impose] any solution on the parties. The U.S. is trying to be faithful to this policy."

The speech was Bush's first opportunity to directly address the Israeli public after eight months of U.S. diplomacy characterized by a low profile and backroom negotiations.

Bush wants to inspire trust not only in Shamir but also in an Israeli public dismayed by Bush's unyielding stance last month in delaying loan guarantees for immigrant housing.

State Department officials say that Israeli public support for compromise is crucial if its leaders are going to make difficult decisions.

In his speech, Bush played down the U.S. role and defined peace in its widest terms. At the same time, he remained faithful to the traditional U.S. commitment on territorial compromise, without belaboring the point.

Bush spoke of what is meant by peace in clear and straightforward terms. The objective must not simply be to "end the state of war in the Middle East and replace it with a state of non-belligerency," Bush said. "This is not enough; this would not last. Rather, we seek real peace. And by real peace, I mean treaties. Security. Diplomatic relations. Economic relations. Trade. Investment. Cultural exchange. Even tourism."

Also, by setting an ambitious definition of peace, Bush suggested that those who pressured for an immediate Israeli withdrawal were unrealistic.

"We come to here to Madrid as realists," Bush said. "We do not expect peace to be negotiated in a day or week or month or even a year. It will take time; indeed it should take time – time for parties to talk to one another, to listen to one another. Time to heal old wounds and build trust. In this quest, time need not be the enemy of progress."

It is also important what Bush did not say. While he has shown a deep personal interest in the settlement issue, Bush did not explicitly mention it this time, let alone call for a settlement freeze at some point in the process.

It would be a misreading, however, to interpret the speech as a U.S. move away from the concerns of Palestinians. Rather, it is keeping with his desire to avoid political mine fields.

Bush couched traditional U.S. policy in carefully plastered terms by deliberately avoiding the term "land for peace." He sought to defuse criticism from the Likud that his goal is to push Israel to the 1967 borders by instead using the phrase "territorial compromise," that only implies that Arabs – and not just Israelis – have to give a little.

But perhaps most important of all, Bush held out a vision of hope to weary rivals: "We have seen too many generations of children whose haunted eyes show only fear – too many funerals for their brothers and sisters, for mothers and fathers who died too soon – too much hatred, too little love. And if we cannot summon a courage to lay down the past for ourselves, let us resolve to do it for the children."

Talks open with pleas to seize the moment

DAVID MAKOVSKY
ALLISON KAPLAN
JOEL GREENBERG
in Madrid

The first comprehensive peace talks between Israel and its Arab neighbors opened here yesterday with pleas to all sides not to pass up the chance for peace.

"Peace in the Middle East need not be a dream," said U.S. President Bush in the centerpiece speech, which seemed to reassure Israeli officials concerned about Washington's role as an honest broker.

"We seek peace, real peace. And by real peace I mean treaties. Security. Diplomatic relations. Economic relations. Trade. Investment. Cultural exchange. Even tourism," Bush added.

Soviet President Gorbachev said: "Today we have a unique opportunity and it would be unforgivable to miss this opportunity. The conference can only succeed if no one seeks any victory for one side over the other, but all seek a shared victory over a cruel past."

Prime Minister Shamir, who will address the conference this morning at 11 o'clock, to be followed by the heads of the Arab delegations, praised Bush's presentation, calling it "a very good speech." For the most part, Israelis and Arabs alike were expressing optimism.

"I think on the whole this has been a very good day for the prospects of peace," Deputy Foreign Minister Binyamin Netanyahu told a news conference.

"We come here with an open heart and an open mind," said Kamel Abu Jaber, the Jordanian foreign minister, at another briefing.

There was little in the way of concrete developments. Israeli eyebrows were raised in surprise when both Bush and Baker called for "territorial compromise" rather than "land for peace."

Shamir aide Yossi Ben-Aharon called their use of the term "balanced, positive." Added Netanyahu: "I hope – this is my interpretation – that since Israel has already given a full 91 percent of the territories, compromise does not mean that it will be asked to give 100 percent, and the other side asked to give zero."

But Palestinians were largely disappointed that Bush made no mention of settlements and did not openly call withdrawal from the territories.

Hanan Ashrawi, spokeswoman for the Palestinian delegation, said that Bush made "deliberate omissions to avoid issues of great contention." Among them – no mention of Jerusalem, Palestinian self-determination or statehood. Her main complaint was Bush's failure to address the settlement issue.

Syria is also reported to have been dissatisfied with Bush's opening speech, especially his failure to reiterate that the U.S. interprets UN resolutions 242 and 338 to apply on all fronts.

Syrian Foreign Minister Farouk Shara is expected to clarify the Syrian position at a press conference today.

James Baker expressed cautious satisfaction with the opening day. "Before we can run, we've got to crawl, and before we can run, we've got to walk," he told a press conference. "And today, we've all begun to crawl."

His caution also stemmed from the continued impasse between Israel and Syria to agree to a venue for the bilateral talks that are to follow the conference at the beginning of next week. Israel has stood strongly by its insistence that the most of these negotiations take place in the region, while Syria has rejected this.

Baker refused to discuss the details of a possible compromise, saying only that there is not yet agreement.

While denying that there were other obstacles to the bilateral talks, Baker appeared concerned they might crop up.

He warned that the U.S. and Soviet Union "hope very much that parties will not impose, or seek to impose, preconditions upon their willingness to sit down face-to-face and discuss these very difficult issues."

Egyptian Foreign Minister Amr Moussa called on Israel to end its control of East Jerusalem so it could become an open, holy city for all faiths.

"The holy city of Jerusalem has its special status. It should remain free, accessible and sacred to all followers of Islam, Christianity and Judaism," he said in his speech.

The introduction of the Jerusalem issue was a surprise move. Egypt has suggested in recent weeks that the problem be postponed to future negotiations.

The other Arab delegations are also expected to bring up the issue during their speeches today.

Moussa said the Golan Heights, Gaza Strip, West Bank and Israel's self-proclaimed "security zone" in southern Lebanon should all be returned to the respective Arab countries.

Yesterday evening, Moussa and Shamir held a 90-minute meeting.

"I cannot report on anything now," Moussa told reporters afterwards. Asked what were the main obstacles for the conference, he said: "A lot."

He said his talks with Moussa were "frank talks, which touched on very many subjects."

31161318

An Israeli film without a message
Entertainment / Page 8

THE JERUSALEM POST
60 1932 - 1992
Vol. LIX, No. 17926 Tuesday, December 17, 1991 • Tevet 10, 5752 • Jomada Tani 11, 1412 NIS 2.70 (Eilat NIS 2.30)

News Highlights

Katyushas destroyed

South Lebanese Army troops yesterday safely destroyed two katyusha rocket launchers inside the security zone in south Lebanon. The soldiers discovered the rocket launchers north of Bint J'bail while they were on routine operational duties in the western sector of the zone.

•

Jordanian journalist decorated

King Hussein yesterday gave an honorary medal to a prominent journalist barred from writing for giving interviews to Israel television during the peace talks.

Sultan Hattab, 39, a native of Hebron, who was expelled from Jordan's Writers Union and Press Association after being accused of attempting to normalize relations with Israel, expressed jubilation at the gesture.

•

Shamir sends condolences

Prime Minister Yitzhak Shamir last night sent Egyptian President Hosni Mubarak a telegram expressing his condolences to Mubarak, the families of the victims, and the Egyptian people over Sunday's Egyptian ferry accident.

(Ferry – page 4)

•

US concerned over Silwan

The US State Department issued a sharp statement yesterday directed at the Israeli government regarding the situation in Silwan, and called on both Israeli settlers and Palestinians in the territories to restrain themselves from acts that could derail the peace process.

(Silwan – Page 14)

•

Conrad Black victorious

A group led by Canadian publisher Conrad Black, owner of *The Jerusalem Post*, has won its extended battle for ownership of Fairfax, Australia's second-largest media group.

(Page 11)

•

Interest rates cut

Just a few days after Finance Minister Yitzhak Moda'i predicted a major drop in interest rates, the commercial banks cut their prime rates by as much as 3 percentage points to as low as 18%. Rates at Bank of Israel tenders had come down sharply earlier in the day. The cuts inspired a 5% surge in share prices on the Tel Aviv Stock Exchange.

(Page 9)

Government reforms exchange rate system; travel tax on way out

ALISA ODENHEIMER

The government last night unveiled a sweeping reform in its foreign currency exchange rate mechanism. The new mechanism, which officials have nicknamed "the diagonal system", is intended to bring about a gradual 14-15% devaluation of the shekel over the next year.

As part of the package, Finance Minister Yitzhak Moda'i and Bank of Israel Governor Jacob Frenkel announced at a Jerusalem news conference that there would be an immediate 3% upward adjustment in the midpoint of the band within which the shekel-basket of currencies exchange rate is permitted to fluctuate.

In addition, the reform calls for the elimination of the travel tax and the surcharge on imported services on December 1, 1992. It also calls for a reduction in "exchange rate insurance" (a type of subsidy for exporters), which will be reduced by 1% on January 1, 1992, and by an additional 1% on July 1, 1992.

The new shekel-basket midpoint will be NIS 2.6288, up from NIS 2.5522 yesterday. Under the new system, this midpoint will be gradually moved upward daily, by a steady increment, that will bring it up by an additional 9% by the end of the year, over and above tomorrow's 3% adjustment.

Just as before, the shekel exchange rate will continue to be permitted to fluctuate up to 5% below and above this moving midpoint, in response to supply and demand for foreign currency generated by the market.

The new system will allow business people to plan ahead, since it will give them a basic idea of where the shekel exchange rate will be during the next 12 months, Frenkel and Moda'i said.

The 3% upward adjustment of the shekel does not necessarily mean that the shekel will actually undergo a devaluation today, or during the next few days, since the current shekel-basket exchange rate is still well within the new band.

Moda'i and Frenkel explained that the new mechanism is intended to put an end to the wave of foreign currency speculation that would frequently plague the market under the old system. They insisted that the new system would not lead to a creeping devaluation since the actual exchange rate would still be set by market forces.

Under the system of a fixed midpoint, businessmen knew that every six months or so the shekel would begin to hit the upper ceiling of the exchange rate bank, and the government would have to make an upward adjustment in the midpoint to allow the exchange rate to continue its upward drift.

UN votes 112:25 to rescind Zionism = racism resolution

Egypt declines to take part

JONATHAN SCHACHTER

UNITED NATIONS – The General Assembly last night overwhelmingly reversed its resolution equating Zionism with racism, ending 16 years of what Israeli diplomats termed their country's "delegitimization" by the world body.

The vote was 111-25, with 13 abstentions. Many of those voting for repeal had also voted for the original resolution. Many of the Arab states and several non-aligned countries voted no.

"This is the day for which we have waited, it is here," said Foreign Minister David Levy shortly before the vote. "This issue was a stain on the escutcheon of this organization, and it is this stain which are removing today."

The original resolution was "a distortion and a misrepresentation, the product of a moment of eclipse within the UN," Levy added. In a reference to the recent celebration last week of Hanukka, he called it "only fitting that in this season we have come here to drive out the darkness."

In presenting the draft resolution, US deputy secretary of state Lawrence Eagleburger called the original resolution "one of this body's most ungenerous acts. It branded the national aspirations of one people, and one people only, as illegitimate – a people which had been homeless, dispersed and exiled for the better part of two millennia. It labelled as racist the national aspirations of the one people more victimized by racism than any other."

The assembly president, Saudi Ambassador Samir Shihabi, was absent when the vote took place. Presiding in his place was his deputy, Honduran Ambassador Roberto Flores Bermudez.

Before the vote, Yemeni Ambassador Abdalla al-Ashtal called for the repeal resolution to be considered an "important question," which requires a two-thirds majority, or 112 votes, to pass. But the proposal was overwhelmingly defeated.

In a move unprecedented in the UN, the repeal was co-sponsored by 85 countries, representing over half of the world body's 166 members. Some 15 of those had voted for the original resolution.

One of the last countries to agree to co-sponsor the repeal was the Soviet Union , which led the 1975 drive to enact the original resolution. "It joined in after some debate," Levy said.

The move for repeal was led by the US, in coordination with Israel and other countries friendly to Israel.

Levy praised the "intense cooperation" between the US and Israel in arranging the worldwide campaign, comparing the effort to a "well-oiled machine" and a "harmonious orchestra."

Ambassador Yoram Aridor said that the move signified Israel's improved standing within the world body. "The proof is the very large number of countries that co-sponsored repeal."

Jewish organizations hailed the repeal. "I think we are 16 years too late, but it is important to do it even now," said Malcolm Hoenlein, executive director of the Conference of Presidents of Major American Jewish Organizations.

The text of the repeal resolution read simply: "The General Assembly decides to revoke the determination contained in its Resolution 3379 of 10 November 1975."

Diplomats said they purposely kept the resolution brief to discourage at tempts at attaching hostile amendments or otherwise tampering with its wording.

The original resolution, sponsored by a coalition of Arab, Islamic, non-aligned and Soviet-bloc states, was adopted after one of the stormiest debates in UN history. The vote was 72-35, with 32 abstentions.

After its adoption, then-UN ambassador Chaim Herzog stood at the rostrum and tore up a copy of the resolution, flinging the pieces at the members of the assembly. Then US delegate Daniel Moynihan told the body that the US "does not acknowledge, it will never abide by, it will never acquiesce in this infamous act."

For more than a decade, efforts by Israel to lobby for the resolution's repeal m et with little success. Israeli diplomats pledged to seek the resolution's reversal as soon as a "comfortable majority" was reached, pointing out that a failed repeal attempt would be more disastrous than none at all. But, until the global changes of the past few months, the numbers weren't even close.

This past September, however, President Bush reaffirmed his intention to push for the repeal, telling the General Assembly that the resolution mocked the principles upon which the UN was founded.

While he did not provide a specific timetable for the repeal, State Department officials later said they hoped it could come by the end of the current assembly session.

Then Soviet foreign minister Boris Pankin broke with previous Soviet policy and echoed Bush's call for

(Continued on Page 2)

Russian President Boris Yeltsin yesterday assured Secretary of State James Baker III that all 27,000 Soviet nuclear weapons will be put under strict control. Yeltsin, deputy prime minister Gennady Bourboulis and Defense Minister Marshall Yevgeni Shaposhnikov, met with Baker and US Ambassador Robert Strauss for four hours and then told reporters at a joint news conference that a "single authority" would take charge of all strategic and nuclear arms. He also said that Ukraine, Byelorussia and Kazakhstan would destroy their nuclear weapons, leaving Russia as the only nuclear state to emerge from the splintering Soviet Union. They also discussed the growing international relief effort to assist the Soviet people through the harsh winter now taking hold. (AFP)

Arabs may ask US to break impasse

ALLISON KAPLAN and DAVID MAKOVSKY

WASHINGTON – Palestinian and Jordanian negotiators threatened yesterday to bring their dispute with Israel to the US to resolve, as it appeared the deadlock over the structure of their bilateral talks was tightening.

"As of today, the entire process is in jeopardy," Palestinian spokeswoman Hanan Ashrawi told an afternoon news briefing, shortly before negotiators returned to the much-worn sofa in the State Department corridor for what was described as a final attempt to reach agreement without American intervention.

Although Israeli officials agreed the negotiations appeared to be moving toward an impasse, they privately expressed confidence the US would not choose to intervene at this stage, even if requested to do so.

The bilateral talks with the Syrian and Lebanese delegations also continued. The Israelis asked the Syrians to recognized Israel's legitimacy as a state, just as Israel recognizes Syria's legitimacy as a state and the Syrians refused, said Yossi Olmert, a member of the Israeli delegation to the Syrian talks.

As he left the meeting, the Syrian spokesman said: "The Israeli delegation is still not budging an inch on its position not to discuss substantive matters."

The pessimism from both the Israeli and the Jordanian-Palestinian delegations was a marked contrast from indications earlier in the day that the differences would be bridged.

Both Ashrawi and Jordanian spokesman Marwan Mu'asher said that they were deeply disappointed that Israel had not accepted either of two proposals submitted in the morning. Both were based on the principle that negotiations between should take place on two tracks – one dealing with Israeli-Palestinian issues and the other with Israeli-Jordanian matters.

"Both proposals were turned down, and we feel this is a way in which the Israeli side is pushing us into an impasse and a deadlock," Ashrawi said.

Mu'asher called the afternoon round of meetings as a "last attempt to reach a solution," and said: "Obviously, if the process reaches a deadlock, we have to go to the co-sponsors."

At the end of the morning round, the Israelis submitted a counterproposal, but there did not appear to be

(Continued on Page 2)

Blast paralyzes London railways

LONDON (Reuter) – A bomb believed to be the work of the IRA exploded on the track near one of the world's busiest railway junctions yesterday, paralyzing London's rail network and causing chaos for up to one million commuters.

The early morning blast near south London's Clapham Junction came minutes after a man claiming to be from the Irish Republican Army telephoned a bomb threat to a television station.

London's eight main rail stations were closed by the threat.

Though the bomb, described by police as small, caused no injuries and only slight damage, it had a devastating effect on businesses in London, where 40% of commuters travel by train.

"It appears they were aiming for disruption rather than destruction," one security source said.

Police could not confirm that the bomb was the work of the IRA, but noted that it followed a pre-Christmas firebomb blitz on stores and other targets in Britain, including one at the weekend at the National Gallery in London's Trafalgar Square.

Commander George Churchill-Coleman, head of the police anti-terrorist branch, urged the public to be "especially vigilant."

Yeltsin: 10 republics to join new Commonwealth of Independent States

News agencies

MOSCOW – The new Commonwealth of Independent States will begin operating by the end of this month with at least 10 of the 12 former Soviet republics as members, Russian President Boris Yeltsin said yesterday.

Speaking to reporters after a four-hour meeting with US Secretary of State James Baker, Yeltsin also said Russia would seek the Soviet Union's "vacant" Security Council seat at the UN and eventually would be the only former Soviet republic with nuclear weapons.

Russia also said it was taking over the Soviet parliament's property and named itself the central legislature's "successor," Interfax news agency said.

His long meeting with Baker, and his authoritative answers at their Kremlin news conference, underlined his position as the country's most powerful politician.

Yeltsin told an Italian newspaper that President Mikhail Gorbachev had no role to play in the reshaped Soviet Union and called on him to resign by the middle of next month.

But Baker did not ignore Gorbachev. They met separately for 2½ hours, after which Baker and Gorbachev also spoke to reporters in the Kremlin.

"These fundamental changes are due, in no small part, to your efforts," Baker said in a tribute to Gorbachev, whose resignation appears nearly inevitable.

Gorbachev has been in power since March 1985.

Baker's remarks indicated the US accepts the change of power in the Soviet Union but retains great respect for Gorbachev and does not want to take sides. He sidestepped questions about the US view of Yeltsin's actions, saying he did not want to interfere in "the political process" in Moscow.

The visit capped another turbulent day as the Soviet Union, beset by food shortages and the threat of chaos, is quickly breaking into a dozen independent states, linked only by the loosely defined commonwealth.

The Russian decree naming itself the legislature's successor, rang the death knell for the Soviet Union's parliamentary democracy, born in 1989 after seven decades of communist rule but now a victim of the collapse of central authority.

Saudis bar Israeli Arabs from visiting holy sites

DAVID RUDGE

HAIFA – A planned pilgrimage by a group of over 1,000 Israeli Moslems to Saudi Arabia has been canceled by the Saudi authorities without explanation.

The "Little Haj" (Umra) to Mecca and Medina had been scheduled to go ahead tomorrow after two months of planning.

Israeli officials expressed shock and disappointment over the decision, especially in light of the peace talks.

The prime minister's adviser on Arab affairs Dr. Alexander Bligh said they took a grave view of the decision by the Saudi authorities.

He pointed out that notification of the cancellation had been received last Thursday, just six days before the visit was to take place.

The message was relayed to Israel via Jordanian officials who had been involved in assisting in the formalities and transport arrangements for the pilgrims.

It simply stated that Israeli Moslems would not be allowed to visit holy sites in Saudi Arabia. The message said reasons for the decision would be forwarded, but have so far not been forthcoming.

Bligh noted that the Saudi decision appeared to conflict with the atmosphere in the Middle East in light of the ongoing peace process.

"Today there is an atmosphere of direct talks and goodwill, at least from Israel's point of view, on various issues which are in dispute," said Bligh.

"This matter, however, is not really in dispute because it primarily relates to freedom of religion," he said.

Compounding the gravity of the decision is the fact that the group of 1,120 Moslems have been informed that their deposits for transport and hotel arrangements, amounting to around NIS 1,000 each, would not be refunded.

The planned trip would have been the fourth "Little Haj" by Israeli Moslems to Saudi Arabia.

There have been suggestions that the question of religious freedom should be raised in the multi-lateral peace talks and a permanent forum established between Israel, Jordan and Saudi Arabia, to deal specifically with travel to holy sites in the three countries.

"I think it would be advisable, in order to prevent disputes, for the governments involved to have some form of direct contact in order to facilitate direct access for pilgrims to holy sites," said Bligh.

17121316

THE JERUSALEM POST

60 1932 - 1992

Vol. LX, No. 17941 Friday, January 3, 1992 • Tevet 27, 5752 • Jomada Tani 27, 1412 NIS 3.90 (Eilat NIS 3.30)

Complete TV, radio listings
Pages 4B-5B

News Highlights

Lynn conducts filibuster

Knesset law committee chairman Uriel Lynn yesterday conducted a two-hour filibuster to prolong debate on the bill calling for direct election of the prime minister, with the aim of postponing the vote until next week. By press time, it was certain the vote would not be held before next week. Lynn did not exercise his prerogative to ask the plenum to withdraw the bill, but said he might do so later on.

•

Air Force head

Herzl Budinger was named OC Air Force yesterday, succeeding Avihu Bin-Nun. Budinger, who was promoted to major-general, was formally named to the post by Chief of General Staff Lieut.-Gen. Ehud Barak and Defense Minister Moshe Arens, in a ceremony at the Tel-Nof Air Force base in central Israel.

•

Tase up sharply

Share prices on the Tel Aviv Stock Exchange rose more than 2% in the first day of trading in the new year. On foreign-currency markets, the shekel gained a slight 0.09% against the dollar, and 0.11% against basket of currencies. **Page 13**

THE JERUSALEM POST

Production difficulties resulting from the heavy snowfall may have caused some shortcomings in this issue. In particular, we were under pressure of a very early deadline. We expect our readers to understand.

We also apologize to subscribers whose paper was not delivered to their door yesterday morning because of distribution problems.

03812321

Floods, blizzard – and now comes ice

Jerusalem residents dodge fallen trees as they walk along Rehov Ben-Yehuda (Zeev Ackerman)

Numerous areas still have no power

Jerusalem Post Staff

Jerusalem, Upper Galilee and the Golan Heights yesterday remained buried under a thick cloak of snow, which cut electricity supplies to over 250,000 homes in the capital and left numerous roads impassable.

The Weather Service said the stormy weather was already easing off last night, and would continue to gradually abate today. Light snow continued to fall in hilly areas above 500 meters in elevation last night. It is to continue this morning, but taper off towards evening, while rain falling over most of the rest of the country is also expected to decrease later today.

The service warned that when snow melted, sub-zero evening temperatures would freeze the resulting slush, making walking and driving extremely hazardous over the next few days. He advised parents to accompany their children to school in snow-affected areas where classes are in session today. Jerusalem schools will be closed.

By last night, some localities had made definite decisions about holding classes today. Schools are slated to be closed in the Jerusalem suburbs of Givat Ze'ev and Mevasseret Yerushalayim, while in Yavne, Arad, Petah Tikva, and Rehovot, schools were scheduled to open.

Other localities were to make final decisions only this morning, so parents are once again advised to keep up with early-morning radio broadcasts.

Many Jerusalem residents prepared to spend a home-bound Shabbat, as snow continued to fall on already covered roads, blocking Electric Corporation workers' attempts to complete repairs. Electric Corp. general manager Moshe Katz said last night power might not be fully restored in Jerusalem for several days.

Energy Minister Yuval Ne'eman demanded Katz present him with a report on the company's plans for repairing storm damage to the nation's power supply. Katz told Ne'eman that demands for power reached unprecedented levels Wednesday, with 4,430 megawatts supplied. He said additional teams from the south were dispatched to Jerusalem to help with repairs, and more teams would be sent today.

Snow flurries remarkably reached as far as Ein Gedi, Yeroham, and Dimona, while in Tel Aviv, hundreds of people flooded out of their homes began sorting out the damage.

Jerusalem's 126,000 pupils were among yesterday's happy throngs of children learning the "three s's" – snowballs, snowmen and sledding – as the worst snowfall in recent memory closed schools across the country.

In sporting fixtures, meanwhile, all National League soccer matches have been postponed until Monday. The local rugby league has announced its intention to play.

Supermarket chains reported that weekly sales figures exceeded the average turnover by up to 80 percent.

The nation's two largest food chains, Supersol and Blue Square Co-Op, said all branches were open.

In the Golan Heights, the snow reached a record depth of two meters. Ski enthusiasts in Safed were busy checking out possible ski slopes.

Attempts were made to keep northern roads open, especially those leading to hospitals, but the continuing snowfall was hampering those efforts. Dozens of cars and trucks including heavy vehicles were stuck in the snow.

Hundreds of soldiers at a Golan Heights base were temporarily moved to the Katzrin gym after rooms on their base were flooded.

Upper Galilee moshavim were completely cut off. Upper Galilee regional council head Aharon Ma'atok said the moshavim had enough food for an extended period, and residents could remain at home without cause for concern.

Only about half the workers in Safed and Upper Galilee showed up for work. Many trees were down in the area, blocking thoroughfares. Safed municipality workers worked all night to remove felled trees.

Snow also fell yesterday on the Jordan Valley hills. Jordan Valley local council head David Levy said snow had not fallen there in at least 23 years, since the beginning of settlement in the area.

The heavy snow sent historians running for their record books.

Veteran residents recalled the storm of 1949-50, which left dozens of centimeters of snow in many parts of the country. In 1967-68, snow swept from Haifa and the Carmel mountain range to the Coastal Plain, dumping the white stuff on the Jezreel and Hula valleys. Heavy snow fell on Jerusalem on Purim of 1980 as well.

December turned out to be one of the wettest in the past several decades. The extremely wet winter has resulted in many locations already surpassing annual average rainfall.

Northern Israel received twice its average rainfall for the month, while in the central region, the areas between Ra'anana and Nablus and between Gaza and Hebron soaked up three to four times the monthly average. The Negev also received a bit more than usual.

In some areas, the rainfall for December was the highest since officials started keeping records there. In Hafetz Haim, 478 mm. of rain fell, the most since 1946. In Gaza, 358 mm. were recorded, the largest amount since 1967.

A time for turtle-necks and hot chocolate

HERB KEINON

Finally, a real snow.

A snow that sticks to the ground, conjures up memories of snow plows, fireplaces, Doris Day movies. A snow that makes you want to shovel walks, trek through the virgin powder.

Serious snow.

Snow measured by the inches, not the flakes. Snow that will be there in the morning, that makes you long for auto anti-freeze, turtle-necks, hot chocolate. Snow that looks lovely as it falls and falls and falls through the orange light given off by street lamps. Snow that sends you to the bookshelves in search of Robert Frost, and to the radio hoping to hear *Winterwonderland*.

Serious snow.

Yesterday's was a flurry that made up for all those years when the only snow in most of this country was a few *nebesch* flakes around Purim. Yesterday's flurry made up for the depressing reality of previous years when snow that fell in the morning melted by the afternoon. Yesterday's flurry made it possible to use the winter-weather training that was pounded into me since I was old enough to shovel the sidewalk in Denver, Colorado.

"Knock the snow off tree branches, boy," my father ordered me after countless snowfalls. "Pump lightly on the car brakes before stopping. And never, never, wear tennis shoes out there."

It was this sage advice that left me so prepared, so damn knowledgable, as I maneuvered my way yesterday through the white streets of the capital. But there I saw branch after branch cracking under the weight of the snow, car after car swerve when stopping at traffic lights, and foot after foot drenched because of a mistep on unshoveled sidewalks.

And I felt smug, a little superior, watching the natives react, dare I say overreact, to the storm.

Now, I know that Jerusalem isn't Denver. I know that Firestone snow tires are not big sellers here; that no one owns a snow shovel; and that hiking boots with the red laces, so nifty and necessary in Rocky Mountain storms, are kind of odd here.

But still, there seems something wrong that, as we approach the 21st century, in a country with reported nuclear capability and the ability to transplant a heart, a good, healthy snow storm would leave much of the city without electricity, without most of its traffic lights, and with stores that don't have bread.

The run on bread is fascinating. It's as if every once in a while we have this urge to feel under siege, stock up on bread and milk, keep the kids home from school, stay home from work. Maybe this is the way we make up for our lack of three-day weekends.

"A storm like this in southern Italy would send the people outside yelling *che bella* (how beautiful)," a colleague noted. "Here it sends them to the stores looking for bread."

Just as fascinating are the school closures. OK, close the schools in Jerusalem, that I can understand. But in Ma'ale Adumim, out there in the Judean desert where the clouds dropped maybe a couple inches of non-stickable snow? What's the point? All it does is give those immigrants from snowy climes the ability to say to their children, as their fathers said to them, "When I was young I walked to school in snow up to my navel."

Yet the country's quirks in dealing with the storm do not detract from the utter beauty of seeing the capital and its landmarks set in snow, not blushed in sunlight. It's picture-perfect, tainted only by the man, with plastic bags covering his tennis shoes, walking through the falling snow holding an open umbrella. If ever there was a metaphor ...

Shas-NRP deal leads to passage of 1992 budget

DAN IZENBERG

Opposition members stalked out of the plenum yesterday evening during the second reading of the 1992 state budget, as the government easily brushed aside their objections and approved the bill following a last-minute agreement between Shas and the National Religious Party.

The oppostion later returned and the budget passed its third reading by a vote of 60-53, with one abstention.

With one eye on the vote on the direct election of prime ministers bill, which was to follow the budget vote, the coalition insisted on a roll-call vote on each objection to the budget to prolong the vote and postpone the debate on the direct election bill.

The opposition demanded that deputy speaker Dan Tichon stop holding roll calls; they left their seats and shouted at him and the Likud benches before finally walking out.

With the opposition seats empty except for MK Charlie Biton (Black Panthers) and the objections of the opposition withdrawn to save time, the coalition steamrolled its way through the second reading and endorsed the proposal exactly as presented by the finance committee.

It was an anti-climactic finish to a week of drama and tension, during which the government was only hours away from asking the plenum to approve a one-month provisional budget, a move which would have been viewed as a serious setback for Prime Minister Shamir.

The Likud was saved from that fate when Shascaved in to NRP demands to eliminate the possibility of special allocations in the 1992 budget.

Shas had demanded the inclusion in the budget of a NIS 40m "safety net" to be allocated by haredi MKs to their cultural institutions, if they were not satisfied with the way the NRP-controlled Religious Affairs Ministry distributed the money.

It had been agreed that the ministry would allocate the funds by objective criteria, but Shas leader Aryeh Deri declared that he did not trust the NRP. On Wednesday, Shamir agreed to the Shas demand and the safety net was approved by the Finance Ministry and included in the budget.

The NRP then announced that it would vote against the budget.

Late Wednesday night, on hearing of Shamir's intention to submit a provisional budget, Shas accepted the NRP demand. In return, Religious Affairs Minister Avner Shaki and Education Minister Zevulun Hammer promised Deri in writing that "we will conduct ourselves with regard to the Tora and haredi cultural institutions in our budgets according to criteria and with complete fairness... Remove from your hearts the fear that [we will create] unfair obstacles or delays. [We will] implement the budget according to its letter and spirit."

SHABBAT	BEGINS	ENDS
Jerusalem	4:11	5:27
Tel Aviv	4:29	5:29
Haifa	4:18	5:26
Beersheba	4:27	5:26
Eilat	4:32	5:33

Terror victim buried; new settlement in Gaza

News agencies

HOLON – Doron Shorshan, the 29-year-old Kfar Darom resident gunned down in a terrorist ambush near Deir el-Balah in the Gaza Strip Wednesday, was buried here yesterday. He left a 29-year-old wife and three children, six, four and three.

Science Minister Yuval Ne'eman represented the government at the funeral, and OC Southern Command Maj.-Gen. Matan Vilnai represented the IDF.

"In the struggle for the Land of Israel, blood, tears, and pain have been wrung out of us in every corner of the land. But this will not prevent our return to our homeland," Ne'eman said.

Vilnai said the IDF and the other security services "would do everything in their power to apprehend the murderers and to protect every resident of the country."

Meanwhile, a settlement was set up outside Deir el-Balah yesterday, and an influential Moslem fundamentalist group renewed a call for attacks on settlers everywhere.

Three mobile homes were placed on the spot outside the refugee camp where unidentified terrorists ambushed Shorshan's car and shot him to death. The settlement was named Doron in his memory. Shorshan was the fourth Israeli shot dead in the territories since October, but the first Israeli civilian killed in the strip since the outbreak of the intifada four years ago.

IDF soldiers last night began to evacuate the caravans, Israel Radio reported, despite opposition by the settlers.

The Doron settlers, a group of about 30, also fixed up a long-deserted railway station, while soldiers stood guard in heavy rains on the coldest day in Gaza in decades.

In a leaflet dated January 3, the Islamic movement Hamas, which is strong in the Gaza Strip, said: "Hamas... urges all our people to attack settlers everywhere."

It was the first Hamas leaflet to advocate violence against settlers since Middle East peace talks started in October.

Shorshan was killed on the 27th anniversary of the first operation against Israel by the the PLO's Fatah faction. The army rounded up 40 Arabs. No one claimed responsibility for the attack.

Angry at the ambushes, settlers have opened fire in Arab villages, damaged Arab property and demanded tougher army measures including the expulsion of Arab activists.

In a statement, Gaza settlers blamed the US and Unrwa workers in Gaza for failing to discourage Hamas from attacking Jews.

But Unrwa spokesman Hashim Abu Sido said:

"This is absolute and utter nonsense. Unrwa staff are there to carry out Unrwa's mandate – providing education, health and relief services to Palestine refugees in the area – and are not involved in such activities."

The settlers demanded the expulsion of Unrwa, set up to handle Palestinians who fled Israel in 1948, and a halt of US funding for the agency.

"We live together, Arabs and Jews, in this small country and probably forever we are going to live together," Yitzhak Amitai, a spokesman for the 3,000 Jews in Gaza, said.

12 picked for deportation

ALON PINKAS

Twelve residents of the territories, all of whom are known to the security forces, were arrested yesterday and steps are underway for their deportation, a defense ministry official said yesterday. The names of the twelve could not be obtained last night. All 12, six of them from the Gaza district, have previously been arrested, and some were apparently released in the Ahmed Jibril prisoner exchange several years ago.

The decision to go ahead with deportations, predicted yesterday by *The Jerusalem Post*, was reached by both the Prime Minister and the Minister of Defense. The official said that Israel expects criticism from the United States, and is resorting to deportation as a last option.

Two committees have been established, one in the central command and one in the southern command. The designated deportees can appeal to those committees and contest the decision to deport them.

Nuclear deterrence and nuclear chaos
Page 1B

THE JERUSALEM POST
60 1932 - 1992
Vol. LX, No. 17959 Friday, January 24, 1992 • Shvat 19, 5752 • Rajab 19, 1412 NIS 3.90 (Eilat NIS 3.30)

News Highlights

US to airlift aid
Secretary of State James Baker said yesterday the US will provide Air Force planes to fly 54 shipments of emergency medicine and food to the former Soviet republics. Baker said the first C5 transports in Operation Provide Hope will leave Frankfurt February 10. He said they would fly to any former Soviet state where their safety could be assured. **Earlier story Page 4.**

•

Building collapse kills 20
A 16-floor luxury apartment building overlooking the sea in the Mediterranean port of Alexandria collapsed at dawn yesterday, killing at least 20 people, a police source said. The source said the suspected reason for the collapse of the 10-year-old building was that its owners illegally added several floors to it.

•

Interest rate warning
Bank of Israel governor Jacob Frenkel suggested that if thecommercial banks do not substantially cut interest rates, he will take administrative steps to achieve that end. **Page 11**

•

Tase drives higher
The Tel Aviv Stock Exchange's main indicator drove up 2.01% on heavy trading yesterday, as investors acted as if the US loan guarantees are in the bag. In foreign-currency markets the shekel lost 0.13% against the dollar. **Page 11**

THE KIBITZER - Foreign Minister David Levy looks over the shoulder of a Chinese card player yesterday during a visit to Beijing's Temple of Heaven. The two card players carried on with their game, unware of the importance of their visitor. (AP)

China-Israel talks today after compact signed

DAVID MAKOVSKY in Beijing

By early this morning, diplomatic relations will have been established between Israel and China, inaugurating a new chapter in Chinese-Israeli relations.

Foreign Ministers Qian Qichen and David Levy are to sign the protocols affirming the new ties this morning at government guesthouse Villa No. 18, near where Levy is staying.

After the ceremony and a festive lunch, Levy is to hold key talks with Chinese Premier Li Peng and Qian. The discussion is to focus on China's arms sales to the Middle East, bilateral issues and China's role in the multilateral talks opening in Moscow next Tuesday, Levy told reporters last night.

On Sunday Levy will meet with Chinese Vice Premier Wu Xuequian and raise the flag at the Israeli embassy. Zev Sufott, Israel's top diplomat in Beijing and currently attached to the Israel's Academy of Sciences and Humanities liaison, will shortly be named Israel's first ambassador to China, senior Israeli officials say.

Last night Levy told reporters traveling with him he would appeal to Chinese leaders to stop arming Israel's enemies in the Mideast. Chinese Foreign Ministry spokesman Wu Jianmin confirmed to Israeli reporters that China sold a research nuclear reactor for "peaceful purposes" to Algeria last year, and another is believed to have been sold to Iran.

There have been widespread reports of China's intention to sell M-9 ballistic missiles to Syria and tanks to Saudi Arabia.

While saying he would appeal to Chinese leaders to halt sales, Levy was far from confident China would act, except in a broader context. Levy said: "China says it is inconceivable that the US and Europe is allowed to sell (arms), and it cannot."

Levy said he would seek Li's support for a total freeze on the sale of both conventional and non-conventional weapons to the Middle East, including Israel. Six months ago, Defense Minister Moshe Arens called for a ban on all conventional weapons sales to the Middle East. "It is time to bring down the curtain on all arms sales to the Middle East, and stop providing any forms of weapons to the region," Levy said.

Levy for the first time tacitly acknowledged Israeli-Chinese arms links over the past decades. When pressed by reporters, Levy responded, "I think this has been grossly exaggerated, but I do not want to get into it. There are a lot of fanciful things published in the media."

While refusing to divulge further information about arms ties, Levy said he believed enhanced trade between the two countries was possible, and he hoped to name a trade

(Continued on Page 14)

Tzomet to support government

SARAH HONIG

The government was assured last night of surviving Monday's no-confidence vote when Tzomet's secretariat decided to support the government.

The Likud, meanwhile, took its first practical steps towards early elections when the party secretariat yesterday scheduled elections for party leader and Knesset candidates for the end of February.

This was done with the full agreement of Housing Minister Ariel Sharon, despite the fact that he is an announced challenger for the leadership.

Sharon's interests would have been better served had the showdown been delayed and held in the arena of a newly elected party convention, rather than the present central committee. The central committee favors Prime Minister Yitzhak Shamir and Defense Minister Moshe Arens.

The fact that Sharon agreed to speedy internal elections is compelling evidence that the Likud believes that early elections are around the corner.

According to the schedule worked out by the secretariat yesterday, the central committee of 3,400 members will meet on February 10 to work out final details.

It will gather again on February 20 to elect the party leader; five days later the committee will elect a panel of Knesset candidates; and two days after that, on February 27, the central committee will rank its Knesset nominees on its list of candidates.

According to one theory, emanating from the prime minister's entourage, the announcement of early elections now hinges on whether the United States will grant Israel the loan guarantee it requested. Should the US comply, the betting in the prime minister's office is that he will coordinate on Sunday an early elections date with Labor.

The ability to choose his options was afforded Shamir by Tzomet, who's action guarantees that Shamir's coalition will have at least 61 votes out of 120, enough to defeat the no-confidence motion.

The Likud believes that Tehiya and Moledet, although they bolted the coalition a few days ago, might also refrain from joining Labor's motion. Sources close to Shamir told the Post that had there been any danger of the Likud government falling in Monday's no-confidence vote, Shamir would not have cooperated with Labor on rescheduling elections.

Sharon, very much resigned to the likelihood of advanced elections, reiterated before students at Tel Aviv's Gymnasiya Herzliya yesterday that he will be challenging Shamir for the Likud's No. 1 one slot.

US, Israel share information on former Soviet scientists

DAVID MAKOVSKY

BEIJING – The US and Israel recently traded information about scientists from the former Soviet republics who may seek to sell their nuclear expertise to help radical Arab states, Foreign Minister David Levy said here last night.

Meanwhile, the US has accepted Israel's request to broaden the scope of categories to be discussed in next week's Moscow multilateral talks on regional issues, Levy announced.

The Jerusalem Post has obtained a Foreign Ministry working paper passed to the US expressing its views on both the structure of the Moscow talks and its outline for progress in technical and regional cooperation.

In a press conference, Levy said he raised the issue of Soviet scientists in a recent letter to Secretary of State James Baker and subsequently, information has been traded on

(Continued on Page 14)

Chinese official here

Chinese deputy minister of industry Pan Li Chen arrived in Israel yesterday with a nine-man delegation to complete negptiations for the establishment of a potash factory on a salt lake in southwestern China, between Tibet and Mongolia.

The project, which is being organized by businessman Shaul Eisenberg, involves a factory expected to initially produce 800,000 tons of potash a year.

The guests are expected to spend 10 days here visiting various industrial sites after spending four days at the Dead Sea Works. Talks on the project will continue in China. (Itim)

Labor bureau to advance primaries

JACOB WIRTSCHAFTER

The Labor Party's top policy making body – the 100-member political bureau – yesterday postponed a final decision on the timing of its internal primaries while throwing water on the fire set by Sunday's bitter exchange between Shimon Peres and Yitzak Rabin.

MK Haim Bar-Lev, who announced that his parliamentary career would come to a close at the end of the current Knesset, was appointed chairman of the elections committee, which will oversee the primaries. The committee is expected to push up the date of the primaries to the second week in April.

While the official agenda of the political bureau included next week's no-confidence vote, to be introduced by Labor over the issue of unemployment, and the timing of the party's internal elections, the Peres-Rabin confrontation was the major concern addressed by the party activists.

"There was an accident this week and damage was caused," said Labor's Secretary General Micha Harish. "We can't let this competition slow down the momentum we've gained since our convention."

While Harish went on to say that "all four of our candidates have a better record to bring to the electorate than Yitzak Shamir," some political bureau members disclosed that the mutual accusations between Rabin and Peres were in fact making them consider whether Labor would be better off with Ora Namir or Yisrael Kessar.

Sarah Honig adds:

The warring Peres and Rabin camps each held campaign rallies yesterday, each ostensibly seeking to lower the level of escalation in the feud between the two arch-rivals.

Addressing his supporters in Beersheba, Yitzhak Rabin appealed to them to "evince as much self-restraint as possible in view of the obvious provocation with which others are seeking to turn this contest."

Peres, speaking to an impressive turnout of supporters at the Eretz Yisrael Museum in Ramat Aviv, all but ignored Rabin save for the crack that "the Yitzhak I am running against is not Rabin but Shamir."

Poll shows Labor is gaining: Page 16

Foreign Minister Levy and Chinese Vice Foreign Minister Yang Fuchang listen to Iman Hajj Daoud yesterday during Levy's visit to the Niujie Mosque, the largest in Beijing. Yang has announced he will represent China at the Middle East talks in Moscow. (Reuter)

Shoval, Baker to meet today on guarantees

ALLISON KAPLAN and news services

WASHINGTON – A crucial meeting between Secretary of State James Baker and Israeli Ambassador Zalman Shoval is scheduled today after being postponed yesterday afternoon.

Baker is expected to outline the portion of $10 billion in absorption loan guarantees which the US is willing to consider. He is also expected to outline the conditions regarding settlement activity that the Bush administration will demand for Israel to receive the guarantees.

No official reason for the postponement was given to the Israeli Embassy, but Baker's crowded schedule has been extremely tight this week.

Meanwhile, Palestinian spokeswoman Hanan Ashrawi said yesterday Palestinians would go ahead with peace talks despite US approval of loan guarantees if the loans were not used to further occupation.

Her remarks after returning from peace talks in Washington seemed to open the way for compromise after Palestinians threatened to walk out of the negotiations over the loan guarantee issue.

"If the US can manage to get conditions and constraints that would eliminate entirely any possibility of these funds being to subsidize the occupation or settlements...that would be none of our business," Ashrawi said.

Bank of Israel governor going to Moscow

Frenkel says loan guarantees 'vital' to country's economy

ALISA ODENHEIMER

The $10 billion in loan guarantees that Israel has requested from the US are "vital" to this country's economy, Bank of Israel Governor Jacob Frenkel said yesterday.

Frenkel, who will be joining the negotiating team for the multilateral talks in Moscow next week, said that without the guarantees, Israel will be unable to borrow the funds necessary to absorb the massive immigration.

The governor's statement comes on the heels of remarks by Finance Minister Yitzhak Moda'i earlier this week that if forced to choose between receiving the guarantees and continuing settlement activity, he would choose the latter.

Frenkel told the Israel-America Chamber of Commerce in Tel Aviv that there is great competition for capital in world markets, and without the guarantees, Israel's ability to borrow money is "limited."

He said he is confident of the country's ability to return the loans as long as the money is used for investment in infrastructure and for the development of industry.

"There have been loans in the past that were wasted – they were used to boost the consumption level and to raise the standard of living. When the morning after came around, the only thing left was a bigger debt and perhaps some good memories of high living, but the tree that should have been bearing fruit wasn't there," Frenkel said.

He warned that the government must fight the temptation to lower unemployment by simply hiring the unemployed. "It will be dangerous if we look for the answer [to the unemployment problem] in solutions that will increase the size of the public sector.

Earlier in the week, Moda'i announced that the government would begin to operate New Deal-type public works programs in selected pockets of high unemployment.

'India role depends on ties'

NEW DELHI (Reuter) India's participation in the peace talks would be welcomed if New Delhi establishes full diplomatic ties with Jerusalem, Bombay-based consul Giora Becher said yesterday.

"The government of Israel will consider favorably India's participation in the multilateral talks [provided] full diplomatic ties are established between the two countries," Becher said.

India has never raised its ties with Israel above the consular level.

But senior government officials said India's Foreign Ministry had approved an exchange of ambassadors and Prime Minister Narasimha Rao was now looking for a suitable occasion to make a formal announcement.

On Tuesday, PLO chief Yasser Arafat told a news conference in New Delhi that an Indian move towards full diplomatic relations with Israel would not harm its ties with the Palestinians.

An Indian Foreign Office spokesman welcomed Arafat's proposal that New Delhi play a role in the peace talks. "We will be happy to play any useful role in the peace talks," the spokesman said.

Military appeals court decides against deporting Palestinian

Only second time an expulsion decision reversed

ALON PINKAS and News Services

The Central Command military appeals committee has recommended that Iyad Judah, selected for deportation by the IDF should not be deported.

The army spokesman added that OC Central Command Maj.-Gen. Danni Yatom has accepted the recommendation.

It was believed to be only the second case where commanders have reversed a deportation decision since Judea and Samaria have been under Israeli control.

The decision involves Eyad Judah, 28, a student at Birzeit University who lives in El Bireh, an army statement said.

Judah, a Popular Front for the Liberation of Palestine member, was among 12 intifada activists from various organizations arrested last month and scheduled to be expelled. Four other residents of Judea and Samaria designated for deportation who also appealed were turned down by the committee.

The statement said the tribunal ruled that in Judah's case, "the Israeli army has less serious means at its disposal than deportation with which to halt his activities."

An army spokesman, speaking on condition of anonymity, said Judah's was apparently the second time in which the military had reversed a deportation decision.

In 1979, a military board overruled plans to expel Bassam Shaka, then mayor of Nablus, who was accused of inciting anti-Israeli violence.

Seven individuals from the Gaza Strip scheduled for expulsion lost their appeals to the committee set up in the Southern Command. All can now petition the High Court of Justice to reverse the decision to expel them.

SHABBAT	BEGINS	ENDS
Jerusalem	4:29	5:44
Tel Aviv	4:47	5:46
Haifa	4:37	5:43
Beersheba	4:46	5:45
Eilat	4:49	5:50

MK Ze'ev Begin, his shirt torn as a symbol of mourning, comforts his sister, Hassia, yesterday at their father's grave. (AFP)

NATION MOURNS BEGIN
75,000 join funeral march to Mount of Olives

BILL HUTMAN

Former prime minister Menachem Begin was buried yesterday on the Mount of Olives in the presence of the nation's leaders and a vast crowd of mourners estimated by police at 75,000.

Begin was buried alongside his wife, Aliza, who died in 1982. At his request, there were no eulogies at the brief, simple service, as well as no military guard of honor and no lying in state.

Begin was given a people's funeral, as thousands of mourners, many in tears, walked the four kilometers from the Sanhedria funeral home to the cemetery. A fleet of 50 buses carried others through streets that had been closed off to traffic.

Israel's sixth prime minister died at 3:30 a.m. yesterday in Ichilov Hospital, a week after suffering a heart attack. All three of his children were present when he died.

President Herzog, Prime Minister Shamir and nearly all the government ministers and Supreme Court justices attended the funeral. The hastily arranged service – Begin was buried at 4:37, 13 hours after his death – did not leave time for foreign dignitaries to fly here, but a number of ambassadors attended, including Egyptian Ambassador Mohammed Bassiouni attended, at the urging of President Hosni Mubarak.

Begin's son, MK Ze'ev Binyamin Begin, recited kaddish in the funeral home, with his sisters Hassia and Lea by his side. The street outside was packed with silent mourners, as thousands of residents in the surrounding neighborhood stood on rooftops and porches to get a view of the funeral procession.

Former Irgun Zvai Leumi (IZL) commanders acted as pallbearers for the 1978 Nobel Peace Prize Laureate.

Many walked to the cemetery, following a route blocked off to traffic by police, up Sderot Eshkol, through Wadi Joz, past the Rockefeller Museum and by the Lions Gate of the Old City to the cemetery.

The procession ran through the heart of eastern Jerusalem, as many

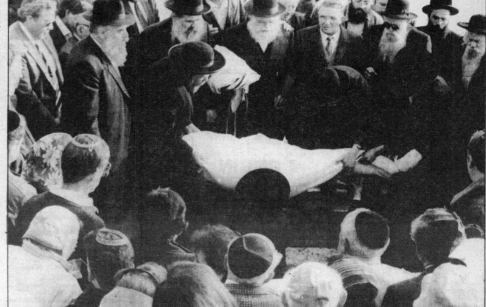

Members of the Jerusalem Burial Society lower the body of Menachem Begin into his grave. (Boris Smartenko/Scoop 80)

Arab residents watched silently from roofs, windows and sidewalks as it passed by. One incident was reported in the Ras El-Amud neighborhood near the cemetery. Stones were thrown at a border police jeep, and one border policeman was slightly injured.

Many of those who came to the funeral couldn't get near the cemetery, and fewer still could see the small area where Begin was laid to rest next to his wife.

Begin's longtime aide, Yehiel Kadishai, recited El male rahamim, and Ze'ev Binyamin Begin read the graveside kaddish. Family members and close friends filled the grave with dirt.

Hassia Begin, her head covered by a scarf, cried uncontrollably during the brief service, which was concluded with the singing of the Betar hymn by many of Begin's old Irgun Zvai Leumi colleagues.

Notably absent at the funeral was Housing Minister Ariel Sharon, who many charged caused Begin's downfall by leading the country into the Lebanon war. Sharon was in New York, on a trip arranged by Israel Bonds in order to raise funds for immigrant absorption.

"To his sorrow and despite all of his efforts, minister Sharon was unable to return in time for Menachem Begin's funeral," said a statement issued by the Housing Ministry.

Begin's oldest comrade-in-arms from his underground days, Ya'acov Meridor, told reporters Begin had stepped down in 1983 because of his sensitivity to the loss of life of Israeli soldiers in Lebanon and because of the anti-war demonstrations held daily outside his home.

It was the first time that a Begin intimate had offered an explanation for his resignation in Begin's own words. Meridor said the demonstrators had even prevented Begin from sleeping at night because of their chanting.

Begin had been a virtual recluse since abruptly resigning from office in 1983 during the Lebanon War, after six years in office. He subsequently emerged once a year, on the anniversary of his wife's death.

His last public appearance was last fall, when he celebrated his granddaughter's wedding.

(Continued on Page 2)

Never before has Jerusalem seen a funeral like this

ABRAHAM RABINOVICH

Menachem Begin completed his eventful journey from Brisk yesterday as he could only have fantasized when he started out – lowered into a grave alongside his beloved wife in a united Jerusalem, with his old comrades singing the Betar anthem and his political opponents paying their respects in a ceremony that did homage to national unity.

A figure of bitter controversy and estrangement from the Zionist mainstream for most of his adult life, Menachem Begin was buried as a national icon.

Jerusalem has probably never seen a funeral like this in its mass spontaneity and confusion. Most of the thousands who streamed to the Mount of Olives did not see the interment or even know where it was being held, as they stumbled through the ancient cemetery for an hour looking for a vantage point. There was simply no place to hold a crowd of that size.

Little sense of bereavement was evident among the crowd, despite the affection and adulation that had plainly brought the extraordinary throng, many of them several kilometers on foot. The mourning for Begin had been internalized by the public during his years of isolation.

They had long since said their painful goodbyes to the vigorous leader who always knew what he wanted and never waivered. It was out of respect for his memory that they came to bury the frail old man yesterday.

In a bus bound for the cemetery, a news photographer pointed out to a colleague the Arabs watching the procession from sidewalks and rooftops in East Jerusalem.

"It almost looks as if they're paying their respects, too," said the colleague.

"Why not?" said the photographer. "Begin gave them more than anyone else. Golda [Meir, former Labor prime minister] said Palestinians don't exist. Begin said he recognized their legitimate rights."

Headgear visible in the closepressed throng told something of its diversity – a white fez of a Druse cleric alongside the turban of the chief Sephardi rabbi and the red paratroop beret of Chief of General Staff Ehud Barak and a moshavnik's kova tembel worn by former CGS and current Tsomet leader MK Rafael "Raful" Eitan.

Yesterday, Menachem Begin was gathered to his own fathers and to the bosom of the nation.

News Highlights

Guyana renews ties
The government of Guyana announced yesterday it is resuming diplomatic relations with Israel 18 years after breaking off ties following the Yom Kippur War. A statement said both governments are now anxious to develop and strengthen ties and will soon begin discussions on naming non-resident representatives.

●

Hussein backs Iceland
Jordan's King Hussein said in Iceland yesterday he favors the North Atlantic island as a possible venue for Arab-Israel peace talks. "It would make an excellent venue for the negotiations," Hussein said. Iceland Premier David Oddsson welcomed the idea that Middle East peace talks take place in Iceland. "If the negotiations become very, very hot then this would be a good place to cool down," he said.

●

Lebanese civil war toll
Beirut police said yesterday that 144,240 people were killed and 197,506 wounded in the 1975-1990 civil war, with 17,415 still missing. The report, the first official statistics on civil war casualties, excluded more than 6,630 people killed and nearly 8,000 wounded in spinoff conflicts involving the Palestinians.

●

Zim slated for sale
Zim is expected to be the next government company to be privatized, as the Treasury announced it has completed the purchase of Hevrat Ha'ovdim's shares in four stateowned firms. Page 11

●

Split market personality
It was a tale of two markets yesterday, as heavily weighted shares lost ground on the Tel Aviv Stock Exchange but smaller issues continued to advance. On foreign currency markets, the shekel slipped 0.04% against the dollar. Page 11

Doctors: Begin was too weak

JACOB WIRTSCHAFTER

Doctors mounted an intensive, but unsuccessful, last-ditch effort to keep Menachem Begin alive.

At 3:15 a.m. yesterday, an emergency team at Ichilov Hospital attempted to resuscitate Begin's failing heart with electric shocks and injections to the cardiac muscle.

But as hospital director Prof. Dan Michaeli described later, Begin – weakened by last week's severe heart attack – lacked the strength to respond to his physician's efforts.

A nurse called Begin's children, who had left the hospital shortly after 10 p.m., and daughter Lea Milo rushed to her father's bedside.

Begin was officially pronounced dead at 3:30 a.m., although his death was not publicly announced for another 90 minutes.

Shortly before 6 a.m., the hospital's cantor arrived at Begin's bedside to recite kaddish, the traditional prayer in Aramaic praising God and justifying his decisions.

At 6:15, IDF burial society (hevra kadisha) members arrived to prepare Begin's body for burial.

Menachem Begin / 1913-1992

Bomb destroys Israel's embassy in Buenos Aires; 5 dead, 81 hurt

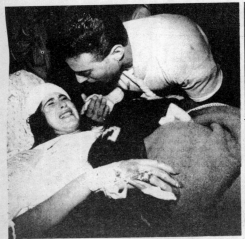

A girl injured in yesterday's terrorist attack in Jaffa is comforted by a friend.
(Israel Sun)

Diplomat's wife among the victims

DAVID MAKOVSKY
and news agencies

A bomb destroyed the Israeli Embassy in Buenos Aires yesterday, killing at least five people and wounding at least 81.

Among those killed was the wife of an Israeli diplomat. Her name was not released last night.

Five embassy staffers were injured and two are still missing, Foreign Minister David Levy reported at midnight.

Police outside the shattered building in a smart Buenos Aires suburb said five people had died and at least 30 victims were believed trapped in the rubble. They said the bomb could have been placed in a car.

Argentine Foreign Minister Guido Ditella told Levy in a telephone call that to the best of his knowledge four of the dead were local electrical technicians working in the building.

When asked if this second attack at an Israeli embassy in the last 10 days constituted a major security lapse, Levy defended security personel. "They are soldiers at the front and they do their job the best they can. It should be recalled that this car-bombing happened in the middle of a busy city."

While admitting Israel had no information yet as to the identity of the bombers, he said: "We have an open account with them which we will close. We cannot coexist with terrorism."

Prime Minister Shamir was notified of the bombing during a dinner he hosted in honor of Bulgarian Prime Minister Filip Dimitrov. In his after dinner remarks Shamir declared: "Arab terrorism continues to rage and kill innocent women and children."

Not referring directly to the killings in Buenos Aires or to those

Firemen remove debris from the Israel Embassy in Buenos Aires after an explosion devastated it yesterday.
(AP)

responsible for it he called on all civilized countries to "outlaw the PLO since it is a terrorist organization."

Argentine President Carlos Menem attributed the blast to neo-Nazis and rebel groups within the army.

"They are Argentine Nazis who see themselves as totally surrounded," he said, adding that the blast was "a product of something that was put down on December 3, 1990," referring to a bloody uprising by military rebels that was crushed by loyal troops.

Dov Kalinsky, an Israeli pulled from the wreckage, said that dozens of injured from the embassy and the surrounding buildings were taken to three hospitals in the area.

He said the rescue work was going very slowly. "The Argentines just don't have the right equipment for the job," he said.

"All over the place there were there were people injured from shattered glass – women, children, pregnant women, old people. I could never imagine a scene like this," said photographer Roberto Decournex, who arrived at the scene within minutes of the blast.

"It was the worst moment of my life. It is just by chance that I am alive," said an Israeli diplomat. "My office was blown apart, and I don't know where my secretary is.

"She must be under the rubble," he said, sobbing. "I can't talk."

Scores of police and civil defense rescue workers evacuated the area and began to search through the rubble of the embassy and adjacent buildings, which were also badly damaged.

Witnesses said they saw an elderly woman being carried from one of the buildings, a wrecked door serving as an improvised stretcher. Among the injured were a dozen children in a school across the street who were hit by flying glass.

Embassy sources said 70 people worked in the offices, which they described as being like a fortress.

Ambassador Yitzhak Shefi was not in the building at the time of the blast, his daughter, Nili Chaminsky,

told Israel Television from Buenos Aires.

No group immediately claimed responsibility for the blast. And Defense Minister Moshe Arens, in Washington on an official visit, said he did not know which group was responsible but that "it's part of a terrorist campaign which is being waged against Israel by all kinds of Moslem holy warriors and Palestinian terrorists."

He speculated that some terrorist activities might be aimed at sabotaging the Middle East peace process, but "as far as we're concerned, it's not going to put an end to the peace talks."

But he added: "It doesn't make it easier."

Machete-wielding terrorist murders two people in Jaffa

MICHAEL ROTEM
and Itim

Violence and fear pushed aside the Purim holiday atmosphere in Jaffa yesterday morning, when a terrorist from Gaza, wielding a machete, killed 19-year-old Ilanit Ohana and Abdel Ghani Karim, 44, a garage owner who tried to come to her rescue. The terrorist was shot to death.

Raed al-Reefi, 22, also managed to injure 16 people, most of them high school pupils from Holon who had come to celebrate Purim in a nearby club.

A passing taxi driver fired one shot from his pistol, wounding the terrorist. A vacationing border policeman then shot him to death. Shortly afterwards, police arrested two Gaza men suspected of being the assailant's accomplices at a roadblock.

Police found Islamic Jihad leaflets and a letter calling Palestinians to follow the path of the slayers of the

soldiers near Galed in the dead terrorist's pockets. He also wrote that he was going on a suicide mission to kill as many Jews as possible. The man had a valid entrance permit to the city, police said.

Karim left a wife and four sons, aged 15 to 22.

"No, we're not looking for revenge; I am not angry at anyone," his eldest son, Abdel Jani Issu, said. "Arabs are attacked just like Jews. Father wanted peace and for this whole situation to end, but he won't live to see it.

"The Jews think all Arabs are bad, but that's not true. There are good people and bad people among both Jews and Arabs. There are also radicals among Jews, and those who want to live in co-existence. The same is true about us. I only hope these will be the last victims in this bloody struggle."

Issu said the first news the family

(Continued on Page 2)

News Highlights

• S.Africans go to polls

South African whites voted yesterday in a critical referendum on President de Klerk's reform process towards power sharing with South Africa's blacks. Voter turnout was estimated at 70 percent as both de Klerk and his right-wing opponents forecast victory in a vote that could result in de Klerk's resignation if his initiative failed to receive voter approval. **Page 4**

• Guarantees 'a must'

Government economist yesterday warned of dire economic and social consequences if the US loan guarantees are not forthcoming, and suggested that Israel would have to be "more accommodating" to the US. **Page 7**

• Tase mixed; shekel up

After sharp morning losses, share prices on the Tel Aviv Stock Exchange moderated as blue chips edged higher but the General Share Index declined. On foreign-currency markets, the shekel gained 0.25% against the dollar. **Page 7**

Purim starts tonight

SURIE ACKERMAN

Purim begins tonight with the reading of the *megilla* (the Book of Esther) in synagogues across the country, except Jerusalem, where the holiday starts tomorrow night, Shushan Purim.

Last year, Purim was celebrated in an atmosphere of euphoria, as the Gulf war and the state of emergency here were declared over on Purim morning, and residents ecstatically packed away their gas masks, dismantled their sealed rooms, and toasted the defeat of Saddam Hussein.

But this week, Saddam's defiance of UN arms-destruction orders has led to the realization that celebrating the destruction of the "Iraqi Haman" last year was premature.

(Continued on Page 3)

Bush rejects guarantees compromise

ALLISON KAPLAN
and **ASHER WALLFISH**

President Bush yesterday rejected a congressional compromise to provide loan guarantees to Israel, key lawmakers said.

"I'm frankly very, very disappointed," said Sen. Patrick Leahy after meeting with Bush to discuss the proposed deal. "This language is not acceptable to the president."

Bush met with Leahy and other lawmakers after saying that Israeli settlements in the territories were "counterproductive to peace."

Just before the meeting, Bush said he did not believe the loan guarantees were "dead" but stressed longstanding US policy on the territories.

"If there's room in that policy to support" Jewish immigrants, "we'll try to support that," he said. "I've said over and over again that we want to help...but we're simply not going to shift and change the foreign policy of this country."

Earlier, US Secretary of State James Baker did not budge from the administration's uncompromising stand on American conditions for

the guarantees in his session with Defense Minister Moshe Arens yesterday.

In Jerusalem, Prime Minister Shamir made it clear he was also not willing to compromise. "There is no reason for us to withdraw our request and we do not propose to make things simpler for anybody by taking it back," he said, speaking to reporters after a gathering of coalition MKs to mark the final week of parliamentary sessions.

Finance Minister Yitzhak Moda'i insisted that Israel could absorb the immigration without the US loan guarantees, and said that he had prepared "alternative tools" for raising the needed capital.

"Israel's continued existence, as well as the continuation of the wave of immigration," he said, "are not completely or even mostly dependent on the willingness of our friends the Americans to give us the guarantees," Moda'i told Israel Radio yesterday.

Israel's congressional supporters and American Jewish leaders yesterday were pessimistic that the gap between the administration's de-

mands and the proposal promoted by Sens. Patrick Leahy and Robert Kasten could be bridged.

"This is a loan guarantee request which is now basically off the table, an issue that will be delayed or withdrawn," said Rep. Mel Levine, in a congressional hearing.

Leahy and Kasten were scheduled to meet with President Bush last night to discuss the issue, but there was little hope that they could reach an agreement which would grant Israel any part of the $10 billion in guarantees it has requested.

That hope was diminished further when State Department spokeswoman Margaret Tutwiler reiterated that the administration had given Senate negotiators a proposal that would grant the guarantees only on the condition "that there be no new housing construction beyond what is already underway."

"We are disappointed by what we have seen and the statements today by Margaret Tutwiler rejecting the efforts of the Senate to reach an accord," Malcolm Hoenlein, executive director of the Conference of Presidents of Major American Jewish Organizations said.

A scooter made for one

Bazaar / Page 10

THE JERUSALEM POST

60 1932 - 1992

2ND. EDITION

Vol. LX, No. 18086 Wednesday, June 24, 1992 • Sivan 23, 5752 • Zul Hijja 23, 1412 NIS 3.00 (Eilat NIS 2.50) 2:20 AM

EGYPT WITH THE EXPERTS

EXCLUSIVE – MIDNIGHT EXPRESS

Daily Bus to Cairo Via Rafah-Taba from $ 20

PANORAMIC TOUR 4 Days $ 73

ECONOMY PACKAGE 7 Days $ 299

NILE CRUISE • SINAI

TWAIG MEDIA

For all information call us:

MAZADA TOURS

TEL AVIV: 141 IBN GVIROL, TEL: 03-5444454, FAX: 5461928

JERUSALEM: 24, BEN-SIRA ST. TEL:/FAX: 02-255454

NAZARETH: PAULUS VI ST. TEL:/FAX: 06-564372

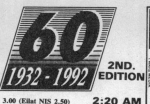

VICTORY FOR LABOR AND LEFT

Labor outpolls Likud; Rabin seen certain to head government

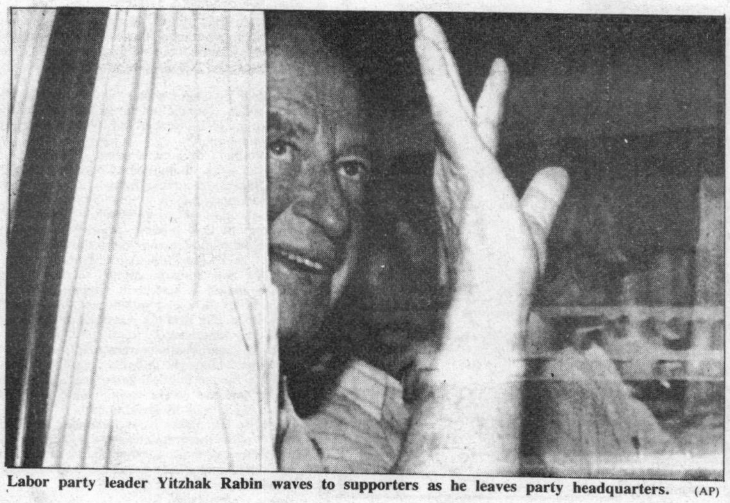

Labor party leader Yitzhak Rabin waves to supporters as he leaves party headquarters. (AP)

DAVID MAKOVSKY

Labor beat Likud by a wide margin last night and appeared headed towards forming a coalition government headed by former Prime Minister Yitzhak Rabin, ending 15 years of Likud rule.

"We will want to include all the positive forces of the people that identify with our path – furthering peace-making while ensuring security," party leader Yitzhak Rabin told cheering supporters after ITV projected Labor winning 45 seats to just 32 for the Likud.

"This will be a coalition of the mainstream. The people have supported our mandate and we will implement it," he added. "I will steer the coalition negotiations. I will decide who the ministers are."

But as the night wore on, the results kept narrowing following ITV's 10 p.m. exit poll projection, which showed Labor and the left sweeping to a bloc of 64 seats – a solid Knesset majority.

At Likud headquarters, initial gloom gave way to hope that Prime Minister Yitzhak Shamir and his right-wing and religious supporters might eventually win enough votes to block Rabin from forming a narrow government.

But if the numbers hold, Rabin will return him to the winner's circle in a stunning comeback after resigning as Prime Minister in 1977.

The partial results gave the bloc of Labor, Meretz and two Arab parties 62 seats, compared to 58 for the Likud, religious and right-wing parties. The Likud was suffering its worst finish since 1969.

"We must not give up. The night is not over," Shamir told Likud enthusiasts early this morning.

Rabin is expected to move speedily and build a coalition with Meretz, which gained 13 seats. Rabin will need three mandates to reach an outright Knesset majority, since he has ruled out a coalition with Arab parties.

The Arabs, who garnered four seats, are expected to support a Labor government from outside the coalition.

Labor headquarters at Tel Aviv's Dan Hotel was a scene of jubiliation, with its leaders promising significant progress on Middle East peace talks, scaling down Likud's settlement program, and improving Israel's ties with the US.

Labor's likeliest coalition partners are either the United Torah Judaism alliance or Shas. Since Labor only needs three mandates, it would be sufficient for only part of the haredi alliance to join.

It is expected that Likud will exert herculanean pressure to prevent either party from joining Labor. Failure for Labor to gain one vote would force the party to turn to the Likud for a national unity government.

Yair Tsaban, number two on the Meretz list, said the left's strong showing meant that the religious parties could only join a coalition if they accept the terms of the majority. He termed any effort by Labor to form a national unity government a "fatal mistake."

The religious emerge from this election somewhat weakened. While Shas and the National Religious Party each gained a seat to seven and six seats respectively, the United Torah Judaism lost three seats.

Observers say that the religious parties cannot afford to be outside of any government, and therefore they may all be fighting to join.

Some insiders say that the religious may justify the move to their own voters as saving the country from a secular party, such as Meretz, which has vowed to roll back religious gains.

The Likud loss is magnified not only by the loss of religious allies but also by the fact that the settler party Tehiya, which had three seats last time, apparently did not even cross the 1½ percent thresshold needed to enter the Knesset.

The only party on the right that sharply boosted its position was Tsomet, which climbed from two to seven seats. The success both of Meretz on the left and Tsomet on the right seemed to indicate a backlash against religious influence in Israeli government.

Both parties favor drafting yeshiva students.

The rise of Tsomet characterizes a new phenomenon: right-wing anti-religious sentiment. But Tsomet leader Rafael Eitan said his party would not go with Labor because it supports "land for peace."

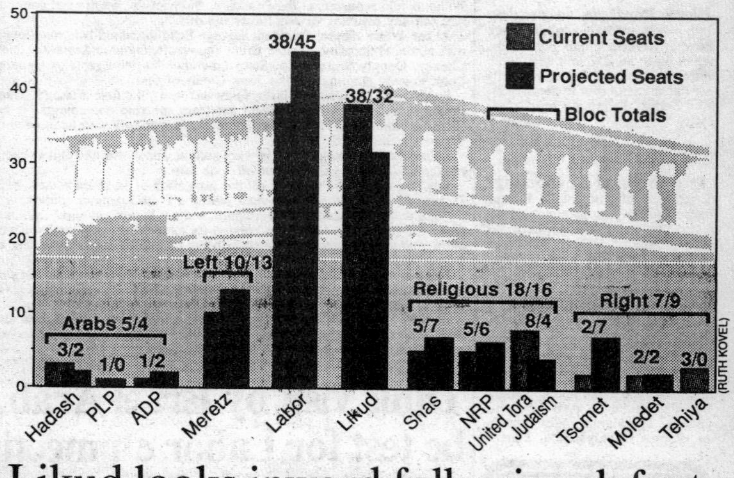
Current Seats
Projected Seats
Bloc Totals
50
40
30
20
10
0
38/45
38/32
Left 10/13
Arabs 5/4
3/2
1/0
1/2
Religious 18/16
5/7
5/6
8/4
Right 7/9
2/7
2/2
3/0
Hadash
PLP
ADP
Meretz
Labor
Likud
Shas
NRP
United Tora Judaism
Tsomet
Moledet
Tehiya
(RUTH KOVEL)

Labor celebrates political upheaval

MICHAL YUDELMAN

Labor supporters at the Dan Hotel erupted in paroxysms of joy, euphoria and singing when Israel Television's exit poll results indicating a political upheaval and a massive Labor victory were announced.

Champagne bottles, stashed in the cellars for over a decade, were opened, and activists and politicians hugged and kissed each other, some with tears in their eyes. People danced on tables and chairs and the entire crowd filling the hall heaved and shook with thunderous singing and dancing.

Cars along Hayarkon Street and the vicinity began hooting their horns, flashing their headlights and their passengers rolled down the windows to shout: "Rabin, Rabin!"

Rabin arrived on the premises shortly after Peres, but kept away from the main hall until he could be sure that the initial sample election results were not a mistake and would not change significantly, as they had in 1981.

In his speech at party headquarters, Rabin said that should he form the next government, he would appoint ministers according to their merit and would not give Shimon Peres's camp representation as such.

Rabin assumed full responsibility for his success or failure and took full credit for his party's winning the elections.

Rabin cautiously noted that his address was based on the assumption that the TV sample would prove accurate or close to correct. But apart from this reservation and his referances to internal party strife, Rabin plunged right into the role of future prime minister.

He began with expressing "my deep appreciation of the people in Israel for a serious, mature election campaign, with no violence and no hatred, characterized by business-like debates, listening to the views of the various parties and their leaders about the issues at stake in the next four years."

Here Rabin could no longer ignore the cries of "Smile, Rabin, smile," from the crowd and broke into a wide grin. His wife, Leah, at his side also smiled. Then he resumed his customary solemnity as he offered his "deepest gratitude to the public which elected me and Labor to lead the state."

Rabin pledged that he saw himself and Labor as having been entrusted by the public with carrying out the policy they had presented to the people and for which they were elected. "This, if the results turn out like the sample and we form the government, we shall implement. I said before the elections that I assume personal responsibility for better or for worse, and I'm glad it turned out for the better.

"There is no responsibility without authority being given to who is responsible. Therefore, I shall steer the coalition negotiations when the final election results are clear. I will decide who will be the ministers. There will be no bargaining. The ministers will be chosen according to their capabilities, not their belonging to one group or another."

Rabin said Labor would strive for a coalition which would reflect the main stream in the nation, "and we will want to take on as partners all the positive forces in the nation who identify with our way, promoting peace while at the same time preserving our security."

Rabin promised to change the national scale of priorities to providing jobs for the unemployed, hope for the younger generation, stopping the freeze in aliya, promoting education providing housing for young couples.

"To do this we shall need to change the allotment of funds in the state and create the conditions to raise resources from without, so that we can make peace and preserve security, and at the same time change things from within," he said.

Rabin thanked all the activists and campaign chiefs who helped Labor's victory and finally mentioned, after prompting from the audience, Peres and Yisrael Kessar.

When Peres earlier arrived at the entrance of the hall, which hundreds of people continued to pour into, he was greeted with thunderous applause and, perhaps for the first time in his life, with the song "Shimon, melech Yisrael (Shimon, King of Israel)."

The crowd closed around Peres, choking him with love and hugs and kisses as he tried to advance towards the voices calling to him from the stage.

"This is the greatest and best thing that could have happened to the State of Israel, to the Jewish people, to the peace, to employment," Peres cried from the stage to the cheering crowd. "I want to congratulate Yitzhak Rabin, the prime minister. I want to congratulate Micha Harish, the campaign chairman. I want to kiss each and every one of you."

Peres noted that "this is not only a great joy for all of us, but a heavy responsibility on our shoulders, to realize all the hopes for peace, for a strong Israel, united and thriving."

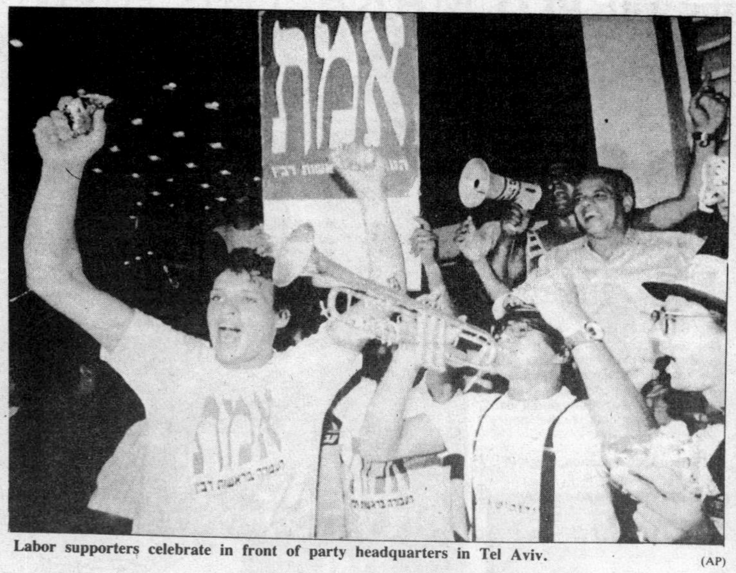
אמת

Labor supporters celebrate in front of party headquarters in Tel Aviv. (AP)

Likud looks inward following defeat

JACOB WIRTSCHAFTER

Prime Minister Yitzhak Shamir stopped just short of conceding his party's defeat late last night at the Likud campaign headquarters at Metzudat Ze'ev in Tel Aviv.

"There will be people in different parts of the world, in the Arab countries, and in other places, that will look at tonight's results and be pleased," Shamir said. "The Likud has gone down, they'll say. But they are wrong. No matter what the actual results, our accomplishments and achievements will continue to be a part of this state."

Housing Minister Ariel Sharon came closer to admitting the electoral defeat, saying the Likud respected the will of the voter and the principles of democracy. But he warned the party would be a vigorous opposition, and would be aggressive in defending the "Greater Land of Israel" by opposing any attempts to hurt the nation's security through terriotiral compromise.

Foreign Minster David Levy, who accompanied Shamir into the campaign headquarters at 1:30 a.m., told the audience of supporters he was proud of the hard work waged in the precincts.

Some Likud leaders said the party's internal strife was responsible for its disastrous showing yesterday, while also claiming the other side had somehow misled the public.

Deputy Minster Binyamin Netanyahu said the public had been confused because during the campaign Labor had hidden its true positions on the crucial issue of negotiations with the Arabs.

"All the polls show that the vast majority of the public supports the Likud's position on the issues," insisted Netanyahu. "What Labor did was take advantage of the internal problems in Likud and told the public, 'Look, we have mostly the same positions they do, without the same problems.'

"I'd like to see the new government commit itself to electoral reform, which will reflect the true opinion of the public on the issues spur reform inside the party," Netanyahu added. He also hinted a national referendum would be necessary on any agreement resulting from peace talks with the Arabs.

MK Michael Kleiner, who headed the Likud's campaign among new immigrants, said he had warned the party's leadership more than a year ago that Labor was doing serious organizing among the Russian speaking newcomers.

"We only began our serious efforts a month ago. But the Histadrut was organizing on the neighborhood level for months, taking advantage of these people's genuine pain."

The few rank and file party members present in the hall said they were expecting bad news all day but were still deeply dissapointed.

"We just weren't on the street and we didn't have the advantage of having a united leadership," said Sholmi Zeeri, a Sharon supporter from South Tel Aviv.

"Arik tried to tell them all along that more had to be done for jobs and housing. Some people in my neighborhood swiched from Likud to Meretz," he said.

Zeeri added he was fearful of what he said was Labor's unclear stance on the future of the territories.

"Rabin says one thing but Burg and the other doves say something else. Still, I'm not so scared of what they'll do. I'm just afraid beacuse I don't know what they'll do."

Rabin holding all coalition cards as national unity gov't seen unlikely

ANALYSIS / Sarah Honig

A national unity government appeared highly unlikely last night considering Labor's impressive – if the final returns do not substantively upset the prediction of Israel Television's exit polls.

Yitzhak Rabin is expected to set up a narrow coalition with Meretz soon, then widen it a bit with possible religious partners.

Barring any radical changes, the Likud is not seen as able to join the new Labor-led government. If the final results do not significantly improve its situation and that of the entire right-wing bloc, it cannot hope to enjoy a position as an equal partner. To enter the coalition with no real clout is as unthinkable for the Likud as it was for Labor in 1977, when it refused to enter the Likud coalition as a junior partner.

The bad news for the Likud of the initial exit poll was somewhat softened by later, actual results. These buoyed spirits considerably in the expectation that a tie between the left and right blocs is still possible despite the fact that the Likud clearly lost to Labor.

Rabin seems to be holding all the coalition cards and can play his winning hand any way he likes. He is not desperate for religious support, though he would like as many Zionist partners and as little dependence on tacit Arab support as possible. He would also not mind weakening Meretz's hand. However, he can bide his time and dictate his terms. Thus, the price which the religious parties can extract is minimal.

"An understanding had already been reached with one of the religious parties," a high-level Labor source told The Jerusalem Post just before election day. The betting among political observers last night was that the party in question is Shas, whose leader Aryeh Deri had been holding meetings on the sly with Labor's Haim Ramon.

Deri last night did not deny that his party might go with Labor. "We did promise our people to go with the Likud, but things change," he said.

He has special reason to wish to team up with Labor, in the hope that coalition clout, with new partners, would help him beat the pending police investigation against him.

There were rumors in Labor last night that Rabin had offered Shas both the Interior and Religious Affairs portfolios. The latter traditionally belongs to the National Religious Party, and would be a tremendous blow to them if lost.

United Tora Judaism sources also did not rule out a deal with Labor, saying that they would have to consult with their Council of Tora Sages. The National Religious Party's Zevulun Hammer deepened the melancholy on the right by saying his party had undertaken to join the Likud in a coalition, but not to follow it into opposition.

Yet the changing tune among the Likud's religious satellites has raised apprehension in Labor's primary partner, Meretz, which fears that in his desire to expand the coalition, Rabin may well – as one Meretz source said – "sell out to the haredim. Rabin will want religious partners and they will want to join, all of which is likely to make Meretz very wary."

Insiders in both large parties are certain that old feuds are sure to be revived in the coming days. In Labor, the various camps are already gearing up for the fight over portfolios.

Shimon Peres is convening his supporters tomorrow morning to back up his demands for the Foreign Ministry, as well as for jobs for his people. Peres' ally Yossi Beilin is convening his Mashov Circle, which is likely to press similar demands.

After absorbing the initial shock of its stinging loss, the Likud is expected to undergo a shattering internecine battle. Without a doubt, the defeat signals the end of Yitzhak Shamir's tenure at the party helm. Israel's longest reigning prime minister will now have to retire, sent home in virtual disgrace by the voters.

His departure will set off a momentous showdown among his would-be heirs. David Levy will blame the rest of the party for ganging up on him in the selection of the Knesset list. But he will be blamed by the rest of the party for the divisiveness which the party sees as the chief reason for its defeat.

Moshe Arens is seen as having little chance after Shamir's fall. Ariel Sharon had prepared an alibi by attacking the party's campaign line, – but he is not seen as having enough support within the party.

If the Likud is not torn asunder by the internal fight, it is likely that the younger generation will put up new leaders like Binyamin Begin or Binyamin Netanyahu. In any event, the next few months will be painful and bloody for the Likud.

The decisive component in the winning Labor formula appeared to be the personal campaign by Rabin. It was a risky gamble which paid off handsomely, and allowed Labor to rob the Likud of many of its grass-roots supporters.

Rabin appeared almost as a hawkish prince of the right and managed to blur his party's differences with the Likud enough to woo a great segment of the electorate away from them. Aiding him was the fact that for years the Likud had been building him up to spite Peres.

The Likud also entered the campaign fatally handicapped by internal strife, and then could not get its campaign act together. The entire political right fielded many lists and lost by its failure to unite, as the left did in Meretz.

But most important of all is the plain fact that the Likud had been in power for 15 years – and that is very long for a democracy. The public had matured considerably since the first three decades of the state, when a change of power was unthinkable. Now it no longer is.

24061001

40 years
of Nasserism

Page 9A

THE JERUSALEM
POST
60
1932 - 1992

Vol. LX, No. 18112 Friday, July 24, 1992 • Tamuz 23, 5752 • Moharram 24, 1413 NIS 4.10 (Eilat NIS 3.50)

News Highlights

Drug lord escapes

BOGOTA – The escape of drug-lord Pablo Escobar and nine associates from a ranch-style jail has raised questions about whether Colombia's corruption-prone system is capable of holding powerful traffickers and stopping their business – even from behind bars. Page 4

•

US road victims buried

Four members of the Korman family, who died in a car accident in the US earlier this week, were buried yesterday in a cemetery near Ramat Hasharon. Daniella Korman and her children Avinoam, Maya and Hen were laid to rest as those in attendance cried bitterly, some of them fainting. Many of those attending the funeral remained behind for over a hour, refusing to leave the cemetery.

•

IAF strikes Hizbullah bases

Israel Air Force planes blasted Hizbullah targets in the Iklim al-Toufah region north of the security zone in south Lebanon yesterday morning. Meanwhile, a close aide to Palestinian terrorist leader Abu Nidal was gunned down and killed in the southern outskirts of Beirut. Page 16

•

Black Panthers surrender

Two prominent leaders of the Black Panther terrorist group gave themselves up to an IDF unit near Jenin yesterday, just one day after a Border Police patrol shot to death Mahmud Zarini, the group's head of security. Page 2

•

Two arrested in shooting

Combined units of police, Border Police and IDF troops yesterday arrested two men in the northern Samaria village of Jilaboun suspected of firing at a car near Kibbutz Meirav, on the slopes of Mount Gilboa, the previous night. The occupants of the car were unhurt. Page 3

•

Tase falls again

The two-sided index fell by 1.4% to 151.4 and the Maof index declined by 1.3% on the Tel Aviv Stock Exchange. The Karam index, however, dropped by only 0.57%. Page 10

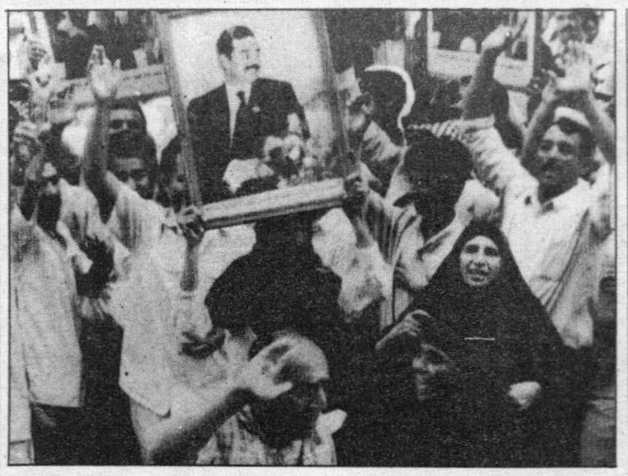

Iraqis rejoice outside the Ministry of Agriculture in Baghdad after the UN team of weapons inspectors ended their 18-day vigil outside the building because of threats against them. (Reuter)

US increases pressure on Iraq as port calls for Med ships canceled

WASHINGTON (Reuter) – The Bush administration yesterday sharply stepped up pressure on Iraq to comply with Gulf War cease-fire resolutions, and said an aircraft carrier battle group has canceled scheduled Mediterranean port calls and will remain at sea.

US Defense Department spokesman Pete Williams said visits next week to Greece and Turkey by the carrier Saratoga, two guided missile cruisers and a destroyer had been canceled. He said the Saratoga was in the central Mediterranean and the carrier Independence was already in the Gulf.

Williams repeated US warnings that Baghdad must stop defying UN arms inspectors. The White House said Wednesday it was keeping open all options, including the use of force, against Iraq.

"Any of our carriers could be called on for any mission anywhere," Williams told reporters at the Pentagon. "Obviously, we are not going to rule out any planning or any future options."

At the White House, President George Bush discussed Iraq over lunch with National Security Adviser Brent Scowcroft, Defence Secretary Dick Cheney, Deputy Secretary of State Lawrence Eagleburger and General Colin Powell, chairman of the Joint Chiefs of Staff.

Presidential spokesman Marlin Fitzwater said "the first message" Iraqi President Saddam Hussein should get from the ship movements "is he should get in compliance with the UN resolutions and allow those inspectors the access they need."

"The second message is we're very serious about this and this is not a matter he (Saddam) should put off," he said.

But Iraq continued to shrug off the possibility of an allied attack, with Deputy Prime Minister Tareq Aziz telling a Baghdad news conference:

"Iraq will not concede its sovereignty, will not accept any insult, will not allow the inspection teams to threaten its national security and will not allow... any other person affiliated with the United Nations to interfere in its internal affairs."

Iraq has refused to allow UN inspectors to enter the Agriculture Ministry in Baghdad despite suspicions by the inspection team that records of Iraqi arms programs might be inside.

In New York, Jose Luis Jesus, the ambassador from Cape Verde and current president of the UN Security Council, said yesterday that a compromise has been proposed to the Iraqis.

No more new houses, roads allowed in areas from today

Building of 10,000 homes to continue despite freeze

BILL HUTMAN

A comprehensive freeze on construction in Judea and Samaria was ordered yesterday, as the new government took its first official step towards reallocating national funds to social and economic projects within the Green Line.

But the go-ahead was also given to finish construction on thousands of new homes in the administered territories, with officials saying cuts promised in there could not be more extensive for fiscal and political reasons.

In addition, preliminary cuts were ordered on new housing starts within the Green Line. More extensive cuts are likely to be announced next week, when officials from the Housing and Finance ministries are scheduled to continue talks on the nation's future building plans.

"It was a difficult decision, but it was taken based on rational economic and political considerations," Finance Minister Avraham Shohat said.

The Judea and Samaria Jewish communities council condemned the plan. It was also criticized by figures ranging from former prime minister Yitzhak Shamir to the spokesman for the Palestinian delegation to the peace talks, Hanan Ashrawi.

Shamir called the decision "a nightmare" and said Israel is giving up territories without negotiating. Ashrawi said Israel's failure to halt all settlement construction is "extremely dangerous."

Meanwhile, a senior Housing Ministry official told *The Jerusalem Post* a survey of housing starts in the territories, with estimates of how much would be halted, was presented to US Secretary of State James Baker during his visit here earlier this week.

Asked about the expected US reaction to the housing cuts, Shohat said, "These numbers [of units frozen and those on which work will continue] were given by the prime minister to the secretary of state."

"Mr. Rabin talked about 10,000 apartments that were in advanced stages of construction. Even the secretary of state understands it's impossible to stop work on a building [in such a late stage of construction]," Shohat said.

Shohat made the remarks during a joint Jerusalem press conference with Housing Minister Binyamin Ben-Eliezer, where the two announced details of the government's plans to curtail housing in the territories, and preliminary plans within the Green Line.

Among the projects being immediately halted are about a dozen highways in the territories, to have cost over NIS 200 million; chief among

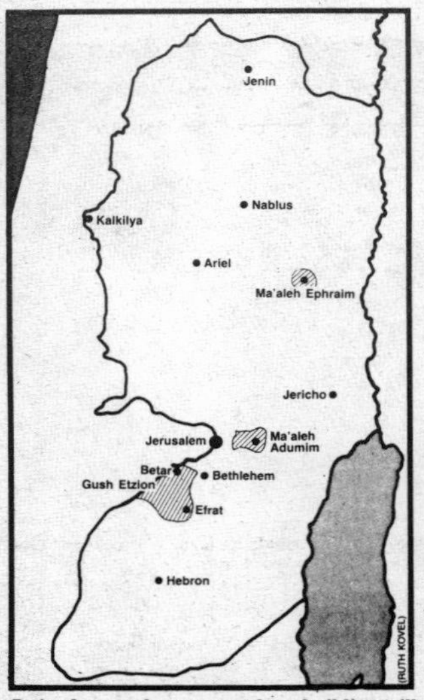

Striped parts show areas where building will not be stopped.

them the widening of the Trans-Samaria Highway and construction of the Nablus bypass road.

Shohat charged that these were "political highways" the Likud government built at the expense of badly needed roadwork in more congested areas of the country.

Plans to build nearly 7,000 new homes in Judea, Samaria, and Gaza were also cancelled, including 3,000 units whose final contracts are still pending and another 3,500 units for which contracts were signed with builders, but only foundation work started.

Yesterday's decision made official temporary freezes ordered early this week. The decision also allowed the moratorium on new home sales the ministry placed on the territories to be lifted.

Ben-Eliezer said a more extensive freeze on housing construction is not possible for "legal and political reasons." Many units under construction have already been sold, he explained, while in some areas, such as areas in the environs of Jerusalem, including Efrat, Betar, Gush Etzion, Ma'aleh Adumim as well as Ma'aleh Ephraim, the government is committed to continued expansion.

The ministers gave the go-ahead to finish some 10,000 homes in the territories, and left open the possibility contractors would be allowed to complete another 2,500 units on which work has just begun.

A final decision on those units and possible cutbacks in construction in other areas of the country are to be worked out by the two ministries next week.

Yesterday's decision to freeze some construction, but allow thousands of other units to be built, prompted attacks from both sides of the political spectrum.

"In the past 44 years there has never been a government that made a priority of stopping construction and leaving destruction and ruin its wake," said Likud MK Ariel Sharon.

Judea and Samaria council leader Aharon Domb issued a statement saying: "We are shocked by the speed with which the ministers decided to give into the demands of the Egyptians and Americans."

Small demonstrations were held near several settlements last night. A banner reading: "Kiryat Arba, a Zionist Political Settlement," was hung at the entrance of the town, where work was halted on several hundred homes.

On the left, Peace Now declared: "The decision to allow the completion of 8,000 units in the territories will mean another 50,000 persons living in settlements, and a waste of another NIS 1 billion."

Asher Wallfish adds:

The Likud chairman of the Knesset interior committee, Yehoshua Matza, said last night his committee would hold an urgent meeting next week to discuss measures to assure the personal safety of the Jewish residents of Judea and Samaria.

Matza said the freeze on building ring-roads around Arab localities would leave these residents at the mercy of Arab terrorists. "The government's decision puts human life in danger. It must be revoked. The settlers must not be compelled to drive through hostile Arab places," Matza said.

Likud MK Michael Eitan, chairman of the Eretz Yisrael caucus in the Knesset, said the gravest blunder of all was the freeze on the Trans-Samaria Highway.

"The highway has a high accident rate and must be improved," said Eitan. "It is vital for military operations, because it links the Jordan Valley with the Coastal Plain. If the highway does not provide safe links with Jewish communities along its course, the implication is that the government wants them to wither away and disappear."

Tunis visit by Israel Arab leaders could be test for Labor on meetings with PLO

DAVID RUDGE

A senior delegation of Israeli Arab leaders is scheduled to leave for Cairo this morning en route to Tunis, the headquarters of the Palestine Liberation Organization, in what could be a test of the Labor party's commitment to repeal the ban on unauthorized meetings with the PLO.

Delegation spokesman Dr. Ahmed Tibi said that the group would not "break Israeli law" during its visit. Still, he noted, that "at least one member" of the delegation, Ahmed Darwish, was expected to meet with a member of the PLO executive, his poet brother, Mahmoud Darwish.

Tibi said meetings between close relatives were allowed under existing law.

Ostensibly, the six-member delegation is traveling to Tunisia at the invitation of the authorities there, to attend the annual cultural festival in the town of Kartaga near the capital of Tunis.

Some political observers said the planned visit was seen as an attempt by Israeli Arab leaders to test the new government especially over the law banning meetings with PLO officials.

But delegation sources denied this was the case.

Several Labor Party members are expected to submit private bills next week that would legalize meetings with PLO officials in cases where state security was not harmed.

The Arab delegation is composed of Tibi, chairman of the Academic Association in the Triangle town of Taba; Ahmed Darwish, from J'daideh village in the Galilee, who is secretary-general of the Progressive List for Peace; Democratic Front for Peace and Equality (Hadash) Knesset member Hashem Mahemeed; Hadash secretary-general and editor of the communist-backed daily *Al Ittihad*, Salem Jubran; Arab Democratic Party member and Kafr Manda council head Muhammed Zaidan; and attorney Ossama Sa'adeh of Araba village in the Galilee.

Tibi said the delegates intended to meet Osama el-Baz, senior political adviser to Egyptian President Hosni Mubarak, as well as leading members of the Palestinian community in Egypt, during their stop-over on route to Tunisia.

The week-long visit is seen as part on ongoing attempts by leaders of the Israeli Arab community to play a more pivotal role in regional matters, and especially the peace process.

Baker visits Lebanon, Page 16

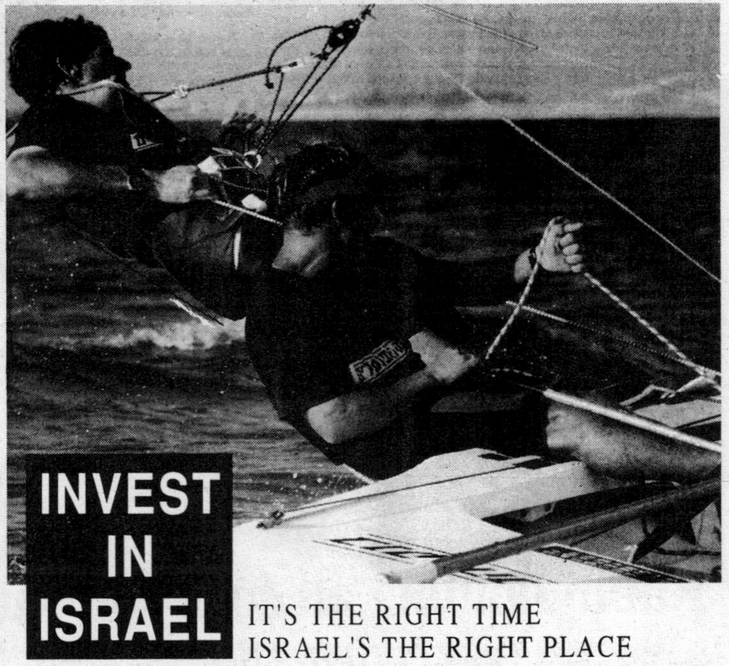

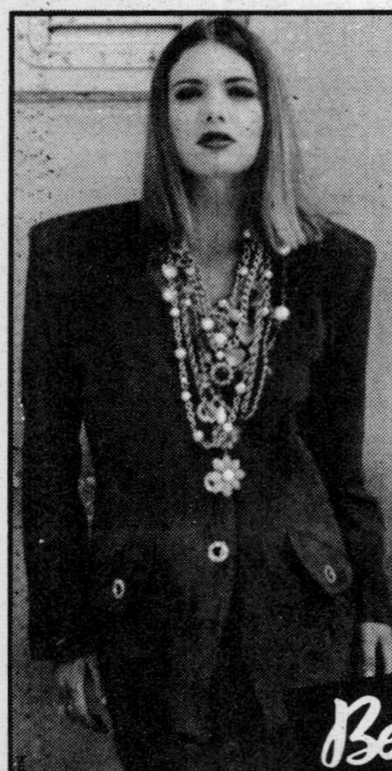

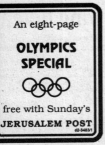

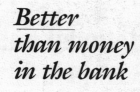

SHABBAT	BEGINS	ENDS
Jerusalem	7:05	8:23
Tel Aviv	7:23	8:25
Haifa	7:17	8:26
Beersheba	7:19	8:16
Eilat	7:16	8:19

Soccer league clubs' debts reach NIS 42m.

Page 11

THE JERUSALEM POST

60 1932 - 1992

Vol. LX, No. 18128 Wednesday, August 12, 1992 • Menahem Av 13, 5752 • Safar 13, 1413 NIS 3.10 (Eilat NIS 2.60)

2nd EDITION

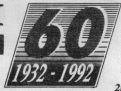

News Highlights

Serbs: mothers, children can go

Serbian forces agreed yesterday to allow mothers and children to begin leaving Sarajevo, officials said. The agreement, signed by a Serbian officer and a representative of the Children's Embassy, a private aid organization in Sarajevo, stipulates that all children under 18 and their mothers can leave the city.

Bosnian camps, Page 4

•

Bulgarian president to visit

Bulgarian president Dr. Zheliyu Zhelev is to pay a three-day state visit to Israel beginning August 31, as the guest of President Chaim Herzog.

•

Gaza man shot dead

Abdel Wahab Ghattas, 49, of Deir El-Balah was shot and killed by masked Palestinians while driving to work yesterday morning, the IDF reported. A squad affiliated with the PLO's mainstream Fatah wing claimed responsibility for the killing, saying Ghattas had cooperated with the authorities. *AP*

•

One dead, eight hurt in crash

One man was killed, two were seriously hurt and six lightly injured when two cars collided head-on yesterday afternoon near Moshav Elifelet, near Rosh Pinna. The injured were taken by helicopter to Haifa's Rambam Hospital. The accident forced the closing of the road for an hour just when cars were making their way to Safed for the opening of the Klezmer Festival.

•

Waterskier hurt in Kinneret

A 17-year-old youth was gravely injured in the head yesterday while waterskiing in the Kinneret near the Dugit Beach. He was taken to Tiberias's Poriya Hospital.

•

Namir: Syrians torpedoed talks

Environment Minister Ora Namir yesterday accused Syria of deliberately disrupting direct talks between Israel, Egypt, Jordan and Saudi Arabia on Red Sea environmental issues. "It appears that, because of Syrian intervention, the meeting of Red Sea coast nations, in which we participated along with Jordan, Egypt and Saudi Arabia, was halted because the Syrians feared we would reach agreements," Namir said yesterday in Haifa. *Yigal Kotzer*

•

Tase turnaround

Prices on the Tel Aviv Stock Exchange reversed course in late trading yesterday, after news of the US loan guarantees. In foreign currency markets, the shekel inched up 0.08% against the dollar. **Page 7**

Bush agrees to $10b. loan guarantees

Asks Rabin to be positive in peace talks

DAVID MAKOVSKY

KENNEBUNKPORT – US President George Bush concluded his summit with Prime Minister Yitzhak Rabin yesterday by declaring an agreement on "basic principles" to provide Israel with up to $10 billion in long-awaited loan guarantees. The president's announcement brought to a close a year of bitter acrimony between the two countries.

Bush said he supports the loan guarantees "enthusiastically" and called on Rabin to be forthcoming when peace talks resume in Washington later this month.

He said that Rabin had "persuaded" him that Israel is genuine about peace.

Both the content and the enthusiastic tone of Bush's statements – including one about the two countries being "strategic partners" – reflected a new warmth in the relationship. Bush denied that this was due to his bid to attract Jewish votes in his deeply troubled reelection campaign.

Later yesterday, Rabin returned to Washington to meet US Secretary of Defense Richard Cheney to discuss strategic cooperation between the two countries.

Some unspecified issues attached to the loan guarantees were left unresolved, but Bush expressed confidence that these issues would be finalized after consultations with the US congressional leadership.

In his prepared remarks yesterday, Bush also encouraged other countries to aid Israel. It is believed that countries such as Germany and even Japan would be willing to provide Israel with additional funds in the form of loan guarantees, now that the US and Israel are working out an accord that trades guarantees for a sharp cutback in Israeli settlement activity in the territories.

Standing alongside Rabin outside his home overlooking the Maine coastline, Bush declared "I am extremely pleased to announce that we are able to reach a an agreement on the basic principles of the government granting up to $10 billion in loan guarantees.

"I am committed to assist Israel with the task of absorbing immigrants. I am delighted that the prime minister and I have agreed to an approach which will assist these new Israelis without frustrating the search for peace. We can pursue these humanitarian goals at the same time."

Asked how much of the loan guarantee deal is finalized, Bush stated, "It is more than just a general agreement. There is enough specifics for me to recommend enthusiastically to the United States Congress and the American people that this is not only in the interest of Israel, but it is in our interest."

While his adamant opposition to settlements is the reason why Bush punished Rabin's predecessor Yitzhak Shamir by withholding the guarantees over the past year, the president made scant reference to settlements yesterday. When asked about Rabin's approach to settlement, Bush responded, "We see a very different approach to settlements. We salute the prime minister. It was not easy. It took courage."

In his remarks, Rabin only obliquely touched on the settlement issue, using instead his election campaign metaphor of "changing the national priorities." Throughout the campaign and since assuming office last month, Rabin has consistently maintained that halting settlement activity is essential to reallocating national resources and not because Israel was yielding to an American ultimatum. Rabin said that receiving the assistance means Israel needs to take the road of economic reform. "We on our part are determined to improve our national economy to a more efficient and privatized system."

Rabin said, "We should also carry as much as possible the financial burden of the guarantees, so as to lessen any costs to the American taxpayer."

Diplomatic sources say an agreement was reached between Rabin and Bush that the US and Israel would split the 7 percent cost of the risk premium, but this could not be confirmed.

The positive tone of Bush's remarks was not limited to loan guarantees. Bush sounded a hopeful note regarding the upcoming peace talks in Washington this month.

"I am optimistic that these talks are about to enter a new more productive phase," Bush said. "Prime Minister Rabin has persuaded me that Israel's new government is committed to making these talks succeed. I call upon the Arab parties to respond in kind."

In response to a question by *The Jerusalem Post* as to whether Israel has strategic importance in the aftermath of the Cold War, Bush replied, "Nobody knows from where the next crises will come. You rely on friends. Israel is not only important as a friend, but has demonstrated strategic reliability. I would just want to reemphasize that our friendship is based not only on democracy, but it is in the interest of the United States. It is in our security interest to retain the kind of relationship we have – militarily and every other way – with Israel."

Finance Minister Avraham Shohat said yesterday the money from the guarantees is earmarked for investment and would not be used to prop up the budget.

But Likud Knesset faction head Moshe Katsav warned that Rabin invited more and more pressure from the Americans.

Katsav said Israel's Arab partners to Middle East peace talks would now make tougher demands and pressure Israel by urging Washington to withhold aid.

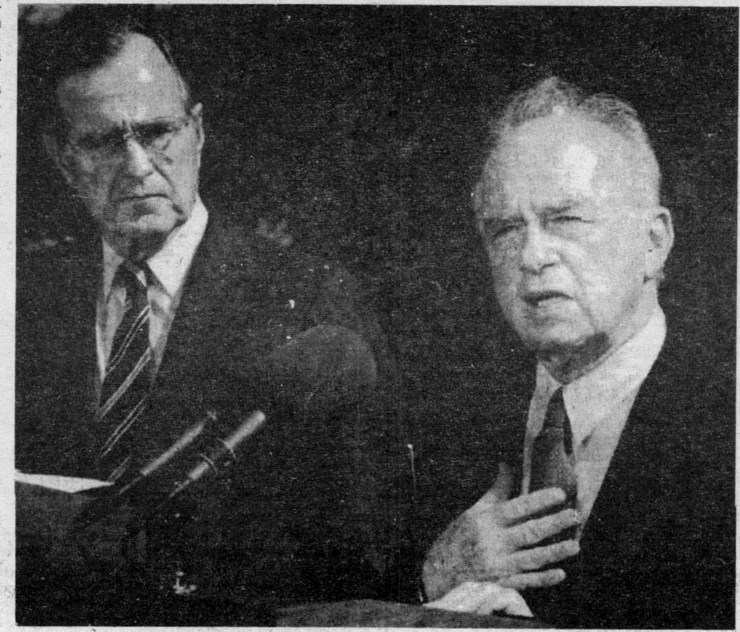

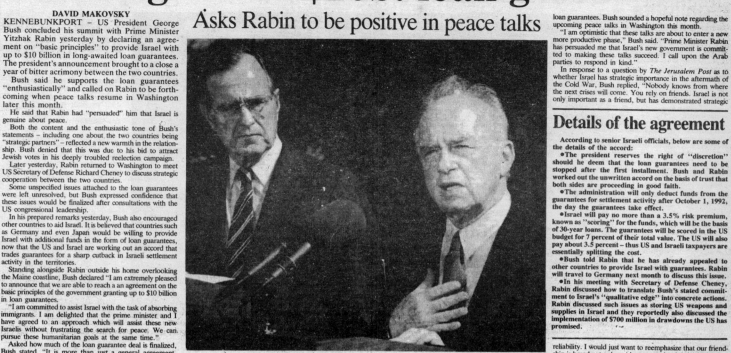

Prime Minister Rabin thanks President Bush at their news conference yesterday, after Bush announced he would recommend the granting of up to $10 billion in loan guarantees. (AFP)

Details of the agreement

According to senior Israeli officials, below are some of the details of the accord:

•The president reserves the right of "discretion" should he deem that the loan guarantees need to be stopped after the first installment. Bush and Rabin worked out the unwritten accord on the basis of trust that both sides are proceeding in good faith.

•The administration will only deduct funds from the guarantees for settlement activity after October 1, 1992, the day the guarantees take effect.

•Israel will pay no more than a 3.5% risk premium, known as "scoring" for the funds, which will be the basis of 30-year loans. The guarantees will be scored in the US budget for 7 percent of their total value. The US will also pay about 3.5 percent – thus US and Israeli taxpayers are essentially splitting the cost.

•Bush told Rabin that he has already appealed to other countries to provide Israel with guarantees. Rabin will travel to Germany next month to discuss this issue.

•In his meeting with Secretary of Defense Cheney, Rabin discussed how to translate Bush's stated commitment to Israel's "qualitative edge" into concrete actions. Rabin discussed such issues as storing US weapons and supplies in Israel and they reportedly also discussed the implementation of $700 million in drawdowns the US has promised.

Washington not ready to resume PLO dialog

News agencies

Washington is not ready to change its policy against a dialog with the Palestine Liberation Organization, despite Israeli moves to legalize contact with the group, a senior U.S. official said on Monday.

The US opened a dialogue with the PLO in December 1989, but suspended the policy in June 1990 when PLO Chief Yasser Arafat refused to denounce the attempted raid on Nitzanim beach by the Palestinian Liberation Front, a radical PLO faction.

A senior U.S. official, briefing reporters on talks between President George Bush and Prime Minister Yitzhak Rabin, was asked if the US planned to relax its policy since Israel might also.

"We are not in the process of changing our position on the PLO – under the basic conditions which President Bush outlined after the terrorist incident in Israel," he said.

"And those conditions would have to be fulfilled before the United States government would contemplate a resumption of the dialogue."

The United States said the dialog would resume only if the PLO condemned the operation and took disciplinary action against PLF leader Mohammed Abbas (Abu Abbas), who was then a member of the PLO's 15-member executive committee.

The PLO responded by condemning all attacks on civilians but did not specifically denounce the raid on Israel. PLO chairman Yasser Arafat obtained Abbas' resignation from the executive committee at the following session of the Palestinian National Council in 1991.

Meanwhile, in Tunis yesterday, a PLO official said Washington's renewed refusal to resume the dialog was an electoral ploy by the administration.

"The conditions have been fulfilled and the problem is over since a long time....There is an attempt [by the U.S. administration] to escape reality," Rabbo said.

"It is only a pretext for electoral considerations," added Rabbo, who was a memberof the PLO's four-man delegation to the short-lived dialog.

US president denies praise of prime minister aimed at Jewish voters

Leaders put new shine on bilateral ties

ALLISON KAPLAN

KENNEBUNKPORT – Standing together yesterday on the rocky Atlantic coast, President George Bush and Prime Minister Yitzhak Rabin were making a conscious effort to turn over a new leaf in US-Israel relations.

The two men were trying to project an atmosphere of friendship and harmony as they concluded their day-and-a-half of talks here.

"This is a special relationship. It is one that is built to endure," Bush said, Rabin standing by his side.

Over the weekend the two had discussed a range of topics, and although most attention was focused on Bush's agreement to grant Israel loan guarantees, the discussions covered everything from arms control in the Middle East to the current strife in Bosnia.

But the main intent of Rabin's invitation to Kennebunkport was to paint the picture of harmony reflected yesterday morning.

Standing along the shore in back of Bush's Walker Point vacation house, the two leaders were flanked by rows of their top aides on one side and a cluster of the Bushes' friends and family on the other. The tableaux included Barbara Bush leaning against a station wagon, cuddling one of her grandchildren.

Bush himself noted that he considered the greatest achievement of the visit not the context of the talks but the "tone."

He said that he related well personally to the Israeli Prime Minister particularly because they were members of "the old ambassadors club," presumably an unofficial diplomatic fraternity

"Our time together can be described as a consultation between close friends and strategic partners, one characterized by trust, warmth, and a commitment " Bush stressed.

When two leaders have such a relationship, he said, "this is strategic cooperation at its very best."

That statement by Bush sums up his philosophy of personal diplomacy. According to that philosophy, Bush's visceral dislike of Prime Minister Yitzhak Shamir had made US-Israel relations as difficult to overcome as any policy differences.

The smoothness of the Rabin stay in Kennebunkport was no less than expected, in what has been described as his "honeymoon" period here following the election.

The extra effort made on Rabin's behalf, however, does not have to do only with the Israeli position on settlements, but with an eye towards the November elections, and Bush's weakened stand with the American Jewish community.

Still, Bush rejected any suggestion that he was trying to win over American Jewry. He protested when asked by *The Jerusalem Post* at the press conference whether the tone of the Rabin visit could mend fences with American Jewish voters, who became angry and alienated from Bush during Shamir's tenure as Prime Minister .

"We're not talking about domestic American politics just as we are not talking about domestic Israeli politics," he said. "We are talking about principle. We are talking about doing what is right."

Even so, his praise of Rabin was extremely generous. He gave Rabin a "salute" for his "courage" on reducing settlements, and not only noted "how much we enjoyed having the Rabins in our home," but suggested he and the entire American people hoped that the Rabins would be "frequent visitors " to the United States.

Rabin responded with his own pleasantries to Bush, thanking him for his role in Soviet and Ethiopian immigration in the past, as well as his decision to recommend the release of the loan guarantees. He told Bush that his "role will not be forgotten" by Israel.

For Bush, the Rabin visit was a bright spot in the difficult and stressful week preceding the Republican convention. His reelection fight cast a shadow over the Rabin press conference when a reporter asked about allegations that Bush had once had a tryst with a former aide.

In addition, he is facing domestic pressure to deal with the crisis in Bosnia, which both he and Rabin mentioned during their remarks yesterday. "The world must work to bring to an end this humanitarian nightmare that exists in what used to be Yugoslavia," said Bush.

Rabin, who has in recent days criticized European inaction regarding the crisis, noted that "the Jewish people having suffered thruout history cannot remain indifferent to such tragedies. The killing must stop."

Tryst report denied. Page 4

FM willing to help Israeli Arabs adopt Bosnian orphans

DAVID RUDGE

The Foreign Ministry is willing in principle to assist Israeli Arabs who want to take in orphaned and wounded Moslem youngsters and refugees from the fighting in Bosnia-Herzegovina, Foreign Ministry director-general Yossi Hadass said yesterday.

This would be part of the general humanitarian aid Israel intends to give to victims of the fighting, regardless of race, creed or religion, he said.

Hadass noted that the ministry had received offers from Umm el-Fahm and the Kibbutz Artzi movement to take in refugees, orphans and wounded.

The numbers of those admitted and how they would be brought to Israel would depend on the ability to absorb and treat them and on the situation in Yugoslavia, said Hadass.

Killer mutant mushrooms in CIS

MOSCOW (Reuter) – Hundreds of people poisoned and dozens killed in Russia and Ukraine this summer may have been victims of "mutant" toadstools taking on the appearance of harmless edible mushrooms, Itar-Tass news agency said.

The agency quoted Russian epidemiological service head Vladimir Chiburayev as saying 600 people had been taken ill and 60 died in Ukraine alone after eating mushrooms they had picked. Dozens more have died in Russia.

Chiburayev said one possible explanation was that people experienced in telling poisonous from edible varieties were being fooled by mutations. "Toadstools may have taken the appearance of edible mushrooms under the influence of natural factors or, to be more precise, ailing ecology," Tass said.

Another possibility was that normally harmless mushrooms were drawing poisonous substances from the soil for lack of moisture in a hot, dry summer.

Peres: 300 Bosnian Jews headed here

BATSHEVA TSUR and ASHER WALLFISH

Three hundred Jews from Bosnia are on their way to Israel, Foreign Minister Shimon Peres reportedly told the Knesset foreign affairs and defense committee yesterday.

According to a source who attended the meeting, Peres said another 200 of the 900 Jews who lived there before the fighting started are currently on their way from Sarajevo to Zagreb in Croatia. The remaining 400 are still in Sarajevo and are not inclined to leave the city, but are anxious to receive aid from Israel, Peres reportedly said.

The source quoted Peres as saying it was impossible to take a position on the claims of the three warring entities, Serbs, Bosnians and Croats. "But we can take a stand on tortures and concentration camps," the Foreign Minister reportedly said.

Meretz MK Yossi Sarid, head of the fact-finding mission on aid to Bosnia, had been unable to get a seat on a United Nations plane to Sarajevo because they were all full with mercy supplies on the way in, and with critically wounded on the way out, Peres reportedly told the committee.

Meanwhile, a senior Kupat Holim physician, Dr. Rami Ditzyan, was due to leave late last night for what was formerly Yugoslavia to hold contacts with the UN and other international bodies aimed at assessing the population's medical needs.

Ditzyan will examine the feasibility of setting up a mobile field hospital or clinics and what the exact nature and location of the humanitarian aid should be. An Israeli Moslem doctor will be included in the staff.

This was decided yesterday at a meeting of senior foreign ministry officials with Jewish Agency, Health Ministry, Magen David Adom and Kupat Holim Clalit representatives.

They also decided that non-Jewish children would be hosted by the Kibbutz Artzi movement and by the Umm el-Fahm municipality, both of which have expressed their desire to help.

(Continued on Page 2)

12081004

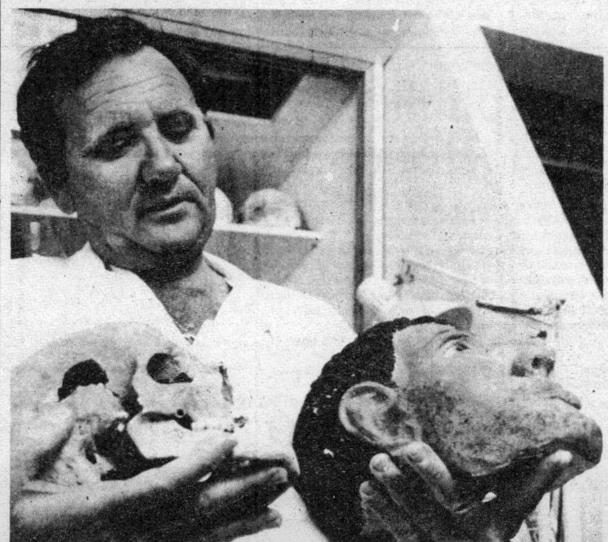

Hadassah University Hospital dental surgeon Dr. Motti Sela displays the 3,000-year-old skull of a Phoenician man alongside a reconstruction of the man's face. (Reuter)

3,000-year-old gets new face

JUDY SIEGEL

A Phoenician who apparently died 3,000 years ago in a fall at Achziv has been given a new face by plastic surgeons at Hadassah-University Hospital's maxillofacial rehabilitation department.

Prof. Patricia Smith of the anatomy department asked Prof. Motti Sela of the rehabilitation department to repair an ancient skull found at the archeological dig at Achziv on the northern coast and restore its facial features. Doing so would give archaeologists a better idea of how ancient Phoenicians looked.

According to Hadassah, Prof. Sela and his colleagues took up the challenge and used techniques meant for restoring the face after tumors are removed or following a traumatic injury. Documentation of the restoration process was accepted for an article by *National Geographic* magazine.

The skull was spongy and broken into four parts when it arrived at the Hadassah lab. To prevent it from falling apart it was coated with hydrocolloid materials. They then repaired the back of the skull, whose injury apparently led to the man's death, and put the four parts together using methyl methacralite, which has a bone-like toughness.

Artist Raviv Genshira then used measurements known to anthropologists and used natural-looking materials to create synthetic soft tissue to make the skull look human. The location and size of various features, including the mouth and nose, were produced by using measurements known in anthropological literature. A plaster cast was made, dried and painted, and hair was added, producing a life-like Phoenician Man.

THE JERUSALEM
POST
60
1932 - 1992

Vol. LX, No. 18173 Monday, October 5, 1992 • Tishrei 8, 5753 • Rabia Tania 8, 1413 NIS 3.10 (Eilat NIS 2.60)

Scores killed in El Al cargo plane crash

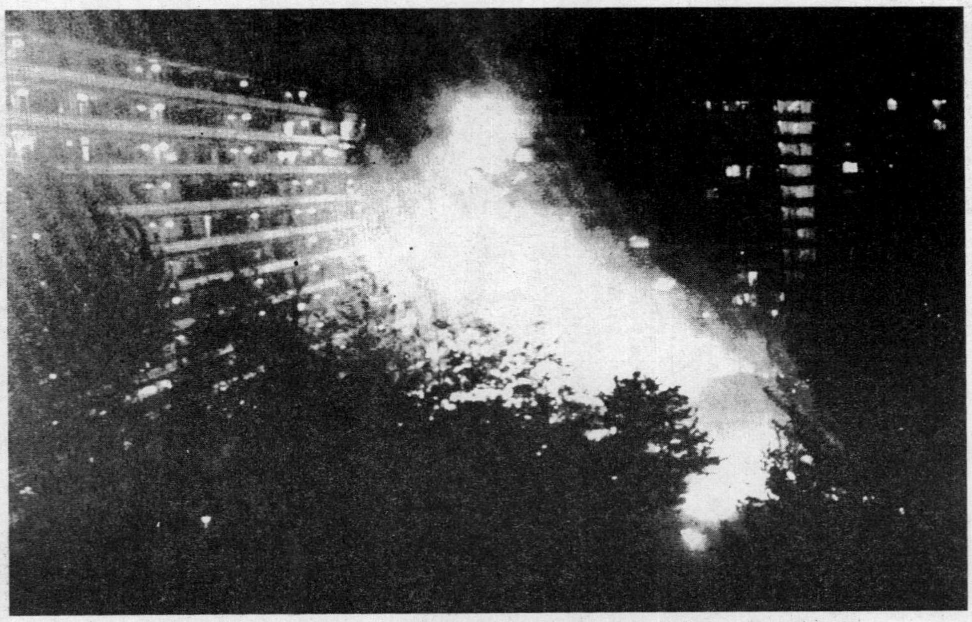

More than 50 apartments are ablaze in an Amsterdam suburb after an apartment complex was hit by an El Al cargo plane. (AFP)

Engine trouble reported after Amsterdam takeoff

News Agencies

An El Al cargo jet crashed into two adjacent apartment buildings on the outskirts of Amsterdam last night, minutes after its pilot reported engine trouble on takeoff from the city's Schiphol airport.

Flaming wreckage from the Boeing 747 scattered widely over a densely populated area near the airport. Dutch television said police feared up to 200 people in or near the buildings may have died in the crash and ensuing fire. By late last night, 12 bodies had been recovered.

Airline officials dismissed early suspicion of a terrorist strike.

Yisrael Cherbin, cargo manager for El Al in Amsterdam, said the plane's captain reported problems with two engines shortly after takeoff and asked to return to the airport, about 15 kilometers south of Amsterdam.

"He's returning to land, and when he said he was landing, it crashed," said Cherbin. He said the Tel Aviv-bound plane, carried "a regular commercial load." He added the plane had carried three crew members and a passenger, who were apparently killed instantly.

The cargo plane crash would be the first loss of an El Al plane to mechanical problems in the airline's 44-year history.

The plane flew over a lake to dump fuel and crashed about 1730 GMT (7:30 p.m. Israel time) on the turn to make a new approach to Schiphol, one of Europe's busiest airfields. A Dutch police officer and at least one witness said the fuel dumping caused fires for several kilometers along the route of the attempted landing.

Mayor Ed van Thijn of the suburb of Duivendrecht said at least 50 apartments had been gutted by the blaze. One of the buildings collapsed after burning for several hours.

Some people jumped out of the windows of their apartments to escape the inferno, Dutch radio reported. Residents searched frantically for family members, as helicopters fitted with strobe lights tried to illuminate the scene for hundreds of rescue workers.

Municipal authorities made an emergency call for blood donations, to help treat the dozens of victims who were rushed to area hospitals.

"I saw the plane going nose-down with the left wing up and the right wing down behind the next flat building," said photographer Peter de Neef, who witnessed the crash. "The engines were smoking ... and then I heard the pilot trying to pull up and then I didn't see it and I saw sparks coming in the air."

"It crashed right into the building. I saw the wings and all ignited. It exploded into one huge sea of fire," said resident Mark van der Linden.

One unidentified man told Dutch radio said he saw the plane flying at low altitude. "It was banked and a pillar of smoke rose from the right wing, then we saw the sky burst into red," he said.

Prime Minister Yitzhak Rabin expressed his shock over the tragedy in a cable to Netherlands Prime Minister Ruud Lubbers.

"I was deeply shocked at the horrible tragedy...Our heart is with you as we mourn the death of Dutch and Israelis alike," Rabin said in the cable released by his office. "We wish a quick recovery to the injured. Please convey my sincere condolences to the people of Holland and to the bereaved families."

Israel's ambassador to Holland, Michael Bavli, visited the crash site.

News Highlights

Preemie deaths

The death of three premature babies at Soroka Hospital was caused by a contaminated intravenous feeding solution. Page 3

•

Bush to debate Clinton

President George Bush and Democrat Bill Clinton will hold their first debate Sunday in St. Louis and latecomer Ross Perot is invited. Bush's staff made the formal announcement of three, 90-minute, nationally televised presidential debates and one vice-presidential debate, all squeezed into nine days. Page 4

•

Fisher, Spassky draw

Bobby Fischer and Boris Spassky played to their third successive draw yesterday in the 15th game of their $5 million chess rematch, leaving Fischer with a 5-3 lead. The players agreed to a draw after 32 moves.

•

Rubinstein to continue

The cabinet yesterday voted to extend the tenure of current cabinet secretary Elyakim Rubinstein for another three months. Rubinstein is also chief negotiator for peace talks with Palestinians and Jordanians. He has served as cabinet secretary for four years during the tenure of prime minister Shamir, and wanted to assume a position as deputy attorney-general. Prime Minister Rabin has refused to let him leave, however, saying he trusts Rubinstein.

•

Records at Tase

Two key stock market indexes rose more than 2% and turnover reached a record NIS 191m. as the public poured more money into mutual funds. Page 7

Unproductive visit to Damascus by Dumas

DAVID MAKOVSKY

French Foreign Minister Roland Dumas apparently made no progress with Syrian President Hafez Assad over the weekend in breaking the logjam in peace talks with Israel.

After talks in Jerusalem yesterday with Prime Minister Rabin and Foreign Minister Shimon Peres, Dumas said that Assad considers the ball to be in Israel's court.

Furthermore, Syria is sticking to its boycott of five different sets of multilateral peace talks on regional issues, Dumas said.

At the same time, Dumas voiced hope. In his meetings yesterday, Dumas cited Assad as favoring quick progress, with a breakthrough preceding the US elections in November.

Dumas said he was concerned – as was Syria – that momentum at the peace table will be lost if both sides wait until a new US administration takes hold in January.

Meanwhile, in a press conference at the conclusion of talks with Peres, Dumas spoke of new warmth in Paris' relationship with Israel. To illustrate the point, he said France's President Francois Mitterrand would be visiting Israel from November 26-28.

Standing alongside Dumas, Peres hailed Mitterrand as a "great friend of Israel".

It was also announced that President Chaim Herzog will be visiting France on October 18.

2 SLA soldiers killed, 3 hurt by Hizbullah

DAVID RUDGE

Two South Lebanese Army soldiers were killed and three others were lightly wounded yesterday in what appeared to be a carefully-planned Hizbullah ambush of an SLA convoy along the northern perimeter of the security zone.

Reports from Lebanon said one of those killed was the SLA's top security chief in the region, Hussein Abdul Nahbi, who had survived previous assassination attempts.

SLA gunners responded by bombarding suspected terrorist targets north of the zone. The village of Tibnin and its environs were hit, although there were no reports of casualties.

It was the second major attack by the Hizbullah following last Wednesday's abortive assault on a SLA outpost near Rashaf village in the western sector of the zone.

Two SLA soldiers were killed and four wounded in that incident, as well as four of the Hizbullah attackers. An Irish Unifil soldier and two Lebanese civilians were also killed in the heavy fighting that erupted at that time.

The incident yesterday afternoon occurred near the Beit Yahoun crossing point on the northern perimeter of the zone, in the central sector, which has been the scene of several Hizbullah attacks on SLA and IDF targets in the past.

Reports from Lebanon said the Hizbullah attacked a SLA convoy carrying Nahbi and his escorts by detonating a roadside bomb alongside the vehicles. The gunmen, at the same time, opened fire with mortars, RPGs and light weapons fire at the convoy.

Second mystery memo on Bush-Nir meeting

MICHAEL ROTEM

An analysis by *The Jerusalem Post* indicates that there are two alleged top secret memoranda, said to have been written by Amiram Nir to then prime minister Shinon Peres, and not one as reported until now.

The documents detail an alleged secret meeting with then American vice-president George Bush.

The first document, dated March 11, was mentioned in *The Jerusalem Post* in a report by David Makovsky on September 27, quoting a still unpublished *US News and World Report* article. That document resurfaced yesterday in a *Ha'aretz* report.

According to that document, which contained a note saying it was one of only two copies, Bush was briefed on July 29, 1986 by Nir, then Peres' adviser on terrorism, about the release of three hostages just one day before then president Ronald Reagan authorized the shipment of 240 Hawk missiles to Iran.

The meeting between Bush and Nir was reportedly set up by Lt.-Col. Oliver North, who headed negotiations on selling arms to Iran. In their meeting, Nir reportedly told Bush and his top aide, Craig Fuller, "that Israel intercepted information from the Iranian government and the hostage holders, and that Israel knew of the Iranian instruction to the kidnapers to release three hostages."

The second document, dated February 9, 1987, was at the center of a Friday night ABC-TV *Nightline report*. It was a memo telling Peres he had explained to Bush that the Iranians involved in the scheme were "clearly the most extreme," *Nightline* reported. It carried a note indicating only four copies of the document had been made.

Bush has said several times that he believed the contacts were with moderate Iranians who might some day be friendly toward the US.

The security authorities suspect at least one of the documents was apparently leaked to the American press by an Israeli.

Many secret documents were stolen from Nir's home in what detectives called a "professional" break-in a few months ago. Nir's widow, Judy, yesterday ruled out that "the document" was "stolen in the burglary," but it was unclear to which document she was referring.

It is still unknown whether Nir, killed in a mysterious plane crash shortly after Bush was elected president, recorded the 25-minute briefing he reportedly had with Bush, as was his habit. Cassette tapes were also taken from Nir's home in the break-in.

Bush has always maintained that he was "out of the loop" during the entire Iran-Contra affair, and that Nir made no mention of trading weapons to Iran for the release of hostages. Published notes of then secretary of state George Shultz and secretary of defense Caspar Weinberger about meetings where Bush was present indicate that Bush's knowledge about Iran-Contra exceeds his public statements.

Operation to replace public's gas masks begins on October 21

MICHAEL ROTEM

Operation Ra'am (Thunder), the large-scale effort to replace the gas masks given to the public before the Gulf war, will start as scheduled on October 21, the Home Front Command announced yesterday.

On that date, the IDF will open six pilot distribution centers, to run through the distribution procedures before centers open nationwide. Notices have already been mailed to some 800 families in Upper Nazareth, Haifa, Or Yehuda, Jerusalem, Beersheba and Rishon Lezion, who are to take part in the pilot distribution.

During the 10-month operation, the IDF will also provide kits for those civilians – new immigrants, recently demobilized soldiers, and babies – who never received one.

The new distribution will differ from the one before the Gulf war, in that each person over age six will have his mask fit to his head.

Residents who have protective kits will be required to pay for parts or items that are broken or missing, the Home Command added yesterday.

Forms to report broken or missing parts are to filled out at post offices, where payment for the items must also be made.

An entire protective kit that has been lost will cost NIS 78, while a missing protective children's hood will cost NIS 256 and a misplaced "Mamat" NIS 256. Costs for other missing or damaged items include NIS 10 for an entropine injector, and NIS 18 for a filter.

The stamped form will have to presented at the distribution center before the kit will be replaced.

Questions regarding gas mask distribution can be addressed to the information being operated by the Home Front Command, at 08-211166.

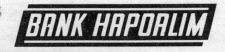

Eban on Balfour declaration
Page 9A

THE JERUSALEM POST
60 1932 - 1992
Vol. LX, No. 18192 Friday, October 30, 1992 • Heshvan 3, 5753 • Jomada Awal 4, 1413 NIS 4.10 (Eilat NIS 3.50)

Jordan makes commitment to negotiate peace treaty

DAVID MAKOVSKY

Jordan has agreed in writing, for the first time, that the aim of its negotiations with Israel is a peace treaty.

The Jerusalem Post has obtained excerpts of the agenda hammered out between the two countries on Wednesday, just before the recess of the current round of Middle East peace talks in Washington. At the end of the document, both sides agree to the following formula: "It is anticipated that the above endeavor will ultimately ... culminate in a peace treaty."

Senior Israeli officials are satisfied that the fifth section of the agenda, listed under the heading of "areas of bilateral cooperation," constitutes the essence of normalization between the two countries.

It must be stressed, however, that such a treaty is not imminent.

It will not be signed until all the bilateral problems between the two countries are worked out, including such thorny issues as dealing with Palestinian refugees in Jordan. Furthermore, while there is no formal link to the talks with the Palestinians, Bush administration officials have said privately they expect a Jordan-Israel peace treaty only after an accord on Palestinian self-rule is reached.

The officials said the agreement on the agenda will only be formalized after King Hussein gives his official stamp of approval. However, it is widely believed that the Jordanian delegates would not have agreed without prior authorization.

In a symbolic gesture, chief Israeli delegate Elyakim Rubinstein and his Jordanian counterpart, Abdelsalam Majali, together informed US assistant secretary of state for Near East affairs Edward Djerejian of the agreement on Wednesday.

The Israeli team returned yesterday for a recess until the talks reconvene after the US elections.

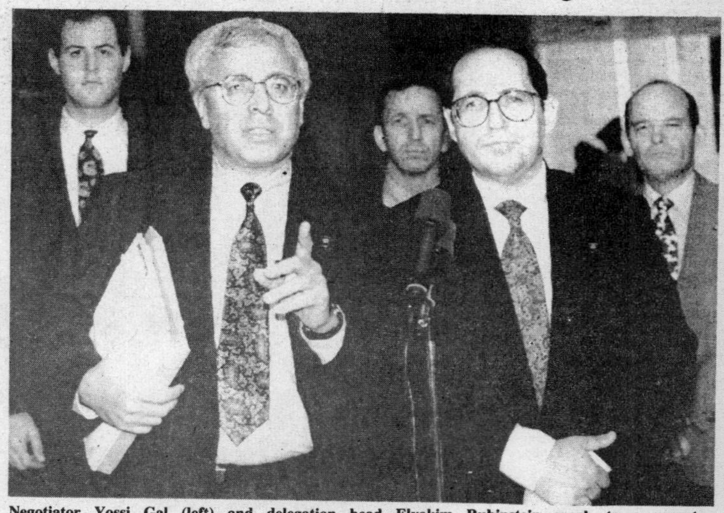

Negotiator Yossi Gal (left) and delegation head Elyakim Rubinstein speak to a reporter yesterday in Washington. (AFP)

The agreement came on the eve of today's first anniversary of the Madrid conference, and marks the only breakthrough in the talks.

Israel has been insisting that Jordan accept the idea of a "peace treaty," but until now Amman only spoke of a "peace settlement" or "peace agreement."

The agenda contains five sections – security, water, refugees, border and territorial issues, and areas of bilateral cooperation. Israeli officials say the Jordanians have asked that when the talks reconvene, first priority be given to the water issue due to the dearth of resources in that country.

The bilateral cooperation section contains four subheadings – natural resources, human resources, infrastructure, and economic cooperation. There are also listings within the subheadings. For example, under human resources, both sides listed health, education, and welfare. Under economic cooperation, tourism is listed. However, there is no subheading on diplomatic relations.

If the other talks, rather modest progress was made with the Palestinians. Both sides held informal discussions on the legal status of different types of land in the territories and exchanged concepts on self-rule. The Palestinians have dropped their insistence on a prior commitment to ultimate withdrawal from the territories.

Israel also submitted a paper to Syria, which for the first time contained the term "withdrawal," but made talks on withdrawal contingent on Syria's detailing its commitment to peace.

Mideast reconstruction bank proposed at Paris multilaterals

DAVID MAKOVSKY
and news agencies

The World Bank suggested establishing a Middle East reconstruction bank, as multilateral talks on development involving 40 nations opened in Paris yesterday.

The idea is modeled on the European Bank for Reconstruction and Development created last year to promote market economies in the former Communist states of eastern Europe. Both Israel and France have been supporters of the idea.

It is understood by all that such ambitious projects are only possible after major progress in the bilateral peace talks in Washington.

Israel boycotted the first round of economic talks in May because a member of the Palestinian National Council was included in the Palestinian delegation. But the PNC member was left out of the delegation to this round as part of a deal by which Israel agreed to negotiate for the first time with Palestinians from outside the occupied territories.

This time, the Palestinian team is headed by businessman Zein Mayasi, a London-based businessman.

"For special reasons, Yussuf Sayegh, the delegation head was not in the room and the Palestinian team was headed by Zein Mayasi and Khalil Hindi," a Palestinian source told Reuters. Hindi is a university professor from Manchester, England, the source said.

The agenda included detailed proposals by Japan, the US, France and the European Community, French officials said.

They said the initial proposals were relatively modest and ranged from developing tourism to university exchanges. The talks are to cover tourism, communications, and job training.

Israel asked that all economic boycotts and arms buildups in the Middle East come to an end.

Bank of Israel Governor Jacob Frenkel, the head of the Israeli delegation, delivered a speech in which he stressed that the Middle East cannot avoid regional cooperation, such as that now under way in Europe, North America and Asia.

"Joint cooperation between the peoples of the region could be the decisive factor" in regional stability and lasting peace, Frenkel said, according to a text of his speech.

"Economic boycotts are therefore economically counterproductive and utterly non-consistent" with the peace process, he said.

In public remarks, Arab officials spoke about proceding along the lines of project studies conducted by non-regional parties such as the UN or EC, thereby averting direct contact with Israelis in subcommittees.

"We cannot make any contact with the Israelis with Arab lands occupied and their people under siege," said Dr. Fayez Tarawneh, head of the joint Jordanian-Palestinian delegation.

Tarawneh, a former Jordanian cabinet minister, said there was a consensus among Arab delegates not to participate in any so-called confidence-building projects if they entailed direct contact with Israelis.

"The Israelis would like to cooperate right now but... we cannot accept this as it would indicate normalization before peace," he said.

"Palestinians could gain some advantages in these talks," one Palestinian source told reporters. "There could be some direct trade, especially in agriculture, between Palestinian territories and the EC and Arab countries."

Palestinian exports through Jordan, which would be the main route for such products, are banned, he said, and Israeli restrictions often result in Palestinian produce rotting before it can be shipped.

The meeting, co-sponsored by Japan and the 12-nation EC, is presided over by David Gore Booth of the British Foreign Office. Britain currently holds the EC's six-month rotating presidency.

Syria and Lebanon stayed away, but Arab states present included Egypt, Jordan and Saudi Arabia, as well as Algeria, Bahrain, Kuwait, Mauritania, Morocco, Oman, Qatar, Tunisia, the United Arab Emirates and Yemen.

The two-day meeting is to end this afternoon. The talks are being held at the Kleber Center, where the Vietnam peace accords were reached.

News Highlights

Not guilty in Brooklyn murder

A New York court acquitted 17-year-old Lemrick Nelson of the murder of Yankel Rosenbaum, an Australian yeshiva student killed during the riots in the Crown Heights section of Brooklyn last year. The verdict, announced after midnight last night Israel time, had been held up for several hours as police massed reinforcements in the neighborhood in anticipation of possible violence.

•

Stones thrown at pupils

A construction worker from the territories was arrested yesterday on suspicion of throwing stones at two Ra'anana pupils. The children told their principal, who in turn alerted police.

•

Netanyahu has best chance

Binyamin Netanyahu has the best chance to lead the Likud to victory in the next election, according to 52.9% of 512 Jewish Israelis 18 and older from across the country surveyed in a Teleseker poll this week.

•

Gasoline prices to drop

The cost of gasoline of all octanes is expected to drop some 3% at midnight tomorrow, according to the Energy Ministry, but diesel fuel and kerosene prices will rise about 2.5%.

•

TASE index climbs

The Tel Aviv Stock Exchange two-sided index rose by 1.13% yesterday to end October at 183.68. The index rose 8% during the month.

Rabin: We want to put an end to bloodshed

MICHAEL ROTEM

Prime Minister Yitzhak Rabin, Chief of General Staff Lt.-Gen. Ehud Barak joined thousands of family members at yesterday's Armored Corps memorial ceremony in Latrun.

"We want to put an end to the fire, the bloodshed and the killing," Rabin said. "We want to see an end to wars, and to know that our children will return home safely. That is why we work and struggle to bring peace. But peace without security is meaningless."

The Armored Corps has lost 4,786 men since the founding of the state, more than any other IDF branch. This week, the names of the three soldiers killed in the recent roadside bomb in Lebanon were added to the memorial wall.

OC Armored Corps Brig.-Gen. Yitzhak Rabin said: "The bravery of the Armored Corps warriors exemplifies the corps' basic values: motivation, professionalism, initiative and discipline. These values have brought us great achievements."

Nehama Israeli, who lost two sons in the Yom Kippur War, spoke on behalf of the bereaved families. Corp. Meirav Katz, 19, of Haifa, a tank instructor at the Armored Corps academy, lit a memorial candle. Her father Lt. Nissan Katz was killed on October 16, 1973, the day she was born.

Batsheva Tsur adds:

"We will not let the enemies of peace block the peace negotiations," Rabin yesterday told the closing session of the Jewish Agency Assembly. "Any attempt to stop the peace process because of terror attacks will only serve as an incentive to increase terror."

But Israel has to take a "calculated risk" in its search for peace with Syria, including territorial concessions, Rabin said. But first Syria must agree to a full peace.

Speaking about unemployment, he said the problem could only be solved through long-term investments and greater exports. But there is an interim solution, too, he said. If Israelis were willing to do all kinds of work, the number of Palestinians from the territories crossing the Green Line to work would be cut in half.

Rabin called on Diaspora Jews to encourage their governments to support Israel, and invest in Israel.

SHABBAT	BEGINS	ENDS
Jerusalem	4:16	5:28
Tel Aviv	4:34	5:30
Haifa	4:25	5:28
Beersheba	4:32	5:29
Eilat	4:34	5:32

Three winners split NIS 9m Lotto jackpot

RAINE MARCUS

Three winners shared yesterday's NIS 9 million Mifal Hapayis jackpot.

A self-employed man from Givatayim won NIS 4,605,970 after buying NIS 924 worth of Lotto cards. He said that this was the first time he had ever entered the lottery, and he chose the numbers based on *gematria,* a system of assigning numerical values to Hebrew letters.

"I had a strong intuition I would win," he said. "I knew I would become a millionaire one day – but I thought I would have to work hard for it."

When he checked his numbers yesterday and realized that he had just become a millionaire, he excitedly woke his wife up. He had not told her earlier that he had bought lottery tickets.

"She thought it was a practical joke at first," he said.

Two Jerusalem kollel teachers, 38 and 32, split NIS 4,548,812, after jointly buying a ticket for NIS 28 during a morning break.

Their friends persuaded them not to check the numbers the following day, saying: "It is better to live under an illusion for a couple of weeks."

Upon visiting their Lotto kiosk, they were astonished to discover that they had won.

Nobel laureate: Israel violating human rights

Nobel Peace Prize winner Rigoberta Menchu accused Israel in an interview yesterday of having violated human rights by aiding Guatemala's army.

The Guatemalan Indian leader, who won the prize this month, told the *Davar* newspaper:

"In the past, the Guatemalan army received very generous aid from Israel. Among other things, it received aid in computers and weaponry.

A defense ministry spokesman said in a statement he rejected Menchu's claims.

(Reuter)

US upbeat on talks, Arabs decry 'lack of progress'

ALLISON KAPLAN

WASHINGTON – The Bush administration yesterday tried to sound positive about the peace process one year after the Madrid conference, but officials upbeat words were undercut by Arab representatives, who complained of inadequate progress.

At a news conference yesterday, marking the conference's anniversary today, Assistant Secretary of State Edward Djerejian, hailed the peace process as having "changed the diplomatic and political map in the region."

Djerejian insisted his assessment was objective, and that his appearance was not timed to give President Bush's image a boost right before the presidential election.

During the six-and-a-half rounds of bilateral talks, he said, "the tough core issues of the conflict – land, peace and security – are being discussed by all the parties." The talks "have survived extreme violence" time after time, he said, and "in each track, there is real engagement and focus on the right issues."

But a far different message was delivered in another news conference yesterday given by the negotiators from Syria, Lebanon, Jordan and the Palestinians. The officials spoke before their departure home, as the current round of talks recessed for the US elections.

Though none of the Arab leaders even came close to threatening to pull out of the talks, as they had on earlier occasions, their tone was pessimistic.

"We are celebrating the first anniversary not in great joy, because whatever progress has been acheived is minimal," said Syrian negotiator Moaffac al-Allaf.

"Israel has always said that the Arabs have never missed an opportunity to miss an opportunity. It seems this time that it is Israel that is missing an opportunity."

Palestinian negotiator Haider Abdel-Shafi complained of a "sense of concern and frustration that we have not been able to acheive our objectives."

The one bright spot was provided by the Jordanian chief negotiator, Abdel Salam Majali, who indicated that he was only awaiting final governmental approval before the joint Jordanian-Israeli agenda for negotiations could be unveiled.

Israeli and US officials agree that Israel and Jordan are on the brink of such a breakthrough. The joint agenda is "a done deal, as long as the governments agree to it at home," said Djerejian.

When Jordanian and Israeli negotiators return to complete the second half of the seventh round of talks on November 9, they will be "ready to delve into key issues," he said. The Israeli-Jordanian example "should inspire all parties to do the same thing," he added.

Djerejian rejected the suggestion that the talks with Syria were stalemated.

"Israel and Syria have engaged in a very significant manner in the core issues of this peace procee – land, peace and security – and they have engaged in a discussion, for the first time, on mutual security and Resolutions 242 and 338, and on the meaning of peace," he said. "That discussion, that engagement, is real. It is different, because they are the issues that are at the heart of the Arab-Israeli conflict."

Djererian was also optimistic about prospects for progress with Palestinians, saying a Palestinian interim self-governing authority could be "in place by May, 1993."

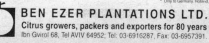

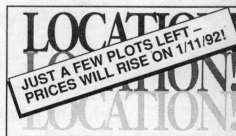

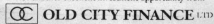

Mystic Mahler

Page 8

THE JERUSALEM POST

60 1932 - 1992

Vol. LX, No. 18201 Tuesday, November 10, 1992 • Heshvan 14, 5753 • Jomada Awal 15, 1413 NIS 3.10 (Eilat NIS 2.60)

Israel-Germany basketball clash tonight

Page 11

Lebanon talks cut short after tense session

ALLISON KAPLAN

WASHINGTON – Talks here yesterday between the Israeli and Lebanese delegations to the peace talks here were tense, and their meeting was cut short after 50 minutes by delegation head Uri Lubrani.

Lubrani said after the meeting he delivered a tough message to the Lebanese, warning of coming retaliation for Sunday night's Katyusha attack on Israel.

"If there is no security on our side of the border, life will become intolerable on your side of the border as well," Lubrani said. "The latest attack will not pass unnoticed."

Although Israel has generally pursued the policy of attempting to separate the peace talks from the violence in the region, Lubrani said yesterday that "the negotiations being held here between our two delegations have been jeopardized and marred by events perpetrated by terrorist activity along our border and into Israel now.

"Therefore, we felt it is absolutely necessary to register our very, very serious view of what is happening. We have said that this is something which can't be left unnoticed."

The issue of the violence in Lebanon was also raised in talks with Syria yesterday, according to delegation spokesman Yossi Gal, because "we wanted to make sure the Israeli message is loud and clear."

The talks with the Syrians yesterday continued to focus on the definitions of withdrawal and peace. Syrian negotiator Moaffac al-Allaf said Israel "promised" to return to the negotiating table with "a new formulation about withdrawal which can better satisfy requirements under resolution 242."

But the head of the team negotiating with the Syrians, Itamar Rabinovich, said that Israel had made no such promise, and that it was resisting pressure coming from Syrian president Hafez Assad to commit itself not just to "withdrawal" but to "full withdrawal."

Meanwhile, despite high expectations, Israeli and Jordanian negotiators failed to agree on a final joint agenda for negotiations yesterday.

Gal said the Jordanians had requested "minor definitional clarifications" on the draft joint agenda, and the document had not yet been finalized. Gal said that the requests were forwarded to Jerusalem, and that Israel would respond today.

It appeared the delay may have been intentional in reaction to other Arab negotiating teams' cpmcerns about a breakthrough.

PLO leader Yasser Arafat yesterday sent a message to Bill Clinton urging him to adopt George Bush's peace plan.

News Highlights

Rabin phones Clinton

US President-elect Bill Clinton pledged his continued support for the Middle East peace talks during a short phone conversation with Prime Minister Yitzhak Rabin yesterday. The first meeting between the two will likely be in March, when Rabin is to visit Washington to address the American-Israel Public Affairs Committee (Aipac) policy conference.

•

1 killed, 2 hurt on roads

David Levy, 32, of Moshav Zanoah, near Beit Shemesh, was killed yesterday when a truck swerved on the Beit Shemesh-Nes Harim road and hit the small truck he was driving.

•

Rape sentence extended

The Supreme Court yesterday accepted the State Attorney's appeal against the verdict and sentence in a Beersheba rape trial. Yosef Alabid had been charged with two counts of rape, but was acquitted of one because of a "slight doubt" as to the victim's accurate identification of him, and sentenced to six years. The judges said the evidence presented was sufficient to have convicted Alabid of the second count, and extended his sentence to 10 years.

17 years for rape, Page 3

A view into the new Supreme Court building in Jerusalem (Isaac Harari)

IDF forces in the north on high alert

DAVID RUDGE

The IDF has beefed up its forces in the north and all troops there have been placed on a high state of alert following Sunday's Katyusha bombardment, a senior IDF source said yesterday.

Forty-six Katyusha rockets were fired towards Israel from north of the security zone in South Lebanon on Sunday night and in the early hours of yesterday morning; 24 fell in various parts of the Galilee.

No one was wounded and no damage was caused.

In response, the US said it would warn Syria once again that Hizbullah should not be allowed to launch Katyusha attacks against Israel. This message was conveyed to Ambassador Zalman Shoval by assistant secretary of state for Near East affairs Edward Djerejian.

According to one senior IDF source, the rockets were aimed at civilian targets.

He noted that in the past the IDF had hit Hizbullah bases and targets, and the terrorists had attacked IDF and South Lebanese Army targets in the security zone.

The change in Hizbullah tactics would not prevent the IDF from hitting terrorists, as in the IAF air strike against a Hizbullah base on Sunday, he stressed.

The IDF, he added, has beefed up its forces in the north in the last few days, and all troops have been placed on a high state of alert.

A tense quiet reigned along the northern border last night, as many residents of front-line towns and villages said they intended to sleep in security rooms and bomb shelters.

Tension was equally high north of the zone, with Hizbullah gunmen and Lebanese Army troops on alert in case of IDF reprisals.

Observers in Lebanon said the situation has changed since Hizbullah's recent declaration that a "Jewish civilian must be killed every time one of our people is killed."

Until earlier in the year, Hizbullah had refrained from firing rockets into Israel because of pressure from the Lebanese government to avoid massive IDF retaliation.

Since entering the Lebanese parliament, however, it has denounced anyone who dares to publicly oppose its "resistance activities" and "right of self-defense and retaliation."

In a statement yesterday, as the funeral of the four "martyrs" was held in the organization's stronghold of Baalbek, Hizbullah said "[Israel] won't have any peace and stability as long as we have men who are willing to die."

Despite the fighting rhetoric, South Lebanon remained relatively quiet, with the exception of two Katyushas being fired towards Kantara village in the western sector of the security zone in the early afternoon. They caused neither injuries nor damage.

The IDF reported that a flare, dropped by the Air Force over south Lebanon, failed to go off in the air and apparently injured several villagers.

The shelling by IDF and SLA gunners of suspected terrorist targets continued sporadically through Sunday night.

A special inner cabinet session was held to discuss the situation in the north. Senior IDF officers briefed ministers on the situation, but no other details were disclosed.

Shoval spoke with Djerjian on Sunday, officials in the Prime Minister's Office said. After last month's attack on Kiryat Shmona in which 14-year-old Vadim Shuchman was killed and four members of his family wounded, the US issued a stiff protest to Syria, believing Damascus would seek to contain Hizbullah attacks to south Leabanon.

At the time, the US also urged Israel to be careful that any retaliation did not cause an unintended confrontation with the Syrians in the Bekaa Valley. Observers believe Djerejian repeated the same point to Shoval.

Meanwhile, Shimon Sheves, director-general of the Prime Minister's Office announced a three-year, NIS 95 million program to improve security facilities and aid residents of "confrontation line" settlements in the north.

The program, a large part of which is expected to be implemented next year, was unveiled at an urgently-arranged meeting of the special committee of ministry directors-general dealing with the subject of confrontation line settlements.

The proposed measures include the construction of security rooms for recently-constructed homes, roads, lighting and fencing.

David Makovsky contributed to this report.

Residents take to shelters, Page 2

Festive opening ceremony today for new Supreme Court building

DAN IZENBERG

Supreme Court President Meir Shamgar, the architects of the Supreme Court building which is due to be inaugurated today, and philanthropist Lord James Rothschild, whose family paid for the structure, exchanged compliments yesterday during a press conference prior to the gala opening.

Meanwhile, construction workers raced against the clock to complete work on the building before the ceremony.

A beaming Shamgar declared that the massive stone structure, located in the government compound near the Knesset "is the most beautiful public building in the country."

Lord Rothschild, whose family foundation, Yad Hanadiv, took complete responsibility for the erection of the building, congratulated architects Ram Carmi and his sister, Ada Carmi-Melamede, and others involved in its design and construction.

He refused to divulge the cost, saying only that it was less than new courthouses being built in Boston, Massachusetts, and southern England.

He added that the Supreme Court compared favorably with three building projects his family his currently financing in England.

Carmi and Carmi-Melamede explained that the building was designed to serve as a link between the eastern and western parts of Jerusalem, along the east-west axis, and to connect the entrance to the capital and the central bus station with the Knesset, along the north-south axis.

They added that the building contained many symbolic elements and some of the mystery of Jerusalem.

Shamgar added that the building managed to bestow the dignity befitting a court of law without overwhelming the individuals it serves. He also expressed the hope that the Supreme Court would serve as a model and inspiration for the improvement of the lower court infrastructure throughout the country.

Rabin ask Kollek to put off retirement

BILL HUTMAN

The early retirement of Jerusalem Mayor Teddy Kollek was aborted yesterday, at least temporarily, at the direct request of Prime Minister Yitzhak Rabin.

"[Rabin] asked me to wait some [before retiring]. He wants to prepare things better than they are now. I agreed to that," Kollek told reporters after the meeting.

But longtime Tel Aviv Mayor Shlomo Lahat yesterday announced that he would not seek another term. **(See story, Page 2)**

Rabin and Kollek, who had planned to step down and allow his hand-picked successor, deputy mayor Amos Mar-Haim, gain public exposure by serving out the remainder of his term, met for over an hour.

But Kollek left open the possibility he would still resign early, and reiterated his support for Mar-Haim.

"I'm still sure the best candidate we have is Amos Mar-Haim, but everyone is not sure of that, so we'll wait another few weeks until the matter is cleared up," Kollek said.

A source close to Kollek, has served as mayor for more than 25 years, said he has apparently put off a final decision on early retirement until the end of next month.

"I'm not promising anything," said Kollek, whose plans to step down have created much concern in the Labor Party, many of whose stalwarts oppose Mar-Haim's candidacy.

Mar-Haim declined to comment on the meeting, to which he was not invited, party sources said, so Rabin, Kollek, and other Jerusalem party leaders could discuss his candidacy freely.

"From the beginning I have said I will not try for another term. At 83, running for another five-year term would be cheating the public," Kollek said.

He said he is primarily interested in ensuring "moderate and rational" leadership in Jerusalem continues after he steps down, blasting the Likud for being a party of "extremists."

Labor's Jerusalem branch is already preparing to set up teams to organize the mayoral campaign, no matter who runs, said party secretary Haim Cohen.

No final date has yet been set for nationwide municipal elections, but they are expected to be held held between November 1993 and February 1994.

Cohen declined to comment on the Kollek-Rabin meeting, which he attended along with acting Religious Affair Minister Uzi Baram, Economics Minister Shimon Shetreet, and MK Dalia Itzik.

UN set to increase investment in areas

SUE FISHKOFF

NEW YORK – The UN Development Program will invest $20 million in projects in Judea, Samaria and Gaza in the coming year.

This will hopefully be increased to $35 million the following year, according to agency head William Draper.

UNDP is responding to Israel's recent request for more UN investment and involvement in economic projects in the territories, specifically development of roads and ports, and providing opportunities for residents to receive vocational training, Draper told UN Ambassador Gad Ya'acobi yesterday.

"It is our intention to increase the activities of the UNDP in the territories in coordination with Israel," Draper reportedly told Ya'acobi.

He said his agency is exploring ways of raising the necessary funds for the project among oil-producing Arab countries and in Western Europe.

Ya'acobi also requested that more Israelis be brought into UNDP operations, primarily in the fields of development of water resources, regional and village development, and agricultural planning.

Violent protests in Germany mark Kristallnacht and fall of Berlin Wall

BERLIN (AP) – Germany had little stomach for celebrating yesterday's third anniversary of the Berlin Wall's fall after a huge rally against right-wing violence and intolerance was spoiled by egg-hurling anarchists.

Yesterday also marked the anniversary of Kristallnacht, noted with the unveiling of a plaque commemorating the Passauer Strasse Synagogue, one the Nazis burned.

The *Frankfurter Rundschau* called Sunday's spoiled rally in Berlin, which was attended by 350,000 people, a "catastrophe" with "disgusting, undignified scenes.

November 9 is known as the "day of fate" in Germany, and Sunday's events could not help but evoke a sense that the lessons of an ugly past have been lost on too many.

President Richard von Weizsaecker, who sponsored the rally, declared that the Weimar Republic had failed "because there were too few democrats for too long. It should never come to that again. It is high time to be on guard. We are all called to action."

East Berliner Doris Schmid, 48, among those who responded to Weizsaecker's call to march, wore a picture of Anne Frank pinned to her jacket. But her assessment of her country's situation was bleak:

"I think it's tragic the situation is so bad that we have to go into the streets. I think it's too late for us."

Rightist violence, at first directed exclusively at refugees, has spread to antisemitic attacks on Holocaust memorials at former concentration camps, upsetting the Jewish community.

At the plague dedication yesterday, the head of Berlin's Jewish community, Jerzy Kanal, said Germany must "be careful that antisemitism doesn't spread and that the Jewish community is given the possibility to live here in peace."

Berlin's honorary citizens, Page 4

THE JERUSALEM POST

VOL. LX, NO. 18230
MONDAY, DECEMBER 14, 1992 • KISLEV 19, 5753 • JOMADA TANI 19, 1413
NIS 3.10 (EILAT NIS 2.60)

Hamas kidnaps border policeman

Police search the area where Nissim Toledano was kidnapped yesterday. (Ilan Osendriver/Israel Sun)

Search continues, territories sealed off

MICHAEL ROTEM and DAVID MAKOVSKY

THE army sealed off the administered territories as security services last night continued the hunt for the terrorists who kidnapped Border Police Sgt.-Maj. Nissim Toledano in Lod yesterday morning.

Yassin, serving a life sentence for organizing terrorist murders, appeared last night on Israel Television's *Mabat* news and appealed to the kidnappers not to kill Toledano.

Prime Minister Rabin convened the inner cabinet at his Defense Ministry office in Tel Aviv last night to update the ministers on the manhunt and discuss related developments. Earlier, he had briefed the Editor's Committee and leaders of the opposition including Yitzhak Shamir, Moshe Katzav and Ariel Sharon. Katzav said later the Likud supported the government's moves in the crisis.

The government, in a prepared statement released by Defense Ministry spokesman Oded Ben-Ami, said it "views very gravely the abduction of... Toledano and demands his immediate release. The Israeli Government regards the kidnappers and those who ordered the attack as responsible for the welfare and release of Toledano. The government warns agains harming him."

Defense sources said the kidnappers have not established contact with the authorities, except for the letter, and a later telephone call to the Associated Press offices. The sources stressed there is no proof Toledano is alive.

The drama started at 4:30 a.m., when Toledano, 29, as usual left his Lod home to walk his job in the services section at Border Police headquarters some two kilometers away.

Toledano, originally from Tirat Carmel, and his wife Rivka, a nurse, have two children, Natalie, five, and Shai, two. Toledano also has 13 brothers and sisters. He has worked for the Border Police since completing his compulsory military service.

After he failed to arrive by 8, the base called his home and was told that he had left for work. Shortly before 10, two masked men entered the Red Crescent offices in Al-Bira, near Ramallah, said they were Hamas members, and left a photocopy of Toledano's ID card and a letter demanding Yassin's release by 9 p.m.

A preliminary investigation indicated that Toledano was apparently grabbed at an intersection some 600 meters from his home. His *kipa* was found near the spot. Police sources said there were no signs of a struggle. They noted that Toledano was armed with a pistol, but said he probably had no chance to use it.

When Red Crescent officials informed police of the letter they had received, a large scale search began in the Lod area and the territories.

Police Inspector-General Ya'acov Terner ordered all police vacations canceled, so the necessary manpower would be available for the search.

The move was also designed to enable police to "respond to disturbances by various groups," which the kidnapping may spark, and to provide manpower to beef up patrols throughout the nation, according to a statement released by the police spokesman.

Nissim Toledano

The decision was taken at a meeting between Terner, Central Region commander Asaf Hefetz, and Commander Gabi Leist, head of the special operations division.

Senior defense sources said that despite the massive searches, the main effort was being concentrated on the intelligence level.

"We cannot rule out the possibility the kidnappers killed Toledano immediately, then made their demand for the release of Sheikh Yassin just to show off," a General Security Service source said.

"We are familiar with many Hamas activists, but the kidnappers must be out of their minds because this will not help their cause.

"Until now, we have treated them as regular terrorists, but if they think they are going to make a habit of kidnapping and killing Israelis in uniform, a very painful blow must be struck to disillusion them."

"There is not much the army can do in such a case," one Central Command officer confessed. "We are not equipped to deal with kidnappers. It's true, we have gained some experience in police work during the intifada, but a modern army is not designed to fight kidnappers. That is the job of the GSS and the police."

A senior Egyptian diplomat voiced the hope that Toledano would not be harmed because of Yassin's televised appeal. The Egyptian Embassy was one of several locations that received a fax announcing the kidnappers' demands that Yassin be released.

The abduction came amid deepening violence in the occupied territories where 11 Palestinians and five Israeli soldiers have been killed in the past two weeks.

"Our group kidnapped one of the officers of the occupation on December 13, 1992," said a statement from the Qassam military wing of Hamas, the Islamic Resistance Movement that has taken responsibility for two machinegun attacks that killed four Israeli soldiers in the past week.

"We are demanding the occupation authorities and Israeli leaders release Sheikh Ahmed Yassin in exchange for releasing this officer," the facsimile statement sent to news offices said.

An hour before the deadline expired, Yassin appeared on Israel television from his jail cell and appealed to the kidnappers not to kill their hostage.

"I say that I am not for killing this person. The authorities must be given the chance to respond to the demands. The kidnappers have a goal and the authorities must come through with them, respond to them, achieve them."

The kidnappers said Yassin must be freed in the presence of representatives of the International Committee of the Red Cross and ambassadors from France, Sweden, Turkey and Egypt. The statement also said he must not rearrested.

Sheikh Yassin, the leader of Hamas, was jailed for life by an Israeli military court in October 1991 for ordering killings of Palestinians suspected of cooperating with Israeli authorities.

Crippled in a sporting accident while a youth, Yassin was originally charged with masterminding the kidnapping and killing of two Israeli soldiers in 1989. Those charges were dropped in a plea-bargain deal.

Yassin was due to have cataract surgery this week, according to Israeli prison authorities. They deny allegations by Yassin's lawyer that his health has worsened since his arrest in May 1989.

In the television interview, Yassin looking frail with a towel wrapped around his shoulders said he was suffering from infections and other health problems in his lungs, ears and eyes.

Shouting slogans like "Rabin is a murderer," and "We don't want bodies, we want soldiers," several hundred people demonstrated near the prime minister's residence in Jerusalem last night, calling for stricter measures to quell the intifada.

About 15 demonstrators were arrested after they overran police barricades and blocked traffic for about 30 minutes at the King George-Keren Hayesod interchange in the middle of town. Dozens of police and border policemen were on hand to control the crowd, and did so with relatively little force.

When one of the demonstrators praised a policeman for his handling of the demonstration, the cop replied: "Look, we're hurting as much as you."

Herb Keinon, Bill Hutman and Raine Marcus contributed to this report.

One soldier killed, 2 wounded in Hebron jeep attack

JON IMMANUEL

ONE soldier was killed and two others wounded Saturday night when gunmen fired on their jeep near Hebron, sending it swerving off the road into a seven-meter deep wadi.

Meanwhile, in the Nusseirat refugee camp in the Gaza Strip, one man was shot dead yesterday and a 10-year-old was badly wounded during disturbances marking the fifth anniversary of the founding of Hamas.

The soldier killed in Hebron was identified as Sgt. (res.) Yuval Tutanji, 24, of Eilat, who was driving.

After surgery at Hadassah-University Hospital, Ein Kerem, Yariv Amran, 21, of Hadera, remained unconscious and in serious condition, with bullet wounds in the head.

Ya'acov Segal, 18, of Kibbutz Nativ, was in moderate condition after being shot in the leg.

Izzadin Kassem, the military wing of Hamas, is considered responsible for the attack.

It bore the markings of two other recent attacks attributed to the group in which local cars overtook army vehicles and sprayed them with bullets before speeding away.

One attack killed three soldiers on the main Gaza highway last Monday.

Another occurred on October 21, less than a kilometer from Saturday's shooting, on the road to Haggai south of Hebron. A soldier and a woman officer narrowly missed being killed in that attack.

A curfew was imposed on Hebron yesterday as security forces searched for the killers. The attack occurred about 9:30, and initially was thought to have been the result of an accident, possibly caused by stone-throwers, until Arab passersby helped contact the Civil Administration after Segal climbed up the hill to report the attack.

Area commander Col. Yossi told reporters two rifles were used in the shooting and sprayed "a large number of bullets."

He likened it to a "hit and run" incident, saying it showed "no great daring. He added that several arrests had been made.

Izzadin Kassem was reported by security authorities to have moved several members from Gaza to train new members in the Ramallah and Hebron areas earlier this year, after several Gazan members were arrested in an apartment in Al-Bireh. It was said they numbered no more than 15 members.

Ringleader Bashir Hamad, 28, from the Jabalya refugee camp, and Talal Saleh, 21, thought reponsible for the Hebron attack on October 21 and another which killed First Sgt. (res) Shmuel Gersh on a roof overlooking the Cave of the Patriarchs on October 25, subsequently escaped to Egypt via Rafiah.

In Gaza yesterday, demonstrations which erupted in the Nusseirat refugee camp led to soldiers shooting dead Shaaban Abu Ayada, 22, and wounding four others, Palestinian surces said.

The IDF confirmed the death and were investigating the circumstances.

Palestinians also reported that Mohammed Abu Shmais, 10, was wounded in the back. Nusseirat is considered a main center of Hamas support, like Sheikh Radwan, where three people were killed by soldiers in disturbances during the past two weeks.

An attempt to hold a pro-Hamas demonstration in Gaza City for the second day yesterday in advance of today's Hamas fifth anniversary, was suppressed with up to 20 wounded, local sources said.

Jabalya, Sheikh Radwan, the Shati refugee camp, Beit Hanoun, and the Bureij refugee camp remained under curfew.

Soldiers near Tel Rumeida in Hebron reported yesterday morning that shots were fired at their vehicle, puncturing a tire.

The army confirmed the report but said that it had not found proof of a shooting.

Hamas's moral victory

ANALYSIS

MICHAEL ROTEM

THE chances of finding Sgt. Maj. Nissim Toledano alive are rather uncertain, to say the least.

The Hamas organization, one of the most murderous, has a record of kidnapping and murdering uniformed Israelis.

Avi Sassportas and Ilan Sa'adon were abducted and murdered in 1989 by Hamas members who disguised themselves as observant Jews, and drove stolen Israeli vehicles.

According to intelligence information, the two soldiers were murdered shortly after they were kidnapped.

A few months ago, Hamas made another attempt to kidnap and murder a soldier in the Gaza Strip, but were foiled, probably by a passing car. The terrorists threw the injured soldier out of their vehicle, but only after taking his weapon and uniform.

Intelligence information indicates that in the past few days many members of the Izzadin Kassem faction escaped to Egypt. Eleven of the most wanted Hamas terrorists are now out of the reach of the security services.

However, army intelligence officials say Hamas took a risk this time by not perpetrating the kidnapping in Gaza – where they could disappear into the alleys within seconds – but rather in Lod, the center of the country.

Intelligence warned that the period beginning December 5, the anniversary of the intifada, would be a difficult time.

The period also included the anniversary of the founding of the PFLP, and the anniversary of the founding of Hamas today.

The IDF can show impressive achievements in its war against terrorism. But all those achievements cannot diminish the fact that the big, mechanized army is helpless when it comes to dealing with daring terrorists who shoot out of speeding vehicles at soldiers or kidnap soldiers.

Even the most experienced intelligence officers admit that any further successes in this terror campaign will be a moral victory for the terrorists and will encourage them to try more brazen attacks.

Until they fail, one should expect more such attacks. Until the government decides what to do and the IDF commanders in the field are able to stop improvising , both soldiers and civilians will be subjected to this painful kind of hit-and-run warfare.

Any delay in forming a policy of crushing this kind of terrorism will cost more lives and further damage the IDF's prestige

Soldier killed in security zone in apparent accident

DAVID RUDGE

THE IDF soldier killed Saturday night inside the security zone was hit by shots apparently fired accidentally by another soldier in his unit, according to an initial IDF inquiry into the incident..

The incident happened while the soldiers were on operational duties in the eastern sector of the zone.

The troops were moving through tangled undergrowth in difficult terrain when shots were fired by one of the soldiers, hitting Corp. Haim Bar-Natan, who was towards the front of the squad.

The paramedic with the unit treated Bar-Natan in the field. Reinforcements, including a doctor, were rushed to the scene together with a helicopter and a rescue team, but efforts to save him failed.

Bar-Natan, 19, of Jerusalem, is to be buried in the military section of the Mt. Herzl cemetery in Jerusalem at 10 this morning.

The investigations unit of the Military Police is continuing inquiries into the cause of the incident.

Angry crowd gathers near Toledano home

RAINE MARCUS

A CROWD of angry youths swarmed out of the Toledano family home on Sprinzak Street last night after the deadline on the life Nissim Toledano expired, shouting "Death to the Arabs" and "Rabin out." Arriving at the junction of Jabotinsky Street and Sderot Yerushalayim, they blocked the traffic, clapping and shouting their slogans.

"I dread to think what's going to happen here. These people are hotheaded," said one local youth. "If they go another 200 meters, that's where all the Lod Arabs live. There are going to be riots here."

Central District Police Commander Assaf Hefetz arrived at the scene, but the crowd continued to shout at him. "The situation is extremely sensitive," he said. "What worries us is that there will be rioting tomorrow."

Hefetz called on residents to show restraint, saying that rioting would only worsen the situation and give terrorists what they want.

Police sources said they would try to disperse the demonstrators with a minimum of force.

Earlier in the evening, supporters gathered outside the home.

"The riots in Bat Yam are nothing compared to what will happen here if he doesn't return alive," screamed one woman.

"We have lived together with Arabs for years," said another. "But we have to ban Arabs from the territories from coming here. In Or Yehuda, they don't let the Arabs in, and they should do the same here."

Neighbor Eli Tevet blamed Rabin for the increasing attacks. "Where is Rabin now?" he shouted angrily. "Where is Meretz? How many have been killed since this government took office? If Toledano is not found alive, we should destroy a complete Arab village. That will show them."

Other enraged residents joined in shouting anti-Arab and anti-Rabin slogans. "I'm afraid to send my kids to school or let them play on the street," said Becky Cohen. "If this can happen near somebody's home in the center of the country, then nowhere is safe."

14121005

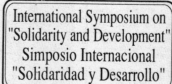

Acid parties
Page 9

THE JERUSALEM POST

VOLUME LX. NUMBER 18234 FRIDAY, DECEMBER 18, 1992 • KISLEV 23, 5753 • JAMAD TANI 23, 1413 NEW ISRAELI SHEKEL 4.10 (EILAT NIS 3.50)

Israel deports over 400 inciters

Court issues 5-2 ruling on deporting activists

HERB KEINON

AFTER nearly 24-hours of furious legal activity, the High Court of Justice ruled late yesterday afternoon that over 400 Hamas and Islamic Jihad members could be temporarily deported.

In its 5-2 decision, the court rescinded a restraining order issued early Thursday morning. That order had held up the 22 buses carrying the deportees in Metulla, en route to Lebanon.

The court also issued a show-cause order giving the government 30 days to explain why it deported the Palestinians.

Court President Meir Shamgar, Deputy President Menahem Elon, and Justices Shoshana Netanyahu, Eliezer Goldberg, and Eliahu Matza voted in favor of going ahead with the deportations; Justices Aharon Barak and Theodor Orr voted against.

Immediately after the decision was handed down, some 418 Palestinians were taken to the border. Because of a "bureaucratic error," the army removed 35 of them from the buses and sent them back to prison. Military sources said another 32 prisoners were flown by helicopter to Lebanon later.

"The decision is unprecedented as a matter of international law generally and Israeli law in particular," internationally known law professor Irwin Cottler told *The Jerusalem Post* last night. "The commencement of the proceedings at 5 a.m., the issuing of a temporary restraining order halting the deportation in its tracks, the temporary character of the deportation order itself, the marathon character of the proceedings, the unusual enlargement of the panel of justices during the hearing itself, and the somewhat quixotic character of a 'final' court order which is itself temporary – all testify to a textbook Socratic case that cannot be found in any textbook."

The legal maneuverings began early Wednesday evening, when Lea Tsemel received calls from the families of some of the 1,600 Hamas members who were arrested earlier, saying that buses were moving out and deportation proceedings were under way.

Tsemel called an official in the State Attorney's Office, who responded "no comment" when asked whether deportations were indeed taking place. Taking this as an affirmative answer, she – along with Andre Rosenthal – gathered the names of some of the 1,600 who were arrested and on their behalf turned to Justice Barak, the duty judge, for a restraining order.

The deportations followed a cabinet decision that read: "In light of the emergency situation and in order to preserve public order, the prime minister and defense minister is empowered to order officers in Judea, Samaria, and Gaza to issue orders for temporary expulsions without prior warning."

The order spelled out that the deportations would not be for more than two years, and that they would directed against those whose actions endanger lives or who incite to such actions. It was determined that committees of appeals, headed by military judges, will be established to hear appeals by the deportee's family members or lawyers within 60 days.

The hearing on the deportations in front of three High Court justices was set for 10 a.m., but because of the urgency was moved up to 5 a.m. The court was later expanded from three to seven justices.

For some 10 hours, the court heard arguments supporting the decision from Attorney-General Yosef Harish, and against the de-

(Continued on Page Two)

The buses wait at the Israeli-Lebanese border yesterday. (AFP)

Truckloads of deportees crossing in to Lebanon

DAVID RUDGE and news agencies

LEBANESE army troops and police were reported to be on full alert last night, after receiving order to prevent the 400 plus Hamas and Islamic Jihad deportees from entering the country.

The Lebanese government also asked Unifil not to allow the deportees to pass through checkpoints in the areas of south Lebanon under its control.

Unifil headquarters said the peacekeeping force would act in accord with the wishes of the Lebanese government, following a direct request from Foreign Minister Farez Bouez.

However, by midnight, the first truckloads of deportees had arrived at the northern border of the security zone. Trucks were waiting for them on the other side. At least 12 truckloads of deportees had passed Norwegian Unifil checkpoints without any interference and were pressing on towards the northern boundary of the security zone.

Reports from Lebanon said Lebanese army troops had sealed off regions close to the zone border and more checkpoints had been set-up through the south.

The Hamas spokesman in Lebanon, Abu Mohammed Mustafa, who was expelled from Israel three years ago, issued a statement in Beirut calling on the UN to prevent the deportations.

As the Lebanese government, which has failed to prevent deportations in the past, continued to make statements, the deportees were being transported into the security zone.

The move began just minutes after the High Court of Justice decided to lift the temporary injunction and allow the deportations to go ahead was announced on the radio shortly before 7 p.m.

The headlights of the buses which had brought the deportees from various detention centers to the border near Metulla more than 14 hours earlier suddenly blazed.

Shortly afterwards, the first batch of buses moved into the security zone where the occupants, blindfolded and bound hand and foot, were transferred from the buses into tents.

Television crews converged on the area, photographing the convoy and catching glimpses of the prisoners inside before the buses parked near the border. The site was declared a closed military area.

Throughout the long, cold and wet day, the buses remained stationary. The prisoners ate breakfast, dinner, and tea in their seats after food, the same given to their IDF guards, was brought to them from a nearby army base.

Prisoners were allowed off the buses, under guard, one at a time to relieve themselves by the side of the road.

When the order came to move, the red-and-white buses, escorted by three armored personnel carriers and several jeeps, headed northeast toward the Zommaraya crossing, one of five gateways linking the security zone with the rest of Lebanon.

Anticipating that the deportees will eventually be allowed to head north, five mosques in Lebanon's port city of Sidon were being readied to accommodate them.

Move complicates search for peace – US

DAVID MAKOVSKY and ALLISON KAPLAN

ISRAEL deported over 400 Hamas and Islamic Jihad activists to Lebanon last night in a move that has raised the ire of the United States, as well as the Arab negotiating teams at the peace talks.

32 of the detainees were flown up by helicopter from the Ketziot prison camp in the Negev, security sources said.

After nearly 24-hours of furious legal activity, the High Court of Justice ruled in the early evening that the activists could be temporarily deported.

In a 5-2 decision, the court rescinded a restraining order issued early yesterday morning that had held up the 22 buses carrying the Hamas and Islamic Jihad members in Metulla for some 15 hours.

While the Bush administration criticized Israel's action in a carefully-worded statement, all the Arab delegations to the Middle East peace talks stayed away from negotiations in protest.

White House spokesman Marlin Fitzwater said Arabs and Israelis "need to form a concerted voice calling for an end to all forms of violence, and avoid reactions such as deportations that risk complicating the search for peace."

The statement, issued shortly after the High Court of Justice decision upholding the deportations, said "actions and statements of the parties away from the table are no less important than the negotiations themselves."

President-elect Bill Clinton said in a news conference that while he sympathizes with the anger and frustration in Israel over the activities of groups like Hamas, he feels the deportation is an overly severe reaction.

In a meeting with Israeli delegates to the peace talks, President George Bush referred to the deportations and "expressed his hope that these temporary roadblocks will not block the road of peace," according to negotiator Elyakim Rubinstein, who said he told Bush Israel had to issue the order.

"These fundamentalist terrorists that we are talking about are not just after the peace process or the peace talks," Rubinstein said. "They are after the physical existence of Jews, Israelis, and the existence of the State of Israel. No government would tolerate it, no government should tolerate it."

Palestinian representatives told reporters they had appealed to Bush to force Israel to reverse its decision, and threatened to leave the peace process if the deportees are not returned.

"If this step will not be stopped, and if those people will not go back to their homes or at least to their land, I believe it will be completely impossible to find any way of continuing our negotiations in this peace process," said Faisal Husseini, head of the Palestinian delegation.

Husseini sat grim-faced in a press conference yesterday next to Palestinian spokesman Hanan Ashrawi, PLO representative and delegation adviser Nabil Sha'ath, and Dr. Haider Abdel Shafi, head of the Palestinian negotiating team.

Shafi, who participated in yesterday's meeting with Bush, said the president had agreed with the Palestinian delegation's charge that Israel's move violated the Geneva Convention, and that the US president "nodded in approval" when he was informed that the Palestinians plan to take their protest to the Security Council.

In Tunis shortly afterward, the PLO said in a statement the Palestinians were suspending their participation in the Middle East peace process until Israel allows the deportees to return.

"The expulsion means a halt of the peace process which cannot be resumed until the international community forces Israel to respect" international conventions related to the treatment of people under occupation, the statement said.

Shafi expressed particular dismay that Meretz ministers had supported the deportation decision. Sha'ath said many Palestinian leaders had asked him repeatedly in disbelief if it were really true Shulamit Aloni had voted for the measure.

Ashrawi and Husseini are scheduled to meet privately today with Secretary of State Eagleburger and President Bush.

The decision of the Palestinian and other Arab delegations not to meet with the Israeli delegation actually preceded the announcement by the High Court.

(Continued on Page Two)

An 'overreaction' to strengthen deterrence

ANALYSIS

GERALD STEINBERG

THE expulsion of over 400 Hamas and Islamic Jihad activists is primarily an attempt to quickly strengthen the level of deterrence through a strong "overreaction."

Israeli strategy has always been based on a policy of rapid and forceful responses to Arab threats and attacks, to demonstrate the ability to act offensively and prevail militarily. The logic of deterrence is based on the assumption tha the other side will realize that it is too weak to continue the conflict, and will back down first.

This strategy was used, with some success, in the 1950s to persuade Jordan to prevent terrorist raids. As defense minister, Moshe Dayan used similar tactics to end a wave of Palestinian terror following the Six-Day War, and against Egypt in the War of Attrition. Eventually, Israel developed a reputation for retaliating strongly, despite international protests, and thereby limiting the willingness of the Arab states to risk another war.

However, at the beginning of the intifada five years ago, large numbers of Palestinians demonstrated a willingness to take unprecedented risks in confronting the army. At the time, Yitzhak Rabin was defense minister, and his initial response was to order the IDF to react strongly and to "break the bones" of the leaders of the intifada.

The process took a long time, and seemed to demonstrate a decline in deterrent capability. In debating the lack of a strong military response to Iraqi missile attacks during the Gulf war, some military analysts feared it would lead to further erosion in the credibility of Israeli deterrence.

In the past few years, the increase in suicide attacks by Hizbullah in Lebanon continued to raise problems with respect to deterrence. Fanatics who are willing, even eager, to sacrifice their lives and those of their families for the cause are difficult to deter. As a result, Israel was forced to raise the level of violence after each Hizbullah attack, showering strongholds with hundreds of mortar rounds and artillery shells, and bringing a large number of tanks and other weapons into southern Lebanon before gaining a temporary halt to the attacks.

As the attacks on soldiers increased over the past few weeks, including this week's kidnapping and murder, both Rabin and Chief of General Staff Lt.-Gen. Ehud Barak feared that without an immediate strong "overreaction," the level of violence would grow, and would lead to other military challenges.

The number of activists expelled is clearly designed to raise the stakes, and to demonstrate that in the long term, Israel will continue to be much more powerful than Palestinian rejectionists and fundamentalists.

The government is aware that the expulsions will not prevent further Hamas attacks, but it is expected that the support its cells receive from the Palestinian community will dry up for fear of provoking further Israeli wrath.

Gerald Steinberg is the research director of the Center for Strategic Studies, Bar-Ilan University.

With today's The Jerusalem Post:

The weekend **MAGAZINE** helps you plan eight days of Hanukka fun. CARL SCHRAG takes a look at the spectacular Moscow Stage Circus.

THE 16-page color **TIME OUT** supplement gives all the vital listings for the coming week: Cable TV, regular TV, radio, theater, cinema, plus reviews and features.

In the paper's main section, Jerusalem Post reporters provide background and analysis on the deportations and the Hamas movement.

AND don't miss: JUDY SIEGEL's medical advice column on Sunday; the incomparable New York Times Weekly Review with Monday's paper; and starting Thursday a new, different, general advice column, 'Dear Ruthie.'

THE JERUSALEM POST
At your service

SHABBAT	BEGINS	ENDS
Jerusalem	4:02	5:17
Tel Aviv	4:20	5:19
Haifa	4:09	5:16
Beersheba	4:18	5:16
Eilat	4:22	5;23

18121001

Health advice column
Page 5

THE JERUSALEM POST

Spying on employees
Page 7

VOLUME LXI, NUMBER 18295 SUNDAY, FEBRUARY 28, 1993 • ADAR 7, 753 • RAMADAN 7 1413 NEW ISRAELI SHEKEL 3.20 (EILAT NIS 2.70)

Police suspect terrorists behind bombing of World Trade Center

Five killed, more than 1,000 injured in Manhattan blast

News agencies

NEW YORK – A massive hunt was underway yesterday for the bombers who killed five people and injured over 1,000 in a powerful blast that rocked the World Trade Center at noon on Friday, shutting down the city's financial center.

Police Commissioner Raymond Kelly, who noted that two people were still unaccounted for, said evidence showed the blast had almost certainly been caused by a bomb. Traces of explosive chemicals and the intensity of the heat generated by the explosion "would buttress our position that we believe it to be a bomb," he told a press conference yesterday.

If the explosion is confirmed to be a bomb blast, it would be one of the largest acts of urban terror in US history.

Kelly said authorities received 19 telephone calls from "all sorts of groups and individuals" claiming to have set off the explosion. One source told The Associated Press that a caller claiming to represent Croatian militants, called 15 minutes before the blast.

"It may be terrorist related," said James Fox, head of the FBI's New York office.

"If indeed this is a terrorist attack... then no one is safe in any city," Mayor David Dinkins said, as news of the tragedy reached him in Osaka, Japan.

In Washington, spokesmen for the Defense Department, State Department and police who guard Congress said security at all these locations had been stepped up.

Pentagon spokesman Lieutenant Colonel P.J. Crowley said that it was likely precautions were being taken at US military installations elsewhere.

The explosion in an underground parking garage turned Friday's lunch hour in the twin 110-story towers into a terrifying test of survival.

About 200 kindergartners and elementary school children were stranded on an observation deck 107 stories high, while 17 more youngsters and their adult chaperones were trapped in an elevator for five hours. A pregnant woman was plucked off the roof by a helicopter. Other people were trapped in elevators, or in rubble in the garage and a train station beneath it.

Kelly said there were three reasons to believe the explosion was caused by a bomb: "The magnitude of the explosion, the fact that a significant amount of heat was generated, and the fact that traces of nitrate were found."

"It looks like a bomb [and] it smells like a bomb," Gov. Mario Cuomo said, although he stressed it was too early to be certain.

Cuomo, who has an office in one of the damaged towers, toured the area for 20 minutes yesterday morning, walking down to the crumpled parking garage to see the enormous crater carved by the blast.

President Bill Clinton promised in his weekly radio address that "the full measure of federal law enforcement resources will be brought to bear on this investigation."

The blast hit at 12:18 p.m., creating a 60-by-30 meter crater in the garage below the center's Vista Hotel. It demolished parked cars – including a fleet of Secret Service vehicles – tossed beams and concrete debris into a commuter train station and jolted both towers, a virtual small city, where some 130,000 people work.

Electricity and heat were cut off to the entire complex. Some broke windows to get air. Others remained stranded for hours in elevators, frozen between floors when the power went out.

One emergency volunteer, Regan Kelly, said he helped revive about nine people who were trapped in an elevator on the 44th floor for more than two hours.

"They looked like corpses when we got to them," he said. "I don't think they could have lasted much longer."

Hundreds poured out of the towers into the streets of lower Manhattan, gasping, their faces black with soot, after groping their way from as high as the 105th floor.

Many hugged each other with joy at having made it out. A businessman in an expensive suit sat on the sidewalk, sobbing in relief. A secretary knelt in prayer.

The elementary school pupils on the observation deck finally walked down to safety. Their schoolmates in the elevator were rescued after five hours, when firefighters pulled them to safety. Twenty-eight people were removed from the roofs of the towers by helicopter.

By late evening, police put the death toll at five. They were identified as four men and one woman, all from the New York City area. All but one were employees of the Port Authority, as were the two still unaccounted for yesterday.

Authorities put the number of injured at 1,042, including 416 who walked into hospitals by themselves. Most were suffering from smoke inhalation and were released after treatment.

A bomb threat four hours later forced the evacuation of the Empire State Building several kilometers uptown, police said. Two bomb threats followed at the United Nations, where the bomb squad was searching the building, a UN source said. Security was also strengthened at all area airports, said Eric Hedrick of the Port Authority.

Police cars and fire trucks line up at the foot of the World Trade Center in New York after Friday's noontime blast. (AP)

Katyusha rockets fall in the north; SLA retaliates

News agencies

A TRAGEDY was narrowly averted early yesterday morning when Katyusha rockets landed only meters from a dormitory where dozens of youths were spending the night in a western Galilee village.

The hail of rockets caused light damage to several vehicles and buildings, mainly in the form of broken glass. There were no injuries.

The attack drew retaliatory fire from the South Lebanese Army in the security zone.

Security sources said Hizbullah fired at least 60 Katyushas, with some 24 of them landing in the north.

The whooshing sound of rockets and the blasts kept most of the security zone's estimated 200,000 residents huddled in basements and bomb shelters.

The rockets were fired from the vicinity of Yater, a Hizbullah stronghold north of the security zone. They hit and damaged a number of houses in the towns of Marjayoun, Khiam, and Ibil al-Saqi.

Almost immediately after the rockets fell on the Galilee village, police, Border Police, and army forces rushed to the area.

Amir, a member of the village administration, said residents had not entered the bomb shelters. The village had been warned of hostile activity, but had not been told to take shelter, he said.

"Katyushas fall in the area all the time," Amir said. "The last time they fell in our village, though, was during the Lebanon War. Unfortunately, this is part of our lives, and we won't change our routine because of such incidents."

Amir complained that the security rooms in residents' homes did not meet their needs, noting they were small rooms of 9 sq.m. that could serve to protect residents for a few hours, but were not suitable for spending long periods should that be necessary.

"We hope the government institutions, that speak a lot about helping towns in the north, will also help us by providing adequate protective devices and security rooms," Amir said.

In the afternoon, O/C Northern Command Maj.-Gen. Yitzhak Mordechai visited the village, saying the IDF was closely following developments north of the border.

"You must remember that in the last month, 12 terrorists have been killed and dozens injured," Mordechai told area residents. "All their attempts to carry out attacks have failed. Even today's attack caused no injuries and minimal damage. We are following events and will take decisive action."

Mordechai relayed the complaints about inadequate security rooms to the director-general of the Prime Minister's Office, Shimon Sheves, who told Mordechai there is a plan to build 2,000 security rooms in northern towns at a cost of NIS 80 million.

In response to the shelling, SLA gunners pounded the terrain north of the zone with 130mm howitzers.

The rocket launchings followed a Friday attack by Israeli helicopters in which a one-story house used by Hizbullah members was destroyed. The house was vacant at the time.

Earlier Friday, three SLA soldiers were wounded in an ambush by unidentified terrorists.

Deportees hope Syria will hold up talks

JON IMMANUEL and news agencies

THE Palestinian deportees in Lebanon said yesterday they were banking on Syria to block any resumption of Middle East peace talks before Israel allowed them to return.

"I am confident Syria will convince all the Arab states not to resume the negotiations before the issue of the deportees is resolved," Abdul Aziz al-Rantisi, spokesman for the 396 exiles, told Reuters at the deportees' tent camp.

After talks with European Community officials and US Secretary of State Warren Christopher in Brussels, Syrian Foreign Minister Farouk Shara said Friday his country would host high-level Arab talks, "to come up with a unified Arab position vis-a-vis the deportation issue and the resumption of the peace talks."

Palestinians here said steps are still being taken to solve the deportee issue before negotiations resume, in talks between the US and Israel and the US and Palestinians.

"The thrust of these [talks] deal with the principles of the illegality of deportations plus reversing steps already taken," and "concrete steps on human rights, a reaffirmation of the terms of reference and other negotiation issues," delegation Hanan Ashrawi said in a statement.

Palestinian sources here have said the deal being discussed includes the return of "a sizeable" proportion of the 1,200 Palestinians deported since 1967. PLO sources in Cairo said the points about terms of reference meant Washington would focus clearly on UN resolutions 242 and 338 and the status of Jerusalem could be discussed.

Christopher's own statements indicate that he is willing to act to bridge differences between Israel and the Palestinians only after they resume talks in Washington. He also said he "is not in the business of pressuring Israel."

Palestinian delegates, however, remain outwardly optimistic about the possibility of a solution "in the near future."

They also denied Christopher told them in their meeting Wednesday that he could not renew the US dialogue with the PLO because it had "terrorist tendencies."

"We reported the usual request for dialogue with the PLO and he repeated the known American position that currently they cannot renew it," said delegate Ghassan Khatib who was at the meeting. "If he had said that we would not have let it pass," Khatib added.

Bombers active across world

WHILE the bomb at New York's World Trade Center dominated the weekend news, the American city was not alone in being targeted by terrorists. The following places were also hit:

LONDON – The IRA bombed a crowded shopping street injuring 14 people. The group earlier admitted responsibility for two bombs that destroyed a huge natural gas storage tank in northwestern England, and a third device that exploded but failed to damage a larger storage facility nearby.

(Story Page 3)

CAIRO – Egypt's main Moslem militant organization denied yesterday it bombed a crowded Cairo coffee bar, killing four people and wounding 16. The Islamic Group has claimed responsibility for a series of attacks on foreign tourists in the last five months.

(Story below)

BELFAST – Constable Reggie Williamson, 46, was fatally injured when a bomb attached to the underside of his car exploded in north Armagh, about 50 km. southwest of Belfast, late Thursday night. No group claimed responsibility.

MEDELLIN – A powerful car bomb went off outside the regional telephone company headquarters injuring 25 people and causing millions of dollars of damage to nearby buildings. A 90-kg. bomb, packed into a milk churn hidden in the back of a stolen car, exploded late Friday in a central square of Colombia's second city. Drug baron Pablo Escobar is suspected.

ZAGREB – Police found a bomb lying in the street opposite the US embassy in the Croatian capital on Friday and defused it without incident, an embassy spokeswoman said. The suitcase-sized bomb, packed with dynamite, was discovered about 12 meters from the embassy entrance on a busy main street in downtown Zagreb.

TBILISI – A bomb derailed a passenger train in eastern Georgia on Friday, injuring a number of people. The blast, triggered by remote control, derailed up to seven cars and destroyed 250 meters of track, officials said.

KUWAIT – A bomb exploded at a Russian circus touring Kuwait on Friday, in at least the third attack on circuses in the past year. A Russian member of the circus was injured in the explosion, caused by a kilogram of dynamite.

Six 'collaborators' killed in Gaza

JON IMMANUEL and Itim

SIX people were killed in the Gaza Strip over the weekend, apparently because they were suspected of informing for the authorities.

Meanwhile, Hava Wechsberg, 11, of Kiryat Arba, died on Friday, two days after after the car she was riding in plunged down a hill in Gush Etzion, apparently following a stoning attack.

Dozens of Kiryat Arba residents attended Wechsberg's funeral. Palestinians in Hebron reported the windows of several Arab cars were smashed.

The IDF said it was investigating whether the accident was the result of an attack. Dr. Blanka Wechsberg, a dentist, said she was driving with her children near Karmei Tzur, when a rock crashed through the windshield and she lost control of the car. She and a son were lightly injured in the accident.

Palestinian sources identified the six Gaza dead as Suleiman Sharatah, 40, from the village of Jabalya, shot in his car on Thursday night; Yusra Salima, 25, a woman from Khan Yunis, shot in the head; Nasser Salim Saleh, 32, from Gaza City, who was stabbed; Ahmed Abdul Karia, of Sheikh Radwan, who was shot Saturday night; Kamal Akhram, of the Muazi refugee camp, who was shot, and Aziz Abu Warda, 39, from the Jabalya refugee camp.

In Akrabe, in the Nablus area, soldiers yesterday wounded two men during clashes following the arrest of a fugitive in an action by undercover troops. Ibrahim Derieh, 29, was captured after being shot and moderately wounded, as he tried to flee across the roofs of several houses. Security forces found three pistols and two pipe bombs in his house. Two others were arrested for sheltering him, the IDF said.

The IDF said Derieh was a Fatah activist and had been wanted for nine months in connection with the murder of several Arabs said to be informers.

Meanwhile, Prime Minister Yitzhak Rabin has accepted the recommendation of Maj.-Gen. Danny Rothschild, coordinator of activities in the territories, that the civil administration budget be made public starting this fiscal year, for the first time since 1967.

The budget, approved by a joint subcommittee of the Knesset foreign affairs and defense and finance committees, has been kept secret since 1967.

Four die, 16 hurt in blast at Cairo cafe

News agencies

CAIRO – Moslem extremists admitted yesterday they detonated a bomb in a crowded Cairo coffee shop that killed a Swede, a Turk and two Egyptians. They vowed to "continue the vendetta with the government."

However, the al-Gamaa al-Islamiya, or Moslem group later denied responsibility in a fax and phone call to an international news agency.

The homemade bomb was packed with TNT and steel nails as projectiles, a classic terror weapon to maim and kill. The Interior Ministry said 16 people were injured in the Friday night attack, including two Americans, a Canadian and a Frenchman.

Police sources said authorities suspect one of the dead Egyptians, identified as Emad Abdel-Baset, may have been involved in the bombing.

The Wadi el-Nil coffee shop is on bustling Tahrir Square, the heart of Cairo where thousands of foreign tourists walk every day. The Egyptian Museum, Cairo's biggest subway station, the Nile Hilton Hotel and the Arab League headquarters are at the square.

"I was sitting in front of our building when I heard a big explosion," said Mahmoud Hamid, janitor of a building next to the coffee shop. "All the buildings around us shook. We saw a lot of smoke coming out of the cafeteria. People were screaming and running. There was blood splattered all over."

Yesterday morning, glass shards and pieces of broken wood were strewn for 10 meters in front of the shop. Most of the furniture and equipment were removed, but a few burned chairs and tables remained inside.

The dead Swede and Turk were the second and third foreigners killed since Moslem militants declared last year they were targeting foreign tourists to undermine Egypt's secular government. The first tourist fatality was a British woman, killed in an attack on a bus in southern Egypt last October.

In the southern city of Assiut, an extremist hotbed 320 km. south of Cairo, militants claimed responsibility and said the bombing was to avenge a government crackdown.

A member of al-Gamaa al-Islamiya relayed the claim orally to local reporters at a mosque.

"Tourism is not the goal but is a means to pressure the regime into releasing members of al-Gamaa al-Islamiya who were unjustly arrested," said the man, known to local reporters as a spokesman for the extremists.

Less than 24 hours after the bombing, police sources said authorities would begin installing walk-through metal detectors today at museums and movie theaters.

The Interior Ministry said the device that caused Friday night's blast was placed behind a column in the coffee shop.

The explosion occurred as Tahrir Square filled with people after iftar, the evening meal that breaks the daytime fast of Ramadan.

Ten of the 16 wounded were Egyptians.

The bomb attack was the most serious in Cairo for many years.

THE JERUSALEM POST
an international newspaper
distributed on 6 continents
in English and French.
Over 500,000 readers
worldwide

THE JERUSALEM POST

VOLUME LXI, NUMBER 18317 THURSDAY, MARCH 25, 1993 • NISAN 3, 5753 • SHAWAL 2, 1413 NEW ISRAELI SHEKEL 3.20 (EILAT NIS 2.70)

Classy hatchback
Page 8

Likud primary turnout seems to favor Netanyahu

SARAH HONIG

THE voter turnout in yesterday's Likud primary – estimated at over 65 percent late last night – appeared to augur well for frontrunner Binyamin Netanyahu, although some of his aides had hoped for a 70 percent turnout.

The turnout is thought to be a reliable indication of the fortunes of the four candidates – Binyamin Netanyahu, David Levy, Ze'ev Begin, and Moshe Katzav. Final results of the balloting are not expected until this evening.

A large turnout would favor Netanyahu, while a small one would benefit Levy.

In all, more than 150,000 Likud members cast ballots during the day.

This in itself is considered an impressive achievement for the party, in which there was no certainty that so large a proportion of the membership would actually go to the polls, especially after after the acrimonious campaign, and the depleted state of the party treasury which made it difficult to properly organize the election.

To win in the first round, one candidate must receive at least 40 percent of the vote. If no one achieves this, a run-off will be held on Wednesday.

As soon as the polls opened at 7:30 a.m., nearly all attention was riveted on the turnout figures. The Netanyahu team took the impressive figures as a good sign, but the more Netanyahu's aides delighted in the numbers, the more Levy's people quoted lower figures.

The Levy faction even openly challenged official turnout figures issued from time to time by party spokesman Gil Samsonov, charging he is a Netanyahu man and therefore not to be trusted.

Since the elections were on a work day, it was unclear how high the turnout would be, especially in the big cities where most of Netanyahu's support is said to be.

Early on it was evident that the turnout in Levy's development town strongholds was considerably higher, but that was only to be expected since these are small localities, with short distances and a cohesive factional affiliations. But the weight these towns would have in the final result depended on the overall turnout. The higher it was in the center of the country, the less the proportional weight of the development towns.

The invective which characterized the campaign remained to the end. Levy charged that Netanyahu had hired people to foment trouble in his strongholds. He also accused Netanyahu of circulating false reports of a Levy-Begin deal.

"First there was the big Bibigate bluff, and now the Bibi-big-deal," he quipped. Begin also accused Netanyahu of being the source of the reports.

Levy reiterated his threat that he would not serve under Netanyahu.

All day, there were reports of local clashes and even fist fights. The altercations were exclusively between Netanyahu's and Levy's people. Some scuffles, however, had nothing to do with the leadership contest, but with local branch elections.

The Levy side complained that a Netanyahu man roughed up a supporter of their's in Tel Aviv, while Netanyahu's people accused two of Levy's sons of having removed the the partitions in the polling booths in their home town of Beit She'an, thus denying voters the guarantee of a secret ballot. The Levy brothers were further accused of handing the voters their father's ballot slips just to make sure.

Later, the Levy family was forced to evacuate its home after receiving an anonymous call saying a bomb had been placed in the house. A police search, however, revealed no explosives.

In Nazareth, Netanyahu's ballots disappeared and election judges Avraham Friedman and Hanna Evenor permitted write-in ballots until new printed ones could be supplied.

(Continued on Page 2)

Ezer Weizman elected seventh president of Israel

President-elect Ezer Weizman speaks to President Chaim Herzog, who called to congratulate him on his election. (Isaac Harari)

Jerusalem Post Staff

ON an unprecedented second ballot, apparently caused by four extra ballot slips unintentionally stuck together, the Knesset yesterday elected Ezer Weizman the seventh president of Israel by a vote of 66 to 53, with one abstention.

Speaking to reporters after the vote, Weizman said he regards the job of president as "the most complicated and difficult one I have ever assumed" and promised "not to take a step without consulting the cabinet, the prime minister, and the foreign minister."

Weizman, 69, who is to be installed on May 13, refrained from political statements, but did refer to the increased attacks by terrorists and the atmosphere of fear and anger they have created.

Prime Minister Yitzhak Rabin said Weizman would have a crucial role to play as a healer and unifier at a time Israel faces "great possibilities and no little danger."

During the day congratulatory messages arrived from French President Francois Mitterrand, Egyptian President Hosni Mubarak, and former American president Jimmy Carter.

In his message Mubarak said Weizman "played an important and essential role in establishing peace between Egypt and Israel" in 1979.

Meanwhile, the working-class town of Or Akiva last night prepared to be the first community to officially welcome the president-elect, who lives in the neighboring resort town of Caesarea.

Local council head Ya'acov Edri brought a huge floral wreath and a cake inscribed "to Reuma and Ezer" from the people of Or Akiva. The children's choir from the local community center was poised to perform a special song for the president-elect when he arrived. Full coverage, Page 3

Egypt extradites suspect in Trade Center bombing

SUE FISHKOFF
NEW YORK

THE suspected ringleader in the World Trade Center bombing was back in the United States last night, following an international manhunt that ended in a Cairo jail.

Mahmud Abu Halima, 33, the fourth suspect arrested so far in connection with the February 26 bombing, was apprehended in Egypt on March 14 and handed over to FBI agents yesterday. An FBI spokesman in Washington confirmed that an agency team flew to Egypt Tuesday and escorted Abu Halima back to New York.

His arrest, sources say, completes the nucleus of the terrorist cell reportedly behind the massive explosion that killed six people, wounded 1,000 and caused more than a billion dollars worth of damage. Abu Halima is expected to be arraigned today in Manhattan Federal Court.

Abu Halima, who disappeared two days after the March 4 arrest of Mohammed Salameh, the man accused of driving the van containing the fatal car-bomb, was originally believed to have fled to Pakistan. It is now learned he flew on March 6 to Johannesburg and later to Egypt, where he, his wife, and four children were taken into custody.

Law enforcement officials declined to give details of his arrest, but one source told reporters it came "during the Egyptian government's crackdown on Moslem fundamentalists who are believed responsible" for a wave of terror bombings inside Egypt.

FBI officials identified Abu Halima two weeks ago as the ringleader of the terrorist cell behind the World Trade Center explosion. He has also been identified as the personal driver for Sheikh Omar Abdel Rahman, a fiery Egyptian cleric who preaches at mosques in New Jersey and Brooklyn, and who is described as the spiritual leader of Islamic fundamentalist groups seeking to overthrow Egyptian President Hosni Mubarak.

Rahman, who was ordered deported from the US last week, denies knowing Abu Halima, and denies any involvement in the Trade Center bombing. He is to be retried in absentia in Egypt on April 6 for the assassination of President Anwar Sadat, a crime for which he was acquitted four years ago.

On Tuesday, Rahman made his first public appearance since the fatal bombing, praying in a Jersey City parking lot with 1,000 followers to mark the end of Ramadan.

Abu Halima today joins two other suspects arraigned in the Trade Center bombing, Salameh, 25, and Nidal Ayyad, a 25-year-old chemical engineer. Also under arrest on charges of obstructing justice is Ibrahim Elgabrowny, 42, an Egyptian contractor who allegedly hit federal agents who searched his Brooklyn apartment the day after Salameh's arrest.

Law enforcement sources predicted that two more suspects would be arrested within the next few days. A spokesman for the FBI in New York declined to confirm this, saying, "We can't predict future arrests, but we certainly hope the case continues to move along as it has so far."

New York FBI spokesman Joe Valiquette refused to comment on a *Daily News* report that the FBI had been investigating Abu Halima for the past two years. Unidentified investigators told reporters that witnesses saw Abu Halima in Salameh's van at dawn the day of the bombing.

Investigators and terrorist experts are drawing more links between the Trade Center bombing and the 1990 assassination of Rabbi Meir Kahane.

Authorities have reopened the Kahane case, and may seek to retry Nosair in federal court on charges of violating Kahane's civil rights. This week's *Village Voice* reports that law enforcement sources are quietly suggesting that the same group may have been behind both the Kahane murder and the World Trade Center bombing.

Sheik calls for Egyptian overthrow, Page 5

Theme park planned for Timna copper mines

HAIM SHAPIRO

THE abandoned copper mines at Timna will be turning out gold if a Disney-style park planned for the site by the Negev Tourism Development Administration is successful.

The park, to be known as King Solomon's Mines, Timna Desert Park, is to include a visitors' center with shops, restaurants, an IMAX (special effects) theater, and rides. It is also to serve as the starting out point for bus, jeep, and camel tours.

An international tender to cover the investment of some $15 million is to be issued shortly, the administration announced yesterday. This week, final plans were authorized by the administration, the Eilot Regional Council, and the Timna National Park. The Tourism Ministry also gave its blessing.

According to the plans, drawn up by ITEC Productions and Management Resources, both of Orlando, Florida, visitors are first to tour the park's attractions in special buses, equipped with audio-visual equipment, in which they will view a video program and listen to a commentary.

From there, they will enter an underground labyrinth where special cars will take them from attraction to attraction. A full range of audio-visual effects will be used to show them mining techniques in recent and in biblical times.

Yeltsin slams 'attempt to restore authoritarian regime'

MOSCOW (AP) – Russia veered between confrontation and compromise yesterday, and President Boris Yeltsin and his legislative opponents ended up no closer to resolving their power struggle.

There had been hopes the sides would be able to resolve the power struggle that has paralyzed Russia's government for weeks and threatened economic reforms.

Yeltsin started the day by softening his claim to special powers but later denounced lawmakers for proceeding with plans for an emergency parliament session to try to oust him. An aide repeated the president's charge that hard-liners want to restore the Communists' authoritarian regime.

Lawmakers demanded that Yeltsin appear at the Congress of People's Deputies tomorrow, when they may vote to remove him from office for declaring emergency rule and calling an April 25 referendum on who the people trust to govern – the president or the legislature.

The parliament is trying "to use any means to remove the lawfully elected president and open the way to power for the forces of revenge and totalitarian restoration," presidential spokesman Vyacheslav Kostikov said.

Yeltsin's aides have said the president would ignore a vote to remove him by the Congress, which was elected before the collapse of the Soviet Union.

The president had seemed to be inching toward compromise with his critics.

He issued the text of his decree calling for a nationwide vote of confidence, and it omitted any reference to the special powers he had claimed during a televised address Saturday.

Yeltsin also met privately with the speaker of parliament and Russia's chief justice to seek a compromise. But they did not reach agreement, and speaker Ruslan Khasbulatov told lawmakers later that the special parliament session on removing Yeltsin would go forward.

The day began with a session of the Supreme Soviet, the standing legislature, which voted 135-34 to convene the 1,033-member Congress tomorrow.

At the same time, Yeltsin's office released the controversial decree, without any reference to a "special order" of rule, the provision that had most alarmed the legislature.

It was not clear whether Yeltsin revised the decree to meet the demands of the Constitutional Court and lawmakers, or whether he exaggerated its harshness during his speech Saturday.

Some Yeltsin critics said he backed down under pressure.

"He removed from the text the most notorious part of his TV speech, the supremacy of the presidential decisions over the Supreme Soviet," said hard-line lawmaker Vladimir Isakov.

Israeli beetles to help save Californian crops

TOM TUGEND
LOS ANGELES

SOME tiny but voracious Israeli beetles have a new assignment: keeping California-grown fruit and vegetables safe from the dreaded silverleaf whitefly, the scourge of crops in the Sunshine State's Imperial Valley.

The Israeli export is the ladybird beetle, which has scored remarkable successes in gobbling up the citrus whitefly, which threatened Israel's fruit crop.

California scientists hope that the beetles will be just as effective in destroying the related silverleaf whitefly, blamed for $200 million worth of damage to fruit and vegetable crops.

Crop damage across the southern US caused by the silverleaf whitefly is put at $750 million, the *Los Angeles Times* reported, and pesticides have proven useless against its predations.

Expert: Russia heading for breakup

STEVE RODAN

THE showdown between President Boris Yeltsin and parliament is plunging Russia toward a breakup, according to Hebrew University Prof. Shlomo Avineri, an expert on the area.

"It's not going to be like Yugoslavia, but it could be close," he said.

Avineri said Russia is in a "deep constitutional crisis and I don't see a constitutional way out. Each side has a part of the constitution that justifies it. There is no Supreme Court. The new Constitutional Court, set up a year ago, did not give Yeltsin what he wanted."

Part of the problem, Avineri said, is that the constitution is a patchwork, with more than 200 amendments added since its approval.

But Avineri said the key question is whether the armed forces will get involved. "So far, they are saying they are neutral," he said. "This is not encouraging."

Avineri says Yeltsin's aim is to stay in power and carry out his radical reform program. "His reform program is totally unsuited to Russian conditions," he said. "There is a very naive feeling that the market can be introduced into Russia in a year or two."

The aim of parliament is to stop the process. It's a battle that cannot be avoided, Avineri said.

"Showdowns can be postponed when both sides go to the brink and they are frightened," he said.

"But I don't think it will hold."

Jews shouldn't be worried more than anybody else, Avineri said.

THE JERUSALEM POST
an international newspaper distributed on 6 continents in English and French.
Over 500,000 readers worldwide

THE JERUSALEM POST

EIGHT PAGES FROM The New York Times WEEKLY REVIEW

VOLUME LXI, NUMBER 18359 MONDAY, MAY 17, 1993 • IYAR 26, 5753 • ZULKIDA 26, 1413 NIS 3.40 (EILAT NIS 2.90)

Terrorists kill four in Gush Katif

Two Jews, two Arabs shot from passing car

JON IMMANUEL

THREE or more gunmen, firing from a passing car, killed two Israelis and two Palestinian vegetable merchants near the settlement of Gadid west of Khan Yunis in the Gaza Strip yesterday.

The victims were identified as Nissim Falas, 33, of Dimona, Avshalom Halfon, 21, of Ofakim, Ziad Abu Zhohab, 25, of Hebron, and Tewfik Abu Gharab, 19, of Khan Yunis, who was their local contact.

Halfon was buried last night.

The attack took place at the end of a secluded lane, off the road from Khan Yunis to the settlement, where a handful of farmers live and raise crops in greenhouses. Access to the area is considered fairly safe, as it is close to a main route to Jewish settlements.

Falas and Halfon arrived in a car with yellow license plates, and Abu Zhohab and Abu Gharab in a van with blue Hebron plates.

Responsibility for the attack, unusual in that it claimed both Arab and Jewish lives, was claimed by a squad of Hamas and Fatah supporters from the Ezzedin al-Kassem and Fatah Hawks groups.

The two groups, which have attacked each other in the past, apparently joined forces for the first time.

A leaflet, signed by both groups and left at the site of the shootings, said the attack was a response to the killing of members of their groups by the IDF.

The victims were buying wholesale produce, prices of which have bottomed out in Gaza due to a glut caused by a good harvest, the difficulty of exporting vegetables during the closure of the territories, and the drop in local demand since the closure has cost many thousands their jobs.

A senior security official said that Falas and Halfon were in the area for more than an hour, which would have given terrorists time to organize an attack.

Military sources said some 15 people, almost everybody living in the area of the greenhouses, were held for questioning. It is believed that someone there may have tipped off the killers that Falas and Halfon were there. It is not clear if the killers knew that Abu Zhohab and Abu Gharab were Palestinians.

One woman in the area said she heard shots and saw a car drive off quickly.

"Ambush would not be a suitable word for the attack, but it was planned," said Deputy Cmdr. Haim Dardik, the Gaza region deputy police chief.

Israeli vegetable dealers come to the area frequently, he noted, adding that Dardik said Falas had been arrested "hundreds of times for smuggling vegetables." A police file had been opened against him last week, after an Israeli snackbar owner in the area complained that he had Arab farmers bring produce to his van near her kiosk.

Vegetable wholesaler Yehezkel Avraham was killed in the same area by Palestinian gunmen on February 9. An Israeli Arab friend who was with him escaped. A year ago, farmer Hani Abdel-Latif saved the lives of two Israeli customers who were attacked near his home in Beit Lahiya. David Cohen, a livestock farmer, was shot dead while trying to buy goats in Beit Lahiya last May.

The commercial temptations are great. One settler in the area said "prices are so low that a dealer from Ashkelon who fills up a van has made his week." Since the closure, vegetable prices have dropped by 50%-75%.

The attack took place on the Hebrew anniversary of the stabbing of Rabbi Shimon Biran, whose memorial service was held shortly after yesterday's murders in the Gush Katif cemetery, about two kilometers away from where the killings took place.

Biran was stabbed last May 27 as he crossed the road from his home at Kfar Darom to the Tora and Land Yeshiva, next to Deir el-Balah. His death precipitated a six-day closure of the Gaza Strip. Dozens of settlers and family members met by the graveside.

Biran is one of four Israelis buried in Gaza. The other three graves are all of children.

Baruch, a resident of Ganei Tal, said the cemetery was a "symbol that God has brought about our return to this part of the Land of Israel."

Zvi Hendel, the head of the Gaza Coast Regional Council, said the murders were to be expected with the end of the current round of peace talks.

"They are trying to pressure us to make more gestures," he said. "If they can't get what they want at the peace talks, they try to pressure us on the street."

Hendel said there are elements in the PLO just as extreme as Hamas who are trying to "burn the ground under the Zionists' feet," as Yasser Arafat called upon them to do two months ago.

Herb Keinon contributed to this report

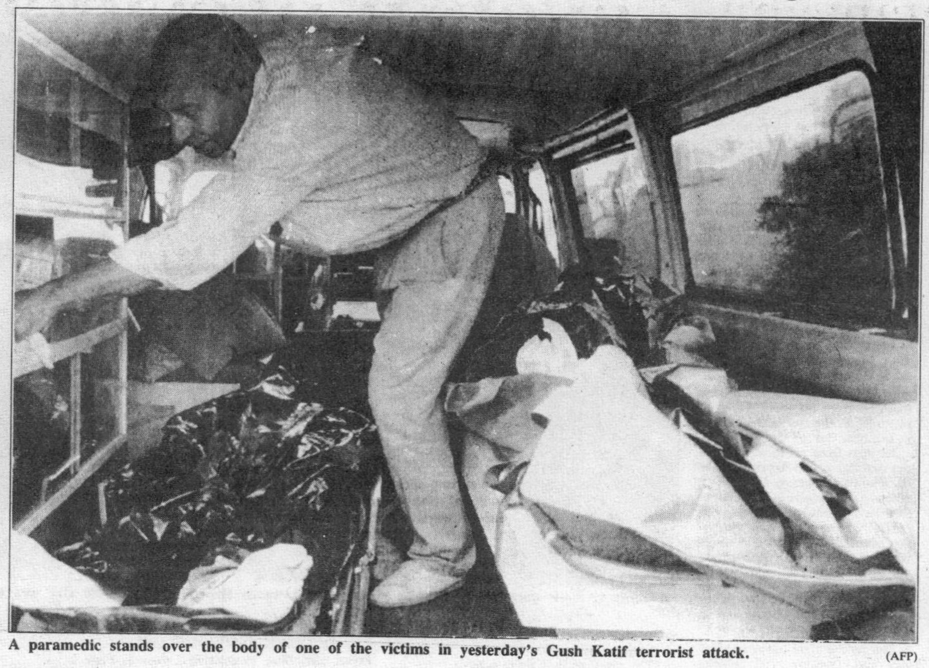

A paramedic stands over the body of one of the victims in yesterday's Gush Katif terrorist attack. (AFP)

Kupat Holim: Nurses in contempt of court

JUDY SIEGEL and JOSE ROSENFELD

KUPAT Holim Clalit's board of directors took its toughest stand yet on the six-day old nurses' strike, declaring last night that the health fund would ask that the union be held in contempt of the Tel Aviv Labor Court.

The strike will continue today.

Contrary to previous announcements, Kupat Holim ruled out placing the health fund into receivership, now or in the foreseeable future.

The labor court, which will hold another hearing today, yesterday called on the nurses to halt their strike. Two weeks ago, it had issued a restraining order barring all work sanctions, but it was ignored by the union.

The health fund "didn't want to push the nurses up against the wall," said a Kupat Holim source, "but given the present dead end, this may be the only alternative."

Meanwhile, the union of government hospital nurses last night threatened to join the strike in an expression of solidarity, but did not set a date.

The Kupat Holim board declared that the five percent cut in all staffers' salaries had been demanded in March by the government, and that it and the Histadrut had no alternative but to go along.

The board authorized chairman Prof. Dan Michaeli and director-general Avigdor Kaplan to close any hospital in which patients lives were in danger because of the strike.

During the past few days, most Kupat Holim hospitals have closed their emergency rooms, referring patients to the nearest government or other public hospital. Occupancy, comprising the most seriously ill patients, has fallen below 40 percent, and all but emergency operations have been canceled.

The board declared that it would carry out any agreement approved by the Knesset if the health fund's recovery program, including state funding, were ensured.

Some 300 nurses were bused to Jerusalem yesterday for a demonstration outside the office of Finance Minister Avraham Shohat. They met with him late last night, without result. Earlier in the day, Shohat held a press conference in which he outlined his opposition to the nurses' proposal that vacation and advanced-training pay be set aside for a few years instead of the five-percent wage cut.

Shohat said this would constitute a precedent, and that the interest would have to exceed the market rate. He suggested a plan that the nurses had suggested on Thursday and he turned down: that no Kupat Holim worker earning less than NIS 3,000 gross a month be subject to the wage cut, and those above that floor would suffer a graduated cut. This was rejected by the nurses.

Rabin: Don't enter territories unnecessarily

DAVID MAKOVSKY

THOSE who do not live in the administered territories should avoid unnecessary travel to and around them, Prime Minister Yitzhak Rabin warned after two Israelis and two Palestinians were killed in Gaza yesterday.

While the statement was motivated by security considerations, Rabin's remarks suggest the latest example of his publicly declared intention of separating the Israeli and Palestinian populations.

Speaking to reporters while visiting new President Ezer Weizman, Rabin urged people to avoid traveling to the territories. "I am not talking about those who live there. There are many visitors, hikers, and workers in the settlements. They are permitted to keep going, but things are happening even when activities are legal. Do not endanger your life to make a few hundred shekels."

At yesterday's weekly cabinet meeting, Absorption Minister Yair Tsaban and Tourism Minister Uzi Baram called for the end of the closure of the territories, which has now lasted longer than it did during the Gulf war.

Convinced up to 80,000 Palestinians will eventually be allowed to return to work in Israel, Tsaban told reporters afterwards: "If the closure is not lifted now, accompanied by controls, it will be dangerous. The territories are already a pressure-cooker."

Tsaban said he was concerned that the continued closure would hurt the Palestinian negotiating team.

But Rabin said the government would make no more unilateral gestures toward the Palestinians, rejecting the idea that such steps are needed to lure them back to the peace table, participants in the meeting said.

Instead of appreciating previous gestures, the Palestinians have complained that they were inadequate and that more was needed, he said.

A senior official in the Prime Minister's Bureau said that gestures would now be predicated upon a Palestinian modification of negotiation positions that have remained unchanged since the start of negotiations and a public call by Palestinian negotiators for a halt to violence against Israelis.

Until now, when pressed, these negotiators will only say that the cycle of violence has to stop on both sides.

In reporting to the cabinet on the peace talks, chief negotiator with the Palestinians Elyakim Rubinstein said violence in the territories has a negative impact on the negotiations. At the same time, he suggested that Palestinian negotiators may have fueled the violence by issuing pessimistic statements.

He said that Israel has offered to appoint human rights liaison officers in every town in the territories. These officers would receive complaints on alleged human rights abuses between negotiating sessions. He said that no response has been received.

In reporting on the talks with Syria, assistant Foreign Ministry director-general for research David Afek said Damascus is still insisting that "every millimeter" of land must be returned in exchange for an end to the state of belligerency, cabinet participants said. But Damascus has not ruled out the possibility of normal relations after all territories are returned. In the past, Damascus has categorically rejected normalization.

Eighteen-month-old boy killed by troops during riot

JON IMMANUEL and ASHER WALLFISH

IDF troops hit and killed an 18-month-old boy, Mohammed Faris al-Kurdi, while shooting to break up a riot by Palestinian stonethrowers in the Jabalya refugee camp yesterday, according to Palestinian sources.

More than 20 wounded were reported in the Shati camp and in Jabalya, which was under curfew for several days last week, following the funeral of Hassan Hamouda, a Hamas gunman shot by troops on the Egyptian border.

Military sources said they were investigating the cause of the death, the 18th in Gaza this month, a total that includes 11 wanted terrorists and three children under 15.

Meanwhile, Knesset law committee chairman Dedi Zucker wrote Prime Minister Rabin in his capacity as defense minister yesterday, urging the appointment of an ombudsman to handle complaints from the Palestinian residents of the territories.

Zucker proposed that the ombudsman deal with complaints against the Civil Administration and against the actions of the IDF in its contact with the population at large, as distinct from its military operations.

"The appointment of a man with legal experience and familiarity with the functioning of the IDF and the Civil Administration might well alter the atmosphere among the local population and among the Israeli soldiers and officials responsible for them," Zucker wrote.

In another development, a firebomb was thrown at the car of a Jewish resident of Dolev, east of Ramallah.

Levy boycotts Likud convention in fit of pique

SARAH HONIG

THE bitter internal feuding which Likud leader Binyamin Netanyahu hopes to eliminate was all too evident yesterday, as his rival, David Levy, boycotted the opening of the first party convention in seven years.

The opening ceremony was held in Katzrin on the Golan Heights, but Levy reportedly sulked at home in Beit She'an to protest what he called Netanyahu's "attitude," as well as the draft of the constitution the Likud chairman plans to present to the convention during today's session.

Levy was badly beaten by Netanyahu in the party's March 24 primary and vowed not to cooperate with the party's new leader.

Levy charged yesterday that Netanyahu "plans to turn the opening ceremony into his own coronation as the party monarch and I have no interest in taking part in that. He will turn the Likud into a dictatorship, unlike any party in the country."

Levy's brother Maxim, who is mayor of Lod and his closest confidant, said his brother continues to be miffed by the fact that "no apology has yet come from Netanyahu for insinuating that Levy was behind an alleged blackmail attempt against him."

The only address at yesterday's convention opening, aside from President Ezer Weizman's greeting, was Netanyahu's.

MK Ariel Sharon was also almost a no-show yesterday. He, too, took Netanyahu to task for "seeking to do away with the party's system of checks and balances."

Sharon had an excuse, however. He had set up a meeting with members of Moshav Neve Ativ on the Golan to discuss their fear of a possible withdrawal from the heights. The appointment coincided with the opening ceremony, and Sharon said he was unsure he would be able to appear.

Sharon finally did arrive, however, after being persuaded by those close to him not to follow Levy's example and inject acrimony into the festivities.

Today's proceedings at the Yad Eliyahu Sports Stadium in Tel Aviv are expected to be the first real test of Netanyahu's leadership. Topping the agenda will be the proposed constitution, in which Netanyahu will seek to do away with what he calls the "feudal manors of Likud factions." He wants a professional executive to run things, who would be hired for his abilities, not appointed because of factional quotas.

In theory, Netanyahu should have the support of a majority of delegates to push through his constitution. However, all those who ran against him last March are staunchly opposed to having him as a strong chairman and are expected to mount a strong challenge.

Tomorrow, the convention's final day, the 3,500 delegates will tackle a host of ideological proposals including suggestions that Jordan be identified as Palestine, that the death penalty be imposed on terrorists, and that the Likud withdraw its endorsement of the autonomy plan.

'No to Golan withdrawal,' Page 2

Eliyahu group buys 60% of Union Bank

GALIT LIPKIS and JOSE ROSENFELD

THE Shlomo Eliyahu group yesterday acquired 60% of Union Bank for $85.5 million as part of government plans to increase competition in the banking system, Finance Minister Avraham Shohat announced yesterday.

Union was purchased from Bank Leumi, which owned 42% of the bank, and the government, which owned the remaining shares. Union specializes in finance for the diamond industry.

The remaining 40% of the bank's shares, 16.8% held by Leumi and 23.2% held by the government, will be offered by tender to the public and the bank's employees, the Treasury announced yesterday.

The group consists of four investors who joined forces about one year ago in order to bid for the bank; Shlomo Eliyahu, chairman of Eliyahu Insurance company (30% share), David Lubinsky, the importer of Peugeot cars (30% share), Joshua Landau, a major shareholder in Sonol (30% share) and the Rotlevi family, involved in the textile sector (10% share).

Complete story on Page 8.

Warshavsky Freilich Dover

YOUR PEACE OF MIND IS OUR BUSINESS.

At Israel Discount Bank, your peace of mind is our business. We are attuned to your special financial requirements. In a fast changing International environment it pays to diversify your investments. Profit from our experience.

When you open a tax free foreign currency account at Israel Discount Bank, you profit in more ways than one:
- Strict confidentiality
- Short & medium term deposits in all major foreign currencies
- Highly competitive interest rates on term deposits
- Deposits convertible into all major foreign currencies
- Interest free of income tax in Israel
- No estate duties in Israel
- Funds transferable worldwide

When you consider to diversify your financial assets, you may invest through the Bank in bonds and stocks, traded on major stock exchanges worldwide and on the Tel-Aviv stock exchange.

When you wish to purchase real estate in Israel, you may receive a loan of up to 50% of the value of the property acquired.

We offer you discretion, diversification and profitability - the opportunity to invest with peace of mind.

For further details please visit any Israel Discount Bank branch or contact any Israel Discount Bank Tourist Center.

Tel Aviv Head Office: 27 Yehuda Halevi St., Tel: (03) 514-5555. Main Foreign Exchange Branch and Tourist Center: 16 Mapu St., Tel: (03) 542-1122.

THE PEOPLE YOU CAN TALK TO.
ISRAEL DISCOUNT BANK

THE JERUSALEM POST
an international newspaper distributed on 6 continents in English and French.
Over 500,000 readers worldwide

THE JERUSALEM POST

EGYPT • SINAI ISRAEL • JORDAN GREECE • TURKEY
TRAVEL WITH THE EXPERTS see last page
For all information call us: MAZADA TOURS
TEL AVIV: 141 IBN GVIROL, TEL: 03-5444454, FAX: 5461928
JERUSALEM: 24, BEN-SIRA ST. TEL/FAX: 02-255454
NAZARETH: PAULUS VI ST. TEL/FAX: 06-564372

VOLUME LXI, NUMBER 18420 | WEDNESDAY, JULY 28, 1993 • AV 10, 5753 • SAFAR 9, 1414 | NIS 3.40 (EILAT NIS 2.90)

Christopher cuts short Asian tour; calls Rabin, Shara

HILLEL KUTTLER and HERB KEINON

US SECRETARY of State Warren Christopher abruptly headed back to Washington from Singapore yesterday, curtailing his visit to the Pacific because of the Israel-Lebanon crisis.

Christopher spoke by telephone with Prime Minister Yitzhak Rabin and Syrian Foreign Minister Farouk Shara to discuss the situation in Lebanon.

Rabin urged Christopher to stick to his plan to visit the region this week, and Christopher assured Rabin he has no intention of changing his plans, the Associated Press reported.

Christopher was said to have also told Shara to "think of ways in which violence may be deescalated," an implicit reference to Syrian sway over Hizbullah and Palestinian groups operating in Lebanese territory under Syrian control. Christopher is due to return to the US today.

Hours after Christopher's announcement, President Bill Clinton held a press conference in which he seemed to go out of his way to praise Syria's position in the developing situation.

"I think the Syrians have shown commendable restraint so far," Clinton told reporters at the White House. "I don't think we should let Hizbullah and all these groups that don't want anything good to happen in the Middle East derail the peace process by what they do."

Foreign Minister Shimon Peres said it is inconceivable that either Israel or the Americans would end or reduce their efforts in the peace process because of Hizbullah.

"We will not put our security, or put peace, in the hands of Hizbullah," Peres said while touring the north yesterday. "I am sure that Christopher understands that. If we divert from the peace process, this would be the biggest victory possible for Hizbullah."

When asked how long Operation Accountability would last, Peres said: "No one can say for certain. But we are not talking about weeks or months."

The Foreign Ministry is concerned the Syrians will condition curbing Hizbullah on Israeli concessions in the peace talks.

Deputy Foreign Minister Yossi Beilin told Army Radio yesterday Christopher's decision to return to Washington before coming here is significant, because it shows that the Lebanon situation is high on the US agenda.

Assistant Secretary of State for Near East Affairs Edward Djerejian told a Congressional panel that recalling Christopher "reflects the gravity with which the administration views the outbreak of hostilities."

Following telephone consultations with Clinton, the decision was made for Christopher to return immediately to Washington to confer with the president and top State Department aides before heading to the Middle East later this week.

Christopher is scheduled to arrive in Cairo Saturday night for a four-day visit to capitals including Jerusalem, Damascus, and Amman, with a view towards getting the next round of Middle East peace talks back on track.

"I have been following the dramatic escalation of violence in Southern Lebanon and Northern Israel with great concern, and I will be discussing the impact of these events on the peace process," Christopher announced prior to his departure from Singapore, where he had participated in a meeting of foreign ministers.

Asked for clarification of Clinton's remarks, a White House official said: "It is clear Syria has not taken action to escalate the seriousness of this situation. At the same time, it is clear we call on all parties to deescalate the situation there ... In the case of Syria: to use their influence with Hizbullah to reduce the tensions there, as well as to get Hizbullah to stop subverting the peace process."

White House spokeswoman Dee Dee Meyers stated that Syria "has not signaled any intention to change their participation" in the peace process as a result of the renewed hostilities.

On Capitol Hill yesterday.

(Continued on Page 2)

150,000 villagers flee south Lebanon

IDF steps up attacks north of security zone

DAVID RUDGE and MICHAEL ROTEM

A MASSIVE flight of Lebanese Shi'ites from villages north of the security zone up the coastal road toward Beirut was reported yesterday, as the IDF maintained its artillery, aerial, and naval bombardment of terrorist targets.

Hizbullah forces continued to launch sporadic Katyusha rocket attacks on parts of the Galilee. Two people were lightly hurt, there was minor damage to property, and fires were started in some areas.

The Katyushas will not stop within the next day or two, IDF Chief of General Staff Lt.-Gen. Ehud Barak said.

"We have hit several Katyusha launchers," he told Israel Radio, "but I think the terrorist organizations have more. They are relatively small and easy to conceal, and I expect they will try to bring in others from the north. I am not planning on the Katyushas ending in the next day or two."

Reports from north of the border said more than 50 people have been killed and nearly 200 wounded since the beginning of Operation Accountability on Sunday.

IDF sources maintained that every effort had been made to hit terrorist targets and to minimize casualties among Lebanese civilians. Nevertheless, reports from Lebanon said the majority of those killed and wounded were in fact civilians.

During the night between Monday and Tuesday, 700 vehicles were sighted on the Lebanese coastal road and another 1,000 or so today. It is estimated that 150,000 Shi'ites have fled the range of IDF gunners.

Their villages, presumed to be empty of civilians, were heavily hit yesterday, following an estimate that Hizbullah terrorists preferred to dig in within these villages.

Lebanese civilians pack pickup trucks as they flee towards Beirut to escape the IDF attacks. (AP)

"The message that we're sending to the Lebanese people, their government, and the governments that assist them is that the time has arrived to put an end to the violent activities of Hizbullah, to stop firing Katyushas at innocent civilians," Prime Minister Yitzhak Rabin said in Kiryat Shmona.

OPERATION ACCOUNTABILITY
Peres: Hizbullah victimizing Lebanon, Page 2
Tourism drops sharply in north, Page 3

Military sources estimated that Hizbullah targets have been hit with some 4,000 155mm shells, including smoke and flares intended to scare off civilians.

Fresh IDF reinforcements also poured into southern Lebanon yesterday. Senior military sources insisted that Israel is not seeking a war, and that everything depends on the other side.

If Hizbullah ceases its attacks on the North, it will have peace, one source said. But if it escalates the situation, the IDF might use some contingency plans which are more aggressive than those used until now.

It was unclear last night whether the ground assault option would be used. As the number of Katyusha rockets hitting the north markedly decreased yesterday, the sources said, it seems the tension is decreasing. Only 14 Katyusha rockets had hit the North by late last night.

"We estimate that the temporary reduction in the number of Katyushas is because Hizbullah is finding it very difficult to reach its stockpiles," a senior military source said. "The terrorists also have a manpower problem, as many of their men have fled north. However, I don't rule out the possibility that after reorganizing, they will attack."

The IAF also continued hitting terrorist sites in Lebanon. Helicopters rocketed terrorist targets in the village of Ya'atar, in the eastern sector, after Katyusha launchers were seen on a rooftop. The building was reportedly destroyed. Other aircraft hit Sidon, and four Palestinians were reportedly wounded in its Ein el-Hilwe refugee camp.

Responding to UN claims that four UNIFIL soldiers were lightly injured when their position was hit by an IAF jet, the senior source said that a preliminary investigation indicated the planes were attacking more than a kilometer and a half away from the UN post. He said the post was probably hit by a Hizbullah Katyusha.

The UNIFIL spokesman said that at about 10 a.m., two IAF planes dropped four bombs on the headquarters of the force's Nepalese battalion in Ein al-Hinniyeh, south of Tyre.

He said that four soldiers were lightly to moderately wounded, and 15 UN vehicles partially or totally destroyed, as were several buildings. He said the hilltop compound was clearly marked as a UN position, and there appeared to be no reason for the attack.

The spokesman added that UNIFIL had launched a "very strong protest" with the IDF.

Officer: We haven't yet seen Hizbullah's full firepower

MICHAEL ROTEM

"HIZBULLAH has not yet demonstrated its full ability to fire Katyushas, I am sure of that," a field-grade officer in the Golani Brigade said yesterday.

"They have truckloads of them, and they have not yet even taken them out of their caches. I believe Hizbullah can fire up to 200 Katyushas a day."

He pointed at the clouds of smoke rising from Shi'ite villages north of his post in the central sector of the security zone, noting that artillery had been firing into them since early morning.

"We watch the villages, and we see no civilians moving around," he noted. "I don't think any civilians remain after the mass exodus which started on Monday."

The warning shells fired by the IDF on Sunday and Monday, and repeated warnings on south Lebanese radio, caused most of the residents to flee.

"On Sunday and Monday, we identified Hizbullah terrorists moving around the villages," the officer said. "But today, we have not seen any of them. It doesn't necessarily mean the terrorists escaped with the residents; it's quite possible they're in hiding right now."

He said his men have seen 12 Katyushas being launched from Shi'ite villages near their post, adding that on Monday two Katyushas were fired at the post.

"During the day it is much more difficult to see the Katyushas being launched; at night, the rockets leave a trail of fire."

The enlisted men at the position have grown accustomed to the demands of the situation.

"Our commanders expect higher performance from us than from other brigades," said Cpl. Zohar. "It took us a few days to adjust to life on this post, but we've gotten into the routine very quickly. We're not rookies; almost everyone here has been in the army for 18 months or two years. We've served in Lebanon before."

Zohar and his friends said they are looking forward to the order to launch a ground assault against the terrorist strongholds.

"If the order is given, all these men that you see will be ready to go within minutes," one officer said proudly.

The senior officer, however, was more cautious.

"I hope we will not reach a situation in which we have to go; I hope the problem can be solved elsewhere," he said.

Rabin: Aim of operation is to move population northward

DAN IZENBERG

THE goal of Operation Accountability is "not just to cause destruction, but to get the [Lebanese] population to move north," Prime Minister Yitzhak Rabin reportedly told the Knesset foreign affairs and defense committee yesterday.

According to a senior official who attended the meeting, Rabin told the MKs that the "movement would hopefully tell the Lebanese authorities something about the [mass of] refugees which can be expected to reach as far as Beirut. We want to create a wave of refugees and attack anyone who is a Hizbullah accomplice."

Rabin said Hizbullah changed the rules of the game in southern Lebanon after the IDF killed its leader, Sheikh Abbas Musawi, in a helicopter attack in February 1992.

The first signs of the change occurred immediately afterwards, when Hizbullah fired Katyusha rockets at Israel and blew up the Israeli Embassy in Argentina with Iranian help.

The dramatic escalation began in January 1993, after the Lebanese elections. According to the "new rules," Hizbullah would retaliate for any IDF attack north of the security zone by firing rockets at Israeli settlements. An additional escalation was the introduction of Iranian-supplied Sagger anti-tank missiles.

As a result, over the past few months IDF retaliatory actions beyond the zone were restricted to artillery fire to minimize attacks on Israeli settlements.

"Hizbullah has hundreds of Katyushas and launchers, a strong infrastructure and hinterland, and Iranian backing," said Rabin. "We know of Hizbullah appeals for more money from Iran. The Islamic movement is loaded with money."

In light of the new situation, Israel faced three choices, according to Rabin:

Prime Minister Rabin briefs MKs yesterday. (Isaac Harari)

• expanding the security zone, even though the terrorists possess 122 mm Katyushas with a range of 22 km;
• accepting the rules of the game as laid down by Hizbullah;
• or making it clear that if Israel does not have quiet, there will not be quiet in Lebanon.

"Hizbullah wants to halt the peace talks," said Rabin. "For them, that would be a greater achievement than hitting our settlements."

Rabin acknowledged that it is difficult to locate the Katyushas before they are fired and that Hizbullah has acquired much experience in operating them.

"But we are operating against them," he continued. "I know that our settlements in the North are undergoing hardship and that life is not easy [these days], but our aim is that Hizbullah will not have an itchy trigger finger for its Katyushas. We have no other goal."

Rabin added that Operation Accountability would also strengthen the Israeli-backed South Lebanese Army.

Ephraim Sneh (Labor) urged imposing a naval blockade on Lebanon, to step up the pressure on Beirut to take action against Hizbullah. Forcing the population to evacuate their villages is insufficient, he said.

Party colleague Haggai Merom and Ran Cohen (Meretz) strongly disagreed. "We shouldn't fight in Lebanon," said Cohen. "We must not turn Operation Accountability into a second Peace for Galilee."

Ariel Sharon (Likud) congratulated Rabin on the military operation and urged making the continuation of the peace talks conditional on Syria taking action against Hizbullah.

Northerners find noise of artillery comforting after crash of Katyushas

DAVID RUDGE

THE sound of IDF artillery fire reverberated along the northern border yesterday, as terrorist targets north of the security zone continued to be pounded on the third day of Operation Accountability.

The constant cannon fire was frequently interspersed with the clatter of northward-bound helicopter gunships passing overhead. Occasionally, jets streaked into Lebanon, presumably to hit Hizbullah and Palestinian terrorist bases.

The noise of the fighting brought comfort to some residents, but did little to ease the tension and concern that has prevailed since Sunday.

According to army sources, most of the shelling was "suppression fire" to hamper the launching of Katyusha rockets. Nonetheless, some Katyushas hit various parts of the Galilee, lightly wounding two people and causing minor damage to property and at least one fire.

On Monday night, a Katyusha exploded near Eli's home as he and his family were sleeping. The blast blew out windows and shutters, damaged a jeep parked outside, and brought down a power line.

Eli said he had intended to send his wife and five children to stay with relatives in Tel Aviv, but had delayed the move on the advice of a neighbor, who said it would be risky for them to travel at night.

"I meant to take them at 7 p.m., and then 4½ hours later, a rocket explodes by our home. My wife and children were very upset, but I managed to calm them down," he said.

Kiryat Shmona resembles a ghost town, with virtually all shops and businesses closed and the remaining residents firmly entrenched in bomb shelters or security rooms.

Hundreds of children have already left the township to be hosted at summer camps in other parts of the country.

Even some veteran residents, who said they had lived through even worse experiences, said that they had decided to send their children away as a precaution and to give them a chance to enjoy a "normal summer vacation."

Among the visitors to the bomb shelters were two hairdressers from Haifa, who gave free haircuts and shampoos, and ministers, MKS, and Tel Aviv Mayor Shlomo Lahat.

Shahak: Katyusha attacks lessening, but more terrorists moving south

RAINE MARCUS

KATYUSHA attacks by Hizbullah have been greatly reduced in the 24 hours ending last night, Deputy Chief of General Staff Maj.-Gen Amnon Shahak said last night at a press briefing, as some 150,000 Lebanese villagers fled the security zone.

When asked how long the IDF bombardments would continue, Shahak said this depends on the intervention by those parties who are in a position to put pressure on Hizbullah.

"From our point of view it could end tomorrow," he said.

On Monday, civilians in southern Lebanon responded to army warnings to evacuate their homes. By last night, large numbers of civilians were still fleeing north, but the villages in the south were nearly empty of civilians, Shahak said.

"This mass exit enabled our forces to strike at targets for a second time, to flush out terrorists," said Air Force Commander Maj.-Gen. Herzl Bodinger.

The IAF has made some 300 sorties since the bombardments started, Bodinger said. Sixty percent of the air strikes were carried out by warplanes and the other 40 percent, particularly those in densely populated areas, by Apache helicopters.

Some 150 targets have been hit by air and artillery fire since Operation Accountability started, he said. "Unfortunately, a small number of civilians were also hit, as were three Unifil soldiers," Bodinger added.

Shahak estimated some 20 civilians have been killed and 60-70 wounded, but stressed those figures have not been confirmed. Twenty terrorists have been killed and some 20 wounded, he added.

Despite the bombardments, Hizbullah is not deserting southern Lebanon, said military intelligence officer Brig.-Gen Ami.

"As 150,000 people are fleeing north, more terrorists are moving into the south," said Ami. "Our toughest problem [during the bombardments] was separating the civilians from the terrorists. As in the past, Hizbullah is using innocent civilians as cover."

As for Syria's role in the conflict, Ami noted: "The Syrian government is capable of ending warfare tomorrow," but is not interested in doing so.

Syria holds the key to the continuing survival of Hizbullah, he explained. Iran sends its arms and ammunition via Damascus and terrorists must pass through Syria on their way to training camps in Iran.

Ami also blamed the Lebanese "puppet" government and its army for not acting to stop the Hizbullah, and for not disarming the Hizbullah when other terrorist organizations were forced to give up their arms.

THE JERUSALEM POST
an international newspaper distributed on 6 continents in English and French. Over 500,000 readers worldwide

THE JERUSALEM POST

Know-nothing newsmen
Page 6

VOLUME LXI, NUMBER 18449 TUESDAY, AUGUST 31, 1993 • ELUL 14, 5753 • RABIA AWAL 14, 1414 NIS 3.40 (EILAT NIS 2.90)

Cabinet approves 'Gaza/Jericho first'

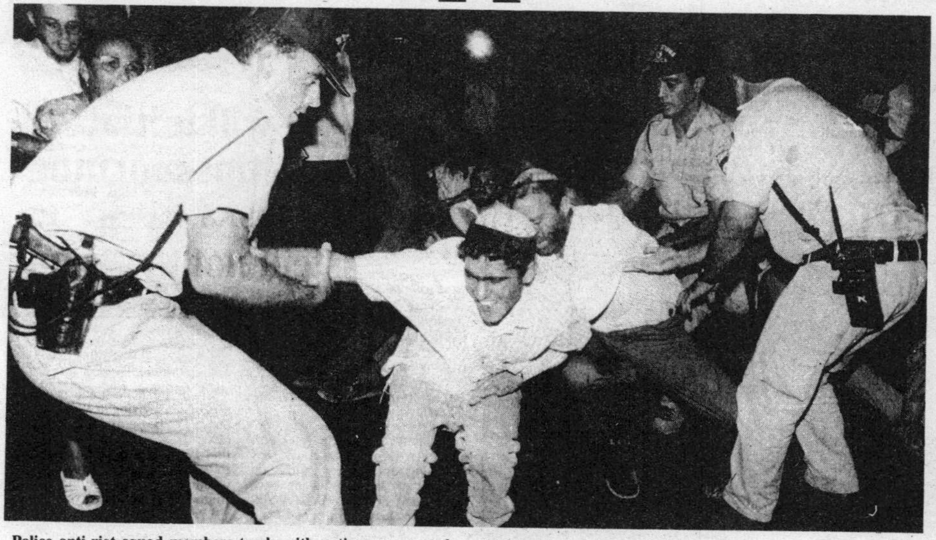

Police anti-riot squad members tussle with anti-government demonstrators last night. (Isaac Harari)

HERB KEINON

THE cabinet last night approved an historic agreement of principles with the PLO, following a marathon session that lasted till after midnight. All the ministers voted in favor, with Interior Minister Aryeh Deri and Economics Minister Shimon Shetreet abstaining. There seemed little doubt the cabinet would ratify the agreement, after a long day during which most ministers read its terms for the first time. The only question was whether any of them would abstain or vote against the agreement.

As the cabinet met, thousands of protesters demonstrated against the agreement outside the Prime Minister's Office last night.

The agreement provides for Palestinian self-rule in Gaza and Jericho as a first step towards autonomy in the rest of the territories.

"Every change has its risks, but the time has come to take a chance for peace," Prime Minister Yitzhak Rabin told coalition members earlier yesterday. "We stand on the verge of a great opportunity."

Likud leader Binyamin Netanyahu blasted the proposed plan, which he said threatens the nation's existence.

"You are much worse than [former British prime minister Neville] Chamberlain, because Chamberlain threatened the security and freedom of another nation, while you are threatening the security and freedom of your own nation," Netanyahu told Foreign Minister Shimon Peres during a special Knesset session.

"I hope [the plan] will be accepted unanimously," Communications Minister Shulamit Aloni told reporters during a break in the cabinet session. "This is a great day. I don't understand the commotion outside, especially since no one raised the idea of uprooting any of the settlements."

Health Minister Haim Ramon was equally sanguine. "It's a very serious discussion," he said. "Everyone realizes the heavy responsibility, but also the great opportunity to come to a peace agreement with the Palestinians once and for all."

Ramon said the ministers are "well aware" of the dangers involved in the agreement, "but all the other alternatives are worse." He said the other alternatives are the continued control of Gaza, or the annexation of two million Palestinians.

Deri reportedly told Rabin that since he is unlikely to be a minister in a few days, he would have difficulty voting for a policy for which he will not share responsibility.

Absorption Minister Yair Tsaban cautioned against rushing to formally recognize the PLO. He noted that "mutual recognition between Israel and the PLO – based on the PLO's acceptance of Israel and renunciation of terrorism – has always been a principle of Meretz." But, he added, this is not the time for formal recognition.

Rabin: Horizons for peace are open
Netanyahu: Bridgehead for destruction of Israel
Page 2

The ministers began arriving at the Prime Minister's Office at 7 p.m. Rabin briefed them on the agreement, as did Chief of General Staff Lt.-Gen. Ehud Barak, who talked about security problems which might ensue.

Among the issues Barak raised was what would happen if the IDF pursued a wanted terrorist who fled into the autonomous region of Gaza or Jericho. Barak also discussed where and how the IDF would redeploy.

Chief negotiator Elyakim Ru-

(Continued on Page 2)

Settlers battle police as cabinet meets

BILL HUTMAN

SETTLEMENT leaders from Judea, Samaria, and Gaza vowed violent protests would escalate, after police and anti-government demonstrators headed by the settlement leaders clashed outside the Prime Minister's Office last night.

The demonstration took place as the cabinet met inside to discuss and to vote on the interim autonomy agreement with the Palestinians.

Dozens of police and Border Police officers blocked the protesters, who shouted "Rabin is a traitor" and "Rabin is a liar."

Twenty one demonstrators were detained, and two police officers were hit by stones and hospitalized by late in the evening, with the protest still going strong, the police spokesman said.

"We are reacting with violence because the government has acted with violence by forcing this agreement on the nation," said Aaron Domb, spokesman for the Council of Settlements in Judea, Samaria, and Gaza.

Several protesters threw stones and eggs at about 50 Peace Now activists demonstrating in support for the peace process and the government.

"We have no doubt the people of Israel are with us," said Peace Now spokeswoman Vered Livne.

Police, including the special anti-riot squad, used a water cannon in an attempt to clear demonstrators from Ruppin Street, but the protesters closed the road for over two hours, despite police efforts.

Senior police officers, however, said their operation was a success, because the protesters were kept far from the Prime Minister's Office.

Thirty carloads of settlers from the Hebron area on their way to the demonstration were reportedly halted late last night by police at the Gilo junction in south Jerusalem.

On the verge of making history

HERB KEINON

"HISTORY" hung heavy in the air at the government complex near the Knesset last night, as the cabinet discussed an agreement of principles with the PLO.

Minister after minister filed into the cabinet wearing a relieved grin that seemed to say, "Peace is really within reach."

But the peace hinged largely on a decision being taken by the leadership of Shas, one building over. In that meeting, there were calls to link the government's diplomatic moves with the future of their embattled leader.

When that leader, Aryeh Deri, emerged from this meeting, he could hear the angry shouts, whistles, and sirens from the settlement demonstration nearby ricocheting off the surrounding office buildings.

The sounds of this demonstration, the first rumblings of what some fear could be a civil insurrection, also smashed through the windows of the cabinet room, and had to dampen – if just a bit – the spirits of the ministers.

For we are a nation divided.

Settlers stood on one hill near the Prime Minister's Office, shouting "traitors" and carrying signs reading "Eretz Yisrael is in danger."

On another hill – across a wide chasm of a boulevard – Peace Now supporters stood holding torches, chanting that Rabin *does* have a mandate, and carrying signs reading "Give Peace a Chance."

If any ministers peered out the window of the cabinet meeting at the demonstrations 100 meters away – at the arrests, the water cannons, the hurtling eggs – they must have realized it will take every bit as much finesse to come to an "agreement of principles" with their own people, as it took to reach such an agreement with the PLO.

Deri decides not to resign

HERB KEINON and MICHAL YUDELMAN

INTERIOR Minister Aryeh Deri has decided not to resign from the cabinet until the High Court of Justice decides whether Prime Minister Yitzhak Rabin has to fire him.

"According to the directives of Rabbi Ovadia Yosef, I will resign only after the High Court's decision," Deri said, after a meeting of the Shas Party's leadership last night. The meeting dealt with both the question of Deri's resignation, and whether Shas will accept the "Gaza/Jericho first" plan.

The High Court of Justice yesterday postponed ruling on whether Rabin must fire Deri, but sent a clear message that it considers a minister under indictment to be a violation of proper public norms. **(See Page 4)**

MK Yosef Azran said Yosef once again renewed his call to Deri to "sit and do nothing." Yosef has long maintained there is no reason for Deri to quit the government on his own initiative, but rather to wait until he is forced out.

Shas faction head Shlomo Benizri said he had also advised Deri not to resign now. "My advice is to see the legal process through until the end. The minute he doesn't do this, he is admitting to all the accusations," he said.

Benizri said that the High Court justices' harsh words for Deri yesterday do not mean they will rule against him. This sentiment was echoed by Azran, who said the fact that the justices asked for more time to rule is proof the outcome is not necessarily cut and dried.

MK Aryeh Gamliel also called upon Deri "not to take the coals out of the fire for anybody, not even the High Court."

That there is concern in the coalition that Shas might quit if Deri resigns or is forced out was evident in coalition Knesset faction head Eli Dayan's presence at the Shas meeting.

"There is no coalition crisis," Dayan said. "But we should not underestimate Shas's problems."

There is fear in Labor that the peace process, now suddenly forced into high gear by the Gaza/Jericho proposals, might collapse if the coalition falls apart.

Health Minister Haim Ramon urged Shas not to leave and by so doing harm the peace process. Shas, Ramon said, "has always spoken of peace and it has been an important part of its platform and its leader Rabbi Ovadia Yosef's position. This is Shas's chance to be part of real, dignified peace, as a partner in a government which brings it about."

Benizri said yesterday that the general consensus in the party is not to pull out of the coalition, even if Deri is forced out of the Interior Ministry. Sources in the Prime Minister's Office expressed a similar view of Shas's intentions.

Nevertheless, Foreign Minister Shimon Peres resumed his contacts with the Agudat Yisrael faction of the United Tora Judaism yesterday, in an attempt to secure Aguda's support for the Gaza/Jericho plan, at least from outside the coalition. Peres met Aguda's MK Menahem Porush and gave him details of the plan.

Porush said he would pass on the information to Aguda's institutions and its Council of Tora Sages, who will ultimately decide what the faction will do. Officially, UTJ is still refusing to join any coalition that includes Meretz.

Will Shas leave the coalition?

ANALYSIS
MICHAL YUDELMAN

THE question most repressed – but most pressing – in the Prime Minister's Office these days is what will happen to the peace process should Shas leave the coalition. If Shas walks out, Prime Minister Yitzhak Rabin's dramatic breakthrough will be jeopardized.

The more rumors there are of Interior Minister Aryeh Deri's possible resignation or suspension – with Shas perhaps following suit – the less anyone is willing to address the question directly. Instead they deny the possibility exists. "We don't know about any such idea," and "Nobody here is talking about such a move," sources in the Prime Minister's Office say when faced with the question.

But Rabin is well aware of how vital a role Shas plays in his peace plan. This, according to sources, is the reason why he has so obstinately clung to Deri's letter – promising to quit if and when an indictment against him is handed down (and not before). This is also the reason why Rabin has refused to suspend Deri in spite of Attorney-General Yosef Harish's advice and has insisted on defending his position before the Supreme Court, even when Harish declined to do so.

Finally, Rabin tried – in vain – to postpone the High Court hearing for a few days, at least until after his "Gaza/Jericho first" plan is approved.

If Shas leaves, Rabin's (Jewish) majority in the Knesset will disappear and and the peace process may grind to a halt. Shas, it is felt, is holding him just where it hurts most if it squeezes. This is why Shimon Peres resumed contact with Agudat Yisrael yesterday. He hopes to secure its support in the Knesset, just in case.

It is also possible that Shas will leave the coalition, but support it from without, as Deri hinted earlier this week. This prospect is far from attractive, rendering the government even more susceptible to Shas's tiniest whim.

However, the growing assessment in Labor is that Shas will not quit, even if both its senior representatives in cabinet, Deri and Deputy Religious Affairs Minister Raphael Pinhasi, are forced out by the High Court.

Shas has too much to lose, Labor ministers say. Its leaders realize that once torn away from the "udders of power," Shas's end as a political movement will be near. It will not be able to fund its many institutions or provide jobs and positions for thousands of its activists and supporters. Finally, Shas would lose its constituency and find itself once again tied to Rabbi Eliezer Schach's apron strings.

However, with a party like Shas, as Labor leaders well know, rational considerations do not always prevail. Shas might react emotionally, as an act of protest against Labor for "abandoning" its leaders. In any case, the final decision is up to Rabbi Ovadia Yosef and, to a large extent, to Deri, Yosef's protege.

Public health nurses to begin wildcat strike

JUDY SIEGEL

SOME 1,000 public health nurses are due to begin a wildcat strike this morning, closing *tipat halav* (family health) centers and reducing the functioning of district health offices to a minimum.

The Health Ministry reacted with "amazement" to the nurses' decision, since on Sunday night deputy director-general Ilan Cohen had requested a week's cooling-off period to study their demands. In view of the unauthorized strike, which is not preceded by the declaration of a work dispute, the ministry said it would "consider its steps."

The strike will halt immunization and health checks of babies, as well as vaccination of local residents exposed to hepatitis A infection and travelers going to disease-endemic areas abroad. There will be no school nurses on hand when classes begin tomorrow, if the strike is not over by then.

The nurses said their decision to strike was backed by the Nurses Union after the Finance and Health ministries rejected their demands on wages and work conditions.

Public health nurses claim they suffer discrimination compared to hospital nurses, and that the number of job slots has not been increased in proportion to an increased workload. They also demand shorter working hours for nurses over 55, higher car allowances and increased recreation pay.

As to their not officially declaring a work dispute, union head Moriah Galili said the nurses were tired of waiting "years" for a response to their demands and saw no benefit in declaring an official strike.

The Health Ministry argues that conditions can never be equalized between public health and hospital nurses, because the latter work shifts late at night and over the weekends under more difficult conditions.

THE JERUSALEM POST

VOLUME LXI, NUMBER 18458   FRIDAY, SEPTEMBER 10, 1993 • ELUL 24, 5753 • RABIA AWAL 24, 1414   NIS 4.40 (EILAT NIS 3.80)

ISRAEL RECOGNIZES THE PLO

Arafat accepts Israel's right to exist in peace and security

US ready to resume dialogue with PLO

HILLEL KUTTLER,
DAVID MAKOVSKY
and news agencies

WASHINGTON

THE US is on the verge of resuming the dialogue with the PLO, suspended in 1990, but an expected official statement by President Bill Clinton to this effect was canceled late last night.

The White House attributed the postponement to the fact that Prime Minister Yitzhak Rabin had not yet initialed Israel's recognition of the PLO.

"The president believed he'd be jumping the gun by making a statement before Rabin had signed the agreement," a White House official said.

The official said Clinton is likely to make his statement this morning.

While visiting Cleveland, Ohio, earlier in the day, Clinton said he was "pleased" and "extremely happy" with the mutual recognition between Israel and the PLO and had called Rabin to offer his congratulations.

Asked if the deal included US recognition of the PLO, Clinton replied: "If the PLO's statement today meets the criteria we have repeatedly set down – renouncing terrorism, acknowledging Israel's right to exist, those things – then we will resume our dialogue with them, and then we'll go forward from there."

Clinton indicated that, depending on the timing of the PLO's executive committee's ratification of the accord, US recognition of the PLO could be offered momentarily.

Meanwhile, senior administration officials said Secretary of State Warren Christopher would "most likely" visit the Middle East next month. They suggested the purpose of the visit is to revive the moribund Israeli-Syrian talks.

Arab diplomats who have met with senior Syrian officials in recent days stress that Damascus will not oppose the deal with the Palestinians, but is looking for signals that Rabin will not neglect Syria.

When request by the US to restrain Arab radicals from torpedoing the Israel-PLO accord, sources said Syria replied it "would try," but fell short of offering a firm commitment.

The official Israeli-PLO signing ceremony is to take place at 9 Monday morning on the White House lawn, in the presence of Clinton. There will be no anthems or national flags, and the signing will be officially witnessed by Christopher and Russian Foreign Minister Andrei Kozyrev. Norwegian Foreign Minister Jorgen Holst, Egyptian Foreign Minister Amr Moussa, and ambassadors representing those present at the 1991 Madrid conference will be among the honored guests.

Past administration officials instrumental in efforts to attain Arab-Israeli peace, perhaps including former secretaries of state James Baker and Henry Kissinger, are also expected.

Asked whether the PLO will now call a halt to the intifada, Palestinian delegation spokeswoman Hanan Ashrawi said: "With the devolution of the conflict, the intifada will end because the causes will end."

However, she stated that the declaration of principles contains "no formulation" to that effect.

Ashrawi told reporters she was filled with "hope, awe, and apprehension, because I recognize the significance of the moment ... I just hope we are up to the challenge of creating a Palestinian state."

(Continued on Page 12)

A feisty Foreign Minister Shimon Peres trades insults with Knesset foes during yesterday's special session. (Story, Page 3)   (AP)

Rabin will initial document this morning

MICHAL YUDELMAN and news agencies

PRIME Minister Yitzhak Rabin is to initial the document of mutual recognition with the PLO at 9 o'clock this morning, following the inner cabinet's approval of it yesterday.

In Tunis, the PLO executive committee last night after midnight empowered chairman Yasser Arafat to sign a letter recognizing Israel, PLO executive committee member Yasser Abed-Rabbo said.

ter's reply were released by the Prime Minister's Office (see Page 2).

The final hitches in the mutual recognition document were ironed out before dawn yesterday by Foreign Ministry Director-General Uri Savir and the ministry's legal adviser, Yoel Singer, at an all-night meeting in Paris with the PLO's Abu Alaf.

Foreign Minister Shimon Peres, who was advised by Savir early yesterday that the two sides had

Main points of agreement

- Recognition of Israel's right to exist in peace and security
- A sharp denunciation of terror and all violence
- A call to the Palestinian people in the territories to refrain from all violence and terror
- Removal of clauses in the PLO convenant that refer to the destruction of Israel
- Establishing a process that will solve in a peaceful manner any problems that might arise.

The full cabinet is to convene Sunday to ratify the document. The next day, both the mutual recognition document and the agreement of principles with the Palestinians are to be signed in Washington, though neither side has apparently decided who will represent them at the signing ceremony.

Today's signing, which had been scheduled for last night, was postponed due to the delay in the arrival here of Norwegian Foreign Minister Johan Jorgen Holst from Tunis. Holst was to bring the recognition document, along with a letter to Rabin signed by PLO Chairman Yasser Arafat.

However, texts of Arafat's letter to Rabin and the prime minis-

reached full agreement, went to Rabin's house to inform him personally.

In the document, the PLO undertakes to renounce all acts of violence and terrorism. Furthermore, Arafat undertakes to call on the Palestinian residents of the territories to refrain from acts of terrorism and to stop the intifada.

"The PLO has changed completely," a triumphant Peres announced after the inner-cabinet meeting yesterday. "Many Israelis had hoped for years for these changes. Israel has achieved in this document all the points it had demanded."

In Tunis, PLO officials said there was heated debate at the executive committee meeting and PLO "foreign minister" Farouk

(Continued on Page 12)

Reactions

FOLLOWING are reactions on yesterday's government announcement of mutual recognition between Israel and the PLO:

Housing Minister Binyamin Ben-Eliezer (Labor):

"After 27 years of fighting Israel's wars in the IDF, I feel this is a good ending to the drama which went on for decades. I'm glad that my generation, which carried the burden of all those wars, is trying to save the next generation from another war ... This is an historic moment. I feel we are closing the door on one era and opening the door to a new one."

Communications Minister Shulamit Aloni (Meretz):

"The PLO has changed the Palestinian Covenant and condemns terrorism and any form of violence and wants to promote peace in the region. This is the biggest achievement possible."

Environment Minister Yossi Sarid (Meretz):

"This is an historic turning point. Today, we mark the day the PLO ceased being the PLO. This is a happy day for me. But I'm not euphoric, I also have worries and

(Continued on Page 12)

THE JERUSALEM POST

POST

an international newspaper
distributed on 6 continents
in English and French.
Over 500,000 readers
worldwide

THE JERUSALEM POST

For your shopping convenience
**THE JERUSALEM POST
BOOK DEPT.**
is open Sun. - Thur.,
9:00 a.m. - 4:00 p.m.
Fridays 9:00 a.m.-1:00 p.m.
10 Harav Kook St.
Downtown Jerusalem.
Tel. 02-241282

VOLUME LXI, NUMBER 18461   TUESDAY, SEPTEMBER 14, 1993 • ELUL 28, 5753 • RABIA AWAL 28, 1414   NIS 3.40 (EILAT NIS 2.90)

'TIME FOR PEACE HAS COME'

Israel, PLO sign accords; Rabin and Arafat shake hands

Prime Minister Yitzhak Rabin and PLO chairman Yasser Arafat shake hands as President Bill Clinton looks on.   (AP)

Peres: Yesterday a dream, today a commitment

DAVID MAKOVSKY

WASHINGTON

PRIME Minister Yitzhak Rabin and PLO chairman Yasser Arafat sealed their peace accord with a handshake at a historic White House ceremony yesterday.

Rabin pledged to do his best to "embark upon a new era in the history of the Middle East," and to end the enmity that has brought wars, terrorism, and decades of ceaseless strife to Israelis and Palestinians.

The premier also cited Ecclesiastes, and concluded: "Ladies and gentlemen, the time for peace has come."

The 3,000 guests at the emotion-laden ceremony on the White House lawn, including former presidents George Bush and Jimmy Carter, heard President Bill Clinton say the occasion put "a peace of the brave within our reach."

Secretary of State Warren Christopher and Russian Foreign Minister Andrei Kozyrev served as official witnesses as Foreign Minister Shimon Peres and senior PLO official Mahmoud Abbas (Abu Mazen) signed the Declaration of Principles for Palestinian self-rule in the territories, beginning with Gaza and Jericho. They also countersigned the letters of recognition Rabin and Arafat signed last week.

Before signing the declaration, Peres said: "It is a revolution: Yesterday a dream, today a commitment."

As applause rang out after the accord was signed, Arafat extended his hand to Rabin, Clinton threw his arm over Rabin's shoulder to draw him closer, and Rabin grabbed Arafat's hand and shook it.

In an uplifting speech, Rabin spoke directly to the Palestinians, saying, "We who have come from a land where parents bury their children, we who have fought against you, the Palestinians, we say to you today in a loud and clear voice: 'Enough of blood and tears, enough!'

"We wish to open a new chapter in the sad book of our lives together, a chapter of mutual recognition, of good neighborliness, of mutual respect, of understanding. We hope to embark on a new era in the history of the Middle East."

Arafat, wearing an olive green military-style uniform and his trademark black-and-white checkered keffiyeh and speaking in Arabic, said: "My people are hoping that this agreement which we are signing today marks the beginning of the end of a chapter of pain and suffering which has lasted throughout this century. My people are hoping that this agreement which we are signing today will usher in an age of peace, coexistence and equal rights.

"The battle for peace is the most difficult battle of our lives. It deserves our utmost efforts because the land of peace, the land of peace yearns for a just and comprehensive peace."

After Arafat finished his speech, he shook Rabin's hand again.

Closing the 70-minute ceremony, Clinton called on the parties to maintain the momentum of the

(Continued on Page 2)

Rabin to Arafat: We're going to have to work very hard

Jerusalem Post Reporter

PRIME Minister Yitzhak Rabin and PLO chief Yasser Arafat spoke to each other at the White House about the hard work needed to make their peace accord succeed, US President Bill Clinton said yesterday.

"Before we came out, Mr. Rabin and Mr. Arafat were alone in the Blue Room upstairs with me and we walked down together, when everyone else had left, and they had not spoken at the time of the reception," Clinton told Israel Television in an interview.

"But they looked at each other, really clearly in the eye, for the first time, and the prime minister said: 'You know we are going to have to work very hard to make this work.'

"And Arafat said: 'I know, and I am prepared to do my part,'" Clinton said.

The US leader said both men immediately exchanged about three sentences – "right to business, no pleasantries.... I thought they were both quite serious."

Clinton said the world saw the two former bitter enemies shake hands on stage, something "a lot of people thought would never happen."

Their two handshakes and an attempt by each leader to speak in their respective addresses "to the people represented by the other" were important gestures, the president said.

Clinton told Arafat yesterday that the Palestinians had to move quickly to implement their new peace agreement with Israel.

Clinton put Arafat on notice at an unscheduled one-on-one meeting after the signing of the peace accord that the US expected rapid results, National Security Council official Martin Indyk said.

"The president made the point with some emphasis that it was absolutely essential to move quickly now to seize the momentum created by this incredible event and to start getting things moving on the ground," Indyk told reporters.

"I am convinced that the United States must bear a very heavy role of responsibility to make this work and implement the agreement," Clinton told a group of prominent Jewish and Arab-Americans who earlier in the day saw the accord signed.

Reactions

FOLLOWING are comments by various public figures on yesterday's ceremony in Washington:

● **Likud chairman Binyamin Netanyahu:** The impetuous rush to embrace an enemy who uses the language of peace for the purposes of war, in the long term will be seen as an historic blunder.

● **Communications Minister Shulamit Aloni:** I feel like it's November 29, 1947. We didn't know then where we were heading, but we knew we were heading for great things... We have battled for years for this step.

● **Former chief rabbi Shlomo Goren:** The signing ceremony in Washington is a day of mourning for the Jewish people and one must tear one's clothes for the destruction of Eretz Yisrael.

● **Henry Kissinger:** This is one of the most moving events I've ever seen... All the substantive issues still have to be resolved. Only the psychological barrier has been passed.

● **Cyrus Vance:** I was doubtful that I would ever live to see this day.

● **George McGovern:** This is a biblical miracle and I'm all for it. I think it is comparable to the Berlin Wall coming down. The cold war in the Middle East can never come back.

● **Prince Bandar, Saudi Arabia's ambassador to the US:** We're fully supporting the peace and will continue until we achieve it... The House of Saud has always come through when [funds for the Palestinians] were needed, but there are no specifics yet.

● **Adolfo Taylhardat of Venezuela, president of the UN Security Council:** The members of the council wish to convey to the leaders of the parties involved...their congratulations on the courage and statesmanship with which they have undertaken the initiatives that have led to this outstanding result.

● **The Vatican:** "The signing of the accord is a courageous and necessary act. The Holy See is aware of the present and future difficulties, but it is convinced the signing of the accord signifies the opening of a path to peace," Vatican chief spokesman Joaquin Navarro-Valls said in a statement.

● **Monsignor Clemente Riva, an official in Italy's National Conference of Catholic Bishops:** The accord will undoubtedly have a strong impact on interreligious dialogue, and in particular on the relationships the Church has with Israel and Islam.

● **US House of Representatives foreign affairs committee chairman Lee Hamilton:** It's a day of great exhilaration for us, but at the same time great apprehension... I've got a lot of questions in my mind about the ability of the Palestinians to implement the accord. It's a fragile agreement even for the Israelis. That's why the event is important – it kind of puts the stamp of approval of the US on the agreement.

Rabin seizes the emotional center

ANALYSIS

DAVID MAKOVSKY/WASHINGTON

WITH two old enemies pledging themselves to trying to forge a peaceful tomorrow, it sounded like the Middle East's past would no longer have to bury its future.

Prime Minister Yitzhak Rabin's stirring speech captured the gravity of the occasion. PLO chairman Yasser Arafat's remarks were conciliatory, but not as uplifting. He did, however, literally extend his hand to Rabin.

Rabin, known for his lack of eloquence, seized the emotional center of the day in one of his best speeches.

He spoke not in euphoric terms, but rather of "hope mixed with apprehension." Rabin spoke briefly, simply and, at times, even poetically, with a magnanimity of spirit. While displaying sensitivity to those who had suffered in the past, he spoke movingly of the nexus between past and future.

Putting the event in human terms, he spelled out the context of the ceremony: The hope for an

(Continued on Page 2)

THE JERUSALEM POST
an international newspaper distributed on 6 continents in English and French. Over 500,000 readers worldwide

THE JERUSALEM POST

New findings on vitamins
Page 5

VOLUME LXI, NUMBER 18503 | SUNDAY, NOVEMBER 7, 1993 • HESHVAN 23, 5754 • JUMAD AL ULA 23, 1414 | NIS 3.40 (EILAT NIS 2.90)

Police search Thursday for more bodies or clues in Australia's Belanglo State Forest, 80 miles southwest of Sydney, where seven bodies of missing tourists have been found. On Thursday, the bodies of two German backpackers were dicovered. (AP)

Hussein, Peres signed 'understandings' in Amman last week

DAVID MAKOVSKY

JORDAN'S King Hussein and Foreign Minister Shimon Peres "signed understandings" during nine hours of talks in Amman last week on economic cooperation, and also discussed the outline of a peace treaty, senior officials told *The Jerusalem Post* last night.

At the same time, King Hussein made clear that Jordan cannot sign a peace treaty with Israel unless Syria does so first, according to officials in the Prime Minister's Office and Foreign Ministry.

Officials indicated that broad cooperation was agreed upon, and that Peres and Hussein actually signed documents. "It is understood that Jordan won't sign a separate agreement, but short of a peace treaty, they agreed to do a lot," one official said.

Another senior official said the sides agreed on "open economic cooperation," among other issues. A third official, however, suggested that all understandings will only go into effect after a peace accord is signed.

Last night, Peres told the opening of a joint Hebrew University-Foreign Ministry conference in Jerusalem that, "We are very, very near to having an agreement with the Jordanians."

It remains unclear if Peres and Hussein reached an understanding on a Jordanian-Palestinian confederation at the end of the five-year interim period of Palestinian self-rule.

The Peres-Hussein sessions began in Amman Tuesday evening and concluded Wednesday morning, the same day that Peres later teased reporters to "remember the third of November." Jordan, which is holding its first multi-party elections tomorrow, has neither confirmed or denied that the meetings took place.

The meetings came on the eve of the first ever Jordan-Israel-US talks on economic cooperation in Paris last Thursday.

Officials in the Prime Minister's Office and Foreign Ministry sought to temper speculation that the Jordanian monarch would attend a White House meeting already scheduled for Friday between President Bill Clinton and Prime Minister Yitzhak Rabin.

According to some who have met the Jordanian monarch recently, Hussein feels secure about Israel's attitude towards the Hashemite Kingdom, after a secret meeting last month between himself and Prime Minister Yitzhak Rabin in Akaba.

Hussein was upset that he was excluded from the Oslo negotiations between Israel and the PLO, and his aides feared that Israel may have planned to help PLO chairman Yasser Arafat gain control of Jordan.

The Hussein-Peres understandings demonstrate a new assertiveness by Jordan, and its diminishing fear of what radicals both inside and outside the country may say or do.

Dr. Asher Susser, an expert on Jordan and director of Tel Aviv University's Dayan Center for Middle East Studies, said: "Jordanians don't want to be left out, politically and economically. Jordanians feel their past passivity didn't pay off."

Jordan's more assertive stance can be seen in recent comments by King Hussein. He recently told an interviewer "some people here say they are afraid. Members of this [radical] school have had their run for years, but they haven't much to show for it. I have no fear whatsoever. This is a period of rapid movement. Still, you can't formulate a peace treaty before we see a resolution of all the problems leading up to that period."

Jordan realizes that unless it takes more open steps for peace, it will not win the international assistance that is now being directed at the Palestinians. International donors have agreed to provide Palestinians in the territories with $2 billion in economic aid over the next several years, while Jordan has received no assistance for the Palestinians living in its country.

Amman also hopes that a pro-peace stance will win it more international sympathy as it seeks aid in both restructuring and erasing part of its estimated $12 billion debt, which is reportedly more than twice its GNP. It hopes Israel will use its lobbying muscle in the US towards this end.

Just two weeks ago, King Hussein told an interviewer: "In the context of peace, I think the possibilities available are unbelievable for joining together to secure a better future for everyone. Obviously, economic [cooperation] is one dimension."

In the short run, Jordan also seeks coordination both with Israel and the PLO in maintaining its currency as legal tender in the territories during self-rule, and the in the reopening of Jordanian banks closed in the territories in 1967.

Beyond economic issues, it is believed that Peres and Hussein discussed security concerns during the period of self-rule. For example, Israeli officials said Jordan favors continued Israeli control of the Allenby and Adam Bridges.

Susser said he believes that, barring an unforeseen surge in support for Moslem fundamentalists, the Jordanian elections tomorrow will not disrupt any understandings between Jerusalem and Amman.

"The fundamentalists now have 40 percent of the seats in Parliament, but this has not stopped Jordan from participating in Middle East peace talks for the past two years. The king has made clear that forging policy is his prerogative," Susser said.

New site for talks sought by Rabin

PRIME Minister Yitzhak Rabin is taking steps to relocate the Taba talks on security issues to a site not accessible to the media.

This issue is believed to have been raised in the meeting Rabin held Thursday with Egyptian Foreign Minister Amr Moussa.

Talks might still be held at Taba, but only for discussions of non-security issues.

Officials in the Prime Minister's Office say the talks are likely to be relocated to another site in Egypt. Speculation has ranged from a secluded part of Cairo to a spot in the Sinai Desert. **D.M.**

Histadrut, Palestinian trade unions sign pact

MICHAL YUDELMAN

THE Histadrut and the Palestinian trade unions reached a cooperation agreement Friday, at a meeting between Histadrut officials and Palestinian trade union leaders.

The meeting was held in the Beit Hanina home of Dr. Ahmed Tibi, special adviser to PLO head Yasser Arafat. It was attended by Histadrut Secretary-General Haim Haberfeld, the head of the labor federation's international department, Grisha Alroi; the head of the Histadrut's "peace team," Binyamin Yas'ur, of Mapam and Histadrut spokesman Eyal Faradis.

The Palestinians who attended included Shaher Sae'd, general-secretary of the General Federation of the United Palestinian Trade Unions, and the chairman of Gaza's trade union, Rassen Biari.

This was the second public meeting between the representatives of the two sides; the first took place in Brussels the previous week. A clandestine meeting between Haberfeld and Sae'd, organized by the German Friedrich Ebert Foundation, took place a year and a half ago in Europe.

Friday's meeting was initiated by Tibi, who met with Haberfeld in his office some two weeks ago at Histadrut headquarters in Tel Aviv.

It was decided at the meeting to set up a joint work team to formulate areas of cooperation including workers' training courses, examination of workers' rights in Israel and consideration of the Palestinians' demand for a return of the deductions made from the wages of Palestinian workers in Israel for the past 26 years.

The head of the Citizens Rights Movement in the Histadrut, MK Ran Cohen, said last week the Histadrut must ensure that the hundreds of millions of shekels deducted from Palestinian workers' wages since 1967 – for severance pay, pension, and national insurance – on which they never received benefits, are placed at the Palestinians disposal.

"There are workers aged 50 and 60 who are eligible to receive pension. If the Histadrut doesn't see to it that they get their benefits, no one else will," Cohen said.

Haberfeld last week blasted foreign trade unions that promised the Palestinian unions financial assistance but failed to come through with the money.

The leaders of the Palestinian unions were invited to an international conference to be held later this month in Tel Aviv, organized by the Histadrut and Labor Party, focusing on "the future relations between the social-democratic parties and the trade unions."

Two IDF soldiers, one SLA member wounded by gunmen in separate attacks in zone

DAVID RUDGE and YIGAL KOTZER

TWO IDF soldiers and a member of the South Lebanese Army were wounded in separate attacks by gunmen in the security zone over the weekend.

The first incident occurred on Friday afternoon when members of the Islamic Resistance, the fighting arm of Hizbullah, fired several mortar rounds towards a joint SLA/IDF post near Soujud village, in the eastern sector of the zone.

At least one of the rounds apparently exploded in the compound, wounding two IDF soldiers. They were treated at the scene and evacuated by helicopter to an IDF first aid station before being subsequently flown to Haifa's Rambam Hospital.

Corp. Ronnie Cohen, aged 19, of Moshav Brachiya, near Ashkelon, was reported to be suffering from serious injuries to the upper part of his spine, while the other soldier, Corp. Alex Sherman, also 19, of Migdal Ha'Emek, had stomach wounds. Cohen was later transferred to the intensive care unit and Sherman to a surgical ward.

Hizbullah claimed responsibility for the long-range attack on the Soujud position. IDF and SLA gunners blasted suspected Hizbullah targets north of the zone with artillery fire in response to the attack.

The Soujud area has become the hottest in the zone with incidents occurring there on an almost daily basis, the majority long-range attacks from hilltops overlooking the SLA and IDF posts.

The area is also favored by terrorists for ambushes and roadside bomb attacks against IDF and SLA patrols because of the hilly, brush-covered terrain which provides plenty of cover for attackers and bomb-planters.

Senior officers in the Northern Command met recently to decide the best way to curb the attacks in the Soujud region.

The SLA soldier was wounded in a mine explosion while troops were on operational duties in the Jezzine enclave, north of the security zone, yesterday morning:

He suffered moderate injuries and after treatment in the field was evacuated by helicopter to Rambam Hospital where he also underwent surgery.

The incidents over the weekend followed fierce artillery exchanges between Hizbullah and IDF and SLA gunners in the Huleh/Shakra area in the central sector of the zone on Thursday.

PLO official allegedly faces execution for spying for Mossad

DOUGLAS DAVIS and news agencies

A TOP PLO official faces likely execution after allegedly confessing to spying for the Mossad, PLO sources said yesterday.

The accused, Adnan Yassin, a consular official for the PLO in Tunis, was flown to Yemen for trial under the personal escort of PLO chairman Yasser Arafat, the sources said. He had been arrested in Tunis on October 25, according to press reports in London.

Yassin, 48, was deputy head of the PLO's diplomatic mission in Tunisia and effectively ran the "embassy." He is also said to have had access to many of the PLO's most intimate secrets.

Palestinian sources described Yassin as a trusted adviser to Arafat who didn't need security clearance before entering the chairman's offices.

The press reports said Arafat has asked for a meeting with Prime Minister Yitzhak Rabin to discuss the matter. According to these reports, Yassin had plotted to detonate a car-bomb outside Arafat's office in Tunis.

The London-based daily *Asharq al-Awsat* reported that before being arrested, Yassin was kept under surveillance for two weeks after he had cleared a Mercedes that had been shipped from France through customs .

French officials reportedly informed their Tunisian counterparts in advance that the vehicle was loaded with Semtex explosives and sophisticated electronic detonators concealed in hidden compartments.

Yassin is said to have broken down at an early stage in his interrogation and to have given a full account of his recruitment by the Mossad, reportedly in a European capital in 1990, and of his activities.

He allegedly admitted the explosives in the Mercedes were intended to be detonated outside Arafat's office at the PLO headquarters in Tunis; that he had bugged the offices of senior PLO officials, including Mahmoud Abbas (Abu Mazen), who signed the September 13 accord with Israel, and that he passed information to the Mossad on secret activities of PLO leaders, including videotapes of their private parties.

PLO sources said listening devices in Abbas's desk may have put the Israelis in earshot of PLO strategy sessions for the Norway talks. Arafat also participated in the sessions.

While Yassin has reportedly confessed to working for the Mossad, he insisted that his 24-year-old son, Hani, who was also arrested, was an unwitting accomplice. It was not clear whether Hani was also taken to Yemen.

There have never before been allegations of an Israeli agent penetrating so high into the organization's hierarchy.

In its Tunis-datelined report, the Saudi-owned *Asharq al-Awsat* said news of the arrest "has caused panic among Palestinians in Tunis and abroad."

"It is common knowledge that Yassin was in charge of many secrets and other files relating to the affairs of the Palestinians in Tunis," the paper said.

"He was also in charge of travel arrangements for Palestinians from the occupied territories who came to Tunis for secret consultations with Arafat, as well as the secret travels of Arafat himself and other PLO leaders," it added.

It said "Palestinian circles" in Tunis believe Yassin may have been involved in the April 1988 assassination of Khali. Wazir (Abu Jihad), who was gunned down at his home in Tunis, allegedly by an Israeli commando unit.

They also believe his arrest may have resolved a number of other security lapses which had baffled PLO officials.

The paper added that PLO leaders have held several meetings to discuss the implications, and that Arafat has set up a commission of inquiry to investigate the affair.

Witnesses who saw Yassin handed over to PLO guards earlier this week described him as gaunt and run-down. He has been kept in solitary confinement.

PLO sources said Arafat made an unscheduled stop with his private jet in Tunis on Friday to pick up Yassin while shuttling from Senegal to the Yemeni capital San'a, seat of the PLO's Revolutionary Court.

However, PLO officials in Yemen denied that Yassin had arrived and insisted he was still in Tunis. Further efforts to trace Yassin's whereabouts were unsuccessful.

The trial before the military-style tribunal is expected to be swift and begin as soon as possible. The PLO sources said the penalty is expected to be execution.

The last PLO official to be executed was Hamza Abu Zaid, a member of the Abu Nidal terrorist faction. Abu Zaid was found guilty of the 1991 assassinations of PLO leaders Salah Khalaf, also known as Abu Iyad, and Hayel Abdul Hamid, or Abu Al-Hul in Tunis.

If convicted, Yassin will likely be killed on a PLO boat off the Yemeni coast. In the past the San'a government has refused to allow the organization to carry out death sentences on Yemeni soil, fearful of reprisals from the group's enemies.

'End of boycott depends on Syria-Israel peace accord'

NEW YORK (Reuter) – Arab leaders have told a US Jewish group the boycott against companies doing business with Israel cannot be formally abandoned until Israel signs a peace accord with Syria, although they admit it is dead in all but name.

American Jewish Congress leader Henry Siegman said Friday this was the message he received last week when he headed a group that met Egypt's President Hosni Murbarak, PLO leader Yasser Arafat, Jordan's King Hussein and Saudi Arabia's foreign minister and chief of intelligence.

It was the first time a Jewish group had met Saudi Arabia's intelligence chief Turki al-Faisal. The delegation members were invited as the guests of the Saudi king, even though he did not meet the 10-member group.

Siegman said the group pressed the case that US businesses would be reluctant to join the international effort to rebuild the economy of territories unless the secondary boycott of companies that do business with Israel was formally lifted.

Anti-boycott legislation in the United States has led to heavy fines on companies that respect the boycott and, in several cases, led to companies losing business because they complied with it.

Therefore, Siegman said, many companies would be hesitant to cooperate in joint ventures with Arab companies and leave themselves open to the risk their new partners complied with the boycott.

He said this argument impressed many Arab leaders, including Murbarak and that Saudi Foreign Minister, Saud al-Faisal, assured him that his country was no longer enforcing the boycott.

Siegman added that the Arab leaders he met expected the boycott to collapse of its own weight, but would not formally abandon it for fear of undercutting Syria in its negotiations with Israel.

He also said that Arab leaders were convinced the peace process would work, and that almost all Arab states would recognize Israel once the Syrian issue was resolved.

4 Hebron Arabs hurt in clashes with Jews

FOUR Arab residents of Hebron, including a woman, were injured over the weekend in clashes between Arabs and Jews in Hebron and Kiryat Arba.

The disturbances began Friday night, when Jews who were stoned while walking to the Machpela Cave to pray responded by smashing windows of cars and houses. They also beat several passing Arabs. Later, settlers threw stones at Arab cars traveling the road between Hebron and Kiryat Arba.

Last night, near the southern gate of Kiryat Arba, Jewish youths smashed the windows of cars that passed through the area.

The IDF arrested a Jerusalem resident. (Itim)